Jane's

FIGHTING SHIPS

Edited by Captain Richard Sharpe OBE RN

One Hundred and Third Edition

2000-2001

Founded in 1897 by Fred T Jane

Bookmark Jane's homepage on
http://www.janes.com

Jane's award-winning web site provides you with continuously updated news and information.
As well as extracts from our world renowned magazines, you can browse the online catalogue,
visit the Press Centre, discover the origins of Jane's, use the extensive glossary,
download our screen saver and much more.

Jane's now offers powerful electronic solutions to meet the rapid changes in your
information requirements. All our data, analysis and imagery is available on CD-ROM
or via a new secure web service – Jane's Online at www.janesonline.com.

Tailored electronic delivery can be provided through Jane's Data Services.
Contact an information consultant at any of our international offices to
find out how Jane's can change the way you work or e-mail us at
info.janes.co.uk *or* info@janes.com

ISBN 0 7106 2018 7
"Jane's" is a registered trade mark

Copyright © 2000 by Jane's Information Group Limited, Sentinel House, 163 Brighton Road, Coulsdon, Surrey CR5 2YH, UK

In the USA and its dependencies
Jane's Information Group Inc, 1340 Braddock Place, Suite 300, Alexandria, Virginia 22314-1651, USA

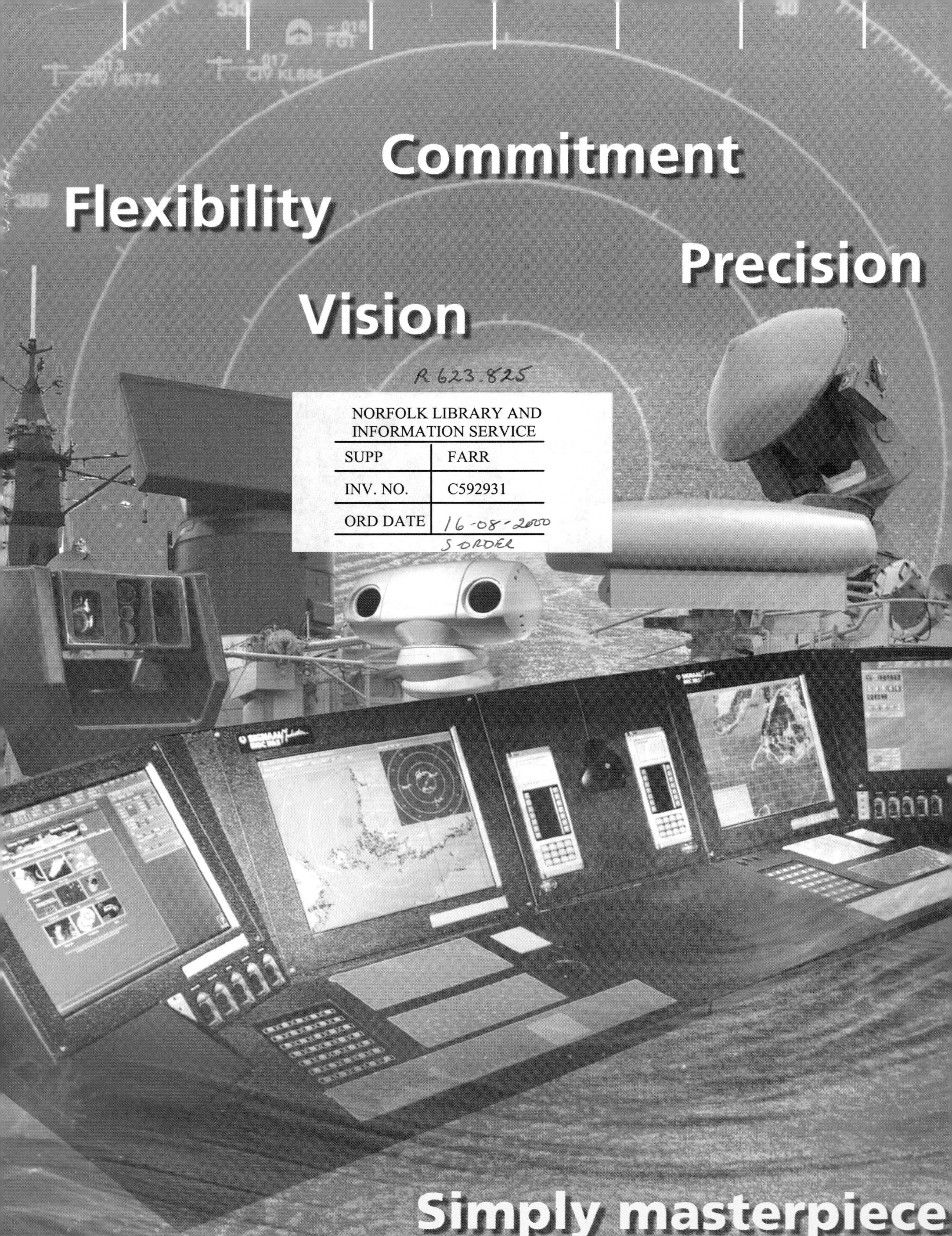

Flexibility

Commitment

Precision

Vision

Simply masterpiece

◆ SIGNAAL

Hollandse Signaalapparaten B.V., subsidiary of Thomson-CSF
P.O. Box 42 7550 GD HENGELO The Netherlands
Phone: +31(0) 74 2488111   Fax: +31(0) 74 2425936
Internet: http://www.signaal.thomson-csf.com

Contents

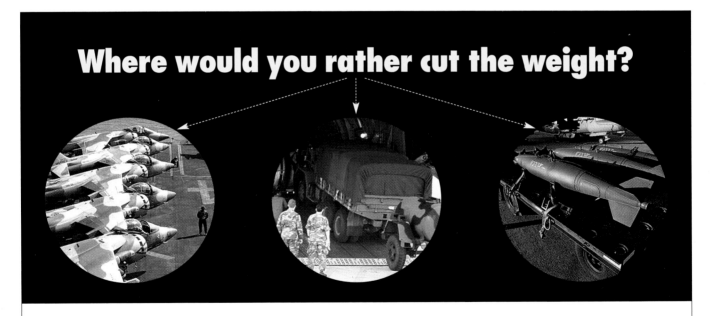

Flying the flag

Many Navies fly our flag: Best quality at the best price.

Join the leading flag, you will not get more for less.

Bazan

Paseo de la Castellana nº 55 - 28046 Madrid.(Spain) • Tel. 34-91 335 84 00 • Fax 34-91 441 50 90 • Web: www.enbazan.es • E-mail: comercial@bazan.es

Glossary

Type abbreviations are listed at head of Pennant List

AAW	Anti-air warfare
ACDS	Advanced combat direction system
ACV	Air cushion vehicle
AEW	Airborne early warning
AIP	Air independent propulsion
ARM	Anti-radiation missile
ASDS	Advanced swimmer delivery system
A/S, ASW	Anti-submarine (warfare)
ASM	Air-to-surface missile
AUV	Autonomous undersea vehicle
BPDMS	Base point defence missile system
Cal	Calibre — the diameter of a gun barrel; also used for measuring length of the barrel eg a 6 in gun 50 calibres long (6 in/50) would be 25 ft long
CEC	Co-operative engagement capability
CIWS	Close-in weapon system
CODAG, CODOG, CODLAG, COGAG, COGOG, COSAG, COGAL	Descriptions of mixed propulsion systems: combined diesel and gas turbine, diesel-electric and gas turbine, diesel or gas turbine, gas turbine and gas turbine, gas turbine or gas turbine, steam and gas turbine, gas turbine and electric
CONAS	Combined nuclear and steam
cp	Controllable pitch (propellers)
DC	Depth charge
DP	Dual purpose (gun) for surface or AA use
Displacement	Basically the weight of water displaced by a ship's hull when floating: (a) Light: without fuel, water or ammunition (b) Normal: used for Japanese MSA ships. Similar to 'standard' (c) Standard: as defined by Washington Naval Conference 1922 — fully manned and stored but without fuel or reserve feed-water (d) Full load: fully laden with all stores, ammunition, fuel and water
DSRV	Deep submergence recovery vessel
dwt	Deadweight tonnage (see tonnage)
ECM	Electronic countermeasures eg jamming
ECCM	Electronic counter-countermeasures
EEZ	Exclusive economic zone

EHF	Extreme high frequency
ELF	Extreme low frequency radio
ELINT	Electronic intelligence eg recording radar, W/T etc
ESM	Electronic support measures eg intercept
EW	Electronic warfare
FAC	Fast attack craft
FLIR	Forward-looking infra-red
FRAM	Fleet rehabilitation and modernisation programme
GCCS	Global Command and Control System
GFCS	Gun fire-control system
GMLS	Guided missile launch system
GPS	Global positioning system
grt	Gross registered tonnage (see tonnage)
HF	High frequency

Horsepower (hp) or (hp(m))	Power developed or applied:
	(a) bhp: brake horsepower = power available at the crankshaft
	(b) shp: shaft horsepower = power delivered to the propeller shaft
	(c) ihp: indicated horsepower = power produced by expansion of gases in the cylinders of reciprocating steam engines
	(d) 1 kW = 1.341 hp = 1.360 metric hp
	   1 hp = 0.746 kW = 1.014 metric hp
	   1 metric hp = 0.735 kW = 0.968 hp
	(e) Sustained horsepower may be different for similar engines in different conditions

IFF	Identification friend/foe
IRST	Infra-red search and track
JTIDS	Joint tactical information distribution system
kT	Kiloton
kW	Kilowatt
LAMPS	Light airborne multipurpose system
LAMS	Local area missile system
Length	Expressed in various ways: (a) oa: overall = length between extremities (b) pp: between perpendiculars = between fore side of the stem and after side of the rudderpost (c) wl: waterline = between extremities on the water-line
LF	Low frequency

SÖDERMANLAND

B Sullivan/0085427

LRMP	Long-range maritime patrol	**SLCM**	Ship-launched cruise missile
MAD	Magnetic Anomaly Detector	**SLEP**	Service Life Extension Programme
MCMV	Mine countermeasures vessel	**SRBOC**	Super rapid blooming offboard chaff
MDF	Maritime defence force	**SSDE/SSE**	Submerged signal and decoy ejector
Measurement	See Tonnage	**SSDS**	Ship self-defence system
MF	Medium frequency	**SSM**	Surface-to-surface missile
MFCS	Missile fire-control system	**STIR**	Surveillance Target Indicator Radar
MG	Machine gun	**STOBAR**	Short take off and barrier arrested recovery
MIRV	Multiple, independently targetable re-entry vehicle	**STOVL**	Short take off and vertical landing
MRV	Multiple re-entry vehicle	**SURTASS**	Surface Towed Array Surveillance System
MSA	Japan Maritime safety agency	**SWATH**	Small waterplane area twin hull
MSC	US Military Sealift Command	**TACAN**	Tactical air navigation beacon
MW	Megawatt	**TACTASS**	Tactical Towed Acoustic Sensor System
NBC	Nuclear, biological and chemical (warfare)	**TAS**	Target Acquisition System
net	Net registered tonnage (see tonnage)	**TASS**	Towed Array Surveillance System
n miles	Nautical miles	**TBMD**	Theatre ballistic missile defence
NTDS	Naval tactical direction system	**Tonnage**	Measurement tons, computed on capacity of a ship's hull rather than its 'displacement' (see above):
oa	Overall length		(a) Gross: the internal volume of all spaces within the
OPV	Offshore patrol vessel		hull and all permanently enclosed spaces above decks
OTC	Officer in Tactical Command		that are available for cargo, stores and accommodation.
PAAMS	Principal anti-air missile system		The result in cubic feet divided by 100 = gross tonnage
PDMS	Point defence missile system		(b) Net: gross minus all those spaces used for machinery,
PWR	Pressurised water reactor		accommodation etc ('non-earning' spaces)
QRCC	Quick reaction combat capability		(c) Deadweight (dwt): the amount of cargo, bunkers,
RAM	Radar absorbent material		stores etc that a ship can carry at her load draught
RAS	Replenishment at sea	**Tonnes**	One ton equals 1.016 tonnes
RBU	Anti-submarine rocket launcher	**UAV**	Unmanned aerial vehicle
RIB	Rigid inflatable boat	**UHF**	Ultra-high frequency
ro-ro	Roll-on/roll-off	**UUV**	Unmanned undersea vehicle
ROV	Remote operated vehicle	**VDS**	Variable depth sonar which is lowered to best listening
rpm	Revolutions per minute		depth. Known as dunking sonar in helicopters.
SAM	Surface-to-air missile		
SAR	Search and rescue	**Vertrep**	Vertical replenishment
SATCOM	Satellite communications	**VLF**	Very low frequency radio
SDV	Swimmer delivery vehicle	**VLS**	Vertical launch system
SES	Surface effect ship	**VSTOL**	Vertical or short take-off/landing
SHF	Super high frequency	**VTOL**	Vertical take-off/landing
SINS	Ship's inertial navigation system	**wl**	Waterline length
SLBM	Submarine-launched ballistic missile		

ANZAC

S Connolly, RAN/0085426

Rodman 101
high performance

Rodman 101, a patrol boat with high performance capabilities.

For surveillance, monitoring, security tasks, etc. Navies, Coast Guards, fishery protection services and marine police forces all over the world rely on Rodman Polyships to design and build their units in order to carry out their operational requirements meeting the highest standards with minimum servicing and crew requirements. Rodman, a wide range of units built with composite materials from 9 to 36 metres.

TECHNICAL FEATURES	
Overall length	30 m.
Mould breadth	6 m.
Draught	1,10 m.
Operating range	600 / 1.000 miles
Crew	9/13 men
Power	1.400 / 2.366 HP
Max. speed	35 knots
Cruising speed	28 knots

pintado et guzmán

Ríos - Teis, s/nº • P. O. BOX 501 • 36200 VIGO - Spain • Tel: +34 986 81 18 11 • Fax: +34 986 81 18 21 • e-mail: vpresidencia@rodman.es

Sea
family of titles

Jane's Amphibious Warfare Capabilities
Evaluate the organisational structure and capabilities of amphibious forces around the globe. Comprehensive information on equipment and logistics, with country by country overviews including recent operations and funding, providing you with both the range and depth of coverage you need.

Jane's Fighting Ships
The ultimate reference source of the world's navies. Provides current information on warships, auxiliaries and paramilitary vessels in service and under construction. Covers complete and up-to-date technical details for each entry from dimensions and main machinery to speed and crew size.

Jane's Marine Propulsion
Detailed information on marine engines currently in production for naval or commercial use. Includes engine, transmission, propellers and drive systems, along with main specifications and development history.

Jane's Merchant Ships
Allows easy recognition and identification of cargo and passenger carrying vessels around the world via use of the revised Talbot-Booth system. Textual details are provided with over 8,000 accompanying illustrations.

Jane's Naval Construction and Retrofit Markets
Helps you to identify market opportunities and trends by detailing naval constructions, retrofitting and major refitting programmes currently being developed, or planned for the future.

Jane's Naval Weapons Systems
Covers new and upgraded weaponry to provide you with a full picture of the current naval weapon technology market. Descriptions range from naval guns and missiles to torpedoes and anti-submarine weapons.

Jane's Underwater Technology
In-depth information on the latest sub-sea equipment, allowing evaluation of underwater hardware, systems, technologies and applications. Over 600 photographs and drawings provide full visual reference in a clear and concise format.

Jane's Underwater Warfare Systems
An indispensable guide to the technologies and systems required to equip modern submarines. Details the current status of equipment, review of potential for refitting and modernisation and evaluation of fleet strengths.

Jane's Naval/Maritime Special Reports
Patrol Craft Markets

Jane's Exclusive Economic Zones
This unique reference source provides you with a global survey of national claims to maritime jurisdiction, together with an assessment of individual country capabilities for securing and protecting their maritime space.

Jane's Survey Vessels
A one-stop source for all the relevant specifications across the entire worldwide fleet of survey vessels.

Other Jane's titles

Magazines
Jane's Airport Review
Jane's Asian Infrastructure Monthly
Jane's Defence Industry
Jane's Defence Upgrades
Jane's Defence Weekly
Jane's Foreign Report
Jane's Intelligence Digest
Jane's Intelligence Review
Jane's International Defense Review
Jane's International Police Review
Jane's Islamic Affairs Analyst
Jane's Missiles and Rockets
Jane's Navy International
Jane's Police Review
Jane's Terrorism and Security Monitor
Jane's Transport Finance

Geopolitical
Jane's Chem-Bio Handbook
Jane's Chemical-Biological Defense Guidebook
Jane's Counter Terrorism
Jane's Intelligence Watch Report
Jane's Sentinel Security Assessments
Jane's Terrorism Watch Report
Jane's Unconventional Weapons
Jane's World Insurgency and Terrorism

Transport
Jane's Air Traffic Control
Jane's Airports and Handling Agents
Jane's Airports, Equipment and Services
Jane's High-Speed Marine Transportation
Jane's Road Traffic Management
Jane's Urban Transport Systems
Jane's World Airlines
Jane's World Railways

Industry
Jane's International ABC Aerospace Directory
Jane's International Defence Directory
Jane's World Defence Industry

Systems
Jane's C⁴I Systems
Jane's Electro-Optic Systems
Jane's Electronic Mission Aircraft
Jane's Military Communications
Jane's Radar and Electronic Warfare Systems
Jane's Simulation and Training Systems
Jane's Strategic Weapon Systems

Land
Jane's Ammunition Handbook
Jane's Armour and Artillery
Jane's Armour and Artillery Upgrades
Jane's High Command
Jane's Infantry Weapons
Jane's Land-Based Air Defence
Jane's Military Vehicles and Logistics
Jane's Mines and Mine Clearance
Jane's Nuclear, Biological and Chemical Defence
Jane's Personal Combat Equipment
Jane's Police and Security Equipment
Jane's World Armies

Air
Jane's 3-D
Jane's Aero-Engines
Jane's Aircraft Component Manufacturers
Jane's Aircraft Upgrades
Jane's Air-Launched Weapons
Jane's All the World's Aircraft
Jane's Avionics
Jane's Helicopter Markets and Systems
Jane's Space Directory
Jane's Unmanned Aerial Vehicles and Targets
Jane's World Air Forces

For more information on any of the above products, please contact one of our sales offices listed below:

Europe, Middle East & Africa
Jane's Information Group
Sentinel House
163 Brighton Road
Coulsdon, Surrey, CR5 2YH, UK
Tel: +44 (0) 20 8700 3700
Fax: +44 (0) 20 8763 1006
e-mail: info@janes.co.uk

The Americas
Jane's Information Group
1340 Braddock Place
Suite 300, Alexandria
Virginia 22314-1657, USA
Tel: (+1 703) 683 37 00
Fax: (+1 703) 836 02 97
e-mail: info@janes.com

Asia
Jane's Information Group
60 Albert Street
15-01 Albert Complex
Singapore 189969
Tel: (+65) 331 62 80
Fax: (+65) 336 99 21
e-mail: janefish@mbox3.singnet.com.sg

Australia
Jane's Information Group
PO Box 3502
Rozelle Delivery Centre
New South Wales 2039, Australia
Tel: (+61 2) 85 87 79 00
Fax: (+61 2) 85 87 79 01
e-mail: info@janes.thomson.com.au

USA West Coast
Jane's Information Group
201 East Sandpoint Avenue
Suite 370
Santa Ana, CA92707, USA
Tel: (+1 714) 850 0585
Fax: (+1 714) 850 0606
e-mail: janeswest@janes.com

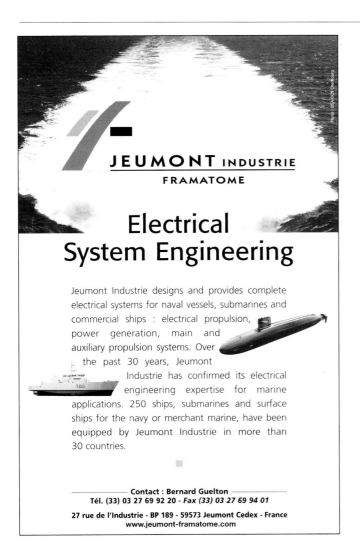
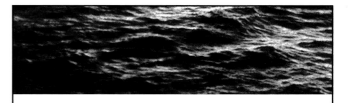

Information Services & Solutions

Jane's is the leading unclassified information provider for military, government and commercial organisations worldwide, in the fields of defence, geopolitics, transportation and law enforcement.

We are dedicated to providing the information our customers need, in the formats and frequency they require. Read on to find out how Jane's information in electronic format can provide you with the best way to access the information you require.

Jane's Online

Search across the complete portfolio of Jane's Information, via the Internet

Created for the professional seeking specific detailed information, this user-friendly service can be customised to suit your ever-changing information needs. Search across any combination of titles to retrieve the information you need quickly and easily. You set the query — Jane's Online finds the answer!

Key benefits of Jane's Online include:
- the most up to date information available from Jane's
- accessible anytime, anywhere
- saves time — research can be carried out quickly and easily
- archives enable you to compare how specifics have changed over time
- accurate analysis at your fingertips
- site licences available
- user-friendly interface
- high-quality images linked to text

Check out this site today: **www.janesonline.com**

Jane's CD-ROM Libraries

Quickly pinpoint the information you require from Jane's

Choose from nine powerful CD-ROM libraries for quick and easy access to the defence, geopolitical, space, transportation and law enforcement information you need. Take full advantage of the information groupings and purchase the entire library.

Libraries available:
Jane's Air Systems Library
Jane's Defence Equipment Library
Jane's Defence Magazines Library
Jane's Geopolitical Library
Jane's Land and Systems Library
Jane's Market Intelligence Library
Jane's Police and Security Library
Jane's Sea and Systems Library
Jane's Transport Library

Key benefits of Jane's CD-ROM include:
- quick and easy access to Jane's information and graphics
- easy-to-use Windows interface with powerful search capabilities
- online glossary and synonym searching
- search across all the titles on each disc, even if you do not subscribe to them, to determine whether you would like to add them to your library
- export and print out text or graphics
- quarterly updates
- full networking capability
- supported by an experienced technical team

CD-Rom enhancements for 2000:
- compatability with Windows NT and Macintosh plaltforms
- annotations
- bookmark facility
- personal viewer
- multi-media support

Jane's Data Service

Jane's information on your intranet or controlled military network

Jane's Data Service brings together more than 200 sources of near-realtime and technical reference information serving defence, intelligence, space, transportation and law enforcement professionals. By making Jane's data (HTML) and images (JPEG) available for integration behind Intranet environments or closed networks, this unique service offers you a way to receive information that is updated frequently and works in tune with your organisation. We can also offer a complete management service where Jane's hosts the information and server for you. The most secure way to access Jane's Information.

Jane's Consultancy

A service as individual as your needs
Whether it is research on your competitors' markets, in-depth analysis or customised content that you require, Jane's Consultancy can offer you a tailored, highly confidential personal service to help you achieve your objectives. However large or small your requirement, contact us in confidence for a free proposal and quotation.

Jane's Consultancy will bring you a variety of benefits:
- expert personnel in a wide variety of disciplines
- a global and well-established information network
- total confidentiality
- objective analysis
- Jane's reputation for accuracy, authority and impartiality

The information you require, delivered in a format to suit your needs.

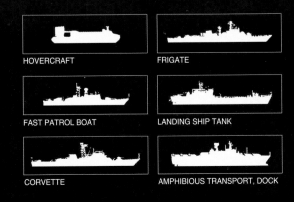

ADMINISTRATION

Publisher:	*Karen Heffer*
Managing Editor:	*Keith Faulkner*
IS Application Support Manager:	*Ruth Simmance*
Content Editing/Prepress Manager:	*Anita Slade*
Team Leaders:	*Joanne Fenwick*
	Stephen McCarthy
Editorial:	*Emma Pond*

EDITORIAL OFFICE

Jane's Information Group Limited, Sentinel House, 163 Brighton Road, Coulsdon, Surrey CR5 2YH, UK
Tel: (+44 20) 87 00 37 00   Fax: (+44 20) 87 00 37 88
e-mail: jfs@janes.co.uk

SALES OFFICE

Send enquiries to: *Jo Moon – Group Sales and Customer Service Manager*
Jane's Information Group Limited, Sentinel House, 163 Brighton Road, Coulsdon, Surrey CR5 2YH, UK
Tel: (+44 20) 87 00 37 00   Fax: (+44 20) 87 63 10 06
e-mail: info@janes.co.uk

Send USA enquiries to: *Robert Loughman – Vice-President Product Sales*
Jane's Information Group Inc, 1340 Braddock Place, Suite 300, Alexandria, Virginia 22314-1651, USA
Tel: (+1 703) 683 37 00   Fax: (+1 703) 836 00 29   Telex: 6819193
Tel: (+1 800) 824 07 68   Fax: (+1 800) 836 02 97
e-mail: order@janes.com

Send Asia enquiries to: *David Fisher – Business Manager*
Jane's Information Group Asia, 60 Albert Street, #15-01 Albert Complex, Singapore 189969
Tel: (+65) 331 62 80   Fax: (+65) 336 99 21
e-mail: janefish@mbox3.singnet.com.sg

Send Australia/New Zealand enquiries to: *Pauline Roberts – Business Manager*
Jane's Information Group, PO Box 3502, Rozelle Delivery Centre, New South Wales 2039, Australia
Tel: (+61 2) 85 87 79 00   Fax: (+61 2) 85 87 79 01
e-mail: pauline.roberts@thomson.com.au

ADVERTISEMENT SALES OFFICES

Australia: *Chris Green* (UK Head Office)

Austria: *Dr Uwe Wehrstedt* (See Germany)

Benelux: *Stephen Judge* (UK Head Office)

Channel Islands: *Steven Soffe* (UK Head Office)

Eastern Europe: *Dr Uwe Wehrstedt* (See Germany)

Egypt: *Stephen Judge* (UK Head Office)

France: *Patrice Février*
BP 418, 35 avenue MacMahon,
F-75824 Paris Cedex 17, France
Tel: (+33 1) 45 72 33 11   Fax: (+33 1) 45 72 17 95
e-mail: patrice.fevrier@wanadoo.fr

Germany: MCW *Dr Uwe Wehrstedt*
Hagenbrite 9, D-06463 Ermsleben, Germany
Tel: (+49 34) 74 36 20 91 Fax: (+49 34) 74 36 20 90

Greece: *Steven Soffe* (UK Head Office)

India: *Chris Green* (UK Head Office)

Ireland: *Chris Green* (UK Head Office)

Israel: *Oreet Ben-Yaacov*
Oreet International Media, 15 Kinneret Street,
IL-51201 Bene Berak, Israel
Tel: (+972 3) 570 65 27   Fax: (+972 3) 570 65 26
e-mail: oreet@oreet-marcom.com

Italy and Switzerland: *Ediconsult Internazionale Srl*
Piazza Fontane Marose 3, I-16123 Genoa, Italy
Tel: (+39 010) 58 36 84   Fax: (+39 010) 56 65 78
e-mail: ediconsult@iol.it

Korea, South: *Young Seoh Chinn*
JES Media International, 2nd Floor ANA Building,
2571 Myungil-Dong, Kangdong-Gu, Seoul 134 070, South Korea
Tel: (+82 2) 481 34 11   Fax: (+82 2) 481 34 14
e-mail: jesmedia@unitel.co.kr

Middle East: *Steven Soffe* (UK Head Office)

Pakistan: *Chris Green* (UK Head Office)

Rest of the World: *Stephen Judge* (UK Head Office)

Russian Federation and Associated States (CIS): *Simon Kay*
33 St John's Street, Crowthorne, Berkshire RG45 7NQ, UK
Tel: (+44 1344) 77 71 23   Fax: (+44 1344) 77 58 85
e-mail: crowkay@msn.com

Saudi Arabia: *Steven Soffe* (UK Head Office)

Scandinavia: *Gillian Thompson*
The Falsten Partnership, PO Box 21175,
London N16 6ZG, UK
Tel: (+44 20) 88 06 23 01   Fax: (+ 44 20) 88 06 81 37
e-mail: falsten@dial.pipex.com

Singapore: *Richard West* (UK Head Office)

South Africa: *Stephen Judge* (UK Head Office)

Spain: *Michael Andrade*
Via Exclusivas SL, Viriato 69SC, E-28010 Madrid, Spain
Tel: (+34 91) 448 76 22   Fax: (+34 91) 446 01 98
e-mail: via@varenga.com

Thailand: *Chris Green* (UK Head Office)

Turkey: *Steven Soffe* (UK Head Office)

United Arab Emirates: *Steven Soffe* (UK Head Office)

UK – London: *Stephen Judge* (UK Head Office)

UK – South, South East, South West, North West, Wales and West Scotland:
Steven Soffe (UK Head Office)

UK – North East, East, East Scotland: *Chris Green* (UK Head Office)

Senior Key Accounts Manager: *Richard West*
Jane's Information Group Limited, Sentinel House, 163 Brighton Road, Coulsdon, Surrey CR5 2YH, UK
Tel: (+44 1892) 72 55 80   Fax: (+44 1892) 72 55 81
e-mail: richard.west@janes.co.uk

Advertising Sales Office Manager: *Brenda DiLieto*
Jane's Information Group Limited, Sentinel House, 163 Brighton Road, Coulsdon, Surrey CR5 2YH, UK
Tel: (+44 20) 87 00 38 50   Fax: (+44 20) 87 00 38 59
e-mail: brenda.dilieto@janes.co.uk

Senior Advertisement Sales Executive: *Stephen Judge*
Jane's Information Group Limited, Sentinel House, 163 Brighton Road, Coulsdon, Surrey CR5 2YH, UK
Tel: (+44 20) 87 00 38 53   Fax: (+44 20) 87 00 37 44
e-mail: stephen.judge@janes.co.uk

Advertising Sales Executive: *Chris Green*
Jane's Information Group Limited, Sentinel House, 163 Brighton Road, Coulsdon, Surrey CR5 2YH, UK
Tel: (+44 20) 87 00 39 63   Fax: (+44 20) 87 00 37 44
e-mail: chris.green@janes.co.uk

Advertising Sales Executive: *Steven Soffe*
Jane's Information Group Limited, Sentinel House, 163 Brighton Road, Coulsdon, Surrey CR5 2YH, UK
Tel: (+44 20) 87 00 39 43   Fax: (+44 20) 87 00 37 44
e-mail: steven.soffe@janes.co.uk

USA and Canada: *Ronald R Lichtinger III*, Advertising Sales Director
Jane's Information Group Inc, 1340 Braddock Place, Suite 300, Alexandria, Virginia 22314-1651, USA
Tel: (+1 703) 683 37 00   Fax: (+1 703) 836 55 37
e-mail: lichtinger@janes.com

North Eastern USA and East Canada: *Harry Carter*
Jane's Information Group Inc, 1340 Braddock Place, Suite 300, Alexandria, Virginia 22314-1651, USA
Tel: (+1 703) 683 37 00   Fax: (+1 703) 836 55 37
e-mail: carter@janes.com

South Eastern USA: *Kristin D Schulze*
5370 Eastbay Drive, Suite 104,
Clearwater, Florida 33764, USA
Tel: (+1 727) 524 77 41   Fax: (+1 727) 524 75 62
e-mail: kristin@intnet.net

Western USA and West Canada: *Richard L Ayer*
127 Avenida del Mar, Suite 2A,
San Clemente, California 92672, USA
Tel: (+1 949) 366 84 55   Fax: (+1 949) 366 92 89
e-mail: ayercomm@earthlink.net

Administration:
USA and Canada: *Maureen Nute*
Jane's Information Group Inc, 1340 Braddock Place, Suite 300, Alexandria, Virginia 22314-1651, USA
Tel: (+1 703) 683 37 00   Fax: (+1 703) 836 00 29
e-mail: nute@janes.com

UK and Rest of World: *Joni Beeden*
Jane's Information Group Limited, Sentinel House, 163 Brighton Road, Coulsdon, Surrey CR5 2YH, UK
Tel: (+44 20) 87 00 37 42   Fax: (+44 20) 87 00 38 59
e-mail: joni.beeden@janes.co.uk

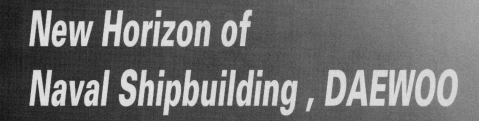

New Horizon of
Naval Shipbuilding , DAEWOO

**As a leading shipbuilder for existing classes
of proven major warships for the ROK Navy,
we`re setting a new pace for the future in
warship technology.**

- **Destroyers, Frigates, Corvettes**
- **OPVs, Patrol boats,**
- **Rescue ship, Various support ships**
- **Submarines**

Alphabetical list of advertisers

PREPARING FOR THE 21ST CENTURY

We know what advanced navies
in the world require to reinforce defense
system for the 21st Century.

HYUNDAI always aims to take initiative in
complying with those requirements with
Top Quality and Cost Efficiency.

Ensigns and Flags of the World's Navies

In cases where countries do not have ensigns their warships normally fly the national flag.

Albania
Ensign

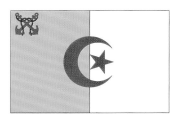

Algeria
Ensign

Angola
National Flag

Anguilla
Ensign

Antigua
National Flag

Argentina
National Flag and Ensign

Australia
Ensign

Austria
Ensign

Azerbaijan
National Flag

Bahamas
Ensign

Bahrain
National Flag

Bangladesh
Ensign

Barbados
Ensign

Belgium
Ensign

Belize
National Flag

Benin
National Flag

Bermuda
National Flag

Bolivia
Ensign

Brazil
National Flag and Ensign

Brunei
Ensign

Bulgaria
Ensign

Burma
National Flag and Ensign

Cambodia
National Flag

Cameroon
National Flag

Canada
National Flag

Cape Verde
National Flag

Chile
National Flag and Ensign

China, People's Republic
Ensign

Colombia
Ensign

Comoro Islands
National Flag

Congo
National Flag

Congo, Democratic Republic
National Flag

Cook Islands
National Flag

Costa Rica
Ensign

Croatia
National Flag

Cuba
National Flag and Ensign

Cyprus, Republic
National Flag

Cyprus, Turkish Republic
(Not recognised by United Nations)
Ensign

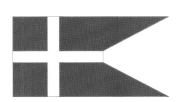

Denmark
Ensign

Djibouti
National Flag

Dominica
National Flag

Dominican Republic
Ensign

Ecuador
National Flag and Ensign

Egypt
Ensign

El Salvador
National Flag and Ensign

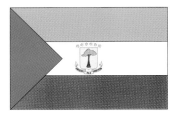

Equatorial Guinea
National Flag

Eritrea
National Flag

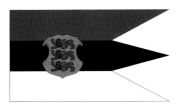

Estonia
Ensign

Falkland Islands
Falkland Islands Flag

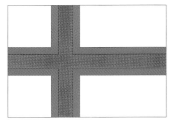

Faroes
The Islands Flag

Fiji
Ensign

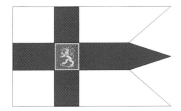

Finland
Ensign

France
National Flag and Ensign

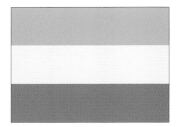

Gabon
National Flag

Gambia
National Flag

Georgia
National Flag

Germany
Ensign

Ghana
Ensign

Greece
National Flag and Ensign

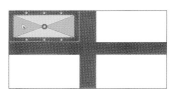

Grenada
Ensign

Guatemala
National Flag and Ensign

Guinea
National Flag

Guinea-Bissau
National Flag

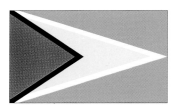

Guyana
National Flag

Haiti
State Flag and Ensign

Honduras
Ensign

Hungary
National Flag

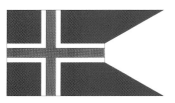

Iceland
Ensign

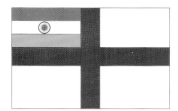

India
Ensign

Indonesia
National Flag and Ensign

Iran
National Flag

Iraq
National Flag

Republic of Ireland
National Flag and Ensign

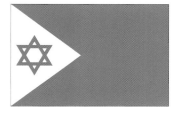

Israel
Ensign

Italy
Ensign

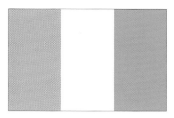

Ivory Coast
National Flag

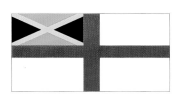

Jamaica
Ensign

Japan
Japan (Navy) Ensign

Japan
Japan (MSA) Ensign

Jordan
Ensign

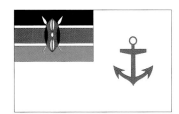

Kenya
Ensign

Korea, North
National Flag

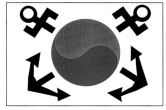

Korea, South
Ensign

Kuwait
National Flag

Laos
National Flag

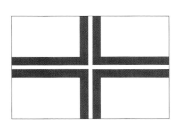

Latvia
Ensign

Lebanon
National Flag

Liberia
National Flag and Ensign

Libya
National Flag

Lithuania
Ensign

Madagascar
National Flag

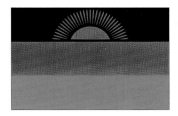

Malawi
National Flag

Malaysia
Ensign

Maldives
National Flag

Mali
National Flag

Malta
National Flag

Mauritania
National Flag

Mauritius
Ensign

Mexico
National Flag and Ensign

Morocco
Ensign

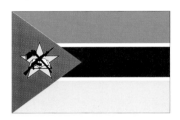

Mozambique
National Flag

NATO
Flag of the North Atlantic Treaty Organization

Netherlands
National Flag and Ensign

New Zealand
Ensign

Nicaragua
National Flag and Ensign

Nigeria
Ensign

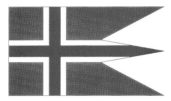

Norway
Ensign

Oman
Ensign

Pakistan
Ensign

Panama
National Flag and Ensign

Papua New Guinea
Ensign

Paraguay
National Flag and Ensign

Paraguay
National Flag and Ensign (reverse)

Peru
Ensign

Philippines
National Flag

Poland
Ensign

Portugal
National Flag and Ensign

Qatar
National Flag

Romania
National Flag and Ensign

Russia
Ensign

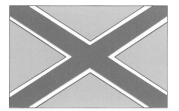

Russia
Border Guard Ensign

St Kitts-Nevis
Ensign

St Lucia
National Flag

St Vincent
National Flag

Saudi Arabia
Ensign

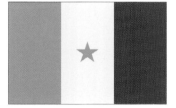

Senegal
National Flag

Seychelles
National Flag

Sierre Leone
Ensign

Singapore
Ensign

Slovenia
Ensign

Solomon Islands
National Flag

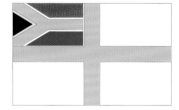

South Africa
Ensign

Spain
National Flag and Ensign

Sri Lanka
Ensign

Sudan
National Flag

Surinam
National Flag

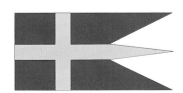

Sweden
Ensign and Jack

Switzerland
National Flag

Syria
National Flag

Taiwan
National Flag and Ensign

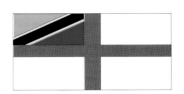

Tanzania
Ensign

Thailand
Ensign

Togo
National Flag

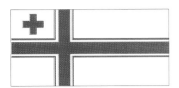

Tonga
Ensign

Trinidad and Tobago
Ensign

Tunisia
National Flag

Turkey
National Flag and Ensign

Uganda
National Flag

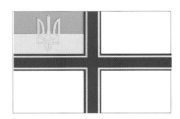

Ukraine
Ensign

United Arab Emirates
National Flag

United Kingdom
Ensign

United States of America
National Flag and Ensign

Uruguay
National Flag and Ensign

Vanuatu
Ensign

Venezuela
National Flag and Ensign

Vietnam
National Flag

Virgin Islands
National Flag

Western Samoa
National Flag

Yemen
National Flag

Yugoslavia
National Flag

Ranks and Insignia of the World's Navies

Where possible, the rank titles are shown in the language of the relevant country followed by the equivalent ranks in English.

The sleeves are drawn to one scale and the shoulder insignia to another allowing respective comparisons of size to be made. The exception to this is Croatia where badges worn on the right breast of the uniforms are depicted.

Albania

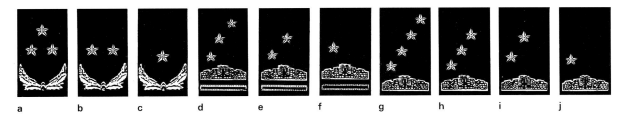

a: *Admiral*, Admiral   **b:** *Nenadmiral*, Vice Admiral   **c:** *Klinderadmiral*, Rear Admiral   **d:** *Kapiten I Rangut Te Pare*, Captain   **e:** *Kapiten I Rangut Te Dyte*, Commander
f: *Kapiten I Rangut Te Trete*, Lieutenant Commander   **g:** *Kapiten Leitnant I Pare*, Senior Lieutenant   **h:** *Kapiten Leitnant*, Lieutenant   **i:** *Leitnant*, Sub Lieutenant
j: *Nen Leitnant*, Acting Sub Lieutanant

Silver stars and gold braid on black. Four lowest ranks have silver stars, all other (higher) ranks have gold stars.

Algeria (Marine de la République Algérienne Démocratique et Populaire)

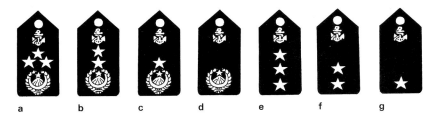

a: *'Amid*, Admiral   **b:** *'Aqid*, Captain   **c:** *Muqaddam*, Commander   **d:** *Ra'id*, Lieutenant Commander
e: *Naqid*, Lieutenant   **f:** *Mulazim Awwal*, Sub Lieutenant
g: *Mulazim*, Acting Sub Lieutenant

Gold on navy blue.

Angola (Marinha di Guerra)

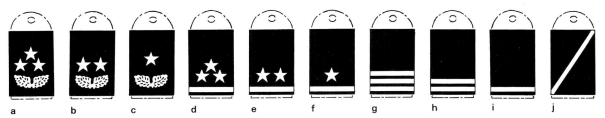

a: *Almirante*, Admiral   **b:** *Vice-Almirante*, Vice Admiral   **c:** *Contra-Almirante*, Rear Admiral   **d:** *Capitão-de-Mar-e-Guerra*, Captain   **e:** *Capitão-de-Fragata*, Commander
f: *Capitão-de-Corveta*, Lieutenant Commander   **g:** *Tenente-de-Navio*, Lieutenant   **h:** *Tenente-de-Fragata*, Sub Lieutenant   **i:** *Tenente-de-Corveta*, Acting Sub Lieutenant
j: *Aspirante*, Cadet

Admiral to Lieutenant Commander, gold on navy blue. Lieutenant to Sub Lieutenant, silver on navy blue. Midshipman and Cadet, light blue on navy blue.

Argentina (Armada República Argentina)

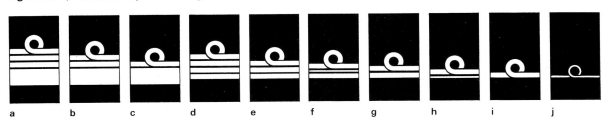

a: *Almirante*, Admiral   **b:** *Vicealmirante*, Vice Admiral   **c:** *Contraalmirante*, Rear Admiral   **d:** *Capitán de Navío*, Captain   **e:** *Capitán de Fragata*, Commander
f: *Capitán de Corbeta*, Lieutenant Commander   **g:** *Teniente de Navío*, Lieutenant   **h:** *Teniente de Fragata*, Sub Lieutenant   **i:** *Teniente de Corbeta*, Acting Lieutenant
j: *Guardiamarina*, Midshipman

Gold on navy blue.

Argentina (Coast Guard) (Prefectura Naval Argentina)

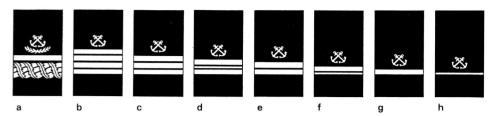

a: *Prefecto General*, Rear Admiral   **b:** *Prefecto Mayor*, Captain   **c:** *Prefecto Principal*, Commander   **d:** *Prefecto*, Lieutenant Commander
e: *Subprefecto*, Lieutenant   **f:** *Oficial Principal*, Sub Lieutenant   **g:** *Oficial Auxiliar*, Acting Sub Lieutenant   **h:** *Oficial Ayudante*, Midshipman

Gold on navy blue.

Australia

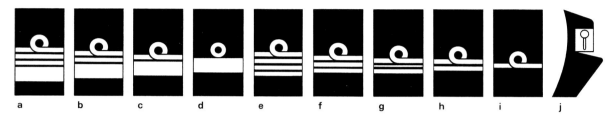

a: Admiral   **b:** Vice Admiral   **c:** Rear Admiral   **d:** Commodore   **e:** Captain   **f:** Commander   **g:** Lieutenant Commander   **h:** Lieutenant
i: Sub Lieutenant   **j:** Midshipman

Gold on navy blue.

Bahamas (Royal Bahamas Defence Force (Naval Division))

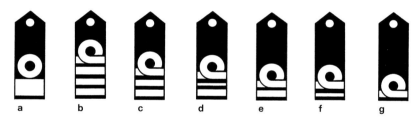

a: Commodore   **b:** Captain   **c:** Commander   **d:** Lieutenant Commander   **e:** Lieutenant
f: Junior Lieutenant   **g:** Sub Lieutenant

Gold on black.

Bahrain Coast Guard

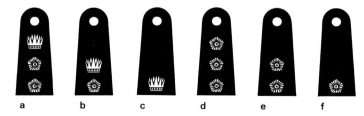

a: *'Aqid*, Colonel   **b:** *Muqaddam*, Lieutenant Colonel   **c:** *Ra'id*, Major   **d:** *Naqib*, Captain
e: *Mulazim Awwal*, Lieutenant   **f:** *Mulazim Thani*, Second Lieutenant

Gold and red on navy blue.

Bangladesh

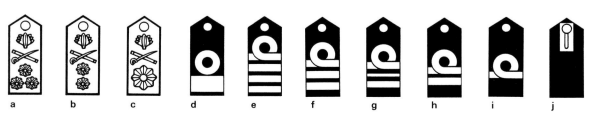

a: Admiral   **b:** Vice Admiral   **c:** Rear Admiral   **d:** Commodore   **e:** Captain   **f:** Commander   **g:** Lieutenant Commander   **h:** Lieutenant
i: Sub Lieutenant   **j:** Midshipman

Gold on navy blue. Flag ranks, gold edged blue. silver devices. White patch on midshipman's shoulder strap.

Barbados (Coast Guard)

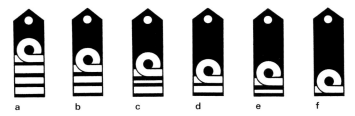

a: Captain   **b:** Commander   **c:** Lieutenant Commander   **d:** Lieutenant
e: Junior Lieutenant   **f:** Sub Lieutenant

Gold on black.

Belgium (Zeemacht/La Force Navale)

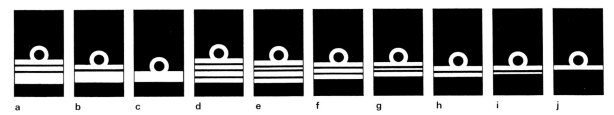

a: *Vice-Admiraal/Vice Amiral*, Vice Admiral   **b:** *Divisie-Admiraal/Amiral de Division*, Rear Admiral   **c:** *Commodore/Commodore*, Commodore
d: *Kapitein-ter-Zee/Capitaine de Vaisseau*, Captain   **e:** *Fregatkapitein/Capitaine de Frégate*, Commander   **f:** *Corvetkapitein/Capitaine de Corvette*,
Lieutenant Commander   **g:** *Luitenant-ter-Zee 1ste Klasse/Lieutenant de Vaisseau 1re Classe*, Senior Lieutenant   **h:** *Luitenant-ter-Zee/Lieutenant de Vaisseau*,
Lieutenant   **i:** *Vaandrig-ter-Zee/Enseigne de Vaisseau*, Sub Lieutenant
j: *Vaandrig-ter-Zee 2e Klasse/Enseigne de Vaisseau 2e Classe*, Acting Sub Lieutenant

Ranks given in Flemish, French and English. Gold on navy blue.

Benin (Marine du Bénin)

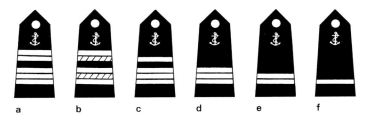

a: *Capitaine de Vaisseau*, Captain   **b:** *Capitaine de Frégate*, Commander   **c:** *Capitaine de Corvette*,
Lieutenant Commander   **d:** *Lieutenant de Vaisseau*, Lieutenant   **e:** *Enseigne de Vaisseau 1re Classe*,
Sub Lieutenant   **f:** *Enseigne de Vaisseau 2e Classe*, Acting Sub Lieutenant

Gold on black. Commander, three gold, two silver stripes.

Bolivia

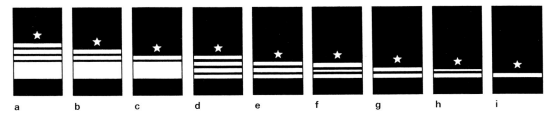

a: *Almirante*, Admiral   **b:** *Vicealmirante*, Vice Admiral   **c:** *Contraalmirante*, Rear Admiral   **d:** *Capitán de Navío*, Captain
e: *Capitán de Fragata*, Commander   **f:** *Capitán de Corbeta*, Lieutenant Commander   **g:** *Teniente de Navío*, Lieutenant
h: *Teniente de Fragata*, Sub Lieutenant   **i:** *Alférez*, Acting Sub Lieutenant

Gold on navy blue.

Brazil (Marinha do Brasil)

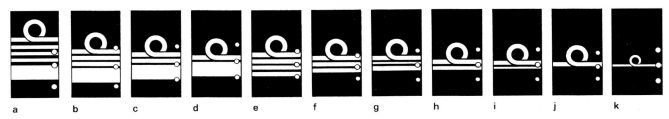

a: *Almirante*, Admiral of the fleet   **b:** *Almirante de Esquadra*, Admiral   **c:** *Vice-Almirante*, Vice Admiral   **d:** *Contra-Almirante*, Rear Admiral   **e:** *Capitão-de-Mar-e-Guerra*,
Captain   **f:** *Capitão-de-Fragata*, Commander   **g:** *Capitão-de-Corveta*, Lieutenant Commander   **h:** *Capitão-Tenente*, Lieutenant   **i:** *Primero Tenente*, Sub Lieutenant
j: *Segundo Tenente*, Acting Sub Lieutenant   **k:** *Guarda-Marinha*, Midshipman

Gold on dark blue.

British Virgin Islands (Police – Marine Branch)

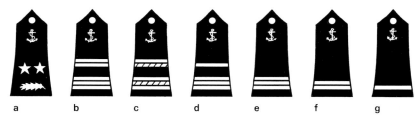

a: Chief Inspector **b:** Inspector **c:** Station Sergeant **d:** Sergeant
e: Constable

Silver on black.

Brunei (Angkatan Tentera Laut Diraja Brunei)

a: *Colonel*, Captain **b:** *Lieutenant Colonel*, Commander **c:** *Major*, Lieutenant Commander
d: *Captain*, Lieutenant **e:** *Lieutenant*, Sub Lieutenant **f:** 2nd *Lieutenant*, Acting Sub Lieutenant
g: *Officer Cadet*, Midshipman

Gold on navy blue.

Bulgaria

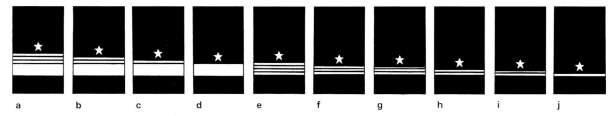

a: *Admiral*, Admiral **b:** *Vitseadmiral*, Vice Admiral **c:** *Kontraadmiral*, Rear Admiral **d:** *Kapitan I Rang*, Captain **e:** *Kapitan II Rang*, Commander
f: *Kapitan III Rang*, Lieutenant Commander **g:** *Kapitan Leytenant*, Lieutenant **h:** *Starshi Leytenant*, Junior Lieutenant **i:** *Leytenant*, Sub Lieutenant
j: *Mladshi Leytenant*, Acting Sub Lieutenant

Burma

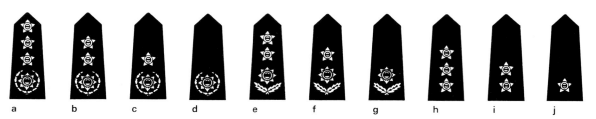

a: Admiral **b:** Vice Admiral **c:** Rear Admiral **d:** Commodore **e:** Captain **f:** Commander **g:** Lieutenant Commander **h:** Lieutenant **i:** Sub Lieutenant
j: Acting Sub Lieutenant

Gold on dark blue. All three services have same rank insignia based on the army.

Cambodia

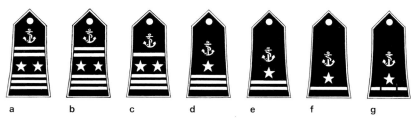

a: *Contre-Amiral*, Rear Admiral **b:** *Capitaine de Vaisseau*, Captain **c:** *Capitaine de Frégate*, Commander
d: *Capitaine de Corvette*, Lieutenant Commander **e:** *Lieutenant de Vaisseau*, Lieutenant
f: *Enseigne de Vaisseau 1re Classe*, Sub Lieutenant **g:** *Enseigne de Vaisseau 2e Classe*, Acting Sub Lieutenant

Silver stars, gold anchor and palm on navy blue.

Cameroon (Marine Nationale République du Cameroun

a: *Capitaine de Vaisseau*, Captain **b:** *Capitaine de Frégate*, Commander **c:** *Capitaine de Corvette*,
Lieutenant Commander **d:** *Lieutenant de Vaisseau*, Lieutenant **e:** *Enseigne de Vaisseau 1re Classe*, Sub Lieutenant
f: *Enseigne de Vaisseau 2e Class*, Acting Sub Lieutenant **g:** *Aspirant*, Midshipman

Gold on navy blue. Top two stripes for Commander, silver. Thin green edging on shoulder straps.

Canada (Maritime Command)

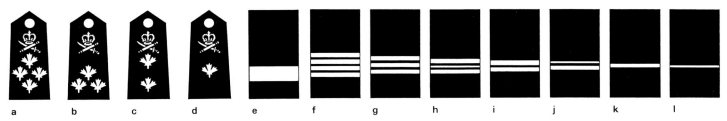

a b c d e f g h i j k l

a: Admiral   **b:** Vice Admiral   **c:** Rear Admiral   **d:** Commodore   **e:** All Flag Ranks   **f:** Captain   **g:** Commander   **h:** Lieutenant Commander   **i:** Lieutenant   **j:** Sub Lieutenant
k: Acting Sub Lieutenant   **l:** Officer Cadet

Gold on black.

Canada (Coast Guard)

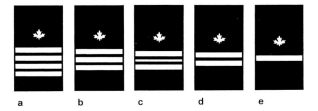

a b c d e

a: Commanding Officer   **b:** Chief Officer   **c:** First Officer   **d:** Second Officer
e: Third Officer Rank structure for large ships only.

Gold on navy blue.

Chile (Armada de Chile)

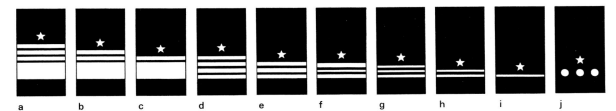

a b c d e f g h i j

a: *Almirante*, Admiral   **b:** *Vicealmirante*, Vice Admiral   **c:** *Contraalmirante*, Rear Admiral   **d:** *Capitán de Navío*, Captain   **e:** *Capitán de Fragata*, Commander
f: *Capitán de Corbeta*, Lieutenant Commander   **g:** *Teniente Primero*, Lieutenant   **h:** *Teniente Segundo*, Junior Lieutenant   **i:** *Sub Teniente*, Sub Lieutenant
j: *Guardia Marina*, Midshipman

Gold on black.

China (People's Liberation Army Navy)

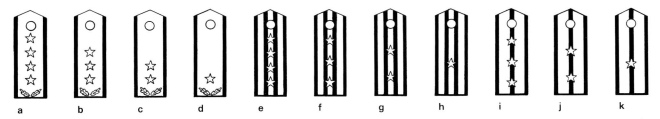

a b c d e f g h i j k

a: *Senior General*, Admiral of the Fleet   **b:** *General*, Admiral   **c:** *Lieutenant General*, Vice Admiral   **d:** *Major General*, Rear Admiral   **e:** *Senior Colonel*, Commodore
f: *Colonel*, Captain   **g:** *Lieutenant Colonel*, Commander   **h:** *Major Colonel*, Lieutenant Commander   **i:** *Captain*, Lieutenant   **j:** *Lieutenant*, Sub Lieutenant
k: *Second Lieutenant*, Acting Sub Lieutenant

Generals, gold edged dark blue. Gold button. Silver stars. Senior Colonel to Major Colonel two dark blue stripes. Captain to Second Lieutenant one dark blue stripe.

Colombia (Armada de la Republica de Colombia)

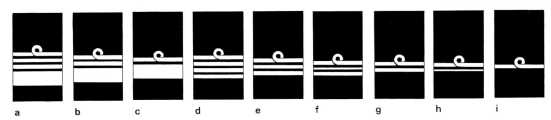

a b c d e f g h i

a: *Almirante*, Admiral   **b:** *Vicealmirante*, Vice Admiral   **c:** *Contraalmirante*, Rear Admiral   **d:** *Capitán de Navío*, Captain   **e:** *Capitán de Fragata*, Commander
f: *Capitán de Corbeta*, Lieutenant Commander   **g:** *Teniente de Navío*, Lieutenant   **h:** *Teniente de Fragata*, Sub Lieutenant   **i:** *Teniente de Corbeta*,
Acting Sub Lieutenant

Gold on black.

Congo

a: *Capitaine de Vaisseau*, Captain   **b:** *Capitaine de Frégate*, Commander   **c:** *Capitaine de Corvette*,
Lieutenant Commander   **d:** *Lieutenant de Vaisseau*, Lieutenant   **e:** *Enseigne de Vaisseau 1re Classe*, Sub Lieutenant
f: *Enseigne de Vaisseau 2e Classe*, Acting Sub Lieutenant

Captain three red stars, Commander one gold over two red stars, Lieutenant Commander one red star, remainder red stars, all on black.

Congo, Democratic Republic

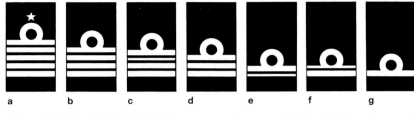

a: *Contre-Amiral*, Rear Admiral   **b:** *Capitaine de Vaisseau*, Captain   **c:** *Capitaine de Frégate*, Commander
d: *Capitaine de Corvette*, Lieutenant Commander   **e:** *Lieutenant de Vaisseau*, Lieutenant   **f:** *Enseigne de
Vaisseau 1re Classe*, Sub Lieutenant   **g:** *Enseigne de Vaisseau 2e Classe*, Acting Sub Lieutenant

Gold on black.

Costa Rica (Guardia Civil Sección Maritime)

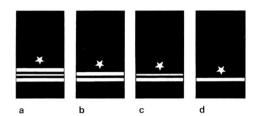

a: *Major*, Lieutenant Commander   **b:** *Capitan*, Lieutenant
c: *Teniente*, Sub Lieutenant   **d:** *Sub Teniente*, Acting Sub Lieutenant

Gold on navy blue.

Croatia (Hrvatska Ratna Mornarica)

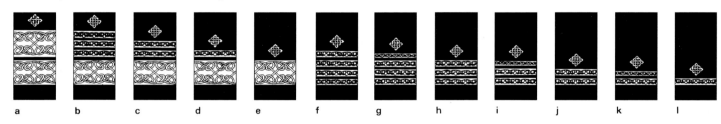

a: *Stožerni Admiral*, Admiral of the Fleet   **b:** *Admiral*, Admiral   **c:** *Viceadmiral*, Vice Admiral   **d:** *Kontraadmiral*, Rear Admiral   **e:** *Komodor*, Commodore   **f:** *Kapetan Bojnog Broda*,
Captain   **g:** *Kapetan Fregate*, Commander   **h:** *Kapetan Korvete*, Lieutenant Commander   **i:** *Poručnik Bojnog Broda*, Lieutenant   **j:** *Poručnik Fregate*, Sub Lieutenant   **k:** *Poručnik
Korvete*, Acting Sub Lieutenant   **l:** *Zastavnik*, Midshipman

Gold on navy blue.

Cuba (Marina de Guerra Revolucionaria)

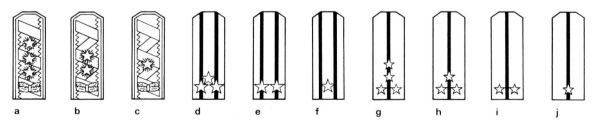

a: *Almirante*, Admiral   **b:** *Vicealmirante*, Vice Admiral   **c:** *Contraalmirante*, Rear Admiral   **d:** *Capitán de Navío*, Captain   **e:** *Capitán de Frégata*, Commander
f: *Capitán de Corbeta*, Lieutenant Commander   **g:** *Teniente de Navío*, Senior Lieutenant   **h:** *Teniente de Frégata*, Lieutenant   **i:** *Teniente de Corbeta*, Sub Lieutenant
j: *Alférez*, Acting Sub Lieutenant

Black stripes. Admirals, gold stars on blue design.

Cyprus

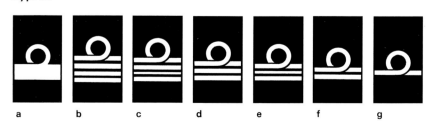

a: *Archipliarchos*, Commodore   **b:** *Pilarchos*, Captain   **c:** *Antipliarchos*, Commander   **d:** *Plotarchis*,
Lieutenant Commander   **e:** *Ypopliarchos*, Lieutenant   **f:** *Anthypopliarchos*, Sub Lieutenant
g: *Simaioforos*, Acting Sub Lieutenant

Gold on navy blue.

Denmark (Søvaernet)

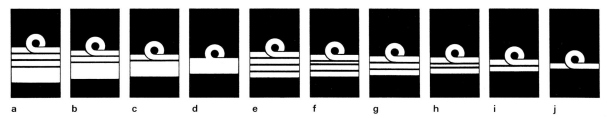

a   b   c   d   e   f   g   h   i   j

a: *Admiral,* Admiral   **b:** *Viceadmiral,* Vice Admiral   **c:** *Kontreadmiral,* Rear Admiral   **d:** *Flotilleadmiral,* Commodore   **e:** *Kommandør,* Captain
f: *Kommandørkaptajn,* Senior Commander   **g:** *Orlogskaptajn,* Commander   **h:** *Kaptajnløjtnant,* Lieutenant Commander   **i:** *Premierløjtnant,* Lieutenant
j: *Løjtnant,* Junior Grade Lieutenant

Gold on black.

Djibouti

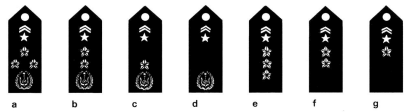

a   b   c   d   e   f   g

a: *Brigadier,* Commodore   **b:** *Colonel,* Captain   **c:** *Lieutenant Colonel,* Commander   **d:** *Major,* Lieutenant Commander
e: *Captain,* Lieutenant   **f:** *Lieutenant,* Sub Lieutenant   **g:** *2nd Lieutenant,* Acting Sub Lieutenant

Gold crest, gold stripes, red star. Rank device silver.

Dominican Republic (Marina de Guerra)

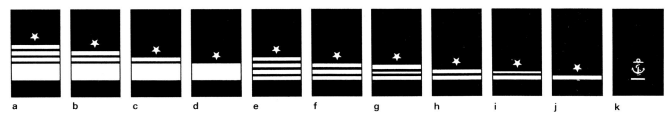

a   b   c   d   e   f   g   h   i   j   k

a: *Almirante,* Admiral   **b:** *Vicealmirante,* Vice Admiral   **c:** *Contraalmirante,* Rear Admiral   **d:** *Comodoro,* Commodore   **e:** *Capitán de Navío,* Captain
f: *Capitán de Fragata,* Commander   **g:** *Capitán de Corbeta,* Lieutenant Commander   **h:** *Teniente de Navío,* Lieutenant   **i:** *Alférez de Navío,* Sub Lieutenant
j: *Alférez de Fragata,* Acting Sub Lieutenant   **k:** *Guardiamarina,* Midshipman

Gold on black.

Ecuador (Armada de Guerra)

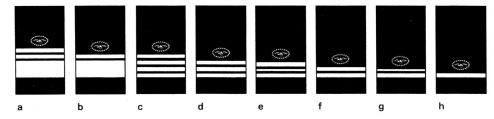

a   b   c   d   e   f   g   h

a: *Vicealmirante,* Vice Admiral   **b:** *Contraalmirante,* Rear Admiral   **c:** *Capitán de Navío,* Captain   **d:** *Capitán de Fragata,* Commander
e: *Capitán de Corbeta,* Lieutenant Commander   **f:** *Teniente de Fragata,* Lieutenant   **g:** *Alférez de Navío,* Sub Lieutenant
h: *Alférez de Fragata,* Acting Sub Lieutenant

Gold on black.

Egypt

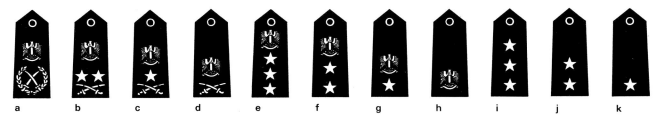

a   b   c   d   e   f   g   h   i   j   k

a: *Mushir,* Admiral of the Fleet   **b:** *Fariq Awwal,* Admiral   **c:** *Fariq,* Vice Admiral   **d:** *Liwa',* Rear Admiral   **e:** *'Amid,* Commodore   **f:** *'Aqid,* Captain
g: *Muqaddam,* Commander   **h:** *Ra'id,* Lieutenant Commander   **i:** *Naqib,* Lieutenant   **j:** *Mulazim Awwal,* Sub Lieutenant   **k:** *Mulazim,* Acting Sub Lieutenant

Gold on black. Shield on eagle's breast black, white and red.

El Salvador (Fuerza Naval de El Salvador)

a: *Vice Almirante,* Vice Admiral   **b:** *Contra Almirante,* Rear Admiral   **c:** *Capitan de Navio,* Captain   **d:** *Capitan de Fragata,* Commander
e: *Capitan de Corbeta,* Lieutenant Commander   **f:** *Teniente de Navio,* Lieutenant   **g:** *Teniente de Fragata,* Sub Lieutenant
h: *Teniente de Corbeta,* Acting Sub Lieutenant

Gold on navy blue. Admirals shoulder straps are gold with navy blue edges. Stars and anchors are silver.

Estonia (Mereväe Ülem)

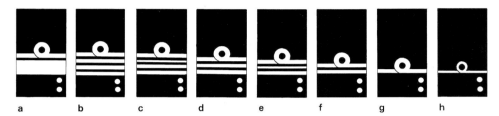

a: *Kontradmiral,* Rear Admiral   **b:** *Mereväe-kapten,* Captain   **c:** *Kapten-leitnant,* Commander   **d:** *Kapten-major,*
Lieutenant Commander   **e:** *Vanem-leitnant,* Senior Lieutenant   **f:** *Leitnant,* Lieutenant   **g:** *Noorem-leitnant,* Sub Lieutenant
h: *Lipnik,* Acting Sub Lieutenant

Fiji (Republic of Fiji Military Forces Navy Element)

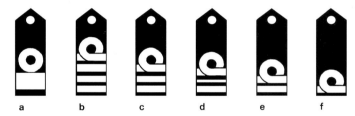

a: Commodore   **b:** Captain   **c:** Commander   **d:** Lieutenant Commander   **e:** Lieutenant   **f:** Sub Lieutenant

Finland (Suomen Merivoimat)

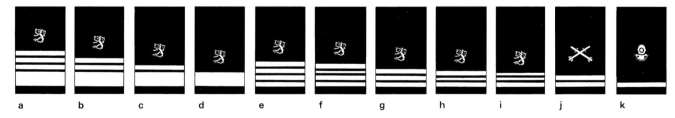

a: *Amiraali,* Admiral   **b:** *Vara-amiraali,* Vice Admiral   **c:** *Kontra-amiraali,* Rear Admiral   **d:** *Lippue-amiraali,* Commodore   **e:** *Kommodori,* Captain   **f:** *Komentaja,*
Commander   **g:** *Komentajakapteeni,* Lieutenant Commander   **h:** *Kapteeniluutnantti,* Senior Lieutenant   **i:** *Yliluutnantti,* Lieutenant   **j:** *Luutnantti,* Junior Lieutenant
k: *Aliluutnantti,* Sub Lieutenant

Gold on black.

France (Marine Nationale)

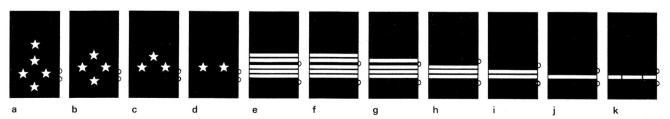

a: *Amiral,* Admiral of the Fleet   **b:** *Vice-Amiral d'Escadre,* Admiral   **c:** *Vice-Amiral,* Vice Admiral   **d:** *Contre-Amiral,* Rear Admiral   **e:** *Capitaine de Vaisseau,* Captain
f: *Capitaine de Frégate,* Commander   **g:** *Capitaine de Corvette,* Lieutenant Commander   **h:** *Lieutenant de Vaisseau,* Lieutenant   **i:** *Enseigne de Vaisseau de 1re Classe,*
Sub Lieutenant   **j:** *Enseigne de Vaisseau de 2e Classe,* Acting Sub Lieutenant   **k:** *Aspirant,* Midshipman

Flag ranks, silver stars. Captain, gold. Commander, three gold two silver. Lieutenant Commander to Midshipman, gold. Vertical stripes on Midshipman's lace, mid blue.
All on dark blue.

Gabon (Marine Gabonaise)

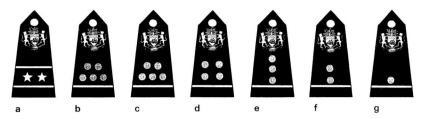

a: *Commodore,* Commodore   **b:** *Colonel,* Captain   **c:** *Lieutenant Colonel,* Commander
d: *Commandant,* Lieutenant Commander   **e:** *Capitaine,* Lieutenant   **f:** *Lieutenant,* Sub Lieutenant
g: *Sous Lieutenant,* Acting Sub Lieutenant

Devices gold on navy blue. Lieutenant Colonel top two discs, silver.

Germany (Deutsche Marine)

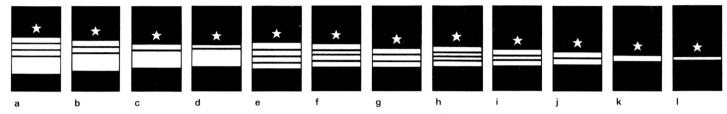

a: *Admiral,* Admiral   **b:** *Viceadmiral,* Vice Admiral   **c:** *Konteradmiral,* Rear Admiral   **d:** *Flottillenadmiral,* Commodore   **e:** *Kapitan zur See,* Captain   **f:** *Fregattenkapitan,*
Commander   **g:** *Korvettenkapitan,* Lieutenant Commander   **h:** *Stabskapitanleutnant,* Senior Lieutenant   **i:** *Kapitanleutnant,* Lieutenant   **j:** *Oberleutnant zur See,*
Sub Lieutenant   **k:** *Leutnant zur See,* Acting Sub Lieutenant   **l:** *Oberfahnrich zur See,* Midshipman

Gold on navy blue.

Germany Coast Guard (Bundesgrenzschutz See)

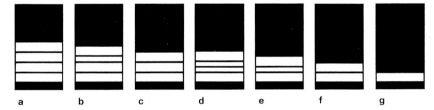

a: *Polizeidirektor im BGS,* Captain   **b:** *Polizeioberrat im BGS,* Commander   **c:** *Polizeirat im BGS,* Lieutenant Commander
d: *Erster Polizeihauptkommissar im BGS,* Senior Lieutenant   **e:** *Polizeihauptkommissar im BGS,* Lieutenant
f: *Polizeioberkommissar im BGS,* Sub Lieutenant   **g:** *Polizeikommissar im BGS,* Acting Sub Lieutenant

Gold on navy blue.

Ghana

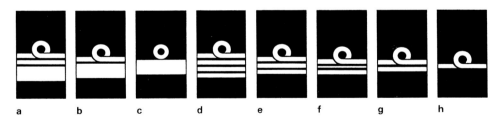

a: Vice Admiral   **b:** Rear Admiral   **c:** Commodore   **d:** Captain   **e:** Commander   **f:** Lieutenant Commander   **g:** Lieutenant
h: Sub Lieutenant

Gold on navy blue.

Greece (Hellenic Navy)

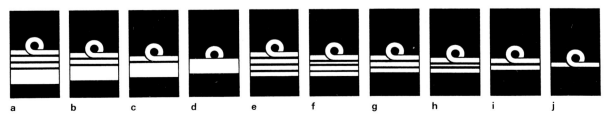

a: *Navarchos,* Admiral   **b:** *Antinavarchos,* Vice Admiral   **c:** *Yponavarchos,* Rear Admiral   **d:** *Archipliarchos,* Commodore   **e:** *Pliarchos,* Captain
f: *Antipliarchos,* Commander   **g:** *Plotarchis,* Lieutenant Commander   **h:** *Ypopliarchos,* Lieutenant   **i:** *Anthypopliarchos,* Sub Lieutenant
j: *Simaioforos, Acting* Sub Lieutenant

Gold on navy blue.

Greece (Coast Guard)

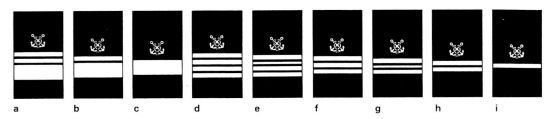

a   b   c   d   e   f   g   h   i

a: *Antinavarchos*, Vice Admiral **b:** *Yponavarchos*, Rear Admiral **c:** *Archipliarchos*, Commodore **d:** *Pliarchos*, Captain
e: *Antipliarchos*, Commander **f:** *Plotarchis*, Lieutenant Commander **g:** *Ypopliarchos*, Lieutenant **h:** *Anthypopliarchos*, Sub Lieutenant
i: *Simaioforos, Acting* Sub Lieutenant

Gold on navy blue.

Guatemala (Marina de Guatemala)

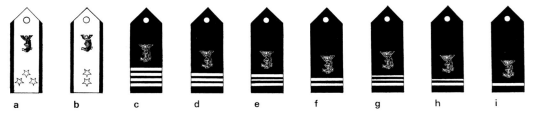

a   b   c   d   e   f   g   h   i

a: *Vicealmirante*, Admiral **b:** *Contraalmirante*, Vice Admiral **c:** *Capitán de Navío*, Captain **d:** *Capitán de Fragata*, Commander
e: *Capitán de Corbeta*, Lieutenant Commander **f:** *Teniente de Navío*, Lieutenant **g:** *Teniente de Fragata*, Sub Lieutenant
h: *Alférez de Navío*, Sub Lieutenant (JG) **i:** *Alférez de Fragata*, Acting Sub Lieutenant

Gold on navy blue. Fouled anchor and quetzal bird gold for officers – silver for admirals.

Guinea (Marine du Guinea)

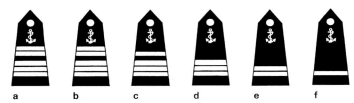

a   b   c   d   e   f

a: *Capitaine de Vaisseau*, Captain **b:** *Capitaine de Frégate*, Commander
c: *Capitaine de Corvette*, Lieutenant Commander **d:** *Lieutenant de Vaisseau*,
Lieutenant **e:** *Enseigne de Vaisseau 1re Classe*, Sub Lieutenant **f:** *Enseigne de
Vaisseau 2e Classe*, Acting Sub Lieutenant

Gold on black. Commander, three gold and two silver stripes.

Guinea-Bissau

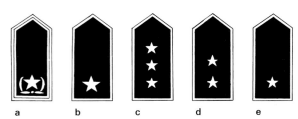

a   b   c   d   e

a: *Comandante*, Commander **b:** *Major*, Lieutenant Commander
c: *Capitao*, Lieutenant **d:** *Tenente*, Sub Lieutenant
e: *Alférez*, Acting Sub Lieutenant

Stars are silver. Piping and wreath in gold. Backing dark blue.

Haiti (Marine du Haiti)

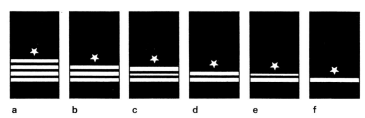

a   b   c   d   e   f

a: *Capitaine de Vaisseau*, Captain **b:** *Commandant*, Commander **c:** *Lieutenant Commandant*,
Lieutenant Commander **d:** *Lieutenant de Vaisseau*, Lieutenant **e:** *Sous Lieutenant de Vaisseau*,
Sub Lieutenant **f:** *Enseigne de Vaisseau*, Acting Sub Lieutenant

Gold on navy blue.

Honduras (Fuerza Naval Republica de Honduras)

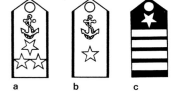

a   b   c   d   e   f   g   h

a: *Almirante*, Vice Admiral **b:** *Contralmirante*, Rear Admiral **c:** *Capitán de Navío*, Captain **d:** *Capitán de Fragata*,
Commander **e:** *Capitán de Corbeta*, Lieutenant Commander **f:** *Teniente de Navío*, Lieutenant **g:** *Teniente de Fragata*,
Sub Lieutenant **h:** *Alferez de Fragata*, Acting Sub Lieutenant

Gold on navy blue. Flag ranks, gold shoulder boards edged blue, silver devices.

Hungary

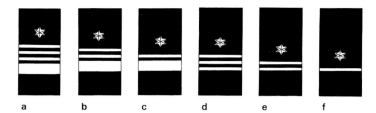

a: *Ezredes*, Captain   b: *Alezredes*, Commander   c: *Örnagy*, Lieutenant Commander
d: *Szazados*, Lieutenant   e: *Föhadnagy*, Sub Lieutenant   f: *Hadnagy*, Acting Sub Lieutenant

Gold lace on dark blue.

Iceland (Coast Guard)

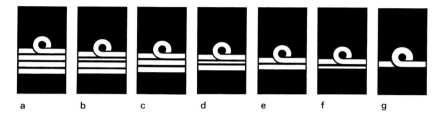

a: *Director General*, Captain   b: *Chief of Operations*, Senior Commander   c: *Captain and Chief Engineer*,
Commander   d: *Chief Mate and First Engineer*, Lieutenant Commander   e: *First Mate and Second Engineer*,
Lieutenant   f: *Second Mate and officers with less than six years' service*, Sub Lieutenant   g: *Officers with less
than two years' service*, Acting Sub Lieutenant

Gold on navy blue.

India

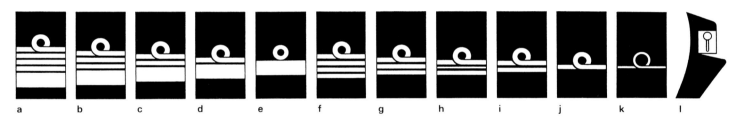

a: Admiral of the Fleet   b: Admiral   c: Vice Admiral   d: Rear Admiral   e: Commodore   f: Captain   g: Commander   h: Lieutenant Commander   i: Lieutenant
j: Sub Lieutenant   k: Commissioned Officer   l: Midshipman (Lapel)

Gold on navy blue.

India (Coast Guard)

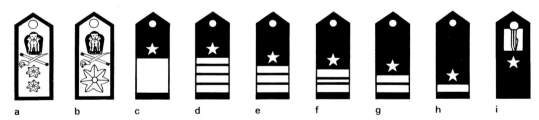

a: *Director General*, Vice Admiral   b: *Inspector General*, Rear Admiral   c: *Deputy Inspector General with 3 years' seniority*, Commodore
d: *Deputy Inspector General*, Captain   e: *Commandant*, Commander   f: *Deputy Commandant*, Lieutenant Commander
g: *Assistant Commandant*, Lieutenant   h: *Assistant Commandant under training after completion of Phase III afloat training and during sub courses*,
Acting Lieutenant   i: *Assistant Commandant under training after completion of Phase II afloat training*, Midshipman

Gold on navy blue. Silver sword crossed with silver baton, silver embroidered star with thin blue edgings.

Indonesia (Tentara Nasional Indonesia Angkatan Laut)

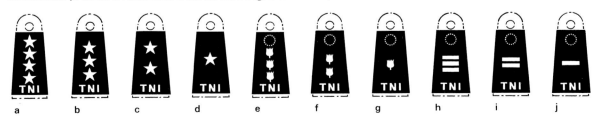

a: *Laksamana*, Admiral   b: *Laksdya*, Vice Admiral   c: *Laksda*, Rear Admiral   d: *Laksma*, Commodore   e: *Kolonel*, Captain   f: *Letnan Kolonel*, Commander
g: *Mayor*, Lieutenant Commander   h: *Kapten*, Senior Lieutenant   i: *Letnan Satu*, Lieutenant   j: *Letnan Dua*, Sub Lieutenant

Gold on medium blue.

Iran

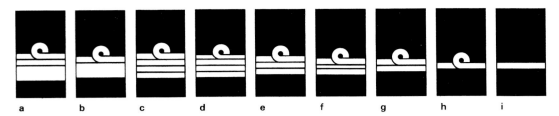

a: *Daryaban*, Vice Admiral **b:** *Daryadar*, Rear Admiral **c:** *Nakhoda Yekom*, Captain **d:** *Nakhoda Dovom*, Commander **e:** *Nakhoda Sevom*, Lieutenant Commander **f:** *Navsarvan*, Lieutenant **g:** *Navban Yekom*, Junior Lieutenant **h:** *Navban Dovom*, Sub Lieutenant **i:** *Navban Sevom*, Midshipman.

Gold on navy blue.

Iraq

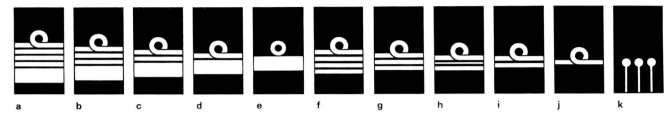

a: *Mushir*, Admiral of the Fleet **b:** *Fariq Awwal*, Admiral **c:** *Fariq*, Vice Admiral **d:** *Liwa'*, Rear Admiral **e:** *'Amid*, Commodore **f:** *'Aqid*, Captain **g:** *Muqaddam*, Commander **h:** *Ra'id*, Lieutenant Commander **i:** *Naqib*, Lieutenant **j:** *Mulazim Awwal*, Sub Lieutenant **k:** *Mulazim*, Midshipman

Gold on navy blue.

Republic of Ireland (An Seirbhis Chabhlaigh)

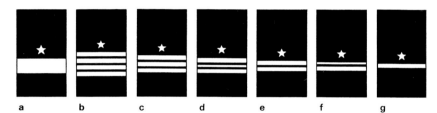

a: Commodore **b:** Captain **c:** Commander **d:** Lieutenant Commander **e:** Lieutenant **f:** Sub Lieutenant **g:** Ensign

Gold on navy blue.

Israel

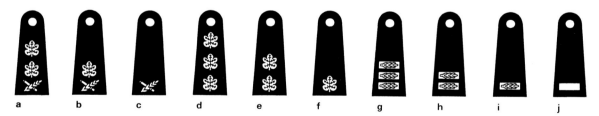

a: *General (Rav-Aluf)*, Admiral **b:** *Major General (Aluf)*, Vice Admiral **c:** *Brigadier (Tat-Aluf)*, Rear Admiral **d:** *Colonel (Alut-Mishneh)*, Captain **e:** *Lieutenant Colonel (Sgan-Aluf)*, Commander **f:** *Major, (Rav-Seren)*, Lieutenant Commander **g:** *Captain (Seren)*, Lieutenant **h:** *First Lieutenant (Segen)*, Sub Lieutenant **i:** *Second Lieutenant (Segen-Mishneh)*, Acting Sub Lieutenant **j:** *Officer Aspirant (Mamak)*, Officer Candidate

Bright brass or gold generally on dark blue or black. Officer Candidate, white bar.

Italy (Marina Militare)

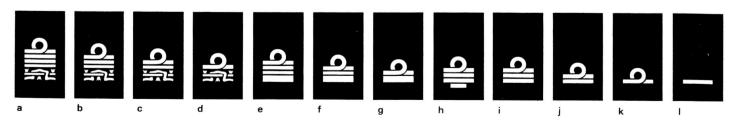

a: *Ammiraglio di Squadra con Incarichi Speciali*, Admiral Commanding Navy **b:** *Ammiraglio di Squadra e Ammiraglio Ispettore Capo*, Admiral and Senior Inspector General (Navy) **c:** *Ammiraglio di Divisione e Ammiraglio Ispettore*, Vice Admiral and Inspector General (Navy) **d:** *Contrammiraglio*, Rear Admiral **e:** *Capitano di Vascello*, Captain **f:** *Capitano di Fregata*, Commander **g:** *Capitano di Corvetta*, Lieutenant Commander **h:** *1° Tenente di Vascello*, First Lieutenant **i:** *Tenente di Vascello*, Lieutenant **j:** *Sottotenente di Vascello*, Sub Lieutenant **k:** *Guardiamarina*, Acting Sub Lieutenant **l:** *Aspirante Guardiamarina*, Midshipman

Gold on dark blue.

Ivory Coast (Marine Côte D'Ivoire)

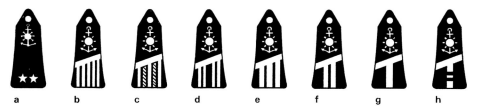

a: *Contre-Amiral,* Rear Admiral   **b:** *Capitaine de Vaisseau,* Captain   **c:** *Capitaine de Frégate,* Commander
d: *Capitaine de Corvette,* Lieutenant Commander   **e:** *Lieutenant de Vaisseau,* Lieutenant
f: *Enseigne de Vaisseau de 1re Classe,* Sub Lieutenant   **g:** *Enseigne de Vaisseau de 2e Classe,*
Acting Sub Lieutenant   **h:** *Aspirant,* Midshipman

Gold on black. Commander, gold and silver on black. Stars, silver.

Jamaica (Defence Force Coast Guard)

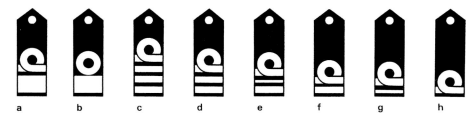

a: Rear Admiral   **b:** Commodore   **c:** Captain   **d:** Commander   **e:** Lieutenant Commander   **f:** Lieutenant
g: Junior Lieutenant   **h:** Ensign

Gold on black.

Japan (Maritime Self Defence Force)

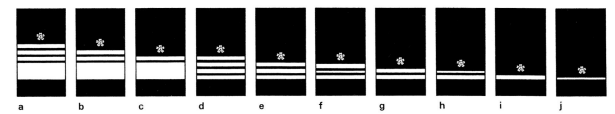

a: Admiral   **b:** Vice Admiral   **c:** Rear Admiral   **d:** Captain   **e:** Commander   **f:** Lieutenant Commander   **g:** Lieutenant   **h:** Sub Lieutenant
i: Acting Sub Lieutenant   **j:** Warrant Officer

Gold on navy blue.

Japan (Maritime Safety Agency)

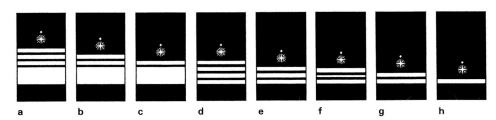

a: Commandant   **b:** Vice Commandant   **c:** Maritime Safety Superintendent First Grade   **d:** Maritime Safety Superintendent Second Grade
e: Maritime Safety Superintendent Third Grade   **f:** Maritime Safety Officer First Grade   **g:** Maritime Safety Officer Second Grade
h: Maritime Safety Officer Third Grade

Gold on navy blue.

Jordan

a: *'Amid,* Commodore   **b:** *'Aqid,* Captain   **c:** *Muqaddam,* Commander   **d:** *Ra'id,* Lieutenant Commander
e: *Naqib,* Lieutenant   **f:** *Mulazim Awwal,* Sub Lieutenant   **g:** *Mulazim,* Acting Sub Lieutenant

Khaki shoulder straps.

Kenya

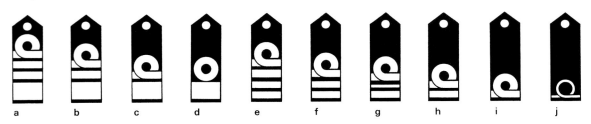

a: *General*, Admiral   **b:** *Lieutenant General*, Vice Admiral   **c:** *Major General*, Rear Admiral   **d:** *Brigadier*, Commodore   **e:** *Colonel*, Captain
f: *Lieutenant Colonel*, Commander   **g:** *Major*, Lieutenant Commander   **h:** *Captain*, Lieutenant   **i:** *Lieutenant*, Sub Lieutenant   **j:** *Second Lieutenant*,
Acting Sub Lieutenant

Gold on black.

Korea, People's Democratic Republic (North)

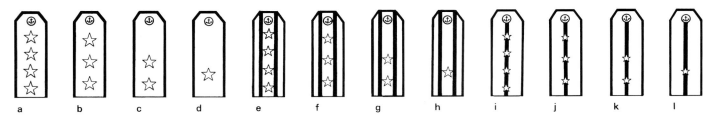

a: Admiral of the Fleet   **b:** Admiral   **c:** Vice Admiral   **d:** Rear Admiral   **e:** Commodore   **f:** Captain   **g:** Commander   **h:** Lieutenant Commander   **i:** Senior Lieutenant
j: Lieutenant   **k:** Sub Lieutenant   **l:** Acting Sub Lieutenant

Black stripes, silver stars on gold.

Korea, Republic (South)

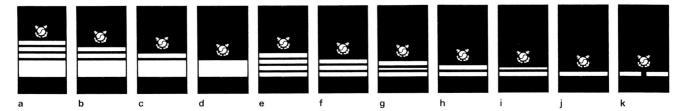

a: Admiral   **b:** Vice Admiral   **c:** Rear Admiral   **d:** Commodore   **e:** Captain   **f:** Commander   **g:** Lieutenant Commander   **h:** Lieutenant   **i:** Sub Lieutenant
j: Acting Sub Lieutenant   **k:** Warrant Officer

Gold on navy blue.

Kuwait

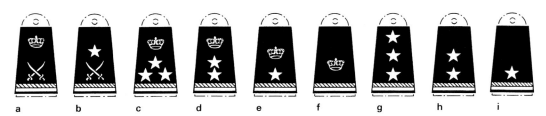

a: *Fariq*, Vice Admiral   **b:** *Liwa'*, Rear Admiral   **c:** *'Amid*, Commodore   **d:** *'Aqid*, Captain   **e:** *Muqaddam*, Commander
f: *Ra'id*, Lieutenant Commander   **g:** *Naqib*, Lieutenant   **h:** *Mulazim Awwal*, Sub Lieutenant   **i:** *Mulazim*, Acting Sub Lieutenant

Usually gold on tan. Can be gold on dark green or dark blue.

Latvia

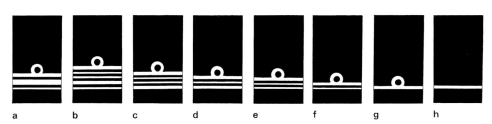

a: *Admirālis*, Admiral   **b:** *Jūraskapteinis*, Captain   **c:** *Komandkapteinis*, Commander Senior Grade   **d:** *Kapteinis*, Commander Junior Grade
e: *Kapteinleitnants*, Lieutenant Commander   **f:** *Virsleitnants*, Lieutenant   **g:** *Leitnants*, Lieutenant Junior Grade   **h:** *Virsniekvietnieks*, Warrant Officer

Lebanon

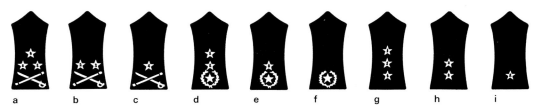

a: *'Imad*, Vice Admiral   **b:** *Liwa'*, Rear Admiral   **c:** *'Amid*, Commodore   **d:** *'Aqid*, Captain   **e:** *Muqaddam*, Commander
f: *Ra'id*, Lieutenant Commander   **g:** *Ra'is*, Lieutenant   **h:** *Mulazim Awwal*, Sub Lieutenant   **i:** *Mulazim*, Acting Sub Lieutenant

Gold on black.

Libya

a: *'Aqid*, Captain   **b:** *Muqaddam*, Commander   **c:** *Ra'id*, Lieutenant Commander   **d:** *Naqib*, Lieutenant
e: *Mulazim Awwal*, Sub Lieutenant   **f:** *Mulazim*, Acting Sub Lieutenant

Gold on navy blue.

Lithuania (Karines Juru Pajegos)

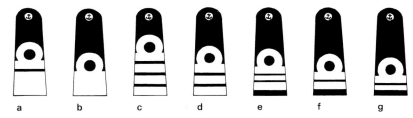

a: *Kontradmirolas*, Rear Admiral   **b:** *Komandoras*, Commodore   **c:** *Komandoras-Leitenantas*, Captain
d: *Jūru Kapitonas*, Commander   **e:** *Kapitonas-Leitenantas*, Lieutenant Commander
f: *Jūru Vyresnysis Leitenantas*, Lieutenant   **g:** *Jūru Leitenantas*, Sub Lieutenant

Gold on black.

Madagascar (Malagasy Republic Marine)

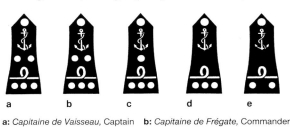

a: *Capitaine de Vaisseau*, Captain   **b:** *Capitaine de Frégate*, Commander
c: *Capitaine de Corvette*, Lieutenant Commander   **d:** *Lieutenant de Vaisseau*,
Lieutenant   **e:** *Enseigne de Vaisseau 1re Classe*, Sub Lieutenant
f: *Enseigne de Vaisseau 2e Classe*, Acting Sub Lieutenant

Gold on black. Commander, top two discs silver.

Malawi

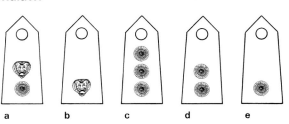

a: *Lieutenant Colonel*, Commander   **b:** *Major*, Lieutenant Commander
c: *Captain*, Lieutenant   **d:** *Lieutenant*, Sub Lieutenant   **e:** *2nd Lieutenant*,
Acting Sub Lieutenant

Black on khaki.

Malaysia (Tentera Laut)

a: *Laksamana Armada*, Admiral of the Fleet   **b:** *Laksamana*, Admiral   **c:** *Laksamana Madya*, Vice Admiral   **d:** *Laksamana Muda*, Rear Admiral   **e:** *Laksamana Pertama*,
Commodore   **f:** *Kapeten*, Captain   **g:** *Komander*, Commander   **h:** *Leftenan Komander*, Lieutenant Commander   **i:** *Leftenan*, Lieutenant   **j:** *Leftenan Madya and Leftenan
Muda*, Sub Lieutenant and Acting Sub Lieutenant   **k:** *Kadet Kanan*, Midshipman   **l:** *Kadet*, Cadet

Vice Admiral to Commodore, silver on gold. Remainder gold on navy blue, plus midshipman's white patch.

Malta (Maritime Squadron, AFM)

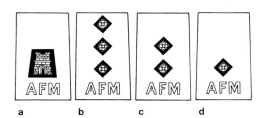

a: *Major*, Lieutenant Commander **b:** *Captain*, Lieutenant **c:** *Lieutenant*, Sub Lieutenant **d:** *2nd Lieutenant*, Acting Sub Lieutenant

White on dark blue.

Mauritania (Marine Mauritanienne)

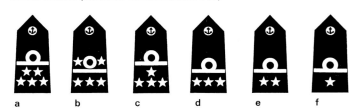

a: *Colonel*, Captain **b:** *Lieutenant Colonel*, Commander **c:** *Major*, Lieutenant Commander **d:** *Captain*, Lieutenant **e:** *Lieutenant*, Sub Lieutenant **f:** *2nd Lieutenant*, Acting Sub Lieutenant

Gold on blue or green. Exception is two silver stars above lace for commander.

Mexico (Armada de Mexico)

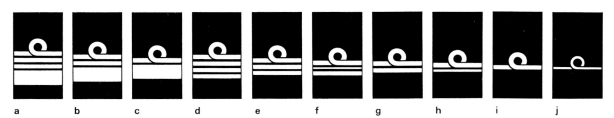

a: *Almirante*, Admiral **b:** *Vicealmirante*, Vice Admiral **c:** *Contraalmirante*, Rear Admiral **d:** *Capitán de Navío*, Captain **e:** *Capitán de Fragata*, Commander **f:** *Capitán de Corbeta*, Lieutenant Commander **g:** *Teniente de Navío*, Lieutenant **h:** *Teniente de Fragata*, Sub Lieutenant **i:** *Teniente de Corbeta*, Acting Sub Lieutenant **j:** *Guardiamarina*, Midshipman

Gold on navy blue.

Morocco (Marine Royale Marocaine)

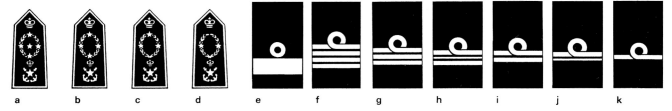

a: *Amiral*, Admiral of the Fleet **b:** *Amiral d'Escadre*, Admiral **c:** *Vice Amiral*, Vice Admiral **d:** *Contre Amiral*, Rear Admiral **e:** *Capitaine de Vaisseau Major*, Commodore **f:** *Capitaine de Vaisseau*, Captain **g:** *Capitaine de Frégate*, Commander **h:** *Capitaine de Corvette*, Lieutenant Commander **i:** *Lieutenant de Vaisseau*, Lieutenant **j:** *Enseigne de Vaisseau 1re Classe*, Sub Lieutenant **k:** *Enseigne de Vaisseau 2e Classe*, Acting Sub Lieutenant

Gold on black. Flag ranks silver stars.

Mozambique

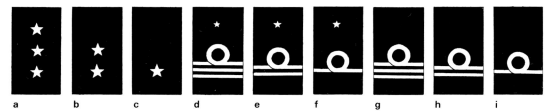

a: *Almirante*, Admiral **b:** *Vice-Almirante*, Vice Admiral **c:** *Contra-Almirante*, Rear Admiral **d:** *Capitão-de-Mar-e-Guerra*, Captain **e:** *Capitão-de-Fragate*, Commander **f:** *Capitão-Tenente*, Lieutenant Commander **g:** *Primerio-Tenente*, Lieutenant **h:** *Segundo-Tenente*, Sub Lieutenant **i:** *Guarda-Marinha*, Midshipman

Gold insignia on dark blue slip-ons.

Netherlands (Koninklijke Marine)

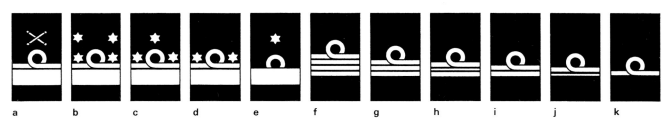

a: *Admiraal*, Admiral of the Fleet **b:** *Luitenant-Admiraal*, Admiral **c:** *Vice-Admiraal*, Vice Admiral **d:** *Schout-bij-nacht*, Rear Admiral **e:** *Commandeur*, Commodore **f:** *Kapitein ter zee*, Captain **g:** *Kapitein-luitenant ter zee*, Commander **h:** *Luitenant ter zee der eerste klasse*, Lieutenant Commander **i:** *Luitenant ter zee der tweede klasse oudste categorie*, Lieutenant **j:** *Luitenant ter zee der tweede klasse*, Sub Lieutenant **k:** *Luitenant ter zee der derde klasse*, Acting Sub Lieutenant

Gold on navy blue. Stars and crossed batons, silver.

New Zealand

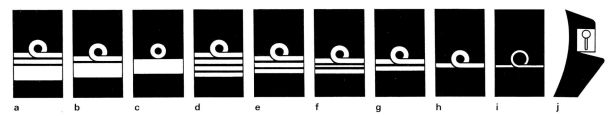

a b c d e f g h i j

a: Vice Admiral **b:** Rear Admiral **c:** Commodore **d:** Captain **e:** Commander **f:** Lieutenant Commander **g:** Lieutenant **h:** Sub Lieutenant
i: Ensign **j:** Midshipman

Gold on navy blue.

Nicaragua (la Fuerza Naval)

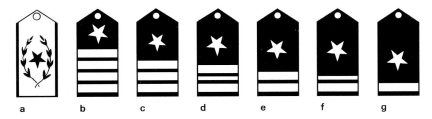

a b c d e f g

a: *Contraalmirante,* Rear Admiral **b:** *Capitán de Navío,* Captain **c:** *Capitán de Fragata,* Commander
d: *Capitán de Corbeta,* Lieutenant Commander **e:** *Teniente de Navío,* Lieutenant **f:** *Teniente de Fragata,*
Sub Lieutenant **g:** *Teniente de Corbeta,* Acting Sub Lieutenant

Gold button and star. Green wreath on gold brocade, navy blue edges. Gold lace and stars on navy blue.

Nigeria

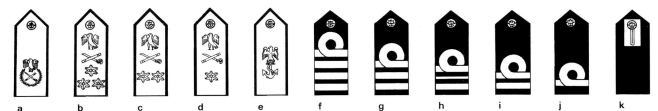

a b c d e f g h i j k

a: Admiral of the Fleet **b:** Admiral **c:** Vice Admiral **d:** Rear Admiral **e:** *Brigadier,* Commodore **f:** *Colonel,* Captain **g:** *Lieutenant Colonel,* Commander
h: *Major,* Lieutenant Commander **i:** *Captain,* Lieutenant **j:** *Lieutenant,* Sub Lieutenant **k:** *Second Lieutenant,* Midshipman

Gold on navy blue. Eagles, red. Stars and crossed battons, silver.

Norway (Sjoforsvaret)

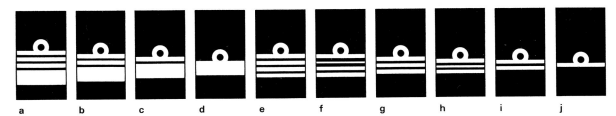

a b c d e f g h i j

a: *Admiral,* Admiral **b:** *Viseadmiral,* Vice Admiral **c:** *Kontreadmiral,* Rear Admiral **d:** *Flaggkommandør,* Commodore **e:** *Kommandør,* Captain
f: *Kommandørkaptein,* Commander Senior Grade **g:** *Orlogskaptein,* Commander **h:** *Kapteinløytnant,* Lieutenant Commander **i:** *Løytnant,* Lieutenant
j: *Fenrik,* Sub Lieutenant

Gold on navy blue.

Oman

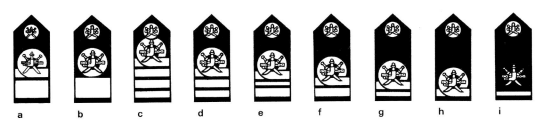

a b c d e f g h i

a: *Liwaa Bahry,* Rear Admiral **b:** *'Amid Bahry,* Commodore **c:** *'Aqid Bahry,* Captain **d:** *Muqaddam Bahry,* Commander **e:** *Ra'id Bahry,*
Lieutenant Commander **f:** *Naqib Bahry,* Lieutenant **g:** *Mulazim Awwal Bahry,* Sub Lieutenant **h:** *Mulazim Tanin Bahry,* Acting Sub Lieutenant
i: *Dabit Murashshah,* Midshipman

Gold on navy blue. White stripe, midshipman.

Pakistan

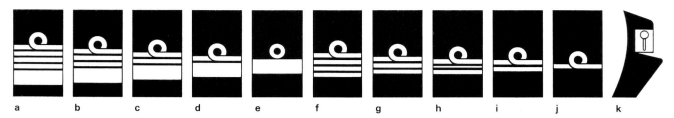

a: Admiral of the Fleet   **b:** Admiral   **c:** Vice Admiral   **d:** Rear Admiral   **e:** Commodore   **f:** Captain   **g:** Commander   **h:** Lieutenant Commander   **i:** Lieutenant
j: Sub Lieutenant   **k:** Midshipman

Gold on navy blue.

Panama (Servicio Maritime Nacional)

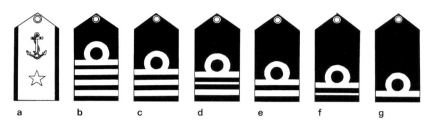

a: *Director General*, Rear Admiral   **b:** *Capitán de Navío*, Captain   **c:** *Capitán de Fragata*, Commander
d: *Capitán de Corbeta*, Lieutenant Commander   **e:** *Teniente de Navío*, Lieutenant   **f:** *Teniente de Fragata*,
Lieutenant (JG)   **g:** *Alférez de Navío*, Sub Lieutenant

Gold on navy blue.

Paraguay (Armada Nacional)

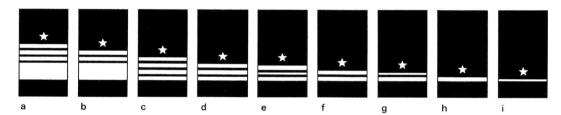

a: *Vicealmirante*, Vice Admiral   **b:** *Contralmirante,* Rear Admiral   **c:** *Capitán de Navío*, Captain   **d:** *Capitán de Fragata*, Commander
e: *Capitán de Corbeta*, Lieutenant Commander   **f:** *Teniente de Navío*, Lieutenant   **g:** *Teniente de Fragata*, Sub Lieutenant
h: *Teniente de Corbeta,* Acting Sub Lieutenant   **i:** *Guardamarinha*, Midshipman

Gold on navy blue.

Peru (Armada Perúana)

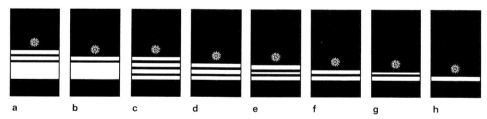

a: *Vicealmirante*, Vice Admiral   **b:** *Contraalmirante*, Rear Admiral   **c:** *Capitán de Navío*, Captain   **d:** *Capitán de Fragata*, Commander
e: *Capitán de Corbeta*, Lieutenant Commander   **f:** *Teniente Primero*, Lieutenant   **g:** *Teniente Segundo*, Sub Lieutenant
h: *Alférez de Fragata*, Acting Sub Lieutenant

Gold on navy blue.

Philippines

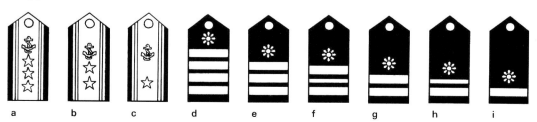

a: Vice Admiral   **b:** Rear Admiral   **c:** Commodore   **d:** Captain   **e:** Commander   **f:** Lieutenant Commander   **g:** Lieutenant
h: Lieutenant Junior Grade   **i:** Ensign

Gold on black. Commodore, dark blue edged, silver devices on gold.

Poland (Marynarka Wojenna)

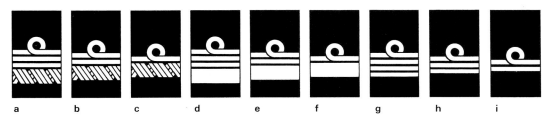

a   b   c   d   e   f   g   h   i

a: *Admiral*, Admiral   **b:** *Vice-Admiral*, Vice Admiral   **c:** *Kontradmiral*, Rear Admiral   **d:** *Komandor*, Captain   **e:** *Komandor Porucznik*, Commander
f: *Komandor Podporucznik*, Lieutenant Commander   **g:** *Kapitan Marynarki*, Lieutenant   **h:** *Porucznik Marynarki*, Sub Lieutenant
i: *Podporucznik Marynarki*, Acting Sub Lieutenant

Gold on dark blue.

Portugal (Marinha Portuguesa)

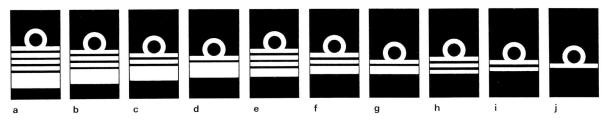

a   b   c   d   e   f   g   h   i   j

a: *Almirante da Armada*, Admiral of the Fleet   **b:** *Almirante*, Admiral   **c:** *Vice-Almirante*, Vice Admiral   **d:** *Contra-Almirante*, Rear Admiral
e: *Capitão-de-Mar-e-Guerra*, Captain   **f:** *Capitão-de-Fragata*, Commander   **g:** *Capitão-Tenente*, Lieutenant Commander   **h:** *Primeiro-Tenente*, Lieutenant
i: *Segundo-Tenente*, Sub Lieutenant   **j:** *Guarda-Marinha-ou-Subtenente*, Midshipman or Acting Sub Lieutenant

Gold on navy blue.

Qatar

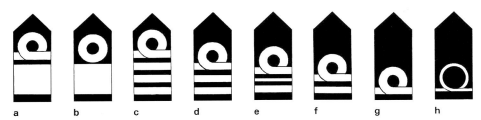

a   b   c   d   e   f   g   h

a: Rear Admiral   **b:** Commodore   **c:** Captain   **d:** Commander   **e:** Lieutenant Commander   **f:** Lieutenant
g: Sub Lieutenant   **h:** Acting Sub Lieutenant

Gold bullion lace on navy blue.

Romania (Marină Română)

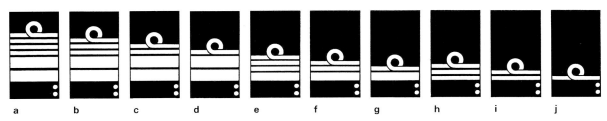

a   b   c   d   e   f   g   h   i   j

a: *Amiral*, Admiral   **b:** *Viceamiral Comandor*, Vice Admiral   **c:** *Viceamiral*, Rear Admiral Upper Half   **d:** *Contraamiral*, Rear Admiral Lower Half
e: *Comandor*, Captain   **f:** *Căpitan Commander*, Commander   **g:** *Locotenent Comandor*, Lieutenant Commander   **h:**

Russia (Rosiyskiy Voennomorsky Flot)

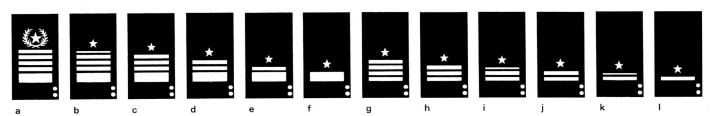

a   b   c   d   e   f   g   h   i   j   k   l

a: *Admiral Flota Rosiyskoy Federatsii*, Admiral of the Fleet of the Russian Federation   **b:** *Admiral Flota*, Admiral of the Fleet   **c:** *Admiral*, Admiral   **d:** *Vitse-Admiral*, Vice Admiral
e: *Kontr-Admiral*, Rear Admiral   **f:** *Kapitan Pervogo Ranga*, Captain   **g:** *Kapitan Vtorogo Ranga*, Commander   **h:** *Kapitan Tretyego Ranga*, Lieutenant Commander
i: *Kapitan-Leytenant*, Lieutenant   **j:** *Starshiy Leytenant*, Junior Lieutenant   **k:** *Leytenant*, Sub Lieutenant   **l:** *Mladshiy Leytenant*, Acting Sub Lieutenant

Gold on black.

Saudi Arabia (Royal Saudi Naval Forces)

a: *Lieutenant General (Navy)*, Vice Admiral   **b:** *Major General (Navy)*, Rear Admiral   **c:** *Brigadier General (Navy)*, Commodore
d: *Colonel (Navy)*, Captain   **e:** *Lieutenant Colonel (Navy)*, Commander   **f:** *Major (Navy)*, Lieutenant Commander
g: *Captain (Navy)*, Lieutenant   **h:** *Lieutenant (Navy)*, Sub Lieutenant   **i:** *Second Lieutenant (Navy)*, Acting Sub Lieutenant

Gold buttons, sabres and Arabic titles, light green stars and crowns on black.

Senegal (Marine Sénégalaise)

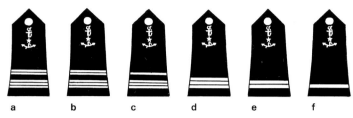

a: *Contre-Amiral*, Rear Admiral   **b:** *Capitaine de Vaisseau*, Captain
c: *Capitaine de Frégate*, Commander   **d:** *Capitaine de Corvette*, Lieutenant Commander
e: *Lieutenant de Vaisseau*, Lieutenant   **f:** *Enseigne de Vaisseau*, Sub Lieutenant

Gold on black. Captain, three gold and two silver stripes.

Seychelles

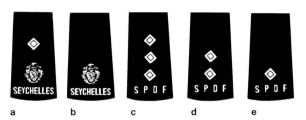

a: *Lieutenant Colonel*, Commander   **b:** *Major*, Lieutenant Commander
c: *Captain*, Lieutenant   **d:** *Lieutenant*, Sub Lieutenant   **e:** *Second Lieutenant*, Acting Sub Lieutenant

Gold embroidered on dark blue.

Singapore (Republic of Singapore Navy)

a: Vice Admiral   **b:** Rear Admiral   **c:** Commodore   **d:** Colonel   **e:** Lieutenant Colonel   **f:** Major   **g:** Captain
h: Lieutenant   **i:** Second Lieutenant

Gold on navy blue. Senior officers only have naval titles.

Slovenia (Slovenski Mornarji)

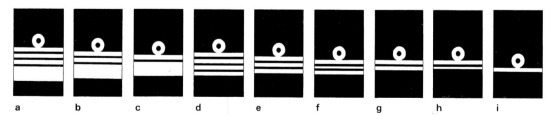

a: *Admiral*, Admiral   **b:** *Viceadmiral*, Vice Admiral   **c:** *Kapitan*, Commodore   **d:** *Kapitan Bojne Ladje*, Captain   **e:** *Kapitan Fregate*, Commander
f: *Kapitan Korvete*, Lieutenant Commander   **g:** *Poročnik Fregate*, Lieutenant   **h:** *Poročnik Korvete*, Sub Lieutenant
i: *Podporočnik*, Acting Sub Lieutenant

Gold on dark blue.

South Africa

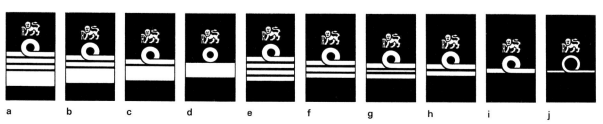

a: Admiral   **b:** Vice Admiral   **c:** Rear Admiral   **d:** Rear Admiral (JG)   **e:** Captain   **f:** Commander   **g:** Lieutenant Commander   **h:** Lieutenant
i: Sub Lieutenant   **j:** Ensign

Gold on navy blue.

Spain (Armada Española)

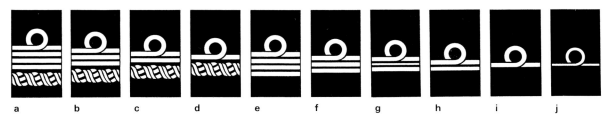

a: *Capitán General*, Admiral of the Fleet   **b:** *Almirante General*, Admiral   **c:** *Vicealmirante*, Vice Admiral   **d:** *Contraalmirante*, Rear Admiral
e: *Capitán de Navío*, Captain   **f:** *Capitán de Fragata*, Commander   **g:** *Capitán de Corbeta*, Lieutenant Commander   **h:** *Teniente de Navío*, Lieutenant
i: *Alférez de Navío*, Sub Lieutenant   **j:** *Alférez de Fragata*, Acting Sub Lieutenant

Gold on navy blue.

Sri Lanka

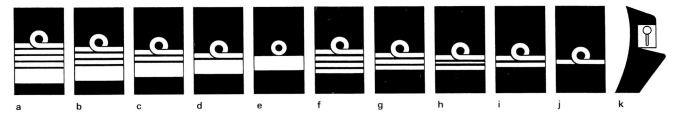

a: Admiral of the Fleet   **b:** Admiral   **c:** Vice Admiral   **d:** Rear Admiral   **e:** Commodore   **f:** Captain   **g:** Commander   **h:** Lieutenant Commander   **i:** Lieutenant
j: Sub Lieutenant   **k:** Midshipman

Gold on navy blue.

Sudan

a: *'Amid*, Commodore   **b:** *'Aqid*, Captain   **c:** *Muqaddam*, Commander   **d:** *Ra'id Lieutenant*,
Commander   **e:** *Naqib*, Lieutenant   **f:** *Mulazim Awwal*, Sub Lieutenant   **g:** *Mulazim Thani*,
Acting Sub Lieutenant

Gold on black.

Surinam

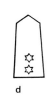

a: *Kapitein Ter Zee*, Commander   **b:** *Kapitein-Luitenant Ter Zee*,
Lieutenant Commander   **c:** *Luitenant Ter Zee Der 1e Klasse*,
Lieutenant   **d:** *Luitenant Ter Zee Der 2e Klasse Oudste Categorie*,
Sub Lieutenant   **e:** *Luitenant Ter Zee Der 3e Klasse*,
Acting Sub Lieutenant

Gold on white.

Sweden (Marinen)

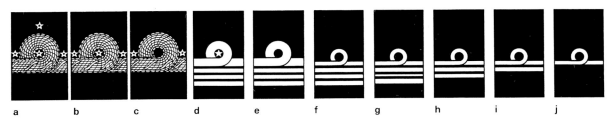

a: *Amiral*, Admiral   **b:** *Viceamiral*, Vice Admiral   **c:** *Konteramiral*, Rear Admiral   **d:** *Kommendör av 1. gr*, Commodore   **e:** *Kommendör*, Captain
f: *Kommendörkapten*, Commander   **g:** *Örlogskapten*, Lieutenant Commander   **h:** *Kapten*, Lieutenant   **i:** *Löjnant*, Sub Lieutenant
j: *Fänrik*, Acting Sub Lieutenant

Gold on dark blue.

Sweden Coast Guard (Kustbevakning)

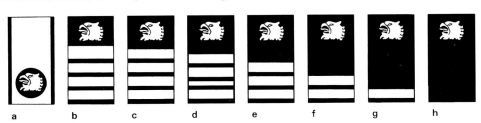

a: *Generaldirektör*, Rear Admiral   **b:** *Kustbevakningsdirektör*, Commodore   **c:** *Kustbevakningsöverinspectör Överingenjör*,
Captain and Senior Engineer Officer   **d:** *Förste Kustbevakningsinspektör*, Commander   **e:** *Kustbevakningsinspektör*,
Lieutenant Commander   **f:** *Kustbevakningassistent*, Lieutenant   **g:** *Kustuppsyningsman*, Sub Lieutenant   **h:** *Kustbevakningsaspirant*, Midshipman

Gold on navy blue.

Syria

a b c d e f g h i

a: *Fariq,* Vice-Admiral   **b:** *Liwa,* Rear Admiral   **c:** *Amid,* Commodor   **d:** *'Aqid,* Captain   **e:** *Muqaddam,* Commander
f: *Ra'id,* Lieutenant Commander   **g:** *Naqib,* Lieutenant   **h:** *Mulazim Awwal,* Sub Lieutenant   **i:** *Mulazim,* Acting Sub Lieutenant

Gold on black.

Taiwan (Republic of China)

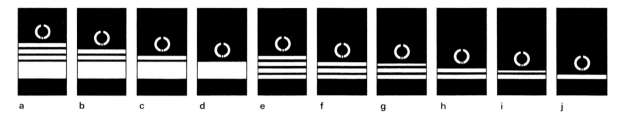

a b c d e f g h i j

a: Admiral   **b:** Vice Admiral   **c:** Rear Admiral   **d:** Commodore   **e:** Captain   **f:** Commander   **g:** Lieutenant Commander   **h:** Lieutenant
i: Lieutenant JG (II)   **j:** Sub Lieutenant

Gold on navy blue.

Tanzania

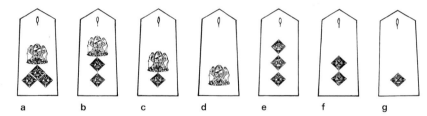

a b c d e f g

a: *Brigadier Head of the Navy,* Commodore   **b:** *Colonel,* Captain   **c:** *Lieutenant Colonel,* Commander
d: *Major,* Lieutenant Commander   **e:** *Captain,* Lieutenant   **f:** *Lieutenant,* Sub Lieutenant
g: *Second Lieutenant,* Acting Sub Lieutenant

Gold coloured devices on light tan shoulder strapes.

Thailand (Royal Thai Navy)

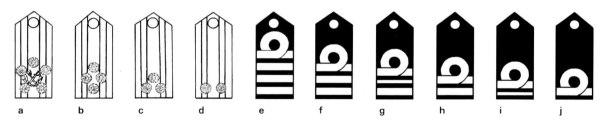

a b c d e f g h i j

a: Admiral of the Fleet   **b:** Admiral   **c:** Vice Admiral   **d:** Rear Admiral   **e:** Captain   **f:** Commander   **g:** Lieutenant Commander   **h:** Lieutenant
i: Sub Lieutenant   **j:** Acting Sub Lieutenant
Admirals wear gold brocaded shoulder straps with silver insignia.

Gold lace and buttons on black.

Togo (Marine du Togo)

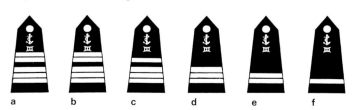

a b c d e f

a: *Capitaine de Vaisseau,* Captain   **b:** *Capitaine de Frégate,* Commander
c: *Capitaine de Corvette,* Lieutenant Commander   **d:** *Lieutenant de Vaisseau,* Lieutenant
e: *Enseigne de Vaisseau 1re Classe,* Sub Lieutenant   **f:** *Enseigne de Vaisseau 2e Classe,*
Acting Sub Lieutenant

Gold on black. Commander, three gold two silver stripes.

Tonga

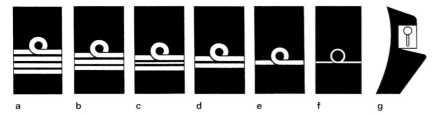

a: Captain **b:** Commander **c:** Lieutenant Commander **d:** Lieutenant **e:** Sub Lieutenant **f:** Ensign
g: Midshipman

Gold on navy blue.

Trinidad and Tobago Coast Guard

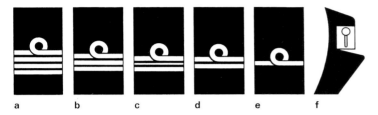

a: Captain **b:** Commander **c:** Lieutenant Commander **d:** Lieutenant **e:** Sub Lieutenant
f: Midshipman

Gold on navy blue.

Tunisia

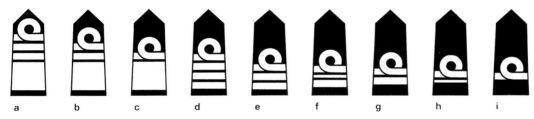

a: *Vice-Amiral d'Escadre*, Admiral **b:** *Vice-Amiral*, Vice Admiral **c:** *Contre-Amiral*, Rear Admiral **d:** *Capitaine de Vaisseau*, Captain
e: *Capitaine de Frégate*, Commander **f:** *Capitaine de Corvette*, Lieutenant Commander **g:** *Lieutenant de Vaisseau*, Lieutenant
h: *Enseigne de Vaisseau 1re Classe*, Sub Lieutenant **i:** *Enseigne de Vaisseau 2e Classe*, Acting Sub Lieutenant

Gold on black.

Turkey (Türk Deniz Kuvvetleri)

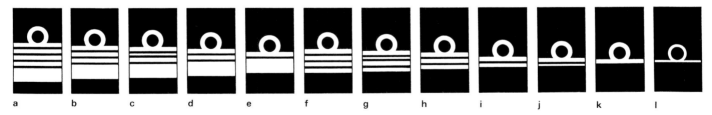

a: *Büyükamiral*, Admiral of the Fleet **b:** *Oramiral*, Admiral **c:** *Koramiral*, Vice Admiral **d:** *Tümamiral*, Rear Admiral **e:** *Tugamiral*, Commodore **f:** *Albay*, Captain
g: *Yarbay*, Commander **h:** *Binbasi*, Lieutenant Commander **i:** *Yüzbasi*, Lieutenant **j:** *Üstegmen*, Sub Lieutenant **k:** *Tegmen*, Acting Sub Lieutenant
l: *Astegmen*, Warrant Officer

Gold on black.

Ukraine

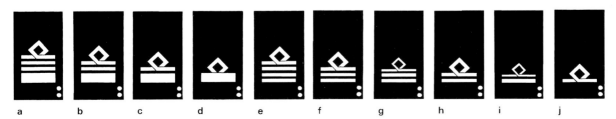

a: *Admiral*, Admiral **b:** *Vitse-Admiral*, Vice Admiral **c:** *Kontr-Admiral*, Rear Admiral **d:** *Kapitan Pervogo Ranga*, Captain **e:** *Kapitan Vtorogo Ranga*,
Commander **f:** *Kapitan Tretyego Ranga*, Lieutenant Commander **g:** *Kapitan-Leytenant*, Lieutenant **h:** *Starshiy-Leytenant*, Junior Lieutenant
i: *Leytenant*, Sub Lieutenant **j:** *Mladshiy-Leytenant*, Acting Sub Lieutenant

Gold on black.

RANKS AND INSIGNIA OF THE WORLD'S NAVIES

United Arab Emirates

a: *'Amid,* Commodore   **b:** *'Aqid,* Captain   **c:** *Muqaddam,* Commander   **d:** *Ra'id,* Lieutenant Commander
e: *Naqib,* Lieutenant   **f:** *Mulazim Awwal,* Sub Lieutenant   **g:** *Mulazim Thani,* Acting Sub Lieutenant

Gold on black.

United Kingdom

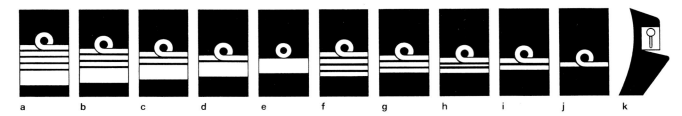

a: Admiral of the Fleet   **b:** Admiral   **c:** Vice Admiral   **d:** Rear Admiral   **e:** Commodore   **f:** Captain   **g:** Commander   **h:** Lieutenant Commander   **i:** Lieutenant
j: Sub Lieutenant   **k:** Midshipman

Gold on navy blue, Rank **a:** is being abolished.

United Kingdom (Royal Fleet Auxiliary)

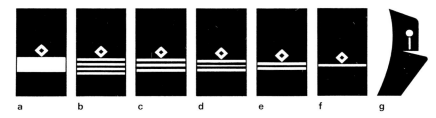

a: Commodore   **b:** Captain   **c:** Chief Officer   **d:** First Officer   **e:** 2nd Officer   **f:** 3rd Officer   **g:** Deck Cadet
Gold on navy blue.

United States

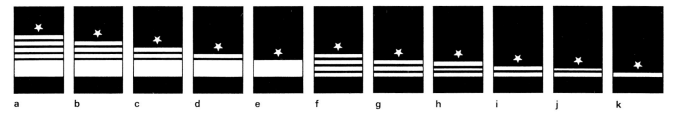

a: *Fleet Admiral,* Admiral of the Fleet   **b:** *Admiral,* Admiral   **c:** *Vice Admiral,* Vice Admiral   **d:** *Rear Admiral (Upper Half),* Rear Admiral   **e:** *Rear Admiral (Lower Half),*
Commodore   **f:** *Captain,* Captain   **g:** *Commander,* Commander   **h:** *Lieutenant Commander,* Lieutenant Commander   **i:** *Lieutenant,* Lieutenant   **j:** *Lieutenant Junior Grade,*
Sub Lieutenant   **k:** *Ensign,* Acting Sub Lieutenant

Gold on navy blue.

United States Coast Guard

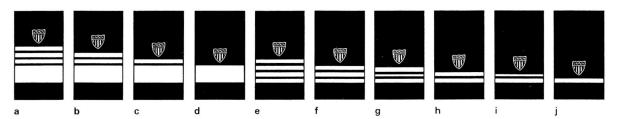

a: *Admiral,* Admiral   **b:** *Vice Admiral,* Vice Admiral   **c:** *Rear Admiral,* Rear Admiral   **d:** *Rear Admiral Lower Half,* Commodore   **e:** *Captain,* Captain
f: *Commander,* Commander   **g:** *Lieutenant Commander,* Lieutenant Commander   **h:** *Lieutenant,* Lieutenant   **i:** *Lieutenant Junior Grade,* Sub Lieutenant
j: *Ensign,* Acting Sub Lieutenant

Gold on navy blue.

Uruguay (Armada Nacional)

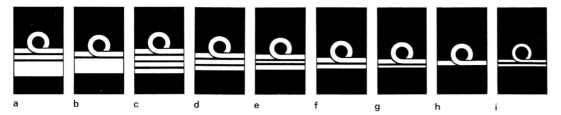

a: *Vicealmirante*, Vice Admiral   **b:** *Contraalmirante*, Rear Admiral   **c:** *Capitán de Navío*, Captain   **d:** *Capitán de Fragata*, Commander
e: *Capitán de Corbeta*, Lieutenant Commander   **f:** *Teniente de Navío*, Lieutenant   **g:** *Alférez de Navío*, Sub Lieutenant   **h:** *Alférez de Fragata*,
Acting Sub Lieutenant   **i:** *Guardiamarina*, Midshipman

Gold on navy blue.

Venezuela (Marina de Guerra de Venezuela)

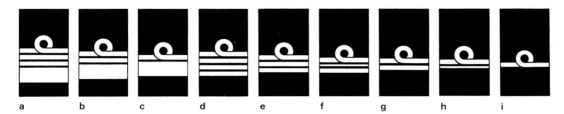

a: *Almirante*, Admiral   **b:** *Vicealmirante*, Vice Admiral   **c:** *Contraalmirante*, Rear Admiral   **d:** *Capitán de Navío*, Captain   **e:** *Capitán de Fragata*,
Commander   **f:** *Capitán de Corbeta*, Lieutenant Commander   **g:** *Teniente de Navío*, Lieutenant   **h:** *Teniente de Fragata*, Sub Lieutenant
i: *Alférez de Navío*, Acting Sub Lieutenant

Gold on navy blue.

Vietnam

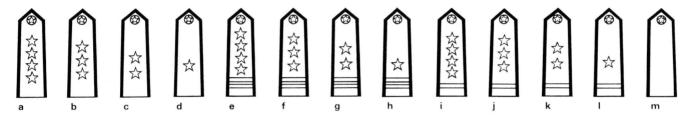

a: *Senior General*, Admiral of the Fleet   **b:** *Colonel General*, Admiral   **c:** *Lieutenant General*, Vice Admiral   **d:** *Major General*, Rear Admiral   **e:** *Senior Colonel*, Commodore
f: *Colonel*, Captain   **g:** *Lieutenant Colonel*, Commander   **h:** *Major*, Lieutenant Commander   **i:** *Senior Captain*, Senior Lieutenant   **j:** *Captain*, Lieutenant
k: *Senior Lieutenant*, Sub Lieutenant   **l:** *2nd Lieutenant*, Acting Sub Lieutenant   **m:** *Student Officer*, Midshipman

Gold shoulder straps. Generals, edged red gold stars. Remainder, silver stars and lace.

Yemen

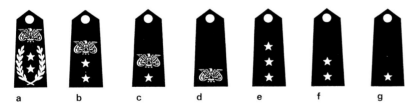

a: *'Amid*, Commodore   **b:** *'Aqid*, Captain   **c:** *Muqaddam*, Commander   **d:** *Ra'id*, Lieutenant Commander
e: *Naqib*, Lieutenant   **f:** *Mulazim Awwal*, Sub Lieutenant   **g:** *Mulazim Thani*, Acting Sub Lieutenant

Gold on black.

Yugoslavia (Jugoslovenska Ratna Mornarica)

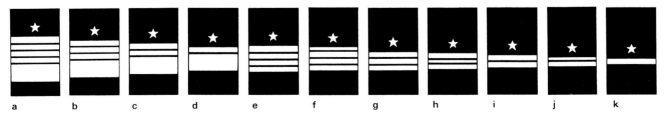

a: *Admiral Flote*, Admiral of the Fleet   **b:** *Admiral*, Admiral   **c:** *Viceadmiral*, Vice Admiral   **d:** *Kontraadmiral*, Rear Admiral   **e:** *Kapetan Bojnog Broda*, Captain
f: *Kapetan Fregate*, Commander   **g:** *Kapetan Korvete*, Lieutenant Commander   **h:** *Poručnik Bojnog Broda*, Lieutenant (Senior)   **i:** *Poručnik Fregate*, Lieutenant
j: *Poručnik Korvete*, Sub Lieutenant   **k:** *Potporučnik*, Acting Sub Lieutenant

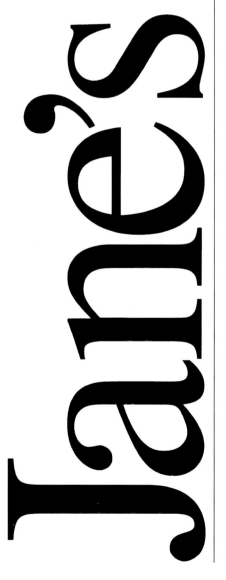

Users' Charter

This publication is brought to you by Jane's Information Group, a global company with more than 100 years of innovation and an unrivalled reputation for impartiality, accuracy and authority.

Our collection and output of information and images is not dictated by any political or commercial affiliation. Our reportage is undertaken without fear of, or favour from, any government, alliance, state or corporation.

We publish information that is collected overtly from unclassified sources, although much could be regarded as extremely sensitive or not publicly accessible.

Our validation and analysis aims to eradicate misinformation or disinformation as well as factual errors; our objective is always to produce the most accurate and authoritative data.

In the event of any significant inaccuracies, we undertake to draw these to the readers' attention to preserve the highly valued relationship of trust and credibility with our customers worldwide.

If you believe that these policies have been breached by this title, you are invited to contact the editor.

A copy of Jane's Information Group's Code of Conduct for its editorial teams is available from the publisher.

INVESTOR IN PEOPLE

Pennant list of major surface ships

Type abbreviations

Note: Guided missile does not denote vessels with surface-to-air missiles only, unless they have some surface-to-surface capabilities.
Country abbreviations follow designations specific to one nationality.

Submarines

AGSS	Submarine, auxiliary (USA)
ASDS	Advanced Swimmer-Seal Delivery System (USA)
SDV	Swimmer delivery vehicle
SNA	Submarine, attack, nuclear-powered (Fra)
SNLE	Ballistic missile nuclear-powered submarine (Fra)
SS	Submarine, general
SSA(N)	Submarine, auxiliary, nuclear-powered
SSA	Submarine with ASW capability (Jpn)
SSB	Ballistic missile submarine (CPR)
SSBN	Ballistic missile nuclear-powered submarine
SSC	Submarine, coastal
SSG (N)	Submarine, surface to surface missile, nuclear-powered
SSK	Submarine with ASW capability
SSN	Submarine, attack, nuclear-powered

Aircraft Carriers

CV (G)	Aircraft carrier (guided missile)
CVH	Helicopter carrier
CVN	Aircraft carrier, nuclear-powered
CVS	Aircraft carrier ASW
PAN	Aircraft carrier, nuclear-powered (Fra)

Cruisers

CG	Guided missile cruiser
CGH	Guided missile helicopter cruiser
CGN	Guided missile cruiser, nuclear-powered
CH	Helicopter cruiser
CLM	Guided missile cruiser (Per)

Destroyers

DD	Destroyer
DDG	Guided missile destroyer
DDK	Destroyer (Jpn)

Frigates

DE	Destroyer escort (Jpn)
DDE	Destroyer escort (Can)
DDH	Destroyer, helicopter (Can)
FF	Frigate
FFG	Guided missile frigate
FFH	Frigate, helicopter (Can)
FS (G)	Corvette (guided missile)

Patrol Forces

CF	River gunboat (Per)
CM	Corvette (guided missile) (Per)
HSIC	High Speed Infiltration Craft
OPV	Offshore patrol vessel
PB (F)(I)(R)	Patrol boat (fast) (inshore) (river)
PBL	Patrol escort, small (Can)
PC (F)(G)(R)	Patrol craft (fast) (guided missile) (river)
PG (F)(G)(R)	Patrol or gunship (fast) (guided missile) (river)
PH (G)(T)	Patrol hydrofoil (guided missile) (torpedo)
PGGA	Patrol air cushion vessel, guided missile
SES	Surface effect ship
SOC	Special operations craft (USA)

Landing Ships

AAAV	Advanced Amphibious Assault Vehicle
ACV	Landing craft air cushion (Rus)
AGC	Amphibious command ship (RoC)
BTS	Amphibious transport, dock (Fra)
EDCG	Landing craft, utility (Brz)
HSS	Helicopter support ship
LCA	Landing craft, assault
LCAC	Landing craft air cushion
LCC	Amphibious command ship
LCH	Landing craft, heavy (Aust)
LCL	Landing craft, logistic (UK)
LCM	Landing craft, mechanical
LCP (L)	Landing craft, personnel (small)
LCT	Landing craft, tank
LCU	Landing craft, utility
LCVP	Landing craft, vehicle/personnel
LHA	Amphibious assault ship general purpose
LHD	Amphibious assault ship (multipurpose)
LKA	Amphibious cargo ship
LPA	Amphibious transport, personnel
LPD	Amphibious transport, dock
LPH	Amphibious assault ship, helicopter
LSD	Landing ship, dock
LSL	Landing ship, logistic
LSM	Landing ship, medium
LST	Landing ship, tank
LSV	Landing ship, vehicle
RCL	Ramped craft, logistic
TCD	Landing ship, dock (Fra)
UCAC	Utility craft air cushion

Mine Warfare Ships

MCAC	Mine countermeasures air cushion vessel
MCD	Mine countermeasures vessel, diving
MCDV	Maritime coast defence vessel (Can)
MCM	Mine countermeasures ship
MCS	Mine countermeasures support ship
MH (I)(C)(O)	Minehunter (inshore) (coastal) (ocean)
MHSC	Minehunter/sweeper coastal
ML (I)(C)(A)	Minelayer (inshore) (coastal) (auxiliary)
MRD	Minehunter, drone
MS (I)(C)(R)	Minesweeper (inshore) (coastal) (river)
MSA (T)	Minesweeper, auxiliary (tug)
MSB	Minesweeper, boat
MSCD	Coastal minesweeper capable of controlling drones
MSD	Minesweeper, drone
MSO	Minesweeper, ocean
MST	Mine countermeasures support ship
SRMH	Single role mine hunter (UK)

Auxiliaries

ABU	Buoy tender
ACM	MCMV tender
ACS	Auxiliary crane ship
AD	Destroyer tender
ADG	Degaussing ship
AE (L)	Ammunition ship (small)
AEM	Missile support ship
AF (L)	Stores ship (small)
AFS (H)	Combat stores ship (helicopter)
AG	Auxiliary miscellaneous
AGB	Icebreaker
AGE	Research ship
AGF	Auxiliary Flag or command ship
AGI	Intelligence collection ship
AGM	Missile range instrumentation ship
AGOB	Polar research ship
AGOR	Oceanographic research ship
AGOS	Ocean surveillance ship
AGP	Patrol craft tender
AGS (C)	Surveying ship (coastal)
AH	Hospital ship
AK (L) (R)	Cargo ship (light) (ro-ro)
AKB	Lash type cargo ship, barge
AKF	Armament stores carrier
AKR	Fast sealift ship
AKS (L)	Stores ship (light)
ANL	Boom defence/cable/netlayer
AO	Replenishment oiler (USA)
AOE	Fast combat support ship
AOR (L)(H)	Replenishment oiler (small) (helicopter)
AOS (R)	Special liquid ship (radiological)
AOT (L)	Transport oiler (small)
AP	Personnel transport
APB	Barracks ship
AR (L)	Repair ship (small)
ARC	Submarine cable repair ship
ARS (D)	Salvage ship (heavy lift)
AS (L)	Submarine tender (small)
ASE	Research ship (Jpn)
ASR	Submarine rescue craft
ASU	Training support and rescue ship
ATA	Auxiliary ocean tug
ATC	Armoured troop carrier
ATF	Fleet ocean tug and supply ship
ATR	Fleet ocean tug (firefighting)
ATS	Salvage and rescue ship
AVB	Aviation support ship
AWT	Water tanker
AX (L)	Training ship (small)
AXS	Sail training ship
AXT	Training tender
TV	Training ship (Jpn)

Service Craft

ASY	Auxiliary yacht (Jpn)
TRV	Torpedo recovery vessel
WFL	Water/fuel lighter (Aust)
YAC	Royal yacht
YAG	Service craft, miscellaneous
YAS	Converted minesweeper tender
YDG	Degaussing craft
YDT	Diving tender
YE	Ammunition lighter
YFB	Ferry boat
YFL	Launch
YFS	Survey launch
YFU	Former LCU used for cargo
YGT	Floating target
YH	Ambulance boat
YNG	Gate craft
YO (G)	Fuel barge (gasolene)
YP	Harbour patrol craft
YPT	Torpedo recovery vessel (Can)
YR	Floating workshop
YT (B)(M)(L)	Harbour tug (large) (medium) (small)
YTR	Harbour fire/rescue craft
YTT	Torpedo trials craft
YW	Water barge

Pennant numbers of major surface ships in numerical order

Number	Ship's name	Type	Country
001	President H I Remeliik	PC	Palau
01	Adelaide	FFG	Australia
01	Pohjanmaa	ML	Finland
01	Tarangau	PC	Papua New Guinea
A 01	Paluma	AGSC	Australia
A 01	Rio Panuco	LST	Mexico
A 01	Contramaestre Casado	AP	Spain
B 01	Durango	AP	Mexico
C 01	Capitán de Navio Sebastian José Holzinger	PG	Mexico
CM 01	Muray Jib	FSG	UAE
E 01	Cuitlahuac	DD	Mexico
F 01	Abu Dhabi	FFG	UAE
FM 01	Presidente Eloy Alfaro	FFG	Ecuador
HQ 01	Pham Ngu Lao	FF	Vietnam
M 01	Viesturs	MSC	Latvia
P 01	Trident	PC	Barbados
P 01	Salamis	PC	Cyprus
P 01	Zibens	PCF	Latvia
P 01	Azteca	PC	Mexico
P 01	Capitan Cabral	PGR	Paraguay
Q 01	Damsah	PCFG	Qatar
S 01	Gladan	AXS	Sweden
SVG 01	Captain Mulzac	PC	St Vincent
02	Canberra	FFG	Australia
02	Hämeenmaa	ML	Finland
02	Dreger	PC	Papua New Guinea
02	Savo	PC	Solomon Islands
02	Tukoro	PC	Vanuatu
A 02	Mermaid	AGSC	Australia
A 02	Rio Papaloapan	LST	Mexico
A 02	Charles Upham	AK/AP/ AX	New Zealand
C 02	Capitán De Navio Blas Godinez Brito	PG	Mexico
CM 02	Das	FSG	UAE
F 02	Al Emirat	FFG	UAE
FM 02	Moran Valverde	FFG	Ecuador
KA 02	Spulga	PC	Latvia
M 02	Imanta	MSC	Latvia
P 02	Waspada	PCFG	Brunei
P 02	Heindrich Dor	PCF	Latvia
P 02	Guaycura	PC	Mexico
P 02	Nanawa	PGR	Paraguay
Q 02	Al Ghariyah	PCFG	Qatar
S 02	Falken	AXS	Sweden
03	Sydney	FFG	Australia
03	Lomor	PC	Marshall Islands
03	Seeadler	PC	Papua New Guinea
03	Lata	PC	Solomon Islands
A 03	Shepparton	AGSC	Australia
A 03	Rio Grijalva	AR	Mexico
C 03	Brigadier José Mariá de la Vega Gonzalez	PG	Mexico
H 03	Alejandro de Humbolt	AGOR	Mexico
KA 03	Cometa	PC	Latvia
M 03	Nemejs	MHC	Latvia
M 03	Visborg	ML/AGF/ AS	Sweden
P 03	Pejuang	PCFG	Brunei
P 03	Nahuatl	PC	Mexico
P 03	Yellow Elder	PCF	Bahamas
Q 03	Rbigah	PCFG	Qatar
04	Darwin	FFG	Australia
04	Karjala	FS	Finland
04	Basilisk	PC	Papua New Guinea
04	Auki	PC	Solomon Islands
A 04	Benalla	AGSC	Australia
A 04	Kahu	AXL	New Zealand
C 04	General Felipe B Berriozábal	PG	Mexico
H 04	Onjuku	AGS	Mexico
M 04	Carlskrona	ML/AXT	Sweden
N 04	Aktion	MLC	Greece
P 04	Port Nelson	PCF	Bahamas
P 04	Seteria	PCFG	Brunei
P 04	Bulta	PCF	Latvia
P 04	Totoran	PC	Mexico
P 04	Teneinte Farina	PGR	Paraguay
Q 04	Barzan	PGFG	Qatar
05	Melbourne	FFG	Australia
05	Uusimaa	ML	Finland
A 05	El Camino Español	AP	Spain
H 05	Altair	AGOR	Mexico
L 05	President El Hadj Omar Bongo	LST	Gabon
N 05	Amvrakia	MLC	Greece
P 05	Samana	PCF	Bahamas
P 05	Papago	PC	Mexico
P 05	Itaipú	PGR	Paraguay

Number	Ship's name	Type	Country
Q 05	Huwar	PGFG	Qatar
R 05	Invincible	CVS	UK
06	Newcastle	FFG	Australia
06	Condell	FFG	Chile
A 06	Edic class	LCT	Spain
H 06	Antares	AGOR	Mexico
P 06	Tarahumara	PC	Mexico
Q 06	Al Udeid	PGFG	Qatar
R 06	Illustrious	CVS	UK
07	Lynch	FFG	Chile
A 07	Cuauhtemoc	AXS	Mexico
A 07	Takapu	AGSC	New Zealand
C 07	Guanajuato	PG	Mexico
P 07	Général d'Armée Ba Oumar	PC	Gabon
P 07	Tepehuan	PC	Mexico
Q 07	Al Deebel	PGFG	Qatar
R 07	Ark Royal	CVS	UK
08	Ministro Zenteno	FFG	Chile
A 08	Aldebaran	AKS	Mexico
A 08	Tarapunga	AGSC	New Zealand
A 08	Edic class	LCT	Spain
H 08	Rio Hondo	AKS	Mexico
P 08	Colonel Djoue Dabany	PC	Gabon
P 08	Mexica	PC	Mexico
A 09	Manawanui	YDT	New Zealand
HQ 09	Petya class	FFL	Vietnam
P 09	Zapoteca	PC	Mexico
1	Uruguay	FFG	Uruguay
1/508	Petya III class	FFL	Syria
A 1	Comandante General Irigoyen	PG	Argentina
AOE 1	Sacramento	AOE	USA
B 1	Al Bushra	OPV	Oman
C 1	Paraguay	PGR	Paraguay
CMH 1	Dat Assawari	MHC	Egypt
D 1	Hercules	DDG	Argentina
FSM 1	Palikir	PC	Micronesia
LHA 1	Tarawa	LHA	USA
LHD 1	Wasp	LHD	USA
MCM 1	Avenger	MCM	USA
PC 1	Cyclone	PCF	USA
RSV 1	Safaga	MSI	Egypt
S 1	Shabab Oman	AXS	Oman
T-AGOS 1	Stalwart	AGOS	USA
Z 1	Baltyk	AORL	Poland
2	General Artigas	FFG	Uruguay
2/508	Petya class	FFL	Syria
A 2	Teniente Olivieri	PG	Argentina
A 2	Al Sultana	AKS	Oman
AOE 2	Camden	AOE	USA
B 2	Al Mansoor	OPV	Oman
C 2	Humaita	PGR	Paraguay
CMH 2	Navarin	MHC	Egypt
D 2	Santisima Trinidad	DDG	Argentina
FSM 2	Micronesia	PC	Micronesia
L 2	Nasr Al Bahr	LSL	Oman
LHA 2	Saipan	LHA	USA
LHD 2	Essex	LHD	USA
MCM 2	Defender	MCM	USA
PC 2	Tempest	PCF	USA
Q 2	Libertad	AXS	Argentina
RSV 2	Abu el Ghoson	MSI	Egypt
3	Montevideo	FFG	Uruguay
A 3	Francisco de Gurruchaga	PG	Argentina
AGF 3	La Salle	AGF	USA
AOE 3	Seattle	AOE	USA
T-AFS 3	Niagara Falls	AFS	USA
B 3	Canal Beagle	AKS	Argentina
B 3	Al Najah	OPV	Oman
CMH 3	Burullus	MHC	Egypt
FSM 3	Paluwlap	PC	Micronesia
LHA 3	Belleau Wood	LHA	USA
LHD 3	Kearsage	LHD	USA
MCM 3	Sentry	MCM	USA
PC 3	Hurricane	PCF	USA
PL 3	Sea Panther	PC	Hong Kong
T-AGOS 3	Vindicator	AGOS	USA
YAC 3	Oriole	AXS	Canada
Z 3	Krab	AOT	Poland
AOE 4	Detroit	AOE	USA
B 4	Bahia San Blas	AKS	Argentina
FSM 4	Constitution	PC	Micronesia
LHA 4	Nassau	LHA	USA
LHD 4	Boxer	LHD	USA
LPD 4	Austin	LPD	USA
MCM 4	Champion	MCM	USA
PC 4	Monsoon	PCF	USA
PL 4	Sea Horse	PC	Hong Kong
5	15 de Noviembre	PC	Uruguay

Number	Ship's name	Type	Country
B 5	Cabo de Hornos	AKS	Argentina
CG 5	Barracuda	PC	Trinidad and Tobago
FSM 5	Independence	PC	Micronesia
LHA 5	Peleliu	LHA	USA
LHD 5	Bataan	LHD	USA
LPD 5	Ogden	LPD	USA
M 5	Chaco	MHC	Argentina
MCM 5	Guardian	MCM	USA
PC 5	Typhoon	PCF	USA
Q 5	Almirante Irizar	AGB	Argentina
T-AFS 5	Concord	AFS	USA
6	25 de Agosto	PC	Uruguay
A 6	Suboficial Castillo	PG	Argentina
AOE 6	Supply	AOE	USA
CG 6	Cascadura	PC	Trinidad and Tobago
LHD 6	Bonhomme Richard	LHD	USA
LPD 6	Duluth	LPD	USA
M 6	Formosa	MHC	Argentina
MCM 6	Devastator	MCM	USA
PC 6	Sirocco	PCF	USA
T-AGOS 6	Persistent	AGOS	USA
7	Comodoro Coé	PC	Uruguay
AOE 7	Rainier	AOE	USA
LHD 7	Iwo Jima	LHD	USA
LPD 7	Cleveland	LPD	USA
MCM 7	Patriot	MCM	USA
P 7	Fort Charles	PC	Jamaica
PC 7	Squall	PCF	USA
T-AFS 7	San Jose	AFS	USA
T-AGOS 7	Indomitable	AGOS	USA
T-ARC 7	Zeus	ARC	USA
AOE 8	Arctic	AOE	USA
FFG 8	McInerney	FFG	USA
L 8	Saba Al Bahr	LCM	Oman
LPD 8	Dubuque	LPD	USA
MCM 8	Scout	MCM	USA
P 8	Paul Bogle	PC	Jamaica
PC 8	Zephyr	PCF	USA
T-AFS 8	Sirius	AFS	USA
T-AGOS 8	Prevail	AGOS	USA
Z 8	Meduza	AOT	Poland
A 9	Alferez Sobral	PG	Argentina
FFG 9	Wadsworth	FFG	USA
LPD 9	Denver	LPD	USA
L 9	Al Doghas	LCM	Oman
MCM 9	Pioneer	MCM	USA
PC 9	Chinook	PCF	USA
T-AFS 9	Spica	AFS	USA
T-AGOS 9	Assertive	AGOS	USA
Z 9	Slimak	AOT	Poland
10	Al Riffa	PCF	Bahrain
10	Colonia	PC	Uruguay
A 10	Comodoro Somellera	PG	Argentina
A 10	Rio Usumacinta	AP/AK/AH	Mexico
AOE 10	Bridge	AOE	USA
B 10	Dhofar	PCFG	Oman
D 10	Almirante Brown	DDG	Argentina
E 10	Ilhuicamina	DD	Mexico
GED 10	Guarapari	EDCG/LCU	Brazil
L 10	Al Temsah	LCM	Oman
L 10	Fearless	LPD	UK
LPD 10	Juneau	LPD	USA
MCM 10	Warrior	MCM	USA
P 10	San Salvador II	PC	Bahamas
P 10	Piratini	PC	Brazil
P 10	Huasteca	PC	Mexico
PC 10	Firebolt	PCF	USA
T-AFS 10	Saturn	AFS	USA
T-AGOS 10	Invincible	AGOS	USA
U 10	Aspirante Nascimento	AX	Brazil
011	Varyag	CG	Russia
11	Hawar	PCF	Bahrain
11	Smeli	FF	Bulgaria
11	Prat	DDG	Chile
11	Kralj Petar Kresimir IV	FSG	Croatia
11	Tuima	MLI	Finland
11	Mahamiru	MHC	Malaysia
11	Rio Negro	PC	Uruguay
A 11	Minas Gerais	CV	Brazil
A 11	Rio Coatzacoalcos	AP/AK/AH	Mexico
A 11	Endeavour	AOR	New Zealand
A 11	Marqués de la Ensenada	AORL	Spain
AGF 11	Coronado	AGF	USA
B 11	Al Sharqiyah	PCFG	Oman
BE 11	Simon Bolivar	AXS	Venezuela
BO 11	Punta Brava	AGOR	Venezuela
C 11	Cadete Virgilio Uribe Robles	PG	Mexico
CF 11	Amazonas	CF/PGR	Peru
CM 11	Esmeraldas	FSG	Ecuador
D 11	La Argentina	DDG	Argentina
E 11	Netzahualcoyotl	DD	Mexico
F 11	Zemaitis	FFL	Lithuania
GED 11	Tambaú	EDCG/LCU	Brazil
HQ 11	Petya class	FFL	Vietnam
K 11	Felinto Perry	ASR	Brazil
K 11	Stockholm	FSG	Sweden
M 11	Styrsö	MSI	Sweden
MCM 11	Gladiator	MCM	USA
MUL 11	Kalvsund	MLC	Sweden
P 11	Pirajá	PC	Brazil
P 11	Mazahua	PC	Mexico
P 11	Barceló	PCF	Spain
PC 11	Whirlwind	PCF	USA
PC 11	Constitutión	PCF	Venezuela
PF 11	Rajah Humabon	FF	Philippines
Q 11	Comodoro Rivadavia	AGS	Argentina
R 11	Gniewko	ATS	Poland
R 11	Principe de Asturias	CVS	Spain
U 11	Guarda Marinha Jensen	AX	Brazil
12	Cochrane	DDG	Chile
12	Kralj Tomislav	FSG	Croatia
12	Tuisku	MLI	Finland
12	Jerai	MHC	Malaysia
12	Paysandu	PC	Uruguay
B 12	Al Bat'nah	PCFG	Oman
C 12	Teniente José Azueta Abad	PG	Mexico
CF 12	Loreto	CF/PGR	Peru
CM 12	Manabi	FSG	Ecuador
D 12	Heroina	DDG	Argentina
F 12	Aukstaitis	FFL	Lithuania
FFG 12	George Philip	FFG	USA
GED 12	Camboriú	EDCG/LCU	Brazil
K 12	Malmö	FSG	Sweden
L 12	Ocean	LPH	UK
LPD 12	Shreveport	LPD	USA
M 12	Spårö	MSI	Sweden
MCM 12	Ardent	MCM	USA
MCS 12	Inchon	MCS	USA
MUL 12	Arkösund	MLC	Sweden
P 12	Pampeiro	PC	Brazil
P 12	Huichol	PC	Mexico
P 12	Laya	PCF	Spain
PC 12	Thunderbolt	PCF	USA
PC 12	Federación	PCFG	Venezuela
Q 12	Punta Alta	ABU	Argentina
R 12	Bolko	ATS	Poland
T-AGOS 12	Bold	AGOS	USA
U 12	Guarda Marinha Brito	AX	Brazil
13	Reshitelni	FS/PCF	Bulgaria
13	Ledang	MHC	Malaysia
13	Vice Admiral Mihai Gavrilescu	FS	Romania
A 13	Tunas Samudera	AXS	Malaysia
C 13	Capitan de Fragata Pedro Sáinz de Baranda Borreyro	PG	Mexico
CF 13	Marañon	CF/PGR	Peru
CM 13	Los Rios	FSG	Ecuador
D 13	Sarandi	DDG	Argentina
FFG 13	Samuel Eliot Morison	FFG	USA
H 13	Mestre João dos Santos	ABU	Brazil
HQ 13	Petya class	FFL	Vietnam
LPD 13	Nashville	LPD	USA
M 13	Skaftö	MSI	Sweden
MCM 13	Dextrous	MCM	USA
MUL 13	Kalmarsund	MLC	Sweden
P 13	Parati	PC	Brazil
P 13	Seri	PC	Mexico
P 13	Javier Quiroga	PCF	Spain
PC 13	Shamal	PCF	USA
PC 13	Independencia	PCF	Venezuela
R 13	Semko	ATS	Poland
14	Bodri	FS/PCF	Bulgaria
14	Tuuli	MLI	Finland
14	Kinabalu	MHC	Malaysia
14	Vice Admiral Ioan Balanescu	FS	Romania
A 14	Resolution	AGS	New Zealand
A 14	Patiño	AOR	Spain
AGOR 14	Melville	AGOR	USA
B 14	Mussandam	PCFG	Oman
C 14	Comodoro Carlos Castillo Bretón Barrero	PG	Mexico
CF 14	Ucayali	CF/PGR	Peru
CM 14	El Oro	FSG	Ecuador
FFG 14	John H Sides	FFG	USA
J 14	Nirupak	AGS	India
L 14	Ghorpad	LSM	India
L 14	Albion	LPD	UK
LPD 14	Trenton	LPD	USA

Number	Ship's name	Type	Country
M 14	Sturkö	MSI	Sweden
MCM 14	Chief	MCM	USA
P 14	Penedo	PC	Brazil
P 14	Antipoploiarchos Anninos	PCFG	Greece
P 14	Yaqui	PC	Mexico
P 14	Ordóñez	PCF	Spain
PC 14	Tornado	PC	USA
PC 14	Libertad	PCFG	Venezuela
R 14	Zbyszko	ARS	Poland
15	Blanco Encalada	DDG	Chile
15	Tyrsky	MLI	Finland
15	Vice Admiral Emil Gregescu	FS	Romania
A 15	Nireehshak	ASR	India
AGOR 15	Knorr	AGOR	USA
C 15	Vicealmirante Othón Blanco Nunez de Caceres	PG	Mexico
CM 15	Los Galapagos	FSG	Ecuador
F 15	Abu Bakr	FF	Bangladesh
FFG 15	Estocin	FFG	USA
G 15	Paraguassú	AKS	Brazil
HQ 15	Petya class	FFL	Vietnam
J 15	Investigator	AGS	India
L 15	Kesari	LSM	India
L 15	Bulwark	LPD	UK
LPD 15	Ponce	LPD	USA
M 15	Aratú	MSC	Brazil
MUL 15	Grundsund	MLC	Sweden
P 15	Poti	PC	Brazil
P 15	Ipoploiarchos Arliotis	PCFG	Greece
P 15	Tlapaneco	PC	Mexico
P 15	Acevedo	PCF	Spain
PC 15	Patria	PCF	Venezuela
Q 15	Cormoran	AGS	Argentina
R 15	Hazirani	PCFG	Iraq
R 15	Macko	ARS	Poland
V 15	Imperial Marinheiro	PG	Brazil
16	Vice Admiral Ioan Georgescu	FS	Romania
C 16	Contralmirante Angel Ortiz Monasterio	PG	Mexico
CM 16	Loja	FSG	Ecuador
F 16	Umar Farooq	FF	Bangladesh
J 16	Jamuna	AGS	India
L 16	Shardul	LSM	India
M 16	Anhatomirim	MSC	Brazil
P 16	Ipoploiarchos Konidis	PCFG	Greece
P 16	Tarasco	PC	Mexico
P 16	Cándido Pérez	PCF	Spain
PC 16	Victoria	PCFG	Venezuela
T-AGOS 16	Capable	AGOS	USA
U 16	Trinidade	ATS	Brazil
F 17	Ali Haider	FF	Bangladesh
G 17	Potengi	AGP	Brazil
HQ 17	Petya class	FFL	Vietnam
J 17	Sutlej	AGS	India
L 17	Sharabh	LSM	India
LPD 17	San Antonio	LPD	USA
M 17	Atalaia	MSC	Brazil
MUL 17	Skramsösund	AG	Sweden
P 17	Ipoploairchos Batsis	PCFG	Greece
P 17	Acolhua	PC	Mexico
U 17	Parnaiba	AG	Brazil
A 18	Perkons	ATA	Latvia
F 18	Osman	FFG	Bangladesh
H 18	Comandante Varella	ABU	Brazil
J 18	Sandhayak	AGS	India
K 18	Bryza	AXL	Poland
L 18	Cheetah	LSM	India
LPD 18	New Orleans	LPD	USA
M 18	Araćatuba	MSC	Brazil
MUL 18	Fårösund	MLC	Sweden
P 18	Armatolos	PG	Greece
P 18	Otomi	PC	Mexico
U 18	Oswaldo Cruz	AH	Brazil
H 19	Tenente Castelo	ABU	Brazil
J 19	Nirdeshak	AGS	India
L 19	Mahish	LSM	India
LCC 19	Blue Ridge	LCC	USA
M 19	Abrolhas	MSC	Brazil
MUL 19	Barösund	MLC	Sweden
P 19	Navmachos	PG	Greece
P 19	Mayo	PC	Mexico
PS 19	Miguel Malvar	FS	Philippines
T-AGOS 19	Victorious	AGOS	USA
AH 19	Mercy	AH	USA
U 19	Carlos Chagas	AH	Brazil
V 19	Caboclo	PG	Brazil
20	Ahmad El Fateh	PCFG	Bahrain
20	Capitan Miranda	AXS	Uruguay
020	Mitrofan Moskalenko	LPD	Russia
A 20	Rio Nautla	AKS	Mexico
A 20	Moawin	AOR	Pakistan
A 20	Neptuno	ATA	Spain

Number	Ship's name	Type	Country
AH 20	Comfort	AH	USA
E 20	Miguel Hidalgo	FF	Mexico
F 20	Godavari	FFG	India
G 20	Custódio de Mello	AKS	Brazil
H 20	Comandante Manhães	ABU	Brazil
L 20	Magar	LST	India
LCC 20	Mount Whitney	LCC	USA
M 20	Albardão	MSC	Brazil
MUL 20	Furusund	MLC	Sweden
P 20	Murature	PG	Argentina
P 20	Pedro Teixera	PBR	Brazil
P 20	Antiploiarchos Laskos	PCFG	Greece
P 20	Deirdre	OPV	Ireland
P 20	Pimas	PC	Mexico
PS 20	Magat Salamat	FS	Philippines
Q 20	Puerto Deseado	AGOB	Argentina
T-AGOS 20	Able	AGOS	USA
U 20	Cisne Branco	AXS	Brazil
V 20	Angostura	PG	Brazil
21	Al Jabiri	PCFG	Bahrain
21	Sibenic	PCFG	Croatia
21	Hejaz	LCT	Iran
21	Sour	LST	Lebanon
21	Vigilant	OPV	Mauritius
21	Sirius	ABU	Uruguay
A 21	Rio Tonala	AKSL	Mexico
A 21	Kalmat	AOTL	Pakistan
A 21	Castor	AGS	Spain
AGOR 21	Gyre	AGOR	USA
ASR 21	Chung Hae Jin	ASR	Korea, South
CM 21	Velarde	CM/PCFG	Peru
E 21	Vincente Guerrero	FF	Mexico
F 21	Gomati	FFG	India
F 21	Mariscal Sucre	FFG	Venezuela
G 21	Ary Parreiras	AKS	Brazil
H 21	Sirius	AGS	Brazil
J 21	Darshak	AGS	India
K 21	Göteborg	FSG	Sweden
L 21	Guldar	LSM	India
LM 21	Quito	PCFG	Ecuador
M 21	Júcar	MSC	Spain
P 21	King	PG	Argentina
P 21	Raposo Tavares	PBR	Brazil
P 21	Plotarhis Blessas	PCFG	Greece
P 21	Emer	OPV	Ireland
P 21	Chichimeca	PC	Mexico
P 21	Anaga	PC	Spain
R 21	Tritão	ATA	Brazil
RP 21	Fernando Gomez	AK	Venezuela
T-AGOS 21	Effective	AGOS	USA
V 21	Bahiana	PG	Brazil
Y 21	Oilpress	AOTL	UK
22	Abdul Rahman Al Fadel	PCFG	Bahrain
22	Karabala	LCT	Iran
22	Damour	LST	Lebanon
22	Oyarvide	AGS	Uruguay
A 22	Rio Lerma	AK	Mexico
A 22	Pollux	AGS	Spain
CM 22	Santillana	CM/PCFG	Peru
E 22	Jose Maria Morelos Y Pavon	FF	Mexico
F 22	Ganga	FFG	India
F 22	Almirante Brión	FFG	Venezuela
G 22	Soares Dutra	AKS	Brazil
J 22	Sarveskhak	AGS	India
K 22	Gävle	FSG	Sweden
L 22	Kumbhir	LSM	India
M 22	Ebro	MSC	Spain
P 22	Ipoploiarchos Mikonios	PCFG	Greece
P 22	Aoife	OPV	Ireland
P 22	Chontal	PC	Mexico
P 22	Tagomago	PC	Spain
PS 22	Sultan Kudarat	FS	Philippines
R 22	Tridente	ATA	Brazil
R 22	Viraat	CV	India
RM 22	Enriquillo	PG/ATA	Dominican Republic
T-AGOS 22	Loyal	AGOS	USA
23	Al Taweelah	PCFG	Bahrain
23	Amir	LCT	Iran
A 23	Antares	AGS	Spain
AGOR 23	Thomas G Thompson	AGOR	USA
CM 23	De los Heros	CM/PCFG	Peru
F 23	General Urdaneta	FFG	Venezuela
G 23	Almirante Gastão Motta	AOR	Brazil
K 23	Kalmar	FSG	Sweden
L 23	Gharial	LST	India
LM 23	Guayaquil	PCFG	Ecuador
P 23	Ipoploiarchos Troupakis	PCFG	Greece
P 23	Aisling	OPV	Ireland
P 23	Mazateco	PC	Mexico
P 23	Marola	PC	Spain
PS 23	Datu Marikudo	FS	Philippines

Number	Ship's name	Type	Country
R 23	Triunfo	ATA	Brazil
T-AGM 23	Observation Island	AGM	USA
T-AGOS 23	Impeccable	AGOS	USA
V 23	Purus	PG	Brazil
24	Farsi	LST	Iran
24	Rahmat	FF/AX	Malaysia
24	Lieutenant Remus Lepri	MSC	Romania
24	Comandante Pedro Campbell	AGOR	Uruguay
A 24	Rio Tehuantepec	AKS	Mexico
A 24	Rigel	AGS	Spain
AGOR 24	Roger Revelle	AGOR	USA
CM 24	Herrera	CM/PCFG	Peru
F 24	General Soublette	FFG	Venezuela
H 24	Castelhanos	ABU	Brazil
K 24	Sundsvall	FSG	Sweden
LM 24	Cuenca	PCFG	Ecuador
M 24	Tajo	MSC	Spain
P 24	Simeoforos Kavaloudis	PCFG	Greece
P 24	Tolteca	PC	Mexico
P 24	Mouro	PC	Spain
R 24	Almirante Guilhem	ATA	Brazil
V 24	Solimões	PG	Brazil
25	Sardasht	LST	Iran
25	Kasturi	FSG	Malaysia
25	Lieutenant Lupu Dinescu	MSC	Romania
AGOR 25	Atlantis	AGOR	USA
AT 25	Ang Pangulo	AP	Philippines
CM 25	Larrea	CM/PCFG	Peru
F 25	General Salom	FFG	Venezuela
H 25	Tenente Boanerges	ABU	Brazil
LM 25	Manta	PCFG	Ecuador
M 25	Genil	MSC	Spain
P 25	Maya	PC	Mexico
P 25	Grosa	PC	Spain
R 25	Almirante Guillobel	ATA	Brazil
26	Sab Sahel	LST	Iran
26	Lekir	FSG	Malaysia
26	Vanguardia	ARS	Uruguay
AGOR 26	Ronald H Brown	AGOR	USA
CM 26	Sanchez Carrillon	CM/PCFG	Peru
F 26	Almirante Garcia	FFG	Venezuela
G 26	Duque de Caxais	LST	Brazil
H 26	Faroleiro Mário Seixas	ABU	Brazil
M 26	Odiel	MSC	Spain
P 26	Dzata	PCF	Ghana
P 26	Ipoploiarchos Degiannis	PCFG	Greece
P 26	Cochimie	PC	Mexico
P 26	Medas	PC	Spain
T-AE 26	Kilauea	AE	USA
27	Banco Ortiz	YTB	Uruguay
A 27	Rio Suchiate	AKS	Mexico
ATS 27	Pyong Taek	ARS/ATS	Korea, South
D 27	Pará	FF	Brazil
G 27	Marajo	AOR	Brazil
H 27	Faroleiro Areas	ABU	Brazil
LM 27	Nuevo Rocafuerte	PCFG	Ecuador
M 27	Sil	MSC	Spain
P 27	Sebo	PCF	Ghana
P 27	Simeoforos Xenos	PCFG	Greece
P 27	Cora	PC	Mexico
P 27	Izaro	PC	Spain
PN 27	Sipa	AOTL	Yugoslavia
T-AE 27	Butte	AE	USA
T-AGS 27	Kane	AGS	USA
U 27	Brasil	AX	Brazil
ATS 28	Kwang Yang	ARS/ATS	Korea, South
D 28	Paraíba	FF	Brazil
FFG 28	Boone	FFG	USA
G 28	Mattoso Maia	LST	Brazil
P 28	Achimota	PCF	Ghana
P 28	Simeoforos Simitzopoulos	PCFG	Greece
P 28	Totonaca	PC	Mexico
P 28	Tabarca	PC	Spain
PS 28	Cebu	FS	Philippines
T-AE 28	Santa Barbara	AE	USA
29	Jebat	FFG	Malaysia
29	Lieutenant Dmitrie Nocolescu	MSC	Romania
D 29	Paraná	FF	Brazil
FFG 29	Stephen W Groves	FFG	USA
M 29	Brecon	MHSC	UK
P 29	Yogaga	PCF	Ghana
P 29	Simeoforos Starakis	PCFG	Greece
P 29	Kondor I class	PC	Malta
P 29	Mixteco	PC	Mexico
P 29	Deva	PC	Spain
PS 29	Negros Occidental	FS	Philippines
30	Casma	PCFG	Chile
30	Lekiu	FFG	Malaysia
30	Sub Lieutenant Alexandru Axente	MSC	Romania
D 30	Pernambuco	FF	Brazil
E 30	Comodoro Manuel Azueta Perillos	FF/AX	Mexico
G 30	Ceará	LSD	Brazil
H 30	Faroleiro Nascimento	ABU	Brazil
M 30	Ledbury	MHSC	UK
P 30	Roirama	PBR	Brazil
P 30	Kondor I class	PC	Malta
P 30	Olmeca	PC	Mexico
P 30	Bergantín	PC	Spain
Q 30	Al Mabrukah	FS/AXL/AGS	Oman
V 30	Inhaúma	FSG	Brazil
31	Drummond	FFG	Argentina
31	Iskar	MSC	Bulgaria
31	Chipana	PCFG	Chile
31	Salamaua	LCM	Papua New Guinea
31	Temerario	MSC	Uruguay
A 31	Malaspina	AGS	Spain
A 31	Ferrol	ATA	Spain
F 31	Brahmaputra	FFG	India
F 31	Descubierta	FFG/FSG	Spain
G 31	Rio de Janeiro	LSD	Brazil
H 31	Argus	AGS	Brazil
LG 31	25 de Julio	PC	Ecuador
M 31	Segura	MHC	Spain
M 31	Gåssten	MSI	Sweden
M 31	Cattistock	MHSC	UK
P 31	Rondônia	PBR	Brazil
P 31	Eithne	OPV	Ireland
P 31	Dzükas	PCF	Lithuania
P 31	Kondor I class	PC	Malta
P 31	Tlahuica	PC	Mexico
P 31	Conejera	PC	Spain
PS 31	Pangasinan	FS	Philippines
Q 31	Qahir Al Amwaj	FSG	Oman
V 31	Jaceguay	FSG	Brazil
32	Guerrico	FFG	Argentina
32	Zibar	MSC	Bulgaria
32	Iquique	PCFG	Chile
32	Buna	LSM	Papua New Guinea
32	Valiente	MSC	Uruguay
32	Podgorica	FFG	Yugoslavia
A 32	Tofiño	AGS	Spain
F 32	Betwa	FFG	India
F 32	Diana	FFG/FSG	Spain
FFG 32	John L Hall	FFG	USA
H 32	Orion	AGS	Brazil
M 32	Sella	MHC	Spain
M 32	Norsten	MSI	Sweden
M 32	Cottesmore	MHSC	UK
P 32	Amapá	PBR	Brazil
P 32	Dragonera	PC	Spain
PS 32	Iloilo	FS	Philippines
Q 32	Al Mua'zzar	FSG	Oman
T-AE 32	Flint	AE	USA
V 32	Julio de Noronha	FSG	Brazil
Y 32	Moorhen	ARS	UK
33	Granville	FFG	Argentina
33	Dobrotich	MSC	Bulgaria
33	Covadonga	PCFG	Chile
33	Fortuna	MSC	Uruguay
33	Kotor	FFG	Yugoslavia
A 33	Hespérides	AGOB	Spain
AW 33	Lake Bulusan	AWT	Philippines
BB 33	Gorgona	AGS	Colombia
F 33	Beas	FFG	India
F 33	Infanta Elena	FFG/FSG	Spain
FFG 33	Jarrett	FFG	USA
J 33	Makar	AGS	India
L 33	Teraban	LCU	Brunei
M 33	Tambre	MHC	Spain
M 33	Viksten	MSI	Sweden
M 33	Brocklesby	MHSC	UK
P 33	Abhay	FS	India
P 33	Espalmador	PC	Spain
RA 33	Miguel Rodriguez	PG/AGS	Venezuela
T-AE 33	Shasta	AE	USA
V 33	Frontin	FSG	Brazil
Y 33	Moorfowl	ARS	UK
34	Evstati Vinarov	MSC	Bulgaria
34	Angamos	PCFG	Chile
34	Kris	PC	Malaysia
34	Audaz	MSC	Uruguay
34	Novi Sad	FFG	Yugoslavia
AW 34	Lake Paoay	AWT	Philippines
F 34	Himgiri	FF	India
F 34	Infanta Cristina	FFG/FSG	Spain
H 34	Almirante Graça Aranha	YAG	Brazil
J 34	Mithun	AGS	India
L 34	Serasa	LCU	Brunei
L 34	Vasco da Gama	LCU	India
M 34	Turia	MHC	Spain

PENNANT LIST

Number	Ship's name	Type	Country
M 34	Middleton	MHSC	UK
P 34	Ajay	FS	India
P 34	Alcanada	PC	Spain
PB 34	Kozara	PG	Yugoslavia
T-AE 34	Mount Baker	AE	USA
V 34	Barroso	FSG	Brazil
BB35	Vis class	PG	Yugoslavia
F 35	Cazadora	FFG/FSG	Spain
H 35	Amorim do Valle	ABU	Brazil
J 35	Meen	AGS	India
LG 35	5 de Agosto	PC	Ecuador
M 35	Dulverton	MHSC	UK
P 35	Akshay	FS	India
PS 35	Emilio Jacinto	FS	Philippines
T-AE 35	Kiska	AE	USA
36	Riquelme	PCFG	Chile
36	Sundang	PC	Malaysia
F 36	Dunagiri	FF	India
F 36	Vencedora	FFG/FSG	Spain
FFG 36	Underwood	FFG	USA
H 36	Taurus	ABU	Brazil
J 36	Mesh	AGS	India
LG 36	27 de Febrero	PC	Ecuador
LSD 36	Anchorage	LSD	USA
P 36	Agray	FS	India
PS 36	Apolinario Mabini	FS	Philippines
37	Orella	PCFG	Chile
37	Badek	PC	Malaysia
FFG 37	Crommelin	FFG	USA
H 37	Garnier Sampaio	ABU	Brazil
LSD 37	Portland	LSD	USA
M 37	Chiddingfold	MHSC	UK
PS 37	Artemio Ricarte	FS	Philippines
38	Serrano	PCFG	Chile
38	Renchong	PC	Malaysia
FFG 38	Curts	FFG	USA
L 38	Midhur	LCU	India
L 38	Galana	LCM	Kenya
M 38	Atherstone	MHSC	UK
39	Uribe	PCFG	Chile
39	Tombak	PC	Malaysia
AS 39	Emory S Land	AS	USA
FFG 39	Doyle	FFG	USA
L 39	Mangala	LCU	India
L 39	Tana	LCM	Kenya
LSD 39	Mount Vernon	LSD	USA
M 39	Hurworth	MHSC	UK
40	Lembing	AXL	Malaysia
A 40	Attock	AWT	Pakistan
AS 40	Frank Cable	AS	USA
E 40	Nicolas Bravo	FF	Mexico
F 40	Niteroi	FFG	Brazil
FFG 40	Halyburton	FFG	USA
H 40	Antares	AGS	Brazil
K 40	Veer	FSG	India
P 40	Grajaú	PG	Brazil
041	Madeleine	PC	Lithuania
41	Espora	FFG	Argentina
41	Brisbane	DDG	Australia
41	Ajeera	AFL	Bahrain
41	Letyashti	FS	Bulgaria
41	Yan Taing Aung	FS	Burma
41	Aquiles	AP	Chile
41	Dubrovnik	PCF/ML	Croatia
41	Serampang	PC	Malaysia
A 41	Vetra	AGOR/AX	Lithuania
F 41	Defensora	FFG	Brazil
F 41	Taragiri	FF	India
FFG 41	McClusky	FFG	USA
H 41	Almirante Câmara	AGOR	Brazil
K 41	Nirbhik	FSG	India
L 41	Hernán Cortés	LST	Spain
LSD 41	Whidbey Island	LSD	USA
M 41	Quorn	MHSC	UK
P 41	Guaiba	PG	Brazil
P 41	Orla	PG	Ireland
PO 41	Espartana	PCF	Colombia
42	Rosales	FFG	Argentina
42	Mashtan	LCU	Bahrain
42	Bditelni	FS	Bulgaria
42	Yan Gyi Aung	FS	Burma
42	Merino	AS	Chile
42	Panah	PC	Malaysia
A 42	Portrero Del Llano	AOT	Mexico
E 42	Hermenegildo Galeana	FF	Mexico
F 42	Constituição	FFG	Brazil
F 42	Vindhyagiri	FF	India
FFG 42	Klakring	FFG	USA
H 42	Barão de Teffé	AGOB	Brazil
K 42	Nipat	FSG	India
L 42	Pizarro	LST	Spain
LSD 42	Germantown	LSD	USA

Number	Ship's name	Type	Country
P 42	Graúna	PG	Brazil
P 42	Ciara	PG	Ireland
P 42	Cabo Corrientes	PC	Mexico
PO 42	Pablo José	PC	Colombia
43	Spiro	FFG	Argentina
43	Rubodh	LCU	Bahrain
43	Bezstrashni	FS	Bulgaria
43	Esmeralda	AXS	Chile
43	Kerambit	AXL	Malaysia
F 43	Liberal	FFG	Brazil
FFG 43	Thach	FFG	USA
K 43	Nishank	FSG	India
LSD 43	Fort McHenry	LSD	USA
M 43	Guadalquivir	MSO	Spain
M 43	Hisingen	MSI/YDT	Sweden
N 43	Lindormen	MLC	Denmark
P 43	Goiana	PG	Brazil
P 43	Cabo Corzo	PC	Mexico
PO 43	Jorge Enrique Marquez Duran	PC	Colombia
44	Parker	FFG	Argentina
44	Suwad	LCU	Bahrain
44	Khrabri	FS	Bulgaria
44	Beladau	AXL	Malaysia
A 44	Bholu	YTB	Pakistan
F 44	Independencia	FFG	Brazil
H 44	Ary Rangel	AGOB	Brazil
K 44	Nirghat	FSG	India
LSD 44	Gunston Hall	LSD	USA
M 44	Blackan	MSI/YDT	Sweden
N 44	Lossen	MLC	Denmark
P 44	Guajará	PG	Brazil
P 44	Kirpan	FSG	India
P 44	Cabo Catoche	PC	Mexico
T 44	Puerto Cabello	AK	Venezuela
45	Robinson	FFG	Argentina
45	Jervis Bay	AP	Australia
45	Kelewang	PC	Malaysia
45	Mikhail Kogalniceanu	PGR	Romania
A 45	Las Chiopas	YOG/YO	Mexico
A 45	Gama	YTB	Pakistan
F 45	União	FFG	Brazil
FFG 45	De Wert	FFG	USA
K 45	Vibhuti	FSG	India
LSD 45	Comstock	LSD	USA
M 45	Dämman	MSI/YDT	Sweden
P 45	Guaporé	PG	Brazil
T-AG 45	Waters	AG	USA
46	Gomez Roca	FFG	Argentina
46	Contralmirante Oscar Viel Toro	AGS	Chile
46	Rentaka	PC	Malaysia
46	I C Bratianu	PGR	Romania
A 46	Amatlan	YOG/YO	Mexico
AE 46	Cape Bojeador	ABU	Philippines
F 46	Greenhalgh	FFG	Brazil
F 46	Krishna	AX	India
FFG 46	Rentz	FFG	USA
K 46	Vipul	FSG	India
LSD 46	Tortuga	LSD	USA
M 46	Galten	MSI/YDT	Sweden
P 46	Kuthar	FSG	India
P 46	Gurupá	PG	Brazil
47	Sri Perlis	AXL	Malaysia
47	Lascar Catargiu	PGR	Romania
A 47	Nasr	AOR	Pakistan
CG 47	Ticonderoga	CG	USA
F 47	Dodsworth	FFG	Brazil
FFG 47	Nicholas	FFG	USA
K 47	Vinash	FSG	India
LSD 47	Rushmore	LSD	USA
P 47	Khanjar	FSG	India
P 47	Gurupi	PG	Brazil
CG 48	Yorktown	CG	USA
F 48	Bosisio	FFG	Brazil
FFG 48	Vandegrift	FFG	USA
K 48	Vidyut	FSG	India
LSD 48	Ashland	LSD	USA
P 48	Guanabara	PG	Brazil
49	Sri Johor	AXL	Malaysia
A 49	Gwadar	AOTL	Pakistan
CG 49	Vincennes	CG	USA
F 49	Rademaker	FFG	Brazil
FFG 49	Robert G Bradley	FFG	USA
LSD 49	Harpers Ferry	LSD	USA
P 49	Guaruja	PG	Brazil
P 49	Khukri	FSG	India
50	Al Manama	FSG	Bahrain
A 50	Alster	AGI	Germany
A 50	Quezalcoatl	ATF	Mexico
ARS 50	Safeguard	ARS	USA
C 50	General Miguel Negrete	OPV	Mexico
CG 50	Valley Forge	CG	USA

Number	Ship's name	Type	Country
E 50	Ignacio Allende	FF	Mexico
FFG 50	Taylor	FFG	USA
L 50	Tobruk	LSL	Australia
LSD 50	Carter Hall	LSD	USA
N 50	Tyr	ML	Norway
P 50	Guaratuba	PG	Brazil
P 50	Hesperos	PCF	Greece
P 50	Sukanya	OPV	India
51	Al Muharraq	FSG	Bahrain
A 51	Huitilopochtli	ATF	Mexico
A 51	Mahón	ATA	Spain
ARS 51	Grasp	ARS	USA
BE 51	Guayas	AXS	Ecuador
C 51	General Manuel Gonzalez	OPV	Mexico
CG 51	Thomas S Gates	CG	USA
D 51	Rajput	DDG	India
DDG 51	Arleigh Burke	DDG	USA
E 51	Mariano Abasolo	FF	Mexico
FFG 51	Gary	FFG	USA
FL 51	Almirante Padilla	FSG	Colombia
FM 51	Carvajal	FFG	Peru
L 51	Kanimbla	LPA/LST	Australia
L 51	Galicia	LPD	Spain
LSD 51	Oak Hill	LSD	USA
MHC 51	Osprey	MHC	USA
P 51	Gravataí	PG	Brazil
P 51	Subhadra	OPV	India
P 51	Roisin	OPV	Ireland
PL 51	Protector	PC	Hong Kong
T-AGS 51	John McDonnell	AGS	USA
052	Vorovsky	FFH	Russia
A 52	Oste	AGI	Germany
A 52	Matanga	ATA	India
A 52	Kukulkan	ATF	Mexico
A 52	Las Palmas	ATA	Spain
ARS 52	Salvor	ARS	USA
C 52	General Manuel E Rincon	OPV	Mexico
CG 52	Bunker Hill	CG	USA
D 52	Rana	DDG	India
DDG 52	Barry	DDG	USA
E 52	Knox class	FF	Mexico
FFG 52	Carr	FFG	USA
FL 52	Caldas	FSG	Colombia
FM 52	Villavicencio	FFG	Peru
L 52	Manoora	LPA/LST	Australia
L 52	Castilla	LPD	Spain
LSD 52	Pearl Harbor	LSD	USA
M 52	Süduvis	MHC	Lithuania
MHC 52	Heron	MHC	USA
N 52	Vidar	ML	Norway
P 52	Suvarna	OPV	India
PL 52	Guardian	PC	Hong Kong
T-AGS 52	Littlehales	AGS	USA
53	Araucano	AOR	Chile
A 53	Oker	AGI	Germany
A 53	Ambika	ATS	India
A 53	Ehacatl	ATF	Mexico
A 53	La Graña	ATA	Spain
ARS 53	Grapple	ARS	USA
C 53	General Felipe Xicotencatl	OPV	Mexico
CG 53	Mobile Bay	CG	USA
D 53	Ranjit	DDG	India
DDG 53	John Paul Jones	DDG	USA
FFG 53	Hawes	FFG	USA
FL 53	Antioquia	FSG	Colombia
FM 53	Montero	FFG	Peru
MHC 53	Pelican	MHC	USA
N 53	Vale	ML	Norway
P 53	Kyklon	PCF	Greece
P 53	Savitri	OPV	India
PL 53	Defender	PC	Hong Kong
54	Raisio	PC	Finland
A 54	Amba	AS	India
A 54	Tonatiuh	ATF	Mexico
C 54	Cadete Augustin Melgar	OPV	Mexico
CG 54	Antietam	CG	USA
D 54	Ranvir	DDG	India
DDG 54	Curtis Wilbur	DDG	USA
FFG 54	Ford	FFG	USA
FL 54	Independiente	FSG	Colombia
FM 54	Mariategui	FFG	Peru
MHC 54	Robin	MHC	USA
P 54	Lelaps	PCF	Greece
P 54	Saryu	OPV	India
PL 54	Preserver	PC	Hong Kong
055	Marshal Ustinov	CG	Russia
55	Röytta	PC	Finland
A 55	Chac	ATF	Mexico
C 55	Teniente Juan De La Barrera	OPV	Mexico
CG 55	Leyte Gulf	CG	USA
D 55	Ranvijay	DDG	India
DDG 55	Stout	DDG	USA
FFG 55	Elrod	FFG	USA
FV 55	Indaw	OPV	Burma
MHC 55	Oriole	MHC	USA
P 55	Sharada	OPV	India
PL 55	Rescuer	PC	Hong Kong
C 56	Cadete Juan Escutia	OPV	Mexico
CG 56	San Jacinto	CG	USA
DDG 56	John S McCain	DDG	USA
FFG 56	Simpson	FFG	USA
FV 56	Inma	OPV	Burma
MHC 56	Kingfisher	MHC	USA
P 56	Tyfon	PCF	Greece
P 56	Sujata	OPV	India
PL 56	Detector	PC	Hong Kong
057	Dzerzhinsky	FFH	Russia
A 57	Shakti	AOR	India
AO 57	Chun Jee	AOR	Korea, South
C 57	Cadete Fernando Montes De Oca	OPV	Mexico
CG 57	Lake Champlain	CG	USA
DDG 57	Mitscher	DDG	USA
FFG 57	Reuben James	FFG	USA
FV 57	Inya	OPV	Burma
MHC 57	Cormorant	MHC	USA
P 57	Pirpolitis	PG	Greece
A 58	Jyoti	AOR	India
AO 58	Dae Chung	AOR	Korea, South
CG 58	Philippine Sea	CG	USA
DDG 58	Laboon	DDG	USA
FFG 58	Samuel B Roberts	FFG	USA
MHC 58	Black Hawk	MHC	USA
A 59	Aditya	AOR/AR	India
AO 59	Hwa Chun	AOR	Korea, South
C 59	Cadete Francisco Marquez	OPV	Mexico
CG 59	Princeton	CG	USA
DDG 59	Russell	DDG	USA
FFG 59	Kauffman	FFG	USA
MHC 59	Falcon	MHC	USA
60	Vidal Gormaz	AGOR	Chile
60	Helsinki	PCFG	Finland
060	Anadyr	FFH	Russia
A 60	Gorch Fock	AXS	Germany
C 60	General Ignacio Zaragoza	OPV	Mexico
CG 60	Normandy	CG	USA
FFG 60	Rodney M Davis	FFG	USA
DDG 60	Paul Hamilton	DDG	USA
M 60	Erato	MSC	Greece
MHC 60	Cardinal	MHC	USA
P 60	Bahamas	OPV	Bahamas
P 60	Bracui	PG	Brazil
T-AGS 60	Pathfinder	AGS	USA
61	Briz	MSC	Bulgaria
61	Mirna class	PCF	Croatia
61	Turku	PCFG	Finland
61	Ashdod	LCT	Israel
C 61	Cadete Vicente Suarez	OIPV	Mexico
CG 61	Monterey	CG	USA
D 61	Delhi	DDG	India
FFG 61	Ingraham	FFG	USA
DDG 61	Ramage	DDG	USA
M 61	Evniki	MSC	Greece
M 61	Pondicherry	MSO	India
MHC 61	Raven	MHC	USA
P 61	Baradero	PC	Argentina
P 61	Nassau	OPV	Bahamas
P 61	Benevente	PG	Brazil
P 61	Polemistis	PG	Greece
P 61	Kora	FSG	India
P 61	Chilreu	PG	Spain
Q 61	Ciudad De Carate	ABU	Argentina
T 61	Capana	LST	Venezuela
T-AGS 61	Sumner	AGS	USA
TR 61	Hualcopo	LST	Ecuador
62	Shkval	MSC	Bulgaria
62	Solta	PCF	Croatia
62	Oulu	PCFG	Finland
CG 62	Chancellorsville	CG	USA
D 62	Mysore	DDG	India
DDG 62	Fitzgerald	DDG	USA
M 62	Porbandar	MSO	India
MHC 62	Shrike	MHC	USA
P 62	Barranqueras	PC	Argentina
P 62	Bocaina	PG	Brazil
P 62	Niki	FS	Greece
P 62	Alboran	PG	Spain
Q 62	Ciudad De Rosario	ABU	Argentina
T 62	Esequibo	LST	Venezuela
T-AGS 62	Bowditch	AGS	USA
TR 62	Calicuchima	AKF	Ecuador
63	Ppiboy	MSC	Bulgaria
63	George Slight Marshall	ABU	Chile
63	Mirna class	PCF	Croatia

Number	Ship's name	Type	Country	Number	Ship's name	Type	Country
63	Kotka	PCFG	Finland	M 72	Arholma	MHC	Sweden
063	Admiral Kuznetsov	CVN	Russia	P 72	Ipopliarchos Votsis	PCFG	Greece
A 63	Torpédistra Hernandez	AWT	Spain	P 72	Centinela	OPV	Spain
CG 63	Cowpens	CG	USA	RM 72	Pedro de Heredia	PG	Colombia
CV 63	Kitty Hawk	CV	USA	T 72	La Orchila	LCU	Venezuela
D 63	Bombay	DDG	India	73	Isaza	PC	Chile
DDG 63	Stethem	DDG	USA	73	Faust Vrančič	ASR	Croatia
M 63	Bedi	MSO	India	73	Naantali	PCFG	Finland
P 63	Clorinda	PC	Argentina	73	Sabalan	FFG	Iran
P 63	Babitonga	PG	Brazil	C 73	Manuel Doblado	PG	Mexico
P 63	Doxa	FS	Greece	CG 73	Port Royal	CG	USA
T 63	Goajira	LST	Venezuela	CVN 73	George Washington	CVN	USA
T-AGS 63	Henson	AGS	USA	DDG 73	Decatur	DDG	USA
TR 63	Atahualpa	AWT	Ecuador	F 73	Cataluña	FFG	Spain
64	Shtorm	MSC	Bulgaria	M 73	Koster	MHC	Sweden
64	Hrvatska Kostajnica	PCF	Croatia	P 73	Antiploiarchos Pezopoulos	PCFG	Greece
CG 64	Gettysburg	CG	USA	P 73	Anjadip	FFL	India
CV 64	Constellation	CV	USA	P 73	Vigia	OPV	Spain
DDG 64	Carney	DDG	USA	RM 73	Sebastion de Belal Calzar	PG	Colombia
M 64	Bhavnagar	MSO	India	74	Morel	PC	Chile
P 64	Concepción de Uruguay	PC	Argentina	74	Hamina	PCFG	Finland
P 64	Eleftheria	FS	Greece	A 74	Aris	AX	Greece
T 64	Los Llanos	LST	Venezuela	A 74	Sagardhwani	AGOR	India
T-AGS 64	Bruce C Heezen	AGS	USA	A 74	La Graciosa	AXS	Spain
TR 64	Quisquis	AWT	Ecuador	C 74	Sebastian Lerdo De Tejada	PG	Mexico
A 65	Marinero Jarano	AWT	Spain	CVN 74	John C Stennis	CVN	USA
CG 65	Chosin	CG	USA	DDG 74	McFaul	DDG	USA
CVN 65	Enterprise	CVN	USA	F 74	Asturias	FFG	Spain
DDG 65	Benfold	DDG	USA	M 74	Kullen	MHC	Sweden
M 65	Alleppey	MSO	India	P 74	Plotarhis Vlahavas	PCFG	Greece
P 65	Carteria	FS	Greece	P 74	Atalaya	OPV	Spain
T-AGS 65	Mary Spears	AGS	USA	PS 74	Rizal	FS	Philippines
TR 65	Taurus	AOTL	Ecuador	AU 75	Bessang Pass	PC	Philippines
66	Galvarino	ATF	Chile	C 75	Santos Degollado	PG	Mexico
A 66	Condestable Zaragoza	AWT	Spain	CVN 75	Harry S Truman	CVN	USA
CG 66	Hue City	CG	USA	DDG 75	Donald Cook	DDG	USA
DDG 66	Gonzalez	DDG	USA	F 75	Extremadura	FFG	Spain
M 66	Ratnagiri	MSO	India	M 75	Vinga	MHC	Sweden
P 66	Agon	FS	Greece	P 75	Plotarhis Maridakis	PCFG	Greece
67	Lautaro	ATF	Chile	P 75	Amini	FFL	India
CG 67	Shiloh	CG	USA	76	Hang Tuah	FF/AX	Malaysia
CV 67	John F Kennedy	CV	USA	C 76	Ignacio De La Llave	PG	Mexico
DDG 67	Cole	DDG	USA	CVN 76	Ronald Reagan	CVN	USA
M 67	Karwar	MSO	India	DDG 76	Higgins	DDG	USA
68	Leucoton	ATF	Chile	M 76	Ven	MHC	Sweden
CG 68	Anzio	CG	USA	P 76	Sea Wolf	PCGF	Singapore
CVN 68	Nimitz	CVN	USA	77	Cabrales	PC	Chile
DDG 68	The Sullivans	DDG	USA	DDG 77	O'Kane	DDG	USA
M 68	Cannanore	MSO	India	C 77	Juan N Alvares	PG	Mexico
CG 69	Vicksburg	CG	USA	F 77	Te Kaha	FF	New Zealand
CVN 69	Dwight D Eisenhower	CVN	USA	M 77	Ulvön	MHC	Sweden
DDG 69	Milius	DDG	USA	P 77	Sea Lion	PCFG	Singapore
M 69	Cuddalore	MSO	India	78	Sibbald	PC	Chile
P 69	Androth	FFL	India	AF 78	Lake Buhi	YO	Philippines
70	Rauma	PCFG	Finland	C 78	Manuel Gutierrez Zamora	PG	Mexico
C 70	Leandro Valle	PG	Mexico	DDG 78	Porter	DDG	USA
CG 70	Lake Erie	CG	USA	F 78	Kent	FFG	UK
CVN 70	Carl Vinson	CVN	USA	P 78	Sea Dragon	PCFG	Singapore
DDG 70	Hopper	DDG	USA	AE 79	Limasawa	ABU	Philippines
M 70	Kakinada	MSO	India	C 79	Valentin Gomez Farias	PG	Mexico
PS 70	Quezon	FS	Philippines	DDG 79	Oscar Austin	DDG	USA
RA 70	Chimborazo	ATF	Ecuador	F 79	Portland	FFG	UK
71	Micalvi	PC	Chile	P 79	Sea Tiger	PCFG	Singapore
71	Raahe	PCFG	Finland	080	Admiral Nahkimov	CGN	Russia
71	Alvand	FFG	Iran	C 80	Ignacio Manuel Altamirano	PG	Mexico
A 71	Juan Sebastian de Elcano	AXS	Spain	DDG 80	Roosevelt	DDG	USA
AT 71	Mangyan	ABU	Philippines	F 80	Grafton	FFG	UK
C 71	Guillermo Prieto	PG	Mexico	M 80	Rushcutter	MHI	Australia
CG 71	Cape St George	CG	USA	P 80	Sea Hawk	PCFG	Singapore
CVN 71	Theodore Roosevelt	CVN	USA	081	Nikolay Vilkov	LST	Russia
DDG 71	Ross	DDG	USA	81	Zhenghe	AX	China
F 71	Baleares	FFG	Spain	81	Cetina	LCT/ML	Croatia
K 71	Vijaydurg	FSG	India	81	Bayandor	FS	Iran
M 71	Kozhikode	MSO	India	A 81	Brambleleaf	AOT	UK
M 71	Landsort	MHC	Sweden	C 81	Francisco Zarco	PG	Mexico
P 71	Serviola	OPV	Spain	CH 81	Almirante Grau	CG/CLM	Peru
RA 71	Cayambe	ATF	Ecuador	DDG 81	Winston Churchill	DDG	USA
T 71	Margarita	LCU	Venezuela	F 81	Santa María	FFG	Spain
72	Ortiz	PC	Chile	F 81	Sutherland	FFG	UK
72	Andrija Mohorovičić	AGS	Croatia	M81	Shoalwater	MHI	Australia
72	Porvoo	PCFG	Finland	N 81	Fyen	ML	Denmark
72	Alborz	FFG	Iran	P 81	Sea Scorpion	PCFG	Singapore
A 72	Arosa	AXS	Spain	P 81	Toralla	PC	Spain
A 72	Cameron	ARS	UK	T 81	Ciudad Bolivar	AK	Venezuela
AF 72	Lake Taal	YO	Philippines	82	Shichang	ATS	China
C 72	Mariano Escobedo	PG	Mexico	82	Krka	LCT/ML	Croatia
CG 72	Vella Gulf	CG	USA	82	Naghdi	FS	Iran
CVN 72	Abraham Lincoln	CVN	USA	82	Resilience	OPV	Singapore
DDG 72	Mahan	DDG	USA	C 82	Ignacio L Vallarta	PG	Mexico
F 72	Andalucia	FFG	Spain	DDG 82	Lassen	DDG	USA
K 72	Sindhudurg	FSG	India	F 82	Victoria	FFG	Spain
M 72	Konkan	MSO	India	F 82	Somerset	FFG	UK

Number	Ship's name	Type	Country
M 82	Huon	MHC	Australia
N 82	Møen	ML	Denmark
P 82	Formentor	PC	Spain
83	Unity	OPV	Singapore
C 83	Jesus Gonzalez Ortega	PG	Mexico
DDG 83	Howard	DDG	USA
F 83	Erinomi	FS	Nigeria
F 83	Numancia	FFG	Spain
F 83	St Albans	FFG	UK
K 83	Nashak	FSG	India
M 83	Hawkesbury	MHC	Australia
M 83	Mahé	MSI	India
84	Sovereignty	OPV	Singapore
C 84	Melchor Ocampo	PG	Mexico
CH 84	Aguirre	CH	Peru
F 84	Enymiri	FS	Nigeria
F 84	Reina Sofía	FFG	Spain
DDG 84	Bulkeley	DDG	USA
M 84	Norman	MHC	Australia
M 84	Malvan	MSI	India
85	Justice	OPV	Singapore
C 85	Juan Aldama	PG	Mexico
DDG 85	McCampbell	DDG	USA
F 85	Navarra	FFG	Spain
F 85	Cumberland	FFG	UK
M 85	Gascoyne	MHC	Australia
M 85	Mangrol	MSI	India
P 85	Intrepida	PCF	Argentina
86	Freedom	OPV	Singapore
A 86	Tir	AX	India
C 86	Mariano Matamoros	PG	Mexico
DDG 86	Shoup	DDG	USA
F 86	Canarias	FFG	Spain
F 86	Campbeltown	FFG	UK
LT 86	Zamboanga del Sur	LST	Philippines
M 86	Diamantina	MHC	Australia
M 86	Malpe	MSI	India
P 86	Indomita	PCF	Argentina
87	Independence	OPV	Singapore
D 87	Newcastle	DDG	UK
DDG 87	Mason	DDG	USA
F 87	Chatham	FFG	UK
LT 87	South Cotabato	LST	Philippines
M 87	Yarra	MHC	Australia
M 87	Mulki	MSI	India
D 88	Glasgow	DDG	UK
DDG 88	Preble	DDG	USA
M 88	Magdala	MSI	India
P 88	Victory	FSG	Singapore
AG 89	Kalinga	AKL	Philippines
D 89	Exeter	DDG	UK
DDG 89	Mustin	DDG	USA
F 89	Aradu	FFG	Nigeria
P 89	Valour	FSG	Singapore
90	Sabha	FFG	Bahrain
90	Elicura	LSM	Chile
AC 90	Mactan	AK	Philippines
D 90	Southampton	DDG	UK
DDG 90	Chaffee	DDG	USA
P 90	Vigilance	FSG	Singapore
ASY 91	Hashidate	ASY/YAC	Japan
B 91	Orion	AGOR	Ecuador
D 91	Nottingham	DDG	UK
K 91	Pralaya	PCFG	India
M 91	Sagar	MSO	Bangladesh
P 91	Valiant	FSG	Singapore
R 91	Charles de Gaulle	CVN/PAN	France
92	Rancagua	LST	Chile
D 92	Liverpool	DDG	UK
P 92	Vigour	FSG	Singapore
93	Valdivia	LST	Chile
P 93	Vengeance	FSG	Singapore
94	Orompello	LSM	Chile
94	Grivita	PGR	Romania
94	Fearless	OPV	Singapore
K 94	Chapal	PCFG	India
95	Chacabuco	LST	Chile
95	Rahova	PGR	Romania
95	Brave	OPV	Singapore
D 95	Manchester	DDG	UK
M 95	Shapla	MSI/PC	Bangladesh
96	Courageous	OPV	Singapore
A 96	Sea Crusader	AK	UK
D 96	Gloucester	DDG	UK
F 96	Sheffield	FFG	UK
K 96	Chatak	PCFG	India
M 96	Shaikat	MSI/PC	Bangladesh
97	Valas	AKSL	Finland
97	Gallant	OPV	Singapore
D 97	Edinburgh	DDG	UK
M 97	Surovi	MSI/PC	Bangladesh
R 97	Jeanne d'Arc	CVH	France

Number	Ship's name	Type	Country
98	Mursu	AKSL	Finland
98	Daring	OPV	Singapore
A 98	Sea Centurion	AK	UK
D 98	York	DDG	UK
F 98	Coventry	FFG	UK
K 98	Prahar	FSG	India
M 98	Shaibal	MSI/PC	Bangladesh
099	Pyotr Velikiy	CGN	Russia
99	Kustaanmiekka	AGF/AGI	Finland
99	Dauntless	OPV	Singapore
F 99	Cornwall	FFG	UK
R 99	Foch	CV	France
AU 100	Tirad Pass	PC	Philippines
101	Mulniya	FSG	Bulgaria
101	Fouque	LSL	Iran
101	Al Hussein	PCF	Jordan
A 101	Mar Caribe	ATF	Spain
C 101	Démocrata	OPV	Mexico
DD 101	Murasame	DDG	Japan
F 101	Alvaro de Bazán	FFG	Spain
FNH 101	Guaymuras	PCF	Honduras
M 101	Sandown	MHC/ SRMH	UK
P 101	Mandume	PC	Angola
PG 101	Kagitingan	PC	Philippines
102	Uragon	PCFG	Bulgaria
102	Al Hussan	PCF	Jordan
A 102	Agnadeen	AOR	Iraq
A 102	Jupiter	YDT	Singapore
DD 102	Harusame	DDG	Japan
F 102	Roger de Lauria	FFG	Spain
FNH 102	Honduras	PCF	Honduras
GC 102	Betelgeuse	PC	Dominican Republic
M 102	Inverness	MHC/ SRMH	UK
P 102	Polar	PC	Angola
PG 102	Bagong Lakas	PC	Philippines
PM 102	Rafael del Castillo y Rada	PC	Colombia
103	Burya	PCFG	Bulgaria
103	King Abdullah	PCF	Jordan
103	Kedrov	FFH	Russia
DD 103	Yuudachi	DDG	Japan
F 103	Blas de Lazo	FFG	Spain
FNH 103	Hibueras	PCF	Honduras
H 103	Guama	AGS	Cuba
M 103	Cromer	MHC/ SRMH	UK
P 103	Atlantico	PC	Angola
P 103	L'Audacieux	PC	Cameroon
PM 103	Jóse Maria Palas	PC	Colombia
Y 103	Al Meks	ATA	Egypt
104	Pskov	FFH	Russia
DD 104	Kirisame	DDG	Japan
F 104	Mendez Nuñez	FFG	Spain
L 104	Inouse	LST	Greece
M 104	Walney	MHC/ SRMH	UK
P 104	Golfinho	PC	Angola
P 104	Bakassi	PCG	Cameroon
PG 104	Bagong Silang	PC	Philippines
PM 104	Medardo Monzon Coronado	PC	Colombia
PVL 104	Tiir	LCU	Estonia
105	Jinan	DDG	China
DD 105	Inazuma	DDG	Japan
L 105	Arromanches	LCL/RCL	UK
M 105	Bedok	MHC	Singapore
M 105	Bridport	MHC/ SRMH	UK
PM 105	Jaime Gómez Castro	PC	Colombia
PVL 105	Torm	PCF	Estonia
Y 105	Al Agami	ATA	Egypt
106	Xian	DDG	China
DD 106	Samidare	DDG	Japan
FNH 106	Copan	PC	Honduras
M 106	Kallang	MHC	Singapore
M 106	Penzance	MHC/ SRMH	UK
PM 106	Juan Nepomuceno Peña	PC	Colombia
PVL 106	Maru	PC	Estonia
107	Yinchuan	DDG	China
DD 107	Ikazuchi	DDG	Japan
FNH 107	Tegucigalpa	PC	Honduras
L 107	Andalsnes	LCL/RCL	UK
M 107	Katong	MHC	Singapore
M 107	Pembroke	MHC/ SRMH	UK
PVL 107	Kou	PC	Estonia
Y 107	Antar	ATA	Egypt
108	Xining	DDG	China
D 108	Cardiff	DDG	UK
M 108	Punggol	MHC	Singapore

Number	Ship's name	Type	Country
M 108	Grimsby	MHC/SRMH	UK
PVL 108	Linda	PG	Estonia
109	Kaifeng	DDG	China
A 109	Valvas	PC	Estonia
A 109	Bayleaf	AOT	UK
L 109	Akyab	LCL/RCL	UK
M 109	Bangor	MHC/SRMH	UK
Y 109	Al Dikhila	ATA	Egypt
110	Anticosti	MSA	Canada
110	Dalian	DDG	China
A 110	Orangeleaf	AOT	UK
L 110	Aachen	LCL/RCL	UK
M 110	Ramsey	MHC/SRMH	UK
N 110	Nusret	ML	Turkey
PG 110	Tomas Batilo	PCF	Philippines
111	Svetkavitsa	PCFG	Bulgaria
111	Al Isar	MSO	Libya
111	Marasesti	DDG	Romania
A 111	Alerta	AGI/AGOR	Spain
A 111	Oakleaf	AOT	UK
F 111	Te Mana	FFG	New Zealand
L 111	Arezzo	LCL/RCL	UK
M 111	Blythe	MHC/SRMH	UK
P 111	Sultanhisar	PG	Turkey
PG 111	Bonny Serrano	PCF	Philippines
Y 111	Al Iskandarani	ATA	Egypt
112	Moresby	MSA	Canada
112	Harbin	DDG	China
112	Typfoon	PCFG	Bulgaria
112	Ibn Al Hadrami	LSM	Libya
112	Eugen Stihi	AG	Romania
M 112	Shoreham	MHC/SRMH	UK
P 112	Demirhisar	PG	Turkey
PG 112	Bienvenido Salting	PCF	Philippines
PM 112	Quita Sueno	PCF	Colombia
113	Smerch	PCFG	Bulgaria
113	Qingdao	DDG	China
113	Al Tiyar	MSO	Libya
113	Ion Ghiculescu	AG	Romania
113	Menzhinsky	FFH	Russia
L 113	Audemer	LCL/RCL	UK
P 113	Yarhisar	PG	Turkey
PM 113	José Maria Garcia y Toledo	PC	Colombia
Y 113	Kalir	ATA	Egypt
114	Grumete Perez	YFB	Chile
P 114	Akhisar	PG	Turkey
PG 114	Salvador Abcede	PCF	Philippines
PM 114	Juan Nepomuceno Eslava	PC	Colombia
115	Ras al Hamman	MSO	Libya
P 115	Sivrihisar	PG	Turkey
PG 115	Ramon Aguirre	PCF	Philippines
PM 115	Tecim Jaime E Cárdenas	PC	Colombia
116	Pisagua	AKS	Chile
116	Ibn Umayaa	LSM	Libya
L 116	Kos	LST	Greece
P 116	Koçhisar	PG	Turkey
117	Ras al Fulaijah	MSO	Libya
118	Ibn Al Farat	LSM	Libya
118	Admiral Glovko	CG	Russia
119	Ras al Qula	MSO	Libya
119	V Gumanenko	MHO	Russia
119	Donetsky Shakhter	LST	Russia
NL 120	Bayraktar	LST/ML	Turkey
121	Vahakari	AKSL	Finland
121	Ras al Madwar	MSO	Libya
121	Moskva	CG	Russia
DDK121	Yuugumo	DD	Japan
J 121	Changxingdao	ASR	China
NL 121	Sancaktar	LST/ML	Turkey
A 122	Olwen	AO	UK
DD 122	Hatsuyuki	DDG	Japan
123	Ras al Massad	MSO	Libya
A 123	Olna	AO	UK
ARB 123	Guardian Rios	ARA/ATF	Peru
DD 123	Shirayuki	DDG	Japan
NL 123	Sarucabey	LST/ML	Turkey
DD 124	Mineyuki	DDG	Japan
NL 124	Karamürselbey	LST/ML	Turkey
125	Ras al Hani	MSO	Libya
DD 125	Sawayuki	DDG	Japan
NL 125	Osman Gazi	LST	Turkey
126	Huangfen class	PCFG	Yemen
DD 126	Hamayuki	DDG	Japan
L 126	Balikpapan	LCH/LSM	Australia
127	Huangfen class	PCFG	Yemen
A 127	Torrent	TRV	UK
DD 127	Isoyuki	DDG	Japan
L 127	Brunei	LCH/LSM	Australia
128	Huangfen class	PCFG	Yemen
DD 128	Haruyuki	DDG	Japan
L 128	Labuan	LCH/LSM	Australia
DD 129	Yamayuki	DDG	Japan
L 129	Tarakan	LCH/LSM	Australia
130	Ibn Al Idrisi	LCT	Libya
A 130	Roebuck	AGS	UK
DD 130	Matsuyuki	DDG	Japan
L 130	Wewak	LCH/LSM	Australia
U 130	Hetman Sagaidachny	FFH	Ukraine
131	Nanjing	DDG	China
131	Ibn Marwan	LCT	Libya
A 131	Scott	AGS	UK
ATC 131	Ilo	AF/ATC	Peru
DD 131	Setoyuki	DDG	Japan
R 131	Norrköping	PCFG	Sweden
132	Hefei	DDG	China
132	Ibn Ouf	LST	Libya
132	El Kobayat	LST	Libya
A 132	Diligence	AR	UK
DD 132	Asayuki	DDG	Japan
R 132	Nynäshamm	PCFG	Sweden
133	Chongqing	DDG	China
L 133	Betano	LCH/LSM	Australia
U 133	Mikolaiv	FF	Ukraine
134	Zunyi	DDG	China
134	Ibn Harissa	LST	Libya
134	Laksamana Hang Nadim	FSG	Malaysia
U 134	Dnipropetrovsk	FF	Ukraine
135	Laksamana Tun Abdul Gamil	FSG	Malaysia
135	Toplivo class	AOTL	Yemen
A 135	Argus	HSS/ATS	UK
136	Laksamana Muhammad Amin	FSG	Malaysia
137	Laksamana Tun Pusmah	FSG	Malaysia
A 138	Herald	AGS	UK
R 138	Piteå	PCFG	Sweden
R 139	Luleå	PCFG	Sweden
140	Toplivo class	AOTL	Yemen
A 140	Tornado	TRV	UK
P 140	Rajshahi	PC	Pakistan
P 140	Girne	PCF	Turkey
PG 140	Emilo Aguinaldo	PC	Philippines
R 140	Halmstad	PCFG	Sweden
DDH 141	Haruna	DDH	Japan
DT 141	Paita	LST	Peru
PG 141	Antonio Luna	PC	Philippines
A 142	Tormentor	TRV	UK
DDH 142	Hiei	DDH	Japan
M 142	Brseč	MSI	Yugoslavia
R 142	Ystad	PCFG	Sweden
DDH 143	Shirane	DDH	Japan
DDH 144	Kurama	DDH	Japan
DT 144	Eten	LST	Peru
NF 146	Guillermo Londoño Vargas	AH	Colombia
148	Ilya Azarov	LST	Russia
150	Anzac	FF	Australia
150	Voronezhsky	LST	Russia
151	Arunta	FF	Australia
DD 151	Asagiri	DDG	Japan
152	Warramunga	FF	Australia
152	Mutiara	AGS	Malaysia
152	Nikolay Filchenkov	LST	Russia
ATP 152	Talara	AOT/ATP	Peru
DD 152	Yamagiri	DDG	Japan
M 152	Podgora	MHSC	Yugoslavia
U 152	Uman	PHG	Ukraine
153	Stuart	FF	Australia
153	Perantau	AGS	Malaysia
BH 153	Quindio	ABU	Colombia
DD 153	Yuugiri	DDG	Japan
M 153	Blitvenica	MHSC	Yugoslavia
U 153	Priluki	PHG	Ukraine
154	Parramatta	FF	Australia
DD 154	Amagiri	DDG	Japan
U 154	Kahovka	PHG	Ukraine
155	Ballarat	FF	Australia
BO 155	Providencia	AGOR	Colombia
DD 155	Hamagiri	DDG	Japan
U 155	Nicopol	FSG	Ukraine
156	Toowoomba	FF	Australia
156	Orel	FFH	Russia
BO 156	Malpelo	AGOR	Colombia
D 156	Nazim	DD	Pakistan
DD 156	Setogiri	DDG	Japan
U 156	Kremenchuk	FSG	Ukraine
157	Perth	FF	Australia
DD 157	Sawagiri	DDG	Japan
P 157	Larkana	PC	Pakistan
158	Yung Chuan	MSC	Taiwan
DD 158	Umigiri	DDG	Japan
ATP 159	Lobitos	AOT	Peru

Number	Ship's name	Type	Country	Number	Ship's name	Type	Country
P 159	Kaparen	PCFG	Sweden	D 186	Shahjahan	DDG/FFG	Pakistan
160	Musytari	OPV	Malaysia	A 187	Salmaid	ARSD	UK
BE 160	Gloria	AXS	Colombia	T-AO 187	Henry J Kaiser	AO	USA
P 160	Väktaren	PCFG	Sweden	188	Zborul	FSG	Romania
161	Changsha	DDG	China	189	Pescarusul	FSG	Romania
161	Marikh	OPV	Malaysia	L 189	Milos	LCT	Greece
BL 161	Cartagena De Indias	ARL	Colombia	T-AO 189	John J Lenthall	AO	USA
FMB 161	Osa II class	PCFG	Eritrea	190	Lastunul	FSG	Romania
P 161	Snapphanen	PCFG	Sweden	191	Chung Cheng	LSD	Taiwan
162	Nanning	DDG	China	193	Shiu Hai	LSD	Taiwan
162	Yung Fu	MSC	Taiwan	T-AO 193	Walter S Diehl	AO	USA
BL 162	Buena Ventura	ARL	Colombia	T-AO 194	John Ericsson	AO	USA
P 162	Spejaren	PCFG	Sweden	195	Vulturul	PCFG	Romania
163	Nanchang	DDG	China	L 195	Serifos	LCM	Greece
163	Yung Ching	MSC	Taiwan	O 195	Westralia	AOR/AOT	Australia
M 163	Muhafiz	MHC	Pakistan	T-AG 195	Hayes	AG	USA
P 163	Styrbjörn	PCFG	Sweden	T-AO 195	Leroy Grumman	AO	USA
164	Guilin	DDG	China	P 196	Andromeda	PCF	Greece
DDA 164	Takatsuki	DDG	Japan	T-AO 196	Kanawha	AO	USA
L 164	Ipoploiarchos Roussen	LSM	Greece	T-AO 197	Pecos	AO	USA
M 164	Mujahid	MSC	Pakistan	198	Eretele	PCFG	Romania
P 164	Starkodder	PCFG	Sweden	P 198	Kyknos	PCF	Greece
165	Zhanjiang	DDG	China	T-AO 198	Big Horn	AO	USA
165	Yung Chung	MSC	Taiwan	199	Albatrosul	PCFG	Romania
DDA 165	Kikuzuki	DDG	Japan	P 199	Pigasos	PCF	Greece
L 165	Ipoploiarchos Krystalidis	LSM	Greece	T-AO 199	Tippecanoe	AO	USA
P 165	Tordön	PCFG	Sweden	200	Yan Lon Aung	YDT	Burma
166	Zhuhai	DDG	China	200	Smolny	AX	Russia
M 166	Munsif	MHC	Pakistan	T-AO 200	Guadelupe	AO	USA
P 166	Tirfing	PCFG	Sweden	201	Kula	PC	Fiji
167	Shenzhen	DDG	China	201	Naluca	PCF	Romania
L 167	Ios	LCU	Greece	201	Chung Hai	LST	Taiwan
DDG 168	Tachikaze	DDG	Japan	201	Natya class	MSO	Yemen
L 168	Sikinos	LCU	Greece	A 201	Orion	AGI	Sweden
T-ATF 168	Catawba	ATF	USA	P 201	Ruposhi Bangla	PC	Bangladesh
DDG 169	Asakaze	DDG	Japan	P 201	Iberia	PC	Georgia
L 169	Irakleia	LCU	Greece	P 201	Neiafu	PC	Tonga
SSV169	Tavriya	AGI	Russia	SSV 201	Priazove	AGI	Russia
T-ATF 169	Navajo	ATF	USA	T-AO 201	Patuxent	AO	USA
DDG 170	Sawakaze	DDG	Japan	UAM 201	Creoula	AXS	Portugal
L 170	Folegrandos	LCU	Greece	202	Dimiter A Dimitrov	AOL	Bulgaria
T-ATF 170	Mohawk	ATF	USA	202	Kikau	PC	Fiji
U 170	Skadovsk	PC	Ukraine	202	Smeul	PCF	Romania
171	Endeavour	AGOR	Canada	L 202	Excellence	LST	Singapore
A 171	Endurance	AGOB	UK	M 202	Atalanti	MSC	Greece
AH 171	Carrasco	AGSC/AH	Peru	P 202	Kutaisi	PC	Georgia
DDG 171	Hatakaze	DDG	Japan	P 202	Pangai	PC	Tonga
T-ATF 171	Sioux	ATF	USA	T-AO 202	Yukon	AO	USA
172	Quest	AGOR	Canada	203	Fremantle	PC	Australia
172	Pohorje	PCF	Yugoslavia	203	Type 650	AOL	Bulgaria
AH 172	Stiglich	AGSC/AH	Peru	203	Kiro	PC	Fiji
DDG 172	Shimakaze	DDG	Japan	203	Viforul	PCF	Romania
T-ATF 172	Apache	ATF	USA	L 203	Intrepid	LST	Singapore
DDG 173	Kongou	DDG	Japan	LDG 203	Bacamarte	LCT/LDG	Portugal
L 173	Chios	LST	Greece	P 203	Savea	PC	Tonga
174	Učka	PCF	Yugoslavia	T-AO 203	Laramie	AO	USA
DDG 174	Kirishima	DDG	Japan	204	Warrnambool	PC	Australia
L 174	Samos	LST	Greece	204	Vijelia	PCF	Romania
175	Grmeč	PCF	Yugoslavia	BH 204	El Idrissi	AGS	Algeria
AH 175	Carrillo	AGSC/AH	Peru	T-AO 204	Rappahannock	AO	USA
DDG 175	Myoukou	DDG	Japan	205	Townsville	PC	Australia
L 175	Ikaria	LST	Greece	205	Viscolul	PCF	Romania
SSV 175	Odograf	AGI	Russia	205	Chung Chien	LST	Taiwan
AH 176	Melo	AGSC/AH	Peru	P 205	Griffin	PC	Georgia
DDG 176	Choukai	DDG	Japan	U 205	Chernigiv	FFL	Ukraine
L 176	Lesbos	LST	Greece	206	Wollongong	PC	Australia
177	Opanez	PGR	Romania	206	Kapitan 1st rank Dimiter Dobrev	ADG/AX	Bulgaria
177	Fruška Gora	PCF	Yugoslavia	206	Virtejul	PCF	Romania
L 177	Rodos	LST	Greece	L 206	Perseverence	LSL	Singapore
178	Smirdan	PGR	Romania	M 206	Faidra	MSC	Greece
178	Kosmaj	PCF	Yugoslavia	U 206	Vinnitsa	FFL	Ukraine
L 178	Naxos	LCU	Greece	207	Launceston	PC	Australia
P 178	Ekpe	PCF	Nigeria	207	Fulgerul	PCF	Romania
179	Posada	PG	Romania	F 207	Bremen	FFG	Germany
179	Zelengora	PCF	Yugoslavia	L 207	Endurance	LPD/LST	Singapore
L 179	Paros	LCU	Greece	P 207	Utique	PC	Tunisia
P 179	Damisa	PCF	Nigeria	U 207	Lutsk	FFL	Ukraine
180	Rovine	PG	Romania	U 207	Uzhgorod	PCF	Ukraine
P 180	Agu	PCF	Nigeria	208	Whyalla	PC	Australia
D 181	Tariq	DD/FF	Pakistan	208	Vintul	PCF	Romania
P 181	Siri	PCFG	Nigeria	208	Chung Shun	LST	Taiwan
D 182	Babur	DDG/FFG	Pakistan	F 208	Niedersachsen	FFG	Germany
P 182	Ayam	PCFG	Nigeria	L 208	Resolution	LPD/LST	Singapore
D 183	Khaibar	DD/FF	Pakistan	P 208	Separacion	FS	Dominican Republic
P 183	Ekun	PCFG	Nigeria	P 208	Jerba	PC	Tunisia
D 184	Badr	DDG/FFG	Pakistan	SSV 208	Kwily	AGI	Russia
A 185	Salmoor	ARSD	UK	U 208	Khmelnitsky	PCF	Ukraine
D 185	Lütjens	DDG	Germany	209	Ipswich	PC	Australia
D 185	Tippu Sultan	DD/FF	Pakistan	209	Vulcanul	PCF	Romania
L 185	Kithera	LCT	Greece	F 209	Rheinland-Pfalz	FFG	Germany
A 186	Salmaster	ARSD	UK				
D 186	Mölders	DDG	Germany				

Number	Ship's name	Type	Country
L 209	Persistence	LPD/LST	Singapore
P 209	Calderas	FS	Dominican Republic
P 209	Kuriat	PC	Tunisia
U 209	Sumy	FFL	Ukraine
210	Cessnock	PC	Australia
210	Furtuna	PCF	Romania
210	Smolny	AX	Russia
A 210	Ayeda 4	AOTL	Egypt
F 210	Emden	FFG	Germany
L 210	Endeavour	LPD/LST	Singapore
M 210	Thalia	MSC	Greece
U 210	Kherson	FFL	Ukraine
211	Bendigo	PC	Australia
211	Parvin	PC	Iran
211	Trasnetul	PCF	Romania
A 211	Maryut	AOTL	Egypt
F 211	Köln	FFG	Germany
M 211	Alkyon	MSC	Greece
P 211	Meghna	PG	Bangladesh
212	Gawler	PC	Australia
212	Bahram	PC	Iran
212	Tornada	PCF	Romania
212	Al Qiaq	YFU	Saudi Arabia
A 212	Al Furat	AOTL	Egypt
A 212	Ägir	YDT	Sweden
F 212	Karlsruhe	FFG	Germany
F 212	Al Hani	FFG	Libya
P 212	Jamuna	PG	Bangladesh
213	Geraldton	PC	Australia
213	Nahid	PC	Iran
A 213	Al Nil	AOTL	Egypt
A 213	Nordanö	YDT	Sweden
F 213	Augsburg	FFG	Germany
F 213	Al Qirdabiyah	FFG	Libya
M 213	Klio	MSC	Greece
214	Dubbo	PC	Australia
214	Akdu	AOTL	Egypt
214	Al Sulayel	YFU	Saudi Arabia
A 214	Akdu	AOTL	Egypt
A 214	Belos III	ARS	Sweden
F 214	Lübeck	FFG	Germany
M 214	Avra	MSC	Greece
215	Geelong	PC	Australia
A 215	Maryut Atbarah	AOTL	Egypt
F 215	Brandenburg	FFG	Germany
216	Gladstone	PC	Australia
216	Al Ula	YFU	Saudi Arabia
216	Chung Kuang	LST	Taiwan
A 216	Ayeda 3	AOTL	Egypt
F 216	Schleswig-Holstein	FFG	Germany
217	Bunbury	PC	Australia
217	Chung Chao	LST	Taiwan
F 217	Bayern	FFG	Germany
218	Afif	YFU	Saudi Arabia
A 218	Al Burullus	AOTL	Egypt
D 218	Kimon	DDG	Greece
F 218	Mecklenburg-Vorpommern	FFG	Germany
219	Kao Hsiung	AGC	Taiwan
D 219	Nearchos	DDG	Greece
F 219	Sachsen	FFG	Germany
D 220	Formion	DDG	Greece
DE 220	Chitose	FF	Japan
F 220	Hamburg	FFG	Germany
221	Jupiter	ATS	Bulgaria
221	Sobat	AFL	Sudan
221	Chung Chuan	LST	Taiwan
D 221	Themistocles	DDG	Greece
DE 221	Niyodo	FF	Japan
F 221	Hessen	FFG	Germany
M 221	T 43 class	MSO	Albania
P 221	Kaman	PGF	Iran
222	Vaarlahti	AKSL	Finland
222	Dinder	AFL	Sudan
DE 222	Teshio	FF	Japan
M 222	T 43 class	MSO	Albania
P 222	Zoubin	PGF	Iran
DE 223	Yoshino	FF	Japan
P 223	Khadang	PGF	Iran
DE 224	Kumano	FF	Japan
DE 225	Noshiro	FF	Japan
M 225	T 301 class	MSI	Albania
226	Chung Chih	LST	Taiwan
DE 226	Ishikari	FFG	Japan
P 226	Falakhon	PGF	Iran
227	Chung Ming	LST	Taiwan
DE 227	Yubari	FFG	Japan
P227	Shamshir	PGF	Iran
M227	T 301 class	MSI	Albania
DE 228	Yubetsu	FFG	Japan
P 228	Toxotis	PCF	Greece
P 228	Gorz	PGF	Iran

Number	Ship's name	Type	Country
A 229	Eldaren	AOTL	Sweden
DE 229	Abukuma	FFG	Japan
F 229	Lancaster	FFG	UK
P 229	Tolmi	PG	Greece
P 229	Gardouneh	PGF	Iran
230	Chung Pang	LST	Taiwan
DE 230	Jintsu	FFG	Japan
F 230	Norfolk	FFG	UK
P 230	Ormi	PG	Greece
P 230	Khanjar	PGF	Iran
231	Chung Yeh	LST	Taiwan
DE 231	Ohyodo	FFG	Japan
F 231	Argyll	FFG	UK
P 231	Neyzeh	PGF	Iran
SSV 231	Pelengator	AGI	Russia
232	Chung Ho	LST	Taiwan
DE 232	Sendai	FFG	Japan
P 232	Tabarzin	PGF	Iran
233	Chung Ping	LST	Taiwan
DE 233	Chikuma	FFG	Japan
F 233	Marlborough	FFG	UK
DE 234	Tone	FFG	Japan
F 234	Iron Duke	FFG	UK
F 235	Monmouth	FFG	UK
F 236	Montrose	FFG	UK
F 237	Westminster	FFG	UK
F 238	Northumberland	FFG	UK
F 239	Richmond	FFG	UK
240	Kaszub	FF	Poland
F 240	Yavuz	FFG	Turkey
M 240	Aidon	MSC	Greece
DBM 241	Silba class	LCT/ML	Yugoslavia
F 241	Turgutreis	FFG	Turkey
M 241	Kichli	MSC	Greece
F 242	Fatih	FFG	Turkey
M 242	Kissa	MSC	Greece
F 243	Yildirim	FFG	Turkey
F 244	Barbaros	FFG	Turkey
A 245	Leeuwin	AGS	Australia
F 245	Orucreis	FFG	Turkey
A 246	Melville	AGS	Australia
F 246	Salihreis	FFG	Turkey
LD 246	Morrosquillo	LCU	Colombia
A 247	Pelikanen	TRV	Sweden
F 247	Kemalreis	FFG	Turkey
LD 247	Urabá	LCU	Colombia
M 247	Dafni	MSC	Greece
A 248	Pingvinen	TRV	Sweden
LD 248	Bahí Honda	LCU	Colombia
M 248	Pleias	MSC	Greece
LD 249	Bahí Portete	LCU	Colombia
F 250	Muavenet	FFG	Turkey
251	Wodnik	AXT	Poland
A 251	Achilles	ATA	Sweden
F 251	Adatepe	FFG	Turkey
LD 251	Bahí Solano	LCU	Colombia
F 252	Kocatepe	FFG	Turkey
FNH 252	Yojoa	ABU	Honduras
LD 252	Bahí Cupica	LCU	Colombia
253	Iskra	AXS	Poland
A 253	Hermes	ATA	Sweden
C 253	Stalwart	PC	St Kitts-Nevis
F 253	Zafer	FFG	Turkey
LD 253	Bahí Utria	LCU	Colombia
F 254	Trakya	FFG	Turkey
LD 254	Bahí Málaga	LCU	Colombia
M 254	Niovi	MSC	Greece
F 255	Karadeniz	FFG	Turkey
F 256	Ege	FFG	Turkey
F 257	Akdeniz	FFG	Turkey
P 258	Leeds Castle	OPV	UK
260	Admiral Petre Barbuneanu	FF	Romania
M 260	Edincik	MHC	Turkey
261	Kopernik	AGS	Poland
261	Vice Admiral Vasile Scodrea	FF	Romania
A 261	Utö	AS	Sweden
M 261	Edremit	MHC	Turkey
262	Navigator	AGI	Poland
262	Vice Admiral Vasile Urseanu	FF	Romania
A 262	Skredsvik	YDT	Sweden
F 262	Zulfiquar	FF	Pakistan
M 262	Enez	MHC	Turkey
263	Hydrograf	AGI	Poland
263	Vice Admiral Eugeniu Rosca	FF	Romania
A 263	Galö	ARL	Sweden
F 263	Shamser	FF	Pakistan
M 263	Erdek	MHC	Turkey
264	Contre Admiral Eustatiu Sebastian	FF	Romania
A 264	Trossö	ARL	Sweden
M 264	Erdemli	MHC	Turkey
265	Heweliusz	AGS	Poland

Number	Ship's name	Type	Country
265	Admiral Horia Macellaru	FF	Romania
P 265	Dumbarton Castle	OPV	UK
266	Arctowski	AGS	Poland
P 268	Knossos	PC	Greece
A 269	Grey Rover	AOL	UK
271	Warszawa	DDG	Poland
271	Vice Admiral Ioan Murgescu	ML/MCS	Romania
A 271	Gold Rover	AOL	UK
272	Kampela 2	LCU/AKSL	Finland
272	General Kazimierz Pulawski	FFG	Poland
273	Kosciuizkol	FFG	Poland
A 273	Black Rover	AOL	UK
274	Vice Admiral Constantin Balescu	ML/MCS	Romania
P 277	Anglesey	OPV	UK
P 278	Alderney	OPV	UK
280	Iroquois	DDG	Canada
281	Huron	DDG	Canada
281	Piast	ARS	Poland
281	Constanta	AE	Romania
282	Athabaskan	DDG	Canada
282	Lech	ARS	Poland
283	Algonquin	DDG	Canada
283	Midia	AE	Romania
P 286	Diopos Antoniou	PCF	Greece
P 287	Kelefstis Stamou	PCF	Greece
295	Automatica	ADG	Romania
296	Electronica	AGI	Romania
297	Energetica	ADG	Romania
P 297	Guernsey	OPV	UK
298	Magnetica	ADG	Romania
P 298	Shetland	OPV	UK
Y 298	Bandicoot	MSA(T)	Australia
Y 299	Wallaroo	MSA(T)	Australia
P 300	Lindisfarne	OPV	UK
W 300	Nornen	OPV	Norway
Y 300	Barsø	PC	Denmark
301	Polnochny A class	LSM	Egypt
301	Shahrokh	MSC	Iran
301	Teanoai	PC	Kiribati
A 301	Drakensberg	AOR	South Africa
A 301	Lomipeau	AOTL	Tonga
F 301	Bergen	FFG	Norway
MSO 301	Yaeyama	MSO	Japan
P 301	Batumi	PCF	Georgia
P 301	Inttisar	PC	Kuwait
P 301	Panquiaco	PC	Panama
P 301	Bizerte	PC	Tunisia
P 301	Kozlu	PCF	Turkey
Y 301	Drejø	PC	Denmark
302	Atiya	AOL	Bulgaria
302	Simorgh	MSC	Iran
302	Okba	PC	Morocco
A 302	Outeniqua	AOR	South Africa
F 302	Trondheim	FFG	Norway
J 302	Chongmingdao	ASR	China
MSO 302	Tsushima	MSO	Japan
P 302	Tbilisi	PHG	Georgia
P 302	Aman	PC	Kuwait
P 302	Ligia Elena	PC	Panama
P 302	Horria	PC	Tunisia
P 302	Kuşadasi	PCF	Turkey
Y 302	Romsø	PC	Denmark
303	Polnochny A class	LSM	Egypt
303	Karkas	MSC	Iran
303	Triki	PC	Morocco
MSO 303	Hachijuo	MSO	Japan
P 303	Maimon	PC	Kuwait
P 303	Naos	PC	Panama
W 303	Svalbard	OPV	Norway
Y 303	Samsø	PC	Denmark
304	El Khattabi	PCFG	Morocco
304	Stevan Filipović Steva	PCFG	Yugoslavia
F 304	Narvik	FFG	Norway
OR 304	Success	AOR	Australia
P 304	Mobark	PC	Kuwait
P 304	Flamenco	PC	Panama
P 304	Monastir	PC	Tunisia
Y 304	Thurø	PC	Denmark
305	Polnochny A class	LSM	Egypt
305	Commandant Boutouba	PCFG	Morocco
305	Žikica Jovanović-Španac	PCFG	Yugoslavia
P 305	Al Shaheed	PC	Kuwait
P 305	Escudo De Veraguas	PC	Panama
P 305	AG 5	ABU	Turkey
Y 305	Vejrø	PC	Denmark
306	Commandant El Harty	PCFG	Morocco
306	Nikola Martinović	PCFG	Yugoslavia
P 306	Bayan	PC	Kuwait
P 306	AG 6	ABU	Turkey
Y 306	Farø	PC	Denmark
307	Commandant Azougghar	PCFG	Morocco

Number	Ship's name	Type	Country
307	Josip Mažar Sosa	PCFG	Yugoslavia
A 307	Thetis	ANL	Greece
Y 307	Laesø	PC	Denmark
308	El Hahiq	PC	Morocco
308	Karlo Rojc	PCFG	Yugoslavia
Y 308	Rømø	PC	Denmark
309	El Tawfiq	PC	Morocco
310	L V Rabhi	PC	Morocco
U 310	Zhovti Vody	MSO	Ukraine
311	Errachiq	PC	Morocco
311	Prabparapak	PCFG	Thailand
P 311	Bishkhali	PC	Bangladesh
P 311	Weeraya	PCF	Sri Lanka
U 311	Cherkasy	MSO	Ukraine
312	El Akid	PC	Morocco
312	Hanhak Sattru	PCFG	Thailand
P 312	Padma	PC	Bangladesh
P 312	Ranakamee	PCF	Sri Lanka
313	El Maher	PC	Morocco
313	Suphairin	PCFG	Thailand
P 313	Surma	PC	Bangladesh
314	El Majid	PC	Morocco
P 314	Karnaphuli	PC	Bangladesh
315	El Bachir	PC	Morocco
C 315	Late	LCM	Tonga
P 315	Tista	PC	Bangladesh
316	El Hamiss	PC	Morocco
P 316	Jagatha	PCF	Sri Lanka
317	El Karib	PC	Morocco
A 317	Bulldog	AGS	UK
318	Raïs Bargach	PC	Morocco
319	Raïs Britel	PC	Morocco
A 319	Beagle	AGS	UK
320	Raïs Charkaoui	PC	Morocco
W 320	Nordkapp	OPV	Norway
321	Pauk II class	FS	Cuba
321	Raïs Maaninou	PC	Morocco
321	Ratcharit	PCFG	Thailand
P 321	Denizkuşu	PCF	Turkey
W 321	Senja	OPV	Norway
322	Raïs Al Mounastiri	PC	Morocco
322	Witthayakhom	PCFG	Thailand
A 322	Heros	ATA	Sweden
F 322	Kronshtadt class	PG	Albania
P 322	Ranarisi	PCF	Sri Lanka
P 322	Atmaca	PCF	Turkey
W 322	Andenes	OPV	Norway
323	Vänö	AKSL	Finland
323	Udomdet	PCFG	Thailand
A 323	Hercules	ATA	Sweden
P 323	Şahin	PCF	Turkey
A 324	Protea	AGS	South Africa
A 324	Hera	ATA	Sweden
P 324	Kartal	PCF	Turkey
P 326	Pelikan	PCF	Turkey
P 327	Albatros	PCF	Turkey
P 328	Şimşek	PCF	Turkey
P 329	Kasirga	PCF	Turkey
330	Halifax	FFH/FFG	Canada
F 330	Vasco da Gama	FFG	Portugal
P 330	Ranajaya	PCF	Sri Lanka
P 330	Kiliç	PCF	Turkey
U 330	Mezitopol	MHSC	Ukraine
331	Vancouver	FFH/FFG	Canada
331	Martha Kristina Tiyahahu	FF	Indonesia
331	Chon Buri	PCF	Thailand
F 331	Alvares Cabral	FFG	Portugal
P 331	Ranadeera	PCF	Sri Lanka
P 331	Kalkan	PCF	Turkey
U 331	Mariupol	MHSC	Ukraine
332	Ville de Québec	FFH/FFG	Canada
332	W Zakarias Yohannes	FF	Indonesia
332	Songkhla	PCF	Thailand
F 332	Corte Real	FFG	Portugal
P 332	Ranawickrama	PCF	Sri Lanka
P 332	Mizrak	PCF	Turkey
333	Toronto	FFH/FFG	Canada
333	Hasanuddin	FF	Indonesia
333	Phuket	PCF	Thailand
334	Regina	FFH/FFG	Canada
335	Calgary	FFH/FFG	Canada
336	Montreal	FFH/FFG	Canada
337	Fredericton	FFH/FFG	Canada
338	Winnipeg	FFH/FFG	Canada
339	Charlottetown	FFH/FFG	Canada
P 339	Bora	PGF	Turkey
340	St John's	FFH/FFG	Canada
M 340	Oksøy	MHSC	Norway
P 340	Doğan	PCFG	Turkey
341	El Yadekh	PC	Algeria
341	Ottawa	FFH/FFG	Canada
341	Samadikun	FF	Indonesia

Number	Ship's name	Type	Country
341	Mei Chin	LSM	Taiwan
M 341	T 43 class	MSO	Albania
M 341	Karmøy	MHSC	Norway
P 341	Marti	PCFG	Turkey
342	El Mourakeb	PC	Algeria
342	Martadinata	FF	Indonesia
M 342	Maløy	MHSC	Norway
P 342	Tayfun	PCFG	Turkey
343	El Kechef	PC	Algeria
343	Monginsidi	FF	Indonesia
A 343	Sleipner	AKL	Sweden
AS 343	T 301	MSI	Albania
M 343	Hinnøy	MHSC	Norway
P 343	Volkan	PCFG	Turkey
344	El Moutarid	PC	Algeria
344	Ngurahrai	FF	Indonesia
A 344	Loke II	AKL	Sweden
P 344	Rüzgar	PCFG	Turkey
345	El Rassed	PC	Algeria
P 345	Poyraz	PCFG	Turkey
346	El Djari	PC	Algeria
P 346	Gurbet	PCFG	Turkey
347	El Saher	PC	Algeria
347	Mei Sung	LSM	Taiwan
P 347	Firtina	PCFG	Turkey
348	El Moukadem	PC	Algeria
P 348	Yildiz	PCFG	Turkey
349	Kebir class	PC	Algeria
P 349	Karayel	PCFG	Turkey
M 350	Alta	MHSC	Norway
351	Djebel Chinoise	FS	Algeria
351	Ahmed Yani	FFG	Indonesia
351	Grozny	PC	Poland
351	Al Jouf	PCF	Saudi Arabia
M 351	Otra	MHSC	Norway
P 351	Parakramabahu	PCF	Sri Lanka
352	El Chihab	FS	Algeria
352	Slamet Riyadi	FFG	Indonesia
352	Wytrwaly	PC	Poland
352	Turaif	PCF	Saudi Arabia
M 352	Rauma	MHSC	Norway
353	Yos Sudarso	FFG	Indonesia
353	Hail	PCF	Saudi Arabia
353	Mei Ping	LSM	Taiwan
M 353	Orkla	MHSC	Norway
353	Zreczny	PC	Poland
354	El Mayher	PC	Algeria
354	Oswald Siahann	FFG	Indonesia
354	Zwinny	PC	Poland
354	Najran	PCF	Saudi Arabia
F 354	Niels Juel	FFG	Denmark
M 354	Glomma	MHSC	Norway
355	Abdul Halim Perdanakusuma	FFG	Indonesia
355	Zwrotny	PC	Poland
F 355	Olfert Fischer	FFG	Denmark
356	Karel Satsuitubun	FFG	Indonesia
356	Zawziety	PC	Poland
356	Mei Lo	LSM	Taiwan
F 356	Peter Tordenskiold	FFG	Denmark
357	Nieugiety	PC	Poland
F 357	Thetis	FF	Denmark
358	Czujny	PC	Poland
F 358	Triton	FF	Denmark
P 358	Hessa	AXL	Norway
D 359	Peyk	FF	Turkey
F 359	Vaedderen	FF	Denmark
P 359	Vigra	AXL	Norway
F 360	Hvidbjørnen	FF	Denmark
U 360	Genichesk	MHC	Ukraine
361	Fatahillah	FFG	Indonesia
362	Malahayati	FFG	Indonesia
363	Nala	FFG	Indonesia
364	Ki Hajar Dewantara	FFG/AX	Indonesia
A 367	Newton	ANL/AGOR	UK
A 368	Warden	YAG	UK
P 370	Rio Minho	PCR	Portugal
371	Kampela 1	LCU/AKSL	Finland
371	Kapitan Patimura	FS	Indonesia
HQ 371	Tarantul class	FSG	Vietnam
M 371	Ohue	MHSC	Nigeria
372	Untung Suropati	FS	Indonesia
HQ 372	Tarantul class	FSG	Vietnam
M 372	Marabai	MHSC	Nigeria
373	Nuku	FS	Indonesia
A 373	Hermis	AGI	Greece
HQ 373	Tarantul class	FSG	Vietnam
374	Lambung Mangkurat	FS	Indonesia
HQ 374	Tarantul class	FSG	Vietnam
375	Cut Nyak Dien	FS	Indonesia
A 375	Zeus	AOTL	Greece
376	Sultan Thaha Syaifuddin	FS	Indonesia
A 376	Orion	AOTL	Greece
377	Sutanto	FS	Indonesia
A 377	Arethusa	AOT	Greece
378	Sutedi Senoputra	FS	Indonesia
A 378	Kinterbury	AKF	UK
379	Wiratno	FS	Indonesia
380	Memet Sastrawiria	FS	Indonesia
381	Tjiptadi	FS	Indonesia
382	Hasan Basri	FS	Indonesia
A 382	Arrochar	ASL	UK
383	Iman Bonjol	FS	Indonesia
384	Pati Unus	FS	Indonesia
385	Teuku Umar	FS	Indonesia
A 385	Fort Rosalie	AFS	UK
386	Silas Papare	FS	Indonesia
A 386	Fort Austin	AFS	UK
Y 386	Agdlek	PC	Denmark
A 387	Fort Victoria	AOR	UK
Y 387	Agpa	PC	Denmark
A 388	Fort George	AOR	UK
Y 388	Tulugaq	PC	Denmark
A 389	Wave Knight	AO	UK
A 390	Wave Ruler	AO	UK
U 400	Rivne	LST	Ukraine
401	Admiral Branimir Ormanov	AGS	Bulgaria
401	Lieutenant Malghagh	LCT	Morocco
401	Ho Chi	LCU	Taiwan
401	Rade Končar	PCFG	Yugoslavia
L 401	Al Soumood	LCM/AKL	Kuwait
L 401	Ertuğrul	LST	Turkey
P 401	Cassiopea	OPV	Italy
402	Daoud Ben Aicha	LST	Morocco
402	Ho Huei	LCU	Taiwan
L 402	Al Tahaddy	LCM/AKL	Kuwait
L 402	Serdar	LST	Turkey
P 402	Libra	OPV	Italy
U 402	Konstantin Olshansky	LST	Ukraine
403	Ahmed Es Sakali	LST	Morocco
403	Ho Yao	LCU	Taiwan
403	Ramiz Sadiku	PCFG	Yugoslavia
ASR 403	Chihaya	ASR	Japan
P 403	Spica	OPV	Italy
404	Abou Abdallah El Ayachi	LST	Morocco
404	Hasan Zafirovič-Laca	PCFG	Yugoslavia
P 404	Vega	OPV	Italy
405	Jordan Nikolov Orce	PCFG	Yugoslavia
AS 405	Chiyoda	AS	Japan
P 405	Esploratore	PC	Italy
406	El Aigh	AKS	Morocco
406	Bezuderzhny	DDG	Russia
406	Ho Chao	LCU	Taiwan
406	Ante Banina	PCFG	Yugoslavia
P 406	Sentinella	PC	Italy
407	Sidi Mohammed Ben Abdallah	LST	Morocco
P 407	Vedetta	PC	Italy
408	Dakhla	AKS	Morocco
P 408	Staffetta	PC	Italy
409	Moroz	FSG	Russia
411	Kangan	AWT	Iran
411	Tachin	FF	Thailand
C 411	Tobruk	AX	Libya
P 411	El Nasr	PC	Mauritania
412	Taheri	AWT	Iran
412	Prasae	FF	Thailand
M 412	Sulev	OPV	Estonia
MSC 412	Addriyah	MSC	Saudi Arabia
413	Pin Klao	FF	Thailand
A 414	Ariadne	AOT	Greece
M 414	Kalev	MSI	Estonia
MSC 414	Al Quysumah	MSC	Saudi Arabia
A 415	Evros	AKF	Greece
M 415	Olev	MSI	Estonia
416	Tariq Ibn Ziyad	FSG	Libya
A 416	Ouranos	AOTL	Greece
M 416	Wambola	MHC	Estonia
MSC 416	Al Wadeeah	MSC	Saudi Arabia
417	Ean Al Gazala	FSG	Libya
A 417	Hyperion	AOTL	Greece
418	Ean Zara	FSG	Libya
MSC 418	Safwa	MSC	Saudi Arabia
A 419	Pandora	AP	Greece
420	Parainen	ATA	Finland
420	Al Jawf	MHC	Saudi Arabia
A 420	Pandrosos	AP	Greece
U 420	Donetsk	ACV	Ukraine
421	Olev Blagoev	AX	Bulgaria
421	Bandar Abbas	AORL	Iran
421	Orkan	FSG	Poland
421	Naresuan	FFG	Thailand
AOE 421	Sagami	AOE/AOR	Japan
F 421	Canterbury	FF	New Zealand
422	Boushehr	AORL	Iran

Number	Ship's name	Type	Country	Number	Ship's name	Type	Country
422	Piorun	FSG	Poland	F 480	Comandante João Belo	FF	Portugal
422	Shaqra	MHC	Saudi Arabia	481	Ho Shun	LCU	Taiwan
422	Taksin	FFG	Thailand	A 481	St Likoudis	ABU	Greece
AOE 422	Towada	AOE/AOR	Japan	F 481	Comandante Hermenegildo Capelo	FF	Portugal
U 422	Kramatorsk	ACV	Ukraine	ARC 482	Muroto	ARC	Japan
423	Grom	FSG	Poland	F 483	Comandante Sacadura Cabral	FF	Portugal
423	Smerch	FSG	Russia	484	Ho Chung	LCU	Taiwan
A 423	Heraklis	ATA	Greece	F 484	Augusto de Castilho	FS	Portugal
AOE 423	Tokiwa	AOE/AOR	Japan	F 485	Honorio Barreto	FS	Portugal
U 423	Gorlivka	ACV	Ukraine	F 486	Baptista de Andrade	FS	Portugal
424	Al Kharj	MHC	Saudi Arabia	F 487	João Roby	FS	Portugal
A 424	Iason	ATA	Greece	488	Ho Shan	LCU	Taiwan
AOE 424	Hamana	AOE/AOR	Japan	F 488	Afonso Cerqueira	FS	Portugal
U 424	Artemivsk	ACV	Ukraine	489	Ho Chuan	LCU	Taiwan
A 425	Odisseus	ATA	Greece	F 489	Oliveira E Carmo	FS	Portugal
427	Puck	PCFG	Poland	490	Ho Seng	LCU	Taiwan
428	Ustka	PCFG	Poland	F 490	Gaziantep	FFG	Turkey
429	Oksywie	PCFG	Poland	491	Ho Meng	LCU	Taiwan
430	Al Nour	PCF	Egypt	F 491	Giresun	FFG	Turkey
430	Darlowo	PCFG	Poland	492	Ho Mou	LCU	Taiwan
431	Kharg	AOR	Iran	F 492	Gemlik	FFG	Turkey
431	Swinoujscie	PCFG	Poland	493	Ho Shou	LCU	Taiwan
431	Tapi	FF	Thailand	F 493	Gelibolu	FFG	Turkey
432	Dziwnów	PCFG	Poland	494	Ho Chun	LCU	Taiwan
432	Inez	FSG	Russia	F 494	Gökçeada	FFG	Turkey
432	Khirirat	FF	Thailand	495	Ho Yung	LCU	Taiwan
A 432	Laine	AK	Estonia	P 495	Bambù	OPV	Italy
433	Al Hady	PCF	Egypt	496	Ho Chien	LCU	Taiwan
433	Wladyslawowo	PCFG	Poland	A 498	Lana	AGS	Nigeria
433	Makut Rajakumarn	FF/AX	Thailand	Y 498	Mario Marino	YDT	Italy
434	Gornik	FSG	Poland	Y 499	Alcide Pedretti	YDT	Italy
434	Besstrashny	DDG	Russia	500	Grozavu	ATA	Romania
435	Hutnik	FSG	Poland	M 500	Foça	MSI	Turkey
436	Al Hakim	PCF	Egypt	P 500	Palma	OPV	Italy
436	Metalowiec	FSG	Poland	501	Gharbiya	MSO	Egypt
437	Rolnik	FSG	Poland	501	Teluk Langsa	LST	Indonesia
439	Al Wakil	PCF	Egypt	501	Eilat	FSG	Israel
441	Yan Sit Aung	PC	Burma	501	Lieutenant Colonel Errhamani	FFG	Morocco
441	Rattanakosin	FSG	Thailand	501	La Galité	PCFG	Tunisia
442	Yan Myat Aung	PC	Burma	HQ 501	Da Nang	LST	Vietnam
442	Al Qatar	PCF	Egypt	LT 501	Laguna	LST	Philippines
442	Sukothai	FSG	Thailand	M 501	Fethiye	MSI	Turkey
443	Yan Nyein Aung	PC	Burma	502	Teluk Bajur	LST	Indonesia
444	Yan Khwin Aung	PC	Burma	502	Lahav	FSG	Israel
445	Yan Min Aung	PC	Burma	502	Tunis	PCFG	Tunisia
445	Al Saddam	PCF	Egypt	HQ 502	Qui Nonh	LST	Vietnam
446	Yan Ye Aung	PC	Burma	M 502	Fatsa	MSI	Turkey
447	Yan Paing Aung	PC	Burma	503	Teluk Amboina	LST	Indonesia
448	Yan Win Aung	PC	Burma	503	Hanit	FSG	Israel
448	Al Salam	PCF	Egypt	503	Carthage	PCFG	Tunisia
449	Yan Aye Aung	PC	Burma	HQ 503	Vung Tau	LST	Vietnam
450	Yan Zwe Aung	PC	Burma	M 503	Finike	MSI	Turkey
450	Razliv	FSG	Russia	504	Sharkiya	MSO	Egypt
F 450	Elli	FFG	Greece	504	Teluk Kau	LST	Indonesia
451	Al Rafia	PCF	Egypt	504	T 43 class	MSO	Syria
F 451	Limnos	FFG	Greece	LT 504	Lanao del Norte	LST	Philippines
F 452	Hydra	FFG	Greece	J 506	Yongxingdao	ASR	China
F 453	Spetsai	FFG	Greece	507	Daqahliya	MSO	Egypt
BM 454	Prestol	PG	Dominican Republic	507	Hsin Lung	AOTL	Taiwan
F 454	Psara	FFG	Greece	LT 507	Benguet	LST	Philippines
455	Chao Phraya	FFG	Thailand	508	Teluk Tomini	LST	Indonesia
F 455	Salamis	FFG	Greece	509	Chang De	FFG	China
456	Bangpakong	FFG	Thailand	509	Teluk Ratai	LST	Indonesia
C 456	Almirante Juan Alexandro Acosta	PG/WMEC	Dominican Republic	AOR 509	Protecteur	AOR	Canada
F 456	Epirus	FFG	Greece	510	Shaoxing	FFG	China
457	Kraburi	FFG	Thailand	510	Bahariya	MSO	Egypt
F 457	Thrace	FFG	Greece	510	Teluk Saleh	LST	Indonesia
458	Saiburi	FFG	Thailand	AOR 510	Preserver	AOR	Canada
F 459	Adrias	FFG	Greece	M 510	Samsun	MSC	Turkey
F 460	Aegean	FFG	Greece	U 510	Slavutich	AGF	Ukraine
461	Phuttha Yotfa Chulalok	FFG	Thailand	511	Nantong	FFG	China
F 461	Navarinon	FFG	Greece	511	Teluk Bone	LST	Indonesia
462	Phuttha Loetia Naphalai	FFG	Thailand	511	Hengam	LSL	Iran
F 462	Kountouriotis	FFG	Greece	511	Al Katum	PCFG	Libya
MST 463	Uraga	MST/ML	Japan	511	Al Siddiq	PCFG	Saudi Arabia
A 464	Axios	AR/AOT	Greece	A 511	Shaheed Ruhul Amin	AX	Bangladesh
MST 464	Bungo	MST/ML	Japan	A 511	Elbe	ARL	Germany
A 470	Aliakmon	AR/AOT	Greece	HQ 511	Polnochny class	LSM	Vietnam
471	Polnochny B class	LSM	Algeria	M 511	Sinop	MSC	Turkey
F 471	Antonio Enes	FS	Portugal	U 511	Simferopol	AGS	Ukraine
472	Kalaat Beni Hammad	LSL	Algeria	512	Wuxi	FFG	China
473	Kalaat Beni Rached	LSL	Algeria	512	Teluk Semangka	LST	Indonesia
A 474	Pytheas	AGS	Greece	512	Larak	LSL	Iran
F 475	João Coutinho	FS	Portugal	A 512	Shahayak	YR	Bangladesh
A 476	Strabon	AGSC	Greece	A 512	Mosel	ARL	Germany
F 476	Jacinto Candido	FS	Portugal	HQ 512	Polnochny class	LCM	Vietnam
F 477	General Pereira d'Eça	FS	Portugal	M 512	Sümene	MSC	Turkey
A 478	Naftilos	AGS	Greece	513	Huayin	FFG	China
A 479	I Karavoyiannos Theophilopoulos	ABU	Greece	513	Sinai	MSO	Egypt
				513	Teluk Penju	LST	Indonesia
				513	Tonb	LSL	Iran

Number	Ship's name	Type	Country	Number	Ship's name	Type	Country
513	Tral class	FS	Korea, North	533	Longlom	FS	Thailand
513	Al Zuara	PCFG	Libya	A 533	Norge	YAC	Norway
A 512	Shahayak	YR	Bangladesh	U 533	Kolomiya	AEM	Ukraine
513	Al Farouq	PCFG	Saudi Arabia	534	Jinhua	FFG	China
A 513	Shahjalal	AG	Bangladesh	534	Teluk Berau	LSM	Indonesia
A 513	Rhein	ARL	Germany	534	Shafak	PCFG	Libya
HQ 513	Polnochny class	LSM	Vietnam	535	Huangshi	FFG	China
M 513	Seddülbahir	MSC	Turkey	535	Teluk Peleng	LSM	Indonesia
514	Zhenjiang	FFG	China	A 535	Valkyrien	AKS/ATS	Norway
514	Teluk Mandar	LST	Indonesia	SSV 535	Kareliya	AGI	Russia
514	Lavan	LSL	Iran	536	Wuhu	FFG	China
A 514	Werra	ARL	Germany	536	Qena	MSO	Egypt
M 514	Silifke	MSC	Turkey	536	Teluk Sibolga	LSM	Indonesia
515	Xiamen	FFG	China	536	Bark	PCFG	Libya
515	Teluk Sampit	LST	Indonesia	537	Zhoushan	FFG	China
515	Al Ruha	PCFG	Libya	537	Teluk Manado	LSM	Indonesia
515	Abdul Aziz	PCFG	Saudi Arabia	538	Teluk Hading	LSM	Indonesia
515	Lung Chuan	AOTL	Taiwan	538	Rad	PCFG	Libya
A 515	Khan Jahan Ali	AOT	Bangladesh	539	Anqing	FFG	China
A 515	Main	ARL	Germany	539	Sohag	MSO	Egypt
M 515	Saros	MSC	Turkey	539	Teluk Parigi	LSM	Indonesia
516	Jiujiang	FFG	China	540	Huainan	FFG	China
516	Assiout	MSO	Egypt	540	Teluk Lampung	LSM	Indonesia
516	Teluk Banten	LST	Indonesia	A 540	Dannebrog	YAC	Denmark
A 516	Donau	ARL	Germany	A 540	Hansaya	LCP	Sri Lanka
LT 516	Kalinga Apayao	LST	Philippines	U 540	Chernivici	AXL	Ukraine
M 516	Sigacik	MSC	Turkey	541	Huaibei	FFG	China
517	Nanping	FFG	China	541	Teluk Jakarta	LSM	Indonesia
517	Teluk Ende	LST	Indonesia	541	Hua Hin	PC	Thailand
517	Al Baida	PCFG	Libya	A 541	Lihiniya	LCP	Sri Lanka
517	Faisal	PCFG	Saudi Arabia	P 541	Aboubekr Ben Amer	OPV	Mauritania
M 517	Sapanca	MSC	Turkey	U 541	Suvar	AXL	Ukraine
518	Jian	FFG	China	542	Tongling	FFG	China
518	Sharaba	PCFG	Libya	542	Teluk Sangkulirang	LSM	Indonesia
M 518	Sariyer	MSC	Turkey	542	Laheeb	PCFG	Libya
519	Changzhi	FFG	China	542	Klaeng	PC	Thailand
519	Al Nabha	PCFG	Libya	U 542	Akar	AXL	Ukraine
519	Kahlid	PCFG	Saudi Arabia	543	Dandong	FFG	China
520	Rassvet	FSG	Russia	543	Teluk Cirebon	AK	Indonesia
A 520	Sagres	AXS	Portugal	543	Marshal Shaposhnikov	DDG	Russia
M 520	Karamürsel	MSC	Turkey	543	Si Racha	PC	Thailand
SSV 520	Meridian	AGI	Russia	544	Siping	FFG	China
521	Hai	AGOR	China	544	Teluk Sabang	AK	Indonesia
521	Al Safhra	PCFG	Libya	545	Linfen	FFG	China
521	Amyr	PCFG	Saudi Arabia	P 546	Rodsteen	PCFG	Denmark
521	Sattahip	PC	Thailand	P 547	Sehested	PCFG	Denmark
A 521	Schultz Xavier	ABU	Portugal	548	Admiral Panteleyev	DDG	Russia
M 521	Kerempe	MSC	Turkey	548	Ta Tung	ATF/ARS	Taiwan
P 521	Vigilante	PC	Cape Verde	549	Ta Peng	ARS	Taiwan
522	Jiangwei II class	FFG	China	550	Ta De	ARS	Taiwan
522	Wahag	PCFG	Libya	A 550	Elbjørn	AGB	Denmark
522	Klongyai	PC	Thailand	C 550	Vittorio Veneto	CGH	Italy
A 522	D Carlos I	AGS	Portugal	D 550	Ardito	DDG	Italy
M 522	Kilimli	MSC	Turkey	LC 550	Bacolod City	LSV	Philippines
523	Jiangwei II class	FFG	China	LSM 550	Pung To	ML	Korea, South
523	Al Fikah	PCFG	Libya	P 550	Flyvefisken	PG/MH/	Denmark
523	Tariq	PCFG	Saudi Arabia			ML/AGS	
523	Wan An	AK/AP	Taiwan	551	Maoming	FFG	China
523	Takbai	PC	Thailand	551	Liven	FSG	Russia
A 523	Almirante Gago Coutinho	AGS	Portugal	551	Ta Wan	ATF/ARS	Taiwan
524	Shehab	PCFG	Libya	551	Ta Tuen	ARS	Taiwan
524	Yuen Feng	AK	Taiwan	A 551	Danbjørn	AGB	Denmark
524	Kantang	PC	Thailand	B 551	Voum-Legleita	PG	Mauritania
525	Al Mathur	PCFG	Libya	C 551	Giuseppe Garibaldi	CVS	Italy
525	Oqbah	PCFG	Saudi Arabia	D 551	Audace	DDG	Italy
525	Wu Kang	AK	Taiwan	F 551	Minerva	FS	Italy
525	Thepha	PC	Thailand	LC 551	Dagupan City	LSV	Philippines
526	Nakat	FSG	Russia	MSC 551	Kum San	MSC	Korea, South
526	Hsin Kang	AK	Taiwan	P 551	Hajen	PG/MH/	Denmark
526	Taimuang	PC	Thailand			ML/AGS	
527	Al Mosha	PCFG	Libya	552	Yibin	FFG	China
527	Abu Obaidah	PCFG	Saudi Arabia	552	Ta Hu	ARS	Taiwan
528	Shouaiai	PCFGG	Libya	A 552	Isbjørn	AGB	Denmark
529	Al Sakab	PCFG	Libya	F 552	Urania	FS	Italy
530	Giza	MSO	Egypt	MSC 552	Ko Hung	MSC	Korea, South
530	Wu Yi	AOE	Taiwan	P 552	Havkatten	PG/MH/	Denmark
A 530	Horten	ASL	Norway			ML/AGS	
P 530	Trabzon	PG/AGI	Turkey	553	Shaoguan	FFG	China
531	Teluk Gilimanuk	LSM	Indonesia	553	Ta Han	ATF/ARS	Taiwan
531	Najin class	FFG	Korea, North	A 553	Thorbjørn	AGB	Denmark
531	Al Bitar	PCFG	Libya	F 553	Danaide	FS	Italy
531	Khamronsin	FS	Thailand	MSC 553	Kum Kok	MSC	Korea, South
P 531	Terme	PG/AGI	Turkey	P 553	Laxen	PG/MH/	Denmark
532	Teluk Celukan Bawang	LSM	Indonesia			ML/AGS	
532	Shoula	PCFG	Libya	554	Anshun	FFG	China
532	Sonya class	MSC	Syria	554	Ta Kang	ATF/ARS	Taiwan
532	Thayanchon	FS	Thailand	F 554	Sfinge	FS	Italy
A 532	Ahti	AGF	Estonia	P 554	Makrelen	PG/MH/	Denmark
533	Ningpo	FFG	China			ML/AGS	
533	Aswan	MSO	Egypt	555	Zhaotong	FFG	China
533	Teluk Cendrawasih	LSM	Indonesia	555	Geyzer	FSG	Russia
533	Al Sadad	PCFG	Libya	555	Ta Fung	ATF/ARS	Taiwan

Number	Ship's name	Type	Country
F 555	Driade	FS	Italy
MSC 555	Nam Yang	MSC	Korea, South
P 555	Støren	PG/MH/ ML/AGS	Denmark
F 556	Chimera	FS	Italy
MSC 556	Ha Dong	MSC	Korea, South
P 556	Svaerdfisken	PG/MH/ ML/AGS	Denmark
557	Jishou	FFG	China
F 557	Fenice	FS	Italy
MSC 557	Sam Kok	MSC	Korea, South
P 557	Glenten	PG/MH/ ML/AGS	Denmark
558	Zigong	FFG	China
F 558	Sibilla	FS	Italy
MSC 558	Yong Dong	MSC	Korea, South
P 558	Gribben	PG/MH/ ML/AGS	Denmark
559	Kangding	FFG	China
A 559	Sleipner	AKS	Denmark
MSC 559	Ok Cheon	MSC	Korea, South
P 559	Lommen	PG/MH/ ML/AGS	Denmark
560	Dongguan	FFG	China
560	Won San	ML	Korea, South
560	Zyb	FSG	Russia
D 560	Luigi Durand de La Penne	DDG	Italy
P 560	Ravnen	PGG/MH/ ML/AGS	Denmark
561	Shantou	FFG	China
561	Multatuli	AGF	Indonesia
561	Kang Kyeong	MHC	Korea, South
D 561	Francesco Mimbelli	DDG	Italy
P 561	Skaden	PG/MH/ ML/AGS	Denmark
562	Jiangmen	FFG	China
562	Kang Jing	MHC	Korea, South
562	Priliv	FSG	Russia
P 562	Viben	PG/MH/ ML/AGS	Denmark
563	Zhaoqing	FFG	China
563	Ko Ryeong	MHC	Korea, South
563	Ta Tai	ATF/ARS	Taiwan
P 563	Søløven	PG/MH/ ML/AGS	Denmark
Y 563	Proserpina	YDT	Spain
564	Admiral Tributs	DDG	Russia
F 564	Lupo	FFG	Italy
565	Kim Po	MHC	Korea, South
F 565	Sagittario	FFG	Italy
566	Ko Chang	MHC	Korea, South
566	Burun	FSG	Russia
F 566	Perseo	FFG	Italy
567	Kum Wha	MHC	Korea, South
F 567	Orsa	FFG	Italy
A 569	Skinfaxe	AOTL	Denmark
570	Sonya class	MSC/MH	Cuba
570	Passat	FSG	Russia
A 570	Taşkizak	AOL	Turkey
F 570	Maestrale	FFG	Italy
571	Yang Yang Ham	MHC	Korea, South
A 571	Albay Hakki Burak	AOL	Turkey
F 571	Grecale	FFG	Italy
SSV 571	Belomore	AGI	Russia
572	Admiral Vinogradov	DDG	Russia
A 572	Yuzbasi Ihsan Tolunay	AOL	Turkey
F 572	Libeccio	FFG	Italy
A 573	Binbaşi Saadettin Gürçan	AOL	Turkey
F 573	Scirocco	FFG	Italy
F 574	Aliseo	FFG	Italy
575	Pyhäranta	MLI	Finland
575	Samum	PGGF/ PGGA	Russia
A 575	Inebolu	AOT	Turkey
F 575	Euro	FFG	Italy
X 575	Taicang	AOR	China
576	Pansio	MLI	Finland
A 576	Değirmendere	ATA	Turkey
F 576	Espero	FFG	Italy
577	Storm	FSG	Russia
A 577	Sokullu Mehmet Paşa	AX	Turkey
F 577	Zeffiro	FFG	Italy
578	Sonya class	MSC/MH	Cuba
A 578	Darica	ATR	Turkey
A 579	Cezayirli Gazi Hasan Pasa	AX	Turkey
580	Dore	LCU	Indonesia
A 580	Akar	AOR	Turkey
A 581	Çinar	AWT	Turkey
F 581	Carabiniere	AG	Italy
582	Kupang	LCU	Indonesia
F 582	Artigliere	FFG	Italy
583	Dili	LCU	Indonesia

Number	Ship's name	Type	Country
F 583	Aviere	FFG	Italy
584	Nusuntara	LCU	Indonesia
A 582	Kemer	AGS	Turkey
A 584	Kurtaran	ASR	Turkey
F 584	Bersagliere	FFG	Italy
A 585	Akin	ASR	Turkey
F 585	Granatiere	FFG	Italy
PGM 586	Pae Ku 56	PCFG	Korea, South
A 587	Gazal	ATF	Turkey
PGM 587	Pae Ku 57	PCFG	Korea, South
PGM 588	Pae Ku 58	PCFG	Korea, South
A 589	Işin	ARS	Turkey
PGM 589	Pae Ku 59	PCFG	Korea, South
590	Meteor	FSG	Russia
A 590	Yunus	AGI	Turkey
SSV 590	Krym	AGI	Russia
A 591	Çesme	AGS	Turkey
PGM 591	Pae Ku 61	PCFG	Korea, South
SSV 591	Kavkaz	AGI	Russia
A 592	Karadeniz Ereğlisi	AKS	Turkey
A 593	Eceabat	AWT	Turkey
A 594	Çubuklu	AGS	Turkey
A 595	Yarbay Kudret Güngör	AOR	Turkey
A 596	Ulubat	AWT	Turkey
A 597	Van	AWT	Turkey
A 598	Söğüt	AWT	Turkey
A 600	Kavak	AWT	Turkey
601	Lung Chiang	PCFG	Taiwan
601	Ras El Blais	PC	Tunisia
A 601	Monge	AGE	France
A 601	Tekirdağ	AGI	Turkey
P 601	Jayesagara	OPV	Sri Lanka
602	Sui Chang	PCFG	Taiwan
602	Ras Ajdir	PC	Tunisia
D 602	Suffren	DDG	France
603	Aiyar Lulin	LCU	Burma
603	Jin Chiang	PGG	Taiwan
603	Ras el Edrak	PC	Tunisia
D 603	Duquesne	DDG	France
U 603	Alchevsk	AGS	Ukraine
604	Aiyar Mai	LCU	Burma
604	Ras El Manoura	PC	Tunisia
Y 604	Ariel	YFB	France
605	Aiyar Maung	LCU	Burma
605	Andromache	PC	Seychelles
605	Tan Chiang	PGG	Taiwan
605	Ras Enghela	PC	Tunisia
605	Admiral Levchenko	DDG	Russia
606	Aiyar Minthamee	LCU	Burma
606	Hsin Chiang	PGG	Taiwan
607	Aiyar Minthar	LCU	Burma
607	Fong Chiang	PGG	Taiwan
A 607	Meuse	AOR	France
608	Tseng Chiang	PGG	Taiwan
A 608	Var	AOR	France
609	Kao Chiang	PGG	Taiwan
610	Sechelt	YDT	Canada
610	Nastoychivy	DDG	Russia
610	Svyazist	MSO	Russia
610	Hsiang Chiang	PGG	Taiwan
A 610	Ile d'Oléron	AGE	France
D 610	Tourville	DDG	France
611	Sikanni	YTT/YPT	Canada
611	Tsi Chiang	PGG	Taiwan
LCF 611	Solgae	LCAC	Korea, South
M 611	Vulcain	MCD	France
P 611	Tawheed	PC	Bangladesh
612	Sooke	YDT	Canada
612	Badr	FSG	Saudi Arabia
612	Po Chiang	PGG	Taiwan
612	Bangkeo	MSC	Thailand
D 612	De Grasse	DDG	France
P 612	Tawfiq	PC	Bangladesh
613	Stikine	YTT/YPT	Canada
613	Chan Chiang	PGG	Taiwan
613	Donchedi	MSC	Thailand
A 613	Achéron	MCD	France
P 613	Tamjeed	PC	Bangladesh
Y 613	Faune	YFB	France
614	Al Yarmook	FSG	Saudi Arabia
D 614	Cassard	DDG	France
M 614	Styx	MCD	France
P 614	Tanveer	PC	Bangladesh
615	Bora	PGGF/ PGGA	Russia
615	Chu Chiang	PGG	Taiwan
A 615	Loire	AG	France
D 615	Jean Bart	DDG	France
X 615	Dongyun	AOR	China
616	Hitteen	FSG	Saudi Arabia
617	Miras	FSG	Russia
AP 617	Yakal	AR	Philippines

Number	Ship's name	Type	Country	Number	Ship's name	Type	Country
618	Tabuk	FSG	Saudi Arabia	661	Letuchy	FFG	Russia
619	Severomorsk	DDG	Russia	MSC 661	Takashima	MHSC	Japan
620	Bespokoiny	DDG	Russia	Y 661	Korrigan	YFB	France
620	Shtyl	FSG	Russia	MSC 662	Nuwajima	MHSC	Japan
A 620	Jules Verne	AD	France	Y 662	Dryade	YFB	France
621	Mandau	PCFG	Indonesia	663	Storozhevoy	FF	Russia
621	Briz	FSG	Russia	MSC 663	Etajima	MHSC	Japan
621	Thalang	MST	Thailand	A 664	Malabar	ATA	France
A 621	Rhin	AG/AR	France	MSC 664	Kamishima	MHSC	Japan
622	Rencong	PCFG	Indonesia	MSC 665	Himeshima	MHSC	Japan
622	Rybitwa	MHSC	Poland	MSC 666	Ogishima	MHSC	Japan
M 622	Pluton	MCD	France	MSC 667	Moroshima	MHSC	Japan
623	Badik	PCFG	Indonesia	Y 667	Tupa	ABU	France
623	Mewa	MHSC	Poland	MSC 668	Yurishima	MHSC	Japan
624	Keris	PCFG	Indonesia	A 669	Tenace	ATA	France
624	Czajka	MHSC	Poland	MSC 669	Hikoshima	MHSC	Japan
625	TR 25	MSC	Poland	670	Ramadan	PCFG	Egypt
626	TR 26	MSC	Poland	MSC 670	Awashima	MHSC	Japan
630	Goplo	MSC	Poland	671	Tral class	FS	Korea, North
A 630	Marne	AOR	France	A 671	Le Fort	YTM	France
631	Najin class	FFG	Korea, North	LST 671	Un Bong	LST	Korea, South
631	Gardno	MSC	Poland	MSC 671	Sakushima	MHSC	Japan
631	Bang Rachan	MHSC	Thailand	P 671	Glaive	PC	France
A 631	Somme	AOR	France	672	Khyber	PCFG	Egypt
632	Bukowo	MSC	Poland	MSC 672	Uwajima	MHSC	Japan
632	Nongsarai	MHSC	Thailand	P 672	Épée	PC	France
633	Dabie	MSC	Poland	A 673	Lutteur	YTM	France
633	Lat Ya	MHSC	Thailand	MSC 673	Ieshima	MHSC	Japan
A 633	Taape	AG	France	674	El Kadessaya	PCFG	Egypt
634	Jamno	MSC	Poland	MSC 674	Tsukishima	MHSC	Japan
634	Tha Din Daeng	MHSC	Thailand	MSC 675	Maejima	MHSC	Japan
A 634	Rari	AFL	France	LST 675	Kae Bong	LST	Korea, South
635	Mielno	MSC	Poland	A 675	Fréhel	YTM	France
A 635	Revi	AFL	France	676	El Yarmouk	PCFG	Egypt
636	Wicko	MSC	Poland	A 676	Saire	YTM	France
A 636	Maroa	YTM	France	LST 676	Wee Bong	LST	Korea, South
U 635	Skvyra	AGS	Ukraine	MSC 676	Kumejima	MHSC	Japan
637	Resko	MSC	Poland	P 676	Flamant	PC	France
A637	Maito	YTM	France	A 677	Armen	YTM	France
638	Sarbsko	MSC	Poland	LST 677	Su Yong	LST	Korea, South
A 638	Manini	YTM	France	MSC 677	Makishima	MHSC	Japan
Y 638	Lardier	YTM	France	P 677	Cormoran	PC	France
639	Necko	MSC	Poland	678	Badr	PCFG	Egypt
Y 639	Giens	YTM	France	678	Admiral Kharlamov	DDG	Russia
640	Naklo	MSC	Poland	A 678	La Houssaye	YTM	France
D 640	Georges Leygues	DDG	France	LST 678	Buk Han	LST	Korea, South
Y 640	Mengam	YTM	France	MSC 678	Tobishima	MHSC	Japan
641	Druzno	MSC	Poland	P 678	Pluvier	PC	France
D 641	Dupleix	DDG	France	A 679	Kéréon	YTM	France
M 641	Éridan	MHC	France	MSC 679	Yugeshima	MHSC	Japan
Y 641	Balaguier	YTM	France	LST 679	Hwa San	LST	Korea, South
642	Hancza	MSC	Poland	P 679	Grèbe	PC	France
642	Natya class	MSC/AGOR	Syria	680	Hettein	PCFG	Egypt
				A 680	Sicié	YTM	France
D 642	Montcalm	DDG	France	MSC 680	Nagashima	MHSC	Japan
M 642	Cassiopée	MHC	France	P 680	Sterne	PC	France
Y 642	Taillat	YTM	France	LST 681	Kojoon Bong	LST	Korea, South
643	Mamry	MHSC	Poland	A 681	Taunoa	YTM	France
D 643	Jean de Vienne	DDG	France	MSC 681	Sugashima	MSC	Japan
M 643	Andromède	MHC	France	P 681	Albatros	PG	France
644	Wigry	MHSC	Poland	LST 682	Biro Bong	LST	Korea, South
D 644	Primauguet	DDG	France	MSC 682	Notojima	MSC	Japan
M 644	Pégase	MHC	France	P 682	L'Audacieuse	PC	France
645	Sniardwy	MHSC	Poland	LST 683	Hyangro Bong	LST	Korea, South
D 645	La Motte-Picquet	DDG	France	MSC 683	Tsunoshima	MSC	Japan
M 645	Orion	MHC	France	P 683	La Boudeuse	PC	France
646	Wdzydze	MHSC	Poland	P 684	La Capricieuse	PC	France
D 646	Latouche-Treville	DDG	France	MSC 684	Naoshima	MSC	Japan
M 646	Croix du Sud	MHC	France	LST 685	Seongin Bong	LST	Korea, South
M 647	Aigle	MHC	France	P 685	La Fougueuse	PC	France
M 648	Lyre	MHC	France	P 686	La Glorieuse	PC	France
A 649	L'Etoile	AXS	France	687	Marshal Vasilevsky	DDG	Russia
M 649	Persée	MHC	France	P 687	La Gracieuse	PC	France
650	Admiral Chabanenko	DDG	Russia	P 688	La Moqueuse	PC	France
A 650	La Belle Poule	AXS	France	P 689	La Railleuse	PC	France
M 650	Sagittaire	MHC	France	P 690	La Rieuse	PC	France
651	Singa	PC	Indonesia	P 691	La Tapageuse	PC	France
M 651	Verseau	MHC	France	Y 692	Telenn Mor	ABU	France
A 652	Mutin	AXS	France	693	Haijiu class	PG	China
M 652	Céphée	MHC	France	A 693	Acharné	YTM	France
653	Houxin class	PGG	China	A 695	Bélier	YTB	France
653	Ajak	PC	Indonesia	A 696	Buffle	YTB	France
M 653	Capricorne	MHC	France	Y 696	Alphée	YFB	France
654	Houxin class	PGG	China	697	Haijiu class	PG	China
655	Houxin class	PGG	China	A 697	Bison	YTB	France
656	Houxin class	PGG	China	Y 698	Calmar	ABU	France
657	Houxin class	PGG	China	700	Kingston	MCDV	Canada
LSM 657	Wol Mi	LSM	Korea, South	A 700	Khaireddine	AGS	Tunisia
658	Houxin class	PGG	China	Y 700	Néréide	YFB	France
LSM 658	Ki Rin	LSM	Korea, South	701	Sirius	LSM	Bulgaria
659	Houxin class	PGG	China	701	Glace Bay	MCDV	Canada
MSC 660	Hahajima	MHSC	Japan	701	Pulau Rani	MSO	Indonesia

Number	Ship's name	Type	Country	Number	Ship's name	Type	Country
A 701	N N O Salammbo	AGOR/AX	Tunisia	754	Houxin class	PGG	China
U 701	Krab	YDT	Ukraine	754	Bezboyazenny	DDG	Russia
Y 701	Ondine	YFB	France	754	Druzhny	FF	Russia
702	Antares	LSM	Bulgaria	A 754	Tigre	AXL	France
702	Nanaimo	MCDV	Canada	U 754	Dzhankoi	AR	Ukraine
702	Pulau Ratewo	MSO	Indonesia	755	Houxin class	PGG	China
702	Abu El Barakat Al Barbari	AGOR	Morocco	755	An Yang	FS	Korea, South
702	Pylky	FF	Russia	A 755	Lion	AXL	France
702	Madina	FFG	Saudi Arabia	U 755	Yalta	AGS	Ukraine
Y 702	Naiade	YFB	France	756	Houxin class	PGG	China
703	Edmonton	MCDV	Canada	756	Po Hang	FS/FSG	Korea, South
704	Shawinigan	MCDV	Canada	A 756	L'Espérance	AGS	France
704	Hofouf	FFG	Saudi Arabia	U 756	Sudak	AWT	Ukraine
705	Whitehorse	MCDV	Canada	757	Houxin class	PGG	China
706	Yellowknife	MCDV	Canada	757	Kun San	FS/FSG	Korea, South
706	Abha	FFG	Saudi Arabia	A 757	D'Entrecasteaux	AGOR	France
U 706	Izyaslav	ATS/PG	Ukraine	U 757	Makivka	AOR	Ukraine
707	Goose Bay	MCDV	Canada	758	Houxin class	PGG	China
708	Moncton	MCDV	Canada	758	Kyong Ju	FS/FSG	Korea, South
708	Taif	FFG	Saudi Arabia	U 758	Kerch	AOL	Ukraine
709	Saskatoon	MCDV	Canada	759	Houxin class	PGG	China
710	Brandon	MCDV	Canada	759	Mok Po	FS/FSG	Korea, South
F 710	La Fayette	FFG	France	760	Houxin class	PGG	China
711	Summerside	MCDV	Canada	L 760	Flunder	LCU	Germany
711	Pulau Rengat	MHC	Indonesia	761	Kim Chon	FS/FSG	Korea, South
711	Zeltin	AR/LSD	Libya	761	Mataphon	LCU	Thailand
711	Podchorazy	AXL	Poland	762	Chung Ju	FS/FSG	Korea, South
711	Kerch	CG	Russia	762	Rawi	LCU	Thailand
F 711	Surcouf	FFG	France	L 762	Lachs	LCU	Germany
P 711	Barkat	PC	Bangladesh	763	Jin Ju	FS/FSG	Korea, South
712	Pulau Rupat	MHC	Indonesia	763	Adang	LCU	Thailand
712	Kadet	AXL	Poland	L 763	Plötze	LCU	Germany
712	Neustrashimy	FFG	Russia	764	Houxin class	PGG	China
712	Chang	LST	Thailand	764	Phetra	LCU	Thailand
F 712	Courbet	FFG	France	765	Houxin class	PGG	China
713	Elew	AXL	Poland	765	Yo Su	FS/FSG	Korea, South
713	Pangan	LST	Thailand	L 765	Schlei	LCU	Germany
F 713	Aconit	FFG	France	766	Houxin class	PGG	China
714	Lanta	LST	Thailand	766	Jin Hae	FS/FSG	Korea, South
F 714	Guépratte	FFG	France	766	Talibong	LCU	Thailand
715	Bystry	DDG	Russia	767	Houxin class	PGG	China
715	Prathong	LST	Thailand	767	Sun Chon	FS/FSG	Korea, South
718	Semen Roshak	MSO	Russia	768	Houxin class	PGG	China
719	Desantnik	MSO	Russia	768	Yee Ree	FS/FSG	Korea, South
721	Pulau Rote	MSC	Indonesia	A 768	Élan	AG	France
721	Sichang	LST	Thailand	769	Houxin class	PGG	China
A 721	Khadem	ATA	Bangladesh	769	Won Ju	FGS/FSG	Korea, South
722	Pulau Raas	MSC	Indonesia	L 769	Zander	LCU	Germany
722	Al Munjed	ARS	Libya	770	Houjian class	PGG	China
722	Surin	LST	Thailand	A 770	Glycine	AXL	France
A 722	Sebak	YTM	Bangladesh	M 770	Antares	MHI	France
A 722	Poséidon	YAG	France	771	Houjian class	PGG	China
MCL 722	Niijima	MST/MCL	Japan	771	An Dong	FS/FSG	Korea, South
U 722	Borshev	YTR	Ukraine	771	Thong Kaeo	LCU	Thailand
723	Pulau Romang	MSC	Indonesia	A 771	Eglantine	AXL	France
MCL 723	Yakushima	MST/MCL	Japan	M 771	Altair	MHI	France
724	Pulau Rimau	MSC	Indonesia	772	Houjian class	PGG	China
725	Pulau Rondo	MSC	Indonesia	772	Chon An	FS/FSG	Korea, South
725	Sariwon class	FS	Korea, North	772	Thong Lang	LCU	Thailand
726	Pulau Rusa	MSC	Indonesia	M 772	Aldebaran	MHI	France
726	Sariwon class	FS	Korea, North	773	Houjian class	PGG	China
727	Pulau Rangsang	MSC	Indonesia	773	Song Nam	FS/FSG	Korea, South
727	Sariwon class	FS	Korea, North	773	Wang Nok	LCU	Thailand
728	Pulau Raibu	MSC	Indonesia	P 773	Njambuur	PC	Senegal
U 728	Evpatoria	YTR	Ukraine	774	Houjian class	PGG	China
729	Pulau Rempang	MSC	Indonesia	774	Wang Nai	LCU	Thailand
F 730	Floréal	FFG	France	A 774	Chevreuil	AG	France
731	Neukrotimy	FFG	Russia	775	Houjian class	PGG	China
731	Kut	LSM	Thailand	775	Bu Chon	FS/FSG	Korea, South
F 731	Prairial	FFG	France	775	Man Nok	LCU	Thailand
732	Kram	LSM	Thailand	A 775	Gazelle	AG	France
F 732	Nivôse	FFG	France	776	Jae Chon	FS/FSG	Korea, South
F 733	Ventôse	FFG	France	776	Man Klang	LCU	Thailand
F 734	Vendémiaire	FFG	France	A 776	Isard	AG	France
F 735	Germinal	FFG	France	777	Porkkala	MLI	Finland
738	Zaryad	MSO	Russia	777	Dae Chon	FS/FSG	Korea, South
741	Prab	LCM	Thailand	777	Man Nal	LCU	Thailand
742	Satakut	LCM	Thailand	778	Sok Cho	FS/FSG	Korea, South
A 743	Denti	AGE	France	778	Burny	DDG	Russia
A 748	Léopard	AXL	France	779	Yong Ju	FS/FSG	Korea, South
A 749	Panthère	AXL	France	781	Nam Won	FS/FSG	Korea, South
A 750	Jaguar	AXL	France	782	Kwan Myong	FS/FSG	Korea, South
751	Houxin class	PGG	China	783	Sin Hung	FS/FSG	Korea, South
751	Dong Hae	FS	Korea, South	785	Kong Ju	FS/FSG	Korea, South
751	Nakha	LSL	Thailand	A 785	Thétis	AGE	France
A 751	Lynx	AXL	France	F 788	Second Maître Le Bihan	FFG	France
752	Houxin class	PGG	China	F 789	Lieutenant de Vaisseau Le Hénaff	FFG	France
752	Su Won	FS	Korea, South	A 790	Coralline	AGE	France
A 752	Guépard	AXL	France	F 790	Lieutenant de Vaisseau Lavallée	FFG	France
753	Houxin class	PGG	China	A 791	Lapérouse	AGS	France
753	Kang Reung	FS	Korea, South	F 791	Commandant l'Herminier	FFG	France
A 753	Chacal	AXL	France				

PENNANT LIST

Number	Ship's name	Type	Country	Number	Ship's name	Type	Country
A 792	Borda	AGS	France	847	Sibarau	PC	Indonesia
F 792	Premier Maitre L'Her	FFG	France	PG 847	Leopoldo Regis	PCF	Philippines
A 793	Laplace	AGS	France	848	Siliman	PC	Indonesia
F 793	Commandant Blaison	FFG	France	PG 848	Leon Tadina	PCF	Philippines
F 794	Enseigne de Vaisseau Jacoubet	FFG	France	PG 849	Loreto Danipog	PCF	Philippines
A 795	Arago	AGS	France	M 850	Alkmaar	MHC	Netherlands
F 795	Commandant Ducuing	FFG	France	851	KD-11	LCU	Poland
F 796	Commandant Birot	FFG	France	A 851	Cerberus	YDT	Netherlands
F 797	Commandant Bouan	FFG	France	HQ 851	Yurka class	MSO	Vietnam
799	Hylje	AOS	Finland	M 851	Delfzyl	MHC	Netherlands
L 800	Rotterdam	LPD/ATS	Netherlands	PG 851	Apollo Tiano	PCF	Philippines
801	Rais Hamidou	FSG	Algeria	U 851	Novy Bug	ARC	Ukraine
801	Thu Tay Thi	AGS	Burma	852	KD-12	LCU	Poland
801	Pandrong	PC	Indonesia	A 852	Argus	YDT	Netherlands
801	Ladny	FF	Russia	M 852	Dordrecht	MHC	Netherlands
A 801	Pelikaan	ARL	Netherlands	853	KD-13	LCU	Poland
F 801	De Zeven Provincien	DDG	Netherlands	853	Rin	YTB	Thailand
802	Salah Rais	FSG	Algeria	A 853	Nautilus	YDT	Netherlands
802	(ex-Changi)	AGS	Burma	M 853	Haarlem	MHC	Netherlands
802	Sura	PC	Indonesia	PG 853	Sulpicio Hernandez	PCF	Philippines
F 802	De Ruyter	DDG	Netherlands	854	Rang	YTB	Thailand
803	Rais Ali	FSG	Algeria	A 854	Hydra	YDT	Netherlands
803	Todak	PC	Indonesia	M 854	Harlingen	MHC	Netherlands
F 803	Tromp	FFG	Netherlands	855	Machinist	MSO	Russia
U 803	Krasnodon	AR	Ukraine	855	Samaesan	YTB	Thailand
804	Hiu	PC	Indonesia	M 855	Scheveningen	MHC	Netherlands
804	Sderzhanny	DDG	Russia	856	Raet	YTB	Thailand
F 804	Evertsen	DDG	Netherlands	M 856	Maasluis	MHC	Netherlands
805	Layang	PC	Indonesia	857	Sigalu	PC	Indonesia
806	Dorang	PC	Indonesia	M 857	Makkum	MHC	Netherlands
806	Motorist	MSO	Russia	858	Silea	PC	Indonesia
F 806	De Ruyter	FFG	Netherlands	M 858	Middelburg	MHC	Netherlands
808	Pytlivy	FFG	Russia	859	Siribua	PC	Indonesia
810	Cedynia	LCT	Poland	M 859	Hellevoetsluis	MHC	Netherlands
810	Smetlivy	DDG	Russia	M 860	Schiedam	MHC	Netherlands
811	Kakap	PC	Indonesia	Y 860	Schwedeneck	AG	Germany
811	Grunwald	LCT	Poland	861	Kled Keo	AK	Thailand
811	Chanthara	AGS	Thailand	M 861	Urk	MHC	Netherlands
U 811	Balta	YDG	Ukraine	Y 861	Kronsort	AG	Germany
812	Kerapu	PC	Indonesia	862	Siada	PC	Indonesia
812	Arriyad	FFG	Saudi Arabia	M 862	Zierikzee	MHC	Netherlands
812	Suk	AGS	Thailand	Y 862	Helmsand	AG	Germany
F 812	Jacob van Heemskerck	FFG	Netherlands	863	Sikuda	PC	Indonesia
P 812	Nirbhoy	PC	Bangladesh	M 863	Vlaardingen	MHC	Netherlands
U 812	Severodonetsk	AGS	Ukraine	Y 863	Stollergrund	AG	Germany
813	Tongkol	PC	Indonesia	864	Sigurot	PC	Indonesia
F 813	Witte de With	FFG	Netherlands	HQ 864	Sonya class	MSC	Vietnam
814	Barakuda	PC	Indonesia	M 864	Willemstad	MHC	Netherlands
L 820	Yunnan class	LCU	Sri Lanka	Y 864	Mittelgrund	AG	Germany
821	Lublin	LCT/ML	Poland	Y 865	Kalkgrund	AG	Germany
821	Suriya	AGOR	Thailand	Y 866	Breitgrund	AG	Germany
L 821	Yunnan class	LCU	Sri Lanka	Y 867	Bant	AG	Germany
822	Gniezno	LCT/ML	Poland	871	Similan	AOR	Thailand
823	Soho class	FFG	Korea, North	874	Voronesh	AEM	Russia
823	Krakow	LCT/ML	Poland	A 874	Linge	YTB	Netherlands
F 823	Philips van Almonde	FFG	Netherlands	A 875	Regge	YTB	Netherlands
824	Poznan	LCT/ML	Poland	A 876	Hunze	YTB	Netherlands
824	Navodchik	MSO	Russia	877	Kampela 3	LCU/AKSL	Finland
F 824	Bloys van Treslong	FFG	Netherlands	A 877	Rotte	YTB	Netherlands
825	Torun	LCT/ML	Poland	879	Volga	AS	Russia
F 825	Jan van Brakel	FFG	Netherlands	L 880	Shakthi	LSM	Sri Lanka
826	Isku	MLI	Finland	HQ 885	Yurka class	MSO	Vietnam
F 826	Pieter Florisz	FFG	Netherlands	U 891	Dagushan	ARL	China
F 827	Karel Doorman	FFG	Netherlands	Y 891	Altmark	APB	Germany
F 828	Van Speijk	FFG	Netherlands	Y 895	Wische	APB	Germany
F 829	Willem van der Zaan	FFG	Netherlands	899	Halli	AOS	Finland
F 830	Tjerk Hiddes	FFG	Netherlands	A 900	Mercuur	ASL/TRV	Netherlands
U 830	Korets	ATR	Ukraine	L 900	Shah Amanat	LSL	Bangladesh
831	Chula	AOR	Thailand	901	Mourad Rais	FFG	Algeria
F 831	Van Amstel	FFG	Netherlands	901	Balikpapan	AOTL	Indonesia
U 831	Kovel	ATR	Ukraine	901	A Zheleznyakov	MHO	Russia
832	Samui	YO	Thailand	F 901	Sharm el Sheikh	FFG	Egypt
A 832	Zuiderkruis	AOR	Netherlands	L 901	Shah Poran	LCU	Bangladesh
F 832	Abraham van der Hulst	FFG	Netherlands	902	Rais Kellich	FFG	Algeria
833	Prong	YO	Thailand	902	Sambu	AOTL	Indonesia
F 833	Van Nes	FFG	Netherlands	902	Boraida	AOR	Saudi Arabia
834	Polemetchik	MSO	Russia	A 902	Van Kinsbergen	AXL	Netherlands
834	Proet	YW	Thailand	L 902	Shah Makhdum	LCU	Bangladesh
F 834	Van Galen	FFG	Netherlands	P 902	Liberation	PBR	Belgium
835	Samed	YW	Thailand	903	Rais Korfou	FFG	Algeria
A 836	Amsterdam	AOR	Netherlands	903	Arun	AOR	Indonesia
L 836	Ranavijaya	LCM	Sri Lanka	A 903	Zeefakkel	AX	Netherlands
L 839	Ranagaja	LCM	Sri Lanka	904	Yunbou	AOR	Saudi Arabia
PG 840	Conrado Yap	PCF	Philippines	A 906	Tydeman	AGOR	Netherlands
841	Karabane	LCT	Senegal	F 906	Toushka	FFG	Egypt
841	Chuang	YW	Thailand	907	Fu Yang	DDG	Taiwan
PG 842	Tedorico Dominado Jr	PCF	Philippines	M 908	G Truffaut	MSO	Belgium
PG 843	Cosme Acosta	PCF	Philippines	909	Turbinist	MSO	Russia
844	Barentsevo More	MCS	Russia	F 910	Wielingen	FFG	Belgium
PG 844	Jose Artiaga Jr	PCF	Philippines	911	Sorong	AOT	Indonesia
PG 846	Nicanor Jimenez	PCF	Philippines	911	Zhukov	MSO	Russia
				911	Chakri Naruebet	CVS	Thailand

Number	Ship's name	Type	Country	Number	Ship's name	Type	Country
F 911	Westdiep	FFG	Belgium	966	Rasheed	FFG	Egypt
F 911	Mubarak	FFG	Egypt	DD 966	Hewitt	DDG	USA
P 911	Madhumati	PC/OPV	Bangladesh	DD 967	Elliott	DDG	USA
912	Chien Yang	DD	Taiwan	DD 968	Arthur W Radford	DDG	USA
F 912	Wandelaar	FFG	Belgium	DD 969	Peterson	DDG	USA
913	Snaypr	MSO	Russia	DD 970	Caron	DDG	USA
914	Vinogradov	MSO	Russia	DDG 971	King Kwanggaeto	DDG	Korea, South
M 915	Aster	MHC	Belgium	971	Tarantul class	FSG	Yemen
DD 916	Jeong Buk	DDG	Korea, South	DD 971	David R Ray	DDG	USA
F 916	Taba	FFG	Egypt	972	Tanjung Oisina	AP	Indonesia
M 916	Bellis	MHC	Belgium	DDG 972	Euljimundok	DDG	Korea, South
917	Nan Yang	DDG	Taiwan	DD 972	Oldendorf	DDG	USA
M 917	Crocus	MHC	Belgium	DD 973	John Young	DDG	USA
VM 917	Al Manoud	YDT	Libya	DDG 973	Yangmanchun	DDG	Korea, South
DD 919	Taejon	DDG	Korea, South	DD 975	O'Brien	DDG	USA
920	Dazhi	AS	China	DD 977	Briscoe	DDG	USA
921	El Fateh	DD	Egypt	DD 978	Stump	DDG	USA
921	Jaya Wijaya	AR	Indonesia	DD 980	Moosbrugger	DDG	USA
921	Liao Yang	DD	Taiwan	DD 981	John Hancock	DDG	USA
DD 921	Kwang Ju	DDG	Korea, South	DD 982	Nicholson	DDG	USA
M 921	Lobelia	MHC	Belgium	DD 985	Cushing	DDG	USA
922	Rakata	ATA	Indonesia	P 986	Hauk	PCFG	Norway
DD 922	Kang Won	DDG	Korea, South	DD 987	O'Bannon	DDG	USA
M 922	Myosotis	MHC	Belgium	P 987	Ørn	PCFG	Norway
923	Soputan	ATF	Indonesia	DD 988	Thorn	DDG	USA
923	Shen Yang	DD	Taiwan	P 988	Terne	PCFG	Norway
M 923	Narcis	MHC	Belgium	DD 989	Deyo	DDG	USA
924	Kai Yang	DDG	Taiwan	P 989	Tjeld	PCFG	Norway
M 924	Primula	MHC	Belgium	P 990	Skarv	PCFG	Norway
925	Te Yang	DD	Taiwan	991	Yuting class	LST	China
DD 925	Jeon Ju	DDG	Korea, South	DD 991	Fife	DDG	USA
926	Shuei Yang	DDG	Taiwan	P 991	Teist	PCFG	Norway
927	Yukan class	LST	China	DD 992	Fletcher	DDG	USA
927	Yun Yang	DD	Taiwan	P 992	Jo	PCFG	Norway
928	Yukan class	LST	China	P 993	Lom	PCFG	Norway
928	Chen Yang	DD	Taiwan	P 994	Stegg	PCFG	Norway
929	Yukan class	LST	China	P 995	Falk	PCFG	Norway
929	Shao Yang	DD	Taiwan	P 996	Ravn	PCFG	Norway
930	Yukan class	LST	China	DD 997	Hayler	DDG	USA
930	Legky	FFG	Russia	P 997	Gribb	PCFG	Norway
931	Yukan class	LST	China	P 998	Geir	PCFG	Norway
931	Burujulasad	AGOR	Indonesia	P 999	Erle	PCFG	Norway
932	Yukan class	LST	China	P 1022	Jalalat	PCFG	Pakistan
932	Dewa Kembar	AGS	Indonesia	P 1024	Shujaat	PCFG	Pakistan
932	Chin Yang	FFG	Taiwan	P 1026	Dehshat	PCFG	Pakistan
933	Yukan class	LST	China	P 1027	Himmat	PCFG	Pakistan
933	Jalanidhi	AGOR	Indonesia	P 1028	Quwwat	PCFG	Pakistan
933	Fong Yang	FFG	Taiwan	GC 1051	Kukulkán	PCF	Guatemala
934	Yuting class	LST	China	M 1052	Mühlhausen	MCD	Germany
934	Lampo Batang	YTM	Indonesia	M 1058	Fulda	MHC	Germany
934	Feng Yang	FFG	Taiwan	M 1059	Weilheim	MHC	Germany
935	Yuting class	LST	China	1060	Barkat	OPV	Pakistan
935	Tambora	YTM	Indonesia	M 1060	Weiden	MHC	Germany
935	Yen Yang	FFG	Taiwan	1061	Rehmat	OPV	Pakistan
936	Yuting class	LST	China	M 1061	Rottweil	MHC	Germany
936	Bromo	YTM	Indonesia	1062	Nusrat	OPV	Pakistan
936	Hae Yang	FFG	Taiwan	M 1062	Sulzbach-Rosenberg	MHC	Germany
937	Yuting class	LST	China	1063	Vehdat	OPV	Pakistan
937	Hwai Yang	FFG	Taiwan	M 1063	Bad Bevensen	MHC	Germany
938	Yuting class	LST	China	M 1064	Grömitz	MHC	Germany
938	Ning Yang	FFG	Taiwan	M 1065	Dillingen	MHC	Germany
939	Yi Yang	FFG	Taiwan	1066	Sabqat	PCF	Pakistan
F 941	El Suez	FFG	Egypt	M 1066	Frankenthal	MHC	Germany
F 946	Abu Qir	FFG	Egypt	M 1067	Bad Rappenau	MHC	Germany
951	Dayun class	AK	China	1068	Rafaqat	PCF	Pakistan
951	Najim al Zaffer	FFG	Egypt	M 1068	Datteln	MHC	Germany
FF 951	Ulsan	FFG	Korea, South	1069	Pishin	PCF	Pakistan
952	Dayun class	AK	China	M 1069	Homburg	MHC	Germany
952	Nusa Telu	AK	Indonesia	1070	Bahawalpur	PCF	Pakistan
FF 952	Seoul	FFG	Korea, South	M 1073	Schleswig	MSC	Germany
953	Nancang	AOR/AK	China	M 1079	Düren	MSC	Germany
953	Chung Nam	FFG	Korea, South	M 1081	Konstanz	MSC	Germany
955	Zadorny	FF	Russia	M 1082	Wolfsburg	MSC	Germany
FF 955	Masan	FFG	Korea, South	M 1090	Pegnitz	MSC	Germany
956	El Nasser	FFG	Egypt	M 1091	Kulmbach	MSC	Germany
FF 956	Kyong Buk	FFG	Korea, South	M 1092	Hameln	MSC	Germany
FF 957	Chon Nam	FFG	Korea, South	M 1093	Auerbach	MSC	Germany
A 958	Zenobe Gramme	AXS	Belgium	M 1094	Ensdorf	MSC	Germany
FF 958	Che Ju	FFG	Korea, South	M 1095	Überherrn	MSC	Germany
959	Teluk Mentawai	AK	Indonesia	M 1096	Passau	MSC	Germany
FF 959	Busan	FFG	Korea, South	M 1097	Laboe	MSC	Germany
960	Karimata	AK	Indonesia	M 1098	Siegburg	MSC	Germany
A 960	Godetia	AGF	Belgium	M 1099	Herten	MSC	Germany
961	Damyat	FFG	Egypt	1101	Cheng Kung	FFG	Taiwan
A 961	Zinnia	AGF	Belgium	1102	Brolga	MSA(S)	Australia
P 960	Skjold	PCFG	Norway	1103	Cheng Ho	FFG	Taiwan
FF 961	Chung Ju	FFG	Korea, South	1105	Chi Kuang	FFG	Taiwan
A 962	Belgica	AGOR	Belgium	1106	Yueh Fei	FFG	Taiwan
A 963	Stern	ARL	Belgium	1107	Tzu-I	FFG	Taiwan
DD 963	Spruance	DDG	USA	1108	Pan Chao	FFG	Taiwan
DD 964	Paul F Foster	DDG	USA	1109	Chang Chien	FFG	Taiwan
DD 965	Kinkaid	DDG	USA	1110	Tien Tan	FFG	Taiwan

PENNANT LIST

Number	Ship's name	Type	Country	Number	Ship's name	Type	Country
1131	Stenka class	PCF	Cambodia	1608	Fresia	PC	Chile
1134	Stenka class	PCF	Cambodia	Y 1643	Bottsand	AOTL	Germany
P 1140	Cacine	PG	Portugal	Y 1644	Eversand	AOTL	Germany
P 1141	Cunene	PG	Portugal	C 2001	Justo Sierra Mendez	PG	Mexico
M 1142	Umzimkulu	MHC	South Africa	C 2002	Benito Juarez	PG	Mexico
P 1143	Rovuma	PG	Portugal	M 2011	Orwell	MSC/AXL	UK
P 1144	Cuanza	PG	Portugal	M 2658	Frauenlob	MSI	Germany
P 1145	Geba	PG	Portugal	M 2660	Gefion	MSI	Germany
P 1146	Zaire	PG	Portugal	M 2661	Medusa	MSI	Germany
P 1147	Zambeze	PG	Portugal	M 2662	Undine	MSI	Germany
P 1150	Argos	PC	Portugal	M 2665	Loreley	MSI	Germany
P 1151	Dragão	PC	Portugal	L 3004	Sir Bedivere	LSL	UK
P 1152	Escorpião	PC	Portugal	L 3005	Sir Galahad	LSL	UK
P 1153	Cassiopeia	PC	Portugal	L 3027	Sir Geraint	LSL	UK
P 1154	Hidra	PC	Portugal	L 3036	Sir Percivale	LSL	UK
P 1155	Centauro	PC	Portugal	P 3100	Mamba	PCG	Kenya
P 1156	Orion	PC	Portugal	P 3121	Madaraka	PCG	Kenya
P 1157	Pegaso	PC	Portugal	P 3126	Nyayo	PCFG	Kenya
P 1158	Sagitario	PC	Portugal	P 3127	Umoja	PCFG	Kenya
P 1160	Limpopo	PG	Portugal	3144	Sri Sabah	PC	Malaysia
P 1161	Save	PG	Portugal	3145	Sri Sarawak	PC	Malaysia
P 1162	Albatroz	PC	Portugal	3146	Sri Negri Sembilan	PC	Malaysia
P 1163	Açor	PC	Portugal	3147	Sri Melaka	PC	Malaysia
P 1164	Andorinha	PC	Portugal	P 3148	Fleur	YDT	South Africa
P 1165	Aguia	PC	Portugal	P 3301	Ardhana	PC	UAE
P 1167	Cisne	PC	Portugal	P 3302	Zurara	PC	UAE
LST 1184	Frederick	LST	USA	P 3303	Murban	PC	UAE
LST 1194	La Moure County	LST	USA	P 3304	Al Ghullan	PC	UAE
1202	Kang Ding	FFG	Taiwan	P 3305	Radoom	PC	UAE
1203	Si Ning	FFG	Taiwan	P 3306	Ghanadhah	PC	UAE
1205	Kun Ming	FFG	Taiwan	3501	Perdana	PCFG	Malaysia
1206	Di Hua	FFG	Taiwan	A 3501	Annad	YTB	UAE
1207	Wu Chang	FFG	Taiwan	3502	Serang	PCFG	Malaysia
1209	Chen Te	FFG	Taiwan	3503	Ganas	PCFG	Malaysia
M 1212	Umhloti	MHC	South Africa	3504	Ganyang	PCFG	Malaysia
M 1213	Umgeni	MHC	South Africa	3505	Jerong	PCF	Malaysia
M 1214	Walvisbaai	MSC	South Africa	L 3505	Sir Tristram	LSL	UK
M 1215	East London	MSC	South Africa	3506	Todak	PCF	Malaysia
1301	Yung Feng	MHC	Taiwan	3507	Paus	PCF	Malaysia
1302	Yung Chia	MHC	Taiwan	3508	Yu	PCF	Malaysia
1303	Yung Ting	MHC	Taiwan	TV 3508	Kashima	AX/TV	Japan
1305	Yung Shun	MHC	Taiwan	3509	Baung	PCF	Malaysia
1306	Yung Yang	MSO	Taiwan	3510	Pari	PCF	Malaysia
1307	Yung Tzu	MSO	Taiwan	3511	Handalan	PCFG	Malaysia
1308	Yung Ku	MSO	Taiwan	3512	Perkasa	PCFG	Malaysia
1309	Yung Teh	MSO	Taiwan	TV 3512	Aokumo	AX/TV	Japan
LST 1312	Ambe	LST	Nigeria	3513	Pendekar	PCFG	Malaysia
LST 1313	Ofiom	LST	Nigeria	TV 3513	Shimayuki	AX/TV	Japan
A 1401	Eisvogel	AGB	Germany	3514	Gempita	PCFG	Malaysia
A 1405	FW 5	AWT	Germany	TV 3514	Akigumo	AX/TV	Japan
A 1409	Wilhelm Pullwer	AG	Germany	P 3553	Moa	PC	New Zealand
A 1411	Berlin	AOR	Germany	P 3554	Kiwi	PC	New Zealand
A 1412	Frankfurt	AOR	Germany	P 3555	Wakakura	PC	New Zealand
A 1413	Freiburg	ARL	Germany	P 3556	Hinau	PC	New Zealand
A 1414	Glücksburg	ARL	Germany	P 3711	Um Almaradim	PCFG	Kuwait
A 1418	Meersburg	ARL	Germany	P 3113	Ouha	PCFG	Kuwait
A 1424	Walchensee	AOL	Germany	P 3715	Failaka	PCFG	Kuwait
A 1425	Ammersee	AOL	Germany	P 3717	Maskan	PCFG	Kuwait
A 1426	Tegernsee	AOL	Germany	P 3719	Al-Ahmadi	PCFG	Kuwait
A 1427	Westensee	AOL	Germany	P 3721	Alfahaheel	PCFG	Kuwait
A 1435	Westerwald	AEL	Germany	P 3723	Al Yarmouk	PCFG	Kuwait
A 1436	Odenwald	AEL	Germany	P 3725	Garoh	PCFG	Kuwait
A 1439	Baltrum	AX	Germany	LST 4001	Osumi	LST/LPD	Japan
A 1440	Juist	AX	Germany	LST 4103	Nemuro	LST	Japan
A 1441	Langeoog	AX	Germany	LST 4152	Ojika	LST	Japan
A 1442	Spessart	AOL	Germany	LST 4153	Satsuma	LST	Japan
A 1443	Rhön	AOL	Germany	LSU 4171	Yura	LSU/LCU	Japan
A 1450	Planet	AGE	Germany	LSU 4172	Noto	LSU/LCU	Japan
A 1451	Wangerooge	ATR	Germany	P 4401	Mubarraz	PCFG	UAE
A 1452	Spiekeroog	ATR	Germany	ATS 4202	Kurobe	AXT/ATS	Japan
A 1455	Norderney	ATR	Germany	P 4402	Makasib	PCFG	UAE
A 1456	Alliance	AGOR	NATO	ATS 4203	Tenryu	AS/ASU	Japan
A 1458	Fehmarn	ATS	Germany	P 4501	Ban Yas	PCFG	UAE
FNH 1491	Punta Caxinas	LCU	Honduras	L 4502	Reinøysund	LCT	Norway
M 1499	Umkomaas	MHC	South Africa	P 4502	Marban	PCFG	UAE
1503	Sri Indera Sakti	AOR/ AE/AX	Malaysia	L 4503	Sørøysund	LCT	Norway
				P 4503	Rodqm	PCFG	UAE
1504	Mahawangsa	AOR/AE/ AX	Malaysia	L 4504	Maursund	LCT	Norway
				P 4504	Shaheen	PCFG	UAE
1505	Sri Inderapura	LST	Malaysia	L 4505	Rotsund	LCT	Norway
P 1563	Adam Kok	PCFG	South Africa	P 4505	Al Sanbouk	PCFG	Kuwait
P 1565	Isaac Dyobha	PCFG	South Africa	P 4505	Sagar	PCFG	UAE
P 1566	René Sethren	PCFG	SouthAfrica	L 4506	Tjeldsund	LCT	Norway
P 1567	Galeshewe	PCFG	South Africa	P 4506	Tarif	PCFG	UAE
P 1568	Job Maseko	PCFG	South Africa	AGB 5002	Shirase	AGB	Japan
P 1569	Makhanda	PCFG	South Africa	AGS 5102	Futami	AGS	Japan
1601	Ta Kuan	AGS	Taiwan	AGS 5103	Suma	AGS	Japan
1603	Alacalufe	PC	Chile	AGS 5104	Wakasa	AGS	Japan
1604	Hallef	PC	Chile	AGS 5105	Nichinan	AGS/AGI	Japan
1605	Quidora	PC	Chile	AOS 5201	Hibiki	AOS	Japan
1606	Tegualda	PC	Chile	AOS 5202	Harima	AOS	Japan
1607	Guacolda	PC	Chile	A 5203	Andromeda	AGS	Portugal

Number	Ship's name	Type	Country	Number	Ship's name	Type	Country
A 5205	Auriga	AGS	Portugal	ASE 6102	Asuka	ASE/AGS	Japan
A 5210	Bérrio	AOL	Portugal	P 6111	Albatros	PCFG	Germany
A 5305	Ammiraglio Magnaghi	AGS	Italy	P 6112	Falke	PCFG	Germany
A 5305	Murena	AGE	Italy	P 6113	Geier	PCFG	Germany
A 5306	Mirto	AGS	Italy	P 6114	Bussard	PCFG	Germany
A 5309	Anteo	ARS	Italy	P 6115	Sperber	PCFG	Germany
A 5310	Proteo	ARS	Italy	P 6116	Greif	PCFG	Germany
A 5311	Palinuro	AXS	Italy	P 6117	Kondor	PCFG	Germany
A 5312	Amerigo Vespucci	AXS	Italy	P 6118	Seeadler	PCFG	Germany
A 5315	Raffaele Rossetti	AG/AGOR	Italy	P 6119	Habicht	PCFG	Germany
A 5317	Atlante	ATR	Italy	P 6120	Kormoran	PCFG	Germany
A 5318	Prometeo	ATR	Italy	P 6121	Gepard	PCFG	Germany
A 5319	Ciclope	ATR	Italy	P 6122	Puma	PCFG	Germany
A 5320	Vincenzo Martellotta	AGE	Italy	P 6123	Hermelin	PCFG	Germany
A 5324	Titano	ATR	Italy	P 6124	Nerz	PCFG	Germany
A 5325	Poliferno	ATR	Italy	P 6125	Zobel	PCFG	Germany
A 5326	Etna	AOR	Italy	P 6126	Frettchen	PCFG	Germany
A 5327	Stromboli	AOR	Italy	P 6127	Dachs	PCFG	Germany
A 5328	Gigante	ATR	Italy	P 6128	Ozelot	PCFG	Germany
A 5329	Vesuvio	AOR	Italy	P 6129	Wiesel	PCFG	Germany
A 5330	Saturno	ATR	Italy	P 6130	Hyäne	PCFG	Germany
A 5347	Gorgona	AKL	Italy	P 6145	Leopard	PCFG	Germany
A 5348	Tremiti	AKL	Italy	P 6146	Fuchs	PCFG	Germany
A 5349	Caprera	AKL	Italy	P 6147	Jaguar	PCFG	Germany
A 5351	Pantellaria	AKL	Italy	P 6148	Löwe	PCFG	Germany
A 5352	Lipari	AKL	Italy	P 6150	Panther	PCFG	Germany
A 5353	Capri	AKL	Italy	P 6155	Alk	PCFG	Germany
A 5356	Basento	AWT	Italy	P 6156	Dommel	PCFG	Germany
A 5357	Bradano	AWT	Italy	P 6157	Weihe	PCFG	Germany
A 5358	Brenta	AWT	Italy	P 6158	Pinguin	PCFG	Germany
A 5359	Bormida	AWT	Italy	P 6159	Reiher	PCFG	Germany
A 5364	Ponza	ABU	Italy	ASU 7020	Hayase	AS/ASU	Japan
A 5365	Tenace	ATR	Italy	P 8111	Durbar	PCFG	Bangladesh
A 5366	Levanzo	ABU	Italy	P 8112	Duranta	PCFG	Bangladesh
A 5367	Tavolara	ABU	Italy	P 8113	Durvedya	PCFG	Bangladesh
A 5368	Palmaria	ABU	Italy	P 8114	Durdam	PCFG	Bangladesh
A 5375	Simeto	AWT	Italy	P 8125	Durdharsha	PCFG	Bangladesh
A 5376	Ticino	AWT	Italy	P 8126	Durdanta	PCFG	Bangladesh
A 5377	Tirso	AWT	Italy	P 8127	Durnibar	PCFG	Bangladesh
A 5378	Aragosta	AXL	Italy	P 8128	Dordanda	PCFG	Bangladesh
A 5379	Astice	AXL	Italy	P 8131	Anirban	PCFG	Bangladesh
A 5380	Mitilo	AXL	Italy	P 8141	Uttal	PCFG	Bangladesh
A 5381	Polipo	AXL	Italy	L 9011	Foudre	TCD/LSD	France
A 5382	Porpora	AXL	Italy	L 9012	Siroco	TCD/LSD	France
A 5383	Procida	ABU	Italy	L 9021	Ouragan	TCD/LSD	France
A 5384	Alpino	MCS	Italy	L 9022	Orage	TCD/LSD	France
L 5401	Al Feyi	LSL	UAE	L 9030	Champlain	LST	France
L 5402	Dayyinah	LSL	UAE	L 9031	Francis Garnier	LST	France
L 5403	Jananah	LSL	UAE	L 9032	Dumont D'Urville	LST	France
S 5509	Qaruh	AG	Kuwait	L 9033	Jacques Cartier	LST	France
M 5550	Lerici	MHSC	Italy	L 9034	La Grandière	LST	France
M 5551	Sapri	MHSC	Italy	L 9051	Sabre	LCT	France
M 5552	Milazzo	MHSC	Italy	L 9052	Dague	LCT	France
M 5553	Vieste	MHSC	Italy	L 9061	Hallebarde	LCT	France
M 5554	Gaeta	MHSC	Italy	L 9062	Rapière	LCT	France
M 5555	Termoli	MHSC	Italy	L 9077	Bougainville	BTS/LPD	France
M 5556	Alghero	MHSC	Italy	L 9090	Gapeau	LSL	France
M 5557	Numana	MHSC	Italy	LTC 9501	EDIC class	LST	Eritrea
M 5558	Crotone	MHSC	Italy	LTC 9502	EDIC class	LST	Eritrea
M 5559	Viareggio	MHSC	Italy	JW 9867	Mzizi	PCF	Tanzania
M 5560	Chioggia	MHSC	Italy	JW 9868	Mzia	PCF	Tanzania
M 5561	Rimini	MHSC	Italy	L 9892	San Giorgio	LPD	Italy
P 5702	Istiqlal	PCFG	Kuwait	L 9893	San Marco	LPD/AG	Italy
ASE 6101	Kurihama	ASE/AGS	Japan	L 9894	San Giusto	LPD	Italy

DONALD COOK

FINCANTIERI INSTINCT OF THE SEA

Advanced technology and great experience, accumulated in more than 200 years of activity and the building of hundreds of ships for the Italian and foreign navies: these are the main features of the naval vessels built by Fincantieri, an integrated Group, in the forefront the world over, able to satisfy every requirement of those concerned with defence and security.

FINCANTIERI
NAVAL vessels

Naval Vessel Business Unit:
Via Cipro, 11
16129 Genova (Italy)
Tel. +39 010 59951
Fax +39 010 5995379
Telex 270168 FINCGE I
www.fincantieri.com

Foreword

Introduction

There is something rotten in the continent of Europe, when the combined armed forces of NATO's European allies are unable to conduct a military campaign against a country the size of Serbia without massive assistance from the United States.

The reason is that western Europe has lived for so long under the shelter of an American defence umbrella that the political will to spend money on real armed forces, as opposed to making declining contributions to an alliance, has withered and been replaced by social self indulgence. Only in the US is there still strong political and popular support for interventionist forces capable of supporting diplomacy worldwide.

No longer is it the first duty of a European state government to defend the realm and protect its interests. Foreign policy now comes a very poor second in political priority to the redistribution of state income within a predominantly domestic agenda. So narrow is this vision that there is little popular consciousness of just how much effort is being made by the US to retain a worldwide presence and influence, and not surprisingly, no political inclination to inform the public. With a few exceptions, the mass media in Europe would rather criticise American activity than draw attention to Europe's increasingly inadequate contribution in defence of its own strategic interests.

If that sounds like an overstatement, it is only necessary to study the latest figures for the percentage of GDP being spent on defence by European nations. Of 5,000 aircraft in NATO Europe suitable for air strikes, less than 500 are fitted with precision-guided land attack weapons and most of those have to be escorted into battle zones by US aircraft providing both air-to-air and EW defences. Europe can muster just one fixed-wing aircraft carrier and five STOVL carriers, while the United States has twelve of each type. The decision not to use ground forces to prevent the ethnic cleansing of Kosovo in 1999 was mostly driven by the reluctance of European nations to act without the involvement of the US Army and Marines, even though total air supremacy was assured. In command, control and intelligence satellite systems, the US has 64 military satellites, Europe has five. Last year alone the US budget for military Research and Development was nine times greater than the combined total of all NATO European countries.

The logical conclusions that might be drawn from this unhappy state are that US strength is in part responsible for Europe's weakness, and Europe should create an effective collaborative defence force to ease its dependence on the United States. Both conclusions have a sort of tendentious symmetry, but the first one is a distorted rationalisation and the second a recipe for further failure.

Europe is a continent comprising several rich states, many of which can afford to maintain balanced forces in their own right if they choose to do so. In a league table of international wealth the USA and Japan are followed by Germany, UK, France and Italy. Each of these European countries has slipped far behind the US in the proportion of national income spent on defence. Adequate investment ought to provide independent professional armed services which could be brought together either under NATO, or in *ad hoc* contact groups when circumstances dictate that it is in the national interest to do so. US leadership will remain an important factor in a mix of continental nations which has no superior power or even *primus inter pares*, and whose historically different foreign policy perspectives remain powerful factors in their instinctive responses to every crisis, either in Europe or anywhere else in the world. These differences cannot just be air-brushed into oblivion by those with federalist ambitions.

Symbolic Eurocorps-style forces are political not military units, and the attempt at creating a Euro Rapid Reaction Force with air and naval support may look good on paper, but the various elements will always be vulnerable to national veto prior to their usage in war. So the pursuit of a European military identity using existing forces and equipment becomes once again a method of trying to obscure institutional national weakness, rather than spending the money to correct it. Europe's overall defence spending has actually declined by about ten per cent in each of the last two years, whereas it has increased almost everywhere else, including the US, China, India, Japan and even Russia.

European nations need to wake up, stop the gesture politics and re-build their armed forces before operational standards decay beyond the point of redemption. The problem lies not so much in the number of men in uniform, but the equipment they have to use, their ability to deploy with adequate logistic support and the lack of modern command and control systems. There is no sign that the political will exists to halt this long-term unilateral disarmament, and perhaps it is time for the US Congress to turn its occasional mutterings of discontent (why should 250 million Americans pay for the security of 530 million rich Europeans?) into a concerted effort to make European states once again invest adequate funds to support their own national strategic interests.

There are other democratic nations worldwide taking a similar free ride on the back of the United States, but in most cases there is a more plausible rationale than exists in Europe.

United States

In spite of the overwhelming maritime superiority of the US Navy, it would be sensible not to forget that US expenditure on defence has also declined in the last decade, and that this has generated much internal stress within the military establishment.

Last year five carrier battle groups and two amphibious formations were involved in active campaigns in the Balkans and the Gulf. This was the highest level of commitment since Desert Storm in 1991. Thirty per cent of all commissioned warships were on six month overseas deployments at any one time throughout the year. The post-Cold War draw-down in terms of both numbers of ships and personnel numbers has ended. The target force levels of 305 surface warships and 50 attack submarines are now likely to be revised in the 2001 Quadrennial Defence Review as being too low to meet current operational requirements. Also under review is the planned shipbuilding programme which does not even sustain these levels in the medium term.

With thousands of missions over Kosovo and Iraq in the last year, naval air squadrons are even more stretched than the ships. A measure of the aircraft carrier domination of the Fleet is that it takes up nearly 40 per cent of the Navy's total sea-going manpower. Trials are being done in *Nimitz* in an attempt to introduce smart ship technology to reduce crew size.

Research and Development and investment in new equipment programmes is streets ahead of anything which is going on in the rest of the world's navies. The communications revolution continues with the installation of a data and video package *Information Technology for the 21st Century* (IT 21). This uses Internet-type technology to provide two local area networks, one for classified and one for unclassified exchanges of information. It is easy to grow weary of the endless, sometimes evangelical claims of the Network enthusiast, but this system is claimed to have largely replaced individual messages and radio communications for such things as tasking orders and targeting data. The aim is to fit every ship by the end of 2002. Inevitably there is a manning requirement to work the equipment 24 hours a day, and IT 21 further exacerbates the problem of communications interoperability with other nations' navies. "The gap that exists with our allies is a resource gap", one Admiral is reported to have commented. "They need to make the commitment to buy the equipment". For those navies whose main rationale is being able to contribute to US-led operations, this is a statement with which there can be no argument.

In the expanding field of combat data exchange it is no surprise that there are also local interoperability problems between the Combat Engagement Capability (CEC) and some versions of the Advanced Command Direction System (ACDS) and Aegis command systems. CEC is a high-bandwidth network able to pass tracks at a faster rate than tactical datalinks (Links 11 and 16). This leads to multiple reports of a single track. This is not a new datalink problem and it can be alleviated by disciplined procedures while a more technical fix is being found.

CARL VINSON

C E Castle / 0084441

Attack submarines, like naval aircraft, are also being over-worked and current intentions to reduce SSN numbers to 50 hulls are being denounced as a cut too far. Four of the eight C4-fitted Trident SSBNs have started conversion to the D5 missile and there is a strong lobby to convert the other four C4 ships to cruise missile carriers. Each could carry up to 154 Tomahawk SLCMs as well as having two missile tubes for use by special forces. The third and last 'Seawolf' class attack submarine has been delayed by two years so that she can be given an extensive fit for special operations including amphibious assault.

For surface warfare, the year has seen the introduction of the first helicopter-fitted Aegis destroyer of the 'Arleigh Burke' Flight IIA class and these will continue to be built at about three a year until superseded by the more futuristic DD 21 stealth ship, which will not be in service until the end of this decade. One decision though that has already been made is that the design will include an electric drive propulsion system. This eliminates reduction gearing and the traditional long propeller shaft, allowing propulsion power generators to be situated anywhere in the ship.

The first of the amphibious transport (LPD) 'San Antonio' class will be launched next year and is to have a derivative of the enclosed mast sensor system which has been doing trials in a 'Spruance' class destroyer. All major amphibious ships, and those destroyers and frigates with flight decks, are to be capable of operating unmanned aerial vehicles (UAV). A common design is expected to start entering service in 2002. As with all unmanned devices at sea, reliability of launch and recovery will be the single most important factor in their success or failure.

The US Navy's commitment to the nuclear-powered fixed-wing aircraft carrier is absolute, and although there will be some changes in CVN 77 which is due to be launched in 2006, the design will vary little from the familiar shape of the 'Nimitz' class. CVN 78 may show more radical changes.

The value of dedicated EW aircraft to jam enemy radar and communications was highlighted once again during air attacks on Serbian military installations in 1999. This capability has emerged from a period of neglect to assume vital importance in the future.

The primary threats to this all-powerful Fleet, which is increasingly orientated towards littoral deployments in support of land attack operations, comes from submarines or mines in coastal regions and missiles fired from fast coastal craft, mobile shore batteries and land-based aircraft. Retribution would be swift and massive against the nation which fired at the US Navy or its allies, but warships are no more exempt from this type of attack than are aircraft or main battle tanks. That no warship has been damaged during high-intensity conflicts in recent years is a major achievement, and there is no complacency amongst those who have operated in the narrow confines of places like the Adriatic or the Gulf.

Defences range over the whole spectrum of advance intelligence, layered hard kill weapons, jammers and electronic decoys. But the primary advantage of the warship is mobility. Precision-guided weapons and GPS guidance has sounded the death knell of any fixed installations such as air bases, static headquarters or commercial infrastructures. Although weapon homing technology continues to improve, it is still infinitely easier to hit a fixed target than one which moves.

The battle for resources between those whose priority is more offensive capabilities at sea and those who would prefer to spend the money on self-defence, is never going to be resolved to both sides' satisfaction. There are persuasive arguments for better stand-off weapons and a greater use of tactical options to limit the risk of counter attack.

The issue of National Missile Defence (NMD) generates more political heat than effective hardware. Defence against ballistic missiles is the aim of the extended range Standard SAM programme. In military terms protagonists argue that some defence is better than none at all. The problem is that a very limited capability may not be worth the adverse political fallout.

One of the more astonishing features of the 1999 NATO Serbia campaign was the total lack of casualties amongst the NATO forces. It has been commented that there is something vaguely distasteful, even cowardly, about killing enemies without serious risk to your own side. The description used is ''fly-by warfare''. It has also raised the question once again as to whether the US is any longer prepared to fight if casualties are inevitable.

This attitude is rightly scorned by the military themselves, and opinion polls have revealed that the general public in America is much more resilient on this issue than has been assumed. The problem seems to be in the upper echelons of the politico-military establishment in Washington. While it is their job not to risk lives unnecessarily, a perception that they might lack the guts for a real war would undermine the whole point of having armed forces deployed around the world.

To inject a more light-hearted note into a deadly serious subject, there is a story of a naval officer candidate who, at interview, said he had been assured by the recruiter that under no circumstances would he have to go to sea. He could not understand why this made his application unacceptable. Commanders who give the impression of not being prepared to risk the lives of their subordinates should not be part of the military chain of command.

On the manpower side, some of the shortfalls of a year ago have been alleviated not least by an injection of more money for better pay and conditions. People don't join navies for the money, but remuneration must keep pace with whatever the civilian world is prepared to pay for particular skills.

Having reached the lower targets set by the requirements to man a smaller Fleet, the Navy for the first time in a decade now has to recruit one man or woman for anyone who opts out early or reaches the end of their service career. With today's high levels of employment in the US it is a daunting task, but at least US servicemen know they will get the wholehearted support of the nation.

Russia

There is a danger of forgetting that Russia still has considerable naval firepower, particularly in its submarine force. The sudden and unexpected deployment of a Northern Fleet 'Oscar' class SSGN *Kursk* to the Mediterranean last September was reported in the Russian press with obvious approval.

Nor has the shipbuilding capability gone away. China and India are both in the process of receiving major warships and submarines from Russian yards. There appear to be no inhibitions about selling the latest military equipment to anyone who can pay some fairly modest prices.

The declared economy may be no more than that of Mexico or Denmark, but much activity is obscured by commercial barter, and the recent rise in the price of oil has revived the revenues received by the state. Nonetheless, some estimates suggest that Russia has reduced its spending on defence by 80 per cent in the last decade,

Get connected ...

LPD(R) for the Royal Navy

(artist impression)

... to this Naval Power from Wärtsilä NSD

Wärtsilä NSD supplies a wide range of engines and power systems in the marine industry. Recent naval and fleet auxiliary installations with Integrated Full Electric Propulsion, offering — improved flexibility — optimised redundancy — competitive Through Life Costs — IMO emissions compliance —, are powered by our engines. We have a complete diesel engine portfolio, covering high-, medium- and low-speed engines and complete propulsion systems under the Wärtsilä and Sulzer brands from 720 to 66,000 kW (980 – 90,000 bhp). This range, combined with our worldwide network of sales and service companies, makes Wärtsilä NSD the partner you can truly rely on.

WÄRTSILÄ
SULZER

WÄRTSILÄ NSD
CORPORATION

hence the inclination by the rest of the world to ignore what is left of a once formidable superpower.

The country is entering the next century with a new leader and a strong feeling of resentment about the expansion of NATO and the perceived lack of support from the West during the last turbulent decade.

Although naval activity, apart from strategic submarine deployments, has been at a minimum in the last year, there has been some movement in the shipyards with the completion of an Akula II SSN and the resumption of refit activity on some major surface ships. In spite of this, almost no work is being done on new designs for the Russian Fleet, and that includes both the new 'Borey' class SSBN and 'Severodvinsk' class SSN.

In February this year the Commander-in-Chief stated the intention to deploy an aircraft carrier group to the Mediterranean within the next twelve months. This assumes that the carrier can be brought up to the required mechanical and operational standards. He also predicted the launching of more submarine ballistic missiles, some with low trajectories, from the high latitudes of the Arctic Ocean, targeting ranges in Kamchatka and the North.

Closer links are being forged with China, and early indications from the new regime are that opportunities may be taken to antagonise western military forces and if necessary complicate their operations. It needs no imagination from those familiar with aircraft carrier flying operations to calculate the effect of a Russian naval force including *Kuznetsov* appearing in the Adriatic or the Gulf during intensive air attacks against shore targets. Russia and China in coalition remains an unpleasant prospect, as does Russian expansion south into the Caucasus. If Russia's military ambitions seem to be a thing of the past, the overwhelming support of the population for the war against Chechnya might serve as a warning for the future.

United Kingdom

The Royal Navy is almost impossible to help in the political battle for adequate resources. Most elected governments respond to popular pressure, but in the UK every time the informed media begin to express concern about the lack of investment in defence, the Navy can be guaranteed to put out a public response to say how splendidly it is adapting to change.

One rationale for this curious behaviour may be that senior officers are fearful of the effects that public scrutiny might have on the morale of the service. This seems to suggest a belief in the power of exhortation over the visible evidence plainly apparent to every sailor down to the rank of Able Seaman. It also indicates a traditional loyalty to a form of politics now almost defunct, and an equally outdated dependence on the power of persuasion within the offices of Whitehall. This last was more effective in the days when Cabinet ministers and senior civil servants had served in uniform, but none now has the necessary experience to understand fully the case being made and some have barely concealed their hostility to the armed forces. Nor do the focus groups, around which so many political priorities are first tested, know any better unless they are kept informed of the true state of their Navy, Army and Air Force.

One result of all this is more than three years without a single warship order being placed, existing shipbuilding programmes falling behind schedule (to the delight of the Treasury), a withering of the naval logistic support service, the hiving-off of naval fixed-wing and commando helicopter flying into joint service organisations, cancellation of planned exercises due to inadequate operating budgets and the laying up or selling of some ships which have barely reached their planned half lives.

It is a measure of the stranglehold joint service thinking has got on the UK armed forces that the second edition of *British Maritime Doctrine* launched last year has as one of its conclusions that ''There is no doubt at all that aircraft are best and most easily operated from properly equipped land bases.'' This is contentious even allowing for the qualifying statement that such bases ''are not always available''. A properly equipped mobile aircraft carrier has a number of operating advantages over a fixed air field at the end of a long logistic supply line, and it is to be hoped that a properly argued comparison is featured in the next edition.

The most peculiar feature of the current failure to invest adequately in the Navy is that there is a UK defence strategy which broadly advocates the deployment of rapid reaction forces in support of allies (mostly the US), which has a strong maritime flavour.

The strategy is defined, but sufficient funding is not, because like every other European nation, ultimate reliance on the US is embedded in the defence debate.

Nor is the Navy alone with its problems. All the UK armed services have been subjected to a cultural and structural blitzkrieg based on European human rights legislation which is threatening to undermine the foundations of a disciplined force able to survive the stresses of war. To paraphrase Nelson's famous signal at Trafalgar, ''Europe expects that every man and woman will claim their human rights.''

The Navy is adjusting, as it always has, to these new circumstances, and at unit level remains highly competent within the limitations of its equipment and logistic deficiencies. A traditional sense of duty takes a long time to undermine, although it can be argued that the European Court's interpretation of military discipline is doing its best.

The good news is that LPDs and Fleet tankers ordered over three years ago are now approaching first of class launch dates, and building work has started on a new class of SSN. The UK has finally withdrawn from the always ill-conceived air-defence destroyer project with France and Italy, and a new national design has a prime contractor. So many years have been wasted, first with a NATO-wide collaborative project and then with the trilateral Horizon, that the new air-defence destroyer will not be in service until 2007, by which time the ship it is designed to replace will be nearly 30 years old. The hidden cost of a decade of the wrong sort of collaboration lies in the prolonged delays of introducing a modern capability in this most vital of all warfare disciplines. The older the ship, the more expensive it is to maintain.

The versatility of the aircraft carrier was again demonstrated last year when one carrier flew operational sorties against both Iraq and Serbia during the same deployment from the UK.

All British SSNs are being fitted with Tomahawk cruise missiles, as a result of successful firings in support of NATO operations against Serbia. Work is being done on a torpedo tube-launched version of the latest SLCM variant, the so-called Tactical Tomahawk

SEA HARRIERS   0084442

which is fired from vertical tubes in US ships. Submarine operations are reported as being hampered by a zero defects mentality within the nuclear safety executive. Any apparatchik can tighten safety regulations far beyond the point of sensible return, and to the detriment of operational capability. It requires real technical and political leadership, and courage, to stop or reverse this dangerous process.

With new aircraft carriers projected, and interesting design developments for a next-generation frigate in the pipeline, the future looks bright, but only if the Navy places public support as its highest priority, and the nation decides that dependence on the United States has gone far enough. The time has also come for America to demand a greater contribution from its closest allies.

Europe

There are two Europes — one real, the other largely imagined. The imaginary version lives in the minds of visionaries who add together European nations' individual assets and conclude that the continent could be a real force in the world if only it had a central government empowered to control everything from financial policy to defence.

The real Europe, as represented by the European Union, has a bureaucracy which has been shown to be corrupt, a high tax and spend interventionist social agenda which works against competitive business practices, a low workforce mobility and a strong nationalist instinct below the level of the political establishment. It also continues to believe in milking a peace dividend which has long since run out of substance.

The UK withdrew from the collaborative Anglo/French/Italian destroyer project in spite of the highest level of political support in London because, according to a Ministry of Defence memorandum to the House of Commons Defence Committee "The very wide range of companies involved could not agree on one of them becoming an effective leader. This prevented the nomination of an empowered prime contractor taking full responsibility for the project, which is fundamental to best procurement principles." In other words, the rigid structure of the project, which aimed to force each navy to accept identical equipment, was unworkable in practice.

On the other hand the German and Dutch Navies, liaising in the same timescale but within a much looser arrangement, are well into the process of launching ships which share some common equipment, but only where there are clear operational and commercial advantages.

The lesson here is clear. Collaboration between disparate nations works when it is flexible and mutually advantageous, but not when it is politically driven in the face of reasoned and practical objections.

The latest attempt at generating an EU defence identity has been an agreement at the Helsinki summit in December last year to create a deployable peacekeeping force of some 60,000 soldiers within three years. Even this modest total is proving difficult to put together from Europe's static and ill-equipped armies. The high ratio of talk to action in Europe is set to go even higher. The risk is that this will alienate the United States and weaken its commitment to NATO.

The one good piece of news is that military doctrines in the major European countries are showing signs of recognising the need for rapid reaction forces and the ability to deploy, but it will take a marked increase in defence spending to translate the doctrine into useful capability.

In the NATO campaign against Serbia, European navies were active, led by a French fixed-wing aircraft carrier flying strike attack missions. Operations in the Adriatic were under threat from the Yugoslav Navy based in Montenegran ports. Submarines, mines and surface-to-surface missiles were all potential dangers and the coastline was kept under constant observation by maritime aircraft and submarines from France, Italy and the Netherlands as well as the US and UK. NATO's multinational standing naval frigate forces were also deployed in the area to monitor shipping and provide ASW defences to high value units. Similarly, NATO's standing MCM forces were used to dispose of ordnance dumped at sea by aircraft unable to complete their targeting missions. USN heavy lift helicopters from the MCM depot ship *Inchon* were extensively used for logistic support ashore and afloat.

The Yugoslav Navy, although moving around, kept a low profile and was not attacked in harbour because of NATO's sensitivity to dragging Montenegro into the campaign. Had Yugoslav ships and submarines ventured out of territorial waters they would have been

LE TRIOMPHANT   *Marine Nationale* / 0084443

sunk without hesitation. The supremacy at sea of the US and her allies has been one of the great military enabling factors for all operations on land in the last decade. Marine amphibious groups were also readily available, had the decision been made to send in ground forces before Serbia withdrew her army from Kosovo. Growing tensions between Serbia and Montenegro may lead to further fighting in this unstable region.

Equipment developments in the last year have seen Norway become the second nation after Spain to opt for an Aegis air defence system to be fitted in new frigates. France which up to now has been more resilient than her continental partners in maintaining her defence equipment budget, has joined most of the rest in making further cuts. The move to all volunteer forces is proving expensive. The CVN *Charles de Gaulle* is this year replacing the forty-year old *Foch* as the sole French aircraft carrier, and new LPD's are about to be built.

The only European navies where there is no shrinkage are those of Greece and Turkey. The giant earthquake of August last year caused extensive damage to the main Turkish naval base and shipyard at Golçuk, and facilities had to be transferred to Pendik. Emergency aid from Greece and the lifting of long-standing objections to Turkey joining the EU have caused a thaw in relations between the two old adversaries, but the purchase by Greece of four Pormornik (Zubr) hovercraft from Russia and the Ukraine is unlikely to have been favourably received in Ankara. These are amongst the largest

SKJOLD   *H M Steele* / 0063932

military hovercraft in the world and are capable of carrying 170 tons of cargo or ten APCs and 230 troops. With speeds of up to 60 kt they are ideal for rapid reinforcement within the Aegean archipelago. This is also the first major purchase by a NATO navy of seagoing equipment originally built for the former Soviet Union.

Indian Ocean and Gulf

The Balkans may have been the focus of much international attention in the past year, but the Gulf and the China Seas remain the maritime areas of greatest strategic interest.

For the first time for some years the recent increases in the price of oil have been a reminder of the dependence of world trade on cheap Gulf oil. Much has been made of the more relaxed attitude of a new Iranian regime, but the acquisition of yet more missile-armed fast patrol craft from China reinforces the West's military analysis that Iran has the means to blockade the Straits of Hormuz, should the US and her allies' naval presence be relaxed.

The oil price hike has also fuelled another burst of military equipment procurement by the Gulf states. With the exception of Oman, Gulf navies are not particularly impressive in operational performance, but the new investment is a necessary preamble to increasing the levels of competence of these emerging navies. It is also a factor in helping to keep alive some of those western industries involved in defence who are not being supported in their own countries.

The steady attrition of Iraqi air defence systems and the enforcement of no-fly zones has continued without receiving much coverage in the western press. Combined with sanctions operations, this is another 'fly-by' war, but justified by the need to contain this pariah state from developing weapons of mass destruction.

With Iraq to the left and Iran to the right, the narrow waters of the Gulf remain a testing environment in which to operate surface warships of frigate size and above. Some half-hearted efforts by Iraq to resurrect its defunct Navy are being watched with interest.

The largest single annual increase in India's defence budget follows last year's border war with Pakistan in the Kargil region of Kashmir. Some commentators have credited the Navy's strategic manoeuvres in the Arabian Sea off the Pakistan coast in mid-1999 as hastening the end of that burst of fighting, and as a result some of the budget increase has been directed at the Navy.

To an independent observer it is surprising that after six years of deliberation the decision seems finally to have been made to accept a 15-year old Russian aircraft carrier, which never really worked and has been laid up for much of the last decade. The conversion of the ship to a genuine fixed-wing carrier with both an angled deck and a ski jump bow has started at Severodvinsk and is forecast to take three years. Although India is reported as having been gifted the ship and is only paying for the conversion, this project must be rated as high risk if it goes ahead to completion. At the same time, approval has been given to build an indigenous air defence ship to serve as a second aircraft carrier platform in the longer term.

Submarines are refitting and taking on the latest design of torpedo-launched SSMs in Russian shipyards both at Severodvinsk and St Petersburg, and frigates are being built at St Petersburg. The Navy is committed to buying MiG aircraft. There is also a slow-moving indigenous shipbuilding programme which owes much to Russian equipment.

If you buy another nation's ships and equipment and send officers to its staff colleges, inevitably you absorb some of that nation's influence, operating philosophies and attitudes. Excessive secrecy, centralised command and control, and reluctance to liaise closely with other navies are all Russian characteristics which are becoming more apparent in Indian naval operations. Only the Indians can judge whether this is in their best interests in the longer term. Limited exercises are still carried out with task groups deployed by other major navies in transit in the Indian Ocean, and it is to be hoped that these contacts will be maintained.

If it were not for the heavy US naval presence in the region, the Indian Navy could dominate the waters of southern Asia from the Straits of Malacca to the Gulf of Aden.

China

China's increasing obsession over Taiwan is casting a growing shadow over the whole of east Asia. Worldwide, there are comparable disputes over the sovereignty of adjacent and much smaller territories and these are not just confined to totalitarian regimes. Spain and Gibraltar, Argentina and the Falkland Islands are two other examples where the normal conventions of modern diplomacy have been overtaken by militant action.

KORA   *GRSE* / 0084444

Taiwan is different because although an offshore island and constitutionally still linked with the mainland, it is a considerable state in its own right, and one that has the qualified support of the United States. This year's ritualistic threat from China in the run-up to Taiwanese elections, had a harder edge to it than usual, effectively threatening America with 'extreme long-range strikes', should it seek to intervene to defend Taiwan from an attack by the mainland.

As was shown last year in Serbia, even small countries can withstand 'fly-by' bombing and cruise missile attacks with non-nuclear warheads. To capture Taiwan, China would need either to resort to nuclear weapons or to have sufficient amphibious and airlift capacity to invade with ground forces. The third option is economic blockade. All three courses of action would serve as a severe test of the willingness of America to demonstrate its commitment to being the power broker in the region, and only a fool would try and predict the outcome.

Some commentators still doubt whether China has the amphibious lift to invade, and if the lesser option is taken, sufficient naval superiority over Taiwan to blockade its ports. Neither action would be possible in the event of the US becoming militarily involved, but those who still question China's naval capability should take a hard look at the four different submarine building programmes, at the massive inventory of surface-to-surface and air-to-surface missiles of all types, at the growing amphibious lift capability, which could be augmented by civilian transports, and at the large stocks of 'intelligent' mines. Total military lift by sea is now assessed at 11,000 troops and 250 main battle tanks. This is increasing each year, and in the narrow Straits of Taiwan the turnaround time for amphibious ships and craft would be very short.

Although amphibious operations would play a central role in the event of war between the two countries, the present international trend of assuming that the modern rationale for most navies is support of land forces would quickly be shown to be overdue for review. Anti-submarine warfare would become a major priority for Taiwan.

Highlights of the Chinese naval year have included the arrival of the first of two (possibly four) Russian-built 'Sovremenny' class destroyers with supersonic Sunburn SSMs. This first ship completed sea trials in the Baltic at the end of last year, and it had been expected that a task group would be sent half way across the world to escort her home. In the event the potentially historic opportunity for Chinese warships to be seen in northern European waters was missed, and the ship sailed alone with the crew augmented by Russians. A tanker rendezvous in the Gulf of Aden, and a destroyer escort in the South China Sea was as far abroad as the Navy was prepared to send other ships. Such timidity is still a feature of this Fleet. For this reason, laudable attempts by the US Commander-in-Chief Pacific to draw China into humanitarian local exercises seem most unlikely to succeed. China is a country that makes a virtue out of its military isolation, but is not above seeking political and technical support from Russia, or of buying and reverse-engineering western technology.

The second issue in the region over which China continues to flex its maritime muscles is in the disputed Spratly Islands. China currently occupies 12 islands, Vietnam 25, the Philippines eight, Malaysia four and Taiwan one. China, Taiwan and Vietnam claim sovereignty over the whole lot, while the other nations' claims, including those of Brunei are more modest.

The last major row was in 1988 when China sank three Vietnamese vessels. Since then, China has developed seven permanent military outposts on the islands, and the whole dispute is a running sore strategically placed in the vicinity of the vital international shipping routes across the South China Sea. Further enforcement of Chinese claims seems inevitable in the future.

East Asia

If Europe is doing its best to reduce spending on defence, Asia is once again heading firmly in the opposite direction. After a couple of lean years from 1997, defence budgets are all rising in line with economic recovery.

In every part of East Asia there is the potential for sudden and violent military activity whether in Korea, Taiwan or Indonesia. China looms over the whole area, Theatre Missile Defence (TMD) is a divisive issue embracing Japan and possibly Taiwan, and any successes in ethnic separatism in Indonesia could encourage similar

BANGPAKONG   0084445

movements in the Philippines or Thailand, to name just two countries that are vulnerable. The ASEAN Regional Forum (ARF) offers opportunities for co-operation in defence, but even if the political will and leadership existed, the ethnic crisis in East Timor revealed the inability of Southeast Asia's armed forces rapidly to deploy and command a multinational force, even for peacekeeping.

Thailand and The Philippines have a number of amphibious transport ships and aircraft theoretically capable of long-range operational deployments, but availability is poor due to reduced manning and ineffective logistic support. Australia was criticised for taking too active a role in the East Timor crisis, but this was the only country able to fill the vacuum as ASEAN defaulted, handing over responsibility to the US and her allies. Even when the UN authorised the use of a peacekeeping force, it became clear that an ASEAN initiative lacked both the credibility and the experience needed to organise an international operation.

Individually the navies of Southeast Asia are all on the move. Indonesia intends to expand by 20,000 sailors and 10,000 marines within the next five years. Security of the archipelago is said to be the first national priority.

After months of working up under Swedish control in the Baltic, Singapore's first submarine was transported to its home base in April this year. The second is to follow in 2001. There could be no greater contrast in diesel submarine operating conditions than those found in the Baltic and the South China Sea. It will be interesting to see how the latest navy to acquire submarines develops its conduct of submarine operations. Although battery cooling has been fitted, there will still be limits on dived performance in tropical conditions.

In the north of the region, Japan is edging towards the wider security role more compatible with its economic strength and dependence on international shipping. A year ago guidelines were revised to embrace a greater role for Japan in bilateral co-operation with the US, and this process is set to continue with a further rise in defence spending.

The impact of two North Korean spy-ships penetrating Japanese waters last year has also had an effect on public opinion, as did the over-flight of a North Korean test missile. Japan has changed its defence posture to allow pre-emptive action against enemy missile bases, and the Navy now has the right of hot pursuit in international waters.

Taiwan and South Korea are also spending more, both on new ships and high-technology equipment. The United States may be becoming irritated by the failure of its European allies to maintain defences consistent with their national wealth, but in the shadow of China and North Korea there is no such reluctance in this region.

The Russian Pacific Fleet is a decaying giant, but elements could be made available in support of China to disrupt US naval operations, just as Russia did its best to complicate NATO troop deployments in Kosovo last year.

Routine clashes between North and South Korean navies no longer receive much attention from the world's media, but in the middle of last year a fourteen-minute exchange of fire along the unofficial border to the west of the peninsula led to the sinking of at least one North Korean patrol craft and damage to others. The DPRK spends much of its naval equipment budget on large numbers of coastal and mini submarines and high-speed infiltration craft of various types.

Endemic to east Asia is the growth of piracy on the high seas which shows no signs of levelling off, although a Peking initiative has deterred attacks in Chinese waters. The execution of 13 convicted pirates in Shanghai earlier this year, and better control of China's proliferating naval paramilitary units has had a salutary effect.

Worldwide there were 285 recorded incidents last year, the highest figure since the Piracy Reporting Centre in Kuala Lumpur started recording in 1991. Those in Indonesian waters doubled from 60 in 1998 to 113 in 1999. Other attacks on merchant ships were carried out in the Straits of Singapore (18), Malaysian waters (18) and Bangladesh (23). Other regions badly infected with this scourge are sea areas off Somalia and Nigeria, and to a lesser extent Latin America.

As many ship owners are reluctant to report minor incidents for fear of having ships and cargoes held in foreign ports during investigations, the overall number of attacks is known to be far higher. The policy of leaving policing action to the countries where most incidents are recorded is clearly not working and the UN Security Council is being lobbied with a view to setting up a Piracy Response Team under the UN flag. Practical operating difficulties and high costs are likely to discourage effective UN action, at least while Marine Insurers are prepared to pay the bills for lost cargoes. A major environmental disaster caused by a pirated ship running aground might help concentrate the minds of the international community. On the scale of atrocities being committed worldwide, the murder of a few merchant seamen does not seem to merit too much attention.

Rest of the World

One immediate side effect of the East Timor crisis was the revoking of Indonesia's four-year-old defence treaty with Australia, pitching relationships between the two neighbours to a new low and knocking out a central plank of Australia's national strategy.

The reluctance of Australia to invest adequately in defence mirrors those countries in western Europe and with even less excuse. The US is a powerful ally, but the Seventh Fleet operates mostly in the

WALLER, LOS ANGELES, FARNCOMB

S Connolly, RAN / 0084446

LIVERPOOL   0084447

northern hemisphere. The Australian Navy's impending loss of a medium-range air defence capability is a serious blow, with no obvious solution in sight other than buying discarded US destroyers with all the logistic and manpower problems that would entail.

Much public commentary on the Navy has centred on the 'Collins' class submarines. Flow noise, cavitation inception and automated combat data systems are being incrementally improved. As there are no absolute standards, it is a matter of judgement as to what is essential as opposed to being 'nice to have'. The arcane subject of acoustic vulnerability has been so simplified by the defence press as to be almost meaningless. All submarines are stealthy, it is just a matter of degree. They do not divide into categories listed as 'noisy' or 'quiet'.

More serious are exhaust back-pressure stresses when the submarine is snorting in rough weather, and questions over the reserve of buoyancy and righting moment when surface running or diving in a seaway. Watertight integrity doubts have also been raised. These are issues fundamental to the operation of the submarine, and it is not encouraging that the Navy is far short of the trained numbers

needed to man six submarines, although this probably has much to do with stationing them at Fleet Base West at the nether end of the continent.

This is a resourceful navy with high operating standards. If Australia wants to keep it that way, it is going to have to inject more money, particularly now that the carefully constructed accord with Indonesia has been so brutally shattered.

The nations of Central and Southern Africa are understandably fed up with being indiscriminately reported in the western press as irredeemable basket cases, but for various reasons most navies are being starved of adequate investment, and it is difficult to be optimistic about operational capabilities. South Africa remains the only exception with approval for new corvettes and submarines to be built in Germany. The surface ships are to be fitted out in South Africa. Foreign deployments and major exercises are still programmed, but not all the ships in the current official order of battle are still available for active service.

By contrast with most of the rest of the world, South America's potential for violent conduct in the last year has been comparatively subdued. It is a crude yardstick, but when did the US Navy last have to send a carrier battle group to the waters of this sub-continent for operational reasons?

The much improved relationship between Argentina and Chile is reflected in Argentina sending one of its Type 42 destroyers to a Chilean shipyard for conversion of the after end to carry Sea King helicopters. As well as resurrecting its own frigate building programme, Argentina has been active in the second-hand market, acquiring a fleet replenishment ship from France, and a couple of minor auxiliaries and a small patrol craft from the US. There are also rumours of the possibility of more Type A 69 frigates from France and more Sea King helicopters from the US. One submarine is being refitted in Brazil, US Mk 48 submarine-launched torpedoes are being acquired to replace the obsolete Mk 37, and Sea King helicopters are being fitted with Exocet missiles. Chartered merchant ships are also being used for military purposes. Argentina's diplomatic claims to the sovereignty of the Falkland Islands remain as vociferous as ever.

Chile's former close links with the UK have been ruptured by General Pinochet's enforced stay in England in response to a Spanish request for his extradition to be tried for crimes against humanity. Although now back in his own country, the reverberations in international law on the vulnerability of former heads of state travelling abroad are likely to be considerable.

The Chilean Navy has selected a German MEKO design for construction in a local shipyard, and already has two submarines building in France. Ex-Netherlands frigates are another option. The Seaslug SAM has finally gone out of service and is likely to be followed this year by the last destroyer to be fitted with the system. This comparatively trivial piece of information reflects the Editor's personal interest in this 'County' class destroyer.

Brazil has been offered the French aircraft carrier *Foch*, but having just spent a considerable amount of money updating the *Minas Gerais*, acquisition is unlikely unless there are problems operating the newly acquired AF1 Skyhawk aircraft. Of the 23 aircraft acquired last year, only 12 are operational and the rest are being used for spares.

After years of neglecting its armed forces there is some confidence in Canada that the government may have to respond to mounting political concern. An increase in the defence budget has been announced for this year, but it is not enough to prevent some changes to the force structure. A decision to replace the Sea King helicopters is long overdue.

An acknowledgement that the Navy can no longer maintain all its ships at the same level of technical readiness has led to the introduction of a three-tier structure. This means that only half the Fleet remains at high readiness for deployments, some of the others are only capable of routine domestic operations and all the remainder are alongside doing extended maintenance.

Such a system appears to have disadvantages in terms of crew morale. The effect on an ambitious officer of being appointed to a ship at extended readiness does not need elaborating. On the other hand there are those who will welcome more time alongside. The contrast with the US Navy and its current attempts to increase operational numbers of ships could not be more stark. Canada is yet another country taking a free ride on the US taxpayer.

In Conclusion

This has been a year of reappraisal for those who advocate the merits of multinational alliances for fighting wars. The Kosovo campaign revealed the inherent weakness in NATO's political command and control and the limitation of European nations to deploy usable armed forces. At the same time the operation in East Timor showed up ASEAN's inability to take any form of effective military action even for peacekeeping purposes.

By contrast, US-led activities in the Gulf, Indian Navy deployments off Pakistan and the US Navy presence off Taiwan have all had the effect of calming, at least for the time being, potentially more explosive developments. Chinese naval and military action against Taiwan remains a major and immediate threat for the foreseeable future.

Operationally, navies have done well, flying carrier-borne aircraft strikes and enforcing maritime sanctions against Iraq and Serbia, containing the Yugoslav Navy, supporting deployed forces with the sealift of equipment and stores to ground forces in all theatres and backing up those forces with amphibious capabilities. Sea-launched cruise missiles were used in large numbers against Serbia.

In Europe, there is a slow movement towards more integrated armed forces in an attempt to conceal growing equipment and structural weaknesses. Far from achieving this aim, these amalgamations merely add confused political command to the military inadequacies.

The difficulty of achieving a consensus from sixteen different nations on daily targeting lists during the NATO war with Serbia, has been revealed in detail by the NATO air commander, as have problems with operational security. The ground forces commander has written that NATO's machinery for decision making in war is ''Not up to the job.'' How much worse would it be in an all-European force which has no acknowledged leading nation? The political reluctance to deploy ground forces in this operation also revealed institutional weaknesses, and included the supreme military folly of telling your enemy in advance what you did not intend to do.

Every armed intervention worldwide highlights the extent of the growing gap between US equipment and that of both its allies and enemies. The technology to remain abreast of US developments is available to the rich countries of western Europe but the will to pay for it is not. The dangers are obvious. US operational commanders will prefer to act without the support of allies that cannot communicate adequately or contribute modern firepower, and the US forces may themselves grow arrogant and complacent in the knowledge of their obvious superiority. Complacency is unlikely to exist in the front line where commanders at sea are all too aware of the dangers posed by air flight missiles, submarines and mines, which are the preferred weapons of even quite small nations. The problem lies more in Washington where the successes of 'fly-by' warfare and US superiority in cyberspace control systems could breed a 'go it alone' mentality.

There is no revolution in military affairs, but the US is making radical changes in mission, force structure, tactics and doctrine to shift towards a more co-ordinated form of warfare. In spite of the hype, information technology is not as decisive in changing the nature of war as has been the case in the past with the introduction of aircraft, submarines or weapons of mass destruction. Communications do not kill, but they do enable weapons to be used more effectively.

The concentration on technology and the attempt to diminish the role of people in fighting wars has actually reduced capability against unsophisticated opponents such as small units able to avoid surveillance.

Major attacks against communications systems in the future are inevitable, either by physical disruption of satellites or by cyber warfare. Data deluge and misinterpretation of instant communications are both obvious dangers. So is the potential inability to respond when the networks fail.

To the question ''What is the biggest single change in military affairs in democratic countries since the Second World War?'' the answer is not space-based electronic systems, long-range precision-guided weapons or even nuclear proliferation. It is the lack of first-hand experience of serving in the armed forces by almost every politician and civilian who now makes decisions about how these forces should be recruited, trained, equipped and used.

In many western countries, growing affluence and a decade of no longer being physically threatened by war have reinforced the complacency of those who think they live out of range of the effects of worldwide asymmetric threats. The steady devaluation of military ethics and the replacement of duties by rights is another factor undermining fighting effectiveness. The trend towards greater joint service training has merit at staff level, but weakens individual expertise and *esprit de corps* if taken too far down the chain of command. Joint service logistics, the civilianisation of support organisations and amalgamated international groupings are all ways of trying to conceal the under-funding of effective national forces. Lean and mean, better value for money and smart procurement are amongst the many euphemisms deployed to cover up inadequate investment.

If industrialised nations want to continue to enjoy their affluence, they have got to make a stronger contribution to the stabilising efforts of the United States. The post-Cold War peace dividend has been sucked dry.

Richard Sharpe   **April 2000**

Acknowledgements

As the tidal wave of electronic information sweeps along, it is a pleasure to report that the hard-copy product retains a strong reserve of buoyancy. Both types of publication are complimentary. The computer screen is ideal for focusing on individual data searches, while the printed page is better for absorbing quickly a wider spread of information. Where the computer has the advantage is in the ease with which the database can be regularly updated.

This year we have taken the major leap forward into full colour availability for all 4,000+ photographs, although a few older ones still linger on in black and white until replacements can be found. Reflecting the different shades of light at sea, colour prints are variable in quality and there can be problems with some pictures sent by Internet or on disk which have been scanned at source with inadequate definition for the printed page. Some of these electronic photographs are also fairly second rate on screen. Nonetheless the overall effect of colour is a huge improvement in presentation, revealing details that were often hidden in monochrome prints. The next stage is to introduce video sequences into the electronic product, although the practicalities of collection may limit this innovation to the larger ships of the major navies.

The business of collecting information and recording change has always been a continuous process, but up to a couple of years ago its presentation had been cyclical. *Jane's Fighting Ships* hard-copy book remains annual, but for those users more impatient for change as it happens, the online product is ideal. The main limitations of online updating are the willingness of contributors to provide information on a continuous basis. Government and industrial web-sites are fine as far as they go, but they too suffer from the same cyclical updating problem and are a poor second best to the well-informed individual contributor.

To the literally hundreds of anonymous people in government and industry who make data collection such a pleasure, my warmest thanks. We are not interested in secrets, but only in ensuring that open discussion on defence is based on reliable facts.

The importance of the US Navy in maritime affairs merits a special contributor in Tom Philpott who is the editor of *Military Update* in Washington. Ian Sturton's excellent scale line drawings and Mike Forder's detailed Indexes have long become major features of the publication. Navies continue to adjust their Ranks and Insignia, and changes in that section are provided by W Maitland Thornton, who is an international expert, with artwork by Derek Ballington.

Other individual contributors who are at the heart of the updating process, and who wish to be acknowledged include:

Captain M Annati, Monsieur G de Bakker, Mr J Bamber, Mr D Boey, Mr C Borgenstam, Herr S Breyer, Mr J Brodie, Mr J L M van der Burg, Señor C Busquets i Vilanova, Señor A Campanera i Rovira, Señor D Quevedo Carmona, Herr H Carstens, Mr C Castle, Dr C Chung, Mr J Cislak, Mr P Cornelis, Senhor S Baptista da Costa, Lieutenant Commander M Cropper, Mr J W Currie, Mr G Davies, Mr M Declerck, Mr D Dervissis, Herr H Ehlers, Mr S Emre, Herr F Findler, Commander A Fraccaroli, Dr Z Freivogel, Señor A E Galarce, Signor G Ghiglione, Mr L van Ginderen, Colonel W Globke, Captain J Goldrick, Commander A W Grazebrook, Mr J Grima, Mr T Hollingsbee, Mr P Jackson, Mr V Jeffery, Mr M Kadota, Herr G Koop, Mr P Körnefeldt, Colonel J Kürsener, Mr E Laursen, Mr M Laursen, Mr C D Maginley, Monsieur P Marsan, Mr R Montchai, Mr J Montes, Captain J E Moore, Mr S Morison, Mr J Mortimer, Mr H Nakai, Mr L-G Nilsson, Herr M Nitz, Mr P O'Keeffe, Mr R Pabst, Mr I J Plokker, Mr F Phillips, Mr M Prendergast, Mr A J R Risseeuw, Commander L Robbins, Monsieur J Y Robert, Mr F Sadek, Mr S San, Mr W Sartori, Mr C Sattler, Monsieur G Schaeffer, Mr M Schiele, Dr A Sharma, Monsieur A Sheldon-Duplaix, Herr N A Sifferlinger, Mr H M Steele, Mr B Sullivan, Captain T Tamura, Herr F Themann, Mr G Toremans, Mr N Trudeau, Mr M Verschaeve, Mr N Wallace, Mr J Webber, Dr A Wessels, Herr M Winter, Mr C D Yaylali, Señor L O Zunino.

Jane's staff continuity at Coulsdon eases the production process, and no praise can be high enough for Emma Pond (editorial) and Jack Brenchley (page composition) who once again have borne with skill and humour the brunt of the principal updating process. Others involved include Ruth Simmance, Jane Lawrence, Chris Jessup, Kevan Box, Sharon Jackson, Lynette Murphy, Barry Compton,

Harriet Harding and Frank Baker. Closer to home, my wife Joanna is an essential member of the year-round editorial and administrative effort.

Cross referencing to other Jane's publications is made easy by the Defence Equipment Library CD-ROM which includes *Jane's All the World's Aircraft, Jane's Strategic Weapon Systems, Jane's Naval Weapon Systems, Jane's Radar and EW Systems, Jane's Underwater Warfare Systems* and *Jane's Amphibious Warfare Capabilities*. Jane's magazines include *International Defense Review, Jane's Navy International, Jane's Intelligence Review* and *Jane's Defence Weekly*. Amongst many other publications the Japanese magazine *Ships of the World* is also a source of useful data, as is the *Asia Pacific Defence Reporter* and Ed Walsh's *Naval Systems Update*.

The focus of *Jane's Fighting Ships* remains the man at sea, whether on the bridge or in the operations room. The aim is to provide the operational capabilities of a ship or navy in a consistent and concise format. Individual entries are composed so that there is no need to turn a page or cross-refer to other sections. It is always a pleasure to get feedback and updating information from those at sea.

All updating material should be sent to:

> Captain Richard Sharpe
> Foundry House
> Kingsley
> Bordon
> Hampshire GU35 9LY
> United Kingdom
>
> Fax number: (+44 1420) 47 78 33
> e-mail: jfs@janes.co.uk

Note: No illustration from this book may be reproduced without the publisher's permission, but the press may reproduce information and governmental photographs, provided that *Jane's Fighting Ships* is acknowledged as the source. Photographs credited to other than official organisations must not be reproduced without permission from the originator.

Biographical note: The editor

In 34 years in the Royal Navy the editor travelled all over the world. He has commanded nuclear and conventional submarines as well as a guided missile destroyer which was for some of the time the Flagship of NATO's Standing Naval Force Atlantic. He has also served in several appointments at the Ministry of Defence in London, including one in Naval Intelligence, and has been the Operations Officer for the UK Submarine Flotilla. In his last job before taking over as editor of *Jane's Fighting Ships* he was responsible for the selection of RN officers.

The editor on board a Russian 'Kilo' class submarine   0084448

How to use *Jane's Fighting Ships*

(see also Glossary and Type abbreviations)

1) Details of major warships are grouped under six separate non-printable headings. These are:-

(a) **Number and Class name**. Totals of vessels per class are listed as 'active + building (proposed)' or 'active + transfer (proposed)'.

(b) **Building programme**. This includes builders' names and key dates. In general the 'laid down' column reflects keel laying but modern shipbuilding techniques make it difficult to be specific about the start date of actual construction. Launching and christening can be similarly confusing, now that many ships are lowered into the water and formally christened some time later. Some nations commission their ships on completion of building, others after the ships have completed trials. In this edition any date after March 2000 is projected or estimated and therefore liable to change.

(c) **Hull**. This section tends to have only specification and performance parameters and contains little free text. Hull related details such as **Military lift** and **Cargo capacity** may be included when appropriate. **Displacement** and **Measurement** tonnages, **Dimensions**, **Horsepower** etc are defined in the Glossary. Throughout the life of a ship its displacement tends to creep upwards as additional equipment is added and redundant fixtures and fittings are left in place. For the same reasons, ships of the same class, active in different navies, frequently have different displacements and other dissimilar characteristics. Unless otherwise stated the lengths and widths given are overall and the draught is at full load. Sustained maximum horsepower is given where the information is available and may not be the same for similar engines operating in different hulls under different conditions. **Speed** is the maximum obtainable under trials conditions.

(d) **Weapon systems**. This section contains operational details and some free text on weapons and sensors which are laid out in a consistent order using the same subheadings throughout the book. The titles are:- **Missiles** (subdivided into SLBM, SSM, SAM, A/S); **Guns** (numbers of barrels are given and the rate of fire is 'per barrel' unless stated otherwise); **Torpedoes**; **A/S mortars**; **Depth charges**; **Mines**; **Countermeasures**; **Combat data systems**; **Weapons control**; **Radars**; **Sonars**. The Weapons control heading is used for weapons' direction equipment. In most cases the performance specifications are those of the manufacturer and may therefore be considered to be at the top end of the spectrum of effective performance. So-called 'operational effectiveness' is difficult to define, depends upon many variables and in the context of range may be considerably less than the theoretical maximum. Numbers inserted in the text refer to similar numbers included on line drawings.

(e) **Aircraft**. Only the types and numbers are included here. Where appropriate each country has a separate section listing overall numbers and operational parameters of front-line shipborne and land-based maritime aircraft, normally included after the Frigate section if there is one.

(f) **General comments**. A maximum of six sub-headings are used to sweep up the variety of additional information which is available but has no logical place in the other sections. These headings are: **Programmes**; **Modernisation**; **Structure**; **Operational**; **Sales** and **Opinion**. The last of these allows space for informed comment. Some ships remain theoretically in the order of battle in some navies even though they never go to sea and could be more accurately described as in reserve. Where this is known comment is made under **Operational**.

2) Minor or less important ship entries follow the same format except that there is often much less detail in the first four headings and all additional remarks are put together under the single heading of **Comment**. The distinction between major and minor depends upon editorial judgement and is primarily a function of firepower. The age of the ship or class and its relative importance within the Navy concerned is also taken into account.

3) The space devoted to front-line maritime aircraft reflects the importance of air power as an addition to the naval weapon systems armoury, but the format used is necessarily brief and covers only numbers, roles and operational characteristics. Greater detail can be found in *Jane's All the World's Aircraft* and the appropriate volume of the *Jane's Weapon Systems* series.

4) Other than for coastal navies, tables are included at the front of each country section with such things as strength of the fleet, senior appointments, personnel numbers, bases and so on. There is also a list of pennant numbers and a deletions column covering the previous three years. If you cannot find your favourite ship, always look in the **Deletions** list first.

5) No addenda is included because modern typesetting technology allows changes to the main text to be made up to a few weeks before publication.

6) Shipbuilding companies and weapons manufacturers frequently change their names by merger or takeover. As far as possible the published name shows the title when the ship was built or weapon system installed. It is therefore historically accurate.

7) Like many descriptive terms in international naval nomenclature, differences between Coast Guards, Maritime Police, Customs and other paramilitary maritime forces are often indistinct and particular to an individual nation. Such vessels are usually included if they have a paramilitary function and are armed.

8) When selecting photographs for inclusion, priority is given to those that have been taken most recently. A glossy picture five years old may look nice but often does not show the ship as it is now.

9) The Navies by country section is geared to the professional user who needs to be able to make an assessment of the fighting characteristics of a Navy or class of ship without having to cross refer to other Navies and sections of the book. Much effort has also been made to prevent entries spilling across from one page to another.

10) Regular updates can be found on Jane's online.

11) To help users of this title evaluate the published data, entries have been divided into three categories:

(a) *VERIFIED* The editor has made a detailed examination of the entry's content checking its relevancy and accuracy for publication to the new edition to the best of his knowledge.

(b) *UPDATED* During the verification process, changes to content or photographs have been made to reflect the latest position known to Jane's at time of publication.

(c) *NEW ENTRY* A ship class appearing for the first time in the title.

(d) Photographs are dated and where * appears a new or re-scanned photograph has been substituted or added. Many are followed by a seven digit number to ease identification.

DPA
DIRECTORY & DATABASE
PUBLISHERS ASSOCIATION
M E M B E R

British Library Cataloguing-in-Publication Data.
A catalogue record for this book is available from the British Library.

Printed and bound in Great Britain by Bath Press, Bath and Glasgow

WORLD NAVIES

A — Z

ALBANIA

Headquarters Appointments

Commander of the Navy:
Rear Admiral Kudret Çela

Personnel

2000:   Numbers uncertain but still falling. Training is being done in Albania by the Italian Navy.

Bases

Districts: Durres, Vlore.
Bases: Tirana (HQ), Shengyin, Himara, Sarande.

General

All operational units sailed to Italian ports in early 1997. Some of these were made seaworthy again and were returned to Albania from late 1997 until December 1998, when the last batch sailed. Those ships which were not repairable were returned under tow.

Mercantile Marine

Lloyd's Register of Shipping:
33 vessels of 21,362 tons gross

DELETIONS

Submarines

1997   4 'Whiskey V' class

Patrol Forces

1997   2 Kronshtadt, 12 Huchuan, 4 Shanghai II
1998   1 Huchuan, 1 Shanghai II, 2 PO 2

Auxiliaries

1997   *Patos*
1998   *Semani*

PATROL FORCES

1 KRONSHTADT CLASS (LARGE PATROL CRAFT) (PG)

F 322

Displacement, tons: 303 standard; 335 full load
Dimensions, feet (metres): 170.9 × 21.3 × 6.9 *(52.1 × 6.5 × 2.1)*
Main machinery: 3 Kolomna Type 9-D-8 diesels; 3,000 hp(m) *(2.2 MW)* sustained; 3 shafts
Speed, knots: 18. **Range, miles:** 1,400 at 12 kt
Complement: 51 (4 officers)

Guns: 1—3.5 in *(85 mm)*/52; 18 rds/min to 15.5 km *(8.5 n miles)*; weight of shell 9.5 kg.
1—37 mm/63; 160 rds/min to 4 km *(2.2 n miles)*; weight of shell 0.7 kg.
6—12.7 mm (3 vertical twin) MGs.
A/S mortars: 2 RBU 1200 five-tubed rocket launchers; range 1,200 m; warhead 34 kg.
Depth charges: 2 projectors; 2 racks.
Mines: 2 rails; approx 8 mines.
Radars: Surface search: Ball Gun; E/F-band.
Navigation: Neptun; I-band.
IFF: High Pole.

Programmes: Four were transferred from the USSR in 1958. This sole survivor was returned by Italy in late 1998. A second of class was beyond repair and was towed back at the same time.
VERIFIED

KRONSHTADT   1989

10 HUCHUAN (TYPE 025/026) CLASS
(FAST ATTACK HYDROFOIL—TORPEDO) (PHT)

| S 101 | S 201 | S 210 | S 305 | S 307 |
| S 102 | S 209 | S 214 | S 306 | S 406 |

Displacement, tons: 39 standard; 45 full load
Dimensions, feet (metres): 71.5 × 20.7 × 11.8 (hullborne) *(21.8 × 6.3 × 3.6)*
Main machinery: 3 Type M 50F diesels; 3,300 hp(m) *(2.4 MW)* sustained; 3 shafts
Speed, knots: 50 foilborne. **Range, miles:** 500 at 30 kt
Complement: 11
Guns: 4—14.5 mm (2 twin) MGs.
Torpedoes: 2—21 in *(533 mm)* tubes; Yu-1; 9.2 km *(5 n miles)* at 39 kt; warhead 400 kg.
Radars: Surface search/fire control: Skin Head; I-band.

Comment: Built in Shanghai and transferred from China as follows; six in 1968, 15 in 1969, two in 1970, seven in 1971, two in June 1974. Not all have foils but those that do have them forward while the stern planes on the surface. One escaped to Italy in May 1991 and was seized by the Italian authorities but handed back in October 1991. These last 10 escaped to Italy in early 1997 and were the only ones capable of being made seaworthy. They were returned in batches in 1998, together with two others which were beyond repair.
UPDATED

HUCHUAN S 209   2/1996* / 0056445

3 SEA SPECTRE Mk 111 (PC)

Displacement, tons: 41 full load
Dimensions, feet (metres): 65 × 18 × 5.9 *(19.8 × 5.5 × 1.8)*
Main machinery: 3 Detroit 8V-71 diesels; 690 hp *(515 kW)* sustained; 3 shafts
Speed, knots: 28. **Range, miles:** 450 at 25 kt
Complement: 9
Guns: 2—25 mm. 2—12.7 mm MGs.
Radars: Surface search: Raytheon; I-band.

Comment: Transferred from the US on 27 February 1999.   *NEW ENTRY*

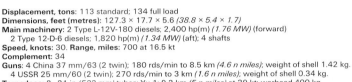

SEA SPECTRE   4/1991*, Giorgio Arra / 0056446

1 SHANGHAI II CLASS (FAST ATTACK CRAFT—GUN) (PCF)

P 123

Displacement, tons: 113 standard; 134 full load
Dimensions, feet (metres): 127.3 × 17.7 × 5.6 *(38.8 × 5.4 × 1.7)*
Main machinery: 2 Type L-12V-180 diesels; 2,400 hp(m) *(1.76 MW)* (forward)
2 Type 12-D-6 diesels; 1,820 hp(m) *(1.34 MW)* (aft); 4 shafts
Speed, knots: 30. **Range, miles:** 700 at 16.5 kt
Complement: 34
Guns: 4 China 37 mm/63 (2 twin); 180 rds/min to 8.5 km *(4.6 n miles)*; weight of shell 1.42 kg.
4 USSR 25 mm/60 (2 twin); 270 rds/min to 3 km *(1.6 n miles)*; weight of shell 0.34 kg.
Torpedoes: 2—21 in *(533 mm)* tubes; Yu-1; 9.2 km *(5 n miles)* at 39 kt; warhead 400 kg.
Depth charges: 2 projectors; 8 depth charges in lieu of torpedo tubes.
Mines: Rails can be fitted; probably only 10 mines.
Radars: Surface search/fire control: Skin Head; I-band.
Sonars: Hull-mounted set probably fitted.

Comment: Four transferred from China in mid-1974 and two in 1975. Has torpedo tubes on the stern taken from deleted 'Huchuan' class. This last ship escaped to Italy in early 1997 and was returned in early 1998.   *UPDATED*

SHANGHAI II (China colours)   6/1992* / 0081445

3 PO 2 CLASS (COASTAL PATROL CRAFT) (PC)

A 151   A 252   A 253

Displacement, tons: 56 full load
Dimensions, feet (metres): 70.5 × 11.5 × 3.3 *(21.5 × 3.5 × 1)*
Main machinery: 1 Type 3-D-12 diesel; 300 hp(m) *(220 kW)* sustained; 1 shaft
Speed, knots: 12
Complement: 8
Guns: 2—12.7 mm MGs. At least one of the class has a twin 25 mm/60.
Radars: Surface search: I-band.

Comment: Three have survived from a total of 11 transferred from USSR 1957-60. Previous minesweeping gear has been removed and the craft are used for utility roles. All escaped to Italy in early 1997 and returned, two in early 1998 and one in late 1998. Two others were towed back as being beyond repair. One other *A 451* was sunk in a collision with an Italian corvette in March 1997.   *UPDATED*

PO 2 (old number)   7/1992*, Terje Nilsen / 0056447

2 COASTAL PATROL CRAFT (PB)

Displacement, tons: 18 full load
Dimensions, feet (metres): 45.6 × 13 × 3 *(13.9 × 4 × 0.9)*
Main machinery: 2 diesels; 1,300 hp *(942 kW)*; 2 waterjets
Speed, knots: 34. **Range, miles:** 200 at 30 kt
Complement: 4
Guns: 2—12.7 mm MGs.
Radars: Surface search: Raytheon; I-band.

Comment: Transferred from the US on 27 February 1999.

NEW ENTRY

CPC (US colours)   *6/1994*, PBI* / 0056448

MINE WARFARE FORCES

3 T 301 CLASS (MINESWEEPERS—INSHORE) (MSI)

M 225   M 227   AS 343

Displacement, tons: 146 standard; 170 full load
Dimensions, feet (metres): 124.6 × 18.7 × 5.2 *(38 × 5.7 × 1.6)*
Main machinery: 3—6-cyl diesels; 900 hp(m) *(661 kW)*; 3 shafts
Speed, knots: 14. **Range, miles:** 2,200 at 9 kt
Complement: 25
Guns: 2—37 mm/63; 160 rds/min to 8.5 km *(5 n miles)*; weight of shell 0.7 kg.
   4—14.5 mm (2 twin) MGs.
Mines: Mine rails fitted for 18.

Comment: Transferred from the USSR—two in 1957, two in 1959 and two in 1960. Those deleted have been cannibalised for spares. These three escaped to Italy in early 1997 were repaired and returned in 1998.

VERIFIED

T 301 (old number)   *1991*

3 T 43 CLASS (MINESWEEPERS—OCEAN) (MSO)

M 221   M 222   M341

Displacement, tons: 500 standard; 580 full load
Dimensions, feet (metres): 190.2 × 27.6 × 6.9 *(58 × 8.4 × 2.1)*
Main machinery: 2 Kolomna Type 9-D-8 diesels; 2,000 hp(m) *(1.47 MW)* sustained; 2 shafts
Speed, knots: 15. **Range, miles:** 3,000 at 10 kt; 2,000 at 14 kt
Complement: 65
Guns: 4—37 mm/63 (2 twin); 160 rds/min to 9 km *(5 n miles)*; weight of shell 0.7 kg.
   8—12.7 mm MGs.
Depth charges: 2 projectors.
Mines: 16.
Radars: Air/surface search: Ball End; E/F-band.
Navigation: Neptun; I-band.
Sonars: Stag Ear; hull-mounted set probably fitted.

Comment: Transferred from USSR in 1960. All escaped to Italy in early 1997 and were returned in 1998.

UPDATED

M 221   *5/1996** / 0056449

AUXILIARIES

Note: The only additional auxiliaries confirmed as having survived are a survey ship of 20 tons and an old ex-USSR 'Shalanda' class tender. A 'Khobi' class oiler and a tug were beyond repair and were towed back from Italy in late 1998.

1 LCT 3 CLASS (REPAIR SHIP) (ARL)

— (ex-*MOC 1203*)

Displacement, tons: 640 full load
Dimensions, feet (metres): 192 × 31 × 7 *(58.6 × 9.5 × 2.1)*
Main machinery: 2 diesels; 1,000 hp *(746 kW)*; 2 shafts
Speed, knots: 8
Complement: 24

Comment: 1943 built LCT converted in Italian use as a repair craft. Refitted in Italy and transferred in 1999.

UPDATED

LCT 3 (Italian colours)   *10/1998*, Diego Quevedo* / 0017507

ALGERIA
MARINE DE LA REPUBLIQUE ALGERIENNE

Headquarters Appointments

Commander of the Navy:
   General Brahim Dadci
Inspector General of the Navy:
   General Major Abdelmadjid Taright

Personnel

(a) 2000: 7,800 (500 officers) (Navy) (includes 600 naval infantry); 500 (Coast Guard)
(b) Voluntary service

Bases

Algiers (1st Region), Mers-el-Kebir (2nd Region), Jijel (3rd Region), Annaba (CG HQ)

Coast Defence

Four batteries of truck-mounted SS-C-3 Styx twin launchers. Permanent sites at Algiers, Mers-el-Kebir and Jijel linked by radar.

Mercantile Marine

Lloyd's Register of Shipping:
   148 vessels of 1,004,690 tons gross

DELETIONS

1996-97   *Yavdezan,* 2 Baglietto Type 20, 6 Mangusta

SUBMARINES

Note: One decommissioned 'Romeo' class is used for training.

2 KILO CLASS (TYPE 877E) (SSK)

Name	No	Builders	Laid down	Launched	Commissioned
RAIS HADJ MUBAREK	012	Admiralty Yard, Leningrad	1985	1986	Oct 1987
EL HADJ SLIMANE	013	Admiralty Yard, Leningrad	1985	1987	Jan 1988

Displacement, tons: 2,325 surfaced; 3,076 dived
Dimensions, feet (metres): 238.2 × 32.5 × 21.7
(72.6 × 9.9 × 6.6)
Main machinery: Diesel-electric; 2 diesels; 3,650 hp(m)
(2.68 MW); 2 generators; 1 motor; 5,900 hp(m) *(4.34 MW);*
1 shaft; 2 auxiliary MT-168 motors; 204 hp(m) *(150 kW);*
1 economic speed motor; 130 hp(m) *(95 kW)*
Speed, knots: 17 dived; 10 surfaced; 9 snorting
Range, miles: 6,000 at 7 kt snorting; 400 at 3 kt dived
Complement: 52 (13 officers)

Torpedoes: 6—21 in *(533 mm)* tubes. Combination of Russian
TEST-71ME; anti-submarine active/passive homing to 15 km
(8.2 n miles) at 40 kt; warhead 205 kg and 53-65; anti-surface
ship passive wake homing to 19 km *(10.3 n miles)* at 45 kt;
warhead 300 kg. Total of 18 weapons.
Mines: 24 in lieu of torpedoes.
Countermeasures: ESM: Brick Pulp; radar warning.
Weapons control: MVU 110 TFCS.
Radars: Surface search: Snoop Tray; I-band.
Sonars: MGK 400 Shark Teeth/Shark Fin; hull-mounted;
passive/active search and attack; medium frequency.
MG 519 Mouse Roar; active attack; high frequency.

Programmes: New construction hulls, delivered as replacements
for the 'Romeo' class.
Structure: Diving depth, 790 ft *(240 m).* 9,700 kWh batteries.
Pressure hull 169.9 ft *(51.8 m).* May be fitted with SA-N-5/8
portable SAM launcher.
Operational: One in refit at St Petersburg from June 1993,
returned to service in May 1995. Second in refit in late 1993
and back in March 1996. Both are active.
UPDATED

RAIS HADJ MUBAREK

3/1996* / 0056450

FRIGATES

3 MOURAD RAIS (KONI) CLASS (TYPE 1159.2) (FF)

Name	No	Builders	Commissioned
MOURAD RAIS	901	Zelenodolsk Shipyard	20 Dec 1980
RAIS KELLICH	902	Zelenodolsk Shipyard	24 Mar 1982
RAIS KORFOU	903	Zelenodolsk Shipyard	3 Jan 1985

Displacement, tons: 1,440 standard; 1,900 full load
Dimensions, feet (metres): 316.3 × 41.3 × 11.5
(96.4 × 12.6 × 3.5)
Main machinery: CODAG; 1 SGW, Nikolayev, M8B gas turbine
(centre shaft); 18,000 hp(m) *(13.25 MW)* sustained; 2 Russki
B-68 diesels; 15,820 hp(m) *(11.63 MW)* sustained; 3 shafts
Speed, knots: 27 gas; 22 diesel. **Range, miles:** 1,800 at 14 kt
Complement: 130

Missiles: SAM: SA-N-4 Gecko twin launcher ❶; semi-active radar
homing to 15 km *(8 n miles)* at 2.5 Mach; height envelope
9-3,048 m *(29.5-10,000 ft);* warhead 50 kg; 20 missiles. Some
anti-surface capability.
Guns: 4—3 in *(76 mm)*/60 (2 twin) ❷; 90 rds/min to 15 km *(8 n
miles);* weight of shell 6.8 kg.
4—30 mm/65 (2 twin) ❸; 500 rds/min to 5 km *(2.7 n miles);*
weight of shell 0.54 kg.
A/S mortars: 2—12-barrelled RBU 6000 ❹; range 6,000 m;
warhead 31 kg.
Depth charges: 2 racks.
Mines: Rails; capacity 22.
Countermeasures: Decoys: 2 PK 16 chaff launchers.
ESM: Watch Dog. Cross Loop D/F.
Weapons control: 3P-60 UE.
Radars: Air/surface search: Strut Curve ❺; F-band.

RAIS KORFOU

(Scale 1 : 900), Ian Sturton

Navigation: Don 2; I-band.
Fire Control: Hawk screech ❻; I-band (for guns).
Drum tilt ❼; H/I-band (for search and acquisition).
Pop Group ❽; F/H/I-band (for missile control).
IFF: High Pole B. 2 Square Head.
Sonars: Hercules (MG 322) hull-mounted; active search and
attack; medium frequency.

Programmes: New construction ships built in USSR with hull
numbers 5, 7 and 10 in sequence. Others of the class built for
Cuba, Yugoslavia, East Germany and Libya. Interest was

shown in ex-GDR ships in 1991 but sale was rejected by the
German government.
Modernisation: New generators fitted 1992-94. *Mourad Rais* in
refit at Kronstadt from 1997 to late 1999. To be followed by
second of class in 2000. Updated command and control
facilities included in the refit.
Structure: The deckhouse aft in Type II Konis houses air
conditioning machinery. No torpedo tubes.
Operational: All have been used for Training cruises.
UPDATED

RAIS KORFOU

8/1997 / 0017509

CORVETTES

2 + 1 DJEBEL CHINOISE (C 58) CLASS (TYPE 802) (FS)

Name	No	Builders	Launched		Commissioned
DJEBEL CHINOISE	351	ECRN, Mers-el-Kebir	3 Feb	1985	Nov 1988
EL CHIHAB	352	ECRN, Mers-el-Kebir	Feb	1990	June 1995
—	353	ECRN, Mers-el-Kebir	2000		2001

Displacement, tons: 496 standard; 540 full load
Dimensions, feet (metres): 191.6 × 27.9 × 8.5 *(58.4 × 8.5 × 2.6)*
Main machinery: 3 MTU 20V 538 TB92 diesels; 12,800 hp(m) *(9.4 MW)*; 3 shafts
Speed, knots: 31
Complement: 52 (6 officers)

Missiles: SSM: 4 China C 802 (2 twin); active radar homing to 120 km *(86 n miles)* at 0.9 Mach; warhead 165 kg.
Guns: 1 Russian 3 in *(76 mm)*/60; 90 rds/min to 15 km *(8 n miles)*; weight of shell 6.8 kg.
2 Breda 40 mm/70 (twin); 300 rds/min to 12.5 km *(6.8 n miles)*; weight of shell 0.96 kg.
4 USSR 23 mm (2 twin).
Weapons control: Optronic director.
Radars: Surface search: Racal Decca 1226; I-band.

Programmes: Ordered July 1983. Project 802 built with Bulgarian assistance. First one completed trials in 1988. Work on the second of class was suspended in 1992 due to shipyard debt problems but the ship completed in 1995 without main guns. The projected third of class is now to be completed after suffering similar delays.
Modernisation: Both earlier ships being fitted with main armaments comprising SSMs and 76 mm guns. To be completed by 2001.
Structure: Hull size suggests association with 'Bazán Cormoran' class.   ***UPDATED***

EL CHIHAB (without main armament)   *5/1995*, Diego Quevedo /* 0056451

3 NANUCHKA II (BURYA) CLASS (TYPE 1234)
(MISSILE CORVETTES) (FSG)

Name	No	Builders	Commissioned
RAIS HAMIDOU	801	Petrovsky, Leningrad	4 July 1980
SALAH RAIS	802	Petrovsky, Leningrad	9 Feb 1981
RAIS ALI	803	Petrovsky, Leningrad	8 May 1982

Displacement, tons: 660 full load
Dimensions, feet (metres): 194.5 × 38.7 × 8.5 *(59.3 × 11.8 × 2.6)*
Main machinery: 6 M 504 diesels; 26,112 hp(m) *(19.2 MW)*; 3 shafts
Speed, knots: 33. Range, miles: 2,500 at 12 kt; 900 at 31 kt
Complement: 42 (7 officers)

Missiles: SSM: 4 SS-N-2C; active radar or IR homing to 46 km *(25 n miles)* at 0.9 Mach; warhead 513 kg or 16 SS-N-25 (Kh 35 Uran) (4 quad); active radar homing to 130 km *(70.2 n miles)* at 0.9 Mach; warhead 145 kg.
SAM: SA-N-4 Gecko twin launcher; semi-active radar homing to 15 km *(8 n miles)* at 2.5 Mach; height envelope 9-3,048 m *(29.5-10,000 ft)*; warhead 50 kg; 20 missiles. Some anti-surface capability.
Guns: 2—57 mm/80 (twin); 120 rds/min to 6 km *(3.3 n miles)*; weight of shell 2.8 kg.
Countermeasures: Decoys: 2 PK 16 16-barrelled chaff launchers.
ESM: Bell Tap. Cross Loop; D/F.
Radars: Surface search: Square Tie (Radome); I-band.
Navigation: Don 2; I-band.
Fire control: Pop Group; F/H/I-band (SA-N-4). Muff Cob; G/H-band. Plank Shave; I/J-band (SS-N-25).
IFF: Two Square Head. High Pole.

Programmes: Delivered as new construction.
Modernisation: First one refitted at Kronstadt 1997-99 with refurbished diesels and a replacement SSM system. Second pair to follow in 2000/2001.   ***UPDATED***

SALAH RAIS (with SS-N-2C)   *6/1997* /* 0017510

LAND-BASED MARITIME AIRCRAFT

Numbers/Type: 2 Beechcraft Super King Air 200T.
Operational speed: 282 kt *(523 km/h)*.
Service ceiling: 35,000 ft *(10,670 m)*.
Range: 2,030 n miles *(3,756 km)*.
Role/Weapon systems: Operated by air force for close-range EEZ operations. Sensors: Weather radar only. Weapons: Unarmed.   ***VERIFIED***

Numbers/Type: 3 Fokker F27-400/600.
Operational speed: 250 kt *(463 km/h)*.
Service ceiling: 25,000 ft *(7,620 m)*.
Range: 2,700 n miles *(5,000 km)*.
Role/Weapon systems: Visual reconnaissance duties in support of EEZ, particularly offshore platforms. Sensors: Weather radar and visual means only. Weapons: Limited armament.   ***VERIFIED***

PATROL FORCES

9 OSA II CLASS (TYPE 205)
(FAST ATTACK CRAFT—MISSILE) (PCFG)

644-652

Displacement, tons: 245 full load
Dimensions, feet (metres): 126.6 × 24.9 × 8.8 *(38.6 × 7.6 × 2.7)*
Main machinery: 3 Type M 504 diesels; 10,800 hp(m) *(7.94 MW)* sustained; 3 shafts
Speed, knots: 37. Range, miles: 500 at 35 kt
Complement: 30

Missiles: SSM: 4 SS-N-2B; active radar or IR homing to 46 km *(25 n miles)* at 0.9 Mach; warhead 513 kg.
Guns: 4—30 mm/65 (2 twin); 500 rds/min to 5 km *(2.7 n miles)*; weight of shell 0.54 kg.
Radars: Surface search: Square Tie; I-band.
Fire control: Drum Tilt; H/I-band.
IFF: 2 Square Head. High Pole B.

Programmes: Osa II transferred 1976-77 (four), fifth in September 1978, sixth in December 1978, next pair in 1979 and one from the Black Sea on 7 December 1981.
Modernisation: Plans to re-engine were reported as starting in late 1992 but there has been no confirmation.
Operational: At least six Osa IIs are active.   ***UPDATED***

OSA 652   *1989*

11 + 2 (1) KEBIR CLASS (FAST ATTACK CRAFT—GUN) (PC)

EL YADEKH 341	EL RASSED 345	EL MOUKADEM 348
EL MOURAKEB 342	EL DJARI 346	349-350
EL KECHEF 343	EL SAHER 347	EL MAYHER 354
EL MOUTARID 344		

Displacement, tons: 166 standard; 200 full load
Dimensions, feet (metres): 123 × 22.6 × 5.6 *(37.5 × 6.9 × 1.7)*
Main machinery: 2 MTU 12V 538 TB92 diesels; 5,110 hp(m) *(3.8 MW)*; 2 shafts (see *Structure*)
Speed, knots: 27. Range, miles: 3,300 at 12 kt; 2,600 at 15 kt
Complement: 27 (3 officers)

Guns: 1 OTO Melara 3 in *(76 mm)*/62 compact (341-342); 85 rds/min to 16 km *(9 n miles)* anti-surface; 12 km *(6.5 n miles)* anti-aircraft; weight of shell 6 kg.
4 USSR 25 mm/60 (2 twin) (remainder); 270 rds/min to 3 km *(1.6 n miles)*; weight of shell 0.34 kg.
2 USSR 14.5 mm (twin) (in first five).
Weapons control: Lawrence Scott optronic director (in 341 and 342).
Radars: Surface search: Racal Decca 1226; I-band.

Programmes: Design and first pair ordered from Brooke Marine in June 1981. First left for Algeria without armament in September 1982, second arrived Algiers 12 June 1983. A further seven were then assembled or built at ECRN, Mers-el-Kebir. 346 commissioned 10 November 1985. 347-349 ordered June 1986, and delivered by 1993. After a delay 349 was completed in late 1997 followed by 354 in 1998. A total of 15 is expected in due course.
Structure: Same hull as Barbados *Trident*. There are some variations in armament.
Operational: A major refit programme is being done locally. Six of the class have been transferred to the Coast Guard.   ***UPDATED***

EL MOURAKEB and EL YADEKH   *5/1990* /* 0056452

KEBIR 350 (with 25 mm guns)   *6/1998 /* 0017511

AMPHIBIOUS FORCES

2 LANDING SHIPS (LOGISTIC) (LSL)

Name	No	Builders	Commissioned
KALAAT BENI HAMMAD	472	Brooke Marine, Lowestoft	Apr 1984
KALAAT BENI RACHED	473	Vosper Thornycroft, Woolston	Oct 1984

Displacement, tons: 2,450 full load
Dimensions, feet (metres): 305 × 50.9 × 8.1 *(93 × 15.5 × 2.5)*
Main machinery: 2 MTU 16V 1163 TB82 diesels; 8,880 hp(m) *(6.5 MW)* sustained; 2 shafts
Speed, knots: 15. **Range, miles:** 3,000 at 12 kt
Complement: 81
Military lift: 240 troops; 7 MBTs and 380 tons other cargo; 2 ton crane with athwartships travel

Guns: 2 Breda 40 mm/70 (twin); 300 rds/min to 12.5 km *(6.8 n miles)*; weight of shell 0.96 kg.
  4 USSR 25 mm/60 (2 twin); 270 rds/min to 3 km *(1.6 n miles)*; weight of shell 0.34 kg.
Countermeasures: Decoys: Wallop Barricade double layer chaff launchers.
ESM: Racal Cutlass; intercept.
ECM: Racal Cygnus; jammer.
Weapons control: CSEE Naja optronic.
Radars: Navigation: Racal Decca TM 1226; I-band.
Fire control: Marconi S 800; J-band.

Helicopters: Platform only for one Sea King.

Programmes: First ordered in June 1981, and launched 18 May 1983; second ordered 18 October 1982 and launched 15 May 1984. Similar hulls to Omani *Nasr El Bahr*.
Structure: These ships have a through tank deck closed by bow and stern ramps. The forward ramp is of two sections measuring length 18 m (when extended) × 5 m breadth, and the single section stern ramp measures 4.3 × 5 m with the addition of 1.1 m finger flaps. Both hatches can support a 60 ton tank and are winch operated. In addition, side access doors are provided on each side forward. The tank deck side bulkheads extend 2.25 m above the upper deck between the forecastle and the forward end of the superstructure, and provide two hatch openings to the tank deck below. Additional 25 mm guns have been fitted either side of the bridge.

VERIFIED

KALAAT BENI HAMMAD   *8/1998, Diego Quevedo /* 0017513

1 POLNOCHNY B CLASS (TYPE 771) (LSM)

471

Displacement, tons: 760 standard; 834 full load
Dimensions, feet (metres): 246.1 × 31.5 × 7.5 *(75 × 9.6 × 2.3)*
Main machinery: 2 Kolomna Type 40-D diesels; 4,400 hp(m) *(3.2 MW)* sustained; 2 shafts
Speed, knots: 18. **Range, miles:** 1,000 at 18 kt
Complement: 42
Military lift: 180 troops; 350 tons including up to 6 tanks
Guns: 2—30 mm/65 (twin) AK 230; 500 rds/min to 5 km *(2.7 n miles)*; weight of shell 0.54 kg.
  2—140 mm 18-tubed rocket launchers.
Radars: Navigation: Don 2; I-band.
Fire control: Drum Tilt; H/I-band.
IFF: Square Head. High Pole B.

Comment: Class built in Poland 1968-70. Transferred from USSR in August 1976. Tank deck covers 2,000 m². Still operational, but rarely seen at sea.

UPDATED

POLNOCHNY 471   *1990, van Ginderen Collection*

MINE WARFARE FORCES

Notes: (1) The Coast Guard support ship *El Mourafik* may have a minelaying capability.
(2) Two MCMV are expected to be out to tender in due course.

SURVEY SHIPS

1 SURVEY SHIP (AGS)

EL IDRISSI BH 204 (ex-A 673)

Displacement, tons: 540 full load
Complement: 28 (6 officers)

Comment: Built by Matsukara, Japan and delivered 17 April 1980. Based at Algiers.

UPDATED

EL IDRISSI   *9/1990* /* 0056453

RAS TARSA   ALIDADE

Comment: Both are survey craft. *Ras Tarsa* is of 16 tons displacement, built in 1980 and has a crew of four. *Alidade* is of 20 tons, built in 1983 and has a crew of eight.

VERIFIED

AUXILIARIES

Note: A training ship was put out to tender in 1998. Order expected in due course.

1 POLUCHAT I CLASS (TRV)

A 641

Displacement, tons: 70 standard; 100 full load
Dimensions, feet (metres): 97.1 × 19 × 4.8 *(29.6 × 5.8 × 1.5)*
Main machinery: 2 Type M 50F diesels; 2,200 hp(m) *(1.6 MW)* sustained; 2 shafts
Speed, knots: 20. **Range, miles:** 1,500 at 10 kt
Complement: 15

Comment: Transferred from USSR in early 1970s. Has been used for SAR.

VERIFIED

POLUCHAT   *1989*

TUGS

Note: There are a number of harbour tugs of about 265 tons. These include *Kader* A 210, *El Chadid* A 211 and *Mazafran* 1-4 Y 206-Y 209.

MAZAFRAN 4   *6/1994* /* 0056454

COAST GUARD

Notes: (1) Six 'Kebir' class were transferred from the Navy for Coast Guard duties but may have naval crews.
(2) There is also an unknown number of small fishery protection vessels in the GC 301 series.

1 SUPPORT SHIP

EL MOURAFIK GC 261

Displacement, tons: 600 full load
Dimensions, feet (metres): 193.6 × 27.6 × 6.9 *(59 × 8.4 × 2.1)*
Main machinery: 2 diesels; 2,200 hp(m) *(1.6 MW)*; 2 shafts
Speed, knots: 14
Complement: 54
Guns: 2—12.7 mm MGs.
Radars: Surface search: I-band.

Comment: Delivered by transporter ship from China in April 1990. The design appears to be a derivative of the T43 minesweeper but with a stern gantry. May have a minelaying capability. Based at Algiers. *UPDATED*

EL MOURAFIK *9/1995*, van Ginderen Collection / 0056455

7 EL MOUDERRIB (CHUI-E) CLASS

EL MOUDERRIB I-VII GC 251-GC 257

Displacement, tons: 388 full load
Dimensions, feet (metres): 192.8 × 23.6 × 7.2 *(58.8 × 7.2 × 2.2)*
Main machinery: 3 PCR/Kolomna diesels; 6,600 hp(m) *(4.92 MW)*; 3 shafts
Speed, knots: 24. **Range, miles:** 1,400 at 15 kt
Complement: 42 including 25 trainees
Guns: 4 China 14.5 mm (2 twin).
Radars: Surface search: Type 756; I-band.

Comment: Two delivered by transporter ship from China in April 1990 and described as training vessels. Two more acquired in January 1991, the last three in July 1991. 'Hainan' class hull with modified propulsion and superstructure similar to some Chinese paramilitary vessels. Used for training when boats are carried aft in place of the second 14.5 mm gun. *UPDATED*

EL MOUDERRIB I *6/1992*, Diego Quevedo / 0056456

5 BAGLIETTO TYPE 20

GC 321   EL HAMIL GC 325   El ASSAD GC 326   MARKHAD GC 327   ETAIR GC 328

Displacement, tons: 44 full load
Dimensions, feet (metres): 66.9 × 17.1 × 5.5 *(20.4 × 5.2 × 1.7)*
Main machinery: 2 CRM 18DS diesels; 2,660 hp(m) *(2 MW)*; 2 shafts
Speed, knots: 36. **Range, miles:** 445 at 20 kt
Complement: 11 (3 officers)
Guns: 1 Oerlikon 20 mm.

Comment: The first pair delivered by Baglietto, Varazze in August 1976 and the remainder in pairs at two monthly intervals. Fitted with radar and optical fire control. Three others of the class cannibalised for spares. *VERIFIED*

BAGLIETTO 20 GC CRAFT *1978, Baglietto*

4 EL MOUNKID CLASS

EL MOUNKID I-IV   GC 231-GC 234

Comment: First three delivered by transporter ship from China which arrived in Algiers in April 1990, a fourth followed a year later. Used for SAR. *UPDATED*

GC 231-GC 233 *1991* / 0056457

CUSTOMS

Note: The Customs service is a paramilitary organisation employing a number of patrol craft armed with small MGs. These include *Bouzagza, Djurdjura, Hodna, Aures* and *Hoggar.* The first three are 'P 1200' class 39 ton craft capable of 33 kt. The next pair are 'P 802' class. They were built by Watercraft, Shoreham and delivered in November 1985.

ANGOLA
MARINHA DE GUERRA

Headquarters Appointments	General	Personnel	Bases	Mercantile Marine
Chief of the Navy: Admiral Gaspar Santos Rufino *Deputy Chief of the Navy:* Vice Admiral Feleciano Antonio Dos Santos *Chief of Staff:* Vice Admiral Augusto da Silva Cunha	By early 2000 there were no operational vessels in the Navy. The most modern craft are still listed but there have been no orders for equipment or spares to put them back in service. All may now be beyond economical repair.	(a) 2000: 3,000 (b) Voluntary service	Luanda, Lobito, Namibe. (There are other good harbours available on the 1,000 mile coastline.) Naval HQ at Luanda on Ila de Luanda is in an old fort, as is Namibe.	*Lloyd's Register of Shipping:* 124 vessels of 65,749 tons gross

PATROL FORCES

Note: One Rodman 52 in 1990, and four Rodman 38 in 1993, harbour patrol craft were acquired by the Police.

3 COASTAL PATROL CRAFT (PC)

PATRULHEIRO   TEMERARIO   PRESERVADOR

Dimensions, feet (metres): 63.3 × 18.4 × 3 *(19.3 × 5.6 × 0.9)*
Main machinery: 2 Baudouin V12 BTI diesels; 1,680 hp(m) *(1.25 MW)*; 2 shafts
Speed, knots: 25. **Range, miles:** 1,000 at 18 kt
Complement: 8
Guns: 1—12.7 mm MG.
Radars: Surface search: Furuno; I-band.

Comment: Built by Couach, Arachon, France and delivered in 1994 for Fishery Protection duties. Funded by France. All are non-operational. *UPDATED*

PATRULHEIRO *6/1994*, Couach / 0056458

4 MANDUME CLASS (COASTAL PATROL CRAFT) (PC)

MANDUME P 101	POLAR P 102	ATLANTICO P 103	GOLFINHO P 104

Displacement, tons: 110 full load
Dimensions, feet (metres): 103.7 × 19.5 × 4.9 *(31.6 × 5.9 × 1.5)*
Main machinery: 2 Paxman Vega 16CM diesels; 3,840 hp *(2.86 MW)* sustained; 2 shafts
Speed, knots: 27. **Range, miles:** 8,000 at 15 kt
Complement: 11 (1 officer)
Guns: 1 Oerlikon GAM-BO1 20 mm. 2—12.7 mm MGs.
Radars: Surface search: Racal Decca; I-band.

Comment: Ordered 27 March 1991. First two laid down November 1991 at Bazán Shipyard, San Fernando; launched 11 September 1992. First one handed over in April 1993, the others at three month intervals. This is an Alcotan 30 design with steel hulls and an aluminium superstructure. These craft have a controlled clutch hydraulic drive system for slow speed operations. All are non-operational.

VERIFIED

POLAR

3/1993, Bazán

ANGUILLA

Headquarters Appointments	Personnel	Mercantile Marine
Commissioner of Police: Mitchell D Harrington	2000: 32	*Lloyd's Register of Shipping:* 5 vessels of 1,387 tons gross

POLICE

1 HALMATIC M160 CLASS (INSHORE PATROL CRAFT) (PB)

DOLPHIN

Displacement, tons: 18 light
Dimensions, feet (metres): 52.5 × 15.4 × 4.6 *(16 × 4.7 × 1.4)*
Main machinery: 2 Detroit 6V-92TA diesels; 520 hp *(390 kW)* sustained; 2 shafts
Speed, knots: 27. **Range, miles:** 500 at 17 kt
Complement: 8
Guns: 1—12.7 mm MG.
Radars: Surface search: Furuno 1941; I-band.

Comment: Built by Halmatic and delivered 22 December 1989. Identical craft to British Virgin Islands and Turks and Caicos Islands. GRP hulls. Rigid inflatable boat launched by gravity davit.
UPDATED

1 BOSTON WHALER (INSHORE PATROL CRAFT) (PB)

LAPWING

Displacement, tons: 2.2 full load
Dimensions, feet (metres): 27 × 10 × 1.5 *(8.2 × 3 × 0.5)*
Main machinery: 2 Evinrude outboards; 350 hp *(261 kW)*
Speed, knots: 35
Complement: 3

Comment: Delivered in 1990 and re-engined in 1992.

UPDATED

DOLPHIN

8/1999*, Anguilla Police / 0056459

LAPWING

8/1999*, Anguilla Police / 0056460

ANTIGUA and BARBUDA

Headquarters Appointments	General	Personnel	Bases	Mercantile Marine
Commanding Officer, Coast Guard: Lieutenant Paul W Wright	The Defence Force took over the Coast Guard on 1 May 1995. The Commanding Officer of the Coast Guard is seconded from Jamaica.	2000: 54 (6 officers)	HQ: Deepwater Harbour, St Johns. Repairs: Camp Blizzard	*Lloyd's Register of Shipping:* 664 vessels of 3,621,890 tons gross

COAST GUARD

Note: (1) In addition there is a Hurricane RIB, *CG 081* with a speed of 35 kt and two Boston Whalers, *CG 071-2,* with speeds of 30 kt. All were acquired in 1988/90.

1 POINT CLASS (PC)

Name	No	Builders	Commissioned
HERMITAGE (ex-*Point Steel*)	P 03	Coast Guard Yard, Curtis Bay	26 Apr 1967

Displacement, tons: 66 full load
Dimensions, feet (metres): 83 × 17.2 × 5.8 *(25.3 × 5.2 × 1.8)*
Main machinery: 2 Caterpillar 3412 diesels; 1,600 hp *(1.19 MW)*; 2 shafts
Speed, knots: 23. **Range, miles:** 1,500 at 8 kt
Complement: 10
Guns: 2—7.62 mm MGs.
Radars: Surface search: Raytheon SPS-64(V)1; I-band.

Comment: Ex-US Coast Guard ship of the C series acquired as a gift and transferred on 17 July 1998. Recommissioned 4 September 1998.

UPDATED

HERMITAGE

9/1999*, Antigua Coast Guard / 0056461

1 SWIFT 65 ft CLASS (PC)

Name	No	Builders	Commissioned
LIBERTA	P 01	Swiftships, Morgan City	30 Apr 1984

Displacement, tons: 36 full load
Dimensions, feet (metres): 65.5 × 18.4 × 5 *(20 × 5.6 × 1.5)*
Main machinery: 2 Detroit Diesel 12V-71TA diesels; 840 hp *(616 kW)* sustained; 2 shafts
Speed, knots: 22. **Range, miles:** 250 at 18 kt
Complement: 9
Guns: 1—12.7 mm MG. 2—7.62 mm MGs.
Radars: Surface search: Furuno; I-band.

Comment: Ordered in November 1983. Aluminium construction. Funded by USA. Refitted in 1996 when the colour of the ship was changed to grey.

UPDATED

1 DAUNTLESS CLASS (PC)

Name	No	Builders	Commissioned
PALMETTO	P 02	SeaArk Marine, Monticello	7 July 1995

Displacement, tons: 11 full load
Dimensions, feet (metres): 40 × 14 × 4.3 *(12.2 × 4.3 × 1.3)*
Main machinery: 2 Caterpillar 3208TA diesels; 870 hp *(650 kW)* sustained; 2 shafts
Speed, knots: 27. **Range, miles:** 600 at 18 kt
Complement: 4
Guns: 1—7.62 mm MG.
Radars: Surface search: Raytheon R40; I-band.

Comment: Funded by USA. Similar craft delivered to several Caribbean countries in 1994-98.

UPDATED

LIBERTA   *9/1999*, Antigua Coast Guard /* 0056462

PALMETTO   *9/1999*, Antigua Coast Guard /* 0056463

ARGENTINA
ARMADA REPUBLICA

Headquarters Appointments

Chief of Naval General Staff:
   Admiral Joaquin Edgardo Stella
Deputy Chief of Naval Staff:
   Vice Admiral Alvaro Vasquez
Naval Aviation Commander:
   Rear Admiral Julio Alberto Covarrubias
Commander Marine Infantry:
   Rear Admiral Oscar Alfredo Monnereau
Naval Operations Commander:
   Vice Admiral Alberto Valerio Pico

Senior Appointments

Commander Fleet:
   Vice Admiral Julio Vara
Naval Area South:
   Rear Admiral Hector Agustin Tebaldi

Personnel

2000: 16,000 (2,500 officers)

Organisation

Naval Area South covers coastal area from latitude 39° to 60° south.
Naval Areas Atlantic and Fluvial have been discarded. Naval Area Antarctica is in force when *Almirante Irizar* deploys.

Special Forces Command

Consists of frogmen who operate from submarines and other naval units, and amphibious commandos who are trained in parachuting and behind the lines operations. Total of about 150 officers and NCOs.

Bases

Buenos Aires (Dársena Norte): Some naval training.
Rio Santiago (La Plata): Schools.
Mar del Plata: Submarine base plus two frigates.
Puerto Belgrano: Main naval base, schools.
Ushuaia, Deseado, Dársena Sur, Zárate, Caleta Paula; Small naval bases.

Coast Guard (Prefectura Naval Argentina)

In January 1992 the Coast Guard was limited to operations inside 12 mile territorial seas but this legislation was then cancelled in favour of the previous 200 mile operating zone. In May 1994 a Community Protection Secretariat was formed to include the Coast Guard, Border Guard and Federal Police. In June 1996 the Coast Guard and Border Guard were placed under the Interior Ministry.

Prefix to Ships' Names

ARA (Armada Republica Argentina)

Naval Aviation

Personnel: 2,500
1st Naval Air Wing (Punta del Indio Naval Air Base): Naval Aviation School with Beech T-34Cs, Turbo Mentor.
2nd Naval Air Wing (Comandante Espora Naval Air Base): Anti-Submarine Squadron with Grumman S-2T Turbo Trackers; 2nd Naval Helicopter Squadron with Agusta/Sikorsky SH-3D and S-61D. 3rd Squadron for UH-1H.
3rd Naval Air Wing (Comandante Espora Naval Air Base): 2nd Naval Fighter/Attack Squadron with Super Etendards; 1st Naval Helicopter Squadron with Alouette III and Fennecs.
4th Naval Air Wing (Punta Indio Naval Air Base): 1st Naval Attack Squadron with Embraer EMB-326 Xavantes; Naval Aerophotographic Squadron with Beech King Air 200s.
5th Naval Air Wing (Almirante Irizar Naval Air Base): 2nd Naval Logistic Support Squadron with Fokker F28s.
6th Naval Air Wing (Almirante Irizar Naval Air Base): Naval Reconnaissance Squadron with Orion, Lockheed Electra L-188E, Pilatus PC-6, and Super King Airs.
There are plans to move the naval air command to Puerto Belgrano.

Marine Corps

Organisation and Deployment

Personnel: 2,800
2nd Marine Infantry Battalion (Puerto Belgrano)
3rd Marine Infantry Battalion (Zarate)
4th Marine Infantry Battalion (Río Gallegos)
5th Marine Infantry Battalion (Ushuaia)

Marine Field Artillery Battalion (Puerto Belgrano)
Command and Logistics Support Battalion (Puerto Belgrano)
Amphibious Vehicles Battalion (Puerto Belgrano)
Communications Battalion (Puerto Belgrano)
Marine A/A Battalion (Puerto Belgrano)
Amphibious Engineers Company (Puerto Belgrano)
Amphibious Commandos Group (Puerto Belgrano)
There are Marine Security Companies at Naval Bases in Buenos Aires, Mar del Plata, Trelew, Puerto Belgrano, Ushuaia, Rio Gallegos, and Caleta Olivia.

Strength of the Fleet

Type	Active (Reserve)	Building
Patrol Submarines	3	—
Destroyers	6	—
Frigates	7	2 (3)
Patrol Ships	8	—
Fast Attack Craft (Gun/Missile)	2	—
Coastal Patrol Craft	6	—
Minehunters	2	—
Survey/Oceanographic Ships	3	—
Survey Launches	2	—
Transports/Tankers	11	—
Training Ships	4	—

Mercantile Marine

Lloyd's Register of Shipping:
   493 vessels of 477,254 tons gross

DELETIONS

Aircraft Carriers

1997   *Veinticinco de Mayo*

Amphibious Forces

1997   *Cabo San Antonio*

Mine Warfare Forces

1997   *Neuquen, Rio Negro*

Auxiliaries

1997   *Sanaviron, San Nicolas, Capitan Tulio Panigadi, Chirguano, Huarpe, Tonocote, Perhuenche*
1998   *Rio Gallegos*

PENNANT LIST

Submarines		41		Espora	P 64	Concepcion del Uruguay	Q 11	Comodoro Rivadavia
		42		Rosales	P 65	Punta Mogotes	Q 12	Punta Alta
S 31	Salta	43		Spiro	P 85	Intrepida	Q 15	Cormoran
S 41	Santa Cruz	44		Parker	P 86	Indomita	Q 16	Petrel
S 42	San Juan	45		Robinson (bldg)			Q 20	Puerto Deseado
		46		Gomez Roca (bldg)		**Mine Warfare Forces**	Q 61	Ciudad de Carate
							Q 62	Ciudad de Rosario
Destroyers					M 5	Chaco	Q 73	Itati
					M 6	Formosa	Q 74	Fortuna I
D 1	Hercules	**Patrol Forces**					Q 75	Fortuna II
D 2	Santisima Trinidad						R 2	Querandi
D 10	Almirante Brown	A 1		Comandante General Irigoyen	**Auxiliaries**		R 3	Tehuelche
D 11	La Argentina	A 2		Teniente Olivieri			R 4	Mataco
D 12	Heroina	A 3		Francisco de Gurruchaga	B 1	Patagonia	R 5	Mocovi
D 13	Sarandi	A 6		Suboficial Castillo	B 3	Canal Beagle	R 6	Calchaqui
		A 9		Alferez Sobral	B 4	Bahia San Blas	R 7	Ona
Frigates		A 10		Comodoro Somellera	B 5	Cabo de Hornos	R 8	Toba
		P 20		Murature	B 8	Astra Federico	R 10	Chulupi
31	Drummond	P 21		King	B 9	Astra Valentina	R 16	Capayan
32	Guerrico	P 61		Baradero	B 13	Ingeniero Julio Krause	R 18	Chiquilyan
33	Granville	P 62		Barranqueras	Q 2	Libertad	R 19	Morcoyan
		P 63		Clorinda	Q 5	Almirante Irizar		

SUBMARINES

Note: Cosmos and Havas underwater chariots in service. Cosmos types are capable of carrying limpet or ground mines.

2 SANTA CRUZ (TR 1700) CLASS (SSK)

Name	No	Builders	Laid down	Launched	Commissioned
SANTA CRUZ	S 41	Thyssen Nordseewerke	6 Dec 1980	28 Sep 1982	18 Oct 1984
SAN JUAN	S 42	Thyssen Nordseewerke	18 Mar 1982	20 June 1983	19 Nov 1985

Displacement, tons: 2,116 surfaced; 2,264 dived
Dimensions, feet (metres): 216.5 × 23.9 × 21.3
(66 × 7.3 × 6.5)
Main machinery: Diesel-electric; 4 MTU 16V 652 MB81 diesels;
6,720 hp(m) *(4.94 MW)* sustained; 4 alternators; 4.4 MW;
1 Siemens Type 1HR4525 + 1HR 4525 4-circuit DC motor;
6.6 MW; 1 shaft
Speed, knots: 15 surfaced; 12 snorting; 25 dived
Range, miles: 12,000 at 8 kt surfaced; 20 at 25 kt; 460 at 6 kt
dived
Complement: 29 (5 officers)

Torpedoes: 6—21 in *(533 mm)* bow tubes. 22 AEG SST 4; wire-
guided; active/passive homing to 12/28 km *(6.5/15 n miles)*
at 35/23 kt; warhead 260 kg; automatic reload in 50 seconds
or US Mk 37; wire-guided; active/passive homing to 8 km
(4.4 n miles) at 24 kt; warhead 150 kg. Swim-out discharge.
Mk 48 to replace Mk 37 in 2000/01.
Mines: Capable of carrying 34 ground mines.
Countermeasures: ESM: Sea Sentry III; radar warning.
Weapons control: Signaal Sinbads; can handle 5 targets and
3 torpedoes simultaneously.
Radars: Navigation: Thomson-CSF Calypso IV; I-band.
Sonars: Atlas Elektronik CSU 3/4; active/passive search and
attack; medium frequency.
Thomson Sintra DUUX 5; passive ranging.

Programmes: Contract signed 30 November 1977 with Thyssen
Nordseewerke for two submarines to be built at Emden with
parts and overseeing for four more boats to be built in
Argentina by Astilleros Domecq Garcia, Buenos Aires. In early
1996 S 43 was 52 per cent complete, S 44 30 per cent
complete but no further work was being done. The dockyard
was sold in February 1996 and both were then cannibalised

SAN JUAN   *7/1999 *, A E Galarce /* 0056464

for spares. Equipment for numbers five and six also used for
spares.
Modernisation: *Santa Cruz* mid-life update in Brazil started
September 1999 for two years. Refit includes new main
motors and sonar upgrade. Mk 48 torpedoes are replacing the
Mk 37.

Structure: Diving depth, 270 m *(890 ft).*
Operational: Maximum endurance is 70 days. Both can be used
for Commando insertion operations. They are based at Mar del
Plata.

UPDATED

1 SALTA (209) (TYPE 1200) CLASS (SSK)

Name	No	Builders	Laid down	Launched	Commissioned
SALTA	S 31	Howaldtswerke, Kiel	30 Apr 1970	9 Nov 1972	7 Mar 1974

Displacement, tons: 1,248 surfaced; 1,440 dived
Dimensions, feet (metres): 183.4 × 20.5 × 17.9
(55.9 × 6.3 × 5.5)
Main machinery: Diesel-electric; 4 MTU 12V 493 AZ80 diesels;
2,400 hp(m) *(1.76 MW)* sustained; 4 alternators; 1.7 MW;
1 motor; 4,600 hp(m) *(3.36 MW)*; 1 shaft
Speed, knots: 10 surfaced; 22 dived; 11 snorting
Range, miles: 6,000 at 8 kt surfaced; 230 at 8 kt; 400 at 4 kt
dived
Complement: 31 (5 officers)

Torpedoes: 8—21 in *(533 mm)* bow tubes. 14 AEG SST 4 Mod 1;
wire-guided; active/passive homing to 12/28 km *(6.5/15 n
miles)* at 35/23 kt; warhead 260 kg or US Mk 37; wire-guided;
active/passive homing to 8 km *(4.4 n miles)* at 24 kt; warhead
150 kg. Swim-out discharge.
Mines: Capable of carrying ground mines.
Countermeasures: ESM: DR 2000; radar warning.
Weapons control: Signaal M8 digital; computer-based; up to
3 targets engaged simultaneously.
Radars: Navigation: Thomson-CSF Calypso II.
Sonars: Atlas Elektronik CSU 3 (AN 526/AN 5039/41); active/
passive search and attack; medium frequency.
Thomson Sintra DUUX 2C and DUUG 1D; passive ranging.

Programmes: Ordered in 1968. Built in sections by
Howaldtswerke Deutsche Werft AG, Kiel from the IK 68 design
of Ingenieurkontor, Lübeck. Sections were shipped to
Argentina for assembly at Tandanor, Buenos Aires.
Modernisation: *Salta* completed a mid-life modernisation at the
Domecq Garcia Shipyard. New engines, weapons and
electrical systems fitted and the ship was relaunched on
4 October 1994 and recommissioned in May 1995.
Structure: Diving depth, 250 m *(820 ft).*
Operational: Operational and based at Mar del Plata. Second of
class cannibalised for spares.   *UPDATED*

SALTA   *5/1998 *, A E Galarce /* 0056465

DESTROYERS

4 ALMIRANTE BROWN (MEKO 360) CLASS (DDG)

Name	No	Builders	Laid down	Launched	Commissioned
ALMIRANTE BROWN	D 10	Blohm + Voss, Hamburg	8 Sep 1980	28 Mar 1981	26 Jan 1983
LA ARGENTINA	D 11	Blohm + Voss, Hamburg	30 Mar 1981	25 Sep 1981	4 May 1983
HEROINA	D 12	Blohm + Voss, Hamburg	24 Aug 1981	17 Feb 1982	31 Oct 1983
SARANDI	D 13	Blohm + Voss, Hamburg	9 Mar 1982	31 Aug 1982	16 Apr 1984

Displacement, tons: 2,900 standard; 3,360 full load
Dimensions, feet (metres): 413.1 × 46 × 19 (screws)
  (125.9 × 14 × 5.8)
Main machinery: COGOG; 2 RR Olympus TM3B gas turbines;
  50,000 hp *(37.4 MW)* sustained;
  2 RR Tyne RM1C gas turbines; 9,900 hp *(7.4 MW)* sustained;
  2 shafts; cp props
Speed, knots: 30.5; 20.5 cruising. **Range, miles:** 4,500 at 18 kt
Complement: 200 (26 officers)

Missiles: SSM: 8 Aerospatiale MM 40 Exocet (2 quad) launchers
  ❶; inertial cruise; active radar homing to 70 km *(40 n miles)*;
  warhead 165 kg; sea-skimmer.
SAM: Selenia/Elsag Albatros octuple launcher ❷; 24 Aspide;
  semi-active homing to 13 km *(7 n miles)* at 2.5 Mach; height
  envelope 15-5,000 m *(49.2-16,405 ft)*; warhead 30 kg.

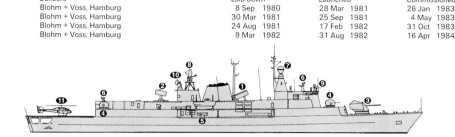

ALMIRANTE BROWN

(Scale 1 : 1,200), Ian Sturton / 0017516

Guns: 1 OTO Melara 5 in *(127 mm)*/54 automatic ❸; 45 rds/min
  to 16 km *(8.7 n miles)* anti-surface; 7 km *(3.6 n miles)* anti-
  aircraft; weight of shell 32 kg; also fires chaff and illuminants.
  8 Breda/Bofors 40 mm/70 (4 twin) ❹; 300 rds/min to

12.6 km *(6.8 n miles)* anti-surface; 4 km *(2.2 n miles)* anti-
  aircraft; weight of shell 0.96 kg; 2 Oerlikon 20 mm.
Torpedoes: 6—324 mm ILAS 3 (2 triple) tubes ❺. Whitehead
  A 244; anti-submarine; active/passive homing to 7 km *(3.8 n
  miles)* at 33 kt; warhead 34 kg (shaped charge); 18 reloads.
Countermeasures: Decoys: CSEE Dagaie double mounting;
  Graseby G1738 towed torpedo decoy system.
  2 Breda 105 mm SCLAR chaff rocket launchers; 20 tubes per
  launcher; can be trained and elevated; chaff to 5 km *(2.7 n
  miles)*; illuminants to 12 km *(6.6 n miles)*.
ESM/ECM: Sphinx/Scimitar.
Combat data systems: Signaal SEWACO; Link 10/11. SATCOMs
  can be fitted.
Weapons control: 2 Signaal LIROD radar/optronic systems ❻
  each controlling 2 twin 40 mm mounts; Signaal WM25 FCS ❼.
Radars: Air/surface search: Signaal DA08A ❽; F-band; range
  204 km *(110 n miles)* for 2 m² target.
Surface search: Signaal ZW06 ❾; I-band.
Navigation: Decca 1226; I-band.
Fire control: Signaal STIR ❿; I/J/K-band; range 140 km *(76 n
  miles)* for 1 m² target.
Sonars: Atlas Elektronik 80 (DSQS-21BZ); hull-mounted; active
  search and attack; medium frequency.

Helicopters: AS 555 Fennec ⓫.

Programmes: Six were originally ordered in 1978, but later
  restricted to four when Meko 140 frigates were ordered in
  1979.
Modernisation: Block II Exocet MM 40 may be fitted when funds
  are available.
Operational: *Almirante Brown* took part in allied Gulf operations
  in late 1990. Fennec helicopters delivered in 1996 which
  improves ASW capability and provides over the horizon
  targeting for SSMs. All are operational and based at Puerto
  Belgrano. All can be used as Flagships. Half life refits are
  needed.

UPDATED

LA ARGENTINA
7/1999*, A E Galarce / 0056466

SARANDI

7/1998, A E Galarce / 0017518

2 HERCULES (TYPE 42) CLASS (DDG)

Name	No
HERCULES	D 1 (ex-28)
SANTISIMA TRINIDAD	D 2

	Builders	Laid down	Launched	Commissioned
	Vickers, Barrow	16 June 1971	24 Oct 1972	12 July 1976
	AFNE, Rio Santiago	11 Oct 1971	9 Nov 1974	July 1981

SANTISIMA TRINIDAD   (Scale 1 : 1,200), Ian Sturton / 0017520

Displacement, tons: 3,150 standard; 4,100 full load
Dimensions, feet (metres): 412 × 47 × 19 (screws)
   (125.6 × 14.3 × 5.8)
Main machinery: COGOG; 2 RR Olympus TM3B gas turbines;
   50,000 hp (37.3 MW) sustained;
   2 RR Tyne RM1A gas-turbines; 9,900 hp (7.4 MW) sustained;
   2 shafts; cp props
Speed, knots: 29; 18 (Tynes). **Range, miles:** 4,000 at 18 kt
Complement: 280

Missiles: SSM: 4 Aerospatiale MM 38 Exocet ❶; inertial cruise;
   active homing to 42 km (23 n miles) at 0.9 Mach; warhead
   165 kg; sea-skimmer.
   SAM: British Aerospace Sea Dart Mk 30 twin launcher ❷; semi-
   active radar homing to 40 km (21.5 n miles) at 2 Mach; height
   envelope 100-18,300 m (328-60,042 ft); 22 missiles; limited
   anti-ship capability.
Guns: 1 Vickers 4.5 in (115 mm)/55 Mk 8 automatic ❸; 25 rds/
   min to 22 km (12 n miles); weight of shell 21 kg; also fires chaff
   and illuminants.
   2 Oerlikon 20 mm Mk 7 ❹. 2—12.7 mm MGs.
Torpedoes: 6—324 mm ILAS 3 (2 triple) tubes ❺. Whitehead
   A 244/S; anti-submarine; active/passive homing to 7 km
   (3.8 n miles) at 33 kt; warhead 34 kg (shaped charge).
Countermeasures: Decoys; Graseby towed torpedo decoy.
   Knebworth Corvus 8-tubed trainable launchers for chaff ❻.
   ESM: Racal RDL 257; radar intercept.
   ECM: Racal RCM 2 (Hercules only); jammer.
Combat data systems: Plessey-Ferranti ADAWS-4; Link 10.
Radars: Air search: Marconi Type 965P with double AKE2 array
   and 1010/1011 IFF ❼; A-band.
   Surface search: Marconi Type 992Q ❽; E/F-band.
   Navigation, HDWS and helicopter control: Kelvin Hughes Type
   1006; I-band.
   Fire control: Two Marconi Type 909 ❾; I/J-band (for Sea Dart
   missile control).
Sonars: Graseby Type 184M; hull-mounted; active search and
   attack; medium frequency 6-9 kHz.
   Kelvin Hughes Type 162M classification set; sideways looking;
   active; high frequency.

Helicopters: 1 SA 319B Alouette III ❿ or platform for 2 Sea
   King.

Programmes: Contract signed 18 May 1970 between the
   Argentine government and Vickers Ltd.
Modernisation: Combat Data Systems have been improved with
   local modifications. Hercules refitting in Chile from November
   1999 to make flight deck Sea King capable. The plan was to
   clear the area aft of the mainmast to fit a double hangar,
   removing the after 909 radar. This may now be done later.
   Santisima Trinidad may also be similarly converted in due
   course.

HERCULES (before conversion)   7/1999*, A E Galarce / 0056467

Operational: Although laid up for some time between 1983 and
1986, both ships were at sea for short periods in 1987 and
back with the Fleet from 1988. By 1996 Santisima Trinidad
had become little more than a hulk providing spares, but the
plan is to bring her back into service in 2000 after ten years in
reserve. Based at Puerto Belgrano. SAM and Type 909 fire-
control radars are non-operational.

                                                            UPDATED

FRIGATES

3 + (3) DRUMMOND (TYPE A 69) CLASS (FFG)

Name	No	Builders	Laid down	Launched	Completed
DRUMMOND (ex-Good Hope, ex-Lieutenant de Vaisseau le Hénaff F 789)	31	Lorient Naval Dockyard	12 Mar 1976	5 May 1977	Mar 1978
GUERRICO (ex-Transvaal, ex-Commandant l'Herminier F 791)	32	Lorient Naval Dockyard	1 Oct 1976	13 Sep 1977	Oct 1978
GRANVILLE	33	Lorient Naval Dockyard	1 Dec 1978	28 June 1980	22 June 1981

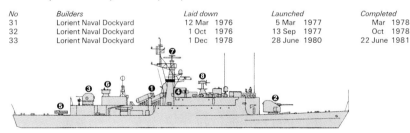

GRANVILLE   (Scale 1 : 900), Ian Sturton

Displacement, tons: 950 standard; 1,170 full load
Dimensions, feet (metres): 262.5 × 33.8 × 9.8; 18 (sonar)
   (80 × 10.3 × 3; 5.5)
Main machinery: 2 SEMT-Pielstick 12 PC2.2 V 400 diesels;
   12,000 hp(m) (8.82 MW) sustained; 2 shafts; acbLIPS cp
   props
Speed, knots: 23. **Range, miles:** 4,500 at 15 kt; 3,000 at 18 kt
Complement: 93 (10 officers)

Missiles: SSM: 4 Aerospatiale MM 38 Exocet (2 twin) launchers
   ❶; inertial cruise; active radar homing to 42 km (23 n miles);
   warhead 165 kg; sea-skimmer.
Guns: 1 Creusot-Loire 3.9 in (100 mm)/55 Mod 1953 ❷; 80°
   elevation; 60 rds/min to 17 km (9 n miles) anti-surface; 8 km
   (4.4 n miles) anti-aircraft; weight of shell 13.5 kg.
   2 Breda 40 mm/70 (twin) ❸; 300 rds/min to 12.5 km (6.8 n
   miles); weight of shell 0.96 kg; ready ammunition 736 (or 444)
   using AP tracer, impact or proximity fuzing.
   2 Oerlikon 20 mm ❹. 2—12.7 mm MGs.
Torpedoes: 6—324 mm Mk 32 (2 triple) tubes ❺. Whitehead
   A 244; anti-submarine; active/passive homing to 7 km (3.8 n
   miles) at 33 kt; warhead 34 kg.
Countermeasures: Decoys: CSEE Dagaie double mounting; 10
   or 6 replaceable containers; trainable; chaff to 12 km (6.5 n
   miles); illuminants to 4 km (2.2 n miles); decoys in H- to J-bands
   or Corvus sextuple launchers for chaff.
   ESM: DR 2000/DALIA 500; radar warning.
   ECM: Thomson-CSF Alligator; jammer.
Weapons control: Thomson-CSF Vega system. CSEE Panda
   Mk 2 optical director ❻. Naja optronic director (for 40 mm
   guns).
Radars: Air/surface search: Thomson-CSF DRBV 51A ❼ with
   UPX12 IFF; G-band.
   Navigation: Decca 1226; I-band.
   Fire control: Thomson-CSF DRBC 32E ❽; I/J-band (for 100 mm
   gun).
Sonars: Thomson Sintra Diodon; hull-mounted; active search
   and attack.

Programmes: The first pair was originally built for the French
Navy and sold to the South African Navy in 1976 while under
construction. As a result of a UN embargo on arms sales to
South Africa this sale was cancelled. Purchased by Argentina
in Autumn 1978. Both arrived in Argentina 2 November 1978

DRUMMOND   7/1999*, A E Galarce / 0056469

(third ship being ordered some time later) and all have proved
very popular ships in the Argentine Navy. Three more of the
class have been offered by the French Navy for possible
transfer in 2000.
Modernisation: Drummond has had her armament updated to
the same standard as the other two, replacing the Bofors
40/60. It is reported that a SENIT combat data system may
have been installed but this is not confirmed.
Operational: Endurance, 15 days. Very economical in fuel
consumption. Assisted in UN operations off Haiti in 1994. All
based at Puerto Belgrano but two are expected to move to
Caleta Paula in due course.   **UPDATED**

4 + 2 ESPORA (MEKO 140) CLASS (FFG)

Name	No	Builders	Laid down		Launched		Commissioned	
ESPORA	41	AFNE, Rio Santiago	3 Oct	1980	23 Jan	1982	5 July	1985
ROSALES	42	AFNE, Rio Santiago	1 July	1981	4 Mar	1983	14 Nov	1986
SPIRO	43	AFNE, Rio Santiago	4 Jan	1982	24 June	1983	24 Nov	1987
PARKER	44	AFNE, Rio Santiago	2 Aug	1982	31 Mar	1984	17 Apr	1990
ROBINSON	45	AFNE, Rio Santiago	8 June	1983	15 Feb	1985	Dec	2000
GOMEZ ROCA	46	AFNE, Rio Santiago	1 Dec	1983	14 Nov	1986	Sep	2002

Displacement, tons: 1,470 standard; 1,790 full load
Dimensions, feet (metres): 299.1 × 36.4 × 11.2
(91.2 × 11.1 × 3.4)
Main machinery: 2 SEMT-Pielstick 16 PC2-5 V 400 diesels;
20,400 hp(m) *(15 MW)* sustained; 2 shafts
Speed, knots: 27. **Range, miles:** 4,000 at 18 kt
Complement: 93 (11 officers)

Missiles: SSM: 4 Aerospatiale MM 38 Exocet ❶ inertial cruise;
active radar homing to 42 km *(23 n miles)*; warhead 165 kg;
sea-skimmer.
Guns: 1 OTO Melara 3 in *(76 mm)*/62 compact ❷; 85 rds/min to
16 km *(8.7 n miles)* anti-surface; 12 km *(6.5 n miles)* anti-
aircraft; weight of shell 6 kg; also fires chaff and illuminants.
4 Breda 40 mm/70 (2 twin) ❸; 300 rds/min to 12.5 km *(6.8 n
miles)*; weight of shell 0.96 kg; ready ammunition 736 (or 444)
using AP tracer, impact or proximity fuzing.
2—12.7 mm MGs.
Torpedoes: 6—324 mm ILAS 3 (2 triple) tubes ❹. Whitehead
A 244/S; anti-submarine; active/passive homing to 7 km
(3.8 n miles) at 33 kt; warhead 34 kg (shaped charge).
Countermeasures: Decoys: CSEE Dagaie double mounting; 10
or 6 replaceable containers; trainable; chaff to 12 km *(6.5 n
miles)*; illuminants to 4 km *(2.2 n miles)*; decoys in H- to
J-bands.
ESM: Racal RQN-3B; radar warning.
ECM: Racal TQN-2X; jammer.
Combat data systems: Signaal SEWACO.
Weapons control: Signaal WM22/41 integrated system;
1 LIROD 8 optronic director ❺ (plus 2 sights—1 on each bridge
wing).
Radars: Air/surface search: Signaal DA05 ❻; E/F-band; range
137 km *(75 n miles)* for 2 m² target.
Navigation: Decca TM 1226; I-band.
Fire control: Signaal WM28 ❼; I/J-band; range 46 km *(25 n
miles)*.
IFF: Mk 10.
Sonars: Atlas Elektronik ASO 4; hull-mounted; active search and
attack; medium frequency.

Helicopters: 1 SA 319B Alouette III or AS 555 Fennec ❽ (in 44-
46).

Programmes: A contract was signed with Blohm + Voss on
1 August 1979 for this group of ships which are scaled down
Meko 360s. All have been fabricated in AFNE, Rio Santiago.
The last pair were to have been scrapped, but on 8 May 1997 a

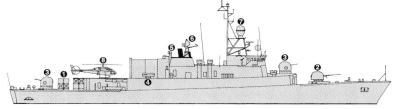

PARKER   *(Scale 1 : 900), Ian Sturton / 0012007*

SPIRO   *7/1999*, A E Galarce / 0056470*

decision was taken to try and complete them some 14 years
after each was first launched. A formal restart ceremony was
held on 18 July 1997 but progress since then has been
restricted by lack of funds. Latest reports indicate that the late
2000 completion date may be achieved for *Robinson*.
Modernisation: Plans to fit MM 40 Exocet from Meko 360. Flight
deck extensions for AS 555 helicopters.

Structure: *Parker* fitted with a telescopic hangar which is
planned to be retrofitted in first three and is being built into the
last pair. Fitted with stabilisers.
Operational: Mostly used for offshore patrol and fishery
protection duties but *Spiro* and *Rosales* sent to the Gulf in
1990-91. First pair based at Mar del Plata, second pair at
Puerto Belgrano.   ***UPDATED***

ROSALES   *7/1998*, A E Galarce / 0056471*

PARKER   *4/1997, Michael Nitz / 0017523*

SHIPBORNE AIRCRAFT

Numbers/Type: 5 Aerospatiale SA 319B Alouette III.
Operational speed: 113 kt *(210 km/h).*
Service ceiling: 10,500 ft *(3,200 m).*
Range: 290 n miles *(540 km).*
Role/Weapon systems: ASW Helicopter; used for liaison in peacetime; wartime role includes commando assault and ASW/ASVW. Sensors: Nose-mounted search radar. Weapons: ASW; 2 × Mk 44 torpedoes. ASV; 2 × AS12 missiles.
UPDATED

ALOUETTE III   *7/1999*, A E Galarce /* 0056472

Numbers/Type: 4 Aerospatiale AS 555 Fennec.
Operational speed: 121 kt *(225 km/h).*
Service ceiling: 13,125 ft *(4,000 m).*
Range: 389 n miles *(722 km).*
Role/Weapon systems: ASW version with OTHT capability in surface-to-surface role. Delivered in 1996. More are wanted. Sensors: Bendix RDR 1500 radar; Mk 3 MAD. Weapons: ASW; 2 × A 244 torpedoes to be fitted or 4 depth bombs.
UPDATED

FENNEC   *7/1999*, A E Galarce /* 0056473

Numbers/Type: 5/2 Agusta-Sikorsky ASH-3H/AS-61D Sea King.
Operational speed: 120 kt *(222 km/h).*
Service ceiling: 12,205 ft *(3,720 m).*
Range: 630 n miles *(1,165 km).*
Role/Weapon systems: ASW Helicopter; with limited surface search capability. Can operate from *Hercules.* Sensors: APS-705 search radar, Bendix AQS 18 sonar. Weapons: ASW; up to 4 × A 244 torpedoes or 4 × depth bombs. ASV: 1 AM 39 Exocet ASM.
UPDATED

SEA KING (with AM 39)   *7/1999*, A E Galarce /* 0056475

Numbers/Type: 8 Bell UH-1H.
Operational speed: 110 kt *(204 km/h).*
Service ceiling: 15,000 ft *(4,570 m).*
Range: 250 n miles *(463 km).*
Role/Weapon systems: First pair acquired for the Marines in 1999. Six more in 2000. Sensors: none. Weapons: 2—7.62 mm MGs.
NEW ENTRY

LAND-BASED MARITIME AIRCRAFT

Notes: (1) In addition there are three Fokker F28 for Logistic Support; one Pilatus PC-6B for reconnaissance and 10 Beech T-34 Turbo Mentor training aircraft.
(2) Thirty-four ex-US Navy A4M Skyhawk with radar APG-66 acquired by the Air Force by July 1998. First 18 delivered in crates in 1995-96 and remainder modernised before delivery in 1997-98.

Numbers/Type: 5 (6) Dassault-Breguet Super Etendard.
Operational speed: Mach 1.
Service ceiling: 44,950 ft *(13,700 m).*
Range: 920 n miles *(1,700 km).*
Role/Weapon systems: Strike Fighter with anti-shipping ability. In the past have flown from US or Brazilian aircraft carriers. Five aircraft are operational out of a total of eleven. Strike, air defence and ASV roles. Hi-lo-hi combat radius 460 n miles *(850 km).* Sensors: Thomson-CSF Agave multimode radar, ECM. Weapons: Strike; 2.1 tons of 'iron' bombs. ASVW; 1 AM 39 Exocet or 1 × Martin Pescador missiles. Self-defence; 2 × Magic AAMs. Standard; 2 × 30 mm cannon.
UPDATED

SUPER ETENDARD   *7/1999*, A E Galarce /* 0056474

Numbers/Type: 6 Grumman S-2ET Tracker.
Operational speed: 130 kt *(241 km/h).*
Service ceiling: 25,000 ft *(7,620 m).*
Range: 1,350 n miles *(2,500 km).*
Role/Weapon systems: Used for MR and EEZ patrol. One shipped to Israel in 1989 for Garrett turboprop installation. Prototype for fleet conversion in Argentina which completed in 2000. Sensors: EL/M-2022 search radar up to 32 sonobuoys, ALD-2B or AES 210/E ESM, echo-ranging depth charges. Weapons: ASW; A 244 torpedoes, bombs and depth charges.
UPDATED

TRACKER   *7/1998, A E Galarce /* 0017527

Numbers/Type: 8 Aermacchi MB-326GB.
Operational speed: 468 kt *(867 km/h).*
Service ceiling: 47,000 ft *(14,325 m).*
Range: 1,320 n miles *(2,446 km).*
Role/Weapon systems: Light Attack; supplements anti-shipping/strike; also has training role. Weapons: ASV; 1.8 tons of 'iron' bombs. Strike; 6 × rockets. Recce; underwing camera pod.
UPDATED

Numbers/Type: 1 Lockheed L-188E Electra.
Operational speed: 389 kt *(721 km/h).*
Service ceiling: 28,400 ft *(8,655 m).*
Range: 3,000 n miles *(5,570 km).*
Role/Weapon systems: Converted from transport aircraft for overwater Elint/EW role. Sensors: Radar APS-70; various EW systems including Elisra ESM. Weapons: Unarmed.
UPDATED

Numbers/Type: 4 Beechcraft B 200T Cormoran.
Operational speed: 260 kt *(482 km/h).*
Service ceiling: 31,000 ft *(9,448 m).*
Range: 2,000 n miles *(3,705 km).*
Role/Weapon systems: Multipurpose converted to Cormoran version for maritime patrol. There are three other unconverted aircraft. Sensors: Search radar. Weapons: Unarmed.
UPDATED

Numbers/Type: 6 Lockheed P-3B Orions.
Operational speed: 410 kt *(760 km/h).*
Service ceiling: 28,300 ft *(8,625 m).*
Range: 4,000 m *(7,410 km).*
Role/Weapon systems: Two acquired in 1997 from US; four more in 1998, and two for spares in 1999. Sensors: APS-115 radar; ESM. Weapons: ASW equipment may be carried in due course. ASV weapons are embargoed by US.
UPDATED

ORION   *6/1999* /* 0056476

PATROL FORCES

3 CHEROKEE CLASS (PATROL SHIPS) (PG)

Name	No	Builders	Commissioned
COMANDANTE GENERAL IRIGOYEN (ex-*Cahuilla*)	A 1	Charleston SB and DD Co	10 Mar 1945
FRANCISCO DE GURRUCHAGA (ex-*Luiseno* ATF 156)	A 3	Charleston SB and DD Co	16 June 1945
SUBOFICIAL CASTILLO (ex-*Takelma* ATF 113)	A 6	United Engineering Co, Alameda	3 Aug 1944

Displacement, tons: 1,235 standard; 1,731 full load
Dimensions, feet (metres): 205 × 38.5 × 17 *(62.5 × 11.7 × 5.2)*
Main machinery: Diesel-electric; 4 GM 12-278 diesels; 4,400 hp *(3.28 MW)*; 4 generators; 1 motor; 3,000 hp *(2.24 MW)*; 1 shaft
Speed, knots: 16. **Range, miles:** 6,500 at 15 kt; 15,000 at 8 kt
Complement: 85
Guns: 1 or 2 Bofors 40/60. 2 Oerlikon 20 mm.
Radars: Surface search: Racal Decca 626; I-band.
Navigation: Racal Decca 1230; I-band.

Comment: Fitted with powerful pumps and other salvage equipment. *Comandante General Irigoyen* transferred by the US at San Diego, California, on 9 July 1961. Classified as a tug until 1966 when she was rerated as patrol ship. *Francisco De Gurruchaga* transferred on 1 July 1975 by sale, *Suboficial Castillo* on 30 September 1993 by grant aid. All operational. Armament has been reduced.

VERIFIED

SUBOFICIAL CASTELLO   *9/1998* / 0017529

2 KING CLASS (PATROL SHIPS) (PG)

Name	No	Builders	Launched	Commissioned
MURATURE	P 20	Base Nav Rio Santiago	5 July 1943	12 Apr 1945
KING	P 21	Base Nav Rio Santiago	2 Nov 1943	28 July 1946

Displacement, tons: 913 standard; 1,000 normal; 1,032 full load
Dimensions, feet (metres): 252.7 × 29.5 × 13.1 *(77 × 9 × 4)*
Main machinery: 2 Werkspoor diesels; 2,500 hp(m) *(1.8 MW)*; 2 shafts
Speed, knots: 18. **Range, miles:** 9,000 at 12 kt
Complement: 130
Guns: 3 Vickers 4 in *(105 mm)*/45; 16 rds/min to 19 km *(10 n miles)*; weight of shell 16 kg.
4 Bofors 40 mm/60 (1 twin, 2 single); 120 rds/min/barrel to 10 km *(5.5 n miles)*; weight of shell 0.89 kg.
5—12.7 mm MGs.
Radars: Surface search: Racal Decca 1226; I-band.

Comment: Named after Captain John King, an Irish follower of Admiral Brown, who distinguished himself in the war with Brazil, 1826-28; and Captain Jose Murature, who performed conspicuous service against the Paraguayans at the Battle of Cuevas in 1865. *King* laid down June 1938. *Murature* March 1940. Both operational and used for cadet training.

VERIFIED

KING   *1/1998, Hartmut Ehlers* / 0017530

1 OLIVIERI CLASS (PATROL SHIP) (PG)

Name	No	Builders	Commissioned
TENIENTE OLIVIERI (ex-*Marsea 10*)	A 2	Quality SB, Louisiana	1981

Displacement, tons: 1,640 full load
Dimensions, feet (metres): 184.8 × 40 × 14 *(56.3 × 12.2 × 4.3)*
Main machinery: 2 GM/EMD 16-645 E6; 3,230 hp *(2.4 MW)* sustained; 2 shafts; bow thruster
Speed, knots: 14. **Range, miles:** 2,800 at 10 kt
Complement: 15 (4 officers)
Guns: 2—12.7 mm MGs.

Comment: Built by Quality Shipyards, New Orleans, as an oilfield support ship but rated as an Aviso. Acquired from US Maritime Administration 15 November 1987. Capable of carrying 600 tons of stores and 800 tons of liquids. Based at Puerto Belgrano.

UPDATED

TENIENTE OLIVIERI   *7/1999*, *A E Galarce* / 0056477

2 SOTOYOMO CLASS (PATROL SHIPS) (PG/ATA)

Name	No	Builders	Commissioned
ALFEREZ SOBRAL (ex-*Salish* ATA 187)	A 9	Levingstone, Orange	9 Sep 1944
COMODORO SOMELLERA (ex-*Catawba* ATA 210)	A 10	Levingstone, Orange	7 Dec 1944

Displacement, tons: 800 full load
Dimensions, feet (metres): 143 × 33.9 × 13 *(43.6 × 10.3 × 4)*
Main machinery: Diesel-electric; 2 GM 12-278A diesels; 2,200 hp *(1.64 MW)*; 2 generators; 1 motor; 1,500 hp *(1.12 MW)*; 1 shaft
Speed, knots: 12.5. **Range, miles:** 16,500 at 8 kt
Complement: 49
Guns: 1 Bofors 40 mm/60. 2 or 4 Oerlikon 20 mm.
Radars: Surface search: Decca 1226; I-band.

Comment: Former US ocean tugs transferred on 10 February 1972. *Alferez Sobral* was paid off in 1987 but was back in service by 1996. *Comodoro Somellera* sunk in collision at Ushuaia in August 1998 but was refloated and has been repaired. Armament on both ships has been reduced.

UPDATED

ALFEREZ SOBRAL   *10/1998* / 0017531

2 INTREPIDA CLASS (TYPE TNC 45)
(FAST ATTACK CRAFT—GUN/MISSILE) (PCF/PCFG)

Name	No	Builders	Launched	Commissioned
INTREPIDA	P 85	Lürssen, Bremen	2 Dec 1973	20 July 1974
INDOMITA	P 86	Lürssen, Bremen	8 Apr 1974	12 Dec 1974

Displacement, tons: 268 full load
Dimensions, feet (metres): 147.3 × 24.3 × 7.9 *(44.9 × 7.4 × 2.4)*
Main machinery: 4 MTU MD 16V 538 TB90 diesels; 12,000 hp(m) *(8.82 MW)*; 4 shafts
Speed, knots: 38. **Range, miles:** 1,450 at 20 kt
Complement: 39 (5 officers)
Missiles: SSM: 2 Aerospatiale Exocet MM 38; *(Intrepida)*; active radar homing to 42 km *(23 n miles)*; warhead 165 kg.
Guns: 1 OTO Melara 3 in *(76 mm)*/62 compact; 85 rds/min to 16 km *(9 n miles)* anti-surface; 12 km *(6.5 n miles)* anti-aircraft; weight of shell 6 kg.
1 or 2 Bofors 40 mm/70; 330 rds/min to 12 km *(6.5 n miles)* anti-surface; 4 km *(2.2 nm)* anti-aircraft; weight of shell 0.89 kg.
2 Oerlikon 81 mm rocket launchers for illuminants.
Torpedoes: 2—21 in *(533 mm)* launchers. AEG SST-4; wire-guided; active/passive homing to 28 km *(15 n miles)* at 23 kt; warhead 250 kg.
Countermeasures: ESM: Racal RDL 1; radar warning.
Weapons control: Signaal WM22 optronic for guns/missiles. Signaal M11 for torpedo guidance and control.
Radars: Surface search: Decca 626; I-band.

Comment: These two vessels were ordered in 1970. Both are painted with a brown/green camouflage. Exocet SSM fitted vice the forward of the two Bofors guns in *Intrepida* in 1998. No indication of second of class being similarly refitted.

VERIFIED

INDOMITA (without SSM)   *6/1994* / 0052042

4 BARADERO (DABUR) CLASS (COASTAL PATROL CRAFT) (PC)

Name	No	Builders	Commissioned
BARADERO	P 61	Israel Aircraft Industries	1978
BARRANQUERAS	P 62	Israel Aircraft Industries	1978
CLORINDA	P 63	Israel Aircraft Industries	1978
CONCEPCIÓN DEL URUGUAY	P 64	Israel Aircraft Industries	1978

Displacement, tons: 33.7 standard; 39 full load
Dimensions, feet (metres): 64.9 × 18 × 5.8 *(19.8 × 5.5 × 1.8)*
Main machinery: 2 GM 12V-71TA diesels; 840 hp *(627 kW)* sustained; 2 shafts
Speed, knots: 19. **Range, miles:** 450 at 13 kt
Complement: 9
Guns: 2 Oerlikon 20 mm. 2—12.7 mm MGs.
Depth charges: 2 portable rails.
Radars: Navigation: Decca 101; I-band.

Comment: Of all-aluminium construction. Employed in 1991 and 1992 as part of the UN Central American peacekeeping force. Based at Ushuaia.

VERIFIED

BARADERO   *1/1998 /* 0017532

1 POINT CLASS (PC)

Name	No	Builders	Commissioned
PUNTA MOGOTES (ex-*Point Hobart*)	P 65 (ex-82377)	J Martinac, Tacoma	13 July 1970

Displacement, tons: 67 full load
Dimensions, feet (metres): 83 × 17.2 × 15.8 *(25.3 × 5.2 × 1.8)*
Main machinery: 2 Caterpillar diesels; 1,600 hp *(1.19 MW)*; 2 shafts
Speed, knots: 22. **Range, miles:** 1,200 at 8 kt
Complement: 10
Guns: 2—12.7 mm MGs.
Radars: Surface search: Raytheon SPS 64; I-band.

Comment: Transferred from US Coast Guard on 8 July 1999. More of the class may follow.

NEW ENTRY

PUNTA MOGOTES   *11/1999*, A E Galarce /* 0056478

AMPHIBIOUS FORCES

Notes: (1) An ex-US 'Newport' class LST was nominated in 1996 for possible transfer, and funds are still being sought. Marine Corps future was thought to depend on the lease of this ship but this is no longer true.
(2) Marine Corps acquired two Piranha Boston Whalers in October 1999 and two more in February 2000. Powered by twin 150 hp Johnson outboards. Carry 1—12.7 mm MG and 4—7.62 mm MGs, Raytheon radar.

PIRANHA   *12/1999*, A E Galarce /* 0056479

4 LCM 6 CLASS (LCM) and 16 LCVPs

EDM 1, 2, 3, 4   EDVP 30-37   + 8

Displacement, tons: 56 full load
Dimensions, feet (metres): 56 × 14 × 3.9 *(17.1 × 4.3 × 1.2)*
Main machinery: 2 Gray 64 HN9 diesels; 330 hp *(246 kW)* sustained; 2 shafts
Speed, knots: 11. **Range, miles:** 130 at 10 kt
Military lift: 30 tons
Guns: 2—12.7 mm MGs.

Comment: Details given are for the LCMs acquired from the USA in June 1971. The LCVPs are split between those acquired from the USA in 1970 and a smaller variant built locally since 1971.

VERIFIED

MINE WARFARE FORCES

2 NEUQUEN (TON) CLASS (COASTAL MINEHUNTERS) (MHC)

Name	No	Builders	Launched
CHACO (ex-*Rennington*)	M 5	Richards	27 Nov 1958
FORMOSA (ex-*Ilmington*)	M 6	Camper & Nicholson	8 Mar 1954

Displacement, tons: 360 standard; 440 full load
Dimensions, feet (metres): 153 × 28.9 × 8.2 *(46.6 × 8.8 × 2.5)*
Main machinery: 2 Paxman Deltic/Mirrlees JVSS-12 diesels; 3,000 hp *(2.24 MW)*; 2 shafts
Speed, knots: 15. **Range, miles:** 2,500 at 12 kt
Complement: 36

Guns: 1 or 2 Bofors 40 mm/60; 120 rds/min to 10 km *(5.5 n miles)* anti-surface; 3 km *(1.6 n miles)* anti-aircraft; weight of shell 0.89 kg.
Radars: Navigation: Decca 45; I-band.
Sonars: Plessey Type 193; active minehunting; 100/300 kHz.

Programmes: Former British coastal minesweepers of the 'Ton' class. Purchased in 1967.
Modernisation: In 1968 both were converted into minehunters in HM Dockyard, Portsmouth. Of composite wooden and non-magnetic metal construction.
Operational: Four of the class paid off in 1996/97 but these last two are still active at Puerto Belgrano.

VERIFIED

FORMOSA   *7/1998 /* 0017533

SURVEY AND RESEARCH SHIPS

Note: There are also two Fisheries Research Ships employed by the government. These are *Oca Balda* and *Eduardo Holmberg*.

Name	No	Builders	Commissioned
PUERTO DESEADO	Q 20 (ex-Q 8)	Astarsa, San Fernando	26 Feb 1979

Displacement, tons: 2,133 standard; 2,400 full load
Dimensions, feet (metres): 251.9 × 51.8 × 21.3 *(76.8 × 15.8 × 6.5)*
Main machinery: 2 Fiat-GMT diesels; 3,600 hp(m) *(2.65 MW)*; 1 shaft
Speed, knots: 15. **Range, miles:** 12,000 at 12 kt
Complement: 61 (12 officers) plus 20 scientists
Radars: Navigation: Decca 1629; I-band.

Comment: Laid down on 17 March 1976 for Consejo Nacional de Investigaciones Tecnicas y Scientificas. Launched on 4 December 1976. For survey work fitted with: four Hewlett-Packard 2108-A, gravimeter, magnetometer, seismic systems, high-frequency sonar, geological laboratory. Omega and NAVSAT equipped. Painted with an orange hull in late 1996 for Antarctic deployments.

UPDATED

PUERTO DESEADO   *10/1996*, Luis Oscar Zunino /* 0056480

Name	No	Builders	Commissioned
COMODORO RIVADAVIA	Q 11	Mestrina, Tigre	6 Dec 1974

Displacement, tons: 820 full load
Dimensions, feet (metres): 171.2 × 28.9 × 8.5 *(52.2 × 8.8 × 2.6)*
Main machinery: 2 Stork Werkspoor RHO-218K diesels; 1,160 hp(m) *(853 kW)*; 2 shafts
Speed, knots: 12. **Range, miles:** 6,000 at 12 kt
Complement: 34 (8 officers)

Comment: Laid down on 17 July 1971 and launched on 2 December 1972. Used for research.
VERIFIED

COMODORO RIVADAVIA   *8/1988, van Ginderen Collection*

Name	No	Builders	Commissioned
CORMORAN	Q 15	AFNE, Rio Santiago	20 Feb 1964

Displacement, tons: 102 full load
Dimensions, feet (metres): 83 × 16.4 × 5.9 *(25.3 × 5 × 1.8)*
Main machinery: 2 GM 6-71 diesels; 440 hp(m) *(323 kW)*; 2 shafts
Speed, knots: 11
Complement: 19 (3 officers)
Radars: Navigation: I-band.

Comment: Launched 10 August 1963. Classified as a coastal launch.
UPDATED

CORMORAN   *7/1999*, A E Galarce /* 0056481

Name	No	Builders	Commissioned
PETREL	Q 16	Cadenazzi, Tigre	4 Nov 1965

Displacement, tons: 50 full load
Dimensions, feet (metres): 64.8 × 14.8 × 5.6 *(19.7 × 4.5 × 1.7)*
Main machinery: 2 GM 6-71 diesels; 340 hp(m) *(250 kW)*; 2 shafts
Speed, knots: 9
Complement: 9 (2 officers)

Comment: Built using hull of EM 128 transferred from Prefectura Naval. Classified as a coastal launch. Non operational in early 1999 but is to be refitted.
VERIFIED

PETREL   *1/1998, Hartmut Ehlers /* 0017534

TRAINING SHIPS

Note: There are also three small yachts: *Itati* (Q 73), *Fortuna I* (Q 74) and *Fortuna II* (Q 75) plus a 25 ton yawl *Tijuca* acquired in 1993.

1 SAIL TRAINING SHIP (AXS)

Name	No	Builders	Commissioned
LIBERTAD	Q 2	AFNE, Rio Santiago	28 May 1963

Displacement, tons: 3,025 standard; 3,765 full load
Dimensions, feet (metres): 262 wl; 301 oa × 45.3 × 21.8 *(79.9; 91.7 × 13.8 × 6.6)*
Main machinery: 2 Sulzer diesels; 2,400 hp(m) *(1.76 MW)*; 2 shafts
Speed, knots: 13.5 under power. **Range, miles:** 12,000
Complement: 220 crew plus 90 cadets
Guns: 4 Hotchkiss 47 mm saluting guns.
Radars: Navigation: Decca; I-band.

Comment: Launched 30 May 1956. She set record for crossing the North Atlantic under sail in 1966. Sail area, 26,835 m². Based at Puerto Belgrano.
UPDATED

LIBERTAD   *7/1999*, M Declerck /* 0056482

AUXILIARIES

1 DURANCE CLASS (AOR)

Name	No	Builders	Launched	Commissioned
PATAGONIA	B 1 (ex-A 629)	Brest Naval Dockyard	6 Sep 1975	1 Dec 1976
(ex-*Durance*)				

Displacement, tons: 17,900 full load
Dimensions, feet (metres): 515.9 × 69.5 × 38.5 *(157.3 × 21.2 × 10.8)*
Main machinery: 2 SEMT-Pielstick 16 PC2.5 V 400 diesels; 20,800 hp(m) *(15.3 MW)* sustained; 2 shafts; acbLIPS cp props
Speed, knots: 19. **Range, miles:** 9,000 at 15 kt
Complement: 164 (10 officers) plus 29 spare
Cargo capacity: 9,000 tons fuel; 500 tons Avcat; 130 distilled water; 170 victuals; 150 munitions; 50 naval stores
Guns: 3 Breda/Mauser 30 mm/70; 800 rds/min; weight of shell 0.37 kg. 4—12.7 mm MGs.
Countermeasures: ESM/ECM.
Radars: Navigation: 2 Racal Decca 1226; I-band.
Helicopters: 1 Alouette III.

Comment: Acquired from France on 12 July 1999 having been in reserve for two years. Being refitted in Argentina and expected to return to service in an amphibious support role in 2000. The 30 mm guns may be replaced by the original 40 and 20 mm weapons. There are four beam transfer positions and two astern.
NEW ENTRY

PATAGONIA (French colours)   *6/1997*, van Ginderen Collection /* 0063464

3 CHARTERED SHIPS (AKS/AOTL)

Name	No	Builders	Completed	Chartered
INGENIERO JULIO KRAUSE	B 13	Astarsa, Tigre	1981	1992
ASTRA FEDERICO	B 8	Astarsa, Tigre	1981	1992
ASTRA VALENTINA	B 9	Astarsa, Tigre	1982	1992

Comment: Taken over by the Navy but also used for commercial trading. *Krause* is a 10,000 ton oiler, the other pair are 30,000 ton cargo ships. All have civilian crews.
UPDATED

ASTRA FEDERICO   *12/1997, Hartmut Ehlers /* 0017536

3 COSTA SUR CLASS (TRANSPORT) (AKS)

Name	No	Builders	Commissioned
CANAL BEAGLE	B 3	Astillero Principe y Menghi SA	29 Apr 1978
BAHIA SAN BLAS	B 4	Astillero Principe y Menghi SA	27 Nov 1978
CABO DE HORNOS	B 5	Astillero Principe y Menghi SA	28 June 1979
(ex-Bahia Camarones)			

Measurement, tons: 5,800 dwt; 4,600 gross
Dimensions, feet (metres): 390.3 × 57.4 × 21 *(119 × 17.5 × 6.4)*
Main machinery: 2 AFNE-Sulzer diesels; 6,400 hp(m) *(4.7 MW)*; 2 shafts
Speed, knots: 15
Complement: 36

Comment: Ordered December 1975. Laid down 10 January 1977, 11 April 1977 and 29 April 1978. Launched 19 October 1977, 29 April 1978 and 4 November 1978. Used to supply offshore research installations in Naval Area South. One operated in the Gulf in 1991. Painted grey in 1998 indicating a more active naval role in amphibious support operations.
UPDATED

BAHIA SAN BLAS   6/1999* / 0056483

CANAL BEAGLE   8/1999*, P Marsan / 0081446

3 RED CLASS (BUOY TENDERS)

Name	No	Builders	Launched
PUNTA ALTA (ex-Red Birch)	Q 12 (ex-WLM 687)	CG Yard, Maryland	19 Feb 1965
CIUDAD DE ZARATE	Q 61 (ex-WLM 688)	CG Yard, Maryland	1 Aug 1970
(ex-Red Cedar)			
CIUDAD DE ROSARIO	Q 62 (ex-WLM 685)	CG Yard, Maryland	4 Apr 1964
(ex-Red Wood)			

Displacement, tons: 536 full load
Dimensions, feet (metres): 157 × 33 × 6 *(47.9 × 10.1 × 1.8)*
Main machinery: 2 diesels; 1,800 hp *(1.34 MW)*; 2 shafts; cp props; bow thruster
Speed, knots: 12. **Range, miles:** 2,248 at 11 kt
Complement: 31 (6 officers)

Comment: Ex-USCG buoy tenders. First one transferred on 10 June 1998 and recommissioned on 17 November 1998. Two more transferred 30 July 1999. Strengthened hull for light ice breaking. Equipped with a 10 ton boom. *Punta Alta* used as supply ship in the southern archipelago. The other pair are used as river supply ships.
UPDATED

PUNTA ALTA   7/1999*, A E Galarce / 0056484

2 FLOATING DOCKS

Number	Dimensions, feet (metres)	Capacity, tons
Y 1 (ex-ARD 23)	492 × 88.6 × 56 *(150 × 27 × 17.1)*	3,500
3	215.8 × 46 × 45.5 *(65.8 × 14 × 13.7)*	750

Comment: First one is at Mar del Plata naval base, the second at Puerto Belgrano. The ex-USN ARD was transferred 8 September 1993 by grant aid. All other docks have been sold.
UPDATED

ICEBREAKERS

Name	No	Builders	Launched	Commissioned
ALMIRANTE IRIZAR	Q 5	Wärtsilä, Helsinki	3 Feb 1978	15 Dec 1978

Displacement, tons: 14,900 full load
Dimensions, feet (metres): 392 × 82 × 31.2 *(119.3 × 25 × 9.5)*
Main machinery: Diesel-electric; 4 Wärtsilä-SEMT-Pielstick 8 PC2.5 L diesels; 18,720 hp(m) *(13.77 MW)* sustained; 4 generators; 2 Stromberg motors; 16,200 hp(m) *(11.9 MW)*; 2 shafts
Speed, knots: 16.5
Complement: 133 ship's company plus 100 passengers
Guns: 2 Bofors 40 mm/70; 300 rds/min to 12 km *(6.5 n miles)* anti-surface; 4 km *(2.2 n miles)* anti-aircraft; weight of shell 0.96 kg.
Radars: Air/surface search: Plessey AWS 2; E/F-band.
Navigation: 2 Decca; I-band.
Helicopters: 2 ASH-3H Sea King.

Comment: Fitted for landing craft with two 16 ton cranes, fin stabilisers, Wärtsilä bubbling system and a 60 ton towing winch. RAST helicopter securing system. Red hull with white upperworks and red funnel. Designed for Antarctic support operations and able to remain in polar regions throughout the Winter with 210 people aboard. Used as a transport to South Georgia in December 1981 and as a hospital ship during the Falklands campaign April to June 1982. Has been used as a Patagonian supply ship, and for other activities associated with the Navy in the region.
UPDATED

ALMIRANTE IRIZAR   7/1999*, A E Galarce / 0056485

TUGS

5 COASTAL and 6 HARBOUR TUGS (YTB/YTL)

QUERANDI R 2	MOCOVI R 5	TOBA R 8	CHIQUILYAN R 18
TEHUELCHE R 3	CALCHAQUI R 6	CHULUPI R 10	MORCOYAN R 19
MATACO R 4	ONA R 7	CAPAYAN R 16	

Comment: R 2-4 and R 7-8 are coastal tugs of about 250 tons. The remainder are harbour tugs transferred from the USA.
UPDATED

MATACO   3/1997*, van Ginderen Collection / 0012016

PREFECTURA NAVAL ARGENTINA
(COAST GUARD)

Headquarters Appointments

Commander:
Prefecto General Juan José Beltritti
Vice Commander:
Prefecto General Julio Alberto Castiglia

Personnel

2000: 11,900 (1,600 officers)

History

The Spanish authorities in South America established similar organisations to those in Spain. In 1756 the Captainship of the Port came into being in Buenos Aires—in 1810 the Ship Registry office was added to this title. On 29 October 1896 the title of Capitania General de Puertos was established by Act of Congress, the beginning of the PNA. Today, as a security and safety force, it has responsibilities throughout the rivers of Argentina, the ports and harbours as well as within territorial waters out to the 200 mile EEZ. An attempt was made in January 1992 to restrict operations to a 12 mile limit but the legislation was cancelled.

Tasks

Under the General Organisation Act the PNA is charged with:
(a) Enforcement of Federal Laws on the high seas and waters subject to the Argentine Republic.
(b) Enforcement of environmental protection laws in Federal waters.
(c) Safety of ships in EEZ. Search and Rescue.
(d) Security of waterfront facilities and vessels in port.
(e) Operation of certain Navaids.
(f) Operation of some Pilot Services.
(g) Management and operation of Aviation Service; Coastguard Vessels; Salvage, Fire and Anti-Pollution Service; Yachtmaster School; National Diving School; several Fire Brigades and Anti-Narcotics Department.
(h) Operation of some Customs activities.

Organisation

Formed in 10 districts; High Parana River, Upper Parana and Paraguay Rivers, Lower Parana River, Upper Uruguay River, Lower Uruguay River, Delta, River Plate, Northern Argentine Sea, Southern Argentine Sea, Lakes and Comahue.

Identity markings

Two unequal blue stripes with, superimposed, crossed white anchors followed by the title Prefectura Naval.

Strength of Prefectura

Patrol Ships	6
Large Patrol Craft	4
Coastal Patrol Craft	60
Training Ships	4
Pilot Stations	1
Pilot and Patrol Craft	5

PATROL FORCES (PC)

Note: In addition to the ships and craft listed below the PNA operates 400 craft, including floating cranes, runabouts and inflatables of all types. A firefighting vessel was acquired in August 1993 and renamed *Rodolfo D'Agostini*.

1 PATROL SHIP (PG)

Name	No	Builders	Completed
DELFIN	GC 13	Ijsselwerf, Netherlands	14 May 1957

Displacement, tons: 700 standard; 1,000 full load
Dimensions, feet (metres): 193.5 × 29.8 × 13.8 *(59 × 9.1 × 4.2)*
Main machinery: 2 MAN diesels; 2,300 hp(m) *(1.69 MW)*; 2 shafts
Speed, knots: 15. **Range, miles:** 6,720 at 10 kt
Complement: 27
Guns: 1 Oerlikon 20 mm. 2—12.7 mm Browning MGs.
Radars: Navigation: Decca; I-band.

Comment: Whaler acquired for PNA in 1969. Commissioned 23 January 1970.
UPDATED

DELFIN   *11/1999*, Prefectura Naval /* 0056486

2 LYNCH CLASS (LARGE PATROL CRAFT) (PC)

Name	No	Builders	Commissioned
LYNCH	GC 21	AFNE, Rio Santiago	20 May 1964
TOLL	GC 22	AFNE, Rio Santiago	7 July 1966

Displacement, tons: 100 standard; 117 full load
Dimensions, feet (metres): 98.4 × 21 × 6.9 *(30 × 6.4 × 2.1)*
Main machinery: 2 MTU Maybach diesels; 2,700 hp(m) *(1.98 MW)*; 2 shafts
Speed, knots: 22. **Range, miles:** 2,000
Complement: 14 (3 officers)
Guns: 1 Oerlikon 20 mm (can be carried).
Radars: Surface search: Decca; I-band.
UPDATED

LYNCH   *1/1997*, Prefectura Naval /* 0012018

5 HALCON (TYPE B 119) CLASS (PG)

Name	No	Builders	Commissioned
MANTILLA	GC 24	Bazán, El Ferrol	20 Dec 1982
AZOPARDO	GC 25	Bazán, El Ferrol	28 Apr 1983
THOMPSON	GC 26	Bazán, El Ferrol	20 June 1983
PREFECTO FIQUE	GC 27	Bazán, El Ferrol	29 July 1983
PREFECTO DERBES	GC 28	Bazán, El Ferrol	20 Nov 1983

Displacement, tons: 910 standard; 1,084 full load
Dimensions, feet (metres): 219.9 × 34.4 × 13.8 *(67 × 10.5 × 4.2)*
Main machinery: 2 Bazán-MTU 16V 956 TB91 diesels; 7,500 hp(m) *(5.52 MW)* sustained; 2 shafts
Speed, knots: 20. **Range, miles:** 5,000 at 18 kt
Complement: 33 (10 officers)
Guns: 1 Breda 40 mm/70; 300 rds/min to 12.5 km *(7 n miles)*; weight of shell 0.96 kg.
2—12.7 mm MGs.
Radars: Navigation: Decca 1226 ARPA; I-band.
Helicopters: Platform for 1 Dauphin 2.

Comment: Ordered in 1979 from Bazán, El Ferrol, Spain. All have helicopter hangar and Magnavox MX 1102 SATNAV. Hospital with four beds. Carry one rigid rescue craft *(6 m)* with a 90 hp MWM diesel powering a Hamilton water-jet and a capacity for 12 and two inflatable craft *(4.1 m)* with Evinrude outboard.
UPDATED

THOMPSON   *10/1999*, H J Diaz /* 0056487

1 LARGE PATROL CRAFT (PG)

Name	No	Builders	Commissioned
MANDUBI	GC 43	Base Naval Rio Santiago	1940

Displacement, tons: 270 full load
Dimensions, feet (metres): 108.9 × 20.7 × 6.2 *(33.2 × 6.3 × 1.9)*
Main machinery: 2 MAN G6V-23.5/33 diesels; 500 hp(m) *(367 kW)*; 1 shaft
Speed, knots: 14. **Range, miles:** 800 at 14 kt; 3,400 at 10 kt
Complement: 12
Guns: 2—12.7 mm Browning MGs.
Radars: Surface search: Decca; I-band.

Comment: Since 1986 has acted as training craft for PNA Cadets School carrying 20 cadets.
UPDATED

MANDUBI   *8/1994*, Mario Diaz /* 0056488

1 RIVER PATROL SHIP (ARS)

Name	No	Builders	Commissioned
TONINA	GC 47	SANYM SA San Fernando, Argentina	30 June 1978

Displacement, tons: 103 standard; 153 full load
Dimensions, feet (metres): 83.8 × 21.3 × 10.1 *(25.5 × 6.5 × 3.3)*
Main machinery: 2 GM 16V-71TA diesels; 1,000 hp *(746 kW)* sustained; 2 shafts
Speed, knots: 10. **Range, miles:** 2,800 at 10 kt
Complement: 11 (3 officers)
Guns: 1 Oerlikon 20 mm.
Radars: Navigation: Decca 1226; I-band.

Comment: Served as training ship for PNA Cadets School until 1986. Now acts as salvage ship with salvage pumps and recompression chamber. Capable of operating divers and underwater swimmers. Also used as a patrol ship.   ***VERIFIED***

TONINA   *1/1998, Hartmut Ehlers /* 0017541

18 MAR DEL PLATA CLASS (COASTAL PATROL CRAFT) (PC)

MAR DEL PLATA GC 64	**RIO DE LA PLATA** GC 70	**INGENIERO WHITE** GC 76
MARTIN GARCIA GC 65	**LA PLATA** GC 71	**GOLFO SAN MATIAS** GC 77
RIO LUJAN GC 66	**BUENOS AIRES** GC 72	**MADRYN** GC 78
RIO URUGUAY GC 67	**CABO CORRIENTES** GC 73	**RIO DESEADO** GC 79
RIO PARAGUAY GC 68	**RIO QUEQUEN** GC 74	**USHUAIA** GC 80
RIO PARANA GC 69	**BAHIA BLANCA** GC 75	**CANAL DE BEAGLE** GC 81

Displacement, tons: 81 full load
Dimensions, feet (metres): 91.8 × 17.4 × 5.2 *(28 × 5.3 × 1.6)*
Main machinery: 2 MTU 8V-331-TC92 diesels; 1,770 hp(m) *(1.3 MW)* sustained; 2 shafts
Speed, knots: 22. **Range, miles:** 1,200 at 12 kt; 780 at 18 kt
Complement: 14 (3 officers)
Guns: 1 Oerlikon 20 mm. 2—12.7 mm Browning MGs.
Radars: Navigation: Decca 1226; I-band.

Comment: Ordered 24 November 1978 from Blohm + Voss to a Z-28 design. First delivered in June 1979 and then at monthly intervals. Steel hulls. GC 82 and 83 were captured by the British Forces in 1982.   ***UPDATED***

RIO PARAGUAY   *12/1998*, Prefectura Naval /* 0056489

1 COASTAL PATROL CRAFT (PC)

Name	No	Builders	Commissioned
DORADO	GC 101	Base Naval, Rio Santiago	17 Dec 1939

Displacement, tons: 43 full load
Dimensions, feet (metres): 69.5 × 14.1 × 4.9 *(21.2 × 4.3 × 1.5)*
Main machinery: 2 GM 6071-6A diesels; 360 hp *(268 kW)*; 1 shaft
Speed, knots: 12. **Range, miles:** 1,550
Complement: 7 (1 officer)
Radars: Navigation: Furuno; I-band.

UPDATED

DORADO   *12/1999*, R O Rivero /* 0056490

33 SMALL PATROL CRAFT (PB)

GC 48-61   GC 88-95   GC 102-108   GC 111-114

Displacement, tons: 15 full load
Dimensions, feet (metres): 41 × 11.8 × 3.6 *(12.5 × 3.6 × 1.1)*
Main machinery: 2 GM diesels; 514 hp *(383 kW)*; 2 shafts
Speed, knots: 20. **Range, miles:** 400 at 18 kt
Complement: 3
Guns: 12.7 mm Browning MG.
Radars: Navigation; I-band.

Comment: First delivered September 1978. First 14 built by Cadenazzi, Tigre 1977-79, most of the remainder by Ast Belen de Escobar 1984-86. *GC 102-114* are slightly smaller.   ***VERIFIED***

GC 89   *1/1998 /* 0017543

1 BAZAN TYPE (PB)

GC 142

Displacement, tons: 14.5 full load
Dimensions, feet (metres): 39 × 12.4 × 2.2 *(11.9 × 3.8 × 0.7)*
Main machinery: 2 MAN D2848 LXE diesels; 1,360 hp(m) *(1 MW)* sustained; 2 Hamilton 362 waterjets
Speed, knots: 38. **Range, miles:** 300 at 25 kt
Complement: 4
Guns: 1—12.7 mm MG.
Radars: Navigation: Furuno; I-band.

Comment: Acquired in 1997 from Bazán, San Fernando. Similar to Spanish 'Bazán 39' class for Spanish Maritime Police. More may be acquired.   ***UPDATED***

GC 142   *1/1997*, Fernando Murillo /* 0012020

3 + 7 ALUCAT 1050 CLASS (PB)

GC 137-139

Displacement, tons: 9 full load
Dimensions, feet (metres): 37.7 × 12.5 × 2 *(11.5 × 3.8 × 0.6)*
Main machinery: 2 Volvo 61 ALD; 577 hp(m) *(424 kW)*; 2 Hamilton 273 waterjets
Speed, knots: 18
Complement: 4
Radars: Navigation: Furuno 12/24; I-band.

Comment: Damen Alucat 1050s delivered in August 1994. Seven more ordered in 1999.   ***UPDATED***

GC 138   *11/1995*, Prefectura Naval /* 0056491

22 + 5 ALUCAT 850 CLASS (PB)

LS 9201-LS 9222

Displacement, tons: 7 full load
Dimensions, feet (metres): 30.2 × 10.8 × 2 *(9.2 × 3.3 × 0.6)*
Main machinery: 2 Volvo TAMD 41B; 400 hp(m) *(294 kW)*; 2 waterjets
Speed, knots: 26
Complement: 4
Radars: Navigation: Furuno; I-band.

Comment: 'Alucat 850' class built by Damen. First six delivered in 1995, six more in February 1996, five more in December 1996 and five in December 1997. Five more ordered in 1999.
UPDATED

LS 9205 *11/1995*, Prefectura Naval / 0012021

4 TRAINING SHIPS (AXL/AXS)

| ESPERANZA | ADHARA II | TALITA II | DR BERNARDO HOUSSAY (ex-*El Austral*) |

Displacement, tons: 33.5 standard
Dimensions, feet (metres): 62.3 × 14.1 × 8.9 *(19 × 4.3 × 2.7)*
Main machinery: 1 VM diesel; 90 hp(m) *(66 kW)*; 1 shaft
Speed, knots: 6; 15 sailing
Complement: 6 plus 6 cadets

Comment: Details given are for *Esperanza* built by Ast Central de la PNA. Launched and commissioned 20 December 1968 as a sail training ship. The 30 ton training craft *Adhara II* and *Talita II* are of similar dimensions. *Dr Bernardo Houssay* is a Danish-built ketch built in 1930. Displacement 460 tons and has a crew of 25 (five officers). Acquired by the PNA in 1996.
UPDATED

TALITA II *6/1998, Prefectura Naval / 0017545*

DR BERNARDO HOUSSAY *11/1998*, A B Casabelle / 0056493

6 HARBOUR TUGS (YTL) and 2 FIREFIGHTING SHIPS (YTR)

| CANAL EMILIO MITRE SB 8 | SB 3, 4, 5, 9 and 10 | SI 1 | SI 3 |

Comment: *Canal Emilio Mitre* is of 53 tons full load, it has a speed of 10 kt and was built by Damen Shipyard, Netherlands in 1982. *SI 1* is a firefighting ship commissioned in 1960 and *SI 3*, a second one, was built in 1953 and commissioned in the PNA in 1993.
UPDATED

SI 3 *6/1995*, Prefectura Naval / 0056492

PILOT VESSELS

1 PILOT STATION

Name	No	Builders	Commissioned
RECALADA (ex-*Rio Limay*)	DF 15	Astillero Astarsa	30 May 1972

Displacement, tons: 10,070 full load
Dimensions, feet (metres): 482.3 × 65.6 × 28 *(147 × 20 × 8.5)*
Speed, knots: 13
Complement: 28 (3 officers)

Comment: Commissioned as a Coast Guard ship 24 December 1991. Painted red with a white superstructure. Has a helicopter deck forward and a 20 bed hospital. After an extensive conversion and refit the ship replaced *Lago Lacar* in 1995.
UPDATED

RECALADA *8/1994*, Marcelo Campodonico / 0056494

5 PILOT AND 17 PATROL CRAFT

ALUMINE GC 118 (ex-SP 14)	BUENOS AIRES GC 125 (ex-SP 22)	FUTALAUFQUEN GC 133 (ex-SP 30)
TRAFUL GC 119 (ex-SP 15)	FAGNANO SP 23	FALKNER GC 134 (ex-SP 31)
COLHUE GC 129 (ex-SP 16)	LACAR GC 120 (ex-SP 24)	FONTANA GC 121 (ex-SP 32)
MASCARDI GC 122 (ex-SP 17)	CARDIEL SP 25	COLHUE HUAPI GC 136 (ex-SP 33)
MARIA L PENDO GC 130 (ex-SP 18)	MUSTERS GC 126 (ex-SP 26)	HUECHULAFQUEN GC 135 (ex-SP 34)
NAHUEL HUAPI SP 19	QUILLEN SP 27	YEHUIN SP 30 (ex-SP 35)
VIEDMA GC 123 (ex-SP 20)	ROCA GC 131 (ex-SP 28)	
SAN MARTIN GC 124 (ex-SP 21)	PUELO GC 132 (ex-SP 29)	

(All names preceded by **LAGO**)

Comment: There are five different types of named pilot and patrol craft. SP 14-15 of 33.7 tons built in 1981; SP 16-18 of 47 tons built since 1981; SP 19-23 of 51 tons built since 1981; SP 25-27 of 20 tons built in 1981; SP 28-30 of 16.5 m built in 1983; SP 31-35 of 7 tons built in 1986-1991. Most built by Damen SY, Netherlands. The last one built by Astillero Mestrina, Tigre. No armament. Six were transferred to patrol duties in 1993 and 11 more in 1995 and all have GC numbers. SP 19, 23, 25, 27 and 30 are the pilot craft.
VERIFIED

HUECHULAFQUEN *12/1997, Hartmut Ehlers / 0017546*

LAND-BASED MARITIME AIRCRAFT

Note: In addition to the aircraft listed, there are two Piper Warrior II/Archer II training aircraft, two Schweizer 269C training helicopters, and one Piper Azteca.

Numbers/Type: 2 Aerospatiale SA 330 Super Puma.
Operational speed: 151 kt *(279 km/h)*.
Service ceiling: 15,090 ft *(4,600 m)*.
Range: 335 n miles *(620 km)*.
Role/Weapon systems: Support and SAR helicopter for patrol work. Both updated in France in 1996. Sensors: Omera search radar. Weapons: Can carry pintle-mounted machine guns but are usually unarmed.
UPDATED

SUPER PUMA *11/1996*, Luis O Zunino / 0056495

Numbers/Type: 2 Aerospatiale AS 365 Dauphin 2.
Operational speed: 150 kt (278 km/h).
Service ceiling: 15,000 ft (4,575 m).
Range: 410 n miles (758 km).
Role/Weapon systems: Acquired in 1995-96 to replace the Super Puma during the latter's update but have been retained. Sensors: Agrion search radar. Weapons: Unarmed.

UPDATED

Numbers/Type: 2/3 CASA C-212 S 68/A 68 Aviocar.
Operational speed: 190 kt (353 km/h).
Service ceiling: 24,000 ft (7,315 m).
Range: 1,650 n miles (3,055 km).
Role/Weapon systems: Two S 68 acquired in 1989, three A 68 in 1990. Medium-range reconnaissance and coastal surveillance duties in EEZ. Sensors: Bendix RDS 32 surface search radar. Omega Global GNS-500. Weapons: ASW; can carry torpedoes, depth bombs or mines. ASV; 2 × rockets or machine gun pods not normally fitted.

VERIFIED   DAUPHIN 2

10/1996*, Prefectura Naval / 0012022

AUSTRALIA

Headquarters Appointments

Chief of Navy:
 Vice Admiral D J Shackleton
Deputy Chief of Navy:
 Rear Admiral G F Smith, AM
Head of Capability Systems:
 Rear Admiral C A Ritchie, AM
Head of Systems Acquisition:
 Rear Admiral R Lamacrat

Senior Appointments

Maritime Commander, Australia:
 Rear Admiral J R Lord, AM
Support Commander Navy:
 Rear Admiral K J Scarce, CSC
Director General Coastwatch
 Rear Admiral R E Shalders, CSC
Commodore Flotillas:
 Commodore J Shackleton

Diplomatic Representation

Naval Attaché in Jakarta:
 Captain D J Ramsay
Naval Adviser in London:
 Captain R Longbottom
Defence Attaché in Washington:
 Commodore J H McCaffrie, AM, CSM
Defence Attaché in Seoul:
 Captain J S Moore, AM
Defence Adviser in Singapore:
 Captain G D Kennedy
Defence Attaché in Bonn:
 Captain MacKinnell, CSC
Defence Attaché in Southern Europe:
 Captain K B Taylor, CSC

Personnel

(a) 2000: 13,900 officers and ratings
(b) 6,300 reserves

RAN Reserve

The Naval Reserve is integrated into the Permanent Force. Personnel are either Active Reservists with regular commitments or Inactive Reservists with periodic or contingent duty. The missions undertaken by the Reserve include Naval Control of Shipping, Aviation, MCM, Intelligence, Diving and patrol boat/landing craft operations. In addition, members of the Ready Reserve (a component of the Active Reserve) are shadow posted to selected major fleet units.

Shore Establishments

Sydney: Maritime Headquarters, Fleet Base East (Garden Island), *Waterhen* (Mine Warfare), *Watson* (Warfare Training), *Penguin* (Diving, Hospital, Staff College), *Kuttabul* (Administration).
Jervis Bay Area: *Albatross* (Air Station), *Creswell* (Naval College and Fleet Support), Jervis Bay Range Facility.
Cockburn Sound (WA): Fleet Base West, *Stirling* (Administration and Maintenance Support, Submarines).
Darwin: Minor warship base, *Coonawarra* (Communications Station).
Cairns: Headquarters Patrol Boat Force, *Cairns* (Minor warship base).
Canberra: Navy Headquarters, *Harman* (Communications Station).
Westernport: *Cerberus* (Major training facility).
North West Cape: Harold E Holt Communications Station.

Fleet Deployment

Fleet Base East (and other Sydney bases): 1 DDG, 3 FFG, 1 AOR, 2 LPA, 1 LSH, 1 ASR, 2 MHI, 3 MSA, 2 LCH, 2 PTF.
Fleet Base West: 4 SS, 3 FFG, 1 AO, 2 PTF.
Darwin Naval Base: 6 PTF, 1 LCH.
Cairns: 5 PTF, 2 LCH, 4 AGS.

Fleet Air Arm (see *Shipborne Aircraft* section).

Squadron	Aircraft
HC-723	Squirrel AS 350B, Utility, FFG embarked flights, SAR HS 748, Fixed-wing, EW operations and training Bell 206B, survey support
HS-817	Sea King Mk 50, Utility
HS-816	Seahawk S-70B-2, ASW, ASST

Prefix to Ships' Names

HMAS.   Her Majesty's Australian Ship

Mercantile Marine

Lloyd's Register of Shipping
 621 vessels of 2,084,180 tons gross

Strength of the Fleet

Type	Active	Building (Projected)
Patrol Submarines	4	2
Destroyers	1	(4)
Frigates (FFG)	6	—
Frigates (FF)	3	5
Minehunters (Coastal)	3	3
Minehunters (Inshore)	2	—
Minesweepers (Auxiliary)	3	—
Large Patrol Craft	15	—
Amphibious Heavy Lift Ship	1	—
Amphibious Transports	3	—
Landing Craft	9 (1)	—
Survey Ships	6	—
Replenishment Ships	2	—
Training Ships	1	—

DELETIONS

Submarines

1999   *Onslow, Otama* (reserve)

Destroyers

1999   *Perth*
2000   *Hobart*

Frigates

1998   *Torrens*

Patrol Forces

1999   *Ardent* (museum)

Mine Warfare Forces

2000   *Koraaga, Bermagui*

Auxiliaries

1997   *Moresby*
1998   *Protector* (civilian), *Flinders*

PENNANT LIST

Submarines	
73	Collins
74	Farncomb
75	Waller
76	Dechaineux
77	Sheean
78	Rankin

Destroyers	
41	Brisbane

Frigates	
01	Adelaide
02	Canberra
03	Sydney
04	Darwin
05	Melbourne
06	Newcastle
150	Anzac
151	Arunta
152	Warramunga
153	Stuart
154	Parramatta (bldg)
155	Ballarat (bldg)
156	Toowoomba (bldg)
157	Perth (bldg)

Mine Warfare Forces	
M 80	Rushcutter
M 81	Shoalwater
M 82	Huon
M 83	Hawkesbury
M 84	Norman
M 85	Gascoyne (bldg)
M 86	Diamantina (bldg)
M 87	Yarra (bldg)
Y 298	Bandicoot
Y 299	Wallaroo
1102	Brolga

Patrol Forces	
203	Fremantle
204	Warrnambool
205	Townsville
206	Wollongong
207	Launceston
208	Whyalla
209	Ipswich
210	Cessnock
211	Bendigo
212	Gawler
213	Geraldton
214	Dubbo
215	Geelong
216	Gladstone
217	Bunbury

Amphibious Forces	
45	Jervis Bay
L 50	Tobruk
L 51	Kanimbla
L 52	Manoora
L 126	Balikpapan
L 127	Brunei
L 128	Labuan
L 129	Tarakan
L 130	Wewak
L 133	Betano

Survey Ships	
A 01	Paluma
A 02	Mermaid
A 03	Shepparton
A 04	Benalla
A 245	Leeuwin
A 246	Melville

Auxiliaries	
O 195	Westralia
OR 304	Success

SUBMARINES

Notes: (1) Stirling 4V-275R (75 kW) engines supplied for AIP trials ashore.
(2) *Remora* is a commercially operated DSRV completed in December 1995 and capable of diving to 547 m *(1,800 ft)* and taking off nine survivors.

4 + 2 COLLINS CLASS (SSK)

Name	No	Builders	Laid down		Launched		Commissioned	
COLLINS	73	Australian Submarine Corp, Adelaide	14 Feb	1990	28 Aug	1993	27 July	1996
FARNCOMB	74	Australian Submarine Corp, Adelaide	1 Mar	1991	15 Dec	1995	31 Jan	1998
WALLER	75	Australian Submarine Corp, Adelaide	19 Mar	1992	14 Mar	1997	10 July	1999
DECHAINEUX	76	Australian Submarine Corp, Adelaide	4 Mar	1993	12 Mar	1998	June	2000
SHEEAN	77	Australian Submarine Corp, Adelaide	17 Feb	1994	3 May	1999	Oct	2000
RANKIN	78	Australian Submarine Corp, Adelaide	12 May	1995	May	2000	June	2001

Displacement, tons: 3,051 surfaced; 3,353 dived
Dimensions, feet (metres): 255.2 × 25.6 × 23
(77.8 × 7.8 × 7)
Main machinery: Diesel-electric; 3 Hedemora/Garden Island Type V18B/14 diesels; 6,020 hp *(4.42 MW)*; 3 Jeumont Schneider generators; 4.2 MW; 1 Jeumont Schneider motor; 7,344 hp(m) *(5.4 MW)*; 1 shaft; 1 MacTaggart Scott DM 43006 hydraulic motor for emergency propulsion
Speed, knots: 10 surfaced; 10 snorting; 20 dived
Range, miles: 9,000 at 10 kt (snort); 11,500 at 10 kt (surfaced) 400 at 4 kt (dived)
Complement: 42 (6 officers)

Missiles: SSM: McDonnell Douglas Sub Harpoon; active radar homing to 130 km *(70 n miles)* at 0.9 Mach; warhead 227 kg.
Torpedoes: 6—21 in *(533 mm)* fwd tubes. Gould Mk 48 Mod 4; dual purpose; wire-guided; active/passive homing to 38 km *(21 n miles)* at 55 kt or 50 km *(27 n miles)* at 40 kt; warhead 267 kg. Air turbine pump discharge. Total of 22 weapons including Mk 48 and Sub Harpoon.
Mines: 44 in lieu of torpedoes.
Countermeasures: Decoys: 2 SSE.
ESM: Argo AR 740; radar warning.
Weapons control: Boeing/Rockwell integrated system. Link 11.
Radars: Navigation: Kelvin Hughes Type 1007; I-band.

Sonars: Thomson Sintra Scylla active/passive bow array and passive flank, intercept and ranging arrays.
GEC-Marconi Kariwara (first pair) or Thomson Marconi Narama or Allied Signal TB 23; retractable passive towed array.

Programmes: Contract signed on 3 June 1987 for construction of six Swedish-designed Kockums Type 471. Fabrication work started in June 1989; bow and midships (escape tower) sections of the first submarines built in Sweden.
Structure: Stirling air independent propulsion (AIP) has been tested on a shore rig. Scylla is an updated Eledone sonar suite. Diving depth, 300 m *(984 ft)*. Anechoic tiles are fitted during build to all but *Collins* which is retrofitted. Pilkington Optronics CK 43 search and CH 93 attack periscopes fitted. Plans for an external mine belt have been abandoned.
Operational: All to be based at Fleet Base West with one or two deploying regularly to the east coast. Full operational service delayed to mid-2000 because of setting to work command data systems software and other first of class problems. These include speed related radiated noise levels which are to be corrected by a redesign of the casing and a new bow fairing.
UPDATED

WALLER
5/1999*, P Lewis, RAN
0056496

WALLER
7/1998, S Farrow, RAN / 0038005

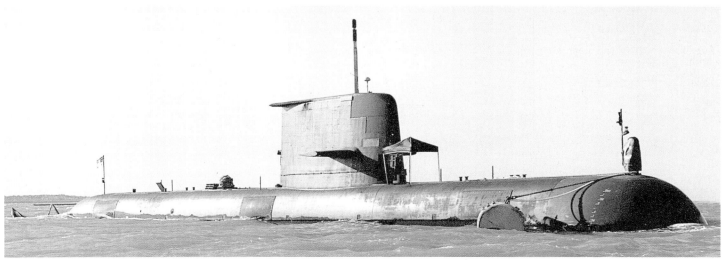

FARNCOMB
8/1998*, John Mortimer / 0081447

DESTROYERS

Note: The acquisition of four ex-US 'Kidd' class DDGs has been investigated.

1 PERTH (MODIFIED CHARLES F ADAMS) CLASS (DDG)

Name	No	Builders	Laid down	Launched	Commissioned
BRISBANE	41	Defoe Shipbuilding Co, Bay City, Michigan	15 Feb 1965	5 May 1966	16 Dec 1967

Displacement, tons: 3,370 standard; 4,618 full load
Dimensions, feet (metres): 440.8 × 47.1 × 20.1
  (134.3 × 14.3 × 6.1)
Main machinery: 4 Foster-Wheeler boilers; 1,200 psi *(84.37 kg/cm²)*, 950°F *(510°C)*; 2 GE turbines; 70,000 hp *(52 MW)*; 2 shafts
Speed, knots: 30+. **Range, miles:** 6,000 at 15 kt; 2,000 at 30 kt
Complement: 310 (25 officers)

Missiles: SSM: McDonnell Douglas Harpoon (fitted for but not with).
  SAM: 40 GDC Pomona Standard SM-1MR; Mk 13 Mod 6 launcher ❶; command guidance; semi-active radar homing to 46 km *(25 n miles)* at 2 Mach; height 45.7-18,288 m *(150-60,000 ft)*. Dual capability launcher for SSM.
Guns: 2 FMC 5 in *(127 mm)*/54 Mk 42 Mod 10 automatic ❷; 40 rds/min to 24 km *(13 n miles)* anti-surface; 14 km *(8 n miles)* anti-aircraft; weight of shell 32 kg.
  2 GE/GDC 20 mm Mk 15 Vulcan Phalanx ❸; 6 barrels per mounting; 3,000 rds/min combined to 1.5 km. Can be carried.
  Up to 6—12.7 mm MGs.
Torpedoes: 6—324 mm Mk 32 Mod 5 (2 triple) tubes ❹. Honeywell Mk 46 Mod 5; anti-submarine; active/passive homing to 11 km *(5.9 n miles)* at 40 kt; warhead 44 kg.
Countermeasures: Decoys: 2 Loral Hycor SRBOC 6-barrelled fixed Mk 36; chaff and IR flares to 1-4 km *(0.6-2.2 n miles)*. Nulka quad expendable decoy launcher.
  SLQ-25; towed torpedo decoy.
ESM/ECM: WLR-1H; intercept. ULQ-6; jammer.
Combat data systems: NCDS with NTDS consoles and Univac UYK-7 computers; Link 11. OE-2 SATCOM ❺.
Weapons control: GFCS Mk 68. Missile control Mk 74 Mod 13. Electro-optic sights may be fitted.
Radars: Air search: Hughes SPS-52C ❻; E/F-band.
  Lockheed SPS-40C ❼; E/F-band.
Surface search: Norden SPS-67V ❽; G-band.
Fire control: Two Raytheon SPG-51C ❾; G/I-band (for Standard).
  Western Electric SPG-53F ❿; I/J-band (for guns).
IFF: AIMS Mk 12.
Tacan: URN 25.
Sonars: Sangamo SQS-23KL; hull-mounted; active; medium frequency; with limited bottom bounce capability.

Modernisation: Major equipment upgraded: search and fire-control radars, naval combat data system, gun systems, the Mk 13 missile launcher (to take Harpoon). Missile modernisation included decoy and improved ECM equipment; three-dimensional radar SPS-52B upgraded to SPS-52C. In 1990 fitted for Phalanx CIWS. To accommodate Phalanx the ship's boat was replaced by a RIB. Ikara launcher and magazine removed. Nulka standoff decoys may be carried.
Operational: Operational deployments include communications enhancements and portable RAM panels. Complement numbers have been reduced as a result of the withdrawal of Ikara. Expected to pay off in 2001.

UPDATED

BRISBANE (Gulf fit)   *(Scale 1 : 1,200), Ian Sturton /* 0056499

BRISBANE   *8/1999*, John Mortimer /* 0056497

BRISBANE   *8/1999*, John Mortimer /* 0056498

FRIGATES

3 + 5 ANZAC (MEKO 200) CLASS (FF)

Name	No	Builders	Laid down		Launched		Commissioned	
ANZAC	150	Transfield, Williamstown	5 Nov	1993	16 Sep	1994	13 May	1996
ARUNTA (ex-Arrernte)	151	Transfield, Williamstown	22 July	1995	28 June	1996	12 Dec	1998
WARRAMUNGA (ex-Warumungu)	152	Transfield, Williamstown	26 July	1997	23 May	1998	Feb	2001
STUART	153	Tenix Defence Systems, Williamstown	23 July	1998	17 Apr	1999	Dec	2001
PARRAMATTA	154	Tenix Defence Systems, Williamstown	24 Apr	1999	June	2000	Sep	2002
BALLARAT	155	Tenix Defence Systems, Williamstown	May	2000	Feb	2001	June	2003
TOOWOOMBA	156	Tenix Defence Systems, Williamstown	Mar	2001	Feb	2002	May	2004
PERTH	157	Tenix Defence Systems, Williamstown	Feb	2002	Dec	2002	Apr	2005

Displacement, tons: 3,600 full load
Dimensions, feet (metres): 387.1 oa; 357.6 wl × 48.6 × 14.3
(118; 109 × 14.8 × 4.35)
Main machinery: CODOG: 1 GE LM 2500 gas turbine; 30,172 hp
(22.5 MW) sustained; 2 MTU 12V 1163 TB83 diesels;
8,840 hp(m) *(6.5 MW)* sustained; 2 shafts; cp props
Speed, knots: 27. **Range, miles:** 6,000 at 18 kt
Complement: 163 (22 officers)

Missiles: SSM: 8 McDonnell Douglas Harpoon to be fitted.
SAM: Raytheon Sea Sparrow RIM-7NP; Lockheed Martin Mk 41
Mod 5 octuple vertical launcher ❶; semi-active radar homing
to 14.6 km *(8 n miles)* at 2.5 Mach; warhead 39 kg. 8 missiles
total. Quadpack Evolved Sea Sparrow for 32 missiles in 153
onwards.
Guns: 1 United Defense 5 in (127 mm)/54/62 Mk 45 Mod 2/4
❷; 20 rds/min to 23 km *(12.6 n miles)* or 115 km *(62 n miles)*
(Mod 4); weight of shell 32 kg. 2—12.7 mm MGs.
Torpedoes: 6—324 mm (2 triple) Mk 32 Mod 5 tubes ❸ fitted
after ship acceptance into the Navy. Mk 46 Mod 5; anti-
submarine; active/passive homing to 11 km *(5.9 n miles)* at
40 kt; warhead 44 kg.
Countermeasures: Decoys: G & D Aircraft SRBOC Mk 36 Mod 1
decoy launchers ❹ for SRBOC/NATO Sea Gnat. 4 BAe Nulka
quad expendable decoy launchers.
FEL SLQ-25A towed torpedo decoy.
ESM: Racal Thorn modified Sceptre A; radar intercept.
Telefunken PST-1720 Telegon 10.
ECM: Jammer (to be fitted).
Combat data systems: CelsiusTech 9LV 453 Mk 3. Link 11.
Weapons control: CelsiusTech 9LV 453 optronic director with
Raytheon CW Mk 73 Mod 1 (for SAM).
Radars: Air search: Raytheon SPS-49(V)8 ANZ ❺; C/D-band.
Air/surface search: CelsiusTech 9LV 453 TIR (Ericsson Tx/Rx) ❻;
G-band.
Navigation: Atlas Elektronik 9600 ARPA; I-band.
Fire control: CelsiusTech 9LV 453 ❼; J-band.
IFF: Cossor AIMS Mk XII.
Sonars: Thomson Sintra Spherion B Mod 5; hull-mounted; active
search and attack; medium frequency. Provision for Kariwara
towed array; passive search; very low frequency (may be
fitted). Mine avoidance sonar may be fitted first in 152.

Helicopters: 1 S-70B-2 Seahawk ❽ or SH-2G Seasprite.

Programmes: Contract signed with Australian Marine
Engineering Consolidated on 10 November 1989 to build eight
Blohm + Voss designed MEKO 200 ANZ frigates for Australia
and two for New Zealand, which has an option for two more.
First ship started construction 27 March 1992. Modules are
being constructed at Newcastle and Whangarei and shipped
to Williamstown for assembly. The second and fourth ships of
the class have been delivered to New Zealand.
Modernisation: Underwater and surface warfare capability
enhancements are being included under Phase 3 of the
ANZAC Ship Project and include fitting of Harpoon surface-to-
surface missiles, introduction of a mine avoidance sonar
system, full integration of the ship launched torpedo tubes into

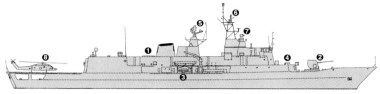

ANZAC   *(Scale 1 : 1,200), Ian Sturton / 0056501*

ARUNTA   *4/1999 *, Sattler/Steele / 0056500*

the combat system and a torpedo self-defence system. Air
warfare enhancements are being undertaken under a
Warfighting Improvement Program which has been scaled
back to include only anti-ship missile defences. Plans to include
area air defence were shelved in late 1999. It is currently
planned to incorporate the Evolved Seasparrow Missile from
Stuart during production and to backfit the first three ships.
Another development under the Evolved Seasparrow Missile
Project is a "Quadpack" capability which will allow each cell of
the eight cell Vertical Launching System to be capable of
storing and firing four missiles, rather than the current single
missile capability. Other possible upgrades in the longer term

are the Mk 45 gun to Mod 4 status to allow firing of guided
munitions, and incorporation of MILSATCOM.
Structure: 'Space and weight' reserved for a CIWS, Harpoon
SSM, an additional octuple VLS, second channel of fire for VLS,
towed array sonar, offboard active ECM, extended ESM
frequency coverage, Helo datalink and SATCOM. Stealth
features are incorporated in the design. All-steel construction.
Fin stabilisers. Torpedo tubes are being taken from older
classes and fitted after ship acceptance from the builders. Indal
RAST helicopter recovery system. Sperry Mk 49 SINS.
Operational: The helicopter is to be ASM missile fitted in due
course. Two RHIBs are carried.   ***UPDATED***

ANZAC   *2/1999 *, Sattler/Steele / 0056502*

6 ADELAIDE (OLIVER HAZARD PERRY) CLASS (FFG)

Name	No	Builders	Laid down	Launched	Commissioned
ADELAIDE	01	Todd Pacific Shipyard Corporation, Seattle, USA	29 July 1977	21 June 1978	15 Nov 1980
CANBERRA	02	Todd Pacific Shipyard Corporation, Seattle, USA	1 Mar 1978	1 Dec 1978	21 Mar 1981
SYDNEY	03	Todd Pacific Shipyard Corporation, Seattle, USA	16 Jan 1980	26 Sep 1980	29 Jan 1983
DARWIN	04	Todd Pacific Shipyard Corporation, Seattle, USA	3 July 1981	26 Mar 1982	21 July 1984
MELBOURNE	05	Australian Marine Eng (Consolidated), Williamstown	12 July 1985	5 May 1989	15 Feb 1992
NEWCASTLE	06	Australian Marine Eng (Consolidated), Williamstown	21 July 1989	21 Feb 1992	11 Dec 1993

Displacement, tons: 4,100 full load
Dimensions, feet (metres): 453 × 45 × 24.5 (sonar); 14.8 (keel) *(138.1 × 13.7 × 7.5; 4.5)*
Main machinery: 2 GE LM 2500 gas turbines; 41,000 hp *(30.6 MW)* sustained; 1 shaft; cp prop; 2 auxiliary electric retractable propulsors fwd; 650 hp *(490 kW)*
Speed, knots: 29 (4 on propulsors). **Range, miles:** 4,500 at 20 kt
Complement: 184 (15 officers) plus aircrew

Missiles: SSM: 8 McDonnell Douglas Harpoon; active radar homing to 130 km *(70 n miles)* at 0.9 Mach; warhead 227 kg.
SAM: GDC Pomona Standard SM-1MR; Mk 13 Mod 4 launcher for both SAM and SSM systems **❶**; command guidance; semi-active radar homing to 46 km *(25 n miles)* at 2 Mach; height 45.7-18,288 m *(150-60,000 ft)*; 40 missiles (combined SSM and SAM). 2 Mk 41 quad pack VLS for ESSM from 2003.
Guns: 1 OTO Melara 3 in *(76 mm)*/62 US Mk 75 compact **❷**; 85 rds/min to 16 km *(9 n miles)* anti-surface; 12 km *(6.5 n miles)* anti-aircraft; weight of shell 6 kg. Guns for 05 and 06 manufactured in Australia.
1 General Electric/GDC 20 mm Mk 15 Vulcan Phalanx **❸**; anti-missile system with 6 barrels; 4,500 rds/min combined to 1.5 km.
Up to 6—12.7 mm MGs.
Torpedoes: 6—324 mm Mk 32 (2 triple) tubes **❹**. Honeywell Mk 46 Mod 5; anti-submarine; active/passive homing to 11 km *(5.9 n miles)* at 40 kt; warhead 44 kg. Some Mk 44 torpedoes are still in service.
Countermeasures: Decoys: 2 Loral Hycor SRBOC Mk 36 chaff and IR decoy launchers; fixed 6-barrelled system; range 1-4 km. 4 BAe Nulka quad expendable decoy launchers being fitted.
SLQ-25; towed torpedo decoy or TMS Sea Defender torpedo countermeasures (from 2003).
ESM/ECM: Raytheon SLQ-32C **❺**; intercept and jammer. Elbit EA-2118 jammer.
Combat data systems: NCDS using NTDS consoles and UYK 7 and/or UYK 43 computers. OE-2 SATCOM; Link 11. Link 16 (from 2003).
Weapons control: Sperry Mk 92 Mod 2 (Mod 12 from 2003) gun and missile control (Signaal derivative). Radamec 2500 optronic director with TV, laser and IR imager fitted from 1999.
Radars: Air search: Raytheon SPS-49 **❻**; C-band.
Surface search/navigation: ISC Cardion SPS-55 **❼**; I-band.
Fire control: Lockheed SPG-60 **❽**; I/J-band; range 110 km *(60 n miles)*; Doppler search and tracking.
Sperry Mk 92 **❾**; I/J-band.
IFF: AIMS Mk XII.
Tacan: URN 25.
Sonars: Raytheon SQS-56 or EMI/Honeywell Mulloka (05 and 06); hull-mounted; active; medium frequency. To be replaced by Thomson Marconi TMS 4131 with Petrel mine avoidance from 2003.
Towed active/passive array from 2001.

Helicopters: 2 Sikorsky S-70B-2 Seahawks **❿** or 1 Seahawk and 1 Squirrel.

Programmes: US numbers: *Adelaide* FFG 17; *Canberra* FFG 18; *Sydney* FFG 35; *Darwin* FFG 44.
Modernisation: *Adelaide* in November 1989, *Sydney* February 1989 and *Canberra* December 1991 completed a 12 month Helicopter Modification Programme to allow operation of Seahawk helicopters. The modification, fitted to *Darwin* during construction, involved angling the transom (increasing the ship's overall length by 8 ft) and fitting the RAST helo recovery system. *Melbourne* and *Newcastle* fitted during construction which also included longitudinal strengthening and buoyancy upgrades. Radamec 2500 optronic director being fitted. Contract signed 1 June 1999 with Transfield to upgrade Mk 92 weapons control system and SPS 49 radar; and to fit 8 cell

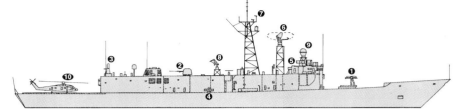

ADELAIDE *(Scale 1 : 1,200), Ian Sturton /* 0056503

ADELAIDE *1/1999*, S Connolly, RAN /* 0056504

quad pack VLS for ESSM, Link 16 and improved EW and torpedo countermeasures. Work on *Adelaide* starts in 2002.
Operational: *Adelaide, Darwin* and *Canberra* based at Fleet Base West. The remainder are based at Fleet Base East. For operational tasks ships are fitted with enhanced communications, electro-optical sights, rigid inflatable boats and portable RAM panels. All ships are fighter control capable.
UPDATED

DARWIN *8/1999*, John Mortimer /* 0056505

SHIPBORNE AIRCRAFT

Note: There are also five Bell 206B Kiowa utility helicopters in service.

KIOWA   10/1998*, Hachiro Nakai / 0056506

Numbers/Type: 11 Kaman Seasprite SH-2G(A).
Operational speed: 130 kt (241 km/h).
Service ceiling: 22,500 ft (6,860 m)
Range: 540 n miles (1,000 km).
Role/Weapon systems: Contract placed in June 1997 for eleven aircraft for Anzac frigates. To be delivered from 2001-2003. Sensors: Telephonics APS 143(V)3 radar; Raytheon AAQ-27 FLIR; AAR 54/AES 210/LWS 20 ESM; ALE 47 chaff and IR flares; Elisra APS 143B(V)3 ECM; Link 11. Weapons: ASW; 2 Mk 46 torpedoes. ASV: Penguin Mk 2 Mod 7; 1—7.62 mm MG.
UPDATED

SEASPRITE SH-2G(A)   1/2000*, Kaman / 0067399

Numbers/Type: 7 Westland Sea King HAS 50/50A.
Operational speed: 125 kt (230 km/h).
Service ceiling: 10,500 ft (3,200 m).
Range: 630 n miles (1,165 km).
Role/Weapon systems: Utility helicopter; embarked periodically for operations from Afloat Support Ships. Life extension to 2008 completed in November 1996 for six aircraft. One more acquired from UK in 1996 and upgraded to 50LEP standard. Sensors: MEL 5955 radar. Weapons: Disarmed in 1992 but still capable of torpedo weapon drops.
VERIFIED

SEA KING   4/1996, RAN / 0017555

Numbers/Type: 16 Sikorsky S-70B-2 Seahawk.
Operational speed: 135 kt (250 km/h).
Service ceiling: 12,000 ft (3,810 m).
Range: 600 n miles (1,110 km).
Role/Weapon systems: Seahawk SH-60F derivative aircraft designed by Sikorsky to meet RAN specifications for ASW and ASST operations. Eight assembled by ASTA in Victoria. Helicopters embarked in FFG-7 and used temporarily in ANZAC frigates. Upgrades from 2002 to include Raytheon AAQ 27 FLIR, Tracor ALE 47 countermeasures and Elisra AES 210 ESM. Sensors: MEL Surface surveillance radar, CDC Sonobuoy Processor and Barra Side Processor, and CAE Magnetic Anomaly Detector Set controlled by a versatile Tactical Display/Management System. Weapons: ASW; two Mk 46 Mod 5 torpedoes. ASV; two Mag 58 MGs, possibly ASM after 2003.
VERIFIED

SEAHAWK   10/1998, Hachiro Nakai / 0017554

Numbers/Type: 6 Aerospatiale AS 350B Squirrel.
Operational speed: 125 kt (232 km/h).
Service ceiling: 10,000 ft (3,050 m).
Range: 390 n miles (720 km).
Role/Weapon systems: Support helicopter for utility tasks and training duties. Regularly embarked at sea. Sensors: None. Weapons: ASV; two Mag 58 MGs.
VERIFIED

SQUIRREL   1996, RAN / 0012035

LAND-BASED MARITIME AIRCRAFT

Note: Six Britten Islanders, one Shrike Aero Commander, three Dash 8-200 and three Reims F406 used by Coastwatch for Customs duties.

Numbers/Type: 2 BAe HS 748.
Operational speed: 140 kt (259 km/h).
Service ceiling: 25,000 ft (7,620 m).
Range: 2,675 n miles (4,950 km).
Role/Weapon systems: EW training aircraft also used as VIP transports operated by Squadron RAN HC 723 specially equipped by Sanders Associates, USA. Sensors: Complete EW suite.
VERIFIED

Numbers/Type: 17/4/15 General Dynamics F-111C/RF-111C/F-111G.
Operational speed: 793 kt (1,469 km/h).
Service ceiling: 60,000 ft (18,290 m).
Range: 2,540 n miles (4,700 km).
Role/Weapon systems: Air Force operates the F-111 for anti-shipping strike and its small force of RF-111 for coastline surveillance duties using EW/ESM and photographic equipment underwing. Sensors: GE AN/APG-144, podded EW. Weapons: ASV; 4 × Harpoon missiles. Strike; 4 × Snakeye bombs. Self-defence; 2 × AIM-9P.
VERIFIED

Numbers/Type: 18 Lockheed P-3C/Update II Orion.
Operational speed: 410 kt (760 km/h).
Service ceiling: 28,300 ft (8,625 m).
Range: 4,000 n miles (7,410 km).
Role/Weapon systems: Operated by Air Force for long-range ocean surveillance and ASW. CSC UVS 503 acoustic processors, ASQ-212 data management and IAI ESM system. Three more aircraft (plus one for spare parts) without armament or sensors acquired for training. Sensors: Elta EL/M-2022A(V)3 radar, AQS-901 processor, AQS-81 MAD, ECM, Elta/IAI, ALR 2001 ESM, 80 × BARRA sonobuoys. Weapons: ASW; 8 × Mk 46 (Mod 5 after upgrade) torpedoes, Mk 25 mines, 8 × Mk 54 depth bombs. ASV; up to 6 AGM-84A/C Harpoon.
UPDATED

Numbers/Type: 68 McDonnell Douglas F/A-18 Hornet.
Operational speed: 1,032 kt (1,910 km/h).
Service ceiling: 50,000 ft (15,240 m).
Range: 1,000 n miles (1,829 km).
Role/Weapon systems: Air defence and strike aircraft operated by Air Force but with fleet defence and anti-shipping secondary roles. Sensors: APG-65 attack radar, AAS-38 FLIR/ALR-67 radar warning receiver. Weapons: ASV; 4 × Harpoon missiles. Strike; 1 × 20 mm cannon, up to 7.7 tons of 'iron' bombs. Fleet defence; 4 × AIM-7 Sparrow and 4 × AIM-9L Sidewinder.
UPDATED

AMPHIBIOUS FORCES

Note: See Army section for details of LCM 8s.

2 NEWPORT CLASS (LPA/LST)

Name	No	Builders	Laid down	Launched	Commissioned	Recommissioned
KANIMBLA (ex-Saginaw)	L 51 (ex-1188)	National Steel & Shipbuilding	24 May 1969	7 Feb 1970	23 Jan 1971	29 Aug 1994
MANOORA (ex-Fairfax County)	L 52 (ex-1193)	National Steel & Shipbuilding	28 Mar 1970	19 Dec 1970	16 Oct 1971	25 Nov 1994

Displacement, tons: 4,975 light; 8,450 full load
Dimensions, feet (metres): 552 × 69.5 × 17.5 (aft)
(168.2 × 21.2 × 5.3)
Main machinery: 6 ALCO 16-251 diesels; 16,500 hp *(12.3 MW)*
sustained; 2 shafts; cp props; bow thruster
Speed, knots: 20. **Range, miles:** 14,000 at 15 kt
Complement: 180 (12 officers) plus 18 Army
Military lift: 450 troops (25 officers); 2 LCM 8; 250 tons aviation
fuel

Guns: 1 General Electric/General Dynamics 20 mm Vulcan
Phalanx Mk 15 can be fitted. 2—12.7 mm MGs.
Countermeasures: 2 SRBOC Mk 36 chaff and IR launchers.
Radars: Surface search: Kelvin Hughes 1007; F/G-band.
Navigation: Kelvin Hughes; I-band.

Helicopters: 4 Army Black Hawks or 3 Sea Kings or 1 Chinook.

MANOORA   *12/1999*, Sattler/Steele /* 0081448

Programmes: Acquired by sale from USA on 25 August and
27 September 1994.
Modernisation: Both ships modified by fitting a hangar to take
four Black Hawk helicopters, to incorporate a third landing spot
forward, to increase aviation fuel capacity and to dispense with
the bow landing ramp. The after flight deck is Chinook capable.

A stern gate to the tank deck is retained. Two Army LCMs are
carried on the deck forward of the bridge and handled by a
70 ton crane. Both ships have enhanced command and control
facilities. A classroom and improved medical facilities are
installed. Contract placed with Forgacs Shipbuilding,
Newcastle in May 1996.

Operational: Operational range is increased. Complement
reduced from the 250 in US service. The ships can carry a
small battalion with armoured vehicles and artillery. *Manoora*
started sea trials 10 December 1999 and moved to Fleet Base
East. Both ships should be in service by end 2000.

UPDATED

MANOORA   *12/1999*, Sattler/Steele /* 0081449

1 HEAVY LIFT SHIP (LSL)

Name	No	Builders	Laid down	Launched	Commissioned
TOBRUK	L 50	Carrington Slipways Pty Ltd	7 Feb 1978	1 Mar 1980	23 Apr 1981

Displacement, tons: 3,300 standard; 5,700 full load
Dimensions, feet (metres): 417 × 60 × 16
(127 × 18.3 × 4.9)
Main machinery: 2 Mirrlees Blackstone KDMR8 diesels;
9,600 hp *(7.2 MW)*; 2 shafts
Speed, knots: 18. **Range, miles:** 8,000 at 15 kt
Complement: 144 (13 officers)
Military lift: 350-500 troops; 1,300 tons cargo; 70 tons capacity
derrick; 2—4.25 ton cranes; 2 LCVP; 2 LCM

Guns: 2 Bofors 40 mm/60. 2—12.7 mm MGs.
Radars: Surface search: Kelvin Hughes Type 1006; I-band.
Navigation: Kelvin Hughes 1007; I-band.

Helicopters: Platform only for up to 4 Sea Kings.

Structure: The design is an update of the British 'Sir Bedivere'
class and provides facilities for the operation of helicopters,
landing craft, amphibians or side-carried pontoons for ship-to-
shore movement. A special feature is the ship's heavy lift

derrick system for handling heavy loads. Able to embark a
squadron of Leopard tanks plus a number of wheeled vehicles
and artillery in addition to its troop lift. Bow and stern ramps are
fitted. Carries two 20 kt LCVPs at davits. Fitted for side-carrying
two NLE pontoons. Two LCM 8 carried on deck. Helicopters
can be operated from the well-deck or the after platform.
Operational: A comprehensive communication fit and minor
hospital facilities are provided. Can operate all in-service
helicopters. Based at Sydney.

UPDATED

TOBRUK   *10/1999*, John Mortimer /* 0056508

6 LANDING CRAFT (HEAVY) (LCH/LSM)

Name	No	Builders	Commissioned
BALIKPAPAN	L 126	Walkers Ltd, Queensland	8 Dec 1971
BRUNEI	L 127	Walkers Ltd, Queensland	5 Jan 1973
LABUAN	L 128	Walkers Ltd, Queensland	9 Mar 1973
TARAKAN	L 129	Walkers Ltd, Queensland	15 June 1973
WEWAK	L 130	Walkers Ltd, Queensland	10 Aug 1973
BETANO	L 133	Walkers Ltd, Queensland	8 Feb 1974

Displacement, tons: 310 light; 503 full load
Dimensions, feet (metres): 146 × 33 × 6.5 *(44.5 × 10.1 × 2)*
Main machinery: 2 GM 6-71 diesels; 348 hp *(260 kW)* sustained; 2 shafts
Speed, knots: 10. **Range, miles:** 3,000 at 10 kt
Complement: 13 (2 officers)
Military lift: 3 medium tanks or equivalent
Guns: 2—7.62 mm MGs.
Radars: Navigation: Racal Decca Bridgemaster; I-band.

Comment: Originally this class was ordered for the Army but only *Balikpapan* saw Army service until being commissioned into the Navy on 27 September 1974. The remainder were built for the Navy. *Brunei* and *Betano* act as diving tenders at Cairns. *Labuan* at Cairns and *Balikpapan* at Darwin are both operational. *Tarakan* operates from Cairns in a survey ship role and for general duties. All are available for amphibious duties. All are to be given a life extension refit, starting with *Wewak* in 2000, for retention to at least 2007. *Buna* and *Salamaua* transferred to Papua New Guinea Defence Force in November 1974.

UPDATED

BRUNEI *3/1996*, van Ginderen Collection / 0080559*

1 INCAT CLASS

Name	No	Builders	Commissioned
JERVIS BAY	45	Incat, Hobart	10 June 1999

Displacement, tons: 1,250 full load
Dimensions, feet (metres): 284.1 × — × 12.1 *(86.6 × — × 3.7)*
Main machinery: 4 Ruston 20RK270 diesels; 3,852 hp(m) *(2.83 MW)*; 4 acbLIPS 145/3 waterjets
Speed, knots: 43. **Range, miles:** 1,000 at 40 kt
Complement: 20
Military lift: 500 fully equipped troops plus vehicles or 380 tons

Comment: Leased for two years from Incat, Hobart. Based at Darwin with combined Navy/Army crews. Others of the class are in civilian service.

NEW ENTRY

JERVIS BAY *6/1999*, D Pawlenko, RAN / 0056510*

JERVIS BAY *7/1999*, Sattler/Steele / 0069034*

4 LANDING CRAFT (LIGHT) (LCVP)

T 4-T 7

Displacement, tons: 6.5 full load
Dimensions, feet (metres): 43.3 × 11.5 × 2.3 *(13.2 × 3.5 × 0.7)*
Main machinery: 2 Volvo Penta Sterndrives; 400 hp(m) *(294 kW)*
Speed, knots: 22; 15 (fully laden)
Complement: 3
Military lift: 4.5 tons cargo or 1 Land Rover or 36 troops

Comment: Prototype built by Geraldton, Western Australia. Trials conducted in late 1992. Three more delivered in July 1993. Two for *Tobruk*, one for *Success* (T 7) and one spare attached to *Penguin.*

UPDATED

LCVPs *2/1997*, Nikolaus Sifferlinger / 0012044*

PATROL FORCES

Note: A decision is expected in 2000 to build a new class of patrol vessels to replace the 'Fremantle' class.

15 FREMANTLE CLASS (LARGE PATROL CRAFT) (PC)

Name	No	Builders	Commissioned
FREMANTLE	203	Brooke Marine, Lowestoft	17 Mar 1980
WARRNAMBOOL	204	NQEA Australia, Cairns	14 Mar 1981
TOWNSVILLE	205	NQEA Australia, Cairns	18 July 1981
WOLLONGONG	206	NQEA Australia, Cairns	28 Nov 1981
LAUNCESTON	207	NQEA Australia, Cairns	1 Mar 1982
WHYALLA	208	NQEA Australia, Cairns	3 July 1982
IPSWICH	209	NQEA Australia, Cairns	13 Nov 1982
CESSNOCK	210	NQEA Australia, Cairns	5 Mar 1983
BENDIGO	211	NQEA Australia, Cairns	28 May 1983
GAWLER	212	NQEA Australia, Cairns	27 Aug 1983
GERALDTON	213	NQEA Australia, Cairns	10 Dec 1983
DUBBO	214	NQEA Australia, Cairns	10 Mar 1984
GEELONG	215	NQEA Australia, Cairns	2 June 1984
GLADSTONE	216	NQEA Australia, Cairns	8 Sep 1984
BUNBURY	217	NQEA Australia, Cairns	15 Dec 1984

Displacement, tons: 245 full load
Dimensions, feet (metres): 137.1 × 23.3 × 5.9 *(41.8 × 7.1 × 1.8)*
Main machinery: 2 MTU 16V 538 TB91 diesels; 6,140 hp(m) *(4.5 MW)* sustained; 2 shafts
Speed, knots: 30. **Range, miles:** 1,450 at 30 kt
Complement: 24 (4 officers)

Guns: 1 Bofors AN 4—40 mm/60; 120 rds/min to 10 km *(5.5 n miles)*. The 40 mm mountings were designed by Australian Government Ordnance Factory and although the guns are of older manufacture, this mounting gives greater accuracy particularly in heavy weather. 1—81 mm mortar. 3—12.7 mm MGs.
Countermeasures: ESM: AWA Defence Industries Type 133 PRISM.
Radars: Navigation: Kelvin Hughes Type 1006; I-band.

Programmes: The decision to buy these patrol craft was announced in September 1977. The design is by Brooke Marine, Lowestoft which built the lead ship.
Modernisation: Original 15 year life was extended to 19 years and is now extended again. ESM added in 1994-95. The cruise diesel on a centre line shaft has been deleted.
Operational: Bases: Cairns—P 205, 208, 209, 211, 216. Darwin—P 206, 207, 210, 212, 214, 215. Sydney—P 203, 204. Fremantle—P 213, 217.

UPDATED

GAWLER *8/1999*, John Mortimer / 0056511*

MINE WARFARE FORCES

Note: A new class of six minesweepers is planned. They are to use locally developed sweeps.

3 + 3 HUON (GAETA) CLASS (MINEHUNTERS COASTAL) (MHC)

Name	No	Builders	Launched		Commissioned	
HUON	82	Intermarine/ADI, Newcastle	25 July	1997	15 May	1999
HAWKESBURY	83	ADI, Newcastle	24 Apr	1998	12 Feb	2000
NORMAN	84	ADI, Newcastle	3 May	1999	Aug	2000
GASCOYNE	85	ADI, Newcastle	11 Mar	2000	Apr	2001
DIAMANTINA	86	ADI, Newcastle	Nov	2000	Feb	2002
YARRA	87	ADI, Newcastle	Sep	2001	Sep	2002

Displacement, tons: 720 full load
Dimensions, feet (metres): 172.2 × 32.5 × 9.8 *(52.5 × 9.9 × 3.0)*
Main machinery: 1 Fincantieri GMT diesel; 1,986 hp(m) *(1.46 MW)*; 1 shaft; acbLIPS cp prop; 3 Isotta Fraschini 1300 diesels; 1,440 hp(m) *(1,058 kW)*; 3 electrohydraulic motors; 506 hp(m) *(372 kW)*; Riva Calzoni retractable/rotatable APUs
Speed, knots: 14 diesel; 6 APUs. **Range, miles:** 1,600 at 12 kt
Complement: 38 (6 officers) plus 11 spare

Guns: 1 MSI DS 30B 30 mm/75. 650 rds/min to 10 km *(5.4 n miles)* anti-surface; 3 km *(1.6 n miles)* anti-aircraft; weight of shell 0.36 kg.
Countermeasures: MCM systems: 2 Bofors SUTEC Double-Eagle Mk 2 mine disposal vehicles with DAMDIC charges; ADI double Oropesa mechanical sweep and capable of towing the Australian developed Mini-Dyad influence sweep.
Decoys: 2 MEL Aviation Super Barricade; chaff launchers.
ESM: AWADI Prism.
Combat data systems: GEC-Marconi Nautis 2M with Link 11 receive only.
Weapons control: Radamec 1000N optronic surveillance system.
Radars: Navigation: Kelvin Hughes 1007; I-band.
Sonars: GEC-Marconi Type 2093; VDS; VLF-VHF multifunction with five arrays; mine search and classification.

Programmes: The Force Structure Review of May 1991 recommended the acquisition of coastal minehunters of proven design. These ships would be required to operate in deeper and more exposed waters, to achieve lower transit times and remain on station longer than the two inshore minehunters currently in service. A contract was signed with Australian Defence Industries (ADI) on 12 August 1994 to build six Intermarine designed 'Gaeta' class derivatives. The hull of the first ship was constructed at Intermarine's Sarzana Shipyard in Italy and arrived in Australia as deck cargo on 31 August 1995 for fitting out in Newcastle, where the remaining five ships are being built at ADI's Throsby Basin. Local content for this project is about 69 per cent.
Structure: Monocoque GRP construction. A recompression chamber, one RIB and an inflatable diving boat are carried to support a six-man diving team.
Operational: This class which is named after Australian rivers, is based at HMAS *Waterhen* in Sydney.

UPDATED

HAWKESBURY   *8/1999*, Sattler/Steele /* 0056512

2 MINESWEEPERS AUXILIARY (TUGS) (MSA(T))

BANDICOOT (ex-*Grenville VII*) Y 298   WALLAROO (ex-*Grenville V*) Y 299

Displacement, tons: 412 full load
Dimensions, feet (metres): 95.8 × 28 × 11.3 *(29.6 × 8.5 × 3.4)*
Main machinery: 2 Stork Werkspoor diesels; 2,400 hp(m) *(1.76 MW)*; 2 shafts
Speed, knots: 11. **Range, miles:** 6,300 at 10 kt
Complement: 10
Radars: Navigation: Furuno 7040D; I-band.

Comment: Built in Singapore 1982 and operated by Maritime (PTE) Ltd. Purchased by the RAN and refurbished prior to delivery 11 August 1990. Used for minesweeping trials towing large AMASS influence and mechanical sweeps. No side scan sonar. Also used as berthing tugs. Bollard pull, 30 tons.

UPDATED

BANDICOOT   *10/1999*, John Mortimer /* 0056513

2 BAY CLASS (MINEHUNTERS—INSHORE) (MHI)

Name	No	Builders	Launched		Commissioned	
RUSHCUTTER	M 80	Carrington Slipways	3 May	1986	1 Nov	1986
SHOALWATER	M 81	Carrington Slipways	20 June	1987	10 Oct	1987

Displacement, tons: 178 full load
Dimensions, feet (metres): 101.7 × 29.5 × 6.6 *(30.9 × 9 × 2)*
Main machinery: 2 Poyaud 520-V8-S2 diesel generators; 650 hp(m) *(478 kW)*; 2 Schottel hydraulic transmission and steering systems (one to each hull)
Speed, knots: 10. **Range, miles:** 1,500 at 10 kt
Complement: 13 (3 officers)

Guns: 2—12.7 mm MGs can be carried.
Countermeasures: MCM: STN Atlas Elektronic MWS80-5 minehunting system (containerised variant of MWS80-4 fitted to German *Frankenthal*); ECA 38 mine disposal system with two PAP 104 Mk 3 vehicles; Syledis and GPS precision navigation systems.
Radars: Navigation: Kelvin Hughes Type 1006; I-band.
Sonars: Atlas Elektronik DSQS-11M; hull-mounted; minehunting; high frequency.

Programmes: Ordered January 1983. Both ships finally accepted into full service in June 1994 after extensive evaluation.
Structure: The catamaran hull form was chosen as it provides stability, a large deck area, greater manoeuvrability than a monohull and reduction in signatures by placing heavy machinery high in the ship. Each hull is 3 m beam with 3 m space between. GRP sandwich construction was adopted and a policy of repair by replacement. *Shoalwater* fitted with two funnels in 1992 to assess impact on noise reduction; *Rushcutter* similarly modified in 1993.
Operational: Due to performance deficiencies of the original variant of MWS 80 minehunting weapon system, comparative trials were conducted in 1992 between the Atlas MWS 80-5 and the Thomson Sintra Ibis V Mk 2 systems. The Atlas system was selected. The two ships are based in Sydney and used to cover the whole eastern seaboard with forward support. The DSQS-11M sonar operates on three frequencies (40, 100 and 200 kHz). These ships are uncomfortable seaboats.

UPDATED

SHOALWATER   *2/1999*, van Ginderen Collection /* 0056514

1 MINESWEEPER AUXILIARY (SMALL) (MSA(S))

BROLGA (ex-*Lumen*) 1102

Displacement, tons: 268 full load
Dimensions, feet (metres): 93.2 × 26.6 × 11.5 *(28.4 × 8.1 × 3.5)*
Main machinery: 1 Mirrlees Blackstone diesel; 540 hp *(403 kW)*; 1 shaft; cp prop
Speed, knots: 10
Complement: 8 (1 officer)
Radars: Navigation: I-band.

Comment: Launched in 1975. Acquired from the Department of Transport on 10 February 1988 for the COOP programme. The COOP tow a magnetic body and acoustic noise makers for influence minesweeping, a mechanical sweep to counter moored mines and a Klein side scan sonar for route surveillance.

UPDATED

BROLGA   *10/1997*, van Ginderen Collection /* 0017560

3 MINESWEEPING DRONES (MSD)

MSD 01-03

Dimensions, feet (metres): 24 × 9.2 × 2 *(7.3 × 2.8 × 0.6)*
Main machinery: 2 Yamaha outboards; 300 hp(m) *(221 kW)*
Speed, knots: 45; 8 (sweeping)

Comment: Built by Hamil Haven in 1991-92. Remote-controlled drones. GRP hulls made by Hydrofield. Used for sweeping ahead of the MSA craft. Differential GPS navigation system with Syledis Vega back-up.   *UPDATED*

MSD 03   *11/1992, John Mortimer*

SURVEY SHIPS (HYDROGRAPHIC SURVEY)

Note: In addition to the ships listed below there are four civilian survey vessels; *Icebird*, *Franklin*, *Rig Seismic* and *Lady Franklin*. Also an arctic supply ship *Aurora Australis* started operating in the Antarctic in 1990; this vessel carries 70 scientists and has a helicopter hangar.

AURORA AUSTRALIS   *12/1994*, van Ginderen Collection / 0056515*

2 LEEUWIN CLASS (AGS)

Name	No	Builders	Launched	Commissioned
LEEUWIN	A 245	NQEA, Cairns	19 July 199	June 2000
MELVILLE	A 246	NQEA, Cairns	23 June 1998	June 2000

Displacement, tons: 2,170 full load
Dimensions, feet (metres): 233.6 × 49.9 × 14.4 *(71.2 × 15.2 × 4.4)*
Main machinery: Diesel-electric; 4 GEC Alsthom 6RK 215 diesel generators; 2,176 mph *(1.6 MW)* sustained; 2 motors; 2 MW; 2 shafts; bow thruster
Speed, knots: 14. **Range, miles:** 8,000 at 12 kt
Complement: 50 plus 14 spare
Radars: Navigation: STN Atlas 9600 ARPA; I-band.
Sonars: C-Tech CMAS 36/39; hull mounted; high frequency active.
Helicopters: 1 light

Comment: Contract awarded 2 April 1996 to North Queensland Engineers & Agents (NQEA). STN Atlas supplied the hydrographic systems. Klein 2000 towed side scan sonar and STN Atlas multibeam and single-beam echo sounders are installed. The ships carry three SMBs, one inflatable boat and light utility boats. Based at Cairns.   *UPDATED*

LEEUWIN   *7/1998, RAN / 0017563*

4 PALUMA CLASS (AGSC)

Name	No	Builders	Commissioned
PALUMA	A 01	Eglo, Adelaide	27 Feb 1989
MERMAID	A 02	Eglo, Adelaide	4 Dec 1989
SHEPPARTON	A 03	Eglo, Adelaide	24 Jan 1990
BENALLA	A 04	Eglo, Adelaide	20 Mar 1990

Displacement, tons: 320 full load
Dimensions, feet (metres): 118.9 × 45.3 × 6.2 *(36.6 × 13.8 × 1.9)*
Main machinery: 2 Detroit 12V-92TA diesels; 1,020 hp *(760 kW)* sustained; 2 shafts
Speed, knots: 12. **Range, miles:** 3,500 at 11 kt
Complement: 12 (2 officers)
Radars: Navigation: JRC JMA-3710-6; I-band.
Sonars: Skipper S113; hull-mounted; active; high frequency. ELAC LAZ 72; hull-mounted side scan; active; high frequency.

Comment: Catamaran design based on 'Prince' class ro-ro passenger ferries. Steel hulls and aluminium superstructure. Contract signed in November 1987. Although she commissioned in February 1989, *Paluma* was not accepted into service until September 1989 because of noise problems. As a result other members of the class were about six months late completing. Qubit Hydlaps data logging and processing system fitted. All are based at Cairns and are fitted out for operations in shallow waters of Northern Australia. Normally operate in pairs.   *VERIFIED*

SHEPPARTON   *7/1993, Ian Edwards*

9 SURVEY MOTOR BOATS

FANTOME	DUYFKEN	JOHN GOWLLAND	GEOGRAPHE
MEDA	TOM THUMB	WYATT EARP	CASURINA
INVESTIGATOR			

Dimensions, feet (metres): 35.1 × 9.5 × 5.6 *(10.7 × 2.9 × 1.7)*
Main machinery: 2 Volvo Penta AQAD-41A diesel stern drives; 400 hp(m) *(294 kW)*; 2 props
Speed, knots: 29. **Range, miles:** 300 at 12 kt
Complement: 4 (1 officer)
Radars: Navigation: JRC; I-band.

Comment: Survey motor boats built by Pro Marine, Victoria between October 1992 and July 1993. Aluminium hulls. Equipment includes Hydlaps data logging and processing, a JRC radar and a side scan sonar towfish. Equipment upgrades include multi- and single-beam echo sounders. Six of the class are allocated to the 'Leeuwin' class, two to *Penguin*, the Hydrographic School, and one is attached to the Antarctic Survey Unit (HODSU). Side numbers 1004-1012.   *VERIFIED*

MEDA   *3/1998, van Ginderen Collection / 0017564*

TUGS

Note: In addition the two MSA(T) ships are used as tugs. Details under Mine Warfare Forces.

6 HARBOUR TUGS

TAMMAR DT 2601	**JOE MANN** AT 2700	**CURRAWONG** HTS 502
QUOKKA DT 1801	**BRONZEWING** HTS 501	**MOLLYMAWK** HTS 504

Comment: *Tammar* has a bollard pull of 35 tons and is based at *Stirling*; *Quokka* bollard pull 8 tons, is based at Darwin. *Joe Mann* is an Army firefighting tug based at Sydney. The three HTS vessels have a bollard pull of 5 tons. Run as part of the commercial support programme from 1997.   *UPDATED*

QUOKKA   *8/1999*, John Mortimer / 0056521*

TRAINING SHIPS

Notes: In addition to *Young Endeavour* there are five 'Fleet' class yachts. Of 36.1 ft *(11 m)*. GRP yachts named *Charlotte of Cerberus, Friendship of Leeuwin, Scarborough of Cerberus, Lady Penrhyn of Nirimba* and *Alexander of Creswell*. The names are a combination of Australia's first colonising fleet and the training base to which each yacht is allocated.

1 SAIL TRAINING SHIP (AXS)

Name	Builders	Launched	Commissioned
YOUNG ENDEAVOUR	Brooke Yachts, Lowestoft	2 June 1987	25 Jan 1988

Displacement, tons: 239 full load
Dimensions, feet (metres): 144 × 26 × 13 *(44 × 7.8 × 4)*
Main machinery: 2 Perkins V8 diesels; 334 hp *(294 kW)*; 2 shafts
Speed, knots: 14 sail; 10 diesel. **Range, miles:** 2,500 at 7 kt
Complement: 33 (9 RAN, 24 youth)

Comment: Built to Lloyds 100 AI LMC yacht classification by Brooke Yachts, Lowestoft. Sail area 707.1 m². Presented to Australia by UK Government as a bicentennial gift. Operated by RAN on behalf of the Young Endeavour Youth Scheme.   ***VERIFIED***

YOUNG ENDEAVOUR   *12/1994, van Ginderen Collection*

1 TRAINING SHIP (AXL)

Name	No	Builders	Launched
SEAHORSE MERCATOR	—	Tenix Shipbuilding, Henderson WA	15 Oct 1998

Displacement, tons: 165 full load
Dimensions, feet (metres): 103.3 × 26.9 × 7.9 *(31.5 × 8.2 × 2.4)*
Main machinery: 2 Caterpillar 3412 diesels; 2 shafts
Speed, knots: 16. **Range, miles:** 2,700 at 10 kt
Complement: 8 plus 18 trainees

Comment: Operated by Defence Maritime Services as a Navigation training ship based at Sydney. Similar to Pacific Forum patrol craft and has replaced *Ardent*.   ***UPDATED***

SEAHORSE MERCATOR   *10/1999*, DMS / 0081450*

AUXILIARIES

Note: *Westralia* and *Success* are the only two naval auxiliaries. Since 1998 all other support vessels have been contracted to the Defence Maritime Services. These craft have blue hulls and buff superstructures, and are chartered as required.

2 TRIALS AND SAFETY VESSELS (ASR)

Name	No	Builders	Commissioned
SEAHORSE STANDARD	—	Marystown Shipyard, Newfoundland	1980
SEAHORSE SPIRIT	—	Marystown Shipyard, Newfoundland	1980

Measurement, tons: 2,090 grt; 1,635 dwt
Dimensions, feet (metres): 236.2 × 52.5 × 17.4 *(72 × 16 × 5.3)*
Main machinery: 2 MLW-ALCO Model 251 V-12 diesels; 5,480 hp(m) *(4.03 MW)*; 1 shaft; cp prop; 2 stern and 2 bow thrusters
Speed, knots: 12
Complement: 20 plus 44 spare

Comment: Acquired 2 December 1998 by Defence Maritime Services to support RAN trials in Western and Southern Australian waters. Dynamic Positioning system.   ***UPDATED***

SEAHORSE STANDARD   *8/1999*, John Mortimer / 0056516*

1 TRIALS AND SAFETY VESSEL (ASR)

Name	No	Builders	Commissioned
SEAHORSE HORIZON (ex-*Protector*, ex-*Blue*, *Nabilla*, ex-*Osprey*)	ASR 241	Stirling Marine Services, WA	1984

Displacement, tons: 670 full load
Dimensions, feet (metres): 140.1 × 31.2 × 9.8 *(42.7 × 9.5 × 3)*
Main machinery: 2 Detroit 12V-92TA diesels; 1,020 hp *(760 kW)* sustained; 2 Heimdal cp props
Speed, knots: 11.5. **Range, miles:** 10,000 at 11 kt
Complement: 13
Radars: Navigation: JRC 310; I-band. Decca RM 970BT; I-band.
Sonars: Klein; side scan; high frequency.
Helicopters: Platform for 1 light.

Comment: A former National Safety Council of Australia vessel commissioned into the Navy in November 1990. Used to support contractor's sea trials of the 'Collins' class submarines, and for mine warfare trials and diving operations. acbLIPS dynamic positioning, two ROVs and a recompression chamber. Helicopter deck and a submersible were removed in 1992. Based at Adelaide to support submarine sea trials in South Australian waters. Decommissioned in early 1998 and run as part of the commercial support programme.   ***UPDATED***

SEAHORSE HORIZON   *10/1999*, DMS / 0081451*

3 FISH CLASS (TORPEDO RECOVERY VESSELS) (TRV)

TUNA TRV 801   **TREVALLY** TRV 802   **TAILOR** TRV 803

Displacement, tons: 91.6 full load
Dimensions, feet (metres): 88.5 × 20.9 × 4.5 *(27 × 6.4 × 1.4)*
Main machinery: 3 GM diesels; 890 hp *(664 kW)*; 3 shafts
Speed, knots: 13
Complement: 9
Radars: Navigation: I-band.

Comment: All built at Williamstown completed between January 1970 and April 1971. Can transport eight torpedoes. Based at Jervis Bay, Sydney and Fleet Base West respectively. Run as part of the commercial support programme from 1997. Blue hulls and buff superstructures.   ***VERIFIED***

TREVALLY   *11/1998*, van Ginderen Collection / 0017569*

1 LEAF CLASS (UNDER WAY REPLENISHMENT TANKER) (AOR/AOT)

Name	No	Builder	Laid down	Launched	Commissioned
WESTRALIA (ex-*Hudson Cavalier*, ex-*Appleleaf*)	O 195 (ex-A 79)	Cammell Laird, Birkenhead	1974	24 July 1975	Nov 1979

Displacement, tons: 40,870 full load
Measurement, tons: 20,761 gross; 10,851 net; 33,595 dwt
Dimensions, feet (metres): 560 × 85 × 38.9
  (170.7 × 25.9 × 11.9)
Main machinery: 2 SEMT-Pielstick 14 PC2.2 V 400 diesels;
  14,000 hp(m) *(10.3 MW)* sustained; 1 shaft
Speed, knots: 16 (11 on 1 engine). **Range, miles:** 7,260 at 15 kt
Complement: 61 (8 officers) plus 9 spare berths
Cargo capacity: 20,000 tons dieso; 3,000 tons aviation fuel;
  1,500 tons water
Countermeasures: ESM: Matilda; radar warning.
Radars: Navigation: 2 Kelvin Hughes; 1007 ARPA (I-band) and
  Radpak (E/F-band).

Comment: Part of an order by the Hudson Fuel and Shipping Co which was subsequently cancelled. Leased by the RN from 1979 until transferred on 9 October 1989 on a five year lease to the RAN, arriving in Fremantle 20 December 1989. Purchased in 1994. Has three 3 ton cranes and two 5 ton derricks. Hospital facilities. Two beam replenishment stations. Stern refuelling restored in 1995. Based at *Stirling*. Saab RBS 70 SAM systems (with Army detachment) and 4—12.7 mm MGs may be embarked for operations. Also modified to provide a large Vertrep platform aft. Lifeboats have been replaced by liferafts. Being fitted for Phalanx CIWS in due course. Engine room fire in 1998 caused extensive damage. Repairs completed and the ship back on sea trials in December 1999.

UPDATED   WESTRALIA   *12/1999*, S Connolly, RAN / 0056517*

1 DURANCE CLASS (UNDERWAY REPLENISHMENT TANKER) (AOR)

Name	No	Builders	Laid down	Launched	Commissioned
SUCCESS	OR 304	Cockatoo Dockyard, Sydney	9 Aug 1980	3 Mar 1984	19 Feb 1986

Displacement, tons: 17,933 full load
Dimensions, feet (metres): 515.7 × 69.5 × 30.6
  (157.2 × 21.2 × 8.6)
Main machinery: 2 SEMT-Pielstick 16 PC2.5 V 400 diesels;
  20,800 hp(m) *(15.3 MW)* sustained; 2 shafts; acbLIPS
  cp props
Speed, knots: 20. **Range, miles:** 8,616 at 15 kt
Complement: 205 (25 officers)
Cargo capacity: 10,200 tons: 8,707 dieso; 975 Avcat; 116
  distilled water; 57 victuals; 250 munitions including SM1
  missiles and Mk 46 torpedoes; 95 naval stores and spares

Guns: 2 Vulcan Phalanx Mk 15 CIWS. 3 Bofors 40 mm/60.
  4—12.7 mm MGs.
Radars: Navigation. 2 Kelvin Hughes Type 1006; I-band.
Helicopters: 1 AS 350B Squirrel, Sea King or Seahawk.

Comment: Based on French 'Durance' class design. Replenishment at sea from four beam positions (two having heavy transfer capability) and vertrep. One LCVP is carried on the starboard side aft. Hangar modified to take Sea Kings. Phalanx guns fitted aft in 1997.

VERIFIED   SUCCESS   *8/1997, John Mortimer / 0017567*

4 SELF-PROPELLED LIGHTERS (WFL/AOTL)

WARRIGAL WFL 8001	**WOMBAT** WFL 8003
WALLABY WFL 8002	**WYULDA** WFL 8004

Displacement, tons: 265 light; 1,206 full load
Dimensions, feet (metres): 124.6 × 33.5 × 12.5 *(38 × 10.2 × 3.8)*
Main machinery: 2 Harbourmaster outdrives (1 fwd, 1 aft)
Speed, knots: 8

Comment: First three were laid down at Williamstown in 1978. The fourth, for HMAS *Stirling*, was ordered in 1981 from Williamstown Dockyard. Used for water/fuel transport. Steel hulls with twin, swivelling, outboard propellers. Based at Jervis Bay and Cockburn Sound (WFL 8001, 8004), other pair at Garden Island, Sydney. Run as part of the commercial support operation from 1997.

UPDATED

HARBOUR CRAFT

OTTER NWBD 1281	**DOLPHIN** NWBD 1286	**WATTLE** CSL 01
WALRUS NWBD 1282	**DUGONG** NWBD 1287	**BORONIA** CSL 02
BEAVER NWBD 1283	**TURTLE** NWBD 1292	**TELOPEA** CSL 03
GRAMPUS NWBD 1285	**AWB 400-445**	**AWL** CSL 04

Comment: Those with NWBD numbers are work boats. There are four hydrofoil Cheetah remote-controlled surface targets capable of 35 kt. Those with CSL numbers are self-propelled lighters. There are also some naval Shark Cat craft, pennant numbers in the 0901 series. Run as part of the commercial support operation from 1997.

UPDATED

WOMBAT   *1/1999*, van Ginderen Collection / 0056519*

AWB 444   *4/1999*, van Ginderen Collection / 0056520*

3 DIVING TENDERS (YDT)

SEAL 2001   **MALU BAIZAM** 2003   **SHARK** 2004

Displacement, tons: 22 full load
Dimensions, feet (metres): 65.5 × 18.5 × 4.6 *(20 × 5.6 × 1.4)*
Main machinery: 2 diesels; 2 shafts
Speed, knots: 28. **Range, miles:** 350 at 18 kt
Complement: 6 plus 16 divers

Comment: Built by Geraldton Boat Builders, Western Australia and completed in August 1993. Carry 2 tons of diving equipment to support 24 hour diving operations in depths of 54 m. *Shark* based at *Stirling*, *Seal* in Sydney, *Malu Baizam* at Thursday Island. One of the class grounded in 1995 and was assessed as being beyond economical repair. Replacement built in 1996. Run as part of the commercial support operation from 1997.

UPDATED

SEAL   *11/1997, John Mortimer /* 0012048

ARMY

Notes: (1) Operated by Royal Australian Army Corps of Transport. Personnel: About 300 as required.
(2) In addition to the craft listed below there are some 140 assault boats 16.4 ft *(5 m)* in length and capable of 30 kt. Can carry 12 troops or 1,200 kg of equipment.
(3) New LCMs have been approved to enter service by 2002/03. Must be capable of recovery by the LPAs 70 ton derricks.

15 LCM 8 CLASS

AB 1050, 1051, 1053, 1055, 1056, 1058-1067

Displacement, tons: 116 full load
Dimensions, feet (metres): 73.5 × 21 × 5.2 *(22.4 × 6.4 × 1.6)*
Main machinery: 2 8V92GM diesels; 720 hp *(547 kW)*; 2 shafts
Speed, knots: 11. **Range, miles:** 290 at 10 kt
Complement: 4-5
Military lift: 55 tons
Guns: 2—12.7 mm MGs.

Comment: Built by North Queensland Engineers, Cairns and Dillinghams, Fremantle to US design. Based at Townsville and Darwin. *AB 1057* transferred to Tonga 1982, *AB 1052* and *AB 1054* sold to civilian use in 1992. All upgraded to Mod 2 standard by late 1999 with new engines and with endurance increased. Additional LCMs are to be built by 2003.

UPDATED

AB 1067 (aboard *Manoora*)   *11/1999 *, N A Sifferlinger /* 0056522

1 + (1) SAFCOL CRAFT

CORAL SNAKE AM 1353

Comment: Built at Geraldton Boat Builders and delivered in late 1994 as a Special Action Forces Craft Offshore Large (SAFCOL). The launch is 65.4 ft *(20 m)* and is operated by SASR in Western Australia. A second vessel, AM 1354, is to be ordered in due course.

VERIFIED

9 EXPRESS SHARK CAT CLASS

AM 237-244   428

Comment: Built by NoosaCat, Queensland and delivered by 1995. Trailer transportable. Similar craft in service with Navy and Police. Multihulls 30.8 ft *(9.4 m)* in length overall with twin Johnson outboards; 450 hp *(336 kW)* total power output, giving 40 kt maximum speed.

UPDATED

AM 243   *11/1997 *, van Ginderen Collection /* 0012946

NON-NAVAL PATROL CRAFT

Notes: (1) In addition to the commecial support craft already listed, various State and Federal agencies, including some fishery departments, have built offshore patrol craft up to 25 m and 26 kt.
(2) Cocos Island patrol carried out by *Sir Zelman Cowan* of 47.9 × 14 ft *(14.6 × 4.3 m)* with two Cummins diesels; 20 kt, range 400 n miles at 17 kt, complement 13 (3 officers). Operated by West Australian Department of Harbours and Lights.
(3) The Naval Police operate four 'Shark Cat' class (0801-0804) which are similar to Army and Naval versions. These craft are based at Sydney and Rockingham.
(4) All previously listed RAAF craft have been sold for civilian use.

CUSTOMS

8 BAY CLASS

131-138

Measurement, tons: 28 dwt
Dimensions, feet (metres): 125.3 × 23.6 × 7.9 *(38.2 × 7.2 × 2.4)*
Main machinery: 2 MTU 16V 2000M 70 diesels; 2,856 hp(m) *(2.1 MW)* sustained; 2 shafts
Speed, knots: 21. **Range, miles:** 1,000 at 20 kt
Complement: 12
Radars: Surface search: Racal Decca; E/F- and I-band.

Comment: Built by Austal Ships and delivered from August 1999 to August 2000. Named after Australian bays. The craft carry two RIBs capable of 25 kt.   *NEW ENTRY*

ROEBUCK BAY   *8/1999 *, Austal Ships /* 0056523

AUSTRIA
ÖSTERREICHISCHE MARINE

Commanding Officer

Major Manfred Zemsauer

Diplomatic Representation

Defence Attaché in London:
Brigadier W Plasche

Personnel

(a) 2000: 35 (cadre personnel and national service), plus a small shipyard unit
(b) 8 months' national service

Bases

Marinekaserne Tegetthof, Wien-Kuchelau (under command of Austrian School of Military Engineering)

Mercantile Marine

Lloyd's Register of Shipping:
22 vessels of 71,069 tons gross

PATROL FORCES

Notes: (1) Orders for two new patrol craft of 30 m planned for 2001.
(2) In addition to two ships listed, there are 10 M-Boot 80 work boats.

1 RIVER PATROL CRAFT (PBR)

Name	No	Builders	Commissioned
OBERST BRECHT	A 601	Korneuberg Werft AG	14 Jan 1958

Displacement, tons: 10 full load
Dimensions, feet (metres): 40.3 × 8.2 × 2.5 *(12.3 × 2.5 × 0.75)*
Main machinery: 2 MAN 6-cyl diesels; 290 hp(m) *(213 kW)*; 2 shafts
Speed, knots: 18
Complement: 5
Guns: 1—12.7 mm MG. 1—84 mm PAR 66 Carl Gustav AT mortar.

Comment: Planned to be replaced in 2002 by first of the new 30 m craft.   ***UPDATED***

OBERST BRECHT   6/1995*, Austrian Government / 0056524

1 RIVER PATROL CRAFT (PCR)

Name	No	Builders	Launched	Commissioned
NIEDERÖSTERREICH	A 604	Korneuberg Werft AG	26 July 1969	16 Apr 1970

Displacement, tons: 78 full load
Dimensions, feet (metres): 96.8 × 17.8 × 3.6 *(29.4 × 5.4 × 1.1)*
Main machinery: 2 MWM V16 diesels; 1,640 hp(m) *(1.2 MW)*; 2 shafts
Speed, knots: 22
Complement: 9 (1 officer)
Guns: 1 Oerlikon 20 mm SPz Mk 66. 1—12.7 mm MG. 1—7.62 mm MG. 1—84 mm PAR 66 'Carl Gustav' AT mortar.

Comment: Fully welded. Only one built of a projected class of 12. Re-engined in 1985.
UPDATED

NIEDERÖSTERREICH   6/1995*, Austrian Government / 0056525

AZERBAIJAN

Headquarters Appointments

Commander of Navy:
   Captain Rafik Akerov

General

Coast Guard formed in July 1992 with ships transferred from the Russian Caspian Flotilla and Border Guard. By 1995 overall control had been resumed by the Russians in order to provide adequate maintenance and support. The aim is to be independent again in due course. Details of all listed classes can be found in the Russian section. About four of the listed ships are assessed as being operational.

Personnel

2000: 2,200

Bases

Baku

Mercantile Marine

Lloyd's Register of Shipping:
   286 vessels of 654,183 tons gross

Strength of the Fleet (1 January 2000)

Patrol Forces: 2 Stenka (205P), 1 Svetlyak (1140); 1 Osa II (without SSM), 1 Zhuk
Mine Warfare Forces: 3 Sonya (12650), 2 Yevgenya (1258)
Amphibious Forces: 2 Polnochny B (771); 2 Vydra (106K)
Training Ship: 1 Wodnik II (Luga)
Survey Ships: 1 Vadim Popov, 2 Valerian Uryvayev
Auxiliaries: 1 Finik, 1 Kamenka, 1 Emba

Note: These ships are either laid up or under the control of the Russian Caspian Sea Flotilla. The Stenkas, Svetlyak and Zhuk belong to the Border Guard.

SVETLYAK   6/1997* / 0012051

BAHAMAS

Headquarters Appointments

Commander Royal Bahamas Defence Force:
   Commodore Davy F Rolle
Squadron Commanding Officer:
   Commander Albert Armbrister

Bases

HMBS *Coral Harbour* (New Providence Island)
HMBS *Matthew Town Inagua* (Great Inagua Island)

Personnel

2000: 886

Prefix to Ships' Names

HMBS

Mercantile Marine

Lloyd's Register of Shipping:
   1,294 vessels of 29,482,531 tons gross

DELETIONS

Patrol forces

1999   *Marlin, Fort Fincastle*

Auxiliaries

1998   *Fort Charlotte*

PATROL FORCES

Note: There is an option on four 140 ft *(42.7 m)* 'Nassau' class patrol craft to be built by Halter Marine if the option is taken up.

1 CAPE CLASS (PC)

Name	No	Builders	Commissioned
SAN SALVADOR II (ex-*Fox*)	P 10	USCG Yard, Curtis Bay	22 Aug 1955

Displacement, tons: 98 standard; 148 full load
Dimensions, feet (metres): 95 × 20.2 × 6.6 *(28.9 × 6.2 × 2)*
Main machinery: 2 Detroit 16V-149TI diesels; 2,322 hp *(1.73 MW)* sustained; 2 shafts
Speed, knots: 20. **Range, miles:** 2,500 at 10 kt
Complement: 18 (2 officers)
Guns: 2—12.7 mm MGs.
Radars: Navigation: Furuno; I-band.

Comment: Modernisation in 1980 included new engines, electronics and improved habitability. Commissioned into the Bahamian Defence Force in November 1989. Designed for port security and search and rescue, the survivor of six originally transferred and being replaced by the 'Bahamas' class OPVs. One RIB is carried and can be launched by a jib on the after mast. One more is used as a firefighting training school.   *UPDATED*

SAN SALVADOR II   *6/1998, RBDF /* 0017572

2 BAHAMAS CLASS (OPV)

Name	No	Builders	Commissioned
BAHAMAS	P 60	Moss Point Marine, Escatawpa	Jan 2000
NASSAU	P 61	Moss Point Marine, Escatawpa	Jan 2000

Displacement, tons: 375 full load
Dimensions, feet (metres): 198.8 × 29.2 × 8.5 *(60.6 × 8.9 × 2.6)*
Main machinery: 3 Caterpillar 3516B diesels; 6,600 hp(m) *(4.85 MW)*; 3 shafts
Speed, knots: 24. **Range, miles:** 3,000 at 10 kt
Complement: 62
Guns: 1 Bushmaster 25 mm. 3—12.7 mm MGs.
Radars: Surface search: I-band.
Navigation: Litton Bridgemaster C181; I-band.

Comment: Order placed 14 March 1997 with Halter Marine Group. Aluminium superstructures fabricated at Equitable Shipyards while hulls are building at Moss Point. The design is an adapted Vosper International Europatrol 250 with a RIB and launching crane at the stern.   *UPDATED*

BAHAMAS   *1999*, Halter Marine /* 0056526

3 PROTECTOR CLASS (PCF)

Name	No	Builders	Commissioned
YELLOW ELDER	P 03	Fairey Marine, Cowes	20 Nov 1986
PORT NELSON	P 04	Fairey Marine, Cowes	20 Nov 1986
SAMANA	P 05	Fairey Marine, Cowes	20 Nov 1986

Displacement, tons: 110 standard; 180 full load
Dimensions, feet (metres): 108.3 × 22 × 6.9 *(33 × 6.7 × 2.1)*
Main machinery: 3 Detroit 16V-149TI diesels; 3,483 hp *(2.6 MW)* sustained; 3 shafts
Speed, knots: 30. **Range, miles:** 300 at 24 kt; 600 at 14 kt on 1 engine
Complement: 20 (3 officers) plus 5 spare
Guns: 1 Rheinmetall 20 mm. 3—7.62 mm MGs.
Radars: Surface search: Furuno; I-band.

Comment: Ordered December 1984. Steel hulls. One RIB is carried and can be launched by a trainable crane.   *UPDATED*

SAMANA   *4/1996*, RBDF /* 0056527

1 CHALLENGER CLASS (PB)

P 41

Displacement, tons: 8 full load
Dimensions, feet (metres): 27 × 5.5 × 1 *(8.2 × 1.7 × 0.3)*
Main machinery: 2 Evinrude outboards; 450 hp *(330 kW)*
Speed, knots: 26
Complement: 4
Guns: 1—7.62 mm MG.

Comment: Built by Boston Whaler Edgewater, Florida and delivered in September 1995.   *UPDATED*

P 41   *9/1996*, RBDF /* 0056530

BAHAMAS   *1/2000*, RBDF /* 0081452

1 ELEUTHERA (KEITH NELSON) CLASS (PC)

Name	No	Builders	Commissioned
INAGUA	P 27	Vosper Thornycroft	10 Dec 1979

Displacement, tons: 30 standard; 37 full load
Dimensions, feet (metres): 60 × 15.8 × 4.6 *(18.3 × 4.8 × 1.4)*
Main machinery: 2 Caterpillar 3408BTA diesels; 1,070 hp *(800 kW)* sustained; 2 shafts
Speed, knots: 20. **Range, miles:** 650 at 16 kt
Complement: 11
Guns: 3—7.62 mm MGs.
Radars: Surface search: Furuno; I-band.

Comment: The survivor of a class of five. Light machine guns mounted in sockets either side of the bridge. One more is used as a museum.

UPDATED

INAGUA   *6/1998*, RBDF / 0017574

2 DAUNTLESS CLASS (INSHORE PATROL CRAFT) (PB)

P 42   P 43

Displacement, tons: 11 full load
Dimensions, feet (metres): 40.4 × 14 × 4.3 *(12.3 × 4.3 × 1.3)*
Main machinery: 2 Caterpillar 3208TA diesels; 870 hp *(650 kW)* sustained; 2 shafts
Speed, knots: 25. **Range, miles:** 600 at 18 kt
Complement: 5
Guns: 2—7.62 mm MGs.
Radars: Surface search: Furuno 1761; I-band.

Comment: Built by SeaArk Marine, Monticello, Arkansas and delivered in January 1996. Used primarily for medium-range search and rescue missions.

UPDATED

P43   *6/1999*, RBDF / 0081453

P 42   *9/1996*, RBDF / 0056529

4 BOSTON WHALERS

P 110-111   P 112-113

Displacement, tons: 1.5 full load
Dimensions, feet (metres): 20 × 7.2 × 1.1 *(6.1 × 2.2 × 0.4)*
Main machinery: 2 Evinrude outboards; 180 hp *(134 kW)* (P 110-111); 2 Mariner outboards; 150 hp *(120 kW)* (P 112-113)
Speed, knots: 45 *(P 110-111)*; 38 *(P 112-113)*
Complement: 3

Comment: P 112 and 113 are Impact designs commissioned 25 September 1995. P 110 and 111 are Wahoo types commissioned 23 October 1995.

UPDATED

P 110 and P 111   *9/1997*, RBDF / 0012053

P113   *6/1999*, RBDF / 0081454

AUXILIARIES

1 SUPPLY CRAFT (YFU)

FORT MONTAGUE A 01

Displacement, tons: 90 full load
Dimensions, feet (metres): 94 × 23 × 6 *(28.6 × 7 × 1.8)*
Main machinery: 2 Detroit 12V-71 diesels; 680 hp *(508 kW)* sustained; 2 shafts
Speed, knots: 13. **Range, miles:** 3,000 at 10 kt
Complement: 16
Guns: 2—7.62 mm MGs.
Radars: Navigation: Furuno; I-band.

Comment: Acquired 6 August 1980.

UPDATED

FORT MONTAGUE   *1991*, RBDF / 0056531

BAHRAIN

Headquarters Appointments

Chief of Staff:
Major General Shaikh Abdullah Bin Salman Bin Khalid Al Khalifa
Commander of Navy:
Lieutenant Colonel Yusuf Ahmad Malullah
Director of Coast Guard:
Colonel Abdul Ghaffar Abdul Aziz Mohammed

Personnel

(a) 2000: 1,300 (Navy), 260 (Coast Guard—seagoing)
(b) Voluntary service

Bases

Mina Sulman (Navy), Al-Hadd (CG)

Coast Guard

This unit is under the direction of the Ministry of the Interior.

Mercantile Marine

Lloyd's Register of Shipping:
120 vessels of 291,714 tons gross

FRIGATES

1 OLIVER HAZARD PERRY CLASS (FFG)

Name	No	Builders	Laid down	Launched	Commissioned	Recommissioned
SABHA (ex-*Jack Williams*)	90 (ex-FFG 24)	Bath Iron Works	25 Feb 1980	30 Aug 1980	19 Sep 1981	25 Feb 1997

Displacement, tons: 2,750 light; 3,638 full load
Dimensions, feet (metres): 445 × 45 × 14.8; 24.5 (sonar)
  (135.6 × 13.7 × 4.5; 7.5)
Main machinery: 2 GE LM 2500 gas turbines; 41,000 hp
  (30.59 MW) sustained; 1 shaft; cp prop
  2 auxiliary retractable props; 650 hp *(484 kW)*
Speed, knots: 29. **Range, miles:** 4,500 at 20 kt
Complement: 206 (13 officers) including 19 aircrew

Missiles: SSM: 4 McDonnell Douglas Harpoon; active radar
  homing to 130 km *(70 n miles)* at 0.9 Mach; warhead 227 kg.
  SAM: 36 GDC Standard SM-1MR; command guidance; semi-
  active radar homing to 46 km *(25 n miles)* at 2 Mach.
  1 Mk 13 Mod 4 launcher for both SSM and SAM missiles ❶.
Guns: 1 OTO Melara 3 in *(76 mm)*/62 Mk 75 ❷; 85 rds/min to
  16 km *(8.7 n miles)* anti-surface; 12 km *(6.6 n miles)* anti-
  aircraft; weight of shell 6 kg.
  1 General Electric/General Dynamics 20 mm/76 6-barrelled
  Mk 15 Vulcan Phalanx ❸; 3,000 rds/min (4,500 in Block 1)
  combined to 1.5 km.
  4—12.7 mm MGs.
Torpedoes: 6—324 mm Mk 32 Mod 7 (2 triple) tubes ❹. 24
  Honeywell Mk 46; anti-submarine; active/passive homing to
  11 km *(5.9 n miles)* at 40 kt; warhead 44 kg.
Countermeasures: Decoys: 2 Loral Hycor SRBOC 6-barrelled
  fixed Mk 36 ❺; IR flares and chaff to 4 km *(2.2 n miles)*.
  SLQ-25 Nixie; torpedo decoy.
ESM/ECM: SLQ-32(V)2 ❻; radar warning. Sidekick modification
  adds jammer and deception system.

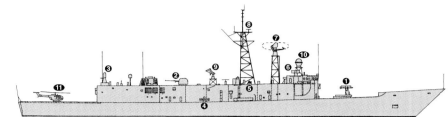

SABHA

(Scale 1 : 1,200), Ian Sturton / 0056532

Combat data systems: NTDS with Link 14.
Weapons control: SWG-1 Harpoon LCS. Mk 92 (Mod 4). The
  Mk 92 is the US version of the Signaal WM28 system. Mk 13
  weapon direction system. 2 Mk 24 optical directors.
Radars: Air search: Raytheon SPS-49(V)4 ❼; C/D-band; range
  457 km *(250 n miles)*.
  Surface search: ISC Cardion SPS-55 ❽; I-band.
  Fire control: Lockheed STIR (modified SPG-60) ❾; I/J-band;
  range 110 km *(60 n miles)*.
  Sperry Mk 92 (Signaal WM28) ❿; I/J-band.
  Tacan: URN 25.
Sonars: Raytheon SQS-56; hull-mounted; active search and
  attack; medium frequency.

Helicopters: 1 Eurocopter BO 105 ⓫. Space for 2 SH-2G.

Programmes: Transferred from the USA by grant 18 September
  1996. Arrived in the Gulf in June 1997 for a work-up and
  training period.
Structure: Apart from the removal of the US SATCOM aerials
  there are no visible changes from US service.
Operational: A transfer of helicopters is required if the ASW
  potential of the ship is to be realised.

UPDATED

SABHA

3/1999*, Maritime Photographic / 0056533

SABHA

3/1999*, Maritime Photographic / 0056534

CORVETTES

2 AL MANAMA (MGB 62) CLASS (FSG)

Name	No	Builders	Commissioned
AL MANAMA	50	Lürssen	14 Dec 1987
AL MUHARRAQ	51	Lürssen	3 Feb 1988

Displacement, tons: 632 full load
Dimensions, feet (metres): 206.7 × 30.5 × 9.5
    (63 × 9.3 × 2.9)
Main machinery: 4 MTU 20V 538 TB92 diesels; 12,820 hp(m)
    (9.42 MW) sustained; 4 shafts
Speed, knots: 32. **Range, miles:** 4,000 at 16 kt
Complement: 43 (7 officers)

Missiles: SSM: 4 Aerospatiale MM 40 Exocet launchers (2 twin)
    ❶; inertial cruise; active radar homing to 70 km *(40 n miles)* at
    0.9 Mach; warhead 165 kg; sea-skimmer.
Guns: 1 OTO Melara 3 in *(76 mm)*/62 compact **❷**; 85 rds/min to
    16 km *(8.7 n miles)* anti-surface; 12 km *(6.5 n miles)* anti-
    aircraft; weight of shell 6 kg.

2 Breda 40 mm/70 (twin) **❸**; 300 rds/min to 12.5 km *(6.8 n
    miles)*; weight of shell 0.96 kg.
2 Oerlikon GAM-BO1 20 mm/93.
Countermeasures: Decoys: CSEE Dagaie **❹**; chaff and IR flares.
ESM/ECM: Racal Decca Cutlass/Cygnus **❺**; intercept and
    jammer.
Weapons control: CSEE Panda Mk 2 optical director. Philips
    TV/IR optronic director **❻**.
Radars: Air/surface search: Philips Sea Giraffe 50 HC **❼**; G-band.
    Navigation: Racal Decca 1226; I-band.
    Fire control: Philips 9LV 331 **❽**; J-band.

Helicopters: 1 Eurocopter BO 105 **❾**.

Programmes: Ordered February 1984.
Modernisation: Upgrade planned to include a SAM self-defence
    system.
Structure: Similar to Abu Dhabi, Singapore and UAE designs.
    Steel hull, aluminium superstructure. Fitted with a helicopter
    platform which incorporates a lift to lower the aircraft into the
    hangar.
Operational: Planned SA 365F helicopters were not acquired.
    UPDATED

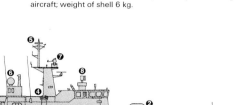

AL MANAMA

(Scale 1 : 600), Ian Sturton / 0056535

AL MANAMA

3/1999*, Maritime Photographic / 0056536

AL MANAMA

3/1999*, C E Castle / 0056537

PATROL FORCES

4 AHMAD EL FATEH (TNC 45) CLASS
(FAST ATTACK CRAFT—MISSILE) (PCFG)

Name	No	Builders	Commissioned
AHMAD EL FATEH	20	Lürssen	5 Feb 1984
AL JABIRI	21	Lürssen	3 May 1984
ABDUL RAHMAN AL FADEL	22	Lürssen	10 Sep 1986
AL TAWEELAH	23	Lürssen	25 Mar 1989

Displacement, tons: 228 half load; 259 full load
Dimensions, feet (metres): 147.3 × 22.9 × 8.2 *(44.9 × 7 × 2.5)*
Main machinery: 4 MTU 16V 538 TB92 diesels; 13,640 hp(m) *(10 MW)* sustained; 4 shafts
Speed, knots: 40. **Range, miles:** 1,600 at 16 kt
Complement: 36 (6 officers)

Missiles: SSM: 4 Aerospatiale MM 40 Exocet (2 twin); inertial cruise; active radar homing to 70 km *(40 n miles)* at 0.9 Mach; warhead 165 kg; sea-skimmer.
Guns: 1 OTO Melara 3 in *(76 mm)*/62; dual purpose; 85 rds/min to 16 km *(8.7 n miles)* anti-surface; 12 km *(6.5 n miles)* anti-aircraft; weight of shell 6 kg.
  2 Breda 40 mm/70 (twin); 300 rds/min to 12.5 km *(6.8 n miles)*; weight of shell 0.96 kg.
  3—7.62 mm MGs.
Countermeasures: Decoys: CSEE Dagaie launcher; trainable mounting; 10 containers firing chaff decoys and IR flares.
ESM: RDL 2 ABC; radar warning.
ECM: Racal Cygnus (not in 20 and 21); jammer.
Weapons control: 1 Panda optical director for 40 mm guns.
Radars: Air/surface search: Philips Sea Giraffe 50 HC; G-band.
Fire control: Philips 9LV 226/231; J-band.
Navigation: Racal Decca 1226; I-band.

Programmes: First pair ordered in 1979, second pair in 1985. Similar craft in service with Ecuador, Kuwait and UAE navies.
Structure: Only the second pair have the communication radome on the after superstructure.
Operational: Refits from 2000 by Lürssen at Abu Dhabi.   ***UPDATED***

AL JABIRI   *3/1999*, Maritime Photographic /* 0056538

AL TAWEELAH   *3/1999*, C E Castle /* 0056539

2 AL RIFFA (FPB 38) CLASS (FAST ATTACK CRAFT—GUN) (PCF)

Name	No	Builders	Commissioned
AL RIFFA	10	Lürssen	3 Mar 1982
HAWAR	11	Lürssen	3 Mar 1982

Displacement, tons: 188 half load; 205 full load
Dimensions, feet (metres): 126.3 × 22.9 × 7.2 *(38.5 × 7 × 2.2)*
Main machinery: 2 MTU 16V 538 TB92 diesels; 6,810 hp(m) *(5 MW)* sustained; 2 shafts
Speed, knots: 32. **Range, miles:** 1,100 at 16 kt
Complement: 27 (3 officers)
Guns: 2 Breda 40 mm/70 (twin); dual purpose; 300 rds/min to 12 km *(6.5 n miles)* anti-surface; 4 km *(2.2 n miles)*; weight of shell 0.96 kg.
  1—57 mm Starshell rocket launcher.
Mines: Mine rails fitted.
Countermeasures: Decoys: 1 Wallop Barricade chaff launcher.
ESM: Racal RDL-2 ABC; radar warning.
Weapons control: CSEE Lynx optical director with Philips 9LV 126 optronic system.
Radars: Surface search: Philips 9GR 600; I-band.
Navigation: Racal Decca 1226; I-band.

Comment: Ordered in 1979. *Al Riffa* launched April 1981. *Hawar* launched July 1981.   ***UPDATED***

AL RIFFA   *6/1995* /* 0056540

2 AL JARIM (FPB 20) CLASS (FAST ATTACK CRAFT—GUN) (PCF)

Name	No	Builders	Commissioned
AL JARIM	30	Swiftships, Morgan City	9 Feb 1982
AL JASRAH	31	Swiftships, Morgan City	26 Feb 1982

Displacement, tons: 33 full load
Dimensions, feet (metres): 63 × 18.4 × 6.5 *(19.2 × 5.6 × 2)*
Main machinery: 2 Detroit 12V-71TA diesels; 840 hp(m) *(627 kW)* sustained; 2 shafts
Speed, knots: 30. **Range, miles:** 1,200 at 18 kt
Guns: 1 Oerlikon GAM-BO1 20 mm.
Radars: Surface search: Decca 110; I-band.

Comment: Aluminium hulls.
                                              VERIFIED

AL JARIM   *1991, J Bouvia, USN*

SHIPBORNE AIRCRAFT

Note: SH-2G helicopters may be acquired for the frigate in due course.

Numbers/Type: 2 Eurocopter BO 105.
Operational speed: 113 kt *(210 km/h)*.
Service ceiling: 9,845 ft *(3,000 m)*.
Range: 407 n miles *(754 km)*.
Role/Weapon systems: Acquired in August 1994 as the first aircraft of a Naval Air Arm. Sensors: Search radar. Weapons: Unarmed.
                                              UPDATED

BO 105   *6/1995* /* 0056541

AUXILIARIES

Note: There are also two RTK Medevac boats and one Diving Boat (512).

1 AJEERA CLASS (SUPPLY SHIPS) (AFL)

Name	No	Builders	Commissioned
AJEERA	41	Swiftships, Morgan City	21 Oct 1982

Displacement, tons: 420 full load
Dimensions, feet (metres): 129.9 × 36.1 × 5.9 *(39.6 × 11 × 1.8)*
Main machinery: 2 Detroit 16V-71 diesels; 811 hp *(605 kW)* sustained; 2 shafts
Speed, knots: 13. **Range, miles:** 1,500 at 10 kt
Complement: 21
Guns: 2—12.7 mm MGs.
Radars: Navigation: Racal Decca; I-band.

Comment: Used as general purpose cargo ships and can carry up to 200 tons of fuel and water. Built to an LCU design with a bow ramp and 15 ton crane.
                                              UPDATED

AJEERA   *9/1990*

3 LCU 1466 CLASS (LCU)

MASHTAN 42   **RUBODH** 43   **SUWAD** 44

Displacement, tons: 360 full load
Dimensions, feet (metres): 119 × 34 × 6 *(36.3 × 10.4 × 1.8)*
Main machinery: 3 Gray Marine 64 YTL diesels; 675 hp *(504 kW)*; 3 shafts
Speed, knots: 8. **Range, miles:** 800 at 8 kt
Complement: 15
Cargo capacity: 167 tons
Guns: 2—12.7 mm MGs.
Radars: Navigation: Racal Decca; I-band.

Comment: Transferred from US in 1991.

UPDATED

LCU 1466 (Colombian colours)   *6/1995, Hartmut Ehlers /* 0017579

COAST GUARD

Notes: (1) In addition to the craft listed below about 10 small open fibreglass boats are used for patrol duties.
(2) Three 3.5 ton Cheverton craft are still in service. Names are *Noon* (15), *Askar* (16) and *Suwad* (17).
(3) 'Tiger' class hovercraft *Nejood* deleted in 1998, *Dera'a 1* in 1999.

1 WASP 30 METRE CLASS

AL MUHARRAQ

Displacement, tons: 90 standard; 103 full load
Dimensions, feet (metres): 98.5 × 21 × 5.5 *(30 × 6.4 × 1.6)*
Main machinery: 2 Detroit 16V-149TI diesels; 2,322 hp *(1.73 MW)* sustained; 2 shafts
Speed, knots: 25. **Range, miles:** 500 at 22 kt
Complement: 9
Guns: 1—30 mm. 2—7.62 mm MGs.
Radars: Surface search: Racal Decca; I-band.

Comment: Ordered from Souters, Cowes, Isle of Wight in 1984. Laid down November 1984, launched 12 August 1985, shipped 21 October 1985. GRP hull. Sometimes used as a Presidential Yacht.

UPDATED

AL MUHARRAQ   *3/1997*, Maritime Photographic /* 0012060

4 HALMATIC 20 METRE CLASS

DERA'A 2, **6**, **7** and **8**

Displacement, tons: 31.5 full load
Dimensions, feet (metres): 65.9 × 19.4 × 5.1 *(20.1 × 5.9 × 1.5)*
Main machinery: 2 Detroit 12V-71TA diesels; 840 hp *(626 kW)* sustained; 2 shafts
Speed, knots: 25. **Range, miles:** 500 at 20 kt
Complement: 7
Guns: 2—7.62 mm MGs.

Comment: Three delivered in late 1991, the last in early 1992. GRP hulls.

UPDATED

DERA'A 8   *7/1998*, Bahrain Coast Guard /* 0017580

2 WASP 20 METRE CLASS

DERA'A 4 and **5**

Displacement, tons: 36.3 full load
Dimensions, feet (metres): 65.6 × 16.4 × 4.9 *(20 × 5 × 1.5)*
Main machinery: 2 Detroit 12V-71TA diesels; 840 hp *(626 kW)* sustained; 2 shafts
Speed, knots: 24.5. **Range, miles:** 500 at 20 kt
Complement: 8
Guns: 2—7.62 mm MGs.
Radars: Surface search: Racal Decca; I-band.

Comment: Built by Souters, Cowes, Isle of Wight. Delivered 1983. GRP hulls.

VERIFIED

DERA'A 4   *9/1995, Bahrain Coast Guard*

1 TRACKER CLASS

DERA'A 1

Displacement, tons: 31 full load
Dimensions, feet (metres): 64 × 16 × 5 *(19.5 × 4.9 × 1.5)*
Main machinery: 2 General Motors diesels; 1,120 hp *(823 kW)*; 2 shafts
Speed, knots: 22
Complement: 5
Guns: 1—7.62 mm MG.
Radars: Surface search: Furuno; I-band.

Comment: Built by Fairey Marine Ltd in 1980. Survivor of three of the class.

UPDATED

DERA'A 1   *12/1993*, Bahrain Coast Guard /* 0056542

6 HALMATIC 160 CLASS

SAIF 5, **6**, **7**, **8**, **9** and **10**

Displacement, tons: 17 full load
Dimensions, feet (metres): 47.2 × 12.8 × 3.9 *(14.4 × 3.9 × 1.2)*
Main machinery: 2 Detroit 6V-92TA diesels; 520 hp *(388 kW)* sustained; 2 shafts
Speed, knots: 27. **Range, miles:** 500 at 22 kt
Complement: 4
Guns: 1—7.62 mm MG.
Radars: Surface search: Furuno; I-band.

Comment: Delivered in 1990-91. GRP hulls.

VERIFIED

SAIF 9   *7/1998, Bahrain Coast Guard /* 0017581

4 FAIREY SWORD CLASS

SAIF 1, 2, 3 and **4**

Displacement, tons: 15
Dimensions, feet (metres): 44.9 × 13.4 × 4.3 *(13.7 × 4.1 × 1.3)*
Main machinery: 2 GM 8V-71 diesels; 590 hp *(440 kW)* sustained; 2 shafts
Speed, knots: 22
Complement: 6
Radars: Navigation: Furuno; I-band.

Comment: Purchased in 1980. Built by Fairey Marine Ltd. *UPDATED*

SAIF 3   *11/1999*, Bahrain Coast Guard* / 0056543

3 WASP 11 METRE CLASS

SAHAM 1   SAHAM 2   SAHAM 3

Displacement, tons: 7 full load
Dimensions, feet (metres): 36.1 × 10.5 × 2.6 *(11 × 3.2 × 0.8)*
Main machinery: 2 Yamaha outboards; 400 hp(m) *(294 kW)*
Speed, knots: 25. **Range, miles:** 125 at 20 kt
Complement: 3
Radars: Navigation: Koden; I-band.

Comment: Built by Souters, Cowes in 1983. *Saham 2* re-engined with outboards and recommissioned in August 1997. *Saham 1* similarly back in service in 1998, and *Saham 3* in 2000. *UPDATED*

SAHAM 2   *10/1997*, Bahrain Coast Guard* / 0012061

1 SUPPORT CRAFT

SAFRA 3

Displacement, tons: 165 full load
Dimensions, feet (metres): 85 × 25.9 × 5.2 *(25.9 × 7.9 × 1.6)*
Main machinery: 2 Detroit 16V-92TA diesels; 1,380 hp *(1.03 MW)*; 2 shafts
Speed, knots: 13. **Range, miles:** 700 at 12 kt
Complement: 6
Radars: Navigation: Racal Decca; I-band.

Comment: Built by Halmatic, Havant and delivered in early 1992. Logistic support work boat equipped for towing and firefighting. Can carry 15 tons. *VERIFIED*

SAFRA 3   *10/1998, Bahrain Coast Guard* / 0017582

1 LANDING CRAFT

SAFRA 2

Displacement, tons: 150 full load
Measurement, tons: 90 dwt
Dimensions, feet (metres): 73.9 × 24.9 × 4 *(22.5 × 7.5 × 1.2)*
Main machinery: 2 Detroit 12V-71 diesels; 680 hp *(508 kW)* sustained; 2 shafts
Speed, knots: 8
Complement: 8
Radars: Navigation: Furuno; I-band.

Comment: Built by Fairey Marine and delivered in 1981. Based at Al-Hadd. *UPDATED*

SAFRA 2   *12/1993*, Bahrain Coast Guard* / 0056544

BANGLADESH

Headquarters Appointments

Chief of Naval Staff:
  Rear Admiral Abu Taher
Assistant Chief of Naval Staff (Operations):
  Commodore Abu Zafer Mohammed Abdul Moquit
Assistant Chief of Naval Staff (Personnel):
  Commodore Harunur Rashid
Assistant Chief of Naval Staff (Logistics):
  Commodore Emdadul Islam
Assistant Chief of Naval Staff (Material):
  Commodore Mohammad Anwarul Haque

Senior Appointments

Commodore Commanding BN Flotilla:
  Commodore Khurshed Alam
Commodore Commanding Chittagong:
  Commodore Abul Kalam Mohammad Azad
Commodore Commanding Khulna:
  Commodore Khondker Moyeenuddin Ahmed
Director General Coast Guard:
  Commodore Shafiq-ur-Rahman

Personnel

(a) 2000: 11,282 (1,007 officers)
(b) Voluntary service

Strength of the Fleet

Type	Active	Building
Frigates	4	1
Fast Attack Craft (Missile)	10	—
Fast Attack Craft (Torpedo)	8	—
Fast Attack Craft (Gun)	4	1
Large Patrol Craft	4	—
Coastal Patrol Craft	7	—
Riverine Patrol Craft	5	—
Minesweepers	5	(3)
Training Ships	1	—
Repair Ship	1	—
Tankers	2	—
Survey Craft	3	—

Bases

Chittagong (BNS *Issa Khan*, BN Dockyard, BNS *Ulka*). Naval Academy (BNS *Patenga*); (BNS *Bhatiary*, Nucox's Bazar).
Kaptai (BNS *Shaheed Moazzam*).
Dhaka (BNS *Haji Mohsin*).
Khulna (BNS *Titumir*, *Nu Mongla* and *Hiron Point*).

Coast Guard

Formed on 19 December 1995 with two ships on loan from the Navy. Bases at Chittagong (East Zone) and Khulna (West Zone). Personnel 270 (20 officers). Colours thick red and thin blue diagonal stripes on hull with COAST GUARD on ships side. New ship acquired in 1999.

Prefix to Ships' Names

BNS

Mercantile Marine

Lloyd's Register of Shipping:
  306 vessels of 377,722 tons gross

PENNANT LIST

Frigates				Mine Warfare Forces				
		P 115	Bogra	P 911	Madhumati		A 515	Khan Jahan Ali
		P 201	Ruposhi Bangla	P 8111	Durbar		A 516	Imam Gazzali
F 15	Abu Bakr	P 211	Meghna	P 8112	Duranta	M 91	Sagar	A 581	Darshak
F 16	Umar Farooq	P 212	Jamuna	P 8113	Durvedya	M 95	Shapla	A 582	Tallashi
F 17	Ali Haider	P 311	Bishkhali	P 8114	Durdam	M 96	Shaikat	A 583	Agradoot
F 18	Osman	P 312	Padma	P 8125	Durdharsha	M 97	Surovi	A 711	Sundarban
		P 313	Surma	P 8126	Durdanta	M 98	Shaibal	A 721	Khadem
		P 314	Karnaphuli	P 8127	Durnibar			A 722	Sebak
		P 315	Tista	P 8128	Dordanda			A 731	Balaban
Patrol Forces		P 611	Tawheed (CG)	P 8131	Anirban			L 900	Shah Amanat
		P 612	Tawfiq	P 8141	Uttal	**Auxiliaries**		L 901	Shah Paran
P 111	Pabna (CG)	P 613	Tamjeed	P 8235	TB 35			L 902	Shah Makhdum
P 112	Noakhali	P 614	Tanveer	P 8236	TB 36	A 511	Shaheed Ruhul Amin		
P 113	Patuakhali	P 711	Barkat	P 8237	TB 37	A 512	Shahayak		
P 114	Rangamati	P 812	Nirbhoy	P 8238	TB 38	A 513	Shahjalal		

FRIGATES

Note: Tenders for a new frigate up to 3,000 tons opened on 21 November 1995 and were re-issued in August 1996 after a poor response. Daewoo selected in March 1998 to build a modified 'Ulsan' class of 2,300 tons armed with four SSMs, a 76 mm gun, two twin 40 mm guns, ASW and mining capabilities and a helicopter. Signaal radar and Racal EW. SEMT-Pielstick diesels have been selected. The launch is scheduled for June 2000 with delivery in June 2001.

1 OSMAN (JIANGHU I) CLASS (TYPE 053 H1) (FFG)

Name	No	Builders	Laid down	Launched	Commissioned
OSMAN (ex-*Xiangtan*)	F 18 (ex-556)	Hudong Shipyard, Shanghai	1986	Dec 1988	4 Nov 1989

Displacement, tons: 1,425 standard; 1,702 full load
Dimensions, feet (metres): 338.6 × 35.4 × 10.2
(103.2 × 10.7 × 3.1)
Main machinery: 2 Type 12 E 390V diesels; 14,400 hp(m)
(10.6 MW) sustained; 2 shafts
Speed, knots: 26. **Range, miles:** 2,700 at 18 kt
Complement: 300 (27 officers)

Missiles: SSM: 4 Hai Ying 2 (2 twin) launchers ❶; active radar or IR homing to 80 km *(43.2 n miles)* at 0.9 Mach; warhead 513 kg.
Guns: 4 China 3.9 in *(100 mm)*/56 (2 twin) ❷; 18 rds/min to 22 km *(12 n miles)*; weight of shell 15.9 kg.
8 China 37 mm/76 (4 twin) ❸; 180 rds/min to 8.5 km *(4.6 n miles)* anti-aircraft; weight of shell 1.42 kg.
A/S mortars: 2 RBU 1200 5-tubed fixed launchers ❹; range 1,200 m; warhead 34 kg.
Depth charges: 2 BMB-2 projectors; 2 racks.
Mines: Can carry up to 60.
Countermeasures: Decoys: 2 Loral Hycor SRBOC Mk 36 6-barrelled chaff launchers.
ESM: Watchdog; radar warning.
Weapons control: Wok Won director (752A) ❺.

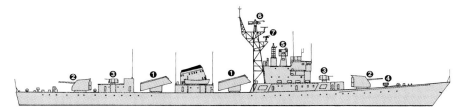

OSMAN (Scale 1 : 900), Ian Sturton / 0056545

Radars: Air/surface search: MX 902 Eye Shield (922-1) ❻; E-band.
Surface search/fire control: Square Tie (254) ❼; I-band.
Navigation: Fin Curve (352); I-band.
IFF: High Pole A.
Sonars: Echo Type 5; hull-mounted; active search and attack; medium frequency.

Programmes: Transferred 26 September 1989 from China, arrived Bangladesh 8 October 1989. Second order expected in 1991 was cancelled.
Structure: This is a Jianghu Type I (version 4) hull with twin 100 mm guns (vice the 57 mm in the ships sold to Egypt), Wok Won fire-control system and a rounded funnel.
Operational: Damaged in collision with a merchant ship in August 1991. One 37 mm mounting uprooted and SSM and RBU mountings misaligned. Repaired in 1992-93. **UPDATED**

OSMAN 12/1999*, Sattler/Steele / 0081498

1 SALISBURY CLASS (TYPE 61) (FF)

Name	No	Builders	Laid down	Launched	Commissioned
UMAR FAROOQ (ex-*Llandaff*)	F 16	Hawthorn Leslie Ltd	27 Aug 1953	30 Nov 1955	11 Apr 1958

Displacement, tons: 2,170 standard; 2,408 full load
Dimensions, feet (metres): 339.8 × 40 × 15.5 (screws)
(103.6 × 12.2 × 4.7)
Main machinery: 8 VVS ASR 1 diesels; 12,380 hp *(9.2 MW)*
sustained; 2 shafts
Speed, knots: 24. **Range, miles:** 2,300 at 24 kt; 7,500 at 16 kt
Complement: 237 (14 officers)

Guns: 2 Vickers 4.5 in *(115 mm)*/45 (twin) Mk 6 ❶; dual purpose; 20 rds/min to 19 km *(10 n miles)* anti-surface; 6 km *(3.3 n miles)* anti-aircraft; weight of shell 25 kg.
2 Bofors 40 mm/60 Mk 9 ❷; 120 rds/min to 3 km *(1.6 n miles)* anti-aircraft; 10 km *(5.5 n miles)* maximum.
A/S mortars: 1 triple-barrelled Squid Mk 4 ❸; fires pattern of 3 depth charges to 300 m ahead of ship.

Countermeasures: Decoys: Corvus chaff launchers.
Weapons control: 1 Mk 6M gun director. Link Y.
Radars: Air search: Marconi Type 965 with double AKE 2 array ❹; A-band.
Air/surface search: Plessey Type 993 ❺; E/F-band.
Heightfinder: Type 278M ❻; E-band.
Surface search: Decca Type 978 ❼; I-band.
Navigation: Decca Type 978; I-band.
Fire control: Type 275 ❽; F-band.
Sonars: Type 174; hull-mounted; active search; medium frequency.
Graseby Type 170B; hull-mounted; active attack; 15 kHz.

Programmes: Transferred from UK at Royal Albert Dock, London 10 December 1976.
Operational: The radar Type 982 aerial is still retained on the after mast but the set is non-operational. The ship has been refitted to remain in service for as long as possible.
UPDATED

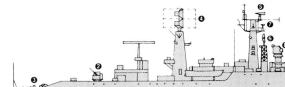

UMAR FAROOQ (Scale 1 : 900), Ian Sturton

UMAR FAROOQ 10/1998 / 0017585

2 LEOPARD CLASS (TYPE 41) (FF)

Name	No	Builders	Laid down	Launched	Commissioned
ABU BAKR (ex-*Lynx*)	F 15	John Brown & Co Ltd, Clydebank	13 Aug 1953	12 Jan 1955	14 Mar 1957
ALI HAIDER (ex-*Jaguar*)	F 17	Wm Denny & Bros Ltd, Dumbarton	2 Nov 1953	30 July 1957	12 Dec 1959

Displacement, tons: 2,300 standard; 2,520 full load
Dimensions, feet (metres): 339.8 × 40 × 15.5 (screws)
  (103.6 × 12.2 × 4.7)
Main machinery: 8 VVS ASR 1 diesels; 12,380 hp *(9.2 MW)*
  sustained; 2 shafts
Speed, knots: 24. **Range, miles:** 2,300 at full power; 7,500 at
  16 kt
Complement: 235 (15 officers)

Guns: 4 Vickers 4.5 in *(115 mm)*/45 (2 twin) Mk 6 ❶; dual
  purpose; 20 rds/min to 19 km *(10 n miles)* anti-surface; 6 km
  (3.3 n miles) anti-aircraft; weight of shell 25 kg.
  1 Bofors 40 mm/60 Mk 9 ❷; 120 rds/min to 3 km *(1.6 n miles)*
  anti-aircraft; 10 km *(5.5 n miles)*.
Countermeasures: Decoys: Corvus chaff launchers.
  ESM: Radar warning.
Weapons control: Mk 6M gun director. Link Y.
Radars: Air search: Marconi Type 965 with single AKE 1 array ❸;
  A-band.
  Air/surface search: Plessey Type 993 ❹; E/F-band.
  Navigation: Decca Type 978; Kelvin Hughes 1007; I-band.
  Fire control: Type 275 ❺; F-band.

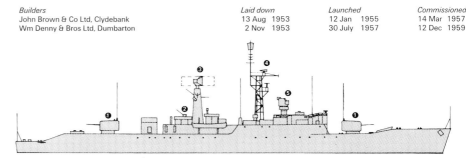

ABU BAKR   *(Scale 1 : 900), Ian Sturton*

Programmes: *Ali Haider* transferred from UK 16 July 1978 and
  Abu Bakr on 12 March 1982. *Ali Haider* refitted at Vosper
  Thornycroft August-October 1978. *Abu Bakr* extensively
  refitted in 1982.
Structure: All welded. Fitted with stabilisers. Sonars removed
  while still in service with RN. Fuel tanks have a water
  compensation system to improve stability.

Operational: Designed as air defence ships. *Abu Bakr* may
  remain in service for several years as a Training Ship. *Ali Haider*
  is expected to be paid off when the new frigate completes in
  2001, but may be retained as a hulk for alongside training.
                                                          UPDATED

ABU BAKR   *3/1998 / 0017588*

PATROL FORCES

1 MADHUMATI (SEA DRAGON) CLASS (PC/OPV)

Name	No	Builders	Commissioned
MADHUMATI	P 911	Hyundai, Ulsan	18 Feb 1998

Displacement, tons: 635 full load
Dimensions, feet (metres): 199.5 × 26.2 × 8.9 *(60.8 × 8 × 2.7)*
Main machinery: 2 SEMT-Pielstick 12 PA6 diesels; 9,600 hp(m) *(7.08 MW)* sustained; 2 shafts
Speed, knots: 24. **Range, miles:** 6,000 at 15 kt
Complement: 43 (7 officers)
Guns: 1 Bofors 57 mm/70 Mk 1; 220 rds/min to 17 km *(9.3 n miles)*; weight of shell 2.4 kg.
  1 Bofors 40 mm/70. 2 Oerlikon 20 mm.
Weapons control: Optronic director.
Radars: Surface search: Kelvin Hughes KH 1007; I-band.
  Navigation: GEM Electronics SPN 753B; I-band.

Comment: Ordered in 1995 and delivered in October 1997. Very similar to the South Korean Coast
  Guard vessels, but with improved fire-control equipment. Vosper stabilisers. Classified as an
  OPV. Total of six required but no further orders are projected yet.
                                                          UPDATED

5 DURDHARSHA (HUANGFEN) CLASS (TYPE 021)
(FAST ATTACK CRAFT—MISSILE) (PCFG)

DURDHARSHA P 8125	DURNIBAR P 8127	ANIRBAN P 8131
DURDANTA P 8126	DORDANDA P 8128	

Displacement, tons: 171 standard; 205 full load
Dimensions, feet (metres): 126.6 × 24.9 × 8.9 *(38.6 × 7.6 × 2.7)*
Main machinery: 3 Type 42-160 diesels; 12,000 hp(m) *(8.8 MW)*; 3 shafts
Speed, knots: 35. **Range, miles:** 800 at 30 kt
Complement: 35 (5 officers)
Missiles: SSM: 4 HY-2; active radar or IR homing to 80 km *(43.2 n miles)* at 0.9 Mach; warhead
  513 kg.
Guns: 4 USSR 30 mm/65 (2 twin).
Radars: Surface search: Square Tie; I-band.
  Fire control: Rice Lamp; H/I-band.
  IFF: High Pole A.

Comment: Built in China. First four commissioned in Bangladesh Navy on 10 November 1988.
  Chinese equivalent of the Soviet 'Osa' class which started building in 1985. All damaged in April
  1991 typhoon but recovered and repaired. A fifth vessel *Anirban* was delivered in June 1992.
                                                          UPDATED

MADHUMATI   *2/1998, Bangladesh Navy / 0017589*   DURDHARSHA   *3/1996*, Bangladesh Navy / 0056546*

5 DURBAR (HEGU) CLASS (TYPE 024)
(FAST ATTACK CRAFT—MISSILE) (PCFG)

DURBAR P 8111	**DURVEDYA** P 8113	**UTTAL** P 8141
DURANTA P 8112	**DURDAM** P 8114	

Displacement, tons: 68 standard; 79.2 full load
Dimensions, feet (metres): 88.6 × 20.7 × 4.3 *(27 × 6.3 × 1.3)*
Main machinery: 4 Type L-12V-180 diesels; 4,800 hp(m) *(3.53 MW)*; 4 shafts
Speed, knots: 37.5. **Range, miles:** 400 at 30 kt
Complement: 17 (4 officers)
Missiles: SSM: 2 SY-1; active radar or IR homing to 45 km *(24.3 n miles)* at 0.9 Mach; warhead 513 kg.
Guns: 2—25 mm/80 (twin); 270 rds/min to 3 km *(1.6 n miles)*; weight of shell 0.34 kg.
Radars: Surface search: Square Tie; I-band.

Comment: Built in China. First pair commissioned in Bangladesh Navy on 6 April 1983, second pair on 10 November 1983. Two badly damaged in April 1991 typhoon but were repaired. *Uttal* was delivered in June 1992. Missiles are seldom embarked.   **VERIFIED**

UTTAL   *3/1998 /* 0017590

4 HUCHUAN CLASS (TYPE 026)
(FAST ATTACK CRAFT—TORPEDO) (PHT)

TB 35 T 8235	**TB 36** T 8236	**TB 37** T 8237	**TB 38** T 8238

Displacement, tons: 46 full load
Dimensions, feet (metres): 73.8 × 16.4 × 6.9 (foil) *(22.5 × 5 × 2.1)*
Main machinery: 3 Type L-12V-180 diesels; 3,600 hp(m) *(2.64 MW)*; 3 shafts
Speed, knots: 50. **Range, miles:** 500 at 30 kt
Complement: 23 (3 officers)
Guns: 4 China 14.5 mm (2 twin); 600 rds/min to 7 km *(3.8 km)*.
Torpedoes: 2—21 in *(533 mm)* China YU-1; anti-ship; to 9.2 km *(5 n miles)* at 39 kt or 3.7 km *(2.1 n miles)* at 51 kt; warhead 400 kg.
Radars: Surface search: China Type 753; I-band.

Comment: Chinese 'Huchuan' class. Two damaged in April 1991 typhoon but were repaired. At least two are non-operational.   **UPDATED**

TB 35   *4/1988 * /* 0056547

1 DURJOY (HAINAN) (TYPE 037) CLASS
(LARGE PATROL CRAFT) (PC)

NIRBHOY P 812

Displacement, tons: 375 standard; 392 full load
Dimensions, feet (metres): 192.8 × 23.6 × 7.2 *(58.8 × 7.2 × 2.2)*
Main machinery: 4 PCR/Kolomna Type 9-D-8 diesels; 4,000 hp(m) *(2.94 MW)* sustained; 4 shafts
Speed, knots: 30.5. **Range, miles:** 1,300 at 15 kt
Complement: 70
Guns: 4 China 57 mm/70 (2 twin); 120 rds/min to 12 km *(6.5 n miles)*; weight of shell 6.31 kg.
4—25 mm/60 (2 twin); 270 rds/min to 3 km *(1.6 n miles)* anti-aircraft.
A/S mortars: 4 RBU 1200 fixed 5-barrelled launchers; range 1,200 m; warhead 34 kg.
Depth charges: 2 racks; 2 throwers. 18 DCs.
Mines: Fitted with rails for 12 mines.
Radars: Surface search: Pot Head; I-band.
IFF: High Pole.
Sonars: Tamir II; hull-mounted; short-range attack; high frequency.

Comment: Transferred from China and commissioned 1 December 1985. Forms part of Escort Squadron 81 at Chittagong. Some previous confusion over numbers of this class. A second of class damaged beyond repair in 1995.   **UPDATED**

NIRBHOY   *6/1996 *, Bangladesh Navy /* 0056548

4 SHAHEED (SHANGHAI II) (TYPE 062) CLASS
(FAST ATTACK CRAFT—GUN) (PC)

TAWHEED P 611	**TAWFIQ** P 612	**TAMJEED** P 613	**TANVEER** P 614

Displacement, tons: 113 standard; 134 full load
Dimensions, feet (metres): 127.3 × 17.7 × 5.6 *(38.8 × 5.4 × 1.7)*
Main machinery: 4 Type M 50 diesels; 4,400 hp(m) *(3.2 MW)* sustained; 4 shafts
Speed, knots: 30. **Range, miles:** 800 at 16.5 kt
Complement: 36 (4 officers)
Guns: 4—37 mm/63 (2 twin); 180 rds/min to 8.5 km *(4.6 n miles)*; weight of shell 1.4 kg.
4—25 mm/80 (2 twin); 270 rds/min to 3 km *(1.6 n miles)* anti-aircraft.
Depth charges: 2 throwers; 8 charges.
Mines: 10 can be carried.
Radars: Surface search: Skin Head/Pot Head; I-band.
Sonars: Hull-mounted; active; short range; high frequency. Some reported to have VDS.

Comment: Transferred from China March 1982. Different engine arrangement from Chinese craft. Based at Chittagong form Patrol Squadron 41. *Tawheed* leased to the Coast Guard from December 1995 but has retained its pennant number. Four others of the class are used for spares.   **UPDATED**

TAMJEED   *3/1998 /* 0017591

TAWHEED   *6/1996 *, Bangladesh Coast Guard /* 0056549

1 RUPOSHI BANGLA CLASS (COASTAL PATROL CRAFT) (PC)

Name	*No*	*Builders*	*Launched*	*Commissioned*
RUPOSHI BANGLA	P 201	Hong Leong-Lürssen	28 June 1999	Oct 1999

Displacement, tons: 195 full load
Dimensions, feet (metres): 126.3 × 23 × 13.5 *(38.5 × 7 × 4.1)*
Main machinery: 2 Paxman 12VP 185 diesels; 6,729 hp(m) *(4.95 MW)* sustained; 2 shafts
Speed, knots: 30
Complement: 27 (5 officers)
Guns: 1 Otobreda 25 mm KBA. 2—7.62 mm MGs.
Radars: Surface search: Furuno; I-band.

Comment: Ordered in June 1998 and laid down 11 August 1998. Based on the PZ design for the Malaysian Police. Operated by the Coast Guard.   **NEW ENTRY**

RUPOSHI BANGLA   *10/1999 *, Hong Leong-Lürssen /* 0064625

1 HAIZHUI (TYPE 062/1) CLASS (COASTAL PATROL CRAFT) (PC)

BARKAT P 711

Displacement, tons: 139 full load
Dimensions, feet (metres): 127.2 × 17.7 × 5.6 *(38.8 × 5.4 × 1.7)*
Main machinery: 4 Chinese L12-180A diesels; 4,800 hp(m) *(35.3 MW)*; 4 shafts
Speed, knots: 28. **Range, miles:** 750 at 17 kt
Complement: 43 (4 officers)
Guns: 4 China 37 mm/63 (2 twin); 180 rds/min to 8.5 km *(4.6 n miles)*; weight of shell 1.42 kg.
    4 China 25 mm/80 (2 twin).
Depth charges: 2 rails.
Radars: Surface search: Anitsu 726; I-band.
Sonars: Stag Ear; active; high frequency.

Comment: Acquired from China in 1995. This is the Shanghai III, the larger and slower version of the Shanghai II which in Chinese service has anti-submarine mortars. An inclined pole mast and platform behind the bridge are distinguishing features.
UPDATED

BARKAT   *3/1998 /* 0017592

2 KARNAPHULI (KRALJEVICA) CLASS
(LARGE PATROL CRAFT) (PC)

Name	No	Builders	Commissioned
KARNAPHULI (ex-*PBR 502*)	P 314	Yugoslavia	1956
TISTA (ex-*PBR 505*)	P 315	Yugoslavia	1956

Displacement, tons: 195 standard; 245 full load
Dimensions, feet (metres): 141.4 × 20.7 × 5.7 *(43.1 × 6.3 × 1.8)*
Main machinery: 2 MAN V8V 30/38 diesels; 3,300 hp(m) *(2.42 MW)*; 2 shafts
Speed, knots: 24. **Range, miles:** 1,500 at 12 kt
Complement: 44 (4 officers)
Guns: 2 Bofors 40 mm/70. 4 Oerlikon 20 mm. 2—128 mm rocket launchers (5 barrels per mounting).
Depth charges: 2 racks; 2 Mk 6 projectors.
Radars: Surface search: Decca 1229; I-band.
Sonars: QCU 2; hull-mounted; active; high frequency.

Comment: Transferred and commissioned 6 June 1975. *Karnaphuli* re-engined in 1995, *Tista* in 1998.
UPDATED

TISTA   *6/1999*, Bangladesh Navy /* 0056550

2 AKSHAY CLASS (COASTAL PATROL CRAFT) (PC)

Name	No	Builders	Commissioned
PADMA (ex-*Akshay*)	P 312	Hooghly D & E Co, Calcutta	Jan 1962
SURMA (ex-*Ajay*)	P 313	Hooghly D & E Co, Calcutta	Apr 1962

Displacement, tons: 120 standard; 150 full load
Dimensions, feet (metres): 117.2 × 20 × 5.5 *(35.7 × 6.1 × 1.7)*
Main machinery: 2 Paxman YHAXM diesels; 1,100 hp *(820 kW)*; 2 shafts
Speed, knots: 18. **Range, miles:** 500 at 12 kt
Complement: 35 (3 officers)
Guns: 4 or 8 Oerlikon 20 mm 1 or (2 quad). 2 Bofors 40 mm/60 (twin) *(Surma)*.
Radars: Surface search: Racal Decca; I-band.

Comment: Transferred from India and commissioned 12 April 1973 and 26 July 1974 respectively. *Surma* has a 40 mm gun aft vice the second quad 20 mm.
UPDATED

PADMA   *6/1997*, Bangladesh Navy /* 0012065

2 MEGHNA CLASS (COASTAL PATROL CRAFT) (PG)

Name	No	Builders	Launched
MEGHNA	P 211	Vosper Private, Singapore	19 Jan 1984
JAMUNA	P 212	Vosper Private, Singapore	19 Mar 1984

Displacement, tons: 410 full load
Dimensions, feet (metres): 152.5 × 24.6 × 6.6 *(46.5 × 7.5 × 2)*
Main machinery: 2 Paxman Valenta 12CM diesels; 5,000 hp *(3.73 MW)* sustained; 2 shafts
Speed, knots: 20. **Range, miles:** 2,000 at 16 kt
Complement: 47 (3 officers)
Guns: 1 Bofors 57 mm/70 Mk 1; 200 rds/min to 17 km *(9.3 n miles)*; weight of shell 2.4 kg.
    1 Bofors 40 mm/70; 300 rds/min to 12 km *(6.5 n miles)*; weight of shell 0.96 kg.
    2—7.62 mm MGs; launchers for illuminants on the 57 mm gun.
Weapons control: Selenia NA 18 B optronic system.
Radars: Surface search: Decca 1229; I-band.

Comment: Built for EEZ work under the Ministry of Agriculture. Both completed late 1984. Both damaged in April 1991 typhoon but have been repaired.
UPDATED

MEGHNA   *6/1996*, Bangladesh Navy /* 0056551

4 TYPE 123K (CHINESE P4) CLASS
(FAST ATTACK CRAFT—TORPEDO) (PHT)

TB 1 T 8221   **TB 2** T 8222   **TB 3** T 8223   **TB 4** T 8224

Displacement, tons: 25 full load
Dimensions, feet (metres): 62.3 × 10.8 × 3.3 *(19 × 3.3 × 1)*
Main machinery: 2 Type L-12V-180 diesels; 2,400 hp(m) *(1.76 MW)*; 2 shafts
Speed, knots: 50. **Range, miles:** 410 at 30 kt
Complement: 12 (1 officer)
Guns: 2—14.5 mm (twin) MG.
Torpedoes: 2—17.7 in *(450 mm)*; anti-ship.

Comment: Transferred from China 6 April 1983. Reported to have paid off in 1989 when the class became confused with the 'Huchuan' class, but have remained in service throughout.
UPDATED

TB 1   *6/1994*, Bangladesh Navy /* 0056552

1 RIVER CLASS (COASTAL PATROL CRAFT) (PC)

Name	No	Builders	Commissioned
BISHKHALI (ex-*Jessore*)	P 311	Brooke Marine Ltd	20 May 1965

Displacement, tons: 115 standard; 143 full load
Dimensions, feet (metres): 107 × 20 × 6.9 *(32.6 × 6.1 × 2.1)*
Main machinery: 2 MTU 12V 538 TB90 diesels; 4,500 hp(m) *(3.3 MW)* sustained; 2 shafts
Speed, knots: 24
Complement: 30
Guns: 2 Breda 40 mm/70; 300 rds/min to 12.5 km *(6.8 n miles)*; weight of shell 0.96 kg.
Radars: Surface search: Racal Decca; I-band.

Comment: PNS *Jessore*, which was sunk during the 1971 war, was salvaged and extensively repaired at Khulna Shipyard and recommissioned as *Bishkhali* on 23 November 1978.
UPDATED

BISHKHALI   *6/1996*, Bangladesh Navy /* 0056554

5 PABNA CLASS (RIVERINE PATROL CRAFT) (PBR)

Name	No	Builders	Commissioned
PABNA	P 111	DEW Narayangonj, Dhaka	12 June 1972
NOAKHALI	P 112	DEW Narayangonj, Dhaka	8 July 1972
PATUAKHALI	P 113	DEW Narayangonj, Dhaka	7 Nov 1974
RANGAMATI	P 114	DEW Narayangonj, Dhaka	11 Feb 1977
BOGRA	P 115	DEW Narayangonj, Dhaka	15 July 1977

Displacement, tons: 69.5 full load
Dimensions, feet (metres): 75 × 20 × 3.5 *(22.9 × 6.1 × 1.1)*
Main machinery: 2 Cummins diesels; 2 shafts
Speed, knots: 10.8. **Range, miles:** 700 at 8 kt
Complement: 33 (3 officers)
Guns: 1 Bofors 40 mm/60 or Oerlikon 20 mm.

Comment: The first indigenous naval craft built in Bangladesh. Form River Patrol Squadron 11 at Mongla. *Pabna* leased to the newly formed Coast Guard in December 1995.

UPDATED

PABNA 6/1997*, Bangladesh Coast Guard / 0056553

RANGAMATI 1984, Bangladesh Navy

MINE WARFARE FORCES

4 SHAPLA (RIVER) CLASS
(MINESWEEPERS/PATROL CRAFT) (MSI/PC)

Name	No	Builders	Commissioned
SHAPLA (ex-*Waveney*)	M 95	Richards, Lowestoft	12 July 1984
SHAIKAT (ex-*Carron*)	M 96	Richards, Great Yarmouth	30 Sep 1984
SUROVI (ex-*Dovey*)	M 97	Richards, Great Yarmouth	30 Mar 1985
SHAIBAL (ex-*Helford*)	M 98	Richards, Great Yarmouth	7 June 1985

Displacement, tons: 890 full load
Dimensions, feet (metres): 156 × 34.5 × 9.5 *(47.5 × 10.5 × 2.9)*
Main machinery: 2 Ruston 6RKC diesels; 3,100 hp *(2.3 MW)* sustained; 2 shafts
Speed, knots: 14. **Range, miles:** 4,500 at 10 kt
Complement: 30 (7 officers)
Guns: 1 Bofors 40 mm/60 Mk 3.
Radars: Navigation: 2 Racal Decca TM 1226C; I-band.

Comment: These ships are four of a class of 12 of which seven are in service with Brazil. Transferred from the UK on 3 October 1994 and recommissioned on 27 April 1995. Steel hulled for deep-armed team sweeping with wire sweeps, and intended for use both as minesweepers and as patrol craft. Fitted with Racal Integrated Minehunting System. Magnetic and acoustic sweeps to be fitted in due course. *Shaibal* converted for survey duties but retains minesweeping gear. A second of class may follow. Towed side scan sonars may be fitted.

VERIFIED

SUROVI 3/1998 / 0017593

1 + (3) SAGAR (T 43) CLASS (MINESWEEPERS) (MSO)

Name	No	Builders	Commissioned
SAGAR	M 91	Wuhan Shipyard	27 Apr 1995

Displacement, tons: 520 standard; 590 full load
Dimensions, feet (metres): 196.8 × 27.6 × 6.9 *(60 × 8.8 × 2.3)*
Main machinery: 2 PCR/Kolomna Type 9-D-8 diesels; 2,000 hp(m) *(1.47 MW)*; 2 shafts
Speed, knots: 14. **Range, miles:** 3,000 at 10 kt
Complement: 70 (10 officers)

Guns: 4 China 37 mm/63 (2 twin); 180 rds/min to 8.5 km *(4.6 n miles)*; weight of shell 1.42 kg.
4—25 mm/60 (2 twin); 270 rds/min to 3 km *(1.6 n miles)*.
4 China 14.5 mm/93 (2 twin); 600 rds/min to 7 km *(3.8 n miles)*.
Depth charges: 2 BMB-2 projectors; 20 depth charges.
Mines: Can carry 12-16.
Countermeasures: MCMV; MPT-1 paravanes; MPT-3 mechanical sweep; acoustic and magnetic gear.
Radars: Surface search: Fin Curve; I-band.
Sonars: Celcius Tech CMAS 36/39; active high frequency mine detection.

Programmes: Ordered from China in 1993. First of class handed over 18 December 1994 but subsequent planned deliveries have been delayed by lack of funds.
Modernisation: New sonar fitted in 1998.
Structure: This is a new build ship almost identical to those in service in the Chinese Navy.
Operational: Used mostly as a patrol ship.

UPDATED

SAGAR 3/1998 / 0017594

TRAINING SHIPS

1 ISLAND CLASS (AX)

Name	No	Builders	Commissioned
SHAHEED RUHUL AMIN (ex-*Jersey*)	A 511 (ex-P 295)	Hall Russell, Aberdeen	15 Oct 1976

Displacement, tons: 925 standard; 1,260 full load
Dimensions, feet (metres): 176 wl; 195.3 oa × 36 × 15 *(53.7; 59.5 × 11 × 4.5)*
Main machinery: 2 Ruston 12RKC diesels; 5,640 hp *(4.21 MW)* sustained; 1 shaft; cp prop
Speed, knots: 16.5. **Range, miles:** 7,000 at 12 kt
Complement: 39
Guns: 1 Bofors 40 mm/60 Mk 3. 2 FN 7.62 mm MGs.
Countermeasures: ESM: Orange Crop; intercept.
Combat data systems: Racal CANE DEA-1 action data automation.
Radars: Navigation: Kelvin Hughes Type 1006; I-band.

Comment: First sale agreed with the UK in December 1993. Sailed for Bangladesh in February 1994 and has replaced the old training ship of the same name. A second of class *Orkney* was to have transferred in May 1999 but the sale was not concluded. This class has been fitted with enlarged keels, stabilisers and water ballast arrangements to damp down motion in a seaway.

UPDATED

SHAHEED RUHUL AMIN 6/1996*, Bangladesh Navy / 0056555

AUXILIARIES

1 FLOATING DOCK and 1 FLOATING CRANE

Comment: Floating Dock A 711 (*Sundarban*) acquired from Brodogradiliste Joso Lozovina-Mosor, Trogir, Yugoslavia in 1980; capacity 3,500 tons. Has a complement of 85 (5 officers). Floating crane A 731 (*Balaban*) is self-propelled at 9 kt and has a lift of 70 tons; built at Khulna Shipyard and commissioned 18 May 1988, she has a complement of 29 (two officers).

UPDATED

1 TANKER (AOT)

KHAN JAHAN ALI A 515

Displacement, tons: 2,900 full load
Measurement, tons: 1,343 gross
Dimensions, feet (metres): 250.8 × 37.5 × 18.4 *(76.4 × 11.4 × 5.6)*
Main machinery: 1 diesel; 1,350 hp(m) *(992 kW)*; 1 shaft
Speed, knots: 12
Complement: 26 (3 officers)
Cargo capacity: 1,500 tons
Guns: 2 Oerlikon 20 mm.

Comment: Completed in Japan in 1983. Can carry out stern replenishment at sea but is seldom used in this role.

VERIFIED

KHAN JAHAN ALI   3/1998 / 0017595

1 TANKER (AOT)

IMAN GAZZALI A 516

Displacement, tons: 213 full load
Dimensions, feet (metres): 146.8 × 23 × 11.2 *(44.8 × 7 × 3.4)*
Main machinery: 1 Cummins diesel; 1 shaft
Speed, knots: 8
Complement: 30 (2 officers)

Comment: An oil tanker of some 600,000 litres capacity acquired in 1996.

NEW ENTRY

IMAN GAZZALI   6/1999*, Bangladesh Navy / 0056556

1 REPAIR SHIP (YR)

SHAHAYAK A 512

Displacement, tons: 477 full load
Dimensions, feet (metres): 146.6 × 26.2 × 6.6 *(44.7 × 8 × 2)*
Main machinery: 1 Cummins 12 VTS 6 diesel; 425 hp *(317 kW)*; 1 shaft
Speed, knots: 11.5. **Range, miles:** 3,800 at 11.5 kt
Complement: 45 (1 officer)
Guns: 1 Oerlikon 20 mm.

Comment: Re-engined and modernised at Khulna Shipyard and commissioned in 1978 to act as repair vessel.

UPDATED

SHAHAYAK   6/1996*, Bangladesh Navy / 0056557

1 TENDER (AG)

SHAHJALAL A 513

Displacement, tons: 600 full load
Dimensions, feet (metres): 131.8 × 29.7 × 12.6 *(40.2 × 9.1 × 3.8)*
Main machinery: 1 V 16-cyl type diesel; 1 shaft
Speed, knots: 12. **Range, miles:** 7,000 at 12 kt
Complement: 55 (3 officers)
Guns: 2 Oerlikon 20 mm.

Comment: Ex-Thai fishing vessel SMS *Gold 4*. Probably built in Tokyo. Commissioned on 15 January 1987 and used as a patrol craft for a time but is now in use as a tender.

UPDATED

SHAHJALAL   6/1996*, Bangladesh Navy / 0056558

1 HARBOUR TENDER

SANKET

Displacement, tons: 80 full load
Dimensions, feet (metres): 96.5 × 20 × 5.9 *(29.4 × 6.1 × 1.8)*
Main machinery: 2 Deutz diesels; 2,400 hp(m) *(1.76 MW)*; 2 shafts
Speed, knots: 16. **Range, miles:** 1,000 at 16 kt
Complement: 16 (1 officer)
Guns: 1 Oerlikon 20 mm.

Comment: A former MFV taken over in 1989 and used as a utility harbour craft. No pennant number has been allocated. A second vessel of this type *Shamikha* is in civilian service.

UPDATED

SANKET   3/1996* / 0056559

1 LANDING CRAFT LOGISTIC (LSL)

SHAH AMANAT L 900

Displacement, tons: 366 full load
Dimensions, feet (metres): 154.2 × 34.1 × 8 *(47 × 10.4 × 2.4)*
Main machinery: 2 Caterpillar D 343 diesels; 730 hp *(544 kW)* sustained; 2 shafts
Speed, knots: 9.5
Complement: 31 (3 officers)
Military lift: 150 tons
Guns: 2—12.7 mm MGs.

Comment: LSL delivered in 1988 for civilian use. Transferred to the Navy in 1990. A second of class is still in civilian service.

UPDATED

SHAH AMANAT   6/1996*, Bangladesh Navy / 0056562

2 LCU 1512 CLASS (LCU)

SHAH PARAN (ex-*Cerro Gordo*) L 901   **SHAH MAKHDUM** (ex-*Cadgel*) L 902

Displacement, tons: 375 full load
Dimensions, feet (metres): 134.9 × 29 × 6.1 *(41.1 × 8.8 × 1.9)*
Main machinery: 4 Detroit 6-71 diesels; 696 hp *(508 kW)* sustained; 2 shafts
Speed, knots: 11. **Range, miles:** 1,200 at 8 kt
Complement: 14 (2 officers)
Military lift: 170 tons
Guns: 2—12.7 mm MGs.
Radars: Navigation: LN 66; I-band.

Comment: Ex-US Army landing craft transferred in April 1991 and commissioned 16 May 1992 after refit.

UPDATED

SHAH MAKHDUM   6/1996*, Bangladesh Navy / 0056563

5 YUCH'IN CLASS (TYPE 068/069) (LCU/LCP)

DARSHAK A 581	**TALLASHI** A 582	
L 101	L 102	L 104

Displacement, tons: 85 full load
Dimensions, feet (metres): 81.2 × 17.1 × 4.3 *(24.8 × 5.2 × 1.3)*
Main machinery: 2 Type 12V 150 diesels; 600 hp(m) *(440 kW)*; 2 shafts
Speed, knots: 11.5. **Range, miles:** 450 at 11.5 kt
Complement: 23
Military lift: Up to 150 troops *(L 101-104)*
Guns: 4 China 14.5 mm (2 twin) MGs can be carried.

Comment: Named craft transferred from China in 1983 and used as an inshore survey craft. Second pair transferred 4 May 1986; third pair 1 July 1986. Probably built in the late 1960s. Two badly damaged in April 1991 typhoon and one of these has subsequently been scrapped.
UPDATED

DARSHAK (survey)   6/1984*, Bangladesh Navy / 0056560

L 101   2/1992*, Bangladesh Navy / 0056561

3 LCVP

L 011	L 012	L 013

Displacement, tons: 83 full load
Dimensions, feet (metres): 69.9 × 17.1 × 4.9 *(21.3 × 5.2 × 1.5)*
Main machinery: 2 Cummins diesels; 730 hp *(544 kW)*; 2 shafts
Speed, knots: 12
Complement: 10 (1 officer)

Comment: First two built at Khulna Shipyard and *013* at DEW Narayangong; all completed in 1984.
UPDATED

L 011   6/1996*, Bangladesh Navy / 0056564

TUGS

1 HUJIU CLASS (OCEAN TUG) (ATA)

KHADEM A 721

Displacement, tons: 1,472 full load
Dimensions, feet (metres): 197.5 × 38 × 16.1 *(60.2 × 11.6 × 4.9)*
Main machinery: 2 LVP 24 diesels; 1,800 hp(m) *(1.32 MW)*; 2 shafts
Speed, knots: 14. **Range, miles:** 7,200 at 14 kt
Complement: 56 (7 officers)
Guns: 2—12.7 mm MGs.
Radars: Navigation: China Type 756; I-band.

Comment: Commissioned 6 May 1984 after transfer from China.
UPDATED

KHADEM   6/1996*, Bangladesh Navy / 0056565

1 COASTAL TUG (YTM)

SEBAK A 722

Comment: Built at Dhaka in 1993. Commissioned in 1995.
UPDATED

SEBAK   6/1996*, Bangladesh Navy / 0056566

BARBADOS

Headquarters Appointments

Chief of Staff, Barbados Defence Force:
   Colonel H D Maynard
Commanding Officer Coast Guard Squadron:
   Lieutenant Commander D A Dowridge

Personnel

(a) 2000: 96 (11 officers)
(b) Voluntary service

Coast Guard

This was formed early in 1973. In 1979 it became the naval arm of the Barbados Defence Force.

Bases

Bridgetown (HMBS *Willoughby Fort*)

Prefix to Ships' Names

HMBS

Mercantile Marine

Lloyd's Register of Shipping:
   77 vessels of 724,797 tons gross

DELETIONS

Patrol Forces

1999   *T T Lewis, Commander Marshall, J T C Ramsey*

PATROL FORCES

1 KEBIR CLASS (LARGE PATROL CRAFT) (PC)

Name	No	Builders	Launched	Commissioned
TRIDENT	P 01	Brooke Marine	14 Apr 1981	Nov 1981

Displacement, tons: 155.5 standard; 190 full load
Dimensions, feet (metres): 123 × 22.6 × 5.6 *(37.5 × 6.9 × 1.7)*
Main machinery: 2 Paxman Valenta 12CM diesels; 5,000 hp *(3.73 MW)* sustained; 2 shafts
Speed, knots: 29. **Range, miles:** 3,000 at 12 kt
Complement: 28
Guns: 2—12.7 mm MGs. 2—12.7 mm MGs.
Radars: Surface search: Racal Decca Bridgemaster; I-band.

Comment: Refitted by Bender Shipyard in 1990 when the old guns were removed. Refitted again by Cable Marine in 1998 after a main engine seized. Same hull as Algerian 'Kebir' class.
UPDATED

TRIDENT   *1/1992* / 0056567

1 + 2 DAUNTLESS CLASS (INSHORE PATROL CRAFT) (PB)

Name	No	Builders	Commissioned
ENDEAVOUR	P 04	SeaArk Marine, Monticello	Dec 1997

Displacement, tons: 11 full load
Dimensions, feet (metres): 40 × 14 × 4.3 *(12.2 × 4.3 × 1.3)*
Main machinery: 2 Caterpillar 3208 TA diesels; 870 hp *(650 kW)*; 2 shafts
Speed, knots: 27. **Range, miles:** 600 at 18 kt
Complement: 4
Guns: 1—12.7 mm MG. 1—7.62 mm MG.
Radars: Surface search: Raytheon R40; I-band.

Comment: Aluminium construction. Two more to follow the first by mid-2000.
UPDATED

DAUNTLESS (Trinidad colours)   *5/1995*, SeaArk Marine / 0056568

4 INSHORE PATROL CRAFT (PB)

Comment: Two Boston Whaler *(P 08* and *P 09)* 22 ft craft; speed 25 kt; commissioned early 1989. One Zodiac Hurricane 24 ft, speed 25 kt commissioned July 1995. A third *(PO 10)* Boston Whaler acquired in late 1996. All used for law enforcement.
VERIFIED

BELGIUM

Headquarters Appointments

Chief of Naval Staff:
Rear Admiral M Verhulst
Deputy Chief of Naval Staff:
Captain W Goethals

Diplomatic Representation

Defence Attaché in London:
Captain A Kockx

Personnel

(a) 2000: 2,453
(b) Voluntary service

Bases

Zeebrugge: Frigates, MCMV, Reserve Units, Training Ships, Logistics, Diving Centre.
Oostende: Logistics, Mine Warfare Operational Sea Test centre (MOST).
Koksijde: Naval aviation.
Brugge: Naval training centre.

Mercantile Marine

Lloyd's Register of Shipping:
184 vessels of 132,084 tons gross

DELETIONS

Mine Warfare Forces

1997   *De Brouwer* (reserve), *F Bovesse* (reserve)
1998   *Merksem*
1999   *A F Dufour* (reserve)

Auxiliaries

1997   *Ekster*
1998   *Hommel*
1999   *Bij*

FRIGATES

WANDELAAR   *4/1999*, Michael Nitz / 0056570

3 WIELINGEN CLASS (TYPE E-71) (FFG)

Name	No	Builders	Laid down	Launched	Commissioned
WIELINGEN	F 910	Boelwerf, Temse	5 Mar 1974	30 Mar 1976	20 Jan 1978
WESTDIEP	F 911	Cockerill, Hoboken	2 Sep 1974	8 Dec 1975	20 Jan 1978
WANDELAAR	F 912	Boelwerf, Temse	28 Mar 1975	21 June 1977	27 Oct 1978

Displacement, tons: 1,940 light; 2,430 full load
Dimensions, feet (metres): 349 × 40.3 × 18.4
  (106.4 × 12.3 × 5.6)
Main machinery: CODOG; 1 RR Olympus TM3B gas-turbine;
  25,440 hp *(19 MW)* sustained; 2 Cockerill 240 CO V 12
  diesels; 6,000 hp(m) *(4.4 MW)*; 2 shafts; acbLIPS; cp props
Speed, knots: 26; 15 on 1 diesel; 20 on 2 diesels
Range, miles: 4,500 at 18 kt; 6,000 at 15 kt
Complement: 159 (13 officers)

Missiles: SSM: 4 Aerospatiale MM 38 Exocet (2 twin) launchers
  ❶; inertial cruise; active radar homing to 42 km *(23 n miles)* at
  0.9 Mach; warhead 165 kg; sea-skimmer.
  SAM: Raytheon Sea Sparrow Mk 29 octuple launcher ❷; semi-
  active radar homing to 14.6 km *(8 n miles)* at 2.5 Mach;
  warhead 39 kg.
Guns: 1 Creusot-Loire 3.9 in *(100 mm)*/55 Mod 68 ❸; 80 rds/
  min to 17 km *(9 n miles)* anti-surface; 8 km *(4.4 n miles)* anti-
  aircraft; weight of shell 13.5 kg.
Torpedoes: 2—21 in *(533 mm)* launchers. ECAN L5 Mod 4; anti-
  submarine; active/passive homing to 9.5 km *(5 n miles)* at
  35 kt; warhead 150 kg; depth to 550 m *(1,800 ft)*.
A/S Mortars: 1 Creusot-Loire 375 mm 6-barrelled trainable
  launcher ❹; Bofors rockets to 1,600 m; warhead 107 kg.
Countermeasures: Decoys: 2 Tracor MBA SRBOC 6-barrelled
  Mk 36 launchers; chaff decoys and IR flares to 4 km *(2.2 n
  miles)*.
  Nixie SLQ-25; towed anti-torpedo decoy.
  ESM: Thomson-CSF DR 2000 or Argos AR 900; intercept.
Combat data systems: Signaal SEWACO IV action data
  automation; Link 11. SATCOM.
Weapons control: 2 CSEE DMAb optical directors ❺ or Sagem
  Vigy 105 optronic director (from mid-2000).
Radars: Air/surface search: Signaal DA05 ❻; E/F-band.
  Surface search/fire control: Signaal WM25 ❼; I/J-band.
  Navigation: Signaal Scout; I/J-band.
  IFF: Mk XII.
Sonars: Computing Devices Canada SQS 510; hull-mounted;
  active search and attack; medium frequency.

Programmes: This compact, well-armed class of frigate was
  designed by the Belgian Navy and built in Belgian yards. The
  programme was approved on 23 June 1971 and an order
  placed in October 1973.
Modernisation: Plans to fit a CIWS were abandoned in 1993, but
  Sea Sparrow has been updated from 7M to 7P. In addition
  WM25 radar has been updated to improve ECCM and MTI
  qualities and a new navigation radar fitted. New sonars and
  ESM fitted from 1998. Optronic director, IFF and
  communications updates are being done to each ship from
  mid-2000 until 2002. *Wandelaar* is the last to complete.
Structure: Fully air conditioned. Fin stabilisers fitted.
Operational: Based at Zeebrugge. Two of the three remaining
  ships of this class are kept in an operational status and one is
  laid up in rotation.   ***UPDATED***

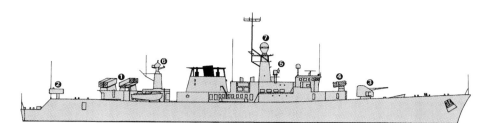

WIELINGEN   *(Scale 1 : 900), Ian Sturton*

WANDELAAR   *6/1999*, G Toremans / 0056569*

MINE WARFARE FORCES

7 FLOWER CLASS (TRIPARTITE)
(MINEHUNTERS—COASTAL) (MHC)

Name	No	Builders	Launched	Commissioned
ASTER	M 915	Beliard, Ostend	6 June 1985	17 Dec 1985
BELLIS	M 916	Beliard, Ostend	14 Feb 1986	14 Aug 1986
CROCUS	M 917	Beliard, Ostend	6 Aug 1986	5 Feb 1987
LOBELIA	M 921	Beliard, Ostend	6 Jan 1988	9 May 1989
MYOSOTIS	M 922	Beliard, Ostend	4 Aug 1988	14 Dec 1989
NARCIS	M 923	Beliard, Ostend	30 Mar 1990	27 Sep 1990
PRIMULA	M 924	Beliard, Ostend	17 Dec 1990	29 May 1991

Displacement, tons: 562 standard; 595 full load
Dimensions, feet (metres): 168.9 × 29.2 × 8.2 *(51.5 × 8.9 × 2.5)*
Main machinery: 1 Stork Wärtsilä A-RUB 215W-12 diesel; 1,860 hp(m) *(1.37 MW)* sustained;
  1 shaft; acbLIPS cp prop; 2 motors; 240 hp(m) *(176 kW)*; 2 active rudders; 2 bow thrusters
Speed, knots: 15. **Range, miles:** 3,000 at 12 kt
Complement: 46 (5 officers)

Guns: 1 DCN 20 mm/20; 720 rds/min to 10 km *(5.5 n miles)*. 1—12.7 mm MG.
Countermeasures: MCM: 2 PAP 104 remote-controlled mine locators; 39 charges.
  Mechanical sweep gear (medium depth).
Radars: Navigation: Racal Decca 1229; I-band.
Sonars: Thomson Sintra DUBM 21B; hull-mounted; active minehunting; 100 kHz ± 10 kHz.

Programmes: Developed in co-operation with France and the Netherlands. A 'ship factory' for the
  hulls was built at Ostend and the hulls were towed to Rupelmonde for fitting out. Each country
  built its own hulls but for all 35 ships. France provided MCM gear and electronics, Belgium
  electrical installation and the Netherlands the engine room equipment.
Modernisation: Propulsion system upgrade completed in 1999 for all of the class. Capability
  upgrade planned for 2001-04.
Structure: GRP hull fitted with active tank stabilisation, full NBC protection and air conditioning.
  Has automatic pilot and buoy tracking.
Operational: A 5 ton container can be carried, stored for varying tasks—HQ support, research,
  patrol, extended diving, drone control. The ship's company varies from 23 to 46 depending on
  the assigned task. Six divers are carried when minehunting. All of the class are based at
  Zeebrugge. *Myosotis* has been modified as an ammunition transport.
Sales: Three of the class paid off for sale in July 1993 and were bought by France in 1997.
                                                    UPDATED

NARCIS   *10/1998*, Selim San / 0081499*

MYSOTIS   *7/1999*, J Cislak / 0056572*

0 + 1 (3) KMV MINESWEEPERS (COASTAL) (MSC)

M 926-M 929

Displacement, tons: 644 full load
Dimensions, feet (metres): 170.6 × 31.5 × 11.2 *(52 × 9.6 × 3.4)*
Main machinery: 2 diesels; 2,176 hp(m) *(1.6 MW)* sustained; 2 shafts; cp props
Speed, knots: 15; 10 (sweeping). **Range, miles:** 3,000 at 12 kt
Complement: 27 plus 5 spare

Guns: 1—30 mm, 2—12.7 mm MGs.
Countermeasures: MCM: Thomson Sintra Sterne multi-influence sweep. M9 mechanical sweep.
Decoys: Chaff launcher.
ESM: Radar intercept.
Combat data systems: SEWACO.
Weapons control: Optronic director.
Radars: Navigation: ARPA; I-band.
Sonars: Active; moored mine detection; high frequency.

Programmes: Memorandum of Understanding signed 6 April 1989 for a joint Belgium/ Netherlands minesweeper project. Design contract awarded November 1990 to van der Giessen-de Noord Marinebouw in a joint venture with Beliard Polyship NV, completed in August 1992. Portugal joined the venture as an observer in 1991. In early 1993 the Netherlands pulled out due to budget restraints and Portugal had other priorities. Belgium therefore continues the project alone with four hulls authorised on 25 February 1994. Delays have been caused by arguments over prime contractorship and shipyard problems. An engineering contract placed with SKB Antwerp was completed in October 1999. The first of class is scheduled to be in service in 2003. The remaining three hulls are to be built from 2003 to 2007.
Structure: GRP hulls. An A frame is fitted on the stern.
Operational: The ship is to be fitted with a sophisticated combined influence sweeping gear capable of operating in what is called a Target Simulation Sweeping Mode. The gear will simulate the different characteristic influences of the ships or shipping to be protected. Following influences will be generated: magnetic, acoustic, extremely low frequency electromagnetic (ELFE) and underwater electrical potential (UEP). The gear is composed of six different bodies, interconnected and towed in array. The requirement is to be able to sweep mines which cannot be detected by hunters.

UPDATED

KMV   *(not to scale), Ian Sturton / 0056571*

1 AGGRESSIVE CLASS (OCEAN MINESWEEPER) (MSO)

Name	No	Builders	Commissioned
G TRUFFAUT	M 908	Tampa Marine, Tampa, FL	21 Sep 1956

Displacement, tons: 720 standard; 780 full load
Dimensions, feet (metres): 172.5 × 35.1 × 14.1 *(52.6 × 10.7 × 4.3)*
Main machinery: 4 GM 8-268A diesels; 1,760 hp *(1.3 MW)*; 2 shafts; acbLIPS; cp props
Speed, knots: 14. **Range, miles:** 2,400 at 12 kt; 3,000 at 10 kt
Complement: 40 (3 officers)

Guns: 2—12.7 mm MGs (twin).
Radars: Navigation: Racal Decca 1229; I-band.
Sonars: GE SQQ-14; VDS; minehunting; high frequency.

Programmes: Transferred from US; 12 October 1956.
Structure: Wooden hull and non-magnetic structure. Capable of sweeping mines of all types. Diesels of non-magnetic stainless steel alloy.
Operational: Based at Zeebrugge as the trials ship for Thomson Marconi Sterne multi-influence sweep. Three others of the class, M 903, M 904 and M 909, are in reserve but unlikely to go to sea again.

UPDATED

G TRUFFAUT   *6/1998, G Toremans / 0017599*

PATROL FORCES

Notes: (1) Three 7 m RIC were acquired in May 1994 from RIBTEC, Swanwick.
(2) Four Griffon Hovercraft belong to the Army.

1 RIVER PATROL CRAFT (PBR)

Name	No	Builders	Launched	Commissioned
LIBERATION	P 902	Hitzler, Regensburg	29 July 1954	4 Aug 1954

Displacement, tons: 45 full load
Dimensions, feet (metres): 85.5 × 13.1 × 3.2 *(26.1 × 4 × 1)*
Main machinery: 2 MWM diesels; 440 hp(m) *(323 kW)*; 2 shafts
Speed, knots: 19
Complement: 7
Guns: 2—12.7 mm MGs.
Radars: Navigation: Racal Decca; I-band.

Comment: Laid down 12 March 1954. Paid off 12 June 1987 but put back in active service 15 September 1989 after repairs. Last of a class of 10. Replacement planned when funds are available.

UPDATED

LIBERATION   *7/1999*, van Ginderen Collection / 0056573*

SHIPBORNE AIRCRAFT

Numbers/Type: 3 Aerospatiale SA 316B Alouette III.
Operational speed: 113 kt *(210 km/h)*.
Service ceiling: 10,500 ft *(3,200 m)*.
Range: 290 n miles *(540 km)*.
Role/Weapon systems: CG helicopter; used for close-range search and rescue and support for commando forces. Sensors: Carries Thomson-CSF search radar. Weapons: Unarmed.

UPDATED

ALOUETTE III   *7/1999*, M Declerck / 0056574*

LAND-BASED MARITIME AIRCRAFT

Numbers/Type: 5 Westland Sea King Mk 48.
Operational speed: 140 kt *(260 km/h)*.
Service ceiling: 10,500 ft *(3,200 m)*.
Range: 630 n miles *(1,165 km)*.
Role/Weapon systems: SAR helicopter; operated by air force; used for surface search and combat rescue tasks. Upgraded in 1995 with new radar, FLIR and GPS. Sensors: Bendix RDR 1500B search radar. FLIR 2000F. Weapons: Unarmed.

UPDATED

SEA KING   *7/1999*, van Ginderen Collection / 0056575*

AUXILIARIES

1 COMMAND AND SUPPORT SHIP (AGF)

Name	No	Builders	Launched	Commissioned
ZINNIA	A 961	Cockerill, Hoboken	6 May 1967	22 Sep 1967

Displacement, tons: 1,705 light; 2,620 full load
Dimensions, feet (metres): 324.7 × 45.9 × 11.8 *(99 × 14 × 3.6)*
Main machinery: 2 Cockerill Ougree 240 CO 12 TR diesels; 5,000 hp(m) *(3.68 MW)*; 1 shaft; cp prop
Speed, knots: 18. **Range, miles:** 14,000 at 12.5 kt
Complement: 102 (8 officers)
Guns: 2 Bofors 40 mm/60.
Radars: Surface search: Racal Decca 1229; I-band.
Helicopters: 1 Alouette III.

Comment: Laid down 8 November 1966. Design includes a telescopic hangar. Rated as Command and Logistic Support Ship with an oil fuel capacity of 500 tons. Fitted with chaff launchers for prolonged operations. Based at Zeebrugge and inactive since 1995. May be replaced by a second-hand RoRo ship. *VERIFIED*

ZINNIA　　　　10/1998, van Ginderen Collection / 0017603

1 COMMAND AND SUPPORT SHIP (AGF)

Name	No	Builders	Launched	Commissioned
GODETIA	A 960	Boelwerf, Temse	7 Dec 1965	23 May 1966

Displacement, tons: 2,000 standard; 2,260 full load
Dimensions, feet (metres): 301 × 46 × 11.5 *(91.8 × 14 × 3.5)*
Main machinery: 4 ACEC-MAN diesels; 5,400 hp(m) *(3.97 MW)*; 2 shafts; cp props
Speed, knots: 19. **Range, miles:** 8,700 at 12.5 kt
Complement: 105 (8 officers)
Guns: 6—12.7 mm MGs.
Radars: Surface search: Racal Decca 1229; I-band.
Helicopters: Platform for 1 Alouette III.

Comment: Laid down 15 February 1965. Rated as Command and Logistic Support Ship. Refit (1979-80) and mid-life conversion (1981-82) included helicopter deck and replacement cranes. Refitted again in 1992. Minesweeping cables fitted either side of helo deck are being removed. Can also serve as a Royal Yacht. *UPDATED*

GODETIA　　　　11/1999*, van Ginderen Collection / 0056576

1 SUPPORT SHIP (ARL)

Name	No	Builders	Commissioned
STERN (ex-*KBV 171*)	A 963	Karlskronavarvet	3 Sep 1980

Displacement, tons: 375 full load
Dimensions, feet (metres): 164 × 27.9 × 7.9 *(50 × 8.5 × 2.4)*
Main machinery: 2 Hedemora V16A diesels; 4,480 hp(m) *(3.28 MW)* sustained; 2 shafts; cp props
Speed, knots: 18. **Range, miles:** 3,000 at 12 kt
Complement: 18
Radars: Navigation: 2 Kelvin Hughes; E/F- and I-band.
Helicopters: Platform for 1 light.

Comment: Transferred from Swedish Coast Guard on 6 October 1998. GRP hull indentical to 'Landsort' class. In Swedish service the ship carried a 20 mm gun, and had a Subsea sonar. Used for fishery protection and SAR duties. *UPDATED*

STERN　　　　7/1999*, van Ginderen Collection / 0056577

1 HARBOUR LAUNCH (YP)

SPIN A 997

Comment: Harbour launch of 32 tons built in Netherlands 1958. Based at Zeebrugge. A second launch *Avila* became a museum exhibit in 1996. *UPDATED*

SPIN　　　　7/1999*, van Ginderen Collection / 0056578

TUGS

6 COASTAL/HARBOUR TUGS (YTM/YTL)

VALCKE (ex-*Steenbank*, ex-*Astroloog*) A 950	ALBATROS (ex-*Westgat*) A 996　WESP A 952	KREKEL A 956　MIER A 955	ZEEMEEUW A 954

Displacement, tons: 183 full load
Dimensions, feet (metres): 99.7 × 24.9 × 11.8 *(30.4 × 7.6 × 3.6)*
Main machinery: Diesel-electric; 2 Deutz diesel generators; 1,240 hp(m) *(911 kW)*; 1 shaft
Speed, knots: 12
Complement: 12

Comment: Details given are for A 950. A 952 and A 955 are 195 tons, A 954 is 146 tons, A 996 is 206 tons, and A 956 is 60 tons. All were launched between 1960 (A 950) and 1971 (A 954) and all are capable of about 12 kt. *UPDATED*

WESP　　　　7/1999*, G Toremans / 0056581

ALBATROS　　　　7/1999*, van Ginderen Collection / 0056580

SURVEY AND RESEARCH SHIPS

Note: In addition to *Belgica* there are five small civilian manned survey craft: *Ter Streep*, *Scheldewacht II*, *De Parel II*, *Veremans* and *Prosper*.

Name	No	Builders	Launched	Commissioned
BELGICA	A 962	Boelwerf, Temse	6 Jan 1984	5 July 1984

Displacement, tons: 1,085 full load
Dimensions, feet (metres): 167 × 32.8 × 14.4 *(50.9 × 10 × 4.4)*
Main machinery: 1 ABC 6M DZC diesel; 1,600 hp(m) *(1.18 MW)* sustained; 1 Kort nozzle prop
Speed, knots: 13.5. **Range, miles:** 5,000 at 12 kt
Complement: 26 (11 civilian)
Radars: Navigation: Racal Decca 1229; I-band.

Comment: Ordered 1 December 1982. Laid down 17 October 1983. Used for hydrography, oceanography, meteorology and fishery control. Marisat fitted. Based at Zeebrugge. Painted white.

UPDATED

BELGICA   *7/1999*, van Ginderen Collection /* 0056579

TRAINING SHIPS

1 SAIL TRAINING VESSEL (AXS)

Name	No	Builders	Commissioned
ZENOBE GRAMME	A 958	Boel and Zonen, Temse	27 Dec 1961

Displacement, tons: 149 full load
Dimensions, feet (metres): 92 × 22.5 × 7 *(28 × 6.8 × 2.1)*
Main machinery: 1 MWM diesel; 200 hp(m) *(147 kW)*; 1 shaft
Speed, knots: 10
Complement: 14 (2 officers)
Radars: Navigation: Racal Decca; I-band.

Comment: Auxiliary sail ketch. Laid down 7 October 1960 and launched 23 October 1961. Designed for scientific research but now only used as a training ship.

UPDATED

ZENOBE GRAMME   *7/1999*, Per Kornefeldt /* 0056582

BELIZE

Headquarters Appointments

Commanding Officer Defence Force Maritime Wing:
   Major F Teck

Personnel

(a) 2000: 39 (4 officers)
(b) The Maritime Wing of the Belize Defence Force comprises volunteers from the Army.

Bases

Ladyville, Hunting Caye

General

The Maritime Wing, which may become a Coast Guard in 2000/01, comprises:
(a) Two Halmatic 22 ft RIBs with twin Yamaha 115 hp outboards. Names *Stingray Commando* and *Blue Marlin Ranger.*
(b) Two Pelikan 35 ft craft with twin Yamaha 200 hp outboards. Built at Bradleys Boatyard in 1996 and called *Ocean Sentinel* and *Reef Sniper.*
(c) Four Colombian 32 ft skiffs with twin Yamaha 200 hp outboards, confiscated and commissioned in service 1995-97.

Maritime Patrol

Two Pilatus Britten-Norman Defenders are used for maritime surveillance.

Mercantile Marine

Lloyd's Register of Shipping:
   1,631 vessels of 2,368,152 tons gross

DELETIONS

Patrol Forces

1997   *Charcoal Warrior* (sold), *Barracuda Guardsman* (sold), *Shark Invaders* (Monza) (sold), *Sharan* (not acquired)
1999   *Dangriga, Toledo* (both sold)

BENIN

Headquarters Appointments

Commander Navy:
   Lieutenant Colonel Prosper Beré Kiando

General

In 1978 a decision was taken to found a naval force. As the coastline of Benin is no more than 75 miles long the Patrol Craft can cover the whole coast in a little over two hours.

Aircraft

Dornier Do 128 and a DHC-6 Twin Otter reconnaissance aircraft are used for surveillance.

Bases

Cotonou

Personnel

1999: 50

Mercantile Marine

Lloyd's Register of Shipping:
   7 vessels of 1,118 tons gross

PATROL FORCES

Note: Four 'Zhuk' class patrol craft are derelict.

PATROLE   *9/1992, French Navy*

1 PR 360T COASTAL PATROL CRAFT (PC)

PATRIOTE

Displacement, tons: 70 full load
Dimensions, feet (metres): 124.7 × 22.3 × 4.3 *(38 × 6.8 × 1.3)*
Main machinery: 3 Baudouin 12P15.2SR diesels; 3,000 hp(m) *(2.2 MW)* sustained; 3 water-jets
Speed, knots: 35. **Range, miles:** 1,500 at 16 kt
Complement: 23
Guns: 1 Oerlikon 20 mm. 2—12.7 mm MGs.
Radars: Surface search: Decca; I-band.

Comment: Laid down by Société Bretonne de Construction Navale (Loctudy) in October 1986. Launched January 1988 and completed 15 May 1988. Has a wood/epoxy resin composite hull. Endurance 10 days. The craft was damaged shortly after delivery and was not operational again until early 1992. Operational status doubtful, but may still be seaworthy.

VERIFIED

BERMUDA

Headquarters Appointments

Commanding Officer:
Inspector Mark Bothello

General

A small group operated by the Bermuda Police. There are also two tugs, *Powerful* and *Faithful*, operated by the Department of Marine and Port Services.

Bases

Hamilton

Mercantile Marine

Lloyd's Register of Shipping:
140 vessels of 6,186,973 tons gross

POLICE

BLUE HERON

Comment: Donated by the US Drug Enforcement Agency in May 1996 to replace the original craft of the same name. 46 ft *(14 m)* in length and fitted with a Furuno radar. Complement six. The craft is used by the Joint Marine Interdiction Team to patrol inshore waters to intercept drug runners.

UPDATED

HERON I   HERON II   HERON III

Comment: *Heron I,* delivered in July 1997 to replace the previous craft of the same name, and *Heron III* delivered in June 1992 are 22 ft Boston Whalers fitted with twin Yamaha 225 hp and twin Yamaha 115 hp outboards, respectively. *Heron II* delivered in August 1996 to replace the previous craft of the same name, is a 27 ft Boston Whaler with twin Yamaha 250 hp(m) outboard engines.

UPDATED

HERON II   6/1997*, *Bermuda Police* / 0012079

RESCUE I   RESCUE II

Comment: *Rescue II* delivered May 1988 by Osborne Rescue Boats Ltd. An 'Arctic' rigid hull inflatable. Of 1.45 tons, 24 ft with twin Yamaha 115 hp outboard engines. Complement three. *Rescue I* replaced the craft of the same name in November 1998. She is a Halmatic 24 ft Arctic RIB with twin 200 hp Yamaha outboards and a complement of three.

VERIFIED

BLUE HERON   5/1996*, *Bermuda Police* / 0056583

BOLIVIA
ARMADA BOLIVIANA

Headquarters Appointments

Commander in Chief, Navy:
Admiral Luis Adolfo Guillen Tejada

Personnel

(a) 2000: 5,000 (including Marines)
(b) 12 months' selective military service

General

Used for patrolling Lake Titicaca and the Beni, Madre de Dios, Mamoré and Paraguay river systems. Founded in 1963, receiving its present name in 1982. These rivers cover over 10,000 miles. Most of the advanced training of officers and senior ratings is carried out in Argentina and Peru. The junior ratings are almost entirely converted soldiers.

Organisation

The country is divided into six naval districts, each with one flotilla.
1st Naval District at *Bague* (HQ Riberalta). Patrol craft and two BTL logistic vessels on the Beni/Mamoré river system.
2nd Naval District at *Tocopilla* (HQ Trinidad). Patrol craft and two BTL logistic vessels on the northern portion of Lake Titicaca.
3rd Naval District at *Mejillones* (HQ Puerto Guayaramerin). Four patrol craft and two BTL logistic vessels on the Madre de Dios river.
4th Naval District at *Independencia* and *Alianza* (HQ San Pedro de Tiquina). Patrol craft and the hospital ship on the southern portion of Lake Titicaca.
5th Naval District at *Calama* (HQ Puerto Quijarro). Three patrol craft and one BTL logistic vessel on the upper Paraguay river.
6th Naval District at *Columna Porvenir* (HQ Cobija). Patrol craft.

Prefix to Ships' Names

ARB

Marine Corps

Infanteria de Marina of 2,000 men based at Tiquina with detachments at Riberalta, Trinidad, Puerto Guayaramerin, Quijarro and Cobija.

Aviation

One Cessna 402C are used for reconnaissance and transport. Six SA 315B helicopters are owned by the Air Force but used for marine operations.

Mercantile Marine

Lloyd's Register of Shipping:
60 vessels of 178,937 tons gross

PATROL FORCES

4 LAKE PATROL CRAFT (PBF)

CAPITAN PALOMEQUE PR 21	ANTOFAGASTA PR 32
PRESIDENTE PAZ ZAMORA PR 11	GENERAL BANZER P 31

Displacement, tons: 8 full load
Dimensions, feet (metres): 42.7 × 10.5 × 1.6 *(13 × 3.2 × 0.5)*
Main machinery: 2 diesels; 2 shafts
Speed, knots: 27
Complement: 4
Guns: 1—7.62 mm MG.

Comment: Details given are for *Capitan Palomeque* acquired in 1993. The others are similar in appearance and all are less than ten years old. Operate in the 1st, 2nd and 3rd Districts.

UPDATED

CAPITAN PALOMEQUE   1996*, *Bolivian Navy* / 0056585

1 SANTA CRUZ CLASS (PBR)

SANTA CRUZ DE LA SIERRA PR 51

Displacement, tons: 46 full load
Dimensions, feet (metres): 68.9 × 19 × 3.9 *(21 × 5.8 × 1.2)*
Main machinery: 2 Detroit diesels; 2 shafts
Speed, knots: 20. **Range, miles:** 800 at 16 kt
Complement: 10
Guns: 2—12.7 mm MGs.
Radars: Surface search: Furuno; I-band.

Comment: Built by Hope Shipyards, Louisiana, in 1985. Used both as a patrol craft and supply ship. Operates in the 5th District on the river Paraguay.

UPDATED

SANTA CRUZ DE LA SIERRA   *1996*, Bolivian Navy /* 0056584

11 BOSTON WHALERS (PBR)

COMANDO LP 401	MARISCAL DE ZAPITA LP 409	SANTA ROSA LP 604
INTI LP 404	COBIJA LP 601	PORVENIR LP 605
MALLCU LP 405	RAPIRRAN LP 602	ACRE LP 606
AUXILIAR LP 408	PUERTO RICO LP 603	

Displacement, tons: 2 full load
Dimensions, feet (metres): 22.3 × 7.5 × 2.3 *(6.8 × 2.3 × 0.7)*
Main machinery: 2 outboards; 360 hp *(267 kW)*
Speed, knots: 40
Complement: 2
Guns: 1—12.7 mm MG.

Comment: The survivors of 15 craft delivered under US Grant Aid in 1989-91. Augmented by Rodman craft in February 1999.

UPDATED

COMANDO   *1996*, Bolivian Navy /* 0056586

6 CAPITAN BRETEL CLASS (PBR)

CAPITAN BRETEL LP 410	T F BACARREZA LP 412	GUAQUI LA 414
TENIENTE SOLIZ LP 411	COPACABANA LP 413	CHAGUAYA LP 415

Displacement, tons: 5 full load
Dimensions, feet (metres): 42.3 × 12.7 × 3.3 *(12.9 × 3.9 × 1)*
Main machinery: 2 diesels; 2 shafts
Speed, knots: 15
Complement: 5
Guns: 1—12.7 mm MG.
Radars: Surface search: Raytheon; I-band.

Comment: *Guaqui* is used as logistic craft. All operate in the 4th District.

UPDATED

CAPITAN BRETEL alongside TENIENTE SOLIZ   *1996*, Bolivian Navy /* 0056587

32 PIRANA Mk II and 26 RODMAN CLASS (PBR)

LP 01-LP 32

Comment: The Piranas were delivered from 1992 onwards. Fitted with one 12.7 mm MG and has twin outboards. The Rodmans are a mixture of 17 m, 11 m and 8 m craft, were delivered on 11 February 1999 and are used for transport.

UPDATED

PIRANA Mk II   *1996*, Bolivian Navy /* 0056588

15 LOGISTIC SUPPORT and PATROL CRAFT (AFL/PBR)

GENERAL PANDO BTL-01	V A H UGARTECHE BTL-06	TRINIDAD M-224
NICOLAS SUAREZ BTL-02	ALMIRANTE GRAU M-101	J CHAVEZ SUAREZ M-225
MARISCAL CRUZ BTL-03	COMANDANTE ARANDIA M-103	ING PALACIOS M-315
MAX PAREDES BTL-04	MANURIPI M-105 (ex-BTL-07)	ING GUMUCIO M-341
CAPITAN OLMOS BTL-05	LIBERTADOR M-223	SUAREZ ARANA M-510

Displacement, tons: 70 full load
Dimensions, feet (metres): 78.7 × 21.3 × 4.6 *(24 × 6.5 × 1.4)*
Speed, knots: 12. **Range, miles:** 500 at 12 kt
Complement: 11
Radars: Navigation: Raytheon; I-band.

Comment: Details given are for *Ing Gumucio* which is a troop transport and supply ship. The craft with BTL numbers are river tankers and have a liquid cargo capacity of 250,000 litres and a displacement of 40 tons. The remainder are logistic craft of various types, some acquired from China.

UPDATED

ING GUMUCIO   *1996*, Bolivian Navy /* 0056589

4 AUXILIARIES

Name	No	Tonnage
JULIAN APAZA	AH 01	150
BOLIVIAMAR	LT 02	30
PIONERA	LH 01	30
XAVIER PINTO TELLERIA	TNBH 01	—

Comment: AH 01 is a hospital ship given by the USA in 1972, LT 01 a transport vessel, LH 01 a survey ship and *Telleria* a hospital ship built in 1997 for the 2nd and 3rd naval districts.

UPDATED

BRAZIL
MARINHA DO BRASIL

Headquarters Appointments

Commander of the Navy:
Admiral Sergio Gitirana Florêncio Chagasteles
Chief of Naval Staff:
Admiral Arlindo Vianna Filho
Chief of Naval Operations:
Admiral José Alberto Accioly Fragelli
Chief of Naval Personnel:
Admiral Roberto de Guimaräes Carvalho
Commandant General Brazilian Marines:
Admiral (Marine Corps) Carlos Augusto Costa
General Director of Material:
Admiral Airton Ronaldo Longo
General Secretary of Navy:
Admiral Marcos Augusto Leal de Azevedo
Vice Chief of Naval Staff:
Vice Admiral Miguel Angelo Davena

Senior Officers

Commander-in-Chief, Fleet:
Vice Admiral Jeronymo MacDowell Gonçalves
Commander, Fleet Marine Force:
Vice Admiral (Marine Corps) Marcelo Gaya Cardoso Tosta
Commander, I Naval District:
Vice Admiral Mauro Magalhäes de Souza Pinto
Commander, II Naval District:
Vice Admiral Rayder Alencar da Silveira
Commander, III Naval District:
Vice Admiral Marcio Mortello Assumpcao Taveira
Commander, IV Naval District:
Vice Admiral José Alfredo Lourenço Dos Santos
Commander, V Naval District:
Vice Admiral Izidério de Almeida Mendes
Commander, VI Naval District:
Rear Admiral Lucio Franco de Sa Fernandez
Commander, VII Naval District:
Rear Admiral Julio Saboya de Aranjo Jorge
Commander, VIII Naval District
Vice Admiral Euclides Duncan Janot de Matos
Commander, Occidental Amazonia Naval Command:
Rear Admiral Murillo de Moraes Rego Correa Barbosa

Diplomatic Representation

Naval Attaché in England, Sweden and Norway:
Captain Ariel Certano Franco
Naval Attaché in Uruguay:
Captain Francisco Cesar Augusto Texeira Villaça
Naval Attaché in France and Belgium:
Captain Carlos Afonso Fernandez Testoni
Naval Attaché in Italy:
Captain Bernardo José Pierantoni Gambôa
Naval Attaché in Paraguay:
Captain Celso Lehnemann
Naval Attaché in Germany and Netherlands:
Captain Paulo Cezar Garcia Brandão
Naval Attaché in South Africa:
Captain Vinicius Fréire Japlassu
Naval Attaché in Bolivia:
Captain Werner Gripp
Naval Attaché in Argentina:
Captain Ney Zanella Dos Santos
Naval Attaché in Venezuela:
Captain Arnon Lima Barbosa
Naval Attaché in Peru:
Captain Luiz Roberto de Moraes Passos
Naval Attaché in Portugal:
Captain Marcos Perdiglo Bernardes
Naval Attaché in Chile:
Captain Marcos Augusto Dias Ferreira

Naval Attaché in USA and Canada:
Rear Admiral Alvaro Luiz Pinto
Defence Attaché in Spain:
Captain Sergio Baptista Soares
Defence Attaché in Japan and Indonesia:
Captain Teodorico Ferreira Fernandes
Defence Attaché in China and Korea:
Captain Cesar Augusto Lambert de Azevedo

Personnel

(a) 2000: 31,400 (5,900 officers) Navy; (including 1,300 naval air)
15,100 (680 officers) Marines
(b) One year's national service

Bases

Arsenal de Marinha do Rio de Janeiro - Rio de Janeiro (Naval shipyard with three dry docks and one floating dock with graving docks of up to 70,000 tons capacity)
Base Naval do Rio de Janeiro - Rio de Janeiro (Main Naval Base with two dry docks)
Base Almirante Castro e Silva - Rio de Janeiro (Naval Base for submarines)
Base Naval de Aratu - Bahia (Naval Base and repair yard with one dry dock and synchrolift)
Base Naval de Val-de-Cães - Pará (Naval River and repair yard with one dry dock)
Base Naval de Natal - Rio Grande do Norte (Small Naval Base and repair yard with one floating dock)
Base Fluvial de Ladário - Mato Grosso do Sul (Small Naval River Base and repair yard with one dry dock)
Base Aérea Naval de São Pedro d'Aldeia - Rio de Janeiro (Naval Air Station)
Estação Naval do Rio Negro - Amazonas (Small Naval River Station and repair yard with one floating dock)
Estação Naval do Rio Grande - Rio Grande do Sul (Small Naval Station and repair yard)

Organisation

Naval Districts as follows:
I Naval District (HQ Rio de Janeiro)
II Naval District (HQ Salvador)
III Naval District (HQ Natal)
IV Naval District (HQ Belém)
V Naval District (HQ Rio Grande)
VI Naval District (HQ Ladário)
VII Naval District (HQ Brasilia)
VIII Naval District (HQ São Paulo)
Comando Naval de Amazonia Occidental (HQ Manaus)

Naval Aviation

Squadrons: São Pedro da Aldeira; HA-1 Super Lynx; HS-1 Sea King; HI-1 JetRanger; HU-1 Ecureuil 1 and 2; HU-2 Super Puma/Cougar; VF 1 Skyhawk AF1.
Estação Naval do Rio Negro; HU-3 Ecureuil.
Base Fluvial de Ladario; HU-4 Ecureuil.
Estação Naval do Rio Grande; HU-5 Ecureuil.

Prefix to Ships' Names

These vary, indicating the type of ship for example, N Ae L = Aircraft Carrier; CT = Destroyer.

Pennant Numbers

As a result of cuts in Officer numbers, ships are sometimes formally decommissioned from the Navy and lose their pennant numbers. They are then retained in service as tenders to Naval establishments and are commanded by Warrant Officers.

Marines (Corpo de Fuzileiros Navais)

Headquarters at Fort São José, Rio de Janeiro
Divisão Anfibia: 3 Infantry Battalions (Riachuelo, Humaita and Paissandu), 1 Artillery Battalion, 1 HQ Company, 1 Air Defence Battery, 1 Tank Company.
Tropa de Reforço: 1 Engineer Battalion, 1 Amphib Vehicles Battalion, 1 Logistic Battalion.
Special Forces Battalion (Tonelero).
Grupamentos Regionais: One security group in each naval district and command (Rio de Janeiro, Salvador, Natal, Belém, Rio Grande, Ladário, Manaus, Brasilia).

Strength of the Fleet

Type	Active	Building (Planned)
Submarines (Patrol)	5	2
Aircraft Carrier (light)	1	—
Destroyers/Frigates	14	—
Corvettes	4	1 (7)
Patrol Forces	49	— (12)
LSD/LST	4	—
Minesweepers (Coastal)	6	—
Survey and Research Ships	9	—
Buoy Tenders	22	—
S/M Rescue Ship	1	—
Tankers	3	—
Hospital Ships	2	—
Training Ships	8	—

Mercantile Marine

Lloyd's Register of Shipping:
503 vessels of 3,933,327 tons gross

DELETIONS

Submarines

1997 *Riachuelo* (museum)

Destroyers

1997 *Mariz E Barros* (trials)

Patrol Forces

1997 *Forte de Coimbra*
1999 *Mearim*

Auxiliaries and Survey Ships

1997 *Canopus, Belmonte, Atlas, Campos Salles*

PENNANT LIST

Submarines

S 21	Tonelero
S 30	Tupi
S 31	Tamoio
S 32	Timbira
S 33	Tapajo
S 34	Tikuna (bldg)

Aircraft Carriers

A 11	Minas Gerais

Destroyers/Frigates

D 27	Pará
D 28	Paraiba
D 29	Paraná
D 30	Pernambuco
F 40	Niteroi
F 41	Defensora
F 42	Constituição
F 43	Liberal
F 44	Independência
F 45	União
F 46	Greenhalgh
F 47	Dodsworth
F 48	Bosisio
F 49	Rademaker

Corvettes

V 30	Inhaúma
V 31	Jaceguay
V 32	Julio de Noronha
V 33	Frontin
V 34	Barroso (bldg)

Amphibious Forces

G 26	Duque de Caxias
G 28	Mattoso Maia
G 30	Ceará
G 31	Rio de Janeiro
GED 10	Guarapari
GED 11	Tambaú
GED 12	Camboriú

Patrol Forces

V 15	Imperial Marinheiro
V 19	Caboclo
V 20	Angostura
V 21	Bahiana
V 23	Purus
V 24	Solimões
P 10	Piratini
P 11	Pirajá
P 12	Pampeiro
P 13	Parati
P 14	Penedo
P 15	Poti
P 20	Pedro Teixeira
P 21	Raposo Tavares
P 30	Roraima
P 31	Rondônia
P 32	Amapá
P 40	Grajaú
P 41	Guaiba
P 42	Graúna
P 43	Goiana
P 44	Guajará
P 45	Guaporé
P 46	Gurupá
P 47	Gurupi
P 48	Guanabara
P 49	Guaruja
P 50	Guaratuba
P 51	Gravataí
P 60	Bracui
P 61	Benevente
P 62	Bocaina
P 63	Babitonga

Mine Warfare Forces

M 15	Aratú
M 16	Anhatomirim
M 17	Atalaia
M 18	Araçatuba
M 19	Abrolhos
M 20	Albardão

Survey Ships and Tenders

H 13	Mestre João dos Santos
H 18	Comandante Varella
H 19	Tenente Castelo
H 20	Comandante Manhães
H 21	Sirius
H 24	Castelhanos
H 25	Tenente Boanerges
H 26	Faroleiro Mário Seixas
H 27	Faroleiro Areas
H 30	Faroleiro Nascimento
H 31	Argus
H 32	Orion
H 34	AlmiraOnte Graça Aranha
H 35	Amorim do Valle
H 36	Taurus
H 37	Garnier Sampaio
H 40	Antares
H 41	Almirante Câmara
H 42	Barão de Teffé
H 44	Ary Rongel

Auxiliaries

G 15	Paraguassú
G 17	Potengi
G 20	Custódio de Mello
G 21	Ary Parreiras
G 22	Soares Dutra
G 23	Almirante Gastao Motta
G 27	Marajo
K 11	Felinto Perry
R 21	Tritão
R 22	Tridente
R 23	Triunfo
R 24	Almirante Guilhem
R 25	Almirante Guillobel
U 10	Aspirante Nascimento
U 11	Guarda Marinha Jensen
U 12	Guarda Marinha Brito
U 16	Trindade
U 17	Parnaiba
U 18	Oswaldo Cruz
U 19	Carlos Chagas
U 20	Cisne Branco
U 27	Brasil
U 29	Piraim

SUBMARINES

Note: Plans for the construction of nuclear-powered submarines are advancing with a prototype nuclear reactor IPEN/MB-1 built at Aramar, Iperó, São Paulo. A uranium enrichment plant was inaugurated at Iperó in April 1988. The prototype SSN (SNAC-2) *Riachuelo* is to be about 2,825 tons and have a power plant developing 50 MW for a speed of 25 kt. In mid-1995 it was announced that the project was delayed by a decade to 2010.

0 + 1 TIKUNA CLASS (SNAC-1)

Name	No
TIKUNA (ex-*Tocantins*)	S 34

Builders	Laid down	Launched	Commissioned
Arsenal de Marinha, Rio de Janeiro	11 June 1997	Apr 2000	2003

Displacement, tons: 1,850 surfaced; 2,425 dived
Dimensions, feet (metres): 219.7 × 26.2 × 18
 (67 × 8 × 5.5)
Main machinery: Diesel-electric; 4 MTU 12V 396 diesels;
 3,760 hp(m) *(2.76 MW)*; 4 alternators; 1 motor; 1 shaft
Speed, knots: 11 surfaced/snorting; 22 dived
Range, miles: 11,000 at 8 kt surfaced; 400 at 4 kt dived
Complement: 39 (8 officers)

Missiles: SSM: Exocet or Sub Harpoon.
Torpedoes: 8—21 in *(533 mm)* bow tubes. Bofors Torpedo 2000; wire guided active/passive homing to 50 km *(27 n miles)* at 20-50 kt; warhead 250 kg. Swim-out discharge. IPqM designed A/S torpedoes may also be carried; 18 km *(9.7 n miles)* at 45 kt. Total of 16 missiles and torpedoes.
Mines: 32 IPqM/Consub MCF-01/100 carried in lieu of torpedoes.
Countermeasures: ESM: Thomson-CSF DR-4000; intercept.
Weapons control: ISUS 83-13; 2 Kollmorgen Mod 76 periscopes.
Radars: Navigation: Thomson-CSF Calypso III; I-band.
Sonars: Atlas Elektronik CSU-83/1; hull-mounted; passive/active search and attack; medium frequency.

Programmes: Planned intermediate stage between 'Tupi' class and the first SSN. Designed by the Naval Engineering Directorate. Contract effective with HDW in October 1995 for S 34, although the completion date has drifted six years and a projected second of class has been cancelled.
Structure: Improved Tupi design. Diving depth, 300 m *(985 ft)*. Very high-capacity batteries with GRP lead-acid cells by Varta/Saturnia. More powerful engines than *Tupi*, a non-penetrating optronic mast and much improved fire-control system.
Operational: Endurance, 60 days.

UPDATED

4 TUPI CLASS (209 TYPE 1400) (SSK)

Name	No
TUPI	S 30
TAMOIO	S 31
TIMBIRA	S 32
TAPAJÓ (ex-*Tapajós*)	S 33

Builders	Laid down	Launched	Commissioned
Howaldtswerke-Deutsche Werft, Kiel	8 Mar 1985	28 Apr 1987	6 May 1989
Arsenal de Marinha, Rio de Janeiro	15 July 1986	18 Nov 1993	12 Dec 1994
Arsenal de Marinha, Rio de Janeiro	15 Sep 1987	5 Jan 1996	16 Dec 1996
Arsenal de Marinha, Rio de Janeiro	6 Mar 1996	5 June 1998	Apr 2000

Displacement, tons: 1,400 surfaced; 1,550 dived
Dimensions, feet (metres): 200.8 × 20.3 × 18
 (61.2 × 6.2 × 5.5)
Main machinery: Diesel-electric; 4 MTU 12V 493 AZ80 GA31L diesels; 2,400 hp(m) *(1.76 MW)*; 4 alternators; 1.7 MW; 1 Siemens motor; 4,600 hp(m) *(3.36 MW)* sustained; 1 shaft
Speed, knots: 11 surfaced/snorting; 21.5 dived
Range, miles: 8,200 at 8 kt surfaced; 400 at 4 kt dived
Complement: 36 (7 officers)

Torpedoes: 8—21 in *(533 mm)* bow tubes. 16 Marconi Mk 24 Tigerfish Mod 1 or 2; wire-guided; active homing to 13 km *(7 n miles)* at 35 kt; passive homing to 29 km *(15.7 n miles)* at 24 kt; warhead 134 kg. IPqM anti-submarine torpedoes may also be carried; range 18 km *(9.7 n miles)* at 45 kt. Swim-out discharge.
Countermeasures: ESM: Thomson-CSF DR-4000; radar warning.
Weapons control: Ferranti KAFS-A10 action data automation. 2 Kollmorgen Mod 76 periscopes.
Radars: Navigation: Thomson-CSF Calypso III; I-band.
Sonars: Atlas Elektronik CSU-83/1; hull-mounted; passive/active search and attack; medium frequency.

Programmes: Contract signed with Howaldtswerke in February 1984. Financial negotiations were completed with the West German Government in October 1984. Original plans included building four in Brazil followed by two improved Tupis for a total of six. In the end only three were constructed in Brazil.
Modernisation: Retrofit of Bofors 2000 torpedo is planned in due course.
Structure: Hull constructed of HY 80 steel. Diving depth, 250 m *(820 ft)*. Equipped with Sperry Mk 29 Mod 3 SINS.
Operational: Based at Niteroi, Rio de Janeiro.

UPDATED

TUPI

8/1997, van Ginderen Collection / 0017610

1 HUMAITÁ (OBERON) CLASS (SSK)

Name	No
TONELERO	S 21

Builders	Laid down	Launched	Commissioned
Vickers, Barrow	18 Nov 1971	22 Nov 1972	10 Dec 1977

Displacement, tons: 2,030 surfaced; 2,410 dived
Dimensions, feet (metres): 295.2 × 26.5 × 18
 (90 × 8.1 × 5.5)
Main machinery: Diesel-electric; 2 ASR 16 VVS-ASR1 diesels; 3,680 hp *(2.74 MW)*; 2 AEI motors; 6,000 hp *(4.48 MW)*; 2 shafts
Speed, knots: 12 surfaced; 17 dived; 10 snorting
Range, miles: 9,000 surfaced at 12 kt
Complement: 70 (6 officers)

Torpedoes: 8—21 in *(533 mm)* (6 bow, 2 stern) tubes. 20 Marconi Mk 24 Tigerfish Mod 1; wire-guided; active homing to 13 km *(7 n miles)* at 35 kt; passive homing to 29 km *(15.7 n miles)* at 24 kt; warhead 134 kg.
 4 Honeywell Mk 37 Mod 2 (stern tubes); wire-guided; active/passive homing to 8 km *(4.4 n miles)* at 24 kt; warhead 150 kg.
 Some Mk 8 Mod 4 anti-ship torpedoes (4.5 km at 45 kt) are still in service.
Countermeasures: ESM: UA 4; radar warning.
Weapons control: Ferranti DCH tactical data system.
Radars: Navigation: Kelvin Hughes Type 1006; I-band.
Sonars: Atlas Elektronik CSU-90-61; hull-mounted; passive/active search and attack; medium frequency.
 BAC Type 2007; flank array; passive search; low frequency.

Programmes: Two ordered from Vickers in 1969, the third in 1972. Completion of *Tonelero* was much delayed by a serious fire on board originating in the cabling. It was this fire which resulted in re-cabling of all 'Oberon' class under construction.
Modernisation: Contract signed in 1995 with HDW and Ferrostaal to install new hull-mounted sonar.

TONELERO

6/1996, Brazilian Navy / 0012081

Structure: Pilkington Optronics CK 24 search, and CH 74 attack periscopes are fitted.

Operational: This last of class is expected to pay off in 2000.

UPDATED

AIRCRAFT CARRIERS

Note: Interest in the French aircraft carrier *Foch* has been reported. There are also plans for a new 35,000 ton ship to be in service by 2010.

1 COLOSSUS CLASS (CV)

Name	No	Builders	Laid down	Launched	Commissioned
MINAS GERAIS (ex-*Vengeance*)	A 11	Swan Hunter & Wigham Richardson, Ltd, Wallsend on Tyne	16 Nov 1942	23 Feb 1944	15 Jan 1945

Displacement, tons: 15,890 standard; 17,500 normal; 19,890 full load

Dimensions, feet (metres): 695 × 80 × 24.5 *(211.8 × 24.4 × 7.5)*

Flight deck, feet (metres): 690 × 119.6 *(210.3 × 36.4)*

Main machinery: 4 Admiralty boilers; 400 psi *(28.1 kg/cm²)*, 700°F *(371°C)*; 2 Parsons turbines; 40,000 hp *(30 MW)*; 2 shafts

Speed, knots: 24. **Range, miles:** 12,000 at 14 kt; 6,200 at 23 kt

Complement: 1,300 (300 aircrew)

Missiles: SAM: 2 Matra Sadral twin launchers; Mistral; IR homing to 4 km *(2.2 n miles)*; warhead 3 kg. 2—47 mm saluting guns.

Countermeasures: Decoys: Plessey Shield chaff launchers. ESM: Racal Cutlass B-1; radar warning.

Combat data systems: SICONTA system. Ferranti Link YB system compatible with CAAIS fitted ships. SATCOM.

Weapons control: 2 Mk 63 GFCS. 1 Mk 51 Mod 2 GFCS.

Radars: Air search: Lockheed SPS-40E; E/F-band; range 320 km *(175 n miles)*.
Air/surface search: Plessey AWS 4; E/F-band.
Navigation: Scanter Mil and Furuno; I-band.
CCA: Scanter Mil-Par; I-band.

Fixed-wing aircraft: 10 A-4 Skyhawks.

Helicopters: 4-6 Agusta SH-3A/D Sea Kings; 2 Aerospatiale UH-12 Esquilo; 2 Aerospatiale UH-14 Cougar.

Programmes: Served in the UK Navy from 1945 onwards. Fitted out 1948-49 for experimental cruise to the Arctic. Lent to the

MINAS GERAIS   7/1999*, G Toremans / 0056592

RAN early in August 1953, returned to the Royal Navy in 1955. Purchased by the Brazilian Government on 14 December 1956 and commissioned in the Brazilian Navy on 6 December 1960.

Modernisation: During reconstruction in 1957-60 at Rotterdam the steam capacity was increased when the boilers were retubed. New lifts were installed; also included were one MacTaggart-Scott single track steam catapult for launching, and arrester wires for recovering 30,000 lb aircraft at 60 kt. The conversion and overhaul also included the installation of the 8.5° angled deck, mirror-sight deck landing system, armament fire control, a new island and radar equipment. Completed refit in 1981. Further modernisation was undertaken from July 1991 to October 1993. This included new CCA radars, electronics and communications, tactical

control system (SICONTA) incorporating IPqM/Datanav TTI-2700 consoles, datalink YB; retubing of boilers and other major engine overhauls. Guns removed in favour of Sadral twin launchers for Mistral SAM in 1994. Catapult again refurbished in 1999. Some spares acquired from deleted Argentine aircraft carrier *25 de Mayo*.

Structure: Hangar dimensions: length, 135.6 m *(445 ft)*; width, 15.8 m *(52 ft)*; clear depth, 5.3 m *(17.5 ft)*. Aircraft lifts: 13.7 × 10.4 m *(45 × 34 ft)*. The ship's overall length quoted does not include the catapult spur.

Operational: Recommissioned after refit in October 1993. Refit again in 1998/99 for further work on steam catapult prior to Skyhawk Squadron joining in mid-2000.

UPDATED

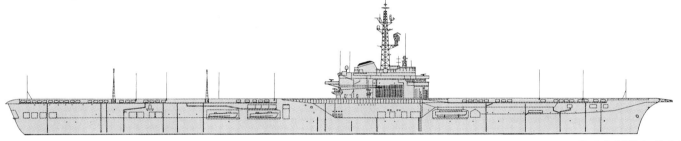

MINAS GERAIS   (Scale 1 : 1,200), Ian Sturton / 0056591

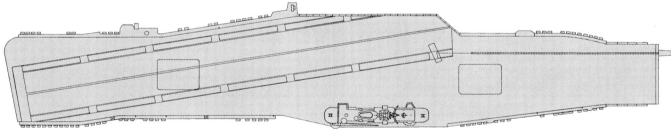

MINAS GERAIS   (Scale 1 : 1,200), Ian Sturton / 0056590

MINAS GERAIS   9/1997, Brazilian Navy / 0012083

FRIGATES

4 BROADSWORD CLASS (TYPE 22) (FFG)

Name	No	Builders	Laid down	Launched	Commissioned	Recommissioned
GREENHALGH (ex-Broadsword)	F 46 (ex-F 88)	Yarrow Shipbuilders, Glasgow	7 Feb 1975	12 May 1976	3 May 1979	30 June 1995
DODSWORTH (ex-Brilliant)	F 47 (ex-F 90)	Yarrow Shipbuilders, Glasgow	25 Mar 1977	15 Dec 1978	15 May 1981	31 Aug 1996
BOSISIO (ex-Brazen)	F 48 (ex-F 91)	Yarrow Shipbuilders, Glasgow	18 Aug 1978	4 Mar 1980	2 July 1982	31 Aug 1996
RADEMAKER (ex-Battleaxe)	F 49 (ex-F 89)	Yarrow Shipbuilders, Glasgow	4 Feb 1976	18 May 1977	28 Mar 1980	30 Apr 1997

Displacement, tons: 3,500 standard; 4,400 full load
Dimensions, feet (metres): 430 oa; 410 wl × 48.5 × 19.9 (screws) *(131.2; 125 × 14.8 × 6)*
Main machinery: COGOG; 2 RR Olympus TM3B gas turbines; 50,000 hp *(37.3 MW)* sustained; 2 RR Tyne RM1C gas turbines; 9,900 hp *(7.4 MW)* sustained; 2 shafts; cp props
Speed, knots: 30; 18 on Tynes
Range, miles: 4,500 at 18 kt on Tynes
Complement: 273 (30 officers)

Missiles: SSM: 4 Aerospatiale MM 40 Block II Exocet ❶; inertial cruise; active radar homing to 70 km *(40 n miles)* at 0.9 Mach; warhead 165 kg; sea-skimmer.
SAM: 2 British Aerospace 6-barrelled Seawolf GWS 25 Mod 4 ❷; command line of sight (CLOS) TV/radar tracking to 5 km *(2.7 n miles)* at 2+ Mach; warhead 14 kg; 32 rounds.
Guns: 2 Bofors 40 mm/70 ❸; 300 rds/min to 12 km *(6.5 n miles)*; weight of shell 0.96 kg.
2 Oerlikon BMARC 20 mm GAM-BO1.
Torpedoes: 6—324 mm Plessey STWS Mk 2 (2 triple) tubes ❹. Marconi Stringray; active/passive homing to 11 km *(5.9 n miles)* at 45 kt; warhead 35 kg.
Countermeasures: Decoys: 4 Sea Gnat 130 mm/102 mm 6-barrelled fixed launchers ❺; for chaff.
Graseby Type 182; towed torpedo decoy.
ESM: MEL UAA-2; intercept.
ECM: Type 670; jammers.
Combat data systems: CAAIS; Link YB being fitted. Inmarsat.
Weapons control: GWS 25 Mod 4 (for SAM); GWS 50.
Radars: Air/surface search: Marconi Type 967/968 ❻; D/E-band.
Navigation: Kelvin Hughes Type 1006; I-band.
Fire control: Two Marconi Type 911 ❼; I/Ku-band (for Seawolf).
Sonars: Plessey Type 2016; hull-mounted; search and attack; medium frequency.

Helicopters: 2 Westland Super Lynx ❽.

Programmes: Contract signed on 18 November 1994 to transfer four Batch I Type 22 frigates from the UK, one in 1995, two in 1996 and one in 1997. It is not planned to buy more Type 22s.
Modernisation: Plans to fit a single 57 mm gun on the bow have been shelved in favour of a 40 mm gun on each beam. These guns are being taken from the 'Niteroi' class. MM 40 being fitted forward.
Structure: Accommodation modified in UK service to take 65 officers under training.
Operational: Primary role is ASW. Form Second Frigate Squadron at Niteroi, Rio de Janeiro.

UPDATED

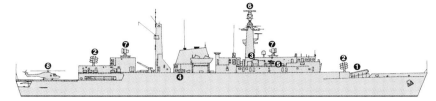

GREENHALGH   *(Scale 1 : 1,200)*, Ian Sturton / 0012084

GREENHALGH   3/1998 / 0017612

GREENHALGH (with Exocet and 40 mm guns)   3/1998 / 0017613

6 NITEROI CLASS (FFG)

Name	No	Builders	Laid down	Launched	Commissioned
NITEROI	F 40	Vosper Thornycroft Ltd	8 June 1972	8 Feb 1974	20 Nov 1976
DEFENSORA	F 41	Vosper Thornycroft Ltd	14 Dec 1972	27 Mar 1975	5 Mar 1977
CONSTITUIÇÃO	F 42	Vosper Thornycroft Ltd	13 Mar 1974	15 Apr 1976	31 Mar 1978
LIBERAL	F 43	Vosper Thornycroft Ltd	2 May 1975	7 Feb 1977	18 Nov 1978
INDEPENDÊNCIA	F 44	Arsenal de Marinha, Rio de Janeiro	11 June 1972	2 Sep 1974	3 Sep 1979
UNIÃO	F 45	Arsenal de Marinha, Rio de Janeiro	11 June 1972	14 Mar 1975	12 Sep 1980

Displacement, tons: 3,200 standard; 3,707 full load
Dimensions, feet (metres): 424 × 44.2 × 18.2 (sonar)
(129.2 × 13.5 × 5.5)
Main machinery: CODOG; 2 RR Olympus TM3B gas turbines;
50,880 hp (37.9 MW) sustained; 4 MTU 16V 956 TB91
diesels; 15,000 hp(m) (11 MW) sustained; 2 shafts; cp props
Speed, knots: 30 gas; 22 diesels. **Range, miles:** 5,300 at 17 kt
on 2 diesels; 4,200 at 19 kt on 4 diesels; 1,300 at 28 kt on gas
Complement: 217 (22 officers)

Missiles: SSM: 4 Aerospatiale MM 40 Exocet (2 twin) launchers
❶; inertial cruise; active radar homing to 70 km (40 n miles) at
0.9 Mach; warhead 165 kg; sea-skimmer.
SAM: 2 Short Brothers' Seacat triple launchers **❷**; optical/radar
guidance to 5 km (2.7 n miles); warhead 10 kg; 60 missiles.
Being replaced by AESN Albatros octuple launcher for Aspide
❸; semi-active radar homing to 13 km (7 n miles) at 2.5 Mach.
A/S: 1 Ikara launcher (Branik standard) (A/S version) **❹**;
command radio/radar guidance to 24 km (13 n miles) at
0.8 Mach; 10 missiles; payload Mk 46 torpedoes. Being
removed. The second gun is mounted aft in place of Ikara in
F 42.
Guns: 1 or 2 (Constituição) Vickers 4.5 in (115 mm)/55 Mk 8 **❺**;
25 rds/min to 22 km (12 n miles) anti-surface; 6 km (3.2 n
miles) anti-aircraft; weight of shell 21 kg.

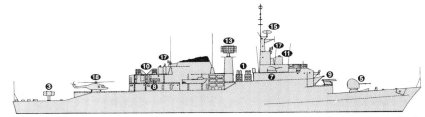

LIBERAL (after modernisation)　　　　(Scale 1 : 1,200), Ian Sturton / 0056593

2 Bofors 40 mm/70 **❻**; 300 rds/min to 12 km (6.5 n miles)
anti-surface; 4 km (2.2 n miles) anti-aircraft; weight of shell
0.96 kg. Being replaced by Bofors SAK 40 mm/70 Mk 3 **❼**
based on Trinity CIWS mounting.
Torpedoes: 6—324 mm Plessey STWS-1 (2 triple) tubes **❽**.
Honeywell Mk 46 Mod 5; anti-submarine; active/passive
homing to 11 km (5.9 n miles) at 40 kt; warhead 44 kg.
A/S mortars: 1 Bofors 375 mm trainable rocket launcher (twin-
tube) **❾**; automatic loading; range 1,600 m.

Depth charges: 1 rail; 5 charges (GP version) can be carried.
Countermeasures: Decoys: 2 Plessey Shield chaff launchers
being replaced by IPqM launchers **❿**.
ESM: SDR-2/7 or Racal Cutlass B-1B; intercept.
ECM: Racal Cygnus or Elebra SLQ-1; jammer.
Combat data systems: Ferranti CAAIS 400 with FM 1600B
computers being replaced by IPqM/Elebra Siconta II. Link YB.
Weapons control: Ikara tracker (A/S version). Saab EOS 450
optronic director **⓫** after modernisation. Ferranti WSA 400
series.
Radars: Air/surface search: Plessey AWS 3 with Mk 10 IFF **⓬**;
E/F-band. Being replaced by AESN RAN 20 S (3L) **⓭**; E-band.
Surface search: Signaal ZW06 **⓮**. Being replaced by Decca TM
1226 **⓯**; I-band.
Fire control: 2 Selenia Orion RTN 10X **⓰**. Being replaced by two
AESN RTN 30X **⓱**; I/J-band.
Navigation: Terma Scanter; I-band.
Sonars: EDO 610E Mod 1; hull-mounted; active search and
attack; medium frequency.
EDO 700E VDS (F 40 and 41); active search and attack;
medium frequency.

Helicopters: 1 Westland Super Lynx SAH-11 **⓲**.

Programmes: A contract announced on 29 September 1970
was signed between the Brazilian Government and Vosper
Thornycroft for the design and building of six Vosper
Thornycroft Mark 10 frigates. Seventh ship with differing
armament was ordered from Navyard, Rio de Janeiro in June
1981 and is used as a training ship.
Modernisation: The modernisation plan first signed in March
1995 included replacing Seacat by Aspide, Plessey AWS 3
radar by Alenia RAN 3L, RTN 10X by RTN 30X, ZW06 radar by
Decca TM 1226, the Bofors gun, Plessey Shield
countermeasures and Racal Cutlass ESM equipment as the
'Inhaúma' class. The Ikara system is to be removed. All the
ships of the class are to be updated with the emphasis on air
defence and new displays and combat data integration
designed by ESCA. Work is being done by Elebra. Liberal is
planned to complete in April 2000, Independência in
September 2000. Defensora in February 2001, União in late
2001, Niteroi and Constituição in late 2001. Plans to replace
the diesel engines have been shelved but a new hull sonar is
still being considered.
Structure: Originally F 40, 41, 44 and 45 were of the A/S
configuration. F 42 and 43 general purpose design. Fitted with
retractable stabilisers.
Operational: Endurance, 45 days' stores, 60 days' provisions.
The helicopter has Sea Skua ASM. Ikara and Sea Cat are
probably non-operational. All are based at Niteroi and form the
First Frigate Squadron.　　　　　　　　　　　　　*UPDATED*

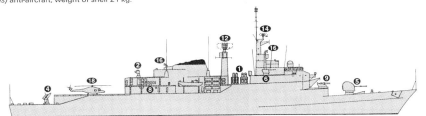

INDEPENDÊNCIA　　　　　　(Scale 1 : 1,200), Ian Sturton / 0056594

INDEPENDÊNCIA　　　　　　　　　　　　　7/1998 / 0017615

DEFENSORA　　　　　　　　　　　3/1999 *, M Declerck / 0056595

4 PARÁ (GARCIA) CLASS (FF)

Name	No	Builders	Laid down	Launched	Commissioned	Recommissioned
PARÁ (ex-*Albert David*)	D 27 (ex-FF 1050)	Lockheed SB & Construction Co	29 Apr 1964	19 Dec 1964	19 Oct 1968	18 Sep 1989
PARAÍBA (ex-*Davidson*)	D 28 (ex-FF 1045)	Avondale Shipyards	20 Sep 1963	2 Oct 1964	7 Dec 1965	25 July 1989
PARANÁ (ex-*Sample*)	D 29 (ex-FF 1048)	Lockheed SB & Construction Co	19 July 1963	28 Apr 1964	23 Mar 1968	24 Aug 1989
PERNAMBUCO (ex-*Bradley*)	D 30 (ex-FF 1041)	Bethlehem Steel, San Francisco	17 Jan 1963	26 Mar 1964	15 May 1965	25 Sep 1989

Displacement, tons: 2,620 standard; 3,560 full load
Dimensions, feet (metres): 414.5 × 44.2 × 24 sonar; 14.5 keel *(126.3 × 13.5 × 7.3; 4.4)*
Main machinery: 2 Foster-Wheeler boilers; 1,200 psi *(83.4 kg/cm²)*; 950°F *(510°C)*; 1 Westinghouse or GE turbine; 35,000 hp *(26 MW)*; 1 shaft
Speed, knots: 27.5. **Range, miles:** 4,000 at 20 kt
Complement: 286 (18 officers) + 25 spare

Missiles: SSM: Harpoon may be fitted in due course.
A/S: Honeywell ASROC Mk 112 octuple launcher ❶; inertial guidance to 1.6-10 km *(1-5.4 n miles)*; payload Mk 46 torpedo. *Pará* and *Paraná* have automatic ASROC reload system.
Guns: 2 USN 5 in *(127 mm)*/38 Mk 30 ❷; 15 rds/min to 17 km *(9.3 n miles)*; weight of shell 25 kg.
Torpedoes: 6—324 mm Mk 32 (2 triple) tubes ❸. 14 Honeywell Mk 46 Mod 5; anti-submarine; active/passive homing to 11 km *(5.9 n miles)* at 40 kt; warhead 44 kg.
Countermeasures: Decoys: 2 Loral Hycor Mk 33 RBOC 6-tubed chaff launchers. T-Mk 6 Fanfare; torpedo decoy system. Prairie/Masker; hull/blade rate noise suppression.
ESM: WLR-1; WLR-6; radar warning.
ECM: ULQ-6; jammer.
Weapons control: Mk 56 GFCS. Mk 114 ASW FCS. SATCOM.
Radars: Air search: Lockheed SPS-40B ❹; E/F-band; range 320 km *(175 n miles)*.
Surface search: Raytheon SPS-10C ❺; G-band.
Navigation: Marconi LN66; I-band.
Fire control: General Electric Mk 35 ❻; I/J-band.
Tacan: SRN 15. IFF: UPX XII.
Sonars: EDO/General Electric SQS-26 AXR (D 29 and 30) or SQS-26B; bow-mounted; active search and attack; medium frequency.

Helicopters: Westland Super Lynx SAH-11 ❼.

Programmes: First three transferred from USA by lease 15 April 1989 and last one 1 October 1989. All arrived in Brazil on 13 December 1989. Classified as Destroyers in the Brazilian Navy. The lease was renewed in 1994.
Modernisation: Harpoon SSM may be fitted subject to US agreement.
Structure: All four have the enlarged hangar capable of taking a helicopter the size of a Sea King but in USN service *Pará* and *Paraná* had the flight deck area converted to take SQR-15 towed array which was removed on transfer.
Operational: Form First Destroyer Squadron at Niteroi, Rio de Janeiro.   **UPDATED**

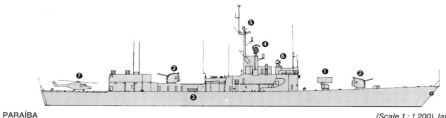
PARAÍBA
(Scale 1 : 1,200), Ian Sturton

PARÁ
10/1994*, Adam Goodrich / 0012089

PARÁ
3/1999* / 0056596

CORVETTES

0 + 1 (7) BARROSO CLASS (FSG)

Name	No	Builders	Laid down	Launched	Commissioned
BARROSO	V 34	Arsenal de Marinha, Rio de Janeiro	21 Dec 1994	Sep 2000	June 2003

Displacement, tons: 1,785 standard; 2,350 full load
Dimensions, feet (metres): 328 × 37.4 × 12.1; 17.4 (sonar) *(100 × 11.4 × 3.7; 5.3)*
Main machinery: CODOG; 1 GE LM 2500 gas turbine; 27,500 hp *(20.52 MW)* sustained; 2 MTU 20V 1163 TB83 diesels; 11,780 hp(m) *(8.67 MW)* sustained; 2 shafts; Kamewa cp props
Speed, knots: 29. **Range, miles:** 4,000 at 15 kt
Complement: 160 (15 officers)

Missiles: SSM: 4 Aerospatiale MM 40 Exocet ❶; inertial cruise; active radar homing to 70 km *(40 n miles)* at 0.90 Mach; warhead 165 kg; sea-skimmer.
Guns: 1 Vickers 4.5 in *(115 mm)* Mk 8 ❷; 55° elevation; 25 rds/min to 22 km *(12 n miles)* anti-surface; 6 km *(3.3 n miles)* anti-aircraft; weight of shell 21 kg.
1 Bofors SAK Sea Trinity CIWS 40 mm/70 Mk 3 ❸; 330 rds/min to 4 km *(2.2 n miles)* anti-aircraft; 2.5 km *(1.4 n miles)* anti-missile; weight of shell 0.96 kg; with '3P' improved ammunition; mounted on the hangar roof.
Torpedoes: 6—324 mm Mk 32 (2 triple) tubes ❹; Honeywell Mk 46 Mod 5; anti-submarine; active/passive homing to 11 km *(5.9 n miles)* at 40 kt; warhead 44 kg.
Countermeasures: Decoys: IPqM chaff launcher ❺.
ESM: IPqM/Elebra ET/SLQ-1A ❻; radar warning.
ECM: IPqM/Elebra ET/SLQ-2 ❼; jammer.

Combat data systems: IPqM/Esca Siconta Mk II with Link YB.
Weapons control: Saab/Combitech EOS-400 FCS with optronic director ❽; two OFDLSE optical directors ❾.
Radars: Surface search: AESN RAN-3L with IFF ❿; D-band.
Navigation: Racal Decca TM 1226C or Terma Scanter; I-band.
Fire control: AESN RTN-30-X ⓫; I/J-band (for Albatross and guns).
Sonars: Atlas Elektronik ASO-4-2; hull-mounted; active; medium frequency.

Helicopters: 1 SAH-11A Westland Super Lynx ⓬.

Programmes: Ordered in 1994 as a follow-on to the Inhauma programme. Second of class projected order in 1997 but this has been delayed.
Structure: The hull is some 4.2 m longer than the 'Inhauma' class to improve sea-keeping qualities and allow extra space in the engine room. The design allows the use of containerised equipment to aid modernisation. Efforts have been made to incorporate stealth technology. Vosper stabilisers.
   UPDATED

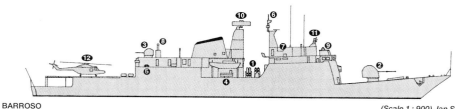
BARROSO
(Scale 1 : 900), Ian Sturton

4 INHAÚMA CLASS (FSG)

Name	No	Builders	Laid down	Launched	Commissioned
INHAÚMA	V 30	Arsenal de Marinha, Rio de Janeiro	23 Sep 1983	13 Dec 1986	12 Dec 1989
JACEGUAY	V 31	Arsenal de Marinha, Rio de Janeiro	15 Oct 1984	8 June 1987	2 Apr 1991
JULIO DE NORONHA	V 32	Verolme, Angra dos Reis	8 Dec 1986	15 Dec 1989	27 Oct 1992
FRONTIN	V 33	Verolme, Angra dos Reis	14 May 1987	6 Feb 1992	11 Mar 1994

Displacement, tons: 1,600 standard; 1,970 full load
Dimensions, feet (metres): 314.2 × 37.4 × 12.1; 17.4 (sonar) *(95.8 × 11.4 × 3.7; 5.3)*
Main machinery: CODOG; 1 GE LM 2500 gas turbine; 27,500 hp *(20.52 MW)* sustained; 2 MTU 16V 396 TB94 diesels; 5,800 hp(m) *(4.26 MW)* sustained; 2 shafts; Kamewa cp props
Speed, knots: 27. **Range, miles:** 4,000 at 15 kt
Complement: 122 (15 officers)

Missiles: SSM: 4 Aerospatiale MM 40 Exocet ❶; inertial cruise; active radar homing to 70 km *(40 n miles)* at 0.9 Mach; warhead 165 kg; sea-skimmer.
Guns: 1 Vickers 4.5 in *(115 mm)* Mk 8 ❷; 55° elevation; 25 rds/min to 22 km *(12 n miles)* anti-surface; 6 km *(3.3 n miles)* anti-aircraft, weight of shell 21 kg.
2 Bofors 40 mm/70 ❸; 300 rds/min to 12 km *(6.5 n miles)* anti-surface; 4 km *(2.2 n miles)* anti-aircraft; weight of shell 0.96 kg.
Torpedoes: 6—324 mm Mk 32 (2 triple) tubes ❹. Honeywell Mk 46 Mod 5; anti-submarine; active/passive homing to 11 km *(5.9 n miles)* at 40 kt; warhead 44 kg.
Countermeasures: Decoys: 2 Plessey Shield chaff launchers ❺; fires chaff and IR flares in distraction, decoy or centroid patterns.
ESM/ECM: Racal Cygnus B1 radar intercept ❻ and IPqM SDR-7 or Elebra SLQ-1; jammer ❼.
Combat data systems: Ferranti CAAIS 450/WSA 421; Link YB.
Weapons control: Saab EOS-400 FCS with optronic director ❽ and two OFDLSE optical ❾ directors.
Radars: Surface search: Plessey AWS 4 ❿; E/F-band.
Navigation: Kelvin Hughes Type 1007; I/J-band.
Fire control: Selenia Orion RTN 10X ⓫; I/J-band.
Sonars: Atlas Elektronik DSQS-21C; hull-mounted; active; medium frequency.

Helicopters: 1 Westland Super Lynx ⓬ or UH-12 Ecureuil.

Programmes: Designed by Brazilian Naval Design Office with advice from West German private Marine Technik design company. Signature of final contract on 1 October 1981. First pair ordered on 15 February 1982 and second pair 9 January 1986. In mid-1986 the government approved, in principle, construction of a total of 16 ships but this was reduced to four.
Modernisation: Plans to fit Simbad SAM have been shelved.
Operational: Form First Corvette Squadron based at Niteroi, Rio de Janeiro.

UPDATED

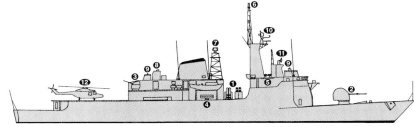

INHAÚMA *(Scale 1 : 900), Ian Sturton /* 0017617

FRONTIN *3/1999* / 0056597*

FRONTIN *6/1998, G Toremans /* 0017618

SHIPBORNE AIRCRAFT (FRONT LINE)

Numbers/Type: 9/3 McDonnell Douglas AF 1/AF 1A Skyhawk.
Operational speed: 560 kt *(1,040 km/h).*
Service ceiling: 45,000 ft *(13,780 m).*
Range: 1,060 n miles *(1,965 km).*
Role/Weapon systems: Acquired from Kuwait Air Force in September 1998 to restore carrier fixed wing flying by mid-2000. Eleven others are used for spares. Sensors: APS-53 radar; ESM/ECM. Weapons: AAM; 4 MAA-1 or 4 AIM 9D/G; 2 Colt 30 mm cannon; ASVW; bombs and rocket pods.
UPDATED

SKYHAWK   *6/1999 * /* 0056598

Numbers/Type: 7/6 Agusta/Sikorsky SH-3D/H Sea King.
Operational speed: 125 kt *(230 km/h).*
Service ceiling: 12,200 ft *(3,720 m).*
Range: 400 n miles *(740 km).*
Role/Weapon systems: ASW helicopter; carrierborne and shore-based for medium-range ASW, ASVW and SAR. Seven SH-3D delivered in 1995. Six ex-USN 3H acquired in mid-1997. Sensors: SMA APS-705(V)II or APS-24 search radar; Bendix AQS 13F or AQS 18(V) dipping sonar. Weapons: ASW; up to 4 × Mk 44/46 torpedoes, or 4 Mk II depth bombs. ASVW; 2 × AM 39 Exocet missiles.
UPDATED

SEA KING (with Exocet)   *8/1992 *, Mário R V Carneiro /* 0056599

Numbers/Type: 5/2 Aerospatiale UH-14 (AS 332F1 Super Puma/AS 532 SC Cougar).
Operational speed: 100 kt *(182 km/h).*
Service ceiling: 20,000 ft *(6,100 m).*
Range: 345 n miles *(635 km).*
Role/Weapon systems: SAR, troop transport and ASVW. Sensors: Thomson-CSF Varan search radar. Weapons: None.
UPDATED

SUPER PUMA   *6/1999 * /* 0056600

Numbers/Type: 14 Westland Super Lynx.
Operational speed: 125 kt *(232 km/h).*
Service ceiling: 12,000 ft *(3,650 m).*
Range: 160 n miles *(296 km).*
Role/Weapon systems: ASW helicopter; additional ASVW role from 1988. First batch upgraded in 1994-97 to Super Lynx standard with Mk 3 radar and Racal Kestrel EW suite. Eleven more Super Lynx delivered in mid-1998. Sensors: Sea Spray Mk 1/Mk 3 radar; Racal MIR 2 ESM. Weapons: ASW; 2 × Mk 46 torpedoes, or Mk II depth bombs. ASV; 4 × BAe/Ferranti Sea Skua missiles.
UPDATED

SUPER LYNX   *6/1998 *, GKN Westland /* 0056602

Numbers/Type: 18 Aerospatiale UH-12 Esquilo (AS-350BA Ecureuil).
Operational speed: 120 kt *(222 km/h).*
Service ceiling: 10,000 ft *(3,050 m).*
Range: 240 n miles *(445 km).*
Role/Weapon systems: Support helicopters for Fleet liaison and Marine Corps transportation. Sensors: None. Weapons: 2 × axial 7.62 mm MGs or 1 × lateral MG or 2 × rocket pods.
UPDATED

ECUREUIL   *6/1990 *, Brazilian Navy /* 0056602

Numbers/Type: 9 (7) Aerospatiale UH-13 Esquilo (AS 355FA Ecureuil 2).
Operational speed: 121 kt *(224 km/h).*
Service ceiling: 11,150 ft *(3,400 m).*
Range: 240 n miles *(445 km).*
Role/Weapon systems: SAR, liaison and utility in support of Marine Corps. Seven more ordered in 1998. Sensors: Search radar. Weapons: 2 × axial 7.62 mm MGs or 1 × lateral MG or 2 × rocket pods.
UPDATED

ECUREUIL 2   *7/1994 *, A Sheldon Duplaix /* 0056603

Numbers/Type: 19 IH-6B (Bell JetRanger III).
Operational speed: 115 kt *(213 km/h).*
Service ceiling: 20,000 ft *(6,100 m).*
Range: 368 n miles *(682 km).*
Role/Weapon systems: Utility and training helicopters. Sensors: None. Weapons: 2 × 7.62 mm MGs or 2 × rocket pods.
UPDATED

JETRANGER   *8/1992 *, Mário R V Carneiro /* 0056604

LAND-BASED MARITIME AIRCRAFT (FRONT LINE)

Numbers/Type: (9) Lockheed P-3 Orion.
Operational speed: 411 kt *(761 km/h)*.
Service ceiling: 28,300 ft *(8,625 m)*.
Range: 4,000 m *(7,410 km)*.
Role/Weapon systems: Twelve P-3 B/A being acquired from US. Nine are to be operated to P-3C standard from 2002. Sensors: APS-115 search radar; MAD; ESM/ECM. Weapons: ASW; four Mk 46 torpedoes; ASVW; four ASMs.   ***NEW ENTRY***

Numbers/Type: 9/10 Bandeirante P-95A/P-95B (EMB-111(B)).
Operational speed: 194 kt *(360 km/h)*.
Service ceiling: 25,500 ft *(7,770 m)*.
Range: 1,590 n miles *(2,945 km)*.
Role/Weapon systems: Air Force operated for coastal surveillance role by four squadrons. Sensors: MEL or APS-128 sea search radar, ECM, searchlight pod on starboard wing, EFIS-74 (electronic flight instrumentation) and Collins APS-65 (autopilot); ESM Thomson-CSF DR2000A/Dalia 1000A Mk II, Marconi Canada CMA-771 Mk III (Omega navigation system). Weapons: 6 or 8 × 127 mm rockets, or up to 28 × 70 mm rockets.   ***UPDATED***

Numbers/Type: 18 A-1 (Embraer/Alenia/Aermacchi) AMX.
Operational speed: 493 kt *(914 km/h)*.
Service ceiling: 42,650 ft *(13,000 m)*.
Range: 1,800 n miles *(3,336 km)*.
Role/Weapon systems: Air Force operated for strike, reconnaissance and anti-shipping attack; shore-based for fleet air defence and ASV primary roles; operated by 3rd/10th Group at Santa Maria Air Base (KS). Sensors: Tecnasa/SMA SCP-01 Scipio radar. ECM suite/ESM flares and chaffs; FLIR; GPS and IFF. Weapons: Strike; up to 3,800 kg of 'IRON' bombs; Self-defence; AAM; 2 × MAA-1 Piranha or 2 × AIM-9 Sidewinder missiles; 2 DEFA 30 mm cannon.   ***UPDATED***

Numbers/Type: 8 Tucano AT-27 (EMB-312).
Operational speed: 247 kt *(457 km/h)*.
Service ceiling: 32,570 ft *(9,936 m)*.
Range: 995 n miles *(1,844 km)*.
Role/Weapon systems: Air Force operated for liaison and attack by 2 ELO. Sensors: None. Weapons: 6 or 8 × 127 mm rockets or bombs and 1 × 7.62 mm MG pod in each wing.   ***VERIFIED***

PATROL FORCES

Note: Tenders for up to 12 OPVs of 1,200 tons issued in 1998. To be built in Brazil.

12 GRAJAÚ CLASS (LARGE PATROL CRAFT) (PC)

Name	No	Builders	Launched		Commissioned	
GRAJAÚ	P 40	Arsenal de Marinha	21 May	1993	1 Dec	1993
GUAIBA	P 41	Arsenal de Marinha	10 Dec	1993	12 Sep	1994
GRAÚNA	P 42	Estaleiro Mauá, Niteroi	10 Nov	1993	15 Aug	1994
GOIANA	P 43	Estaleiro Mauá, Niteroi	26 Jan	1994	26 Feb	1997
GUAJARÁ	P 44	Peenewerft, Germany	24 Oct	1994	28 Apr	1995
GUAPORÉ	P 45	Peenewerft, Germany	23 Jan	1995	29 Aug	1995
GURUPÁ	P 46	Peenewerft, Germany	11 May	1995	8 Dec	1995
GURUPI	P 47	Peenewerft, Germany	6 Sep	1995	23 Mar	1996
GUANABARA	P 48	Inace, Fortalesa	5 Nov	1997	9 July	1999
GUARUJÁ	P 49	Inace, Fortalesa	24 Apr	1998	Mar	2000
GUARATUBA	P 50	Peenewerft, Germany	16 June	1999	13 Oct	1999
GRAVATAÍ	P 51	Peenewerft, Germany	26 Aug	1999	20 Nov	1999

Displacement, tons: 263 full load
Dimensions, feet (metres): 152.6 × 24.6 × 7.5 *(46.5 × 7.5 × 2.3)*
Main machinery: 2 MTU 16V 396 TB94 diesels; 5,800 hp(m) *(4.26 MW)* sustained; 2 shafts
Speed, knots: 22. **Range, miles:** 2,200 at 12 kt
Complement: 31 (5 officers)
Guns: 1 Bofors 40 mm/70. 2 Oerlikon 20 mm (P 40-43). 2 Oerlikon BMARC 20 mm GAM-BO1 (P 44-51).
Weapons control: Radamec optronic director may be fitted in due course.
Radars: Surface search: Racal Decca 1290A; I-band.

Comment: Two ordered in late 1987 to a Vosper QAF design similar to Bangladesh 'Meghna' class. Technology transfer in February 1988 and construction started in July 1988 for the first pair; second pair started construction in September 1990. Class name changed in 1993 when the first four were renumbered to reflect revised delivery dates. Building problems are also reflected in the replacing of the order for the third pair with Peenewerft in November 1993 and the fourth pair in August 1994. Two more ordered from Inace in September 1996 and from Peenewerft in 1998. Used for patrol duties and diver support. Carry one RIB and telescopic launching crane.   ***UPDATED***

GURUPÁ   *3/1998*, I J Plokker /* 0056605

GUAJARÁ   *3/1999* /* 0056606

6 IMPERIAL MARINHEIRO CLASS (COASTAL PATROL SHIPS) (PG)

Name	No	Builders	Commissioned
IMPERIAL MARINHEIRO	V 15	Smit, Kinderdijk, Netherlands	8 June 1955
CABOCLO	V 19	Smit, Kinderdijk, Netherlands	5 Apr 1955
ANGOSTURA	V 20	Smit, Kinderdijk, Netherlands	21 May 1955
BAHIANA	V 21	Smit, Kinderdijk, Netherlands	27 June 1955
PURUS	V 23	Smit, Kinderdijk, Netherlands	17 Apr 1955
SOLIMÕES	V 24	Smit, Kinderdijk, Netherlands	3 Aug 1955

Displacement, tons: 911 standard; 960 full load
Dimensions, feet (metres): 184 × 30.5 × 11.7 *(56 × 9.3 × 3.6)*
Main machinery: 2 Sulzer diesels; 2,160 hp(m) *(1.59 MW)*; 2 shafts
Speed, knots: 16
Complement: 64 (6 officers)
Guns: 1–3 in *(76 mm)*/50 Mk 33; 50 rds/min to 12.8 km *(6.9 n miles)*; weight of shell 6 kg. 2 or 4 Oerlikon 20 mm.
Radars: Surface search: Racal Decca; I-band.

Comment: Fleet tugs classed as corvettes. Equipped for firefighting. *Imperial Marinheiro* has acted as a submarine support ship but gave up the role in 1990. Beginning to be taken out of service.   ***UPDATED***

ANGOSTURA   *2/1996*, van Ginderen Collection /* 0056607

2 PEDRO TEIXEIRA CLASS (RIVER PATROL SHIPS) (PBR)

Name	No	Builders	Launched		Commissioned	
PEDRO TEIXEIRA	P 20	Arsenal de Marinha	14 Oct	1970	17 Dec	1973
RAPOSO TAVARES	P 21	Arsenal de Marinha	11 June	1972	17 Dec	1973

Displacement, tons: 690 standard
Dimensions, feet (metres): 208.7 × 31.8 × 5.6 *(63.6 × 9.7 × 1.7)*
Main machinery: 2 MAN V6 V16/18 TL diesels; 1,920 hp(m) *(1.41 MW)*; 2 shafts
Speed, knots: 16. **Range, miles:** 6,800 at 13 kt
Complement: 60 (6 officers)
Guns: 1 Bofors 40 mm/60; 300 rds/min to 12 km *(6.5 n miles)*. 6–12.7 mm MGs. 2—81 mm Mk 2 mortars.
Radars: Surface search: 2 Racal Decca; I-band.
Helicopters: 1 Bell JetRanger.

Comment: Built in Rio de Janeiro. Belong to Amazon Flotilla. Can carry two armed LCVPs and 85 marines in deck accommodation.   ***UPDATED***

PEDRO TEIXEIRA   *6/1997*, Brazilian Navy /* 0012091

3 RORAIMA CLASS (RIVER PATROL SHIPS) (PBR)

Name	No	Builders	Launched		Commissioned	
RORAIMA	P 30	Maclaren, Niteroi	2 Nov	1972	21 Feb	1975
RONDÔNIA	P 31	Maclaren, Niteroi	10 Jan	1973	3 Dec	1975
AMAPÁ	P 32	Maclaren, Niteroi	9 Mar	1973	12 Jan	1976

Displacement, tons: 340 standard; 365 full load
Dimensions, feet (metres): 151.9 × 27.9 × 4.6 *(46.3 × 8.5 × 1.4)*
Main machinery: 2 MAN V6 V16/18TL diesels; 1,920 hp(m) *(1.41 MW)*; 2 shafts
Speed, knots: 14. **Range, miles:** 6,000 at 12 kt
Complement: 40 (9 officers)
Guns: 1 Bofors 40 mm/60; 300 rds/min to 12 km *(6.5 n miles)*. 2 Oerlikon 20 mm. 2—81 mm mortars. 6—12.7 mm MGs.
Radars: Surface search: 2 Racal Decca; I-band.

Comment: Carry two armed LCVPs. Belong to Amazon Flotilla.   ***UPDATED***

RORAIMA   *6/1998*, Brazilian Navy /* 0017623

4 BRACUI (RIVER) CLASS (COASTAL PATROL CRAFT) (PC)

Name	No	Builders	Commissioned	
BRACUI (ex-Itchen)	P 60 (ex-M 2009)	Richards, Lowestoft	12 Oct	1985
BENEVENTE (ex-Blackwater)	P 61 (ex-M 2008)	Richards, Great Yarmouth	5 July	1985
BOCAINA (ex-Spey)	P 62 (ex-M 2013)	Richards, Lowestoft	4 Apr	1986
BABITONGA (ex-Arun)	P 63 (ex-M 2014)	Richards, Lowestoft	29 Aug	1986

Displacement, tons: 890 full load
Dimensions, feet (metres): 156 × 34.5 × 9.5 (47.5 × 10.5 × 2.9)
Main machinery: 2 Ruston 6 RKC diesels; 3,100 hp(m) (2.3 MW) sustained; 2 shafts
Speed, knots: 14. **Range, miles:** 4,500 at 10 kt
Complement: 36 (6 officers)
Guns: 1 Bofors 40 mm/60.
Radars: Surface search: 2 Racal Decca TM 1226C; I-band.

Comment: Second batch of ex-UK 'River' class minesweepers transferred in 1998. These four were converted as patrol craft in UK service. Recommissioned 6 April, 10 July, 10 July and 9 September respectively. Three others transferred in 1995 are listed under Survey Ships.

UPDATED

POTI   6/1998, Brazilian Navy / 0017624

16 TRACKER II (LPPN-2) CLASS (COASTAL PATROL CRAFT) (PC)

CPCE/CPMA/CPRJ/CPSP   02-17 (ex-P 8002-P 8017)

Displacement, tons: 37 full load
Dimensions, feet (metres): 68.6 × 17 × 4.8 (20.9 × 5.2 × 1.5)
Main machinery: 2 MTU 8V 396 TB83 diesels; 2,100 hp(m) (1.54 MW) sustained; 2 shafts
Speed, knots: 27. **Range, miles:** 600 at 15 kt
Complement: 12 (4 officers)
Guns: 2—12.7 mm MGs.
Radars: Surface search: Racal Decca RM 1070A; I-band.

Comment: First four ordered in February 1987 to a Fairey design and built at Estaleiro Shipyard, Porto Alegre. National input is 60 per cent. First of class completed building 22 February 1990. First four all entered service in May 1991. Plans for more were postponed in 1991 when the shipbuilder went bankrupt, but were resurrected in 1993 with AMRJ assistance. Two more completed in May 1995 and the remaining ten between December 1995 and October 1997. Designed for EEZ patrol, and given CP numbers from 1995.

UPDATED

BOCAINA   7/1998 *, Maritime Photographic / 0056608

6 PIRATINI CLASS (COASTAL PATROL CRAFT) (PC)

Name	No	Builders	Commissioned	
PIRATINI (ex-PGM 109)	P 10	Arsenal de Marinha, Rio de Janeiro	30 Nov	1970
PIRAJÁ (ex-PGM 110)	P 11	Arsenal de Marinha, Rio de Janeiro	8 Mar	1971
PAMPEIRO (ex-PGM 118)	P 12	Arsenal de Marinha, Rio de Janeiro	16 June	1971
PARATI (ex-PGM 119)	P 13	Arsenal de Marinha, Rio de Janeiro	29 July	1971
PENEDO (ex-PGM 120)	P 14	Arsenal de Marinha, Rio de Janeiro	30 Sep	1971
POTI (ex-PGM 121)	P 15	Arsenal de Marinha, Rio de Janeiro	29 Oct	1971

Displacement, tons: 105 standard; 146 full load
Dimensions, feet (metres): 95 × 19 × 6.5 (29 × 5.8 × 2)
Main machinery: 4 Cummins VT-12M diesels; 1,100 hp (820 kW); 2 shafts
Speed, knots: 17. **Range, miles:** 1,700 at 12 kt
Complement: 15 (2 officers)
Guns: 1 Oerlikon 20 mm. 2—12.7 mm MGs.
Radars: Surface search: Racal Decca 1070; I-band.
Navigation: Furuno 3600; I-band.

Comment: Built under offshore agreement with the USA and similar to the US 'Cape' class. 81 mm mortar removed in 1988. Carries an inflatable launch. P 11 and P 15 are based at Fluvial de Ladário, Mato Grosso, the other four at Amazonas.

UPDATED

P 8002 (old number)   1991, Brazilian Navy

AMPHIBIOUS FORCES

1 NEWPORT CLASS (LST)

Name	No	Builders	Laid down	Launched	Commissioned	Recommissioned
MATTOSO MAIA (ex-Cayuga)	G 28 (ex-LST 1186)	National Steel & Shipbuilding Co	28 Sep 1968	12 July 1969	8 Aug 1970	30 Aug 1994

Displacement, tons: 4,975 light; 8,450 full load
Dimensions, feet (metres): 522.3 (hull) × 69.5 × 17.5 (aft) (159.2 × 21.2 × 5.3)
Main machinery: 6 ALCO 16-251 diesels; 16,500 hp (12.3 MW) sustained; 2 shafts; cp props; bow thruster
Speed, knots: 20. **Range, miles:** 2,500 at 14 kt
Complement: 267 (17 officers)
Military lift: 365 troops (15 officers); 500 tons vehicles; 3 LCVPs and 1 LCPL on davits

Guns: 1 General Electric/General Dynamics 20 mm Vulcan Phalanx Mk 15. 8—12.7 mm MGs.
Radars: Surface search: Raytheon SPS-10F; G-band.
Navigation: Raytheon SPS-64(V)6 and Furuno FR 2120; I-band.

Helicopters: Platform only.

Programmes: Transferred from the USN by lease 26 August 1994, arriving in Brazil in late October. Second of class will not now be acquired.

Structure: The ramp is supported by twin derrick arms. A stern gate to the tank deck permits unloading of amphibious tractors into the water, or unloading of other vehicles into an LCU or onto a pier. Vehicle stowage covers 19,000 sq ft. Length over derrick arms is 562 ft (171.3 m); full load draught is 11.5 ft forward and 17.5 ft aft.

UPDATED

MATTOSO MAIA   9/1995 *, Brazilian Navy / 0056609

2 CEARÁ (THOMASTON) CLASS (LSD)

Name	No	Builders	Laid down	Launched	Commissioned	Recommissioned
CEARÁ (ex-Hermitage)	G 30 (ex-LSD 34)	Ingalls, Pascagoula	11 Apr 1955	12 June 1956	14 Dec 1956	28 Nov 1989
RIO DE JANEIRO (ex-Alamo)	G 31 (ex-LSD 33)	Ingalls, Pascagoula	11 Oct 1954	20 Jan 1956	24 Aug 1956	21 Nov 1990

Displacement, tons: 6,880 light; 12,150 full load
Dimensions, feet (metres): 510 × 84 × 19
  (155.5 × 25.6 × 5.8)
Main machinery: 2 Babcock & Wilcox boilers; 580 psi *(40.8 kg/cm²)*; 2 GE turbines; 24,000 hp *(17.9 MW)*; 2 shafts
Speed, knots: 22.5. **Range, miles:** 10,000 at 18 kt
Complement: 345 (20 officers)
Military lift: 340 troops; 21 LCM 6s or 3 LCUs and 6 LCMs or 50 LVTs; 30 LVTs on upper deck
Guns: 6 USN 3 in *(76 mm)*/50 (3 twin) Mk 33; 50 rds/min to 12.8 km *(7 n miles)*; weight of shell 6 kg.
Radars: Surface search: Raytheon SPS-10F; G-band.
Navigation: Raytheon CRP 3100; I-band.
Helicopters: Platform for Super Puma.

Programmes: The original plan to build a 4,500 ton LST was overtaken by the acquisition of these two LSDs from the USA on a five year lease which has been extended.

Structure: Has two 50 ton capacity cranes and a docking well of 391 × 48 ft *(119.2 × 14.6 m)*. SATCOM fitted. Phalanx guns and SRBOC chaff launchers removed before transfer. Air search radars removed. **UPDATED**

CEARA   3/1999* / 0056610

1 DE SOTO COUNTY CLASS (LST)

Name	No	Builders	Launched	Commissioned
DUQUE DE CAXIAS (ex-Grant County LST 1174)	G 26	Avondale, New Orleans	12 Oct 1956	8 Nov 1957

Displacement, tons: 4,164 light; 7,804 full load
Dimensions, feet (metres): 445 × 62 × 17.5
  (135.6 × 18.9 × 5.3)
Main machinery: 4 Fairbanks-Morse 38D8-1/8-12 diesels; 8,500 hp *(6.34 MW)* sustained; 2 shafts; cp props
Speed, knots: 16.5. **Range, miles:** 13,000 at 10 kt
Complement: 175 (11 officers)
Military lift: 575 troops; 75 tons equipment
Guns: 6 FMC 3 in *(76 mm)*/50 (3 twin) Mk 33; 50 rds/min to 12.8 km *(6.9 n miles)*; weight of shell 6 kg.
Weapons control: 1 Mk 51 Mod 5 GFCS.
Radars: Surface search: Raytheon SPS-21; G/H-band.
Navigation: Racal Decca; I-band.

Comment: Transferred from the USA 15 January 1973, purchased 11 February 1980. Four LCVPs carried on davits; helicopter platform.

UPDATED

DUQUE DE CAXIAS   3/1999* / 0056611

3 LCU 1610 CLASS (EDCG/LCU)

Name	No	Builders	Commissioned
GUARAPARI	GED 10 (ex-L 10)	Arsenal de Marinha, Rio de Janeiro	27 Mar 1978
TAMBAÚ	GED 11 (ex-L 11)	Arsenal de Marinha, Rio de Janeiro	27 Mar 1978
CAMBORIÚ	GED 12 (ex-L 12)	Arsenal de Marinha, Rio de Janeiro	6 Jan 1981

Displacement, tons: 390 full load
Dimensions, feet (metres): 134.5 × 27.6 × 6.6 *(41 × 8.4 × 2.0)*
Main machinery: 2 GM 12V-71 diesels; 874 hp *(650 kW)* sustained; 2 shafts; cp props
Speed, knots: 11. **Range, miles:** 1,200 at 8 kt
Military lift: 172 tons
Guns: 3—12.7 mm MGs.
Radars: Navigation: Furuno 3600; I-band.

Comment: Status changed in 1991 when all of the class were reclassified EDCG (landing craft) and lost their pennant numbers having been decommissioned from the Navy. They remain in service based at Niteroi. GED (Group Embarcacoes and Desembarque). **UPDATED**

CAMBORIU   12/1997*, Hartmut Ehlers / 0012952

5 EDVM 17 and 30 EDVP CLASSES (LCM/LCVP)

GED 301-304   GED 306   EDVP 2-31

Displacement, tons: 55 full load
Dimensions, feet (metres): 55.8 × 14.4 × 3.9 *(17 × 4.4 × 1.2)*
Main machinery: 2 Saab Scania diesels; 470 hp(m) *(345 kW)*; 2 shafts
Speed, knots: 9
Complement: 3
Military lift: 80 troops plus 31 tons equipment

Comment: Details given for the five EDVMs which are LCM 6 type acquired from the USA. Based at Niteroi. There are also 30 EDVPs of 13 tons built by BFL, Ladario and capable of carrying 3.7 tons or 37 troops at 10 kt. These are based at Ladario and Manaus. **UPDATED**

5 EDVM 25 CLASS (LCM)

GED 801-805

Displacement, tons: 157 full load
Dimensions, feet (metres): 71 × 21 × 4.8 *(21.7 × 6.4 × 1.5)*
Main machinery: 2 Detroit diesels; 400 hp *(294 kW)* sustained; 2 shafts
Speed, knots: 9. **Range, miles:** 95 at 9 kt
Complement: 5
Military lift: 150 troops plus 72 tons equipment

Comment: First of class launched 18 January 1994 by AMRJ, remainder by Inace. LCM 8 type. Based at Niteroi.

UPDATED

MINE WARFARE FORCES

6 ARATÚ (SCHÜTZE) CLASS (MINESWEEPERS—COASTAL) (MSC)

Name	No	Builders	Commissioned
ARATÚ	M 15	Abeking & Rasmussen, Lemwerder	5 May 1971
ANHATOMIRIM	M 16	Abeking & Rasmussen, Lemwerder	30 Nov 1971
ATALAIA	M 17	Abeking & Rasmussen, Lemwerder	13 Dec 1972
ARAÇATUBA	M 18	Abeking & Rasmussen, Lemwerder	13 Dec 1972
ABROLHOS	M 19	Abeking & Rasmussen, Lemwerder	25 Feb 1976
ALBARDÃO	M 20	Abeking & Rasmussen, Lemwerder	25 Feb 1976

Displacement, tons: 230 standard; 280 full load
Dimensions, feet (metres): 154.9 × 23.6 × 6.9 *(47.2 × 7.2 × 2.1)*
Main machinery: 4 MTU Maybach diesels; 4,500 hp(m) *(3.3 MW)*; 2 shafts; 2 Escher-Weiss cp props
Speed, knots: 24. **Range, miles:** 710 at 20 kt
Complement: 39 (4 officers)
Guns: 1 Bofors 40 mm/70.
Radars: Surface search: Signaal ZW06; I-band.

Comment: Wooden hulled. First four ordered in April 1969 and last pair in November 1973. Same design as the now deleted German 'Schütze' class. Can carry out wire, magnetic and acoustic sweeping. Modernisation expected in due course. Based at Aratu, Bahia.

VERIFIED

EDVM 301   1985, Ronaldo S Olive   ABROLHOS   3/1998, Brazilian Navy / 0017625

SURVEY AND RESEARCH SHIPS

Notes: (1) Survey ships are painted white except for those operating in the Antarctic which have red hulls.
(2) There are also two river buoy tenders *Lufada* and *Piracema*.

1 POLAR RESEARCH SHIP (AGOB)

Name	No	Builders	Commissioned
BARÃO DE TEFFÉ (ex-*Thala Dan*)	H 42	Aalborg Vaerft	8 May 1957

Displacement, tons: 5,500 full load
Measurement, tons: 2,183 gross
Dimensions, feet (metres): 246.6 × 45.2 × 20.8 *(75.2 × 14.2 × 6.3)*
Main machinery: 1 Burmeister & Wain diesel; 1,970 hp(m) *(1.45 MW)*; 1 shaft; cp prop
Speed, knots: 12
Complement: 76 (11 officers)
Helicopters: 2 Aerospatiale UH-13 Ecureuil 2.

Comment: A Danish polar supply ship commissioned into the Navy on 28 September 1982. Strengthened for ice. SATCOM fitted. This ship has a red hull, mast and funnel and a pale brown superstructure. Reclassified as a Lighthouse Tender in 1994. May soon be scrapped.
UPDATED

BARÃO DE TEFFÉ   *12/1997, Hartmut Ehlers /* 0017626

1 POLAR RESEARCH SHIP (AGOB)

Name	No	Builders	Commissioned
ARY RONGEL (ex-*Polar Queen*)	H 44	Eides, Norway	22 Jan 1981

Displacement, tons: 3,670 full load
Dimensions, feet (metres): 247 × 42.7 × 17.4 *(75.3 × 13 × 5.3)*
Main machinery: 2 MAK 6M-453 diesels; 4,500 hp(m) *(3.3 MW)*; 1 shaft; cp prop; 2 bow thrusters; 1 stern thruster
Speed, knots: 14.5. **Range, miles:** 19,500 at 14 kt
Complement: 51 (12 officers)
Cargo capacity: 2,400 m³
Helicopters: Platform for Ecureuil 2.

Comment: Acquired by sale 19 April 1994. Ice-strengthened hull fitted with Simrad Albatross dynamic positioning system. Has a red hull; masts are pale brown.   *UPDATED*

ARY RONGEL   *6/1995 *, Brazilian Navy /* 0056613

1 RESEARCH SHIP (AGS)

Name	No	Builders	Commissioned
ANTARES (ex-M/V *Lady Harrison*)	H 40	Mjellem and Karlsen A/S, Bergen	Aug 1984

Displacement, tons: 1,076 full load
Dimensions, feet (metres): 180.3 × 33.8 × 14.1 *(55 × 10.3 × 4.3)*
Main machinery: 1 Burmeister & Wain Alpha diesel; 1,860 hp(m) *(1.37 MW)*; 1 shaft; bow thruster
Speed, knots: 13.5. **Range, miles:** 10,000 at 12 kt
Complement: 49 (9 officers)
Radars: Navigation: 2 Racal Decca; I-band.

Comment: Research vessel acquired from Racal Energy Resources. Used for seismographic survey. Recommissioned 6 June 1988. Painted white with orange masts and funnels.
UPDATED

ANTARES   *8/1994 *, Peter Humphries /* 0056614

1 ROBERT D CONRAD CLASS (OCEANOGRAPHIC SHIP) (AGOR)

Name	No	Builders	Commissioned
ALMIRANTE CÂMARA (ex-*Sands* T-AGOR 6)	H 41	Marietta Co, Point Pleasant, West Virginia	8 Feb 1965

Displacement, tons: 1,200 standard; 1,380 full load
Dimensions, feet (metres): 208.9 × 40 × 15.3 *(63.7 × 12.2 × 4.7)*
Main machinery: Diesel-electric; 2 Caterpillar diesel generators; 1 motor; 1,000 hp *(746 kW)*; 1 shaft; bow thruster
Speed, knots: 13.5. **Range, miles:** 12,000 at 12 kt
Complement: 36 (7 officers) plus 15 scientists
Radars: Navigation: RCA CRM-NIA-75; I/J-band.

Comment: Built specifically for oceanographic research. Launched 14 September 1963. Equipped for gravimetric, magnetic and geological research. 10 ton crane and 620 hp gas turbine for providing 'quiet power'. Transferred from USA 1 July 1974. Painted white with orange masts and funnel.
VERIFIED

ALMIRANTE CÂMARA   *12/1997, Hartmut Ehlers /* 0012953

1 SIRIUS CLASS (SURVEY SHIP) (AGS)

Name	No	Builders	Launched	Commissioned
SIRIUS	H 21	Ishikawajima Co Ltd, Tokyo	30 July 1957	17 Jan 1958

Displacement, tons: 1,463 standard; 1,800 full load
Dimensions, feet (metres): 255.7 × 39.3 × 12.2 *(78 × 12.1 × 3.7)*
Main machinery: 2 Sulzer 7T6-36 diesels; 2,700 hp(m) *(1.98 MW)*; 2 shafts; cp props
Speed, knots: 15.7. **Range, miles:** 12,000 at 11 kt
Complement: 116 (16 officers) plus 14 scientists
Radars: Navigation: Racal Decca TM 1226C; I-band.
Helicopters: 1 Bell JetRanger.

Comment: Laid down 1955-56. Painted white with orange funnel and masts. Special surveying apparatus, echo-sounders, Raydist equipment, sounding machines installed, and landing craft (LCVP), jeep, and survey launches carried. All living and working spaces are air conditioned.
UPDATED

SIRIUS   *8/1999 * /* 0056615

2 ARGUS CLASS (SURVEY SHIPS) (AGS)

Name	No	Builders	Launched	Commissioned
ARGUS	H 31	Arsenal de Marinha, Rio de Janeiro	6 Dec 1957	29 Jan 1959
ORION	H 32	Arsenal de Marinha, Rio de Janeiro	5 Feb 1958	11 June 1959

Displacement, tons: 250 standard; 343 full load
Dimensions, feet (metres): 146.7 × 21.3 × 9.2 *(44.7 × 6.5 × 2.8)*
Main machinery: 2 Caterpillar D 379 diesels; 1,098 hp *(818 kW)* sustained; 2 shafts
Speed, knots: 15. **Range, miles:** 3,000 at 15 kt
Complement: 42 (6 officers)
Guns: 2 Oerlikon 20 mm (removed).
Radars: Navigation: 2 Racal Decca 1226C; I-band.

Comment: *Orion* re-engined in 1974. White hull and superstructure, orange funnel.
VERIFIED

ARGUS   *6/1998, Brazilian Navy /* 0017628

1 LIGHTHOUSE TENDER

Name	No	Builders	Launched	Commissioned
ALMIRANTE GRAÇA ARANHA	H 34	Ebin, Niteroi	23 May 1974	9 Sep 1976

Displacement, tons: 2,390 full load
Dimensions, feet (metres): 245.3 × 42.6 × 13.8 *(74.8 × 13 × 4.2)*
Main machinery: 1 diesel; 2,440 hp(m) *(1.8 MW)*; 1 shaft; bow thruster
Speed, knots: 14
Complement: 95 (13 officers)
Radars: Navigation: 2 Racal Decca; I-band.
Helicopters: 1 Bell JetRanger.

Comment: Laid down in 1971. Fitted with telescopic hangar, 10 ton crane, two landing craft, GP launch and two Land Rovers. Omega navigation system. White hull and superstructure, orange mast and funnel. **UPDATED**

ALMIRANTE GRAÇA ARANHA   9/1998* / 0056616

3 AMORIM DO VALLE (RIVER) CLASS (BUOY TENDERS) (ABU)

Name	No	Builders	Commissioned
AMORIM DO VALLE (ex-*Humber*)	H 35 (ex-M 2007)	Richards, Lowestoft	7 June 1985
TAURUS (ex-*Helmsdale*)	H 36 (ex-M 2010)	Richards, Lowestoft	1 Mar 1986
GARNIER SAMPAIO (ex-*Ribble*)	H 37 (ex-M 2012)	Richards, Great Yarmouth	19 Feb 1986

Displacement, tons: 890 full load
Dimensions, feet (metres): 156 × 34.5 × 9.5 *(47.5 × 10.5 × 2.9)*
Main machinery: 2 Ruston 6RKC diesels; 3,100 hp *(2.3 MW)* sustained; 2 shafts
Speed, knots: 14. **Range, miles:** 4,500 at 10 kt
Complement: 36 (6 officers)
Radars: Navigation: 2 Racal Decca TM 1226C; I-band.

Comment: Contract signed on 18 November 1994 to transfer three ships from the UK on 31 January 1995. Steel hulled for deep-armed team sweeping with wire sweeps. All minesweeping gear and the 40 mm gun removed on transfer and they are used as light buoy tenders and hydrographic ships. Painted white with orange mast and funnels. *H 36* has a stern gantry and second crane amidships for oceanographic research. Four others of the class transferred in 1998 are listed under Patrol Forces. The class is also in service with the Bangladesh Navy. **VERIFIED**

TAURUS   12/1997, Hartmut Ehlers / 0012954

4 BUOY TENDERS (ABU)

Name	No	Builders	Commissioned
COMANDANTE VARELLA	H 18	Arsenal de Marinha, Rio de Janeiro	20 May 1982
TENENTE CASTELO	H 19	Estanave, Manaus	15 Aug 1984
COMANDANTE MANHÃES	H 20	Estanave, Manaus	15 Dec 1983
TENENTE BOANERGES	H 25	Estanave, Manaus	29 Mar 1985

Displacement, tons: 440 full load
Dimensions, feet (metres): 123 × 28.2 × 8.5 *(37.5 × 8.6 × 2.6)*
Main machinery: 2—8-cyl diesels; 1,300 hp(m) *(955 kW)*; 2 shafts
Speed, knots: 12. **Range, miles:** 2,880 at 10 kt
Complement: 28 (2 officers)
Radars: Navigation: Racal Decca; I-band.

Comment: Dual-purpose minelayers. *Tenente Castelo* is based at Santana, *Tenente Boanerges* at Sao Luiz. White hull and superstructure, orange mast and funnel. **UPDATED**

COMANDANTE VARELLA   4/1998*, I J Plokker / 0056617

5 BUOY TENDERS (ABU)

MESTRE JOÃO DOS SANTOS H 13	FAROLEIRO AREAS H 27
CASTELHANOS H 24	FAROLEIRO NASCIMENTO H 30
FAROLEIRO MÁRIO SEIXAS H 26	
(ex-*Mestre Jerânimo*)	

Displacement, tons: 280 full load
Dimensions, feet (metres): 96.8 × 22.6 × 6.2 *(29.5 × 6.9 × 1.9)*
Main machinery: 1 diesel; 1 shaft
Speed, knots: 6
Complement: 17 (1 or 2 officers)

Comment: Details are given for H 13 and H 24 built by AMRJ. Four taken over 1973—H 26 on 21 January 1984. H 26 launched in 1962; remainder 1954-57. All are white with orange masts and funnels. Planned to pay off in 2003/4. **UPDATED**

CASTELHANOS   12/1997*, Hartmut Ehlers / 0012955

10 LB 20 CLASS BUOY TENDERS (ABU)

ACHERNAR CPSP 02	DENEBOLA SSN 4103	RIGEL SSN 409
ALDEBARAN SSN 201	FOMALHAUT CPPR 05	VEGA SSN 506
BETELGEUSE CPSF 03	REGULUS SSN 4204	POLLUX CAMR 11
CAPELLA CPES 03		

Measurement, tons: 120 grt
Dimensions, feet (metres): 65 × 19.7 × 5.9 *(19.8 × 6 × 1.8)*
Main machinery: 2 Cummins NT 855M diesels; 720 hp(m) *(530 kW)*; 2 shafts
Speed, knots: 10

Comment: Built by Damen, Gorichen and assembled by Wilson, Sao Paolo. First one commissioned 20 December 1995 and the last on 29 December 1997. **UPDATED**

RIGEL   6/1998, Brazilian Navy / 0017629

6 SURVEY LAUNCHES (AGSC)

PARAIBANO (ex-H 11) SSN 411	ITACURUSSÁ (ex-H 15) SSN 415
RIO BRANCO (ex-H 12) SSN 412	CAMOCIM (ex-H 16) DHN 03
NOGUEIRA DA GAMA (ex-*Jaceguai*) (ex-H 14) SSN 414	CARAVELAS (ex-H 17) SSN 615

Displacement, tons: 32 standard; 50 full load
Dimensions, feet (metres): 52.5 × 15.1 × 4.3 *(16 × 4.6 × 1.3)*
Main machinery: 2 GM diesels; 330 hp *(246 kW)*; 2 shafts
Speed, knots: 11. **Range, miles:** 600 at 11 kt
Complement: 10 (1 officer)
Radars: Navigation: Racal Decca 110; I-band.

Comment: First pair commissioned 7 November 1969, second pair 8 March 1971 and last two 22 September 1972. Built by Bormann, Rio de Janeiro. Majority work in Amazon Flotilla. Wooden hulls. All decommissioned in 1991 but retained in service as support to naval establishments and reclassified AvHi (inshore survey craft). H pennant numbers may be restored. There are also four trawler types in service from October 1982; names are *Cabo Branco, Cabo Frio, Cabo Orange* and *Cabo Calcanhar*. SSN (Service Sinalizacao Nautica). **UPDATED**

PARAIBANO   1985, Brazilian Navy

1 OCEAN SURVEY VESSEL (AGS)

Name	No	Builders	Commissioned
SUBOFICIAL OLIVEIRA	CAMR 02 (ex-DHN 02, ex-U 15)	Inace	22 May 1981

Displacement, tons: 170 full load
Dimensions, feet (metres): 116.4 × 22 × 15.7 *(35.5 × 6.7 × 4.8)*
Main machinery: 2 diesels; 740 hp(m) *(544 kW)*; 2 shafts
Speed, knots: 8. **Range, miles:** 1,400 at 8 kt
Complement: 10 (2 officers)
Radars: Navigation: Racal Decca 110; I-band.

Comment: Commissioned at Fortaleza for Naval Research Institute. Decommissioned in 1991 but retained in service as an AvPqOc (ocean survey craft). ***UPDATED***

SUBOFICIAL OLIVEIRA (old number)   *1990*, Brazilian Navy* / 0056618

TRAINING SHIPS

Note: There are 12 small sail training ships.

1 MODIFIED NITEROI CLASS (AX)

Name	No	Builders	Commissioned
BRASIL	U 27	Arsenal de Marinha, Rio de Janeiro	21 Aug 1986

Displacement, tons: 2,548 light; 3,729 full load
Dimensions, feet (metres): 430.7 × 44.3 × 13.8 *(131.3 × 13.5 × 4.2)*
Main machinery: 2 Pielstick/Ishikawajima (Brazil) 6 PC2.5 L 400 diesels; 7,020 hp(m) *(5.17 MW)* sustained; 2 shafts
Speed, knots: 18. **Range, miles:** 7,000 at 15 kt
Complement: 221 (27 officers) plus 200 midshipmen
Guns: 2 Bofors 40 mm/70. 4 saluting guns.
Countermeasures: ESM: Racal RDL-2 ABC; radar intercept.
Weapons control: Saab Scania TVT 300 optronic director.
Radars: Surface search: Racal Decca RMS 1230C; E/F-band.
Navigation: Racal Decca TM 1226C and TMS 1230; I-band.
Helicopters: Platform for 1 Sea King.

Comment: A modification of the Vosper Thornycroft Mk 10 Frigate design ordered in June 1981. Laid down 18 September 1981, launched 23 September 1983. Designed to carry midshipmen and other trainees from the Naval and Merchant Marine Academies. Minimum electronics as required for training. There are four 51 mm launchers for flares and other illuminants. ***UPDATED***

BRASIL   *6/1999*, Findler & Winter* / 0056619

---

3 NASCIMENTO CLASS (AXL)

Name	No	Builders	Commissioned
ASPIRANTE NASCIMENTO	U 10	Ebrasa, Santa Catarina	13 Dec 1980
GUARDA MARINHA JENSEN	U 11	Ebrasa, Santa Catarina	22 July 1981
GUARDA MARINHA BRITO	U 12	Ebrasa, Santa Catarina	22 July 1981

Displacement, tons: 108.5 standard; 130 full load
Dimensions, feet (metres): 91.8 × 21.3 × 5.9 *(28 × 6.5 × 1.8)*
Main machinery: 2 MWM D232V12 diesels; 650 hp(m) *(478 kW)*; 2 shafts
Speed, knots: 10. **Range, miles:** 700 at 10 kt
Complement: 12
Guns: 1—12.7 mm MG.
Radars: Navigation: Racal Decca; I-band.

Comment: Can carry 24 trainees overnight. All of the class are attached to the Naval Academy at Rio de Janeiro. ***VERIFIED***

ASPIRANTE NASCIMENTO   *3/1998* / 0017631

3 ROSCA FINA CLASS (AXL)

ROSCA FINA (ex-U 31) CN 31   **VOGA PICADA** (ex-U 32) CN 32
LEVA ARRIBA (ex-U 33) CN 33

Displacement, tons: 50 full load
Dimensions, feet (metres): 61 × 15.4 × 3.9 *(18.6 × 4.7 × 1.2)*
Main machinery: 1 diesel; 650 hp(m) *(477 kW)*; 1 shaft
Speed, knots: 11. **Range, miles:** 200
Complement: 5 plus trainees
Radars: Navigation: Racal Decca 110; I-band.

Comment: Built by Carbrasmar, Rio de Janeiro. All commissioned 21 February 1984 and attached to the Naval College at Angra dos Reis. Pennant numbers removed in 1989. In addition the former American fishing vessel *Night Hawk* is in use for training at Centro de Instrucao Almirante Braz de Aguiar. ***VERIFIED***

VOGA PICADA   *1984, Brazilian Navy*

1 SAIL TRAINING SHIP (AXS)

Name	No	Builders	Launched	Completed
CISNE BRANCO	U 20	Damen Shipyards, Gorinchem	4 Aug 1999	15 Dec 1999

Displacement, tons: 1,038 full load
Dimensions, feet (metres): 249.3 × 34.4 × 15.7 *(76 × 10.5 × 4.8)*
Main machinery: 1 Caterpillar 3508B DI-TA diesel; 1,015 hp(m) *(746 kW)* sustained; 1 shaft; Berg cp prop; bow thruster; 408 hp(m) *(300 kW)*
Speed, knots: 17 (sail); 11 (diesel)
Complement: 22 (7 officers) plus 58 trainees
Radars: Navigation: Furuno FR 1510 Mk 3; I-band.

Comment: Ordered in 1998. Maximum sail area 2,195 m². ***NEW ENTRY***

CISNE BRANCO (artist's impression)   *1999*, Van der Kloet/Damen* / 0056620

AUXILIARIES

Notes: (1) In addition to the vessels listed below there are (1) three 485 ton water tankers built in 1957 *Dr Gondim* (R 38), *Itapura* (R 42) and *Paulo Afonso* (R 43); (2) two general purpose auxiliaries *Guairia* (R 40) and *Iguacu* (R 41). There are also large numbers of small service craft and river launches.
(2) The USN repair ship *Holland* AS 32 was proposed for transfer in 1998 but was rejected.
(3) *Merrimack* AO 179 was also rejected for transfer from the US in 1999.

1 SUBMARINE RESCUE SHIP (ASR)

Name	No	Builders	Commissioned
FELINTO PERRY	K 11	Stord Verft, Norway	1979
(ex-*Holger Dane*, ex-*Wildrake*)			

Displacement, tons: 1,380 standard; 3,850 full load
Dimensions, feet (metres): 256.6 × 57.4 × 15.1 *(78.2 × 17.5 × 4.6)*
Main machinery: Diesel-electric; 2 BMK KVG B12 and 2 KVG B16 diesels; 11,400 hp(m) *(8.4 MW)*; 2 motors; 7,000 hp(m) *(5.15 MW)*; 2 shafts; cp props; 2 bow thrusters; 2 stern thrusters
Speed, knots: 14.5
Complement: 65 (9 officers)
Radars: Navigation: 2 Raytheon; I-band.
Helicopters: Platform only.

Comment: Former oilfield support ship acquired 28 December 1988. Has an octagonal heliport (62.5 ft diameter) above the bridge. Equipped with a moonpool for saturation diving, and rescue and recompression chambers as the submarine rescue ship. Dynamic positioning system. Based at Niteroi, Rio de Janeiro. ***UPDATED***

FELINTO PERRY   *12/1997*, Hartmut Ehlers /* 0017632

3 BARROSO PEREIRA CLASS (TRANSPORTS) (AKS)

Name	No	Builders	Commissioned
CUSTÓDIO DE MELLO	G 20 (ex-U 26)	Ishikawajima, Tokyo	8 Feb 1955
ARY PARREIRAS	G 21	Ishikawajima, Tokyo	6 Mar 1957
SOARES DUTRA	G 22	Ishikawajima, Tokyo	27 May 1957

Displacement, tons: 4,800 standard; 7,300 full load
Measurement, tons: 4,200 dwt; 4,879 gross (Panama)
Dimensions, feet (metres): 362 pp; 391.8 oa × 52.5 × 20.5 *(110.4; 119.5 × 16 × 6.3)*
Main machinery: 2 Ishikawajima boilers and turbines; 4,800 hp(m) *(3.53 MW)*; 2 shafts
Speed, knots: 15
Complement: 159 (15 officers)
Military lift: 1,972 troops (overload); 497 troops (normal)
Cargo capacity: 425 m³ refrigerated cargo space; 4,000 tons
Guns: 2—3 in *(76 mm)* Mk 33; 50 rds/min to 12.8 km *(6.9 n miles)* anti-aircraft; weight of shell 6 kg.
2 or 4 Oerlikon 20 mm.
Radars: Navigation: Two Racal Decca; I-band.

Comment: Transports and cargo vessels. Details given are for G 21 and G 22. G 20 is larger at 9,464 tons full load although similar to the other pair in appearance. Helicopter landing platform aft except in *Custódio de Mello*. Medical, hospital and dental facilities. Working and living quarters are mechanically ventilated with partial air conditioning. Refrigerated cargo space 15,500 cu ft. *Custódio de Mello* was classified as a training ship in July 1961, replaced by *Brasil* in 1987 and has now reverted to being a transport. All operate commercially from time to time, and may soon be replaced by converted RoRo vessels. ***UPDATED***

ARY PARREIRAS   *12/1997*, Hartmut Ehlers /* 0017633

1 TRANSPORT SHIP (AKS)

Name	No	Builders	Commissioned
PARAGUASSU (ex-*Garapuava*)	G 15	Amsterdam Drydock	1951

Displacement, tons: 285 full load
Dimensions, feet (metres): 131.2 × 23 × 6.6 *(40 × 7 × 2)*
Main machinery: 3 diesels; 2,505 hp(m) *(1.84 MW)*; 1 shaft
Speed, knots: 13. **Range, miles:** 2,500 at 10 kt
Complement: 43 (4 officers)
Military lift: 178 troops
Guns: 6—7.62 mm MGs.
Radars: Navigation: Furuno 3600; I-band.

Comment: Passenger ship converted into a troop carrier in 1957 and acquired on 20 June 1972. ***UPDATED***

PARAGUASSU   *1989*, Brazilian Navy /* 0056621

1 PARNAIBA CLASS (RIVER MONITOR) (AG)

Name	No	Builders	Commissioned
PARNAIBA	U 17 (ex-P 2)	Arsenal de Marinha, Rio de Janeiro	6 Nov 1938

Displacement, tons: 620 standard; 720 full load
Dimensions, feet (metres): 180.5 × 33.3 × 5.1 *(55 × 10.1 × 1.6)*
Main machinery: 2 diesels; 2 shafts
Speed, knots: 12. **Range, miles:** 1,350 at 10 kt
Complement: 90
Guns: 2 Bofors 40 mm/60. 6 Oerlikon 20 mm.
Radars: Surface search: Racal Decca; I-band.
Navigation: Furuno 3600; I-band.
Helicopters: Platform for one Esquilo.

Comment: Laid down 11 June 1936. Launched 2 September 1937. In Mato Grosso Flotilla. Re-armed with new guns in 1960. 3 in *(76 mm)* side armour and partial deck protection. Converted in 1995/96 into a river logistics support ship with improved armament, and with diesel engines replacing the steam reciprocating propulsion plant. Converted again in 1998 with Bofors guns taken from 'Niteroi' class frigates and a helo deck at the stern. Facilities to refuel and re-arm a UH-12 helicopter. Recommissioned 6 May 1999. ***UPDATED***

PARNAIBA   *6/1997, Brazilian Navy /* 0017634

1 RIVER TRANSPORT (AGP)

Name	No	Builders	Commissioned
PIRAIM (ex-*Guaicuru*)	U 29	Estaleiro SNBP, Mato Grosso	10 Mar 1982

Displacement, tons: 91.5 full load
Dimensions, feet (metres): 82.0 × 18.0 × 3.2 *(25.0 × 5.5 × 0.97)*
Main machinery: 2 MWM diesels; 400 hp(m) *(294 kW)*; 2 shafts
Speed, knots: 7. **Range, miles:** 700 at 7 kt
Complement: 17 (2 officers)
Guns: 1—7.62 mm MG.
Radars: Navigation: Furuno 3600; I-band.

Comment: Used as a logistics support ship for the Mato Grosso Flotilla. ***UPDATED***

PIRAIM   *6/1998, Brazilian Navy /* 0017635

2 HOSPITAL SHIPS (AH)

Name	No	Builders	Commissioned
OSWALDO CRUZ	U 18	Arsenal de Marinha, Rio de Janeiro	29 May 1984
CARLOS CHAGAS	U 19	Arsenal de Marinha, Rio de Janeiro	7 Dec 1984

Displacement, tons: 500 full load
Dimensions, feet (metres): 154.2 × 26.9 × 5.9 *(47.2 × 8.5 × 1.8)*
Main machinery: 2 diesels; 714 hp(m) *(525 kW)*; 2 shafts
Speed, knots: 9. **Range, miles:** 4,000 at 9 kt
Complement: 46 (4 officers) plus 21 medical (6 doctors/dentists)
Radars: Navigation: Racal Decca; I-band.
Helicopters: 1 Helibras HB-350B.

Comment: *Oswaldo Cruz* launched 11 July 1983, and *Carlos Chagas* 16 April 1984. Has two sick bays, dental surgery, a laboratory, two clinics and X-ray centre. The design is a development of the 'Roraima' class with which they operate in the Amazon Flotilla. Since 1992 both ships painted grey with dark green crosses on the hull. ***UPDATED***

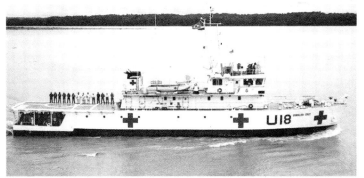

OSWALDO CRUZ   *1992*, Brazilian Navy /* 0056622

1 REPLENISHMENT TANKER (AOR)

Name	No	Builders	Commissioned
ALMIRANTE GASTÃO MOTTA	G 23	Ishibras, Rio de Janeiro	26 Nov 1991

Displacement, tons: 10,320 full load
Dimensions, feet (metres): 442.9 × 62.3 × 24.6 *(135 × 19 × 7.5)*
Main machinery: Diesel-electric; 2 Wärtsilä 12V32 diesel generators; 11,700 hp(m) *(8.57 MW)* sustained; 1 motor; 1 shaft; Kamewa cp prop
Speed, knots: 20. **Range, miles:** 10,000 at 15 kt
Complement: 121 (13 officers)
Cargo capacity: 5,000 tons liquid; 200 tons dry
Guns: 2—12.7 mm MGs.

Comment: Ordered March 1987. Laid down 11 December 1989 and launched 1 June 1990. Fitted for abeam and stern refuelling.

VERIFIED

ALMIRANTE GASTÃO MOTTA   *6/1998, Errol M Cornish /* 0017636

1 REPLENISHMENT TANKER (AOR)

Name	No	Builders	Launched	Commissioned
MARAJO	G 27	Ishikawajima do Brasil	31 Jan 1968	8 Jan 1969

Displacement, tons: 10,500 full load
Dimensions, feet (metres): 440.7 × 63.3 × 24 *(134.4 × 19.3 × 7.3)*
Main machinery: 1 Sulzer GRD 68 diesel; 8,000 hp(m) *(5.88 MW)*; 1 shaft
Speed, knots: 13. **Range, miles:** 9,200 at 13 kt
Complement: 121 (13 officers)
Cargo capacity: 6,600 tons fuel

Comment: Fitted for abeam replenishment with two stations on each side. Was to have been replaced by *Gastão Motta* but has been retained in service until the end of the decade.

UPDATED

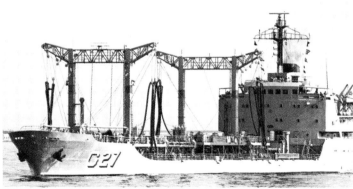

MARAJO   *1/1999 * /* 0056623

1 RIVER TANKER (AGP)

Name	No	Builders	Commissioned
POTENGI	G 17	Papendrecht, Netherlands	28 June 1938

Displacement, tons: 600 full load
Dimensions, feet (metres): 178.8 × 24.5 × 6 *(54.5 × 7.5 × 1.8)*
Main machinery: 2 diesels; 550 hp(m) *(404 kW)*; 2 shafts
Speed, knots: 10. **Range, miles:** 600 at 8 kt
Complement: 19
Cargo capacity: 450 tons dieso and avcat
Radars: Navigation: Furuno 3600; I-band.

Comment: Launched 16 March 1938. Employed in the Mato Grosso Flotilla on river service. Converted to logistic support ship and recommissioned 6 May 1999.

UPDATED

POTENGI   *1992 *, Brazilian Navy /* 0056624

1 TARGET TOWING TUG (ATS)

Name	No	Builders	Commissioned
TRINDADE (ex-*Nobistor*)	U 16	J G Hitzler, Lavenburg	1969

Displacement, tons: 590 light; 1,308 full load
Dimensions, feet (metres): 176.1 × 36.1 × 11.1 *(53.7 × 11 × 3.4)*
Main machinery: 2 MWM diesels; 2,740 hp(m) *(2 MW)* sustained; 2 shafts
Speed, knots: 12.7 kt
Complement: 22 (2 officers)
Guns: 2—12.7 mm MGs.
Radars: Navigation: Furuno 1830; I-band.

Comment: Ex-Panamanian tug seized for smuggling in 1989 and commissioned in the Navy 31 January 1990. Used for target towing.

UPDATED

TRINDADE   *1990 *, Mário R V Carneiro /* 0056625

7 RIO DOCE and RIO PARDO CLASSES (YFB)

RIO REAL (ex-U 23)	RIO PARDO BNAJ 08 (ex-U 40)	RIO CHUI CIAW 14 (ex-U 42)
RIO TURVO (ex-U 24)	RIO NEGRO BNRJ 07 (ex-U 41)	RIO OIAPOQUE BNRJ 09 (ex-U 43)
RIO VERDE (ex-U 25)		

Displacement, tons: 150 full load
Dimensions, feet (metres): 120 × 21.3 × 6.2 *(36.6 × 6.5 × 1.9)*
Main machinery: 2 Sulzer 6TD24; 900 hp(m) *(661 kW)*; 2 shafts
Speed, knots: 14. **Range, miles:** 700 at 14 kt
Complement: 10
Radars: Navigation: Racal Decca 110; I-band.

Comment: Can carry 600 passengers. The first three were built by Holland Nautic, commissioned in 1954 and the second group by Inconav de Niteroi in 1975-76. Pennant numbers removed in 1989.

UPDATED

1 TORPEDO RECOVERY VESSEL (TRV)

Name	No	Builders	Commissioned
ALMIRANTE HESS	COMFORS 02 (ex-BACS 01, ex-U 30)	Inace, Fortaleza	2 Dec 1983

Displacement, tons: 91 full load
Dimensions, feet (metres): 77.4 × 19.7 × 6.6 *(23.6 × 6 × 2)*
Main machinery: 2 diesels; 2 shafts
Speed, knots: 13
Complement: 14
Radars: Navigation: Racal Decca 110; I-band.

Comment: Attached to the Submarine Naval Base. Can transport up to four torpedoes. Decommissioned in 1991 but retained in service as an AvPpCo (coast support craft). BASC (Base Almirante Castro y Silva).

UPDATED

ALMIRANTE HESS (old number)   *6/1997 *, Brazilian Navy /* 0012096

4 FLOATING DOCKS

CIDADE DE NATAL (ex-AFDL 39) G 27	ALMIRANTE JERONIMO GONÇALVES
ALMIRANTE SCHIECK	(ex-*Goiaz* AFDL 4) G 26
ALFONSO PENA (ex-ARD 14)	

Comment: The first two are floating docks loaned to Brazil by US Navy in the mid-1960s and purchased 11 February 1980. Ship lifts of 2,800 tons and 1,000 tons respectively. *Almirante Schieck* of 3,600 tons displacement was built by Arsenal de Marinha, Rio de Janeiro and commissioned 12 October 1989. *Alfonso Pena* acquired from US and based at Rio de Janeiro.

UPDATED

TUGS

Note: In addition to the vessels listed below there are two harbour tugs: *Olga* (CASOP 01) and *Alves Barbosa* (AMRJ 11).

2 ALMIRANTE GUILHEM CLASS (FLEET OCEAN TUGS) (ATA)

Name	No	Builders	Commissioned
ALMIRANTE GUILHEM (ex-*Superpesa 4*)	R 24	Sumitomo, Uraga	1976
ALMIRANTE GUILLOBEL (ex-*Superpesa 5*)	R 25	Sumitomo, Uraga	1976

Displacement, tons: 2,400 full load
Dimensions, feet (metres): 207 × 44 × 14.8 *(63.2 × 13.4 × 4.5)*
Main machinery: 2 GM EMD 20-645F7B diesels; 7,120 hp *(5.31 MW)* sustained; 2 shafts; cp props; bow thruster
Speed, knots: 14
Complement: 40
Guns: 2 Oerlikon 20 mm (not always carried).

Comment: Originally built as civilian tugs. Bollard pull, 84 tons. Commissioned into the Navy 22 January 1981.

VERIFIED

ALMIRANTE GUILLOBEL   *12/1997, Hartmut Ehlers /* 0012956

3 TRITÃO CLASS (FLEET OCEAN TUGS) (ATA)

Name	No	Builders	Commissioned
TRITÃO (ex-*Sarandi*)	R 21	Estanave, Manaus	19 Feb 1987
TRIDENTE (ex-*Sambaiba*)	R 22	Estanave, Manaus	8 Oct 1987
TRIUNFO (ex-*Sorocaba*)	R 23	Estanave, Manaus	5 July 1986

Displacement, tons: 1,680 full load
Dimensions, feet (metres): 181.8 × 38.1 × 11.2 *(55.4 × 11.6 × 3.4)*
Main machinery: 2 diesels; 2,480 hp(m) *(1.82 MW)*; 2 shafts; bow thruster
Speed, knots: 12
Complement: 49
Guns: 2 Oerlikon 20 mm.
Radars: Navigation: 2 Racal Decca; I-band.

Comment: Offshore supply vessels acquired from National Oil Company of Brazil and converted for naval use. Assumed names of previous three ships of 'Sotoyomo' class. Fitted to act both as tugs and patrol vessels. Bollard pull, 23.5 tons. Firefighting capability. Endurance, 45 days.

UPDATED

TRITÃO   *4/1998*, I J Plokker /* 0056626

11 COASTAL TUGS

INTREPIDO BNRJ 16	**COMANDANTE MARROIG** (ex-R 15) BNRJ 03	**LAHMEYER** BNA 01
ARROJADO BNRJ 17	**COMANDANTE DIDIER** (ex-R 16) BNRJ 04	**DNOG** BNA 02
VALENTE BNRJ 18	**TENENTE MAGALHÃES** (ex-R 17) BNRJ 06	**ISAIAS DE NORONHA** BNA 03
IMPAVIDO BNRJ 19	**CABO SCHRAMM** (ex-R 18) BNVC 01	

Comment: BNPJ 16-19 are 200 tons with a bollard pull of 22.5 tons, built in 1992. BNRJ 03-06 and BNVC 01 are 115 tons built in 1982. The last three are 100 tons built in 1972.

UPDATED

IMPAVIDO   *3/1999* /* 0056627

BRUNEI
ANGKATAN TENTERA LAUT DIRAJA BRUNEI

Headquarters Appointments	Personnel	Bases	Prefix to Ships' Names	Mercantile Marine

Commander of the Navy:
  Colonel Abdul Jalil Bin Haji Ahmad
	(a) 2000: 747 (58 officers)
	    This total includes the River Division
	(b) Voluntary service
		Muara	KDB (Kapal Di-Raja Brunei)	*Lloyd's Register of Shipping:*
				  59 vessels of 362,010 tons gross

CORVETTES

0 + 3 BRUNEI CLASS (FSG)

Displacement, tons: 1,940 full load
Dimensions, feet (metres): 311.7 oa; 294.9 wl × 42 × 11.8
(95; 89.9 × 12.8 × 3.6)
Main machinery: 4 Alsthom 20 cyl GEC diesels; 2 shafts
Speed, knots: 30. **Range, miles:** 5,800 at 12 kt
Complement: 62 plus 24 spare

Missiles: SSM: 8 Exocet MM 40 Block II ❶.
SAM: BAe 16 cell VLS ❷. BAe Sea Wolf. 16 missiles.
Guns: Otobreda 76 mm Super Rapid ❸.
  2 GAM-BO1 20 mm ❹.
Torpedoes: 6 Marconi 324 mm (2 triple) tubes ❺.
Countermeasures: Decoys: 2 chaff launchers ❻.
ESM/Marconi Falcon; intercept.
Combat data systems: Nautis Mk 2 with Link Y.
Weapons control: Optronic director ❼.
Radars: Air/surface search: Plessey AWS 9 ❽; E/F-band.
Surface search: Kelvin Hughes 1007 ❾; I-band.
Fire control: 2 Marconi 1802 ❿; I/J-band.
Sonars: Thomson Marconi 4130C1 or FMS 21/3.

Helicopters: Platform for 1 medium.

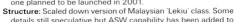

BRUNEI   *(Scale 1 : 900), Ian Sturton /* 0017638

Programmes: Tenders requested on 28 April 1995. Yarrow Shipbuilders selected in August 1995. Detailed design done in 1996 with final contract signed 14 January 1998. First steel cut 16 March 1999, second of class 15 November 1999. First one planned to be launched in 2001.
Structure: Scaled down version of Malaysian 'Lekiu' class. Some details still speculative but ASW capability has been added to the original design. Facilities to land and refuel S-70A and Bell 212 helicopters.
Opinion: This is an ambitious project for a very small navy with training and personnel numbers posing obvious problems.

UPDATED

PATROL FORCES

Note: There are also up to 15 Rigid Raider assault boats operated by the River Division for infantry battalions. These boats are armed with 1—7.62 mm MG.

3 WASPADA CLASS (FAST ATTACK CRAFT—MISSILE) (PCFG)

Name	No	Builders	Launched		Commissioned	
WASPADA	P 02	Vosper (Singapore)	3 Aug	1977	2 Aug	1978
PEJUANG	P 03	Vosper (Singapore)	15 Mar	1978	25 Mar	1979
SETERIA	P 04	Vosper (Singapore)	22 June	1978	22 June	1979

Displacement, tons: 206 full load
Dimensions, feet (metres): 121 × 23.5 × 6 *(36.9 × 7.2 × 1.8)*
Main machinery: 2 MTU 20V 538 TB91 diesels; 7,680 hp(m) *(5.63 MW)* sustained; 2 shafts
Speed, knots: 32. **Range, miles:** 1,200 at 14 kt
Complement: 24 (4 officers)

Missiles: SSM: 2 Aerospatiale MM 38 Exocet; inertial cruise; active radar homing to 42 km *(23 n miles)* at 0.9 Mach; warhead 165 kg.
Guns: 2 Oerlikon 30 mm GCM-B01 (twin); 650 rds/min to 10 km *(5.5 n miles);* weight of shell 1 kg. 2—7.62 mm MGs. 2 MOD(N) 2 in launchers for illuminants.
Countermeasures: ESM: Decca RDL; radar warning.
Weapons control: Sea Archer system with Sperry Co-ordinate Calculator and 1412A digital computer. Radamec 2500 optronic director being fitted.
Radars: Surface search: Kelvin Hughes Type 1007; I-band.

Modernisation: Started in 1988 and included improved gun fire control and ESM equipment. Further improvements in 1998 include Type 1007 radar and a Radamec 2500 optronic director. First ship completed in late 1998, second in 1999.
Structure: Welded steel hull with aluminium alloy superstructure. *Waspada* has an enclosed upper bridge for training purposes.   *UPDATED*

SETERIA   *5/1998* / 0017639

WASPADA   *5/1997** / 0012098

3 PERWIRA CLASS (COASTAL PATROL CRAFT) (PC)

Name	No	Builders	Launched		Commissioned	
PERWIRA	P 14	Vosper (Singapore)	5 May	1974	9 Sep	1974
PEMBURU	P 15	Vosper (Singapore)	30 Jan	1975	17 June	1975
PENYERANG	P 16	Vosper (Singapore)	20 Mar	1975	24 June	1975

Displacement, tons: 38 full load
Dimensions, feet (metres): 71 × 20 × 5 *(21.7 × 6.1 × 1.2)*
Main machinery: 2 MTU MB 12V 331 TC81 diesels; 2,450 hp(m) *(1.8 MW)* sustained; 2 shafts
Speed, knots: 32. **Range, miles:** 600 at 22 kt; 1,000 at 16 kt
Complement: 14 (2 officers)
Guns: 2 Oerlikon/BMARC 20 mm GAM-B01; 800 rds/min to 2 km; weight of shell 0.24 kg. 2—7.62 mm MGs.
Radars: Surface search: Racal Decca RM 1290; I-band.

Comment: Of all-wooden construction on laminated frames. Fitted with enclosed bridges— modified July 1976. A high speed RIB is launched from a stern ramp. New guns fitted in mid-1980s. At least one of this class is reported to be non-operational.   *UPDATED*

PENYERANG   *6/1999**, Royal Brunei Armed Forces / 0056628

AUXILIARIES

2 TARABAN CLASS (LCU)

Name	No	Builders	Commissioned	
TERABAN	33	Transfield, Perth	8 Nov	1996
SERASA	34	Transfield, Perth	8 Nov	1996

Displacement, tons: 220 full load
Dimensions, feet (metres): 119.8 × 26.2 × 4.9 *(36.5 × 8 × 1.5)*
Main machinery: 2 diesels; 2 shafts
Speed, knots: 12
Complement: 12
Military lift: 100 tons
Radars: Navigation: Racal; I-band.

Comment: Ordered in November 1995 and delivered in December 1996. Used as utility transports. Bow and side ramps are fitted.   *UPDATED*

TARABAN   *5/1998**, John Mortimer / 0056629

2 CHEVERTON LOADMASTERS (YFU)

Name	No	Builders	Commissioned
DAMUAN	L 31	Cheverton Ltd, Isle of Wight	May 1976
PUNI	L 32	Cheverton Ltd, Isle of Wight	Feb 1977

Displacement, tons: 60; 64 *(Puni)* standard
Dimensions, feet (metres): 65 × 20 × 3.6 *(19.8 × 6.1 × 1.1)* (length 74.8 *(22.8) Puni)*
Main machinery: 2 Detroit 6-71 diesels; 442 hp *(305 kW)* sustained; 2 shafts
Speed, knots: 9. **Range, miles:** 1,000 at 9 kt
Complement: 8
Military lift: 32 tons
Radars: Navigation: Racal Decca RM 1216; I-band.

UPDATED

DAMUAN   *6/1997**, Royal Brunei Armed Forces / 0012141

LAND-BASED MARITIME AIRCRAFT

Note: There are also BO-105, S-70A and Bell 212 utility helicopters.

Numbers/Type: 3 CASA/IPTN CN-235 MPA.
Operational speed: 240 kt *(445 km/h).*
Service ceiling: 26,600 ft *(8,110 m).*
Range: 669 n miles *(1,240 km).*
Role/Weapon systems: Long-range maritime patrol for surface surveillance and ASW. Sensors: Search radar: Litton AN/APS 504(V)5; MAD; acoustic processors; sonobuoys. Weapons; Mk 46 torpedoes.

UPDATED

CN-235MPA   *1997**, Paul Jackson / 0056630

POLICE

Note: In addition to the vessels listed below there are two Rotork type *Behagia* 07 and *Selamat* 10 and four River Patrol Craft *Aman* 01, *Damai* 02, *Sentosa* 04 and *Sejahtera* 06.

7 INSHORE PATROL CRAFT

PDB 11-15   PDB 63   PDB 68

Displacement, tons: 20 full load
Dimensions, feet (metres): 47.7 × 13.9 × 3.9 *(14.5 × 4.2 × 1.2)*
Main machinery: 2 MAN D 2840 LE diesels; 1,040 hp(m) *(764 kW)* sustained; 2 shafts
Speed, knots: 30. **Range, miles:** 310 at 22 kt
Complement: 7
Guns: 1—7.62 mm MG.
Radars: Surface search: Furuno; I-band.

Comment: Built by Singapore SBEC. First three handed over in October 1987, second pair in 1988, last two in 1996. Aluminium hulls.

UPDATED   PDB 15

3/1999*, John Webber / 0056631

BULGARIA
VOENNOMORSKI SILI

Headquarters Appointments

Commander of the Navy and Chief of Staff:
  Vice Admiral Petar Petrov
First Deputy Chief of Staff:
  Rear Admiral Konstantin Bogdanov
Chief Inspector of the Navy:
  Rear Admiral Mintcho Bakalov

Diplomatic Representation

Defence Attaché, London:
  Lieutenant General Anyo Anguelov

Organisation

Four squadrons: Submarine, Surface, MCMV and Auxiliary, with Headquarters at Varna and Burgas. There is also a Border Guard Unit. About two thirds of all the ships listed are operational.

Personnel

(a) 2000: 6,000 (including 1,990 marines and 260 naval aviation)
(b) 12 months' national service
(c) Reserves 10,000

Bases

Varna; Naval HQ (North Zone), Naval Base, Air Station
Burgas: Naval HQ (South Zone)
Sozopol, Atiya, Balchik, Vidin (Danube); Naval Bases
Higher Naval School *(Nikola Yonkov Vaptsarov)* at Varna.

Coast Defence

One battalion with six truck-mounted SS-C-3 Styx twin launchers. Two Army regiments of coastal artillery with 100 mm and 130 mm guns.

Mercantile Marine

Lloyd's Register of Shipping:
  173 vessels of 1,035,787 tons gross

DELETIONS

Submarines

1998   *Nadezhda*

Patrol Forces

1998   *Grum*

Amphibious Forces

1997/98   13 Vydra

Auxiliaries

1997   *N I Vaptsarov*

SUBMARINES

1 ROMEO CLASS (SS)

SLAVA 84

Displacement, tons: 1,475 surfaced; 1,830 dived
Dimensions, feet (metres): 251.3 × 22 × 16.1
  (76.6 × 6.7 × 4.9)
Main machinery: Diesel-electric; 2 Type 37-D diesels; 4,000 hp (m) *(2.94 MW)*; 2 motors; 2,700 hp(m) *(1.98 MW)*; 2 creep motors; 2 shafts
Speed, knots: 16 surfaced; 13 dived.
Range, miles: 9,000 at 9 kt surfaced
Complement: 54

Torpedoes: 8—21 in *(533 mm)* tubes (6 bow, 2 stern). 14 SAET-60; passive homing to 15 km *(8.1 n miles)* at 40 kt; warhead 400 kg.
Mines: Can carry up to 28 in lieu of torpedoes.
Countermeasures: ESM: Stop Light; radar warning.
Radars: Surface search: Snoop Plate; I-band.
Sonars: Hull-mounted; active/passive search and attack; high frequency.

Programmes: Built in 1961. Transferred from the USSR in 1986. An order for two 'Kilo' class was subsequently cancelled.
Operational: Restricted to diving to about 50 m *(165 ft)*. Based at Varna. Attempts have been made to keep this last boat operational by cannibalising others of the class. It is probably a losing battle.

VERIFIED

SLAVA

6/1997 / 0012100

FRIGATES

1 KONI CLASS (TYPE 1159) (FF)

SMELI (ex-*Delfin*) 11

Displacement, tons: 1,440 standard; 1,900 full load
Dimensions, feet (metres): 316.3 × 41.3 × 11.5
(96.4 × 12.6 × 3.5)
Main machinery: CODAG; 1 SGW, Nikolayev M8B gas turbine
(centre shaft); 18,000 hp(m) *(13.25 MW)* sustained; 2 Russki
B-68 diesels; 15,820 hp(m) *(11.63 MW)* sustained; 3 shafts
Speed, knots: 27 gas; 22 diesel. **Range, miles:** 1,800 at 14 kt
Complement: 110

Missiles: SAM: SA-N-4 Gecko twin launcher ❶; semi-active radar
homing to 15 km *(8 n miles)* at 2.5 Mach; warhead 50 kg;
altitude 9.1-3,048 m *(30-10,000 ft)*; 20 missiles.
Guns: 4—3 in *(76 mm)*/60 (2 twin) ❷; 60 rds/min to 15 km *(8 n miles)*; weight of shell 7 kg.
4—30 mm/65 (2 twin) ❸; 500 rds/min to 5 km *(2.7 n miles)*;
weight of shell 0.54 kg.
A/S mortars: 2 RBU 6000 12-tubed trainable ❹; range 6,000 m;
warhead 31 kg.
Depth charges: 2 racks.
Mines: Capacity for 22.
Countermeasures: Decoys: 2 PK 16 chaff launchers.
ESM: 2 Watch Dog; radar warning.
Radars: Air search: Strut Curve ❺; F-band; range 110 km *(60 n miles)* for 2 m² target.
Surface search: Don 2; I-band.
Fire control: Hawk Screech ❻; I-band (for 76 mm). Drum Tilt ❼;
H/I-band (for 30 mm). Pop Group ❽; F/H/I-band (for SA-N-4).
IFF: High Pole B.
Sonars: Hercules (MG 322); hull-mounted; active search and
attack; medium frequency.

Programmes: First reported in the Black Sea in 1976. Type I
retained by the USSR for training foreign crews but transferred
in February 1990 when the Koni programme terminated.
Others of the class acquired by the former East German Navy
(now deleted), Yugoslavia, Algeria, Cuba and Libya.
Operational: Based at Varna. Marisat fitted in 1996. Poor
operational availability.

UPDATED

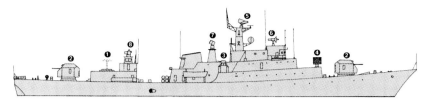

SMELI

(Scale 1 : 900), Ian Sturton

SMELI   *1/1998 /* 0017641

LAND-BASED MARITIME AIRCRAFT (FRONT LINE)

Notes: (1) A number of Air Force MiG-23s have AS-7 Kerry ASMs.
(2) Three Hormone B helicopters are non-operational.

Numbers/Type: 3 Mil Mi-14PL 'Haze A'.
Operational speed: 120 kt *(222 km/h)*.
Service ceiling: 15,000 ft *(4,570 m)*.
Range: 240 n miles *(445 km)*.
Role/Weapon systems: Primary role as inshore/coastal ASW and Fleet support helicopter; one
converted as transport. Coastal patrol and surface search. Sensors: Search radar, MAD,
sonobuoys, dipping sonar. Weapons: ASW; up to 2 × torpedoes, or mines, or depth bombs.

UPDATED

MULNIYA   *9/1999*, E & M Laursen /* 0056633

4 LETYASHTI (POTI) CLASS (FS)

LETYASHTI 41   **BDITELNI** 42   **BEZSTRASHNI** 43   **KHRABRI** 44

Displacement, tons: 545 full load
Dimensions, feet (metres): 196.8 × 26.2 × 6.6 *(60 × 8 × 2)*
Main machinery: CODAG; 2 gas-turbines; 30,000 hp(m) *(22.4 MW)*; 2 Type M 503A diesels;
5,350 hp(m) *(3.91 MW)* sustained; 2 shafts
Speed, knots: 32. **Range, miles:** 3,000 at 18 kt; 500 at 37 kt
Complement: 80

Guns: 2 USSR 57 mm/80 (twin); 120 rds/min to 6 km *(3 n miles)*; weight of shell 2.8 kg.
Torpedoes: 4—16 in *(406 mm)* tubes. SAET-40; anti-submarine; active/passive homing to 10 km
(5.4 n miles) at 30 kt; warhead 100 kg.
A/S mortars: 2 RBU 6000 12-tubed trainable launchers; range 6,000 m; warhead 31 kg.
Countermeasures: ESM: 2 Watch Dog; radar warning.
Radars: Air search: Strut Curve; F-band.
Surface search: Don; I-band.
Fire control: Muff Cob; G/H-band.
IFF: Square Head. High Pole.
Sonars: Hull-mounted; active search and attack; high frequency.

Programmes: Series built at Zelenodolsk between 1961 and 1968. Three transferred from USSR
December 1975, the fourth at the end of 1986 and the last two in 1990. Two deleted in 1993.
Names: 41 Flying, 42 Vigilant, 43 Fearless and 44 Gallant.
Operational: Based at Atiya and probably non-operational.

UPDATED

HAZE   *1994*, A Mladenov /* 0056632

CORVETTES

Note: New corvettes planned to be built at Varna from 2001 if funds are available.

1 TARANTUL II CLASS (TYPE 1241.1M) (FSG)

MULNIYA 101

Displacement, tons: 385 standard; 455 full load
Dimensions, feet (metres): 184.1 × 37.7 × 8.2 *(56.1 × 11.5 × 2.5)*
Main machinery: COGAG; 2 Nikolayev Type DR 77 gas turbines; 16,016 hp(m) *(11.77 MW)*
sustained; 2 Nikolayev Type DR 76 gas turbines with reversible gearboxes; 4,993 hp(m)
(3.67 MW) sustained; 2 shafts
Speed, knots: 36 on 4 turbines. **Range, miles:** 400 at 36 kt; 2,000 at 20 kt
Complement: 34 (5 officers)

Missiles: SSM: 4 Raduga SS-N-2C Styx (2 twin) launchers; active radar or IR homing to 83 km *(45 n
miles)* at 0.9 Mach; warhead 513 kg; sea-skimmer.
SAM: SA-N-5 Grail quad launcher; manual aiming; IR homing to 6 km *(3.2 n miles)* at 1.5 Mach;
altitude to 2,500 m *(8,000 ft)* ; warhead 1.5 kg.
Guns: 1—3 in *(76 mm)*/60; 120 rds/min to 15 km *(8.1 n miles)*; weight of shell 7 kg.
2—30 mm/65; 6 barrels per mounting; 3,000 rds/min to 2 km.
Countermeasures: Decoys: 2 PK 16 chaff launchers.
ESM: 2 Half Hat; intercept.
Weapons control: Hood Wink optronic director. Band Stand datalink for SSM.
Radars: Air/surface search: Plank Shave; E-band.
Navigation: Kivach; I-band.
Fire control: Bass Tilt; H/I-band.
IFF: Square Head. High Pole.

Programmes: Built at Volodarski, Rybinsk. Transferred from USSR in December 1989. Name
means Thunderbolt.
Operational: Based at Sozopol.

UPDATED

LETYASHTI   *6/1996, Bulgarian Navy*

2 RESHITELNI (PAUK I) CLASS (TYPE 1241P) (FS/PCF)

RESHITELNI 13   **BODRI** 14

Displacement, tons: 440 full load
Dimensions, feet (metres): 195.2 × 33.5 × 10.8 *(59.5 × 10.2 × 3.3)*
Main machinery: 2 Type 521 diesels; 16,180 hp(m) *(11.9 MW)* sustained; 2 shafts
Speed, knots: 32. **Range, miles:** 2,200 at 14 kt
Complement: 38

Missiles: SAM: SA-N-5 Grail quad launcher; manual aiming; IR homing to 6 km *(3.2 n miles)* at
    1.5 Mach; altitude to 2,500 m *(8,000 ft)*; warhead 1.5 kg; 8 missiles.
Guns: 1—3 in *(76 mm)*/60; 120 rds/min to 15 km *(8 n miles)*; weight of shell 7 kg.
    1—30 mm/65; 6 barrels; 3,000 rds/min combined to 2 km.
Torpedoes: 4—16 in *(406 mm)* tubes. Type 40; anti-submarine; active/passive homing up to 15 km
    (8 n miles) at up to 40 kt; warhead 100-150 kg.
A/S mortars: 2 RBU 1200 5-tubed fixed; range 1,200 m; warhead 34 kg.
Depth charges: 2 racks (12).
Countermeasures: Decoys: 2 PK 16 chaff launchers.
    ESM: 3 Brick Plug; intercept.
Radars: Air/surface search: Peel Cone; E-band.
    Surface search: Spin Trough; I-band.
    Fire control: Bass Tilt; H/I-band.
Sonars: Foal Tail VDS (mounted on transom); active attack; high frequency.

Programmes: *Reshitelni* transferred from USSR in September 1989, *Bodri* in December 1990.
Operational: Based at Varna. *Reshitelni* is non-operational with propulsion problems.
                              VERIFIED

BODRI   *10/1998, C D Yaylali /* 0017643

PATROL FORCES

Notes: (1) Customs craft operate on the Danube. Vessels include three Boston Whalers donated by
the USA and RIBs given by the UK in 1992-93.
(2) It is reported that one Shershen remains in service with the Border Police, with pennant number
114 and is based at Sozopol.

SHERSHEN 114   *8/1998, E & M Laursen /* 0017644

10 ZHUK (TYPE 1400M) CLASS (COASTAL PATROL CRAFT) (PC)

511-513   515   521-523   531-533

Displacement, tons: 39 full load
Dimensions, feet (metres): 78.7 × 16.4 × 3.9 *(24 × 5 × 1.2)*
Main machinery: 2 Type M 401B diesels; 2,200 hp(m) *(1.6 MW)* sustained; 2 shafts
Speed, knots: 30. **Range, miles:** 1,100 at 15 kt
Complement: 11 (3 officers)
Guns: 4 USSR 14.5 mm (2 twin) MGs.
Radars: Surface search: Spin Trough; I-band.

Comment: Transferred from USSR 1980-81. Belong to the Border Police under the Minister of the
    Interior and have 'Border Guard' insignia on the ships side. Six based at Atiya and four at Varna.
                              VERIFIED

ZHUK 512   *6/1996, Bulgarian Navy*

3 OSA II and 2 OSA I (TYPE 205) CLASSES
(FAST ATTACK CRAFT—MISSILE) (PCFG)

URAGON 102	**SVETKAVITSA** 111	**SMERCH** 113 (Osa I)
BURYA 103 (Osa I)	**TYPFOON** 112	

Displacement, tons: 245 full load; 210 (Osa I)
Dimensions, feet (metres): 126.6 × 24.9 × 8.8 *(38.6 × 7.6 × 2.7)*
Main machinery: 3 Type M 504 diesels; 10,800 hp(m) *(7.94 MW)* sustained; 3 shafts (Osa II)
    3 Type 503A diesels; 8,025 hp(m) *(5.9 MW)* sustained; 3 shafts (Osa I)
Speed, knots: 37 (Osa II); 35 (Osa I). **Range, miles:** 500 at 35 kt
Complement: 26 (3 officers)
Missiles: SSM: 4 SS-N-2A/B Styx; active radar/IR homing to 46 km *(25 n miles)* at 0.9 Mach;
    warhead 513 kg. SS-N-2A in Osa I.
Guns: 4 USSR 30 mm/65 (2 twin); 500 rds/min to 5 km *(2.7 n miles)*; weight of shell 0.54 kg.
Radars: Surface search/fire control: Square Tie; I-band.
    Fire control: Drum Tilt; H/I-band.
    IFF: High Pole. Square Head.

Comment: Osa IIs built between 1965 and 1970, and transferred from USSR between 1977 and
    1982. The Osa Is transferred in 1972 and survived longer than expected. Names: 102 Hurricane,
    103 Storm, 111 Lightning, 112 Typhoon and 113 Tornado. All based at Sozopol and seldom go to
    sea.
                              UPDATED

URAGON   *9/1999*, E & M Laursen /* 0056634

SMERCH   *9/1999*, E & M Laursen /* 0056635

MINE WARFARE FORCES

Note: Six 'Vydra' class (see *Amphibious Forces*) converted to minelayers in 1992-93. Some are in
reserve.

4 BRIZ (SONYA) (TYPE 12650) CLASS
(MINESWEEPERS—COASTAL) (MSC)

BRIZ 61   **SHKVAL** 62   **PPIBOY** 63   **SHTORM** 64

Displacement, tons: 450 full load
Dimensions, feet (metres): 157.4 × 28.9 × 6.6 *(48 × 8.8 × 2)*
Main machinery: 2 Kolomna Type 9-D-8 diesels; 2,000 hp(m) *(1.47 MW)* sustained; 2 shafts
Speed, knots: 15. **Range, miles:** 1,500 at 14 kt
Complement: 43 (5 officers)
Guns: 2 USSR 30 mm/65 (twin); 500 rds/min to 5 km *(2.7 n miles)*; weight of shell 0.54 kg.
    2 USSR 25 mm/80 (twin); 270 rds/min to 3 km *(1.6 n miles)*; weight of shell 0.34 kg.
Mines: 5.
Radars: Surface search/navigation: Kivach; I-band.
    IFF: Two Square Head. High Pole B.
Sonars: MG 69/79; hull-mounted; active minehunting; high frequency.

Comment: Wooden hulled ships transferred from USSR in 1981-84. Based at Atiya.
                              UPDATED

SKHVAL   *7/1997*, Frank Behling /* 0012957

4 ISCAR (VANYA) (TYPE 257D) CLASS
(MINESWEEPERS—COASTAL) (MSC)

ISKAR 31   **ZIBAR** 32   **DOBROTICH** 33   **EVSTATI VINAROV** 34

Displacement, tons: 245 full load
Dimensions, feet (metres): 131.2 × 23.9 × 5.9 (40 × 7.3 × 1.8)
Main machinery: 2 M 870 diesels; 2,502 hp(m) (1.84 MW); 2 shafts; cp props
Speed, knots: 16. **Range, miles:** 2,400 at 10 kt
Complement: 36
Guns: 2 USSR 30 mm/65 (twin); 500 rds/min to 5 km (2.7 n miles); weight of shell 0.54 kg.
Mines: Can carry 8.
Radars: Surface search: Don 2; I-band.
Sonars: MG 69/79; hull-mounted; active minehunting; high frequency.

Comment: Built 1961 to 1973. Transferred from the USSR—two in 1970, two in 1971 and two in 1985. Can act as minehunters. Two paid off in 1992, but back in service in 1994 and then finally scrapped in 1995. Based at Varna.

VERIFIED

DOBROTICH   *2/1998 /* 0017646

4 YEVGENYA (TYPE 1258) CLASS
(MINESWEEPERS—COASTAL) (MHC)

65   66   67   68

Displacement, tons: 77 standard; 90 full load
Dimensions, feet (metres): 80.4 × 18 × 4.6 (24.5 × 5.5 × 1.4)
Main machinery: 2 Type 3-D-12 diesels; 600 hp(m) (440 kW) sustained; 2 shafts
Speed, knots: 11. **Range, miles:** 300 at 10 kt
Complement: 10 (1 officer)
Guns: 2—25 mm/80 (twin).
Mines: 8 racks.
Radars: Surface search: Spin Trough; I-band.
IFF: High Pole.
Sonars: MG-7 lifted over stern; active; high frequency.

Comment: GRP hulls built at Kolpino. Transferred from USSR 1977. Based at Atiya.

VERIFIED

YEVGENYA 66   *6/1996, Bulgarian Navy*

2 PO 2 (501) CLASS (MINESWEEPERS—INSHORE) (MSB)

57   58

Displacement, tons: 56 full load
Dimensions, feet (metres): 70.5 × 11.5 × 3.3 (21.5 × 3.5 × 1)
Main machinery: 1 Type 3-D-12 diesel; 300 hp(m) (220 kW) sustained; 2 shafts
Speed, knots: 12
Complement: 8

Comment: Built in Bulgaria. First units completed in early 1950s and last in early 1960s. Originally a class of 24 and these two are the last to survive. Occasionally carry a 12.7 mm MG, when used for patrol duties. Both based at Balchik.

UPDATED

6 OLYA (TYPE 1259) CLASS (MINESWEEPERS—INSHORE) (MSB)

51   52   53   54   55   56

Displacement, tons: 64 full load
Dimensions, feet (metres): 84.6 × 14.9 × 3.3 (25.8 × 4.5 × 1)
Main machinery: 2 Type 3D 6S11/235 diesels; 471 hp(m) (346 kW) sustained; 2 shafts
Speed, knots: 12. **Range, miles:** 300 at 10 kt
Complement: 15
Guns: 2—12.7 mm MGs (twin).
Radars: Navigation: Pechora; I-band.

Comment: First five built between 1988 and 1992 in Bulgaria to the Russian Olya design. *56* completed in 1996. Minesweeping equipment includes AT-6, SZMT-1 and 3 PKT-2 systems. Based at Balchik.

VERIFIED

OLYA 55   *1992, Bulgarian Navy*

AMPHIBIOUS FORCES

2 POLNOCHNY A (TYPE 770) CLASS (LSM)

SIRIUS (ex-*Ivan Zagubanski*) 701   **ANTARES** 702

Displacement, tons: 750 standard; 800 full load
Dimensions, feet (metres): 239.5 × 27.9 × 5.8 (73 × 8.5 × 1.8)
Main machinery: 2 Kolomna Type 40-D diesels; 4,400 hp(m) (3.2 MW) sustained; 2 shafts
Speed, knots: 19. **Range, miles:** 1,000 at 18 kt
Complement: 40
Military lift: 350 tons including 6 tanks; 180 troops
Guns: 2 USSR 30 mm (twin). 2—140 mm 18-barrelled rocket launchers.
Radars: Navigation: Spin Trough; I-band.

Comment: Built 1963 to 1968. Transferred from USSR 1986-87. Not fitted either with the SA-N-5 Grail SAM system or with Drum Tilt fire-control radars. Plans to convert them to minelayers have been shelved and both are now used as transports. Based at Atiya.

VERIFIED

SIRIUS   *2/1998 /* 0017647

6 VYDRA (TYPE 106K) CLASS (LCU)

703-707   712

Displacement, tons: 425 standard; 550 full load
Dimensions, feet (metres): 179.7 × 25.3 × 6.6 (54.8 × 7.7 × 2)
Main machinery: 2 Type 3-D-12 diesels; 600 hp(m) (440 kW) sustained; 2 shafts
Speed, knots: 12. **Range, miles:** 2,500 at 10 kt
Complement: 20
Military lift: 200 tons or 100 troops or 3 MBTs
Radars: Navigation: Don 2; I-band.
IFF: High Pole.

Comment: Built 1963 to 1969. Ten transferred from the USSR in 1970, the remainder built in Bulgaria between 1974 and 1978. In 1992-93 *703-707* and *712* converted to be used as minelayers. Many deleted. Based at Atiya.

UPDATED

VYDRA 706 (and others)   *7/1995 *, Alexander Mladenov /* 0056636

SURVEY SHIPS

1 MOMA (TYPE 861) CLASS (AGS)

ADMIRAL BRANIMIR ORMANOV 401

Displacement, tons: 1,580 full load
Dimensions, feet (metres): 240.5 × 36.8 × 12.8 *(73.3 × 11.2 × 3.9)*
Main machinery: 2 Zgoda-Sulzer 6TD48 diesels; 3,300 hp(m) *(2.43 MW)* sustained; 2 shafts; cp props
Speed, knots: 17. **Range, miles:** 9,000 at 12 kt
Complement: 37 (5 officers)
Radars: Navigation: 2 Don-2; I-band.

Comment: Built at Northern Shipyard, Gdansk, Poland in 1977. Based at Varna. Two others of the class belonging to Russia were refitted in Bulgaria in 1995-96.

UPDATED

ADMIRAL BRANIMIR ORMANOV   *6/1997* /* 0012104

2 COASTAL SURVEY VESSELS (TYPE 612) (AGSC)

231   331

Displacement, tons: 114 full load
Dimensions, feet (metres): 87.6 × 19 × 4.9 *(26.7 × 5.8 × 1.5)*
Main machinery: 2 Type 3-D-12 diesels; 600 hp(m) (440 kW) sustained; 2 shafts
Speed, knots: 12. **Range, miles:** 600 at 10 kt
Complement: 9 (2 officers)
Radars: Navigation: I-band.

Comment: Built in Bulgaria in 1986 and 1988 respectively. Can carry 2 tons of equipment. *331* is based at Atiya.

VERIFIED

AGSC 331   *6/1996, Bulgarian Navy*

AUXILIARIES

1 SUPPORT TANKER (TYPE 650) (AOL)

203

Displacement, tons: 1,250 full load
Dimensions, feet (metres): 181.8 × 36.1 × 11.5 *(55.4 × 11 × 3.5)*
Main machinery: 2 Sulzer 6AL-20-24 diesels; 1,500 hp(m) *(1.1 MW)*; 2 shafts
Speed, knots: 12. **Range, miles:** 1,000 at 8 kt
Complement: 23
Cargo capacity: 650 tons fuel
Guns: 2 ZU-23-2F Wrobel 23 mm (twin).
Radars: Navigation: I-band.

Comment: Laid down 1989, launched 1993 and completed in 1994 at Burgas Shipyards, Burgas. Second of class may be built when funds are available. Based at Varna.

VERIFIED

203   *1/1998 /* 0017648

2 SUPPORT TANKERS (TYPE 102) (AOL)

DIMITR A DIMITROV (ex-*Mesar*, ex-*Anlene*) 202   ATIYA 302

Displacement, tons: 3,240 full load
Dimensions, feet (metres): 319.8 × 45.6 × 16.4 *(97.5 × 13.9 × 5)*
Main machinery: 2 diesels; 12,000 hp(m) *(8.82 MW)*; 2 shafts
Speed, knots: 18. **Range, miles:** 12,000 at 15 kt
Complement: 32 (6 officers)
Cargo capacity: 1,593 tons
Guns: 4 USSR 30 mm/65 (2 twin).
Radars: Navigation: Two Don 2; I-band.

Comment: Both built in Bulgaria in 1979 and 1987 respectively. Abeam fuelling to port and astern fuelling. Mount 1.5 ton crane amidships. Also carry dry stores. Based at Atiya.

UPDATED

DIMITR A DIMITROV   *8/1997* /* 0056637

1 DIVING TENDER (TYPE 245) (YDT)

223

Displacement, tons: 112 full load
Dimensions, feet (metres): 91.5 × 17.1 × 7.2 *(27.9 × 5.2 × 2.2)*
Main machinery: Diesel-electric; 2 MCK 83-4 diesel generators; 1 motor; 300 hp(m) *(220 kW)*; 1 shaft
Speed, knots: 10. **Range, miles:** 400 at 10 kt
Complement: 6 + 7 divers
Radars: Navigation: Don 2; I-band.

Comment: Built in Bulgaria in mid-1980s. A twin 12.7 mm MG can be fitted. Capable of bell diving to 60 m.

VERIFIED

YDT 223   *6/1998, S Breyer collection /* 0017650

1 BEREZA (TYPE 130) CLASS (ADG/AX)

KAPITAN 1st RANK DIMITER DOBREV 206

Displacement, tons: 2,051 full load
Dimensions, feet (metres): 228 × 45.3 × 13.1 *(69.5 × 13.8 × 4)*
Main machinery: 2 Zgoda-Sulzer 8 AL 25/30 diesels; 2,925 hp(m) *(2.16 MW)* sustained; 2 shafts; cp props
Speed, knots: 13. **Range, miles:** 1,000 at 13 kt
Complement: 48
Radars: Navigation: Kivach; I-band.

Comment: New construction built in Poland and transferred July 1988. Used as a degaussing ship. Fitted with an NBC citadel and upper deck wash-down system. The ship has three laboratories. Has also been used as a training ship. Based at Varna.

UPDATED

KAPITAN 1st RANK DIMITER DOBREV   *6/1997* /* 0012105

1 SALVAGE TUG (ATS)

JUPITER 221

Displacement, tons: 792 full load
Dimensions, feet (metres): 146.6 × 35.1 × 12.7 *(44.7 × 10.7 × 3.9)*
Main machinery: 2—12 KVD 21 diesels; 1,760 hp(m) *(1.3 MW)*; 2 shafts
Speed, knots: 12.5. **Range, miles:** 3,000 at 12 kt
Complement: 39 (6 officers)
Guns: 4—25 mm/70 (2 twin) automatic (can be carried).
Radars: Navigation: I-band.

Comment: Built at Peenewerft Shipyard and completed 20 March 1964. Bollard pull, 16 tons.
Former DDR Type 700. Based at Varna.

UPDATED

8 AUXILIARIES

121	215	216	224	312	313	321	421

Comment: *421* is *Olev Blagoev* which is a survey vessel converted to a training ship. *121* and *215* are torpedo recovery vessels of the same class; *216* a work boat; *312* a tug; *224*, *313* and *321* firefighting vessels. *224* was built in 1996 and replaced the old *224*.

UPDATED

OLEV BLAGOEV   7/1998, C D Yaylali / 0052046

121   3/1999 * / 0056639

JUPITER   8/1996 * / 0056638

BURMA
TATMADAW YAY

Headquarters Appointments

Vice-Chief of Staff, Defence Services (Navy):
  Vice Admiral Than Nyunt
Chief of Naval Staff and Commander in Chief:
  Rear Admiral Tin Aye

Personnel

(a) 2000: 10,000 (including 800 naval infantry)
(b) Voluntary service

General

The title used by the current government is Myanmar. Although some of the hulls are very old, operating in predominantly fresh water has kept corrosion to within containable limits.

Bases

There are three Regions: Arakan, Irrawaddy and Tenasserim. Bases at Bassein, Mergui, Moulmein, Rangoon, Seikyi, Sittwe (Akyab), Sinmalaik, Hanggyi Island, Kyaukpyu, Sandoway.

Naval Infantry

Mostly deployed to Arakan and Tenasserim coastal regions and to the Irawaddy delta for counter-insurgency operations.

Mercantile Marine

Lloyd's Register of Shipping:
  127 vessels of 540,232 tons gross

CORVETTES

Note: Three new corvettes of 1,200 tons reported building at Sinmalaik Shipyard. Based on Chinese hulls with 76 mm guns. First one may complete in 2001/02.

1 PCE 827 CLASS (FS)

Name	No	Builders	Commissioned
YAN TAING AUNG	41	Willamette Iron & Steel Co,	10 Aug 1943
(ex-*Farmington* PCE 894)		Portland, OR	

Displacement, tons: 640 standard; 903 full load
Dimensions, feet (metres): 184 × 33 × 9.5 *(56 × 10.1 × 2.9)*
Main machinery: 2 GM 12-567A diesels; 1,800 hp *(1.34 MW)*; 2 shafts
Speed, knots: 15
Complement: 72

Guns: 1 US 3 in *(76 mm)*/50 Mk 26; 20 rds/min to 12 km *(6.6 n miles)*; weight of shell 6 kg.
  2 Bofors 40 mm/60. 8 Oerlikon 20 mm (4 twin).
Radars: Surface search: Raytheon SPS-5; G/H-band.

Programmes: Laid down on 7 December 1942 and launched on 15 May 1943. Transferred from USA on 18 June 1965.
Operational: All ASW equipment removed. Decommissioned in 1994 but not yet out of the Fleet list, and may remain in operational reserve until new corvettes are in service. *UPDATED*

1 ADMIRABLE CLASS (FS)

Name	No	Builders	Commissioned
YAN GYI AUNG	42	Willamette Iron & Steel Co,	18 Dec 1945
(ex-*Creddock* MSF 356)		Portland, OR	

Displacement, tons: 650 standard; 945 full load
Dimensions, feet (metres): 184.5 × 33 × 9.8 *(56.2 × 10.1 × 3)*
Main machinery: 2 Busch-Sulzer BS-539 diesels; 1,500 hp(m) *(1.1 MW)*; 2 shafts
Speed, knots: 14.8. **Range, miles:** 4,300 at 10 kt
Complement: 73

Guns: 1 US 3 in *(76 mm)*/50 Mk 26; 20 rds/min to 12 km *(6.6 n miles)*; weight of shell 6 kg.
  4 Bofors 40 mm/60 (2 twin). 4 Oerlikon 20 mm (2 twin).
Radars: Surface search: Raytheon SPS-5; G/H-band.

Programmes: Laid down on 10 November 1943 and launched on 22 July 1944. Transferred from USA at San Diego on 31 March 1967.
Operational: Minesweeping gear and ASW equipment removed. Decommissioned in 1994 but not yet out of the Fleet list and may remain in operational reserve until new corvettes are in service. *UPDATED*

YAN TAING AUNG   1987

YAN GYI AUNG   12/1991 * / 0056640

PATROL FORCES

6 HOUXIN (TYPE 037/1G) CLASS
(FAST ATTACK CRAFT—MISSILE) (PGG)

471-476 (ex-*451-456*)

Displacement, tons: 478 full load
Dimensions, feet (metres): 206 × 23.6 × 7.9 *(62.8 × 7.2 × 2.4)*
Main machinery: 4 PR 230ZC diesels; 4,000 hp(m) *(2.94 MW)*; 4 shafts
Speed, knots: 28. **Range, miles:** 1,300 at 15 kt
Complement: 71

Missiles: SSM: 4 YJ-1 (C-801) (2 twin); active radar homing to 40 km *(22 n miles)* at 0.9 Mach; warhead 165 kg; sea skimmer.
Guns: 4—37 mm/63 Type 76A (2 twin); 180 rds/min to 8.5 km *(4.6 n miles)*; weight of shell 1.42 kg.
4—14.5 mm Type 69 (2 twin).
Countermeasures: ESM/ECM: intercept and jammer.
Radars: Surface search: Square Tie; I-band.
Fire control: Rice Lamp; I-band.

Programmes: First pair arrived from China in December 1995, second pair in mid-1996 and last two in late 1997. The first four were wrongly reported as 'Hainan' class.
Structure: Details given are for this class in Chinese service, but the missile fit, although confirmed may include C-802s.
Operational: The fifth of class was damaged in a collision during builders sea trials in August 1996.
UPDATED

HOUXIN (Chinese colours)   *4/1997* * / 0012106

3 OSPREY CLASS (OFFSHORE PATROL VESSELS) (OPV)

Name	No	Builders	Commissioned
INDAW	FV 55	Frederikshavn Dockyard	30 May 1980
INMA	FV 56	Frederikshavn Dockyard	25 Mar 1982
INYA	FV 57	Frederikshavn Dockyard	25 Mar 1982

Displacement, tons: 385 standard; 505 full load
Dimensions, feet (metres): 164 × 34.5 × 9 *(50 × 10.5 × 2.8)*
Main machinery: 2 Burmeister and Wain Alpha diesels; 4,640 hp(m) *(3.4 MW)*; 2 shafts; cp props
Speed, knots: 20. **Range, miles:** 4,500 at 16 kt
Complement: 20 (5 officers)
Guns: 1 Bofors 40 mm/60. 2 Oerlikon 20 mm.

Comment: Operated by Burmese Navy for the People's Pearl and Fishery Department. Helicopter deck with hangar in *Indaw*. Carry David Still craft or RIBs capable of 25 kt.   *UPDATED*

INYA   *1980* * / 0056642

2 MYANMAR CLASS (COASTAL PATROL CRAFT) (PC)

Displacement, tons: 213 full load
Dimensions, feet (metres): 147.3 × 23 × 8.2 *(45 × 7 × 2.5)*
Main machinery: 2 Mercedes-Benz diesels; 2 shafts
Speed, knots: 30+
Complement: 34 (7 officers)
Guns: 2 Bofors 40 mm/60.
Radars: Surface search: I-band.

Comment: Under construction at the Naval Engineering Depot, Rangoon in 1991. Reported as being commissioned on 27 March 1996 but this is not confirmed and the two vessels were reported as still fitting out in late 1998. C-801 missiles may be carried.   *VERIFIED*

FAC(G)   *(not to scale), Ian Sturton*

10 HAINAN (TYPE 037) CLASS (COASTAL PATROL CRAFT) (PC)

Name	No	Name	No	Name	No
YAN SIT AUNG	441	YAN MIN AUNG	445	YAN WIN AUNG	448
YAN MYAT AUNG	442	YAN YE AUNG	446	YAN AYE AUNG	449
YAN NYEIN AUNG	443	YAN PAING AUNG	447	YAN ZWE AUNG	450
YAN KHWIN AUNG	444				

Displacement, tons: 375 standard; 392 full load
Dimensions, feet (metres): 192.8 × 23.6 × 7.2 *(58.8 × 7.2 × 2.2)*
Main machinery: 4 PCR/Kolomna Type 9-D-8 diesels; 4,000 hp(m) *(2.94 MW)* sustained; 4 shafts
Speed, knots: 30.5. **Range, miles:** 1,300 at 15 kt
Complement: 69
Guns: 4 China 57 mm/70 (2 twin); 120 rds/min to 12 km *(6.5 n miles)*; weight of shell 6.31 kg.
4 USSR 25 mm/60 (2 twin); 270 rds/min to 3 km *(1.6 n miles)* anti-aircraft; weight of shell 0.34 kg.
A/S mortars: 4 RBU 1200 5-tubed fixed launchers; range 1,200 m; warhead 34 kg.
Depth charges: 2 BMB-2 projectors; 2 racks.
Mines: Rails fitted.
Countermeasures: ESM: Intercept.
Radars: Surface search: Pot Head; I-band.
Navigation: Raytheon Pathfinder; I-band.
IFF: High Pole.
Sonars: Stag Ear; hull-mounted; active search and attack; high frequency.

Comment: First six delivered from China in January 1991, four more in mid-1993. The first six originally had double figure pennant numbers which have been changed to three figures. These ships are the later variant of this class with tripod masts.   *UPDATED*

YAN WIN AUNG   *9/1993* * / 0056641

YAN KHWIN AUNG   *12/1994, G Toremans*

3 PB 90 CLASS (COASTAL PATROL CRAFT) (PC)

424   **425**   **426**

Displacement, tons: 92 full load
Dimensions, feet (metres): 89.9 × 21.5 × 7.2 *(27.4 × 6.6 × 2.2)*
Main machinery: 3 diesels; 4,290 hp(m) *(3.15 MW)*; 3 shafts
Speed, knots: 32. **Range, miles:** 400 at 25 kt
Complement: 17
Guns: 8—20 mm M75 (two quad). 2—128 mm launchers for illuminants.
Radars: Surface search: Decca 1226; I-band.

Comment: Built by Brodotechnika, Yugoslavia for an African country and completed in 1986-87. Laid up when the sale did not go through and shipped to Burma arriving in October 1990. All are active.
     UPDATED

PB 90 (old number)   *1990* *, Yugoslav FDSP* / 0056643

6 BURMA PGM TYPE (COASTAL PATROL CRAFT) (PC)

PGM 412-PGM 415   THIHAYARZAR I and II

Displacement, tons: 168 full load
Dimensions, feet (metres): 110 × 22 × 6.5 *(33.5 × 6.7 × 2)*
Main machinery: 2 Deutz SBA16MB816 LLKR diesels; 2,720 hp(m) *(2 MW)*; 2 shafts
Speed, knots: 16. **Range, miles:** 1,400 at 14 kt
Complement: 17
Guns: 2 Bofors 40 mm/60.

Comment: Built by Burma Naval Dockyard modelled on the US PGM 401 type. First two completed 1983. Two more craft with identical dimensions and named *Thihayarzar I* and *II* were delivered by Myanma Shipyard to the Customs on 27 June 1993. Both craft are armed and were taken over by the Navy.
UPDATED

PGM 415   *4/1993* / 0056644

6 PGM TYPE (COASTAL PATROL CRAFT) (PC)

PGM 401-PGM 406

Displacement, tons: 141 full load
Dimensions, feet (metres): 101 × 21.1 × 7.5 *(30.8 × 6.4 × 2.3)*
Main machinery: 8 GM 6-71 diesels; 1,392 hp *(1.04 MW)* sustained; 2 shafts
Speed, knots: 17. **Range, miles:** 1,000 at 15 kt
Complement: 17
Guns: 1 Bofors 40 mm/60. 2 Oerlikon 20 mm (twin). 2—12.7 mm MGs.
Radars: Surface search: Raytheon 1500 (PGM 405-406).
    EDO 320 (PGM 401-404); I/J-band.

Comment: First four built by Marinette Marine in 1959; last pair by Peterson Shipbuilders in 1961. Ex-US PGM 43-46, 51 and 52 respectively.
UPDATED

PGM 406   *3/1992* / 0056646

3 SWIFT TYPE PGM (COASTAL PATROL CRAFT) (PC)

PGM 421-PGM 423

Displacement, tons: 128 full load
Dimensions, feet (metres): 103.3 × 23.8 × 6.9 *(31.5 × 7.2 × 3.1)*
Main machinery: 2 MTU 12V 331 TC81 diesels; 2,450 hp(m) *(1.8 MW)* sustained; 2 shafts
Speed, knots: 27. **Range, miles:** 1,800 at 18 kt
Complement: 25
Guns: 2 Bofors 40 mm/60. 2 Oerlikon 20 mm. 2—12.7 mm MGs.
Radars: Surface search: Raytheon 1500; I-band.

Comment: Swiftships construction completed between March and September 1979. Acquired 1980 through Vosper, Singapore.
UPDATED

PGM 421   *6/1991* / 0056645

2 IMPROVED Y 301 CLASS (RIVER GUNBOATS) (PGR)

Y 311   Y 312

Displacement, tons: 250 full load
Dimensions, feet (metres): 121.4 × 24 × 3.9 *(37 × 7.3 × 1.2)*
Main machinery: 2 MTU MB diesels; 1,000 hp(m) *(735 kW)*; 2 shafts
Speed, knots: 12
Complement: 37
Guns: 2 Bofors 40 mm/60. 4 Oerlikon 20 mm.
Radars: Surface search: Raytheon; I-band.

Comment: Built at Simmilak in 1969 and based on similar Yugoslav craft which have been scrapped.
UPDATED

Y 312   *8/1994* / 0056647

10 Y 301 CLASS (RIVER GUNBOATS) (PGR)

Y 301-Y 310

Displacement, tons: 120 full load
Dimensions, feet (metres): 104.8 × 24 × 3 *(32 × 7.3 × 0.9)*
Main machinery: 2 MTU MB diesels; 1,000 hp(m) *(735 kW)*; 2 shafts
Speed, knots: 13
Complement: 29
Guns: 2 Bofors 40 mm/60 or 1 Bofors 40 mm/60 and 1 Vickers 2-pdr.

Comment: All of these boats were completed in 1958 at the Uljanik Shipyard, Pula, Yugoslavia. At least five are reported as active.
UPDATED

Y 304   *1991* / 0056648

4 RIVER GUNBOATS (Ex-TRANSPORTS) (PGR)

SAGU   SEINDA   SHWETHIDA   SINMIN

Displacement, tons: 98 full load
Dimensions, feet (metres): 94.5 × 22 × 4.5 *(28.8 × 6.7 × 1.4)*
Main machinery: 1 Crossley ERL 6-cyl diesel; 160 hp *(119 kW)*; 1 shaft
Speed, knots: 12
Complement: 32
Guns: 1—40 mm/60 *(Sagu)*. 1—20 mm (3 in *Sagu*).

Comment: Built in mid-1950s. *Sinmin*, *Seinda* and *Shwethida* have a roofed-in upper deck with a 20 mm gun forward of the funnel. *Sagu* has an open upper deck aft of the funnel but with a 40 mm gun forward and mountings for 20 mm aft on the upper deck and midships either side on the lower deck. Four other ships of the same type are unarmed and are listed under *Auxiliaries*.
UPDATED

SEINDA   *8/1994* / 0056649

2 CGC TYPE (RIVER GUNBOATS) (PCR)

MGB 102   MGB 110

Displacement, tons: 49 standard; 66 full load
Dimensions, feet (metres): 83 × 16 × 5.5 *(25.3 × 4.9 × 1.7)*
Main machinery: 4 GM diesels; 800 hp *(596 kW)*; 2 shafts
Speed, knots: 11
Complement: 16
Guns: 1 Bofors 40 mm/60. 1 Oerlikon 20 mm.

Comment: Ex-USCG type cutters with new hulls built in Burma. Completed in 1960. Have not been seen recently.
UPDATED

MGB 110

9 RIVER PATROL CRAFT (PBR)

RPC 11–RPC 19

Displacement, tons: 37 full load
Dimensions, feet (metres): 50 × 14 × 3.5 *(15.2 × 4.3 × 1.1)*
Main machinery: 2 Thornycroft RZ 6 diesels; 250 hp *(186 kW)*; 2 shafts
Speed, knots: 10. **Range, miles:** 400 at 8 kt
Complement: 8
Guns: 1 Oerlikon 20 mm or 2—12.7 mm MGs (twin). 1—12.7 mm MG.

Comment: Built by the Naval Engineering Depot, Rangoon. First five in mid-1980s; second batch of a modified design in 1990-91. Sometimes used by the Naval Infantry and can carry up to 35 troops.

VERIFIED

6 RIVER PATROL CRAFT (PBR)

PBR 211-216

Displacement, tons: 9 full load
Dimensions, feet (metres): 32 × 11 × 2.6 *(9.8 × 3.4 × 0.8)*
Main machinery: 2 GM 6V-53 diesels; 348 hp *(260 kW)* sustained; 2 water-jets
Speed, knots: 25. **Range, miles:** 180 at 20 kt
Complement: 4 or 5
Guns: 2—12.7 mm (twin, fwd) MGs. 1—7.9 mm LMG (aft).
Radars: Surface search: Raytheon 1900; I-band.

Comment: Acquired in 1978. Built by Uniflite, Washington. GRP hulls. Not reported as active recently.

UPDATED

PBR 211   1987

25 MICHAO CLASS (PBR)

001-025

Comment: Small craft, 52 ft *(15.8 m)* long, acquired from Yugoslavia in 1965. Also used to ferry troops and two are used as VIP launches.

UPDATED

RPL   5/1995 * / 0056650

6 CARPENTARIA CLASS (RIVER PATROL CRAFT) (PBR)

111-113   117   119-120

Displacement, tons: 26 full load
Dimensions, feet (metres): 51.5 × 15.7 × 4.3 *(15.7 × 4.8 × 1.3)*
Main machinery: 2 MTU 8V 331 TC92 diesels; 1,770 hp(m) *(1.3 MW)* sustained; 2 shafts
Speed, knots: 29. **Range, miles:** 950 at 18 kt
Complement: 10
Guns: 1 Oerlikon 20 mm. 1—12.7 mm MG.

Comment: Built by De Havilland Marine, Sydney. First two delivered 1979, remainder in 1980. Similar to craft built for Indonesia.

UPDATED

CARPENTARIA 113   1991 * / 0056651

AMPHIBIOUS FORCES

Note: As well as the vessels listed below there are three Army Landing Craft (001-003) of about 75 tons.

LANDING CRAFT 003   7/1992 * / 0056652

4 ABAMIN CLASS (LCU)

AIYAR MAI 604	**AIYAR MINTHAMEE** 606
AIYAR MAUNG 605	**AIYAR MINTHAR** 607

Displacement, tons: 250 full load
Dimensions, feet (metres): 125.6 × 29.8 × 4.6 *(38.3 × 9.1 × 1.4)*
Main machinery: 2 Kubota diesels; 600 hp(m) *(441 kW)*; 2 shafts
Speed, knots: 10
Complement: 10
Military lift: 100 tons
Guns: 1—12.7 mm MG.

Comment: All built by Yokohama Yacht in 1969.

UPDATED

AIYAR MAUNG   1991 * / 0056653

1 LCU

AIYAR LULIN 603

Displacement, tons: 360 full load
Dimensions, feet (metres): 119 × 34 × 6 *(36.3 × 10.4 × 1.8)*
Main machinery: 4 GM diesels; 600 hp *(448 kW)*; 2 shafts
Speed, knots: 10. **Range, miles:** 1,200 at 8 kt
Complement: 14
Military lift: 168 tons
Guns: 1—12.7 mm MG.

Comment: Completed in Rangoon in 1966 to the US 1610 design.

UPDATED

AIYAR LULIN   1990 * / 0056654

10 LCM 3 TYPE

LCM 701-710

Displacement, tons: 52 full load
Dimensions, feet (metres): 50 × 14 × 4 *(15.2 × 4.3 × 1.2)*
Main machinery: 2 Gray Marine 64 HN9 diesels; 330 hp *(246 kW)*; 2 shafts
Speed, knots: 9
Complement: 5

Comment: US-built LCM type landing craft. Used as local transports for stores and personnel. Cargo capacity, 30 tons. Guns have been removed.

UPDATED

LCM 704   5/1994 * / 0056655

MINE WARFARE FORCES

Note: Up to two Chinese-built minesweepers are expected to be acquired when funds are available.

SURVEY SHIPS

Note: Thu Tay Thi means 'survey vessel'.

Name	No	Builders	Commissioned
—	801	Brodogradiliste Tito, Belgrade, Yugoslavia	1965

Displacement, tons: 1,059 standard
Dimensions, feet (metres): 204 × 36 × 11.8 *(62.2 × 11 × 3.6)*
Main machinery: 2 MTU 12V 493 TY7 diesels; 2,120 hp(m) *(1.62 MW)* sustained; 2 shafts
Speed, knots: 15
Complement: 99 (7 officers)
Guns: 2 Bofors 40 mm/60. 2 Oerlikon 20 mm (twin).
Radars: Navigation: Racal Decca; I-band.

Comment: Has two surveying motor boats. The after gun can be removed to provide a helicopter platform. This ship is sometimes referred to as Thu Tay Thi which means 'survey vessel'.

VERIFIED

801   6/1993

Name	No	Builders	Commissioned
— (ex-Changi)	802	Miho Shipyard, Shimizu	20 June 1973

Displacement, tons: 880 full load
Dimensions, feet (metres): 154.2 × 28.6 × 11.9 *(47 × 8.7 × 3.6)*
Main machinery: 1 Niigata diesel; 1 shaft
Speed, knots: 13
Complement: 45 (5 officers)
Guns: 2 Oerlikon 20 mm.
Radars: Navigation: I-band.

Comment: A fishery research ship of Singapore origin, arrested on 8 April 1974 and taken into service as a survey vessel in about 1981. Stern trawler type.

UPDATED

802   10/1993* / 0056657

Name	No	Builders	Commissioned
YAY BO	807	Damen, Netherlands	1958

Displacement, tons: 108 full load
Dimensions, feet (metres): 98.4 × 22.3 × 4.9 *(30 × 6.8 × 1.5)*
Main machinery: 2 diesels; 2 shafts
Speed, knots: 10
Complement: 34 (2 officers)
Guns: 1—12.7 mm MG.

Comment: Used for river surveys.

UPDATED

YAY BO   1990* / 0056656

AUXILIARIES

Note: As well as the ships listed below there is a small coastal oil tanker, a harbour tug and several harbour launches and personnel carriers.

1 TRANSPORT VESSEL (AK)

AYIDAWAYA

Displacement, tons: 805 full load
Dimensions, feet (metres): 163.4 × 27.6 × 12.1 *(49.8 × 8.4 × 3.7)*
Main machinery: 1 diesel; 600 hp(m) *(441 kW)*; 1 shaft
Speed, knots: 12
Complement: 30

Comment: Built in Norway in 1975. Acquired in 1991 and used as transport for stores and personnel.

UPDATED

AYIDAWAYA   12/1991* / 0056658

1 TANKER (AOT)

INTERBUNKER

Displacement, tons: 2,900 full load
Dimensions, feet (metres): 232 × 36.1 × 16.1 *(70.7 × 11 × 4.9)*
Main machinery: 2 Daihatsu diesels; 1,860 hp(m) *(1.37 MW)*; 1 shaft
Speed, knots: 11. **Range, miles:** 5,000 at 11 kt
Complement: 15

Comment: Thai owned commercial tanker arrested in October 1991 and taken into the Navy.

UPDATED

INTERBUNKER   12/1991* / 0056659

1 DIVING SUPPORT VESSEL (YDT)

YAN LON AUNG 200

Displacement, tons: 536 full load
Dimensions, feet (metres): 179 × 30 × 8 *(54.6 × 9.1 × 2.4)*
Main machinery: 2 diesels; 2 shafts
Speed, knots: 12
Complement: 88
Guns: 1 Bofors 40 mm/60. 2—12.7 mm MGs.

Comment: Support diving ship acquired from Japan in 1967.

UPDATED

YAN LON AUNG   7/1993* / 0056660

4 TRANSPORT VESSELS (AKL)

SABAN   SETHYA   SHWEPAZUN   SETYAHAT

Displacement, tons: 98 full load
Dimensions, feet (metres): 94.5 × 22 × 4.5 (28.8 × 6.7 × 1.4)
Main machinery: 1 Crossley ERL 6-cyl diesel; 160 hp (119 kW); 1 shaft
Speed, knots: 12
Complement: 30

Comment: These are sister ships to the armed gunboats shown under *Patrol Forces*. It is possible that a 20 mm gun may be mounted on some occasions. **UPDATED**

SHWEPAZUN   1991* / 0056661

1 TRANSPORT VESSEL (AKL)

PYI DAW AYE

Displacement, tons: 850 full load
Dimensions, feet (metres): 160 × 27 × 11 (48.8 × 8.2 × 3.4)
Main machinery: 2 diesels; 600 hp (447 kW); 2 shafts
Speed, knots: 11
Complement: 12

Comment: Completed in about 1975. Dimensions are approximate. Naval manned. **UPDATED**

PYI DAW AYE   1991* / 0056663

7 MFVs

511   521-523   901   905   906

Comment: Armed vessels of approximately 200 tons (901), 80 tons (905, 906) and 50 tons (remainder) with a 12.7 mm or 6.72 mm MG mounted above the bridge in some. All have navigational radars. **UPDATED**

MFVs 905 and 906 (alongside Swift Type PGMs)   4/1996* / 0056664

1 BUOY TENDER (ABU)

HSAD DAN

Displacement, tons: 706 full load
Dimensions, feet (metres): 130.6 × 37.1 × 8.9 (39.8 × 11.3 × 2.7)
Main machinery: 2 Deutz BA8M816 diesels; 1,341 hp(m) (986 kW); 2 shafts
Speed, knots: 10
Complement: 23

Comment: Built by Italthai in 1986. Operated by the Rangoon Port Authority but manned by the Navy. **UPDATED**

HSAD DAN   5/1992* / 0056662

PRESIDENTIAL YACHT

YADANABON

Comment: Built in Burma and used for VIP cruises on the Irrawaddy river and in coastal waters. Armed with 2—7.62 mm MGs and manned by the Navy. **UPDATED**

PRESIDENT'S YACHT   1990* / 0056665

BURUNDI

General	Bases	Personnel
Naval contingent of the Burundi Army	Bujumbura, Lake Tanganyika	2000: 95

PATROL FORCES

2 YULIN CLASS (LAKE PATROL CRAFT) (PBR)

RUVUBU   COHOHA

Displacement, tons: 10 full load
Dimensions, feet (metres): 42.6 × 9.5 × 3.5 (13 × 2.9 × 1.1)
Main machinery: 1 PRC diesel; 300 hp(m) (221 kW); 1 shaft
Speed, knots: 18
Complement: 6
Guns: 4 ZU-23-2 Wrobel 23 mm/87 (2 twin); 400 rds/min to 2 km.
Radars: Surface search: Furuno; I-band.

Comment: Built in Shanghai in the mid-1960s. These two are the survivors of four originally transferred, although one of these two may have been sunk in mid-1998. Re-armed. **UPDATED**

COHOHA and RUVUBU
11/1996* / 0012107

AUXILIARIES

Comment: Two LCTs built locally, and a 40 ton craft *Muhuhura* are used for logistic support. There is also a supply launch *Nicole*, which was built in 1991, and several small LCVPs with Mercury outboards.

UPDATED

LCVP   *11/1996* / 0012109*   NICOLE   *11/1996* / 0012108*

CAMBODIA

Headquarters Appointments

Commander of Navy:
Rear Admiral Ung San Khann

General

In 1992 all naval units were under UN command and painted white, but with the UN withdrawal in November 1993 all were repainted grey.

Personnel

2000: 2,800 (780 officers) including marines

Bases

Ream (ocean), Phnom Penh (river), Kompongson (civil)

Organisation

Ocean Division has nine battalions and the River Division seven battalions. Command HQ is at Phnom Penh.

Mercantile Marine

Lloyd's Register of Shipping:
300 vessels of 998,716 tons gross

DELETIONS

Patrol Forces

1997-98   2 Turya, 4 Shmel, 9 Kano, 2 PCF
1998-99   2 Stenka, 2 Zhuk

Auxiliaries

1997-98   3 T4, 5 LCVP

PATROL FORCES

Note: There are also about 170 motorised and manual canoes.

2 MODIFIED STENKA CLASS (TYPE 205P) (FAST ATTACK CRAFT—PATROL) (PCF)

1131   1134

Displacement, tons: 211 standard; 253 full load
Dimensions, feet (metres): 129.3 × 25.9 × 8.2 *(39.4 × 7.9 × 2.5)*
Main machinery: 3 Caterpillar diesels; 14,000 hp(m) *(10.29 MW)*; 3 shafts
Speed, knots: 37. **Range, miles:** 800 at 24 kt; 500 at 35 kt
Complement: 25 (5 officers)
Guns: 2—23 mm/87 (twin). 2 Bofors 40 mm/60 (twin).
Radars: Surface search: Racal Decca Bridgemaster; I-band.
Fire control: Muff Cob; G/H-band.
Navigation: Racal Decca; I-band.
IFF: High Pole. 2 Square Head.

Comment: Four transferred from USSR in November 1987. Export model without torpedo tubes and sonar. One pair were modernised in Hong Leong Shipyard, Butterworth, from early 1995 to April 1996. New engines, guns and radars were fitted. The second pair similarly refitted by August 1997, and by late 1998 only two were still operational. Pennant numbers were changed for UN operations but changed back again in November 1993.

UPDATED

2 KAOH CLASS (RIVER PATROL CRAFT) (PBR)

KAOH CHHLAM 1105   KAOH RONG 1106

Displacement, tons: 44 full load
Dimensions, feet (metres): 76.4 × 20 × 3.9 *(23.3 × 6.1 × 1.2)*
Main machinery: 2 Deutz/MWM TBD 616 V16 diesels; 2,992 hp(m) *(2.2 MW)*; 2 shafts
Speed, knots: 34. **Range, miles:** 400 at 30 kt
Complement: 13 (3 officers)
Guns: 2—14.5 mm MG (twin). 2—12.7 mm MGs.
Radars: Surface search: Racal Decca Bridgemaster; I-band.

Comment: Ordered from Hong Leong Shipyard, Butterworth to a German design in 1995 and delivered 20 January 1997. Aluminium construction.   *UPDATED*

KAOH CHHLAM   *1/1997*, Hong Leong Shipyard / 0056667*

STENKA 1131   *8/1997*, Hong Leong Shipyard / 0056666*

CAMEROON
MARINE NATIONALE RÉPUBLIQUE

Headquarters Appointments	Personnel	Bases	Mercantile Marine
Chief of Naval Staff: Commander Guillaume Ngouah Ngally	2000: 1,250	Douala (HQ), Limbe, Kribi	*Lloyd's Register of Shipping:* 61 vessels of 13,600 tons gross

PATROL FORCES

Note: Two Rodman 30 m, four Rodman 14 m and ten Rodman 6.5 m craft are to be delivered from late 2000. All have speeds in excess of 25 kt.

1 BIZERTE (TYPE PR 48) CLASS (LARGE PATROL CRAFT) (PC)

Name	No	Builders	Commissioned
L'AUDACIEUX	P 103	SFCN, Villeneuve-La-Garenne	11 May 1976

Displacement, tons: 250 full load
Dimensions, feet (metres): 157.5 × 23.3 × 7.5 *(48 × 7.1 × 2.3)*
Main machinery: 2 SACM 195 V12 CZSHR diesels; 6,000 hp(m) *(4.41 MW)* sustained; 2 shafts; cp props
Speed, knots: 23. **Range, miles:** 2,000 at 16 kt
Complement: 25 (4 officers)
Guns: 2 Bofors 40 mm/70; 300 rds/min to 12.8 km *(7 n miles)*; weight of shell 0.96 kg.

Comment: L'Audacieux ordered in September 1974. Laid down on 10 February 1975, launched on 31 October 1975. Similar to 'Bizerte' class in Tunisia. Operational status doubtful and not reported at sea since 1995. Fitted for SS 12M missiles but these are not embarked. *UPDATED*

BIZERTE (Tunisian colours) 1993*, van Ginderen Collection / 0056668

1 COASTAL PATROL CRAFT (PC)

QUARTIER MAÎTRE ALFRED MOTTO

Displacement, tons: 96 full load
Dimensions, feet (metres): 95.4 × 20.3 × 6.3 *(29.1 × 6.2 × 1.9)*
Main machinery: 2 Baudouin diesels; 1,290 hp(m) *(948 kW)*; 2 shafts
Speed, knots: 14
Complement: 17 (2 officers)
Guns: 2 Oerlikon 20 mm. 2—7.62 mm MGs.
Radars: Surface search: I-band.

Comment: Built at Libreville, Gabon in 1974. Discarded as a derelict hulk in 1990 but refurbished and brought back into service with assistance from the French Navy in 1995-96. *UPDATED*

1 BAKASSI (TYPE P 48S) CLASS (MISSILE PATROL CRAFT) (PCG)

Name	No	Builders	Launched	Commissioned
BAKASSI	P 104	SFCN, Villeneuve-La-Garenne	22 Oct 1982	9 Jan 1984

Displacement, tons: 308 full load
Dimensions, feet (metres): 172.5 × 23.6 × 7.9 *(52.6 × 7.2 × 2.4)*
Main machinery: 2 SACM 195 V16 CZSHR diesels; 8,000 hp(m) *(5.88 MW)* sustained; 2 shafts
Speed, knots: 25. **Range, miles:** 2,000 at 16 kt
Complement: 39 (6 officers)
Guns: 2 Bofors 40 mm/70; 300 rds/min to 12.8 km *(7 n miles)*; weight of shell 0.96 kg.
Weapons control: 2 Naja optronic systems. Racal Decca Cane 100 command system.
Radars: Navigation/surface search: 2 Furuno; I-band.

Comment: Ordered January 1981. Laid down 16 December 1981. Major refit at Lorient completed in August 1999. This included removing the Exocet missile system and EW equipment, and fitting a funnel aft of the mainmast to replace the waterline exhausts. New radars were also installed. *UPDATED*

BAKASSI (old configuration) 1984*, SFCN / 0056669

6 SWIFT PBR CLASS (RIVER PATROL CRAFT) (PBR)

Displacement, tons: 12 full load
Dimensions, feet (metres): 38 × 12.5 × 3.2 *(11.6 × 3.8 × 1)*
Main machinery: 2 Stewart and Stevenson 6V-92TA diesels; 520 hp *(388 kW)* sustained; 2 shafts
Speed, knots: 32. **Range, miles:** 210 at 20 kt
Complement: 4
Guns: 2—12.7 mm MGs. 2—7.62 mm MGs.

Comment: Built by Swiftships and supplied under the US Military Assistance Programme. First 10 delivered in March 1987, second 10 in September 1987 and the remainder in March 1988. These last survivors are used by the gendarmerie. Several others have been cannibalised for spares. *UPDATED*

PR 01 4/1992* / 0056671

QUARTIER MAÎTRE ALFRED MOTTO 2/1996*, French Navy / 0056670

CANADA

Headquarters Appointments

Vice Chief of Defence Staff:
Vice Admiral G L Garnett, CMM
Director General Maritime Doctrine and Operations:
Captain J Dewar

Flag Officers

Chief of Maritime Staff:
Vice Admiral G R Maddison, OMM, MSC
Commander, Maritime Forces, Atlantic:
Rear Admiral D E Miller, OMM
Commander, Maritime Forces, Pacific:
Rear Admiral R D Buck, OMM

Diplomatic Representation

Military Representative, Brussels:
Vice Admiral J A King, CMM
Naval Adviser, London:
Captain K C E Beardmore
Naval Attaché, Moscow:
Commander A T Pinnell
Naval Attaché, Washington:
Captain P Hoes
Naval Attaché, Tokyo:
Captain S F Verran
Naval Attaché, Paris:
Commander R Drolet
Naval Attaché, Canberra:
Captain B R Brown
Naval Attaché, Kiev:
Commander R M Williams

Establishment

The Royal Canadian Navy (RCN) was officially established on 4 May 1910, when Royal Assent was given to the Naval Service Act. On 1 February 1968 the Canadian Forces Reorganisation Act unified the three branches of the Canadian Forces and the title 'Royal Canadian Navy' was dropped.

Personnel

(a) 2000: 8,930 (Regular), 4,010 (Reserves)

Prefix to Ships' Names

HMCS

Bases

Halifax and Esquimalt

Fleet Deployment

Atlantic:
Operations Group One (destroyers, frigates, AOR)
Operations Group Five (maritime warfare forces, submarines and coastal defence districts)

Pacific:
Operations Group Two (destroyers, frigates, AOR)
Operations Group Four (maritime warfare forces and coastal defence districts)

Maritime Air Components (MAC)

Commander MAC (Atlantic)—based in Halifax
Commander MAC (Pacific)—based in Esquimalt

Squadron/ Unit	Base	Aircraft	Function
MP 404	Greenwood, NS	Aurora/ Arcturus	LRMP/ Training
MP 405	Greenwood, NS	Aurora	LRMP
HT 406	Shearwater, NS	Sea King	Training
MP 407	Comox, BC	Aurora	LRMP
MP 415	Greenwood, NS	Aurora	LRMP
MH 423	Shearwater, NS	Sea King	General
MH 443	Victoria, BC	Sea King	General
HOTEF	Shearwater, NS	Sea King	Test
MPEU	Greenwood, NS	Aurora	Test

Notes

(a) Detachments from 423 and 443 meet ships' requirements in Atlantic and Pacific Fleets respectively. Sea King helicopters are now classified as General Purpose vice the former ASW designation.

(b) 413 Squadron based in Greenwood, NS, and 442 Squadron based in Comox, BC, are two maritime search and rescue squadrons under the command of 1 Canadian Air Division (CAD).

(c) 434 Combat Support (CS) Squadron along with 420 Air Reserve Squadron (ARS) located in Greenwood NS, and 414 CS located in Comox BC, are part of 1 Canadian Air Division (CAD) providing services to Maritime Command operations with CT/CE-133 Silver Stars.

Strength of the Fleet

Type	Active	Building
Submarines	2	3
Destroyers	4	—
Frigates	12	—
Mine Warfare Forces	14	—
Survey Ships	2	—
Support Ships	2	(4)

Mercantile Marine

Lloyd's Register of Shipping:
857 vessels of 2,495,904 tons gross

DELETIONS

Submarines

1998   *Ojibwa, Okanagan*

Frigates

1997   *Gatineau* (reserve), *Terra Nova* (reserve)
1998   *Annapolis, Nipigon*

Patrol Forces

1997   *Thunder, Cowichan*
1998   *Miramachi, Chaleur*

Auxiliaries

1997   *YDT 6, 8* and *9, Cormorant*
1998   *Provider*

PENNANT LIST

Submarines

73	Onondaga
876	Victoria
877	Windsor
878	Cornerbrook
879	Chicoutimi

Destroyers

280	Iroquois
281	Huron
282	Athabaskan
283	Algonquin

Frigates

330	Halifax
331	Vancouver
332	Ville de Québec
333	Toronto
334	Regina
335	Calgary
336	Montreal
337	Fredericton
338	Winnipeg
339	Charlottetown
340	St John's
341	Ottawa

Mine Warfare Forces

110	Anticosti
112	Moresby
700	Kingston
701	Glace Bay
702	Nanaimo
703	Edmonton
704	Shawinigan
705	Whitehorse
706	Yellowknife
707	Goose Bay
708	Moncton
709	Saskatoon
710	Brandon
711	Summerside

Auxiliaries

171	Endeavour
172	Quest
509	Protecteur
510	Preserver
610	Sechelt
611	Sikanni
612	Sooke
613	Stikine

SUBMARINES

WINDSOR (UK colours)

6/1994*, B Sullivan / 0081388

1 + 3 VICTORIA (UPHOLDER) CLASS (TYPE 2400) (SSK)

Name	No	Builders	Start date	Launched	Commissioned	Recommissioned
VICTORIA (ex-*Unseen*)	876 (ex-S 41)	Cammell Laird, Birkenhead	Jan 1986	14 Nov 1989	7 June 1991	June 2000
WINDSOR (ex-*Unicorn*)	877 (ex-S 43)	Cammell Laird, Birkenhead (VSEL)	Feb 1989	16 Apr 1992	25 June 1993	June 2001
CORNERBROOK (ex-*Ursula*)	878 (ex-S 42)	Cammell Laird, Birkenhead (VSEL)	Aug 1987	28 Feb 1991	8 May 1992	June 2001
CHICOUTIMI (ex-*Upholder*)	879 (ex-S 40)	Vickers Shipbuilding and Engineering, Barrow	Nov 1983	2 Dec 1986	9 June 1990	July 2002

Displacement, tons: 2,168 surfaced; 2,455 dived
Dimensions, feet (metres): 230.6 × 25 × 17.7 *(70.3 × 7.6 × 5.5)*
Main machinery: Diesel-electric; 2 Paxman Valenta 16SZ diesels; 3,620 hp *(2.7 MW)* sustained; 2 GEC alternators; 2.8 MW; 1 GEC motor; 5,400 hp *(4 MW)*; 1 shaft
Speed, knots: 12 surfaced; 20 dived; 12 snorting
Range, miles: 8,000 at 8 kt snorting
Complement: 48 (7 officers) plus 5 spare

Torpedoes: 6—21 in *(533 mm)* bow tubes. 18 Gould Mk 48 Mod 4; dual purpose; active/passive homing to 50 km *(27 n miles)*/38 km *(21 n miles)* at 40/55 kt; warhead 267 kg. Air turbine pump discharge.
Countermeasures: Decoys: 2 SSE launchers.
ESM: Sperry Guardian Star; intercept.

Weapons control: Loral Librascope TFCS
Radars: Navigation: Kelvin Hughes Type 1007; I-band.
Furuno (portable); I-band.
Sonars: Thomson Sintra Type 2040; hull-mounted; passive search and intercept; medium frequency.
BAe Type 2007; flank array; passive; low frequency.
Hermes Electronics/MUSL; towed array; passive low frequency.
Passive ranging.

Programmes: First ordered 2 November 1983. Further three ordered on 2 January 1986. Laid up after post Cold War defence cuts in 1994 and acquired from the UK own 6 April 1998. Being refitted at Vickers, Barrow, for delivery from June 2000.

Modernisation: Changes for Canadian operations include the transfer of torpedoes from the 'Oberon' class, and the removal of SSMs and mines. The torpedo fire-control system and sonar towed arrays are also the same as the 'Oberon' class. AIP is under consideration for the future.
Structure: Single-skinned NQ1 high tensile steel hull, tear dropped shape 9:1 ratio, five man lock-out chamber in fin. Fitted with elastomeric acoustic tiles. Diving depth, greater than 200 m *(650 ft)*. Fitted with Pilkington Optronics CK 35 search and CH 85 attack optronic periscopes.
Operational: Reactivation and certification for submerged operations is the responsibility of the UK. The first submarine is scheduled to be fully operational by the end of 2000.

UPDATED

CHICOUTIMI (UK colours)

1989, VSEL / 0010824

1 OBERON CLASS (SSK)

Name	No	Builders	Laid down	Launched	Commissioned
ONONDAGA	73	HM Dockyard, Chatham	18 June 1964	25 Sep 1965	22 June 1967

Displacement, tons: 2,030 surfaced; 2,410 dived
Dimensions, feet (metres): 295.2 × 26.5 × 18 *(90 × 8.1 × 5.5)*
Main machinery: Diesel-electric; 2 ASR 16 VVS-ASR1 diesels; 3,680 hp *(2.74 MW)*; 2 AEI motors; 6,000 hp *(4.48 MW)*; 2 shafts
Speed, knots: 12 surfaced; 17 dived; 10 snorting
Range, miles: 9,000 surfaced at 12 kt
Complement: 65 (7 officers)

Torpedoes: 6—21 in *(533 mm)* bow tubes. 20 Gould Mk 48 Mod 4; dual purpose; active/passive homing to 50 km *(27 n miles)*/38 km *(21 n miles)* at 40/55 kt; warhead 267 kg.

Countermeasures: ESM: Sperry Guardian Star; intercept.
Weapons control: Loral Librascope TFCS.
Radars: Navigation: Furuno 1831; I-band.
Sonars: Plessey Triton Type 2051; hull-mounted; passive/active search and attack; medium frequency.
BAC Type 2007 AC; flank array; passive search; long range; low frequency.
BQG 501 Sperry Micropuffs; passive ranging.
Hermes Electronics/MUSL towed array; passive low frequency.

Modernisation: Underwent SOUP (Submarine Operational Update Project) with more modern sonar and fire-control equipment fitted in 1982-84. Starting in 1987 weapon launching and fire-control systems were upgraded to take the US Mk 48 torpedo which replaced the Mk 37. Plessey Triton Type 2051 sonar purchased in 1989. Fitted with towed array sonar in 1995. TFCS updated at the same time.
Structure: Diving depth, 200 m *(656 ft)* but probably now restricted because of the age of the hulls. Stern tubes have been blanked off. Pilkington Optronics CK 24 search, and CH 74 attack, periscopes.
Operational: Planned to pay off on 31 July 2000.

UPDATED

ONONDAGA

6/1998, CDF / 0017652

FRIGATES

Note: *Yukon* (263) is used as an alongside training ship at Esquimalt.

12 HALIFAX CLASS (FFH/FFG)

Name	No	Builders	Laid down		Launched		Commissioned	
HALIFAX	330	Saint John SB Ltd, New Brunswick	19 Mar	1987	30 Apr	1988	29 June	1992
VANCOUVER	331	Saint John SB Ltd, New Brunswick	19 May	1988	8 July	1989	23 Aug	1993
VILLE DE QUÉBEC	332	Marine Industries Ltd, Sorel	17 Jan	1989	16 May	1991	14 July	1994
TORONTO	333	Saint John SB Ltd, New Brunswick	24 Apr	1989	18 Dec	1990	29 July	1993
REGINA	334	Marine Industries Ltd, Sorel	6 Oct	1989	25 Oct	1991	30 Sep	1994
CALGARY	335	Marine Industries Ltd, Sorel	15 June	1991	28 Aug	1992	12 May	1995
MONTREAL	336	Saint John SB Ltd, New Brunswick	8 Feb	1991	28 Feb	1992	21 July	1994
FREDERICTON	337	Saint John SB Ltd, New Brunswick	25 Apr	1992	13 Mar	1993	10 Sep	1994
WINNIPEG	338	Saint John SB Ltd, New Brunswick	19 Mar	1993	5 Dec	1993	23 June	1995
CHARLOTTETOWN	339	Saint John SB Ltd, New Brunswick	5 Dec	1993	10 July	1994	9 Sep	1995
ST JOHN'S	340	Saint John SB Ltd, New Brunswick	24 Aug	1994	12 Feb	1995	26 June	1996
OTTAWA	341	Saint John SB Ltd, New Brunswick	29 Apr	1995	22 Nov	1995	28 Sep	1996

Displacement, tons: 4,770 full load
Dimensions, feet (metres): 441.9 oa; 408.5 pp × 53.8 × 16.4; 23.3 (screws) *(134.7; 124.5 × 16.4 × 5; 7.1)*
Main machinery: CODOG; 2 GE LM 2500 gas turbines; 47,494 hp *(35.43 MW)* sustained 1 SEMT-Pielstick 20 PA6 V 280 diesel; 8,800 hp(m) *(6.48 MW)* sustained; 2 shafts; cp props
Speed, knots: 29
Range, miles: 9,500 at 13 kt (diesel); 3,930 at 18 kt (gas)
Complement: 198 (17 officers) plus 17 (8 officers) aircrew

Missiles: SSM: 8 McDonnell Douglas Harpoon Block 1C (2 quad) launchers ❶; active radar homing to 130 km *(70 n miles)* at 0.9 Mach; warhead 227 kg.
SAM: 2 Raytheon Sea Sparrow Mk 48 octuple vertical launchers ❷; semi-active radar homing to 14.6 km *(8 n miles)* at 2.5 Mach; warhead 39 kg; 28 missiles (16 normally carried).
Guns: 1 Bofors 57 mm/70 Mk 2 ❸; 220 rds/min to 17 km *(9 n miles)*; weight of shell 2.4 kg.
1 GE/GDC 20 mm Vulcan Phalanx Mk 15 Mod 1 ❹; anti-missile; 3,000 rds/min (6 barrels combined) to 1.5 km.
8—12.7 mm MGs.
Torpedoes: 4—324 mm Mk 32 Mod 9 (2 twin) tubes ❺. 24 Honeywell Mk 46 Mod 5; anti-submarine; active/passive homing to 11 km *(5.9 n miles)* at 40 kt; warhead 44 kg.
Countermeasures: Decoys: 4 Plessey Shield Mk 2 decoy launchers ❻; sextuple mountings; fires P8 chaff and P6 IR flares in distraction, decoy or centroid modes. Nulka to be fitted.
Nixie SLQ-25; towed acoustic decoy.
ESM: MEL/Lockheed Canews SLQ-501 ❼; radar intercept; (0.5-18 GHz). SRD 502; intercept.
ECM: MEL/Lockheed Ramses SLQ-503 ❽; jammer.
Combat data systems: UYC-501 SHINPADS action data automation with UYQ-504 and UYK-505 or 507 (336-341) processors. Links 11 and 14.
Weapons control: AHWCS for Harpoon. CDC UYS-503(V); sonobuoy processing system.
Radars: Air search: Raytheon SPS-49(V)5 ❾; C/D-band; range 457 km *(250 n miles)*.
Air/surface search: Ericsson Sea Giraffe HC 150 ❿; G/H-band; range 100 km *(55 n miles)* against missiles in clear conditions.
Fire control: Two Signaal SPG-503 (STIR 1.8) ⓫; K/I-band; range 140 km *(76 n miles)* for 1 m² target.
Navigation: Sperry Mk 340 being replaced by Kelvin Hughes 1007; I-band.
Tacan: URN 25. IFF Mk XII.
Sonars: Westinghouse SQS-510; hull-mounted; active search and attack; medium frequency.
CDC SQR-501 CANTASS towed array (uses part of Martin Marietta SQR-19 TACTASS). TIAPS in due course.

Helicopters: 1 CH-124A ASW or 1 CH-124B Heltas Sea King ⓬.

Programmes: On 29 June 1983 Saint John Shipbuilding Ltd won the competition for the first six of a new class of patrol frigates. Combat system design and integration was subcontracted to Loral Canada (formerly Paramax, a subsidiary of Unisys). Three ships were subcontracted to Marine Industries Ltd in Lauzon and Sorel. On 18 December 1987 six

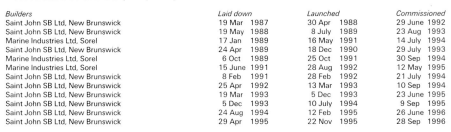

HALIFAX   *(Scale 1 : 1,200), Ian Sturton / 0012116*

MONTREAL   *9/1998*, E & M Laursen / 0056672*

additional ships of the same design were ordered from Saint John SB Ltd.
Modernisation: Sonar upgraded to SQS-510 in all of the class by 1999. There are plans to fit a towed integrated active/passive sonar (TIAPS) from 2002 if the new build destroyer (CADRE) is delayed. It is also reported but not confirmed that four of the class may be converted to air defence ships from 2002. Conversion to include Signaal APAR and possibly Standard SAM and Extended Range Sea Sparrow.

Structure: Much effort has gone into stealth technology. Gas turbine engines are raft mounted. Dresball IR suppression is fitted. Indal RAST helicopter handling system.
Operational: Problems on first of class trials included higher than designed radiated noise levels which are reported as speed associated. These have been rectified and the ships are stable and quiet in all sea conditions. *Vancouver, Regina, Calgary, Winnipeg* and *Ottawa* are Pacific based.

UPDATED

CALGARY   *6/1999*, Sattler/Steele / 0056674*

ST JOHN'S   *4/1999*, M Declerck* / 0056676

CHARLOTTETOWN   *9/1999*, G Toremans* / 0056675

TORONTO   *4/1999*, M Declerck* / 0056673

DESTROYERS

Note: There are provisional plans for a new Air Defence destroyer (CADRE), with a projected in service date of 2007.

4 IROQUOIS CLASS (DDG)

Name	No	Builders	Laid down	Launched	Commissioned
IROQUOIS	280	Marine Industries Ltd, Sorel	15 Jan 1969	28 Nov 1970	29 July 1972
HURON	281	Marine Industries Ltd, Sorel	15 Jan 1969	3 Apr 1971	16 Dec 1972
ATHABASKAN	282	Davie Shipbuilding, Lauzon	1 June 1969	27 Nov 1970	30 Sep 1972
ALGONQUIN	283	Davie Shipbuilding, Lauzon	1 Sep 1969	23 Apr 1971	3 Nov 1973

Displacement, tons: 5,300 full load

Dimensions, feet (metres): 398 wl; 426 oa × 50 × 15.5 keel/21.5 screws *(121.4; 129.8 × 15.2 × 4.7/6.6)*

Main machinery: COGOG; 2 Pratt & Whitney FT4A2 gas turbines; 50,000 hp *(37 MW)*; 2 GM Allison 570-KF gas turbines; 12,700 hp *(9.5 MW)* sustained; 2 shafts; acbLIPS cp props

Speed, knots: 27. **Range, miles:** 4,500 at 15 kt (cruise turbines)

Complement: 255 (23 officers) plus 30 (9 officers) aircrew

Missiles: SAM: 1 Martin Marietta Mk 41 VLS ❶ for 29 GDC Standard SM-2MR Block III; command/inertial guidance; semi-active radar homing to 73 km *(40 n miles)* at Mach 2.

Guns: 1 OTO Melara 3 in *(76 mm)*/62 Super Rapid ❷; 120 rds/min to 16 km *(8.7 n miles)*; weight of shell 6 kg. 6—12.7 mm MGs.

1 GE/GDC 20 mm/76 6-barrelled Vulcan Phalanx Mk 15 ❸; 3,000 rds/min combined to 1.5 km.

Torpedoes: 6—324 mm Mk 32 (2 triple) tubes ❹. Honeywell Mk 46 Mod 5; anti-submarine; active/passive homing to 11 km *(5.9 n miles)* at 40 kt; warhead 44 kg.

Countermeasures: Decoys: 4 Plessey Shield Mk 2 6-tubed fixed launchers ❺. P 8 chaff or P 6 IR flares.

BAe Nulka offboard decoys in quad pack launchers from 1999. SLQ-25 Nixie; torpedo decoy.

ESM: MEL SLQ-501 Canews ❻; radar warning.

SRD 503 Ramses; intercept.

ECM: BAe Nulka.

Combat data systems: SHINPADS, automated data handling with UYQ-504 and UYK-507 processors. Links 11 and 14. Link 16 in 2000. Link 22 by 2006. JMCIS and Marconi Matra SHF SATCOM ❼ (DDG 280 and 282).

Weapons control: Signaal LIROD 8 ❽ optronic director. UYS-503(V) sonobuoy processor.

Radars: Air search: Signaal SPQ-502 (LW08) ❾; D-band.

Surface search: Signaal SPQ-501 (DA08) ❿; E/F-band.

Fire control: 2 Signaal SPG-501 (STIR 1.8) ⓫; I/J-band.

Navigation: 2 Raytheon Pathfinder; I-band.

Koden MD 373 *(Iroquois* only, on hangar roof); I-band.

Tacan: URN 26.

Sonars: Westinghouse SQS-510; combined VDS and hull-mounted; active search and attack. 2 sets.

Helicopters: 2 CH-124A Sea King ASW ⓬.

Modernisation: A contract for the Tribal Class Update and Modernisation Project (TRUMP) was awarded to Litton Systems Canada Limited in June 1986. The equipment reflected the changing role of the ship and replaced systems that did not meet the air defence requirement. *Algonquin* started modernisation in November 1987 at Mil Davie, Quebec, and completed October 1991, followed by *Iroquois,* started November 1988, and completed May 1992. *Athabaskan* entered the yard in September 1991 and

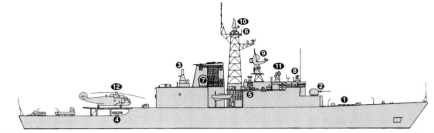

IROQUOIS   *(Scale 1 : 1,200), Ian Sturton /* 0056677

IROQUOIS   *12/1999*, van Ginderen Collection /* 0056678

completed in August 1994; *Huron* started in June 1992 and completed 17 January 1995. Sonar upgraded from 1998. Nulka system has replaced ULQ-6 in 1999. JMCIS has been fitted vice JOTS II, with SHF SATCOM in DDG 280 and 282, and the others in due course. Canews II EW upgrade planned. Link 16 is planned for 2000, Link 22 by 2006.

Structure: These ships are also fitted with a landing deck equipped with double hauldown and Beartrap, pre-wetting system to counter NBC conditions, enclosed citadel and bridge control of machinery. The flume type anti-roll tanks have been replaced during modernisation with a water displaced fuel system. Design weight limit has been reached.

Operational: Helicopters can carry 12.7 mm MGs and ESM/FLIR instead of ASW gear. *Algonquin* and *Huron* are based in the Pacific.

UPDATED

ATHABASKAN   *7/1999*, M Declerck /* 0056679

SHIPBORNE AIRCRAFT

Note: The Maritime Helicopter Project to procure up to 28 new aircraft awaits government approval. An order for 15 Agusta Westland Cormorant SAR helicopters was placed in January 1998.

Numbers/Type: 24/6 Sikorsky CH-124A ASW/CH-124B Heltas Sea King.
Operational speed: 110 kt *(203 km/h).*
Service ceiling: 17,000 ft *(5,150 m).*
Range: 410 n miles *(760 km).*
Role/Weapon systems: ASW, surface surveillance and support; carried by escorts and AORs; 'Iroquois' class carry 2 helicopters, AORs 3. CH-124B Heltas Sea Kings dedicated to 'Halifax' class ships. Sensors: CH-124A ASW - APS-503 radar, sonobuoys, AQS-502 dipping sonar. Some modified for FLIR. During Gulf operations, FLIR modified aircraft were also fitted with APR-39, ALE-37 chaff dispenser and ALQ-144 IR countermeasures. CH-124B Heltas - APS-503 radar, UYS-503 sonobuoy processor, GPS and ASQ-504 MAD. Weapons: Two Mk 46 Mod 5 torpedoes for both aircraft types.

UPDATED

LAND-BASED MARITIME AIRCRAFT (FRONT LINE)

Numbers/Type: 18/3 Lockheed CP-140 Aurora/CP-140A Arcturus.
Operational speed: 410 kt *(760 km/h).*
Service ceiling: 34,000 ft *(9,930 m).*
Range: 4,000 n miles *(7,410 km).*
Role/Weapon systems: Aurora operated for long-range maritime surveillance over Atlantic, Pacific and Arctic Oceans; roles include ASW/ASV and SAR; Arcturus for unarmed Arctic patrol, maritime surveillance, SAR and training. Arcturus fitted with same equipment as Aurora but without the ASW fit. Lockheed Martin Spotlight synthetic aperture radar fitted in 1999 for trials. Incremental modernisation programme planned over next several years. Aurora sensors: APS-506 radar, IFF, ALR-502 ESM, ECM, FLIR OR 5008, ASQ-502 MAD, OL 5004 acoustic processor. Weapons: 8 Mk 46 Mod 5 torpedoes. Arcturus sensors: APS-507 radar, IFF.

UPDATED

SEA KING   *4/1999*, Winter & Findler /* 0056683

AURORA   *6/1998*, Canada DND /* 0081501

MINE WARFARE FORCES

Note: A remote minehunting system (RMS) based on the Dolphin unmanned submersible started trials in October 1996 for the 'Kingston' class. The RMS is powered by a Caterpillar 3116TA diesel engine giving 350 hp which maintains a speed of 12 kt (maximum 19 kt) when towing a side scan sonar at 180 m. Endurance is 16 hours increasing to 28 hours with the sonar at 60 m or 48 hours when not towing. The system is being developed by MacDonald Dettwiler.

12 KINGSTON CLASS (MCDV)

Name	No	Builders	Laid down	Launched	Commissioned
KINGSTON	700	Halifax Shipyards	15 Dec 1994	12 Aug 1995	21 Sep 1996
GLACE BAY	701	Halifax Shipyards	28 Apr 1995	22 Jan 1996	26 Oct 1996
NANAIMO	702	Halifax Shipyards	11 Aug 1995	17 May 1996	10 May 1997
EDMONTON	703	Halifax Shipyards	8 Dec 1995	16 Aug 1996	21 June 1997
SHAWINIGAN	704	Halifax Shipyards	26 Apr 1996	15 Nov 1996	14 June 1997
WHITEHORSE	705	Halifax Shipyards	26 July 1996	24 Feb 1997	17 Apr 1998
YELLOWKNIFE	706	Halifax Shipyards	7 Nov 1996	5 June 1997	18 Apr 1998
GOOSE BAY	707	Halifax Shipyards	22 Feb 1997	4 Sep 1997	26 July 1998
MONCTON	708	Halifax Shipyards	31 May 1997	5 Dec 1997	12 July 1998
SASKATOON	709	Halifax Shipyards	5 Sep 1997	30 Mar 1998	21 Nov 1998
BRANDON	710	Halifax Shipyards	6 Dec 1997	3 Sep 1998	5 June 1999
SUMMERSIDE	711	Halifax Shipyards	28 Mar 1998	4 Oct 1998	18 July 1999

Displacement, tons: 962 full load
Dimensions, feet (metres): 181.4 × 37.1 × 11.2 *(55.3 × 11.3 × 3.4)*
Main machinery: Diesel-electric; 4 Wärtsilä UD 23V12 diesels; 4 Jeumont ANR-53-50 alternators; 7.2 MW; 2 Jeumont CI 560L motors; 3,000 hp(m) *(2.2 MW);* 2 acbLIPS Z drive azimuth thrusters
Speed, knots: 15; 10 sweeping. **Range, miles:** 5,000 at 8 kt
Complement: 31 (Patrol); 37 (MCM)

Guns: 1 Bofors 40 mm/60 Mk 5C. 2—12.7 mm MGs.

Countermeasures: MCM: 1 of 3 modular payloads: (a) Indal Technologies SLQ 38 (single and double Oropesa sweeps); (b) Route survey system; (c) Mine inspection Sutec ROV.
Radars: Surface search: Kelvin Hughes 6000; E/F-band.
Navigation: Kelvin Hughes; I-band.
Sonars: MacDonald Dettwiler towed side scan; high frequency active; minehunting.

Programmes: Contract awarded to Fenco MacLaren on 15 May 1992. Halifax Shipyards is owned by Saint John Shipbuilding. Known as Maritime Coastal Defence Vessels (MCDV) combining MCM with general patrol duties.

Structure: MacDonald Dettwiler combat systems integration, MCM systems and integrated logistics support. Modular payloads comprising two MMS, four Route Survey and one ISE Trail Blazer 25 ROV. The Z drives can be rotated through 360°. Options for diving and minehunting equipment are being considered.
Operational: Predominantly manned by reservists. Six on each coast (700, 701, 704, 707, 708 and 711 Atlantic and St Lawrence, remainder Pacific). The St Lawrence vessels are based at Quebec from May to November. Two of the class are at extended readiness on a rotational basis.

UPDATED

KINGSTON   *5/1999*, W Sartori /* 0056680

2 MINESWEEPERS AUXILIARY (MSA)

Name	No	Builders	Commissioned
ANTICOSTI (ex-*Jean Tide*)	MSA 110	Allied SB, Vancouver	7 May 1989
MORESBY (ex-*Joyce Tide*)	MSA 112	Allied SB, Vancouver	7 May 1989

Displacement, tons: 2,205 full load
Dimensions, feet (metres): 191 × 43 × 17 *(58.2 × 13.1 × 5.2)*
Main machinery: 4 Wärtsilä Nohab Polar SF 16RS diesels; 4,600 hp(m) *(3.38 MW)*; 2 shafts; Gil Jet bow thruster; 575 hp *(429 kW)*
Speed, knots: 13. **Range, miles:** 12,000 at 13 kt
Complement: 41 (5 officers)
Guns: 2—7.62 mm MGs.
Countermeasures: MCM: BAJ Mk 9 mechanical sweep with WSMF (monitoring equipment).
Radars: Navigation: 2 Brighttrack 502; I-band.
Sonars: Side scan towed VDS; high frequency.

Comment: Former offshore towing/supply vessels Ice class 3, suitable for navigation in light ice. Built in 1973 and purchased in March 1988. Each ship has a triple drum towing winch of 300,000 lb pull. *Anticosti* fitted with astern refuelling in mid-1995. Both ships converted again by January 1997 as Fleet Support vessels for the MCDVs providing fuel, water, stores and extra accommodation. *Moresby* transferred to the Pacific in February 1997 for Group 4; *Anticosti* in the Atlantic with Group 5. Both may be paid off in 2000.

UPDATED

ANTICOSTI   *5/1999*, W Sartori* / 0056681

3 MCM DIVING TENDERS (YDT/YAG)

YDT 10   YDT 11, 12

Displacement, tons: 70; 110 *(YDT 11-12)*
Dimensions, feet (metres): 78 × 18.5 × 8.5 *(22.9 × 5.6 × 2.6) (YDT 10)*
99 × 20 × 8.5 *(27.3 × 6.2 × 2.6) (YDT 11-12)*
Main machinery: 2 GM diesels; 165 hp *(123 kW)*; 228 hp *(170 kW) (YDT 11-12)*; 2 shafts
Speed, knots: 11
Complement: 9 (1 officer); 13 (2 officers) *(YDT 11-12)*
Radars: Navigation: Racal Decca; I-band.

Comment: *YDT 10* of wooden construction, *11-12* of steel. *11-12* have recompression chambers, a side scan sonar and are capable of deploying 100 m surface supplied diving systems. Divers carry hand-held sonars and use MCM diving sets for their primary role. *YDT 10* is a general purpose craft with all diving gear removed. See also 'Sechelt' class under *Auxiliaries*.

UPDATED

YDT 12   *11/1995*, CDF* / 0056682

TRAINING SHIPS

1 SAIL TRAINING SHIP (AXS)

Name	No	Builders	Launched
ORIOLE	YAC 3	Owens	4 June 1921

Displacement, tons: 92 full load
Dimensions, feet (metres): 102 × 19 × 9 *(31.1 × 5.8 × 2.7)*
Main machinery: 1 Cummins diesel; 165 hp *(123 kW)*; 1 shaft
Speed, knots: 8
Complement: 6 (1 officer) plus 18 trainees

Comment: Commissioned in the Navy in 1948 and based at Esquimalt. Sail area (with spinnaker) 11,000 sq ft. Height of mainmast 94 ft *(28.7 m)*, mizzen 55.2 ft *(16.8 m)*.

UPDATED

ORIOLE   *12/1997*, van Ginderen Collection* / 0017662

SURVEY AND RESEARCH SHIPS

Name	No	Builders	Launched	Commissioned
QUEST	AGOR 172	Burrard, Vancouver	9 July 1968	21 Aug 1969

Displacement, tons: 2,130 full load
Dimensions, feet (metres): 235 × 42 × 15.5 *(71.6 × 12.8 × 4.6)*
Main machinery: Diesel-electric; 4 Fairbanks-Morse 38D8-1/8-9 diesel generators; 4.37 MW sustained; 2 GE motors; 2 shafts; cp props
Speed, knots: 16. **Range, miles:** 10,000 at 12 kt
Complement: 55
Helicopters: Platform only.

Comment: Built for the Naval Research Establishment of the Defence Research Board for acoustic, hydrographic and general oceanographic work. Capable of operating in heavy ice in the company of an icebreaker. Launched on 9 July 1968. Based at Halifax and does line array acoustic research in the straits of the northern archipelago. Mid-life update in 1997-99 included new communications and navigation equipment and improved noise insulation. Planned to conduct TIAPS trials (towed integrated active/passive sonar) in 2000.

UPDATED

QUEST   *8/1994, van Ginderen Collection* / 0056684

Name	No	Builders	Launched	Commissioned
ENDEAVOUR	AGOR 171	Yarrows Ltd, Esquimalt	17 Aug 1961	9 Mar 1965

Displacement, tons: 1,560 full load
Dimensions, feet (metres): 236 × 38.5 × 13 *(71.9 × 11.7 × 4)*
Main machinery: Diesel-electric; 4 Fairbanks-Morse 38D8-1/8-9 diesel generators; 4.36 MW; 2 GE motors; 2 shafts; cp props
Speed, knots: 16. **Range, miles:** 10,000 at 12 kt
Complement: 50 (10 officers, 13 scientists, 2 aircrew)
Radars: Navigation: Racal Decca 1229 and 1630C; I-band.
Helicopters: Platform for 1 light.

Comment: A naval research ship designed primarily for anti-submarine research. Flight deck 48 × 31 ft *(14.6 × 9.4 m)*. Stiffened for operating in ice-covered areas. Able to turn in 2.5 times her own length. Two 9 ton Austin-Weston telescopic cranes are fitted. There are two oceanographical winches each holding 5,000 fathoms of wire, two bathythermograph winches and a deep-sea anchoring and coring winch. She has acoustic insulation in her machinery spaces.

UPDATED

ENDEAVOUR   *6/1999*, CDF* / 0056685

AUXILIARIES

2 PROTECTEUR CLASS (AOR)

Name	No	Builders	Laid down	Launched	Commissioned
PROTECTEUR	AOR 509	St John Dry Dock Co, NB	17 Oct 1967	18 July 1968	30 Aug 1969
PRESERVER	AOR 510	St John Dry Dock Co, NB	17 Oct 1967	29 May 1969	30 July 1970

Displacement, tons: 8,380 light; 24,700 full load
Dimensions, feet (metres): 564 × 76 × 33.3
  (171.9 × 23.2 × 10.1)
Main machinery: 2 Babcock & Wilcox boilers; 1 GE Canada
  turbine; 21,000 hp (15.7 MW); 1 shaft; bow thruster
Speed, knots: 21
Range, miles: 4,100 at 20 kt; 7,500 at 11.5 kt
Complement: 365 (27 officers) including 45 aircrew
Cargo capacity: 14,590 tons fuel; 400 tons aviation fuel; 1,048
  tons dry cargo; 1,250 tons ammunition; 2 cranes (15 ton lift)
Guns: 2 GE/GDC 20 mm/76 6-barrelled Vulcan Phalanx Mk 15.
  6—12.7 mm MGs.
Countermeasures: Decoys: 4 Loral Hycor SRBOC chaff
  launchers.
ESM: Racal Kestrel SLQ-504; radar warning.
Combat data systems: EDO Link 11; SATCOM WSC-3(V).
Radars: Surface search: Norden SPS-502 with Mk XII IFF.
Navigation: Racal Decca 1630 and 1629; I-band.
Tacan: URN 20.
Helicopters: 3 CH-124A ASW or CH-124B Heltas Sea King.

Comment: Four replenishment positions. Both have been used
as Flagships and troop carriers. They can carry anti-submarine
helicopters, military vehicles and bulk equipment for sealift
purposes; also four LCVPs. For the Gulf deployment in 1991,
the 76 mm gun was remounted, two Vulcan Phalanx and two
Bofors 40/60 guns were fitted, four Plessey Shield chaff

PRESERVER   4/1999*, Michael Nitz / 0056686

launchers and ESM equipment were provided for *Protecteur*.
Additionally, all helicopters carried 12.7 mm MGs and ESM/
FLIR equipment instead of ASW gear. Bofors, 76 mm guns and
hull mounted sonars later removed from both ships and are
unlikely to be fitted again. *Protecteur* transferred to the Pacific
Fleet November 1992.

UPDATED

0 + (2) MULTIROLE SUPPORT VESSELS (ALSC)

Displacement, tons: 30,000 full load
Dimensions, feet (metres): 656.2 × 105 × 27.9 (200 × 32 × 8.5)
Main machinery: 2 diesels or 2 gas turbines; 1 shaft; podded propulsion; bow thruster
Speed, knots: 21. **Range, miles:** 10,800 at 15 kt
Complement: 180
Cargo capacity: 8,000 tons fuel; 510 tons aviation fuel; 300 tons ammunition; 200 × 20 ft
  containers; 2,500 m ro-ro space
Guns: 2 Vulcan Phalanx CIWS.
Countermeasures: Decoys: Chaff launchers. Towed torpedo decoy.
ESM/ECM: Canews intercept and jammer.
Radars: Air/surface search: E/F-band.
Navigation: I-band.
Helicopters: 3-5 Sea King size.

Comment: Speculative details given for a projected new class of afloat logistics and sealift
capability (ALSC) ship to replace current AORs between 2008 and 2010. Combines the features
of a tanker with a ro-ro ship. Two RAS stations each side. Stern and side ramp. The after
superstructure is on the starboard side of the flight deck. Up to four of the class may be built.

UPDATED

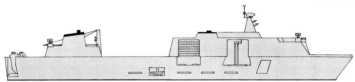

ALSC   (not to scale), Ian Sturton / 0056687

4 SECHELT CLASS (YTT/YPT/YDT)

Name	No	Builders	Commissioned
SECHELT	YDT 610	West Coast Manly	10 Nov 1990
SIKANNI	YPT 611	West Coast Manly	10 Nov 1990
SOOKE	YDT 612	West Coast Manly	10 Nov 1990
STIKINE	YPT 613	West Coast Manly	10 Nov 1990

Displacement, tons: 290 full load
Dimensions, feet (metres): 108.5 × 27.8 × 7.8 (33.1 × 8.5 × 2.4)
Main machinery: 2 Caterpillar 3412T diesels; 1,080 hp (806 kW) sustained; 2 shafts
Speed, knots: 12.5
Complement: 4 or 12 (610 and 612)

Comment: Based at the Nanoose Bay Maritime Experimental and Test Range. *Sechelt* and *Sooke*
converted to diving tenders in 1997 with a recompression chamber or a workshop container
embarked. Diving operations supported to 80 m. *Sechelt* on west coast, *Sooke* on east coast.

UPDATED

SECHELT   6/1999*, CDF / 0056688

TUGS AND TENDERS

13 COASTAL TUGS (YTB/YTL)

GLENDYNE YTB 640	LAWRENCEVILLE YTL 590	FIREBIRD YTR 561
GLENDALE YTB 641	PARKSVILLE YTL 591	FIREBRAND YTR 562
GLENEVIS YTB 642	LISTERVILLE YTL 592	TILLICUM YTM 555
GLENBROOK YTB 643	MERRICKVILLE YTL 593	
GLENSIDE YTB 644	MARYSVILLE YTL 594	

Comment: 'Glen' class are 255 ton tugs built in the mid-1970s. 'Ville' class are 70 ton tugs built in
1974. The two YTRs are firefighting craft of 130 tons. The YTM is a 140 ton tug.   ***UPDATED***

GLENBROOK   5/1994*, N A Sifferlinger / 0056689

4 DIVING SUPPORT VESSELS (DSV)

Displacement, tons: 2.2 full load
Dimensions, feet (metres): 39 × 12.5 × 2.3 (11.9 × 3.8 × 0.7)
Main machinery: 2 Caterpillar 3126TA diesels; 740 hp(m) (548 kW); 2 WMC 357 waterjets
Speed, knots: 36. **Range, miles:** 600 at 29 kt
Complement: 3 plus 14 divers

Comment: Built by Celtic Shipyards and delivered in early 1997, two to each coast. Landing craft
bows for launching unmanned submersibles. Bollard pull 6,560 lb.   ***VERIFIED***

DSVs   6/1997, CDF / 0012131

COAST GUARD

Administration

Commissioner Canadian Coast Guard/Assistant Deputy Minister Marine:
   John Adams

Establishment

In January 1962 all ships owned and operated by the Federal Department of Transport, with the exception of pilotage and canal craft, were amalgamated into the Canadian Coast Guard Fleet. On 1 April 1995 ships of the Fisheries and Oceans department merged with the Coast Guard under the direction of the Minister of Fisheries and Oceans. Its headquarters are in Ottawa while field operations are administered from five regional offices located in Vancouver, British Columbia (Pacific Region); Winnipeg, Manitoba (Central & Arctic Region); Quebec, Quebec (Laurentian Region); Dartmouth, Nova Scotia (Maritimes Region); and St John's, Newfoundland (Newfoundland Region).

Flag and Identity Markings

The Canadian Coast Guard has its own distinctive jack, a red maple leaf on a white ground at the hoist and two gold dolphins on a blue ground at the fly. The colour scheme for all ships is being changed, as they become due for refit, to: red hull with a white diagonal stripe, white upperworks and a red maple leaf on the funnel.

Missions

The Canadian Coast Guard carries out the following missions:
(a) Icebreaking and Escort. Icebreaking and escort of commercial ships is carried out in waters off the Atlantic seaboard, in the Gulf of St Lawrence, St Lawrence River and the Great Lakes in Winter and in Arctic waters in Summer.
(b) Aids to Navigation. Installation, supply and maintenance of fixed and floating aids to navigation in Canadian waters.
(c) Organise and provide icebreaker escort to commercial shipping in support of the annual Northern Sealift which supplies bases and settlements in the Canadian Arctic, Hudson Bay and Foxe Basin.
(d) Provide and operate a wide range of marine search and rescue vessels.
(e) Provide and operate Hydrographic survey, Oceanographic and Fishery Research vessels.
(f) Carry out Fishery Patrol and enforcement of fishery regulations.

Shipborne Aircraft

A total of 26 helicopters can be embarked in ships with aircraft facilities. These include five Bell 206, five Bell 212, 15 MBB BO 105s and a long range Sikorsky S-61N. All have Coast Guard markings.

Small Craft

In addition to the ships listed there are numerous lifeboats, surfboats, self-propelled barges and other small craft which are carried on board the larger vessels. Also excluded are shore-based work boats, floating oil spill boats, oil slick-lickers or any of the small boats which are available for use at the various Canadian Coast Guard Bases and lighthouse stations.

DELETIONS

1997   *Tupper, James Sinclair, Avocet, Rosmarus, Chebucto, Robert Foulis*
1998   *Louis M Lauzier* (charter), *Miskanaw, Caligus, CG 039*
1999   *Cap Goéland, Narwhal, Montmagny*
2000   *Hudson*

HEAVY GULF ICEBREAKERS

1 GULF CLASS (Type 1300)

Name	Builders	Launched		Commissioned	
LOUIS S ST LAURENT	Canadian Vickers Ltd, Montreal	3 Dec	1966	Oct	1969

Displacement, tons: 14,500 full load
Measurement, tons: 11,441 grt; 5,370 net
Dimensions, feet (metres): 392.7 × 80.1 × 32.2 *(119.7 × 24.4 × 9.8)*
Main machinery: Diesel-electric; 5 Krupp MaK 16 M 453C diesels, 39,400 hp(m) *(28.96 MW)*; 5 Siemens alternators; 3 GE motors; 27,000 hp(m) *(19.85 MW)*; 3 shafts; bow thruster
Speed, knots: 18. **Range, miles:** 23,000 at 17 kt
Complement: 47 (13 officers) plus 38 scientists
Radars: Navigation: 3 Kelvin Hughes; I-band.
Helicopters: 2 BO 105CBS.

Comment: Larger than any of the former Coast Guard icebreakers. Two 49.2 ft *(15 m)* landing craft embarked. Mid-life modernisation July 1988 to early 1993 included replacing main engines with a diesel-electric system, adding a more efficient *Henry Larsen* type icebreaking bow (adds 8 m to length) with an air bubbler system and improving helicopter facilities with a fixed hangar. In addition the complement was reduced. Based in the Maritimes Region at Dartmouth, NS. On 22 August 1994 became the first Canadian ship to reach the North Pole, in company with USCG *Polar Sea*.   ***UPDATED***

LOUIS S ST LAURENT   *6/1998, Harald Carstens /* 0017665

LOUIS S ST LAURENT   *6/1998*, Harald Carstens /* 0056691

MEDIUM GULF/RIVER ICEBREAKERS

3 R CLASS (Type 1200)

Name	Builders	Launched		Commissioned	
PIERRE RADISSON	Burrard, Vancouver	3 June	1977	June	1978
SIR JOHN FRANKLIN	Burrard, Vancouver	10 Mar	1978	Mar	1979
DES GROSEILLIERS	Port Weller, Ontario	20 Feb	1982	Aug	1982

Displacement, tons: 6,400 standard; 8,180 (7,594, *Des Groseilliers*) full load
Measurement, tons: 5,910 gross; 1,678 net
Dimensions, feet (metres): 322 × 64 × 23.6 *(98.1 × 19.5 × 7.2)*
Main machinery: Diesel-electric; 6 Montreal Loco 251V-16F diesels; 17,580 hp *(13.1 MW)*; 6 GEC generators; 11.1 MW sustained; 2 motors; 13,600 hp *(10.14 MW)*; 2 shafts; bow thruster
Speed, knots: 16. **Range, miles:** 15,000 at 13.5 kt
Complement: 38 (12 officers)
Radars: Navigation: Sperry; E/F- and I-band.
Helicopters: 1 Bell 212.

Comment: *Franklin* is based at St John's, Newfoundland but may move to the Great Lakes for winter 2000/01. The other two based in the Laurentian Region at Quebec.   ***UPDATED***

DES GROSEILLIERS   *1/1996*, van Ginderen Collection /* 0056690

1 MODIFIED R CLASS (Type 1200)

Name	Builders	Launched		Commissioned	
HENRY LARSEN	Versatile Pacific SY, Vancouver, BC	3 Jan	1987	29 June	1988

Displacement, tons: 5,798 light; 8,290 full load
Measurement, tons: 6,172 gross; 1,756 net
Dimensions, feet (metres): 327.3 × 64.6 × 24 *(99.8 × 19.7 × 7.3)*
Main machinery: Diesel-electric; 3 Wärtsilä Vasa 16V32 diesel generators; 17.13 MW/60 Hz sustained; 3 motors; 16,320 hp(m) *(12 MW)*; 3 shafts
Speed, knots: 16. **Range, miles:** 15,000 at 13.5 kt
Complement: 52 (15 officers) plus 20 spare berths
Radars: Navigation: Racal Decca Bridgemaster; I-band.
Helicopters: 1 Bell 212.

Comment: Contract date 25 May 1984, laid down 23 August 1985. Although similar in many ways to the 'R' class she has a different hull form particularly at the bow and a very different propulsion system. Fitted with Wärtsilä air bubbling system. Based in Newfoundland Region. Engine room fire in 1998 put her out of commission for some time.   ***UPDATED***

HENRY LARSEN   *3/1999*, Canadian Coast Guard /* 0056707

HEAVY ICEBREAKER/SUPPLY TUG

Name	Builders	Launched	Commissioned
TERRY FOX	Burrard Yarrow, Vancouver	1982	1983

Displacement, tons: 7,100 full load
Measurement, tons: 4,233 gross; 1,955 net
Dimensions, feet (metres): 288.7 × 58.7 × 27.2 (88 × 17.9 × 8.3)
Main machinery: 4 Werkspoor 8-cyl 4SA diesels; 23,200 hp(m) (17 MW); 2 shafts; cp props; bow and stern thrusters
Speed, knots: 16. **Range, miles:** 1,920 at 15 kt
Complement: 23 (10 officers)
Radars: Navigation: 2 Racal Decca ARPA; 1 Furuno 1411; E/F- and I-bands.

Comment: Initially leased for two years from Gulf Canada Resources during the completion of *Louis S St Laurent* conversion but has now been retained. Commissioned in Coast Guard colours 1 November 1991 and purchased 1 November 1993. Based in the Maritimes Region at Dartmouth. **UPDATED**

TERRY FOX 7/1997*, M B MacKay / 0012133

MAJOR NAVAIDS TENDERS/LIGHT ICEBREAKERS
(Type 1100)

Name	Builders	Commissioned
MARTHA L BLACK	Versatile Pacific, Vancouver, BC	30 Apr 1986
GEORGE R PEARKES	Versatile Pacific, Vancouver, BC	17 Apr 1986
EDWARD CORNWALLIS	Marine Industries Ltd, Tracy, Quebec	14 Aug 1986
SIR WILLIAM ALEXANDER	Marine Industries Ltd, Tracy, Quebec	13 Feb 1987
SIR WILFRID LAURIER	Canadian Shipbuilding Ltd, Ontario	15 Nov 1986
ANN HARVEY	Halifax Industries Ltd, Halifax, NS	29 June 1987

Displacement, tons: 4,662 full load
Measurement, tons: 3,818 (Martha L Black); 3,809 (George R Pearkes); 3,812 (Sir Wilfrid Laurier); 3,727 (Edward Cornwallis and Sir William Alexander); 3,823 (Ann Harvey) gross
Dimensions, feet (metres): 272.2 × 53.1 × 18.9 (83 × 16.2 × 5.8)
Main machinery: Diesel-electric; 3 Bombardier/Alco 12V-251 diesels; 8,019 hp (6 MW) sustained; 3 Canadian GE generators; 6 MW; 2 Canadian GE motors; 7,040 hp (5.25 MW); 2 shafts; bow thrusters
Speed, knots: 15.5. **Range, miles:** 6,500 at 15 kt
Complement: 25 (10 officers)
Radars: Navigation: Racal Decca Bridgemaster; I-band.
Helicopters: 1 light type, such as Bell 206L.

Comment: *Black*, and *Pearkes* based in the Laurentian Region at Quebec, *Cornwallis* and *Alexander* in the Maritimes Region at Dartmouth, *Ann Harvey* in the Newfoundland Region at St Johns and *Laurier* in the Pacific Region at Victoria. *Cornwallis* converted as a survey ship in 1997/98. **UPDATED**

SIR WILLIAM ALEXANDER 8/1998, M B MacKay / 0017668

GEORGE R PEARKES 4/1996*, van Ginderen Collection / 0056692

Name	Builders	Commissioned
GRIFFON	Davie Shipbuilding, Lauzon	Dec 1970

Displacement, tons: 3,096 full load
Measurement, tons: 2,212 gross; 752 net
Dimensions, feet (metres): 233.9 × 49 × 15.5 (71.3 × 14.9 × 4.7)
Main machinery: Diesel-electric; 4 Fairbanks-Morse 38D8-1/8-12 diesel generators; 5.8 MW sustained; 2 motors; 3,982 hp(m) (2.97 MW); 2 shafts
Speed, knots: 14. **Range, miles:** 5,500 at 10 kt
Complement: 25 (9 officers)
Radars: Navigation: 2 Kelvin Hughes; I-band.
Helicopters: Platform for 1 light type, such as Bell 206L.

Comment: Based in the Central and Arctic Region at Prescott, Ontario. **VERIFIED**

GRIFFON 7/1998, van Ginderen Collection / 0017669

Name	Builders	Commissioned
J E BERNIER	Davie Shipbuilding, Lauzon	Aug 1967

Displacement, tons: 3,096 full load
Measurement, tons: 2,457 gross; 705 net
Dimensions, feet (metres): 231 × 49 × 16 (70.5 × 14.9 × 4.9)
Main machinery: Diesel-electric; 4 Fairbanks-Morse 4SA 8-cyl diesels; 5,600 hp (4.12 MW); 4 generators; 3.46 MW; 2 motors; 4,250 hp (3.13 MW); 2 shafts
Speed, knots: 13.5. **Range, miles:** 4,000 at 11 kt
Complement: 21 (9 officers)
Radars: Navigation: 2 Kelvin Hughes; I-band.
Helicopters: 1 Bell 206L/L-1.

Comment: Based in Newfoundland Region at St Johns. Probably to be paid off in 2001. **UPDATED**

J E BERNIER 7/1996*, van Ginderen Collection / 0056693

Name	Builders	Commissioned
SIR HUMPHREY GILBERT	Davie Shipbuilding, Lauzon	June 1959

Displacement, tons: 3,056 full load
Measurement, tons: 2,152 gross; 728 net
Dimensions, feet (metres): 237.9 × 48 × 16.3 (72.5 × 14.6 × 5)
Main machinery: Diesel-electric; 4 Fairbanks-Morse 2SA 8-cyl diesels; 5,120 hp (3.77 MW); 4 generators; 3.46 MW; 2 motors; 4,240 hp (3.13 MW); 2 shafts
Speed, knots: 13. **Range, miles:** 10,000 at 11 kt
Complement: 25
Radars: Navigation: 2 Sperry; I-band.
Helicopters: 1 Bell 206L/L-1.

Comment: First Canadian Coast Guard vessel to be fitted with an air-bubbling system. In 1984-85 completed a major refit which included a diesel-electric a/c-a/c propulsion system, the fitting of a new bow and a new derrick. Based in Newfoundland Region at St Johns. **UPDATED**

SIR HUMPHREY GILBERT 3/1999*, Canadian Coast Guard / 0056705

MEDIUM NAVAIDS TENDERS/LIGHT ICEBREAKERS
(Type 1050)

Name	Builders	Commissioned
SAMUEL RISLEY	Vito Construction Ltd, Delta, BC	4 July 1985
EARL GREY	Pictou Shipyards Ltd, Pictou, NS	30 May 1986

Displacement, tons: 2,935 full load
Measurement, tons: 1,988 gross *(Grey)*; 1,967 gross *(Risley)*; 642 net *(Grey)*; 649.5 net *(Risley)*
Dimensions, feet (metres): 228.7 × 44.9 × 19 *(69.7 × 13.7 × 5.8)*
Main machinery: Diesel-electric; 4 Wärtsilä 4SA 12-cyl diesels; 8,644 hp(m) *(6.4 MW)* *(Samuel Risley)*; 4 Deutz 4SA 9-cyl diesels; 8,836 hp(m) *(6.5 MW)* *(Earl Grey)*; 2 shafts; cp props
Speed, knots: 13. **Range:** 18,000 at 12 kt
Complement: 22
Radars: Navigation: 2 Racal Decca; I-band.

Comment: *Risley* based in the Central and Arctic Region at Thunder Bay, Ontario, *Grey* in the Maritimes Region at Charlottetown, PEI.

UPDATED

SAMUEL RISLEY   *4/1993*, Canadian Coast Guard* / 0056694

MEDIUM NAVAIDS TENDERS/ICE STRENGTHENED
(Type 1000)

Name	Builders	Commissioned
SIMON FRASER	Burrard Dry Dock Co, Vancouver	Feb 1960

Displacement, tons: 1,375 full load
Measurement, tons: 1,358 gross; 431 net
Dimensions, feet (metres): 204.5 × 42 × 15.1 *(62.4 × 12.8 × 4.6)*
Main machinery: Diesel-electric; 2 Alco 4SA 12-cyl diesels; 3,330 hp *(2.45 MW)*; 2 generators; 2.3 MW; 2 motors; 1,900 hp *(2.16 MW)*; 2 shafts
Speed, knots: 13. **Range, miles:** 5,000 at 10 kt
Complement: 24 (10 officers)
Radars: Navigation: 2 Racal Decca; I-band.
Helicopters: Platform for 1 Bell 206L/L-1.

Comment: Based in the Maritimes Region.

VERIFIED

Name	Builders	Commissioned
BARTLETT	Marine Industries, Sorel	Dec 1969
PROVO WALLIS	Marine Industries, Sorel	Oct 1969

Displacement, tons: 1,620 full load *(Bartlett)*
Measurement, tons: 1,317 gross; 491 net
Dimensions, feet (metres): 189.3; 209 *(Provo Wallis)* × 42.5 × 15.4 *(57.7; 63.7 × 13 × 4.7)*
Main machinery: 2 National Gas 6-cyl diesels; 2,100 hp *(1.55 MW)*; 2 shafts; acbLIPS cp props
Speed, knots: 12.5. **Range, miles:** 3,300 at 11 kt
Complement: 24 (9 officers)
Radars: Navigation: 2 Kelvin Hughes; I-band.

Comment: *Bartlett* based in Pacific Region at Victoria, *Provo Wallis* in the Maritimes Region at Saint Johns, New Brunswick. *Bartlett* was modernised in 1988 and *Provo Wallis* completed one year modernisation at Marystown, Newfoundland at the end of 1990. Work included lengthening the hull by 6 m, installing new equipment and improving accommodation.

UPDATED

BARTLETT   *5/1999*, Hartmut Ehlers* / 0056695

0 + (3) TYPE 1000

Displacement, tons: 2,013 full load
Dimensions, feet (metres): 213.3 × 45.9 × 11.8 *(65 × 14 × 3.6)*
Main machinery: 2 diesels; 2 shafts
Speed, knots: 14. **Range, miles:** 6,000 at 12 kt
Complement: 34

Comment: Designated as a shallow draft, multitaskable utility vessel. The plan is to order three first followed by four more to replace all existing Type 1000 ships. Contract in 2002 at the earliest.

UPDATED

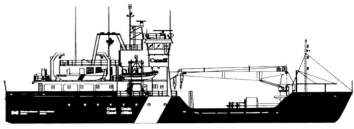

TYPE 1000   *1998, Canadian Coast Guard* / 0017670

Name	Builders	Commissioned
TRACY	Port Weller Drydocks, Ontario	17 Apr 1968

Displacement, tons: 1,300 full load
Measurement, tons: 963 gross; 290 net
Dimensions, feet (metres): 181.1 × 38 × 12.1 *(55.2 × 11.6 × 3.7)*
Main machinery: Diesel-electric; 2 Fairbanks-Morse 38D8-1/8-8 diesel generators; 1.94 MW sustained; 2 motors; 2,000 hp *(1.49 MW)*; 2 shafts
Speed, knots: 13. **Range, miles:** 5,000 at 11 kt
Complement: 23 (8 officers)
Radars: Navigation: Kelvin Hughes; I-band.

Comment: Based in Laurentian Region at Sorel.

UPDATED

TRACY   *4/1999*, Canadian Coast Guard* / 0056716

Name	Builders	Commissioned
SIMCOE	Canadian Vickers Ltd, Montreal	Oct 1962

Displacement, tons: 1,390 full load
Measurement, tons: 961 gross; 361 net
Dimensions, feet (metres): 179.5 × 38 × 12.5 *(54.7 × 11.6 × 3.8)*
Main machinery: Diesel-electric; 2 Paxman 4SA 12-cyl diesels; 3,000 hp *(2.24 MW)*; 2 motors; 2,000 hp *(1.49 MW)*; 2 shafts
Speed, knots: 13. **Range, miles:** 5,000 at 10 kt
Complement: 27 (10 officers)
Radars: Navigation: 2 Kelvin Hughes; I-band.

Comment: Based in Central and Arctic Region at Prescott, Ontario. Modernised in 1988.

UPDATED

SIMCOE   *4/1999*, Canadian Coast Guard* / 0056712

SMALL NAVAIDS TENDERS/ICE STRENGTHENED
(Type 900)

Name	Builders	Commissioned
NAMAO	Riverton Boat Works, Manitoba	1975

Displacement, tons: 380 full load
Measurement, tons: 318 gross; 107 net
Dimensions, feet (metres): 110 × 28 × 7 *(33.5 × 8.5 × 2.1)*
Main machinery: 2 Detroit 12V-71 diesels; 1,350 hp *(1 MW)*; 2 shafts
Speed, knots: 12. **Range, miles:** 2,000 at 12 kt
Complement: 11 (4 officers)
Radars: Navigation: Racal Decca; I-band.

Comment: Based in the Central and Arctic Region on Lake Winnipeg at Selkirk. Planned to pay off in 1996 but kept in service until at least 2002. **UPDATED**

NAMAO *4/1999*, Canadian Coast Guard /* 0056710

SMALL NAVAIDS TENDERS (Type 800)

Name	Builders	Commissioned
COVE ISLE	Canadian D and D, Kingston, Ontario	1980
GULL ISLE	Canadian D and D, Kingston, Ontario	1980
TSEKOA II	Allied Shipbuilders, Vancouver	1984
PARTRIDGE ISLAND	Breton Industries, Port Hawkesbury, NS	31 Oct 1985
ILE DES BARQUES	Breton Industries, Port Hawkesbury, NS	26 Nov 1985
ILE SAINT-OURS	Breton Industries, Port Hawkesbury, NS	15 May 1986
CARIBOU ISLE	Breton Industries, Port Hawkesbury, NS	16 June 1986

Displacement, tons: 138 full load
Measurement, tons: 92 gross; 36 net
Dimensions, feet (metres): 75.5 × 19.7 × 4.4 *(23 × 6 × 1.4)*
Main machinery: 2 Detroit 8V-92 diesels; 475 hp *(354 kW)*; 2 shafts
Speed, knots: 11. **Range, miles:** 1,800 at 11 kt
Complement: 5
Radars: Navigation: Sperry 1270; I-band.

Comment: Details given are for the last four. *Cove Isle* and *Gull Isle* are 3 m less in length; *Tsekoa II* is 3.7 m longer. *Cove Isle* and *Gull Isle* are based in the Central and Arctic Region at Parry Sound and Amherstburg respectively. *Tsekoa II* is based in the Pacific. *Partridge Island* and *Ile des Barques* based in the Maritimes Region at Saint Johns, New Brunswick, *Caribou Isle* in the Central and Arctic Region at Sault Ste Marie, Ontario, and the other one in the Laurentian Region at Sorel. Can carry 20 tons of stores. **UPDATED**

ILE SAINT-OURS *9/1994*, van Ginderen Collection /* 0056696

SPECIAL RIVER NAVAIDS TENDERS (Type 700)

Name	Builders	Commissioned
NAHIDIK	Allied Shipbuilders Ltd, N Vancouver	1974

Displacement, tons: 1,125 full load
Measurement, tons: 856 gross; 392 net
Dimensions, feet (metres): 175.2 × 49.9 × 6.6 *(53.4 × 15.2 × 2)*
Main machinery: 2 Detroit diesels; 4,290 hp *(3.2 MW)*; 2 shafts
Speed, knots: 14. **Range, miles:** 5,000 at 10 kt
Complement: 15

Comment: Based in Central and Arctic Region at Hay River, North West Territories. **UPDATED**

NAHIDIK *10/1997*, Canadian Coast Guard /* 0056709

Name	Builders	Commissioned
DUMIT	Allied Shipbuilders Ltd, N Vancouver	July 1979

Displacement, tons: 629 full load
Measurement, tons: 569 gross; 176 net
Dimensions, feet (metres): 160.1 × 40 × 5.2 *(48.8 × 12.2 × 1.6)*
Main machinery: 2 Caterpillar 3512TA; 2,420 hp *(1.8 MW)* sustained; 2 shafts
Speed, knots: 12. **Range, miles:** 8,500 at 10 kt
Complement: 10

Comment: Similar to *Eckaloo*. Based in Central and Arctic Region at Hay River, North West Territories. **UPDATED**

DUMIT *7/1996*, Canadian Coast Guard /* 0017671

Name	Builders	Commissioned
TEMBAH	Allied Shipbuilders Ltd, N Vancouver	Oct 1963

Measurement, tons: 189 gross; 58 net
Dimensions, feet (metres): 123 × 25.9 × 3 *(37.5 × 7.9 × 0.9)*
Main machinery: 2 Cummins diesels; 500 hp *(373 kW)*; 2 shafts
Speed, knots: 12. **Range:** 1,300 at 10 kt
Complement: 9

Comment: Based in Central and Arctic Region at Hay River, North West Territories. **UPDATED**

TEMBAH *4/1999*, Canadian Coast Guard /* 00∷∷14

Name	Builders	Commissioned
ECKALOO	Vancouver SY Ltd	31 Aug 1988

Displacement, tons: 534 full load
Measurement, tons: 661 gross; 213 net
Dimensions, feet (metres): 160.8 × 44 × 4 *(49 × 13.4 × 1.2)*
Main machinery: 2 Caterpillar 3512TA; 2,420 hp *(1.8 MW)* sustained; 2 shafts
Speed, knots: 13. **Range:** 2,500 at 12 kt
Complement: 10
Helicopters: Platform for 1 Bell 206L/L-1.

Comment: Replaced vessel of the same name. Similar design to *Dumit*. Based in Central and Arctic Region at Hay River, North West Territories. **UPDATED**

ECKALOO *9/1994*, van Ginderen Collection /* 0056697

OFFSHORE MULTITASK PATROL CUTTERS
(Type 600)

Note: In addition there are two others, *Arrow Post* and *E P Le Québécois*.

Name	Builders	Commissioned
SIR WILFRED GRENFELL	Marystown SY, Newfoundland	1987

Displacement, tons: 3,753 full load
Measurement, tons: 2,403 gross; 664.5 net
Dimensions, feet (metres): 224.7 × 49.2 × 16.4 *(68.5 × 15 × 5)*
Main machinery: 4 Deutz 4SA (2—16-cyl, 2—9-cyl) diesels; 12,862 hp(m) *(9.46 MW)*; 2 shafts; cp props
Speed, knots: 16. **Range:** 11,000 at 14 kt
Complement: 20

Comment: Built on speculation in 1984-85. Modified to include an 85 tonne towing winch and additional SAR accommodation and equipment. Ice strengthened hull. Based the Newfoundland Region at St John's.   **UPDATED**

SIR WILFRED GRENFELL   8/1997*, *M B MacKay* / 0012137

Name	Builders	Commissioned
MARY HICHENS	Marystown SY, Newfoundland	19 Apr 1985

Displacement, tons: 3,262 full load
Measurement, tons: 1,684 gross; 696 net
Dimensions, feet (metres): 210 × 45 × 19.7 *(64 × 13.8 × 6)*
Main machinery: 2 Burmeister & Wain Alpha 18 V 28/32-VO diesels; 10,800 hp(m) *(7.94 MW)* sustained; 2 shafts; 2 acbLIPS cp props; bow thrusters
Speed, knots: 15. **Range, miles:** 15,000 at 14 kt
Complement: 20

Comment: Based in the Maritimes Region at Dartmouth. Offshore oil rig supply ship built for firefighting and SAR. Ice strengthened hull. To be scrapped in 2000.   **UPDATED**

MARY HICHENS   7/1997*, *M B MacKay* / 0012138

Name	Builders	Commissioned
LEONARD J COWLEY	Manly Shipyard, RivTow Ind, Vancouver BC	June 1985

Displacement, tons: 2,080 full load
Measurement, tons: 2,244 grt; 655 net
Dimensions, feet (metres): 236.2 × 45.9 × 16.1 *(72 × 14 × 4.9)*
Main machinery: 2 Wärtsilä Nohab F 312A diesels; 2,325 hp(m) *(1.71 MW)*; 1 shaft; bow thruster
Speed, knots: 12. **Range, miles:** 12,000 at 12 kt
Complement: 20
Guns: 2—12.7 mm MGs.
Radars: Surface search: Sperry 340; E/F-band.
Navigation: Sperry ARPA; I-band.
Helicopters: Capability for 1 light.

Comment: Based in Newfoundland. Marisat fitted.   **UPDATED**

LEONARD J COWLEY   9/1996*, *D Maginley* / 0056698

Name	Builders	Commissioned
CYGNUS	Marystown SY, Newfoundland	May 1981
CAPE ROGER	Ferguson Industries, Pictou NS	Aug 1977

Displacement, tons: 1,465 full load
Measurement, tons: 1,255 grt; 357 net
Dimensions, feet (metres): 205 × 40 × 13 *(62.5 × 12.2 × 4.1)*
Main machinery: 2 Wärtsilä Nohab F 212V diesels, 4,461 hp(m) *(3.28 MW)*; 1 shaft; bow thruster
Speed, knots: 13. **Range, miles:** 10,000 at 12 kt
Complement: 19
Guns: 2—12.7 mm MGs.
Helicopters: Capability for 1 light.

Comment: *Cygnus* based in Nova Scotia, *Cape Roger* in Newfoundland. Half-life refits completed in 1995-97.   **UPDATED**

CYGNUS   9/1999*, *Canadian Coast Guard* / 0056704

INTERMEDIATE MULTITASK PATROL CUTTERS
(Type 500)

Name	Builders	Commissioned
TANU	Yarrows Ltd, Victoria BC	Sep 1968

Displacement, tons: 925 full load
Measurement, tons: 746 grt; 203 net
Dimensions, feet (metres): 164.3 × 3.2 × 15.1 *(50.1 × 9.8 × 4.6)*
Main machinery: 2 Fairbanks-Morse diesels; 2,624 hp *(1.96 MW)*; 1 shaft
Speed, knots: 11. **Range, miles:** 4,000 at 11 kt
Complement: 18 plus 16 spare
Guns: 2—12.7 mm MGs.

Comment: Based in Pacific Region. Expected to pay off in late 2000.   **UPDATED**

TANU (old colours)   11/1994*, *van Ginderen Collection* / 0056699

Name	Builders	Commissioned
LOUISBOURG	Breton Industries, Port Hawkesbury, NS	1977

Displacement, tons: 460 full load
Measurement, tons: 295 grt; 65 net
Dimensions, feet (metres): 125 × 27.2 × 8.5 *(38.1 × 8.3 × 2.6)*
Main machinery: 2 MTU 12V 538 TB91 diesels; 4,600 hp(m) *(3.38 MW)*; 2 shafts
Speed, knots: 13. **Range, miles:** 6,200 at 12 kt
Complement: 14
Guns: 2—12.7 mm MGs.

Comment: Based in the Laurentian Region.   **UPDATED**

LOUISBOURG   9/1999*, *Canadian Coast Guard* / 0056708

Name	Builders	Commissioned	
GORDON REID	Versatile Pacific, Vancouver	Oct	1990
JOHN JACOBSON	Versatile Pacific, Vancouver	Nov	1990

Measurement, tons: 836 gross; 247 net
Dimensions, feet (metres): 163.9 × 36.1 × 13.1 *(49.9 × 11 × 4)*
Main machinery: 4 Deutz SBV-6M-628 diesels; 2,475 hp(m) *(1.82 MW)* sustained; 2 shafts; bow thruster; 400 hp *(294 kW)*
Speed, knots: 15. **Range, miles:** 2,500 at 15 kt
Complement: 14 plus 8 spare

Comment: Designed for long-range patrols along the British Columbian coast out to 200 mile limit. They have a stern ramp for launching Zodiac Hurricane 733 rigid inflatables in up to Sea State 6. The Zodiac has a speed of 50 kt and is radar equipped. Both based in the Pacific Region at Victoria.

UPDATED

GORDON REID *1992, Canadian Coast Guard /* 0056711

SMALL MULTITASK CUTTERS (Type 400)

Note: In addition there are *Atlin Post, Chilco Post, Comox Post, Cumella, Estevan Reef, Kitimat II, Lewis Reef, Robson Reef* and *Sooke Post.*

Name	Builders	Commissioned
ADVENT	Alloy Manufacturing, Qu	1972
POINT HENRY	Breton Industrial and Machinery	1980
ISLE ROUGE	Breton Industrial and Machinery	1980
POINT RACE	Pt Hawkesbury, NS	1982
CAPE HURD	Pt Hawkesbury, NS	1982

Displacement, tons: 97 full load
Measurement, tons: 57 gross; 14 net
Dimensions, feet (metres): 70.8 × 18 × 5.6 *(21.6 × 5.5 × 1.7)*
Main machinery: 2 MTU 8V 396 TC82 diesels; 1,740 hp(m) *(1.28 MW)* sustained; 2 shafts
Speed, knots: 20. **Range, miles:** 950 at 12 kt
Complement: 5

Comment: Aluminium alloy hulls. *Point Henry* and *Point Race* based in Pacfic Region, *Cape Hurd* and *Advent* in Central and Arctic Region; *Isle Rouge* in the Laurentian Region. *Advent* is slightly larger at 23.5 m and has a top speed of 10 kt.

UPDATED

POINT HENRY *7/1994*, van Ginderen Collection /* 0056701

SMALL SAR CUTTERS/ICE STRENGTHENED
(Type 200)

Name	Builders	Commissioned	
HARP	Georgetown SY, PEI	12 Dec	1986
HOOD	Georgetown SY, PEI	12 Dec	1986

Displacement, tons: 225 full load
Measurement, tons: 179 gross; 69 net
Dimensions, feet (metres): 76.1 × 24.9 × 8.2 *(23.2 × 7.6 × 2.5)*
Main machinery: 2 Caterpillar 3408 diesels; 850 hp *(634 kW)*; 2 Kort nozzle props
Speed, knots: 10. **Range, miles:** 500 at 10 kt
Complement: 7 plus 10 spare berths
Radars: Navigation: Sperry Mk 1270; I-band.

Comment: Ordered 26 April 1985. Ice strengthened hulls. Based in Newfoundland.

UPDATED

HOOD *3/1999*, Canadian Coast Guard /* 0056706

SMALL SAR UTILITY CRAFT (Type 100)

Note: There are also at least 15 Inshore Rescue boats with CG numbers.

Name	Builders	Commissioned	
CG 119	Eastern Equipment, Montreal		1973
SORA	Eastern Equipment, Montreal		1968
BITTERN	Canadian Dredge, Kingston		1982
MALLARD	Matsumoto Shipyard, Vancouver, BC	Feb	1986
SKUA	Matsumoto Shipyard, Vancouver, BC	Mar	1986
OSPREY	Matsumoto Shipyard, Vancouver, BC	May	1986
STERNE	Matsumoto Shipyard, Vancouver, BC	Mar	1987

Measurement, tons: 15 gross
Dimensions, feet (metres): 40.8 × 13.2 × 4.2 *(12.4 × 4.1 × 1.3)*
Main machinery: 2 Mitsubishi diesels; 637 hp *(475 kW)*; 2 shafts
Speed, knots: 26. **Range, miles:** 200 at 16 kt
Complement: 3

Comment: First three based in Central and Arctic Region; *Sterne* based at Quebec, remainder in Pacific Region. There are some structural differences and the two older craft are slower.

VERIFIED

CG 119 *1990, van Ginderen Collection*

MULTITASK LIFEBOATS (Type 300)

Name	Builders	Commissioned
BAMFIELD	McKay Cormack Ltd, Victoria, BC	1970
TOFINO	McKay Cormack Ltd, Victoria, BC	1970
PORT HARDY (ex-*Bull Harbour*)	McKay Cormack Ltd, Victoria, BC	1970
TOBERMORY	Georgetown SY, PEI	1974
WESTFORT (ex-*Thunder Bay*)	Georgetown SY, PEI	1974
SHIPPEGAN	Eastern Equipment, Montreal, Quebec	1975
CG 141 (ex-*Cap Aux Meules*)	Georgetown SY, PEI	1982
SOURIS	Hike Metal Products Ltd, Ontario	1985
CGR 100	Hurricane Rescue Craft, Richmond, BC	1986

Measurement, tons: 10 gross
Dimensions, feet (metres): 44.1 × 12.7 × 3.4 *(13.5 × 3.9 × 1)*
Main machinery: 2 diesels; 485 hp *(362 kW)*; 2 shafts
Speed, knots: 12.5; 26 *(CGR 100)*
Complement: 3 or 4

Comment: Four Type 300A based in the Maritimes Region, three in the Pacific Region, two in the Central and Arctic Region. *CGR 100* is a self-righting Medina lifeboat (Type 300B) and has a speed of 26 kt. Three others *CG 107, CG 117* and *CG 118* serve as tenders to the Coast Guard Training College. Being replaced by new craft.

UPDATED

TOFINO *4/1999*, Canadian Coast Guard /* 0056715

Name	Builders	Commissioned
BICKERTON	Halmatic, Havant	Aug 1989
SPINDRIFT	Georgetown, PEI	Oct 1993
SPRAY	Industrie Raymond, Quebec	Sep 1994
SPUME	Industrie Raymond, Quebec	Oct 1994
W JACKMAN (ex-*Cap Aux Meules*)	Industrie Raymond, Quebec	Sep 1995
W G GEORGE	Industrie Raymond, Quebec	Sep 1995
CAP AUX MEULES	Hike Metal Products Ltd, Ontario	Oct 1996
CLARK'S HARBOUR	Hike Metal Products Ltd, Ontario	Sep 1996
SAMBRO	Hike Metal Products Ltd, Ontario	Jan 1997
WESTPORT	Hike Metal Products Ltd, Ontario	May 1997
CAPE SUTIL	Metalcraft Marine, Kingston	Dec 1998
CAPE CALVERT	Metalcraft Marine, Kingston	Aug 1999
CAPE ST JAMES	Metalcraft Marine, Kingston	Nov 1999

Measurement, tons: 34 gross
Dimensions, feet (metres): 52 × 17.5 × 4.6 *(15.9 × 5.3 × 1.5)*
Main machinery: 2 Caterpillar 3408BTA diesels; 1,070 hp *(786 kW)* sustained; 2 shafts
Speed, knots: 16-20. **Range:** 100-150 m
Complement: 5
Radars: Navigation: Furuno; I-band.

Comment: Details given are for the first 10 Arun Type 300B high-endurance lifeboats. Four based in Martimes Region, two in Central and Arctic Region, two in Newfoundland Region, two in Laurentian Region. *Bickerton* has GRP hull, remainder aluminium. From *Cape Sutil* onwards the hulls are slightly smaller and the speed is increased to 25 kt. These three are based in the Pacific. More expected to complete in 2000.

UPDATED

CLARK'S HARBOUR   8/1996*, Kathy Johnson / 0056702

HOVERCRAFT

1 SRN 6 TYPE

CG 045

Displacement, tons: 10.9 full load
Dimensions, feet (metres): 48.5 × 23 × 3.9 (skirt) *(14.8 × 7 × 1.2)*
Main machinery: 1 RR Gnome 1050 gas turbine; 1,050 hp *(783 kW)* sustained
Speed, knots: 50. **Range, miles:** 170 at 30 kt
Complement: 3

Comment: Built in 1977. Based at Sea Island in the Pacific Region. Can carry up to 6 tons of equipment. Second of class cannibalised for spares in late 1998.

VERIFIED

SRN 6 Type   1986, Canadian Coast Guard

1 API-88/200 TYPE

Name	Builders	Commissioned
WABAN-AKI	Westland Aerospace	15 July 1987

Displacement, tons: 47.6 light
Dimensions, feet (metres): 80.4 × 36.7 × 19.6 *(24.5 × 11.2 × 6.6)* (height on cushion)
Main machinery: 4 Deutz diesels; 2,394 hp(m) *(1.76 MW)*
Speed, knots: 50; 35 cruising
Complement: 3
Cargo capacity: 12 tons

Comment: *Waban-Aki* is based at Quebec and capable of year round operation as a Navaid Tender for flood control operations in the St Lawrence. Fitted with a hydraulic crane. The name means People of the Dawn.

UPDATED

WABAN-AKI   4/1999*, Canadian Coast Guard / 0056717

2 AP. I-88/400 TYPE

SIPU MUIN   SIYAY

Displacement, tons: 69 full load
Dimensions, feet (metres): 93.5 × 39.4 *(28.5 × 12)*
Main machinery: 4 Caterpillar 3412 TTA diesels; 3,650 hp(m) *(2.68 MW)* sustained
Speed, knots: 50; 35 cruising
Complement: 4
Cargo capacity: 22.6 tons

Comment: Contract awarded to GKN Westland in May 1996. Built at Hike Metal Products, Wheatley, Ontario and completed in August and December 1998 respectively. Well-deck size 8.2 × 4.6 m. There is a 5,000 kg load crane. The first craft is based in the St Lawrence and the second at Vancouver.

VERIFIED

SIPU MUIN   5/1998, Canada Coast Guard / 0017672

FISHERY RESEARCH SHIPS

Name	Commissioned	Based	Measurement, tons
ALFRED NEEDLER	Aug 1982	Maritimes Region	925 grt
WILFRED TEMPLEMAN	Mar 1982	Maritimes Region	925 grt
W E RICKER (ex-*Callistratus*)	Dec 1978	Pacific Region	1,040 grt
TELEOST	1996	Newfoundland Region	
PANDALUS III	1986	Maritimes Region	13 grt
SHAMOOK	1975	Newfoundland Region	187 grt
NAVICULA	1968	Maritimes Region	106 grt
OPILIO	1989	Maritimes Region	74 grt
SHARK	1971	Central and Arctic Region	19 grt
CALANUS II	1991	Laurentian Region	160 grt
J L HART	1974	Maritimes Region	93 grt

Comment: First four are classified as Offshore Fishery Research vessels, remainder as Inshore Fishery Research vessels. *Ricker* is expected to pay off in 2001.

UPDATED

TELEOST   4/1999*, Canadian Coast Guard / 0056713

SURVEY AND RESEARCH SHIPS

Name	Commissioned	Based	Displacement, tons
MATTHEW	1990	Maritimes Region	950
F C G SMITH	1986	Laurentian Region	300
JOHN P TULLY	1985	Pacific Region	1,800
PARIZEAU	1967	Maritimes Region	1,787
VECTOR	1967	Pacific Region	520
LIMNOS	1968	Central and Arctic	—
R B YOUNG	1990	Pacific Region	330
FREDERICK G CREED	1988	Laurentian Region	81

Comment: The one ship in the Central and Arctic Region is employed on Limnology, and the remainder on Oceanographic Research. *Hudson, Tully* and *Parizeau* are classified as Offshore vessels, and the remainder are Coastal. *Smith* and *Creed* are multihulled. *R B Young* is in reserve, and *Tully* and *Vector* only operate for part of the year.

UPDATED

F C G SMITH   *7/1998, C D Maginley /* 0017673

CAPE VERDE

Personnel	Bases	Maritime Aircraft	Mercantile Marine
2000: 130	Praia, main naval base. Porto Grande (Isle de Sao Vicente), naval repair yard.	One EMB-111 and one Dornier Do 328 are used for maritime surveillance.	*Lloyd's Register of Shipping:* 40 vessels of 20,523 tons gross

PATROL FORCES

Note: One 'Zhuk' class may still be in service but seldom goes to sea.

1 KONDOR I CLASS (COASTAL PATROL CRAFT) (PC)

Name	No	Builders	Commissioned
VIGILANTE (ex-*Kühlungsborn*)	P 521 (ex-BG 32, ex-GS 07)	Peenewerft, Wolgast	1970

Displacement, tons: 377 full load
Dimensions, feet (metres): 170.3 × 23.3 × 7.2 *(51.9 × 7.1 × 2.2)*
Main machinery: 2 Russki/Kolomna Type 40DM diesels; 4,408 hp(m) *(3.24 MW)* sustained; 2 shafts; cp props
Speed, knots: 20. **Range, miles:** 1,800 at 15 kt
Complement: 25 (3 officers)
Guns: 2—25 mm (twin).
Radars: Surface search: Racal Decca; I-band.

Comment: Former GDR minesweeper taken over by the German Coast Guard, and then acquired by Cape Verde in September 1998. Armament is uncertain. Being refitted in Germany in 1999/2000.

UPDATED

1 ESPADARTE CLASS (PETERSON Mk 4 TYPE)
(COASTAL PATROL CRAFT) (PC)

Name	No	Builders	Commissioned
ESPADARTE	P 151	Peterson Builders Inc	19 Aug 1993

Displacement, tons: 22 full load
Dimensions, feet (metres): 51.3 × 14.8 × 4.3 *(15.6 × 4.5 × 1.3)*
Main machinery: 2 Detroit 6V-92TA diesels; 520 hp *(388 kW)* sustained; 2 shafts
Speed, knots: 24. **Range, miles:** 500 at 20 kt
Complement: 6 (2 officers)
Guns: 2—12.7 mm MGs (twin). 2—7.62 mm MGs.
Radars: Surface search: Raytheon; I-band.

Comment: Ordered from Peterson Builders Inc, under FMS programme on 25 September 1992. Option on three more not taken up. Aluminium hulls. The 12.7 mm mounting is aft with the smaller guns on the bridge roof.

UPDATED

KONDOR I (Malta colours)   *6/1997*, Robert Pabst /* 0017674

Mk 4 CPC (US colours)   *11/1993, Peterson Builders /* 0081500

CAYMAN ISLANDS

POLICE

Note: There is also a Grady White fast launch with a Johnson 40 hp outboard, and a Customs craft with twin outboards.

1 DAUNTLESS CLASS (PB)

CAYMAN PROTECTOR

Displacement, tons: 17 full load
Dimensions, feet (metres): 47.9 × 14.1 × 3.3 *(14.6 × 4.3 × 1)*
Main machinery: 2 Caterpillar 3208 TA diesels; 720 hp(m) *(529 kW)* sustained; 2 shafts
Speed, knots: 26. **Range, miles:** 400 at 20 kt
Complement: 4
Guns: 2—7.62 mm MGs.
Radars: Surface search: Raytheon R40; I-band.

Comment: Built by SeaArk Marine, Monticello and acquired in July 1994.

UPDATED

CAYMAN PROTECTOR   *4/1996*, W H Clements /* 0017675

CHILE
ARMADA DE CHILE

Headquarters Appointments

Commander-in-Chief:
  Admiral Jorge Patricio Arancibia
Chief of the Naval Staff:
  Vice Admiral Jorge Swett
Director General, Naval Personnel:
  Vice Admiral Andres Swett
Director General, Naval Services:
  Vice Admiral Onofre Torres
Director General Maritime Territory and Merchant Marine:
  Vice Admiral Jorge Arancibia
Director General of Naval Finances:
  Vice Admiral Miguel Vergara
Flag Officer, Fleet:
  Rear Admiral Alex Waghorn
Flag Officer, Submarines:
  Rear Admiral Rodolfo Soria
Flag Officer, 1st Naval Zone:
  Rear Admiral Felipe Howard
Flag Officer, 2nd Naval Zone:
  Rear Admiral Juan Patillo
Flag Officer, 3rd Naval Zone:
  Rear Admiral Oscar Manzano
Flag Officer, 4th Naval Zone:
  Rear Admiral Rodolfo Codina

Diplomatic Representation

Naval Attaché in London:
  Captain Juan Schilling
Naval Attaché in Washington:
  Rear Admiral Alfredo Giuliano
Naval Attaché in Paris:
  Captain José Valdivia
Naval Attaché in Buenos Aires:
  Captain Cristian Millar
Naval Attaché in Brasilia:
  Captain Carlos Mackenney
Naval Attaché in Seoul:
  Captain Arturo Ojeda
Naval Attaché in Tel Aviv:
  Captain Gonzalo Villalon
Naval Attaché in Lima:
  Captain Eugenio Arellano
Naval Attaché in Madrid:
  Captain Pedro Urrutia
Naval Attaché in Bogotá:
  Captain Percy Richter

Personnel

(a) 2000: 22,055 (1,807 officers)
(b) 3,380 Marines
(c) 2 years' national service

Command Organisation

1st Naval Zone. HQ at Valparaiso. From 26°S to Topocalma Point (33°S).
2nd Naval Zone. HQ at Talcahuano. From Topocalma Point to 47°S.
3rd Naval Zone. HQ at Punta Arenas. From 47°S to South Pole including Beagle Naval District.
4th Naval Zone. HQ at Iquique. From Peruvian frontier to 26°S.
Coast Guard is fully integrated with the Navy.

Naval Air Stations and Organisation

Having won the battle to own all military aircraft flying over the sea, a fixed-wing squadron of about 20 CASA/ENAER Halcón is envisaged when finances permit.
Viña del Mar (Valparaiso); *Almirante Von Schroeders* (Punta Arenas); *Guardiamarina Zañartu* (Puerto Williams).
Four Squadrons: VP1: EMB-111, P-3A
  HA1: NAS 332C Cougar
  VC1: EMB-110, CASA 212, PC-7
  HU1: Bell 206B, BO 105C
  VP1: Mod Skymaster

Infanteria de Marina

Organisation: 4 detachments each comprising Amphibious Warfare, Coast Defence and Local Security. Also embarked are detachments of commandos, engineering units and a logistic battalion.
1st Marine Infantry Detachment 'Patricio Lynch'. At Iquique.
2nd Marine Infantry Detachment 'Miller'. At Viña del Mar.
3rd Marine Infantry Detachment 'Sargento Aldea'. At Talcahuano.
4th Marine Infantry Detachment 'Cochrane'. At Punta Arenas.
51 Commando Group. At Valparaiso.
Some embarked units, commando and engineering units and a logistics battalion.

Bases

Valparaiso. Main naval base, schools, repair yard. HQ 1st Naval Zone. Air station.
Talcahuano. Naval base, schools, major repair yard (two dry docks, three floating docks), two floating cranes. HQ 2nd Naval Zone. Submarine base.
Punta Arenas. Naval base. Dockyard with slipway having building and repair facilities. HQ 3rd Naval Zone. Air station.
Iquique. Small naval base. HQ 4th Naval Zone.
Puerto Montt. Small naval base.
Puerto Williams (Beagle Channel). Small naval base. Air station.
Dawson Island (Magellan Straits). Small naval base.

Strength of the Fleet (including Coast Guard)

Type	Active	Building
Patrol Submarines	4	2
Destroyers	3	—
Frigates	3	(4)
Landing Ships (Tank)	3	—
Landing Craft	2	—
Fast Attack Craft (Missile)	9	—
Large Patrol Craft	4	(4)
Coastal Patrol Craft	34	(2)
Survey Ships	3	—
Training Ships	1	—
Transports	1	—
Tankers	1	(1)
Tenders	3	—

Mercantile Marine

Lloyd's Register of Shipping:
  472 vessels of 819,990 tons gross

DELETIONS

Destroyers

1998   *Latorre*

Frigates

1998   *General Baquedano*

Patrol Forces

1997   *Pillan* (CG), *Tronador* (CG)
1998   *Papudo, Llaima* (CG), *Antuco* (CG), *Choshuenko* (CG), *Rio Rinihue* (CG), *Chadmo* (CG), *Rio Bueno* (CG)
1999   *Rano Kau* (CG), *Villarica* (CG), *Corcovado* (CG)

Amphibious Forces

1998   *Maipo*

Auxiliaries

1997   *Piloto Pardo*
1998   *Almirante Jorge Montt, Guardian Brito, Janequeo, Colo Colo, Yelcho, Castor* (CG), *Cape Odger* (CG), *Cirujano Videla* (CG)

PENNANT LIST

Note: From 1997 pennant numbers have been painted on major warship hulls.

Submarines

20	Thomson
21	Simpson
22	O'Brien
23	Hyatt

Destroyers

11	Prat
12	Cochrane
15	Blanco Encalada

Frigates

06	Condell
07	Lynch
08	Ministro Zenteno

Patrol Forces

30	Casma
31	Chipana
32	Iquique
33	Covadonga
34	Angamos
36	Riquelme
37	Orella
38	Serrano
39	Uribe
71	Micalvi
72	Ortiz
73	Isaza
74	Morel
77	Cabrales
78	Sibbald
1601	Ona
1602	Yagan
1603	Alacalufe
1604	Hallef
1605	Quidora
1606	Tegualda
1607	Guacolda
1608	Fresia
1701	Kimitahi
1808	Osorno
1810	Copahue
1811	Guale
1814	Diaz
1815	Bolados
1816	Salinas
1817	Tellez
1818	Bravo
1819	Campos
1820	Machado
1821	Johnson
1822	Troncoso
1823	Hudson
1901	Maule
1902	Rapel
1903	Aconcagua
1904	Lauca
1905	Isluga
1906	Loa
1907	Maullín
1908	Copiapó
1909	Cau-Cau
1910	Pudeto
1911	Robinson Crusoe
1916	Petrohue

Survey Ships

46	Contralmirante Oscar Viel Toro
60	Vidal Gormaz
63	George Slight Marshall

Training Ships

43	Esmeralda

Amphibious Forces

90	Elicura
92	Rancagua
93	Valdivia
94	Orompello
95	Chacabuco

Auxiliaries

41	Aquiles
42	Merino
53	Araucano
YFB 114	Grumete Perez
BSG 116	Pisagua

Tugs/Supply Ships

ATF 66	Galvarino
ATF 67	Lautaro
ATF 68	Leucoton

SUBMARINES

Note: There are some Swimmer Delivery Vehicles French Havas Mk 8 in service. This is the two-man version.

0 + 2 SCORPENE CLASS (SSK)

Name	No	Builders	Laid down	Launched	Commissioned
HYATT	—	DCN Cherbourg	18 Nov 1999	2003	2004
O'BRIEN	—	Bazán, Cartagena	Sep 2000	2004	2006

Displacement, tons: 1,650 surfaced; 1,908 dived
Dimensions, feet (metres): 208.3 × 20.3 × 19
  (63.5 × 6.2 × 5.8)
Main machinery: Diesel electric; 4 MTU 16V 396 SE84 diesels; 2,992 hp(m) *(2.2 MW)*; 1 Jeumont Schneider motor; 3,808 hp (m) *(2.8 MW)*; 1 shaft
Speed, knots: 20 dived; 12 surfaced
Range, miles: 550 at 4 kt dived; 6,500 at 8 kt surfaced
Complement: 31 (6 officers)

Torpedoes: 6—21 in *(533 mm)* tubes. 18 A 184 Mod 1 torpedoes.
Countermeasures: ESM; Argos AR 900; intercept.
Weapons control: UDS International SUBTICS.
Radars: Navigation: Sagem; I-band.
Sonars: Hull mounted; active/passive search and attack, medium frequency.

Programmes: Project Neptune. Contract awarded to DCN and Bazán on 17 December 1997 and became effective in April 1998. First one being built in France and second in Spain. First steel cut July 1998 for first of class and August 1999 for the second.
Structure: Not all details have been confirmed. Sagem provides the APS attack periscope and an SMS optronic search periscope. SISDEF is fitting a datalink terminal. Diving depth more than 300 m *(984 ft)*. AIP is not required.

UPDATED

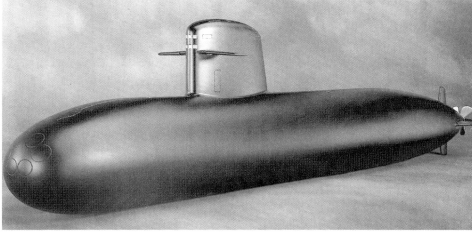

SCORPENE (computer graphic)   *1998, DCN /* 0017689

2 THOMSON (TYPE 209) CLASS (TYPE 1300) (SSK)

Name	No	Builders	Laid down	Launched	Commissioned
THOMSON	20	Howaldtswerke	1 Nov 1980	28 Oct 1982	31 Aug 1984
SIMPSON	21	Howaldtswerke	15 Feb 1982	29 July 1983	18 Sep 1984

Displacement, tons: 1,260 surfaced; 1,390 dived
Dimensions, feet (metres): 195.2 × 20.3 × 18
  (59.5 × 6.2 × 5.5)
Main machinery: Diesel-electric; 4 MTU 12V 493 AZ80 GA31L diesels; 2,400 hp(m) *(1.76 MW)* sustained; 4 Piller alternators; 1.7 MW; 1 Siemens motor; 4,600 hp(m) *(3.38 MW)* sustained; 1 shaft
Speed, knots: 11 surfaced; 21.5 dived
Range, miles: 400 at 4 kt dived; 16 at 21.5 kt dived; 8,200 at 8 kt snorkel
Complement: 32 (5 officers)

Torpedoes: 8—21 in *(533 mm)* bow tubes. 14 AEG SUT Mod 1; wire-guided; active homing to 12 km *(6.5 n miles)* at 35 kt; passive homing to 28 km *(15 n miles)* at 23 kt; warhead 250 kg.
Countermeasures: ESM: Thomson-CSF DR 2000U; radar warning.
Radars: Surface search: Thomson-CSF Calypso II; I-band.
Sonars: Atlas Elektronik CSU 3; hull-mounted; active/passive search and attack; medium frequency.

Programmes: Ordered from Howaldtswerke, Kiel in 1980.
Modernisation: *Thomson* refit completed at Talcahuano in late 1990, *Simpson* in 1991. Refit duration about 10 months each. CSU 90 sonar is to be transferred from the 'Oberon' class when they pay off.
Structure: Fin and associated masts lengthened by 50 cm to cope with wave size off Chilean coast.

VERIFIED

SIMPSON   *1992, Chilean Navy /* 0012143

2 OBERON CLASS (SSK)

Name	No	Builders	Laid down	Launched	Commissioned
O'BRIEN	22	Scott-Lithgow	17 Jan 1971	21 Dec 1972	15 Apr 1976
HYATT (ex-*Condell*)	23	Scott-Lithgow	10 Jan 1972	26 Sep 1973	27 Sep 1976

Displacement, tons: 2,030 surfaced; 2,410 dived
Dimensions, feet (metres): 295.2 × 26.5 × 18.1
  (90 × 8.1 × 5.5)
Main machinery: Diesel-electric; 2 ASR 16 VVS-ASR1 diesels; 3,680 hp *(2.74 MW)*; 2 AEI motors; 6,000 hp *(4.48 MW)*; 2 shafts
Speed, knots: 12 surfaced; 17 dived; 10 snorting
Complement: 65 (7 officers)

Torpedoes: 8—21 in *(533 mm)* tubes (6 bow, 2 stern). 22 AEG SUT; wire-guided; active homing to 12 km *(6.5 n miles)* at 35 kt; passive homing to 28 km *(15 n miles)* at 23 kt; warhead 250 kg.
Countermeasures: ESM: Thomson-CSF DR 2000U; radar warning.
Weapons control: STN Atlas Elektronik TFCS.
Radars: Navigation: Kelvin Hughes Type 1006; I-band.
Sonars: BAC Type 2007; flank array; passive; long range; low frequency.
  Atlas Elektronik CSU 90; bow-mounted; passive/active search and attack; medium frequency.

O'BRIEN   *8/1997, Chilean Navy /* 0012144

Programmes: Ordered from Scott's Shipbuilding & Engineering Co Ltd, Greenock, late 1969. Both suffered delays in fitting out due to recabling and a minor explosion in *Hyatt* in January 1976.

Modernisation: STN fire-control system fitted in 1992. Atlas Elektronik CSU 90 has replaced Type 187. Pilkington Optronics CK 24 search and CH 74 attack periscopes.
Operational: Stern tubes are no longer used. These submarines are to be deleted when the 'Scorpene' class enter service.

UPDATED

DESTROYERS

3 PRAT (COUNTY) CLASS (DDG)

Name	No	Builders	Laid down	Launched	Commissioned
PRAT (ex-Norfolk)	11	Swan Hunter, Wallsend	15 Mar 1966	16 Nov 1967	7 Mar 1970
COCHRANE (ex-Antrim)	12	Fairfield SB & Eng Co Ltd, Govan	20 Jan 1966	19 Oct 1967	14 July 1970
BLANCO ENCALADA (ex-Fife)	15	Fairfield SB & Eng Co Ltd, Govan	1 June 1962	9 July 1964	21 June 1966

Displacement, tons: 5,440 standard; 6,200 full load
Dimensions, feet (metres): 520.5 × 54 × 20.5
(158.7 × 16.5 × 6.3)
Main machinery: COSAG; 2 Babcock & Wilcox boilers; 700 psi
(49.2 kg/cm²); 950°F *(510°C)*; 2 AEI steam turbines;
30,000 hp *(22.4 MW)*; 4 English Electric G6 gas turbines;
30,000 hp *(22.4 MW)*; 2 shafts
Speed, knots: 30. **Range, miles:** 3,500 at 28 kt
Complement: 470 (36 officers)

Missiles: SSM: 4 Aerospatiale MM 38 Exocet ❶; inertial cruise;
active radar homing to 42 km *(23 n miles)* at 0.9 Mach;
warhead 165 kg; sea-skimmer. MM 40 in due course.
SAM: Short Brothers Seaslug Mk 2 *(Prat only)* ❷; non-
operational.
2 octuple IAI/Rafael Barak I ❸ command line of sight radar or
optical guidance to 10 km *(5.5 n miles)* at 2 Mach; warhead
22 kg.
Guns: 2 Vickers 4.5 in *(115 mm)* Mk 6 semi-automatic (twin) ❹;
20 rds/min to 19 km *(10.3 n miles)* anti-surface; 6 km *(3.2 n
miles)* anti-aircraft; weight of shell 25 kg.
2 or 4 Oerlikon 20 mm Mk 9 ❺; 800 rds/min to 2 km.
Torpedoes: 6—324 mm Mk 32 (2 triple) tubes ❻; Honeywell Mk
46 Mod 2; active/passive homing to 11 km *(5.9 n miles)* at
40 kt; warhead 44 kg.
Countermeasures: Decoys: 2 Corvus 8-barrelled trainable chaff
launchers ❼; distraction or centroid patterns to 1 km.
2 Wallop Barricade double layer chaff launchers ❽; 6 sets
triple-barrelled with 4 modes of fire.
ESM: Elisra 9003, intercept. Elta IR sensor.
ECM: Type 667; jammer.
Combat data systems: Sisdef Imagen SP 100 with datalink.
SATCOM.
Weapons control: Gunnery MRS 3 system.
Radars: Air search: Marconi Type 966 *(Blanco Encalada)* ❾;
A-band.
Admiralty Type 277 M *(Prat)* ❿; E-band.
Elta LM 2228S ⓫; E/F-band (for Barak).
Surface search: Marconi Type 992 Q or R ⓬; E/F-band; range
55 km *(30 n miles)*.
Navigation: Decca Type 978/1006; I-band.
Fire control: Plessey Type 903 ⓭; I-band (for Guns).
Marconi Type 901 *(Prat)* ⓮; G/H-band.
Two Elta EL/M-2221GM ⓯; I/J/K-band (for Barak).
Sonars: Kelvin Hughes Type 162 M; hull-mounted; sideways
looking classification; high-frequency.
Graseby Type 184 M; hull-mounted; active search and attack;
medium range; 7 to 9 kHz.

Helicopters: 1 Bell 206B *(Prat)* ⓰. 2 NAS 332SC Cougar
(others) ⓱.

Programmes: Transferred from UK 6 April 1982 *(Prat)*, 22 June
1984 *(Cochrane)*, and 12 August 1987 *(Blanco Encalada)*.
Extensive refits carried out after transfer. Although all are
named after senior officers, the titles Almirante and Capitan
are not used.
Modernisation: Blanco Encalada converted at Talcahuano into
helicopter carrier for two Super Pumas completed May 1988;
Cochrane similar conversion completed in May 1994. Prat
serves as Flagship. All of the class fitted with the Israeli Barak I
and new communications, optronic directors and EW
equipment. Imagen combat data system fitted in 1993 to Blanco Encalada, and
remainder by 1997. Indal Assist helo recovery system also
fitted and magazine stowage increased. MM 40 is planned to
be fitted to replace Exocet MM 38.
Structure: Blanco Encalada and Cochrane are markedly different
in appearance from Prat with a greatly enlarged flight deck
(617 m²) continued right aft to accommodate two large

PRAT   *(Scale 1 : 1,500), Ian Sturton /* 0017690

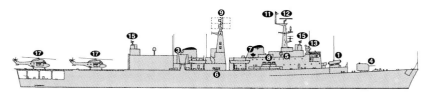

BLANCO ENCALADA   *(Scale 1 : 1,500), Ian Sturton /* 0017691

BLANCO ENCALADA   *10/1997, Winter & Findler /* 0017692

helicopters simultaneously, making them effectively flush-
decked. The hangar has also been completely rebuilt
(dimensions 16.9 × 11.7 m) and the foremast extended. Indal
ASIST helo handling system.

Operational: Fourth ship of the class paid off in late 1998. The
Seaslug SAM system is not operational and Prat's planned refit
was cancelled in 1999. The ship may soon be scrapped.
UPDATED

PRAT   *10/1996, Chilean Navy /* 0017694

BLANCO ENCALADA *2/1998* / 0017693

BLANCO ENCALADA *10/1997, Julio Montes* / 0012146

COCHRANE *3/1997, van Ginderen Collection* / 0012149

FRIGATES

Note: Project Tridente is the plan for four new MEKO 200 frigates with CODOG propulsion. These are to be built at ASMAR, Talcahuano.

3 LEANDER CLASS (FFG)

Name	No	Builders	Laid down	Launched	Commissioned
CONDELL	06	Yarrow & Co, Scotstoun	5 June 1971	12 June 1972	21 Dec 1973
LYNCH	07	Yarrow & Co, Scotstoun	6 Dec 1971	6 Dec 1972	25 May 1974
MINISTRO ZENTENO (ex-*Achilles*)	08 (ex-F 12)	Yarrow & Co, Scotstoun	1 Dec 1967	21 Nov 1968	9 July 1970

Displacement, tons: 2,500 standard; 2,962 full load
Dimensions, feet (metres): 372 oa; 360 wl × 43 × 18 (screws)
  (113.4; 109.7 × 13.1 × 5.5)
Main machinery: 2 Babcock & Wilcox boilers; 550 psi *(38.7 kg/ cm²)*; 850°F *(450°C)*; 2 White/English Electric turbines; 30,000 hp *(22.4 MW)*; 2 shafts
Speed, knots: 29. **Range, miles:** 4,500 at 12 kt
Complement: 263 (20 officers)

Missiles: SSM: 4 Aerospatiale MM 40 Exocet or MM 38 *(Zenteno)* ❶; inertial cruise; active radar homing to 70 km *(40 n miles)* (MM 40) or 42 km *(23 n miles)* (MM 38) at 0.9 Mach; warhead 165 kg; sea-skimmer.
SAM: Short Brothers Seacat GWS 22 quad launcher ❷; optical/radar guidance to 5 km *(2.7 n miles)*; warhead 10 kg; 16 reloads.
Guns: 2 Vickers 4.5 in *(115 mm)*/45 Mk 6 (twin) semi-automatic ❸; 20 rds/min to 19 km *(10 n miles)* anti-surface; 6 km *(3.2 n miles)* anti-aircraft; weight of shell 25 kg.
4 Oerlikon 20 mm Mk 9 (2 twin) ❹; 800 rds/min to 2 km.

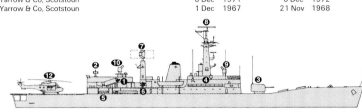

CONDELL *(Scale 1 : 1,200), Ian Sturton /* 0012150

Torpedoes: 6—324 mm Mk 32 (2 triple) tubes ❺. Honeywell Mk 46 Mod 2; active/passive homing to 11 km *(5.9 n miles)* at 40 kt; warhead 44 kg. To be replaced by Murene in due course.
Countermeasures: Decoys: 2 Corvus 8-barrelled trainable chaff rocket launchers ❻; distraction or centroid patterns to 1 km. Wallop Barricade double layer chaff launchers.
ESM/ECM: Elta EW system; intercept and jammer.

Combat data systems: Sisdef Imagen SP 100 includes datalink. Link 11 receive (06 and 07).
Weapons control: MRS 3 system for gunnery. GWS 22 system for Seacat.
Radars: Air search: Marconi Type 965/966 ❼; A-band.
Surface search: Marconi Type 992 Q or Plessey Type 994 *(Zenteno)* ❽; E/F-band.
Navigation: Kelvin Hughes Type 1006; I-band.
Fire control: Plessey Type 903 ❾; I-band (for guns).
Plessey Type 904 ❿; I-band (for Seacat).
Sonars: Graseby Type 184 M/P; hull-mounted; active search and attack; medium frequency (6/9 kHz).
Graseby Type 170 B; hull-mounted; active attack; high frequency (15 kHz).
Kelvin Hughes Type 162 M; hull-mounted; sideways-looking classification; high frequency.

Helicopters: 1 Bell 206B *(Zenteno)* ⓫ or Cougar ⓬.

Programmes: First two ordered from Yarrow & Co Ltd, Scotstoun in the late 1960s. Third ship purchased from UK in September 1990.
Modernisation: In 1989 *Lynch* was considerably modified at Talcahuano Dockyard with two twin MM 40 Exocet launchers being mounted on each side of the hangar (instead of the MM 38 aft) and by moving the torpedo tubes down one deck. The enlarged flight deck can now take a Cougar aircraft. Other modifications include improvements to the fire-control radars and Israeli EW systems. Plans to fit Barak SAM have been shelved. *Condell* completed a similar modernisation to *Lynch* in 1993 but with the addition of a new combat data system which has now been fitted in *Lynch*. The increased hangar size has led to the flight deck being extended to the stern of the ship and the stern gear moved down a deck. Indal Assist helicopter recovery system is fitted. *Ministro Zenteno* modified in 1997 with MM 38 launchers and a new foremast. The flight deck can take a Cougar helicopter but the hangar has not been enlarged.
Operational: A fourth of class paid off in 1998.

UPDATED

MINISTRO ZENTENO *(Scale 1 : 1,200), Ian Sturton /* 0012151

MINISTRO ZENTENO 6/1998 / 0017697

CONDELL 6/1998, van Ginderen Collection / 0017695

LYNCH 1/1997, Chilean Navy / 0017696

SHIPBORNE AIRCRAFT

Numbers/Type: 7 Nurtanio (Aerospatiale) NAS 332C Cougar.
Operational speed: 151 kt *(279 km/h)*.
Service ceiling: 15,090 ft *(4,600 m)*.
Range: 335 n miles *(620 km)*.
Role/Weapon systems: ASV/ASW helicopters for DLG conversions; surface search and SAR secondary roles. Sensors: Thomson-CSF Varam radar and Thomson Sintra HS-312 dipping sonar. DR 2000 ESM. Weapons: ASW; 2 × Alliant Mk 46 Mod 2 torpedoes or depth bombs. ASV; 1 or 2 × Aerospatiale AM 39 Exocet missiles.

UPDATED

COUGAR   *10/1997*, Julio Montes /* 0012155

Numbers/Type: 6 MBB BO 105C.
Operational speed: 113 kt *(210 km/h)*.
Service ceiling: 9,845 ft *(3,000 m)*.
Range: 407 n miles *(754 km)*.
Role/Weapon systems: Coastal patrol helicopter for patrol, training and liaison duties; SAR as secondary role. Sensors: Bendix search radar. Weapons: Unarmed.

UPDATED

BO 105C   *6/1992*, Chilean Navy /* 0056719

Numbers/Type: 6 Bell 206B JetRanger.
Operational speed: 115 kt *(213 km/h)*.
Service ceiling: 13,500 ft *(4,115 m)*.
Range: 368 n miles *(682 km)*.
Role/Weapon systems: Some tasks and training carried out by torpedo-armed liaison helicopter; emergency war role for ASW. Weapons: ASW; 1 × Mk 46 torpedo or 2 depth bombs.

UPDATED

JETRANGER   *6/1993*, Chilean Navy /* 0056720

LAND-BASED MARITIME AIRCRAFT (FRONT LINE)

Notes: (1) In addition there are EMB-110, and Casa Aviocar 212 support aircraft.
(2) The Air Force has one Boeing 707 converted for AEW duties.

Numbers/Type: 4 Embraer EMB-111 Bandeirante.
Operational speed: 194 kt *(360 km/h)*.
Service ceiling: 25,500 ft *(7,770 m)*.
Range: 1,590 n miles *(2,945 km)*.
Role/Weapon systems: Designated EMB-111N for peacetime EEZ and wartime MR. Sensors: Eaton-AIL AN/APS-128 search radar, Thomson-CSF DR 2000 ESM, searchlight. Weapons: Strike; 6 × 127 mm or 28 × 70 mm rockets.

UPDATED

EMB-111   *3/1994*, Mario R V Carneiro /* 0056721

Numbers/Type: 9 Pilatus PC-7 Turbo-Trainer.
Operational speed: 270 kt *(500 km/h)*.
Service ceiling: 32,000 ft *(9,755 m)*.
Range: 1,420 n miles *(2,630 km)*.
Role/Weapon systems: Training includes simulated attacks to exercise ships' AA defences; emergency war role for strike operations. Sensors: None. Weapons: 4 × 127 mm or similar rockets and machine gun pods.

UPDATED

Numbers/Type: 6 Lockheed P-3A Orion.
Operational speed: 410 kt *(760 km/h)*.
Service ceiling: 28,300 ft *(8,625 m)*.
Range: 4,000 n miles *(7,410 km)*.
Role/Weapon systems: Long-range MR for surveillance and SAR. First one delivered from USA in March 1993 followed by seven more of which two are used for spares. Sensors: To be fitted with new radar, ESM and FLIR in due course. APS-115 radar. Weapons: Weapon systems removed but to be replaced in due course including ASMs.

UPDATED

ORION   *3/1994*, Mario R V Carneiro /* 0056722

Numbers/Type: 6 0-2A Skymaster.
Operational speed: 130 kt *(241 km/h)*.
Service ceiling: 5,000 ft *(1,524 m)*.
Range: 550 n miles *(1,019 km)*.
Role/Weapon systems: Maritime coastal patrol and training acquired in 1998/99. Sensors: None. Weapons: May be equipped with 4 weapons stations in due course.

NEW ENTRY

SKYMASTER   *6/1999*, Chilean Navy /* 0056723

PATROL FORCES

Note: Project Zonamar is the planned building of four 90 m offshore patrol vessels with a helo deck and light gun. Orders have been delayed by lack of funds, but the requirement is still in force.

3 CASMA (SAAR 4) CLASS
(FAST ATTACK CRAFT—MISSILE) (PCFG)

Name	No	Builders	Commissioned
CASMA (ex-*Romah*)	LM 30	Haifa Shipyard	Mar 1974
CHIPANA (ex-*Keshet*)	LM 31	Haifa Shipyard	Oct 1973
ANGAMOS (ex-*Reshef*)	LM 34	Haifa Shipyard	Apr 1973

Displacement, tons: 415 standard; 450 full load
Dimensions, feet (metres): 190.6 × 25 × 8 *(58 × 7.8 × 2.4)*
Main machinery: 4 MTU 16V 538 TB82 diesels; 11,880 hp(m) *(8.74 MW)* sustained (30 and 31);
4 MTU 16V 596 TB91 diesels; 15,000 hp(m) *(11.3 MW)* (34); 4 shafts
Speed, knots: 32. **Range, miles:** 1,650 at 30 kt; 4,000 at 17.5 kt
Complement: 51 (8 officers)

Missiles: SSM: 4 IAI Gabriel I or II; radar or optical guidance; semi-active radar homing to 20 km *(10.8 n miles)* (I) or 36 km *(20 n miles)* (II); at 0.7 Mach; warhead 75 kg HE.
Guns: 2 OTO Melara 3 in *(76 mm)*/62 compact; 85 rds/min to 16 km *(8.7 n miles)* anti-surface;
12 km *(6.5 n miles)* anti-aircraft; weight of shell 6 kg.
2 Oerlikon 20 mm; 800 rds/min to 2 km.
Countermeasures: Decoys: 4 Rafael LRCR chaff decoy launchers.
ESM: Elta Electronics MN-53; intercept.
ECM: Elta Rattler; jammer.
Radars: Surface search: Thomson-CSF THD 1040 Neptune; E/F-band; range 110 km *(60 n miles)*.
Navigation: Raytheon 20X; I-band.
Fire control: Elta Electronics M-2221 or Selenia Orion RTN 10X; I/J-band; range 40 km *(22 n miles)*.

Programmes: One transferred from Israel December 1979 and second in January 1981 for refit and deployment to Beagle Channel. Two more acquired from Israel 1 June 1997.
Structure: The second pair were modernised in Israeli service.
Operational: The poor condition of the second pair on transfer meant that one (ex-*Tarshish*) had to be cannibalised for spares in 1998. **VERIFIED**

CASMA   6/1998 / 0017698

CHIPANA   2/1997, Chilean Navy / 0012156

2 IQUIQUE (SAAR 3) CLASS
(FAST ATTACK CRAFT—MISSILE) (PCFG)

Name	No	Builders	Commissioned
IQUIQUE (ex-*Hamit*)	LM 32	CMN Cherbourg	1969
COVADONGA (ex-*Hefz*)	LM 33	CMN Cherbourg	1969

Displacement, tons: 220 standard; 250 full load
Dimensions, feet (metres): 147.6 × 23 × 8.2 *(45 × 7 × 2.5)*
Main machinery: 4 MTU MD 16V 537 TB80 diesels; 10,000 hp(m) *(7.35 MW)* sustained; 4 shafts
Speed, knots: 40+. **Range, miles:** 2,500 at 15 kt; 1,600 at 20 kt; 1,000 at 30 kt
Complement: 35-40 (5 officers)

Missiles: SSM: Up to 6 IAI Gabriel II; active radar or optical TV guidance; semi-active radar homing to 36 km *(20 n miles)* at 0.7 Mach; warhead 75 kg.
Guns: 1 OTO Melara 3 in *(76 mm)*/62 DP; 65 rds/min to 8 km *(4.4 n miles)*; weight of shell 6 kg.
2—12.7 mm MGs.
Countermeasures: Decoys: 6—24-tube, 4 single-tube chaff launchers.
ESM: Elta Electronics MN-53; intercept.
ECM: Elta Rattler; jammer.
Radars: Air/surface search: Thomson-CSF TH-D 1040 Neptune; G-band; range 33 km *(18 n miles)* for 2 m² target.
Fire control: Selenia Orion RTN 10X; I/J-band.

Programmes: Both acquired from Israel in December 1988 and commissioned into the Chilean Navy 3 May 1989. **VERIFIED**

IQUIQUE   6/1998, Chilean Navy / 0017703

4 RIQUELME (TIGER) CLASS (TYPE 148)
(FAST ATTACK CRAFT—MISSILE) (PCFG)

Name	No	Builders	Commissioned
RIQUELME (ex-*Wolf*)	LM 36 (ex-P 6149)	CMN Cherbourg	26 Feb 1974
ORELLA (ex-*Elster*)	LM 37 (ex-P 6154)	CMN Cherbourg	14 Nov 1974
SERRANO (ex-*Tiger*)	LM 38 (ex-P 6141)	CMN Cherbourg	30 Oct 1972
URIBE (ex-*Luchs*)	LM 39 (ex-P 6143)	CMN Cherbourg	9 Apr 1973

Displacement, tons: 234 standard; 265 full load
Dimensions, feet (metres): 154.2 × 23 × 8.9 *(47 × 7 × 2.7)*
Main machinery: 4 MTU MD 16V 538 TB90 diesels; 12,000 hp(m) *(8.82 MW)* sustained; 4 shafts
Speed, knots: 36. **Range, miles:** 570 at 30 kt; 1,600 at 15 kt
Complement: 30 (4 officers)

Missiles: SSM: 4 Aerospatiale MM 38 Exocet (2 twin) launchers; inertial cruise; active radar homing to 42 km *(23 n miles)* at 0.9 Mach; warhead 165 kg; sea-skimmer.
Guns: 1 OTO Melara 3 in *(76 mm)*/62 compact; 85 rds/min to 16 km *(8.6 n miles)* anti-surface; 12 km *(6.5 n miles)* anti-aircraft; weight of shell 6 kg.
1 Bofors 40 mm/70; 330 rds/min to 12 km *(6.5 n miles)* anti-surface; 4 km *(2.2 n miles)* anti-aircraft; weight of shell 0.96 kg; fitted with GRP dome (1984).
Mines: Laying capability.
Countermeasures: Decoys: Wolke chaff launcher.
Combat data systems: PALIS and Link 11.
Weapons control: CSEE Panda optical director. Thomson-CSF Vega PCET system, controlling missiles and guns.
Radars: Air/surface search: Thomson-CSF Triton; G-band; range 33 km *(18 n miles)* for 2 m² target.
Navigation: SMA 3 RM 20; I-band; range 73 km *(40 n miles)*.
Fire control: Thomson-CSF Castor; I/J-band.

Programmes: First pair transferred from Germany on 27 August 1997 and sailed in a transport ship on 2 September. Four more transferred on 22 September 1998 and sailed 11 October. These four were all damaged during a storm in transit, and the two best were taken into service, with the other pair *(Pelikan* and *Kranich)* being used for spares. The ship names have prefixed ranks but these are not used.
Structure: Similar to Combattante II craft. EW equipment was removed prior to transfer.
Operational: Operate in the Beagle channel. Exocet missiles were not part of the transfer but have been acquired separately. **UPDATED**

SERRANO   10/1998, Findler & Winter / 0017701

RIQUELME   6/1998, Chilean Navy / 0017700

10 GRUMETE DIAZ (DABUR) CLASS
(COASTAL PATROL CRAFT) (PC)

DIAZ 1814	BRAVO 1818	JOHNSON 1821
BOLADOS 1815	CAMPOS 1819	TRONCOSO 1822
SALINAS 1816	MACHADO 1820	HUDSON 1823
TELLEZ 1817		

Displacement, tons: 39 full load
Dimensions, feet (metres): 64.9 × 18 × 5.9 *(19.8 × 5.5 × 1.8)*
Main machinery: 2 Detroit 12V 71TA diesels; 840 hp *(627 kW)* sustained; 2 shafts
Speed, knots: 19. **Range, miles:** 450 at 13 kt
Complement: 8 (2 officers)
Guns: 2 Oerlikon 20 mm.
Radars: Surface search: Racal Decca Super 101 Mk 3; I-band.

Comment: First six transferred from Israel and commissioned 3 January 1991. Second batch of four more transferred and commissioned 17 March 1995. A fast inflatable boat is carried on the stern. Deployed in the Fourth Naval Zone. All have LPC numbers and Grumete precedes the ships' names. **VERIFIED**

GRUMETE DIAZ   3/1998 / 0017704

6 MICALVI CLASS (LARGE PATROL CRAFT) (PC/AEML)

Name	No	Builders	Launched	Commissioned
MICALVI	PSG 71	ASMAR, Talcahuano	12 Sep 1992	30 Mar 1993
ORTIZ	PSG 72	ASMAR, Talcahuano	23 July 1993	15 Dec 1993
ISAZA	PSG 73	ASMAR, Talcahuano	7 Jan 1994	31 May 1994
MOREL	PSG 74	ASMAR, Talcahuano	21 Apr 1994	11 Aug 1994
CABRALES	PSG 77	ASMAR, Talcahuano	4 Apr 1996	29 June 1996
SIBBALD	PSG 78	ASMAR, Talcahuano	5 June 1996	29 Aug 1996

Displacement, tons: 518 full load
Dimensions, feet (metres): 139.4 × 27.9 × 9.5 *(42.5 × 8.5 × 2.9)*
Main machinery: 2 Caterpillar 3512 TA diesels; 2,560 hp(m) *(1.88 MW)* sustained; 2 shafts
Speed, knots: 15. **Range, miles:** 4,200 at 12 kt
Complement: 23 (5 officers) plus 10 spare
Guns: 1 Bofors 40 mm/60. 2 Oerlikon 20 mm.
Radars: Surface search: Racal Decca; I-band.

Comment: First four built under design project Taitao. Last pair built for export but bought by the Navy. Multipurpose patrol vessels with a secondary mission of transport and servicing navigational aids. Provision for bow thruster, sonar and mine rails. Can carry 35 tons cargo in holds and 18 tons in containers. Crane lift of 2.5 tons. The ships' names all have prefixed ranks but these are not used. *Micalvi* and *Ortiz* were classified as missile tenders in 1999 and are listed as auxiliaries. ***UPDATED***

CABRALES   *1/1999*, van Ginderen Collection /* 0056725

MICALVI   *2/1998 /* 0017702

4 GUACOLDA CLASS (COASTAL PATROL CRAFT) (PC)

Name	No	Builders	Commissioned
GUACOLDA	1607 (ex-80)	Bazán, San Fernando	30 July 1965
FRESIA	1608 (ex-81)	Bazán, San Fernando	9 Dec 1965
QUIDORA	1605 (ex-83)	Bazán, San Fernando	28 Mar 1966
TEGUALDA	1606 (ex-84)	Bazán, San Fernando	1 July 1966

Displacement, tons: 134 full load
Dimensions, feet (metres): 118.1 × 18.4 × 7.2 *(36 × 5.6 × 2.2)*
Main machinery: 2 MTU MB 16V 652 SB60 diesels; 3,200 hp(m) *(2.35 MW)* sustained; 2 shafts
Speed, knots: 22. **Range, miles:** 1,500 at 15 kt
Complement: 20
Guns: 1 Bofors 40 mm/70.
Radars: Navigation: Decca 505; I-band.

Comment: Built to West German Lürssen design from 1963 to 1966. First launched 1964. By mid-1998 all four had been converted to coastal patrol craft with torpedo tubes and after gun removed. ***UPDATED***

GUACOLDA   *6/1999* /* 0056724

SURVEY SHIPS

1 TYPE 1200 CLASS (AGS)

Name	No	Builders	Commissioned
CONTRALMIRANTE OSCAR VIEL TORO	AP 46	Canadian Vickers, Montreal	Oct 1960
(ex-*Norman McLeod Rogers*)			

Displacement, tons: 6,320 full load
Measurement, tons: 4,179 gross; 1,847 net
Dimensions, feet (metres): 294.9 × 62.5 × 20 *(89.9 × 19.1 × 6.1)*
Main machinery: 4 Fairbanks-Morse 38D8-1/8-12 diesels; 8,496 hp *(6.34 MW)* sustained; 4 GE generators; 4.8 MW; 2 Ruston RK3CZ diesels; 7,250 hp *(5.6 MW)* sustained; 2 GE generators; 2.76 MW; 2 GE motors; 12,000 hp *(8.95 MW)*; 2 shafts
Speed, knots: 15. **Range, miles:** 12,000 at 12 kt
Complement: 33
Guns: 2 Oerlikon 20 mm.
Helicopters: 1 BO 105C.

Comment: Acquired from the Canadian Coast Guard on 16 February 1995. The ship was formerly based on the west coast at Victoria, BC, and was laid up in 1993. Has replaced the deleted *Piloto Pardo* as the Antarctic patrol and survey ship. Red painted hull and pale yellow superstructure. ***UPDATED***

CONTRALMIRANTE OSCAR VIEL TORO   *4/1996* /* 0056728

1 ROBERT D CONRAD CLASS (AGOR)

Name	No	Builders	Commissioned
VIDAL GORMAZ	60 (ex-AGOR 10)	Marinette Marine, WI	27 Sep 1965
(ex-*Thomas Washington*)			

Displacement, tons: 1,370 full load
Dimensions, feet (metres): 208.9 × 40 × 15.3 *(63.7 × 12.2 × 4.7)*
Main machinery: Diesel-electric; 2 Cummins diesel generators; 1 motor; 1,000 hp *(746 kW)*; 1 shaft
Speed, knots: 13.5. **Range, miles:** 12,000 at 12 kt
Complement: 41 (9 officers, 15 scientists)
Guns: 2 Oerlikon 20 mm.
Radars: Navigation: TM 1660/12S; I-band.

Comment: Transferred from USA on 28 September 1992. This is the first class of ships designed and built by the US Navy for oceanographic research. Fitted with instrumentation and laboratories to measure gravity and magnetism, water temperature, sound transmission in water, and the profile of the ocean floor. Special features include 10 ton capacity boom and winches for handling over-the-side equipment; 620 hp gas turbine (housed in funnel structure) for providing 'quiet' power when conducting experiments; can propel the ship at 6.5 kt. Ships of this class are in service with several other navies. ***UPDATED***

VIDAL GORMAZ   *1/1999*, van Ginderen Collection /* 0056729

1 BUOY TENDER (ABU)

Name	No	Builders	Commissioned
GEORGE SLIGHT MARSHALL (ex-*M V Vigilant*)	BRS 63	Netherlands	July 1978

Displacement, tons: 816 full load
Dimensions, feet (metres): 173.9 × 36.7 × 11.5 *(53 × 11.2 × 3.5)*
Main machinery: 2 Ruston 6AP230 diesels; 1,360 hp *(1 MW)*; 2 shafts; bow thruster
Speed, knots: 12
Complement: 20
Guns: 2 Oerlikon 20 mm.

Comment: Acquired from the UK Mersey Harbour Board and recommissioned 5 February 1997. Carries a 15 ton derrick. ***VERIFIED***

GEORGE SLIGHT MARSHALL   *1/1999*, van Ginderen Collection /* 0050081

AMPHIBIOUS FORCES

1 NEWPORT CLASS (LST)

Name	No	Builders	Laid down	Launched	Commissioned	Recommissioned
VALDIVIA (ex-San Bernardino)	93 (ex-LST 1189)	National Steel & Shipbuilding Co	12 July 1969	28 Mar 1970	27 Mar 1971	30 Sep 1995

Displacement, tons: 4,975 light; 8,450 full load
Dimensions, feet (metres): 522.3 (hull) × 69.5 × 17.5 (aft)
  (159.2 × 21.2 × 5.3)
Main machinery: 6 ALCO 16-251 diesels; 16,500 hp *(12.3 MW)*
  sustained; 2 shafts; cp props; bow thruster
Speed, knots: 20. **Range, miles:** 2,500 at 14 kt
Complement: 257 (13 officers)
Military lift: 400 troops; 500 tons vehicles; 3 LCVPs and 1 LCPL
  on davits

Guns: 1 General Electric/General Dynamics 20 mm Vulcan
  Phalanx Mk 15.
Radars: Surface search: Raytheon SPS-67; G-band.
Navigation: Marconi LN66; I/J-band.

Helicopters: Platform only.

Programmes: Transferred from the US by lease on
  30 September 1995. A second of class was offered but not
  accepted due to its poor condition.
Structure: The hull form required to achieve 20 kt would not
  permit bow doors, thus these ships unload by a 112 ft ramp
  over their bow. The ramp is supported by twin derrick arms. A
  ramp just forward of the superstructure connects the lower
  tank deck with the main deck and a vehicle passage through
  the superstructure provides access to the parking area
  amidships. A stern gate to the tank deck permits unloading of

VALDIVIA   *1/1999*, van Ginderen Collection* / 0056726

amphibious tractors into the water, or unloading of other
vehicles into an LCU or on to a pier. Vehicle stowage covers
19,000 sq ft. Length over derrick arms is 562 ft *(171.3 m)*; full
load draught is 11.5 ft forward and 17.5 ft aft. Bow thruster
fitted to hold position offshore while unloading amphibious
tractors.

Operational: Damaged by grounding in mid-1997, but
  subsequently repaired.
                                                UPDATED

2 MAIPO (BATRAL) CLASS (LST)

Name	No	Builders	Launched	Commissioned
RANCAGUA	92	ASMAR, Talcahuano	6 Mar 1982	8 Aug 1983
CHACABUCO	95 (ex-93)	ASMAR, Talcahuano	16 July 1985	15 Apr 1986

Displacement, tons: 873 standard; 1,409 full load
Dimensions, feet (metres): 260.4 × 42.7 × 8.2 *(79.4 × 13 × 2.5)*
Main machinery: 2 SEMT-Pielstick 12 PA4 V 185 VG; 4,012 hp(m) *(2.95 MW)* sustained; 2 shafts;
  cp props
Speed, knots: 16. **Range, miles:** 3,500 at 13 kt
Complement: 43 (5 officers)
Military lift: 180 troops; 12 vehicles; 350 tons
Guns: 2 Bofors 40 mm/60. 1 Oerlikon 20 mm. 2—81 mm mortars.
Radars: Navigation: Decca 1229; I/J-band.
Helicopters: Platform for 1 Cougar.

Comment: First laid down in 1980 to standard French design with French equipment. Have 40 ton
  bow ramps and vehicle stowage above and below deck.   *UPDATED*

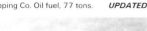

CHACABUCO   *6/1999*, Chilean Navy* / 0056727

2 ELICURA CLASS (LSM)

Name	No	Builders	Commissioned
ELICURA	90	Talcahuano	10 Dec 1968
OROMPELLO	94	Dade Dry Dock Co, MI	15 Sep 1964

Displacement, tons: 290 light; 750 full load
Dimensions, feet (metres): 145 × 34 × 12.8 *(44.2 × 10.4 × 3.9)*
Main machinery: 2 Cummins VT-17-700M diesels; 900 hp *(660 kW)*; 2 shafts
Speed, knots: 10.5. **Range, miles:** 2,900 at 9 kt
Complement: 20
Military lift: 350 tons
Guns: 3 Oerlikon 20 mm (can be carried).
Radars: Navigation: Raytheon 1500B; I/J-band.

Comment: Two of similar class operated by Chilean Shipping Co. Oil fuel, 77 tons.   *UPDATED*

ELICURA   *4/1997*, Chilean Navy* / 0017706

TRAINING SHIPS

Note: There is also a 32 ton yacht *Blanco Estela* commissioned 25 January 1978.

1 SAIL TRAINING SHIP (AXS)

Name	No	Builders	Commissioned
ESMERALDA (ex-Don Juan de Austria)	43	Bazán, Cadiz	15 June 1954

Displacement, tons: 3,420 standard; 3,754 full load
Dimensions, feet (metres): 269.2 pp; 360 oa × 44.6 × 23 *(82; 109.8 × 13.1 × 7)*
Main machinery: 1 Fiat diesel; 1,400 hp(m) *(1.03 MW)*; 1 shaft
Speed, knots: 11. **Range, miles:** 8,000 at 8 kt
Complement: 271 plus 80 cadets
Guns: 2 Hotchkiss saluting guns.

Comment: Four-masted schooner originally intended for the Spanish Navy. Near sister ship of *Juan
  Sebastian de Elcano* in the Spanish Navy. Refitted Saldanha Bay, South Africa, 1977. Sail area,
  26,910 sq ft.   *UPDATED*

ESMERALDA   *1/1999*, van Ginderen Collection* / 0056730

AUXILIARIES

1 TRANSPORT SHIP (AP)

Name	No	Builders	Launched	Commissioned
AQUILES	AP 41	ASMAR, Talcahuano	4 Dec 1987	15 July 1988

Displacement, tons: 2,767 light; 4,550 full load
Dimensions, feet (metres): 337.8 × 55.8 × 18 *(103 × 17 × 5.5 (max))*
Main machinery: 2 Krupp MaK 8 M 453B diesels; 7,080 hp(m) *(5.10 MW)* sustained; 1 shaft; bow
  thruster
Speed, knots: 18
Complement: 80
Military lift: 250 troops
Helicopters: Platform for up to Cougar size.

Comment: Ordered 4 October 1985. Can be converted rapidly to act as hospital ship.

                                                UPDATED

AQUILES   *3/1997* / 0012166

1 ÄLVSBORG CLASS (SUPPORT SHIP) (AS)

Name	No	Builders	Launched	Commissioned
MERINO (ex-Älvsborg)	42 (ex-A 234, ex-M 02)	Karlskronavarvet	11 Nov 1969	6 Apr 1971

Displacement, tons: 2,660 full load
Dimensions, feet (metres): 303.1 × 48.2 × 13.2 (92.4 × 14.7 × 4)
Main machinery: 2 Nohab-Polar 112 VS diesels; 4,200 hp(m) (3.1 MW); 1 shaft; cp prop; bow thruster; 350 hp(m) (257 kW)
Speed, knots: 16
Complement: 52 (accommodation for 205)
Guns: 3 Bofors 40 mm/70 SAK 48.
Countermeasures: Decoys: 2 Philax chaff/IR launchers.
Radars: Surface search: Raytheon; E/F-band.
Fire control: Philips 9LV 200 Mk 2; I/J-band.
Navigation: Terma Scanter 009; I-band.
Helicopters: Platform for 1 medium.

Comment: Ordered in 1968 as a minelayer. Transferred from the Swedish Navy in November 1996, having been paid off in 1995. Recommissioned 7 February 1997. Originally designed as a minelayer with a capacity of 300 mines. Converted to act as a general support ship with improved accommodation and workshops. Acts as a depot ship for submarines and attack craft. The full name is *Almirante José Toribio Merino Castro*.
VERIFIED

MERINO   6/1998 / 0017709

1 REPLENISHMENT SHIP (AOR)

Name	No	Builders	Commissioned
ARAUCANO	AO 53	Burmeister & Wain, Copenhagen	10 Jan 1967

Displacement, tons: 23,000 full load
Dimensions, feet (metres): 497.6 × 74.9 × 28.8 (151.7 × 22.8 × 8.8)
Main machinery: 1 Burmeister & Wain Type 62 VT 2BF140 diesel; 10,800 hp(m) (7.94 MW); 1 shaft
Speed, knots: 17. **Range, miles:** 12,000 at 15.5 kt
Complement: 130 (14 officers)
Cargo capacity: 21,126 m³ liquid; 1,444 m³ dry
Guns: 8 Bofors 40 mm/60 (4 twin).
Radars: Navigation: Racal Decca; I-band.

Comment: Launched on 21 June 1966.
VERIFIED

ARAUCANO   6/1998, Chilean Navy / 0017710

1 HARBOUR TRANSPORT (YFB)

Name	No	Builders	Commissioned
GRUMETE PEREZ	YFB 114	ASMAR, Talcahuano	12 Dec 1975

Displacement, tons: 165 full load
Dimensions, feet (metres): 80 × 22 × 8.5 (24.4 × 6.7 × 2.6)
Main machinery: 1 diesel; 370 hp(m) (272 kW); 1 shaft
Speed, knots: 10
Complement: 6
Guns: 1 Oerlikon 20 mm can be carried.
Radars: Navigation: Furuno; I-band.

Comment: Transferred to Seaman's School as harbour transport. Modified fishing boat design.
UPDATED

GRUMETE PEREZ   8/1997*, Chilean Navy / 0012168

1 SUPPLY SHIP (AKS)

Name	No	Builders	Commissioned
PISAGUA	116	SIMAR, Santiago	11 July 1995

Displacement, tons: 195 full load
Dimensions, feet (metres): 73.2 × 19.7 × 4.9 (22.3 × 6 × 1.5)
Main machinery: 1 diesel; 1 shaft
Speed, knots: 8. **Range, miles:** 500 at 8 kt
Cargo capacity: 50 tons
Radars: Navigation: Furuno; I-band.

Comment: LCU design operated by the Seaman's School, Quiriquina Island as a general purpose stores ship.
UPDATED

PISAGUA   8/1997*, Chilean Navy / 0012169

3 FLOATING DOCKS

Name	No	Lift	Commissioned
INGENIERO MERY (ex-ARD 25)	131	3,000 tons	1944 (1973)
MUTILLA (ex-ARD 32)	132	3,000 tons	1944 (1960)
TALCAHUANO (ex-ARD 5)	133	3,000 tons	1944 (1999)

Comment: There is also a Floating Dock *Marinero Gutierrez* with a 1,200 ton lift. Built in 1991.
UPDATED

TUGS

Note: Small harbour tugs *Reyes*, *Cortés* (both 100 tons and built in 1960) and *Galvez* (built in 1975), and the small personnel transport *Buzo Sobenes* BRT 112 are also in commission.

BUZO SOBENES   7/1997*, Chilean Navy / 0012170

1 SMIT LLOYD CLASS (TUG/SUPPLY VESSEL) (ATF)

Name	No	Builders	Commissioned
LEUCOTON (ex-Smit Lloyd 44)	ATF 68	de Waal, Zaltbommel	1972

Displacement, tons: 1,750 full load
Dimensions, feet (metres): 174.2 × 39.4 × 14.4 (53.1 × 12 × 4.4)
Main machinery: 2 Burmeister & Wain Alpha diesels; 4,000 hp(m) (2.94 MW); 2 shafts
Speed, knots: 13
Complement: 12
Guns: 2 Bofors 40 mm/60.
Radars: Surface search: E/F-band.

Comment: Acquired in February 1991. Modified at Punta Arenas and now used mainly as a supply ship.
UPDATED

LEUCOTON   6/1993*, Chilean Navy / 0056732

2 VERITAS CLASS (TUG/SUPPLY VESSELS) (ATF)

Name	No	Builders	Commissioned
GALVARINO (ex-*Maersk Traveller*)	ATF 66	Aukra Bruk, Aukra	1974
LAUTARO (ex-*Maersk Tender*)	ATF 67	Aukra Bruk, Aukra	1973

Displacement, tons: 941 light; 2,380 full load
Dimensions, feet (metres): 191.3 × 41.4 × 12.8 *(58.3 × 12.6 × 3.9)*
Main machinery: 2 Krupp MaK 8 M 453AK diesels; 6,400 hp(m) *(4.7 MW)*; 2 shafts; cp props; bow thruster
Speed, knots: 14
Complement: 11 plus 12 spare berths
Cargo capacity: 1,400 tons
Guns: 1 Bofors 40 mm/60 can be carried.
Radars: Navigation: Terma Pilot 7T-48; Furuno FR 240; I-band.

Comment: First one delivered from Maersk and commissioned into Navy 26 January 1988. Third one delivered in 1991. Bollard pull, 70 tonnes; towing winch, 100 tons. Fully air conditioned. Designed for towing large semi-submersible platform in extreme weather conditions. Ice strengthened.   ***UPDATED***

GALVARINO   *6/1994* */ 0056731

COAST GUARD

Note: There are also large numbers of harbour and SAR craft.

2 + (2) PROTECTOR CLASS (PC)

ALACALUFE LEP 1603   **HALLEF** LEP 1604

Displacement, tons: 107 full load
Dimensions, feet (metres): 107.3 × 22 × 6.6 *(32.7 × 6.7 × 2)*
Main machinery: 2 MTU diesels; 5,200 hp(m) *(3.82 MW)*; 2 shafts
Speed, knots: 20. **Range, miles:** 1,000 at 15 kt
Complement: 16

Comment: Built under licence from FBM at ASMAR, Talcahuano, in conjunction with FBM Marine. First commissioned 24 June 1989; options on six more were not taken up but two more gun armed versions may be authorised in due course. Manned by the Navy for patrol and Pilot Service duties in the Magellan Straits.   ***UPDATED***

HALLEF   *6/1999* *, *Chilean Navy* / 0056733

4 COASTAL PATROL CRAFT (PC)

KIMITAHI LPC 1701   **OSORNO** LPC 1808   **GUALE** LPC 1811   **COPAHUE** LPC 1810

Displacement, tons: 43 full load
Dimensions, feet (metres): 61 × 17.3 × 5.6 *(18.6 × 5.3 × 1.7)*
Main machinery: 2 MTU 8V 331 TC82 diesels; 1,740 hp(m) *(1.28 MW)* sustained; 2 shafts
Speed, knots: 30. **Range, miles:** 700 at 15 kt
Guns: 2 Oerlikon 20 mm; 800 rds/min.
Depth charges: 2 racks.

Comment: Details given are for the last three built by Maclaren, Niteroi, Brazil. Ordered 1977. GRP hulls. Completed between August 1979 and November 1982. There are some minor superstructure differences. Eight have been deleted so far. LPC 1701 is bigger at 48 tons and was built in 1980 by Asenav, Valdivia. She is capable of only 22 kt.   ***UPDATED***

CPC (old number)   *1991* *, *Chilean Navy* / 0056734

---

2 COASTAL PATROL CRAFT (PC)

ONA LEP 1601   **YAGAN** LEP 1602

Displacement, tons: 79 full load
Dimensions, feet (metres): 80.7 × 17.4 × 9.5 *(24.6 × 5.3 × 2.9)*
Main machinery: 2 MTU 6V 331 TC82 diesels; 1,300 hp(m) *(960 kW)* sustained; 2 shafts
Speed, knots: 22
Complement: 5
Guns: 2—12.7 mm MGs.

Comment: Built by Asenav and commissioned in 1980.   ***UPDATED***

ONA   *4/1994* *, *Chilean Navy* / 0056736

12 INSHORE PATROL CRAFT (PBI)

MAULE LPM 1901	**ISLUGA** LPM 1905	**CAU-CAU** LPM 1909
RAPEL LPM 1902	**LOA** LPM 1906	**PUDETO** LPM 1910
ACONCAGUA LPM 1903	**MAULLIN** LPM 1907	**ROBINSON CRUSOE** LPM 1911
LAUCA LPM 1904	**COPIAPÓ** LPM 1908	**PETROHUE** LPM 1916

Displacement, tons: 14 full load
Dimensions, feet (metres): 43.3 × 11.5 × 3.5 *(13.2 × 3.5 × 1.1)*
Main machinery: 2 MTU 6V 331 TC82 diesels; 1,300 hp(m) *(960 kW)* sustained; 2 shafts
Speed, knots: 18
Guns: 1—12.7 mm MG.
Radars: Surface search: I-band.

Comment: LPM 1901-1910 ordered in August 1981. Completed by Asenav 1982-83. Remainder built in the late 1980s. One wrecked in 1994, three more deleted in 1998.   ***UPDATED***

ACONCAGUA   *3/1997* *, *van Ginderen Collection* / 0012173

18 RODMAN 800 CLASS (PBI)

PM 2031-PM 2048

Dimensions, feet (metres): 29.2 × 9.8 × 3.6 *(8.9 × 3 × 0.8)*
Main machinery: 2 Volvo diesels; 300 hp(m) *(220 kW)*; 2 shafts
Speed, knots: 28. **Range, miles:** 150 at 25 kt
Complement: 3
Guns: 1—12.7 mm MG.

Comment: Built by Rodman Polyships, Vigo and all delivered by 17 May 1996.   ***UPDATED***

PM 2032   *1/1999* *, *van Ginderen Collection* / 0056735

CHINA
PEOPLE'S LIBERATION ARMY NAVY (PLAN)

Headquarters Appointments

Commander-in-Chief of the Navy:
   Admiral Shi Yunsheng
Political Commissar of the Navy:
   Vice Admiral Yang Huaiqing
Deputy Commanders-in-Chief of the Navy:
   Vice Admiral Zhang Dingfa
   Vice Admiral He Peng Fei
   Vice Admiral Shen Binyi
Chief of Naval Staff:
   Rear Admiral Wang Yucheng
Commander Naval Air Forces:
   Rear Admiral M A Bingzhi

Fleet Commanders

North Sea Fleet:
   Vice Admiral Yao Xinyuan
East Sea Fleet:
   Vice Admiral Zhao Guojun
South Sea Fleet:
   Vice Admiral Wang Yongguo

Personnel

(a) 2000: 268,000 officers and men, including 25,000 naval air force, 7,000 marines (28,000 in time of war) and 28,000 for coastal defence
(b) 3 years' national service for sailors afloat; 3 years for those in shore service. Some stay on for up to 15 years. 41,000 conscripts

Operational Numbers

Because numbers of vessels are kept in operational reserve, the Chinese version of the order of battle tends to show fewer ships than are counted by Western observers.

Bases

North Sea Fleet. Major bases: Qingdao (HQ), Huludao, Jianggezhuang, Guzhen Bay, Lushun, Xiaopingdao. Minor bases: Weihai Wei, Qingshan, Luda, Lien Yun, Ling Shan, Ta Ku Shan, Changshandao, Liuzhuang, Dayuanjiadun, Dalian
East Sea Fleet. Major bases: Ningbo (HQ), Zhoushan, Shanghai, Daxie, Fujan. Minor bases: Zhenjiangguan, Wusong, Xinxiang, Wenzhou, Sanduao, Xiamen, Xingxiang, Quandou, Wen Zhou SE, Wuhan, Dinghai, Jiaotou
South Sea Fleet. Major bases: Zhanjiang (HQ), Yulin, Huangfu, Hong Kong, Guangzhou (Canton). Minor bases: Haikou, Shantou, Humen, Kuanchuang, Tsun, Kuan Chung, Mawai, Beihai, Ping Tan, San Chou Shih, Tang-Chiah Huan, Longmen, Bailong, Dongcun, Baimajing, Xiachuandao, Yuchi

Organisation

Each of the North, East and South Sea Fleets has two submarine divisions, three DD/FF divisions and one MCMV division. The North also has one Amphibious Division, and the other Fleets have two each. The South has a Marine Infantry Brigade.

Coast Defence

A large number of HY-2 (CSSC-3) and HY-3 (CSSC-301) SSMs in 20 semi-fixed armoured sites. 35 Coastal Artillery regiments.

Equipment Procurement

Although often listed under the name of the designer, equipment has not necessarily been supplied direct from the parent company. It may have been acquired from a third party or by reverse engineering.

Training

The main training centres are:

Dalian: First Surface Vessel Academy, Political School
Canton: Second Surface Vessel Academy
Qingdao: Submarine Academy, Aviation School
Wuhan: Engineering College
Nanjing: Naval Staff College, Medical School, Electronic Engineering College
Yan Tai: Aviation Engineering College

Marines

There are two brigades based at Heieu and subordinate to the Navy. Each has three Infantry regiments and one Artillery regiment.

Naval Air Force

With 25,000 officers and men and over 800 aircraft, this is a considerable naval air force primarily land-based. There is a total of eight Divisions with 27 Regiments split between the three Fleets. Some aircraft are laid up unrepaired.

Air bases include:

North Sea Fleet: Dalian, Qingdao, Jinxi, Jiyuan, Laiyang, Jiaoxian, Xingtai, Laishan, Anyang, Changzhi, Liangxiang and Shan Hai Guan
East Sea Fleet: Danyang, Daishan, Shanghai, Ningbo, Luqiao, and Shitangqiao
South Sea Fleet: Foluo, Haikou, Lingshui, Sanya, Guiping, Jialaishi and Lingling

Strength of the Fleet

Type	Active (Reserve)	Building (Planned)
Aircraft Carrier	0	(1)
SSBN	1	(1)
SSB	1	—
SSN	5	1
SSG	1	—
Patrol Submarines	56 (8)	3 (2)
Destroyers	20	1 (1)
Frigates	41	2
Fast Attack Craft (Missile)	87	(1)
Fast Attack Craft (Gun)	98	—
Fast Attack Craft (Torpedo)	15	—
Fast Attack Craft (Patrol)	117	—
Patrol Craft	15	2
Minesweepers (Ocean)	27 (13)	—
Minesweepers (Coastal)	8	1
Mine Warfare Drones	4 (42)	—
Minelayer	1	—
Hovercraft	10	—
LSTs	18	1
LSMs	37	3
LCMs—LCUs	44 (230)	—
Training Ships	2	—
Troop Transports (AP/AH)	6	—
Submarine Support Ships	6	—
Salvage and Repair Ships	3	1
Supply Ships	29+	3
Fleet Replenishment Ships	3	3
Icebreakers	4	—

Mercantile Marine

Lloyd's Register of Shipping:
   3,288 vessels of 16,318,172 tons gross

DELETIONS

Submarines

1998	1 Romeo
1999	5 Romeo

Patrol Forces

1995-97	2 Haijiu, 26 Huangfen, 16 Houku, 5 Hainan, 48 Huchuan (some may be in unmaintained reserve)
1998-99	4 Huangfen, 5 Houku, 3 Hainan
2000	4 Huangfen, 5 Shanghai II

Amphibious Vessels

1997	5 Shan, 3 Yudao
1998-99	9 Yuliang

Major Auxiliaries

1997	3 Jinyou, 2 Mettawee

PENNANT LIST

Destroyers

105	Jinan
106	Xian
107	Yinchuan
108	Xining
109	Kaifeng
110	Dalian
112	Harbin
113	Qingdao
131	Nanjing
132	Hefei
133	Chongqing
134	Zunyi
136	Hangzhou
161	Changsha
162	Nanning
163	Nanchang
164	Guilin
165	Zhanjiang
166	Zhuhai
167	Shenzhen

Frigates

509	Chang De
510	Shaoxing
511	Nantong
512	Wuxi
513	Huayin
514	Zhenjiang
515	Xiamen
516	Jiujiang
517	Nanping
518	Jian
519	Changzhi
521	—
522	—
523	—
524	—
533	Ningpo
534	Jinhua
535	Huangshi
536	Wuhu
537	Zhoushan
539	Anqing
540	Huainan
541	Huaibei
542	Tongling
543	Dandong
544	Siping
545	Linfen

551	Maoming
552	Yibin
553	Shaoguan
554	Anshun
555	Zhaotong
557	Jishou
558	Zigong
559	Kangding
560	Dongguan
561	Shantou
562	Jiangmen
563	Zhaoqing

Principal Auxiliaries

81	Zhenghe
82	Shichang
920	Dazhi
121	Changxingdao
302	Chongmingdao
506	Yongxingdao
891	Dagushan
575	Taicang
615	Dongyun
953	Nancang

SUBMARINES

Strategic Missile Submarines

Note: A new design Type 094 is being developed with 16 tubes for the JL-2 (CSS-NX-5) missile. The first of a class of four is expected to start building at Huludao in 2000, but may be held up until the JL-2 missile has been fully developed.

1 XIA CLASS (TYPE 092) (SSBN)

Name	No	Builders	Laid down	Launched	Commissioned
XIA	406	Huludao Shipyard	1978	30 Apr 1981	1987

Displacement, tons: 6,500 dived
Dimensions, feet (metres): 393.6 × 33 × 26.2
    (120 × 10 × 8)
Main machinery: Nuclear; turbo-electric; 1 PWR; 90 MW; 1 shaft
Speed, knots: 22 dived
Complement: 140

Missiles: SLBM: 12 JL-1 (CSS-N-3); inertial guidance to 2,150 km *(1,160 n miles)*; warhead single nuclear 250 kT.
Torpedoes: 6—21 in *(533 mm)* bow tubes. Yu-3 (SET-65E); active/passive homing to 15 km *(8.1 n miles)* at 40 kt; warhead 205 kg.
Countermeasures: ESM: Type 921-A; radar warning.
Radars: Surface search: Snoop Tray; I-band.
Sonars: Trout Cheek; hull-mounted; active/passive search and attack; medium frequency.

Programmes: A second of class was reported launched in 1982 and an unconfirmed report suggests that one of the two was lost in an accident in 1985. A new design Type 094 is being developed with a longer range missile.
Modernisation: Started major update in late 1995 at Huludao, thought to include fitting improved JL-1A missile with increased range but this has not been confirmed.
Structure: Diving depth 300 m *(985 ft)*.
Operational: First test launch of the JL-1 missile took place on 30 April 1982 from a submerged pontoon near Huludao (Yellow Sea). Second launched on 12 October 1982, from the 'Golf' class trials submarine. The first firing from *Xia* was in 1985 and was unsuccessful (delaying final acceptance into service of the submarine) and it was not until 27 September 1988 that a satisfactory launch took place. Based in the North Sea Fleet at Huludao, but in refit until late 1998. Expected to be fully operational again sometime in 2000.

UPDATED   XIA

1988, Chinese Gazette

XIA   *1990 /* 0012177

1 GOLF CLASS (SSB)

200

Displacement, tons: 2,350 surfaced; 2,950 dived
Dimensions, feet (metres): 319.9 × 28.2 × 21.7
    (97.5 × 8.6 × 6.6)
Main machinery: Diesel-electric; 3 Type 37-D diesels; 6,000 hp (m) *(4.41 MW)*; 3 motors; 5,500 hp(m) *(4 MW)*; 3 shafts

Speed, knots: 17 surfaced; 13 dived
Range, miles: 6,000 surfaced at 15 kt
Complement: 86 (12 officers)

Missiles: SLBM: 1 JL-2 (CSS-NX-5); 2 or 3-stage solid fuel; inertial guidance to 8,000 km *(4,320 n miles)*; warhead 3 or 4 MIRV nuclear 90 kT or single nuclear 250 kT or 650 kT.

Torpedoes: 10—21 in *(533 mm)* tubes (6 bow, 4 stern). 12 Type Yu-4 (SAET-60); passive homing to 15 km *(8.1 n miles)* at 40 kt; warhead 400 kg.
Radars: Navigation: Snoop Plate; I-band.
Sonars: Pike Jaw; hull-mounted; active/passive search; medium frequency.

Programmes: Ballistic missile submarine similar but not identical to the deleted USSR 'Golf' class. Built at Dalian and launched in September 1966.
Modernisation: Refitted in 1995 to take the JL-2 missile.
Operational: This was the trials submarine for the JL-1 ballistic missile which was successfully launched to 1,800 km in October 1982. Continues to be available as a trials platform for the successor missile JL-2. Based in the Northern Fleet.

UPDATED

GOLF (with JL-2)   *(Scale 1 : 900), Ian Sturton /* 0012176

Attack Submarines (SSN)

Note: There are unconfirmed reports of Chinese interest in acquiring two Russian 'Akula' class SSNs.

0 + 1 (1) TYPE 093 (SSN)

Displacement, tons: 6,000 dived
Dimensions, feet (metres): 351 × 36 × 24.6
(107 × 11 × 7.5)
Main machinery: Nuclear: 2 PWR; 150 MW; 2 turbines; 1 shaft
Speed, knots: 30 dived
Complement: 100

Missiles: SLCM; SSM.
Torpedoes: 6—21 in *(533 mm tubes).*
Countermeasures: Decoys: ESM.
Radars: Surface search.
Sonars: Hull mounted passive/active; flank and towed arrays.

Programmes: Designed in conjunction with Russian experts. Prefabrication started in late 1994 and the first launch is expected in 2003 from Huludao shipyard. First in-service date 2005 with second of class to follow two years later. The programme dates may be affected, and therefore delayed, by the need to complete 'Han' class refits first.

Structure: Details given are speculative, based on the Russian Victor III design from which this submarine is reported to be derived. *UPDATED*

TYPE 093

1997, US Navy / 0012178

5 HAN CLASS (TYPE 091) (SSN)

No	Builders	Laid down	Launched	Commissioned
401	Huludao Shipyard	1967	26 Dec 1970	1 Aug 1974
402	Huludao Shipyard	1974	1977	Jan 1980
403	Huludao Shipyard	1980	1983	21 Sep 1984
404	Huludao Shipyard	1984	1987	Nov 1988
405	Huludao Shipyard	1987	8 Apr 1990	Dec 1990

Displacement, tons: 4,500 surfaced; 5,550 dived
Dimensions, feet (metres): 321.5; 347.8 *(403* onwards) × 32.8 × 24.2 *(98; 106 × 10 × 7.4)*
Main machinery: Nuclear; turbo-electric; 1 PWR; 90 MW; 1 shaft
Speed, knots: 25 dived; 12 surfaced
Complement: 75

Missiles: SSM YJ-82 (C-801); inertial cruise; active radar homing to 40 km *(22 n miles)* at 0.9 Mach; warhead 165 kg; sea-skimmer may be carried.
Torpedoes: 6—21 in *(533 mm)* bow tubes; combination of Yu-3 (SET-65E); active/passive homing to 15 km *(8.1 n miles)* at 40 kt; warhead 205 kg and Yu-1 (Type 53-51) to 9.2 km *(5 n miles)* at 39 kt or 3.7 km *(2 n miles)* at 51 kt; warhead 400 kg. 20 weapons.
Mines: 36 in lieu of torpedoes.
Countermeasures: ESM: Type 921-A; radar warning.
Radars: Surface search: Snoop Tray; I-band.
Sonars: Trout Cheek; hull-mounted; active/passive search and attack; medium frequency.
DUUX-5; passive ranging and intercept; low frequency.

Programmes: First of this class delayed by problems with the power plant. Although completed in 1974 she was not fully operational until the 1980s.
Modernisation: The basic Russian ESM equipment was replaced by a French design. A French intercept sonar set has been fitted.
Structure: From *403* onwards the hull has been extended by some 8 m although this was not to accommodate missile tubes as previously reported. SSMs may be fired from the torpedo tubes. Diving depth 300 m *(985 ft).*
Operational: In North Sea Fleet based at Jianggezhuang. The first pair were thought to be non-operational for a time in the late 1980s but have been extensively refitted and are back in service. Torpedoes are a combination of older straight running and more modern Russian homing types. *403* and *404* started mid-life refits in 1998 which completed in early 2000. The class has been more active in recent years and four are now operational. *UPDATED*

HAN 404

5/1996, Ships of the World

HAN 402

1990

Patrol Submarines

Notes: (1) The Russian 'Amur' class is a possible follow-on to the Kilos.
(2) An unknown number of midget submarines are reported building.

SONG 320

6/1999*, Ships of the World / 0056737

2 + 2 SONG CLASS (TYPE 039) (SSG)

No	Builders	Laid down	Launched	Commissioned
320	Wuhan Shipyard	1991	May 1994	1999
321	Wuhan Shipyard	1995	Nov 1999	2000
322	Wuhan Shipyard	1996	June 2000	2001
323	Wuhan Shipyard	1998	2001	2002

Displacement, tons: 1,700 surfaced; 2,250 dived
Dimensions, feet (metres): 246 × 27.6 × 17.5
(74.9 × 8.4 × 5.3)
Main machinery: Diesel-electric; 4 MTU 16V 396 SE; 6,092 hp
(m) *(4.48 MW)* diesels; 4 alternators; 1 motor; 1 shaft
Speed, knots: 15 surfaced; 22 dived
Complement: 60 (10 officers)

Missiles: SSM: YJ-82 (C-801); radar active homing to 40 km
(22 n miles) at 0.9 Mach; warhead 165 kg.
Torpedoes: 6—21 in *(533 mm)* tubes. Combination of
Yu-4 (SAET-60); passive homing to 15 km *(8.1 n miles)*
at 40 kt; warhead 400 kg and Yu-1 (Type 53-51) to
9.2 km *(5 n miles)* at 39 kt or 3.7 km *(2.1 n miles)* at 51 kt;
warhead 400 kg. Possible Shkval to be fitted.
Mines: In lieu of torpedoes.
Countermeasures: ESM: Type 921-A; radar warning.
Radars: Surface search: I-band.
Sonars: Bow-mounted; passive/active search and attack;
medium frequency.
Flank array; passive search; low frequency.

Programmes: First of class started sea trials in August 1995.
Second of class is expected to be an improvement as a result of
these trials. In series production.

SONG 320   6/1997, PLA(N) / 0012179

Structure: Comparable in size to 'Ming' class but with a single
skew propeller and an integrated spherical bow sonar. The
forward hydroplanes are mounted below the bridge which is
on a step lower than the part of the fin that contains the masts.
Some of the details are still speculative and later hulls of the
class may benefit from experience gained with the Kilos. The
diesel engines are likely to be reverse engineered. Sonars are
reported to be of French design.
Operational: The YJ-82 is the submarine launched version of the
C-801 and is fired from torpedo tubes. Reports of an anti-
submarine CY-1 air flight weapon are not confirmed. The Russian
Shkval 200 kT torpedo may be acquired.   ***UPDATED***

4 + (2) KILO CLASS (TYPE 877EKM/636) (SSK)

364	365	366	367

Displacement, tons: 2,325 surfaced; 3,076 dived
Dimensions, feet (metres): 242.1 × 32.5 × 21.7
(73.8 × 9.9 × 6.6)
Main machinery: Diesel-electric; 2 diesels; 3,650 hp(m)
(2.68 MW); 2 generators; 1 motor; 5,900 hp(m) *(4.34 MW)*;
1 shaft; 2 auxiliary motors; 204 hp(m) *(150 kW)*; 1 economic
speed motor; 130 hp(m) *(95 kW)*
Speed, knots: 17 dived; 10 surfaced
Complement: 52 (13 officers)

Torpedoes: 6—21 in *(533 mm)* tubes. 18 torpedoes.
Combination of TEST 71/96; wire-guided; active/passive
homing to 15 km *(8.1 n miles)* at 40 kt; warhead 205 kg and
53-65; passive wake homing to 19 km *(10.3 n miles)* at 45 kt;
warhead 300 kg.
Mines: 24 in lieu of torpedoes.
Countermeasures: ESM: Squid Head or Brick Pulp; radar warning.

Weapons control: MVU-119 EM Murena TFCS.
Radars: Surface search: Snoop Tray; I-band.
Sonars: Shark Teeth; hull-mounted; passive/active search and
attack; medium frequency.
Mouse Roar; hull-mounted; active attack; high frequency.

Programmes: Four of the class were ordered in mid-1993. First
one arrived by transporter ship in February 1995 having left
the Baltic six weeks earlier. Second one transported by the
same method arriving in November 1995. These first two were
Type 877 hulls built for a former Warsaw Pact country and
subsequently cancelled. The third and fourth are of the newer
Type 636 design built at Admiralty Yard, St Petersburg and
launched on 24 April 1997 and 18 June 1998 respectively.
The first of these two left the Baltic by transporter in November
1997 and arrived in January 1998. The second followed in
December 1998 arriving on 1 February 1999. Follow-on
orders are more likely to involve the newer 'Amur' class or Type
636M possibly with SS-N-27.

Structure: Latest export version of the elderly Kilo design and
has better weapon systems co-ordination and improved
accommodation than the earlier ships of the class. Normal
diving depth is 240 m with 300 m available in emergency. At
least two torpedo tubes can fire wire-guided weapons. An SA-
N-8 SAM launcher may be fitted on top of the fin. Some
modifications have been carried out after arrival in China
including a possible new ESM. SSMs may be fitted in due
course.
Operational: Based at Xiangshan in the East Sea Fleet. The
torpedoes are far more advanced than those previously
available to China. The first pair have been reported as having
propulsion/battery problems, due to Chinese cost cutting in
the initial fitting of equipment.
Opinion: This programme complements the 'Song' and 'Ming'
classes, allowing a more rapid replacement of the ageing
Romeos than could be achieved with indigenous build
alone.

UPDATED

KILO 367   6/1998, V Osintsev / 0017711

KILO 364   6/1998 / 0017712

18 + 1 MING CLASS (TYPE 035) (SS)

232	342	352	353	354	356	357	358	359
360	361	362	363	305	306	307	308	309

Displacement, tons: 1,584 surfaced; 2,113 dived
Dimensions, feet (metres): 249.3 × 24.9 × 16.7
(76 × 7.6 × 5.1)
Main machinery: Diesel-electric; 2 diesels; 5,200 hp(m)
(3.82 MW); 2 shafts
Speed, knots: 15 surfaced; 18 dived; 10 snorting
Range, miles: 8,000 at 8 kt snorting; 330 at 4 kt dived
Complement: 57 (10 officers)

Torpedoes: 8—21 in *(533 mm)* (6 fwd, 2 aft) tubes. Combination of Yu-4 (SAET-60); passive homing to 15 km *(8.1 n miles)* at

40 kt; warhead 400 kg, and Yu-1 (53-51) to 9.2 km *(5 n miles)* at 39 kt or 3.7 km *(2.1 n miles)* at 51 kt; warhead 400 kg; 16 weapons.
Mines: 32 in lieu of torpedoes.
Radars: Surface search: Snoop Tray; I-band.
Sonars: Pike Jaw; hull-mounted; active/passive search and attack; medium frequency.
DUUX 5; passive ranging and intercept; low frequency.

Programmes: First three completed between 1971 and 1979 one of which was scrapped after a fire. These were Type ES5C/D. Building resumed at Wuhan Shipyard in 1987 at the rate of one per year to a modified design ES5E. The programme was thought to have ended with

hull number 14 *(363)* launched in May 1996, but 305 was launched in June 1997 followed by 306 in September 1997, 307 in May 1998, 308 in October 1998 and 309 in November 1999. One more is expected to complete in 2000.
Structure: Diving depth, 300 m *(985 ft)*. Only the later models have the DUUX 5 sonar.
Operational: Thirteen are based in the North Sea Fleet at Lushun, Qingdao and Xiapingdao. From 305 onwards, based in the South Sea Fleet. Fitted with Magnavox SATNAV.
UPDATED

MING 359
12/1998*, Ships of the World / 0056738

1 MODIFIED ROMEO CLASS (TYPE 033G) (SSG)

351

Displacement, tons: 1,650 surfaced; 2,100 dived
Dimensions, feet (metres): 251.3 × 22 × 17.1
(76.6 × 6.7 × 5.2)
Main machinery: Diesel-electric; 2 Type 37-D diesels; 4,000 hp (m) *(2.94 MW)*; 2 motors; 2,700 hp(m) *(1.98 MW)*; 2 creep motors; 2 shafts
Speed, knots: 13 dived; 15 surfaced; 10 snorting
Complement: 54 (10 officers)

Missiles: SSM: 6 YJ-1 (Eagle Strike) (C-801); three launchers either side of fin; inertial cruise; active radar homing to 40 km *(22 n miles)* at 0.9 Mach; warhead 165 kg; sea-skimmer. May be replaced by C-802 in due course.
Torpedoes: 8—21 in *(533 mm)* (6 bow, 2 stern) tubes.
Mines: 28 in lieu of torpedoes.
Radars: Surface search: Snoop Plate and Snoop Tray; I-band.
Sonars: Hercules or Pike Jaw; hull-mounted; active/passive search and attack; medium frequency.

Programmes: This design, designated ES5G, is a modified Romeo (Wuhan) rebuilt as a trials SSM platform.

MOD ROMEO 351
6/1987, Xinhua

Structure: The six missile tubes are built into the casing abreast the fin and elevate to fire. To provide target acquisition an additional radar mast (Snoop Tray) is mounted between the two periscopes.
Operational: Has to surface to fire missiles although trials are reported to include an encapsulated missile which is launched

from a torpedo tube while dived. Based in the North Sea Fleet and reported still doing trials in 1999. Clearly there is no intention to fit this type of missile tube in other classes, and the submarine may soon be scrapped.
UPDATED

32 (+ 8 RESERVE) ROMEO CLASS (TYPE 033) (SS)

256-260	268-272	275-280	
286-287	291-304	343-349	355

Displacement, tons: 1,475 surfaced; 1,830 dived
Dimensions, feet (metres): 251.3 × 22 × 17.1
(76.6 × 6.7 × 5.2)
Main machinery: Diesel-electric; 2 Type 37-D diesels; 4,000 hp (m) *(2.94 MW)*; 2 motors; 2,700 hp(m) *(1.98 MW)*; 2 creep motors; 2 shafts
Speed, knots: 15.2 surfaced; 13 dived; 10 snorting
Range, miles: 9,000 at 9 kt surfaced
Complement: 54 (10 officers)

Torpedoes: 8—21 in *(533 mm)* (6 bow, 2 stern) tubes. Combination of Yu-4 (SAET-60); passive homing to 15 km

(8.1 n miles) at 40 kt; warhead 400 kg and Yu-1 (53-51) to 9.2 km *(5 n miles)* at 39 kt or 3.7 km *(2.1 n miles)* at 55 kt; warhead 400 kg. 14 weapons.
Mines: 28 in lieu of torpedoes.
Radars: Surface search: Snoop Plate or Snoop Tray; I-band.
Sonars: Hercules or Tamir 5; hull-mounted; active/passive search and attack; high frequency.
Thomson Sintra DUUX 5 intercept in some of the class.

Programmes: The first boats of this class were built at Jiangnan SY, Shanghai in mid-1962 with Wuhan being used later. The basic 'Romeo' class design has evolved from the Type 031 (ES3B). Construction stopped around 1987 with the resumption of the 'Ming' class programme. A total of 84 was built.

Modernisation: Battery refits are being done and the more modern boats have French passive ranging sonar.
Structure: Diving depth, 300 m *(984 ft)*. There are probably some dimensional variations between newer and older ships of the class.
Operational: Operational numbers are declining rapidly as large numbers of these obsolete submarines are being scrapped. Few are now kept in reserve. ASW capability is virtually non-existent. The submarines are split between the three Fleets.
Sales: Seven to North Korea in 1973-75. Two to Egypt in 1982, two in 1984. All new construction.
UPDATED

ROMEO 272
3/1995, van Ginderen Collection

AIRCRAFT CARRIERS

Note: After six years of discussions and negotiations about a new aircraft carrier, the Russian Nevskoye Design Bureau was given a contract in about 1994 to design an aircraft carrier based on Chinese requirements. Preparatory work may have started at Dalian Shipyard in August 1996 and it was reported in a Hong Kong newspaper in February 2000 that a 48,000 ton ship was to be built to enter service in 2005. The ship is to carry 24 Russian-built Flanker aircraft if the report is correct.

DESTROYERS

1 + 1 (2) SOVREMENNY CLASS (TYPE 956E) (DDG)

Name	No	Builders	Laid down	Launched	Commissioned
HANGZHOU (ex-*Vazhny*, ex-*Yekaterinbugr*)	136 (ex-698)	North Yard, St Petersburg	4 Nov 1988	23 May 1994	25 Dec 1999
— (ex-*Alexandr Nevsky*)	—	North Yard, St Petersburg	22 Feb 1989	16 Apr 1999	Dec 2000

Displacement, tons: 7,940 full load
Dimensions, feet (metres): 511.8 × 56.8 × 21.3
(156 × 17.3 × 6.5)
Main machinery: 4 KVN boilers; 2 GTZA-674 turbines;
99,500 hp(m) *(73.13 MW)* sustained; 2 shafts; bow thruster
Speed, knots: 32. **Range, miles:** 2,400 at 32 kt; 6,500 at 20 kt;
14,000 at 14 kt
Complement: 296 (25 officers) plus 60 spare

Missiles: SSM: 8 Raduga SS-N-22 Sunburn (Moskit 3M-80E)
(2 quad) launchers ❶; active/passive radar homing to 160 km
(87 n miles) at 2.5 *(4.5 for attack)* Mach; warhead 300 kg; sea-
skimmer.
SAM: 2 SA-N-7 Gadfly (Uragan) ❷ 9M38M1 Smerch; command/
semi-active radar and IR homing to 25 km *(13.5 n miles)* at
3 Mach; warhead 70 kg; altitude 15-14,020 m *(50-46,000 ft)*;
44 missiles. Multiple channels of fire.
Guns: 4—130 mm/70 (2 twin) AK 130 ❸; 35-45 rds/min to
29.5 km *(16 n miles)*; weight of shell 33.4 kg.
4—30 mm/65 AK 630 ❹; 6 barrels per mounting; 3,000 rds/
min combined to 2 km.
Torpedoes: 4—21 in *(533 mm)* (2 twin) tubes ❺.
A/S mortars: 2 RBU 1000 6-barrelled ❻; range 1,000 m;
warhead 55 kg; 120 rockets carried. Torpedo
countermeasure.
Mines: Mine rails for up to 40.
Countermeasures: Decoys: 8 PK 10 and 2 PK 2 chaff launchers.
ESM/ECM: 4 Foot Ball. 6 Half Cup laser warner.
Weapons control: 1 China optronic director and laser
rangefinder ❼. Band Stand ❽ datalink for SS-N-22. Bell Nest,
2 Light Bulb and 2 Tee Pump datalinks.
Radars: Air search: Top Plate ❾; 3D; D/E-band.
Surface search: 3 Palm Frond ❿; I-band.
Fire control: 6 Front Dome ⓫; F-band (for SA-N-7). Kite Screech
⓬; H/I/K-band (for 130 mm guns). 2 Bass Tilt ⓭; H/I-band
(for 30 mm guns).
Sonars: Bull Horn (Platina) and Whale Tongue; hull-mounted;
active search and attack; medium frequency.

Helicopters: 2 Harbin Zhi-9A Haitun ⓮ or Kamov KA-28 Helix.

Programmes: After prolonged negotiations, a contract was
signed in September 1996 for two uncompleted Russian
'Sovremenny' class destroyers. These are hulls 18 and 19.
A third of class may also be acquired in due course. Progress
was held up for a time because China wanted KA-28
helicopters included, and the Russians demanded extra

payment for the aircraft. Deleted Russian units of the class may
have been cannibalised for some equipment.
Structure: These are the first Chinese warships to have a data
system link. The optronic director is probably a Chinese version
of Squeeze Box.

Operational: First one arrived Dinghai on 16 February 2000.
Opinion: A lack of area air defence is one of the greatest PLAN
weaknesses and these ships are needed to provide escorts for
heavy units, as well as providing China with supersonic SSMs.
UPDATED

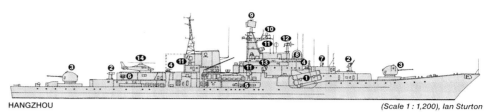

HANGZHOU   *(Scale 1 : 1,200), Ian Sturton*

HANGZHOU   1/2000*, *Curt Borgenstam* / 0056739

HANGZHOU   1/2000*, *Curt Borgenstam* / 0056740

HANGZHOU   1/2000*, *Curt Borgenstam* / 0056741

2 LUHU (TYPE 052) CLASS (DDG)

Name	No
HARBIN	112
QINGDAO	113

Builders	Laid down	Launched	Commissioned
Jiangnan Shipyard	Nov 1990	Oct 1991	July 1994
Jiangnan Shipyard	Jan 1993	Oct 1993	Mar 1996

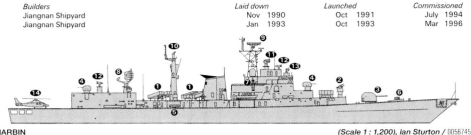

HARBIN   (Scale 1 : 1,200), Ian Sturton / 0056745

Displacement, tons: 4,600 full load
Measurement, tons: 472.4 × 52.5 × 16.7
   (144 × 16 × 5.1)
Main machinery: CODOG: 2 GE LM 2500 gas turbines
   (112); 55,000 hp *(41 MW)* sustained or 2 Ukraine gas
   turbines (113) 48,600 hp(m) *(35.7 MW)*; 2 MTU 12V 1163
   TB83 diesels; 8,840 hp(m) *(6.5 MW)* sustained; 2 shafts; cp
   props
Speed, knots: 31. **Range, miles:** 5,000 at 15 kt
Complement: 260 (40 officers)

Missiles: SSM: 8 YJ-1 (Eagle Strike) (C-801) (CSS-N-4 Sardine) **❶**;
   active radar homing to 40 km *(22 n miles)* (or 120 km *(66 n
   miles)* for C-802 (CSS-N-8 Saccade)) at 0.9 Mach; warhead
   165 kg; sea-skimmer.
SAM: 1 HQ-7 (Crotale) octuple launcher **❷**; CSA-4; line of sight
   guidance to 13 km *(7 n miles)* at 2.4 Mach; warhead 14 kg.
Guns: 2—3.9 in *(100 mm)*/56 (twin) **❸**; 18 rds/min to 22 km
   (12 n miles); weight of shell 15 kg.
   8—37 mm/63 Type 76A (4 twin) **❹**; 180 rds/min to 8.5 km
   (4.6 n miles) anti-aircraft; weight of shell 1.42 kg.
Torpedoes: 6—324 mm Whitehead B515 (2 triple) tubes **❺**. Yu-2
   (Mk 46 Mod 1); active/passive homing to 11 km *(5.9 n miles)*
   at 40 kt; warhead 44 kg.
A/S mortars: 2 FQF 2500 **❻** 12-tubed fixed launchers; range
   1,200 m; warhead 34 kg. 120 rockets.
Countermeasures: Decoys: 2 SRBOC Mk 36; 6-barrelled chaff
   launchers. 2 China 26-barrelled chaff launchers.

ESM/ECM: BM 8610; (Signaal Rapids/Ramses); intercept and
   jammer.
Combat data systems: Thomson-CSF TAVITAC; action data
   automation. SATCOM. Link W.
Weapons control: 2 GDG-775 optronic directors **❼**.
Radars: Air search: Hai Ying or God Eye **❽**; G-band.
Air/surface search: Thomson-CSF TSR 3004 Sea Tiger **❾**;
   E/F-band.
Surface search: China ESR 1 **❿**; I-band.
Navigation: Racal Decca 1290; I-band.
Fire control: Type 347G **⓫**; I-band (for SSM and 100 mm).
   Two EFR 1 Rice Lamp **⓬**; I-band (for 37 mm).
   Thomson-CSF Castor II **⓭**; I/J-band (for Crotale).
Sonars: DUBV-23; Hull-mounted; active search and attack;
   medium frequency.
DUBV-43 VDS; active attack; medium frequency.

Helicopters: 2 Harbin Zhi-9A Haitun **⓮**.

Programmes: Class of two ordered in 1985 but delayed by
   priority being given to export orders for Thailand.
Structure: The most notable features are the SAM launcher,
   improved radar and fire-control systems and a modern
   100 mm gun. Gas turbines for the second of class came from
   the Ukraine. The HQ-7 launcher is a Chinese copy of Crotale.
   DCN Samahe 110N helo handling system.
Operational: First of class based in North Sea Fleet at Guzhen
   Bay, second in the East Sea Fleet at Jianggezhuang.

UPDATED

HARBIN   8/1999*, Ships of the World / 0056746

QINGDAO   5/1998 / 0017715

QINGDAO   5/1998*, Sattler/Steele / 0056747

QINGDAO   5/1998*, Sattler/Steele / 0056748

15 LUDA I/II (TYPE 051) CLASS (DDG)

Name	No	Name	No	Name	No
JINAN	105 (Type II)	DALIAN	110 (Type II)	CHANGSHA	161
XIAN	106	NANJING	131	NANNING	162
YINCHUAN	107	HEFEI	132	NANCHANG	163
XINING	108	CHONGQING	133	GUILIN	164
KAIFENG	109	ZUNYI	134	ZHANJIANG	165

Displacement, tons: 3,250 standard; 3,670 full load
Dimensions, feet (metres): 433.1 × 42 × 15.1
(132 × 12.8 × 4.6)
Main machinery: 2 or 4 boilers; 2 turbines; 72,000 hp(m)
(53 MW); 2 shafts
Speed, knots: 32. **Range, miles:** 2,970 at 18 kt
Complement: 280 (45 officers)

Missiles: SSM: 6 HY-2 (C-201) (CSS-C-3A Seersucker) (2 triple)
launchers ❶; active radar or IR homing to 95 km *(51 n miles)* at
0.9 Mach; warhead 513 kg or 8 C-802 (CSS-N-8 Saccade)
(Kaifeng) ❷; active radar homing to 120 km *(66 n miles)* at
0.9 Mach; warhead 165 kg; sea skimmer.
SAM: HQ-7 (Crotale) octuple launcher *(Kaifeng and Xian)* ❸
CSA-4; line of sight guidance to 13 km *(7 n miles)* at 2.4 Mach;
warhead 14 kg.
Guns: 4 (Type I) or 2 (Type II) USSR 5.1 in *(130 mm)*/58 (2 twin)
(Type I) ❹; 17 rds/min to 29 km *(16 n miles)*; weight of shell
33.4 kg.
8 China 57 mm/70 (4 twin); 120 rds/min to 12 km *(6.5 n
miles)*; weight of shell 6.31 kg. These guns are fitted in some of
the class, the others have 37 mm.
8 China 37 mm/63 (4 twin) (some Type I) ❺; 180 rds/min to
8.5 km *(4.6 n miles)*; weight of shell 1.42 kg.
8 USSR 25 mm/60 (4 twin) ❻; 270 rds/min to 3 km *(1.6 n
miles)* anti-aircraft; weight of shell 0.34 kg.
Torpedoes: 6—324 mm Whitehead B515 (2 triple tubes) (fitted
in some Type I); Yu-2 (Mk 46 Mod 1); active/passive homing to
11 km *(5.9 n miles)* at 40 kt; warhead 44 kg.
A/S mortars: 2 FQF 2500 12-tubed fixed launchers ❼;
120 rockets; range 1,200 m; warhead 34 kg. Similar in design
to the RBU 1200.
Depth charges: 2 or 4 BMB projectors; 2 or 4 racks (Type I).
Mines: 38.
Countermeasures: Decoys: Chaff launchers (fitted to some).
ESM: Jug Pair (RW-23-1); 2-18 GHz; radar warning.
Combat data systems: Thomson-CSF TAVITAC with Vega FCS
(in some).
Radars: Air search: Knife Rest or Cross Slot; A-band or Bean
Sticks or Pea Sticks ❽; E/F-band.
Rice Screen ❾ (on mainmast in some); 3D; G-band. Similar to
Hughes SPS-39A.
Surface search: Eye Shield ❿; E-band or Thomson-CSF Sea
Tiger; E/F-band.
Square Tie (not in all); I-band.
Navigation: Fin Curve or Racal Decca 1290; I-band.
Fire control: Wasp Head (also known as Wok Won) or Type 343
Sun Visor B (series 2) ⓫; G/H-band.
2 Rice Lamp (series 2) or 2 Type 347G ⓬; I-band.
Thomson-CSF Castor II ⓭; I/J-band (for Crotale).
IFF: High Pole.
Sonars: Pegas 2M and Tamir 2; hull-mounted; active search and
attack; high frequency.
Helicopters: 2 Harbin Z-9A (Dauphin) ⓮ (Type II).

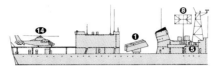

TYPE I   *(Scale 1 : 1,200), Ian Sturton* / 0056749

TYPE II   *(Scale 1 : 1,200), Ian Sturton* / 0056750   KAIFENG   *(Scale 1 : 1,200), Ian Sturton* / 0056751

HEFEI   *6/1999*, Ships of the World* / 0056752

Programmes: The first Chinese-designed destroyers of such a
capability to be built. First of class completed in 1971. 105 to
110 built at Luda; 131 to 134 at Shanghai and 161 to 165 at
Dalian. Similar to the deleted USSR 'Kotlin' class. The
programme was much retarded after 1971 by drastic cuts in
the defence budget. In early 1977 building of series two of this
class was put in hand and includes those after 109, with the
latest 164 completed in April 1990, and 165 in October 1991.
The order of completion was 105, 160 (scrapped), 106, 161,
107, 162, 131, 108, 132, 109, 163, 110, 133, 134, 164 and
165. Subsequent ships are Type III and merit a separate entry.
Modernisation: First of class 105 completed a major refit in
1987 as a Type II trials ship, with the after armament replaced
by a twin helicopter hangar and deck. Second converted to
Type II was 110 in 1996. Most Type I may be fitted with HQ-7

SAM in due course although newer classes of destroyer are
being given the priority. C-802 missiles retrofitted in *Kaifeng*
and probably in others to come.
Structure: Electronics vary in later ships. Some ships have
57 mm guns, others 37 mm. Type II may have Alcatel
'Safecopter' landing aid. Thomsea combat data system
including Vega FCS has been installed in at least two of the
class and SAM is fitted in *Kaifeng* and *Xian* in X gun position.
Operational: Capable of foreign deployment, although
command and control is limited. Underway refuelling is
practised. Deployment; 105 series in North Sea Fleet at Yuchi;
131 series in East Sea Fleet at Dalian; 161 series in South Sea
Fleet at Zhanjiang. 160 was damaged by an explosion in 1978,
and was scrapped.

UPDATED

JINAN   *1/1994** / 0056753

YINCHUAN   *8/1999*, Ships of the World* / 0056754

1 LUDA III CLASS (DDG)

Name	No	Builders	Laid down	Launched	Commissioned
ZHUHAI	166 (168 out of area)	Dalian Shipyard	Aug 1988	Oct 1990	Oct 1991

Displacement, tons: 3,250 standard; 3,730 full load
Dimensions, feet (metres): 433.1 × 42 × 15.3
(132 × 12.8 × 4.7)
Main machinery: 2 boilers; 2 turbines; 72,000 hp(m) *(53 MW)*;
2 shafts
Speed, knots: 32. **Range, miles:** 2,970 at 18 kt
Complement: 280 (45 officers)

Missiles: SSM: 8 YJ-1 (Eagle Strike) (C-801) (CSS-N-4
Sardine) (4 twin) launchers **❶**; active radar homing to
40 km *(22 n miles)* at 0.9 Mach; warhead 165 kg; sea-
skimmer.
A/S: The after set of launchers may also be used in due course for
CY-1 anti-submarine missiles; range 8-15 km *(4.4-8.3 n miles)*;
payload anti-submarine torpedoes.
Guns: 4 USSR 5.1 in *(130 mm)*/58 (2 twin) **❷**; 17 rds/min to
29 km *(16 n miles)*; weight of shell 33.4 kg.
8 China 37 mm/63 Type 76A (4 twin) **❸**; 180 rds/min to
8.5 km *(4.6 n miles)*; weight of shell 1.42 kg.
Torpedoes: 6—324 mm Whitehead B515 (2 triple tubes) **❹**; Yu-2
(Mk 46 Mod 1); active/passive homing to 11 km *(5.9 n miles)*
at 40 kt; warhead 44 kg.
A/S mortars: 2 FQF 2500 12-tubed fixed launchers **❺**;
120 rockets; range 1,200 m; warhead 34 kg. Similar in design
to the RBU 1200.

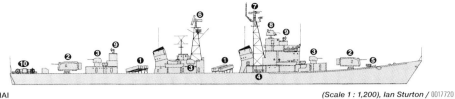

ZHUHAI
(Scale 1 : 1,200), Ian Sturton / 0017720

Countermeasures: Decoys: 2—15 tubed fixed launchers for
chaff and IR decoys.
ESM: Jug Pair (RW-23-1); radar warning.
Combat data systems: Thomson-CSF TAVITAC.
Radars: Air search: Rice Screen **❻**; 3D; G-band. Similar to Hughes
SPS-39A.
Surface search: China ESR 1 **❼**; I-band.
Navigation: Racal Decca 1290; I-band.
Fire control: Type 343 Sun Visor B **❽**; G/H-band.
2 Type 347G **❾**; I-band.
IFF: High Pole.
Sonars: DUBV 23; hull-mounted; active search and attack;
medium frequency.

DUBV 43 VDS **❿**; active search and attack; medium
frequency.

Programmes: Updated Luda design.
Structure: Modified after SSM launchers which may fire the CY-1
anti-submarine missile in due course. The VDS sonar is a copy
of DUBV 43.
Operational: South Seas Fleet based at Zhanjiang. There have
long been reports of a ballistic trajectory ASW weapon CY-1
and the different types of SSM launchers in *Zhuhai* indicate
that the weapon may be developed in due course. Different
pennant number used for foreign deployments.
UPDATED

ZHUHAI
12/1998*, Ships of the World / 0056755

ZHUHAI
5/1997, US Navy / 0012181

1 + (1) LUHAI CLASS (DDG)

Name	No
SHENZHEN	167

Builders	Laid down	Launched	Commissioned
Dalian Shipyard	July 1996	16 Oct 1997	4 Jan 1999

Displacement, tons: 6,000 full load
Dimensions, feet (metres): 502 × 54.1 × 19.7
(153 × 16.5 × 6)
Main machinery: CODOG; 2 Ukraine gas turbines; 48,600 hp(m)
(35.7 MW); 2 MTU 12V 1163 TB 83 diesels; 8,840 hp(m)
(6.5 MW) sustained; 2 shafts; cp props
Speed, knots: 29. **Range, miles:** 14,000 at 15 kt
Complement: 250 (42 officers)

Missiles: SSM: 16 C-802 (CSS-N-8 Saccade) ❶; active radar
homing to 120 km *(66 n miles)* at 0.9 Mach; warhead 165 kg;
sea skimmer.

SAM: 1 HQ-7 (Crotale) octuple launcher ❷; CSA-N-4 line of sight
guidance to 13 km *(7 n miles)* at 2.4 Mach; warhead 14 kg.
Possible reloading hatch aft of the HQ-7 launcher.
Guns: 2—3.9 in *(100 mm)*/56 (twin) ❸; 18 rds/min to 22 km
(12 n miles); weight of shell 15 kg.
8—37 mm/63 Type 76A (4 twin) ❹; 180 rds/min to 8.5 km
(4.6 n miles) anti-aircraft; weight of shell 1.42 kg.
Torpedoes: 6—324 mm B515 (2 triple) tubes ❺ Yu-2/5/6;
active/passive homing to 11 km *(5.9 n miles)* at 40 kt;
warhead 44 kg.
Countermeasures: Decoys 2 Mk 36 SRBOC; chaff launchers ❻.
ESM/ECM. China intercept and jammer.

Combat data systems: Thomson CSF TAVITAC; SATCOM.
Radars: Air search: Rice Screen ❼ 3D; G-band.
Air/surface search: China Type 363 ❽; E/F-band.
Fire control: Type 347G ❾; I-band (for SSM and 100 mm).
2 EFR-1 Rice Lamp ❿; I-band (for 37 mm).
China Castor II ⓫; I/J-band (for HQ-7).
Sonars: DUBV-23; hull mounted; active search and attack;
medium frequency.

Helicopters: 2 Harbin Zhi-9A Haitun ⓬ or Kamov Ka-28 Helix.

Programmes: Follow-on from the 'Luhu' class. Expected second
of class had not started building by early 2000.
Structure: Apart from the second funnel and octuple SSM
launchers, there are broad similarities with the smaller Luhu.
Anti-aircraft guns are all mounted aft allowing more space in
front of the bridge which seems to show a reloading hatch for
HQ-7.
Operational: Sea trials started in September 1998 having been
delayed by damage caused to the starboard side of the ship
while alongside in gale force winds. Based at Zhanjiang in
South Sea Fleet.

UPDATED

SHENZHEN
(Scale 1 : 1,200), Ian Sturton / 0056742

SHENZHEN
5/1999*, Ships of the World / 0056743

FRIGATES

6 + 2 JIANGWEI II CLASS (FFG)

Name	No
—	521 (ex-597)
—	522
—	523
—	524
—	564
—	565
—	—
—	—

Builders	Laid down	Launched	Commissioned
Hudong Shipyard	Oct 1996	10 Aug 1997	Nov 1998
Hudong Shipyard	Dec 1996	8 Aug 1997	Feb 1999
Hudong Shipyard	June 1997	10 Aug 1998	Oct 1999
Hudong Shipyard	Dec 1997	Dec 1998	Nov 1999
Huangpu Shipyard	Dec 1997	Oct 1998	Dec 1999
Huangpu Shipyard	May 1998	Apr 1999	Mar 2000
Hudong Shipyard	Dec 1999	Feb 2001	Dec 2001
Huangpu Shipyard	Mar 2000	Mar 2001	Jan 2002

Displacement, tons: 2,250 full load
Dimensions, feet (metres): 366.5 × 40.7 × 15.7
(111.7 × 12.4 × 4.8)
Main machinery: 2 Type 18E 390 diesels; 24,000 hp(m)
(17.65 MW) sustained; 2 shafts
Speed, knots: 27. **Range, miles:** 4,000 at 18 kt
Complement: 170

Missiles: SSM: 6 or 8 YJ-1 (Eagle Strike) (C-801) (CSS-N-4
Sardine) or C-802 (2 triple) launchers ❶; active radar homing to

40 km *(22 n miles)* or 120 km *(66 n miles)* (C-802) at 0.9 Mach;
warhead 165 kg; sea-skimmer.
SAM: 1 HQ-7 (Crotale) octuple launcher ❷; CSA-N-4 line of sight
guidance to 13 km *(7 n miles)* at 2.4 Mach; warhead 14 kg.
Guns: 2 China 3.9 in *(100 mm)*/56 (twin) ❸; 18 rds/min to
22 km *(12 n miles)*; weight of shell 15.9 kg.
8 China 37 mm/63 Type 76A (4 twin) ❹; 180 rds/min to
8.5 km *(4.6 n miles)* anti-aircraft; weight of shell 1.42 kg.
A/S mortars: 2 RBU 1200 ❺; 5-tubed fixed launchers; range
1,200 m; warhead 34 kg.
Countermeasures: Decoys: 2 SRBOC Mk 36 6-barrelled chaff
launchers ❻; 2 China 26-barrelled chaff launchers ❼.
ESM: RWD8; intercept.
ECM: NJ81-3; jammer. Similar to Scimitar.
Radars: Air/surface search: Type 360 ❽; E/F-band.
Fire control: Type 347G ❾; I-band (for SSM and 100 mm).
China Castor II ❿; I/J-band (for SAM). EFR-1 ⓫; I/J-band (for
37 mm).
Navigation: Type 360.
Sonars: Echo Type 5; hull-mounted; active search and attack;
medium frequency.

Helicopters: 2 Harbin Z-9A (Dauphin) ⓬.

Programmes: Follow-on to the 'Jiangwei' class, building some
four years later. Production has been increased with the
inclusion of a second shipyard. The first two ships were
intended for Pakistan but funding was not completed in
time and later ships of the class may replace them for
transfer.
Structure: An improved SAM system, updated fire-control radars
and a redistribution of the after anti-aircraft guns are the
obvious differences from the original Jiangwei. First two ships
have two quad SSM launchers.
Sales: Probably two for Pakistan in due course, but with some
changes in equipment fitted.

UPDATED

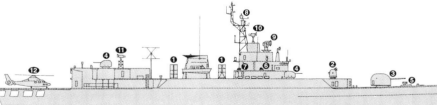

JIANGWEI II
(Scale 1 : 900), Ian Sturton / 0056756

JIANGWEI II
4/1999*, John Webber / 0056757

4 JIANGWEI I (TYPE 053 H2G) CLASS (FFG)

Name	No	Builders	Laid down	Launched	Completed
ANQING	539	Hudong Shipyard	Nov 1990	July 1991	Dec 1991
HUAINAN	540 (548 out of area)	Hudong Shipyard	Jan 1991	Oct 1991	July 1992
HUAIBEI	541	Hudong Shipyard	July 1992	Apr 1993	Aug 1993
TONGLING	542	Hudong Shipyard	Dec 1992	Sep 1993	Apr 1994

Displacement, tons: 2,250 full load
Dimensions, feet (metres): 366.5 × 40.7 × 15.7
(111.7 × 12.4 × 4.8)
Main machinery: 2 Type 18E 390 diesels; 24,000 hp(m)
(17.65 MW) sustained; 2 shafts
Speed, knots: 27. **Range, miles:** 4,000 at 18 kt
Complement: 170

Missiles: SSM: 6 YJ-1 (Eagle Strike) (C-801) (CSS-N-4 Sardine) or
C-802 (2 triple) launchers **1**; active radar homing to 40 km
(22 n miles) or 120 km *(66 n miles)* (C-802) at 0.9 Mach;
warhead 165 kg; sea-skimmer.
SAM: 1 HQ-61 sextuple launcher **2**; RF 61 (CSA-N-2); semi-active
radar homing to 10 km *(5.5 n miles)* at 2 Mach. Similar to Sea
Sparrow. May be replaced in due course.
Guns: 2 China 3.9 in *(100 mm)*/56 (twin) **3**; 18 rds/min to
22 km *(12 n miles)*; weight of shell 15.9 kg.
8 China 37 mm/63 Type 76A (4 twin) **4**; 180 rds/min to
8.5 km *(4.6 n miles)* anti-aircraft; weight of shell 1.42 kg.
A/S mortars: 2 RBU 1200 **5**; 5-tubed fixed launchers; range
1,200 m; warhead 34 kg.
Countermeasures: Decoys: 2 SRBOC Mk 36 6-barrelled chaff
launchers **6**. 2 China Type 945 26-barrelled chaff launchers
7.
ESM: RWD8; intercept.
ECM: NJ81-3; jammer. Similar to Scimitar.
Radars: Air/surface search: Knife Rest **8**; G-band.
Fire control: Sun Visor (with Wasp Head B) **9**; I-band.
Fog Lamp **10**; I/J-band (for SAM). Rice Lamp **11**; I/J-band.
Navigation: Racal Decca 1290 and China Type 360; I-band.
Sonars: Echo Type 5; hull-mounted; active search and attack;
medium frequency.

Helicopters: 2 Harbin Z-9A (Dauphin) **12**.

Programmes: Programme started in 1988. First one conducted
sea trials in late 1991. Four of the class built before the design
moved on to the Jiangwei II.
Modernisation: SAM system has been unsatisfactory and may
be replaced in due course.

ANQING   *(Scale 1 : 900), Ian Sturton*

HUAINAN   6/1999 * / 0056759

Structure: The sextuple launcher is a multiple launch
SAM system using the CSA-N-2 missile. Early reports indicated
a possible ASW capability but this was not correct.
There is a possibility that CY-1 A/S missiles may in due
course also be launched from the YJ-1 launchers as in
Luda III.
Operational: All based in the East Sea Fleet at Dinghai.
UPDATED

HUAIBEI   6/1999 *, Ships of the World / 0056760

HUAINAN   6/1994, Ships of the World

27 JIANGHU I (TYPE 053) CLASS (FFG)

Name	No	Name	No	Name	No	Name	No
CHANG DE	509	JIUJIANG	516	LINFEN	545	ZIGONG	558
SHAOXING	510	NANPING	517	MAOMING	551	KANGDING	559
NANTONG	511	JIAN	518	YIBIN	552	DONGGUAN	560
WUXI	512	CHANGZHI	519	SHAOGUAN	553	SHANTOU	561
HUAYIN	513	NINGPO	533	ANSHUN	554	JIANGMEN	562
ZHENJIANG	514	JINHUA	534	ZHAOTONG	555	ZHAOQING	563
XIAMEN	515	DANDONG	543	JISHOU	557		

Displacement, tons: 1,425 standard; 1,702 full load
Dimensions, feet (metres): 338.5 × 35.4 × 10.2
(103.2 × 10.8 × 3.1)
Main machinery: 2 Type 12E 390V diesels; 14,400 hp(m)
(10.6 MW) sustained; 2 shafts
Speed, knots: 26. **Range, miles:** 4,000 at 15 kt; 2,700 at 18 kt
Complement: 200 (30 officers)

Missiles: SSM: 4 HY-2 (C-201) (CSSC-3 Seersucker) (2 twin)
launchers ❶; active radar or IR homing to 80 km *(43.2 n miles)*
at 0.9 Mach; warhead 513 kg.
Guns: 2 or 4 China 3.9 in *(100 mm)*/56 (2 single ❷ or 2 twin ❸);
18 rds/min to 22 km *(12 n miles)*; weight of shell 15.9 kg.
12 China 37 mm/63 (6 twin) ❹ (8 (4 twin), in some); 180 rds/
min to 8.5 km *(4.6 n miles)* anti-aircraft; weight of shell 1.42 kg.
A/S mortars: 2 RBU 1200 5-tubed fixed launchers (4 in some) ❺;
range 1,200 m; warhead 34 kg.
Depth charges: 2 BMB-2 projectors; 2 racks (in some).
Mines: Can carry up to 60.
Countermeasures: Decoys: 2 RBOC Mk 33 6-barrelled chaff
launchers or 2 China 26-barrelled launchers.
ESM: Jug Pair or Watchdog; radar warning.
Weapons control: Wok Won director (in some) ❻.
Radars: Air/surface search: MX 902 Eye Shield (Type 354) ❼;
E/F-band.
Rice Screen/Shield ❽ (*Zigong* onwards); G-band.
Surface search/fire control: Square Tie (Type 352) ❾; I-band.
Navigation: Don 2 or Fin Curve or Racal Decca; I-band.
Fire control: Rice Lamp (in some) ❿; I/J-band.
Sun Visor (with Wasp Head) (in some) ⓫; I-band.
IFF: High Pole A. Yard Rake or Square Head.
Sonars: Echo Type 5; hull-mounted; active search and attack;
medium frequency.

Programmes: Pennant numbers changed in 1979. All built in
Shanghai starting in the mid-1970s at the Hudong, Jiangnan
and Huangpu shipyards. Ships were completed in the following
order: 515, 516, 517, 511, 512, 513, 514, 518, 509, 510, 519,
520, 551, 552, 533, 534, two for Egypt, 543, 553, 554, 555,
545, 556 (to Bangladesh), 557, 544, 558, 560, 561, 559, 562
and 563. The last of class 563 completed in February 1996.
Reports that construction had restarted in 1997 were incorrect.
Modernisation: Fire control and electronics equipment are being
modernised. Sun Visor and Rice Lamp have been seen on
newly refitted Type Is. Possible VDS or sonar towed array may
be fitted in one of the class. The latest ships starting with
Zigong have gunhouses on the 37 mm guns and a new air/
surface search radar.
Structure: All of the class have the same hull dimensions.
Previously reported Type numbers have been superseded by
the following designations:
Type I has at least five versions. Version 1 has an oval funnel
and square bridge wings; version 2 a square funnel with
bevelled bridge face; version 3 an octagonal funnel; version 4
reverts back to the oval funnel and version 5 has a distinctive
fluting arrangement with cowls on the funnel, as well as
gunhouses on the 37 mm guns. Some have bow bulwarks.
Type II. See separate entry.
Types III and IV. See separate entry.
Operational: 520 paid off in 1993. Ten are based in the Eastern
Fleet, three in the North and the remainder in the South.
Sales: Two have been transferred to Egypt, one in September
1984, the other in March 1985, and one, *Xiangtan* 556, to
Bangladesh in November 1989. **UPDATED**

ZHENJIANG (single 100 mm gun)   *(Scale 1 : 900), Ian Sturton*

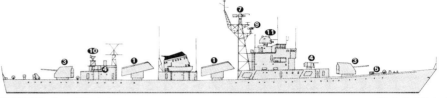

NINGPO (Rice Lamp FC radar)   *(Scale 1 : 900), Ian Sturton*

DONGGUAN (37 mm gunhouses)   *(Scale 1 : 900), Ian Sturton*

JIUJIANG   *6/1999 *, Ships of the World / 0056761*

CHANG DE   *5/1997, Maritime Photographic / 0017724*

YIBIN
6/1997* / 0056762

KANGDING
1/1999*, 92 Wing RAAF / 0056763

CHANG DE
6/1997* / 0056764

3 JIANGHU III and IV (TYPE 053 HT) CLASS (FFG)

HUANGSHI 535 (Type III)   **WUHU** 536 (Type III)   **ZHOUSHAN** 537 (Type IV)

Displacement, tons: 1,924 full load
Dimensions, feet (metres): 338.5 × 35.4 × 10.2
(103.2 × 10.8 × 3.1)
Main machinery: 2 Type 18E 390V diesels; 14,400 hp(m)
(10.6 MW) sustained; 2 shafts
Speed, knots: 28. **Range, miles:** 4,000 at 15 kt; 2,700 at 18 kt
Complement: 200 (30 officers)

Missiles: SSM: 8 YJ-1 (Eagle Strike) (C-801) (CSS-N-4 Sardine) ❶;
active radar homing to 40 km *(22 n miles)* at 0.9 Mach;
warhead 165 kg. Type IV is fitted with C-802 (CSS-N-8
Saccade) with an extended range to 120 km *(66 n miles)*.
Guns: 4 China 3.9 in *(100 mm)*/56 (2 twin) ❷; 18 rds/min to
22 km *(12 n miles)*; weight of shell 15.9 kg.
8 China 37 mm/63 (4 twin) ❸; 180 rds/min to 8.5 km *(4.6 n
miles)* anti-aircraft; weight of shell 1.42 kg. See *Modernisation*.
A/S mortars: 2 RBU 1200 5-tubed fixed launchers ❹; range
1,200 m; warhead 34 kg.
Depth charges: 2 BMB-2 projectors; 2 racks.
Mines: Can carry up to 60.
Countermeasures: Decoys: 2 China 26-barrelled chaff
launchers.
ESM: Elettronica Newton; radar warning.
ECM: Elettronica 929 (Type 981); jammer.
Radars: Air/surface search: MX 902 Eye Shield ❺; E-band.
Surface search/fire control: Square Tie ❻; I-band.
Navigation: Fin Curve; I-band.
Fire control: Rice Lamp ❼; I/J-band.
Sun Visor B (with Wasp Head) ❽; I-band.
IFF: High Pole A. Square Head.
Sonars: Echo Type 5; hull-mounted; active search and attack;
medium frequency.

Programmes: These ships are Jianghu hulls 27, 28 and 30 and
are referred to as New Missile Frigates. *Huangshi*
commissioned 14 December 1986, *Wuhu* in 1987, and
Zhoushan completed in 1989. A fourth of class 538 was
reported in 1991 but may have been confused with one of the
Thai ships.
Modernisation: It has been reported that a CIWS mounting PL
8H may be fitted in place of some of the twin 37 mm guns. This
is a combined 37 mm gun and SAM system, the missiles using
IR homing. No sign of this change by late 1998.

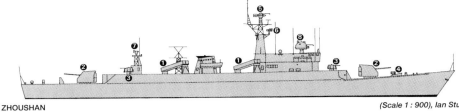

ZHOUSHAN   *(Scale 1 : 900), Ian Sturton*

WUHU   *10/1992*, Ships of the World /* 0056765

Structure: The main deck is higher in the midships section and
the lower part of the mast is solid. Type IV has an improved
SSM missile which is probably the turbojet C-802. The
arrangement of the launchers is side by side, as opposed to the
staggered pairings in Type III. These are the first all-enclosed,
air conditioned ships built in China.
Operational: Based in East Sea Fleet at Dinghai.
Sales: Four modified Type III to Thailand in 1991-92.   ***UPDATED***

ZHOUSHAN   *10/1992*, Ships of the World /* 0056766

WUHU   *5/1992*

1 JIANGHU II (TYPE 053) CLASS (FFG)

Name	No	Builders	Laid down	Launched	Commissioned
SIPING	544	Hudong Shipyard, Shanghai	1984	Sep 1985	Nov 1986

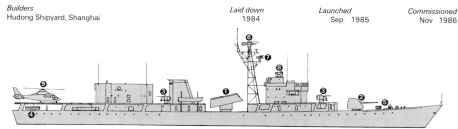

SIPING

(Scale 1 : 900), Ian Sturton

Displacement, tons: 1,550 standard; 1,865 full load
Dimensions, feet (metres): 338.5 × 35.4 × 10.2
(103.2 × 10.8 × 3.1)
Main machinery: 2 Type 12E 390V diesels; 14,400 hp(m)
(10.6 MW) sustained; 2 shafts
Speed, knots: 26. **Range, miles:** 4,000 at 15 kt; 2,700 at 18 kt
Complement: 185 (30 officers)

Missiles: SSM: 2 HY-2 (C-201) (CSSC-3 Seersucker) (twin)
launchers ❶; active radar or IR homing to 80 km *(43.2 n miles)*
at 0.9 Mach; warhead 513 kg.
Guns: 1 Creusot-Loire 3.9 in *(100 mm)*/55 ❷; 60-80 rds/min to
17 km *(9.3 n miles)*; weight of shell 13.5 kg.
8 China 37 mm/63 (4 twin) ❸; 180 rds/min to 8.5 km *(4.6 n
miles)* anti-aircraft; weight of shell 1.42 kg.
Torpedoes: 6—324 mm ILAS (2 triple) tubes ❹. Yu-2 (Mk 46
Mod 1) active/passive homing to 11 km *(5.9 n miles)* at 40 kt;
warhead 44 kg.
A/S mortars: 2 RBU 1200 5-tubed fixed launchers ❺; range
1,200 m; warhead 34 kg.
Countermeasures: Decoys: 2 SRBOC Mk 33 6-barrelled chaff
launchers or 2 China 26-barrelled launchers.
ESM: Jug Pair or Watchdog; radar warning.

Weapons control: CSEE Naja optronic director for 100 mm gun.
Radars: Air/surface search: MX 902 Eye Shield ❻; possible
E-band.
Surface search/fire control: Square Tie ❼; I-band.
Navigation: Don 2 or Fin Curve; I-band.
Fire control: Sun Visor B (with Wasp Head) ❽; I/J-band.
IFF: High Pole A. Yard Rake or Square Head.
Sonars: Echo Type 5; hull-mounted; active search and attack;
medium frequency.

Helicopters: Harbin Z-9A (Dauphin) ❾.

Programmes: Built as a standard Jianghu I and then converted
before being commissioned.
Structure: The after part of the ship has been rebuilt to take a
hangar and flight deck for a single helicopter. Alcatel
'Safecopter' landing aid. This ship also has a French 100 mm
gun and optronic director, and Italian triple torpedo tubes
mounted on the quarterdeck.
Operational: Based in North Sea Fleet at Guzhen Bay.
Opinion: More of the class were expected to be converted, but
this may have been a one-off helicopter trials ship for the Luhu
and Jiangwei designs   *UPDATED*

SIPING   *6/1990* / 0056758*

SHIPBORNE AIRCRAFT

Note: Six Racal Searchwater radars ordered in 1996.

Numbers/Type: 6 Aerospatiale SA 321G/Zhi-8 Super Frelon.
Operational speed: 134 kt *(248 km/h)*.
Service ceiling: 10,000 ft *(3,100 m)*.
Range: 440 n miles *(815 km)*.
Role/Weapon systems: ASW helicopter; SA 321G delivered from France but supplemented by
locally built Zhi-8, of which the first operational aircraft was delivered in late 1991. Thomson
Sintra HS-12 in four SA 321Gs for SSBN escort role. Sensors: HS-12 dipping sonar and processor,
some have French-built search radar. Weapons: ASW; Whitehead A244 or Yu-2 (Mk 46 Mod 1)
torpedo. ASV: C-802K ASM.
                                                              UPDATED

HAITUN   *7/1997 / 0012193*

Numbers/Type: 6/4 Kamov Ka 28PL/Ka 28PS Helix.
Operational speed: 135 kt *(250 km/h)*.
Service ceiling: 19,685 ft *(6,000 m)*.
Range: 432 n miles *(800 km)*.
Role/Weapon systems: First pair are ASW helicopters acquired in 1997 for evaluation. Four more
ASW versions and four for SAR delivered in late 1999. Sensors: Splash Drop radar; VGS-3
dipping sonar; MAD; ESM. Weapons: three torpedoes or depth bombs or mines.
                                                              UPDATED

SUPER FRELON   *6/1995* / 0012766*

Numbers/Type: 10 Harbin Zhi-9A Haitun (Dauphin 2).
Operational speed: 140 kt *(260 km/h)*.
Service ceiling: 15,000 ft *(4,575 m)*.
Range: 410 n miles *(758 km)*.
Role/Weapon systems: About 10 are available to be embarked in latest Chinese escorts. China
has an option to continue building. Sensors: Thomson-CSF Agrion; HS-12 dipping sonar; Crouzet
MAD. Weapons: ASV; up to four locally built radar-guided anti-ship missiles and Whitehead
A244 torpedoes or Yu-2 (Mk 46 Mod 1).
                                                    VERIFIED

HELIX A (Russian colours)   *7/1997*, van Ginderen Collection / 0012194*

LAND-BASED MARITIME AIRCRAFT (FRONT LINE)

Notes: (1) JH-7 Fencer type may be in naval service in due course. Carry two C-801 ASM.
(2) Russian AWACS A 40 aircraft are being acquired by the Air Force and an IL-76 aircraft is fitted with a Phalcon AEW radar.
(3) In addition to those listed there are about 170 training and transport aircraft.

Numbers/Type: 95 Sukhoi Su-27 Flanker.
Operational speed: 1,345 kt (2,500 km/h).
Service ceiling: 59,000 ft (18,000 m).
Range: 2,160 n miles (4,000 km).
Role/Weapon systems: Air Force manned air defence fighter first one acquired in 1991 for trials. 25 more purchased in 1992 and 24 more including two trainers in 1995-96. More being built under license to a planned total of 300 by 2015. Sensors: Doppler radar. Weapons: One 30 mm cannon; 10 AAMs.
UPDATED

Numbers/Type: 7 Harbin SH-5.
Operational speed: 243 kt (450 km/h).
Service ceiling: 23,000 ft (7,000 m).
Range: 2,563 n miles (4,750 km).
Role/Weapon systems: Multipurpose amphibian introduced into service in 1986. Final total of about 20 planned with ASW and avionics upgrade. Sensors: Doppler radar; MAD; sonobuoys. Weapons: ASV; four C 101, two gun turret, bombs. ASW; Yu-2 (Mk 46 Mod 1) torpedoes, mines, depth bombs.
UPDATED

Numbers/Type: 6 Hanzhong Y-8MPA Cub.
Operational speed: 351 kt (650 km/h).
Service ceiling: 34,120 ft (10,400 m).
Range: 3,020 n miles (5,600 km).
Role/Weapon systems: Maritime patrol version of Y-8 (AN-12) transport; first flown 1985; evaluated to replace Be-6 for ASW and AEW roles. Sensors: Litton APSO-504(V)3 search radar in undernose radome. Two Litton LTN 72R INS and Omega/Loran. Weapons: No weapons carried.
UPDATED

CUB
7/1997 */ 0012195

Numbers/Type: 45 Harbin H-5 (Il-28 Beagle).
Operational speed: 487 kt (902 km/h).
Service ceiling: 40,350 ft (12,300 m).
Range: 1,175 n miles (2,180 km).
Role/Weapon systems: Overwater strike aircraft with ASW/ASVW roles. Being phased out and some moved into second line roles such as target towing and ECM training. Weapons: ASW; two torpedoes or four depth bombs. ASVW; one torpedo + mines. Standard; four 23 mm cannon.
UPDATED

Numbers/Type: 18/15 Shenyang J-8-I/II Finback A/B.
Operational speed: 701 kt (1,300 km/h).
Service ceiling: 65,620 ft (20,000 m).
Range: 1,187 n miles (2,200 km).
Role/Weapon systems: Dual role, all-weather fighter introduced into service in 1990 and production continues. There are at least 50 more in service with the Air Force. Weapons: 23 mm twin-barrel cannon; PL-2/7 AAM; ASM. PL-2 has some ASM capability.
UPDATED

Numbers/Type: 40 Nanchang A-5 (Fantan A) (MiG-19).
Operational speed: 643 kt (1,190 km/h).
Service ceiling: 52,500 ft (16,000 m).
Range: 650 n miles (1,188 km).
Role/Weapon systems: Strike aircraft developed from Shenyang J-6; operated in the beachhead and coastal shipping attack role. A-5M version adapted to carry two torpedoes or C-801 ASM. Weapons: Two 23 mm cannon, two cluster bombs, one or two air-to-air missiles. Capable of carrying 1 ton warload.
VERIFIED

Numbers/Type: 320 Shenyang F-6 (MiG-19 Farmer).
Operational speed: 831 kt (1,540 km/h).
Service ceiling: 58,725 ft (17,900 m).
Range: 1,187 n miles (2,200 km).
Role/Weapon systems: Strike fighter for Fleet air defence and anti-shipping strike. Weapons: Fleet air defence role; four AA-1 ('Alkali') beam-riding missiles. Attack; some 1,000 kg of underwing bombs or depth charges, PL-2 missile has anti-ship capability.
UPDATED

Numbers/Type: 14 Xian B-6/6D (Tu-16 Badger).
Operational speed: 535 kt (992 km/h).
Service ceiling: 40,350 ft (12,300 m).
Range: 2,605 n miles (4,800 km).
Role/Weapon systems: Bomber and maritime reconnaissance aircraft. Sensors: Search/attack radar; ECM. Weapons: ASV; two underwing anti-shipping missiles of local manufacture, including C-801. Up to five 23 mm cannon; bombs.
VERIFIED

Numbers/Type: 30 Xian F-7 Fishbed C/E.
Operational speed: 1,175 kt (2,175 km/h).
Service ceiling: 61,680 ft (18,800 m).
Range: 804 n miles (1,490 km).
Role/Weapon systems: Land-based Fleet air defence fighter with limited strike role against enemy shipping or beachhead. Numbers reducing. Sensors: Search attack radar, some ECM. Weapons: ASV; 500 kg bombs or 36 rockets. Standard; two 30 mm cannon. AD; two 'Atoll' AAMs.
UPDATED

PATROL FORCES

Notes: (1) Many patrol craft carry the HN-5 shoulder-launched Chinese version of the SA-N-5 SAM.
(2) More Patrol Craft are listed under Paramilitary vessels at the end of the Chinese section.

26 HOUXIN (TYPE 037/1G) CLASS
(FAST ATTACK CRAFT—MISSILE) (PGG)

751-760   764-769   653-659

Displacement, tons: 478 full load
Dimensions, feet (metres): 203.4 × 23.6 × 7.5 (62.8 × 7.2 × 2.4)
Main machinery: 4 China PR 230ZC diesels; 4,000 hp(m) (2.94 MW); 4 shafts
Speed, knots: 28. **Range, miles:** 750 at 18 kt
Complement: 71

Missiles: SSM: 4 YJ-1 (Eagle Strike) (C-801) (CSS-N-4 Sardine) (2 twin); active radar homing to 40 km (22 n miles) at 0.9 Mach; warhead 165 kg; sea-skimmer. C-802 in due course.
Guns: 4—37 mm/63 (Type 76A) (2 twin); 180 rds/min to 8.5 km (4.6 n miles) anti-aircraft; weight of shell 1.42 kg
4—14.5 mm (Type 69) (2 twin); 600 rds/min to 7 km (3.8 n miles).
Countermeasures: ESM/ECM: Intercept and jammer.
Radars: Surface search: Square Tie; I-band.
Fire control: Rice Lamp; I-band.
Navigation: Anritsu Type 723; I-band.

Programmes: First seen in 1991 and built at the rate of up to three per year at Qiuxin and Huangpu Shipyards to replace the 'Houku' class and for export. Building may have stopped in mid-1999.
Structure: This is a missile armed version of the 'Hainan' class. There are some variations in the bridge superstructure in later ships of the class.
Operational: Split between the East and South Sea Fleets.
Sales: Two to Burma in December 1995, two in July 1996 and two in late 1997.
UPDATED

HOUXIN 756
5/1997, Maritime Photographic / 0017726

HOUXIN 759
6/1999, Ships of the World* / 0056767

2 HAIJIU CLASS (LARGE PATROL CRAFT) (PG)

693   697

Displacement, tons: 490 full load
Dimensions, feet (metres): 210 × 23.6 × 7.2 (64 × 7.2 × 2.2)
Main machinery: 4 diesels; 8,800 hp(m) (6.47 MW); 4 shafts
Speed, knots: 28. **Range, miles:** 750 at 18 kt
Complement: 72
Guns: 4 China 57 mm/70 (2 twin); 120 rds/min to 12 km (6.5 n miles); weight of shell 6.31 kg.
4 USSR 30 mm/65 (2 twin); 500 rds/min to 5 km (2.7 n miles) anti-aircraft; weight of shell 0.54 kg.
A/S mortars: 4 RBU 1200 5-tubed fixed launchers; range 1,200 m; warhead 34 kg.
Depth charges: 2 rails.
Radars: Surface search: Pot Head; I-band.
Fire control: Round Ball; I-band.
Sonars: Stag Ear or Thomson Sintra SS 12.

Comment: A lengthened version of the 'Hainan' class probably used as a prototype for the 'Houxin' class. 697 seen with a Thomson Sintra SS 12 VDS Sonar. Both in East Sea Fleet. Two others have been scrapped.
UPDATED

HAIJIU (old number)
4/1990, John Mapletoft* / 0056768

6 + (1) HOUJIAN (OR HUANG) (TYPE 037/2) CLASS
(FAST ATTACK CRAFT—MISSILE) (PGG)

No	Builders	Launched	Commissioned
770	Huangpu Shipyard	Jan 1991	May 1991
771	Huangpu Shipyard	July 1994	Feb 1995
772	Huangpu Shipyard	Feb 1995	Apr 1995
773	Huangpu Shipyard	May 1995	July 1995
774	Huangpu Shipyard	Sep 1998	Feb 1999
775	Huangpu Shipyard	Apr 1999	Nov 1999

Displacement, tons: 520 standard
Dimensions, feet (metres): 214.6 × 27.6 × 7.9 *(65.4 × 8.4 × 2.4)*
Main machinery: 3 SEMT-Pielstick 12 PA6 280 diesels; 15,840 hp(m) *(11.7 MW)* sustained; 3 shafts
Speed, knots: 32. **Range, miles:** 1,800 at 18 kt
Complement: 75

Missiles: SSM: 6 YJ-1 (Eagle Strike) (C-801) (CSS-N-4 Sardine) (2 triple); inertial cruise; active radar homing to 40 km *(22 n miles)* at 0.9 Mach; warhead 165 kg or C-802 (CSS-N-8 Saccade); range 120 km *(66 miles)*.
Guns: 2—37 mm/63 (twin) Type 76A; 180 rds/min to 8.5 km *(4.6 n miles)* anti-aircraft; weight of shell 1.42 kg.
4—30 mm/65 (2 twin) Type 69; 500 rds/min to 5 km *(2.7 n miles)*; weight of shell 0.54 kg.
Countermeasures: ESM/ECM: Intercept and jammer.
Weapons control: China Type 88C optronic director.
Radars: Surface search: Square Tie; I-band.
Fire control: Rice Lamp; I-band.
Navigation: Type 765; I-band.

Programmes: First of class laid down in 1989 and built in a very short time. Sometimes called the 'Huang' class.
Operational: Based in South Sea Fleet at Hong Kong from mid-1997. One possibly sunk in late 1997.
UPDATED

HOUJIAN 770   *5/1993* / 0012767*

95 HAINAN (TYPE 037) CLASS
(FAST ATTACK CRAFT—PATROL) (PC)

Nos 275-285, 290, 302, 305, 609, 610, 618-622, 626-629, 636-643, 646-681, 683-687, 689-692, 695-699, 701, 707, 723-733, 740-742

Displacement, tons: 375 standard; 392 full load
Dimensions, feet (metres): 192.8 × 23.6 × 7.2 *(58.8 × 7.2 × 2.2)*
Main machinery: 4 PCR/Kolomna Type 9-D-8 diesels; 4,000 hp(m) *(2.94 MW)* sustained; 4 shafts
Speed, knots: 30.5. **Range, miles:** 1,300 at 15 kt
Complement: 78

Missiles: Can be fitted with 4 YJ-1 launchers in lieu of the after 57 mm gun.
Guns: 4 China 57 mm/70 (2 twin); 120 rds/min to 12 km *(6.5 n miles)*; weight of shell 6.31 kg.
4 USSR 25 mm/60 (2 twin); 270 rds/min to 3 km *(1.6 n miles)* anti-aircraft; weight of shell 0.34 kg.
A/S mortars: 4 RBU 1200 5-tubed fixed launchers; range 1,200 m; warhead 34 kg.
Depth charges: 2 BMB-2 projectors; 2 racks. 18 DCs.
Mines: Rails fitted for 12.
Radars: Surface search: Pot Head or Skin Head; I-band.
IFF: High Pole.
Sonars: Stag Ear; hull-mounted; active search and attack; high frequency.
Thomson Sintra SS 12 (in some); VDS.

Programmes: A larger Chinese-built version of the former Soviet SO 1. Low freeboard. Programme started 1963-64 and continued with new hulls replacing the first ships of the class. There are at least six variants with minor differences.
Structure: Later ships have a tripod or solid foremast in place of a pole and a short stub mainmast. Two trials SS 12 sonars fitted in 1987.
Operational: Divided between the three Fleets.
Sales: Two to Bangladesh, one in 1982 and one in 1985; eight to Egypt in 1983-84; six to North Korea 1975-78; four to Pakistan, two in 1976 and two in 1980; six to Burma in 1991 and four in 1993.
UPDATED

HAINAN 677   *10/1997 / 0017728*

HAINAN 680   *6/1999*, Ships of the World / 0056770*

30 HUANGFEN (TYPE 021) (OSA I TYPE) and 1 HOLA CLASS
(FAST ATTACK CRAFT—MISSILE) (PCFG)

3100 series	6100 series	7100 series

Displacement, tons: 171 standard; 205 full load
Dimensions, feet (metres): 126.6 × 24.9 × 8.9 *(38.6 × 7.6 × 2.7)*
Main machinery: 3 Type 42-160 diesels; 12,000 hp(m) *(8.8 MW)* sustained; 3 shafts
Speed, knots: 35. **Range, miles:** 800 at 30 kt
Complement: 28

Missiles: SSM: 4 HY-2 (CSS-N-3 Seersucker) (2 twin) launchers; active radar or IR homing to 80 km *(43.2 n miles)* at 0.9 Mach; warhead 513 kg.
Guns: 4 USSR 25 mm/60 (2 twin); 270 rds/min to 3 km *(1.6 n miles)* anti-aircraft.
Replaced in some by 4 USSR 30 mm/65 (2 twin) AK 230.
Radars: Surface search: Square Tie; I-band.
Fire control: Round Ball or Rice Lamp; H/I-band.
IFF: 2 Square Head; High Pole A.

Programmes: First reported in 1985.
Structure: The only 'Hola' class has a radome aft, four launchers, no guns, slightly larger dimensions (137.8 ft *(42 m)* long) and a folding mast. This radome is also fitted in others which carry 30 mm guns. Pennant numbers: Hola, 5100 and the remainder 3100/7100 series.
Operational: China credits this class with a speed of 39 kt. Split between the Fleets. Numbers have been radically reduced.
Sales: Four to North Korea, 1980; four to Pakistan, 1984; four to Bangladesh, 1988; and one more in 1992. Three of a variant called the 'Hounan' class were transferred to Yemen in May 1995, delivery having been delayed by the Yemen civil war. A variant called the 'Hudong' class has been built for Iran. Five delivered to Iran in September 1994, five more in March 1996.
UPDATED

HUANGFEN 6119   *6/1999*, Ships of the World / 0056769*

25 HOUKU (TYPE 024) CLASS
(FAST ATTACK CRAFT—MISSILE) (PCFG)

Displacement, tons: 68 standard; 79.2 full load
Dimensions, feet (metres): 88.6 × 20.7 × 4.3 *(27 × 6.3 × 1.3)* (28.6 m—'Hema' class)
Main machinery: 4 Type L-12V-180 diesels; 4,800 hp(m) *(3.53 MW)*; 4 shafts
Speed, knots: 37.5. **Range, miles:** 400 at 30 kt
Complement: 17 (2 officers)

Missiles: SSM: 2 SY-1 (CSS-N-1 Scrubbrush); inertial cruise; active radar homing to 45 km *(24.3 n miles)* at 0.9 Mach; warhead 513 kg. 1 C-801 in one of the class.
Guns: 2 USSR 25 mm/60 (twin) (4 (2 twin) in 'Hema' class); 270 rds/min to 3 km *(1.6 n miles)* anti-aircraft; weight of shell 0.34 kg.
Radars: Surface search: Square Tie; I-band; range 73 km *(40 n miles)*.
IFF: High pole A.

Programmes: The Komars delivered from the USSR in the 1960s have been deleted. They were followed by a building programme of 10 a year of a Chinese variant of the Komar with a steel hull instead of wooden. Pennant numbers; 1100 and 3100 series as some of the 'Huangfen' class.
Modernisation: Plans to replace the missiles with C-801 have been shelved although a few may be fitted. One craft is a trials platform for the C-101 and has a single launcher on the stern. This is an SSM designed for FACs but may have been overtaken by the C-801.
Structure: The chief external difference is the siting of the launchers clear of the bridge and further inboard, eliminating sponsons and use of pole instead of lattice mast. A hydrofoil variant, the 'Hema' class, has a semi-submerged foil forward. The extra 6 ft length allows for the mounting of a second twin 25 mm abaft the missile launchers.
Operational: Numbers are declining. Half are based in the North Sea Fleet, remainder split between East and South.
Sales: Four to Pakistan, 1981; four to Bangladesh, February 1983 and one more in 1992; six to Egypt, 1984.
UPDATED

HOUKU   *4/1988, A Sheldon Duplaix*

22 HAIQING (TYPE 037/1) CLASS
(FAST ATTACK CRAFT—PATROL) (PC)

710-717, 743-744, 761-765, 787-792

Displacement, tons: 478 full load
Dimensions, feet (metres): 206 × 23.6 × 7.9 *(62.8 × 7.2 × 2.4)*
Main machinery: 4 Chinese PR 230ZC diesels; 4,000 hp(m) *(2.94 MW)* sustained; 4 shafts
Speed, knots: 28. **Range, miles:** 1,300 at 15 kt
Complement: 71

Guns: 4 China 37 mm/63 (2 twin) Type 76. 4 China 14.5 mm (2 twin) Type 69.
A/S mortars: 2 Type 87 6-tubed launchers.
Radars: Surface search: Anritsu RA 723; I-band.
Sonars: Hull mounted; active search and attack; medium frequency Thomson Sintra SS 12; VDS.

Programmes: Starting building at Qiuxin Shipyard in 1992 and replaced the 'Hainan' class programme. First one completed in November 1993. Production continued at Qingdao, Chongqing and Huangpu as well as Qiuxin.
Structure: Based on the 'Hainan' class, but the large A/S mortars suggest a predominantly ASW role, and this may explain the rapid building rate.
Operational: In service in all three Fleets.
Sales: One to Sri Lanka in December 1995.

UPDATED

HAIQING 762 and 763   *6/1996* / 0012771*

15 + 2 HAIZHUI/SHANGHAI III (TYPE 062/1) CLASS
(COASTAL PATROL CRAFT) (PC)

2327   2329   4340   4341   +11

Displacement, tons: 170 full load
Dimensions, feet (metres): 134.5 × 17.4 × 5.9 *(41 × 5.3 × 1.8)*
Main machinery: 4 Chinese L12-180A diesels; 4,400 hp(m) *(3.22 MW)* sustained; 4 shafts
Speed, knots: 25. **Range, miles:** 750 at 17 kt
Complement: 43

Guns: 4 China 37 mm/63 (2 twin); 180 rds/min to 8.5 km *(4.6 n miles)*; weight of shell 1.42 kg. 4 China 14.5 mm (2 twin) Type 69 or 4 China 25 mm (2 twin).
A/S mortars: 3 RBU 1200 5-tubed fixed launchers; range 1,200 m; warhead 34 kg (in some).
Radars: Surface search: Pot Head or Anritsu 726; I-band.
Sonars: Stag Ear; hull-mounted; active search; high frequency (in some).

Programmes: First seen in 1992 but now in series production for China and for export. Sometimes referred to as Shanghai III class when not fitted with ASW equipment.
Structure: Lengthened Shanghai II hull. Inclined pole mast and a pronounced step at the back of the bridge superstructure are recognition features. Much reduced top speed.
Operational: So far only based in the North and East Sea Fleets.
Sales: Three to Sri Lanka in August 1995, three more in May 1996 and three more in August 1998. One to Bangladesh in mid-1996.

UPDATED

HAIZHUI 4341   *2/1999* / 0056771*

HAIZHUI 4340   *5/1997 / 0017731*

15 HUCHUAN (TYPE 025/026) CLASS
(FAST ATTACK CRAFT—TORPEDO) (PHT)

205, 207-209, 248, 1247, 2201, 2203, 3206, 3214, 6218, 7230 +3

Displacement, tons: 39 standard; 45.8 full load
Dimensions, feet (metres): 71.5 × 20.7 oa × 11.8 (hullborne) *(21.8 × 6.3 × 3.6)*
Main machinery: 3 Type M 50 diesels; 3,300 hp(m) *(2.42 MW)* sustained; 3 shafts
Speed, knots: 50 foilborne. **Range, miles:** 500 at 30 kt
Complement: 16

Guns: 4 China 14.5 mm (2 twin); 600 rds/min to 7 km *(3.8 n miles)*.
Torpedoes: 2—21 in *(533 mm)* tubes. Yu-1; anti-ship; to 9.2 km *(5 n miles)* at 39 kt or 3.7 km *(2.1 n miles)* at 51 kt; warhead 400 kg.
Radars: Surface search: Skin Head or China Type 753; I-band.

Programmes: Hydrofoils designed and built by China, in the Hudong yard, Shanghai. Construction started in 1966. Construction discontinued in 1988-89 and numbers are now declining rapidly although four more were reported as being completed in 1994.
Structure: Of all-metal construction with a bridge well forward and a low superstructure extending aft. Forward pair of foils can be withdrawn into recesses in the hull. There are two variants. Older boats have a twin mounting amidships and one aft with the front of the bridge well forward of the lips of the tubes. Newer versions have the front of the bridge in line with the lips of the tubes and the first mounting on the forecastle and have differences in their electronics. Not all are hydrofoil fitted.
Operational: These last survivors are based in the North Sea Fleet.
Sales: 32 to Albania, four to Pakistan (passed on to Bangladesh), four to Tanzania, three to Romania plus additional craft of indigenous construction. Four to Bangladesh in 1989. Some have been deleted.

UPDATED

HUCHUAN   *6/1994*, CSSC / 0012198*

98 SHANGHAI II (TYPE 062) CLASS
(FAST ATTACK CRAFT—GUN) (PC)

Displacement, tons: 113 standard; 134 full load
Dimensions, feet (metres): 127.3 × 17.7 × 5.6 *(38.8 × 5.4 × 1.7)*
Main machinery: 2 Type L-12V-180 diesels; 2,400 hp(m) *(1.76 MW)* (forward); 2 Type 12-D-6 diesels; 1,820 hp(m) *(1.34 MW)* (aft); 4 shafts
Speed, knots: 30. **Range, miles:** 700 at 16.5 kt on 1 engine
Complement: 38

Guns: 4 China 37 mm/63 (2 twin); 180 rds/min to 8.5 km *(4.6 n miles)*; weight of shell 1.42 kg. 4 USSR 25 mm/60 (2 twin); 270 rds/min to 3 km *(1.6 n miles)* anti-aircraft; weight of shell 0.34 kg.
Some are fitted with a twin 57 mm/70, some have a twin 75 mm Type 56 recoilless rifle mounted forward and some have a twin 14.5 mm MG.
Depth charges: 2 projectors; 8 weapons.
Mines: Mine rails can be fitted for 10 mines.
Radars: Surface search: Skin Head or Pot Head; I-band.
IFF: High Pole.
Sonars: Hull-mounted active sonar or VDS in some.

Programmes: Construction began in 1961 and continued at Shanghai and other yards at rate of about 10 a year for 30 years before being replaced by the Type 062/1G 'Haizhui' class.
Structure: The five versions of this class vary slightly in the outline of their bridges. A few of the class have been reported as fitted with RBU 1200 anti-submarine mortars.
Operational: Evenly divided between the three Fleets. Reported but not confirmed that up to 20 have been converted to sweep mines. All Shanghai I's have been scrapped.
Sales: Eight to North Vietnam in May 1966, plus Romanian craft of indigenous construction. Seven to Tanzania in 1970-71, six to Guinea, 12 to North Korea, 12 to Pakistan, five to Sri Lanka in 1972, two to Tunisia in 1977, six to Albania, eight to Bangladesh in 1980-82, three to Congo, four to Egypt in 1984, three to Sri Lanka in 1991, two to Tanzania in 1992, three more of a variant to Tunisia in 1994. One to Sierra Leone in 1997. Many of the earlier craft have since been deleted.

UPDATED

SHANGHAI II (Sri Lankan colours)   *1992* / 0012374*

4 HARBOUR PATROL CRAFT (PBI)

Displacement, tons: 80 full load
Dimensions, feet (metres): 82 × 13.3 × 4.5 *(25 × 4.1 × 1.4)*
Main machinery: 2 diesels; 2 shafts
Speed, knots: 28
Guns: 2—14.5 mm (twin).
Radars: Surface search: I-band.

Comment: Four new patrol craft arrived at Hong Kong on 1 July 1997. There may be more of the class, which are similar to some of the paramilitary patrol craft, but much faster.
NEW ENTRY

PB 7360   *6/1999*, Ships of the World /* 0056772

MINE WARFARE FORCES

Note: There are also some 50 auxiliary minesweepers of various types including trawlers and motor-driven junks. Up to 20 'Shanghai II' class may be used.

27 (+13 RESERVE) T 43 CLASS (TYPE 010)
(MINESWEEPERS—OCEAN) (MSO)

364-6, 377-9, 386-9, 396-9, 801-3, 807-9, 821-3, 829-832, 853-4, 863, 994-6 *et al*

Displacement, tons: 520 standard; 590 full load
Dimensions, feet (metres): 196.8 × 27.6 × 6.9 *(60 × 8.8 × 2.3)*
Main machinery: 2 PCR/Kolomna Type 9-D-8 diesels; 2,000 hp(m) *(1.47 MW)*; 2 shafts
Speed, knots: 14. **Range, miles:** 3,000 at 10 kt
Complement: 70 (10 officers)

Guns: 2 or 4 China 37 mm/63 (1 or 2 twin) (3 of the class have a 65 mm/52 forward instead of one twin 37 mm/63); dual purpose; 180 rds/min to 8.5 km *(4.6 n miles)*; weight of shell 1.42 kg.
    4 USSR 25 mm/60 (2 twin); 270 rds/min to 3 km *(1.6 n miles)*.
    4 China 14.5 mm/93 (2 twin); 600 rds/min to 7 km *(3.8 n miles)*.
    Some also carry 1—85 mm/52 Mk 90K; 18 rds/min to 15 km *(8 n miles)*; weight of shell 9.6 kg.
Depth charges: 2 BMB-2 projectors; 20 depth charges.
Mines: Can carry 12-16.
Countermeasures: MCMV; MPT-1 paravanes; MPT-3 mechanical sweep; acoustic and magnetic gear.
Radars: Surface search: Fin Curve or Type 756; I-band.
IFF: High Pole or Yard Rake.
Sonars: Tamir II; hull-mounted; active search and attack; high frequency.

Programmes: Started building in 1956 and continued intermittently until the late 1980s at Wuhan and at Guangzhou.
Structure: Based on the USSR T 43s, some of which transferred in the mid-1950s but have all now been deleted.
Operational: Ten in North Sea Fleet, nine in East Sea Fleet and eight in South Sea Fleet. Some are used as patrol ships with sweep gear removed. Three units reported as having a 65 mm/52 gun forward. Thirteen of the class are in reserve.
Sales: One to Bangladesh in 1995.
UPDATED

T 43 830   *6/1995* /* 0056774

T 43 830   *10/1997, van Ginderen Collection /* 0017732

T 43 829   *5/1994* /* 0056773

1 WOLEI CLASS (MINELAYER) (ML/MST)

814

Displacement, tons: 3,100 full load
Dimensions, feet (metres): 307.7 × 47.2 × 13.1 *(93.8 × 14.4 × 4)*
Main machinery: 4 diesels; 6,400 hp(m) *(4.7 MW)*; 2 shafts
Speed, knots: 18. **Range, miles:** 7,000 at 14 kt
Complement: 180
Guns: 8 China 37 mm/63 (4 twin); 180 rds/min to 8.5 km *(4.6 n miles)*; weight of shell 1.42 kg.
Mines: 300.
Radars: Surface search. Fire control. Navigation.

Comment: Built at Dalian Shipyard and completed successful sea trials in 1988. Resembles the deleted Japanese 'Souya' class and may be used as a support ship as well as a minelayer. Based in the North Sea Fleet.
VERIFIED

SOUYA (Japanese colours)   *10/1994, Hachiro Nakai*

8 + 1 WOSAO CLASS (MINESWEEPER—COASTAL) (MSC)

4422   4423   +6

Displacement, tons: 320 full load
Dimensions, feet (metres): 147 × 22.3 × 7.5 *(44.8 × 6.8 × 2.3)*
Main machinery: 4 M 50 diesels; 4,400 hp(m) *(3.23 MW)*; 4 shafts
Speed, knots: 25. **Range, miles:** 500 at 15 kt
Complement: 40 (6 officers)
Guns: 4 China 25 mm/60 (2 twin); 270 rds/min to 3 km *(1.6 n miles)*.
Mines: 6.
Countermeasures: Acoustic, magnetic and mechanical sweeps.
Radars: Navigation: China Type 753; I-band.
Sonars: Hull-mounted; active minehunting.

Comment: Building started in 1986. First of class commissioned in 1988 and has continued at about one every 18 months. Steel hull with low magnetic properties. Based in the East Sea Fleet.
UPDATED

WOSAO   *6/1998 /* 0017733

WOSAO   *10/1997, van Ginderen Collection /* 0017734

4 (+ 42 RESERVE) FUTI CLASS (TYPE 312)
(DRONE MINESWEEPERS) (MSB)

Displacement, tons: 47 standard
Dimensions, feet (metres): 68.6 × 12.8 × 6.9 *(20.9 × 3.9 × 2.1)*
Main machinery: Diesel-electric; 1 Type 12V 150C diesel generator; 300 hp(m) *(220 kW)*; 1 motor; cp prop
Speed, knots: 12. **Range, miles:** 144 at 12 kt
Complement: 3

Comment: A large number of these craft, similar to the German Troikas, has been built since the early 1970s. Fitted to carry out magnetic and acoustic sweeping under remote control up to 5 km *(2.7 n miles)* from shore control station. Most are kept in reserve.   **UPDATED**

DRONE Type 312   *1988*, CSSC /* 0056775

AMPHIBIOUS FORCES

Notes: (1) In addition to the ships listed below there are up to 500 minor LCM/LCVP types used to transport stores and personnel.
(2) Eight 'Yuchai' class (USSR T 4 design) and ten T4 LCMs are still in reserve in the South Sea Fleet.
(3) A 20 m WIG (wing-in-ground effect) craft assembled at Shanghai and completed in late 1997. Resembles Russian Volga II passenger ferry and may enter naval service if it proves to be reliable.

3 US 1-511 (SHAN) CLASS (LST)

Displacement, tons: 1,653 standard; 4,080 full load
Dimensions, feet (metres): 328 × 50 × 14 *(100 × 15.3 × 4.3)*
Main machinery: 2 GM 12-567A diesels; 1,800 hp(m) *(1.32 MW)*; 2 shafts
Speed, knots: 11. **Range, miles:** 1,500 at 11 kt
Complement: 115
Military lift: 165 troops; 2,100 tons cargo; 2 LCVP
Guns: 2—76 mm/50; dual purpose; 18 rds/min to 12.8 km *(7 n miles)*; weight of shell 5.92 kg.
9 China 37 mm/63 (3 twin, 3 single); 180 rds/min to 8.5 km *(4.6 n miles)*; weight of shell 1.42 kg.
Mines: All capable of minelaying.

Comment: The survivors of large class being replaced by more modern designs. Some other ex-US LSTs are in the merchant service or used as tenders. Some armed with rocket launchers. All built between 1942 and 1945. Based in the North Sea Fleet.   **UPDATED**

SHAN 926   *8/1995*, Paul Beaver /* 0056779

1 YUDENG (TYPE 073) CLASS (LSM)

No	Builders	Launched	Commissioned
990	Zhonghua Shipyard	Mar 1991	Aug 1994

Displacement, tons: 1,850 full load
Dimensions, feet (metres): 285.4 × 42.7 × 12.5 *(87 × 13 × 3.8)*
Main machinery: 2 diesels; 2 shafts
Speed, knots: 14
Complement: 35
Military lift: 500 troops; 9 tanks
Guns: 2 China 57 mm/50 (twin). 4—25 mm (2 twin).
Radars: Navigation: China Type 753; I-band.

Comment: The only one of the class. Based in the South Sea Fleet. Production may have been for export or the design was overtaken by the smaller 'Wuhu-A' class.   **VERIFIED**

YUDENG 990   *8/1995, Paul Beaver*

8 + 1 YUTING (TYPE 074) CLASS (LST)

No	Builders	Launched	Commissioned
991	Zhonghua Shipyard	Sep 1991	Sep 1992
934	Zhonghua Shipyard	Apr 1995	Sep 1995
935	Zhonghua Shipyard	July 1995	Dec 1995
936	Zhonghua Shipyard	Dec 1995	May 1996
937	Zhonghua Shipyard	Apr 1996	Aug 1996
938	Zhonghua Shipyard	Aug 1996	Jan 1997
939	Zhonghua Shipyard	Nov 1999	Apr 2000
—	Zhonghua Shipyard	May 2000	Oct 2000

Displacement, tons: 3,770 standard; 4,800 full load
Dimensions, feet (metres): 426.5 × 52.5 × 10.5 *(130 × 16 × 3.2)*
Main machinery: 2 diesels; 2 shafts
Speed, knots: 17. **Range, miles:** 3,000 at 14 kt
Complement: 120
Military lift: 250 troops; 10 tanks; 4 LCVP
Guns: 6 China 37 mm/63 (3 twin); 180 rds/min to 8.5 km *(4.6 n miles)*; weight of shell 1.42 kg.
Radars: Navigation: 2 China Type 753; I-band.
Helicopters: Platform for 2 medium.

Comment: To augment amphibious lift capabilities and provide helicopter lift. Bow and bridge structures are very similar to the 'Yukan' class but there is a large helicopter deck. All based in the South Sea Fleet. It is possible that hull number 8 may be the first of an improved class.   **UPDATED**

YUTING 991   *6/1995* /* 0056777

YUTING 938   *11/1999* /* 0056776

7 YUKAN (TYPE 072) CLASS (LST)

927   928   929   930   931   932   933

Displacement, tons: 3,110 standard; 4,170 full load
Dimensions, feet (metres): 393.6 × 50 × 9.5 *(120 × 15.3 × 2.9)*
Main machinery: 2 Type 12E 390 diesels; 14,400 hp(m) *(10.6 MW)* sustained; 2 shafts
Speed, knots: 18. **Range, miles:** 3,000 at 14 kt
Complement: 109
Military lift: 200 troops; 10 tanks; 2 LCVP; total of 500 tons
Guns: 8 China 57 mm/50 (4 twin) (some carry 4—57 mm (2 twin) and 4—37 mm (2 twin));
120 rds/min to 12 km *(6.5 n miles)*; weight of shell 6.31 kg.
4—25 mm/60 (2 twin) (some also have 4—25 mm (2 twin) mountings amidships above the tank deck); 270 rds/min to 3 km *(1.6 n miles)*.
Radars: Navigation: 2 China Type 753; I-band.

Comment: First completed in 1980 at Wuhan Shipyard. Building appeared to terminate in November 1995. Bow and stern ramps fitted. Carry two LCVPs. Bow ramp maximum load 50 tons, stern ramp 20 tons. Five based in the East and two in South Sea Fleets.   **UPDATED**

YUKAN 928   *11/1999* /* 0056778

YUKAN 933   *11/1997 /* 0017736

22 YULIANG (TYPE 079) CLASS (LSM)

Displacement, tons: 1,100 full load
Dimensions, feet (metres): 206.7 × 32.8 × 7.9 *(63 × 10 × 2.4)*
Main machinery: 2 diesels; 2 shafts
Speed, knots: 14
Complement: 60
Military lift: 3 tanks
Guns: 4—25 mm/60 (2 twin); 270 rds/min to 3 km *(1.6 n miles).*
  2 BM 21 MRL rocket launchers; range about 9 km *(5 n miles).*
Radars: Navigation: Fin Curve; I-band.

Comment: Series production started in 1980 in three or four smaller shipyards. Numbers have been overestimated in the past and production stopped in favour of 'Wuhu-A' class. Four in the North Sea Fleet, remainder based in the South Sea Fleet.

UPDATED

YULIANG
1/1996 * / 0012204

13 + 3 YUHAI (TYPE 074) (WUHU-A) CLASS (LSM)

| 481 | 6562 | 7579 | +10 |

Displacement, tons: 799 full load
Dimensions, feet (metres): 191.6 × 34.1 × 8.9 *(58.4 × 10.4 × 2.7)*
Main machinery: 2 MAN-8L 20/27 diesels; 4,900 hp(m) *(3.6 MW)*; 2 shafts
Speed, knots: 14
Complement: 56
Military lift: 2 tanks; 250 troops
Guns: 10—14.5 mm/93 (5 twin).
Radars: Navigation: I-band.

Comment: First one completed in Wuhu Shipyard in 1995. Building at up to six a year in Wuhu and Qingdao yards. One sold to Sri Lanka in December 1995. Three based in the North, four in the East and six in the South Sea Fleet.

UPDATED

YUHAI 481
2/1999 * / 0056780

36 (+ 200 RESERVE) YUNNAN CLASS (TYPE 067) (LCU)

Displacement, tons: 135 full load
Dimensions, feet (metres): 93.8 × 17.7 × 4.9 *(28.6 × 5.4 × 1.5)*
Main machinery: 2 diesels; 600 hp(m) *(441 kW)*; 2 shafts
Speed, knots: 12. Range, miles: 500 at 10 kt
Complement: 12
Military lift: 46 tons
Guns: 4—14.5 mm (2 twin) MGs.
Radars: Navigation: Fuji; I-band.

Comment: Built in China 1968-72 although a continuing programme was reported in 1982. Pennant numbers in 3000 series (3313, 3321, 3344 seen). 5000 series (5526 seen) and 7000 series (7566 and 7568 seen). The majority of the operational hulls are based in the South Sea Fleet. One to Sri Lanka in 1991 and a second in 1995. Two to Tanzania in 1995. Numbers have been overestimated in the past but another 200 are probably in reserve. Some may have 12.7 mm MGs. Twelve in the East Sea Fleet, remainder in the South.

UPDATED

YUNNAN
5/1998, Ships of the World / 0017737

1 YUDAO CLASS (LSM)

965

Displacement, tons: 1,650 full load
Dimensions, feet (metres): 253.9 × 34.1 × 9.8 *(77.4 × 10.4 × 3)*
Speed, knots: 18. Range, miles: 1,000 at 16 kt
Complement: 60
Guns: 8—25 mm/60 (2 quad); 270 rds/min to 3 km *(1.6 n miles).*
Radars: Navigation: Fin Curve; I-band.

Comment: First entered service in early 1980s. *965* is the only one left and is in the East Fleet.

UPDATED

YUDAO 965
6/1995 * / 0056781

8 (+ 30 RESERVE) YUCH'IN (TYPE 068/069) CLASS (LCU/LCP)

Displacement, tons: 58 standard; 85 full load
Dimensions, feet (metres): 81.2 × 17.1 × 4.3 *(24.8 × 5.2 × 1.3)*
Main machinery: 2 Type 12V 150C diesels; 600 hp(m) *(441 kW)*; 2 shafts
Speed, knots: 11.5. Range, miles: 450 at 11.5 kt
Complement: 12
Military lift: Up to 150 troops
Guns: 4—14.5 mm (2 twin) MGs.

Comment: Built in Shanghai 1962-72. Smaller version of 'Yunnan' class with a shorter tank deck and longer poop deck. Primarily intended for personnel transport. Based in South Sea Fleet. Six sold to Bangladesh.

UPDATED

YUCH'IN
1987 * / 0056782

10 JINGSAH II CLASS (HOVERCRAFT)

| 452 | +9 |

Displacement, tons: 70
Dimensions, feet (metres): 72.2 × 26.2 *(22 × 8)*
Main machinery: 2 propulsion motors; 2 lift motors
Speed, knots: 55
Military lift: 15 tons
Guns: 4—14.5 mm (2 twin) MGs.

Comment: The prototype was built at Dagu in 1979. This may now have been scrapped and this improved version is in series production although it may be replaced by a WIG (see *Note* at head of section) if the prototype is successful. Has a bow door for disembarkation. Numbers are uncertain.

UPDATED

JINGSAH II
1993 *, Ships of the World / 0056783*

TRAINING SHIPS

1 SHICHANG CLASS (ATS)

Name	No	Builders	Launched	Commissioned
SHICHANG	82	Qiuxin, Shanghai	Apr 1996	27 Jan 1997

Displacement, tons: 10,000 full load
Dimensions, feet (metres): 393.7 × 59.1 × 23 *(120 × 18 × 7)*
Main machinery: 2 diesels; 2 shafts
Speed, knots: 17.5. **Range, miles:** 8,000 at 17 kt
Complement: 170 plus 200 trainees
Military lift: 300 containers
Helicopters: 2 Zhi-9A Haitun.

Comment: China's first air training ship described officially as a defence mobilisation vessel which can be used for civilian freight, for helicopter or navigation training, or as a hospital ship. The vessel looks like a scaled down version of the UK *Argus* with the bridge superstructure forward and an after funnel on the starboard side of the flight deck. There are two landing spots. Based in the South Sea Fleet and deployed to Australia in mid-1998.   *VERIFIED*

1 DAXIN CLASS (AX)

Name	No	Builders	Launched	Commissioned
ZHENGHE	81	Qiuxin, Shanghai	12 July 1986	27 Apr 1987

Displacement, tons: 5,470 full load
Dimensions, feet (metres): 390.4 × 51.8 × 15.7 *(119 × 15.8 × 4.8)*
Main machinery: 2 6PC2-5L diesels; 7,800 hp(m) *(5.73 MW)*; 2 shafts
Speed, knots: 15. **Range, miles:** 5,000 at 15 kt
Complement: 170 plus 30 instructors plus 200 Midshipmen
Guns: 4 China 57 mm/70 (2 twin). 4—30 mm AK 230 (2 twin). 4—12.7 mm MGs.
A/S mortars: 2 FQF 2500 fixed 12-tubed launchers; range 1,200 m; warhead 34 kg.
Radars: Air/surface search: Eye Shield; E-band.
Surface search: China Type 756; I-band.
Navigation: Racal Decca 1290; I-band.
Fire control: Round Ball; I-band.
Sonars: Echo Type 5; hull-mounted; active; high frequency.
Helicopters: Platform only.

Comment: Resembles a small cruise liner. Subordinate to the Naval Academy and replaced *Huian*. Based in the North Sea Fleet.   *VERIFIED*

SHICHANG   *5/1998, Sattler/Steele /* 0017738

ZHENGHE   *1/1994, 92 Wing RAAF*

SHICHANG   *5/1998, RAN /* 0017739

AUXILIARIES

2 FUQING CLASS (REPLENISHMENT SHIPS) (AOR)

TAICANG 575   **DONGYUN** (ex-*Fenfcang*) 615

Displacement, tons: 7,500 standard; 21,750 full load
Dimensions, feet (metres): 552 × 71.5 × 30.8 *(168.2 × 21.8 × 9.4)*
Main machinery: 1 Sulzer 8RL B66 diesel; 15,000 hp(m) *(11 MW)* sustained; 1 shaft
Speed, knots: 18. **Range, miles:** 18,000 at 14 kt
Complement: 130 (24 officers)
Cargo capacity: 10,550 tons fuel; 1,000 tons dieso; 200 tons feed water; 200 tons drinking water; 4 small cranes
Guns: 8—37 mm (4 twin) (fitted for but not with).
Radars: Navigation: Fin Curve or Racal Decca 1290; I-band.
Helicopters: Platform for 1 medium.

Comment: Operational in late 1979. This is the first class of ships built for underway replenishment in the Chinese Navy. Helicopter platform but no hangar. All built at Dalian. Two liquid replenishment positions each side with one solid replenishment position each side by the funnel. A third of the class *Hongcang* (X 950) was converted to merchant use in 1989 and renamed *Hai Lang*, registered at Dalian. A fourth (X 350) was sold to Pakistan in 1987. One based in the North and one in the East.   *UPDATED*

DONGYUN   *11/1997* * / 0012210

1 NANYUN CLASS (REPLENISHMENT SHIP) (AOR/AK)

Name	No	Builders	Launched	Commissioned
NANCANG (ex-*Vladimir Peregudov*)	953	Kherson/Dalian	Apr 1992	2 June 1996

Displacement, tons: 37,000 full load
Measurement, tons: 28,750 dwt
Dimensions, feet (metres): 586.9 × 83 × 36.1
(178.9 × 25.3 × 11)
Main machinery: 1 B&W diesel; 11,600 hp(m) *(8.53 MW)*; 1 shaft
Speed, knots: 16
Complement: 125
Cargo capacity: 9,630 tons fuel
Helicopters: 1 Super Frelon.

Comment: One of a class of 11 built at Kherson Shipyard, Crimea. Laid down in January 1989. Sailed from Ukraine to Dalian Shipyard in 1993. Completed fitting out in China and joined the South Sea Fleet. RAS rigs on both sides and stern refuelling. Similar to Indian *Jyoti* but with better helicopter facilities.

UPDATED

NANCANG
5/1998, John Mortimer / 0017741

NANCANG   *5/1998, Sattler/Steele /* 0017742

6 QIONGSHA CLASS (4 AP + 2 AH)

Y 830	Y 831	Y 832	Y 833	Y 834	Y 835

Displacement, tons: 2,150 full load
Dimensions, feet (metres): 282.1 × 44.3 × 13.1 *(86 × 13.5 × 4)*
Main machinery: 3 SKL 8 NVD 48 A-2U diesels; 3,960 hp(m) *(2.91 MW)* sustained; 3 shafts
Speed, knots: 16
Complement: 59
Military lift: 400 troops; 350 tons cargo
Guns: 8 China 14.5mm/93 (4 twin); 600 rds/min to 7 km *(3.8 n miles)*.
Radars: Navigation: Fin Curve; I-band.

Comment: Personnel attack transports begun about 1980. Previous numbers of this class were overestimated. All South Sea Fleet. Has four sets of davits, light cargo booms serving forward and aft. No helicopter pad. Twin funnels. Carries a number of LCAs. Two converted to Hospital Ships (AH) and painted white.

UPDATED

3 DAJIANG CLASS (SUBMARINE SUPPORT SHIPS) (ASR)

CHANGXINGDAO J 121	CHONGMINGDAO J 302	YONGXINGDAO J 506

Displacement, tons: 11,975 full load
Dimensions, feet (metres): 511.7 × 67.2 × 22.3 *(156 × 20.5 × 6.8)*
Main machinery: 2 MAN K9Z60/105E diesels; 9,000 hp(m) *(6.6 MW)*; 2 shafts
Speed, knots: 20
Complement: 308
Guns: Light MGs. Can carry 6—37 mm (3 twin).
Radars: Surface search: Eye Shield; E-band.
Navigation: 2 Fin Curve; I-band.
Helicopters: 2 Aerospatiale SA 321G Super Frelon.

Comment: Submarine support and salvage ships built at Shanghai. First launched in mid-1973, operational in 1976. *Yongxingdao* has a smoke deflector on funnel. Provision for DSRV on forward well-deck aft of launching crane. A fourth and fifth of the class are listed under *Research Ships*. Foremast on *Yongxingdao* suggests secondary use as a research ship role with long-range communications similar to Russian ships. One based in each Fleet. *UPDATED*

QIONGSHA 831   *2/1999* * */* 0056784

CHANGXINGDAO   *6/1994* *, Ships of the World /* 0056785

YONGXINGDAO   *6/1996* * */* 0012206

1 DAZHI CLASS (SUBMARINE SUPPORT SHIP) (AS)

DAZHI 920

Displacement, tons: 5,600 full load
Dimensions, feet (metres): 350 × 50 × 20 *(106.7 × 15.3 × 6.1)*
Main machinery: Diesel-electric; 2 diesel generators; 3,500 hp(m) *(2.57 MW)*; 2 shafts
Speed, knots: 14. **Range, miles:** 6,000 at 14 kt
Complement: 290
Cargo capacity: 500 tons dieso
Guns: 4 China 37 mm/63 (2 twin). 4—25 mm/60 (2 twin).
Radars: Navigation: Fin Curve; I-band.

Comment: Built at Hudong, Shanghai 1963-65. Has four electrohydraulic cranes. Carries large stock of torpedoes and stores. Based in East Sea Fleet and seldom goes to sea.

VERIFIED

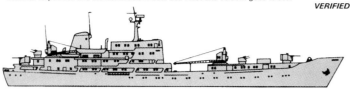

DAZHI   (not to scale)

1 DADONG and 1 DADAO CLASS (SALVAGE SHIPS) (ARS)

304   +1

Displacement, tons: 1,500 full load
Dimensions, feet (metres): 269 × 36.1 × 8.9 *(82 × 11 × 2.7)*
Main machinery: 2 diesels; 7,400 hp(m) *(5.44 MW)*; 2 shafts
Speed, knots: 18
Complement: 150
Guns: 4—25 mm/80 (2 twin).
Radars: Navigation: Type 756; I-band.

Comment: *304* reported to have been built at Hudong. Has a large and conspicuous crane aft. Principal role is wreck location and salvage. A similar ship called the 'Dadao' class was launched in January 1986. This vessel is slightly larger (84 × 12.4 m) and is civilian manned. Both ships are in the East Sea Fleet.

UPDATED

'DADAO' class   1989, Gilbert Gyssels

4 DALANG CLASS (SUBMARINE SUPPORT SHIPS) (ASR)

503   122   911   428

Displacement, tons: 3,700 standard; 4,200 full load
Dimensions, feet (metres): 367 × 47.9 × 14.1 *(111.9 × 14.6 × 4.3)*
Main machinery: 2 diesels; 4,000 hp(m) *(2.94 MW)*; 2 shafts
Speed, knots: 16. **Range, miles:** 8,000 at 14 kt
Complement: 180
Guns: 8 China 37 mm/63 (4 twin). 4 or 8 China 14.5 mm/93 (2 or 4 twin) MGs.
Radars: Navigation: Fin Curve; I-band.

Comment: Details given are for the first two built at Guangzhou Shipyard. *503* commissioned November 1975, *122* in 1986. *911* built at Wuhu Shipyard, commissioning in late 1986, and *428* was launched in June 1996. Sometimes called 'Dalang I' and 'Dalang II' classes. Have been used as AGIs.

UPDATED

DALANG 911   9/1997* / 0012207

DALANG 428   6/1997*, A Sharma / 0017743

2 DAZHOU CLASS (SUBMARINE TENDERS) (ASL)

502   504

Displacement, tons: 1,100 full load
Dimensions, feet (metres): 259.2 × 31.2 × 8.5 *(79 × 9.5 × 2.6)*
Main machinery: 2 diesels; 2 shafts
Speed, knots: 18
Complement: 130
Guns: 2 China 37 mm/63 (twin). 4—14.5 mm/93 (2 twin).
Radars: Navigation: Fin Curve; I-band.

Comment: Built in 1976-77. One in South Sea Fleet, one in the North and both have been used as AGIs.

UPDATED

DAZHOU 504   12/1990, DTM

1 HUDONG CLASS (SUBMARINE RESCUE SHIP) (ASR)

HAIJUI 512 (ex-J 301)

Displacement, tons: 4,500 standard; 4,900 full load
Dimensions, feet (metres): 308.5 × 55.8 × 15.1 *(94 × 17 × 4.6)*
Main machinery: 2 diesels; 3,600 hp(m) *(2.64 MW)*; 2 shafts
Speed, knots: 16. **Range, miles:** 5,000 at 12 kt
Complement: 225 (est)
Guns: 4 China 37 mm/63 (2 twin). 4 China 14.5 mm/93 (2 twin).
Radars: Navigation: Fin Curve; I-band.

Comment: Built at Hudong Shipyard, Shanghai. Laid down 1965, launched 1967. Design revised before completion. Has two bow and two stern anchors. Two 5 ton booms and stern gantry for submarine rescue bell. Second of class probably scrapped in 1994. Based in the East Sea Fleet.

VERIFIED

HAIJUI 512   1987

2 DSRV (SALVAGE SUBMARINES)

Displacement, tons: 35 full load
Dimensions, feet (metres): 48.9 × 8.5 × 8.5 *(14.9 × 2.6 × 2.6)*
Main machinery: 2 silver-zinc batteries; 1 mortar; 1 shaft
Speed, knots: 4. **Range, miles:** 40 at 2 kt
Complement: 3

Comment: First tested in 1986 and can be carried on large salvage ships. Capable of 'wet' rescue at 200 m and of diving to 600 m. Capacity for six survivors. Underwater TV, high-frequency active sonar and a manipulator arm are all fitted. Life support duration is 1,728 man-hours.

UPDATED

DSRV   1991*, CSSC / 0056786

2 YANTAI CLASS (AK)

800   801

Displacement, tons: 3,330 full load
Dimensions, feet (metres): 393.6 × 50 × 9.8 *(120 × 15.3 × 3)*
Main machinery: 2 diesels; 9,600 hp(m) *(7.06 MW)*; 2 shafts
Speed, knots: 17. **Range, miles:** 3,000 at 16 kt
Complement: 100
Guns: 2 China 37 mm/63 (twin).
Radars: Navigation: Type 756; I-band.

Comment: First seen in 1992. Based in South Sea Fleet.

UPDATED

YANTAI 800   6/1996* / 0056789

1 ACHELOUS CLASS (REPAIR SHIP) (ARL)

DAGUSHAN (ex-*Hsiang An*, ex-*Achilles* ARL 41, ex-LST 455) U 891

Displacement, tons: 1,625 light; 4,325 full load
Dimensions, feet (metres): 328 × 50 × 14 *(100 × 15.2 × 4.3)*
Main machinery: 2 GM 12-567A diesels; 1,800 hp *(1.34 MW)*; 2 shafts
Speed, knots: 12
Complement: 270
Guns: 12 China 37 mm/63 (6 twin). 4 China 14.5 mm/93 (2 twin).
Radars: Navigation: Fin Curve; I-band.

Comment: Launched on 17 October 1942. Transferred to Nationalist China from the USA as *Hsiang An* in September 1947. Burned and grounded in 1949, salvaged and refitted. Has 60 ton A-frame and 25 ton crane. Based in East Sea Fleet. **UPDATED**

DAGUSHAN 7/1985*, Fischer/Donko / 0056787

2 DAYUN (TYPE 904) CLASS (AK)

951   952

Displacement, tons: 8,500 full load
Dimensions, feet (metres): 407.5 × 42 × 12.5 *(124.2 × 12.8 × 3.8)*
Main machinery: 2 diesels; 9,000 hp(m) *(6.6 MW)*; 2 shafts
Speed, knots: 22
Complement: 240
Guns: 4—37 mm/63 (2 twin). 4—25 mm/80 (2 twin).
Radars: Navigation: 2 Type 756; I-band.
Helicopters: 2 SA 321 Super Frelon.

Comment: First of class completed at Hudong Shipyard in March 1992, second in August 1992. Similar to 'Dajiang' class support ships and with a similar crane on the foredeck. Four landing craft are embarked. Both based in South Sea Fleet. A reported third of class was in fact the first of the larger 'Nanyun' class. **UPDATED**

DAYUN 952 12/1998*, Ships of the World / 0056788

13 DANLIN CLASS (AK/AOT)

| 531 | 591 | 592 | 594 | 794 | 972 | 975 | +3 |
| 827 | 834 | 835 |

Displacement, tons: 1,290 full load
Dimensions, feet (metres): 198.5 × 29.5 × 13.1 *(60.5 × 9 × 4)*
Main machinery: 1 USSR/PRC Type 6DRN 30/50 diesel; 750 hp(m) *(551 kW)*; 1 shaft
Speed, knots: 15
Complement: 35
Cargo capacity: 750-800 tons
Guns: 4—25 mm/80 (2 twin). 4—14.5 mm (2 twin).
Radars: Navigation: Fin Curve or Skin Head; I-band.

Comment: Built in China in early 1960-62. The six AKs have refrigerated stores capability and serve in the South Sea Fleet. The seven AOTs are split between the Fleets. **UPDATED**

DANLIN 794 5/1992*, Henry Dodds / 0056790

3 DANDAO CLASS (AK/AOT)

201   599   803

Displacement, tons: 1,600 full load
Dimensions, feet (metres): 215.6 × 41 × 13 *(65.7 × 12.5 × 4)*
Main machinery: 1 diesel; 1 shaft
Speed, knots: 12
Complement: 40
Guns: 4 China 37 mm/63 (2 twin). 4 China 14.5 mm/93 (2 twin).
Radars: Navigation: Fin Curve; I-band.

Comment: Built in the late 1970s. Similar to the 'Danlin' class. Two in the North and one in the East Sea Fleet. **UPDATED**

DANDAO 803 12/1998* / 0056792

5 HONGQI CLASS (AK)

443   528   755   756   771

Displacement, tons: 1,950 full load
Dimensions, feet (metres): 203.4 × 39.4 × 14.4 *(62 × 12 × 4.4)*
Main machinery: 1 diesel; 1 shaft
Speed, knots: 14. **Range, miles:** 2,500 at 11 kt
Complement: 35
Guns: 4 China 25/80 (2 twin).

Comment: Used to support offshore military garrisons. A further ship, L 202, appears to be similar but carries no armament. Others of this type in civilian use. Three in the North, two in the East Sea Fleet. **UPDATED**

HONGQI 756 11/1997* / 0012208

9 LEIZHOU CLASS (AWT/AOT)

| 728 | 736 | 792 | 793 | 823 |
| 826 | 828 | 973 | 974 |

Displacement, tons: 900 full load
Dimensions, feet (metres): 173.9 × 32.2 × 10.5 *(53 × 9.8 × 3.2)*
Main machinery: 1 diesel; 500 hp(m) *(367 kW)*; 1 shaft
Speed, knots: 12. **Range, miles:** 1,200 at 10 kt
Complement: 25-30
Cargo capacity: 450 tons
Guns: 4—14.5 mm/93 (2 twin).
Radars: Navigation: Skin Head; I-band.

Comment: Built in late 1960s at Qingdao and Wudong. Split between the Fleets. Some have been converted to carry water, others carry oil. Many deleted or in civilian use. **UPDATED**

LEIZHOU 838 6/1996, Giorgio Arra / 0012209

8 FULIN CLASS (REPLENISHMENT SHIPS) (AWT)

Displacement, tons: 2,300 standard
Dimensions, feet (metres): 216.5 × 42.6 × 13.1 *(66 × 13 × 4)*
Main machinery: 1 diesel; 600 hp(m) *(441 kW)*; 1 shaft
Speed, knots: 10. **Range, miles:** 1,500 at 8 kt
Complement: 30
Guns: 4—25 mm/80 (2 twin).
Radars: Navigation: Fin Curve; I-band.

Comment: A total of 20 of these ships built at Hudong, Shanghai, beginning 1972. Naval ships painted grey. Both in South Sea Fleet. Many others of the class are civilian but may carry pennant numbers. **VERIFIED**

FULIN 6/1998 / 0017744

2 SHENGLI CLASS (AOT)

620   621

Displacement, tons: 3,300 standard; 4,950 full load
Dimensions, feet (metres): 331.4 × 45.3 × 18 *(101 × 13.8 × 5.5)*
Main machinery: 1 6 ESDZ 43/82B diesel; 2,600 hp(m) *(1.91 MW)*; 1 shaft
Speed, knots: 14. **Range, miles:** 2,400 at 11 kt
Complement: 48
Cargo capacity: 3,400 tons dieso
Guns: 2—37 mm/63 (twin). 4—25 mm/80 (2 twin).
Radars: Navigation: Fin Curve; I-band.

Comment: Built at Hudong SY, Shanghai in late 1970s. Others of the class in commercial service.
UPDATED

SHENGLI 621   *11/1997* / 0012213*

7 FUZHOU CLASS (AWT)

Displacement, tons: 2,100 full load
Dimensions, feet (metres): 208.3 × 41.3 × 12.5 *(63.5 × 12.6 × 3.8)*
Main machinery: 1 diesel; 600 hp(m) *(441 kW)*; 1 shaft
Speed, knots: 11
Complement: 35
Cargo capacity: 600 tons
Guns: 4—25 mm/80 (2 twin). 4—14.5 mm/93 (2 twin).
Radars: Navigation: Fin Curve; I-band.

Comment: Built 1964-70. At least 18 others of the class are civilian but may carry pennant numbers.
UPDATED

FUZHOU 940   *7/1997* / 0056791*

5 GUANGZHOU CLASS (AOTL/AWTL)

Displacement, tons: 530 full load
Dimensions, feet (metres): 160.8 × 24.6 × 9.8 *(49 × 7.5 × 3)*
Main machinery: 1 diesel; 1 shaft
Speed, knots: 10
Complement: 19
Guns: 4—14.5 mm/93 (2 twin).

Comment: Coastal tankers built in the 1970s and 1980s. At least 18 others of the class are civilian but may carry pennant numbers.
VERIFIED

GUANGZHOU   *6/1998* / 0017745

3 YEN PAI CLASS (ADG)

735   746   863

Displacement, tons: 746 standard
Dimensions, feet (metres): 213.3 × 29.5 × 8.5 *(65 × 9 × 2.6)*
Main machinery: Diesel-electric; 2 12VE 230ZC diesels; 2,200 hp(m) *(1.62 MW)*; 2 ZDH-99/57 motors; 2 shafts
Speed, knots: 16. **Range, miles:** 800 at 15 kt
Complement: 55
Guns: 4—37 mm/63 (2 twin). 4—25 mm/80 (2 twin).
Radars: Navigation: Type 756; I-band.

Comment: Enlarged version of T 43 MSF with larger bridge and funnel amidships. Reels on quarterdeck for degaussing function. Not all the guns are embarked.
UPDATED

YEN PAI 735   *12/1998* / 0056793*

SURVEY AND RESEARCH SHIPS

Notes: (1) In addition to the naval ships shown in this section there are large numbers of civilian marine survey ships. The majority belong to the **National Marine Bureau** and have funnel markings of a red star with light blue wave patterns on either side. There are about 37 ships with names *Zhong Guo Hai Jian* or *Xiang Yang Hong* followed by a pennant number. The **National Land Resources Department** has two Geological Survey Squadrons and these ships have a red star and light blue ring on a white or yellow background. The **State Education Department** Science section owns ships with funnel markings of yellow and blue lines either side of a circular blue design. Also there are a few nationalised companies such as the **China Marine Oil Company** which have a band of light blue round the top of the funnel.
(2) There are some 80 fishing trawlers converted for offshore surveillance.

AGI 201 (converted trawler)   *6/1997*, A Sharma* / 0017746

XIANG YANG HONG 09 (National Marine Bureau)   *7/1997* / 0012223*

ZHONG GUO HAI JIAN 47 (National Marine Bureau)   *10/1995*, van Ginderen Collection* / 0056794

FENDOU SHIHAO (National Land Resources)   *6/1999*, Ships of the World* / 0056795

DONG FANG HONG 2 (State Education Department)   *6/1999*, Ships of the World* / 0056796

HAI YING 12 HAO (China Marine Oil Company)   *6/1997*, A Sharma* / 0006690

1 DAHUA CLASS (AGOR/AGE)

970 (ex-909)

Displacement, tons: 6,000 full load
Dimensions, feet (metres): 433.1 × 58.1 × 23 *(132 × 17.7 × 7)*
Main machinery: 2 diesels; 2 shafts
Speed, knots: 20
Complement: 80

Comment: Launched on 9 March 1997 with pennant number 909 at Zhonghua, and completed in August 1997 with new pennant number. There is a helicopter deck aft and the ship is probably being used for weapon systems trials, including a VLS missile.

UPDATED

DAHUA 970   *6/1999* */ 0056797*

4 SPACE EVENT SHIPS (AGM/AGI)

YUAN WANG 1	YUAN WANG 2	YUAN WANG 3	YUAN WANG 4	+1

Displacement, tons: 17,100 standard; 18,400 full load
Dimensions, feet (metres): 610.2 × 74.1 × 24.6 *(186 × 22.6 × 7.5)*
Main machinery: 1 Sulzer diesel; 17,400 hp(m) *(12.78 MW)*; 1 shaft
Speed, knots: 20. **Range, miles:** 18,000 at 20 kt
Complement: 470

Comment: Details given are for the four. Built by Shanghai Jiangnan Yard. First two commissioned in 1979, the third in April 1995 and a fourth in late 1996. Have helicopter platform but no hangar. Extensive communications, SATNAV and meteorological equipment fitted in the first pair in Jiangnan SY in 1986-87. Both refitted in 1991-92. Third and fourth of class have some structural differences. Based in the East Sea Fleet, but all belong to the National Marine Bureau.

UPDATED

YUAN WANG 1   *6/1995* */ 0056799*

YUAN WANG 3   *11/1999* *, Robert Pabst / 0056798*

1 SPACE EVENT SHIP (AGM/AGI)

SHIYAN

Displacement, tons: 6,000 full load
Dimensions, feet (metres): 426.5 × 53.8 × 21.3 *(130 × 16.4 × 6.5)*
Main machinery: 2 diesels; 2 shafts
Speed, knots: 20
Complement: 250

Comment: First seen fitting out in 1999. A larger version of 'Dadie' class with extensive space monitoring equipment. Expected to be in service in 2000, probably with the National Marine Bureau. The name is unconfirmed.

NEW ENTRY

SHIYAN   *6/1999* *, Ships of the World / 0056800*

1 DADIE CLASS (AGI)

BEIDIAO 841

Displacement, tons: 2,550 full load
Dimensions, feet (metres): 308.4 × 37.1 × 13.1 *(94 × 11.3 × 4)*
Main machinery: 2 diesels; 2 shafts
Speed, knots: 17
Complement: 170 (18 officers)
Guns: 4 China 37 mm/63 (2 twin).
Radars: Navigation: 2 Type 753; I-band.

Comment: Built at Wuhan shipyard, Wuchang and commissioned in 1986. North Sea Fleet and seen regularly in Sea of Japan and East China Sea.

VERIFIED

BEIDIAO   *10/1997 / 0017748*

2 KAN CLASS (AGOR)

101	102

Displacement, tons: 1,100 full load
Dimensions, feet (metres): 225 × 22.5 × 9 *(68.6 × 6.9 × 2.7)*
Main machinery: 2 diesels; 2 shafts
Speed, knots: 18
Complement: 150
Radars: Navigation: Fin Curve; I-band.

Comment: Details given are for *102* which is believed built in 1985-87, possibly at Shanghai. Large open stern area. Aft main deck area covered and may have cable reel system. *101* is similar but slightly larger and may have been built in 1965 as an ASR. Operate in East China Sea and Sea of Japan.

VERIFIED

KAN 102   *9/1990, G Jacobs*

2 YANQIAN CLASS (AGOR)

V 231	V 232

Displacement, tons: 1,325 full load
Dimensions, feet (metres): 229.3 × 34.4 × 11.8 *(69.9 × 10.5 × 3.6)*
Main machinery: 2 Type 8300 ZC diesels; 2,200 hp(m) *(1.62 MW)*; 2 shafts
Speed, knots: 13.5. **Range, miles:** 2,400 at 13 kt
Complement: 110

Comment: Former 'Kansha' class, built at Chunghua SY, Shanghai in 1980-81. Trials July 1981. Designed by Chinese Marine Design and Research Institute. Carries one French SM-358-S DSRV (deep submergence recovery vehicle), 7 m long with a crew of five and an operating depth of 985 ft *(300 m)*. Ship has one 5 ton crane fwd and a 2 ton crane aft. Based in South Sea Fleet.

VERIFIED

1 HAI CLASS (AGOR)

HAI 521

Displacement, tons: 550 full load
Dimensions, feet (metres): 164 × 32.8 × 11.5 *(50 × 10 × 3.5)*
Main machinery: 2 Niigata Type 6M26KHHS diesels; 1,600 hp(m) *(1.18 MW)*; 2 shafts; bow thruster
Speed, knots: 14. **Range, miles:** 5,000 at 11 kt
Complement: 15 (7 officers) plus 25 scientists
Radars: Navigation: Japanese AR-M31; I-band.

Comment: Built by Niigata Engineering Co, Niigata (Japan) in 1974-75. Launched 10 March 1975. Commissioned July 1975. First operated by the China National Machinery Export-Import Corporation on oceanographic duties. Operates on East and South China research projects but based in North Sea Fleet. For small vessel, has cruiser stern with raked bow and small funnel well aft. Capability to operate single DSRV and the Chinese Navy has a number of Japanese-built KSWB-300 submersibles. Painted white. This ship may belong to the China Marine Oil Company.

UPDATED

HAI 521   *4/1996* */ 0056801*

1 SHUGUANG CLASS (ex T-43) (AGOR/AGS)

203

Displacement, tons: 500 standard; 570 full load
Dimensions, feet (metres): 190.3 × 28.9 × 11.5 *(58 × 8.8 × 3.5)*
Main machinery: 2 PRC/Kolomna Type 9-D-8 diesels; 2,000 hp(m) *(1.47 MW)* sustained; 2 shafts
Speed, knots: 15. **Range, miles:** 5,300 at 8 kt
Complement: 55-60

Comment: Converted from ex-Soviet T43 minesweeper in late 1960s. Painted white. This last survivor is based in the North Sea Fleet. *UPDATED*

SHUGUANG 203   *10/1997*, van Ginderen Collection /* 0012980

1 GANZHU CLASS (AGS)

420

Displacement, tons: 1,000 full load
Dimensions, feet (metres): 213.2 × 29.5 × 9.7 *(65 × 9 × 3)*
Main machinery: 4 diesels; 4,400 hp(m) *(3.23 MW)*; 2 shafts
Speed, knots: 20
Complement: 125
Guns: 4—37 mm/63 (2 twin); 4—14.5 mm (2 twin).

Comment: Built at Zhujiang in 1973-75. Long refit in 1996 for up to two years. *NEW ENTRY*

GANZHU 420   *8/1998* /* 0056802

5 YENLAI CLASS (AGS)

200	226	420	427	943

Displacement, tons: 1,040 full load
Dimensions, feet (metres): 241.8 × 32.1 × 9.7 *(73.7 × 9.8 × 3)*
Main machinery: 2 PRC/Kolomna Type 9-D-8 diesels; 2,000 hp(m) *(1.47 MW)* sustained; 2 shafts
Speed, knots: 16. **Range, miles:** 4,000 at 14 kt
Complement: 25
Guns: 4 China 37 mm/63 (2 twin). 4—25 mm/80 (2 twin).
Radars: Navigation: Fin Curve; I-band.

Comment: Built at Zhonghua Shipyard, Shanghai in early 1970s. Carries four survey motor boats. *UPDATED*

YENLAI 427   *6/1997*, Giorgio Arra /* 0012225

6 YANNAN CLASS (AGS)

124	263	463	982	983	B-22

Displacement, tons: 1,750 standard
Dimensions, feet (metres): 237.2 × 38.7 × 13.1 *(72.3 × 11.8 × 4)*
Main machinery: 2 diesels; 2,640 hp(m) *(1.94 MW)*; 2 shafts
Speed, knots: 12
Complement: 95
Guns: 4 China 37 mm/63 (2 twin). 4 China 14.5 mm/93 (2 twin).
Radars: Navigation: Fin Curve; I-band.

Comment: Built 1978-79; commissioned 1980. *UPDATED*

YANNAN B-22   *9/1997*, Fafio /* 0056803

ICEBREAKERS

1 YANBING (MOD YANHA) CLASS (AGB/AGI)

723

Displacement, tons: 4,420 full load
Dimensions, feet (metres): 334.6 × 56 × 19.5 *(102 × 17.1 × 5.9)*
Main machinery: Diesel-electric; 2 diesel generators; 2 motors; 2 shafts
Speed, knots: 17
Complement: 95
Guns: 8—37 mm/63 Type 61/74 (4 twin).
Radars: Navigation: 2 Fin Curve; I-band.

Comment: Enlarged version of 'Yanha' class icebreaker, built in 1982, with greater displacement, longer and wider hull, added deck level and curved upper funnel. In October 1990, painted white while operating in Sea of Japan. Used as an AGI in the North Sea Fleet. *UPDATED*

YANBING 723   *5/1999*, Ships of the World /* 0056804

3 YANHA CLASS (AGB/AGI)

519	721	722

Displacement, tons: 3,200 full load
Dimensions, feet (metres): 290 × 53 × 17 *(88.4 × 16.2 × 5.2)*
Main machinery: Diesel-electric; 2 diesel generators; 1 motor; 1 shaft
Speed, knots: 17.5
Complement: 90
Guns: 8—37 mm/63 Type 61/74 (4 twin). 4—25 mm/80 Type 61.
Radars: Navigation: Fin Curve; I-band.

Comment: *721* and *722* built in 1969-70. *519* commissioned in 1989. Used as AGIs in the North Sea Fleet. *VERIFIED*

519   *10/1991, G Jacobs*

TUGS

Note: The vessels below represent a cross-section of the craft available.

4 TUZHONG CLASS (ATA)

154	710	830	890

Displacement, tons: 3,600 full load
Dimensions, feet (metres): 278.5 × 46 × 18 *(84.9 × 14 × 5.5)*
Main machinery: 2 10 ESDZ 43/82B diesels; 8,600 hp(m) *(6.32 MW)*; 2 shafts
Speed, knots: 18.5
Complement: 120
Radars: Navigation: Fin Curve; I-band.

Comment: Built in late 1970s. Can be fitted with twin 37 mm AA armament and at least one of the class *(710)* has been fitted with a Square Tie radar. 35 ton towing winch. One in each Fleet and one in reserve. *UPDATED*

TUZHONG   *11/1996*, A Sharma /* 0012228

1 DAOZHA CLASS (ATA)

Displacement, tons: 4,000 full load
Dimensions, feet (metres): 275.6 × 41.3 × 17.7 *(84 × 12.6 × 5.4)*
Main machinery: 2 diesels; 8,600 hp(m) *(6.32 MW)*; 2 shafts
Speed, knots: 18
Complement: 125

Comment: Built in 1993-94 probably as a follow-on to the 'Tuzhong' class. Based in South Sea Fleet.   ***VERIFIED***

DAOZHA   *9/1993, Hachiro Nakai*

17 GROMOVOY CLASS (ATA)

149	156	166	167	680	683	684	716	802
809	811	813	814	817	822	824	827	

Displacement, tons: 795 standard; 890 full load
Dimensions, feet (metres): 149.9 × 31.2 × 15.1 *(45.7 × 9.5 × 4.6)*
Main machinery: 2 diesels; 1,300 hp(m) *(956 kW)*; 2 shafts
Speed, knots: 11. **Range, miles:** 7,000 at 7 kt
Complement: 25-30 (varies)
Guns: 4—14.5 mm (2 twin) or 12.7 mm (2 twin) MGs.
Radars: Navigation: Fin Curve or OKI X-NE-12 (Japanese); I-band.

Comment: Built at Luda Shipyard and Shanghai International, 1958-62. Four in North Sea Fleet, nine in East Sea Fleet and four in South Sea Fleet.   ***UPDATED***

GROMOVOY 802   *5/1992*, Henry Dodds /* 0056805

9 HUJIU CLASS (ATA)

147	155	622	711	717	837	842	843	875

Displacement, tons: 1,470 full load
Dimensions, feet (metres): 197.5 × 38.1 × 14.4 *(60.2 × 11.6 × 4.4)*
Main machinery: 2 LVP 24 diesels; 1,800 hp(m) *(1.32 MW)*; 2 shafts
Speed, knots: 15. **Range, miles:** 7,200 at 14 kt
Complement: 56
Radars: Navigation: Fin Curve or Type 756; I-band.

Comment: Built at Wuhu in 1980s. One sold to Bangladesh in 1984 and a second in 1995. Three based in the North and East, three in the South Sea Fleet.   ***UPDATED***

HUJIU 875   *6/1999* /* 0056806

19 ROSLAVL CLASS (ATA/ARS)

153	159	161-164	168	518	604	613
618	646	707	852-854	862	863	867

Displacement, tons: 670 full load
Dimensions, feet (metres): 149.9 × 31 × 15.1 *(45.7 × 9.5 × 4.6)*
Main machinery: Diesel-electric; 2 diesel generators; 1,200 hp(m) *(882 kW)*; 1 motor; 1 shaft
Speed, knots: 12. **Range, miles:** 6,000 at 11 kt
Complement: 28
Guns: 4—14.5 mm (2 twin) MGs.

Comment: Built in China in mid-1960s to the USSR design. One carries diving bell and submarine rescue gear on stern and is classified as ARS. Split evenly between the fleets.   ***VERIFIED***

ROSLAVL 854   *6/1998 /* 0017752

MARITIME MILITIA (MBDF)

Notes: (1) China has four regular paramilitary maritime Security Forces: the Customs Service *(Hai Guan)*; the maritime section of the Public Security Bureau *(Hai Gong)*; the maritime command *(Gong Bian)* of the Border Security Force (which is itself a part of the PLA-subordinated People's Armed Police); and the Border Defence *(Bian Jian)*.

These four organisations patrol extensively with a variety of vessels. In recent years the better disciplined and centrally controlled *Hai Guan* has received a significant number of new vessels, many of them with offshore capabilities. A number of Haitun helicopters are also in service.

There have been many reports of Chinese paramilitary vessels committing acts of piracy in the South China Sea, particularly *Gong Bian* vessels. *Gong Bian* and *Hai Guan* patrol vessels have been operating as far as the coasts of Luzon and Taiwan.
(2) Types of vessels vary from Huxins, Shanghai IIs and Huludaos to a number of other designs spread across all forces. For example 'Huxin' and 'Huludao' classes can show the markings of all four services.
(3) Chinese characters used on pennant numbers are:

a. 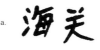   HAI GUAN (HOI KWAN) — CUSTOMS

b.   HAI GONG (HOI KUNG) — MARITIME POLICE

c. 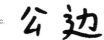   GONG BIAN (KUNG BIN) — BORDER SECURITY

d. 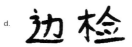   BIAN JIAN (PIN KAM) — BORDER DEFENCE

(4) From December 1999 pennant numbers have been standardised to show the vessels' legitimate operating area. This is an attempt to crack down on illegal activities by making it easier for merchant ships to report violations to the Maritime Police (Hai Gong), who have taken overall responsibility.

BORDER SECURITY FORCE
MARITIME COMMAND (GONG BIAN)

HUXIN CLASS

Displacement, tons: 165 full load
Dimensions, feet (metres): 91.9 × 13.8 × 5.2 *(28 × 4.2 × 1.6)*
Main machinery: 2 diesels; 1,000 hp(m) *(735 kW)*; 2 shafts
Speed, knots: 13. **Range, miles:** 400 at 10 kt
Complement: 26
Guns: 2 China 14.5 mm/93 (twin).
Radars: Surface search: Skin Head; I-band.

Comment: This is a class of modified Huangpu design with a greater freeboard and a slightly larger displacement. First seen in 1989 and now in series production. Huxin 178 is a modified command vessel with a forward superstructure extension.   ***VERIFIED***

HUXIN   *4/1998 /* 0017753

COASTAL PATROL CRAFT (NEW)

Displacement, tons: 58 full load
Dimensions, feet (metres): 73.8 × 15.7 × 5.2 *(22.5 × 4.8 × 1.6)*
Main machinery: 2 diesels; 1,600 hp(m) *(1.18 MW)*; 2 shafts
Speed, knots: 22. **Range, miles:** 850 at 11 kt
Complement: 13
Guns: 2—14.5 mm (twin).
Radars: Surface search: I-band.

Comment: Large numbers of this type in all Fleet areas. Frequently involved in piracy and other illegal activities, although whether as official policy or as a result of private enterprise is unknown. Armaments vary.

UPDATED

GONG BIAN 4401   6/1999* / 0056807

GONG BIAN 4407   6/1997 / 0017754

COASTAL PATROL CRAFT (OLD)

Displacement, tons: 82 full load
Dimensions, feet (metres): 82 × 13.5 × 4.6 *(25 × 4.1 × 1.4)*
Main machinery: 2 diesels; 900 hp(m) *(662 kW)*; 2 shafts
Speed, knots: 14. **Range, miles:** 900 at 11 kt
Complement: 12
Guns: 4—14.5 mm/93 2 (twin).
Radars: Surface search: Fin Curve; I-band.

Comment: Large numbers of this type still extensively used although numbers are declining in favour of Huxin and the newer CPC design.

UPDATED

GONG BIAN 1301   3/1995*, van Ginderen Collection / 0056808

STEALTH CRAFT

Comment: Since 1996 large numbers of low profile stealth craft have been active in the South Sea areas, and have been reported as far away as the Philippines. Sizes vary from 30 to 60 m in length and many are capable of speeds in excess of 30 kt. Most are paramilitary vessels but some may be privately owned.

UPDATED

STEALTH   8/1996* / 0012232

INSHORE PATROL CRAFT

Displacement, tons: 32 full load
Dimensions, feet (metres): 62 × 13.1 × 3.6 *(18.9 × 4 × 1.1)*
Main machinery: 2 diesels; 900 hp(m) *(662 kW)*; 2 shafts
Speed, knots: 15
Complement: 5
Guns: 1—12.7 mm MG.

Comment: Details given are for the standard small patrol craft. In addition there are a number of speedboats confiscated from smugglers and used for interception duties.

UPDATED

GONG BIAN 3110   4/1998 / 0017755

GONG BIAN SPEEDBOAT   2/1995*, T Hollingsbee / 0056809

CUSTOMS (HAI GUAN) AND PUBLIC SECURITY BUREAU (HAI GONG) AND BORDER DEFENCE (BIAN JIAN)

HULUDAO CLASS (TYPE 206)
(FAST ATTACK CRAFT—PATROL) (PC)

Displacement, tons: 180 full load
Dimensions, feet (metres): 147.6 × 21 × 5.6 *(45 × 6.4 × 1.7)*
Main machinery: 3 MWM TBD604BV12 diesels; 5,204 hp(m) *(3.82 MW)* sustained; 3 shafts
Speed, knots: 29. **Range, miles:** 1,000 at 15 kt
Complement: 24 (6 officers)
Guns: 6 China 14.5 mm Type 82 (3 twin); 600 rds/min to 7 km *(3.8 n miles)*; weight of shell 1.42 kg.

Comment: EEZ patrol craft first seen at Wuxi Shipyard in 1988. The craft is sometimes referred to as the 'Wuting' class.

UPDATED

HAI GONG HULUDAO   6/1995* / 0056810

7 TYPE P 58E (COMMAND SHIPS)

901-907

Displacement, tons: 435 full load
Dimensions, feet (metres): 190.3 × 24.9 × 7.5 *(58 × 7.6 × 2.3)*
Main machinery: 4 MTU diesels; 8,720 hp(m) *(6.4 MW)* sustained; 4 shafts
Speed, knots: 27. **Range, miles:** 1,500 at 12 kt
Complement: 50
Guns: 2 China 14.5 mm/93 (twin) MGs.
Radars: Surface search: I-band.

Comment: First one built at Guangzhou in 1990, last one in 1998. Less well armed but similar to those in service with Pakistan's MSA. Used as command ships. *UPDATED*

HAI GUAN 901   *1993*, T Hollingsbee* / 0056811

42 COASTAL PATROL CRAFT (NEW)

801   812   836

Displacement, tons: 98 full load
Dimensions, feet (metres): 101.7 × 15.4 × 4.6 *(31 × 4.7 × 1.4)*
Main machinery: 2 diesels; 2 shafts
Speed, knots: 32
Complement: 15
Guns: 2 China 14.5 mm/93 (twin).
Radars: Surface search: Racal Decca ARPA; I-band.

Comment: Building in Shanghai at about six a year since 1992. More may follow. *UPDATED*

HAI GUAN 812   *1993, T Hollingsbee*

COASTAL PATROL CRAFT (OLD)

Comment: Shanghai type hull but with a different superstructure. Two twin 14.5 mm MGs. Being phased out and replaced by the 800 series of patrol craft.
UPDATED

HAI GUAN 62   *6/1995** / 0056812

2 COMBATBOAT 90E

Displacement, tons: 9 full load
Dimensions, feet (metres): 39 × 9.5 × 2.3 *(11.9 × 2.9 × 0.7)*
Main machinery: 1 Scania AB DSI 14 diesel; 398 hp(m) *(293 kW)*; waterjet
Speed, knots: 40
Complement: 2

Comment: Two delivered to Hai Guan in April 1997. This is the transport version of the Swedish raiding craft and can lift two tons of stores or 6-10 troops.
UPDATED

COMBATBOAT 90E (Swedish colours)   *5/1999*, Per Kornefeldt* / 0056813

COLOMBIA
ARMADA DE LA REPUBLICA

Headquarters Appointments

Fleet Commander:
   Admiral Sergio Garcia Torres
Deputy Fleet Commander:
   Vice Admiral Pedro Monsalve Angarita
Chief of Naval Operations:
   Rear Admiral William Porras Ferreira
Commander Atlantic Force:
   Rear Admiral Jairo Cardona Forero
Commander Pacific Force:
   Rear Admiral Jamie Jaramillo Gómez
Commander Marine Corps:
   Brigadier General Luis Eduardo Peñuela Anzola

Personnel

(a) 2000: 7,500 (Navy); 11,050 (Marines); 200 (Coast Guard);
     100 (Aircrew)
(b) 2 years' national service (few conscripts in the Navy)

Bases

ARC Bolivar, Cartagena, Main naval base (floating dock, 1 slipway), schools.
ARC Bahía Málaga: Major Pacific base.
ARC Barranquilla: Naval training base.
ARC Puerto Leguízamo: Putumayo River base.
ARC Leticia: Minor River base.
Puerto López: Minor River base.
Puerto Carreño: Minor River base.
Barrancabermeja: Minor River base.
San Andrés y Providencia: Specific Command

Dimar

Maritime authority in charge of hydrography and navigational aids.

Organisation

Atlantic Force Command: HQ at Cartagena.
Pacific Force Command: HQ at Bahia Malaga.
Naval Force South: HQ at Puerto Leguízamo.
Riverine Brigade: HQ at Santafé de Bogotá.
Coast Guard: HQ at Bogotá.

Marine Corps

Organisation: First Brigade (Sincelejo):
No. 3 Battalion (Malaga)
No. 21 MP Battalion (Cartagena de Indias)
No. 5 Battalion (Corozal)
No. 43 Training Battalion, (Coveñas)
No. 23 MP Battalion (Coveñas)
No. 41 Training Battalion (Coveñas)
Specials Forces Battalion (Cartagena de Indias)
Nos. 31-33 Battalions (Sincelejo)
Second Brigade (Buenaventura).
No. 6 Battalion (Bahía Solano)
No. 40 training Battalion (Tumaco)
No. 2 Battalion (Tumaco)
No. 4 Battalion (Puerto Leguizamo)

Coast Guard and Customs (DIAN)

The Coast Guard was established in 1979 but then gave way to the Customs Service before being re-established in January 1992 under the control of the Navy. Headquarters at Bogotá. Main bases are Cartagena, Buenaventura y Turbo and Valle. Ships have a red and yellow diagonal stripe on the hull and patrol craft have a PM number. Customs craft were absorbed into the Coast Guard but by 1995 were again independent as part of the DIAN (Direccion de Impuestos y Aduanas Nacionales). Customs craft have Aduana written on the ship's side, a thick and two thin diagonal stripes and have AN numbers.

Strength of the Fleet

Type	Active
Patrol Submarines	2
Midget Submarines	2
Frigates	4
Patrol Ships and Fast Attack Craft (Gun)	12
Coast Patrol Craft	46
Amphibious Forces	11
River Patrol Craft	33
River Patrol Craft Support	9
River Assault Boats	150
Survey Vessels	7
Auxiliaries	27
Training Ships	4

Prefix to Ships' Names

ARC (Armada Republica de Colombia)

Mercantile Marine

Lloyd's Register of Shipping:
   113 vessels of 96,886 tons gross

DELETIONS

Patrol Forces

1999 *Rodrigo de Bastidas*

Auxiliaries

1997 *Nestor Ospina*

PENNANT LIST

Submarines		PB 438	Alpheraz	PRF 190	Río Putumayo	DF 170	Mayor Jaime Arias Arango
		PB 439	Bellatrix	PRF 191	Río Caqueta	NF 601	Filigonio Hichamon
SO 28	Pijao	PB 440	Canopus	PRF 192	Río Orinoco	NF 602	SSIM Manuel Antonio Moyar
SO 29	Tayrona	PB 441	Procycom	PRF 193	Río Orteguaza	NF 603	Igaraparaná
ST 20	Intrépido	PB 442	Tulcán	PRF 194	Río Vichada	NF 604	SSIM Julio Correa Hernández
ST 21	Indomable	PB 443	Halley	PRF 195	Río Guaviare	NF 605	Manacacías
		PB 444	Orca			NF 606	Cotuhe
		PB 445	Hooker Bay			NF 131	Socorro
Frigates		PB 446	Isla Bolívar	Amphibious Forces		NF 132	Hernando Gutiérrez
		PB 447	Capella			NF 146	CPCIM Guillermo Londoño
FL 51	Almirante Padilla	PC 451	Andrómeda	LD 240	Bahía Zapzurro		Vargas
FL 52	Caldas	PC 452	Casiopea	LD 241	Bahía Humbolt		
FL 53	Antioquia	PC 453	Centauro	LD 242	Bahía Octavia	Survey Vessels	
FL 54	Independiente	PC 454	Dragón	LD 246	Morrosquillo		
		PC 455	Vela	LD 247	Urabá	BO 155	Providencia
		PC 456	Polaris	LD 248	Bahía Honda	BO 156	Malpelo
Patrol Forces		PC 457	Fenix	LD 249	Bahía Portete	BH 153	Quindio
		PC 458	Regulus	LD 251	Bahía Solano	BB 31	Capitán Binney
PO 41	Espartana	PC 459	Aquila	LD 252	Bahía Cupica	BB 33	Gorgona
PO 42	Capitán Pablo José de Porto	PC 460	Perseus	LD 253	Bahía Utría	BB 34	Ciénaga de Mayorquin
PO 43	Capitán Jorge Enrique Márques	PC 461	Ramadan	LD 254	Bahía Málaga	BB 35	Abadía Médez
	Durán	PC 462	Apolo				
PM 102	Rafael del Castillo y Rada	PC 463	Zeus			Training Ships	
PM 103	TN José María Palas	PC 464	Sagitario	Auxiliaries			
PM 104	CN Medardo Monzón	PC 465	Cáncer			BE 160	Gloria
PM 105	S2 Jaime Gómez Castro	PF 135	Riohacha	BL 161	Cartagena de Indias	YT 230	Comodoro
PM 106	S2 Juan Nepomuceno Peña	PF 136	Leticia	BL 162	Buenaventura	YT 231	Tridente
PM 112	Quitasueño	PF 137	Arauca	TM 501	Bocachica	YT 232	Cristina
PM 113	José María García y Toledo	PF 121	Diligente	TM 502	Arturus		
PM 114	Juan Nepomuceno Eslava	PF 122	Juan Lucio	TM 503	Pedro David Salas		
PM 115	TECIM Jaime E Cárdenas	PF 123	Alfonso Vargas	TM 504	Sirius	Tugs	
PG 401	Altair	PF 124	Fritz Hagale	TM 506	Tolú		
PG 402	Castor	PF 125	Vengadora	TM 507	Calima	RM 72	Pedro de Heredia
PG 403	Pollux	PF 126	Humberto Cortez	TM 508	Bahí Santa Catalina	RM 73	Sebastián de Belalcázar
PG 404	Vega	PF 127	Ariarí	TM 509	Móvil I	RM 75	Andagoya
PB 421	Antares	PF 128	Carlos Galindo	TM 510	Móvil II	RM 76	Josué Alvarez
PB 422	Capricornio	PF 129	Capitán Jaime Rook	TM 511	Renacer del Pacifico	RF 81	Capitán Castro
PB 423	Acuario	PF 130	Manuela Saenz	TM 512	Jhonny Cay	RF 83	Joves Fiallo
PB 424	Picis	PRF 176	Magdalena	TM 513	Punta Evans	RF 84	Capitán Alvaro Ruiz
PB 425	Aries	PRF 177	Río Cauca	TB 542	Playa Blanca	RF 85	Miguel Silva
PB 426	Tauro	PRF 178	Río Atrato	TB 543	Tierra Bomba	RF 86	Capitán Rigoberto Giraldo
PB 427	Géminis	PRF 179	Río Sinú	TB 544	Bell Salter	RF 87	Vladimir Valek
PB 428	Deneb	PRF 180	Río San Jorge	TB 545	Maldonado	RF 88	Teniente Luis Bernal
PB 429	Rigel	PRF 181	Tenerife	TB 546	Orion	RF 91	TN Alejandro Baldomero
PB 430	Júpiter	PRF 182	Tarapaca	TB 547	Pegasso		Salgado
PB 431	Leo	PRF 183	Mompox	TB 548	Almirante I	RF 92	Carlos Rodríguez
PB 432	Aldebarán	PRF 184	Orocué	TB 549	Almirante II	RF 93	Sejeri
PB 433	Neptuno	PRF 185	Calamar	TB 550	Ara	RF 94	Ciudad de Puerto López
PB 434	Spica	PRF 186	Magangue	TB 551	Valerosa	RF 96	Inirida
PB 435	Denebola	PRF 187	Monclart	TB 552	Luchadora		
PB 436	Libra	PRF 188	Caucaya	TB 553	Azul		
PB 437	Escorpión	PRF 189	Mitú	TB 554	Portete		

SUBMARINES

2 PIJAO (209 TYPE 1200) CLASS (SS)

Name	No	Builders	Laid down	Launched	Commissioned
PIJAO	SO 28	Howaldtswerke, Kiel	1 Apr 1972	10 Apr 1974	18 Apr 1975
TAYRONA	SO 29	Howaldtswerke, Kiel	1 May 1972	16 July 1974	16 July 1975

Displacement, tons: 1,180 surfaced; 1,285 dived
Dimensions, feet (metres): 183.4 × 20.5 × 17.9
(55.9 × 6.3 × 5.4)
Main machinery: Diesel-electric; 4 MTU 12V 493 AZ80 diesels;
2,400 hp(m) *(1.76 MW)* sustained; 4 AEG alternators; 1.7 MW; 1
Siemens motor; 4,600 hp(m) *(3.38 MW)* sustained; 1 shaft
Speed, knots: 22 dived; 11 surfaced
Range, miles: 8,000 at 8 kt surfaced; 4,000 at 4 kt dived
Complement: 34 (7 officers)

Torpedoes: 8—21 in *(533 mm)* bow tubes. 14 AEG SUT; dual
purpose; wire-guided; active/passive homing to 12 km *(6.5 n
miles)* at 35 kt; 28 km *(15 n miles)* at 23 kt; warhead 250 kg.
Swim-out discharge.
Countermeasures: ESM: Thomson-CSF DR 2000; intercept.
Weapons control: Signaal M8/24 TFCS.
Radars: Surface search: Thomson-CSF Calypso II; I-band.
Sonars: Atlas Elektronik CSU 3-2; hull-mounted; active/passive
search and attack; medium frequency.
Atlas Elektronik PRS 3-4; passive ranging; integral with CSU 3.

Programmes: Ordered in 1971. Both refitted by HDW at Kiel;
Pijao completed refit in July 1990 and *Tayrona* in September
1991. Main batteries were replaced.
Structure: Diving depth, 820 ft *(250 m)*.
Operational: Being refitted 1999-2002.   ***UPDATED***

TAYRONA   *4/1999*, Michael Nitz / 0056814

2 MIDGET SUBMARINES

Name	No	Builders	Launched	Commissioned
INTREPIDO	ST 20	Cosmos, Livorno	1 Jan 1972	17 Apr 1973
INDOMABLE	ST 21	Cosmos, Livorno	1 Jan 1972	17 Apr 1973

Displacement, tons: 58 surfaced; 70 dived
Dimensions, feet (metres): 75.5 × 13.1 *(23 × 4)*
Main machinery: Diesel-electric; 1 diesel; 1 motor; 300 hp(m)
(221 kW); 1 shaft
Speed, knots: 11 surfaced; 6 dived
Range, miles: 1,200 surfaced; 60 dived
Complement: 4
Mines: 6 Mk 21 with 300 kg warhead. 8 Mk 50 with 50 kg
warhead.

Comment: They can carry eight swimmers with 2 tons of
explosive as well as two swimmer delivery vehicles (SDVs).
Built by Cosmos, Livorno and commissioned at 40 tons, but
subsequently enlarged in the early 1980s. Listed by the Navy
as 'Tactical Submarines'.

UPDATED   INDOMABLE

2/1997* / 0012233

FRIGATES

4 ALMIRANTE PADILLA CLASS (TYPE FS 1500) (FL)

Name	No	Builders	Laid down	Launched	Commissioned
ALMIRANTE PADILLA	FL 51	Howaldtswerke, Kiel	17 Mar 1981	6 Jan 1982	31 Oct 1983
CALDAS	FL 52	Howaldtswerke, Kiel	14 June 1981	23 Apr 1982	14 Feb 1984
ANTIOQUIA	FL 53	Howaldtswerke, Kiel	22 June 1981	28 Aug 1982	30 Apr 1984
INDEPENDIENTE	FL 54	Howaldtswerke, Kiel	22 June 1981	21 Jan 1983	24 July 1984

Displacement, tons: 1,500 standard; 2,100 full load

Dimensions, feet (metres): 325.1 × 37.1 × 12.1
(99.1 × 11.3 × 3.7)

Main machinery: 4 MTU 20V 1163 TB92 diesels; 23,400 hp(m)
(17.2 MW) sustained; 2 shafts; cp props

Speed, knots: 27; 18 on 2 diesels

Range, miles: 7,000 at 14 kt; 5,000 at 18 kt

Complement: 94

Missiles: SSM: 8 Aerospatiale MM 40 Exocet ❶; inertial cruise; active radar homing to 70 km *(40 n miles)* at 0.9 Mach; warhead 165 kg; sea-skimmer.
SAM: ❷ To be fitted forward of the bridge when funds become available.

Guns: 1 OTO Melara 3 in *(76 mm)*/62 compact ❸; 85 rds/min to 16 km *(8.7 n miles)*; weight of shell 6 kg.
2 Breda 40 mm/70 (twin) ❹; 300 rds/min to 12.5 km *(6.8 n miles)* anti-surface; weight of shell 0.96 kg.
4 Oerlikon 30 mm/75 Mk 74 (2 twin); 650 rds/min to 10 km *(5.5 n miles)*; 950 ready use rounds.

Torpedoes: 6—324 mm Mk 32 (2 triple) tubes ❺; anti-submarine.

Countermeasures: Decoys: 1 CSEE Dagaie double mounting; IR flares and chaff decoys (H- to J-band).
ESM: Argo AC672; radar warning.
ECM: Racal Scimitar; jammer.

Combat data systems: Thomson-CSF TAVITAC action data automation. Possibly Link Y fitted.

Weapons control: 2 Canopus optronic directors. Thomson-CSF Vega II GFCS.

Radars: Air/surface search: Thomson-CSF Sea Tiger ❻; E/F-band; range 110 km *(60 n miles)* for 2 m² target.
Navigation: Furuno; I-band.
Fire control: Castor II B ❼; I/J-band; range 15 km *(8 n miles)* for 1 m² target.
IFF: Mk 10.

Sonars: Atlas Elektronik ASO 4-2; hull-mounted; active attack; medium frequency.

Helicopters: 1 Eurocopter AS 555 Fennec ❽ or 1 Bell 412.

Programmes: Order for four Type FS 1500 placed late 1980. Reclassified as light frigates in 1999. Similar to Malaysian frigates.

Modernisation: No confirmation of SAM fit. Albatros/Aspide, Crotale and Barak have all been mentioned. A modernisation

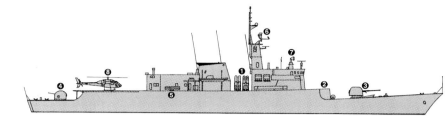

ALMIRANTE PADILLA   *(Scale 1 : 900), Ian Sturton /* 0056815

ALMIRANTE PADILLA   *4/1999*, Michael Nitz /* 0056816

programme remains the top priority and plans to replace the engines were reported in 1994, but so far no funds have been earmarked. Helicopter deck lengthened by 2 m to take Bell

412 aircraft. There have also been minor modifications to ship systems and superstructure.

UPDATED

ALMIRANTE PADILLA   *4/1999*, Michael Nitz /* 0056817

SHIPBORNE AIRCRAFT

Note: There are also two Air Force Cessna V-206G and one Beech King Air C90 land-based aircraft, used for maritime surveillance.

Numbers/Type: 3 MBB BO 105CB.
Operational speed: 113 kt *(210 km/h)*.
Service ceiling: 9,854 ft *(3,000 m)*.
Range: 407 n miles *(754 km)*.
Role/Weapon systems: Surface search and limited ASW helicopter. Sensors: Search/weather radar. Weapons: ASW; provision to carry depth bombs. ASV; light attack role with machine gun pods.

UPDATED

BO 105
1990*, Colombian Navy / 0056818

Numbers/Type: 2 Eurocopter AS 555 Fennec.
Operational speed: 121 kt *(225 km/h)*.
Service ceiling: 13,125 ft *(4,000 m)*.
Range: 389 n miles *(722 km)*.
Role/Weapon systems: OTHT capability for surface-to-surface role. Also used for logistic support. More are being acquired. Sensors: Bendix RDR 1500B radar. Weapons: Torpedoes may be fitted in due course.

NEW ENTRY

Numbers/Type: 6 Bell 412.
Operational speed: 122 kt *(226 km/h)*.
Service ceiling: 6,300 ft *(1,920 m)*.
Range: 402 n miles *(744 km)*.
Role/Weapon systems: Multipurpose used mostly for surveillance, troop transport and logistic support. Sensors: Weather radar. Weapons: ASV 7.62 mm MG can be carried.

NEW ENTRY

FENNEC   *4/1999 *, Michael Nitz /* 0056819

BELL 412   *6/1999 *, Colombian Navy /* 0056820

PATROL FORCES

2 LAZAGA CLASS (FAST ATTACK CRAFT—GUN)

Name	No	Builders	Commissioned
PABLO JOSÉ DE PORTO (ex-*Recalde*)	PO 42 (ex-PM 116, ex-P 06)	Bazán, La Carraca	17 Dec 1977
JORGE ENRIQUE MARQUEZ DURAN (ex-*Cadarso*)	PO 43 (ex-PM 117, ex-P 03)	Bazán, La Carraca	10 July 1976

Displacement, tons: 393 full load
Dimensions, feet (metres): 190.6 × 24.9 × 8.5 *(58.1 × 7.6 × 2.6)*
Main machinery: 2 MTU/Bazán 16V 956 TB 91 diesels; 7,500 hp(m) *(5.5 MW)* sustained; 2 shafts
Speed, knots: 26. **Range, miles:** 2,400 at 15 kt
Complement: 40 (4 officers)
Guns: 1 Breda 40 mm/70. 1 Oerlikon 20 mm L85. 1—12.7 mm MG.
Weapons control: CSEE optical director.
Radars: Surface search: Furuno; E/F-band.
Navigation: Furuno; I-band.

Comment: Paid off from the Spanish Navy in 1993 and put into reserve. Acquired by Colombia in March 1997 for extensive refurbishment at Bazán, San Fernando. Recommissioned 25 April 1998 and 25 June 1998 respectively. Radars have been changed and the 76 mm gun replaced by a 20 mm cannon. These ships may be used to carry troops. Four more of the class are available and more may be acquired in due course.

UPDATED

PABLO JOSÉ DE PORTO (old number)   *5/1998, Diego Quevedo /* 0017758

1 CORMORAN CLASS (FAST ATTACK CRAFT—GUN) (PCF)

Name	No	Builders	Commissioned
ESPARTANA (ex-*Cormoran*)	PO 41	Bazán, San Fernando	27 Oct 1989

Displacement, tons: 358 full load
Dimensions, feet (metres): 185.7 × 24.7 × 6.5 *(56.6 × 7.5 × 2)*
Main machinery: 3 MTU-Bazán 16V 956 TB91 diesels; 11,250 hp(m) *(8.27 MW)* sustained; 3 shafts
Speed, knots: 32. **Range, miles:** 2,500 at 15 kt
Complement: 31 (5 officers)
Guns: 1 Bofors 40/70 SP 48. 1 Oerlikon 20 mm.
Weapons control: Alcor C optronic director.
Radars: Surface search: Raytheon; I-band.

Comment: Built with overseas sales in mind, this ship was launched in October 1985, but from 1989 served in the Spanish Navy until April 1994 when she was laid up at Cartagena. Transferred in September 1995, she was then refitted at Cadiz, before sailing for Colombia in mid-1996. Based at San Andres Island and belongs to the Coast Guard.

UPDATED

3 ARAUCA CLASS (RIVER GUNBOATS) (PG)

Name	No	Builders	Commissioned
RIOHACHA	PF 135 (ex-35)	Union Industrial de Barranquilla	6 Sep 1956
LETICIA	PF 136 (ex-36)	Union Industrial de Barranquilla	6 Sep 1956
ARAUCA	PF 137 (ex-37)	Union Industrial de Barranquilla	6 Sep 1956

Displacement, tons: 275 full load
Dimensions, feet (metres): 163.5 × 27.2 × 8.9 *(49.9 × 8.3 × 2.7)*
Main machinery: 2 Caterpillar diesels; 916 hp *(683 kW)*; 2 shafts
Speed, knots: 14. **Range, miles:** 1,890 at 14 kt
Complement: 43; 39 plus 6 orderlies *(Leticia)*
Guns: 2 USN 3 in *(76 mm)*/50 Mk 26. 4 Oerlikon 20 mm (not *Leticia*).

Comment: Launched in 1955. *Leticia* has been equipped as a hospital ship with six beds and been disarmed although she has retained her pennant number.

UPDATED

ARAUCA   *1991 *, Colombian Navy /* 0056821

2 JOSÉ MARIA PALAS (SWIFT 110) CLASS
(LARGE PATROL CRAFT) (PC)

Name	No	Builders	Commissioned
JOSÉ MARIA PALAS	PM 103 (ex-GC 103)	Swiftships Inc, Berwick	Sep 1989
MEDARDO MONZON CORONADO	PM 104 (ex-GC 104)	Swiftships Inc, Berwick	July 1990

Displacement, tons: 99 full load
Dimensions, feet (metres): 109.9 × 24.6 × 6.6 *(33.5 × 7.5 × 2)*
Main machinery: 4 Detroit 12V-71TI diesels; 2,400 hp *(1.79 MW)*; 4 shafts
Speed, knots: 25. **Range, miles:** 2,250 at 15 kt
Complement: 19 (3 officers)
Guns: 1 Bofors 40 mm/60 Mk 3. 1—12.7 mm MG. 2—7.62 mm MGs.
Radars: Surface search: Raytheon; I-band.

Comment: Acquired under US FMS programme. These ships belong to the Coast Guard.

UPDATED

ESPARTANA   *10/1996 *, Colombian Navy /* 0056822

JOSÉ MARIA PALAS   *1/1996 *, van Ginderen Collection /* 0056824

2 CHEROKEE CLASS (PATROL SHIPS) (PG)

Name	No	Builders	Commissioned
PEDRO DE HEREDIA (ex-*Choctaw*)	RM 72	Charleston SB	21 Apr 1943
SEBASTION DE BELAL CALZAR (ex-*Carib*)	RM 73	Charleston SB	24 July 1943

Displacement, tons: 1,235 standard; 1,675 full load
Dimensions, feet (metres): 205 × 38.5 × 17 *(62.5 × 11.7 × 5.2)*
Main machinery: Diesel-electric; 4 GM 12-278 diesels; 4,400 hp *(3.28 MW)*; 4 generators; 1 motor; 3,000 hp *(2.24 MW)*; 1 shaft
Speed, knots: 15. **Range, miles:** 7,000 at 15 kt
Complement: 75
Guns: 1 USN 3 in *(76 mm)*/50 Mk 22.

Comment: *Pedro De Heredia* transferred from the US on loan in 1961 and by sale 31 March 1978. Second one transferred by sale on 15 March 1979. Both paid off in 1987. Reactivated in 1990. Originally built as tugs but used as patrol ships. A third of class was scrapped in 1999.
UPDATED

SEBASTION DE BELAL CALZAR   *4/1993* * / 0056823

1 ASHEVILLE CLASS (FAST ATTACK CRAFT—GUN) (PCF)

Name	No	Builders	Commissioned
QUITA SUENO (ex-*Tacoma*)	PM 112	Tacoma Boat Building	14 July 1969

Displacement, tons: 225 standard; 245 full load
Dimensions, feet (metres): 164.5 × 23.8 × 9.5 *(50.1 × 7.3 × 2.9)*
Main machinery: CODOG; 2 Cummins VT12-875M diesels; 1,450 hp *(1.08 MW)*; 1 GE LM 1500 gas turbine; 13,300 hp *(9.92 MW)*; 2 shafts; cp props
Speed, knots: 40. **Range, miles:** 1,700 at 16 kt on diesels; 325 at 37 kt
Complement: 24
Guns: 1 US 3 in *(76 mm)*/50 Mk 34; 50 rds/min to 12.8 km *(7 n miles)*; weight of shell 6 kg. 1 Bofors 40 mm/56; 160 rds/min to 11 km *(5.9 n miles)* anti-aircraft; weight of shell 0.96 kg. 2—12.7 mm (twin) MGs.
Radars: Surface search: Marconi LN66/LP; I-band.

Comment: Transferred from US by lease 16 May 1983 and recommissioned 6 September 1983 and by sale August 1989. Fire-control system removed. Unreliable propulsion system prevented further transfers of this class and it is unlikely the gas turbine is operational, which reduces the top speed to 16 kt. Belongs to the Coast Guard.
UPDATED

QUITA SUENO   *6/1998, van Ginderen Collection* / 0017759

2 TOLEDO CLASS (LARGE PATROL CRAFT) (PC)

Name	No	Builders	Commissioned
JOSÉ MARIA GARCIA Y TOLEDO	PM 113	Bender Marine, Mobile	15 July 1994
JUAN NEPOMUCENO ESLAVA	PM 114	Bender Marine, Mobile	25 May 1994

Displacement, tons: 142 full load
Dimensions, feet (metres): 116 × 24.9 × 7 *(35.4 × 7.6 × 2.1)*
Main machinery: 2 MTU 12V 396 TE94 diesels; 8,240 hp(m) *(6.1 MW)*; 2 shafts
Speed, knots: 25. **Range, miles:** 1,200 at 15 kt
Complement: 25 (5 officers)
Guns: 1 Bushmaster 25 mm/87 Mk 96. 2—12.7 mm MGs.
Radars: Surface search: Raytheon; I-band.

Comment: Acquired under US FMS programme. These ships belong to the Coast Guard.
UPDATED

JOSÉ MARIA GARCIA Y TOLEDO   *1/1996* *, van Ginderen Collection* / 0056825

2 RAFAEL DEL CASTILLO Y RADA (SWIFT 105) CLASS
(LARGE PATROL CRAFT) (PC)

Name	No	Builders	Commissioned
RAFAEL DEL CASTILLO Y RADA	PM 102 (ex-GC 102, ex-AN 202)	Swiftships Inc, Berwick	Feb 1983
TECIM JAIME E CÁRDENAS GOMEZ (ex-*Olaya Herrera*)	PM 115 (ex-AN 21, ex-AN 201)	Swiftships Inc, Berwick	16 Oct 1981

Displacement, tons: 115 full load
Dimensions, feet (metres): 105 × 22 × 7 *(31.5 × 6.7 × 2.1)*
Main machinery: 4 MTU 12V 331 TC92 diesels; 5,320 hp(m) *(3.97 MW)* sustained; 4 shafts
Speed, knots: 25. **Range, miles:** 1,200 at 18 kt
Complement: 19 (3 officers)
Guns: 1 Bofors 40 mm/60 Mk 3 (PM 102). 2—12.7 mm MGs.
Radars: Surface search: Raytheon; I-band.

Comment: Delivered for the Customs service. PM 102 is part of the Coast Guard. PM 115 was paid off, but returned unarmed as part of the resurrected Customs service until being transferred back to the Coast Guard in 1997.
UPDATED

RAFAEL DEL CASTILLO Y RADA   *6/1999* *, Colombian Navy* / 0056826

2 JAIME GÓMEZ (Mk III PB) CLASS
(COASTAL PATROL CRAFT) (PC)

Name	No	Builders	Commissioned
JAIME GÓMEZ CASTRO	PM 105 (ex-GC 105)	Peterson Builders	1975
JUAN NEPOMUCENO PEÑA	PM 106 (ex-GC 106)	Peterson Builders	1977

Displacement, tons: 34 full load
Dimensions, feet (metres): 64.9 × 18 × 5.1 *(19.8 × 5.5 × 1.6)*
Main machinery: 3 Detroit 8V-71 diesels; 690 hp *(515 kW)* sustained; 3 shafts
Speed, knots: 28. **Range, miles:** 450 at 26 kt
Complement: 7 (1 officer)
Guns: 2—12.7 mm MGs. 2—7.62 mm MGs. 1 Mk 19 grenade launcher.
Radars: Surface search: Raytheon; I-band.

Comment: Acquired from the USA. Recommissioned in December 1989 and February 1990 respectively. Original 40 mm and 20 mm guns replaced by lighter armament. Both based in the Atlantic under Coast Guard control.
UPDATED

JAIME GÓMEZ CASTRO   *1990* *, Colombian Navy* / 0056827

2 ROTORK 412 CRAFT (RIVER PATROL CRAFT) (PBR)

CAPITÁN JAIME ROOK PF 129 (ex-PM 107)   **MANUELA SAENZ** PF 130 (ex-PM 108)

Displacement, tons: 9 full load
Dimensions, feet (metres): 41.7 × 10.5 × 2.3 *(12.7 × 3.2 × 0.7)*
Main machinery: 2 Caterpillar diesels; 240 hp *(179 kW)*; 2 shafts
Speed, knots: 25
Complement: 4
Military lift: 4 tons or 8 marines
Guns: 1—12.7 mm MG. 2—7.62 mm MGs.
Radars: Surface search: Raytheon; I-band.

Comment: Acquired in 1989-90. Capable of transporting eight fully equipped marines but used as river patrol craft.
UPDATED

CAPITÁN JAIME ROOK   *1990* *, Colombian Navy* / 0056828

9 TENERIFE CLASS (RIVER PATROL CRAFT) (PBR)

TENERIFE PRF 181	OROCUE PRF 184	MONCLART PRF 187
TARAPACA PRF 182	CALAMAR PRF 185	CAUCAYA PRF 188
MOMPOX PRF 183	MAGANGUE PRF 186	MITU PRF 189

Displacement, tons: 12 full load
Dimensions, feet (metres): 40.7 × 9.5 × 2 *(12.4 × 2.9 × 0.6)*
Main machinery: 2 Caterpillar 3208 TA diesels; 850 hp *(634 kW)* sustained; 2 shafts
Speed, knots: 29. **Range, miles:** 530 at 15 kt
Complement: 5 plus 12 troops
Guns: 3—12.7 mm MGs (1 twin, 1 single). 1 Mk 19 grenade launcher. 1—7.62mm MGs.
Radars: Surface search: Raytheon 1900; I-band.

Comment: Built by Bender Marine, Mobile, Alabama. Acquired in October 1993 for anti-narcotics patrols. Aluminium hulls. Can be transported by aircraft.   *UPDATED*

TENERIFE   *1/1999* / 0012235

25 INSHORE PATROL CRAFT (PBI)

ALTAIR PG 401	ISLA BOLIVAR PB 446	REGULUS PC 458
CASTOR PG 402	ANDROMEDA PC 451	AQUILA PC 459
POLLUX PG 403	CASIOPEA PC 452	PERSEUS PC 460
VEGA PG 404	CENTAURO PC 453	RAMADAN PC 461
JUPITER PB 430	DRAGON PC 454	APOLO PC 462
NEPTUNO PB 433	VELA PC 455	ZEUS PC 463
HALLEY PB 443	POLARIS PC 456	SAGITARIO PC 464
ORCA PB 444	FENIX PC 457	CANCER PC 465
HOOKER BAY PB 445		

Comment: All are of about 10 tons. PG 401-404 have a speed of 10 kt and are armed with 2—7.62 mm MGs. The remainder have outboard engines and are capable of speeds in excess of 30 kt.   *NEW ENTRY*

VEGA   *6/1999*, Columbian Navy / 0056830

11 RIO CLASS (RIVER PATROL CRAFT) (PBR)

RIO MAGDALENA PRF 176	RIO SAN JORGE PRF 180	RIO ORTEGUAZA PRF 193
RIO CAUCA PRF 177	RIO PUTUMAYO PRF 190	RIO VICHADA PRF 194
RIO SINÚ PRF 178	RIO CAQUETÁ PRF 191	RIO GUAVIARE PRF 195
RIO ATRATO PRF 179	RIO ORINOCO PRF 192	

Displacement, tons: 9 full load
Dimensions, feet (metres): 31 × 11.1 × 2 *(9.8 × 3.5 × 0.6)*
Main machinery: 2 Detroit 6V-53 diesels; 296 hp *(221 kW)* sustained; 2 water-jets
Speed, knots: 24. **Range, miles:** 150 at 22 kt
Complement: 4
Guns: 2—12.7 mm (twin) MGs. 1—7.62 mm MG. 1—60 mm mortar.
Radars: Surface search: Raytheon 1900; I-band.

Comment: Acquired in 1989-90. Ex-US PBR Mk II built by Uniflite in 1970. All recommissioned in September 1990. GRP hulls.   *UPDATED*

RIO SAN JORGE   *11/1990, Hartmut Ehlers*

8 RIVER PATROL CRAFT (PBR)

DILIGENTE PF 121 (ex-LR 138)	ALFONSO VARGAS PF 123	VENGADORA PF 125 (ex-LR 139)	ARIARI PF 127
JUAN LUCIO PF 122	FRITZ HAGALE PF 124	HUMBERTO CORTES PF 126	CARLOS GALINDO PF 128

Comment: PF 127 is of 234 tons, PF 125 of 122 tons and the remainder between 31 and 40 tons. Various designs and ages, but all are armed with two 12.7 mm MGs and most have 7.62 mm MGs as well.   *UPDATED*

JUAN LUCIO   *1991*, Colombian Navy / 0056829

21 DELFIN CLASS (PBR)

ANTARES PB 421	GEMINIS PB 427	SPICA PB 434	BELLATRIX PB 439
CAPRICORNIO PB 422	DENEB PB 428	DENEBOLA PB 435	CANOPUS PB 440
ACUARIO PB 423	RIGEL PB 429	LIBRA PB 436	PROCYON PB 441
PISCIS PB 424	LEO PB 431	ESCORPIÓN PB 437	TULCÁN PB 442
ARIES PB 425	ALDEBARAN PB 432	ALPHERAZ PB 438	CAPELLA PB 447
TAURO PB 426			

Displacement, tons: 5.4 full load
Dimensions, feet (metres): 25.9 × 8.5 × 3.1 *(7.9 × 2.6 × 0.9)*
Main machinery: 2 Evinrude outboards; 400 hp *(294 kW)*
Speed, knots: 40
Complement: 4
Guns: 1—12.7 mm MG. 2—7.62 mm MGs.
Radars: Surface search: Raytheon; I-band.

Comment: First two built by Mako Marine, Miami and delivered in December 1992. Remainder acquired locally from 1993-94. Together with the two Rotorks and four of the LCUs, these craft are used to patrol the inland waterways (Aguas Interiores).   *UPDATED*

LIBRA   *10/1996* / 0056831

AMPHIBIOUS FORCES

35 PIRANA CRAFT (PBR)

Comment: These are 6.8 m river assault boats acquired from Boston Whaler for use by Marines. Armed with 1—12.7 mm and 2—7.62 mm MGs. 14 patrol units each operate with one 'Rio' or 'Tenerife' class and three Piranas. Capable of 25 to 30 kt depending on load. Some have been damaged beyond repair. There are also about 110 small river assault boats.   *UPDATED*

1 LCM 8 and 2 LCM 6

BAHÍA ZAPZURRO LD 240	BAHÍA HUMBOLT LD 241	BAHÍA OCTAVIA LD 242

Displacement, tons: 125 full load
Dimensions, feet (metres): 71.9 × 20.7 × 9.9 *(21.9 × 6.3 × 3)*
Main machinery: 1 diesel; 285 hp *(213 kW)*; 1 shaft
Speed, knots: 12
Complement: 5
Military lift: 60 tons or 200 troops

Comment: Details given are for LD 240. The other pair are smaller LCM 6s. All acquired for the US in 1993/94.   *NEW ENTRY*

BAHÍA ZAPZURRO   *6/1999*, Colombian Navy / 0056832

8 MORROSQUILLO (LCU 1466A) CLASS (LCU)

MORROSQUILLO LD 246	**BAHIA PORTETE** LD 249	**BAHIA UTRIA** LD 253
URABA LD 247	**BAHIA SOLANO** LD 251	**BAHIA MALAGA** LD 254
BAHIA HONDA LD 248	**BAHIA CUPICA** LD 252	

Displacement, tons: 347 full load
Dimensions, feet (metres): 119 × 34 × 6 *(36.3 × 10.4 × 1.8)*
Main machinery: 3 Detroit 6-71 diesels; 522 hp *(389 kW)* sustained; 3 shafts
Speed, knots: 7. **Range, miles:** 700 at 7 kt
Complement: 14
Cargo capacity: 167 tons or 300 troops
Guns: 2—12.7 mm MGs.
Radars: Navigation: Raytheon; I-band.

Comment: Former US Army craft built in 1954 and transferred in 1991 and 1992 with new engines. Used as inshore transports. Speed quoted is fully laden. Four based on each coast.
UPDATED

MORROSQUILLO *1/1993* * / 0056833

SURVEY SHIPS

Note: There are also three small buoy tenders: *Capitán Binney* BB 31, *Ciénaga de Mayorquin* BB 34, and *Abadia Mendez* BB 35.

Name	No	Builders	Commissioned
PROVIDENCIA	BO 155	Martin Jansen SY, Leer	24 July 1981
MALPELO	BO 156	Martin Jansen SY, Leer	24 July 1981

Displacement, tons: 1,040 full load
Dimensions, feet (metres): 164.3 × 32.8 × 13.1 *(50.3 × 10 × 4)*
Main machinery: 2 MAN-Augsburg diesels; 1,570 hp(m) *(1.15 MW)*; 1 Kort nozzle prop; bow thruster
Speed, knots: 13. **Range, miles:** 15,000 at 12 kt
Complement: 48 (5 officers) plus 6 scientists
Radars: Navigation: Raytheon; I-band.

Comment: Both launched in January 1981. *Malpelo* employed on fishery research and *Providencia* on geophysical research. Both are operated by DIMAR, the naval authority in charge of hydrographic, pilotage, navigational and ports services. Painted white. *UPDATED*

MALPELO *1992, Colombian Navy /* 0056834

Name	No	Builders	Commissioned
QUINDIO (ex-*YFR 443*)	BH 153	Niagara SB Corporation	11 Nov 1943

Displacement, tons: 600 full load
Dimensions, feet (metres): 131 × 29.8 × 9 *(40 × 9.1 × 2.7)*
Main machinery: 2 Union diesels; 600 hp *(448 kW)*; 2 shafts
Speed, knots: 10
Complement: 17 (2 officers)

Comment: Transport ship transferred by lease from the USA in July 1964 and by sale on 31 March 1979. Used as a buoy tender. *UPDATED*

QUINDIO *11/1990, Hartmut Ehlers*

Name	No	Builders	Commissioned
GORGONA	BB 33 (ex-BO 154, ex-BO 161, ex-FB 161)	Lidingoverken, Sweden	28 May 1954

Displacement, tons: 574 full load
Dimensions, feet (metres): 135 × 29.5 × 9.3 *(41.2 × 9 × 2.8)*
Main machinery: 2 Wärtsilä Nohab diesels; 910 hp(m) *(669 kW)*; 2 shafts
Speed, knots: 13
Complement: 45 (2 officers)

Comment: Paid off in 1982 but after a complete overhaul at Cartagena naval base was back in service in late 1992. *UPDATED*

GORGONA (old number) *1993, Colombian Navy /* 0056835

AUXILIARIES

2 LUNEBURG CLASS (TYPE 701) (SUPPORT SHIPS) (ARL)

Name	No	Builders	Commissioned
CARTAGENA DE INDIAS (ex-*Luneburg*)	BL 161 (ex-A 1411)	Flensburger	31 Jan 1966
BUENA VENTURA (ex-*Nienburg*)	BL 162 (ex-A 1416)	Bremer Vulcan	1 Aug 1968

Displacement, tons: 3,483 full load
Dimensions, feet (metres): 341.2 × 43.3 × 13.8 *(104 × 13.2 × 4.2)*
Main machinery: 2 MTU MD 16V 538 TB90 diesels; 6,000 hp(m) *(4.1 MW)* sustained; 2 shafts; cp props; bow thruster
Speed, knots: 16. **Range, miles:** 3,200 at 14 kt
Complement: 70 (9 officers)
Cargo capacity: 1,100 tons
Guns: 4 Bofors 40 mm/70 (2 twin).
Radars: Navigation: I-band.

Comment: BL 161 paid off from the German Navy in 1994. Taken inland for refit by HDW, Kiel in August 1997. Recommissioned on 2 November 1997. Guns were cocooned in German service. The ship acts as a depot ship for patrol craft. BL 162 paid off and was transferred the same day on 27 March 1998. She is now based at Cartagena. *UPDATED*

BUENA VENTURA *5/1998 *, Michael Nitz /* 0056836

2 TRANSPORTS (YAG)

Name	No	Builders	Commissioned
HERNANDO GUTIERREZ	NF 132 (ex-BD 35, ex-TF 52)	Ast Naval, Cartagena	1955
SOCORRO (ex-*Alberto Gomez*)	NF 131 (ex-BD 33, ex-TF 53)	Ast Naval, Cartagena	1956

Displacement, tons: 190 full load
Dimensions, feet (metres): 98.4 × 18 × 3.9 *(30 × 5.5 × 1.2)*
Main machinery: 2 Lister 8KB FRAPIL diesels; 260 hp *(194 kW)*; 2 shafts
Speed, knots: 6. **Range, miles:** 650 at 9 kt
Complement: 20 plus berths for 48 troops and medical staff
Guns: 2—12.7 mm MGs.

Comment: River transports. Named after Army officers. *Socorro* was converted in July 1967 into a floating surgery. *Hernando Gutierrez* was converted into a dispensary ship in 1970. Both used as support river patrol craft. *UPDATED*

HERNANDO GUTIERREZ *10/1990, Hartmut Ehlers*

7 SUPPORT SHIPS (YDT/YAG)

GUILERMO LONDOÑO VARGAS NF 146	**JULIO CORREA HERNANDEZ** NF 604 (ex-NF 143)
FILOGONIO HICHAMÓN NF 601 (ex-NF 141)	**MANACACIAS** NF 605
MANUEL A MOYAR NF 602 (ex-NF 144)	**COTUHE** NF 606
IGARAPARANA NF 603	

Comment: Various characteristics. All used as river patrol craft command and support ships. NF 146 is a hospital ship. *UPDATED*

JULIO CORREA HERNANDEZ (old number)   *6/1999*, Colombian Navy / 0056837*

12 TRANSPORTS

BOCACHICA TM 501	**TOLÚ** TM 506	**MÓVIL II** TM 510
ARTURUS TM 502	**CALIMA** TM 507 (ex-TM 49)	**RENACER DEL PACIFICO** TM 511
PEDRO DAVID SALAS TM 503 (ex-TM 101)	**BAHÍA SANTA CATALINA** TM 508	**JHONNY CAY** TM 512
SIRIUS TM 504 (ex-TM 62)	**MÓVIL I** TM 509	**PUNTA EVANS** TM 513

Comment: Small supply ships of various characteristics from 300 tons (TM 506) to 3 tons (TM 508-513). The others are mostly about 30 tons with a speed of 10 kt. *UPDATED*

CALIMA   *6/1999*, Colombian Navy / 0056838*

13 BAY SUPPORT CRAFT

PLAYA BLANCA TB 542	**PEGASSO** TB 547	**VALEROSA** TB 551
TIERRA BOMBA TB 543	**ALMIRANTE I** TB 548	**LUCHADORA** TB 552
BELL SALTER TB 544	**ALMIRANTE II** TB 549	**AZUL** TB 553
MALDONADO TB 545	**ARA** TB 550	**PORTETE** TB 554
ORION TB 546		

Comment: Mostly small craft of less than 10 tons. The largest is TB 544 which is 87 tons and has previously been listed as an Admiral's Yacht. *NEW ENTRY*

BELL SALTER   *6/1999*, Colombian Navy / 0056840*

1 DEPOT SHIP (ASL)

MAYOR JAIME ARIAS ARANGO DF 170 (ex-DF 41, ex-170)

Comment: Capacity of 165 tons, length 140 ft *(42.7 m)*, displacement 700 tons. Used as a non-self-propelled depot ship for the midget submarines. *UPDATED*

MAYOR JAIME ARIAS ARANGO   *6/1999*, Colombian Navy / 0056839*

TUGS

14 RIVER TUGS (YTL)

PASCUAL DE ANDAGOYA RM 75	**TENIENTE VLADIMIR VALEK** RF 87
JOSUE ALVAREZ RM 76	**TENIENTE LUIS BERNAL BAQUERO** RF 88
CAPITAN CASTRO RF 81	**TENIENTE BALDOMERO** RF 91
JOVES FIALLO RF 83	**CARLOS RODRIGUEZ** RF 92
CAPITAN ALVARO RUIZ RF 84	**SEJERI** RF 93
TENIENTE MIGUEL SILVA RF 85	**CIUDAD DE PUERTO LÓPEZ** RF 94
CAPITAN RIGOBERTO GIRALDO RF 86	**INIRIDA** RF 96

Comment: River craft of various types all described as 'Remolcadores'. Used for transport and ferry duties in harbours and rivers. RM 75 and RM 76 are harbour tugs. *UPDATED*

JOSUE ALVAREZ   *6/1999*, Colombian Navy / 0056841*

TRAINING SHIPS

Note: There are also three sail training yachts *Comodoro* YT 230, *Tridente* YT 231 and *Cristina* YT 232.

1 SAIL TRAINING SHIP (AXS)

Name	No	Builders	Launched	Commissioned
GLORIA	BE 160	AT Celaya, Bilbao	6 Sep 1966	16 May 1969

Displacement, tons: 1,250 full load
Dimensions, feet (metres): 249.3 oa; 211.9 wl; × 34.8 × 21.7 *(76; 64.6 × 10.6 × 6.6)*
Main machinery: 1 auxiliary diesel; 530 hp(m) *(389 kW)*; 1 shaft
Speed, knots: 10.5
Complement: 51 (10 officers) plus 88 trainees

Comment: Sail training ship. Barque rigged. Hull is entirely welded. Sail area, 1,675 sq yds *(1,400 sq m)*. Endurance, 60 days. Similar to Ecuador, Mexico and Venezuelan vessels. *UPDATED*

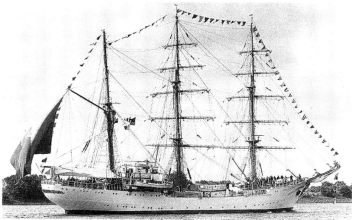

GLORIA   *8/1994, Harald Carstens*

COMORO ISLANDS

General

Three of the four main islands of this group joined in a unilateral Declaration of Independence in July 1975. This has been legitimised by France.

Bases

Moroni.

Mercantile Marine

Lloyd's Register of Shipping:
3 vessels of 744 tons gross

PATROL FORCES

2 YAMAYURI CLASS (PBI)

Name	No	Builders	Commissioned
KARTHALA	—	Ishihara Dockyard Co Ltd	Oct 1981
NTRINGUI	—	Ishihara Dockyard Co Ltd	Oct 1981

Displacement, tons: 26.5 standard; 41 full load
Dimensions, feet (metres): 59 × 14.1 × 3.6 *(18 × 4.3 × 1.1)*
Main machinery: 2 Nissan RD10TA06 diesels; 900 hp(m) *(661 kW)* maximum; 2 shafts
Speed, knots: 20
Complement: 6
Guns: 2—12.7 mm (twin) MGs.
Radars: Surface search: FRA 10; I-band.

Comment: These two patrol vessels of the MSA type (steel-hulled), supplied under Japanese Government co-operation plan. Used for fishery protection services. Due to be replaced.

UPDATED   KARTHALA

10/1981*, Ishihara DY / 0056842

CONGO

General

This country has been in chaos for some years and it is unlikely that any of the naval craft are seaworthy. A number of small boats may have survived on the rivers.

Bases

Pointe-Noire, Brazzaville, Mossaka.

Mercantile Marine

Lloyd's Register of Shipping:
20 vessels of 3,788 tons gross

DELETIONS

Note: Some of these craft may be recoverable in due course.

1997   Zhuks 301-303, Piraña 601-603

CONGO
DEMOCRATIC REPUBLIC

Headquarters Appointments

Chief of the Navy:
Major General Lowanga Mata Yamunyiga

General

Formerly Zaire. New name declared in 1997. Civil war cease fire declared in September 1999.

Personnel

(a)   2000: 1,000 (70 officers)
(b)   Voluntary service

Organisation

There are three commands which came under the Army in 1997: Matadi (coastal), Kinshasa (riverine), Kalémié (lake). Kalémié was in rebel hands by mid-1998 and Moba by mid-1999.

Bases

Boma, Kinshasa, Kalémié (Lake Tanganyika), Moba.

Coast Defence

A few coast launched HY-2 Silkworm SSMs. Probably non-operational.

Mercantile Marine

Lloyd's Register of Shipping:
20 vessels of 12,918 tons gross

DELETIONS

Patrol Forces

1997-98   Shanghai II 102, *Luadia, Mboko*

PATROL FORCES

4 SHANGHAI II CLASS (FAST ATTACK CRAFT—GUN) (PCF)

P 103-106

Displacement, tons: 113 standard; 134 full load
Dimensions, feet (metres): 127.3 × 17.7 × 5.6 *(38.8 × 5.4 × 1.7)*
Main machinery: 2 Type L12-180 diesels; 2,400 hp(m) *(1.76 MW)* forward; 2 Type L12-180Z diesels; 1,820 hp(m) *(1.34 MW)* aft; 4 shafts
Speed, knots: 30. **Range, miles:** 700 at 17 kt

Complement: 34
Guns: 4—37 mm/65 (2 twin). 4—25 mm/80 (2 twin).
Radars: Surface search: Furuno; I-band.

Comment: First four delivered from China in 1976-78. All were thought to be beyond repair by 1985 but two of the four were patched up, two replacements were delivered in February 1987 and one more has been recovered since then. New radars and communications fitted in 1990. *P 101* sunk at moorings in mid-1990. No lake patrols were reported after the 1997 coup. One of these craft reported captured by rebels in 1998. Operational status unknown.   *UPDATED*

SHANGHAI II 104 and 105

6/1996 / 0017761

COOK ISLANDS

PATROL FORCES

1 PACIFIC FORUM TYPE
(LARGE PATROL CRAFT) (PC)

Name	Builders	Commissioned
TE KUKUPA	Australian Shipbuilding Industries	1 Sep 1989

Displacement, tons: 162 full load
Dimensions, feet (metres): 103.3 × 26.6 × 6.9
(31.5 × 8.1 × 2.1)
Main machinery: 2 Caterpillar 3516TA diesels; 2,820 hp
(2.1 MW) sustained; 2 shafts
Speed, knots: 20. **Range, miles:** 2,500 at 12 kt
Complement: 17 (3 officers)
Radars: Surface search: Furuno 1011; I-band.

Comment: Laid down 16 May 1988 and launched 27 January 1989. Cost, training and support provided by Australia under defence co-operation. Acceptance date was 9 March 1989 but the handover was deferred another six months because of the change in local government. Has Furuno D/F equipment, SATNAV and a Stressl seaboat with a 40 hp outboard engine.

VERIFIED   TE KUKUPA   6/1995, van Ginderen Collection

COSTA RICA

GUARDIA CIVIL SECCIÓN MARITIMO

Personnel	Bases	Mercantile Marine	DELETIONS
(a) 2000: 350 officers and men (b) Voluntary service	Pacific: Golfito, Punta Arenas, Cuajiniquil, Quepos. Atlantic: Limon, Moin.	*Lloyd's Register of Shipping:* 15 vessels of 5,732 tons gross	1998-99 *Donna Margarita, Punta Burica*

PATROL FORCES

Note: A total of 13 Boston Whalers of 18 ft were delivered in 1993. Most have been deleted.

1 CAPE CLASS (LARGE PATROL CRAFT) (PC)

Name	No	Builders	Commissioned
ASTRONAUTA FRANKLIN CHANG (ex-*Cape Henlopen*)	95-1	Coast Guard Yard, Curtis Bay	5 Dec 1958

Displacement, tons: 98 standard; 148 full load
Dimensions, feet (metres): 94.8 × 20.3 × 6.6 *(28.9 × 6.2 × 2)*
Main machinery: 2 Detroit 16V-149TI diesels; 2,070 hp *(1.54 MW)* sustained; 2 shafts
Speed, knots: 20. **Range, miles:** 2,500 at 10 kt
Complement: 14 (1 officer)
Guns: 2—12.7 mm MGs.
Radars: Surface search: Raytheon SPS-64(V)1; I-band.

Comment: Transferred from US Coast Guard 28 September 1989 after a refit by Bender SB and Repair Co. Painted white in 1989. Based at Punta Arenas.

UPDATED

ASTRONAUTA FRANKLIN CHANG   6/1989*, Bender Shipbuilding / 0056843

1 SWIFT 105 ft CLASS (FAST PATROL CRAFT) (PCF)

Name	No	Builders	Commissioned
ISLA DEL COCO	1055	Swiftships, Morgan City	Feb 1978

Displacement, tons: 118 full load
Dimensions, feet (metres): 105 × 23.3 × 7.2 *(32 × 7.1 × 2.2)*
Main machinery: 3 MTU 12V 1163 TC92 diesels; 10,530 hp(m) *(7.74 MW)*; 3 shafts
Speed, knots: 33. **Range, miles:** 1,200 at 18 kt; 2,000 at 12 kt
Complement: 17 (3 officers)
Guns: 1—12.7 mm MG. 4—7.62 mm (2 twin) MGs. 1—60 mm mortar.
Radars: Navigation: Furuno; I-band.

Comment: Refitted in 1985-86 under FMS funding. The twin MGs are fitted abaft the bridge and the mortar is on the stern. Based at Punta Arenas.   *UPDATED*

ISLA DEL COCO   2/1989* / 0056844

2 POINT CLASS (COASTAL PATROL CRAFT) (PC)

Name	No	Builders	Commissioned
COLONEL ALFONSO MONGE (ex-*Point Hope*)	82-1 (ex-82302)	US Coast Guard Yard, Curtis Bay	5 Oct 1960
SANTAMARIA (ex-*Point Camden*)	82-2 (ex-82373)	J Martinac, Tacoma	4 May 1970

Displacement, tons: 67 full load
Dimensions, feet (metres): 83 × 17.2 × 5.8 *(25.3 × 5.2 × 1.8)*
Main machinery: 2 Caterpillar 3412 diesels; 1,600 hp *(1.19 MW)*; 2 shafts
Speed, knots: 23. **Range, miles:** 1,200 at 8 kt
Complement: 10
Guns: 2—12.7 mm MGs.
Radars: Navigation: Raytheon SPS-64/Hughes SPS-73; I-band.

Comment: First one transferred from USCG 3 May 1991. Based at Limon. Second transferred 15 December 1999.   *UPDATED*

COLONEL ALFONSO MONGE   1/1996*, van Ginderen Collection / 0056845

3 SWIFT 65 ft CLASS (COASTAL PATROL CRAFT) (PC)

CABO VELAS 656   **ISLA UVITA** 652   **CABO BLANCO** 653

Displacement, tons: 35 full load
Dimensions, feet (metres): 65.5 × 18.4 × 6.6 *(20 × 5.6 × 2)*
Main machinery: 2 MTU 8V 331 TC92 diesels; 1,770 hp(m) *(1.3 MW)*; 2 shafts
Speed, knots: 23. **Range, miles:** 500 at 18 kt
Complement: 7 (2 officers)
Guns: 1—12.7 mm MG. 4—7.62 mm (2 twin) MGs. 1—60 mm mortar.
Radars: Navigation: Furuno; I-band.

Comment: Built by Swiftships, Morgan City in 1979. Refitted 1985-86 under FMS funding. *653* is
    based at Limon. All are in poor condition.   ***UPDATED***

ISLA UVITA   *12/1987 * / 0056846*

2 SWIFT 36 ft CLASS (INSHORE PATROL CRAFT) (PB)

TELAMANCA 361   **CARIARI** 362

Displacement, tons: 11 full load
Dimensions, feet (metres): 36 × 10 × 2.6 *(11 × 3.1 × 0.8)*
Main machinery: 2 Detroit diesels; 500 hp *(373 kW)*; 2 shafts
Speed, knots: 24. **Range, miles:** 250 at 18 kt
Complement: 4 (1 officer)
Guns: 1—12.7 mm MG. 1—60 mm mortar.
Radars: Navigation: Raytheon 1900; I-band.

Comment: Built by Swiftships, Morgan City and completed in March 1986.   ***UPDATED***

CARIARI   *1991 * / 0056847*

CROATIA
HRVATSKA RATNA MORNARICA

Headquarters Appointments

Commander of the Navy:
    Vice Admiral Vid Stipetić
Chief of Staff:
    Captain Ivica Supić

Personnel

2000: 2,800 (180 officers) (including reserves)

General

The Navy was established on 12 September 1991. Ships
captured from the Yugoslav Federation form the bulk of the Fleet.
The main task is the protection and defence of territorial waters.
The Navy is largely inactive due to shortage of fuel.

Bases and Organisation

Headquarters: Lora-Split.
Main base: Split.
Minor bases: Sibenik, Pula, Ploce.
River Patrol Flotillas: Osijek (Drava) and Sisak (Sava).
There are three coastal command sectors: North, Middle and
South Adriatic. Radar surveillance stations and coastal batteries
are established on key islands and peninsulas. All the bases and
naval installations of the former federal Navy were taken over
with the exception of those in the Bay of Cattaro.

Coast Defence

Three mobile RBS 15 batteries on trucks. Total of 10 coastal
artillery batteries. Jadran command system for coastal defence
using Italian built radars.

Naval Infantry

Headquarters in Split. Companies deployed to Pula, Sibenik and
Ploce.

Mercantile Marine

Lloyd's Register of Shipping:
    257 vessels of 868,894 tons gross

SUBMARINES

Note: Three R-2 and R-2N 'Mala' class Swimmer Delivery Vehicles were captured and are in use. There are also a number of locally built manned SDVs including R-1 which is a 3.7 m craft capable of
2.8 kt down to 50 m diving depth, and R-2M a 5 m craft capable of 3 kt down to 80 m. Both types carry demolition charges either on board or in a towed waterproof container. Plans to build a 120 ton
midget have been shelved.

1 + 1 MODIFIED UNA CLASS (MIDGET SUBMARINE)

Name	No	Builders	Commissioned	Recommissioned
VELEBIT (ex-*Soča*)	P 01 (ex-P914)	Split	May 1985	17 Sep 1996
—	P 02	Split	2000	

Displacement, tons: 88 surfaced; 99 dived
Dimensions, feet (metres): 68.6 × 8.9 × 7.9 *(20.9 × 2.7 × 2.4)*
Main machinery: 1 MTU 6R 009TA diesel generator; 143 hp(m) *(105 kW)*; 2 Koncar motors; 54 hp
    (m) *(40 kW)*; 1 shaft

Speed, knots: 6 surfaced; 7 dived. **Range, miles:** 200 at 4 kt dived
Complement: 4 (1 officer) plus 6 divers
Sonars: Atlas Elektronik; RIZ PP1OM; passive/active search; high frequency.

Comment: Exit/re-entry capability with mining capacity. Can carry six combat swimmers, plus four
    Swimmer Delivery Vehicles (SDV) with 12 limpet mines or four ground mines. Diving depth,
    120 m *(394 ft)*. In 1993 the submarine was cut in half in order to insert a diesel generator.
    Access is through the conning tower. The forward fairing has a periscope. The diesel exhaust is
    on the after casing just aft of the fin. The others of the class are in the Yugoslav Navy but have no
    diesel. A second of class is building.   ***UPDATED***

VELEBIT   *7/1997, Dario Vuljanić / 0017762*

CORVETTES

1 + 1 KRALJ (TYPE R-03) CLASS (FSG)

Name	No	Builders	Launched	Commissioned
KRALJ PETAR KRESIMIR IV	RTOP 11	Kraljevica Shipyard	21 Mar 1992	7 July 1992
KRALJ TOMISLAV (?)	RTOP 12	Kraljevica Shipyard	—	—

Displacement, tons: 385 full load
Dimensions, feet (metres): 175.9 × 27.9 × 7.5
  (53.6 × 8.5 × 2.3)
Main machinery: 3 M 504B-2 diesels; 12,500 hp(m) *(9.2 MW)*
  sustained; 3 shafts
Speed, knots: 36. **Range, miles:** 1,800 at 18 kt
Complement: 33 (5 officers)

Missiles: SSM: 4 or 8 Saab RBS 15B (2 or 4 twin) ❶; active radar
  homing to 70 km *(37.8 n miles)* at 0.8 Mach; warhead 83 kg.
Guns: 1 Bofors 57 mm/70 ❷; 200 rds/min to 17 km *(9.3 n
  miles)*; weight of shell 2.4 kg. Launchers for illuminants on side
  of mounting.
  1—30 mm/65 AK 630M ❸; 6 barrels; 3,000 rds/min
  combined to 2 km.
  2 Oerlikon 20 mm or 2—12.7 mm MGs ❹.
Mines: 4 AIM-70 magnetic or 6 SAG-1 acoustic in lieu of SSMs.
Countermeasures: Decoys: 2 Wallop Barricade chaff/IR
  launchers.
Weapons control: BEAB 9LV 249 Mk 2 director.
  Kolonka for AK 630M.
Radars: Surface search: Racal BT 502 ❺; E/F-band.
  Fire control: BEAB 9LV 249 Mk 2 ❻; I/J-band.
  Navigation: Racal 1290A; I-band.
Sonars: RIZ PP10M; hull-mounted; active search; high frequency.

Programmes: The building of this class (formerly called Kobra by
  NATO) was officially announced as 'suspended' in 1989 but
  was restarted in 1991. Progress on the second of class had
  stopped by late 1999 due to shortage of funds. Projected
  numbers are uncertain after the first two but a more modern
  design is likely. Designated as a missile Gunboat.
Structure: Derived from the 'Koncar' class with a stretched hull
  and a new superstructure. Either missiles or mines may be
  carried. The second of class has a command bridge and may
  also be fitted with a SAM system.
Operational: Based at Split.

UPDATED

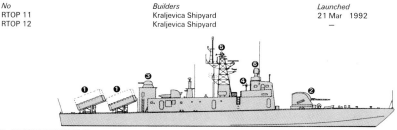

KRALJ PETAR KRESIMIR IV   *(Scale 1 : 600), Ian Sturton*

KRALJ PETAR KRESIMIR IV
6/1997*, Dario Vuljaniç / 0012239

KRALJ PETAR KRESIMIR IV   *6/1997, Croatian Navy / 0017763*

PATROL FORCES

Note: There is a stated need for four new coastal patrol craft. Requirements include 10—18 m, two
diesels and 20 kt.

1 KONČAR (TYPE R-02) CLASS
(FAST ATTACK CRAFT—MISSILE) (PCFG)

Name	No	Builders	Launched	Commissioned
ŠIBENIK (ex-*Vlado Četković*)	RTOP 21 (ex-*402*)	Tito SY, Kraljevica	20 Aug 1977	Mar 1978

Displacement, tons: 260 full load
Dimensions, feet (metres): 147.6 × 27.6 × 8.5 *(45 × 8.4 × 2.6)*
Main machinery: CODAG; 2 RR Proteus 52-M558 gas turbines; 7,200 hp *(5.37 MW)* sustained;
  2 MTU 16V 538 TB91 diesels; 7,200 hp(m) *(5.29 MW)* sustained; 4 shafts; cp props
Speed, knots: 38; 23 (diesels). **Range, miles:** 500 at 35 kt; 880 at 23 kt (diesels)
Complement: 30 (5 officers)

Missiles: SSM: 4 Saab RBS 15B; active radar homing to 70 km *(37.8 n miles)* at 0.8 Mach;
  warhead 83 kg.
Guns: 1 Bofors 57 mm/70; 200 rds/min to 17 km *(9.3 n miles)*; weight of shell 2.4 kg. 128 mm
  rocket launcher for illuminants.
  1—30 mm/65 AK 630M; 6 barrels; 3,000 rds/min to 2 km.
Countermeasures: Decoys: 2 Wallop Barricade double layer chaff launchers.
Weapons control: PEAB 9LV 202 GFCS.

Radars: Surface search: Decca 1226; I-band.
  Fire control: Philips TAB; I/J-band.

Programmes: Type name, Raketna Topovnjaca. Recommissioned into the Croatian Navy on
  28 September 1991. Others of the class serve with the Yugoslav Navy.
Modernisation: The original Styx missiles have been replaced by RBS 15 and the after 57 mm gun
  by a 30 mm AK 630. Fire-control radar was updated in 1994.
Structure: Aluminium superstructure. Designed by the Naval Shipping Institute in Zagreb based on
  Swedish 'Spica' class with bridge amidships like Malaysian boats.
Operational: Based at Split.

UPDATED

ŠIBENIK   *7/1997*, Dario Vuljanić / 0012240*

1 MODIFIED OSA I (TYPE 205) CLASS (PCF/ML)

DUBROVNIK (ex-*Mitar Acev*) OBM 41 (ex-310)

Displacement, tons: 171 standard; 210 full load
Dimensions, feet (metres): 126.6 × 24.9 × 8.8 *(38.6 × 7.6 × 2.7)*
Main machinery: 3 Type M 503A diesels; 8,025 hp(m) *(5.9 MW)* sustained; 3 shafts
Speed, knots: 35. **Range, miles:** 400 at 34 kt
Complement: 30 (4 officers)
Guns: 4 USSR 30 mm/65 AK 230 (2 twin); 500 rds/min to 5 km *(2.7 n miles)*; weight of shell 0.54 kg.
Mines: 14-30 mines.
Radars: Surface search: Square Tie (Ramgut); I-band.
IFF: High Pole. 2 Square Head.

Comment: Two of these ex-USSR vessels captured from the Yugoslav Navy. First commissioned in 1970. *Dubrovnik* was badly damaged and nearly scrapped, but eventually repaired at Sibenik. Converted to a minelayer in 1995. The second of class paid off in 1994 and was used as a target. **UPDATED**

DUBROVNIK   5/1997*, *Dario Vuljanić* / 0012241

1 RLM-301 CLASS (RIVER PATROL CRAFT) (PB)

SLAVONAC PB 91

Displacement, tons: 48 full load
Dimensions, feet (metres): 63.6 × 14.4 × 3.3 *(19.4 × 4.4 × 1)*
Main machinery: 2 Torpedo B 536 diesels; 280 hp(m) *(206 kW)*; 2 shafts
Speed, knots: 12
Complement: 9
Guns: 1 Bofors 40 mm/70. 4—14.5 mm (quad) MGs; 2—12.7 mm (twin) MG.
Radars: Surface search: Racal Decca; I-band.

Comment: Former minesweeper launched in 1952 at Mačvanska, Mitrovica. Used as a river patrol vessel. **VERIFIED**

SLAVONAC   12/1996, *Croatian Navy* / 0017764

5 RIVER PATROL CRAFT (PB)

BREKI   **PB 92**   **VUKOVAR 91**   **DOMAGOJ**   **TOMISLAV**

Displacement, tons: 48 full load
Dimensions, feet (metres): 59.4 × 13.4 × 3.4 *(19.5 × 4.4 × 3.4)*
Main machinery: 2 Torpedo B 538 diesels; 345 hp(m) *(254 kW)*; 2 shafts
Speed, knots: 8
Guns: 1 Bofors 40 mm/70. 4—14.5 mm (quad) MGs. 2—12.7 mm MGs.

Comment: Details given are for *PB 92*. *Breki* and *Tomislav* are of similar size but unarmed, *Vukovar 91* and *Domagoj* are of 30 tons and capable of 6 kt. *Vukovar 91* has a 40 mm/70 gun. **VERIFIED**

PB 92   12/1996, *Croatian Navy* / 0017765

4 MIRNA (TYPE 140) CLASS
(FAST ATTACK CRAFT—PATROL) (PCF)

Name	No	Builders	Launched
— (ex-*Biokovo*)	PB 61 (ex-171)	Kraljevica Shipyard	18 Dec 1980
SOLTA (ex-*Mukos*)	PB 62 (ex-176)	Kraljevica Shipyard	11 Nov 1982
— (ex-*Cer*)	PB 63 (ex-180)	Kraljevica Shipyard	27 Sep 1984
HRVATSKA KOSTAJNICA (ex-*Durmitor*)	PB 64 (ex-181)	Kraljevica Shipyard	10 Jan 1985

Displacement, tons: 142 full load
Dimensions, feet (metres): 104.9 × 22 × 7.5 *(32 × 6.7 × 2.3)*
Main machinery: 2 SEMT-Pielstick 12 PA4 200 VGDS diesels; 5,292 hp(m) *(3.89 MW)* sustained; 2 shafts
Speed, knots: 25. **Range, miles:** 500 at 24 kt
Complement: 19 (3 officers)
Missiles: SAM: 1 SA-N-5 Grail quad mounting; manual aiming; IR homing to 6 km *(3.2 n miles)* at 1.5 Mach; altitude to 2,500 m *(8,000 ft)*; warhead 1.5 kg.
Guns: 1 Bofors 40 mm/70. 4 Hispano 20 mm (quad) Type M75. 2—128 mm illuminant launchers.
Depth charges: 8 DCs.
Countermeasures: Decoys: chaff launcher.
Radars: Surface search: Racal Decca 1216C; I-band.
Sonars: Simrad SQS-3D/SF; active high frequency.

Comment: An electric outboard motor has been removed. Two were captured after sustaining heavy damage, one by a missile fired from Brac island and the other by a torpedo. Both fully repaired and all four are operational. *61* and *63* have no names. **UPDATED**

HRVATSKA KOSTAJNICA   6/1996*, *Gordan Laušić* / 0012242

AMPHIBIOUS FORCES

2 CETINA (SILBA) CLASS (LCT/ML)

Name	No	Builders	Launched	Commissioned
CETINA	DBM 81	Brodosplit, Split	18 July 1992	19 Feb 1993
KRKA	DBV 82	Brodosplit, Split	17 Sep 1994	9 Mar 1995

Displacement, tons: 880 full load
Measurement, tons: 163.1 oa; 144 wl × 40 × 10.5 *(49.7; 43.9 × 12.2 × 3.2)*
Main machinery: 2 Alpha 10V23L-VO diesels; 3,100 hp(m) *(2.28 MW)* sustained; 2 shafts; cp props
Speed, knots: 12. **Range, miles:** 1,200 at 12 kt
Complement: 33 (3 officers)
Military lift: 460 tons or 6 medium tanks or 7 APCs or 4—130 mm guns plus towing vehicles or 300 troops with equipment
Missiles: SAM: 1 SA-N-5 Grail quad mounting *(Cetina)*.
Guns: 1 Bofors 40 mm/70 *(Krka)* or 4—30 mm/65 (2 twin) AK 230 *(Cetina)*. 2 or 4 Hispano 20 mm M71.
Mines: 94 Type SAG-1.
Radars: Surface search: Racal Decca 1290A; I-band.

Comment: Ro-ro design with bow and stern ramps. *Krka*'s 40 mm gun is mounted at the bow; *Cetina*'s two 30 mm guns are either side of the bridge. Can be used for minelaying, transporting weapons or equipment and personnel. *Krka* is being used as a water carrier. Based at Split. Plans for a third of class have been shelved. **UPDATED**

CETINA   6/1996* / 0056848

KRKA   10/1998 / 0017766

2 TYPE 21 and 3 TYPE 11 (LCU)

DJC 101-103   DJC 104   DJC 107

Displacement, tons: 32 full load
Dimensions, feet (metres): 69.9 × 15.7 × 5.2 *(21.3 × 4.8 × 1.6)*
Main machinery: 1 MTU 12V 331 TC81 diesel; 1,450 hp(m) *(1.07 MW)*; 1 shaft
Speed, knots: 21. **Range, miles:** 320 at 22 kt
Complement: 6
Military lift: 6 tons or 40 troops
Guns: 1 or 2—20 mm M71. 2—30 mm grenade launchers.
Radars: Navigation: Decca 1213; I-band.

Comment: Built at Greben Shipyard 1987-88. *DJC 101-103* are Type 11 and the other pair Type 21.
UPDATED

DJC 103   *5/1997*, Dario Vuljanić /* 0012246

1 DTM TYPE (LCT/MINELAYER) (LCT/ML)

DTM 219

Displacement, tons: 458 full load
Dimensions, feet (metres): 151 × 27.3 × 5.1 *(49.8 × 9.0 × 1.7)*
Main machinery: 3 Torpedo diesels, 260 hp(m) *(191 kW)*; 3 shafts
Speed, knots: 7
Complement: 20 (2 officers)
Military lift: 200 troops or 3 heavy tanks
Missiles: SAM 1 SA-N-5 Grail.
Guns: 4—20 mm M75 (quad); 2 Hispano 20 mm M71.
Mines: Can carry 100.
Radars: Navigation: Decca 1216; I-band.

Comment: Can also act as a minelayer. Armament has been changed. Based at Split. DTM (DesantniTenkonosac/Minopolagac means landing ship tank/minelayer). A second of class is a civilian ship named *Trebinje*.
UPDATED

DTM 219   *6/1997, Dario Vuljanić /* 0017767

1 TYPE 22 (LCU)

DJC 106 (ex-624)

Displacement, tons: 48 full load
Dimensions, feet (metres): 73.2 × 15.7 × 3.3 *(22.3 × 4.8 × 1)*
Main machinery: 2 MTU diesels; 1,740 hp(m) *(1.28 MW)*; 2 water-jets
Speed, knots: 35. **Range, miles:** 320 at 22 kt
Complement: 8
Military lift: 40 troops or 15 tons cargo
Guns: 2 Hispano 20 mm.
Radars: Navigation: Decca 101; I-band.

Comment: Built at Greben Shipyard in 1987 of polyester and glass fibre. A second of class belongs to the Fire Brigade.
VERIFIED

DJC 106   *8/1998, N A Sifferlinger /* 0038489

1 DSM 501 TYPE (LCT/MINELAYER) (LCT/ML)

DSM 110 (ex-*PDS 110*)

Displacement, tons: 260 full load
Dimensions, feet (metres): 78.2 × 41.5 × 3.6 *(25.8 × 13.7 × 1.2)*
Main machinery: 2 Mercedes diesels; 200 hp(m) *(147 kW)*; 2 shafts
Speed, knots: 8
Complement: 20 (2 officers)
Military lift: 100 tons
Guns: 6 Hispano 20 mm (1 quad and 2 single).
Mines: 64 type SAG-2 or 28 type AiM M70.

Comment: Built at Pula in late 1950s. Unlike other tank landing craft in that the centre part of the bow drops to form a ramp down which the tanks go ashore, the vertical section of the bow being articulated to form outer end of ramp. Can also act as a minelayer. Armament has been changed. Based at Split. A second of class is in reserve.
UPDATED

DSM 110   *6/1996*, Tomislav Brandt /* 0012244

MINE WARFARE FORCES

0 + 1 MPMB CLASS (MINEHUNTER—INSHORE) (MHI)

Name	No	Builders	Launched
—	—	Greben, Vela Luka	—

Displacement, tons: 173 full load
Dimensions, feet (metres): 84.3 × 22.3 × 8.5 *(25.7 × 6.8 × 2.6)*
Main machinery: 2 MTU 8V 183TE62 diesels; 993 hp(m) *(730 kW)*; 2 Holland Roerpropeler stern azimuth thrusters; bow thruster; 190 hp(m) *(140 kW)*
Speed, knots: 11
Complement: 14
Guns: 1—20 mm M71.
Countermeasures: Minehunting: 1 ECA38 PAP 104; 1 Super Sea Rover (Benthos); Minesweeping: MDL3 mechanical sweep.
Radars: Navigation: Kelvin Hughes 5000 ARPA, NINAS Mod.
Sonars: Reson mine avoidance; active; high frequency.
Klein 2000 side scan; active for route survey; high frequency.

Comment: Ordered in 1995. The ship has a trawler appearance with a gun on the forecastle and a hydraulic crane on the sweep deck. GRP hull. Due to a shortage of funds, building had stopped by late 1999 and the hull was 'preserved' in the Greben Shipyard.
UPDATED

TRAINING SHIPS

Note: A sail training ship is to be acquired in due course.

1 MOMA (TYPE 861) CLASS (AGS)

Name	No	Builders	Commissioned
ANDRIJA MOHOROVIČIČ	PT 72 (ex-PH 33)	Northern Shipyard, Gdansk	1972

Displacement, tons: 1,514 full load
Dimensions, feet (metres): 240.5 × 33.5 × 12.8 *(73.3 × 10.2 × 3.9)*
Main machinery: 2 Zgoda-Sulzer 6TD48 diesels; 3,300 hp(m) *(2.4 MW)* sustained; 2 shafts; cp props
Speed, knots: 17. **Range, miles:** 9,000 at 11 kt
Complement: 30 (4 officers)
Radars: Navigation: Racal Decca BT 506; I-band.

Comment: Built in 1971 for the Yugoslav Navy as a survey vessel. Based at Split. Has a 5 ton crane and carries a launch. Used as the Naval Academy training ship.
UPDATED

ANDRIJA MOHOROVIČIČ   *6/1996* /* 0056849

AUXILIARIES

Note: In addition there are two harbour tugs *LR-71* and *LR 73*, two diving tenders *BRM-51* and *BRM-83*, auxiliary transport ship *PDS-713* (similar to *DSM-110*), five harbour transport boats *BMT-1/5*, and two yachts *Učka* (ex-*Podgorka*) and *Jadranka* (ex-civilian *Smile*).

1 SPASILAC CLASS (ASR)

Name	No	Builders	Commissioned
FAUST VRANČIČ (ex-*Spasilac*)	PT-73 (ex-PS 12)	Tito Shipyard, Belgrade	10 Sep 1976

Displacement, tons: 1,590 full load
Dimensions, feet (metres): 182 × 39.4 × 14.1 *(55.5 × 12 × 4.3)*
Main machinery: 2 diesels; 4,340 hp(m) *(3.19 MW)*; 2 shafts; Kort nozzle props; bow thruster
Speed, knots: 13. **Range, miles:** 4,000 at 12 kt
Complement: 53 plus 19 spare berths
Cargo capacity: 490 tons fuel; 250 tons deck cargo
Radars: Navigation: Kelvin Hughes Nucleus 5000R; I-band.

Comment: Fitted for firefighting and fully equipped for salvage work. Decompression chamber and can support a German built manned rescue submersible. Can be fitted with two quadruple M 75 and two single M 71 20 mm guns. Based at Split.   ***VERIFIED***

FAUST VRANČIČ   *2/1997, van Ginderen Collection* / 0012248

1 PT 71 TYPE (TRANSPORT) (AKL)

PT 71 (ex-*Meduza*)

Displacement, tons: 710 full load
Dimensions, feet (metres): 152.2 × 23.6 × 17.1 *(46.4 × 7.2 × 5.2)*
Main machinery: 1 Burmeister & Wain diesel; 930 hp(m) *(684 kW)*; 1 shaft
Speed, knots: 10
Complement: 17 (2 officers)
Guns: 1 Bofors 40 mm/70. 2 Hispano 20 mm M71 can be carried.
Radars: Navigation: Racal Decca 1216A; I-band.

Comment: Built in 1953.

UPDATED

PT 71   *6/1996** / 0056850

POLICE

Notes: (1) Plans to form a Coast Guard were eventually shelved in favour of a strengthened Harbour Police Force. Police craft have Policija marked on the hull and usually carry MGs.
(2) In addition there are civilian registered base port craft with PU (Pula), SB (Sibenic) and so on markings.

POLICIJA P-12   *6/1998, W Clements* / 0017768

2-PU   *8/1998, N Sifferlinger* / 0017769

CUBA
MARINA DE GUERRA REVOLUCIONARIA

General

As a separate organisation the Navy remains in disarray. Most ships lack spares and fuel and seldom go to sea, and at least half are in a state where they are unlikely to become operational again. Manpower figures have been radically reduced.

Personnel

2000: 2,500 (including 500 marines)

Command Organisation

Western Naval District (HQ Cabanas).
Eastern Naval District (HQ Holguin).

Coast Defence

Truck mounted SS-N-2B Styx.

Bases

Cabanas, Nicaro, Cienfuegos, Havana, Santiago de Cuba, Banes.

Mercantile Marine

Lloyd's Register of Shipping:
100 vessels of 130,108 tons gross

DELETIONS

Note: Some of these vessels have been disposed of. Others are decaying alongside in harbour.

Submarines

1997	Foxtrot 729
1998	Foxtrot 725

Frigates

1998	Koni 383 (sunk for tourists), Koni 350

Patrol Forces

1997	2 Osa IIs
1998	5 Osa IIs (one sunk for tourists)
1999	1 Osa I

Mine Warfare Forces

1995-97	2 Sonya, 8 Yevgenya

Auxiliaries

1996-97	Polnochny 690, Yelva B-015
1998	*Isla de la Juventud* (civilian)

CORVETTES

1 PAUK II CLASS (TYPE 1241PE) (FS)

321

Displacement, tons: 440 full load
Dimensions, feet (metres): 189 × 33.5 × 11.2 *(57.6 × 10.2 × 3.4)*
Main machinery: 2 Type M 521 diesels; 16,184 hp(m) *(11.9 MW)* sustained; 2 shafts
Speed, knots: 32. **Range, miles:** 2,400 at 14 kt
Complement: 32
Missiles: SAM: SA-N-5 quad launcher; manual aiming, IR homing to 10 km *(5.4 n miles)* at 1.5 Mach; warhead 1.1 kg.
Guns: 1 USSR 76 mm/60; 120 rds/min to 7 km *(3.8 n miles)*; weight of shell 16 kg.
1—30 mm/65; 6 barrels, 3,000 rds/min combined to 2 km. 4—25 mm (2 twin).
A/S mortars: 2 RBU 1200 5-tubed fixed; range 1,200 m; warhead 34 kg.
Countermeasures: 2 PK 16 chaff launchers.
Radars: Air/surface search: Positive E; E/F-band.
Navigation: Pechora; I-band.
Fire control: Bass Tilt; H/I-band.
Sonars: Rat Tail; VDS (on transom); attack; high frequency.

Comment: Built at Yaroslav Shipyard in the USSR and transferred in May 1990. Similar to the ships built for India. Has a longer superstructure than the Pauk I and electronics with a radome similar to the 'Parchim II' class. Torpedo tubes removed. Two twin 25 mm guns fitted on the stern. Still operational.   ***UPDATED***

PAUK II (Indian colours)   *2/1998* / 0052339

PATROL FORCES

6 OSA II CLASS (TYPE 205)
(FAST ATTACK CRAFT—MISSILE) (PCFG)

261   262   267   268   271   274

Displacement, tons: 171 standard; 245 full load
Dimensions, feet (metres): 126.6 × 24.9 × 8.8 *(38.6 × 7.6 × 2.7)*
Main machinery: 3 Type M 504 diesels; 10,800 hp(m) *(7.94 MW)* sustained; 3 shafts
Speed, knots: 37. **Range, miles:** 500 at 35 kt
Complement: 30
Missiles: SSM: 4 SS-N-2B Styx; active radar or IR homing to 46 km *(25 n miles)* at 0.9 Mach; warhead 513 kg.
Guns: 4—30 mm/65 (2 twin); 500 rds/min to 5 km *(2.7 n miles)*; weight of shell 0.54 kg.
Radars: Surface search: Square Tie; I-band.
Fire control: Drum Tilt; H/I-band.
IFF: Square Head. High Pole B.

Comment: One Osa II delivered in mid-1976, one in January 1977 and one in March 1978. Further two delivered in December 1978, one in April 1979, one in October 1979, two from Black Sea November 1981, four in February 1982. Some have been cannibalised for spares and all have had their missiles disembarked for use in shore batteries. One was sunk as a tourist attraction in 1998. All Osa Is scrapped by 1999.   ***UPDATED***

OSA II (Bulgarian colours)   *8/1998*, *E & M Laursen* / 0017645

MINE WARFARE FORCES

Note: No MCM exercises have been reported since 1990.

2 SONYA CLASS (TYPE 1265)
(MINESWEEPERS/HUNTERS) (MSC/MH)

570   578

Displacement, tons: 450 full load
Dimensions, feet (metres): 157.4 × 28.9 × 6.6 *(48 × 8.8 × 2)*
Main machinery: 2 Kolomna Type 9-D-8 diesels; 2,000 hp(m) *(1.47 MW)* sustained; 2 shafts
Speed, knots: 15. **Range, miles:** 3,000 at 10 kt
Complement: 43
Guns: 2—30 mm/65 (twin); 500 rds/min to 5 km *(2.7 n miles)*; weight of shell 0.54 kg.
2—25 mm/80 (twin); 270 rds/min to 3 km *(1.6 n miles)*.
Mines: Can carry 8.
Radars: Navigation: Don 2; I-band.
IFF: 2 Square Head. High Pole B.
Sonars: MG 69/79; hull-mounted; active minehunting; high frequency.

Comment: Transferred from USSR in January and December 1985. Two others are non-operational but these two were reported at sea in 1998/99.   ***UPDATED***

SONYA (Russian colours)   *5/1990** / 0056851

4 YEVGENYA CLASS (TYPE 1258) (MINEHUNTERS) (MHC)

501 series

Displacement, tons: 77 standard; 90 full load
Dimensions, feet (metres): 80.7 × 18 × 4.9 *(24.6 × 5.5 × 1.5)*
Main machinery: 2 Type 3-D-12 diesels; 600 hp(m) *(440 kW)* sustained; 2 shafts
Speed, knots: 11. **Range, miles:** 300 at 10 kt
Complement: 10
Guns: 2—14.5 mm (twin) MGs.
Countermeasures: Minehunting gear is lowered on a crane at the stern.
Radars: Navigation: Don 2; I-band.
Sonars: MG 7 lifted over the stern.

Comment: First pair transferred from USSR in November 1977, one in September 1978, two in November 1979, two in December 1980, two from the Baltic on 10 December 1981, one in October 1982 and four on 1 September 1984. There are two squadrons, one central and one west. These last four are the only seaworthy units.   ***VERIFIED***

YEVGENYA (Russian colours)   *1991*

SURVEY SHIPS

Notes: (1) In addition there are five other vessels: *Hatuey* H 107 of 430 tons, *Baconao* H 73 of 226 tons, H 75 of 283 tons, *Siboney* H 101 of 535 tons and used for cadet training, and a buoy tender *Tanio* H 102 of 1,123 tons. None are active.
(2) The 'Pelym' class, ADG 40, which paid off in 1997 may return to service as a training ship in 2000.

1 BIYA (TYPE 871) CLASS (AGS)

GUAMA H 103

Displacement, tons: 766 full load
Dimensions, feet (metres): 180.4 × 32.1 × 8.5 *(55 × 9.8 × 2.6)*
Main machinery: 2 diesels; 1,200 hp(m) *(882 kW)*; 2 shafts; cp props
Speed, knots: 13. **Range, miles:** 4,700+ at 11 kt
Complement: 29 (7 officers)
Radars: Navigation: Don 2; I-band.

Comment: Has laboratory facilities, one survey launch and a 5 ton crane. Built in Poland and acquired from USSR in November 1980. Subordinate to Institute of Hydrography. Last deployed in 1993, but is used locally as a buoy tender.   ***UPDATED***

BIYA (Russian colours)   *10/1993, van Ginderen Collection*

BORDER GUARD

Notes: (1) A 5,000 strong force which operates under the Ministry of the Interior at a higher state of readiness than the Navy. Pennant numbers painted in red.
(2) Three ex-North Korean 'Sin Hung' class patrol craft were reported in 1997. These are possibly former USSR P6 craft brought back in to service.

3 STENKA (TARANTUL) CLASS (TYPE 205P)
(FAST ATTACK CRAFT—PATROL) (PCF)

Displacement, tons: 211 standard; 253 full load
Dimensions, feet (metres): 129.3 × 25.9 × 8.2 *(39.4 × 7.9 × 2.5)*
Main machinery: 3 M 583A diesels; 12,172 hp(m) *(8.95 MW)*; 3 shafts
Speed, knots: 34. **Range, miles:** 2,250 at 14 kt
Complement: 25 (5 officers)
Guns: 4—30 mm/65 (2 twin) AK 230; 500 rds/min to 5 km *(2.7 n miles)*; weight of shell 0.54 kg.
Radars: Surface search: Pot Drum; H/I-band.
Fire control: Muff Cob; G/H-band.
IFF: High Pole. Square Head.

Comment: Similar to class operated by Russian border guard with torpedo tubes and sonar removed. Transferred from USSR in February 1985 (two) and August 1985 (one). At least two are operational.   *UPDATED*

STENKA   *1990* */ 0056852*

18 ZHUK (GRIF) CLASS (TYPE 199)
(COASTAL PATROL CRAFT) (PC)

Displacement, tons: 39 full load
Dimensions, feet (metres): 78.7 × 16.4 × 3.9 *(24 × 5 × 1.2)*
Main machinery: 2 Type M 401B diesels; 2,200 hp(m) *(1.6 MW)* sustained; 2 shafts
Speed, knots: 30. **Range, miles:** 1,100 at 15 kt
Complement: 11 (3 officers)
Guns: 4—14.5 mm (2 twin) MGs.
Radars: Surface search: Spin Trough; I-band.

Comment: A total of 40 acquired since 1971. Last batch of two arrived December 1989. Some transferred to Nicaragua. The total has been reduced to allow for wastage. In some of the class the after gun has been removed. Most of the remaining vessels are still active.   *UPDATED*

ZHUK (Yemen colours)   *11/1989* */ 0056853*

CYPRUS, Republic

Headquarters Appointments

Chief of Marine National Guard:
    Captain Loucas Souchlas
Head of Naval Operations:
    Commander A Ioannides

Bases

Limassol

General

In November 1983 Turkey set up an independent republic in the northern part of the island. Subsequently the UN declared this to be illegal. *Raif Denktas* and *SG 102-103* are patrol craft permanently based at Kyrenia (Girne) flying the North Cyprus flag. For details of these vessels see Turkey Coast Guard section.

Coast Defence

Twenty-four Exocet MM 40 Block 2. Truck-mounted in batteries of four.

Mercantile Marine

Lloyd's Register of Shipping:
    1,556 vessels of 23,641,000 tons gross

PATROL FORCES

Notes: (1) The Greek 'Dilos' class patrol craft *Kerinia* (ex-*Knossos*) is to be acquired in 2000.
(2) There are also three launches and a number of RIBs in use by the Underwater Diving section of the Navy.

1 MODIFIED PATRA CLASS (PC)

Name	No	Builders	Commissioned
SALAMIS	P 01	Chantiers de l'Esterel	24 May 1983

Displacement, tons: 98 full load
Dimensions, feet (metres): 105.3 × 21.3 × 5.9 *(32.1 × 6.5 × 1.8)*
Main machinery: 2 SACM 195 CZSHRY12 diesels; 4,680 hp(m) *(3.44 MW)* sustained; 2 shafts
Speed, knots: 30. **Range, miles:** 1,200 at 15 kt
Complement: 22
Missiles: SAM: 2 Matra Simbad twin launchers; Mistral; IR homing to 4 km *(2.2 n miles)*; warhead 3 kg.
Guns: 1 Breda 40 mm/70; 300 rds/min to 12.5 km *(6.8 n miles)* anti-surface; weight of shell 0.96 kg.
1 Rheinmetall Wegmann 20 mm. 2—12.7 mm MGs.
Radars: Surface search: Decca 1226; I-band.

Comment: Laid down in December 1981 for Naval Command of National Guard.   *UPDATED*

SALAMIS   *10/1999*, E & M Laursen / 0056854

POLICE

Notes: (1) In addition there are five Fletcher Malibu speed boats, *Astrapi I-V,* of 5.3 m with 200 hp engines built in Cyprus in 1986.
(2) Personnel numbers in 2000 are 330 Maritime Police.

1 PLASCOA TYPE (PC)

Name	No	Builders	Commissioned
KIMON	PL 2	Archachon, France	16 June 1979

Displacement, tons: 45 full load
Dimensions, feet (metres): 58.1 × 17.1 × 4.9 *(17.7 × 5.2 × 1.5)*
Main machinery: 2 Poyaud V12 diesels; 2 shafts
Speed, knots: 17. **Range, miles:** 300 at 15 kt
Complement: 6
Guns: 1—12.7 mm MG. 1—7.62 mm MG.
Radars: Surface search: Decca; I-band.

Comment: GRP hull. Second of class deleted in 1991.   *UPDATED*

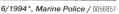

KIMON   *6/1994*, Marine Police / 0056857

5 SAB 12 TYPE (PB)

KARPASIA PL 11 (ex-G 50/GS 10)
ILARION PL 12 (ex-G 52/GS 25)
KOURION PL 13 (ex-G 54/GS 27)

DIONYSOS PL 14 (ex-G 55/GS 12)
AKAMAS PL 15 (ex-G 57/GS 28)

Displacement, tons: 14 full load
Dimensions, feet (metres): 41.3 × 13.1 × 3.6 *(12.6 × 4 × 1.1)*
Main machinery: 2 Volvo Penta diesels; 539 hp(m) *(396 kW)*; 2 shafts
Speed, knots: 16. **Range, miles:** 300 at 15 kt
Complement: 5
Guns: 1—7.62 mm MG.
Radars: Surface search: Raytheon; I-band.

Comment: Built in 1979 by Veb Yachwerft, Berlin. Harbour patrol craft of the former GDR 'MAB 12' class transferred in December 1992. New radars fitted.

UPDATED

PV 22

10/1999*, E & M Laursen / 0056855

ILARION

10/1999*, E & M Laursen / 0056858

1 SHALDAG CLASS (PCF)

Name	No	Builders	Commissioned
—	PV 22	Israel Shipyards	4 Sep 1997

Displacement, tons: 56 full load
Dimensions, feet (metres): 81.4 × 19.7 × 3.9 *(24.8 × 6 × 1.2)*
Main machinery: 2 MTU 12V 396TE diesels; 3,560 hp(m) *(2.62 MW)* sustained; 2 Kamewa waterjets
Speed, knots: 45. **Range, miles:** 850 at 16 kt
Complement: 15
Guns: 1 Oerlikon 20 mm; 2—7.62 mm MGs.
Weapons control: Optronic director.
Radars: Surface search: Raytheon; I-band.

Comment: Similar to craft in service with Sri Lankan Navy.

UPDATED

2 POSEIDON CLASS (PC)

Name	No	Builders	Commissioned
POSEIDON	PV 20	Brodotehnika SY, Belgrade	21 Nov 1991
EVAGORAS	PV 21	Brodotehnika SY, Belgrade	21 Nov 1991

Displacement, tons: 58 full load
Dimensions, feet (metres): 80.7 × 18.7 × 3.9 *(24.6 × 5.7 × 1.2)*
Main machinery: 2 MTU 12V 396 TE94 diesels; 3,560 hp(m) *(2.62 MW)* sustained; 2 Kamewa 56 water-jets
Speed, knots: 42. **Range, miles:** 600 at 20 kt
Complement: 9
Guns: 1 Breda KVA 25 mm; ISBRS rocket launcher. 2—12.7 mm MGs.
Radars: Surface search: JRC; I-band.

Comment: Designated as FAC-23 Jets. Aluminium construction. New radars fitted.   *UPDATED*

EVAGORAS

10/1999*, E & M Laursen / 0056856

LAND-BASED MARITIME AIRCRAFT

Note: There are also three Bell 206 utility helicopters.

Numbers/Type: 1 Pilatus Britten-Norman Maritime Defender BN-2A.
Operational speed: 150 kt *(280 km/h)*.
Service ceiling: 18,900 ft *(5,760 m)*.
Range: 1,500 n miles *(2,775 km)*.
Role/Weapon systems: Operated around southern coastline of Cyprus to prevent smuggling and terrorist activity. Sensors: Search radar, searchlight mounted on wings. Weapons: ASV; various machine gun pods and rockets.   *VERIFIED*

DENMARK
DET KONGELIGE DANSKE SØVAERN

Headquarters Appointments

Admiral Fleet:
  Rear Admiral K H Winther
Inspector Naval Home Guard:
  Captain P A Andersen

Diplomatic Representation

Defence Attaché, Berlin and The Hague:
  Colonel F Rytter
Defence Attaché, London and Dublin:
  Captain U Haagen-Olsen
Defence Attaché, Helsinki and Tallin:
  Lieutenant Colonel S H Hartov
Defence Attaché, Warsaw:
  Colonel F Carlsson
Defence Attaché, Washington and Ottawa:
  Brigadier E T Pedersen
Defence Attaché, Paris:
  Colonel C L L Scheel
Defence Attaché, Moscow and Minsk:
  Major General K J Moeller
Defence Attaché, Kiev:
  Lieutenant Colonel C Mathiesen
Defence Attaché, Riga:
  Lieutenant Colonel N M Moesgaard
Defence Attaché, Vilnius:
  Lieutenant Colonel S B Andersen

Personnel

(a) 2000: 5,900 (913 officers) including 496 national service
    Reserves: 7,300.
    Naval Home Guard: 4,400.
(b) 9 months' national service

Bases

Korsør (Corvettes, FACs, Stanflex), Frederikshavn (Submarines, MCMV, Fishery Protection Ships), Grønnedal (Greenland)

Naval Air Arm

Naval helicopters owned and operated by Navy in naval squadron based at Värlöse near Copenhagen. All servicing and maintenance by Air Force. LRMP are flown by the Air Force.

Naval Home Guard

Established in 1952. Duties include guarding naval installations, surveillance, harbour patrol and search and rescue operations.

Coast Defence

Nine radar stations and a number of coast watching stations. There are also two mobile batteries linked by a Terma command and control system; each consists of three trailers, one for command and two for carrying quadruple Harpoon launchers.

Command and Control

The Royal Danish Navy, on behalf of the Ministry of Defence, runs and maintains the icebreakers. Likewise, the Navy runs and maintains two environmental protection divisions based in Copenhagen and Korsør respectively. From 1998 responsibility for environmental survey of maritime areas around Denmark was transferred to the Ministry of Defence. The execution of this responsibility is vested with the Royal Danish Navy. Survey ships are run by the Farvandsdirektoratet Nautisk Afdeling (Administration of Navigation and Hydrography) under the Ministry of Defence, and the Ministry of Fisheries has four rescue vessels.

Appearance

Ships are painted in six different colours as follows:
Grey: frigates, corvettes and patrol frigates.
Olive green: FACs and tankers.
Black: submarines.
Orange: survey vessels.
White: Royal Yacht and the sail training yawls.
Black/yellow: service vessels, tugs and ferryboats.

Strength of the Fleet

Type	Active	Building (Projected)
Submarines (Coastal)	5	(4)
Frigates	7	(4)
Fast Attack Craft (Missile)	2	—
Large Patrol Craft	26	—
Coastal Patrol Craft	1	—
Naval Home Guard	32	2
Minelayers	4	—
Minehunters (Drones)	10	(10)
Support Ships	—	(2)
Transport Ship	1	—
Tankers (Small)	1	—
Icebreakers	4	—
Royal Yacht	1	—

Prefix to Ships' Names

HDMS

Mercantile Marine

Lloyd's Register of Shipping:
  914 vessels of 5,809,166 tons gross

DELETIONS

Frigates

2000   *Beskytteren*

Patrol Forces

1999   *Bille, Bredal, Hammer, Huitfeldt, Krieger, Norby*
2000   *Suenson, Willemoes, Lunden*

Naval Home Guard

1997   *Hercules* (old), Y 375, *Betelgeuse* (old), *Baunen* (old)
1998   Y 376, *Budstikken* (old)
1999   *Cassiopeia, Enø, Lyø*
2000   *Manø, Patrioten* (old), *Kureren* (old)

Mine Warfare Forces

1997   *Gronsund*
2000   *Falster, Sjaelland*

Auxiliaries

1997   *Graspurven, Snespurven, Jenspurven*
1999   *Rimfaxe*

PENNANT LIST

Submarines		**Patrol Forces**					**Auxiliaries**	
S 320	Narhvalen	P 546	Rodsteen	Y 301	Drejø		A 540	Dannebrog
S 321	Nordkaperen	P 547	Sehested	Y 302	Romsø		A 550	Elbjørn
S 322	Tumleren	P 550	Flyvefisken	Y 303	Samsø		A 551	Danbjørn
S 323	Saelen	P 551	Hajen	Y 304	Thurø		A 552	Isbjørn
S 324	Springeren	P 552	Havkatten	Y 305	Vejrø		A 553	Thorbjørn
		P 553	Laxen	Y 306	Farø		A 559	Sleipner
		P 554	Makrelen	Y 307	Laesø		A 569	Skinfaxe
		P 555	Støren	Y 308	Rømø		TO 8	Hugin
Frigates		P 556	Svaerdfisken	Y 386	Agdlek		TO 9	Munin
		P 557	Glenten	Y 387	Agpa		TO 10	Mimer
F 354	Niels Juel	P 558	Gribben	Y 388	Tulugaq		—	MSA 4
F 355	Olfert Fischer	P 559	Lommen				Y 101	Svanen
F 356	Peter Tordenskiold	P 560	Ravnen	**Mine Warfare Forces**			Y 102	Thyra
F 357	Thetis	P 561	Skaden					
F 358	Triton	P 562	Viben	N 43	Lindormen			
F 359	Vaedderen	P 563	Søløven	N 44	Lossen			
F 360	Hvidbjørnen	Y 300	Barsø	N 81	Fyen			
				N 82	Møen			

SUBMARINES

Notes: (1) Viking collaborative project with Norway and Sweden is partially funded. Four of a 45 m class may be built at Karlskrona with a first in-service date of 2007.
(2) Two Swedish Vastergötland class may be leased as a stop-gap measure to keep a total of three boats operational, and two others at a lower state of readiness.

3 TUMLEREN (KOBBEN) (TYPE 207) CLASS (SSK)

Name	No	Builders	Laid down	Launched	Commissioned	Recommissioned
TUMLEREN (ex-*Utvaer*)	S 322	Rheinstahl-Nordseewerke, Emden	24 Mar 1965	30 July 1965	1 Dec 1965	20 Oct 1989
SAELEN (ex-*Uthaug*)	S 323	Rheinstahl-Nordseewerke, Emden	31 May 1965	3 Oct 1965	16 Feb 1966	5 Oct 1990
SPRINGEREN (ex-*Kya*)	S 324	Rheinstahl-Nordseewerke, Emden	26 May 1963	20 Feb 1964	15 Jan 1964	10 Oct 1991

Displacement, tons: 459 surfaced; 524 dived
Dimensions, feet (metres): 155.5 × 15 × 14
(47.4 × 4.6 × 4.3)
Main machinery: Diesel-electric; 2 MTU 12V 493 AZ80 diesels; 1,200 hp(m) *(880 kW)*; 1 motor; 1,700 hp(m) *(1.25 MW)*; 1 shaft
Speed, knots: 12 surfaced; 18 dived
Range, miles: 5,000 at 8 kt snorting
Complement: 24 (7 officers)

Torpedoes: 8—21 in *(533 mm)* bow tubes. FFV Type 613; anti-surface; wire-guided; passive homing to 25 km *(13.7 n miles)*

at 30/45 kt; warhead 240 kg.
Countermeasures: ESM: Racal Sea Lion; radar warning.
Weapons control: Terma Tactic TFCS.
Radars: Surface search: Furuno 805; I-band.
Sonars: Atlas Elektronik PSU NU; passive search and attack; medium frequency.

Programmes: First two acquired from Norway in 1986 for modernisation; the third in late 1989.
Modernisation: Work done at Urivale Shipyard, Bergen between 1987 and 1991 included lengthening by 5.2 ft *(1.6 m)* (which has increased displacement) and new communications, ESM,

navigation and fire-control equipment. New sonar fitted in 1992/93.
Structure: Diving depth, 200 m *(650 ft)*. Pilkington Optronics CK 34 search periscope.
Operational: *Saelen* sank in the Kattegat while unmanned and under tow in December 1990. Salvaged and repaired using spares taken from the ex-Norwegian *Kaura*, which was purchased for cannibalisation. Back in service in August 1993.

UPDATED

SPRINGEREN

11/1999 *, J Cislak / 0056860

2 NARHVALEN CLASS (SSK)

Name	No	Builders	Laid down		Launched		Commissioned	
NARHVALEN	S 320	Royal Dockyard, Copenhagen	16 Feb	1965	10 Sep	1968	27 Feb	1970
NORDKAPEREN	S 321	Royal Dockyard, Copenhagen	4 Mar	1966	18 Dec	1969	22 Dec	1970

Displacement, tons: 420 surfaced; 450 dived
Dimensions, feet (metres): 145.3 × 15 × 13.8
(44.3 × 4.6 × 4.2)
Main machinery: Diesel-electric; 2 MTU 12V 493 TY7; 2,250 hp
(m) *(1.62 MW)*; 1 motor; 1,200 hp(m) *(882 kW)*; 1 shaft
Speed, knots: 12 surfaced; 17 dived
Complement: 24 (7 officers)

Torpedoes: 8—21 in *(533 mm)* bow tubes. Combination of FFV
Type 613; wire-guided; passive homing to 25 km *(13.7 n
miles)* anti-surface at 30/45 kt; warhead 240 kg.
Countermeasures: ESM: Racal Sea Lion; radar warning.
Weapons control: Terma Tactic TFCS.
Radars: Surface search: Furuno 805; I-band.
Sonars: Atlas Elektronik PSU NU; hull-mounted; passive search
and attack; medium frequency.

Programmes: These coastal submarines are similar to the West
German Improved Type 205 and were built under licence at
the Royal Dockyard, Copenhagen with modifications for
Danish needs.
Modernisation: Equipment update similar to the 'Tumleren' class
to enable both submarines to serve until replaced. Work

started on *Narhvalen* in late 1993 and completed in February
1995. Work on *Nordkaperen* started in mid-1995 and
completed in mid-1998. It included new periscopes, a Sagem

optronic mast, Racal upgrade ESM, and improved radar and
sonar.

6/1999*, Royal Danish Navy / 0056859

NARHVALEN

UPDATED

FRIGATES

Note: Four patrol ships with a design based on the Multi-Role Support Ship are planned to be ordered from 2005. At about 4,000 tons the patrol ships are similar to the 'Thetis' class but slightly larger.

3 NIELS JUEL CLASS (FFG)

Name	No	Builders	Laid down		Launched		Commissioned	
NIELS JUEL	F 354	Aalborg Vaerft	20 Oct	1976	17 Feb	1978	26 Aug	1980
OLFERT FISCHER	F 355	Aalborg Vaerft	6 Dec	1978	10 May	1979	16 Oct	1981
PETER TORDENSKIOLD	F 356	Aalborg Vaerft	3 Dec	1979	30 Apr	1980	2 Apr	1982

Displacement, tons: 1,320 full load
Dimensions, feet (metres): 275.5 × 33.8 × 10.2
(84 × 10.3 × 3.1)
Main machinery: CODOG; 1 GE LM 2500 gas turbine;
24,600 hp *(18.35 MW)* sustained; 1 MTU 20 V 956 TB82
diesel; 5,210 hp(m) *(3.83 MW)* sustained; 2 shafts
Speed, knots: 28, gas; 20, diesel
Range, miles: 2,500 at 18 kt
Complement: 94 (15 officers)

Missiles: SSM: 8 McDonnell Douglas Harpoon (2 quad)
launchers **❶**; active radar homing to 130 km *(70 n miles)* at
0.9 Mach; warhead 227 kg.
SAM: 12 (2 sextuple) Raytheon Sea Sparrow Mk 48 Mod 3

VLS modular launchers **❷**; semi-active radar homing to
14.6 km *(8 n miles)* at 2.5 Mach; warhead 39 kg; 12 missiles.
4 Stinger mountings (2 twin) **❸**.
Guns: 1 OTO Melara 3 in *(76 mm)*/62 compact **❹**; 85 rds/min to
16 km *(8.7 n miles)* anti-surface; 12 km *(6.6 n miles)* anti-
aircraft; weight of shell 6 kg.
4 Oerlikon 20 mm (1 each side of the funnel and 2 abaft the
mast) **❺**.
2—12.7 mm MGs to replace the 20 mm abaft the mast in due
course.
Depth charges: 1 rack.
Countermeasures: Decoys: 2 DL-12T Sea Gnat 12-barrelled
chaff launchers **❻**.
ESM: Racal Cutlass; radar warning.

Combat data systems: CelciusTech 9LV Mk 3. Link 11.
SATCOMs (can be fitted forward or aft of the funnel).
Weapons control: Philips 9LV 200 Mk 3 GFCS with TV tracker.
Raytheon Mk 91 Mod 1 MFCS with two directors. Harpoon to
1A(V) standard.
Radars: Air search: DASA TRS-3D **❼**; G/H-band.
Surface search: Philips 9GR 600 **❽**; I-band.
Fire control: 2 Mk 95 **❾**; I/J-band (for SAM).
Philips 9LV 200 Mk 1 Rakel 203C **❿**; J-band (for guns and
SSM).
Navigation: Burmeister & Wain Elektronik Scanter Mil 009;
E/I-band.
Sonars: Plessey PMS 26; hull-mounted; active search and attack;
10 kHz.

Programmes: YARD Glasgow designed the class to Danish
order.
Modernisation: Mid-life update from 1996-2000, including a
NATO Sea Sparrow VLS, and new communications. Air search
radar replaced by TST TRS-3D. Improved combat data system
fitted. F 356 completed in May 1998, F 354 in April 1999
F 355 in June 2000. Stinger SAM mounted each side of the
funnel.
Operational: Normally only one sextuple SAM launcher is
carried, but the second set can be embarked in a few hours.

PETER TORDENSKIOLD

(Scale 1 : 900), Ian Sturton / 0056861

UPDATED

PETER TORDENSKIOLD

8/1999*, J Cislak / 0056864

PETER TORDENSKIOLD
8/1999* / 0056862

NIELS JUEL
9/1999*, Findler & Winter / 0056863

4 THETIS CLASS (FF)

Name	No	Builders	Laid down	Launched	Commissioned
THETIS	F 357	Svenborg Vaerft	10 Oct 1988	14 July 1989	1 July 1991
TRITON	F 358	Svenborg Vaerft	27 June 1989	16 Mar 1990	2 Dec 1991
VAEDDEREN	F 359	Svenborg Vaerft	19 Mar 1990	21 Dec 1990	9 June 1992
HVIDBJØRNEN	F 360	Svenborg Vaerft	2 Jan 1991	11 Oct 1991	30 Nov 1992

Displacement, tons: 2,600 standard; 3,500 full load
Dimensions, feet (metres): 369.1 oa; 327.4 wl × 47.2 × 19.7
(112.5; 99.8 × 14.4 × 6.0)
Main machinery: 3 MAN/Burmeister & Wain Alpha 12V 28/
32A diesels; 10,800 hp(m) *(7.94 MW)* sustained; 1 shaft;
Kamewa cp prop; bow and azimuth thrusters; 880 hp(m)
(647 kW), 1,100 hp(m) *(800 kW)*
Speed, knots: 20; 8 on thrusters
Range, miles: 8,500 at 15.5 kt
Complement: 60 (12 officers) plus 12 spare berths

Guns: 1 OTO Melara 3 in *(76 mm)*/62; Super Rapid ❶; dual
purpose; 120 rds/min to 16 km *(8.7 n miles)*; weight of shell
6 kg.
1 or 2 Oerlikon 20 mm.
Depth charges: 2 Rails (door in stern).
Countermeasures: Decoys: 2 Sea Gnat DL-12T 12-barrelled
launchers for chaff and IR flares.
ESM: Racal Cutlass; intercept.
ECM: Racal Scorpion; jammer.
Combat data systems: Terma TDS; SATCOM ❷.
Weapons control: Bofors 9LV 200 Mk 3 director. FSI Safire
surveillance director ❸.
Radars: Air/surface search: Plessey AWS 6 ❹; G-band.
Surface search: Terma Scanter Mil; I-band.
Navigation: Furuno FR1505DA; I-band.
Fire control: CelsiusTech 9LV Mk 3 ❺; I/J-band.
Sonars: Thomson Sintra TSM 2640 Salmon; VDS; active search
and attack; medium frequency.
C-Teck; hull-mounted; active search; medium frequency.

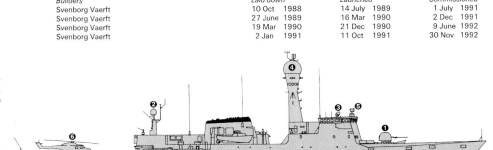

THETIS   *(Scale 1 : 900), Ian Sturton / 0012258*

Helicopters: 1 Westland Lynx Mk 91 ❻.

Programmes: Preliminary study by YARD in 1986 led to Dwinger
Marine Consultants being awarded a contract for a detailed
design completed in mid-1987. All four ordered in October
1987.
Modernisation: There are plans for a new air search radar and
SAM in due course.
Structure: The hull is some 30 m longer than the 'Hvidbjørnen'
class to improve sea-keeping qualities and allow considerable
extra space for additional armament. The design allows the use
of containerised equipment to be shipped depending on role
and there is some commonality with the Flex 300 ships. The
hull is ice strengthened to enable penetration of 1 m thick ice

and efforts have been made to incorporate stealth technology,
for instance by putting anchor equipment, bollards and
winches below the upper deck. There is a double skin up to 2 m
below the waterline. The flight deck (28 × 14 m) is
strengthened to take Sea King or Merlin helicopters. A rigid
inflatable boarding craft plumbed by a hydraulic crane is fitted
alongside the fixed hangar. The bridge and ops room are
combined. *Thetis* has a modified stern for seismological
equipment.
Operational: Primary role is fishery protection. *Thetis* is
employed for three to four months a year doing seismological
surveys in the Greenland EEZ. A 4,000 m towed array is used
to receive signals generated by pneumatic noise guns towed
800 m astern.   **UPDATED**

THETIS   *6/1999*, Maritime Photographic / 0056865*

HVIDBJØRNEN   *6/1998, Michael Nitz / 0017775*

SHIPBORNE AIRCRAFT

Numbers/Type: 8 Westland Lynx Mk 91.
Operational speed: 125 kt *(232 km/h)*.
Service ceiling: 12,500 ft *(3,810 m)*.
Range: 320 n miles *(593 km)*.
Role/Weapon systems: Shipborne helicopter for EEZ and surface search tasks. Being upgraded to Super Lynx standard from 1999. Sensors: Ferranti Seaspray; Racal Kestrel ESM; FLIR 2000. Weapons: Unarmed.

VERIFIED

GULFSTREAM III   *5/1999*, H M Steele /* 0056866

Numbers/Type: 7 Sikorsky S-61A-1 Sea King.
Operational speed: 118 kt *(219 km/h)*.
Service ceiling: 14,700 ft *(4,480 m)*.
Range: 542 n miles *(1,005 km)*.
Role/Weapon systems: Land-based SAR helicopter for combat rescue and surface search. Sensors: Bendix weather radar; GEC Avionics FLIR. Weapons: unarmed.

UPDATED

LYNX   *6/1997, Michael Nitz /* 0017777

LAND-BASED MARITIME AIRCRAFT

Numbers/Type: 2 Gulfstream Aerospace SMA-3 Gulfstream III.
Operational speed: 500 kt *(926 km/h)*.
Service ceiling: 45,000 ft *(13,720 m)*.
Range: 3,940 n miles *(7,300 km)*.
Role/Weapon systems: MR and liaison aircraft; flown on EEZ patrol around Greenland coast and in Danish sea areas in Baltic; EW work undertaken. Sensors: APS-127 surveillance radar. Weapons: Unarmed.

UPDATED

SEA KING   *5/1999*, H M Steele /* 0056867

Numbers/Type: 1 Challenger 604.
Operational speed: 470 kt *(870 km/h)*.
Service ceiling: 41,000 ft *(12,497 m)*.
Range: 3,769 n miles *(6,980 km)*.
Role/Weapon systems: Maritime reconnaissance for EEZ patrol in the Baltic and off Greenland. Sensors: Terma SLAR radar; IR/UV scanner. Weapons: unarmed.   *NEW ENTRY*

PATROL FORCES

Notes: (1) Two patrol vessels (Arctic) with helicopter platforms to be ordered for an in-service date of 2005/06.
(2) Six minor patrol vessels are to be ordered to replace the 'Ø' class. First in-service date in 2004, then at six month intervals.

2 WILLEMOES CLASS (FAST ATTACK CRAFT—MISSILE) (PGFG)

Name	No	Builders	Commissioned
RODSTEEN	P 546	Frederikshavn V and F	16 Feb 1978
SEHESTED	P 547	Frederikshavn V and F	19 May 1978

Displacement, tons: 260 full load
Dimensions, feet (metres): 151 × 24 × 8.2 *(46 × 7.4 × 2.5)*
Main machinery: CODOG; 3 RR 52M/544 gas turbines; 12,750 hp *(9.51 MW)*; 2 GM 8V-71 diesels for cruising on wing shafts; 460 hp *(343 kW)* sustained; 3 shafts; cp props
Speed, knots: 38 (12 on diesels)
Complement: 25 (4 officers)

Missiles: SSM: 4 or 8 McDonnell Douglas Harpoon; active radar homing to 130 km *(70 n miles)* at 0.9 Mach; warhead 227 kg. Numbers carried depend on task and numbers of torpedoes.
SAM: Dual Stinger mounting can be carried.
Guns: 1 OTO Melara 3 in *(76 mm)*/62 compact; 85 rds/min to 16 km *(8.7 n miles)*; weight of shell 6 kg.
2 triple 103 mm illumination rocket launchers.
Torpedoes: 2 or 4—21 in *(533 mm)* tubes. FFV Type 61; wire-guided; passive homing to 25 km *(13.7 n miles)* at 45 kt; warhead 240 kg.
Countermeasures: Decoys: Sea Gnat DL-6T 6-barrelled chaff and IR flares.
ESM: Racal Cutlass; radar warning.
Combat data systems: Terma action data automation.
Radars: Air/surface search: 9GA 208; E/F-band.
Navigation: Terma Elektronik 20T 48 Super; E/I-band.
Fire control: Philips 9LV 200; J-band.

Programmes: Designed by Lürssen to Danish order. Original order to Frederikshavn for four boats, increased to eight and finally 10.
Modernisation: Terma combat data system replaced EPLO. Dual Stinger missiles from 1997. Sea Gnat decoy launchers were fitted in 1991-92.
Operational: Patrols do not normally exceed 36 hours. The mix of weapons varies. These last two survivors are probably to pay off in 2001.

UPDATED

RODSTEEN   *5/1999*, H M Steele /* 0056869

2 VTS CLASS (COASTAL PATROL CRAFT) (PC)

VTS 3   VTS 4

Displacement, tons: 34 full load
Dimensions, feet (metres): 55.8 × 16.1 × 6.9 *(17 × 4.9 × 2.1)*
Main machinery: 2 MWM TBD 616 V12 diesels; 979 hp(m) *(720 kW)*; 2 waterjets
Speed, knots: 33. **Range, miles:** 300 at 30 kt
Complement: 3
Guns: 1—7.62 mm MG can be carried.
Radars: Surface search: Furuno FR 1505 Mk 2; I-band.
Navigation: Furuno M1831; I-band.

Comment: Built by Mulder & Rijke, Netherlands. Completed in 1997 and 1998 to replace Botved type.

UPDATED

RODSTEEN   *5/1999*, Findler & Winter /* 0056868

VTS 3   *6/1999*, Royal Danish Navy /* 0056874

14 FLYVEFISKEN CLASS (LARGE PATROL/ATTACK CRAFT AND MINEHUNTERS/LAYERS) (PG/MHC/MLC/AGSC)

Name	No	Builders	Commissioned
FLYVEFISKEN	P 550	Danyard A/S, Aalborg	19 Dec 1989
HAJEN	P 551	Danyard A/S, Aalborg	19 July 1990
HAVKATTEN	P 552	Danyard A/S, Aalborg	1 Nov 1990
LAXEN	P 553	Danyard A/S, Aalborg	22 Mar 1991
MAKRELEN	P 554	Danyard A/S, Aalborg	1 Oct 1991
STØREN	P 555	Danyard A/S, Aalborg	24 Apr 1992
SVAERDFISKEN	P 556	Danyard A/S, Aalborg	1 Feb 1993
GLENTEN	P 557	Danyard A/S, Aalborg	29 Apr 1993
GRIBBEN	P 558	Danyard A/S, Aalborg	1 July 1993
LOMMEN	P 559	Danyard A/S, Aalborg	21 Jan 1994
RAVNEN	P 560	Danyard A/S, Aalborg	17 Oct 1994
SKADEN	P 561	Danyard A/S, Aalborg	10 Apr 1995
VIBEN	P 562	Danyard A/S, Aalborg	15 Jan 1996
SØLØVEN	P 563	Danyard A/S, Aalborg	28 May 1996

Displacement, tons: 480 full load
Dimensions, feet (metres): 177.2 × 29.5 × 8.2 *(54 × 9 × 2.5)*
Main machinery: CODAG; 1 GE LM 500 gas turbine (centre shaft); 5,450 hp *(4.1 MW)* sustained; 2 MTU 16V 396 TB94 diesels (outer shafts); 5,800 hp(m) *(4.26 MW)* sustained; 3 shafts; cp props on outer shafts; bow thruster. Auxiliary propulsion by hydraulic motors on outer gearboxes; hydraulic pumps driven by 1 GM 12V-71 diesel; 500 hp *(375 kW)*
Speed, knots: 30; 20 on diesels; 10 on hydraulic propulsion. **Range, miles:** 2,400 at 18 kt
Complement: 19-29 (depending on role) (4 officers)

Missiles: SSM: 8 McDonnell Douglas Harpoon ❶; active radar homing to 130 km *(70 n miles)* at 0.9 Mach; warhead 227 kg. Attack role only. Block II from 2001 gives land attack option.
SAM: 3 Mk 48 Mod 3 twin launchers ❷; 6 Sea Sparrow; semi-active radar homing to 14.6 km *(8 n miles)* at 2.5 Mach; warhead 32 kg. 12 missiles from 2002. Fitted for Attack, MCM and Minelaying roles.
Guns: 1 OTO Melara 3 in *(76 mm)*/62 Super Rapid ❸; dual purpose; 120 rds/min to 16 km *(8.7 n miles)*; weight of shell 6 kg.
2—12.7 mm MGs.
Torpedoes: 2—21 in *(533 mm)* tubes ❹; FFV Type 613; wire-guided passive homing to 15 km *(8.2 n miles)* at 45 kt; warhead 240 kg. Attack role only. Eurotorp Mu 90 Impact from 2001.
Depth charges: 4.
Mines: 60. Minelaying role only ❺.
Countermeasures: MCMV: Ibis 43 minehunting system with Thomson Sintra 2061 tactical system and 2054 side scan sonar towed by SAV (see *Mine Warfare Forces* section). Bofors Double Eagle ROV Mk I or II. Minehunting role only.
Decoys: 2 Sea Gnat 130 mm DL-6T 6-barrelled launcher for chaff and IR flares.
ESM: Racal Sabre; radar warning.
ECM: Racal Cygnus; jammer.

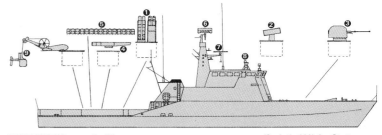

FLYVEFISKEN (composite fit)   *(Scale 1 : 600), Ian Sturton*

Combat data systems: Terma/CelsiusTech TDS. Link 11 being fitted.
Weapons control: CelsiusTech 9LV Mk 3 optronic director. Harpoon to 1A(V) standard or AHWCS with Block II.
Radars: Air/surface search: Plessey AWS 6 (550-556); G-band; or Telefunken SystemTechnik TRS-3D (557-563) ❻; G/H-band.
Surface search: Terma Scanter Mil ❼; I-band.
Navigation: Furuno; I-band.
Fire control: CelsiusTech 9LV 200 Mk 3 ❽; Ku/J-band.
Sonars: CelsiusTech CTS-36/39; hull-mounted; active search; high frequency.
Thomson Sintra TSM 2640 Salmon ❾; VDS; medium frequency. For ASW only.

Programmes: Standard Flex 300 which has replaced 'Daphne' class (seaward defence craft) and 'Søløven' class (fast attack craft torpedo), and will replace 'Sund' (MCM) class. First batch of seven with option on a further nine contracted with Danyard on 27 July 1985. Second batch of six ordered 14 June 1990 and last one authorised in 1993 to a total of 14 which is two less than originally planned.
Modernisation: Mk 48 Mod 3 SAM launchers to become dual pack with 12 weapons from 2002. Block II Harpoon with GPS from 2001. Link 11 being fitted.
Structure: GRP sandwich hulls. Four positions prepared to plug in armament and equipment containers in combinations meeting the requirements of the various roles. Torpedo tubes and minerails detachable. Combat data system modular with standard consoles of which three to six are embarked depending on the role. SAV control aerials are mounted on the bridge. TRS-3D radar fitted in last seven, remainder in due course.
Operational: All vessels can be fitted out as patrol craft; the number of outfits for the other roles are: attack role 10; MCMV five; minelayer 14; ASW four. In general outfits can be changed within a few hours. Outfits for non-military tasks such as pollution control and hydrographic survey have also been developed. The Double Eagle ROV carries Reson SeaBat 6012 sonar, TV camera, and a mine disposal charge.

UPDATED

HAVKATTEN   *6/1999*, Maritime Photographic /* 0056871

SKADEN   *5/1999*, H M Steele /* 0056872

3 AGDLEK CLASS (LARGE PATROL CRAFT) (PC)

Name	No	Builders	Commissioned
AGDLEK	Y 386	Svendborg Vaerft	12 Mar 1974
AGPA	Y 387	Svendborg Vaerft	14 May 1974
TULUGAQ	Y 388	Svendborg Vaerft	26 June 1979

Displacement, tons: 300; 330 (Y 388) full load
Dimensions, feet (metres): 103 × 25.3 × 11.2 *(31.4 × 7.7 × 3.4)*
Main machinery: 1 Burmeister & Wain Alpha A08-26 VO diesel; 800 hp(m) *(588 kW)*; 1 shaft
Speed, knots: 12
Complement: 14 (3 officers)
Guns: 2 Oerlikon 20 mm.
Radars: Surface search: Terma 20T 48 Super; E/I-band.
Navigation: Skanter 009; I-band.

Comment: Designed for service off Greenland. Ice strengthened. SATCOM fitted. To be replaced from 2005 by two new patrol vessels. **UPDATED**

TULUGAQ *6/1999*, Royal Danish Navy* / 0056870

9 Ø CLASS (LARGE PATROL CRAFT) (PC)

Name	No	Builders	Commissioned
BARSØ	Y 300	Svendborg Vaerft	13 June 1969
DREJØ	Y 301	Svendborg Vaerft	1 July 1969
ROMSØ	Y 302	Svendborg Vaerft	21 July 1969
SAMSØ	Y 303	Svendborg Vaerft	15 Aug 1969
THURØ	Y 304	Svendborg Vaerft	12 Sep 1969
VEJRØ	Y 305	Svendborg Vaerft	17 Oct 1969
FARØ	Y 306	Svendborg Vaerft	17 May 1973
LAESØ	Y 307	Svendborg Vaerft	23 July 1973
ROMØ	Y 308	Svendborg Vaerft	3 Sep 1973

Displacement, tons: 155 full load
Dimensions, feet (metres): 84 × 19.7 × 9.2 *(25.6 × 6 × 2.8)*
Main machinery: 1 diesel; 385 hp(m) *(283 kW)*; 1 shaft
Speed, knots: 11
Complement: 19 (2 officers)
Guns: 2 Oerlikon 20 mm (not always fitted). 1—12.7 mm MG.
Radars: Navigation: Terma Skanter 009; I-band.

Comment: Rated as patrol cutters. *Laesø* acts as diver support ship with a recompression chamber and towed acoustic array. The last three have a wheelhouse which extends over the full beam. Replacement programme planned based on the manned MRD drone, to be in service starting in 2004. **UPDATED**

FARØ *9/1999*, E & M Laursen* / 0056873

NAVAL HOME GUARD

1 KUTTER CLASS (COASTAL PATROL CRAFT) (PC)

CRUX MHV 64

Displacement, tons: 35 full load
Dimensions, feet (metres): 60.4 × 17.1 × 7.5 *(18.4 × 5.2 × 2.3)*
Main machinery: 1 diesel; 165 hp(m) *(121 kW)*; 1 shaft
Speed, knots: 9
Guns: 2—7.62 mm MGs.
Radars: Navigation: Raytheon RM 1290S; I-band.

Comment: Veteran of the Second World War. This last of class pays off in 2001. **UPDATED**

CRUX *6/1999*, Royal Danish Navy* / 0056875

16 + 2 MHV 800 CLASS (COASTAL PATROL CRAFT) (PC)

Name	No	Builders	Commissioned
ALDEBARAN	MHV 801	Soby Shipyard	9 July 1992
CARINA	MHV 802	Soby Shipyard	30 Sep 1992
ARIES	MHV 803	Soby Shipyard	30 Mar 1993
ANDROMEDA	MHV 804	Soby Shipyard	30 Sep 1993
GEMINI	MHV 805	Soby Shipyard	28 Feb 1994
DUBHE	MHV 806	Soby Shipyard	1 July 1994
JUPITER	MHV 807	Soby Shipyard	30 Nov 1994
LYRA	MHV 808	Soby Shipyard	30 May 1995
ANTARES	MHV 809	Soby Shipyard	30 Nov 1995
LUNA	MHV 810	Soby Shipyard	30 May 1996
APOLLO	MHV 811	Soby Shipyard	30 Nov 1996
HERCULES	MHV 812	Soby Shipyard	28 May 1997
BAUNEN	MHV 813	Soby Shipyard	17 Dec 1997
BUDSTIKKEN	MHV 814	Soby Shipyard	30 Aug 1998
KUREREN	MHV 815	Soby Shipyard	30 May 1999
PATRIOTEN	MHV 816	Soby Shipyard	25 Feb 2000
PARTISAN	MHV 817	Soby Shipyard	Nov 2000
SABOTØREN	MHV 818	Soby Shipyard	Aug 2001

Displacement, tons: 83 full load
Dimensions, feet (metres): 77.8 × 18.4 × 6.6 *(23.7 × 5.6 × 2)*
Main machinery: 2 Saab Scania DSI-14 diesels; 900 hp(m) *(661 kW)*; 2 shafts
Speed, knots: 13. **Range, miles:** 990 at 11 kt
Complement: 8 + 4 spare
Guns: 2—7.62 mm MGs. 2—20 mm (can be fitted).
Radars: Navigation: Furuno 1505; I-band.

Comment: First six ordered in April 1991, second six in July 1992, six more in 1997. Steel hulls with a moderate ice capability. **UPDATED**

LUNA *8/1999*, L-G Nilsson* / 0056876

6 MHV 90 CLASS (COASTAL PATROL CRAFT) (PC)

BOPA MHV 90	HOLGER DANSKE MHV 92	RINGEN MHV 94
BRIGADEN MHV 91	HVIDSTEN MHV 93	SPEDITØREN MHV 95

Displacement, tons: 85 full load
Dimensions, feet (metres): 64.9 × 18.7 × 8.2 *(19.8 × 5.7 × 2.5)*
Main machinery: 1 Burmeister & Wain diesel; 400 hp(m) *(294 kW)*; 1 shaft
Speed, knots: 11
Complement: 10
Guns: 2—7.62 mm MGs.
Radars: Navigation: Furuno 1505; I-band.

Comment: Built between 1973 and 1975. New radars fitted. **UPDATED**

HOLGER DANSKE *6/1999*, Michael Nitz* / 0056877

4 MHV 80 CLASS (COASTAL PATROL CRAFT) (PC)

Name	No	Builders	Commissioned
FAENØ (ex-MHV 69, ex-MS 6)	MHV 80	Denmark	July 1941
ASKØ (ex-Y 386, ex-M 560, ex-MS 2)	MHV 81	Denmark	1 Aug 1941
BAAGØ (ex-Y 387, ex-M 561, ex-MS 3)	MHV 84	Denmark	9 Aug 1941
HJORTØ (ex-Y 389, ex-M 564, ex-MS 7)	MHV 85	Denmark	24 Sep 1941

Displacement, tons: 80 full load
Dimensions, feet (metres): 80.1 × 15.1 × 5.2 *(24.4 × 4.6 × 1.6)*
Main machinery: 1 diesel; 350 hp(m) *(257 kW)*; 1 shaft
Speed, knots: 11
Complement: 10
Guns: 2—7.62 mm MGs.
Radars: Navigation: Raytheon RM 1290S; I-band.

Comment: Of wooden construction. All launched in 1941. Former inshore minesweepers.
UPDATED

ASKØ   *7/1997*, Findler & Winter /* 0017783

3 MHV 70 CLASS (COASTAL PATROL CRAFT) (PC)

SATURN MHV 70   **SCORPIUS** MHV 71   **SIRIUS** MHV 72

Displacement, tons: 125 full load
Dimensions, feet (metres): 64 × 16.7 × 8.2 *(19.5 × 5.1 × 2.5)*
Main machinery: 1 diesel; 200 hp(m) *(147 kW)*; 1 shaft
Speed, knots: 10
Complement: 9
Guns: 2—7.62 mm MGs.
Radars: Navigation: Raytheon RM 1290S; I-band.

Comment: Patrol boats and training craft for the Naval Home Guard. Built in the Royal Dockyard, Copenhagen and commissioned in 1958. Formerly designated DMH, but allocated MHV numbers in 1969.
UPDATED

SCORPIUS   *6/1999*, Royal Danish Navy /* 0056878

2 MHV 20 CLASS (COASTAL PATROL CRAFT) (PC)

PARTISAN MHV 23   **SABOTØREN** MHV 25

Displacement, tons: 60 full load
Dimensions, feet (metres): 54.1 × 13.8 × 4.9 *(16.5 × 4.2 × 1.5)*
Main machinery: 2 MTU diesels; 500 hp(m) *(367 kW)*; 2 shafts
Speed, knots: 15
Complement: 9
Guns: 2—7.62 mm MGs.
Radars: Navigation: Terma 9T48/9; I-band.

Comment: Built of GRP by Ejvinds Plastikbodevaerft, Svendborg between 1978 and 1981. Used for patrols in The Sound. MHV 23 to be deleted in November 2000 and the last one in 2001.
UPDATED

MHV 24 (old number)   *8/1999*, L-G Nilsson /* 0056879

MINE WARFARE FORCES

Note: See also 'Flyvefisken' class under *Patrol Forces*.

2 FALSTER CLASS (MINELAYERS) (ML)

Name	No	Builders	Commissioned
FYEN	N 81	Frederikshavn Vaerft	18 Sep 1963
MØEN	N 82	Frederikshavn Vaerft	29 Apr 1964

Displacement, tons: 1,880 full load
Dimensions, feet (metres): 252.6 × 42 × 11.8 *(77 × 12.8 × 3.6)*
Main machinery: 2 GM/EMD 16-567D3 diesels; 4,800 hp *(3.58 MW)* sustained; 2 shafts
Speed, knots: 17
Complement: 74 (10 officers) plus 59 cadets

Missiles: SAM: Three twin Stinger launchers can be carried in lieu of 20 mm guns.
Guns: 2 US 3 in *(76 mm)*/50 Mk 33 (twin); 25 rds/min to 12.8 km *(7 n miles)*; weight of shell 6 kg.
    4 Oerlikon 20 mm.
Mines: 4 rails; 400.
Countermeasures: Decoys: 2 Sea Gnat DL-6T six-barrelled launchers; chaff and IR flare launchers.
ESM: Racal Cutlass; radar warning.
Combat data systems: Terma TDS.
Radars: Air/surface search: 9 GR 608; E/F-band.
Fire control: CGS 1; I-band.
Surface search: NWS 2; I-band.
Navigation: Terma Pilot; E/I-band.

Programmes: Ordered in 1960-61 and launched 1962-63. Named after Danish islands. Similar to Turkish *Nusret*.
Modernisation: Terma command and control system. Mine stocks updated in collaboration with Germany. Twin Stinger SAM mountings can be fitted. Fitted with new radars and chaff launchers in 1997/98, when the mainmast was removed.
Structure: The steel hull is flush-decked with a raking stem, a full stern and a prominent knuckle forward. The hull has been specially strengthened for ice navigation. In 1991 *Fyen* main mast was raised, *Møen* in 1993. The mast was subsequently removed in *Fyen*.
Operational: Both ships can be employed for midshipmen's training.
UPDATED

MØEN   *6/1999*, Maritime Photographic /* 0056880

FYEN (no mainmast)   *8/1998, L-G Nilsson /* 0017785

4 + (10) MSF MK 1 CLASS (MRD)

MSF 1-MSF 4

Displacement, tons: 125 full load
Dimensions, feet (metres): 86.9 × 23 × 6.9 *(26.5 × 7 × 2.1)*
Main machinery: 2 Scania DSI 14 diesels; 1,000 hp(m) *(736 kW)*; 2 Schottel waterjets or 2 Schottel azimuth thrusters
Speed, knots: 12
Complement: 4
Combat data systems: IN-SNEC/INFOCOM.
Radars: Navigation: Raytheon 40 or Terma; I-band.
Sonars: Thomson Marconi STS 2054 side scan active; high frequency.

Comment: MSF (Minor Standard Vessel). First batch of four ordered in January 1997 from Danyard, Aalborg, and delivered June 1998 to January 1999. Fitted out as MCMV drones. GRP hulls. IN-SNEC is a high data rate sonar/TV link. INFOCOM is a low data rate command link. Further ten planned for 2004-2007. Role outfits for Batch 2 ships are planned as follows: training ships two; torpedo recovery vessels three; survey vessels four; coastal patrol one. Outfits can be changed between hulls.
UPDATED

MSF 1   *8/1999*, L-G Nilsson /* 0056882

2 LINDORMEN CLASS (COASTAL MINELAYERS) (MLC)

Name	No	Builders	Launched	Commissioned
LINDORMEN	N 43	Svendborg Vaerft	7 June 1977	16 Feb 1978
LOSSEN	N 44	Svendborg Vaerft	11 Oct 1977	14 June 1978

Displacement, tons: 570 full load
Dimensions, feet (metres): 146 × 29.5 × 8 *(44.5 × 9 × 2.6)*
Main machinery: 2 Frichs diesels; 1,600 hp(m) *(1.2 MW)*; 2 shafts
Speed, knots: 14
Complement: 27 (4 officers)
Guns: 3 Oerlikon 20 mm.
Mines: 50-60 (depending on type).
Radars: Navigation: NWS 3; I-band.

Comment: Controlled Minelayers.

UPDATED

LINDORMEN   *9/1997*, van Ginderen Collection /* 0012267

6 SAV CLASS (MINEHUNTER—DRONES) (MRD)

MRD 1 (ex-*MRF 1*)   **MRD 2** (ex-*MRF 2*)   **MRD 3-6**

Displacement, tons: 32 full load
Dimensions, feet (metres): 59.7 × 15.6 × 3.9 *(18.2 × 4.8 × 1.2)*
Main machinery: 1 Detroit diesel; 350 hp(m) *(257 kW)*; 1 Schottel waterjet propulsor
Speed, knots: 12
Complement: 4
Combat data systems: Terma link to 'Flyvefisken' class (in MCMV configuration).
Radars: Navigation: Furuno; I-band.
Sonars: Thomson Sintra TSM 2054 side scan; active minehunting; high frequency.

Comment: Built by Danyard with GRP hulls. First one completed in March 1991, second in December 1991. Four more ordered in mid-1994 and delivered in 1996. The vessels are robot drones (or Surface Auxiliary Vessels (SAV)) operated in pairs by the 'Flyvefisken' class in MCMV configuration. Hull is based on the 'Hugin' class TRVs with low noise propulsion. The towfish with side scan sonar is lowered and raised from the stern-mounted gantry. The first two craft have slightly different funnel designs. ADI Dyad influence sweeps trials in 1999/2000.

UPDATED

MRD 1   *4/1998*, Winter & Findler /* 0056881

AUXILIARIES

Note: There is a roadborne support unit (MOBA) for the Attack Craft with two sections. The first, of eight vehicles with radar, W/T and control offices is MOBA (Ops) and the second, of 25 vehicles for stores, fuel, provisions, torpedoes and workshops is M-LOG.

0 + (2) MULTIROLE SUPPORT SHIP

Comment: The larger variant of a Standard Ship design to provide flexible support for multirole operators. First contract to be placed in 2002 for delivery in late 2004. The ships are to be of about 6,000 tons. Four ships of a 4,000 ton smaller version are subsequently to be built as Patrol Ships.

NEW ENTRY

MULTIROLE SUPPORT SHIP   *1999*, Royal Danish Navy /* 0056883

1 TRANSPORT SHIP (AKS)

Name	No	Builders	Commissioned
SLEIPNER	A 559	Åbenrå Vaerft og A/S	18 July 1986

Displacement, tons: 465 full load
Dimensions, feet (metres): 119.6 × 24.9 × 8.8 *(36.5 × 7.6 × 2.7)*
Main machinery: 1 Callesen diesel; 575 hp(m) *(423 kW)*; 1 shaft
Speed, knots: 11. **Range, miles:** 2,400 at 11 kt
Complement: 7 (1 officer)
Cargo capacity: 150 tons
Radars: Navigation: Scanter Mil 009; I-band.

UPDATED

SLEIPNER   *2/1995*, Erik Laursen /* 0056884

1 YO 65 CLASS (TANKERS) (AOTL)

Name	No	Builders	Commissioned
SKINFAXE (ex-US YO 229)	A 569	Jefferson Bridge & Machine Co, USA	7 Dec 1945

Displacement, tons: 1,400 full load
Dimensions, feet (metres): 174 × 32.9 × 13.3 *(53.1 × 10 × 4.1)*
Main machinery: 1 GM diesel; 560 hp *(418 kW)*; 1 shaft
Speed, knots: 10. **Range, miles:** 2,100 at 10 kt
Complement: 13 (3 officers)
Cargo capacity: 900 tons fuel
Guns: 1 Oerlikon 20 mm.
Radars: Navigation: NWS 3; I-band.

Comment: Transferred from the USA on 2 August 1962. Acts as tender for the 'Willemoes' class.

UPDATED

SKINFAXE   *5/1999*, Per Kornefeldt /* 0056885

1 ROYAL YACHT (YAC)

Name	No	Builders	Commissioned
DANNEBROG	A 540	R Dockyard, Copenhagen	20 May 1932

Displacement, tons: 1,130 full load
Dimensions, feet (metres): 246 × 34 × 12.1 *(75 × 10.4 × 3.7)*
Main machinery: 2 Burmeister & Wain Alpha T23L-KVO diesels; 1,800 hp(m) *(1.32 MW)*; 2 shafts; cp props
Speed, knots: 14
Complement: 54 (12 officers)
Guns: 2—40 mm saluting guns.
Radars: Navigation: Scanter Mil 009; I-band.

Comment: Laid down 2 January 1931, launched on 10 October 1931. Major refit 1980 included new engines and electrical gear. Marisat fitted in 1992.

UPDATED

DANNEBROG   *5/1999*, Per Kornefeldt /* 0056886

1 MINE TRANSPORT (YE)

Name	No	Builders	Commissioned
MSA 4	— (ex-MK 5, ex-Y 383)	Holbaek Bädevaerft	1949

Displacement, tons: 34 full load
Dimensions, feet (metres): 62.3 × 13.8 × 4.9 *(19 × 4.2 × 1.5)*
Main machinery: 1 diesel; 150 hp(m) *(110 kW)*; 1 shaft
Speed, knots: 8
Complement: 4
Radars: Navigation: Furuno; I-band.   **UPDATED**

MSA 4   *10/1995**, Erik Laursen* / 0056887

3 HUGIN CLASS (TORPEDO RECOVERY VESSELS) (TRV)

HUGIN TO 8   **MUNIN** TO 9   **MIMER** TO 10

Displacement, tons: 23 full load
Dimensions, feet (metres): 53.1 × 13.8 × 3.9 *(16.2 × 4.2 × 1.2)*
Main machinery: 1 MWM diesel; 450 hp(m) *(330 kW)*; 1 shaft
Speed, knots: 15
Complement: 4

Comment: Built by Ejvinds, Svenborg. The same hull, slightly lengthened, is the basis of the SAV
class robot boats.   **UPDATED**

HUGIN   *6/1997**, Royal Danish Navy* / 0056888

2 POLLUTION CONTROL CRAFT (AOTL)

MILJØ 101 and **102**

Displacement, tons: 16 full load
Dimensions, feet (metres): 53.8 × 14.4 × 7.1 *(16.2 × 4.2 × 2.2)*
Main machinery: 1 MWM TBD232V12 diesel; 454 hp(m) *(334 kW)* sustained; 1 shaft
Speed, knots: 15. **Range, miles:** 350 at 8 kt
Complement: 3 (1 officer)

Comment: Built by Ejvinds Plastikbodevaerft, Svendborg. Carry derricks and booms for framing oil
slicks and dispersant fluids. Naval manned. Delivered 1 November and 1 December 1977.
UPDATED

MILJØ 101   *6/1999**, Royal Danish Navy* / 0056890

4 RESCUE VESSELS (ATR)

NORDJYLLAND   NORDSØEN   VESTKYSTEN   JENS VAEVER

Displacement, tons: 475; 657 *(Vestkysten)*; 141 *(Jens Vaever)*
Dimensions, feet (metres): 134.5 × 32.8 × 13 *(41 × 10 × 4)*
     163.7 × 32.8 × 10.8 *(49.9 × 10 × 3.3)* (Vestkysten)
     95.1 × 19.7 × 9.8 *(29 × 6 × 3)* (Jens Vaever)

Comment: Three for the North Sea, one for the Baltic. *Jens Vaever* commissioned 1960;
Nordjylland 1967 and *Nordsøen* 1968. *Vestkysten* commissioned in 1987 and replaced the old
ship of the same name. All are capable of about 12 kt sustained speed. Used for fishery
protection.
UPDATED

NORDSØEN   *1/1999**, Harald Carstens* / 0056889

2 SEA TRUCKS (AKL)

METTE MILJØ   MARIE MILJØ

Displacement, tons: 157 full load
Dimensions, feet (metres): 97.7 × 26.2 × 5.2 *(29.8 × 8 × 1.6)*
Main machinery: 2 Grenaa diesels; 660 hp(m) *(485 kW)*; 2 shafts
Speed, knots: 10
Complement: 9 (1 officer)

Comment: Built by Carl B Hoffmann A/S, Esbjerg and Søren Larsen & Sønners Skibsvaerft A/S,
Nykøbing Mors. Delivered 22 February 1980. Have orange and yellow superstructure.
UPDATED

METTE MILJØ   *6/1999**, van Ginderen Collection* / 0056891

2 OIL POLLUTION CRAFT (AOTL/ABU)

GUNNAR THORSON   GUNNAR SEIDENFADEN

Displacement, tons: 750 full load
Dimensions, feet (metres): 183.7 × 40.3 × 12.8 *(56 × 12.3 × 3.9)*
Main machinery: 2 Burmeister and Wain Alpha 8V23L-VO diesels; 2.320 hp(m) *(1.7 MW)*;
2 shafts; cp props; bow thruster
Speed, knots: 12.5
Complement: 16 (7 officers)

Comment: Built by Ørnskov Stålskibsvaerft, Frederikshavn. Delivered 8 May and 2 July 1981
respectively. *G Thorson* at Copenhagen, *G Seidenfaden* at Korsør. Carry firefighting equipment.
Large hydraulic crane fitted in 1988 for the secondary task of buoy tending. Orange painted
hulls.
VERIFIED

GUNNAR THORSON   *7/1998, M Declerck* / 0017790

1 RESEARCH SHIP

DANA

Displacement, tons: 3,700 full load
Dimensions, feet (metres): 257.5 × 48.6 × 19.7 *(78.5 × 14.8 × 6)*
Main machinery: 2 Burmeister and Wain Alpha 16V23-LU diesels; 4,960 hp(m) *(3.65 MW)*; 1 shaft cp prop; bow and stern thrusters
Speed, knots: 15. **Range, miles:** 8,000 at 14 kt
Complement: 27 plus 12 scientists

Comment: Built by Dannebrog, Aarhus in 1982. Used mostly for Fisheries survey and research. Has an ice-strengthened hull and three 6 ton cranes.

VERIFIED

DANA   *10/1994, van Ginderen Collection*

ICEBREAKERS

Note: Icebreakers, are controlled by the Navy but have a combined naval and civilian crew. Maintenance is done at Frederikshavn in Summer. During Summer period one icebreaker may be employed on surveying duties in Danish waters for the Administration of Navigation and Hydrography.

Name	No	Builders	Commissioned
THORBJØRN	A 553	Svendborg Vaerft	June 1981

Displacement, tons: 2,344 full load
Dimensions, feet (metres): 221.4 × 50.2 × 15.4 *(67.5 × 15.3 × 4.7)*
Main machinery: Diesel-electric; 4 Burmeister & Wain Alpha 16U28L-VO diesels; 6,800 hp(m) *(5 MW)*; 2 motors; 2 shafts
Speed, knots: 16.5. **Range, miles:** 22,000 at 16 kt
Complement: 22 (7 officers)

Comment: No bow thruster. Side rolling tanks. Fitted for surveying duties in non-ice periods.

UPDATED

THORBJØRN   *6/1994*, *Mikael Laursen* / 0056892

Name	No	Builders	Commissioned
DANBJØRN	A 551	Lindø Vaerft, Odense	1965
ISBJØRN	A 552	Lindø Vaerft, Odense	1966

Displacement, tons: 3,685 full load
Dimensions, feet (metres): 252 × 56 × 20 *(76.8 × 17.1 × 6.1)*
Main machinery: Diesel-electric; 6 Burmeister and Wain 12-26MT-40V diesels; 10,500 hp(m) *(7.72 MW)*; 8 motors; 5,240 hp(m) *(38.5 MW)*; 4 shafts
Speed, knots: 14. **Range, miles:** 11,500 at 14 kt
Complement: 25 (9 officers)

Comment: Two of the four propellers are positioned forward, two aft.

UPDATED

DANBJØRN   *7/1995*, *Harald Carstens* / 0056893

Name	No	Builders	Commissioned
ELBJØRN	A 550	Frederikshavn Vaerft	1966

Displacement, tons: 893 standard; 1,400 full load
Dimensions, feet (metres): 156.5 × 40.3 × 14.5 *(47 × 12.1 × 4.4)*
Main machinery: Diesel-electric; 3 Frichs diesel generators; 3,600 hp(m) *(2.64 MW)*; 3 motors; 3 shafts
Speed, knots: 12
Complement: 24 (8 officers)

Comment: Used for survey duties during non-ice periods.

UPDATED

ELBJØRN   *2/1999*, *van Ginderen Collection* / 0056894

TRAINING SHIPS

Note: There are two small Sail Training Ships, *Svanen* Y 101 and *Thyra* Y 102. Of 32 tons they have a sail area of 480 m² and an auxiliary diesel of 72 hp(m) *(53 kW)*. Built in 1960.

SVANEN   *6/1999*, *van Ginderen Collection* / 0056895

SURVEY SHIPS

Note: *Thorbjorn* and *Elbjørn* are also used as survey ships.

6 SURVEY LAUNCHES (YFS)

SKA 11   12   13   14   15   16

Displacement, tons: 52 full load
Dimensions, feet (metres): 65.6 × 17.1 × 6.9 *(20 × 5.2 × 2.1)*
Main machinery: 1 GM diesel; 540 hp *(403 kW)*; 1 shaft
Speed, knots: 12
Complement: 6 (1 officer)
Radars: Navigation: Skanter Mil 009; I-band.

Comment: GRP hulls. Built 1981-84 by Rantsausminde. Have red hulls and white superstructures. Survey motor launches.

UPDATED

SKA 16   *7/1997, E & M Laursen* / 0012275

DJIBOUTI

Personnel	Bases	French Navy	Mercantile Marine	DELETIONS
2000: 120	Djibouti	The permanent French naval contingent usually includes up to three frigates and a repair ship.	Lloyd's Register of Shipping: 13 vessels of 4,356 tons gross	1997 Zena

PATROL FORCES

Notes: (1) One Zhuk and one Boghammar patrol craft were transferred from Ethiopia in 1996. Neither are operational.
(2) Up to six RIBs are in use. Zodiac and Avon types.

2 PLASCOA CLASS (COASTAL PATROL CRAFT) (PB)

Name	No	Builders	Commissioned
MOUSSA ALI	P 10	Plascoa, Cannes	8 June 1985
MONT ARREH	P 11	Plascoa, Cannes	16 Feb 1986

Displacement, tons: 35 full load
Dimensions, feet (metres): 75.5 × 18 × 4.9 *(23 × 5.5 × 1.5)*
Main machinery: 2 SACM Poyaud V12-520 M25 diesels; 1,700 hp(m) *(1.25 MW)*; 2 shafts
Speed, knots: 25. **Range, miles:** 750 at 12 kt
Complement: 15
Guns: 1 Giat 20 mm. 1—12.7 mm MG.
Radars: Navigation: Decca 36; I-band.

Comment: Ordered in October 1984 and transferred as a gift from France. GRP hulls. Refitted in 1988 and 1994. *UPDATED*

5 SAWARI CLASS (INSHORE PATROL CRAFT) (PBR)

5-7   12-13

Comment: All acquired from Iraq in 1989. Can be armed with MGs and rocket launchers. Outboard engines give speeds up to 25 kt in calm conditions. *5* to *7* are the 13 m type and *12* and *13* are 21 m. *VERIFIED*

MONT ARREH   *1986*, Plascoa /* 0056896

DOMINICA

Headquarters Appointments	General	Personnel	Bases	Mercantile Marine
Head of Coast Guard: Inspector O Frederick	An independent island in the British Commonwealth situated north of Martinique.	2000: 32	Roseau	Lloyd's Register of Shipping: 7 vessels of 2,233 tons gross

COAST GUARD

1 SWIFT 65 ft CLASS (PB)

Name	No	Builders	Commissioned
MELVILLE	D 4	Swiftships, Morgan City	1 May 1984

Displacement, tons: 33 full load
Dimensions, feet (metres): 64.9 × 18.4 × 6.6 *(19.8 × 5.6 × 2)*
Main machinery: 2 Detroit 12V-71TA diesels; 840 hp *(616 kW)* sustained; 2 shafts
Speed, knots: 23. **Range, miles:** 250 at 18 kt
Complement: 10
Guns: 1—7.62 mm MG.
Radars: Surface search: Furuno; I/J-band.

Comment: Ordered in November 1983. Similar craft supplied to Antigua and St Lucia. *VERIFIED*

MELVILLE   *11/1993, Maritime Photographic*

1 DAUNTLESS CLASS (PB)

Name	No	Builders	Commissioned
UKALE	D 05	SeaArk Marine	8 Nov 1995

Displacement, tons: 11 full load
Dimensions, feet (metres): 40 × 14 × 4.3 *(12.2 × 4.3 × 1.3)*
Main machinery: 2 Caterpillar 3208TA diesels; 870 hp *(650 kW)* sustained; 2 shafts
Speed, knots: 27. **Range, miles:** 600 at 18 kt
Complement: 6
Guns: 1—7.62 mm MG (can be carried).
Radars: Surface search: Raytheon; I-band.

Comment: Similar to craft delivered by the USA to many Caribbean Coast Guards under FMS. *UPDATED*

UKALE   *11/1995*, SeaArk /* 0056897

3 PATROL CRAFT (PBR)

VIGILANCE   OBSERVER   RESCUER

Displacement, tons: 2.4 full load
Dimensions, feet (metres): 27 × 8.4 × 1 *(8.2 × 2.6 × 0.3)*
Main machinery: 1 Evinrude outboard; 225 hp *(168 kW)* sustained or 2 Johnson outboards *(Rescuer)*; 280 hp *(205 kW)*
Speed, knots: 28 or 45 *(Rescuer)*
Complement: 3

Comment: First two are Boston Whalers acquired in 1988. *Rescuer* is of similar size but is an RHIB acquired in 1994. *VERIFIED*

OBSERVER   *11/1993, Maritime Photographic*

DOMINICAN REPUBLIC
MARINA DE GUERRA

Headquarters Appointments

Chief of Naval Staff:
Vice Admiral Victor F Garcia Alecont
Vice Chief of Naval Staff:
Rear Admiral Juan Thomas Diaz Polanco

Personnel

(a) 2000: 3,800 officers and men (including naval infantry)
(b) Selective military service

Bases

27 de Febrero, Santo Domingo: HQ of CNS, Naval School. Supply base.
Las Calderas, Las Calderas, Bani: Naval dockyard, 700 ton synchrolift. Training centre. Supply base.
Haina: Dockyard facility. Supply base.
Puerto Plata. Small naval base.

Mercantile Marine

Lloyd's Register of Shipping:
22 vessels of 10,078 tons gross

DELETIONS

Note: *Melia* still flies an ensign as a museum ship.

Corvettes   **Auxiliaries**

1997 *Cambiaso*   1999 *Neptuno*

Patrol Forces

1997 *Tortuguero*

PATROL FORCES

2 COHOES CLASS (PG)

Name	No	Builders	Commissioned
SEPARACION (ex-*Passaconaway* AN 86)	P 208	Marine SB Co	27 Apr 1945
CALDERAS (ex-*Passaic* AN 87)	P 209	Leatham D Smith SB Co	6 Mar 1945

Displacement, tons: 855 full load
Dimensions, feet (metres): 162.3 × 33.8 × 11.7 *(49.5 × 10.3 × 3.6)*
Main machinery: Diesel-electric; 2 Busch-Sulzer BS-539 diesels; 1,500 hp(m) *(1.1 MW)*; 2 generators; 1 motor; 1 shaft
Speed, knots: 12
Complement: 64 (5 officers)
Guns: 2—3 in *(76 mm)*/50 Mk 26. 3 Oerlikon 20 mm.
Radars: Surface search: Raytheon SPS-64; I-band.

Comment: Ex-netlayers laid up in reserve in USA in 1963. Transferred by sale on 29 September 1976. Now used for patrol duties. 208 modified in 1980 with the removal of the bow horns. P 209 has only one 76 mm gun and is used as a survey ship.   **UPDATED**

SEPARACION   5/1999*, A Sheldon Duplaix / 0056898

1 BALSAM CLASS (PG/WMEC)

Name	No	Builders	Commissioned
ALMIRANTE JUAN ALEXANDRO ACOSTA (ex-*Citrus*)	C 456 (ex-WMEC 300)	Marine Iron, Duluth	30 May 1943

Displacement, tons: 1,034 full load
Dimensions, feet (metres): 180 × 37 × 12 *(54.9 × 11.3 × 3.8)*
Main machinery: Diesel-electric; 2 Cooper Bessemer diesels; 1,402 hp *(1.06 MW)*; 2 motors; 1,200 hp *(895 kW)*; 1 shaft; bow thruster
Speed, knots: 13
Complement: 54 (4 officers)
Guns: 2—12.7 mm MGs.
Radars: Surface search: Raytheon SPS-64(V)1; I-band.

Comment: Built as a buoy tender but served as a US Coast Guard cutter from 1979 to 1994. Transferred by gift on 16 September 1995 and recommissioned in January 1996 after a short refit.   **UPDATED**

ALMIRANTE JUAN ALEXANDRO ACOSTA   8/1997*, A Sheldon Duplaix / 0012277

1 ADMIRABLE CLASS (PG)

Name	No	Builders	Launched
PRESTOL (ex-*Separacion*, ex-*Skirmish* MSF 303)	C 454	Associated SB	16 Aug 1943

Displacement, tons: 650 standard; 905 full load
Dimensions, feet (metres): 184.5 × 33 × 14.4 *(56.3 × 10.1 × 4.4)*
Main machinery: 2 Cooper-Bessemer GSB8 diesels; 1,710 hp *(1.28 MW)*; 2 shafts
Speed, knots: 15. **Range, miles:** 4,300 at 10 kt
Complement: 90 (8 officers)
Guns: 1—3 in *(76 mm)*/50 Mk 26. 2 Bofors 40 mm/60. 6 Oerlikon 20 mm.
Radars: Surface search: Raytheon SPS-64(V)9; I-band.

Comment: Former US fleet minesweeper. Purchased on 13 January 1965. Sweep-gear removed. Classified as Cañoneros.   **UPDATED**

PRESTOL   6/1997*, A Sheldon Duplaix / 0012278

1 SOTOYOMO CLASS (PG/ATA)

Name	No	Builders	Commissioned
ENRIQUILLO (ex-*Stallion* ATA 193)	RM 22	Levington SB Co, Orange, TX	26 Feb 1945

Displacement, tons: 534 standard; 860 full load
Dimensions, feet (metres): 143 × 33.9 × 13 *(43.6 × 10.3 × 4)*
Main machinery: Diesel-electric; 2 GM 12-278A diesels; 2,200 hp *(1.64 MW)*; 2 generators; 1 motor; 1,500 hp *(1.12 MW)*; 1 shaft
Speed, knots: 13. **Range, miles:** 8,000 at 10kt
Complement: 45
Guns: 1 US 3 in *(76 mm)*/50 Mk 26. 2 Oerlikon 20 mm.
Radars: Surface search: Raytheon SPS-5D; G/H-band.

Comment: Leased from USA 30 October 1980, renewed 15 June 1992 and approved for transfer 10 June 1997.   **UPDATED**

ENRIQUILLO   9/1999*, A Sheldon Duplaix / 0056899

1 PGM 71 CLASS (LARGE PATROL CRAFT) (PC)

Name	No	Builders	Commissioned
BETELGEUSE (ex-*PGM* 77)	GC 102	Peterson, USA	1966

Displacement, tons: 130 standard; 145 full load
Dimensions, feet (metres): 101.5 × 21 × 5 *(30.9 × 6.4 × 1.5)*
Main machinery: 2 Caterpillar D 348 diesels; 1,450 hp *(1.08 MW)* sustained; 2 shafts
Speed, knots: 21. **Range, miles:** 1,500 at 10 kt
Complement: 20 (3 officers)
Guns: 1 Oerlikon 20 mm. 2—12.7 mm MGs.
Radars: Surface search: Raytheon; I-band.

Comment: Built in the USA and transferred to the Dominican Republic under the Military Aid Programme on 14 January 1966. Re-engined in 1980.   **UPDATED**

BETELGEUSE   8/1997*, A Sheldon Duplaix / 0012280

2 CANOPUS (SWIFTSHIPS 110 ft) CLASS (LARGE PATROL CRAFT)

Name	No	Builders	Commissioned
CRISTOBAL COLON (ex-*Canopus*)	GC 107	Swiftships, Morgan City	June 1984
ORION	GC 109	Swiftships, Morgan City	Aug 1984

Displacement, tons: 93.5 full load
Dimensions, feet (metres): 109.9 × 23.9 × 5.9 *(33.5 × 7.3 × 1.8)*
Main machinery: 3 Detroit 12V-92TA diesels; 1,020 hp *(760 kW)* sustained; 3 shafts
Speed, knots: 23. **Range, miles:** 1,500 at 12 kt
Complement: 19 (3 officers)
Guns: 1 Bofors 40 mm/60 Mk 3. 2—12.7 mm MGs.
Radars: Surface search: Raytheon; I-band.

Comment: Built of aluminium.

UPDATED

CRISTOBAL COLON   *9/1999*, A Sheldon Duplaix /* 0056900

2 POINT CLASS (PC)

Name	No	Builders	Commissioned
ARIES (ex-*Point Martin*)	PB 101 (ex-82379)	J Martinac, Tacoma	20 Aug 1970
ANTARES (ex-*Point Batan*)	— (ex-82340)	CG Yard, Maryland	21 Nov 1962

Displacement, tons: 67 full load
Dimensions, feet (metres): 83 × 17.2 × 5.8 *(25.3 × 5.2 × 1.8)*
Main machinery: 2 Caterpillar diesels; 1,600 hp *(1.19 MW)*; 2 shafts
Speed, knots: 22. **Range, miles:** 1,200 at 8 kt
Complement: 10
Guns: 2—12.7 mm MGs.
Radars: Surface search: Hughes/Furuno SPS-73; I-band.

Comment: Transferred from US Coast Guard 1 October 1999. These ships are widely spread throughout the Caribbean navies.

NEW ENTRY

ARIES   *12/1999*, A Sheldon Duplaix /* 0056901

4 BELLATRIX CLASS (COASTAL PATROL CRAFT) (PC)

Name	No	Builders	Commissioned
PROCION	GC 103	Sewart Seacraft Inc, Berwick, LA	1967
ALDEBARÁN	GC 104	Sewart Seacraft Inc, Berwick, LA	1972
BELLATRIX	GC 106	Sewart Seacraft Inc, Berwick, LA	1967
CAPELLA	GC 108	Sewart Seacraft Inc, Berwick, LA	1968

Displacement, tons: 60 full load
Dimensions, feet (metres): 85 × 18 × 5 *(25.9 × 5.5 × 1.5)*
Main machinery: 2 GM 16V-71 diesels; 811 hp *(605 kW)* sustained; 2 shafts
Speed, knots: 18.7. **Range, miles:** 800 at 15 kt
Complement: 12
Guns: 3—12.7 mm MGs.
Radars: Surface search: Raytheon SPS-64; I-band.

Comment: Transferred to the Dominican Navy by the USA. *Procion* was taken out of service in 1995 but returned in 1997 after a long refit.

UPDATED

BELLATRIX   *1/1998*, M Mokrus /* 0017793

BELLATRIX and ORION   *5/1999*, A Sheldon Duplaix /* 0080648

AUXILIARIES

Note: There is also a dredger manned by the Navy.

DREDGER   *10/1998*, A Sheldon Duplaix /* 0056902

1 HARBOUR TANKER (YO)

Name	No	Builders	Commissioned
CAPITAN BEOTEGUI (ex-*YO 215*)	BT 5	Ira S Bushey, Brooklyn	17 Dec 1945

Displacement, tons: 422 light; 1,400 full load
Dimensions, feet (metres): 174 × 32.9 × 13.3 *(53.1 × 10 × 4.1)*
Main machinery: 1 Union diesel; 525 hp *(392 kW)*; 1 shaft
Speed, knots: 8
Complement: 23
Cargo capacity: 6,570 barrels
Guns: 2 Oerlikon 20 mm.

Comment: Former US self-propelled fuel oil barge. Lent by the USA in April 1964. Lease renewed 31 December 1980 and again 5 August 1992 and approved for transfer 10 June 1997.

UPDATED

CAPITAN BEOTEGUI   *1/1998*, M Mokrus /* 0017794

1 WHITE SUMAC CLASS (ABU)

Name	No	Builders	Commissioned
TORTUGUERO (ex-*White Holly*)	BA 1 (ex-WLM 543)	Basalt Rock, Napa	8 Apr 1944

Displacement, tons: 485 full load
Dimensions, feet (metres): 133 × 31 × 9 *(40.5 × 9.5 × 2.7)*
Main machinery: 2 Caterpillar diesels; 600 hp *(448 kW)*; 2 shafts
Speed, knots: 9
Complement: 24

Comment: Transferred from US Coast Guard in 1999. Fitted with a 10 ton capacity boom.

NEW ENTRY

TORTUGUERO   *12/1999*, A Sheldon Duplaix /* 0056903

2 FLOATING DOCKS

ENDEAVOR   DF 1 (ex-AFDL 1)   **DF 2** (ex-AFDM 2)

Comment: DF 1 lift, 1,000 tons. Commissioned in 1943. Transferred from US on loan 8 March 1986 and approved for transfer 10 June 1997. DF 2 lift, 12,000 tons. Commissioned in 1942. Transferred from US in 1999.   ***UPDATED***

TUGS

5 COASTAL/HARBOUR TUGS (YTM/YTS)

HERCULES (ex-*R 2*) RP 12
GUACANAGARIX (ex-*R 5*) RP 13
OCOA LPD 303
BOHECHIO (ex-*YTL 600*) RP 16
CAYACCA RP 19

Displacement, tons: 200 full load
Dimensions, feet (metres): 70 × 15.6 × 9 *(21.4 × 4.8 × 2.7)*
Main machinery: 1 Caterpillar diesel; 500 hp *(373 kW)*; 1 shaft
Complement: 8

Comment: Details given are for RP 12 and 13 built in 1960. RP 16 and 19 are small harbour tugs of about 70 tons. *Ocoa* is an LCU type used as a tug.   ***UPDATED***

HERCULES   5/1999 *, A Sheldon Duplaix / 0056904

LAND-BASED MARITIME AIRCRAFT (FRONT LINE)

Numbers/Type: 2 Aerospatiale SA 316B Alouette III.
Operational speed: 113 kt *(210 km/h)*.
Service ceiling: 10,500 ft *(3,200 m)*.
Range: 290 n miles *(540 km)*.
Role/Weapon systems: Operated by Air Force liaison and SAR tasks. Sensors: None. Weapons: 7.62 mm MG.
   VERIFIED

Numbers/Type: 5 Cessna T-41D.
Operational speed: 102 kt *(188 km/h)*.
Service ceiling: 13,100 ft *(3,995 m)*.
Range: 535 n miles *(990 km)*.
Role/Weapon systems: Inshore/coastal reconnaissance reporting role; also used for training. Operated by Air Force. Sensors: Hand-held cameras only. Weapons: Unarmed.
   VERIFIED

TRAINING SHIPS

Note: In addition to those listed below there are various tenders mostly acquired 1986-88: *Cojinoa* BA 01, *Bonito* BA 02, *Beata* BA 14, *Albacora* BA 18, *Salinas* BA 19, *Carey* BA 20.

5 SAIL TRAINING SHIPS (AXS)

Name	No	Builders	Commissioned
CARITE	BA 3	Ast Navales Dominicanos	1975
ATÚN	BA 6	Ast Navales Dominicanos	1975
PICÚA	BA 9	Ast Navales Dominicanos	1975
JUREL	BA 15	Ast Navales Dominicanos	1975
NUBE DEL MAR	BA 7	Ast Navales Dominicanos	1979

Displacement, tons: 24
Dimensions, feet (metres): 45 × 13 × 6.6 *(13.7 × 4 × 1.9)*
Main machinery: 1 GM diesel; 101 hp *(75 kW)*; 1 shaft
Speed, knots: 9
Complement: 4
Guns: 1—7.62 mm MG.

Comment: The first four are auxiliary sailing craft with a sail area of 750 sq ft and a cargo capacity of 7 tons. There may be more of this class. *Nube del Mar* is an auxiliary yacht used for sail training at the Naval School and is slightly smaller.
   VERIFIED

ECUADOR
ARMADA DE GUERRA

Headquarters Appointments

Commander-in-Chief of the Navy:
   Vice Admiral Enrique Monteverde Nimbriotis
Chief of Naval Staff:
   Vice Admiral Miguel Saona Roca
Chief of Naval Operations:
   Vice Admiral Fernando Donoso Moran
Chief of Naval Materiel:
   Vice Admiral Jorge Endara Troncoso

Diplomatic Representation

Naval Attaché in Rome:
   Captain Carlos Ayala Baidal
Naval Attaché in London and Paris:
   Captain R Samaniego Granja
Naval Attaché in Washington:
   Captain José Olmedo Morán

Personnel

(a) 2000: 6,500 (including 1,500 marines and 375 naval aviation)
(b) 1 year's selective national service

Bases

Guayaquil (main naval base), Jaramijo, Salinas.
San Lorenzo, Galapagos Islands.
Guayaquil air base.

Establishments

The Naval Academy and Merchant Navy Academy in Salinas; Naval War College in Guayaquil.

Naval Infantry

A force of marines is based at Guayaquil, Esmeraldas San Lorenzo, Galapagos and Jaramijo.

Coast Guard

Small force formed in 1980. Hull markings include diagonal thick and thin red stripes on the hull.

Prefix to Ships' Names

BAE

Mercantile Marine

Lloyd's Register of Shipping:
   175 vessels of 309,223 tons gross

DELETIONS

Patrol Forces

1998   *Tulcan* (sunk)

Coast Guard

1997   24 De Mayo (old)
1999   *10 de Agosto, 3 de Noviembre*

Auxiliaries

1999   *Cayambe, Putumayo*

PENNANT LIST

Submarines

S 101	Shyri
S 102	Huancavilca

Frigates

FM 01	Presidente Eloy Alfaro
FM 02	Moran Valverde

Corvettes

CM 11	Esmeraldas
CM 12	Manabi
CM 13	Los Rios
CM 14	El Oro
CM 15	Los Galapagos
CM 16	Loja

Patrol Forces

LM 21	Quito
LM 23	Guayaquil
LM 24	Cuenca
LM 25	Manta
LM 27	Nuevo Rocafuerte

Amphibious Forces

TR 61	Hualcopo

Survey/Research Vessels

BI 91	Orion
LH 94	Rigel

Tugs

RA 70	Chimborazo
RB 72	Sangay
RB 73	Cotopaxi
RB 75	Iliniza
RB 76	Altar
RB 78	Quilotoa

Auxiliaries

TR 62	Calicuchima
TR 63	Atahualpa
TR 64	Quisquis
TR 65	Taurus
BE 91	Guayas
DF 81	Amazonas
DF 82	Napo

UT 111	Isla de la Plata
UT 112	Isla Puná

Coast Guard

LG 31	25 de Julio
LG 35	5 de Agosto
LG 36	27 de Febrero
LG 37	9 de Octubre
LG 38	27 de Octubre
LG 41	Rio Puyango
LG 42	Rio Mataje
LG 43	Rio Zarumilla
LG 44	Rio Chone
LG 45	Rio Daule
LG 46	Rio Babahoyo

SUBMARINES

Note: The expected transfer of three ex-Israeli 'Gal' class submarines did not take place in 1999.

2 TYPE 209 CLASS (TYPE 1300) (SSK)

Name	No	Builders	Laid down	Launched	Commissioned
SHYRI	S 101 (ex-S 11)	Howaldtswerke, Kiel	5 Aug 1974	6 Oct 1976	5 Nov 1977
HUANCAVILCA	S 102 (ex-S 12)	Howaldtswerke, Kiel	2 Jan 1975	15 Mar 1977	16 Mar 1978

Displacement, tons: 1,285 surfaced; 1,390 dived
Dimensions, feet (metres): 195.1 × 20.5 × 17.9 *(59.5 × 6.3 × 5.4)*
Main machinery: Diesel-electric; 4 MTU 12V 493 AZ80 GA31L diesels; 2,400 hp(m) *(1.76 MW)* sustained; 4 Siemens alternators; 1.7 MW; 1 Siemens motor; 4,600 hp(m) *(3.38 MW)* sustained; 1 shaft
Speed, knots: 11 surfaced/snorting; 21.5 dived
Complement: 33 (5 officers)

Torpedoes: 8—21 in *(533 mm)* bow tubes. 14 AEG SUT; dual purpose; wire-guided; active/passive homing to 28 km *(15 n miles)* at 23 kt; 12 km *(6.5 n miles)* at 35 kt; warhead 250 kg.
Countermeasures: ESM: Thomson-CSF DR 2000U; intercept.
Weapons control: Signaal M8 Mod 24.
Radars: Surface search: Thomson-CSF Calypso; I-band.
Sonars: Atlas Elektronik CSU 3; hull-mounted; active/passive search and attack; medium frequency.
Thomson Sintra DUUX 2; passive ranging.

Programmes: Ordered in March 1974. *Shyri* underwent major refit in West Germany in 1983; *Huancavilca* in 1984. Second refits by ASMAR, Chile starting with *Shyri* in 1999/2000.
Operational: Based at Guayaquil.

UPDATED

SHYRI

6/1998 / 0017796

FRIGATES

2 LEANDER CLASS (FFG)

Name	No	Builders	Laid down	Launched	Commissioned
PRESIDENTE ELOY ALFARO (ex-*Penelope*)	FM 01 (ex-F 127)	Vickers Armstrong, Newcastle	14 Mar 1961	17 Aug 1962	31 Oct 1963
MORAN VALVERDE (ex-*Danae*)	FM 02 (ex-F 47)	HM Dockyard, Devonport	16 Dec 1964	31 Oct 1965	7 Sep 1967

Displacement, tons: 2,450 standard; 3,200 full load
Dimensions, feet (metres): 360 wl; 372 oa × 41 × 14.8 (keel); 19 (screws) *(109.7; 113.4 × 12.5 × 4.5; 5.8)*
Main machinery: 2 Babcock & Wilcox boilers; 38.7 kg/cm²; 850°F *(450°C)*; 2 English Electric/White turbines; 30,000 hp *(22.4 MW)*; 2 shafts
Speed, knots: 28. **Range, miles:** 4,000 at 15 kt
Complement: 248 (20 officers)

Missiles: SSM: 4 Aerospatiale MM 38 Exocet ❶; inertial cruise; active radar homing to 42 km *(23 n miles)* at 0.9 Mach; warhead 165 kg.
SAM: 3 twin Matra Simbad launchers ❷ for Mistral; IR homing to 4 km *(2.2 n miles)*; warhead 3 kg.

Guns: 2 Bofors 40 mm/60 Mk 9 ❸; 120 rds/min to 10 km *(5.4 n miles)* anti-surface; 3 km *(1.6 n miles)* anti-aircraft; weight of shell 0.89 kg.
2 Oerlikon/BMARC 20 mm GAM-BO1 can be fitted midships or aft.
6—324 mm ILAS-3 (2 triple) tubes ❹ Whitehead A 244; anti-submarine; pattern running to 7 km *(3.8 n miles)* at 33 kt; warhead 34 kg shaped charge.
Countermeasures: Decoys: Graseby Type 182; towed torpedo decoy.
2 Vickers Corvus 8-barrelled trainable launchers ❺. 2 Mk 36 SRBOC; chaff and IR launchers.
ESM: UA-8/9; radar warning.
ECM: Type 667/668; jammer.

Combat data systems: SISDEF. Link Y.
Radars: Air search: Marconi Type 966 ❻; A-band.
Surface search: Plessey Type 994 ❼; E/F-band.
Navigation: Kelvin Hughes Type 1006; I-band.
Fire control: Selenia ❽ I/J-band.
Sonars: Kelvin Hughes Type 162M; hull-mounted; bottom classification; 50 kHz.
Graseby Type 184P; hull-mounted; active search and attack; 7-9 kHz.

Helicopters: 1 Bell 412EP ❾.

Programmes: Both ships acquired from UK 25 April 1991 and sailed for Ecuador after working up in July and August respectively.
Modernisation: Chilean SISDEF command system is being installed. Simbad launchers have replaced Seacat, and the torpedo tubes restored. ASMAR is investigating replacing the steam turbines by diesel engines.
Structure: These are Batch 2 Exocet conversions completed in 1980 and 1982. SRBOC chaff launchers fitted after transfer.
Operational: Both ships have propulsion problems. New helicopters acquired in late 1998.

UPDATED

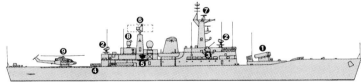

PRESIDENTE ELOY ALFARO

(Scale 1 : 1,200), Ian Sturton / 0056906

PRESIDENTE ELOY ALFARO

6/1998 / 0017799

CORVETTES

6 ESMERALDAS CLASS (FSG)

Name	No
ESMERALDAS	CM 11
MANABI	CM 12
LOS RIOS	CM 13
EL ORO	CM 14
LOS GALAPAGOS	CM 15
LOJA	CM 16

Builders	Laid down	Launched	Commissioned
Fincantieri Muggiano	27 Sep 1979	1 Oct 1980	7 Aug 1982
Fincantieri Ancona	19 Feb 1980	9 Feb 1981	21 June 1983
Fincantieri Muggiano	5 Dec 1979	27 Feb 1981	9 Oct 1983
Fincantieri Ancona	20 Mar 1980	9 Feb 1981	11 Dec 1983
Fincantieri Muggiano	4 Dec 1980	4 July 1981	26 May 1984
Fincantieri Ancona	25 Mar 1981	27 Feb 1982	26 May 1984

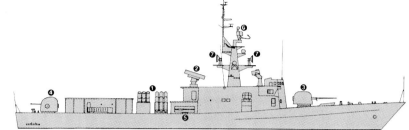

Displacement, tons: 685 full load
Dimensions, feet (metres): 204.4 × 30.5 × 8
(62.3 × 9.3 × 2.5)
Main machinery: 4 MTU 20V 956 TB92 diesels; 22,140 hp(m)
(16.27 MW) sustained; 4 shafts
Speed, knots: 37. **Range, miles:** 4,400 at 14 kt
Complement: 51

Missiles: SSM: 6 Aerospatiale MM 40 Exocet (2 triple) launchers
❶; inertial cruise; active radar homing to 70 km *(40 n miles)* at
0.9 Mach; warhead 165 kg; sea-skimmer.
SAM: Selenia Elsag Albatros quad launcher ❷; Aspide; semi-
active radar homing to 13 km *(7 n miles)* at 2.5 Mach; height
envelope 15-5,000 m *(49.2-16,405 ft)*; warhead 30 kg.
Guns: 1 OTO Melara 3 in *(76 mm)*/62 compact ❸; 85 rds/min to
16 km *(8.7 n miles)*; weight of shell 6 kg.
2 Breda 40 mm/70 (twin) ❹; 300 rds/min to 12.5 km *(6.8 n
miles)* anti-surface; weight of shell 0.96 kg.
Torpedoes: 6—324 mm ILAS-3 (2 triple) tubes ❺; Whitehead
Motofides A244; anti-submarine; self-adaptive patterns to
7 km *(3.8 n miles)* at 33 kt; warhead 34 kg shaped charge. Not
fitted in all.
Countermeasures: Decoys: 1 Breda 105 mm SCLAR launcher;
chaff to 5 km *(2.7 n miles)*; illuminants to 12 km *(6.6 n miles)*.
ESM/ECM: Elettronika Gamma ED; radar intercept and jammer.
Combat data systems: Selenia IPN 10 action data automation.
Link Y.
Weapons control: 2 Selenia NA21 with C03 directors.
Radars: Air/surface search: Selenia RAN 10S ❻; E/F-band; range
155 km *(85 n miles)*.
Navigation: SMA 3 RM 20; I-band.
Fire control: 2 Selenia Orion 10X ❼; I/J-band; range 40 km *(22 n
miles)*.
Sonars: Thomson Sintra Diodon; hull-mounted; active search
and attack; 11, 12 or 13 kHz.

Helicopters: Platform for 1 Bell 206B.

Programmes: Ordered in 1979. *El Oro* out of commission for two
years from mid-1985 after a bad fire.
Modernisation: Contracts for updating command and weapons
control systems placed in 1993-94 but no funds are available.
Operational: Torpedo tubes removed from two of the class to
refit in frigates.   ***UPDATED***

ESMERALDAS   *(Scale 1 : 600), Ian Sturton*

EL ORO   *6/1998 /* 0017800

MANABI   *6/1998 /* 0017801

LAND-BASED MARITIME AIRCRAFT (FRONT LINE)

Numbers/Type: 3 Beech T-34C-1 Turbo-Mentor.
Operational speed: 150 kt *(278 km/h)*.
Service ceiling: 20,000 ft *(6,060 m)*.
Range: 650 n miles *(1,205 km)*.
Role/Weapon systems: Operated for training and surveillance tasks. Sensors: None. Weapons:
Underwing pylons for rockets, cannon and bombs.
VERIFIED

Numbers/Type: 1 Beech Super King Air 200T.
Operational speed: 250 kt *(450 km/h)*.
Service ceiling: 30,000 ft *(9,090 m)*.
Range: 2,030 n miles *(3,756 km)*.
Role/Weapon systems: Maritime reconnaissance and drug interdiction. Sensors: Weather radar.
Weapons: Unarmed.
VERIFIED

SHIPBORNE AIRCRAFT

Numbers/Type: 2 Bell 412EP Sentinel.
Operational speed: 124 kt *(230 km/h).*
Service ceiling: 6,800 ft *(2,070 m).*
Range: 402 n miles *(745 km).*
Role/Weapon systems: Upgraded by Heli Dyne Systems and delivered in late 1998 and early 1999. Sensors: Allied Systems RDR 1500B radar; Wescam 16 DS(W) optronics; datalink; Ocean Systems AQS-18A dipping sonar. Weapons: 2 Mk 46 torpedoes; ASV: 2 Penguin Mk 2 Mod 7 in due course. **UPDATED**

BELL 412   *1/1999*, Heli Dyne /* 0056907

Numbers/Type: 4 Bell 206B JetRanger.
Operational speed: 115 kt *(213 km/h).*
Service ceiling: 13,500 ft *(4,115 m).*
Range: 368 n miles *(682 km).*
Role/Weapon systems: Support helicopter for afloat reconnaissance and SAR. Navalised Bell 230s acquired in 1995. Sensors: None. Weapons: None. **UPDATED**

JETRANGER   *6/1998 /* 0017802

PATROL FORCES

Note: Three 34 m OPVs are required when funds are available.

3 QUITO (LÜRSSEN 45) CLASS
(FAST ATTACK CRAFT—MISSILE) (PCFG)

Name	No	Builders	Launched	Commissioned
QUITO	LM 21	Lürssen, Vegesack	20 Nov 1975	13 July 1976
GUAYAQUIL	LM 23	Lürssen, Vegesack	5 Apr 1976	22 Dec 1977
CUENCA	LM 24	Lürssen, Vegesack	6 Dec 1976	17 July 1977

Displacement, tons: 255
Dimensions, feet (metres): 147.6 × 23 × 8.1 *(45 × 7 × 2.5)*
Main machinery: 4 MTU 16V 396 diesels; 13,600 hp(m) *(10 MW)* sustained; 4 shafts
Speed, knots: 40. **Range, miles:** 700 at 40 kt; 1,800 at 16 kt
Complement: 35

Missiles: SSM: 4 Aerospatiale MM 38 Exocet; inertial cruise; active radar homing to 42 km *(23 n miles)* at 0.9 Mach; warhead 165 kg; sea-skimmer.
Guns: 1 OTO Melara 3 in *(76 mm)*/62 compact; 85 rds/min to 16 km *(8.7 n miles)*; weight of shell 6 kg.
2 Oerlikon 35 mm/90 (twin); 550 rds/min to 6 km *(3.3 n miles)*; weight of shell 1.55 kg.
Countermeasures: ESM: Thomson-CSF DR 2000; intercept.
Weapons control: Thomson-CSF Vega system.
Radars: Air/surface search: Thomson-CSF Triton; G-band; range 33 km *(18 n miles)* for 2 m² target.
Fire control: Thomson-CSF Pollux; I/J-band; range 31 km *(17 n miles)* for 2 m² target.
Navigation: Racal Decca 1226; I-band.

Modernisation: New engines fitted during refits in 1994-95 at Guayaquil.
Operational: *Quito* may be laid up. **VERIFIED**

GUAYAQUIL   *6/1998 /* 0017803

2 MANTA CLASS (FAST ATTACK CRAFT—MISSILE) (PCFG)

Name	No	Builders	Commissioned
MANTA	LM 25	Lürssen, Vegesack	11 June 1971
NUEVO ROCAFUERTE	LM 27	Lürssen, Vegesack	23 June 1971

Displacement, tons: 119 standard; 134 full load
Dimensions, feet (metres): 119.4 × 19.1 × 6 *(36.4 × 5.8 × 1.8)*
Main machinery: 3 Mercedes-Benz diesels; 9,000 hp(m) *(6.61 MW)*; 3 shafts
Speed, knots: 42. **Range, miles:** 700 at 30 kt; 1,500 at 15 kt
Complement: 19

Missiles: SSM: 4 IAI Gabriel II; radar or optical guidance; semi-active radar homing to 36 km *(19.4 n miles)* at 0.7 Mach; warhead 75 kg.
Guns: 2 Emerson Electric 30 mm (twin); 1,200 rds/min combined to 6 km *(3.3 n miles)*; weight of shell 0.35 kg.
Countermeasures: ESM: Thomson-CSF DR 2000S; intercept.
Weapons control: Thomson-CSF Vega system.
Radars: Fire control: Thomson-CSF Pollux; I/J-band; range 31 km *(17 n miles)* for 2 m² target.
Navigation: I-band.

Modernisation: Rearmed in 1980 with new electronic fit and missiles. Torpedo tubes removed.
Structure: Similar design to the Chilean 'Guacolda' class with an extra diesel, 3 kt faster.
Operational: Missiles are not carried when used on EEZ surveillance. A third of class sank in September 1998 after a collision with a tug. **VERIFIED**

MANTA   *6/1997, Ecuador Navy /* 0012284

AMPHIBIOUS FORCES

1 512-1152 CLASS (LST)

Name	No	Builders	Commissioned
HUALCOPO	TR 61	Chicago Bridge and	9 June 1945
(ex-*Summit County* LST 1146)	(ex-T 61)	Iron Co	

Displacement, tons: 1,653 standard; 4,080 full load
Dimensions, feet (metres): 328 × 50 × 14 *(100 × 16.1 × 4.3)*
Main machinery: 2 GM 12-567A diesels; 1,800 hp *(1.34 MW)*; 2 shafts
Speed, knots: 11.6. **Range, miles:** 7,200 at 10 kt
Complement: 119
Military lift: 147 troops
Guns: 8 Bofors 40 mm. 2 Oerlikon 20 mm.
Radars: Navigation: I-band.

Comment: Purchased from USA on 14 February 1977. Commissioned in November 1977 after extensive refit. Plans for replacement not yet realised. The ship had a bad fire in July 1998 and may still be non-operational. **UPDATED**

HUALCOPO (old number)   *10/1984, R E Parkinson*

SURVEY AND RESEARCH SHIPS

Name	No	Builders	Commissioned
RIGEL	LH 94 (ex-LH 92)	Halter Marine	1975

Displacement, tons: 50 full load
Dimensions, feet (metres): 64.5 × 17.1 × 3.6 *(19.7 × 5.2 × 1.1)*
Main machinery: 2 diesels; 2 shafts
Speed, knots: 10
Complement: 10 (2 officers)

Comment: Used for inshore oceanographic work. **VERIFIED**

Name	No	Builders	Commissioned
ORION (ex-*Dometer*)	BI 91 (ex-HI 91, ex-HI 92)	Ishikawajima, Tokyo	10 Nov 1982

Measurement, tons: 1,105 gross
Dimensions, feet (metres): 210.6 pp × 35.1 × 11.8 *(64.2 × 10.7 × 3.6)*
Main machinery: Diesel-electric; 3 Detroit 16V-92TA diesel generators; 2,070 hp *(1.54 MW)* sustained; 2 motors; 1,900 hp *(1.42 MW)*; 1 shaft
Speed, knots: 12.6. **Range, miles:** 6,000 at 12 kt
Complement: 45 (6 officers) plus 14 civilians
Radars: Navigation: 2 Decca 1226; I-band.

Comment: Research vessel for oceanographic, hydrographic and meteorological work.
VERIFIED

ORION (old number)   3/1990, T J Gander

TRAINING SHIPS

1 SAIL TRAINING SHIP (AXS)

Name	No	Builders	Commissioned
GUAYAS	BE 91 (ex-BE 01)	Ast Celaya, Spain	23 July 1977

Measurement, tons: 234 dwt; 934 gross
Dimensions, feet (metres): 264 × 33.5 × 13.4 *(80 × 10.2 × 4.2)*
Main machinery: 1 GM 12V-149T diesel; 875 hp *(652 kW)* sustained; 1 shaft
Speed, knots: 11.3
Complement: 50 plus 80 trainees

Comment: Three masted. Launched 23 September 1976. Has accommodation for 180. Similar to ships in service with Colombia, Mexico and Venezuela.
UPDATED

GUAYAS   4/1992*, van Ginderen Collection / 0056908

AUXILIARIES

Notes: (1) One uncompleted 'Henry J Kaiser' class oiler (T-AO 192) has been offered by the USA for possible transfer if funds are available.
(2) There are also two small harbour utility craft *Isla la Plata* UT 111 and *Isla Puna* UT 112.

1 YW CLASS (WATER TANKER) (AWT)

Name	No	Builders	Commissioned
ATAHUALPA (ex-*YW 131*)	TR 63	Leatham D Smith SB Co	17 Sep 1945

Displacement, tons: 415 light; 1,235 full load
Dimensions, feet (metres): 174 × 32 × 15 *(53.1 × 9.8 × 4.6)*
Main machinery: 2 GM 8-278A diesels; 1,500 hp *(1.12 MW)*; 2 shafts
Speed, knots: 11.5
Complement: 20
Cargo capacity: 930 tons

Comment: Acquired from the USA on 2 May 1963. Purchased on 1 December 1977. Paid off in 1988 but back in service in 1990 to provide water for the Galapagos Islands.
VERIFIED

1 OIL TANKER (AOTL)

Name	No	Builders	Commissioned
TAURUS	TR 65 (ex-T 66)	Astinave, Guayaquil	1985

Measurement, tons: 1,175 dwt; 1,110 gross
Dimensions, feet (metres): 174.2 × 36 × 14.4 *(53.1 × 11 × 4.4)*
Main machinery: 2 GM diesels; 1,050 hp *(783 kW)*; 1 shaft
Speed, knots: 11
Complement: 20

Comment: Acquired for the Navy in 1987.
VERIFIED

1 ARMAMENT STORES CARRIER (AKF)

Name	No	Builders	Commissioned
CALICUCHIMA (ex-*Throsk*)	TR 62 (ex-A 379)	Cleland SB Co, Wallsend	20 Sep 1977

Displacement, tons: 2,207 full load
Dimensions, feet (metres): 231.2 × 39 × 15 *(70.5 × 11.9 × 4.6)*
Main machinery: 2 Mirrlees-Blackstone diesels; 3,000 hp *(2.2 MW)*; 1 shaft
Speed, knots: 14.5. **Range, miles:** 4,000 at 11 kt
Complement: 24 (8 officers)
Cargo capacity: 785 tons
Radars: Navigation: Kelvin Hughes 1006; I-band.

Comment: Acquired from the UK in November 1991. Recommissioned 24 March 1992.
UPDATED

CALICUCHIMA   2/1992*, A J Moorey / 0080649

1 + (1) WATER CLASS (WATER TANKER) (AWT)

Name	No	Builders	Commissioned
QUISQUIS (ex-*Waterside*)	TR 64 (ex-Y 20)	Drypool Engineering, Hull	1968

Measurement, tons: 285 gross
Dimensions, feet (metres): 131.5 × 24.8 × 8 *(40.1 × 7.5 × 2.4)*
Main machinery: 1 Lister-Blackstone ERS-8-MCR diesel; 660 hp *(492 kW)*; 1 shaft
Speed, knots: 11. **Range, miles:** 1,500 at 11 kt
Complement: 8
Cargo capacity: 150 tons
Radars: Navigation: Decca; I-band.

Comment: Acquired from the UK in November 1991. Second of class *Watercourse* may be acquired from the UK when funds are available.
UPDATED

QUISQUIS   2/1992*, A J Moorey / 0056909

2 + 1 ARD 12 CLASS (FLOATING DOCKS)

Name	No	Builders	Commissioned
AMAZONAS (ex-*ARD 17*)	DF 81 (ex-DF 121)	USA	1944
NAPO (ex-*ARD 24*)	DF 82	USA	1944

Dimensions, feet (metres): 492 × 81 × 17.7 *(150 × 24.7 × 5.4)*

Comment: *Amazonas* leased from USA in 1961 and bought outright in 1982; *Napo* bought in 1988. Suitable for docking ships up to 3,200 tons. *Alamogordo* (ARDM 2) may be acquired from the US in 2000.
UPDATED

TUGS

5 HARBOUR TUGS (YTM/YTL)

SANGAY RB 72	ILINIZA RB 75	QUILOTOA RB 78
COTOPAXI RB 73	ALTAIR RB 76	

Comment: Mostly built in the 1950s and 1960s.
UPDATED

1 CHEROKEE CLASS (ATF)

Name	No	Builders	Commissioned
CHIMBORAZO	RA 70 (ex-R 710,	Charleston SB	21 Feb 1945
(ex-*Chowanoc* ATF 100)	ex-R 71, ex-R 105)	& DD Co	

Displacement, tons: 1,235 standard; 1,640 full load
Dimensions, feet (metres): 205 × 38.5 × 17 *(62.5 × 11.7 × 5.2)*
Main machinery: Diesel-electric; 4 Busch-Sulzer BS-539 diesels; 4 generators; 1 motor; 3,000 hp
(2.24 MW); 1 shaft
Speed, knots: 16.5. **Range, miles:** 7,000 at 15 kt
Complement: 85
Guns: 1—3 in *(76 mm)*. 2 Bofors 40 mm. 2 Oerlikon 20 mm (not all fitted).

Comment: Launched 20 August 1943 and transferred 1 October 1977.

UPDATED

CHEROKEE (old number)   *1970, Ecuadorean Navy*

COAST GUARD

Note: In addition to the vessels listed below, there are up to 40 river patrol launches operated by both the Coast Guard and the Army.

2 ESPADA CLASS (LARGE PATROL CRAFT) (PC)

Name	No	Builders	Commissioned
5 DE AGOSTO	LG 35	Moss Point Marine, Escatawpa	May 1991
27 DE FEBRERO	LG 36	Moss Point Marine, Escatawpa	Nov 1991

Displacement, tons: 190 full load
Dimensions, feet (metres): 112 × 22.5 × 7 *(34.1 × 6.9 × 2.1)*
Main machinery: 2 Detroit 16V-149TI diesels; 2,322 hp *(1.73 MW)* sustained; 1 Detroit 16V-92TA;
690 hp *(514 kW)* sustained; 3 shafts
Speed, knots: 27. **Range, miles:** 1,500 at 14 kt
Complement: 19 (5 officers)
Guns: 1 Bofors 40 mm/60. 2—12.7 mm MGs.
Radars: Surface search: Racal Decca; I-band.

Comment: Built under FMS programme. Steel hulls and aluminium superstructure. Accommodation is air conditioned. Carry a 10-man RIB and launching crane on the stern.

VERIFIED

5 DE AGOSTO   *6/1998* / 0017804

2 SWIFTSHIPS CLASS (RIVER PATROL CRAFT) (PBR)

Name	No	Builders	Commissioned
9 DE OCTUBRE	LG 37	Swiftships, Morgan City	1 Oct 1992
27 DE OCTUBRE	LG 38	Swiftships, Morgan City	1 Oct 1992

Displacement, tons: 17 full load
Dimensions, feet (metres): 45.5 × 11.8 × 1.8 *(13.9 × 3.6 × 0.6)*
Main machinery: 2 Detroit 6V-92TA diesels; 900 hp *(671 kW)*; 2 Hamilton water-jets
Speed, knots: 22. **Range, miles:** 600 at 22 kt
Complement: 4
Guns: 2 M2HB 12.7 mm MGs; 2 M60D 7.62 mm MGs.
Radars: Surface search: Raytheon 40; I-band.

Comment: Transferred from USA under MAP to the Navy and thence to the Coast Guard. Hard chine modified V hull form. Can carry up to eight troops. Used as command craft for river flotillas.

UPDATED

9 DE OCTUBRE   *9/1992*, Swiftships* / 0056910

1 POINT CLASS (COASTAL PATROL CRAFT) (PC)

Name	No	Builders	Commissioned
24 DE MAYO (ex-*Point Richmond*)	LG 32 (ex-82370)	CG Yard, Curtis Bay	25 Aug 1967

Displacement, tons: 66 full load
Dimensions, feet (metres): 83 × 17.2 × 5.8 *(25.3 × 5.2 × 1.8)*
Main machinery: 2 Caterpillar 3412 diesels; 1,600 hp *(1.19 MW)*; 2 shafts
Speed, knots: 23. **Range, miles:** 1,500 at 8 kt
Complement: 10
Radars: Navigation: Raytheon SPS 64(V)1; I-band.

Comment: Transferred from US Coast Guard on 22 August 1997.

VERIFIED

24 DE MAYO   *6/1998* / 0017806

6 RIO PUYANGO CLASS (RIVER PATROL CRAFT) (PBR)

Name	No	Builders	Commissioned
RIO PUYANGO	LG 41 (ex-LGC 40)	Halter Marine, New Orleans	15 June 1986
RIO MATAGE	LG 42 (ex-LGC 41)	Halter Marine, New Orleans	15 June 1986
RIO ZARUMILLA	LG 43 (ex-LGC 42)	Astinave, Guayaquil	11 Mar 1988
RIO CHONE	LG 44 (ex-LGC 43)	Astinave, Guayaquil	11 Mar 1988
RIO DAULE	LG 45 (ex-LGC 44)	Astinave, Guayaquil	17 June 1988
RIO BABAHOYO	LG 46 (ex-LGC 45)	Astinave, Guayaquil	17 June 1988

Displacement, tons: 17
Dimensions, feet (metres): 44 × 13.5 × 3.5 *(13.4 × 4.1 × 1.1)*
Main machinery: 2 Detroit 8V-71 diesels; 460 hp *(343 kW)* sustained; 2 shafts
Speed, knots: 26. **Range, miles:** 500 at 18 kt
Complement: 5 (1 officer)
Guns: 1—12.7 mm MG. 2—7.62 mm MGs.
Radars: Surface search: Furuno 2400; I-band.

Comment: Two delivered by Halter Marine in June 1986. Four more ordered in February 1987; assembled under licence at Astinave shipyard, Guayaquil. Used mainly for drug interdiction and all are very active.

UPDATED

RIO PUYANGO (old number)   *1/1988*, Halter Marine* / 0056911

1 PGM-71 CLASS (LARGE PATROL CRAFT) (PC)

Name	No	Builders	Commissioned
25 DE JULIO (ex-*Quito*)	LG 31 (ex-LGC 31, ex-LC 71)	Peterson, USA	30 Nov 1965

Displacement, tons: 130 standard; 146 full load
Dimensions, feet (metres): 101.5 × 21 × 5 *(30.9 × 6.4 × 1.5)*
Main machinery: 4 MTU diesels; 3,520 hp(m) *(2.59 MW)*; 2 shafts
Speed, knots: 21. **Range, miles:** 1,000 at 12 kt
Complement: 15
Guns: 1 Bofors 40 mm/60. 4 Oerlikon 20 mm (2 twin). 2—12.7 mm MGs.
Radars: Surface search: Raytheon; I-band.

Comment: Transferred from USA to the Navy under MAP on 30 November 1965 and then to the Coast Guard in 1980. Paid off into reserve in 1983 and deleted from the order of battle. Refitted with new engines in 1988-89. Second of class deleted in 1997.

VERIFIED   25 DE JULIO   *6/1998* / 0017805

EGYPT

Headquarters Appointments

Commander of Naval Forces:
  Vice Admiral Ahmed Salim
Chief of Naval Staff:
  Rear Admiral Mohammad Farag Ali Lofty
Chief of Operations:
  Rear Admiral Tamer Abdul Halim Isma'il

Personnel

(a) 2000: 19,000 officers and men, including 2,000 Coast Guard and 10,000 conscripts (Reserves of 14,000)
(b) 1 to 3 years' national service (depending on educational qualifications)

Bases

Alexandria (HQ Med), Port Said, Mersa Matru, Abu Qir, Suez. Safaqa and Hurghada (HQ Red Sea) on the Red Sea.
Naval Academy: Abu Qir.

Coast Defence

There are three batteries of Border Guard Otomat truck-mounted SSMs (two twin launchers each) with targeting by Plessey radars (fixed) and Thomson-CSF radars (mobile). Two Artillery brigades, under naval co-operative control, are armed with 100, 130 and 152 mm guns.

Maritime Air

Although the Navy has no air arm the Air Force has a number of E-2Cs, ASW Sea Kings and Gazelles with an ASM capability (see *Land-based Maritime Aircraft* section). The Sea Kings and Seasprite helicopters are controlled by the Anti-Submarine Brigade and have some naval aircrew.

Prefix to Ships' Name

ENS

Strength of the Fleet

Type	Active	Building (Projected)
Submarines (Patrol)	4	(2)
Destroyers	1	—
Frigates	10	—
Fast Attack Craft (Missile)	21	(6)
Fast Attack Craft (Gun)	10	—
Fast Attack Craft (Patrol)	8	—
LSMs/LST	3	(2)
LCUs	9	—
Minesweepers (Ocean)	10	—
Minehunters (Coastal)	3	—
Route Survey Vessels	2	—

Mercantile Marine

Lloyd's Register of Shipping:
  374 vessels of 1,368,036 tons gross

DELETIONS

Frigates

1999	*Tariq*

Patrol Forces

| 1996-97 | 2 Osa I |
| 1998 | 1 Hegu |

Amphibious Forces

| 1996-97 | 2 SMB |

Auxiliaries

| 1997 | *Al Mazilla* |

PENNANT LIST

Destroyers

D 921	El Fateh

Frigates

F 901	Sharm el Sheikh
F 906	Toushka
F 911	Mubarak
F 916	Taba
F 941	El Suez
F 946	Abu Qir
F 951	Najim al Zaffer
F 956	El Nasser
F 961	Damyat
F 966	Rasheed

Patrol Forces

P 430	Al Nour
P 433	Al Hady
P 436	Al Hakim
P 439	Al Wakil
P 442	Al Qatar
P 445	Al Saddam
P 448	Al Salam
P 451	Al Rafia
P 670	Ramadan
P 672	Khyber
P 674	El Kadessaya
P 676	El Yarmouk
P 678	Badr
P 680	Hettein

Mine Warfare Forces

CMH 1	Dat Assawari
CMH 2	Navarin
CMH 3	Burullus
M 501	Gharbiya
M 504	Sharkiya
M 507	Daqahliya
M 510	Bahariya
M 513	Sinai
M 516	Assiout
M 530	Giza
M 533	Aswan
M 536	Qena
M 539	Sohag
RSV 1	Safaga
RSV 2	Abu el Ghoson

Auxiliaries

A 210	Ayeda 4
A 211	Maryut
A 212	Al Furat
A 213	Al Nil
A 214	Akdu
A 215	Maryut Atbarah
A 216	Ayeda 3
A 218	Al Burullus
Y 103	Al Meks
Y 105	Al Agami
Y 107	Antar
Y 109	Al Dikhila
Y 111	Al Iskandarani
Y 113	Kalir

SUBMARINES

Notes: (1) The most recent attempt to acquire new submarines is based on the building by RDM of two 'Moray' class hulls, to be fitted out by Litton Ingalls using FMS funds.
(2) Some two-man Swimmer Delivery Vehicles (SDVs) of Italian CF2 FX 100 design are in service.

4 IMPROVED ROMEO CLASS (TYPE 033) (SSK)

849	852	855	858

Displacement, tons: 1,475 surfaced; 1,830 dived
Dimensions, feet (metres): 251.3 × 22 × 16.1 *(76.6 × 6.7 × 4.9)*
Main machinery: Diesel-electric; 2 Type 37-D diesels; 4,000 hp (m) *(2.94 MW)*; 2 motors; 2,700 hp(m) *(1.98 MW)*; 2 creep motors; 2 shafts
Speed, knots: 16 surfaced; 13 dived
Range, miles: 9,000 at 9 kt surfaced
Complement: 54 (8 officers)

Missiles: SSM: McDonnell Douglas Sub Harpoon; active radar homing to 130 km *(70 n miles)* at 0.9 Mach; warhead 227 kg.
Torpedoes: 8—21 in *(533 mm)* tubes (6 bow, 2 stern). 14 Alliant Mk 37F Mod 2; wire-guided; active/passive homing to 18 km *(9.7 n miles)* at 32 kt; warhead 148 kg.
Mines: 28 in lieu of torpedoes.
Countermeasures: ESM: Argo Phoenix AR-700-S5; radar warning.
Weapons control: Singer Librascope Mk 2. Datalink.
Radars: Surface search: I-band.
Sonars: Atlas Elektronik CSU 83; bow-mounted; active/passive; medium frequency.
  Loral; hull-mounted; active attack; high frequency.

ROMEO 852   *2/1998* / 0017807

Programmes: Two transferred from China 22 March 1982. Second pair arrived from China 3 January 1984, commissioned 21 May 1984.
Modernisation: In early 1988 a five year contract was signed with Tacoma, Washington to retrofit Harpoon, and Mk 37 wire-guided torpedoes; weapon systems improvements to include Loral active sonar, Atlas Elektronik passive sonar and fire-control system. New air conditioning was also installed. The US Congress did not give approval to start work until July 1989 and then Tacoma went bankrupt and the work was not taken over by Loral/Lockheed Martin until April 1992. Towed communications wire and GPS are fitted. Kollmorgen 76 and 86 periscopes. Optronic masts to be fitted 2000/02.
Operational: *855* was the first to complete modernisation and was active again in late 1994. The remainder completed by mid-1996 although *849* has not been reported active since then. All based at Alexandria. The ex-USSR submarines of this class have paid off but are still alongside at Alexandria.   **UPDATED**

DESTROYERS

1 Z CLASS (DD)

Name	No	Builders	Laid down	Launched	Commissioned
EL FATEH (ex-*Zenith*, ex-*Wessex*)	921	Wm Denny & Bros, Dumbarton	19 May 1942	5 June 1944	22 Dec 1944

Displacement, tons: 1,730 standard; 2,575 full load
Dimensions, feet (metres): 362.8 × 35.7 × 16
(110.6 × 10.9 × 4.9)
Main machinery: 2 Admiralty boilers; 2 Parsons turbines;
40,000 hp *(30 MW)*; 2 shafts
Speed, knots: 24. **Range, miles:** 2,800 at 20 kt
Complement: 186

Missiles: SAM: 2 SA-N-5 mountings.
Guns: 4 Vickers 4.5 in *(115 mm)*/45 hand-loaded Mk 5
mounting; 50° elevation; 14 rds/min to 17 km *(9.3 n miles)*;
weight of shell 25 kg.
8 China 37 mm/63 (4 twin); 180 rds/min to 8.5 km *(4.6 n
miles)*; weight of shell 1.42 kg.
2 Bofors 40 mm/60 (twin).
Torpedoes: 8—21 in *(533 mm)* (2 quad) tubes.
Depth charges: 4 projectors.
Weapons control: Fly 4 director.
Radars: Air/surface search: Marconi SNW 10; D-band.
Navigation: Racal Decca 916; I-band.
Fire control: Marconi Type 275; F-band.

EL FATEH   *4/1994, van Ginderen Collection /* 0017808

Programmes: Purchased from the UK in 1955.
Modernisation: Bofors replaced by Chinese 37 mm guns. Sonars
removed. Boilers renewed in 1993 and SA-N-5 mountings fitted.

Operational: Used primarily for harbour training, and the
intention is to keep the ship in service until at least the end of
2000. Last seen at sea in 1994.   **UPDATED**

FRIGATES

Note: The 1940s vintage 'Black Swan' class *Tariq* 931 still has a limited training role.

4 OLIVER HAZARD PERRY CLASS (FFG)

Name	No	Builders	Laid down	Launched	Commissioned
MUBARAK (ex-*Copeland*)	F 911 (ex-FFG 25)	Todd Shipyards, San Pedro	24 Oct 1979	26 July 1980	7 Aug 1982
TABA (ex-*Gallery*)	F 916 (ex-FFG 26)	Bath Iron Works	17 May 1980	20 Dec 1980	5 Dec 1981
SHARM EL SHEIKH (ex-*Fahrion*)	F 901 (ex-FFG 22)	Todd Shipyards, Seattle	1 Dec 1978	24 Aug 1979	16 Jan 1982
TOUSHKA (ex-*Lewis B Puller*)	F 906 (ex-FFG 23)	Todd Shipyards, San Pedro	23 May 1979	15 Mar 1980	17 Apr 1982

Displacement, tons: 2,750 light; 3,638 full load
Dimensions, feet (metres): 445 × 45 × 14.8; 24.5 (sonar)
(135.6 × 13.7 × 4.5; 7.5)
Main machinery: 2 GE LM 2500 gas turbines; 41,000 hp
(30.59 MW) sustained; 1 shaft; cp prop
2 auxiliary retractable props; 650 hp *(484 kW)*
Speed, knots: 29. **Range, miles:** 4,500 at 20 kt
Complement: 206 (13 officers) including 19 aircrew

Missiles: SSM: 4 McDonnell Douglas Harpoon; active radar
homing to 130 km *(70 n miles)* at 0.9 Mach; warhead 227 kg.
SAM: 36 GDC Standard SM-1MR; command guidance; semi-
active radar homing to 46 km *(25 n miles)* at 2 Mach.
1 Mk 13 Mod 4 launcher for both SSM and SAM missiles ❶.
Guns: 1 OTO Melara 3 in *(76 mm)*/62 Mk 75 ❷; 85 rds/min to
16 km *(8.7 n miles)* anti-surface; 12 km *(6.6 n miles)* anti-
aircraft; weight of shell 6 kg.
1 General Electric/General Dynamics 20 mm/76 6-barrelled
Mk 15 Vulcan Phalanx ❸; 3,000 rds/min combined to 1.5 km.
4—12.7 mm MGs.
Torpedoes: 6—324 mm Mk 32 (2 triple) tubes ❹. 24 Alliant
Mk 46 Mod 5; anti-submarine; active/passive homing to
11 km *(5.9 n miles)* at 40 kt; warhead 44 kg.
Countermeasures: Decoys: 2 Loral Hycor SRBOC 6-barrelled
fixed Mk 36 ❺; IR flares and chaff to 4 km *(2.2 n miles)*.
T—Mk-6 Fanfare/SLQ-25 Nixie; torpedo decoy.
ESM/ECM: Elettronica ❻ intercept and jammer.
Combat data systems: Link Y.
Weapons control: SWG-1 Harpoon LCS. Mk 92 (Mod 4). Mk 13
weapon direction system. 2 Mk 24 optical directors.
Radars: Air search: Raytheon SPS-49(V)4 ❼; C/D-band.
Surface search: ISC Cardion SPS-55 ❽; I-band.
Fire control: Lockheed STIR (modified SPG-60) ❾; I/J-band;
range 110 km *(60 n miles)*.
Sperry Mk 92 (Signaal WM28) ❿; I/J-band.
Navigation: Furuno; I-band. JRC; I-band.
Tacan: URN 25. IFF Mk XII AIMS UPX-29.
Sonars: Raytheon SQS-56; hull-mounted; active search and
attack; medium frequency.

Helicopters: 2 Kaman SH-2G Seasprite ⓫.

Programmes: First one acquired from USA on 18 September
1996, second on 28 September 1996, third on 31 March
1998, and fourth on 30 September 1998.
Modernisation: EW suite replaced after transfer. JRC radar fitted
on hangar roof.
Operational: First pair arrived in Egypt in mid-1997 after working up, third in late 1998 and fourth in 1999. At least one of the
class operates in the Red Sea.   **UPDATED**

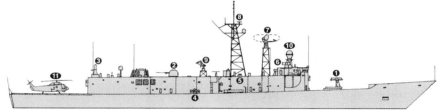
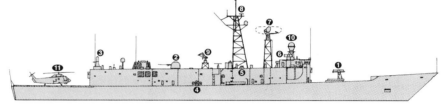

MUBARAK   *(Scale 1 : 1,200), Ian Sturton /* 0012290

TABA   *6/1998, G Toremans /* 0017809

MUBARAK   *5/1999*, *C D Yaylali /* 0056912

2 KNOX CLASS (FFG)

Name	No	Builders	Laid down	Launched	Commissioned	Recommissioned
DAMYAT (ex-*Jesse L Brown*)	961 (ex-FF 1089)	Avondale Shipyard	8 Apr 1971	18 Mar 1972	17 Feb 1973	1 Oct 1994
RASHEED (ex-*Moinester*)	966 (ex-FF 1097)	Avondale Shipyard	25 Aug 1972	12 May 1973	2 Nov 1974	1 Oct 1994

Displacement, tons: 3,011 standard; 4,260 full load
Dimensions, feet (metres): 439.6 × 46.8 × 15; 24.8 (sonar) *(134 × 14.3 × 4.6; 7.8)*
Main machinery: 2 Combustion Engineering/Babcock & Wilcox boilers; 1,200 psi *(84.4 kg/cm²)*; 950°F *(510°C)*; 1 turbine; 35,000 hp *(26 MW)*; 1 shaft
Speed, knots: 27. **Range, miles:** 4,000 at 22 kt on 1 boiler
Complement: 288 (17 officers)

Missiles: SSM: 8 McDonnell Douglas Harpoon; active radar homing to 130 km *(70 n miles)* at 0.9 Mach; warhead 227 kg.
A/S: Honeywell ASROC Mk 16 octuple launcher with reload system (has 2 cells modified to fire Harpoon) ❶; inertial guidance to 1.6-10 km *(1-5.4 n miles)*; payload Mk 46.
Guns: 1 FMC 5 in *(127 mm)*/54 Mk 42 Mod 9 ❷; 20-40 rds/min to 24 km *(13 n miles)* anti-surface; 14 km *(7.7 n miles)* anti-aircraft; weight of shell 32 kg.
1 General Electric/General Dynamics 20 mm/76 6-barrelled Mk 15 Vulcan Phalanx ❸; 3,000 rds/min combined to 1.5 km.
Torpedoes: 4—324 mm Mk 32 (2 twin) fixed tubes ❹. 22 Alliant Mk 46 Mod 5; anti-submarine; active/passive homing to 11 km *(5.9 n miles)* at 40 kt; warhead 44 kg.
Countermeasures: Decoys: 2 Loral Hycor SRBOC 6-barrelled fixed Mk 36 ❺; IR flares and chaff to 4 km *(2.2 n miles)*. T Mk 6 Fanfare/SLQ-25 Nixie; torpedo decoy. Prairie Masker hull and blade rate noise suppression.
ESM/ECM: Elettronica ❻ intercept and jammer.
Combat data systems: FFISTS mini NTDS with Link Y.

Weapons control: SWG-1A Harpoon LCS. Mk 68 GFCS. Mk 114 ASW FCS. Mk 1 target designation system.
Radars: Air search: Lockheed SPS-40B ❼; E/F-band; range 320 km *(175 n miles)*.
Surface search: Raytheon SPS-10 or Norden SPS-67 ❽; G-band.
Navigation: Marconi LN66; I-band.
Fire control: Western Electric SPG-53A/D/F ❾; I/J-band.
Tacan: SRN 15.
Sonars: EDO/General Electric SQS-26 CX; bow-mounted; active search and attack; medium frequency.

Helicopters: 1 Kaman SH-2G Seasprite ❿.

Programmes: Lease agreed from USA in mid-1993 and signed 27 July 1994 when both ships sailed for Egypt. Two others were transferred for spares in 1996. Ships of this class have been transferred to Greece, Taiwan, Turkey and Thailand.
Modernisation: Vulcan Phalanx fitted in the mid-1980s. There are plans to fit quadruple Harpoon launchers and possibly to remove the ASROC launcher. EW suite replaced.
Structure: Four torpedo tubes are fixed in the midship superstructure, two to a side, angled out at 45°. A lightweight anchor is fitted on the port side and an 8,000 lb anchor fits in to the after section of the sonar dome.
Operational: These ships have had boiler problems in Egyptian service, and refits are planned with US assistance when funds are available.

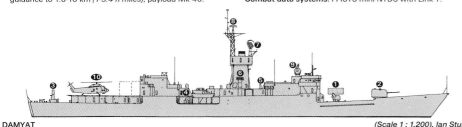

DAMYAT *(Scale 1 : 1,200), Ian Sturton* **UPDATED**

RASHEED and DAMYAT *2/1996 / 0017810*

2 DESCUBIERTA CLASS (FFG)

Name	No	Builders	Laid down	Launched	Commissioned
ABU QIR (ex-*Serviola*)	F 946	Bazán, Ferrol	28 Feb 1979	20 Dec 1979	27 Oct 1984
EL SUEZ (ex-*Centinela*)	F 941	Bazán, Ferrol	31 Oct 1978	6 Oct 1979	21 May 1984

Displacement, tons: 1,233 standard; 1,479 full load
Dimensions, feet (metres): 291.3 × 34 × 12.5 *(88.8 × 10.4 × 3.8)*
Main machinery: 4 MTU-Bazán 16V 956 TB91 diesels; 15,000 hp(m) *(11 MW)* sustained; 2 shafts; cp props
Speed, knots: 25.5; 28 trials. **Range, miles:** 4,000 at 18 kt
Complement: 116 (10 officers)

Missiles: SSM: 8 McDonnell Douglas Harpoon (2 quad) launchers ❶; active radar homing to 130 km *(70 n miles)* at 0.9 Mach; warhead 227 kg.
SAM: Selenia Elsag Albatros octuple launcher ❷; 24 Aspide; semi-active radar homing to 13 km *(7 n miles)* at 2.5 Mach; height envelope 15-5,000 m *(49.2-16,405 ft)*; warhead 30 kg.
Guns: 1 OTO Melara 3 in *(76 mm)*/62 compact ❸; 85 rds/min to 16 km *(8.7 n miles)*; weight of shell 6 kg.
2 Bofors 40 mm/70 ❹; 300 rds/min to 12.5 km *(6.8 n miles)*; weight of shell 0.96 kg.
Torpedoes: 6—324 mm Mk 32 (2 triple) tubes ❺. MUSL Stingray; anti-submarine; active/passive homing to 11 km *(5.9 n miles)* at 45 kt; warhead 35 kg (shaped charge); depth to 750 m *(2,460 ft)*.
A/S mortars: 1 Bofors 375 mm twin-barrelled trainable launcher ❻; automatic loading; range 1,600 or 3,600 m depending on type of rocket.
Countermeasures: ESM/ECM: Elettronica SpA Beta; intercept and jammer.
Prairie Masker; acoustic signature suppression.
Combat data systems: Signaal SEWACO action data automation. Link Y.
Radars: Air/surface search: Signaal DA05 ❼; E/F-band; range 137 km *(75 n miles)* for 2 m² target.
Navigation: Signaal ZW06; I-band.
Fire control: Signaal WM25 ❽; I/J-band.
Sonars: Raytheon 1160B; hull-mounted; active search and attack; medium frequency.
Raytheon 1167 ❾; VDS; active search; 12-7.5 kHz.

Programmes: Ordered September 1982 from Bazán, Spain. The two Spanish ships *Centinela* and *Serviola* were sold to Egypt prior to completion and transferred after completion at Ferrol and modification at Cartagena. *El Suez* completed 28 February 1984 and *Abu Qir* on 31 July 1984.
Modernisation: The combat data system, air search and fire-control radars were updated in 1995-96.
Operational: Stabilisers fitted. Modern noise insulation of main and auxiliary machinery. Both are active. **UPDATED**

EL SUEZ *(Scale 1 : 900), Ian Sturton*

ABU QIR *10/1999* / 0085001*

2 JIANGHU I CLASS (FFG)

Name	No	Builders	Commissioned
NAJIM AL ZAFFER	951	Hudong, Shanghai	27 Oct 1984
EL NASSER	956	Hudong, Shanghai	16 Apr 1985

Displacement, tons: 1,425 standard; 1,702 full load
Dimensions, feet (metres): 338.5 × 35.4 × 10.2
(103.2 × 10.8 × 3.1)
Main machinery: 2 Type 12 E 390V diesels; 14,400 hp(m)
(10.6 MW) sustained; 2 shafts
Speed, knots: 26. **Range, miles:** 4,000 at 15 kt
Complement: 195

Missiles: SSM: 4 Hai Ying 2 (Flying Dragon) (2 twin) ❶; active
radar or passive IR homing to 80 km *(43.2 n miles)* at
0.9 Mach; warhead 513 kg.
Guns: 4 China 57 mm/70 (2 twin) ❷; 120 rds/min to 12 km
(6.5 n miles); weight of shell 6.31 kg.
12 China 37 mm/63 (6 twin) ❸; 180 rds/min to 8.5 km *(4.6 n
miles)*; weight of shell 1.42 kg.
A/S mortars: 2 RBU 1200 5-tubed fixed launchers ❹; range
1,200 m; warhead 34 kg.
Depth charges: 4 projectors.
Mines: Up to 60.
Countermeasures: ESM/ECM: Elettronica SpA Beta or Litton
Triton; intercept and jammer.
Radars: Air search: Type 765 ❺.
Surface search: Eye Shield ❻; E-band.
Surface search/gun direction: Square Tie; I-band.

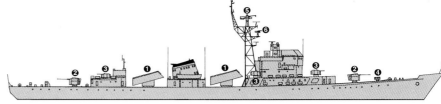

NAJIM AL ZAFFER   *(Scale 1 : 900), Ian Sturton /* 0056914

Fire control: Fog Lamp.
Navigation: Decca RM 1290A; I-band.
Sonars: China Type E5; hull-mounted; active search and attack;
high frequency.

Programmes: Ordered from China in 1982. This is a 'Jianghu I'
class modified with 57 mm guns vice the standard 100 mm.
These were the 17th and 18th hulls of the class.
Modernisation: Combat data system to be fitted together
with CSEE Naja optronic fire-control directors. There are also

plans, confirmed in October 1994, to remove the after
superstructure and guns and build a flight deck for an SH-2G
Seasprite helicopter. No sign yet of any of this work being
done.
Structure: The funnel is the rounded version of the 'Jianghu'
class.
Operational: Both ships are very active in the Red Sea.

VERIFIED

NAJIM AL ZAFFER   *5/1996, Camil Busquets i Vilanova /* 0017812

SHIPBORNE AIRCRAFT

Numbers/Type: 10 Kaman SH-2G(E) Seasprite.
Operational speed: 130 kt *(241 km/h)*.
Service ceiling: 22,500 ft *(6,860 m)*.
Range: 367 n miles *(679 km)*.
Role/Weapon systems: Total of 10 upgraded SH-2F aircraft transferred under FMS by September
1998 with six more needed. New engines and avionics. Sensors: LN66/HP radar; ALR-66 ESM;
ALE-39 ECM; ARN-118 Tacan; Ocean Systems AQS-18A dipping sonar. Possible mine detection
optronic sensor. Weapons: 2 × Mk 46 torpedoes or a depth bomb.

UPDATED

SEASPRITE   *1995*, Kaman /* 0056915

LAND-BASED MARITIME AIRCRAFT (FRONT LINE)

Note: There are also 2/4 Westland Commando Mk 2B/2E helicopters. Some refitted in 1997/98.

Numbers/Type: 11 Aerospatiale SA 342L Gazelle.
Operational speed: 142 kt *(264 km/h)*.
Service ceiling: 14,105 ft *(4,300 m)*.
Range: 407 n miles *(755 km)*.
Role/Weapon systems: Air Force helicopter for coastal anti-shipping strike, particularly against
FAC and insurgents. Sensors: SFIM sight. Weapons: ASV; 2 × AS-12 wire-guided missiles.

UPDATED

Numbers/Type: 5 Grumman E-2C Hawkeye.
Operational speed: 323 kt *(598 km/h)*.
Service ceiling: 37,000 ft *(11,278 m)*.
Range: 1,540 n miles *(2,852 km)*.
Role/Weapon systems: Air Force airborne early warning and control tasks; capable of handling up
to 30 tracks over water or land. Sensors: APS-138 search/warning radar being upgraded to
APS-148 from 2002; various ESM/ECM systems. Weapons: Unarmed.   ***UPDATED***

Numbers/Type: 5 Westland Sea King Mk 47.
Operational speed: 112 kt *(208 km/h)*.
Service ceiling: 14,700 ft *(4,480 m)*.
Range: 664 n miles *(1,230 km)*.
Role/Weapon systems: Air Force helicopter for ASW and surface search; secondary role as SAR
helicopter. Airframe and engine refurbishment in 1990 for first five. Four more are in reserve and
out of service. Sensors: MEL search radar. Weapons: ASW; 4 × Mk 46 or Stingray torpedoes or
depth bombs. ASV; Otomat.   ***VERIFIED***

Numbers/Type: 2 Beechcraft 1900C.
Operational speed: 267 kt *(495 km/h)*.
Service ceiling: 25,000 ft *(7,620 m)*.
Range: 1,569 n miles *(2,907 km)*.
Role/Weapon systems: Two (of six) Air Force aircraft acquired in 1988 and used for maritime
surveillance. Sensors: Litton search radar; Motorola multimode SLAMMR radar; Singer S-3075
ESM; Datalink Y. Weapons: Unarmed.   ***VERIFIED***

PATROL FORCES

Note: ITT proposed in late 1999 for up to six new FACs. Specifications include 300-500 tons, SSMs, CIWS, 76 mm gun. Speeds up to 38 kt on four diesels. If acquired under FMS funding a variant of the US 'Cyclone' class would be a contender.

6 RAMADAN CLASS (FAST ATTACK CRAFT—MISSILE) (PCFG)

Name	No	Builders	Launched		Commissioned	
RAMADAN	670	Vosper Thornycroft	6 Sep	1979	20 July	1981
KHYBER	672	Vosper Thornycroft	31 Jan	1980	15 Sep	1981
EL KADESSAYA	674	Vosper Thornycroft	19 Feb	1980	6 Apr	1982
EL YARMOUK	676	Vosper Thornycroft	12 June	1980	18 May	1982
BADR	678	Vosper Thornycroft	17 June	1981	17 June	1982
HETTEIN	680	Vosper Thornycroft	25 Nov	1980	28 Oct	1982

Displacement, tons: 307 full load
Dimensions, feet (metres): 170.6 × 25 × 7.5 *(52 × 7.6 × 2.3)*
Main machinery: 4 MTU 20V 538 TB91 diesels; 15,360 hp(m) *(11.29 MW)* sustained; 4 shafts
Speed, knots: 40. **Range, miles:** 1,600 at 18 kt
Complement: 30 (4 officers)

Missiles: SSM: 4 OTO Melara/Matra Otomat Mk 1; active radar homing to 80 km *(43.2 n miles)* at 0.9 Mach; warhead 210 kg.
Guns: 1 OTO Melara 3 in *(76 mm)* compact; 85 rds/min to 16 km *(8.7 n miles)*; weight of shell 6 kg. 2 Breda 40 mm/70 (twin); 300 rds/min to 12.5 km *(6.8 n miles)* anti-surface; weight of shell 0.96 kg.
Countermeasures: Decoys: 4 Protean fixed launchers each with 4 magazines containing 36 chaff decoy and IR flare grenades.
ESM: Racal Cutlass; radar intercept.
ECM: Racal Cygnus; jammer.
Combat data systems: Ferranti CAAIS action data automation.
Weapons control: Marconi Sapphire System with 2 radar/TV and 2 optical directors.
Radars: Air/surface search: Marconi S 820; E/F-band; range 73 km *(40 n miles)*.
Navigation: Marconi S 810; I-band.
Fire control: 2 Marconi ST 802; I-band.

Programmes: The contract was carried out at the Porchester yard of Vosper Thornycroft Ltd with some hulls built at Portsmouth Old Yard, being towed to Porchester for fitting out.
Modernisation: The intention was to double the SSM capability with eight lightweight Otomat or Harpoon but this now seems unlikely. EW upgrade started in 1995-96.
Operational: Portable SAM SA-N-5 sometimes carried. *El Kadessaya* in poor condition and may be scrapped.

UPDATED

KHYBER   3/1996 * / 0056916

4 OSA I (TYPE 205) CLASS
(FAST ATTACK CRAFT—MISSILE) (PCFG)

631   633   641   643

Displacement, tons: 171 standard; 210 full load
Dimensions, feet (metres): 126.6 × 24.9 × 8.9 *(38.6 × 7.6 × 2.7)*
Main machinery: 3 MTU diesels; 12,000 hp(m) *(8.82 MW)*; 3 shafts
Speed, knots: 35. **Range, miles:** 400 at 34 kt
Complement: 30

Missiles: SSM: 4 SS-N-2A Styx; active radar or IR homing to 46 km *(25 n miles)* at 0.9 Mach; altitude preset up to 300 m *(984.3 ft)*; warhead 513 kg.
SAM: SA-N-5 Grail; manual aiming; IR homing to 6 km *(3.2 n miles)* at 1.5 Mach; altitude to 2,500 m *(8,000 ft)*; warhead 1.5 kg.
Guns: 4 USSR 30 mm/65 (2 twin); 500 rds/min to 5 km *(2.7 n miles)* anti-aircraft; weight of shell 0.54 kg.
2—12.7 mm MGs.
Countermeasures: ESM: Thomson-CSF DR 875; radar warning.
ECM: Racal; jammer.
Radars: Air/surface search: Kelvin Hughes; I-band.
Navigation: Racal Decca 916; I-band.
Fire control: Drum Tilt; H/I-band.
IFF: High Pole. Square Head.

Programmes: Thirteen reported to have been delivered to Egypt by the Soviet Navy in 1966-68 but some were sunk in war with Israel, October 1973. Four of the remainder were derelict in 1989 but one more was back in service in 1991 and two more in 1993 and the last of the four in 1995.
Modernisation: Refitted with MTU diesels, two machine guns, improved radars and EW equipment.
Operational: All of those listed were active in 1999. Two more *637* and *639* are laid up.

UPDATED

OSA 633   1986

6 OCTOBER CLASS (FAST ATTACK CRAFT—MISSILE) (PCFG)

781   783   785   787   789   791

Displacement, tons: 82 full load
Dimensions, feet (metres): 84 × 20 × 5 *(25.5 × 6.1 × 1.3)*
Main machinery: 4 CRM 12 D/SS diesels; 5,000 hp(m) *(3.67 MW)* sustained; 4 shafts
Speed, knots: 38. **Range, miles:** 400 at 30 kt
Complement: 20

Missiles: SSM: 2 OTO Melara/Matra Otomat Mk 1; active radar homing to 80 km *(43.2 n miles)* at 0.9 Mach; warhead 210 kg; can be carried.
Guns: 4 BMARC/Oerlikon 30 mm/75 (2 twin); 650 rds/min to 10 km *(5.5 n miles)* anti-surface; 3 km *(1.6 n miles)* anti-aircraft; weight of shell 1 kg and 0.36 kg mixed.
Countermeasures: Decoys: 2 Protean fixed launchers each with 4 magazines containing 36 chaff decoy and IR flare grenades.
ESM: Racal Cutlass; radar warning.
Weapons control: Marconi Sapphire radar/TV system.
Radars: Air/surface search: Marconi S 810; range 48 km *(25 n miles)*.
Fire control: Marconi/ST 802; I-band.

Programmes: Built in Alexandria 1975-76. Hull of same design as USSR 'Komar' class. Refitted by Vosper Thornycroft, completed 1979-81. *791* was washed overboard on return trip, recovered and returned to Portsmouth for refit. Left UK after repairs on 12 August 1982. Probably Link fitted.
Operational: *783* and *785* refitted in 1998.

VERIFIED

OCTOBER 789   2/1997 / 0012291

5 HEGU CLASS (FAST ATTACK CRAFT—MISSILE) (PCFG)

609   611   613   615   617

Displacement, tons: 68 standard; 79.2 full load
Dimensions, feet (metres): 88.6 × 20.7 × 4.3 *(27 × 6.3 × 1.3)*
Main machinery: 4 Type L-12V-180 diesels; 4,800 hp(m) *(3.53 MW)*; 4 shafts
Speed, knots: 37.5. **Range, miles:** 400 at 30 kt
Complement: 17 (2 officers)

Missiles: SSM: 2 SY-1; active radar or passive IR homing to 40 km *(22 n miles)* at 0.9 Mach; warhead 513 kg.
Guns: 2—23 mm (twin); locally constructed to fit 25 mm mounting.
Countermeasures: ESM: Litton Triton; radar intercept.
Radars: Air/surface search: Square Tie; I-band.
IFF: High Pole A.

Programmes: Acquired from China and commissioned in Egypt on 27 October 1984. The Hegu is the Chinese version of the deleted Komar.
Modernisation: ESM fitted in 1995-96.
Operational: A sixth of class 619 is laid up.

VERIFIED

HEGU 617   2/1998, M Verschaeve / 0017813

HEGU 609   7/1995 / 0050086

6 SHERSHEN CLASS (FAST ATTACK CRAFT—GUN) (PCF)

| 751 | 753 | 755 | 757 | 759 | 761 |

Displacement, tons: 145 standard; 170 full load
Dimensions, feet (metres): 113.8 × 22 × 4.9 *(34.7 × 6.7 × 1.5)*
Main machinery: 3 Type M 503A diesels; 8,025 hp(m) *(5.9 MW)* sustained; 3 shafts
Speed, knots: 45. **Range, miles:** 850 at 30 kt
Complement: 23

Missiles: SAM: SA-N-5 Grail *(755-761)*; manual aiming; IR homing to 6 km *(3.2 n miles)* at 1.5 Mach; warhead 1.5 kg.
Guns: 4 USSR 30 mm/65 (2 twin); 500 rds/min to 5 km *(2.7 n miles)*; weight of shell 0.54 kg.
2 USSR 122 mm rocket launchers (*755-761* in lieu of torpedo tubes); 20 barrels per launcher; range 9 km *(5 n miles)*.
Depth charges: 12.
Countermeasures: ESM: Thomson-CSF DR 875; radar warning.
Radars: Surface search: Pot Drum; H/I-band.
Fire control: Drum Tilt, H/I-band (in some).
IFF: High Pole.

Programmes: Five delivered from USSR in 1967 and two more in 1968. One deleted. *753* completed an extensive refit at Ismailia in 1987; *751* in 1988.
Structure: The last four have had their torpedo tubes removed to make way for multiple BM21 rocket launchers and one SA-N-5 Grail, which are not always carried. Some have Drum Tilt radars removed. The first two have also had their torpedo tubes removed but these may be replaced.
Operational: Based at Alexandria, Port Said and Mersa Matru. All are active.

VERIFIED

SHERSHEN 751   *5/1997 /* 0012293

8 HAINAN CLASS (FAST ATTACK CRAFT—PATROL) (PCF)

| AL NOUR 430 | AL HADY 433 | AL HAKIM 436 | AL WAKIL 439 |
| AL QATAR 442 | AL SADDAM 445 | AL SALAM 448 | AL RAFIA 451 |

Displacement, tons: 375 standard; 392 full load
Dimensions, feet (metres): 192.8 × 23.6 × 7.2 *(58.8 × 7.2 × 2.2)*
Main machinery: 4 PRC/Kolomna Type 9-D-8 diesels; 4,000 hp *(2.94 MW)* sustained; 4 shafts
Speed, knots: 30.5. **Range, miles:** 1,300 at 15 kt
Complement: 69

Guns: 4 China 57 mm/70 (2 twin); 120 rds/min to 12 km *(6.5 n miles)*; weight of shell 6.31 kg.
4—23 mm (2 twin); locally constructed to fit the 25 mm mountings.
Torpedoes: 6—324 mm (2 triple) tubes (in two of the class). Mk 44 or MUSL Stingray.
A/S mortars: 4 RBU 1200 fixed 5-tubed launchers; range 1,200 m; warhead 34 kg.
Depth charges: 2 projectors; 2 racks. 18 DCs.
Mines: Rails fitted. 12 mines.
Radars: Surface search: Pot Head or Skin Head; I-band.
Navigation: Decca; I-band.
IFF: High Pole.
Sonars: Stag Ear; hull-mounted; active search and attack; high frequency.

Programmes: First pair transferred from China in October 1983, next three in February 1984 (commissioned 21 May 1984) and last three late 1984.
Modernisation: Two fitted with torpedo tubes and with Singer Librascope fire control. No sign of the remainder being similarly equipped.
Operational: Based at Alexandria.

VERIFIED

AL NOUR   *1/1998 /* 0017814

4 SHANGHAI II CLASS (FAST ATTACK CRAFT—GUN) (PCF)

| 793 | 795 | 797 | 799 |

Displacement, tons: 113 standard; 131 full load
Dimensions, feet (metres): 127.3 × 17.7 × 5.6 *(38.8 × 5.4 × 1.7)*
Main machinery: 2 Type L12-180 diesels; 2,400 hp(m) *(1.76 MW)* (forward); 2 Type L12-180Z diesels; 1,820 hp(m) *(1.34 MW)* (aft); 4 shafts
Speed, knots: 30. **Range, miles:** 700 at 16.5 kt
Complement: 34

Guns: 4 China 37 mm/63 (2 twin); 180 rds/min to 8.5 km *(4.6 n miles)*; weight of shell 1.42 kg.
4—23 mm (2 twin); locally constructed to fit the 25 mm mountings.
Mines: Rails can be fitted for 10 mines.
Countermeasures: ESM: Thomson-CSF; radar warning.
Radars: Surface search: Decca; I-band.
IFF: High Pole.

Programmes: Transferred from China in 1984.
Operational: Three based at Suez and one at Mersa Matru. *795* refitted in 1998.

UPDATED

SHANGHAI 797   *6/1997, J W Currie /* 0012295

AMPHIBIOUS FORCES

Notes: (1) Two ex-US 'Newport' class LSTs have been approved for transfer in 2000, but may not be taken up. The ships are the *Barbour County* 1195 and *Peoria* 1183.
(2) Ro-ro ferries are chartered for amphibious exercises.
(3) Rigid Raiders with Johnson outboards are also in service.

3 POLNOCHNY A (TYPE 770) CLASS (LSM)

| 301 | 303 | 305 |

Displacement, tons: 800 full load
Dimensions, feet (metres): 239.5 × 27.9 × 5.8 *(73 × 8.5 × 1.8)*
Main machinery: 2 Kolomna Type 40-D diesels; 4,400 hp(m) *(3.2 MW)* sustained; 2 shafts
Speed, knots: 19. **Range, miles:** 1,000 at 18 kt
Complement: 40
Military lift: 6 tanks; 350 tons
Guns: 2 USSR 30 mm/65 (twin); 500 rds/min to 5 km *(2.7 n miles)*; weight of shell 0.54 kg.
2—140 mm rocket launchers; 18 barrels to 9 km *(4.9 n miles)*.
Radars: Surface search: Decca; I-band.
Fire control: Drum Tilt; H/I-band.

Comment: Built at Northern Shipyard, Gdansk and transferred from USSR 1973-74. All used for Gulf logistic support in 1990-91. SA-N-5 may be carried. Radar updated. All are active.

UPDATED

POLNOCHNY 303   *10/1998, F Sadek /* 0017816

8 SEAFOX TYPE (SWIMMER DELIVERY CRAFT) (PB)

| 21 | 23 | 25 | 26 | 27 | 28 | 29 | 30 |

Displacement, tons: 11.3 full load
Dimensions, feet (metres): 36.1 × 9.8 × 2.6 *(11 × 3 × 0.8)*
Main machinery: 2 GM 6V-92TA diesels; 520 hp *(388 kW)* sustained; 2 shafts
Speed, knots: 30. **Range, miles:** 200 at 20 kt
Complement: 3
Guns: 2—12.7 mm MGs. 2—7.62 mm MGs.
Radars: Surface search: LN66; I-band.

Comment: Ordered from Uniflite, Washington in 1982. GRP construction painted black. There is a strong underwater team in the Egyptian Navy which is also known to use commercial two-man underwater chariots. Based at Abu Qir and all took part in the 1998 Fleet review. Two others have been deleted. RIBs are also in service.

UPDATED

SEAFOX   *1999* / 0056917

9 VYDRA CLASS (LCU)

330	332	334	336	338	340	342	344	346

Displacement, tons: 425 standard; 600 full load
Dimensions, feet (metres): 179.7 × 25.3 × 6.6 *(54.8 × 7.7 × 2)*
Main machinery: 2 Type 3-D-12 diesels; 600 hp(m) *(440 kW)* sustained; 2 shafts
Speed, knots: 11. **Range, miles:** 2,500 at 10 kt
Complement: 20
Military lift: 200 troops; 250 tons.
Guns: 2 or 4—37 mm/63 (1 or 2 twin) (may be fitted).
Radars: Navigation: Decca; I-band.

Comment: Built in late 1960s, transferred from USSR 1968-69. For a period after the Israeli war of October 1973 several were fitted with rocket launchers and two 37 or 40 mm guns, some of which have now been removed. All still in service. **VERIFIED**

VYDRA 338   *9/1998, van Ginderen Collection /* 0017817

MINE WARFARE FORCES

4 YURKA CLASS (MINESWEEPERS—OCEAN) (MSO)

GIZA 530	ASWAN 533	QENA 536	SOHAG 539

Displacement, tons: 540 full load
Dimensions, feet (metres): 171.9 × 30.8 × 8.5 *(52.4 × 9.4 × 2.6)*
Main machinery: 2 Type M 503 diesels; 5,350 hp(m) *(3.91 MW)* sustained; 2 shafts
Speed, knots: 17. **Range, miles:** 1,500 at 12 kt
Complement: 45
Guns: 4 USSR 30 mm/65 (2 twin); 500 rds/min to 5 km *(2.7 n miles)*; weight of shell 0.54 kg.
Mines: Can lay 10.
Radars: Navigation: Don; I-band.
Sonars: Stag Ear; hull-mounted; active search; high frequency.

Comment: Steel-hulled minesweepers transferred from the USSR in 1969. Built 1963-69. Egyptian 'Yurka' class do not carry Drum Tilt radar and have a number of ship's-side scuttles. The plan to equip them with VDS sonar has been shelved. At least one operates an ROV. *Qena* is in refit. **VERIFIED**

ASWAN   *10/1998, F Sadek /* 0017818

2 SWIFTSHIPS TYPE (ROUTE SURVEY VESSELS) (MSI)

Name	No	Builders	Commissioned
SAFAGA	RSV 1	Swiftships	1 Oct 1994
ABU EL GHOSON	RSV 2	Swiftships	1 Oct 1994

Displacement, tons: 165 full load
Dimensions, feet (metres): 90 × 24.8 × 8 *(27.4 × 7.6 × 2.4)*
Main machinery: 2 MTU 12V 183 TA61 diesels; 928 hp(m) *(682 kW)*; 2 shafts; bow thruster; 60 hp(m) *(44 kW)*
Speed, knots: 12. **Range, miles:** 1,500 at 10 kt
Complement: 16 (2 officers)
Guns: 1—12.7 mm MG.
Radars: Navigation: Furuno 2020; I-band.
Sonars: EG & G side scan; active; high frequency.

Comment: Route survey vessels ordered from Swiftships in November 1990 and delivered in September 1993. Two more are planned to be built in Egyptian yards in due course. Unisys improved SYQ-12 command system. Provision for both shallow and deep towed bodies. The names have been taken from the obsolete 'K 8' class. **UPDATED**

SAFAGA   *9/1993*, Swiftships /* 0080650

3 SWIFTSHIPS TYPE (COASTAL MINEHUNTERS) (MHC)

Name	No	Builders	Launched		Commissioned	
DAT ASSAWARI	CMH 1	Swiftships, Morgan City	4 Oct	1993	13 July	1997
NAVARIN	CMH 2	Swiftships, Morgan City	13 Nov	1993	13 July	1997
BURULLUS	CMH 3	Swiftships, Morgan City	4 Dec	1993	13 July	1997

Displacement, tons: 203 full load
Dimensions, feet (metres): 111 × 27 × 8 *(33.8 × 8.2 × 2.3)*
Main machinery: 2 MTU 12V 183 TE61 diesels; 1,068 hp(m) *(786 kW)*; 2 Schottel steerable props; 1 White Gill thruster; 300 hp *(224 kW)*
Speed, knots: 12.4. **Range, miles:** 2,000 at 10 kt
Complement: 25 (5 officers)
Guns: 2—12.7 mm MGs.
Radars: Navigation: Sperry; I-band.
Sonars: Thoray/Thomson Sintra TSM 2022; hull-mounted; active minehunting; high frequency.

Comment: MCM vessels with GRP hulls ordered from Swiftships in December 1990 with FMS funding. First one acceptance trials in June 1994 and completion in August. Fitted with a Unisys command data handling system which is an improved version of SYQ-12. GPS and line of sight navigation system. Dynamic positioning. A side scan sonar body and Gaymarine Pluto ROV can be streamed from a deck crane. Portable decompression chamber carried. Two delivered 29 November 1995 and the third in April 1996. All were finally commissioned after delays caused by problems with the minehunting equipment. **UPDATED**

DAT ASSAWARI   *1/1995*, Swiftships /* 0056918

NAVARIN   *4/1996* /* 0056919

6 T 43 CLASS (MINESWEEPERS—OCEAN) (MSO)

GHARBIYA 501	DAQAHLIYA 507	SINAI 513
SHARKIYA 504	BAHARIYA 510	ASSIOUT 516

Displacement, tons: 580 full load
Dimensions, feet (metres): 190.2 × 27.6 × 6.9 *(58 × 8.4 × 2.1)*
Main machinery: 2 Kolomna Type 9-D-8 diesels; 2,000 hp(m) *(1.47 MW)* sustained; 2 shafts
Speed, knots: 15. **Range, miles:** 3,000 at 10 kt
Complement: 65
Guns: 4—37 mm/63 (2 twin); 160 rds/min to 9 km *(5 n miles)*; weight of shell 0.7 kg.
8—12.7 mm (4 twin) MGs.
Mines: Can carry 20.
Radars: Navigation: Don 2; I-band.
Sonars: Stag Ear; hull-mounted; active search; high frequency.

Comment: Delivered in the early 1970s from the USSR. Others of the class have been sunk or used as targets or cannibalised for spares. The plan to fit them with VDS sonars and ROVs has been shelved. All still in service except *Sharkiya* and *Daqahlilya* which are in refit. **UPDATED**

SINAI   *10/1997* /* 0012299

AUXILIARIES

Notes: (1) There are also two survey launches *Misaha 1* and *2* with a crew of 14. Both were commissioned in 1991.
(2) An ex-trawler *Amira Rama* was acquired by the Navy in 1987 and is used as lighthouse tender.
(3) Two Poluchat I TRVs are also in service.

8 TOPLIVO 2 CLASS (TANKERS) (AOTL/AWTL)

AYEDA 4 210	**AL FURAT** 212	**AKDU** 214	**AYEDA 3** 216
MARYUT 211	**AL NIL** 213	**MARYUT ATBARAH** 215	**AL BURULLUS** 218

Displacement, tons: 1,029 full load
Dimensions, feet (metres): 176.2 × 31.8 × 10.5 *(53.7 × 9.7 × 3.2)*
Main machinery: 1 6DR 30/50-5 diesel; 600 hp(m) *(441 kW)*; 1 shaft
Speed, knots: 10. **Range, miles:** 400 at 7 kt
Complement: 16
Cargo capacity: 500 tons diesel or water (211-215)
Radars: Navigation: Spin Trough; I-band.

Comment: Built in Alexandria in 1972-77 to a USSR design. Another of the class 217 is laid up.
UPDATED

AL FURAT   *6/1999* * / 0080651

TUGS

Note: There are also four Coast Guard harbour tugs built by Damen in 1982. Names *Khoufou*, *Khafra*, *Ramses* and *Kreir*. Two other harbour tugs were delivered in 1998. Names *Ajmi* and *Jihad*.

6 OKHTENSKY CLASS (ATA)

AL MEKS 103	**ANTAR** 107	**AL ISKANDARANI** 111
AL AGAMI 105	**AL DIKHILA** 109	**KALIR** 113

Displacement, tons: 930 full load
Dimensions, feet (metres): 156.1 × 34 × 13.4 *(47.6 × 10.4 × 4.1)*
Main machinery: Diesel-electric; 2 BM diesel generators; 1 motor; 1,500 hp(m) *(1.1 MW)*; 1 shaft
Speed, knots: 13. **Range, miles:** 6,000 at 13 kt
Complement: 38

Comment: Two transferred from USSR in 1966, others assembled at Alexandria. Replacements are needed.
UPDATED

AL AGAMI   *2/1998, M Verschaeve* / 0017822

COAST GUARD

Notes: (1) The Coast Guard is controlled by the Navy.
(2) There are four obsolete P 6 craft; pennant numbers 222, 246, 253 and 201.
(3) There are also some Bollinger type craft of 8 tons building at the Suez Canal Authority yards. Twin diesel engines. Carry a 7.62 mm MG.

9 TYPE 83 CLASS (LARGE PATROL CRAFT)

46-54

Displacement, tons: 85 full load
Dimensions, feet (metres): 83.7 × 21.3 × 5.6 *(25.5 × 6.5 × 1.7)*
Main machinery: 2 diesels; 2 shafts
Speed, knots: 24
Complement: 12
Guns: 2—23 mm (twin). 1 Oerlikon 20 mm.
Radars: Surface search: Furuno; I-band.

Comment: Two of this class commissioned 13 July 1997 but overall numbers are uncertain. Built locally, these craft are similar to the Swiftships 93 ft class.
UPDATED

---

22 TIMSAH CLASS (LARGE PATROL CRAFT) (PC)

01-02   04-22

Displacement, tons: 106 full load
Dimensions, feet (metres): 101.8 × 17 × 4.8 *(30.5 × 5.2 × 1.5)*
Main machinery: 2 MTU 8V 331 TC92 diesels; 1,770 hp *(1.3 MW)* sustained; 2 shafts *(01-06)*;
2 MTU 12V 331 TC92 diesels; 2,660 hp(m) *(1.96 MW)* sustained; 2 shafts *(07-19)*
Speed, knots: 25. **Range, miles:** 600 at 18 kt
Complement: 13
Guns: 2 Oerlikon 30 mm (twin) or 2 Oerlikon 20 mm.
Radars: Surface search: Racal Decca; I-band.

Comment: First three completed December 1981, second three December 1982 at Timsah SY, Ismailia. Further six ordered in January 1985 and completed in 1988-89 with a different type of engine and with waterline exhaust vice a funnel. Last of this batch in service in 1992, followed by ten more by 1999. *03* sunk in late 1993. Building at about one a year.
UPDATED

TIMSAH 21   *8/1996* *, A Sharma* / 0056921

TIMSAH 02 (with funnel)   *6/1995* *, Ships of the World* / 0056922

9 SWIFTSHIPS 93 ft CLASS (LARGE PATROL CRAFT) (PC)

35-43

Displacement, tons: 102 full load
Dimensions, feet (metres): 93.2 × 18.7 × 4.9 *(28.4 × 5.7 × 1.5)*
Main machinery: 2 MTU 12V 331 TC92 diesels; 2,660 hp(m) *(1.96 MW)* sustained; 2 shafts
Speed, knots: 27. **Range, miles:** 900 at 12 kt
Complement: 14 (2 officers)
Guns: 2—23 mm (twin); 1 Oerlikon 20 mm or 1—14.5 mm MG.
Radars: Surface search: Furuno; I-band.

Comment: Ordered November 1983. First three built in USA, remainder assembled by Osman Shipyard, Ismailia. First four commissioned 16 April 1985, five more in 1986. Armament upgraded with 23 mm guns fitted forward in some of the class.
UPDATED

SWIFTSHIPS 43   *12/1998* * / 0056920

6 CRESTITALIA 70 ft CLASS (COASTAL PATROL CRAFT) (PBF)

Displacement, tons: 36 full load
Dimensions, feet (metres): 68.9 × 17.4 × 3 *(21 × 5.3 × 0.9)*
Main machinery: 2 MTU 12V 331 TC92 diesels; 2,660 hp(m) *(1.96 MW)* sustained; 2 shafts
Speed, knots: 35. **Range, miles:** 500 at 32 kt
Complement: 10 (1 officer)
Guns: 2 Oerlikon 30 mm A32 (twin). 1 Oerlikon 20 mm.
Radars: Surface search: Racal Decca; I-band.

Comment: Ordered 1980—GRP hulls. Naval manned but still employed on Coast Guard duties.
VERIFIED

CRESTITALIA 70 ft   *1980, Crestitalia*

12 SPECTRE CLASS (COASTAL PATROL CRAFT) (PB)

Displacement, tons: 37 full load
Dimensions, feet (metres): 64.9 × 18 × 5.9 *(19.8 × 5.5 × 1.8)*
Main machinery: 3 GM 8V-71TI diesels; 1,800 hp *(1.3 MW)*; 3 shafts
Speed, knots: 29. **Range, miles:** 450 at 25 kt
Complement: 9 (1 officer)
Guns: 2—12.7 mm MGs.
Radars: Surface search: Raytheon; I-band.

Comment: PB Mk III type built by Peterson, Sturgeon Bay and delivered in 1980-81. Used for Customs duties.
UPDATED

SPECTRE   *1981*, Peterson Builders / 0056924*

9 PETERSON TYPE (COASTAL PATROL CRAFT) (PB)

71-79

Displacement, tons: 18 full load
Dimensions, feet (metres): 45.6 × 13 × 3 *(13.9 × 4 × 0.9)*
Main machinery: 2 MTU 8V 183 TE92 diesels; 1,314 hp(m) *(966 kW)* sustained; Hamilton 362 water-jets
Speed, knots: 34. **Range, miles:** 200 at 30 kt
Complement: 4
Guns: 2—12.7 mm MGs.
Radars: Surface search: Raytheon; I-band.

Comment: Built by Peterson Shipbuilders, Sturgeon Bay and delivered between June and October 1994 under FMS. Replaced Bertram type and used as pilot boats.
UPDATED

PETERSON 72 (US colours)   *6/1994*, PBI / 0056925*

5 NISR CLASS (LARGE PATROL CRAFT) (PC)

NISR 713	THAR 701	NUR 703	NIMR 719	AL BAHR

Displacement, tons: 110 full load
Dimensions, feet (metres): 102 × 18 × 4.9 *(31 × 5.2 × 1.5)*
Main machinery: 2 Maybach diesels; 3,000 hp(m) *(2.2 MW)*; 2 shafts
Speed, knots: 24
Complement: 15
Guns: 2 or 4—23 mm (twin). 1 BM 21 122 mm 8-barrelled rocket launcher.
Radars: Surface search: Racal Decca 1230; I-band.

Comment: Built by Castro, Port Said on P6 hulls. First three launched in May 1963. Two more completed 1983. The rocket launcher and after 23 mm guns are interchangeable. 701 and 703 were refitted in 1998. Naval manned but employed on Coast Guard duties.
UPDATED

NISR (with BM 21)   *1991*

NIMR (with 2 twin 23 mm guns)   *10/1995* / 0056923*

3 PETERSON TYPE (COASTAL PATROL CRAFT) (PB)

80-82

Displacement, tons: 20 full load
Dimensions, feet (metres): 51 × 12 × 3 *(15.5 × 3.7 × 0.9)*
Main machinery: 2 MTU diesels; 2,266 hp(m) *(1.66 MW)*; Hamilton 391 water-jets
Speed, knots: 45. **Range, miles:** 320 at 30 kt
Complement: 5
Guns: 2—12.7 mm MGs.
Radars: Surface search: Raytheon; I-band.

Comment: Built by Peterson Shipbuilders, Sturgeon Bay and delivered between October and December 1996 under FMS. Aluminium construction. Used mostly as pilot boats.   *UPDATED*

PETERSON 80   *8/1996*, PBI / 0056926*

29 DC 35 TYPE (YFL)

Displacement, tons: 4 full load
Dimensions, feet (metres): 35.1 × 11.5 × 2.6 *(10.7 × 3.5 × 0.8)*
Main machinery: 2 Perkins T6-354 diesels; 390 hp *(287 kW)*; 2 shafts
Speed, knots: 25
Complement: 4

Comment: Built by Dawncraft, Wroxham, UK, from 1977. Harbour launches. One destroyed in September 1994. About half are laid up at Port Said.   *UPDATED*

DC 35   *8/1994*, F Sadek / 0056927*

TRAINING SHIPS

Notes: *Al Kousser* is a 1,000 ton vessel belonging to the Naval Academy. *Intishat* is a 500 ton training ship. Pennant number 160 is a USSR 'Sekstan' class used as a cadet training ship. Two YSB training craft acquired from the USA in 1989. A 3,300 ton training ship *Aida IV* presented by Japan in 1988 for delivery in March 1992 belongs to the Arab Maritime Transport Academy.

1 PRESIDENTIAL YACHT

Name	Builders	Commissioned
EL HORRIYA (ex-*Mahroussa*)	Samuda, Poplar	1865

Displacement, tons: 4,560 full load
Dimensions, feet (metres): 479 × 42.6 × 17.4 *(146 × 13 × 5.3)*
Main machinery: 3 boilers; 3 turbines; 5,500 hp *(4.1 MW)*; 3 shafts
Speed, knots: 16
Complement: 160

Comment: Became a museum in 1987 but was reactivated in 1992. Used as a training ship as well as a Presidential Yacht.   *UPDATED*

EL HORRIYA   *8/1997* / 0012301

EL SALVADOR
FUERZA NAVAL DE EL SALVADOR

Senior Officer	Personnel	Bases	Mercantile Marine
Commander of the Navy: Captain Milton Mauricio Perla Sorto	(a) 2000: 800 (including 150 Naval Infantry) (b) Voluntary service	Acajutla, La Libertad, El Triunfo y La Union	*Lloyd's Register of Shipping:* 13 vessels of 1,598 tons gross

PATROL FORCES

3 CAMCRAFT TYPE (COASTAL PATROL CRAFT) (PC)

GC 6,   GC 7,   GC 8

Displacement, tons: 100 full load
Dimensions, feet (metres): 100 × 21 × 4.9 *(30.5 × 6.4 × 1.5)*
Main machinery: 3 Detroit 12V-71TA diesels; 1,260 hp *(939 kW)* sustained; 3 shafts
Speed, knots: 25. **Range, miles:** 780 at 24 kt
Complement: 10
Guns: 1 Oerlikon 20 mm or 1—12.7 mm MG. 2—7.62 mm MGs. 1—81 mm mortar.
Radars: Surface search: Furuno; I-band.

Comment: Delivered 24 October, 8 November and 3 December 1975. Refitted in 1986 at Lantana Boatyard. Sometimes carry a combined 12.7 mm MG/81 mm mortar mounting in the stern. New radars fitted in 1995. Difficult to maintain and may be replaced by ASMAR 'Protector' class by 2001.   *UPDATED*

GC 6 and GC 7   *1/1998, Julio Montes* / 0017823

1 SWIFTSHIPS 77 ft CLASS (COASTAL PATROL CRAFT) (PC)

GC 11

Displacement, tons: 48 full load
Dimensions, feet (metres): 77.1 × 20 × 4.9 *(23.5 × 6.1 × 1.5)*
Main machinery: 3 Detroit 12V-71TA diesels; 1,260 hp *(939 kW)* sustained; 3 shafts
Speed, knots: 26
Complement: 7
Guns: 2—12.7 mm MGs. Aft MG combined with 81 mm mortar.
Radars: Surface search: Furuno; I-band.

Comment: Aluminium hull. Delivered by Swiftships, Morgan City 6 May 1985.   *UPDATED*

GC 11   *1993*, Julio Montes* / 0056929

1 SWIFTSHIPS 65 ft CLASS (COASTAL PATROL CRAFT) (PC)

GC 10

Displacement, tons: 36 full load
Dimensions, feet (metres): 65.6 × 18.3 × 5 *(20 × 6 × 1.5)*
Main machinery: 2 Detroit 12V-71TA diesels; 840 hp *(626 kW)* sustained; 2 shafts
Speed, knots: 23. **Range, miles:** 600 at 18 kt
Complement: 6
Guns: 1 Oerlikon 20 mm. 1 or 2—12.7 mm MGs. 1—81 mm mortar.
Radars: Surface search: Furuno; I-band.

Comment: Aluminium hull. Delivered by Swiftships, Morgan City 14 June 1984. Was laid up for a time in 1989-90 but became operational again in 1991. Refitted in 1996.   *UPDATED*

GC 10   *2/1996*, Julio Montes* / 0056928

0 + 2 ASMAR PROTECTOR CLASS (PC)

Displacement, tons: 107 full load
Dimensions, feet (metres): 107.3 × 22 × 6.6 *(32.7 × 6.7 × 2)*
Main machinery: 2 diesels; 5,200 hp(m) *(3.82 MW)*; 2 shafts
Speed, knots: 20. **Range, miles:** 1,000 at 15 kt
Complement: 16
Guns: 2 Oerlikon 20 mm.
Radars: Surface search: I-band.

Comment: Contract with ASMAR in September 1999, replacing the 'Alcotan' class proposal which was cancelled. To be delivered in 2000/01. Similar to those craft in service with the Chilean Coast Guard.
UPDATED

4 PIRANHA CLASS (RIVER PATROL CRAFT) (PBR)

LOF 021-026

Displacement, tons: 8.2 full load
Dimensions, feet (metres): 36 × 10.1 × 1.6 *(11 × 3.1 × 0.5)*
Main machinery: 2 Caterpillar 3208TA diesels; 680 hp *(507 kW)* sustained; 2 shafts
Speed, knots: 26
Complement: 5
Guns: 2—12.7 mm (twin) MGs. 2—7.62 mm (twin) MGs.
Radars: Surface search: Furuno 3600; I-band.

Comment: Riverine craft with Kevlar hulls used by the Naval Infantry. Completed in March 1987 by Lantana Boatyard, Florida. Same type supplied to Honduras. Two deleted in 1997.
UPDATED

LOF 022   *1/1994*, Julio Montes / 0056930

8 PROTECTOR CLASS (RIVER PATROL CRAFT) (PBR)

LP 03 01-03 10

Displacement, tons: 9 full load
Dimensions, feet (metres): 40.4 × 13.4 × 1.4 *(12.3 × 4 × 0.4)*
Main machinery: 2 Caterpillar 3208TA diesels; 680 hp *(507 kW)* sustained; 2 shafts
Speed, knots: 28. **Range, miles:** 350 at 20 kt
Complement: 4
Guns: 2—12.7 mm MGs. 2—7.62 mm MGs.
Radars: Surface search: Furuno 3600; I-band.

Comment: Ordered in December 1987 from SeaArk Marine (ex-MonArk). Four delivered in December 1988 and the remainder in February and March 1989. Two deleted in 1997.
UPDATED

LP 03 06   *1/1994*, Julio Montes / 0056932

PROTECTORS   *6/1997*, Julio Montes / 0012303

10 MERCOUGAR RIVERINE CRAFT (PBR)

LP 04 1-5   LR 1-5

Comment: Five 40 ft monohulls *(LP)* and five 35 ft catamarans *(LR)* completed by Mercougar, Miami in 1988-89. Both types are powered by two Ford Merlin diesels, 600 hp *(448 kW)*, giving speeds up to 40 kt. The 40 ft craft have a range of 556 km *(300 n miles)* which extends to 741 km *(400 n miles)* in the 35 ft version. All are radar fitted. One 40 ft craft is equipped as a hospital vessel. There are also some Boston Whalers and some locally built catamarans in service. All these craft can be transported by road.
UPDATED

CATAMARAN   *9/1999*, Julio Montes / 0056931

AUXILIARIES

3 LCM

LD 02   LD 04   LD 05

Displacement, tons: 45 full load
Dimensions, feet (metres): 64.7 × 14 × 5 *(21.5 × 4.6 × 1.6)*
Main machinery: 2 Detroit 12V 71TA diesels; 840 hp *(626 kW)* sustained; 2 shafts
Speed, knots: 15
Complement: 6
Guns: 2—12.7 mm MGs. 2—7.62 mm MGs.
Radars: Navigation: Furuno; I-band.

Comment: First one delivered by SeaArk Marine in January 1987, second pair in May 1996.
NEW ENTRY

LD 05   *10/1999*, El Salvador Navy / 0056933

POLICE

10 RODMAN 800 (PBR)

Dimensions, feet (metres): 29.2 × 9.8 × 3.6 *(8.9 × 3 × 0.8)*
Main machinery: 2 Volvo diesels; 300 hp(m) *(220 kW)*; 2 shafts
Speed, knots: 28. **Range, miles:** 150 at 25 kt
Complement: 3
Guns: 1—7.62 mm MG.
Radars: Surface search: I-band.

Comment: Ten craft delivered by Rodman in September 1998. These are for the newly formed Policia National Civile.
UPDATED

RODMAN 800   *6/1999*, El Salvador Police / 0056934

EQUATORIAL GUINEA

Bases

Malabo (Fernando Po), Bata (Rio Muni)

Patrol Forces

Two craft remain. One is *Rowele* 034 and the other is *Isla de Bioko* 037. Neither is seaworthy and both may be beyond economical repair.

Mercantile Marine

Lloyd's Register of Shipping:
   67 vessels of 43,916 tons gross

ERITREA

Headquarters Appointments

Commander Eritrean Navy:
   Major General Hummed Ahmed Karikari

Ethiopia

All vessels of the former Ethiopian Navy were put up for sale at Djibouti from 16 September 1996. All were either taken over by Eritrea, sold to civilian firms or scrapped (see *Deletions*).

Personnel

2000:   700 including 500 conscripts

Bases

Massawa, Dahlak.

Mercantile Marine

Lloyd's Register of Shipping:
   10 vessels of 15,913 tons gross

DELETIONS

Patrol Forces

1997   4 Boghammar (sold civilian), Mol 111 (scrap)
1998   1 Osa II

Mine Warfare Forces

1997   Natya 402, Sonya 401 (both sold civilian)

Auxiliaries

1997   Toplivo 502 (sold civilian)
1999   LTC 9501

PATROL FORCES

Note: There are also about 50 rigid raiding craft.

1 OSA II CLASS (FAST ATTACK CRAFT—MISSILE) (PCFG)

FMB 161

Displacement, tons: 245 full load
Dimensions, feet (metres): 126.6 × 24.9 × 8.8 *(38.6 × 7.6 × 2.7)*
Main machinery: 3 Type M 504 diesels; 10,800 hp(m) *(7.94 MW)* sustained; 3 shafts
Speed, knots: 37. **Range, miles:** 800 at 30 kt
Complement: 30

Missiles: SSM: 4 SS-N-2B Styx; active radar or IR homing to 46 km *(25 n miles)* at 0.9 Mach; warhead 513 kg.
Guns: 4—30 mm/65 (2 twin); 500 rds/min to 5 km *(2.7 n miles)* anti-aircraft; weight of shell 0.54 kg.
Radars: Surface search: Square Tie; I-band.
Fire control: Drum Tilt; H/I-band.
IFF: Square Head. High Pole B.

Programmes: Acquired from USSR on 13 January 1981. The rest of the class has been sunk or scuttled. *FMB 161* was refitted from October 1994 to January 1995 and taken over by Eritrea. A second of class *FMB 163* was acquired by sale in 1997 for spares. Probably non-operational.
UPDATED

FMB 161   *1/1998 / 0017824*

2 ZHUK CLASS (COASTAL PATROL CRAFT) (PC)

P 206 (ex-*PC 17*)   **P 207**

Displacement, tons: 39 full load
Dimensions, feet (metres): 78.7 × 16.4 × 3.9 *(24 × 5 × 1.2)*
Main machinery: 2 Type M 401B diesels; 2,200 hp(m) *(1.6 MW)* sustained; 2 shafts
Speed, knots: 30. **Range, miles:** 1,100 at 15 kt
Complement: 12 (3 officers)
Guns: 2—14.5 mm (twin) MGs.
Radars: Surface search: Spin Trough; I-band.

Comment: First two delivered from USSR 9 October 1982 in Fizik Korchatov. Second pair arrived in Assad on 9 June 1990. These last two are at Massawa and are probably non-operational.
UPDATED

P 206 (old number)   *1985*

4 SUPER DVORA CLASS (FAST ATTACK CRAFT—GUN) (PCF)

P 114   **+3**

Displacement, tons: 58 full load
Dimensions, feet (metres): 82 × 18.7 × 3 *(25 × 5.7 × 0.9)*
Main machinery: 2 MTU 8V 396 TE 94 diesels; 3,046 hp(m) *(2.24 MW)*; 2 shafts; ASD 14 surface drives
Speed, knots: 40. **Range, miles:** 1,200 at 17 kt
Complement: 10 (1 officer)
Guns: 2—23 mm (twin). 2—12 mm MGs.
Depth charges: 1 rail.
Weapons control: Optronic sight.
Radars: Surface search: Raytheon; I-band.

Comment: Built by Israel Aircraft Industries and delivered from July 1993 to a modified Super Dvora design. The original order may have been for six of the class. All are based at Massawa and all are active.
UPDATED

SUPER DVORA (Israeli colours)   *6/1996* / *0056935*

3 SWIFTSHIPS 105 ft CLASS (LARGE PATROL CRAFT) (PC)

P 151   P 152   P 153

Displacement, tons: 118 full load
Dimensions, feet (metres): 105 × 23.6 × 6.5 *(32 × 7.2 × 2)*
Main machinery: 2 MTU MD 16V 538 TB90 diesels; 6,000 hp(m) *(4.41 MW)* sustained; 2 shafts
Speed, knots: 30. **Range, miles:** 1,200 at 18 kt
Complement: 21
Guns: 4 Emerlec 30 mm (2 twin) *(P 201)*; 600 rds/min to 6 km *(3.3 n miles)*; weight of shell 0.35 kg.
4—23 mm/60 (2 twin) *(P 203/204)*. 2—12.7 mm (twin).
Radars: Surface search: Decca RM 916; I-band.

Comment: Six ordered in 1976 of which four were delivered in April 1977 before the cessation of US arms sales to Ethiopia. Built by Swiftships, Louisiana. One deserted to Somalia and served in that Navy for a time. Based at Massawa and in reasonable condition. All are active.
                                                                                                  UPDATED

P 153   1/1998 / 0017825

AMPHIBIOUS FORCES

Notes: (1) Two commercial LSTs are owned and operated by the Maritime Transit Service between Gizan, Berbera, Massawa, Assab and Djibouti. One is named *Chamo*. Both are armed with 23 mm guns and have been used by the Navy.
(2) Two obsolete ex-USSR T4 LCUs are in harbour service at Massawa.

1 EDIC CLASS (LST)

LTC 9502 (ex-*1036*)

Displacement, tons: 250 standard; 670 full load
Dimensions, feet (metres): 193.5 × 39.2 × 4.2 *(59 × 12 × 1.3)*
Main machinery: 2 SACM MGO 175 V12 diesels; 1,200 hp(m) *(882 kW)* sustained; 2 shafts
Speed, knots: 12. **Range, miles:** 1,800 at 8 kt
Complement: 16 (1 officer)
Military lift: 5 heavy vehicles or 11 personnel carriers
Guns: 4 DCN 20 mm (1 twin and 2 single).

Comment: Two of the class completed by SFCN, Villeneuve la Garenne, France in May 1977. Cargo deck space 28.5 × 5 m *(93.5 × 16.4 ft)*. This last one was repaired in 1997 and taken over by Eritrea.   *UPDATED*

LTC 9502   1990, Ethiopian Navy

ESTONIA
MEREVÄE ÜLEM

Headquarters Appointments

Commander of the Navy:
   Captain Jaan Kapp
Chief of Staff:
   Commander Ahti Piirimägi
General Director, Border Guard:
   Rear Admiral Tarmo Kõuts

General

The Navy was founded in 1918, but absorbed by the Soviet Baltic Fleet in 1940, and re-established on 22 April 1994. The Border Guard comes under the Department of the Interior and is responsible for SAR.

Personnel

(a) 2000: 300 (30 officers)
(b) 12 months' national service
(c) Border Guard: 300

Bases

Major: Miinisadam (Tallinn), Kopli (Tallinn) (Border Guard)
Minor: Põhjasadam (Paldiski)

Mercantile Marine

Lloyd's Register of Shipping:
   219 vessels of 452,648 tons gross

DELETIONS

Patrol Forces

1999   *Leopard*
2000   *Vambola*

Auxiliaries

1998   *Eva 311* (civilian)
2000   *Mardus*

PATROL FORCES

Note: Seven small inshore patrol boats are being built in Tallinn.

1 ZHUK CLASS (TYPE 1400) (COASTAL PATROL CRAFT) (PC)

GRIF P 401

Displacement, tons: 50 full load
Dimensions, feet (metres): 75.4 × 17 × 6.2 *(23 × 5.2 × 1.9)*
Main machinery: 2 Type M 50 diesels; 2,200 hp(m) *(1.6 MW)* sustained; 2 shafts
Speed, knots: 30. **Range, miles:** 1,100 at 15 kt
Complement: 15
Guns: 1—12.7 mm MG.
Radars: Surface search: Spin Trough; I-band.
Navigation: Furuno; I-band.

Comment: Built in 1976, acquired from Russia in December 1991 and commissioned 1 February 1994. A second of class has been cannibalised for spares.   *UPDATED*

GRIF   9/1996*, Hartmut Ehlers / 0056936

2 RIHTNIEMI CLASS (PC)

Name	No	Builders	Commissioned
RISTNA (ex-*Rihtniemi*)	P 422 (ex-51)	Rauma-Repola	21 Feb 1957
SUUROP (ex-*Rymättylä*)	P 423 (ex-52)	Rauma-Repola	20 May 1957

Displacement, tons: 91 standard; 112 full load
Dimensions, feet (metres): 101.7 × 18.7 × 5.9 *(31 × 5.6 × 1.8)*
Main machinery: 2 MTU MB diesels; 2,500 hp(m) *(1.84 MW)*; 2 shafts; cp props
Speed, knots: 18
Complement: 20
Guns: 4 USSR 23 mm/87 (2 twin).
A/S mortars: 2 RBU 1200 fixed 5-tubed launchers.
Mines: Can lay mines.
Radars: Navigation: Decca 1226; I-band.
Sonars: Simrad; hull-mounted; active search and attack; high frequency.

Comment: Transferred from Finland 8 July 1999. Both ships were modernised for ASW in 1981, but it is likely that the mortars and sonar are to be removed in Estonian service.   *NEW ENTRY*

SUUROP   7/1999*, Estonian Navy / 0056937

1 KONDOR CLASS (OPV)

Name	No	Builders	Commissioned
SULEV (ex-*Meteor*)	M 412	Peenewerft, Wolgast	13 May 1972

Displacement, tons: 377 full load
Dimensions, feet (metres): 170.3 × 23.3 × 7.2 *(51.9 × 7.1 × 2.2)*
Main machinery: 2 Russki Kolomna diesels; 4,408 hp(m) *(3.24 MW)* sustained; 2 shafts
Speed, knots: 20
Complement: 30
Guns: 2—25 mm/80 (twin). 2—14.5 mm (twin) MG.
Radars: Surface search: TSR 333; I-band.
Navigation: Racal Decca; I-band.

Comment: Former GDR intelligence collection vessel. Delivered in May 1994 and rearmed. Used as offshore patrol vessel. A twin MG mounting has been fitted aft of the funnel. Second of class cannibalised for spares.

UPDATED

SULEV   6/1997*, Findler & Winter / 0012304

MINE WARFARE FORCES

2 FRAUENLOB (TYPE 394) CLASS (MSI)

Name	No	Builders	Commissioned
KALEV (ex-*Minerva*)	M 414 (ex-M 2663)	Krogerwerft, Rendsburg	16 June 1967
OLEV (ex-*Diana*)	M 415 (ex-M 2664)	Krogerwerft, Rendsburg	21 Sep 1967

Displacement, tons: 246 full load
Dimensions, feet (metres): 124.6 × 26.9 × 6.6 *(38 × 8.2 × 2)*
Main machinery: 2 MTU MB 12V 493 TY70 diesels; 2,200 hp(m) *(1.62 MW)* sustained; 2 shafts
Speed, knots: 12. **Range, miles:** 700 at 14 kt
Complement: 25
Guns: 1 Bofors 40 mm/70.
Mines: Laying capability.
Radars: Navigation: Atlas Elektronik; I-band.

Comment: Transferred in April and June 1997 having paid off from the German Navy in 1995. May be fitted with Sea Eagle ROV in due course.

UPDATED

KALEV   6/1999*, J Cislak / 0056939

OLEV   9/1999*, Michael Nitz / 0056940

1 LINDAU (TYPE 331) CLASS (MHC)

Name	No	Builders	Commissioned
WAMBOLA (ex-*Cuxhaven*)	M 416 (ex-M 1078)	Burmeister, Bremen	11 Mar 1959

Displacement, tons: 463 full load
Dimensions, feet (metres): 154.5 × 27.2 × 9.8 (9.2 Troika) *(47.1 × 8.3 × 3) (2.8)*
Main machinery: 2 MTU MD diesels; 4,000 hp(m) *(2.94 MW)*; 2 shafts
Speed, knots: 16.5. **Range, miles:** 850 at 16.5 kt
Complement: 43 (5 officers)
Guns: 1 Bofors 40 mm/70; 330 rds/min to 12 km *(6.5 n miles)*; weight of shell 0.96 kg.
Radars: Navigation: Raytheon SPS 64; I-band.
Sonars: Atlas Elektronik DSQS-11; minehunting; high frequency.

Comment: Transferred from Germany in January 2000. Two PAP 104 ROVs were included in the transfer.

NEW ENTRY

LINDAU (German colours)   6/1999*, van Ginderen Collection / 0056938

AUXILIARIES

1 TRANSPORT SHIP (AK)

LAINE (ex-*Revalia*) A 432

Displacement, tons: 87 full load
Dimensions, feet (metres): 60.4 × 17.7 × 5.2 *(18.4 × 5.4 × 1.6)*
Main machinery: 1 diesel; 235 hp(m) *(173 kW)*; 1 shaft
Speed, knots: 9
Complement: 14 (3 officers)
Radars: Navigation: Mius; I-band.

Comment: Built in Kaliningrad in 1986. Acquired in 1994 from Russia and used as a tender and navigation training vessel. Transferred to the Defence Reserve Force on 3 September 1999.

UPDATED

LAINE   9/1996, Hartmut Ehlers

1 MAAGEN CLASS (AGF)

Name	No	Builders	Commissioned
AHTI (ex-*Mallemukken*)	A 532 (ex-A 431, ex-Y 385)	Helsingor Dockyard	19 May 1960

Displacement, tons: 190 full load
Dimensions, feet (metres): 88.6 × 23.6 × 9.5 *(27 × 7.2 × 2.9)*
Main machinery: 1 diesel; 385 hp(m) *(283 kW)*; 1 shaft
Speed, knots: 10
Complement: 11
Guns: 2—25 mm/80 (twin).
Radars: Surface search: Pechora; I-band.
Navigation: Skanter 009; I-band.

Comment: Handed over at Tallinn on 29 March 1994, having decommissioned from the Danish Navy in 1992. Serves as a patrol craft. Pennant number changed 1 January 2000.

UPDATED

AHTI (old number)   8/1995*, Estonian Navy / 0056941

BORDER GUARD (EESTI PIIRIVALVE)

Note: The letters PV are visible on the national flag which is defaced with green and yellow markings.

1 BALSAM CLASS (WLB)

Name	No	Builders	Commissioned
VALVAS (ex-*Bittersweet*)	A 109 (ex-WLB 389)	Duluth Shipyard, Minnesota	11 May 1944

Displacement, tons: 1,034 full load
Dimensions, feet (metres): 180 × 37 × 12 *(54.9 × 11.3 × 3.8)*
Main machinery: Diesel electric; 2 diesels; 1,402 hp *(1.06 MW)*; 1 motor; 1,200 hp *(895 kW)*; 1 shaft; bow thruster
Speed, knots: 13. **Range, miles:** 8,000 at 12 kt
Complement: 53
Guns: 2—12.7 mm MG.
Radars: Navigation: Raytheon SPS-64(V)1.

Comment: Transferred from the US Coast Guard and recommissioned as a Border Guard Headquarters ship on 5 September 1997. ***UPDATED***

VALVAS   *6/1999*, Estonian Border Guard /* 0056943

1 SILMÄ CLASS (LARGE PATROL CRAFT) (PC)

Name	No	Builders	Commissioned
KOU (ex-*Silmä*)	PVL 107	Laivateollisuus, Turku	19 Aug 1963

Displacement, tons: 530 full load
Dimensions, feet (metres): 158.5 × 27.2 × 14.1 *(48.3 × 8.3 × 4.3)*
Main machinery: 1 Werkspoor diesel; 1,800 hp(m) *(1.32 MW)*; 1 shaft
Speed, knots: 15
Complement: 10
Guns: 2—25 mm/80 (twin).
Radars: Surface search: I-band.
Sonars: Simrad SS105; active scanning; 14 kHz.

Comment: Transferred from Finland Frontier Guard in January 1995. ***UPDATED***

KOU   *6/1999*, Maritime Photographic /* 0056944

1 VIIMA CLASS (COASTAL PATROL CRAFT) (PC)

Name	No	Builders	Commissioned
MARU (ex-*Viima*)	PVL 106	Laivateollisuus, Turku	12 Oct 1964

Displacement, tons: 134 full load
Dimensions, feet (metres): 117.1 × 21.7 × 7.5 *(35.7 × 6.6 × 2.3)*
Main machinery: 3 MTU MB diesels; 4,050 hp(m) *(2.98 MW)*; 3 shafts; cp props
Speed, knots: 23
Complement: 9
Guns: 2—14.5 mm MGs (twin). 1—7.62 mm MG.
Radars: Surface search: I-band.

Comment: Acquired from Finland Frontier Guard in January 1995. ***UPDATED***

MARU   *6/1996*, Michael Nitz /* 0056942

3 KOSKELO CLASS (COASTAL PATROL CRAFT) (PC)

PVL 100 (ex-*Telkkä*)	**PVL 101** (ex-*Kuikka*)	**PVL 102** (ex-*Kaakkuri*)

Displacement, tons: 95 full load
Dimensions, feet (metres): 95.1 × 16.4 × 6.2 *(29 × 5 × 1.9)*
Main machinery: 2 MTU MB diesels; 2,700 hp(m) *(1.98 MW)*; 2 shafts
Speed, knots: 21
Complement: 8
Guns: 1—12.7 mm MG.
Radars: Surface search: I-band.

Comment: Acquired from the Finnish Coast Guard 16 November 1992 and transferred on 15 September 1993. Steel hulled craft built between 1955 and 1958 and modernised in 1973. ***UPDATED***

PVL 101   *10/1995*, Estonian Navy /* 0056945

1 PIKKER CLASS (COASTAL PATROL CRAFT) (PC)

Name	No	Builders	Launched	Commissioned
PIKKER	PVL 103	Talinn	23 Dec 1995	Apr 1996

Displacement, tons: 90 full load
Dimensions, feet (metres): 98.4 × 19 × 4.9 *(30 × 5.8 × 1.5)*
Main machinery: 2 12YH 18/20 diesels; 2,700 hp(m) *(1.98 MW)* sustained; 2 shafts
Speed, knots: 23
Complement: 5
Guns: 2—14.5 mm MGs (twin). 2—7.62 mm MGs.
Radars: Surface search: I-band.

Comment: Carries an RIB with a hydraulic launch crane aft. Intended to be the first of a series of 10 of which the other nine may be funded in due course. ***UPDATED***

PIKKER   *6/1999*, Estonian Border Guard /* 0056946

1 KEMIO CLASS (PG)

LINDA (ex-*Kemio*) PVL 108 (ex-93)

Displacement, tons: 340 full load
Dimensions, feet (metres): 118.1 × 29.5 × 9.8 *(36 × 9 × 3)*
Main machinery: 1 diesel; 670 hp(m) *(492 kW)*; 1 shaft
Speed, knots: 11
Complement: 8
Guns: 2—25 mm/60 (twin).

Comment: Built in 1958 as a buoy tender and converted to a command ship in 1983. Transferred in December 1992 having paid off from the Finnish Navy. Armament changed in 1988. Used by the Marine Education Seamanship School and also by the Border Guard as a patrol craft and transport. Based in Tallinn. ***UPDATED***

LINDA   *6/1999*, Estonian Border Guard /* 0056947

1 STORM CLASS (PCF)

Name	No	Builders	Launched
TORM (ex-*Arg*)	PVL 105 (ex-P968)	Bergens Mek, Verksteder	24 May 1966

Displacement, tons: 100 standard; 135 full load
Dimensions, feet (metres): 120 × 20 × 5 *(36.5 × 6.1 × 1.5)*
Main machinery: 2 MTU MB 16V 538 TB90 diesels; 6,000 hp(m) *(4.41 MW)* sustained; 2 shafts
Speed, knots: 32. **Range, miles:** 800 at 25 kt
Complement: 8
Guns: 2—25 mm/80 (twin). 2—14.5 mm MGs (twin).
Radars: Surface search: Racal Decca TM 1226; I-band.

Comment: Built in 1966 and paid off from the Norwegian Navy in 1991. Transferred 16 December 1994 stripped of all weapons and associated sensors. Rearmed in 1995 with light guns.
UPDATED

TORM   *6/1999*, Estonian Border Guard /* 0056948

1 SERNA CLASS (LCU)

Name	No	Builders	Commissioned
TIIR	PVL 104	Volga Shipyard, Russia	Oct 1994

Displacement, tons: 105 full load
Dimensions, feet (metres): 86.3 × 19 × 5.6 *(26.3 × 5.8 × 1.7)*
Main machinery: 2 M 503 A3 diesels; 5,522 hp(m) *(4.06 MW)*; 2 shafts
Speed, knots: 30. **Range, miles:** 600 at 22 kt
Complement: 6
Military lift: 45 tons or 100 troops

Comment: Same type is in service in the Russian Navy, and sold to the UAE commercially.
UPDATED

TIIR   *8/1996*, H Kajando /* 0012308

3 INSHORE PATROL CRAFT (PC)

PVK 001 (ex-*KBV 257*)   **PVK 002** (ex-*KBV 259*)   **PVK 003** (ex-*KBV 246*)

Displacement, tons: 17 full load
Dimensions, feet (metres): 63 × 13.1 × 4.3 *(19.2 × 4 × 1.3)*
Main machinery: 2 Volvo Penta TAMD120A diesels; 700 hp(m) *(515 kW)*; 2 shafts
Speed, knots: 22
Complement: 5
Guns: 1—7.62 mm MG.

Comment: Transferred on 4 April 1992, 20 October 1993 and 6 December 1993. Former Swedish Coast Guard vessel built in 1970. Similar craft to Latvia and Lithuania.
UPDATED

PVK 003   *8/1995*, Erki Holm /* 0056949

19 INSHORE PATROL CRAFT (PC)

PVK 006-008   **PVK 013-015**   **PVK 017-019**   **PVK 025**   **+9**

Comment: These are all launches of various types over 12 m except *PVK 017* (ex-*EVA 203*) which is a 44 ton MFV type of vessel built in Finland in 1963. *PVK 019* (ex-*EVA 206*) is a diving boat, *PVK 018* (ex-*EVA 204*) is a 22 kt craft built in Finland in 1993 and *PVK 006-008* and *013-015* are 13.7 ton icebreaking launches acquired from Finland. *PVK 008* and *013* are based on Lake Peipus. There is also a Jet Combi 10 power boat based on Lake Peipus. A further nine craft under 12 m have numbers *PVK 004-005, 009-012, 016, 020-021*. *PVK 025* is an ex-Swedish craft acquired in 1998.
UPDATED

PVK 006   *8/1994*, Erki Holm /* 0056950

PVK 015   *8/1995*, Estonian Navy /* 0056951

1 GRIFFON 2000 TDX Mk II (HOVERCRAFT)

PVH 1

Displacement, tons: 6.8 full load
Dimensions, feet (metres): 36.1 × 15.1 *(11 × 4.6)*
Main machinery: 1 Deutz BF8L 513 diesel; 320 hp *(293 kW)* sustained
Speed, knots: 33. **Range, miles:** 300 at 25 kt
Complement: 2
Military lift: 16 troops or 2 tons
Guns: 1—7.62 mm MG.

Comment: Similar to craft supplied to Finland. Acquired in 1999.
NEW ENTRY

PVH 1   *8/1999*, Estonian Border Guard /* 0056952

NATIONAL MARITIME BOARD (EVA)

Note: The board was re-established in 1991. Main base, also housing the logistic infrastructure and buoy storage areas, is in Tallin's harbour basin adjacent to the Estonian Naval Base. The EVA vessels have a blue hull and white superstructure. The majority of the vessels are former Russian naval units and not all are operational:

EVA 200 (ex-*Reet*), Russian research ship
EVA 307 (ex-*Zenit*), Russian survey ship 'Samara' class
EVA 308 (ex-*GS-108*, ex-*Vern'er*), Russian survey ship 'Kamenka' class
EVA 309-310, Russian inshore survey vessels type GPB 480
EVA 312-315, Russian inshore survey launch types
EVA 316 (ex-*Lonna*), Finnish 'Seili' class survey ship/buoy tender, built 1980
Tarmo, Finnish 'Tarmo' class icebreaker, built 1963, acquired 1994.
Karu, Finnish 'Karhu' class icebreaker acquired in 1993.

FAEROES

Headquarters Appointments

Head of Coast Guard:
  Captain Elmar Hojgaard

General

The Coast Guard and Fisheries come under the Landsstyri which is the islands' local government. Vessels work closely with the Danish Navy.

Personnel

2000: 60

Bases

Tórshavn (Isle of Streymoy)

Mercantile Marine

Lloyd's Register of Shipping:
  143 vessels of 103,659 tons gross

DELETIONS

1997   *Ólavur Halgi* (sold)
1999   *Nolsoyar Pall*

COAST GUARD

Note: A 36 m former Danish vessel *Gorm* (ex-*Naleraq*) is on charter in 2000. It is to be replaced by a new trawler type building in Norway in late 2000.

1 PATROL SHIP (PG)

TJALDRID

Displacement, tons: 650 full load
Dimensions, feet (metres): 146 × 33.1 × 10.5
  (44.5 × 10.1 × 3.2)
Main machinery: 2 MWM diesels; 2,400 hp(m) *(1.76 MW)*; 2 shafts
Speed, knots: 14.5
Complement: 18 plus 4 divers
Guns: 1 Oerlikon 20 mm can be carried.
Radars: Surface search: Raytheon TM/TCPA; I-band.

Comment: Originally a commercial tug built in 1976 by Svolvaer, Verksted and acquired by the local government in 1987. The old 57 mm gun has been replaced. A decompression chamber can be carried.

UPDATED

TJALDRID
12/1999*, Faeroes CG / 0080652

FALKLAND ISLANDS

General

A dependent territory of the United Kingdom. The capital and principal town is at Stanley. In 1986 Britain declared a fishing zone off the Falklands within which only licensed ships may work. On 26 December 1990 a further outer zone was declared, extending the original zones to 200 miles where possible.

Maritime Aircraft

There are two Pilatus Britten-Norman Defender unarmed maritime surveillance aircraft.

Mercantile Marine

Lloyd's Register of Shipping:
  24 vessels of 45,333 tons gross

DELETIONS

Patrol Forces

1997   *Fox*
1998   *Cordella*

PATROL FORCES

1 FISHERY PATROL SHIP

CRISCILLA

Measurement, tons: 924 grt
Dimensions, feet (metres): 175.9 × 37.1 × 24 *(53.62 × 11.31 × 7.32)*
Main machinery: 1 GEC Alsthom Ruston diesel; 2,500 hp *(1,865 MW)*; 1 shaft; cp prop
Speed, knots: 15
Complement: 15
Radars: Surface search: 1 Koden MD 3210; 1 Furuno 2110 ARPA; I-band.

Comment: Built in 1972. Chartered from Marr, Hull in April 1998 until May 2000 but may be renewed. Ship has red hull and white superstructure. Carries two RIBs capable of 30 kt.

UPDATED

1 FISHERY PATROL SHIP

DORADA

Measurement, tons: 2,360 grt
Dimensions, feet (metres): 249.3 × 47.9 × 20 *(76 × 14.6 × 6.1)*
Main machinery: 1 Sulzer-Cegielski diesel; 3,900 hp(m) *(2.87 MW)*; 1 shaft; cp prop; 1 ABB bow thruster; 340 hp *(250 kW)*
Speed, knots: 15.5. **Range, miles:** 14,000 at 12 kt
Complement: 15
Guns: 1 Oerlikon Mk VII A 20 mm.
Radars: Surface search: 2 Furuno 2120; I-band.

Comment: Stern trawler built in Poland in 1991 and refitted in New Zealand. Chartered in August 1997 for ten years from Dorada Marine. Has a red hull and white superstructure. Carries two RIBs capable of over 30 kt. Gun fitted in May 1999 but may not be carried all year round.

UPDATED

CRISCILLA   *6/1998, van Ginderen Collection /* 0017830

DORADA   *1/1998*, Falkland Islands /* 0012983

FIJI

Headquarters Appointments

Commander, Navy:
Captain J V Bainimarama

Personnel

2000: 300

Prefix to Ships' Names

RFNS (Republic of Fiji naval ship)

General

On 12 June 1975 the then Royal Fiji Military Forces were authorised to raise a Naval Division to carry out Fishery Protection, Surveillance, Hydrographic Surveying and Coast Guard duties. On 14 May 1987 a military coup overthrew the government and Fiji became a Republic on 10 October 1987. The Fiji Navy comes under the authority of the Minister of Home Affairs, and has been accountable to the CinC Military Forces since June 1989. Hydrography is a civilian responsibility.

Bases

RFNS *Viti,* at Togalevu (Training).
RFNS *Stanley Brown.*
Operation base at Walu Bay, Suva.

Mercantile Marine

Lloyd's Register of Shipping:
51 vessels of 28,668 tons gross

PATROL FORCES

Notes: (1) It is reported that two 45 m craft are required.
(2) *Cagi Donu* was civilianised in 1995 but has been taken back in the Navy as the President's Yacht.

3 PACIFIC FORUM CLASS (LARGE PATROL CRAFT) (PC)

Name	No	Builders	Commissioned
KULA	201	Transfield Shipbuilding	28 May 1994
KIKAU	202	Transfield Shipbuilding	27 May 1995
KIRO	203	Transfield Shipbuilding	14 Oct 1995

Displacement, tons: 162 full load
Dimensions, feet (metres): 103.3 × 26.6 × 6.9 *(31.5 × 8.1 × 2.1)*
Main machinery: 2 Caterpillar 3516TA diesels; 2,820 hp *(2.09 MW)* sustained; 2 shafts
Speed, knots: 20. **Range, miles:** 2,500 at 12 kt
Complement: 17 (4 officers)
Guns: 1—12.7 mm MG.
Radars: Surface search: Furuno; I-band.

Comment: Ordered in December 1992. These are hulls 17, 19 and 20 of the class offered by the Australian Government under Defence Co-operation Programme.   ***VERIFIED***

LAUTOKA   *8/1996*, Fiji Navy* / 0056953

4 VAI (DABUR) CLASS (COASTAL PATROL CRAFT) (PC)

VAI 301   **OGO** 302   **SAKU** 303   **SAQA** 304

Displacement, tons: 39 full load
Dimensions, feet (metres): 64.9 × 18 × 5.8 *(19.8 × 5.5 × 1.8)*
Main machinery: 4 GM 12V-71TA diesels; 1,680 hp *(1.25 MW)* sustained; 4 shafts
Speed, knots: 19. **Range, miles:** 450 at 13 kt
Complement: 9 (2 officers)
Guns: 2 Oerlikon 20 mm. 2—7.62 mm MGs.
Radars: Surface search: Racal Decca Super 101 Mk 3; I-band.

Comment: Built in mid-1970s by Israel Aircraft Industries and transferred from Israel 22 November 1991. ASW equipment is not fitted. Reported as being no longer required by the Navy and may be used by other government departments.   ***UPDATED***

KIRO   *9/1998, van Ginderen Collection* / 0017831

2 COASTAL PATROL CRAFT (PC)

Name	No	Builders	Recommissioned
LEVUKA	101	Beaux's Bay Craft, Louisiana	22 Oct 1987
LAUTOKA	102	Beaux's Bay Craft, Louisiana	28 Oct 1987

Displacement, tons: 97 full load
Dimensions, feet (metres): 110 × 24 × 5 *(33.8 × 7.4 × 1.5)*
Main machinery: 4 GM 12V-71TA diesels; 1,680 hp *(1.25 MW)* sustained; 4 shafts
Speed, knots: 12
Complement: 12 (2 officers)
Guns: 1—12.7 mm MG.
Radars: Surface search: Racal Decca; I-band.

Comment: Built in 1979-80 as oil rig support craft. Purchased in September 1987. All aluminium construction.   ***UPDATED***

SAQA   *6/1995** / 0056954

FINLAND
SUOMEN MERIVOIMAT

Headquarters Appointments

Commander-in-Chief Finnish Navy:
Rear Admiral Esko Illi
Chief of Staff FNHQ:
Captain Pertti Malmburg

Diplomatic Representation

Defence Attaché in London:
Commander I Bergholm
Defence Attaché in Moscow:
Captain Pertti Inkinen
Defence Attaché in Paris:
Colonel Arto-Pekka Nurminen

Personnel

(a) 2000: 2,350 regulars (after merger with Coastal Artillery in 1998)
(b) 5,100 conscripts (6-12 months' national service)

Fleet Organisation

Gulf of Finland Naval Command; main base Uppinniemi, Helsinki.
Archipelago Sea Naval Command; main base at Pansio, near Turku.
Kotka Coastal Command at Kotka.
Uusimaa Jaeger Brigade at Tammisaari.
Not all ships are fully manned all the time but all are rotated on a regular basis.

Coast Defence

Coastal Artillery and naval infantry troops. RBS 15 truck-mounted quadruple SSM launchers. 155 mm, 130 mm and 100 mm fixed and mobile guns.

Frontier Guard

All Frontier Guard vessels come under the Ministry of the Interior. The ships have dark green hulls with a thick red diagonal stripe superimposed by a thin white stripe. Superstructure is painted grey. Personnel numbers: 600.

Icebreakers

Icebreakers work for the Board of Navigation.

Mercantile Marine

Lloyd's Register of Shipping:
   279 vessels of 1,658,401 tons gross

DELETIONS

Corvettes

2000   *Turunmaa*

Patrol Forces

1997   *Kihu* (to Lithuania)
1999   *Rihtniemi, Rymättylä* (both to Estonia), *Tiira* (possibly to Latvia)

PENNANT LIST

Corvettes		72	Porvoo
		73	Naantali
04	Karjala	74	Hamina

	Mine Warfare Forces	
	01	Pohjanmaa
	02	Hämeenmaa
	05	Uusimaa
	11	Tuima
Patrol Forces	12	Tuisku
	14	Tuuli
30	Hurja (training)	15	Tyrsky
54	Raisio	21-26	Kuha 21-26
55	Röytta	521-	
56	Kajava (training)	527	Kiiski 1-7
57	Lokki (training)	575	Pyhäranta
60	Helsinki	576	Pansio
61	Turku	777	Porkkala
62	Oulu	826	Isku
63	Kotka		
70	Rauma		
71	Raahe		

Auxiliaries			339	Hästö
91	Viiri		371	Kampela 1
92	Putsaari		420	Parainen
96	Pikkala		430	Högsåra
97	Valas		431	Hakuni
98	Mursu		436	Houtskar
99	Kustaanmiekka		452	Lohm
121	Vahakari		511	Jymy
133	Havouri		521	Raju
171	Kala 1		531	Syöksy
222	Vaarlahti		541	Vinha
232	Hauki		731	Haukipää
235	Hirsala		776	Kala 6
237	Hila		799	Hylje
238	Harun		831	Kallanpää
241	Askeri		874	Kala 6
251	Lohi		877	Kampela 3
272	Kampela 2		899	Halli
323	Vänö		992	Träskö
334	Hankoniemi		993	Torsö

CORVETTES

1 TURUNMAA CLASS (FS)

Name	No	Builders	Laid down	Launched	Commissioned
KARJALA	04	Wärtsilä, Helsinki	Mar 1967	16 Aug 1967	21 Oct 1968

Displacement, tons: 660 standard; 770 full load
Dimensions, feet (metres): 243.1 × 25.6 × 7.9
   (74.1 × 7.8 × 2.4)
Main machinery: CODOG; 1 RR Olympus TM1A gas turbine; 15,000 hp *(11.2 MW)* sustained; 3 MTU MB diesels; 3,000 hp (m) *(2.2 MW)*; 3 shafts; cp props
Speed, knots: 35; 17 diesel. **Range, miles:** 2,500 at 14 kt
Complement: 70

Guns: 1 Bofors 4.7 in *(120 mm)*/46 ❶; 80 rds/min to 18.5 km *(10 n miles)*; weight of shell 21 kg. 6—103 mm rails for illuminants are fitted on the side of the mounting.
   2 Bofors 40 mm/70 ❷; 300 rds/min to 12 km *(6.6 n miles)*; weight of shell 0.96 kg.
   4 USSR 23 mm/87 (2 twin) ❸.
A/S mortars: 2 RBU 1200 5-tubed fixed launchers ❹ (mounted inside main deck superstructure abaft the pennant number); range 1,200 m; warhead 34 kg.
Depth charges: 2 racks.
Countermeasures: Decoys: Wallop Barricade double chaff launcher.
ESM: Argo ❺; radar intercept.
Weapons control: SAAB EOS-400 optronic director ❻.
Radars: Surface search: Terma 20T 48 Super ❼; E/F-band.
Fire control: Signaal WM22 ❽; I/J-band.
Navigation: Raytheon ARPA; I-band.
Sonars: Simrad; hull-mounted; active search and attack; high frequency. Optimised for operations in archipelago waters.

Programmes: Ordered on 18 February 1965.
Modernisation: Completed refit at the Wärtsilä Shipyard, Turku in 1986. New equipment included radar, EW and sonar.
Structure: Flush decked. Fitted with Vosper Thornycroft fin stabiliser equipment. The exhaust system is trunked on either side of the quarter-deck, the two plumes coalescing some 50 ft abaft the stern. These trunks are sometimes mistaken for torpedo tubes.
Operational: Second of class in reserve in 1999 and unlikely to go to sea again.

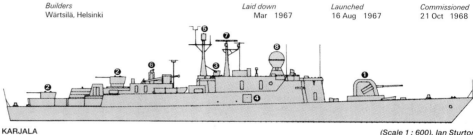

KARJALA   *(Scale 1 : 600), Ian Sturton*

UPDATED   KARJALA   *6/1995*, E & M Laursen* / 0069865

PATROL FORCES

2 RUISSALO CLASS (LARGE PATROL CRAFT) (PC)

Name	No	Builders	Commissioned
RAISIO	54	Laivateollisuus, Turku	12 Sep 1959
RÖYTTA	55	Laivateollisuus, Turku	14 Oct 1959

Displacement, tons: 110 standard; 130 full load
Dimensions, feet (metres): 108.9 × 18.5 × 5.9 *(33 × 5.6 × 1.8)*
Main machinery: 2 MTU MB diesels; 2,500 hp(m) *(1.84 MW)*; 2 shafts; cp props
Speed, knots: 17
Complement: 20
Guns: 4 USSR 23 mm/87 (2 twin).
A/S mortars: 2 RBU 1200 fixed 5-tubed launchers; range 1,200 m; warhead 34 kg.
Mines: Can lay mines.
Radars: Navigation: Decca 1226; I-band.
Sonars: Simrad; hull-mounted; active search and attack; high frequency.
Finnyards Sonac/PTA towed array; passive search; low frequency.

Comment: Ordered in January 1958. Launched on 2 June and 2 July 1959. Both modernised in 1980. Fitted with towed arrays in 1993 but have retained the after gun. Mostly used for navigation training.

UPDATED   RAISIO (with towed array)   *8/1993, Finnish Navy*

1 + (1) HAMINA CLASS (FAST ATTACK CRAFT—MISSILE) (PCFG)

Name	No	Builders	Commissioned
HAMINA	74	Aker Finnyards, Rauma	24 Aug 1998

Displacement, tons: 270 full load
Dimensions, feet (metres): 164 × 26.2 × 6.2 *(50.8 × 8.3 × 2)*
Main machinery: 2 MTU 16V 538 TB93 diesels; 7,510 hp(m) *(5.52 MW)* sustained; 2 Kamewa 90SII waterjets
Speed, knots: 32. **Range, miles:** 500 at 30 kt
Complement: 21 (5 officers)

Missiles: SSM: 6 Saab RBS 15SF; active radar homing to 150 km *(80 n miles)* at 0.8 Mach; warhead 200 kg.
SAM: 1 sextuple launcher; Matra Mistral; IR homing to 4 km *(2.2 n miles)*; warhead 3 kg.
Guns: Bofors 40 mm/70; 300 rds/min to 12 km *(6.6 n miles)*; weight of shell 0.96 kg.
  6—103 mm rails for rocket illuminants. 2—12.7 mm MGs.
  2 Sako 23 mm/87 (twin); can be fitted instead of Mistral launcher.
A/S mortars: 4 Saab Elma LLS-920 9-tubed launchers; range 300 m; warhead 4.2 kg shaped charge.
Depth charges: 1 rail.
Countermeasures: Decoys: Philax chaff and IR flares.
ESM: MEL Matilda; radar intercept.
Combat data systems: Signaal TACTICOS (trial in 2000).
Weapons control: Saab Dynamics EOS-400 optronic director.
Radars: Surface search: Signaal Scout; I-band.
Fire control: Bofors Electronic 9LV 225; J-band.
Navigation: Raytheon ARPA; I-band.
Sonars: Simrad Subsea Toadfish sonar; search and attack; active high frequency.
  Finnyards Sonac/PTA towed array; low frequency.

Programmes: Ordered on 31 December 1996. One more is planned. The original requirement for seven has been overtaken in favour of hovercraft orders.
Structure: A continuation of the Rauma design with greater use of composite materials. Aluminium hull. Signature reduction is aided by RAM coatings on the superstructure, submerged engine exhausts, upper deck pre-wetting, resilient mountings for all machinery, waterjet propulsion and conductive sealings on doors and hatches to prevent electromagnetic leakage.
A Signaal CDS system is under trial from February to August 2000.

UPDATED

HAMINA   8/1998*, Aker Finnyards / 0069866

4 RAUMA CLASS (FAST ATTACK CRAFT—MISSILE) (PCFG)

Name	No	Builders	Commissioned
RAUMA	70	Hollming, Rauma	18 Oct 1990
RAAHE	71	Hollming, Rauma	20 Aug 1991
PORVOO	72	Finnyards, Rauma	27 Apr 1992
NAANTALI	73	Finnyards, Rauma	23 June 1992

Displacement, tons: 215 standard; 248 full load
Dimensions, feet (metres): 157.5 × 26.2 × 4.5 *(48 × 8 × 1.5)*
Main machinery: 2 MTU 16V 538 TB93 diesels; 7,510 hp(m) *(5.52 MW)* sustained; 2 Riva Calzoni IRC 115 water-jets
Speed, knots: 30
Complement: 19 (5 officers)

Missiles: SSM: 6 Saab RBS 15SF (could embark 8); active radar homing to 150 km *(80 n miles)* at 0.8 Mach; warhead 200 kg.
SAM: 1 sextuple launcher; Matra Mistral; IR homing to 4 km *(2.2 n miles)*; warhead 3 kg.
Guns: 1 Bofors 40 mm/70; 300 rds/min to 12 km *(6.6 n miles)*; weight of shell 0.96 kg.
  6—103 mm rails for rocket illuminants. 2—12.7 mm MGs.
  2 Sako 23 mm/87 (twin); can be fitted instead of Mistral launcher.
A/S mortars: 4 Saab Elma LLS-920 9-tubed launchers; range 300 m; warhead 4.2 kg shaped charge.
Depth charges: 1 rail.
Countermeasures: Decoys: Philax chaff and IR flares.
ESM: MEL Matilda; radar intercept.
Weapons control: Bofors Electronic 9LV Mk 3 optronic director with TV camera; infra-red and laser telemetry.
Radars: Surface search: 9GA 208; I-band.
Fire control: Bofors Electronic 9LV 225; J-band.
Navigation: Raytheon ARPA; I-band.
Sonars: Simrad Subsea Toadfish sonar; search and attack; active high frequency.
  Finnyards Sonac/PTA towed array; low frequency.

Programmes: Ordered 27 August 1987.
Structure: Developed from 'Helsinki' class. Hull and superstructure of light alloy. SAM and 23 mm guns are interchangeable within the same Sako barbette which has replaced the ZU mounting.
Operational: Primary function is the anti-ship role but there is some ASW capability. Mine rails can be fitted in place of the missile launchers. Towed array cable is 78 m with 24 hydrophones and can be used at speeds between 3 and 12 kt.

UPDATED

4 HELSINKI CLASS (FAST ATTACK CRAFT—MISSILE) (PCFG)

Name	No	Builders	Commissioned
HELSINKI	60	Wärtsilä, Helsinki	1 Sep 1981
TURKU	61	Wärtsilä, Helsinki	3 June 1985
OULU	62	Wärtsilä, Helsinki	1 Oct 1985
KOTKA	63	Wärtsilä, Helsinki	16 June 1986

Displacement, tons: 280 standard; 300 full load
Dimensions, feet (metres): 147.6 × 29.2 × 9.9 *(45 × 8.9 × 3)*
Main machinery: 3 MTU 16V 538 TB92 diesels; 10,230 hp(m) *(7.52 MW)* sustained; 3 shafts
Speed, knots: 30
Complement: 30

Missiles: SSM: 8 Saab RBS 15; inertial guidance; active radar homing to 70 km *(37.8 n miles)* at 0.8 Mach; warhead 150 kg; sea-skimmer.
SAM: 2 sextuple launchers; Matra Mistral; IR homing to 4 km *(2.2 n miles)*; warhead 3 kg.
Guns: 1 Bofors 57 mm/70; 200 rds/min to 17 km *(9.3 n miles)*; weight of shell 2.4 kg. 6—103 mm rails for rocket illuminants.
  4 Sako 23 mm/87 (2 twin); can be fitted in place of Mistral launcher.
Depth charges: 2 rails.
Countermeasures: Decoys: Philax chaff and IR flare launcher.
ESM: Argo; radar intercept.
Weapons control: Saab EOS 400 optronic director.
Radars: Surface search: 9GA 208; I-band.
Fire control: Philips 9LV 225; J-band.
Navigation: Raytheon ARPA; I-band.
Sonars: Simrad Marine SS 304; high-resolution active scanning.
  Finnyards Sonac/PTA towed array; low frequency.

OULU   6/1998, Michael Nitz / 0052001

RAUMA   6/1999*, Maritime Photographic / 0069867   KOTKA   6/1996*, Michael Nitz / 0012315

0 + 1 (3) HOVERCRAFT

Displacement, tons: 84 full load
Dimensions, feet (metres): 89.9 × 50.5 *(27.4 × 15.4)*
Main machinery: 4 gas turbines (2 drive, 2 lift); 12,240 hp(m) *(9 MW)*; 2 cp air props
Speed, knots: 50
Complement: 10
Missiles: SSM, SAM.
Guns: 1—20 mm.
Torpedoes: or mines.
Radars: Surface search.

Comment: Ordered 9 July 1999 from Aker Finnyards as a prototype for a class of four to be put up for competitive tender. US assistance being given with hovercraft technology. This first craft to be delivered in September 2001. Armament will vary, depending upon task.
NEW ENTRY

MULTIPURPOSE HOVERCRAFT (artist's impression)
1999*, Aker Finnyards / 0069868

MINE WARFARE FORCES

Notes: (1) A new class of light minehunters may be built in due course.
(2) In addition there are two 130 ton minelaying dumb barges (721 and 821) built in 1987.

2 HÄMEENMAA CLASS (MINELAYERS) (ML)

Name	No	Builders	Laid down	Launched	Commissioned
HÄMEENMAA	02	Finnyards, Rauma	2 Apr 1991	11 Nov 1991	15 Apr 1992
UUSIMAA	05	Finnyards, Rauma	12 Nov 1991	June 1992	2 Dec 1992

Displacement, tons: 1,330 full load
Dimensions, feet (metres): 252.6 oa; 228.3 wl × 38.1 × 9.8 *(77; 69.6 × 11.6 × 3)*
Main machinery: 2 Wärtsilä 16V22 diesels; 6,300 hp(m) *(4.64 MW)* sustained; 2 Kamewa cp props; bow thruster; 247 hp(m) *(184 kW)*
Speed, knots: 19
Complement: 70

Missiles: SAM: 1 sextuple launcher; Matra Mistral; IR homing to 4 km *(2.2 n miles)*; warhead 3 kg.
Guns: 2 Bofors 40 mm/70; 300 rds/min to 12 km *(6.6 n miles)*; weight of shell 0.96 kg.
4 or 6 Sako 23 mm/87 (2 or 3 twin) (the third mounting is interchangeable with Mistral launcher).
A/S mortars: 2 RBU 1200 fixed 5-tubed launchers; range 1,200 m; warhead 34 kg.
Depth charges: 2 racks for 16 DCs.
Mines: 4 rails for 100-150.
Countermeasures: Decoys: 2 ML/Wallop Superbarricade multichaff and IR launchers.
ESM: MEL Matilda; intercept.
Weapons control: Radamec System 2400 optronic director; 2 Galileo optical directors.
Radars: Surface search and Navigation: 3 Selesmar ARPA; I-band.

UUSIMAA   *6/1999*, Maritime Photographic /* 0069869

Sonars: Simrad; hull-mounted; active mine detection; high frequency.

Programmes: First one ordered 29 December 1989 after the original order in July from Wärtsilä had been cancelled. Second ordered 13 February 1991. Dual role as a transport and support ship.

Structure: Steel hull and alloy superstructure. Ice strengthened (Ice class 1A) and capable of breaking up to 40 mm ice. Ramps in bow and stern. The Mistral launcher is mounted at the stern. SAM system can be replaced by a third twin 23 mm mounting within the same barbette.
UPDATED

1 MINELAYER (ML)

Name	No	Builders	Laid down	Launched	Commissioned
POHJANMAA	01	Wärtsilä, Helsinki	4 May 1978	28 Aug 1978	8 June 1979

Displacement, tons: 1,000 standard; 1,100 full load
Dimensions, feet (metres): 255.8 × 37.7 × 9.8 *(78.2 × 11.6 × 3)*
Main machinery: 2 Wärtsilä Vasa 16V22 diesels; 6,300 hp(m) *(4.64 MW)* sustained; 2 shafts; cp props; bow thruster
Speed, knots: 19. **Range, miles:** 3,500 at 15 kt
Complement: 90

Missiles: SAM: 2 sextuple launchers; Matra Mistral; IR homing to 4 km *(2.2 n miles)*; warhead 3 kg.
Guns: 1 Bofors 57 mm/70; 200 rds/min to 17 km *(9.3 n miles)*; weight of shell 2.4 kg.
6—103 mm launchers for illuminants fitted to the mounting.
2 Bofors 40 mm/70; 300 rds/min to 12 km *(6.6 n miles)*; weight of shell 0.96 kg.
4 Sako 23 mm/87 (2 twin). 2—12.7 mm MGs.
A/S mortars: 2 RBU 1200 fixed 5-tubed launchers; range 1,200 m; warhead 34 kg.
Depth charges: 2 rails.
Mines: 120 including UK Stonefish.
Countermeasures: Decoys: Philax chaff and IR flare launcher.
ESM: Argo; radar intercept.
Radars: Air search: Signaal DA05; E/F-band.
Fire control: Phillips 9LV 220; J-band.
Navigation: I-band.

POHJANMAA   *5/1998, Per Kornefeldt /* 0052005

Sonars: Simrad; hull-mounted; active search and attack; high frequency.
Bottom classification; search; high frequency.

Programmes: Design completed 1976. Ordered late 1977.
Modernisation: In 1992 the forward 23 mm guns were replaced by 12.7 mm MGs. Major refit in 1996-98 to replace the main gun, improve air defences and minelaying capability. The SAM mounting is interchangeable with 23 mm guns.
Operational: Also serves as training ship. Carries 70 trainees accommodated in Portakabins on the mine deck. Helicopter area on quarterdeck but no hangar.
VERIFIED

3 PANSIO CLASS (MINELAYERS—LCU TYPE) (MLI)

Name	No	Builders	Commissioned
PANSIO	576 (ex-876)	Olkiluoto Shipyard	25 Sep 1991
PYHÄRANTA	575 (ex-475)	Olkiluoto Shipyard	26 May 1992
PORKKALA	777	Olkiluoto Shipyard	29 Oct 1992

Displacement, tons: 450 standard
Dimensions, feet (metres): 144.3 oa; 128.6 wl × 32.8 × 6.6 *(44; 39.2 × 10 × 2)*
Main machinery: 2 MTU 12V 183 TE62 diesels; 1,500 hp(m) *(1.1 MW)*; 2 shafts; bow thruster
Speed, knots: 10
Complement: 12
Guns: 2 ZU 23 mm/87 (twin). 1—12.7 mm MG.
Mines: 50.
Radars: Navigation: Raytheon ARPA; I-band.

Comment: Ordered in May 1990. Used for inshore minelaying and transport with a capacity of 100 tons. Ice strengthened with ramps in bow and stern. Has a 15 ton crane fitted aft.
UPDATED

PYHÄRANTA   *9/1999*, E & M Laursen /* 0069870

4 TUIMA (MODIFIED OSA II) CLASS (MINELAYERS) (MLI)

TUIMA 11   **TUISKU** 12   **TUULI** 14   **TYRSKY** 15

Displacement, tons: 245 full load
Dimensions, feet (metres): 110.2 × 24.9 × 8.8 *(33.6 × 7.6 × 2.7)*
Main machinery: 3 Type M 504 diesels; 10,800 hp(m) *(7.94 MW)* sustained; 3 shafts
Speed, knots: 35. **Range, miles:** 500 at 35 kt
Complement: 28
Guns: 4 USSR 30 mm/65 (2 twin).
Mines: 30.
Radars: Surface search: Raytheon ARPA; I-band.

Comment: Ex-USSR Osa IIs purchased in 1974. Converted in 1993 *(Tuima)* and 1994 *(Tuuli)* to minelayers with missile systems removed and a new radar fitted. The other pair had their missiles removed by the end of 1995 and similarly converted in 1996. An hydraulic crane is used for RIB launch and recovery.

VERIFIED

TUIMA   *4/1994, van Ginderen Collection*

1 TRIALS SHIP (MLI)

Name	No	Builders	Launched	Commissioned
ISKU	826 (ex-16)	Reposaaron Konepaja	4 Dec 1969	1970

Displacement, tons: 180 full load
Dimensions, feet (metres): 108.5 × 28.5 × 5.9 *(33 × 8.7 × 1.8)*
Main machinery: 4 Type M 50 diesels; 4,400 hp(m) *(3.3 MW)* sustained; 4 shafts
Speed, knots: 18
Complement: 25
Radars: Navigation: Raytheon ARPA; I-band.

Comment: Formerly a missile experimental craft, now used for various equipment trials. Modernised in 1989-90 by Uusikaupunki Shipyard and lengthened by 7 m. Can quickly be converted to a minelayer.

VERIFIED

ISKU   *1990, Finnish Navy*

6 KUHA CLASS (MINESWEEPERS—INSHORE) (MSI)

Name	No	Builders	Commissioned
KUHA 21—26	21—26	Laivateollisuus, Turku	1974-75

Displacement, tons: 90 full load
Dimensions, feet (metres): 87.2; 104 × 22.7 × 6.6 *(26.6; 31.7 × 6.9 × 2)*
Main machinery: 2 Cummins MT-380M diesels; 600 hp(m) *(448 kW)*; 1 shaft; cp prop; active rudder
Speed, knots: 12
Complement: 15 (3 officers)
Guns: 2 ZU 23 mm/60 (twin). 1—12.7 mm MG.
Radars: Navigation: Decca; I-band.
Sonars: Reson Seabat 6012 mine avoidance; active high frequency.

Comment: All ordered 1972. First one completed 28 June 1974, and last on 13 November 1975. Fitted for magnetic, acoustic and pressure-mine clearance. Hulls are of GRP. May carry a Pluto ROV. Four of the class were lengthened in 1997/98 to take a new minesweeping control system, and new magnetic and acoustic sweeps. New sonars installed.

UPDATED

KUHA 24 (lengthened)   *9/1999 *, E & M Laursen / 0069871*

7 KIISKI CLASS (MINESWEEPERS—INSHORE) (MSI)

Name	No	Builders	Commissioned
KIISKI 1-7	521-527	Fiskars, Turku	1983-84

Displacement, tons: 20 full load
Dimensions, feet (metres): 49.9 × 13.4 × 3.3 *(15.2 × 4.1 × 1.2)*
Main machinery: 2 Valmet 611 CSMP diesels; 340 hp(m) *(250 kW)*; 2 Hamilton water-jets
Speed, knots: 11. **Range, miles:** 260 at 11 kt
Complement: 4

Comment: Ordered January 1983. All completed by 24 May 1984. GRP hull. Built to be used with 'Kuha' class for unmanned teleguided sweeping, but this was not successful and they are now used for manned magnetic and acoustic sweeping operations with crew of four.

UPDATED

KIISKI 5   *5/1993 *, van Ginderen Collection / 0069872*

ICEBREAKERS

Note: Controlled by Board of Navigation which also operates 13 transport ships and nine oil recovery vessels. There is also the German-owned, Finnish-manned, icebreaker *Hansa*, of the 'Karhu' class, completed on 25 November 1966, which operates off Germany in Winter and off Finland at other times.

2 KARHU 2 CLASS (AGB)

OTSO   KONTIO

Measurement, tons: 9,200 dwt
Dimensions, feet (metres): 324.7 × 79.4 × 26.2 *(99 × 24.2 × 8)*
Main machinery: Diesel-electric; 4 Wärtsilä Vasa 16V32 diesel generators; 22.84 MW 60 Hz sustained; 2 motors; 17,700 hp(m) *(13 MW)*; 2 shafts; 2 thrusters
Speed, knots: 18.5
Complement: 28
Helicopters: 1 light.

Comment: First ordered from Wärtsilä 29 March 1984, completed 30 January 1986. Second ordered 29 November 1985, delivered 29 January 1987. Fitted with Wärtsilä bubbler system. One other transferred to Estonia in 1993.

UPDATED

KONTIO   *1/1987 *, Wärtsilä / 0069873*

2 URHO CLASS (AGB)

URHO   SISU

Displacement, tons: 7,800 *Urho* (7,900, *Sisu*) standard; 9,500 full load
Dimensions, feet (metres): 343.1 × 78.1 × 27.2 *(104.6 × 23.8 × 8.3)*
Main machinery: Diesel-electric; 5 Wärtsilä-SEMT-Pielstick diesel generators; 25,000 hp(m) *(18.37 MW)*; 4 motors; 22,000 hp(m) *(16.2 MW)*; 4 shafts (2 fwd, 2 aft (cp props))
Speed, knots: 18
Complement: 47
Helicopters: 1 light.

Comment: Built by Wärtsilä and commissioned on 5 March 1975 and 28 January 1976 respectively. Fitted with two screws aft, taking 60 per cent of available power and two forward, taking the remainder. Similar to Swedish 'Atle' class.
UPDATED

SISU   *4/1994*, van Ginderen Collection /* 0069874

1 TARMO CLASS (AGB)

APU

Displacement, tons: 4,890 full load
Dimensions, feet (metres): 281 × 71 × 23.9 *(85.7 × 21.7 × 7.3)*
Main machinery: Diesel-electric; 4 Wärtsilä-Sulzer diesel generators; 12,000 hp(m) *(8.82 MW)*; 4 shafts (2 screws fwd, 2 aft)
Speed, knots: 17. **Range, miles:** 7,000 at 17 kt
Complement: 45-55
Helicopters: 1 light.

Comment: Built by Wärtsilä and commissioned in 1970. Two others transferred to Latvia and Estonia in 1994.
UPDATED

APU   *2/1994*, van Ginderen Collection /* 0069875

2 FENNICA CLASS (AGB)

FENNICA   NORDICA

Measurement, tons: 1,650 (Winter); 3,900 (Arctic); 4,800 (Summer) dwt
Dimensions, feet (metres): 380.5 × 85.3 × 27.6 *(116 × 26 × 8.4)*
Main machinery: Diesel-electric; 2 Wärtsilä Vasa 16V32D/ABB Strömberg diesel generators; 12 MW; 2 Wärtsilä Vasa 12V32D/ABB Strömberg diesel generators; 9 MW; 2 ABB Strömberg motors; 2 Aquamaster US ARC 1 nozzles; 20,400 hp(m) *(15 MW)*; 3 Brunvoll bow thrusters; 6,120 hp(m) *(4.5 MW)*
Speed, knots: 16
Complement: 16 + 80 passengers
Radars: Navigation: 2 Selemar; I-band.
Helicopters: 1 light.

Comment: First of class ordered in October 1991, second in May 1992, from Finnyards, Rauma. *Fennica* launched 10 September 1992 and completed 15 March 1993. *Nordica* launched July 1993 and completed January 1994. Bollard pull 230 tons. Capable of 8 kt at 0.8 m level ice and continuous slow speed at 1.8 m arctic level ice. 115 ton A frame and two deck cranes of 15 and 5 tons each. Combination of azimuth propulsion units and bow thrusters gives full dynamic positioning capability.
UPDATED

FENNICA   *5/1994*, Erik Laursen /* 0069876

TRAINING SHIPS

Note: *Hurja* 30, a patrol craft, is used by the Naval Reserve.

2 LOKKI CLASS (AX)

Name	No	Builders	Commissioned
LOKKI	57	Valmet/Lavateollisuus	28 Aug 1986
KAJAVA	56	Valmet/Lavateollisuus	3 Oct 1981

Displacement, tons: 59 *(Lokki)*; 64
Dimensions, feet (metres): 87.9 × 18 × 6.2 *(26.8 × 5.5 × 1.9)*
    87.9 × 17.1 × 8.5 *(26.8 × 5.2 × 2.1) (Lokki)*
Main machinery: 2 MTU 8V 396 TB82 diesels; 1,740 hp(m) *(1.28 MW)* sustained *(Lokki)*
    2 MTU 8V 396 TB84 diesels; 2,100 hp(m) *(1.54 MW)* sustained; 2 shafts
Speed, knots: 25
Complement: 6
Guns: 2 ZU 23 mm/60 can be carried.
Sonars: Simrad SS 242; hull-mounted; active search; high frequency.

Comment: Transferred from the Frontier Guard to the Navy in 1999 and used as training vessels. Built in light metal alloy. *Lokki* has a V-shaped hull. A third of class to Lithuania in 1997, and possibly a fourth to Latvia in 2000.
UPDATED

LOKKI (old colours)   *6/1990*, van Ginderen Collection /* 0069877

3 TRAINING SHIPS (AX)

681   683   685

Comment: Naval Academy training ships.
UPDATED

681   *5/1997*, N A Sifferlinger /* 0012319

AUXILIARIES

1 KEMIO CLASS (COMMAND SHIP) (AGF/AGI)

KUSTAANMIEKKA (ex-*Valvoja III*) 99

Displacement, tons: 340 full load
Dimensions, feet (metres): 118.1 × 29.5 × 9.8 *(36 × 9 × 3)*
Main machinery: 1 Burmeister & Wain diesel; 670 hp(m) *(492 kW)*; 1 shaft
Speed, knots: 11
Complement: 10
Guns: 2—12.7 mm MGs (not always carried).

Comment: Completed in 1963. Former buoy tender transferred from Board of Navigation and converted by Hollming, Rauma in 1989. Bofors 40 mm gun removed in 1988. A ship of the same class transferred to Estonia in 1992.
UPDATED

KUSTAANMIEKKA   *4/1994, van Ginderen Collection*

5 VALAS CLASS (GP TRANSPORTS) (AKSL)

VALAS 97   **MURSU** 98   **VAHAKARI** 121   **VAARLAHTI** 222   **VANO** 323

Displacement, tons: 285 full load
Dimensions, feet (metres): 100.4 × 26.5 × 10.4 *(30.6 × 8.1 × 3.2)*
Main machinery: 1 Wärtsilä Vasa 8V22 diesel; 1,576 hp(m) *(1.16 MW)* sustained; 1 shaft
Speed, knots: 12
Complement: 11
Military lift: 35 tons or 150 troops
Guns: 2—23 mm/60 (twin). 1—12.7 mm MG.
Mines: 28 can be carried.
Radars: Navigation: Decca 1226; I-band.

Comment: Completed 1979-80. *Mursu* acts as a diving tender. Funnel is offset to starboard. Can be used as minelayers or transport/cargo carriers and are capable of breaking thin ice. *UPDATED*

VALAS   *7/1998*, van Ginderen Collection /* 0069878

3 KAMPELA CLASS (LCU TRANSPORTS) (LCU/AKSL)

Name	No	Builders	Commissioned
KAMPELA 1	371	Enso Gutzeit	29 July 1976
KAMPELA 2	272	Enso Gutzeit	21 Oct 1976
KAMPELA 3	877	Finnmekano	23 Oct 1979

Displacement, tons: 90 light; 260 full load
Dimensions, feet (metres): 106.6 × 26.2 × 4.9 *(32.5 × 8 × 1.5)*
Main machinery: 2 Scania diesels; 460 hp(m) *(338 kW)*; 2 shafts
Speed, knots: 9
Complement: 10
Guns: 2 or 4 ZU 23 mm/60 (1 or 2 twin).
Mines: About 20 can be carried.

Comment: Can be used as amphibious craft, transports, minelayers or for shore support. Armament can be changed to suit role. *UPDATED*

KAMPELA 2   *5/1993*, A Sheldon Duplaix /* 0069879

3 KALA CLASS (LCU TRANSPORTS) (LCU/AKSL)

KALA 1 171   **KALA 4** 874   **KALA 6** 776

Displacement, tons: 60 light; 200 full load
Dimensions, feet (metres): 88.6 × 26.2 × 6 *(27 × 8 × 1.8)*
Main machinery: 2 Valmet diesels; 360 hp(m) *(265 kW)*; 2 shafts
Speed, knots: 9
Complement: 10
Guns: 2 Oerlikon 20 mm (not in all).
Mines: 34.
Radars: Navigation: Decca 1226; I-band.

Comment: Completed between 20 June 1956 *(Kala 1)* and 4 December 1959 *(Kala 6)*. Can be used as coastal transports, amphibious craft, minelayers or for shore support. Armament can be changed to suit role. Pennant numbers changed in 1990. *UPDATED*

KALA 6   *7/1988*, A Sheldon Duplaix /* 0069880

6 HAUKI CLASS (TRANSPORTS) (AKSL)

HAVOURI 133	**HIRSALA** 235	**HAKUNI** 431
HAUKI 232	**HANKONIEMI** 334	**HOUTSKÄR** 436

Displacement, tons: 45 full load
Dimensions, feet (metres): 47.6 × 15.1 × 7.2 *(14.5 × 4.6 × 2.2)*
Main machinery: 2 Valmet 611 CSM diesels; 586 hp(m) *(431 kW)*; 1 shaft
Speed, knots: 12
Complement: 4
Cargo capacity: 6 tons or 40 passengers
Radars: Navigation: I-band.

Comment: Completed 1979. Ice strengthened; two serve isolated island defences. Four converted in 1988 as tenders to the Marine War College, but from 1990 back in service as light transports. *VERIFIED*

HOUTSKÄR   *9/1996, Hartmut Ehlers /* 0012318

4 HILA CLASS (TRANSPORTS) (AKSL)

HILA 237   **HARUN** 238   **HÄSTÖ** 339   **HÖGSÅRA** 430

Displacement, tons: 50 full load
Dimensions, feet (metres): 49.2 × 13.1 × 5.9 *(15 × 4 × 1.8)*
Main machinery: 2 diesels; 416 hp(m) *(306 kW)*; 2 shafts
Speed, knots: 12
Complement: 4

Comment: Ordered from Kotkan Telakka in August 1990. Second pair completed in 1994. Ice strengthened. *UPDATED*

HILA   *10/1991* /* 0069881

2 LOHI CLASS (LCU TRANSPORTS) (LCU)

LOHI 251   **LOHM** 452

Displacement, tons: 38 full load
Dimensions, feet (metres): 65.6 × 19.7 × 3 *(20 × 6 × 0.9)*
Main machinery: 2 WMB diesels; 1,200 hp(m) *(882 kW)*; 2 water-jets
Speed, knots: 20. **Range, miles:** 240 at 20 kt
Complement: 4
Guns: 2 ZU 23 mm/60 (twin). 1—14.5 mm MG.

Comment: Commissioned September 1984. Used as troop carriers and for light cargo. Guns not always carried. *UPDATED*

LOHM   *7/1988*, A Sheldon Duplaix /* 0069882

2 TRANSPORT and COMMAND LAUNCHES (YFB)

ASKERI 241   VIIRI 91

Displacement, tons: 25 full load
Dimensions, feet (metres): 52.6 × 14.5 × 4.5 *(16 × 4.4 × 1.4)*
Main machinery: 2 Volvo Penta diesels; 1,100 hp(m) *(808 kW)*; 2 shafts
Speed, knots: 22
Complement: 6
Radars: Surface search: I-band.
Navigation: Raytheon; I-band.

Comment: Both completed in 1992. Closely resemble Spanish 'PVC II' class.
                                                          VERIFIED

VIIRI   *12/1994, Finnish Navy*

7 VIHURI CLASS (COMMAND LAUNCHES) (YFB)

JYMY 511   SYÖKSY 531   TRÄSKÖ 992   ALSKÄR 994
RAJU 512   VINHA 541   TORSÖ 993

Displacement, tons: 13 full load
Dimensions, feet (metres): 42.7 × 13.1 × 3 *(13 × 4 × 0.9)*
Main machinery: 2 diesels; 772 hp(m) *(567 kW)*; 2 water-jets
Speed, knots: 30
Complement: 6
Radars: Surface search: I-band.

Comment: First of class *Vihuri* delivered in 1988, the next five in 1991 and the last pair in 1993. *Träskö, Torsö* and *Alskär* act as fast transports. The remainder are command launches for Navy squadrons. *Vihuri* was destroyed by fire in late 1991.   **UPDATED**

VINHA   *5/1993*, van Ginderen Collection / 0069883

29 MERIUISKO CLASS (LCP)

Displacement, tons: 10 full load
Dimensions, feet (metres): 36 × 11.5 × 2.9 *(11 × 3.5 × 0.9)*
Main machinery: 2 Volvo TAMD70E diesels; 418 hp(m) *(307 kW)* sustained; 2 Hamilton water-jets
Speed, knots: 36; 30 full load
Complement: 3
Military lift: 48 troops
Radars: Navigation (U 401 series): I-band.

Comment: First batch of 11 completed by Alumina Varvet from 1983 to 1986. Last four ordered in 1989. Constructed of light alloy. Two of the class equipped with cable handling system for boom defence work. Batch one has smaller cabins.   **UPDATED**

MERIUISKO   *8/1994*, E & M Laursen / 0069884

1 SUPPORT SHIP (ATA)

PARAINEN (ex-*Pellinki*, ex-*Meteor*) 420 (ex-210)

Displacement, tons: 404 full load
Dimensions, feet (metres): 126.3 × 29.5 × 14.8 *(38.5 × 9 × 4.5)*
Main machinery: 1 diesel; 1,800 hp(m) *(1.32 MW)*; 1 shaft
Speed, knots: 13
Complement: 17
Guns: 1 Madsen 20 mm can be carried.
Radars: Navigation: I-band.

Comment: Built as a tug in 1960. Acquired late 1980 from Oy Neptun Ab and modernised in 1987 by Teijon Telakka.
                                             UPDATED

PARAINEN   *2/1999*, van Ginderen Collection / 0069885

1 CABLE SHIP (ANL)

PUTSAARI 92

Displacement, tons: 45
Dimensions, feet (metres): 149.5 × 28.6 × 8.2 *(45.6 × 8.7 × 2.5)*
Main machinery: 1 Wärtsilä diesel; 510 hp(m) *(375 kW)*; 1 shaft; active rudder; bow thruster
Speed, knots: 10
Complement: 20

Comment: Built by Rauma-Repola, Rauma, launched on 15 December 1965 and commissioned in 1966. Modernised by Wärtsilä in 1987. Fitted with two 10 ton cable winches. Strengthened for ice operations.
                                           VERIFIED

PUTSAARI   *1992, Finnish Navy*

1 SUPPORT CRAFT (YFB)

PIKKALA (ex-*Fenno*) 96

Displacement, tons: 66 full load
Dimensions, feet (metres): 75.5 × 14.4 × 6.6 *(23 × 4.4 × 2)*
Main machinery: 1 Valmet diesel; 177 hp(m) *(130 kW)*; 1 shaft
Speed, knots: 10
Complement: 5

Comment: Used for utility and transport roles at Helsinki. Commissioned in June 1946 at Turhu.
                                           VERIFIED

PIKKALA   *9/1996, Hartmut Ehlers*

2 POLLUTION CONTROL VESSELS (AOS)

HYLJE 799 **HALLI** 899

Displacement, tons: 1,500 *(Hylje)*; 1,600 *(Halli)* full load
Dimensions, feet (metres): 164; 198.5 *(Halli)* × 41 × 9.8 *(50; 60.5 × 12.5 × 3)*
Main machinery: 2 Saab diesels; 680 hp(m) *(500 kW)*; 2 shafts; active rudders; bow thruster *(Hylje)*
2 Wärtsilä diesels; 2,650 hp(m) *(19.47 MW)*; 2 shafts; active rudders *(Halli)*
Speed, knots: 7 *(Hylje)*; 13 *(Halli)*

Comment: Painted grey. Strengthened for ice. Owned by Ministry of Environment, civilian-manned but operated by Navy from Turku. *Hylje* commissioned 3 June 1981, *Halli* in January 1987. Capacity is about 550 m³ *(Hylje)* and 1,400 m³ *(Halli)* of contaminated seawater. The ships have slightly different superstructure lines aft.

UPDATED

HALLI *5/1993*, van Ginderen Collection /* 0069886

TUGS

2 HARBOUR TUGS (YTM)

HAUKIPÄÄ 731 **KALLANPÄÄ** 831

Displacement, tons: 38 full load
Dimensions, feet (metres): 45.9 × 16.4 × 7.5 *(14 × 5 × 2.3)*
Main machinery: 2 diesels; 360 hp(m) *(265 kW)*; 2 shafts
Speed, knots: 9
Complement: 2

Comment: Delivered by Teijon Telakka Oy in December 1985. Similar to 'Hauki' class. Also used as utility craft.

UPDATED

KALLANPÄÄ *5/1993*, van Ginderen Collection /* 0069887

FRONTIER GUARD

1 IMPROVED TURSAS CLASS (OFFSHORE PATROL VESSEL) (OPV)

MERIKARHU

Displacement, tons: 1,100 full load
Dimensions, feet (metres): 189.6 × 36.1 × 15.1 *(57.8 × 11 × 4.6)*
Main machinery: 2 Wärtsilä Vasa 8R26 diesels; 3,808 hp(m) *(2.8 MW)* sustained; 1 shaft; cp prop; bow and stern thrusters
Speed, knots: 15. **Range, miles:** 2,000 at 15 kt
Complement: 30
Guns: 2—23 mm/87 (twin) can be carried.
Radars: Surface search. Navigation.

Comment: Ordered 17 June 1993 from Finnyards, and completed 28 October 1994. Capable of 5 kt in 50 cm of ice. Used as an all-weather patrol ship in the Baltic, capable of Command, SAR, tug work with 30 ton bollard pull, and environmental pollution cleaning up. Carries an RIB launched from a hydraulic crane.

UPDATED

MERIKARHU *6/1999*, van Ginderen Collection /* 0069888

2 TURSAS CLASS (OFFSHORE PATROL VESSELS) (OPV)

TURSAS **UISKO**

Displacement, tons: 730 full load
Dimensions, feet (metres): 160.8 × 34.1 × 13.1 *(49 × 10.4 × 4)*
Main machinery: 2 Wärtsilä Vasa 8R22 diesels; 3,152 hp(m) *(2.32 MW)* sustained; 2 shafts
Speed, knots: 16
Complement: 32
Guns: 2 Sako 23 mm/60 (twin).
Sonars: Simrad SS105; active scanning; 14 kHz.

Comment: First ordered from Rauma-Repola on 21 December 1984, launched 31 January 1986 and delivered 6 June 1986. Second ordered 20 March 1986, launched 19 June 1986 and delivered 27 January 1987. Operate as offshore patrol craft and can act as salvage tugs. Ice strengthened. *UPDATED*

UISKO *5/1994, van Ginderen Collection*

1 IMPROVED VALPAS CLASS (OFFSHORE PATROL VESSEL) (OPV)

TURVA

Displacement, tons: 550 full load
Dimensions, feet (metres): 159.1 × 28 × 12.8 *(48.5 × 8.6 × 3.9)*
Main machinery: 2 Wärtsilä diesels; 2,000 hp(m) *(1.47 MW)*; 1 shaft
Speed, knots: 15
Complement: 23
Guns: 1 Oerlikon 20 mm.
Sonars: Simrad SS105; active scanning; 14 kHz.

Comment: Built by Laivateollisuus, Turku and commissioned 15 December 1977. Armament changed in 1992. *UPDATED*

TURVA *6/1993*, van Ginderen Collection /* 0069889

1 + 2 TELKKÄ CLASS (OPV)

TELKKÄ

Displacement, tons: 400 full load
Dimensions, feet (metres): 160.8 × 24.6 × 11.8 *(49 × 7.5 × 3.6)*
Main machinery: 2 diesels; 6,120 hp(m) *(4.5 MW)*; 2 shafts
Speed, knots: 20
Complement: 17
Guns: 1—20 mm.
Sonars: Sonac PTA; towed array; low frequency.

Comment: First of class entered service in July 1999. Two more being built. *NEW ENTRY*

1 VALPAS CLASS (OFFSHORE PATROL VESSEL) (OPV)

VALPAS

Displacement, tons: 545 full load
Dimensions, feet (metres): 159.1 × 27.9 × 12.5 *(48.5 × 8.5 × 3.8)*
Main machinery: 1 Werkspoor diesel; 2,000 hp(m) *(1.47 MW)*; 1 shaft; cp prop
Speed, knots: 15
Complement: 18
Guns: 1 Oerlikon 20 mm.
Sonars: Simrad SS105; active scanning; 14 kHz.

Comment: An improvement on the *Silmä* design. Built by Laivateollisuus, Turku, and commissioned 21 July 1971. Ice strengthened. **UPDATED**

VALPAS   *1/1990*, van Ginderen Collection / 0069890

2 KIISLA CLASS (COASTAL PATROL CRAFT) (PC)

KIISLA   KURKI

Displacement, tons: 270 full load
Dimensions, feet (metres): 158.5 × 28.9 × 7.2 *(48.3 × 8.8 × 2.2)*
Main machinery: 2 MTU 16V 538 TB93 diesels; 7,510 hp(m) *(6.9 MW)* sustained; 2 Kamewa 90 water-jets
Speed, knots: 25
Complement: 10
Guns: 2 USSR 23 mm/60 (twin) or 1 Madsen 20 mm.
Weapons control: Radamec 2100 optronic director.
Sonars: Simrad SS304 hull-mounted and VDS; active search; high frequency.

Comment: First ordered from Hollming on 23 November 1984 and commissioned 25 May 1987 after lengthy trials. Three more of an improved type ordered 22 November 1988, the first of which was laid down 3 August 1989 and commissioned in November 1990. Work on the last pair was cancelled. The design allows for rapid conversion to attack craft, ASW craft, minelayer, minesweeper or minehunter. A central telescopic crane over the engine room casing is used to launch a 5.7 m rigid inflatable sea boat. A fire monitor is mounted in the bows. The Kamewa steerable water-jets extend the overall hull length by 2 m. **UPDATED**

KIISLA   *7/1997*, M Enqvist / 0069891

4 SLINGSBY SAM 2200 (HOVERCRAFT)

Displacement, tons: 5.5 full load
Dimensions, feet (metres): 34.8 × 13.8 *(10.6 × 4.2)*
Main machinery: 1 Cummins 6CTA-8-3M-1 diesel; 300 hp *(224 kW)*
Speed, knots: 40. **Range, miles:** 400 at 30 kt
Complement: 2
Military lift: 2.2 tons or 12 troops
Guns: 1—12.7 mm MG.
Radars: Navigation: Raytheon R41; I-band.

Comment: First one acquired from Slingsby Amphibious Hovercraft Company in March 1993. Three more ordered in February 1998 and delivered in late 1999. **UPDATED**

SLINGSBY 2200   *1993*, Slingsby / 0069892

3 GRIFFON 2000 TDX(M) (HOVERCRAFT)

Displacement, tons: 6.8 full load
Dimensions, feet (metres): 36.1 × 15.1 *(11 × 4.6)*
Main machinery: 1 Deutz BF8L513 diesel; 320 hp *(239 kW)* sustained
Speed, knots: 33. **Range, miles:** 300 at 25 kt
Complement: 2
Military lift: 16 troops or 2 tons
Guns: 1—7.62 mm MG.
Radars: Navigation: I-band.

Comment: First two acquired from Griffon, UK and commissioned 1 December 1994; third one bought in June 1995. Can be embarked in an LCU. Speed indicated is at Sea State 3 with a full load. Similar to those in service with the UK Navy. **UPDATED**

GRIFFON 2000   *1993*, G Hydes / 0080653

39 INSHORE PATROL CRAFT AND TENDERS (PB)

Class	Total	Tonnage	Speed	Commissioned
RV	15	12-18	10	1961-74
RV 390	10	25	12	1992-96
PV 113	14	10	28	1984-90
				UPDATED

PV 306   *6/1993* / 0069894

LAND-BASED MARITIME AIRCRAFT

Numbers/Type: 2 Agusta AB 412 Griffon.
Operational speed: 122 kt *(226 km/h)*.
Service ceiling: 17,000 ft *(5,180 m)*.
Range: 354 n miles *(656 km)*.
Role/Weapon systems: Operated by Coast Guard/Frontier force for patrol and SAR. Sensors: Radar and FLIR. Weapons: Unarmed at present but mountings for machine guns. **UPDATED**

GRIFFON   *5/1993*, A Sheldon Duplaix / 0069895

Numbers/Type: 3 Eurocopter AS 332L1 Super Puma.
Operational speed: 130 kt *(240 km/h)*.
Service ceiling: 15,090 ft *(4,600 m)*.
Range: 672 n miles *(1,245 km)*.
Role/Weapon systems: Coastal patrol, surveillance and SAR helicopters. Sensors: Surveillance radar, FLIR, tactical navigation systems and SAR equipment. Weapons: Unarmed. **UPDATED**

Numbers/Type: 2 Agusta AB 206B JetRanger.
Operational speed: 116 kt *(215 km/h)*.
Service ceiling: 13,500 ft *(4,120 m)*.
Range: 364 n miles *(674 km)*.
Role/Weapon systems: Coastal patrol and inshore surveillance helicopters. Sensors: Visual means only. FLIR may be fitted in due course. Weapons: Unarmed. **VERIFIED**

Numbers/Type: 2 Dornier Do 228-212.
Operational speed: 223 kt *(413 km/h)*.
Service ceiling: 29,600 ft *(9,020 m)*.
Range: 939 n miles *(1,740 km)*.
Role/Weapon systems: Maritime surveillance, SAR and pollution control. Acquired in 1995. Sensors: GEC-Marconi Seaspray radar; Terma Side scan radar; FLIR/TV, SLAR and IR/UV scanner. Weapons: Unarmed. **VERIFIED**

FRANCE
MARINE NATIONALE

Headquarters Appointments

Chief of the Naval Staff:
  Amiral Jean-Luc Delaunay
Inspector General of the Navy:
  Vice-Amiral Lucien Uzan
Director of Personnel:
  Vice-Amiral d'Escadre Alain Béreau
Major General of the Navy:
  Vice-Amiral Jean-Louis Battet

Senior Appointments

C-in-C Atlantic Theatre (CECLANT):
  Vice-Amiral d'Escadre Yves Naquet-Radiguet
C-in-C Mediterranean Theatre (CECMED):
  Vice-Amiral d'Escadre Paul Habert
Flag Officer, French Forces Polynesia (ALPACI):
  Vice-Amiral Jean Moulin
Flag Officer, Naval Forces Indian Ocean (ALINDIEN):
  Contre-Amiral Patrice du Puy-Montbrun
Flag Officer, Lorient:
  Contre-Amiral Patrice Dupeyron
Flag Officer, Cherbourg:
  Contre-Amiral Yves Laganne
Flag Officer, Submarines (ALFOST):
  Vice-Amiral d'Escadre Bernard Capart
Flag Officer, Naval Action Force (ALFAN):
  Vice-Amiral d'Escadre Alain Witrand
Flag Officer ASW Action Group (ALGASM):
  Contre-Amiral Jean-François Got
Flag Officer Mine Warfare Force (ALMINES):
  Contre-Amiral Jean-Luc Masuy
Flag Officer Naval Aviation (ALAVIA):
  Contre-Amiral Pierre Toubon
Commandant Marines:
  Capitaine de Vaisseau Olivier Aubrun

Diplomatic Representation

Defence and Naval Attaché in London:
  Contre-Amiral P Sabatié-Garat
Defence and Naval Attaché in Ryad:
  Contre-Amiral Jean-Louis Baillot
Military Delegate to WEU:
  Contre-Amiral Bernard Oliveau
Military Attaché to SACLANT:
  Contre-Amiral Raymond Masson
Military Attaché to CINCSOUTH:
  Contre-Amiral Jérôme Denavit
Naval Attaché in Washington:
  Capitaine de Vaisseau Philippe Alquier

Personnel

(a) 2000: 49,490 (4,350 officers)
(b) 10 months' national service (7,000) (ends in 2002)

Bases

Brest: Main Atlantic base. SSBN base
Toulon: Mediterranean Command base
Cherbourg: Channel base
Bayonne: Landes firing range
Small bases at Papeete (Tahiti), Fort-de-France (Martinique),
  Nouméa (New Caledonia), Degrad-des-Cannes (French
  Guiana), Port-des-Galets (La Réunion).

Shipyards (Naval)

Cherbourg: Submarines and Fast Attack Craft (private shipyard)
Brest: Major warships and refitting
Lorient: Destroyers and Frigates, MCMVs, Patrol Craft
Toulon: Major refits.

Dates

Armement pour essais: After launching when the ship is
sufficiently advanced to allow a crew to live on board, and the
commanding officer has joined. From this date the ship hoists the
French flag and is ready to undertake her first harbour trials.
Armement définitif: On this date the ship has received her full
complement and is able to undergo sea trials.
Clôture d'armement: Trials are completed and the ship is now
able to undertake her first endurance cruise.
Croisière de longue durée or *traversée de longue durée:* The
endurance cruise follows the *clôture d'armement* and lasts until
the ship is accepted with all systems fully operational.
Admission au service actif: Commissioning date.

Reserve

A ship in 'Reserve Normale' has no complement but is available
at short notice. 'Reserve Speciale' means that a refit will be
required before the ship can go to sea again. 'Condamnation' is
the state before being broken up or sold; at this stage a Q number
is allocated.

Prefix to Ships' Names

FS is used in NATO communications but is not official.

Mercantile Marine

Lloyd's Register of Shipping:
  822 vessels of 4,925,003 tons gross

Strength of the Fleet

Type	Active (Reserve)	Building (Projected)
Submarines (SSBN)	4	1 (1)
Submarines (SSN)	6	(6)
Submarines (SSK)	2	—
Aircraft Carriers	2	(1)
Helicopter Carrier	1	—
Destroyers	13	2 (2)
Frigates	20	1
Public Service Force	6	—
Patrol Craft	10	—
LSDs	5	(2)
LST/LCT	9	—
LCMs	17	—
Route Survey Vessels	3	—
Minehunters	13	—
Diving Tenders	4	—
Survey/Research Ships	10	1 (1)
Tankers (AOR)	4 (1)	—
Maintenance Ships	1	—
Depot Ships	2	—
Boom Defence Vessels	1	—
Supply Tenders	7	—
Transports	9	—
Training Ships	16	—

DELETIONS

Submarines

1997 *Agosta* (reserve), *Sirène, Le Foudroyant*
1998 *Bévéziers, Psyché*
1999 *Le Tonnant*

Aircraft Carriers

1997 *Clemenceau*

Destroyers

1997 *Aconit* (old)
1999 *Duguay-Trouin*

Frigates

1997 *Détroyat*
1999 *D'Estienne d'Orves, Amyot d'Inville, Jean Moulin*
2000 *Drogou, Quartier Maître Anquetil, Commandant de
      Pimodan*

Patrol Forces

1997 *Pertuisane* (GM), *Mascareigne* (GM), *Karukéra* (GM)
1998 *Vétiver* (GM) (to Mayotte)

Mine Warfare Forces

1997 *Cybèle, Calliope, Clio, Circé, Cérès* (all to Turkey)

Amphibious Forces

1998 2 CTMs
1999 *Javeline* (to Senegal), 7 CTMs

Auxiliaries

1997 *Rhône, L'Archéonaute* (civilian), *Durance* (to Argentina),
      La Fidèle (sunk), *Sylphe*
1998 *Girelle*
1999 *Morgane, Merlin, Mélusine, Berry, Tianée*
2000 *Garonne, La Prudente*

Tugs

1998 *Travailleur, Laborieux, Centaure* (to Turkey)
1999 *L'Utile, Efficace, Goéland, Merisier, Paletuvier, Macreuse,
      P 7-P 10*

Fleet Air Arm Bases

Embarked Squadrons

Base/Squadron No	Aircraft	Task
Lann Bihoué/4F	E-2C Hawkeye	AEW
Landivisiau/11F	Super Étendard	Assault
Landivisiau/12F	Rafale	Air Defence
Landivisiau/17F	Super Étendard	Assault
St Mandrier/31F	Lynx	ASW
Lanvéoc-Poulmic/34F	Lynx	ASW
St Mandrier/36F	Panther	Surveillance

Support Squadrons

Hyères/ERCE/10S	Various	Research
Lanvéoc-Poulmic/22S	Alouette III	Support Atlantic Region
Lanvéoc-Poulmic 32F	Super Frelon, Dauphin 2	Support, SAR
St Mandrier/35F	Super Frelon Dauphin 2, Alouette	Support, SAR
Landivisiau/57S	Falcon 10 MER/Paris	Support, Training

Maritime Patrol Squadrons

Lann Bihoué/23F	Atlantique Mk 2	MP
Lann Bihoué/24F	Falcon 50/20 Gardian	Surveillance, SAR
Hyères/28F	Nord 262/Xingu	Surveillance, SAR

Training Squadrons

Nîmes Garons/56S	Nord 262E	Flying School
Lanvéoc-Poulmic/50S	MS 880 Rallye/ CAP 10	Initial Flying School, Recreational

Approximate Fleet Dispositions 1 April 2000

	FAN	GASM	FOST	FGM	Mediterranean	Atlantic	Channel	Indian Ocean	Pacific	Antilles
Carriers	1	—	—	—	—	1 (hel)	—	—	—	—
SSBN	—	—	4	—	—	—	—	—	—	—
SSN	—	—	6	—	—	—	—	—	—	—
SS	—	—	2	—	—	—	—	—	—	—
DDG/DDH	8	4	—	—	—	1	—	—	—	—
FFG	3	9	—	—	7	1	—	2	2	1
MCMV (incl tenders)	—	—	—	13	5	—	1	—	—	—
Patrol Forces	—	—	—	—	1	17	4	4	5	6
LPD/LSD	3	—	—	—	—	—	—	—	1	—
LST/LCT	4	—	—	—	1	—	—	2	3	1
AOR	3	—	—	—	—	—	—	1	—	—

FAN = Force d'Action Navale (based at Toulon). All foreign operational deployments
GASM = Groupe d'Action Sous-Marine (based at Brest)
FOST = Force Océanique Stratégique (HQ at Houilles, near Paris). SSBNs based at l'Ile Longue near Brest. All SSNs based at Toulon.
FGM = Force de Guerre des Mines (HQ and main base at Brest). One diving tender based at Cherbourg. Three MHCs and one diving tender at Toulon. Remainder plus one tender and one trials ship at Brest

PENNANT LIST

Submarines		F 791	Commandant l'Herminier	P 708	Gendarme Perez	A 621	Rhin
		F 792	Premier Maître l'Her	P 709	MDLC Richard	A 630	Marne
S 601	Rubis	F 793	Commandant Blaison	P 710	General Delfosse	A 631	Somme
S 602	Saphir	F 794	Enseigne de Vaisseau Jacoubet	P 711	Gentiane	A 633	Taape
S 603	Casabianca	F 795	Commandant Ducuing	P 712	Fuschia	A 634	Rari
S 604	Émeraude	F 796	Commandant Birot	P 713	Capitaine Moulié (GM)	A 635	Revi
S 605	Améthyste	F 797	Commandant Bouan	P 714	Lieut Jamet (GM)	A 636	Maroa
S 606	Perle			P 715	Bellis (GM)	A 637	Maito
S 613	L'Indomptable	**Mine Warfare Forces**		P 716	MDLC Jacques (GM)	A 638	Manini
S 615	L'Inflexible			P 717	Lavande (GM)	A 649	L'Étoile
S 616	Le Triomphant	M 611	Vulcain	P 720	Géranium (GM)	A 650	La Belle Poule
S 617	Le Téméraire	M 614	Styx	P 721	Jonquille (GM)	A 652	Mutin
S 618	Le Vigilant (bldg)	M 622	Pluton	P 722	Violette (GM)	A 653	La Grande Hermine
S 622	La Praya	M 641	Éridan	P 723	Jasmin (GM)	A 664	Malabar
S 623	Ouessant	M 642	Cassiopée	P 740	Fulmar (GM)	A 669	Tenace
		M 643	Andromède	P 760	Pétulante (GM)	A 671	Le Fort
Aircraft and Helicopter Carriers		M 644	Pégase	P 761	Mimosa (GM)	A 673	Lutteur
		M 645	Orion	P 764	—	A 675	Fréhel
R 91	Charles de Gaulle	M 646	Croix du Sud	P 772	Oeillet (GM)	A 676	Saire
R 97	Jeanne d'Arc	M 647	Aigle	P 774	Camélia (GM)	A 677	Armen
R 99	Foch	M 648	Lyre	P 775	Stellis (GM)	A 678	La Houssaye
		M 649	Persée	P 776	Sténia (GM)	A 679	Kéréon
		M 650	Sagittaire	P 778	Réséda (GM)	A 680	Sicié
Destroyers		M 651	Verseau	P 789	Mellia (GM)	A 681	Taunoa
		M 652	Céphée	P 791	Hortensia (GM)	A 693	Acharné
D 602	Suffren	M 653	Capricorne			A 695	Bélier
D 603	Duquesne	M 770	Antarès	GM = Gendarmerie Maritime		A 696	Buffle
D 610	Tourville	M 771	Altaïr			A 697	Bison
D 612	De Grasse	M 772	Aldébaran	**Amphibious Forces**		A 712	Athos
D 614	Cassard					A 713	Aramis
D 615	Jean Bart	**Patrol Forces**		L 9011	Foudre	A 714	Tourmaline
D 640	Georges Leygues			L 9012	Siroco	A 722	Poséidon
D 641	Dupleix	P 671	Glaive (GM)	L 9021	Ouragan	A 743	Denti
D 642	Montcalm	P 672	Épée (GM)	L 9022	Orage	A 748	Léopard
D 643	Jean de Vienne	P 676	Flamant	L 9030	Champlain	A 749	Panthère
D 644	Primauguet	P 677	Cormoran	L 9031	Francis Garnier	A 750	Jaguar
D 645	La Motte-Picquet	P 678	Pluvier	L 9032	Dumont D'Urville	A 751	Lynx
D 646	Latouche-Tréville	P 679	Grèbe	L 9033	Jacques Cartier	A 752	Guépard
		P 680	Sterne	L 9034	La Grandière	A 753	Chacal
		P 681	Albatros	L 9051	Sabre	A 754	Tigre
Frigates		P 682	L'Audacieuse	L 9052	Dague	A 755	Lion
		P 683	La Boudeuse	L 9061	Hallebarde	A 756	L'Espérance
F 710	La Fayette	P 684	La Capricieuse	L 9062	Rapière	A 757	D'Entrecasteaux
F 711	Surcouf	P 685	La Fougueuse	L 9077	Bougainville	A 768	Élan
F 712	Courbet	P 686	La Glorieuse	L 9090	Gapeau	A 770	Glycine
F 713	Aconit	P 687	La Gracieuse			A 771	Églantine
F 714	Guépratte (bldg)	P 688	La Moqueuse			A 774	Chevreuil
F 730	Floréal	P 689	La Railleuse	**Major Auxiliaries Survey and Support Ships**		A 775	Gazelle
F 731	Prairial	P 690	La Rieuse			A 776	Isard
F 732	Nivôse	P 691	La Tapageuse	A 601	Monge	A 785	Thétis
F 733	Ventôse	P 703	Lilas	A 607	Meuse	A 790	Coralline
F 734	Vendémiaire	P 704	Bégonia	A 608	Var	A 791	Lapérouse
F 735	Germinal	P 705	Pivoine	A 610	Ile d'Oléron	A 792	Borda
F 788	Second Maître Le Bihan	P 706	Nymphéa	A 613	Achéron	A 793	Laplace
F 789	Lieutenant de Vaisseau le Hénaff	P 707	MDLC Robet	A 615	Loire	A 795	Arago
F 790	Lieutenant de Vaisseau Lavallée			A 620	Jules Verne		

SUBMARINES

Strategic Missile Submarines (SSBN/SNLE)

2 L'INFLEXIBLE M4 CLASS (SSBN/SNLE)

Name	No	Builders	Laid down		Launched		Operational	
L'INDOMPTABLE	S 613	DCN, Cherbourg	4 Dec	1971	17 Sep	1974	23 Dec	1976
L'INFLEXIBLE	S 615	DCN, Cherbourg	21 Mar	1980	23 June	1982	1 Apr	1985

Displacement, tons: 8,080 surfaced; 8,920 dived
Dimensions, feet (metres): 422.1 × 34.8 × 32.8 *(128.7 × 10.6 × 10)*
Main machinery: Nuclear; turbo-electric; 1 PWR; 2 turbo-alternators; 1 Jeumont Schneider motor; 16,000 hp(m) *(11.76 MW)*; twin SEMT-Pielstick/Jeumont Schneider 8 PA4 V 185 SM diesel-electric auxiliary propulsion; 1.5 MW; 1 emergency motor; 1 shaft
Speed, knots: 25 dived; 20 surfaced
Range, miles: 5,000 at 4 kt on auxiliary propulsion only
Complement: 130 (15 officers) (2 crews)

Missiles: SLBM: 16 Aerospatiale M4/TN 71; 3-stage solid fuel rockets; inertial guidance to 5,300 km *(2,860 n miles)*; thermonuclear warhead with 6 MRV each of 150 kT. M 45/TN 75 missiles are to be carried in S 613 by 2002.
SSM: Aerospatiale SM 39 Exocet; launched from 21 in *(533 mm)* torpedo tubes; inertial cruise; active radar homing to 50 km *(27 n miles)* at 0.9 Mach; warhead 165 kg.

Torpedoes: 4—21 in *(533 mm)* tubes. ECAN L5 Mod 3; dual purpose; active/passive homing to 9.5 km *(5.1 n miles)* at 35 kt; warhead 150 kg; depth to 550 m *(1,800 ft)*; and ECAN F17 Mod 2; wire-guided; active/passive homing to 20 km *(10.8 n miles)* at 40 kt; warhead 250 kg; depth 600 m *(1,970 ft)*; total of 18 torpedoes and SSM carried in a mixed load.
Countermeasures: ESM: Thomson-CSF ARUR 13/DR 3000U; intercept.
Weapons control: SAD (Système d'Armes de Dissuasion) strategic data system (for SLBMs); SAT (Système d'Armes Tactique) tactical data system and DLA 1A weapon control system (for SSM and torpedoes).
Radars: Navigation: Thomson-CSF DRUA 33; I-band.
Sonars: Thomson Sintra DSUX 21 'multifunction' passive bow and flank arrays.
DUUX 5; passive ranging and intercept; low frequency.
DSUV 61; towed array.

Programmes: With the paying off of *Le Redoutable* in December 1991, the remaining submarines of the class became known as 'L'Inflexible' class SNLE M4.
Modernisation: Fitted with M4 missiles. *L'Inflexible* on build and *L'Indomptable* 1 July 1989. As well as replacing the missile system, work included an improved reactor core, noise reduction efforts, updating sonar and other equipment to the same standard as *L'Inflexible* on build. M 45/TN 75 missiles to be retrofitted in *L'Indomptable* by 2002.
Structure: Diving depth, 250 m *(820 ft)* approx. Improved streamlining of M4 conversion changed the silhouette to that of *L'Inflexible*.
Operational: Next to go will be *L'Indomptable* by July 2004. *L'Inflexible* is planned to pay off in July 2006 but this may be extended to 2010. A third of class *Le Tonnant* paid off to reserve in 1999 by may be used as a trials platform for SLCM.
UPDATED

L'INFLEXIBLE

2 + 1 (1) LE TRIOMPHANT CLASS (SSBN/SNLE-NG)

Name	No	Builders	Launched		Commissioned	
LE TRIOMPHANT	S 616	DCN, Cherbourg	13 July	1993	21 Mar	1997
LE TÉMÉRAIRE	S 617	DCN, Cherbourg	8 Aug	1997	23 Dec	1999
LE VIGILANT	S 618	DCN, Cherbourg	Mar	2002	July	2004
—	S 619	DCN, Cherbourg	Nov	2005	July	2008

Displacement, tons: 12,640 surfaced; 14,120 dived
Dimensions, feet (metres): 453 × 41; 55.8 (aft planes) × 41
(138 × 12.5; 17 × 12.5)
Main machinery: Nuclear; turbo-electric; 1 PWR Type K15
(enlarged CAS 48); 150 MW; 2 turbo-alternators; 1 motor;
41,500 hp(m) *(30.5 MW)*; diesel-electric auxiliary propulsion;
2 SEMT-Pielstick 8 PA4 V 200 SM diesels; 900 kW;
1 emergency motor; 1 shaft; pump jet propulsor
Speed, knots: 25 dived
Complement: 111 (15 officers) (2 crews)

Missiles: SLBM: 16 Aerospatiale M45/TN 75; 3-stage solid fuel
rockets; inertial guidance to 5,300 km *(2,860 n miles)*;
thermonuclear warhead with 6 MRV each of 150 kT. To be
replaced by M51/TN 75 which has a planned range of
8,000 km *(4,300 n miles)* and 6 MRVs. To be fitted first in
S 619.
SSM: Aerospatiale SM 39 Exocet; launched from 21 in *(533 mm)*
torpedo tubes; inertial cruise; active radar homing to 50 km
(27 n miles) at 0.9 Mach; warhead 165 kg.

Torpedoes: 4—21 in *(533 mm)* tubes. ECAN L5 Mod 3; dual
purpose; active/passive homing to 9.5 km *(5.1 n miles)* at
35 kt; warhead 150 kg; depth to 550 m *(1,800 ft)*; total of 18
torpedoes and SSM carried in a mixed load.
Countermeasures: ESM: Thomson-CSF ARUR 13/DR 3000U;
intercept.
Weapons control: SAD (Système d'Armes de Dissuasion)
strategic data system (for SLBMs); SAT (Système d'Armes
Tactique) tactical data system and DLA 4A weapon control
system (for SSM and torpedoes).
Radars: Search: Dassault; I-band.
Sonars: Thomson Sintra DMUX 80 'multifunction' passive bow
and flank arrays; passive ranging and intercept; low frequency.
Towed array; very low frequency.

Programmes: *Le Triomphant* ordered 10 March 1986 with first
steel cut 30 October 1986. Complete hull transferred to dock
13 July 1993. Floated in November 1993 when the reactor
started to operate. *Le Téméraire* ordered 18 October 1989.
Le Vigilant ordered 27 May 1993 with first steel cut

9 December. Fourth of the class to be ordered in 2000. Class
of six originally planned, but reduced to four after the end of the
Cold War. Sous-marins Nucléaires Lanceurs d'Engins-Nouvelle
Génération (SNLE-NG).
Modernisation: Development of the M5 missile discontinued in
favour of the less expensive M51 which is planned to equip
S 619 in 2008 and then be retrofitted to the others. Warhead
TN O is to replace TN 75 by 2015.
Structure: Built of HLES 100 steel capable of withstanding
pressures of more than 100 kg/mm². Diving depth 500 m
(1,640 ft). Height from keel to top of fin is 21.3 m *(69.9 ft)*.
Plans to lengthen the hull in later ships of the class have been
shelved.
Operational: Sea trials of *Le Triomphant* started 15 April 1994,
with official trials starting 1 July 1994. First sea cruise 16 July
to 22 August 1995. First submerged M45 launch on
14 February 1996, second on 19 September 1996.
Le Téméraire official trials started April 1998, first submerged
M 45 launch 4 May 1999. Based at Brest.

UPDATED

LE TRIOMPHANT   *6/1998, French Navy* / 0052009

LE TÉMÉRAIRE   *6/1999*, H M Steele* / 0069898

LE TÉMÉRAIRE

6/1999*, French Navy / 0069897

Attack Submarines (SSN/SNA)

Note: A new generation SSN (Project Barracuda) has been funded under the 1997-2002 budget. Operational requirements passed to DCN on 20 December 1996. The submarine is to displace about 4,000 tons, have a vertical launch SSM system, and is planned to be ordered in 2001 and to start sea trials in 2008. One to be built every two years to a total of six, to replace the 'Rubis' class.

6 RUBIS AMÉTHYSTE CLASS (SSN/SNA)

Name	No	Builders	Laid down	Launched	Operational
RUBIS	S 601	Cherbourg Naval Dockyard	11 Dec 1976	7 July 1979	23 Feb 1983
SAPHIR	S 602	Cherbourg Naval Dockyard	1 Sep 1979	1 Sep 1981	6 July 1984
CASABIANCA	S 603	Cherbourg Naval Dockyard	19 Sep 1979	22 Dec 1984	13 May 1987
ÉMERAUDE	S 604	Cherbourg Naval Dockyard	4 Mar 1981	12 Apr 1986	15 Sep 1988
AMÉTHYSTE	S 605	Cherbourg Naval Dockyard	31 Oct 1983	14 May 1988	20 Mar 1992
PERLE	S 606	Cherbourg Naval Dockyard	27 Mar 1987	22 Sep 1990	7 July 1993

Displacement, tons: 2,410 surfaced; 2,670 dived

Dimensions, feet (metres): 241.5 × 24.9 × 21
(73.6 × 7.6 × 6.4)

Main machinery: Nuclear; turbo-electric; 1 PWR CAS 48; 48 MW; 2 turbo-alternators; 1 motor; 9,500 hp(m) *(7 MW)*; SEMT-Pielstick/Jeumont Schneider 8 PA4 V 185 SM diesel-electric auxiliary propulsion; 450 kW; 1 emergency motor; 1 shaft

Speed, knots: 25

Complement: 66 (8 officers) (2 crews)

Missiles: SSM: Aerospatiale SM 39 Exocet; launched from 21 in *(533 mm)* torpedo tubes; inertial cruise; active radar homing to 50 km *(27 n miles)* at 0.9 Mach; warhead 165 kg.

Torpedoes: 4—21 in *(533 mm)* tubes. ECAN L5 Mod 3; dual purpose; active/passive homing to 9.5 km *(5.1 n miles)* at 35 kt; warhead 150 kg; depth to 550 m *(1,800 ft)*; and ECAN F17 Mod 2; wire-guided; active/passive homing to 20 km *(10.8 n miles)* at 40 kt; warhead 250 kg; depth 600 m *(1,970 ft)*. Total of 14 torpedoes and missiles carried in a mixed load.

Mines: Up to 32 FG 29 in lieu of torpedoes.

Countermeasures: ESM: Thomson-CSF ARUR 13/DR 3000U; intercept.

Combat data systems: TIT (Traitement des Informations Tactiques) data system; OPSMER command support system; Syracuse 2 SATCOM.

Weapons control: LAT (Lancement des Armes Tactiques) system.

Radars: Navigation: Kelvin Hughes 1007; I-band.

Sonars: Thomson Sintra DMUX 20 multifunction; passive search; low frequency.
DSUV 62C; towed passive array; very low frequency.

Programmes: The programme was terminated early by defence economies with the seventh of class *Turquoise* and eighth of class *Diamant* being cancelled.

Modernisation: Between 1989 and 1995 the first four of this class converted under operation Améthyste (AMÉlioration Tactique HYdrodynamique Silence Transmission Ecoute) to bring them to the same standard of ASW (included new sonars) efficiency as the later boats rather than that required for the original anti-surface ship role. Two F17 torpedoes can be guided simultaneously against separate targets. *Saphir* recommissioned 1 July 1991; *Rubis* in February 1993; *Casabianca* in June 1994 and *Émeraude* in March 1996. A new radar added on a telescopic mast.

Structure: Diving depth, greater than 300 m *(984 ft)*. There has been a marked reduction in the size of the reactor compared with the 'L'Inflexible' class. On completion of the modernisation programme, all six of the class are virtually identical.

Operational: All operational SSNs are based at Toulon but frequently deploy to the Atlantic. Endurance rated at 45 days, limited by amount of food carried. *Rubis* collided with a tanker on 17 July 1993 and has undergone extensive repairs. *Émeraude* had a bad steam leak on 30 March 1994 which caused casualties amongst the crew.

UPDATED

CASABIANCA　　　　　　　　　　　　　6/1997, B Sullivan / 0012322

PERLE　　　　　　　　　　10/1999 *, van Ginderen Collection / 0069900

ÉMERAUDE　　　　　　　　　　　　　5/1997, S G Gaya / 0012323

Patrol Submarines (SSK)

2 AGOSTA CLASS (SSK)

Name	No
LA PRAYA	S 622
OUESSANT	S 623

Builders	Laid down	Launched	Commissioned
Cherbourg Naval Dockyard	1974	15 May 1976	9 Mar 1978
Cherbourg Naval Dockyard	1974	23 Oct 1976	27 July 1978

Displacement, tons: 1,230 standard; 1,510 surfaced; 1,760 dived

Dimensions, feet (metres): 221.7 × 22.3 × 17.7 (67.6 × 6.8 × 5.4)

Main machinery: Diesel-electric; 2 SEMT-Pielstick 16 PA4 V 185 VG diesels; 3,600 hp(m) (2.65 MW); 2 alternators; 1.7 MW; 1 motor; 4,600 hp(m) (3.4 MW); 1 cruising motor; 31 hp(m) (23 kW); 1 shaft

Speed, knots: 12 surfaced; 20 dived

Range, miles: 8,500 at 9 kt snorting; 350 at 3.5 kt dived

Complement: 54 (7 officers)

Missiles: SSM: Aerospatiale SM 39 Exocet; launched from 21 in (533 mm) tubes; inertial cruise; active radar homing to 50 km (27 n miles) at 0.9 Mach; warhead 165 kg.

Torpedoes: 4—21 in (533 mm) bow tubes. ECAN L5 Mod 3; dual purpose; active/passive homing to 9.5 km (5.1 n miles) at 35 kt; warhead 150 kg; depth to 550 m (1,800 ft) and ECAN F17 Mod 2; wire-guided; active/passive homing to 20 km (10.8 n miles) at 40 kt; warhead 250 kg; depth 600 m (1,970 ft). Total of 20 torpedoes and missiles carried in a mixed load.

Mines: Up to 36 in lieu of torpedoes.

Countermeasures: ESM: ARUR, ARUD; intercept and warning.

Weapons control: DLA 2A weapon control system.

Radars: Search: Thomson-CSF DRUA 33; I-band.

Sonars: Thomson Sintra DSUV 22; passive search; medium frequency.
DUUA 2D; active search and attack; 8 kHz.
DUUA 1D; active search. DUUX 2; passive ranging.
DSUV 62A; passive towed array; very low frequency.

Modernisation: Included fitting of SM 39 Exocet and better torpedo discharge and reloading. Completed in 1987.

Structure: First diesel submarines in the French Navy to be fitted with 21 in (533 mm) tubes. Diving depth, 320 m (1,050 ft).

Operational: Based at Brest from 1 July 1995 and assigned to GESMAT (Groupe des Sous-Marins d'Attaque de l'Atlantique). Endurance, 45 days. Ouessant to pay off in late 2000 when GESMAT is to be disbanded. La Praya is a testbed for the Project Barracuda SSN new equipment and is to stay in service until 2005.

Sales: Four built at Cartagena for Spanish Navy and two for Pakistan by Dubigeon, with three more for Pakistan ordered 21 September 1994.   **UPDATED**

LA PRAYA   11/1999*, Michael Nitz / 0069899

HELICOPTER CARRIERS (CVH)

1 JEANNE D'ARC CLASS (CVH)

Name	No
JEANNE D'ARC (ex-La Résolue)	R 97

Builders	Laid down	Launched	Commissioned
Brest Naval Dockyard	7 July 1960	30 Sep 1961	16 July 1964

Displacement, tons: 10,000 standard; 13,270 full load

Dimensions, feet (metres): 597.1 × 78.7 hull × 24 (182 × 24 × 7.3)

Flight deck, feet (metres): 203.4 × 68.9 (62 × 21)

Main machinery: 4 boilers; 640 psi (45 kg/cm²); 840°F (450°C); 2 Rateau-Bretagne turbines; 40,000 hp(m) (29.4 MW); 2 shafts

Speed, knots: 26.5. **Range, miles:** 6,000 at 15 kt

Complement: 455 (25 officers) plus 12 instructors and 140 cadets

Missiles: SSM: 6 Aerospatiale MM 38 Exocet (2 triple) ❶; inertial cruise; active radar homing to 42 km (23 n miles) at 0.9 Mach; warhead 165 kg; sea-skimmer.

Guns: 4 DCN 3.9 in (100 mm)/55 Mod 1964 CADAM automatic ❷; 80 rds/min to 17 km (9 n miles) anti-surface; 8 km (4.4 n miles) anti-aircraft; weight of shell 13.5 kg.
4—12.7 mm MGs.

Countermeasures: Decoys: 2 CSEE/VSEL Syllex 8-barrelled trainable launchers for chaff (may not be fitted).
ESM: Thomson-CSF ARBR 16/ARBX 10; intercept.

Weapons control: 3 C T Analogiques; 2 Sagem DMAa optical sights. SATCOM ❸.

Radars: Air search: Thomson-CSF DRBV 22D ❹; D-band; range 366 km (200 n miles).
Air/surface search: DRBV 50 (51 in due course) ❺; G-band.
Navigation: 2 DRBN 34A (Racal-Decca); I-band.
Fire control: 3 Thomson-CSF DRBC 32A ❻; I-band.
Tacan: SRN-6.

Sonars: Thomson Sintra DUBV 24C; hull-mounted; active search; medium frequency; 5 kHz.

Helicopters: 4 Dauphin. War inventory includes 8 Super Frelon and Lynx.

Modernisation: Long refits in the summers of 1989 and 1990 have allowed equipment to be updated to enable the ship to continue well into the next century. SENIT 2 combat data system was to have been fitted but this was cancelled as a cost-saving measure. DRBV 51 radar is to be fitted in due course.

Structure: Flight deck lift has a capacity of 12 tons. Some of the hangar space is used to accommodate officers under training. The ship is almost entirely air conditioned. Carries two LCVPs. Topmast can be removed for passing under bridges or other obstructions.

Operational: Used for training officer cadets. After rapid modification, she could be used as a commando ship, helicopter carrier or troop transport with commando equipment and a battalion of 700 men. Flagship of the Training Squadron for an Autumn/Spring cruise with Summer refit.

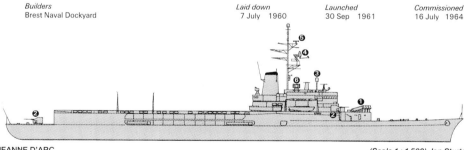

JEANNE D'ARC   (Scale 1 : 1,500), Ian Sturton

JEANNE D'ARC   7/1999*, Per Kornefeldt / 0069909

Army helicopters Super Puma/Cougar and Gazelle are embarked during training cruises. Thirty-three training cruises completed by April 1997 when the ship was docked for extensive propulsion machinery repairs which completed in July 1998. Planned to stay in service until 2005.   **UPDATED**

AIRCRAFT CARRIERS

1 CHARLES DE GAULLE CLASS (CVN/PAN)

Name	No	Builders	Laid down	Launched	Commissioned
CHARLES DE GAULLE	R 91	DCN, Brest	14 Apr 1989	7 May 1994	Oct 2000

Displacement, tons: 36,600 standard; 40,578 full load
Dimensions, feet (metres): 857.7 oa; 780.8 wl × 211.3 oa; 103.3 wl × 27.8 *(261.5; 238 × 64.4; 31.5 × 8.5)*
Flight deck, feet (metres): 857.7 × 211.3 *(261.5 × 64.4)*
Main machinery: Nuclear; 2 PWR Type K15; 300 MW; 2 GEC Alsthom turbines; 76,200 hp(m) *(56 MW)* sustained; 2 shafts
Speed, knots: 28
Complement: 1,150 ship's company plus 550 aircrew plus 50 Flag Staff; (accommodation for 1,950) (plus temporary 800 marines)

Missiles: SAM: 4 EUROSAAM VLS octuple launchers **❶**; Aerospatiale ASTER 15; anti-missile system with inertial guidance and mid-course update; active radar homing at 4.5 Mach to 15 km *(8.1 n miles)*; warhead 13 kg. 32 weapons.
2 Matra Sadral PDMS sextuple launchers **❷**; Mistral; IR homing to 4 km *(2.2 n miles)*; warhead 3 kg; anti-sea-skimmer; able to engage targets down to 10 ft above sea level.
Guns: 8 Giat 20F2 20 mm; 720 rds/min to 8 km *(4.3 n miles)*; weight of shell: 0.25 kg.
Countermeasures: Decoys: 4 CSEE Sagaie 10-barrelled trainable launchers **❸**; medium range; chaff to 8 km *(4.3 n miles)*; IR flares to 3 km *(1.6 n miles)*. Dassault LAD offboard decoys. SLAT torpedo decoys from 2002.
ESM: Thomson-CSF ARBR 21; intercept. 2 SAT DIBV 2A Vampir MB; (IRST) **❹**.
ECM: 2 ARBB 33 **❺**; jammers.
Combat data systems: SENIT 8; Links 11, 14 and 16. Syracuse 2 FLEETSATCOM **❻**. AIDCOMER command support system.
Weapons control: 2 Sagem VIGY-105 optronic directors.
Radars: Air search: Thomson-CSF DRBJ 11B **❼**; 3D; E/F-band; range 366 km *(200 n miles)* for aircraft.
Thomson-CSF DRBV 26D Jupiter **❽**; D-band; range 183 km *(100 n miles)* for 2 m² target.
Air/surface search: Thomson-CSF DRBV 15D Sea Tiger Mk 2 **❾**; E/F-band; range 110 km *(60 n miles)* for 2 m² target.
Navigation: Two Racal 1229 (DRBN 34A) **❿**; I-band.
Fire control: Thomson-CSF Arabel 3D **⓫**; I/J-band (for SAAM); range 70 km *(38 n miles)* for 2 m² target.
Tacan: NRBP 20A **⓬**.
Sonars: To include SLAT torpedo attack warning.

Fixed-wing aircraft: 24 Super Étendard, 2 E-2C Hawkeye. 10 Rafale F1 by 2002.
Helicopters: 2 AS 565 Panther or 2 AS 322 Cougar (AF).

Programmes: On 23 September 1980 the Defence Council decided to build two nuclear-propelled carriers to replace *Clemenceau* in 1996 and *Foch* some years later. First of class ordered 4 February 1986, first metal cut 24 November 1987. Hull floated for technical trials on 19 December 1992, and back in dock on 8 January 1993. Second ship, if built, will probably be called *Richelieu* or *Clemenceau* and was to have been ordered in 1992 but a decision will not be taken until 2003. A 19.8 m *(65 ft)* long one-twelfth scale model was used for hydrodynamic trials. Building programme delayed three years due to defence budget cuts.
Modernisation: From October 1999 to March 2000 modifications included additional radiation shielding, and lengthening of angled flight deck by 4.4 m.
Structure: Two lifts 62.3 × 41 ft *(19 × 12.5 m)* of 36 tons capacity. Hangar for 20-25 aircraft; dimensions 454.4 × 96.5 × 20 ft *(138.5 × 29.4 × 6.1 m)*. Angled deck 8.5° and 639.8 ft *(195 m)* overall length. Catapults: 2 USN Type C13-3; length

CHARLES DE GAULLE

5/1999*, French Navy / 0069901

246 ft *(75 m)* for Super Étendards and up to 22 tonne aircraft. Enhanced weight capability of flight deck to allow operation of AEW aircraft. Island placed well forward so that both lifts can be protected from the weather. CSEE Dallas (Deck Approach and Landing Laser System) fitted, later to be replaced by MLS system. Active fin stabilisers.

Operational: Five years continuous steaming at 25 kt available before refuelling (same reactors as *Le Triomphant*). Both reactors self-sustaining by 10 June 1998. Sea trials started 26 January 1999. Trials planned to complete in June 2000 followed by a long cruise. First Rafale Squadron is to be embarked in 2002 and a third Hawkeye in 2003. **UPDATED**

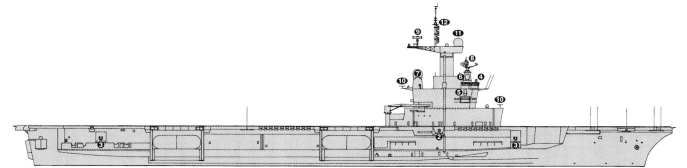

CHARLES DE GAULLE

(Scale 1 : 1,500), Ian Sturton / 0069903

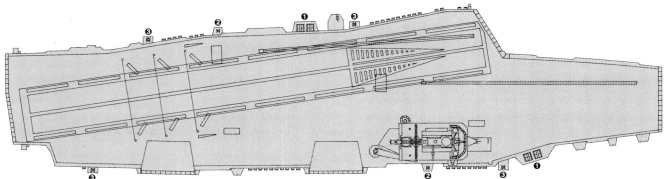

CHARLES DE GAULLE

(Scale 1 : 1,500), Ian Sturton / 0069902

CHARLES DE GAULLE

5/1999*, French Navy / 0069904

CHARLES DE GAULLE

9/1999*, French Navy / 0069905

CHARLES DE GAULLE

5/1999*, H M Steele / 0069906

1 CLEMENCEAU CLASS (CV)

Name	No	Builders	Laid down	Launched	Commissioned
FOCH	R 99	Chantiers de l'Atlantique, St. Nazaire	15 Feb 1957	28 July 1960	15 July 1963

Displacement, tons: 27,307 standard; 32,780 full load
Dimensions, feet (metres): 869.4 oa; 780.8 pp × 104.1 hull (168 oa) × 28.2 (265; 238 × 31.7 (51.2) × 8.6)
Flight deck, feet (metres): 543 × 96.8 (165.5 × 29.5)
Main machinery: 6 boilers; 640 psi (45 kg/cm²); 840°F (450°C); 2 GEC Alsthom turbines; 126,000 hp(m) (93 MW); 2 shafts
Speed, knots: 32. **Range, miles:** 7,500 at 18 kt; 4,800 at 24 kt; 3,500 at full power
Complement: 1,017 (47 officers) plus 672 aircrew (70 officers)

Missiles: SAM: 2 Thomson-CSF Crotale EDIR octuple launchers ❶; 18 missiles per magazine; radar and IR line of sight guidance to 13 km (7 n miles) at 2.4 Mach; warhead 14 kg.
2 Matra Sadral PDMS sextuple launchers ❷; Mistral; IR homing to 4 km (2.2 n miles); warhead 3 kg.
Guns: Several M2 12.7 mm MGs.
Countermeasures: Decoys: 2 CSEE Sagaie 10-barrelled trainable launchers ❸; medium-range decoy rockets; chaff to 8 km (4.3 n miles); IR flares to 3 km (1.6 n miles). Dassault LAD offboard decoys.
ESM: ARBR 17; radar warning.
ECM: ARBB 33; jammer.
Combat data systems: SENIT 2/8 tactical data automation system; Links 11 and 14; Syracuse 2; Inmarsat; FLEETSATCOM; AIDCOMER and JMCIS/NTCS command support system.
Weapons control: 2 C T Analogiques; 2 Sagem DMAa optical sights.
Radars: Air search: Thomson-CSF DRBV 23B ❹; D-band; range 201 km (110 n miles).
Air/surface search: 2 DRBI 10 ❺; E/F-band. Thomson-CSF DRBV 15 ❻; E/F-band.
Navigation: Racal Decca 1226; I-band.
Fire control: 2 Thomson-CSF DRBC 32B ❼ (for Sadral); I-band; two Crotale ❶ (for SAM); I-band.
Tacan: SRN-6.
Landing approach control: NRBA 51 ❽; I-band.
Sonars: Westinghouse SQS-505; hull-mounted; active search; medium frequency; 7 kHz.

Fixed-wing aircraft: 24 Super Étendard; 7 Alizé.
Helicopters: 2 SA 365F Dauphin 2.

Modernisation: In 1995-97 more work done enabling the carrier to operate Rafale M aircraft. A foldable mini ski-jump has been fitted to both catapults. The jet deflectors are enlarged (this implies reducing the area of the forward lift). Fitted with two Sadral SAM systems in 1996 when the last of the 100 mm guns were removed.
Structure: Flight deck, island superstructure and bridges, hull (over machinery spaces and magazines) are all armour plated. There are three bridges: Flag, Command and Aviation.
Two Mitchell-Brown steam catapults; Mk BS 5; able to launch 20 ton aircraft at 110 kt. The flight deck is angled at 8°. Two lifts 52.5 × 36 ft (16 × 10.97 m) one of which is on the starboard deck edge. Dimensions of the hangar are 590.6 × 78.7 × 23 ft (180 × 24 × 7 m).

Operational: Oil fuel capacity is 3,720 tons. The aircraft complement for the helicopter carrier role includes between 30 and 40 with a mixture of Super Frelon, Lynx, Super Puma, Puma and Gazelle (the last three types being army owned). Crusaders refitted to stay in service until replaced by Rafale. Deck trials of Rafale M aircraft were first carried out in April/May 1993, and again in 1994. Total of 35 aircraft are normally carried. The ship is to be paid off when *Charles de Gaulle* becomes fully operational in late 2000.
Sales: May be sold to Brazil.

UPDATED

FOCH   *6/1999*, French Navy /* 0069907

FOCH   *6/1999*, French Navy /* 0069908

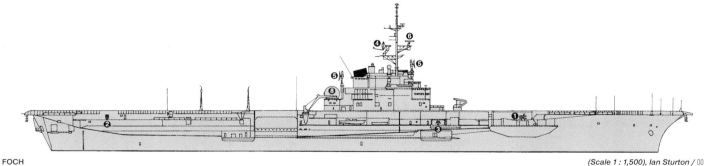

FOCH   *(Scale 1 : 1,500), Ian Sturton /* 0012331

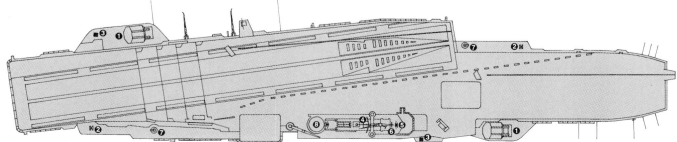

FOCH   *(Scale 1 : 1,500), Ian Sturton /* 0012332

DESTROYERS

Note: A new programme is planned with a common hull and machinery for two classes, one dedicated to ASW, replacing the 'Tourville' and 'Georges Leygues' classes, and a class of general purpose frigates to replace the avisos and supplement the La Fayettes, with the emphasis on land attack capabilities. These ships might be able to launch a derivative of the Matra BAe Dynamics Scalp/Storm Shadow ASM. These new ships should displace between 4,000 and 6,000 tons. First of class should start sea trials in 2008 to be commissioned in 2010.

0 + 2 (2) HORIZON CLASS (DDG)

Displacement, tons: 6,500 full load
Dimensions, feet (metres): 486.9 oa; 459.3 wl × 65.3 × 15.7
(148.4; 140 × 19.9 × 4.8)
Main machinery: CODOG: 2 GE LM 2500 gas turbines; 43 MW;
2 diesels; 8 MW; 2 shafts; cp props
Speed, knots: 29. **Range, miles:** 7,000 at 18 kt
Complement: 200 plus 35 spare

Missiles: SSM: 8 (2 quad) Aerospatiale Exocet MM 40 Block II ❶.
SAM: DCN Sylver VLS ❷ PAAMS (principal anti-air missile
system); 64 cells for Aster 15 and Aster 30 weapons.
2 Sadral launchers ❸.
Guns: 2 Otobreda 76 mm/62 Super Rapid ❹.
2 Breda Mauser 30 mm ❺.
Torpedoes: 4 (2 twin) fixed launchers ❻. Eurotorp Mu 90 Impact
torpedoes.
Countermeasures: Decoys: 4 Matra Defense chaff/IR flare
launchers ❼. SLAT torpedo defence system.
ESM/ECM. Elettronica JANEWS ❽.
Combat data systems: SENIT 8; Link 16. SATCOM ❾.
Weapons control: Sagem Vampir.
Radars: Air/surface search: Thomson-CSF/Plessey DRBV 27
(S 1850M) Astral ❿; D-band.
Surveillance/fire control: Alenia EMPAR ⓫; G-band;
multifunction.
Surface search ⓬.
Fire control: Alenia Marconi NA 25 ⓭.

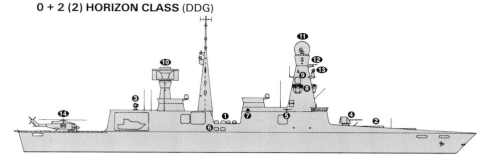

HORIZON   *(Scale 1 : 1,200), Ian Sturton /* 0069915

Sonars: Thomson Marconi 4110CL; hull-mounted; active search
and attack; medium frequency.

Helicopters: 1 Marine Nationale NH 90 ⓮ or AS 565 MA
Panther.

Programmes: Three-nation project for a new air defence ship
with Italy, France and UK. Joint project office established in
1993. Memorandum of Understanding for joint development
signed 11 July 1994. After UK withdrew in April 1999, an
agreement was signed on 7 September 1999 between France
and Italy to continue. Contracts expected for first pair to start
building at DCN Lorient in 2001 for a first in service date of
2005 and second in 2007. These ships are intended to replace
the 'Suffren' class. A second pair are planned to be included in
the 2003-08 budget.
Structure: Details given are subject to change. 48 cells of the
Sylver VLS system are provided by six octuple launchers with a
further 16 cells added on in French ships only.
UPDATED

2 CASSARD CLASS (TYPE F 70 (A/A)) (DDG)

Name	No	Builders	Laid down	Launched	Commissioned
CASSARD	D 614	Lorient Naval Dockyard	3 Sep 1982	6 Feb 1985	28 July 1988
JEAN BART	D 615	Lorient Naval Dockyard	12 Mar 1986	19 Mar 1988	21 Sep 1991

Displacement, tons: 4,230 standard; 4,730 full load
Dimensions, feet (metres): 455.9 × 45.9 × 21.3 (sonar)
(139 × 14 × 6.5)
Main machinery: 4 SEMT-Pielstick 18 PA6 V 280 BTC diesels;
43,200 hp(m) *(31.75 MW)* sustained; 2 shafts
Speed, knots: 29. **Range, miles:** 5,800 at 14 kt.
Complement: 225 (25 officers) accommodation for 251

Missiles: SSM: 8 Aerospatiale MM 40 Exocet ❶; inertial cruise;
active radar homing to 70 km *(40 n miles)* at 0.9 Mach;
warhead 165 kg; sea-skimmer.
SAM: 40 GDC Pomona Standard SM-1MR; Mk 13 Mod 5
launcher ❷; semi-active radar homing to 46 km *(25 n miles)* at
2 Mach; height envelope 45-18,288 m *(150-60,000 ft)*.
Launchers taken from T 47 (DDG) ships. To be replaced by
Aster 30 in due course.
2 Matra Sadral PDMS sextuple launchers ❸; 39 Mistral;
IR homing to 4 km *(2.2 n miles)*; warhead 3 kg; anti-sea-
skimmer; able to engage targets down to 10 ft above sea level.
Guns: 1 DCN/Creusot-Loire 3.9 in *(100 mm)*/55 Mod 68
CADAM automatic ❹; 80 rds/min to 17 km *(9 n miles)* anti-
surface; 8 km *(4.4 n miles)* anti-aircraft; weight of shell 13.5 kg.
2 Oerlikon 20 mm ❺; 720 rds/min to 10 km *(5.5 n miles)*.
4—12.7 mm MGs.
Torpedoes: 2 fixed launchers model KD 59E ❻. 10 ECAN L5 Mod
4; anti-submarine; active/passive homing to 9.5 km *(5.1 n
miles)* at 35 kt; warhead 150 kg; depth to 550 m *(1,800 ft)*.
Countermeasures: Decoys: 2 CSEE AMBL 1B Dagaie ❼ and 2
AMBL 2A Sagaie 10-barrelled trainable launchers ❽; fires a
combination of chaff and IR flares. Dassault LAD offboard
decoys. Nixie; towed torpedo decoy.
ESM: Thomson-CSF ARBR 17B ❾; radar warning. DIBV 1A
Vampir ❿; IR detector (integrated with search radar for
active/passive tracking in all weathers). Saigon radio intercept
at masthead.
ECM: Thomson-CSF ARBB 33; jammer; H-, I- and J-bands.

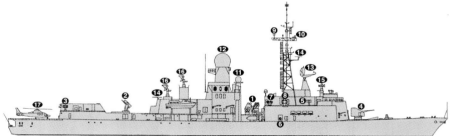

CASSARD   *(Scale 1 : 1,200), Ian Sturton*

Combat data systems: SENIT 6 action data automation; Links 11
and 14. SENIT 8 and Link 16 from 2001. Syracuse 2 SATCOM
⓫. OPSMER command support system.
Weapons control: DCN CTMS optronic/radar system with DIBC
1A Piranha II IR/TV tracker; CSEE Najir optronic secondary
director.
Radars: Air search: Thomson-CSF DRBJ 11B ⓬; 3D; E/F-band;
range 366 km *(200 n miles)*.
Air/surface search: Thomson-CSF DRBV 26C ⓭; D-band.
Navigation: 2 Racal DRBN 34A; I-band (1 for close-range
helicopter control ⓮).
Fire control: Thomson-CSF DRBC 33A ⓯; I-band (for guns).
2 Raytheon SPG-51C ⓰; G/I-band (for missiles).
Sonars: Thomson Sintra DUBA 25A (D 614) or DUBV 24C
(D 615); hull-mounted; active search and attack; medium
frequency.

Helicopters: 1 AS 565SA Panther ⓱.

Programmes: The building programme was considerably slowed
down by finance problems and doubts about the increasingly
obsolescent Standard SM 1 missile system. Service lives: First,
2013; second, 2015. Re-rated F 70 (ex-C 70) on 6 June 1988,
officially 'frégates anti-aériennes (FAA)'.
Modernisation: Aster 30 was planned to replace SM-1MR during
mid-life refits but this is likely to be cancelled in favour of
replacement of the ships by 'Horizon' class destroyers. DRBJ
15 radar initially fitted in *Cassard* but this was replaced in 1992
by DRBJ 11. Panther has replaced Lynx helicopter. Plans to fit
DSBV 62 towed array sonar are probably to be shelved. Link 16
being fitted with SENIT 8 nucleus.
Structure: Samahe 210 helicopter handling system.
Operational: Helicopter used for third party targeting for the
SSM. Both ships are based at Toulon.
UPDATED

JEAN BART   *6/1999*, H M Steele /* 0069914

7 GEORGES LEYGUES CLASS (TYPE F 70 (ASW)) (DDG)

Name	No	Builders	Laid down		Launched		Commissioned	
GEORGES LEYGUES	D 640	Brest Naval Dockyard	16 Sep	1974	17 Dec	1976	10 Dec	1979
DUPLEIX	D 641	Brest Naval Dockyard	17 Oct	1975	2 Dec	1978	13 June	1981
MONTCALM	D 642	Brest Naval Dockyard	5 Dec	1975	31 May	1980	28 May	1982
JEAN DE VIENNE	D 643	Brest Naval Dockyard	26 Oct	1979	17 Nov	1981	25 May	1984
PRIMAUGUET	D 644	Brest Naval Dockyard	17 Nov	1981	17 Mar	1984	5 Nov	1986
LA MOTTE-PICQUET	D 645	Brest Naval Dockyard/Lorient	12 Feb	1982	6 Feb	1985	18 Feb	1988
LATOUCHE-TRÉVILLE	D 646	Brest Naval Dockyard/Lorient	15 Feb	1984	19 Mar	1988	16 July	1990

Displacement, tons: 3,830 standard; 4,300 (D 640-643); 4,580 (D 644-646) full load
Dimensions, feet (metres): 455.9 × 45.9 × 18.7 *(139 × 14 × 5.7)*
Main machinery: CODOG; 2 RR Olympus TM3B gas turbines; 46,200 hp *(34.5 MW)* sustained; 2 SEMT-Pielstick 16 PA6 V280 diesels; 12,800 hp(m) *(9.41 MW)* sustained; 2 shafts; acbLIPS cp props
Speed, knots: 30; 21 on diesels
Range, miles: 8,500 at 18 kt on diesels; 2,500 at 28 kt
Complement: 218 (16 officers); 171 (D 640)

Missiles: SSM: 4 Aerospatiale MM 38 Exocet (MM 40 in D 642-646) **❶**; inertial cruise; active radar homing to 42 km *(23 n miles)* at 0.9 Mach (MM 38); active radar homing to 70 km *(40 n miles)* at 0.9 Mach (MM 40); warhead 165 kg; sea-skimmer. 4 additional Exocet missiles can be carried as a warload (D 644-646).
SAM: Thomson-CSF Crotale Naval EDIR octuple launcher **❷**; command line of sight guidance; radar/IR homing to 13 km *(7 n miles)* at 2.4 Mach; warhead 14 kg; 26 missiles.
2 Matra Simbad twin launchers may be mounted in lieu of 20 mm guns (D 644-646); 2 Matra Sadral sextuple launchers being fitted to D 640-643; Mistral; IR homing to 4 km *(2.2 n miles)*; warhead 3 kg.
Guns: 1 DCN/Creusot-Loire 3.9 in *(100 mm)*/55 Mod 68 CADAM automatic **❸**; dual purpose; 78 rds/min to 17 km *(9 n miles)* anti-surface; 8 km *(4.4 n miles)* anti-aircraft; weight of shell 13.5 kg.
2 Breda/Mauser 30 mm guns being fitted (D 640-643) **❹**. 800 rds/min to 3 km; weight of shell 0.37 kg.
2 Oerlikon 20 mm **❺**; 720 rds/min to 10 km *(5.5 n miles)*. 4 M2HB 12.7 mm MGs.

Torpedoes: 2 fixed launchers. 10 ECAN L5; anti-submarine; active/passive homing to 9.5 km *(5.1 n miles)* at 35 kt; warhead 150 kg; depth to 550 m *(1,800 ft)*. 12 Honeywell Mk 46 or Eurotorp Mu 90 Impact for helicopters (in due course).
Countermeasures: Decoys: 2 CSEE Dagaie Mk 1 or 2 10-barrelled double trainable launcher **❻**; chaff and IR flares; H- to J-band. Dassault LAD offboard decoys.
ESM: ARBR 17 **❼**; radar warning. Sagem DIBV 2A Vampir MB IRST (D 641-643).
ECM: ARBB 32B or Dassault ARBB 36 (D 641-643); jammer.
Combat data systems: SENIT 4; STIDAV based on SENIT 8 being added (D 640-643) action data automation; Links 11 and 14. Syracuse 2 SATCOM **❽**. OPSMER command support system.

Weapons control: Thomson-CSF Vega (D 640-643) and DCN CTMS (D 644-646) optronic/radar systems. SAT Murène IR tracker being added to CTMS and Vega systems. CSEE Panda optical director. 2 Sagem VIGY-105 optronic systems (for 30 mm guns) fitted 1995-97. DLT L4 (D 640-643) and DLT L5 (D 644-646) torpedo control system. OPS-100F acoustic processor being fitted.
Radars: Air search: Thomson-CSF DRBV 26A (D 640-643) **❾**; D-band; range 182 km *(100 n miles)* for 2 m² target.
Air/surface search: Thomson-CSF DRBV 51C **❿** (DRBV 15A **⓫** in D 644-646); G-band; range 120 km *(65 n miles)* for 2 m² target.
Navigation: 2 Decca 1226; I-band (1 for close-range helicopter control).
Fire control: Thomson-CSF Vega with DRBC 32E (D 640-643) **⓬**; I-band; DRBC 33A (D 644-646) **⓭**; I-band.
Crotale **⓮**; I-band (for SAM).
Sonars: Thomson Sintra DUBV 23D (DUBV 24C in D 644-646); bow-mounted; active search and attack; 5 kHz.
DUBV 43B (43C in D 643-646) **⓯**; VDS; search; medium frequency; paired with DUBV 23D/24; tows at 24 kt down to 200 m *(650 ft)*, *(700 m (3,000 ft)* for 43C). Length of tow 600 m *(2,000 ft)*; being upgraded to 43C.
DSBV 61B (in D 644 onward); passive linear towed array; very low frequency; 365 m *(1,200 ft)*. ATBF 2 lightweight towed array may be fitted in due course.

Helicopters: 2 Lynx Mk 4 **⓰** (except D 640).

Programmes: First three were in the 1971-76 new construction programme, fourth in 1978 estimates, fifth in 1980 estimates, sixth in 1981 estimates, seventh in 1983 estimates. D 645 and 646 were towed from Brest to Lorient for completion. Service lives: *Georges Leygues*, 2010; *Dupleix* and *Montcalm*, 2006; *Jean de Vienne*, 2008; *Primauguet*, 2011; *La Motte-Picquet*, 2012; *Latouche-Tréville*, 2014. Re-rated F 70 'frégates anti-sous-marines (FASM)' (ex-C 70) on 6 June 1988.
Modernisation: Air defence upgrade (Opération Amélioration Autodéfense Antimissiles, OP3A) for three of the class, with *Jean de Vienne* conducting sea trials in 1996. *Dupleix* September 1998 to May 1999. *Montcalm* in 2000. Large command structure fitted above the bridge, two Matra Sadral sextuple launchers, two Breda/Mauser 30 mm gun mounts controlled by Sagem Vigy 105 optronic sights, Vampir MB IRST and ARBB 36 jammers (replacing ARBB 32). ASW modernisation of the last six of the class planned but this may be overtaken by priorities being given to new ships. Plans to fit Milas ASW missiles have been shelved. *Georges Leygues* hangar converted for training role in 1999 and crew reduced.
Structure: Bridge raised one deck in the last three of the class. Inmarsat aerial can be fitted forward of the funnel or between the Syracuse domes.
Operational: *Primauguet* and *Latouche-Tréville* allocated to GASM, remainder to FAN, except *Georges Leygues* which from 1999 acts as a tender to *Jeanne d'Arc* for training cruises.

UPDATED

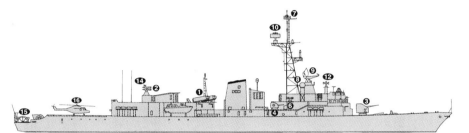

LA MOTTE-PICQUET   *(Scale 1 : 1,200), Ian Sturton*

JEAN DE VIENNE   *(Scale 1 : 1,200), Ian Sturton /* 0052146

JEAN DE VIENNE   *2/1999*, M Declerck /* 0069910

LATOUCHE-TRÉVILLE   *6/1999*, Maritime Photographic /* 0069911

DUPLEIX
6/1999*, H M Steele / 0069912

LATOUCHE-TRÉVILLE
6/1999*, H M Steele / 0069913

2 SUFFREN CLASS (DDG)

Name	No	Builders	Laid down	Launched	Commissioned
SUFFREN	D 602	Lorient Naval Dockyard	21 Dec 1962	15 May 1965	20 July 1968
DUQUESNE	D 603	Brest Naval Dockyard	1 Feb 1965	12 Feb 1966	1 Apr 1970

Displacement, tons: 5,090 standard; 6,910 full load
Dimensions, feet (metres): 517.1 × 50.9 × 20 *(157.6 × 15.5 × 6.1)*
Main machinery: 4 boilers; 640 psi *(45 kg/cm²)*; 842°F *(450°C)*; 2 Rateau turbines; 72,500 hp(m) *(53 MW)*; 2 shafts
Speed, knots: 34. **Range, miles:** 5,100 at 18 kt; 2,400 at 29 kt
Complement: 355 (23 officers)

Missiles: SSM: 4 Aerospatiale MM 38 Exocet ❶; inertial cruise; active radar homing to 42 km *(23 n miles)* at 0.9 Mach; warhead 165 kg; sea-skimmer.
SAM: ECAN Ruelle Masurca twin launcher ❷; Mk 2 Mod 3 semi-active radar homers; range 55 km *(30 n miles)*; warhead 98 kg; 48 missiles.
Guns: 2 DCN/Creusot-Loire 3.9 in *(100 mm)*/55 Mod 1964 CADAM automatic ❸; 80 rds/min to 17 km *(9 n miles)* anti-surface; 8 km *(4.4 n miles)* anti-aircraft; weight of shell 13.5 kg.
4 or 6 Oerlikon 20 mm ❹; 720 rds/min to 10 km *(5.5 n miles)*. 2—12.7 mm MGs.
Torpedoes: 4 launchers (2 each side) ❺. 10 ECAN L5; anti-submarine; active/passive homing to 9.5 km *(5.1 n miles)* at 35 kt; warhead 150 kg; depth to 550 m *(1,800 ft)*.
Countermeasures: Decoys: 2 CSEE Sagaie 10-barrelled trainable launchers; chaff to 8 km *(4.4 n miles)* and IR flares to 3 km *(1.6 n miles)*. 2 Dagaie launchers ❻. Dassault LAD offboard decoys.
ESM: ARBR 17 ❼; intercept.
ECM: ARBB 33; jammer.
Combat data systems: SENIT 2 action data automation; Links 11 and 14. Syracuse 2 SATCOM ❽. OPSMER command support system. Marisat.
Weapons control: DCN CTMS radar/optronic control system with SAT DIBC 1A Piranha IR and TV tracker. 2 Sagem DMA optical directors.
Radars: Air search (radome): DRBI 23 ❾; D-band.
Air/surface search: DRBV 15A ❿; E/F-band.
Navigation: Racal Decca 1229 (DRBN 34A); I-band.
Fire control: 2 Thomson-CSF DRBR 51 ⓫; G/I-band (for Masurca).
Thomson-CSF DRBC 33A ⓬; I-band (for guns).
Tacan: URN 20.
Sonars: Thomson Sintra DUBV 23; hull-mounted; active search and attack; 5 kHz.
DUBV 43 ⓭; VDS; medium frequency 5 kHz; tows at up to 24 kt at 200 m *(656 ft)*.

Programmes: Ordered under the 1960 programme.
Modernisation: MM 38 Exocet fitted in 1977 *(Duquesne)* and 1979 *(Suffren)*; Masurca modernised in 1984-85 *(Duquesne)* and 1988-89 *(Suffren)*, with new computers. DRBV 15A radars replaced DRBV 50. *Suffren* had a major refit from May 1988 to September 1989 and *Duquesne* from June 1990 to March 1991: modernisation of the DRBI-23 radar; new computers for the SENIT combat data system; new CTMS fire-control system

for 100 mm guns fitted (with DRBC-33A radar, TV camera and DIBC-1A Piranha IR tracker). New ESM/ECM suite: ARBR 17 radar interceptor, ARBB 33 jammer and Sagaie decoy launchers. Two 20 mm guns fitted either side of DRBC 33A.
Structure: Equipped with gyro-controlled stabilisers operating three pairs of non-retractable fins. NBC citadel fitted during modernisation. Air conditioning of accommodation and operational areas. Excellent sea boats and weapon platforms.

Operational: Both ships are based at Toulon. Officially frégates lance-missiles (FLM). *Duquesne* in refit from September 1998 to July 1999, and *Suffren* from July 1999 to June 2000. *Malafon* removed having been non-operational since 1997. Being kept in service to 2005 which is longer than planned due to delays in Horizon project.

UPDATED

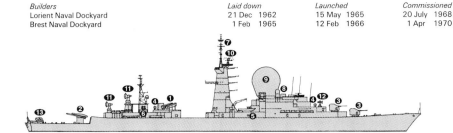

DUQUESNE
(Scale 1 : 1,500), Ian Sturton / 0069916

DUQUESNE
*10/1999 *, van Ginderen Collection /* 0069917

DUQUESNE
*9/1999 *, H M Steele /* 0069904

PARTNERING NAVIES

Scorpène SSK: a unique combination of modular design and state-of-the-art technologies

La Fayette-class stealthy frigates: a world reference

SENIT CMS: 30 years of experience in tactical data processing

DCN INTERNATIONAL

19-21, rue du colonel Pierre-Avia - 75015 Paris - FRANCE
Tel.: + 33 (0)1 41 08 71 71 - Fax.: + 33 (0)1 41 08 00 27
www.dcnintl.com

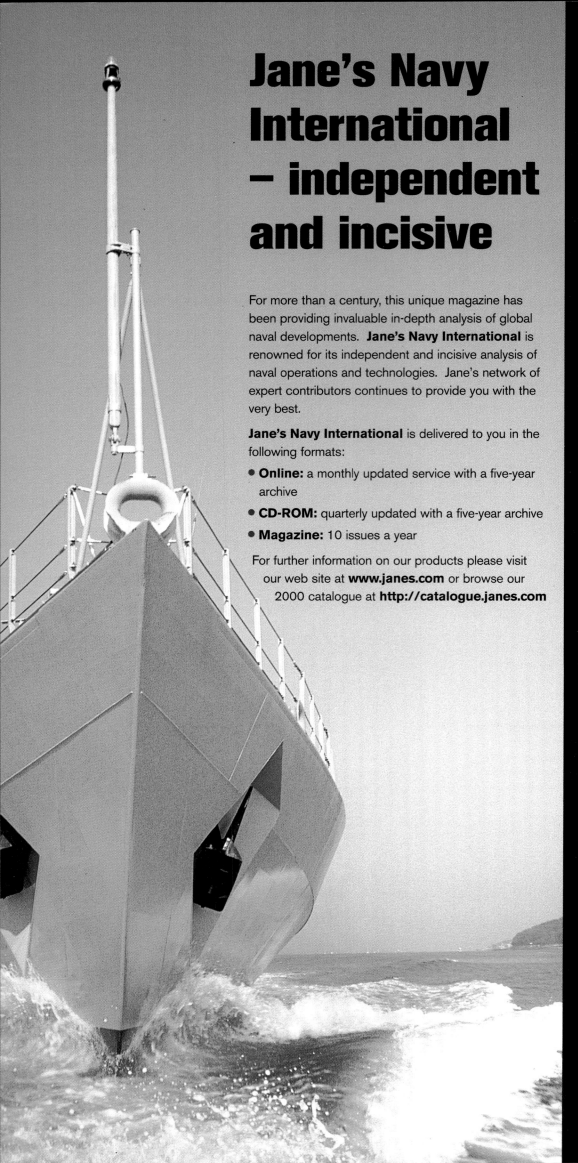

2 TOURVILLE CLASS (TYPE F 67) (DDG)

Name	No	Builders	Laid down	Launched	Commissioned
TOURVILLE	D 610	Lorient Naval Dockyard	16 Mar 1970	13 May 1972	21 June 1974
DE GRASSE	D 612	Lorient Naval Dockyard	14 June 1972	30 Nov 1974	1 Oct 1977

Displacement, tons: 4,580 standard; 5,950 full load
Dimensions, feet (metres): 501.6 × 52.4 × 18.7
  (152.8 × 16 × 5.7)
Main machinery: 4 boilers; 640 psi *(45 kg/cm²)*; 840°F *(450°C)*;
  2 Rateau turbines; 58,000 hp(m) *(43 MW)*; 2 shafts
Speed, knots: 32. **Range, miles:** 5,000 at 18 kt
Complement: 301 (21 officers)

Missiles: SSM: 6 Aerospatiale MM 38 Exocet ❶; inertial cruise;
  active radar homing to 42 km *(23 n miles)* at 0.9 Mach;
  warhead 165 kg; sea-skimmer.
SAM: Thomson-CSF Crotale Naval EDIR octuple launcher ❷;
  command line of sight guidance; radar/IR homing to 13 km
  (7 n miles) at 2.4 Mach; warhead 14 kg.
Guns: 2 DCN/Creusot-Loire 3.9 in *(100 mm)*/55 Mod 68
  CADAM automatic ❸; dual purpose; 80 rds/min to 17 km *(9 n
  miles)* anti-surface; 8 km *(4.4 n miles)* anti-aircraft; weight of
  shell 13.5 kg.
  2 Giat 20 mm ❹.
Torpedoes: 2 launchers ❺. 10 ECAN L5; anti-submarine; active/
  passive homing to 9.5 km *(5.1 n miles)* at 35 kt; warhead
  150 kg; depth to 550 m *(1,800 ft)*. Honeywell Mk 46 or
  Eurotorp Mu 90 Impact torpedoes for helicopters.
Countermeasures: Decoys: 2 CSEE/VSEL Syllex 8-barrelled
  trainable launcher (to be replaced by 2 Dagaie systems) ❻;
  chaff to 1 km in centroid and distraction patterns.
ESM: ARBR 16; radar warning.
ECM: ARBB 32; jammer.
Combat data systems: SENIT 3 action data automation; Links 11
  and 14. Syracuse 2 SATCOM ❼. OPSMER command support
  system. Inmarsat.
Weapons control: SENIT 3 radar/TV tracker (possibly SAT
  Murène in due course). 2 Sagem DMAa optical directors.
  OPS-100F acoustic processor.
Radars: Air search: DRBV 26 ❽; D-band; range 182 km *(100 n
  miles)* for 2 m² target.
Air/surface search: Thomson-CSF DRBV 51B ❾; G-band; range
  29 km *(16 n miles)*.
Navigation: 2 Racal Decca Type 1226; I-band (1 for helicopter
  control).
Fire control: Thomson-CSF DRBC 32D ❿; I-band.
  Crotale ⓫; J-band (for SAM).
Sonars: Thomson Sintra DUBV 23; bow-mounted; active search
  and attack; medium frequency.
  Thomson Sintra DSBX 1A (ATBF) VDS ⓬; active 1 kHz
  transmitter and 5 kHz transceiver in same 10 tonne towed
  body.
  Thomson Sintra DSBV 62C; passive linear towed array; very
  low frequency.

Helicopters: 2 Lynx Mk 4 ⓭.

Programmes: Originally rated as corvettes but reclassified as
  'frégates anti-sous-marins (FASM)' on 8 July 1971 and given D
  pennant numbers.
Modernisation: Major communications and combat data
  systems updates. The SLASM ASW combat suite installed in
  Tourville from March 1994 to April 1995, *De Grasse* from May
  1995 to September 1996. This included new signal processing
  for the bow sonar, plus LF and MF towed active sonar with
  separate towed passive array including torpedo warning.
  Acoustic processor for helo borne sonobuoys. Milas ASW
  missile cancelled. Passive towed arrays fitted in 1990. Malafon
  removed from *Tourville* in 1994 and *De Grasse* in 1996.
Operational: Assigned to GASM. Helicopters are now used
  primarily in the ASW role with sonar or sonobuoy dispenser,
  and ASW weapons.

UPDATED

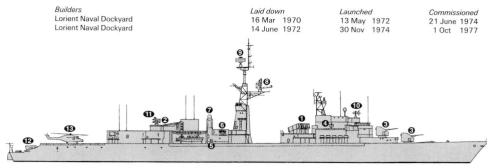

TOURVILLE   *(Scale 1 : 1,200), Ian Sturton /* 0052151

DE GRASSE   *6/1999*, H M Steele /* 0069919

DE GRASSE   *10/1999*, Diego Quevedo /* 0069920

TOURVILLE   *6/1999*, H M Steele /* 0069921

FRIGATES

4 + 1 LA FAYETTE CLASS (FFG)

Name	No	Builders	Laid down	Launched	Commissioned
LA FAYETTE	F 710	DCN, Lorient	15 Dec 1990	13 June 1992	23 Mar 1996
SURCOUF	F 711	DCN, Lorient	3 July 1992	3 July 1993	7 Feb 1997
COURBET	F 712	DCN, Lorient	15 Sep 1993	12 Mar 1994	1 Apr 1997
ACONIT (ex-Jauréguiberry)	F 713	DCN, Lorient	1 Aug 1996	8 June 1997	10 June 1999
GUÉPRATTE	F 714	DCN, Lorient	1 Oct 1998	3 Mar 1999	June 2002

Displacement, tons: 3,700 full load
Dimensions, feet (metres): 407.5 oa; 377.3 pp × 50.5 × 19.4 (screws) *(124.2; 115 × 15.4 × 5.9)*
Main machinery: CODAD; 4 SEMT-Pielstick 12 PA6 V 280 STC diesels; 21,107 hp(m) *(15.52 MW)* sustained; 2 shafts; acbLIPS cp props; bow thruster
Speed, knots: 25. **Range, miles:** 7,000 at 15 kt; 9,000 at 12 kt
Complement: 139 (15 officers) plus 12 aircrew plus 12 Marines

Missiles: SSM: 8 Aerospatiale MM 40 Block 2 Exocet ❶; inertial cruise; active radar homing to 70 km *(40 n miles)* at 0.9 Mach; warhead 165 kg; sea-skimmer.
SAM: Thomson-CSF Crotale Naval CN 2 (EDIR with V3 in *La Fayette* to be retrofitted with CN 2 in due course) octuple launcher ❷; VT 1; command line of sight guidance; radar/IR homing to 13 km *(7 n miles)* at 3.5 Mach; warhead 14 kg. 24 missiles. May be replaced by SAAM VLS ❸ with 16 Aster 15 missiles in mid-life modernisation.
Guns: 1 DCN 3.9 in *(100 mm)*/55 TR ❹; 80 rds/min to 17 km *(9 n miles)*; weight of shell 13.5 kg.
2 Giat 20F2 20 mm ❺; 720 rds/min to 10 km *(5.5 n miles)*.
2—12.7 mm MGs.
Countermeasures: Decoys: 2 CSEE Dagaie Mk 2 ❻ 10-barrelled trainable launchers; chaff and IR flares.
ESM: Thomson-CSF ARBR 21 (DR 3000-S) ❼ or ARBR 17 *(La Fayette)*; radar intercept.
DIBV 10 Vampir ❽; IR detector (can be fitted).
ECM: Dassault ARBB 33; jammer (can be fitted).
Combat data systems: Thomson-CSF TAVITAC 2000. Links 11 and 14. Syracuse 2 SATCOM ❾. OPSMER command support system.
Weapons control: Thomson-CSF CTM radar/IR system. Sagem TDS 90 VIGY optronic system.
Radars: Air/surface search: Thomson-CSF Sea Tiger Mk 2 (DRBV 15C) ❿; E/F-band; range 110 km *(60 n miles)* for 2 m² target.
Navigation: 2 Racal Decca 1229 (DRBN 34A) ⓫; I-band. One set for helicopter control.
Fire control: Thomson-CSF Castor 2J ⓬; J-band; range 17 km *(9.2 n miles)* for 1 m² target.
Crotale ⓭; J-band (for SAM).
Arabel for SAAM ⓮ (after modernisation).

Helicopters: 1 Aerospatiale AS 565 MA Panther ⓯ or platform for 1 Super Frelon. NH 90 ⓰ in due course.

Programmes: Originally described as 'Frégates Légères' but this was changed in 1992 to 'Frégates type La Fayette'. First three ordered 25 July 1988; three more 24 September 1992 but the last of these was cancelled in May 1996. The construction timetable has been delayed by several months because of funding problems. First steel cut for each hull about 14 months before the keel is laid.
Structure: Constructed from high-tensile steel with a double skin from waterline to upper deck. 10 mm plating protects vital spaces. Space left for two octuple SAAM VLS launchers forward of the bridge which may replace Crotale CN 2 in mid-life modernisation. This might mean putting the Arabel fire-control radar on top of a more solid looking foremast once Crotale is removed. Superstructure inclines at 10° to the vertical to reduce radar echoing area. External equipment such as capstans, bollards and so on, either 'hidden' or installed as low as possible. Radar absorbent paint is used extensively. Sensitive areas are armour-plated. SLAT anti-torpedo system may be fitted when available. Plans to fit sonar have been dropped but in the future an ASW version of the ship could be built with hull and towed array sonars, K 69 lightweight torpedo launchers, and an ASW configured helicopter. DCN Samahe helo handling system.

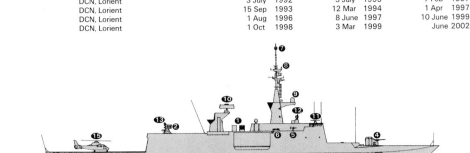

LA FAYETTE *(Scale 1 : 1,200), Ian Sturton*

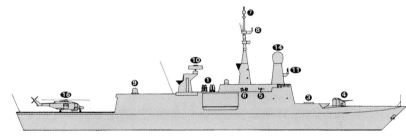

LA FAYETTE (after mid-life modernisation) *(Scale 1 : 1,200), Ian Sturton*

SURCOUF *3/1998 / 0052156*

Operational: *La Fayette* started sea trials 27 September 1993, *Surcouf* 4 July 1994, *Courbet* 14 September 1995 and *Aconit* 14 April 1998. These frigates are designed for out of area operations on overseas stations and the first three are assigned to FAN for the Indian Ocean. Super Frelon helicopters can land on the flight deck. NH 90 prototype trials in *Courbet* in 1998. The ship can launch inflatable boats from a hatch in the stern which hinges upwards. The Vampir IR detector and ARBB 33 jammer are fitted 'for but not with'.
Sales: Three of an improved design to Saudi Arabia for completion from 1999, and six for Taiwan.

UPDATED

ACONIT *5/1999*, B Sullivan / 0069922*

10 D'ESTIENNE D'ORVES (TYPE A 69) CLASS (FFG)

Name	No	Builders	Laid down		Launched		Commissioned	
SECOND MAÎTRE LE BIHAN	F 788	Lorient Naval Dockyard	1 Nov	1976	13 Aug	1977	7 July	1979
LIEUTENANT DE VAISSEAU LE HÉNAFF	F 789	Lorient Naval Dockyard	21 Mar	1977	16 Sep	1978	13 Feb	1980
LIEUTENANT DE VAISSEAU LAVALLÉE	F 790	Lorient Naval Dockyard	30 Nov	1977	11 May	1979	8 Oct	1980
COMMANDANT L'HERMINIER	F 791	Lorient Naval Dockyard	29 May	1979	7 Mar	1981	19 Jan	1986
PREMIER MAÎTRE L'HER	F 792	Lorient Naval Dockyard	15 Dec	1978	28 June	1980	5 Dec	1981
COMMANDANT BLAISON	F 793	Lorient Naval Dockyard	15 Nov	1979	7 Mar	1981	26 Apr	1982
ENSEIGNE DE VAISSEAU JACOUBET	F 794	Lorient Naval Dockyard	June	1980	28 Sep	1981	23 Oct	1982
COMMANDANT DUCUING	F 795	Lorient Naval Dockyard	1 Oct	1980	26 Sep	1981	17 Mar	1983
COMMANDANT BIROT	F 796	Lorient Naval Dockyard	23 Mar	1981	22 May	1982	14 Mar	1984
COMMANDANT BOUAN	F 797	Lorient Naval Dockyard	12 Oct	1981	23 Apr	1983	1 Nov	1984

COMMANDANT L'HERMINIER   (Scale 1 : 900), Ian Sturton

Displacement, tons: 1,175 standard; 1,250 (1,330, later ships) full load

Dimensions, feet (metres): 264.1 × 33.8 × 18 (sonar) (80.5 × 10.3 × 5.5)

Main machinery: 2 SEMT-Pielstick 12 PC2 V 400 diesels; 12,000 hp(m) (8.82 MW); 2 shafts; acbLIPS cp props
2 SEMT-Pielstick 12 PA6 V 280 BTC diesels; 14,400 hp(m) (10.6 MW) sustained; 2 shafts; acbLIPS cp props (Commandant L'Herminier)

Speed, knots: 23. **Range, miles:** 4,500 at 15 kt

Complement: 90 (7 officers) plus 18 marines (in some)

Missiles: SSM: 4 Aerospatiale MM 40 (or 2 MM 38) Exocet ❶; inertial cruise; active radar homing to 70 km (40 n miles) (or 42 km (23 n miles)) at 0.9 Mach; warhead 165 kg; sea-skimmer. Most will get dual fit capability ITL in due course (see Modernisation) but a few only have MM 38 capability (ITS) and some none at all.
SAM: Matra Simbad twin launcher for Mistral; IR homing to 4 km (2.2 n miles); warhead 3 kg.

Guns: 1 DCN/Creusot-Loire 3.9 in (100 mm)/55 Mod 68 CADAM automatic ❷; 80 rds/min to 17 km (9 n miles) anti-surface; 8 km (4.4 n miles) anti-aircraft; weight of shell 13.5 kg.
2 Giat 20 mm ❸; 720 rds/min to 10 km (5.5 n miles).
4—12.7 mm MGs.

Torpedoes: 4 fixed tubes ❹. ECAN L5; dual purpose; active/passive homing to 9.5 km (5.1 n miles) at 35 kt; warhead 150 kg; depth to 550 m (1,800 ft).

A/S mortars: 1 Creusot-Loire 375 mm Mk 54 6-tubed trainable launcher ❺; range 1,600 m; warhead 107 kg. Removed from F 792, F 793, F 794, F 796 and others in due course.

Countermeasures: Decoys: 2 CSEE Dagaie 10-barrelled trainable launchers ❻; chaff and IR flares; H- to J-band.
Nixie torpedo decoy.
ESM: ARBR 16; radar warning.

Combat data systems: Syracuse 2 SATCOM (F 792, F 793, F 794, F 796, F 797 and others in due course). OPSMER command support system with Link 11 and Syracuse SATCOM in MM 40 ships.

Weapons control: Thomson-CSF Vega system; CSEE Panda optical secondary director.

Radars: Air/surface search: Thomson-CSF DRBV 51A ❼; G-band.
Navigation: Racal Decca 1226; I-band.
Fire control: Thomson-CSF DRBC 32E ❽; I-band.

Sonars: Thomson Sintra DUBA 25; hull-mounted; search and attack; medium frequency.

Programmes: Classified as 'Avisos'.

Modernisation: In 1985 Commandant L'Herminier, F 791, fitted with 12PA6 BTC Diesels Rapides as trial for Type F 70. Most have dual MM 38/MM 40 ITL (Installation de Tir Légère) capability. Weapon fit depends on deployment and operational requirement. Those without ITL are being retrofitted with ITS (Installation de Tir Standard). Syracuse 2 SATCOM fitted in Commandant Blaison and Enseigne de Vaisseau Jacoubet in 1993, Premier Maître l'Her in 1994 and Commandant Birot in 1999, vice the A/S mortar, and accommodation provided for commandos. Others of the class may be similarly modified in due course. Matra Simbad launchers have been fitted aft of the A/S mortar/Syracuse SATCOM for operations.

Operational: Endurance, 30 days and primarily intended for coastal A/S operations. Also available for overseas patrols. F 794-797 assigned to Commander Mediterranean Flotilla or abroad. Remainder to GASM. Toulon-based ships have MM 40 Exocet. By 2002 the plan is to have six at Brest for GASM and the remaining three at Toulon.

Sales: The original Lieutenant de Vaisseau Le Hénaff and Commandant l'Herminier sold to South Africa in 1976 while under construction. As a result of the UN embargo on arms sales to South Africa, they were sold to Argentina in September 1978 followed by a third, specially built. Three more decommissioned in 2000 and may be transferred to Argentina.   **UPDATED**

PREMIER MAÎTRE L'HER   11/1999*, Camil Busquets i Vilanova / 0069923

COMMANDANT L'HERMINIER   8/1999*, Michael Nitz / 0069924

COMMANDANT BOUAN   6/1999*, H M Steele / 0069925

6 FLORÉAL CLASS (FFG)

Name	No	Builders	Laid down		Launched		Commissioned	
FLORÉAL	F 730	Chantiers de l'Atlantique, St Nazaire	2 Apr	1990	6 Oct	1990	27 May	1992
PRAIRIAL	F 731	Chantiers de l'Atlantique, St Nazaire	11 Sep	1990	23 Mar	1991	20 May	1992
NIVÔSE	F 732	Chantiers de l'Atlantique, St Nazaire	16 Jan	1991	10 Aug	1991	16 Oct	1992
VENTÔSE	F 733	Chantiers de l'Atlantique, St Nazaire	28 June	1991	14 Mar	1992	5 May	1993
VENDÉMIAIRE	F 734	Chantiers de l'Atlantique, St Nazaire	17 Jan	1992	29 Aug	1992	20 Oct	1993
GERMINAL	F 735	Chantiers de l'Atlantique, St Nazaire	17 Aug	1992	13 Mar	1993	17 May	1994

Displacement, tons: 2,600 standard; 2,950 full load
Dimensions, feet (metres): 306.8 × 45.9 × 14.1
(93.5 × 14 × 4.3)
Main machinery: CODAD; 4 SEMT-Pielstick 6 PA6 L 280 diesels;
8,820 hp(m) *(6.5 MW)* sustained; 2 shafts; acbLIPS cp props;
bow thruster; 340 hp(m) *(250 kW)*
Speed, knots: 20. **Range, miles:** 10,000 at 15 kt
Complement: 86 (10 officers) (including aircrew) plus 24
Marines + 13 spare

Missiles: SSM: 2 Aerospatiale MM 38 Exocet ❶; inertial cruise;
active radar homing to 42 km *(23 n miles)* at 0.9 Mach;
warhead 165 kg; sea-skimmer.
SAM: 1 or 2 Matra Simbad twin launchers can replace 20 mm
guns or Dagaie launcher.
Guns: 1 DCN 3.9 in *(100 mm)*/55 Mod 68 CADAM ❷; 80 rds/
min to 17 km *(9 n miles)*; weight of shell 13.5 kg.
2 Giat 20 F2 20 mm ❸; 720 rds/min to 10 km *(5.5 n miles).*
Countermeasures: Decoys: 1 or 2 CSEE Dagaie Mk II; 10-
barrelled trainable launchers ❹; chaff and IR flares.
ESM: Thomson-CSF ARBR 17 ❺; radar intercept.
Weapons control: CSEE Najir optronic director ❻. Syracuse 2
SATCOM ❼.
Radars: Air/surface search: Thomson-CSF Mars DRBV 21A ❽;
D-band.
Navigation: 2 Racal Decca 1229 (DRBN 34A); I-band (1 for
helicopter control ❾).

Helicopters: 1 AS 565 MA Panther or platform for 1 AS 332F
Super Puma ❿.

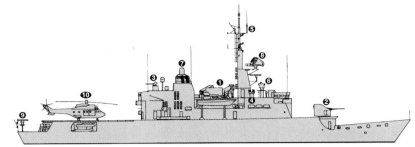

FLORÉAL   *(Scale 1 : 900), Ian Sturton / 0012348*

Programmes: Officially described as 'Frégates de Surveillance'
or 'Ocean capable patrol vessel' and designed to operate in the
offshore zone in low-intensity operations. First two ordered on
20 January 1989; built at Chantiers de l'Atlantique, St Nazaire,
with weapon systems fitted by DCAN Lorient. Second pair
ordered 9 January 1990; third pair in January 1991. Named
after the months of the Revolutionary calendar.
Structure: Built to merchant passenger marine standards with
stabilisers and air conditioning. New funnel design improves
air flow over the flight deck. Has one freight bunker aft for
about 100 tons cargo. Second-hand Exocet MM 38 has been
fitted instead of planned MM 40.

Operational: Endurance, 50 days. Range proved to be better
than expected during sea trials. Able to operate a helicopter up
to Sea State 5. Stations as follows: *Floreal* in South Indian
Ocean, *Ventose* in Antilles, *Germinal* at Toulon, *Prairial* and
Vendémiaire in Tahiti, *Nivôse* in Nouméa.
Sales: Two ordered by Morocco in 1998.

UPDATED

PRAIRIAL   *2/1999 *, Hachiro Nakai / 0069926*

SHIPBORNE AIRCRAFT

Note: First 11 NH 90 helicopters funded in 1997-2002 budget. First deck trials in *Courbet* in July
1998. First production model is expected to be in service in 2005. Total of 27 required of which 14
are allocated for 1st rate frigates.

Numbers/Type: 4 Dassault Aviation ACM Rafale M.
Operational speed: Mach 2.
Service ceiling: 50,000 ft *(15,240 m).*
Range: 1,800 n miles *(3,335 km).*
Role/Weapon systems: Total procurement of up to 60, with first production aircraft delivered
7 July 1999. First batch of 12 aircraft to be delivered by 2002: Air defence role, with some air-to-
ground capabilities. Second batch of aircraft to be delivered from 2005 as true multirole aircraft
(all aircraft to be brought to this standard later on). First naval prototype flown 12 December
1992. Deck trials in *Foch* from 1993. Sensors: Thomson-CSF/Dassault Electronique RBE2
multirole radar, SPECTRA EW/IR countermeasure suite, MIDS-LVT voice/data (Link 16),
Thomson-CSF/SAT OSF optronic surveillance and target acquisition device and optional recce
pod (multirole). Weapons: Giat M 791 30 mm cannon, eight AAMs, Matra MICA/EM medium
range and Magic 2 short range (for air defence role); MICA/IR AAM, Matra Apache weapon
dispenser and Aerospatiale AS 30L laser-guided standoff ASM (for air-to-ground role);
Aerospatiale ASMP nuclear ASM, Matra SCALP standoff precision-guided ASM, AASM general
use standoff modular ASM and AM 39 anti-ship missiles (multirole). Up to eight tons of weapon
load, limited to six tons for carrier operations.

UPDATED   RAFALE M

1995, Dassault Aviation / 0012961

Numbers/Type: 50 Dassault-Bréguet Super Étendard.
Operational speed: Mach 1 (approximately).
Service ceiling: 45,000 ft *(13,700 m)*.
Range: 920 n miles *(1,682 km)*.
Role/Weapon systems: Carrierborne strike fighter with nuclear strike capabilities and limited air defence role; tactical recce role to be added from 2000. All aircraft still in inventory modernised 1994-1999 to standard 3. Four aircraft to standard 4 for reconnaissance from 2000. Standard 5 from 2002 includes FLIR. Sensors: Dassault Electronique Anémone radar, Thomson-CSF Sherloc ESM (standard 4), SAGEM UAT 90 computer, Thomson-CSF Barracuda jammer, Phimat chaff dispenser, Alkan IR decoy dispenser; photo/optronic chassis in development (standard 4) to be installed in place of the cannon chassis (according to the mission). Weapons: air defence and self protection: two Matra BAe Dynamic Magic 2 short range AAMs and two DEFA 30 mm cannon; nuclear strike: one Aerospatiale ASMP nuclear ASM; air-to-surface: one Aerospatiale AM 39 Exocet anti-ship missile; air-to-ground: bombs, and (standard 3 aircraft) laser guided bombs (Paveway) or one Aerospatiale AS 30L laser guided missile. ***UPDATED***

SUPER ÉTENDARD   *6/1999 *, French Navy /* 0069927

Numbers/Type: 2 (1) Grumman E-2C Hawkeye Group 2.
Operational speed: 320 kt *(593 km/h)*.
Service ceiling: 37,000 ft *(11,278 m)*.
Range: 1,540 n miles *(2,852 km)*.
Role/Weapon systems: Used for AEW, and direction of AD and strike operations; total of three aircraft anticipated, with first pair ordered in May 1995 and delivered in April and December 1998 respectively. Third in 2003. To equip *Charles de Gaulle* but not *Foch*. Sensors: APS-145 radar, ESM, ALR-73 PDS, ALQ-108 airborne tactical data system with Links 11 and 16. Weapons: Unarmed. ***UPDATED***

HAWKEYE   *9/1999 *, J Corless /* 0033626

Numbers/Type: 15 Aerospatiale SA 321G Super Frelon.
Operational speed: 148 kt *(275 km/h)*.
Service ceiling: 10,170 ft *(3,100 m)*.
Range: 442 n miles *(820 km)*.
Role/Weapon systems: Formerly ASW helicopter; only six are operational and are now used for assault and support tasks embarked on carriers and LSDs; radar updated; provision for 27 passengers. Sensors: Omera ORB search radar. Weapons: Provision for 20 mm gun. ***UPDATED***

SUPER FRELON (on *Jeanne d'Arc*)   *2/1999 *, Hachiro Nakai /* 0069928

Numbers/Type: 31 Westland Lynx Mk 4 (FN).
Operational speed: 125 kt *(232 km/h)*.
Service ceiling: 12,500 ft *(3,810 m)*.
Range: 320 n miles *(593 km)*.
Role/Weapon systems: Sole French ASW helicopter, all now of the Mk 4 variant; embarked in destroyers and deployed on training tasks. Sensors: Omera 31 search radar, Alcatel (DUAV 4) dipping sonar, sonobuoys, Sextant Avionique MAD. Weapons: ASW: two Mk 46 Mod 1 (or Mu 90 Impact in due course) torpedoes, or depth charges. ASV: 1—7.62 mm MG. ***UPDATED***

LYNX   *1/2000 *, A Sharma /* 0081932

Numbers/Type: 30 Aerospatiale SA 319B Alouette III.
Operational speed: 113 kt *(210 km/h)*.
Service ceiling: 10,500 ft *(3,200 m)*.
Range: 290 n miles *(540 km)*.
Role/Weapon systems: General purpose helicopter; replaced by Lynx for ASW; now used for trials, surveillance and training tasks. Sensors: Some radar. Weapons: Unarmed. ***UPDATED***

ALOUETTE III   *6/1993, Albert Campanera i Rovira /* 0012964

Numbers/Type: 3/5/15 Aerospatiale SA 365F Dauphin 2/SA 365SN Dauphin 2/AS 565MA Panther.
Operational speed: 165 kt *(305 km/h)*.
Service ceiling: 16,700 ft *(5,100 m)*.
Range: 483 n miles *(895 km)*.
Role/Weapon systems: SA 365F Dauphin 2s procured to replace Alouette III for carrierborne SAR. Four more used for SAR role from various locations in metropolitan France. Three of these aircraft taken over by the Navy from civilian companies, last one being an ex-Air Force machine. Total of 15 AS 565MA Panthers ordered in several batches for 'Cassard' class DDGs, 'La Fayette' class and 'Floréal' class frigates. Total of 24 required. Sensors: Thomson-CSF Varan radar (AS-565 MA). FLIR to be fitted. Weapons: 7.62 mm MG (AS-565 MA). ASM in due course. ***UPDATED***

DAUPHIN 2   *7/1997, H M Steele /* 0012353

PANTHER   *9/1998, M Declerck /* 0052167

LAND-BASED MARITIME AIRCRAFT (FRONT LINE)

Numbers/Type: 4 Dassault Falcon 50.
Operational speed: 370 kt *(685 km/h)*.
Service ceiling: 49,000 ft *(14,930 m)*.
Range: 2,700 n miles *(5,000 km)*.
Role/Weapon systems: Maritime reconnaissance and SAR roles in the Atlantic and overseas stations (replaced deleted Atlantic Mk 1). Second-hand business jets acquired and modified to Navy requirements. Sensors: Thomson-CSF/DASA Ocean Master 100 radar, Thomsom-CSF (TRT) Défense Chlio FLIR. Weapons: Unarmed. ***UPDATED***

Numbers/Type: 4 Boeing E-3F Sentry AWAC.
Operational speed: 460 kt *(853 km/h)*.
Service ceiling: 30,000 ft *(9,145 m)*.
Range: 870 n miles *(1,610 km)*.
Role/Weapon systems: Air defence early warning aircraft with secondary role to provide coastal AEW for the Fleet; 6 hours endurance at the range given above. Sensors: Westinghouse APY-2 surveillance radar, Bendix weather radar, Mk XII IFF, Yellow Gate, ESM, ECM. Weapons: Unarmed. Operated by the Air Force. ***VERIFIED***

Numbers/Type: 28 Dassault Aviation Atlantique Mk 2.
Operational speed: 355 kt *(658 km/h).*
Service ceiling: 32,800 ft *(10,000 m).*
Range: 8 hours patrol at 1,000 n miles from base; 4 hours patrol at 1,500 n miles from base.
Role/Weapon systems: Maritime reconnaissance. ASW, ASV, COMINT/ELINT roles. Last one delivered in January 1998. Six aircraft are in long-term storage. Sensors: Thomson-CSF Iguane radar, ARAR 13 ESM, ECM, FLIR, MAD, sonobuoys (with DSAX-1 Thomson-CSF Sadang processing equipment). Link 11 (being fitted in all). COMINT/ELINT equipment optional. Integrated sensor/weapon system built around a CIMSA 15/125X computer. Weapons: Two AM 39 Exocet ASMs in ventral bay, or up to eight lightweight torpedoes (Mk 46 and later Mu 90), or depth charges, mines or bombs. *VERIFIED*

ATLANTIQUE   *6/1998, J Cislak /* 0052168

Numbers/Type: 6 Dassault-Bréguet Falcon 10MER.
Operational speed: 492 kt *(912 km/h).*
Service ceiling: 35,500 ft *(10,670 m).*
Range: 1,920 n miles *(3,560 km).*
Role/Weapon systems: Primary aircrew/ECM training role but also has overwater surveillance role. Sensors: Search radar. Weapons: Unarmed. *UPDATED*

Numbers/Type: 5 Dassault-Bréguet Gardian.
Operational speed: 470 kt *(870 km/h).*
Service ceiling: 45,000 ft *(13,715 m).*
Range: 2,425 n miles *(4,490 km).*
Role/Weapon systems: Maritime reconnaissance role in Atlantic and overseas stations. To return to France by 2001. Sensors: Thomson-CSF Varan radar, Omega navigation, ECM/ESM pods. Weapons: Unarmed. *UPDATED*

Numbers/Type: 15 Aerospatiale N262E.
Operational speed: 226 kt *(420 km/h).*
Service ceiling: 26,900 ft *(8,200 m).*
Role/Weapon systems: Crew training and EEZ surveillance role. Used by Escadrille 56S in training role and can be used for EEZ surveillance. Modified N262A aircraft. Sensors: Omera ORB 32 radar; photo pod. Weapons: Unarmed. Target towing capability. *UPDATED*

AMPHIBIOUS FORCES

Note: A new LSD/LPD rated as an NTCD (Nouveau Transport de Chlands de Débarquement) is to be ordered from Alsthom Atlantique, St Nazaire in 2000 for delivery in 2004 with a second to be delivered in 2006. At 19,000 tons these will be cheaper ships than the NIMIS or BIP which had been proposed in 1996. The emphasis is to be on helicopter operations, amphibious command and control, and SES craft.

1 BOUGAINVILLE CLASS (BTS/LPD/AGI)

Name	No	Builders	Launched		Commissioned
BOUGAINVILLE	L 9077	Chantier Dubigeon, Nantes	3 Oct	1986	25 June 1988

Displacement, tons: 4,876 standard; 5,195 full load
Dimensions, feet (metres): 372.3; 344.4 wl × 55.8 × 14.1 *(113.5; 105 × 17 × 4.3)*
Flight deck, feet (metres): 85.3 × 55.8 *(26 × 17)*
Main machinery: 2 SACM AGO 195 V12 RVR diesels; 4,410 hp(m) *(3.24 MW)* sustained; 2 shafts; acbLIPS cp props; bow thruster; 400 hp(m) *(294 kW)*
Speed, knots: 15. **Range, miles:** 6,000 at 12 kt
Complement: 53 (5 officers) plus 10 staff
Military lift: 500 troops for 8 days; 1,180 tons cargo; 2 LCU in support or 10 LCP plus 2 LCM for amphibious role

Missiles: SAM: 2 Matra Simbad twin launchers (may be fitted).
Guns: 2—12.7 mm MGs.
Radars: Navigation: 2 Decca 1226; I-band.

Helicopters: Platform for 2 Super Frelon.

Programmes: Ordered November 1984 for the Direction du Centre d'Experimentations Nucléaires (DIRCEN). As Chantier Dubigeon closed down after her launch she was completed by Chantiers de l'Atlantique of the Alsthom group. Bâtiment de Transport et de Soutien (BTS).
Modernisation: Conversion 30 November 1998, Syracuse II SATCOM and communications intercept equipment fitted.
Structure: Well size is 78 × 10.2 m *(256 × 33.5 ft)*. It can receive tugs and one BSR or two CTMs, a supply tender of the 'Chamois' class, containers, mixed bulk cargo. Has extensive repair workshops and repair facilities for helicopters. Can act as mobile crew accommodation and has medical facilities. Storerooms for spare parts, victuals and ammunition. Hull to civilian standards. Carries a 37 ton crane.
Operational: Returned to France from Papeete in November 1998. Can dock a 500 ton ship. Based at Toulon since November 1999 and is used as an AGI, replacing *Berry*. *UPDATED*

BOUGAINVILLE   *9/1999*, L-G Nilsson /* 0069929

5 BATRAL TYPE (LIGHT TRANSPORTS and LANDING SHIPS) (LST)

Name	No	Builders	Commissioned
CHAMPLAIN	L 9030	Brest Naval Dockyard	5 Oct 1974
FRANCIS GARNIER	L 9031	Brest Naval Dockyard	27 Oct 1974
DUMONT D'URVILLE	L 9032	Français de l'Ouest	5 Feb 1983
JACQUES CARTIER	L 9033	Français de l'Ouest	23 Sep 1983
LA GRANDIÈRE	L 9034	Français de l'Ouest	20 Jan 1987

Displacement, tons: 750 standard; 1,330 (1,409, second pair) full load
Dimensions, feet (metres): 262.4 × 42.6 × 7.9 *(80 × 13 × 2.4)*
Main machinery: 2 SACM AGO 195 V12 diesels; 3,600 hp(m) *(2.65 MW)* sustained; 2 shafts; cp props
Speed, knots: 16. **Range, miles:** 4,500 at 13 kt
Complement: 43 (5 officers)
Military lift: 138 troops (180 in second pair); 12 vehicles; 350 tons load; 10 ton crane

Missiles: SAM: 2 Matra Simbad twin launchers (may be fitted).
Guns: 2 Bofors 40 mm/60 (L 9030, L 9031). 2 Giat 20F2 20 mm (L 9032, L 9033). 1—81 mm mortar. 2—12.7 mm MGs.
Radars: Navigation: DRBN 32; I-band.

Helicopters: 1 SA 319B Alouette III.

Programmes: Classified as Batral 3F. Bâtiments d'Assaut et de TRAnsport Légers (BATRAL). First two launched 17 November 1973. *Dumont D'Urville* floated out 27 November 1981. *Jacques Cartier* launched 28 April 1982 and *La Grandière* 15 December 1985.
Structure: 40 ton bow ramp; stowage for vehicles above and below decks. One LCVP and one LCPS carried. Helicopter landing platform. Last three of class have bridge one deck higher, a larger helicopter platform and a crane replaces the boom on the cargo deck.
Operational: Deployment: *Champlain*, Toulon (FAN); *F Garnier*, Antilles/French Guiana; *D D'Urville*, Papeete; *J Cartier*, New Caledonia; *La Grandière*, Indian Ocean.
Sales: Ships of this class built for Chile, Gabon, Ivory Coast and Morocco. *La Grandière* was also built for Gabon under Clause 29 arrangements but funds were not available. *UPDATED*

CHAMPLAIN   *9/1999*, H M Steele /* 0069934

3 EDIC 700 CLASS (LCT)

Name	No	Builders	Commissioned
SABRE	L 9051	SFCN, Villeneuve la Garenne	13 June 1987
DAGUE	L 9052	SFCN, Villeneuve la Garenne	19 Dec 1987

Displacement, tons: 736 full load
Dimensions, feet (metres): 193.6 × 38.1 × 5.8 *(59 × 11.6 × 1.7)*
Main machinery: 2 SACM Uni Diesel UD 30 V12 M1 diesels; 1,200 hp(m) *(882 kW)* sustained; 2 shafts
Speed, knots: 12. **Range, miles:** 1,800 at 12 kt
Complement: 17
Military lift: 350 tons
Guns: 2 Giat 20F2 20 mm. 2—12.7 mm MGs.
Radars: Navigation: Racal Decca 1229; I-band.

Comment: Ordered 10 March 1986. Given names on 29 April 1999. Rated as Engins de Débarquement d'Infanterie et Chars (EDIC III). Based at Toulon (*L 9051*) and Djibouti (*L 9052*). One more of the class to Senegal for the second time in February 1999. *UPDATED*

DAGUE   *9/1994*, van Ginderen Collection /* 0081933

2 CDIC CLASS (LCT)

Name	No	Builders	Commissioned
HALLEBARDE	L 9061	SFCN, Villeneuve la Garenne	19 Oct 1988
RAPIÈRE	L 9062	SFCN, Villeneuve la Garenne	2 Mar 1989

Displacement, tons: 380 light; 710 full load
Dimensions, feet (metres): 194.9 × 39 × 5.9 *(59.4 × 11.9 × 1.8)*
Main machinery: 2 SACM Uni Diesel UD 30 V12 M1 diesels; 1,200 hp(m) *(882 kW)* sustained; 2 shafts
Speed, knots: 10.5. **Range, miles:** 1,000 at 10 kt
Complement: 12 (1 officer)
Military lift: 336 tons
Guns: 2 Giat 20F2 20 mm. 2—12.7 mm MGs.
Radars: Navigation: Racal Decca 1229; I-band.

Comment: CDIC (Chaland de Débarquement d'Infanterie et de Chars) built to work with 'Foudre' class. The wheelhouse can be lowered to facilitate docking manoeuvres in the LPDs. Assigned to FAN at Toulon. Given names on 21 July 1997. *UPDATED*

RAPIÈRE   *2/1998, van Ginderen Collection /* 0052166

2 OURAGAN CLASS (LANDING SHIPS DOCK) (TCD/LSD)

Name	No	Builders	Laid down	Launched	Commissioned
OURAGAN	L 9021	Brest Naval Dockyard	June 1962	9 Nov 1963	1 June 1965
ORAGE	L 9022	Brest Naval Dockyard	June 1966	22 Apr 1967	1 Apr 1968

Displacement, tons: 5,800 light; 8,500 full load; 15,000 when fully docked down

Dimensions, feet (metres): 488.9 × 75.4 × 17.7 (28.5 flooded) *(149 × 23 × 5.4 (8.7))*

Main machinery: 2 SEMT-Pielstick diesels; 8,600 hp(m) *(6.32 MW)*; 2 shafts; acbLIPS cp props

Speed, knots: 17. **Range, miles:** 9,000 at 15 kt

Complement: 236 (14 officers)

Military lift: 343 troops (plus 129 short haul only); 2 LCTs (EDIC) with 11 light tanks each or 8 loaded CTMs; logistic load 1,500 tons; 2 cranes (35 tons each)

Missiles: SAM: 2 Matra Simbad twin launchers; Mistral; IR homing to 4 km *(2.2 n miles)*; warhead 3 kg; anti-sea-skimmer.

Guns: 2—4.7 in *(120 mm)* mortars; 42 rds/min to 20 km *(10.8 n miles)*; weight of shell 24 kg.
   2 Bofors 40 mm/60; 300 rds/min to 12 km *(6.5 n miles)* or 2 Breda/Mauser 30 mm/70. 4—12.7 mm MGs.

Weapons control: Sagem VIGY-105 optronic system (in due course for 30 mm guns).

Radars: Air/surface search: Thomson-CSF DRBV 51A; G-band.
Navigation: 2 Racal Decca 1226; I-band.

Helicopters: 4 SA 321G Super Frelon or 10 SA 319B Alouette III.

Programmes: Service lives extended until new LSD/LPDs are commissioned in 2004/06.

Modernisation: Simbad SAM and new search radars fitted in 1993. Sagem VIGY-105 optronic fire-control system and 30 mm guns are being fitted to replace the 40 mm. *Ouragan* sonar has been removed. *Orage* has an enclosed Flag bridge.

Structure: Normal helicopter platform for operating three Super Frelon or 10 Alouette III plus a portable platform for a further one Super Frelon or three Alouette III. Bridge is on the starboard side. Three LCVPs can also be carried. Extensive workshops. Flight deck is 900 m²; docking well 120 × 13.2 m with 3 m of water. Two 35 ton cranes.

OURAGAN   *6/1998*, Schaeffer/Marsan* / 0069932

Operational: Typical loads—18 Super Frelon or 80 Alouette III helicopters or 120 AMX 10 APCs, or 84 DUKWs or 340 Jeeps or 12—50 ton barges. A 400 ton ship can be docked. Command facilities for directing amphibious and helicopter operations. Both ships assigned to FAN and based in Toulon.

Typical loads: one CDIC, four CTM, 10 AMX 10RC armoured cars and 21 vehicles or total of 150 to 170 vehicles (without landing craft).

UPDATED

ORAGE   *6/1998*, Schaeffer/Marsan* / 0069933

2 FOUDRE CLASS (LANDING SHIPS DOCK) (TCD 90/LSD)

Name	No	Builders	Laid down	Launched	Commissioned
FOUDRE	L 9011	DCN, Brest	26 Mar 1986	19 Nov 1988	7 Dec 1990
SIROCO	L 9012	DCN, Brest	2 Oct 1994	14 Dec 1996	21 Dec 1998

Displacement, tons: 8,190 light; 12,400 full load; 17,200 flooded

Dimensions, feet (metres): 551 × 77.1 × 17 (30.2 flooded) *(168 × 23.5 × 5.2 (9.2))*

Main machinery: 2 SEMT-Pielstick 16 PC2.5 V 400 diesels; 20,800 hp(m) *(15.3 MW)* sustained; 2 shafts; acbLIPS cp props; bow thruster; 1,000 hp(m) *(735 kW)*

Speed, knots: 21. **Range, miles:** 11,000 at 15 kt

Complement: 215 (17 officers)

Military lift: 467 troops plus 1,880 tons load; 2 CDIC or 10 CTM or 1 EDIC/CDIC plus 4 CTMs

Missiles: SAM: 2 Matra Simbad twin launchers ❶; Mistral; IR homing to 4 km *(2.2 n miles)*; warhead 3 kg.

Guns: 1 Bofors 40 mm/60 ❷ *(Foudre)*. 2 Giat 20F2 20 mm guns ❸ *(Foudre)*. 2—12.7 mm MGs.
3 Breda/Mauser 30 mm/70 *(Siroco)*. Also to replace guns in *Foudre*.

Countermeasures: ESM/ECM: Dassault Electronique (to be fitted).

Combat data systems: Syracuse SATCOM ❹. OPSMER command support system.

Weapons control: 2 Sagem VIGY-105 optronic systems (for 30 mm guns).

Radars: Air/surface search: Thomson-CSF DRBV 21A Mars ❺; D-band.
Surface search: Racal Decca 2459 ❻; I-band.
Navigation: 2 Racal Decca RM 1229; I-band (1 for helo control) ❼.

Helicopters: 4 AS 332F Super Puma ❽ or 2 Super Frelon.

Programmes: First ordered 5 November 1984, second 11 April 1994. Transports de Chalands de Débarquement (TCD).

Modernisation: Sadral SAM replaced by two lightweight Simbad SAMs either side of bridge. New air search radar. 30 mm guns to replace 40 mm and 20 mm in *Foudre* and fitted on build in *Siroco*. Sagem optronic fire control fitted in 1997. ESM/ECM to be acquired.

Structure: Designed to take a mechanised regiment of the Rapid Action Force and act as a logistic support ship. Extensive command (OPSMER and other systems) and hospital facilities (500 m²) include two operating suites and 47 beds. Modular field hospital may be embarked on *Siroco*. Well dock of 122 × 14 m *(1,640 m²)* which can be used to dock a 400 tons ship. Crane of 37 tons and lift of 52 tons *(Foudre)* or 38 tons *(Siroco)*. Flight deck of *Foudre* 1,450 m² with two landing spots (one fitted with landing grid and SAMAHE helo handling system). Additional landing spot on the (removable) well rolling cover. *Siroco* landing deck extended aft up to the lift to give a 1,740 m² area. Flume stabilisation fitted in 1993 to *Foudre*.

Operational: Two landing spots on flight deck plus one on deck well rolling cover. Can operate Super Frelons or Super Pumas. Could carry up to 1,600 troops in emergency. Endurance, 30 days (with 700 persons aboard). Assigned to FAN and based at Toulon. Typical loads: one CDIC, four CTM, 10 AMX 10RC armoured cars and 50 vehicles or total of 180 to 200 vehicles (without landing craft). *Siroco* deployed to East Timor in 1999.

UPDATED

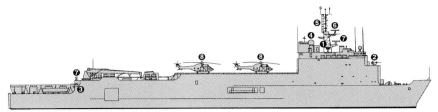

FOUDRE
(Scale 1 : 1,500), Ian Sturton

SIROCO
6/1999*, French Navy / 0069930

FOUDRE
6/1999*, H M Steele / 0069931

15 CTMs and 2 LCM 6 (LCM)

CTM 17-31   1057, 1058

Displacement, tons: 56 standard; 150 full load
Dimensions, feet (metres): 78 × 21 × 4.2 *(23.8 × 6.4 × 1.3)*
Main machinery: 2 Poyaud 520 V8 diesels; 225 hp(m) *(165 kW)*; 2 shafts
Speed, knots: 9.5. **Range, miles:** 350 at 8 kt
Complement: 6
Military lift: 90 tons (maximum); 48 tons (normal)

Comment: Details given for the CTMs. First series of 16 built 1966-70 and so far nine have been deleted. Second series *(CTM 17-31)* built at CMN, Cherbourg 1982-92. All have a bow ramp but the second series has a different shaped pilot-house. Chalands de Transport de Matériel (CTM). Ten are assigned to FAN. Others based at naval bases as service craft or deployed overseas as amphibious/service craft. Six others of the class operated by the French Army Transport Corps include L 14-16 and L 924-925. *1057* and *1058* are LCM 6's built at Réunion and completed in March 1983. Two to Ivory Coast and one to Senegal in 1999.   **UPDATED**

L 924 (Army)   *9/1997, van Ginderen Collection /* 0012352

CTM 29   *12/1999*, Sattler/Steele /* 0081934

PATROL FORCES

10 P 400 CLASS (LARGE PATROL CRAFT) (PC)

Name	No	Builders	Commissioned	
L'AUDACIEUSE	P 682	CMN, Cherbourg	18 Sep	1986
LA BOUDEUSE	P 683	CMN, Cherbourg	15 Jan	1987
LA CAPRICIEUSE	P 684	CMN, Cherbourg	13 Mar	1987
LA FOUGUEUSE	P 685	CMN, Cherbourg	13 Mar	1987
LA GLORIEUSE	P 686	CMN, Cherbourg	18 Apr	1987
LA GRACIEUSE	P 687	CMN, Cherbourg	17 July	1987
LA MOQUEUSE	P 688	CMN, Cherbourg	18 Apr	1987
LA RAILLEUSE	P 689	CMN, Cherbourg	16 May	1987
LA RIEUSE	P 690	CMN, Cherbourg	13 June	1987
LA TAPAGEUSE	P 691	CMN, Cherbourg	11 Feb	1988

Displacement, tons: 406 standard; 477 full load
Dimensions, feet (metres): 178.6 × 26.2 × 8.5 *(54.5 × 8 × 2.5)*
Main machinery: 2 SEMT-Pielstick 16 PA4 200 VGDS diesels; 8,000 hp(m) *(5.88 MW)* sustained; 2 shafts
Speed, knots: 24.5. **Range, miles:** 4,200 at 15 kt
Complement: 26 (3 officers) plus 20 passengers

Guns: 1 Bofors 40 mm/60; 1 Giat 20F2 20 mm; 2—12.7 mm MGs.
Radars: Surface search: Racal Decca 1226; I-band.

Programmes: First six ordered in May 1982, with further four in March 1984. The original propulsion system was unsatisfactory. Modifications were ordered and construction slowed. This class relieved the Patra fast patrol craft which have all transferred to the Gendarmerie.
Structure: Steel hull and superstructure protected by an upper deck bulwark. Design modified from original missile craft configuration. Now capable of transporting personnel with appropriate store rooms. Of more robust construction than previously planned and used as overseas transports. Can be converted for missile armament (MM 38) with dockyard assistance and Sadral PDMS has been considered. *L'Audacieuse* has done trials with a VDS-12 sonar. Twin funnels replaced the unsatisfactory submerged diesel exhausts in 1990-91.
Operational: Deployments: Antilles/French Guiana; P 684, 687, Fort de France; P 685. Nouméa; P 686, 688. La Réunion; P 683, 690. Tahiti; P 689, 691. Cherbourg; P 682. Endurance, 15 days with 45 people aboard. All are receiving a six month refit in Lorient which means some switching of deployments.
Sales: To Gabon and Oman.   **VERIFIED**

L'AUDACIEUSE   *10/1998, H M Steele /* 0052169

FORCE DE SURFACE A MISSIONS CIVILES—FSMC

Note: This designation is applied to a programme of ships and craft designed for offshore and coastal patrol, fishery protection, maritime traffic surveillance, anti-pollution duties and search and rescue, all being manned by the Navy. All vessels are Public Service Special Patrol Craft (PSSP).

1 TRAWLER TYPE (PG)

Name	No	Builders	Commissioned
ALBATROS (ex-*Névé*)	P 681	Ch de la Seine Maritime	1967

Displacement, tons: 2,800 full load
Dimensions, feet (metres): 278.1 × 44.3 × 18.4 *(84.8 × 13.5 × 5.6)*
Main machinery: Diesel-electric; 2 SACM UD 33 V12 M6 diesel generators; 4,410 hp(m) *(3.24 MW)* sustained; 2 motors; 3,046 hp(m) *(2.24 MW)*; 1 shaft; 2 cruise motors; 500 hp(m) *(368 kW)*
Speed, knots: 15. **Range, miles:** 12,000 at 15 kt
Complement: 46 (5 officers) plus 16 passengers
Guns: 1 Bofors 40 mm/60. 2—12.7 mm MGs.
Radars: Surface search: 2 Decca; I-band.
Helicopters: Platform for Alouette III.

Comment: Former trawler bought in April 1983 from Compagnie Nav. Caennaise for conversion into a patrol ship. Commissioned 19 May 1984. Conducts patrols from Réunion to Kerguelen, Crozet, St Paul and Amsterdam Islands with occasional deployments to South Pacific. Can carry 200 tons cargo, has extensive sick berth arrangements and VIP accommodation. Major refit in Lorient from June 1990 to March 1991 which included new diesel-electric propulsion. Service life: 2015.   **VERIFIED**

ALBATROS   *6/1996, Robert Pabst*

1 STERNE CLASS (PC)

Name	No	Builders	Commissioned
STERNE	P 680	La Perrière, Lorient	20 Oct 1980

Displacement, tons: 380 full load
Dimensions, feet (metres): 160.7 × 24.6 × 9.2 *(49 × 7.5 × 2.8)*
Main machinery: 2 SACM 195 V12 CZSHR diesels; 4,340 hp(m) *(3.19 MW)* sustained; electrohydraulic auxiliary propulsion on starboard shaft; 150 hp(m) *(110 kW)*; 2 shafts
Speed, knots: 20; 6 on auxiliary propulsion. **Range, miles:** 4,900 at 12 kt; 1,500 at 20 kt
Complement: 18 (3 officers); 2 crews
Guns: 2—12.7 mm MGs.
Radars: Navigation: Racal Decca; I-band.

Comment: *Sterne* was the first ship for the FSMC. Has active tank stabilisation. Launched 31 October 1979 and completed 18 July 1980 for the 'Affaires Maritimes' but then transferred and is now manned and operated by the Navy from Brest.   **UPDATED**

STERNE   *9/1999*, L-G Nilsson /* 0069939

1 GRÈBE CLASS (PC)

Name	No	Builders	Commissioned
GRÈBE	P 679	SFCN, Villeneuve La Garenne	6 Apr 1991

Displacement, tons: 410 full load
Dimensions, feet (metres): 170.6 × 32.2 × 9 *(52 × 9.8 × 2.8)*
Main machinery: 2 Wärtsilä UD 33 V12 M6D diesels; 4,410 hp(m) *(3.24 MW)*; diesel-electric auxiliary propulsion; 245 hp(m) *(180 kW)*; 2 shafts; cp props
Speed, knots: 23; 7.5 on auxiliary propulsion. **Range, miles:** 4,500 at 12 kt
Complement: 19 (4 officers); accommodation for 24; 2 crews
Guns: 2—12.7 mm MGs.
Radars: Navigation: Racal Decca; I-band.

Comment: Type Espadon 50 ordered 17 July 1988 and launched 16 November 1989. Serter 'Deep V' hull; stern ramp for craft handling. Large deck area (8 × 8 m) for Vertrep operations. Pollution control equipment and remotely operated water-jet gun for firefighting. Based at Toulon from November 1997.   **UPDATED**

GRÈBE   *9/1999*, J Y Robert /* 0069940

3 FLAMANT (OPV 54) CLASS (PC)

Name	No	Builders	Launched		Commissioned	
FLAMANT	P 676	CMN, Cherbourg	24 Apr	1995	18 Dec	1997
CORMORAN	P 677	Leroux & Lotz, Lorient	15 May	1995	29 Oct	1997
PLUVIER	P 678	CMN, Cherbourg	2 Dec	1996	18 Dec	1997

Displacement, tons: 374 full load
Dimensions, feet (metres): 179.8 × 32.8 × 7.2 *(54.8 × 10 × 2.2)*
Main machinery: CODAD; 2 Deutz/MWM 16V TBD 620 diesels; 6,093 hp(m) *(4.48 MW)* sustained; 2 MWM 12V TBD 234 diesels; 1,860 hp(m) *(1.37 MW)* sustained; 2 shafts; acbLIPS cp props
Speed, knots: 22. **Range, miles:** 4,500 at 12 kt
Complement: 19 (3 officers)
Guns: 2—12.7 mm MGs.
Radars: Surface search: 2 Racal Decca Bridgemaster 250; I-band.

Comment: Authorised in July 1992 and ordered in August 1993 to a Serter design. Has a stern door for a 7 m EDL 700 fast assault craft or a Zodiac Hurricane RIB, capable of 30 kt. Two passive stabilisation tanks are fitted, and a remotely operated water-jet gun for firefighting. Deck area of 12 × 9 m for Vertrep. Similar to craft built for Mauritania in 1994. *Flamant* based at Cherbourg, the other two at Brest. **UPDATED**

CORMORAN   *4/1999*, W Sartori /* 0069941

MINE WARFARE FORCES

13 ÉRIDAN (TRIPARTITE) CLASS (MINEHUNTERS) (MHC)

Name	No	Laid down		Launched		Commissioned	
ÉRIDAN	M 641	20 Dec	1977	2 Feb	1979	16 Apr	1984
CASSIOPÉE	M 642	26 Mar	1979	26 Sep	1981	5 May	1984
ANDROMÈDE	M 643	6 Mar	1980	22 May	1982	18 Oct	1984
PÉGASE	M 644	22 Dec	1980	23 Apr	1983	30 May	1985
ORION	M 645	17 Aug	1981	6 Feb	1985	14 Jan	1986
CROIX DU SUD	M 646	22 Apr	1982	6 Feb	1985	14 Nov	1986
AIGLE	M 647	2 Dec	1982	8 Mar	1986	1 July	1987
LYRE	M 648	13 Oct	1983	14 Nov	1986	16 Dec	1987
PERSÉE	M 649	30 Oct	1984	19 Apr	1988	4 Nov	1988
SAGITTAIRE	M 650	1 Feb	1993	14 Jan	1995	2 Apr	1996
VERSEAU (ex-*Iris*)	M 651	20 May	1986	21 June	1987	6 Oct	1988
CÉPHÉE (ex-*Fuchsia*)	M 652	28 Oct	1985	23 Oct	1987	18 Feb	1988
CAPRICORNE (ex-*Dianthus*)	M 653	17 Apr	1985	26 Feb	1987	14 Aug	1987

Displacement, tons: 562 standard; 605 full load
Dimensions, feet (metres): 168.9 × 29.2 × 8.2 *(51.5 × 8.9 × 2.5)*
Main machinery: 1 Stork Wärtsilä A-RUB 215X-12 diesel; 1,860 hp(m) *(1.37 MW)* sustained; 1 shaft; acbLIPS cp prop
Auxiliary propulsion; 2 motors; 240 hp(m) *(179 kW)*; 2 active rudders; 2 bow thrusters
Speed, knots: 15; 7 on auxiliary propulsion. **Range, miles:** 3,000 at 12 kt
Complement: 46 (5 officers)

Guns: 1 Giat 20F2 20 mm; 1—12.7 mm MG.
Countermeasures: MCM: 2 PAP 104 ROVs; OD3 mechanical sweep gear. AP-4 acoustic sweep. Double Eagle ROV from 2001.
Combat data systems: TSM 2061 being fitted.
Radars: Navigation: Racal Decca 1229; I-band.
Sonars: Thomson Sintra DUBM 21B or 21D (M 650); being replaced from 2001 by Thomson Marconi 2022 Mk 3; hull-mounted; active; high frequency.

Programmes: All built in Lorient. Belgium, France and the Netherlands each agreed to build 15 (10 in Belgium with option on five more). Subsequently the French programme was cut to 10. Belgium provided all the electrical installations, France all the minehunting gear and some electronics and the Netherlands the propulsion systems. Replacement for the last of class (sold to Pakistan) was ordered in January 1992. Three Belgian ships of the class acquired between March and August 1997 after being in reserve since 1990.
Modernisation: New sonar in M 643 in mid-2001, then the remainder of the class at four a year. This sonar operates with a ROV propelled VDS stationed 500 m ahead of the ship. New data system being fitted based on the TSM 2061.
Structure: GRP hull. Equipment includes: autopilot and hovering; automatic radar navigation; navigation aids by Loran and Syledis; Evec data system.
Operational: Minehunting, minesweeping, patrol, training, directing ship for unmanned mine-sweeping, HQ ship for diving operations and pollution control. Prepacked 5 ton modules of equipment embarked for separate tasks. M 641-646 and M 651-653 based at Brest, remainder at Toulon. Chasseurs de Mines Tripartites (CMT).
Sales: The original tenth ship of the class, completed in 1989, was transferred to Pakistan 24 September 1992 as part of an order for three; the second built in Lorient, the third in Karachi. **UPDATED**

CÉPHÉE   *6/1999*, H M Steele /* 0069936

AIGLE   *4/1999*, Giorgio Ghiglione /* 0069937

3 ANTARÈS (BRS) CLASS (ROUTE SURVEY VESSELS) (MHI)

Name	No	Builders	Commissioned	
ANTARÈS	M 770	Socarenam, Boulogne	15 Dec	1993
ALTAÏR	M 771	Socarenam, Boulogne	30 July	1994
ALDÉBARAN	M 772	Socarenam, Boulogne	10 Mar	1995

Displacement, tons: 340 full load
Dimensions, feet (metres): 92.8 × 25.3 × 13.1 *(28.3 × 7.7 × 4)*
Main machinery: 1 Baudouin 12P15-2SR diesel; 800 hp(m) *(590 kW)*; 1 shaft; cp prop; bow thruster
Speed, knots: 10. **Range, miles:** 3,600 at 10 kt
Complement: 25 (1 officer)
Guns: 1—12.7 mm MG.
Radars: Navigation: 2 Racal-Decca; I-band.
Sonars: 2 Thomson Sintra DUBM 41B; towed side scan; active search; high frequency.

Comment: Has replaced the 'Aggressive' class for route survey at Brest. BRS Bâtiments Remorqueurs de Sonars. Trawler type similar to 'Glycine' class (see *Training Ships* section). The DUBM 41B towed bodies have been taken from the older MSOs. A mechanical sweep is also carried. There are two 4.5 ton hydraulic cranes. Original dual navigation training role has been lost. **UPDATED**

ALTAIR   *2/1999*, van Ginderen Collection /* 0069935

4 MCM DIVING TENDERS (MCD)

Name	No	Builders	Launched		Commissioned	
VULCAIN	M 611	La Perrière, Lorient	17 Jan	1986	11 Oct	1986
PLUTON	M 622	La Perrière, Lorient	13 May	1986	10 Dec	1986
ACHÉRON	A 613	CMN, Cherbourg	9 Nov	1986	21 Apr	1987
STYX	M 614	CMN, Cherbourg	3 Mar	1987	22 July	1987

Displacement, tons: 375 standard; 505 full load
Dimensions, feet (metres): 136.5 × 24.6 × 12.5 *(41.6 × 7.5 × 3.8)*
Main machinery: 2 SACM MGO 175 V16 ASHR diesels; 2,200 hp(m) *(1.62 MW)*; 2 shafts; bow thruster; 70 hp(m) *(51 kW)*
Speed, knots: 13.7. **Range, miles:** 2,800 at 13 kt; 7,400 at 9 kt
Complement: 14 (1 officer) plus 12 divers
Guns: 1—12.7 mm MG.
Radars: Navigation: Decca 1226; I-band.

Comment: First pair ordered in December 1984. Second pair ordered July 1985. Designed to act as support ships for clearance divers. (Bâtiments Bases pour Plongeurs Démineurs - BBPD). *Vulcain* based at Cherbourg, *Pluton* at Toulon, *Achéron* at Toulon as a diving school tender and *Styx* at Brest. Modified 'Chamois' (BSR) class design. 5 ton hydraulic crane. **UPDATED**

VULCAIN   *8/1999*, Michael Nitz /* 0069938

SURVEY AND RESEARCH SHIPS

Notes: (1) These ships are painted white. A total of about 100 officers and technicians with oceanographic and hydrographic training is employed in addition to the ships' companies listed here. They occupy the extra billets marked as 'scientists'.

(2) In addition to the ships listed below there is a civilian-manned 25 m trawler *L'Aventurière II* (launched July 1986) operated by GESMA, Brest for underwater research which comes under DCN.

(3) A new survey ship to replace *L'Espérance* was out to tender on 7 April 1998. Details include 3,500 tons, diesel-electric propulsion, speed 12, accommodation for 50 for 45 days continuous operations. Planned in service date of 2002. A second to replace *D'Entrecasteaux* planned for 2006.

4 LAPÉROUSE (BH2) CLASS (AGS)

Name	No	Builders	Launched		Commissioned	
LAPÉROUSE	A 791	Lorient Naval Dockyard	14 Nov	1986	20 Apr	1988
BORDA	A 792	Lorient Naval Dockyard	14 Nov	1986	18 June	1988
LAPLACE	A 793	Lorient Naval Dockyard	9 Nov	1988	5 Oct	1989
ARAGO	A 795	Lorient Naval Dockyard	6 Nov	1989	9 July	1991

Displacement, tons: 970 standard; 1,100 full load
Dimensions, feet (metres): 193.5 × 35.8 × 11.9 *(59 × 10.9 × 3.6)*
Main machinery: 2 Wärtsilä UD 30 V12 M6D diesels; 2,500 hp(m) *(1.84 MW)*; 2 cp props; bow thruster; auxiliary electric motor (A 791)
Speed, knots: 15. **Range, miles:** 6,000 at 12 kt
Complement: 27 (2 officers) plus 11 scientists plus 7 spare berths
Radars: Navigation: Decca 1226; I-band.
Sonars: Thomson Sintra DUBM 42 or DUBM 21C (A 791); active search; high frequency.

Comment: Ordered under 1982 and 1986 estimates, first two on 24 July 1984, third 22 January 1986 and fourth 12 April 1988. BH2 (Bâtiments Hydrographiques de 2e classe). Two variants: BH2A (A 791)—Carry Thomson Sintra DUBM 21C sonar for detection of underwater obstacles. Carry two VH8 survey launches for hydrographic work. *Borda* has the TSM 5260 Lennermor multipath echo-sounder. Auxiliary electric propulsion fitted in *Lapérouse* in 1994. *Arago* based in the Pacific. The other three at Brest from mid-1999.
UPDATED

LAPÉROUSE   *8/1998*, J Y Robert / 0069943*

Name	No	Builders	Commissioned	
D'ENTRECASTEAUX	A 757	Brest Naval Dockyard	8 Oct	1971

Displacement, tons: 2,400 full load
Dimensions, feet (metres): 292 × 42.7 × 14.4 *(89 × 13 × 4.4)*
Main machinery: Diesel-electric; 2 diesel generators; 2,720 hp(m) *(2 MW)*; 2 motors; 2 shafts; acbLIPS cp props; auxiliary propulsion; 2 Schottel trainable and retractable props
Speed, knots: 15. **Range, miles:** 10,000 at 12 kt
Complement: 76 (8 officers) plus 36 scientific staff
Radars: Navigation: 2 Racal Decca 1226; I-band.
Helicopters: 1 SA 319B Alouette III.

Comment: This ship was specially designed for oceanographic surveys capable of working to 6,000 m *(19,686 ft)*. Bâtiment Océanographique (BO). Carries one LCP and three survey launches. Telescopic hangar. In 1994 fitted with Inmarsat A, an acoustic Doppler current profiler and Sea Soar towed system for oceanographic collection. Propulsion modernised at the same time. Based at Brest from September 1995.
UPDATED

D'ENTRECASTEAUX   *5/1999*, H M Steele / 0069942*

Name	No	Builders	Commissioned	
L'ESPÉRANCE (ex-*Jacques Coeur*)	A 756	Gdynia	25 June	1969

Displacement, tons: 956 standard; 1,360 full load
Dimensions, feet (metres): 209.3 × 32.1 × 19.4 *(63.8 × 9.8 × 5.9)*
Main machinery: 2 MAN diesels; 1,850 hp(m) *(1.36 MW)*; 1 shaft; bow thruster
Speed, knots: 13. **Range, miles:** 7,000 at 13 kt
Complement: 32 (3 officers) plus 14 scientists

Comment: Former trawler first commissioned 18 July 1962 at Gdynia and purchased by the Navy in 1968. Adapted as survey ship. Refitted in 1992-93. Survey launches and crane removed in 1997. Based in Atlantic. Has a Simrad EM 12D multipath echo-sounder. Scheduled to pay off in 2002 and be replaced by a new class of ship.
UPDATED

L'ESPÉRANCE   *6/1996, van Ginderen Collection*

Name	No	Builders	Commissioned	
MONGE	A 601	Chantiers de l'Atlantique, St Nazaire	5 Nov	1992

Displacement, tons: 21,040 full load
Dimensions, feet (metres): 753.3 × 81.4 × 25.3 *(229.6 × 24.8 × 7.7)*
Main machinery: 2 SEMT-Pielstick 8 PC2.5 L 400 diesels; 10,400 hp(m) *(7.65 MW)* sustained; 1 shaft; acbLIPS cp props; bow thruster; 1,360 hp(m) *(1 MW)*
Speed, knots: 15. **Range, miles:** 15,000 at 15 kt
Complement: 120 (10 officers) plus 100 military and civilian technicians
Guns: 2 Giat F2 20 mm. 2—12.7 mm MGs.
Combat data systems: Tavitac 2000 for trials.
Radars: Air search: Thomson-CSF DRBV 15C; E/F-band.
Missile tracking: Thomson-CSF Stratus; L-band; Gascogne; two Armor; Savoie; two Antarès.
Navigation: Two Racal Decca (one for helo control); I-band.
Helicopters: 2 Super Frelon or Alouette III.

Comment: Ordered 25 November 1988. Rated as a BEM (Bâtiment d'Essais et de Mesures). Laid down 26 March 1990, and launched 6 October 1990. She has 14 telemetry antennas; optronic tracking unit; LIDAR; Syracuse SATCOM. Flume tank stabilisation restricts the ship to a maximum of 9° roll at slow speed in Sea State 6. Flagship of the Trials Squadron. Used for space surveillance by the French Space Agency (CNES). May be placed in special reserve in 2000.
UPDATED

MONGE   *7/1999*, H M Steele / 0069944*

Name	No	Builders	Commissioned	
ILE D'OLÉRON (ex-*München*, ex-*Mür*)	A 610	Weser, Bremen	Apr	1939

Displacement, tons: 5,500 standard; 6,500 full load
Dimensions, feet (metres): 378 × 50.6 × 21.3 *(115.2 × 15.5 × 6.5)*
Main machinery: 2 MAN 6-cyl diesels; 3,500 hp(m) *(2.57 MW)*; 1 shaft
Speed, knots: 14.5. **Range, miles:** 7,200 at 12 kt
Complement: 195 (12 officers)
Radars: Various, according to experiments (DRBV 22C, DRBV 50, Arabel).
Navigation: Racal Decca 1226; I-band.

Comment: Taken as a war prize. Commissioned in French Navy 29 August 1945. Formerly rated as a transport. Converted to experimental guided missile ship in 1957-58 by Chantiers de Provence and l'Arsenal de Toulon. Commissioned early in 1959. Fitted with one launcher for target planes. Has been fitted with various equipment and weapon systems for trials: Masurca, Crotale, Otomat, MM 40 Exocet, Sadral, 100 mm gun with CTMS fire-control system, Crotale Modulaire, Sagaie, Simbad. Fitted for sea trials of Milas in 1992 (ASW torpedo delivery missile with a range of 50 km). Modified in 1995-96 for the trials of the SAAM/SAMP short/medium-range SAM system, with prototype Sylver launcher for VLS Aster 15 PDMS and Aster 30 area SAMs fitted on the foredeck and a large lattice mast structure on the after deck for the Arabel multifunction radar. Trials of SAAM continue in 1999. Planned to pay off in 2000, but this may be postponed if Aster trials have not been completed. Based at Toulon.
UPDATED

ILE D'OLÉRON   *9/1999*, H M Steele / 0069945*

Name	No	Builders		Commissioned
THÉTIS (ex-*Nereide*)	A 785	Lorient Naval Dockyard		9 Nov 1988

Name	No	Builders	Launched	Commissioned
DENTI	A 743	DCAN Toulon	7 Oct 1975	15 July 1976

Displacement, tons: 720 standard; 1,000 full load
Dimensions, feet (metres): 185.4 × 35.8 × 11.8 *(56.5 × 10.9 × 3.6)*
Main machinery: 2 Uni Diesel UD 30 V16 M4 diesels; 2,710 hp(m) *(1.99 MW)* sustained; 1 shaft; cp prop
Speed, knots: 15. **Range, miles:** 6,000
Complement: 36 (2 officers) plus 7 passengers
Guns: 2—12.7 mm MGs.
Radars: Navigation: Racal Decca 1226; I-band.
Sonars: VDS; Thomson Sintra DUBM 42 and DUBM 60A; active search; high frequency.

Comment: Same hull as 'Lapérouse' class. Classified as Bâtiment Experimental Guerre de Mines (BEGM). Operated by the Centre d'Études, d'Instruction et d'Entraînement de la Guerre des Mines (CETIEGM) in Brest. Launched 19 March 1988. Renamed to avoid confusion with Y 700. Equipped to conduct trials on all underwater weapons and sensors for mine warfare. Can lay mines. Can support six divers. Fitted with the Thomson Sintra Lagadmor mine warfare combat system designed for the cancelled 'Narvik' class. Also used for experiments with Propelled Variable Depth Sonar system.   *UPDATED*

Displacement, tons: 190 full load
Dimensions, feet (metres): 113.8 × 21.6 × 7.5 *(34.7 × 6.6 × 2.3)*
Main machinery: 2 Baudouin DP8 diesels; 960 hp(m) *(706 kW)*; 2 shafts; cp props
Speed, knots: 12. **Range, miles:** 800 at 12 kt
Complement: 6 (2 officers) plus 6 scientists
Radars: Navigation: Decca; I-band.

Comment: Employed on ammunition trials for DCN off Toulon.

UPDATED

THÉTIS   *6/1999*, H M Steele /* 0069946

DENTI   *11/1999*, van Ginderen Collection /* 0081935

AUXILIARIES

Notes: (1) The Flotte Auxiliaire Occasionnelle (FAO) consists of civilian ships taken up as required by the Navy for transport and other duties. Those on long-term charter include two salvage tugs *Abeille Flandre* (based at Brest) and *Abeille Languedoc* (based at Cherbourg), and four offshore supply vessels *Alcyon* and *Ailette* (based at Brest) and *Carangue* and *Mérou* (based at Toulon).

(2) *Captain Martin* is a tanker of the FAO fitted for replenishment at sea.
(3) *Abeille Supporter* is used by DGA to support missile firings and has a ROV and UUVs for underwater recovery operations. *Langevin* is occasionally chartered for submarine associated trials.

CARANGUE   *8/1997, Giorgio Ghiglione /* 0012365

MÉROU   *10/1998, J Y Robert /* 0052179

4 DURANCE CLASS (UNDERWAY REPLENISHMENT TANKERS) (AOR)

Name	No	Builders	Laid down	Launched	Commissioned
MEUSE	A 607	Brest Naval Dockyard	2 June 1977	2 Dec 1978	21 Nov 1980
VAR	A 608	Brest Naval Dockyard	8 May 1979	1 June 1981	29 Jan 1983
MARNE	A 630	Brest Naval Dockyard	4 Aug 1982	2 Feb 1985	16 Jan 1987
SOMME	A 631	Normed, la Seyne	3 May 1985	3 Oct 1987	7 Mar 1990

Displacement, tons: 17,900 full load
Dimensions, feet (metres): 515.9 × 69.5 × 38.5 *(157.3 × 21.2 × 10.8)*
Main machinery: 2 SEMT-Pielstick 16 PC2.5 V 400 diesels; 20,800 hp(m) *(15.3 MW)* sustained; 2 shafts; acbLIPS cp props
Speed, knots: 19. **Range, miles:** 9,000 at 15 kt
Complement: 164 (10 officers) plus 29 spare
Cargo capacity: 5,000 tons FFO; 3,200 diesel; 1,800 TR5 Avcat; 130 distilled water; 170 victuals; 50 naval stores *(Meuse)*. 5,090 tons FFO; 3,310 diesel; 1,090 TR5 Avcat; 260 distilled water; 180 munitions; 15 stores *(Var, Somme and Marne)*

Missiles: SAM: 2 Matra Simbad twin launchers; Mistral; IR homing to 4 km *(2.2 n miles)*; warhead 3 kg.
Guns: 3 Breda/Mauser 30 mm/70; 800 rds/min; weight of shell 0.37 kg. 4—12.7 mm MGs.
Countermeasures: ESM/ECM.
Combat data systems: Syracuse 2 SATCOM. OPSMER command support system (fitted for BCR ships).
Radars: Navigation: 2 Racal Decca 1226; I-band.

Helicopters: 1 Dauphin or Alouette III or Lynx Mk 4.

Programmes: One classed as Pétroliers Ravitailleurs d'Escadres (PRE). Three classed as Bâtiments de Commandement et de Ravitaillement (BCR; Command and Replenishment Ships).
Modernisation: 40 and 20 mm guns replaced by 30 mm and EW equipment fitted to improve air defences under the 3A programme in 1996-99. Simbad SAM may be carried at bridge deck level.
Structure: Four beam transfer positions and two astern, two of the beam positions having heavy transfer capability. *Var, Marne* and *Somme* differ from *Meuse* in several respects. The bridge extends further aft, boats are located either side of the funnel and a crane is located between the gantries. Also fitted with Syracuse SATCOM.
Operational: *Var, Marne* and *Somme* are designed to carry a Maritime Zone staff or Commander of a Logistic Formation and

MEUSE   *11/1999*, G Toremans /* 0069947

MARNE   *7/1999*, M Declerck /* 0069948

a commando unit of up to 45 men. Capable of accommodating 250 men. Assigned to FAN with one of the three BCR ships deployed to the Indian Ocean as a Flagship.

Sales: One to Australia built locally; two of similar but smaller design to Saudi Arabia. One to Argentina in July 1999.

UPDATED

1 MAINTENANCE and REPAIR SHIP (AD)

Name	No	Builders	Commissioned
JULES VERNE (ex-Achéron)	A 620	Brest Naval Dockyard	17 Sep 1976

Displacement, tons: 6,485 standard; 10,250 full load
Dimensions, feet (metres): 482.2 × 70.5 × 21.3 *(147 × 21.5 × 6.5)*
Main machinery: 2 SEMT-Pielstick 12 PC2.2 V 400 diesels; 12,000 hp(m) *(8.8 MW)* sustained; 1 shaft
Speed, knots: 19. **Range, miles:** 9,500 at 17 kt
Complement: 130 plus 135 for support
Guns: 2 Bofors 40 mm/60. 4—12.7 mm MGs.
Radars: Navigation: 2 Racal Decca 1226; I-band.
Helicopters: 3 SA 319B Alouette III.

Comment: Ordered in 1961 budget, originally as an Armament Supply Ship. Role and design changed whilst building—now rated as Engineering and Electrical Maintenance Ship. Launched 30 May 1970. Serves in Indian Ocean, providing general support for all ships. Carries stocks of torpedoes and ammunition. Refit in France November 1988/June 1989 and another refit at Brest from January to June 1995. Based at Toulon from December 1997 and assigned to FAN. Refitted in 1998 after a collision with *Var*. Super Frelon and Cougar helicopters can be landed on the flight deck.   ***UPDATED***

JULES VERNE   *4/1999*, A Sharma /* 0069949

2 RHIN CLASS (SUPPORT SHIP) (AG/AR)

Name	No	Builders	Commissioned
LOIRE	A 615	Lorient Naval Dockyard	10 Oct 1967
RHIN	A 621	Lorient Naval Dockyard	1 Mar 1964

Displacement, tons: 2,445 full load
Dimensions, feet (metres): 331.5 × 43 × 12.1 *(101.1 × 13.1 × 3.7)*
Main machinery: 2 SEMT-Pielstick 12 PA4 V 400 diesels; 4,000 hp(m) *(2.94 MW)*; 1 shaft
Speed, knots: 16.5. **Range, miles:** 13,000 at 13 kt
Complement: 156 (12 officers)
Guns: 3 Bofors 40 mm/60. 3—12.7 mm MGs.
Radars: Air/surface search: Thomson-CSF DRBV 50; D-band.
Navigation: Racal Decca 1226; I-band.
Helicopters: 1-3 SA 310B Alouette III *(Loire)*.

Comment: *Loire* has a 5 ton crane and carries two LCPs. Used for minesweeper support at Brest. *Rhin* based at Martinique until shore support facilities have been completed.   ***UPDATED***

LOIRE   *1/1999*, M Declerck /* 0069950

5 CHAMOIS CLASS (SUPPLY TENDERS) (AG)

Name	No	Builders	Commissioned
TAAPE	A 633	La Perrière, Lorient	2 Nov 1983
ÉLAN	A 768	La Perrière, Lorient	7 Apr 1978
CHEVREUIL	A 774	La Perrière, Lorient	7 Oct 1977
GAZELLE	A 775	La Perrière, Lorient	13 Jan 1978
ISARD	A 776	La Perrière, Lorient	15 Dec 1978

Displacement, tons: 495 (500, *Taape*) full load
Dimensions, feet (metres): 136.1 × 24.6 × 10.5 *(41.5 × 7.5 × 3.2)*
Main machinery: 2 SACM AGO 175 V16 diesels; 2,700 hp(m) *(1.98 MW)*; 2 shafts; cp props; bow thruster
Speed, knots: 14.2. **Range, miles:** 6,000 at 12 kt
Complement: 13 plus 7 spare berths
Radars: Navigation: Racal Decca 1226; I-band.

Comment: Similar to the standard fish oil rig support ships. Can act as tugs, oil pollution vessels, salvage craft (two 30 ton and two 5 ton winches), coastal and harbour controlled minelaying, torpedo recovery, diving tenders and a variety of other tasks. Bollard pull 25 tons. Can carry 100 tons of stores on deck or 125 tons of fuel and 40 tons of water or 65 tons of fuel and 120 tons of water. *Taape* ordered in March 1982 from La Perrière—of improved design but basically similar with bridge one deck higher. *Élan* based at Cherbourg, remainder at Toulon. *Isard* serves as a special diving support ship with an extra deckhouse. Two paid off so far, one of which transferred to Madagascar in May 1996.   ***UPDATED***

ÉLAN   *11/1999*, Harald Carstens /* 0069951

2 RR 4000 TYPE (SUPPLY TENDERS) (AFL)

Name	No	Builders	Commissioned
RARI	A 634	Breheret, Conéron	21 Feb 1985
REVI	A 635	Breheret, Conéron	9 Mar 1985

Displacement, tons: 900 light; 1,450 full load
Dimensions, feet (metres): 167.3 × 41.3 × 13.1 *(51 × 12.6 × 4)*
Main machinery: 2 SACM AGO 195 V12 diesels; 4,410 hp(m) *(3.24 MW)*; 2 shafts; cp props; 2 bow thrusters
Speed, knots: 14.5. **Range, miles:** 6,000 at 12 kt
Complement: 22 plus 18 passengers
Radars: Navigation: Racal Decca 1226; I-band.

Comment: Two 'remorqueurs ravitailleurs' built for le Centre d'Expérimentation du Pacifique. Can carry 400 tons of cargo on deck. Bollard pull 47 tons. *Revi* based at Papeete and *Rari* at Brest.   ***VERIFIED***

RARI   *12/1998, Diego Quevedo /* 0052185

1 TRANSPORT LANDING SHIP (LSL)

Name	No	Builders	Commissioned
GAPEAU	L 9090	Chantier Serra, la Seyne	2 Oct 1987

Displacement, tons: 509 standard; 1,058 full load
Dimensions, feet (metres): 216.5 × 40 × 11.2 *(66 × 12.2 × 3.4)*
Main machinery: 2 diesels; 550 hp(m) *(404 kW)*; 2 shafts
Speed, knots: 10
Complement: 6 + 30 scientists
Cargo capacity: 460 tons
Radars: Navigation: Racal Decca 1226; I-band.

Comment: Supply ship with bow doors. Operates for Centre d'Essais de la Mediterranée, Levant Island (missile range).   ***UPDATED***

GAPEAU   *7/1999*, M Declerck /* 0069952

1 NETLAYER (ANL)

Name	No	Builders	Launched	Commissioned
LA PERSÉVÉRANTE	Y 750	AC La Rochelle	14 May 1968	3 Mar 1969

Displacement, tons: 626 full load
Dimensions, feet (metres): 142.8 × 32.8 × 9.2 *(43.5 × 10 × 2.8)*
Main machinery: Diesel-electric; 2 Baudouin diesels; 620 hp(m) *(441 kW)*; 1 shaft
Speed, knots: 10. **Range, miles:** 4,000 at 10 kt
Complement: 30 (1 officer)
Radars: Navigation: Racal Decca 1226; I-band.

Comment: Has a 25 ton lift. Based at Toulon. A second of class is in reserve at Brest.   ***UPDATED***

LA PERSÉVÉRANTE   *6/1998*, Schaeffer/Marsan /* 0069953

3 MOORING VESSELS (ABU)

TUPA Y 667　　**TELENN MOR** Y 692　　**CALMAR** Y 698

Comment: 292 tons with 210 hp(m) *(154 kW)* diesel. *Tupa* commissioned 16 March 1974, *Telenn Mor* on 16 January 1986. *Tupa* based at Brest, *Telenn Mor* at Brest. *Calmar* is a converted harbour tug of 270 tons commissioned 12 August 1970 and is based at Lorient.
UPDATED

TELENN MOR　　　　　　　　　　　8/1998*, J Y Robert / 0069954

9 ARIEL CLASS (TRANSPORTS) (YFB)

ARIEL Y 604	**DRYADE** Y 662	**ONDINE** Y 701
FAUNE Y 613	**ALPHÉE** Y 696	**NAIADE** Y 702
KORRIGAN Y 661	**NEREIDE** Y 700	**ELFE** Y 741

Displacement, tons: 195 standard; 225 full load
Dimensions, feet (metres): 132.8 × 24.5 × 10.8 *(40.5 × 7.5 × 3.3)*
Main machinery: 2 SACM MGO or Poyaud diesels; 1,640 hp(m) *(1.21 MW)* or 1,730 hp(m) *(1.27 MW)*; 2 shafts
Speed, knots: 15.3. **Range, miles:** 940 at 14 kt
Complement: 9
Radars: Navigation: Racal Decca 1226; I-band.

Comment: All built by Société Française de Construction Naval (ex-Franco-Belge) except for *Nereide, Ondine* and *Naiade* by DCAN Brest. *Ariel* in service 1964, *Elfe* in 1980; the remainder at approximately two year intervals. Can carry 400 passengers (250 seated). *Naiade* and *Ariel* based with CEM Toulon, remainder at Brest.
UPDATED

FAUNE　　　　　　　　　　　　　9/1999*, L-G Nilsson / 0069955

5 TENDERS (YAG)

POSÉIDON A 722

Displacement, tons: 220 full load
Dimensions, feet (metres): 132.9 × 23.6 × 7.3 *(40.5 × 7.2 × 2.2)*
Main machinery: 1 diesel; 600 hp(m) *(441 kW)*; 1 shaft
Speed, knots: 13
Complement: 15 (1 officer) plus 27 swimmers
Radars: Navigation: Racal Decca 1226; I-band.

Comment: Base ship for assault swimmers at Toulon. Built in St Malo and completed 6 August 1975.
UPDATED

POSÉIDON　　　　　　　　4/1999*, Schaeffer/Marsan / 0069956

TOURMALINE A 714

Displacement, tons: 45 full load
Dimensions, feet (metres): 88 × 16.8 × 4.8 *(26.8 × 5.1 × 1.5)*
Main machinery: 2 diesels; 480 hp(m) *(353 kW)*; 2 shafts
Speed, knots: 15
Complement: 6
Radars: Navigation: Racal Decca 1226; I-band.

Comment: Commissioned 14 February 1974. Built by Chantiers Navals de L'Esterel. Attached to Mediterranean Test Range. Civilian-manned and conducted trials firing of MM 15 missiles in 1994. Based at Port Pothau near Toulon and classified as a range safety craft from July 1995.
VERIFIED

TOURMALINE　　　　　　　　　　　9/1995, B Sullivan

ATHOS A 712　　**ARAMIS** A 713

Displacement, tons: 100 full load
Dimensions, feet (metres): 105.3 × 21.3 × 6.2 *(32.1 × 6.5 × 1.9)*
Main machinery: 2 SACM diesels; 4,400 hp(m) *(3.23 MW)*; 2 shafts
Speed, knots: 32. **Range, miles:** 1,500 at 15 kt
Complement: 12 plus 6 passengers
Guns: 1 Oerlikon 20 mm. 2—12.7 mm MGs.
Radars: Navigation: Racal Decca 1226; I-band.

Comment: Built by Chantiers Navals de l'Esterel for Missile Trials Centre of Les Landes (CEL). Based at Bayonne, forming Groupe des Vedettes de l'Adour. Commissioned 1980. Classified as Range Safety Craft from July 1995.
VERIFIED

ATHOS　　　　　　　　　　9/1983, van Ginderen Collection

Y 732

Displacement, tons: 260 full load
Dimensions, feet (metres): 125.3 × 14.1 × 7.2 *(38.2 × 4.3 × 2.2)*
Main machinery: 1 diesel; 380 hp(m) *(279 kW)*; 1 shaft
Speed, knots: 9
Complement: 5

Comment: Built in Lorient. Commissioned 3 March 1979. Based at Brest. Designated 'Station de Démagnétisation No 3'.
VERIFIED

Y 732　　　　　　　　　　4/1998, M Declerck / 0052189

10 DIVING TENDERS (YDT)

CORALLINE A 790	LISERON Y 793	GENÊT Y 796
DIONÉE Y 790	MAGNOLIA Y 794	GIROFLÉE Y 797
MYOSOTIS Y 791	AJONC Y 795	ACANTHE Y 798
GARDÉNIA Y 792		

Displacement, tons: 44 full load
Dimensions, feet (metres): 68.9 × 14.8 × 3.6 *(21 × 4.5 × 1.1)*
Main machinery: 2 diesels; 264 hp(m) *(194 kW)*; 2 shafts
Speed, knots: 13
Complement: 4 plus 14 divers

Comment: Diving tenders built at Lorient. First one delivered in February 1990. *Coralline* is used for radioactive monitoring in Cherbourg. *Y 794* and *Y 798* based at Cherbourg. *Y 790*, *Y 791*, *Y 792*, *Y 795* and *Y 797* based at Toulon. *Y 793* and *Y 796* based at Brest. Rated as 'Vedettes d'Instruction Plongée (VIP)', divers training craft, and 'Vedettes d'Intervention Plongeurs-Démineurs (VIPD)', clearance diving team support craft.

UPDATED

AJONC   11/1999*, G Toremans / 0069957

19 HARBOUR CRAFT (YFL/YP/YTR)

Y 753-755	Y 776-777	Y 783-785
Y 762-765	Y 779-781	Y 786-789

Displacement, tons: 18-21 full load
Dimensions, feet (metres): 47.9 × 15.1 × 3.3 *(14.6 × 4.6 × 1)*
Main machinery: 2 Baudouin diesels; 1,000-750 hp(m) *(735-551 kW)*; 2 shafts
Speed, knots: 25-17. **Range, miles:** 400 at 11 kt
Complement: 4

Comment: All except *Y 783-785* built between 1988 and 1992. *Y 762-765* are patrol craft and can carry one 12.7 mm MG; *Y 779-781* are pilot craft; *Y 753-755* and *Y 786-789* are transport craft. *Y 783-785* were completed in 1993-94 by Alan Sibiril Shipyard, Carentec and are for firefighting; *Y 776-777* are radiological monitoring craft and have smaller engines. *Y 755* carries a 12.7 mm MG.

UPDATED

Y 780   1/1999*, M Declerck / 0069959

Y 783   8/1998*, J Y Robert / 0069960

2 PHAÉTON CLASS (TOWED ARRAY TENDERS)

PHAÉTON Y 656   MACHAON Y 657

Displacement, tons: 69 full load
Dimensions, feet (metres): 61 × 15.7 × 5.6 *(18.6 × 4.8 × 1.7)*
Main machinery: 1 diesel; 660 hp(m) *(485 kW)*; waterjet
Speed, knots: 8
Complement: 4

Comment: 18.6 m catamarans built in 1993-94 at Brest. Water-jet propulsion, speed 8 kt. Hydraulic crane and winch to handle submarine towed arrays. *Phaéton* based at Toulon, the second at Brest.

UPDATED

PHAÉTON   10/1999*, van Ginderen Collection / 0069958

85 HARBOUR SUPPORT CRAFT

Comment: There are 35 oil barges (CIM, CIG, CIC, CIGH and CICGH), one of which is of 1,200 tonnes and the rest between 100 and 800 tonnes, 16 400 tonne oily bilge barges (CIEM), four anti-pollution barges (800 tonne BAPM, and 400 tonne CIEP), and nine water barges (CIE, 120 to 400 tonnes). Some self-propelled. Also 19 self-propelled YFUs (CHA), and two 15 m Sea Truck craft.

UPDATED

CHA 30   10/1999*, van Ginderen Collection / 0069961

1 FLOATING DOCK and 6 FLOATING CRANES

Comment: The dock is of 3,800 tons capacity, built at Brest in 1975. Based at Papeete. 150 × 33 m. The cranes have lifts up to 15 tons and are self-propelled. Based at Brest, Toulon and Cherbourg.

VERIFIED

TRAINING SHIPS

Note: In addition there are two naval school tenders of 100 tons, *Chimère* Y 706 and *Farfadet* Y 711, built in 1971, and an ex-fishing vessel built in 1932, *La Grande Hermine* A 653 which works for the navigation school.

2 GLYCINE CLASS (AXL)

Name	No	Builders	Commissioned
GLYCINE	A 770	Socarenam, Boulogne	11 Apr 1992
EGLANTINE	A 771	Socarenam, Boulogne	9 Sep 1992

Displacement, tons: 295 full load
Dimensions, feet (metres): 92.8 × 25.3 × 12.5 *(28.3 × 7.7 × 3.8)*
Main machinery: 1 Baudouin 12P15-2SR diesel; 800 hp(m) *(588 kW)*; 1 shaft; cp prop
Speed, knots: 10. **Range, miles:** 3,600 at 10 kt
Complement: 10 + 16 trainees
Radars: Navigation: 2 Furuno; I-band.

Comment: Trawler type. Three more built in 1995-96 as route survey craft (included under *Mine Warfare Forces* section).

VERIFIED

EGLANTINE   11/1998, John Brodie / 0052192

8 LÉOPARD CLASS (AXL)

Name	No	Builders	Commissioned
LÉOPARD	A 748	ACM, St Malo	4 Dec 1982
PANTHÈRE	A 749	ACM, St Malo	4 Dec 1982
JAGUAR	A 750	ACM, St Malo	18 Dec 1982
LYNX	A 751	La Perrière, Lorient	18 Dec 1982
GUÉPARD	A 752	ACM, St Malo	1 July 1983
CHACAL	A 753	ACM, St Malo	10 Sep 1983
TIGRE	A 754	La Perrière, Lorient	1 July 1983
LION	A 755	La Perrière, Lorient	10 Sep 1983

Displacement, tons: 463 full load
Dimensions, feet (metres): 141 × 27.1 × 10.5 *(43 × 8.3 × 3.2)*
Main machinery: 2 SACM MGO 175 V16 ASHR diesels; 2,200 hp(m) *(1.62 MW)*; 2 shafts
Speed, knots: 15. **Range, miles:** 4,100 at 12 kt
Complement: 14 plus 21 trainees
Guns: 2 Oerlikon 20 mm.
Radars: Navigation: Racal Decca 1226; I-band.

Comment: First four ordered May 1980. Further four ordered April 1981. Form 20ème Divec (Training division) for shiphandling training and occasional EEZ patrols.   *UPDATED*

CHACAL   *7/1999*, J Cislak /* 0069962

2 LA BELLE POULE CLASS (AXS)

L'ÉTOILE A 649   **LA BELLE POULE** A 650

Displacement, tons: 275 full load
Dimensions, feet (metres): 127 × 24.3 × 12.1 *(37.5 × 7.4 × 3.7)*
Main machinery: 1 Sulzer diesel; 300 hp(m) *(220 kW)*; 1 shaft
Speed, knots: 9 (diesel)
Complement: 20 (1 officer) plus 20 trainees

Comment: Auxiliary sail vessels. Built by Chantiers de Normandie (Fécamp) and launched 7 July 1932 and 8 February 1932 respectively. Accommodation for three officers, 30 cadets, five petty officers, 12 men. Sail area 450 m². Attached to Naval School. A 649 major overhaul in 1994.   *UPDATED*

L'ÉTOILE   *6/1999*, Findler & Winter /* 0069963

1 SAIL TRAINING SHIP (AXS)

Name	No	Builders	Launched
MUTIN	A 652	Chaffeteau, Les Sables d'Olonne	18 Mar 1927

Displacement, tons: 57 full load
Dimensions, feet (metres): 108.3 × 21 × 11.2 *(33 × 6.4 × 3.4)*
Main machinery: 1 diesel; 112 hp(m) *(82 kW)*; 1 auxiliary prop
Speed, knots: 6 (diesel). **Range, miles:** 860 at 6 kt
Complement: 12 + 6 trainees

Comment: Attached to the Navigation School. Has a sail area of 312 m². This is the oldest ship in the French Navy. Used by the SOE during the Second World War.   *UPDATED*

MUTIN   *8/1996*, van Ginderen Collection /* 0081936

TUGS

2 OCEAN TUGS (ATA)

MALABAR A 664   **TENACE** A 669

Displacement, tons: 1,080 light; 1,454 full load
Dimensions, feet (metres): 167.3 × 37.8 × 18.6 *(51 × 11.5 × 5.7)*
Main machinery: 2 Krupp MaK 9 M 452 AK diesels; 4,600 hp(m) *(3.38 MW)*; 1 shaft; Kort nozzle
Speed, knots: 15. **Range, miles:** 9,500 at 13 kt
Complement: 56 (2 officers)
Radars: Navigation: Racal Decca RM 1226; I-band.
  Racal Decca 060; I-band.

Comment: *Malabar* and *Tenace* built by J. Oelkers, Hamburg. *Tenace* commissioned 15 November 1973, and *Malabar* on 3 February 1976. Based at Brest. Carry firefighting equipment. Bollard pull, 60 tons. One of the class to Turkey in 1999.   *VERIFIED*

MALABAR   *5/1998, John Brodie /* 0052194

3 BÉLIER CLASS (YTB)

BÉLIER A 695   **BUFFLE** A 696   **BISON** A 697

Displacement, tons: 500 standard; 800 full load
Dimensions, feet (metres): 104.9 × 28.9 × 10.5 *(32 × 8.8 × 3.2)*
Main machinery: 2 SACM AGO 195 V8 CSHR diesels; 2,600 hp(m) *(1.91 MW)*; 2 Voith-Schneider props
Speed, knots: 11
Complement: 12

Comment: Built at Cherbourg. *Bélier* commissioned 10 July 1980, *Buffle* on 19 July 1980, *Bison* on 16 April 1981. All based at Toulon but *Buffle* detached to Brest for sea trials of *Charles de Gaulle* in 1999/2000. Bollard pull, 25 tons.   *UPDATED*

BÉLIER   *11/1999*, van Ginderen Collection /* 0069964

3 MAROA CLASS (YTM)

MAROA A 636   **MAITO** A 637   **MANINI** A 638

Displacement, tons: 280 full load
Dimensions, feet (metres): 90.5 × 27.2 × 11.5 *(27.6 × 8.9 × 3.5)*
Main machinery: 2 SACM diesels; 1,280 hp(m) *(941 kW)*; 2 Voith-Schneider props
Speed, knots: 11. **Range, miles:** 1,200 at 10 kt
Complement: 10

Comment: Built by SFCN and Villeneuve La Garonne (A 638) and formerly used at the CEP Nuclear Test Range. *Maito* commissioned 25 July 1984, *Maroa* 28 July 1984, *Manini* 12 September 1985. Bollard pull, 12 tons.   *UPDATED*

MAROA   *1/1999*, M Declerck /* 0069965

15 + 1 FRÉHEL CLASS (COASTAL TUGS) (YTM)

FRÉHEL A 675	KÉRÉON (ex-Sicie) A 679	SICIÉ Y 680	NIVIDIC Y 643
SAIRE A 676	LARDIER Y 638	BALAGUIER Y 641	LE FOUR Y 647
ARMEN A 677	MENGAM Y 640	TAILLAT Y 642	PORT CROS Y 649
LA HOUSSAYE A 678	GIENS Y 639	TAUNOA A 681	+ 1

Displacement, tons: 259 full load
Dimensions, feet (metres): 82 × 27.6 × 11.2 (25 × 8.4 × 3.4)
Main machinery: 2 diesels; 1,280 hp(m) (941 kW) (1,320 hp(m) (970 kW) in later vessels); 2 Voith-Schneider props
Speed, knots: 10. **Range, miles:** 800 at 10 kt
Complement: 8 (coastal); 5 (harbour)

Comment: Building at Lorient Naval et Industries shipyard (formerly Chantiers et Ateliers de la Perrière, now part of Leroux et Lotz) and at Boulogne by SOCARENAM. Fréhel in service 23 May 1989, based at Cherbourg, Saire 16 October 1989 at Cherbourg, Armen 6 December 1991 at Brest, La Houssaye 30 October 1992 at Lorient, Kereon 5 December 1992 at Brest. Mengam 6 October 1994 at Brest, Giens 2 December 1994 at Toulon, Lardier March 1995 at Toulon, Sicié 6 October 1994 at Toulon, Balaguier 8 July 1995 at Toulon, Taillat 18 October 1995 at Toulon. Taunoa completed 9 March 1996 at Brest, Nividic on 12 December 1996 at Brest, Port Cros on 21 June 1997 at Toulon, Le Four on 13 March 1998 at Brest. Bollard pull 12 tons. Those with 'A' numbers have a crew of eight.

UPDATED

PORT CROS   6/1999*, G Toremans / 0069966

HARBOUR TUGS (YTL/YTR)

MOUETTE Y 617	FRÈNE Y 644	EIDER Y 729	LORIOT Y 747
CHATAIGNER Y 620	HEVEA Y 655	ARA Y 730	GÉLINOTTE Y 748
MÉSANGE Y 621	PIVERT Y 694	NOYER Y 739	P 3-P 5
BONITE Y 630	ÉBÈNE Y 717	PAPAYER Y 740	P 11-P 38
ROUGET Y 634	SANTAL Y 720	AIGUIÈRE Y 745	P 102-P 104
MARTINET Y 636	MARABOUT Y 725	EMBRUN Y 746	

Comment: All between 65 and 100 tons. Those without names are pusher tugs. At least seven others in reserve. One to Senegal in 1998, two to Ivory Coast in 1999.

UPDATED

EMBRUN   4/1998, M Declerck / 0052199

P 102   4/1998, M Declerck / 0052200

3 ACTIF CLASS (YTM)

LE FORT A 671 (12 July 1971)	ACHARNÉ A 693 (5 July 1974)
LUTTEUR A 673 (19 July 1963)	

Displacement, tons: 230 full load
Dimensions, feet (metres): 92 × 26 × 13 (28.1 × 7.9 × 4)
Main machinery: 1 SACM MGO diesel; 1,050 hp(m) (773 kW) or 1,450 hp(m) (1.07 MW) (later ships); 1 shaft
Speed, knots: 11. **Range, miles:** 2,400 at 10 kt
Complement: 15

Comment: Commissioning dates in brackets. Bollard pull, 13 tons. Two at Toulon and Acharné at Cherbourg. One more, Hercule, sold to a commercial company, and four others in reserve.

UPDATED

ACHARNÉ   10/1999*, van Ginderen Collection / 0069967

GOVERNMENT MARITIME FORCES
RESEARCH SHIPS

Note: Eleven civilian research ships are run by three state controlled agencies. These are Ifremer, Orstom (Tropics) and TAAF (Antarctic). The ships are named Marion Dufresne, L'Atalante, Thalassa, Nadir, Le Suroît, L'Europe, Antea, Alis, La Curieuse, Thalia, Gwen Drez.

THALASSA   10/1999*, van Ginderen Collection / 0069968

POLICE (GENDARMERIE MARITIME)

Note: These ships are operated and maintained by the Navy but are manned by Gendarmes. Tasked to protect naval bases and establishments ashore.

2 PATRA CLASS (COASTAL PATROL CRAFT) (PC)

Name	No	Builders	Commissioned
GLAIVE	P 671	Auroux, Arcachon	2 Apr 1977
ÉPÉE	P 672	CMN, Cherbourg	9 Oct 1976

Displacement, tons: 115 standard; 147.5 full load
Dimensions, feet (metres): 132.5 × 19.4 × 5.2 (40.4 × 5.9 × 1.6)
Main machinery: 2 SACM AGO 195 V12 diesels; 4,410 hp(m) (3.24 MW); 2 shafts; cp props
Speed, knots: 26. **Range, miles:** 1,750 at 10 kt; 750 at 20 kt
Complement: 18 (1 officer)
Guns: 1 Bofors 40 mm/60. 1 or 2—12.7 mm MGs.
Radars: Surface search: Racal Decca 1226; I-band.

Comment: Glaive based at Cherbourg and Épée at Lorient. Two others paid off in 1996.

UPDATED

GLAIVE   4/1999*, van Ginderen Collection / 0069969

2 STELLIS CLASS (COASTAL PATROL CRAFT) (PC)

Name	No	Builders	Commissioned
STELLIS	P 775	DCN, Lorient	5 Sep 1992
STÉNIA	P 776	DCN, Lorient	1 Mar 1993

Displacement, tons: 60 full load
Dimensions, feet (metres): 81.7 × 20 × 5.6 *(24.9 × 6.1 × 1.7)*
Main machinery: 3 diesels; 2,500 hp(m) *(1.8 MW)*; 2 shafts; 1 water-jet
Speed, knots: 28; 10 (water-jet only). **Range, miles:** 700 at 22 kt
Complement: 8
Guns: 1—12.7 mm MG. 2—7.62 mm MGs.
Radars: Navigation: Racal Decca 1226; I-band.

Comment: Both based at Degrad-des-Cannes in French Guiana. GRP hulls.   *VERIFIED*

STELLIS   *8/1992, DCN*

4 GERANIUM CLASS (PC)

Name	No	Builders	Commissioned
GÉRANIUM	P 720	DCN, Lorient	19 Feb 1997
JONQUILLE	P 721	Chantiers Guy Couach Plascoa	15 Nov 1997
VIOLETTE	P 722	DCN, Lorient	4 Dec 1997
JASMIN	P 723	Chantiers Guy Couach Plascoa	15 Nov 1997

Displacement, tons: 99 full load
Dimensions, feet (metres): 112.9 × 20 × 5.9 *(34.4 × 6.1 × 1.8)*
Main machinery: 3 Deutz/MWM TRD 616 V16(2) or V12(1) diesels; 4,352 hp(m) *(3.2 MW)*; 2 shafts; 1 Hamilton 422 water-jet
Speed, knots: 28. **Range, miles:** 1,200 at 15 kt
Complement: 12 (2 officers)
Guns: 1—12.7 mm MG. 2—7.62 mm MGs.
Radars: Navigation: Racal Bridgemaster II; E/F-band.

Comment: There are some minor differences between the DCN and the Plascoa craft. *Géranium* based at Cherbourg; *Jonquille* at Réunion Island; *Violette* at Pointe-à-Pitre, Guadeloupe; *Jasmin* at Papeete, Tahiti. Two similar craft built for Affaires Maritimes.   *UPDATED*

GÉRANIUM   *11/1999*, Harald Carstens /* 0069970

7 VSC 14 CLASS (PB)

PÉTULANTE P 760	RÉSÉDA P 778	VÉTIVER P 790
MIMOSA P 761	MELLIA P 789	HORTENSIA P 791
— P 764		

Displacement, tons: 21 full load
Dimensions, feet (metres): 47.9 × 15.1 × 3.3 *(14.6 × 4.6 × 1)*
Main machinery: 2 Baudouin 12 F11 SM diesels; 800 hp(m) *(588 kW)*; 2 shafts
Speed, knots: 20. **Range, miles:** 360 at 18 kt
Guns: 2—12.7 mm MGs.
Radars: Navigation: Furuno; I-band.

Comment: Type V14 SC. Built 1985-87 except P 791 in 1990. Similar to naval tenders with Y pennant numbers. Based at Nouméa, Ajaccio, Bayonne, Toulon, Port-des-Galets and Brest. P 790 based at Mayotte in October 1997.   *UPDATED*

P 764   *1/1998*, Schaeffer/Marsan /* 0069971

1 FULMAR CLASS (COASTAL PATROL CRAFT) (PC)

FULMAR (ex-*Jonathan*) P 740

Displacement, tons: 680 full load
Dimensions, feet (metres): 131.2 × 27.9 × 15.4 *(40 × 8.5 × 4.7)*
Main machinery: 1 diesel; 1,200 hp(m) *(882 kW)*; 1 shaft
Speed, knots: 12. **Range, miles:** 3,500 at 12 kt
Complement: 8 (1 officer)
Guns: 1—12.7 mm MG.
Radars: Surface search: 2 Furuno; I-band.

Comment: Former trawler built in 1990, acquired in October 1996 and converted for patrol duties by April 1997. Recommissioned 28 October 1997 and is based at St Pierre for western Atlantic Fishery Protection duties.   *VERIFIED*

2 TECIMAR CLASS (PB)

OEILLET P 772   **CAMÉLIA** P 774

Displacement, tons: 14 full load
Dimensions, feet (metres): 43.6 × 13.5 × 3.6 *(13.3 × 4.1 × 1.1)*
Main machinery: 2 diesels; 440 hp(m) *(323 kW)*; 2 shafts
Speed, knots: 25
Guns: 1—12.7 mm MG. 2—7.62 mm MGs.
Radars: Navigation: Furuno; I-band.

Comment: Tecimar Volte 43 class. Commissioned in 1975 and based at Brest.   *VERIFIED*

CAMÉLIA   *4/1998, M Declerck /* 0052202

15 VSC 10 CLASS (PB)

LILAS P 703	GENDARME PEREZ P 708	CAPITAINE MOULIÉ P 713
BÉGONIA P 704	MDLC RICHARD P 709	LIEUT JAMET P 714
PIVOINE P 705	GENERAL DELFOSSE P 710	BELLIS P 715
NYMPHÉA P 706	GENTIANE P 711	MDLS JACQUES P 716
MDLC ROBET P 707	FUSCHIA P 712	LAVANDE P 717

Comment: 10 m craft capable of 25 kt built 1985-95. Based at Dunkirk, Rochefort, Saint-Raphaël, Boulogne, Saint-Malo, Sète, Marseilles, Sables d'Olonnes, Port Vendres, Dieppe and Pornichet. Four more are planned.   *UPDATED*

NYMPHÉA   *6/1998*, P Marsan /* 0069972

CUSTOMS (DOUANES FRANÇAISES)

Note: The French customs service has a number of tasks not normally associated with such an organisation. In addition to the usual duties of dealing with ships entering either its coastal area or ports it also has certain responsibilities for rescue at sea, control of navigation, fishery protection and pollution protection. For these purposes 650 officers and men operate a number of craft of various dimensions: Class I of 30 m, 24 kt and a range of 1,200 miles; Class II of 27 m, 24 kt and with a range of 900 miles; Class III of 17 to 20 m, 24 kt and a range of 400 miles; Class IV of 12 to 17 m, 24 kt and a range of 400 miles. All vessels have DF numbers painted on the bow. There are also four Cessna 404 Titan, and 12 Reims-Cessna F406 Caravan II maritime patrol aircraft and six AS 350B1 Ecureuil helicopters.

DF 40   *8/1999*, van Ginderen Collection /* 0069973

AFFAIRES MARITIMES

Note: A force of some 37 patrol ships and craft of varying sizes. The vessels are unarmed and manned by civilians on behalf of the Préfectures Maritimes. Their duties mainly involve fishery protection, pollution control, navigation and pilotage supervision as well as search and rescue. All have PM numbers painted on the bow and Affaires Maritime written on the superstructure in the vicinity of the bridge. The Thomson-CSF demonstrator craft *Iris* was acquired in 1997.

ORIGAN PM 31   4/1999*, P Marsan / 0069976

IRIS PM 40   7/1999*, P Marsan / 0069974

GABON
MARINE GABONAISE

Bases	Personnel	Mercantile Marine	DELETIONS
Port Gentil, Mayumba	2000: 500 (60 officers)	*Lloyd's Register of Shipping:* 47 vessels of 15,711 tons gross	1997 *Manga* 1999 *General Nazaire Boulingui*

PATROL FORCES

2 PATRA CLASS (LARGE PATROL CRAFT) (PC)

Name	No	Builders	Commissioned
GÉNÉRAL d'ARMÉE BA-OUMAR	P 07	CMN, Cherbourg	27 June 1988
COLONEL DJOUE-DABANY	P 08	CMN, Cherbourg	14 Sep 1990

Displacement, tons: 446 full load
Dimensions, feet (metres): 179 × 26.2 × 8.5 *(54.6 × 8 × 2.5)*
Main machinery: 2 Wärtsilä UD 33 V16 diesels; 8,000 hp(m) *(5.88 MW)* sustained; 2 shafts; cp props
Speed, knots: 24. **Range, miles:** 4,200 at 15 kt
Complement: 32 (4 officers)
Military lift: 20 troops
Guns: 1 Bofors 57 mm/70 SAK 57 Mk 2 (P 07); 220 rds/min to 17 km *(9 n miles)*; weight of shell 2.4 kg. Not in P 08 which has a second Oerlikon 20 mm.
2 Giat F2 20 mm (twin) (P 08).
Weapons control: CSEE Naja optronic director (P 07).
Radars: Surface search: Racal Decca 1226C; I-band.

Programmes: Contract signed May 1985 with CMN Cherbourg. First laid down 2 July 1986, launched 18 December 1987 and arrived in Gabon 6 August 1988 for a local christening ceremony. Second ordered in February 1989 and launched 29 March 1990.
Structure: There is space on the quarterdeck for two MM 40 Exocet surface-to-surface missiles. These craft are similar to the French vessels but with different engines. *Ba-Oumar* had twin funnels fitted in 1992, similar to French 'P 400' class conversions. The second of class may be similarly converted but this now seems unlikely.

UPDATED

P 400 (French colours)   10/1998*, H M Steele / 0052169

LAND-BASED MARITIME AIRCRAFT

Note: In addition there are also two EMB-110s.

Numbers/Type: 1 Embraer EMB-111 Bandeirante.
Operational speed: 194 kt *(360 km/h).*
Service ceiling: 25,500 ft *(7,770 m).*
Range: 1,590 n miles *(2,945 km).*
Role/Weapon systems: Air Force coastal surveillance and EEZ protection tasks are primary roles. Sensors: APS-128 search radar, limited ECM, searchlight. Weapons: ASV; 8 × 127 mm rockets or 28 × 70 mm rockets.

VERIFIED

AMPHIBIOUS FORCES

1 BATRAL TYPE (LST)

Name	No	Builders	Launched	Commissioned
PRESIDENT EL HADJ OMAR BONGO	L 05	Français de l'Ouest, Rouen	16 Apr 1984	26 Nov 1984

Displacement, tons: 770 standard; 1,336 full load
Dimensions, feet (metres): 262.4 × 42.6 × 7.9 *(80 × 13 × 2.4)*
Main machinery: 2 SACM Type 195 V12 CSHR diesels; 3,600 hp(m) *(2.65 MW)*; 2 shafts; cp props
Speed, knots: 16. **Range, miles:** 4,500 at 13 kt
Complement: 39
Military lift: 188 troops; 12 vehicles; 350 tons cargo
Guns: 1 Bofors 40 mm/60; 300 rds/min to 12 km *(6.5 n miles)*; weight of shell 0.89 kg.
2—81 mm mortars. 2 Browning 12.7 mm MGs. 1—7.62 mm MG.
Radars: Surface search: Racal Decca 1226; I-band.
Helicopters: Capable of operating up to SA 330 Puma size.

Comment: Sister to French *La Grandière*. Carries one LCVP and one LCP. Started refit by Denel, Cape Town in April 1996, and returned to service in 1997 with bow doors welded shut.

UPDATED

PRESIDENT EL HADJ OMAR BONGO   6/1993*, Gabon Navy / 0069977

2 SEA TRUCKS (LCVP)

Comment: Built by Tanguy Marine, Le Havre in 1985. One of 12.2 m with two Volvo Penta 165 hp (m) *(121 kW)* engines and one of 10.2 m with one engine. *VERIFIED*

POLICE

Note: The Police have about 12—6.8 m LCVPs and Simmoneau 11 m patrol craft, 10 of which were delivered in 1989.

SIMMONEAU SM 360   1989*, Simmoneau Marine / 0069978

GAMBIA

Headquarters Appointments

Commander, Navy:
Captain M B Sarr

Personnel

(a) 2000: 95
(b) Voluntary service

General

On 1 February 1982 the two countries of Senegal and Gambia united to form the confederation of Senegambia, which included merging the armed forces. Confederation was cancelled on 30 September 1989 and the forces again became national and independent of each other. The patrol craft came under 3 Marine Company of the National Army until 30 July 1996 when a Navy was established.

Bases

Banjul

Mercantile Marine

Lloyd's Register of Shipping:
8 vessels of 1,884 tons gross

DELETIONS

1998   *Gunjur, Brufut*

PATROL FORCES

Note: Replacements are needed for the two deleted Shanghai IIs. Funds are not available.

1 FAIREY MARINE TRACKER 2 CLASS
(COASTAL PATROL CRAFT) (PC)

Name	No	Builders	Commissioned
JATO	P 12	Fairey Marine, Cowes	Dec 1978

Displacement, tons: 31.5 full load
Dimensions, feet (metres): 65.7 × 17 × 4.8 *(20 × 5.2 × 1.5)*
Main machinery: 2 GM 12V-71TA diesels; 840 hp *(617 kW)* sustained; 2 shafts
Speed, knots: 29. **Range, miles:** 650 at 20 kt
Complement: 11
Guns: 1 Oerlikon 20 mm. 2—7.62 mm MGs.
Radars: Surface search: Racal Decca; I-band.

Comment: Hull and superstructure of GRP. Air conditioned accommodation. Re-engined in 1991. Used for fishery patrol. The other two of the class returned to Senegal in September 1989.
UPDATED

1 FAIREY MARINE LANCE CLASS (COASTAL PATROL CRAFT) (PC)

Name	No	Builders	Commissioned
SEA DOG	P 11	Fairey Marine, Cowes	28 Oct 1976

Displacement, tons: 17 full load
Dimensions, feet (metres): 48.7 × 15.3 × 4.3 *(14.8 × 4.7 × 1.3)*
Main machinery: 2 GM 8V-71TA diesels; 650 hp *(485 kW)* sustained; 2 shafts
Speed, knots: 24. **Range, miles:** 500 at 16 kt
Complement: 9
Guns: 2—7.62 mm MGs (not carried).
Radars: Surface search: Racal Decca 110; I-band.

Comment: Delivered 28 October 1976. Unarmed and used for training. Still seaworthy.
UPDATED

SEA DOG   *1/1990*, E Grove* / 0069980

1 PETERSON MK 4 CLASS (PC)

Name	No	Builders	Commissioned
BALONGKANTA	P 14	Peterson Builders, Sturgeon Bay	15 Oct 1993

Displacement, tons: 24 full load
Dimensions, feet (metres): 50.9 × 14.8 × 4.3 *(15.5 × 4.5 × 1.3)*
Main machinery: 2 Detroit 6V-92TA diesels; 520 hp *(388 kW)* sustained; 2 shafts
Speed, knots: 24. **Range, miles:** 500 at 20 kt
Complement: 6
Guns: 2—12.7 mm MGs.
Radars: Surface search: Raytheon R4IX; I-band.

Comment: Similar craft in service in Egypt, Cape Verde, Guinea Bissau and Senegal.   *UPDATED*

JATO   *8/1993** / 0069979

PETERSON Mk 4 (Senegal colours)   *1/1998** / 0050096

GEORGIA

Headquarters Appointments

Commander of the Navy:
  Colonel Zurab Iramadze
Commander of the Border Guard:
  Major General Chkheidze

Personnel

2000: 3,100

General

Naval and Coast Guard Forces formed 7 July 1993 but are under different command. The Border Guard is much the better funded of the two maritime services.

Bases

Poti (HQ), Batumi.

Mercantile Marine

Lloyd's Register of Shipping:
  104 vessels of 132,235 tons gross

PATROL FORCES

Notes: (1) In addition to the vessels listed there are five former trawlers armed with 40 mm guns, and up to 16 harbour craft of various types.
(2) Four 'Yevgenya' class MSCs and up to six LCT/LCMs have also been reported but are not confirmed as being operational.
(3) Romania may donate a corvette in 2000.

1 + (2) LINDAU (TYPE 331) CLASS (PC)

Name	No	Builders	Commissioned
AYETY (ex-*Minden*)	— (ex-*M1085*)	Burmester, Bremen	22 Jan 1960

Displacement, tons: 463 full load
Dimensions, feet (metres): 154.5 × 27.2 × 9.8 *(47.1 × 8.3 × 2.8)*
Main machinery: 2 MTU MD diesels; 4,000 hp(m) *(2.94 MW)*; 2 shafts
Speed, knots: 16. **Range, miles:** 850 at 16 kt
Complement: 43
Guns: 1 Bofors 40 mm/70. 2—12.7 mm MGs.
Radars: Surface search: Atlas Elektronik TRS; I-band.

Comment: Paid off from German Navy in 1997 and transferred 22 October 1998 to the Coast Guard. Former minehunter refitted as a patrol craft in Germany before transfer. Two more *(Lindau* and *Marburg)* may follow but this is unlikely.
UPDATED

AYETY   *10/1998, Michael Nitz* / 0052206

1 TURK CLASS (PC)

Name	No	Builders	Commissioned
KUTAISI (ex-*AB 30*)	P 202 (ex-*P 130*)	Haliç Shipyard	21 Feb 1969

Displacement, tons: 170 full load
Dimensions, feet (metres): 132 × 21 × 5.5 *(40.2 × 6.4 × 1.7)*
Main machinery: 4 SACM-AGO V16 CSHR diesels; 9,600 hp(m) *(7.06 MW)*; 2 cruise diesels; 300 hp(m) *(220 kW)*; 2 shafts
Speed, knots: 22
Complement: 31
Guns: 1 Bofors 40 mm/70. 1 Oerlikon 20 mm.
Radars: Surface search: Racal Decca; I-band.

Comment: Transferrred from Turkish Navy on 5 December 1998 to the Navy. May retain its active sonar and ASW rocket launcher but this is unlikely.
UPDATED

TURK (Turkish colours)   *3/1996, Selim San* / 0052207

1 STENKA (TYPE 205P) CLASS (PCF)

BATUMI (ex-*PSKR 638*)   P 301 (ex-*692*)

Displacement, tons: 253 full load
Dimensions, feet (metres): 129.3 × 25.9 × 8.2 *(39.4 × 7.9 × 2.5)*
Main machinery: 3 diesels; 14,100 hp(m) *(10.36 MW)*; 3 shafts
Speed, knots: 37. **Range, miles:** 2,300 at 14 kt
Complement: 25
Guns: 2 Bofors 40 mm/60.
Radars: Surface search: Pot Drum; H/I-band.
Fire control: Drum Tilt; H/I-band.
Navigation: Palm Frond; I-band.

Comment: Transferred from Ukraine in 1998. This unit is the Navy's craft. A second of class for the Coast Guard is laid up. ASW gear is non-operational and guns have been changed.
UPDATED

STENKA (Russian colours)   *7/1993, Hartmut Ehlers* / 0052208

1 MATKA (TYPE 206MP) CLASS (PHG)

TBILISI P 302

Displacement, tons: 225 standard; 260 full load
Dimensions, feet (metres): 129.9 × 24.9 (41 over foils) × 6.9 (13.1 over foils) *(39.6 × 7.6 (12.5) × 2.1 (4))*
Main machinery: 3 Type M 504 diesels; 10,800 hp(m) *(7.94 MW)* sustained; 3 shafts
Speed, knots: 40. **Range, miles:** 600 at 35 kt foilborne; 1,500 at 14 kt hullborne
Complement: 33
Missiles: SSM: 2 SS-N-2C/D Styx; active radar or IR homing to 83 km *(45 n miles)* at 0.9 Mach; warhead 513 kg; sea-skimmer at end of run.
Guns: 1—3 in *(76 mm)*/60; 120 rds/min to 15 km *(8 n miles)*; weight of shell 7 kg.
  1—30 mm/65 AK 630; 6 barrels per mounting; 3,000 rds/min to 2 km.
Countermeasures: Decoys: 2 PK 16 chaff launchers.
ESM: Clay Brick; intercept.
Weapons control: Hood Wink optronic directors.
Radars: Air/surface search: Plank Shave; E-band.
Navigation: SRN-207; I-band.
Fire control: Bass Tilt; H/I-band.

Comment: Acquired from Ukraine in 1999 with full armament. A second of class may follow.
NEW ENTRY

MATKA (Ukraine colours)   *4/1997* / 0019341

1 ZHUK CLASS (PC)

TOLIA P 101

Displacement, tons: 39 full load
Dimensions, feet (metres): 78.7 × 16.4 × 3.9 *(25 × 5 × 1.2)*
Main machinery: 2 Type 401B diesels; 2,200 hp(m) *(1.6 MW)* sustained; 2 shafts
Speed, knots: 30. **Range, miles:** 1,000 at 15 kt
Complement: 11
Guns: 2—14.5 mm (twin) MGs. 1—12.7 mm MG.
Radars: Surface search: Spin Trough; I-band.

Comment: Two former Russian and three Ukrainian vessels were acquired in 1996/97. Pennant numbers P 101-P 105. This is the only operational hull but two other Border Guard units may be refurbished in due course.

UPDATED

DILOS (Greek colours)   7/1989*, D Dervissis / 0052209

ZHUK (Russian colours)   11/1996, MoD Bonn / 0019041

2 COASTAL PATROL CRAFT (PC)

P 206 (ex-SG 48)   **P 207** (ex-SG 40)

Displacement, tons: 25 full load
Dimensions, feet (metres): 49 × 14.8 × 2.4 *(14.9 × 4.5 × 0.7)*
Main machinery: 2 GM diesels; 450 hp *(335 kW)*; 2 shafts
Speed, knots: 12. **Range, miles:** 200 at 12 kt
Complement: 7
Guns: 1—12.7 mm MG.

Comment: Transferred from the Turkish Coast Guard 27 February 1998. Former US Mk 5 craft built in the 1940s.

UPDATED

2 DILOS CLASS (PC)

Name	No	Builders	Commissioned
IBERIA (ex-*Lindos*)	P 201 (ex-P 269)	Hellenic Shipyard, Skaramanga	1978
GRIFFIN (ex-*Dilos*)	P 205 (ex-P 267)	Hellenic Shipyard, Skaramanga	1978

Displacement, tons: 86 full load
Dimensions, feet (metres): 95.1 × 16.2 × 5.6 *(29 × 5 × 1.7)*
Main machinery: 2 MTU 12V 331 TC92 diesels; 2,660 hp(m) *(1.96 MW)* sustained; 2 shafts
Speed, knots: 27. **Range, miles:** 1,600 at 24 kt
Complement: 15
Guns: 2 Rheinmetall 20 mm.
Radars: Surface search: Racal Decca 1226C; I-band.

Comment: First one transferred from the Greek Navy in February 1998, second in September 1999.

UPDATED

SG 40 (Turkish colours)   6/1995*, Turkish Coast Guard / 0017322

GERMANY
DEUTSCHE MARINE

Headquarters Appointments

Chief of Naval Staff:
   Vice Admiral Hans Lüssow
Chief of Staff:
   Rear Admiral Bernd Heise

Commander-in-Chief

Commander-in-Chief, Fleet:
   Vice Admiral Lutz Feldt
Deputy Commander-in-Chief, Fleet:
   Rear Admiral Ulrich Otto

Diplomatic Representation

Defence Attaché in London:
   Rear Admiral H Hass
Naval Attaché in Washington:
   Captain R Himstedt
Naval Attaché in Paris:
   Captain G W von Maltzan
Defence Attaché in Jakarta:
   Commander G Eschle
Defence Attaché in Teheran:
   Commander P Hausmann
Naval and Military Attaché in Rome:
   Commander Dr F Ganseuer
Defence Attaché in Tokyo:
   Captain R Wallner
Defence Attaché in Riga:
   Commander G Rettinghaus
Defence Attaché in Kuala-Lumpur:
   Commander J Detlefsen
Defence Attaché in Oslo:
   Commander V Brügmann
Defence Attaché in Lima:
   Commander G Gelitzki
Defence Attaché in Stockholm:
   Commander G Bruch
Naval Attaché in Madrid:
   Commander W Anders
Naval Attaché in Ankara:
   Commander B Schmidt
Naval Attaché in Kiev:
   Commander J Freund
Defence Attaché in Abu Dhabi:
   Commander W J Oelsner

Personnel

(a) 2000: 21,600 (5,017 officers) (including naval air arm) plus 5,600 conscripts
(b) 10 months' national service

Fleet Disposition

Submarine Flotilla (Eckernförde)
1st and 3rd Squadrons; Type 206A and Type 205

Destroyer Flotilla (Wilhelmshaven)
1st Destroyer Squadron; 'Lütjens' class
1st Frigate Squadron 'Sachsen' class (from 2001)
2nd and 4th Frigate Squadron; 'Bremen' class
6th Frigate Squadron; 'Brandenburg' class

Mine Warfare Flotilla (Olpenitz)
1st, 3rd and 5th Squadrons: 'Frankenthal', 'Frauenlob' and 'Hameln' classes

Mine Warfare Flotilla (Wilhelmshaven)
6th Squadron 'Lindau' class

FPB Flotilla
2nd and 7th Squadrons (Warnemünde) Type 143
5th Squadron (Olpenitz) Type 148

Bases

C-in-C Fleet: Glücksburg. Flag Officer Naval Command: Rostock.
Baltic: Kiel, Olpenitz (all mine warfare forces in due course), Flensburg*, Neustadt*, Warnemünde (all patrol craft in due course). Eckernförde (all submarines in due course).
North Sea: Wilhelmshaven.
Naval Arsenal: Wilhelmshaven, Kiel.
Training (other than in Bases above): Bremerhaven, Glückstadt, List/Sylt, Plön, Grossenbrode*, Parow.

The administration of the bases is vested in the Naval Support Command at Wilhelmshaven. Those marked with an asterisk are to close by 2000 although Neustadt may retain some minor support facilities.

Prefix to Ships' Names

Prefix FGS is used in communications.

Naval Air Arm

MFG (Marine Flieger Geschwader)
MFG 2 (Fighter-Bomber and Reconnaissance Wing at Eggebek)
      PA 200 Tornado
MFG 3 'Graf Zeppelin' (LRMP Wing at Nordholz)
      Breguet Atlantic of which 4 converted for Sigint, Sea Lynx (landbased for embarkation and maintenance). Dornier Do 228 (for pollution control)
MFG 5 (SAR and Liaison Wing at Kiel). To be evacuated and returned to civil use in due course
      Sea King Mk 41

Strength of the Fleet

Type	Active	Building (Projected)
Submarines—Patrol	14	4
Destroyers	2	—
Frigates	12	3
Corvettes	—	(5)
Fast Attack Craft—Missile	30	—
LCM/LCU	13	—
Minehunters	11	—
Minesweepers—Coastal	15	—
Minesweepers—Inshore	5	—
Minesweepers—Drones	18	—
Tenders	6	—
Support Ships	4	1
Replenishment Tankers	6	—
Ammunition Transports	2	—
Tugs—Icebreaking	1	—
AGIs	3	—
Sail Training Ships	2	—

Hydrographic Service

This service, under the direction of the Ministry of Transport, is civilian-manned with HQ at Hamburg. Survey ships are listed at the end of the section.

Mercantile Marine

Lloyd's Register of Shipping:
   1,028 vessels of 6,513,775 tons gross

DELETIONS

Submarines

1997 *U 13, U 14*
1998 *U 19, U 21*

Destroyers

1999 *Rommel*

Patrol Forces

1997 *Wolf, Elster* (both to Chile)
1998 *Tiger, Luchs, Pelikan, Kranich* (all to Chile)

Mine Warfare Vessels

1997 *Göttingen, Tübingen, Minden* (to Georgia)
1999 *Koblenz* (to Lithuania), *Volklingen* (to Latvia), *Ulm*
2000 *Paderborn* (possibly to South Africa), *Cuxhaven*
      (to Estonia), *Lindau, Marburg* (both possibly to Georgia)

Auxiliaries

1997 *Eisbär, Neuwerk* (to Greece), *Helgoland*
1998 *Nienburg, LP 3, MT 1, Heppens* (to Greece)
2000 *Vogtland, Uckermark*

Coast Guard

1997 *Boltenhagen* (to Malta), *Ahrenshoop* (to Tunisia),
      Kühlungsborn (to Cape Verde)
1999 *Sellin, Rosenheim, Rettin*

PENNANT LIST

Submarines

S 171	U 22
S 172	U 23
S 173	U 24
S 174	U 25
S 175	U 26
S 177	U 28
S 178	U 29
S 179	U 30
S 181	U 31 (bldg)
S 182	U 32 (bldg)
S 183	U 33 (proj)
S 184	U 34 (proj)
S 190	U 11
S 191	U 12
S 194	U 15
S 195	U 16
S 196	U 17
S 197	U 18

Destroyers

D 185	Lütjens
D 186	Mölders

Frigates

F 207	Bremen
F 208	Niedersachsen
F 209	Rheinland-Pfalz
F 210	Emden
F 211	Köln
F 212	Karlsruhe
F 213	Augsburg
F 214	Lübeck
F 215	Brandenburg
F 216	Schleswig-Holstein
F 217	Bayern
F 218	Mecklenburg-Vorpommern
F 219	Sachsen (bldg)
F 220	Hamburg (bldg)
F 221	Hessen (bldg)

Patrol Forces

P 6111	S 61 Albatros
P 6112	S 62 Falke
P 6113	S 63 Geier
P 6114	S 64 Bussard
P 6115	S 65 Sperber
P 6116	S 66 Greif
P 6117	S 67 Kondor
P 6118	S 68 Seeadler
P 6119	S 69 Habicht
P 6120	S 70 Kormoran
P 6121	S 71 Gepard
P 6122	S 72 Puma
P 6123	S 73 Hermelin
P 6124	S 74 Nerz
P 6125	S 75 Zobel
P 6126	S 76 Frettchen
P 6127	S 77 Dachs
P 6128	S 78 Ozelot
P 6129	S 79 Wiesel
P 6130	S 80 Hyäne
P 6145	S 45 Leopard
P 6146	S 46 Fuchs
P 6147	S 47 Jaguar
P 6148	S 48 Löwe
P 6150	S 50 Panther
P 6155	S 55 Alk
P 6156	S 56 Dommel
P 6157	S 57 Weihe
P 6158	S 58 Pinguin
P 6159	S 59 Reiher

Mine Warfare Forces

M 1052	Mühlhausen
M 1058	Fulda
M 1059	Weilheim
M 1060	Weiden
M 1061	Rottweil
M 1062	Sulzbach-Rosenberg
M 1063	Bad Bevensen
M 1064	Grömitz
M 1065	Dillingen
M 1066	Frankenthal
M 1067	Bad Rappenau
M 1068	Datteln
M 1069	Homburg
M 1073	Schleswig
M 1079	Düren
M 1081	Konstanz
M 1082	Wolfsburg
M 1090	Pegnitz
M 1091	Kulmbach
M 1092	Hameln
M 1093	Auerbach
M 1094	Ensdorf
M 1095	Überherrn
M 1096	Passau
M 1097	Laboe
M 1098	Siegburg
M 1099	Herten
M 2658	Frauenlob
M 2660	Gefion
M 2661	Medusa
M 2662	Undine
M 2665	Loreley

Amphibious Forces

L 760	Flunder
L 762	Lachs
L 763	Plötze
L 765	Schlei
L 769	Zander

Auxiliaries

A 50	Alster
A 52	Oste
A 53	Oker
A 60	Gorch Fock
A 511	Elbe
A 512	Mosel
A 513	Rhein
A 514	Werra
A 515	Main
A 516	Donau
A 1401	Eisvogel
A 1405	FW 5
A 1409	Wilhelm Pullwer
A 1411	Berlin
A 1412	Frankfurt (bldg)
A 1413	Freiburg
A 1414	Glücksburg
A 1418	Meersburg
A 1424	Walchensee
A 1425	Ammersee
A 1426	Tegernsee
A 1427	Westensee
A 1435	Westerwald
A 1436	Odenwald
A 1439	Baltrum
A 1440	Juist
A 1441	Langeoog
A 1442	Spessart
A 1443	Rhön
A 1450	Planet
A 1451	Wangerooge
A 1452	Spiekeroog
A 1455	Norderney
A 1458	Fehmarn
Y 811	Knurrhahn
Y 812	Lütje Hörn
Y 814	Knechtsand
Y 815	Scharhorn
Y 816	Vogelsand
Y 817	Nordstrand
Y 819	Langeness
Y 834	Nordwind
Y 835	Todendorf
Y 836	Putlos
Y 837	Baumholder
Y 838	Bergen
Y 839	Munster
Y 842	Schwimmdock A
Y 855	TF 5
Y 856	TF 6
Y 860	Schwedeneck
Y 861	Kronsort
Y 862	Helmsand
Y 863	Stollergrund
Y 864	Mittelgrund
Y 865	Kalkgrund
Y 866	Breitgrund
Y 867	Bant
Y 875	Hiev
Y 876	Griep
Y 879	Schwimmdock B
Y 891	Altmark
Y 895	Wische
Y 1643	Bottsand
Y 1644	Eversand
Y 1656	Wustrow
Y 1658	Dranske
Y 1671	AK 1
Y 1672	AK 3
Y 1674	AM 6
Y 1675	AM 8
Y 1676	MA 2
Y 1677	MA 3
Y 1678	MA 1
Y 1679	AM 7
Y 1680	Neuende
Y 1683	AK 6
Y 1685	Aschau
Y 1686	AK 2
Y 1687	Borby
Y 1689	Bums

SUBMARINES

U 24

5/1999*, Michael Nitz / 0081937

0 + 4 (8) TYPE 212A (SSK)

Name	No
U 31	S 181
U 32	S 182
U 33	S 183
U 34	S 184

Builders	Laid down	Launched	Commissioned
HDW, Kiel	Nov 1999	Oct 2001	Sep 2003
TNSW, Emden	Jan 2002	Nov 2003	May 2005
HDW, Kiel	Oct 2002	Sep 2004	Jan 2006
TNSW, Emden	June 2003	May 2005	Sep 2006

Displacement, tons: 1,450 surfaced; 1,830 dived
Dimensions, feet (metres): 183.4 × 23 × 19.7
(55.9 × 7 × 6)
Main machinery: Diesel-electric; 1 MTU 16V 396 diesel;
4,243 hp(m) *(3.12 MW)*; 1 alternator; 1 Siemens Permasyn
motor; 3,875 hp(m) *(2.85 MW)*; 1 shaft; 9 Siemens/HDW PEM
fuel cell (AIP) modules; 306 kW; sodium sulphide high-energy
batteries
Speed, knots: 20 dived; 12 surfaced
Range, miles: 8,000 at 8 kt surfaced
Complement: 27 (8 officers)

Torpedoes: 6—21 in *(533 mm)* bow tubes; water ram discharge;
STN (formerly AEG) DM 2A4. Total 12 weapons.
Mines: Containers similar to those on the Type 206A.
Countermeasures: Decoys: TAU 2000 (C 303) torpedo
countermeasures.
ESM: DASA FL 1800U; radar warning.
Weapons control: Kongsberg MSI-90U weapons control
system.
Radars: Navigation: Kelvin Hughes 1007; I-band.
Sonars: STN Atlas Elektronik DBQS-40; passive ranging and
intercept; FAS-3 flank and TAS-3 clip on passive towed array.
STN Atlas Elektronik MOA 3070 or Allied Signal ELAK; mine
detection; active; high frequency.

Programmes: Design phase first completed in 1992 by ARGE
212 (HDW/TNSW) in conjunction with IKL. Authorisation for
the first four of the class was given on 6 July 1994, but the first
steel cut was delayed to 1 July 1998 because of modifications
needed to achieve commonality with the Italian Navy, which is
building two identical hulls. Changes included greater diving
depth, improved habitability and possibly an optronic mast.
HDW Kiel, and TNSW Emden, are sharing the work with the
forward half being built by HDW and the back end by TNSW
with final assembly alternating between the shipyards.
Structure: Equipped with a hybrid fuel cell/battery propulsion
based on the Siemens PEM fuel cell technology. The
submarine is designed with a partial double hull which has a
larger diameter forward. This is joined to the after end by a
short conical section which houses the fuel cell plant. Two LOX
tanks and hydrogen stored in metal cylinders are carried
around the circumference of the smaller hull section. Zeiss
search and attack periscopes.

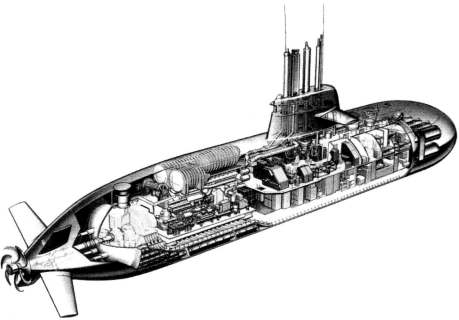

U 31

1998, HDW / 0052211

Operational: Maximum speed on AIP is 8 kt without use of main
battery. All to be based at Eckenförde as part of the First
Submarine Squadron.
Sales: Two identical submarines are being built in Italy.
Opinion: A period of time has been set aside to ensure prototype
testing of the first of class from 2002. This is a sensible

precaution given the inherent operating dangers associated
with AIP technology even though in this case the AIP system
was tested for reliability in a Type 205 submarine in 1988/89.
UPDATED

2 TYPE 205 (SSA)

Name	No
U 11	S 190
U 12	S 191

Builders	Laid down	Launched	Commissioned
Howaldtswerke, Kiel	1 Apr 1966	9 Feb 1968	21 June 1968
Howaldtswerke, Kiel	1 Sep 1966	10 Sep 1968	14 Jan 1969

Displacement, tons: 419 surfaced; 450 dived
Dimensions, feet (metres): 144 × 15.1 × 14.1
(43.9 × 4.6 × 4.3)
Main machinery: Diesel-electric; 2 MTU 12V 493 AZ80 GA 31L
diesels; 1,200 hp(m) *(882 kW)* sustained; 2 alternators;
810 kW; 1 Siemens motor; 1,800 hp(m) *(1.32 MW)* sustained;
1 shaft
Speed, knots: 10 surfaced; 17 dived
Complement: 22 (4 officers)

Torpedoes: 8—21 in *(533 mm)* tubes.
Countermeasures: ESM: Radar warning.
Weapons control: Signaal Mk 8.
Radars: Surface search: Thomson-CSF Calypso II; I-band.
Sonars: Atlas Elektronik SRS M1H; passive/active search and
attack; high frequency.

Programmes: Built in floating docks. First submarines designed
and built by West Germany after the Second World War.
Structure: Diving depth, 159 m *(490 ft)*. Hulls of steel alloys with
non-magnetic properties. *U 11* (Type 205A) converted as a
padded target in 1988; *U 12* (Type 205B) acts as a sonar trials
platform.
Operational: Based at Eckernförde. *U 11* is to be deleted in
2003, and *U 12* in 2006.

UPDATED

U 11

4/1998, M Declerck / 0052212

U 12

6/1998, Michael Nitz / 0052213

LÜRSSEN

PARTNER TO YOUR NAVY

Most Modern Facilities – High-Tech Products

Lürssen is producing the most successful high tech products with years of experience on the development of custom designed Corvettes and Mine Counter-measure Vessels. Our engineers, naval architects, own specialists in system integration and craftsmen together with state-of-the-art-facilities guarantee an unequalled quality and performance of our ships. Complete logistic support is offered by Lürssen´s logistic department: documentation, spare parts managing and own training centre fulfill all requirements regarding systems´ operation and maintenance.

Fr. Lürssen Werft (GmbH & Co.) Ph. (+49)421- 6604-0 · Fax (+49)421- 6604-443

SIEMENS

Reliability When and Where You Need It

Reliability is decisive for every fleet´s readiness for action – reliability of the crew and of the technology.

Siemens technology is reliable. Irrespective of whether we are talking about innovative separate systems for automation, propulsion and shipboard power supply, or sub-systems, or a single integrated system.

All of them are our strong points – reliable technology, including integration into complete systems. We´ll bear overall responsibility for all shipboard electrical and electronic systems – from the project speci-fication phase through to handing over and beyond. And including definition of all interfaces.

Latest examples of this approach are the ANZAC frigates, the class 212 submarines and the new German naval supply vessels class 702.

And we offer complete refit schemes to bring ships of the older generation up to modern standard.

Siemens AG
Marine Engineering
Lindenplatz 2
D-20099 Hamburg
Tel. +49-40-28 89-27 00
Fax +49-40-28 89-36 80
e-mail: marine.engineering
@hbg.siemens.de
www.marine-engineering.de

Industrial Projects
and Technical Services

your success is our goal

PUBLICIS MCD 159U464697

12 TYPE 206A (SSK)

Name	No	Builders	Laid down	Launched	Commissioned
U 15	S 194	Howaldtswerke, Kiel	1 June 1970	15 June 1972	17 July 1974
U 16	S 195	Rheinstahl Nordseewerke, Emden	1 Nov 1970	29 Aug 1972	9 Nov 1973
U 17	S 196	Howaldtswerke, Kiel	1 Oct 1970	10 Oct 1972	28 Nov 1973
U 18	S 197	Rheinstahl Nordseewerke, Emden	1 Apr 1971	31 Oct 1972	19 Dec 1973
U 22	S 171	Rheinstahl Nordseewerke, Emden	18 Nov 1971	27 Mar 1973	26 July 1974
U 23	S 172	Rheinstahl Nordseewerke, Emden	5 Mar 1972	25 May 1974	2 May 1975
U 24	S 173	Rheinstahl Nordseewerke, Emden	20 Mar 1972	26 June 1973	16 Oct 1974
U 25	S 174	Howaldtswerke, Kiel	1 July 1971	23 May 1973	14 June 1974
U 26	S 175	Rheinstahl Nordseewerke, Emden	14 July 1972	20 Nov 1973	13 Mar 1975
U 28	S 177	Rheinstahl Nordseewerke, Emden	4 Oct 1972	22 Jan 1974	18 Dec 1974
U 29	S 178	Howaldtswerke, Kiel	10 Jan 1972	5 Nov 1973	27 Nov 1974
U 30	S 179	Rheinstahl Nordseewerke, Emden	5 Dec 1972	26 Mar 1974	13 Mar 1975

Displacement, tons: 450 surfaced; 498 dived
Dimensions, feet (metres): 159.4 × 15.1 × 14.8
 (48.6 × 4.6 × 4.5)
Main machinery: Diesel-electric; 2 MTU 12V 493 AZ80 GA
 31L diesels; 1,200 hp(m) *(882 kW)* sustained; 2 alternators;
 810 kW; 1 Siemens motor; 1,800 hp(m) *(1.32 MW)* sustained;
 1 shaft
Speed, knots: 10 surfaced; 17 dived
Range, miles: 4,500 at 5 kt surfaced
Complement: 22 (4 officers)

Torpedoes: 8—21 in *(533 mm)* bow tubes. STN Atlas DM 2A3;
 wire-guided; active homing to 13 km *(7 n miles)* at 35 kt;
 passive homing to 28 km *(15 n miles)* at 23 kt; warhead
 260 kg.
Mines: GRP container secured outside hull each side. Each
 container holds 12 mines, carried in addition to the normal
 torpedo or mine armament (16 in place of torpedoes).
Countermeasures: ESM: Thomson-CSF DR 2000U with THORN
 EMI Sarie 2; intercept.
Weapons control: SLW 83 (TFCS).
Radars: Surface search: Thomson-CSF Calypso II; I-band.
Sonars: Atlas Elektronik DBQS-21D; passive/active search and
 attack; medium frequency.
 Thomson Sintra DUUX 2; passive ranging.

Programmes: Authorised on 7 June 1969.
Modernisation: Mid-life conversion of the class was a very
 extensive one, including the installation of new sensors (sonar
 DBQS-21D with training simulator STU-5), periscopes,
 weapon control system (LEWA), ESM, weapons (torpedo
 Seeal), GPS navigation, and a comprehensive refitting of the
 propulsion system, as well as habitability improvements.
 Conversion work was shared between Thyssen Nordseewerke
 (U 23, 30, 22, 27, 15, 26) at Emden and HDW *(U 29, 16, 25,
 28, 17, 18)* at Kiel. The work started in mid-1987 and
 completed in February 1992.
Structure: Hulls are built of high-tensile non-magnetic steel.
Operational: First and third squadrons based at Eckernförde.
Sales: Two unmodernised (Type 206) were to have been
 acquired by Indonesia but the sale was cancelled in late 1998.
 UPDATED

U 24   *5/1999*, Michael Nitz /* 0069981

U 23   *6/1999*, Maritime Photographic /* 0069982

U 17   *3/1999*, John Brodie /* 0069983

DESTROYERS

2 LÜTJENS (MODIFIED CHARLES F ADAMS) CLASS (TYPE 103B) (DDG)

Name	No	Builders	Laid down	Launched	Commissioned
LÜTJENS (ex-US DDG 28)	D 185	Bath Iron Works Corporation	1 Mar 1966	11 Aug 1967	22 Mar 1969
MÖLDERS (ex-US DDG 29)	D 186	Bath Iron Works Corporation	12 Apr 1966	13 Apr 1968	20 Sep 1969

Displacement, tons: 3,370 standard; 4,500 full load
Dimensions, feet (metres): 437 × 47 × 20
 (133.2 × 14.3 × 6.1)
Main machinery: 4 Combustion Engineering boilers; 1,200 psi
 (84.4 kg/cm²); 950°F *(510°C)*; 2 turbines; 70,000 hp
 (52.2 MW); 2 shafts
Speed, knots: 32. **Range, miles:** 4,500 at 20 kt
Complement: 337 (19 officers)

Missiles: SSM: McDonnell Douglas Harpoon; active radar
 homing to 130 km *(70 n miles)* at 0.9 Mach; warhead 227 kg.
 Combined Mk 13 single-arm launcher with SAM system ❶.
 SAM: GDC Pomona Standard SM-1MR; Mk 13 Mod 0 launcher;
 command guidance; semi-active radar homing to 46 km *(25 n
 miles)* at 2 Mach; 40 missiles—combined SSM and SAM.
 2 RAM 21 cell Mk 49 launchers ❷; passive IR/anti-radiation
 homing to 9.6 km *(5.2 n miles)* at 2 Mach; warhead 9.1 kg.
 A/S: Honeywell ASROC Mk 112 octuple launcher ❸; inertial
 guidance to 1.6-10 km *(1-5.4 n miles)*; payload Mk 46 torpedo.
Guns: 2 FMC 5 in *(127 mm)*/54 Mk 42 Mod 10 automatic ❹;
 20 rds/min to 23 km *(12.4 n miles)* anti-surface; 15 km *(8 n
 miles)* anti-aircraft; weight of shell 32 kg.
 2 Rheinmetall 20 mm Rh 202.
Torpedoes: 6—324 mm US Mk 32 (2 triple) tubes ❺. Honeywell
 Mk 46 Mod 2; anti-submarine; active/passive homing to 11 km
 (5.9 n miles) at 40 kt; warhead 44 kg.
Depth charges: 1 projector ❻.
Countermeasures: Decoys: Loral Hycor Mk 36 SRBOC
 6-barrelled chaff launcher; range 1-4 km *(0.6-2.2 n miles)*.
 ESM/ECM: AEG FL-1800S; Stage II; intercept and jammer.
Combat data systems: SATIR 1 action data automation; Link 11.
 SATCOM.
Weapons control: Mk 86 GFCS. Mk 74 MFCS.
Radars: Air search: Lockheed SPS-40 ❼; B-band.
 Hughes SPS-52 ❽; 3D; E/F-band.
 Surface search: Raytheon SPS-67 ❾; G-band.
 Fire control: 2 Raytheon SPG-51 ❿; G/I-band (for missiles).
 Lockheed SPQ-9 ⓫; I/J-band.
 Lockheed SPG-60 ⓬; I/J-band.
Tacan: URN 20 ⓭.
Sonars: Atlas Elektronik DSQS-21B; hull-mounted; active search
 and attack; medium frequency.

Programmes: Modified to suit West German requirements and
 practice. 1965 contract.
Modernisation: The Type 103B modernisation and other
 modifications included: modification of Mk 13 launcher for
 Standard SAM and Harpoon SSM; improved fire control with
 digital in place of analogue computers; higher superstructure
 abaft bridge with SPG-60 and SPQ-9 on a mast platform.
 Carried out by Naval Arsenal, Kiel and Howaldtswerke, Kiel:
 Mölders completed 29 March 1984, *Lütjens* 16 December
 1986. RAM launchers fitted in front of the bridge and aft of the
 Mk 13 launcher. First operational in *Mölders* in December
 1993, then *Lütjens* in June 1995. EW update and new boiler
 tubes fitted in 1996-99.
Structure: Some differences from Charles F Adams in W/T
 aerials and general outline, particularly the funnels.
Operational: First one paid off in June 1999 having been
 deactivated in October 1998 so that some equipment could be
 transferred to first of 'Sachsen' class. These last two are
 planned to pay off in 2002/03.

UPDATED

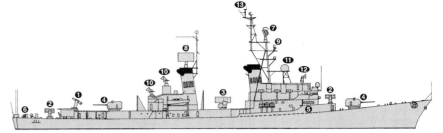

MÖLDERS   *(Scale 1 : 1,200), Ian Sturton / 0069984*

MÖLDERS   *4/1999*, M Declerck / 0069985*

LÜTJENS   *2/1999*, John Brodie / 0069986*

MÖLDERS   *4/1999*, Michael Nitz / 0069987*

FRIGATES

4 BRANDENBURG CLASS (TYPE 123) (FFG)

Name	No
BRANDENBURG	F 215
SCHLESWIG-HOLSTEIN	F 216
BAYERN	F 217
MECKLENBURG-VORPOMMERN	F 218

Builders	Laid down		Launched		Commissioned	
Blohm + Voss, Hamburg	11 Feb	1992	28 Aug	1992	14 Oct	1994
Howaldtswerke, Kiel	1 July	1993	8 June	1994	2 Nov	1995
Thyssen Nordseewerke, Emden	16 Dec	1993	30 June	1994	15 June	1996
Bremer Vulkan/Thyssen Nordseewerke	23 Nov	1993	8 July	1995	6 Dec	1996

Displacement, tons: 4,900 full load

Dimensions, feet (metres): 455.7 oa; 416.3 wl × 54.8 × 22.3 *(138.9; 126.9 × 16.7 × 6.8)*

Main machinery: CODOG; 2 GE 7LM2500SA-ML gas turbines; 51,000 hp *(38 MW)* sustained; 2 MTU 20V 956 TB92 diesels; 11,070 hp(m) *(8.14 MW)* sustained; 2 shafts; Escher Weiss; cp props

Speed, knots: 29; 18 on diesels. **Range, miles:** 4,000 at 18 kt

Complement: 199 (27 officers) plus 19 aircrew

Missiles: SSM: 4 Aerospatiale MM 38 Exocet (2 twin) ❶ (from Type 101A); inertial cruise; active radar homing to 42 km *(23 n miles)* at 0.9 Mach; warhead 165 kg; sea-skimmer.
SAM: Martin Marietta VLS Mk 41 Mod 3 ❷ for 16 NATO Sea Sparrow; semi-active radar homing to 14.6 km *(8 n miles)* at 2.5 Mach; warhead 39 kg.
2 RAM 21 cell Mk 49 launchers ❸; passive IR/anti-radiation homing to 9.6 km *(5.2 n miles)* at 2 Mach; warhead 9.1 kg; 32 missiles.

Guns: 1 OTO Melara 3 in *(76 mm)*/62 Mk 75 ❹; 85 rds/min to 16 km *(8.6 n miles)* anti-surface; 12 km *(6.5 n miles)* anti-aircraft; weight of shell 6 kg.
2 Rheinmetall 20 mm Rh 202 to be replaced by Mauser 27 mm.

Torpedoes: 4—324 mm Mk 32 Mod 9 (2 twin) tubes ❺; anti-submarine. Honeywell Mk 46 Mod 2; anti-submarine; active/passive homing to 11 km *(5.9 n miles)* at 40 kt; warhead 44 kg. To be replaced by Eurotorp Mu 90 Impact in due course.

Countermeasures: Decoys: 2 Breda SCLAR ❻. Chaff and IR flares.
ESM/ECM: TST FL 1800S Stage II; intercept and jammers.

Combat data systems: Atlas Elektronik/Paramax SATIR action data automation with Unisys UYK 43 computer; Link 11. Matra Marconi SCOT 3 SATCOM ❼.

Weapons control: Signaal MWCS. 2 optical sights. STN Atlas Elektronic WBA optronic sensor.

Radars: Air search: Signaal LW08 ❽; D-band.
Air/Surface search: Signaal SMART; 3D; F-band.
Fire control: 2 Signaal STIR 180 trackers ❿.
Navigation: 2 Raytheon Raypath; I-band.

Sonars: Atlas Elektronik DSQS-23BZ; hull-mounted; active search and attack; medium frequency.
Towed array (provision only); active; low frequency.

Helicopters: 2 Westland Sea Lynx Mk 88 or 88A ⓫.

Programmes: Formerly 'Deutschland' class. Four ordered 28 June 1989. Developed by Blohm + Voss whose design was selected in October 1988. Replaced deleted 'Hamburg' class.

Modernisation: LFASS (low frequency active sonar system) towed array to be fitted from 2003. SCOT 3 SATCOM and STN optronic sensor fitted from 1998.

Structure: The design is a mixture of MEKO and improved serviceability Type 122 having the same propulsion as the

BRANDENBURG

(Scale 1 : 1,200), Ian Sturton / 0069988

BAYERN

7/1999*, M Declerck / 0069989

Type 122. Contemporary stealth features. All steel. Fin stabilisers. Space allocated for a Task Group Commander and Staff.

Operational: 6th Frigate Squadron based at Wilhelmshaven. One RIB may be carried for boarding operations.

UPDATED

BRANDENBURG

2/1999*, Michael Nitz / 0069990

8 BREMEN CLASS (TYPE 122) (FFG)

Name	No	Builders	Laid down		Launched		Commissioned	
BREMEN	F 207	Bremer Vulkan	9 July	1979	27 Sep	1979	7 May	1982
NIEDERSACHSEN	F 208	AG Weser/Bremer Vulkan	9 Nov	1979	9 June	1980	15 Oct	1982
RHEINLAND-PFALZ	F 209	Blohm + Voss/Bremer Vulkan	29 Sep	1979	3 Sep	1980	9 May	1983
EMDEN	F 210	Thyssen Nordseewerke, Emden/Bremer Vulkan	23 June	1980	17 Dec	1980	7 Oct	1983
KÖLN	F 211	Blohm + Voss/Bremer Vulkan	16 June	1980	29 May	1981	19 Oct	1984
KARLSRUHE	F 212	Howaldtswerke, Kiel/Bremer Vulkan	10 Mar	1981	8 Jan	1982	19 Apr	1984
AUGSBURG	F 213	Bremer Vulkan	4 Apr	1987	17 Sep	1987	3 Oct	1989
LÜBECK	F 214	Thyssen Nordseewerke, Emden/Bremer Vulkan	1 June	1987	15 Oct	1987	19 Mar	1990

Displacement, tons: 3,680 full load
Dimensions, feet (metres): 426.4 × 47.6 × 21.3
(130 × 14.5 × 6.5)
Main machinery: CODOG; 2 GE LM 2500 gas turbines;
51,000 hp *(38 MW)* sustained; 2 MTU 20V 956 TB92 diesels;
11,070 hp(m) *(8.14 MW)* sustained; 2 shafts; cp props
Speed, knots: 30; 20 on diesels. **Range, miles:** 4,000 at 18 kt
Complement: 219 (26 officers)

Missiles: SSM: 8 McDonnell Douglas Harpoon (2 quad)
launchers **❶**; active radar homing to 130 km *(70 n miles)* at
0.9 Mach; warhead 227 kg.
SAM: 16 Raytheon NATO Sea Sparrow; Mk 29 octuple launcher
❷; semi-active radar homing to 14.6 km *(8 n miles)* at
2.5 Mach; warhead 39 kg.
2 GDC RAM 21 cell **❸**; passive IR/anti-radiation homing to
9.6 km *(5.2 n miles)* at 2 Mach; warhead 9.1 kg.
2 Rheinmetall or Oerlikon 20 mm (can be fitted at bridge level
abreast the foremast). To be replaced by Mauser 27 mm.
Guns: 1 OTO Melara 3 in *(76 mm)*/62 Mk 75 **❹**; 85 rds/min to
16 km *(8.6 n miles)* anti-surface; 12 km *(6.5 n miles)* anti-
aircraft; weight of shell 6 kg.
2 Rheinmetall 20 mm Rh 202, to be replaced by Mauser
27 mm.
Torpedoes: 4—324 mm Mk 32 (2 twin) tubes **❺**. 8 Honeywell
Mk 46 Mod 2; anti-submarine; active/passive homing to 11 km
(5.9 n miles) at 40 kt; warhead 44 kg. To be replaced by
Eurotorp Mu 90.
Countermeasures: Decoys: 4 Loral Hycor SRBOC **❻** 6-barrelled
fixed Mk 36; chaff and IR flares to 4 km *(2.2 n miles)*.
SLQ-25 Nixie; towed torpedo decoy. Prairie bubble noise
reduction.
ESM/ECM: TST 1800S **❼**; radar warning and jammers.
Combat data systems: SATIR action data automation; Link 11;
Matra Marconi SCOT 1A SATCOM **❽** (3 sets for the class).
Weapons control: Signaal WM25/STIR. STN Atlas Elektronic
WBA optronic sensor.
Radars: Air/surface search: DASA TRS-3D/32 **❾**; C-band.
Navigation: SMA 3 RM 20; I-band.
Fire control: Signaal WM25 **❿**; I/J-band.
Signaal STIR **⓫**; I/J/K-band; range 140 km *(76 n miles)* for
1 m² target.
Sonars: Atlas Elektronik DSQS-21BZ (BO); hull-mounted; active
search and attack; medium frequency.

Helicopters: 2 Westland Sea Lynx Mk 88 or 88A **⓬**.

Programmes: Approval given in early 1976 for first six of this
class, a modification of the Netherlands 'Kortenaer' class.
Replaced the deleted 'Fletcher' and 'Köln' classes. Equipment
ordered February 1986 after order placed 6 December 1985
for last pair. Hulls and some engines provided in the five
building yards. Ships were then towed to the prime contractor
Bremer Vulkan where weapon systems and electronics were
fitted and trials conducted. The three names for F 210-212
were changed from the names of Länder to take the well
known town names of the 'Köln' class as they were paid off.
Modernisation: RAM fitted from 1993-1996: Updated EW fit
from 1994. 20 mm guns, taken from Type 520 LCUs, fitted aft
of the bridge on each side. TRS-3D/32 radar is replacing
DA08. Fitting programme: F 210 in 1997; F 212 in 1998; the
remainder in 1999 except F 209 in 2000. STN optronic sensor
being fitted from 1998. 27 mm guns to replace 20 mm in due
course.
Operational: Form 2nd and 4th Frigate Squadrons. Three
containerised SCOT 1A terminals acquired in 1988 and when
fitted are mounted on the hangar roof.

UPDATED

EMDEN   *(Scale 1 : 1,200), Ian Sturton /* 0012400

EMDEN   *5/1999*, Findler & Winter /* 0069991

KÖLN   *7/1999*, Findler & Winter /* 0069992

AUGSBURG   *10/1999*, A Campanera i Rovira /* 0069993

0 + 3 SACHSEN CLASS (TYPE 124) (FFG)

Name	No	Builders	Laid down	Launched	Commissioned
SACHSEN	F 219	Blohm + Voss, Hamburg	1 Feb 1999	1 Dec 1999	Dec 2002
HAMBURG	F 220	Howaldtswerke, Kiel	July 2001	Mar 2002	Dec 2004
HESSEN	F 221	Thyssen Nordseewerke, Emden	July 2002	Mar 2003	Dec 2005

Displacement, tons: 5,600 full load
Dimensions, feet (metres): 469.2 oa; 433.7 wl × 57.1 × 14.4 *(143; 132.2 × 17.4 × 4.4)*
Main machinery: CODAG; 1 GE LM 2500 gas turbine; 31,514 hp *(23.5 MW)*; 2 MTU 20V 1163 TB 93 diesels; 20,128 hp(m) *(14.8 MW)*; 2 shafts; cp props
Speed, knots: 29. **Range, miles:** 4,000 at 18 kt
Complement: 255 (39 officers)

Missiles: SSM: 8 Harpoon ❶ 2 (quad).
SAM: Mk 41 VLS ❷ 32 cells for Standard SM 2 Block IIIA and Evolved Sea Sparrow.
2 RAM launchers ❸. 21 cells each.
Guns: 1 Otobreda 76 mm/62 compact ❹.
2 Mauser 27 mm ❺.
Torpedoes: 4—324 mm Schubert tubes ❻. Eurotorp Mu 90 Impact.
Countermeasures: Decoys: 6 SRBOC 130 mm chaff launchers ❼.
ESM/ECM: DASA FI 1800S-II; intercept ❽ and jammer.
Combat data systems: SEWACO FD; Link 11/16.
Weapons control: MSP optronic director ❾.
Radars: Air search: SMART L ❿ 3D; D-band.
Air/surface search: Signaal APAR phased array ⓫.
Surface search: Triton G ⓬; I-band.
Navigation: 2 sets; I-band.
IFF: Mk XII Mod 4.
Sonars: Atlas DSQS-24B; bow-mounted; active search; medium frequency.
Active towed array; low frequency.

Helicopters: 2 NFH 90 ⓭ or 2 Lynx 88A.

Programmes: Type 124 air defence ships are needed to replace the 'Lütjens' class. A collaborative design with the Netherlands has evolved with a common AAW system based on the Evolved Sea Sparrow missile. A Memorandum of Understanding (MoU) was signed in October 1993 between Blohm + Voss, Royal Schelde and Bazán shipyards. A contract to build three ships was authorised on 12 June 1996 with an option on a fourth *(Thüringen)* which is unlikely to be taken up. First steel cut 27 February 1998 for *Sachsen*.
Structure: Based on the Type 123 hull with improved stealth features. MBB-FHS helo handling system.

UPDATED

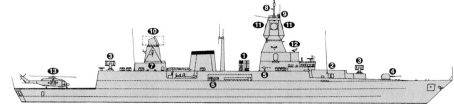

SACHSEN   *(Scale 1 : 1,200), Ian Sturton /* 0069994

SACHSEN (computer graphic)   *1999*, Blohm + Voss /* 0069995

SHIPBORNE AIRCRAFT

Notes: (1) NH 90s are required in due course to replace Sea Kings and Lynx aircraft.
(2) Dasa Seamos UAV being developed for K130 corvette.

Numbers/Type: 15/7 Westland Sea Lynx Mk 88/Super Lynx Mk 88A.
Operational speed: 125 kt *(232 km/h)*.
Service ceiling: 12,500 ft *(3,010 m)*.
Range: 320 n miles *(593 km)*.
Role/Weapon systems: Shipborne ASW/ASV role. Seven Mk 88A ordered in 1996 for delivery in 1999. Mid-life upgrade for the Mk 88 aircraft to Super Lynx standard placed in mid-1998 to complete in 2003. Sensors: Ferranti Sea Spray Mk 1 or GEC Marine Sea Spray 3000 and FLIR (Mk 88A) radar and Bendix AQS-18 dipping sonar. Weapons: ASW; up to two Mk 46 Mod 2 (or Eurotorp Mu 90 Impact in due course) torpedoes or depth charges. ASV; BAe Sea Skua (Mk 88A). *UPDATED*

SUPER LYNX   *7/1999*, GKN Westland /* 0069996

LAND-BASED MARITIME AIRCRAFT (FRONT LINE)

Numbers/Type: 4 Dornier Do 228-212.
Operational speed: 156 kt *(290 km/h)*.
Service ceiling: 20,700 ft *(6,300 m)*.
Range: 667 n miles *(1,235 km)*.
Role/Weapon systems: Liaison and transport. Two converted for pollution control. Sensors: Weather radar; converted aircraft also has SLAR, IR/UR scanner, microwave radiometer, LLL TV camera and data downlink. Weapons: Unarmed. *UPDATED*

DORNIER 228   *4/1999*, Diego Quevedo /* 0069997

Numbers/Type: 22 Westland Sea King Mk 41 KWS.
Operational speed: 140 kt *(260 km/h)*.
Service ceiling: 10,500 ft *(3,200 m)*.
Range: 630 n miles *(1,165 km)*.
Role/Weapon systems: Role change from primary combat rescue helicopter to ASV started in 1988 with new camouflage appearance and an update programme by MBB with BAe/Ferranti support which completed in 1995. Sensors: Ferranti Sea Spray Mk 3 radar, ALR 68 ESM, chaff and flare dispenser. Weapons: ASV; four BAe Sea Skua missiles. *VERIFIED*

SEA KING   *8/1998, N A Sifferlinger /* 0052227

Numbers/Type: 14/4 Breguet Atlantic 1.
Operational speed: 355 kt *(658 km/h)*.
Service ceiling: 32,800 ft *(10,000 m)*.
Range: 4,850 n miles *(8,990 km)*.
Role/Weapon systems: Long-range/endurance MR tasks carried out in North and Baltic Seas, also Atlantic Ocean; four aircraft allocated to Elint/SIGINT tasks. 16 being upgraded by Raytheon with GPS, FLIR, new ESM and radar by 2001. Sensors: APS-134 radar, Loral ESM, MAD, sonobuoys. Weapons: ASW; eight torpedoes (Mk 46 or Mu 90 Impact in due course) or mines or depth bombs. *UPDATED*

ATLANTIC   *10/1998, Michael Nitz /* 0052228

Numbers/Type: 50 Panavia Tornado IDS.
Operational speed: Mach 2.2.
Service ceiling: 80,000 ft *(24,385 m)*.
Range: 1,500 n miles *(2,780 km)*.
Role/Weapon systems: Swing-wing strike and recce; shore-based for fleet air defence and ASV strike primary roles; update with Kormoran 2 and Texas Instruments HARM. Sensors: Texas Instruments nav/attack system, MBB/Alenia multisensor recce pod. Weapons: ASV; four Kormoran 2 missiles. Fleet AD; two 27 mm cannon, four AIM-9L Sidewinder. *VERIFIED*

PATROL FORCES

Note: Vessels in this section have an 'S' number as part of their name as well as a 'P' pennant number. The 'S' number is shown in the Pennant List at the front of this country.

10 ALBATROS CLASS (TYPE 143B)
(FAST ATTACK-CRAFT—MISSILE) (PCFG)

Name	No	Builders	Commissioned
ALBATROS	P 6111	Lürssen, Vegesack	1 Nov 1976
FALKE	P 6112	Lürssen, Vegesack	13 Apr 1976
GEIER	P 6113	Lürssen, Vegesack	2 June 1976
BUSSARD	P 6114	Lürssen, Vegesack	14 Aug 1976
SPERBER	P 6115	Kröger, Rendsburg	27 Sep 1976
GREIF	P 6116	Lürssen, Vegesack	25 Nov 1976
KONDOR	P 6117	Kröger, Rendsburg	17 Dec 1976
SEEADLER	P 6118	Lürssen, Vegesack	28 Mar 1977
HABICHT	P 6119	Kröger, Rendsburg	23 Dec 1977
KORMORAN	P 6120	Lürssen, Vegesack	29 July 1977

Displacement, tons: 398 full load
Dimensions, feet (metres): 189 × 25.6 × 8.5 *(57.6 × 7.8 × 2.6)*
Main machinery: 4 MTU 16V 956 TB91 diesels; 17,700 hp(m) *(13 MW)* sustained; 4 shafts
Speed, knots: 40. **Range, miles:** 1,300 at 30 kt
Complement: 40 (4 officers)

Missiles: SSM: 4 Aerospatiale MM 38 Exocet (2 twin) launchers; inertial cruise; active radar homing to 42 km *(23 n miles)* at 0.9 Mach; warhead 165 kg; sea-skimmer.
Guns: 2 OTO Melara 3 in *(76 mm)*/62 compact; 85 rds/min to 16 km *(8.6 n miles)* anti-surface; 12 km *(6.5 n miles)* anti-aircraft; weight of shell 6 kg.
2—12.7 mm MGs (may be fitted).
Torpedoes: 2—21 in *(533 mm)* aft tubes. AEG Seeal; wire-guided; active homing to 13 km *(7 n miles)* at 35 kt; passive homing to 28 km *(15 n miles)* at 23 kt; warhead 260 kg.
Countermeasures: Decoys: Buck-Wegmann Hot Dog/Silver Dog; IR/chaff dispenser.
ESM/ECM: Racal Octopus (Cutlass intercept, Scorpion jammer).
Combat data systems: AEG/Signaal command and fire-control system; Link 11.
Weapons control: ORG7/3 optronics GFCS. STN Atlas WBA optronic sensor to be fitted.
Radars: Surface search/fire control: Signaal WM27; I/J-band.
Navigation: SMA 3 RM 20; I-band.

Programmes: AEG-Telefunken main contractor. Ordered in 1972.
Modernisation: *Habicht* started trials with RAM-ASDM mounting in 1983. Plans for major modernisation were reduced to fitting a new EW system, Racal Octopus, which completed in 1995 and a Signaal update to the command system which completed in 1999. 12.7 mm MGs may be fitted for deployments.
Structure: Wooden hulled craft.
Operational: Form 2nd Squadron based on tender *Donau* at Warnemünde.

UPDATED

GEIER *9/1999*, Findler & Winter / 0056955*

HABICHT *6/1999*, John Brodie / 0056956*

FALKE *9/1999*, Michael Nitz / 0056957*

10 GEPARD CLASS (TYPE 143 A)
(FAST ATTACK CRAFT—MISSILE) (PCFG)

Name	No	Builders	Launched		Commissioned	
GEPARD	P 6121	AEG/Lürssen	25 Sep	1981	13 Dec	1982
PUMA	P 6122	AEG/Lürssen	8 Feb	1982	24 Feb	1983
HERMELIN	P 6123	AEG/Kröger	8 Dec	1981	5 May	1983
NERZ	P 6124	AEG/Lürssen	18 Aug	1982	14 July	1983
ZOBEL	P 6125	AEG/Lürssen	30 June	1982	25 Sep	1983
FRETTCHEN	P 6126	AEG/Lürssen	26 Jan	1983	15 Dec	1983
DACHS	P 6127	AEG/Kröger	14 Dec	1982	22 Mar	1984
OZELOT	P 6128	AEG/Lürssen	7 June	1983	3 May	1984
WIESEL	P 6129	AEG/Lürssen	8 Aug	1983	12 July	1984
HYÄNE	P 6130	AEG/Lürssen	5 Oct	1983	13 Nov	1984

Displacement, tons: 391 full load
Dimensions, feet (metres): 190 × 25.6 × 8.5 *(57.6 × 7.8 × 2.6)*
Main machinery: 4 MTU MA 16V 956 SB80 diesels; 13,200 hp(m) *(9.7 MW)* sustained; 4 shafts
Speed, knots: 40. **Range, miles:** 2,600 at 16 kt; 600 at 33 kt
Complement: 34 (4 officers)

Missiles: SSM: 4 Aerospatiale MM 38 Exocet; inertial cruise; active radar homing to 42 km *(23 n miles)* at 0.9 Mach; warhead 165 kg; sea-skimmer.
SAM: GDC RAM 21 cell point defence system; passive IR/anti-radiation homing to 9.6 km *(5.2 n miles)* at 2 Mach; warhead 9.1 kg.
Guns: 1 OTO Melara 3 in *(76 mm)*/62 compact; 85 rds/min to 16 km *(8.6 n miles)* anti-surface; 12 km *(6.5 n miles)* anti-aircraft; weight of shell 6 kg.
Mines: Can lay mines.
Countermeasures: Decoys: Buck-Wegmann Hot Dog/Silver Dog; IR/chaff dispenser.
ESM/ECM: Dasa FL 1800 Mk 2; radar intercept and jammer.
Combat data systems: AEG AGIS with Signaal update; Link 11.
Weapons control: STN Atlas WBA optronic sensor being fitted.
Radars: Surface search/fire control: Signaal WM27; I/J-band; range 46 km *(25 n miles)*.
Navigation: SMA 3 RM 20; I-band.

Programmes: Ordered mid-1978 from AEG-Telefunken with subcontracting to Lürssen (P 6121, 6122, 6124-6128) and Kröger (P 6123, 6129, 6130).
Modernisation: Updated EW fit in 1994-95. RAM fitted in *Puma* in 1992, and to the rest from 1993-98. Combat data system update completed in 1999. Improved EW aerials being fitted from 1999.
Structure: Wooden hulls on aluminium frames.
Operational: Form 7th Squadron based on the tender *Elbe* at Warnemünde.

UPDATED

HERMELIN *9/1999*, Michael Nitz / 0069998*

HYÄNE *9/1999*, Curt Borgenstam / 0069999*

OZELOT *6/1999*, B Sullivan / 0070000*

10 TIGER CLASS (TYPE 148)
(FAST ATTACK CRAFT—MISSILE) (PCFG)

Name	No	Builders	Commissioned
LEOPARD	P 6145	CMN, Cherbourg	21 Aug 1973
FUCHS	P 6146	CMN, Cherbourg	17 Oct 1973
JAGUAR	P 6147	CMN, Cherbourg	13 Nov 1973
LÖWE	P 6148	CMN, Cherbourg	9 Jan 1974
PANTHER	P 6150	CMN, Cherbourg	27 Mar 1974
ALK	P 6155	CMN, Cherbourg	7 Jan 1975
DOMMEL	P 6156	CMN, Cherbourg	12 Feb 1975
WEIHE	P 6157	CMN, Cherbourg	3 Apr 1975
PINGUIN	P 6158	CMN, Cherbourg	22 May 1975
REIHER	P 6159	CMN, Cherbourg	24 June 1975

Displacement, tons: 234 standard; 265 full load
Dimensions, feet (metres): 154.2 × 23 × 8.9 *(47 × 7 × 2.7)*
Main machinery: 4 MTU MD 16V 538 TB90 diesels; 12,000 hp(m) *(8.82 MW)* sustained; 4 shafts
Speed, knots: 36. **Range, miles:** 570 at 30 kt; 1,600 at 15 kt
Complement: 30 (4 officers)

Missiles: SSM: 4 Aerospatiale MM 38 Exocet (2 twin) launchers; inertial cruise; active radar homing to 42 km *(23 n miles)* at 0.9 Mach; warhead 165 kg; sea-skimmer.
Guns: 1 OTO Melara 3 in *(76 mm)*/62 compact; 85 rds/min to 16 km *(8.6 n miles)* anti-surface; 12 km *(6.5 n miles)* anti-aircraft; weight of shell 6 kg.
  1 Bofors 40 mm/70; 330 rds/min to 12 km *(6.5 n miles)* anti-surface; 4 km *(2.2 n miles)* anti-aircraft; weight of shell 0.96 kg; fitted with GRP dome (1984) (see *Modernisation*).
Mines: Laying capability.
Countermeasures: Decoys: Wolke chaff launcher. Hot Dog IR launcher.
ESM/ECM: Racal Octopus (Cutlass B1 radar intercept and Scorpion jammer).
Combat data systems: PALIS and Link 11.
Weapons control: CSEE Panda optical director. Thomson-CSF Vega PCET system, controlling missiles and guns.
Radars: Air/surface search: Thomson-CSF Triton; G-band; range 33 km *(18 n miles)* for 2 m² target.
Navigation: SMA 3 RM 20; I-band; range 73 km *(40 n miles)*.
Fire control: Thomson-CSF Castor; I/J-band.

Programmes: Ordered in December 1970 from DTCN as main contractors. Some hulls contracted to Lürssen (P 6146, 6148, 6150, 6156, 6158, 6160) but all fitted out in France.
Modernisation: Triton search and Castor fire-control radars fitted to the whole class; also Racal EW systems as part of a mid-life update. *Dommel* had the 40 mm/70 gun replaced by a Mauser Vierling Taifun CIWS for trials in September 1991. The gun is to replace 40 mm and 20 mm guns in the Fleet from 1999.
Structure: Steel-hulled craft. Similar to Combattante II craft.
Operational: 5th Squadron at Olpenitz based on tender *Main*. The remainder are to be deleted in 2003 and 2004.
Sales: Two paid off in 1992 and transferred to Greece in 1993; two more in 1994 transferred to Greece in March 1995. Two in 1997 to Chile, followed by four in 1998 including two for spares. Two more for Greece planned in 2000.

UPDATED

WEIHE *6/1999*, Maritime Photographic /* 0056958

JAGUAR *7/1999*, Michael Nitz /* 0081938

PANTHER *10/1999*, Harald Carstens /* 0056959

CORVETTES

0 + (5) K130 CLASS (FSG)

Displacement, tons: 1,480 full load
Dimensions, feet (metres): 303.5 × 41.7 × 10.5 *(92.5 × 12.7 × 3.2)*
Main machinery: 2 gas turbines; 2 diesels; total of 20,400 hp(m) *(15 MW)*; 2 shafts
Speed, knots: 26. **Range, miles:** 2,500 at 15 kt
Complement: 60
Missiles: SSM: 4 Harpoon.
SAM: 8 Polyphem. 2 RAM launchers ❶.
Guns: 1 Otobreda 76 mm/62 ❷; 2 Mauser 27 mm ❸.
Countermeasures: ESM: FI 1800 S ❹; intercept.
Radars: Air/surface search: TRS-3D ❺; C-band.
Surface search: ❻ E/F-band.
Fire control: ❼ I/J-band.
Helicopters: VTOL drone.

Programmes: Invitations to tender accepted at the end of 1998. Decision on funding to be taken in 2000 with a possible construction start date in 2001. Numbers could increase to a total of 15 with the first in service in 2004 and the last in 2015, if the project goes ahead.
Structure: Details are all speculative based on the stated requirement. *UPDATED*

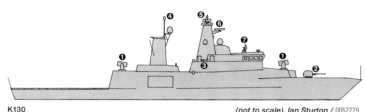

K130 *(not to scale), Ian Sturton /* 0052229

AMPHIBIOUS FORCES

8 TYPE 521 (LCM)

SARDELLE LCM 14	**AUSTER** LCM 24	**GARNELE** LCM 27
HUMMER LCM 21	**MUSCHEL** LCM 25	**LANGUSTE** LCM 28
KRABBE LCM 23	**KORALLE** LCM 26	

Displacement, tons: 168 full load
Dimensions, feet (metres): 77.4 × 20.9 × 4.9 *(23.6 × 6.4 × 1.5)*
Main machinery: 2 MWM 8-cyl diesels; 685 hp(m) *(503 kW)*; 2 shafts
Speed, knots: 10.5
Complement: 7
Military lift: 60 tons or 50 troops
Radars: Navigation: Atlas Elektronik; I-band.

Comment: Built by Rheinwerft, Walsam. Completed in 1964-67 and later placed in reserve. All are rated as 'floating equipment' without permanent crews. Three are based at Kiel, one at Warnemünde, three at Wilhelmshaven, one at Borkum. The design is similar to US LCM 8. LCM 1-11 sold to Greece in April 1991. All but three of the class paid off in 1993-94 but six were brought back into service in 1995 and one paid off again in 1996. In addition LCM 17 is used by the Bremerhaven Fire Brigade. A new class of LCM is being designed but is not yet funded. *UPDATED*

MUSCHEL *6/1998*, E & M Laursen /* 0052236

5 TYPE 520 (LCU)

FLUNDER L 760	**LACHS** L 762	**PLÖTZE** L 763	**SCHLEI** L 765	**ZANDER** L 769

Displacement, tons: 430 full load
Dimensions, feet (metres): 131.2 × 28.9 × 7.2 *(40 × 8.8 × 2.2)*
Main machinery: 2 MWM 12-cyl diesels; 1,020 hp(m) *(750 kW)*; 2 shafts
Speed, knots: 11
Complement: 17
Military lift: 150 tons

Comment: Similar to the US LCU (Landing Craft Utility) type. Provided with bow and stern ramp. Built by Howaldtswerke, Hamburg, 1965-66. Two sold to Greece in November 1989 and six more in 1992. Based at Olpenitz with Minesweeper Squadron 3. Guns have been removed. *UPDATED*

LACHS *7/1999*, Michael Nitz /* 0056960

MINE WARFARE FORCES

12 FRANKENTHAL CLASS (TYPE 332)
(MINEHUNTERS—COASTAL) (MHC)

Name	No	Builders	Launched		Commissioned	
FRANKENTHAL	M 1066	Lürssenwerft	6 Feb	1992	16 Dec	1992
WEIDEN	M 1060	Abeking & Rasmussen	14 May	1992	30 Mar	1993
ROTTWEIL	M 1061	Krögerwerft	12 Mar	1992	7 July	1993
BAD BEVENSEN	M 1063	Lürssenwerft	21 Jan	1993	9 Dec	1993
BAD RAPPENAU	M 1067	Abeking & Rasmussen	3 June	1993	19 Apr	1994
GRÖMITZ	M 1064	Krögerwerft	29 Apr	1993	23 Aug	1994
DATTELN	M 1068	Lürssenwerft	27 Jan	1994	8 Dec	1994
DILLINGEN	M 1065	Abeking & Rasmussen	26 May	1994	25 Apr	1995
HOMBURG	M 1069	Krögerwerft	21 Apr	1994	26 Sep	1995
SULZBACH-ROSENBERG	M 1062	Lürssenwerft	27 Apr	1995	23 Jan	1996
FULDA	M 1058	Abeking & Rasmussen	29 Sep	1997	16 June	1998
WEILHEIM	M 1059	Lürssenwerft	26 Feb	1998	3 Dec	1998

Displacement, tons: 650 full load
Dimensions, feet (metres): 178.8 × 30.2 × 8.5 *(54.5 × 9.2 × 2.6)*
Main machinery: 2 MTU 16V 396 TB84 diesels; 5,550 hp(m) *(4.08 MW)* sustained; 2 shafts; cp props; 1 motor (minehunting)
Speed, knots: 18
Complement: 37 (5 officers)

Missiles: SAM: 2 Stinger quad launchers.
Guns: 1 Bofors 40 mm/70; being replaced by Mauser 27 mm.
Combat data systems: STN MWS 80-4.
Radars: Navigation: Raytheon SPS-64; I-band.
Sonars: Atlas Elektronik DSQS-11M; hull-mounted; high frequency.

Programmes: First 10 ordered in September 1988 with STN Systemtechnik Nord as main contractor. M 1066 laid down at Lürssen 6 December 1989. Last pair ordered 16 October 1995.
Structure: Same hull, similar superstructure and high standardisation as Type 343. Built of amagnetic steel. Two STN Systemtechnik Nord Pinguin-B3 drones with sonar, TV cameras and two countermining charges, but not Troika control and minelaying capabilities.
Sales: Six of the class being built for Turkey from late 1999.   *UPDATED*

DILLINGEN   *4/1999 *, Michael Nitz /* 0056961

4 LINDAU CLASS (TYPE 351, TROIKA)
(MINESWEEPERS—COASTAL) (MSC)

Name	No	Builders	Commissioned	
SCHLESWIG	M 1073	Burmester, Bremen	30 Oct	1958
DÜREN	M 1079	Burmester, Bremen	22 Apr	1959
KONSTANZ	M 1081	Burmester, Bremen	23 July	1959
WOLFSBURG	M 1082	Burmester, Bremen	8 Oct	1959

Displacement, tons: 465 full load
Dimensions, feet (metres): 154.5 × 27.2 × 9.2 *(47.1 × 8.3 × 2.8)*
Main machinery: 2 MTU MD 16V 538 TB90 diesels; 5,000 hp(m) *(3.68 MW)*; 2 shafts
Speed, knots: 16.5. Range, miles: 850 at 16.5 kt
Complement: 44 (4 officers)

Guns: 1 Bofors 40 mm/70; 330 rds/min to 12 km *(6.5 n miles)*; weight of shell 0.96 kg.
Radars: Navigation: Kelvin Hughes 14/9, or Atlas Elektronik TRS N, or Raytheon. SPS 64; I-band.
Sonars: Atlas Elektronik DSQS-11; minehunting; high frequency.

Modernisation: Converted as guidance ships for Troika between 1981 and 1983. Each guide three of these unmanned minesweeping vehicles as well as maintaining their moored minesweeping capabilities. *Schleswig* was modified with a lower bridge in 1958. All were lengthened by 6.8 ft *(2.07 m)* in 1960-64. New gun mountings fitted in 1992.
Structure: The hull is of wooden construction, laminated with plastic glue. The engines are of non-magnetic materials.
Operational: Form 6th Squadron at Wilhelmshaven. The survivors of this class are scheduled to pay off by December 2000 and are being replaced by converted Type 343s.
Sales: One transferred to Latvia in March 1999 and one to Lithuania in June 1999. One to Estonia in January 2000, possibly two to South Africa in due course. These are all minehunter variants.   *UPDATED*

DÜREN   *6/1999 *, J Cislak /* 0056965

10 HAMELN CLASS (TYPE 343)
(MINESWEEPERS/HUNTERS—COASTAL) (MSC/MHC)

Name	No	Builders	Launched		Commissioned	
HAMELN*	M 1092	Lürssenwerft	15 Mar	1988	29 June	1989
ÜBERHERRN	M 1095	Abeking & Rasmussen	30 Aug	1988	19 Sep	1989
LABOE	M 1097	Krögerwerft	13 Sep	1988	7 Dec	1989
PEGNITZ*	M 1090	Lürssenwerft	13 Mar	1989	9 Mar	1990
KULMBACH	M 1091	Abeking & Rasmussen	15 June	1989	24 Apr	1990
SIEGBURG*	M 1098	Krögerwerft	14 Apr	1989	17 July	1990
ENSDORF*	M 1094	Lürssenwerft	8 Dec	1989	25 Sep	1990
PASSAU	M 1096	Abeking & Rasmussen	1 Mar	1990	18 Dec	1990
HERTEN	M 1099	Krögerwerft	22 Dec	1989	26 Feb	1991
AUERBACH*	M 1093	Lürssenwerft	18 June	1990	7 May	1991

* Troika (after conversion)

Displacement, tons: 635 full load
Dimensions, feet (metres): 178.5 × 30.2 × 8.2 *(54.4 × 9.2 × 2.5)*
Main machinery: 2 MTU 16V 538 TB91 diesels; 6,140 hp(m) *(4.5 MW)* sustained; 2 shafts; cp props
Speed, knots: 18
Complement: 37 (4 officers)

Missiles: SAM: 2 Stinger quad launchers.
Guns: 2 Bofors 40 mm/70. To be replaced by Mauser 27 mm.
Mines: 60.
Countermeasures: Decoys: 2 Silver Dog chaff rocket launchers.
ESM: Thomson-CSF DR 2000; radar warning.
Combat data systems: STN MWS 80-4 (for minehunters).
Radars: Surface Search/fire control: Signaal WM20/2; I/J-band.
Navigation: Raytheon SPS-64; I-band.
Sonars: Atlas Elektronik DSQS-11M; hull-mounted; high frequency (see *Modernisation*).
MAS 90 mine avoidance; active high frequency.

Programmes: On 3 January 1985 an STN Systemtechnik Nord-headed consortium was awarded the order. The German designation of 'Schnelles Minenkampfboot' was changed in 1989 to 'Schnelles Minensuchboot'.
Modernisation: Five being modernised to improve SDG-31 mechanical sweeps and to control improved Troika drones and redesignated HL 352. Remainder, being converted to minehunters and redesignated MJ 333. Programme for Troika conversions: M 1094 in April 2000, M 1093 by September 2000, M 1092 by January 2001, M 1090 by May 2001 and M 1098 by November 2001. For minehunter conversions M 1091 in September 1999, M 1095 in February 2000, M 1099 in June 2000, M 1097 by January 2001 and M 1096 by August 2001. All conversions take about a year and some have been delayed. All to have the full DSQS-11M sonar. Disposable ROV Sea Fox I can be used for inspection or countermining. It has a range of 500 m at 6 kt and uses a shaped charge.
Structure: Ships built of amagnetic steel adapted from submarine construction. Signaal M 20 System removed from the deleted 'Zobel' class fast attack craft. PALIS active link.   *UPDATED*

KULMBACH (minehunter conversion)   *10/1999 *, Harald Carstens /* 0056963

18 TROIKA (MINESWEEPERS—DRONES)

SEEHUND 1-18

Displacement, tons: 99 full load
Dimensions, feet (metres): 88.5 × 15 × 4.5 *(26.9 × 4.6 × 1.4)*
Main machinery: 1 Deutz MWM D602 diesel; 446 hp(m) *(328 kW)*; 1 shaft
Speed, knots: 10. Range, miles: 520 at 9 kt
Complement: 3 (passage crew)

Comment: Built by MaK, Kiel and Blohm + Voss, Hamburg between August 1980 and May 1982. Operated in groups of three with converted Type 351 parent vessels or in groups of four with converted Type 343. Remote control using magnetic and acoustic sweeping gear. A modified version MCM-C2 (Siepford) is being developed with the Netherlands.   *UPDATED*

SEEHUND 1   *11/1999 *, Michael Nitz /* 0056964

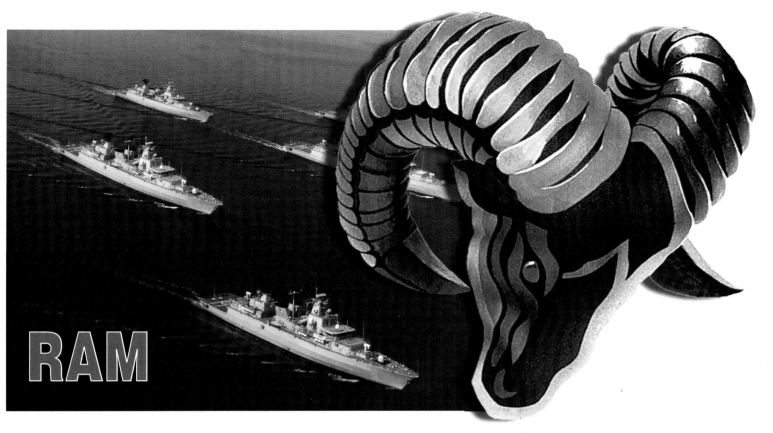

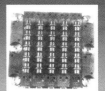

5 FRAUENLOB CLASS (TYPE 394)
(MINESWEEPERS—INSHORE) (MSI)

Name	No	Builders	Commissioned
FRAUENLOB	M 2658	Krögerwerft, Rendsburg	27 Sep 1966
GEFION	M 2660	Krögerwerft, Rendsburg	17 Feb 1967
MEDUSA	M 2661	Krögerwerft, Rendsburg	17 Feb 1967
UNDINE	M 2662	Krögerwerft, Rendsburg	20 Mar 1967
LORELEY	M 2665	Krögerwerft, Rendsburg	29 Mar 1968

Displacement, tons: 246 full load
Dimensions, feet (metres): 124.6 × 26.9 × 6.6 *(38 × 8.2 × 2)*
Main machinery: 2 MTU MB 12V 493 TY70 diesels; 2,200 hp(m) *(1.62 MW)* sustained; 2 shafts
Speed, knots: 12+. **Range, miles:** 700 at 14 kt
Complement: 25 (2 officers)
Guns: 1 Bofors 40 mm/70; 330 rds/min to 12 km *(6.5 n miles)* anti-surface; 4 km *(2.2 n miles)* anti-aircraft; weight of shell 0.96 kg.
Mines: Laying capability.
Radars: Navigation: Atlas Elektronik; I-band.

Comment: Launched in 1965-67. Originally designed Coast Guard boats with W numbers. Rated as inshore minesweepers in 1968 with the M numbers. All subsequently allocated Y numbers and later reallocated M numbers. New guns fitted in 1992. Some have paid off and two transferred to Estonia in 1997.
UPDATED

MEDUSA   *7/1999*, Michael Nitz /* 0056962

1 DIVER SUPPORT SHIP (TYPE 742) (MCD)

Name	No	Builders	Commissioned
MÜHLHAUSEN	M 1052	Burmester, Bremen	21 Dec 1967
(ex-*Walther von Ledebur*)	(ex-A 1410, ex-Y 841)		

Displacement, tons: 775 standard; 825 full load
Dimensions, feet (metres): 206.6 × 34.8 × 8.9 *(63 × 10.6 × 2.7)*
Main machinery: 2 Maybach MTU 16-cyl diesels; 5,200 hp(m) *(3.82 MW)*; 2 shafts
Speed, knots: 19
Complement: 11 plus 10 trials party
Radars: Navigation: I-band.

Comment: Wooden hulled vessel. Launched on 30 June 1966 as a prototype minesweeper but completed as a trials ship. Paid off in April 1994 but reactivated as a diver support ship. Recommissioned in its new role 6 April 1995.
UPDATED

MÜHLHAUSEN   *6/1999*, van Ginderen Collection /* 0056966

AUXILIARIES

1 + 1 BERLIN CLASS (TYPE 702) (AOR)

Name	No	Builders	Launched	Commissioned
BERLIN	A 1411	Flensburger	30 Apr 1999	Sep 2000
FRANKFURT	A 1412	Flensburger	Dec 2000	May 2002

Displacement, tons: 20,240 full load
Dimensions, feet (metres): 569.9 oa; 527.6 wl × 78.7 × 24.3 *(173.7; 160.8 × 24 × 7.4)*
Main machinery: 2 MAN 12V 32/40 diesels; 14,388 hp(m) *(10.58 MW)* sustained; 2 shafts; cp props; bow thruster; 1,000 hp(m) *(735 kW)*
Speed, knots: 20
Complement: 139 plus 94 spare
Cargo capacity: 9,540 tons fuel; 450 tons water; 280 tons cargo; 160 tons ammunition
Missiles: SAM: 2 RAM launchers fitted for but not with.
Guns: 4 Rheinmetall 20 mm Mk 202 to be replaced by 4 Mauser 27 mm.
Radars: Navigation and aircraft control; I-band.
Helicopters: 2 NH 90 or Sea Kings.

Comment: Four EGV combat support ships in two batches were projected. First one ordered 15 October 1997, and second 3 July 1998. Hulls built by FSG, superstructure by Kröger and electronics by Lürssen. First steel cut 24 September 1998. First keel laid down 4 January 1999, second planned for September 2000. MBB-FHS helo handling system. Two RAS beam status and stern refuelling. Two portable SAM launchers are carried. EW equipment may be fitted. These ships are designed to support UN type operations abroad. A containerised hospital unit for 50 can be embarked. First ship to be based at Wilhelmshaven and second at Kiel. A second pair of ships are projected for 2010.
UPDATED

BERLIN   *7/1999*, Michael Nitz /* 0056967

6 ELBE CLASS (TYPE 404) (TENDERS) (ARL)

Name	No	Builders	Launched	Commissioned
ELBE	A 511	Bremer Vulkan	24 June 1992	28 Jan 1993
MOSEL	A 512	Bremer Vulkan	22 Apr 1993	22 July 1993
RHEIN	A 513	Flensburger Schiffbau	11 Mar 1993	22 Sep 1993
WERRA	A 514	Flensburger Schiffbau	17 June 1993	9 Dec 1993
MAIN	A 515	Lürssen/Krögerwerft	15 June 1993	23 June 1994
DONAU	A 516	Lürssen/Krögerwerft	24 Mar 1994	22 Nov 1994

Displacement, tons: 3,586 full load
Dimensions, feet (metres): 329.7 oa; 285.4 wl × 50.9 × 13.5 *(100.5; 87 × 15.5 × 4.1)*
Main machinery: 1 Deutz MWM 8V 12M 628 diesel; 3,335 hp(m) *(2.45 MW)*; 1 shaft; bow thruster
Speed, knots: 15. **Range, miles:** 2,000 at 15 kt
Complement: 40 (4 officers) plus 12 squadron staff plus 38 maintainers
Cargo capacity: 450 tons fuel; 150 tons water; 11 tons luboil; 130 tons ammunition
Missiles: SAM: 2 Stinger (Fliegerfaust 2) quad launchers.
Guns: 2 Rheinmetall 20 mm or Mauser 27 mm.
Radars: Navigation: I-band.
Helicopters: Platform for 1 Sea King.

Comment: Funds released in November 1990 for the construction of six ships to replace the 'Rhein' class. Containers for maintenance and repairs, spare parts and supplies for fast attack craft and minesweepers. Waste disposal capacity: 270 m³ liquids, 60 m³ solids. The use of the 'Darss' class (all sold in 1991) was investigated as an alternative but rejected on the grounds of higher long-term costs because of the age of the ships. Allocated as follows: *Elbe* to 7th Squadron FPBs, *Mosel* to 5th Squadron MSC, *Rhein* to 6th Squadron MSC, *Werra* to 1st Squadron MSC, *Main* to 5th Squadron FPBs, *Donau* to 2nd Squadron FPBs. 20 mm guns are fitted at the break of the forecastle. Converted with helicopter refuelling facilities from July 1996 to July 1997.
UPDATED

WERRA   *5/1999*, Harald Carstens /* 0056968

2 REPLENISHMENT TANKERS (TYPE 704) (AOL)

Name	No	Builders	Commissioned
SPESSART (ex-*Okapi*)	A 1442	Kröger, Rendsburg	1974
RHÖN (ex-*Okene*)	A 1443	Kröger, Rendsburg	1974

Displacement, tons: 14,169 full load
Measurement, tons: 6,103 grt; 10,800 dwt
Dimensions, feet (metres): 427.1 × 63.3 × 26.9 *(130.2 × 19.3 × 8.2)*
Main machinery: 1 MaK 12-cyl diesel; 8,000 hp(m) *(5.88 MW)*; 1 shaft; cp prop
Speed, knots: 16. **Range, miles:** 7,400 at 16 kt
Complement: 42
Cargo capacity: 11,000 m³ fuel; 400 m³ water
Radars: Navigation: I-band.

Comment: Completed for Terkol Group as tankers. Acquired in 1976 for conversion *(Spessart* at Bremerhaven, *Rhön* at Kröger)*. The former commissioned for naval service on 5 September 1977 and the latter on 23 September 1977. Has two portable SAM positions. Civilian manned.
UPDATED

SPESSART   *6/1999*, Michael Nitz /* 0056969

4 WALCHENSEE CLASS (TYPE 703)
(REPLENISHMENT TANKERS) (AOL)

Name	No	Builders	Commissioned
WALCHENSEE	A 1424	Lindenau, Kiel	29 June 1966
AMMERSEE	A 1425	Lindenau, Kiel	2 Mar 1967
TEGERNSEE	A 1426	Lindenau, Kiel	23 Mar 1967
WESTENSEE	A 1427	Lindenau, Kiel	6 Oct 1967

Displacement, tons: 2,191 full load
Dimensions, feet (metres): 243.4 × 36.7 × 14.8 *(74.2 × 11.2 × 4.5)*
Main machinery: 2 MWM 12-cyl diesels; 1,370 hp(m) *(1 MW)*; 1 Kamewa prop
Speed, knots: 12.6. **Range, miles:** 3,250 at 12 kt
Complement: 21
Radars: Navigation: Kelvin Hughes; I-band.

Comment: Civilian manned.   *UPDATED*

WALCHENSEE   *6/1999*, J Cislak* / 0056972

3 LÜNEBURG CLASS (TYPE 701) (SUPPORT SHIPS) (ARL)

Name	No	Builders	Commissioned
FREIBURG	A 1413	Blohm + Voss	27 May 1968
GLÜCKSBURG	A 1414	Bremer Vulkan/Flensburger Schiffbau	9 July 1968
MEERSBURG	A 1418	Bremer Vulkan/Flensburger Schiffbau	25 June 1968

Displacement, tons: 3,709 full load
Dimensions, feet (metres): 374.9 × 43.3 × 13.8 *(114.3 × 13.2 × 4.2)*
388.1 ft *(118.3 m)* for *Freiburg*
Main machinery: 2 MTU MD 16V 538 TB90 diesels; 6,000 hp(m) *(4.1 MW)* sustained; 2 shafts;
cp props; bow thruster
Speed, knots: 17. **Range, miles:** 3,200 at 14 kt
Complement: 71 (9 officers)
Cargo capacity: 1,100 tons
Guns: 2 or 4 Bofors 40 mm/70 (1 or 2 twin).
Countermeasures: Decoys: 2 Breda 105 mm SCLAR chaff launchers.

Comment: Modernised to serve the missile installations of fast attack craft and destroyers, including MM 38 Exocet maintenance. *Freiburg* was lengthened in 1984 by 46.9 ft *(14.3 m)*, has a helicopter deck, port side larger crane and acts as support ship for 'Bremen' class carrying nine spare Harpoons. *Meersburg* is the depot ship for 1st Submarine Squadron. Two others of the class sold to Greece, two to Colombia. *Glücksburg* is planned to pay off when *Berlin* enters service in late 2000, and *Freiburg* is to be replaced by *Frankfurt* in 2002.   *UPDATED*

MEERSBURG   *10/1998*, Diego Quevedo* / 0056970

FREIBURG   *7/1999*, Findler & Winter* / 0056971

1 KNURRHAHN CLASS (TYPE 730) (APB)

Name	No	Builders	Commissioned
KNURRHAHN	Y 811	Sietas, Hamburg	Nov 1989

Displacement, tons: 1,424 full load
Dimensions, feet (metres): 157.5 × 45.9 × 5.9 *(48 × 14 × 1.8)*

Comment: Accommodation for 200 people.   *UPDATED*

KNURRHAHN   *4/1999*, Michael Nitz* / 0056974

2 WESTERWALD CLASS (TYPE 760)
(AMMUNITION TRANSPORTS) (AEL)

Name	No	Builders	Commissioned
WESTERWALD	A 1435	Orenstein and Koppel, Lübeck	11 Feb 1967
ODENWALD	A 1436	Orenstein and Koppel, Lübeck	23 Mar 1967

Displacement, tons: 3,460 standard; 4,042 full load
Dimensions, feet (metres): 344.4 × 46 × 15.1 *(105 × 14 × 4.6)*
Main machinery: 2 MTU MD 16V 538 TB90 diesels; 6,000 hp(m) *(4.1 MW)* sustained; 2 shafts;
cp props; bow thruster
Speed, knots: 17. **Range, miles:** 3,500 at 17 kt
Complement: 31
Cargo capacity: 1,080 tons ammunition
Guns: 2 Bofors 40 mm (cocooned).
Countermeasures: Decoys: 2 Breda SCLAR 105 mm chaff launchers are carried in A 1436.
Radars: Navigation: Kelvin Hughes; I-band.

Comment: Both based at Wilhelmshaven. Civilian manned.

UPDATED

WESTERWALD   *6/1999*, Michael Nitz* / 0056973

1 TYPE 705 (WATER TANKER) (AWT)

FW 5 A 1405 (ex-Y 868)

Displacement, tons: 626 full load
Dimensions, feet (metres): 144.4 × 25.6 × 8.2 *(44.1 × 7.8 × 2.5)*
Main machinery: 1 MWM diesel; 230 hp(m) *(169 kW)*; 1 shaft
Speed, knots: 9.5
Complement: 6
Cargo capacity: 340 tons

Comment: Originally class of six built in pairs by Schiffbarges, Unterweser, Bremerhaven; H. Rancke, Hamburg and Jadewerft, Wilhelmshaven, in 1963-64. *FW 2* (3 December 1975) and *FW 4* (12 April 1991) to Turkey; *FW 3* (22 April 1976) and *FW 6* (5 March 1991) to Greece. *FW 1* to Turkey in February 1996.

UPDATED

FW 5   *6/1999*, Michael Nitz* / 0056975

2 OHRE CLASS (ACCOMMODATION SHIPS) (APB)

ALTMARK Y 891 (ex-H 11)   **WISCHE** (ex-*Harz*) Y 895 (ex-H 31)

Displacement, tons: 1,320 full load
Dimensions, feet (metres): 231 × 39.4 × 5 *(70.4 × 12 × 1.6)*

Comment: Ex-GDR Type 162 built by Peenewerft, Wolgast. One hydraulic 8 ton crane fitted. First commissioned 1985. Classified as 'Schwimmende Stuetzpunkte'. Propulsion and armament has been removed and they are used as non-self-propelled accommodation ships for crews of vessels in refit. Civilian manned. Both modernised for service beyond 2000 at Wilhelmshaven. Two others paid off in 2000 later than expected.

UPDATED

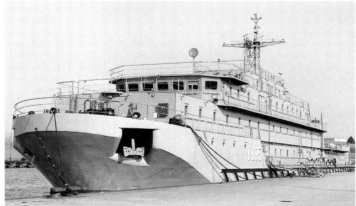

WISCHE   *4/1999*, Harald Carstens* / 0056976

2 BATTERY CHARGING CRAFT (TYPE 718) (YAG)

LP 1   LP 2

Displacement, tons: 234 full load
Dimensions, feet (metres): 90.6 × 23 × 5.2 (27.6 × 7.0 × 1.6)
Main machinery: 1 MTU MB diesel; 250 hp(m) (184 kW); 1 shaft
Speed, knots: 9
Complement: 6

Comment: Built in 1964. Have diesel charging generators for submarine batteries.   *UPDATED*

LP 1   6/1996*, Michael Nitz / 0056977

7 LAUNCHES (TYPE 946/945) (YFL)

AK 1 Y 1671   MA 3 Y 1677   ASCHAU Y 1685
AK 3 Y 1672   MA 1 Y 1678   BORBY Y 1687
MA 2 Y 1676

Dimensions, feet (metres): 39.4 × 12.8 × 6.2 (12.0 × 3.9 × 1.9)
Main machinery: 1 MAN D2540MTE diesel; 366 hp(m) (269 kW); 1 shaft

Comment: Built by Hans Boost, Trier. All completed in 1985 except *MA 1* and *Aschau* which are larger at 16.2 m and completed in 1992. AK prefix indicates Kiel, and MA Wilhelmshaven.   *UPDATED*

AK 1   8/1999*, Michael Nitz / 0056978

6 LAUNCHES (TYPES 743, 744, 744A, 1344) (YFL)

AM 6 Y 1674   AM 7 Y 1679   AK 2 Y 1686
AM 8 Y 1675   AK 6 Y 1683   A 41

Dimensions, feet (metres): 52.5 × 13.1 × 3.9 (16 × 4 × 1.2) approx
Main machinery: 1 or 2 diesels

Comment: For personnel transport and trials work. Types 744 (AK 6) and 744A (AK 2) are radio calibration craft. AM prefix indicates Eckernförde, and AK Kiel. A 41 is a former GDR tug (Type 1344) used as a diving boat at Warnemünde.   *UPDATED*

AK 6   6/1999*, Findler & Winter / 0056979

23 PERSONNEL TENDERS (TYPES 934 and GDR 407) (YFL)

V 3-V 21   B 11   B 33   B 34   B 83

Comment: *V 3-V 21* built in 1987-88 by Hatecke. The B series are ex-GDR craft built by Yachtwerft, Berlin.   *UPDATED*

V 11   6/1999*, Findler & Winter / 0056980

5 RANGE SAFETY CRAFT (TYPE 905) (YAG)

Name	No	Builders	Commissioned
TODENDORF	Y 835	Lürssen, Vegesack	25 Nov 1993
PUTLOS	Y 836	Lürssen, Vegesack	24 Feb 1994
BAUMHOLDER	Y 837	Lürssen, Vegesack	30 Mar 1994
BERGEN	Y 838	Lürssen, Vegesack	19 May 1994
MUNSTER	Y 839	Lürssen, Vegesack	14 July 1994

Displacement, tons: 126 full load
Dimensions, feet (metres): 91.2 × 19.7 × 4.6 (27.8 × 6 × 1.4)
Main machinery: 2 KHD TBD 234 diesels; 2,054 hp(m) (1.51 MW); 2 shafts
Speed, knots: 16
Complement: 15

Comment: Replaced previous Types 369 and 909 craft. Funded by the Army and manned by the Navy.   *UPDATED*

MUNSTER   6/1999*, Harald Carstens / 0056981

2 OIL RECOVERY SHIPS (TYPE 738) (AOTL)

Name	No	Builders	Commissioned
BOTTSAND	Y 1643	Lühring, Brake	24 Jan 1985
EVERSAND	Y 1644	Lühring, Brake	11 June 1988

Measurement, tons: 500 gross; 650 dwt
Dimensions, feet (metres): 151.9 × 39.4 (137.8, bow opened) × 10.2 (46.3 × 12 (42) × 3.1)
Main machinery: 1 Deutz BA12M816 diesel; 1,000 hp(m) (759 kW) sustained; 2 shafts
Speed, knots: 10
Complement: 6

Comment: Built with two hulls which are connected with a hinge in the stern. During pollution clearance the bow is opened. Ordered by Ministry of Transport but taken over by West German Navy. Normally used as tank cleaning vessels and harbour oilers. Civilian manned. *Bottsand* based at Warnemünde, *Eversand* at Wilhelmshaven. A third of class *Thor* belongs to the Ministry of Transport.   *UPDATED*

BOTTSAND   6/1999*, Winter & Findler / 0056982

5 FLOATING DOCKS (TYPES 712-715) and 2 CRANES (TYPE 711)

SCHWIMMDOCK A   Y 842   HIEV   Y 875
SCHWIMMDOCK B   Y 879   GRIEP   Y 876
2 and 3 and C

Comment: Dock lift capacity: 3 (8,000 tons); B (4,500 tons); A and 2 (1,000 tons). C is used for submarine pressure tests. Cranes (100 tons) are self-propelled.   *VERIFIED*

2 TORPEDO RECOVERY VESSELS (TYPE 430A) (TRV)

TF 5 Y 855   **TF 6** Y 856

Comment: Built in 1966 of approximately 56 tons. Provided with stern ramp for torpedo recovery. Two to Greece in 1989 and two more in 1991. One to Netherlands in 1998.

UPDATED

TF 5   *6/1999*, Maritime Photographic /* 0056983

INTELLIGENCE VESSELS

3 OSTE CLASS (TYPE 423) (AGI)

Name	No	Builders	Commissioned
ALSTER	A 50	Schiffsbaugesellschaft, Flensburg	5 Oct 1989
OSTE	A 52	Schiffsbaugesellschaft, Flensburg	30 June 1988
OKER	A 53	Schiffsbaugesellschaft, Flensburg	10 Nov 1988

Displacement, tons: 3,200 full load
Dimensions, feet (metres): 273.9 × 47.9 × 13.8 *(83.5 × 14.6 × 4.2)*
Main machinery: 2 Deutz-MWM BV16M728 diesels; 8,980 hp(m) *(6.6 MW)* sustained; 2 shafts; 2 motors (for slow speed)
Speed, knots: 21 (diesels); 8 (motors)
Complement: 36 plus 40 specialists or 51 plus 36 specialists
Missiles: SAM: 2 Stinger launchers.
Guns: 2—12.7 mm Mauser MGs.

Comment: Ordered in March 1985 and December 1986 and have replaced the Radar Trials Ships of the same name (old *Oker* and *Alster* transferred to Greece and Turkey respectively). *Oste* launched 15 May 1987, *Oker* 24 September 1987, *Alster* 4 November 1988. Carry Atlas Elektronik passive sonar and optical ELAM and electronic surveillance equipment. Particular attention has been given to accommodation standards. Reduced to one crew only for each ship in 1994. All being modified in 1999/2000 for overseas deployments, including light armament and RAS gear.

UPDATED

OKER   *8/1999*, Michael Nitz /* 0056984

SURVEY AND RESEARCH SHIPS

Note: A 12 ton midget submarine *Narwal* was recommissioned in April 1996 for research. Originally built by Krupp Atlas as an SDV.

0 + (1) TYPE 751 (AG)

Displacement, tons: 3,290 full load
Dimensions, feet (metres): 236.2 × 82 × 21.3 *(72 × 25 × 6.5)*
Main machinery: Diesel electric; 1 motor; 7,344 hp(m) *(5.4 MW)*; 1 shaft
Speed, knots: 15. **Range, miles:** 5,000 at 15 kt
Complement: 25 plus 20 trials personnel

Comment: Ex-Type 752 SWATH design to replace *Planet*. First authorised in April 1998 and contract placed with TNSW, Emden, but then delayed indefinitely. May be ordered in 2001 if funds are available. The ship is to have a sonar well, and carry five 20 ton containers.

UPDATED

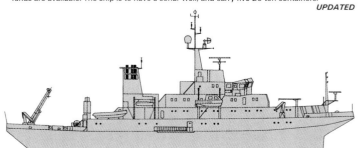

TYPE 751   *(not to scale), Ian Sturton /* 0056987

---

3 SCHWEDENECK CLASS (TYPE 748) (MULTIPURPOSE) (AG)

Name	No	Builders	Commissioned
SCHWEDENECK	Y 860	Krögerwerft, Rendsburg	20 Oct 1987
KRONSORT	Y 861	Elsflether Werft	2 Dec 1987
HELMSAND	Y 862	Krögerwerft, Rendsburg	4 Mar 1988

Displacement, tons: 1,018 full load
Dimensions, feet (metres): 185.3 × 35.4 × 17 *(56.5 × 10.8 × 5.2)*
Main machinery: Diesel-electric; 3 MTU 6V 396 TB53 diesel generators; 1,485 kW 60 Hz sustained; 1 motor; 1 shaft
Speed, knots: 13. **Range, miles:** 2,400 at 13 kt
Complement: 13 plus 10 trials parties
Radars: Navigation: 2 Raytheon; I-band.

Comment: Order for first three placed in mid-1985. One more was planned after 1995 to replace *Mühlhausen* (ex-*Walther von Ledebur*) but was not funded. Based at Eckernförde.

UPDATED

KRONSORT   *6/1999*, W Sartori /* 0056985

---

5 STOLLERGRUND CLASS (TYPE 745) (MULTIPURPOSE) (AG)

Name	No	Builders	Commissioned
STOLLERGRUND	Y 863	Krögerwerft	31 May 1989
MITTELGRUND	Y 864	Elsflether Werft	23 Aug 1989
KALKGRUND	Y 865	Krögerwerft	23 Nov 1989
BREITGRUND	Y 866	Elsflether Werft	19 Dec 1989
BANT	Y 867	Krögerwerft	28 May 1990

Displacement, tons: 450 full load
Dimensions, feet (metres): 126.6 × 30.2 × 10.5 *(38.6 × 9.2 × 3.2)*
Main machinery: 1 Deutz-MWM BV6M628 diesel; 1,690 hp(m) *(1.24 MW)* sustained; 1 shaft; bow thruster
Speed, knots: 12. **Range, miles:** 1,000 at 12 kt
Complement: 7 plus 6 trials personnel

Comment: Five ordered from Lürssen in November 1987; two subcontracted to Elsflether. Equipment includes two I-band radars and an intercept sonar. The first four are based at the Armed Forces Technical Centre, Eckernförde; *Bant* at Wilhelmshaven.

UPDATED

BANT   *5/1999*, Findler & Winter /* 0056986

---

1 RESEARCH SHIP (TYPE 750) (AG)

Name	No	Builders	Commissioned
PLANET	A 1450	Norderwerft, Hamburg	15 Apr 1967

Displacement, tons: 1,943 full load
Dimensions, feet (metres): 263.8 × 41.3 × 13.1 *(80.4 × 12.6 × 4)*
Main machinery: Diesel-electric; 4 MWM diesel generators; 1 motor; 1,390 hp(m) *(1.02 MW)*; 1 shaft; bow thruster
Speed, knots: 13. **Range, miles:** 9,400 at 13 kt
Complement: 39 plus 22 scientists
Radars: Navigation: Two Raytheon; I-band.
Sonars: Hull-mounted; high-frequency search.
Helicopters: 1 Bell 206B or MBB BO 105CB can be embarked.

Comment: Weapons research ship launched 23 September 1965. To be replaced by SWATH type ship (Type 751) in due course but funding is uncertain.

UPDATED

PLANET   *7/1998, Michael Nitz /* 0052257

1 TRIALS SHIP (TYPE 741) (AG)

Name	No	Builders	Commissioned
WILHELM PULLWER	A 1409 (ex-Y 838)	Schürenstadt, Bardenfleth	22 Dec 1967

Displacement, tons: 160 full load
Dimensions, feet (metres): 103.3 × 24.6 × 7.2 (31.5 × 7.5 × 2.2)
Main machinery: 2 MTU MB diesels; 700 hp(m) (514 kW); 2 Voith-Schneider props
Speed, knots: 12.5
Complement: 17

Comment: Wooden hulled trials ship for barrage systems. **UPDATED**

WILHELM PULLWER 3/1999*, Findler & Winter / 0056988

1 TRIAL BOAT (TYPE 740) (AG)

Name	No	Builders	Commissioned
BUMS	Y 1689	Howaldtswerke, Kiel	16 Feb 1970

Dimensions, feet (metres): 86.6 × 22.3 × 4.9 (26.4 × 6.8 × 1.5)

Comment: Single diesel engine. Has a 3 ton crane. Based at Eckernförde. **UPDATED**

BUMS 8/1997*, N Sifferlinger / 0012437

TRAINING SHIPS

Note: In addition to the two listed below there are 54 other sail training vessels (Types 910-915).

Name	No	Builders	Commissioned
GORCH FOCK	A 60	Blohm + Voss, Hamburg	17 Dec 1958

Displacement, tons: 2,006 full load
Dimensions, feet (metres): 293 × 39.2 × 16.1 (89.3 × 12 × 4.9)
Main machinery: Auxiliary 1 Deutz MWM BV6M628 diesel; 1,690 hp(m) (1.24 MW) sustained; 1 shaft; Kamewa cp prop
Speed, knots: 11 power; 15 sail. **Range, miles:** 1,990 at 10 kt
Complement: 206 (10 officers, 140 cadets)

Comment: Sail training ship of the improved Horst Wessel type. Barque rig. Launched on 23 August 1958. Sail area, 21,141 sq ft. Major modernisation in 1985 at Howaldtswerke. Second major refit in 1991 at Motorenwerke, Bremerhaven included a new propulsion engine and three diesel generators, which increased displacement. **UPDATED**

GORCH FOCK 6/1999*, Harald Carstens / 0056989

Name	No	Builders	Commissioned
NORDWIND	Y 834 (ex-W 43)	–	1944

Displacement, tons: 110
Dimensions, feet (metres): 78.8 × 21.3 × 8.5 (24 × 6.5 × 2.6)
Main machinery: 1 Demag diesel; 150 hp(m) (110 kW); 1 shaft
Speed, knots: 8. **Range, miles:** 1,200 at 7 kt
Complement: 10

Comment: Ketch rigged. Sail area, 2,037.5 sq ft. Ex-Second World War patrol craft. Taken over from Border Guard in 1956. **VERIFIED**

NORDWIND 7/1998, Michael Nitz / 0052261

TUGS

10 HARBOUR TUGS (TYPES 725, 724, 660) (YTM)

Name	No	Builders	Commissioned
VOGELSAND	Y 816	Orenstein und Koppel, Lübeck	14 Apr 1987
NORDSTRAND	Y 817	Orenstein und Koppel, Lübeck	20 Jan 1987
LANGENESS	Y 819	Orenstein und Koppel, Lübeck	5 Mar 1987
LÜTJE HORN	Y 812	Husumer Schiffswerft	31 May 1990
KNECHTSAND	Y 814	Husumer Schiffswerft	16 Nov 1990
SCHARHÖRN	Y 815	Husumer Schiffswerft	1 Oct 1990
NEUWERK	Y 823	Schichau, Bremerhaven	5 Apr 1963
WUSTROW (ex-Zander)	Y 1656	VEB Yachtwerft, Berlin	25 May 1989
DRANKSE (ex-Kormoran)	Y 1658	VEB Yachtwerft, Berlin	12 Dec 1989
NEUENDE	Y 1680	Schichau, Bremerhaven	27 Oct 1971

Displacement, tons: 445 full load
Dimensions, feet (metres): 99.3 × 29.8 × 8.5 (30.3 × 9.1 × 2.6)
Main machinery: 2 Deutz MWM BV6M628 diesels; 3,360 hp(m) (2.47 MW) sustained; 2 Voith-Schneider props
Speed, knots: 12
Complement: 10

Comment: Details given are for the Type 725 (Y 812-Y 819) which have a bollard pull of 23 tons. Y 1656 and Y 1658 are Type 660 former GDR vessels of 320 tons. The remainder are Type 724. One to Greece in 1998. **UPDATED**

NORDSTRAND 4/1999*, Findler & Winter / 0056990

NEUENDE 4/1999*, Harald Carstens / 0056991

1 HELGOLAND CLASS (TYPE 720B) (ATS)

Name	No	Builders	Commissioned
FEHMARN	A 1458	Unterweser, Bremerhaven	1 Feb 1967

Displacement, tons: 1,310 standard; 1,643 full load
Dimensions, feet (metres): 223.1 × 41.7 × 14.4 *(68 × 12.7 × 4.4)*
Main machinery: Diesel-electric; 4 MWM 12-cyl diesel generators; 2 motors; 3,300 hp(m) *(2.43 MW)*; 2 shafts
Speed, knots: 17. **Range, miles:** 6,400 at 16 kt
Complement: 34
Mines: Laying capacity.
Radars: Navigation: Raytheon; I-band.
Sonars: High definition, hull-mounted for wreck search.

Comment: Launched on 9 April 1965. Carry firefighting equipment and has an ice-strengthened hull. Employed as safety ship for the submarine training group. Twin 40 mm guns removed. One of the class to Uruguay in 1998.

UPDATED

FEHMARN   6/1999*, W Sartori / 0056992

6 WANGEROOGE CLASS (3 TYPE 722 and 3 TYPE 754) (ATR/AX)

Name	No	Builders	Commissioned
WANGEROOGE	A 1451	Schichau, Bremerhaven	9 Apr 1968
SPIEKEROOG	A 1452	Schichau, Bremerhaven	14 Aug 1968
NORDERNEY	A 1455	Schichau, Bremerhaven	15 Oct 1970
BALTRUM	A 1439	Schichau, Bremerhaven	8 Oct 1968
JUIST	A 1440	Schichau, Bremerhaven	1 Oct 1971
LANGEOOG	A 1441	Schichau, Bremerhaven	14 Aug 1968

Displacement, tons: 854 standard; 1,024 full load
Dimensions, feet (metres): 170.6 × 39.4 × 12.8 *(52 × 12.1 × 3.9)*
Main machinery: Diesel-electric; 4 MWM 16-cyl diesel generators; 2 motors; 2,400 hp(m) *(1.76 MW)*; 2 shafts
Speed, knots: 14. **Range, miles:** 5,000 at 10 kt
Complement: 24 plus 33 trainees (A 1439-1441)
Guns: 1 Bofors 40 mm/70 (cocooned in some, not fitted in all).

Comment: First three are salvage tugs with firefighting equipment and ice-strengthened hulls. *Wangerooge* sometimes used for pilot training and *Spiekeroog* and *Norderney* as submarine safety ships. The second three were converted 1974-78 to training ships with *Baltrum* and *Juist* being used as diving training vessels at Neustadt, with recompression chambers and civilian crews.

UPDATED

WANGEROOGE   6/1999*, Michael Nitz / 0056993

ICEBREAKERS

1 EISVOGEL CLASS (TYPE 721) (AGB)

Name	No	Builders	Commissioned
EISVOGEL	A 1401	J G Hitzler, Lauenburg	11 Mar 1961

Displacement, tons: 640 full load
Dimensions, feet (metres): 125.3 × 31.2 × 15.1 *(38.2 × 9.5 × 4.6)*
Main machinery: 2 Maybach 12-cyl diesels; 2,400 hp(m) *(1.76 MW)*; 2 Kamewa cp props
Speed, knots: 13. **Range, miles:** 2,000 at 12 kt
Complement: 16
Radars: Navigation: Kelvin Hughes; I-band.

Comment: Launched on 28 April 1960. Icebreaking tug of limited capability. Civilian manned. Fitted for but not with one Bofors 40 mm/70.

VERIFIED

EISVOGEL   8/1998, Michael Nitz / 0052267

ARMY

Note: Four companies of River Engineers are located along the River Rhine at Krefeld, Koblenz, Neuwied and Wiesbaden. Each company is provided with Bodan Landing Craft. There are also large numbers of M-Boot type work boats. All other landing craft and patrol boats have been paid off.

12 BODAN CLASS (RIVER LANDING CRAFT) (LCM)

Displacement, tons: 148 full load
Dimensions, feet (metres): 98.4 × 19 *(30 × 5.8)* (loading area)
Main machinery: 4 diesels; 596 hp(m) *(438 kW)*; 4 Schottel props
Speed, knots: 6
Guns: 1 Oerlikon 20 mm.

Comment: Built of 12 pontoons, provided with bow and stern ramp. Can carry 90 tons. These are the only Army LCMs still in service.

VERIFIED

BODAN   6/1992, Horst Dehnst

1 RIVER TUG (YTL)

Dimensions, feet (metres): 91.8 × 19.4 × 3.9 *(28 × 5.9 × 1.2)*
Main machinery: 2 KHD SBF 12M716 diesels; 760 hp(m) *(559 kW)*; 2 shafts
Speed, knots: 11
Complement: 7
Guns: 2—7.62 mm MGs.

Comment: The only survivor of a class of four.

UPDATED

T 821   4/1995*, van Ginderen Collection / 0056994

COAST GUARD
(Bundesgrenschutzamt—See)

Notes: (1) This BGSAMT force consists of about 600 men. Headquarters at Neustadt and bases at Warnemünde and Cuxhaven. There are three Flotillas; one each at Neustadt, Cuxhaven and Warnemünde.
(2) A maritime section of the anti-terrorist force GSG 9 is attached to the Bundesgrenzschutz.
(3) Craft have dark blue hulls and white superstructures. Since 1 July 1994 black/red/yellow stripes have been added to the hull and the inscription Küstenwache painted on the ship's side.
(4) The BGSAMT-See has a total of some nine ships and eight helicopters taken from various agencies including Fishery Protection, Customs and Maritime Traffic Control. BGSAMT-Rostock has eight small craft and BGSAMT-Frankfurt has four.
(5) All 40 mm guns removed in 1997.

1 BREDSTEDT CLASS (TYPE PB 60)

Name	No	Builders	Commissioned
BREDSTEDT	BG 21	Elsflether Werft	24 May 1989

Displacement, tons: 673 full load
Dimensions, feet (metres): 214.6 × 30.2 × 10.5 *(65.4 × 9.2 × 3.2)*
Main machinery: 1 MTU 20V 1163 TB93 diesel; 8,325 hp(m) *(6.12 MW)* sustained; 1 shaft; bow thruster; 1 auxiliary diesel generator; 1 motor
Speed, knots: 25 (12 on motor). **Range, miles:** 2,000 at 25 kt; 7,000 at 10 kt
Complement: 17 plus 4 spare
Guns: 2—7.62 mm MGs.
Radars: Surface search: Racal AC 2690 BT; I-band.
Navigation: 2 Racal ARPA; I-band.
Helicopters: Platform for 1 light.

Comment: Ordered 27 November 1987, laid down 3 March 1988 and launched 18 December 1988. An Avon Searider rigid inflatable craft can be lowered by a stern ramp. A second RIB on the port side is launched by crane. 40 mm gun removed in 1997. Based at Cuxhaven.
UPDATED

BREDSTEDT   *4/1998, Michael Nitz /* 0052268

2 SASSNITZ CLASS (TYPE PB 50 ex-TYPE 153) (PC)

Name	No	Builders	Commissioned
NEUSTRELITZ (ex-*Sassnitz*)	BG 22 (ex-P 6165, ex-591)	Peenewerft, Wolgast	31 July 1990
BAD DÜBEN (ex-*Binz*)	BG 23 (ex-593)	Peenewerft, Wolgast	23 Dec 1990

Displacement, tons: 369 full load
Dimensions, feet (metres): 160.4 oa; 147.6 wl × 28.5 × 7.2 *(48.9; 45 × 8.7 × 2.2)*
Main machinery: 2 MTU 12V 595 TE90 diesels; 8,800 hp(m) *(6.48 MW)* sustained; 2 shafts
Speed, knots: 25. **Range, miles:** 2,400 at 20 kt
Complement: 33 (7 officers)
Guns: 2—7.62 mm MGs.
Radars: Surface search: Racal AC 2690 BT; I-band (BG 22 and 23).
Navigation: Racal ARPA; I-band (BG 22 and 23).

Comment: Ex-GDR designated Balcom 10 and seen for the first time in the Baltic in August 1988. The original intention was to build up to 50 for the USSR, Poland and the GDR. In 1991 the first three were transferred to the Border Guard, based at Neustadt. *Neustrelitz* fitted with German engines and electronics in 1992-93 and accommodation improved. *Bad Düben* similarly modified at Peenewerft in 1995-96. The original design had the SS-N-25 SSM and three engines. The third of class, *Sellin*, had been on loan to WTD 71 (weapons trials) at Eckernförde but was sold in 1999 .
UPDATED

NEUSTRELITZ   *9/1999*, van Ginderen Collection /* 0056995

6 NEUSTADT CLASS (PC)

NEUSTADT BG 11	DUDERSTADT BG 14	ALSFELD BG 16
BAD BRAMSTEDT BG 12	ESCHWEGE BG 15	BAYREUTH BG 17

Displacement, tons: 218 full load
Dimensions, feet (metres): 127.1 × 23 × 5 *(38.5 × 7 × 2.2)*
Main machinery: 2 MTU MD diesels; 6,000 hp(m) *(4.41 MW)*; 1 MWM diesel; 685 hp(m) *(500 kW)*; 3 shafts
Speed, knots: 30. **Range, miles:** 450 at 27 kt
Complement: 17
Guns: 2—7.62 mm MGs.
Radars: Surface search: Selenia ARP 1645; I-band.
Navigation: Racal Decca Bridgemaster MA 180/4; I-band.

Comment: All built between 1969 and late 1970 by Lürssen, Vegesack. BG 13 was sold to Mauritania in February 1990. 40 mm guns removed.
UPDATED

BAYREUTH   *6/1998, Harald Carstens /* 0052270

4 BREMSE CLASS (TYPE GB 23)

PRIGNITZ	BG 61 (ex-G 20, ex-GS 31)	ALTMARK	BG 63 (ex-G 21, ex-GS 21)
UCKERMARK	BG 62 (ex-G 34, ex-GS 23)	BÖRDE	BG 64 (ex-G 35, ex-GS 50)

Displacement, tons: 42 full load
Dimensions, feet (metres): 74.1 × 15.4 × 3.6 *(22.6 × 4.7 × 1.1)*
Main machinery: 2 DM 6VD 18/5 AL-1 diesels; 1,020 hp(m) *(750 kW)*; 2 shafts
Speed, knots: 14
Complement: 6
Radars: Navigation: TSR 333; I-band.

Comment: Built in 1971-72 for the ex-GDR GBK. Five of the class sold to Tunisia, two to Malta and two to Jordan, all in 1992. BG 61 and 62 were based on the Danube for WEU embargo operations in 1994-96. All belong to BGSAMT-Rostock.
UPDATED

PRIGNITZ   *6/1998, E & M Laursen /* 0052271

4 SCHWEDT CLASS

SCHWEDT BG 41	FRANKFURT/ODER BG 43
KUSTRIN-KIEZ BG 42	AURITH BG 44

Displacement, tons: 6 full load
Dimensions, feet (metres): 33.5 × 10.5 × 2.6 *(10.2 × 3.2 × 0.8)*
Main machinery: 2 Volvo Penta TAMD 42 WJ; 462 hp(m) *(340 kW)*; 2 Hamilton 211 waterjets
Speed, knots: 32. **Range, miles:** 200 at 25 km
Complement: 3
Guns: 1—7.62 mm MG.
Radars: Navigation: I-band.

Comment: River patrol craft which belong to the BGSAMT-Frankfurt/Oder since 1994.
UPDATED

FRANKFURT/ODER   *12/1998*, BGSAMT /* 0056996

4 TYPE SAB 12

VOGTLAND	BG 51 (ex-G 56, ex-GS 17)	SPREEWALD	BG 53 (ex-G 51, ex-GS 16)
RHÖN	BG 52 (ex-G 53, ex-GS 26)	ODERBRUCH	BG 54

Displacement, tons: 14 full load
Dimensions, feet (metres): 41.3 × 13.1 × 3.6 *(12.6 × 4 × 1.1)*
Main machinery: 2 Volvo Penta diesels; 539 hp(m) *(396 kW)*; 2 shafts
Speed, knots: 16
Complement: 5

Comment: Ex-GDR MAB 12 craft based at Karnin, Stralsund and Frankfurt/Oder. Five sold to Cyprus in 1992. Belong to BGSAMT-Rostock.

UPDATED

RHÖN   *6/1998, Hartmut Ehlers* / 0052272

FISHERY PROTECTION AND RESEARCH SHIPS

Note: Operated by Ministry of Agriculture and Fisheries.

MEERKATZE of 2,250 tons and 15 kt. Completed December 1977
SEEFALKE of 1,820 tons gross and 20 kt. Completed August 1981
WARNEMÜNDE of 399 tons and 18 kt. Ex-'Kondor I' class completed 1969
SOLEA of 340 tons and 12 kt. Completed May 1974
UTHÖRN of 200 tons and 10 kt. Completed June 1982
WALTHER HERWIG of 2,500 tons and 15 kt. Completed October 1972
HEINCKE of 1,322 tons gross and 13 kt. Completed in June 1990

Comment: First two are Fishery Protection ships serving the fleet in the North Atlantic; *Warnemünde* serves in the Baltic. *Seefalcke* has a helicopter platform. The remainder are research ships carrying scientists. Most have Küstenwache colours.

UPDATED

SEEFALKE   *5/1999*, van Ginderen Collection* / 0056997

POLICE

Notes: (1) Under the control of regional governments. Blue hulls with red, white and blue diagonal stripes on the superstructure. Most have Küstenwache markings.
(2) There are 13 seaward patrol craft: *WSP 1, 4, 5* and *7, Bremen 2, 3* and *9, Helgoland, Sylt, Fehmarn, Birknack, Falshöft, Staberhuk.*
(3) Harbour craft include *Dithmarschen, Probstei, Schwansen, Vossbrook, Angeln, Brunswick, Habicht.*
(4) There are nine 'Stoltera' class patrol craft in service for Mecklenburg-Vorpommern.

WSP 1   *4/1999*, Findler & Winter* / 0079470

CIVILIAN SURVEY AND RESEARCH SHIPS

Note: The following ships operate for the Bundesamt für Seeschiffahrt und Hydrographie (BSH), either under the Ministry of Transport or the Ministry of Research and Technology (*Polarstern, Meteor, Poseidon, Sonne* and *Alkor*).

KOMET (survey and research) 64.2 × 12.5 × 3.6 m completed in October 1998.
ATAIR (survey), **ALKOR** (research), **WEGA** (survey) 1,050 tons, diesel-electric, 11.5 kt. Complement 16 plus 6 scientists. Built by Krögerwerft, completed 3 August 1987, 2 May 1990 and 26 October 1990 respectively
METEOR (research) 97.5 × 16.5 × 4.8 m, diesel-electric, 14 kt, range 10,000 n miles. Complement 33 plus 29 research staff. Completed by Schlichting, Travemünde 15 March 1986
GAUSS (survey and research) 1,813 grt, completed 6 May 1980 by Schlichting, speed 13.5 kt. Complement 19 plus 12 scientists. Modernised 1985
DENEB (survey) completed 24 November 1994 by Peenewerft, 1,100 tons, speed 11 kt, complement 16 plus 7 scientists.
POLARSTERN (polar research) 10,878 grt. Completed 1982
POSEIDON (research) 1,049 grt. Completed 1976
SONNE (research) 1,200 grt. Completed 1990
MERCATOR (survey) ex-GDR. Completed 1983. 167 grt. Complement 19.
BESSEL (survey) ex-GDR. Completed 1981. 20 grt. Complement 4.

ALKOR   *6/1999*, van Ginderen Collection* / 0056998

POLARSTERN   *12/1995*, Robert Pabst* / 0056999

GAUSS   *2/1999*, van Ginderen Collection* / 0081939

POSEIDON   *6/1998*, van Ginderen Collection* / 0052274

CUSTOMS

Notes: (1) Operated by Ministry of Finance with a total of over 100 craft. Green hulls with grey superstructure and sometimes carry machine guns. Some have Küstenwache markings.
(2) Seaward patrol craft include *Hamburg, Bremerhaven, Schleswig-Holstein, Emden, Kniepsand, Alte Liebe, Priwall, Glückstadt, Helgoland, Oldenburg, Laboe, Neu Darchau, Hohwacht, Hiddensee,* and *Kalkgrund.*

SCHLESWIG-HOLSTEIN   *9/1999*, Michael Nitz /* 0079468

KALKGRUND   *6/1999*, Maritime Photographic /* 0079469

WATER AND NAVIGATION BOARD

Notes: (1) Comes under the Ministry of Transport. Most ships have black hulls with black/red/yellow stripes. Some have Küstenwache markings.
(2) Two icebreakers: *Max Waldeck* and *Stephan Jantzen* (ex-GDR).
(3) Nine buoy tenders: *Walter Körte, Kurt Burkowitz, Otto Treplin, Gustav Meyer, Bruno Illing, Konrad Meisel, Barsemeister Brehme, J G Repsold, Buk* (ex-GDR).
(4) Six oil recovery ships: *Scharhörn, Oland, Nordsee, Mellum, Kiel, Neuwerk.*
(5) Seven SKB 64 and 601 types (ex-GDR). *Golwitz, Ranzow, Landtief, Grasort, Gellen, Darsser Ort, Arkona.*

MELLUM   *4/1999*, Harald Carstens /* 0079471

GHANA

Headquarters Appointments

Commander, Navy:
  Rear Admiral Osei Owusu-Ansah
Western Naval Command:
  Commodore J Y Adoko
Eastern Naval Command:
  Captain A R S Nuno

Bases

Burma Camp, Accra (Headquarters)
Sekondi (Western Naval Command)
Tema (near Accra) (Eastern Naval Command)

Mercantile Marine

Lloyd's Register of Shipping:
  205 vessels of 117,504 tons gross

Personnel

(a) 2000: 1,212 (132 officers)
(b) Voluntary service

Maritime Aircraft

Four Defender aircraft are available for maritime surveillance but only one is used.

PATROL FORCES

Note: The ex-UK 'Island' class OPV *Orkney* may be acquired in 2000.

2 LÜRSSEN FPB 45 CLASS (FAST ATTACK CRAFT—GUN) (PCF)

Name	No	Builders	Commissioned
DZATA	P 26	Lürssen, Vegesack	25 July 1980
SEBO	P 27	Lürssen, Vegesack	25 July 1980

Displacement, tons: 269 full load
Dimensions, feet (metres): 147.3 × 23 × 8.9 *(44.9 × 7 × 2.7)*
Main machinery: 2 MTU 16V 538 TB91 diesels; 6,140 hp(m) *(4.5 MW)* sustained; 2 shafts
Speed, knots: 27. **Range, miles:** 1,800 at 16 kt; 700 at 25 kt
Complement: 45 (5 officers)
Guns: 2 Bofors 40 mm/70; 300 rds/min to 12.5 km *(6.8 n miles)*; weight of shell 0.96 kg.
Radars: Surface search: Decca TM 1226C; I-band.

Comment: Ordered in 1976. *Dzata* completed a major overhaul at Swan Hunter's Wallsend, Tyneside yard on 8 May 1989. *Sebo* started a similar refit at CMN Cherbourg in May 1991 which completed in August 1992. Employed in Fishery Protection role. *Dzata* being refitted in 2000 at Sekondi.

UPDATED

DZATA   *6/1999*, Ghana Navy /* 0064750

2 LÜRSSEN PB 57 CLASS (FAST ATTACK CRAFT—GUN) (PCF)

Name	No	Builders	Commissioned
ACHIMOTA	P 28	Lürssen, Vegesack	27 Mar 1981
YOGAGA	P 29	Lürssen, Vegesack	27 Mar 1981

Displacement, tons: 389 full load
Dimensions, feet (metres): 190.6 × 25 × 9.2 *(58.1 × 7.6 × 2.8)*
Main machinery: 3 MTU 16V 538 TB91 diesels; 9,210 hp(m) *(6.78 MW)* sustained; 3 shafts
Speed, knots: 30
Complement: 55 (5 officers)
Guns: 1 OTO Melara 3 in *(76 mm)* compact; 85 rds/min to 16 km *(8.6 n miles)* anti-surface; 12 km *(6.5 n miles)* anti-air; weight of shell 6 kg; 250 rounds.
  1 Breda 40 mm/70; 300 rds/min to 12.5 km *(6.8 n miles)* anti-surface; weight of shell 0.96 kg.
Weapons control: LIOD optronic director.
Radars: Surface search/fire control: Thomson-CSF Canopus A; I/J-band.
Navigation: Decca TM 1226C; I-band.

Comment: Ordered in 1977. *Yogaga* completed a major overhaul at Swan Hunter's Wallsend, Tyneside yard 8 May 1989. *Achimota* started a similar refit at CMN Cherbourg in May 1991 and was joined by *Yogaga* for repairs in late 1991. Both completed by August 1992. Employed on Fishery Protection duties. *Yogaga* being refitted at Sekondi in 2000.

UPDATED

ACHIMOTA   *3/1997* /* 0079472

GREECE
HELLENIC NAVY

Headquarters Appointments

Chief of the Hellenic Navy:
  Vice Admiral G Ioannidis
Deputy Chief of Staff:
  Rear Admiral D Kanelakis
Commander, Navy Training Command:
  Rear Admiral A Antoniadis
Commander, Navy Logistics Command:
  Rear Admiral M Kyriazanos

Fleet Command

Commander of the Fleet:
  Vice Admiral G Theodoroulakis

Diplomatic Representation

Naval Attaché in Ankara:
  Commander J Miaris
Naval Attaché in Bonn:
  Captain B Martzoukos
Naval Attaché in Cairo:
  Captain G Panagiotakopoulos
Naval Attaché in London:
  Captain N G Louloudis
Naval Attaché in Paris:
  Captain P Kiritsis-Spiromilios
Naval Attaché in Washington:
  Captain J Egolfopoulos
Naval Attaché in Madrid:
  Captain N Manatos

Personnel

(a) 2000: 19,950 (3,692 officers) including 7,408 conscripts
(b) 21 months' national service

Bases

Salamis and Suda Bay

Naval Commands

Commander of the Fleet has under his flag all combatant ships. Navy Logistic Command is responsible for the bases at Salamis and Suda Bay, the Supply Centre and all auxiliary ships. Navy Training Command is in charge of the Naval Officers' Academy, Petty Officers' School, three training centres and a training ship.

Naval Districts

Aegean, Ionian and Northern Greece

Naval Aviation

Alouette III helicopters (Training).
AB 212ASW helicopters (No 1 Squadron).
S-70B-6 Seahawk (No 2 Squadron).
P-3B Orion are operated under naval command by mixed Air Force and Navy crews.

Strength of the Fleet

Type	Active	Building (Planned)
Patrol Submarines	8	3 (1)
Destroyers	4	—
Frigates	12	—
Corvettes	5	—
Fast Attack Craft—Missile	17	5
Fast Attack Craft—Torpedo	8	—
Large Patrol Craft	6	4
Coastal Patrol Craft	5	—
LST/LSD/LSM	9	—
LCUs	6	—
LCTs	2	—
Hovercraft	—	4
Minelayers—Coastal	2	—
Minesweepers—Coastal	14	2
Survey and Research Ships	5	—
Support Ships	2	—
Training Ships	5	—
Tankers	12	1
Auxiliary Transports	2	—
Ammunition Ship	1	—

Prefix to Ships' Names

HS (Hellenic Ship)

Mercantile Marine

Lloyd's Register of Shipping:
  1,491 vessels of 24,833,280 tons gross

DELETIONS

Note: Some of the deleted ships are in unmaintained reserve in anchorages.

Destroyers

1997 *Tompazis* (reserve)

Frigates

1998 *Makedonia*

Patrol Forces

1998 *Lindos* (to Georgia)
1999 *Dilos* (to Georgia)

Amphibious Forces

1997 *Rodos* (old)
1998 *Ikaria* (old)
1999 *Siros*
2000 *Kriti, Nafkratoussa*

PENNANT LIST

Submarines

S 110 Glavkos
S 111 Nereus
S 112 Triton
S 113 Proteus
S 116 Poseidon
S 117 Amphitrite
S 118 Okeanos
S 119 Pontos

Destroyers

D 218 Kimon
D 219 Nearchos
D 220 Formion
D 221 Themistocles

Frigates

F 450 Elli
F 451 Limnos
F 452 Hydra
F 453 Spetsai
F 454 Psara
F 455 Salamis
F 456 Epirus
F 457 Thrace
F 459 Adrias
F 460 Aegean
F 461 Navarinon
F 462 Kountouriotis

Corvettes

P 62 Niki
P 63 Doxa
P 64 Eleftheria
P 65 Carteria
P 66 Agon

Patrol Forces

P 14 Antipoploiarchos Anninos
P 15 Ipoploiarchos Arliotis
P 16 Ipoploiarchos Konidis
P 17 Ipoploiarchos Batsis
P 18 Armatolos
P 19 Navmachos
P 20 Antiploiarchos Laskos
P 21 Plotarhis Blessas
P 22 Ipoploiarchos Mikonios
P 23 Ipoploiarchos Troupakis
P 24 Simeoforos Kavaloudis
P 26 Ipoploiarchos Degiannis
P 27 Simeoforos Xenos
P 28 Simeoforos Simitzopoulos
P 29 Simeoforos Starakis
P 50 Hesperos
P 53 Kyklon
P 54 Lelaps
P 56 Tyfon
P 57 Pirpolitis
P 61 Polemistis
P 72 Ipoploiarchos Votsis
P 73 Antiploiarchos Pezopoulos
P 74 Plotarhis Vlahavas
P 75 Plotarhis Maridakis
P 196 Andromeda
P 198 Kyknos
P 199 Pigasos
P 228 Toxotis
P 229 Tolmi
P 230 Ormi
P 268 Knossos
P 286 Diopos Antoniou
P 287 Kelefstis Stamou

Amphibious Forces

L 104 Inouse
L 116 Kos
L 164 I Roussen
L 165 I Krystallidis
L 167 Ios
L 168 Sikinos
L 169 Irakleia
L 170 Folegandros
L 173 Chios
L 174 Samos
L 175 Ikaria
L 176 Lesbos
L 177 Rodos
L 178 Naxos
L 179 Paros
L 185 Kithera
L 189 Milos
L 195 Serifos

Minelayers

N 04 Aktion
N 05 Amvrakia

Minesweepers/Hunters

M 60 Erato
M 61 Evniki
M 202 Atalanti
M 206 Faidra
M 210 Thalia
M 211 Alkyon
M 213 Klio
M 214 Avra
M 240 Aidon
M 241 Kichli
M 242 Kissa
M 247 Dafni
M 248 Pleias
M 254 Niovi

Auxiliaries, Training and Survey Ships

A 74 Aris
A 233 Maistros
A 234 Sorokos
A 307 Thetis
A 359 Ostria
A 373 Hermis
A 375 Zeus
A 376 Orion
A 377 Arethusa
A 407 Antaios
A 408 Atlas
A 409 Acchileus
A 410 Atromitos-Nikiforos
A 411 Adamastos
A 412 Aias
A 413 Pilefs
A 414 Ariadne
A 415 Evros
A 416 Ouranos
A 417 Hyperion
A 419 Pandora
A 420 Pandrosos
A 422 Kadmos
A 423 Heraklis
A 424 Iason
A 425 Odisseus
A 426 Cyclops
A 427 Danaos
A 428 Nestor
A 430 Perseus
A 431 Titan
A 432 Gigas
A 433 Kerkini
A 434 Prespa
A 435 Kekrops
A 436 Minos
A 437 Pelias
A 438 Aegeus
A 439 Atrefs
A 440 Diomidis
A 441 Theseus
A 460 Evrotas
A 461 Arachthos
A 462 Strymon
A 463 Nestos
A 464 Axios
A 466 Trichonis
A 467 Doirani
A 468 Kalliroe
A 469 Stimfalia
A 470 Aliakmon
A 474 Pytheas
A 476 Strabon
A 478 Naftilos
A 479 I Karavoyiannos Theophilopoulos
A 481 St Likoudis

SUBMARINES

0 + 3 (1) KATSONIS (TYPE 214) CLASS (SSK)

Displacement, tons: 1,700 (surfaced); 1,980 (dived)
Dimensions, feet (metres): 213.3 × 20.7 × 19.7
(65 × 6.3 × 6)
Main machinery: 2 MTU 16V 396 diesels; 8,486 hp(m)
(6.24 MW); 1 Siemens Permasyn motor; 1 shaft; 2 HDW PEM
fuel cells; 240 kW
Speed, knots: 20 dived; 12 surfaced
Complement: 27 (5 officers)

Missiles: SSM: Sub Harpoon.
Torpedoes: 8—21 in *(533 mm)* bow tubes; four fitted for Sub
Harpoon discharge; total of 16 weapons.
Countermeasures: Decoys: ESM.
Weapons control: STN Atlas.
Radars: Surface search: I-band.
Sonars: Bow, flank and towed arrays.

Programmes: Decision taken on 24 July 1998 and announced
on 9 October to order three HDW designed submarines with
an option on a fourth. The plan is to build the first of class at Kiel
and subsequent hulls at Hellenic, Skaramanga. Contracts to
build signed 16 February 2000.
Structure: Details given are mainly for the Type 214 as
advertised by HDW but there may be changes before the first
steel is cut. Diving depth 400 m *(1,300 ft)*. Optronic mast to be
fitted.

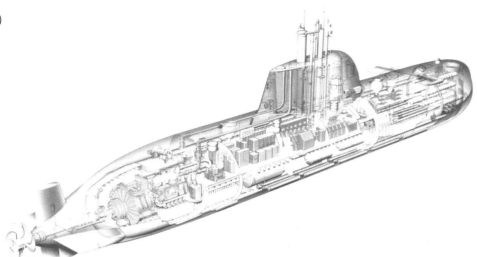

UPDATED   KATSONIS   *1998, HDW /* 0033227

8 GLAVKOS CLASS (209 TYPES 1100 and 1200) (SSK)

Name	No	Builders	Laid down	Launched	Commissioned
GLAVKOS	S 110	Howaldtswerke, Kiel	1 Sep 1968	15 Sep 1970	6 Sep 1971
NEREUS	S 111	Howaldtswerke, Kiel	15 Jan 1969	7 June 1971	10 Feb 1972
TRITON	S 112	Howaldtswerke, Kiel	1 June 1969	14 Oct 1971	8 Aug 1972
PROTEUS	S 113	Howaldtswerke, Kiel	1 Oct 1969	1 Feb 1972	8 Aug 1972
POSEIDON	S 116	Howaldtswerke, Kiel	15 Jan 1976	21 Mar 1978	22 Mar 1979
AMPHITRITE	S 117	Howaldtswerke, Kiel	26 Apr 1976	14 June 1978	14 Sep 1979
OKEANOS	S 118	Howaldtswerke, Kiel	1 Oct 1976	16 Nov 1978	15 Nov 1979
PONTOS	S 119	Howaldtswerke, Kiel	25 Jan 1977	21 Mar 1979	29 Apr 1980

Displacement, tons: 1,100 surfaced; 1,285 dived
Dimensions, feet (metres): 183.4 × 20.3 × 17.9
(55.9 × 6.2 × 5.5)
Main machinery: Diesel-electric; 4 MTU 12V 493 AZ80 diesels;
2,400 hp(m) *(1.76 MW)* sustained; 4 Siemens alternators;
1.7 MW; 1 Siemens motor; 4,600 hp(m) *(3.38 MW)* sustained;
1 shaft
Speed, knots: 11 surfaced; 21.5 dived
Complement: 31 (6 officers)

Missiles: McDonnell Douglas Sub Harpoon; active radar homing
to 130 km *(70 n miles)* at 0.9 Mach; warhead 258 kg. Can be
discharged from 4 tubes only.
Torpedoes: 8—21 in *(533 mm)* bow tubes. 14 AEG SUT Mod 0;
wire-guided; active/passive homing to 12 km *(6.5 n miles)* at
35 kt; warhead 250 kg. Swim-out discharge.
Countermeasures: ESM: Argo AR-700-S5; radar warning.
Weapons control: Signaal Sinbads (S 116-S 119). Unisys/
Kanaris with UYK-44 computers (S 110-113).
Radars: Surface search: Thomson-CSF Calypso II; I-band.
Sonars: Atlas Elektronik CSU 83-90 (DBQS-21); (S 110-113);
Atlas Elektronik CSU 3-4 (S 116-119); hull-mounted; active/
passive search and attack; medium frequency.
Atlas Elektronik PRS-3-4; passive ranging.

Programmes: Designed by Ingenieurkontor, Lübeck for
construction by Howaldtswerke, Kiel and sale by Ferrostaal,
Essen all acting as a consortium.
Modernisation: Contract signed 5 May 1989 with HDW and
Ferrostaal to implement a Neptune update programme to

NEREUS   *1/2000 *, A Sharma /* 0079473

bring first four up to an improved standard and along the same
lines as the German 'S 206A' class. Included Sub Harpoon,
flank array sonar, Unisys FCS, Sperry Mk 29 Mod 3 inertial
navigation system, Magnavox GPS, Omega and SATNAV, and
Argo ESM. *Triton* completed refit at Kiel in May 1993, *Proteus*
at Salamis in December 1995, *Glavkos* in November 1997,
and *Nereus* in December 1999. A modernisation programme
is scheduled on the last four between 2001 and 2008.

Structure: A single-hull design with two ballast tanks and
forward and after trim tanks. Fitted with snort and remote
machinery control. The single screw is slow revving. Very high-
capacity batteries with GRP lead-acid cells and battery
cooling—by Wilh Hagen and VARTA. Diving depth, 250 m
(820 ft). Fitted with two periscopes.
Operational: Endurance, 50 days. A mining capability is reported
but not confirmed.   *UPDATED*

GLAVKOS   *7/1998, Michael Nitz /* 0050677

DESTROYERS

Note: Plans to lease the four ex-US 'Kidd' class DDGs were shelved.

4 KIMON (CHARLES F ADAMS) CLASS (DDG)

Name	No	Builders	Laid down	Launched	Commissioned	Recommissioned
KIMON (ex-Semmes)	D 218 (ex-DDG 18)	Avondale Marine Ways	18 Aug 1960	20 May 1961	10 Dec 1962	12 Sep 1992
NEARCHOS (ex-Waddell)	D 219 (ex-DDG 24)	Todd Shipyards	6 Feb 1962	26 Feb 1963	28 Aug 1964	1 Oct 1992
FORMION (ex-Miltiadis, ex-Strauss)	D 220 (ex-DDG 16)	New York Shipbuilding	27 Dec 1960	9 Dec 1961	20 Apr 1963	1 Oct 1992
THEMISTOCLES (ex-Konon, ex-Berkeley)	D 221 (ex-DDG 15)	New York Shipbuilding	1 June 1960	29 July 1961	15 Dec 1962	1 Oct 1992

Displacement, tons: 3,370 standard; 4,825 full load
Dimensions, feet (metres): 437 × 47 × 15.6; 21 (sonar)
(133.2 × 14.3 × 4.8; 6.4)
Main machinery: 4 boilers (Foster-Wheeler in D 219, Combustion Engineering in D 218, 220 and 221); 2 turbines (General Electric in D 218, 220 and 221, Westinghouse in D 219); 70,000 hp *(52.2 MW)*; 2 shafts
Speed, knots: 30
Range, miles: 6,000 at 15 kt; 1,600 at 30 kt
Complement: 340 (22 officers)

Missiles: SSM: 6 McDonnell Douglas Harpoon; active radar homing to 130 km *(70 n miles)* at 0.9 Mach; warhead 227 kg.
SAM: 34 GDC Standard SM-1MR; command guidance; semi-active radar homing to 46 km *(25 n miles)* at 2 Mach; height 150-60,000 ft (45.7-18,288 m).
1 single Mk 13 launcher ❶; can load, direct and fire about 6 missiles/min. There are 40 missiles carried. 6 Harpoons are stored in the magazines as part of the load.
A/S: Honeywell ASROC Mk 16 octuple launcher ❷; inertial guidance to 1.6-10 km *(1-5.4 n miles)*; payload Mk 46.
Guns: 2 FMC 5 in *(127 n miles)*/54 Mk 42 ❸; 20-40 rds/min to 24 km *(13 n miles)*; weight of shell 32 kg.
4—12.7 mm MGs.
Torpedoes: 6—324 mm Mk 32 (2 triple) tubes ❹. Honeywell Mk 46 Mod 5; anti-submarine; active/passive homing to 11 km *(5.9 n miles)* at 40 kt; warhead 44 kg.
Countermeasures: Decoys: 4 Loral Hycor SRBOC 6-barrelled fixed Mk 36; IR flares and chaff to 4 km *(2.2 n miles)*.
T—Mk 6 Fanfare; torpedo decoy.
ESM/ECM: SLQ-32V(2); intercept. Sidekick jammer and deception system.
Combat data systems: Signaal MITDS/STACOS. Links 11 and 14.
Weapons control: Mk 68 GFCS. Mk 4 WDS. Mk 74 MFCS. Mk 114 FCS ASW. SYS-1 IADT.
Radars: Air search: Hughes SPS-39 ❺; 3D; E/F-band.
Lockheed SPS-40B/D ❻; E/F-band.
Surface search: Raytheon SPS-10D/F or SPS-64 ❼; G-band.
Navigation: Marconi LN66; I-band.
Fire control: 2 Raytheon SPG-51D ❽; G/I-band.
Lockheed SPG-53A ❾; K-band.
Tacan: URN 25/SRN 6.
Sonars: Sangamo or Raytheon DE 1191; hull-mounted (bow-mounted SQQ-23 Pair in D 219); active search and attack; medium frequency.

Programmes: Leased as part of the Defence Co-operation Agreement signed with the USA on 8 July 1990. *Kimon* recommissioned at Salamis, the remainder in San Diego prior to sailing for Greece in late 1992. Leases renewed in 1997 and gifted by grant aid in 1999. A fifth of class *Richard E Byrd*

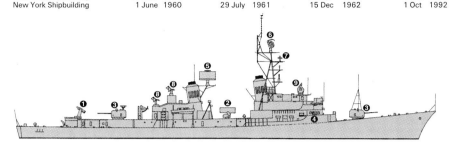

NEARCHOS *(Scale 1 : 1,200), Ian Sturton*

THEMISTOCLES *6/1999*, van Ginderen Collection / 0079474*

(DDG 23) was towed to Salamis on 12 October 1993 where she is used for spares.
Modernisation: DE 1191 sonars and an updated command system fitted.

Structure: *Nearchos* has a stem anchor because of the sonar Pair arrangement.

UPDATED

THEMISTOCLES *6/1999*, Camil Busquets i Vilanova / 0079475*

FRIGATES

4 HYDRA CLASS (MEKO 200HN) (FFG)

Name	No	Builders	Laid down		Launched		Commissioned	
HYDRA	F 452	Blohm + Voss, Hamburg	17 Dec	1990	25 June	1991	12 Nov	1992
SPETSAI	F 453	Hellenic Shipyards, Skaramanga	11 Aug	1992	9 Dec	1993	24 Oct	1996
PSARA	F 454	Hellenic Shipyards, Skaramanga	12 Dec	1993	20 Dec	1994	30 Apr	1998
SALAMIS	F 455	Hellenic Shipyards, Skaramanga	20 Dec	1994	15 May	1997	16 Dec	1998

Displacement, tons: 2,710 light; 3,350 full load
Dimensions, feet (metres): 383.9; 357.6 (wl) × 48.6 × 19.7
(117; 109 × 14.8 × 6)
Main machinery: CODOG; 2 GE LM 2500 gas turbines;
60,000 hp *(44.76 MW)* sustained; 2 MTU 20V 956 TB82
diesels; 10,420 hp(m) *(7.66 MW)* sustained; 2 shafts; cp props
Speed, knots: 31 gas; 20 diesel. **Range, miles:** 4,100 at 16 kt
Complement: 173 (22 officers) plus 16 flag staff

Missiles: SSM: 8 McDonnell Douglas Harpoon Block 1C; 2 quad
launchers ❶; active radar homing to 130 km *(70 n miles)* at
0.9 Mach; warhead 227 kg.
SAM: Raytheon NATO Sea Sparrow Mk 48 Mod 2 vertical
launcher ❷; 16 missiles; semi-active radar homing to 14.6 km
(8 n miles) at 2.5 Mach; warhead 39 kg.
Guns: 1 FMC 5 in *(127 mm)*/54 Mk 45 Mod 2A ❸ 20 rds/min to
24 km *(13 n miles)* anti-surface; 14 km *(7.7 n miles)* anti-
aircraft; weight of shell 32 kg.

2 GD/GE Vulcan Phalanx 20 mm Mk 15 Mod 12 ❹; 6 barrels
per mounting; 3,000 rds/min combined to 1.5 km.
Torpedoes: 6—324 mm Mk 32 Mod 5 (2 triple) tubes ❺.
Honeywell Mk 46 Mod 5; anti-submarine; active/passive
homing to 11 km *(5.9 n miles)* at 40 kt; warhead 44 kg.
Countermeasures: Decoys: 4 Mk 36 Mod 2 SRBOC chaff
launchers ❻.
SLQ-25 Nixie; torpedo decoy.
ESM: Argo AR 700; Telegon 10; intercept.
ECM: Argo APECS II; jammer.
Combat data systems: Signaal STACOS Mod 2; Links 11 and 14.
Weapons control: 2 Signaal Mk 73 Mod 1 (for SAM). Vesta Helo
transponder with datalink for OTHT. SAR-8 IR search. SWG 1
A(V) Harpoon LCS.
Radars: Air search: Signaal MW08 ❼; 3D; F/G-band.
Air Surface search: Signaal/Magnavox; DA08 ❽, F-band.
Navigation: Racal Decca 2690 BT; ARPA; I-band.
Fire Control: 2 Signaal STIR ❾; I/J/K-band.
IFF: Mk XII Mod 4.
Sonars: Raytheon SQS-56/DE 1160; hull-mounted and VDS.

Helicopters: 1 Sikorsky S-70B-6 Aegean Hawk ❿.

Programmes: Decision to buy four Meko 200 Mod 3HN
announced on 18 April 1988. West German Government
'offset' of tanks and aircraft went with the sale, and the
electronics and some of the weapon systems secured through
US FMS credits. The first ship ordered 10 February 1989 built
by Blohm + Voss, Hamburg and the remainder ordered 10
May 1989 at Hellenic Shipyards, Skaramanga. Programme was
delayed by financial problems at Hellenic Shipyards in 1992
and some of the prefabrication of *Spetsai* was done in
Hamburg.
Structure: The design follows the Portuguese 'Vasco da Gama'
class. All steel fin stabilisers.
Operational: Aegean Hawk carried from 1995.   *UPDATED*

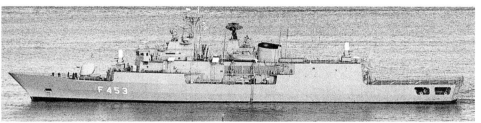

HYDRA   (Scale 1 : 1,200), Ian Sturton / 0052282

SPETSAI   3/1998, John Brodie / 0052283

SALAMIS   12/1998 *, Hellenic Shipyard / 0079476

PSARA   12/1998, B Sullivan / 0052284

6 ELLI (KORTENAER) CLASS (FFG)

Name	No	Builders	Laid down	Launched	Commissioned
ELLI (ex-*Pieter Florisz* F 812)	F 450	Koninklijke Maatschappij de Schelde, Flushing	1 July 1977	15 Dec 1979	10 Oct 1981
LIMNOS (ex-*Witte de With* F 813)	F 451	Koninklijke Maatschappij de Schelde, Flushing	13 June 1978	27 Oct 1979	18 Sep 1982
AEGEAN (ex-*Banckert* F 810)	F 460	Koninklijke Maatschappij de Schelde, Flushing	25 Feb 1976	13 July 1978	29 Oct 1980
ADRIAS (ex-*Callenburgh* F 808)	F 459	Koninklijke Maatschappij de Schelde, Flushing	30 June 1975	12 Mar 1977	26 July 1979
NAVARINON (ex-*Van Kinsbergen* F 809)	F 461	Koninklijke Maatschappij de Schelde, Flushing	2 Sep 1975	16 Apr 1977	24 Apr 1980
KOUNTOURIOTIS (ex-*Kortenaer* F 807)	F 462	Koninklijke Maatschappij de Schelde, Flushing	8 Apr 1975	18 Dec 1976	26 Oct 1978

Displacement, tons: 3,050 standard; 3,630 full load
Dimensions, feet (metres): 428 × 47.9 × 20.3 (screws) *(130.5 × 14.6 × 6.2)*
Main machinery: COGOG; 2 RR Olympus TM3B gas turbines; 50,880 hp *(39.7 MW)* sustained; 2 RR Tyne RM1C gas turbines; 9,900 hp *(7.4 MW)* sustained; 2 shafts; acbLIPS cp props
Speed, knots: 30. **Range, miles:** 4,700 at 16 kt
Complement: 176 (17 officers)

Missiles: SSM: 8 McDonnell Douglas Harpoon (2 quad) launchers ❶; active radar homing to 130 km *(70 n miles)* at 0.9 Mach; warhead 227 kg.
SAM: Raytheon NATO Sea Sparrow ❷; 24 missiles; semi-active radar homing to 14.6 km *(8 n miles)* at 2.5 Mach; warhead 39 kg.
Portable Redeye; shoulder-launched; short range.
Guns: 1 or 2 OTO Melara 3 in *(76 mm)*/62 compact ❸; 85 rds/min to 16 km *(8.6 n miles)* anti-surface; 12 km *(6.5 n miles)* anti-aircraft; weight of shell 6 kg.

1 or 2 GE/GD Vulcan Phalanx 20 mm Mk 15 6-barrelled ❹; 3,000 rds/min combined to 1.5 km. One mounting only on hangar roof in F 459-462.
Torpedoes: 4—324 mm Mk 32 (2 twin) tubes ❺. 16 Honeywell Mk 46 Mod 5; anti-submarine; active/passive homing to 11 km *(5.9 n miles)* at 40 kt; warhead 44 kg. Can be fitted.
Countermeasures: Decoys: 2 Loral Hycor Mk 36 SRBOC chaff launchers.
ESM: Elettronika Sphinx and MEL Scimitar; intercept.
ECM: ELT 715; jammer.
Combat data systems: Signaal SEWACO II action data automation; Links 10, 11 and 14.
Radars: Air search: Signaal LW08 ❻; D-band; range 264 km *(145 n miles)* for 2 m² target.
Surface search: Signaal ZW06 ❼; I-band.
Fire control: Signaal WM25 ❽; I/J-band; range 46 km *(25 n miles)*.
Signaal STIR ❾; I/J/K-band; range 39 km *(21 n miles)* for 1 m² target.
Sonars: Canadian Westinghouse SQS-505; hull-mounted; active search and attack; 7 kHz.

Helicopters: 2 AB 212ASW ❿.

Programmes: A contract was signed with the Netherlands on 15 September 1980 for the purchase of one of the 'Kortenaer' class building for the Netherlands' Navy, and an option on a second of class, which was taken up 7 June 1981. A second contract, signed on 9 November 1992, transferred three more of the class. Recommissioning dates for the second batch are *Aegeon* 14 May 1993, *Adrias* 30 March 1994 and *Navarinon* 1 March 1995. *Kountouriotis*, the sixth ship to transfer, recommissioned on 15 December 1997.
Modernisation: The original plan was to fit one Phalanx CIWS in place of the after 76 mm gun but for Gulf deployments in 1990-91 the gun was retained and two Phalanx fitted on the deck above the torpedo tubes. Corvus chaff launchers replaced by SRBOC (fitted either side of the bridge). The second batch of three ships were to be similarly modified but the original plan of one Phalanx vice the after 76 mm has been used as a cheaper alternative. Future proposed modifications include strengthening some flight decks for Aegean Hawks, fitting Scout radars, upgrading sonars to SQS 510 standard, fitting an optronic radar, and possibly RAM CIWS in last four of the class.
Structure: Hangar is 2 m longer than in Netherlands' ships to accommodate AB 212ASW helicopters.

UPDATED

ELLI   *(Scale 1 : 1,200), Ian Sturton*

KOUNTOURIOTIS   *3/1998, John Brodie* / 0052285

ADRIAS   *7/1997* / 0012462

LIMNOS (with twin Phalanx)   *6/1997, Giorgio Ghiglione* / 0012463

2 EPIRUS (KNOX) CLASS (FFG)

Name	No	Builders	Laid down	Launched	Commissioned	Recommissioned
EPIRUS (ex-*Connole*)	F 456 (ex-FF 1056)	Avondale Shipyards	23 Mar 1967	20 July 1968	30 Aug 1969	30 Aug 1992
THRACE (ex-*Trippe*)	F 457 (ex-FF 1075)	Avondale Shipyards	29 July 1968	1 Nov 1969	19 Sep 1970	30 July 1992

Displacement, tons: 3,011 standard; 3,877 full load
Dimensions, feet (metres): 439.6 × 46.8 × 15; 24.8 (sonar) *(134 × 14.3 × 4.6; 7.8)*
Main machinery: 2 Babcock & Wilcox boilers; 1,200 psi *(84.4 kg/cm²); 950°F (510°C)*; 1 turbine; 35,000 hp *(26 MW)*; 1 shaft
Speed, knots: 27. **Range, miles:** 4,000 at 22 kt on 1 boiler
Complement: 288 (17 officers)

Missiles: SSM: 8 McDonnell Douglas Harpoon; active radar homing to 130 km *(70 n miles)* at 0.9 Mach; warhead 227 kg.
SAM: 4 Stinger or Redeye posts fitted.
A/S: Honeywell ASROC Mk 16 octuple launcher with reload system (has 2 cells modified to fire Harpoon) **❶**; inertial guidance to 1.6-10 km *(1-5.4 n miles)*; payload Mk 46.
Guns: 1 FMC 5 in *(127 mm)*/54 Mk 42 Mod 9 **❷**; 20-40 rds/min to 24 km *(13 n miles)* anti-surface; 14 km *(7.7 n miles)* anti-aircraft; weight of shell 32 kg.

1 General Electric/General Dynamics 20 mm/76 6-barrelled Mk 15 Vulcan Phalanx **❸**; 3,000 rds/min combined to 1.5 km.
2 Rheinmetall 20 mm. 4—12.7 mm MGs.
Torpedoes: 4—324 mm Mk 32 (2 twin) fixed tubes **❹**. 22 Honeywell Mk 46 Mod 5; anti-submarine; active/passive homing to 11 km *(5.9 n miles)* at 40 kt; warhead 44 kg.
Mines: Rail for 8 mines can be fitted.
Countermeasures: Decoys: 2 Loral Hycor SRBOC 6-barrelled fixed Mk 36 **❺**; IR flares and chaff to 4 km *(2.2 n miles)*. T Mk 6 Fanfare/SLQ-25 Nixie; torpedo decoy. Prairie Masker hull and blade rate noise suppression.
ESM/ECM: SLQ-32(V)2 **❻**; radar warning. Sidekick modification adds jammer and deception system.
Combat data systems: FISTS; Link 14 receive only.
Weapons control: SWG-1A Harpoon LCS. Mk 68 GFCS. Mk 114 ASW FCS. Mk 1 target designation system. MMS target acquisition sight (for mines, small craft and low-flying aircraft).

Radars: Air search: Lockheed SPS-40D **❼**; E/F-band; range 320 km *(175 n miles)*.
Surface search: Raytheon SPS-10F **❽**; G-band.
Navigation: Marconi LN66; I-band.
Fire control: Western Electric SPG-53 **❾**; I/J-band.
Tacan: SRN 15. IFF: UPX-12.
Sonars: EDO/General Electric SQS-26 CX; bow-mounted; active search and attack; medium frequency.
EDO SQS-35; independent VDS.

Helicopters: 1 AB 212ASW **❿**.

Programmes: Announced on 11 February 1992 that three 'Knox' class would be leased from the USA and then transferred to the Hellenic Navy. *Thrace* arrived at Salamis 15 September 1992 and *Epirus* 12 February 1993. *Hepburn* FF 1055 acquired for spares in December 1998. Leases being renewed.
Modernisation: From 1972 to 1976 they were modified to accommodate the Seasprite anti-submarine helicopter; hangar and flight deck were enlarged. In 1979 a programme was initiated to fit 3.5 ft bow bulwarks and spray strakes adding 9.1 tons to the displacement. Sea Sparrow SAM replaced by Phalanx 1982-88. A mine rail was placed on the stern in 1997.
Structure: Improved ASROC-torpedo reloading capability (note slanting face of bridge structure immediately behind ASROC). Four Mk 32 torpedo tubes are fixed in the midships superstructure, two to a side, angled out at 45°. The arrangement provides improved loading capability over exposed triple Mk 32 torpedo tubes. A 4,000 lb lightweight anchor is fitted on the port side and an 8,000 lb anchor fits into the after section of the sonar dome. Four SAM launchers for Stinger.
Operational: One more of the class paid off in December 1998.

UPDATED

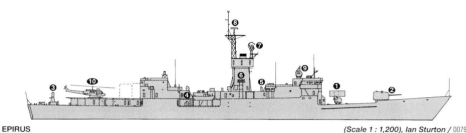

EPIRUS
(Scale 1 : 1,200), Ian Sturton / 0079477

EPIRUS
11/1999*, Giorgio Ghiglione / 0079478

THRACE
10/1999*, Camil Busquets i Vilanova / 0079484

SHIPBORNE AIRCRAFT

Note: There are also two Alouette IIIs used for SAR and training.

Numbers/Type: 8 Sikorsky S-70B-6 Aegean Hawk.
Operational speed: 135 kt *(250 km/h).*
Service ceiling: 10,000 ft *(3,050 m).*
Range: 600 n miles *(1,110 km).*
Role/Weapon systems: Five ordered 25 July 1991. First one delivered 14 October 1994, remainder in July 1995. The option was taken up on one more which was delivered in 1997, and two more in 1998. Sensors: Telephonica APS 143(V)3 search radar, AlliedSignal AQS 18(V)3 dipping sonar, MAD, Litton ALR 606(V)2 ESM, Litton ASN 150(V) tactical data system with CD22 or Link 11. Weapons: ASV; Kongsberg Penguin Mk 2 Mod 7, two AS 12. ASW; two Mk 46 torpedoes.
VERIFIED

AEGEAN HAWK   *6/1997, Hellenic Navy /* 0012466

Numbers/Type: 8/2 Agusta AB 212ASW/EW.
Operational speed: 106 kt *(196 km/h).*
Service ceiling: 14,200 ft *(4,330 m).*
Range: 230 n miles *(425 km).*
Role/Weapon systems: Shipborne ASW, Elint and surface search role from escorts. Sensors: Selenia APS-705 radar, ESM/ECM (Elint version), AlliedSignal AQS-18 dipping sonar (ASW version). Weapons: ASV; two AS 12. ASW; two Mk 46 or two A244/S homing torpedoes.
VERIFIED

AB 212ASW   *9/1994, A Campanera i Rovira /* 0012467

LAND-BASED MARITIME AIRCRAFT

Note: A squadron of Air Force Mirage 2000 EG fighters is assigned to the naval strike role using Exocet AM 39 ASMs.

Numbers/Type: 6 Lockheed P-3B Orion.
Operational speed: 410 kt *(760 km/h).*
Service ceiling: 28,300 ft *(8,625 m).*
Range: 4,000 n miles *(7,410 km).*
Role/Weapon systems: Four P-3A transferred from the USN in 1992-93 as part of the Defence Co-operation. Four P-3B acquired in 1996 plus two more P-3A. Two more P-3B in 1997. The four P-3B are operational; two P-3A are used for ground training only and the remainder for spares. Sensors: APS 115 radar; sonobuoys; ESM. Weapons: ASW; Mk 46 torpedoes, depth bombs and mines.
UPDATED

ORION   *6/1997, Hellenic Navy /* 0012468

CORVETTES

Note: Up to four corvettes capable of carrying an Aegean Hawk helicopter may be ordered in 1999. Ingalls 'SAAR 5' class are being evaluated.

5 NIKI (THETIS) (TYPE 420) CLASS (GUNBOATS) (FS/PG)

Name	No	Commissioned	Recommissioned
NIKI (ex-*Thetis*)	P 62 (ex-P 6052)	1 July 1961	6 Sep 1991
DOXA (ex-*Najade*)	P 63 (ex-P 6054)	12 May 1962	6 Sep 1991
ELEFTHERIA (ex-*Triton*)	P 64 (ex-P 6055)	10 Nov 1962	7 Sep 1992
CARTERIA (ex-*Hermes*)	P 65 (ex-P 6053)	16 Dec 1961	7 Sep 1992
AGON (ex-*Andreia*, ex-*Theseus*)	P 66 (ex-P 6056)	15 Aug 1963	8 Nov 1993

Displacement, tons: 575 standard; 732 full load
Dimensions, feet (metres): 229.7 × 26.9 × 8.6 *(70 × 8.2 × 2.7)*
Main machinery: 2 MAN V84V diesels; 6,800 hp(m) *(5 MW)*; 2 shafts
Speed, knots: 19.5. **Range, miles:** 2,760 at 15 kt
Complement: 64 (4 officers)

Guns: 4 Breda 40 mm/70 (2 twin); 300 rds/min to 12.5 km *(6.7 n miles)*; weight of shell 0.96 kg. 2—12.7 mm MGs.
Torpedoes: 6—324 mm Mk 32 (2 triple) tubes; 4 Honeywell Mk 46 Mod 5; active/passive homing to 11 km *(5.9 n miles)* at 40 kt; warhead 44 kg.
Depth charges: 2 rails.
Countermeasures: ESM: Thomson-CSF DR 2000S; intercept.
Weapons control: Signaal Mk 9 TFCS.
Radars: Surface search: Thomson-CSF TRS 3001; E/F-band.
Navigation: Kelvin Hughes 14/9; I-band.
Sonars: Atlas Elektronik ELAC 1 BV; hull-mounted; active search and attack; high frequency.

Programmes: All built by Rolandwerft, Bremen, and transferred from Germany.
Modernisation: The A/S mortars have been replaced by a second 40 mm gun and single torpedo tubes by triple mountings.
Structure: *Doxa* has a deckhouse before bridge for sick bay.
VERIFIED

NIKI   *5/1998 /* 0052288

PATROL FORCES

Note: *Panagopoulos II* and *III* paid off in 1993, but are back in service as Divers launches working with the MYK (Underwater Demolition Unit).

0 + 3 (4) SUPER VITA CLASS
(FAST ATTACK CRAFT—MISSILE) (PGFG)

Displacement, tons: 580 full load
Dimensions, feet (metres): 203.4 × 31.2 × 8.5 *(62 × 9.5 × 2.6)*
Main machinery: 4 MTU 16V 595 TE 90 diesels; 4 shafts
Speed, knots: 34. **Range, miles:** 1,800 at 12 kt
Complement: 45

Missiles: SSM: Exocet MM 40 ❶.
SAM: RAM ❷.
Guns: 1 Otobreda 76 mm/62 Super Rapid ❸.
2 Otobreda 30 mm ❹.
Countermeasures: Decoys ❺.
ESM: DR 2000 SLW ❻ intercept.
Radars: Air/surface search ❼.
Fire control ❽.

Programmes: Design selected 21 September 1999 based on Vosper Thornycroft Super Vita. Contract signed 7 January 2000. Building started at Eleusis Shipyard in March 2000.
Structure: The SSM type is speculative. Two 21 in torpedo tubes may be fitted. Signaal TACTICOS command data system is likely to be included.
NEW ENTRY

SUPER VITA   *(not to scale), Ian Sturton /* 0079485

9 LASKOS (LA COMBATTANTE III) CLASS
(FAST ATTACK CRAFT—MISSILE) (PGFG)

Name	No	Builders	Commissioned
ANTIPLOIARCHOS LASKOS	P 20	CMN Cherbourg	20 Apr 1977
PLOTARHIS BLESSAS	P 21	CMN Cherbourg	7 July 1977
IPOPLOIARCHOS MIKONIOS	P 22	CMN Cherbourg	10 Feb 1978
IPOPLOIARCHOS TROUPAKIS	P 23	CMN Cherbourg	8 Nov 1977
SIMEOFOROS KAVALOUDIS	P 24	Hellenic Shipyards, Skaramanga	14 July 1980
IPOPLOIARCHOS DEGIANNIS	P 26	Hellenic Shipyards, Skaramanga	Dec 1980
SIMEOFOROS XENOS	P 27	Hellenic Shipyards, Skaramanga	31 Mar 1981
SIMEOFOROS SIMITZOPOULOS	P 28	Hellenic Shipyards, Skaramanga	June 1981
SIMEOFOROS STARAKIS	P 29	Hellenic Shipyards, Skaramanga	12 Oct 1981

Displacement, tons: 359 standard; 425 full load (P 20-23)
329 standard; 429 full load (P 24-29)
Dimensions, feet (metres): 184 × 26.2 × 7 *(56.2 × 8 × 2.1)*
Main machinery: 4 MTU 20V 538 TB92 diesels; 17,060 hp(m) *(12.54 MW)* sustained; 4 shafts (P 20-23)
4 MTU 20V 538 TB91 diesels; 15,360 hp(m) *(11.29 MW)* sustained; 4 shafts (P 24-29)
Speed, knots: 36 (P 20-23); 32.5 (P 24-29). **Range, miles:** 700 at 32 kt; 2,700 at 15 kt
Complement: 42 (5 officers)

Missiles: SSM: 4 Aerospatiale MM 38 Exocet (P 20-P 23); inertial cruise; active radar homing to 42 km *(23 n miles)* at 0.9 Mach; warhead 165 kg.
6 Kongsberg Penguin Mk 2 (P 24-P 29); inertial/IR homing to 27 km *(15 n miles)* at 0.8 Mach; warhead 120 kg.
Guns: 2 OTO Melara 3 in *(76 mm)*/62 compact; 85 rds/min to 16 km *(8.6 n miles)* anti-surface; 12 km *(6.5 n miles)* anti-aircraft; weight of shell 6 kg.
4 Emerson Electric 30 mm (2 twin); multipurpose; 1,200 rds/min combined to 6 km *(3.2 n miles)*; weight of shell 0.35 kg.
Torpedoes: 2—21 in *(533 mm)* aft tubes. AEG SST-4; anti-surface; wire-guided; active homing to 12 km *(6.5 n miles)* at 35 kt; passive homing to 28 km *(15 n miles)* at 23 kt; warhead 250 kg.
Countermeasures: Decoys: Wegmann chaff launchers.
ESM: Thomson-CSF DR 2000S; intercept.
Weapons control: 2 CSEE Panda optical directors for 30 mm guns. Thomson-CSF Vega I or II system (P 20-P 23). NFT PFCS-2 (P 24-P 29).
Radars: Surface search: Thomson-CSF Triton; G-band; range 33 km *(18 n miles)* for 2 m² target.
Navigation: Decca 1226C; I-band.
Fire control: Thomson-CSF Castor II; I/J-band; range 31 km *(17 n miles)* for 2 m² target.
Thomson-CSF Pollux; I/J-band; range 31 km *(17 n miles)* for 2 m² target.

Programmes: First four ordered in September 1974. Second group of six ordered 1978.
Structure: First four fitted with SSM Exocet; remainder have Penguin.
Operational: P 25 sunk after collision with a ferry in November 1996.

VERIFIED

IPOPLOIARHOS MIKONIOS   *9/1998, van Ginderen Collection /* 0052290

IPOPLOIARHOS TROUPAKIS   *9/1998, van Ginderen Collection /* 0052291

SIMEFOROS STARAKIS (with Penguin)   *9/1998, van Ginderen Collection /* 0052292

4 + 2 VOTSIS (LA COMBATTANTE IIA) (TYPE 148) CLASS
(FAST ATTACK CRAFT—MISSILE) (PCFG)

Name	No	Builders	Commissioned
IPOPLOIARCHOS VOTSIS (ex-*Iltis*)	P 72 (ex-P 51)	CMN, Cherbourg	8 Jan 1973
ANTIPLOIARCHOS PEZOPOULOS (ex-*Storch*)	P 73 (ex-P 30)	CMN, Cherbourg	17 July 1974
PLOTARHIS VLAHAVAS (ex-*Marder*)	P 74	CMN, Cherbourg	14 June 1973
PLOTARHIS MARIDAKIS (ex-*Häher*)	P 75	CMN, Cherbourg	12 June 1974

Displacement, tons: 265 full load
Dimensions, feet (metres): 154.2 × 23 × 8.9 *(47 × 7 × 2.7)*
Main machinery: 4 MTU MD 16V 538 TB90 diesels; 12,000 hp(m) *(8.82 MW)* sustained; 4 shafts
Speed, knots: 36. **Range, miles:** 570 at 30 kt; 1,600 at 15 kt
Complement: 30 (4 officers)

Missiles: SSM: 4 Aerospatiale MM 38 Exocet (2 twin) launchers (P 72-73); inertial cruise; active radar homing to 42 km *(23 n miles)* at 0.9 Mach; warhead 165 kg; sea-skimmer.
4 McDonnell Douglas Harpoon (2 twin) launchers (P 74-75); active radar homing to 130 km *(70 n miles)* at 0.9 Mach; warhead 227 kg.
Guns: 1 OTO Melara 3 in *(76 mm)*/62 compact; 85 rds/min to 16 km *(8.6 n miles)* anti-surface; 12 km *(6.5 n miles)* anti-aircraft; weight of shell 6 kg.
1 Bofors 40 mm/70; 330 rds/min to 12 km *(6.5 n miles)* anti-surface; 4 km *(2.2 n miles)* anti-aircraft; weight of shell 0.96 kg; fitted with GRP dome (1984).
Mines: Laying capability.
Countermeasures: Decoys: Wolke chaff launcher.
ESM: Thomson-CSF DR 2000S; intercept.
Combat data systems: PALIS and Link 11.
Weapons control: CSEE Panda optical director. Thomson-CSF Vega PCET system, controlling missiles and guns.
Radars: Air/surface search: Thomson-CSF Triton; G-band; range 33 km *(18 n miles)* for 2 m² target.
Navigation: SMA 3 RM 20; I-band.
Fire control: Thomson-CSF Castor; I/J-band.

Programmes: First pair transferred from Germany in September 1993 and recommissioned 17 February 1994. Two more transferred 16 March 1995 and recommissioned 30 June 1995. Two more planned for 2000.
Modernisation: Mid-life updates in 1980s. P 74-75 fitted with Harpoon. New ESM fitted after transfer.
Structure: Steel hulls. Similar to 'Combattante II' class.   *UPDATED*

ANTIPLOIARCHOS PEZOPOULOS   *6/1998, Hellenic Navy /* 0052289

4 ANNINOS (LA COMBATTANTE II) CLASS
(FAST ATTACK CRAFT—MISSILE) (PCFG)

Name	No	Builders	Commissioned
ANTIPOPLOIARCHOS ANNINOS (ex-*Navsithoi*)	P 14	CMN Cherbourg	June 1972
IPOPLOIARCHOS ARLIOTIS (ex-*Evniki*)	P 15	CMN Cherbourg	Apr 1972
IPOPLOIARCHOS KONIDIS (ex-*Kymothoi*)	P 16	CMN Cherbourg	July 1972
IPOPLOIARCHOS BATSIS (ex-*Calypso*)	P 17	CMN Cherbourg	Dec 1971

Displacement, tons: 234 standard; 255 full load
Dimensions, feet (metres): 154.2 × 23.3 × 8.2 *(47 × 7.1 × 2.5)*
Main machinery: 4 MTU MD 16V 538 TB90 diesels; 12,000 hp(m) *(8.82 MW)* sustained; 4 shafts
Speed, knots: 36.5. **Range, miles:** 850 at 25 kt
Complement: 40 (4 officers)

Missiles: SSM: 4 Aerospatiale MM 38 Exocet; inertial cruise; active radar homing to 42 km *(23 n miles)* at 0.9 Mach; warhead 165 kg; sea-skimmer.
Guns: 4 Oerlikon 35 mm/90 (2 twin); 550 rds/min to 6 km *(3.2 n miles)* anti-surface; 5 km *(2.7 n miles)* anti-aircraft; weight of shell 1.55 kg.
Torpedoes: 2—21 in *(533 mm)* tubes. AEG SST-4; wire-guided; active homing to 12 km *(6.5 n miles)* at 35 kt; passive homing to 28 km *(15 n miles)* at 23 kt; warhead 250 kg.
Countermeasures: ESM: Thomson-CSF DR 2000S; intercept.
Weapons control: Thomson-CSF Vega system.
Radars: Surface search: Thomson-CSF Triton; G-band.
Navigation: Decca 1226C; I-band.
Fire control: Thomson-CSF Pollux; I/J-band.
IFF: Plessey Mk 10.

Programmes: Ordered in 1969. P 15 launched 8 September 1971; P 14 on 20 December 1971; P 17 on 27 April 1971; P 16 on 26 January 1972.
Modernisation: Plans to modernise include updating the fire-control system.   *UPDATED*

IPOPLOIARCHOS BATSIS   *1989*, Hellenic Navy /* 0079486

4 HESPEROS (JAGUAR) CLASS
(FAST ATTACK CRAFT—TORPEDO) (PCF)

Name	No	Builders	Commissioned
HESPEROS (ex-*Seeadler* P 6068)	P 50	Lürssen, Vegesack	29 Aug 1958
KYKLON (ex-*Greif* P 6071)	P 53	Lürssen, Vegesack	3 Mar 1959
LELAPS (ex-*Kondor* P 6070)	P 54	Lürssen, Vegesack	24 Feb 1959
TYFON (ex-*Geier* P 6073)	P 56	Lürssen, Vegesack	3 June 1959

Displacement, tons: 160 standard; 190 full load
Dimensions, feet (metres): 139.4 × 23.6 × 7.9 *(42.5 × 7.2 × 2.4)*
Main machinery: 4 MTU MD 16V 538 TB90 diesels; 12,000 hp(m) *(8.82 MW)* sustained; 4 shafts
Speed, knots: 42. **Range, miles:** 500 at 40 kt; 1,000 at 32 kt
Complement: 39
Guns: 2 Bofors 40 mm/70; 300 rds/min to 12 km *(6.5 n miles)* anti-surface; 4 km *(2.2 n miles)* anti-aircraft; weight of shell 2.4 kg.
Torpedoes: 4—21 in *(533 mm)* tubes. AEG SST-4; anti-surface; wire-guided; passive homing to 28 km *(15.3 n miles)* at 23 kt; active homing to 12 km *(6.6 n miles)* at 35 kt; warhead 250 kg.
Mines: 2 in lieu of each torpedo.
Radars: Surface search: Decca 1226; I-band.

Comment: Transferred from Germany 1976-77. P 53 and P 56 commissioned in Hellenic Navy 12 December 1976. P 50 and P 54 on 24 March 1977, P 52 and P 55 on 22 May 1977. Three others (ex-*Albatros*, ex-*Bussard*, and ex-*Sperber*) transferred at same time for spares.

VERIFIED

LELAPS   *9/1998, van Ginderen Collection /* 0052293

4 NASTY CLASS (FAST ATTACK CRAFT—TORPEDO) (PCF)

Name	No	Builders	Commissioned
ANDROMEDA	P 196	Mandal, Norway	Nov 1966
KYKNOS	P 198	Mandal, Norway	Feb 1967
PIGASOS	P 199	Mandal, Norway	Apr 1967
TOXOTIS	P 228	Mandal, Norway	May 1967

Displacement, tons: 72 full load
Dimensions, feet (metres): 80.4 × 24.6 × 6.9 *(24.5 × 7.5 × 2.1)*
Main machinery: 2 MTU 12V 331 TC92 diesels; 2,660 hp(m) *(1.96 MW)* sustained; 2 shafts
Speed, knots: 25. **Range, miles:** 676 at 17 kt
Complement: 20
Guns: 1 Bofors 40 mm/70. 1 Rheinmetall 20 mm.
Torpedoes: 4—21 in *(533 mm)* tubes. AEG SST-4; wire-guided; active homing to 12 km *(6.5 n miles)* at 35 kt; passive homing to 28 km *(15 n miles)* at 23 kt; warhead 250 kg.
Radars: Surface search: Decca 1226; I-band.

Comment: Six of the class acquired from Norway in 1967 and paid off into reserve in the early 1980s. Four re-engined and brought back into service in 1988. These craft are not very active and top speed has been markedly reduced.

UPDATED

ANDROMEDA   *6/1999*, N A Sifferlinger /* 0079487

2 ARMATOLOS (OSPREY 55) CLASS (LARGE PATROL CRAFT) (PG)

Name	No	Builders	Commissioned
ARMATOLOS	P 18	Hellenic Shipyards, Skaramanga	27 Mar 1990
NAVMACHOS	P 19	Hellenic Shipyards, Skaramanga	15 July 1990

Displacement, tons: 555 full load
Dimensions, feet (metres): 179.8; 166.7 (wl) × 34.4 × 8.5 *(54.8; 50.8 × 10.5 × 2.6)*
Main machinery: 2 MTU 16V 1163 TB63 diesels; 10,000 hp(m) *(7.3 MW)* sustained; 2 shafts; Kamewa cp props
Speed, knots: 25. **Range, miles:** 500 at 25 kt, 2,800 at 12 kt
Complement: 36 plus 25 troops
Missiles: SSM: 4 McDonnell Douglas Harpoon (can be fitted).
Guns: 1 OTO Melara 3 in *(76 mm)*/62 compact; 85 rds/min to 16 km *(8.6 n miles)* anti-surface; 12 km *(6.6 n miles)* anti-aircraft; weight of shell 6 kg.
1 Bofors 40 mm/70.
Mines: Rails.
Countermeasures: Decoys: 2 chaff launchers.
ESM: Thomson-CSF DR 2000S; intercept.
Weapons control: Selenia Elsag NA 21.
Radars: Surface search: Thomson-CSF Triton; G-band.
Fire control: Selenia RTNX; I/J-band.

Comment: Built in co-operation with Danyard A/S. Ordered in March 1988. First one laid down 8 May 1989 and launched 19 December 1989. Second laid down 9 November 1989 and launched 16 May 1990. Armament is of modular design and therefore can be changed. 76 mm guns replaced the Bofors 40 mm in 1995, after being taken from decommissioned 'Gearing' class destroyers. Options on more of the class were shelved in favour of the Hellenic 56 design.

UPDATED

NAVMACHOS   *6/1997*, Hellenic Navy /* 0012472

2 + 4 PIRPOLITIS (HELLENIC 56) CLASS
(LARGE PATROL CRAFT) (PG)

Name	No	Builders	Commissioned
PIRPOLITIS	P 57	Hellenic Shipyard, Skaramanga	4 May 1993
POLEMISTIS	P 61	Hellenic Shipyard, Skaramanga	16 June 1994

Displacement, tons: 555 full load
Dimensions, feet (metres): 185.4 × 32.8 × 8.9 *(56.5 × 10 × 2.7)*
Main machinery: 2 Wärtsilä Nohab 16V25 diesels; 9,200 hp(m) *(6.76 MW)* sustained; 2 shafts
Speed, knots: 24. **Range, miles:** 2,470 at 15 kt; 900 at 24 kt
Complement: 36 (6 officers) plus 23 spare
Missiles: SSM: 4 McDonnell Douglas Harpoon (can be fitted).
Guns: 1 OTO Melara 3 in *(76 mm)*/62 compact; 85 rds/min to 16 km *(8.6 n miles)* anti-surface; 12 km *(6.6 n miles)* anti-aircraft; weight of shell 6 kg.
1 Bofors 40 mm/70. 2 Rheinmetall 20 mm.
Mines: 2 rails.
Weapons control: Selenia Elsag NA 21.
Radars: Surface search: Thomson-CSF Triton; I-band.

Comment: First pair ordered 20 February 1990. This is a design by the Hellenic Navy which uses the modular concept so that weapons and sensors can be changed as required. Appearance is similar to 'Osprey 55' class. *Pirpolitis* launched 16 September 1992, *Polemistis* 21 June 1993. Completion delayed by the shipyard's financial problems. Alternative guns and Harpoon SSM can be fitted. 25 fully equipped troops can be carried. Engines are resiliently mounted. Four more of this class were proposed on 9 February 1998 from Hellenic with authorisation in December 1998, and a contract to build on 21 December 1999. Building started in February 2000. First one is planned to be in service in April 2002.

UPDATED

POLEMISTIS   *2/1998, van Ginderen Collection /* 0052294

POLEMISTIS   *6/1994*, Hellenic Shipyard /* 0079488

2 TOLMI (ASHEVILLE) CLASS (COASTAL PATROL CRAFT) (PC/PG)

Name	No	Builders	Commissioned
TOLMI (ex-Green Bay)	P 229	Peterson, Wisconsin	5 Dec 1969
ORMI (ex-Beacon)	P 230	Peterson, Wisconsin	21 Nov 1969

Displacement, tons: 225 standard; 245 full load
Dimensions, feet (metres): 164.5 × 23.8 × 9.5 (50.1 × 7.3 × 2.9)
Main machinery: 2 Cummins VT12-875 diesels; 1,450 hp (1.07 MW); 2 shafts
Speed, knots: 16. **Range, miles:** 1,700 at 16 kt
Complement: 24 (3 officers)
Missiles: SSM: 4 Aerospatiale SS 12M; wire-guided to 5.5 km (3 n miles) subsonic; warhead 30 kg.
Guns: 1 USN 3 in (76 mm)/50 Mk 34; 50 rds/min to 12.8 km (7 n miles); weight of shell 6 kg.
   1 Bofors 40 mm/56 Mk 10. 4—12.7 mm (2 twin) MGs.
Weapons control: Mk 63 GFCS.
Radars: Surface search: Sperry SPS-53; I/J-band.
Fire control: Western Electric SPG-50; I/J-band.

Comment: Transferred from the USA in mid-1990 after a refit and recommissioned 18 June 1991. Both were in reserve from April 1977 having originally been built for the Cuban crisis. Similar craft in Turkish, Colombian and South Korean navies. Gas-turbine propulsion engine removed prior to transfer. Reclassified as coastal patrol craft.

UPDATED

ORMI   8/1999*, van Ginderen Collection / 0079490

2 COASTAL PATROL CRAFT (PCF)

Name	No	Builders	Commissioned
DIOPOS ANTONIOU	P 286	Ch N de l'Esterel	4 Dec 1975
KELEFSTIS STAMOU	P 287	Ch N de l'Esterel	28 July 1975

Displacement, tons: 115 full load
Dimensions, feet (metres): 105 × 19 × 5.3 (32 × 5.8 × 1.6)
Main machinery: 2 MTU 12V 331 TC81 diesels; 2,610 hp(m) (1.92 MW) sustained; 2 shafts
Speed, knots: 30. **Range, miles:** 1,500 at 15 kt
Complement: 17
Missiles: SSM: 4 Aerospatiale SS 12M; wire-guided to 5.5 km (3 n miles) subsonic; warhead 30 kg.
Guns: 1 Rheinmetall 20 mm. 1—12.7 mm MG.
Radars: Surface search: Decca 1226; I-band.

Comment: Originally ordered for Cyprus, later transferred to Greece. Wooden hulls. Fast RIB carried on the stern.

UPDATED

DIOPOS ANTONIOU   6/1990*, Hellenic Navy / 0079489

1 DILOS CLASS (COASTAL PATROL CRAFT) (PC)

KNOSSOS P 268

Displacement, tons: 74.5 standard; 86 full load
Dimensions, feet (metres): 95.1 × 16.2 × 5.6 (29 × 5 × 1.7)
Main machinery: 2 MTU 12V 331 TC92 diesels; 2,660 hp(m) (1.96 MW) sustained; 2 shafts
Speed, knots: 27. **Range, miles:** 1,600 at 24 kt
Complement: 15
Guns: 2 Rheinmetall 20 mm.
Radars: Surface search: Racal Decca 1226C; I-band.

Comment: Ordered from Hellenic Shipyards, Skaramanga in May 1976 to a design by Abeking & Rasmussen. The Navy used this craft for air-sea rescue duties with an A number. Reverted to P number in 1997. Based at the National SAR centre. Four more of this class serve in Coast Guard and three in Customs service. One to Georgia in February 1998, and a second in September 1999. This ship is to be transferred to Cyprus in 2000.

UPDATED

KNOSSOS   6/1998, E M Cornish / 0052296

AMPHIBIOUS FORCES

Note: There is a number of paid off LSTs and LSMs in unmaintained reserve at Salamis.

5 JASON CLASS (LST)

Name	No	Builders	Launched	Commissioned
CHIOS	L 173	Eleusis Shipyard	16 Dec 1988	30 May 1996
SAMOS	L 174	Eleusis Shipyard	6 Apr 1989	20 May 1994
LESBOS	L 176	Eleusis Shipyard	5 July 1990	28 Feb 1999
IKARIA	L 175	Eleusis Shipyard	22 Oct 1998	6 Oct 1999
RODOS	L 177	Eleusis Shipyard	6 Oct 1999	May 2000

Displacement, tons: 4,400 full load
Dimensions, feet (metres): 380.5 × 50.2 × 11.3 (116 × 15.3 × 3.4)
Main machinery: 2 Wärtsilä Nohab 16V25 diesels; 9,200 hp(m) (6.76 MW) sustained; 2 shafts
Speed, knots: 16
Military lift: 300 troops plus vehicles; 4 LCVPs
Guns: 1 OTO Melara 76 mm/62 Mod 9 compact; 100 rds/min to 16 km (8.6 n miles) anti-surface;
   12 km (6.5 n miles) anti-aircraft; weight of shell 6 kg.
   2 Breda 40 mm/70; 300 rds/min to 12 km (6.5 n miles); weight of shell 0.96 kg.
   4 Rheinmetall 20 mm (2 twin).
Weapons control: 1 CSEE Panda optical director. Thomson-CSF Canopus GFCS.
Radars: Thomson-CSF Triton; G-band.
Fire control: Thomson-CSF Pollux; I/J-band.
Navigation: Kelvin Hughes Type 1007; I-band.
Helicopters: Platform for one medium.

Comment: Contract for construction of five LSTs by Eleusis Shipyard signed 15 May 1986. Bow and stern ramps, drive through design. First laid down 18 April 1987, second in September 1987, third in May 1988, fourth April 1989 and fifth November 1989. Completion of all five and in particular the last three, severely delayed by shipyard financial problems. The shipyard was privatised in October 1997 and progress has markedly improved since then. Combat data system is a refurbished German system.

UPDATED

SAMOS   6/1994*, Hellenic Navy / 0079491

CHIOS   5/1998, Diego Quevedo / 0052297

2 TERREBONNE PARISH CLASS (LST)

Name	No	Builders	Commissioned
INOUSE (ex-Terrell County LST 1157)	L 104	Bath Iron Works Corporation	19 Mar 1953
KOS (ex-Whitfield County LST 1169)	L 116	Christy Corporation	14 Sep 1954

Displacement, tons: 2,590 light; 5,800 full load
Dimensions, feet (metres): 384 × 55 × 17 (117.1 × 16.8 × 5.2)
Main machinery: 4 GM 16-278A diesels; 6,000 hp (4.48 MW); 2 shafts; cp props
Speed, knots: 15
Complement: 115
Military lift: 400 troops; 4 LCVPs
Guns: 6 USN 3 in (76 mm)/50 Mk 21 (3 twin); 20 rds/min to 12 km (6.5 n miles) anti-surface;
   9 km (4.9 n miles) anti-aircraft; weight of shell 6 kg.
   3 Rheinmetall 20 mm S 20.
Weapons control: 2 Mk 63 GFCS.
Radars: Surface search: Raytheon/Sylvania SPS-10; G-band.
Fire control: 2 Western Electric Mk 34; I/J-band.
Navigation: Decca; I-band.

Comment: Part of class of 16 of which these two were transferred from USA 17 March 1977 by sale.

UPDATED

KOS   9/1997*, van Ginderen Collection / 0012475

0 + 4 POMORNIK (ZUBR) (TYPE 1232) HOVERCRAFT (ACV)

Displacement, tons: 550 full load
Dimensions, feet (metres): 189 × 84 (57.6 × 25.6)
Main machinery: 5 Type NK-12MV gas-turbines; 2 for lift, 23,672 hp(m) (17.4 MW) nominal; 3 for drive, 35,508 hp(m) (26.1 MW) nominal
Speed, knots: 60. **Range, miles:** 300 at 55 kt
Complement: 27 (4 officers)
Military lift: 3 MBT or 10 APC plus 230 troops (total 130 tons)
Guns: 2—30 mm/65 AK 630; 6 barrels per mounting.
   2 retractable 122 mm rocket launchers.
Mines: 2 rails can be carried for 80.
Countermeasures: ESM: intercept.
Weapons control: Optronic director.
Radars: Air/surface search: Cross Dome; I-band.
Fire control: Bass Tilt; H/I-band.

Comment: Two ordered from Russia and two from Ukraine on 24 January 2000. All to be delivered in 2001. Details given are for the hovercraft in service in Russian and Ukraine navies.
NEW ENTRY

POMORNIK (Russian colours)   8/1994 *, W Globke / 0079493

2 LSM 1 CLASS

Name	No	Builders	Commissioned
IPOPLOIARCHOS ROUSSEN (ex-*LSM 399*)	L 164	Charleston Navy Yard	13 Aug 1945
IPOPLOIARCHOS KRYSTALLIDIS (ex-*LSM 541*)	L 165	Brown SB Co, Houston	7 Dec 1945

Displacement, tons: 743 beaching; 1,095 full load
Dimensions, feet (metres): 203.5 × 34.2 × 8.3 (62.1 × 10.4 × 2.5)
Main machinery: 2 Fairbanks-Morse 38D8-1/8-10 diesels; 3,540 hp (2.64 MW) sustained; 2 shafts (L 161, 163 and 165); 4 GM 16-278A diesels; 3,000 hp (2.24 MW); 2 shafts (L 164)
Speed, knots: 13. **Range, miles:** 4,900 at 12 kt
Complement: 60
Guns: 2 Bofors 40 mm/60 (twin). 8 Oerlikon 20 mm.
Radars: Navigation: Decca; I-band.

Comment: *LSM 541* was handed over by USA at Salamis on 30 October 1958 and *LSM 399* at Portsmouth, Virginia on 3 November 1958. Both were renamed after naval heroes killed during the Second World War.
UPDATED

IPOPLOIARCHOS ROUSSEN   1/2000 *, A Sharma / 0079492

2 LCTs

KITHERA (ex-*LCT 1198*) L 185   **MILOS** (ex-*LCT 1300*) L 189

Displacement, tons: 400 full load
Dimensions, feet (metres): 187.2 × 38.7 × 4.3 (57 × 11.8 × 1.3)
Main machinery: 2 Paxman diesels; 1,000 hp (746 kW); 2 shafts
Speed, knots: 7. **Range, miles:** 3,000 at 7 kt
Complement: 12
Military lift: 350 tons
Guns: 2 Oerlikon 20 mm.

Comment: The survivors of a class of 12 acquired in 1946 from the UK.
VERIFIED

KITHERA   6/1993, Hellenic Navy

6 TYPE 520 (LCU)

NAXOS (ex-*Renke*) L 178	**IOS** (ex-*Barbe*) L 167	**IRAKLEIA** (ex-*Forelle*) L 169
PAROS (ex-*Salm*) L 179	**SIKINOS** (ex-*Dorsch*) L 168	**FOLEGANDROS** (ex-*Delphin*) L 170

Displacement, tons: 430 full load
Dimensions, feet (metres): 131.2 × 28.9 × 7.2 (40 × 8.8 × 2.2)
Main machinery: 2 MWM 12-cyl diesels; 1,020 hp(m) (750 kW); 2 shafts
Speed, knots: 11. **Range, miles:** 1,200 at 11 kt
Complement: 17
Military lift: 150 tons
Guns: 2 Rheinmetall 20 mm.
Radars: Navigation: Kelvin Hughes; I-band.

Comment: First two transferred from Germany 16 November 1989, remainder on 31 January 1992. Built by HDW, Hamburg in 1966. Bow and stern ramps similar to US Type. Two others (ex-*Rochan* and *Murane*) used for spares.
UPDATED

IOS   9/1997, van Ginderen Collection / 0052299

FOLEGANDROS   11/1999 * / 0081940

10 TYPE 521 (LCM)

SERIFOS L 195   + 9

Displacement, tons: 168 full load
Dimensions, feet (metres): 77.4 × 20.9 × 4.9 (23.6 × 6.4 × 1.5)
Main machinery: 2 MWM 8-cyl diesels; 685 hp(m) (503 kW); 2 shafts
Speed, knots: 10.5. **Range, miles:** 700 at 10 kt
Complement: 7
Military lift: 60 tons or 50 troops

Comment: Built in 1964-67 but spent much of their time in reserve. Transferred from Germany in April 1991 and numbered ABM 20-30.
VERIFIED

LCM OA 21   9/1994, van Ginderen Collection

11 LCM + 29 LCVP + 12 LCP + 7 LCA

Displacement, tons: 56 full load
Dimensions, feet (metres): 56 × 14.4 × 3.9 (17 × 4.4 × 1.2)
Main machinery: 2 Gray Marine 64 HN9 diesels; 330 hp (264 kW); 2 shafts
Speed, knots: 10. **Range, miles:** 130 at 10 kt
Military lift: 30 tons

Comment: Details given are for the LCMs transferred from the USA in 1956-58. The LCVPs were also transferred from the USA 1956-71 and the remainder were built in Greece from 1977.
VERIFIED

MINE WARFARE FORCES

0 + 2 HUNT CLASS (MSC/MSH)

Name	No	Builders	Commissioned
— (ex-Berkeley)	— (ex-M 40)	Vosper Thornycroft	14 Jan 1988
— (ex-Bicester)	— (ex-M 36)	Vosper Thornycroft	20 Mar 1986

Displacement, tons: 750 full load
Dimensions, feet (metres): 187 wl; 197 oa × 32.8 × 9.5 (keel); 11.2 (screws) *(57; 60 × 10 × 2.9; 3.4)*
Main machinery: 2 Ruston-Paxman 9-59K Deltic diesels; 1,900 hp *(1.42 MW)*; 1 Deltic Type 9-55B diesel for pulse generator and auxiliary drive; 780 hp *(582 kW)*; 2 shafts; bow thruster
Speed, knots: 15 diesels; 8 hydraulic drive. **Range, miles:** 1,500 at 12 kt
Complement: 45 (5 officers)
Guns: 1 DES/MSI DS 30B 30 mm/75; 650 rds/min to 10 km *(5.4 n miles)* anti-surface; 3 km *(1.6 n miles)* anti-aircraft; weight of shell 0.36 kg.
2 Oerlikon/BMARC 20 mm GAM-CO1 (enhancement); 900 rds/min to 2 km.
2—7.62 mm MGs.
Countermeasures: MCM: 2 PAP 104/105 remotely controlled submersibles, MS 14 magnetic loop, Sperry MSSA Mk 1 Towed Acoustic Generator and conventional Mk 8 Oropesa sweeps.
Decoys: Outfit DLK; 2 Barricade Mk III; 6 sets of triple barrels per mounting.
2 Irvin Replica RF; passive decoys.
ESM: MEL Matilda UAR 1.
Combat data systems: CAAIS DBA 4 action data automation.
Radars: Navigation: Kelvin Hughes Type 1006; I-band.
Sonars: Plessey 193M Mod 1; hull-mounted; minehunting; 100/300 kHz.
Mil Cross mine avoidance sonar; hull-mounted; active; high frequency.
Type 2059 to track PAP 104/105.

Comment: Planned to pay off from UK Navy in mid-2000 (M 36) and early 2001 (M 40) and to transfer after short refits. Details given are as in UK service and there may be some changes.
NEW ENTRY

HUNT (UK colours)   *8/1999*, Harald Carstens /* 0079494

6 ADJUTANT CLASS
(MINESWEEPERS/HUNTERS—COASTAL) (MSC)

ATALANTI (ex-St Truiden M 919, ex-MSC 169) M 202 ERATO (ex-Castagno M 5504) M 60
FAIDRA (ex-Malmedy M 922, ex-MSC 154) M 206   EVNIKI (ex-Gelso M 5509) M 61
THALIA (ex-Blankenberge M 923, ex-MSC 170) M 210
NIOVI (ex-Laroche M 924, ex-MSC 171) M 254

Displacement, tons: 330 standard; 402 full load
Dimensions, feet (metres): 145 × 27.9 × 8 *(44.2 × 8.5 × 2.4)*
Main machinery: 2 GM 8-268A diesels; 880 hp *(656 kW)*; 2 shafts
Speed, knots: 14. **Range, miles:** 2,500 at 10 kt
Complement: 38 (4 officers)
Guns: 1 Oerlikon 20 mm.
Radars: Navigation: Decca or SMA 3RM 20R; I-band.
Sonars: SQQ-14 or UQS-1D; active; high frequency.

Comment: First four originally supplied by the USA to Belgium under MDAP; built in 1954 in the USA— M 202, M 210 and M 254 by Consolidated SB Corp, Morris Heights and M 206 by Hodgson Bros, Goudy and Stevens, East Booth Bay. Subsequently returned to the USA and simultaneously transferred to Greece as follows: 29 July 1969 *(St Truiden)* and 26 September 1969 *(Laroche, Malmedy and Blankenberge)*. Two more bought from Italy on 10 October 1995. M 60 and 61 are classed as minehunters.
UPDATED

EVNIKI   *6/1997*, J W Currie /* 0012477

FAIDRA   *8/1998, A Sharma /* 0052300

2 AKTION CLASS (COASTAL MINELAYERS) (MLC)

Name	No	Builders	Commissioned
AKTION (ex-LSM 301, ex-MMC 6)	N 04	Charleston Naval Shipyard	1 Jan 1945
AMVRAKIA (ex-LSM 303, ex-MMC 7)	N 05	Charleston Naval Shipyard	6 Jan 1945

Displacement, tons: 720 standard; 1,100 full load
Dimensions, feet (metres): 203.5 × 34.5 × 8.3 *(62.1 × 10.5 × 2.5)*
Main machinery: 2 GM 16-278A diesels; 3,000 hp *(2.24 MW)*; 2 shafts
Speed, knots: 12.5. **Range, miles:** 3,000 at 12 kt
Complement: 65
Guns: 8 Bofors 40 mm/60 (4 twin). 6 Oerlikon 20 mm.
Mines: Capacity 100-130; 2 rails.
Weapons control: 4 Mk 51 optical directors for 40 mm guns.
Radars: Navigation: Decca; I-band.

Comment: Former US 'LSM 1' class. N 04 was launched on 1 January 1945 and N 05 on 14 November 1944. Converted in the USA into minelayers for the Hellenic Navy. Underwent extensive rebuilding from the deck up. Twin rudders. Transferred on 1 December 1953.
UPDATED

AKTION   *7/1993*, van Ginderen Collection /* 0079495

8 ALKYON (MSC 294) CLASS (MINESWEEPERS—COASTAL) (MSC)

Name	No	Builders	Commissioned
ALKYON (ex-MSC 319)	M 211	Peterson Builders	3 Dec 1968
KLIO (ex-Argo, ex-MSC 317)	M 213	Peterson Builders	7 Aug 1968
AVRA (ex-MSC 318)	M 214	Peterson Builders	3 Oct 1968
AIDON (ex-MSC 314)	M 240	Peterson Builders	22 June 1967
KICHLI (ex-MSC 308)	M 241	Peterson Builders	14 July 1964
KISSA (ex-MSC 309)	M 242	Peterson Builders	1 Sep 1964
DAFNI (ex-MSC 307)	M 247	Peterson Builders	23 Sep 1964
PLEIAS (ex-MSC 310)	M 248	Peterson Builders	13 Oct 1964

Displacement, tons: 320 standard; 370 full load
Dimensions, feet (metres): 144 × 28 × 8.2 *(43.3 × 8.5 × 2.5)*
Main machinery: 2 GM-268A diesels; 1,760 hp *(1.3 MW)*; 2 shafts
Speed, knots: 13. **Range, miles:** 2,500 at 10 kt
Complement: 39 (4 officers)
Guns: 2 Oerlikon 20 mm (twin).
Radars: Navigation: Decca; I-band.
Sonars: UQS-1D; active; high frequency.

Comment: Built in the USA for Greece, wooden hulls. Modernisation programme from 1990 to 1995 with replacement main engines and navigation radar. New sonar under consideration but unlikely to be funded.
UPDATED

AVRA   *10/1999*, Diego Quevedo /* 0079496

SURVEY AND RESEARCH SHIPS

Name	No	Builders	Commissioned
HERMIS (ex-Oker, ex-Hoheweg)	A 373	Unterweser, Bremen	19 Oct 1960

Displacement, tons: 1,497 full load
Dimensions, feet (metres): 237.8 × 34.4 × 16.1 *(72.5 × 10.5 × 4.9)*
Main machinery: Diesel-electric: 1 KHD diesel; 1,800 hp(m) *(1.32 MW)*
1 KHD auxiliary diesel; 400 hp(m) *(294 kW)*; 1 shaft
Speed, knots: 15
Complement: 60 (10 officers)

Comment: First converted in 1972 to serve as an AGI in the West German Navy. Transferred 12 February 1988 and now based at Suda Bay. Serves as an AGI.
UPDATED

HERMIS   *9/1989*, Hellenic Navy /* 0079498

Name	No	Builders	Commissioned
NAFTILOS	A 478	Annastadiades Tsortanides, Perama	3 Apr 1976

Displacement, tons: 1,470 full load
Dimensions, feet (metres): 207 × 38 × 13.8 *(63.1 × 11.6 × 4.2)*
Main machinery: 2 Burmeister & Wain SS28LM diesels; 2,640 hp(m) *(1.94 MW)*; 2 shafts
Speed, knots: 15
Complement: 74 (8 officers)

Comment: Launched 19 November 1975. Of similar design to the two lighthouse tenders.
UPDATED

NAFTILOS   9/1999*, van Ginderen Collection / 0079497

Name	No	Builders	Commissioned
PYTHEAS	A 474	Annastadiades Tsortanides, Perama	15 Dec 1983

Displacement, tons: 670 standard; 840 full load
Dimensions, feet (metres): 164.7 × 31.5 × 21.6 *(50.2 × 9.6 × 6.6)*
Main machinery: 2 Detroit 12V-92TA diesels; 1,020 hp *(760 kW)* sustained; 2 shafts
Speed, knots: 14
Complement: 58 (8 officers)

Comment: *Pytheas* ordered in May 1982. Launched 19 September 1983. A similar ship, *Aegeon*, was constructed to Navy specification in 1984 but now belongs to the Maritime Research Institute.
VERIFIED

PYTHEAS   3/1998, M Verschaeve / 0052301

Name	No	Builders	Commissioned
STRABON	A 476	Emanuil-Maliris, Perama	27 Feb 1989

Displacement, tons: 252 full load
Dimensions, feet (metres): 107.3 × 20 × 8.2 *(32.7 × 6.1 × 2.5)*
Main machinery: 1 MAN D2842LE; 571 hp(m) *(420 kW)* sustained; 1 shaft
Speed, knots: 12.5
Complement: 20 (2 officers)

Comment: Ordered in 1987, launched September 1988. Used as coastal survey vessel.
UPDATED

STRABON   10/1994*, van Ginderen Collection / 0079499

OLYMPIAS

Dimensions, feet (metres): 121.4 × 17.1 × 4.9 *(37 × 5.2 × 1.5)*
Main machinery: 170 oars (85 each side in three rows)
Speed, knots: 8
Complement: 180

Comment: Construction started in 1985 and completed in 1987. Made of Oregon pine. Built for historic research and as a reminder of the naval hegemony of ancient Greeks. Part of the Hellenic Navy. Refit in 1992-93.
UPDATED

OLYMPIAS   6/1996*, Hellenic Navy / 0079500

TRAINING SHIPS

1 TRAINING SHIP (AX)

Name	No	Builders	Launched	Commissioned
ARIS	A 74	Salamis	4 Oct 1978	10 Jan 1980

Displacement, tons: 3,532 full load
Dimensions, feet (metres): 328 × 48.2 × 14.8 *(100 × 14.7 × 4.5)*
Main machinery: 2 MAK Mk 8 diesels; 10,000 hp(m) *(7.35 MW)*; 2 shafts
Speed, knots: 18
Complement: 500 (21 officers, up to 360 cadets)
Guns: 1 US 3 in *(76 mm)* Mk 26; 50 rds/min to 12 km *(6.5 n miles)*; weight of shell 6 kg.
    2 Bofors 40 mm/70 (twin); 300 rds/min to 12 km *(6.5 n miles)* anti-surface; 4 km *(2.2 n miles)* anti-aircraft; weight of shell 0.96 kg.
    2 Rheinmetall 20 mm. 2 Oerlikon 20 mm.
Radars: Surface search: 2 Racal Decca 1226C; I-band.
Helicopters: 1 Aerospatiale SA 319B Alouette III.

Comment: Laid down October 1976 at Salamis. Hangar reactivated in 1986. The 76 mm guns are mounted on sponsons forward of the funnel. Can be used as transport or hospital ship.
UPDATED

ARIS   7/1999*, van Ginderen Collection / 0079501

3 SAIL TRAINING CRAFT (AXS)

MAISTROS A 233   **SOROKOS** A 234   **OSTRIA** A 359

Displacement, tons: 12 full load (A 233 and 234)
Dimensions, feet (metres): 48.6 × 12.8 × 6.9 *(14.8 × 3.9 × 2.1)*

Comment: Sail training ships acquired in 1983-84 (A 233-234) and 1989 (A 359). A 359 is slightly smaller at 12.1 × 3.6 m.
VERIFIED

AUXILIARIES

2 FLOATING DOCK and 5 FLOATING CRANES

Comment: One floating dock is 45 m *(147.6 ft)* in length and has a 6,000 ton lift. Built at Eleusis with Swedish assistance and launched 5 May 1988; delivered 1989. The second is the ex-US AFDM 2 transferred in 1999. This dock was built in 1942 and has a 12,000 ton lift. The cranes were all built in Greece.
UPDATED

0 + 1 ETNA CLASS (AOR)

Name	No	Builders	Commissioned
—	—	Eleusis Shipyard	2004

Displacement, tons: 13,400 full load
Dimensions, feet (metres): 480.6 × 68.9 × 24.3 (146.5 × 21 × 7.4)
Flight deck, feet (metres): 91.9 × 68.9 (28 × 21)
Main machinery: 2 Sulzer 12 ZAV 40S diesels; 22,400 hp(m) (16.46 MW) sustained; 2 shafts; bow thruster
Speed, knots: 21. **Range, miles:** 7,600 at 18 kt
Complement: 160 plus 83 spare
Cargo capacity: 6,350 tons gas oil; 1,200 tons JP5; 2,100 m³ ammunition and stores
Guns: 1 OTO Melara 76 mm/62. 2 Breda Oerlikon 25 mm/93.
Radars: Surface search: SMA SPS-702(V)3; I-band.
Navigation: GEM SPN-753; I-band.
Helicopters: Aegean Hawk or 2 AB 212.

Comment: Ordered in August 1999 from Fincantieri and from Eleusis on 7 January 2000. Construction started in March 2000. Details given are for the ship in service in the Italian Navy and there may be some changes to the equipment fitted. There are two RAS stations on each side. *NEW ENTRY*

ETNA (Italian colours)   *5/1999*, Giorgio Ghiglione /* 0079502

2 LÜNEBURG (TYPE 701) CLASS (SUPPORT SHIPS) (AR/AOT)

Name	No	Builders	Commissioned	Recommissioned
AXIOS	A 464	Bremer Vulcan	9 July 1968	30 Sep 1991
(ex-*Coburg*)	(ex-A 1412)			
ALIAKMON	A 470	Blohm + Voss	30 July 1968	19 Oct 1994
(ex-*Saarburg*)	(ex-A 1415)			

Displacement, tons: 3,709 full load
Dimensions, feet (metres): 374.9 × 43.3 × 13.8 (114.3 × 13.2 × 4.2)
Main machinery: 2 MTU MD 16V 538 TB90 diesels; 6,000 hp(m) (4.41 MW) sustained; 2 shafts; cp props; bow thruster
Speed, knots: 17. **Range, miles:** 3,200 at 14 kt
Complement: 71
Cargo capacity: 640 tons fuel; 200 tons ammunition; 130 tons water
Guns: 4 Bofors 40 mm/70 (2 twin); 300 rds/min to 12 km (6.5 n miles); weight of shell 0.96 kg.
Radars: Navigation: Decca; I-band.

Comment: Both ships are being converted as Fleet oilers by Hellenic Shipyards. Contract signed 21 December 1999 and conversion is expected to complete by the end of 2000. *UPDATED*

ALIAKMON   *9/1995*, D Dervissis /* 0079503

2 PATAPSCO CLASS (SUPPORT TANKERS) (AOT)

Name	No	Builders	Commissioned
ARETHUSA (ex-*Natchaug* AOG 54)	A 377	Cargill Inc, Savage	11 June 1945
ARIADNE (ex-*Tombigbee* AOG 11)	A 414	Cargill Inc, Savage	12 July 1944

Displacement, tons: 1,850 light; 4,335 full load
Measurement, tons: 2,575 dwt
Dimensions, feet (metres): 292 wl; 310.8 oa × 48.5 × 15.7 (89.1; 94.8 × 14.8 × 4.8)
Main machinery: 2 GM 16-278A diesels; 3,000 hp (2.24 MW); 2 shafts
Speed, knots: 14
Complement: 43 (6 officers)
Cargo capacity: 2,040 tons fuel
Guns: 1 USN 3 in (76 mm)/50 Mk 26; 20 rds/min to 12 km (6.6 n miles); weight of shell 6 kg.
2 Rheinmetall 20 mm/85.
Weapons control: Mk 26 system for guns.
Radars: Surface search: Westinghouse SPS-5; G/H-band.
Navigation: Decca; I-band.

Comment: Former US petrol carriers. A 377 laid down on 15 August 1944. Launched on 16 December 1944. Transferred from the USA under the Mutual Defense Assistance Program in July 1959. A 414 transferred 7 July 1972 and sold 11 July 1978. Original armament much reduced. *VERIFIED*

ARETHUSA   *8/1998, A Sharma /* 0052303

4 OURANOS CLASS (AOTL)

Name	No	Builders	Commissioned
OURANOS	A 416	Kinosoura Shipyard	27 Jan 1977
HYPERION	A 417	Kinosoura Shipyard	27 Apr 1977
ZEUS	A 375 (ex-A 490)	Hellenic Shipyards	21 Feb 1989
ORION	A 376	Hellenic Shipyards	5 May 1989

Displacement, tons: 2,100 full load
Dimensions, feet (metres): 219.8; 198.2 (wl) × 32.8 × 13.8 (67; 60.4 × 10 × 4.2)
Main machinery: 1 MAN-Burmeister & Wain 12V 20/27 diesel; 1,632 hp(m) (1.2 MW) sustained; 1 shaft
Speed, knots: 11
Complement: 28
Cargo capacity: 1,300 tons oil or petrol
Guns: 2 Rheinmetall 20 mm.

Comment: First two are oil tankers. The others were ordered from Hellenic Shipyards, Skaramanga in December 1986 and are used as petrol tankers. There are some minor superstructure differences between the first two and the last two which have a forward crane instead of kingposts. *UPDATED*

ZEUS   *8/1999*, van Ginderen Collection /* 0079504

HYPERION   *5/1997*, E & M Laursen /* 0012480

6 WATER TANKERS (AWT)

KERKINI (ex-German *FW 3*) A 433   **TRICHONIS** (ex-German *FW 6*) A 466   **KALLIROE** A 468
PRESPA A 434   **DOIRANI** A 467   **STIMFALIA** A 469

Comment: All built between 1964 and 1990. Capacity, 600 tons except A 433 and A 466 which can carry 300 tons and A 469 which can carry 1,000 tons. Three in reserve. *Stimfalia* is similar to *Ouranos*. *VERIFIED*

TRICHONIS   *9/1998, M Declerck /* 0052302

1 NETLAYER (ANL)

Name	No	Builders	Commissioned
THETIS (ex-*AN 103*)	A 307	Kröger, Rendsburg	Apr 1960

Displacement, tons: 680 standard; 805 full load
Dimensions, feet (metres): 169.5 × 33.5 × 11.8 (51.7 × 10.2 × 3.6)
Main machinery: Diesel-electric; 1 MAN GTV-40/60 diesel generator; 1 motor; 1,470 hp(m) (1.08 MW); 1 shaft
Speed, knots: 12. **Range, miles:** 6,500 at 10 kt
Complement: 48 (5 officers)
Guns: 1 Bofors 40 mm/60. 3 Rheinmetall 20 mm.
Radars: Navigation: Decca; I-band.

Comment: US offshore order. Launched in 1959. Some guns not always embarked. *VERIFIED*

THETIS   *9/1998, A Sharma /* 0052305

1 AMMUNITION SHIP (AKF)

Name	No	Builders	Commissioned
EVROS (ex-Schwarzwald, ex-Amaltheé)	A 415	Ch Dubigeon Nantes	7 June 1956

Displacement, tons: 2,400 full load
Measurement, tons: 1,667 gross
Dimensions, feet (metres): 263.1 × 39 × 15.1 (80.2 × 11.9 × 4.6)
Main machinery: 1 Sulzer 6SD60 diesel; 3,000 hp(m) (2.2 MW); 1 shaft
Speed, knots: 15. **Range, miles:** 4,500 at 15 kt
Guns: 4 Bofors 40 mm/60.

Comment: Bought by FDR from Société Navale Caënnaise in February 1960. Transferred to Greece 6 June 1976.

VERIFIED

EVROS   1987, Hellenic Navy

2 AUXILIARY TRANSPORTS (AP)

Name	No	Builders	Commissioned
PANDORA	A 419	Perama Shipyard	26 Oct 1973
PANDROSOS	A 420	Perama Shipyard	1 Dec 1973

Displacement, tons: 390 full load
Dimensions, feet (metres): 153.5 × 27.2 × 6.2 (46.8 × 8.3 × 1.9)
Main machinery: 2 diesels; 2 shafts
Speed, knots: 12
Military lift: 500 troops
Radars: Navigation: Racal Decca; I-band.

Comment: Launched 1972 and 1973.

VERIFIED

PANDORA   5/1998, E & M Laursen / 0052306

4 TYPE 430A (TORPEDO RECOVERY VESSELS) (TRV)

EVROTAS (ex-TF 106) A 460 (ex-Y 872)   STRYMON (ex-TF 107) A 462 (ex-Y 873)
ARACHTHOS (ex-TF 108) A 461 (ex-Y 874)   NESTOS (ex-TF 4) A 463 (ex-Y 854)

Comment: First two acquired from Germany on 16 November 1989, second pair on 5 March 1991. Of about 56 tons with stern ramps for torpedo recovery. Built in 1966.

UPDATED

TYPE 430A (German colours)   6/1998, Michael Nitz / 0052255

2 LIGHTHOUSE TENDERS (ABU)

Name	No	Builders	Commissioned
I KARAVOYIANNOS THEOPHILOPOULOS	A 479	Perama Shipyard	17 Mar 1976
ST LIKOUDIS	A 481	Perama Shipyard	2 Jan 1976

Displacement, tons: 1,450 full load
Dimensions, feet (metres): 207.3 × 38 × 13.1 (63.2 × 11.6 × 4)
Main machinery: 1 Deutz MWM TBD5008UD diesel; 2,400 hp(m) (1.76 MW); 1 shaft
Speed, knots: 15
Complement: 40
Radars: Navigation: Racal Decca; I-band.
Helicopters: Platform for 1 light.

Comment: Similar to Naftilos, the survey ship.

UPDATED

I KARAVOYIANNOS THEOPHILOPOULOS   1/1999*, van Ginderen Collection / 0064674

TUGS

22 HARBOUR TUGS (YTM/YTL)

Name	No	Commissioned
ANTAIOS (ex-Busy YTM 2012)	A 407	1947
ATLAS (ex-Mediator)	A 408	1944
ACCHILEUS (ex-Confident)	A 409	1947
ATROMITOS-NIKIFOROS	A 410	1968
ADAMASTOS	A 411	1968
AIAS (ex-Ankachak YTM 767)	A 412	1972
PILEFS (ex-German)	A 413	1991
KADMOS (ex-US)	A 422	1989
CYCLOPS	A 426	1947
DANAOS (ex-US)	A 427	1989
NESTOR (ex-US)	A 428	1989
PERSEUS	A 429	1989
PELOPS	A 430	1989
TITAN	A 431	1962
GIGAS	A 432	1961
KEKROPS	A 435	1989
MINOS (ex-German)	A 436	1991
PELIAS (ex-German)	A 437	1991
AEGEUS (ex-German)	A 438	1991
ATREFS (ex-Ellerbek)	A 439	1971
DIOMIDIS (ex-Neuwerk)	A 440	1963
THESEUS (ex-Heppens)	A 441	2000

Comment: Some may be armed.

UPDATED

NESTOR   9/1998*, M Declerck / 0064675

PELIAS   1/2000*, A Sharma / 0064676

3 COASTAL TUGS (ATA)

HERAKLIS A 423   **IASON** A 424   **ODISSEUS** A 425

Displacement, tons: 345 full load
Dimensions, feet (metres): 98.5 × 26 × 11.3 *(30 × 7.9 × 3.4)*
Main machinery: 1 Deutz MWM diesel; 1,200 hp(m) *(882 kW)*; 1 shaft
Speed, knots: 12

Comment: Laid down 1977 at Perama Shipyard. Commissioned 6 April, 6 March and 28 June 1978 respectively.

UPDATED

IASON (with *Gigas*)   *8/1997*, A Sharma / 0012482*

COAST GUARD (Limenikon Soma)

Senior Officers

Commander-in-Chief:
  Vice Admiral T Papakonstantinou
Deputy Commanders-in-Chief:
  Rear Admiral N Kypriadakis
  Rear Admiral A Syrigos

Personnel

2000: 4,000 (1,055 officers)

Bases

HQ: Piraeus
Main bases: Piraeus, Eleusis, Thessalonika, Volos, Patra, Corfu, Rhodes, Mytilene, Heraklion (Crete), Chios, Kavala, Chalcis, Igoumenitsa, Rafina
Minor bases: Every port and island of Greece

Ships and Craft

In general very similar in appearance to naval ships, being painted grey. Since 1990 pennant numbers have been painted white and on both sides of the hull they carry a blue and white band with two crossed anchors. From 1993 ships have been given grey hulls and white superstructures.

General

This force consists of about 150 patrol craft and anti-pollution vessels including 24 inflatables for the 48 men Underwater Missions Squad and 12 anti-pollution vessels. Administration in peacetime is by the Ministry of Merchant Marine. In wartime it would be transferred to naval command.
Officers are trained at the Naval Academy and ratings at two special schools.
The pennant numbers are all preceded as in the accompanying photographs by Greek 'Lambda Sigma' for Limenikon Soma.

Pennant Numbers

OPV: 010-090   FPB: 101-199   FPO: 210-299

Duties

The policing of all Greek harbours, coasts and territorial waters, navigational safety, SAR operations, anti-pollution surveillance and operations, supervision of port authorities, merchant navy training, inspection of Greek merchant ships worldwide.

Coast Guard Air Service

In October 1981 the Coast Guard acquired two Cessna Cutlass 172 RG aircraft and in July 1988 two Socata TB 20s. Maintenance and training by the Air Force. Based at Dekelia air base. Four Eurocopter Super Pumas AS 322C1 ordered in August 1998. First pair delivered in December 1999, second pair in May 2000. Being operated by mixed Air Force and Coast Guard crews. Bendix radar fitted. Three Reims Cessna Vigilant aircraft ordered in July 1999.

4 DILOS CLASS

LS 010-040 (ex-*80-83*)

Displacement, tons: 86 full load
Dimensions, feet (metres): 95.1 × 16.2 × 5.6 *(29 × 5 × 1.7)*
Main machinery: 2 MTU 12V 331 TC92 diesels; 2,660 hp(m) *(1.96 MW)* sustained; 2 shafts
Speed, knots: 27. **Range, miles:** 1,600 at 24 kt
Complement: 18
Guns: 2 Rheinmetall 20 mm.
Radars: Surface search: Racal Decca 1226C; I-band.

Comment: Same Abeking and Rasmussen design as the three naval craft and built at Hellenic Shipyards in the early 1980s. Three more of the class are in service with Customs.   *UPDATED*

LS 030   *1/1999*, van Ginderen Collection / 0064677*

44 COLVIC CRAFT

LS 114-LS 119   **LS 121-LS 123**   **LS 125-LS 158**

Displacement, tons: 24 full load
Dimensions, feet (metres): 54.1 × 15.4 × 4.6 *(16.5 × 4.7 × 1.4)*
Main machinery: 2 MAN D2840 LE 401 diesels; 1,644 hp(m) *(1.21 MW)* sustained; 2 shafts
Speed, knots: 34. **Range, miles:** 500 at 25 kt
Complement: 5 (1 officer)
Guns: 1—12.7 mm MG. 1—7.62 mm MG.
Radars: Surface search: Raytheon; I-band.

Comment: Ordered from Colvic Craft, Colchester in 1993. Shipped to Motomarine, Glifada for engine and electronics installation. First 12 completed in mid-1994. The remainder delivered at about 12 per year from 1995. GRP hulls with a stern platform for recovery of divers. Two have been lost in accidents.   *UPDATED*

LS 125   *6/1996*, Motomarine / 0064678*

3 COMBATBOAT 90H

LS 135-LS 137

Displacement, tons: 19 full load
Dimensions, feet (metres): 52.2 × 12.5 × 2.6 *(15.9 × 3.8 × 0.8)*
Main machinery: 2 Volvo Penta TAMD 163P diesels; 1,500 hp(m) *(1.1 MW)*; 2 waterjets
Speed, knots: 45. **Range, miles:** 240 at 30 kt
Complement: 3
Guns: 3—12.7 mm MGs.
Radars: Surface search: I-band.

Comment: Built by Dockstavarvet in Sweden and delivered 6 July 1998. Same design as Swedish naval craft but with more powerful engines.   *VERIFIED*

LS 135   *9/1998, van Ginderen Collection / 0052310*

13 OL 44 CLASS

LS 101-113

Displacement, tons: 14 full load
Dimensions, feet (metres): 44.9 × 14.4 × 2 *(13.7 × 4.4 × 0.6)*
Main machinery: 2 diesels; 630 hp(m) *(463 kW)*; 2 shafts
Speed, knots: 23
Complement: 4
Guns: 1—7.62 mm MG.
Radars: Surface search: JRC; I-band.

Comment: Built by Olympic Marine. GRP hulls.   *VERIFIED*

LS 110   *10/1998, Diego Quevedo / 0052311*

12 LS 51 CLASS

LS 151-LS 155   LS 158-LS 164

Displacement, tons: 13 full load
Dimensions, feet (metres): 44 × 11.5 × 3.3 *(13.4 × 3.5 × 1)*
Main machinery: 2 diesels; 630 hp(m) *(463 kW)*; 2 shafts
Speed, knots: 25. **Range, miles:** 400 at 18 kt
Complement: 4
Guns: 1—7.62 mm MG.
Radars: Surface search: Racal Decca; I-band.

Comment: Built by Olympic Marine. GRP hulls.

VERIFIED

LS 161   *6/1998, E M Cornish /* 0052312

60 COASTAL CRAFT and 22 CRISS CRAFT

Comment: Included in the total are 20 of 8.2 m, 17 of 7.9 m, 26 of 5.8 m and 19 ex-US Criss craft. In addition the Coast Guard operates 24 Inflatable craft, and 10 SAR craft *(LS 509-518)*.
UPDATED

LS 166   *1/1999*, van Ginderen Collection /* 0064679

0 + 2 SLINGSBY SAM 2200 (HOVERCRAFT)

Displacement, tons: 5.5 full load
Dimensions, feet (metres): 34.8 × 13.8 *(10.6 × 4.2)*
Main machinery: 1 diesel; 300 hp(m) *(224 kW)*
Speed, knots: 40. **Range, miles:** 400 at 30 kt
Complement: 2
Military lift: 2.2 tons
Guns: 1—12.7 mm MG.
Radars: Surface search: I-band.

Comment: Ordered in September 1999 for delivery by mid-2000.

NEW ENTRY

4 POLLUTION CONTROL SHIPS

LS 413-415   LS 401

Displacement, tons: 230 full load
Dimensions, feet (metres): 95.1 × 20.3 × 8.2 *(29 × 6.2 × 2.5)*
Main machinery: 2 CAT 3512 DITA diesels; 2,560 hp(m) *(1.88 MW)* sustained; 2 shafts
Speed, knots: 15. **Range, miles:** 500 at 13 kt
Complement: 12
Radars: Navigation: Furuno; I-band.

Comment: Details given are for *LS 413-415*. Built by Astilleros Gondan, Spain in collaboration with Motomarine. Delivered in 1993-94. *LS 401* is an older pollution control ship.
UPDATED

LS 413   *10/1996*, van Ginderen Collection /* 0012487

CUSTOMS

Note: The Customs service also operates large numbers of coastal and inshore patrol craft including 3 'Dilos' class with the same characteristics as the Coast Guard. The craft have a distinctive Alpha Lambda (A/Λ) on the hull and are sometimes armed with 7.62 mm MGs.

DILOS AL 16   *9/1997*, van Ginderen Collection /* 0012486

1 VOSPER EUROPATROL 250 Mk 1

AL 50

Displacement, tons: 240 full load
Dimensions, feet (metres): 155.2 × 24.6 × 7.9 *(47.3 × 7.5 × 2.4)*
Main machinery: 3 GEC/Paxman Valenta 16CM diesels; 13,328 hp(m) *(9.8 MW)*; 3 shafts
Speed, knots: 40. **Range, miles:** 2,000 at 16 kt
Complement: 21
Radars: Surface search: Racal Decca; I-band.

Comment: Ordered from McTay Marine, Bromborough in July 1993 and completed in November 1994. This is a Vosper International design with a steel hull and aluminium superstructure. Replenishment at sea facilities are provided by light jackstay and the ship carries a 45 kt RIB with water-jet propulsion. A continuous patrol speed of 4 kt is achievable using the centre shaft. Air conditioned accommodation. Similar craft built for the Bahamas. Fitted for a 40 mm gun but this is not carried.
UPDATED

AL 50   *11/1994*, McTay Marine /* 0064680

GRENADA

Headquarters Appointments	**Bases**	**Mercantile Marine**
Coast Guard Commander: Superintendent Charles	Prickly Bay (main), St George, Grenville, Hillsborough	*Lloyd's Register of Shipping:* 6 vessels of 1,009 tons gross
Personnel	**General**	
2000: 60	Coast Guard craft are operated under the direction of the Commissioner of Police.	

COAST GUARD

1 GUARDIAN CLASS (COASTAL PATROL CRAFT) (PC)

Name	No	Builders	Commissioned
TYRREL BAY	PB 01	Lantana, Florida	21 Nov 1984

Displacement, tons: 90 full load
Dimensions, feet (metres): 105 × 20.6 × 7 *(32 × 6.3 × 2.1)*
Main machinery: 3 Detroit 12V-71TA diesels; 1,260 hp *(939 kW)* sustained; 3 shafts
Speed, knots: 24. **Range, miles:** 1,500 at 18 kt
Complement: 15 (2 officers)
Guns: 2—12.7 mm MGs. 2—7.62 mm MGs.
Radars: Surface search: Furuno 1411 Mk II; I-band.

Comment: Similar to Jamaican and Honduras vessels. Refit in 1995/96.

UPDATED

LEVERA   *9/1995*, SeaArk Marine /* 0064683

2 BOSTON WHALERS (PB)

Displacement, tons: 1.3 full load
Dimensions, feet (metres): 22.3 × 7.4 × 1.2 *(6.7 × 2.3 × 0.4)*
Main machinery: 2 outboards; 240 hp *(179 kW)*
Speed, knots: 40+
Complement: 4
Guns: 1—12.7 mm MG.

Comment: Acquired in 1988-89.

UPDATED

TYRREL BAY   *11/1990*, Bob Hanlon /* 0064681

1 DAUNTLESS CLASS (PB)

Name	No	Builders	Commissioned
LEVERA	PB 02	SeaArk Marine	8 Sep 1995

Displacement, tons: 11 full load
Dimensions, feet (metres): 40 × 14 × 4.3 *(12.2 × 4.3 × 1.3)*
Main machinery: 2 Caterpillar 3208TA diesels; 870 hp *(650 kW)* sustained; 2 shafts
Speed, knots: 27. **Range, miles:** 600 at 18 kt
Complement: 5
Guns: 1—7.62 mm MG.
Radars: Surface search: Raytheon R40X; I-band.

Comment: One of many of this type, provided by the USA, throughout the Caribbean navies.

UPDATED

BOSTON WHALER   *11/1990*, Bob Hanlon /* 0064682

GUATEMALA

Headquarters Appointments	Personnel	Bases	Mercantile Marine
Commander Caribbean Naval Region: Captain Alfredo Herrera Cabrera *Commander Pacific Naval Region:* Captain Julio Alberto Yon Rivera	(a) 2000: 1,250 (130 officers) including 650 Marines (2 battalions) (mostly volunteers) (b) 2¼ years' national service	Santo Tomás de Castillas (Caribbean); Sipacate and Puerto Quetzal (Pacific)	*Lloyd's Register of Shipping:* 8 vessels of 4,561 tons gross

PATROL FORCES

Notes: (1) There is also a naval manned Ferry *15 de Enero* (T 691) and a 69 ft launch *Orca* which was built locally in 1996/97.
(2) A 'Dauntless' class patrol craft name *Iximche* planned for delivery in 1997, may have been cancelled.

1 BROADSWORD CLASS (COASTAL PATROL CRAFT) (PCF)

Name	No	Builder	Commissioned
KUKULKÁN	GC 1051 (ex-P 1051)	Halter Marine	4 Aug 1976

Displacement, tons: 90.5 standard; 110 full load
Dimensions, feet (metres): 105 × 20.4 × 6.3 *(32 × 6.2 × 1.9)*
Main machinery: 2 Detroit 8V 92TA Model 91; 1,300 hp *(970 kW)*; 2 shafts
Speed, knots: 22. **Range, miles:** 1,150 at 20 kt
Complement: 20 (5 officers)
Guns: 2 Oerlikon GAM/204 GK 20 mm. 2—7.62 mm MGs.
Radars: Surface search: Furuno; I-band.

Comment: As the flagship she used to rotate between Pacific and Atlantic bases every two years but has remained in the Pacific since 1989. Rearmed with 20 mm guns in 1989. These were replaced by GAM guns in 1990-91 when the ship received a new radar. Refitted again in 1996 with new engines.

VERIFIED

2 SEWART CLASS (COASTAL PATROL CRAFT) (PC)

Name	No	Builders	Commissioned
UTATLAN	GC 851 (ex-P 851)	Sewart, Louisiana	May 1967
SUBTENIENTE OSORIO SARAVIA	GC 852 (ex-P 852)	Sewart, Louisiana	Nov 1972

Displacement, tons: 54 full load
Dimensions, feet (metres): 85 × 18.7 × 7.2 *(25.9 × 5.7 × 2.2)*
Main machinery: 2 Detroit 8V 92TA Model 91; 1,300 hp *(970 kW)*; 2 shafts
Speed, knots: 22. **Range, miles:** 400 at 12 kt
Complement: 17 (4 officers)
Guns: 2 Oerlikon GAM/204 GK 20 mm. 2—7.62 mm MGs.
Radars: Surface search: Furuno; I-band.

Comment: Aluminium superstructure. Both rearmed with 20 mm guns, and 75 mm recoilless removed in 1990. P 851 is based in the Atlantic; P 852 in the Pacific. Refitted in 1995-96 with new engines.

VERIFIED

KUKULKÁN   *2/1998 /* 0052314

SUBTENIENTE OSORIO SARAVIA   *2/1998 /* 0052315

6 CUTLASS CLASS
(5 COASTAL PATROL CRAFT AND 1 SURVEY CRAFT) (PC)

Name	No	Builders	Commissioned
TECUN UMAN	GC 651 (ex-P 651)	Halter Marine	26 Nov 1971
KAIBIL BALAM	GC 652 (ex-P 652)	Halter Marine	8 Feb 1972
AZUMANCHE	GC 653 (ex-P 653)	Halter Marine	8 Feb 1972
TZACOL	GC 654 (ex-P 654)	Halter Marine	10 Mar 1976
BITOL	GC 655 (ex-P 655)	Halter Marine	4 Aug 1976
GUCUMAZ	GC-H-656 (ex-BH 656)	Halter Marine	15 May 1981

Displacement, tons: 45 full load
Dimensions, feet (metres): 64.5 × 17 × 3 *(19.7 × 5.2 × 0.9)*
Main machinery: 2 Detroit 8V 92TA Model 91 diesels; 1,300 hp *(970 kW)*; 2 shafts
Speed, knots: 25. **Range, miles:** 400 at 15 kt
Complement: 10 (2 officers)
Guns: 2 Oerlikon GAM/204 GK 20 mm. 2 or 3—12.7 mm MGs.
Radars: Surface search: Furuno; I-band.

Comment: First five rearmed with 20 mm guns in 1991. P 651, 654 and 655 are in the Atlantic, remainder in the Pacific. Aluminium hulls. *Gucumaz* was used as a survey craft but by 1996 was again serving as a patrol craft with three MGs. 654 and 656 refitted in 1994-95, remainder in 1995-97. New engines fitted.

UPDATED

BITOL   *12/1997, A Campanera i Rovira / 0052316*

GUCUMAZ   *2/1999* / 0064684*

6 VIGILANTE CLASS (PB)

GC 271-276

Displacement, tons: 3.5 full load
Dimensions, feet (metres): 26.6 × 10 × 1.8 *(8.1 × 3 × 0.5)*
Main machinery: 2 Evinrude outboards; 600 hp *(448 kW)*
Speed, knots: 40+
Complement: 4
Guns: 1—12.7 mm MG.
Radars: Surface search: Furuno; I-band.

Comment: Ordered in 1993 from Boston Whaler. Delivered in 1994 and divided three to each coast.

UPDATED

GC 273   *2/1996*, Julio Montes / 0064685*

20 RIVER PATROL CRAFT (PBR)

Group A	Group B	Group C	Group D
DENEB	LAGO DE ATITLAN	CHOCHAB	MERO
SIRIUS	MAZATENANGO	ALIOTH	SARDINA
PROCYON	RETALHULEU	MIRFA	PAMPANA
VEGA	ESCUINTLA	SCHEDAR	MAVRO-I
POLUX		COMAMEFA	
SPICA			
STELLA MARIS			

Comment: Group A are wooden hull craft with a speed of 19 kt. Group B have aluminium hulls and a speed of 28 kt. Group C are probably of Israeli design and Group D are commerical craft caught smuggling and confiscated. All can be armed with 7.62 mm MGs and are used by Marine battalions as well as the Navy.

UPDATED

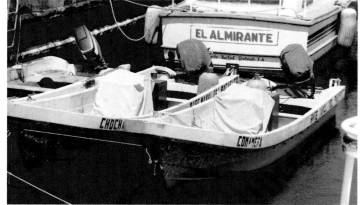

COMAMEFA   *2/1996*, Julio Montes / 0064686*

GUINEA

Personnel	Mercantile Marine	Bases	DELETIONS
(a) 2000: 400 officers and men	*Lloyd's Register of Shipping:*	Conakry, Kakanda	**Note:** These craft are all laid up alongside in various states of decay.
(b) 2 years' conscript service	31 vessels of 10,653 tons gross		

1997-98   3 Bogomol, 2 Zhuk, 2 Stinger
1999   *Vigilante, Intrepide*

GUINEA-BISSAU

Personnel	Base	Maritime Aircraft	Mercantile Marine	DELETIONS
(a) 2000: 350 officers and men	Bissau	A Cessna 337 patrol aircraft is used for offshore surveillance, when serviceable.	*Lloyd's Register of Shipping:* 24 vessels of 6,350 tons gross	1997-98 1 Kondor I, 1 Bogomol, 1 SDB Mk 3
(b) Voluntary service				

PATROL FORCES

1 PETERSON MK 4 CLASS (PC)

Name	No	Builders	Commissioned
ILHA DE CAIO	LF 03	Peterson Builders, WI	22 Oct 1993

Displacement, tons: 22 full load
Dimensions, feet (metres): 51.3 × 14.8 × 4.3 *(15.6 × 4.5 × 1.3)*
Main machinery: 2 Detroit 6V-92TA diesels; 520 hp *(358 kW)* sustained; 2 shafts
Speed, knots: 24. **Range, miles:** 500 at 20 kt
Complement: 6
Guns: 2—12.7 mm MGs (twin). 2—7.62 mm MGs (twin).
Radars: Surface search: Furuno; I-band.

Comment: Similar to craft built for Egypt, Cape Verde, Senegal and Gambia. Carries an RIB.
UPDATED

2 ALFEITE TYPE (COASTAL PATROL CRAFT) (PC)

Name	No	Builders	Commissioned
CACINE	LF 01	Arsenal do Alfeite	9 Mar 1994
CACHEU	LF 02	Arsenal do Alfeite	9 Mar 1994

Displacement, tons: 55 full load
Dimensions, feet (metres): 64.6 × 19 × 10.6 *(19.7 × 5.8 × 3.2)*
Main machinery: 3 MTU 12V 183 TE92 diesels; 3,000 hp(m) *(2.2 MW)* maximum; 3 Hamilton MH 521 water-jets
Speed, knots: 28
Complement: 9 (1 officer)
Radars: Navigation: Furuno FR 2010; I-band.

Comment: Ordered from Portugal in 1991. GRP hulls. Used for fishery protection patrols and are the only vessels regularly reported at sea.
UPDATED

PETERSON Mk 4 (US colours)   *1993*, Peterson Builders /* 0064687

CACHEU   *3/1994*, Arsenal do Alfeite /* 0064688

GUYANA

Headquarters Appointments	Personnel	Bases	General	Mercantile Marine
Commanding Officer, Coast Guard: Lieutenant Commander B Best	(a) 2000: 30 plus 160 reserves (b) Voluntary service	Georgetown, Benab (Corentyne)	All craft were non-operational by late 1998. No change since then.	*Lloyd's Register of Shipping:* 61 vessels of 14,030 tons gross

HAITI

General	Personnel	Bases	Mercantile Marine
The Defence Force has been abolished. All craft are derelict except for four 28 kt Boston Whalers provided by the US in 1996 for the Coast Guard. All four were refitted in Miami in 1999.	2000: 40	Main: Port Au Prince Secondary: Les Cayes, Port de Paix	*Lloyd's Register of Shipping:* 4 vessels of 1,172 tons gross

HONDURAS
FUERZA NAVAL REPUBLICA

Personnel	Bases	Mercantile Marine	DELETIONS
2000: 900 including 350 marines	Puerto Cortés (Atlantic HQ), Amapala (Pacific HQ), Puerto Castilla, La Ceiba, Puerto Trujillo, Teguiligalpa	*Lloyd's Register of Shipping:* 1,551 vessels of 1,219,554 tons gross	1997 *Chamelecon*

PATROL FORCES

Note: In addition there may be three Piranha river craft still in limited service.

3 SWIFT 105 ft CLASS (FAST ATTACK CRAFT—GUN) (PCF)

GUAYMURAS FNH 101   **HONDURAS** FNH 102   **HIBUERAS** FNH 103

Displacement, tons: 111 full load
Dimensions, feet (metres): 105 × 20.6 × 7 *(32 × 6.3 × 2.1)*
Main machinery: 2 MTU 16V 538 TB90 diesels; 6,000 hp(m) *(4.4 MW)* sustained; 2 shafts
Speed, knots: 30. **Range, miles:** 1,200 at 18 kt
Complement: 17 (3 officers)
Guns: 6 Hispano-Suiza 20 mm (2 triple). 2—12.7 mm MGs.
Weapons control: Kollmorgen 350 optronic director.
Radars: Surface search: Furuno; I-band.

Comment: First delivered by Swiftships, Morgan City in April 1977 and last two in March 1980. Aluminium hulls. Armament changed 1996-98.
UPDATED

HONDURAS   *4/1991* /* 0064689

2 GUARDIAN CLASS (COASTAL PATROL CRAFT) (PC)

COPAN FNH 106   **TEGUCIGALPA** FNH 107

Displacement, tons: 94 full load
Dimensions, feet (metres): 106 × 20.6 × 7 *(32.3 × 6.3 × 2.1)*
Main machinery: 3 Detroit 16V-92TA diesels; 2,070 hp *(1.54 MW)* sustained; 3 shafts
Speed, knots: 30. **Range, miles:** 1,500 at 18 kt
Complement: 17 (3 officers)
Guns: 1 General Electric Sea Vulcan 20 mm Gatling.
    3 Hispano Suiza 20 mm (1 triple). 2—12.7 mm MGs.
Weapons control: Kollmorgen 350 optronic director.
Radars: Surface search: Furuno; I-band.

Comment: Delivered by Lantana Boatyard, Florida in January 1983 and August 1986. A third of the class, completed in May 1984, became the Jamaican *Paul Bogle*. Aluminium hulls.   ***VERIFIED***

COPAN   *7/1986, Giorgio Arra*

5 SWIFT 65 ft CLASS (COASTAL PATROL CRAFT) (PC)

NACAOME (ex-*Aguan*, ex-*Gral*) FNH 651   **ULUA** FNH 654
GOASCORAN (ex-*General J T Cabanas*) FNH 652   **CHOLUTECA** FNH 655
PETULA FNH 653

Displacement, tons: 33 full load
Dimensions, feet (metres): 69.9 × 17.1 × 5.2 *(21.3 × 5.2 × 1.6)*
Main machinery: 2 GM 12V-71TA diesels; 840 hp *(627 kW)* sustained; 2 shafts (FNH 651-2)
    2 MTU 8V 396 TB93 diesels; 2,180 hp(m) *(1.6 MW)* sustained; 2 shafts (FNH 653-5)
Speed, knots: 25 (FNH 651-2); 36 (FNH 653-5). **Range, miles:** 2,000 at 22 kt (FNH 651-2)
Complement: 9 (2 officers)
Guns: 1 Oerlikon 20 mm. 2—12.7 mm (twin) MGs. 2—7.62 MGs.
Radars: Surface search: Racal Decca; I-band.

Comment: First pair built by Swiftships, Morgan City originally for Haiti. Contract cancelled and Honduras bought the two that had been completed in 1973-74. Delivered in 1977. Last three ordered in 1979 and delivered 1980.   ***UPDATED***

PETULA   *5/1993*, / 0064690*

10 OUTRAGE CLASS (RIVER PATROL CRAFT) (PBR)

Displacement, tons: 2.2 full load
Dimensions, feet (metres): 24.9 × 7.9 × 1.3 *(7.6 × 2.4 × 0.4)*
Main machinery: 2 Evinrude outboards; 300 hp *(224 kW)*
Speed, knots: 30. **Range, miles:** 200 at 30 kt
Complement: 4
Guns: 1—12.7 mm MG. 2—7.62 mm MGs.
Radars: Navigation: Furuno 3600; I-band.

Comment: Built by Boston Whaler in 1982. Two deleted so far. Radar is sometimes embarked.   ***UPDATED***

OUTRAGE   *10/1997*, Julio Montes / 0012491*

12 RIVER CRAFT (PBR)

Comment: Acquired from Taiwan in 1996. Four based at Castilla, two at Cortes, three at Amapala and the remainder at Teguiligalpa. Single Mercury outboard engine. Carry a 7.62 mm MG. Three sunk in 1998.   ***UPDATED***

PBR   *10/1997*, R Torrento / 0012492*

AUXILIARIES

Note: In addition there are three ex-US LCM 8 (*Warunta* FNH 7401, *Tansin* FNH 7402, *Caratasca* FNH 7403) transferred in 1987, and six ex-Fishing Boats (*Juliana* FNH 7501, *San Rafael* FNH 7502, *Carmen* FNH 7503, *Mairy* FNH 7504, *Yosuro* FNH 7505, *Gregori* FNH 7506). All are used as transport vessels.

1 HOLLYHOCK CLASS (BUOY TENDER) (ABU)

YOJOA (ex-*Walnut*) FNH 252

Displacement, tons: 989 full load
Dimensions, feet (metres): 175.2 × 34.1 × 12.1 *(53.4 × 10.4 × 3.7)*
Main machinery: 2 diesels; 1,350 hp *(1 MW)*; 2 shafts
Speed, knots: 12. **Range, miles:** 6,500 at 12 kt
Complement: 40 (4 officers)

Comment: Transferred from USA in July 1982. Built by Moore Drydock Co, Maryland, and completed 27 June 1939. Has a 20 ton crane.   ***UPDATED***

YOJOA   *8/1989*, / 0064692*

1 LANDING CRAFT (LCU)

PUNTA CAXINAS FNH 1491

Displacement, tons: 625 full load
Dimensions, feet (metres): 149 × 33 × 6.5 *(45.4 × 10 × 2)*
Main machinery: 3 Caterpillar 3412 diesels; 1,821 hp *(1.4 MW)* sustained; 3 shafts
Speed, knots: 14. **Range, miles:** 3,500 at 12 kt
Complement: 18 (3 officers)
Cargo capacity: 100 tons equipment or 50,000 gallons dieso plus 4 standard containers
Radars: Navigation: Furuno 3600; I-band.

Comment: Ordered in 1986 from Lantana, Florida, and commissioned in May 1988.   ***UPDATED***

PUNTA CAXINAS   *6/1997*, / 0064691*

HONG KONG
POLICE MARINE REGION

Headquarters Appointments

Regional Commander:
 Foo Tsun-Kong
Deputy Regional Commander:
 Ng Chee-Kin
Chief Superintendent, Marine Region:
 Au Hok-Lam

Organisation

Marine Police Regional HQ, Sai Wan Ho
Bases at Ma Liu Shui, Tui Min Hoi, Tai Lam Chung, Aberdeen, Sai Wan Ho

General

All the listed craft are operated by the Marine Region of the Hong Kong Police Force. This is a Coast Guard Force responsible for maintaining the integrity of the sea boundary and territorial waters of Hong Kong, enforcing the laws of Hong Kong in territorial waters, prevention of illegal immigration by sea, SAR in territorial and adjacent waters, and casualty evacuation. The role of the Marine Police has not been affected by the change of sovereignty to China in July 1997.

Personnel

(a) 2000: 2,600
(b) Voluntary service

Mercantile Marine

Lloyd's Register of Shipping:
 479 vessels of 7,972,555 tons gross

DELETIONS

1997 *PV 30-37, PV 10-12*
1999 *PL 57-PL 59*

POLICE

Note: The naming of new craft was discontinued in 1999.

2 COMMAND VESSELS (PC)

SEA PANTHER PL 3   **SEA HORSE** PL 4

Displacement, tons: 420 full load
Dimensions, feet (metres): 131.2 × 28.2 × 10.5 *(40 × 8.6 × 3.2)*
Main machinery: 2 Caterpillar 3512TA diesels; 2,420 hp *(1.81 MW)* sustained; 2 shafts
Speed, knots: 14. **Range, miles:** 1,500 at 14 kt
Complement: 33
Radars: Surface search: 2 Racal Decca ARPA C342/8; I-band.

Comment: Built by Hong Kong SY, PL 3 completed 27 July 1987, PL 4 on 29 September 1987. Both commissioned 1 February 1988. Steel hulls. Racal Cane command system replaced by ARPA and GPS Electronic Chart system because of withdrawal of Hyperfix. 12.7 mm MGs removed in mid-1997. Can carry up to 30 armed police for short periods.   *UPDATED*

SEA PANTHER   *6/1993*, Hong Kong Police /* 0064693

14 DAMEN Mk III CLASS (PATROL CRAFT) (PC)

KING LAI PL 70	**KING DAI** PL 74	**KING CHI** PL 78	**KING YAN** PL 82
KING YEE PL 71	**KING CHUNG** PL 75	**KING TAI** PL 79	**KING YUNG** PL 83
KING LIM PL 72	**KING SHUN** PL 76	**KING KWAN** PL 80	**KING KAN** PL 84
KING HAU PL 73	**KING TAK** PL 77		

Displacement, tons: 95 full load
Dimensions, feet (metres): 87 × 19 × 6 *(26.5 × 5.8 × 1.8)*
Main machinery: 2 MTU 12V 396 TC82 diesels; 2,610 hp(m) *(1.92 MW)* sustained; 2 shafts
 1 Mercedes-Benz OM 424A 12V diesel; 341 hp(m) *(251 kW)* sustained; 1 Kamewa 45 water-jet
Speed, knots: 26 on 3 diesels; 8 on water-jet and cruising diesel. **Range, miles:** 600 at 14 kt
Complement: 17
Radars: Surface search: Racal Decca; I-band.

Comment: Steel-hulled craft constructed by Chung Wah SB & Eng Co Ltd, 1984-85. 12.7 mm MGs removed in mid-1997.   *UPDATED*

KING HAU   *11/1996*, Hong Kong Police /* 0064695

6 PROTECTOR (ASI 315) CLASS
(COMMAND/PATROL CRAFT) (PC)

PROTECTOR PL 51	**DEFENDER** PL 53	**RESCUER** PL 55
GUARDIAN PL 52	**PRESERVER** PL 54	**DETECTOR** PL 56

Displacement, tons: 170 full load
Dimensions, feet (metres): 107 × 26.9 × 5.2 *(32.6 × 8.2 × 1.6)*
Main machinery: 2 Caterpillar 3516TA diesels; 4,400 hp *(3.28 MW)* sustained; 2 shafts; 1 Caterpillar 3412TA; 1,860 hp *(1.24 MW)* sustained; Hamilton jet (centreline); 764 hp *(570 kW)*
Speed, knots: 24. **Range, miles:** 600 at 18 kt
Complement: 18
Weapons control: GEC V3901 optronic director.
Radars: Surface search: Racal Decca; I-band.

Comment: Ordered from Australian Shipbuilding Industries in August 1991. Completed 23 October 1992, 20 January 1993, 4 March 1993, 2 April 1993, 9 June 1993 and 19 July 1993. As well as patrol work, the craft provide command platforms for Divisional commanders. Guns removed in 1996 and the optronic director is used for surveillance only.   *UPDATED*

DEFENDER   *3/1993*, ASI /* 0064694

8 DAMEN Mk I CLASS (PATROL CRAFT) (PC)

PL 60-61   PL 63-68

Displacement, tons: 86 full load
Dimensions, feet (metres): 85.9 × 19.4 × 5.5 *(26.2 × 5.9 × 1.7)*
Main machinery: 2 MTU 12V 396 TC82 diesels; 2,610 hp(m) *(1.92 MW)* sustained; 2 shafts
 1 MAN D2566 diesel; 195 hp(m) *(143 kW)*; Schottel prop (centreline)
Speed, knots: 23 MTU; 6 MAN. **Range, miles:** 600 at 14 kt
Complement: 13 *(PL 60-68)*
Radars: Surface search: Racal Decca; I-band.

Comment: Designed by Damen SY, Netherlands. Steel-hulled craft built by Chung Wah SB & Eng Co Ltd. Delivered February 1980 to January 1981. PL 62 transferred to Customs in 1995. 12.7 mm MGs removed in mid-1997. Planned for replacement from 2001 to 2003.   *UPDATED*

PL 68   *12/1996, Giorgio Arra /* 0012495

7 PETREL CLASS (HARBOUR PATROL CRAFT) (PB)

PETREL PL 11	**GULL** PL 13	**SKUA** PL 15	**GANNET** PL 17
AUK PL 12	**TERN** PL 14	**PUFFIN** PL 16	

Displacement, tons: 36 full load
Dimensions, feet (metres): 52.5 × 15.1 × 4.9 *(16 × 4.6 × 1.5)*
Main machinery: 2 Cummins NTA-855-M diesels; 700 hp *(522 kW)* sustained; 2 water-jets
Speed, knots: 12
Complement: 7
Radars: Surface search: Racal Decca; I-band.

Comment: Built by Chung Wah SB & Eng Co Ltd in 1986-87.

UPDATED

AUK   *1/1999*, van Ginderen Collection* / 0064696

5 SEA STALKER 1500 CLASS (HARBOUR PATROL CRAFT) (PB)

PL 85-PL 89

Displacement, tons: 7.5 full load
Dimensions, feet (metres): 48.6 × 9.5 × 2.6 *(14.8 × 2.9 × 0.8)*
Main machinery: 3 Mercruiser Bulldog V8; 1,500 hp(m) *(1.1 MW)*; 3 shafts
Speed, knots: 55; 45 in Sea State 3
Complement: 8
Radars: Surface search: Raytheon; I-band.

Comment: Ordered from Damen, Gorinchem in February 1998 and delivered in mid-1999. Can be armed with two 12.7 mm MGs. Used by the Anti-Smuggling Task Force.

UPDATED

SEA STALKER   *5/1999*, Damen* / 0064697

3 JET CLASS (SHALLOW WATER PATROL CRAFT) (PB)

JETSTREAM PL 6	**SWIFTSTREAM** PL 7	**TIDESTREAM** PL 8

Displacement, tons: 24 full load
Dimensions, feet (metres): 53.8 × 14.8 × 2.8 *(16.4 × 4.5 × 0.8)*
Main machinery: 2 Daimler-Benz OM 422A 8V diesels; 490 hp(m) *(434 kW)* sustained; 2 Hamilton 421 water-jets
Speed, knots: 18. **Range, miles:** 300 at 15 kt
Complement: 8
Radars: Surface search: Racal Decca; I-band.

Comment: Fibreglass hull built by Choy Lee Shipyards Limited. Completed April 1986 *(Jetstream)*, May 1986 *(Swiftstream)* and June 1986 *(Tidestream)*.

UPDATED

SWIFTSTREAM   *9/1993*, Hong Kong Police* / 0064698

4 SEASPRAY CLASS (LOGISTIC CRAFT) (YFB)

PL 46-49

Dimensions, feet (metres): 37.4 × 13.8 × 3.9 *(11.4 × 4.2 × 1.2)*
Main machinery: 2 Caterpillar 3208TA diesels; 550 hp *(410 kW)* sustained; 2 shafts
Speed, knots: 32
Complement: 4 + 16 fully equipped men
Radars: Navigation: Koden; I-band.

Comment: Built by Seaspray Boats, Fremantle. First one in service in June 1992, remainder by the end of the year. Catamaran hulls capable of carrying six people in VIP conditions or 16 for operational purposes.

UPDATED

PL 49   *5/1997*, Jack Brenchley* / 0012497

11 SEASPRAY CLASS (INSHORE PATROL CRAFT) (PB)

PL 22-32

Dimensions, feet (metres): 32.5 × 13.8 × 4.3 *(9.9 × 4.2 × 1.3)*
Main machinery: 2 Caterpillar 3208TA diesels; 680 hp *(508 kW)*; 2 shafts
Speed, knots: 35
Complement: 4
Radars: Surface search: Koden; I-band.

Comment: Built by Seaspray Boats, Fremantle. First three delivered in mid-1992, remainder in early 1993.

UPDATED

PL 29   *3/1993*, Hong Kong Police* / 0064699

15 INSHORE PATROL CRAFT (PB)

PL 20-21	PL 40-45	PL 90-92	PL 93-96

Displacement, tons: 4.5
Dimensions, feet (metres): 27 × 9.2 × 1.6 *(8.3 × 2.8 × 0.5)*
Main machinery: 2 outboards; 540 hp *(403 kW)*
Speed, knots: 40+
Complement: 4
Radars: Surface search: Koden; I-band.

Comment: Details given are for *PL 20-20* which are of catamaran construction, commissioned in October 1988. *PL 90-92* are Boston Whaler Guardians with 2 Johnson 115 hp outboards, and *PL 93-96* are Boston Whaler Vigilants with 2 Johnson 250 hp outboards. The Whalers were all delivered in April 1997 and are capable of speeds in excess of 33 kt. *PL 40-45* built by Cheoy Lee, Kowloon and delivered by July 2000. These are 35 kt craft powered by 2 MAN diesels driving waterjets.

UPDATED

PL 20   *9/1993*, Hong Kong Police* / 0064700

8 HIGH SPEED INTERCEPTORS

PV 30-37

Displacement, tons: 2.7 full load
Dimensions, feet (metres): 28.3 × 8.7 × 2.4 *(8.5 × 2.6 × 0.7)*
Main machinery: 2 Mercury outboards; 500 hp *(373 kW)*
Speed, knots: 51
Complement: 3

Comment: Built by Queensland Ships and delivered in September 1997. These craft replaced earlier high speed craft.

UPDATED

PV 34   *10/1997*, Hong Kong Police /* 0012498

CUSTOMS

Note: Among other craft three Damen 26 m Sector command launches were completed in 1986 by Chung Wah SB & Eng Co Ltd, Kowloon. In all essentials these craft are sisters of the 14 operated by the Royal Hong Kong Police with the exception of the latter's slow speed water-jet. Names: *Sea Glory* (Customs 6), *Sea Guardian* (Customs 5), *Sea Leader* (Customs 2). Damen Mk I *PL 62* transferred from the Police in 1993. Two 32 m craft were ordered in 1999.

SEA GUARDIAN   *4/1999*, G Toremans /* 0064701

LAND-BASED MARITIME AIRCRAFT

Notes: (1) All aircraft belong to the Government Flying Service.
(2) There are also three Black Hawk S-70A and two BAe Jetstream J 41 aircraft used for transport and SAR.

Numbers/Type: 4/2 Sikorsky S-76 A/C.
Operational speed: 145 kt *(269 km/h)*.
Service ceiling: 10,800 ft *(3,565 m)*.
Range: 430 n miles *(798 km)*.
Role/Weapon systems: Coastal surveillance/SAR and transport helicopters acquired in 1993-95. Sensors: FLIR. Weapons: Unarmed.

UPDATED

BLACK HAWK   *10/1998, Hong Kong Police /* 0052317

HUNGARY

Headquarters Appointments	**Personnel**	**Mercantile Marine**
Head of Maritime Wing: Colonel Gábor Hajdú	(a) 2000: 300 officers and men (b) 9 months' national service	*Lloyd's Register of Shipping:* 1 vessels of 11,869 tons gross
Diplomatic Representation		
Defence Attaché in London: Colonel I Lakatos	**Bases**	
	Budapest (to patrol 420 km of the Danube).	

MINE WARFARE FORCES

6 NESTIN CLASS (RIVER MINESWEEPERS) (MSR)

ÚJPEST AM 11	**SZÁZHALOMBATTA** AM 21	**DUNAÚJVÁROS** AM 31
BAJA AM 12	**ÓBUDA** AM 22	**DUNAFOLDVAR** AM 32

Displacement, tons: 72.3 full load
Dimensions, feet (metres): 88.6 × 21.3 × 3.9 *(27 × 6.5 × 1.2)*
Main machinery: 2 Torpedo 12-cyl diesels; 520 hp(m) *(382 kW)*; 2 shafts
Speed, knots: 15. **Range, miles:** 860 at 11 kt
Complement: 17 (1 officer)
Guns: 6 Hispano 20 mm (1 quad M75 fwd, 2 single M70 aft).
Mines: 24 ground mines.
Radars: Navigation: Decca 101; I-band.

Comment: Built by Brodotehnika, Belgrade in 1979-80. Full magnetic/acoustic and wire sweeping capabilities. Kram minesweeping system employs a towed sweep at 200 m.

UPDATED

ÓBUDA   *10/1998*, Hungary Maritime Wing /* 0064703

45 AN-2 CLASS MINE WARFARE/PATROL CRAFT (MSR/PBR)

542-001 to 542-053

Displacement, tons: 10 full load
Dimensions, feet (metres): 44 × 12.5 × 2 *(13.4 × 3.8 × 0.6)*
Main machinery: 2 diesels; 220 hp(m) *(162 kW)*; 2 shafts
Speed, knots: 12.6
Complement: 7
Guns: 2—12.7 mm (twin) MGs.

Comment: Aluminium hulls built between 1955 and 1965. Act as MCMV/patrol craft using mechanical sweeps and countermining. About 30 are active each summer, being laid up in the winter. Can be taken by road transport to the Tisza river. One of the craft, *542-004*, acts as a diving tender. Can lay ground mines but this is not exercised.

UPDATED

542-017   *6/1999*, Hungary Maritime Wing /* 0064702

ICELAND
LANDHELGISGAESLAN

Headquarters Appointments

Director of Coast Guard:
  Hafsteinn Hafsteinsson

Duties

The Coast Guard Service deals with fishery protection, salvage, rescue, hydrographic research, surveying and lighthouse duties. All ships have at least double the number of berths required for the complement.

Personnel

2000: 128 officers and men

Colours

In 1990 all vessels were marked with red, white and blue diagonal stripes on the ships' side and the Coast Guard name (Landhelgisgaeslan).

Bases

Reykjavik

Research Ships

A number of government Research Ships bearing RE pennant numbers operate off Iceland.

Maritime Aircraft

Maritime aircraft include a Fokker Friendship plus AS 332 Super Puma, Dauphin 2 and Ecureuil helicopters

Mercantile Marine

Lloyd's Register of Shipping:
  308 vessels of 192,091 tons gross

COAST GUARD

Note: A new vessel is to be built to replace *Odinn*. Contract planned for 2000.

Name	No	Builders	Commissioned
AEGIR	—	Aalborg Vaerft, Denmark	1968
TYR	—	Dannebrog Vaerft, Denmark	15 Mar 1975

Displacement, tons: 1,200 (1,300 *Tyr*) standard; 1,500 full load
Dimensions, feet (metres): 231.3 × 33 × 14.8 *(70.5 × 10 × 4.6)*
Main machinery: 2 MAN/Burmeister & Wain 8L 40/54 diesels; 13,200 hp(m) *(9.68 MW)* sustained; 2 shafts; cp props
Speed, knots: 19 *(Aegir)*; 20 *(Tyr)*. **Range, miles:** 9,000 at 18 kt
Complement: 19
Guns: 1 Bofors 40 mm/60 Mk 3.
Radars: Surface search: Sperry; E/F-band.
Navigation: Furuno; I-band.
Sonars: Hull-mounted; active search; high frequency *(Tyr)*.
Helicopters: 1 Dauphin 2.

Comment: Similar ships but *Tyr* has a slightly improved design and *Aegir* has no sonar. The hangar is between the funnels. In 1994 a large crane was fitted on the starboard side at the forward end of the flight deck. In 1997 the helicopter deck was extended and a radome fitted on the top of the tower. ***UPDATED***

AEGIR   *9/1997*, Iceland Coast Guard* / 0012501

Name	No	Builders	Commissioned
BALDUR	—	Vélsmiöja Seyöisfjaröar	8 May 1991

Displacement, tons: 54 full load
Dimensions, feet (metres): 65.6 × 17.1 × 5.6 *(20 × 5.2 × 1.7)*
Main machinery: 2 Caterpillar 3406TA diesels; 640 hp *(480 kW)*; 2 shafts
Speed, knots: 12
Complement: 5
Radars: Navigation: Furuno; I-band.

Comment: Built in an Icelandic Shipyard. Used for survey work. ***UPDATED***

BALDUR   *1993*, Iceland Coast Guard* / 0064705

Name	No	Builders	Commissioned
ODINN	—	Aalborg Vaerft, Denmark	Jan 1960

Displacement, tons: 1,200 full load
Dimensions, feet (metres): 210 × 33 × 13 *(64 × 10 × 4)*
Main machinery: 2 MAN/Burmeister & Wain diesels; 5,700 hp(m) *(4.19 MW)*; 2 shafts
Speed, knots: 18. **Range, miles:** 9,500 at 17 kt
Complement: 19
Guns: 1 Bofors 40 mm/60 Mk 3.
Radars: Surface search: Sperry; E/F-band.
Navigation: Furuno; I-band.
Helicopters: Platform for 1 Dauphin 2.

Comment: Refitted in Denmark by Aarhus Flydedock AS late 1975. Has twin funnels and helicopter hangar. A large crane was fitted in 1989 on the starboard side at the forward end of the flight deck. The original 57 mm gun has been replaced. ***UPDATED***

ODINN   *6/1996*, Iceland Coast Guard* / 0064704

INDIA

Headquarters Appointments

Chief of Naval Staff:
Admiral Sushil Kumar, PVSM, UYSM, AVSM, NM
Vice Chief of Naval Staff:
Vice Admiral P J Jacob, AVSM, VSM
Deputy Chief of Naval Staff:
Vice Admiral Harinder Singh, AVSM
Chief of Material:
Vice Admiral A S Krishnan, AVSM, VSM

Senior Appointments

Flag Officer Commanding Western Naval Command:
Vice Admiral Madhvendra Singh, PVSM, AVSM
Flag Officer Commanding Eastern Naval Command:
Vice Admiral V Pasricha, AVSM, NM
Flag Officer Commanding Southern Naval Command:
Vice Admiral R N Ganesh AVSM, NM
Flag Officer Commanding Western Fleet:
Rear Admiral S C Mehta, AVSM
Flag Officer Commanding Eastern Fleet:
Rear Admiral K V Bharathan, VSM
Fortress Commander, Andaman and Nicobar Islands:
Vice Admiral Raman Puri
Flag Officer, Naval Aviation and Goa Area (at Goa):
Rear Admiral K Mohanan
Flag Officer, Submarines (Vishakapatnam):
Rear Admiral A K Singh, AVSM, NM

Personnel

(a) 2000: 53,000 (7,500 officers) (including 5,000 Naval Air Arm and 1,000 Marines)
(b) Voluntary service
(c) The Marine Commando Force was formed in 1986.

Naval Air Arm

Squadron	Aircraft	Role
300 (Goa)	Sea Harrier FRS. Mk 51	Fighter/Strike
	Sea Harrier T Mk 60	Trainer
310 (Goa)	Dornier 228	MRMP
312 (Madras)	Tu-142M 'Bear F'	LRMP/ASW
315 (Goa)	Il-38 May	LRMP/ASW
318 (Goa)	PBN Defender	Utility
321 (Goa)	HAL Chetak	Utility/SAR
330 (Kochi)	Sea King Mk 42B	ASW
331 (Kochi)	HAL Chetak	Utility/SAR
333 (ships) (Goa)	Kamov Ka-28 'Helix'	ASW
336 (Kochi)	Sea King Mk 42/42A	ASW
339 (Mumbai)	Sea King Mk 42C	ASW/ASVW
550 (Kochi)	Defender, Islander, Deepak	Training
551 (Goa)	HAL HJT-16 Kiran	Training (OCU)
561 (Kochi)	HAL Chetak	Training
562 (Kochi)	Hughes 300, Chetak	Training

Air Stations

Name	Location	Role
INS *Kunjali*	Bombay	Helicopters
INS *Garuda*	Willingdon Island, Kochi	Helicopters
INS *Hansa*	Goa	HQ Flag Officer Naval Air Stations, LRMP, Strike/Fighter
INS *Sea Bird*	Karwar	Fleet Support (in due course)
INS *Utkrosh*	Port Blair, Andaman Isles	Maritime Patrol
	Uchipuli, Tamil Nadu	Maritime Patrol
	Ramanathuram	Maritime Patrol
INS *Dega*	Vishakapatnam	Fleet support and maritime patrol
	Tiruchirapalli	
INS *Rajali*	Arakonam	LRMP, Helo Training
INS *Ramnad*	Bangalore	LRMP Naval Air Technical School

Prefix to Ships' Names

INS

Bases and Establishments

Note: Bombay is now referred to as Mumbai, Cochin as Kochi and Madras as Chennai.

New Delhi, HQ (INS *India*)
Bombay, C-in-C **Western Command**, barracks and main Dockyard; with one 'Carrier' dock. Submarine base (INS *Vajrabahu*). Supply school (INS *Hamla*). The region includes Mazagon and Goa shipyards.
Vishakapatnam, C-in-C **Eastern Command**, submarine base (INS *Virbahu*), submarine school (INS *Satyavahana*) and major dockyard built with Soviet support and being extended. Naval Air Station (INS *Dega*). New entry training (INS *Chilka*). At Vijayaraghavapuram is the submarine VLF W/T station completed in September 1986. Facilities at Chennai and Calcutta. The region includes Hindustan and Garden Reach shipyards.
Kochi, C-in-C **Southern Command**, Naval Air Station, and professional schools (INS *Venduruthy*) (all naval training comes under Southern Command). Ship repair yard. Trials establishment (INS *Dronacharya*).
Goa is HQ Flag Officer Naval Air Stations.
Karwar (near Goa) has been selected as the site for a new naval base; first phase due for completion in 2003. Alongside berthing for Aircraft Carriers and a naval air station are planned. At Lakshadweep in the Laccadive Islands there is a patrol craft base. There are also limited support facilities including a floating dock at Port Blair (INS *Jarawa*) in the Andaman Islands.
Shipbuilding: Mumbai (submarines, destroyers, frigates, corvettes); Calcutta (frigates, corvettes, LSTs, auxiliaries); Goa (patrol craft, LCU, MCMV facility planned).

Coast Defence

Truck-mounted SS-3-C Styx missiles. At least seven fixed sites.

Strength of the Fleet

Type	Active	Building (Projected)
Attack Submarine (SSN)	—	1
Patrol Submarines	18	2
Attack Carriers (Medium)	1	1
Destroyers	8	—
Frigates	11	5 (3)
Corvettes	23	3 (4)
Patrol Ships	7	—
Fast Attack Craft—Missile	3	—
Patrol Craft	8	4 (15)
Landing Ships	10	1 (3)
LCUs	10	—
Minesweepers—Ocean	12	—
Minesweepers—Inshore	6	—
Minehunters	—	(6)
Research and Survey Ships	13	—
Training Ships	4	—
Submarine Tender	1	—
Diving Support/Rescue Ship	1	—
Replenishment Tankers	3	(1)
Transport Ships	2	—
Support Tankers	6	—
Water Carriers	2	—
Ocean Tugs	2	—

Mercantile Marine

Lloyd's Register of Shipping:
971 vessels of 6,914,780 tons gross

DELETIONS

Submarines

1998   *Vagsheer*
1999   *Vagir*

Frigates

1998   *Udaygiri*
1999   *Arnala*

Corvettes

1999   *Hosdurg*

Patrol Forces

1997   *Charag*
1998   *T 57*
1999   *Prachand, Prabal*

PENNANT LIST

Submarines

S 20	Kursura
S 21	Karanj
S 40	Vela
S 41	Vagir
S 42	Vagli
S 44	Shishumar
S 45	Shankush
S 46	Shalki
S 47	Shankul
S 55	Sindhughosh
S 56	Sindhudhvaj
S 57	Sindhuraj
S 58	Sindhuvir
S 59	Sindhuratna
S 60	Sindhukesari
S 61	Sindhukirti
S 62	Sindhuvijay
S 63	Sindhurakshak
S 64	Sindhushastra

Aircraft Carriers

R 22	Viraat

Destroyers

D 61	Delhi
D 62	Mysore
D 63	Bombay
D 51	Rajput
D 52	Rana
D 53	Ranjit
D 54	Ranvir
D 55	Ranvijay

Frigates

—	Talwar (bldg)
—	Trishull (bldg)
F 20	
F 20	Godavari
F 21	Gomati
F 22	Ganga
F 31	Brahmaputra
F 32	Betwa (bldg)
F 33	Beas (bldg)
F 34	Himgiri
F 36	Dunagiri
F 41	Taragiri
F 42	Vindhyagiri
F 46	Krishna (training)
P 69	Androth
P 73	Anjadip
P 75	Amini

Corvettes

P 33	Abhay
P 34	Ajay
P 35	Akshay
P 36	Agray
P 44	Kirpan
P 46	Kuthar
P 47	Khanjar
P 49	Khukri
P 61	Kora
—	Kirch (bldg)
—	Kulish (bldg)
—	Karmukh (bldg)
K 40	Veer
K 41	Nirbhik
K 42	Nipat
K 43	Nishank
K 44	Nirghat
K 45	Vibhuti
K 46	Vipul
K 47	Vinash
K 48	Vidyut
K 71	Vijaydurg
K 72	Sindhudurg
K 83	Nashak
K 98	Prahar

Patrol Forces

P 50	Sukanya
P 51	Subhadra
P 52	Suvarna
P 53	Savitri
P 54	Saryu
P 55	Sharada
P 56	Sujata
K 91	Pralaya
K 94	Chapal
K 96	Chatak

Toofan (bldg)

Mine Warfare Forces

M 61	Pondicherry
M 62	Porbandar
M 63	Bedi
M 64	Bhavnagar
M 65	Alleppey
M 66	Ratnagiri
M 67	Karwar
M 68	Cannanore
M 69	Cuddalore
M 70	Kakinada
M 71	Kozhikode
M 72	Konkan
M 83	Mahé
M 84	Malvan
M 85	Mangrol
M 86	Malpe
M 87	Mulki
M 88	Magdala

Amphibious Forces

L 14	Ghorpad
L 15	Kesari
L 16	Shardul
L 17	Sharabh
L 18	Cheetah
L 19	Mahish
L 20	Magar
L 21	Guldar
L 22	Kumbhir
L 23	Gharial
L 34	Vasco da Gama
L 38	Midhur
L 39	Mangala

Auxiliaries and Survey Ships

—	Nicobar
—	Andamans
A 59	Aditya
A 15	Nireekshak
A 52	Matanga
A 53	Ambika
A 54	Amba
A 57	Shakti
A 58	Jyoti
A 74	Sagardhwani
A 86	Tir
J 14	Nirupak
J 15	Investigator
J 16	Jamuna
J 17	Sutlej
J 18	Sandhayak
J 19	Nirdeshak
J 21	Darshak
J 22	Sarveskhak
J 33	Makar
J 34	Mithun
J 35	Meen
J 36	Mesh

SUBMARINES

Notes: (1) The ex-Soviet 'Charlie' class nuclear-powered submarine *Chakra* was leased for three years from January 1988. Plans are now advanced to build nuclear-propelled submarines in India. For this purpose there is a project called the Advanced Technology Vessel (ATV) which is well funded and has facilities in Delhi, Hyderabad, Vishakapatnam and Kalpakkam. A Navy-Defence Research and Development Organisation (DRDO) runs the project and since 1985 has had a Vice Admiral in charge. The submarine is a development of a Russian design with an Indo/Russian PWR, generating about 190 MW. The nuclear propulsion system has been tested ashore. Fabrication has started at Vishakapatnam with a laid down date projected for 2002. Weapon systems integration will be at Mazagon. Launch date is currently projected as around 2007. The hull is of 6,000 tons displacement and, given the degree of Russian technical assistance, could resemble the 'Severodvinsk' class in that it will have VLS tubes capable of firing multiple weapons. The plan is for a class of five fitted with Sargarika or Russian cruise missiles. The ATV is taking money from all other naval programmes.
(2) One of the two 'Amur' class SSKs building at St Petersburg may be exported to India. Launch date is projected for late 2000.
(3) In spite of many negotiations, India has not acquired midget submarines. In 1991 11 Cosmos CE2F/FX100 swimmer delivery vessels were acquired. These are two-man underwater chariots for commando operations. They have not been seen in recent years.

4 + 2 SHISHUMAR (209) CLASS (TYPE 1500) (SSK)

Name	No	Builders	Laid down	Launched	Commissioned
SHISHUMAR	S 44	Howaldtswerke, Kiel	1 May 1982	13 Dec 1984	22 Sep 1986
SHANKUSH	S 45	Howaldtswerke, Kiel	1 Sep 1982	11 May 1984	20 Nov 1986
SHALKI	S 46	Mazagon Dock Ltd, Bombay	5 June 1984	30 Sep 1989	7 Feb 1992
SHANKUL	S 47	Mazagon Dock Ltd, Bombay	3 Sep 1989	21 Mar 1992	28 May 1994
—	S 48	Mazagon Dock Ltd, Bombay	2001	2004	2006
—	S 49	Mazagon Dock Ltd, Bombay	2003	2006	2008

Displacement, tons: 1,450 standard; 1,660 surfaced; 1,850 dived
Dimensions, feet (metres): 211.2 × 21.3 × 19.7 *(64.4 × 6.5 × 6)*
Main machinery: Diesel-electric; 4 MTU 12V 493 AZ80 GA31L diesels; 2,400 hp(m) *(1.76 MW)* sustained; 4 Siemens alternators; 1.8 MW; 1 Siemens motor; 4,600 hp(m) *(3.38 MW)* sustained; 1 shaft
Speed, knots: 11 surfaced; 22 dived
Range, miles: 8,000 snorting at 8 kt; 13,000 surfaced at 10 kt
Complement: 36 (8 officers)

Missiles: SSM: *S 48* and *S 49* only.
Torpedoes: 8—21 in *(533 mm)* tubes. 14 AEG SUT Mod 1; wire-guided; active/passive homing to 28 km *(15.3 n miles)* at 23 kt; 12 km *(6.6 n miles)* at 35 kt; warhead 250 kg.
Mines: External 'strap-on' type for 24 mines.
Countermeasures: Decoys: C 303 acoustic decoys.
ESM: Argo Phoenix II AR 700 or Kollmorgen Sea Sentry; radar warning.
Weapons control: Singer Librascope Mk 1.
Radars: Surface search: Thomson-CSF Calypso; I-band.
Sonars: Atlas Elektronik CSU 83; active/passive search and attack; medium frequency. TSM 2272 to be fitted.
Thomson Sintra DUUX-5; passive ranging and intercept.

Programmes: Howaldtswerke concluded an agreement with the Indian Navy on 11 December 1981. This was in four basic parts: the building in West Germany of two Type 1500 submarines; the supply of 'packages' for the building of two more boats at Mazagon, Bombay; training of various groups of specialists for the design and construction of the Mazagon pair; logistic services during the trials and early part of the commissions as well as consultation services in Bombay. In 1984 it was announced that a further two submarines would

SHALKI *6/1999* / 0064706*

be built at Mazagon for a total of six but this was overtaken by events in 1987-88 and the agreement with HDW terminated at four. This was reconsidered in 1992, again in 1997 and government approval was given in mid-1997. These two are called Project 75 (modified 'Shishumar' class) and are to be fitted with SSMs. Work started in December 1999.
Modernisation: Thomson Sintra Eledone sonars may be fitted in due course.

Structure: The Type 1500 has a central bulkhead and an IKL designed integrated escape sphere which can carry the full crew of up to 40 men, has an oxygen supply for 8 hours, and can withstand pressures at least as great as those that can be withstood by the submarine's pressure hull. Diving depth 260 m *(853 ft)*.
Operational: *Shishumar* mid-life refit started in 1999.
UPDATED

10 SINDHUGHOSH (KILO) (TYPE 877EM/636) CLASS (SSK)

Name	No	Builders	Commissioned
SINDHUGHOSH	S 55	Sudomekh, Leningrad	30 Apr 1986
SINDHUDHVAJ	S 56	Sudomekh, Leningrad	12 June 1987
SINDHURAJ	S 57	Sudomekh, Leningrad	20 Oct 1987
SINDHUVIR	S 58	Sudomekh, Leningrad	16 May 1988
SINDHURATNA	S 59	Sudomekh, Leningrad	19 Nov 1988
SINDHUKESARI	S 60	Sudomekh, Leningrad	19 Dec 1988
SINDHUKIRTI	S 61	Sudomekh, Leningrad	9 Dec 1990
SINDHUVIJAY	S 62	Sudomekh, Leningrad	17 Dec 1990
SINDHURAKSHAK	S 63	Sudomekh, St Petersburg	24 Dec 1997
SINDHUSHASTRA	S 64	Sudomekh, St Petersburg	June 2000

Displacement, tons: 2,325 surfaced; 3,076 dived
Dimensions, feet (metres): 238.2 × 32.5 × 21.7 *(72.6 × 9.9 × 6.6)*
Main machinery: Diesel-electric; 2 Model 4-2AA-42M diesels; 3,650 hp(m) *(2.68 MW)*; 2 generators; 1 motor; 5,900 hp(m) *(4.34 MW)*; 1 shaft; 2 MT-168 auxiliary motors; 204 hp(m) *(150 kW)*; 1 economic speed motor; 130 hp(m) *(95 kW)*
Speed, knots: 10 surfaced; 17 dived; 9 snorting
Range, miles: 6,000 at 7 kt snorting; 400 at 3 kt dived
Complement: 52 (13 officers)

Missiles: SLCM: Novator Alfa Klub SS-N-27 (3M-54E1) (S 57, 58, 59 and 64); active radar homing to 180 km *(97.2 n miles)* at 0.7 Mach (cruise) and 2.5 Mach (attack); warhead 450 kg.
SAM: SA-N-8 portable launcher; IR homing to 3.2 n miles *(6 km)*.
Torpedoes: 6—21 in *(533 mm)* tubes. Combination of Type 53-65; passive wake homing to 19 km *(10.3 n miles)* at 45 kt; warhead 305 kg and TEST 71/96; anti-submarine; active/passive homing to 15 km *(8.1 n miles)* at 40 kt or 20 km *(10.8 n miles)* at 25 kt; warhead 220 kg. Total of 18 weapons. Wire-guided on 2 tubes.
Mines: 24 DM-1 in lieu of torpedoes.
Countermeasures: ESM: Squid Head; radar warning.
Weapons control: Uzel MVU-119EM TFCS.
Radars: Navigation: Snoop Tray; MRP-25; I-band.
Sonars: Shark Teeth/Shark Fin; MGK-400; hull-mounted; active/passive search and attack; medium frequency.
Mouse Roar; MG-519; hull-mounted; active search; high frequency.

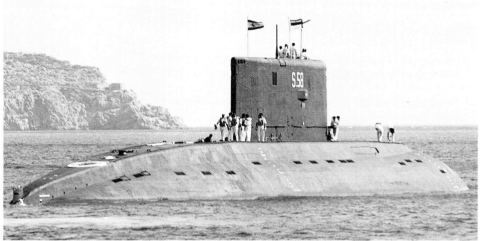

SINDHUVIR (after Russian refit) *9/1999*, Diego Quevedo / 0064707*

Programmes: The 'Kilo' class was launched in the former Soviet Navy in 1979 and although India was the first country to acquire one they have since been transferred to Algeria, Poland, Romania, Iran and China. Because of the slowness of the S 209 programme, the original order in 1983 for six 'Kilo' class expanded to 10 but was then cut back again to eight. Plans to manufacture the class under licence in India have been resurrected and in January 1997 it was announced that two more of the class would be purchased from Russia. The Russian order was confirmed in May 1997 and S 63 was a spare Type 877 hull built for the Russian Navy, but never purchased. S 64 may be a Type 636 and is fitted with SLCM. She was launched on 14 October 1999.
Modernisation: An engine change is probable during major refits in Russia which started in 1997. A tube launched SLCM capability is also part of the refit but full weapon systems integration may not be available until 2002. A German designed main battery with a five year life has replaced Russian batteries in all of the class. Battery cooling has been improved.
Structure: Diving depth, 300 m *(985 ft)*. Reported that from *Sindhuvir* onwards these submarines have an SA-N-8 SAM capability. The launcher is shoulder held and stowed in the fin for use when the submarine is surfaced. Two torpedo tubes can fire wire-guided torpedoes and four tubes have automatic reloading. Anechoic tiles are fitted on casings and fins.
Operational: First four form the 11th Submarine Squadron. Based at Vishakapatnam and the remainder of the 10th Squadron based at Mumbai. *Sindhuvir* completed major refit at Severodvinsk from June 1997 to April 1999. *Sindhuraj* and *Sindhukesari* started similar refits at Admiralty Yard, St Petersburg in May 1999, and *Sindhuratna* at Severodvinsk in May 2000. *Sindhughosh* started refit at Vishakapatnam in 1997.
UPDATED

4 FOXTROT (TYPE 641) CLASS (SS)

Name	No	Builders	Commissioned
KURSURA	S 20	Sudomekh, Leningrad	Dec 1970
KARANJ	S 21	Sudomekh, Leningrad	Oct 1970
VELA	S 40	Sudomekh, Leningrad	Aug 1973
VAGLI	S 42	Sudomekh, Leningrad	Aug 1974

Displacement, tons: 1,952 surfaced; 2,475 dived
Dimensions, feet (metres): 299.5 × 24.6 × 19.7 *(91.3 × 7.5 × 6)*
Main machinery: Diesel-electric; 3 Type 37-D diesels; 6,000 hp (m) *(4.4 MW)*; 3 motors (1 × 2,700 and 2 × 1,350); 5,400 hp (m) *(3.97 MW)*; 3 shafts; 1 auxiliary motor; 140 hp(m) *(103 kW)*
Speed, knots: 16 surfaced; 15 dived
Range, miles: 20,000 at 8 kt surfaced; 380 at 2 kt dived
Complement: 75 (8 officers)

Torpedoes: 10—21 in *(533 mm)* (6 fwd, 4 aft) tubes. 22 SET-65E/SAET-60; active/passive homing to 15 km *(8.1 n miles)* at 40 kt; warhead 205 kg.
Mines: 44 in lieu of torpedoes.
Countermeasures: ESM: Stop Light; radar warning.
Radars: Surface search: Snoop Tray; I-band.
Sonars: Herkules/Fenik; bow-mounted; passive search and attack; medium frequency.

Structure: Diving depth 250 m *(820 ft)*, reducing with age.

FOXTROT   *8/1997 /* 0012502

Operational: Survivors of an original eight of the class. *Vela* is in a refit which may not be completed. *Karanj* is used as a trials platform for the ATV command systems including Pachendriya sonar and Rani radar equipment. The plan is to extend the lives of these four until 2010 but this seems unlikely to be achieved. Form 8th Submarine Squadron at Vishakapatnam, except *Vagli* which is based at Mumbai.

UPDATED

AIRCRAFT CARRIERS

0 + (1) MODIFIED KIEV CLASS (TYPE 1143.4) (CVG)

Name	Builders	Laid down	Launched	Commissioned
ADMIRAL GORSHKOV (ex-*Baku*)	Nikolayev South	17 Feb 1978	1 Apr 1982	11 Dec 1987

Displacement, tons: 44,900 full load
Dimensions, feet (metres): 928.5 oa; 818.6 wl × 167.3 oa; 107.3 wl ×32.8 *(283; 249.5 × 51; 32.7 × 10)*
Main machinery: 8 KWG 4 boilers; 4 GTZA 674 turbines; 200,000 hp(m) *(147 MW)*; 4 shafts
Speed, knots: 30. **Range, miles:** 7,160 at 18 kt
Complement: 1,200 plus aircrew

Missiles: SAM: 2 SA-N-9 Gauntlet sextuple vertical launchers.
Guns: 8—30 mm/65 AK 630. 6 barrels per mounting.
Countermeasures: Decoys: ESM/ECM.
Weapons control: 3 Optronic trackers. SATCOM.

Radars: Air search: Plate Steer.
Surface search: 2 Strut Pair.
Navigation: Aircraft control.
Fire control: 4 Bass Tilt (for guns); 2 Cross Sword (for SAM).
Sonars: Horse Jaw; hull-mounted; active search; medium frequency.

Fixed-wing aircraft: Up to 24 MiG-29K or Sea Harrier FRS Mk 51.
Helicopters: 6 Helix 27/28/31.

Programmes: First offered for sale to India by Russia in 1994. By 1999 the proposal was to gift the ship as long as India pays for the modifications. Work started at Severodvinsk in early 2000, after the ship had been laid up for several years.
Structure: Details given show the ship as it was in service with Russia but with all the forward weapon systems replaced by an extended flight deck with ski jump. There may also be changes to other armaments and sensors. The aircraft complement is also speculative.
Operational: The refit is expected to take up to three years.
Opinion: This is a high risk venture to restore a two-carrier Fleet.

NEW ENTRY

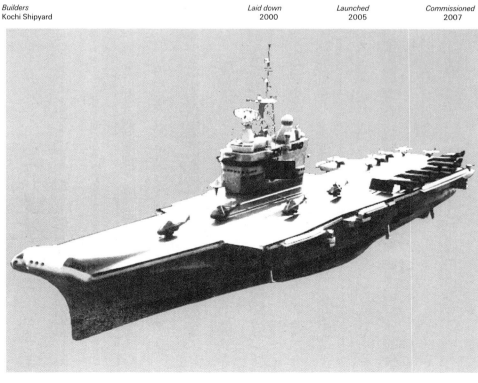

GORSHKOV   *(Scale 1 : 1,500), Ian Sturton /* 0081931

0 + 1 AIRCRAFT CARRIER (CV)

Name	No	Builders	Laid down	Launched	Commissioned
—	—	Kochi Shipyard	2000	2005	2007

Displacement, tons: 32,000 full load
Dimensions, feet (metres): 820.2 × 137.8 × 39.4 *(250 × 42 × 12)*
Speed, knots: 32
Complement: 1,350
Missiles: SAM.
Guns: CIWS.
Radars: Air search; surface search; fire control.
Fixed-wing aircraft: 16 MiG 29s and Sea Harriers.
Helicopters: 20 Helix and Sea King and ALH.

Programmes: The plan announced in 1989 was to build two new aircraft carriers, the first to replace *Vikrant* in 1997. A design study contract was signed with DCN (France) for a ship of about 28,000 tons and with a speed in excess of 30 kt. Size restricted by available construction dock capacity. Options included ski jump and CTOL. The Indian Naval Design Organisation was to translate the design study into the production model with construction to start at Kochi in 1993. However in mid-1991 the Committee on Defence Expenditure told the Navy to abandon plans for large carriers and shift the design effort to Italian *Garibaldi* type. Government funding approved for an Air Defence Ship in June 1999 and the plan is to lay the keel as soon as *Viraat* has cleared the dock in 2000.
Structure: All details are still speculative. Short take off with ski jump, and arrested recovery on an angled deck (STOBAR), are the Navy's stated preferred option for aircraft operations. Operational MiG 29s may be part of the acquisition deal.

NEW ENTRY

AIRCRAFT CARRIER (artist's impression)
1999*, Indian Navy / 0048490

1 HERMES CLASS (CV)

Name	No	Builders	Laid down	Launched	Commissioned
VIRAAT (ex-*Hermes*)	R 22	Vickers Shipbuilding Ltd, Barrow-in-Furness	21 June 1944	16 Feb 1953	18 Nov 1959

Displacement, tons: 23,900 standard; 28,700 full load
Dimensions, feet (metres): 685 wl; 744.3 oa × 90; 160 oa × 28.5 *(208.8; 226.9 × 27.4; 48.8 × 8.7)*
Main machinery: 4 Admiralty boilers; 400 psi *(28 kg/cm²)*; 700°F *(370°C)*; 2 Parsons geared turbines; 76,000 hp *(57 MW)*; 2 shafts
Speed, knots: 28
Complement: 1,350 (143 officers)

Missiles: SAM/Guns: 2 CADS-N-1 (Kashtan) CIWS may be fitted by 2002.
Guns: 2 Bofors 40 mm/60 ❶.
2 USSR 30 mm AK 230 Gatlings ❷.
Countermeasures: Decoys: 2 Knebworth Corvus chaff launchers ❸.
ESM: Bharat Ajanta; intercept ❹.
Combat data systems: CAAIS action data automation. SATCOM ❺.
Radars: Air search: Marconi Type 966 ❻; A-band with IFF 1010.
Air/surface search: Signaal DA05 ❼; E/F-band.
Navigation: 2 Racal Decca 1006; I-band.
Tacan: FT 13-S/M.
Sonars: Graseby Type 184M; hull-mounted; active search and attack; 6-9 kHz.

Fixed-wing aircraft: 12 Sea Harriers FRS Mk 51 ❽ (capacity for 30).
Helicopters: 7 Sea King Mk 42B/C ❾ ASW/ASV/Vertrep and Ka-27 Helix. Ka-31 Helix by 2000.

Programmes: Purchased in May 1986 from the UK, thence to an extensive refit in Devonport Dockyard. Life extension of at least 10 years. Commissioned in Indian Navy 20 May 1987.
Modernisation: UK refit included new fire-control equipment, navigation radars and deck landing aids. Boilers were converted to take distillate fuel and the ship was given improved NBC protection. New search radar in 1995. In 1996 single 40 mm guns fitted on starboard bow and forward of the island; AK 230 Gatlings on the sponsons previously occupied by Seacat SAM. Further modernisation in current refit may include Kashtan CIWS, improved radars and EW equipment, and new communications.
Structure: Fitted with 12° ski jump. Reinforced flight deck (0.75 in); 1 to 2 in of armour over magazines and machinery spaces. Four LCVP on after davits. Magazine capacity includes 80 lightweight torpedoes.
Operational: The Sea Harrier complement is normally no more than 12 or 18 aircraft leaving room for a greater mix of Sea King and Helix helicopters. The engine room was flooded in September 1993, taking the ship out of service for several months. Back in service in 1995. Life extension refit started in July 1999 with the ship docked at Kochi and then moved to Mazagon Dock in 2000. Based at Mumbai.

UPDATED   VIRAAT

2/1998 * / 0064708*

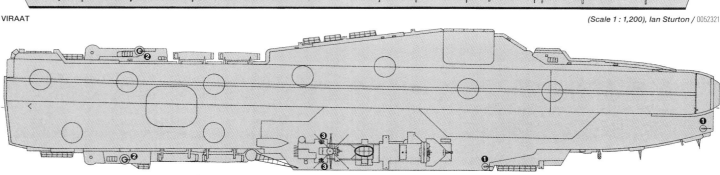

VIRAAT

(Scale 1 : 1,200), Ian Sturton / 0052321

VIRAAT

(Scale 1 : 1,200), Ian Sturton

VIRAAT

2/1997, Roland Harries / 0012509

DESTROYERS

5 RAJPUT (KASHIN II) CLASS (TYPE 61ME) (DDG)

Name	No	Builders	Launched		Commissioned	
RAJPUT (ex-*Nadiozny*)	D 51	Kommuna, Nikolayev	Sep	1977	4 May	1980
RANA (ex-*Gubitielny*)	D 52	Kommuna, Nikolayev	Oct	1978	19 Feb	1982
RANJIT (ex-*Lovky*)	D 53	Kommuna, Nikolayev	June	1979	15 Sep	1983
RANVIR (ex-*Twiordy*)	D 54	Kommuna, Nikolayev	Mar	1983	21 Apr	1986
RANVIJAY (ex-*Tolkovy*)	D 55	Kommuna, Nikolayev	Feb	1986	21 Dec	1987

Displacement, tons: 3,950 standard; 4,974 full load
Dimensions, feet (metres): 480.5 × 51.8 × 15.7
 (146.5 × 15.8 × 4.8)
Main machinery: COGAG; 4 Ukraine gas turbines; 72,000 hp(m)
 (53 MW); 2 shafts
Speed, knots: 35. **Range, miles:** 4,500 at 18 kt; 2,600 at 30 kt
Complement: 320 (35 officers)

Missiles: SSM: 4 SS-N-2D Mod 2 Styx ❶; IR homing to 83 km
 (45 n miles) at 0.9 Mach; warhead 513 kg; sea-skimmer at end
 of run.
 SAM: 2 SA-N-1 Goa twin launchers ❷; command guidance to
 31.5 km *(17 n miles)* at 2 Mach; height 91-22,860 m *(300-
 75,000 ft)*; warhead 60 kg; 44 missiles. Some SSM capability.
Guns: 2—3 in *(76 mm)*/60 (twin, fwd) ❸; 90 rds/min to 15 km
 (8 n miles); weight of shell 6.8 kg.
 8—30 mm/65 (4 twin) AK 230 *(Rajput, Rana and Ranjit)* ❹;
 500 rds/min to 5 km *(2.7 n miles)*; weight of shell 0.54 kg.
 4—30 mm/65 ADG 630 (6 barrels per mounting) *(Ranvir and
 Ranvijay)*; 3,000 rds/min combined to 2 km.
Torpedoes: 5—21 in *(533 mm)* (quin) tubes ❺. Combination of
 SET-65E; anti-submarine; active/passive homing to 15 km
 (8.1 n miles) at 40 kt; warhead 205 kg and Type 53-65;
 passive wake homing to 19 km *(10.3 n miles)* at 45 kt;
 warhead 305 kg.
A/S mortars: 2 RBU 6000 12-tubed trainable ❻; range 6,000 m;
 warhead 31 kg.
Countermeasures: 4 PK 16 chaff launchers for radar decoy and
 distraction.
 ESM: 2 Bell Squat/Bell Shroud (last pair); Bell Clout/Bell Slam/
 Bell Tap (first three); intercept.
 ECM: 2 Top Hat; jammers.
Radars: Air search: Big Net A ❼; C-band; range 183 km *(100 n
 miles)* for 2 m² target.
 Air/surface search: Head Net C ❽; 3D; E-band.
 Navigation: 2 Don Kay; I-band.
 Fire control: 2 Peel Group ❾; H/I-band; range 73 km *(40 n miles)*
 for 2 m² target.
 Owl Screech ❿; G-band.
 2 Drum Tilt ⓫ or 2 Bass Tilt *(Ranvir and Ranvijay)*; H/I-band.
 IFF: 2 High Pole B.
Sonars: Vycheda MG 311; hull-mounted; active search and
 attack; medium frequency.
 Mare Tail VDS; active search; medium frequency.

Helicopters: 1 Ka-27/28 Helix ⓬.

Programmes: First batch of three ordered in the mid-1970s.
 Ranvir was the first of the second batch ordered on
 20 December 1982.
Modernisation: New EW equipment fitted in 1993-94. There are
 plans for modernisation with Ukrainian assistance.
Structure: All built as new construction for India at Nikolayev
 with considerable modifications to the Kashin design.
 Helicopter hangar, which is reached by a lift from the flight
 deck, replaces after 76 mm twin mount and the SS-N-2D
 launchers are sited forward of the bridge. *Ranvir and Ranvijay*

RANA *(Scale 1 : 1,200), Ian Sturton*

RANJIT *10/1998*, Indian Navy / 0064709*

RANVIJAY *3/1998, G Toremans / 0052327*

differ from previous ships in class by being fitted with
ADGM-630 30 mm guns and two Bass Tilt fire-control radars.
It is possible that an Italian combat data system compatible
with Selenia IPN-10 is installed. Inmarsat fitted.

Operational: First three based at Vishakapatnam, last pair at
Mumbai.

UPDATED

RANVIJAY *3/1996 / 0052328*

3 DELHI CLASS (DDG)

Name	No	Builders	Laid down	Launched	Commissioned
DELHI	D 61	Mazagon Dock Ltd, Bombay	14 Nov 1987	1 Feb 1991	15 Nov 1997
MYSORE	D 62	Mazagon Dock Ltd, Bombay	2 Feb 1991	4 June 1993	2 June 1999
BOMBAY	D 63	Mazagon Dock Ltd, Bombay	14 Dec 1992	20 Mar 1995	Sep 2000

Displacement, tons: 6,700 full load
Dimensions, feet (metres): 534.8 × 55.8 × 21.3
(163 × 17 × 6.5)
Main machinery: CODOG; 2 AM-50 Ukraine gas turbines; 54,000 hp(m) *(39.7 MW)*; 2 Bergen/Garden Reach KVM-18 diesels; 9,920 hp(m) *(7.29 MW)* sustained; 2 shafts; cp props
Speed, knots: 28
Complement: 360 (40 officers)

Missiles: SSM: 16 Zvezda SS-N-25 (4 quad) (KH 35 Uran) ❶ active radar homing to 130 km *(70.2 n miles)* at 0.9 Mach; warhead 145 kg; sea skimmer.
SAM: 2 SA-N-7 Gadfly (Kashmir/Uragan) ❷ command, semi-active radar and IR homing to 25 km *(13.5 n miles)* at 3 Mach; warhead 70 kg. Total of 48 missiles.
Guns: 1 USSR 3.9 in *(100 mm)*/59 ❸. AK 100; 60 rds/min to 15 km *(8.2 n miles)*; weight of shell 16 kg.
4 USSR 30 mm/65 ❹ AK 630; 6 barrels per mounting; 3,000 rds/min combined to 2 km.
Torpedoes: 5 PTA 21 in *(533 mm)* (quin) tubes ❺. Combination of SET 65E; anti-submarine; active/passive homing to 15 km *(8.1 n miles)* at 40 kt; warhead 205 kg and Type 53-65; passive wake homing to 19 km *(10.3 n miles)* at 45 kt; warhead 305 kg.
A/S mortars: 2 RBU 6000 ❻; 12 tubed trainable; range 6,000 m; warhead 31 kg.
Depth charges: 2 rails.
Countermeasures: Decoys: 2 PK2 chaff launchers.
ESM: Bharat Ajanta Mk 2; intercept.
ECM: Elettronica TQN-2; jammer.
Combat data systems: Bharat IPN Shikari (IPN 10).
Radars: Air search: Bharat/Signaal RAWL/P318Z (LW08) ❼; D-band.
Air/Surface search: Half Plate (C391A) ❽; E-band.
Fire control: 6 Front Dome ❾; F-band (for SAM); Kite Screech ❿; H/I/K-band (for 100 mm); 2 Bass Tilt ⓫; H/I/J-band (for 30 mm); Plank Shave (Granit Harpun B) ⓬ (for SSM); I/J-band.
Navigation: Bharat Rashmi; 3 Palm Frond; I-band.
Sonars: Bharat APSOH; hull-mounted; active search; medium frequency.
Indal/Garden Reach Model 15-750 VDS.

Helicopters: 2 Westland Sea Kings Mk 42B ⓭ or 2 Hindustan Aeronautics ALH.

Programmes: Built with Russian Severnoye Design Bureau assistance. *Delhi* ordered in March 1986. Programme is called Project 15. Much delay was caused by the breakdown in the central control of Russian export equipment. The name of the third ship may be changed to *Mumbai* in due course but only if the Navy is directed to make the change. Three more of the class are projected but with more western weapon systems.
Structure: The design is described as a 'stretched *Rajput*' with some *Godavari* features. A combination of Russian and Indian

DELHI   *(Scale 1 : 1,500)*, Ian Sturton / 0052325

DELHI   *3/1999 * / 0064710

weapon systems fitted. Missile blast deflectors indicate an original intention to fit SS-N-22 Sunburn. Samahé helo handling system.

Operational: After nine years being built, the first of class started sea trials in February 1997, second of class in September 1998. Based at Mumbai. Has Flag facilities.   **UPDATED**

DELHI   *9/1997 *, Mazagon Dock / 0012515

DELHI   *4/1998 *, Indian Navy / 0064711

DELHI

4/1998, Indian Navy / 0052326

FRIGATES

0 + 3 (3) TALWAR (TYPE 1135.6/PROJECT 17) CLASS (FFG)

Name	No	Builders	Laid Down	Launched	Commissioned
TALWAR	—	Northern Shipyard, St Petersburg	10 Mar 1999	Sep 2000	2002
TRISHULL	—	Northern Shipyard, St Petersburg	28 July 1999	Apr 2001	2003
TOOFAN	—	Northern Shipyard, St Petersburg	Apr 2000	Oct 2001	2003

Displacement, tons: 3,850 full load
Dimensions, feet (metres): 408.5 × 49.9 × 13.8
(124.5 × 15.2 × 4.2)
Main machinery: COGAG; 2 (AM-50) gas turbines; 54,000 hp(m)
(39.7 MW); 2 gas turbines; 13,600 hp(m) *(10 MW)*; 2 shafts
Speed, knots: 32. **Range, miles:** 4,600 at 20 kt; 1,600 at 30 kt
Complement: 180 (18 officers)

Missiles: SSM: 8 SS-N-27 Novator Alfa Klub (3M-54E1) ❶ active
radar homing to 180 km *(97.2 n miles)* at 0.7 Mach (cruise)
and 2.5 Mach (attack); warhead 450 kg. VLS silo.
SAM: SA-N-7 Gadfly (Kashmir/Uragan) ❷ command, semi-active
radar and IR homing to 25 km *(13.5 n miles)* at 3 Mach;
warhead 70 kg.
SAM/Guns: 2 CADS-N-1 (Kortik) ❸ each has twin 30 mm Gatling
combined with 8 SA-N-11 (Grisson) and Hot Flash/Hot Spot
radar/optronic director. Laser beam guidance for missiles to
8 km *(4.4 n miles)* warhead 9 kg; 9,000 rds/min (combined) to
1.5 km for guns.
Guns: 1—100 mm/59 A 190 ❹ 60 rds/min to 15 km *(8.2 n
miles)*; weight of shell 16 kg.
Torpedoes: 4 PTA-53 21 in *(533 mm)* (2 twin) fired launchers ❺.
A/S mortars: 1 RBU 6000 ❻ range 6 km; warhead 31 kg.

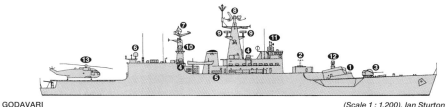

TALWAR *(Scale 1 : 1,200), Ian Sturton /* 0064712

Countermeasures: Decoys: 2 PK 2 chaff launchers.
ESM: Bharat Ajanta; intercept.
ECM: ASOR 11356; jammer.
Radars: Air/surface search: Top Plate ❼ 3D; D/E-band.
Surface search: Palm Frond ❽ I-band.
Fire control: 4 Front Dome ❾ (for SA-N-7); Kite Screech B ❿ (for
SSM and 100 mm gun).
Sonars: Bharat APSOH; hull-mounted; active search and attack;
medium frequency.
VDS; active search; medium frequency.

Helicopters: 1 Ka-28/Ka 31 Helix ⓫ or ALH.

Programmes: Contract placed in 1997 for three Improved Krivak
IIIs. Three more designated Project 17 ships are planned to
start building in 2000 at Mazagon. These later ships may not
be identical to *Talwar*.
Structure: Some weapon systems details are still speculative.
The design of the first three is based on the Northern Design
Bureau initiative. The second three may owe more to the *Delhi*
design. ***UPDATED***

3 GODAVARI CLASS (FFG)

Name	No	Builders	Laid down	Launched	Commissioned
GODAVARI	F 20	Mazagon Dock Ltd, Bombay	2 June 1978	15 May 1980	10 Dec 1983
GOMATI	F 21	Mazagon Dock Ltd, Bombay	1981	19 Mar 1984	16 Apr 1988
GANGA	F 22	Mazagon Dock Ltd, Bombay	1980	21 Oct 1981	30 Dec 1985

Displacement, tons: 3,850 full load
Dimensions, feet (metres): 414.9 × 47.6 × 14.8 (29.5 sonar)
(126.5 × 14.5 × 4.5 (9))
Main machinery: 2 Babcock & Wilcox boilers; 550 psi *(38.7 kg/
cm²)*; 850°F *(450°C)*; 2 turbines; 30,000 hp *(22.4 MW)*;
2 shafts
Speed, knots: 27. **Range, miles:** 4,500 at 12 kt
Complement: 313 (40 officers including 13 aircrew)

Missiles: SSM: 4 SS-N-2D Styx ❶; active radar (Mod 1) or IR (Mod
2) homing to 83 km *(45 n miles)* at 0.9 Mach; warhead 513 kg;
sea-skimmer at end of run. Indian designation.
SAM: SA-N-4 Gecko twin launcher ❷; semi-active radar homing
to 15 km *(8 n miles)* at 2.5 Mach; height 9.1-3,048 m *(130-
10,000 ft)*; warhead 50 kg; limited surface-to-surface
capability; 20 missiles.
Guns: 2—57 mm/70 (twin) ❸; 120 rds/min to 8 km *(4.4 n miles)*;
weight of shell 2.8 kg.
8—30 mm/65 (4 twin) AK 230 ❹; 500 rds/min to 5 km *(2.7 n
miles)*; weight of shell 0.54 kg.
Torpedoes: 6—324 mm ILAS 3 (2 triple) tubes ❺. Whitehead
A244S; anti-submarine; active/passive homing to 7 km *(3.8 n
miles)* at 33 kt; warhead 34 kg (shaped charge). *Godavari* has
tube modifications for the Indian NST 58 version of A244S.
Countermeasures: Decoys: 2 chaff launchers (Super Barricade
in due course). Graseby G738 towed torpedo decoy.
ESM/ECM: Selenia INS-3 (Bharat Ajanta and Elettronica TQN-2);
intercept and jammer.
Combat data systems: Selenia IPN-10 action data automation.
Inmarsat communications (JRC) ❻.
Weapons control: MR 301 MFCS. MR 103 GFCS.
Radars: Air search: Signaal LW08 ❼; D-band.
Air/surface search: Head Net C ❽; 3D; E/F-band.
Navigation/helo control: 2 Signaal ZW06 ❾; or Don Kay; I-band.
Fire control: 2 Drum Tilt ❿; H/I-band (for 30 mm).
Pop Group ⓫; F/H/I-band (for SA-N-4).
Muff Cob ⓬; G/H-band (for 57 mm).
Sonars: Bharat APSOH; hull-mounted; active panoramic search
and attack; medium frequency.
Fathoms Oceanic VDS.
Thomson Sintra DSBV 62 (in *Ganga*); passive towed array; very
low frequency.
Type 162M; bottom classification; high frequency.

Helicopters: 2 Sea King or 1 Sea King and 1 Chetak ⓭.

Structure: A further modification of the original Leander design
with an indigenous content of 72 per cent and a larger hull.
Poor welding is noticeable in *Godavari*. *Gomati* is the first

GODAVARI *(Scale 1 : 1,200), Ian Sturton /* 0052330

GOMATI *3/1998, G Toremans /* 0052331

Indian ship to have digital electronics in her combat data
system.
Operational: French Samahé helicopter handling equipment is
fitted. Usually only one helo is carried with more than one
crew. These ships have a unique mixture of Russian, Western
and Indian weapon systems which has inevitably led to some
equipment compatibility problems. ***VERIFIED***

GODAVARI *6/1997 /* 0012519

1 + 2 MOD GODAVARI CLASS (FFG)

Name	No	Builders	Laid down	Launched	Commissioned
BRAHMAPUTRA	F 31	Garden Reach SY, Calcutta	1989	29 Jan 1994	Apr 2000
BETWA	F 32	Garden Reach SY, Calcutta	1994	26 Feb 1998	2001
BEAS	F 33	Garden Reach SY, Calcutta	1996	2002	2004

Displacement, tons: 3,850 full load
Dimensions, feet (metres): 414.9 × 47.6 × 14.8 (29.5 sonar)
(126.5 × 14.5 × 4.5 (9))
Main machinery: 2 boilers; 550 psi (38.7 kg/cm²); 850°F
(450°C); 2 Bhopal turbines; 30,000 hp (22.4 MW); 2 shafts
Speed, knots: 27. **Range, miles:** 4,500 at 12 kt
Complement: 313 (40 officers including 13 aircrew)

Missiles: SSM: 16 SS-N-25 (4 quad) (KH-35 Uran) ❶; active radar
homing to 130 km (70.2 n miles) at 0.9 Mach; warhead
145 kg; sea skimmer.
SAM: Trishul launcher ❷ command line of sight guidance, radar
homing to 9 km (4.9 n miles) at 2.5 Mach; warhead 50 kg.

Guns: OTO Melara 76 mm/62 ❸; 65 rds/min to 8 km (4.4 n
miles) weight of shell 6 kg.
4—30 mm/65 AK 630 ❹; 6 barrels per mounting; 3,000 rds/
min combined to 2 km.
Torpedoes: 6—324 mm ILAS 3 (2 triple) tubes ❺. Whitehead
A244S; anti-submarine; active/passive homing to 7 km (3.8 n
miles) at 33 kt; warhead 34 kg (shaped charge).
Countermeasures: Decoys: 2 chaff launchers (Super Barricade
in due course). Graseby G738 towed torpedo decoy.
ESM/ECM: Selenia INS-3 (Bharat Ajanta and Elettronica TQN-2)
❻; intercept and jammer.
Combat data systems: Selenia IPN-10 action data automation.
Inmarsat communications (JRC).

Weapons control: MR 103 GFCS.
Radars: Air search: Signaal LW08/Bharat RAWL (PLN 517) ❼;
D-band.
Air/surface search: Head Net C ❽ or Bharat RAWS 03 (PFN 513);
E/F-band.
Navigation/helo control: I-band.
Fire control: 2 Contraves Seaguard ❾ (for 76 mm and SSM).
Bharat Aparna (for SAM).
2 Bass Tilt ❿ (for AK 630) H/I/J-band.
Sonars: Bharat APSOH (Spherion); hull-mounted; active
panoramic search and attack; medium frequency.
Fathoms Oceanic VDS.

Helicopters: 2 Sea King or 1 Sea King and 1 Chetak ⓫.

Programmes: Project 16A. Progress has been very slow.
Structure: Some of the details are still speculative but the main
difference is the replacement of the Godavari SS-N-2 by SS-
N-25 and the introduction of the Trishul SAM system. Gun
armament has also improved.
Operational: First of class basin trials started in December 1998
but full sea trials have been badly delayed. Trishul may not be
operational for some time.

UPDATED

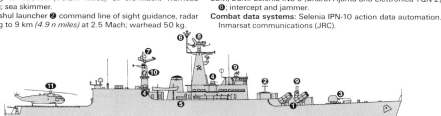

BRAHMAPUTRA   *(Scale 1 : 1,200), Ian Sturton /* 0052329

BRAHMAPUTRA   *12/1999*, GRSE /* 0081941

4 NILGIRI (LEANDER) CLASS (FF)

Name	No	Builders	Laid down	Launched	Commissioned
HIMGIRI	F 34	Mazagon Dock Ltd, Bombay	4 Nov 1968	6 May 1970	23 Nov 1974
DUNAGIRI	F 36	Mazagon Dock Ltd, Bombay	25 Jan 1973	9 Mar 1974	5 May 1977
TARAGIRI	F 41	Mazagon Dock Ltd, Bombay	15 Oct 1975	25 Oct 1976	16 May 1980
VINDHYAGIRI	F 42	Mazagon Dock Ltd, Bombay	5 Nov 1976	12 Nov 1977	8 July 1981

Displacement, tons: 2,682 standard; 2,962 full load
Dimensions, feet (metres): 372 × 43 × 18
(113.4 × 13.1 × 5.5)
Main machinery: 2 Babcock & Wilcox boilers; 550 psi (38.7 kg/
cm²); 850°F (450°C); 2 turbines; 30,000 hp (22.4 MW);
2 shafts
Speed, knots: 27; 28 (Taragiri and Vindhyagiri)
Range, miles: 4,500 at 12 kt
Complement: 267 (17 officers)

Guns: 2 Vickers 4.5 in (114 mm)/45 (twin) Mk 6 ❶; 20 rds/min
to 19 km (10.4 n miles) anti-surface; 6 km (3.3 n miles) anti-
aircraft; weight of shell 25 kg.
4—30 mm/65 (2 twin) AK 230 ❷; 500 rds/min to 5 km (2.7 n
miles); weight of shell 0.54 kg. Replaced Seacat.
2 Oerlikon 20 mm/70 ❸; 800 rds/min to 2 km.
Torpedoes: 6—324 mm ILAS 3 (2 triple) tubes (Taragiri and
Vindhyagiri) ❹. Whitehead A244S or Indian NST 58 version;
anti-submarine; active/passive homing to 7 km (3.8 n miles) at
33 kt; warhead 34 kg (shaped charge).
A/S mortars: 1 Bofors 375 mm twin-tubed launcher (Taragiri
and Vindhyagiri) ❺; range 1,600 m.
1 Limbo Mk 10 triple-tubed launcher (remainder); range
1,000 m; warhead 92 kg.
Countermeasures: Decoys: Graseby 738; towed torpedo decoy.
ESM: Bharat Ajanta; intercept. FH5 Telegon D/F.
ECM: Racal Cutlass; jammer.
Radars: Air search: Signaal LW08 ❻; D-band.
Surface search: Signaal ZW06 ❼; I-band.
Navigation: Decca 1226; I-band.
Signaal M 45 ❽; I/J-band.
IFF: Type 944; 954M.
Sonars: Westinghouse SQS-505; Graseby 750 (APSOH fitted in
Himgiri as trials ship); hull-mounted; active search and attack;
medium frequency. Type 170; active attack; high frequency.
Westinghouse VDS (first two only); active; medium frequency.
Thomson Sintra VDS in Taragiri and Vindhyagiri.

Helicopters: 1 Chetak or 1 Sea King Mk 42 (in Taragiri and
Vindhyagiri) ❾.

Programmes: The first major warships built in Indian yards to a
UK design with a 60 per cent indigenous component. An ex-UK
'Leander' class was acquired in 1995 and is listed under
Training Ships.
Modernisation: The VDS arrays are installed inside towed bodies
built by Fathom Oceanology Ltd of Canada. The transducer
elements in both cases are identical. AK 230 guns have
replaced the obsolete Seacat in all but one of the class.

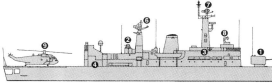

VINDHYAGIRI   *(Scale 1 : 1,200), Ian Sturton*

DUNAGIRI   *6/1998, R Bedi /* 0052332

Structure: In the first two the hangar was provided with
telescopic extension to take the Alouette III helicopter while in
the last pair, a much-changed design, the Mk 10 Mortar has
been removed as well as VDS and the aircraft space increased
to make way for a Sea King helicopter with a telescopic hangar
and Canadian Beartrap haul-down gear. In these two an open

deck has been left below the flight deck for handling mooring
gear and there is a cut-down to the stern.
Operational: Vindhyagiri and Taragiri have more powerful
engines than the remainder. Dunagiri still has a Seacat
launcher but the system is non-operational.

UPDATED

3 ARNALA (PETYA II) CLASS (FFL)

ANDROTH P 69   **ANJADIP** P 73   **AMINI** P 75

Displacement, tons: 950 standard; 1,100 full load
Dimensions, feet (metres): 270 × 29.9 × 10.5
  (82.3 × 9.1 × 3.2)
Main machinery: CODOG; 2 gas turbines; 30,000 hp(m)
  (22 MW); 1 Type 6I-V3 diesel (centre shaft); 5,400 hp(m)
  (3.97 MW) sustained; 3 shafts
Speed, knots: 32. **Range, miles:** 4,000 at 20 kt
Complement: 98

Guns: 4 USSR 3 in *(76 mm)*/60 (2 twin) AK 276 ❶; 90 rds/min
  to 15 km *(8 n miles);* weight of shell 6.8 kg.
Torpedoes: 3—21 in *(533 mm)* (triple) tubes ❷.
A/S mortars: 4 RBU 2500 16-tubed trainable launchers ❸; range
  2,500 m; warhead 21 kg.
Depth charges: 2 racks.
Mines: 2 rails.

Radars: Surface search: Slim Net ❹; E/F-band.
  Navigation: Don 2; I-band.
  Fire control: Hawk Screech ❺; I-band.
  IFF: High Pole B.
Sonars: Herkules; hull-mounted; active search and attack;
  medium/high frequency.

Programmes: A USSR export version of 'Petya II' class with
  simplified communications. Transfers: *Androth* (built at
  Kaliningrad) August 1972; *Anjadip* (built at Khabarovsk)
  February 1973; *Amini* (built at Khabarovsk) March 1974.
Operational: Form 32nd Frigate Squadron based at
  Vishakapatnam. *Andaman* (P 74) sank in heavy weather in the
  Bay of Bengal 22 August 1990. Six others deleted so far, and
  these last three are being replaced as the 'Kora' class
  commissions.
UPDATED

ANDROTH   *(Scale 1 : 900), Ian Sturton*

AMINI   *4/1998, Indian Navy /* 0052333

SHIPBORNE AIRCRAFT

Note: MiG 29 K aircraft may be acquired in due course.

Numbers/Type: 14/3/2 British Aerospace Sea Harrier FRS. Mk 51/Mk 60 (trainers)/T Mk 4
  (in 1999).
Operational speed: 640 kt *(1,186 km/h).*
Service ceiling: 51,200 ft *(15,600 m).*
Range: 800 n miles *(1,480 km).*
Role/Weapon systems: Fleet air defence, strike and reconnaissance STOVL fighter; mid-life
  update planned when funds are available with Elta M-2032 or GEC-Marconi Blue Vixen radar.
  Three more acquired from UK in 1999 to make good losses. Sensors: Ferranti Blue Fox air
  interception radar, limited ECM/RWR (Elta 8420 in due course). Weapons: Air defence; two
  Magic AAMs (possibly ASRAAM in due course), two 30 mm Aden cannon. Strike; two Sea Eagle
  missiles or 3.6 tons of 'iron' bombs.   *UPDATED*

SEA HARRIER   *1994, Indian Navy /* 0012970

Numbers/Type: 5/18/6 Westland Sea King Mks 42A/42B/42C.
Operational speed: 112 kt *(208 km/h).*
Service ceiling: 11,500 ft *(3,500 m).*
Range: 664 n miles *(1,230 km).*
Role/Weapon systems: Mk 42A has primary ASW and 42B primary ASV capability; Mk 42C for
  commando assault/vertrep. Not all aircraft are operational. Sensors: MEL Super Searcher radar,
  Thomson Sintra H/S-12 dipping sonar (Mk 42A and B), AQS 902B acoustic processor (Mk 42B);
  Marconi Hermes ESM (Mk 42B); Bendix weather radar (Mk 42C). Weapons: ASW; 2 Whitehead
  A244S or USSR APR-2 torpedoes; Mk 11 depth bombs, mines (Mk 42B only). ASV; two Sea
  Eagle (Mk 42B only). Unarmed (Mk 42C).   *UPDATED*

SEA KING 42B   *3/1996 /* 0012971

Numbers/Type: 13/5/4 Kamov Ka-27/28/31 Helix A/B/C.
Operational speed: 110 kt *(204 km/h).*
Service ceiling: 12,000 ft *(3,660 m).*
Range: 270 n miles *(500 km).*
Role/Weapon systems: ASW helicopter embarked in large escorts. Has replaced Ka-25. Four
  Kamov Ka-31 AEW acquired in 1999/2000. Sensors: Splash Drop search radar; Oko E-801
  surveillance radar (in Ka 31); VGS-3 dipping sonar, sonobuoys. Weapons: ASW; two Whitehead
  A244S or USSR APR-2 torpedoes or four depth bombs.
UPDATED

HELIX   *2/1996 /* 0012972

Numbers/Type: 23 Aerospatiale (HAL) SA 319B Chetak (Alouette III).
Operational speed: 113 kt *(210 km/h).*
Service ceiling: 10,500 ft *(3,200 m).*
Range: 290 n miles *(540 km).*
Role/Weapon systems: Several helicopter roles performed including embarked ASW and carrier-
  based SAR, utility and support to commando forces. 15 aircraft are operated by Coast Guard.
  Weapons: ASW; two Whitehead A244S torpedoes.
VERIFIED

CHETAK   *8/1997 /* 0012522

Numbers/Type: 6 HAL Advanced Light Helicopter (ALH).
Operational speed: 156 kt *(290 km/h).*
Service ceiling: 9,850 ft *(3,000 m).*
Range: 216 n miles *(400 km).*
Role/Weapon systems: Full production expected in due course to replace Chetak. The naval variant started trials in March 1995 and may be sold to the Coast Guard. Sensors: Dipping sonar, ECM. Weapons: ASW; torpedoes, depth charges. ASV; Sea Eagle ASM.   *UPDATED*

ALH   *4/1998, Indian Navy /* 0052340

LAND-BASED MARITIME AIRCRAFT (FRONT LINE)

Numbers/Type: 24 (7) Dornier 228.
Operational speed: 200 kt *(370 km/h).*
Service ceiling: 28,000 ft *(8,535 m).*
Range: 940 n miles *(1,740 km).*
Role/Weapon systems: Coastal surveillance and EEZ protection duties for Navy and Coast Guard (14 aircraft). Seven more ordered for Coast Guard in late 1999. Sensors: MEL Marec or THORN EMI Super Marec search radar with FLIR, cameras and searchlight. Weapons: Unarmed, but may carry anti-ship missiles in due course.   *UPDATED*

Numbers/Type: 5 Ilyushin Il-38 (May).
Operational speed: 347 kt *(645 km/h).*
Service ceiling: 32,800 ft *(10,000 m).*
Range: 3,887 n miles *(7,200 km).*
Role/Weapon systems: Shore-based long-range ASW reconnaissance into Indian Ocean. Replacements needed. Sensors: Wet Eye search radar, MAD, sonobuoys, ESM. Weapons: ASW; various torpedoes, mines and depth bombs.   *VERIFIED*

Numbers/Type: 11 Pilatus Britten-Norman Maritime Defender.
Operational speed: 150 kt *(280 km/h).*
Service ceiling: 18,900 ft *(5,760 m).*
Range: 1,500 n miles *(2,775 km).*
Role/Weapon systems: Coastal and short-range reconnaissance tasks undertaken in support of Navy (6) and Coast Guard. Six upgraded with turboprop engines 1996-97. Sensors: Search radar, camera. Weapons: Unarmed.   *VERIFIED*

Numbers/Type: 8 (8) Tupolev Tu-142M (Bear F).
Operational speed: 500 kt *(925 km/h).*
Service ceiling: 45,000 ft *(13,720 m).*
Range: 6,775 n miles *(12,550 km).*
Role/Weapon systems: First entered service in April 1988 for long-range surface surveillance and ASW. Air Force manned. Eight more may be acquired by 2001. Sensors: Wet Eye search and attack radars, MAD, cameras. 75 active and passive sonobuoys. Weapons: ASW; 12 torpedoes, depth bombs. ASV possibly AX-S-20 (air-launched SS-N-25) in due course; two 23 mm cannon; possibly Sea Eagle. ASM. Novator Alfa in due course.   *UPDATED*

Numbers/Type: 8 SEPECAT/HAL Jaguar International.
Operational speed: 917 kt *(1,699 km/h)* (max).
Service ceiling: 36,000 ft *(11,000 m).*
Range: 760 n miles *(1,408 km).*
Role/Weapon systems: A maritime strike squadron. Air Force operated. Sensors: Thomson-CSF Agave radar. Weapons: ASV; 2 BAe Sea Eagle; 2 DEFA 30 mm cannon or up to 8—1,000 lb bombs. Can carry 2 Magic AAM overwing.   *UPDATED*

CORVETTES

2 + 2 KORA CLASS (PROJECT 25A) (FSG)

Name	No	Builders	Laid down		Launched		Commissioned
KORA	P 61	Garden Reach SY, Calcutta	10 Jan	1990	23 Sep	1992	10 Aug 1998
KIRCH	—	Garden Reach SY, Calcutta/Mazagon Dock	31 Jan	1990	28 Sep	1995	2000
KULISH	—	Garden Reach SY, Calcutta	4 Oct	1995	18 Aug	1997	2001
KARMUKH	—	Garden Reach SY, Calcutta/Mazagon Dock	27 Aug	1997	June	2000	2003

Displacement, tons: 1,350 full load
Dimensions, feet (metres): 298.9 × 34.4 × 14.8
(91.1 × 10.5 × 4.5)
Main machinery: 2 SEMT-Pielstick/Kirloskar 18 PA6 V 280 diesels; 14,400 hp(m) *(10.58 MW)* sustained; 2 shafts; acbLIPS cp props
Speed, knots: 25. **Range, miles:** 4,000 at 16 kt
Complement: 134 (14 officers)

Missiles: SSM: 16 Zvezda SS-N-25 (4 quad) (Kh 35 Uran) ❶; active radar homing to 130 km *(70.2 n miles)* at 0.9 Mach; warhead 145 kg; sea skimmer.
SAM: 2 SA-N-5 Grail ❷; manual aiming; IR homing to 6 km *(3.2 n miles)* at 1.5 Mach; altitude to 2,500 m *(8,000 ft)*; warhead 1.5 kg.
Guns: 1 USSR 3 in *(76 mm)/*60 AK 176 ❸; 90 rds/min to 15 km *(8 n miles)*; weight of shell 7 kg.
2—30 mm/65 AK 630 ❹; 6 barrels per mounting; 3,000 rds/min to 2 km.
Countermeasures: Decoys: 4 PK 10 chaff launchers ❺. 2 NPOL; towed torpedo decoys.
ESM: Bharat Ajanta P Mk II intercept ❻.
Combat data systems: Bharat Vympal IPN-10.
Radars: Air search: Cross Dome ❼; E/F-band; range 130 km *(70 n miles)*.
Air/surface search: Plank Shave (Granit Harpun B) ❽; I/J-band.
Fire control: Bass Tilt ❾; H/I-band.
Navigation: Bharat 1245; I-band.
IFF: Square Head.

Helicopters: Platform only ❿ for Chetak (to be replaced by Hindustan Aeronautics ALH in due course).

Programmes: First pair ordered in April 1990 and second pair in October 1994. Programme slowed by delays in provision of Russian equipment.
Structure: Very similar to the original 'Khukri' class except that SS-N-25 has replaced SS-N-2. It is possible that Trishul SAM may replace the 76 mm gun in later units of the class. Stabilizers fitted.
Operational: Sea trials for *Kirch* and *Kulish* both scheduled for 2000. All 16 SS-N-25 can be fired in one salvo.   *UPDATED*

KORA   *(Scale 1 : 900), Ian Sturton /* 0064715

KORA   *10/1998*, Maritime Photographic /* 0053466

KORA   *3/1999* /* 0064716

4 KHUKRI CLASS (PROJECT 25) (FSG)

Name	No	Builders	Laid down	Launched	Commissioned
KHUKRI	P 49	Mazagon Dock Ltd, Bombay	27 Sep 1985	3 Dec 1986	23 Aug 1989
KUTHAR	P 46	Mazagon Dock Ltd, Bombay	13 Sep 1986	15 Apr 1989	7 June 1990
KIRPAN	P 44	Garden Reach SY, Calcutta	15 Nov 1985	16 Aug 1988	12 Jan 1991
KHANJAR	P 47	Garden Reach SY, Calcutta	15 Nov 1985	16 Aug 1988	22 Oct 1991

Displacement, tons: 1,350 full load
Dimensions, feet (metres): 298.9 × 34.4 × 13.1 *(91.1 × 10.5 × 4)*
Main machinery: 2 SEMT-Pielstick/Kirloskar 18 PA6 V 280 diesels; 14,400 hp(m) *(10.58 MW)* sustained; 2 shafts; acbLIPS cp props
Speed, knots: 25. **Range, miles:** 4,000 at 16 kt
Complement: 79 (10 officers)

Missiles: SSM: 4 SS-N-2D Mod 1 Styx (2 twin) launchers ❶; IR homing to 83 km *(45 n miles)* at 0.9 Mach; warhead 513 kg.
SAM: SA-N-5 Grail ❷; manual aiming; IR homing to 6 km *(3.2 n miles)* at 1.5 Mach; altitude to 2,500 m *(8,000 ft)*; warhead 1.5 kg.
Guns: 1 USSR 3 in *(76 mm)*/60 AK 176 ❸; 120 rds/min to 15 km *(8 n miles)*; weight of shell 7 kg.
2—30 mm/65 AK 630 ❹; 6 barrels per mounting; 3,000 rds/min to 2 km.
Countermeasures: Decoys: 2 PK 16 chaff launchers ❺. NPOL; towed torpedo decoy.
ESM: Bharat Ajanta P; intercept.
Combat data systems: Selenia IPN-10 *(Khukri)*; Bharat Vympal IPN-10 (remainder).
Radars: Air search: Cross Dome ❻; E/F-band; range 130 km *(70 n miles)*.
Air/surface search: Plank Shave ❼; I-band.
Fire control: Bass Tilt ❽; H/I-band.
Navigation: Bharat 1245; I-band.

Helicopters: Platform only ❾ for Chetak (to be replaced by Hindustan Aeronautics ALH in due course).

Programmes: First two ordered December 1983, two in 1985. The diesels are assembled in India under licence by Kirloskar. Indigenous content of the whole ship is about 65 per cent.
Structure: The reported plan was to make the first four ASW ships, and the remainder anti-aircraft or general purpose. However *Khukri* has neither torpedo tubes nor a sonar (apart from an Atlas Elektronik echo-sounder), so if the plan is correct these ships will rely on an ALH helicopter which has dunking sonar and ASW torpedoes and depth charges. All have fin stabilisers and full air conditioning.
Operational: All based at Vishakapatnam. The advanced light helicopter (ALH) to have Sea Eagle SSM, torpedoes and dipping sonar.

UPDATED

KHUKRI

(Scale 1 : 900), Ian Sturton / 0064714

KHANJAR

10/1998, John Mortimer / 0052335

KIRPAN

5/1999*, van Ginderen Collection / 0064714

KUTHAR

3/1996 / 0012974

4 ABHAY (PAUK II) CLASS (FS)

Name	No	Builders	Commissioned
ABHAY	P 33	Volodarski	10 Mar 1989
AJAY	P 34	Volodarski	24 Jan 1990
AKSHAY	P 35	Volodarski	10 Dec 1990
AGRAY	P 36	Volodarski	30 Jan 1991

Displacement, tons: 485 full load
Dimensions, feet (metres): 189 × 33.5 × 10.8
(57.6 × 10.2 × 3.3)
Main machinery: 2 Type M 521 diesels; 16,184 hp(m) (11.9 MW)
sustained; 2 shafts
Speed, knots: 32. **Range, miles:** 2,400 at 14 kt
Complement: 32 (6 officers)

Missiles: SAM: SA-N-5/8 Grail quad launcher; manual aiming,
IR homing to 6 km (3.2 n miles) at 1.5 Mach; warhead 1.5 kg.
Guns: 1 USSR 3 in (76 mm)/60; 120 rds/min to 15 km (8 n
miles); weight of shell 7 kg.
1—30 mm/65 AK 630; 6 barrels; 3,000 rds/min combined to
2 km.
Torpedoes: 4—21 in (533 mm) (2 twin) tubes. SET-65E; active/
passive homing to 15 km (8.1 n miles) at 40 kt; warhead
205 kg.
A/S mortars: 2 RBU 1200 5-tubed fixed; range 1,200 m;
warhead 34 kg.
Countermeasures: 2 PK 16 chaff launchers.
Radars: Air/Surface search: Cross Dome; E/F-band.
Navigation: Pechora; I-band.
Fire Control: Bass Tilt; H/I-band.
Sonars: Rat Tail VDS (on transom); attack; high frequency.

AJAY 2/1998 / 0052339

Programmes: 'Modified Pauk II' class built in the USSR at
Volodarski, Rybinsk for export. Original order in late 1983 but
completion of the first delayed by lack of funds and the order
for the others was not reinstated until 1987. Names associated
with former coastal patrol craft.

Structure: Has a longer superstructure than the Pauk I, larger
torpedo tubes and improved electronics.
Operational: Classified as ASW ships. All based at Mumbai.
UPDATED

11 + 1 (4) VEER (TARANTUL I) CLASS (TYPE 1241RE) (FSG)

Name	No	Builders	Laid down	Launched	Commissioned
VEER	K 40	Volodarski, Rybinsk	1984	Oct 1986	26 Mar 1987
NIRBHIK	K 41	Volodarski, Rybinsk	1985	Oct 1987	21 Dec 1987
NIPAT	K 42	Volodarski, Rybinsk	1986	Nov 1988	5 Dec 1988
NISHANK	K 43	Volodarski, Rybinsk	1987	June 1989	2 Sep 1989
NIRGHAT	K 44	Volodarski, Rybinsk	1988	Mar 1990	4 June 1990
VIBHUTI	K 45	Mazagon Dock, Bombay	Mar 1988	26 Apr 1990	3 June 1991
VIPUL	K 46	Mazagon Dock, Bombay	July 1988	3 Jan 1991	16 Mar 1992
VINASH	K 47	Goa Shipyard	Jan 1989	24 Jan 1992	20 Nov 1993
VIDYUT	K 48	Goa Shipyard	Mar 1990	12 Dec 1992	16 Jan 1995
NASHAK	K 83	Mazagon Dock, Bombay	Jan 1991	12 Nov 1993	29 Dec 1994
PRAHAR	K 98	Goa Shipyard	Nov 1991	26 Aug 1995	1 Mar 1997
—	—	Mazagon Dock, Bombay	Aug 1998	Sep 2000	June 2001

Displacement, tons: 385 standard; 455 full load
Dimensions, feet (metres): 184.1 × 37.7 × 8.2
(56.1 × 11.5 × 2.5)
Main machinery: COGOG; 2 Nikolayev Type DR 77 gas turbines;
16,016 hp(m) (11.77 MW) sustained; 2 Nikolayev Type DR 76
gas turbines with reversible gearboxes; 4,993 hp(m)
(3.67 MW) sustained; 2 shafts
Speed, knots: 36. **Range, miles:** 2,000 at 20 kt; 400 at 36 kt
Complement: 41 (5 officers)

Missiles: SSM: 4 SS-N-2D Mod 1 Styx; IR homing to 83 km (45 n
miles) at 0.9 Mach; warhead 513 kg; sea-skimmer at end of
run. May be replaced by SS-N-25 in a modified version.
SAM: SA-N-5 Grail quad launcher; manual aiming; IR homing to
6 km (3.2 n miles) at 1.5 Mach; warhead 1.5 kg.
Guns: 1 USSR 3 in (76 mm)/60; 120 rds/min to 15 km (8 n
miles); weight of shell 7 kg.
2—30 mm/65 AK 630; 6 barrels per mounting; 3,000 rds/min
combined to 2 km.
Countermeasures: Decoys: PK 16 chaff launcher.
ESM: Bharat Ajanta; intercept.
Weapons control: Hood Wink optronic director.
Radars: Air/surface search: Plank Shave; I-band.
Navigation: Mius; I-band.
Fire control: Bass tilt; H/I-band.
IFF: Salt Pot, Square Head A. Fire control: Bass tilt: H/I-band.

Programmes: First five are USSR 'Tarantul I' class built for export.
Remainder of this type built in India. Four more of a modified
type reported ordered but this is not confirmed.
Structure: Variations in the Indian-built ships were to include
CODOG propulsion (with one gas turbine and two diesels) but
this has not been confirmed.
Operational: All form the 22nd Squadron at Mumbai.
UPDATED

VINASH 11/1993, Goa Shipyard / 0012976

2 DURG (NANUCHKA II) CLASS (FSG)

Name	No	Commissioned
VIJAYDURG	K 71	Apr 1976
SINDHUDURG	K 72	Sep 1977

Displacement, tons: 660 full load
Dimensions, feet (metres): 194.5 × 38.7 × 8.5
(59.3 × 11.8 × 2.6)
Main machinery: 6 M 504 diesels; 26,112 hp(m) (19.2 MW)
sustained; 3 shafts
Speed, knots: 33. **Range, miles:** 2,500 at 12 kt; 900 at 31 kt
Complement: 42 (7 officers)

Missiles: SSM: 4 SS-N-2C Styx; active radar or IR homing to
83 km (45 n miles) at 0.9 Mach; warhead 513 kg.
SAM: SA-N-4 Gecko twin launcher; semi-active radar homing to
15 km (8 n miles) at 2.5 Mach; height envelope 9-3,048 m
(29.5-10,000 ft); warhead 50 kg; 20 missiles.
Guns: 2 USSR 57 mm/80 (twin); 120 rds/min to 8 km (4.4 n
miles); weight of shell 2.8 kg.
Countermeasures: 2 PK 16 chaff launchers.
ESM: Bell Tap; radar warning.
Radars: Air/surface search: Square Tie; I-band; range 73 km
(40 n miles) (mounted in radome).
Fire control: Pop Group; F/H/I-band (for SAN-4).
Muff Cob; G/H-band.
Navigation: Don 2; I-band.
IFF: High Pole. 2 Square Head.

VIJAYDURG 6/1996, van Ginderen Collection / 0012977

Programmes: Built at Leningrad and transferred from the USSR
in March 1977 and August 1977.
Structure: The radome is mounted lower than in Russian ships of
this class due to the absence of Fish Bowl because of the use of
SS-N-2 missiles in place of SS-N-9.

Operational: Based at Mumbai. One other of the class paid off in
June 1999.
UPDATED

PATROL FORCES

7 SUKANYA CLASS (OPV)

Name	No	Builders	Launched	Commissioned
SUKANYA	P 50	Korea Tacoma, Masan	1989	31 Aug 1989
SUBHADRA	P 51	Korea Tacoma, Masan	1989	25 Jan 1990
SUVARNA	P 52	Korea Tacoma, Masan	22 Aug 1990	4 Apr 1991
SAVITRI	P 53	Hindustan SY, Vishakapatnam	23 May 1989	27 Nov 1990
SARYU	P 54	Hindustan SY, Vishakapatnam	16 Oct 1989	8 Oct 1991
SHARADA	P 55	Hindustan SY, Vishakapatnam	22 Aug 1990	27 Oct 1991
SUJATA	P 56	Hindustan SY, Vishakapatnam	25 Oct 1991	3 Nov 1993

Displacement, tons: 1,890 full load
Dimensions, feet (metres): 331.7 oa; 315 wl × 37.7 × 14.4 *(101.1; 96 × 11.5 × 4.4)*
Main machinery: 2 SEMT-Pielstick 16 PA6 V 280 diesels; 12,800 hp(m) *(9.41 MW)* sustained; 2 shafts
Speed, knots: 21. **Range, miles:** 5,800 at 15 kt
Complement: 140 (15 officers)

Guns: 1 Bofors 40 mm/60. May be replaced by a 76 mm in due course. 4—12.7 mm MGs.
Radars: Surface search: Racal Decca 2459; I-band.
Navigation: Bharat 1245; I-band.

Helicopters: 1 Chetak.

Programmes: First three ordered in March 1987 from Korea Tacoma to an 'Ulsan' class design. Second four ordered in August 1987. The Korean-built ships commissioned at Masan and then sailed for India where the armament was fitted. Three others of a modified design have been built for the Coast Guard.
Structure: Lightly armed and able to 'stage' helicopters, they are fitted out for offshore patrol work only but have the capacity to be much more heavily armed. Fin stabilisers fitted. Firefighting pump on hangar roof aft.
Operational: These ships are used for harbour defence, protection of offshore installations and patrol of the EEZ. Potential for role change is considerable. *Subhadra* modified in early 2000 to test fire Dhanush (naval version of Prithvi) SSM from her flight deck. Missile range is 250 km *(134.9 n miles)*, warhead 500 kg. First three based at Mumbai, last pair at Kochi, the other two at Vishakapatnam.

UPDATED   SUVARNA   *6/1997 /* 0012526

3 OSA II CLASS (FAST ATTACK CRAFT—MISSILE) (PCFG)

PRALAYA K 91   **CHAPAL** K 94   **CHATAK** K 96

Displacement, tons: 245 full load
Dimensions, feet (metres): 126.6 × 24.9 × 8.6 *(38.6 × 7.6 × 2.7)*
Main machinery: 3 Type M 504 diesels; 10,800 hp(m) *(7.94 MW)* sustained; 3 shafts
Speed, knots: 37. **Range, miles:** 800 at 25 kt
Complement: 30

Missiles: SSM: 4 SS-N-2B Styx; active radar or IR homing to 46 km *(25 n miles)* at 0.9 Mach; warhead 513 kg.
Guns: 4 USSR 30 mm/65 (2 twin); 500 rds/min to 5 km *(2.7 n miles)*; weight of shell 0.54 kg.
Radars: Surface search: Square Tie; I-band.
Fire control: Drum Tilt; H/I-band.

Programmes: Eight 'Osa II' class delivered from USSR January 1976/September 1977.
Operational: Five deleted so far and cannibalised for spares. Missile tubes may be removed. Based at Vishakapatnam.

UPDATED

T 61   *1994*, Goa Shipyard /* 0064717

2 + 2 (15) SUPER DVORA Mk II CLASS (PCF)

No	Builders	Commissioned
T 80	Ramta, IAI	24 June 1998
T 81	Ramta, IAI	14 June 1999
T 82	Goa Shipyard	2000
T 83	Goa Shipyard	2001

Displacement, tons: 60 full load
Dimensions, feet (metres): 82 × 18.4 × 4.9 *(25 × 5.6 × 1.5)*
Main machinery: 2 MTU 12V 396 TE94 diesels; 4,570 hp(m) *(3.36 MW)*; 2 surface drives
Speed, knots: 50. **Range, miles:** 700 at 42 kt
Complement: 10 (1 officer)
Guns: 1 Oerlikon 20 mm. 2—12.7 mm MGs.
Weapons control: Elop MSIS optronic director.
Radars: Surface search: Koden; I-band.

Comment: First pair ordered 2 December 1996. Two more building under licence at Goa, with a further fifteen projected, some possibly for the Coast Guard.

UPDATED

OSA II (old number)   *4/1998, Indian Navy /* 0052341

6 + 2 SDB Mk 3/T 62 CLASS (LARGE PATROL CRAFT) (PC)

T 58-T 61   **T 62-T 65**

Displacement, tons: 210 full load
Dimensions, feet (metres): 124 × 24.6 × 6.2 *(37.8 × 7.5 × 1.9)*
Main machinery: 2 MTU 16V 538 TB92 diesels; 6,820 hp(m) *(5 MW)* sustained; 2 shafts
Speed, knots: 30
Complement: 32
Guns: 2 Bofors 40 mm/60; 120 rds/min to 10 km *(5.5 n miles)*; weight of shell 0.89 kg.
Radars: Surface search: Bharat 1245; I-band.

Comment: First batch built at Garden Reach and Goa and completed 1984-86. Second batch of four *(T 62-T 65)* started building in 1997 with the first two launched in March and November 1999 at Garden Reach. This later group may have some differences in design. Some of the earlier ships have been paid off.

UPDATED

T 80   *6/1998*, IAI /* 0064718

AMPHIBIOUS FORCES

2 + 1 (3) MAGAR CLASS (LST)

Name	No	Builders	Launched	Commissioned
MAGAR	L 20	Hindustan/Garden Reach	7 Nov 1984	15 July 1987
GHARIAL	L 23	Hindustan/Garden Reach	1 Apr 1991	14 Feb 1997
—	—	Hindustan/Garden Reach	2002	2008

Displacement, tons: 5,655 full load
Dimensions, feet (metres): 409.4 oa; 393.7 wl × 57.4 × 13.1 *(124.8; 120 × 17.5 × 4)*
Main machinery: 2 SEMT-Pielstick 12 PA6 V280 diesels; 8,560 hp(m) *(6.29 MW)* sustained; 2 shafts
Speed, knots: 15. **Range, miles:** 3,000 at 14 kt
Complement: 136 (16 officers)
Military lift: 15 tanks plus 8 APC plus 500 troops
Guns: 4 Bofors 40 mm/60. 2—122 mm multibarrel rocket launchers at the bow.
Countermeasures: ESM: Bharat Ajanta; intercept.
Radars: Navigation: Bharat; I-band.
Helicopters: 1 Sea King 42C; platform for 2.

Comment: Based on the *Sir Lancelot* design. *Gharial* ordered in 1985. Built at Hindustan Shipyard but fitted out at Garden Reach. A third of class with some major design changes was laid down in July 1996. Based on previous performance with this class, it should be completed in 12 years. More may be built at Mazagon. Carries four LCVPs on davits. Bow door. Can beach on gradients 1 in 40 or more. *Magar* refitted in 1995. Both based at Vishakapatnam.

UPDATED

MAGAR   *10/1990, 92 Wing RAAF*

10 Mk 3 LANDING CRAFT (LCU/LSM)

VASCO DA GAMA L 34	MIDHUR L 38	MANGALA L 39
L 31-33	L 35-37	L 40

Displacement, tons: 500 full load
Dimensions, feet (metres): 188.6 oa; 174.5 pp × 26.9 × 5.2 *(57.5; 53.2 × 8.2 × 1.6)*
Main machinery: 3 Kirloskar-MAN V8V 17.5/22 AMAL diesels; 1,686 hp(m) *(1.24 MW)*; 3 shafts
Speed, knots: 11. **Range, miles:** 1,000 at 8 kt
Complement: 167
Military lift: 250 tons; 2 PT 76 or 2 APC. 120 troops.
Guns: 2 Bofors 40 mm/60 (aft).
Mines: Can be embarked.
Radars: Navigation: Decca 1229; I-band.

Comment: L 34 and L 35 built by Hooghly D and E Co and remainder at Goa Shipyard. First craft *(Vasco da Gama)* commissioned 28 January 1980 and the last one commissioned 25 March 1987. L 35-L 40 have a considerably modified superstructure and a higher bulwark on the cargo deck.

UPDATED

L 36   *2/1999*, 92 Wing RAAF / 0064719*

L 31   *3/1995* / 0064720*

8 POLNOCHNY C (TYPE 773) and D CLASS (LSM)

GHORPAD L 14	SHARDUL L 16	CHEETAH L 18	GULDAR L 21
KESARI L 15	SHARABH L 17	MAHISH L 19	KUMBHIR L 22

Displacement, tons: 1,120 standard; 1,305 (D class); 1,150 full load
Dimensions, feet (metres): 266.7; 275.3 (D class) × 31.8 × 7.9 *(81.3; 83.9 × 9.7 × 2.4)*
Main machinery: 2 Kolomna Type 40-D diesels; 4,400 hp(m) *(3.2 MW)* sustained; 2 shafts
Speed, knots: 18. **Range, miles:** 2,600 at 12 kt
Complement: 108 (12 officers)
Military lift: 350 tons including 6 tanks; 180 troops
Guns: 4—30 mm (2 twin). 2—140 mm 18-tubed rocket launchers.
Radars: Navigation: Don 2 or Krivach (SRN 745); I-band.
Fire control: Drum Tilt; H/I-band (in D class).
Helicopters: Platform only (in D class).

Comment: All new construction direct from Naval Shipyard, Gdynia. *Ghorpad* and *Kesari* transferred in March 1975, *Shardul* and *Sharabh* in February 1976, *Cheetah* in February 1985, *Mahish* in July 1985, *Guldar* in March 1986 and *Kumbhir* in November 1986. The last four are Polnochny Ds with the flight deck forward of the bridge and different radars. All are being restricted operationally through lack of spares, but all are seaworthy. Based at Vishakapatnam.

UPDATED

KUMBHIR   *4/1998, Indian Navy / 0052343*

MINE WARFARE FORCES

Note: A need for at least 10 minehunters has been accepted with the lead vessels to be built overseas and the remainder at Goa. An alternative is to build all 10 to a Russian design. Hulls to be of GRP. In 1990 it was reported that six (M 89-M 94) of 800 tons and 50 m in length were to be ordered from Goa Shipyard which is installing GRP facilities, but no order has been placed.

12 PONDICHERRY (NATYA I) CLASS (TYPE 266M)
(MINESWEEPERS—OCEAN) (MSO)

Name	No	Builders	Commissioned
PONDICHERRY	M 61	Isora, Leningrad	2 Feb 1978
PORBANDAR	M 62	Isora, Leningrad	19 Dec 1978
BEDI	M 63	Isora, Leningrad	27 Apr 1979
BHAVNAGAR	M 64	Isora, Leningrad	27 Apr 1979
ALLEPPEY	M 65	Isora, Leningrad	10 June 1980
RATNAGIRI	M 66	Isora, Leningrad	10 June 1980
KARWAR	M 67	Isora, Leningrad	14 July 1986
CANNANORE	M 68	Isora, Leningrad	17 Dec 1987
CUDDALORE	M 69	Isora, Leningrad	29 Oct 1987
KAKINADA	M 70	Isora, Leningrad	23 Dec 1986
KOZHIKODE	M 71	Isora, Leningrad	19 Dec 1988
KONKAN	M 72	Isora, Leningrad	8 Oct 1988

Displacement, tons: 804 full load
Dimensions, feet (metres): 200.1 × 33.5 × 10.8 *(61 × 10.2 × 3)*
Main machinery: 2 Type 504 diesels; 5,000 hp(m) *(3.67 MW)* sustained; 2 shafts; cp props
Speed, knots: 16. **Range, miles:** 3,000 at 12 kt
Complement: 82 (10 officers)

Guns: 4—30 mm/65 (2 twin); 500 rds/min to 5 km *(2.7 n miles)*; weight of shell 0.54 kg.
4—25 mm/70 (2 twin); 270 rds/min to 3 km *(1.6 n miles)*.
A/S mortars: 2 RBU 1200 5-tubed fixed; range 1,200 m; warhead 34 kg.
Mines: Can carry 10.
Countermeasures: MCM: 1 GKT-2 contact sweep; 1 AT-2 acoustic sweep; 1 TEM-3 magnetic sweep.
Radars: Navigation: Don 2; I-band.
Fire control: Drum Tilt; H/I-band.
IFF: 2 Square Head. High Pole B.
Sonars: MG 69/79; hull-mounted; active mine detection; high frequency.

Programmes: Built for export. Last six were delivered out of pennant number order.
Structure: Steel hulls but do not have stern ramp as in Russian class.
Operational: Some are fitted with two quad SA-N-5 systems. *Pondicherry* was painted white and used as the Presidential yacht for the Indian Fleet Review by President R Venkataramen on 15 February 1989; she reverted to her normal role and colour on completion. One serves as an AGI. First six based at Mumbai, remainder at Vishakapatnam.

UPDATED

BEDI   *1/1996*, van Ginderen Collection / 0064721*

6 MAHÉ (YEVGENYA) CLASS (TYPE 1258)
(MINESWEEPERS—INSHORE) (MSI)

MAHÉ M 83	MANGROL M 85	MULKI M 87
MALVAN M 84	MALPE M 86	MAGDALA M 88

Displacement, tons: 90 full load
Dimensions, feet (metres): 80.7 × 18 × 4.9 *(24.6 × 5.5 × 1.5)*
Main machinery: 2 Type 3-D-12 diesels; 600 hp(m) *(440 kW)* sustained; 2 shafts
Speed, knots: 11. **Range, miles:** 300 at 10 kt
Complement: 10 (1 officer)
Guns: 2 USSR 25 mm/80 (twin).
Radars: Navigation: Spin Trough; I-band.
Sonars: MG 7 small transducer streamed over the stern on a crane.

Comment: First three commissioned 16 May 1983 and second three on 10 May 1984. A mid-1960s design with GRP hulls built at Kolpino. All based at Kochi and reported as likely to be paid off soon.
UPDATED

MULKI   6/1994* / 0064722

SURVEY AND RESEARCH SHIPS

Note: The National Institute of Oceanography operates several research and survey ships including *Sagar Kanya, Samudra Manthan, Sagar Sampada, Samudra Sarvekshak, Samudra Nidhi* and *Samudra Sandhari.*

8 SANDHAYAK CLASS (SURVEY SHIPS) (AGS)

Name	No	Builders	Launched		Commissioned	
SANDHAYAK	J 18	Garden Reach, Calcutta	6 Apr	1977	1 Mar	1981
NIRDESHAK	J 19	Garden Reach, Calcutta	16 Nov	1978	4 Oct	1982
NIRUPAK	J 14	Garden Reach, Calcutta	10 July	1981	14 Aug	1985
INVESTIGATOR	J 15	Garden Reach, Calcutta	8 Aug	1987	11 Jan	1990
JAMUNA	J 16	Garden Reach, Calcutta	4 Sep	1989	31 Aug	1991
SUTLEJ	J 17	Garden Reach, Calcutta	1 Dec	1991	19 Feb	1993
DARSHAK	J 21	Goa Shipyard	3 Mar	1999	June 2000	
SARVESKHAK	J 22	Goa Shipyard	24 Nov	1999	Nov 2000	

Displacement, tons: 1,929 full load
Dimensions, feet (metres): 288 × 42 × 11.1 *(87.8 × 12.8 × 3.4)*
Main machinery: 2 GRSE/MAN 66V 30/45 ATL diesels; 7,720 hp(m) *(5.67 MW)* sustained; 2 shafts; active rudders
Speed, knots: 16. **Range, miles:** 6,000 at 14 kt; 14,000 at 10 kt
Complement: 178 (18 officers) plus 30 scientists
Guns: 1 or 2 Bofors 40 mm/60.
Countermeasures: ESM: Telegon IV HF D/F.
Radars: Navigation: Racal Decca 1629; I-band.
Helicopters: 1 Chetak.

Comment: Telescopic hangar. Fitted with three echo-sounders, side scan sonar, extensively equipped laboratories, and carries four GRP survey launches on davits amidships. Painted white with yellow funnels. An active rudder with a DC motor gives speeds of up to 5 kt. First three based at Vishakapatnam and have been used as troop transports. *Investigator* is at Mumbai and *Jamuna* and *Sutlej* at Kochi. The last pair were laid down in May and August 1995 and have a secondary role as casualty holding ships.
UPDATED

SANDHAYAK   8/1997* / 0012527

---

1 SAGARDHWANI CLASS (RESEARCH SHIP) (AGOR)

Name	No	Builders	Commissioned
SAGARDHWANI	A 74	Garden Reach, Calcutta	30 July 1994

Displacement, tons: 2,050 full load
Dimensions, feet (metres): 279.2 × 42 × 12.1 *(85.1 × 12.8 × 3.7)*
Main machinery: 2 GRSE/MAN 66V 30/45 ATL diesels; 3,860 hp(m) *(2.84 MW)* sustained; 2 shafts; 2 auxiliary thrusters
Speed, knots: 16. **Range, miles:** 6,000 at 16 kt
Complement: 80 (10 officers) plus 16 scientists
Radars: Navigation: Racal Decca 1629; I-band.
Helicopters: Platform for Alouette III.

Comment: Marine Acoustic Research Ship (MARS) launched in May 1991. The hull and main machinery are very similar to the 'Sandhayak' class survey ships, but there are marked superstructure differences with the bridge positioned amidships and a helicopter platform forward. Aft there are two large cranes and a gantry for deploying and recovering research equipment. The vessel is designed to carry out acoustic and geological research and special attention has been paid to noise reduction. The ship is painted white except for the lift equipment and two boats which are orange. Employed in advanced torpedo trials and missile range support. Based at Kochi.
UPDATED

SAGARDHWANI   4/1998, Indian Navy / 0052344

---

4 MAKAR CLASS (SURVEY SHIPS) (AGS)

MAKAR J 33	MITHUN J 34	MEEN J 35	MESH J 36

Displacement, tons: 210 full load
Dimensions, feet (metres): 123 × 24.6 × 6.2 *(37.5 × 7.5 × 1.9)*
Main machinery: 2 diesels; 1,124 hp(m) *(826 kW)*; 2 shafts
Speed, knots: 12. **Range, miles:** 1,500 at 12 kt
Complement: 36 (4 officers)
Guns: 1 Bofors 40 mm/60.
Radars: Navigation: Decca 1629; I-band.

Comment: Launched at Goa in 1981-82. Similar hulls to deleted 'SDB Mk 2' class but with much smaller engines. Two based at Kochi and two at Chennai.
UPDATED

MAKAR   4/1992* / 0064723

TRAINING SHIPS

1 TIR CLASS (TRAINING SHIP) (AX)

Name	No	Builders	Launched		Commissioned	
TIR	A 86	Mazagon Dock Ltd, Bombay	15 Apr	1983	21 Feb	1986

Displacement, tons: 3,200 full load
Dimensions, feet (metres): 347.4 × 43.3 × 15.7 *(105.9 × 13.2 × 4.8)*
Main machinery: 2 Crossley-Pielstick 8 PC2 V Mk 2 diesels; 7,072 hp(m) *(5.2 MW)* sustained; 2 shafts
Speed, knots: 18. **Range, miles:** 6,000 at 12 kt
Complement: 239 (35 officers) plus 120 cadets
Guns: 2 Bofors 40 mm/60 (twin) with launchers for illuminants. 4 saluting guns.
Countermeasures: ESM: Telegon IV D/F.
Radars: Navigation: Bharat/Decca 1245; I-band.
Helicopters: Platform for Alouette III.

Comment: Second of class reported ordered May 1986 but was cancelled as an economy measure. Built to commercial standards, Decca collision avoidance plot and SATNAV. Can carry up to 120 cadets and 20 instructors. Based at Kochi.
UPDATED

TIR   4/1997*, H M Steele / 0012528

1 LEANDER (BATCH 3A) CLASS (AX)

Name	No	Builders	Commissioned
KRISHNA (ex-*Andromeda*)	F 46 (ex-F 57)	Portsmouth Dockyard	2 Dec 1968

Displacement, tons: 2,960 full load
Dimensions, feet (metres): 372 × 43 × 18 (screws) *(113.4 × 13.1 × 5.5)*
Main machinery: 2 Babcock & Wilcox boilers; 550 psi *(38.7 kg/cm²)*; 850°F *(454°C)*; 2 White/ English Electric turbines; 30,000 hp *(22.4 MW)*; 2 shafts
Speed, knots: 28. **Range, miles:** 4,000 at 15 kt
Complement: 260 (19 officers)
Guns: 2 Bofors 40 mm/60. 2 Oerlikon 20 mm.
Radars: Air/surface search: Marconi Type 968; D/E-band.
Navigation: Kelvin Hughes Type 1006; I-band.
Helicopters: 1 Chetak.

Comment: Laid down 25 May 1966 and launched 24 May 1967. Acquired from the UK in April 1995 having paid off in June 1993 to a state of extended readiness. Refitted by DML, Devonport, before recommissioning 22 August 1995. The original 114 mm gun turret, Seacat SAM and ASW Limbo mortar were removed in 1979-80 when Exocet SSM, Seawolf SAM, STWS torpedo tubes and facilities for a Lynx helicopter were fitted. Acquired for training purposes to supplement the *Tir*. Armament has been reduced to the minimum required for the training role, and now includes 40 mm guns on either side, aft of the funnel. Based at Kochi.
UPDATED

KRISHNA   *8/1995*, H M Steele* / 0064724

2 SAIL TRAINING SHIPS (AXS)

VARUNA   TARANGINI

Displacement, tons: 420 full load
Dimensions, feet (metres): 177.2 × 27.9 × 13.1 *(54 × 8.5 × 4)*
Main machinery: 2 diesels; 640 hp(m) *(470 kW)*; 2 shafts; acbLIPS props
Speed, knots: 10 (diesels)
Complement: 15 (6 officers) plus 45 cadets

Comment: *Varuna* completed in April 1981 by Alcock-Ashdown, Bhavnagar. Can carry 26 cadets. Details given are for *Tarangini* which is based on a Lord Nelson design by Colin Mudie of Lymington and has been built by Goa Shipyard. Launched on 23 December 1995, and completed in December 1997. Three masted barque, square rigged on forward and main mast and 'fore and aft' rigged on mizzen mast. Based at Mumbai.
UPDATED

TARANGINI   *3/1998*, Ships of the World* / 0052347

AUXILIARIES

Note: There is also a small hospital ship *Lakshadweep* of 865 tons and a crew of 35 including 16 medics.

1 UGRA CLASS (SUBMARINE TENDER) (AS)

Name	No	Builders	Launched	Commissioned
AMBA	A 54	Nikolayev Shipyard	18 Jan 1968	28 Dec 1968

Displacement, tons: 6,750 standard; 9,650 full load
Dimensions, feet (metres): 462.6 × 57.7 × 23 *(141 × 17.6 × 7)*
Main machinery: Diesel-electric; 4 Kolomna Type 2-D-42 diesel generators; 2 motors; 8,000 hp(m) *(5.88 MW)*; 2 shafts
Speed, knots: 17. **Range, miles:** 21,000 at 10 kt
Complement: 400
Guns: 4 USSR 3 in *(76 mm)*/60 (2 twin).
Radars: Air/surface search: Slim Net; E/F-band.
Fire control: 2 Hawk Screech; I-band.
Navigation: Don 2; I-band.
IFF: 2 Square Head. High Pole A.

Comment: Acquired from the USSR in 1968. Provision for helicopter. Can accommodate 750. Two cranes, one of 6 tons and one of 10 tons. Differs from others of the class by having 76 mm guns. Rarely goes to sea. Based at Vishakapatnam.
UPDATED

AMBA   *2/1998* / 0052348

1 JYOTI CLASS (REPLENISHMENT TANKER) (AOR)

Name	No	Builders	Launched	Commissioned
JYOTI	A 58	Admiralty Yard, St Petersburg	8 Dec 1995	20 July 1996

Displacement, tons: 35,900 full load
Dimensions, feet (metres): 587.3 × 72.2 × 26.2 *(179 × 22 × 8)*
Main machinery: 1 Burmeister & Wain diesel; 10,948 hp(m) *(8.05 MW)*; 1 shaft
Speed, knots: 15. **Range, miles:** 12,000 at 15 kt
Complement: 92 (16 officers)
Cargo capacity: 25,040 tons diesel
Guns: May be fitted in due course.
Radars: Navigation: I-band.
Helicopters: Platform for 1 medium.

Comment: This was the third of a class of merchant tankers, modified for naval use for the Indian Navy and acquired in 1995. The ship was laid down in September 1993. Based at Mumbai where she arrived in November 1996. May be fitted with armament during refit at Vishakapatnam in 1999/2000. There are two replenishment positions on each side and stern refuelling is an option. Similar ship sold to China and two others are in commercial service.
UPDATED

JYOTI   *3/1999** / 0064725

1 DEEPAK CLASS (REPLENISHMENT TANKER) (AOR)

Name	No	Builders	Commissioned
SHAKTI	A 57	Bremer-Vulkan	31 Dec 1975

Displacement, tons: 6,785 light; 15,828 full load
Measurement, tons: 12,013 gross
Dimensions, feet (metres): 552.4 × 75.5 × 30 *(168.4 × 23 × 9.2)*
Main machinery: 2 Babcock & Wilcox boilers; 1 BV/BBC steam turbine; 16,500 hp(m) *(12.13 MW)*; 1 shaft
Speed, knots: 18.5. **Range, miles:** 5,500 at 16 kt
Complement: 169
Cargo capacity: 1,280 tons diesel; 12,624 tons FFO; 1,495 tons avcat; 812 tons FW
Guns: 4 Bofors 40 mm/60. 2 Oerlikon 20 mm can be carried.
Countermeasures: ESM: Telegon IV HF D/F.
Radars: Navigation: 2 Decca 1226; I-band.
Helicopters: 1 Chetak.

Comment: Automatic tensioning fitted to replenishment gear. Heavy and light jackstays. Stern fuelling as well as alongside. DG fitted. Based at Mumbai.
VERIFIED

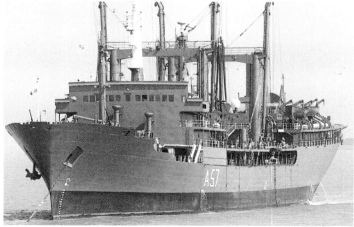

SHAKTI   *2/1998* / 0052350

1 MODIFIED DEEPAK CLASS
(REPLENISHMENT AND REPAIR SHIP) (AOR/AR)

Name	No	Builders	Launched	Commissioned
ADITYA (ex-*Rajaba Gan Palan*)	A 59	Garden Reach, Calcutta	15 Nov 1993	July 2000

Displacement, tons: 24,600 full load
Measurement, tons: 17,000 dwt
Dimensions, feet (metres): 564.3 × 75.5 × 29.9 *(172 × 23 × 9.1)*
Main machinery: 2 MAN/Burmeister & Wain 16V 40/45 diesels; 23,936 hp(m) *(17.59 MW)* sustained; 1 shaft
Speed, knots: 20. **Range, miles:** 10,000 at 16 kt
Complement: 191 plus 6 aircrew
Cargo capacity: 14,200 m³ diesel and avcat; 2,250 m³ water; 2,170 m³ ammunition and stores
Guns: 3 Bofors 40 mm/60.
Helicopters: 1 Chetak or Sea King.

Comment: Ordered in July 1987 to a Bremer-Vulkan design. Lengthened version of 'Deepak' class but with a multipurpose workshop. Four RAS stations alongside. Fully air conditioned. Building progress was very slow and sea trials in September 1999 were curtailed by propulsion problems.
UPDATED

ADITYA   8/1999*, GRSE / 0081942

1 DIVING SUPPORT SHIP (ASR)

Name	No	Builders	Commissioned
NIREEKSHAK	A 15	Mazagon Dock Ltd, Bombay	8 June 1989

Displacement, tons: 2,160 full load
Dimensions, feet (metres): 231.3 × 57.4 × 16.4 *(70.5 × 17.5 × 5)*
Main machinery: 2 Bergen KRM-8 diesels; 4,410 hp(m) *(3.24 MW)* sustained; 2 shafts; cp props; 2 bow thrusters; 2 stern thrusters; 990 hp(m) *(727 kW)*
Speed, knots: 12
Complement: 63 (15 officers)

Comment: Laid down in August 1982 and launched January 1984. Acquired on lease with an option for purchase which was taken up in March 1995, and the ship was recommissioned on 15 September 1995. The vessel was built for offshore support operations but has been modified for naval requirements. Two DSRV, capable of taking 12 men to 300 m, are carried together with two six-man recompression chambers and one three-man bell. Kongsberg ADP-503 Mk II. Dynamic positioning system. The ship is used for submarine SAR. Based at Mumbai.
UPDATED

NIREEKSHAK   1991* / 0064727

2 TRANSPORT SHIPS (AP)

Name	No	Builders	Launched
NICOBAR	—	Hindustan Shipyard	Apr 1998
ANDAMANS (ex-*Swaraj Dweep*)	—	Hindustan Shipyard	Apr 2000

Displacement, tons: 19,000 full load
Dimensions, feet (metres): 515.1 × 68.9 × 24.6 *(157 × 21 × 7.5)*
Main machinery: 2 diesels; 2 shafts
Speed, knots: 16
Complement: 160
Cargo capacity: 1,200 troops
Helicopters: Platform for 1 medium.

Comment: Merchant ships requisitioned while still building at Vishakapatnam. Have large davits for LCVPs. Details are not confirmed, and although the names suggest resupply of the Nicobar and Andaman Islands is the main purpose, there could be a more general role.
UPDATED

NICOBAR   2/1999, 92 Wing RAAF, DETA crew 1/11 Sqdn / 0053441

6 SUPPORT TANKERS (AOTL)

POSHAK   PURAN   PUSHPA   PRADHAYAK   PURAK   PALAN

Comment: First two built at Mazagon Dock Ltd, Bombay. *Poshak* completed April 1982, and *Puran* in November 1988. *Pushpa* built at Goa Shipyard and completed in 1990. *Pradhayak, Purak* and *Palan* built at Rajabagan Shipyard, Bombay, the first two in 1977 and *Palan* in May 1986. Cargo capacities vary from 200 to 376 tons. Civilian manned.
UPDATED

PUSHPA   1990*, Goa Shipyard / 0064728

2 WATER CARRIERS (AWT)

AMBUDA   COCHIN

Comment: First laid down Rajabagan Shipyard 18 January 1977. Second built at Mazagon Dock Ltd, Bombay. Civilian manned.
UPDATED

AMBUDA   4/1992* / 0064729

3 TORPEDO RECOVERY VESSELS (TRV)

A 71   A 72   ASTRAVAHINI

Displacement, tons: 110 full load
Dimensions, feet (metres): 93.5 × 20 × 4.6 *(28.5 × 6.1 × 1.4)*
Main machinery: 2 Kirloskar V12 diesels; 720 hp(m) *(529 kW)*; 2 shafts
Speed, knots: 11
Complement: 13

Comment: Details above apply only to *A 71* and *A 72*. First completed early 1980, second 1981 at Goa Shipyard. *Astravahini* completed in 1984 at Vishakapatnam. All based at Vishakapatnam.
UPDATED

TRV A 72   2/1989, G Jacobs

3 DIVING TENDERS (YDT)

Displacement, tons: 36 full load
Dimensions, feet (metres): 48.9 × 14.4 × 3.9 *(14.9 × 4.4 × 1.2)*
Main machinery: 2 diesels; 130 hp(m) *(96 kW)*; 2 shafts
Speed, knots: 12

Comment: Built at Cleback Yard. First completed 1979; second and third in 1984.
UPDATED

YDT   9/1996* / 0012531

TUGS

2 TUGS (OCEAN) (ATA/ATS)

MATANGA A 52   **AMBIKA** A 53

Measurement, tons: 1,313 grt
Dimensions, feet (metres): 222.4 × 40.4 × 13.1 *(67.8 × 12.3 × 4)*
Main machinery: 2 GRSE/MAN G7V diesels; 3,920 hp(m) *(2.88 MW)*; 2 shafts
Speed, knots: 15. **Range, miles:** 4,000 at 15 kt
Complement: 78 (8 officers)
Guns: 1 Bofors 40 mm/60.
Radars: Navigation: I-band.

Comment: Built by Garden Reach SY. *Matanga* launched 29 October 1977 and *Ambika* completed in 1994. Bollard pull of 40 tons and capable of towing a 20,000 ton ship at 8 kt. *Ambika* carries a diving rescue system and decompression chamber.

UPDATED

AMBIKA   6/1996*, van Ginderen Collection / 0064730

13 HARBOUR TUGS (YTM/YTL)

AGARAL   ARJUN   BALSHIL   RAJAJI   BALRAM   BAJRANG   ANAND   + 6

Measurement, tons: 216 grt
Dimensions, feet (metres): 96.1 × 27.9 × 8.5 *(29.3 × 8.5 × 2.6)*
Main machinery: 2 SEMT-Pielstick 8 PA4 V 200 diesels; 3,200 hp(m) *(2.35 MW)*; 2 shafts
Speed, knots: 11
Complement: 12

Comment: First three built by Mazagon Dock Ltd, Bombay in 1973-74. Five more delivered in 1988-89, and four more in 1991 from Mazagon Dock Ltd, Goa. Details given are for *Balram* and *Bajrang*; *Rajaji* is of comparable size built in 1982; the others are smaller and of varying types.

UPDATED

HARBOUR TUG   4/1992* / 0064731

COAST GUARD

Senior Appointments

Director General:
Vice Admiral J C de Silva, AVSM
Deputy Director General:
Inspector General R Singh, PTM

Personnel

2000:   4,400 (760 officers)

General

The Coast Guard was constituted as an independent paramilitary service on 19 August 1978. It functions under the Ministry of Defence.

Responsibilities include:
(a) Ensuring the safety and protection of artificial islands, offshore terminals and other installations in the Maritime Zones.
(b) Measures for the safety of life and property at sea including assistance to mariners in distress.
(c) Measures to preserve and protect the marine environment and control marine pollution.
(d) Assisting the Customs and other authorities in anti-smuggling operations.
(e) Enforcing the provisions of enactments in force in the Maritime Zones.

Bases

The Headquarters of the Coast Guard is located in Delhi with Regional Headquarters in Mumbai, Chennai and Port Blair. West Coast District Headquarters at Mumbai, New Mangalore, Goa, Porbandar, Kochi. East Coast District/Headquarters at Vishakapatnam, Chennai, Paradip and Haldia. Andaman and Nicobar District Headquarters at Campbell Bay and Diglipur. Stations at Vadinar, Mandapam, Okha and Tuticorin.

Aviation

Air Squadrons at Daman CGAS 750 (8 Dorniers 228); Chennai CGAS 744 (7 Dorniers 228); Calcutta CGAS 700 (1 Dornier 228), Port Blair CGAS 745 (1 Dornier 228); Daman CGAS 841 (3 Chetaks); Mumbai CGAS 842 (4 Chetaks); Goa CGAS 800 (4 Chetaks); Chennai CGAS 848 (3 Chetaks); Port Blair (1 Chetak). 7 more Dornier 228s ordered in 1999.

DELETIONS

1997   *Rajshree*

PATROL FORCES

Note: Patrol Hovercraft are planned to be ordered in 2000/01.

3 + 1 SAMAR CLASS (OFFSHORE PATROL VESSELS) (OPV)

Name	No	Builders	Laid down	Launched		Commissioned	
SAMAR	42	Goa Shipyard	1990	26 Aug	1992	14 Feb	1996
SANGRAM	43	Goa Shipyard	1992	18 Mar	1995	29 Mar	1997
SARANG	44	Goa Shipyard	1993	8 Mar	1997	15 May	1999

Displacement, tons: 2,005 full load
Dimensions, feet (metres): 334.6 oa; 315 wl × 37.7 × 11.5 *(102; 96 × 11.5 × 3.5)*
Main machinery: 2 SEMT-Pielstick 16 PA6 V 280 diesels; 12,800 hp(m) *(9.41 MW)* sustained; 2 shafts; acbLIPS cp props
Speed, knots: 22. **Range, miles:** 7,000 at 15 kt
Complement: 124 (12 officers)

Guns: 1 OTO Melara 3 in *(76 mm)*/62; 60 rds/min to 16 km *(8.7 n miles)*; weight of shell 6 kg.
1 Bofors 40 mm/60.
Weapons control: Bharat/Radamec optronic 2400 director.
Radars: Surface search: Decca 2459; F/I-band.
Navigation: Bharat 1245; I-band.

Helicopters: 1 Sea King or Cheetak.

Programmes: First three ordered in April 1991. The original plan was for six of the class but a new design is likely to replace this one possibly with the fourth of class.
Structure: Similar to the Navy's 'Sukanya' class but more heavily armed and carrying a helicopter capable of transporting a Marine contingent. Telescopic hangar.

UPDATED

SAMAR   8/1997* / 0012532

9 VIKRAM CLASS (OFFSHORE PATROL VESSELS) (OPV)

Name	No	Builders	Launched		Commissioned	
VIKRAM	33	Mazagon Dock, Bombay	26 Sep	1981	19 Dec	1983
VIJAYA	34	Mazagon Dock, Bombay	5 June	1982	12 Apr	1985
VEERA	35	Mazagon Dock, Bombay	30 June	1984	3 May	1986
VARUNA	36	Mazagon Dock, Bombay	28 Jan	1986	27 Feb	1988
VAJRA	37	Mazagon Dock, Bombay	3 Jan	1987	22 Dec	1988
VIVEK	38	Mazagon Dock, Bombay	5 Nov	1987	19 Aug	1989
VIGRAHA	39	Mazagon Dock, Bombay	27 Sep	1988	12 Apr	1990
VARAD	40	Goa Shipyard	3 Sep	1989	19 July	1990
VARAHA	41	Goa Shipyard	5 Nov	1990	11 Mar	1992

Displacement, tons: 1,224 full load
Dimensions, feet (metres): 243.1 × 37.4 × 10.5 *(74.1 × 11.4 × 3.2)*
Main machinery: 2 SEMT-Pielstick 16 PA6 V 280 diesels; 12,800 hp(m) *(9.41 MW)* sustained; 2 shafts; cp props
Speed, knots: 22. **Range, miles:** 4,000 at 16 kt
Complement: 96 (11 officers)
Guns: 1 Bofors 40 mm/60. 2—7.62 mm MGs.
Weapons control: Lynx optical sights.
Radars: Navigation: 2 Decca 1226; I-band.
Helicopters: 1 HAL (Aerospatiale) Chetak or 1 Sea King.

Comment: Owes something to a NEVESBU (Netherlands) design, being a stretched version of its 750 ton offshore patrol vessels. Ordered in 1979. Fin stabilisers. Diving equipment. 4.5 ton deck crane. External firefighting pumps. Has one GRP boat and two inflatable craft. This class is considered too small for its required task and hence the need for the larger 'Samar' class. ***UPDATED***

VARAD   *12/1997*, Indian Coast Guard /* 0052351

14 TARA BAI MOD 1 and PRIYADARSHINI CLASSES
(COASTAL PATROL CRAFT) (PC)

Name	No	Builders	Commissioned	
TARA BAI	71	Singapore SBEC	26 June	1987
AHALYA BAI	72	Singapore SBEC	9 Sep	1987
LAKSHMI BAI	73	Garden Reach, Calcutta	20 Mar	1989
AKKA DEVI	74	Garden Reach, Calcutta	9 Aug	1989
NAIKI DEVI	75	Garden Reach, Calcutta	19 Mar	1990
GANGA DEVI	76	Garden Reach, Calcutta	19 Nov	1990
PRIYADARSHINI	221	Garden Reach, Calcutta	25 May	1992
RAZYA SULTANA	222	Garden Reach, Calcutta	18 Nov	1992
ANNIE BESANT	223	Goa Shipyard	7 Dec	1992
KAMLA DEVI	224	Goa Shipyard	20 May	1992
AMRIT KAUR	225	Goa Shipyard	20 Mar	1993
KANAK LATA BAURA	226	Garden Reach, Calcutta	27 Mar	1997
BHIKAJI CAMA	227	Garden Reach, Calcutta	24 Sep	1997
SUCHETA KRIPALANI	228	Garden Reach, Calcutta	16 Mar	1998

Displacement, tons: 306 full load
Dimensions, feet (metres): 147.3 × 24.6 × 8.5 *(44.9 × 7.5 × 2.6)*
Main machinery: 2 MTU 12V 538 diesels; 4,025 hp(m) *(2.96 MW)* sustained; 2 shafts
Speed, knots: 23. **Range, miles:** 2,400 at 12 kt
Complement: 34 (7 officers)
Guns: 1 Bofors 40 mm/60. 2—7.62 mm MGs.
Radars: Surface search: Racal Decca 1226 or BEL 1245/6X (221-225); I-band.

Comment: Two ordered in June 1986, four more laid down in 1987 followed by a further batch of five more. Last three ordered in 1995. Lürssen 45 design which is a 'follow-on' class to the Type 956. First six are known as 'Tarabai Mod 1' class and remainder as 'Priyadarshini' class. ***UPDATED***

ANNIE BESANT   *6/1998*, Indian Coast Guard /* 0052352

7 JIJA BAI MOD 1 CLASS (TYPE 956)
(COASTAL PATROL CRAFT) (PC)

Name	No	Builders	Commissioned	
JIJA BAI	64	Sumidagawa, Tokyo	22 Feb	1984
CHAND BIBI	65	Sumidagawa, Tokyo	22 Feb	1984
KITTUR CHENNAMMA	66	Sumidagawa, Tokyo	21 Oct	1983
RANI JINDAN	67	Sumidagawa, Tokyo	21 Oct	1983
HABBAH KHATUN	68	Garden Reach, Calcutta	27 Apr	1985
RAMADEVI	69	Garden Reach, Calcutta	3 Aug	1985
AVVAIYYAR	70	Garden Reach, Calcutta	19 Oct	1985

Displacement, tons: 181 full load
Dimensions, feet (metres): 144.3 × 24.3 × 7.5 *(44 × 7.4 × 2.3)*
Main machinery: 2 MTU 12V 538 TB82 diesels; 5,940 hp(m) *(4.37 MW)* sustained; 2 shafts
Speed, knots: 25. **Range, miles:** 2,375 at 14 kt
Complement: 34 (7 officers)
Guns: 1 Bofors 40 mm/60. 2—7.62 mm MGs.
Radars: Surface search: Racal Decca 1226; I-band.

Comment: All were ordered in 1981. ***UPDATED***

RANI JINDAN   *6/1996*, Indian Coast Guard /* 0064732

7 SWALLOW 65 CLASS (PB)

C 01-02   C 04-06   C 62-63

Displacement, tons: 32 full load
Dimensions, feet (metres): 65.6 × 15.4 × 5 *(20 × 4.7 × 1.5)*
Main machinery: 2 Detroit 12V-71TA diesels; 840 hp *(627 kW)* sustained; 2 shafts
Speed, knots: 20. **Range, miles:** 400 at 20 kt
Complement: 8
Guns: 1—7.62 mm MG.
Radars: Navigation: I-band.

Comment: Built by Swallow Craft Co, Pusan, South Korea. First six commissioned 24 September 1980 (one deleted so far), and two on 27 May 1982 having been taken over from India Oil Corporation. ***UPDATED***

C 63   *1982*, Swallow Craft /* 0012534

9 + 1 (6) INSHORE PATROL CRAFT (PB)

C 131-139

Displacement, tons: 49 full load
Dimensions, feet (metres): 68.2 × 19 × 5.9 *(20.8 × 5.8 × 1.8)*
Main machinery: 2 Deutz MWM TBD234V12 diesels; 1,646 hp(m) *(1.21 MW)* sustained; 1 Deutz MWM TBD234V8 diesel; 550 hp(m) *(404 kW)* sustained; 3 Hamilton 402 water-jets
Speed, knots: 40. **Range, miles:** 600 at 15 kt
Complement: 10 (4 officers)
Guns: 1 Oerlikon 20 mm. 1—7.62 mm MG.
Radars: Navigation: Furuno; I-band.

Comment: Ordered from Anderson Marine, Goa in September 1990 to a P-2000 design by Amgram, similar to British 'Archer' class. GRP hull. Official description is 'Interceptor Boats'. Half built at Goa and half at Kochi. Commissioned: *C 131-132* on 16 November 1993, *C 133-134* on 20 May 1994, *C 135-136* on 25 March 1995, *C 137-138* on 4 September 1996, and *C 139* on 16 October 1997. One more building at Goa with an option on six more. ***UPDATED***

C 32 (old number)   *1/1994*, Anderson Marine /* 0064733

INDONESIA
TENTARA NASIONAL

Headquarters Appointments

Chief of the Naval Staff:
Admiral Achmad Sutjipto
Deputy Chief of the Naval Staff:
Vice Admiral Mudjito
Inspector General of the Navy:
Major General Sudarsono Kasdi

Fleet Command

Commander-in-Chief Western Fleet (Barat):
Rear Admiral Indroko Sastowiryono
Commander-in-Chief Eastern Fleet (Timur):
Rear Admiral Adi Haryond
Commandant of Navy Marine Corps:
Major General Hari Triono

Personnel

(a) 2000: 47,500 (including 15,000 Marine Commando Corps and 1,000 Naval Air Arm)
(b) Selective national service

Bases

Tanjung Priok (North Jakarta), Ujung (Surabaya), Sabang, Belawan (North Sumatera), Ujung Pandang (South Sulawesi), Balikpapan (East Kalimantan), Jayapura (Irian Jaya), Tanjung Pinang, Bitung (North Sulawesi), Teluk Ratai (South Sumatera), Banjarmasin, South Kalmantan. Naval Air Base at Juanda (Surabaya), Biak (Irian Jaya), Pekan Baru, Sam Ratulangi (North Sulawesi), Sabang, Natuna, P Aru.

Command Structure

Eastern Command (Surabaya)
Western Command (Teluk Ratai)
Training Command
Military Sea Communications Command (Maritime Security Agency)
Military Sealift Command (Logistic Support)

Marine Corps

Planned re-organisation in 2000 creates an Eastern Area Force at Surabaya, and a Western Area at Teluk Ratai, Sumatra. Four brigades of three battalions each. Equipment includes amphibious tanks, field artillery and anti-aircraft missiles and guns. Three more battalions are planned. As of 2000 numbers total 15,000 of which 12,000 are combat troops. The plan is to expand the Corps to 22,800.

Strength of the Fleet

Type	Active	Building (Projected)
Patrol Submarines	2	—
Frigates	17	—
Corvettes	16	—
Fast Attack Craft—Missile	4	—
Large Patrol Craft	16	4
LST/LSM	26	(1)
MCMV	13	—
Survey and Research Ships	8	(1)
Command Ship	1	—
Repair Ship	1	—
Replenishment Tankers	2	—
Coastal Tankers	3	—
Support Ships	7	—
Transports	1	(1)
Sail Training Ships	2	—

Prefix to Ships' Names

KRI (Kapal di Republik Indonesia)

Mercantile Marine

Lloyd's Register of Shipping:
2,369 vessels of 3,241,462 tons gross

PENNANT LIST

Submarines

401 Cakra
402 Nanggala

Frigates

331 Martha Khristina Tiyahahu
332 W Zakarias Yohannes
333 Hasanuddin
341 Samadikun
342 Martadinata
343 Monginsidi
344 Ngurahrai
351 Ahmed Yani
352 Slamet Riyadi
353 Yos Sudarso
354 Oswald Siahann
355 Abdul Halim Perdanakusuma
356 Karel Satsiutubun
361 Fatahillah
362 Malahayati
363 Nala
364 Ki Hajar Dewantara

Corvettes

371 Kapitan Patimura
372 Untung Suropati
373 Nuku

374 Lambung Mangkurat
375 Cut Nyak Dien
376 Sultan Thaha Syaifuddin
377 Sutanto
378 Sutedi Senoputra
379 Wiratno
380 Memet Sastrawiria
381 Tjiptadi
382 Hasan Basri
383 Iman Bonjol
384 Pati Unus
385 Teuku Umar
386 Silas Papare

Patrol Forces

621 Mandau
622 Rencong
623 Badik
624 Keris
651 Singa
653 Ajak
801 Pandrong
802 Sura
803 Todak (bldg)
804 Hiu (bldg)
805 Layang (bldg)
806 Dorang (bldg)
811 Kakap
812 Kerapu
813 Tongkol

814 Barakuda
847 Sibarau
848 Siliman
857 Sigalu
858 Silea
859 Siribua
862 Siada
863 Sikuda
864 Sigurot

Amphibious Forces

501 Teluk Langsa
502 Teluk Bajur
503 Teluk Amboina
504 Teluk Kau
508 Teluk Tomini
509 Teluk Ratai
510 Teluk Saleh
511 Teluk Bone
512 Teluk Semangka
513 Teluk Penju
514 Teluk Mandar
515 Teluk Sampit
516 Teluk Banten
517 Teluk Ende
531 Teluk Gilimanuk
532 Teluk Celukan Bawang
533 Teluk Cendrawasih
534 Teluk Berau
535 Teluk Peleng

536 Teluk Sibolga
537 Teluk Manado
538 Teluk Hading
539 Teluk Parigi
540 Teluk Lampung
541 Teluk Jakarta
542 Teluk Sangkulirang
580 Dore
582 Kupang
583 Dili
584 Nusantara

Survey Ships

931 Burujulasad
932 Dewa Kembar
933 Jalanidhi

Mine Warfare Forces

701 Pulau Rani
702 Pulau Ratawo
711 Pulau Rengat
712 Pulau Rupat
721 Pulau Rote
722 Pulau Raas
723 Pulau Romang
724 Pulau Rimau
725 Pulau Rondo
726 Pulau Rusa

727 Pulau Rangsang
728 Pulau Raibu
729 Pulau Rempang

Auxiliaries

543 Teluk Cirebon
544 Teluk Sabang
561 Multatuli
901 Balikpapan
902 Sambu
903 Arun
906 Gerong
911 Sorong
921 Jaya Wijaya
922 Rakata
923 Soputan
934 Lampo Batang
935 Tambora
936 Bromo
952 Nusa Telu
959 Teluk Mentawai
960 Karimata
961 Waigeo
972 Tanjung Oisina

SUBMARINES

Note: Two ex-German Type 206 submarines were taken over on 25 September 1997 with plans to refit them, followed by three others. Funds ran out in June 1998 and the whole project was then cancelled.

2 CAKRA (209) CLASS (1300 TYPE) (SSK)

Name	No	Builders	Laid down	Launched	Commissioned
CAKRA	401	Howaldtswerke, Kiel	25 Nov 1977	10 Sep 1980	19 Mar 1981
NANGGALA	402	Howaldtswerke, Kiel	14 Mar 1978	10 Sep 1980	6 July 1981

Displacement, tons: 1,285 surfaced; 1,390 dived
Dimensions, feet (metres): 195.2 × 20.3 × 17.9 *(59.5 × 6.2 × 5.4)*
Main machinery: Diesel-electric; 4 MTU 12V 493 AZ80 GA31L diesels; 2,400 hp(m) *(1.76 MW)* sustained; 4 Siemens alternators; 1.7 MW; 1 Siemens motor; 4,600 hp(m) *(3.38 MW)* sustained; 1 shaft

Speed, knots: 11 surfaced; 21.5 dived
Range, miles: 8,200 at 8 kt
Complement: 34 (6 officers)

Torpedoes: 8—21 in *(533 mm)* bow tubes. 14 AEG SUT Mod 0; dual purpose; wire-guided; active/passive homing to 12 km *(6.5 n miles)* at 35 kt; 28 km *(15 n miles)* at 23 kt; warhead 250 kg.

Countermeasures: ESM: Thomson-CSF DR 2000U; radar warning.
Weapons control: Signaal Sinbad system.
Radars: Surface search: Thomson-CSF Calypso; I-band.
Sonars: Atlas Elektronik CSU 3-2; active/passive search and attack; medium frequency.
PRS-3/4; (integral with CSU) passive ranging.

Programmes: Ordered on 2 April 1977. Designed by Ingenieurkontor, Lübeck for construction by Howaldtswerke, Kiel and sale by Ferrostaal, Essen—all acting as a consortium.
Modernisation: Major refits at HDW spanning three years from 1986 to 1989. These refits were expensive and lengthy and may have discouraged further orders at that time. *Cakra* refitted again at Surabaya from 1993 completing in April 1997, including replacement batteries and updated Sinbad TFCS. *Nanggala* received a similar refit from October 1997 to mid-1999.
Structure: Have high-capacity batteries with GRP lead-acid cells and battery cooling supplied by Wilhelm Hagen AG. Diving depth, 240 m *(790 ft)*.
Operational: Endurance, 50 days. Both are fully operational.

NANGGALA

8/1995*, van Ginderen Collection / 0080001

UPDATED

FRIGATES

Note: Interest is being shown in buying the two Dutch 'Tromp' class, when they become available.

6 AHMAD YANI (VAN SPEIJK) CLASS (FFG)

Name	No	Builders	Laid down	Launched	Commissioned
AHMAD YANI (ex-*Tjerk Hiddes*)	351	Nederlandse Dok en Scheepsbouw Mij, Amsterdam	1 June 1964	17 Dec 1965	16 Aug 1967
SLAMET RIYADI (ex-*Van Speijk*)	352	Nederlandse Dok en Scheepsbouw Mij, Amsterdam	1 Oct 1963	5 Mar 1965	14 Feb 1967
YOS SUDARSO (ex-*Van Galen*)	353	Koninklijke Maatschappij de Schelde, Flushing	25 July 1963	19 June 1965	1 Mar 1967
OSWALD SIAHAAN (ex-*Van Nes*)	354	Koninklijke Maatschappij de Schelde, Flushing	25 July 1963	26 Mar 1966	9 Aug 1967
ABDUL HALIM PERDANAKUSUMA (ex-*Evertsen*)	355	Koninklijke Maatschappij de Schelde, Flushing	6 July 1965	18 June 1966	21 Dec 1967
KAREL SATSUITUBUN (ex-*Isaac Sweers*)	356	Nederlandse Dok en Scheepsbouw Mij, Amsterdam	5 May 1965	10 Mar 1967	15 May 1968

Displacement, tons: 2,225 standard; 2,835 full load
Dimensions, feet (metres): 372 × 41 × 13.8
(113.4 × 12.5 × 4.2)
Main machinery: 2 Babcock & Wilcox boilers; 550 psi *(38.7 kg/cm²)*; 850°F *(450°C)*; 2 Werkspoor/English Electric turbines; 30,000 hp *(22.4 MW)*; 2 shafts
Speed, knots: 28.5. **Range, miles:** 4,500 at 12 kt
Complement: 180

Missiles: SSM: 8 McDonnell Douglas Harpoon ❶; active radar homing to 130 km *(70 n miles)* at 0.9 Mach; warhead 227 kg.
SAM: 2 Short Brothers Seacat quad launchers.
Being replaced by 2 Matra Simbad twin launchers for Mistral ❷; IR homing to 4 km *(2.2 n miles)*; warhead 3 kg.
Guns: 1 OTO Melara 3 in *(76 mm)*/62 compact ❸; 85 rds/min to 16 km *(8.7 n miles)* anti-surface; 12 km *(6.6 n miles)* anti-aircraft; weight of shell 6 kg. 2—12.7 mm MGs.
Torpedoes: 6—324 mm Mk 32 (2 triple) tubes ❹. Honeywell Mk 46; anti-submarine; active/passive homing to 11 km *(5.9 n miles)* at 40 kt; warhead 44 kg.
Countermeasures: Decoys: 2 Knebworth Corvus 8-tubed trainable; radar distraction or centroid chaff to 1 km.
ESM: UA 8/9; UA 13 (355 and 356); radar warning. FH5 D/F.
Combat data systems: SEWACO V action data automation and Daisy data processing.
Weapons control: Signaal LIOD optronic director. Mk 2 fitted in 354, 353 and 356. SWG-1A Harpoon LCS.
Radars: Air search: Signaal LW03 ❺; D-band; range 219 km *(120 n miles)* for 2 m² target.
Air/surface search: Signaal DA05 ❻; E/F-band; range 137 km *(75 n miles)* for 2 m² target.
Navigation: Racal Decca 1229; I-band.
Fire control: Signaal M 45 ❼; I/J-band (for 76 mm gun and SSM).
2 Signaal M 44; I/J-band (for Seacat) (being removed).
Sonars: Signaal CWE 610; hull-mounted; active search and attack; medium frequency. VDS; medium frequency.

Helicopters: 1 Westland Wasp ❽ or NBO 105C.

Programmes: On 11 February 1986 agreement signed with the Netherlands for transfer of two of this class with an option on two more. Transfer dates:—*Tjerk Hiddes*, 31 October 1986; *Van Speijk*, 1 November 1986; *Van Galen*, 2 November 1987; *Van Nes*, 31 October 1988. Contract of sale for the last two of the class signed 13 May 1989. *Evertsen* transferred 1 November 1989 and *Isaac Sweers* 1 November 1990. Ships provided with all spare parts but not towed arrays or helicopters.
Modernisation: This class underwent mid-life modernisation at Rykswerf Den Helder from 1976. This included replacement of

AHMAD YANI (with Simbad)   *(Scale 1 : 1,200), Ian Sturton /* 0012535

YOS SUNDARSO   8/1995 * / 0080002

4.5 in turret by 76 mm, A/S mortar by torpedo tubes, new electronics and electrics, updating combat data system, improved communications, extensive automation with reduction in complement, enlarged hangar for Lynx and improved habitability. Harpoon for first two only initially because there was no FMS funding for the others. However

the USN then provided sufficient SWG 1A panels for all of the class to be retrofitted with Harpoon missiles. LIOD optronic directors Mk 2 fitted in 354, 353 and 356 in 1996-97. Seacat which is non-operational is being replaced by Simbad twin launchers when funds are available.

UPDATED

3 KHRISTINA TIYAHAHU (TRIBAL CLASS) (FF)

Name	No	Builders	Laid down	Launched	Commissioned
MARTHA KHRISTINA TIYAHAHU (ex-*Zulu*)	331	Alex Stephen & Sons Ltd, Govan	13 Dec 1960	3 July 1962	17 Apr 1964
WILHELMUS ZAKARIAS YOHANNES (ex-*Gurkha*)	332	J I Thornycroft Ltd, Woolston	3 Nov 1958	11 July 1960	13 Feb 1963
HASANUDDIN (ex-*Tartar*)	333	HM Dockyard, Devonport	22 Oct 1959	19 Sep 1960	26 Feb 1962

Displacement, tons: 2,300 standard; 2,700 full load
Dimensions, feet (metres): 350 wl; 360 oa × 42.5 × 18 (screws), 12.5 (keel) *(106.7; 109.7 × 13 × 5.5, 3.8)*
Main machinery: COSAG; 1 Babcock & Wilcox boiler; 550 psi *(38.7 kg/cm²)*; 850°F *(450°C)*; 1 Parsons Metrovick turbine; 12,500 hp *(9.3 MW)*; 2 Yarrow/AEI G-6 gas turbines; 7,500 hp *(5.6 MW)*; 1 shaft; cp prop
Speed, knots: 25; 17 gas-turbines. **Range, miles:** 5,400 at 12 kt
Complement: 267 (24 officers)

Missiles: 2 Matra Simbad twin launchers ❶ for Mistral; IR homing to 4 km *(2.2 n miles)*; warhead 3 kg.
Guns: 2 Vickers 4.5 in *(114 mm)* ❷; 14 rds/min to 17 km *(9.3 n miles)*; weight of shell 25 kg.
2 Oerlikon 20 mm ❸; 800 rds/min to 2 km anti-aircraft.
2—12.7 mm MGs.
A/S mortars: 1 Limbo 3-tubed Mk 10 ❹; range 1,000 m; warhead 92 kg.
Countermeasures: Decoys: 2 Knebworth Corvus 8-tubed chaff launchers; distraction or centroid modes to 1 km.
ESM: UA 9; radar warning.
Weapons control: MRS 3 (for guns). 2 GWS 21 ❽ optical directors (for SAM).
Radars: Air search: Marconi Type 965 ❺; A-band.
Surface search: Type 993 ❻; E/F-band.
Navigation: Decca 978; I-band.
Fire control: Plessey Type 903 ❼; I-band (for guns).
Sonars: Graseby Type 177; hull-mounted; active search; 7-9 kHz.
Graseby Type 170 B; hull-mounted; active attack; 15 kHz.
Kelvin Hughes Type 162; classification; 50 kHz.

Helicopters: 1 Westland Wasp ❽ or NBO 105C.

Programmes: Refitted by Vosper Thornycroft before transfer from UK. 331 commissioned in Indonesian Navy on 2 May 1985, 332 on 16 October 1985 and 333 on 3 April 1986.
Modernisation: Simbad launchers are replacing the obsolete Seacat system.
Structure: Helicopter descends by flight deck lift and is covered by portable panels. MGs fitted just aft of the GWS 21 directors.
Operational: All used for EEZ patrols and probably the only operational armament is the guns and SAM system.

UPDATED

HASANUDDIN   *(Scale 1 : 1,200), Ian Sturton /* 0012536

HASANUDDIN   8/1995 * / 0080003

3 FATAHILLAH CLASS (FFG)

Name	No	Builders	Laid down	Launched	Commissioned
FATAHILLAH	361	Wilton Fijenoord, Schiedam	31 Jan 1977	22 Dec 1977	16 July 1979
MALAHAYATI	362	Wilton Fijenoord, Schiedam	28 July 1977	19 June 1978	21 Mar 1980
NALA	363	Wilton Fijenoord, Schiedam	27 Jan 1978	11 Jan 1979	4 Aug 1980

Displacement, tons: 1,200 standard; 1,450 full load
Dimensions, feet (metres): 276 × 36.4 × 10.7
 (84 × 11.1 × 3.3)
Main machinery: CODOG; 1 RR Olympus TM3B gas turbine;
 25,440 hp *(19 MW)* sustained; 2 MTU 20V 956 TB92 diesels;
 11,070 hp(m) *(8.14 MW)* sustained; 2 shafts; acbLIPS cp props
Speed, knots: 30. **Range, miles:** 4,250 at 16 kt
Complement: 89 (11 officers)

Missiles: SSM: 4 Aerospatiale MM 38 Exocet ❶; inertial cruise;
 active radar homing to 42 km *(23 n miles)* at 0.9 Mach;
 warhead 165 kg; sea-skimmer.

Guns: 1 Bofors 4.7 in *(120 mm)*/46 ❷; 80 rds/min to 18.5 km
 (10 n miles); weight of shell 21 kg.
 1 or 2 Bofors 40 mm/70 (2 in *Nala*) ❸; 300 rds/min to 12 km
 (6.6 n miles); weight of shell 0.96 kg.
 2 Rheinmetall 20 mm; 1,000 rds/min to 2 km anti-aircraft;
 weight of shell 0.24 kg.
Torpedoes: 6—324 mm Mk 32 or ILAS 3 (2 triple) tubes (none in
 Nala) ❹. 12 Mk 46 (or A244S); anti-submarine; active/passive
 homing to 11 km *(5.9 n miles)* at 40 kt; warhead 44 kg.
A/S mortars: 1 Bofors 375 mm twin-barrelled trainable ❺; 54
 Erika; range 1,600 m and Nelli; range 3,600 m.
Countermeasures: Decoys: 2 Knebworth Corvus 8-tubed

trainable chaff launchers ❻; radar distraction or centroid
 modes to 1 km. 1 T-Mk 6; torpedo decoy.
ESM: MEL Susie 1 (UAA-1); radar intercept.
Combat data systems: Signaal SEWACO-RI action data
 automation.
Weapons control: Signaal LIROD optronic director.
Radars: Air/surface search: Signaal DA05 ❼; E/F-band; range
 137 km *(75 n miles)* for 2 m² target.
 Surface search: Racal Decca AC 1229 ❽; I-band.
 Fire control: Signaal WM28 ❾; I/J-band; range 46 km *(25 n
 miles)*.
Sonars: Signaal PHS-32; hull-mounted; active search and attack;
 medium frequency.

Helicopters: 1 Westland Wasp (*Nala* only) ❿.

Programmes: Ordered August 1975. Officially rated as
 Corvettes.
Structure: NEVESBU design. *Nala* is fitted with a folding hangar/
 landing deck.

UPDATED

NALA

FATAHILLAH   *(Scale 1 : 1,200), Ian Sturton*

NALA   8/1999*, John Mortimer / 0080004

1 KI HAJAR DEWANTARA CLASS (FFG/AX)

Name	No	Builders	Laid down	Launched	Commissioned
KI HAJAR DEWANTARA	364	Split SY, Yugoslavia	11 May 1979	11 Oct 1980	31 Oct 1981

Displacement, tons: 2,050 full load
Dimensions, feet (metres): 317.3 × 36.7 × 15.7
 (96.7 × 11.2 × 4.8)
Main machinery: CODOG; 1 RR Olympus TM3B gas turbine;
 24,525 hp *(18.3 MW)* sustained; 2 MTU 16V 956 TB92
 diesels; 11,070 hp(m) *(8.14 MW)* sustained; 2 shafts; cp props
Speed, knots: 26 gas; 20 diesels
Range, miles: 4,000 at 18 kt; 1,150 at 25 kt
Complement: 76 (11 officers) plus 14 instructors and 100 cadets

Missiles: SSM: 4 Aerospatiale MM 38 Exocet ❶; inertial cruise;
 active radar homing to 42 km *(23 n miles)* at 0.9 Mach;
 warhead 165 kg; sea-skimmer.
Guns: 1 Bofors 57 mm/70 ❷; 200 rds/min to 17 km *(9.3 n
 miles)*; weight of shell 2.4 kg.
 2 Rheinmetall 20 mm ❸.
Torpedoes: 2—21 in *(533 mm)* tubes ❹. AEG SUT; dual purpose;
 wire-guided; active/passive homing to 28 km *(15 n miles)* at
 23 kt; 12 km *(6.5 n miles)* at 35 kt; warhead 250 kg.
Depth charges: 1 projector/mortar.
Countermeasures: Decoys: 2—128 mm twin-tubed flare
 launchers.
ESM: MEL Susie; radar intercept.
Combat data systems: Signaal SEWACO-RI action data
 automation.
Radars: Surface search: Racal Decca 1229 ❺; I-band.
Fire control: Signaal WM28 ❻; I/J-band.
Sonars: Signaal PHS-32; hull-mounted; active search and attack;
 medium frequency.

Helicopters: Platform ❼ for 1 NBO 105 helicopter.

Programmes: First ordered 14 March 1978 from Split SY,
 Yugoslavia where the hull was built and engines fitted.
 Armament and electronics fitted in the Netherlands and
 Indonesia.
Structure: For the training role there is a classroom and
 additional wheelhouse, navigation and radio rooms. Torpedo
 tubes are fixed in the stern transom. Two LCVP type ships
 boats are carried.
Operational: Used for training and troop transport. War roles
 include escort, ASW and troop transport.

UPDATED

KI HAJAR DEWANTARA
12/1992 / 0080005*

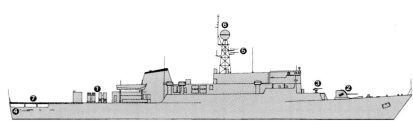

KI HAJAR DEWANTARA   *(Scale 1 : 900), Ian Sturton*

4 SAMADIKUN (CLAUD JONES) CLASS (FF)

Name	No	Builders	Laid down		Launched		Commissioned	
SAMADIKUN (ex-*John R Perry* DE 1034)	341	Avondale Marine Ways	1 Oct	1957	29 July	1958	5 May	1959
MARTADINATA (ex-*Charles Berry* DE 1035)	342	American SB Co, Toledo, OH	29 Oct	1958	17 Mar	1959	25 Nov	1959
MONGINSIDI (ex-*Claud Jones* DE 1033)	343	Avondale Marine Ways	1 June	1957	27 May	1958	10 Feb	1959
NGURAHRAI (ex-*McMorris* DE 1036)	344	American SB Co, Toledo, OH	5 Nov	1958	26 May	1959	4 Mar	1960

Displacement, tons: 1,720 standard; 1,968 full load
Dimensions, feet (metres): 310 × 38.7 × 18
(95 × 11.8 × 5.5)
Main machinery: 2 Fairbanks-Morse 38TD 8-1/8-12 diesels (not in 343); 7,000 hp *(5.2 MW)* sustained; 1 shaft
Speed, knots: 22. **Range, miles:** 3,000 at 18 kt
Complement: 171 (12 officers)

Guns: 1 or 2 US 3 in *(76 mm)*/50 Mk 34; 50 rds/min to 12.8 km *(7 n miles)*; weight of shell 6 kg.
   2 USSR 37 mm/63 (twin); 160 rds/min to 9 km *(5 n miles)*; weight of shell 0.7 kg.
Torpedoes: 6—324 mm Mk 32 (2 triple) tubes. Honeywell Mk 46; anti-submarine; active/passive homing to 11 km *(5.9 n miles)* at 40 kt; warhead 44 kg.
Depth charges: 2 DC throwers.
Countermeasures: ESM: WLR-1C (except *Samadikun*); radar warning.
Weapons control: Mk 70 Mod 2 for guns.
Radars: Air search: Westinghouse SPS-6E; D-band; range 146 km *(80 n miles)* (for fighter).
Surface search: Raytheon SPS-5D; G/H-band; range 37 km *(20 n miles)*.
   Raytheon SPS-4 *(Ngurahrai)*; G/H-band.
Navigation: Racal Decca 1226; I-band.
Fire control: Lockheed SPG-52; K-band.
Sonars: EDO *(Samadikun)*; SQS-45V *(Martadinata)*; SQS-39V *(Monginsidi)*; SQS-42V *(Ngurahrai)*; hull-mounted; active search and attack; medium/high frequency.

Programmes: *Samadikun* transferred from USA 20 February 1973; *Martadinata*, 31 January 1974; *Monginsidi* and *Ngurahrai*, 16 December 1974. All refitted at Subic Bay 1979-82.

MONGINSIDI   *10/1998* * / 0080006

Modernisation: The Hedgehog A/S mortars have been removed, as have the 25 mm guns. Some have a second 76 mm gun vice the 37 mm.

Operational: It was planned that the 'Van Speijk' class would replace these ships but all are still in service, although much time is spent in maintenance.   ***UPDATED***

CORVETTES

16 KAPITAN PATIMURA (PARCHIM I) CLASS (TYPE 133.1) (FS)

Name	No	Builders	Commissioned		Recommissioned	
KAPITAN PATIMURA (ex-*Prenzlau*)	371 (ex-231)	Peenewerft, Wolgast	11 May	1983	23 Sep	1993
UNTUNG SUROPATI (ex-*Ribnitz*)	372 (ex-233)	Peenewerft, Wolgast	29 Oct	1983	23 Sep	1993
NUKU (ex-*Waren*)	373 (ex-224)	Peenewerft, Wolgast	23 Nov	1982	15 Dec	1993
LAMBUNG MANGKURAT (ex-*Angermünde*)	374 (ex-214)	Peenewerft, Wolgast	26 July	1985	12 July	1994
CUT NYAK DIEN (ex-*Lübz*)	375 (ex-P 6169, ex-221)	Peenewerft, Wolgast	12 Feb	1982	25 Feb	1994
SULTAN THAHA SYAIFUDDIN (ex-*Bad Doberan*)	376 (ex-222)	Peenewerft, Wolgast	30 June	1982	25 Feb	1995
SUTANTO (ex-*Wismar*)	377 (ex-P 6170, ex-241)	Peenewerft, Wolgast	9 July	1981	10 Mar	1995
SUTEDI SENOPUTRA (ex-*Parchim*)	378 (ex-242)	Peenewerft, Wolgast	9 Apr	1981	19 Sep	1994
WIRATNO (ex-*Perleberg*)	379 (ex-243)	Peenewerft, Wolgast	19 Sep	1981	19 Sep	1994
MEMET SASTRAWIRIA (ex-*Bützow*)	380 (ex-244)	Peenewerft, Wolgast	30 Dec	1981	2 June	1995
TJIPTADI (ex-*Bergen*)	381 (ex-213)	Peenewerft, Wolgast	1 Feb	1985	10 May	1996
HASAN BASRI (ex-*Güstrow*)	382 (ex-223)	Peenewerft, Wolgast	10 Nov	1982	10 May	1996
IMAN BONJOL (ex-*Teterow*)	383 (ex-P 6168, ex-234)	Peenewerft, Wolgast	27 Jan	1984	26 Apr	1994
PATI UNUS (ex-*Ludwiglust*)	384 (ex-232)	Peenewerft, Wolgast	4 July	1983	21 July	1995
TEUKU UMAR (ex-*Grevesmühlen*)	385 (ex-212)	Peenewerft, Wolgast	21 Sep	1984	27 Oct	1996
SILAS PAPARE (ex-*Gadebusch*)	386 (ex-P 6167, ex-211)	Peenewerft, Wolgast	31 Aug	1984	27 Oct	1996

Displacement, tons: 769 standard
Dimensions, feet (metres): 246.7 × 32.2 × 11.5
(75.2 × 9.8 × 3.5)
Main machinery: 3 Type M 504A diesels; 10,812 hp(m) *(7.95 MW)* sustained; 3 shafts; centreline cp prop
Speed, knots: 24. **Range, miles:** 1,750 at 18 kt
Complement: 64 (9 officers)

Missiles: SAM: SA-N-5/8 launchers fitted in some. May be replaced by twin Simbad launchers.
Guns: 2 USSR 57 mm/80 (twin) ❶ automatic; 120 rds/min to 6 km *(3.2 n miles)*; weight of shell 2.8 kg.
   2—30 mm (twin) ❷; 500 rds/min to 5 km *(2.7 n miles)* anti-aircraft; weight of shell 0.54 kg.
Torpedoes: 4—400 mm tubes ❸.
A/S mortars: 2 RBU 6000 12-barrelled trainable launchers ❹; automatic loading; range 6,000 m; warhead 31 kg.
Depth charges: 2 racks.
Mines: Mine rails fitted.
Countermeasures: Decoys: 2 PK 16 chaff rocket launchers.
ESM: 2 Watch Dog; radar warning.
Radars: Air/surface search: Strut Curve ❺; F-band; range 110 km *(60 n miles)* for 2 m² target.
Navigation: TSR 333; I-band.
Fire control: Muff Cob ❻; G/H-band.
IFF: High Pole B.
Sonars: MG 332T; hull-mounted; active search and attack; high frequency.
   Elk Tail; VDS system on starboard side (in some hulls).

Programmes: Ex-GDR ships mostly paid off in 1991. Formally transferred on 4 January 1993 and became Indonesian ships on 25 August 1993. First three arrived Indonesia in November 1993.
Modernisation: All refitted prior to sailing for Indonesia. Range increased and air conditioning added to accommodation. SAM launchers can be carried. May be re-engined with MTU diesels when funds are available.
Structure: Basically very similar to Russian 'Grisha' class but with a higher freeboard and different armament.
Operational: Engine problems have been experienced, and a few of the class have probably been cannibalised for spares. Maximum speed has been reduced.

UPDATED

KAPITAN PATIMURA   *(Scale 1 : 600), Ian Sturton*

PATI UNUS   *7/1997* / 0012538

SHIPBORNE AIRCRAFT

Notes: One NB 412 helicopter acquired in August 1996.

Numbers/Type: 12 (3) Nurtanio (MBB) NBO 105C.
Operational speed: 113 kt *(210 km/h).*
Service ceiling: 9,845 ft *(3,000 m).*
Range: 407 n miles *(754 km).*
Role/Weapon systems: Embarked for liaison and support duties. Three more to be delivered in 2001. A further eight are planned. Sensors: Thomson-CSF Oceanmaster or APS-115 radar and FLIR in some. Weapons: Unarmed.

UPDATED

NBO 105C   11/1990 * / 0080007

Numbers/Type: 1 Nurtanio (Aerospatiale) NAS-332 Super Puma.
Operational speed: 151 kt *(279 km/h).*
Service ceiling: 15,090 ft *(4,600 m).*
Range: 335 n miles *(620 km).*
Role/Weapon systems: ASW and assault operations with secondary role in utility and SAR; ASVW development possible with Exocet or similar. More are required. Sensors: Thomson-CSF Omera radar and Alcatel dipping sonar in some. Weapons: ASW; two Mk 46 torpedoes or depth bombs.

UPDATED

SUPER PUMA (French colours)   6/1994 * / 0080008

Numbers/Type: 3 Westland Wasp (HAS Mk 1).
Operational speed: 96 kt *(177 km/h).*
Service ceiling: 12,200 ft *(3,720 m).*
Range: 263 n miles *(488 km).*
Role/Weapon systems: Shipborne ASW helicopter weapons carrier and reconnaissance; SAR and utility as secondary roles. Becoming difficult to maintain and these are the only survivors. Preferred replacement is Westland Navy Lynx. Sensors: None. Weapons: ASW; two Mk 44 or one Mk 46 torpedoes, depth bombs or mines.

UPDATED

WASP (NZ colours)   4/1997, Maritime Photographic / 0012537

LAND-BASED MARITIME AIRCRAFT (FRONT LINE)

Note: Six IPTN NC-212 may be acquired in 2001.

Numbers/Type: 5 Boeing 737-200 Surveiller.
Operational speed: 462 kt *(856 km/h).*
Service ceiling: 50,000 ft *(15,240 m).*
Range: 2,530 n miles *(4,688 km).*
Role/Weapon systems: Land-based for long-range maritime surveillance roles. Air Force manned. Sensors upgraded in 1993-94 to include IFF. Sensors: Motorola APS-135(v) SLAM MR radar, Thomson-CSF Oceanmaster radar. Weapons: Unarmed.

VERIFIED

Numbers/Type: 29/6 GAF Searchmaster Nomad B/L.
Operational speed: 168 kt *(311 km/h).*
Service ceiling: 21,000 ft *(6,400 m).*
Range: 730 n miles *(1,352 km).*
Role/Weapon systems: Nomad type built in Australia. Short-range maritime patrol, EEZ protection and anti-smuggler duties. 20 more acquired from Australian Army in August 1997 for use in maritime role. Not all are operational and NC-212 replacements are planned. Sensors: Nose-mounted search radar. Weapons: Unarmed.

UPDATED

Numbers/Type: 9 Northrop F-5E Tiger II.
Operational speed: 940 kt *(1,740 km/h).*
Service ceiling: 51,800 ft *(15,790 m).*
Range: 300 n miles *(556 km).*
Role/Weapon systems: Fleet air defence and strike fighter, formed 'naval co-operation unit'. Planned to be replaced by BAe Hawk 200 in due course. Sensors: AI radar. Weapons: AD; two AIM-9 Sidewinder, two 20 mm cannon. Strike; 3,175 tons of underwing stores.

UPDATED

Numbers/Type: 11 CASA/Nurtanio/IPTN CN-235 MPA.
Operational speed: 240 kt *(445 km/h).*
Service ceiling: 26,600 ft *(8,110 m).*
Range: 669 n miles *(1,240 km).*
Role/Weapon systems: Medium-range maritime reconnaissance role. Five added to the original six in 1997-98. 12 transport variants also in service. Sensors: Litton APS 504 and APS 134 radar or Thomson-CSF Oceanmaster radar. FLIR. Weapons: ASV; may have Exocet AM 39.

VERIFIED

PATROL FORCES

4 DAGGER CLASS (FAST ATTACK CRAFT—MISSILE) (PCFG)

Name	No	Builders	Commissioned
MANDAU	621	Korea Tacoma, Masan	20 July 1979
RENCONG	622	Korea Tacoma, Masan	20 July 1979
BADIK	623	Korea Tacoma, Masan	Feb 1980
KERIS	624	Korea Tacoma, Masan	Feb 1980

Displacement, tons: 270 full load
Dimensions, feet (metres): 164.7 × 23.9 × 7.5 *(50.2 × 7.3 × 2.3)*
Main machinery: CODOG; 1 GE LM 2500 gas turbine; 23,000 hp *(17.16 MW)* sustained; 2 MTU 12V 331 TC81 diesels; 2,240 hp(m) *(1.65 MW)* sustained; 2 shafts; cp props
Speed, knots: 41 gas; 17 diesel. **Range, miles:** 2,000 at 17 kt
Complement: 43 (7 officers)
Missiles: SSM: 4 Aerospatiale MM 38 Exocet; inertial cruise; active radar homing to 42 km *(23 n miles)* at 0.9 Mach; warhead 165 kg; sea-skimmer.
Guns: 1 Bofors 57 mm/70 Mk 1; 200 rds/min to 17 km *(9.3 n miles)*; weight of shell 0.96 kg. Launchers for illuminants on each side.
1 Bofors 40 mm/70; 300 rds/min to 12 km *(6.6 n miles)*; weight of shell 2.4 kg.
2 Rheinmetall 20 mm.
Countermeasures: ESM: Thomson-CSF DR 2000S (in 623 and 624); radar intercept.
Weapons control: Selenia NA-18 optronic director.
Radars: Surface search: Racal Decca 1226; I-band.
Fire control: Signaal WM28; I/J-band.

Programmes: PSMM Mk 5 type craft ordered in 1975.
Structure: Shorter in length and smaller displacement than South Korean units. *Mandau* has a different shaped mast with a tripod base.

UPDATED

RENCONG   10/1998 * / 0052358

4 SINGA (PB 57) CLASS (NAV I and II) (LARGE PATROL CRAFT) (PC)

Name	No	Builders	Commissioned
SINGA	651	Lürssen/PT Pal Surabaya	Apr 1988
AJAK	653	Lürssen/PT Pal Surabaya	5 Apr 1989
PANDRONG	801	PT Pal Surabaya	1992
SURA	802	PT Pal Surabaya	1993

Displacement, tons: 447 full load (NAV I); 428 full load (NAV II)
Dimensions, feet (metres): 190.6 × 25 × 9.2 *(58.1 × 7.6 × 2.8)*
Main machinery: 2 MTU 16V 956 TB92 diesels; 8,850 hp(m) *(6.5 MW)* sustained; 2 shafts
Speed, knots: 27. **Range, miles:** 6,100 at 15 kt; 2,200 at 27 kt
Complement: 42 (6 officers)
Guns: 1 Bofors SAK 57 mm/70 Mk 2; 220 rds/min to 14 km *(7.6 n miles)*; weight of shell 2.4 kg.
    1 Bofors SAK 40 mm/70; 300 rds/min to 12 km *(6.6 n miles)*; weight of shell 0.96 kg.
    2 Rheinmetall 20 mm (NAV II).
Torpedoes: 2—21 in *(533 mm)* Toro tubes (NAV I). AEG SUT; anti-submarine; wire-guided; active/
    passive homing to 12 km *(6.6 n miles)* at 35 kt; 28 km *(15 n miles)* at 23 kt; warhead 250 kg.
Countermeasures: Decoys: CSEE Dagaie single trainable launcher; automatic dispenser for IR
    flares and chaff; H/J-band.
    ESM: Thomson-CSF DR 2000 S3 with Dalia analyser; intercept. DASA Telegon VIII D/F.
Weapons control: Signaal LIOD 73 Ri optronic director. Signaal WM22 72 Ri WCS (NAV I).
Radars: Surface search: Racal Decca 2459; I-band; Signaal Scout; H/I-band (NAV II).
    Fire control: Signaal WM22; I/J-band (NAV I).
Sonars: Signaal PMS 32 (NAV I); active search and attack; medium frequency.

Comment: Class ordered from Lürssen in 1982. First launched and shipped incomplete to PT Pal
    Surabaya for fitting out in January 1984. Second shipped July 1984. The first two are NAV I ASW
    versions with torpedo tubes and sonars. The second pair are NAV II AAW versions with an
    augmented gun armament, an improved surveillance and fire-control radar, but without torpedo
    tubes and sonars and completed later than expected in 1992-93. Vosper Thornycroft fin
    stabilisers are fitted.

UPDATED

SINGA (NAV I)   5/1999*, G Toremans / 0080009

AJAK (NAV I)   5/1998, John Mortimer / 0052359

PANDRONG (NAV II)   12/1999*, Sattler/Steele / 0080010

4 KAKAP (PB 57) CLASS (NAV III and IV) (LARGE PATROL CRAFT) (PC)

Name	No	Builders	Commissioned
KAKAP	811	Lürssen/PT Pal Surabaya	29 June 1988
KERAPU	812	Lürssen/PT Pal Surabaya	5 Apr 1989
TONGKOL	813	PT Pal Surabaya	Dec 1993
BARAKUDA (ex-*Bervang*)	814	PT Pal Surabaya	Aug 1995

Displacement, tons: 423 full load
Dimensions, feet (metres): 190.6 × 25 × 9.2 *(58.1 × 7.6 × 2.8)*
Main machinery: 2 MTU 16V 956 TB92 diesels; 8,850 hp(m) *(6.5 MW)* sustained; 2 shafts
Speed, knots: 28. **Range, miles:** 6,100 at 15 kt; 2,200 at 27 kt
Complement: 49 plus 8 spare berths
Guns: 1 Bofors 40 mm/60; 240 rds/min to 12.6 km *(6.8 n miles)*; weight of shell 0.96 kg.
    2—12.7 mm MGs.
Countermeasures: ESM: Thomson-CSF DR 3000 S1; intercept.
Radars: Surface search: Racal Decca 2459; I-band.
    Navigation: KH 1007; I-band.
Helicopters: Platform for 1 NBO 105.

Comment: Ordered in 1982. First pair shipped from West Germany and completed at PT Pal
    Surabaya. Second pair assembled at Surabaya taking longer than expected to complete. The first
    three are NAV III SAR and Customs versions and by comparison with NAV I are very lightly armed
    and have a 13 × 7.1 m helicopter deck in place of the after guns and torpedo tubes. Vosper
    Thornycroft fin stabilisers are fitted. Can be used for Patrol purposes as well as SAR, and can
    transport two rifle platoons. There is also a fast seaboat with launching crane at the stern and
    two water guns for firefighting. The single NAV IV version has some minor variations and is used
    as Presidential Yacht manned by a special unit.

UPDATED

KAKAP (NAV III)   8/1995*, van Ginderen Collection / 0080011

BARAKUDA (NAV IV)   8/1995*, van Ginderen Collection / 0080012

0 + 4 PB 57 CLASS (NAV V) (LARGE PATROL CRAFT) (PC)

Name	No	Builders	Commissioned
TODAK	803	PT Pal Surabaya	2001
HIU	804	PT Pal Surabaya	2002
LAYANG	805	PT Pal Surabaya	2003
DORANG	806	PT Pal Surabaya	2004

Displacement, tons: 447 full load
Dimensions, feet (metres): 190.6 × 25 × 9.2 *(58.1 × 7.6 × 2.8)*
Main machinery: 2 MTU 16V 956 TB92 diesels; 8,850 hp(m) *(6.5 MW)* sustained; 2 shafts
Speed, knots: 27. **Range, miles:** 6,100 at 15 kt; 2,200 at 27 kt
Complement: 42
Guns: 1 Bofors SAK 57 mm/70 Mk 2 ❶; 220 rds/min to 14 km *(7.6 n miles)*; weight of shell 2.4 kg.
    1 Bofors SAK 40 mm/70 ❷; 300 rds/min to 12 km *(6.6 n miles)*; weight of shell 0.96 kg.
    2 Rheinmetall 20 mm ❸.
Countermeasures: Decoys: CSEE Dagaie chaff launchers.
    ESM: Thomson-CSF DR 3000 S1; intercept.
Combat data systems: TACTICOS type.
Weapons control: Signaal LIOD 73 Ri Mk 2 optronic director ❹.
Radars: Surface search: Signaal Scout variant ❺; E/F-band.
    Fire control: Signaal LIROD Mk 2 ❻; K-band.
    Navigation: Kelvin Hughes KH 1007 ❼; I-band.

Comment: Ordered in mid-1993 from PT Pal Surabaya. Weapon systems ordered in November
    1994. Much improved combat data system is fitted. The after gun was intended to be a second
    57 mm but this has been changed. Funding problems have slowed down construction. The first
    launch is expected in 2000/01.

UPDATED

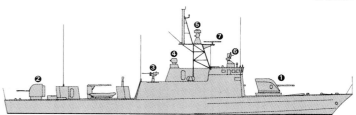

TODAK   (not to scale), Ian Sturton

8 SIBARAU (ATTACK) CLASS (LARGE PATROL CRAFT) (PC)

Name	No	Builders	Commissioned
SIBARAU (ex-*Bandolier*)	847	Walkers, Australia	14 Dec 1968
SILIMAN (ex-*Archer*)	848	Walkers, Australia	15 May 1968
SIGALU (ex-*Barricade*)	857	Walkers, Australia	26 Oct 1968
SILEA (ex-*Acute*)	858	Evans Deakin	24 Apr 1968
SIRIBUA (ex-*Bombard*)	859	Walkers, Australia	5 Nov 1968
SIADA (ex-*Barbette*)	862	Walkers, Australia	16 Aug 1968
SIKUDA (ex-*Attack*)	863	Evans Deakin	17 Nov 1967
SIGUROT (ex-*Assail*)	864	Evans Deakin	12 July 1968

Displacement, tons: 146 full load
Dimensions, feet (metres): 107.5 × 20 × 7.3 *(32.8 × 6.1 × 2.2)*
Main machinery: 2 Paxman 16YJCM diesels; 4,000 hp *(2.98 MW)* sustained; 2 shafts
Speed, knots: 21. **Range, miles:** 1,220 at 13 kt
Complement: 19 (3 officers)
Guns: 1 Bofors 40 mm/60. 1—12.5 mm MG.
Countermeasures: ESM: DASA Telegon VIII; intercept.
Radars: Surface search: Decca 916; I-band.

Comment: Transferred from Australia after refit—*Bandolier* 16 November 1973, *Archer* in 1974, *Barricade* March 1982, *Acute* 6 May 1983, *Bombard* September 1983, *Attack* 22 February 1985 (recommissioned 24 May 1985), *Barbette* February 1985, *Assail* February 1986. All carry rocket/flare launchers. Two similar craft with pennant numbers 860 and 861 were built locally in 1982/83 but have not been reported for some years.

UPDATED

SIGALU   *4/1999* * / 0080013

AMPHIBIOUS FORCES

Notes: (1) This section includes some vessels of the Military Sealift Command—Kolinlamil.
(2) A troop transport is required, possibly from a South Korean shipyard. Military lift 700 troops.

7 LST 1-511 and 512-1152 CLASSES (LST)

Name	No	Builders	Commissioned
TELUK LANGSA (ex-*LST 1128*)	501	Chicago Bridge	9 Mar 1945
TELUK BAJUR (ex-*LST 616*)	502	Chicago Bridge	29 May 1944
TELUK KAU (ex-*LST 652*)	504	Chicago Bridge	1 Jan 1945
TELUK TOMINI (ex-*Inagua Crest*, ex-*Brunei*, ex-*Bledsoe County, LST 356*)	508	Charleston, NY	22 Dec 1942
TELUK RATAI (ex-*Inagua Shipper*, ex-*Presque Isle*, APB 44, ex-*LST 678*, ex-*Teluk Sindoro*)	509	American Bridge, PA	30 June 1944
TELUK SALEH (ex-*Clark County, LST 601*)	510	Chicago Bridge	25 Mar 1944
TELUK BONE (ex-*Iredell County, LST 839*)	511	American Bridge, PA	6 Dec 1944

Displacement, tons: 1,653 standard; 4,080 full load
Dimensions, feet (metres): 328 × 50 × 14 *(100 × 15.2 × 4.3)*
Main machinery: 2 GM 12-567A diesels; 1,800 hp *(1.34 MW)*; 2 shafts
Speed, knots: 11.6. **Range, miles:** 11,000 at 10 kt
Complement: 119 (accommodation for 266)
Military lift: 2,100 tons
Guns: 7—40 mm. 2—20 mm *(Teluk Langsa)*. 6—37 mm (remainder).
Radars: Surface search: SPS-21 *(Teluk Tomini, Teluk Sindoro)*. SPS-53 *(Teluk Saleh, Teluk Bone)*. SO-1 *(Teluk Kau)*. SO-6 *(Teluk Langsa)*.

Comment: *Teluk Bajur*, *Teluk Saleh* and *Teluk Bone* transferred from USA in June 1961 (and purchased 22 February 1979). *Teluk Kau* and *Teluk Langsa* in July 1970. These ships are used as transports and stores carriers. It was anticipated that they would decay in reserve Fleet anchorages once the 'Frosch' class were in service, but all remain active. *Bajur* and *Tomini* serve with the Military Sealift Command.

UPDATED

TELUK BONE   *8/1995* *, John Mortimer / 0080014

6 TACOMA TYPE (LST)

Name	No	Builders	Commissioned
TELUK SEMANGKA	512	Korea-Tacoma, Masan	20 Jan 1981
TELUK PENJU	513	Korea-Tacoma, Masan	20 Jan 1981
TELUK MANDAR	514	Korea-Tacoma, Masan	July 1981
TELUK SAMPIT	515	Korea-Tacoma, Masan	June 1981
TELUK BANTEN	516	Korea-Tacoma, Masan	May 1982
TELUK ENDE	517	Korea-Tacoma, Masan	2 Sep 1982

Displacement, tons: 3,750 full load
Dimensions, feet (metres): 328 × 47.2 × 13.8 *(100 × 14.4 × 4.2)*
Main machinery: 2 diesels; 12,800 hp(m) *(9.41 MW)* sustained; 2 shafts
Speed, knots: 15. **Range, miles:** 7,500 at 13 kt
Complement: 90 (13 officers)
Military lift: 1,800 tons (including 17 MBTs); 2 LCVPs; 200 troops
Guns: 2 or 3 Bofors 40 mm/70. 2 Rheinmetall 20 mm.
Radars: Surface search: Raytheon; E/F-band *(Teluk Banten* and *Teluk Ende)*.
Navigation: Racal Decca; I-band.
Helicopters: 1 Westland Wasp; 3 NAS-332 Super Pumas can be carried in last pair.

Comment: First four ordered in June 1979, last pair June 1981. No hangar in *Teluk Semangka* and *Teluk Mandar*. Two hangars in *Teluk Ende*. The last pair differ in silhouette having drowned exhausts in place of funnels and having their LCVPs carried forward of the bridge. They also have only two 40 mm guns and an additional radar fitted above the bridge. Battalion of marines can be embarked if no tanks are carried. *Teluk Ende* and *Teluk Banten* act as Command ships, the former also serving as a hospital ship.

UPDATED

TELUK SEMANGKA (no hangar)   *8/1995* *, van Ginderen Collection / 0080015

TELUK BANTEN (command ship)   *8/1995* *, van Ginderen Collection / 0080016

TELUK ENDE (hospital ship)   *8/1995* * / 0080017

1 LST

Name	No	Builders	Commissioned
TELUK AMBOINA	503	Sasebo, Japan	June 1961

Displacement, tons: 2,378 standard; 4,200 full load
Dimensions, feet (metres): 327 × 50 × 15 *(99.7 × 15.3 × 4.6)*
Main machinery: 2 MAN V6V 22/30 diesels; 3,425 hp(m) *(2.52 MW)*; 2 shafts
Speed, knots: 13.1. **Range, miles:** 4,000 at 13.1 kt
Complement: 88
Military lift: 212 troops; 2,100 tons; 4 LCVP on davits
Guns: 6—37 mm; anti-aircraft.

Comment: Launched on 17 March 1961 and transferred from Japan in June 1961. A faster copy of US 'LST 511' class with 30 ton crane forward of bridge. Serves with the Military Sealift Command.

UPDATED

TELUK AMBOINA   *8/1995* *, van Ginderen Collection / 0080018

12 FROSCH I CLASS (TYPE 108) (LSM)

Name	No	Commissioned	Recommissioned
TELUK GILIMANUK	531 (ex-611)	12 Nov 1976	12 July 1994
(ex-Hoyerswerda)			
TELUK CELUKAN BAWANG	532 (ex-632)	1 Dec 1976	25 Feb 1994
(ex-Hagenow)			
TELUK CENDRAWASIH	533 (ex-613)	2 Feb 1977	9 Dec 1994
(ex-Frankfurt/Oder)			
TELUK BERAU	534 (ex-634)	28 May 1977	10 Mar 1995
(ex-Eberswalde-Finow)			
TELUK PELENG (ex-Lübben)	535 (ex-631)	15 Mar 1978	23 Sep 1993
TELUK SIBOLGA (ex-Schwerin)	536 (ex-612)	19 Oct 1977	15 Dec 1993
TELUK MANADO	537 (ex-633)	28 Dec 1977	2 June 1995
(ex-Neubrandenburg)			
TELUK HADING (ex-Cottbus)	538 (ex-614)	26 May 1978	12 July 1994
TELUK PARIGI (ex-Anklam)	539 (ex-635)	14 July 1978	21 July 1995
TELUK LAMPUNG (ex-Schwedt)	540 (ex-636)	7 Sep 1979	26 Apr 1994
TELUK JAKARTA	541 (ex-615)	4 Jan 1979	19 Sep 1994
(ex-Eisenhüttenstadt)			
TELUK SANGKULIRANG	542 (ex-616)	4 Jan 1979	9 Dec 1994
(ex-Grimmen)			

Displacement, tons: 1,950 full load
Dimensions, feet (metres): 321.5 × 36.4 × 9.2 *(98 × 11.1 × 2.8)*
Main machinery: 2 diesels; 5,000 hp(m) *(3.68 MW)*; 2 shafts
Speed, knots: 18
Complement: 46
Military lift: 600 tons
Guns: 1—40 mm/60. 4—37 mm/63 (2 twin). 4—25 mm (2 twin).
Mines: Can lay 40 mines through stern doors.
Countermeasures: Decoys: 2 PK 16 chaff launchers.
Radars: Air/surface search: Strut Curve; F-band.
Navigation: TSR 333; I-band.

Comment: All built by Peenewerft, Wolgast. Former GDR ships transferred from Germany on 25 August 1993. Demilitarised with all guns removed, but 37 mm guns have replaced the original 57 mm and 30 mm twin guns. All refitted in Germany prior to sailing. First two arrived Indonesia in late 1993, remainder throughout 1994 and 1995. *Teluk Lampung* damaged by heavy seas during transit in June 1994 but was repaired.

UPDATED

TELUK BERAU   *8/1995*, van Ginderen Collection* / 0075855

TELUK LAMPUNG   *8/1995** / 0080019

4 LCUs and 50 LCM/LCVPs

DORE 580   **KUPANG** 582   **DILI** 583   **NUSANTARA** 584

Displacement, tons: 400 full load
Dimensions, feet (metres): 140.7 × 29.9 × 4.6 *(42.9 × 9.1 × 1.4)*
Main machinery: 4 diesels; 2 shafts
Speed, knots: 12. **Range, miles:** 700 at 11 kt
Complement: 17
Military lift: 200 tons

Comment: Details given are for 582-584 built at Naval Training Centre, Surabaya in 1978-80. Military Sealift Command. 580 is a smaller ship at 275 tons and built in 1968. About 20 LCM 6 type and 30 LCVPs are also in service.

UPDATED

LCVP   *8/1995*, van Ginderen Collection* / 0080020

MINE WARFARE FORCES

2 PULAU RENGAT (TRIPARTITE) CLASS (MHC)

Name	No	Builders	Launched	Commissioned
PULAU RENGAT	711	van der Giessen-de Noord	23 July 1987	26 Mar 1988
PULAU RUPAT	712	van der Giessen-de Noord	27 Aug 1987	26 Mar 1988

Displacement, tons: 502 standard; 568 full load
Dimensions, feet (metres): 168.9 × 29.2 × 8.2 *(51.5 × 8.9 × 2.5)*
Main machinery: 2 MTU 12V 396 TC82 diesels; 2,610 hp(m) *(1.92 MW)* sustained; 1 shaft; acbLIPS cp prop; auxiliary propulsion; 3 Turbomeca gas-turbine generators; 2 motors; 2,400 hp (m) *(1.76 MW)*; 2 retractable Schottel propulsors; 2 bow thrusters; 150 hp(m) *(110 kW)*
Speed, knots: 15; 7 auxiliary propulsion. **Range, miles:** 3,000 at 12 kt
Complement: 46 plus 4 spare berths

Guns: 2 Rheinmetall 20 mm. Matra Simbad SAM launcher may be added for patrol duties or a third 20 mm gun.
Countermeasures: MCM: OD3 Oropesa mechanical sweep gear; Fiskars F-82 magnetic and SA Marine AS 203 acoustic sweeps; Ibis V minehunting system; 2 PAP 104 Mk 4 mine disposal systems.
Combat data systems: Signaal SEWACO-RI action data automation.
Radars: Navigation: Racal Decca AC 1229C; I-band.
Sonars: Thomson Sintra TSM 2022; active minehunting; high frequency.

Programmes: First ordered on 29 March 1985, laid down 22 July 1985, second ordered 30 August 1985 and laid down 15 December 1985. More were to have been built in Indonesia up to a total of 12 but this programme was cancelled by lack of funds.
Structure: There are differences in design between these ships and the European Tripartites, apart from their propulsion. Deckhouses and general layout are different as they are required to act as minehunters, minesweepers and patrol ships. Hull construction is GRP shock-proven.
Operational: Endurance, 15 days. Automatic operations, navigation and recording systems, Thomson-CSF Naviplot TSM 2060 tactical display. A 5 ton container can be shipped, stored for varying tasks—research; patrol; extended diving; drone control.

UPDATED

PULAU RUPAT   *8/1995** / 0080022

9 KONDOR II (TYPE 89) CLASS
(MINESWEEPERS—COASTAL) (MSC)

Name	No	Builders	Commissioned
PULAU ROTE (ex-Wolgast)	721 (ex-V 811)	Peenewerft, Wolgast	1 June 1971
PULAU RAAS (ex-Hettstedt)	722 (ex-353)	Peenewerft, Wolgast	22 Dec 1971
PULAU ROMANG (ex-Pritzwalk)	723 (ex-325)	Peenewerft, Wolgast	26 June 1972
PULAU RIMAU (ex-Bitterfeld)	724 (ex-332, ex-M 2672)	Peenewerft, Wolgast	7 Aug 1972
PULAU RONDO (ex-Zerbst)	725 (ex-335)	Peenewerft, Wolgast	30 Sep 1972
PULAU RUSA (ex-Oranienburg)	726 (ex-341)	Peenewerft, Wolgast	1 Nov 1972
PULAU RANGSANG (ex-Jüterbog)	727 (ex-342)	Peenewerft, Wolgast	7 Apr 1973
PULAU RAIBU (ex-Sömmerda)	728 (ex-311, ex-M 2670)	Peenewerft, Wolgast	9 Aug 1973
PULAU REMPANG (ex-Grimma)	729 (ex-336)	Peenewerft, Wolgast	10 Nov 1973

Displacement, tons: 310 full load
Dimensions, feet (metres): 186 × 24.6 × 7.9 *(56.7 × 7.5 × 2.4)*
Main machinery: 2 Russki Kolomna Type 40-DM diesels; 4,408 hp(m) *(3.24 MW)* sustained; 2 shafts; cp props
Speed, knots: 17. **Range, miles:** 2,000 at 14 kt
Complement: 31 (6 officers)
Guns: 6—25 mm/80 (3 twin).
Mines: 2 rails.
Radars: Navigation: TSR 333; I-band.
Sonars: Bendix AQS 17 VDS; minehunting; active; high frequency (in some).

Comment: Former GDR minesweepers transferred from Germany in Russian dockship *Trans-Shelf* arriving 22 October 1993. MCM is secondary role with EEZ patrol taking priority. ADI Dyads can be embarked for MCM. *Pulau Rondo* was used for trials.

UPDATED

PULAU RUSA   *8/1995*, van Ginderen Collection* / 0080021

2 T 43 CLASS (MINESWEEPERS—OCEAN) (MSO)

PULAU RANI 701   **PULAU RATAWO** 702

Displacement, tons: 580 full load
Dimensions, feet (metres): 190.2 × 27.6 × 6.9 *(58 × 8.4 × 2.1)*
Main machinery: 2 Kolomna 9-D-8 diesels; 2,000 hp(m) *(1.6 MW)* sustained; 2 shafts
Speed, knots: 15. **Range, miles:** 3,000 at 10 kt
Complement: 77
Guns: 4—37 mm/63 (2 twin). 8—12.7 mm (4 twin) MGs.
Depth charges: 2 projectors.
Radars: Navigation: Decca 110; I-band.
Sonars: Stag Ear; hull-mounted; active search and attack; high frequency.

Comment: Transferred from USSR in 1964. Mostly used as patrol craft. Both are still in service but not very active.

VERIFIED

PULAU RANI   *1983, W Sartori*

SURVEY AND RESEARCH SHIPS

4 RESEARCH SHIPS (AGS/AGOR)

Name	No	Builders	Commissioned
BARUNA JAYA I	KAL-IV-02	CMN, Cherbourg	10 Aug 1989
BARUNA JAYA II	KAL-IV-03	CMN, Cherbourg	25 Sep 1989
BARUNA JAYA III	KAL-IV-04	CMN, Cherbourg	3 Jan 1990
BARUNA JAYA IV	KAL-IV-05	CMN, Cherbourg	2 Nov 1995

Displacement, tons: 1,180 (1,425 IV) full load
Dimensions, feet (metres): 198.2 × 39.7 × 13.8 *(60.4 × 12.1 × 4.2)*
Main machinery: 2 Niigata/SEMT-Pielstick 5 PA5 L 255 diesels; 2,990 hp(m) *(2.2 MW)* sustained; 1 shaft; cp prop; bow thruster
Speed, knots: 14. **Range, miles:** 7,500 at 12 kt
Complement: 37 (8 officers) plus 26 scientists

Comment: First three ordered from La Manche, Dieppe in February 1985 by the office of Technology, Ministry of Industry and Research. Badly delayed by the closing down of the original shipbuilders (ACM, Dieppe) and construction taken over by CMN at Cherbourg. Fourth of class ordered in 1993 to a slightly enlarged design and with a more enclosed superstructure. *Baruna Jaya 1* is employed on hydrography, the second on oceanography and the third combines both tasks. *Baruna Jaya IV* is operated by the Agency responsible for developing new technology. All are part of the Naval Auxiliary Service.

UPDATED

BARUNA JAYA II   *4/1998, John Mortimer /* 0052362

BARUNA JAYA IV   *11/1995*, van Ginderen Collection /* 0080023

1 HECLA CLASS (SURVEY SHIP) (AGS)

Name	No	Builders	Commissioned
DEWA KEMBAR (ex-*Hydra*)	932	Yarrow and Co, Blythswood	5 May 1966

Displacement, tons: 1,915 light; 2,733 full load
Dimensions, feet (metres): 260.1 × 49.1 × 15.4 *(79.3 × 15 × 4.7)*
Main machinery: Diesel-electric; 3 Paxman 12YJCZ diesels; 3,780 hp *(2.82 MW)*; 3 generators; 1 motor; 2,000 hp(m) *(1.49 MW)*; 1 shaft; bow thruster
Speed, knots: 14. **Range, miles:** 12,000 at 11 kt
Complement: 123 (14 officers)
Guns: 2—12.7 mm MGs.
Radars: Navigation: Kelvin Hughes Type 1006; I-band.
Helicopters: 1 Westland Wasp.

Comment: Transferred from UK 18 April 1986 for refit. Commissioned in Indonesian Navy 10 September 1986. SATCOM fitted. Two survey launches on davits.

UPDATED

DEWA KEMBAR   *11/1997*, van Ginderen/C Sattler /* 0012542

0 + (1) RESEARCH SHIP (AGOR)

Name	No	Builders	Commissioned
BARUNA JAYA V	KAL-IV-06	CMN, Cherbourg	2002

Displacement, tons: 1,350 full load
Dimensions, feet (metres): 218.2 × 39.4 × 14.8 *(66.5 × 12 × 4.5)*
Main machinery: 2 diesels; 1 shaft; bow thruster
Speed, knots: 13. **Range, miles:** 7,500 at 12 kt
Complement: 41 (11 officers) plus 23 scientists

Comment: Order confirmed as part of a French inter-governmental finance scheme in December 1997 but may be cancelled by lack of funds. This ship is to specialise in seismic research for oil and gas in the EEZ, but will be capable of geological activities as well.

UPDATED

2 SURVEY SHIPS (AGS)

BARUNA JAYA VII   **BARUNA JAYA VIII**

Comment: Survey vessels reported ordered in November 1995.

VERIFIED

BARUNA JAYA VIII   *9/1998, Maritime Photographic /* 0044067

BARUNA JAYA VII   *9/1998, S Tattam, RAN /* 0050681

1 RESEARCH SHIP (AGOR)

Name	No	Builders	Commissioned
BURUJULASAD	931	Schlichting, Lübeck-Travemünde	1967

Displacement, tons: 2,165 full load
Dimensions, feet (metres): 269.5 × 37.4 × 11.5 *(82.2 × 11.4 × 3.5)*
Main machinery: 4 MAN V6V 22/30 diesels; 6,850 hp(m) *(5.03 MW)*; 2 shafts
Speed, knots: 19.1. **Range, miles:** 14,500 at 15 kt
Complement: 108 (15 officers) plus 28 scientists
Guns: 4—12.7 mm (2 twin) MGs.
Radars: Surface search: Decca TM 262; I-band.
Helicopters: 1 Bell 47J.

Comment: *Burujulasad* was launched in August 1965; her equipment includes laboratories for oceanic and meteorological research and a cartographic room. Carries one LCVP and three surveying motor boats. A 37 mm gun was added in 1992 but by 1998 had been removed again. *VERIFIED*

BURUJULASAD   *4/1998, John Mortimer /* 0052361

1 RESEARCH SHIP (AGOR)

Name	No	Builders	Commissioned
JALANIDHI	933	Sasebo Heavy Industries	12 Jan 1963

Displacement, tons: 985 full load
Dimensions, feet (metres): 176.8 × 31.2 × 14.1 *(53.9 × 9.5 × 4.3)*
Main machinery: 1 MAN G6V 30/42 diesel; 1,000 hp(m) *(735 kW)*; 1 shaft
Speed, knots: 11.5. **Range, miles:** 7,200 at 10 kt
Complement: 87 (13 officers) plus 26 scientists
Radars: Navigation: Nikkon Denko; I-band. Furuno; I-band.

Comment: Launched in 1962. Oceanographic research ship with hydromet facilities and weather balloons. 3 ton boom aft. Operated by the Navy for the Hydrographic Office. *UPDATED*

JALANIDHI   *8/1995*, van Ginderen Collection /* 0080024

AUXILIARIES

Notes: (1) The 'Don' class depot ship *Ratulangi* 400 is in use as a floating workshop at Surabaya naval base, but is not seaworthy.
(2) An 'Akademik Fersman' class civilian ship was reported acquired from Russia in July 1997. To be used for troop transport duties, but this is not confirmed.
(3) There is also a small oiler *Sungai Gerong* 906.

1 COMMAND SHIP (AGF)

Name	No	Builders	Launched	Commissioned
MULTATULI	561	Ishikawajima-Harima	15 May 1961	Aug 1961

Displacement, tons: 3,220 standard; 6,741 full load
Dimensions, feet (metres): 365.3 × 52.5 × 23 *(111.4 × 16 × 7)*
Main machinery: 1 Burmeister & Wain diesel; 5,500 hp(m) *(4.04 MW)*; 1 shaft
Speed, knots: 18.5. **Range, miles:** 6,000 at 16 kt
Complement: 135
Guns: 6 USSR 37 mm/63 (2 twin, 2 single); 160 rds/min to 9 km *(5 n miles)*; weight of shell 0.7 kg. 8—12.7 mm MGs.
Radars: Surface search: Ball End; E/F-band.
Navigation: I-band.
Helicopters: 1 Bell 47J.

Comment: Built as a submarine tender. Original after 76 mm mounting replaced by helicopter deck with a hangar added in 1998. Living and working spaces air conditioned. Capacity for replenishment at sea (fuel oil, fresh water, provisions, ammunition, naval stores and personnel). Medical and hospital facilities. Used as fleet flagship (Eastern Force) and is fitted with ICS-3 communications. *UPDATED*

MULTATULI   *8/1995*, van Ginderen Collection /* 0080025

1 REPLENISHMENT TANKER (AOT)

Name	No	Builders	Commissioned
SORONG	911	Trogir SY, Yugoslavia	Apr 1965

Displacement, tons: 8,400 full load
Dimensions, feet (metres): 367.4 × 50.5 × 21.6 *(112 × 15.4 × 6.6)*
Main machinery: 1 diesel; 1 shaft
Speed, knots: 15
Complement: 110
Cargo capacity: 4,200 tons fuel; 300 tons water
Guns: 4—12.7 mm (2 twin) MGs.
Radars: Navigation: Don; I-band.

Comment: Has limited underway replenishment facilities on both sides and stern refuelling. *UPDATED*

SORONG   *8/1995*, van Ginderen Collection /* 0080026

1 ROVER CLASS (REPLENISHMENT TANKER) (AOR)

Name	No	Builders	Commissioned
ARUN (ex-*Green Rover*)	903	Swan Hunter, Tyneside	15 Aug 1969

Displacement, tons: 4,700 light; 11,522 full load
Dimensions, feet (metres): 461 × 63 × 24 *(140.6 × 19.2 × 7.3)*
Main machinery: 2 SEMT-Pielstick 16 PA4 diesels; 15,360 hp(m) *(11.46 MW)*; 1 shaft; Kamewa cp prop; bow thruster
Speed, knots: 19. **Range, miles:** 15,000 at 15 kt
Complement: 49 (16 officers)
Cargo capacity: 6,600 tons fuel
Guns: 2 Bofors 40 mm/60. 2 Oerlikon 20 mm.
Radars: Navigation: Kelvin Hughes Type 1006; I-band.
Helicopters: Platform for Super Puma.

Comment: Transferred from UK in September 1992 after a refit. Small fleet tanker designed to replenish ships at sea with fuel, fresh water, limited dry cargo and refrigerated stores under all conditions while under way. No hangar but helicopter landing platform is served by a stores lift, to enable stores to be transferred at sea by 'vertical lift'. Capable of HIFR. Used as the Flagship for the Training Commander. *UPDATED*

ARUN   *8/1995*, van Ginderen Collection /* 0080027

2 KHOBI CLASS (COASTAL TANKERS) (AOTL)

BALIKPAPAN 901   **SAMBU** 902

Displacement, tons: 1,525 full load
Dimensions, feet (metres): 206.6 × 33 × 14.8 *(63 × 10.1 × 4.5)*
Main machinery: 2 diesels; 1,600 hp(m) *(1.18 MW)*; 2 shafts
Speed, knots: 13. **Range, miles:** 2,500 at 12 kt
Complement: 37 (4 officers)
Cargo capacity: 550 tons dieso
Guns: 4—14.5 mm (2 twin) MGs. 2—12.7 mm MGs.
Radars: Navigation: Neptun; I-band.

Comment: *Balikpapan* and *Sambu* are Japanese copies of the 'Khobi' class built in the 1960s. *UPDATED*

SAMBU   *8/1995*, van Ginderen Collection /* 0080028

1 ACHELOUS CLASS (REPAIR SHIP) (AR)

Name	No	Builders	Commissioned
JAYA WIJAYA (ex-Askari, ex-ARL 30, ex-LST 1131)	921	Chicago Bridge and Iron Co	15 Mar 1945

Displacement, tons: 4,325 full load
Dimensions, feet (metres): 328 × 50 × 14 (100 × 15.3 × 4.3)
Main machinery: 2 GM 12-567A diesels; 1,800 hp (1.34 MW); 2 shafts
Speed, knots: 12. **Range, miles:** 17,000 at 7 kt
Complement: 180 (11 officers)
Cargo capacity: 300 tons; 60 ton crane
Guns: 8 Bofors 40 mm/56 (2 quad); 160 rds/min to 11 km (5.9 n miles); weight of shell 0.9 kg.
Radars: Air/surface search: Sperry SPS-53; I/J-band.
Navigation: Raytheon 1900; I/J-band.
IFF: UPX 12B.

Comment: In reserve from 1956-66. She was recommissioned and reached Vietnam in 1967 to support River Assault Flotilla One. She was used by the USA Navy and Vietnamese Navy working up the Mekong in support of the Cambodian operations in May 1970. Transferred from USA on lease to Indonesia at Guam on 31 August 1971 and purchased 22 February 1979. Bow doors welded shut. Carries two LCVPs.
VERIFIED

JAYA WIJAYA
9/1988, 92 Wing RAAF

2 FROSCH II CLASS (TYPE 109) (SUPPORT SHIPS) (AK/AR)

Name	No	Builders	Commissioned
TELUK CIREBON (ex-Nordperd)	543 (ex-E 171)	Peenewerft, Wolgast	3 Oct 1979
TELUK SABANG (ex-Südperd)	544 (ex-E 172)	Peenewerft, Wolgast	26 Feb 1980

Displacement, tons: 1,700 full load
Dimensions, feet (metres): 297.6 × 36.4 × 9.2 (90.7 × 11.1 × 2.8)
Main machinery: 2 diesels; 4,408 hp(m) (3.24 MW) sustained; 2 shafts
Speed, knots: 18
Cargo capacity: 650 tons
Guns: 4—37 mm/63 (2 twin). 4—25 mm (2 twin).
Countermeasures: Decoys: 2 PK 16 chaff launchers.
Radars: Air/surface search: Strut Curve; F-band.
Navigation: I-band.

Comment: Ex-GDR ships disarmed and transferred from Germany 25 August 1993. 5 ton crane amidships. In GDR service these ships had two twin 57 mm and two twin 25 mm guns plus Muff Cob fire-control radar. Both refitted at Rostock and recommissioned 25 April 1995. 37 mm guns fitted after transfer. Rocket launchers are mounted forward of the bridge.
UPDATED

TELUK SABANG
5/1995*, Frank Behling / 0075856

4 TISZA CLASS (SUPPORT SHIPS) (AK)

NUSA TELU 952	TELUK MENTAWAI 959	KARIMATA 960	WAIGEO 961

Displacement, tons: 2,400 full load
Dimensions, feet (metres): 258.4 × 35.4 × 15.1 (78.8 × 10.8 × 4.6)
Main machinery: 1 MAN diesel; 1,000 hp(m) (735 kW); 1 shaft
Speed, knots: 12. **Range, miles:** 3,000 at 11 kt
Complement: 26
Cargo capacity: 875 tons dry; 11 tons liquid
Guns: 4—14.5 mm (2 twin) MGs.
Radars: Navigation: Spin Trough; I-band.

Comment: Built in Hungary. Transferred in 1963-64. Military Sealift Command since 1978. The survivors of a larger class. There are minor structural differences.
UPDATED

NUSA TELU
8/1995*, van Ginderen Collection / 0080029

1 TRANSPORT (AP)

TANJUNG OISINA (ex-Princess Irene) 972

Measurement, tons: 8,456 grt
Dimensions, feet (metres): 459 × 61.7 × 28.9 (139.9 × 18.8 × 8.8)
Main machinery: 1 diesel; 8,800 hp(m) (6.47 MW); 1 shaft
Speed, knots: 16
Complement: 94
Radars: Navigation: Decca 1226; I-band.

Comment: Passenger liner built in the 1940s and purchased in 1978. Ex-Mecca pilgrim transport now used for troop transfers between islands. Unarmed. Military Sealift Command. A second of class is an alongside hulk.
UPDATED

TANJUNG OISINA
4/1998, John Mortimer / 0052363

TRAINING SHIPS

1 SAIL TRAINING SHIP (AXS)

Name	No	Builders	Commissioned
DEWARUCI	—	HC Stülcken & Sohn, Hamburg	9 July 1953

Displacement, tons: 810 standard; 1,500 full load
Dimensions, feet (metres): 136.2 pp; 191.2 oa × 31.2 × 13.9 (41.5; 58.3 × 9.5 × 4.2)
Main machinery: 1 MAN diesel; 600 hp(m) (441 kW); 1 shaft
Speed, knots: 10.5
Complement: 110 (includes 78 midshipmen)

Comment: Barquentine of steel construction. Sail area, 1,305 sq yards (1,091 sq m). Launched on 24 January 1953.
VERIFIED

DEWARUCI
1/1998, van Ginderen Collection / 0052364

1 SAIL TRAINING SHIP (AXS)

Name	Builders	Launched	Commissioned
ARUNG SAMUDERA	Hendrik Oosterbroek, Tauranga	July 1991	9 Jan 1996
(ex-Adventurer)			

Measurement, tons: 96 grt
Dimensions, feet (metres): 128 oa; 103.7 wl × 21.3 × 8.5 (39; 31.6 × 6.5 × 2.6)
Main machinery: 2 Ford 2725E diesels; 292 hp (218 kW); 2 shafts
Speed, knots: 10 (diesels)
Complement: 20 (includes trainees)

Comment: Three masted schooner acquired from New Zealand. Sail area 433.8 m².

VERIFIED

ARUNG SAMUDERA   1/1998, van Ginderen Collection / 0052365

TUGS

Note: Two 'BIMA VIII' class of 423 tons completed in 1991 are not naval. Names *Merapi* and *Merbabu*.

1 CHEROKEE CLASS (ATA/PG)

Name	No	Builders	Commissioned
RAKATA (ex-Menominee ATF 73)	922	United Engineering, Alameda	25 Sep 1942

Displacement, tons: 1,235 standard; 1,640 full load
Dimensions, feet (metres): 205 × 38.5 × 17 (62.5 × 11.7 × 5.2)
Main machinery: Diesel-electric; 4 GM 12-278 diesels; 4,400 hp (3.28 MW); 4 generators; 1 motor; 3,000 hp (2.24 MW); 1 shaft
Speed, knots: 15. **Range, miles:** 6,500 at 15 kt
Complement: 67
Guns: 1 US 3 in (76 mm)/50. 2 Bofors 40 mm/60 aft. 4—25 mm (2 twin) (bridge wings).
Radars: Surface search: Racal Decca; I-band.

Comment: Launched on 14 February 1942. Transferred from USA at San Diego in March 1961. Used mostly as a patrol ship.

UPDATED

RAKATA   8/1995*, John Mortimer / 0080030

3 HARBOUR TUGS (YTM)

Name	No	Builders	Commissioned
LAMPO BATANG	934	Ishikawajima-Harima	Sep 1961
TAMBORA (Army)	935	Ishikawajima-Harima	June 1961
BROMO	936	Ishikawajima-Harima	Aug 1961

Comment: All of 250 tons displacement. There are a number of other naval tugs in the major ports.

VERIFIED

1 NFI CLASS (ATF)

Name	No	Builders	Commissioned
SOPUTAN	923	Dae Sun SB & Eng, Busan	11 Aug 1995

Measurement, tons: 1,279 grt
Dimensions, feet (metres): 217.2 × 39 × 17.1 (66.2 × 11.9 × 5.2)
Main machinery: Diesel-electric; 4 SEMT-Pielstick diesel generators; 1 motor; 12,240 hp(m) (9 MW); 1 shaft; bow thruster
Speed, knots: 13.5
Complement: 42
Radars: Navigation: Racal Decca; I-band.

Comment: Ocean Cruiser class NFI. Bollard pull 120 tons.

UPDATED

SOPUTAN   8/1995*, van Ginderen Collection / 0080031

CUSTOMS

Note: Identified by BP (Tax and Customs) preceding the pennant number.

14 COASTAL PATROL CRAFT (PC)

BC 2001-2007   BC 3001-3007

Displacement, tons: 70.3 full load
Dimensions, feet (metres): 93.5 × 17.7 × 5.5 (28.5 × 5.4 × 1.7)
Main machinery: 2 MTU 12V 331 TC92 diesels; 2,660 hp(m) (1.96 MW) sustained; 2 shafts
Speed, knots: 28-34
Complement: 19
Guns: 1—20 mm or 1—12.7 mm MG.

Comment: Built CMN Cherbourg. Delivered in 1980 and 1981.

UPDATED

BC 2007   1/1990, 92 Wing RAAF

10 LÜRSSEN VSV 15 CLASS (PBF)

BC 1601-1610

Displacement, tons: 11 full load
Dimensions, feet (metres): 52.5 × 9.2 × 3.3 (16 × 2.8 × 1)
Main machinery: 2 MTU diesels; 600 hp(m) (441 kW); 2 shafts
Speed, knots: 50. **Range, miles:** 750 at 30 kt
Complement: 5 (1 officer)
Guns: 1—7.62 mm MG.

Comment: Built in Germany and delivered between November 1998 and June 1999.

NEW ENTRY

BC 1608   5/1999*, Lürssen / 0080032

53 LÜRSSEN 28 METRE TYPE (PC)

BC 4001-3, 5001-3, 6001-24, 7001-6, 8001-6, 9001-6

Displacement, tons: 68 full load
Dimensions, feet (metres): 91.8 × 17.7 × 5.9 *(28 × 5.4 × 1.8)*
Main machinery: 2 Deutz diesels; 2,720 hp(m) *(2 MW)*; or 2 MTU diesels; 2,260 hp(m) *(1.66 MW)*; 2 shafts
Speed, knots: 30. **Range, miles:** 1,100 at 15 kt; 860 at 28 kt
Complement: 19 (6 officers)
Guns: 1—12.7 mm MG.

Comment: Lürssen design, some built by Fulton Marine and Scheepswerven van Langebrugge of Belgium, some by Lürssen Vegesack and some by PT Pal Surabaya (which also assembled most of them). Programme started in 1980. Some of these craft are operated by the Navy, the Police and the Maritime Security Agency.
UPDATED

BC 4001   8/1995*, van Ginderen Collection / 0080033

5 LÜRSSEN NEW 28 METRE TYPE (PC)

BC 10001-10002   BC 20001-20003

Displacement, tons: 85 full load
Dimensions, feet (metres): 92.5 × 21.7 × 4.6 *(28.2 × 6.6 × 1.4)*
Main machinery: 2 MTU 16V 396 TE94 diesels; 2,955 hp(m) *(2.14 MW)* sustained; 2 shafts
Speed, knots: 40. **Range, miles:** 1,100 at 30 kt
Complement: 11 (3 officers)
Guns: 2—7.62 mm MGs.
Radars: Surface search: Furuno FR 8731; I-band.

Comment: First pair built in Germany and delivered between May 1999 and November 1999. Last three built by PT Pal Surabaya and delivered between September 1999 and November 1999. Aluminium construction.
NEW ENTRY

BC 10001   5/1999*, Lürssen / 0080034

BC 20001   9/1999*, PT Pal / 0075857

COAST AND SEAWARD DEFENCE COMMAND

Notes: (1) Established in 1978 as the Maritime Security Agency to control the 200 mile EEZ and to maintain navigational aids. Comes under the Military Sea Communications Agency. Some craft have blue hulls with a diagonal thick white and thin red stripe plus KPLP on the superstructure. In addition to the craft listed there are large numbers of small harbour boats.
(2) There are also a number of civilian manned vessels used for transport and servicing navigational aids.

5 KUJANG CLASS (SAR CRAFT)

| KUJANG 201 | PARANG 202 | CELURIT 203 | CUNDRIK 204 | BELATI 205 |

Displacement, tons: 162 full load
Dimensions, feet (metres): 125.6 × 19.6 × 6.8 *(38.3 × 6 × 2.1)*
Main machinery: 2 AGO SACM 195 V12 CZSHR diesels; 4,410 hp(m) *(3.24 MW)*; 2 shafts
Speed, knots: 28. **Range, miles:** 1,500 at 18 kt
Complement: 18
Guns: 1—12.7 mm MG.

Comment: Built by SFCN, Villeneuve la Garenne. Completed April 1981 *(Kujang and Parang)*, August 1981 *(Celurit)*, October 1981 *(Cundrik)*, December 1981 *(Belati)*. Pennant numbers are preceded by PAT.
VERIFIED

CUNDRIK   11/1998, van Ginderen Collection / 0052366

4 GOLOK CLASS (SAR CRAFT)

| GOLOK 206 | PANAN 207 | PEDANG 208 | KAPAK 209 |

Displacement, tons: 190 full load
Dimensions, feet (metres): 123 pp × 23.6 × 6.6 *(37.5 × 7.2 × 2)*
Main machinery: 2 MTU 16V 652 TB91 diesels; 4,610 hp(m) *(3.39 MW)* sustained; 2 shafts
Speed, knots: 25. **Range, miles:** 1,500 at 18 kt
Complement: 18
Guns: 1 Rheinmetall 20 mm.

Comment: All launched 5 November 1981. First pair completed 12 March 1982. Last pair completed 12 May 1982. Built by Deutsche Industrie Werke, Berlin. Fitted out by Schlichting, Travemünde. Used for SAR and have medical facilities. Pennant numbers preceded by PAT.
VERIFIED

KAPAK   11/1998, van Ginderen Collection / 0052367

15 HARBOUR PATROL CRAFT (PB)

PAT 01-PAT 15

Displacement, tons: 12 full load
Dimensions, feet (metres): 40 × 14.1 × 3.3 *(12.2 × 4.3 × 1)*
Main machinery: 1 Renault diesel; 260 hp(m) *(191 kW)*; 1 shaft
Speed, knots: 14
Complement: 4
Guns: 1—7.62 mm MG.

Comment: First six built at Tanjung Priok Shipyard 1978-79. Four more of a similar design built in 1993-94 by Mahalaya Utama Shipyard and delivered from 1995.
VERIFIED

PB   11/1998, van Ginderen Collection / 0052368

NAVAL AUXILIARY SERVICE

Note: This is a paramilitary force of non-commissioned craft. They have KAL pennant numbers. About 24 vessels operate in the eastern Fleet and 47 in the western Fleet, and three belong to the Naval Academy. In addition, the Baruna Jaya ships listed under Survey Ships are also part of the NAS.

KAL   *4/1999* / 0080035

65 KAL KANGEAN CLASS (COASTAL PATROL CRAFT) (PC)

Displacement, tons: 44.7 full load
Dimensions, feet (metres): 80.4 × 14.1 × 3.3 *(24.5 × 4.3 × 1)*
Main machinery: 2 diesels; 2 shafts
Speed, knots: 18
Guns: 2 USSR 25 mm/80 (twin). 2 USSR 14.5 mm (twin) MGs.

Comment: Ordered from Tanjung Uban Navy Yard in about 1984 and completed between 1987 and 1996. Numbers are uncertain. Have four figure pennant numbers in the 1101 series.
VERIFIED

KAL KANGEAN 1112   *10/1988, Trevor Brown*

6 CARPENTARIA CLASS (COASTAL PATROL CRAFT) (PC)

201-206

Displacement, tons: 27 full load
Dimensions, feet (metres): 51.5 × 15.7 × 4.3 *(15.7 × 4.8 × 1.3)*
Main machinery: 2 MTU 8V 331 TC92 diesels; 1,770 hp(m) *(1.3 MW)* sustained; 2 shafts
Speed, knots: 29. **Range, miles:** 950 at 18 kt
Complement: 10
Guns: 2—12.7 mm MGs.
Radars: Surface search: Decca; I-band.

Comment: Built 1976-77 by Hawker de Havilland, Australia. Endurance, four to five days. Transferred from the Navy in the mid-1980s to the Police and now with the Naval Auxiliary Service.
UPDATED

CARPENTARIA 203   *8/1995*, van Ginderen Collection* / 0080036

ARMY

Note: The Army (ADRI) craft have mostly been transferred to the Military Sealift Command (Logistic Support).

27 LANDING CRAFT LOGISTICS (LCL)

ADRI XXXII-ADRI LVIII

Displacement, tons: 580 full load
Dimensions, feet (metres): 137.8 × 35.1 × 5.9 *(42 × 10.7 × 1.8)*
Main machinery: 2 Detroit 6-71 diesels; 348 hp(m) *(260 kW)* sustained; 2 shafts
Speed, knots: 10. **Range, miles:** 1,500 at 10 kt
Complement: 15
Military lift: 122 tons equipment

Comment: Built in Tanjung Priok Shipyard 1979-82. XXXI sank in February 1993.
UPDATED

ADRI XXXIII   *10/1999*, David Boey* / 0080037

POLICE

Note: The police operate about 85 craft of varying sizes including 14 'Bango' class of 194 tons and 32 Hamilton water-jet craft of 7.9 m, 234 hp giving a speed of 28 kt. Lürssen type (619-623) are identical to Customs craft.

POLICE 622   *8/1995* / 0080038

POLICE 620   *3/1997, A Sharma* / 0012545

IRAN

Headquarters Appointments

Commander of Navy:
  Rear Admiral Abbas Mohtaj
Head of Naval Equipment:
  Rear Admiral Mohammed Hossein Shafii
Head of IRCG(N) (Sepah):
  Major General Ali Akbar Ahmadian

Personnel

2000: 18,000 Navy (including 2,000 Naval Air and Marines),
20,000 IRGCN

Bases

Persian Gulf: Bandar Abbas (MHQ and 1st Naval District),
Boushehr (2nd Naval District and also a Dockyard), Kharg Island,
Qeshm Island, Bandar Lengeh
Indian Ocean: Chah Bahar (3rd Naval District and forward base)
Caspian Sea: Bandar Anzali (4th Naval District)
Pasdaran: Al Farsiyah, Halileh, Sirri, Abu Musa, Larak

Coast Defence

Three Navy and one IRGCN brigades with many fixed
installations and command posts. 300 CSSC-2 (Silkworm) being
replaced by C 802 and 100 CSSC-3 (Seersucker) Chinese SSMs
in at least four sites plus up to 12 Russian SS-N-22 Sunburn in
mobile trucks.

Mines

Stocks of up to 3,000 mines are reported including Chinese
rising mines.

Strength of the Fleet

Type	Active	Building
Submarines	3	—
Midget Submarines	3	(3)
Frigates	3	—
Corvettes	2	3
Fast Attack Craft—Missile	20	—
Large Patrol Craft	8	—
Coastal Patrol Craft	123+	12
Landing Ships (Logistic)	7	—
Landing Ships (Tank)	6	—
Hovercraft	6	—
Minesweepers—Coastal	3	—
Replenishment Ship	1	—
Supply Ships	1 (1)	—
Support Ships	7	—
Water Tankers	4	—
Tenders	13	—

Prefix to Ships' Names

IS

Mercantile Marine

Lloyd's Register of Shipping:
  380 vessels of 3,546,243 tons

DELETIONS

Destroyers

1996-97   *Babr, Palang* (both reserve)

Patrol Forces

1998   Osa II, 3 Zafar

Amphibious Forces

1996   4 Rotork

Mine Warfare Forces

1999   *Harischi, Riazi* (both reserve)

Auxiliaries

1997-98   *Kish, Hamzeh* (old)

PENNANT LIST

Submarines			Patrol Forces					Amphibious Warfare Forces and Auxiliaries	
901	Tareq		211	Parvin	P 313-4	Ra'd		101	Fouque
902	Noor		212	Bahram	P 313-5	Fajr		411	Kangan
903	Yunes		213	Nahid	P 313-6	Shams		412	Taheri
			P 221	Kaman	P 313-7	Me'raj		421	Bandar Abbas
Frigates			P 222	Zoubin	P 313-8	Falaq		422	Boushehr
			P 223	Khadang	P 313-9	Hadid		431	Kharg
71	Alvand		P 226	Falakhon	P 313-10	Qadr		511	Hengam
72	Alborz		P 227	Shamshir				512	Larak
73	Sabalan		P 228	Gorz				513	Tonb
			P 229	Gardouneh				514	Lavan
			P 230	Khanjar					
Corvettes			P 231	Neyzeh	**Mine Warfare Forces**				
			P 232	Tabarzin					
			P 313-1	Fath	301	Hamzeh			
81	Bayandor		P 313-2	Nasr	302	Simorgh			
82	Naghdi		P 313-3	Saf	303	Karkas			

SUBMARINES

Note: There are also about six swimmer delivery vessels (SDVs).

3 KILO CLASS (TYPE 877 EKM) (SSK)

Name	No	Builders	Laid down	Launched	Commissioned
TAREQ	901	Admiralty Yard, St Petersburg	1988	1991	21 Nov 1992
NOOR	902	Admiralty Yard, St Petersburg	1989	1992	6 June 1993
YUNES	903	Admiralty Yard, St Petersburg	1990	1993	25 Nov 1996

Displacement, tons: 2,356 surfaced; 3,076 dived
Dimensions, feet (metres): 238.2 × 32.5 × 21.7
  (72.6 × 9.9 × 6.6)
Main machinery: Diesel-electric; 2 diesels; 3,650 hp(m)
  (2.68 MW); 2 generators; 1 motor; 5,500 hp(m) *(4.05 MW)*;
  1 economic speed motor; 130 hp(m) *(95 kW)*; 1 shaft;
  2 auxiliary propulsion motors; 204 hp(m) *(150 kW)*
Speed, knots: 17 dived; 10 surfaced; 9 snorting
Range, miles: 6,000 at 7 kt snorting; 400 at 3 kt dived
Complement: 53 (12 officers)

Torpedoes: 6—21 in *(533 mm)* tubes; combination of
TEST-71/96; wire-guided active/passive homing to 15 km
(8.1 n miles) at 40 kt; warhead 220 kg and 53-65; passive
wake homing to 19 km *(10.3 n miles)* at 45 kt; warhead
350 kg. Total of 18 weapons.
Mines: 24 in lieu of torpedoes.

Countermeasures: ESM: Squid Head; radar warning. Quad Loop
D/F.
Weapons control: MVU-119EM Murena TFCS.
Radars: Surface search: Snoop Tray MRP-25; I-band.
Sonars: Sharks Teeth MGK-400; hull-mounted; passive/active
search and attack; medium frequency.
  Mouse Roar MG-519; active attack; high frequency.

Programmes: Contract signed in 1988 for three of the class. The
first submarine to be transferred sailed from the Baltic in
October 1992 flying the Russian flag and with a predominantly
Russian crew. The second sailed in June 1993. The third
completed in 1994 but delivery delayed by funding problems.
She arrived in Iran in mid-January 1997.
Modernisation: Chinese YJ-1 or Russian Novator Alfa SSMs may
be fitted in due course.

Structure: Diving depth, 240 m *(787 ft)* normal. Has a
9,700 kW/h battery. SA-N-10 SAM system may be fitted, but
this is not confirmed.
Operational: Initially based at Bandar Abbas but planned to
move to Chah Bahar which is outside the Persian Gulf on the
northern shore of the Gulf of Oman. Training is being done with
assistance from India and Russia. Problems with battery
cooling and air conditioning have been resolved using Indian
batteries. *Tareq* may return to Russia for refit in due course. As
this has been delayed, the second and third class may be
refitted in Iran.
Opinion: The northern Gulf of Oman and the few deep water
parts of the Persian Gulf are notoriously bad areas for anti-
submarine warfare. These submarines will be vulnerable to
attack when alongside in harbour but pose a severe threat to
merchant shipping either with torpedoes or mines.
UPDATED

YUNES

3 + (3) MIDGET SUBMARINES

Displacement, tons: 76 surfaced; 90 dived
Dimensions, feet (metres): 62.3 × 9.2 *(19 × 2.8)*
Main machinery: 2 diesels; 320 hp(m) *(236 kW)*; 1 shaft
Speed, knots: 12 surfaced; 8 dived
Range, miles: 1,200 at 6 kt
Complement: 3 + 7 divers

Programmes: Initial submarine constructed in Iran and assembled at Bandar Abbas, combining Japanese and German Second World War design drawings with locally available fabrication and imported equipment. Initially completed in May 1987 but shipped to Tehran in late 1988 for modifications, as diving tests were unsuccessful. This programme seems to have been overtaken by midget submarines of North Korean (DPRK) design of which one was delivered in June 1988. The reported total so far probably includes some from Croatia, bearing in mind the former Yugoslavia's involvement with the North Korean programme. Local construction again reported in 1996 but this may not have been followed through, and foreign purchase may be taken up again.

Structure: The listed characteristics are based on the Korean design. Diving depth, approximately 100 m *(328 ft)*. There is a 'wet and dry' compartment for divers.
Operational: Based at Boushehr. Side cargoes can be released from inside the hull but limpet mines require a diver to exit, attach the mines to the target and then re-enter. Successful operation will require a very high level of training and support, and there is insufficient evidence that this is being achieved, or that these submarines are operational.

UPDATED

FRIGATES

3 ALVAND (VOSPER Mk 5) CLASS (FFG)

Name	No
ALVAND (ex-*Saam*)	71
ALBORZ (ex-*Zaal*)	72
SABALAN (ex-*Rostam*)	73

Builders	Laid down	Launched	Commissioned
Vosper Thornycroft, Woolston	22 May 1967	25 July 1968	20 May 1971
Vickers, Barrow	3 Mar 1968	25 July 1969	1 Mar 1971
Vickers, Newcastle & Barrow	10 Dec 1967	4 Mar 1969	28 Feb 1972

Displacement, tons: 1,350 full load
Dimensions, feet (metres): 310 × 36.4 × 14.1 (screws) *(94.5 × 11.1 × 4.3)*
Main machinery: CODOG; 2 RR Olympus TM2A gas turbines; 40,000 hp *(29.8 MW)* sustained; 2 Paxman 16YJCM diesels; 3,800 hp *(2.83 MW)* sustained; 2 shafts; cp props
Speed, knots: 39 gas; 18 diesel
Range, miles: 3,650 at 18 kt; 550 at 36 kt
Complement: 125 (accommodation for 146)

Missiles: SSM: 4 China C-802 (2 twin) *(Alborz* and *Sabalan)* ❶; active radar homing to 120 km *(66 n miles)* at 0.9 Mach; warhead 165 kg; sea-skimmer.
1 Sistel Sea Killer II quin launcher *(Alvand)*; beam-rider radio command or optical guidance to 25 km *(13.5 n miles)* at 0.8 Mach; warhead 70 kg. Has been modified by removal of top row of cassettes to incorporate a BM-21 MRL.
Guns: 1 Vickers 4.5 in *(114 mm)*/55 Mk 8 ❷; 25 rds/min to 22 km *(12 n miles)* anti-surface; 6 km *(3.3 n miles)* anti-aircraft; weight of shell 21 kg.
2 Oerlikon 35 mm/90 (twin) ❸; 550 rds/min to 6 km *(3.3 n miles)*; weight of shell 1.55 kg.
3 Oerlikon GAM-BO1 20 mm ❹. 2—12.7 mm MGs.
A/S mortars: 1—3-tubed Limbo Mk 10 ❺; automatic loading; range 1,000 m; warhead 92 kg.
Countermeasures: Decoys: 2 UK Mk 5 rocket flare launchers.
ESM: Decca RDL 2AC; radar warning. Racal FH 5-HF/DF.
Radars: Air/surface search: Plessey AWS 1 ❻; E/F-band; range 110 km *(60 n miles)*.
Surface search: Racal Decca 1226 ❼; I-band.
Navigation: Decca 629; I-band.
Fire control: Contraves Sea Hunter ❽; I/J-band.
IFF: UK Mk 10.
Sonars: Graseby 174; hull-mounted; active search; medium/high frequency.
Graseby 170; hull-mounted; active attack; high frequency.

Programmes: Ordered on 25 August 1966.
Modernisation: Major refits including replacement of 4.5 in Mk 5 gun by Mk 8 completed 1977. Modifications in 1988 included replacing Seacat with a 23 mm gun and boat davits with minor armaments. By mid-1991 the 23 mm and both boats had been replaced by GAM-BO1 20 mm guns and the SSM launcher had effectively become a twin launcher. In 1996/97 two of the class had the Sea Killer SSM replaced by C-802 launchers and a new communications mast fitted between the two fire-control radars. The third is likely to be similarly modified.
Structure: Air conditioned throughout. Fitted with Vosper stabilisers.

ALBORZ

(Scale 1 : 900), Ian Sturton / 0012550

SABALAN (with C-802)

2/1998 / 0052371

Operational: *Sahand* sunk by USN on 18 April 1988. *Sabalan* had her back broken by a laser-guided bomb in the same skirmish but was out of dock by the end of 1990 and was operational again in late 1991. ASW equipment is probably unserviceable. All are active.

UPDATED

ALVAND

5/1997 / 0012551

CORVETTES

Note: Three new corvettes of about 1,200 tons are being built at Bandar Abbas. First one planned to be launched in 2002/03.

2 BAYANDOR (PF 103) CLASS (FS)

Name	No	Builders	Laid down	Launched	Commissioned
BAYANDOR (ex-US *PF 103*)	81	Levingstone Shipbuilding Co, Orange, TX	20 Aug 1962	7 July 1963	18 May 1964
NAGHDI (ex-US *PF 104*)	82	Levingstone Shipbuilding Co, Orange, TX	12 Sep 1962	10 Oct 1963	22 July 1964

Displacement, tons: 900 standard; 1,135 full load
Dimensions, feet (metres): 275.6 × 33.1 × 10.2
  (84 × 10.1 × 3.1)
Main machinery: 2 Fairbanks-Morse 38TD8-1/8-9 diesels;
  5,250 hp *(3.92 MW)* sustained; 2 shafts
Speed, knots: 20. **Range, miles:** 2,400 at 18 kt; 4,800 at 12 kt
Complement: 140

Guns: 2 US 3 in *(76 mm)*/50 Mk 34 ❶; 50 rds/min to 12.8 km
  (7 n miles); weight of shell 6 kg.
  1 Bofors 40 mm/60 (twin) ❷; 120 rds/min to 10 km *(5.5 n miles)*; weight of shell 0.89 kg.
  2 Oerlikon GAM-BO1 20 mm ❸. 2—12.7 mm MGs.
Weapons control: Mk 63 for 76 mm gun. Mk 51 Mod 2 for
  40 mm guns.
Radars: Air/surface search: Westinghouse SPS-6C ❹; D-band;
  range 146 km *(80 n miles)* (for fighter).
Surface search: Racal Decca ❺; I-band.
Navigation: Raytheon 1650 ❻; I/J-band.
Fire control: Western Electric Mk 36 ❼; I/J-band.
IFF: UPX-12B.
Sonars: EDO SQS-17A; hull-mounted; active attack; high
  frequency.

Programmes: Transferred from the USA to Iran under the Mutual
  Assistance programme in 1964.
Modernisation: *Naghdi* change of engines and reconstruction of
  accommodation completed in mid-1988. 23 mm gun and
  depth charge racks replaced by 20 mm guns in 1990.
Operational: *Milanian* and *Khanamuie* sunk in 1982 during war
  with Iraq. Both remaining ships are very active.

VERIFIED

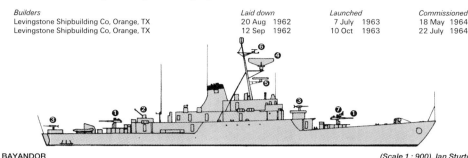

BAYANDOR *(Scale 1 : 900), Ian Sturton*

BAYANDOR *2/1998 / 0052372*

SHIPBORNE AIRCRAFT

Numbers/Type: 6 Agusta AB 204ASW/212.
Operational speed: 104 kt *(193 km/h)*.
Service ceiling: 11,500 ft *(3,505 m)*.
Range: 332 n miles *(615 km)*.
Role/Weapon systems: Mainly engaged in ASV operations in defence of oil installations. Numbers
  are uncertain. Sensors: APS 705 search radar, dipping sonar (if carried). Weapons: ASW; two
  China YU-2 torpedoes. ASV: two AS 12 missiles.

UPDATED

Numbers/Type: 6 Agusta-Sikorsky ASH-3D Sea King.
Operational speed: 120 kt *(222 km/h)*.
Service ceiling: 12,200 ft *(3,720 m)*.
Range: 630 n miles *(1,165 km)*.
Role/Weapon systems: Shore-based ASW helicopter to defend major port and oil installations.
  Can be embarked in *Kharg*. Sensors: Selenia search radar, dipping sonar. Weapons: ASW; four
  A244/S torpedoes or depth bombs.

VERIFIED

SEA KING *3/1997 / 0012549*

LAND-BASED MARITIME AIRCRAFT (FRONT LINE)

Notes: (1) The Air Force also has six F-4 Phantoms equipped with C 8DIK ASMs for the maritime
role.
(2) Five F-27 Fokker Friendship aircraft are used in a utility MPA role.
(3) Five Dornier 228 are also in service with five more under construction.

Numbers/Type: 3 Sikorsky RH/MH-53D Sea Stallion.
Operational speed: 125 kt *(232 km/h)*.
Service ceiling: 11,100 ft *(3,385 m)*.
Range: 405 n miles *(750 km)*.
Role/Weapon systems: Surface search helicopter which could be used for mine clearance but so
  far has only been used for Logistic purposes. Can be carried on 'Hengam' class flight deck.
  Sensors: Weather radar. Weapons: Unarmed.

UPDATED

Numbers/Type: 5 Lockheed C-130H-MP Hercules.
Operational speed: 325 kt *(602 km/h)*.
Service ceiling: 33,000 ft *(10,060 m)*.
Range: 4,250 n miles *(7,876 km)*.
Role/Weapon systems: Long-range maritime reconnaissance role by Air Force which has a total
  of 25 of these aircraft. Sensors: Search/weather radar. Weapons: Unarmed.

VERIFIED

Numbers/Type: 6 Lockheed P-3F Orion.
Operational speed: 410 kt *(760 km/h)*.
Service ceiling: 28,300 ft *(8,625 m)*.
Range: 4,000 n miles *(7,410 km)*.
Role/Weapon systems: Air Force manned. One of the remaining aircraft can be used for early
  warning and control duties for strikes. All reported non-operational through lack of spares.
  Sensors: Search radar, sonobuoys. Weapons: ASW; various weapons can be carried. ASV; C-802
  SSM.

UPDATED

ORION *3/1998, A Sharma / 0052373*

PATROL FORCES

6 MIG-S-2600 CLASS (PCF)

Displacement, tons: 85 full load
Dimensions, feet (metres): 80 × 20.3 × 4.6 *(26.2 × 6.2 × 1.4)*
Main machinery: 4 diesels; 4,000 hp(m) *(2.94 MW)*; 4 shafts
Speed, knots: 35
Complement: 12
Guns: 2—23 mm/80 (twin). 1—12-barrelled 107 mm MRL.
Radars: Surface search: I-band.

Comment: Numbers are uncertain. Built by Joolaee Marine Industries, Tehran, to a similar
  specification as the North Korean 'Zafar' (Chaho) class but with a different superstructure and a
  raised mast to give an improved radar horizon. Pasdaran manned.

UPDATED

MIG-S-2600 *1996, Joolaee Marine Industries*

10 KAMAN (COMBATTANTE II) CLASS
(FAST ATTACK CRAFT—MISSILE) (PGF)

Name	No	Builders	Commissioned
KAMAN	P 221	CMN, Cherbourg	12 Aug 1977
ZOUBIN	P 222	CMN, Cherbourg	12 Sep 1977
KHADANG	P 223	CMN, Cherbourg	15 Mar 1978
FALAKHON	P 226	CMN, Cherbourg	31 Mar 1978
SHAMSHIR	P 227	CMN, Cherbourg	31 Mar 1978
GORZ	P 228	CMN, Cherbourg	22 Aug 1978
GARDOUNEH	P 229	CMN, Cherbourg	11 Sep 1978
KHANJAR	P 230	CMN, Cherbourg	1 Aug 1981
NEYZEH	P 231	CMN, Cherbourg	1 Aug 1981
TABARZIN	P 232	CMN, Cherbourg	1 Aug 1981

Displacement, tons: 249 standard; 275 full load
Dimensions, feet (metres): 154.2 × 23.3 × 6.2 *(47 × 7.1 × 1.9)*
Main machinery: 4 MTU 16V 538 TB91 diesels; 12,280 hp(m) *(9.03 MW)* sustained; 4 shafts
Speed, knots: 37.5. **Range, miles:** 2,000 at 15 kt; 700 at 33.7 kt
Complement: 31

Missiles: SSM: 2 or 4 China C-802 (1 or 2 twin); active radar homing to 120 km *(66 n miles)* at 0.9 Mach; warhead 165 kg; sea-skimmer or 4 McDonnell Douglas Harpoon (2 twin); active radar homing to 40 km *(22 n miles)* at 0.9 Mach; warhead 165 kg; sea-skimmer or Standard SM1-MR box launchers *(Gorz)*.
Guns: 1 OTO Melara 3 in *(76 mm)*/62 compact; 85 rds/min to 16 km *(8.7 n miles)* anti-surface; 12 km *(6.6 n miles)* anti-aircraft; weight of shell 6 kg; 320 rounds.
1 Breda Bofors 40 mm/70; 300 rds/min to 12 km *(6.6 n miles)*; weight of shell 0.96 kg; 900 rounds. Some have a 23 mm or 20 mm gun in place of the 40 mm.
2—12.7 mm MGs.
Countermeasures: ESM: Thomson-CSF TMV 433 Dalia; radar intercept.
ECM: Thomson-CSF Alligator; jammer.
Radars: Surface search/fire control: Signaal WM28; I/J-band.
Navigation: Racal Decca 1226; I-band.
IFF: UPZ-27N/APX-72.

Programmes: Ordered in February 1974. The transfer of the last three craft was delayed by the French Government after the Iranian revolution. On 12 July 1981 France decided to hand them over. This took place on 1 August—on 2 August they sailed and soon after *Tabarzin* was seized by a pro-Royalist group off Cadiz. After the latter surrendered to the French in Toulon further problems were prevented by sending all three to Iran in a merchant ship.
Modernisation: Most of the class fitted with C-802 SSM in 1996-98. *Gorz* has been used for trials, first with Harpoon, and now with SM 1 launchers taken from the deleted 'Sumner' class destroyers, together with the missile fire-control system.
Structure: Portable SA-7 launchers may be embarked in some.
Operational: *Peykan* was sunk in 1980 by Iraq; *Joshan* in April 1988 by the USN.

UPDATED

KHANJAR   6/1998 / 0052374

FALAKHON (with Harpoon)   3/1999 * / 0080040

TABARZIN (with C-802)   10/1997 / 0012554

10 THONDOR (HOUDONG) CLASS
(FAST ATTACK CRAFT—MISSILE) (PCFG)

FATH	P 313-1	FAJR	P 313-5	FALAQ	P 313-8
NASR	P 313-2	SHAMS	P 313-6	HADID	P 313-9
SAF	P 313-3	ME'RAJ	P 313-7	QADR	P 313-10
RA'D	P 313-4				

Displacement, tons: 171 standard; 205 full load
Dimensions, feet (metres): 126.6 × 22.3 × 8.9 *(38.6 × 6.8 × 2.7)*
Main machinery: 3 diesels; 8,025 hp(m) *(7.94 MW)* sustained; 3 shafts
Speed, knots: 35. **Range, miles:** 800 at 30 kt
Complement: 28 (3 officers)

Missiles: SSM: 4 China C-802; active radar homing to 120 km *(66 n miles)* at 0.9 Mach; warhead 165 kg; sea-skimmer.
Guns: 2—30 mm/65 (twin) AK 230. 2—23 mm/87 (twin).
Radars: Surface search: China SR-47A; I-band.
Navigation: China RM 1070A; I-band.
Fire control: Rice Lamp Type 341; I/J-band.

Programmes: Negotiations for sale started in 1991 but were held up by arguments over choice of missile. Built at Zhanjiang Shipyard. First five delivered in September 1994 by transporter vessel, second batch in March 1996. Original pennant numbers 301-310. More may be built in Iran under licence.
Structure: The hull is similar to the standard Huangfen but the superstructure has a lattice mast to support two I-band radars and there is a separate director plinth for the fire-control system. A twin 23 mm gun is being fitted aft of the mast.
Operational: Manned by the Pasdaran.

UPDATED

SAF   10/1997 / 0052375

ME'RAJ   6/1998 / 0052376

3 PARVIN (PGM-71) CLASS (LARGE PATROL CRAFT) (PC)

Name	No	Builders	Commissioned
PARVIN (ex-*PGM 103*)	211	Peterson Builders Inc	1967
BAHRAM (ex-*PGM 112*)	212	Peterson Builders Inc	1969
NAHID (ex-*PGM 122*)	213	Peterson Builders Inc	1970

Displacement, tons: 98 standard; 148 full load
Dimensions, feet (metres): 101 × 21.3 × 8.3 *(30.8 × 6.5 × 2.5)*
Main machinery: 8 GM 6-71 diesels; 2,040 hp *(1.52 MW)* sustained; 2 shafts
Speed, knots: 22. **Range, miles:** 1,140 at 17 kt
Complement: 20
Guns: 1 Bofors 40 mm/60. 1 GAM-BO1 20 mm. 2—12.7 mm MGs.
Depth charges: 4 racks (8 US Mk 6).
Radars: Surface search: I-band.
Sonars: SQS-17B; hull-mounted active attack; high frequency.

Comment: The heavier 40 mm gun is mounted aft and the 20 mm forward to compensate for the large SQS-17B sonar dome under the bows. Mousetrap A/S mortar removed. Beginning to be difficult to maintain in an operational state.

UPDATED

BAHRAM   3/1997 / 0012556

50 MIG-S-1800 CLASS (COASTAL PATROL CRAFT) (PC)

Displacement, tons: 60 full load
Dimensions, feet (metres): 61.3 × 18.9 × 3.4 *(18.7 × 5.8 × 1.1)*
Main machinery: 2 MWM TBD 234 V12 diesels; 1,646 hp(m) *(1.21 MW)*; 2 shafts
Speed, knots: 18
Complement: 10
Guns: 1 Oerlikon 20 mm. 2—7.62 mm MGs.
Radars: Surface search: I-band.

Comment: Assembled in Iran as general purpose patrol craft. Numbers uncertain but large. Pasdaran craft.

UPDATED

MIG-S-1800   *1996, Joolaee Marine Industries*

9 US Mk III CLASS (COASTAL PATROL CRAFT) (PB)

Displacement, tons: 41.6 full load
Dimensions, feet (metres): 65 × 18.1 × 6 *(19.8 × 5.5 × 1.8)*
Main machinery: 3 GM 8V-71TI diesels; 690 hp *(515 kW)* sustained; 3 shafts
Speed, knots: 30. **Range, miles:** 500 at 28 kt
Complement: 8
Guns: 1—20 mm GAM-BO1. 1—12.7 mm MG.
Radars: Surface search: RCA LN66; I-band.

Comment: Twenty ordered from Marinette Marine Corporation, Wisconsin, USA; the first delivered in December 1975 and the last in December 1976. A further 50 were ordered in 1976 to be shipped out and completed in Iran. It is not known how many were finally assembled. Six lost in the Gulf War, others have been scrapped. These last nine are based at Boushehr and Bandar Abbas.

UPDATED

US Mk III   *5/1999* / 0080041*

10 MIG-G-1900 CLASS (COASTAL PATROL CRAFT) (PC)

Displacement, tons: 30 full load
Dimensions, feet (metres): 64 × 13.8 × 3 *(19.5 × 4.2 × 0.9)*
Main machinery: 2 MWM TBD 234 V12 diesels; 1,646 hp(m) *(1.21 MW)*; 2 shafts
Speed, knots: 36
Complement: 8
Guns: 2—23 mm/80 (twin).
Radars: Surface search: I-band.

Comment: Building in Iran to a modified US Mk II design. Numbers uncertain. Pasdaran craft.

UPDATED

MIG-G-1900   *1992*, Iranian Marine Industries / 0080042*

6 US Mk II CLASS (COASTAL PATROL CRAFT) (PC)

Displacement, tons: 22.9 full load
Dimensions, feet (metres): 49.9 × 15.1 × 4.3 *(15.2 × 4.6 × 1.3)*
Main machinery: 2 GM 8V-71TI diesels; 460 hp *(343 kW)* sustained; 2 shafts
Speed, knots: 28. **Range, miles:** 750 at 26 kt
Complement: 8
Guns: 2—12.7 mm MGs.
Radars: Surface search: SPS-6; I-band.

Comment: Twenty-six ordered from Peterson, USA in 1976-77. Six were for the Navy and the remainder for the Imperial Gendarmerie. All were built in association with Arvandan Maritime Corporation, Abadan. The six naval units operate in the Caspian Sea. Of the remaining 20, six were delivered complete and the others were only 65 per cent assembled on arrival in Iran. Some were lost when the Iraqi Army captured Koramshahr. Others have been lost at sea. Numbers uncertain.

UPDATED

US Mk II   *3/1996* / 0080043*

30 PBI TYPE (COASTAL PATROL CRAFT) (PC)

Displacement, tons: 20.1 full load
Dimensions, feet (metres): 50 × 15 × 4 *(15.2 × 4.6 × 1.2)*
Main machinery: 2 GM 8V-71TI diesels; 460 hp *(343 kW)* sustained; 2 shafts
Speed, knots: 28. **Range, miles:** 750 at 26 kt
Complement: 5 (1 officer)
Missiles: SSM: Tigercat; range 6 km *(3.2 n miles)*.
Guns: 2—12.7 mm MGs.
Radars: Surface search: I-band.

Comment: Ordered by Iranian Arvandan Maritime Company. First 19 completed by Petersons and remainder shipped as kits for completion in Iran. The SSM is crude and unguided. Numbers are approximate.

UPDATED

PBI   *4/1995* / 0080044*

20 BOGHAMMAR CRAFT (PBI)

Displacement, tons: 6.4 full load
Dimensions, feet (metres): 41.2 × 8.6 × 2.3 *(13 × 2.7 × 0.7)*
Main machinery: 2 Seatek 6-4V-9 diesels; 1,160 hp *(853 kW)*; 2 shafts
Speed, knots: 46. **Range, miles:** 500 at 40 kt
Complement: 5/6
Guns: 3—12.7 mm MGs. 1 RPG-7 rocket launcher or 106 mm recoilless rifle. 1—12-barrelled 107 mm rocket launcher (MRL).
Radars: Surface search: I-band.

Comment: Ordered in 1983 and completed in 1984-85 for Customs Service. Total of 51 delivered. Used extensively by the Pasdaran. Maximum payload 450 kg. Speed is dependent on load carried. They can be transported by Amphibious Lift Ships and can operate from bases at Farsi, Sirri and Abu Musa Islands with a main base at Bandar Abbas. Re-engined with Seatek diesels from 1991. There are also a further 10—11 m craft with similar characteristics. Known as TORAGH boats and manned by the Pasdaran and the Navy.

UPDATED

TORAGH   *5/1997* / 0012557*

12 + 12 CHINA CAT CLASS (PCF)

Displacement, tons: 19 full load
Dimensions, feet (metres): 45.9 × 13.1 × 3.4 *(14 × 4 × 1)*
Main machinery: 2 diesels; 2 shafts
Speed, knots: 40
Complement: 10
Missiles: SSM: China type; range 37 km *(20 n miles).*
Guns: 2 China 25 mm (twin).
Radars: Surface search: I-band.

Comment: First one reported in late 1999. Catamaran hulls. Large numbers are expected. The SSM
launcher is on the stern. Details are speculative.
UPDATED

RIVER ROADSTEAD PATROL AND HOVERCRAFT (PBR)

Comment: Numerous craft used by the Revolutionary Guard include:
Type 2: Dimensions, feet (metres): 22.0 × 7.2 *(6.7 × 2.2)*; single outboard engine; 1—12.7 mm
MG.
Type 3: Dimensions, feet (metres): 16.4 × 5.2 *(5.0 × 1.6)*; single outboard engine; small arms.
Type 4: Dimensions, feet (metres): 13.1-26.2 × 7.9 *(4-8 × 1.6)*; two outboard engines; small arms.
Type 5: Dimensions, feet (metres): 24.6 × 9.2 *(7.5 × 2.8)*; assault craft.
Type 6: Dimensions, feet (metres): 30.9 × 11.8 *(9.4 × 3.6)*; single outboard engine; 1—12.7 mm
MG.
Dhows: Dimensions, feet (metres): 77.1 × 20 *(23.5 × 6.1)*; single diesel engine; mine rails.
Yunus: Dimensions, feet (metres): 27.6 × 9.8 *(8.4 × 3)*; speed 32 kt.
Ashoora: Dimensions, feet (metres): 26.6 × 7.9 *(8.1 × 2.4)*; two outboards; speed 42 kt;
1—7.62 mm MG.
Jet Skis; RPGs.
UPDATED

Type 4   *5/1997* */ 0012558*

ASHOORA   *6/1994* */ 0080045*

JET SKI (with RPG)   *5/1999* */ 0080046*

20 BOSTON WHALER CRAFT (TYPE 1) (PBI)

Displacement, tons: 1.3 full load
Dimensions, feet (metres): 22.3 × 7.4 × 1.2 *(6.7 × 2.3 × 0.4)*
Main machinery: 2 outboards; 240 hp *(179 kW)*
Speed, knots: 40+
Complement: 4
Guns: Various, but can include 1—12-barrelled 107 mm MRL or 1—12.7 mm MG.

Comment: Designed for coastal law enforcement by Boston Whaler Inc, USA. GRP hulls.
Numerous indigenously constructed hulls. Numbers uncertain. Manned by the Pasdaran and the
Navy.
VERIFIED

BOSTON WHALER   *1988*

MINE WARFARE FORCES

3 MSC 268/292 CLASS (MINESWEEPERS—COASTAL) (MSC)

Name	No	Builders	Commissioned
HAMZEH (ex-*Shahrokh*, ex-*MSC 276*)	301	Bellingham Shipyard	1960
SIMORGH (ex-*MSC 291*)	302	Tacoma Boat	1962
KARKAS (ex-*MSC 292*)	303	Peterson Builders	1959

Displacement, tons: 384 full load
Dimensions, feet (metres): 145.8 × 28 × 8.3 *(44.5 × 8.5 × 2.5)*
Main machinery: 4 GM 6-71 diesels; 696 hp *(519 kW)* sustained; 2 shafts
Speed, knots: 13. **Range, miles:** 2,400 at 10 kt
Complement: 40 (6 officers)
Guns: 2 Oerlikon 20 mm (twin).
Radars: Surface search: Decca; I-band.

Comment: Originally class of four. Of wooden construction with mechanical, acoustic and
magnetic sweeps. Transferred from the USA under MAP in 1959-62. *Karkas* still active but rarely
seen at sea. *Simorgh* paid off some years ago but reactivated in 1992. Both are based at
Boushehr. None of these ships exercises in the minesweeping role. *Hamzeh* in the Caspian Sea
was reported scrapped, but has re-emerged as a diving tender with the new name of the former
Royal Yacht.
UPDATED

MSC 268 (Spanish colours)   *4/1999* *, Diego Quevedo / 0080047*

AMPHIBIOUS FORCES

Notes: (1) There is also a troop carrier *Iran Javad*, details not known.
(2) Commercial LSLs are being built at Bandar Abbas. These include two 1,151 grt ships, *Chavoush*
launched in December 1995 and *Chalak* in June 1996.

3 IRAN HORMUZ 21 CLASS (LST)

HEJAZ 21   **KARABALA** 22   **AMIR** 23

Displacement, tons: 1,280 full load
Measurement, tons: 750 dwt
Dimensions, feet (metres): 213.3 × 39.4 × 8.5 *(65 × 12 × 2.6)*
Main machinery: 2 MAN V12V-12.5/14 or 2 MWM TBD 604 V12 diesels; 1,460 hp(m) *(1.07 MW)*;
2 shafts
Speed, knots: 9
Complement: 12
Military lift: 600 tons

Comment: Officially ordered for 'civilian use' and built by Ravenstein, Netherlands in 1984-85.
21 and 22 are manned by the Pasdaran. A local version is assembled as the MIG-S-5000 for
commercial use. One was launched in mid-1995 at Boushehr and a second in 1997.
UPDATED

4 HENGAM CLASS (LSL)

Name	No	Builders	Commissioned
HENGAM	511	Yarrow (Shipbuilders) Ltd, Clyde	12 Aug 1974
LARAK	512	Yarrow (Shipbuilders) Ltd, Clyde	12 Nov 1974
TONB	513	Yarrow (Shipbuilders) Ltd, Clyde	21 Feb 1985
LAVAN	514	Yarrow (Shipbuilders) Ltd, Clyde	16 Jan 1985

Displacement, tons: 2,540 full load
Dimensions, feet (metres): 305 × 49 × 7.3 *(93 × 15 × 2.4)*
Main machinery: 4 Paxman 12YJCM diesels *(Hengam, Larak)*; 3,000 hp *(2.24 MW)* sustained;
  2 shafts. 4 MTU 16V 652 TB81 diesels *(Tonb, Lavan)*; 4,600 hp(m) *(3.38 MW)* sustained;
  2 shafts
Speed, knots: 14.5. **Range, miles:** 4,000+ at 12 kt
Complement: 80
Military lift: Up to 9 tanks depending on size; 600 tons cargo; 227 troops; 10 ton crane

Guns: 4 Bofors 40 mm/60 *(Hengam* and *Larak)*. 8 USSR 23 mm/80 (4 twin) *(Tonb* and *Lavan)*.
  2—12.7 mm MGs.
  1 BM-21 multiple rocket launcher.
Countermeasures: Decoys: 2 UK Mk 5 rocket flare launchers.
Radars: Navigation: Racal Decca 1229; I-band.
IFF: SSR 1520 *(Hengam* and *Larak)*.
Tacan: URN 25.

Helicopters: Can embark 1 Sikorsky MH-53D.

Programmes: Named after islands in the Gulf. First two ordered 25 July 1972. Four more ordered
  20 July 1977. The material for the last two ships of the second order had been ordered by
  Yarrows when the order was cancelled in early 1979. *Tonb* carried out trials in October 1984
  followed by *Lavan* later in the year and both were released by the UK in 1985 as 'Hospital Ships'.
Structure: Smaller than British *Sir Lancelot* design with no through tank deck. Rocket launcher
  mounted in the bows.
Operational: Two LCVPs and a number of small landing craft can be carried. Can act as Depot
  Ships for MCMV and small craft and have been used to ferry Pasdaran small craft around the
  Gulf.

UPDATED

LAVAN   *3/1997* / 0012559*

LARAK   *3/1997*, Maritime Photographic / 0052378*

3 IRAN HORMUZ 24 CLASS (LST)

FARSI 24   **SARDASHT** 25   **SAB SAHEL** 26

Displacement, tons: 2,014 full load
Dimensions, feet (metres): 239.8 × 46.6 × 8.2 *(73.1 × 14.2 × 2.5)*
Main machinery: 2 Daihatsu 6DLM-22 diesels; 2,400 hp(m) *(1.76 MW)*; 2 shafts
Speed, knots: 12
Complement: 30 plus 110 berths
Military lift: 9 tanks, 140 troops

Comment: Built at Inchon, South Korea in 1985-86 and as with the Iran 'Hormuz 21' class officially
  classed as Merchant Ships. Have been used to support Pasdaran activities.

UPDATED

IRAN HORMUZ 24   *5/1999* / 0080048*

3 FOUQUE (MIG-S-3700) CLASS (LSL)

FOUQUE 101   **102**   **103**

Displacement, tons: 276 full load
Dimensions, feet (metres): 121.4 × 26.2 × 4.9 *(37 × 8 × 1.5)*
Main machinery: 2 MWM TBD 234 V8 diesels; 879 hp(m) *(646 kW)*; 2 shafts
Speed, knots: 10. **Range, miles:** 400 at 10 kt
Complement: 8
Military lift: 140 tons of vehicles

Comment: *Fouque* assembled in Iran by Martyr Darvishi Marine, Bandar Abbas. Launched in June
  1998. Others of the class are in commercial service and more can be taken over by the Navy if
  required. Two others for the Navy were launched in September 1995.

UPDATED

FOUQUE   *1994*, Iranian Marine Industries / 0080049*

6 + 6 WELLINGTON (BH.7) CLASS (HOVERCRAFT)

101-106

Displacement, tons: 53.8 full load
Dimensions, feet (metres): 78.3 × 45.6 × 5.6 (skirt) *(23.9 × 13.9 × 1.7)*
Main machinery: 1 RR Proteus 15 M/541 gas turbine; 4,250 hp *(3.17 MW)* sustained
Speed, knots: 70; 30 in Sea State 5 or more. **Range, miles:** 620 at 66 kt
Guns: 2 Browning 12.7 mm MGs.
Radars: Surface search: Decca 1226; I-band.

Comment: First pair are British Hovercraft Corporation 7 Mk 4 commissioned in 1970-71 and the
  next four are Mk 5 craft commissioned in 1974-75. Mk 5 craft fitted for, but not with Standard
  missiles. Some refitted in UK in 1984. Can embark troops and vehicles or normal support
  cargoes. The Iranian Aircraft Manufacturing Industries (HESA) is reported to be able to maintain
  these craft in service and is building a new class based on the same design. The older design
  'SR.N6' class have not been reported and are assumed to be inoperable, although they are still
  claimed to be in service by Iran.

UPDATED

WELLINGTON   *6/1998*, HESA / 0033385*

AUXILIARIES

Note: There is also an inshore survey vessel *Abnegar*.

2 FLOATING DOCKS

400 (ex-US *ARD 29*, ex-*FD 4*)   **DOLPHIN**

Dimensions, feet (metres): 487 × 80.2 × 32.5 *(149.9 × 24.7 × 10)* *(400)*
  786.9 × 172.1 × 58.4 *(240 × 52.5 × 17.8)* *(Dolphin)*

Comment: *400* is an ex-US 'ARD 12' class built by Pacific Bridge, California and transferred in
  1977; lift 3,556 tons. *Dolphin* built by MAN-GHH Nordenham, West Germany and completed in
  November 1985; lift 28,000 tons.

VERIFIED

1 REPLENISHMENT SHIP (AOR)

Name	No	Builders	Commissioned
KHARG	431	Swan Hunter Ltd, Wallsend	5 Oct 1984

Displacement, tons: 11,064 light; 33,014 full load
Measurement, tons: 9,367 dwt; 18,582 gross
Dimensions, feet (metres): 679 × 86.9 × 30 *(207.2 × 26.5 × 9.2)*
Main machinery: 2 Babcock & Wilcox boilers; 2 Westinghouse turbines; 26,870 hp *(19.75 MW)*; 1 shaft
Speed, knots: 21.5
Complement: 248
Guns: 1 OTO Melara 76 mm/62 compact. 4 USSR 23 mm/80 (2 twin). 2—12.7 mm MGs.
Radars: Navigation: Decca 1229; I-band.
Tacan: URN 20.
Helicopters: 3 Sea Kings (twin hangar).

Comment: Ordered October 1974. Laid down 27 January 1976. Launched 3 February 1977. Ship handed over to Iranian crew on 25 April 1980 but remained in UK. In 1983 Iranian Government requested this ship's transfer. The UK Government delayed approval until January 1984. On 10 July 1984 began refit at Tyne Ship Repairers. Trials began 4 September 1984 and ship was then delivered without guns which were subsequently fitted. A design incorporating some of the features of the British 'Ol' class but carrying ammunition and dry stores in addition to fuel. Inmarsat fitted.

VERIFIED

KHARG   *5/1997 /* 0052379

KHARG   *6/1998 /* 0052380

2 FLEET SUPPLY SHIPS (AORL)

Name	No	Builders	Commissioned
BANDAR ABBAS	421	C Lühring Yard, Brake, West Germany	Apr 1974
BOUSHEHR	422	C Lühring Yard, Brake, West Germany	Nov 1974

Displacement, tons: 4,673 full load
Measurement, tons: 3,250 dwt; 3,186 gross
Dimensions, feet (metres): 354.2 × 54.4 × 14.8 *(108 × 16.6 × 4.5)*
Main machinery: 2 MAN 6L 52/55 diesels; 12,060 hp(m) *(8.86 MW)* sustained; 2 shafts
Speed, knots: 20. **Range, miles:** 3,500 at 16 kt
Complement: 59
Guns: 3 GAM-BO1 20 mm can be carried. 2—12.7 mm MGs.
Radars: Navigation: 2 Decca 1226; I-band.
Helicopters: 1 AB 212.

Comment: *Bandar Abbas* launched 11 August 1973, *Boushehr* launched 23 March 1974. Combined tankers and store-ships carrying victualling, armament and general stores. Telescopic hangar. Both carry 2 SA-7 portable SAM and 20 mm guns have replaced the former armament. *Bandar Abbas* damaged by an explosion in early 1999 and may not be repairable.

UPDATED

BOUSHEHR   *5/1999* / 0080050

4 KANGAN CLASS (WATER TANKERS) (AWT)

KANGAN 411	TAHERI 412	SHAHID MARJANI —	AMIR —

Displacement, tons: 12,000 full load
Measurement, tons: 9,430 dwt
Dimensions, feet (metres): 485.6 × 70.5 × 16.4 *(148 × 21.5 × 5)*
Main machinery: 1 MAN 7L52/55A diesel; 7,385 hp(m) *(5.43 MW)* sustained; 1 shaft
Speed, knots: 15
Complement: 14
Cargo capacity: 9,000 m³ of water
Guns: 2 USSR 23 mm/80 (twin). 2—12.7 mm MGs.
Radars: Navigation: Decca 1229; I-band.

Comment: The first two were built in Mazagon Dock, Bombay in 1978 and 1979. The second pair to a slightly modified design was acquired in 1991-92 but may be civilian manned. Some of the largest water tankers afloat and are used to supply remote coastal towns and islands. Accommodation is air conditioned. All have a 10 ton boom crane.

VERIFIED

TAHERI   *5/1989*

12 HENDIJAN CLASS (TENDERS) (AG)

HENDIJAN	GENAVEH	BAHREGAN (ex-*Geno*)	NAYBAND
KALAT	SIRIK	MOGAM	MACHAM
KONARAK	GAVATAR	ROSTANI	KORAMSHAHR

Displacement, tons: 460 full load
Dimensions, feet (metres): 166.7 × 28.1 × 11.5 *(50.8 × 8.6 × 3.5)*
Main machinery: 2 Mitsubishi S16MPTK diesels; 7,600 hp(m) *(5.15 MW)*; 2 shafts
Speed, knots: 25
Complement: 15 plus 90 passengers
Cargo capacity: 40 tons on deck; 95 m³ of liquid/solid cargo space
Guns: 2—12.7 mm MGs.
Radars: Navigation: Racal Decca or China RM 1070A; I-band.

Comment: First eight built by Damen, Netherlands 1988-91. Remainder built at Bandar Abbas under the MIG-S-4700 programme. Last pair launched on 25 November 1995. Reports of three more being built may be caused by confusion with new corvettes. Variously described in the Iranian press as 'frigates' or 'patrol ships', they can be used for coastal surveillance. One is used as a training ship. Pennant numbers in the 1400 series.

UPDATED

HENDIJAN 1409   *6/1998 /* 0052381

10 DAMEN 1550 (PILOT CRAFT)

Displacement, tons: 25 full load
Dimensions, feet (metres): 52.5 × 15.1 × 4.6 *(16 × 4.6 × 1.4)*
Main machinery: 2 MTU diesels; 2 shafts
Speed, knots: 19
Complement: 3
Radars: Navigation: Furuno; I-band.

Comment: Ordered from Damen, Gorinchen in February 1993. Steel hull and aluminium superstructure. Used primarily as pilot craft.

UPDATED

DAMEN 1550   *1993*, Damen Shipyards / 0080051

7 DELVAR CLASS (SUPPORT SHIPS) (AEL/AKL/AWT)

CHARAK (AKL)	CHIROO (AKL)	DELVAR (AEL)	DILIM (AWT)
SOURU (AKL)	SIRJAN (AEL)	DAYER (AWT)	

Measurement, tons: 890 gross; 765 dwt
Dimensions, feet (metres): 210 × 34.4 × 10.9 *(64 × 10.5 × 3.3)*
Main machinery: 2 MAN G6V 23.5/33ATL diesels; 1,560 hp(m) *(1.15 MW)*; 2 shafts
Speed, knots: 11
Complement: 20
Guns: 1 GAM-BO1 20 mm. 2—12.7 mm MGs.
Radars: Navigation: Decca 1226; I-band.

Comment: All built by Karachi SY in 1980-82. *Delvar* and *Sirjan* are ammunition ships, *Dayer* and *Dilim* water carriers and the other three are general cargo ships. The water carriers have only one crane (against two on the other types), and have rounded sterns (as opposed to transoms). Re-armed.   **UPDATED**

DELVAR 491   *3/1997* * / 0012562

CHARAK   *10/1997* * / 0012563

TUGS

17 HARBOUR TUGS (YTB/YTM)

HAAMOON	ALBAN	ASLAM	DARYAVAND II
HIRMAND	SEFID-RUD	DEHLORAN	KHANDAG
MENAB	ATRAK	ILAM	ARVAND
HARI-RUD	ABAD	HANGAM	KARKHEH
ARAS			

Comment: All between 70 and 90 ft in length, built since 1984.   **VERIFIED**

IRAQ

Bases

Basra, Khor Az Zubayr, Umm Qasr (new naval base)

Coast Defence

Five CSSC-3 missile batteries back in operation by 1999.

General

Recent signs of some activity with a new base being built at Umm Qasr and at least one patrol craft now operational. If sanctions are lifted the two Italian corvettes at La Spezia and the oiler at Alexandria could be reclaimed.

Maritime Aircraft

Air Force F-1s can be Exocet AM 39 fitted. A few Bell AB-212 and A-103A helicopters may be operational.

Mercantile Marine

Lloyd's Register of Shipping:
98 vessels of 510,618 tons

DELETIONS

Note: Some of the vessels could become active again, but all are laid up as shown.

Corvettes

Mussa Ben Nussair, Tariq Bin Ziad (at La Spezia)

Patrol Forces

6 Vosper PBR (at Basra), 1 Bogomol (at Zubayr), 2 PB-90 (at Zubayr), 2 Zhuk (at Zubayr), 3 SRN-6 (at Zubayr)

Mine Warfare Forces

2 Nestin (at Zubayr), 2 Yevgenya (at Basra)

Auxiliaries

Agnadeen (at Alexandria), 5 Harbour craft (at Basra)

PATROL FORCES

Note: In addition to the Osa I reported back at sea in 1999, there are about 80 Sawari open boats of about 12 m, and capable of speeds up to 25 kt powered by outboard motors. Some have 30 mm cannon and MGs.

1 OSA I (TYPE 205) CLASS (FAST ATTACK CRAFT—MISSILE)

HAZIRANI R 15

Displacement, tons: 210 full load
Dimensions, feet (metres): 126.6 × 24.9 × 8.8 *(38.6 × 7.6 × 2.7)*
Main machinery: 3 Type 503A diesels; 8,025 hp(m) *(5.9 MW)*; 3 shafts
Speed, knots: 35. **Range, miles:** 500 at 35 kt
Complement: 26
Missiles: SSM: 4 SS-N-2A Styx; active radar/IR homing to 46 km *(25 n miles)* at 0.9 Mach; warhead 513 kg.
Guns: 4 USSR 30 mm/65 (2 twin).
Radars: Surface search/fire control: Square Tie; I-band.
Fire control: Drum Tilt; H/I-band.

Comment: Built in early 1970s. Out of action after 1991 but reported back in service in 1999. Missile system may be inoperable.   **NEW ENTRY**

HAZIRANI   *1980* * / 0080052

REPUBLIC OF IRELAND
AN SEIRBHIS CHABHLAIGH

Headquarters Appointments

Flag Officer Commanding Naval Service:
Commodore J J Kavanagh

Bases

Haulbowline Island, Cork Harbour—HQ, and Dockyard

Personnel

(a) 2000: 1,050 (115 officers)
(b) Voluntary service
(c) Reserves: 455 (two companies in Dublin and one each in Waterford, Cork and Limerick)

Prefix to Ships' Names

LÉ (Long Éirennach = Irish Ship)

Fishery Protection

All ships are fitted with NS designed Fishery Protection Information System (FPIS) and Fishery Legislation Expert System (FLES). The FPIS and FLES are accessed through the ship's computer network and the FPIS, which is a database of all known information regarding fishing vessels, is updated on a daily basis from the Naval Supervisory Centre by satellite link.

Mercantile Marine

Lloyd's Register of Shipping:
153 vessels of 218,882 tons gross

PATROL FORCES

1 EITHNE CLASS (OPV)

Name	No	Builders	Laid down	Launched	Commissioned
EITHNE	P 31	Verolme, Cork	15 Dec 1982	19 Dec 1983	7 Dec 1984

Displacement, tons: 1,760 standard; 1,910 full load
Dimensions, feet (metres): 265 × 39.4 × 14.1
  (80.8 × 12 × 4.3)
Main machinery: 2 Ruston 12RKC diesels; 6,800 hp *(5.07 MW)*
  sustained; 2 shafts; cp props
Speed, knots: 20+; 19 normal. **Range, miles:** 7,000 at 15 kt
Complement: 73 (10 officers) plus 8 (2 officers) aircrew

Guns: 1 Bofors 57 mm/70 Mk 1; 200 rds/min to 17 km *(9.3 n
  miles)*; weight of shell 2.4 kg.
  2 Rheinmetall 20 mm/20. 2—7.62 mm MGs.
  2 Wallop 57 mm launchers for illuminants.
Weapons control: Signaal LIOD director. 2 Signaal optical
  sights.
Radars: Air/surface search: Signaal DA05 Mk 4; E/F-band; range
  137 km *(75 n miles)* for 2 m² target.
  Surface search: Racal Decca 1629C; I-band.
  Navigation: Racal Decca 1229C; I-band.
  Tacan: MEL RRB transponder.
Sonars: Plessey PMS 26; hull-mounted; lightweight; active
  search and attack; 10 kHz.

Helicopters: 1 SA 365F Dauphin 2.

Programmes: Ordered 23 April 1982 from Verolme, Cork, this
  was the last ship to be built at this yard.
Structure: Fitted with retractable stabilisers. Closed circuit TV for
  flight deck operations. Satellite navigation and
  communications. Kelvin Hughes integrated bridge system
  being fitted in 1999.
Operational: Helicopter fully operational from 1993. Two Avon
  RIBs with 90 hp outboards are carried. Long refit (SLEP) in
  1998/99.

UPDATED

EITHNE   *6/1999*, Michael Nitz /* 0080054

1 + 1 ROISIN CLASS (OPV)

Name	No	Builders	Laid down	Launched	Commissioned
ROISIN	P 51	Appledore Shipbuilders, Bideford	Dec 1998	12 Aug 1999	15 Dec 1999

Displacement, tons: 1,700 full load
Dimensions, feet (metres): 255.9 × 45.9 × 12.8
  (78 × 14 × 3.9)
Main machinery: 2 Wärtsilä 16V26 diesels; 6,800 hp(m)
  (5 MW) sustained; 2 shafts; cp props; bow thruster; 462 hp(m)
  (340 kW)
Speed, knots: 23. **Range, miles:** 6,000 at 15 kt
Complement: 44 (6 officers)
Guns: 1 OTO Melara 3 in *(76 mm)*/62; 85 rds/min to 16 km
  (8.6 n miles); weight of shell 6 kg.
  2—12.7 mm MGs. 4—7.62 mm MGs.
Weapons control: Radamec 1500 optronic director.
Radars: Surface search: Kelvin Hughes; E/F/I-band.
  Navigation: Kelvin Hughes; I-band.

Comment: Contract signed on 16 December 1997 with 65 per
  cent of EU funding. The ship was delivered in late October
  1999. Option on a second of class is to be taken up by
  mid-2000. The design is a modification of the Mauritius ship
  Vigilant but without the hangar or flight deck. Main armament
  fitted after delivery. Two Delta 6.5 m and one Avon 5.4 m RIBs
  are carried. *UPDATED*

ROISIN   *1/2000*, Republic of Ireland Navy /* 0080053

4 P 21 and DEIRDRE CLASSES
(OFFSHORE PATROL VESSELS) (OPV)

Name	No	Builders	Launched	Commissioned
DEIRDRE	P 20	Verolme, Cork	29 Dec 1971	19 June 1972
EMER	P 21	Verolme, Cork	4 Aug 1977	16 Jan 1978
AOIFE	P 22	Verolme, Cork	12 Apr 1979	29 Nov 1979
AISLING	P 23	Verolme, Cork	3 Oct 1979	21 May 1980

Displacement, tons: 972 *(Deirdre)*; 1,019.5 (remainder)
Dimensions, feet (metres): 184.3 pp × 34.1 × 14.4 *(56.2 × 10.4 × 4.4) (Deirdre)*
  213.7 × 34.4 × 14 *(65.2 × 10.5 × 4.4)* (remainder)
Main machinery: 2 British Polar SF112 VS-F diesels; 4,200 hp *(3.13 MW)*; 1 shaft *(Deirdre)*
  2 SEMT-Pielstick 6 PA6 L 280 diesels; 4,800 hp *(3.53 MW)*; 1 shaft (remainder); bow thruster
  (Aoife and Aisling)
Speed, knots: 17. **Range, miles:** 4,000 at 17 kt; 6,750 at 12 kt
Complement: 47 (6 officers)

Guns: 1 Bofors 40 mm/60 Mk 22; 120 rds/min to 10 km *(5.4 n miles)*; weight of shell 0.89 kg.
  2 GAM-B01 20 mm (except *Deirdre*); 900 rds/min to 2 km.
  2—12.7 mm MGs *(Deirdre)*. 2—7.62 mm MGs.
Radars: Surface search: Kelvin Hughes Mk VI; F-band.
  Navigation: Racal Decca 1226 *(Deirdre)*; Kelvin Hughes Mk IV (remainder); I-band.
Sonars: Simrad Marine; hull-mounted; active search; 34 kHz.

Programmes: *Deirdre* was the first vessel built for the Naval Service in Ireland.
Modernisation: New search radars were fitted in 1994-95.
Structure: Stabilisers fitted. *Aoife* and *Aisling* are equipped with a bow thruster. Inmarsat SATCOM
  fitted.
Operational: The practice of keeping one in reserve and rotating every six months was stopped at
  the end of 1990. *Emer* refitted in 1995, *Aoife* in 1996/97 and *Aisling* in 1997/98. *Deirde* is to
  stay in service until the second 'Roisin' class completes in about 2002.

UPDATED

AISLING   *10/1994*, Diego Quevedo /* 0075859   DEIDRE   *7/1999*, P Marsan /* 0080055

2 P 41 PEACOCK CLASS (COASTAL PATROL VESSELS) (PG)

Name	No	Builders	Commissioned
ORLA (ex-*Swift*)	P 41	Hall Russell, Aberdeen	3 May 1985
CIARA (ex-*Swallow*)	P 42	Hall Russell, Aberdeen	17 Oct 1984

Displacement, tons: 712 full load
Dimensions, feet (metres): 204.1 × 32.8 × 8.9 *(62.6 × 10 × 2.7)*
Main machinery: 2 Crossley SEMT-Pielstick 18 PA6 V 280 diesels; 14,400 hp(m) *(10.58 MW)* sustained; 2 shafts; auxiliary drive; Schottel prop; 181 hp(m) *(133 kW)*
Speed, knots: 25. **Range, miles:** 2,500 at 17 kt
Complement: 39 (5 officers)

Guns: 1—3 in (76 mm)/62 OTO Melara compact; 85 rds/min to 16 km *(8.6 n miles)*; weight of shell 6 kg.
2—12.7 mm MGs. 4—7.62 mm MGs.
Weapons control: BAe Sea Archer optronic director (for 76 mm).
Radars: Surface search: Kelvin Hughes Mk IV; I-band.
Navigation: Kelvin Hughes 500A; I-band.

Programmes: *Orla* launched 11 September 1984 and *Ciara* 31 March 1984. Both served in Hong Kong from mid-1985 until early 1988. Acquired from UK and commissioned 21 November 1988. Others of the class acquired by the Philippines in 1997.
Modernisation: New radars fitted in 1993. These have a Nucleus 6000A which interfaces with the Weapons Control System.
Structure: Can carry Sea Rider craft. Have loiter drive. Displacement increased after building by the addition of more electronic equipment.   *UPDATED*

CIARA   *3/1999*, B Risseeuw /* 0080056

SHIPBORNE AIRCRAFT

Numbers/Type: 5 Aerospatiale SA 365F Dauphin 2.
Operational speed: 140 kt *(260 km/h).*
Service ceiling: 15,000 ft *(4,575 m).*
Range: 410 n miles *(758 km).*
Role/Weapon systems: Embarked helicopter for MR/SAR tasks in *Eithne*; some shore land-based training by Army Air Corps and SAR. Sensors: Bendix RDR 1500 radar. Weapons: Unarmed.
VERIFIED

DAUPHIN 2   *6/1993, John Daly*

LAND-BASED MARITIME AIRCRAFT

Note: Two civilian operated Sikorsky S-61 helicopters provide long-range SAR services.

Numbers/Type: 2 Casa CN-235 Persuader.
Operational speed: 210 kt *(384 km/h).*
Service ceiling: 24,000 ft *(7,315 m).*
Range: 2,000 n miles *(3,218 km).*
Role/Weapon systems: EEZ surveillance. First one delivered in June 1992 but returned to Spain in 1995. Two more delivered in December 1994. Sensors: Search radar Bendix APS 504(V)5; FLIR. Weapons: Unarmed.
UPDATED

PERSUADER   *6/1994* /* 0080057

AUXILIARIES

Notes: (1) In addition there are a number of mostly civilian manned auxiliaries including: *Seabhac* a small tug acquired in 1983; *Fainleog*, *David F* (built in 1962) and *Fiachdubh* passenger craft, the last two taken over after lease in 1988 and the first in 1983; *Tailte* a Dufour 35 ft sail training yacht bought in 1979 and two elderly training yachts *Nancy Bet* and *Creidne*. An ex-Dutch yacht *Brime* of 65 ft was awarded to the Navy in March 1994 and may be used for training.
(2) *Granuaile* is a lighthouse tender operated by the Commissioners of Irish Lights.

GRANUAILE   *7/1996, van Ginderen Collection*

ISRAEL
HEYL YAM

Headquarters Appointments

Commander-in-Chief:
  Rear Admiral Yadidia Ya'ari

Personnel

(a) 2000: 6,500 (880 officers) of whom 2,500 are conscripts. Includes a Naval Commando of 300
(b) 3 years' national service for Jews and Druzes

Note: An additional 5,000 Reserves available on mobilisation.

Bases

Haifa, Ashdod, Eilat
(The repair base at Eilat has a synchrolift)

Coast Defence

There are ten integrated coastal radar stations.

Prefix to Ships' Names

INS (Israeli Naval Ship)

Mercantile Marine

Lloyd's Register of Shipping:
  52 vessels of 728,435 tons gross

DELETIONS

Submarines

1999-2000 *Gal, Tanin, Rahav*

Patrol Forces

1997	*Tarshish* (old), *Reshef* (both to Chile)
1998	2 *Dabur*
1999	1 *Super Dvora*

Amphibious Forces

1997-98 *Ashkelon, Achziv*

SUBMARINES

3 DOLPHIN (TYPE 800) CLASS (SSK)

Name	No	Builders	Laid down	Launched	Commissioned
DOLPHIN	—	Howaldtswerke/Thyssen Nordseewerke	7 Oct 1994	12 Apr 1996	37 July 1999
LEVIATHAN	—	Howaldtswerke/Thyssen Nordseewerke	13 Apr 1995	25 Apr 1997	15 Nov 1999
TEKUMA	—	Howaldtswerke/Thyssen Nordseewerke	12 Dec 1996	26 June 1998	June 2000

Displacement, tons: 1,640 surfaced; 1,900 dived
Dimensions, feet (metres): 188 × 22.3 × 20.3
  (57.3 × 6.8 × 6.2)
Main machinery: 3 MTU 16V 396 SE 84 diesels; 4,243 hp(m)
  (3.12 MW) sustained; 3 alternators; 2.91 MW; 1 Siemens
  motor; 3,875 hp(m) *(2.85 MW)* sustained; 1 shaft
Speed, knots: 20 dived; 11 snorting
Range, miles: 8,000 at 8 kt surfaced; 420 at 8 kt dived
Complement: 30 (6 officers)

Missiles: SSM/SLCM: Sub Harpoon; UGM-84C; active radar or
  GPS homing to 130 km *(70 n miles)* at 0.9 Mach; warhead
  227 kg or nuclear.
SAM: Fitted for Triten anti-helicopter system.
Torpedoes: 4—25.6 in *(650 mm)* and 6—21 in *(533 mm)* bow
  tubes. STN Atlas DM2A4 Sechelt; wire-guided active homing
  to 13 km *(7 n miles)* at 35 kt; passive homing to 28 km *(15 n
  miles)* at 23 kt; warhead 260 kg. Total of 16 torpedoes and 5
  SSMs. The four 650 mm tubes may be for SDVs, but could
  carry torpedoes if liners are fitted.
Mines: In lieu of torpedoes.
Countermeasures: ESM: Elbit Timnex 4CH(V)2; intercept.
Weapons control: STN/Atlas Elektronik ISUS 90-1 TCS.
Radars: Surface search: Elta; I-band.
Sonars: Atlas Elektronik CSU 90; hull-mounted; passive/active
  search and attack.
  Atlas Elektronik PRS-3; passive ranging.
  FAS-3; flank array; passive search.

Programmes: In mid-1988 Ingalls Shipbuilding Division of Litton
  Corporation was chosen as the prime contractor for two IKL-
  designed 'Dolphin' class submarines to be built in West
  Germany with FMS funds by HDW in conjunction with Thyssen
  Nordseewerke. Funds approved in July 1989 with an effective
  contract date of January 1990 but the project was cancelled in
  November 1990 due to pressures on defence funds. After the
  Gulf War in April 1991 the contract was resurrected, this time
  with German funding for two submarines with an option on a
  third taken up in July 1994.
Structure: Diving depth, 350 m *(1,150 ft)*. Similar to German
  Type 212 in design but with a 'wet and dry' compartment for
  underwater swimmers. Two Kollmorgen periscopes. Probably
  fitted for Triten anti-helicopter SAM system.
Operational: Endurance, 30 days. Used for interdiction,
  surveillance and special boat operations. Painted blue/green
  to aid concealment in the eastern Mediterranean. Some other
  NT 37E torpedoes are embarked until full Sechelt outfits are
  available. Harpoon has GPS homing for the SLCM land attack
  role.

UPDATED   DOLPHIN   6/1999*, Michael Nitz / 0080058

LEVIATHAN   10/1999*, Michael Nitz / 0080059

CORVETTES

3 EILAT (SAAR 5) CLASS (FSG)

Name	No	Builders	Laid down	Launched	Completed
EILAT	501	Ingalls, Pascagoula	24 Feb 1992	9 Feb 1993	24 May 1994
LAHAV	502	Ingalls, Pascagoula	25 Sep 1992	20 Aug 1993	23 Sep 1994
HANIT	503	Ingalls, Pascagoula	5 Apr 1993	4 Mar 1994	7 Feb 1995

Displacement, tons: 1,075 standard; 1,227 full load
Dimensions, feet (metres): 283.5 oa; 251.3 wl × 39 × 10.5
  (86.4; 76.6 × 11.9 × 3.2)
Main machinery: CODOG; 1 GE LM 2500 gas turbine; 30,000 hp *(22.38 MW)* sustained; 2 MTU 12V 1163 TB82 diesels; 6,600 hp(m) *(4.86 MW)* sustained; 2 shafts; Kamewa cp props

Speed, knots: 33 gas; 20 diesels. **Range, miles:** 3,500 at 17 kt
Complement: 64 (16 officers) plus 10 (4 officers) aircrew

Missiles: SSM: 8 McDonnell Douglas Harpoon (2 quad) launchers ❶; active radar homing to 130 km *(70 n miles)* at 0.9 Mach; warhead 227 kg.

SAM: 2 Israeli Industries Barak I (vertical launch) ❷; 2 × 32 cells; command line of sight radar or optical guidance to 10 km *(5.5 n miles)* at 2 Mach; warhead 22 kg (see *Operational*).
Guns: OTO Melara 3 in *(76 mm)*/62 compact ❸; 85 rds/min to 16 km *(8.7 n miles)*; weight of shell 6 kg.
  The main gun is interchangeable with a Bofors 57 mm gun or Vulcan Phalanx CIWS ❹.
  2 Sea Vulcan 25 mm CIWS ❺; range 1 km.
Torpedoes: 6—324 mm Mk 32 (2 triple) tubes ❻. Honeywell Mk 46; anti-submarine; active/passive homing to 11 km *(5.9 n miles)* at 40 kt; warhead 44 kg. Mounted in the superstructure.
Countermeasures: Decoys: 3 Elbit/Deseaver 72-barrelled chaff and IR launchers ❼; Rafael ATC-1 towed torpedo decoy.
ESM: Elisra NS 9003; intercept. Tadiran NATACS.
ECM: 2 Rafael 1010; Elisra NS 9005; jammers.
Combat data systems: Elbit NTCCS using Elta EL/S-9000 computers. Reshet datalink.
Weapons control: 2 Elop MSIS optronic directors ❽.
Radars: Air search: Elta EL/M-2218S ❾; E/F-band.
Surface search: Cardion SPS-55 ❿; I-band.
Navigation: I-band.
Fire control: 3 Elta EL/M-2221 GM STGR ⓫; I/K/J-band.
Sonars: EDO Type 796 Mod 1; hull-mounted; search and attack; medium frequency.
  Rafael towed array (fitted for).

Helicopters: 1 Dauphin SA 366G ⓬ or Sea Panther can be carried.

Programmes: A design by John J McMullen Associates Inc for Israeli Shipyards, Haifa in conjunction with Ingalls Shipbuilding Division of Litton Corporation which was authorised to act as main contractor using FMS funding. Contract awarded 8 February 1989. An option for a fourth was not taken up. All delivered to Israel for combat system installation, first two completed in 1996 and last one in mid-1997.
Structure: Steel hull and aluminium superstructure. Stealth features including resilient mounts for main machinery, funnel exhaust cooling, radar absorbent material (RAM), NBC washdown and Prairie Masker Bubbler system. A secondary operations room is fitted aft. There are some Flag capabilities. Plans to carry Gabriel SSMs have been scrapped because of topweight problems. The planned third MSIS director has not yet been seen on the platform aft of the air search radar.
Operational: Endurance, 20 days. The main role is to counter threats in shipping routes. ICS-2 integrated communications system. The position of the satellite aerial suggests that the SAM after VLS launchers are not used. Barak has still to be installed, because of lack of funds. For the same reason the normal Harpoon load may be reduced to four.

UPDATED

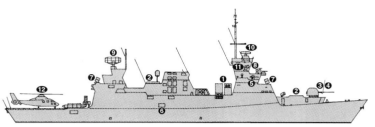

EILAT

(Scale 1 : 900), Ian Sturton / 0012570

EILAT
10/1999 */ 0075860*

EILAT

6/1999 */ 0080062*

PATROL FORCES

Notes: (1) There are about 12 'Firefish' type fast attack boats in service with Special Forces.
(2) A 50 ft *(15.2 m)* shallow draft Stealth craft has been built in a Vancouver Shipyard and delivered in late 1998. A second completed by Oregon Iron Works, Portland in 1999 and painted dark green. Two diesels giving 35 kt and a Rafael optronic surveillance system are included. Crew of five.
(3) The 'Saar 2' class are no longer operational although at least one is kept for trials and training.

6 HETZ (SAAR 4.5) CLASS (FAST ATTACK CRAFT—MISSILE) (PGF)

Name	Builders	Launched	Commissioned
ROMAT	Israel Shipyards, Haifa	30 Oct 1981	Oct 1981
KESHET	Israel Shipyards, Haifa	Oct 1982	Nov 1982
HETZ (ex-*Nirit*)	Israel Shipyards, Haifa	Oct 1990	Feb 1991
KIDON	Israel Shipyards, Haifa	—	7 Feb 1994
TARSHISH	Israel Shipyards, Haifa	—	June 1995
YAFFO	Israel Shipyards, Haifa	—	1 July 1998

Displacement, tons: 488 full load
Dimensions, feet (metres): 202.4 × 24.9 × 8.2 *(61.7 × 7.6 × 2.5)*
Main machinery: 4 MTU 16V 538 TB93 or 4 MTU 16V 396 TE diesels; 16,600 hp(m) *(12.2 MW)*; 4 shafts
Speed, knots: 31. **Range, miles:** 3,000 at 17 kt; 1,500 at 30 kt
Complement: 53

Missiles: SSM: 4 McDonnell Douglas Harpoon; active radar homing to 130 km *(70 n miles)* at 0.9 Mach; warhead 227 kg.
6 IAI Gabriel II; radar or optical guidance; semi-active radar plus anti-radiation homing to 36 km *(19.4 n miles)* at 0.7 Mach; warhead 75 kg.
SAM: Israeli Industries Barak I (vertical launch); 32 or 16 cells in 2— or 4—8 pack launchers; command line of sight radar or optical guidance to 10 km *(5.5 n miles)* at 2 Mach; warhead 22 kg. Most fitted for but not with.

Guns: 1 OTO Melara 3 in *(76 mm)*/62; 85 rds/min to 16 km *(8.7 n miles)*; weight of shell 6 kg.
2 Oerlikon 20 mm; 800 rds/min to 2 km.
1 General Electric/General Dynamics Vulcan Phalanx 6-barrelled 20 mm Mk 15; 3,000 rds/min combined to 1.5 km anti-missile.
2 or 4—12.7 mm (twin or quad) MGs.
Countermeasures: Decoys: Elbit/Deseaver 72-barrelled launchers for chaff and IR flares.
ESM/ECM: Elisra NS 9003/5; intercept and jammer.
Combat data systems: IAI Reshet datalink.
Weapons control: Galileo OG 20 optical director; Elop MSIS optronic director.
Radars: Air/surface search: Thomson-CSF TH-D 1040 Neptune; G-band.
Fire control: 2 Elta EL/M-2221 GM STGR; I/K/J-band.

Programmes: *Hetz* started construction in 1984 as the fifth of the class but was not completed, as an economy measure. Taken in hand again in 1989 and fitted out as the trials ship for some of the systems installed in the 'Eilat' class.
Modernisation: *Romat* and *Keshet* are modernised to same standard as *Hetz* in what is called the Nirit programme, but the Barak system has caused delays and timings are uncertain. The Saar 4s are also being modernised to Nirit standards using new hulls with some new equipment and some taken from the old SAAR 4 class. Some confusion has been caused by old names being transferred to new hulls.
Structure: The CIWS is mounted in the eyes of the ship replacing the 40 mm gun. The eight pack Barak launchers are fully containerised and require no deck penetration or onboard maintenance. They are fitted aft in place of two of the Gabriel launchers. The fire-control system for Barak is fitted on the platform aft of the bridge on the port side.
Operational: Davits can be installed aft of the Penguin missiles for special forces boats. Barak SAM is only operational in one of the class.   *UPDATED*

KESHET   *10/1999 *, C E Castle* / 0075861

KIDON   *4/1999 *, C E Castle* / 0080064

2 ALIYA (SAAR 4.5) CLASS (FAST ATTACK CRAFT—MISSILE) (PGF)

Name	Builders	Launched	Commissioned
ALIYA	Israel Shipyards, Haifa	11 July 1980	Aug 1980
GEOULA	Israel Shipyards, Haifa	Oct 1980	31 Dec 1980

Displacement, tons: 498 full load
Dimensions, feet (metres): 202.4 × 24.9 × 8.2 *(61.7 × 7.6 × 2.5)*
Main machinery: 4 MTU/Bazán 16V 956 TB91 diesels; 15,000 hp(m) *(11.03 MW)* sustained; 4 shafts
Speed, knots: 31. **Range, miles:** 3,000 at 17 kt; 1,500 at 30 kt
Complement: 53

Missiles: SSM: 4 McDonnell Douglas Harpoon; active radar homing to 130 km *(70 n miles)* at 0.9 Mach; warhead 227 kg.
  4 IAI Gabriel II; radar or optical guidance; semi-active radar plus anti-radiation homing to 36 km *(19.4 n miles)* at 0.7 Mach; warhead 75 kg.
Guns: 2 Oerlikon 20 mm; 800 rds/min to 2 km.
  1 General Electric/General Dynamics Vulcan Phalanx 6-barrelled 20 mm Mk 15; 3,000 rds/min combined to 1.5 km anti-missile.
  2 or 4—12.7 mm (twin or quad) MGs.
Countermeasures: Decoys: 1—45-tube, 4—24-tube, 4 single-tube chaff launchers.
ESM/ECM: Elisra NS 9003/5; intercept and jammer.
Combat data systems: IAI Reshet datalink.
Radars: Air/surface search: Thomson-CSF TH-D 1040 Neptune; G-band.
Fire control: Selenia Orion RTN-10X; I/J-band.

Programmes: First two of the original class of five Saar 4.5s, before conversions from Saar 4s started.
Structure: The CIWS mounted in the eyes of the ship replaced the 40 mm gun. Others of the class extensively modernised under the Nirit programme.
Operational: The Hellstar RPV project has been cancelled. The davits aft are for special forces boats, and replace the former helicopter capability.

UPDATED

ALIYA 6/1997* / 0080067

15 DABUR CLASS (COASTAL PATROL CRAFT) (PC)

860-920 series

Displacement, tons: 39 full load
Dimensions, feet (metres): 64.9 × 18 × 5.8 *(19.8 × 5.5 × 1.8)*
Main machinery: 2 GM 12V-71TA diesels; 840 hp *(627 kW)* sustained; 2 shafts
  About 8 have more powerful GE engines.
Speed, knots: 19; 30 (GE engines). **Range, miles:** 450 at 13 kt
Complement: 6/9 depending on armament

Guns: 2 Oerlikon 20 mm; 800 rds/min to 2 km.
  2—12.7 mm MGs. Carl Gustav 84 mm portable rocket launchers.
Torpedoes: 2—324 mm tubes. Honeywell Mk 46; anti-submarine; active/passive homing to 11 km *(5.9 n miles)* at 40 kt; warhead 44 kg.
Depth charges: 2 racks in some.
Weapons control: Elop optronic director.
Radars: Surface search: Decca Super 101 Mk 3 or HDWS; I-band.
Sonars: Active search and attack; high frequency.

Programmes: Twelve built by Sewart Seacraft USA and remainder by Israel Aircraft Industries (RAMTA) between 1973 and 1977. Final total of 34.
Structure: Aluminium hull. Several variations in the armament. Up to eight of the class are fitted with more powerful General Electric engines to increase speed to 30 kt.
Operational: These craft have been designed for overland transport. Good rough weather performance. Portable rocket launchers are carried for anti-terrorist purposes. Not considered fast enough to cope with modern terrorist speedboats and some have been sold as Super Dvoras commissioned. Two based at Eilat, remainder at Ashdod.
Sales: Four to Argentina in 1978; four to Nicaragua in 1978 and three more in 1996; two to Sri Lanka in 1984; four to Fiji, six to Chile in 1991 and four more in 1995. Five also given to Lebanon Christian Militia in 1976 but these were returned.

UPDATED

DABUR 12/1998* / 0075862

4 RESHEF (SAAR 4) CLASS (FAST ATTACK CRAFT—MISSILE)

Name	Builders	Launched	Commissioned
NITZHON	Israel Shipyards, Haifa	10 July 1978	Sep 1978
ATSMOUT	Israel Shipyards, Haifa	3 Dec 1978	Feb 1979
MOLEDT	Israel Shipyards, Haifa	22 Mar 1979	May 1979
KOMEMIUT	Israel Shipyards, Haifa	19 July 1978	Aug 1980

Displacement, tons: 415 standard; 450 full load
Dimensions, feet (metres): 190.6 × 25 × 8 *(58 × 7.8 × 2.4)*
Main machinery: 4 MTU/Bazán 16V 956 TB91 diesels; 15,000 hp(m) *(11.03 MW)* sustained; 4 shafts
Speed, knots: 32. **Range, miles:** 1,650 at 30 kt; 4,000 at 17.5 kt
Complement: 45

Missiles: SSM: 2-4 McDonnell Douglas Harpoon (twin or quad) launchers; active radar homing to 130 km *(70 n miles)* at 0.9 Mach; warhead 227 kg.
  4-6 Gabriel II; radar or TV optical guidance; semi-active radar plus anti-radiation homing to 36 km *(20 n miles)* at 0.7 Mach; warhead 75 kg.
  Harpoons fitted with Israeli homing systems. The Gabriel II system carries a TV camera which can transmit a homing picture to the firing ship beyond the radar horizon. The missile fit currently varies in training boats—2 Harpoon, 5 Gabriel II.
Guns: 1 or 2 OTO Melara 3 in *(76 mm)*/62 compact; 85 rds/min to 16 km *(8.7 n miles)*; weight of shell 6 kg. Adapted for shore bombardment.
  2 Oerlikon 20 mm; 800 rds/min to 2 km.
  1 General Electrics/General Dynamics Vulcan Phalanx 6-barrelled 20 mm Mk 15; 3,000 rds/min combined to 1.5 km anti-missile.
  2—12.7 mm MGs.
Countermeasures: Decoys: 1—45-tube, 4— or 6—24-tube, 4 single-tube chaff launchers.
ESM/ECM: Elisra NS 9003/5; intercept and jammer.
Combat data systems: IAI Reshet datalink.
Radars: Air/surface search: Thomson-CSF TH-D 1040 Neptune; G-band; range 33 km *(18 n miles)* for 2 m² target.
Fire control: Selenia Orion RTN 10X; I/J-band.
Sonars: EDO 780; VDS; occasionally fitted in some of the class.

Modernisation: Some of the class modernised to Nirit standards and transferred to the 'Saar 4.5' class. Gabriel III SSM did not go into production. This programme continues.
Sales: Nine built for South Africa in Haifa and Durban. One transferred to Chile late 1979, one in February 1981, and two more in June 1997. Two are planned to go to Sri Lanka in 2000.

UPDATED

SAAR 4 (deleted SAAR 2 in background) 6/1995* / 0080065

SAAR 4 10/1999* / 0075863

SAAR 4 (with VDS) 2/1999* / 0080066

13 SUPER DVORA CLASS (FAST ATTACK CRAFT—GUN) (PCF)

811-819 (Mk I)   **820-823 (Mk II)**

Displacement, tons: 54 full load
Dimensions, feet (metres): 71 × 18 × 5.9 screws *(21.6 × 5.5 × 1.8)* (Mk I)
   82 × 18.4 × 3.6 *(25 × 5.6 × 1.1)* (Mk II)
Main machinery: 2 Detroit 16V-92TA diesels; 1,380 hp *(1.03 MW)* sustained; 2 shafts (Mk I)
   2 MTU 12V 396 TE94 diesels; 4,175 hp(m) *(3.07 MW)* sustained; 2 ASD 16 drives (Mk II)
Speed, knots: 36 or 46 (Mk II). **Range, miles:** 1,200 at 17 kt
Complement: 10 (1 officer)

Missiles: SSM Hellfire; range 8 km *(4.3 n miles)*; can be carried.
Guns: 2 Oerlikon 20 mm/80 or Bushmaster 25 mm/87 Mk 96 or 3 Typhoon 12.7 mm (triple) MGs.
   2—12.7 or 7.62 mm MGs. 1—84 mm rocket launcher.
Depth charges: 2 racks.
Weapons control: Elop MSIS optronic director.
Radars: Surface search: Raytheon; I-band.

Programmes: An improvement on the Dabur design ordered in March 1987 from Israel Aircraft Industries (RAMTA). First started trials in November 1988, and first two commissioned in June 1989. First 10 are Mk I. From 820 onwards the ships are fitted with more powerful engines for a higher top speed and surface drives which greatly reduce maximum draft. First Mk II commissioned in 1993. The three engined Mk III design was cancelled.
Structure: All gun armament and improved speed and endurance compared with the prototype Dvora. SSM, depth charges, torpedoes or a 130 mm MRL can be fitted if required.
Operational: Two (Mk II) are based at Eilat, the remainder at Haifa. The 25 mm or 12.7 mm Gatling guns can be operated by joystick control from the bridge. Hellfire SSM is sometimes carried.
Sales: Six Mk I sold to Sri Lanka in 1988 and four to Eritrea in 1993. One Mk II to Sri Lanka in 1995 and three more in 1996. One to Slovenia in 1996 and a second in 1997. Two to India in 1997, with more building under licence in India.

UPDATED

SUPER DVORA Mk II 820   *1995*, IAI /* 0080068

SUPER DVORA 819   *4/1996* /* 0080069

SUPER DVORA 815 (with Typhoon gun)   *1997, General Dynamics*

3 BOBCAT (COASTGUARD) CLASS (PB)

Displacement, tons: 36 full load
Dimensions, feet (metres): 72.2 × 23 × 3 *(22 × 7 × 0.9)*
Main machinery: 2 ADE 444 TI 12V diesels; 2,000 hp *(1.5 MW)*; 2 Castoldi water-jets
Speed, knots: 32. **Range, miles:** 530 at 22 kt
Complement: 16 (1 officer)
Guns: 1 Oerlikon 20 mm.
Radars: Surface search: I-band.

Comment: Ordered in November 1997 from T Craft International, Cape Town. One in service by mid-1998 and two more by late 1998. Catamaran hulls capable of carrying 15 troops. Can carry an RIB in the stern well. Based at Eilat and may replace Daburs in the Gulf of Aqaba.

UPDATED

COASTGUARD (SAN colours)   *8/1996*, South African Navy /* 0012578

AUXILIARIES

Notes: (1) Two new construction landing ships are planned by the Navy to transport large numbers of troops. No funds available. A 'Newport' class *Peoria* LST 1183 has been authorised for lease from the US but this has not been confirmed.
(2) A ro-ro ship *Queshet* is used for research and development. Built in Japan in 1979 and formerly used as a general purpose cargo ship.
(3) Two former merchant ships *Nir* and *Naharya* are used as alongside tenders in Haifa and Eilat respectively.

1 ASHDOD CLASS (LCT)

Name	No	Builders	Commissioned
ASHDOD	61	Israel Shipyards, Haifa	1966

Displacement, tons: 400 standard; 730 full load
Dimensions, feet (metres): 205.5 × 32.8 × 5.8 *(62.7 × 10 × 1.8)*
Main machinery: 3 MWM diesels; 1,900 hp(m) *(1.4 MW)*; 3 shafts
Speed, knots: 10.5
Complement: 20
Guns: 2 Oerlikon 20 mm.

Comment: Used as a trials ship for Barak VLS. Based at Ashdod but refitted at Eilat in 1999.

UPDATED

ASHDOD   *3/1989* /* 0080070

SHIPBORNE AIRCRAFT

Numbers/Type: 1 Aerospatiale SA 366G Dauphin.
Operational speed: 140 kt *(260 km/h)*.
Service ceiling: 15,000 ft *(4,575 m)*.
Range: 410 n miles *(758 km)*.
Role/Weapon systems: Air Force SAR/MR helicopters acquired in 1985 and primarily SAR/MR. Sensors: Israeli-designed radar/FLIR systems. Integrated Elop MSIS for OTHT. Weapons: Unarmed. *VERIFIED*

Numbers/Type: 4 Eurocopter AS 565SA Sea Panther.
Operational speed: 165 kt *(305 km/h)*.
Service ceiling: 16,700 ft *(5,100 m)*.
Range: 483 n miles *(895 km)*.
Role/Weapon systems: Built by American Eurocopter in Texas. Three delivered by October 1998 with one more in 1999. Sensors: Telephonics search radar; Elop MSIS for OTHT. Weapons: Unarmed. *UPDATED*

LAND-BASED MARITIME AIRCRAFT

Notes: (1) Army helicopters can be used including Cobras.
(2) Two C-130 aircraft used for maritime surveillance.

Numbers/Type: 17 Bell 212.
Operational speed: 100 kt *(185 km/h)*.
Service ceiling: 13,200 ft *(4,025 m)*.
Range: 224 n miles *(415 km)*.
Role/Weapon systems: SAR and coastal helicopter surveillance tasks undertaken. Sensors: IAI EW systems. Weapons: Unarmed except for self-defence machine guns. *UPDATED*

Numbers/Type: 3 IAI 1124N Sea Scan.
Operational speed: 471 kt *(873 km/h)*.
Service ceiling: 45,000 ft *(13,725 m)*.
Range: 2,500 n miles *(4,633 km)*.
Role/Weapon systems: Air Force manned. Coastal surveillance tasks with long endurance; used for intelligence gathering. Sensors: Elta EL/M-2022 radar, IFF, MAD, Sonobuoys, and various EW systems of IAI manufacture. *VERIFIED*

ITALY
MARINA MILITARE

Headquarters Appointments

Chief of Defence Staff:
Admiral Guido Venturoni
Chief of Naval Staff:
Admiral Umberto Guarnieri
Vice Chief of Naval Staff:
Admiral Quinto Gramellini
Chief of Joint Military Intelligence:
Admiral Gianfranco Battelli
Chief of Procurement:
Engineer Admiral Ennio Piantini

Flag Officers

Commander, Allied Naval Forces, Southern Europe (Naples):
Admiral Luigi Lillo
Commander-in-Chief of Fleet (and Comedcent):
Admiral Marcello de Donno
Commander, Tyrrhenian Sea (La Spezia):
Admiral Manlio Galliccia
Commander, Ionian Sea (Taranto):
Admiral Paolo Mancinelli
Commander, Adriatic Sea (Ancona):
Vice Admiral Elio Bolongaro
Commander, Sicily (Augusta):
Vice Admiral Oreste Guglielmino
Commander, Sardinia (Cagliari):
Rear Admiral Giancarlo Porchiazzo
Commander, High Seas Fleet (COMFORAL):
Vice Admiral Roberto Cesaretti
Commander, Naval Group (COMGRUPNAVIT) (Taranto):
Rear Admiral Sergio Magarelli
Commander, Naval Group (COMGRUPNAV) (La Spezia):
Rear Admiral Luigi Binelli Mantelli
Commander, MCM Forces (MARICODRAG) (La Spezia):
Rear Admiral Gino Bizzari
Commander, Landing Force (COMFORSBA) (Brindisi):
Rear Admiral Roberto Paperini
Commander, Training Command (MARICENTADD) (Taranto):
Vice Admiral Francesco Ricci
Commander, Patrol Forces (COMFORPAT) (Augusta):
Captain Michele Saponaro
Commander, Naval Air Force (COMFORAER) (Rome):
Captain Giuseppe de Giorgi
Commander Submarine Force (COMFORSUB) (Taranto):
Captain Adriano Bugliari
Naval Commandos and Special Naval Group (COMFORSUB) (La Spezia):
Rear Admiral Giancarlo Cicchetti
Commander Coast Guard:
Vice Admiral Eugenio Sicurezza

Prefix to Ships' Names

MM (Marina Militare)

Diplomatic Representation

Naval Attaché in Bonn:
Captain Dalmazio Sauro
Naval Attaché in London:
Rear Admiral A Campregher
Naval Attaché in Moscow:
Captain Pio Bracco
Naval Attaché in Paris:
Captain Andrea Porto
Naval Attaché in Washington:
Captain Giovanni Bortolato

Bases

Regional Commands: La Spezia (Tyrrhenian Sea), Taranto (Ionian Sea), Ancona (Adriatic Sea), Messina (Sicily), La Maddalena (Sardinia).
Main bases (Major Arsenals/Navy Shipyards): Taranto, La Spezia.
Secondary base (Minor Arsenal/Navy Shipyard): Augusta.
Minor bases: Brindisi, La Maddalena, Messina.

Organisation

High-Sea Forces Command (COMFORAL) including all Major and Amphibious Ships. Based in Taranto with subordinated command (deputy) in La Spezia.
Coastal Forces Command (COMFORCOS) Corvettes and OPVs. Based in Augusta.
Naval Air Command. Based at Santa Rosa, Rome.
Submarine Force Command. Based at Taranto.
Mine Countermeasures Command. Based at La Spezia.
Special Forces Command (COMSUBIN) Commandos and support craft. Based near La Spezia.

Strength of the Fleet

Type	Active	Building (Planned)
Submarines	8	2
Aircraft Carriers	1	—
Cruisers	1	—
Destroyers	4	2 (2)
Frigates	16	—
Corvettes	8	—
Offshore Patrol Vessels	8	4 (3)
Coastal Patrol Craft	3	1
LPD/LHA	3	1
Minehunters/sweepers	12	—
Survey/Research Ships	7	1
Replenishment Tankers	3	—
Harbour Tankers	14	—
Fleet Support Ship	1	—
Coastal Transports	8	—
Sail Training Ships	7	—
Training Ships	5	—
Lighthouse Tenders	5	—
Salvage Ships	2	—
Repair Ships	3	—

Personnel

(a) 2000: 40,000 (4,950 officers) including 1,550 naval air and 2,100 naval infantry (amphib) and 1,800 (security)
(b) 1 year's national service (about 10,600 are conscripts)

Naval Air Arm

1 LRMP squadron—Bréguet Atlantic (No 41, Catania); operated by Navy with Air Force support and maintenance
2 SH-3D/H helicopter squadrons (1st and 3rd based at Luni and Catania respectively)
3 AB 212 helicopter squadrons (2nd, 4th and 5th based at Luni, Taranto and Catania respectively)
1 AV-8B Harrier II squadron at Grottaglie, Taranto (2 TAV-8B plus 16 AV-8B)
1 amphibious squadron at Taranto (AB 212 and SH-3D)

Naval Infantry

A Landing Force Command was established in 1998 including a collaborative Spanish/Italian amphibious brigade (SIAF). Landing Force Command is based at Brindisi and comprises the San Marco assault regiment (two assault battalions), the Carlotto support regiment (one logistic and one training battalion) and a Landing Craft Group. The Amphibious assault air squadron has seven modified SH-3D and eight modified AB-212 helicopters.

Mercantile Marine

Lloyd's Register of Shipping:
1,389 vessels of 8,048,464 tons gross

DELETIONS

Patrol Forces

1997 *Gheppio*
1998 *Falcone, Astore, Mogano*
1999 *Grifone, Condor*

Survey Ships

1999 *Pioppo*

Auxiliaries

1999 *Piave, MOC 1203* (to Albania), *1202, 1205, Paolucci*

PENNANT LIST

Submarines

S 518	Nazario Sauro
S 519	Fecia di Cossato
S 520	Leonardo da Vinci
S 521	Guglielmo Marconi
S 522	Salvatore Pelosi
S 523	Giuliano Prini
S 524	Primo Longobardo
S 525	Gianfranco Gazzana Priaroggia

Light Aircraft Carriers

C 551	Giuseppe Garibaldi

Cruisers

C 550	Vittorio Veneto

Destroyers

D 550	Ardito
D 551	Audace
D 560	Luigi Durand de la Penne
D 561	Francesco Mimbelli

Frigates

F 564	Lupo
F 565	Sagittario
F 566	Perseo
F 567	Orsa
F 570	Maestrale
F 571	Grecale
F 572	Libeccio
F 573	Scirocco
F 574	Aliseo
F 575	Euro
F 576	Espero
F 577	Zeffiro
F 581	Carabiniere
F 582	Artigliere
F 583	Aviere
F 584	Bersagliere
F 585	Granatiere

Corvettes

F 551	Minerva
F 552	Urania
F 553	Danaide
F 554	Sfinge
F 555	Driade
F 556	Chimera
F 557	Fenice
F 558	Sibilla

Patrol Forces

P 401	Cassiopea
P 402	Libra
P 403	Spica
P 404	Vega
P 405	Esploratore
P 406	Sentinella
P 407	Vedetta
P 408	Staffetta (bldg)
P 495	Bambu
P 500	Palma
5431	Storione
5433	Squalo

Minehunters

M 5550	Lerici
M 5551	Sapri
M 5552	Milazzo
M 5553	Vieste
M 5554	Gaeta
M 5555	Termoli
M 5556	Alghero
M 5557	Numana
M 5558	Crotone
M 5559	Viareggio
M 5560	Chioggia
M 5561	Rimini

Amphibious Forces

L 9892	San Giorgio
L 9893	San Marco
L 9894	San Giusto

Survey and Research Ships

A 5303	Ammiraglio Magnaghi
A 5305	Murena
A 5306	Mirto
A 5315	Raffaele Rossetti
A 5320	Vincenzo Martellotta
A 5353	Aretusa
A 5354	Galatea

Auxiliaries

A 5302	Caroly
A 5309	Anteo
A 5310	Proteo
A 5311	Palinuro
A 5312	Amerigo Vespucci
A 5313	Stella Polare
A 5316	Corsaro II
A 5317	Atlante
A 5318	Prometeo
A 5319	Ciclope
A 5322	Capricia
A 5323	Orsa Maggiore
A 5324	Titano
A 5325	Polifemo
A 5326	Etna
A 5327	Stromboli
A 5328	Gigante
A 5329	Vesuvio
A 5330	Saturno
A 5331	MOC 1201
S 5334	MOC 1204
A 5347	Gorgona
A 5348	Tremiti
A 5349	Caprera
A 5351	Pantelleria
A 5352	Lipari
A 5353	Capri
A 5356	Basento
A 5357	Bradano
A 5358	Brenta
A 5359	Bormida
A 5364	Ponza
A 5365	Tenace
A 5366	Levanzo
A 5367	Tavolara
A 5368	Palmaria
A 5370-3	MCC 1101-4
A 5375	Simeto (reserve)
A 5376	Ticino
A 5377	Tirso
A 5378	Aragosta
A 5379	Astice
A 5380	Mitilo
A 5381	Polipo
A 5382	Porpora
A 5383	Procida
A 5384	Alpino
Y 413	Porto Fossone
Y 416	Porto Torres
Y 417	Porto Corsini
Y 421	Porto Empedocle
Y 422	Porto Pisano
Y 423	Porto Conte
Y 425	Portoferraio
Y 426	Portovenere
Y 428	Porto Salvo
Y 443	Riva Trigoso
Y 498	Mario Marino
Y 499	Alcide Pedretti
Y 0240	Porto d'Ischia

SUBMARINES

0 + 2 (2) TYPE 212A (SSK)

Name	No	Builders	Laid down	Launched	Commissioned
—	S 526	Fincantieri, Muggiano	Jan 2001	Nov 2002	Feb 2005
—	S 527	Fincantieri, Muggiano	Apr 2002	Apr 2004	May 2006

Displacement, tons: 1,450 surfaced; 1,830 dived
Dimensions, feet (metres): 183.4 × 23 × 19.7
 (55.9 × 7 × 6)
Main machinery: Diesel-electric; 1 MTU 16V 396 diesel;
 4,243 hp(m) *(3.12 MW)*; 1 alternator; 1 Siemens PEM motor;
 3,875 hp(m) *(2.85 MW)*; 1 shaft; Siemens/HDW PEM 9 fuel
 cell (AIP) modules; 306 kW; sodium sulphide high-energy
 batteries
Speed, knots: 20 dived; 12 surfaced
Range, miles: 8,000 at 8 kt surfaced; 420 at 8 kt dived
Complement: 27 (8 officers)

Torpedoes: 6—21 in *(533 mm)* bow tubes; water ram discharge;
 Whitehead A184 Mod 3 and STN DM 2A4. Total 12 weapons.
Mines: In lieu of torpedoes.
Countermeasures: Decoys: C 303 Torpedo countermeasures.
 ESM: Elettronica BLD 727 or DASA FL 1800U; intercept.
Weapons control: Kongsberg MSI-90U TFCS.
Radars: Navigation: BPS 704; I-band.
Sonars: STN Atlas Elektronik DBQS-40; passive ranging and
 intercept; FAS-3 Flank and TAS-3 clip on passive towed array.
 STN Atlas Moa 3070, mine detection, active, high frequency.

Programmes: German design phase first completed in 1992 by
 ARGE 212 (HDW/TNSW) in conjunction with IKL. MoU signed
 with Germany 22 April 1996 for a common design. First pair
 ordered from Fincantieri in August 1997. First steel cut for first
 of class 19 July 1999, and for second in July 2000.
Structure: Equipped with a hybrid fuel cell/battery propulsion
 based on the Siemens PEM fuel cell technology. The
 submarine is designed with a partial double hull which has a
 larger diameter forward. This is joined to the after end by a
 short conical section which houses the fuel cell plant. Two LOX
 tanks and hydrogen stored in metal cylinders are carried
 around the circumference of the smaller hull section. Italian
 requirements included a greater diving depth, improved
 external communications, and better submerged escape
 facilities. The final design is identical to the German
 submarines.
Operational: Dived speeds up to 8 kt are projected, without use
 of main battery.

UPDATED

TYPE 212A (model)   *1996, HDW /* 0012579

4 SAURO (TYPE 1081) CLASS (SSK)

Name	No	Builders	Laid down	Launched	Commissioned
NAZARIO SAURO	S 518	Italcantieri, Monfalcone	27 June 1974	9 Oct 1976	12 Feb 1980
FECIA DI COSSATO	S 519	Italcantieri, Monfalcone	15 Nov 1975	16 Nov 1977	5 Nov 1979
LEONARDO DA VINCI	S 520	Italcantieri, Monfalcone	8 June 1978	20 Oct 1979	23 Oct 1981
GUGLIELMO MARCONI	S 521	Italcantieri, Monfalcone	23 Oct 1979	20 Sep 1980	11 Sep 1982

Displacement, tons: 1,456 surfaced; 1,631 dived
Dimensions, feet (metres): 210 × 22.5 × 18.9
 (63.9 × 6.8 × 5.7)
Main machinery: Diesel-electric; 3 Fincantieri GMT 210.16 NM
 diesels; 3,350 hp(m) *(2.46 MW)* sustained; 3 alternators;
 2.16 MW; 1 motor; 3,210 hp(m) *(2.36 MW)*; 1 shaft. AIP trial
 in *Fecia di Cossato*
Speed, knots: 11 surfaced; 19 dived; 12 snorting
Range, miles: 11,000 surfaced at 11 kt; 250 dived at 4 kt
Complement: 49 (6 officers) plus 4 trainees

Torpedoes: 6—21 in *(533 mm)* bow tubes. 12 Whitehead A184
 Mod 3; dual purpose; wire-guided; active/passive homing to
 25 km *(13.7 n miles)* at 24 kt; 17 km *(9.2 n miles)* at 38 kt;
 warhead 250 kg. Swim-out discharge.
Countermeasures: ESM: Elettronica BLD 727; radar warning.

Weapons control: SMA BSN 716(V)1 SACTIS data processing
 and computer-based TMA. CCRG FCS.
Radars: Search/navigation: SMA BPS 704; I-band.
Sonars: Selenia Elsag IPD 70/S; linear passive array;
 200 Hz-7.5 kHz; active and UWT transducers in bow (15 kHz).
 Selenia Elsag MD 100; passive ranging.
 Thomson Sintra towed array; passive; low frequency.

Programmes: Two of this class were originally ordered in 1967
 but were cancelled in the following year. Reinstated in the
 building programme in 1972. Second pair provided for in
 Legge Navale and ordered 12 February 1976.
 The discrepancy in commissioning dates of *N Sauro* and *F di
 Cossato* was due to problems over the main batteries. *F di
 Cossato* was provided with a new CGA battery which was
 satisfactory. *N Sauro* was then similarly fitted.

Modernisation: All modernised. *Fecia di Cossato* in 1990,
 Nazario Sauro in 1991, *Guglielmo Marconi* in 1992 and
 Leonardo da Vinci in 1993. New batteries have greater
 capacity, some auxiliary machinery replaced and habitability
 improved. A clip-on towed array and new weapons control
 system evaluated in *Nazario Sauro*. STN Atlas ISUS-90 TFCS to
 be fitted in all from 2002.
Structure: Diving depth, 300 m *(985 ft)* (max) and 250 m
 (820 ft) (normal). Periscopes: Pilkington Optronics CK 31
 search and CH 81 attack.
Operational: Endurance, 35 days. Reliability improved by the
 mid-life modernisation programme. *Nazario Sauro* is being
 used as a trials boat with a reduced crew and is not combat
 qualified.

UPDATED

LEONARDO DA VINCI   *5/1997, H M Steele /* 0012581

4 IMPROVED SAURO CLASS (SSK)

Name	No	Builders	Laid down	Launched	Commissioned
SALVATORE PELOSI	S 522	Fincantieri, Monfalcone	24 May 1984	29 Dec 1986	14 July 1988
GIULIANO PRINI	S 523	Fincantieri, Monfalcone	30 May 1985	12 Dec 1987	11 Nov 1989
PRIMO LONGOBARDO	S 524	Fincantieri, Monfalcone	19 Dec 1991	20 June 1992	20 May 1994
GIANFRANCO GAZZANA PRIAROGGIA	S 525	Fincantieri, Monfalcone	12 Nov 1992	26 June 1993	12 Apr 1995

Displacement, tons: 1,476 (1,653, S 524-5) surfaced; 1,662 (1,862, S 524-5) dived
Dimensions, feet (metres): 211.2 (217.8 S 524-5) × 22.3 × 18.4 *(64.4 (66.4) × 6.8 × 5.6)*
Main machinery: Diesel-electric; 3 Fincantieri GMT 210.16 SM diesels; 3,672 hp(m) *(2.7 MW)* sustained; 3 generators; 2.16 MW; 1 motor; 3,128 hp(m) *(2.3 MW)*; 1 shaft
Speed, knots: 11 surfaced; 19 dived; 12 snorting
Range, miles: 11,000 at 11 kt surfaced; 250 at 4 kt dived
Complement: 50 (7 officers)

Missiles: Capability to launch Harpoon or Exocet being considered (for S 524-5).
Torpedoes: 6—21 in *(533 mm)* bow tubes. 12 Whitehead A184 Mod 3; dual purpose; wire-guided; active/passive homing to

25 km *(13.7 n miles)* at 24 kt; 17 km *(9.2 n miles)* at 38 kt; warhead 250 kg. Swim-out discharge.
Countermeasures: ESM: Elettronica BLD-727; radar warning; 2 aerials—1 on a mast, second in search periscope.
Weapons control: SMA BSN 716(V)2 SACTIS including Link 11 (receive only) or STN Atlas ISUS 90-20.
Radars: Search/navigation: SMA BPS 704; I-band; also periscope radar for attack ranging.
Sonars: Selenia Elsag IPD 70/S; linear passive array; 200 Hz-7.5 kHz; active and UWT transducers in bow (15 kHz). Selenia Elsag MD 100S; passive ranging.

Programmes: The first two were ordered in March 1983 and the second pair in July 1988.

Modernisation: Last pair being fitted with STN Atlas ISUS 90-20 integrated sonar and upgraded SACTIS by 2001, followed by first pair starting in 2002.
Structure: Pressure hull of HY 80 steel with a central bulkhead for escape purposes. Diving depth, 300 m *(985 ft)* (test) and 600 m *(1,970 ft)* (crushing). The second pair has a slightly longer hull to give space for SSMs.
Periscopes: Kollmorgen; S 76 Mod 322 with laser rangefinder and ESM—attack; S 76 Mod 323 with radar rangefinder and ESM—search. Wave contour snort head has a very low radar profile. The last pair have anechoic tiles.
Operational: Litton Italia PL 41 inertial navigation; Ferranti autopilot (in S 522-3) or Sepa autopilot (S 524-5) Omega and Transit. Endurance, 45 days possibly increased in second pair.
UPDATED

GIULIANO PRINI   10/1999 *, B Sullivan / 0080071

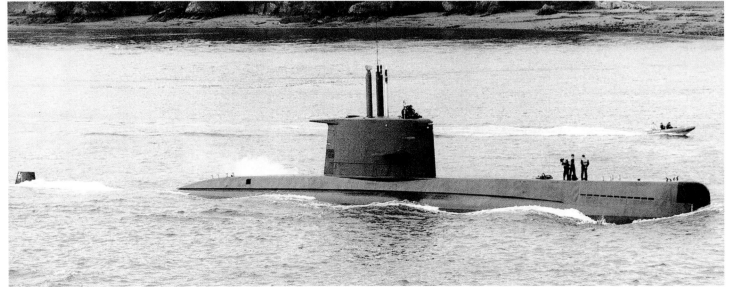

GIULIANO PRINI   9/1999 *, John Brodie / 0080072

AIRCRAFT CARRIERS

1 GARIBALDI CLASS (CVS)

Name	No	Builders	Laid down	Launched	Commissioned
GIUSEPPE GARIBALDI	C 551	Italcantieri, Monfalcone	26 Mar 1981	4 June 1983	30 Sep 1985

Displacement, tons: 10,100 standard; 13,850 full load
Dimensions, feet (metres): 591 × 110.2 × 22
(180 × 33.4 × 6.7)
Flight deck, feet (metres): 570.2 × 99.7 (173.8 × 30.4)
Main machinery: COGAG; 4 Fiat/GE LM 2500 gas turbines; 81,000 hp (60 MW) sustained; 2 shafts
Speed, knots: 30. **Range, miles:** 7,000 at 20 kt
Complement: 550 ship plus 230 air group (accommodation for 825 including Flag and staff)

Missiles: SSM: 8 OTO Melara Teseo Mk 2 (TG 2) ❶; active radar homing to 180 km (98.4 n miles) at 0.9 Mach; warhead 210 kg; sea-skimmer for last 4 km (2.2 n miles). Mk 3 with radar/IR homing to 300 km (162 n miles); warhead 160 kg can be carried.
SAM: 2 Selenia Elsag Albatros octuple launchers ❷; 48 Aspide; semi-active radar homing to 13 km (7 n miles) at 2.5 Mach; height envelope 15-5,000 m (49.2-16,405 ft); warhead 30 kg.
Guns: 6 Breda 40 mm/70 (3 twin) MB ❸; 300 rds/min to 12.5 km (6.8 n miles) anti-surface; 4 km (2.2 n miles) anti-aircraft; weight of shell 0.96 kg.
Torpedoes: 6—324 mm B-515 (2 triple) tubes ❹. Honeywell Mk 46; anti-submarine; active/passive homing to 11 km (5.9 n miles) at 40 kt; warhead 44 kg. Being replaced by new A 290.
Countermeasures: Decoys: SLQ-25 Nixie; noisemaker.
2 Breda SCLAR 105 mm 20-barrelled launchers; trains and elevates; chaff to 5 km (2.7 n miles); illuminants to 12 km (6.6 n miles). SLAT in 2002.
ESM/ECM: Elettronica Nettuno SLQ-732; integrated intercept and jamming system.

Combat data systems: IPN 20 (SADOC 2) action data automation including Links 11 and 14. SATCOM ❺.
Weapons control: 3 Alenia NA 30E electro-optical back-up for SAM. 3 Dardo NA21 for guns.
Radars: Long-range air search: Hughes SPS-52C ❻; 3D; E/F-band; range 440 km (240 n miles).
Air search: Selenia SPS-768 (RAN 3L) ❼; D-band; range 220 km (120 n miles).
SMA SPN-728; I-band; range 73 km (40 n miles); TV indicator.
Air/surface search: Selenia SPS-774 (RAN 10S) ❽; E/F-band.
Surface search/target indication: SMA SPS-702 UPX; 718 beacon; I-band.
Navigation: SMA SPN-749(V)2; I-band.
Fire control: 3 Selenia SPG-75 (RTN 30X) ❾; I/J-band; range 15 km (8 n miles) (for Albatros).
3 Selenia SPG-74 (RTN 20X) ❿; I/J-band; range 13 km (7 n miles) (for Dardo).
CCA: Selenia SPN-728(V)1; I-band.
Sonars: Raytheon DE 1160 LF; bow-mounted; active search; medium frequency.

Fixed-wing aircraft: 16 AV-8B Harrier II.
Helicopters: 18 SH-3D Sea King or EH 101 Merlin helicopters (12 in hangar, 6 on deck). The total capacity is either 16 Harriers or 18 helicopters, but this leaves no space for movement. In practice a combination is embarked (see Operational).

Programmes: Contract awarded 21 November 1977. The design work completed February 1980. Started sea trials 3 December 1984.
Modernisation: Sonar to be improved to NGS 2000 standard for LF multistatic operations in due course. Command and control installed for CJTF and CATF in 1999.
Structure: Six decks with 13 vertical watertight bulkheads. Fitted with 6.5° ski-jump and VSTOL operating equipment. Two 15 ton lifts 18 × 10 m (59 × 32.8 ft). Hangar size 110 × 15 × 6 m (361 × 49.2 × 19.7 ft). Hangar capacity is for 10 Harriers or 12 Sea Kings. Has a slightly narrower flight deck than UK 'Invincible' class. Two 'MEN' class fast personnel launches (capacity 250) can be embarked for amphibious operations or disaster relief.
Operational: Fleet Flagship. Equipped for Joint Task Force command and control. The long standing dispute between the Navy and the Air Force concerning the former's operation of fixed-wing aircraft (dating back to pre-Second World War legislation) was finally resolved by legislation passed on 29 January 1989. Embarked aircraft are operated by the Navy with the Air Force providing evaluation and maintenance. The carrier has operated in the assault role with seven SH-3D, four AB 212 and Army helicopters including six AB 205, three A 129 and two CH-47. First operational Harriers embarked for permanent duty in December 1994.

UPDATED

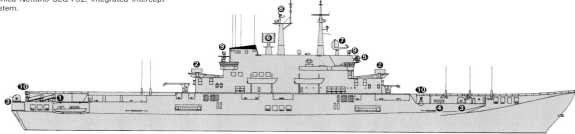

GIUSEPPE GARIBALDI
(Scale 1 : 1,200), Ian Sturton

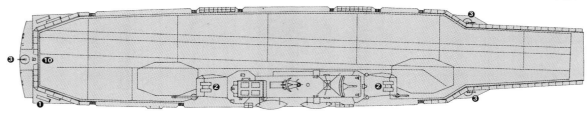

GIUSEPPE GARIBALDI
(Scale 1 : 1,200), Ian Sturton

GIUSEPPE GARIBALDI
6/1999 *, M Declerck / 0080073

GIUSEPPE GARIBALDI

5/1997, H M Steele / 0016622

GIUSEPPE GARIBALDI

6/1999*, M Declerck / 0080074

GIUSEPPE GARIBALDI

11/1998, Camil Busquets i Vilanova / 0053287

CRUISERS

1 VITTORIO VENETO CLASS (CGH)

Name	No	Builders	Laid down	Launched	Commissioned
VITTORIO VENETO	C 550	Italcantieri, Castellammare	10 June 1965	5 Feb 1967	12 July 1969

Displacement, tons: 7,500 standard; 9,500 full load
Dimensions, feet (metres): 589 × 63.6 × 19.7
(179.6 × 19.4 × 6)
Flight deck, feet (metres): 131 × 61 *(40 × 18.6)*
Main machinery: 4 Foster-Wheeler boilers (Ansaldo); 700 psi
(50 kg/cm²); 850°F *(450°C)*; 2 Tosi turbines; 73,000 hp(m)
(54 MW); 2 shafts
Speed, knots: 32. **Range, miles:** 5,000 at 17 kt
Complement: 557 (53 officers)

Missiles: SSM: 4 OTO Melara Teseo Mk 2 (TG 2) **❶**; inertial
cruise; active radar homing to 180 km *(98.4 n miles)* at
0.9 Mach; warhead 210 kg; sea-skimmer.
SAM: GDC Pomona Standard SM-1ER; Aster twin Mk 10 Mod 9
launcher **❷**; capacity for 60 missiles (including ASROC) on 3
drums; command guidance; semi-active radar homing to
64 km *(35 n miles)* at 2.5 Mach.
A/S: Honeywell ASROC; inertial guidance to 1.6-10 km *(1-5.4 n
miles)*; payload Mk 46 torpedo.
Guns: 8 OTO Melara 3 in *(76 mm)*/62 MMK **❸**; 55-65 rds/min to
8 km *(4.4 n miles)*; weight of shell 6 kg.
6 Breda 40 mm/70 (3 twin) **❹**; 300 rds/min to 12.5 km *(6.8 n
miles)* anti-surface; 4 km *(2.2 n miles)* anti-aircraft; weight of
shell 0.96 kg.
Torpedoes: 6—324 mm US Mk 32 (2 triple) tubes **❺**. Honeywell
Mk 46; anti-submarine; active/passive homing to 11 km *(5.9 n
miles)* at 40 kt; warhead 44 kg.
Countermeasures: Decoys: 2 Breda SCLAR 105 mm 20-
barrelled trainable **❻**; chaff to 5 km *(2.7 n miles)*; illuminants to
12 km *(6.6 n miles)*. SLQ-25 Nixie; towed torpedo decoy.
ESM: SLR 4; intercept.
ECM: 3 SLQ-B; 2 SLQ-C; jammers.
Combat data systems: SADOC 1 action data automation;
Link 11. SATCOM.
Weapons control: 4 Argo 10 systems for 76 mm guns. 2 Dardo
systems for 40 mm guns.
Radars: Long range air search: Hughes SPS-52C **❼**; 3D; E/F-
band.
Air search: Selenia SPS-768 (RAN 3L) **❽**; D-band.
Surface search/target indication: SMA SPS-702 **❾**; I-band.
Navigation: SMA SPS-748; I-band.
Fire control: 4 Selenia SPG-70 (RTN 10X) **❿**; I/J-band; range
40 km *(22 n miles)* (for Argo).
2 Selenia SPG-74 (RTN 20X) **⓫**; I/J-band; range 13 km *(7 n
miles)* (for Dardo).
2 Sperry/RCA SPG-55C **⓬**; G/H-band; range 51 km *(28 n
miles)* (for Standard).
IFF: Mk XII. Tacan: URN 20.
Sonars: Sangamo SQS-23G; bow-mounted; active search and
attack; medium frequency.

Helicopters: 6 AB 212ASW **⓭**.

Programmes: Projected under the 1959-60 New Construction
Programme, but her design was recast several times. Started
trials 30 April 1969. Defined as a Guided Missile Helicopter
Cruiser.

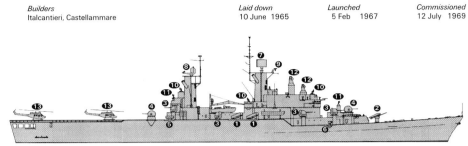

VITTORIO VENETO   *(Scale 1 : 1,500), Ian Sturton / 0010759*

VITTORIO VENETO   *3/1997, C D Yaylali / 0012583*

Modernisation: In hand from 1981 to early 1984 for
modernisation which included the four Teseo launchers and
the three twin Breda compact 40 mm.
Structure: Developed from the 'Andrea Doria' class but with
much larger helicopter squadron and improved facilities

for anti-submarine operations. Fitted with two sets of
stabilisers.
Operational: This ship is to be replaced by the LHA *Luigi Einaudi*
in 2007.

UPDATED

DESTROYERS

0 + 2 (2) HORIZON CLASS (DDG)

Displacement, tons: 6,500 full load
Dimensions, feet (metres): 497.4 oa; 464.9 wl × 57.4 × 16.7
(151.6; 141.7 × 17.5 × 5.1)
Main machinery: CODOG: 2 GE LM 2500 gas turbines;
58,480 hp(m) *(43 MW)*; 2 diesels 10,880 hp(m) *(8 MW)*; 2
shafts; cp props
Speed, knots: 29. **Range, miles:** 7,000 at 18 kt
Complement: 200 plus 35 spare

Missiles: SSM: 8 (2 quad) Teseo Mk 2 **❶**.
SAM: DCN Sylver VLS **❷** PAAMS (principal anti-air missile
system); 48 cells for Aster 15 and Aster 30 weapons.
Guns: 3 Otobreda 76 mm/62 Super Rapid **❸**.
2 Breda Oerlikon 25 mm/80 **❹**.
Torpedoes: 4 (2 twin) fixed launchers **❺**. Eurotorp Mu 90 Impact
torpedoes.

Countermeasures: Decoys: 2 Otobreda Schlar H chaff/IR flare
launchers
❻. SLAT torpedo defence system.
ESM/ECM. Elettronica JANEWS **❼**.
Combat data systems: DCN/Alenia Senit 8; Link 16.
SATCOM **❽**.
Weapons control: Sagem Vampir optronic director.
Radars: Air/surface search: S 1850M **❾**; D-band.
Surveillance/fire control: Alenia EMPAR **❿**; G-band;
multifunction.
Surface search: Alenia RASS **⓫**; E/F-band.
Fire control: 2 Alenia Marconi RTN 25X **⓬**.
Navigation: Alenia SPN 753(V)4; I-band.
Sonars: Thomson Marconi 4110CL; hull-mounted; active search
and attack; medium frequency.

Helicopters: 1 Augusta/Westland EH 101 Merlin **⓭**.

Programmes: Three-nation project for a new air defence ship
with Italy, France and UK. Joint project office established in
1993. Memorandum of Understanding for joint development
signed 11 July 1994. After UK withdrew in April 1999, an
agreement was signed on 7 September 1999 between France
and Italy to continue. Contracts expected in 2000 for a first in
service date of 2005 and second in 2007. A second pair are
planned.
Structure: Details given are subject to change. 48 cells of the
Sylver VLS system are provided by six octuple launchers. It is
possible that a VLS Mk 41 for Standard SM 2 and SM 3 may be
incorporated in the Italian ships forward of Sylver.

UPDATED

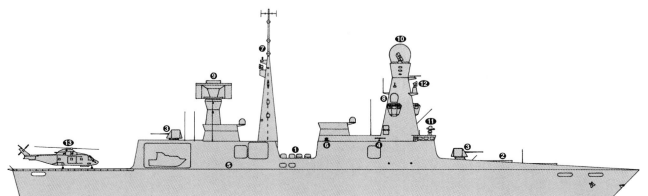

HORIZON   *(Scale 1 : 900), Ian Sturton / 0080077*

2 DE LA PENNE (ex-ANIMOSO) CLASS (DDG)

Name	No	Builders	Laid down	Launched	Commissioned
LUIGI DURAND DE LA PENNE (ex-*Animoso*)	D 560	Fincantieri, Riva Trigoso/Muggiano	20 Jan 1988	29 Oct 1989	18 Mar 1993
FRANCESCO MIMBELLI (ex-*Ardimentoso*)	D 561	Fincantieri, Riva Trigoso/Muggiano	15 Nov 1989	13 Apr 1991	19 Oct 1993

Displacement, tons: 4,330 standard; 5,400 full load
Dimensions, feet (metres): 487.4 × 52.8 × 28.2 (sonar)
 (147.7 × 16.1 × 8.6)
Flight deck, feet (metres): 78.7 × 42.7 *(24 × 13)*
Main machinery: CODOG; 2 Fiat/GE LM 2500 gas turbines;
 54,000 hp *(40.3 MW)* sustained; 2 GMT BL 230.20 DVM
 diesels; 12,600 hp(m) *(9.3 MW)* sustained; 2 shafts; cp props
Speed, knots: 31 (21 on diesels). **Range, miles:** 7,000 at 18 kt
Complement: 377 (32 officers)

Missiles: SSM: 4 or 8 OTO Melara/Matra Teseo Mk 2 (TG 2) (2 or
 4 twin) ❶; mid-course guidance; active radar homing to
 180 km *(98.4 n miles)* at 0.9 Mach; warhead 210 kg; sea-
 skimmer.
 Mk 3 with radar/IR homing to 300 km *(162 n miles)*; warhead
 160 kg in due course.
 A/S: OTO Melara/Matra Milas launcher; inertial guidance with
 command update to 55 km *(29.8 n miles)* at 0.9 Mach;
 payload Mk 46 Mod 5 or Mu 90 torpedo; 4 weapons (see
 Modernisation).
 SAM: 40 GDC Pomona Standard SM-1MR; Mk 13 Mod 4
 launcher ❷; command guidance; semi-active radar homing to
 46 km *(25 n miles)* at 2 Mach.
 Selenia Albatros Mk 2 octuple launcher for Aspide ❸; semi-
 active radar homing to 13 km *(7 n miles)* at 2.5 Mach; 16
 missiles. Automatic reloading.
Guns: 1 OTO Melara 5 in *(127 mm)*/54 ❹; 45 rds/min to 16 km
 (8.7 n miles); weight of shell 32 kg.
 3 OTO Melara 3 in *(76 mm)*/62 Super Rapid ❺; 120 rds/min to
 16 km *(8.7 n miles)*; weight of shell 6 kg. 2—20 mm.
Torpedoes: 6—324 mm B-515 (2 triple) tubes ❻. Honeywell
 Mk 46; anti-submarine; active/passive homing to 11 km *(5.9 n
 miles)* at 40 kt; warhead 44 kg. May be replaced by Whitehead
 Mu 90 in due course.
Countermeasures: Decoys: 2 CSEE Sagaie chaff launchers ❼.
 1 SLQ-25 Nixie anti-torpedo system.
ESM/ECM: Elettronica SLQ-732 Nettuno ❽; integrated intercept
 and jamming system. SLC 705.
Combat data systems: Selenia Elsag IPN 20 (SADOC 2); Links 11
 and 14. SATCOM.
Weapons control: 4 Dardo E systems (3 channels for Aspide).
 Milas TFCS.
Radars: Long-range air search: Hughes SPS-52C; 3D ❾; E/F-
 band.
 Air search: Selenia SPS-768 (RAN 3L) ❿; D-band.
 Air/surface search: Selenia SPS-774 (RAN 10S) ⓫; E/F-band.
 Surface search: SMA SPS-702 ⓬; I-band.
 Fire control: 4 Selenia SPG-76 (RTN 30X) ⓭; I/J-band (for
 Dardo).
 2 Raytheon SPG-51D ⓮; G/I-band (for SAM).
 Navigation: SMA SPN-748; I-band.
IFF: Mk X/XII. Tacan: SRN-15A.
Sonars: Raytheon DE 1164 LF-VDS; integrated bow and VDS;
 active search and attack; medium frequency (3.75 kHz (hull);
 7.5 kHz (VDS)).

Helicopters: 2 AB 212ASW ⓯; SH-3D Sea King and EH 101
 Merlin capable.

Programmes: Order placed 9 March 1986 with Riva Trigoso. All
 ships built at Riva Trigoso are completed at Muggiano after
 launching. Names changed on 10 June 1992 to honour former
 naval heroes. Acceptance dates were delayed by reduction
 gear radiated noise problems which have been resolved.
Modernisation: Both ships were to have been fitted with Milas
 ASW launchers by 2002. The project was cancelled by France
 in 1998 and is being reconsidered by Italy. New sonar dome
 being fitted in D 560 in 2000 increases draft by 1.5 m.
Structure: Kevlar armour fitted. Steel alloys used in
 superstructure. Prairie Masker noise suppression system. The
 127 mm guns are ex-'Audace' class B turrets. Fully stabilised.
 Hangar is 18.5 m in length.
Operational: GPS and Meteosat receivers fitted. The three Super
 Rapid 76 mm guns are used as a combined medium-range
 anti-surface armament and CIWS against missiles.

UPDATED

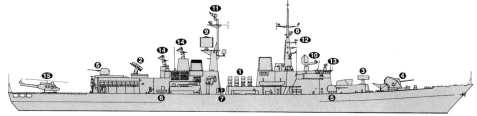

LUIGI DURAND DE LA PENNE   *(Scale 1 : 1,200), Ian Sturton /* 0052393

LUIGI DURAND DE LA PENNE   *5/1998, John Brodie /* 0052394

FRANCESCO MIMBELLI   *6/1999*, A Sharma /* 0080075

FRANCESCO MIMBELLI   *6/1999*, B Sullivan /* 0080076

2 AUDACE CLASS (DDG)

Name	No	Builders	Laid down	Launched	Commissioned
ARDITO	D 550	Italcantieri, Castellammare	19 July 1968	27 Nov 1971	5 Dec 1972
AUDACE	D 551	Fincantieri, Riva Trigoso/Muggiano	27 Apr 1968	2 Oct 1971	16 Nov 1972

Displacement, tons: 3,600 standard; 4,400 full load
Dimensions, feet (metres): 448 × 46.6 × 15.1
(136.6 × 14.2 × 4.6)
Main machinery: 4 Foster-Wheeler boilers; 600 psi *(43 kg/cm²)*;
850°F *(450°C)*; 2 turbines; 73,000 hp(m) *(54 MW)*; 2 shafts
Speed, knots: 34. **Range, miles:** 3,000 at 20 kt
Complement: 380 (30 officers)

Missiles: SSM: 8 OTO Melara/Matra Teseo Mk 2 (TG 2) (4 twin)
❶; mid-course guidance; active radar homing to 180 km
(98.4 n miles) at 0.9 Mach; warhead 210 kg; sea-skimmer.
SAM: 40 GDC Pomona Standard SM-1MR; Mk 13 Mod 4
launcher ❷; command guidance; semi-active radar homing to
46 km *(25 n miles)* at 2 Mach; height envelope 45.7 to
18,288 m *(150 to 60,000 ft)*.
Selenia Albatros octuple launcher for Aspide ❸; semi-active
radar homing to 13 km *(7 n miles)* at 2.5 Mach.
Guns: 1 OTO Melara 5 in *(127 mm)*/54 ❹; 45 rds/min to 16 km
(8.7 n miles) anti-surface; 7 km *(3.8 n miles)* anti-aircraft;
weight of shell 32 kg.
3 OTO Melara 3 in *(76 mm)*/62 Compact (*Ardito*) and 1
(*Ardito*) or 4 (*Audace*) Super Rapid ❺; 85 rds/min (Compact) or
120 rds/min (Super Rapid) to 16 km *(8.7 n miles)* anti-surface;
12 km *(6.6 n miles)* anti-aircraft; weight of shell 6 kg.
Torpedoes: 6—324 mm US Mk 32 (2 triple) tubes ❻. Honeywell
Mk 46; anti-submarine; active/passive homing to 11 km *(5.9 n
miles)* at 40 kt; warhead 44 kg. Transom tubes have been
removed.
Countermeasures: Decoys: 2 Breda 105 mm SCLAR 20-
barrelled trainable; chaff to 5 km *(2.7 n miles)*; illuminants to
12 km *(6.6 n miles)*. SLQ-25 Nixie; towed torpedo decoy.
ESM/ECM: Elettronica SLQ-732 Nettuno; integrated intercept
and jammer.
Combat data systems: Selenia Elsag IPN-20 SADOC 2 action
data automation; Links 11 and 14. SATCOM ❼.
Weapons control: 3 Dardo E FCS (3 channels for Aspide).
Selenia NA 30 optronic director. Mk 74 Mod 13 MFCS.
Radars: Long-range air search: Hughes SPS-52C ❽; 3D; E/F-
band.
Air search: Selenia SPS-768 (RAN 3L) ❾; D-band.
Air/surface search: Selenia SPS-774 (RAN 10S) ❿; E/F-band.
Surface search: SMA SPQ-2D ⓫; I-band.
Navigation: SMA SPN-748; I-band.
Fire control: 3 Selenia SPG-76 (RTN 30X) ⓬; I/J-band; range
40 km *(22 n miles)* (for Dardo E).
2 Raytheon SPG-51 ⓭; G/I-band; (for Standard).
IFF: Mk XII.
Tacan: SRN-15A.
Sonars: CWE 610; hull-mounted; active search and attack;
medium frequency.

Helicopters: 2 AB 212ASW ⓮ or EH 101 Merlin.

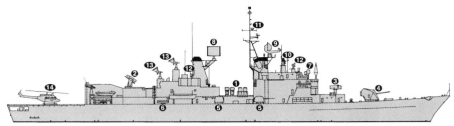

ARDITO   *(Scale 1 : 1,200), Ian Sturton* / 0012585

ARDITO   *6/1998, A Sharma* / 0052397

Programmes: It was announced in April 1966 that two new
guided missile destroyers would be built. They are basically
similar to, but an improvement in design on, that of the
'Impavido' class (now deleted).
Modernisation: B gun has been replaced by Albatros PDMS.
Stern torpedo tubes removed. *Audace* fitted with four and
Ardito one Super Rapid guns vice the 76 mm Compacts. Plans
to give *Ardito* three more by 1994 were shelved. *Ardito*
completed modernisation in March 1988 and *Audace* in early
1991. Improved EW equipment also fitted.
Structure: Both fitted with stabilisers.
Operational: First deck landing trials of EH 101 helicopters were
carried out on 14 May 1992.

VERIFIED

AUDACE   *8/1998, Giorgio Ghiglione* / 0052396

FRIGATES

8 MAESTRALE CLASS (FFG)

Name	No	Builders	Laid down		Launched		Commissioned	
MAESTRALE	F 570	Fincantieri, Riva Trigoso	8 Mar	1978	2 Feb	1981	6 Mar	1982
GRECALE	F 571	Fincantieri, Muggiano	21 Mar	1979	12 Sep	1981	5 Feb	1983
LIBECCIO	F 572	Fincantieri, Riva Trigoso	1 Aug	1979	7 Sep	1981	5 Feb	1983
SCIROCCO	F 573	Fincantieri, Riva Trigoso	26 Feb	1980	17 Apr	1982	20 Sep	1983
ALISEO	F 574	Fincantieri, Riva Trigoso	10 Aug	1980	29 Oct	1982	7 Sep	1983
EURO	F 575	Fincantieri, Riva Trigoso	15 Apr	1981	25 Apr	1983	24 Jan	1984
ESPERO	F 576	Fincantieri, Riva Trigoso	29 July	1982	19 Nov	1983	4 May	1984
ZEFFIRO	F 577	Fincantieri, Riva Trigoso	15 Mar	1983	19 May	1984	4 May	1985

Displacement, tons: 2,500 standard; 3,200 full load
Dimensions, feet (metres): 405 × 42.5 × 15.1
(122.7 × 12.9 × 4.6)
Flight deck, feet (metres): 89 × 39 *(27 × 12)*
Main machinery: CODOG; 2 Fiat/GE LM 2500 gas turbines; 50,000 hp *(37.3 MW)* sustained; 2 GMT BL 230.20 DVM diesels; 12,600 hp(m) *(9.3 MW)* sustained; 2 shafts; acbLIPS cp props
Speed, knots: 32 gas; 21 diesels. **Range, miles:** 6,000 at 16 kt
Complement: 232 (24 officers)

Missiles: SSM: 4 OTO Melara Teseo Mk 2 (TG 2) ❶; mid-course guidance; active radar homing to 180 km *(98.4 n miles)*; warhead 210 kg; sea-skimmer. Mk 3 with radar/IR homing to 300 km *(162 n miles)*; warhead 160 kg in due course.
SAM: Selenia Albatros octuple launcher; 16 Aspide ❷; semi-active homing to 13 km *(7 n miles)* at 2.5 Mach; height envelope 15-5,000 m *(49.2-16,405 ft)*; warhead 30 kg.
Guns: 1 OTO Melara 5 in *(127 mm)*/54 automatic ❸; 45 rds/min to 16 km *(8.7 n miles)* anti-surface; 7 km *(3.8 n miles)* anti-aircraft; weight of shell 32 kg; fires chaff and illuminants.
4 Breda 40 mm/70 (2 twin) compact ❹; 300 rds/min to 12.5 km *(6.8 n miles)* anti-surface; 4 km *(2.2 n miles)* anti-aircraft; weight of shell 0.96 kg.
2 Oerlikon 20 mm fitted for Gulf deployments in 1990-91.
2 Breda Oerlikon 25 mm/90 (twin) tested in *Espero*.
Torpedoes: 6—324 mm US Mk 32 (2 triple) tubes ❺. Honeywell Mk 46; anti-submarine; active/passive homing to 11 km *(5.9 n miles)* at 40 kt; warhead 44 kg.
2—21 in *(533 mm)* B516 tubes in transom ❻. Whitehead A184; dual purpose; wire-guided; active/passive homing to 17 km *(9.2 n miles)* at 38 kt; 25 km *(13.7 n miles)* at 24 kt; warhead 250 kg.
Countermeasures: Decoys: 2 Breda 105 mm SCLAR 20-tubed trainable chaff rocket launchers ❼; chaff to 5 km *(2.7 n miles)*; illuminants to 12 km *(6.6 n miles)*. 2 Dagaie chaff launchers.
SLQ-25; towed torpedo decoy. Prairie Masker; noise suppression system.
ESM: Elettronica SLR-4; intercept.
ECM: 2 SLQ-D; jammers.
Combat data systems: IPN 20 (SADOC 2) action data automation; Link 11. SATCOM ❽.
Weapons control: NA 30 for Albatros and 5 in guns. 2 Dardo for 40 mm guns.
Radars: Air/surface search: Selenia SPS-774 (RAN 10S) ❾; E/F-band.
Surface search: SMA SPS-702 ❿; I-band.
Navigation: SMA SPN-703; I-band.
Fire control: Selenia SPG-75 (RTN 30X) ⓫; I/J-band (for Albatros and 12.7 mm gun).
2 Selenia SPG-74 (RTN 20X) ⓬; I/J-band; range 15 km *(8 n miles)* (for Dardo).
IFF: Mk XII.

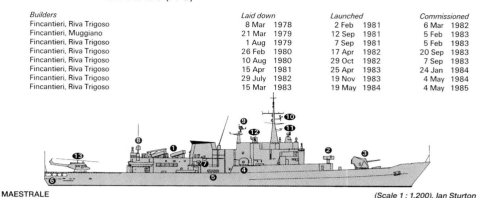

MAESTRALE   *(Scale 1 : 1,200), Ian Sturton*

MAESTRALE   *4/1999*, Giorgio Ghiglione /* 0080080

Sonars: Raytheon DE 1164; hull-mounted; VDS; active/passive attack; medium frequency. VDS can be towed at up to 28 kt. Maximum depth 300 m. Modified to include mine detection active high frequency.

Helicopters: 2 AB 212ASW ⓭.

Programmes: First six ordered December 1976 and last pair in October 1980. All Riva Trigoso ships completed at Muggiano after launch.

Modernisation: Hull and VDS sonars modified from 1994 to give better shallow water performance and a mine detection capability.
Structure: There has been a notable increase of 34 ft in length and 5 ft in beam over the 'Lupo' class to provide for the fixed hangar and VDS, the result providing more comfortable accommodation but a small loss of top speed. Fitted with stabilisers.
Operational: A towed passive LF array may be attached to the VDS body. F 576 fitted in 1991 with an Oerlikon Breda KBA 25 mm gun for evaluation. ***UPDATED***

EURO   *3/1999*, Maritime Photographic /* 0080081

4 LUPO CLASS (FFG)

Name	No	Builders	Laid down	Launched	Commissioned
LUPO	F 564	Fincantieri, Riva Trigoso	11 Oct 1974	29 July 1976	12 Sep 1977
SAGITTARIO	F 565	Fincantieri, Riva Trigoso	4 Feb 1976	22 June 1977	18 Nov 1978
PERSEO	F 566	Fincantieri, Riva Trigoso	28 Feb 1977	12 July 1978	1 Mar 1980
ORSA	F 567	Fincantieri, Muggiano	1 Aug 1977	1 Mar 1979	1 Mar 1980

Displacement, tons: 2,208 standard; 2,525 full load
Dimensions, feet (metres): 371.3 × 37.1 × 12.1
 (113.2 × 11.3 × 3.7)
Main machinery: CODOG; 2 Fiat/GE LM 2500 gas turbines;
 50,000 hp *(37.3 MW)* sustained; 2 GMT BL 230.20 M diesels;
 10,000 hp(m) *(7.3 MW)* sustained; 2 shafts; acbLIPS cp props
Speed, knots: 35 turbines; 21 diesels
Range, miles: 4,350 at 16 kt
Complement: 185 (16 officers)

Missiles: SSM: 16 OTO Melara Teseo Mk 2 (TG 2) (8 twin
 launchers) ❶; mid-course guidance; active radar homing to
 180 km *(98.4 n miles)* at 0.9 Mach; warhead 210 kg; sea-
 skimmer.
 SAM: Raytheon NATO Sea Sparrow Mk 29 octuple launcher ❷;
 semi-active radar homing to 14.6 km *(8 n miles)* at 2.5 Mach;
 warhead 39 kg. 8 reloads. Updated for RIM-7M and can fire
 either Aspide or RIM-7M missiles.

Guns: 1 OTO Melara 5 in *(127 mm)*/54 ❸; 45 rds/min to 16 km
 (8.7 n miles) anti-surface; 7 km *(3.8 n miles)* anti-aircraft;
 weight of shell 32 kg.
 4 Breda 40 mm/70 (2 twin) compact ❹; 300 rds/min to
 12.5 km *(6.8 n miles)* anti-surface; 4 km *(2.2 n miles)* anti-
 aircraft; weight of shell 0.96 kg.
 2 Oerlikon 20 mm can be fitted.
Torpedoes: 6—324 mm US Mk 32 tubes ❺. Honeywell Mk 46;
 anti-submarine; active/passive homing to 11 km *(5.9 n miles)*
 at 40 kt; warhead 44 kg.
Countermeasures: Decoys: 2 Breda 105 mm SCLAR 20-tubed
 trainable ❻; chaff to 5 km *(2.7 n miles)*; illuminants to 12 km
 (6.6 n miles).
 SLQ-25 Nixie; towed torpedo decoy.
 ESM: SLR-4; intercept.
 ECM: 2 SLQ-D; jammers.
Combat data systems: IPN 20 (SADOC 2) action data
 automation; Link 11. SATCOM.

Weapons control: Argo NA10 Mod 2 for missiles and 5 in gun.
 2 Dardo for 40 mm guns.
Radars: Air search: Selenia SPS-774 (RAN 10S) ❼; E/F-band.
 Surface search/target indication: SMA SPS-702 ❽; I-band.
 Surface search: SMA SPQ-2F ❾; I-band.
 Navigation: SMA SPN-748; I-band.
 Fire control: Selenia SPG-70 (RTN 10X) ❿; I/J-band; range
 40 km *(22 n miles)* (for Argo).
 2 Selenia SPG-74 (RTN 20X) ⓫; I/J-band; range 15 km *(8 n
 miles)* (for Dardo).
 US Mk 95 Mod 1 (for SAM) ⓬; I-band.
 IFF: Mk XII.
Sonars: Raytheon DE 1160B; hull-mounted; active search and
 attack; medium frequency.

Helicopters: 1 AB 212ASW ⓭.

Modernisation: Mid-life update started in 1991 and included
 low-altitude CORA SPS-702 search radar (radome on bridge
 roof), new gyros and improved communications including
 SATCOM. All completed by early 1994. SSM launchers have
 been strengthened to take two missiles each.
Structure: 14 watertight compartments; fixed-fin stabilisers;
 telescopic hangar.
Sales: Similar ships built for Peru (4), Venezuela (6) and Iraq (4).
 Iraqi ships not delivered and transferred to the Italian Navy on
 20 January 1992 (see 'Artigliere' class).
Operational: The CORA SPS 702 radar is able to exploit ducting
 conditions allowing OTHT for SSM.

UPDATED

LUPO   *(Scale 1 : 1,200), Ian Sturton*

PERSEO   *5/1999*, A Sharma /* 0080078

PERSEO   *6/1999*, M Declerck /* 0080079

4 ARTIGLIERE (LUPO) CLASS (FLEET PATROL SHIPS) (FFG)

Name	No	Builders	Laid down	Launched	Commissioned
ARTIGLIERE (ex-Hittin)	F 582 (ex-F 14)	Fincantieri, Ancona	31 Mar 1982	27 July 1983	28 Oct 1994
AVIERE (ex-Thi Qar)	F 583 (ex-F 15)	Fincantieri, Ancona	3 Sep 1982	19 Dec 1984	4 Jan 1995
BERSAGLIERE (ex-Al Yarmouk)	F 584 (ex-F 17)	Fincantieri, Riva Trigoso	12 Mar 1984	18 Apr 1985	8 Nov 1995
GRANATIERE (ex-Al Qadisiya)	F 585 (ex-F 16)	Fincantieri, Ancona	1 Dec 1983	1 June 1985	20 Mar 1996

Displacement, tons: 2,208 standard; 2,525 full load
Dimensions, feet (metres): 371.3 × 37.1 × 12.1
(113.2 × 11.3 × 3.7)
Main machinery: CODOG; 2 Fiat/GE LM 2500 gas turbines;
50,000 hp *(37.3 MW)* sustained; 2 GMT BL 230.20 M diesels;
10,000 hp(m) *(7.3 MW)* sustained; 2 shafts; acbLIPS cp props
Speed, knots: 35 turbines; 21 diesels
Range, miles: 4,350 at 16 kt on diesels
Complement: 185 (16 officers)

ARTIGLIERE

(Scale 1 : 1,200), Ian Sturton

Missiles: SSM: 8 OTO Melara Teseo Mk 2 (TG 2) **❶**; mid-course
guidance; active radar homing to 180 km *(98.4 n miles)* at
0.9 Mach; warhead 210 kg; sea-skimmer.
SAM: Selenia Elsag Aspide octuple launcher **❷**; semi-active radar
homing to 14.6 km *(8 n miles)* at 2.5 Mach; warhead 39 kg.
8 reloads.
Guns: 1 OTO Melara 5 in *(127 mm)*/54 **❸**; 45 rds/min to 16 km
(8.7 n miles) anti-surface; 7 km *(3.8 n miles)* anti-aircraft;
weight of shell 32 kg.
4 Breda 40 mm/70 (2 twin) compact **❹**; 300 rds/min to
12.5 km *(6.8 n miles)* anti-surface; 4 km *(2.2 n miles)* anti-
aircraft; weight of shell 0.96 kg.
2 Oerlikon 20 mm can be fitted.
Countermeasures: Decoys: 2 Breda 105 mm SCLAR 20-tubed
trainable **❺**; chaff to 5 km *(2.7 n miles)*; illuminants to 12 km
(6.6 n miles).
ESM/ECM: Selenia SLQ-747 (INS-3M); intercept and jammer.
Combat data systems: IPN 10 mini SADOC action data
automation; Link 11. SATCOM.

Weapons control: 2 Elsag Mk 10 Argo with NA 21 directors for
missiles and 5 in gun. 2 Dardo for 40 mm guns.
Radars: Air search: Selenia SPS-774 (RAN 10S) **❻**; E/F-band.
Surface search: Selenia SPQ-712 (RAN 12 L/X) **❼**; I-band.
Navigation: SMA SPN-703; I-band.
Fire control: 2 Selenia SPG-70 (RTN 10X) **❽**; I/J-band; range
40 km *(22 n miles)* (for Argo).
2 Selenia SPG-74 (RTN 20X) **❾**; I/J-band; range 15 km *(8 n
miles)* (for Dardo).
IFF: Mk XII.

Helicopters: 1 AB 212 **❿**.

Programmes: On 20 January 1992 it was decided to transfer the
four ships built for Iraq to the Italian Navy. The original sale to
Iraq was first delayed by payment problems and then

cancelled in 1990 when UN embargoes were placed on
military sales to Iraq. After several attempts by the Italian
Defence Committee to cancel the project, finance was finally
authorised in July 1993.
Modernisation: The details given are for the ships as modernised
for Italian service. All ASW equipment removed, new combat
and communications systems to Italian standards and a major
upgrading of damage control and accommodation facilities.
One unit is to be fitted with the lightweight 127 mm/54 gun
for trials.
Operational: The first two commissioned with only machinery,
damage control and accommodation upgraded. The weapon
systems' changes were made during 1995. The last pair
entered service fully modified. Official designation is Fleet
Patrol Ships. All based at La Spezia.

UPDATED

GRANATIERE

*5/1999 *, Giorgio Ghiglione / 0080082*

2 ALPINO CLASS (MCS/AG)

Name	No	Builders	Laid down	Launched	Commissioned
ALPINO (ex-Circe)	A 5384 (ex-F 580)	Fincantieri, Riva Trigoso	27 Feb 1963	10 June 1967	14 Jan 1968
CARABINIERE (ex-Climene)	F 581	Fincantieri, Riva Trigoso	9 Jan 1965	30 Sep 1967	28 Apr 1968

Displacement, tons: 2,400 standard; 2,700 full load
Dimensions, feet (metres): 371.7 × 43.6 × 12.7
(113.3 × 13.3 × 3.9)
Main machinery: 4 Tosi OTV-320 diesels; 16,800 hp(m)
(12.35 MW); 2 shafts
Speed, knots: 20. **Range, miles:** 3,500 at 18 kt
Complement: 163 (13 officers)

Missiles: SAM: Alenia/DCN 8-cell VLS for Aster 15 trials
(Carabiniere); radar homing to 30 km *(16.2 n miles)* at
4.5 Mach; warhead 13 kg.
A/S: OTO Melara/Matra Milas launcher *(Carabiniere)*; command
guidance to 55 km *(29.8 n miles)* at Mach 0.9; payload Mu 90
or Mk 46 Mod 5 torpedo.
Guns: 3 *(Alpino)* or 1 *(Carabiniere)* OTO Melara 3 in *(76 mm)*/62;
60 rds/min to 16 km *(8.7 n miles)*; weight of shell 6 kg. OTO
Melara 5 in *(125 mm)*/54 to replace the 76 mm in A gun
position in *Carabiniere* in due course.
Torpedoes: 6—324 mm Whitehead (2 triple tubes) *(Carabiniere)*.
Countermeasures: ESM/ECM: Selenia SLQ-747; integrated
intercept and jammer.
Combat data systems: SADOC 3 for EMPAR trials *(Carabiniere)*.
Weapons control: 2 Argo 'O' for 3 in guns.
Radars: Air search: RCA SPS-12; D-band.
Surface search: SMA SPS-702(V)3; I-band.
Navigation: SMA SPN-748; I-band.
Fire control: 2 Selenia SPG-70 (RTN 10X); I/J-band.
Alenia/Marconi EMPAR SPY 790 *(Carabiniere)*; for PAAMS;
G-band; range 50 km *(27 n miles)* for 0.1 m² target.

Helicopters: 1 AB 212ASW *(Alpino)*.

Modernisation: *Carabiniere* modified as a trials ship. B gun turret
and the Whitehead mortar have been replaced by Milas
launchers and the Aster 15 SAAM system. An oil rig type mast
on the flight deck carries the SAAM/PAAMS system radar SPY
790 installed in early 1995. *Alpino* modified as an MCMV
command and support ship 1996-97. Gun armament reduced,
A/S mortar, torpedo tubes, sonars and chaff launchers
removed. A 2.5 ton crane has been put in B gun position and a
recompression chamber embarked. Both ships have gas
turbines removed.
Structure: Stabilisers fitted.
Operational: *Alpino* is used as an MCMV command and support
ship and will remain in service to 2008. *Carabiniere* carrying
out trial firings of the complete SAAM system. *UPDATED*

CARABINIERE

3/1998, Giorgio Ghiglione / 0052403

ALPINO

*3/1999 *, Giorgio Ghiglione / 0053496*

CORVETTES

Note: 'Albatros' class *Alcione* F 544 and *Airone* F 545 are used only for harbour training.

8 MINERVA CLASS (FS)

Name	No	Builders	Laid down		Launched		Commissioned	
MINERVA	F 551	Fincantieri, Riva Trigoso	11 Mar	1985	3 Apr	1986	10 June	1987
URANIA	F 552	Fincantieri, Riva Trigoso	4 Apr	1985	21 June	1986	1 June	1987
DANAIDE	F 553	Fincantieri, Muggiano	26 June	1985	18 Oct	1986	9 Sep	1987
SFINGE	F 554	Fincantieri, Muggiano	2 Sep	1986	16 May	1987	13 Feb	1988
DRIADE	F 555	Fincantieri, Riva Trigoso	18 Mar	1988	11 Mar	1989	19 Apr	1990
CHIMERA	F 556	Fincantieri, Riva Trigoso	21 Dec	1988	7 Apr	1990	15 Jan	1991
FENICE	F 557	Fincantieri, Riva Trigoso	6 Sep	1988	9 Sep	1989	11 Sep	1990
SIBILLA	F 558	Fincantieri, Muggiano	16 Oct	1989	15 Sep	1990	16 May	1991

Displacement, tons: 1,029 light; 1,285 full load
Dimensions, feet (metres): 284.1 × 34.5 × 10.5
(86.6 × 10.5 × 3.2)
Main machinery: 2 Fincantieri GMT BM 230.20 DVM diesels; 12,600 hp(m) *(9.26 MW)* sustained; 2 shafts; cp props
Speed, knots: 24. **Range, miles:** 3,500 at 18 kt
Complement: 123 (10 officers)

Missiles: SSM: Fitted for but not with 4 or 6 Teseo Otomat between the masts.
SAM: Selenia Elsag Albatros octuple launcher **①**; 8 Aspide; semi-active radar homing to 13 km *(7 n miles)* at 2.5 Mach; height envelope 15-5,000 m *(49.2-16,405 ft)*; warhead 30 kg. Capacity for larger magazine.
Guns: 1 OTO Melara 3 in *(76 mm)*/62 Compact **②**; 85 rds/min to 16 km *(8.7 n miles)* anti-surface; 12 km *(6.6 n miles)* anti-aircraft; weight of shell 6 kg.
Torpedoes: 6—324 mm Whitehead B 515 (2 triple) tubes **③**. Honeywell Mk 46; active/passive homing to 11 km *(5.9 n miles)* at 40 kt; warhead 44 kg. Being replaced by Whitehead Mu 90.
Countermeasures: Decoys: 2 Wallop Barricade double layer launchers for chaff and IR flares. SLQ-25 Nixie; towed torpedo decoy.
ESM/ECM: Selenia SLQ-747 intercept and jammer.

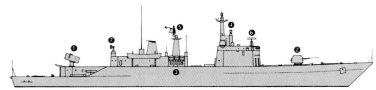

MINERVA   *(Scale 1 : 900), Ian Sturton*

Combat data systems: Selenia IPN 10 Mini SADOC action data automation; Link 11. SATCOM.
Weapons control: 1 Elsag Dardo E system. Selenia/Elsag NA 18L Pegaso optronic director **④**. Elmer TLC system.
Radars: Air/surface search: Selenia SPS-774 (RAN 10S) **⑤**; E/F-band.
Navigation: SMA SPN-728(V)2 **⑥**; I-band.
Fire control: Selenia SPG-76 (RTN 30X) **⑦**; I/J-band (for Albatros and gun).
Sonars: Raytheon/Elsag DE 1167; hull-mounted; active search and attack; 7.5-12 kHz.

Programmes: First four ordered in November 1982, second four in January 1987. A third four were planned, but this plan was overtaken by the acquisition of the 'Artigliere' class.
Structure: The funnels remodelled to reduce turbulence and IR signature. Two fin stabilisers.
Operational: Omega transit fitted. Intended for a number of roles including EEZ patrol, fishery protection and Commanding Officers' training. All based at Augusta, Sicily.

UPDATED

SIBILLA   *5/1999*, H M Steele /* 0080083

SFINGE   *6/1998, Maritime Photographic /* 0052407

SHIPBORNE AIRCRAFT

Note: 56 NH 90s planned in due course.

Numbers/Type: 16/2 AV-8B/TAV-8B Harrier II Plus.
Operational speed: 562 kt *(1,041 km/h)*.
Service ceiling: 50,000 ft *(15,240 m)*.
Range: 800 n miles *(1,480 km)*.
Role/Weapon systems: Two trainers delivered in July 1991 plus 16 front-line aircraft from 1994 to December 1997. Sensors: Radar derived from Hughes APG-65, FLIR, ALQ-164 ESM. Weapons: Maverick ASM; AMRAAM AIM-120 AAM; bombs and 25 mm cannon.

VERIFIED

HARRIER 5/1992, Giorgio Ghiglione / 0012978

Numbers/Type: 4 Agusta/Westland EH 101 Merlin.
Operational speed: 160 kt *(296 km/h)*.
Service ceiling: 15,000 ft *(4,572 m)*.
Range: 550 n miles *(1,019 km)*.
Role/Weapon systems: Primary anti-submarine role with secondary anti-surface and troop carrying capabilities. 16 ordered in October 1995 and approved in July 1997 for delivery which started for the first four ASW versions by July 2000. Total of eight for ASW, four for AEW and four utility/assault by 2004. 18 more ordered in 2000 (10 ASW, 8 utility/assault). Sensors: Eliradar APS-784 (E in AEW version) radar, Bendix dipping sonar, Galileo FLIR, ALR 735 ESM, ELT 156X ESM, Marconi RALM 1 decoys, Link 11, sonobuoy acoustic processor. Weapons: ASW; four Mk 46 or Mu 90 torpedoes. ASV; four Marte ASM capability for guidance of ship-launched SSM.

UPDATED

MERLIN 12/1999*, EH Industries / 0067279

Numbers/Type: 51 Agusta-Bell 212.
Operational speed: 106 kt *(196 km/h)*.
Service ceiling: 17,000 ft *(5,180 m)*.
Range: 360 n miles *(667 km)*.
Role/Weapon systems: ASW/ECM/Assault helicopter; mainly deployed to escorts, but also shore-based for ASW support duties and nine used for assault. Five are for EW. Sensors: Selenia APS 705 (APS 707 in five 'Artigliere' class aircraft) search/attack radar, AQS-13B dipping sonar or GUFO (not in Artigliere aircraft) ESM/ECM. Weapons: ASW; two Mk 46 torpedoes. Assault aircraft have an armoured cabin, no sensors and are armed with two 7.62 mm MGs and two 70 mm MRLs.

UPDATED

BELL 212 6/1999*, M Declerck / 0080084

Numbers/Type: 26 Agusta-Sikorsky SH-3D/H Sea King.
Operational speed: 120 kt *(222 km/h)*.
Service ceiling: 12,200 ft *(3,720 m)*.
Range: 630 n miles *(1,165 km)*.
Role/Weapon systems: ASW helicopter; embarked in larger ASW ships, including CVL; also shore-based for medium ASV-ASW in Mediterranean Sea; nine are fitted for ASV, 12 with ASW and EW equipment, six transport/assault. Sensors: Selenia APS 705 search radar, AQS-13B dipping sonar, sonobuoys. ESM/ECM. Weapons: ASW; four Mk 46 torpedoes. ASV; two Marte 2 missiles. Assault aircraft have armoured cabins, no sensors, and are armed with two 7.62 mm MGs.

UPDATED

SEA KING 4/1998, Diego Quevedo / 0052405

LAND-BASED MARITIME AIRCRAFT

Note: Collaboration with Germany for a replacement MPA. MoU signed in 1996 to develop either Atlantique 2 or Orion P-3C airframes with own avionics.

Numbers/Type: 17 Bréguet Atlantic 1.
Operational speed: 355 kt *(658 km/h)*.
Service ceiling: 32,800 ft *(10,000 m)*.
Range: 4,855 n miles *(8,995 km)*.
Role/Weapon systems: Air Force shore-based for long-range MR and shipping surveillance; wartime role includes ASW support to helicopters. Sensors: Thomson-CSF Iguane radar, ECM/ESM, MAD, sonobuoys; Marconi ASQ-902 acoustic system. Weapons: ASW; nine torpedoes (including Mk 46 torpedoes) or depth bombs or mines.

VERIFIED

Numbers/Type: 16 Panavia Tornado IDS.
Operational speed: 2.2 Mach.
Service ceiling: 80,000 ft *(24,385 m)*.
Range: 1,500 n miles *(2,780 km)*.
Role/Weapon systems: Air Force swing wing strike and recce; part of a force of a total of 100 aircraft of which 16 are used for maritime operations based near Bari. Sensors: Texas instruments nav/attack systems. Weapons: ASV; four Kormoran missiles; two 27 mm cannon. AD; four AIM-9L Sidewinder.

VERIFIED

PATROL FORCES

2 BAMBU (AGAVE) CLASS (OFFSHORE PATROL VESSELS) (OPV)

BAMBU P 495 (ex-M 5521)   **PALMA** P 500 (ex-M 5525)

Displacement, tons: 375 standard; 405 full load
Dimensions, feet (metres): 144 × 25.6 × 8.5 *(43 × 7.8 × 2.6)*
Main machinery: 2 GM 8-268A diesels; 880 hp *(656 kW)*; 2 shafts
Speed, knots: 13.5. **Range, miles:** 2,500 at 10 kt
Complement: 38 (5 officers)
Guns: 2 Oerlikon 20 mm (twin).
Radars: Navigation: SPN-750; I-band.

Comment: Non-magnetic minesweepers of composite wooden and alloy construction similar to those transferred from the USA but built in Italian yards; all completed November 1956-April 1957. Originally class of 19. *Mirto* now used for surveying. These two were converted for patrol duties with UN force in Red Sea, carry P numbers and are painted white. Being replaced by 'Esploratore' class and are scheduled to pay off in late 2000.

UPDATED

BAMBU 6/1999*, F Sadek / 0080086

0 + 4 (3) OFFSHORE PATROL VESSELS (OPV)

Displacement, tons: 1,500 full load
Dimensions, feet (metres): 291 × 40 × 10.8
(88.7 × 12.2 × 3.3)
Main machinery: 2 diesels; 9,000 hp(m) *(6.6 MW)*; 2 shafts;
cp props
Speed, knots: 25. Range 3,500 at 14 kt
Complement: 70 (8 officers)

Guns: 1 OTO Melara 3 in *(76 mm)*/62 compact ❶ taken from
'Sparviero' class.
2 Oerlikon 25 mm ❷ or 7.62 mm MGs.
Weapons control: 1 optronic director ❸.
Radars: Surface search ❹.
Fire control ❺.
Navigation.

Helicopters: 1 AB 212 ❻ or NH 90 in due course.

OPV   *(Scale 1 : 900), Ian Sturton /* 0052774

Programmes: First four for the Navy, and three more for the Ministry of Transport, to be manned by the Navy, but equipped with more simple command data systems. First of class scheduled to be launched in 2000 and to start sea trials in early 2001 followed by the others at about six month intervals. This programme may be delayed.

Structure: Some details are still speculative but stealth features include IR suppression and reduced radar cross section. The M of T ships are to have less powerful engines, no hangar and MGs vice 25 mm guns.

UPDATED

4 CASSIOPEA CLASS (OFFSHORE PATROL VESSELS) (OPV)

Name	No	Builders	Laid down		Launched		Commissioned	
CASSIOPEA	P 401	Fincantieri, Muggiano	16 Dec	1987	20 July	1988	6 July	1989
LIBRA	P 402	Fincantieri, Muggiano	17 Dec	1987	27 July	1988	28 Nov	1989
SPICA	P 403	Fincantieri, Muggiano	5 Sep	1988	27 May	1989	3 May	1990
VEGA	P 404	Fincantieri, Muggiano	20 June	1989	24 Feb	1990	25 Oct	1990

Displacement, tons: 1,002 standard; 1,475 full load
Dimensions, feet (metres): 261.8 × 38.7 × 11.5
(79.8 × 11.8 × 3.5)
Flight deck, feet (metres): 72.2 × 26.2 *(22 × 8)*
Main machinery: 2 Fincantieri/GMT BL 230.16 M diesels;
7,940 hp(m) *(5.84 MW)* sustained; 2 shafts; acbLIPS cp props
Speed, knots: 20. Range, miles: 3,300 at 17 kt
Complement: 78 (8 officers)

Guns: 1 OTO Melara 3 in *(76 mm)*/62; 60 rds/min to 16 km
(8.7 n miles); weight of shell 6 kg. Breda Oerlikon 25 mm/90.
2—12.7 mm MGs.
Weapons control: Argo NA 10.
Radars: Surface search: SMA SPS-702(V)2; I-band.
Navigation: SMA SPN-748(V)2; I-band.
Fire control: Selenia SPG-70 (RTN 10X); I/J-band.

Helicopters: 1 AB 212ASW.

Programmes: Ordered in December 1986 for operations in EEZ. Officially 'pattugliatori marittimi'. Funded by the Ministry of Transport but all operated by the Navy.
Structure: Fitted for firefighting, rescue and supply tasks. Telescopic hangar. The 20 mm guns were old stock taken from deleted 'Bergamini' class and have been replaced by 25 mm guns. There is a 500 m³ tank for storing oil polluted water.
Operational: All based at Messina.

UPDATED

VEGA
7/1999, van Ginderen Collection / 0080085

2 AGGRESSIVE CLASS (OFFSHORE PATROL VESSELS) (OPV)

Name	No	Builders	Commissioned
STORIONE (ex-*MSO 506*)	5431	Martinolich SB Co	23 Feb 1956
SQUALO (ex-*MSO 518*)	5433	Tampa Marine Co	20 June 1957

Displacement, tons: 665 standard; 720 full load
Dimensions, feet (metres): 172 × 36 × 13.6 *(52.4 × 11 × 4.1)*
Main machinery: 4 GM 8-268A diesels; 1,760 hp *(1.31 MW)*; 2 shafts; cp props
Speed, knots: 14. Range, miles: 2,400 at 10 kt
Complement: 62 (4 officers)
Guns: 1 US/Bofors 40 mm/56.
Radars: Navigation: SMA SPN-703; I-band; range 73 km *(40 n miles)*.
Sonars: GE UQS-1; active mine detection; high frequency.

Comment: Built in the USA. Converted to offshore patrol vessels in 1992-93. Pennant numbers retained without the M prefix. All minesweeping gear removed. New bridges fitted. Scheduled to be paid off in late 2000.

UPDATED

3 + 1 ESPLORATORE CLASS (PC)

Name	No	Builders	Launched		Commissioned	
ESPLORATORE	P 405	Coinaval, La Spezia	4 Nov	1996	26 June	1997
SENTINELLA	P 406	Coinaval, La Spezia	13 Nov	1997	10 July	1998
VEDETTA	P 407	Coinaval, La Spezia	11 Jan	1997	29 July	1999
STAFFETTA	P 408	Coinaval, La Spezia	Apr	1999	Dec	2000

Displacement, tons: 165 full load
Dimensions, feet (metres): 122 × 23.3 × 6.2 *(37.2 × 7.1 × 1.9)*
Main machinery: 2 Isotta Fraschini M1712T2 diesels; 3,810 hp(m) *(2.8 MW)*; 2 shafts
Speed, knots: 20. Range, miles: 1,200 at 20 kt
Complement: 14 (2 officers)
Guns: 1 Breda Oerlikon 25 mm/90. 2—7.62 mm MGs.
Weapons control: AESN Medusa optronic director to be fitted.
Radars: Surface search: 2 SPS-753B/C; I-band.

Comment: Ordered from Ortona Shipyard in December 1993 but the contract was then transferred to Coinaval Yards, La Spezia in 1994 which caused inevitable delays and construction did not start until 1995. An option on a fourth of class, was taken up in February 1998. Replacing the 'Bambu' class for UN patrols in the Red Sea, and for anti-illegal immigration operations in the southern Adriatic. Based at Brindisi. Red Sea ships are painted white.

UPDATED

SQUALO
1/1997, van Ginderen Collection / 0012598

SENTINELLA
10/1999, Giorgio Ghiglione / 0080087

AMPHIBIOUS FORCES

Notes: (1) A RoRo ship MV *Major* built in 1984 is on long term charter to the Army Mobility and Transport Command. 6,830 tons displacement with 1,240 m of vehicle lanes. Can carry 3,955 tons of cargo.
(2) There are also 45 Rigid Raider Craft in service with Amphibious Forces.

3 SAN GIORGIO CLASS (LPD)

Name	No	Builders	Laid down	Launched	Commissioned
SAN GIORGIO	L 9892	Fincantieri, Riva Trigoso	27 June 1985	25 Feb 1987	9 Oct 1987
SAN MARCO	L 9893	Fincantieri, Riva Trigoso	28 June 1986	21 Oct 1987	18 Mar 1988
SAN GIUSTO	L 9894	Fincantieri, Riva Trigoso	30 Nov 1992	2 Dec 1993	9 Apr 1994

Displacement, tons: 6,687 standard; 7,665 (7,950 *San Giusto*) full load
Dimensions, feet (metres): 449.5 *(San Giusto)*; 437.2 × 67.3 × 17.4 *(137; 133.3 × 20.5 × 5.3)*
Flight deck, feet (metres): 328.1 × 67.3 *(100 × 20.5)*
Main machinery: 2 Fincantieri GMT A 420.12 diesels; 16,800 hp (m) *(12.35 MW)* sustained; 2 shafts; acbLIPS cp props; bow thruster
Speed, knots: 21. **Range, miles:** 7,500 at 16 kt; 4,500 at 20 kt
Complement: 163 (17 officers); 196 (16 officers) *(San Giusto)*
Military lift: Battalion of 400 plus 30-36 APCs or 30 medium tanks. 3 LCMs in stern docking well. 3 LCVPs on upper deck. 1 LCPL

Guns: 1 OTO Melara 3 in *(76 mm)*/62 (Compact in *San Giusto*); 60 rds/min to 16 km *(8.7 n miles)*; weight of shell 6 kg. 2 Breda Oerlikon 25 mm/90. 2—12.7 mm MGs.
Countermeasures: ESM: SLR 730; intercept.
ESM/ECM: SLQ-747 *(San Giusto)*.
Combat data systems: Selenia IPN 20 *(San Giusto)*. Marisat.

Weapons control: Elsag NA 10.
Radars: Surface search: SMA SPS-702; I-band.
Navigation: SMA SPN-748; I-band.
Fire control: Selenia SPG-70 (RTN 10X); I/J-band.

Helicopters: 3 SH-3D Sea King or EH 101 Merlin or 5 AB 212.

Programmes: *San Giorgio* ordered 26 November 1983, *San Marco* on 5 March 1984 and *San Giusto* 1 March 1991. Launching dates of the first two are slightly later than the 'official' launching ceremony because of poor weather and for the third because of industrial problems.
Modernisation: 25 mm guns replace 20 mm from 1999. From early 2001 *San Giorgio* is being modified with the removal of the 76 mm gun, LCVPs to move from davits to a new sponson, and the flight deck lengthened and enlarged to allow two Merlin and two AB 212 to operate simultaneously on deck. Bow doors are to be removed. *San Marco* will be similarly modernised in 2002.

Structure: Aircraft carrier type flight deck with island to starboard. Three landing spots. Bow ramp (except *San Giusto*) for amphibious landings. Stern docking well 20.5 × 7 m. Fitted with a 30 ton lift and two 40 ton travelling cranes for LCMs. *San Giusto* is 300 tons heavier, of similar design except for more accommodation, a slightly longer island and different LCVP davit arrangement. Also no bow doors and therefore no beaching capability. Davits are placed in a sponson on the port side, freeing the whole flight deck for cargo and flight operations.
Operational: *San Marco* was paid for by the Ministry of Civil Protection, is specially fitted for disaster relief but is run by the Navy. All are based at Brindisi and assigned to the Third Naval Division. *San Giusto* is attached to the Naval Academy at Livorno during the annual three month Summer cruise.

UPDATED

SAN GIORGIO and SAN MARCO

6/1998, H M Steele / 0052410

SAN GIUSTO

12/1999*, Vic Jeffery, RAN / 0080089

0 + 1 LUIGI EINAUDI CLASS (LHA)

Name	No	Builders	Laid down	Launched	Commissioned
LUIGI EINAUDI	552	Fincantieri, Riva Trigoso	2001	2005	2007

Displacement, tons: 22,500 full load
Dimensions, feet (metres): 721.8 oa; 664 wl × 128 oa; 96.8 wl × 21.7 *(220; 202.4 × 39; 29.5 × 6.6)*
Flight deck, feet (metres): 603.7 × 111.5 *(184 × 34)*
Main machinery: COGAG 4 GE/Fiat LM 2500 gas turbines; 11,968 hp(m) *(88 MW)*; 2 shafts; cp props; bow thruster; 4 diesel generators for auxiliary electric propulsion by 2 motors
Speed, knots: 28; 9 on motors
Complement: 430 plus 203 aircrew plus 140 Flag staff
Military lift: 4 LCM 6 or 2 LCM 60 or 1 LCAC; 612 troops; 26 MBT or 50 trucks (in lieu of aircraft). 4 LCVP on davits.

Missiles: SAM: 4 Sylver 8 cell VLS for Aster 15.
Guns: 3—3 in *(76 mm)*/62 Super Rapid.
Countermeasures: Decoys: SLAT torpedo decoy. ESM/ECM.
Radars: Air search: EMPAR; surface search.

Fixed-wing aircraft: 8 AV-8B Harrier II or JSF.
Helicopters: 12 EH 101 Merlin.

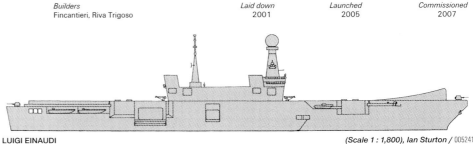

LUIGI EINAUDI

(Scale 1 : 1,800), Ian Sturton / 0052411

Programmes: UMPA (Unita Maggiore Per Operazione Anfibie) planned for contract. To replace *Vittorio Veneto* in 2007. Approved for design definition on 10 December 1997.
Structure: Designed with a hangar/garage to take various combinations of aircraft and marine equipment. Six helicopter spots on the flight deck with provision made for a 6° ski-jump.

Two lifts, one forward of the island, the second starboard side aft. Docking well 25 × 15 m. Some details are still speculative and may include long term plans to operate a Joint Strike Fighter (JSF).

UPDATED

2 PEDRETTI CLASS (COMMANDO SUPPORT CRAFT) (YDT)

Name	No	Builders	Commissioned
ALCIDE PEDRETTI	Y 499 (ex-MEN 213)	Crestitalia-Ameglia	23 Oct 1984
MARIO MARINO	Y 498 (ex-MEN 214)	Crestitalia-Ameglia	21 Dec 1984

Displacement, tons: 75.4 (*Alcide Pedretti*), 69.5 (*Mario Marino*) full load
Dimensions, feet (metres): 86.6 × 22.6 × 3.3 *(26.4 × 6.9 × 1)*
Main machinery: 2 Isotta Fraschini ID 36 SS 12V diesels; 2,640 hp(m) *(1.94 MW)* sustained; 2 shafts
Speed, knots: 25. **Range, miles:** 450 (*Alcide Pedretti*), 250 (*Mario Marino*) at 23 kt
Complement: 6 (1 officer)
Radars: Navigation: I-band.

Comment: Both laid down 8 September 1983. For use by assault swimmers of COMSUBIN. Both have decompression chambers. *Alcide Pedretti* has a floodable dock aft and is used for combat swimmers and special operations, while *Mario Marino* is fitted for underwater work and rescue missions. Based at Varignano, La Spezia. A similar but more heavily equipped vessel serves with the UAE Navy.

UPDATED

ALCIDE PEDRETTI

10/1999*, Giorgio Ghiglione / 0080088

9 MTM 217 CLASS (LCM)

MEN 217-222   **MEN 227-228**   **MEN 551**

Displacement, tons: 64.6 full load
Dimensions, feet (metres): 60.7 × 16.7 × 3 *(18.5 × 5.1 × 0.9)*
Main machinery: 2 Fiat diesels; 560 hp(m) *(412 kW)*; 2 shafts
Speed, knots: 9. **Range, miles:** 300 at 9 kt
Complement: 3
Military lift: 30 tons

Comment: First six built at Muggiano, La Spezia by Fincantieri. Three completed 9 October 1987 for *San Giorgio*, three completed 8 March 1988 for *San Marco*. Three more ordered in March 1991 from Balzamo Shipyard and completed in 1993 for *San Giusto*. Others of this class are also in service with the Army.

UPDATED

MEN 220

9/1991, van Ginderen Collection

17 MTP 96 CLASS (LCVP)

MDN 94-104   **MDN 108-109**   **MDN 114-117**

Displacement, tons: 14.3 full load
Dimensions, feet (metres): 44.9 × 12.5 × 2.3 *(13.7 × 3.8 × 0.7)*
Main machinery: 2 diesels; 700 hp(m) *(515 kW)*; 2 shafts or 2 water-jets
Speed, knots: 29 or 22. **Range, miles:** 100 at 12 kt
Complement: 3

Comment: Built by Technomatic Ancona in 1985 (two), Technomatic Bari in 1987-88 (six) and Technoplast Venezia 1991-94 (nine). Can carry 45 men or 4.5 tons of cargo. These craft have Kevlar armour. The most recent versions have water-jet propulsion which gives a top speed of 29 kt (22 kt fully laden). This is being backfitted to all GRP LCVPs.

VERIFIED

MDN 95

8/1994, van Ginderen Collection

SURVEY AND RESEARCH SHIPS

0 + 1 ALLIANCE TYPE (AGS/AGOR)

Name	No	Builders	Commissioned
—	—	Fincantieri, Muggiano	Dec 2002

Displacement, tons: 3,180 full load
Dimensions, feet (metres): 305.1 × 49.9 × 17.1 *(93 × 15.2 × 5.2)*
Main machinery: Diesel electric; 2 shafts; bow thruster
Speed, knots: 16. **Range, miles:** 7,200 at 11 kt
Complement: 24 (10 officers)
Radars: Navigation: I-band.

Comment: Ordered on 1 December 1999 with construction starting in March 2000. The design is very similar to NATO *Alliance* but with updated research and survey equipment.

NEW ENTRY

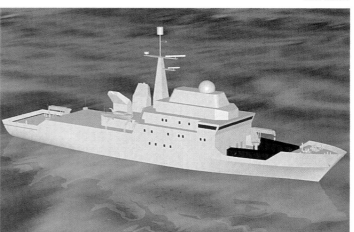

ALLIANCE TYPE (artist's impression)

1/2000*, Fincantieri / 0049974

1 SURVEY SHIP (AGS)

Name	No	Builders	Commissioned
AMMIRAGLIO MAGNAGHI	A 5303	Fincantieri, Riva Trigoso	2 May 1975

Displacement, tons: 1,700 full load
Dimensions, feet (metres): 271.3 × 44.9 × 11.5 *(82.7 × 13.7 × 3.5)*
Main machinery: 2 GMT B 306 SS diesels; 3,000 hp(m) *(2.2 MW)*; 1 shaft; cp prop; auxiliary motor; 240 hp(m) *(176 kW)*; bow thruster
Speed, knots: 16. **Range, miles:** 6,000 at 12 kt (1 diesel); 4,200 at 16 kt (2 diesels)
Complement: 148 (14 officers, 15 scientists)
Guns: 1 Breda 40 mm/70 (not fitted).
Radars: Navigation: SMA 3 RM 20; I-band.
Helicopters: Platform only.

Comment: Ordered under 1972 programme. Laid down 13 June 1973. Launched 11 October 1974. Full air conditioning, bridge engine controls, flume-type stabilisers. Equipped for oceanographical studies including laboratories and underwater TV. Two Qubit Trac V integrated navigation and logging systems and a Chart V data processing system installed in 1992 to augment the existing Trac 100-based HODAPS. Carries six surveying motor boats.
UPDATED

AMMIRAGLIO MAGNAGHI   6/1999*, Giorgio Ghiglione / 0080094

1 AGAVE CLASS (AGS)

Name	No	Builders	Commissioned
MIRTO	A 5306	Breda, Porta Marghera	4 Aug 1956

Displacement, tons: 405 full load
Dimensions, feet (metres): 144 × 25.6 × 8.5 *(43 × 7.8 × 2.6)*
Main machinery: 2 GM 8-268A diesels; 880 hp *(656 kW)*; 2 shafts
Speed, knots: 13. **Range, miles:** 2,500 at 10 kt
Complement: 40 (4 officers)
Radars: Navigation: SPN-750; I-band.

Comment: Converted for surveying duties. To be replaced by two new construction ships in 2000.
UPDATED

MIRTO   5/1999*, van Ginderen Collection / 0080095

2 SURVEY SHIPS (AGS)

Name	No	Builders	Commissioned
ARETUSA	A 5353	Intermarine	Oct 2000
GALATEA	A 5354	Intermarine	Dec 2000

Displacement, tons: 390 full load
Dimensions, feet (metres): 128.6 × 41.3 × 7.9 *(39.2 × 12.6 × 2.4)*
Main machinery: Diesel electric; 2 Isotta Fraschini V170812 ME diesels; 2 ABB generators 1,904 hp(m) *(1.4 MW)*; 2 shafts; Schottel props; 2 bow thrusters
Speed, knots: 13. **Range, miles:** 1,700 at 13 kt
Complement: 31 (4 officers)
Guns: 1 Breda Oerlikon 25 mm/90; 2—7.62 mm MGs.
Radars: 2 Navigation; I-band.

Comment: Ordered in January 1998. GRP catamaran design. To replace *Mirto* and *Pioppo*.
UPDATED

ARETUSA   (not to scale), Ian Sturton / 0012606

3 RESEARCH SHIPS (AG/AGOR)

Name	No	Builders	Launched	Commissioned
RAFFAELE ROSSETTI	A 5315	Picchiotti, Viareggio	12 July 1986	20 Dec 1986

Displacement, tons: 320 full load
Dimensions, feet (metres): 146.3 × 25.9 × 6.9 *(44.6 × 7.9 × 2.1)*
Main machinery: 2 Fincantieri Isotta Fraschini ID 36 N 12V diesels; 1,320 hp(m) *(970 kW)* sustained; 2 shafts; cp props; bow thruster
Speed, knots: 17.5. **Range, miles:** 700 at 15 kt
Complement: 17 (1 officer, 8 technicians)

Comment: Five different design torpedo tubes fitted for above and underwater testing and trials. Other equipment for research into communications, surface and air search as well as underwater weapons. There is a stern doorway which is partially submerged and the ship has a set of 96 batteries to allow 'silent' propulsion. Operated by the Permanent Commission for Experiments of War Materials at La Spezia.
VERIFIED

RAFFAELE ROSSETTI   3/1998, Giorgio Ghiglione / 0052416

Name	No	Builders	Commissioned
VINCENZO MARTELLOTTA	A 5320	Picchiotti, Viareggio	22 Dec 1990

Displacement, tons: 340 full load
Dimensions, feet (metres): 146.3 × 25.9 × 7.5 *(44.6 × 7.9 × 2.3)*
Main machinery: 2 Fincantieri Isotta Fraschini ID 36 SS 16V diesels; 3,520 hp(m) *(2.59 MW)* sustained; 2 shafts; cp props; bow thruster
Speed, knots: 17. **Range, miles:** 700 at 15 kt
Complement: 9 (1 officer) plus 8 scientists

Comment: Launched on 28 May 1988. Has one 21 in *(533 mm)* and three 12.75 in *(324 mm)* torpedo tubes and acoustic equipment to operate a 3D tracking range for torpedoes or underwater vehicles. Like *Rossetti* she is operated by the Commission for Experiments at La Spezia.
UPDATED

VINCENZO MARTELLOTTA   10/1999*, Giorgio Ghiglione / 0080096

Name	No	Builders	Commissioned
MURENA (ex-*Scampo*)	A 5305 (ex-M 5466)	Apuana	1957

Displacement, tons: 188 full load
Dimensions, feet (metres): 106 × 21 × 6 *(32.5 × 6.4 × 1.8)*
Main machinery: 2 Fiat/MTU MB 12V 493 TY7 diesels; 2,200 hp(m) *(1.62 MW)* sustained; 2 shafts
Speed, knots: 14. **Range, miles:** 2,000 at 9 kt
Complement: 16 (4 officers)
Radars: Navigation: I-band.

Comment: Converted 'Aragosta' class MSI used as a torpedo launching and support vessel. Has one triple 324 mm ILAS mounting and a crane for overside recovery of torpedoes.
VERIFIED

MURENA   9/1993, Marina Fraccaroli

MINE WARFARE FORCES

Note: The Navy is studying a 'Gaeta plus' design which will include hunting, sweeping and clearance diving.

4 LERICI and 8 GAETA CLASS (MINEHUNTERS/SWEEPERS) (MHC/MSC)

Name	No	Builders	Launched		Commissioned	
LERICI	M 5550	Intermarine, Sarzana	3 Sep	1982	22 Mar	1985
SAPRI	M 5551	Intermarine, Sarzana	5 Apr	1984	4 June	1985
MILAZZO	M 5552	Intermarine, Sarzana	4 Jan	1985	6 Aug	1985
VIESTE	M 5553	Intermarine, Sarzana	18 Apr	1985	2 Dec	1985
GAETA	M 5554	Intermarine, Sarzana	28 July	1990	3 July	1992
TERMOLI	M 5555	Intermarine, Sarzana	15 Dec	1990	13 Nov	1992
ALGHERO	M 5556	Intermarine, Sarzana	11 May	1991	31 Mar	1993
NUMANA	M 5557	Intermarine, Sarzana	26 Oct	1991	30 July	1993
CROTONE	M 5558	Intermarine, Sarzana	11 Apr	1992	19 Jan	1994
VIAREGGIO	M 5559	Intermarine, Sarzana	3 Oct	1992	1 July	1994
CHIOGGIA	M 5560	Intermarine, Sarzana	9 May	1994	19 May	1996
RIMINI	M 5561	Intermarine, Sarzana	17 Sep	1994	26 Nov	1996

Displacement, tons: 620 (697, *Gaeta* onwards) full load
Dimensions, feet (metres): 164 (172.1 *Gaeta*) × 32.5 × 8.6
(50 (52.5) × 9.9 × 2.6)
Main machinery: 1 Fincantieri GMT BL 230.8 M diesel (passage);
1,985 hp(m) *(1.46 MW)* sustained; 1 shaft; acbLIPS cp prop; 3
Isotta Fraschini ID 36 SS 6V diesels (hunting); 1,481 hp(m)
(1.1 MW) sustained; 3 hydraulic 360° rotating thrust props;
506 hp(m) *(372 kW)* (1 fwd, 2 aft)
Speed, knots: 14; 6 hunting. **Range, miles:** 1,500 at 14 kt
Complement: 47 (4 officers) including 7 divers

Guns: 1 Oerlikon 20 mm/70 or 2 Oerlikon 20 mm/70 (twin)
(*Gaeta* onwards) or 2 Breda Oerlikon 25 mm/90. 2 additional
20 mm guns added for deployments.
Countermeasures: Minehunting: 1 MIN 77 or MIN Mk 2 (*Gaeta*
onwards) ROV; 1 Pluto mine destruction system; diving
equipment and recompression chamber.
Minesweeping: Oropesa Mk 4 wire sweep.
Combat data systems: Motorola MRS III/GPS Eagle precision
navigation system with Datamat SMA SSN-714V(2) automatic
plotting and radar indicator IP-7113.
Radars: Navigation: SMA SPN-728V(3); I-band.
Sonars: FIAR SQQ-14(IT) VDS (lowered from keel forward of
bridge); classification and route survey; high frequency.

Programmes: First four ordered 7 January 1978 under Legge
Navale. Next six ordered from Intermarine 30 April 1988 and
two more in 1991. From No 5 onwards ships are 2 m longer
and are of an improved design. Construction of Gaetas started
in 1988. The last pair delayed by budget cuts but re-ordered on
17 September 1992.
Modernisation: Improvements to 'Gaeta' class include a better
minehunting sonar system which was backfitted to the 'Lerici'
class in 1991. Other Gaeta upgrades include a third hydraulic
system, improved electrical generators, ROV with better
endurance and equipment, a new type of recompression
chamber, and a reduced magnetic signature. 25 mm guns are
replacing all 20 mm from 1999.
Structure: Of heavy GRP throughout hull, decks and bulkheads,
with frames eliminated. All machinery is mounted on vibration
dampers and main engines made of amagnetic material. Fitted
with Galeazzi two man compression chambers and a
telescopic crane for launching Callegari frogmen boats.
Operational: Endurance, 12 days. For long passages passive roll-
stabilising tanks can be used for extra fuel increasing range to
4,000 miles at 12 kt.
Sales: Four to Malaysia, two to Nigeria. 12 of a modified design
built by the USA, six by Australia and two by Thailand.

UPDATED

LERICI
11/1999, Giorgio Ghiglione / 0080090*

CHOGGIA
5/1999, G Toremans / 0080091*

CROTONE
5/1998, Giorgio Ghiglione / 0080092*

AUXILIARIES

1 ETNA CLASS (REPLENISHMENT TANKER) (AOR)

Name	No	Builders	Laid down	Launched	Commissioned
ETNA	A 5326	Fincantieri, Riva Trigoso	4 July 1995	12 July 1997	29 Aug 1998

Displacement, tons: 13,400 full load
Dimensions, feet (metres): 480.6 × 68.9 × 24.3
(146.5 × 21 × 7.4)
Flight deck, feet (metres): 91.9 × 68.9 *(28 × 21)*
Main machinery: 2 Sulzer 12 ZAV 40S diesels; 22,400 hp(m)
(16.46 MW) sustained; 2 shafts; bow thruster
Speed, knots: 21. **Range, miles:** 7,600 at 18 kt
Complement: 160 plus 83 spare
Cargo capacity: 6,350 tons gas oil; 1,200 tons JP5; 2,100 m³
ammunition and stores
Guns: 1 OTO Melara 76 mm/62. 2 Breda Oerlikon 25 mm/93.
Radars: Surface search: SMA SPS-702(V)3; I-band.
Navigation: GEM SPN-753; I-band.
Helicopters: 1 EH 101 Merlin or SH-3D or 2 AB 212.

Comment: Details revised in 1992 for an order 29 July 1994.
Construction authorised on 3 January 1995. The main gun is
not fitted, and the specification includes a CIWS on the hangar
roof. Two RAS stations on each side.

UPDATED

ETNA
8/1998*, Fincantieri / 0080097

2 STROMBOLI CLASS (REPLENISHMENT TANKERS) (AOR)

Naame	No	Builders	Launched	Commissioned
STROMBOLI	A 5327	Fincantieri, Riva Trigoso	20 Feb 1975	20 Nov 1975
VESUVIO	A 5329	Fincantieri, Muggiano	4 June 1977	18 Nov 1978

Displacement, tons: 3,556 light; 8,706 full load
Dimensions, feet (metres): 423.1 × 59 × 21.3 *(129 × 18 × 6.5)*
Main machinery: 2 GMT C428 SS diesels; 9,600 hp(m) *(7.06 MW)*; 1 shaft; acbLIPS cp prop
Speed, knots: 18.5. **Range, miles:** 5,080 at 18 kt
Complement: 115 (9 officers)
Cargo capacity: 3,000 tons FFO; 1,000 tons dieso; 400 tons JP5; 300 tons other stores
Guns: 1 OTO Melara 3 in *(76 mm)*/62.
2 Breda Oerlikon 25 mm/93.
Weapons control: Argo NA 10 system.
Radars: Surface search: SMA SPQ-2; I-band.
Navigation: SMA SPN-748; I-band.
Fire control: Selenia SPG-70 (RTN 10X); I/J-band.
Helicopters: Platform for 1 medium.

Comment: *Vesuvio* was the first large ship to be built at Muggiano (near La Spezia) since the
Second World War and the first with funds under Legge Navale 1975. Beam and stern refuelling
stations for fuel and stores. Also Vertrep. The two ships have different midships crane
arrangements. Similar ship built for Iraq and laid up in Alexandria since 1986. 20 mm guns
replaced by 25 mm from 1999.

UPDATED

VESUVIO
5/1999*, Giorgio Ghiglione / 0080098

3 BASENTO CLASS (WATER TANKERS) (AWT)

Name	No	Builders	Commissioned
BASENTO	A 5356	Inma di La Spezia	19 July 1971
BRADANO	A 5357	Inma di La Spezia	29 Dec 1971
BRENTA	A 5358	Inma di La Spezia	18 Apr 1972

Displacement, tons: 1,914 full load
Dimensions, feet (metres): 225.4 × 33.1 × 12.8 *(68.7 × 10.1 × 3.9)*
Main machinery: 2 Fiat LA 230 diesels; 1,730 hp(m) *(1.27 MW)*; 2 shafts
Speed, knots: 13. **Range, miles:** 1,650 at 12 kt
Complement: 24 (3 officers)
Cargo capacity: 1,200 tons
Guns: 2 Oerlikon 20 mm.
Radars: Navigation: SPN-703; I-band.

Comment: Guns to be replaced by 25 mm. Not always fitted.

UPDATED

BRENTA
7/1999*, M Declerck / 0080099

1 BORMIDA CLASS (WATER TANKER) (AWT)

BORMIDA (ex-*GGS 1011*) A 5359

Displacement, tons: 736 full load
Dimensions, feet (metres): 131.9 × 23.6 × 10.5 *(40.2 × 7.2 × 3.2)*
Main machinery: 1 diesel; 130 hp(m) *(95.6 kW)*; 1 shaft
Speed, knots: 7
Complement: 11 (1 officer)
Cargo capacity: 260 tons

Comment: Converted at La Spezia in 1974.

VERIFIED

BORMIDA
6/1998, Giorgio Ghiglione / 0052419

4 MCC 1101 CLASS (WATER TANKERS) (AWT)

MCC 1101 A 5370	**MCC 1102** A 5371	**MCC 1103** A 5372	**MCC 1104** A 5373

Displacement, tons: 898 full load
Dimensions, feet (metres): 155.2 × 32.8 × 10.8 *(47.3 × 10 × 3.3)*
Main machinery: 2 Fincantieri Isotta Fraschini ID 36 SS 6V diesels; 1,320 hp(m) *(970 kW)*
sustained; 2 shafts
Speed, knots: 13. **Range, miles:** 1,500 at 12 kt
Complement: 12 (2 officers)
Cargo capacity: 550 tons
Radars: Navigation: SPN-753; I-band.

Comment: Built by Ferrari, La Spezia and completed one in 1986, two in May 1987, one in
May 1988.

UPDATED

MCC 1104
5/1999*, A Sharma / 0080100

3 SIMETO CLASS (WATER TANKERS) (AWT)

Name	No	Builders	Commissioned
SIMETO	A 5375	Cinet, Molfetta	9 July 1988
TICINO	A 5376	Poli Shipyard, Pellestrina	10 June 1994
TIRSO	A 5377	Poli Shipyard, Pellestrina	12 Mar 1994

Displacement, tons: 1,858 full load; 1,968 (*Ticino* and *Tirso*) full load
Dimensions, feet (metres): 229 × 33.1 × 14.4 (*69.8 × 10.1 × 4.1*)
Main machinery: 2 GMT B 230.6 BL diesels; 2,530 hp(m) (*1.86 MW*) sustained; 2 shafts; cp props; bow thruster; 300 hp(m) (*220 kW*)
Speed, knots: 13. **Range, miles:** 1,800 at 12 kt
Complement: 36 (3 officers)
Cargo capacity: 1,130 tons; 1,200 (*Ticino* and *Tirso*)
Guns: 1—20 mm/70. 2—7.62 mm MGs can be carried.
Radars: Navigation: 2 SPN-753B(V); I-band.

Comment: Second two units of a slightly improved version ordered in November 1993. Guns are not normally carried. *Simeto* was in reserve in 1997.
UPDATED

TICINO 4/1999 *, Flottenkommando / 0080102

7 DEPOLI CLASS TANKERS (AOTL/AWT)

GGS 1012-1014   GRS/G 1010-1012   GRS/J 1013

Dimensions, feet (metres): 128.3 × 27.9 × 10.2 (*39.1 × 8.5 × 3.1*)
Main machinery: 2 diesels; 748 hp(m) (*550 kW*); 2 shafts
Speed, knots: 11
Complement: 12
Cargo capacity: 500 m³ liquids
Radars: Navigation: I-band.

Comment: Built by DePoli and delivered between February 1990 and February 1991. The GGS series is for water, GRS/G for fuel and GRS/J for JP5.
UPDATED

DEPOLI 5/1999 *, A Sharma / 0080101

6 MTC 1011 CLASS (RAMPED TRANSPORTS) (AKL)

Name	No	Builders	Commissioned
GORGONA (1011)	A 5347	CN Mario Marini	23 Dec 1986
TREMITI (1012)	A 5348	CN Mario Marini	2 Mar 1987
CAPRERA (1013)	A 5349	CN Mario Marini	10 Apr 1987
PANTELLERIA (1014)	A 5351	CN Mario Marini	26 May 1987
LIPARI (1015)	A 5352	CN Mario Marini	10 July 1987
CAPRI (1016)	A 5353	CN Mario Marini	16 Sep 1987

Displacement, tons: 631 full load
Dimensions, feet (metres): 186 × 32.8 × 8.2 (*56.7 × 10 × 2.5*)
Main machinery: 2 CRM 12D/SS diesels; 1,760 hp(m) (*1.29 MW*); 2 shafts
Speed, knots: 14.5. **Range, miles:** 1,500 at 14 kt
Complement: 32 (4 officers)
Guns: 1 Oerlikon 20 mm (fitted for). 2—7.62 mm MGs.
Radars: Navigation: SMA SPN-748; I-band.

Comment: As well as transporting stores, oil or water they can act as support ships for Light Forces, salvage ships or minelayers. Stern ramp fitted. 1015 and 1016 are attached to the Italian Naval Academy at Livorno, 1011 based at La Spezia, 1012 at Ancona, 1013 at La Maddalena and 1014 at Taranto.
UPDATED

TREMITI 6/1994 *, Aldo Fraccaroli / 0075864

1 SALVAGE SHIP (ARS)

Name	No	Builders	Commissioned
PROTEO (ex-*Perseo*)	A 5310	Cantieri Navali Riuniti, Ancona	24 Aug 1951

Displacement, tons: 1,865 standard; 2,147 full load
Dimensions, feet (metres): 248 × 38 × 21 (*75.6 × 11.6 × 6.4*)
Main machinery: 2 Fiat diesels; 4,800 hp(m) (*3.53 MW*); 1 shaft
Speed, knots: 16. **Range, miles:** 7,500 at 13 kt
Complement: 122 (8 officers)
Guns: 2—3.9 in (twin). 2 Oerlikon 20 mm.
Radars: Navigation: SMA SPN-748; I-band.

Comment: Laid down at Cantieri Navali Riuniti, Ancona, in 1943. Suspended in 1944. Seized by Germans and transferred to Trieste. Construction restarted at Cantieri Navali Riuniti, Ancona, in 1949. Formerly mounted one 3.9 in gun which was replaced in 1999.
UPDATED

PROTEO 7/1999 *, van Ginderen Collection / 0080103

1 SALVAGE SHIP (ARS)

Name	No	Builders	Launched	Commissioned
ANTEO	A 5309	C N Breda-Mestre	11 Nov 1978	31 July 1980

Displacement, tons: 3,200 full load
Dimensions, feet (metres): 322.8 × 51.8 × 16.7 (*98.4 × 15.8 × 5.1*)
Main machinery: 2 GMT A 230.12 diesels; 5,000 hp(m) (*3.68 MW*); 2 motors; 6,000 hp(m) (*4.41 MW*); 1 shaft; 2 bow thrusters; 1,000 hp(m) (*735 kW*)
Speed, knots: 20. **Range, miles:** 4,000 at 14 kt
Complement: 121 (including salvage staff)
Guns: 2 Breda Oerlikon 25 mm/90 fitted during deployments.
Radars: Surface search: SMA SPN-751; I-band.
Navigation: SMA SPN-748; I-band.
Helicopters: 1 AB 212.

Comment: Ordered mid-1977. Comprehensively fitted with flight deck and hangar, extensive salvage gear, including rescue bell and recompression chambers. Carries four lifeboats of various types. Three firefighting systems. Full towing equipment. Carries midget submarine, *Usel*, of 13.2 tons dived with dimensions 26.2 × 6.2 × 8.9 ft (*8 × 1.9 × 2.7 m*). Carries two men and can dive to 600 m. Endurance, 120 hours at 5 kt. Also has a McCann rescue chamber.
UPDATED

ANTEO 6/1999 *, Harald Carstens / 0080104

5 PONZA CLASS (LIGHTHOUSE TENDERS) (ABU)

Name	No	Builders	Commissioned
PONZA	A 5364	Morini Yard, Ancona	9 Dec 1988
LEVANZO	A 5366	Morini Yard, Ancona	24 Jan 1989
TAVOLARA	A 5367	Morini Yard, Ancona	12 Apr 1989
PALMARIA	A 5368	Morini Yard, Ancona	12 May 1989
PROCIDA	A 5383	Morini Yard, Ancona	14 Nov 1990

Displacement, tons: 608 full load
Dimensions, feet (metres): 186 × 35.4 × 8.2 (*56.7 × 10.8 × 2.5*)
Main machinery: 2 Fincantieri Isotta Fraschini ID 36 SS 8V diesels; 1,760 hp(m) (*1.29 MW*) sustained; 2 shafts; cp props; bow thruster; 120 hp(m) (*88 kW*)
Speed, knots: 14.5. **Range, miles:** 1,500 at 14 kt
Complement: 34 (2 officers)
Guns: 2—7.62 mm MGs.
Radars: Navigation: SPN-732; I-band.

Comment: MTF 1304-1308. Similar to 'MTC 1011' class.
UPDATED

PROCIDA 7/1999 *, Giorgio Ghiglione / 0080105

2 LCT 3 CLASS (REPAIR SHIPS) (ARL)

MOC 1201 A 5331 **MOC 1204** A 5334

Displacement, tons: 350 standard; 640 full load
Dimensions, feet (metres): 192 × 31 × 7 *(58.6 × 9.5 × 2.1)*
Main machinery: 2 diesels; 1,000 hp *(746 kW)*; 2 shafts
Speed, knots: 8
Complement: 24 (3 officers)
Guns: 2 Bofors 40 mm/70. 2 Oerlikon 20 mm.
 2 ships have 2—40 mm and 1 ship has 3—20 mm.

Comment: Built in 1943 to a UK design. Originally converted as repair craft. Other duties have been taken over—*MOC 1201* is used for torpedo trials. One of the class transferred to Albania in 1999.
VERIFIED

MOC 1201 *1/1998, A Sharma /* 0052426

1 MEN 212 CLASS (TRV)

MEN 212

Displacement, tons: 32 full load
Dimensions, feet (metres): 58.4 × 16.7 × 3.3 *(17.8 × 5.1 × 1)*
Main machinery: 2 HP diesels; 1,380 hp(m) *(1.01 MW)*; 2 shafts
Speed, knots: 22. **Range, miles:** 250 at 20 kt
Complement: 4
Radars: Navigation: SPN-732; I-band.

Comment: Torpedo Recovery Vessel completed in October 1983 by Crestitalia. GRP construction with a stern ramp. Capacity for up to three torpedoes.
UPDATED

MEN 212 *8/1994*, Nikolaus Sifferlinger /* 0080106

2 MEN 215 CLASS (YFU/YFB)

MEN 215 **MEN 216**

Displacement, tons: 82 full load
Dimensions, feet (metres): 89.6 × 23 × 3.6 *(27.3 × 7 × 1.1)*
Main machinery: 2 Isotta Fraschini ID 36 SS 12V diesels; 2,640 hp(m) *(1.94 MW)* sustained; 2 shafts
Speed, knots: 28. **Range, miles:** 250 at 14 kt
Complement: 4
Radars: Navigation: SPN-732; I-band.

Comment: Fast personnel launches completed in June 1986 by Crestitalia. Can also be used for amphibious operations or disaster relief. One is based at La Spezia and one in Taranto, where they are used as local ferries.
VERIFIED

MEN 216 *3/1998, Giorgio Ghiglione /* 0052424

HARBOUR CRAFT

Comment: There are large numbers of naval manned harbour craft with MDN, MCN, MBN and MEN numbers. There is also a ferry *Cheradi* Y 402 at Taranto. Craft with VF numbers are non-naval.
UPDATED

MDN *5/1999*, A Sharma /* 0080107

MDN *6/1998*, Georgio Ghiglione /* 0052427

19 FLOATING DOCKS

Number	Date	Capacity-tons	Number	Date	Capacity-tons
GO 1	1942	1,000	GO 18B	1920	600
GO 5	1893	100	GO 20	1935	1,600
GO 8	1904	3,800	GO 22-23	1935	1,000
GO 10	1900	2,000	GO 51	1971	2,000
GO 11	1920	2,700	GO 52-54	1988-93	6,000
GO 17	1917	500	GO 55-57	1995-96	850
GO 18A	1920	800	GO 58	1995	2,000

Comment: Stationed at La Spezia *(GO 52)*, Augusta *(GO 53)* and Taranto *(GO 54)*.
VERIFIED

TRAINING SHIPS

Notes: (1) In addition to the ships listed the LPD *San Giusto* is used in a training role.
(2) A new class of four GRP training ships are to be ordered in 2000 to replace the 'Aragosta' class.

1 SAIL TRAINING SHIP (AXS)

Name	No	Builders	Commissioned
AMERIGO VESPUCCI	A 5312	Castellammare	15 May 1931

Displacement, tons: 3,543 standard; 4,146 full load
Dimensions, feet (metres): 229.5 pp; 270 oa hull; 330 oa bowsprit × 51 × 22 *(70; 82.4; 100 × 15.5 × 7)*
Main machinery: Diesel-electric; 2 Fiat B 306 ESS diesel generators; 2 Marelli motors; 2,000 hp (m) *(1.47 MW)*; 1 shaft
Speed, knots: 10. **Range, miles:** 5,450 at 6.5 kt
Complement: 243 (13 officers)
Radars: Navigation: 2 SMA SPN-748; I-band.

Comment: Launched on 22 March 1930. Hull, masts and yards are of steel. Sail area, 22,604 sq ft. Extensively refitted at La Spezia Naval Dockyard in 1973 and again in 1984. Used for Naval Academy Summer cruise with up to 150 trainees.
UPDATED

AMERIGO VESPUCCI *8/1999*, Michael Nitz /* 0080108

1 SAIL TRAINING SHIP (AXS)

Name	No	Builders	Commissioned
PALINURO (ex-*Commandant Louis Richard*)	A 5311	Ch Dubigeon, Nantes	1934

Displacement, tons: 1,042 standard; 1,450 full load
Measurement, tons: 858 gross
Dimensions, feet (metres): 193.5 × 32.8 × 15.7 *(59 × 10 × 4.8)*
Main machinery: 1 MAN G8V diesel; 450 hp(m) *(331 kW)*; 1 shaft
Speed, knots: 7.5. **Range, miles:** 5,390 at 7.5 kt
Complement: 47 (4 officers)
Radars: Navigation: SPN-748; I-band.

Comment: Barquentine launched in 1934. Purchased in 1951. Rebuilt in 1954-55 and commissioned in Italian Navy on 1 July 1955. Sail area, 1,152 sq ft. She was one of the last two French Grand Bank cod-fishing barquentines. Owned by the Armement Glâtre she was based at St Malo until bought by Italy. Used for seamanship basic training.
UPDATED

5/1998, A Campanera i Rovira / 0052429

PALINURO   *7/1999*, Per Kornefeldt /* 0080109

5 ARAGOSTA (HAM) CLASS (AXL)

ARAGOSTA A 5378	MITILO A 5380	PORPORA A 5382
ASTICE A 5379	POLIPO A 5381	

Displacement, tons: 188 full load
Dimensions, feet (metres): 106 × 21 × 6 *(32.5 × 6.4 × 1.8)*
Main machinery: 2 Fiat-MTU 12V 493 TY7 diesels; 2,200 hp(m) *(1.62 MW)* sustained; 2 shafts
Speed, knots: 14. **Range, miles:** 2,000 at 9 kt
Complement: 15 (2 officers)
Radars: Navigation: BX 732; I-band.

Comment: Builders: CRDA, Monfalcone: *Aragosta, Astice*. Picchiotti, Viareggio: *Mitilo*. Costaguta, Voltri: *Polipo, Porpora*. Similar to the late UK 'Ham' class. All constructed to the order of NATO in 1955-57. Designed armament of one 20 mm gun not mounted. Originally class of 20. Remaining five converted for training 1986. *Polipo* and *Porpora* used by the Naval Academy. *Aragosta* has large deckhouse aft as support ship for frogmen. Others of the class include *Murena* the experimental ship and GLS 501-502 ferries. To be replaced in 2002/03 by a new class.
UPDATED

PORPORA   *7/1999*, Giorgio Ghiglione /* 0080110

5 SAIL TRAINING YACHTS (AXS)

Name	No	Builders	Commissioned
CAROLY	A 5302	Baglietto, Varazze	1948
STELLA POLARE	A 5313	Sangermani, Chiavari	8 Oct 1965
CORSARO II	A 5316	Costaguta, Voltri	5 Jan 1961
CAPRICIA	A 5322	Bengt-Plym	1963
ORSA MAGGIORE	A 5323	Tencara, Venezia	1994

Comment: The first three are sail training yachts between 40 and 60 tons with a crew including trainees of about 16. *Capricia* is a yawl of 55 tons and was donated by the Agnelli foundation as replacement for *Cristoforo Colombo II* which was not completed when the shipyard building her went bankrupt. *Capricia* commissioned in the Navy 23 May 1993. *Orsa Maggiore* is a ketch of 70 tons.
UPDATED

TUGS

8 OCEAN TUGS (ATR)

ATLANTE A 5317	TITANO A 5324	SATURNO A 5330
PROMETEO A 5318	POLIFEMO A 5325	TENACE A 5365
CICLOPE A 5319	GIGANTE A 5328	

Displacement, tons: 658 full load
Dimensions, feet (metres): 127.6 × 32.5 × 12.1 *(38.9 × 9.9 × 3.7)*
Main machinery: 2 GMT B 230.8 M diesels; 3,970 hp(m) *(2.02 MW)* sustained; 2 shafts; acbLIPS cp props
Speed, knots: 14.5. **Range, miles:** 3,000 at 14 kt
Complement: 12
Radars: Navigation: SPN-748; I-band.

Comment: Details given are for all except A 5317/8. Built by CN Ferrari, La Spezia. Completed *Ciclope*, 5 September 1985; *Titano*, 7 December 1985; *Polifemo*, 21 April 1986; *Gigante*, 18 July 1986; *Saturno* 5 April 1988 and *Tenace* 9 July 1988. All fitted with firefighting equipment and two portable submersible pumps. Bollard pull 45 tons. *Atlante* and *Prometeo* were completed 14 August 1975 and are slightly larger at 746 tons and have single engine propulsion.
UPDATED

SATURNO   *7/1999*, van Ginderen Collection /* 0080111

11 COASTAL TUGS (YTB)

PORTO EMPEDOCLE Y 421	PORTO VENERE Y 426	PORTO CORSINI Y 417
PORTO PISANO Y 422	PORTO SALVO Y 428	PORTO D'ISCHIA Y 436
PORTO CONTE Y 423	PORTO FOSSONE Y 413	RIVA TRIGOSO Y 443
PORTO FERRAIO Y 425	PORTO TORRES Y 416	

Displacement, tons: 412 full load
Measurement, tons: 122 dwt
Dimensions, feet (metres): 106.3 × 27.9 × 12.8 *(32.4 × 8.5 × 3.9)*
Main machinery: 1 GMT B 230.8 M diesels; 1,600 hp(m) *(1.18 MW)* sustained; 1 shaft; cp prop
Speed, knots: 12.7. **Range, miles:** 4,000 at 12 kt
Complement: 13
Radars: Navigation: GEM BX 132; I-band.

Comment: Details given are for all except Y 436 and 443. Six ordered from CN De Poli (Pellestrina) and further three from Ferbex (Naples) in 1986.
Delivery dates *Porto Salvo* (13 September 1985), *Porto Pisano* (22 October 1985), *Porto Ferraio* (20 July 1985), *Porto Conte* (21 November 1985), *Porto Empedocle* (19 March 1986), *Porto Venere* (16 May 1989), *Porto Fossone* (24 September 1990), *Porto Torres* (16 January 1991) and *Porto Corsini* (4 March 1991).
Fitted for firefighting and anti-pollution. Carry a 1 ton telescopic crane. Based at Taranto, La Spezia, Augusta and La Maddalena. *Porto d'Ischia* and *Riva Trigoso* are slightly smaller with single diesels and were built in 1970.
UPDATED

PORTO D'ISCHIA   *9/1999*, Giorgio Ghiglione /* 0080112

32 HARBOUR TUGS (YTM)

RP 101 Y 403 (1972)	RP 113 Y 463 (1978)	RP 125 Y 478 (1983)
RP 102 Y 404 (1972)	RP 114 Y 464 (1980)	RP 126 Y 479 (1983)
RP 103 Y 406 (1974)	RP 115 Y 465 (1980)	RP 127 Y 480 (1984)
RP 104 Y 407 (1974)	RP 116 Y 466 (1980)	RP 128 Y 481 (1984)
RP 105 Y 408 (1974)	RP 118 Y 468 (1980)	RP 129 Y 482 (1984)
RP 106 Y 410 (1974)	RP 119 Y 470 (1980)	RP 130 Y 483 (1985)
RP 108 Y 452 (1975)	RP 120 Y 471 (1980)	RP 131 Y 484 (1985)
RP 109 Y 456 (1975)	RP 121 – (1984)	RP 132 Y 485 (1985)
RP 110 Y 458 (1975)	RP 122 Y 473 (1981)	RP 133 Y 486 (1985)
RP 111 Y 460 (1975)	RP 123 Y 467 (1981)	RP 134 Y 487 (1985)
RP 112 Y 462 (1975)	RP 124 Y 477 (1981)	

Comment: *RP 126* by Cantieri Navali Vittoria of Adria and *RP 121* by Baia, Naples. *RP 127-131* and *134* built by Ferrari Yard, La Spezia. *RP 132* and *133* built by CINET Yard, Molfetta. *RP 113-126* are of slightly larger dimensions and differ somewhat in appearance. *RP 127-134* are larger and slower. **UPDATED**

RP 106   *5/1999*, A Sharma* / 0080113

ARMY

Note: The following units are operated by the 'Serenissima Amphibious Regiment' in the Venice Lagoons area. EIG means Italian Army Craft and is part of the hull number. Four LCM (EIG 29, 30, 31, 32), 60 tons; two LCVP (EIG 26, 27), 13 tons; four recce craft (EIG 3, 48, 49, 206), 5 tons; two command craft (EIG 208, 210), 21.5 tons; one rescue tug (EIG 209), 45 tons; one inshore tanker (EIG 44), 95 tons; one ambulance and rescue craft (EIG 28) and about 70 minor craft (ferries, barges, river boats, rigid inflatable raiders).

ARMY   *7/1993*, van Ginderen Collection* / 0075865

GOVERNMENT MARITIME FORCES

Note: Consideration has been given to combine all these forces into one Coast Guard.

CUSTOMS (SERVIZIO NAVALE GUARDIA DI FINANZA)

Notes: (1) This force is operated by the Ministry of Finance but in time of war would come under the command of the Marina Militare. It is divided into 19 areas, 28 operational sectors and 26 squadrons. Their task is to patrol ports, lakes and rivers. The total manpower is 5,400. Nearly all the larger craft are armed. There are 12 P-166 and 4 ATR 42 patrol aircraft plus 61 Hughes NH 500, 21 Agusta A 109 and 14 Agusta Bell AB 412 helicopters, all radar and FLIR fitted.
(2) In addition to the classes detailed below there are:
(a) 180 inshore patrol craft of between 27 and 3 tons and 23 to 64 kt, including seized smugglers craft.
(b) 100 lake patrol craft.
(3) Three V6000 superfast craft (70 kt) entered service in 1999 and a further 11 are on order from Intermarine for 2000/01.

3 ANTONIO ZARA CLASS

Name	No	Builders	Commissioned
ANTONIO ZARA	P 01	Fincantieri, Muggiano	23 Feb 1990
GIUSEPPE VIZZARI	P 02	Fincantieri, Muggiano	27 Apr 1990
DENARO	P 03	Fincantieri, Muggiano	20 Mar 1998

Displacement, tons: 340 full load
Dimensions, feet (metres): 167 × 24.6 × 6.2 *(51 × 7.5 × 1.9)*
Main machinery: 2 GMT BL 230.12 M diesels; 5,956 hp(m) *(4.38 MW)* sustained; 2 shafts
    4 MTU 16V 396 TB94 diesels; 13,029 hp(m) *(9.58 MW)* sustained; 2 shafts (P 03)
Speed, knots: 27; 35 (P 03). **Range, miles:** 3,800 at 15 kt
Complement: 33 (3 officers)
Guns: 1 or 2 Breda 30 mm/70 (single or twin). 2—7.62 mm MGs.
Weapons control: Selenia Pegaso or AESN Medusa (P 03) optronic director.
Radars: Surface search: Gemant 2 ARPA and SPN 749; I-band.

Comment: Similar to the 'Ratcharit' class built for Thailand in 1976-79. First pair ordered in August 1987. One more ordered in October 1995 with more powerful engines and with a modified armament of a single 30 mm gun with a Medusa optronic director. **UPDATED**

ANTONIO ZARA   *8/1999*, Giorgio Ghiglione* / 0080114

2 MAZZEI CLASS

Name	No	Builders	Commissioned
MAZZEI	—	Intermarine, Sarzana	Apr 1998
VACCARO	—	Intermarine, Sarzana	May 1998

Displacement, tons: 115 full load
Dimensions, feet (metres): 116.5 × 24.8 × 3.6 *(35.5 × 7.6 × 1.1)*
Main machinery: 2 MTU 16V 396 TB94 diesels; 5,800 hp(m) *(4.26 MW)* sustained; 2 shafts
Speed, knots: 35. **Range, miles:** 700 at 18 kt
Complement: 17 plus 18 trainees
Guns: 1 Breda Mauser 30 mm/70. 2—7.62 mm MGs.
Weapons control: Elsag Medusa optronic director.
Radars: Surface search: GEM 3072A ARPA; I-band.
Navigation: GEM 1410; I-band.

Comment: Based on the 'Bigliani' class but with an extended hull. Mainly used as training ships. **UPDATED**

MAZZEI   *10/1998*, Giorgio Ghiglione* / 0080115

12 BIGLIANI CLASS

BIGLIANI G 80	**MACCHI** G 83	**BUONOCORE** G 86	**LA MALFA** G 88
CAVAGLIA G 81	**SMALTO** G 84	**SQUITIERI** G 87	**ROSATI** G 89
GALIANO G 82	**FORUNA** G 85	**BARLETTA** G 79	**OTTONELLI** G 78

Displacement, tons: 87 full load
Dimensions, feet (metres): 86.6 × 23 × 3.6 *(26.4 × 7 × 1.1)*
Main machinery: 2 MTU 16V 396 TB94 diesels; 5,800 hp(m) *(4.26 MW)* sustained; 2 shafts
Speed, knots: 42. **Range, miles:** 770 at 18 kt
Complement: 11 (1 officer)
Guns: 1 Breda Mauser 30 mm/70. 2—7.62 mm MGs.
Weapons control: Elsag Medusa Mk 3 optronic director.
Radars: Surface search: GEM 3072A ARPA; I-band.
Navigation: GEM 1410; I-band.

Comment: First eight built by Crestitalia and delivered from October 1987 to September 1992. Three more were ordered from Crest-Italia/Intermarine in October 1994 and were delivered from December 1996 to April 1997. A fourth was delivered in late 1999. There are minor structural differences between the first series (G 80-81), the second (G 82-87) and the third series (G 78-79, G 88-89). **UPDATED**

OTTONELLI   *1/2000*, Giorgio Ghiglione* / 0075866

26 + 8 CORRUBIA CLASS

CORRUBIA G 90	FAIS G 97	APRUZZI G 104	LETIZIA G 110
GIUDICE G 91	FELICIANI G 98	BALLALI G 105	MAZZARELLA G 111
ALBERTI G 92	GARZONI G 99	BOVIENZO G 106	NIOI G 112
ANGELINI G 93	LIPPI G 100	CARRECA G 107	PARTIPILO G 113
CAPPELLETTI G 94	LOMBARDI G 101	CONVERSANO G 108	PULEO G 114
CIORLIERI G 95	MICCOLI G 102	INZERILLI G 109	ZANNOTTI G 115
D'AMATO G 96	TREZZA G 103		

Displacement, tons: 92 full load
Dimensions, feet (metres): 87.9 × 24.9 × 3.9 *(26.8 × 7.6 × 1.2)*
Main machinery: 2 Isotta Fraschini ID 36 SS 16V diesels; 6,400 hp(m) *(4.7 MW)*; 2 shafts (G 90-91)
2 MTU 16V 396 TB94; 5,800 hp(m) *(4.26 MW)* sustained; 2 shafts (G 92-103)
Speed, knots: 43. **Range, miles:** 700 at 20 kt
Complement: 12 (1 officer)
Guns: 1 Breda Mauser 30 mm/70 (G 90-103). 1 Astra 20 mm (G 104-115). 2—7.62 mm MGs.
Weapons control: Elsag Medusa optronic director.
Radars: Surface search: GEM 3072A ARPA; I-band.
Navigation: GEM 1210; I-band.

Comment: First two built by Cantieri del Golfo, Gaeta and delivered in 1990. Others built by Cantieri del Golfo (G 92-100), and Crest-Italia (G 101-103), and Intermarine from 1995 onwards. G 115 completed in 1999. There are minor structural differences between the first series (G 90-91), the second series (G 92-103) and the third batch (G 104-115). Another batch of eight ordered in 2000.   ***UPDATED***

LETIZIA   *11/1998*, Giorgio Ghiglione / 0080116

44 MEATINI CLASS

G 13-G 66 series

Displacement, tons: 40 full load
Dimensions, feet (metres): 65.9 × 17.1 × 3.3 *(20.1 × 5.2 × 1)*
Main machinery: 2 CRM diesels; 2,500 hp(m) *(1.84 MW)*; 2 shafts
Speed, knots: 34. **Range, miles:** 550 at 20 kt
Complement: 11 (1 officer)
Guns: 1 Oerlikon 20 mm. 2—7.62 mm MGs.
Radars: Surface search: 1 GEM 1210; I-band.

Comment: Fifty-six of the class built from 1970 to 1978. Numbers are reducing.   ***UPDATED***

MEATINI   *6/1998, Guardia di Finanza / 0052439*

COAST GUARD (GUARDIA COSTIERA—CAPITANERIE DI PORTO)

Note: This is a force which is affiliated with the Marina Militare under whose command it would be placed in an emergency. The Coast Guard denomination was given after the Sea Protection Law in 1988. All vessels have a red diagonal stripe painted on the white hull and many are armed with 7.62 mm MGs. There are some 5,000 naval personnel including 800 officers of which about half are doing national service. Ranks are the same as the Navy.
(a) SAR craft; *Saettia* CP 901 (391 tons); *Giulio Ingianni* CP 409 (180 tons); CP 401-408 (136 tons). *Michelle Fiorillo* CP 307 (84 tons); *Bruno Gregoretti* CP 312 (65 tons); *Dante Novaro* CP 313; CP 314-318 (43 tons); CP 302-306, 309-311 (29 tons). 25 CP 800 class built 1996-98.
(b) Fast patrol craft; CP 254-260 (22.5 tons), CP 244-253 (21.5 tons), CP 231-238 (14 tons).
(c) Inshore patrol craft; 98 craft of between 4 and 15 tons. There are also 27 airport rescue craft.
(d) Aircraft include 14 Piaggio P 166 DL3 and two ATR 42MP maritime patrol, and 12 Griffon AB 412SP helicopters.
(e) CP 451 is a 1,278 ton training ship (ex-US ATF *Bannock*). C 452 is a former naval Safety Range patrol craft. *Barbara* recommissioned in late 1999.

CP 451 (training)   *7/1999*, Giorgio Ghiglione / 0080119

CP 250 (patrol)   *1/1999*, van Ginderen Collection / 0080120

1 + 3 (1) SAETTIA CLASS

SAETTIA CP 901

Displacement, tons: 391 full load
Dimensions, feet (metres): 169.6 × 26.6 × 6.6 *(51.7 × 8.1 × 2)*
Main machinery: 4 MTU 16V 538 TB93 diesels; 17,598 hp(m) *(12.94 MW)*; 4 shafts
Speed, knots: 40. **Range, miles:** 1,800 at 18 kt
Guns: 1 Otobreda 25 mm.
Weapons control: Eurocontrol optronic sensor.
Radars: Surface search: SPN 753; I-band.

Comment: Built in 1984 by Fincantieri as an attack missile craft demonstrator. Modified for use as an SAR craft and taken over by the Coast Guard 20 July 1999. Based at Messina. Three more of the class with smaller engines ordered in 2000. Two RIBs are carried together with a ROV and side scan sonar.
                                                                                 NEW ENTRY

SAETTIA (SAR)   *7/1999*, Fincantieri / 0080121

POLICE (SERVIZIO NAVALE CARABINIERI)

Notes: (1) The Carabinieri established its maritime force in 1969. This currently numbers 179 craft in service or building which operate in coastal waters within the 3 mile limit and in inshore waters. The following are typical of the craft concerned; 27—800 class of 26 tons building 1996-1999; 6—700 class of 22 tons; 23—600 class of 12 tons; 30 N 500 class of 6 tons; 3 S 500 class of 7 tons; 2 T 120 class of 7.5 tons; 90—100/200/300 classes of 2 tons.
Most are capable of 20 to 25 kt except the 800 class at 35 kt.
(2) There is also a Sea Police Force of the State. All craft have POLIZIA written on the side. Vessels include 28 'Squalo' class of 14 tons, 4 'Nelson' class of 11 tons, 7 'Intermarine' class of 8.4 tons, 37 'Crestitalia' class of 6 tons and 25 'Aquamaster/Drago' classes of 3 tons. Speeds vary between 23 and 45 kt.

500 class   *11/1998*, Per Kornefeldt / 0080117

POLIZIA craft   *5/1999*, A Sharma / 0080118

IVORY COAST
MARINE CÔTE D'IVOIRE

Headquarters Appointments	Bases	Personnel	Mercantile Marine	**DELETIONS**
Chief of Naval Staff: Capitaine de Frigate Diomande Megna	Use made of ports at Locodjo (Abidjan), Sassandra, Tabouand San-Pédro	2000: 950 (75 officers)	*Lloyd's Register of Shipping:* 35 vessels of 9,508 tons gross	1997 *Le Vigilant*

PATROL FORCES

Note: Two Rodman 800 craft delivered in late 1997 for the Police.

2 PATRA CLASS (LARGE PATROL CRAFT) (PC)

Name	No	Builders	Launched	Commissioned
L'ARDENT	—	Auroux, Arcachon	21 July 1978	6 Oct 1978
L'INTRÉPIDE	—	Auroux, Arcachon	21 July 1978	6 Oct 1978

Displacement, tons: 147.5 full load
Dimensions, feet (metres): 132.5 × 19.4 × 5.2 *(40.4 × 5.9 × 1.6)*
Main machinery: 2 SACM AGO 195 V12 CZSHR diesels; 4,340 hp(m) *(3.19 MW)* sustained; 2 shafts; cp props
Speed, knots: 26. **Range, miles:** 1,750 at 10 kt; 750 at 20 kt
Complement: 19 (2 officers)
Guns: 1 Breda 40 mm/70. 1 Oerlikon 20 mm. 2—7.62 mm MGs.
Radars: Surface search: Racal Decca 1226; I-band.

Comment: Of similar design to French 'Patra' class. Laid down 7 July 1977 *(Intrépide)* and 7 May 1977 *(Ardent)*. Patrol endurance of five days. Both in need of refits but still seaworthy. SS-12M missiles are no longer carried.

UPDATED

L'ARDENT   *3/1994* * / 0080123

1 FRANCO-BELGE TYPE (LARGE PATROL CRAFT) (PG)

Name	No	Builders	Launched	Commissioned
LE VALEUREUX	—	SFCN, Villeneuve	8 Mar 1976	25 Oct 1976

Displacement, tons: 235 standard; 250 full load
Dimensions, feet (metres): 155.8 × 23.6 × 7.5 *(47.5 × 7 × 2.3)*
Main machinery: 2 AGO diesels; 4,220 hp(m) *(3 MW)*; 2 shafts *(Valeureux)*
2 MGO diesels; 2,400 hp(m) *(1.76 MW)*; 2 shafts *(Vigilant)*
Speed, knots: 22 *(Valeureux)*; 18.5 *(Vigilant)*. **Range, miles:** 2,000 at 15 kt
Complement: 34 (4 officers)
Guns: 2 Breda 40 mm/70. 2—12.7 mm MGs.
Radars: Surface search: Racal Decca 1226; I-band.

Comment: Received new engines in 1987. Second of class *Le Vigilant* (see picture) was beyond economical repair by 1998.

UPDATED

LE VIGILANT   *10/1994* * / 0080122

1 BATRAL TYPE (LIGHT TRANSPORT) (LST)

Name	No	Builders	Commissioned
L'ÉLÉPHANT	—	Chantier Naval Querqueville	2 Feb 1977

Displacement, tons: 750 standard; 1,330 full load
Dimensions, feet (metres): 262.4 × 42.6 × 7.9 *(80 × 13 × 2.4)*
Main machinery: 2 SACM Type 195 V12 diesels; 3,600 hp(m) *(2.65 MW)*; 2 shafts; cp props
Speed, knots: 16. **Range, miles:** 4,500 at 13 kt
Complement: 47 (5 officers)
Military lift: 180 troops; 12 vehicles; 350 tons cargo
Guns: 2 Breda 40 mm/70. 2—81 mm mortars.
Radars: Surface search: Racal Decca 1226; I-band.
Helicopters: Platform only.

Comment: Ordered 20 August 1974. Laid down 1975. In poor condition but reported at sea under civilian charter.

UPDATED

L'ÉLÉPHANT   *10/1994* * / 0080124

2 CTM (LCM)

CTM 15   CTM 16

Displacement, tons: 150 full load
Dimensions, feet (metres): 78 × 21 × 4.2 *(23.8 × 6.4 × 1.3)*
Main machinery: 2 Poyaud 520 V8 diesels; 225 hp(m) *(165 kW)*; 2 shafts
Speed, knots: 9.5. **Range, miles:** 350 at 8 kt
Complement: 6
Military lift: 48 tons

Comment: Transferred from France in March 1999. Built in about 1968. Bow ramps are fitted.

NEW ENTRY

CTM (French colours)   *6/1995* * / 0012960

AUXILIARIES

Notes: There are also some Rotork 412 craft supplied in 1980. Some are naval, some civilian.
(2) Two French harbour tugs *Meusier* and *Meronnior* were acquired in September 1999.

JAMAICA

Headquarters Appointments	Bases	**DELETIONS**
Commanding Officer Coast Guard: Commander H M Lewin	Main: *Cagway*, Port Royal Coastguard: Discovery Bay, Pedro Cays	1998 *Holland Bay, Manatee Bay*

Personnel

(a) 2000: 195 (26 officers) Regulars
(b) 55 (16 officers) Reserve Forces

Mercantile Marine

Lloyd's Register of Shipping:
9 vessels of 3,647 tons gross

COAST GUARD

Note: There are also two Boston Whalers, CG 091 and CG 092 built in 1992.

1 FORT CLASS (PC)

Name	No	Builders	Commissioned
FORT CHARLES	P 7	Sewart Seacraft Inc, Berwick	Sep 1974

Displacement, tons: 130 full load
Dimensions, feet (metres): 115 × 24 × 7 *(34.5 × 7.3 × 2.1)*
Main machinery: 2 MTU 16V 396 diesels; 6,000 hp(m) *(4.41 MW)* sustained; 2 shafts
Speed, knots: 32. **Range, miles:** 1,500 at 18 kt
Complement: 20 (4 officers)
Guns: 1 Oerlikon 20 mm. 2—12.7 mm MGs.
Radars: Surface search: Sperry 4016; I-band.

Comment: Of all-aluminium construction, launched July 1974. Underwent refit at Jacksonville, Florida, in 1980-81 which included extensive modifications to the bow resulting in increased length. Refitted again in 1987-88. A third refit is planned including new engines. Accommodation for 18 soldiers and may be used as 18-bed mobile hospital in an emergency. ***UPDATED***

FORT CHARLES   *6/1999*, JDFCG / 0080125*

1 HERO CLASS (PC)

Name	No	Builders	Commissioned
PAUL BOGLE	P 8	Lantana Boatyard Inc, FL	17 Sep 1985

Displacement, tons: 93 full load
Dimensions, feet (metres): 105 × 20.6 × 7 *(32 × 6.3 × 2.1)*
Main machinery: 3 MTU 8V 396 TB93 diesels; 3,270 hp(m) *(2.4 MW)* sustained; 3 shafts
Speed, knots: 32
Complement: 20 (4 officers)
Guns: 1 Oerlikon 20 mm. 2—12.7 mm MGs.
Radars: Surface search: Furuno 2400; I-band.
Navigation: Sperry 4016; I-band.

Comment: Of all-aluminium construction, launched in 1984. *Paul Bogle* was originally intended for Honduras as the third of the 'Guardian' class. Similar to patrol craft in Honduras and Grenada navies. Refitted in March 1998 at Network Marine, Louisiana. ***UPDATED***

PAUL BOGLE   *6/1999*, JDFCG / 0080126*

2 POINT CLASS (PC)

Name	No	Builders	Commissioned
SAVANNAH POINT (ex-*Point Nowell*)	CG 251 (ex-82363)	CG Yard, Maryland	1 June 1967
BELMONT POINT (ex-*Point Barnes*)	CG 252 (ex-82371)	J Martinac, Tacoma	21 Apr 1970

Displacement, tons: 67 full load
Dimensions, feet (metres): 83 × 17.2 × 5.8 *(25.3 × 5.3 × 1.8)*
Main machinery: 2 Caterpillar diesels; 1,600 hp *(1.19 MW)*; 2 shafts
Speed, knots: 22. **Range, miles:** 1,200 at 8 kt
Complement: 10
Guns: 2—12.7 mm MGs.
Radars: Surface search: Hughes/Furuno SPS-73; I-band.

Comment: Transferred from US Coast Guard on 15 October and 21 January 2000 respectively. These ships are spread throughout the Caribbean navies. ***NEW ENTRY***

SAVANNAH POINT   *10/1999*, JDFCG / 0080127*

4 DAUNTLESS CLASS (INSHORE PATROL CRAFT) (PB)

CG 121   CG 122   CG 123   CG 124

Displacement, tons: 11 full load
Dimensions, feet (metres): 40 × 14 × 4.3 *(12.2 × 4.3 × 1.3)*
Main machinery: 2 Caterpillar 3208TA diesels; 870 hp *(650 kW)*; 2 shafts
Speed, knots: 27. **Range, miles:** 600 at 18 kt
Complement: 5
Guns: 1—7.62 mm MG (can be carried).
Radars: Surface search: Raytheon 40X; I-band.

Comment: Delivered in September and November 1992, January 1993 and May 1994. Built by SeaArk Marine, Monticello. Aluminium construction. Craft of this class have been distributed throughout the Caribbean under FMS funding. ***UPDATED***

CG 121   *6/1999*, JDFCG / 0080128*

3 OFFSHORE PERFORMANCE TYPE (INSHORE PATROL CRAFT) (PBI)

CG 101   CG 102   CG 103

Displacement, tons: 3 full load
Dimensions, feet (metres): 33 × 8 × 1.8 *(10.1 × 2.4 × 0.6)*
Main machinery: 2 Johnson OMC outboards; 450 hp *(336 kW)*
Speed, knots: 48
Complement: 3
Guns: 1—7.62 mm MG (can be carried).
Radars: Surface search: Raytheon 40X; I-band.

Comment: Delivered in April 1992. Built by Offshore Performance Marine, Miami. Used in the anti-narcotics role. ***VERIFIED***

CG 102   *5/1992*, JDFCG

JAPAN
MARITIME SELF-DEFENCE FORCE (MSDF)
KAIJOH JIEI-TAI

Headquarters Appointments

Chief of Staff, Maritime Self-Defence Force:
   Admiral Kousei Fujita
Commander-in-Chief, Self-Defence Fleet:
   Admiral Kataru Hasegawa

Senior Appointments

Commander Fleet Escort Force:
   Vice Admiral Hiraku Katsuyama
Commander Submarine Force:
   Vice Admiral Mitsumori Akeno

Diplomatic Representation

Defence (Naval) Attaché in London:
   Captain Keiichi Kuno

Personnel

2000: 45,752 (including Naval Air) plus 3,735 civilians

District Flotillas

In addition to the Escort Force there are two Submarine Flotillas (Kure and Yokosuka), one Minesweeper Flotilla (Yokosuka) which are to be merged and five District Flotillas (Yokosuka, Maizuru, Ohminato, Sasebo and Kure). The District Flotillas are made up of up to five destroyers, an LST and a number of MSC and patrol craft.

Bases

Naval—Yokosuka, Kure, Sasebo, Maizuru, Ohminato
Naval Air—Atsugi, Hachinohe, Iwakuni, Kanoya, Komatsujima, Naha, Ozuki, Ohminato, Ohmura, Shimofusa, Tateyama, Tokushima, Ioujima

Organisation of the Major Surface Units of Japan (MSDF)

Four Escort Flotillas each consisting of DDH (Flagship); two Air Defence ships and five ASW/general purpose ships.

Escort Force (Yokosuka)
   Tachikaze (DDG 168) Flagship

Escort Flotilla 1 (Yokosuka)
   Shirane (DDH 143)
1st Destroyer Division (Y)
   Murasame (DD 101)
   Harusame (DD 102)
5th Destroyer Division (Y)
   Yuugiri (DD 153)
   Amagiri (DD 154)
   Umigiri (DD 158)
61st Destroyer Division (Y)
   Kirishima (DDG 174)
   Hatakaze (DDG 171)

Escort Flotilla 3 (Maizuru)
   Haruna (DDH 141)
3rd Destroyer Division (M)
   Mineyuki (DD 124)
   Hamayuki (DD 126)
7th Destroyer Division (O)
   Sawayuki (DD 125)
   Hamagiri (DD 155)
   Setogiri (DD 156)
63rd Destroyer Division (M)
   Shimakaze (DDG 172)
   Myoukou (DDG 175)

Escort Flotilla 2 (Sasebo)
   Kurama (DDH 144)
2nd Destroyer Division (S)
   Asagiri (DD 151)
   Yamagiri (DD 152)
   Sawagiri (DD 157)
6th Destroyer Division (S)
   Yuudachi (DD 103)
   Kirisame (DD 104)
62nd Destroyer Division (S)
   Sawakaze (DDG 170)
   Kongou (DDG 173)

Escort Flotilla 4 (Kure)
   Hiei (DDH 142)
4th Destroyer Division (K)
   Inazuma (DD 105)
   Samidare (DD 106)
8th Destroyer Division (K)
   Yamayuki (DD 129)
   Matsuyuki (DD 130)
   Setoyuki (DD 131)
64th Destroyer Division (S)
   Asakaze (DDG 169)
   Choukai (DDG 176)

Coast Defence

The Army controls 78 SSM-1 truck-mounted sextuple launchers.

Strength of the Fleet (1 April 2000)

Type	Active (Auxiliary)	Building (Projected)
Submarines—Patrol	16 (2)	4 (1)
Destroyers	41	7 (1)
Frigates	12	—
Patrol Forces	3	4
LSTs	4	2
LCUs	4	—
LCACs	2	2 (2)
Landing Craft (LCM)	11	—
MCM Tenders/Controllers	4	—
Minesweepers—Ocean	3	—
Minesweepers—Coastal	24	4 (2)
Major Auxiliaries	27	1

New Construction Programme (Warships)

1997	2—4,400 ton DD, 1—2,700 ton SS, 1—510 ton MSC, 1—2,400 ton ATS, 1—400 ton ASY.
1998	2—4,600 ton DD, 1—2,700 ton SS, 1—510 ton MSC, 1—8,900 ton LST.
1999	1—4,600 ton DD, 1—2,700 ton SS, 2—510 ton MSC, 1—8,900 ton LST, 1—980 ton AMS, 2—200 ton PG.
2000	1—4,600 ton DD, 1—2,700 ton SS, 1—510 ton MSC, 2—200 ton PG, 1—13,500 ton AOE.

Naval Air Force

17 Air Patrol Sqns: P-3C, HSS-2B, SH-60J
Six Air Training Sqns: P-3C, YS-11, TC-90, KM-2, T-5, OH-6D, HSS-2B, SH-60J
One Air Training Support Squadron: U-36A, EP-3
One Transport Sqn: YS-11, LC-90
One MCM Sqn: MH-53E
Air Training Command (Shimofusa)
Air Wings at Kanoya (Wing 1), Hachinohe (Wing 2), Atsugi (Wing 4), Naha (Wing 5), Tateyama (Wing 21), Ohmura (Wing 22), Iwakuni (Wing 31)

Mercantile Marine

Lloyd's Register of Shipping:
   8,462 vessels of 17,062,556 tons gross

PENNANT LIST

Submarines—Patrol

SS 576	Okishio
SS 577	Nadashio
SS 578	Hamashio
SS 579	Akishio
SS 580	Takeshio
SS 581	Yukishio
SS 582	Sachishio
SS 583	Harushio
SS 584	Natsushio
SS 585	Hayashio
SS 586	Arashio
SS 587	Wakashio
SS 588	Fuyushio
SS 590	Oyashio
SS 591	Michishio
SS 592	Uzushio
SS 593	Makishio (bldg)

Submarines—Auxiliary

TSS 3601	Asashio
TSS 3602	Setoshio

Destroyers

DD 101	Murasame
DD 102	Harusame
DD 103	Yuudachi
DD 104	Kirisame
DD 105	Inazuma
DD 106	Samidare
DD 107	Ikazuchi (bldg)
DD 110	—
DD 111	—
DDK 121	Yuugumo
DD 122	Hatsuyuki
DD 123	Shirayuki
DD 124	Mineyuki
DD 125	Sawayuki
DD 126	Hamayuki
DD 127	Isoyuki
DD 128	Haruyuki
DD 129	Yamayuki
DD 130	Matsuyuki
DD 131	Setoyuki
DD 132	Asayuki
DDH 141	Haruna
DDH 142	Hiei
DDH 143	Shirane
DDH 144	Kurama
DD 151	Asagiri
DD 152	Yamagiri
DD 153	Yuugiri
DD 154	Amagiri
DD 155	Hamagiri
DD 156	Setogiri
DD 157	Sawagiri
DD 158	Umigiri
DDA 164	Takatsuki
DDA 165	Kikuzuki
DDG 168	Tachikaze
DDG 169	Asakaze
DDG 170	Sawakaze
DDG 171	Hatakaze
DDG 172	Shimakaze
DDG 173	Kongou
DDG 174	Kirishima
DDG 175	Myoukou
DDG 176	Choukai

Frigates

DE 220	Chitose
DE 221	Niyodo
DE 222	Teshio
DE 223	Yoshino
DE 224	Kumano
DE 225	Noshiro
DE 226	Ishikari
DE 227	Yubari
DE 228	Yubetsu
DE 229	Abukuma
DE 230	Jintsu
DE 231	Ohyodo
DE 232	Sendai
DE 233	Chikuma
DE 234	Tone

Patrol Forces

PG 821-823	PG 01-03

Minehunters/Sweepers—Ocean

MSO 301	Yaeyama
MSO 302	Tsushima
MSO 303	Hachijou

Minesweepers—Coastal

MSC 660	Hahajima
MSC 661	Takashima
MSC 662	Nuwajima
MSC 663	Etajima
MSC 664	Kamishima
MSC 665	Himeshima
MSC 666	Ogishima
MSC 667	Moroshima
MSC 668	Yurishima
MSC 669	Hikoshima
MSC 670	Awashima
MSC 671	Sakushima
MSC 672	Uwajima
MSC 673	Ieshima
MSC 674	Tsukishima
MSC 675	Maejima
MSC 676	Kumejima
MSC 677	Makishima
MSC 678	Tobishima
MSC 679	Yugeshima
MSC 680	Nagashima
MSC 681	Sugashima
MSC 682	Notojima
MSC 683	Tsunoshima
MSC 684	Naoshima (bldg)

MCM Tenders/Control Ships

MST 463	Uraga
MST 464	Bungo
MLC 722	Niijima
MLC 723	Yakushima

Amphibious Forces

LST 4001	Osumi
LST 4103	Nemuro
LST 4152	Ojika
LST 4153	Satsuma
LSU 4171	Yura
LSU 4172	Noto

Submarine Depot/Rescue Ships

AS 405	Chiyoda
ASR 403	Chihaya

Fleet Support Ships

AOE 421	Sagami
AOE 422	Towada
AOE 423	Tokiwa
AOE 424	Hamana

Training Ships

TV 3508	Kashima
TV 3512	Aokumo
TV 3513	Shimayuki
TV 3514	Akigumo

Training Support Ships

ATS 4202	Kurobe
ATS 4203	Tenryu
ASU 7020	Hayase

Cable Repair Ship

ARC 482	Muroto

Icebreakers

AGB 5002	Shirase

Survey and Research Ships

AGS 5102	Futami
AGS 5103	Suma
AGS 5104	Wakasa
AGS 5105	Nichinan
ASE 6101	Kurihama
ASE 6102	Asuka

Ocean Surveillance Ships

AOS 5201	Hibiki
AOS 5202	Harima

Tenders

ASU 83-85	—
ASY 91	Hashidate
YAS 98	Hatsushima
YAS 01	Ninoshima
YAS 02	Miyajima

DELETIONS and CONVERSIONS

Submarines		Frigates		Mine Warfare Forces		Auxiliaries	
1997	*Mochishio* (converted)	1997	*Mikuma*	1997	*Ooshima, Niijima* (both converted), 2 MSB	1997	ASU 81, *Takami, Muzuki, Iwai, Hashira*
1998	*Setoshio* (converted), *Yuushio*	1998	*Tokachi, Iwase*	1998	*Hayase* (converted), *Fukue* (converted)	1998	*Asagumo, Katori, Yokose, Sakate*, ASU 82
2000	*Okishio* (converted), *Mochishio, Asashio*	1999	*Chitose, Nyodo*	1999	*Narushima, Yakushima* (converted), *Fukue*	1999	*Akashi, Minegumo, Natsugumo, Mochizuki,*
	(converted)	2000	*Teshio*	2000	*Chichijima, Torishima*		*Azuma, Hyodori, Oumi*
						2000	*Fushimi, Murakumo, Okitsu*

Destroyers				Amphibious Forces	
1998	*Murakumo* (converted)	**Patrol Forces**		1998	*Atsumi*
1999	*Aokumo* (converted), *Shimayuki* (converted)	1998	*PB 25, PB 26*	1999	*Motobu*
2000	*Akigumo* (converted), *Murakumo*	1999	*PB 27*	2000	*Miura*

SUBMARINES

3 + 4 (1) OYASHIO CLASS (SSK)

Name	No	Builders	Laid down		Launched		Commissioned	
OYASHIO	SS 590	Kawasaki, Kobe	26 Jan	1994	15 Oct	1996	16 Mar	1998
MICHISHIO	SS 591	Mitsubishi, Kobe	16 Feb	1995	18 Sep	1997	10 Mar	1999
UZUSHIO	SS 592	Kawasaki, Kobe	6 Mar	1996	26 Nov	1998	9 Mar	2000
MAKISHIO	SS 593	Mitsubishi, Kobe	26 Mar	1997	22 Sep	1999	Mar	2001
—	SS 594	Kawasaki, Kobe	9 Mar	1998	Sep	2000	Mar	2002
—	SS 595	Mitsubishi, Kobe	2 Apr	1999	Nov	2001	Mar	2003
—	SS 596	Kawasaki, Kobe	26 Mar	2000	Nov	2002	Mar	2004

Displacement, tons: 2,700 standard; 3,000 dived
Dimensions, feet (metres): 268 × 29.2 × 25.9
(81.7 × 8.9 × 7.9)
Main machinery: Diesel-electric; 2 Kawasaki 12V25S diesels; 5,520 hp(m) *(4.1 MW)*; 2 Kawasaki alternators; 3.7 MW; 2 Fuji motors; 7,750 hp(m) *(5.7 MW)*; 1 shaft
Speed, knots: 12 surfaced; 20 dived
Complement: 69 (10 officers)

Missiles: SSM: McDonnell Douglas Sub-Harpoon; active radar homing to 130 km *(70 n miles)* at 0.9 Mach; warhead 227 kg.
Torpedoes: 6—21 in *(533 mm)* tubes; Type 89; wire guided; active/passive homing to 50 km *(27 n miles)*/38 km *(21 n miles)* at 40/55 kt; warhead 267 kg and Type 80 ASW. Total of 20 SSM and torpedoes.
Countermeasures: ESM: ZLR 7; radar warning.
Weapons control: SMCS type TFCS.
Radars: Surface search: JRC ZPS 6; I-band.
Sonars: Hughes/Oki ZQQ 5B/6; hull and flank arrays; active/ passive search and attack; medium/low frequency.
ZQR 1 (BQR 15) towed array; passive search; very low frequency.

Programmes: First of a new class approved in the 1993 budget and then one a year up to FY2000.
Structure: Fitted with large flank sonar arrays which are reported as the reason for the increase in displacement over the 'Harushio' class. Double hull sections forward and aft and anechoic tiles on the fin. A new type of deck casing and faired fin are other distinguishing features.

OYASHIO   *11/1999*, *Hachiro Nakai* / 0080130

Opinion: Experiments have been done by Kawasaki Heavy Industries with an 800 hp Stirling engine under agreement with Kockums, with fuel cells and, on a commercial basis, with MHD propulsion. The Technical Research and Development Institute is conducting tests on the Stirling engine with two delivered by March 1995. It seems unlikely that AIP will be fitted until the next class is ordered.

UPDATED

7 HARUSHIO CLASS (SSK)

Name	No	Builders	Laid down		Launched		Commissioned	
HARUSHIO	SS 583	Mitsubishi, Kobe	21 Apr	1987	26 July	1989	30 Nov	1990
NATSUSHIO	SS 584	Kawasaki, Kobe	8 Apr	1988	20 Mar	1990	20 Mar	1991
HAYASHIO	SS 585	Mitsubishi, Kobe	9 Dec	1988	17 Jan	1991	25 Mar	1992
ARASHIO	SS 586	Kawasaki, Kobe	8 Jan	1990	17 Mar	1992	17 Mar	1993
WAKASHIO	SS 587	Mitsubishi, Kobe	12 Dec	1990	22 Jan	1993	1 Mar	1994
FUYUSHIO	SS 588	Kawasaki, Kobe	12 Dec	1991	16 Feb	1994	7 Mar	1995
ASASHIO	TSS 3601 (ex-SS 589)	Mitsubishi, Kobe	24 Dec	1992	12 July	1995	12 Mar	1997

Displacement, tons: 2,450 (2,560, SS 589) standard; 2,750 (2,850, SS 589) dived
Dimensions, feet (metres): 252.6; 255.9 (SS 589) × 32.8 × 25.3 *(77; 78 × 10 × 7.7)*
Main machinery: Diesel-electric; 2 Kawasaki 12V25/25S diesels; 5,520 hp(m) *(4.1 MW)*; 2 Kawasaki alternators; 3.7 MW; 2 Fuji motors; 7,200 hp(m) *(5.3 MW)*; 1 shaft
Speed, knots: 12 surfaced; 20 dived
Complement: 74 (10 officers); 71 (10 officers) (SS 589)

Missiles: SSM: McDonnell Douglas Sub-Harpoon; active radar homing to 130 km *(70 n miles)* at 0.9 Mach; warhead 227 kg.

Torpedoes: 6—21 in *(533 mm)* tubes. Japanese Type 89; wire-guided (option); active/passive homing to 50 km *(27 n miles)*/38 km *(21 n miles)* at 40/55 kt; warhead 267 kg; depth to 900 m, and Type 80 ASW. Total of 20 SSM and torpedoes.
Countermeasures: ESM: ZLR 3-6; radar warning.
Radars: Surface search: JRC ZPS 6; I-band.
Sonars: Hughes/Oki ZQQ 5B; hull-mounted; active/passive search and attack; medium/low frequency.
ZQR 1 towed array similar to BQR 15; passive search; very low frequency.

Programmes: First approved in 1986 estimates and then one per year until 1992.
Structure: The slight growth in all dimensions is a natural evolution from the 'Yuushio' class and includes more noise reduction, towed sonar and wireless aerials, as well as anechoic coating. Double hull construction. The last of this class has a slightly larger displacement and a small cutback in the crew as a result of greater systems automation for machinery and snorting control. Diving depth 350 m *(1,150 ft)*.
Operational: A remote periscope viewer is fitted in *Asashio*. *Asashio* converted to a training submarine in 2000.

UPDATED

ASASHIO   *7/1999*, *Hachiro Nakai* / 0080131

8 YUUSHIO CLASS (SSK/SSA)

Name	No	Builders	Laid down	Launched	Commissioned
SETOSHIO	TSS 3602 (ex-ATS 8008, ex-SS 575)	Mitsubishi, Kobe	17 Apr 1979	10 Feb 1981	17 Mar 1982
OKISHIO	SS 576	Kawasaki, Kobe	17 Apr 1980	5 Mar 1982	1 Mar 1983
NADASHIO	SS 577	Mitsubishi, Kobe	16 Apr 1981	27 Jan 1983	6 Mar 1984
HAMASHIO	SS 578	Kawasaki, Kobe	8 Apr 1982	1 Feb 1984	5 Mar 1985
AKISHIO	SS 579	Mitsubishi, Kobe	15 Apr 1983	22 Jan 1985	5 Mar 1986
TAKESHIO	SS 580	Kawasaki, Kobe	3 Apr 1984	19 Feb 1986	3 Mar 1987
YUKISHIO	SS 581	Mitsubishi, Kobe	11 Apr 1985	23 Jan 1987	11 Mar 1988
SACHISHIO	SS 582	Kawasaki, Kobe	11 Apr 1986	17 Feb 1988	24 Mar 1989

Displacement, tons: 2,200; 2,250 (SS 574 and 577-582); 2,300 (SS 576) standard; 2,450 dived
Dimensions, feet (metres): 249.3 × 32.5 × 24.3 (76 × 9.9 × 7.4)
Main machinery: Diesel-electric; 2 Kawasaki V8V24/30ATL diesels; 6,800 hp(m) (5 MW); 2 Fuji motors; 7,200 hp(m) (5.3 MW); 1 shaft
Speed, knots: 12 surfaced; 20 dived
Complement: 75 (10 officers)

Missiles: SSM: McDonnell Douglas Sub-Harpoon; active radar homing to 130 km (70 n miles) at 0.9 Mach; warhead 227 kg.

Torpedoes: 6—21 in (533 mm) tubes amidships. Japanese Type 89; active/passive homing to 50 km (27 n miles)/38 km (21 n miles) at 40/55 kt; warhead 267 kg; depth to 900 m and Type 80 ASW. Total of 20 SSM and torpedoes.
Countermeasures: ESM: ZLR 3-6; radar warning.
Radars: Surface search: JRC ZPS 6; I-band.
Sonars: Hughes/Oki ZQQ 5 (modified BQS 4); bow-mounted; passive/active search and attack; medium/low frequency. ZQR 1 towed array similar to BQR 15 (in most of the class); passive search; very low frequency.

Programmes: First one approved in FY75, then one per year from 1977 until 1985.
Modernisation: Towed sonar array fitted in Okishio in 1987 and now backfitted to others in the class. ZQQ 5 retrofitted.
Structure: An enlarged version of the 'Uzushio' class with improved diving depth to 275 m (900 ft). Double hull construction. The towed array is stowed in a conduit on the starboard side of the casing.
Operational: Setoshio became a training submarine on 10 March 1999. Okishio is planned to follow in 2000.
UPDATED

SETOSHIO (old number) *5/1999*, Hachiro Nakai /* 0080132

AKISHIO *7/1999*, Hachiro Nakai /* 0080133

DESTROYERS

4 KONGOU CLASS (DDG)

Name	No	Builders	Laid down		Launched		Commissioned	
KONGOU	DDG 173	Mitsubishi, Nagasaki	8 May	1990	26 Sep	1991	25 Mar	1993
KIRISHIMA	DDG 174	Mitsubishi, Nagasaki	7 Apr	1992	19 Aug	1993	16 Mar	1995
MYOUKOU	DDG 175	Mitsubishi, Nagasaki	8 Apr	1993	5 Oct	1994	14 Mar	1996
CHOUKAI	DDG 176	Ishikawajima Harima, Tokyo	29 May	1995	27 Aug	1996	20 Mar	1998

Displacement, tons: 7,250 standard; 9,485 full load
Dimensions, feet (metres): 528.2 × 68.9 × 20.3; 32.7 (sonar) *(161 × 21 × 6.2; 10)*
Main machinery: COGAG; 4 GE LM 2500 gas turbines; 102,160 hp *(76.21 MW)* sustained; 2 shafts; cp props
Speed, knots: 30. **Range, miles:** 4,500 at 20 kt
Complement: 307 (27 officers)

Missiles: SSM: 8 McDonnell Douglas Harpoon (2 quad) ❶ launchers; active radar homing to 130 km *(70 n miles)* at 0.9 Mach; warhead 227 kg.
SAM: GDC Pomona Standard SM-2MR (SM-3 in due course). FMC Mk 41 VLS (29 cells) forward ❷. Martin Marietta Mk 41 VLS (61 cells) aft ❸; command/inertial guidance; semi-active radar homing to 73 km *(40 n miles)* at 2 Mach. Total of 90 Standard and ASROC weapons.

A/S: Vertical launch ASROC; inertial guidance to 1.6-10 km *(1-5.4 n miles)*; payload Mk 46 Mod 5 Neartip.
Guns: 1 OTO Melara 5 in *(127 mm)*/54 Compatto ❹; 45 rds/min to 16 km *(8.7 n miles)*; weight of shell 32 kg.
2 GE/GD 20 mm/76 Mk 15 Vulcan Phalanx ❺. 6 barrels per mounting; 3,000 rds/min combined to 1.5 km.
Torpedoes: 6—324 mm (2 triple) HOS 302 tubes ❻. Honeywell Mk 46 Mod 5 Neartip; anti-submarine; active/passive homing to 11 km *(5.9 n miles)* at 40 kt; warhead 44 kg.
Countermeasures: Decoys: 4 Mk 36 SRBOC ❼ 6-barrelled Mk 36 chaff launchers; SLQ-25 towed torpedo decoy.
ESM/ECM: Melko NOLQ 2; intercept/jammer.
Combat data systems: Aegis NTDS with Links 11 and 14. Link 16 in due course. SATCOM WSC-3/OE-82C ❽. SQQ-28 helicopter datalink ❾.

Weapons control: 3 Mk 99 Mod 1 MFCS. Type 2-21 GFCS. Mk 116 Hitachi OYQ 102 (Mod 7 for ASW).
Radars: Air search: RCA SPY 1D ❿; 3D; F-band.
Surface search: JRC OPS-28D ⓫; G-band.
Navigation: JRC OPS-20; I-band.
Fire control: 3 SPG-62 ⓬; 1 Mk 2/21 ⓭; I/J-band.
IFF: UPX 29.
Sonars: Nec OQS 102 (SQS-53B/C) bow-mounted; active search and attack.
Oki OQR 2 (SQR-19A (V)) TACTASS; towed array; passive; very low frequency.

Helicopters: Platform ⓮ and fuelling facilities for SH-60J Seahawk.

Programmes: Proposed in the FY87 programme; first one accepted in FY88 estimates, second in FY90, third in FY91, fourth in FY93. Designated as destroyers but these ships are of cruiser size. The combination of cost and US Congressional reluctance to release Aegis technology slowed the programme down.
Structure: This is an enlarged and improved version of the USN *Arleigh Burke* with a lightweight version of the Aegis system. There are two missile magazines. OQS 102 plus OQR 2 towed array is the equivalent of SQQ-89. Prairie-Masker acoustic suppression system.
Operational: As well as air defence of the Fleet, these ships contribute to the air defences of mainland Japan. Standard SM-3 Block 0 to be fitted in due course.

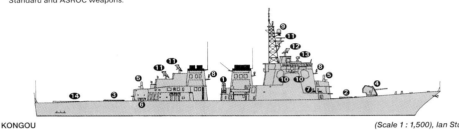

KONGOU   *(Scale 1 : 1,500), Ian Sturton*   **UPDATED**

MYOUKOU   *10/1998, G Toremans /* 0052448

CHOUKAI   *10/1999*, Hachiro Nakai /* 0080134

2 HATAKAZE CLASS (DDG)

Name	No	Builders	Laid down	Launched	Commissioned
HATAKAZE	DDG 171	Mitsubishi, Nagasaki	20 May 1983	9 Nov 1984	27 Mar 1986
SHIMAKAZE	DDG 172	Mitsubishi, Nagasaki	30 Jan 1985	30 Jan 1987	23 Mar 1988

Displacement, tons: 4,600 (4,650, DDG 172) standard; 5,500 full load

Dimensions, feet (metres): 492 × 53.8 × 15.7
(150 × 16.4 × 4.8)

Main machinery: COGAG; 2 RR Olympus TM3B gas turbines; 49,400 hp *(36.8 MW)* sustained; 2 RR Spey SM1A gas turbines; 26,650 hp *(19.9 MW)* sustained; 2 shafts; Kamewa cp props

Speed, knots: 30

Complement: 260 (23 officers)

Missiles: SSM: 8 McDonnell Douglas Harpoon ❶; active radar homing to 130 km *(70 n miles)* at 0.9 Mach; warhead 227 kg.
SAM: 40 GDC Pomona Standard SM-1MR; Mk 13 Mod 4 launcher ❷; command guidance; semi-active radar homing to 46 km *(25 n miles)* at 2 Mach; height envelope 45-18,288 m *(150-60,000 ft)*.
A/S: Honeywell ASROC Mk 112 octuple launcher ❸; inertial guidance to 1.6-10 km *(1-5.4 n miles)* at 0.9 Mach; payload Mk 46 Mod 5 Neartip. Reload capability.

Guns: 2 FMC 5 in *(127 mm)*/54 Mk 42 automatic ❹; 20-40 rds/min to 24 km *(13 n miles)* anti-surface; 14 km *(7.6 n miles)* anti-aircraft; weight of shell 32 kg.
2 General Electric/General Dynamics 20 mm Phalanx Mk 15 CIWS ❺; 6 barrels per mounting; 3,000 rds/min combined to 1.5 km.

Torpedoes: 6—324 mm Type 68 (2 triple) tubes ❻. Honeywell Mk 46 Mod 5 Neartip; anti-submarine; active/passive homing to 11 km *(5.9 n miles)* at 40 kt; warhead 44 kg.

HATAKAZE

(Scale 1 : 1,200), Ian Sturton

Countermeasures: Decoys: 2 Loral Hycor SRBOC 6-barrelled Mk 36 chaff launchers; range 4 km *(2.2 n miles)*.
ESM/ECM: Melco NOLQ 1/3; intercept/jammer. Fujitsu OLR 9B; intercept.
Combat data systems: OYQ-4 Mod 1 action data automation; Links 11 and 14. SATCOM ❼.
Weapons control: Type 2-21C for 127 mm guns. General Electric Mk 74 Mod 13 for Standard.
Radars: Air search: Hughes SPS-52C ❽; 3D; E/F-band.
Melco OPS-11C ❾; B-band.
Surface search: JRC OPS-28B ❿; G/H-band.
Fire control: 2 Raytheon SPG-51C ⓫; G-band.
Melco 2-21 ⓬; I/J-band. Type 2-12 ⓭; I-band.

Sonars: Nec OQS 4 Mod 1; bow-mounted; active search and attack; medium frequency.

Helicopters: Platform for 1 SH-60J Seahawk ⓮.

Programmes: DDG 171 provided for in 1981 programme. DDG 172 provided for in 1983 programme, ordered 29 March 1984.

UPDATED

HATAKAZE

4/1999, Hachiro Nakai* / 0080135

0 + 3 (1) IMPROVED MURASAME CLASS (DDG/DD)

Name	No	Builders	Laid down	Launched	Commissioned
—	DD 110	Sumitomo, Uraga	Apr 2000	Aug 2001	Mar 2003
—	DD 111	Mitsubishi, Nagasaki	May 2000	Sep 2001	Mar 2003
—	DD 112	—	May 2001	Sep 2002	Mar 2004

Displacement, tons: 4,600 standard; 5,150 full load

Dimensions, feet (metres): 495.4 × 57.1 × 17.4
(151 × 17.4 × 5.3)

Main machinery: COGAG; 2 RR Spey SM1C gas turbines; 41,630 hp *(31 MW)* sustained; 2 GE LM 2500 gas turbines; 43,000 hp *(32.08 MW)* sustained; 2 shafts

Speed, knots: 30

Complement: 170

Missiles: SSM: 8 SSM-1B ❶ (Harpoon); active radar homing to 130 km *(70 n miles)* at 0.9 Mach; warhead 227 kg.
SAM: Mk 41 VLS 32 cells ❷ Sea Sparrow; semi-active radar homing to 14.6 km *(8 n miles)* at 2.5 Mach; warhead 39 kg and VL ASROC.

Guns: 1 Otobreda 5 in *(127 mm)*/54 ❸ 45 rds/min to 16 km *(8.7 n miles)*; weight of shell 32 kg.
2 General Electric/General Dynamics 20 mm Phalanx Mk 15 CIWS ❹; 6 barrels per mounting; 3,000 rds/min combined to 1.5 km.

Torpedoes: 6—324 mm Type 68 (2 triple) tubes ❺ Mk 46 Mod 5; anti-submarine; active/passive homing to 11 km *(5.9 n miles)* at 40 kt; warhead 44 kg.

Countermeasures: Decoys: 4 Mk 36 SRBOC chaff launchers ❻. SLQ-25 Nixie towed torpedo decoy.
ESM/ECM: Nec NOLQ 2/3; intercept and jammer.

IMPROVED MURASAME

(Scale 1 : 1,200), Ian Sturton) / 0080138

Combat data systems: OYQ-7 with Link 11. SQQ-28 helicopter datalink ❼.
Weapons control: Hitachi OYQ-103 ASW control system.
Radars: Air search: Melco OPS-24 ❽; 3D; D-band.
Surface search: JRC OPS-28D ❾; G-band.
Fire control: Two FCS 3 ❿.
Navigation: OPS-20; I-band.
Sonars: Hull-mounted; active search and attack; low frequency.
OQR-1 towed array; passive search; very low frequency.

Helicopters: 1 SH-60J Seahawk ⓫.

Programmes: First two approved in FY98, one in FY99 and one in FY2000.
Structure: 'Murasame' class modified to fit a Mk 41 VLS, improved missile fire control and new sonar.

NEW ENTRY

6 + 3 MURASAME CLASS (DDG/DD)

Name	No	Builders	Laid down		Launched		Commissioned	
MURASAME	DD 101	Ishikawajima Harima, Tokyo	18 Aug	1993	23 Aug	1994	12 Mar	1996
HARUSAME	DD 102	Mitsui, Tamano	24 Aug	1994	16 Oct	1995	24 Mar	1997
YUUDACHI	DD 103	Marine United, Uraga	18 Mar	1996	19 Aug	1997	4 Mar	1999
KIRISAME	DD 104	Mitsubishi, Nagasaki	3 Apr	1996	21 Aug	1997	18 Mar	1999
INAZUMA	DD 105	Mitsubishi, Nagasaki	8 May	1997	9 Sep	1998	15 Mar	2000
SAMIDARE	DD 106	Ishikawajima Harima, Tokyo	11 Sep	1997	24 Sep	1998	21 Mar	2000
IKAZUCHI	DD 107	Hitachi, Maizuru	25 Feb	1998	24 June	1999	Mar	2001
—	DD 108	Ishikawajima Harima, Tokyo	29 Oct	1999	Sep	2000	Mar	2002
—	DD 109	Mitsubishi, Nagasaki	18 May	1999	Sep	2000	Mar	2002

Displacement, tons: 4,550 standard; 5,100 full load
Dimensions, feet (metres): 495.4 × 57.1 × 17.1
 (151 × 17.4 × 5.2)
Main machinery: COGAG; 2 RR Spey SM1C gas turbines;
 41,630 hp *(31 MW)* sustained; 2 GE LM 2500 gas turbines;
 43,000 hp *(32.08 MW)* sustained; 2 shafts
Speed, knots: 30
Complement: 166

Missiles: SSM: 8 SSM-1B ❶ (Harpoon); active radar homing to
 130 km *(70 n miles)* at 0.9 Mach; warhead 227 kg.
 SAM: Raytheon Mk 48 VLS 16 cells ❷ Sea Sparrow; semi-active
 radar homing to 14.6 km *(8 n miles)* at 2.5 Mach; warhead
 39 kg.
 A/S: Mk 41 VL ASROC 16 cells ❸. Total of 29 missiles can be
 carried.
Guns: 1 OTO Melara 3 in *(76 mm)*/62 compact ❹; 85 rds/min to
 16 km *(8.6 n miles)* anti-surface; 12 km *(6.5 n miles)* anti-
 aircraft; weight of shell 6 kg.
 2 General Electric/General Dynamics 20 mm Phalanx Mk 15
 CIWS ❺; 6 barrels per mounting; 3,000 rds/min combined to
 1.5 km.

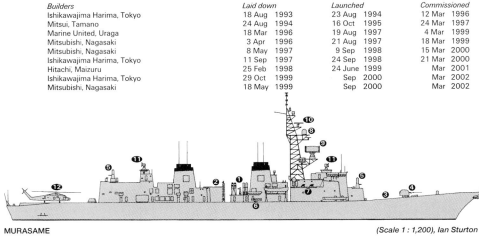

(Scale 1 : 1,200), Ian Sturton

MURASAME

Torpedoes: 6—324 mm Type 68 (2 triple) tubes ❻ Mk 46 Mod 5;
 anti-submarine; active/passive homing to 11 km *(5.9 n miles)*
 at 40 kt; warhead 44 kg.
Countermeasures: Decoys: 4 Mk 36 SRBOC chaff launchers ❼.
 SLQ-25 Nixie towed torpedo decoy.
 ESM/ECM: Nec NOLQ 2/3; intercept and jammer.

Combat data systems: OYQ-7 with Link 11. SQQ-28 helicopter
 datalink ❽.
Weapons control: Hitachi OYQ-103 ASW control system.
Radars: Air search: Melco OPS-24 ❾; 3D; D-band.
 Surface search: JRC OPS-28D ❿; G-band.
 Fire control: Two Type 2-31 ⓫.
 Navigation: OPS-20; I-band.
Sonars: Mitsubishi OQS-5; hull-mounted; active search and
 attack; low frequency.
 OQR-1 towed array; passive search; very low frequency.

Helicopters: 1 SH-60J Seahawk ⓬.

Programmes: First one approved in FY91 as an addition to the
 third Aegis type destroyer. Second approved in FY92. Two
 more approved in FY94 and again in FY95 and two in FY97.
 The programme has been given added priority by the 'Kongou'
 class being reduced to four ships because of the cost of Aegis.
Structure: More like a mini-Kongou than an enlarged 'Asagiri'
 class, with VLS and a much reduced complement. Stealth
 features are evident in sloping sides and rounded
 superstructure. Indal RAST helicopter hauldown.
Operational: ASROC missiles are not carried.

UPDATED

YUUDACHI

4/1999*, Hachiro Nakai / 0080137

HARUSAME

5/1998, Hachiro Nakai / 0052452

8 ASAGIRI CLASS (DDG/DD)

Name	No	Builders	Laid down		Launched		Commissioned	
ASAGIRI	DD 151	Ishikawajima Harima, Tokyo	13 Feb	1985	19 Sep	1986	17 Mar	1988
YAMAGIRI	DD 152	Mitsui, Tamano	5 Feb	1986	8 Oct	1987	25 Jan	1989
YUUGIRI	DD 153	Sumitomo, Uraga	25 Feb	1986	21 Sep	1987	28 Feb	1989
AMAGIRI	DD 154	Ishikawajima Harima, Tokyo	3 Mar	1986	9 Sep	1987	17 Mar	1989
HAMAGIRI	DD 155	Hitachi, Maizuru	20 Jan	1987	4 June	1988	31 Jan	1990
SETOGIRI	DD 156	Sumitomo, Uraga	9 Mar	1987	12 Sep	1988	14 Feb	1990
SAWAGIRI	DD 157	Mitsubishi, Nagasaki	14 Jan	1987	25 Nov	1988	6 Mar	1990
UMIGIRI	DD 158	Ishikawajima Harima, Tokyo	31 Oct	1988	9 Nov	1989	12 Mar	1991

Displacement, tons: 3,500 (3,550, DD 155-158) standard; 4,200 full load

Dimensions, feet (metres): 449.4 × 48 × 14.6 *(137 × 14.6 × 4.5)*

Main machinery: COGAG; 4 RR Spey SM1A gas turbines; 53,300 hp *(39.8 MW)* sustained; 2 shafts; cp props

Speed, knots: 30+

Complement: 220

Missiles: SSM: 8 McDonnell Douglas Harpoon (2 quad) launchers ❶; active radar homing to 130 km *(70 n miles)* at 0.9 Mach; warhead 227 kg.
SAM: Raytheon Sea Sparrow Mk 29 (Type 3/3A) octuple launcher ❷; semi-active radar homing to 14.6 km *(8 n miles)* at 2.5 Mach; warhead 39 kg; 20 missiles.
A/S: Honeywell ASROC Mk 112 octuple launcher ❸; inertial guidance to 1.6-10 km *(1-5.4 n miles)* at 0.9 Mach; payload Mk 46 Mod 5 Neartip. Reload capability.
Guns: 1 OTO Melara 3 in *(76 mm)*/62 compact ❹; 85 rds/min to 16 km *(8.6 n miles)* anti-surface; 12 km *(6.5 n miles)* anti-aircraft; weight of shell 6 kg.
2 General Electric/General Dynamics 20 mm Phalanx Mk 15 CIWS ❺; 6 barrels per mounting; 3,000 rds/min combined to 1.5 km.

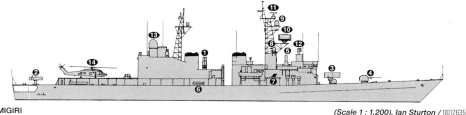

UMIGIRI

(Scale 1 : 1,200), Ian Sturton / 0012635

Torpedoes: 6—324 mm Type 68 (2 triple) HOS 301 tubes ❻. Honeywell Mk 46 Mod 5 Neartip; anti-submarine; active/ passive homing to 11 km *(5.9 n miles)* at 40 kt; warhead 44 kg.
Countermeasures: Decoys: 2 Loral Hycor SRBOC 6-barrelled Mk 36 chaff launchers ❼; range 4 km *(2.2 n miles)*.
1 SLQ-51 Nixie or Type 4; towed torpedo decoy.
ESM: Nec NOLR 6C or NOLR 8 (DD 152) ❽; intercept.
ECM: Fujitsu OLT-3; jammer.
Combat data systems: OYQ-6 data automation; Link 11/14. SATCOM. SQQ-28 helicopter datalink ❾ for SH-60J.

Radars: Air search: Melco OPS-14C (DD 151-154); D-band. Melco OPS-24 (DD 155-158) ❿; 3D; D-band.
Surface search: JRC OPS-28C ⓫; G-band (DD 151, 152, 155-158).
JRC OPS-28C-Y; G-band (DD 153-154).
Fire control: Type 2-22 (for guns) ⓬. Type 2-12E (for SAM) (DD 151-154); Type 2-12G (for SAM) ⓭ (DD 155-158).
Tacan: ORN-6D (URN 25).
Sonars: Mitsubishi OQS 4A (II); hull-mounted; active search and attack; low frequency.
OQR-1; towed array; passive search; very low frequency.

Helicopters: 1 SH-60J Seahawk ⓮.

Programmes: DD 151 in 1983 estimates, DD 152-154 in 1984, DD 155-157 in 1985 and DD 158 in 1986.
Modernisation: The last four were fitted on build with improved air search radar, updated fire-control radars and a helicopter datalink. Plans to fit the first four may have been postponed. *Umigiri* also commissioned with a sonar towed array which has been fitted to the rest of the class.
Structure: Because of the enhanced IR signature and damage to electronic systems on the mainmast caused by after funnel gases there have been modifications to help contain the problem. The mainmast is now slightly higher than originally designed and has been offset to port, more so in the last four of the class. The forward funnel is also offset slightly to port and the after funnel to the starboard side of the superstructure. The hangar structure is asymmetrical extending to the after funnel on the starboard side but only to the mainmast to port. SATCOM is fitted at the after end of the hangar roof.
Operational: Beartrap helicopter hauldown system. Sea Kings have been phased out.

UPDATED

SETOGIRI

10/1998, G Toremans / 0052453

HAMAGIRI

*5/1999 *, John Mortimer /* 0080139

HAMAGIRI

4/1998, Hachiro Nakai / 0052454

11 HATSUYUKI CLASS (DDG/DD)

Name	No	Builders	Laid down		Launched		Commissioned	
HATSUYUKI	DD 122	Sumitomo, Uraga	14 Mar	1979	7 Nov	1980	23 Mar	1982
SHIRAYUKI	DD 123	Hitachi, Maizuru	3 Dec	1979	4 Aug	1981	8 Feb	1983
MINEYUKI	DD 124	Mitsubishi, Nagasaki	7 May	1981	19 Oct	1982	26 Jan	1984
SAWAYUKI	DD 125	Ishikawajima Harima, Tokyo	22 Apr	1981	21 June	1982	15 Feb	1984
HAMAYUKI	DD 126	Mitsui, Tamano	4 Feb	1981	27 May	1982	18 Nov	1983
ISOYUKI	DD 127	Ishikawajima Harima, Tokyo	20 Apr	1982	19 Sep	1983	23 Jan	1985
HARUYUKI	DD 128	Sumitomo, Uraga	11 Mar	1982	6 Sep	1983	14 Mar	1985
YAMAYUKI	DD 129	Hitachi, Maizuru	25 Feb	1983	10 July	1984	3 Dec	1985
MATSUYUKI	DD 130	Ishikawajima Harima, Tokyo	7 Apr	1983	25 Oct	1984	19 Mar	1986
SETOYUKI	DD 131	Mitsui, Tamano	26 Jan	1984	3 July	1985	11 Dec	1986
ASAYUKI	DD 132	Sumitomo, Uraga	22 Dec	1983	16 Oct	1985	20 Feb	1987

Displacement, tons: 2,950 (3,050 from DD 129 onwards) standard; 3,700 (3,800) full load
Dimensions, feet (metres): 426.4 × 44.6 × 13.8 (14.4 from 129 onwards) *(130 × 13.6 × 4.2) (4.4)*
Main machinery: COGOG; 2 Kawasaki-RR Olympus TM3B gas turbines; 49,400 hp *(36.8 MW)* sustained; 2 RR Type RM1C gas turbines; 9,900 hp *(7.4 MW)* sustained; 2 shafts; cp props
Speed, knots: 30; 19 cruise
Complement: 195 (200, DD 124 onwards)

Missiles: SSM: 8 McDonnell Douglas Harpoon (2 quad) launchers ❶; active radar homing to 130 km *(70 n miles)* at 0.9 Mach; warhead 227 kg.
SAM: Raytheon Sea Sparrow Mk 29 Type 3A launcher ❷; semi-active radar homing to 14.6 km *(8 n miles)* at 2.5 Mach; warhead 39 kg; 12 missiles.
A/S: Honeywell ASROC Mk 112 octuple launcher ❸; inertial guidance to 1.6-10 km *(1-5.4 n miles)* at 0.9 Mach; payload Mk 46 Mod 5 Neartip.
Guns: 1 OTO Melara 3 in *(76 mm)*/62 compact ❹; 85 rds/min to 16 km *(8.6 n miles)* anti-surface; 12 km *(6.5 n miles)* anti-aircraft; weight of shell 6 kg.

HATSUYUKI

(Scale 1 : 1,200), Ian Sturton

2 General Electric/General Dynamics 20 mm Phalanx Mk 15 CIWS ❺; 6 barrels per mounting; 3,000 rds/min combined to 1.5 km.
Torpedoes: 6—324 mm Type 68 (2 triple) tubes ❻. Honeywell Mk 46 Mod 5 Neartip; anti-submarine; active/passive homing to 11 km *(5.9 n miles)* at 40 kt; warhead 44 kg.

Countermeasures: Decoys: 2 Loral Hycor SRBOC 6-barrelled Mk 36 chaff launchers; range 4 km *(2.2 n miles)*.
ESM: Nec NOLR 6C or NOLR 8 (DD 131-133); intercept.
ECM: Fujitsu OLT 3; jammer.
Combat data systems: OYQ-5 action data automation; Link 14 (receive only). SATCOM.
Radars: Air search: Melco OPS-14B ❼; D-band.
Surface search: JRC OPS-18-1 ❽; G-band.
Fire control: Type 2-12 A ❾; I/J-band (for SAM).
2 Type 2-21/21A ❿; I/J-band (for guns).
Tacan: ORN-6C-Y (DD 122, 125 and 132); ORN-6C (remainder).
Sonars: Nec OQS 4A (II) (SQS-23 type); bow-mounted; active search and attack; low frequency.
OQR 1 TACTASS (in some); passive; low frequency.

Helicopters: 1 SH-60J Seahawk ⓫.

Modernisation: *Shirayuki* retrofitted with Phalanx in early 1992, and the rest of the class by 1996. *Matsuyuki* first to get sonar towed array in 1990 and *Hatsuyuki* in 1994; the others are being fitted. All of the class converted to carry Seahawk helicopters.
Structure: Fitted with fin stabilisers. Steel in place of aluminium alloy for bridge etc after DD 129 which increased displacement.
Operational: Canadian Beartrap helicopter landing aid. Improved ECM equipment in the last two of the class. Last of class *Shimayuki* converted to a training ship 18 March 1999.

UPDATED

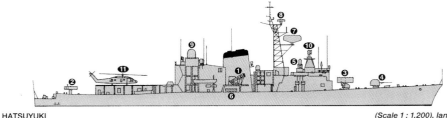

SETOYUKI

4/1999*, Hachiro Nakai / 0080140

2 TAKATSUKI CLASS (DDG/DDA)

Name	No	Builders	Laid down		Launched		Commissioned	
TAKATSUKI	DDA 164	Ishikawajima Harima, Tokyo	8 Oct	1964	7 Jan	1966	15 Mar	1967
KIKUZUKI	DDA 165	Mitsubishi, Nagasaki	15 Mar	1966	25 Mar	1967	27 Mar	1968

Displacement, tons: 3,250 standard
Dimensions, feet (metres): 446.1 × 44 × 14.8 *(136 × 13.4 × 4.5)*

Main machinery: 2 boilers; 600 psi *(60 kg/cm²)*; 850°F *(454°C)*; 2 Mitsubishi turbines; 70,000 hp(m); *(51.5 MW)*; 2 shafts
Speed, knots: 31. **Range, miles:** 7,000 at 20 kt
Complement: 260

Missiles: SSM: 8 McDonnell Douglas Harpoon (2 quad) launchers ❶; active radar homing to 130 km *(70 n miles)* at 0.9 Mach; warhead 227 kg.
SAM: Raytheon Sea Sparrow Type 3 or 3A octuple launcher ❷; semi-active radar homing to 14.6 km *(8 n miles)* at 2.5 Mach; warhead 39 kg; 16 missiles.
A/S: Honeywell ASROC Mk 112 octuple launcher ❸; inertial guidance to 10 km *(5.4 n miles)* at 0.9 Mach; payload Mk 46 Mod 5 Neartip.
Guns: 1 FMC 5 in *(127 mm)*/54 Mk 42 automatic ❹; 20-40 rds/min to 24 km *(13 n miles)* anti-surface; 14 km *(7.6 n miles)* anti-aircraft; weight of shell 32 kg.
1 General Electric/General Dynamics 20 mm Phalanx CIWS Mk 15 (DDA 165) ❺; 6 barrels per mounting; 3,000 rds/min combined to 1.5 km.
Torpedoes: 6—324 mm Type 68 (2 triple) tubes ❻. Honeywell Mk 46 Mod 5 Neartip; anti-submarine; active/passive homing to 11 km *(5.9 n miles)* at 40 kt; warhead 44 kg.
A/S mortars: 1—375 mm Bofors Type 71 4-barrelled trainable rocket launcher ❼; automatic loading; range 1.6 km.
Countermeasures: Decoys: 2 Loral Hycor SRBOC 6-barrelled Mk 36 chaff launchers; range 4 km *(2.2 n miles)*.
ESM: Nec NOLR 6C (NOLR 9 in DDA 165); intercept.
ECM: Fujitsu OLT 3; jammer.
Combat data systems: OYQ-5 action data automation; Link 14. SATCOM.
Weapons control: US Mk 56 or GFCS-1 for 127 mm guns. Type 2-12B for Sea Sparrow system.
Radars: Air search: Melco OPS-11B-Y ❽; D-band.
Surface search: JRC OPS-17 ❾; G-band.
Fire control: Type 2-12B ❿; I/J-band.
2 General Electric Mk 35 ⓫; I/J-band.
Sonars: Nec SQS-35J; hull-mounted; active search and attack; low frequency.
EDO SQR-18 TACTASS; passive; low frequency.

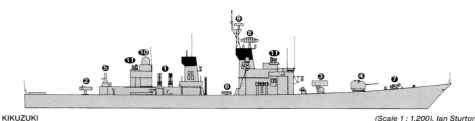

KIKUZUKI

(Scale 1 : 1,200), Ian Sturton

Modernisation: From 1 April 1984 to 31 October 1985 DDA 164 taken in hand for modifications to include removal of after 5 in gun and Dash hangar, fitting of Harpoon and Sea Sparrow, removal of VDS and its replacement by TASS, installation of FCS-2, and fittings for one 20 mm Phalanx mounting on after superstructure. Similar alterations carried out in DDA 165 from May 1985 to December 1986 except that Phalanx has been fitted. NOLR 9 installed in DDA 165 for trials in 1991-92.
Operational: An unmodified ship of this class was converted to a Special Service Auxiliary vessel on 1 April 1995 but has since been deleted.

UPDATED

KIKUZUKI

3/1999*, Hachiro Nakai / 0080136

3 TACHIKAZE CLASS (DDG)

Name	No
TACHIKAZE	DDG 168
ASAKAZE	DDG 169
SAWAKAZE	DDG 170

Builders	Laid down	Launched	Commissioned
Mitsubishi, Nagasaki	19 June 1973	17 Dec 1974	26 Mar 1976
Mitsubishi, Nagasaki	27 May 1976	15 Oct 1977	27 Mar 1979
Mitsubishi, Nagasaki	14 Sep 1979	4 June 1981	30 Mar 1983

Displacement, tons: 3,850 (3,950, DDG 170) standard
Dimensions, feet (metres): 469 × 47 × 15.1
(143 × 14.3 × 4.6)
Main machinery: 2 Mitsubishi boilers; 600 psi (60 kg/cm²);
850°F (454°C); 2 Mitsubishi turbines; 70,000 hp(m);
(51.5 MW); 2 shafts
Speed, knots: 32
Complement: 250-270

Missiles: SSM: 8 McDonnell Douglas Harpoon; active radar
homing to 130 km (70 n miles) at 0.9 Mach; warhead 227 kg
HE (DDG 170 only).
SAM: GDC Pomona Standard SM-1MR; Mk 13 Mod 1 or 4
launcher ❶; command guidance; semi-active radar homing to
46 km (25 n miles) at 2 Mach; height envelope 45-18,288 m
(150-60,000 ft); 40 missiles (SSM and SAM combined).
A/S: Honeywell ASROC Mk 112 octuple launcher ❷; inertial
guidance to 1.6-10 km (1-5.4 n miles) at 0.9 Mach; payload
Mk 46 Mod 5 Neartip. Reloads in DDG 170 only.
Guns: 1 or 2 FMC 5 in (127 mm)/54 Mk 42 automatic ❸; 20-40
rds/min to 24 km (13 n miles) anti-surface; 14 km (7.6 n miles)
anti-aircraft; weight of shell 32 kg.
2 General Electric/General Dynamics 20 mm Phalanx CIWS
Mk 15 ❹; 6 barrels per mounting; 3,000 rds/min combined to
1.5 km.
Torpedoes: 6—324 mm Type 68 (2 triple) tubes ❺. Honeywell
Mk 46 Mod 5 Neartip; anti-submarine; active/passive homing to
11 km (5.9 n miles) at 40 kt; warhead 44 kg.
Countermeasures: Decoys: 4 Loral Hycor SRBOC Mk 36
multibarrelled chaff launchers. SLQ-25 towed torpedo decoy.
ESM: Nec NOLR 6 (DDG 168); Nec NOLQ 1 (others); intercept.
ECM: Fujitsu OLT 3; jammer.
Combat data systems: OYQ-1B (DDG 168), OYQ-2B (DDG 169),
OYQ-4 (DDG 170) action data automation; Links 11 and 14.
SATCOM.
Weapons control: 2 Mk 74 Mod 13 missile control directors. US
Mk 114 ASW control. GFCS-2-21 for gun (DDG 170).
GFCS-72-1A for gun (others).
Radars: Air search: Melco OPS-11C ❻; B-band.
Hughes SPS-52B ❼ or 52C (DDG 170); 3D; E/F-band.
Surface search: JRC OPS-16D ❽; G-band (DDG 168).
JRC OPS-28 (DDG 170); G-band.
JRC OPS-18-3; G-band (DDG 169).
Fire control: 2 Raytheon SPG-51 ❾; G/I-band.
Type 2 FCS ❿; I/J-band.
IFF: US Mk 10.
Sonars: Nec OQS-3A (Type 66); bow-mounted; active search and
attack; low frequency.

Modernisation: Harpoon and CIWS added to DDG 168 in 1983,
DDG 169 and 170 in 1987. After gun removed to allow
increased Flag accommodation in *Tachikaze* in 1998.
Operational: *Tachikaze* is the Escort Force Flagship.

UPDATED

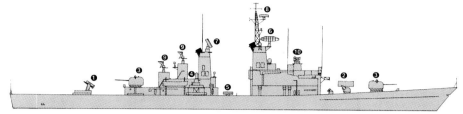

ASAKAZE *(Scale 1 : 1,200), Ian Sturton*

TACHIKAZE *4/1999*, Hachiro Nakai / 0080141*

SAWAKAZE *4/1999*, Hachiro Nakai / 0080142*

2 SHIRANE CLASS (DD/DDH)

Name	No
SHIRANE	DDH 143
KURAMA	DDH 144

Builders	Laid down	Launched	Commissioned
Ishikawajima Harima, Tokyo	25 Feb 1977	18 Sep 1978	17 Mar 1980
Ishikawajima Harima, Tokyo	17 Feb 1978	20 Sep 1979	27 Mar 1981

Displacement, tons: 5,200 standard
Dimensions, feet (metres): 521.5 × 57.5 × 17.5
(159 × 17.5 × 5.3)
Main machinery: 2 IHI boilers; 850 psi (60 kg/cm²); 900°F
(480°C); 2 IHI turbines; 70,000 hp(m) (51.5 MW); 2 shafts
Speed, knots: 31
Complement: 350; 360 (DDH 144) plus 20 staff

Missiles: SAM: Raytheon Sea Sparrow Mk 25 octuple launcher
❶; semi-active radar homing to 14.6 km (8 n miles) at
2.5 Mach; warhead 39 kg; 24 missiles.
A/S: Honeywell ASROC Mk 112 octuple launcher ❷; inertial
guidance to 10 km (5.4 n miles) at 0.9 Mach; payload Mk 46
Mod 5 Neartip.
Guns: 2 FMC 5 in (127 mm)/54 Mk 42 automatic ❸; 20-40 rds/
min to 24 km (13 n miles) anti-surface; 14 km (7.6 n miles) anti-
aircraft; weight of shell 32 kg.
2 General Electric/General Dynamics 20 mm Phalanx Mk 15
CIWS ❹; 6 barrels per mounting; 3,000 rds/min combined to
1.5 km.
Torpedoes: 6—324 mm Type 68 (2 triple) tubes ❺. Honeywell
Mk 46 Mod 5 Neartip; anti-submarine; active/passive homing
to 11 km (5.9 n miles) at 40 kt; warhead 44 kg.
Countermeasures: Decoys: 4 Mk 36 SRBOC chaff launchers.
Prairie Masker; blade rate suppression system.
ESM/ECM: Melco NOLQ 1; intercept/jammer. Fujitsu OLR 9B;
intercept.
Combat data systems: OYQ-3; Links 11 and 14. SATCOM ❻.
Weapons control: Singer Mk 114 for ASROC and TFCS; Type
72-1A GFCS.
Radars: Air search: Nec OPS-12 ❼; 3D; F-band.
Surface search: JRC OPS-28 ❽; G-band.
Navigation: Koden OFS-2D; I-band.
Fire control: Signaal WM25 ❾; I/J-band; range 46 km (25 n
miles).
2 Type 72-1A FCS ❿; I/J-band.
Tacan: ORN-6C/6C-Y.
Sonars: EDO/Nec SQS-35(J); VDS; active/passive search;
medium frequency.
Nec OQS 101; bow-mounted; low frequency.
EDO/Nec SQR-18A; towed array; passive; very low frequency.

Helicopters: 3 SH-60J Seahawk ⓫.

Programmes: One each in 1975 and 1976 programmes.
Modernisation: DDH 143 refit in 1989-90. Both fitted with CIWS
and towed array sonars by mid-1990.

SHIRANE *(Scale 1 : 1,500), Ian Sturton / 0012639*

SHIRANE *8/1999*, Hachiro Nakai / 0080143*

Structure: Fitted with Vosper Thornycroft fin stabilisers. The
after funnel is set to starboard and the forward one to port. The
crane is on the starboard after corner of the hangar. Bear Trap
helicopter hauldown gear.

Operational: Both ships carry Seahawk helicopters. *Shirane* is
the Flagship of Escort Flotilla One at Yokosuka, and *Kurama* of
Escort Flotilla Two at Sasebo.

UPDATED

2 HARUNA CLASS (DD/DDH)

Name	No
HARUNA	DDH 141
HIEI	DDH 142

Builders	Laid down	Launched	Commissioned
Mitsubishi, Nagasaki	19 Mar 1970	1 Feb 1972	22 Feb 1973
Ishikawajima Harima, Tokyo	8 Mar 1972	13 Aug 1973	27 Nov 1974

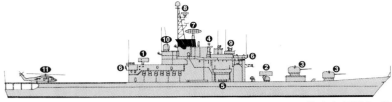

HARUNA   (Scale 1 : 1,500), Ian Sturton / 0012641

Displacement, tons: 4,950 (5,050, DD 142) standard
Dimensions, feet (metres): 502 × 57.4 × 17.1
(153 × 17.5 × 5.2)
Main machinery: 2 Mitsubishi (DDH 141) or IHI (DDH 142)
boilers; 850 psi *(60 kg/cm²)*; 900°F *(480°C)*; 2 Mitsubishi
(DDH 141) or IHI (DDH 142) turbines; 70,000 hp *(51.5 MW)*;
2 shafts
Speed, knots: 31
Complement: 370 (360, DDH 142) (36 officers)

Missiles: SAM: Raytheon Sea Sparrow Mk 29 (Type 3A) octuple
launcher ❶; semi-active radar homing to 14.6 km *(8 n miles)* at
2.5 Mach; warhead 39 kg; 24 missiles.
A/S: Honeywell ASROC Mk 112 octuple launcher ❷; inertial
guidance to 1.6-10 km *(1-5.4 n miles)* at 0.9 Mach; payload
Mk 46 Mod 5 Neartip.
Guns: 2 FMC 5 in *(127 mm)*/54 Mk 42 automatic ❸; 20-40 rds/
min to 24 km *(13 n miles)* anti-surface; 14 km *(7.6 n miles)* anti-
aircraft; weight of shell 32 kg.
2 General Electric/General Dynamics 20 mm Phalanx Mk 15
CIWS ❹; 6 barrels per mounting; 3,000 rds/min combined to
1.5 km.
Torpedoes: 6—324 mm Type 68 (2 triple) tubes ❺. Honeywell
Mk 46 Mod 5 Neartip; anti-submarine; active/passive homing
to 11 km *(5.9 n miles)* at 40 kt; warhead 44 kg.
Countermeasures: Decoys: 4 Loral Hycor SRBOC Mk 36
multibarrelled chaff launchers.
ESM/ECM: Melco NOLQ 1; intercept/jammer. Fujitsu OLR 9;
intercept.

Combat data systems: OYQ-7 *(Hiei)* or OYQ-6 action data
automation; Links 11 and 14; US SATCOM ❻.
Weapons control: 2 Type 2-12 FCS (1 for guns, 1 for SAM).
Radars: Air search: Melco OPS-11C ❼; B-band.
Surface search: JRC OPS-28C/28C-Y ❽; G-band.
Fire control: 1 Type 1A ❾; I/J-band (guns).
1 Type 2-12 ❿; I/J-band (SAM).
Navigation: Koden OPN-11; I-band.
IFF: US Mk 10.
Tacan: Nec ORN-6D/6C.
Sonars: Sangamo/Mitsubishi OQS 3; bow-mounted; active
search and attack; low frequency with bottom bounce.

Helicopters: 3 SH-60J Seahawk ⓫.

Programmes: Ordered under the third five-year defence
programme (from 1967-71).
Modernisation: DDH 141 taken in hand from 31 March 1986 to
31 October 1987 for FRAM at Mitsubishi, Nagasaki; DDH 142
received FRAM from 31 August 1987 to 30 March 1989 at IHI,
Tokyo; included Sea Sparrow, two CIWS and chaff launchers.
Structure: The funnel is offset slightly to port. Fitted with fin
stabilisers. A heavy crane has been fitted on the top of the
hangar, starboard side.
Operational: Fitted with Canadian Beartrap hauldown gear.
Haruna is the Flagship of Escort Flotilla Three at Maizuru and
Hiei of Escort Flotilla Four at Kure.
UPDATED

HARUNA   7/1999*, Hachiro Nakai / 0080144

1 YAMAGUMO CLASS (DD/DDK)

Name	No
YUUGUMO	DDK 121

Builders	Laid down	Launched	Commissioned
Sumitomo, Uraga	4 Feb 1976	31 May 1977	24 Mar 1978

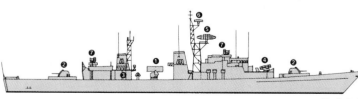

YUUGUMO   (Scale 1 : 1,200), Ian Sturton

Displacement, tons: 2,150 standard
Dimensions, feet (metres): 377.2 × 38.7 × 13.1
(114.9 × 11.8 × 4)
Main machinery: 6 Mitsubishi 12UEV30/40N diesels;
21,600 hp(m) *(15.9 MW)*; 2 shafts
Speed, knots: 27. **Range, miles:** 7,000 at 20 kt
Complement: 220 (19 officers)

Missiles: A/S: Honeywell ASROC Mk 112 octuple launcher ❶;
inertial guidance to 1.6-10 km *(1-5.4 n miles)* at 0.9 Mach;
payload Mk 46 Mod 5 Neartip.
Guns: 4 USN 3 in *(76 mm)*/50 Mk 33 (2 twin) ❷; 50 rds/min to
12.8 km *(6.9 n miles)*; weight of shell 6 kg.
Torpedoes: 6—324 mm Type 68 (2 triple) tubes ❸. Honeywell
Mk 46 Mod 5 Neartip; anti-submarine; active/passive homing
to 11 km *(5.9 n miles)* at 40 kt; warhead 44 kg.
A/S mortars: 1 Bofors 375 mm Type 71 4-barrelled trainable
rocket launcher ❹; automatic loading; range 1.6 km.
Countermeasures: ESM: Nec NOLR 6; radar intercept.
Weapons control: Japanese GFCS-1 for 76 mm guns.
Radars: Air search: Melco OPS-11B/11C ❺; B-band.
Surface search: JRC OPS-18-3 ❻; G-band.
Fire control: 2 General Electric Mk 35 ❼; I/J-band.
IFF: US Mk 10.
Sonars: Nec OQS 3A; hull-mounted; active search and attack;
medium frequency.
EDO SQS-35(J); VDS; active/passive search; medium
frequency.

Operational: The first two of the class were converted to Training
Ships on 20 June 1991 but were deleted in 1995 and the third
became a Submarine Support Ship on 18 October 1993,
before being deleted in 1998. Three more were converted to
Training Ships on 16 March 1998, 18 March 1999 and March
2000 respectively.
UPDATED

YUUGUMO   10/1997, Hachiro Nakai / 0012630

FRIGATES

Note: The MSDF classifies these ships as Destroyer Escorts.

6 ABUKUMA CLASS (FFG/DE)

Name	No	Builders	Laid down	Launched	Commissioned
ABUKUMA	DE 229	Mitsui, Tamano	17 Mar 1988	21 Dec 1988	12 Dec 1989
JINTSU	DE 230	Hitachi, Maizuru	14 Apr 1988	31 Jan 1989	28 Feb 1990
OHYODO	DE 231	Mitsui, Tamano	8 Mar 1989	19 Dec 1989	23 Jan 1991
SENDAI	DE 232	Sumitomo, Uraga	14 Apr 1989	26 Jan 1990	15 Mar 1991
CHIKUMA	DE 233	Hitachi, Maizuru	14 Feb 1991	25 Jan 1992	24 Feb 1993
TONE	DE 234	Sumitomo, Uraga	8 Feb 1991	6 Dec 1991	8 Feb 1993

Displacement, tons: 2,050 standard; 2,550 full load
Dimensions, feet (metres): 357.6 × 44 × 12.5
(109 × 13.4 × 3.8)
Main machinery: CODOG; 2 RR Spey SM1A gas turbines;
26,650 hp *(19.9 MW)* sustained; 2 Mitsubishi S12U-MTK
diesels; 6,000 hp(m) *(4.4 MW)*; 2 shafts
Speed, knots: 27
Complement: 120

Missiles: SSM: 8 McDonnell Douglas Harpoon (2 quad)
launchers ❶; active radar homing to 130 km *(70 n miles)* at
0.9 Mach; warhead 227 kg.

A/S: Honeywell ASROC Mk 112 octuple launcher ❷; inertial
guidance to 1.6-10 km *(1-5.4 n miles)* at 0.9 Mach; payload
Mk 46 Mod 5 Neartip.
Guns: 1 OTO Melara 3 in *(76 mm)*/62 compact ❸; 85 rds/min to
16 km *(8.6 n miles)* anti-surface; 12 km *(6.5 n miles)* anti-
aircraft; weight of shell 6 kg.
1 General Electric/General Dynamics 20 mm Phalanx CIWS
Mk 15 ❹; 6 barrels per mounting; 3,000 rds/min combined to
1.5 km.
Torpedoes: 6—324 mm Type 68 (2 triple) tubes ❺. Honeywell
Mk 46 Mod 5 Neartip; anti-submarine; active/passive homing
to 11 km *(5.9 n miles)* at 40 kt; warhead 44 kg.

Countermeasures: Decoys: 2 Loral Hycor SRBOC 6-barrelled
Mk 36 chaff launchers ❻.
ESM: Nec NOLQ-6C; intercept.
ECM: Fujitsu OLT-3; jammer.
Combat data systems: OYQ-6. SATCOM.
Weapons control: Type 2-21; GFCS.
Radars: Air search: Melco OPS-14C ❻; D-band.
Surface search: JRC OPS-28D (DE 233-234); JRS OPC-28C
(remainder) ❼; G-band.
Fire control: Type 2-21 ❽.
Sonars: Hitachi OQS-8; hull-mounted; active search and attack;
medium frequency.
SQR-19A towed passive array in due course.

Programmes: First pair of this class approved in 1986 estimates,
ordered March 1987; second pair in 1987 estimates, ordered
February 1988; last two in 1989 estimates, ordered
24 January 1989. The name of the first of class was last used
for a light cruiser which was sunk in the battle of Leyte Gulf in
October 1944.
Structure: Stealth features include non-vertical and rounded
surfaces. German RAM PDMS may be fitted later, although this
now seems unlikely, and space has been left for a towed sonar
array. SATCOM fitted aft of the after funnel.

UPDATED

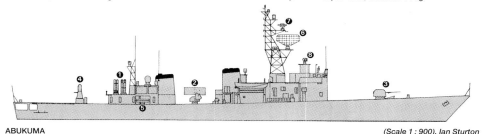

ABUKUMA   *(Scale 1 : 900), Ian Sturton*

TONE   *8/1999*, Hachiro Nakai /* 0080145

1 ISHIKARI AND 2 YUUBARI CLASS (FFG/DE)

Name	No	Builders	Laid down	Launched	Commissioned
ISHIKARI	DE 226	Mitsui, Tamano	17 May 1979	18 Mar 1980	28 Mar 1981
YUUBARI	DE 227	Sumitomo, Uraga	9 Feb 1981	22 Feb 1982	18 Mar 1983
YUUBETSU	DE 228	Hitachi, Maizuru	14 Jan 1982	25 Jan 1983	14 Feb 1984

Displacement, tons: 1,470 (1,290 (DE 226)) standard; 1,690
(1,450 (DE 226)) full load
Dimensions, feet (metres): 298.5; 278.8 (DE 226) × 35.4 × 11.8
(91; 85 × 10.8 × 3.6)
Main machinery: CODOG; 1 Kawasaki/RR Olympus TM3B gas
turbine; 24,700 hp *(18.4 MW)* sustained; 1 Mitsubishi/MAN
6DRV diesel; 4,700 hp(m) *(3.45 MW)*; 2 shafts; cp props
Speed, knots: 25
Complement: 95

Missiles: SSM: 8 McDonnell Douglas Harpoon (2 quad)
launchers ❶; active radar homing to 130 km *(70 n miles)* at
0.9 Mach; warhead 227 kg.
Guns: 1 OTO Melara 3 in *(76 mm)*/62 compact ❷; 85 rds/min to
16 km *(8.6 n miles)* anti-surface; 12 km *(6.5 n miles)* anti-
aircraft; weight of shell 6 kg.
1 General Electric/General Dynamics 20 mm Phalanx CIWS
Mk 15 (not yet fitted) ❸; 6 barrels per mounting; 3,000 rds/
min combined to 1.5 km.
Torpedoes: 6—324 mm Type 68 (2 triple) tubes ❹. Honeywell
Mk 46 Mod 5 Neartip; anti-submarine; active/passive homing
to 11 km *(5.9 n miles)* at 40 kt; warhead 44 kg.
A/S mortars: 1—375 mm Bofors Type 71 4 to 6-barrelled
trainable rocket launcher ❺; automatic loading; range 1.6 km.
Countermeasures: Decoys: 2 Loral Hycor SRBOC 6-barrelled
Mk 36 chaff launchers ❻; range 4 km *(2.2 n miles)*.
ESM: Nec NOLQ 6C ❼; intercept.
ECM: Fujitsu OLT 3; jammer.
Combat data systems: OYQ-5.
Weapons control: Type 2-21 system for 76 mm gun.
Radars: Surface search: JRC OPS-28B/28-1 ❽; G-band.
Navigation: Fujitsu OPS-19B; I-band.
Fire control: Type 2-21 ❾; I/J-band.
Sonars: Nec SQS-36J; hull-mounted; active/passive; medium
frequency.

Programmes: *Yuubari* is a slightly longer version of *Ishikari*.

YUUBARI   *(Scale 1 : 900), Ian Sturton*

YUUBETSU   *7/1998, Hachiro Nakai /* 0052458

Structure: The increased space for the same weapons systems
as *Ishikari* has meant improved accommodation and an
increase in fuel oil carried. It now seems unlikely that Phalanx
will be fitted.

UPDATED

3 CHIKUGO CLASS (FF/DE)

Name	No	Builders	Laid down	Launched	Commissioned
YOSHINO	DE 223	Mitsui, Tamano	28 Sep 1973	22 Aug 1974	6 Feb 1975
KUMANO	DE 224	Hitachi, Maizuru	29 May 1974	24 Feb 1975	19 Nov 1975
NOSHIRO	DE 225	Mitsui, Tamano	27 Jan 1976	23 Dec 1976	30 June 1977

Displacement, tons: 1,500 standard
Dimensions, feet (metres): 305 × 35.5 × 11.5
(93 × 10.8 × 3.5)
Main machinery: 4 Mitsubishi-Burmeister & Wain 12UEV30/
40N diesels; 16,000 hp(m) *(11.8 MW)* (Hitachi ship)
4 Matsui 1228 V 3BU-38V diesels; 16,000 hp(m) *(11.8 MW)*
(Mitsui ships); 2 shafts

Speed, knots: 24. **Range, miles:** 10,900 at 12 kt
Complement: 160 (12 officers)

Missiles: A/S: Honeywell ASROC Mk 112 octuple launcher ❶;
inertial guidance to 1.6-10 km *(1-5.4 n miles)* at 0.9 Mach;
payload Mk 46 Mod 5 Neartip.
Guns: 2 USN 3 in *(76 mm)*/50 Mk 33 (twin) ❷; 50 rds/min to
12.8 km *(6.9 n miles)*; weight of shell 6 kg.

2 Bofors 40 mm/60 Mk 1 (twin) ❸; 120 rds/min to 10 km
(5.4 n miles) anti-surface; 3 km *(1.6 n miles)* anti-aircraft;
weight of shell 0.89 kg.
Torpedoes: 6—324 mm Type 68 (2 triple) tubes ❹. Honeywell
Mk 46 Mod 5 Neartip; anti-submarine; active/passive homing
to 11 km *(5.9 n miles)* at 40 kt; warhead 44 kg.
Countermeasures: ESM: Nec NORL 5 ❺; intercept.
Weapons control: GFCS-1 for 76 mm gun. Mk 51 GFCS for
40 mm gun.
Radars: Air search: Melco OPS-14/14B ❻; D-band.
Surface search: JRC OPS-16C/16D/18-3 ❼; G-band.
Fire control: Type 1B ❽; I/J-band.
IFF: US Mk 10.
Sonars: Hitachi OQS 3A; hull-mounted; active search and attack;
medium frequency.
EDO SPS-35(J); VDS; active/passive search; medium
frequency.

Structure: These are the smallest warships to mount ASROC.
Operational: Being paid off at the rate of about two a year.

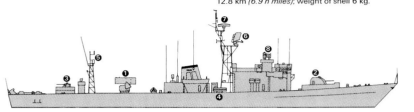

TESHIO   *(Scale 1 : 900), Ian Sturton*   **UPDATED**

KUMANO   *4/1999*, Hachiro Nakai /* 0080146

SHIPBORNE AIRCRAFT

Note: Sea Harrier VSTOL aircraft may be acquired in due course.

Numbers/Type: 56 Sikorsky/Mitsubishi SH-60J (Seahawk).
Operational speed: 135 kt *(250 km/h)*.
Service ceiling: 12,500 ft *(3,810 m)*.
Range: 600 n miles *(1,110 km)*.
Role/Weapon systems: ASW helicopter; started replacing HSS-2B in July 1991; built in Japan;
prototypes fitted by Mitsubishi with Japanese avionics and mission equipment. Total of 48
authorised at the end of 1992 for seaborne use, plus six more in 1997 for landbased operations
plus two more in 1997/98 as prototypes for upgrades. Sensors: Texas Instruments APS 124
search radar; sonobuoys plus datalink; Bendix AQS 18/Nippon HQS 103 dipping sonar, ECM,
HLR 108 ESM. Weapons: ASW; two Mk 46 torpedoes or depth bombs.

VERIFIED

SEAHAWK   *10/1998, Hachiro Nakai /* 0052459

LAND-BASED MARITIME AIRCRAFT (FRONT LINE)

Note: Aircraft type names are not used by the MSDF.

Numbers/Type: 86/5/1/1 Kawasaki P-3C/EP-3/UP-3/UP-3D Update II/III (Orion).
Operational speed: 410 kt *(760 km/h)*.
Service ceiling: 28,300 ft *(8,625 m)*.
Range: 4,000 n miles *(7,410 km)*.
Role/Weapon systems: Long-range MR/ASW and surface surveillance and attack. Most maritime
surveillance is done by these aircraft. Four EW version EP-3. Sensors: APS-115 radar, ASQ-81
MAD, AQA 7 processor, Unisys CP 2044 computer; IFF, ECM, ALQ 78, ESM, ALR 66; sonobuoys.
Weapons: ASW; eight Mk 46 torpedoes, depth bombs or mines, 10 underwing stations for
Harpoon and ASM-1.   **VERIFIED**

Numbers/Type: 30 Mitsubishi SH-3A (HSS-2B) (Sea King).
Operational speed: 120 kt *(222 km/h)*.
Service ceiling: 12,200 ft *(3,720 m)*.
Range: 630 n miles *(1,165 km)*.
Role/Weapon systems: ASW helicopter and surface search. Production completed in 1990. All
land-based since 1996 but can still be embarked at sea. Numbers declining. Sensors: Search
radar, ESM ALR 66(V)1, Bendix AQS-13/18 dipping sonar. Weapons: ASW; four Mk 46
torpedoes or depth bombs.

UPDATED

SEA KING   *8/1998, Hachiro Nakai /* 0052461

Numbers/Type: 10 Sikorsky/Mitsubishi S-80M-1 (Sea Dragon) (MH53E).
Operational speed: 170 kt *(315 km/h)*.
Service ceiling: 18,500 ft *(5,640 m)*.
Range: 1,120 n miles *(2,000 km)*.
Role/Weapon systems: Three-engined AMCM helicopter tows Mk 106 (ALQ 166) MCM sweep
equipment; self-deployed. Sensors: dipping sonar can be carried; Weapons: Two 12.7 mm guns
for self-defence.

UPDATED

SEA DRAGON   *7/1999*, Hachiro Nakai /* 0080147

AMPHIBIOUS FORCES

1 + 2 OSUMI CLASS (LPD/LST)

Name	No	Builders	Laid down	Launched	Commissioned
OSUMI	LST 4001	Mitsui, Tamano	6 Dec 1995	18 Nov 1996	11 Mar 1998
—	LST 4002	Mitsui, Tamano	12 Dec 1999	Nov 2000	Mar 2002
—	LST 4003	Mitsui, Tamano	15 Mar 2000	Nov 2001	Mar 2003

Displacement, tons: 8,900 standard
Dimensions, feet (metres): 584 × 84.6 × 19.7
(178 × 25.8 × 6)
Flight deck, feet (metres): 426.5 × 75.5 *(130 × 23)*
Main machinery: 2 Mitsui 16V42MA diesels; 27,600 hp(m)
(20.29 MW); 2 shafts; 2 bow thrusters
Speed, knots: 22

Complement: 135
Military lift: 330 troops; 2 LCAC; 10 Type 90 tanks or 1,400 tons cargo

Guns: 2 GE/GD 20 mm Vulcan Phalanx Mk 15 ❶. 6 barrels per mounting; 3,000 rds/min combined to 1.5 km.
Countermeasures: ESM/ECM.

Radars: Air search: Mitsubishi OPS-14C ❷; C-band.
Surface search: JRC OPS-28D ❸; G-band.
Navigation: JRC OPS-20; I-band.

Helicopters: Platform for 2 CH-47J.

Programmes: A 5,500 ton LST was requested and not approved in the 1989 or 1990 estimates. The published design resembled the Italian San Giorgio with a large flight deck and a stern dock. No further action was taken for two years but the FY93 request included a larger ship showing the design of a USN LPH, although smaller in size. This vessel, with some modifications, was authorised in the 1993 estimates. A second of class approved in FY98 new construction programme and third in FY99.
Structure: Through deck, flight deck and stern docking well make this more like a mini LHA than an LST, except that the ship is described as providing only 'platform and refuelling facilities for helicopters'.
Opinion: The forward end of the flight deck looks unfinished, as though a ski-jump may be intended in due course.

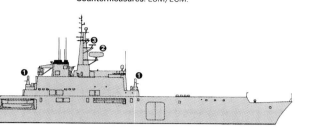

OSUMI

(Scale 1 : 1,500), Ian Sturton / 0012652

UPDATED

OSUMI

3/1998, JMSDF / 0052464

OSUMI

9/1999, Hachiro Nakai / 0080150*

2 MIURA CLASS (LST)

Name	No	Builders	Commissioned
OJIKA	LST 4152	Ishikawajima Harima, Tokyo	22 Mar 1976
SATSUMA	LST 4153	Ishikawajima Harima, Tokyo	17 Feb 1977

Displacement, tons: 2,000 standard
Dimensions, feet (metres): 321.4 × 45.9 × 9.8 *(98 × 14 × 3)*
Main machinery: 2 Kawasaki-MAN V8V22/30ATL diesels; 4,000 hp(m) *(2.94 MW)*; 2 shafts
Speed, knots: 14
Complement: 115
Military lift: 200 troops; 2 LCMs; 2 LCVPs; 10 Type 74 main battle tanks
Guns: 2 USN 3 in *(76 mm)*/50 Mk 33 (twin); 50 rds/min to 12.8 km *(6.9 n miles)*; weight of shell 6 kg.
   2 Bofors 40 mm/70 (twin); 300 rds/min to 12 km *(6.5 n miles)* anti-surface; 4 km *(2.2 n miles)* anti-aircraft; weight of shell 0.96 kg.
Weapons control: US Mk 63 for 76 mm guns. US Mk 51 Mod 2 for 40 mm guns.
Radars: Air search: Melco OPS-14/14B; D-band.
Surface search: JRS OPS-18; G-band.

Comment: Used primarily for logistic support.   **UPDATED**

OJIKA   *5/1999*, Hachiro Nakai /* 0080148

1 ATSUMI CLASS (LST)

Name	No	Builders	Commissioned
NEMURO	LST 4103	Sasebo Heavy Industries	27 Oct 1977

Displacement, tons: 1,550 standard
Dimensions, feet (metres): 291.9 × 42.6 × 8.9 *(89 × 13 × 2.7)*
Main machinery: 2 Kawasaki-MAN V8V22/30ATL diesels; 4,000 hp(m) *(2.94 MW)*; 2 shafts
Speed, knots: 13. **Range, miles:** 9,000 at 12 kt
Complement: 95
Military lift: 130 troops; 400 tons cargo including 5 Type 74 tanks; 2 LCVPs
Guns: 4 Bofors 40 mm/70 Mk 1 (2 twin); 300 rds/min to 12 km *(6.5 n miles)*; weight of shell 0.96 kg.
Weapons control: 2 US Mk 51 for 40 mm guns.
Radars: Navigation: Fujitsu OPS-9; I-band.

Comment: Has an electric crane at the after end of the cargo deck. This last survivor is expected to be deleted in 2000.   **UPDATED**

NEMURO   *5/1999*, Hachiro Nakai /* 0080149

2 YURA CLASS (LSU/LCU)

Name	No	Builders	Commissioned
YURA	LSU 4171	Sasebo Heavy Industries	27 Mar 1981
NOTO	LSU 4172	Sasebo Heavy Industries	27 Mar 1981

Displacement, tons: 590 standard
Dimensions, feet (metres): 190.2 × 31.2 × 5.6 *(58 × 9.5 × 1.7)*
Main machinery: 2 Fuji 6L27.5XF diesels; 3,250 hp(m) *(2.39 MW)*; 2 shafts; cp props
Speed, knots: 12
Complement: 31
Military lift: 70 troops
Guns: 1 GE 20 mm/76 Sea Vulcan 20; 3 barrels per mounting; 1,500 rds/min combined to 4 km *(2.2 n miles)*.
Radars: Navigation: Fujitsu OPS-9B; I-band.

Comment: Both laid down 23 April 1980. 4171 launched 15 October 1980 and 4172 on 12 November 1980.   **UPDATED**

NOTO   *7/1999*, Hachiro Nakai /* 0080151

2 YUSOTEI CLASS (LCU)

Name	No	Builders	Commissioned
YUSOTEI-ICHI-GO	LCU 2001	Sasebo Heavy Industries	17 Mar 1988
YUSOTEI-NI-GO	LCU 2002	Sasebo Heavy Industries	11 Mar 1992

Displacement, tons: 420 standard
Dimensions, feet (metres): 170.6 × 28.5 × 5.2 *(52 × 8.7 × 1.6)*
Main machinery: 2 Mitsubishi S6U-MTK diesels; 3,040 hp(m) *(2.23 MW)*; 2 shafts
Speed, knots: 12
Complement: 28
Guns: 1 GE 20 mm/76 Sea Vulcan; 3 barrels per mounting; 1,500 rds/min combined to 4 km *(2.2 n miles)*.
Radars: Navigation: OPS-19B/26; I-band.

Comment: First approved in 1986 estimates, laid down 11 May 1987, launched 9 October 1987. Second approved in FY90 estimates, laid down 17 May 1991, launched 7 October 1991; plans for a third have been scrapped. Official names are *LCU 01* and *LCU 02*.   **UPDATED**

YUSOTEI-NI-GO   *5/1999*, Hachiro Nakai /* 0080152

2 + 2 (2) LANDING CRAFT AIR CUSHION (LCAC)

LCAC 01   LCAC 02

Displacement, tons: 87.2 light; 170-182 full load
Dimensions, feet (metres): 88 oa (on cushion) (81 between hard structures) × 47 beam (on cushion) (43 beam hard structure) × 2.9 draught (off cushion) *(26.8 (24.7) × 14.3 (13.1) × 0.9)*
Main machinery: 4 Avco-Lycoming TF-40B gas turbines; 2 for propulsion and 2 for lift; 16,000 hp *(12 MW)* sustained; 2 shrouded reversible-pitch airscrews (propulsion); 4 double entry fans, centrifugal or mixed flow (lift)
Speed, knots: 40 (loaded). **Range, miles:** 300 at 35 kt; 200 at 40 kt
Complement: 5
Military lift: 24 troops; 1 MBT or 60-75 tons
Radars: Navigation: LN-66; I-band.

Comment: Approval for sale given by USA on 8 April 1994. First one authorised in FY93, second in the FY95 budget and ordered from Textron Marine, New Orleans. Delivered in 1997 and both are embarked in *Osumi*. Third and fourth authorised in FY99 budget. Cargo space capacity is 1,809 sq ft.   **UPDATED**

LCAC 01   *7/1999*, Hachiro Nakai /* 0080153

11 LCM TYPE

YF 2075	2121	2124-25	2127-29	2132	2135	2138	2141

Displacement, tons: 25 standard
Dimensions, feet (metres): 56.2 × 14 × 3.9 *(17.1 × 4.3 × 1.2)*
Main machinery: 2 Isuzu E120-MF6R diesels; 480 hp(m) *(353 kW)*; 2 shafts
Speed, knots: 10. **Range, miles:** 130 at 9 kt
Complement: 3
Military lift: 34 tons or 80 troops

Comment: Built in Japan. These are in addition to the six LCMs carried in the 'Miura' class which do not have pennant numbers. *YF 2127-29* commissioned in March 1992, *2132* in March 1993, *2135* in March 1995, *2138* in March 1996 and *2141* in March 1997.   **UPDATED**

YF 2124   *12/1999*, Hachiro Nakai /* 0075867

MINE WARFARE FORCES

2 URAGA CLASS (MINESWEEPER TENDERS) (MST/ML)

Name	No	Builders	Launched	Commissioned
URAGA	MST 463	Hitachi, Maizura	22 May 1996	19 Mar 1997
BUNGO	MST 464	Mitsui, Tamano	24 Apr 1997	23 Mar 1998

Displacement, tons: 5,700 standard
Dimensions, feet (metres): 462.6 × 72.2 × 17.7 *(141 × 22 × 5.4)*
Main machinery: 2 Mitsui 12V42MA diesels; 19,500 hp(m) *(14.33 MW)*; 2 shafts
Speed, knots: 22
Complement: 170
Guns: 1 OTO Melara 3 in *(76 mm)*/62 compact; 85 rds/min to 16 km *(8.6 n miles)*; weight of shell 6 kg.
Mines: Laying capability; 4 rails (Type 3).
Radars: Fire control: Type 2–21; I/J-band.
Navigation: JRC OPS-39C; I-band.
Helicopters: Platform for 1 MH 53E.

Comment: First one authorised 15 February 1994 and laid down 19 May 1995; second authorised in FY95 and laid down 4 July 1996. Capable of laying mines, from twelve internal rails. Phalanx is planned to be fitted forward of the bridge and on the superstructure aft of the funnel.
UPDATED

BUNGO   *1/1999*, Hachiro Nakai /* 0080155

3 YAEYAMA CLASS (MINESWEEPERS—OCEAN) (MSO)

Name	No	Builders	Launched	Commissioned
YAEYAMA	MSO 301	Hitachi Zosen, Kanagawa	29 Aug 1991	16 Mar 1993
TSUSHIMA	MSO 302	Nippon Koukan, Tsurumi	20 Sep 1991	23 Mar 1993
HACHIJOU	MSO 303	Nippon Koukan, Tsurumi	15 Dec 1992	24 Mar 1994

Displacement, tons: 1,000 standard; 1,275 full load
Dimensions, feet (metres): 219.8 × 38.7 × 10.2 *(67 × 11.8 × 3.1)*
Main machinery: 2 Mitsubishi 6NMU-TA1 diesels; 2,400 hp(m) *(1.76 MW)*; 2 shafts; 1 hydrojet bow thruster; 350 hp(m) *(257 kW)*
Speed, knots: 14
Complement: 60
Guns: 1 JM-61 20 mm/76 Sea Vulcan; 3 barrels per mounting; 1,500 rds/min combined to 4 km *(2.2 n miles)*.
Radars: Surface search: Fujitsu OPS-39B; I-band.
Sonars: Raytheon SQQ-32 VDS; high frequency; active.

Comment: First two approved in 1989 estimates, third in 1990. First laid down 30 August 1990, second 20 July 1990 and third 17 May 1991. Wooden hulls. Fitted with S 7 deep sea minehunting system, S 8 (SLQ-48) deep sea moored minesweeping equipment and ADI Dyad sweeps. Appears to be a derivative of the USN 'Avenger' class. An integrated tactical system is fitted. Termination of the programme at three of the class suggests similar problems to US ships of the same class.
UPDATED

HACHIJOU   *2/1999*, Hachiro Nakai /* 0080156

12 HATSUSHIMA and 9 UWAJIMA CLASSES
(MINEHUNTERS/SWEEPERS—COASTAL) (MHC/MSC)

Name	No	Builders	Commissioned
HAHAJIMA	MSC 660	Nippon Koukan, Tsurumi	18 Dec 1984
TAKASHIMA	MSC 661	Hitachi Zosen, Kanagawa	18 Dec 1984
NUWAJIMA	MSC 662	Hitachi Zosen, Kanagawa	12 Dec 1985
ETAJIMA	MSC 663	Nippon Koukan, Tsurumi	12 Dec 1985
KAMISHIMA	MSC 664	Nippon Koukan, Tsurumi	16 Dec 1986
HIMESHIMA	MSC 665	Hitachi Zosen, Kanagawa	16 Dec 1986
OGISHIMA	MSC 666	Hitachi Zosen, Kanagawa	19 Dec 1987
MOROSHIMA	MSC 667	Nippon Koukan, Tsurumi	19 Dec 1987
YURISHIMA	MSC 668	Nippon Koukan, Tsurumi	15 Dec 1988
HIKOSHIMA	MSC 669	Hitachi Zosen, Kanagawa	15 Dec 1988
AWASHIMA	MSC 670	Hitachi Zosen, Kanagawa	13 Dec 1989
SAKUSHIMA	MSC 671	Nippon Koukan, Tsurumi	13 Dec 1989
UWAJIMA	MSC 672	Nippon Koukan, Tsurumi	19 Dec 1990
IESHIMA	MSC 673	Hitachi Zosen, Kanagawa	19 Dec 1990
TSUKISHIMA	MSC 674	Hitachi Zosen, Kanagawa	17 Mar 1993
MAEJIMA	MSC 675	Hitachi Zosen, Kanagawa	15 Dec 1993
KUMEJIMA	MSC 676	Nippon Koukan, Tsurumi	12 Dec 1994
MAKISHIMA	MSC 677	Hitachi Zosen, Kanagawa	12 Dec 1994
TOBISHIMA	MSC 678	Nippon Koukan, Tsurumi	10 Mar 1995
YUGESHIMA	MSC 679	Hitachi Zosen, Kanagawa	11 Dec 1996
NAGASHIMA	MSC 680	Nippon Koukan, Tsurumi	25 Dec 1996

Displacement, tons: 440 (490, MSC 670 onwards) standard; 510 full load
Dimensions, feet (metres): 180.4 (189.3, MSC 670 onwards) × 30.8 × 7.9 (9.5) *(55 (57.7) × 9.4 × 2.4 (2.9))*
Main machinery: 2 Mitsubishi YV122C-15/20 diesels (MSC 658-665); 1,440 hp(m) *(1.06 MW)*; 2 Mitsubishi 6NMU-TAI diesels (MSC 666 onwards); 1,400 hp(m) *(1.03 MW)*; 2 shafts
Speed, knots: 14
Complement: 45; 40 (MSC 675 onwards)

Guns: 1 JM-61 20 mm/76 Sea Vulcan 20; 3 barrels per mounting; 1,500 rds/min combined to 4 km *(2.2 n miles)*.
Radars: Surface search: Fujitsu OPS-9 or OPS-39 (MSC 674 onwards); I-band.
Sonars: Nec/Hitachi ZQS 2B or ZQS 3 (MSC 672 onwards); hull-mounted; minehunting; high frequency.

Programmes: First ordered in 1976. Last two authorised in FY94. Because of the new sonar and mine detonating equipment vessels from MSC 672 onwards are known as the 'Uwajima' class.
Structure: From MSC 670 onwards the hull is lengthened by 2.7 m in order to improve the sleeping accommodation from three tier to two tier bunks. Hulls are made of wood. The last pair has more powerful engines developing 1,800 hp(m) *(1.32 MW)*.
Operational: Fitted with S 4 (S 7 from MSC 672 onwards) mine detonating equipment, a remote-controlled counter-mine charge. Four clearance divers are carried. MSC 668, 669, 670 and 671 formed the Minesweeper Squadron to deploy to the Gulf in 1991. Earlier vessels of the class converted to drone control (MSC 655) or to tenders or paid off.
UPDATED

MAKISHIMA   *8/1999*, Hachiro Nakai /* 0080157

ETAJIMA   *2/1999*, Hachiro Nakai /* 0080158

NAGASHIMA   *1/1999*, Hachiro Nakai /* 0075868

3 + 4 (2) SUGASHIMA CLASS (MINESWEEPER (COASTAL)) (MSC)

Name	No	Builders	Launched		Commissioned	
SUGASHIMA	MSC 681	NKK, Tsurumi	25 Aug	1997	16 Mar	1999
NOTOJIMA	MSC 682	Hitachi Zosen, Kanagawa	3 Sep	1997	16 Mar	1999
TSUNOSHIMA	MSC 683	Hitachi Zosen, Kanagawa	22 Oct	1998	Mar	2000
NAOSHIMA	MSC 684	NKK, Tsurumi	7 Oct	1999	Mar	2001
—	MSC 685	Hitachi Zosen, Kanagawa	June	2000	Mar	2002
—	MSC 686	—	Sep	2001	Mar	2003
—	MSC 687	—	Sep	2001	Mar	2003

Displacement, tons: 510 standard
Dimensions, feet (metres): 180.1 × 30.8 × 8.2 *(54.9 × 9.4 × 2.5)*
Main machinery: 2 Mitsubishi 6 NMU-TA1 diesels; 1,800 hp(m) *(1.33 MW)*; 2 shafts; bow thrusters
Speed, knots: 14
Complement: 40
Guns: 1 JM-61 20 mm/76 Sea Vulcan; 3 barrels for mounting; 1,500 rds/min combined to 4 km *(2 n miles)*.
Combat data systems: GEC/NEC Nautis-M type MCM control system.
Radars: Surface search: Fujitsu OPS-39B; I-band.
Sonars: Hitachi/Thomson/Marconi GEC Type 2093 VDS; high frequency; active.

Comment: First pair authorised in FY95 and laid down 8 May 1996. Third of class authorised in FY96 and laid down 7 August 1997, fourth in FY97 and laid down 17 April 1998 and fifth in FY98 and laid down 26 April 1998, and two more authorised in FY99. Hull is similar to *Uwajima* but the upper deck is extended aft to provide more stowage for mine disposal gear, and there are twin funnels. PAP 104 Mk 5 ROVs are carried and ADI Dyad minesweeping gear fitted. Class of up to 12 could be built in due course.   **UPDATED**

SUGASHIMA   *8/1999*, Hachiro Nakai /* 0080159

2 HATSUSHIMA CLASS (DRONE CONTROL SHIPS) (MCL)

Name	No	Builders	Commissioned
NIIJIMA	MCL 722 (ex-MSC 655)	Nippon Koukan, Tsurumi	26 Nov 1981
YAKUSHIMA	MCL 723 (ex-MSC 686)	Nippon Koukan, Tsurumi	17 Dec 1982

Displacement, tons: 440 standard; 510 full load
Dimensions, feet (metres): 180.4 × 30.8 × 7.9 *(55 × 9.4 × 2.4)*
Main machinery: 2 Mitsubishi 12ZC diesels; 1,440 hp(m) *(1.06 MW)*; 2 shafts
Speed, knots: 14
Complement: 28
Guns: 1 GE 20 mm/76 Sea Vulcan 20; 3 barrels per mounting; 1,500 rds/min combined to 4 km *(2.2 n miles)*.
Radars: Surface search: Fujitsu OPS-9B; I-band.

Comment: Converted in 1998 when both ships were redesignated as Minesweeper Control Ships (MCLs) and equipped to operate SAM remote controlled drones. All minesweeping gear removed.   **UPDATED**

YAKUSHIMA   *7/1999*, Hachiro Nakai /* 0080154

6 SAM CLASS (MCM DRONES)

SAM 01-SAM 06

Displacement, tons: 20 full load
Dimensions, feet (metres): 59.1 × 20 × 5.2 *(18 × 6.1 × 1.6)*
Main machinery: 1 Volvo Penta TAMD 70D diesel; 210 hp(m) *(154 kW)*; 1 Schottel prop
Speed, knots: 8. **Range, miles:** 330 at 8 kt

Comment: First pair acquired from Karlskronavarvet, Sweden in February 1998 followed by two more in December 1998 and two more in 2000. Remote controlled magnetic and acoustic catamaran sweepers operated by *Nijima*.   **UPDATED**

SAM 02   *7/1999*, Hachiro Nakai /* 0080160

PATROL FORCES

0 + 4 PG CLASS (PG)

Displacement, tons: 200 standard
Main machinery: 3 LM 500 gas turbines; 3 shafts
Speed, knots: 40
Complement: 20
Missiles: 4 Mitsubishi SSM-1B ❶.
Guns: 1 OTO Melara 3 in *(76 mm)*/62 compact ❷. 2—12.7 mm MGs.
Countermeasures: Decoys: chaff launchers ❸. ESM/ECM.
Radars: Surface search ❹. Fire control ❺. Navigation.

Comment: First pair authorised in FY99 budget, second pair in FY2000. Catamaran hulls.
                                NEW ENTRY

PG   *(not to scale), Ian Sturton /* 0080161

3 PG 01 (SPARVIERO) CLASS
(FAST ATTACK HYDROFOIL—MISSILE) (PHG/PG)

Name	No	Builders	Launched		Commissioned	
PG 01	821	Sumitomo, Uraga	17 July	1992	25 Mar	1993
PG 02	822	Sumitomo, Uraga	17 July	1992	25 Mar	1993
PG 03	823	Sumitomo, Uraga	15 June	1994	13 Mar	1995

Displacement, tons: 50 standard
Dimensions, feet (metres): 71.5 × 22.9 × 4.6 *(21.8 × 7 × 1.4)* (hull) 80.7 × 23.1 × 14.4 *(24.6 × 7 × 4.4)* (foilborne)
Main machinery: 1 GE/IHI LM 500 gas turbine; 5,522 hp *(4.12 MW)* sustained; 1 pumpjet (foilborne); 1 diesel; 1 retractable prop (hullborne)
Speed, knots: 46; 8 (diesel). **Range, miles:** 400 at 45 kt; 1,200 at 8 kt
Complement: 11 (3 officers)
Missiles: SSM: 4 Mitsubishi SSM-1B (derivative of land-based system); range 150 km *(81 n miles)*.
Guns: 1 GE 20 mm/76 Sea Vulcan; 3 barrels per mounting; 1,500 rds/min combined to 4 km *(2.2 n miles)*.
Countermeasures: Decoys: 2 Loral Hycor Mk 36 SRBOC chaff launchers.
ESM/ECM: intercept and jammer.
Combat data systems: Link 11.
Radars: Surface search: JRC OPS-28-2; G-band.

Comment: Classified as Patrol Guided Missile Boats. First two approved in FY90 and both laid down 25 March 1991. One more approved in FY92, laid down 8 March 1993. A fourth was asked for but not authorised in FY95 and the programme is now complete. Built with Italian assistance from Fincantieri. Planned to improve the Navy's interceptor capabilities, this was an ambitious choice of vessel bearing in mind the falling popularity of the hydrofoil in the few navies (US, Italy and Russia) that have built them up to now.
                                UPDATED

PG 03   *7/1998*, Hachiro Nakai /* 0080162

AUXILIARIES

2 + 1 300 TON CLASS (EOD TENDERS) (YDT)

YDT 1   YDT 2   YDT 3

Displacement, tons: 300 standard
Dimensions, feet (metres): 150.9 × 28.2 × 7.2 *(46 × 8.6 × 2.2)*
Main machinery: 2 diesels; 1,500 hp(m) *(1.1 MW)*; 2 shafts
Speed, knots: 15
Complement: 15 plus 15 divers

Comment: First pair approved in FY98 and one more in FY99. First two completed in March 2000. Used as diving tenders.   **NEW ENTRY**

1 MINEGUMO and 1 YAMAGUMO CLASS
(TRAINING SHIPS) (AX/TV)

Name	No	Builders	Commissioned
AOKUMO	TV 3512 (ex-DD 119)	Sumitomo, Uraga	25 Nov 1972
AKIGUMO	TV 3514 (ex-DDK 120)	Sumitomo, Uraga	24 July 1974

Displacement, tons: 2,150 standard
Dimensions, feet (metres): 373.9 × 38.7 × 13.1 *(114 × 11.8 × 4)*
Main machinery: 6 Mitsui Burmeister & Wain diesels; 21,600 hp(m) *(15.9 MW)* sustained; 2 shafts
Speed, knots: 27. **Range, miles:** 7,000 at 20 kt
Complement: 120 plus 36 trainees
Missiles: A/S: Honeywell ASROC Mk 112 octuple launcher.
Guns: 2 or 4 USN 3 in *(76 mm)*/50 Mk 33 (twin); 50 rds/min to 12.8 km *(6.9 n miles)*; weight of shell 6 kg.
    1 OTO Melara 3 in *(76 mm)*/62 Mk 65.
Torpedoes: 6—324 mm Type 68 (2 triple) tubes. Honeywell Mk 46 Mod 5 Neartip; anti-submarine; active/passive homing to 11 km *(5.9 n miles)* at 40 kt; warhead 44 kg.
A/S mortars: 1 Bofors 375 mm Type 71 4-barrelled trainable rocket launcher; automatic loading; range 1.6 km.
Countermeasures: ESM: Nec NOLR 6; radar intercept.
Weapons control: Type 2 for 76 mm guns.
Radars: Air search: Melco OPS-11B/11C; B-band.
Surface search: JRC Type 2/OPS 16D; G-band.
Fire control: 2 Type 1A; I/J-band.
IFF: US Mk 10.
Sonars: Sangamo SQS-23/Nec OQS 3A; hull-mounted; active search and attack; low frequency.
EDO SQS-35(J); VDS; active/passive search; medium frequency.

Comment: Converted as training ships in March 1999 and March 2000 respectively. Lecture room added under ASROC, chart room on the signal deck and accommodation for women.
UPDATED

AOKUMA　　　　　　　　　　　　　　*1/2000*, Hachiro Nakai /* 0080164

1 HATSUYUKI CLASS (TRAINING SHIP) (ATS/TV)

Name	No	Builders	Commissioned
SHIMAYUKI	TV 3513 (ex-DD 133)	Mitsubishi, Nagasaki	17 Feb 1987

Displacement, tons: 3,050 standard; 3,800 full load
Dimensions, feet (metres): 426.4 × 44.6 × 14.4 *(130 × 13.6 × 4.4)*
Main machinery: COGOG; 2 Kawasaki-RR Olympus TM3B gas turbines; 49,400 hp *(36.8 MW)* sustained; 2 RR Type RM1C gas turbines; 9,900 hp *(7.4 MW)* sustained; 2 shafts; cp props
Speed, knots: 30; 19 cruise
Complement: 200
Missiles: SSM: 8 McDonnell Douglas Harpoon (2 quad) launchers; active radar homing to 130 km *(70 n miles)* at 0.9 Mach; warhead 227 kg.
SAM: Raytheon Sea Sparrow Mk 29 Type 3A launcher; semi-active radar homing to 14.6 km *(8 n miles)* at 2.5 Mach; warhead 39 kg; 12 missiles.
A/S: Honeywell ASROC Mk 112 octuple launcher; inertial guidance to 1.6-10 km *(1-5.4 n miles)* at 0.9 Mach; payload Mk 46 Mod 5 Neartip.
Guns: 1 OTO Melara 3 in *(76 mm)*/62 compact; 85 rds/min to 16 km *(8.6 n miles)* anti-surface; 12 km *(6.5 n miles)* anti-aircraft; weight of shell 6 kg.
    2 General Electric/General Dynamics 20 mm Phalanx Mk 15 CIWS; 6 barrels per mounting; 3,000 rds/min combined to 1.5 km.
Torpedoes: 6—324 mm Type 68 (2 triple) tubes. Honeywell Mk 46 Mod 5 Neartip; anti-submarine; active/passive homing to 11 km *(5.9 n miles)* at 40 kt; warhead 44 kg.
Countermeasures: Decoys: 2 Loral Hycor SRBOC 6-barrelled Mk 36 chaff launchers; range 4 km *(2.2 n miles)*.
ESM: NOLR 8; intercept.
ECM: Fujitsu OLT 3; jammer.
Combat data systems: OYQ-5 action data automation; Link 14 (receive only). SATCOM.
Radars: Air search: Melco OPS-14B; D-band.
Surface search: JRC OPS-18-1; G-band.
Fire control: Type 2-12 A; I/J-band (for SAM).
    2 Type 2-21/21A; I/J-band (for guns).
Tacan: ORN-6C/6C-Y.
Sonars: Nec OQS 4A (II) (SQS-23 type); bow-mounted; active search and attack; low frequency.
OQR 1 TACTASS (in some); passive; low frequency.
Helicopters: 1 SH-60J Seahawk.

Comment: Converted to training ship in March 1999. Lecture room added to helicopter hangar.
UPDATED

SHIMAYUKI　　　　　　　　　　*5/1999*, Hachiro Nakai /* 0080163

1 TENRYU CLASS (TRAINING SUPPORT SHIP) (AS/ATS)

Name	No	Builders	Launched	Commissioned
TENRYU	ATS 4203	Sumitomo, Uraga	14 Apr 1999	17 Mar 2000

Displacement, tons: 2,400 standard
Dimensions, feet (metres): 347.8 × 54.1 × 13.5 *(106 × 16.5 × 4.1)*
Main machinery: 4 diesels; 12,500 hp(m) *(9.19 MW)* sustained; 2 shafts
Speed, knots: 22
Complement: 150
Guns: 1 OTO Melara 3 in *(76 mm)*/62 compact; 85 rds/min to 16 km *(8.6 n miles)*; weight of shell 6 kg.
Radars: Air/surface search: Melco OPS-14; D-band.
Navigation: Fujitsu OPS-19; I-band.
Fire control: Type 2-22; I/J-band.
Helicopters: 1 medium.

Comment: Authorised in 1997 budget as a replacement for *Azuma* and laid down 19 June 1998. Carries four BQM-34J drones and four Northrop Chukar III drones used for evaluating performance of ships SAM systems. Improved *Kurobe* design.
UPDATED

TENRYU　　　　　　　　　　*12/1999*, Hachiro Nakai /* 0080165

1 KASHIMA CLASS (TRAINING SHIP) (AX/TV)

Name	No	Builders	Launched	Commissioned
KASHIMA	TV 3508	Hitachi, Maizuru	23 Feb 1994	26 Jan 1995

Displacement, tons: 4,050 standard
Dimensions, feet (metres): 469.2 × 59.1 × 15.1 *(143 × 18 × 4.6)*
Main machinery: CODOG; 2 RR Spey SM1C gas-turbines; 26,650 hp *(19.9 MW)* sustained; 2 Mitsubishi S16U-MTK diesels; 8,000 hp(m) *(5.88 MW)*; 2 shafts
Speed, knots: 25. **Range, miles:** 7,000 at 18 kt
Complement: 389 (includes 140 midshipmen)
Guns: 1 OTO Melara 76 mm/62. 2—40 mm saluting guns.
Torpedoes: 6—324 mm (2 triple) tubes.
Radars: Air/surface search: Melco OPS-14C; D-band.
Surface search: JRC OPS-18-1; D-band.
Navigation: Fujitsu OPS-19; I-band.
Fire control: Type 2-22; I/J-band.
Sonars: Hull-mounted; active search and attack; medium frequency.
Helicopters: Platform for 1 medium.

Comment: Approved in FY91 as a dedicated training ship but the project postponed to FY92 as a budget saving measure. Laid down 20 April 1993. The ship deployed for a world tour in 1995.
UPDATED

KASHIMA　　　　　　　　　　*5/1999*, John Mortimer /* 0080166

1 KUROBE CLASS (TRAINING SUPPORT SHIP) (AXT/ATS)

Name	No	Builders	Commissioned
KUROBE	ATS 4202	Nippon Koukan, Tsurumi	23 Mar 1989

Displacement, tons: 2,270 standard; 3,200 full load
Dimensions, feet (metres): 331.4 × 54.1 × 13.1 *(101 × 16.5 × 4)*
Main machinery: 4 Fuji 8L27.5XF diesels; 8,700 hp(m) *(6.4 MW)*; 2 shafts; cp props
Speed, knots: 20
Complement: 156 (17 officers)
Guns: 1 FMC/OTO Melara 3 in *(76 mm)*/62 Mk 75; 85 rds/min to 16 km *(8.6 n miles)* anti-surface; 12 km *(6.5 n miles)* anti-aircraft; weight of shell 6 kg.
Radars: Air search: Melco OPS-14C; D-band.
Surface search: JRC OPS-18-1; G-band.
Fire control: Type 2-21; I/J-band.

Comment: Approved under 1986 estimates, laid down 31 July 1987, launched 23 May 1988. Carries four BQM-34AJ high-speed drones and four Northrop Chukar II drones with two stern launchers. Used for training crews in anti-aircraft operations and evaluating the effectiveness and capability of ships' anti-aircraft missile systems.
UPDATED

KUROBE　　　　　　　　　　*9/1998*, Hachiro Nakai /* 0080167

1 HAYASE CLASS (TRAINING SUPPORT SHIP) (AS/ASU)

Name	No	Builders	Commissioned
HAYASE	ASU 7020 (ex-MST 462)	Ishikawajima Harima, Tokyo	6 Nov 1971

Displacement, tons: 2,000 standard
Dimensions, feet (metres): 324.8 × 47.6 × 13.8 *(99 × 14.5 × 4.2)*
Main machinery: 4 Kawasaki-MAN V6V22/30ATL diesels; 6,400 hp(m) *(4.7 MW)*; 2 shafts
Speed, knots: 18
Complement: 180
Guns: 2 USN 3 in *(76 mm)*/50 Mk 33 (twin); 50 rds/min to 12.8 km *(6.9 n miles)*; weight of shell 6 kg.
2 GE 20 mm/76 Vulcan; 3 barrels per mounting; 1,500 rds/min to 4 km *(2 n miles)*.
Torpedoes: 6—324 mm Type 68 (2 triple) tubes. Honeywell Mk 46 Mod 5 Neartip; anti-submarine; active/passive homing to 11 km *(5.9 n miles)* at 40 kt; warhead 44 kg.
Mines: 5 internal rails; 116 buoyant mines.
Weapons control: US Mk 63 for 76 mm guns.
Radars: Air search: Melco OPS-14; D-band.
Surface search: JRC OPS-16; D-band.
Fire control: Western Electric Mk 34; I/J-band.
Sonars: SQS-11A; hull-mounted; active search and attack; medium frequency.
Helicopters: Platform for 1 Sea Dragon.

Comment: Flagship of historic Gulf deployment in 1991. Paid off in 1997 and converted as a support ship for the submarine flotilla in 1998.

UPDATED

HAYASE   *1/1999*, Hachiro Nakai* / 0080168

1 CHIYODA CLASS (SUBMARINE DEPOT AND RESCUE SHIP) (AS)

Name	No	Builders	Launched	Commissioned
CHIYODA	AS 405	Mitsui, Tamano	7 Dec 1983	27 Mar 1985

Displacement, tons: 3,650 standard; 4,450 full load
Dimensions, feet (metres): 370.6 × 57.7 × 15.1 *(113 × 17.6 × 4.6)*
Main machinery: 2 Mitsui 8L42M diesels; 10,540 hp(m) *(8.8 MW)*; 2 shafts; cp props; bow and stern thrusters
Speed, knots: 17
Complement: 120
Radars: Navigation: JRC OPS-18-1; G-band.
Helicopters: Platform for up to MH-53 size.

Comment: Laid down 19 January 1983. Carries a Deep Submergence Rescue Vehicle (DSRV), built by Kawasaki Heavy Industries, Kobe, of 40 tons, 40.7 × 10.5 × 14.1 ft *(12.4 × 3.2 × 4.3 m)* with a 30 hp(m) *(22 kW)* electric motor and speed of 4 kt, it has space for 12 people. Flagship Second Submarine Flotilla based at Yokosuka.

UPDATED

CHIYODA   *9/1999*, Hachiro Nakai* / 0080169

1 CHIHAYA CLASS (SUBMARINE RESCUE SHIP) (ASR)

Name	No	Builders	Launched	Commissioned
CHIHAYA	ASR 403	Mitsui, Tamano	8 Oct 1998	23 Mar 2000

Displacement, tons: 5,450 standard
Dimensions, feet (metres): 419.9 × 65.6 × 16.7 *(128 × 20 × 5.1)*
Main machinery: 2 Mitsui 12V 42M-A diesels; 19,500 hp(m) *(14.33 MW)*; 2 shafts; 2 bow and 2 stern thrusters
Speed, knots: 21
Complement: 125
Radars: Navigation: I-band.
Helicopters: Platform for up to MH-53 size.

Comment: Authorisation approved in the 1996 budget as a replacement for *Fushimi*. Laid down 13 October 1997. Fitted with a search sonar and carries a 40 ton DSRV. Also used as a hospital ship.

UPDATED

CHIHAYA   *10/1999*, Hachiro Nakai* / 0080170

3 TOWADA CLASS (FAST COMBAT SUPPORT SHIPS) (AOE/AOR)

Name	No	Builders	Launched	Commissioned
TOWADA	AOE 422	Hitachi, Maizuru	25 Mar 1986	24 Mar 1987
TOKIWA	AOE 423	Ishikawajima Harima, Tokyo	23 Mar 1989	12 Mar 1990
HAMANA	AOE 424	Hitachi, Maizuru	18 May 1989	29 Mar 1990

Displacement, tons: 8,150 standard; 15,850 full load
Dimensions, feet (metres): 547.8 × 72.2 × 26.9 *(167 × 22 × 8.2)*
Main machinery: 2 Mitsui 16V42MA diesels; 23,950 hp(m) *(17.6 MW)*; 2 shafts
Speed, knots: 22
Complement: 140
Cargo capacity: 5,700 tons
Countermeasures: Decoys: 2 chaff launchers can be fitted.
Radars: Surface search: JRC OPS-18-1/28C; G-band.
Helicopters: Platform for 1 Sea King size.

Comment: First approved under 1984 estimates, laid down 17 April 1985. Second and third of class in 1987 estimates. AOE 423 laid down 12 May 1988, and AOE 424 8 July 1988. Two replenishment at sea positions on each side (one fuel only, one fuel or stores).

UPDATED

TOKIWA   *9/1999*, Hachiro Nakai* / 0080171

1 SAGAMI CLASS (FAST COMBAT SUPPORT SHIP) (AOE/AOR)

Name	No	Builders	Launched	Commissioned
SAGAMI	AOE 421	Hitachi, Maizuru	4 Sep 1978	30 Mar 1979

Displacement, tons: 5,000 standard; 11,600 full load
Dimensions, feet (metres): 478.9 × 62.3 × 24 *(146 × 19 × 7.3)*
Main machinery: 2 Type 12DRV diesels; 18,000 hp(m) *(13.23 MW)*; 2 shafts
Speed, knots: 22. Range, miles: 9,500 at 18 kt
Complement: 130
Cargo capacity: 5,000 tons
Radars: Surface search: JRC OPS-18-1; G-band.
Helicopters: Platform for 1 Sea King size.

Comment: Merchant type hull. Ordered December 1976. Laid down 28 September 1977, launched 4 September 1978. Two fuel stations each side. No armament but can be fitted. Based at Sasebo.

UPDATED

SAGAMI   *8/1999*, Hachiro Nakai* / 0080172

36 HARBOUR TANKERS (YO/YW/YG)

Comment: There are: 17 of 490 tons (YO 14, 21-27, 29-31, 33-38); eight of 310 tons (YW 17-24); two of 290 tons (YO 12-13); seven of 270 tons (YO 28, 32 and YG 201-205); two of 160 tons (YW 15-16).

UPDATED

YO 38   *10/1999*, Hachiro Nakai* / 0080173

3 HATSUSHIMA CLASS (EOD TENDERS) (YAS)

HATSUSHIMA	NINOSHIMA	MIYAJIMA
(ex-*MSC 649*) YAS 98	(ex-*MSC 650*) YAS 01	(ex-*MSC 651*) YAS 02

Displacement, tons: 440 standard
Dimensions, feet (metres): 180.4 × 30.8 × 7.9 *(55 × 9.4 × 2.4)*
Main machinery: 2 Mitsubishi YV12ZC-15/20 diesels; 1,440 hp(m) *(1.06 MW)*; 2 shafts
Speed, knots: 14
Complement: 43
Guns: 1 JM-61 Sea Vulcan 20 mm.

Comment: Transferred after conversion to Explosive Ordnance Disposal (EOD) Unit (Mine Hunting Diver) duties which includes removal of two generators used for minesweeping in order to provide for divers' room and equipment. One 'Takami' class *Oumi* YAS 95 may still be used as a noise range support ship.
UPDATED

HATSUSHIMA   *11/1999*, Hachiro Nakai* / 0080174

1 MUROTO CLASS (CABLE REPAIR SHIP) (ARC)

Name	No	Builders	Launched	Commissioned
MUROTO	ARC 482	Mitsubishi, Shimonoseki	25 July 1979	27 Mar 1980

Displacement, tons: 4,544 standard
Dimensions, feet (metres): 436.2 × 57.1 × 18.7 *(133 × 17.4 × 5.7)*
Main machinery: 4 Kawasaki-MAN V8V22/30ATL diesels; 8,000 hp(m) *(5.88 MW)*; 2 shafts; bow thruster
Speed, knots: 18
Complement: 135
Radars: Navigation: Fujitsu OPS-9B; I-band.

Comment: Ocean survey capability. Laid down 28 November 1978. Similar vessels in civilian use.
UPDATED

MUROTO   *3/1999*, Hachiro Nakai* / 0080176

3 ASU 81 CLASS (ASU)

Name	Laid down	Launched	Commissioned
ASU 83	2 Apr 1971	24 May 1971	30 Sep 1971
ASU 84	4 Feb 1972	15 June 1972	13 Sep 1972
ASU 85	20 Feb 1973	16 July 1973	19 Sep 1973

Displacement, tons: 500 *(ASU 85)*, 490 *(ASU 83-84)*, standard
Dimensions, feet (metres): 170.6 × 32.8 × 8.3 *(52 × 10 × 2.5)*
Main machinery: 2 Akasaka diesels; 1,600 hp(m) *(1.18 MW)*; 2 shafts
Speed, knots: 14
Complement: 25; 35 *(ASU 83)*
Radars: Navigation: OPS-9B/10/19B; I-band.

Comment: Training support and rescue. The after deck crane is able to lift a helicopter. To be replaced by new class from 2000/01.
UPDATED

ASU 85   *7/1999*, Hachiro Nakai* / 0080177

0 + 1 980 TON CLASS (AMS)

Displacement, tons: 980 standard
Main machinery: 2 diesels; 2 shafts
Speed, knots: 15
Complement: 40

Comment: Training support ship authorised in FY99 as replacement for ASU 83. Equipped with torpedo launch and recovery.
NEW ENTRY

1 HASHIDATE CLASS (ASY/YAC)

Name	No	Builders	Launched	Commissioned
HASHIDATE	ASY 91	Hitachi, Kanagawa	26 July 1999	30 Nov 1999

Displacement, tons: 400 standard
Dimensions, feet (metres): 203.4 × 30.8 × 6.6 *(62 × 9.4 × 2.0)*
Main machinery: 2 Niigata 16V 16FX diesels; 5,500 hp(m) *(4.04 MW)*; 2 shafts
Speed, knots: 20. **Range, miles:** 1,000 at 12 kt
Complement: 29 plus 130 passengers

Comment: Authorised in FY97 budget. Laid down 28 October 1998. Has replaced *Hiyodori*.
UPDATED

HASHIDATE   *12/1999*, Hachiro Nakai* / 0080175

SURVEY AND RESEARCH SHIPS

Notes: (1) The SES trials ship *Merguro II* does not belong to the MSDF.
(2) Survey ships are also included in the Maritime Safety Agency section.

2 HIBIKI CLASS (AOS)

Name	No	Builders	Launched	Commissioned
HIBIKI	AOS 5201	Mitsui, Tamano	27 July 1990	30 Jan 1991
HARIMA	AOS 5202	Mitsui, Tamano	11 Sep 1991	10 Mar 1992

Displacement, tons: 2,850 standard
Dimensions, feet (metres): 219.8 × 98.1 × 24.6 *(67 × 29.9 × 7.5)*
Main machinery: Diesel-electric; 4 Mitsubishi 6SU diesels; 6,700 hp(m) *(4.93 MW)*; 4 generators; 2 motors; 3,000 hp(m) *(2.2 MW)*; 2 shafts
Speed, knots: 11 (3 towing). **Range, miles:** 3,800 at 10 kt
Complement: 40
Radars: Surface search: JRC OPS-18-1; G-band.
Navigation: Koden OPS-20; I-band.
Sonars: UQQ 2 SURTASS; passive surveillance.
Helicopters: Platform only.

Comment: First authorised 24 January 1989, laid down 28 November, second approved in FY90, laid down 26 December 1990. Auxiliary Ocean Surveillance (AOS) ships to a SWATH design similar to USN 'TAGOS-19' class. A data collection station is based at Yokosuka Bay using WSC-6 satellite data relay to the AOS.
UPDATED

HIBIKI   *2/1999*, Hachiro Nakai* / 0080178

1 NICHINAN CLASS (AGS/AGI)

Name	No	Builders	Launched	Commissioned
NICHINAN	AGS 5105	Mitsubishi, Shimonoseki	11 June 1998	24 Mar 1999

Displacement, tons: 3,300 standard
Dimensions, feet (metres): 364.2 × 55.8 × 14.8 *(111 × 17 × 4.5)*
Main machinery: Diesel-electric; 2 Mitsubishi S16U diesel generators; 2 motors; 5,800 hp(m) *(4.26 MW)*; 2 shafts
Speed, knots: 18
Complement: 80

Comment: Authorisation approved in 1996 budget. Has replaced *Akashi* as an AGI. Laid down in August 1997.
UPDATED

NICHINAN   *1/1999*, Hachiro Nakai* / 0080179

1 SUMA CLASS (AGS)

Name	No	Builders	Launched	Commissioned
SUMA	AGS 5103	Hitachi, Maizuru	1 Sep 1981	30 Mar 1982

Displacement, tons: 1,180 standard
Dimensions, feet (metres): 236.2 × 42 × 11.1 *(72 × 12.8 × 3.4)*
Main machinery: 2 Fuji 6L27.5XF diesels; 3,250 hp(m) *(2.39 MW)*; 2 shafts; cp props; bow thruster
Speed, knots: 15
Complement: 65

Comment: Laid down 24 September 1980. Carries an 11 m launch for surveying work.

UPDATED

SUMA   *2/1999*, Hachiro Nakai* / 0080180

2 FUTAMI CLASS (AGS)

Name	No	Builders	Launched	Commissioned
FUTAMI	AGS 5102	Mitsubishi, Shimonoseki	9 Aug 1978	27 Feb 1979
WAKASA	AGS 5104	Hitachi, Maizuru	21 May 1985	25 Feb 1986

Displacement, tons: 2,050 standard; 3,175 full load
Dimensions, feet (metres): 318.2 × 49.2 × 13.8 *(97 × 15 × 4.2)*
Main machinery: 2 Kawasaki-MAN V8V22/30ATL diesels; 4,000 hp(m) *(2.94 MW)* (AGS 5102);
2 Fuji 8L27.5XF diesels; 3,250 hp(m) *(2.39 MW)* (AGS 5104); 2 shafts; cp props; bow thruster
Speed, knots: 16
Complement: 105
Radars: Navigation: JRC OPS-18-3; G-band.

Comment: AGS 5102 laid down 20 January 1978, AGS 5104 21 August 1984. Built to merchant marine design. Carry an RCV-225 remote-controlled rescue/underwater survey submarine. *Wakasa* has a slightly taller funnel.

UPDATED

FUTAMI   *10/1998*, Hachiro Nakai* / 0075869

1 KURIHAMA CLASS (ASE/AGS)

Name	No	Builders	Launched	Commissioned
KURIHAMA	ASE 6101	Sasebo Heavy Industries	20 Sep 1979	8 Apr 1980

Displacement, tons: 950 standard
Dimensions, feet (metres): 223 × 37.9 × 9.8 (screws) *(68 × 11.6 × 3)*
Main machinery: 2 Fuji 6S30B diesels; 4,800 hp(m) *(3.5 MW)*; 2 shafts; 2 cp props; 2 auxiliary electric props; bow thruster
Speed, knots: 15
Complement: 40 plus 12 scientists
Radars: Navigation: Fujitsu OPS-9B; I-band.

Comment: Experimental ship built for the Technical Research and Development Institute and used for testing underwater weapons and sensors.

VERIFIED

KURIHAMA   *10/1998, Hachiro Nakai* / 0052492

1 ASUKA CLASS (ASE/AGS)

Name	No	Builders	Launched	Commissioned
ASUKA	ASE 6102	Sumitomo, Uraga	21 June 1994	22 Mar 1995

Displacement, tons: 4,250 standard
Dimensions, feet (metres): 495.4 × 56.8 × 16.4 *(151 × 17.3 × 5)*
Main machinery: COGLAG; 2 IHI/GE LM 2500 gas turbines; 43,000 hp *(31.6 MW)*; 2 shafts; cp props
Speed, knots: 27
Complement: 72 plus 100 scientists
Missiles: SAM: 8 cell VLS.
Weapons control: Type 3 FCS.
Radars: Air search: SPY-1D type; E/F-band.
Air/surface search: Melco OPS-14B; D-band.
Surface search: JRC OPS-18-1; G-band.
Fire control: Type 3; I/J-band.
Sonars: Bow-mounted; active search; medium frequency.
Towed passive/active array in due course.
Helicopters: Platform for 1 SH-60J Seahawk.

Comment: Included in the FY92 programme and laid down 21 April 1993. For experimental and weapon systems testing which started with the FCS 3 in 1996. The bow sonar dome extends aft to the bridge. The VLS system is on the forecastle. Surveillance and countermeasures systems are also being evaluated.

UPDATED

ASUKA   *10/1998*, Hachiro Nakai* / 0080181

ICEBREAKERS

1 SHIRASE CLASS (AGB)

Name	No	Builders	Launched	Commissioned
SHIRASE	AGB 5002	Nippon Koukan, Tsurumi	11 Dec 1981	12 Nov 1982

Displacement, tons: 11,600 standard; 19,000 full load
Dimensions, feet (metres): 439.5 × 91.8 × 32.2 *(134 × 28 × 9.8)*
Main machinery: Diesel-electric; 6 Mitsui 12V42M diesels; 53,900 hp(m) *(39.6 MW)*; 6 generators; 6 motors; 30,000 hp(m) *(22 MW)*; 3 shafts
Speed, knots: 19. **Range, miles:** 25,000 at 15 kt
Complement: 170 (37 officers) plus 60 scientists
Cargo capacity: 1,000 tons
Radars: Surface search: JRC OPS-18-1; G-band.
Navigation: OPS-22; I-band.
Tacan: ORN-6 (URN 25).
Helicopters: 2 Mitsubishi S-61A; 1 Kawasaki OH-6D.

Comment: Laid down 5 March 1981. Fully equipped for marine and atmospheric research. Stabilised. The dome covers a weather radar.

UPDATED

SHIRASE   *8/1998, Hachiro Nakai* / 0052493

TUGS

19 + 1 OCEAN TUGS (ATA/YT)

YT 58	YT 63-74	YT 78-79	YT 81	YT 84	YT 86

Displacement, tons: 260 standard
Dimensions, feet (metres): 93 × 28 × 8.2 *(28.4 × 8.6 × 2.5)*
Main machinery: 2 Niigata 6L25B diesels; 1,800 hp(m) *(1.32 MW)*; 2 shafts
Speed, knots: 11
Complement: 10

Comment: YT 58 entered service on 31 October 1978, YT 63 on 27 September 1982, YT 64 on 30 September 1983, YT 65 on 20 September 1984, YT 66 on 20 September 1985, YT 67 on 4 September 1986, YT 68 on 9 September 1987, YT 69 on 16 September 1987, YT 70 on 2 September 1988, YT 71 on 28 July 1989, YT 72 on 28 July 1990, YT 73 on 31 July 1991, YT 74 on 30 September 1991, YT 78 in July 1994, YT 79 on 29 September 1994, YT 81 on 8 July 1996, YT 84 on 30 September 1998, YT 86 in March 2000. Two more approved in FY99 budget. All built by Yokohama Yacht.

UPDATED

24 COASTAL AND HARBOUR TUGS (YTM/YTB)

YT 44-46	YT 48-49	YT 53-57	YT 75-77	YT 82-83
YT 51	YT 59-62	YT 80	YT 85	YT 87-88

Displacement, tons: 190 standard
Dimensions, feet (metres): 84.8 × 23 × 7.5 *(25.7 × 7 × 2.3)*
Main machinery: 2 Kubota M6D20BUCS diesels; 1,500 hp(m) *(1.1 MW)*; 2 shafts
Speed, knots: 11
Complement: 10

Comment: Details given are for YT 53 and YT 55-57 built 1975-77. There are also four of 100 tons *(YT 44-46, YT 48)*; nine of 50 tons *(YT 75-77, YT 80, YT 82-83, YT 85 and YT 87-88)*; two of 35 tons *(YT 60-61)*; and the rest are of 29 tons.

UPDATED

YT 73   7/1999*, Hachiro Nakai / 0080182

YT 60   12/1999*, Hachiro Nakai / 0080183

MARITIME SAFETY AGENCY
KAIJOH HOANCHO

Headquarters Appointments

Commandant of the MSA:
  Shingo Arai

Establishment

Established in May 1948 as an external organisation of the Ministry of Transport to carry out patrol and rescue duties as well as hydrographic and navigation aids services. Since then a very considerable organisation with HQ in Tokyo has been built up. The Academy for the Agency is in Kure and the School in Maizuru.
The main operational branches are the Guard and Rescue, the Hydrographic and the Aids to Navigation Departments. Regional Maritime Safety offices control the 11 districts with their location as follows (airbases in brackets): RMS 1—Otaru (Chitose, Hakodate, Kushiro); 2—Shiogama (Sendai); 3—Yokohama (Haneda); 4—Nagoya (Ise); 5—Kobe (Yao); 6—Hiroshima (Hiroshima); 7—Kitakyushu (Fukuoka); 8—Maizuru (Miho); 9—Niigata (Niigata); 10—Kagoshima (Kagoshima); 11—Naha (Naha, Ishigaki). This organisation includes, as well as the RMS HQ, 66 MS offices, 51 MS stations, 14 MS air stations, 11 district communication centres, six traffic advisory service centres, four hydrographic observatories, 79 aids to navigation offices, one Special Rescue station, one Special Security station and one National Strike Team station.

Personnel

2000: 12,247 (2,630 officers)

Strength of the Fleet

Type	Active	Building
GUARD AND RESCUE SERVICE		
Patrol Vessels:		
Large with helicopter (PLH)	12	1
Large (PL)	40	1
Medium (PM)	47	—
Small (PS)	19	—
Firefighting Vessels (FL)	5	—
Patrol Craft:		
Patrol Craft (PC)	58	1
Patrol Craft (CL)	165	—
Firefighting Craft (FM)	9	—
Special Service Craft:		
Monitoring Craft (MS)	3	—
Guard Boats (GS)	2	—
Surveillance Craft (SS)	40	1
Oil Recovery Craft (OR)	5	—
Oil Skimming Craft (OS)	3	—
Oil Boom Craft (OX)	19	—

Type	Active	Building
HYDROGRAPHIC SERVICE		
Surveying Vessels:		
Large (HL)	5	—
Small (HS)	6	—
AIDS TO NAVIGATION SERVICE		
Aids to Navigation Research Vessel (LL)	1	—
Buoy Tenders:		
Large (LL)	3	—
Medium (LM)	1	—
Aids to Navigation Tenders:		
Medium (LM)	10	—
Small (LS)	48	—

DELETIONS

1997 *Mutsuki, Ayabane, Izu* (old), *Hiryu* (old), *CL 142-150, SS 13, SS 15, Katsuren* (old)
1998 *Shoyo* (old), *Miura* (old), *Kunashiri* (old), *Minabe* (old), *LS 116-118, LS 141-143, HS 11, LS 137*
1999 *Tamanami, Minegumo, CL 152-156, CL 218-221, CL 224, CL 229, Otowa, HS 32-34, LS 116-118, LS 141, LS 143, LS 204, LS 206, SS 12, SS 16, SS 19-20, SS 22, SS 26, SS 28-29, SS 31.*
2000 *Uranami, HS 35*

LARGE PATROL VESSELS

1 SHIKISHIMA CLASS (PLH)

Name	No	Builders	Laid down	Launched	Commissioned
SHIKISHIMA	PLH 31	Ishikawajima Harima, Tokyo	24 Aug 1990	27 June 1991	8 Apr 1992

Displacement, tons: 6,500 standard; 9,350 full load
Dimensions, feet (metres): 492.1 × 55.8 × 19.7 *(150 × 17 × 6)*
Main machinery: 2 SEMT-Pielstick 16 PC2.5 V 400; 20,800 hp (m) *(15.29 MW)*; 2 shafts; bow thruster
Speed, knots: 25. **Range, miles:** 20,000 at 18 kt
Complement: 110 plus 30 aircrew
Guns: 4 Oerlikon 35 mm/90 Type GDM-C (2 twin); 1,100 rds/ min to 6 km *(3.2 n miles)*; weight of shell 1.55 kg.
  2 JM-61 MB 20 mm Gatling.
Radars: Air/surface search: Melco Ops 14; D/E-band.
  Surface search: JMA 1576; I-band.
  Navigation: JMA 1596; I-band.
  Helo control: JMA 3000; I-band.
  Tacan: ORN-6 (URN 25).
Helicopters: 2 Bell 212 or 2 Super Puma.

Comment: Authorised in the FY89 programme in place of the third 'Mizuho' class. Used to escort the plutonium transport ship. SATCOM fitted.

VERIFIED

SHIKISHIMA   6/1998, E M Cornish / 0052497

2 MIZUHO CLASS (PLH)

Name	No	Builders	Launched	Commissioned
MIZUHO	PLH 21	Mitsubishi, Nagasaki	5 June 1985	19 Mar 1986
YASHIMA	PLH 22	Nippon Koukan, Tsurumi	20 Jan 1988	1 Dec 1988

Displacement, tons: 4,900 standard; 5,204 full load
Dimensions, feet (metres): 426.5 × 50.9 × 17.7 *(130 × 15.5 × 5.4)*
Main machinery: 2 SEMT-Pielstick 14 PC2.5 V 400 diesels; 18,200 hp(m) *(13.38 MW)* sustained; 2 shafts; cp props; bow thruster
Speed, knots: 23. **Range, miles:** 8,500 at 22 kt
Complement: 100 plus 30 aircrew
Guns: 1 Oerlikon 35 mm/90; 550 rds/min to 6 km *(3.2 n miles)* anti-surface; 5 km *(2.7 n miles)* anti-aircraft; weight of shell 1.55 kg.
  1 JM-61 MB 20 mm Gatling.
Radars: Surface search: JMA 8303; I-band.
Navigation and helo control: 2 JMA 3000; I-band.
Helicopters: 2 Fuji-Bell 212.

Comment: PLH 21 ordered under the FY83 programme laid down 27 August 1984. PLH 22 in 1986 estimates, laid down 3 October 1987. Two sets of fixed electric fin stabilisers that have a lift of 26 tons × 2 and reduce rolling by 90 per cent at 18 kt. Employed in search and rescue outside the 200 mile economic zone.

UPDATED

YASHIMA   *4/1999*, Hachiro Nakai /* 0080184

9 + 1 SOYA CLASS (PLH)

Name	No	Builders	Commissioned
SOYA	PLH 01	Nippon Kokan, Tsurumi	22 Nov 1978
TSUGARU	PLH 02	IHI, Tokyo	17 Apr 1979
OOSUMI	PLH 03	Mitsui Tamano	18 Oct 1979
HAYATO (ex-*Uraga*)	PLH 04	Hitachi, Maizuru	5 Mar 1980
ZAO	PLH 05	Mitsubishi, Nagasaki	19 Mar 1982
CHIKUZEN	PLH 06	Kawasaki, Kobe	28 Sep 1983
SETTSU	PLH 07	Sumitomo, Oppama	27 Sep 1984
ECHIGO	PLH 08	Mitsui Tamano	28 Feb 1990
RYUKYU	PLH 09	Mitsubishi, Nagasaki	Apr 2000
—	PLH 10	Nippon Kokan, Tsurumi	Sep 2001

Displacement, tons: 3,200 normal; 3,744 full load
Dimensions, feet (metres): 323.4 × 51.2 × 17.1 *(98.6 × 15.6 × 5.2)* (PLH 01) 345.8 × 47.9 × 15.7 *(105.4 × 14.6 × 4.8)*
Main machinery: 2 SEMT-Pielstick 12 PC2.5 V 400 diesels; 15,604 hp(m) *(11.47 MW)* sustained; 2 shafts; cp props; bow thruster
Speed, knots: 21 (PLH 01); 22 (others). **Range, miles:** 5,700 at 18 kt
Complement: 71 (PLH 01-04); 69 (others)
Guns: 1 Bofors 40 mm or Oerlikon 35 mm. 1 Oerlikon 20 mm (PLH 01, 02, 05-07).
Radars: Surface search: JMA 1576; I-band.
Navigation: JMA 1596; I-band.
Helo control: JMA 1596; I-band.
Helicopters: 1 Fuji-Bell 212.

Comment: PLH 01 has an icebreaking capability while the other ships are only ice strengthened. Fitted with both fin stabilisers and anti-rolling tanks of 70 tons capacity. The fixed electric hydraulic fins have a lift of 26 tons × 2 at 18 kt which reduces rolling by 90 per cent at that speed. At slow speed the reduction is 50 per cent, using the tanks. PLH 04 name changed on 27 March 1997. PLH 10 laid down 8 March 1999.

UPDATED

OOSUMI   *4/1999*, Hachiro Nakai /* 0080185

1 IZU CLASS (PL)

Name	No	Builders	Launched	Commissioned
IZU	PL 31	Kawasaki, Sakaide	7 Feb 1997	25 Sep 1997

Displacement, tons: 3,500 normal
Dimensions, feet (metres): 360.9 × 49.2 × 17.4 *(110 × 15 × 5.3)*
Main machinery: 2 diesels; 12,000 hp(m) *(8.82 MW)*; 2 shafts; bow thruster
Speed, knots: 20
Complement: 40 plus 70 spare
Guns: 1 JM-61 MB 20 mm Gatling.
Radars: Surface search: I-band.
Navigation: I-band.
Helicopters: Platform for 1 Fuji-Bell 212.

Comment: Authorised in the FY95 programme. Laid down 22 March 1996. Replaced the former *Izu* in 1998, taking the same name and pennant number. Carries two launches.

UPDATED

IZU   *4/1998*, Hachiro Nakai /* 0080186

1 MIURA CLASS (PL)

Name	No	Builders	Launched	Commissioned
MIURA	PL 22	Sumitomo, Uraga	11 Mar 1998	28 Oct 1998

Displacement, tons: 3,000 normal
Dimensions, feet (metres): 377.3 × 45.9 × 15.7 *(115 × 14 × 4.8)*
Main machinery: 2 diesels; 8,000 hp(m) *(5.88 MW)*; 2 shafts; cp props
Speed, knots: 18
Complement: 40 plus 10 spare
Guns: 1—20 mm JM 61-B Gatling.

Comment: Authorised in FY96 programme. Laid down in October 1996. Has replaced ship of the same name.

UPDATED

MIURA   *2/1999*, Hachiro Nakai /* 0080187

1 KOJIMA CLASS (PL)

Name	No	Builders	Commissioned
KOJIMA	PL 21	Hitachi, Maizuru	11 Mar 1993

Displacement, tons: 2,650 normal; 2,950 full load
Dimensions, feet (metres): 377.3 × 45.9 × 16.4 *(115 × 14 × 5)*
Main machinery: 2 diesels; 8,000 hp(m) *(5.9 MW)*; 2 shafts; cp props
Speed, knots: 18. **Range, miles:** 7,000 at 15 kt
Complement: 118
Guns: 1 Oerlikon 35 mm/90. 1—20 mm JM-61B Gatling. 1—12.7 mm MG.
Radars: Navigation: Two JMA 1596; I-band.
Helicopters: Platform for 1 medium.

Comment: Authorised in the FY90 programme and ordered in March 1991. Laid down 7 November 1991, launched 10 September 1992. Training ship which has replaced the old ship of the same name and pennant number. SATCOM fitted.

UPDATED

KOJIMA   *4/1999*, Hachiro Nakai /* 0080188

1 NOJIMA CLASS (PL)

Name	No	Builders	Commissioned
OKI (ex-*Nojima*)	PL 01	Ishikawajima Harima, Tokyo	21 Sep 1989

Displacement, tons: 1,500 normal
Dimensions, feet (metres): 285.4 × 34.4 × 11.5 *(87 × 10.5 × 3.5)*
Main machinery: 2 Fuji 8S40B diesels; 8,120 hp(m) *(5.97 MW)*; 2 shafts
Speed, knots: 19
Complement: 34
Guns: 1 Oerlikon 35 mm/90. 1—20 mm JM-61B Gatling.
Radars: Navigation: 2 JMA 1596; I-band.
Helicopters: Platform for 1 Bell 212.

Comment: Laid down 16 August 1988 and launched 30 May 1989. Equipped as surveillance and rescue command ship. SATCOM fitted. Name changed on 30 November 1997.   ***UPDATED***

OKI   *6/1999*, Hachiro Nakai /* 0080189

28 SHIRETOKO CLASS (PL)

Name	No	Builders	Commissioned
SHIRETOKO	PL 101	Mitsui Tamano	8 Nov 1978
ESAN	PL 102	Sumitomo	16 Nov 1978
WAKASA	PL 103	Kawasaki, Kobe	29 Nov 1978
SHIMANTO (ex-*Yahiko*)	PL 104	Mitsubishi, Shimonoseki	16 Nov 1978
MOTOBU	PL 105	Sasebo	29 Nov 1978
RISHIRI	PL 106	Shikoku	12 Sep 1979
MATSUSHIMA	PL 107	Tohoku	14 Sep 1979
IWAKI	PL 108	Naikai	10 Aug 1979
SHIKINE	PL 109	Usuki	20 Sep 1979
SURUGA	PL 110	Kurushima	28 Sep 1979
REBUN	PL 111	Narasaki	21 Nov 1979
CHOKAI	PL 112	Nihonkai	30 Nov 1979
NOJIMA (ex-*Ashizuri*)	PL 113	Sanoyasu	31 Oct 1979
TOSA (ex-*Oki*)	PL 114	Tsuneishi	16 Nov 1979
NOTO	PL 115	Miho	30 Nov 1979
YONAKUNI	PL 116	Hayashikane	31 Oct 1979
KURIKOMA (ex-*Kudaka*, ex-*Daisetsu*)	PL 117	Hakodate	31 Jan 1980
SHIMOKITA	PL 118	Ishikawajima, Kakoki	12 Mar 1980
SUZUKA	PL 119	Kanazashi	7 Mar 1980
KUNISAKI	PL 120	Kouyo	29 Feb 1980
GENKAI	PL 121	Oshima	31 Jan 1980
GOTO	PL 122	Onomichi	29 Feb 1980
KOSHIKI	PL 123	Kasado	25 Jan 1980
HATERUMA	PL 124	Osaka	12 Mar 1980
KATORI	PL 125	Tohoku	21 Oct 1980
KUNIGAMI	PL 126	Kanda	17 Oct 1980
ETOMO	PL 127	Naikai	17 Mar 1982
AMAGI (ex-*Mashu*)	PL 128	Shiikoku	12 Mar 1982

Displacement, tons: 974 normal; 1,360 full load
Dimensions, feet (metres): 255.8 × 31.5 × 10.5 *(78 × 9.6 × 3.2)*
Main machinery: 2 Fuji 8S40B; 8,120 hp(m) *(5.97 MW)*; or 2 Niigata 8MA40 diesels; 2 shafts; cp props
Speed, knots: 20. **Range, miles:** 4,400 at 17 kt
Complement: 41
Guns: 1 Bofors 40 mm or 1 Oerlikon 35 mm. 1 Oerlikon 20 mm (PL 101-105, 127 and 128).
Radars: Surface search: JMA 1576; I-band.
Navigation: JMA 1596; I-band.

Comment: Average time from launch to commissioning was about four to five months. Designed for EEZ patrol duties. PL 117 changed her name on 1 April 1988 and again 1 August 1994. PL 128 changed 1 April 1997, and PL 104 on 28 September 1999.   *UPDATED*

SHIMANTO   *10/1999*, Hachiro Nakai* / 0080190

2 DAIO CLASS (PL)

Name	No	Builders	Commissioned
DAIO	PL 15	Hitachi, Maizuru	28 Sep 1973
MUROTO	PL 16	Naikai	30 Nov 1974

Displacement, tons: 1,206 normal
Dimensions, feet (metres): 251.3 × 31.5 × 10.7 *(76.6 × 9.6 × 3.3)*
Main machinery: 2 Fuji 8S40B; 8,120 hp(m) *(5.97 MW)*; 2 shafts; cp props
Speed, knots: 20. **Range, miles:** 4,400 at 18 kt
Complement: 50
Guns: 1 Oerlikon 20 mm. 1 Bofors 40 mm.
Radars: Navigation: JMA 1576. JMA 1596.

Comment: Based at Kushiro (PL 15) and Aburatsu (PL 16).   *VERIFIED*

MUROTO   *12/1996, Hachiro Nakai*

6 + 1 OJIKA CLASS (PL)

Name	No	Builders	Launched	Commissioned
OJIKA	PL 02	Mitsui, Tamano	23 Apr 1991	31 Oct 1991
KUDAKA	PL 03	Hakodate Dock	10 May 1994	25 Oct 1994
YAHIKO (ex-*Satsuma*)	PL 04	Sumitomo, Uraga	3 June 1995	26 Oct 1995
HAKATA	PL 05	Ishikawajima, Tokyo	6 July 1998	26 Nov 1998
DEJIMA	PL 06	Mitsui, Tamano	28 June 1999	29 Oct 1999
SATAUMA	PL 07	Kawasaki, Kobe	3 June 1999	29 Oct 1999
—	PL 08	Sasebo Heavy Industries	June 2000	Oct 2000

Displacement, tons: 1,883 normal
Dimensions, feet (metres): 299.9 × 36.1 × 11.5 *(91.4 × 11 × 3.5)*
Main machinery: 2 Fuji 8S40B diesels; 7,000 hp(m) *(5.15 MW)*; 2 shafts; cp props; 2 bow thrusters
Speed, knots: 18. **Range, miles:** 4,400 at 15 kt
Complement: 38
Guns: 1 Oerlikon 35 mm/90. 1—20 mm JM-61B Gatling.
Radars: Navigation: JMA 1596; I-band.
Helicopters: Platform for 1 Bell 212 or Super Puma.

Comment: Equipped as SAR command ships. SATCOM fitted. 30 ton bollard pull. Stern dock for RIB. PL 04 name changed 28 September 1999.   *UPDATED*

HAKATA   *8/1999*, Hachiro Nakai* / 0080191

SHIPBORNE AIRCRAFT

Numbers/Type: 4 Aerospatiale AS 332L1 Super Puma.
Operational speed: 151 kt *(279 km/h)*.
Service ceiling: 15,090 ft *(4,600 m)*.
Range: 335 n miles *(620 km)*.
Role/Weapon systems: Medium lift, support and SAR. Sensors: Search radar. Weapons: Unarmed.   *UPDATED*

SUPER PUMA   *4/1999*, Hachiro Nakai* / 0080192

Numbers/Type: 27/5 Bell 212/412.
Operational speed: 100 kt *(185 km/h)*.
Service ceiling: 10,000 ft *(3,048 m)*.
Range: 412 n miles *(763 km)*.
Role/Weapon systems: Liaison, medium-range support and SAR. Sensors: Search radar. Weapons: Unarmed.   *UPDATED*

BELL 212   *10/1999*, Hachiro Nakai* / 0080193

Numbers/Type: 4 Sikorsky S-76C.
Operational speed: 145 kt *(269 km/h)*.
Service ceiling: 11,800 ft *(3,505 m)*.
Range: 430 n miles *(798 km)*.
Role/Weapon systems: Utility aircraft acquired in 1994-98. Up to 20 required to replace Bell 212s. Sensors: Search radar. Weapons: Unarmed.   *UPDATED*

S-76C   *2/1999*, JMSA* / 0080194

LAND-BASED MARITIME AIRCRAFT (FRONT LINE)

Note: There are also two SABB 340B utility aircraft.

Numbers/Type: 14/2/5 Beech Super King Air 200T/B200T/350.
Operational speed: 245 kt *(453 km/h).*
Service ceiling: 35,000 ft *(10,670 m).*
Range: 1,460 n miles *(2,703 km).*
Role/Weapon systems: Visual reconnaissance in support of EEZ. Two are trainers. Sensors: Weather/search radar. Weapons: Unarmed.   ***UPDATED***

Numbers/Type: 5 NAMC YS-11A.
Operational speed: 230 kt *(425 km/h).*
Service ceiling: 21,600 ft *(6,580 m).*
Range: 1,960 n miles *(3,629 km).*
Role/Weapon systems: Maritime surveillance and associated tasks. Sensors: Weather/search radar. Weapons: Unarmed.   ***VERIFIED***

Numbers/Type: 2 Dassault Falcon 900.
Operational speed: 428 kt *(792 km/h).*
Service ceiling: 51,000 ft *(15,544 m).*
Range: 4,170 n miles *(7,722 km).*
Role/Weapon systems: Maritime surveillance. Sensors: Weather/search radar. Weapons: Unarmed.   ***VERIFIED***

MEDIUM PATROL VESSELS

14 TESHIO CLASS (PM)

Name	No	Builders	Commissioned
NATSUI (ex-*Teshio*)	PM 01	Shikoku	30 Sep 1980
OIRASE	PM 02	Naikai	29 Aug 1980
ECHIZEN	PM 03	Usuki	30 Sep 1980
TOKACHI	PM 04	Narazaki	24 Mar 1981
HITACHI	PM 05	Tohoku	19 Mar 1981
OKITSU	PM 06	Usuki	17 Mar 1981
ISAZU	PM 07	Naikai	18 Feb 1982
CHITOSE	PM 08	Shikoku	15 Mar 1983
KUWANO	PM 09	Naikai	10 Mar 1983
SORACHI	PM 10	Tohoku	30 Aug 1984
YUBARI	PM 11	Usuki	28 Nov 1985
MOTOURA	PM 12	Shikoku	21 Nov 1986
KANO	PM 13	Naikai	13 Nov 1986
SENDAI	PM 14	Shikoku	1 June 1988

Displacement, tons: 630 normal; 670 full load
Dimensions, feet (metres): 222.4 × 25.9 × 6.6 *(67.8 × 7.9 × 2.7)*
Main machinery: 2 Fuji 6S32F or Arakata 6M31E diesels; 3,650 hp(m) *(2.69 MW);* 2 shafts
Speed, knots: 18. **Range, miles:** 3,200 at 16 kt
Complement: 33
Guns: 1 JN-61B 20 mm Gatling.
Radars: Navigation: 2 JMA 159B; I-band.

Comment: First three built under FY79 programme and second three under FY80, seventh under FY81, PM 08-09 under FY82, PM 10 under FY83, PM 11 under FY84, PM 12-13 under FY85, PM 14 under FY87. *Isazu* has an additional structure aft of the mainmast which is used as a classroom.   ***UPDATED***

OKITSU   *7/1999*, Hachiro Nakai /* 0080195

2 TAKATORI CLASS (PM)

Name	No	Builders	Commissioned
TAKATORI	PM 89	Naikai	24 Mar 1978
KUMANO	PM 94	Namura	23 Feb 1979

Displacement, tons: 634 normal
Dimensions, feet (metres): 152.5 × 30.2 × 9.3 *(46.5 × 9.2 × 2.9)*
Main machinery: 2 Niigata 6M31EX diesels; 3,000 hp(m) *(2.21 MW);* 2 shafts; cp props
Speed, knots: 15. **Range, miles:** 700 at 14 kt
Complement: 34
Radars: Navigation: JMA 1596 and JMA 1576; I-band.

Comment: SAR vessels equipped for salvage and firefighting.   ***UPDATED***

TAKATORI   *4/1999*, Mitsuhiro Kadota /* 0080196

20 BIHORO CLASS (350-M4 TYPE) (PM)

Name	No	Builders	Commissioned
BIHORO	PM 73	Tohoku	28 Feb 1974
KUMA	PM 74	Usuki	28 Feb 1974
FUJI	PM 75	Usuki	7 Feb 1975
KABASHIMA	PM 76	Usuki	25 Mar 1975
SADO	PM 77	Tohoku	7 Feb 1975
ISHIKARI	PM 78	Tohoku	13 Mar 1976
ABUKUMA	PM 79	Tohoku	30 Jan 1976
ISUZU	PM 80	Naikai	10 Mar 1976
KIKUCHI	PM 81	Usuki	6 Feb 1976
KUZURYU	PM 82	Usuki	18 Mar 1976
HOROBETSU	PM 83	Tohoku	27 Jan 1977
SHIRAKAMI	PM 84	Tohoku	24 Mar 1977
SAGAMI	PM 85	Naikai	30 Nov 1976
TONE	PM 86	Usuki	30 Nov 1976
YOSHINO	PM 87	Usuki	28 Jan 1977
KUROBE	PM 88	Shikoku	15 Feb 1977
CHIKUGO	PM 90	Naikai	27 Jan 1978
YAMAKUNI	PM 91	Usuki	26 Jan 1978
KATSURA	PM 92	Shikoku	15 Feb 1978
SHINANO	PM 93	Tohoku	23 Feb 1978

Displacement, tons: 615 normal; 636 full load
Dimensions, feet (metres): 208 × 25.6 × 8.3 *(63.4 × 7.8 × 2.5)*
Main machinery: 2 Niigata 6M31EX diesels; 3,000 hp(m) *(2.21 MW);* 2 shafts; cp props
Speed, knots: 18. **Range, miles:** 3,200 at 16 kt
Complement: 34
Guns: 1 USN 20 mm/80 Mk 10.
Radars: Navigation: JMA 1596 and JMA 1576; I-band.

Comment: Average time from launch to commissioning, four months.   ***UPDATED***

FUJI   *10/1999*, Hachiro Nakai /* 0080197

5 KUNASHIRI CLASS (350-M3 TYPE) (PM)

Name	No	Builders	Commissioned
SAROBETSU	PM 67	Hitachi, Maizuru	30 Mar 1971
KAMISHIMA	PM 68	Usuki	31 Jan 1972
MIYAKE	PM 70	Tohoku	25 Jan 1973
AWAJI	PM 71	Usuki	25 Jan 1973
YAEYAMA	PM 72	Usuki	20 Dec 1972

Displacement, tons: 498 normal
Dimensions, feet (metres): 190.4 × 24.3 × 7.9 *(58 × 7.4 × 2.4)*
Main machinery: 2 Niigata 6MF32H or 6M31EX (PM 70-72) diesels; 2,600 hp(m) *(1.91 MW)* or 3,000 hp(m) *(2.21 MW)* (PM 70-72); 2 shafts; cp props (PM 72)
Speed, knots: 17 or 18. **Range, miles:** 3,000 at 16 kt
Complement: 40
Guns: 1 USN 20 mm Mk 10.
Radars: Navigation: JMA 1576 or 1596 (PM 70-72).

Comment: The last three have slightly more powerful diesels and a top speed of 18 kt. Being paid off.   ***UPDATED***

YAEYAMA   *5/1997*, Hachiro Nakai /* 0012683

4 AMAMI CLASS (PM)

Name	No	Builders	Commissioned
AMAMI	PM 95	Hitachi, Kanagawa	28 Sep 1992
MATSUURU	PM 96	Hitachi, Kanagawa	24 Nov 1995
KUNASHIRI	PM 97	Mitsubishi, Shimonoseki	26 Aug 1998
MINABE	PM 98	Mitsubishi, Shimonoseki	26 Aug 1998

Displacement, tons: 230 normal
Dimensions, feet (metres): 183.7 × 24.6 × 6.6 *(56 × 7.5 × 2)*
Main machinery: 2 Fuji 8S40B diesels; 8,120 hp(m) *(5.97 MW)*; 2 shafts; cp props
Speed, knots: 25
Guns: 1—20 mm JM-61B Gatling.
Radars: Navigation: I-band.

Comment: First one authorised in the FY91 programme; laid down 22 October 1991. Second authorised in FY93 programme; laid down 7 October 1994. Last pair authorised in FY96 programme and both laid down 30 September 1997. Stern ramp for launching RIB.

UPDATED

MATSUURU   *4/1999*, Hachiro Nakai* / 0080198

1 TESHIO CLASS (ICEBREAKER) (PM)

Name	No	Builders	Commissioned
TESHIO	PM 15	Nippon Koukan, Tsurumi	19 Oct 1995

Displacement, tons: 550 normal
Dimensions, feet (metres): 180.4 × 34.8 × 12.8 *(55 × 10.6 × 3.9)*
Main machinery: 2 diesels; 3,600 hp(m) *(2.65 MW)*; 2 shafts; bow thruster
Speed, knots: 14.5
Complement: 35
Guns: 1—20 mm JM-61B Gatling.
Radars: Navigation: 2 sets; I-band.

Comment: Authorised in FY93; laid down 7 October 1994, launched 20 April 1995. Has an icebreaker bow.

VERIFIED

TESHIO   *10/1995, JMSA*

1 YAHAGI CLASS (350 TYPE) (PM)

Name	No	Builders	Commissioned
MISASA (ex-*Okinawa*)	PM 69	Usuki	23 Oct 1970

Displacement, tons: 376 normal
Dimensions, feet (metres): 164.9 × 24 × 7.4 *(50.3 × 7.3 × 2.3)*
Main machinery: 2 Ikegai MSB31S diesels; 1,400 hp(m) *(1.03 MW)*; 2 shafts
Speed, knots: 15.5. **Range, miles:** 2,900 at 14 kt
Complement: 44
Guns: 1 USN 20 mm Mk 10.
Radars: Navigation: 1 set.

Comment: Transferred to MSA in 1972. Name changed 1 April 1988.

VERIFIED

MISASA   *1988, JMSA*

SMALL PATROL VESSELS

Note: A new 180 ton type was laid down at Mitsui, Tamano in March 1999 and is to complete in August 2000.

10 MIHASHI CLASS (PS)

Name	No	Builders	Commissioned
AKIYOSHI (ex-*Mihashi*)	PS 01	Mitsubishi, Shimonoseki	9 Sep 1988
SAROMA	PS 02	Hitachi, Kanagawa	24 Nov 1989
INASA	PS 03	Mitsubishi, Shimonoseki	31 Jan 1990
KIRISHIMA	PS 04	Hitachi, Kanagawa	22 Mar 1991
KAMUI	PS 05	Mitsubishi, Shimonoseki	31 Jan 1994
BANNA (ex-*Bizan*)	PS 06	Hitachi, Kanagawa	31 Jan 1994
ASHITAKI	PS 07	Mitsui, Tamano	30 Sep 1994
KURAMA	PS 08	Mitsubishi, Shimonoseki	29 Aug 1995
ARASE	PS 09	Mitsubishi, Shimonoseki	29 Jan 1997
SANBE	PS 10	Hitachi, Kanagawa	29 Jan 1997

Displacement, tons: 195 normal
Dimensions, feet (metres): 141.1 × 24.6 × 5.6 *(43 × 7.5 × 1.7)*
Main machinery: 2 SEMT-Pielstick 16 PA4 V 200 VGA diesels; 7,072 hp(m) *(5.2 MW)*; 2 shafts
1 SEMT-Pielstick 12 PA4 V 200 VGA diesel; 2,720 hp(m) *(2 MW)*; Kamewa 80 water-jet
Speed, knots: 35. **Range, miles:** 650 at 34 kt
Complement: 34
Guns: 1—12.7 mm MG.
Radars: Navigation: Furuno; I-band.

Comment: Last pair authorised in FY95 programme. Capable of 15 kt on the water-jet alone. PS 01 name changed 28 January 1997, PS 06 on 17 April 1999.

UPDATED

INASA   *8/1999*, Hachiro Nakai* / 0080200

7 AKAGI CLASS (PS)

Name	No	Builders	Commissioned
AKAGI	PS 101	Sumidagawa	26 Mar 1980
TSUKUBA	PS 102	Sumidagawa	24 Feb 1982
KONGOU	PS 103	Ishihara	16 Mar 1987
KATSURAGI	PS 104	Ishihara	24 Mar 1988
HIROMINE	PS 105	Yokohama Yacht Co	24 Mar 1988
SHIZUKI	PS 106	Sumidagawa	24 Mar 1988
TAKACHIHO	PS 107	Sumidagawa	24 Mar 1988

Displacement, tons: 115 full load
Dimensions, feet (metres): 114.8 × 20.7 × 4.3 *(35 × 6.3 × 1.3)*
Main machinery: 2 Pielstick 16 PA4 V 185 diesels; 5,344 hp(m) *(3.93 MW)* sustained; 2 shafts
Speed, knots: 28. **Range, miles:** 500 at 20 kt
Complement: 22
Guns: 1 Browning 12.7 mm MG.
Radars: Navigation: 1 set; I-band.

Comment: Carry a 25-man inflatable rescue craft. The last four were ordered on 31 August 1987 and commissioned less than seven months later.

UPDATED

KATSURAGI   *10/1999*, Hachiro Nakai* / 0080199

2 TAKATSUKI CLASS (PS)

Name	No	Builders	Commissioned
TAKATSUKI	PS 108	Mitsubishi, Shimonoseki	23 Mar 1992
NOBARU	PS 109	Hitachi, Kanagawa	22 Mar 1993

Displacement, tons: 115 normal; 180 full load
Dimensions, feet (metres): 114.8 × 22 × 4.3 *(35 × 6.7 × 1.3)*
Main machinery: 2 MTU 16V 396 TB94 diesels; 5,200 hp(m) *(3.82 MW)*; 2 Kamewa 71 water-jets
Speed, knots: 35
Complement: 13
Guns: 1—12.7 mm MG.
Radars: Navigation: I-band.

Comment: First authorised in the FY91 programme, second in FY92. Aluminium hulls.
VERIFIED

TAKATSUKI   *6/1996, Hachiro Nakai*

COASTAL PATROL CRAFT

23 MURAKUMO CLASS (PC)

Name	No	Builders	Commissioned
MURAKUMO	PC 201	Mitsubishi, Shimonoseki	24 Mar 1978
KITAGUMO	PC 202	Hitachi, Kanagawa	17 Mar 1978
YUKIGUMO	PC 203	Hitachi, Kanagawa	27 Sep 1978
ASAGUMO	PC 204	Mitsubishi, Shimonoseki	21 Sep 1978
HAYAGUMO	PC 205	Mitsubishi, Shimonoseki	30 Jan 1979
AKIGUMO	PC 206	Hitachi, Kanagawa	28 Feb 1979
YAEGUMO	PC 207	Mitsubishi, Shimonoseki	16 Mar 1979
NATSUGUMO	PC 208	Hitachi, Kanagawa	22 Mar 1979
YAMAGIRI	PC 209	Hitachi, Kanagawa	29 June 1979
KAWAGIRI	PC 210	Hitachi, Kanagawa	27 July 1979
BIZAN (ex-*Teruzuki*)	PC 211	Mitsubishi, Shimonoseki	26 June 1979
NATSUZUKI	PC 212	Mitsubishi, Shimonoseki	26 July 1979
MIYAZUKI	PC 213	Hitachi, Kanagawa	13 Mar 1980
NIJIGUMO	PC 214	Mitsubishi, Shimonoseki	29 Jan 1981
TATSUGUMO	PC 215	Mitsubishi, Shimonoseki	19 Mar 1981
HAMAYUKI	PC 216	Hitachi, Kanagawa	27 Feb 1981
ISONAMI	PC 217	Mitsubishi, Shimonoseki	19 Mar 1981
NAGOZUKI	PC 218	Hitachi, Kanagawa	29 Jan 1981
YAEZUKI	PC 219	Hitachi, Kanagawa	19 Mar 1981
YAMAYUKI	PC 220	Hitachi, Kanagawa	16 Feb 1982
KOMAYUKI	PC 221	Mitsubishi, Shimonoseki	10 Feb 1982
UMIGIRI	PC 222	Hitachi, Kanagawa	17 Feb 1983
ASAGIRI	PC 223	Mitsubishi, Shimonoseki	23 Feb 1983

Displacement, tons: 85 normal
Dimensions, feet (metres): 98.4 × 20.7 × 7.2 *(30 × 6.3 × 2.2)*
Main machinery: 2 Ikegai MTU MB 16V 652 SB70 diesels; 4,400 hp(m) *(3.23 MW)* sustained; 2 shafts
Speed, knots: 30. **Range, miles:** 350 at 28 kt
Complement: 13
Guns: 1—12.7 mm MG.
Radars: Navigation: I-band.

Comment: PC 211 name changed on 17 April 1999.
UPDATED

YUKIGUMO   *4/1999*, Hachiro Nakai* / 0080202*

10 AKIZUKI CLASS (PC)

Name	No	Builders	Commissioned
URAYUKI	PC 72	Mitsubishi, Shimonoseki	31 May 1975
ISEYUKI	PC 73	Mitsubishi, Shimonoseki	31 July 1975
HATAGUMO	PC 75	Mitsubishi, Shimonoseki	21 Feb 1976
MAKIGUMO	PC 76	Mitsubishi, Shimonoseki	19 Mar 1976
HAMAZUKI	PC 77	Mitsubishi, Shimonoseki	29 Nov 1976
ISOZUKI	PC 78	Mitsubishi, Shimonoseki	18 Mar 1977
SHIMANAMI	PC 79	Mitsubishi, Shimonoseki	23 Dec 1977
YUZUKI	PC 80	Mitsubishi, Shimonoseki	22 Mar 1979
TAMANAMI (ex-*Hanayuki*)	PC 81	Mitsubishi, Shimonoseki	27 Mar 1981
AWAGIRI	PC 82	Mitsubishi, Shimonoseki	24 Mar 1983

Displacement, tons: 77 normal
Dimensions, feet (metres): 85.3 × 20.7 × 6.9 *(26 × 6.3 × 2.1)*
Main machinery: 3 Mitsubishi 12DM20MTK diesels; 3,000 hp(m) *(2.21 MW)*; 3 shafts
Speed, knots: 22. **Range, miles:** 220 at 21.5 kt
Complement: 10
Radars: Navigation: FRA 10 Mk 2; I-band.

Comment: Aluminium hulls. Used mostly for SAR. Being paid off.
UPDATED

AWAGIRI   *11/1999*, Hachiro Nakai / 0080201*

3 SHIMAGIRI CLASS (PC)

Name	No	Builders	Commissioned
SHIMAGIRI	PC 83	Hitachi, Kanagawa	7 Feb 1985
SETOGIRI	PC 84	Hitachi, Kanagawa	22 Mar 1985
HAYAGIRI	PC 85	Mitsubishi, Shimonoseki	22 Feb 1985

Displacement, tons: 51 normal
Dimensions, feet (metres): 75.5 × 17.4 × 6.2 *(23 × 5.3 × 1.9)*
Main machinery: 2 Ikegai 12V 175 RTC diesels; 3,000 hp(m) *(2.21 MW)*; 2 shafts
Speed, knots: 30
Complement: 10
Guns: 1—12.7 mm MG (not in all).
Radars: Navigation: FRA 10 Mk 2; I-band.

Comment: Aluminium hulls.
VERIFIED

SHIMAGIRI   *8/1998, Hachiro Nakai* / 0052511*

1 MATSUNAMI CLASS (PC)

Name	No	Builders	Commissioned
MATSUNAMI	PC 01	Mitsubishi, Shimonoseki	22 Feb 1995

Displacement, tons: 165 normal
Dimensions, feet (metres): 114.8 × 26.2 × 10.8 *(35 × 8 × 3.3)*
Main machinery: 2 diesels; 5,200 hp(m) *(3.82 MW)*; 2 water-jets
Speed, knots: 25
Complement: 30
Radars: Navigation: I-band.

Comment: Has replaced old craft of the same name. Laid down 10 May 1994. Used for patrol and for VIPs.
VERIFIED

MATSUNAMI   *4/1998, Hachiro Nakai* / 0052508*

3 SHIKINAMI CLASS (PC)

Name	No	Builders	Commissioned
KIYONAMI	PC 69	Mitsubishi, Shimonoseki	30 Oct 1973
OKINAMI	PC 70	Hitachi, Kanagawa	8 Feb 1974
ASOYUKI	PC 74	Hitachi, Kanagawa	16 June 1975

Displacement, tons: 46 normal
Dimensions, feet (metres): 69 × 17.4 × 3.3 *(21 × 5.3 × 1)*
Main machinery: 2 MTU MB 12V 493 TY7 diesels; 2,200 hp(m) *(1.62 MW)* sustained; 2 shafts
Speed, knots: 26. **Range, miles:** 230 at 23.8 kt
Complement: 10
Radars: Navigation: MD 806; I-band.

Comment: Built completely of light alloy. Being paid off.

UPDATED

ASOYUKI   *12/1996, Hachiro Nakai*

14 + 1 HAYANAMI CLASS (PC)

Name	No	Builders	Commissioned
HAYANAMI	PC 11	Sumidagawa	25 Mar 1993
SHIKINAMI	PC 12	Sumidagawa	24 Mar 1994
MIZUNAMI	PC 13	Ishihara	24 Mar 1994
IYONAMI	PC 14	Sumidagawa	30 June 1994
KURINAMI	PC 15	Sumidagawa	30 Jan 1995
HAMANAMI	PC 16	Sumidagawa	28 Mar 1996
SHINONOME	PC 17	Ishihara	29 Feb 1996
HARUNAMI	PC 18	Ishihara	28 Mar 1996
KIYOZUKI	PC 19	Sumidagawa	23 Feb 1996
AYANAMI	PC 20	Yokohama Yacht	28 Mar 1996
TOKINAMI	PC 21	Yokohama Yacht	28 Mar 1996
HAMAGUMO	PC 22	Sumidagawa	27 Aug 1999
AWANAMI	PC 23	Sumidagawa	27 Aug 1999
URANAMI	PC 24	Sumidagawa	Jan 2000
—	PC 25	Sumidagawa	Oct 2000

Displacement, tons: 110 normal; 190 full load
Dimensions, feet (metres): 114.8 × 20.7 × 7.5 *(35 × 6.3 × 2.3)*
Main machinery: 2 diesels; 4,000 hp(m) *(2.94 MW)*; 2 shafts
Speed, knots: 25
Guns: 1—12.7 mm MG.
Radars: Navigation: I-band.

Comment: One more authorised in FY99 budget. From PC 22 onwards these craft are equipped for firefighting.

UPDATED

HAMAGUMO   *9/1999*, *Hachiro Nakai* / 0080203

2 NATSUGIRI CLASS (PC)

Name	No	Builders	Commissioned
NATSUGIRI	PC 86	Sumidagawa	29 Jan 1990
SUGANAMI	PC 87	Sumidagawa	29 Jan 1990

Displacement, tons: 68 normal
Dimensions, feet (metres): 88.6 × 18.4 × 3.9 *(27 × 5.6 × 1.2)*
Main machinery: 2 diesels; 3,000 hp(m) *(2.21 MW)*; 2 shafts
Speed, knots: 27
Complement: 10
Radars: Navigation: I-band.

Comment: Built under FY88 programme. Steel hulls.

UPDATED

SUGANAMI   *9/1999*, *Hachiro Nakai* / 0080204

5 ASOGIRI CLASS (PC)

Name	No	Builders	Commissioned
ASOGIRI	PC 101	Yokohama Yacht	19 Dec 1994
MUROZUKI	PC 102	Ishihara	27 July 1995
WAKAGUMO	PC 103	Ishihara	17 July 1996
NAOZUKI	PC 104	Sumidagawa	23 Jan 1997
KAGAYUKI	PC 105	Mitsubishi	24 Dec 1999

Displacement, tons: 88 normal
Dimensions, feet (metres): 108.3 × 20.7 × 4.6 *(33 × 6.3 × 1.4)*
Main machinery: 2 diesels; 5,200 hp(m) *(3.82 MW)*; 2 shafts
Speed, knots: 30
Complement: 10

Comment: First pair authorised in FY93 programme, third and fourth in FY95. PC 105 is slightly different with a centreline waterjet and a top speed of 36 kt. She carries a 12.7 mm MG.

UPDATED

WAKAGUMO   *4/1999*, *Hachiro Nakai* / 0080205

183 COASTAL PATROL AND RESCUE CRAFT (CL)

CL 01-04, 11-113, 201-217, 222-223, 225-228, 230-264   GS 01-02   SS 51-66

Comment: Some have firefighting capability. Built by Shigi, Ishihara, Sumidagawa, Yokohama Yacht Co and Yamaha. For coastal patrol and rescue duties. Built of high tensile steel.

UPDATED

SS 51   *7/1999*, *Hachiro Nakai* / 0080206

FIREFIGHTING VESSELS AND CRAFT

1 MODIFIED HIRYU CLASS (FL)

Name	No	Builders	Launched	Commissioned
HIRYU	FL 01	NKK, Tsurumi	5 Sep 1997	24 Dec 1997

Displacement, tons: 280 normal
Dimensions, feet (metres): 114.8 × 40 × 8.9 *(35 × 12.2 × 2.7)*
Main machinery: 2 diesels; 4,000 hp(m) *(2.94 MW)*; 2 shafts
Speed, knots: 14
Complement: 15

Comment: Authorised in FY96 programme. Catamaran design. Has replaced ship of the same name and pennant number.

VERIFIED

HIRYU   *4/1998, Hachiro Nakai /* 0052514

4 HIRYU CLASS (FL)

Name	No	Builders	Commissioned
SHORYU	FL 02	Nippon Kokan, Tsurumi	4 Mar 1970
NANRYU	FL 03	Nippon Kokan, Tsurumi	4 Mar 1971
KAIRYU	FL 04	Nippon Kokan, Tsurumi	18 Mar 1977
SUIRYU	FL 05	Yokohama Yacht Co	24 Mar 1978

Displacement, tons: 215 normal
Dimensions, feet (metres): 90.2 × 34.1 × 7.2 *(27.5 × 10.4 × 2.2)*
Main machinery: 2 Ikegai MTU MB 12V 493 TY7 diesels; 2,200 hp(m) *(1.62 MW)* sustained; 2 shafts
Speed, knots: 13.2. **Range, miles:** 300 at 13 kt
Complement: 14

Comment: Catamaran type fire boats designed and built for firefighting services to large tankers.

UPDATED

NANRYU   *11/1999*, Hachiro Nakai /* 0080207

9 NUNOBIKI CLASS (FM)

Name	No	Builders	Commissioned
NUNOBIKI	FM 01	Yokohama Yacht Co	25 Feb 1974
YODO	FM 02	Sumidagawa	30 Mar 1975
SHIRAITO	FM 04	Yokohama Yacht Co	25 Feb 1975
KOTOBIKI	FM 05	Yokohama Yacht Co	31 Jan 1976
NACHI	FM 06	Sumidagawa	14 Feb 1976
KEGON	FM 07	Yokohama Yacht Co	29 Jan 1977
MINOO	FM 08	Sumidagawa	27 Jan 1978
RYUSEI	FM 09	Yokohama Yacht Co	24 Mar 1980
KIYOTAKI	FM 10	Sumidagawa	25 Mar 1981

Displacement, tons: 89 normal
Dimensions, feet (metres): 75.4 × 19.7 × 5.2 *(23 × 6 × 1.6)*
Main machinery: 1 MTU MB 12V 493 TY7 diesel; 1,100 hp(m) *(810 kW)* sustained; 1 shaft
2 Nissan diesels; 500 hp(m) *(515 kW)*; 3 shafts
Speed, knots: 14. **Range, miles:** 180 at 13.5 kt
Complement: 12
Radars: Navigation: FRA 10; I-band.

Comment: Equipped for chemical firefighting.

UPDATED

KIYOTAKI   *8/1999*, Hachiro Nakai /* 0080208

SURVEY SHIPS

Name	No	Builders	Launched	Commissioned
SHOYO	HL 01	Mitsui, Tamano	23 June 1997	20 Mar 1998

Displacement, tons: 3,000 normal
Dimensions, feet (metres): 321.5 × 49.9 × 11.8 *(98 × 15.2 × 3.6)*
Main machinery: Diesel-electric; 2 diesels; 8,100 hp(m) *(5.95 MW)*; 2 motors; 5,712 hp(m) *(4.2 MW)*; 2 shafts; cp props
Speed, knots: 17
Complement: 60

Comment: Authorised in FY95 programme. Laid down 4 October 1996. Has replaced former *Shoyo*.

UPDATED

SHOYO   *4/1999*, Hachiro Nakai /* 0080209

Name	No	Builders	Commissioned
TENYO	HL 04	Sumitomo, Oppama	27 Nov 1986

Displacement, tons: 770 normal
Dimensions, feet (metres): 183.7 × 32.2 × 9.5 *(56 × 9.8 × 2.9)*
Main machinery: 2 Akasaka diesels; 1,300 hp(m) *(955 kW)*; 2 shafts
Speed, knots: 13. **Range, miles:** 5,400 at 12 kt
Complement: 43 (18 officers)
Radars: Navigation: 2 JMA 1596; I-band

Comment: Laid down 11 April 1986, launched 5 August 1986. Based at Tokyo.

VERIFIED

TENYO   *1986, MSA*

Name	No	Builders	Commissioned
TAKUYO	HL 02	Nippon Kokan, Tsurumi	31 Aug 1983

Displacement, tons: 3,000 normal
Dimensions, feet (metres): 314.9 × 46.6 × 15.1 *(96 × 14.2 × 4.6)*
Main machinery: 2 Fuji 6S40B diesels; 6,090 hp(m) *(4.47 MW)*; 2 shafts; cp props
Speed, knots: 17. **Range, miles:** 12,000 at 16 kt
Complement: 60 (24 officers)
Radars: Navigation: 2 sets; I-band.

Comment: Laid down on 14 April 1982, launched on 24 March 1983. Based at Tokyo. Side scan sonar fitted. Two survey launches.   *UPDATED*

TAKUYO   *2/1999*, JMSA /* 0080210

Name	No	Builders	Commissioned
MEIYO	HL 03	Kawasaki, Kobe	24 Oct 1990
KAIYO	HL 05	Mitsubishi, Shimonoseki	7 Oct 1993

Displacement, tons: 550 normal
Dimensions, feet (metres): 196.9 × 34.4 × 10.2 *(60 × 10.5 × 3.1)*
Main machinery: 2 Daihatsu 6 DLM-24 diesels; 3,000 hp(m) *(2.2 MW)*; 2 shafts; bow thruster
Speed, knots: 15. **Range, miles:** 5,280 at 11 kt
Complement: 25 + 13 scientists
Radars: Navigation: 2 sets; I-band.

Comment: *Meiyo* laid down 24 July 1989 and launched 29 June 1990; *Kaiyo* laid down 7 July 1992 and launched 26 April 1993. Have anti-roll tanks and resiliently mounted main machinery. Has a 12 kHz bottom contour sonar. A large survey launch is carried on the port side.   *UPDATED*

KAIYO   *4/1999*, Hachiro Nakai /* 0080211

Name	No	Builders	Commissioned
HAMASHIO	HS 21	Yokohama Yacht	25 Mar 1991
ISOSHI	HS 22	Yokohama Yacht	25 Mar 1993
UZUSHIO	HS 23	Yokohama Yacht	22 Dec 1995
OKISHIO	HS 24	Ishihara	4 Mar 1999
ISESHIO	HS 25	Ishihara	10 Mar 1999
HAYASHIO	HS 26	Ishihara	10 Mar 1999

Displacement, tons: 42 normal
Dimensions, feet (metres): 66.6 × 14.8 × 3.9 *(20.3 × 4.5 × 1.2)*
Main machinery: 3 diesels; 1,015 hp(m) *(746 kW)*; 3 shafts
Speed, knots: 15
Complement: 10
Radars: Navigation: I-band.

Comment: Survey launches.   *UPDATED*

UZUSHIO   *10/1999*, Hachiro Nakai /* 0080212

AIDS TO NAVIGATION SERVICE

Name	No	Builders	Commissioned
TSUSHIMA	LL 01	Mitsui, Tamano	9 Sep 1977

Displacement, tons: 1,950 normal
Dimensions, feet (metres): 246 × 41 × 13.8 *(75 × 12.5 × 4.2)*
Main machinery: 1 Fuji-Sulzer 8S40C diesel; 4,200 hp(m) *(3.09 MW)*; 1 shaft; cp prop; bow thruster
Speed, knots: 15.5. **Range, miles:** 10,000 at 15 kt
Complement: 54

Comment: Lighthouse Supply Ship launched 7 April 1977. Fitted with tank stabilisers. Equipped with modern electronic instruments for carrying out research on electronic aids to navigation.   *UPDATED*

TSUSHIMA   *6/1997*, Hachiro Nakai /* 0080213

Name	No	Builders	Commissioned
HOKUTO	LL 11	Sasebo	29 June 1979
KAIO	LL 12	Sasebo	11 Mar 1980
GINGA	LL 13	Kawasaki, Kobe	18 Mar 1980

Displacement, tons: 700 normal
Dimensions, feet (metres): 180.4 × 34.8 × 8.7 *(55 × 10.6 × 2.7)*
Main machinery: 2 Asakasa MH23R diesels; 1,030 hp(m) *(757 kW)*; 2 shafts
Speed, knots: 12. **Range, miles:** 3,900 at 12 kt
Complement: 31 (9 officers)

Comment: Used as buoy tenders.   *VERIFIED*

KAIO   *12/1998, Hachiro Nakai /* 0052518

Name	No	Builders	Commissioned
MYOJO	LM 11	Nippon Kokan, Tsurumi	25 Mar 1974

Displacement, tons: 303 normal
Dimensions, feet (metres): 88.6 × 39.4 × 8.8 *(27 × 12 × 2.7)*
Main machinery: 2 Niigata 6M9 16HS diesels; 600 hp(m) *(441 kW)*; 2 shafts; cp props
Speed, knots: 10.5. **Range, miles:** 1,360 at 10.5 kt
Complement: 18

Comment: Catamaran type buoy tender, this ship is employed in maintenance and position adjustment service to floating aids to navigation.   *UPDATED*

MYOJO   *10/1998*, Hachiro Nakai /* 0080214

AIDS TO NAVIGATION TENDERS

Name	No	Builders	Commissioned
ZUIUN	LM 101	Usuki	27 July 1983

Displacement, tons: 370 normal
Dimensions, feet (metres): 146.3 × 24.6 × 7.2 *(44.6 × 7.5 × 2.2)*
Main machinery: 2 Mitsubishi-Asakasa MH23R diesels; 1,030 hp(m) *(757 kW)*; 2 shafts
Speed, knots: 13.5. **Range, miles:** 1,000 at 13 kt
Complement: 20

Comment: Classed as a medium tender and used to service lighthouses. Can carry 85 tons of stores.

VERIFIED

ZUIUN   *1988, JMSA*

Name	No	Builders	Commissioned
HAKUUN	LM 106	Sumidagawa	28 Feb 1978
TOUN	LM 107	Sumidagawa	14 Mar 1979
TOKUUN	LM 114	Yokohama Yacht Co	23 Mar 1981
SHOUN	LM 201	Sumidagawa	26 Mar 1986
SEIUN	LM 202	Sumidagawa	22 Feb 1989
SEKIUN	LM 203	Ishihara	12 Mar 1991
HOUUN	LM 204	Ishihara	22 Feb 1991
REIUN	LM 205	Ishihara	28 Feb 1992
GENUN	LM 206	Wakamatsu	19 Mar 1996

Displacement, tons: 58 full load
Dimensions, feet (metres): 75.5 × 19.7 × 3.3 *(23 × 6 × 1)*
Main machinery: 2 GM 12V-71TA diesels; 840 hp *(627 kW)* sustained; 2 shafts
Speed, knots: 14. **Range, miles:** 250 at 14 kt
Complement: 9
Radars: Navigation: FRA 10 Mk III; I-band.

UPDATED

GENUN   *8/1999*, Hachiro Nakai /* 0080215

48 SMALL TENDERS

LS 144-146, 148-149, 154-155, 157-158, 160-161, 164-170, 181, 185-195, 205, 207-221, 231-232

Displacement, tons: 25 full load
Dimensions, feet (metres): 54.4 × 14.1 × 2.6 *(17.5 × 4.3 × 0.9)*
Main machinery: 2 diesels; 560 hp(m) *(412 kW)*; 2 shafts
Speed, knots: 15. **Range, miles:** 230 at 14.5 kt
Complement: 8

Comment: Details given are for *LS 204-221*. Others with varying characteristics.

UPDATED

LS 231   *10/1999*, Hachiro Nakai /* 0080216

ENVIRONMENT MONITORING CRAFT

Note: In addition to those listed there are three oil skimmers OS 01-03.

Name	No	Builders	Commissioned
KINUGASA	MS 01	Ishihara, Takasago	31 Jan 1992
SAIKAI	MS 02	Ishihara, Takasago	4 Feb 1994
KATSUREN	MS 03	Sumidagawa	18 Dec 1997

Displacement, tons: 39 normal
Dimensions, feet (metres): 59.1 × 29.5 × 4.3 *(18 × 9 × 1.3)*
Main machinery: 2 diesels; 1,000 hp(m) *(735 kW)*; 2 shafts
Speed, knots: 15
Complement: 8

Comment: Details given are for *Kinugasa* which has a catamaran hull. *Sakai* and *Katsuren* are monohulls of 26 tons. Used for monitoring pollution.   *UPDATED*

KINUGASA   *9/1997*, Hachiro Nakai /* 0012693

SHIRASAGI OR 01	**MIZUNANGI** OR 03	**ISOSHIGI** OR 05
SHIRATORI OR 02	**CHIDORI** OR 04	

Displacement, tons: 153 normal
Dimensions, feet (metres): 72.3 × 21 × 2.6 *(22 × 6.4 × 0.9)*
Main machinery: 2 Nissan UD626 diesels; 360 hp(m) *(265 kW)*; 2 shafts
Speed, knots: 6. **Range, miles:** 160 at 6 kt
Complement: 7

Comment: Completed by Sumidagawa (OR 01), Shigi (OR 02 and 04) and Ishihara (OR 03 and 05) between 31 January 1977 and 23 March 1979. Used for oil recovery.   *UPDATED*

SHIRASAGI   *4/1998*, Hachiro Nakai /* 0080217

JORDAN

Headquarters Appointments	Organisation	Bases	Personnel	Mercantile Marine
Commander Naval Forces: Brigadier Hussein Ali Mahmoud Al Khasawneh *Deputy Commander:* Colonel Attalla Muhammed Fandi	The Royal Jordanian Naval Force comes under the Director of Operations at General Headquarters.	Dead Sea, Aqaba	(a) 2000: 655 officers and men (b) Voluntary service	*Lloyd's Register of Shipping:* 10 vessels of 42,100 tons gross

PATROL FORCES

Note: In addition to the craft listed, there are also four 17 ft launches and four 14 ft GRP boats used by the Underwater Swimmer unit.

3 AL HUSSEIN (HAWK) CLASS (FAST ATTACK CRAFT—GUN) (PC)

AL HUSSEIN 101   **AL HASSAN** 102   **KING ABDULLAH** 103

Displacement, tons: 124 full load
Dimensions, feet (metres): 100 × 22.5 × 4.9 *(30.5 × 6.9 × 1.5)*
Main machinery: 2 MTU 16V 396 TB94 diesels; 5,800 hp(m) *(4.26 MW)* sustained; 2 shafts
Speed, knots: 32. **Range, miles:** 750 at 15 kt; 1,500 at 11 kt
Complement: 16 (3 officers)
Guns: 2 Oerlikon GCM-A03 30 mm (twin). 1 Oerlikon GAM-BO1 20 mm. 2—12.5 mm MGs.
Countermeasures: Decoys: 2 Wallop Stockade chaff launchers.
Combat data systems: Racal Cane 100.
Weapons control: Radamec Series 2000 optronic director for 30 mm gun.
Radars: Surface search: Kelvin Hughes 1007; I-band.

Comment: Ordered from Vosper Thornycroft in December 1987. GRP structure. First one on trials in May 1989 and completed December 1989. Second completed in March 1990 and the third in early 1991. All transported to Aqaba in September 1991.

UPDATED

FAYSAL   *10/1996* */ 0080218*

3 HASHIM (ROTORK) CLASS (PB)

HASHIM   **FAISAL**   **HAMZA**

Displacement, tons: 9 full load
Dimensions, feet (metres): 41.7 × 10.5 × 3 *(12.7 × 3.2 × 0.9)*
Main machinery: 2 Deutz diesels; 240 hp *(179 kW)*; 2 shafts
Speed, knots: 28
Complement: 5
Military lift: 30 troops
Guns: 1—12.7 mm MG. 1—7.62 mm MG.
Radars: Surface search: Furuno; I-band.

Comment: Delivered in late 1990 for patrolling the Dead Sea. These craft are kept out of the water except when on patrol.

UPDATED

AL HASSAN   *5/1997* */ 0012694*

4 FAYSAL CLASS (INSHORE PATROL CRAFT) (PB)

FAYSAL   **HUSSEIN** (ex-*Han*)   **HASSAN** (ex-*Hasayu*)   **MUHAMMED**

Displacement, tons: 8 full load
Dimensions, feet (metres): 38 × 13.1 × 1.6 *(11.6 × 4 × 0.5)*
Main machinery: 2 6M 8V715 diesels; 600 hp *(441 kW)*; 2 shafts
Speed, knots: 22. **Range, miles:** 240 at 20 kt
Complement: 8
Guns: 1—12.7 mm MG. 1—7.62 mm MG.
Radars: Surface search: Decca; I-band.

Comment: Acquired from Bertram, Miami in 1974. Still operational and no replacements are planned yet.

UPDATED

HASHIM   *5/1997*, *Royal Jordanian Navy / 0003116*

KAZAKHSTAN

Headquarters Appointments	General	Bases	Personnel	Mercantile Marine
Commander, Navy: Rear Admiral Ratmir Komratov	A decision was taken in June 1993 to have a naval Flotilla which was inaugurated on 17 August 1996. The plan was to absorb about 30 of the former USSR Caspian Flotilla, but many of these craft are derelict.	Aktau (Caspian) (HQ) Aralsk (Aral Sea), Bautino (Caspian)	2000: 200	*Lloyd's Register of Shipping:* 18 vessels of 9,253 tons gross

PATROL FORCES

Notes: (1) There is also an ex-trawler *Tyulen II* of 39 m with a single diesel of 578 hp(m) *(425 kW)* capable of 10 kt. Acquired in 1997.
(2) Five Customs cutters acquired from the UAE in 1998. At least one sunk in transit.
(3) Five 'Guardian' class Boston Whalers delivered in November 1995 are unseaworthy.

4 KW 15 (TYPE 369) CLASS (PC)

ALMATY (ex-*KW 15*) 2013 (ex-201)   **ATYRAU** (ex-*KW 17*) 2033 (ex-203)
AKTAU (ex-*KW 16*) 2023 (ex-202)   **SCHAMBYL** (ex-*KW 20*) 2043 (ex-204)

Displacement, tons: 70 full load
Dimensions, feet (metres): 93.5 × 15.4 × 4.9 *(28.9 × 4.7 × 1.5)*
Main machinery: 2 Mercedes-Benz diesels; 2,000 hp(m) *(1.47 MW)*; 2 shafts
Speed, knots: 25
Complement: 17
Guns: 2—20 mm can be fitted.
Radars: Surface search: Kelvin Hughes 14/9; I-band.

Comment: Transferred from Germany at Wilhelmshaven on 23 August 1996. Built in Germany 1952-53 and paid off in 1994, having been used for river patrols and later as range safety craft. Disarmed on transfer. Reported as being non-operational.

UPDATED

ALMATY (old pennant number)   *8/1996*, *Michael Nitz / 0080219*

1 + 1 ZHUK (TYPE 1400) CLASS (PB)

Displacement, tons: 39 full load
Dimensions, feet (metres): 78.7 × 16.4 × 3.9 *(24 × 5 × 1.2)*
Main machinery: 2 Type M401B diesels; 2,200 hp(m) *(1.6 MW)* sustained; 2 shafts
Speed, knots: 30. **Range, miles:** 1,100 at 15 kt
Complement: 11
Guns: 2—14.5 mm (twin); 1—12.7 mm MG.
Radars: Surface search: Spin Trough; I-band.

Comment: Built at Uralsk Shipyard. First one commissioned 15 July 1998 and the second one is expected to complete in 2000.

UPDATED

ZHUK (Russian colours)   *11/1996, MoD Bonn /* 0019041

1 DAUNTLESS CLASS (PB)

Displacement, tons: 11 full load
Dimensions, feet (metres): 42 × 14 × 4.3 *(12.8 × 4.3 × 1.3)*
Main machinery: 2 Detroit 8V-92TA diesels; 1,270 hp *(935 kW)*; 2 shafts
Speed, knots: 35. **Range, miles:** 600 at 18 kt
Complement: 5
Guns: 1—12.7 mm MG. 2—7.62 mm MGs.
Radars: Surface search: Furuno; I-band.

Comment: Ordered under US funding in November 1995. Built by SeaArk, Monticello. Used to interdict the smuggling of nuclear materials across the Caspian Sea.

UPDATED

DAUNTLESS   *7/1996*, SeaArk Marine /* 0080220

2 SAYGAK (TYPE 1408) CLASS (PB)

Displacement, tons: 13 full load
Dimensions, feet (metres): 46.3 × 11.5 × 3 *(14.1 × 3.5 × 0.9)*
Main machinery: 1 diesel; 980 hp(m) *(720 kW)*; 1 water-jet
Speed, knots: 35. **Range, miles:** 135 at 35 kt
Complement: 6
Guns: 2—7.62 mm MGs.
Radars: Surface search: I-band.

Comment: Russian-built small craft primarily found on the Amur river. Built in 1995 and acquired in early 1996.

VERIFIED

SAYGAK (Russian colours)   *7/1996, Hartmut Ehlers /* 0052520

KENYA

Headquarters Appointments

Commander, Navy:
  Major General Aboud Adalla Rafrouf
Fleet Commander:
  Colonel S J Mwathethe

Personnel

(a) 2000: 1,200 plus 120 marines
(b) Voluntary service

Bases

Mombasa, Manda, Malindi, Lamu, Kisumu (Lake Victoria)

Coast Defence

There are nine Masura coastal radar stations spread along the coast. Each station has 30 ft fast boats to investigate contacts.

Customs/Police

There are some 14 Customs and Police patrol craft of between 12 and 14 m. Mostly built by Cheverton, Performance Workboats and Fassmer in the 1980s. One Cheverton 18 m craft acquired in early 1997.

Mercantile Marine

Lloyd's Register of Shipping:
  38 vessels of 20,589 tons gross

DELETIONS

Patrol Forces

1999   *Jamhuri, Harambee*
2000   *Simba*

PATROL FORCES

Note: There are also five Spanish built inshore patrol craft of 16 m armed with 12.7 mm MGs and driven by twin 538 hp diesels for a speed of 16 kt. Acquired in 1995 and have pennant numbers P 943-P 947.

2 NYAYO CLASS (FAST ATTACK CRAFT—MISSILE) (PCFG)

Name	No	Builders	Launched	Commissioned
NYAYO	P 3126	Vosper Thornycroft	20 Aug 1986	23 July 1987
UMOJA	P 3127	Vosper Thornycroft	5 Mar 1987	16 Sep 1987

Displacement, tons: 310 light; 430 full load
Dimensions, feet (metres): 186 × 26.9 × 7.9 *(56.7 × 8.2 × 2.4)*
Main machinery: 4 Paxman Valenta 18CM diesels; 15,000 hp *(11.19 MW)* sustained; 4 shafts; 2 motors (slow speed patrol); 100 hp *(74.6 kW)*
Speed, knots: 40. **Range, miles:** 2,000 at 18 kt
Complement: 40

Missiles: SSM: 4 OTO Melara/Matra Otomat Mk 2 (2 twin); active radar homing to 160 km *(86.4 n miles)* at 0.9 Mach; warhead 210 kg; sea-skimmer for last 4 km *(2.2 n miles)*.
Guns: 1 OTO Melara 3 in *(76 mm)*/62; 85 rds/min to 16 km *(8.7 n miles)* anti-surface; 12 km *(6.5 n miles)* anti-aircraft; weight of shell 6 kg.
  2 Oerlikon/BMARC 30 mm GCM-AO2 (twin); 650 rds/min to 10 km *(5.4 n miles)* anti-surface; 3 km *(1.6 n miles)* anti-aircraft; weight of shell 0.36 kg.
  2 Oerlikon/BMARC 20 mm A41A; 800 rds/min to 2 km; weight of shell 0.24 kg.
Countermeasures: Decoys: 2 Wallop Barricade 18-barrelled launchers; Stockade and Palisade rockets.
ESM: Racal Cutlass; radar warning.
ECM: Racal Cygnus; jammer.
Weapons control: CAAIS 450 including Signaal 423.

NYAYO   *4/1997, Robert Pabst /* 0052521

Radars: Surface search: Plessey AWS 4; E/F-band; range 101 km *(55 n miles)*.
Navigation: Decca AC 1226; I-band.
Fire control: Marconi/Ericsson ST802; I-band.

Programmes: Ordered in September 1984. Sailed in company from the UK, arriving at Mombasa 30 August 1988. Similar to Omani 'Province' class.
Operational: First live Otomat firing in February 1989. RIB carried right aft. Form Squadron 86. Both in good condition and attended South African review in April 1997 at Cape Town. In need of improved command systems.

UPDATED

1 MADARAKA CLASS (LARGE PATROL CRAFT) (PCG)

Name	No	Builders	Commissioned
MADARAKA	P 3121	Brooke Marine, Lowestoft	16 June 1975

Displacement, tons: 120 standard; 145 full load
Dimensions, feet (metres): 107 × 20 × 5.6 *(32.6 × 6.1 × 1.7)*
Main machinery: 2 Paxman Valenta 16CM diesels; 6,650 hp *(4.96 MW)* sustained; 2 shafts
Speed, knots: 25.5. **Range, miles:** 2,500 at 12 kt
Complement: 21 (3 officers)

Missiles: SSM: 4 IAI Gabriel II.
Guns: 2 Oerlikon/BMARC 30 mm GCM (twin); 650 rds/min to 10 km *(5.4 n miles)* anti-surface; 3 km *(1.6 n miles)* anti-aircraft; weight of shell 0.36 kg.
Weapons control: Elop optronic director.
Radars: Navigation: Decca AC 1226; I-band.
Fire control: Selenia RTN 10X; I/J-band.

Programmes: Ordered 10 May 1973. Launched 28 January 1975.
Modernisation: Received SSM, new guns and an optronic director in the early 1980s.
Operational: *Madaraka* started a long refit at Vosper Thornycroft, Portchester, on 4 May 1989 and completed in August 1990. The Gabriel SSM system is non-operational.   *UPDATED*

MADARAKA   *2/1998 /* 0052522

1 MAMBA CLASS (LARGE PATROL CRAFT) (PCG)

Name	No	Builders	Commissioned
MAMBA	P 3100	Brooke Marine, Lowestoft	7 Feb 1974

Displacement, tons: 125 standard; 160 full load
Dimensions, feet (metres): 123 × 22.5 × 5.2 *(37.5 × 6.9 × 1.6)*
Main machinery: 2 Paxman 16YJCM diesels; 4,000 hp *(2.98 MW)* sustained; 2 shafts
Speed, knots: 25. **Range, miles:** 3,300 at 13 kt
Complement: 25 (3 officers)

Missiles: SSM: 4 IAI Gabriel II.
Guns: 2 Oerlikon/BMARC 30 mm GCM-A02 (twin); 650 rds/min to 10 km *(5.4 n miles)* anti-surface; 3 km *(1.6 n miles)* anti-aircraft; weight of shell 0.36 kg.
Radars: Navigation: Decca AC 1226; I-band.
Fire control: Selenia RTN 10X; I/J-band; range 40 km *(22 n miles)*.

Programmes: Laid down 17 February 1972, launched 6 November 1973.
Modernisation: In 1982 missiles, new gunnery equipment and an optronic director fitted.
Operational: Arrived Vosper Thornycroft, Portchester on 4 May 1989 for a long refit. Returned to Kenya with *Madaraka* on 7 November 1990. Gabriel SSM system is non-operational.   *UPDATED*

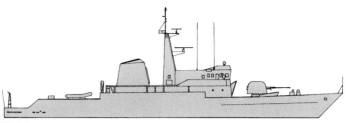

MAMBA   *8/1995* */* 0080221

2 SHUJAA CLASS (LARGE PATROL CRAFT) (PC)

SHUJAA   SHUPAVU

Displacement, tons: 480 full load
Dimensions, feet (metres): 190.3 × 26.9 × 9.2 *(58 × 8.2 × 2.8)*
Main machinery: 2 diesels; 2 shafts
Speed, knots: 22
Complement: 24
Guns: 1 OTO Melara 3 in *(76 mm)*/62.1 Breda 25 mm KBA.
Weapons control: Breda optronic director.
Radars: Surface search: I-band.

Comment: Built to civilian standards at Astilleros Gondan, Castropol and delivered in 1997 when they were taken over by the Navy. Armament fitted in Kenya.   *UPDATED*

SHUJAA   *(not to scale), Ian Sturton /* 0012697

AUXILIARIES

2 GALANA CLASS (LCM)

Name	No	Builders	Commissioned
GALANA	L 38	Astilleros Gondan, Spain	Feb 1994
TANA	L 39	Astilleros Gondan, Spain	Feb 1994

Displacement, tons: 1,400 full load
Dimensions, feet (metres): 208.3 × 43.6 × 7.9 *(63.5 × 13.3 × 2.4)*
Main machinery: 2 MTU/Bazán diesels; 2,700 hp(m) *(1.98 MW)* sustained; 2 shafts; bow thruster
Speed, knots: 12.5
Complement: 30
Radars: Navigation: Racal Decca; I-band.

Comment: Acquired by Galway Ltd for civilian use and taken over by the Navy for logistic support. The 4 m wide ramp is capable of taking 70 ton loads. Guns may be fitted in due course.   *UPDATED*

TANA   *2/1998 /* 0052523

2 TENDERS

Dimensions, feet (metres): 60 × 15.7 × 4.9 *(18.3 × 4.8 × 1.5)*
Main machinery: 2 Caterpillar 3306B-DIT diesels; 880 hp(m) *(647 kW)*; 2 shafts
Speed, knots: 10. **Range, miles:** 200 at 10 kt
Complement: 2 plus 136 passengers

Comment: Built by Souters, Cowes and deliverd in 1998. Personnel tenders.   *VERIFIED*

KIRIBATI

General

Formerly known as the Gilbert Islands. A group of about 30 atolls on the equator in mid-Pacific.

Mercantile Marine

Lloyd's Register of Shipping: 8 vessels of 4,198 tons gross

PATROL FORCES

1 PACIFIC FORUM TYPE (LARGE PATROL CRAFT) (PC)

Name	No	Builders	Commissioned
TEANOAI	301	Transfield Shipbuilding	22 Jan 1994

Displacement, tons: 165 full load
Dimensions, feet (metres): 103.3 × 26.6 × 6.9 *(31.5 × 8.1 × 2.1)*
Main machinery: 2 Caterpillar 3516TA diesels; 4,400 hp *(3.28 MW)* sustained; 2 shafts
Speed, knots: 18. **Range, miles:** 2,500 at 12 kt
Complement: 18 (3 officers)
Guns: Can carry 1—12.7 mm MG but is unarmed.
Radars: Navigation: Furuno 1011; I-band.

Comment: The 16th of this class to be built by the Australian Government for EEZ patrols of Pacific Islands. Others of the class are in service in Fiji, Papua New Guinea, Vanuatu, Cook Islands, Western Samoa, Marshall Islands, Solomon Islands, Micronesia, Tonga and Tuvalu.   *VERIFIED*

TEANOAI   *6/1998, RAAF /* 0052524

KOREA, NORTH
PEOPLE'S DEMOCRATIC REPUBLIC

Headquarters Appointments

Commander of the Navy:
  Admiral Kim Il-Choi
Deputy Commander:
  Vice Admiral Kim Yun-Sim
Chief of Staff:
  Rear Admiral Kong Seng Ho

Bases

East coast: Toejo (HQ), Mayang-do, Najin, Cha-ho (submarines).
Minor bases: Songjon Pando, Munchon-up, Mayang-do-ri, Mugye-po, Changjon, Puam-Dong.
West coast: Nampo (HQ), Pipa-got (submarines), Sagon-ri.
Minor bases: Tasa-ri, Sohae-ri, Chodo, Sunwi-do, Pupo-ri, Koampo.
A number of these bases has underground berthing facilities.

Personnel

(a) 2000: 46,000 officers and men
(b) 5 years' national service

Maritime Coastal Security Force

In addition to the Navy there is a Coastal and Port Security Police Force which would be subordinate to the Navy in war. It is reported that the strength of this force is one 'Sariwon' class PGF, 10-15 Chong-Jin patrol craft and 130 patrol boats of various types.

Strength of the Fleet

Type	Active
Submarines—Patrol	22
Submarines—Coastal	22
Submarines—Midgets	40
Frigates	3
Corvettes	5
Patrol Forces	500+
Amphibious Craft	129
Hovercraft (LCPA)	135
Minesweepers	24
Depot Ships for Midget Submarines	8
Survey Vessels	4

Coast Defence

Two Regiments (12-15 batteries) with six fixed and several mobile launchers of SS-C-2 and HY-2 missiles. Large numbers of 130 mm and 120 mm guns controlled from radar sites.

Mercantile Marine

Lloyd's Register of Shipping:
  171 vessels of 657,819 tons gross

DELETIONS

Note: Changes to the order of battle represent the most up-to-date information available.

SUBMARINES

Notes: (1) A new 1,000 ton reconnaissance submarine reported building from May 1996 at the Bong Dae Bo shipyard, Sinpo.
(2) There are also four obsolete ex-Soviet 'Whiskey' class based at Pipa-got and used for training. Probably restricted to periscope depth when dived.

22 ROMEO (TYPE 033) CLASS (SS)

Displacement, tons: 1,475 surfaced; 1,830 dived
Dimensions, feet (metres): 251.3 × 22 × 17.1 *(76.6 × 6.7 × 5.2)*
Main machinery: Diesel-electric; 2 Type 37-D diesels; 4,000 hp (m) *(2.94 MW)*; 2 motors; 2,700 hp(m) *(1.98 MW)*; 2 creep motors; 2 shafts
Speed, knots: 15 surfaced; 13 dived
Range, miles: 9,000 at 9 kt surfaced
Complement: 54 (10 officers)

Torpedoes: 8—21 in *(533 mm)* tubes (6 bow, 2 stern). 14 probably SAET-60; passive homing up to 15 km *(8.1 n miles)* at 40 kt; warhead 400 kg. Also some 53-56 may be carried.
Mines: 28 in lieu of torpedoes.
Countermeasures: ESM: China Type 921A Golf Ball (Stop Light); radar warning.
Radars: Surface search: Snoop Plate/Tray; I-band.
Sonars: Pike Jaw; hull-mounted; active.
  Feniks; hull-mounted; passive.

Programmes: Two transferred from China 1973, two in 1974 and three in 1975. First three of class built at Sinpo and Mayang-do shipyards in 1976. Programme ran at about one every 14 months until 1995 when it stopped in favour of the 'Sang-O' class. One reported sunk in February 1985.
Operational: Eighteen are stationed on east coast and occasionally operate in Sea of Japan. Four ex-Chinese units are based on the west coast. By modern standards these are basic attack submarines with virtually no anti-submarine performance or potential.

UPDATED

ROMEO (China colours)   3/1995*, van Ginderen Collection / 0080222

28 + 3 SANG-O CLASS (SSC)

Displacement, tons: 256 surfaced; 277 dived
Dimensions, feet (metres): 116.5 × 12.5 × 12.1 *(35.5 × 3.8 × 3.7)*
Main machinery: 1 Russian diesel generator; 1 North Korean motor; 1 shaft; shrouded prop
Speed, knots: 7.6 surfaced; 7.2 snorting; 8.8 dived
Range, miles: 2,700 at 7 kt
Complement: 19 (2 officers) plus 6 swimmers

Torpedoes: 2 or 4—21 in *(533 mm)* tubes (in some). Probably Russian Type 53-56.
Mines: 16 can be carried (in some).
Radars: Surface search: Furuno; I-band.
Sonars: Russian hull-mounted; passive/active search and attack.

Programmes: Started building in 1991 at Sinpo accelerating up to about four to six a year by 1996. From 1997 this has varied between three and six a year.
Structure: A variation of a reverse engineered Yugoslav design. There are at least two types, one with torpedo tubes and one capable of carrying up to six external bottom mines. There is a single periscope and a VLF radio receiver in the fin. Rocket launchers and a 12.7 mm MG can be carried. Diving depth 180 m *(590 ft)*.
Operational: Used extensively for infiltration operations. The submarine can bottom, and swimmer disembarkation is reported as being normally exercised from periscope depth. One of the class grounded and was captured by South Korea on 18 September 1996. Some crew members may be replaced by guerrillas for short operations.

UPDATED

SANG-O
9/1996* / 0080223

36 YUGO and P-4 CLASS (MIDGET SUBMARINES)

Displacement, tons: 90 surfaced; 110 dived
Dimensions, feet (metres): 65.6 × 10.2 × 15.1
(20 × 3.1 × 4.6)
Main machinery: 2 diesels; 320 hp(m) *(236 kW)*; 1 shaft
Speed, knots: 12 surfaced; 8 dived
Range, miles: 550 at 10 kt surfaced; 50 at 4 kt dived
Complement: 4 plus 6-7 divers
Torpedoes: 2—406 mm tubes.
Radars: Navigation: I-band.

Comment: Built at Yukdaeso-ri shipyard since early 1960s. More
than one design. Details given are for the latest type, at least
one of which has been exported to Iran, and have been
building since 1987 to a Yugoslavian design. Some have two
short external torpedo tubes and some have a snort mast. The
conning tower acts as a wet and dry compartment for divers.
There is a second and smaller propeller for slow speed
manoeuvring while dived. Two of the class are designated P-4s
and belong to the KWP. This type has two internal torpedo
tubes. Operate from eight merchant mother ships (see
Auxiliaries). Some have been lost in operations against South
Korea, the latest in June 1998. Numbers are reducing in favour
of the 'Sang-O' class. Two exported to Vietnam in June 1997.
There are also about 50 two-man submersibles of Italian
design 4.9 × 1.4 m.

UPDATED

YUGO P-4
6/1998, Ships of the World / 0052525

FRIGATES

1 SOHO CLASS (FFG)

Name	No
—	823

Displacement, tons: 1,640 full load
Dimensions, feet (metres): 242.1 × 50.9 × 12.5
(73.8 × 15.5 × 3.8)
Main machinery: 2 diesels; 15,000 hp(m) *(11.03 MW)*; 2 shafts
Speed, knots: 23
Complement: 189 (17 officers)

Missiles: SSM: 4 CSS-N-2 ❶; active radar or IR homing to 46 km
(25 n miles) at 0.9 Mach; warhead 513 kg.
Guns: 1—3.9 in *(100 mm)*/56 ❷; 40° elevation; 15 rds/min to
16 km *(8.6 n miles)*; weight of shell 13.5 kg.
4—37 mm/63 (2 twin) ❸.
4—30 mm/65 (2 twin) ❹. 4—25 mm/60 (2 twin) ❺.
A/S mortars: 2 RBU 1200 5-tubed fixed launchers ❻; range
1,200 m; warhead 34 kg.
Countermeasures: ESM: China RW-23 Jug Pair (Watch Dog);
intercept.
Radars: Surface search: Square Tie ❼; I-band.
Fire control: Drum Tilt ❽; H/I-band.
Navigation: I-band.
Sonars: Stag Horn; hull-mounted; active search and attack; high
frequency.

Helicopters: Platform for 1 medium.

Builders	Laid down	Launched	Commissioned
Najin Shipyard	June 1980	Nov 1981	May 1982

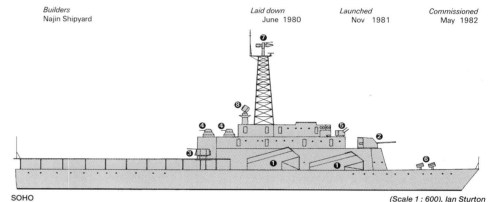

SOHO   *(Scale 1 : 600), Ian Sturton*

Programmes: Planned class of six but only one was ordered.
Structure: One of the largest warships built anywhere with a
twin hull design and a helicopter deck aft. Has a large central
superstructure to carry the heavy gun armament.

Operational: Has been reported as spending some time at sea,
but is probably very weather limited like many catamaran
designs.

UPDATED

2 NAJIN CLASS (FFG)

531	631

Displacement, tons: 1,500 full load
Dimensions, feet (metres): 334.6 × 32.8 × 8.9
(102 × 10 × 2.7)
Main machinery: 3 SEMT-Pielstick Type 16 PA6 280 diesels;
18,000 hp(m) *(13.2 MW)*; 3 shafts
Speed, knots: 24. **Range, miles:** 4,000 at 13 kt
Complement: 180 (16 officers)

Missiles: SSM: 2 CSS-N-1 ❶; active radar or IR homing to 46 km
(25 n miles) at 0.9 Mach; warhead 513 kg HE. Replaced
torpedo tubes on both ships.
Guns: 2—3.9 in *(100 mm)*/56 ❷; 40° elevation; 15 rds/min to
16 km *(8.6 n miles)*; weight of shell 13.5 kg.
4—57 mm/80 (2 twin) ❸; 120 rds/min to 6 km *(3.2 n miles)*;
weight of shell 2.8 kg.
12 or 4—25 mm/60 (6 or 2 twin) ❹ (see *Structure*).
16—14.5 mm (4 quad) ❺ MGs.
A/S mortars: 2 RBU 1200 5-tubed fixed launchers ❻; range
1,200 m; warhead 34 kg (not in *531*).
Depth charges: 2 projectors; 2 racks. 30 weapons.
Mines: 30 (estimated).
Countermeasures: Decoys: 6 chaff launchers.
ESM: China RW-23 Jug Pair (Watch Dog); intercept.
Weapons control: Optical director ❼.
Radars: Air search: Square Tie ❽; I-band.
Surface search: Pot Head ❾; I-band.
Navigation: Pot Drum; H/I-band.
Fire control: Drum Tilt ❿; H/I-band.
IFF: High Pole. Square Head.
Sonars: Stag Horn; hull-mounted; active search; high frequency.

Programmes: Built at Najin and Nampo shipyards. First
completed 1973, second 1975.
Structure: There is some resemblance to the ex-Soviet 'Kola'
class, now deleted. The original torpedo tubes were replaced
by CSS-N-1 missile launchers in the mid-1980s and the RBU
1200 mortars have been removed in at least one of the class.
Gun armaments differ, one having six twin 25 mm while the
other only has one twin 25 mm and four quad 14.5 mm MGs.
Operational: Seldom seen at sea.   ***UPDATED***

NAJIN 631   *(Scale 1 : 900), Ian Sturton*

NAJIN 531   *5/1993*, JMSDF /* 0080224

CORVETTES

3 SARIWON and 2 TRAL CLASS (FS)

513	671	725	726	727

Displacement, tons: 650; 580 (Tral); full load
Dimensions, feet (metres): 203.7 × 23.9 × 7.8
(62.1 × 7.3 × 2.4)
Main machinery: 2 diesels; 3,000 hp(m) *(2.21 MW)*; 2 shafts
Speed, knots: 16. **Range, miles:** 2,700 at 16 kt
Complement: 60 (7 officers)

Guns: 1—85 mm/52 tank turret (Tral) ❶.
4—57 mm/80 (2 twin) (Sariwon).
2 or 4—37 mm/6 (single (Tral) ❷; 2 twin (Sariwon)).
16—14.5 mm ❸; 4 quad.
A/S mortars: 2 RBU 1200 5-tubed fixed launchers (Sariwon 513).
Depth charges: 2 rails.
Mines: 30.

Radars: Surface search: Pot Head or Don 2 ❹; I-band.
Navigation: Model 351; I-band.
IFF: Ski Pole.
Sonars: Stag Horn; hull-mounted; active; high frequency.

Programmes: Three 'Sariwon' class built in Korea in the mid-1960s. The two 'Tral' class were transferred from the USSR in the mid-1950s, were paid off in the early 1980s and returned to service in the early 1990s.
Structure: The Sariwon design is based on the original USSR Fleet minelayer 'Tral' or 'Fugas' class in service in the mid-1930s. Minelaying rails are visible along the whole of upper deck aft of the bridge superstructure. Sariwon 671 is one of the original 'Tral' class built in 1938 and restored to service. Some variations in gun armament and only Sariwon 513 is reported as having sonar and an ASW armament.
Operational: One of the class is the Flagship of the Maritime Coastal Security Forces. There is some doubt about the last three pennant numbers.

UPDATED

TRAL 671   *(Scale 1 : 600), Ian Sturton*

TRAL 671   *5/1993*, JMSDF / 0080225*

PATROL FORCES

8 OSA I (TYPE 205) and 4 HUANGFEN CLASSES
(FAST ATTACK CRAFT—MISSILE) (PCFG)

Displacement, tons: 171 standard; 210 full load
Dimensions, feet (metres): 126.6 × 24.9 × 8.9 *(38.6 × 7.6 × 2.7)*
Main machinery: 3 Type M 503A diesels; 8,025 hp(m) *(5.9 MW)* sustained; 3 shafts
Speed, knots: 35. **Range, miles:** 800 at 30 kt
Complement: 30
Missiles: SSM: 4 SS-N-2A Styx; active radar or IR homing to 46 km *(25 n miles)* at 0.9 Mach; warhead 513 kg.
Guns: 4—30 mm/65 (2 twin) AK 230; 500 rds/min to 5 km *(2.7 n miles)*; weight of shell 0.54 kg.
Countermeasures: ESM: China BM/HZ 8610; intercept ('Huangfen' class).
Radars: Surface search: Square Tie; I-band.
Fire control: Drum Tilt; H/I-band (Osa I).
IFF: High Pole B. Square Head.

Programmes: Twelve 'Osa I' class transferred from USSR in 1968 and four more in 1972-83. Eight deleted so far. Four 'Huangfen' class acquired from China in 1980.

VERIFIED

HUANGFEN (China colours)   *1993*

15 SOJU CLASS (FAST ATTACK CRAFT—MISSILE) (PCFG)

Displacement, tons: 265 full load
Dimensions, feet (metres): 139.4 × 24.6 × 5.6 *(42.5 × 7.5 × 1.7)*
Main machinery: 3 Type M 503A diesels; 8,025 hp(m) *(5.9 MW)* sustained; 3 shafts
Speed, knots: 34. **Range, miles:** 600 at 30 kt
Complement: 32 (4 officers)
Missiles: SSM: 4 SS-N-2 Styx; active radar or IR homing to 46 km *(25 n miles)* at 0.9 Mach; warhead 513 kg.
Guns: 4—30 mm/65 (2 twin) AK 630; 500 rds/min to 5 km *(2.7 n miles)*; weight of shell 0.54 kg.
Countermeasures: ESM: China BM/HZ 8610; intercept.
Radars: Surface search: Square Tie; I-band.
Fire Control: Drum Tilt; H/I-band.

Comment: North Korean built and enlarged version of 'Osa' class. First completed in 1981; built at about one per year at Nampo, Najin and Yongampo shipyards, but the programme terminated in 1996.

VERIFIED

OSA I

6 KOMAR and 6 SOHUNG CLASSES
(FAST ATTACK CRAFT—MISSILE) (PCFG)

| 3224-3229 | 3651-3654 | 3975-3976 |

Displacement, tons: 75 standard; 85 full load
Dimensions, feet (metres): 84 × 24 × 5.9 *(25.6 × 7.3 × 1.8)* (Sohung)
Main machinery: 4 Type M 50 diesels; 4,400 hp(m) *(3.3 MW)* sustained; 4 shafts
Speed, knots: 40. **Range, miles:** 400 at 30 kt
Complement: 19
Missiles: SSM: 2 SS-N-2A Styx or CSS-N-1; active radar or IR homing to 46 km *(25 n miles)* at
  0.9 Mach; warhead 513 kg.
Guns: 2—25 mm/80 (twin); 270 rds/min to 3 km *(1.6 n miles)*; weight of shell 0.34 kg.
  2—14.5 mm (twin) MGs.
Radars: Surface search: Square Tie; I-band.
IFF: Square Head.

Programmes: Ten 'Komar' class transferred by USSR, nine still in service but with wood hulls
  replaced by steel. The 'Sohung' class is a North Korean copy of the 'Komar' class, first built in
  1980-81 and no longer in production.

UPDATED

KOMAR

6 HAINAN CLASS (LARGE PATROL CRAFT) (PC)

| 201-204 | 292-293 |

Displacement, tons: 375 standard; 392 full load
Dimensions, feet (metres): 192.8 × 23.6 × 6.6 *(58.8 × 7.2 × 2)*
Main machinery: 4 Kolomna/PCR Type 9-D-8 diesels; 4,000 hp(m) *(2.94 MW)*; 4 shafts
Speed, knots: 30.5. **Range, miles:** 1,300 at 15 kt
Complement: 69
Guns: 4—57 mm/70 (2 twin); 120 rds/min to 8 km *(4.4 n miles)*; weight of shell 2.8 kg.
  4—25 mm/80 (2 twin); 270 rds/min to 3 km *(1.6 n miles)*; weight of shell 0.34 kg.
A/S mortars: 4 RBU 1200 5-tubed launchers; range 1,200 m; warhead 34 kg.
Depth charges: 2 projectors; 2 racks for 30 DCs.
Mines: Laying capability for 12.
Countermeasures: Decoys: 2 PK 16 chaff launchers.
ESM: China BM/HZ 8610; intercept.
Radars: Surface search: Pot Head (Model 351); I-band.
Sonars: Stag Ear; hull-mounted; active search and attack; high frequency.

Comment: Transferred from China in 1975 (two), 1976 (two), 1978 (two).

UPDATED

HAINAN (China colours) *4/1988 * / 0080226*

19 SO 1 CLASS (LARGE PATROL CRAFT) (PC)

Displacement, tons: 170 light; 215 normal
Dimensions, feet (metres): 137.8 × 19.7 × 5.9 *(42 × 6 × 1.8)*
Main machinery: 3 Kolomna Type 40-D diesels; 6,600 hp(m) *(4.85 MW)* sustained; 3 shafts
Speed, knots: 28. **Range, miles:** 1,100 at 13 kt
Complement: 31
Guns: 1—85 mm/52; 18 rds/min to 15 km *(8 n miles)*; weight of shell 9.5 kg.
  2—37 mm/63 (twin); 160 rds/min to 9 km *(4.9 n miles)*; weight of shell 0.7 kg.
  4 or 6—25 mm/60 (2 or 3 twin); 270 rds/min to 3 km *(1.6 n miles)*; weight of shell 0.34 kg.
  4—14.5 mm/93 MGs.
A/S mortars: 4 RBU 1200 5-tubed launchers; range 1,200 m; warhead 34 kg.
Radars: Surface search: Pot Head (Model 351); I-band.
Navigation: Don 2; I-band.
IFF: Ski Pole or Dead Duck.
Sonars: Stag Ear; hull-mounted; active.

Comment: Eight transferred by the USSR in early 1960s, with RBU 1200 ASW rocket launchers
  and depth charges instead of the 85 mm and 37 mm guns. Remainder built in North Korea to
  modified design. Twelve are fitted out for ASW with sonar and depth charges; the other seven
  are used as gunboats.

VERIFIED

SO 1 (USSR colours) 1988

7 TAECHONG I and 5 TAECHONG II CLASSES
(LARGE PATROL CRAFT) (PC)

Displacement, tons: 385 standard; 410 full load (I); 425 full load (II)
Dimensions, feet (metres): 196.3 (I); 199.5 (II) × 23.6 × 6.6 *(59.8; 60.8 × 7.2 × 2)*
Main machinery: 4 Kolomna Type 40-D diesels; 8,800 hp(m) *(6.4 MW)* sustained; 4 shafts
Speed, knots: 25. **Range, miles:** 2,000 at 12 kt
Complement: 80
Guns: 1—3.9 in *(100 mm)*/56 (Taechong II); 15 rds/min to 16 km *(8.6 n miles)*; weight of shell
    13.5 kg or 1—85 mm/52.
  2—57 mm/70 (twin); 120 rds/min to 8 km *(4.4 n miles)*; weight of shell 2.8 kg.
  4—30 mm/65 (2 twin) (Taechong II). 2—25 mm/60 (twin) (Taechong I).
  16 or 4—14.5 mm MGs (4 quad (Taechong II); 2 twin (Taechong I)).
A/S mortars: 2 RBU 1200 5-tubed fixed launchers; range 1,200 m; warhead 34 kg.
Depth charges: 2 racks.
Radars: Surface search: Pot Head (Model 351); I-band.
Fire control: Drum Tilt; H/I-band.
IFF: High Pole A. Square Head.
Sonars: Stag Ear; hull-mounted; active attack; high frequency.

Comment: North Korean class of mid-1970s design, slightly larger than 'Hainan' class. The first
  seven are 'Taechong I' class. Taechong II built at about one per year at Najin shipyard up to 1995.
  They are slightly longer, and are heavily armed for units of this size.

VERIFIED

TAECHONG *(not to scale)*

TAECHONG II (with *Najin*) 1988

12 SHANGHAI II CLASS (FAST ATTACK CRAFT—GUN) (PCF)

| 381-388 | 391-395 |

Displacement, tons: 113 standard; 131 full load
Dimensions, feet (metres): 126.3 × 17.7 × 5.6 *(38.5 × 5.4 × 1.7)*
Main machinery: 2 Type L12-180 diesels; 2,400 hp(m) *(1.76 MW)* (forward)
  2 Type 12-D-6 diesels; 1,820 hp(m) *(1.34 MW)* (aft); 4 shafts
Speed, knots: 30. **Range, miles:** 700 at 16.5 kt
Complement: 34
Guns: 4—37 mm/63 (2 twin); 160 rds/min to 9 km *(4.9 n miles)*; weight of shell 0.7 kg.
  4—25 mm/60 (2 twin); 270 rds/min to 3 km *(1.6 n miles)*; weight of shell 0.34 kg.
  2—3 in *(76 mm)* recoilless rifles.
Depth charges: 8.
Mines: Rails can be fitted for 10 mines.
Countermeasures: ESM: China BM/HZ 8610; intercept.
Radars: Surface search: Pot Head (Model 351) or Skin Head; I-band.

Comment: Acquired from China since 1967.

UPDATED

SHANGHAI II *1994 * / 0080227*

6 CHONG-JU CLASS (LARGE PATROL CRAFT) (PC)

Displacement, tons: 205 full load
Dimensions, feet (metres): 138.8 × 23.6 × 6.9 *(42.3 × 7.2 × 2.1)*
Main machinery: 4 diesels; 4,406 hp(m) *(3.24 MW)*; 4 shafts
Speed, knots: 20. **Range, miles:** 1,350 at 12 kt
Complement: 48 (7 officers)
Missiles: SSM: 4 CSS-N-1; active radar or IR homing to 46 km *(25 n miles)* at 0.9 Mach; warhead
    513 kg. In three of the class.
Guns: 1—85 mm/52; 18 rds/min to 15 km *(8 n miles)*; weight of shell 9.5 kg.
  4—37 mm/63 (2 twin). 4—25 mm/60 (2 twin).
  4—14.5 mm/93 (2 twin) MGs.
A/S mortars: 2 RBU 1200; 5-tubed launchers; range 1,200 m; warhead 34 kg.
Radars: Surface search: Pot Head (Model 351); I-band.
Sonars: Stag Ear; hull-mounted; active attack; high frequency.

Comment: Built between 1975 and 1989. At least one has been converted to fire torpedoes and
  three others have CSS-N-1 missiles and resemble the 'Soju' class.

VERIFIED

62 CHAHO CLASS (FAST ATTACK CRAFT—GUN) (PCF)

Displacement, tons: 82 full load
Dimensions, feet (metres): 85.3 × 19 × 6.6 *(26 × 5.8 × 2)*
Main machinery: 4 Type M 50 diesels; 4,400 hp(m) *(3.2 MW)* sustained; 4 shafts
Speed, knots: 37. **Range, miles:** 1,300 at 18 kt
Complement: 16 (2 officers)
Guns: 1 BM 21 multiple rocket launcher. 2 USSR 23 mm/87 (twin). 2—14.5 mm (twin) MGs.
Radars: Surface search: Pot Head (Model 351); I-band.

Comment: Building in North Korea since 1974. Based on P 6 hull. Three transferred to Iran in April 1987. Still building and new hulls are replacing the old ones.

VERIFIED

CHAHO (Iranian colours)   *4/1988*

48 CHONG-JIN CLASS (FAST ATTACK CRAFT—GUN)

Displacement, tons: 80 full load
Dimensions, feet (metres): 85.3 × 19 × 5.9 *(26 × 5.8 × 1.8)*
Main machinery: 4 Type M 50 diesels; 4,400 hp(m) *(3.2 MW)* sustained; 4 shafts
Speed, knots: 36. **Range, miles:** 450 at 30 kt
Complement: 17 (3 officers)
Guns: 1—85 mm/52; 18 rds/min to 15 km *(8 n miles)*; weight of shell 9.5 kg. 4 or 8—14.5 mm (2 or 4 twin) MGs.
Radars: Surface search: Skin Head; I-band.
IFF: High Pole B; Square Head.

Comment: Particulars similar to 'Chaho' class of which this is an improved version. Building began about 1975. About one third reported to be a hydrofoil development. Up to 15 are operated by the Coastal Security Force.

UPDATED

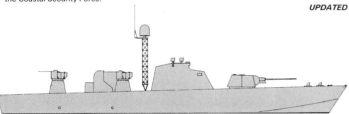

CHONG-JIN   *(not to scale), Ian Sturton*

15 P 6 and SHANTOU CLASS (FAST ATTACK CRAFT—TORPEDO) and 24 SINPO or SINNAM CLASS
(FAST ATTACK CRAFT—GUN) (PCF)

Displacement, tons: 64 standard; 73 full load
Dimensions, feet (metres): 85.3 × 20 × 4.9 *(26 × 6.1 × 1.5)*
Main machinery: 4 Type M 50 diesels; 4,400 hp(m) *(3.2 MW)* sustained; 4 shafts
Speed, knots: 45. **Range, miles:** 450 at 30 kt; 600 at 15 kt
Complement: 15
Guns: 4—25 mm/80 (2 twin) (original). 2—37 mm (others). 6—14.5 mm MGs ('Sinpo' class).
Torpedoes: 2—21 in *(533 mm)* tubes (in some). 'Sinpo' class has no tubes.
Depth charges: 8 in some.
Radars: Surface search: Skin Head; I-band (some have Furuno).
IFF: Dead Duck. High Pole.

Comment: Originally 27 'P 6' class were transferred by the USSR and 15 from China. The Sinpos are locally built versions. Some P 6s have hydrofoils. One P 6 sunk in June 1999.

UPDATED

P 6

SINPO

92 KU SONG, SIN HUNG and MOD SIN HUNG CLASSES
(FAST ATTACK CRAFT—TORPEDO) (PCF)

Displacement, tons: 42 full load
Dimensions, feet (metres): 75.4 × 16.1 × 5.5 *(23 × 4.9 × 1.7)*
Main machinery: 2 Type M 50 diesels; 2,200 hp(m) *(1.6 MW)* sustained; 2 shafts
Speed, knots: 40; 50 (Mod Sin Hung). **Range, miles:** 500 at 20 kt
Complement: 20 (3 officers)
Guns: 4—14.5 mm (2 twin) MGs.
Torpedoes: 2—18 in *(457 mm)* or 2—21 in *(533 mm)* tubes (not fitted in all).
Radars: Surface search: Skin Head; I-band.
IFF: Dead Duck.

Comment: Ku Song and Sin Hung built in North Korea between mid-1950s and 1970s. Frequently operated on South Korean border. A modified version of Sin Hung with hydrofoils built from 1981-85. At least 50 have been scrapped.

UPDATED

SIN HUNG (no torpedo tubes)   *1991*

63 KIMJIN CLASS (COASTAL PATROL CRAFT) (PC)

Displacement, tons: 38 full load
Dimensions, feet (metres): 59.1 × 10.5 × 4.3 *(18 × 3.2 × 1.3)*
Main machinery: 2 diesels; 2,448 hp(m) *(1.8 MW)*; 2 shafts
Speed, knots: 29. **Range, miles:** 350 at 15 kt
Complement: 14 (2 officers)
Guns: 4—14.5 mm/93 (2 twin) MGs.
Radars: Surface search: Furuno; I-band.

Comment: Built in the 1980s. Export versions sold to Nicaragua, Tanzania and Uganda, all deleted.

UPDATED

KIMJIN   *1994*, North Korean Navy / 0080228

45 YONGDO CLASS (COASTAL PATROL CRAFT) (PC)

Displacement, tons: 20 full load
Dimensions, feet (metres): 53.1 × 14.1 × 2.6 *(16.2 × 4.3 × 0.8)*
Main machinery: 2 diesels; 544 hp(m) *(400 kW)*; 2 shafts
Speed, knots: 24
Complement: 7
Guns: 2—14.5 mm (twin) MGs.
Radars: Surface search: Furuno; I-band.

Comment: Built in the 1980s.

UPDATED

MODIFIED FISHING VESSELS (COASTAL PATROL CRAFT) (PB/AGI)

Comment: An unknown number of fishing vessels have been converted for naval use. Some act as patrol craft, others as AGIs. Many are armed.

VERIFIED

MFV 801   *7/1991, G Jacobs*

HIGH-SPEED INFILTRATION CRAFT (HSIC/PBF)

Displacement, tons: 5 full load
Dimensions, feet (metres): 30.5 × 8.2 × 3.1 *(9.3 × 2.5 × 1)*
Main machinery: 1 diesel; 260 hp(m) *(191 kW)*; 1 shaft
Speed, knots: 35
Complement: 2
Guns: 1—7.62 mm MG.
Radars: Navigation: Furuno 701; I-band.

Comment: Large numbers built for Agent infiltration and covert operations. These craft have a very low radar cross-section and 'squat' at high speeds. High rate of attrition. A newer version was reported in 1998. This is 12.8 m in length and has a top speed of about 45 kt. It is alleged to be able to submerge to a depth of 3 m using a snort mast, and to propel dived at 4 kt. More are being built.

UPDATED

HSIC   *1991, J Bermudez*

15 TB 11PA AND 10 TB 40A CLASSES
(INSHORE PATROL CRAFT) (PBF)

Displacement, tons: 8 full load
Dimensions, feet (metres): 36.7 × 8.6 × 3.3 *(11.2 × 2.7 × 1)*
Main machinery: 2 diesels; 520 hp(m) *(382 kW)*; 2 shafts
Speed, knots: 35. **Range, miles:** 200 at 15 kt
Complement: 4
Guns: 1—7.62 mm MG.
Radars: Surface search: Furuno; I-band.

Comment: High-speed patrol boats. Reinforced fibreglass hull. Design closely resembles a number of UK/Western European commercial craft. Larger hull design, known as 'TB 40A' also built. Both classes being operated by the Coastal Security Force.

VERIFIED

AMPHIBIOUS FORCES

10 HANTAE CLASS (LSM)

Displacement, tons: 350 full load
Dimensions, feet (metres): 157.5 × 21.3 × 6.6 *(48 × 6.5 × 2)*
Main machinery: 2 diesels; 4,352 hp(m) *(3.2 MW)*; 2 shafts
Speed, knots: 18. **Range, miles:** 2,000 at 12 kt
Complement: 36 (4 officers)
Military lift: 350 troops plus 3 MBTs
Guns: 8—25 mm/80 (4 twin).

Comment: Built in the early 1980s.

VERIFIED

18 NAMPO A, 73 NAMPO B/C and 4 + 1 NAMPO D CLASSES
(LCP/PC)

Displacement, tons: 75 full load
Dimensions, feet (metres): 85.3 × 19 × 5.6 *(26 × 5.8 × 1.7)*
Main machinery: 4 Type M 50 diesels; 4,400 hp(m) *(3.2 MW)* sustained; 4 shafts
Speed, knots: 36. **Range, miles:** 450 at 30 kt
Complement: 19
Military lift: 35 troops
Guns: 4—14.5 mm (2 twin) MGs.
Radars: Surface search: Skin Head; I-band.

Comment: A class of assault landing craft. Similar to the 'Chong-Jin' class but with a smaller forward gun mounting and with retractable ramp in bows. Building began about 1975. Several have been deleted due to damage. The Mod Nampos have a covered-in deck and most have bow doors welded shut. Four sold to Madagascar in 1979 but now deleted. Latest version is a multihull craft designated Nampo D. First one in service in 1997.

UPDATED

7 HANCHON AND 18 HUNGNAM CLASSES (LCM)

Displacement, tons: 145 full load
Dimensions, feet (metres): 117.1 × 25.9 × 3.9 *(35.7 × 7.9 × 1.2)*
Main machinery: 2 Type 3-D-12 diesels; 600 hp(m) *(443 kW)* sustained; 2 shafts
Speed, knots: 10. **Range, miles:** 600 at 6 kt
Complement: 15 (1 officer)
Military lift: 2 tanks or 300 troops
Guns: 2—14.5 mm/93 (twin) MG.
Radars: Surface search: Skin Head; I-band.

Comment: Details given for the Hanchons, built in the 1980s. The Hungnams are older and half the size.

UPDATED

135 KONGBANG CLASS (HOVERCRAFT) (LCPA)

Comment: Three types: one Type I, 55 Type II and the remainder are Type III. Length 25 m (I), 21 m (II) and 18 m (III). A series of high-speed air cushion landing craft first reported in 1987 and building continued until 1996 and then stopped. Use of air cushion technology is an adoption of commercial technology based on the SRN-6. Kongbang II has twin propellers and can carry up to 50 commandos at 50 kt. Kongbang III has a single propeller and can take about 40 troops at 40 kt. All are radar fitted. Some have Styx SSM missiles. Older craft are being replaced continuously in a high priority programme.

UPDATED

MINE WARFARE FORCES

19 YUKTO I and 5 YUKTO II CLASSES
(COASTAL MINESWEEPERS) (MSC)

Displacement, tons: 60 full load (I); 52 full load (II)
Dimensions, feet (metres): 78.7 × 13.1 × 5.6 *(24 × 4 × 1.7)* (Yukto I)
Main machinery: 2 diesels; 2 shafts
Speed, knots: 18
Complement: 22 (4 officers)
Guns: 1—37 mm/63 or 2—25 mm/80 (twin). 2—14.5 mm/93 (twin) MGs.
Mines: 2 rails for 4.
Radars: Surface search: Skin Head; I-band.

Comment: North Korean design built in the 1980s and replaced the obsolete ex-Soviet 'KN-14' class. Yukto IIs are 3 m shorter (at 21 m length) overall and have no after gun. Wooden construction. One completed mid-1996 but this may have been of a new design.

VERIFIED

SURVEY SHIPS

Note: The Hydrographic Department has four survey ships but also uses a number of converted fishing vessels.

Name	Displacement	Launched	Complement
DONGHAE 101	260 tons	1970	22 (8 officers)
DONGHAE 102	1,100 tons	1979	35 (20 officers)
SOHAI 201	260 tons	1972	22 (14 officers)
SOHAI 202	300 tons	1981	26 (16 officers)

VERIFIED

AUXILIARIES

Notes: (1) Trawlers operate as AGIs on the South Korean border where several have been sunk over the years. In addition many ocean-going commercial vessels are used for carrying weapons and ammunition worldwide in support of international terrorism.
(2) There are also eight ocean cargo ships adapted as mother ships for midget submarines. Their names are *Soo Gun-Ho, Dong Geon Ae Gook-Ho, Dong Hae-Ho, Choong Seong-Ho Number One, Choong Seong-Ho Number Two, Choong Seong-Ho Number Three, Hae Gum Gang-Ho* and the *Song Rim-Ho.*

1 KOWAN CLASS (ASR)

Displacement, tons: 2,010 full load
Dimensions, feet (metres): 275.6 × 46.9 × 12.8 *(84 × 14.3 × 3.9)*
Main machinery: 4 diesels; 8,160 hp(m) *(6 MW)*; 2 shafts
Speed, knots: 16
Complement: 150
Guns: 12—14.5 mm (6 twin) MGs.
Radars: Navigation: Furuno; I-band.

Comment: Used as a submarine rescue ship. Probable catamaran construction.

VERIFIED

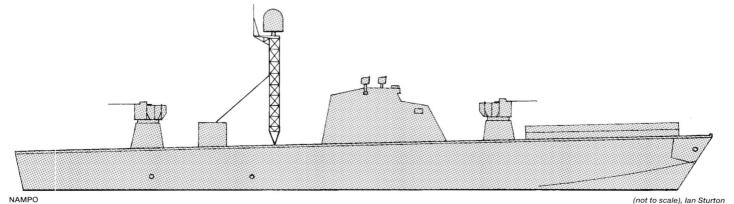

NAMPO   *(not to scale), Ian Sturton*

KOREA, SOUTH
REPUBLIC

Headquarters Appointments

Chief of Naval Operations:
Admiral Lee Soo Yong
Commandant Marine Corps:
Lieutenant General Kim Myung Hwan
Vice Chief of Naval Operations:
Rear Admiral Kim Moo Woong
Chief of Maritime Police:
Kim Sam An

Operational Commands

Commander-in-Chief Fleet:
Vice Admiral Fuh Young Kil
Commander First Fleet:
Rear Admiral Choi Kichul
Commander Second Fleet:
Rear Admiral Nam Hae Il
Commander Third Fleet:
Rear Admiral Kim Sung Man

Diplomatic Representation

Defence Attaché in London:
Captain Lee

Personnel

(a) 2000: Regulars: 33,000 (Navy) and 24,000 (Marines)
Conscripts: 17,000 (Navy and Marines)
(b) 2¼ years' national service for conscripts
(c) Reserves: 9,000

Bases

Major: Chinhae (Fleet HQ and 3rd Fleet), Donghae (1st Fleet), Pyongtaek (2nd Fleet)
Minor: Cheju, Mokpo, Mukho, Pohang, Pusan
Aviation: Pohang (MPA base), Chinhae, Cheju
Marines: Pohang, Kimpo, Pengyongdo

Organisation

In 1986 the Navy was reorganised into three Fleets, each commanded by a Rear Admiral, whereas the Marines retained two Divisions and one brigade plus smaller and support units. From October 1973 the RoK Marine Force was placed directly under the RoK Navy command with a Vice Chief of Naval Operations for Marine Affairs replacing the Commandant of Marine Corps. The Marine Corps was re-established as an independent service on 1 November 1987.

1st Fleet: No 11, 12, 13 DD/FF Sqn; No 101, 102 Coastal Defence Sqn; 181, 191, 111, 121 Coastal Defence Units; 121st Minesweeper Sqn.
2nd Fleet: No 21, 22, 23 DD/FF Sqn; No 201, 202 Coastal Defence Sqn; 211, 212 Coastal Defence Units; 522nd Minesweeper Sqn.
3rd Fleet: 301, 302, 303 DD/FF Sqn; 304, 406th Coastal Defence Units.

Strength of the Fleet

Type	Active (Reserve)	Building (Proposed)
Submarines (Patrol)	8	1 (3)
Submarines (Midget)	11	—
Destroyers	8	1 (2)
Frigates	9	—
Corvettes	28	—
Fast Attack Craft—Missile	5	—
Fast Attack Craft—Patrol	85	—
Minehunters	7	2 (2)
Minesweepers	8	—
Minelayers	2	—
LSTs	10	—
LSMs	3	—
LCU/LCM/LCF	20	—
Logistic Support Ships	3	—

Coast Defence

Three batteries of Marines with truck-mounted quadruple Harpoon SSM launchers.

Pennant Numbers

Numbers ending in 4 are not used as they are unlucky.

Mercantile Marine

Lloyd's Register of Shipping:
2,417 vessels of 5,734,806 tons gross

DELETIONS

Destroyers

1996-97	*Kyong Ki*
2000	*Chung Buk*

Patrol Forces

1997-98	*Pae Ku 52, 53* and *55, PKM 271-272*
1999	3 Sea Dolphin

Amphibious Forces

1997-98	*Ko Mun, Pi An, Nung Ra, Sin Mi, Ul Rung, Bi Bong*

Auxiliaries

1997	*So Yang, Gin Yang, Ku Yong*
1998	*Gumi, Chang Won*

PENNANT LIST

Submarines

061	Chang Bogo
062	Yi Chon
063	Choi Muson
065	Pakui
066	Lee Jongmu
067	Jeongun
068	Lee Sunsin
069	Nadaeyong

Destroyers

DD 916	Jeong Buk
DD 919	Taejon
DD 921	Kwang Ju
DD 922	Kang Won
DD 925	Jeon Ju
DDG 971	King Kwanggaeto
DDG 972	Euljimundok
DDG 973	Yangmanchun
DDG 975	— (bldg)

Frigates

FF 951	Ulsan
FF 952	Seoul
FF 953	Chung Nam
FF 955	Masan
FF 956	Kyong Buk
FF 957	Chon Nam
FF 958	Che Ju
FF 959	Busan
FF 961	Chung Ju

Corvettes

751	Dong Hae
752	Su Won
753	Kang Reung
755	An Yang
756	Po Hang
757	Kun San
758	Kyong Ju
759	Mok Po
761	Kim Chon
762	Chung Ju
763	Jin Ju
765	Yo Su
766	Jin Hae
767	Sun Chon
768	Yee Ree
769	Won Ju
771	An Dong
772	Chon An
773	Song Nam
775	Bu Chon
776	Jae Chon
777	Dae Chon
778	Sok Cho
779	Yong Ju
781	Nam Won
782	Kwan Myong
783	Sin Hung
785	Kong Ju

Mine Warfare Forces

551	Kum San
552	Ko Hung
553	Kum Kok
555	Nam Yang
556	Ha Dong
557	Sam Kok
558	Yong Dong
559	Ok Cheon
560	Won San
561	Kang Kyeong
562	Kang Jing
563	Ko Ryeong
565	Kim Po
566	Ko Chang
567	Kum Wha
571	Yang Yang

Amphibious Forces

LSM 550	Pung To
LCF 611	Solgae
LSM 657	Wol Mi
LSM 658	Ki Rin
LST 671	Un Bong
LST 675	Kae Bong
LST 676	Wee Bong
LST 677	Su Yong
LST 678	Buk Han
LST 679	Hwa San
LST 681	Kojoon Bong
LST 682	Biro Bong
LST 683	Hyangro Bong
LST 685	Seongin Bong

Auxiliaries

ASR 21	Chung Hae Jin
ATS 27	Pyong Taek
ATS 28	Kwang Yang
AO 57	Chun Jee
AO 58	Dae Chung
AO 59	Hwa Chun

SUBMARINES

Notes: (1) Request for Proposals issued in 1999 to seven countries for a design for three 1,500-2,000 ton submarines to be built under licence in South Korea. AIP is a requirement. Contract expected in mid-2000.
(2) Russian 'Kilo' (Type 636) class have been reported as also being considered.

2 KSS-1 TOLGORAE and 9 DOLPHIN (COSMOS) CLASSES (MIDGET SUBMARINES)

052-053 (Tolgorae)

Displacement, tons: 150 surfaced; 175 dived (Tolgorae); 70 surfaced; 83 dived (Cosmos)
Dimensions, feet (metres): 82 × 6.9 *(25 × 2.1)* (Cosmos)
Main machinery: Diesel-electric; 1 diesel generator; 1 motor; 1 shaft
Speed, knots: 9 surfaced; 6 dived
Complement: 6 + 8 swimmers
Torpedoes: 2—406 mm tubes (Tolgorae). 2—533 mm tubes (Cosmos).
Sonars: Atlas Elektronik; hull-mounted; passive search; high frequency.

Comment: Tolgorae in service in 1983. Cosmos type used by Marines. Limited endurance, for use only in coastal waters. Fitted with Pilkington Optronics periscopes (CK 37 in Tolgorae and CK 41 in Cosmos). Numbers of each type confirmed but the 'Tolgorae' class are being replaced by more Cosmos. All are based at Cheju Island. ***UPDATED***

TOLGORAE

11/1985, G Jacobs

8 + 1 (3) CHANG BOGO (TYPE 209) CLASS (1200) (SSK)

Name	No	Builders	Laid down	Launched	Commissioned
CHANG BOGO	061	HDW, Kiel	1989	18 June 1992	2 June 1993
YI CHON	062	Daewoo, Okpo	1990	14 Oct 1992	30 Apr 1994
CHOI MUSON	063	Daewoo, Okpo	1991	25 Aug 1993	27 Feb 1995
PAKUI	065	Daewoo, Okpo	1992	20 May 1994	3 Feb 1996
LEE JONGMU	066	Daewoo, Okpo	1993	17 Apr 1995	29 Aug 1996
JEONGUN	067	Daewoo, Okpo	1994	7 May 1996	29 Aug 1997
LEE SUNSIN	068	Daewoo, Okpo	1995	21 May 1998	15 June 1999
NADAEYONG	069	Daewoo, Okpo	1996	15 June 1999	May 2000
—	071	Daewoo, Okpo	1997	Mar 2000	Mar 2001

Displacement, tons: 1,100 surfaced; 1,285 dived
Dimensions, feet (metres): 183.7 × 20.3 × 18
    (56 × 6.2 × 5.5)
Main machinery: Diesel-electric; 4 MTU 12V 396 SE diesels;
    3,800 hp(m) *(2.8 MW)* sustained; 4 alternators; 1 motor;
    4,600 hp(m) *(3.38 MW)* sustained; 1 shaft
Speed, knots: 11 surfaced/snorting; 22 dived
Range, miles: 7,500 at 8 kt surfaced
Complement: 33 (6 officers)

Torpedoes: 8—21 in *(533 mm)* bow tubes. 14 SystemTechnik
    Nord (STN) SUT Mod 2; wire-guided; active/passive homing to
    12 km *(6.6 n miles)* at 35 kt or 28 km *(15.1 n miles)* at 23 kt;
    warhead 260 kg. Swim-out discharge.

Mines: 28 in lieu of torpedoes.
Countermeasures: ESM: Argo; radar warning.
Weapons control: Atlas Elektronik ISUS 83 TFCS.
Radars: Navigation: I-band.
Sonars: Atlas Elektronik CSU 83; hull-mounted; passive search
    and attack; medium frequency.

Programmes: First three ordered in late 1987, one built at Kiel by
    HDW, and two assembled at Okpo by Daewoo from material
    packages transported from Germany. Second three ordered in
    October 1989 and a further batch of three in January 1994.
    Orders for six more of a stretched type 1500 announced on
    21 November 1997, but this has been delayed until 2000 (see
    Note under *Submarines*).

Modernisation: First refit expected in 2001 when the hulls may
    be stretched to the Type 1400 standard and are to include Sub
    Harpoon SSM.
Structure: Type 1200 similar to those built for the Turkish Navy
    with a heavy dependence on Atlas Elektronik sensors and STN
    torpedoes. Diving depth 250 m *(820 ft)*. A passive towed array
    may be fitted in due course.
Operational: An indigenous torpedo based on the Honeywell
    NP 37 may be available in due course. The plan is to split the
    class between the three Fleets. Operations are being
    conducted off Hawaii from 1997 to improve operating
    standards.

UPDATED

NADAEYONG

3/1999*, van Ginderen Collection / 0081152

LEE JONGMU

3/1999*, van Ginderen Collection / 0081153

DESTROYERS

Note: The KDX-2 programme is likely to be curtailed in favour of KDX-3, which may be an Aegis design based on the Japanese *Kongou* although alternative phased array designs are being investigated.

0 + 1 (2) KDX-2 CLASS (DDG)

Name	No	Builders	Laid down	Launched	Commissioned
—	975	Daewoo, Okpo	2001	2003	2004

Displacement, tons: 4,800 full load
Dimensions, feet (metres): 506.6 × 55.5 × 14.1
  (154.4 × 16.9 × 4.3)
Main machinery: CODOG; 2 GE LM 2500 gas turbines;
  58,200 hp *(43.42 MW)* sustained; 2 MTU 20V 956 TB92
  diesels; 8,000 hp(m) *(5.88 MW)*; 2 shafts
Speed, knots: 29. **Range, miles**: 4,000 at 18 kt
Complement: 200 (18 officers)

Missiles: SSM: 8 Harpoon (Block 1C) (2 quad) ❶.
  SAM: Standard SM-2 MR (Block IIIA); Lockheed Martin Mk 41 32
    cell VLS launcher ❷; Raytheon RAM Mk 49 with Mk 116 Block I
    missiles.
  A/S: ASROC VLS Mk 48.
Guns: 1 United Defense 5 in *(127 mm)*/62 Mk 45 Mod 4 ❸.
  1 Otobreda 3 in *(76 mm)*/62 ❹.
  1 Signaal Goalkeeper 30 mm ❺; 7 barrels per mounting.
Countermeasures: 4 chaff launchers ❻. ESM/ECM.
Combat data systems: BAeSema/Samsung KD COM-2; Link 11.
Weapons control: Marconi Mk 14 weapons direction system.
Radars: Air search: Raytheon SPS-49(V)5 ❼; C/D-band.
  Surface search: Signaal MW08 ❽; G-band.
  Fire control: 2 Signaal STIR 240 ❾; I/J/K-band.
Sonars: DSQS-23; hull-mounted; active search; medium
  frequency. Daewoo Telecom towed array; passive low
  frequency.

Helicopters: 1 Westland Super Lynx Mk 99 ❿.

Programmes: Approval for first three given in late 1996 but the
  final decision was not taken until 1998. Contract to design and
  build the first of class won by Daewoo in November 1999. First
  steel to be cut in late 2000.
Structure: The drawing shows a larger version of 'Okpo' class
  incorporating SM-2 missiles but retaining the same command
  systems. Some details are still speculative as the original
  Hyundai design is being reworked by Daewoo.

UPDATED

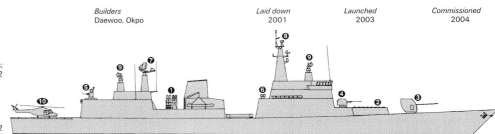

KDX-2   *(Scale 1 : 1,200), Ian Sturton /* 0050080

KDX-2 (computer graphic)   *1996, Hyundai /* 0052538

5 GEARING (FRAM I) CLASS (DDG)

Name	No	Builders	Laid down		Launched		Commissioned	
JEONG BUK (ex-*Everett F Larson* DD 830)	DD 916	Bath Iron Works, Maine	4 Sep	1944	28 Jan	1945	6 Apr	1945
TAEJON (ex-*New* DD 818)	DD 919	Consolidated Steel Corporation	14 Apr	1945	18 Aug	1945	5 Apr	1946
KWANG JU (ex-*Richard E Kraus* DD 849)	DD 921	Bath Iron Works Corporation, Maine	31 July	1945	2 Mar	1946	23 May	1946
KANG WON (ex-*William R Rush* DD 714)	DD 922	Federal SB and DD Co, Newark	19 Oct	1944	8 July	1945	21 Sep	1945
JEON JU (ex-*Rogers* DD 876)	DD 925	Consolidated Steel Corporation	3 June	1944	20 Nov	1944	26 Mar	1945

Displacement, tons: 2,425 standard; 3,470 full load approx
Dimensions, feet (metres): 390.5 × 41.2 × 19
  (119 × 12.6 × 5.8)
Main machinery: 4 Babcock & Wilcox boilers; 600 psi *(43.3 kg/
  cm²)*; 850°F *(454°C)*; 2 GE turbines; 60,000 hp *(45 MW)*;
  2 shafts
Speed, knots: 30
Range, miles: 3,275 at 11 kt; 975 at 32 kt
Complement: 280

Missiles: SSM: 8 McDonnell Douglas Harpoon (2 quad)
  launchers (except DD 925); active radar homing to 130 km
  (70 n miles) at 0.9 Mach; warhead 227 kg.
  A/S: Honeywell ASROC Mk 112 octuple launcher ❶ (DD 925);
  inertial guidance to 1.6-10 km *(1-6 n miles)*; payload Mk 46
  torpedo.
Guns: 4—5 in *(127 mm)*/38 (2 twin) Mk 38 ❷; 15 rds/min to
  17 km *(9 n miles)* anti-surface; 11 km *(5.9 n miles)* anti-aircraft;
  weight of shell 25 kg.
  2 USN/Bofors 40 mm/56 (twin) ❸; 160 rds/min to 11 km
  (5.9 n miles) anti-surface; 6 km *(3.3 n miles)* anti-aircraft;
  weight of shell 0.9 kg.
  2 General Electric/General Dynamics 20 mm Vulcan Gatling
  ❹; 3,000 rds/min to 1.5 km.
Torpedoes: 6—324 mm Mk 32 (2 triple) tubes ❺. Honeywell
  Mk 46; anti-submarine; active/passive homing to 11 km *(5.9 n
  miles)* at 40 kt; warhead 44 kg.

Depth charges: 1 Mk IX rack.
Countermeasures: ESM: WLR-1; radar warning.
Weapons control: 1 Mk 37 GFCS. 1 Mk 51 Mod 2 (for 40 mm).
Radars: Air search: Lockheed SPS-40 ❻ (DD 921 has SPS-37);
  E/F-band.
  Surface search: Raytheon/Sylvania SPS-10 ❼; G-band.
  Fire control: Western Electric Mk 25 ❽; I/J-band.
  IFF: UPX 1-12 (DD 921).
  Tacan: SRN 15.
Sonars: Sangamo SQS-23; hull-mounted; active search and
  attack; medium frequency.

Helicopters: 1 Aerospatiale SA 316B Alouette III or Super Lynx
  (except DD 925).

Programmes: Acquired from USA by sale 1977-81.
Modernisation: All modernised under the US Navy's Fleet
  Rehabilitation and Modernisation (FRAM) programme. Fitted
  with small helicopter hangar and flight deck. The helicopter
  deck has been strengthened. Some have Harpoon SSMs
  mounted amidships with Vulcan Gatlings slightly aft on the
  same platform. *Jeon Ju* has retained her ASROC launcher
  amidships and has the Gatlings on the helicopter platform.
Operational: Last operational survivors. The first pair were paid
  off in the mid-1990s but brought back into service for a training
  role.

UPDATED

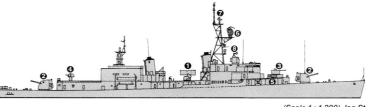

JEON JU   *(Scale 1 : 1,200), Ian Sturton /* 0012699

KANG WON   *10/1997 /* 0052528

3 OKPO CLASS (DDG)

Name	No	Builders	Laid down	Launched	Commissioned
KING KWANGGAETO	971	Daewoo, Okpo	June 1995	28 Oct 1996	24 July 1998
EULJIMUNDOK	972	Daewoo, Okpo	Jan 1996	16 Oct 1997	20 June 1999
YANGMANCHUN	973	Daewoo, Okpo	July 1996	19 Oct 1998	Apr 2000

Displacement, tons: 3,855 full load
Dimensions, feet (metres): 444.2 × 46.6 × 13.8
  (135.4 × 14.2 × 4.2)
Main machinery: CODOG; 2 GE LM 2500 gas turbines;
  58,200 hp *(43.42 MW)* sustained; 2 MTU 20V 956 TB92
  diesels; 8,000 hp(m) *(5.88 MW)*; 2 shafts
Speed, knots: 30. **Range, miles:** 4,000 at 18 kt
Complement: 170 (15 officers)

Missiles: SSM: 8 McDonnell Douglas Harpoon Block 1C (2 quad)
  launchers ❶; active radar homing to 130 km *(70 n miles)* at
  0.9 Mach; warhead 227 kg.
  SAM: Raytheon Sea Sparrow; Mk 48 Mod 2 VLS launcher ❷ for
  16 cells RIM-7P; semi-active radar homing to 14.6 km *(8 n
  miles)* at 2.5 Mach; warhead 39 kg.
Guns: 1 Otobreda 5 in *(127 mm)*/54 ❸; 45 rds/min to 16 km
  (8.7 n miles); weight of shell 32 kg.
  2 Signaal 30 mm Goalkeeper ❹; 7 barrels per mounting;
  4,200 rds/min combined to 2 km.
Torpedoes: 6—324 mm (2 triple) Mk 32 tubes ❺; Alliant
  Techsystems Mk 46 Mod 5; anti-submarine; active/passive
  homing to 11 km *(5.9 n miles)* at 40 kt; warhead 44 kg.
Countermeasures: Decoys: 4 CSEE Dagaie Mk 2 chaff launchers
  ❻. SLQ-25 Nixie towed torpedo decoy.
ESM/ECM: Argo AR 700/APECS II ❼; intercept and jammer.
Combat data systems: BAeSEMA/Samsung SSCS Mk 7; Litton
  NTDS (Link 11).
Radars: Air search: Raytheon SPS-49V5 ❽; C/D-band.
  Surface search: Signaal MW08 ❾; G-band.
  Fire control: 2 Signaal STIR 180 ❿; I/J/K-band.
  Navigation: Daewoo DTR 92 (SPS 55M) ⓫; I-band.
  IFF: UPX-27.
Sonars: Atlas Elektronik DSQS-21BZ; hull-mounted active
  search; medium frequency.
  Daewoo Telecom towed array; passive low frequency.

Helicopters: 1 Westland Super Lynx ⓬.

Programmes: Project KDX-1. A much delayed programme.
The first keel was to have been laid down at Daewoo in late
1992 for completion in 1996, but definition studies extended
to late 1993, when contracts started to be signed for the
weapon systems. First steel cut at Daewoo Okpo in April 1994.

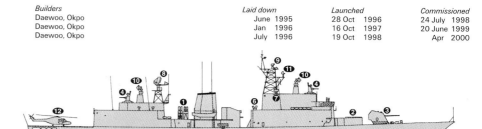

KING KWANGGAETO   *(Scale 1 : 1,200), Ian Sturton / 0081154*

EULJIMUNDOK   *3/1999*, van Ginderen Collection / 0081155*

Structure: Emphasis is on air defence but the design has taken
so long to reach fulfilment that it has been overtaken by the
KDX-2. McTaggart Scott Trigon 5 helo handling system.

Operational: The Goalkeepers are also to be used against
close-in surface threats using FAPDS (Frangible Armour
Penetrating Discarding Sabot).   ***UPDATED***

KING KWANGGAETO   *8/1999*, Hachiro Nakai / 0081156*

KING KWANGGAETO   *8/1999*, Hachiro Nakai / 0081157*

FRIGATES

9 ULSAN CLASS (FFG)

Name	No
ULSAN	FF 951
SEOUL	FF 952
CHUNG NAM	FF 953
MASAN	FF 955
KYONG BUK	FF 956
CHON NAM	FF 957
CHE JU	FF 958
BUSAN	FF 959
CHUNG JU	FF 961

Builders	Laid down	Launched	Commissioned
Hyundai, Ulsan	1979	8 Apr 1980	1 Jan 1981
Hyundai, Ulsan	1982	24 Apr 1984	30 June 1985
Korean SEC, Pusan	1984	26 Oct 1984	1 June 1986
Korea Tacoma	1983	26 Oct 1984	20 July 1985
Daewoo, Okpo	1984	15 Jan 1986	30 May 1986
Hyundai, Ulsan	1986	19 Apr 1988	17 June 1989
Daewoo, Okpo	1986	3 May 1988	1 Jan 1990
Hyundai, Ulsan	1990	20 Feb 1992	1 Jan 1993
Daewoo, Okpo	1990	20 Mar 1992	1 June 1993

Displacement, tons: 1,496 light; 2,180 full load (2,300 for FF 957-961)

Dimensions, feet (metres): 334.6 × 37.7 × 11.5 *(102 × 11.5 × 3.5)*

Main machinery: CODOG; 2 GE LM 2500 gas turbines; 53,640 hp *(40 MW)* sustained; 2 MTU 16V 538 TB82 diesels; 5,940 hp(m) *(4.37 MW)* sustained; 2 shafts; cp props

Speed, knots: 34; 18 on diesels. **Range, miles:** 4,000 at 15 kt

Complement: 150 (16 officers)

Missiles: SSM: 8 McDonnell Douglas Harpoon (4 twin) launchers ❶; active radar homing to 130 km *(70 n miles)* at 0.9 Mach; warhead 227 kg.

Guns: 2—3 in *(76 mm)*/62 OTO Melara compact ❷; 85 rds/min to 16 km *(8.6 n miles)* anti-surface; 12 km *(6.5 n miles)* anti-aircraft; weight of shell 6 kg.
8 Emerson Electric 30 mm (4 twin) (FF 951-955) ❸; 6 Breda 40 mm/70 (3 twin) (FF 956-961) ❹.

Torpedoes: 6—324 mm Mk 32 (2 triple) tubes ❺. Honeywell Mk 46 Mod 1; anti-submarine; active/passive homing to 11 km *(5.9 n miles)* at 40 kt; warhead 44 kg.

Depth charges: 12.

Countermeasures: Decoys: 4 Loral Hycor SRBOC 6-barrelled Mk 36 launchers ❻; range 4 km *(2.2 n miles)*.
SLQ-25 Nixie; towed torpedo decoy.
ESM: ULQ-11K; intercept.

Combat data systems: Samsung/Ferranti WSA 423 action data automation (FF 957-961). Litton systems retrofitted to others. Link 11 in three of the class. WSC-3 SATCOM (F 957).

Weapons control: 1 Signaal Lirod optronic director (FF 951-956) ❼; 1 Radamec System 2400 optronic director (FF 957-961) ❽.

Radars: Air/surface search: Signaal DA05 ❾; E/F-band.
Surface search: Signaal ZW06 (FF 951-956) ❿; Marconi S 1810 (FF 957-961) ⓫; I-band.
Fire control: Signaal WM28 (FF 951-956) ⓬; Marconi ST 1802 (FF 957-961) ⓭; I/J-band.
Navigation: Raytheon SPS-10C (FF 957-961) ⓮; I-band.
Tacan: SRN 15.

Sonars: Signaal PHS-32; hull-mounted; active search and attack; medium frequency.

Modernisation: New sonars fitted. WSC-3 SATCOM fitted in *Chon Nam*.

Structure: Steel hull with aluminium alloy superstructure. There are three versions. The first five ships are the same but *Kyong Buk* has the four Emerson Electric twin 30 mm guns replaced by three Breda twin 40 mm, and the last four of the class have a built-up gun platform aft and a different combination of surface search, target indication and navigation radars. Weapon systems integration caused earlier concern and a Ferranti combat data system has been installed in the last five; Litton Systems Link 11 fitted in three of the class.

Operational: *Che Ju* and *Chung Nam* conducted the first ever deployment of South Korean warships to Europe during a four month tour from September 1991 to January 1992. Trainees were embarked. Three of the class have a shore datalink and act as local area commanders to control attack craft carrying out coastal protection patrols.

UPDATED

ULSAN   *(Scale 1 : 900), Ian Sturton*

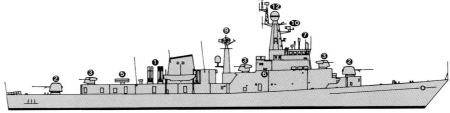

CHE JU   *(Scale 1 : 900), Ian Sturton*

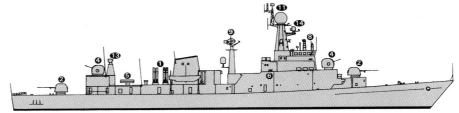

KYONG BUK   *5/1998*, John Mortimer /* 0081159

CHUNG NAM   *8/1999*, Hachiro Nakai /* 0081160

CHON NAM

10/1998, John Mortimer / 0052533

BUSAN

10/1998, John Mortimer / 0052531

MASAN

10/1997 / 0052532

CORVETTES

24 PO HANG CLASS (FS/FSG)

Name	No	Builders	Commissioned
PO HANG	756	Korea SEC, Pusan	Dec 1984
KUN SAN	757	Korea Tacoma	Dec 1984
KYONG JU	758	Hyundai, Ulsan	Nov 1986
MOK PO	759	Daewoo, Okpo	Aug 1986
KIM CHON	761	Korea SEC, Pusan	May 1985
CHUNG JU	762	Korea Tacoma	May 1985
JIN JU	763	Hyundai, Ulsan	June 1988
YO SU	765	Daewoo, Okpo	Nov 1988
JIN HAE	766	Korea SEC, Pusan	Feb 1989
SUN CHON	767	Korea Tacoma	June 1989
YEE REE	768	Hyundai, Ulsan	June 1989
WON JU	769	Daewoo, Okpo	Aug 1989
AN DONG	771	Korea SEC, Pusan	Nov 1989
CHON AN	772	Korea Tacoma	Nov 1989
SONG NAM	773	Daewoo, Okpo	May 1989
BU CHON	775	Hyundai, Ulsan	Apr 1989
JAE CHON	776	Korea SEC, Pusan	May 1989
DAE CHON	777	Korea Tacoma	Apr 1989
SOK CHO	778	Korea SEC, Pusan	Feb 1990
YONG JU	779	Hyundai, Ulsan	Mar 1990
NAM WON	781	Daewoo, Okpo	Apr 1990
KWAN MYONG	782	Korea Tacoma	July 1990
SIN HUNG	783	Korea SEC, Pusan	Mar 1993
KONG JU	785	Korea Tacoma	July 1993

Displacement, tons: 1,220 full load
Dimensions, feet (metres): 289.7 × 32.8 × 9.5 *(88.3 × 10 × 2.9)*
Main machinery: CODOG; 1 GE LM 2500 gas turbine; 26,820 hp *(20 MW)* sustained; 2 MTU 12V 956 TB82 diesels; 6,260 hp(m) *(4.6 MW)* sustained; 2 shafts; Kamewa cp props
Speed, knots: 32. **Range, miles:** 4,000 at 15 kt (diesel)
Complement: 95 (10 officers)

Missiles: SSM: 2 Aerospatiale MM 38 Exocet (756-759) ❶; inertial cruise; active radar homing to 42 km *(23 n miles)* at 0.9 Mach; warhead 165 kg; sea-skimmer.
Guns: 1 or 2 OTO Melara 3 in *(76 mm)*/62 compact ❷; 85 rds/min to 16 km *(8.6 n miles)* anti-surface; 12 km *(6.5 n miles)* anti-aircraft; weight of shell 6 kg.
    4 Emerson Electric 30 mm (2 twin) (756-759) ❸; 4 Breda 40 mm/70 (2 twin) (761 onwards) ❹.
Torpedoes: 6—324 mm Mk 32 (2 triple) tubes ❺. Honeywell Mk 46; anti-submarine; active/passive homing to 11 km *(5.9 n miles)* at 40 kt; warhead 44 kg.

Depth charges: 12 (761 onwards).
Countermeasures: Decoys: 4 MEL Protean fixed launchers; 36 grenades.
    2 Loral Hycor SRBOC 6-barrelled Mk 36 launchers (in some); range 4 km *(2.2 n miles)*.
ESM/ECM: THORN EMI or NobelTech; intercept/jammer.
Combat data systems: Signaal Sewaco ZK (756-759); Ferranti WSA 423 (761 onwards).
Weapons control: Signaal Lirod or Radamec 2400 (766 onwards) optronic director ❻.
Radars: Surface search: Marconi 1810 ❼ and/or Raytheon SPS-64 ❽; I-band.
Fire control: Signaal WM28 ❾; I/J-band; or Marconi 1802 ❿; I/J-band.
Sonars: Signaal PHS-32; hull-mounted; active search and attack; medium frequency.

Programmes: First laid down early 1983. After early confusion, names, pennant numbers and shipbuilders are now correct. The programme terminated in 1993.
Modernisation: The first four of the class have had torpedo tubes installed.
Structure: The first four are Exocet fitted and have a different weapon systems arrangement. The remainder have an improved combat data system with Ferranti/Radamec/Marconi fire-control systems and radars as in the later versions of the 'Ulsan' class.

UPDATED

PO HANG   *(Scale 1 : 900), Ian Sturton /* 0081158

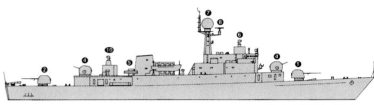

AN DONG   *(Scale 1 : 900), Ian Sturton*

MOK PO   *10/1998, John Mortimer /* 0052541

JIN HAE   *10/1998, G Toremans /* 0052540

4 DONG HAE CLASS (FS)

Name	No	Builders	Commissioned
DONG HAE	751	Korea SEC, Pusan	Aug 1982
SU WON	752	Korea Tacoma	Oct 1983
KANG REUNG	753	Hyundai, Ulsan	Nov 1983
AN YANG	755	Daewoo, Okpo	Dec 1983

Displacement, tons: 1,076 full load
Dimensions, feet (metres): 256.2 × 31.5 × 8.5 *(78.1 × 9.6 × 2.6)*
Main machinery: CODOG; 1 GE LM 2500 gas turbine; 26,820 hp *(20 MW)* sustained; 2 MTU 12V
  956 TB82 diesels; 6,260 hp(m) *(4.6 MW)* sustained; 2 shafts; Kamewa cp props
Speed, knots: 31. **Range, miles:** 4,000 at 15 kt (diesel)
Complement: 95 (10 officers)

Guns: 1 OTO Melara 3 in *(76 mm)*/62 compact ❶; 85 rds/min to 16 km *(8.6 n miles)*; weight of
  shell 6 kg.
  4 Emerson Electric 30 mm (2 twin) ❷. 2 Bofors 40 mm/60 (twin) ❸.
Torpedoes: 6—324 mm Mk 32 (2 triple) tubes ❹. Honeywell Mk 46; anti-submarine; active/
  passive homing to 11 km *(5.9 n miles)* at 40 kt; warhead 44 kg.
Depth charges: 12.
Countermeasures: Decoys: 4 MEL Protean chaff launchers.
ESM/ECM: THORN EMI or NobelTech; intercept and jammer.
Combat data systems: Signaal Sewaco ZK.
Weapons control: Signaal Lirod optronic director ❺.
Radars: Surface search: Raytheon SPS-64 ❻; I-band.
Fire control: Signaal WM28 ❼; I/J-band.
Sonars: Signaal PHS-32; hull-mounted; active search and attack; medium frequency.

Programmes: This was the first version of the corvette series, with four being ordered in 1980, one
  each from the four major warship building yards.
Structure: The design was too small for the variety of different weapons which were intended to be
  fitted for different types of warfare and was therefore discontinued in favour of the 'Po Hang'
  class.

VERIFIED

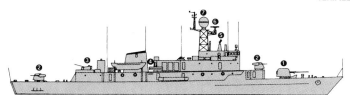

DONG HAE   (Scale 1 : 900), Ian Sturton

DONG HAE   6/1996, D Swetnam

SHIPBORNE AIRCRAFT

Numbers/Type: 17/13 Westland Super Lynx Mk 99/100.
Operational speed: 125 kt *(231 km/h)*.
Service ceiling: 12,000 ft *(3,660 m)*.
Range: 320 n miles *(593 km)*.
Role/Weapon systems: Six ASV helicopters delivered in 1991; 11 ASW versions acquired later
  and 13 more ordered in June 1997 and delivered in 1999/2000. Sensors: Ferranti Sea Spray Mk
  3 radar and Racal ESM. Bendix AQS 18(V) dipping sonar and ASQ 504(V) MAD in ASW versions.
  Weapons: 4 BAe Sea Skua missiles. Mk 46 (Mod 5) torpedo (in ASW version). *UPDATED*

SUPER LYNX   8/1999*, Hachiro Nakai / 0081161

Numbers/Type: 6 Aerospatiale SA 316B/SA 319B Alouette III.
Operational speed: 113 kt *(210 km/h)*.
Service ceiling: 10,500 ft *(3,200 m)*.
Range: 290 n miles *(540 km)*.
Role/Weapon systems: Marine support helicopter; operated by RoK Marine Corps. Sensors:
  None. Weapons: Unarmed. *UPDATED*

ALOUETTE III   1990* / 0081162

LAND-BASED MARITIME AIRCRAFT (FRONT LINE)

Notes: (1) F-16 fighters are capable of firing Harpoon ASV missiles.
(2) There are also 10 UH-60 and 10 UH-1 utility helicopters.

Numbers/Type: 8 Grumman S-2A/F Tracker.
Operational speed: 130 kt *(241 km/h)*.
Service ceiling: 25,000 ft *(7,620 m)*.
Range: 1,350 n miles *(2,500 km)*.
Role/Weapon systems: Maritime surveillance and limited ASW operations; coastal surveillance
  and EEZ patrol. Sensors: Search radar, ECM. Weapons: ASW; torpedoes, depth bombs and
  mines. ASV; underwing 127 mm rockets. HARM missiles may be acquired.

VERIFIED

Numbers/Type: 8 Lockheed P-3C Orion Update III.
Operational speed: 411 kt *(761 km/h)*.
Service ceiling: 28,300 ft *(8,625 m)*.
Range: 4,000 n miles *(7,410 km)*.
Role/Weapon systems: Maritime patrol aircraft ordered in December 1990. First pair delivered
  April 1995, remainder April 1996. Another 8 are required in due course. This is the Update III
  version with ASQ-212 tactical computer. Sensors: APS-134 or 137(V)6 search radar; AAS-36 IR.
  Weapons: four Harpoon ASM.

VERIFIED

Numbers/Type: 5 Rheims-Cessna F 406 Caravan II.
Operational speed: 229 kt *(424 km/h)*.
Service ceiling: 30,000 ft *(9,145 m)*.
Range: 1,153 m *(2,135 km)*.
Role/Weapon systems: Maritime surveillance version ordered in 1997 with first one delivered in
  mid-1999. Sensors: APS 134 radar; Litton FLIR. Weapons: none.

UPDATED

F 406 (Australian colours)   6/1998*, Reims Aviation

PATROL FORCES

5 PAE KU (PSMM 5) CLASS
(FAST ATTACK CRAFT—MISSILE) (PCFG)

Name	No	Builders	Commissioned
PAE KU 56	PGM 586 (ex-PGM 356)	Korea Tacoma Marine	1 Feb 1976
PAE KU 57	PGM 587 (ex-PGM 357)	Korea Tacoma Marine	1977
PAE KU 58	PGM 588 (ex-PGM 358)	Korea Tacoma Marine	1977
PAE KU 59	PGM 589 (ex-PGM 359)	Korea Tacoma Marine	1977
PAE KU 61	PGM 591 (ex-PGM 361)	Korea Tacoma Marine	1978

Displacement, tons: 268 full load
Dimensions, feet (metres): 176.2 × 23.9 × 9.5 *(53.7 × 7.3 × 2.9)*
Main machinery: 6 Avco Lycoming TF-35 gas turbines; 16,800 hp *(12.53 MW)*; 2 shafts; cp props
Speed, knots: 40+. **Range, miles:** 2,400 at 18 kt
Complement: 32 (5 officers)

Missiles: SSM: 4 McDonnell Douglas Harpoon; active radar homing to 130 km *(70 n miles)* at
  0.9 Mach; warhead 227 kg.
Guns: 1 OTO Melara 3 in *(76 mm)*/62 compact; 85 rds/min to 16 km *(8.6 n miles)* anti-surface;
  12 km *(6.5 n miles)* anti-aircraft; weight of shell 6 kg.
  2 Emerson Electric 30 mm (twin); 1,200 rds/min combined to 6 km *(3.2 n miles)*; weight of shell
  0.35 kg.
  2 Browning 12.7 mm MGs.
Countermeasures: Decoys: Loral RBOC 4-barrelled Mk 33 launchers; range 4 km *(2.2 n miles)*.
Weapons control: Honeywell H 930 Mod 0.
Radars: Air search: SPS-58; E/F-band.
Surface search: Marconi Canada HC 75; I-band.
Fire control: Western Electric SPG-50 or Westinghouse W-120; I/J-band.

Programmes: Tacoma design designation was PSMM for multimission patrol ship.
Structure: Aluminium hulls, based on the US Navy's Asheville (PG 84) design, but appearance of
  Korean built ships' superstructure differs.
Operational: One, two, or three turbines can be selected to provide each shaft with a variety of
  power settings. *VERIFIED*

PAE KU 56   10/1998 / 0052542

85 SEA DOLPHIN/WILDCAT CLASS
(FAST ATTACK CRAFT—PATROL) (PCF)

PKM 212-358

Displacement, tons: 148 full load
Dimensions, feet (metres): 121.4 × 22.6 × 5.6 *(37 × 6.9 × 1.7)*
Main machinery: 2 MTU MD 16V 538 TB90 diesels; 6,000 hp(m) *(4.41 MW)* sustained; 2 shafts
Speed, knots: 37. **Range, miles:** 600 at 20 kt
Complement: 31 (5 officers)
Guns: 2 Emerson Electric 30 mm (twin) or USN 3 in *(76 mm)*/50 or Bofors 40 mm/60. 2 GE/GD 20 mm Sea Vulcan Gatlings (in most).
2—12.7 mm MGs. Rocket launchers in lieu of after Gatling in some.
Weapons control: Optical director.
Radars: Surface search: Raytheon 1645; I-band.

Comment: Fifty-four Sea Dolphins built by Korea SEC, and 47 Wildcats by Korea Tacoma. First laid down 1978. The class has some gun armament variations and some minor superstructure changes in later ships of the class. These craft form the basis of the coastal patrol effort against incursions by North Korean amphibious units. Five sold to the Philippines in 1995. Some deleted so far, others are in reserve. *UPDATED*

SEA DOLPHIN 275 (with 30 mm gun)   10/1998 / 0052550

WILDCAT 253   6/1999 * / 0081163

SEA DOLPHIN 372 (with 40 mm gun)   10/1998, L Stephenson / 0052551

AMPHIBIOUS FORCES

3 LSM 1 CLASS (LSM)

PUNG TO (ex-*LSM 54*) LSM 550   **WOL MI** (ex-*LSM 57*) LSM 657   **KI RIN** (ex-*LSM 19*) LSM 658

Displacement, tons: 743 beaching; 1,095 full load
Dimensions, feet (metres): 203.5 × 34.6 × 8.2 *(62 × 10.5 × 2.5)*
Main machinery: 2 Fairbanks-Morse 38D8-1/8-10 diesels; 3,540 hp *(2.64 MW)* sustained; 2 shafts
Speed, knots: 13. **Range, miles:** 5,000 at 7 kt
Complement: 75 plus 50 troops
Military lift: 350 tons
Guns: 2 Bofors 40 mm/60 (twin). 4 Oerlikon 20 mm.

Comment: Former US Navy medium landing ships, completed between June and October 1944 and transferred in 1956. All purchased 15 November 1974. Arrangement of 20 mm guns differs either two single mounts adjacent forward 40 mm mount on forecastle, or 20 mm guns along sides of cargo well. *Pung To* converted to a minelayer. *UPDATED*

PUNG TO   4/1997 * / 0012704

4 ALLIGATOR CLASS (LST)

Name	No	Builders	Launched		Commissioned	
KOJOON BONG	LST 681	Korea Tacoma, Masan	Sep	1992	June	1993
BIRO BONG	LST 682	Korea Tacoma, Masan	Dec	1996	Nov	1997
HYANGRO BONG	LST 683	Korea Tacoma, Masan	Oct	1998	Aug	1999
SEONGIN BONG	LST 685	Korea Tacoma, Masan	Feb	1999	Nov	1999

Displacement, tons: 4,278 full load
Dimensions, feet (metres): 369.1 × 50.2 × 9.8 *(112.5 × 15.3 × 3)*
Main machinery: 2 SEMT-Pielstick 16 PA6 V 280; 12,800 hp(m) *(9.41 MW)* sustained; 2 shafts; cp props
Speed, knots: 16. **Range, miles:** 4,500 at 12 kt
Complement: 169
Military lift: 200 troops; 15 MBT; 6—3 ton vehicles; 4 LCVPs.
Guns: 2 Breda 40 mm/70. 2 Vulcan 20 mm Gatlings.
Countermeasures: Decoys: 1 RBOC chaff launcher.
ESM: radar intercept.
Weapons control: Selenia NA 18. Optronic director. Daeyoung WCS-86.
Radars: Surface search: Raytheon SPS 64; E/F-band.
Navigation: Raytheon SPS 64; I-band.
Helicopters: Platform for 1 UH-60A.

Comment: First one ordered in June 1990 from Korea Tacoma, Masan but delayed by financial problems. Korea Tacoma is now Hanjin Heavy Industries. Design improvements include stern ramp for underway launching of LVTs, helicopter deck, and a lengthened bow ramp. Up to seven may be built in due course. *UPDATED*

KOJOON BONG   11/1997 * / 0081164

KOJOON BONG   10/1998, John Mortimer / 0052552

6 LST 1-510 and 511-1152 CLASSES (LST)

Name	No	Builders	Commissioned	
UN BONG (ex-*LST 1010*)	LST 671	Bethlehem Steel	25 Apr	1944
KAE BONG (ex-*Berkshire County* LST 288)	LST 675	American Bridge	20 Dec	1943
WEE BONG (ex-*Johnson County* LST 849)	LST 676	American Bridge	16 Jan	1945
SU YONG (ex-*Kane County* LST 853)	LST 677	Chicago Bridge	11 Dec	1945
BUK HAN (ex-*Lynn County* LST 900)	LST 678	Dravo, Pittsburg	28 Dec	1944
HWA SAN (ex-*Pender County* LST 1080)	LST 679	Bethlehem Steel	29 May	1945

Displacement, tons: 1,653 standard; 2,366 beaching; 4,080 full load
Dimensions, feet (metres): 328 × 50 × 14 (screws) *(100 × 15.2 × 4.3)*
Main machinery: 2 GM 12-567A diesels; 1,800 hp *(1.34 MW)*; 2 shafts
Speed, knots: 11.6
Complement: 80
Military lift: 2,100 tons including 20 tanks and 2 LCVPs
Guns: 8 Bofors 40 mm (4 twin). 2 Oerlikon 20 mm.

Comment: Former US Navy tank landing ships. Transferred to South Korea between 1955 and 1959. All purchased 15 November 1974. Planned to be replaced by the 'Alligator' class but six reported as still in service. *UPDATED*

HWA SAN   10/1997 * / 0081165

7 FURSEAL CLASS (LCU)

MULKAE 72, 73, 75, 76, 78, 79, 81

Displacement, tons: 415 full load
Dimensions, feet (metres): 134.8 × 28.8 × 5.9 *(41.1 × 8.8 × 1.8)*
Main machinery: 2 GM 6-71 diesels; 348 hp *(260 kW)* sustained; 2 Kort nozzles
Speed, knots: 13. **Range, miles:** 560 at 11 kt
Complement: 14 (2 officers)
Military lift: 150 tons including battle tanks
Guns: 2 Oerlikon 20 mm.

Comment: In service 1979-81. Built by Korea Tacoma Marine Industries Ltd based on US LCU 1610 design.
                                                                    UPDATED

FURSEAL 76   *1987*, Korea Tacoma /* 0081166

1 SOLGAE CLASS (LANDING CRAFT FAST) (LCF)

Name	No	Builders	Launched	Commissioned
SOLGAE	611	Korea Tacoma, Masan	Oct 1989	July 1990

Displacement, tons: 120 full load
Dimensions, feet (metres): 82.7 × 39.4 × 25.6 *(25.2 × 12 × 7.8)*
Main machinery: 2 gas turbines; 5,000 hp(m) *(3.68 MW)* propulsion; 2 gas turbines; 3,000 hp(m) *(2.2 MW)* lift; 2 airscrews
Speed, knots: 65; 40 (loaded). **Range, miles:** 500 at 45 kt
Complement: 8
Military lift: 27 tons; 1 vehicle; 65 troops
Guns: 1 Vulcan 20 mm Gatling.
Radars: Navigation: Raytheon SPS 64(V)2; I-band.

Comment: Strong resemblance to the USN LCAC although developed without consultation with US. Unloaded speed is 65 kt. More may be acquired in due course.
                                                                    UPDATED

SOLGAE   *10/1997, S Tattam, RAN /* 0012705

10 LCM 8 CLASS (LCM)

Displacement, tons: 115 full load
Dimensions, feet (metres): 74.5 × 21 × 4.6 *(22.7 × 6.4 × 1.4)*
Main machinery: 4 GM 6-71 diesels; 696 hp *(519 kW)* sustained; 2 shafts
Speed, knots: 11
Complement: 11
Military lift: 55 tons

Comment: Previously US Army craft. Transferred in September 1978.
                                                                    VERIFIED

LCM 8   *5/1995, David Jordan*

LCVP TYPES

Comment: A considerable number of US type built of GRP in South Korea. In addition there are plans to build up to 20 small hovercraft for special forces; first two reported building in 1994, and one seen on sea trials in May 1995. Also 56 combat support boats of 8 m were ordered from FBM Marine for assembly by Hanjin Heavy Industries.
                                                                    UPDATED

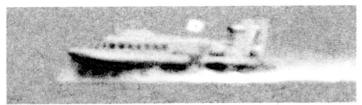

HOVERCRAFT   *5/1995*, David Jordan /* 0081167

MINE WARFARE FORCES

Note: One LSM 1 class (details under *Amphibious Forces*) is used as a minelayer.

6 SWALLOW CLASS (MINEHUNTERS) (MHC)

Name	No	Builders	Commissioned
KANG KYEONG	561	Kangnam Corporation	Dec 1986
KANG JIN	562	Kangnam Corporation	May 1991
KO RYEONG	563	Kangnam Corporation	Nov 1991
KIM PO	565	Kangnam Corporation	Apr 1993
KO CHANG	566	Kangnam Corporation	Oct 1993
KUM WHA	567	Kangnam Corporation	Apr 1994

Displacement, tons: 470 standard; 520 full load
Dimensions, feet (metres): 164 × 27.2 × 8.6 *(50 × 8.3 × 2.6)*
Main machinery: 2 MTU diesels; 2,040 hp(m) *(1.5 MW)* sustained; 2 Voith-Schneider props; bow thruster; 102 hp(m) *(75 kW)*
Speed, knots: 15. **Range, miles:** 2,000 at 10 kt
Complement: 44 (5 officers) plus 4 divers
Guns: 1 Oerlikon 20 mm. 2—7.62 mm MGs.
Countermeasures: MCM: 2 Gaymarine Pluto remote-control submersibles (possibly to be replaced by Double Eagle).
Combat data systems: Racal MAINS 500.
Radars: Navigation: Raytheon SPS 64; I-band.
Sonars: GEC-Marconi 193M Mod 1 or Mod 3; minehunting; high frequency.

Comment: Built to a design developed independently by Kangnam Corporation but similar to the Italian 'Lerici' class. GRP hull. Single sweep gear deployed at 8 kt. Decca/Racal plotting system. First delivered at the end of 1986 for trials. Two more with some modifications ordered in 1988, three more in 1990.
                                                                    UPDATED

KO RYEONG   *10/1998, John Mortimer /* 0052555

3 MSC 268 and 5 MSC 289 CLASSES
(MINESWEEPERS—COASTAL) (MSC)

Name	No	Builders	Commissioned
KUM SAN (ex-*MSC 284*)*	MSC 551	Harbour Boat Building, CA	June 1959
KO HUNG (ex-*MSC 285*)*	MSC 552	Harbour Boat Building, CA	Aug 1959
KUM KOK (ex-*MSC 286*)*	MSC 553	Harbour Boat Building, CA	Oct 1959
NAM YANG (ex-*MSC 295*)	MSC 555	Peterson Builders, WI	Aug 1963
HA DONG (ex-*MSC 296*)	MSC 556	Peterson Builders, WI	Nov 1963
SAM KOK (ex-*MSC 316*)	MSC 557	Peterson Builders, WI	July 1968
YONG DONG (ex-*MSC 320*)	MSC 558	Peterson Builders, WI	Oct 1975
OK CHEON (ex-*MSC 321*)	MSC 559	Peterson Builders, WI	Oct 1975

* 'MSC 268' class

Displacement, tons: 320 light; 370 full load ('268' class)
315 light; 380 full load ('289' class)
Dimensions, feet (metres): 141.1 × 26.2 × 8.5 *(43 × 8 × 2.6)* ('268' class)
145.4 × 27.2 × 12 (screws) *(44.3 × 8.3 × 2.7)* ('289' class)
Main machinery: 2 GM 8-268A diesels; 880 hp *(656 kW)* ('268' class); 2 shafts
4 GM 6-71 diesels; 696 hp *(519 kW)* sustained ('289' class); 2 shafts
Speed, knots: 14. **Range, miles:** 2,500 at 14 kt
Complement: 40
Guns: 2 Oerlikon 20 mm (twin) ('268' class); 2 Oerlikon 20 mm ('289' class).
3 Browning 12.7 mm MGs.
Radars: Navigation: Decca 45; I-band.
Sonars: General Electric UQS-1 or Thomson Sintra 2022; hull-mounted; minehunting; high frequency.

Comment: Built by the USA for transfer under the Military Aid Programme with wooden hulls and non-magnetic metal fittings. MSC 551 transferred to South Korea in June 1959, MSC 552 in September 1959, MSC 553 in November 1959, MSC 555 in September 1963, MSC 556 in November 1963, MSC 557 in July 1968, MSC 558 and 559 on 2 October 1975. The last four may have been retrofitted with Thomson Sintra mine detection sonars. Planned to pay off as 'Swallow' class commission but have been kept going until the follow-on to the Swallows are completed.
                                                                    UPDATED

SAM KOK   *10/1998* /* 0081168

1 WON SAN CLASS (MINELAYER) (ML)

Name	No	Builders	Launched	Commissioned
WON SAN	560	Hyundai, Ulsan	Sep 1996	Sep 1997

Displacement, tons: 3,300 full load
Dimensions, feet (metres): 340.6 × 49.2 × 11.2 (103.8 × 15 × 3.4)
Main machinery: CODAD; 4 SEMT-Pielstick 12 PA6 diesels; 17,200 hp(m) (12.64 MW); 2 shafts
Speed, knots: 22. Range, miles: 4,500 at 15 kt
Complement: 160
Guns: 1 OTO Melara 3 in (76 mm)/62; 85 rds/min to 16 km (8.6 n miles); weight of shell 6 kg.
    2 Breda 40 mm/70.
Torpedoes: 6—324 mm Mk 32 (2 triple) launchers.
Mines: 2 stern launchers. Up to 300.
Countermeasures: Decoys: 2 chaff launchers. ESM/ECM.
Weapons control: Radamec optronic director.
Radars: Air/surface search: E/F-band.
Fire control: Marconi 1802; I/J-band.
Navigation: I-band.
Sonars: Bow-mounted; active search and attack; medium frequency.
Helicopters: Platform only.

Comment: Project design contract ordered October 1991 and completed July 1993 by Hyundai.
    Order to build given in October 1994.

UPDATED

WON SAN   10/1998, G Toremans / 0052554

1 + 2 (2) YANG YANG CLASS (MSC/MHC)

Name	No	Builders	Commissioned
YANG YANG	571	Kangnam Corporation	Dec 1999

Displacement, tons: 880 full load
Dimensions, feet (metres): 195 × 34.4 × 9.8 (59.4 × 10.5 × 3.0)
Main machinery: 2 MTU diesels; 4,000 hp(m) (2.98 MW) sustained; 2 Voith-Schneider props;
    bow thruster; 134 hp(m) (100 kW)
Speed, knots: 15. Range, miles: 3,000 at 12 kt
Complement: 56 (7 officers) plus 5 divers
Guns: 1—20 mm Sea Vulcan Gatling. 2—7.62 mm MGs.
Countermeasures: MCM: BAE Systems deep mechanical and combined influence sweep system.
    2 Gayrobot Pluto plus ROVs.
Combat data systems: Thomson Marconi TSM 2061 Mk 3.
Radars: Navigation: Raytheon; I-band.
Sonars: Thomson Marconi Type 2093 VDS; minehunting; active multifrequency.

Comment: The first one ordered in late 1995. Next two planned to be ordered in mid-2000. Built to
    a design developed by Kangnam Corporation. GRP hull. The integrated navigation and dynamic
    positioning system developed by Kongsberg Simrad.

NEW ENTRY

YANG YANG   12/1999*, Kangnam / 0085026

AUXILIARIES

Notes: (1) The South Korean Navy also operates nine small harbour tugs (designated YTLs). These
include one ex-US Navy craft and five ex-US Army craft. There are also approximately 35 small
service craft in addition to the YO-type tankers listed and the harbour tugs. These craft include open
lighters, floating cranes, diving tenders, dredgers, ferries, non self-propelled fuel barges, pontoon
barges, and sludge removal barges; most are former US Navy craft.
(2) The ex-US Cavallaro high-speed transport (APD 822) is still in service.

1 CHUNG HAE JIN CLASS (ASR)

Name	No	Builders	Launched	Commissioned
CHUNG HAE JIN	21	Daewoo, Okpo	Oct 1995	30 Nov 1996

Displacement, tons: 4,300 full load
Dimensions, feet (metres): 337.3 × 53.8 × 15.1 (102.8 × 16.4 × 4.6)
Main machinery: Diesel-electric; 4 MAN Burmeister & Wain 16V 28/32 diesels; 11,800 hp(m)
    (8.67 MW); 2 motors; 5,440 hp(m) (4 MW); 2 shafts; cp props; 3 bow and 2 stern thrusters
Speed, knots: 18. Range, miles: 9,500 at 15 kt
Complement: 130
Guns: 1 GE/GD 20 mm Vulcan Gatling (can be fitted). 6—12.7 mm MGs.
Radars: Navigation: I-band.
Sonars: Hull-mounted; active search; high frequency.
Helicopters: Platform for 1 light.

Comment: Ordered in 1992. Laid down December 1994. A multipurpose salvage and rescue ship
    which carries a 300 m ROV as well as two LCVPs on davits plus a diving bell for nine men and a
    decompression chamber. Two large hydraulic cranes fore and aft and one towing winch. There
    are also two salvage ships which belong to the Coast Guard.

VERIFIED

CHUNG HAE JIN   10/1998, John Mortimer / 0052558

3 CHUN JEE CLASS (LOGISTIC SUPPORT SHIPS) (AOR)

Name	No	Builders	Launched	Commissioned
CHUN JEE	AO 57	Hyundai, Ulsan	May 1990	Dec 1990
DAE CHUNG	AO 58	Hyundai, Ulsan	Jan 1997	Nov 1997
HWA CHUN	AO 59	Hyundai, Ulsan	July 1997	Mar 1998

Displacement, tons: 7,500 full load
Dimensions, feet (metres): 426.5 × 58.4 × 21.3 (130 × 17.8 × 6.5)
Main machinery: 2 SEMT-Pielstick 16 PA6 V 280 (AO 57) or 12 PC2.5 diesels; 12,800 hp(m)
    (9.4 MW) sustained; 2 shafts
Speed, knots: 20. Range, miles: 4,500 at 15 kt
Cargo capacity: 4,200 tons liquids; 450 tons solids
Guns: 4 Emerlec 30 mm (2 twin) or 2 Breda 40 mm/70. 2 GE/GD 20 mm Vulcan Gatlings.
Radars: Navigation: 2 Racal Decca; I-band.
Helicopters: Platform for 1 medium.

Comment: Chun Jee laid down September 1989. Underway replenishment stations on both sides.
    Helicopter for Vertrep but no hangar. There are three 6 ton lifts. Possibly based on Italian
    'Stromboli' class. Second of class was to have followed on but was eventually ordered together
    with the third in May 1995, to a slightly different design. More may be built when funds are
    available.

UPDATED

CHUN JEE   10/1998, G Toremans / 0052557

DAE CHUNG   10/1997*, Hyundai / 0006557

2 EDENTON CLASS (SALVAGE SHIPS) (ARS/ATS)

Name	No	Builders	Commissioned
PYONG TAEK (ex-*Beaufort*)	ATS 27	Brooke Marine, Lowestoft	22 Jan 1972
KWANG YANG (ex-*Brunswick*)	ATS 28	Brooke Marine, Lowestoft	19 Dec 1972

Displacement, tons: 2,929 full load
Dimensions, feet (metres): 282.6 × 50 × 15.1 *(86.1 × 15.2 × 4.6)*
Main machinery: 4 Paxman 12YJCM diesels; 6,000 hp *(4.48 MW)* sustained; 2 shafts; cp props; bow thruster
Speed, knots: 16. **Range, miles:** 10,000 at 13 kt
Complement: 129 (7 officers)
Guns: 2 Oerlikon 20 mm Mk 68.
Radars: Navigation: Sperry SPS-53; I/J-band.

Comment: Transferred from USA on 29 August 1996. Capable of (1) ocean towing, (2) supporting diver operations to depths of 850 ft, (3) lifting submerged objects weighing as much as 600,000 lb from a depth of 120 ft by static tidal lift or 30,000 lb by dynamic lift, (4) fighting ship fires. Fitted with 10 ton capacity crane forward and 20 ton capacity crane aft. Both recommissioned 28 February 1997.
VERIFIED

PYONG TAEK (US colours)   12/1995, Giorgio Arra

1 TRIALS SUPPORT SHIP (YAG)

Name	No	Builders	Launched	Commissioned
SUNJIN	—	Hyundai, Ulsan	Nov 1992	Apr 1993

Displacement, tons: 320 full load
Dimensions, feet (metres): 113.2 × 49.2 × 12.1 *(34.5 × 15 × 3.7)*
Main machinery: 1 MTU 16V 396 TE74L diesel; 2,680 hp(m) *(2 MW)*; 1 shaft; cp prop; 2 bow thrusters
Speed, knots: 21. **Range, miles:** 600 at 16 kt
Complement: 5 plus 20 scientists
Guns: 1—20 mm Gatling.
Radars: Navigation: I-band.

Comment: Experimental design built by Hyundai. Ordered June 1991, laid down June 1992. Aluminium SWATH hull with dynamic positioning system. Fitted with various trials equipment including an integrated navigation system and torpedo tracking pinger system. VDS and towed arrays. Used by the Defence Development Agency.
UPDATED

SUNJIN   1993*, Hyundai / 0081169

TUGS

Note: In addition to the 'Edenton' class ATS there are a further 10 harbour tugs and numerous port service auxiliaries.

HARBOUR TUG   10/1998, John Mortimer / 0052559

SURVEY SHIPS

PUSAN 801	PUSAN 810	201-204
PUSAN 802	CH'UNGNAM 821	208-209
PUSAN 803	KANGWON 831	215-216
PUSAN 805	PUSAN 806	

Comment: All ships are painted white with a distinctive yellow coloured crest on the funnel. The Hydrographic Service is responsible to the Ministry of Transport.
UPDATED

PUSAN 801   7/1997, van Ginderen Collection / 0012709

203   3/1999*, van Ginderen Collection / 0081170

204   8/1997 / 0012710

MARITIME POLICE

Note: The South Korean Maritime Police operates a number of small ships and several hundred craft including tugs and rescue craft, and has taken over the Coast Guard. The overall colour scheme on all units is a medium blue coloured hull with white superstructure and black block style pennant numbers, with the lettering 'POLICE' in both Korean and English on a prominent space on the superstructure. The colour scheme is further distinguished with a black funnel top where appropriate. Immediately below the funnel top is a thin white band separating a thick lightish green band with the Police logo superimposed. This logo is in gold with the blue and red colours of Korea in the centre. Bell 412 helicopters are being acquired.

1 DAEWOO TYPE (PG)

SUMJINKANG PC 1006

Displacement, tons: 1,650 full load
Dimensions, feet (metres): 275.6 × 34.1 × 11.8 *(84 × 10.4 × 3.6)*
Main machinery: 2 Wärtsilä Nohab 16V25 diesels; 10,000 hp(m) *(7.35 MW)* sustained; 2 shafts
Speed, knots: 21. **Range, miles:** 4,500 at 18 kt
Complement: 57 (7 officers)
Guns: 1—20 mm Sea Vulcan Gatling. 4—12.7 mm MGs.
Radars: Surface search: I-band.

Comment: Ordered in 1997 from Daewoo. Described as a multipurpose patrol ship this is the largest patrol vessel yet built for the Maritime Police. Launched 22 January 1999, and delivered 20 June 1999.
UPDATED

SUMJINKANG   8/1999*, Ships of the World / 0081173

3 MAZINGER CLASS (PG)

PC 1001-PC 1003

Displacement, tons: 1,200 full load
Dimensions, feet (metres): 264.1 × 32.2 × 11.5 *(80.5 × 9.8 × 3.2)*
Main machinery: 2 SEMT-Pielstick 12 PA6 V 280 diesels; 9,600 hp(m) *(7.08 MW)* sustained;
   2 shafts
Speed, knots: 22. **Range, miles:** 7,000 at 18 kt
Complement: 69 (11 officers)
Guns: 1 Bofors 40 mm/70. 4 Oerlikon 20 mm (2 twin).
Radars: Surface search: Raytheon; I-band.

Comment: Ordered 7 November 1980 from Korea Tacoma and Hyundai. *PC 1001* delivered
   29 November 1981. All-welded mild steel construction. Used for offshore surveillance and
   general coast guard duties. *PC 1001* is the Coast Guard Command ship. Only three of this class
   were completed.

VERIFIED

MAZINGER (old colours)   1987, Korea Tacoma

1 HAN KANG CLASS (PG)

HAN KANG PC 1005

Displacement, tons: 1,180 full load
Dimensions, feet (metres): 289.7 × 32.8 × 9.5 *(88.3 × 10 × 2.9)*
Main machinery: CODOG; 1 GE LM 2500 gas turbine; 26,820 hp *(20 MW)* sustained; 2 MTU 12V
   956 TB82 diesels; 6,260 hp(m) *(4.6 MW)* sustained; 3 shafts
Speed, knots: 32. **Range, miles:** 4,000 at 15 kt
Complement: 72 (11 officers)
Guns: 1 OTO Melara 76/62 compact. 1 Bofors 40 mm/70. 2 GE/GD 20 mm Vulcan Gatlings.
Weapons control: Signaal LIOD optronic director.
Radars: Surface search: Raytheon SPS-64(V); I-band.
   Fire control: Signaal WM28; I/J-band.

Comment: Built between May 1984 and December 1985 by Daewoo. Same hull as 'Po Hang' class
   but much more lightly armed. Only one of the class was completed.

UPDATED

HAN KANG   1/1998 * / 0081171

3 HYUNDAI TYPE (PC)

402   403   300

Displacement, tons: 430 full load
Dimensions, feet (metres): 176.2 × 24.3 × 7.9 *(53.7 × 7.4 × 2.4)*
Main machinery: 2 MTU 16V 396 TB83 diesels; 1,990 hp(m) *(1.49 MW)*; 2 shafts; cp props
Speed, knots: 19. **Range, miles:** 2,100 at 17 kt
Complement: 14
Guns: 2 GD/GE 20 mm Vulcan Gatlings. 4—12.7 mm MGs.
Radars: Surface search: Raytheon; I-band.

Comment: Built by Hyundai. First of class delivered in December 1991, second in 1993, third in
   1995. Multipurpose patrol craft.

UPDATED

HYUNDAI 300   3/1996 *, D Swetnam / 0081172

6 SEA DRAGON/WHALE CLASS (PC)

PC 501, 502, 503, 505, 506, 507

Displacement, tons: 640 full load
Dimensions, feet (metres): 199.5 × 26.2 × 8.9 *(60.8 × 8 × 2.7)*
Main machinery: 2 SEMT-Pielstick 12 PA6 V 280 diesels; 9,600 hp(m) *(7.08 MW)* sustained;
   2 shafts
Speed, knots: 24. **Range, miles:** 6,000 at 15 kt
Complement: 40 (7 officers)
Guns: 1 Bofors 40 mm/60. 2 Oerlikon 20 mm. 2 Browning 12.7 mm MGs.
Radars: Navigation: Two sets.

Comment: Delivered 1978-1982 by Hyundai, Korea and Korea Tacoma. Fitted with SATNAV.
   Welded steel hull. Armament varies between ships, one 76 mm gun can be mounted on the
   forecastle. Variant of this class built for Bangladesh and delivered in October 1997.

VERIFIED

SEA DRAGON 507 (old colours)   1987, Korea Tacoma

22 SEA WOLF/SHARK CLASS (PC)

Displacement, tons: 310 full load
Dimensions, feet (metres): 158.1 × 23.3 × 8.2 *(48.2 × 7.1 × 2.5)*
Main machinery: 2 diesels; 7,320 hp(m) *(5.38 MW)*; 2 shafts
Speed, knots: 25. **Range, miles:** 2,400 at 15 kt
Complement: 35 (3 officers)
Guns: 4 Oerlikon 20 mm (2 twin or 1 twin, 2 single). Some have a twin Bofors 40 mm/70 vice the
   twin Oerlikon. 2 Browning 12.7 mm MGs.
Radars: Surface search: I-band.

Comment: First four ordered in 1979-80 from Korea SEC (Sea Shark), Hyundai and Korea Tacoma
   (Sea Wolf). Programme terminated in 1988. Pennant numbers in 200 series up to 277.

UPDATED

SEA WOLF 207   5/1997, van Ginderen Collection / 0012711

4 BUKHANSAN CLASS (PC)

BUKHANSAN 278   CHULMASAN 279   P 281   P 282

Displacement, tons: 380 full load
Dimensions, feet (metres): 174.2 × 24 × 7.2 *(53.1 × 7.3 × 2.2)*
Main machinery: 2 MTU diesels; 8,300 hp(m) *(6.1 MW)* sustained; 2 shafts
Speed, knots: 28. **Range, miles:** 2,500 at 15 kt
Complement: 35 (3 officers)
Guns: 1 Breda 40 mm/70. 1 GE/GD 20 mm Vulcan Gatling. 2—12.7 mm MGs.
Weapons control: Radamec optronic director.
Radars: Surface search: I-band.

Comment: Follow on to 'Sea Wolf' class developed by Hyundai in 1987. Ordered in 1988 from
   Hyundai and Daewoo respectively. First pair in service in 1989, and second pair in 1990.

VERIFIED

CHULMASAN (old colours)   1989, Daewoo

4 HYUNDAI TYPE (PC)

118   **+3**

Displacement, tons: 110 full load
Dimensions, feet (metres): 105.6 × 19.7 × 4.6 *(32.2 × 6 × 1.4)*
Main machinery: 2 diesels; 2 shafts
Speed, knots: 25
Complement: 19
Guns: 1 Rheinmetall 20 mm. 2—12.7 mm MGs.
Radars: Surface search: Furuno; I-band.

Comment: Ordered in 1996 and delivered from June 1997.   *UPDATED*

HYUNDAI 118   *6/1997*, Hyundai /* 0012713

INSHORE PATROL CRAFT (PB)

Displacement, tons: 47 full load
Dimensions, feet (metres): 69.9 × 17.7 × 4.6 *(21.3 × 5.4 × 1.4)*
Main machinery: 2 diesels; 1,800 hp(m) *(1.32 MW)*; 2 shafts
Speed, knots: 22. **Range, miles:** 400 at 12 kt
Complement: 11
Guns: 1 Rheinmetall 20 mm. 3—12.7 mm MGs.
Radars: Surface search: Furuno; I-band.

Comment: Details are for the largest design of patrol craft. There are numbers of this type of vessel used for inshore patrol work. All Police craft have P pennant numbers. Armaments vary. Customs craft have double numbers.   *VERIFIED*

P 01   *7/1997, van Ginderen Collection /* 0012712

CUSTOM 71-810   *6/1996, D Swetnam*

1 SALVAGE SHIP (ARS)

Name	No	Builders	Launched	Commissioned
TAE PUNG YANG I	3001	Hyundai, Ulsan	Oct 1991	18 Feb 1993

Displacement, tons: 3,200 standard; 4,300 full load
Dimensions, feet (metres): 343.5 × 49.2 × 17 *(104.7 × 15 × 5.2)*
Main machinery: 4 Ssangyoung MAN Burmeister & Wain 16V 28/32 diesels; 4,800 hp(m) *(3.53 MW)*; 2 shafts; cp props; bow and stern thrusters
Speed, knots: 21. **Range, miles:** 8,500 at 15 kt
Complement: 121
Guns: 1 GD/GE 20 mm Vulcan Gatling. 6—12.7 mm MGs.
Radars: Navigation: I-band.
Helicopters: 1 light.

Comment: Laid down February 1991. Has a helicopter deck and hangar, an ROV capable of diving to 300 m and a firefighting capability. Dynamic positioning system. Can be used for cable laying. Operates for the Marine Police.   *UPDATED*

TAE PUNG YANG I   *1993*, Hyundai /* 0081174

1 SALVAGE SHIP (ARS)

Name	No	Builders	Commissioned
JAEMIN I	1501	Daewoo, Okpo	28 Dec 1992

Displacement, tons: 2,072 full load
Dimensions, feet (metres): 254.6 × 44.3 × 13.8 *(77.6 × 13.5 × 4.2)*
Main machinery: 2 MTU diesels; 8,000 hp(m) *(5.88 MW)*; 2 shafts; cp props
Speed, knots: 18. **Range, miles:** 4,500 at 12 kt
Complement: 92
Guns: 1 GD/GE 20 mm Vulcan Gatling.
Radars: Navigation: I-band.

Comment: Ordered in 1990. Fitted with diving equipment and has a four point mooring system. Carries two LCVPs.   *VERIFIED*

JAEMIN I   *1992, Daewoo*

1 SALVAGE SHIP (ARS/PG)

Name	No	Builders	Commissioned
TAE PUNG YANG II	3002	Hyundai, Ulsan	Nov 1988

Displacement, tons: 3,900 standard
Dimensions, feet (metres): 362.5 × 50.5 × 16.1 *(110.5 × 15.4 × 4.9)*
Main machinery: 2 diesels; 2 shafts
Speed, knots: 18
Complement: 120
Guns: 2—20 mm Vulcan Gatlings. 6—12.7 mm MGs.
Radars: Surface search: I-band.
Helicopters: Platform for 1 large.

Comment: Ordered from Hyundai in mid-1996. Also used for SAR operations.   *UPDATED*

TAE PUNG YANG II   *8/1999*, Ships of the World /* 0081175

1 SALVAGE SHIP (ARS)

Name	No	Builders	Launched	Commissioned
JAEMIN II	1502	Hyundai, Ulsan	15 July 1995	Apr 1996

Displacement, tons: 2,500 full load
Dimensions, feet (metres): 288.7 × 47.6 × 15.1 *(88 × 14.5 × 4.6)*
Main machinery: 2 MTU diesels; 12,662 hp(m) *(9.31 MW)*; 2 shafts; Kamewa cp props; bow and stern thrusters
Speed, knots: 20. **Range, miles:** 4,500 at 15 kt
Complement: 81
Guns: 1 GE/GD 20 mm Vulcan Gatling.
Radars: Navigation: I-band.

Comment: Ordered in December 1993 for Maritime Police. A general purpose salvage ship capable of towing, firefighting, supply or patrol duties.   *UPDATED*

JAEMIN II   *8/1999*, Ships of the World /* 0081176

KUWAIT

Headquarters Appointments	Personnel	Aviation	Bases	Mercantile Marine
Commander of the Navy: Colonel Ahmed Yousuf Al Mulla *Director of Coast Guard:* Lieutenant Colonel Sayid Al-Buaijan	2000: 2,700 (including 500 Coast Guard)	The Air Force operates four Aerospatiale AS 332F Super Puma helicopters armed with Exocet AM 39 ASMs and 40 F/A-18 Hornets.	Navy: Ras Al Qalayah Coast Guard: Shuwaikh, Umm Al-Hainan, Al-Bida	*Lloyd's Register of Shipping:* 202 vessels of 2,456,457 tons gross

PATROL FORCES

Note: There is a requirement for up to four 88 m OPVs armed with SSMs.

8 UM ALMARADIM (COMBATTANTE I) CLASS (PCFG)

Name	No	Builders	Launched	Commissioned
UM ALMARADIM	P 3711	CMN, Cherbourg	27 Feb 1997	31 July 1998
OUHA	P 3713	CMN, Cherbourg	29 May 1997	31 July 1998
FAILAKA	P 3715	CMN, Cherbourg	29 Aug 1997	19 Dec 1998
MASKAN	P 3717	CMN, Cherbourg	6 Jan 1998	19 Dec 1998
AL-AHMADI	P 3719	CMN, Cherbourg	2 Apr 1998	1 July 1999
ALFAHAHEEL	P 3721	CMN, Cherbourg	16 June 1998	1 July 1999
AL YARMOUK	P 3723	CMN, Cherbourg	3 Mar 1999	May 2000
GAROH	P 3725	CMN, Cherbourg	June 1999	May 2000

Displacement, tons: 245 full load
Dimensions, feet (metres): 137.8 oa; 121.4 wl × 26.9 × 6.2 *(42; 37 × 8.2 × 1.9)*
Main machinery: 2 MTU 16V 538 TB93 diesels; 4,000 hp(m) *(2.94 MW)*; 2 Kamewa water-jets
Speed, knots: 30. **Range, miles:** 1,350 at 14 kt
Complement: 29 (5 officers)

Missiles: SSM: 4 BAe Sea Skua (2 twin). Semi-active radar homing to 15 km *(8.1 n miles)* at 0.9 Mach.
SAM: Sadral sextuple launcher fitted for only.
Guns: 1 Otobreda 40 mm/70; 120 rds/min to 12.5 km *(6.8 n miles)*; weight of shell 0.96 kg.
1 Giat 20 mm M 621. 2—12.7 mm MGs.
Countermeasures: Decoys: 2 Dagaie Mk 2 chaff launchers fitted for only.
ESM: Thomson-CSF DR 3000 S1; intercept.
Combat data systems: Thomson-CSF TAVITAC NT; Link Y.
Weapons control: CS Defence Najir Mk 2 optronic director.
Radars: Air/surface search: Thomson-CSF MRR; 3D; C-band.
Fire control: BAe Seaspray Mk 3; I/J-band (for SSM).
Navigation: Litton Marine 20V90; I-band.

Programmes: Contract signed with CMN Cherbourg on 27 March 1995. First steel cut 9 June 1995. Names are taken from former Kuwaiti patrol craft.
Structure: Late decisions were made on the missile system which has been fitted in the last pair on build and will be to the remainder from 2000. Provision is also made for Simbad SAM and Dagaie decoy launchers, which may be fitted later. Positions of smaller guns are uncertain.
Operational: Training done in France. The aim is to have 10 crews capable of manning the eight ships. First four arrived in the Gulf in mid-August 1999, second four to arrive in mid-2000.
UPDATED

FAILAKA   *12/1998*, CMN Cherbourg /* 0075870

AL-AHMADI   *7/1999*, CMN Cherbourg /* 0075871

1 TNC 45 TYPE (FAST ATTACK CRAFT—MISSILE) (PCFG)

Name	No	Builders	Commissioned
AL SANBOUK	P 4505	Lürssen, Vegesack	26 Apr 1984

Displacement, tons: 255 full load
Dimensions, feet (metres): 147.3 × 23 × 7.5 *(44.9 × 7 × 2.3)*
Main machinery: 4 MTU 16V 538 TB92 diesels; 13,640 hp(m) *(10 MW)* sustained; 4 shafts
Speed, knots: 41. **Range, miles:** 1,800 at 16 kt
Complement: 35 (5 officers)

Missiles: SSM: 4 Aerospatiale MM 40 Exocet; inertial cruise; active radar homing to 70 km *(40 n miles)* at 0.9 Mach; warhead 165 kg; sea-skimmer.
Guns: 1 OTO Melara 3 in *(76 mm)*/62 compact; 85 rds/min to 16 km *(8.6 n miles)* anti-surface; 12 km *(6.5 n miles)* anti-aircraft; weight of shell 6 kg.
2 Breda 40 mm/70 (twin); 300 rds/min to 12.5 km *(6.6 n miles)*; weight of shell 0.96 kg.
Countermeasures: Decoys: CSEE Dagaie; IR flares and chaff; H/J-band.
ESM: Racal Cutlass; intercept.
Weapons control: PEAB 9LV 228 system; Link Y; CSEE Lynx optical sight.
Radars: Air/surface search: Ericsson Sea Giraffe 50HC; G/H-band.
Fire control: Philips 9LV 200; J-band.
Navigation: Decca TM 1226C; I-band.

Programmes: Six ordered from Lürssen in 1980 and delivered in 1983-84.
Operational: *Al Sanbouk* escaped to Bahrain when the Iraqis invaded in August 1990, but the rest of this class was taken over by the Iraqi Navy, and either sunk or severely damaged by Allied forces in February 1991. The ship was refitted by Lürssen in 1995.
VERIFIED

AL SANBOUK   *4/1998 /* 0052560

1 FPB 57 TYPE (FAST ATTACK CRAFT—MISSILE) (PCFG)

Name	No	Builders	Commissioned
ISTIQLAL	P 5702	Lürssen, Vegesack	9 Aug 1983

Displacement, tons: 410 full load
Dimensions, feet (metres): 190.6 × 24.9 × 8.9 *(58.1 × 7.6 × 2.7)*
Main machinery: 4 MTU 16V 956 TB91 diesels; 15,000 hp(m) *(11 MW)* sustained; 4 shafts
Speed, knots: 36. **Range, miles:** 1,300 at 30 kt
Complement: 40 (5 officers)

Missiles: SSM: 4 Aerospatiale MM 40 Exocet; inertial cruise; active radar homing to 70 km *(40 n miles)* at 0.9 Mach; warhead 165 kg; sea-skimmer.
Guns: 1 OTO Melara 3 in *(76 mm)*/62 compact; 85 rds/min to 16 km *(8.6 n miles)* anti-surface; 12 km *(6.5 n miles)* anti-aircraft; weight of shell 6 kg.
2 Breda 40 mm/70 (twin); 300 rds/min to 12.5 km *(6.6 n miles)*; weight of shell 0.96 kg.
Mines: Fitted for minelaying.
Countermeasures: Decoys: CSEE Dagaie trainable mounting; automatic dispenser; IR flares and chaff; H/J-band.
ESM: Racal Cutlass; radar intercept.
ECM: Racal Cygnus; jammer.
Weapons control: PEAB 9LV 228 system; Link Y; CSEE Lynx optical sight.
Radars: Surface search: Marconi S 810 (after radome); I-band; range 43 km *(25 n miles)*.
Navigation: Decca TM 1226C; I-band.
Fire control: Philips 9LV 200; J-band.

Programmes: Two ordered from Lürssen in 1980.
Operational: *Istiqlal* escaped to Bahrain when the Iraqis invaded in August 1990. The second of this class was captured and sunk in February 1991. *Istiqlal* was laid up in 1997 and is probably to be scrapped.
UPDATED

ISTIQLAL   *6/1993* /* 0081177

4 INTTISAR (OPV 310) CLASS (PC)

Name	No	Builders	Commissioned
INTTISAR	P 301	Australian Shipbuilding Industries	20 Jan 1993
AMAN	P 302	Australian Shipbuilding Industries	20 Jan 1993
MAIMON	P 303	Australian Shipbuilding Industries	7 Aug 1993
MOBARK	P 304	Australian Shipbuilding Industries	7 Aug 1993

Displacement, tons: 150 full load
Dimensions, feet (metres): 103.3 oa; 88.9 wl × 21.3 × 6.6 *(31.5; 27.1 × 6.5 × 2)*
Main machinery: 2 MTU 16V 396 TB94 diesels; 5,800 hp(m) *(4.26 MW)* sustained; 2 shafts; 1 MTU 8V 183 TE62 diesel; 750 hp(m) *(550 kW)* maximum; 1 Hamilton 422 water-jet
Speed, knots: 28. **Range, miles:** 300 at 28 kt
Complement: 11 (3 officers)
Guns: 1 Oerlikon 20 mm. 1—12.7 mm MG.
Radars: Surface search: 2 Racal Decca; I-band.

Comment: First two ordered from Australian Shipbuilding Industries in 1991. Second pair ordered in July 1992. Steel hulls, aluminium superstructure. The third engine drives a small water-jet to provide a loiter capability. Carries an RIB. Used by the Coast Guard.
UPDATED

AMAN *1992 *, Australian Shipbuilding Industries /* 0081178

2 AL SHAHEED CLASS (PC)

Name	No	Builders	Commissioned
AL SHAHEED	P 305	OCEA, Les Sables d'Olonne	July 1997
BAYAN	P 306	OCEA, Les Sables d'Olonne	Apr 1999

Displacement, tons: 104 full load
Dimensions, feet (metres): 109.3 × 23 × 4 *(33.3 × 7 × 1.2)*
Main machinery: 2 MTU 12V 396 TE94; 4,352 hp(m) *(3.2 MW)* sustained; 2 shafts
Speed, knots: 30. **Range, miles:** 360 at 25 kt
Complement: 11 (3 officers)
Guns: 1 Oerlikon 20 mm. 2—12.7 mm MGs.
Radars: Surface search: Racal Decca 20V 90 TA; E/F-band.
Navigation: Racal Decca Bridgemaster ARPA; I-band.

Comment: Built by OCEA, France to FPB 100K design. Both craft are operated by the Coast Guard.
UPDATED

AL SHAHEED *10/1997 *, Ships of the World /* 0012718

30 AL-SHAALI TYPE (INSHORE PATROL CRAFT) (PB)

Comment: Ten 33 ft and 23 28 ft patrol craft built by Al-Shaali Marine, Dubai, and delivered in June 1992. Also used by UAE Coast Guard. More Rapid Intervention patrol craft are to be acquired in due course.
VERIFIED

12 MANTA CLASS (INSHORE PATROL CRAFT) (PB)

1B 1501-1B 1523

Displacement, tons: 10 full load
Dimensions, feet (metres): 45.9 × 12.5 × 2.3 *(14 × 3.8 × 0.7)*
Main machinery: 2 Caterpillar 3208 diesels; 810 hp(m) *(595 kW)* sustained; 2 shafts
Speed, knots: 40. **Range, miles:** 180 at 35 kt
Complement: 4
Guns: 3 Herstal M2HB 12.7 mm MGs.
Radars: Surface search: Furuno; I-band.

Comment: Ordered in September 1992 from Simmoneau Marine and delivered in 1993. Aluminium construction. This version has two inboard engines. Pennant numbers are in odd number sequence. May be replaced by more powerful craft from Simmoneau in due course.
UPDATED

MANTA 1501 *11/1996 * /* 0012719

4 COUGAR ENFORCER 40 CLASS (INSHORE PATROL CRAFT) (PB)

Displacement, tons: 5.7 full load
Dimensions, feet (metres): 40 × 9 × 2.1 *(12.2 × 2.8 × 0.8)*
Main machinery: 2 Sabre 380 S diesels; 760 hp(m) *(559 kW)*; 2 Arneson ASD 8 surface drives; 2 shafts
Speed, knots: 45. **Range, miles:** 250 at 35 kt
Complement: 4
Guns: 1—12.7 mm MG.
Radars: Surface search: Koden; I-band.

Comment: First one completed in July 1996 for the Coastguard by Cougar Marine, Warsash. The craft has a V monohull design.
UPDATED

ENFORCER 40 *7/1996 *, Cougar Marine /* 0081179

17 + (6) COUGAR TYPE (INSHORE PATROL CRAFT) (PB)

Comment: Three Cat 900 (32 ft) and six Predator 1100 (35 ft) all powered by two Yamaha outboards (400 hp(m) *(294 kW)*). Four Type 1200 (38 ft) and four Type 1300 (41 ft) all powered by two Sabre diesels (760 hp(m) *(559 kW)*). All based on the high-performance planing hull developed for racing, and acquired in 1991-92. Most have a 7.62 mm MG and a Kroden I-band radar. Used by the Coast Guard. Most have K numbers on the side. More may be ordered.
UPDATED

COUGAR 1200 *1991 *, Cougar Marine /* 0081180

AUXILIARIES

Notes: (1) There are some unarmed craft with Sawahil numbers which are not naval.
(2) A training ship is required.

2 AL TAHADDY CLASS (LCM/AKL)

Name	No	Builders	Commissioned
AL SOUMOOD	L 401	Singapore SBEC	July 1994
AL TAHADDY	L 402	Singapore SBEC	July 1994

Displacement, tons: 215 full load
Dimensions, feet (metres): 141.1 × 32.8 × 6.2 *(43 × 10 × 1.9)*
Main machinery: 2 MTU diesels; 2 shafts
Speed, knots: 13
Complement: 12
Military lift: 80 tons
Radars: Navigation: Racal Decca; I-band.

Comment: Ordered in 1993 and launched on 15 April 1994. Multipurpose supply ships with cargo tanks for fuel, fresh water, refrigerated stores and containers on the main deck. Has 3 ton crane. Capable of beaching. Used by the Coast Guard and have replaced the old Loadmasters.

VERIFIED

1 SUPPORT SHIP (AG)

QARUH S 5509

Measurement, tons: 545 dwt
Dimensions, feet (metres): 181.8 × 31.5 × 6.6 *(55.4 × 9.6 × 2)*
Main machinery: 2 diesels; 2,400 hp(m) *(1.76 MW)*; 2 shafts
Speed, knots: 9
Complement: 40
Guns: 2—12.7 mm MGs.
Radars: Navigation: Racal Decca; I-band.

Comment: This is a 'Sawahil' class oil rig replenishment and accommodation ship which was built in South Korea in 1986 and taken on by the Coast Guard in 1990. She escaped to Bahrain during the Iraqi invasion, and is back in service. High-level helicopter platform aft. Used as a utility transport. Refitted in 1996/97.

UPDATED

AL TAHADDY   *1/1999, Maritime Phototgraphic /* 0053294

QARUH   *11/1997*, Kuwait Navy /* 0012721

LATVIA
LATVIJAS JŪRAS SPĒKI

Headquarters Appointments

Commander of the Navy:
  Captain Ilmārs Lešinskis

Bases

Liepāja, Ventspils, Riga

Personnel

2000: 800 Navy (including Coast Guard)

Coast Guard

These ships have a diagonal thick white and thin white line on the hull, and have KA numbers. They operate as part of the Navy.

Mercantile Marine

Lloyd's Register of Shipping:
  174 vessels of 118,118 tons gross

DELETIONS

Patrol Forces		Auxiliaries	
1998	*Sams*	1999	*Varma* (civilian)

PATROL FORCES

1 STORM CLASS (PCF)

Name	No	Builders	Commissioned
BULTA (ex-*Traust*)	P 04 (ex-P 973)	Bergens Mek Verksteder	1967

Displacement, tons: 135 full load
Dimensions, feet (metres): 120 × 20 × 5 *(36.5 × 6.1 × 1.5)*
Main machinery: 2 MTU MB 872A diesels; 7,200 hp(m) *(5.3 MW)* sustained; 2 shafts
Speed, knots: 32
Complement: 20 (4 officers)
Guns: 1 Bofors 40 mm/60.
Radars: Surface search: Racal Decca TM 1226; I-band.

Comment: Disarmed and acquired from Norway on 13 December 1994 as a gun patrol craft. Recommissioned 1 February 1995 at Liepāja. 40 mm gun fitted aft in 1998. Others of the class given to Lithuania and Estonia.

UPDATED

2 OSA I CLASS (TYPE 205) (PCF)

Name	No	Builders	Commissioned
ZIBENS (ex-*Joseph Schares*)	P 01 (ex-753)	Leningrad	6 Oct 1971
HEINDRICH DOR (ex-*Fritz Gast*)	P 02 (ex-714)	Leningrad	3 Sep 1971

Displacement, tons: 210 full load
Dimensions, feet (metres): 126.6 × 24.9 × 8.8 *(38.6 × 7.6 × 2.7)*
Main machinery: 3 M 503A diesels; 8,025 hp(m) *(5.9 MW)* sustained; 3 shafts
Speed, knots: 35. **Range, miles:** 400 at 34 kt
Complement: 26 (4 officers)
Guns: 2 Wrobel 23 mm Zu-23-2M (twin). 2—30 mm/65 AK 230 (twin).
Radars: Surface search: Square Tie; I-band.

Comment: Three former GDR vessels paid off in 1990 and transferred from Germany on 30 August 1993. All weapon systems were removed before transfer, and the vessels taken to Liepāja for refit and modernisation. First one recommissioned 7 August 1994 at Liepāja. Second one laid up, and the third was cannibalised for spares and then scrapped. Two more of the class transferred June 1995 and one of these has replaced the one laid up in 1993. The second one has not yet become operational and may never go to sea. All the others have been cannibalised. New guns fitted.

UPDATED

BULTA   *6/1999*, J Cislak /* 0081181

ZIBENS   *6/1998, J Cislak /* 0052565

2 RIBNADZOR-4 CLASS (PC)

SPULGA KA 02 (ex-KA 102)   **COMETA** KA 03 (ex-KA 103)

Displacement, tons: 160 full load
Dimensions, feet (metres): 114.8 × 22 × 5.6 *(35 × 6.7 × 1.7)*
Main machinery: 1 40 DMM3 diesel; 2,200 hp(m) *(1.62 MW)*; 1 shaft
Speed, knots: 15
Complement: 17 (3 officers)
Guns: 1—12.7 mm MG.
Radars: Surface search: MIUS; I-band.

Comment: Ex-fishing vessels built in 1974 (KA 02), and 1978 (KA 03) and converted in 1992. *Spulga* recommissioned 5 May 1992 at Liepāja and *Cometa* at Bolderaja. Belong to the Coast Guard. *Cometa* refitted in 1998.   **UPDATED**

COMETA   *8/1994*, E & M Laursen /* 0081182

5 KBV 236 CLASS (PB)

KRISTAPS KA 01 (ex-KBV 244)   **SAULE** KA 08 (ex-KBV 256)
GAISMA KA 06 (ex-KBV 249)   **KLINTS** KA 09 (ex-KBV 250)
AUSMA KA 07 (ex-KBV 260)

Displacement, tons: 17 full load
Dimensions, feet (metres): 63 × 13.1 × 4.3 *(19.2 × 4 × 1.3)*
Main machinery: 2 Volvo Penta TMD 100C diesels; 526 hp(m) *(387 kW)*; 2 shafts
Speed, knots: 20
Complement: 3 (1 officer)
Radars: Navigation: Raytheon or Furuno; I-band.

Comment: Former Swedish Coast Guard vessel built in 1964. First one recommissioned 5 March 1993, second pair 9 November 1993 and last pair 27 April 1994. KA 01, 06 and 09 are based at Bolderaja, 07 at Liepāja and 08 at Ventspils. Not all are identical. All belong to Coast Guard.
                                                          UPDATED

SAULE   *3/1999* /* 0081183

KRISTAPS   *6/1999*, Maritime Photographic /* 0081184

3 HARBOUR PATROL CRAFT (PB)

KA 10   KA 11   GRANATA KA 12

Displacement, tons: 9.6 full load *(KA 10-11)*; 5.4 full load *(KA 12)*
Dimensions, feet (metres): 41.3 × 10.5 × 2 *(12.6 × 3.2 × 0.6)*
Main machinery: 1 3D6C diesel; 150 hp(m) *(110 kW)*; 1 shaft
Speed, knots: 13
Complement: 2
Radars: Navigation: Furuno; I-band.

Comment: Former USSR craft. *KA 10* and *11* were 'Sverdlov' class cruiser boats. *KA 12* is an ex-Border Guard launch of 9 m with a 300 hp(m) *(220 kW)* engine and a speed of 18 kt. All acquired in 1993-94. All belong to Coast Guard.   **UPDATED**

KA 11   *9/1996, Hartmut Ehlers*

MINE WARFARE FORCES

1 LINDAU (TYPE 331) CLASS (MINEHUNTER) (MHC)

Name	No	Builders	Commissioned
NEMĒJS (ex-*Völklingen*)	M 03 (ex-M 1087)	Burmester, Bremen	21 May 1960

Displacement, tons: 463 full load
Dimensions, feet (metres): 154.5 × 27.2 × 9.8 (9.2 Troika) *(47.1 × 8.3 × 3) (2.8)*
Main machinery: 2 MTU MD 871 UM/1D diesels; 4,000 hp(m) *(2.94 MW)*; 2 shafts
Speed, knots: 16.5. **Range, miles:** 850 at 16.5 kt
Complement: 45 (9 officers)
Guns: 1 Bofors 40 mm/70.
Radars: Navigation: Raytheon, SPS 64; I-band.
Sonars: Plessey 193 m; minehunting; high frequency (100/300 kHz).

Comment: Acquired in June 1999 from Germany. Recommissioned 1 October 1999. Hull is of wooden construction. Converted to minehunter 1979. PAP 105 ROV fitted. Based at Lepāja.
                                                          NEW ENTRY

NEMĒJS   *10/1999*, Latvian Navy /* 0081185

2 KONDOR II (TYPE 89.2) CLASS (MINESWEEPERS) (MSC)

Name	No	Builders	Commissioned
VIESTURS (ex-*Kamenz*)	M 01 (ex-351)	Peenewerft, Wolgast	24 July 1971
IMANTA (ex-*Röbel*)	M 02 (ex-324)	Peenewerft, Wolgast	1 Dec 1971

Displacement, tons: 410 full load
Dimensions, feet (metres): 186 × 24.6 × 7.9 *(56.7 × 7.5 × 2.4)*
Main machinery: 2 Type 40D diesels; 4,408 hp(m) *(3.24 MW)*; 2 shafts; cp props
Speed, knots: 17
Complement: 31 (6 officers)
Guns: 2 Wrobel ZU 23-2MR 23 mm (twin). 2 FK 20 20 mm.
Radars: Surface search: Racal Decca; I-band.

Comment: Former GDR vessels transferred from Germany on 30 August 1993. Weapons and minesweeping equipment were removed on transfer. New guns have been fitted and ex-German 'Shultz' class minesweeping gear was installed in 1997. Both recommissioned in April 1994. Based at Liepāja.   **UPDATED**

VIESTURS   *6/1999*, L-G Nilsson /* 0081187

VIESTURS   *5/1999* /* 0081186

AUXILIARIES

1 GOLIAT CLASS (TYPE 667R) (ATA)

PERKONS A 18 (ex-*H 18*)

Displacement, tons: 150 full load
Dimensions, feet (metres): 70.2 × 20 × 8.5 *(21.4 × 6.1 × 2.6)*
Main machinery: 1 Buckau-Wolf 8NVD diesel; 300 hp(m) *(221 kW)*; 1 shaft
Speed, knots: 9
Complement: 8 (2 officers)

Comment: Built at Gdynia in the 1960s and transferred from Poland 16 November 1993 at Liepāja.   *UPDATED*

1 NYRYAT 1 CLASS (DIVING TENDER) (YDT)

LIDAKA (ex-*Gefests*) A 51 (ex-A 101)

Displacement, tons: 92 standard; 116 full load
Dimensions, feet (metres): 93.8 × 17.1 × 5.6 *(28.6 × 5.2 × 1.7)*
Main machinery: 1 6CSP 28/3C diesel; 450 hp(m) *(331 kW)*; 1 shaft
Speed, knots: 11. **Range, miles:** 1,500 at 10 kt
Complement: 18 (3 officers)
Radars: Navigation: SNN-7; I-band.

Comment: Former SAR vessel acquired in 1992. Based at Liepāja.

UPDATED

PERKONS   *4/1995, Hartmut Ehlers*

LIDAKA   *9/1996, Hartmut Ehlers*

LEBANON

Headquarters Appointments	Personnel	Bases	Mercantile Marine
Naval Commander: Rear Admiral Georges Maalouf	2000: 1,250 (47 officers)	Beirut, Jounieh	*Lloyd's Register of Shipping:* 106 vessels of 322,196 tons gross

PATROL FORCES

2 FRENCH EDIC CLASS (LST)

Name	No	Builders	Commissioned
SOUR	21	SFCN, Villeneuve la Garonne	28 Mar 1985
DAMOUR	22	SFCN, Villeneuve la Garonne	28 Mar 1985

Displacement, tons: 670 full load
Dimensions, feet (metres): 193.5 × 39.2 × 4.2 *(59 × 12 × 1.3)*
Main machinery: 2 SACM MGO 175 V12 M1 diesels; 1,200 hp(m) *(882 kW)*; 2 shafts
Speed, knots: 10. **Range, miles:** 1,800 at 9 kt
Complement: 20 (2 officers)
Military lift: 96 troops; 11 trucks or 8 APCs
Guns: 2 Oerlikon 20 mm. 1—81 mm mortar. 2—12.7 mm MGs. 1—7.62 mm MG.
Radars: Navigation: Decca; I-band.

Comment: Both were damaged in early 1990 but repaired in 1991 and are fully operational. Used by the Marine Regiment formed in 1997.

UPDATED

BATROUN   *6/1999*, Lebanese Navy /* 0081188

5 ATTACKER CLASS (COASTAL PATROL CRAFT) (PC)

TRABLOUS 301	**BEIRUT** 305	**JOUNIEH** 307
JBEIL 304	**SAÏDA** 306	

Displacement, tons: 38 full load
Dimensions, feet (metres): 65.6 × 17 × 4.9 *(20 × 5.2 × 1.5)*
Main machinery: 2 Detroit 12V-71TA diesels; 840 hp *(616 kW)* sustained; 2 shafts
Speed, knots: 21. **Range, miles:** 650 at 14 kt
Complement: 10 (1 officer)
Guns: 3—12.7 mm MGs.
Radars: Surface search: Racal Decca 1216; I-band.

Comment: Built at Cowes and Southampton, and commissioned in March 1983. First three transferred from UK 17 July 1992 after serving as patrol craft for the British base in Cyprus. The other two were acquired in 1993. Former names, *Attacker, Hunter, Striker, Chaser* and *Fencer*. All are operational.

UPDATED

DAMOUR   *6/1999*, Lebanese Navy /* 0012725

2 TRACKER Mk 2 CLASS (COASTAL PATROL CRAFT) (PC)

SARAFAND (ex-*Swift*) 302   **BATROUN** (ex-*Safeguard*) 303

Displacement, tons: 31 full load
Dimensions, feet (metres): 63.3 × 16.4 × 4.9 *(19.3 × 5 × 1.5)*
Main machinery: 2 Detroit 12V-71TA diesels; 840 hp *(616 kW)* sustained; 2 shafts
Speed, knots: 25. **Range, miles:** 650 at 20 kt
Complement: 11 (1 officer)
Guns: 3—12.7 mm MGs.
Radars: Surface search: Racal Decca 2690; I-band.

Comment: Two ex-UK Customs Craft first commissioned in 1979 and acquired by Lebanon in late 1993. Fitted with a twin 23 mm gun after transfer but this may have been replaced by a 12.7 mm MG.

UPDATED

TRABLOUS   *6/1998, Lebanese Navy /* 0052570

13 INSHORE PATROL CRAFT (PB/CSB)

Displacement, tons: 6 full load
Dimensions, feet (metres): 26.9 × 8.2 × 2 *(8.2 × 2.5 × 0.6)*
Main machinery: 2 Sabre 212 diesels; 212 hp(m) *(156 kW)*; 2 water-jets
Speed, knots: 22. **Range, miles:** 154 at 22 kt
Complement: 3
Guns: 3—5.56 mm MGs.

Comment: M-boot type used by the US Army on German rivers and 27 were transferred in January 1994. Called Combat Support Boats, there are 13 operational and 14 laid up.   ***UPDATED***

CUSTOMS

2 TRACKER Mk 2 CLASS

LEBANON II   **ARZ II**

Displacement, tons: 31 full load
Dimensions, feet (metres): 63.3 × 16.4 × 4.9 *(19.3 × 5 × 1.5)*
Main machinery: 2 Detroit 12V-71TA diesels; 840 hp *(616 kW)* sustained; 2 shafts
Speed, knots: 25. **Range, miles:** 650 at 20 kt
Complement: 11 (1 officer)
Guns: 2—7.62 mm MGs.
Radars: Surface search: Racal Decca 2690; I-band.

Comment: Built in 1980. Transferred from the Navy to Customs in 1995. 23 mm gun replaced by a 7.62 mm MG.   ***UPDATED***

CSB   6/1998, Lebanese Navy / 0052571

LEBANON II   6/1999*, Lebanese Navy / 0081189

LIBYA

Headquarters Appointments

Chief of Staff Navy:
    Captain Muhammad al Shaybani Ahmad al Suwaihili

Bases

Naval HQ at Al Khums.
Operating Ports at Tripoli, Darnah (Derna) and Benghazi.
Naval bases at Al Khums and Tobruq.
Submarine base at Ras Hilal.
Naval air station at Al Girdabiyah.
Naval infantry battalion at Sidi Bilal.

Personnel

(a) 2000: 7,500 officers and ratings, including Coast Guard
(b) Voluntary service

Coast Defence

Batteries of truck-mounted SS-C-3 Styx missiles.

Mercantile Marine

Lloyd's Register of Shipping:
    142 vessels of 438,871 tons gross

General

Specialist teams in unconventional warfare are a threat and almost any Libyan vessel can lay mines, but overall operational effectiveness is very low, not least because of poor maintenance and stores support. Sanctions imposed by the UN in April 1992 were reported as 'destroying' the Fleet, but the situation improved in late 1995 with mostly Ukrainian technicians being hired on maintenance contracts. More improvements were reported in 1998. Weapon systems are rarely exercised.

SUBMARINES

2 FOXTROT CLASS (TYPE 641) (SS)

AL KHYBER 315   **AL HUNAIN** 316

Displacement, tons: 1,950 surfaced; 2,475 dived
Dimensions, feet (metres): 299.5 × 24.6 × 19.7 *(91.3 × 7.5 × 6)*
Main machinery: Diesel-electric; 3 Type 37-D diesels (1 × 2,700 and 2 × 1,350); 6,000 hp(m) *(4.4 MW)*; 3 motors; 5,400 hp(m) *(3.97 MW)*; 3 shafts; 1 auxiliary motor; 140 hp(m) *(103 kW)*
Speed, knots: 16 surfaced; 15 dived
Range, miles: 20,000 at 8 kt surfaced; 380 at 2 kt dived
Complement: 75 (8 officers)

Torpedoes: 10—21 in *(533 mm)* (6 bow, 4 stern) tubes. SAET-60; passive homing to 15 km *(8.1 n miles)* at 40 kt; warhead 400 kg, and SET-65E; active/passive homing to 15 km *(8.1 n miles)* at 40 kt; warhead 205 kg or Type 53-56. Total of 22 torpedoes.
Mines: 44 in place of torpedoes.
Countermeasures: ESM: Stop Light; radar warning.
Radars: Surface search: Snoop Tray; I-band.
Sonars: Herkules; hull-mounted; active; medium frequency.
    Feniks; hull-mounted; passive.

Programmes: Six of the class originally transferred from USSR; this last one in April 1982.
Operational: Libyan crews trained in the USSR and much of the maintenance was done by Russian personnel. No routine patrols have been seen since 1984. *Al Hunain* is being refitted with Montenegran support with the aim of restoring two operational submarines by mid-2000. *Al Khyber* is reported as conducting very occasional days at sea on the surface.   ***UPDATED***

FOXTROT   6/1992*, van Ginderen Collection / 0081190

FRIGATES

Note: The *Dat Assawari* F 211 is a training hulk alongside in Tripoli.

2 KONI (TYPE 1159) CLASS (FFG)

AL HANI F 212   **AL QIRDABIYAH** F 213

Displacement, tons: 1,440 standard; 1,900 full load
Dimensions, feet (metres): 316.3 × 41.3 × 11.5
(96.4 × 12.6 × 3.5)
Main machinery: CODAG; 1 SGW, Nikolayev, M8B gas turbine
(centre shaft); 18,000 hp(m) *(13.25 MW)* sustained; 2 Russki
B-68 diesels; 15,820 hp(m) *(11.63 MW)* sustained; 3 shafts
Speed, knots: 27 on gas; 22 on diesel
Range, miles: 1,800 at 14 kt
Complement: 120

Missiles: SSM: 4 Soviet SS-N-2C Styx (2 twin) launchers ❶;
active radar/IR homing to 83 km *(45 n miles)* at 0.9 Mach;
warhead 513 kg; sea-skimmer at end of run.
SAM: SA-N-4 Gecko twin launcher ❷; semi-active radar homing
to 15 km *(8 n miles)* at 2.5 Mach; altitude 9.1-3,048 m *(29.5-
10,000 ft)*; warhead 50 kg; 20 missiles.
Guns: 4 USSR 3 in *(76 mm)*/60 (2 twin) ❸; 60 rds/min to 15 km
(8 n miles) anti-surface; 14 km *(7.6 n miles)* anti-aircraft; weight
of shell 16 kg.
4 USSR 30 mm/65 (2 twin) automatic ❹; 500 rds/min to
5 km *(2.7 n miles)*; weight of shell 0.54 kg.
Torpedoes: 4—406 mm (2 twin) tubes amidships ❺. USET-95;
active/passive homing to 10 km *(5.5 n miles)* at 30 kt;
warhead 100 kg.
A/S mortars: 1 RBU 6000 12-tubed trainable launcher ❻;
automatic loading; range 6,000 m; warhead 31 kg.
Depth charges: 2 racks.
Mines: Capacity for 20.
Countermeasures: Decoys: 2—16-barrelled chaff launchers.
Towed torpedo decoys.
ESM: 2 Watch Dog; radar warning.
Radars: Air search: Strut Curve ❼; F-band; range 110 km *(60 n
miles)* for 2 m² target.
Surface search: Plank Shave ❽; I-band.
Navigation: Don 2; I-band.
Fire control: Drum Tilt ❾; H/I-band (for 30 mm).
Hawk Screech ❿; I-band; range 27 km *(15 n miles)* (for
76 mm).
Pop Group ⓫; F/H/I-band (for SAM).
IFF: High Pole B. Square Head.
Sonars: Hercules (MG 322); hull-mounted; active search and
attack; medium frequency.

Programmes: Type III Konis built at Zelenodolsk and transferred
from the Black Sea. 212 commissioned 28 June 1986 and 213
on 24 October 1987.
Structure: SSMs mounted either side of small deckhouse on
forecastle behind gun. A deckhouse amidships contains air

AL HANI   *(Scale 1 : 900), Ian Sturton*

AL HANI   *7/1991*, van Ginderen Collection /* 0081191

conditioning machinery. Changes to the standard Koni include
SSM, four torpedo tubes, only one RBU 6000 and Plank Shave
surface search and target indication radar. Camouflage paint
applied in 1991.

Operational: Both are active and one of the class fired an
exercise Styx missile in September 1999.

UPDATED

CORVETTES

3 NANUCHKA II CLASS (MISSILE CORVETTES) (FSG)

TARIQ IBN ZIYAD (ex-*Ean Mara*) 416   **EAN AL GAZALA** 417   **EAN ZARA** 418

Displacement, tons: 660 full load
Dimensions, feet (metres): 194.5 × 38.7 × 8.5 *(59.3 × 11.8 × 2.6)*
Main machinery: 6 M 504 diesels; 26,112 hp(m) *(19.2 MW)*; 3 shafts
Speed, knots: 33. **Range, miles:** 2,500 at 12 kt; 900 at 31 kt
Complement: 42 (7 officers)

Missiles: SSM: 4 Soviet SS-N-2C Styx launchers; auto-pilot; active radar/IR homing to 83 km *(45 n
miles)* at 0.9 Mach; warhead 513 kg HE; sea-skimmer at end of run.
SAM: SA-N-4 Gecko twin launcher; semi-active radar homing to 15 km *(8 n miles)* at 2.5 Mach;
altitude 9.1-3,048 m *(29.5-10,000 ft)*; warhead 50 kg HE; 20 missiles.
Guns: 2 USSR 57 mm/80 (twin) automatic; 120 rds/min to 6 km *(3.2 n miles)*; weight of shell
2.8 kg.
Countermeasures: Decoys: 2 chaff 16-barrelled launchers.
ESM: Bell Tap; radar warning.
Radars: Surface search: Square Tie; I-band (Bandstand radome).
Navigation: Don 2; I-band.
Fire control: Muff Cob; G/H-band.
Pop Group; F/H/I-band (for SAM).

Programmes: First transferred from USSR in October 1981; second in February 1983; third in
February 1984; fourth in September 1985.
Structure: Camouflage paint applied in 1991 but have been reported as having blue hulls since
1993.
Operational: *Ean Zaquit* (419) sunk on 24 March 1986. *Ean Mara* (416) severely damaged on
25 March 1986 by forces of the US Sixth Fleet; repaired in Leningrad and returned to Libya in
early 1991 as the *Tariq Ibn Ziyad*. All still seaworthy and 416 is still operational. 417 and 418 not
reported at sea recently.   *UPDATED*

TARIQ IBN ZIYAD   *7/1991*, van Ginderen Collection /* 0081192

PATROL FORCES

Notes: (1) More than 50 remote-control explosive craft acquired from Cyprus. Based on Q-Boats
with Q-26 GRP hulls and speed of about 30 kt. Also reported that 15 31 ft craft delivered by
Storebro, and 60 more built locally are similarly adapted. No reports of recent activity.
(2) There is also a Hamelin 37 m patrol craft *Al Ziffa* 206 based at Tripoli.

5 + 7 (RESERVE) OSA II CLASS
(FAST ATTACK CRAFT—MISSILE) (PCFG)

AL KATUM 511	**AL NABHA** 519	**AL MOSHA** 527
AL ZUARA 513	**AL SAFHRA** 521	**AL SAKAB** 529
AL RUHA 515	**AL FIKAH** 523	**AL BITAR** 531
AL BAIDA 517	**AL MATHUR** 525	**AL SADAD** 533

Displacement, tons: 245 full load
Dimensions, feet (metres): 126.6 × 24.9 × 8.8 *(38.6 × 7.6 × 2.7)*
Main machinery: 3 Type M 504 diesels; 10,800 hp(m) *(7.94 MW)* sustained; 3 shafts
Speed, knots: 37. **Range, miles:** 800 at 30 kt; 500 at 35 kt
Complement: 30

Missiles: SSM: 4 Soviet SS-N-2C Styx; active radar or IR homing to 83 km *(45 n miles)* at 0.9 Mach;
warhead 513 kg HE; sea-skimmer at end of run.
Guns: 4 USSR 30 mm/65 (2 twin) automatic; 500 rds/min to 5 km *(2.7 n miles)*; weight of shell
0.54 kg.
Radars: Surface search: Square Tie; I-band; range 73 km *(45 n miles)*.
Fire control: Drum tilt; H/I-band.
IFF: 2 Square Head. High Pole.

Programmes: The first craft arrived from USSR in October 1976, four more in August-October
1977, a sixth in July 1978, three in September-October 1979, one in April 1980, one in May
1980 (521) and one in July 1980 (529).
Structure: Some painted with camouflage stripes in 1991 and some were given blue hulls in 1993.
Operational: These are the warships most frequently seen at sea, but seldom stay out for very long.
Most are based at Tobruk and 513, 515, 523, 525 and 531 are active. One fired an exercise Styx
missile in September 1999.   *UPDATED*

AL MATHUR   *1993*

7 + 2 (RESERVE) COMBATTANTE II G CLASS
(FAST ATTACK CRAFT—MISSILE) (PCFG)

SHARABA (ex-*Beir Grassa*) 518		**SHAFAK** (ex-*Beir Alkrarim*) 534	
WAHAG (ex-*Beir Gzir*) 522		**BARK** (ex-*Beir Alkardmen*) 536	
SHEHAB (ex-*Beir Gtifa*) 524		**RAD** (ex-*Beir Alkur*) 538	
SHOUAIAI (ex-*Beir Algandula*) 528		**LAHEEB** (ex-*Beir Alkuefat*) 542	
SHOULA (ex-*Beir Ktitat*) 532			

Displacement, tons: 311 full load
Dimensions, feet (metres): 160.7 × 23.3 × 6.6 *(49 × 7.1 × 2)*
Main machinery: 4 MTU 20V 538 TB91 diesels; 15,360 hp(m) *(11.29 MW)* sustained; 4 shafts
Speed, knots: 39. **Range, miles:** 1,600 at 15 kt
Complement: 27

Missiles: SSM: 4 OTO Melara/Matra Otomat Mk 2 (TG1); active radar homing to 80 km *(43.2 n miles)* at 0.9 Mach; warhead 210 kg.
Guns: 1 OTO Melara 3 in *(76 mm)*/62 compact; 85 rds/min to 16 km *(8.6 n miles)* anti-surface; 12 km *(6.8 n miles)* anti-aircraft; weight of shell 6 kg.
   2 Breda 40 mm/70 (twin); 300 or 450 rds/min to 12.5 km *(6.8 n miles)* anti-surface; 4 km *(2.2 n miles)* anti-aircraft; weight of shell 0.96 kg.
Weapons control: CSEE Panda director. Thomson-CSF Vega II system.
Radars: Surface search: Thomson-CSF Triton; G-band; range 33 km *(18 n miles)* for 2 m² target.
Fire control: Thomson-CSF Castor IIB; I-band; range 15 km *(8 n miles)* (associated with Vega fire-control system).

Programmes: Ordered from CMN Cherbourg in May 1977. 518 completed February 1982; 522 3 April 1982; 524 29 May 1982; 528 5 September 1982; 532 29 October 1982; 534 17 December 1982; 536 11 March 1983; 538 10 May 1983; 542 29 July 1983.
Structure: Steel hull with alloy superstructure.
Operational: *Waheed* (526) sunk on 24 March 1986 and one other severely damaged on 25 March 1986 by forces of the US Sixth Fleet. All are active except 536 and 538.
UPDATED

SHAFAK   *1993*

LAND-BASED MARITIME AIRCRAFT

Numbers/Type: 2/5 Aerospatiale SA 321 Frelon/SA 324 Super Frelon.
Operational speed: 134 kt *(248 km/h)*.
Service ceiling: 10,000 ft *(3,050 m)*.
Range: 440 n miles *(815 km)*.
Role/Weapon systems: Obsolescent helicopter; Air Force manned but used for naval support tasks. Most are non-operational due to lack of spares. Sensors: None. Weapons: Fitted for Exocet AM 39.
VERIFIED

Numbers/Type: 5 Aerospatiale SA 316B Alouette III.
Operational speed: 113 kt *(210 km/h)*.
Service ceiling: 10,500 ft *(3,200 m)*.
Range: 290 n miles *(540 km)*.
Role/Weapon systems: Support helicopter. Probably non-operational. Another six are used by the Police. Sensors: None. Weapons: Unarmed.
VERIFIED

AMPHIBIOUS FORCES

2 PS 700 CLASS (LST)

Name	No	Builders	Commissioned
IBN OUF	132	CNI de la Mediterranée	11 Mar 1977
IBN HARISSA	134	CNI de la Mediterranée	10 Mar 1978

Displacement, tons: 2,800 full load
Dimensions, feet (metres): 326.4 × 51.2 × 7.9 *(99.5 × 15.6 × 2.4)*
Main machinery: 2 SEMT-Pielstick 16 PA4 V 185 diesels; 5,344 hp(m) *(3.93 MW)* sustained; 2 shafts; cp props
Speed, knots: 15.4. **Range, miles:** 4,000 at 14 kt
Complement: 35
Military lift: 240 troops; 11 tanks
Guns: 6 Breda 40 mm/70 (3 twin). 1—81 mm mortar.
Weapons control: CSEE Panda director.
Radars: Air search: Thomson-CSF Triton; D-band.
Surface search: Decca 1226; I-band.
Helicopters: 1 Aerospatiale SA 316B Alouette III.

Comment: 132 laid down 1 April 1976 and launched 22 October 1976; 134 laid down 18 April 1977, launched 18 October 1977. Both are seaworthy and 134 is active. ***UPDATED***

IBN HARISSA   *1981*

---

1 + 2 (RESERVE) POLNOCHNY D CLASS (TYPE 773U) (LSM)

IBN AL HADRAMI 112	**IBN UMAYAA** 116	**IBN AL FARAT** 118

Displacement, tons: 1,305 full load
Dimensions, feet (metres): 275.3 × 31.8 × 7.9 *(83.9 × 9.7 × 2.4)*
Main machinery: 2 Type 40-D diesels; 4,400 hp(m) *(3.2 MW)* sustained; 2 shafts
Speed, knots: 15. **Range, miles:** 2,900 at 12 kt
Complement: 45
Military lift: 160 troops; 5 MBT or 5 APC or 5 AA guns or 8 trucks
Guns: 4 USSR 30 mm (2 twin). 2—140 mm 18-tubed rocket launchers.
Mines: 100.
Radars: Surface search: Radwar SRN-745; I-band.
Fire control: Drum Tilt; H/I-band.
IFF: Salt Pot A. Square Head.
Helicopters: Platform for 1 medium.

Comment: The first to be transferred from USSR arrived in November 1977. On 14 September 1978 *Ibn Qis* (fourth of the class) was burned out during a landing exercise and was a total loss. 118 and 116 delivered June 1978. All are an export variant of the standard Soviet/Polish 'Polnochny' class but with helicopter deck added. Built at Naval Shipyard, Gdynia. Similar types built for India and Iraq (now deleted). Operational status doubtful but at least one is assessed as seaworthy.
UPDATED

IBN UMAYAA   *6/1990*, van Ginderen Collection /* 0081193

3 TURKISH TYPE (LCT)

IBN AL IDRISI 130	**IBN MARWAN** 131	**EL KOBAYAT** 132

Displacement, tons: 280 standard; 600 full load
Dimensions, feet (metres): 183.7 × 37.8 × 3.6 *(56 × 11.6 × 1.1)*
Main machinery: 3 GM 6-71TI diesels; 930 hp *(694 kW)* maximum; 3 shafts
Speed, knots: 8.5 loaded; 10 max. **Range, miles:** 600 at 10 kt
Complement: 15
Military lift: 100 troops; 350 tons including 5 tanks
Guns: 2—30 mm (twin).

Comment: First two transferred 7 December 1979 (ex-Turkish *C130* and *C131*) from Turkish fleet. Third of class reported in 1991. Previously reported numbers were much exaggerated. Not reported at sea in recent years.
UPDATED

TURKISH LCT (Turkey number)   *10/1991, Harald Carstens*

TRAINING SHIPS

1 VOSPER CLASS (AX)

Name	No	Builders	Commissioned
TOBRUK	C 411	Vosper Thornycroft	20 Apr 1966

Displacement, tons: 500 full load
Dimensions, feet (metres): 177.3 × 28.5 × 13 *(54 × 8.7 × 4)*
Main machinery: 2 Paxman Ventura diesels; 3,800 hp *(2.83 MW)*; 2 shafts
Speed, knots: 18. **Range, miles:** 2,900 at 14 kt
Complement: 63 (5 officers)
Guns: 1 Vickers 4 in *(102 mm)*/33 Mk 52; 2 Bofors 40 mm/70.
Radars: Surface search: Decca TM 1226C; I-band.

Comment: Deleted as a training hulk in 1989 but was seen at sea again in 1992. State apartments are included in the accommodation. The ship is used mostly for training and has not been to sea since early 1996. Still in commission.
VERIFIED

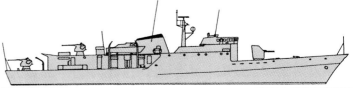

TOBRUK   *(Scale 1 : 600), Ian Sturton*

MINE WARFARE FORCES

5 + 3 (RESERVE) NATYA (TYPE 266ME) CLASS
(OCEAN MINESWEEPERS) (MSO)

AL ISAR (ex-*Ras El Gelais*) 111	**RAS AL FULAIJAH** 117	**RAS AL MASSAD** 123
AL TIYAR (ex-*Ras Hadad*) 113	**RAS AL QULA** 119	**RAS AL HANI** 125
RAS AL HAMMAN 115	**RAS AL MADWAR** 121	

Displacement, tons: 804 full load
Dimensions, feet (metres): 200.1 × 33.5 × 10.8 *(61 × 10.2 × 3)*
Main machinery: 2 Type M 504 diesels; 5,000 hp(m) *(3.67 MW)* sustained; 2 shafts; cp props
Speed, knots: 16. **Range, miles:** 3,000 at 12 kt
Complement: 67
Guns: 4 USSR 30 mm/65 (2 twin) automatic; 500 rds/min to 5 km *(2.7 n miles)*; weight of shell 0.54 kg.
4 USSR 25 mm/60 (2 twin); 270 rds/min to 3 km *(1.6 n miles)*; weight of shell 0.34 kg.
A/S mortars: 2 RBU 1200 5-tubed fixed launchers; elevating; range 1,200 m; warhead 34 kg.
Mines: 10.
Countermeasures: MCM: 1 GKT-2 contact sweep; 1 AT-2 acoustic sweep; 1 TEM-3 magnetic sweep.
Radars: Surface search: Don 2; I-band.
Fire control: Drum Tilt; H/I-band.
IFF: 2 Square Head. 1 High Pole B.
Sonars: Hull-mounted; active search; high frequency.

Comment: First pair transferred from USSR February 1981. Second pair arrived February 1983, one in August 1983, the sixth in January 1984 the seventh in January 1985 and the eighth in October 1986. At least one of the class painted in green striped camouflage in 1991. Others may have blue hulls. Capable of magnetic, acoustic and mechanical sweeping. Mostly used for coastal patrols and never observed minesweeping. 111, 113, 117, 119 and 123 are operational. *Ras Al Massad* has been used for training cruises. ***UPDATED***

RAS AL HANI   2/1988

AUXILIARIES

1 SUPPORT SHIP (AR/LSD)

Name	No	Builders	Commissioned
ZELTIN	711	Vosper Thornycroft, Woolston	23 Jan 1969

Displacement, tons: 2,200 standard; 2,470 full load
Dimensions, feet (metres): 324 × 48 × 10.2 *(98.8 × 14.6 × 3.1)*; 19 *(5.8)* aft when flooded
Main machinery: 2 Paxman 16YJCM diesels; 4,000 hp *(2.98 MW)*; 2 shafts
Speed, knots: 15. **Range, miles:** 3,000 at 14 kt
Complement: 101 (15 officers)
Guns: 2 Bofors 40 mm/70.
Weapons control: Vega II-12 for 40 mm guns.
Radars: Surface search: Thomson-CSF Triton; G-band; range 33 km *(18 n miles)* for 2 m² target (associated with Vega fire control).

Comment: Ordered in January 1967; launched 29 February 1968. Fitted with accommodation for a flag officer or a senior officer and staff. Operational and administrative base of the squadron. Workshops with a total area of approximately 4,500 sq ft are situated amidships with ready access to the dock, and there is a 3 ton travelling gantry fitted with outriggers to cover ships berthed alongside up to 200 ft long. The ship provides full logistic support, including docking maintenance and repair facilities. Craft up to 120 ft can be docked. Used as an alongside tender for Patrol Forces and is probably no longer capable of going to sea. ***UPDATED***

ZELTIN   1969, Vosper Thornycroft

10 TRANSPORTS (AG/ML)

GARYOUNIS (ex-*Mashu*)	**EL TEMSAH**	**DERNA**	**GHAT**
GARNATA (ex-*Monte Granada*)	**TOLETELA** (ex-*Monte Toledo*)	**RAHMA** (ex-*Krol*)	**LA GRAZIETTA**
HANNA	**GHARDIA**		

Measurement, tons: 2,412 gross
Dimensions, feet (metres): 546.3 × 80.1 × 21.3 *(166.5 × 24.4 × 6.5)*
Main machinery: 2 SEMT-Pielstick diesels; 20,800 hp(m) *(15.29 MW)*; 2 shafts; bow thruster
Speed, knots: 20

Comment: Details are for *Garyounis*, a converted ro-ro passenger/car ferry used as a training vessel in 1989. In addition the 117 m *El Temsah* was refitted and another four of these vessels are of ro-ro design. All are in regular civilian service and *Garyounis* is also used by the military. All have minelaying potential. ***UPDATED***

DERNA   6/1998, Diego Quevedo / 0052572

1 SPASILAC CLASS (SALVAGE SHIP) (ARS)

AL MUNJED (ex-*Zlatica*) 722

Displacement, tons: 1,590 full load
Dimensions, feet (metres): 182 × 39.4 × 14.1 *(55.5 × 12 × 4.3)*
Main machinery: 2 diesels; 4,340 hp(m) *(3.19 MW)*; 2 shafts; cp props; bow thruster
Speed, knots: 13. **Range, miles:** 4,000 at 12 kt
Complement: 50
Guns: 4—12.7 mm MGs. Can also be fitted with 8—20 mm (2 quad) and 2—20 mm.
Radars: Surface search: Racal Decca; I-band.

Comment: Transferred from Yugoslavia in 1982. Fitted for firefighting, towing and submarine rescue—carries recompression chamber. Built at Tito SY, Belgrade. Used as the lead vessel for the 1998 training cruise, and is still operational. ***UPDATED***

SPASILAC (Iraq colours)   1988, Peter Jones

1 YELVA CLASS (DIVING TENDER) (YDT)

AL MANOUD VM 917

Displacement, tons: 300 full load
Dimensions, feet (metres): 134.2 × 26.2 × 6.6 *(40.9 × 8 × 2)*
Main machinery: 2 Type 3-D-12A diesels; 630 hp(m) *(463 kW)* sustained; 2 shafts
Speed, knots: 12.5
Complement: 30
Radars: Navigation: Spin trough; I-band.
IFF: High Pole.

Comment: Built in early 1970s. Transferred from USSR December 1977. Carries two 1.5 ton cranes and has a portable decompression chamber. Based at Tripoli and does not go to sea. ***VERIFIED***

YELVA (Russian colours)   7/1996, Hartmut Ehlers

2 FLOATING DOCKS

Comment: One of 5,000 tons capacity at Tripoli. One of 3,200 tons capacity acquired in April 1985. ***VERIFIED***

TUGS

7 COASTAL TUGS (YTB)

RAS EL HELAL A 31	**AL KERIAT**	**A 33-A 35**
AL AHWEIRIF A 32	**AL TABKAH**	

Comment: First four of 34.8 m built in Portugal in 1976-78. Last three of 26.6 m built in the Netherlands in 1979-80. All are in service. ***UPDATED***

LITHUANIA
KARINES JURU PAJEGOS

Headquarters Appointments

Commander of the Navy:
  Rear Admiral Kiestutis Macijauskas
Chief of Staff:
  Commander Oleg Marinic

Personnel

2000: 600

Bases

Klaipeda

State Border Police

Coast Guard Force formed in late 1992. Name changed in 1996 to Border Police. Vessels have one thick and one thin diagonal yellow stripe on the hull.

Mercantile Marine

Lloyd's Register of Shipping:
  192 ships of 424,296 tons gross

DELETIONS

1998 *SK 24*

FRIGATES

2 GRISHA III (ALBATROS) CLASS (TYPE 1124M) (FFL)

Name	No	Builders	Commissioned	Recommissioned
ZEMAITIS	F 11 (ex-MPK 108)	Zelenodolsk Shipyard	1 Oct 1981	6 Nov 1992
AUKSTAITIS	F 12 (ex-MPK 44)	Kiev Shipyard	15 Aug 1980	6 Nov 1992

Displacement, tons: 950 standard; 1,200 full load
Dimensions, feet (metres): 233.6 × 32.2 × 12.1 *(71.2 × 9.8 × 3.7)*
Main machinery: CODAG; 1 gas-turbine; 15,000 hp(m) *(11 MW)*; 2 diesels; 16,000 hp(m) *(11.8 MW)*; 3 shafts
Speed, knots: 30. **Range, miles:** 2,500 at 14 kt diesels; 950 at 27 kt
Complement: 48 (5 officers)

Missiles: SAM: SA-N-4 Gecko twin launcher ❶; semi-active radar homing to 15 km *(8 n miles)* at 2.5 Mach; warhead 50 kg; altitude 9.1-3,048 m *(30-10,000 ft)*; 20 missiles.
Guns: 2—57 mm/80 (twin) ❷; 120 rds/min to 6 km *(3.3 n miles)*; weight of shell 2.8 kg.
  1—30 mm/65 ❸; 6 barrels; 3,000 rds/min combined to 2 km.
A/S mortars: 2 RBU 6000 12-tubed trainable ❹; range 6,000 m; warhead 31 kg.
Depth charges: 2 racks (12).
Mines: Capacity for 18 in lieu of depth charges.
Countermeasures: Decoys: 1 PK-16 (F 11) chaff launcher.
ESM: 2 Watch Dog.
Radars: Air/surface search: Strut Curve ❺; F-band.
Surface search: Racal Decca RM 1290; I-band.
Navigation: Terma Scanter; I-band.
Fire control: Pop Group ❻; F/H/I-band (for SA-N-4). Bass Tilt ❼; H/I-band (for guns).
IFF: High Pole A or B. Square Head. Salt Pot.
Sonars: Bull Nose; hull-mounted; active search and attack; high/medium frequency.

Modernisation: Torpedo tubes removed from F 12 in 1996 and from F 11 in 1997.

UPDATED

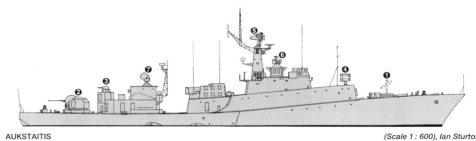

AUKSTAITIS   *(Scale 1 : 600), Ian Sturton*

AUKSTAITIS   *6/1999*, Maritime Photographic /* 0081195

AUKSTAITIS   *6/1999*, L-G Nilsson /* 0081194

PATROL FORCES

1 STORM CLASS (PCF)

Name	No	Builders	Commissioned
DZŪKAS (ex-*Glimt*)	P 31 (ex-P 962)	Bergens Mek Verksteder	1966

Displacement, tons: 135 full load
Dimensions, feet (metres): 120 × 20 × 5 *(36.5 × 6.1 × 1.5)*
Main machinery: 2 MTU MB 16V 538 TB90 diesels; 6,000 hp(m) *(4.41 MW)* sustained; 2 shafts
Speed, knots: 32
Complement: 18 (3 officers)
Guns: Bofors 40 mm/60. 1—12.7 mm MG.
Radars: Surface search: Racal Decca TM 1226; I-band.

Comment: Disarmed and acquired from Norway on 12 December 1994 as a gun patrol craft. Others of the class given to Latvia and Estonia. Re-armed in 1998.   **UPDATED**

DZŪKAS   9/1999*, *Michael Nitz* / 0081197

1 COASTAL PATROL CRAFT (PC)

HK 21 (ex-*Vilnele*)

Displacement, tons: 88 full load
Dimensions, feet (metres): 75.8 × 19 × 5.9 *(23.1 × 5.8 × 1.8)*
Main machinery: 2 diesels; 600 hp(m) *(441 kW)*; 2 shafts
Speed, knots: 12
Complement: 7 (1 officer)

Comment: Acquired in 1992. Former pilot boat and tender to *Vetra*. Used as a hydrographic vessel.   **UPDATED**

HK 21   6/1994*, *Lithuanian Navy* / 0081198

1 KUTTER CLASS

LOKYS (ex-*Apollo*)   SL 07

Displacement, tons: 35 full load
Dimensions, feet (metres): 60.4 × 17.1 × 7.5 *(18.4 × 5.2 × 2.3)*
Main machinery: 1 diesel; 165 hp(m) *(121 kW)*; 1 shaft
Speed, knots: 9
Complement: 7
Guns: 2—7.62 mm MGs.
Radars: Surface search: Raytheon RM 1290S; I-band.

Comment: Built in the 1930s and served with the Danish Naval Home Guard. Transferred in July 1997.   **UPDATED**

LOKYS   9/1997*, *Lithuanian Navy* / 0012732

MINE WARFARE FORCES

1 LINDAU CLASS (TYPE 331) (MINEHUNTER) (MHC)

Name	No	Builders	Commissioned
SÜDUVIS (ex-*Koblenz*)	M 52 (ex-M 1071)	Burmester, Bremen	8 July 1958

Displacement, tons: 463 full load
Dimensions, feet (metres): 154.5 × 27.2 × 9.8 (9.2 Troika) *(47.1 × 8.3 × 3) (2.8)*
Main machinery: 2 MTU MD diesels; 4,000 hp(m) *(2.94 MW)*; 2 shafts
Speed, knots: 16.5. **Range, miles:** 850 at 16.5 kt
Complement: 43 (5 officers)
Guns: 1 Bofors 40 mm/70.
Radars: Navigation: Kelvin Hughes 14/9, or Atlas Elektronik TRS N, or Raytheon. SPS 64; I-band.
Sonars: Plessey 193 m; minehunting; high frequency (100/300 kHz).

Comment: Acquired from Germany in June 1999 and recommissioned 2 December 1999. Converted to minehunter in 1978. Hull is of wooden construction. Full minehunting equipment including PAP 104 ROVs was transferred with the vessel.   **NEW ENTRY**

SÜDUVIS   11/1999*, *Findler & Winter* / 0081199

AUXILIARIES

Notes: (1) *Victoria* 245 is an ex-Swedish Coast Guard vessel now owned by the Fishery Inspection Service.
(2) There is also a personnel launch *Vytis-01* which is similar to Latvian KA 10/11.

1 VALERIAN URYVAYEV CLASS (AGOR/AX)

VETRA (ex-*Rudolf Samoylovich*) A 41

Displacement, tons: 1,050 full load
Dimensions, feet (metres): 180.1 × 31.2 × 13.1 *(54.9 × 9.5 × 4)*
Main machinery: 1 Deutz diesel; 850 hp(m) *(625 kW)*; 1 shaft
Speed, knots: 12
Complement: 34 (8 officers)
Guns: 2—12.7 mm MGs.
Radars: Navigation: Racal Decca RM 1290; I-band.

Comment: Built at Khabarovsk in early 1980s. Transferred from the Russian Navy in 1992 where she was used as a civilian oceanographic research vessel. Now used as the Flag ship for the Baltic States MCMV unit which includes *Olev* and *Kalev* (from Estonia) and *Viesturs* and *Imanta* (from Latvia). A second of class *Vejas* works for the Ministry of Environment.   **UPDATED**

VETRA   6/1997*, *Michael Nitz* / 0012733

POLICE

1 LOKKI CLASS (PC)

KIHU   003

Displacement, tons: 64 full load
Dimensions, feet (metres): 87.9 × 18 × 6.2 *(26.8 × 5.5 × 1.9)*
Main machinery: 2 MTU 8V 396 TB84 diesels; 2,100 hp(m) *(1.54 MW)* sustained; 2 shafts
Speed, knots: 25
Complement: 6

Comment: Acquired from Finland in late 1997. Armament and sonar removed on transfer.   **VERIFIED**

KIHU   1/1998, *Lithuanian Navy* / 0052577

9 SZKWAL CLASS (PB)

101-109 (ex-*SG 101-109*)

Displacement, tons: 27 full load
Dimensions, feet (metres): 38.4 × 15.1 × 5.9 *(11.7 × 4.6 × 1.8)*
Main machinery: 2 M 50F diesels; 2,000 hp(m) *(1.47 MW)* sustained; 2 shafts
Speed, knots: 41. **Range, miles:** 306 at 9 kt
Complement: 5
Guns: 1—7.62 mm MG.
Radars: Surface search: SRN 207; I-band.

Comment: Built at Gdansk between 1983 and 1990. Transferred by gift from Polish Border Guard on 5 August 1996.

UPDATED

MADELEINE   9/1996, Hartmut Ehlers

SG 106 (Polish colours)   8/1996 *, J Cislak / 0081201

1 KBV 101 CLASS (PC)

LILIAN 101 (ex-*KBV 101*)

Displacement, tons: 50 full load
Dimensions, feet (metres): 87.6 × 16.4 × 7.2 *(26.7 × 5 × 2.2)*
Main machinery: 2 Cummins KTA38-M diesels; 2,120 hp(m) *(1.56 MW)*; 2 shafts
Speed, knots: 23. **Range, miles:** 1,000 at 15 kt
Complement: 7
Radars: Surface search: I-band.

Comment: Built in Sweden in 1969. Transferred from Swedish Coast Guard on 24 June 1996. Used in Swedish service as a salvage diving vessel and had a high frequency active hull-mounted sonar.

UPDATED

1 KBV 041 CLASS (PC)

MADELEINE 041 (ex-KBV 041)

Displacement, tons: 70 full load
Dimensions, feet (metres): 60.4 × 17.7 × 4.3 *(18.4 × 5.4 × 1.3)*
Main machinery: 2 diesels; 450 hp(m) *(331 kW)*; 2 shafts
Speed, knots: 8
Complement: 8
Radars: Surface search: I-band.

Comment: Class B sea truck transferred from the Swedish Coast Guard in April 1995. Used for pollution control in Swedish service but now used as patrol craft.

VERIFIED

LILIAN   9/1996 *, Hartmut Ehlers / 0081200

MADAGASCAR
MALAGASY REPUBLIC MARINE

Headquarters Appointments

Head of Navy:
  Rear Admiral Marc Basile Ravelonanosy

Personnel

(a) 2000: 450 officers and men (including Marine Company of 120 men)

Bases

Antsiranana (main), Toamasina, Mahajanga, Toliary, Nosy-Be, Tolagnaro, Manakara.

Mercantile Marine

Lloyd's Register of Shipping:
  101 vessels of 42,553 tons gross

DELETIONS

Patrol Forces

1999   *Malaika*

Amphibious Forces

1999   *Toky*

PATROL FORCES

Note: It is planned to order coastal patrol craft from South Korea in 2001.

AMPHIBIOUS FORCES

1 EDIC CLASS (LCT)

AINA VAO VAO (ex-*L9082*)

Displacement, tons: 250 standard; 670 full load
Dimensions, feet (metres): 193.5 × 39.2 × 4.5 *(59 × 12 × 1.3)*
Main machinery: 2 SACM MGO diesels; 1,000 hp(m) *(753 kW)*; 2 shafts
Speed, knots: 8. **Range, miles:** 1,800 at 8 kt
Complement: 32 (3 officers)
Military lift: 250 tons
Guns: 2 Giat 20 mm.

Comment: Built in 1964 by Chantier Naval Franco-Belge. Transferred from France 28 September 1985 having been paid off by the French Navy in 1981. Repaired by the French and now back in service.

UPDATED

AINA VAO VAO   6/1999 *, Madagascar Navy / 0081202

AUXILIARIES

Notes: (1) Two 'Aigrette' class harbour tugs *Engoulevent* and *Martin-Pêcheur* were acquired from France in May 1996, and two more harbour tugs transported by *Orage* in June 1997.
(2) There is also a coastal tug *Trozona*.

1 CHAMOIS CLASS (SUPPLY TENDER) (AG)

MATSILO (ex-*Chamois*) (ex-A 767)

Displacement, tons: 495 full load
Dimensions, feet (metres): 136.1 × 24.6 × 10.5 *(41.5 × 7.5 × 3.2)*
Main machinery: 2 SACM AGO 175 V16 diesels; 2,700 hp(m) *(1.98 MW)*; 2 shafts; cp props; bow thruster
Speed, knots: 14. **Range, miles:** 6,000 at 12 kt
Complement: 13 plus 7 spare
Cargo capacity: 100 tons cargo; 165 tons of fuel or water
Radars: Navigation: Racal Decca 1226; I-band.

Comment: Built by La Perrière, Lorient and commissioned in the French Navy 24 September 1976. Paid off in 1995 and transferred from France in May 1996. Can act as a tug (bollard pull 25 tons) or for SAR and supply tasks but is mostly used as a patrol craft. There are two 30 ton winches and up to 100 tons of stores can be carried on deck.

UPDATED

MATSILO
6/1999*, Madagascar Navy / 0081203

MALAWI

Headquarters Appointments	Bases	Personnel	Mercantile Marine
Commander of the Navy: Lieutenant Colonel G A Ziyabu	Monkey Bay, Lake Malawi	2000: 225	*Lloyd's Register of Shipping:* 2 vessels of 320 tons gross

PATROL FORCES

Notes: One survey craft built in France in 1988 is operated on Lake Malawi by Department of Surveys.

1 ANTARES CLASS (PC)

KASUNGU (ex-*Chikala*) P 703

Displacement, tons: 41 full load
Dimensions, feet (metres): 68.9 × 16.1 × 4.9 *(21 × 4.9 × 1.5)*
Main machinery: 2 Poyaud 520 V12 M2 diesels; 1,300 hp(m) *(956 kW)*; 2 shafts
Speed, knots: 22. **Range, miles:** 650 at 15 kt
Complement: 16
Guns: 1 MG 21 20 mm. 2—7.62 mm MGs.
Radars: Surface search: Decca; I-band.

Comment: Built in prefabricated sections by SFCN Villeneuve-la-Garenne and shipped to Malawi for assembly on 17 December 1984. Commissioned May 1985. Needs a refit but funds are not available.

VERIFIED

KANING'A   6/1997, Malawi Navy / 0012736

1 ROTORK CLASS (LCU)

CHIKOKO I L 702

Displacement, tons: 9 full load
Dimensions, feet (metres): 41.5 × 10.5 × 1.5 *(12.7 × 3.2 × 0.5)*
Main machinery: 2 Volvo diesels; 260 hp(m) *(191 kW)*; 2 shafts
Speed, knots: 24. **Range, miles:** 3,000 at 15 kt
Complement: 8
Guns: 3—7.62 mm MGs.

Comment: Built by Rotork Marine. Needs a refit but no funds are available.

VERIFIED

KASUNGU   6/1996, Malawi Navy / 0012737

1 NAMACURRA CLASS (PB)

KANING'A (ex-*Y 1520*) P 704

Displacement, tons: 5 full load
Dimensions, feet (metres): 29.5 × 9 × 2.8 *(9 × 2.7 × 0.8)*
Main machinery: 2 BMW 3.3 outboards; 380 hp(m) *(279 kW)*
Speed, knots: 32. **Range, miles:** 180 at 20 kt
Complement: 4
Guns: 1—12.7 mm MG. 2—7.62 mm MGs.
Radars: Surface search: Decca; I-band.

Comment: Delivered by South Africa on 29 October 1988.

VERIFIED

CHIKOKO I   6/1996, Malawi Navy / 0012738

MALAYSIA
TENTERA LAUT DIRAJA

(including Sabah)

Headquarters Appointments

Chief of Navy:
 Vice Admiral Dato Abu Bakar bin Abdul Jamal
Deputy Chief of Navy:
 Rear Admiral Dato Mohd Ramily bin Abubakar
Fleet Commander:
 Rear Admiral Dato Mohd Anwar bin Mohd Nor
Commander Naval Area I (Kuantan):
 Commodore Dato Ilyas bin Hj Din
Commander Naval Area II (Sabah and Sarawak):
 Commodore Tan See Ming

Personnel

(a) 2000: 15,400 (1,450 officers)
(b) Voluntary service
(c) RMNVR: Total, 3,945 officers and sailors
  Divisions at Penang, Selangor and Johore. Target of 7,000 in
  19 port divisions.

Prefix to Ships' Names

The names of Malaysian warships are prefixed by KD (Kapal
DiRaja meaning King's Ship).

Strength of the Fleet

Type	Active	Building (Planned)
Submarines Mini	—	3
Frigates	2	—
Corvettes	6	—
Offshore Patrol Vessels	2	6
Logistic Support Vessels	2	—
Fast Attack Craft—Missile	8	—
Fast Attack Craft—Gun	6	—
Patrol Craft	18	—
Minehunters	4	—
Survey Ships	2	—
LSTs	1	(1)
Training Ships	3	—

Bases

KD *Malaya,* Lumut; (Telok Muroh) Perak
Fleet Operation Command centre, *K D Rajawali*; dockyard and
training centre on west coast. Air Wing 499.
KD *Pelandok,* Lumut (Training Centre)
Pularek Tanjung Pengelih, Johore, Kota Tinggi (Training)
Kuantan—HQ Area 1 (West of 109°E)
Labuan—HQ Area 2 (East of 109°E) KD *Sri Tawau* (ex-*Labuan*),
KD *Sri Sandakan* (ex-*Rejang*)
Penang—HQ Area 3; Kuching, Sarawak—HQ Area 4
Sitiawan, Perak; site for planned new naval air station
Kota Kinabalu, Sabah; naval base in East Malaysia.

Maritime Patrol Craft

There are large numbers of armed patrol craft belonging to the
Police, Customs and Fisheries Departments. Details at the end of
the section.

Mercantile Marine

Lloyd's Register of Shipping:
 828 vessels of 5,244,653 tons gross

DELETIONS

Amphibious Forces

1999 *Sri Banggi, Raja Jarom*

Auxiliaries

1999 *Duyong*

PENNANT LIST

Frigates				Mine Warfare Forces		Amphibious Forces	
29	Jebat	38	Renchong	3505	Jerong	1505	Sri Inderapura
30	Lekiu	39	Tombak	3506	Todak		
		40	Lembing	3507	Paus	**Training Ships**	
Corvettes		41	Serampang	3508	Yu	24	Rahmat
25	Kasturi	42	Panah	3509	Baung	76	Hang Tuah
26	Lekir	43	Kerambit	3510	Pari	A 13	Tunas Samudera
134	Laksamana Hang Nadim	44	Beladau	3511	Handalan		
135	Laksamana Tun Abdul Jamil	45	Kelewang	3512	Perkasa		
136	Laksamana Muhammad Amin	46	Rentaka	3513	Pendekar		
137	Laksamana Tan Pusmah	47	Sri Perlis	3514	Gempita	**Auxiliaries**	
		49	Sri Johor			4	Penyu
		160	Musytari			152	Mutiara
Patrol Forces		161	Marikh			153	Perantau
34	Kris	3144	Sri Sabah			1503	Sri Indera Sakti
36	Sundang	3145	Sri Sarawak			1504	Mahawangsa
37	Badek	3146	Sri Negri Sembilan				
		3147	Sri Melaka	**Mine Warfare Forces**			
		3501	Perdana	11	Mahamiru		
		3502	Serang	12	Jerai		
		3503	Ganas	13	Ledang		
		3504	Ganyang	14	Kinabalu		

SUBMARINES

Note: Contract placed with COSMOS in December 1999 for three 134 ton mini-submarines of a SWATS design. The hull is 29 m, has two torpedo tubes and can carry external SDVs.
Diving depth 150 m, complement six plus 15 swimmers. AIP is likely. First in-service date 2005. Training is being done in Pakistan.

FRIGATES

Note: Two older frigates are listed under Training Ships.

LEKIU

12/1999*, Sattler/Steele / 0081206

2 LEKIU CLASS (FFG)

Name	No	Builders	Laid down	Launched	Commissioned
LEKIU	30	Yarrow (Shipbuilders), Glasgow	Mar 1994	3 Dec 1994	9 Oct 1999
JEBAT	29	Yarrow (Shipbuilders), Glasgow	Nov 1994	27 May 1995	20 Nov 1999

Displacement, tons: 1,845 standard; 2,390 full load
Dimensions, feet (metres): 346 oa; 319.9 wl × 42 × 11.8 *(105.5; 97.5 × 12.8 × 3.6)*
Main machinery: CODAD; 4 MTU 20V 1163 TB93 diesels; 33,300 hp(m) *(24.5 MW)* sustained; 2 shafts; Kamewa cp props
Speed, knots: 28. **Range, miles:** 5,000 at 14 kt
Complement: 146 (18 officers)

Missiles: SSM: 8 Aerospatiale MM 40 Exocet Block II ❶; inertial cruise; active radar homing to 70 km *(40 n miles)* at 0.9 Mach; warhead 165 kg; sea-skimmer.
SAM: British Aerospace VLS Seawolf; 16 launchers ❷; command line of sight (CLOS) radar/TV tracking to 6 km *(3.3 n miles)* at 2.5 Mach; warhead 14 kg.
Guns: 1 Bofors 57 mm/70 SAK Mk 2 ❸; 220 rds/min to 17 km *(9.3 n miles)*; weight of shell 2.4 kg.
2 MSI 30 mm/75 DS 30B ❹; 650 rds/min to 10 km *(5.4 n miles)*; weight of shell 0.36 kg.
Torpedoes: 6 Whitehead B 515 324 mm (2 triple) tubes ❺; anti-submarine; Marconi Stingray; active/passive homing to 11 km *(5.9 n miles)* at 45 kt; warhead 35 kg (shaped charge).
Countermeasures: Decoys: 2 Super Barricade 12-barrelled launchers for chaff ❻; Graseby Sea Siren torpedo decoy.
ESM/ECM: AEG Telefunken/Marconi Mentor/THORN EMI Scimitar; intercept and jammer.
Combat data systems: GEC-Marconi Nautis-F; Signaal Link Y Mk 2.
Weapons control: Radamec 2400 Optronic director ❼. Thomson-CSF ITL 70 (for Exocet); GEC-Marconi Type V 3901 thermal imager.
Radars: Air search: Signaal DA08 ❽; E/F-band.
Surface search: Ericsson Sea Giraffe 150HC ❾; G/H-band.
Navigation: Racal Decca; I-band.
Fire control: 2 Marconi 1802 ❿; I/J-band.
Sonars: Thomson Sintra Spherion; hull-mounted active search and attack; medium frequency.

Helicopters: 1 Westland Super Lynx ⓫.

Programmes: Contract announced 31 March 1992 for two ships originally classed as corvettes but uprated to light frigates. First steel cut in March 1993. *Jebat* is the senior ship and has therefore taken the lower pennant number.

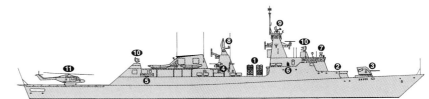

LEKIU *(Scale 1 : 900), Ian Sturton /* 0081204

LEKIU *9/1999*, B Sullivan /* 0081205

Structure: GEC Naval Systems Frigate 2000 design with a modern combat data system and automated machinery control.

Operational: Delivery dates were delayed by weapon system integration problems but both arrived in Malaysia by early 2000. *UPDATED*

CORVETTES

2 KASTURI (TYPE FS 1500) CLASS (FSG)

Name	No	Builders	Laid down	Launched	Commissioned
KASTURI	25	Howaldtswerke, Kiel	3 Jan 1983	14 May 1983	15 Aug 1984
LEKIR	26	Howaldtswerke, Kiel	3 Jan 1983	14 May 1983	15 Aug 1984

Displacement, tons: 1,500 standard; 1,850 full load
Dimensions, feet (metres): 319.1 × 37.1 × 11.5 *(97.3 × 11.3 × 3.5)*
Main machinery: 4 MTU 20V 1163 TB92 diesels; 23,400 hp(m) *(17.2 MW)* sustained; 2 shafts
Speed, knots: 28; 18 on 2 diesels
Range, miles: 3,000 at 18 kt; 5,000 at 14 kt
Complement: 124 (13 officers)

Missiles: SSM: 4 Aerospatiale MM 38 Exocet ❶; inertial cruise; active radar homing to 42 km *(23 n miles)* at 0.9 Mach; warhead 165 kg; sea-skimmer.
Guns: 1 Creusot-Loire 3.9 in *(100 mm)*/55 Mk 2 compact ❷; 20/45/90 rds/min to 17 km *(9.2 n miles)* anti-surface; 6 km *(3.2 n miles)* anti-aircraft; weight of shell 13.5 kg.
1 Bofors 57 mm/70 ❸; 200 rds/min to 17 km *(9.2 n miles)*; weight of shell 2.4 kg. Launchers for illuminants.
4 Emerson Electric 30 mm (2 twin) ❹; 1,200 rds/min combined to 6 km *(3.2 n miles)*; weight of shell 0.35 kg.
A/S mortars: 1 Bofors 375 mm twin trainable launcher ❺; automatic loading; range 3,600 m.
Countermeasures: Decoys: 2 CSEE Dagaie trainable systems; replaceable containers for IR or chaff.
ESM: MEL Rapids; radar intercept.
ECM: MEL Scimitar; jammer.
Combat data systems: Signaal Sewaco-MA. Link Y Mk 2.
Weapons control: 2 Signaal LIOD optronic directors for gunnery.
Radars: Air/surface search: Signaal DA08 ❻; F-band; range 204 km *(110 n miles)* for 2 m² target.
Navigation: Decca TM 1226C; I-band.
Fire control: Signaal WM22 ❼; I/J-band.
IFF: US Mk 10.
Sonars: Atlas Elektronik DSQS-21C; hull-mounted; active search and attack; medium frequency.

Helicopters: Platform for 1 Westland Wasp HAS 1 ❽.

Programmes: First two ordered in February 1981. Fabrication began early 1982. Rated as Corvettes even though they are bigger ships than *Rahmat*.
Modernisation: Plans to fit telescopic hangars have been shelved. Mid-life update planned to include CIWS, and torpedo tubes vice the obsolete ASW mortar. Sewaco combat data system upgraded in 1997-98.
Structure: Near sisters to the Colombian ships with differing armament.
Operational: *Kasturi* is the trials ship for 'smart ship' reduced manning.

UPDATED

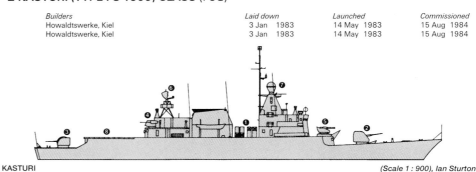

KASTURI *(Scale 1 : 900), Ian Sturton*

LEKIR *11/1999*, Paul Jackson /* 0081209

LEKIR
12/1999*, Sattler/Steele / 0081210

4 LAKSAMANA (ASSAD) CLASS (FSG)

Name	No	Builders	Laid down	Launched	Commissioned
LAKSAMANA HANG NADIM (ex-*Khalid Ibn Al Walid*)	F 134 (ex-F 216)	Fincantieri, Breda, Mestre	3 June 1982	5 July 1983	28 July 1997
LAKSAMANA TUN ABDUL JAMIL (ex-*Saad Ibn Abi Waccade*)	F 135 (ex-F 218)	Fincantieri, Breda, Marghera	17 Sep 1982	2 Dec 1983	28 July 1997
LAKSAMANA MUHAMMAD AMIN (ex-*Abdulla Ben Abi Sarh*)	F 136 (ex-F 214)	Fincantieri, Breda, Mestre	22 Mar 1982	5 July 1983	31 July 1999
LAKSAMANA TAN PUSMAH (ex-*Salahi Ad Deen Alayoori*)	F 137 (ex-F 220)	Fincantieri, Breda, Marghera	17 Sep 1982	30 Mar 1984	31 July 1999

Displacement, tons: 705 full load
Dimensions, feet (metres): 204.4 × 30.5 × 8
(62.3 × 9.3 × 2.5)
Main machinery: 4 MTU 20V 956 TB92 diesels; 20,120 hp(m)
(14.8 MW) sustained; 4 shafts
Speed, knots: 36. **Range, miles:** 2,300 at 18 kt
Complement: 47

Missiles: SSM: 6 OTO Melara/Matra Otomat Teseo Mk 2 (TG 2)
(3 twin) ❶; command guidance; active radar homing to
180 km *(98.4 n miles)* at 0.9 Mach; warhead 210 kg; sea-
skimmer.
SAM: 1 Selenia/Elsag Albatros launcher ❷ (4 cell—2 reloads);
Aspide; semi-active radar homing to 13 km *(7 n miles)* at
2.5 Mach; height envelope 15-5,000 m *(49.2-16,405 ft)*;
warhead 30 kg.

Guns: 1 OTO Melara 3 in *(76 mm)*/62 Super Rapid ❸; 120 rds/
min to 16 km *(8.7 n miles)* anti-surface; 12 km *(6.6 n miles)*
anti-aircraft; weight of shell 6 kg.
2 Breda 40 mm/70 (twin) ❹; 300 rds/min to 12.5 km *(6.8 n
miles)*; weight of shell 0.96 kg.
Torpedoes: 6—324 mm ILAS 3 (2 triple) tubes ❺. Whitehead
A244S; anti-submarine; active/passive homing to 7 km *(3.8 n
miles)*; warhead 34 kg (shaped charge).
Countermeasures: Decoys: 2 Breda 105 mm 6-tubed
multipurpose launchers; chaff to 5 km *(2.7 n miles)*; illuminants
to 12 km *(6.6 n miles)*.
ESM: Selenia INS-3; intercept.
ECM: Selenia TQN-2; jammer.
Combat data systems: Selenia IPN 10; Signaal/AESN Link Y Mk
2.

Weapons control: 2 Selenia NA 21; Dardo.
Radars: Air/surface search: Selenia RAN 12L/X ❻; D/I-band;
range 82 km *(45 n miles)*.
Navigation: Kelvin Hughes 1007; I-band.
Fire control: 2 Selenia RTN 10X ❼; I/J-band; 1 Selenia RTN 20X
❽; I/J-band.
Sonars: Atlas Elektronik ASO 84-41; hull-mounted; active search
and attack.

Programmes: Ordered in February 1981 for the Iraqi Navy and
fell foul of UN sanctions before they could either be paid for or
delivered. Subsequently completed in 1988 and maintained by
Fincantieri. Two near sister ships were paid for by Iraq and
remain laid up in Italian ports. Contract signed on 26 October
1995, and confirmed on 26 July 1996, to transfer two of the
class to the Malaysian Navy after refit at Muggiano and three
months training in Italy. Contract for two more signed on
20 February 1997 for conversion and delivery.
Modernisation: Super Rapid 76 mm gun, datalink, new
navigation radar and GPS fitted in 1996. Bridge wings are
extended to the after gun deck. Second pair were to have been
fitted with IPN 20 combat system but this was shelved. Alenia
Teleguidance Mk 2 mid-course guidance to be fitted for SSM.
Structure: NBC citadel and full air conditioning fitted.
Operational: First pair arrived in Malaysia in September 1997.
Second pair delayed by payment problems but arrived in
September 1999.
Opinion: This is an unusual purchase because of the lack of
equipment commonality with the rest of the Fleet.

UPDATED

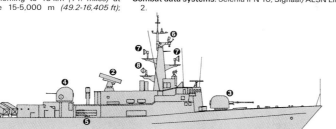

LAKSAMANA HANG NADIM
(Scale 1 : 600), Ian Sturton / 0052581

LAKSAMANA HANG NADIM
11/1999*, Paul Jackson / 0081207

LAKSAMANA TAN PUSMAH
12/1999*, Sattler/Steele / 0081208

SHIPBORNE AIRCRAFT

Note: Sikorsky S-61A Nuri Army support helicopter can be embarked in two Logistic Support Ships and two OPVs.

NURI   6/1997* / 0081211

Numbers/Type: 3 Westland Wasp HAS 1.
Operational speed: 96 kt (177 km/h).
Service ceiling: 12,200 ft (3,720 m).
Range: 268 n miles (488 km).
Role/Weapon systems: First naval air arm helicopter; six acquired in April 1988 and five in 1989-90. Six are used for spares. These last three updated to remain in service to 2004. Sensors: None. Weapons: ASW; 1 or 2 Mk 44 torpedoes, Mk II depth bombs.

UPDATED

Numbers/Type: 4 GKN Westland Super Lynx.
Operational speed: 120 kt (222 km/h).
Service ceiling: 10,000 ft (3,048 m).
Range: 320 n miles (593 km).
Role/Weapon systems: Ordered on 3 September 1999 for delivery 2001-2003. To be used for OTHT and ASW. Sensors: Seaspray radar; ESM. Weapons: ASW; two torpedoes or depth bombs. ASV: 2—12.7 mm MGs; possible ASM in due course.

NEW ENTRY

LYNX (UK colours)   6/1999*, A Sharma / 0081212

LAND-BASED MARITIME AIRCRAFT

Note: The Air Force has eight F/A-18D fighter-bombers with Harpoon ASM, and 28 Hawk fighters with Sea Eagle ASM.

Numbers/Type: 4 Beechcraft B 200T Super King.
Operational speed: 282 kt (523 km/h).
Service ceiling: 35,000 ft (10,670 m).
Range: 2,030 n miles (3,756 km).
Role/Weapon systems: Used for maritime surveillance. Acquired in 1994. Air Force operated. Sensors: Search radar. Weapons: Unarmed.

UPDATED

SUPER KING   6/1993* / 0084007

WASP (New Zealand colours)   6/1996* / 0081213

PATROL FORCES

2 MUSYTARI CLASS (OFFSHORE PATROL VESSELS) (OPV)

Name	No	Builders	Launched	Commissioned
MUSYTARI	160	Korea Shipbuilders, Pusan	20 July 1984	19 Dec 1985
MARIKH	161	Malaysia SB and E Co, Johore	21 Jan 1985	9 Apr 1987

Displacement, tons: 1,300 full load
Dimensions, feet (metres): 246 × 35.4 × 12.1 (75 × 10.8 × 3.7)
Main machinery: 2 SEMT-Pielstick diesels; 12,720 hp(m) (9.35 MW); 2 shafts
Speed, knots: 22. **Range, miles:** 5,000 at 15 kt
Complement: 76 (10 officers)
Guns: 1 Creusot-Loire 3.9 in (100 mm)/55 Mk 2 compact; 20/45/90 rds/min to 17 km (9.2 n miles) anti-surface; 6 km (3.2 n miles) anti-aircraft; weight of shell 13.5 kg.
2 Emerson Electric 30 mm (twin); 1,200 rds/min combined to 6 km (3.2 n miles); weight of shell 0.35 kg.
Countermeasures: ESM: Racal Cutlass; intercept.
Weapons control: PEAB 9LV 230 optronic system.
Radars: Air/surface search: Signaal DA05; E/F-band; range 137 km (75 n miles) for 2 m² target.
Navigation: Racal Decca TM 1226; I-band.
Fire control: Philips 9LV; J-band.

Helicopters: Platform for 1 medium.

Programmes: Ordered in June 1983. Names translate to Jupiter and Mars.
Structure: Flight deck suitable for Sikorsky S-61A Nuri army support helicopter.

VERIFIED

MARIKH
5/1997 / 0052583

0 + 6 MEKO A 100 TYPE (OPV)

Displacement, tons: 1,300 full load
Dimensions, feet (metres): 262.5 × 39.4 × 9.8 *(80 × 12 × 3)*
Main machinery: 2 Caterpillar diesels; 2 shafts
Speed, knots: 22. **Range, miles:** 6,000 at 12 kt
Complement: 72 (11 officers)
Missiles: Fitted for SSM and VLS SAM.
Guns: 1 Otobreda 76 mm/62. 2 Mauser 27 mm.
Countermeasures: ESM/ECM.
Combat data systems: STN Atlas Cosys 110M1.
Weapons control: TMEO optronic director.
Radars: Air/surface search. DASA TRS-3D.
Helicopters: Platform only.

Comment: 27 vessels have been approved to be built over a period of 20 years. First batch of six at
Naval Dockyard, Lumut. Invitation for tenders first issued 30 November 1994. German Naval
Group (GNG) selected in October 1997, and put forward a modified MEKO 100 design. First two
ordered provisionally 6 September 1998 with an option on four more which was confirmed in
August 1999. Hull sections of the first pair are being built in Germany and shipped to Lumut for
fitting out by the Penang Shipbuilding Corporation. First ship is expected to complete in late
2004. May be fitted for but not with SSM and SAM systems. Some details given are speculative.
UPDATED

MEKO A 100 (computer graphic)   *1998, Blohm + Voss* / 0067258

4 HANDALAN (SPICA-M) CLASS
(FAST ATTACK CRAFT—MISSILE) (PCFG)

Name	No	Builders	Commissioned
HANDALAN	3511	Karlskrona, Sweden	26 Oct 1979
PERKASA	3512	Karlskrona, Sweden	26 Oct 1979
PENDEKAR	3513	Karlskrona, Sweden	26 Oct 1979
GEMPITA	3514	Karlskrona, Sweden	26 Oct 1979

Displacement, tons: 240 full load
Dimensions, feet (metres): 142.6 × 23.3 × 7.4 (screws) *(43.6 × 7.1 × 2.4)*
Main machinery: 3 MTU 16V 538 TB91 diesels; 9,180 hp(m) *(6.75 MW)* sustained; 3 shafts
Speed, knots: 34.5. **Range, miles:** 1,850 at 14 kt
Complement: 40 (6 officers)

Missiles: SSM: 4 Aerospatiale MM 38 Exocet; inertial cruise; active radar homing to 42 km *(23 n
miles)* at 0.9 Mach; sea-skimmer.
Guns: 1 Bofors 57 mm/70 Mk 1; 200 rds/min to 17 km *(9.2 n miles)*; weight of shell 2.4 kg.
Illuminant launchers.
1 Bofors 40 mm/70; 300 rds/min to 12 km *(6.5 n miles)* anti-surface; 4 km *(2.2 n miles)* anti-
aircraft; weight of shell 0.96 kg.
Countermeasures: ECM: MEL Susie.
Weapons control: 1 PEAB 9LV212 Mk 2 weapon control system with TV tracking. LME anti-aircraft
laser and TV rangefinder.
Radars: Surface search: Philips 9GR 600; I-band (agile frequency).
Navigation: Racal Decca 1226; I-band.
Fire control: Philips 9LV 212; J-band.

Programmes: Ordered 15 October 1976. All named in one ceremony on 11 November 1978,
arriving in Port Klang on 26 October 1979.
Modernisation: There are plans to replace the MM 38 with MM 40 or Teseo missiles and to update
radar and EW.
Structure: Bridge further forward than in Swedish class to accommodate Exocet. Plans to fit an
ASW capability were shelved and the sonar removed.
Operational: *Handalan* acts as squadron leader.
UPDATED

PERKASA   *12/1999*, Sattler/Steele* / 0081214

4 PERDANA (LA COMBATTANTE II) CLASS
(FAST ATTACK CRAFT—MISSILE) (PCFG)

Name	No	Builders	Launched	Commissioned
PERDANA	3501	CMN, Cherbourg	31 May 1972	21 Dec 1972
SERANG	3502	CMN, Cherbourg	22 Dec 1971	31 Jan 1973
GANAS	3503	CMN, Cherbourg	26 Oct 1972	28 Feb 1973
GANYANG	3504	CMN, Cherbourg	16 Mar 1972	20 Mar 1973

Displacement, tons: 234 standard; 265 full load
Dimensions, feet (metres): 154.2 × 23.1 × 12.8 *(47 × 7 × 3.9)*
Main machinery: 4 MTU MB 870 diesels; 14,000 hp(m) *(10.3 MW)*; 4 shafts
Speed, knots: 36.5. **Range, miles:** 800 at 25 kt; 1,800 at 15 kt
Complement: 30 (4 officers)

Missiles: SSM: 2 Aerospatiale MM 38 Exocet; inertial cruise; active radar homing to 42 km *(23 n
miles)* at 0.9 Mach; warhead 165 kg; sea-skimmer. Not always carried.
Guns: 1 Bofors 57 mm/70; 200 rds/min to 17 km *(9.2 n miles)*; weight of shell 2.4 kg.
1 Bofors 40 mm/70; 300 rds/min to 12 km *(6.5 n miles)* anti-surface; 4 km *(2.2 n miles)* anti-
aircraft; weight of shell 0.96 kg.
Countermeasures: Decoys: 4—57 mm chaff/flare launchers.
ESM: Thomson-CSF DR 2000; intercept.
Weapons control: Thomson-CSF Vega optical for guns.
Radars: Air/surface search: Thomson-CSF TH-D 1040 Triton; G-band; range 33 km *(18 n miles)* for
2 m² target.
Navigation: Racal Decca 616; I-band.
Fire control: Thomson-CSF Pollux; I/J-band; range 31 km *(17 n miles)* for 2 m² target.

Programmes: Left Cherbourg for Malaysia 2 May 1973.
Modernisation: There are plans to replace MM 38 with MM 40 or Teseo SSMs and to update radar
and EW.
Structure: All of basic La Combattante II design with steel hulls and aluminium superstructure.
UPDATED

PERDANA   *12/1999*, Sattler/Steele* / 0081216

18 SABAH and KRIS CLASSES (PATROL CRAFT) (PC)

Name	No	Builders	Commissioned
SRI SABAH	3144	Vosper Ltd, Portsmouth	2 Sep 1964
SRI SARAWAK	3145	Vosper Ltd, Portsmouth	30 Sep 1964
SRI NEGRI SEMBILAN	3146	Vosper Ltd, Portsmouth	28 Sep 1964
SRI MELAKA	3147	Vosper Ltd, Portsmouth	2 Nov 1964
KRIS	34	Vosper Ltd, Portsmouth	1 Jan 1966
SUNDANG	36	Vosper Ltd, Portsmouth	29 Nov 1966
BADEK	37	Vosper Ltd, Portsmouth	15 Dec 1966
RENCHONG	38	Vosper Ltd, Portsmouth	17 Jan 1967
TOMBAK	39	Vosper Ltd, Portsmouth	2 Mar 1967
LEMBING	40*	Vosper Ltd, Portsmouth	12 Apr 1967
SERAMPANG	41	Vosper Ltd, Portsmouth	19 May 1967
PANAH	42	Vosper Ltd, Portsmouth	27 July 1967
KERAMBIT	43*	Vosper Ltd, Portsmouth	28 July 1967
BELADAU	44*	Vosper Ltd, Portsmouth	12 Sep 1967
KELEWANG	45	Vosper Ltd, Portsmouth	4 Oct 1967
RENTAKA	46	Vosper Ltd, Portsmouth	22 Sep 1967
SRI PERLIS	47*	Vosper Ltd, Portsmouth	24 Jan 1968
SRI JOHOR	49*	Vosper Ltd, Portsmouth	14 Feb 1968

* Training

Displacement, tons: 96 standard; 109 full load
Dimensions, feet (metres): 103 × 19.8 × 5.5 *(31.4 × 6 × 1.7)*
Main machinery: 2 Bristol Siddeley or MTU MD 655/18 diesels; 3,500 hp(m) *(2.57 MW)*; 2 shafts
Speed, knots: 27. **Range, miles:** 1,400 (1,660 'Sabah' class) at 14 kt
Complement: 22 (3 officers)
Guns: 2 Bofors 40 mm/70. 2—7.62 mm MGs.
Radars: Surface search: Racal Decca 616 or 707; I-band.

Comment: The four 'Sabah' class were ordered in 1963 for delivery in 1964. The boats of the 'Kris'
class were ordered in 1965 for delivery between 1966 and 1968. All are of prefabricated steel
construction and are fitted with air conditioning and Vosper roll damping equipment. The
differences between the classes are minor, the later ones having improved radar,
communications, evaporators and engines of MTU, as opposed to Bristol Siddeley construction.
All have been refitted to extend their operational lives. Eight are based at Sandakan.
UPDATED

SUNDANG   *4/1997*, Maritime Photographic* / 0012749

SRI NEGRI SEMBILAN   *4/1995** / 0081215

6 JERONG CLASS (FAST ATTACK CRAFT—GUN) (PCF)

Name	No	Builders	Commissioned
JERONG	3505	Hong Leong-Lürssen, Butterworth	27 Mar 1976
TODAK	3506	Hong Leong-Lürssen, Butterworth	16 June 1976
PAUS	3507	Hong Leong-Lürssen, Butterworth	16 Aug 1976
YU	3508	Hong Leong-Lürssen, Butterworth	15 Nov 1976
BAUNG	3509	Hong Leong-Lürssen, Butterworth	11 Jan 1977
PARI	3510	Hong Leong-Lürssen, Butterworth	23 Mar 1977

Displacement, tons: 244 full load
Dimensions, feet (metres): 147.3 × 23 × 8.3 *(44.9 × 7 × 2.5)*
Main machinery: 3 MTU MB 16V 538 TB90 diesels; 9,000 hp(m) *(6.6 MW)* sustained; 3 shafts
Speed, knots: 32. **Range, miles:** 2,000 at 14 kt
Complement: 36 (4 officers)
Guns: 1 Bofors 57 mm/70 Mk 1. 200 rds/min to 17 km *(9.2 n miles)*; weight of shell 2.4 kg.
    1 Bofors 40 mm/70.
Weapons control: CSEE Naja optronic director.
Radars: Surface search: Racal Decca 1226; I-band.

Comment: Lürssen 45 type. Illuminant launchers on both gun mountings.
                                                                                 VERIFIED

PARI   5/1990, John Mortimer / 0081217

MINE WARFARE FORCES

4 MAHAMIRU (LERICI) CLASS (MINEHUNTERS) (MHC)

Name	No	Builders	Launched		Commissioned
MAHAMIRU	11	Intermarine, Italy	23 Feb	1984	11 Dec 1985
JERAI	12	Intermarine, Italy	5 Jan	1984	11 Dec 1985
LEDANG	13	Intermarine, Italy	14 July	1983	11 Dec 1985
KINABALU	14	Intermarine, Italy	19 Mar	1983	11 Dec 1985

Displacement, tons: 610 full load
Dimensions, feet (metres): 167.3 × 32.5 × 9.2 *(51 × 9.9 × 2.8)*
Main machinery: 2 MTU 12V 396 TC82 diesels (passage); 2,605 hp(m) *(1.91 MW)* sustained;
    2 shafts; Kamewa cp props; 3 Fincantieri Isotta Fraschini ID 36 SS 6V diesels; 1,481 hp(m)
    (1.09 MW) sustained; 2 Riva Calzoni hydraulic thrust jets
Speed, knots: 16 diesels; 7 thrust jet. **Range, miles:** 2,000 at 12 kt
Complement: 42 (5 officers)
Guns: 1 Bofors 40 mm/70; 300 rds/min to 12.5 km *(6.8 n miles)*; weight of shell 0.96 kg.
Countermeasures: Thomson-CSF IBIS II minehunting system; 2 improved PAP 104 ROVs.
    Oropesa 'O' MIS-4 mechanical sweep.
Radars: Navigation: Racal Decca 1226; Thomson-CSF Tripartite III; I-band.
Sonars: Thomson Sintra TSM 2022 with Display 2060; minehunting; high frequency.

Comment: Ordered on 20 February 1981. All arrived in Malaysia on 26 March 1986. Heavy GRP
    construction without frames. Snach active tank stabilisers. Draeger Duocom decompression
    chamber. Slightly longer than Italian sisters. Endurance, 14 days. There are plans to upgrade the
    tactical data system. Two based at Lumut and two at Labuan.   *UPDATED*

KINABALU   12/1999*, Sattler/Steele / 0081218

AMPHIBIOUS FORCES

1 NEWPORT CLASS (LST)

Name	No	Builders	Laid down		Launched		Commissioned	
SRI INDERAPURA (ex-*Spartanburg County*)	1505 (ex-1192)	National Steel, San Diego	7 Feb	1970	11 Nov	1970	1 Sep	1971

Displacement, tons: 4,975 light; 8,450 full load
Dimensions, feet (metres): 522.3 (hull) × 69.5 × 17.5 (aft)
    (159.2 × 21.2 × 5.3)

Main machinery: 6 ALCO 16-251 diesels; 16,500 hp *(12.3 MW)*
    sustained; 2 shafts; cp props; bow thruster
Speed, knots: 20. **Range, miles:** 2,500 at 14 kt

Complement: 257 (13 officers)
Military lift: 400 troops (20 officers); 500 tons vehicles; 3 LCVPs
    and 1 LCPL on davits

Guns: 1 General Electric/General Dynamics 20 mm Vulcan
    Phalanx Mk 15.
Radars: Surface search: Raytheon SPS-67; G-band.
    Navigation: Marconi LN66; I/J-band.

Helicopters: Platform only.

Programmes: Transferred by sale from the USN 16 December
    1994, arriving in Malaysia in June 1995. Second authorised for
    transfer by lease in 1998 but this was not confirmed.
Structure: The hull form required to achieve 20 kt would not
    permit bow doors, thus these ships unload by a 112 ft ramp
    over their bow. The ramp is supported by twin derrick arms. A
    ramp just forward of the superstructure connects the lower
    tank deck with the main deck and a vehicle passage through
    the superstructure provides access to the parking area
    amidships. A stern gate to the tank deck permits unloading of
    amphibious tractors into the water, or unloading of other
    vehicles into an LCU or onto a pier. Vehicle stowage covers
    19,000 sq ft. Length over derrick arms is 562 ft *(171.3 m)*; full
    load draught is 11.5 ft forward and 17.5 ft aft.
Operational: 3 in guns removed before transfer. Repeated refits
    in Johore shipyard between late 1995 and 1998.
                                                                 UPDATED

SRI INDERAPURA
5/1995*, Robert Pabst / 0081219

28 LCM/LCP/LCU

LCM 1-5   LCP 1-15   RCP 1-9   LCU 1-4

Displacement, tons: 56 (LCM); 30 (LCU/RCP); 18.5 (LCVP) full load
Main machinery: 2 diesels; 330 hp *(246 kW)* (LCM); 400 hp *(298 kW)* (LCVP); 2 shafts
Speed, knots: 10 (LCM); 16 (LCVP); 17 (LCU/RCP)
Military lift: 30 tons (LCM); 35 troops (LCU/RCP/LCP)

Comment: LCMs and LCPs are Australian built and transferred 1965-70. LCMs have light armour
    on sides and some have gun turrets. RCPs and LCUs are Malaysian built and in service 1974-84.
    Transferred to the Army in 1993.
                                                                 UPDATED

130 DAMEN ASSAULT CRAFT 540

Dimensions, feet (metres): 17.7 × 5.9 × 2 *(5.4 × 1.8 × 0.6)*
Main machinery: 1 outboard; 40 hp(m) *(29.4 kW)*
Speed, knots: 12
Military lift: 10 troops

Comment: First 65 built by Damen Gorinchem, Netherlands in 1986. Remainder built by
    Limbungan Timor SY. Army assault craft. Manportable and similar to Singapore craft. Used by
    the Army. Some have been deleted.   *UPDATED*

LCM 5 (with gun turret)   6/1995* / 0012753

AUXILIARIES

2 LOGISTIC SUPPORT SHIPS (AOR/AE/AX)

Name	No	Builders	Commissioned
SRI INDERA SAKTI	1503	Bremer Vulkan	24 Oct 1980
MAHAWANGSA	1504	Korea Tacoma	16 May 1983

Displacement, tons: 4,300 (1503); 4,900 (1504) full load
Dimensions, feet (metres): 328; 337.9 (1504) × 49.2 × 15.7 *(100; 103 × 15 × 4.8)*
Main machinery: 2 Deutz KHD SBV6M540 diesels; 5,865 hp(m) *(4.31 MW)*; 2 shafts; cp props; bow thruster
Speed, knots: 16.5. **Range, miles:** 4,000 at 14 kt
Complement: 136 (14 officers) plus 65 spare
Military lift: 17 tanks; 600 troops
Cargo capacity: 1,300 tons dieso; 200 tons fresh water (plus 48 tons/day distillers)

Guns: 2 Bofors 57 mm Mk 1 (1 only fwd in 1503). 2 Oerlikon 20 mm.
Weapons control: 2 CSEE Naja optronic directors (1 only in 1503).
Radars: Navigation: Decca TM 1226; I-band.

Helicopters: 1 Sikorsky S-61A Nuri (army support) can be carried.

Programmes: Ordered in October 1979 and 1981 respectively.
Modernisation: 100 mm gun included in original design but used for OPVs.
Structure: Fitted with stabilising system, vehicle deck, embarkation ramps port and starboard, recompression chamber and a stern anchor. Large operations room and a conference room are provided. Transfer stations on either beam and aft, light jackstay on both sides and a 15 ton crane for replenishment at sea. 1504 has additional capacity to transport ammunition and the funnel has been removed to enlarge the flight deck which is also higher in the superstructure.
Operational: Used as training ships for cadets in addition to main roles of long-range support of Patrol Forces and MCM vessels, command and communications and troop or ammunition transport.

UPDATED

SRI INDERA SAKTI   *5/1998, John Mortimer /* 0052588

MAHAWANGSA   *6/1997* /* 0081220

7 COASTAL SUPPLY SHIPS AND TANKERS (AOTL/AKSL)

LANG TIRAM	ENTERPRISE	KEPAH	LANG SIPUT
MELEBAN	JERNIH	TERIJAH	

Comment: Various auxiliaries mostly acquired in the early 1980s. There are also Sabah supply ships identified by M numbers.

VERIFIED

MELEBAN   *4/1997, M A Horsfield, RAN /* 0012757

SURVEY SHIPS

Note: There is also a Survey craft *Penyu* 4 of 465 tons commissioned in 1979. Used as a diving tender. Complement is 26 (two officers).

1 SURVEY VESSEL (AGS)

Name	No	Builders	Commissioned
MUTIARA	152	Hong Leong-Lürssen, Butterworth	12 Jan 1978

Displacement, tons: 1,905 full load
Dimensions, feet (metres): 232.9 × 42.6 × 13.1 *(71 × 13 × 4)*
Main machinery: 2 Deutz SBA12M528 diesels; 4,000 hp(m) *(2.94 MW)*; 2 shafts
Speed, knots: 16. **Range, miles:** 4,500 at 16 kt
Complement: 155 (14 officers)
Guns: 4 Oerlikon 20 mm (2 twin).
Radars: Navigation: 2 Racal Decca 1226/1229; I-band.
Helicopters: Platform only.

Comment: Ordered in early 1975. Carries satellite navigation, auto-data system and computerised fixing system. Davits for six survey launches. Painted white with yellow funnel and mast.

UPDATED

MUTIARA   *12/1997*, John Mortimer /* 0012758

1 SURVEY VESSEL (AGS)

Name	No	Builders	Commissioned
PERANTAU	153	Hong Leong-Lürssen, Butterworth	12 Oct 1998

Displacement, tons: 1,996 full load
Dimensions, feet (metres): 222.4 × 43.6 × 13.1 *(67.8 × 13.3 × 4)*
Main machinery: 2 Deutz/MWM SBV8 M628 diesels; 4,787 hp(m) *(3.52 MW)*; 2 shafts; Berg cp props; Schottel bow thruster
Speed, knots: 16. **Range, miles:** 6,000 at 10 kt
Complement: 94 (17 officers)
Radars: Navigation: STN Atlas; I-band.

Comment: Ordered from Krogerwerft in 1996. The ship is equipped with two survey launches and four multipurpose boats and has three winches and two cranes, including a hoist for a STN Atlas side scan sonar. Full range of hydrographic and mapping equipment embarked.

UPDATED

PERANTAU   *12/1999*, Sattler/Steele /* 0081221

PERANTAU   *10/1998*, Hong Leong-Lürssen /* 0017682

TRAINING SHIPS

1 HANG TUAH (TYPE 41/61) CLASS (FF/AX)

Name	No	Builders	Commissioned
HANG TUAH (ex-*Mermaid*)	76	Yarrow (Shipbuilders), Glasgow	16 May 1973

Displacement, tons: 2,300 standard; 2,520 full load
Dimensions, feet (metres): 339.3 × 40 × 16 (screws) *(103.5 × 12.2 × 4.9)*
Main machinery: 2 Stork Wärtsilä 12SW28 diesels; 9,928 hp(m) *(7.3 MW)* sustained; 2 shafts; cp props
Speed, knots: 24. **Range, miles:** 4,800 at 15 kt
Complement: 210
Guns: 1 Bofors 57 mm/70 Mk 1; 200 rds/min to 17 km *(9.2 n miles)*; weight of shell 2.4 kg.
2 Bofors 40 mm/70; 300 rds/min to 12 km *(6.5 n miles)* anti-surface; 4 km *(2.2 n miles)* anti-aircraft; weight of shell 0.96 kg.
Radars: Air/surface search: Plessey AWS 1; E/F-band.
Navigation: Racal Decca 45; I-band.
Sonars: Graseby Type 170B and Type 174; hull-mounted; active search and attack; 15 kHz.
Helicopters: Platform for 1 Westland Wasp HAS 1 or Super Lynx.

Comment: Originally built for Ghana as a display ship for ex-President Nkrumah but put up for sale after his departure. She was launched without ceremony on 29 December 1966 and completed in 1968. Commissioned in Royal Navy 16 May 1973 and transferred to Royal Malaysian Navy May 1977. Refitted in 1991-92 to become a training ship. Main gun and main engines replaced in 1995-96. The Limbo A/S mortar is non-operational, although the mounting is still fitted.
UPDATED

HANG TUAH   *12/1999*, Sattler/Steele /* 0081222

1 RAHMAT CLASS (FF/AX)

Name	No	Builders	Launched	Commissioned
RAHMAT (ex-*Hang Jebat*)	24	Yarrow, Glasgow	18 Dec 1967	31 Aug 1971

Displacement, tons: 1,250 standard; 1,600 full load
Dimensions, feet (metres): 308 × 34.1 × 14.8 *(93.9 × 10.4 × 4.5)*
Main machinery: CODOG; 1 Bristol Siddeley Olympus TM1B gas turbine; 20,626 hp *(15.4 MW)*; 1 Crossley Pielstick PC2.2 V diesel; 4,000 hp *(2.94 MW)*; 2 shafts; cp props
Speed, knots: 26 gas; 16 diesel
Range, miles: 6,000 at 16 kt; 1,000 at 26 kt
Complement: 140 (12 officers)

Guns: 1 Vickers 4.5 in *(114 mm)*/45 Mk 5 hand-loaded; 14 rds/min to 17 km *(9.2 n miles)* anti-surface; 8 km *(4.4 n miles)* anti-aircraft; weight of shell 25 kg. 103 mm rocket for illuminants on each side of mounting.
3 Bofors 40 mm/70; 300 rds/min to 12 km *(6.5 n miles)* anti-surface; 4 km *(2.2 n miles)* anti-aircraft; weight of shell 0.96 kg.
Countermeasures: Decoys: 2 UK Mk I rail chaff launchers.
ESM: UA-3; radar intercept; FH4 HF D/F.
Combat data systems: Signaal Sewaco-MA. Link Y.
Radars: Surface search: Decca 626; I-band.
Navigation: Kelvin Hughes MS 32; I-band.
Fire control: Signaal M 22; I/J-band; short range.

Programmes: Ordered on 11 February 1966. Arrived on station 23 December 1972.
Modernisation: Seacat system removed during refit in 1982-83 and replaced by an additional Bofors gun. There are plans for further modernisation in due course including new engines as in *Hang Tuah*, to retain the ship as a training vessel.
Operational: Can land helicopter on MacGregor hatch over former Mk 10 well. ASW equipment is all unserviceable and the Air Search radar has been removed and replaced by a 40 mm gun.
UPDATED

RAHMAT   *12/1997*, G Toremans /* 0012740

1 SAIL TRAINING SHIP (AXS)

Name	No	Builders	Commissioned
TUNAS SAMUDERA	A 13	Brooke Yacht, Lowestoft	16 Oct 1989

Displacement, tons: 239 full load
Dimensions, feet (metres): 114.8 × 25.6 × 13.1 *(35 × 7.8 × 4)*
Main machinery: 2 Perkins diesels; 370 hp *(272 kW)*; 2 shafts
Speed, knots: 9
Complement: 10 plus 26 trainees
Radars: Navigation: Racal Decca; I-band.

Comment: Laid down 1 December 1988 and launched 4 August 1989. Two-masted brig manned by the Navy but used for training all sea services.
UPDATED

TUNAS SAMUDERA   *12/1997*, G Toremans /* 0012759

POLICE

14 LANG HITAM CLASS

LANG HITAM PZ 1	BELIAN PZ 6	HARIMAU AKAR PZ 12
LANG MALAM PZ 2	KURITA PZ 7	PERANGAN PZ 13
LANG LEBAH PZ 3	SERANGAN BATU PZ 8	MERSUJI PZ 14
LANG KUIK PZ 4	HARIMAU BINTANG PZ 9	ALU-ALU PZ 15
BALONG PZ 5	HARIMAU BELANG PZ 11	

Displacement, tons: 230 full load
Dimensions, feet (metres): 126.3 × 22.9 × 5.9 *(38.5 × 7 × 1.8)*
Main machinery: 2 MTU 20V 538 TB92 diesels; 8,360 hp(m) *(6.14 MW)* sustained; 2 shafts
Speed, knots: 35. **Range, miles:** 1,200 at 15 kt
Complement: 38 (4 officers)
Guns: 1 Bofors 40 mm/70 (in a distinctive plastic turret).
1 Oerlikon 20 mm. 2 FN 7.62 mm MGs.
Radars: Navigation: Kelvin Hughes; I-band.

Comment: Ordered from Hong Leong-Lürssen, Butterworth, Malaysia in 1979. First delivered August 1980, last in April 1983. One deleted in 1994.
UPDATED

HARIMAU BINTANG   *12/1999*, Sattler/Steele /* 0081223

6 BROOKE MARINE 29 METRE CLASS

SANGITAN PX 28	DUNGUN PX 30	TUMPAT PX 32
SABAHAN PX 29	TIOMAN PX 31	SEGAMA PX 33

Displacement, tons: 114 full load
Dimensions, feet (metres): 95.1 × 19.7 × 5.6 *(29 × 6 × 1.7)*
Main machinery: 2 Paxman Valenta 6CM diesels; 2,250 hp *(1.68 MW)* sustained; 2 shafts
Speed, knots: 36. **Range, miles:** 1,200 at 24 kt
Complement: 18 (4 officers)
Guns: 1 Oerlikon 20 mm. 2—7.62 mm MGs.

Comment: Ordered 1979 from Penang Shipbuilding Co. First delivery June 1981, last pair completed June 1982. Brooke Marine provided lead yard services.
VERIFIED

SANGITAN   *1991, RM Police*

120 INSHORE/RIVER PATROL CRAFT

Comment: Built in several batches and designs since 1964. Some are armed with 7.62 mm MGs. All have PA/PC/PGR/PSC numbers. Included are 23 Simmoneau SM 465 type built between January 1992 and mid-1993.   *UPDATED*

PA 43   *12/1997*, G Toremans /* 0081224

PC 6   *4/1997*, Maritime Photographic /* 0012763

PSC 20   *12/1999*, Sattler/Steele /* 0081225

6 STAN PATROL 1500 CLASS

Dimensions, feet (metres): 48.6 × 8.9 × 2.6 *(14.8 × 2.7 × 0.8)*
Main machinery: 4 diesels; 4,500 hp(m) *(33.1 MW)*; 4 shafts; acbLIPS props
Speed, knots: 55
Complement: 8
Guns: 2—12.7 mm MGs.

Comment: Built in Malaysia and completed in 1998/99. Details are not confirmed.   *UPDATED*

TUGS

11 HARBOUR TUGS AND CRAFT (YTM/YTL)

TUNDA SATU 1-3	KETAM	TERITUP	
SIPUT	BELAWKAS	KEMPONG	
SOTONG	SELAR	TEPURUK	*VERIFIED*

TUNDA SATU   *12/1997, G Toremans /* 0052591

CUSTOMS

Note: In addition there are about 25 interceptor craft of 9 m, and 30 of 13.7 m and some inflatable chase boats.

4 PEMBANTERAS CLASS

Displacement, tons: 58 full load
Dimensions, feet (metres): 94.5 × 19.4 × 6.6 *(28.8 × 5.9 × 2)*
Main machinery: 2 Deutz SBA16M816C diesels; 3,140 hp(m) *(2.31 MW)*; 2 shafts
Speed, knots: 20
Complement: 8

Comment: Built at Limbungan Timor shipyard, Terengganu and completed in 1993.   *VERIFIED*

2 COMBATBOAT 90E

Displacement, tons: 19 full load
Dimensions, feet (metres): 52.2 × 12.5 × 2.6 *(15.9 × 3.8 × 0.8)*
Main machinery: 2 Volvo Penta TAMD 163P diesels; 1,500 hp(m) *(1.1 MW)*; 2 waterjets
Speed, knots: 45. **Range, miles:** 240 at 30 kt
Complement: 3
Radars: Surface search: I-band.

Comment: Ordered from Dockstavarvet in Sweden in April 1997. Have more powerful engines than the boats in Swedish service.   *UPDATED*

COMBATBOAT 90E   *12/1999*, Sattler/Steele /* 0081226

10 VOSPER 32 METRE PATROL CRAFT

JUANG	K 33	—	K 35	BAYU	K 37	—	K 39	— K 41
PULAI	K 34	PERAK	K 36	HIJAU	K 38	JERAI	K 40	— K 42

Displacement, tons: 143 full load
Dimensions, feet (metres): 106.2 × 23.6 × 5.9 *(32.4 × 7.2 × 1.8)*
Main machinery: 2 Paxman Valenta 16CM diesels; 6,650 hp *(5 MW)* sustained; 2 shafts
1 Cummins diesel; 575 hp *(423 kW)*; 1 shaft
Speed, knots: 27; 8 on cruise diesel. **Range, miles:** 2,000 at 8 kt
Complement: 26
Guns: 1 Oerlikon 20 mm. 2—7.62 mm MGs.
Radars: Surface search: Kelvin Hughes; I-band.

Comment: Ordered February 1981 from Malaysia Shipyard and Engineering Company with technical support from Vosper Thornycroft (Private) Ltd, Singapore. Two completed 1982, the remainder in 1983-84. Names are preceded by 'Bahtera'.   *UPDATED*

JERAI   *12/1999*, Sattler/Steele /* 0081227

FISHERIES DEPARTMENT

Note: Patrol craft have distinctive thick blue and thin red diagonal bands on the hull and have been mistaken for a Coast Guard. All have P numbers.

P 204   *12/1999*, Sattler/Steele /* 0081228

PL 65   *12/1999*, Sattler/Steele /* 0081229

MALDIVES

Headquarters Appointments	Bases	Personnel	Mercantile Marine

Chief of Coast Guard:
  Colonel Moosa Ali Jaleel
	Malé	2000: 400	*Lloyd's Register of Shipping:*
			  63 vessels of 89,914 tons gross

COAST GUARD

Notes: (1) All pennant numbers add up to seven.
(2) Two LSLs were ordered from Colombo Dockyard in March 1996 for delivery in 2000.
(3) The ex-UK patrol craft *Kingfisher* was acquired by a civilian company in early 1997. It is painted white and is used as a survey ship.
(4) There are also four RIBs in service.

1 + 1 ISKANDHAR CLASS (PC)

ISKANDHAR

Displacement, tons: 58 full load
Dimensions, feet (metres): 80.1 × 19 × 4.3 *(24.4 × 5.8 × 1.3)*
Main machinery: 2 Paxman diesels; 8,506 hp(m) *(6.26 MW)*; 2 shafts
Speed, knots: 30
Complement: 18
Guns: 2—12.7 mm MGs.
Radars: Surface search: I-band.

Comment: Ordered from Colombo Dockyard in 1997. First one delivered in 1999.
NEW ENTRY

4 TRACKER II CLASS (PC)

KAANI 133 (ex-11)   **KUREDHI** 142 (ex-12)   **MIDHILI** 151 (ex-13)   **NIROLHU** 106 (ex-14)

Displacement, tons: 38 full load
Dimensions, feet (metres): 65.6 × 17.1 × 4.9 *(20 × 5.2 × 1.5)*
Main machinery: 2 Detroit 12V-71TA diesels; 840 hp *(627 kW)* sustained; 2 shafts
Speed, knots: 25. **Range, miles:** 450 at 20 kt
Complement: 10
Guns: 1—12.7 mm MG. 1—7.62 mm MG.
Radars: Surface search: Kroden; I-band.

Comment: First one ordered June 1985 from Fairey Marinteknik and commissioned in April 1987. Three more acquired July 1987 ex-UK Customs craft. GRP hulls. Seven days normal endurance. Used for fishery protection and EEZ patrols.
UPDATED

KAANI   6/1996* / 0081230

1 CHEVERTON CLASS (PC)

BUREVI 115 (ex-7)

Displacement, tons: 24 full load
Dimensions, feet (metres): 55.8 × 14.8 × 3.9 *(17 × 4.5 × 1.2)*
Main machinery: 2 Detroit 8V-71TI diesels; 850 hp *(634 kW)* sustained; 2 shafts
Speed, knots: 22. **Range, miles:** 590 at 18 kt
Complement: 10
Guns: 1—12.7 mm MG. 1—7.62 mm MG.
Radars: Surface search: Kroden; I-band.

Comment: GRP hull and aluminium superstructure. Originally built for Kiribati and subsequently sold to Maldives in 1984. Has a GRP hull.   *UPDATED*

BUREVI (old number)   6/1989*, Maldives CG / 0081231

1 DAGGER CLASS (PB)

FUNA 124

Displacement, tons: 20 full load
Dimensions, feet (metres): 36.8 × 11.2 × 5 *(11.2 × 3.4 × 1.2)*
Main machinery: 2 Sabre diesels; 660 hp *(492 kW)*; 2 shafts
Speed, knots: 35
Complement: 6
Guns: 2—7.62 mm MGs.
Radars: Surface search: Furuno; I-band.

Comment: Built by Fairey Marine at Cowes, Isle of Wight and delivered in 1982.   *UPDATED*

FUNA   6/1993*, Maldives CG / 0081232

MALTA

Headquarters Appointments	General	Personnel	Mercantile Marine	DELETIONS

Officer Commanding Maritime Squadron:
  Major C Spiteri
	A coastal patrol force of small craft was formed in 1971. It is manned by the 2nd Regiment of the Armed Forces of Malta and primarily employed as a Coast Guard.	2000: 220 (9 officers)	*Lloyd's Register of Shipping:*
			  1,574 vessels of 28,205,481 tons gross
				1997 P 29, P 34, P 36, P 37
				1998 P 25, P 27
				1999 P 26

PATROL FORCES

2 BREMSE CLASS (INSHORE PATROL CRAFT) (PC)

P 32 (ex-*G 33/GS 20*)   **P 33** (ex-*G 22/GS 22*)

Displacement, tons: 42 full load
Dimensions, feet (metres): 74.1 × 15.4 × 3.6 *(22.6 × 4.7 × 1.1)*
Main machinery: 2 DM 6VD 18/5 AL-1 diesels; 1,020 hp(m) *(750 kW)*; 2 shafts
Speed, knots: 14
Complement: 6
Guns: 1—12.7 mm MG.
Radars: Surface search: Racal 1290A; I-band.

Comment: Built in 1971-72 for the ex-GDR GBK. Transferred from Germany in mid-1992. Others of the class acquired by Tunisia.
UPDATED

BREMSE P 32   8/1999*, L Dilli/AFM / 0081233

3 KONDOR I CLASS (COASTAL PATROL CRAFT) (PC)

P 30 (ex-*Ückermünde* G 411/GS 01)   **P 29** (ex-*Boltenhagen* BG 31)
P 31 (ex-*Pasewalk* G 423/GS 05)

Displacement, tons: 377 full load
Dimensions, feet (metres): 170.3 × 23.3 × 7.2 *(51.9 × 7.1 × 2.2)*
Main machinery: 2 Russki/Kolomna Type 40DM diesels; 4,408 hp(m) *(3.24 MW)* sustained; 2 shafts; cp props
Speed, knots: 21. **Range, miles:** 1,800 at 15 kt
Complement: 25 (2 officers)
Guns: 4—14.5 mm ZPU-4 (quad) MGs.
Radars: Surface search: Racal Bridgemaster 250/360; I-band.

Comment: First two built by Peenewerft, Wolgast and commissioned 1 July 1969 and 18 October 1969 respectively. Transferred from Germany with armament and sonar removed in July 1992. A quadruple 14.5 mm gun fitted in Malta. Third of class *P 29* transferred from Germany on 24 July 1997 and fitted with 14.5 mm gun in mid-1999. A fourth planned for 1998 was cancelled. Others of the class acquired by Tunisia, Estonia and Cape Verde.
UPDATED

KONDOR P 30   *8/1999*, L Dilli/AFM /* 0081234

2 SWIFT CLASS (HARBOUR PATROL CRAFT) (PB)

P 23 (ex-*C 6823*)   **P 24** (ex-*C 6824*)

Displacement, tons: 22.5 full load
Dimensions, feet (metres): 50 × 13 × 4.9 *(15.6 × 4 × 1.5)*
Main machinery: 2 GM 12V-71 diesels; 680 hp *(507 kW)* sustained; 2 shafts
Speed, knots: 25. **Range, miles:** 400 at 18 kt
Complement: 6
Guns: 3—12.7 mm MG (1 twin, 1 single).
Radars: Surface search: Furuno 1040; I-band.

Comment: Built by Sewart Seacraft Ltd in 1967. Transferred from USA in February 1971. Have an operational endurance of about 24 hours. Modernised in Malta in 1998/99, including the fitting of a twin 12.7 mm MG in both craft in early 2000.
UPDATED

SWIFT P 24   *4/1999*, van Ginderen Collection /* 0081235

2 SUPERVITTORIA 800 CLASS (SAR)

MELITA I   **MELITA II**

Displacement, tons: 12.5 full load
Dimensions, feet (metres): 37.7 × 16.1 × 2.6 *(11.5 × 4.9 × 0.8)*
Main machinery: 2 Cummins 6CTA 8.3 DIAMONS; 840 hp(m) *(618 kW)*; 2 Kamewa FF310 waterjets
Speed, knots: 34. **Range, miles:** 160 at 34 kt
Complement: 4
Radars: Surface search: Raytheon Pathfinder SL 70; I-band.

Comment: Built in 1998 by Vittoria Naval Shipyard, Italy, for the Civil Protection Department of Malta. Transferred to the Armed Forces of Malta (AFM) in May 1999 for search and rescue duties. Although still the property of the Civil Protection Department, the Melita I and II are operated and maintained by the Maritime Squadron of the AFM.
NEW ENTRY

MELITA I   *9/1999*, L Dilli/AFM /* 0069035

1 LCVP

L 1 (ex-*6524*)

Displacement, tons: 13.5 full load
Dimensions, feet (metres): 36 × 10.5 × 1.1 *(11 × 3.2 × 0.3)*
Main machinery: 1 Detroit 64 HN9 diesel; 225 hp *(168 kW)*; 1 shaft
Speed, knots: 10. **Range, miles:** 100 at 10 kt
Complement: 3
Military lift: 3.5 tons or 36 troops

Comment: Built by Gulfstream Co, USA in 1965 and acquired in January 1987.
UPDATED

L 1   *10/1995*, van Ginderen Collection /* 0081236

LAND-BASED MARITIME AIRCRAFT

Note: There are five Alouette III and two Hughes helicopters, plus two BN Islanders. All belong to the AFM.

ALOUETTE III   *6/1992*, R & C Abela/AFM /* 0081237

MARSHALL ISLANDS

Headquarters Appointments

Chief Staff Officer (Sea Patrol):
Lieutenant Commander R A Kehl

Personnel

2000: 30

General

The Marshalls are a group of five main islands which became a self-governing republic on 1 May 1979, but with the USA retaining responsibility for defence.

Bases

Majuro

Mercantile Marine

Lloyd's Register of Shipping:
230 vessels of 6,761,811 tons gross

DELETIONS

1996   *Ionmeto I*

PATROL FORCES

Note: In addition to *Lomor* there are two ex-US LCU/LCMs used as civilian ferries.

1 PACIFIC FORUM TYPE (LARGE PATROL CRAFT) (PC)

Name	No	Builders	Commissioned
LOMOR	03	Australian Shipbuilding Industries	29 June 1991

Displacement, tons: 162 full load
Dimensions, feet (metres): 103.3 × 26.6 × 6.9 *(31.5 × 8.1 × 2.1)*
Main machinery: 2 Caterpillar 3516TA diesels; 4,400 hp *(3.3 MW)* sustained; 2 shafts
Speed, knots: 20. **Range, miles:** 2,500 at 12 kt
Complement: 17 (3 officers)
Guns: 1—12.7 mm MG.
Radars: Surface search: Furuno 1011; I-band.

Comment: The 14th craft to be built in this series for a number of Pacific Island Coast Guards. Ordered in 1989.

UPDATED

PACIFIC FORUM Type   *1988*, Gilbert Gyssels /* 0081238

MAURITANIA
MARINE MAURITANIENNE

Headquarters Appointments	Personnel	Bases	Mercantile Marine	DELETIONS
Commander of Navy: Colonel A Ould Lekwar	(a) 2000: 620 (40 officers) plus 200 marines (b) Voluntary service	Port Etienne, Nouadhibou Port Friendship, Nouakchott	*Lloyd's Register of Shipping:* 143 vessels of 48,581 tons gross	1997-98 *Z'bar, El Vaiz, El Beig, El Kinz*

PATROL FORCES

1 OPV 54 CLASS (OPV)

Name	No	Builders	Launched	Commissioned
ABOUBEKR BEN AMER	P 541	Leroux & Lotz, Lorient	17 Dec 1993	7 Apr 1994

Displacement, tons: 374 full load
Dimensions, feet (metres): 177.2 × 32.8 × 9.2 *(54 × 10 × 2.8)*
Main machinery: 2 MTU 16V 396 TE94 diesels; 5,712 hp(m) *(4.2 MW)* sustained; 2 auxiliary motors; 250 hp(m) *(184 kW)*; 2 shafts; cp props
Speed, knots: 23 (8 on motors). **Range, miles:** 4,500 at 12 kt
Complement: 21 (3 officers)
Guns: 2—12.7 mm MGs.
Radars: Surface search: Racal Decca Bridgemaster 250; I-band.

Comment: Ordered in September 1992. This is the prototype to a Serter design of three similar craft built for the French Navy. Stern ramp for a 30 kt RIB. Option on a second of class not taken up.

UPDATED

EL NASR   *4/1998 /* 0052598

1 LARGE PATROL CRAFT (PG)

Name	No	Builders	Commissioned
VOUM-LEGLEITA (ex-*Poseidon*)	B 551 (ex-A 12)	Bazán	8 Aug 1964

Displacement, tons: 1,069 full load
Dimensions, feet (metres): 183.5 × 32.8 × 13.1 *(55.9 × 10 × 4)*
Main machinery: 2 Sulzer diesels; 3,200 hp *(2.53 MW)*; 1 shaft; cp prop
Speed, knots: 15. **Range, miles:** 4,640 at 14 kt
Complement: 60
Guns: 2 Oerlikon 20 mm.
Radars: Navigation: 2 Decca TM 626; I-band.

Comment: Ocean going tug transferred from Spain in January 2000, about a year later than planned. Expected to be used primarily as an OPV.

NEW ENTRY

ABOUBEKR BEN AMER   *4/1994*, Leroux & Lotz /* 0081239

1 PATRA CLASS (LARGE PATROL CRAFT) (PC)

Name	No	Builders	Commissioned
EL NASR (ex-*Le Dix Juillet*, ex-*Rapière*)	P 411	Auroux, Arcachon	14 May 1982

Displacement, tons: 147.5 full load
Dimensions, feet (metres): 132.5 × 19.4 × 5.2 *(40.4 × 5.9 × 1.6)*
Main machinery: 2 Wärtsilä UD 33 V12 diesels; 4,340 hp(m) *(3.2 MW)* sustained; 2 shafts
Speed, knots: 26.3. **Range, miles:** 1,750 at 10 kt
Complement: 20 (2 officers)
Guns: 1 Bofors 40 mm/60. 1 Oerlikon 20 mm. 2—12.7 mm MGs.
Radars: Surface search: Racal/Decca 1226; I-band.

Comment: Originally built as a private venture by Auroux. Carried out trials with French crew as *Rapière*. Laid down 15 February 1980, launched 3 June 1981, commissioned for trials 1 November 1981. Transferred to Mauritania in 1982. Re-engined in 1993-94.

VERIFIED

VOUM-LEGLEITA   *1/2000*, Diego Quevedo /* 0081240

1 JURA CLASS (PG)

N'MADI (ex-*Criscilla*, ex-*Jura*)

Displacement, tons: 1,285 full load
Dimensions, feet (metres): 195.3 × 35 × 14.4 *(59.6 × 10.7 × 4.4)*
Main machinery: 2 British Polar SP 112VS-F diesels; 4,200 hp *(3.13 MW)*; 1 shaft; cp prop
Speed, knots: 15.5
Complement: 28
Radars: Surface search: Decca; I-band.

Comment: Built by Hall Russell, Aberdeen in 1975. Became a Scottish Fishery Protection vessel but was paid off in 1988 and acquired by J Marr Ltd. On lease from July 1989 for Fishery Patrol duties. Bought by Germany in 1991 and gifted to Mauritania.
UPDATED

JURA (Scottish colours)   *6/1998*, SFPA /* 0053281

4 MANDOVI CLASS (INSHORE PATROL CRAFT) (PB)

Displacement, tons: 15 full load
Dimensions, feet (metres): 49.2 × 11.8 × 2.6 *(15 × 3.6 × 0.8)*
Main machinery: 2 Deutz MWM TBD232V12 Marine diesels; 750 hp(m) *(551 kW)*; 2 Hamilton water-jets
Speed, knots: 24. **Range, miles:** 250 at 14 kt
Complement: 8
Guns: 1—7.62 mm MG.
Radars: Navigation: Furuno FR 8030; I-band.

Comment: Built by Garden Reach, Calcutta and delivered from India in 1990. Same type acquired by Mauritius (see picture).
VERIFIED

LAND-BASED MARITIME AIRCRAFT

Note: There are also two Cessna 337F.

Numbers/Type: 2 Piper Cheyenne II.
Operational speed: 283 kt *(524 km/h)*.
Service ceiling: 31,600 ft *(9,630 m)*.
Range: 1,510 n miles *(2,796 km)*.
Role/Weapon systems: Coastal surveillance and EEZ protection acquired 1981. Sensors: Bendix 1400 weather radar; cameras. Weapons: Unarmed.
VERIFIED

MAURITIUS

Headquarters Appointments	Bases	Personnel	Maritime Aircraft	Mercantile Marine
Commandant Coast Guard: Commander Rajiv Sehgal	Port Louis (plus 12 manned CG stations)	2000: 580 (including some Indian officers)	1 Dornier 228 (MPCG 01).	*Lloyd's Register of Shipping:* 42 vessels of 149,894 tons gross

COAST GUARD

1 GUARDIAN CLASS (OPV)

Name	No	Builders	Launched	Commissioned
VIGILANT	21	Talcahuano Yard, Chile	6 Dec 1995	10 May 1996

Displacement, tons: 1,650 full load
Dimensions, feet (metres): 246.1 × 45.9 × 12.8 *(75 × 14 × 3.9)*
Main machinery: 4 Caterpillar 3516 diesels; 11,530 hp *(8.6 MW)*; 2 shafts; cp props; bow thruster; 671 hp *(500 kW)*
Speed, knots: 22. **Range, miles:** 6,500 at 19 kt
Complement: 57 (11 officers) plus 20 spare
Guns: 1 Bofors 40 mm/70 can be carried. 2—12.7 mm MGs.
Radars: Surface search: Kelvin Hughes; I-band.
Helicopters: 1 light.

Comment: Contract signed with the Western Canada Marine Group in March 1994. Keel was laid in April 1994. All-steel construction. The ship can be operated by a crew of 18. Full helicopter facilities are included in the design which is based on a Canadian Fisheries vessel *Leonard J Cowley*.
UPDATED

VIGILANT   *5/1996, Asmar*

1 SDB Mk 3 CLASS (PC)

Displacement, tons: 210 full load
Dimensions, feet (metres): 124 × 24.6 × 6.2 *(37.8 × 7.5 × 1.9)*
Main machinery: 2 MTU 16V 538 TB92 diesels; 6,820 hp(m) *(5 MW)* sustained; 2 shafts
Speed, knots: 30
Complement: 32
Guns: 2 Bofors 40 mm/60; 120 rds/min to 10 km *(5.5 n miles)*; weight of shell 0.89 kg.
Radars: Surface search: Bharat 1245; I-band.

Comment: Transferred from Indian Navy in 1993. Built by Garden Reach, Calcutta in 1984.
VERIFIED

SDB Mk 3   *4/1998 /* 0052599

2 ZHUK (TYPE 1400M) CLASS (PC)

RESCUER   RETRIEVER

Displacement, tons: 39 full load
Dimensions, feet (metres): 78.7 × 16.4 × 3.9 *(24 × 5 × 1.2)*
Main machinery: 2 M 401B diesels; 2,200 hp(m) *(1.6 MW)* sustained; 2 shafts
Speed, knots: 30. **Range, miles:** 1,100 at 15 kt
Complement: 14
Guns: 4—14.5 mm (2 twin) MGs.
Radars: Surface search: Spin Trough; I-band.

Comment: Acquired from the USSR on 3 December 1989.
UPDATED

RESCUER   *1/1998*, van Ginderen Collection /* 0012775

9 MANDOVI CLASS (INSHORE PATROL CRAFT) (PB)

MARLIN	CASTOR	SIRIUS	CAPELLA	RIGEL
BARRACUDA	POLARIS	POLLUX	CANOPUS	

Displacement, tons: 15 full load
Dimensions, feet (metres): 49.2 × 11.8 × 2.6 *(15 × 3.6 × 0.8)*
Main machinery: 2 Deutz MWM TBD232V12 Marine diesels; 750 hp(m) *(551 kW)*; 2 Hamilton water-jets
Speed, knots: 24. **Range, miles:** 250 at 14 kt
Complement: 8
Guns: 1—7.62 mm MG.
Radars: Navigation: Furuno FR 8030; I-band.

Comment: Ordered 24 July 1987 from Mandovi Marine Private Ltd, courtesy of the Indian Government. First two delivered early in 1989; second batch of three with some modifications on 1 May 1990 and the last four at the end of 1990. SATNAV fitted.
UPDATED

MARLIN   *1990*, Mauritius CG /* 0081241

26 + (18) PATROL BOATS

Comment: Two Rover 663 FPC donated by Australia and 30 Rigid Inflatable craft mostly RHIBS, AVONS and ZODIACS acquired in 1988-89. Two Halmatic RIBs were acquired in 1996 and the plan is to order up to 18 more to replace the earlier craft when funds are available.
UPDATED

PATROL BOAT   *1/1998*, van Ginderen Collection /* 0012776

MEXICO
MARINA NACIONAL

Headquarters Appointments

Secretary of the Navy:
Admiral Jose Ramon Lorenzo Franco
Under-Secretary of the Navy:
Admiral Jaime Felix Perez y Elias
Inspector General of the Navy:
Admiral Miguel Angel Nunez Ehuan
Chief of the Naval Staff:
Admiral Manual Garcia Carmona Santiesteban

Flag Officers

Commander in Chief, Gulf and Caribbean:
Vice Admiral Fernando Meixueiro Ramirez
Commander in Chief, Pacific:
Vice Admiral Manuel Zermeno del Peon

Personnel

(a) 2000: 37,000 officers and men (including 1,100 Naval Air Force and 8,600 Marines)
(b) Voluntary service

Naval Bases and Commands

The Naval Command is split between the Pacific and Gulf areas each with a Commander-in-Chief with HQs at Veracruz (Gulf) and Acapulco (Pacific). Each area has three naval Regions which are further subdivided into Zones (17) and Sectors (16).

Gulf Area

North (First) Naval Region - HQ Tuxpan, Veracruz.
I Naval Zone - HQ Ciudad Madero (State of Tamaupilas).
Naval Sectors - HQ Matamoros, HQ La Pesca.
III Naval Zone - HQ Veracruz (State of Veracruz).
Naval Sectors - HQ Tuxpan, HQ Coatzacoalcos.
East (Third) Naval Region - HQ Frontera.
V Naval Zone - HQ Frontera (State of Tabasco).
VII Naval Zone - HQ Lerma (State of Campeche).
Naval Sectors - HQ Champotón, HQ Ciudad del Cármen.
Caribbean Sea (Fifth) Naval Region - HQ Chetumal.
IX Naval Zone - HQ Yucalpeten (State of Yucatán).
XI Naval Zone - HQ Chetumal (State of Quintana Roo).
Naval Sectors - HQ Isla Mujeres, HQ Isla Cozumel.

Pacific Area

Northwest (Second) Naval Region - HQ Guaymas, Sonora.
II Naval Zone - HQ Ensenada (State of Baja California Norte).
Naval Sector - HQ San Felipe.
IV Naval Zone - HQ La Paz (State of Baja California Sur).
Naval Sectors - HQ Puerto Cortes, HQ Santa Rosalía, HQ San Lucas, HQ Bahia Tortugas.
VI Naval Zone - HQ Guaymas (State of Sonora).
Naval Sector - HQ Puerto Peñasco.
VIII Naval Zone - HQ Mazatlán (State of Sinaloa).
Naval Sector - HQ Topolobampo.
West (Fourth) Naval Region - HQ Manzanillo, Colima.
X Naval Zone - HQ San Blas (State of Nayarit).
XII Naval Zone - HQ Puerto Vallarta (State of Jalisco).
XIV Naval Zone - HQ Manzanillo (State of Colima).
Naval Sector - HQ Isla Socorro.
XVI Naval Zone - HQ Lázaro Cardenas (State of Michoacán).
Southwest (Sixth) Naval Region - HQ Lazaro Cardenas (State of Michoacán).
XVIII Naval Zone - HQ Acapulco (State of Guerrero).
Naval Sector - HQ Ixtapa-Zihuatanejo.
XX Naval Zone - HQ Salina Cruz (State of Oaxaca).
Naval Sector - HQ Puerto Angel.
XXII Naval Zone - HQ Puerto Madero (State of Chiapas).

Naval Air Force

Naval air bases at Mexico City, Campeche, Chetumal, Veracruz, La Paz, Tapachula.

Marine Force

There are three Infantry Brigades, one each based at Veracruz, Acapulco and Manzanillo; one Parachute brigade at Mexico City, and two Artillery battalions one each at Frontera and Puerto Madero. In addition there are separate Infantry Battalions at Mexico City, Ensenada, La Paz, Guaymas, Lerna, Mazatlan, Yucalpeten, Chetumal and Lazaro Cardenas.

General

One of the persistent problems facing the Mexican Navy is the incursion of foreign fishery poachers, frequently highly organised groups working from the USA. In addition there is a requirement for patrolling the Exclusive Economic Zone including the offshore oil fields. The drug smuggling menace takes up much of the Navy's time.

Strength of the Fleet

Type	Active	Building
Destroyers	3	—
Frigates	8	1
Gunships	25	6
Large Patrol Craft/FAC	40	5
Coast Guard	17	—
Coastal and River Patrol Craft	26	20
Survey Ships	5	—
Support Ships	11	—
Tankers	3	—
Sail Training Ship	1	—

Names and Pennant Numbers

Many of the ship names and pennant numbers were changed in early 1994. Destroyers and frigates are named after Aztec emperors and forerunners of the Independence War (1810-1825). Gunboats are named after naval and military heroes.

Mercantile Marine

Lloyd's Register of Shipping:
621 vessels of 917,968 tons gross

DELETIONS

Patrol Forces

1998 *General Pedro Maria Anaya*

Auxiliaries

1997 *Faja de Oro, Tuxpan*
1998 *Rio Balsas*
1999 *Matlalcueye*

DESTROYERS

2 GEARING (FRAM I) CLASS (DD)

Name	No	Builders	Laid down	Launched	Commissioned
ILHUICAMINA (ex-*Quetzalcoatl*, ex-*Vogelgesang* DD 862)	E 10 (ex-E 03)	Bethlehem, Staten Island	3 Aug 1944	15 Jan 1945	28 Apr 1945
NETZAHUALCOYOTL (ex-*Steinaker* DD 863)	E 11 (ex-E 04)	Bethlehem, Staten Island	1 Sep 1944	13 Feb 1945	26 May 1945

Displacement, tons: 3,030 standard; 3,690 full load
Dimensions, feet (metres): 390.2 × 41.9 × 15 *(118.7 × 12.5 × 4.6)*
Main machinery: 4 Babcock & Wilcox boilers; 600 psi *(43.3 kg/cm²)*; 850°F *(454°C)*; 2 GE turbines; 60,000 hp *(45 MW)*; 2 shafts
Speed, knots: 15. **Range, miles:** 5,800 at 15 kt
Complement: 300

Guns: 4 USN 5 in *(127 mm)*/38 (2 twin) Mk 38 ❶; 15 rds/min to 17 km *(9.3 n miles)* anti-surface; 11 km *(5.9 n miles)* anti-aircraft; weight of shell 25 kg.
1 Bofors 57 mm/70 Mk 2 ❷; 220 rds/min to 17 km *(9.3 n miles)*; weight of shell 2.4 kg.
Countermeasures: ESM: WLR-1; radar warning.
Weapons control: Mk 37 GFCS. Mk 112 TFCS.

Radars: Air search: Lockheed SPS-40; E/F-band (E 10). Westinghouse SPS-29 ❸; B/C-band (E 11).
Surface search: Kelvin Hughes 17/9 ❹; I-band.
Navigation: Marconi LN66; I-band.
Fire control: Western Electric Mk 12/22 ❺; I/J-band.

Helicopters: 1 MBB BO 105CB ❻.

Programmes: Transferred from USA by sale 24 February 1982.
Modernisation: A Bofors 57 mm gun was mounted between the torpedo tubes in B gun position in 1993. ASROC, torpedo tubes and sonar removed in 1996, and the flight deck slightly extended. New topmast and search radar also fitted in 1996 in E 11.
Structure: The devices on top of the funnel are to reduce IR signature.
Operational: Top speed much reduced from the original 32 kt. Helicopter seldom carried.

UPDATED

NETZAHUALCOYOTL   *10/1996, van Ginderen Collection*

NETZAHUALCOYOTL   *10/1996, van Ginderen Collection / 0052600*

1 FLETCHER CLASS (DD)

Name	No	Builders	Laid down	Launched	Commissioned
CUITLAHUAC (ex-*John Rodgers* DD 574)	E 01 (ex-E 02, ex-F 2)	Consolidated Steel Corporation	25 July 1941	7 May 1942	9 Feb 1943

Displacement, tons: 2,100 standard; 3,050 full load
Dimensions, feet (metres): 376.5 × 39.4 × 18 *(114.8 × 12 × 5.5)*
Main machinery: 4 Babcock & Wilcox boilers; 600 psi *(43.3 kg/cm²)*; 850°F *(454°C)*; 2 GE turbines; 60,000 hp *(45 MW)*; 2 shafts
Speed, knots: 12. **Range, miles:** 5,000 at 12 kt
Complement: 197 (16 officers)

Guns: 5 USN 5 in *(127 mm)*/38 Mk 30 ❶; 15 rds/min to 17 km *(9.3 n miles)* anti-surface; 8 km *(4.4 n miles)* anti-aircraft; weight of shell 25 kg.
10 Bofors 40 mm/60 (5 twin) Mk 2 ❷; 120 rds/min to 10 km *(5.5 n miles)*; weight of shell 0.89 kg.
Torpedoes: 5—21 in *(533 mm)* (quin) tubes ❸; anti-surface.
Weapons control: Mk 37 GFCS for 127 mm guns. 5 Mk 51 Mod 2 GFCS for 40 mm guns.
Radars: Surface search: Kelvin Hughes 17/9 ❹; I-band.

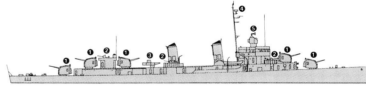

CUITLAHUAC   *(Scale 1 : 1,200), Ian Sturton*

Navigation: Kelvin Hughes 14/9; I-band.
Fire control: Western Electric Mk 25 ❺; I/J-band.

Programmes: Transferred from USA in August 1970.
Modernisation: All anti-submarine equipment has been removed.

Operational: In spite of its age this ship still has a formidable gun armament and is very active in drug enforcement patrols. Top speed has been much reduced from the original 32 kt.

VERIFIED

CUITLAHUAC   *9/1994, Julio Montes / 0052601*

FRIGATES

2 + 1 KNOX CLASS (FF)

Name	No	Builders	Laid down	Launched	Commissioned
IGNACIO ALLENDE (ex-*Stein*)	E 50 (ex-FF 1065)	Lockheed	1 June 1970	19 Dec 1970	8 Jan 1972
MARIANO ABASOLO (ex-*Marvin Shields*)	E 51 (ex-FF 1066)	Todd Shipyards	12 Apr 1968	23 Oct 1969	10 Apr 1971
— (ex-*Roark*)	E 52 (ex-FF 1053)	Todd Shipyards	2 Feb 1966	24 Apr 1967	22 Nov 1969

Displacement, tons: 3,011 standard; 4,260 full load
Dimensions, feet (metres): 439.6 × 46.8 × 15; 24.8 (sonar)
(134 × 14.3 × 4.6; 7.8)
Main machinery: 2 Combustion Engineering/Babcock & Wilcox
boilers; 1,200 psi *(84.4 kg/cm²)*; 950°F *(510°C)*; 1
Westinghouse turbine; 35,000 hp *(26 MW)*; 1 shaft
Speed, knots: 27. **Range, miles:** 4,000 at 22 kt on 1 boiler
Complement: 288 (20 officers)

Missiles: SAM: 1 Mk 25 launcher for Sea Sparrow (in E 50) ❶
(see *Structure*).
A/S: Honeywell ASROC Mk 16 octuple launcher with reload
system (has 2 cells modified to fire Harpoon) ❷; inertial
guidance to 1.6-10 km *(1-5.4 n miles)*; payload Mk 46.
Guns: 1 FMC 5 in *(127 mm)*/54 Mk 42 Mod 9 ❸; 20-40 rds/min
to 24 km *(13 n miles)* anti-surface; 14 km *(7.7 n miles)* anti-
aircraft; weight of shell 32 kg.
Torpedoes: 4—324 mm Mk 32 (2 twin) fixed tubes ❹. 22
Honeywell Mk 46; anti-submarine; active/passive homing to
11 km *(5.9 n miles)* at 40 kt; warhead 44 kg.
Countermeasures: Decoys: 2 Loral Hycor SRBOC 6-barrelled
fixed Mk 36 ❺; IR flares and chaff to 4 km *(2.2 n miles)*. T Mk-6
Fanfare/SLQ-25 Nixie; torpedo decoy. Prairie Masker hull and
blade rate noise suppression.
ESM: SLQ-32(V)2 ❻; intercept.
Weapons control: Mk 68 Mod 3 GFCS. Mk 114 Mod 6 ASW FCS.
Mk 1 target designation system. MMS target acquisition sight
(for mines, small craft and low flying aircraft).
Radars: Air search: Lockheed SPS-40B ❼; E/F-band.
Surface search: Raytheon SPS-10 or Norden SPS-67 ❽; G-band.
Navigation: Marconi LN66; I-band.
Fire control: Western Electric SPG-53D/F ❾; I/J-band.
Tacan: SRN 15.
Sonars: EDO/General Electric SQS-26CX; bow-mounted; active
search and attack; medium frequency.

Helicopters: 1 BO 105CB ❿.

Programmes: First pair decommissioned from USN in 1992/93.
Both transferred on 29 January 1997 and arrived in Mexico
16 August 1997. Both then underwent extensive refits,
entering service on 23 November 1998. Third of class acquired
in 1998. One other, *Whipple*, approved for transfer by sale in
1999, and may be acquired for spares.
Structure: Four Mk 32 torpedo tubes are fixed in the midships
structure, two to a side, angled out at 45°. The original 'Knox'
class SAM launcher has been put back aft, in E 50 only.
Operational: In US service these ships had Harpoon SSM, but it is
reported that these weapons are not carried. **UPDATED**

IGNACIO ALLENDE *(Scale 1 : 1,200), Ian Sturton /* 0052602

MARIANO ABASOLO *4/1999*, Mexican Navy /* 0081243

IGNACIO ALLENDE *11/1998, Mexican Navy /* 0017679

1 EDSALL CLASS (FF/AX)

Name	No	Builders	Laid down	Launched	Commissioned
COMODORO MANUEL AZUETA PERILLOS (ex-*Hurst* DE 250)	E 30 (ex-A 06)	Brown SB Co, Houston, TX	27 Jan 1943	14 Apr 1943	30 Aug 1943

Displacement, tons: 1,400 standard; 1,850 full load
Dimensions, feet (metres): 302.7 × 36.6 × 13
(92.3 × 11.3 × 4)
Main machinery: 4 Fairbanks-Morse 38D8-1/8-10 diesels;
7,080 hp *(5.3 MW)* sustained; 2 shafts
Speed, knots: 12. **Range, miles:** 13,000 at 12 kt
Complement: 216 (15 officers)

Guns: 2 USN 3 in *(76 mm)*/50; 20 rds/min to 12 km *(6.6 n
miles)*; weight of shell 6 kg.
8 Bofors 40 mm/60 (1 quad, 2 twin) Mk 2 and Mk 1; 120 rds/
min to 10 km *(5.5 n miles)*; weight of shell 0.89 kg.
2 Oerlikon 20 mm. 2—37 mm saluting guns.
Weapons control: Mk 52 (for 3 in); Mk 51 Mod 2 (for 40 mm).
Radars: Surface search: Kelvin Hughes Type 17; I-band.
Navigation: Kelvin Hughes Type 14; I-band.

Programmes: Transferred from USA 1 October 1973.
Modernisation: OTO Melara 76 mm gun fitted in 1995 but
subsequently removed and US 3 in gun restored.
Operational: Employed as training ship with Gulf Area
command. A/S weapons and sensors removed. Speed much
reduced.
VERIFIED

COMODORO MANUEL AZUETA PERILLOS *10/1998, E & M Laursen /* 0052604

2 BRONSTEIN CLASS (FF)

Name	No	Builders	Laid down	Launched	Commissioned
HERMENEGILDO GALEANA (ex-Bronstein)	E 42 (ex-FF 1037)	Avondale Shipyards	16 May 1961	31 Mar 1962	16 June 1963
NICOLAS BRAVO (ex-McCloy)	E 40 (ex-FF 1038)	Avondale Shipyards	15 Sep 1961	9 June 1962	21 Oct 1963

Displacement, tons: 2,360 standard; 2,650 full load
Dimensions, feet (metres): 371.5 × 40.5 × 13.5; 23 (sonar) *(113.2 × 12.3 × 4.1; 7)*
Main machinery: 2 Foster-Wheeler boilers; 1 De Laval geared turbine; 20,000 hp *(14.92 MW)*; 1 shaft
Speed, knots: 23.5. **Range, miles:** 3,924 at 15 kt
Complement: 207 (17 officers)

Missiles: A/S: Honeywell ASROC Mk 112 octuple launcher ❶.
Guns: 2 USN 3 in *(76 mm)*/50 (twin) Mk 33 ❷; 50 rds/min to 12.8 km *(7 n miles)*; weight of shell 6 kg, or 1 Bofors 57 mm/70 Mk 2; 220 rds/min to 17 km *(9.3 n miles)*; weight of shell 2.4 kg.
Torpedoes: 6—324 mm US Mk 32 Mod 7 (2 triple) tubes ❸. 14 Honeywell Mk 46; anti-submarine; active/passive homing to 11 km *(5.9 n miles)* at 40 kt; warhead 44 kg.
Countermeasures: Decoys: 2 Loral Hycor 6-barrelled fixed Mk 33; IR flares and chaff to 4 km *(2.2 n miles)*. T—Mk 6 Fanfare; torpedo decoy system.
Weapons control: Mk 56 GFCS. Mk 114 ASW FCS. Mk 1 target designation system. Elsag NA 18 optronic director may be fitted.
Radars: Air search: Lockheed SPS-40D ❹; E/F-band; range 320 km *(175 n miles)*.
Surface search: Raytheon SPS-10F ❺; G-band.
Navigation: Marconi LN66; I-band.
Fire control: General Electric Mk 35 ❻; I/J-band.
Sonars: EDO/General Electric SQS-26 AXR; bow-mounted; active search and attack; medium frequency.

Helicopters: Platform and some facilities but no hangar.

Programmes: Transferred from the USA to Mexico by sale 12 November 1993 having paid off in December 1990.
Modernisation: Bofors 57 mm SAK may be fitted to replace the Mk 33 gun, possibly with an Elsag NA 18 optronic director.
Structure: Position of stem anchor and portside anchor (just forward of gun mount) necessitated by large bow sonar dome. As built, a single 3 in (Mk 34) open mount was aft of the helicopter deck; removed for installation of towed sonar which has since been taken out.
Operational: ASROC is non-operational.

UPDATED

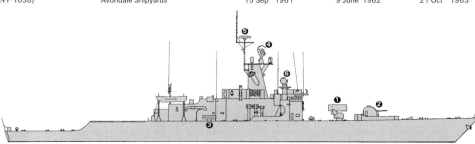

NICOLAS BRAVO   *(Scale 1 : 900), Ian Sturton*

HERMENEGILDO GALEANA
10/1998, Mexican Navy / 0050720

NICOLAS BRAVO

3 CHARLES LAWRENCE and CROSLEY CLASSES (FF)

Name	No	Builders	Laid down	Launched	Commissioned
MIGUEL HIDALGO (ex-*Usumacinta*, ex-*Don O Woods* APD 118, ex-*DE 721*)	E 20 (ex-B 06, ex-H 6)	Consolidated Steel Corporation	1 Dec 1943	19 Feb 1944	28 May 1945
VINCENTE GUERRERO (ex-*Coahuila*, ex-*Rednour* APD 102, ex-*DE 592*)	E 21 (ex-B 07)	Bethlehem SB Co, Hingham, MA	9 Jan 1944	1 Mar 1944	15 Mar 1945
JOSE MARIA MORELOS Y PAVON (ex-*Chihuahua*, ex-*Barber* APD 57, ex-*DE 161*)	E 22 (ex-B 08)	Norfolk Navy Yard, Norfolk, VA	27 Apr 1943	20 May 1943	10 Oct 1943

Displacement, tons: 1,800 standard; 2,130 full load
Dimensions, feet (metres): 306 × 37 × 12.5
   (93.3 × 11.3 × 3.8)
Main machinery: Turbo-electric; 2 Foster-Wheeler boilers; 435 psi *(30.6 kg/cm²)*; 750°F *(399°C)*; 2 GE turbo generators; 12,000 hp *(9 MW)*; 2 motors; 2 shafts
Speed, knots: 13. **Range, miles:** 5,000 at 13 kt
Complement: 221

Guns: 1 USN 5 in *(127 mm)*/38 Mk 30; 15 rds/min to 17 km *(9.3 n miles)*; weight of shell 25 kg.
   6 Bofors 40 mm/60 (3 twin) Mk 1. 6 Oerlikon 20 mm/80.
Weapons control: 3 Mk 51 GFCS for 40 mm guns.
Radars: Surface search: Kelvin Hughes 14/9; I-band.

Programmes: E 20 purchased from USA in December 1963, E 21 in June 1969 and E 22 in December 1969.
Structure: E 21 is the only 'Charles Lawrence' class; the others have a tripod after mast supporting the conspicuous 10 ton boom.
Operational: Speed reduced from the original 18 kt.

VERIFIED

VINCENTE GUERRERO

1/1995, Mexican Navy / 0052605

SHIPBORNE AIRCRAFT

Numbers/Type: 11 MBB BO 105CB/MD 902 Explorer.
Operational speed: 113 kt *(210 km/h)*.
Service ceiling: 9,845 ft *(3,000 m)*.
Range: 407 n miles *(754 km)*.
Role/Weapon systems: Coastal patrol helicopter for patrol, fisheries protection and EEZ protection duties; SAR as secondary role. BO 105s are being replaced by MD 900. Sensors: Bendix search radar. Weapons: MGs or rocket pods.   **UPDATED**

Numbers/Type: 4 Eurocopter AS 555 AF Fennec.
Operational speed: 121 kt *(225 km/h)*.
Service ceiling: 13,120 ft *(4,000 m)*.
Range: 389 n miles *(722 km)*.
Role/Weapon systems: Patrol helicopter for EEZ protection and SAR. More may be acquired when funds are available. Sensors: Bendix 1500 search radar. Weapons: Can carry up to two torpedoes, rocket pods or an MG.

VERIFIED

BO 105CB

9/1994, Mexican Navy / 0052606

AS 555 AF

9/1994, Mexican Navy / 0052607

LAND-BASED MARITIME AIRCRAFT (FRONT LINE)

Notes: (1) A number of confiscated drug-running aircraft are also in service, mostly Cessnas.
(2) Aircraft used for transport and training include five Antonov An-32, 18 Mi-8, three Alouette and four MD 500 helicopters.
(3) Eight Redigos are to be acquired from Finland in due course.

Numbers/Type: 9 CASA C-212 Aviocar.
Operational speed: 190 kt *(353 km/h)*.
Service ceiling: 24,000 ft *(7,315 m)*.
Range: 1,650 n miles *(3,055 km)*.
Role/Weapon systems: Acquired from 1987 and used for Maritime Surveillance. Sensors: Search radar; APS 504. Weapons: Unarmed.

VERIFIED

PATROL FORCES

4 HOLZINGER CLASS (GUNSHIPS) (PG)

Name	No	Builders	Launched	Commissioned
CAPITÁN DE NAVIO SEBASTIAN JOSÉ HOLZINGER (ex-*Uxmal*)	C 01 (ex-GA 01)	Tampico	1 June 1988	23 Nov 1991
CAPITÁN DE NAVIO BLAS GODINEZ BRITO (ex-*Mitla*)	C 02 (ex-GA 02)	Veracruz	1 June 1988	1 Nov 1991
BRIGADIER JOSÉ MARIÁ DE LA VEGA GONZALEZ (ex-*Peten*)	C 03 (ex-GA 03)	Tampico	22 Mar 1992	6 Mar 1994
GENERAL FELIPE B BERRIOZÁBAL (ex-*Anahuac*)	C 04 (ex-GA 04)	Veracruz	21 Apr 1991	5 May 1993

Displacement, tons: 1,290 full load
Dimensions, feet (metres): 244.1 × 34.4 × 11.2
   (74.4 × 10.5 × 3.4)
Main machinery: 2 MTU 20V 956 TB92 diesels; 11,700 hp(m) *(8.6 MW)* sustained; 2 shafts
Speed, knots: 22. **Range, miles:** 3,820 at 16 kt
Complement: 75 (11 officers)

Guns: 1 Bofors 57 mm/70 Mk 3; 220 rds/min to 17 km *(9.3 n miles)*; weight of shell 2.4 kg. At least 2 of the class have a Bofors 40 mm/60 as a temporary measure.
Combat data systems: Elsag 2 CSDA-10.
Weapons control: Elsag NA 18 optronic director.
Radars: Surface search: Raytheon SPS-64(V)6A; I-band.
Navigation: Kelvin Hughes Nucleus; I-band.

Helicopters: 1 MBB BO 105CB.

Programmes: Originally four were ordered from Tampico and Veracruz. First laid down November 1983, second in 1984 but then there were delays caused by financial problems. Named after military heroes.
Structure: An improved variant of the Bazán 'Halcon' (Uribe) class with a flight deck extended to the stern. C 01 and C 02 commissioned with a Bofors 40 mm/60 in lieu of the 57 mm

SEBASTIAN JOSÉ HOLZINGER

7/1997 */* 0012779

and without the optronic director. The Navy describes this as a temporary arrangement, and the bigger guns are to be fitted in due course. Vosper 300 stabilisers being fitted to two of the class.   **UPDATED**

2 + 6 HOLZINGER 2000 CLASS (GUNSHIPS) (PG)

Name	No	Builders	Laid down		Launched		Commissioned
JUSTO SIERRA MENDEZ (ex-Rosas Coria)	C 2001	Tampico, Tamaulipas	19 Jan	1998	1 June	1998	Sep 1999
BENITO JUAREZ	C 2002	Salina Cruz, Oaxaco	19 Jan	1998	23 July	1998	Sep 1999
—	C 2003	Tampico, Tamaulipas	1 June	1998	Mar	1999	2000
—	C 2004	Salina Cruz, Oaxaco	23 July	1998	Mar	1999	2000
—	C 2005	Tampico, Tamaulipas	Mar	1999	2000		2001
—	C 2006	Tampico, Tamaulipas	Mar	1999	2000		2001
—	C 2007	Salina Cruz, Oaxaco	2000		2001		2002
—	C 2008	Salina Cruz, Oaxaco	2000		2001		2002

Displacement, tons: 1,344 full load
Dimensions, feet (metres): 231 × 34.4 × 9.3
  (70.4 × 10.5 × 2.8)
Main machinery: 2 Caterpillar 3616 V16 diesels; 6,197 hp(m)
  (4.55 MW); 2 shafts
Speed, knots: 18
Complement: 76 (10 officers)

Guns: 1 Bofors 57 mm/70 Mk 3; 220 rds/min to 17 km *(9.3 n miles)*; weight of shell 2.4 kg.
Combat data systems: Alenia 2.
Weapons control: Saab EOS 450 optronic director.
Radars: Air/surface search: E/F-band.
Surface search: I-band.

Helicopters: 1 MD 902 Explorer.

Programmes: Follow on to the 'Holzinger' class. First four ordered in 1997, four more on 1 June 1998.
Structure: Virtually the same hull as *Holzinger* but with a markedly different superstructure to improve stability.

UPDATED   JUSTO SIERRA MENDEZ

9/1999*, Mexican Navy / 0084269

6 URIBE CLASS (GUNSHIPS) (PG)

Name	No	Builders	Laid down		Launched		Commissioned
CADETE VIRGILIO URIBE ROBLES	C 11 (ex-GH 01)	Bazán, San Fernando	1 July	1981	12 Nov	1981	2 June 1982
TENIENTE JOSÉ AZUETA ABAD	C 12 (ex-GH 02)	Bazán, San Fernando	7 Sep	1981	12 Dec	1981	30 Aug 1982
CAPITAN de FRAGATA PEDRO SÁINZ de BARANDA BORREYRO	C 13 (ex-GH 03)	Bazán, San Fernando	22 Oct	1981	29 Jan	1982	20 Oct 1982
COMODORO CARLOS CASTILLO BRETÓN BARRERO	C 14 (ex-GH 04)	Bazán, San Fernando	11 Nov	1981	26 Feb	1982	4 Nov 1982
VICEALMIRANTE OTHÓN P BLANCO NUNEZ DE CACERES	C 15 (ex-GH 05)	Bazán, San Fernando	18 Dec	1981	26 Mar	1982	16 Nov 1982
CONTRALMIRANTE ANGEL ORTIZ MONASTERIO	C 16 (ex-GH 06)	Bazán, San Fernando	30 Dec	1981	4 May	1982	17 Dec 1982

Displacement, tons: 988 full load
Dimensions, feet (metres): 219.9 × 34.4 × 11.5
  (67 × 10.5 × 3.5)
Main machinery: 2 MTU-Bazán 16V 956 TB91 diesels; 7,500 hp (m) *(5.52 MW)* sustained; 2 shafts
Speed, knots: 22. **Range, miles:** 5,000 at 13 kt
Complement: 46 (7 officers)

Guns: 1 Bofors 40 mm/70; 300 rds/min to 12.5 km *(6.7 n miles)*; weight of shell 0.96 kg.
Weapons control: Naja optronic director.
Radars: Surface search: Decca AC 1226; I-band.
Navigation: I-band.
Tacan: SRN 15.

Helicopters: 1 MBB BO 105CB.

Programmes: Ordered in 1980 to a 'Halcon' class design. Contracts for a further eight of the class have been shelved. Pennant numbers changed in 1992. Named after naval heroes.
Structure: Flight deck extends to the stern. Similar ships built for Argentina.
Operational: Used for EEZ patrol.

UPDATED   VICEALMIRANTE OTHÓN P BLANCO NUNEZ DE CACERES

6/1994*, van Ginderen Collection / 0081244

17 AUK CLASS (COAST GUARD) (PG)

LEANDRO VALLE (ex-*Pioneer* MSF 105) C 70 (ex-G-01)
GUILLERMO PRIETO (ex-*Symbol* MSF 123) C 71 (ex-G-02)
MARIANO ESCOBEDO (ex-*Champion* MSF 314) C 72 (ex-G-03)
MANUEL DOBLADO (ex-*Defense* MSF 317) C 73 (ex-G-05)
SEBASTIAN LERDO DE TEJADA (ex-*Devastator* MSF 318) C 74 (ex-G-06)
SANTOS DEGOLLADO (ex-*Gladiator* MSF 319) C 75 (ex-G-07)
IGNACIO DE LA LLAVE (ex-*Spear* MSF 322) C 76 (ex-G-08)
JUAN N ALVARES (ex-*Ardent* MSF 340) C 77 (ex-G-09)
MANUEL GUTIERREZ ZAMORA (ex-*Roselle* MSF 379) C 78 (ex-G-10)
VALENTIN GOMEZ FARIAS (ex-*Starling* MSF 64) C 79 (ex-G-11)
IGNACIO MANUEL ALTAMIRANO (ex-*Sway* MSF 120) C 80 (ex-G-12)
FRANCISCO ZARCO (ex-*Threat* MSF 124) C 81 (ex-G-13)
IGNACIO L VALLARTA (ex-*Velocity* MSF 128) C 82 (ex-G-14)
JESUS GONZALEZ ORTEGA (ex-*Chief* MSF 315) C 83 (ex-G-15)
MELCHOR OCAMPO (ex-*Scoter* MSF 381) C 84 (ex-G-16)
JUAN ALDAMA (ex-*Piloti* MSF 104) C 85 (ex-G-18)
MARIANO MATAMOROS (ex-*Hermenegildo Galeana*, ex-*Sage* MSF 111) C 86 (ex-G-19)

Displacement, tons: 1,065 standard; 1,250 full load
Dimensions, feet (metres): 221.2 × 32.2 × 10.8 *(67.5 × 9.8 × 3.3)*
Main machinery: Diesel-electric; 2 GM 278A diesels; 2,200 hp *(1.64 MW)*; 2 generators; 4 Bush Sulzer motors; 2,040 hp *(1.52 MW)*; 2 shafts
Speed, knots: 18. **Range, miles:** 6,900 at 10 kt
Complement: 105 (9 officers)
Guns: 1 USN 3 in *(76 mm)*/50. 4 Bofors 40 mm/60 (2 twin).
  2—12.7 mm MGs (in some on quarterdeck).
Radars: Surface search: Kelvin Hughes 14/9 (in most); I-band.
Helicopters: Platform for 1 BO 105 (C 72, C 73 and C 79 only).

Comment: Transferred from USA six in February 1973, four in April 1973, nine in September 1973. Employed on Coast Guard duties. All built during Second World War. Variations are visible in the mid-ships section where some have a bulwark running from the break of the forecastle to the quarterdeck. Minesweeping gear removed. There is a variety of diesel engines, radars and even shipbuilders for this class. Some carry a Pirana 26 kt motor launch armed with 40 mm grenade launchers and 7.62 mm MGs. C 72, C 73 and C 79 have had helicopter flight decks installed aft. Plans to fit flight decks in the others have been shelved.

SEBASTIAN LERDO DE TEJADA   *3/1998*, van Ginderen Collection / 0081246*

UPDATED   JESUS GONZALEZ ORTEGA   *10/1997, van Ginderen Collection / 0012780*

1 GUANAJUATO CLASS (GUNSHIP) (PG)

Name	No	Builders	Launched	Commissioned
GUANAJUATO	C 07	SECN Ferrol	29 May 1934	19 Mar 1936

Displacement, tons: 1,950 full load
Dimensions, feet (metres): 264 × 37.8 × 13 (80.5 × 11.5 × 4)
Main machinery: 2 Enterprise DMR-38 diesels; 5,000 hp (37.3 MW); 2 shafts
Speed, knots: 14. Range, miles: 3,000 at 12 kt
Complement: 140 (20 officers)
Guns: 2 Vickers 4 in (102 mm)/45; 16 rds/min to 19 km (10.4 n miles); weight of shell 16 kg.
  2 Bofors 40 mm/60. 4 Oerlikon 20 mm.
Radars: Surface search: Kelvin Hughes; I-band.

Comment: Originally used as a gunboat and troop transporter. Steam turbines replaced by diesels in the late 1960s.

UPDATED

GUANAJUATO   *4/1999*, van Ginderen Collection / 0081245

11 ADMIRABLE CLASS (OFFSHORE PATROL VESSELS) (OPV)

Name	No	Recommissioned
GENERAL MIGUEL NEGRETE (ex-Jubilant)	C-50 (ex-D 01)	12 Dec 1962
GENERAL MANUEL GONZALEZ (ex-Execute)	C-51 (ex-D 03)	12 Dec 1962
GENERAL MANUEL E RINCON (ex-Specter)	C-52 (ex-D 04)	21 July 1963
GENERAL FELIPE XICOTENCATL (ex-Scuffle)	C-53 (ex-D 05)	7 Dec 1962
CADETE AUGUSTIN MELGAR (ex-Device)	C-54 (ex-D 11)	30 Mar 1963
TENIENTE JUAN DE LA BARRERA (ex-Ransom)	C-55 (ex-D 12)	30 Mar 1963
CADETE JUAN ESCUTIA (ex-Knave)	C-56 (ex-D 13)	30 Mar 1963
CADETE FERNANDO MONTES DE OCA (ex-Rebel)	C-57 (ex-D 14)	30 Mar 1963
CADETE FRANCISCO MARQUEZ (ex-Diploma)	C-59 (ex-D 17)	30 Mar 1963
GENERAL IGNACIO ZARAGOZA (ex-Invade)	C-60 (ex-D 18)	28 May 1963
CADETE VICENTE SUAREZ (ex-Intrigue)	C-61 (ex-D 19)	27 May 1963

Displacement, tons: 650 standard; 804 full load
Dimensions, feet (metres): 184.5 × 33 × 8.5 (56.3 × 10.1 × 2.6)
Main machinery: 2 Cooper-Bessemer GSB-8 diesels; 1,710 hp (1.28 MW); 2 shafts
Speed, knots: 15. Range, miles: 4,300 at 10 kt
Complement: 104 (8 officers)
Guns: 1 USN 3 in (76 mm)/50 Mk 22; 20 rds/min to 12 km (6.5 n miles) anti-surface; 9 km (4.9 n miles) anti-aircraft; weight of shell 6 kg.
  4 Oerlikon 20 mm (2 twin); 800 rds/min to 2 km; weight of shell 0.24 kg.
Radars: Surface search: Raytheon 1020; I-band.
Helicopters: Platform for 1 BO 105.

Comment: Former US steel hulled fleet minesweepers. All completed in 1943-44. One now fitted for surveying (see *Survey Vessels*). Minesweeping gear removed. Four of the class deleted in 1986. Three others, C 53-C 55, converted in 1991-93, C 56-C 59 in 1994-95, and the remainder in 1996-97 to provide a helicopter platform aft, fit GPS and new electronics. Gun armament changed at the same time. A 22 ft Boston Whaler is carried. One scrapped in 1998 having been replaced by first of 'Centenario' class.

UPDATED

GENERAL FELIPE XICOTENCATL   *4/1994*, Mexican Navy / 0081247

1 + 5 CENTENARIO CLASS (OPV)

Name	No	Builders	Launched	Commissioned
DÉMOCRATA	C 101	Varadero, Guaymas	16 Oct 1997	9 July 1998

Displacement, tons: 450 full load
Dimensions, feet (metres): 172.2 × 29.5 × 8.5 (52.5 × 9 × 2.6)
Main machinery: 2 MTU 20V 956 TB92 diesels; 6,119 hp(m) (4.5 MW); 2 shafts
Speed, knots: 30
Complement: 36 (13 officers)
Guns: 2 Bofors 40 mm/60 (twin).
Radars: Surface search: Racal Decca; E/F-band.

Comment: Large numbers are required to replace the 'Auk' and 'Admirable' classes, and these are to be built in local shipyards as funds become available. A 50 kt Boston Whaler launch is carried at the stern.

UPDATED

DÉMOCRATA   *4/1999*, Mexican Navy / 0081248

3 CAPE (PGM 71) CLASS (LARGE PATROL CRAFT) (PC)

Name	No	Builders	Recommissioned
CABO CORRIENTES	P 42	CG Yard, Curtis Bay	16 Mar 1990
(ex-Jalisco, ex-Cape Carter)			
CABO CORZO	P 43	CG Yard, Curtis Bay	21 Apr 1990
(ex-Nayarit, ex-Cape Hedge)			
CABO CATOCHE	P 44	CG Yard, Curtis Bay	18 Mar 1991
(ex-Cape Hatteras)			

Displacement, tons: 98 standard; 148 full load
Dimensions, feet (metres): 95 × 20.2 × 6.6 (28.9 × 6.2 × 2)
Main machinery: 2 GM 16V-149TI diesels; 2,322 hp (1.73 MW) sustained; 2 shafts
Speed, knots: 20. Range, miles: 2,500 at 10 kt
Complement: 14 (1 officer)
Guns: 2—12.7 mm MGs.
Radars: Navigation: Raytheon SPS-64; I-band.

Comment: All built in 1953; have been re-engined and extensively modernised. Transferred under the FMS programme, having paid off from the US Coast Guard.

UPDATED

CABO CORRIENTES   *6/1992*, Mexican Navy / 0081250

2 POINT CLASS (LARGE PATROL CRAFT) (PC)

Name	No	Builders	Recommissioned
PUNTA MORRO (ex-Point Verde)	P 60 (ex-P 45)	CG Yard, Curtis Bay	12 June 1991
PUNTA MASTUN (ex-Point Herron)	P 61 (ex-P 46)	CG Yard, Curtis Bay	21 June 1991

Displacement, tons: 67 full load
Dimensions, feet (metres): 83 × 17.2 × 5.8 (25.3 × 5.2 × 1.8)
Main machinery: 2 Caterpillar diesels; 1,600 hp (1.19 MW); 2 shafts
Speed, knots: 12. Range, miles: 1,500 at 8 kt
Complement: 10
Guns: 2—12.7 mm MGs (can be carried).
Radars: Surface search: Raytheon SPS-64; I-band.

Comment: Ex-US Coast Guard craft built in 1961. Steel hulls and aluminium superstructures. Speed much reduced from original 23 kt.

UPDATED

PUNTA MASTUN   *6/1994*, Mexican Navy / 0081251

31 AZTECA CLASS (LARGE PATROL CRAFT) (PC)

Name	No	Builders	Commissioned	
AZTECA (ex-Quintana)	P 01	Ailsa Shipbuilding Co Ltd	1 Nov	1974
GUAYCURA (ex-Cordova)	P 02	Scott & Sons, Bowling	22 Oct	1974
NAHUATL (ex-Arizpe)	P 03	Ailsa Shipbuilding Co Ltd	23 Dec	1974
TOTORAN (ex-Izazaga)	P 04	Ailsa Shipbuilding Co Ltd	19 Dec	1974
PAPAGO (ex-Bautista)	P 05	Scott & Sons, Bowling	19 Dec	1974
TARAHUMARA (ex-Rayon)	P 06	Ailsa Shipbuilding Co Ltd	19 Dec	1974
TEPEHUAN (ex-Rejon)	P 07	Ailsa Shipbuilding Co Ltd	4 July	1975
MEXICA (ex-Fuente)	P 08	Ailsa Shipbuilding Co Ltd	4 July	1975
ZAPOTECA (ex-Guzman)	P 09	Scott & Sons, Bowling	7 Apr	1975
HUASTECA (ex-Ramirez)	P 10	Ailsa Shipbuilding Co Ltd	17 July	1975
MAZAHUA (ex-Mariscal)	P 11	Ailsa Shipbuilding Co Ltd	23 Sep	1975
HUICHOL (ex-Jara)	P 12	Ailsa Shipbuilding Co Ltd	7 Nov	1975
SERI (ex-Mata)	P 13	Lamont & Co Ltd	13 Oct	1975
YAQUI (ex-Romero)	P 14	Scott & Sons, Bowling	23 June	1975
TLAPANECO (ex-Lizardi)	P 15	Ailsa Shipbuilding Co Ltd	24 Dec	1975
TARASCO (ex-Mujica)	P 16	Ailsa Shipbuilding Co Ltd	21 Nov	1975
ACOLHUA (ex-Rouaix)	P 17	Scott & Sons, Bowling	7 Nov	1975
OTOMI (ex-Velazco)	P 18	Lamont & Co Ltd	1 Nov	1975
MAYO (ex-Rojas)	P 19	Lamont & Co Ltd	1 Nov	1976
PIMAS (ex-Macias)	P 20	Lamont & Co Ltd	29 Dec	1976
CHICHIMECA (ex-Calderon)	P 21	Lamont & Co Ltd	29 Nov	1976
CHONTAL (ex-Zaragoza)	P 22	Veracruz	1 June	1976
MAZATECO (ex-Tamaulipas)	P 23	Veracruz	18 July	1977
TOLTECA (ex-Yucatan)	P 24	Veracruz	1 Nov	1977
MAYA (ex-Tabasco)	P 25	Veracruz	1 Dec	1978
COCHIMIE (ex-Veracruz)	P 26	Veracruz	1 Dec	1978
CORA (ex-Campeche)	P 27	Veracruz	1 Mar	1980
TOTONACA (ex-Puebla)	P 28	Veracruz	1 June	1982
MIXTECO (ex-Maza)	P 29	Salina Cruz	25 Nov	1976
OLMECA (ex-Vicario)	P 30	Salina Cruz	1 May	1977
TLAHUICA (ex-Ortiz)	P 31	Salina Cruz	1 June	1977

Displacement, tons: 148 full load
Dimensions, feet (metres): 112.7 × 28.3 × 7.2 *(34.4 × 8.7 × 2.2)*
Main machinery: 2 Paxman 12YJCM diesels; 3,000 hp *(2.24 MW)* sustained; 2 shafts
Speed, knots: 24. **Range, miles:** 1,537 at 14 kt
Complement: 24 (2 officers)
Guns: 1 Bofors 40 mm/70; 300 rds/min to 12 km *(6.5 n miles)* anti-surface; 4 km *(2.2 n miles)* anti-aircraft; weight of shell 2.4 kg.
1 Oerlikon 20 mm or 1—7.62 mm MG.
Radars: Surface search: Kelvin Hughes; I-band.

Comment: Ordered by Mexico on 27 March 1973 from Associated British Machine Tool Makers Ltd to a design by TT Boat Designs, Bembridge, Isle of Wight. The first 21 were modernised in 1987 in Mexico with spare parts and equipment supplied by ABMTM Marine Division who supervised the work which included engine refurbishment and the fitting of air conditioning. *UPDATED*

CHONTAL   *4/1999*, van Ginderen Collection /* 0081249

4 ISLA CORONADO CLASS (FAST ATTACK CRAFT) (PCF)

Name	No	Builders	Commissioned	
ISLA CORONADO	P 51	Equitable Shipyards	1 Sep	1993
ISLA LOBOS	P 52	Equitable Shipyards	1 Nov	1993
ISLA GUADALUPE	P 53	Equitable Shipyards	1 Feb	1994
ISLA COZUMEL	P 54	Equitable Shipyards	1 Apr	1994

Displacement, tons: 52 full load
Dimensions, feet (metres): 82 × 17.9 × 4 *(25 × 5.5 × 1.2)*
Main machinery: 3 Detroit diesels; 16,200 hp *(12.9 MW)*; 3 Arneson surface drives
Speed, knots: 50. **Range, miles:** 1,200 at 30 kt
Complement: 9 (3 officers)
Guns: 1—12.7 mm MG. 2—7.62 mm MGs.
Radars: Surface search: Raytheon SPS 69; I-band.
Fire control: Thomson-CSF Agrion; J-band.

Comment: Built by the Trinity Marine Group to an XFPB (extra fast patrol boat) design. Deep Vee hulls with FRP/Kevlar construction. Based at Islas Mujeres in the XI naval zone. Similar craft built for US Navy. May be fitted with MM 15 SSMs in due course and armed with 40 mm or 20 mm guns. *UPDATED*

ISLA LOBOS   *6/1994*, Mexican Navy /* 0081252

7 LAGUNA (ex-POLIMAR) CLASS (COASTAL PATROL CRAFT) (PC)

Name	No	Builders	Commissioned	
TAMIAHUA (ex-Poluno)	P 70 (ex-F 01)	Astilleros de Tampico	1 Oct	1962
LAGARTOS (ex-Poldos)	P 71 (ex-F 02)	Icacas Shipyard, Guerrero	15 July	1968
KANA (ex-Poltres)	P 72 (ex-F 03)	Icacas Shipyard, Guerrero	19 Nov	1968
CUYUTLAN (ex-Polcinco)	P 73 (ex-F 05)	Astilleros de Tampico	2 Sep	1959
MANDINGA (ex-Aspirante Jose V Razcon)	P 74 (ex-F 06)	Astilleros de Tampico	2 Jan	1961
ALVARADO (ex-Polsiete)	P 75 (ex-F 07)	—	1 Jan	1989
CATEMACO (ex-Polocho)	P 76 (ex-F 08)	—	15 Dec	1990

Displacement, tons: 155 full load
Dimensions, feet (metres): 85 × 14.1 × 6.6 *(25.9 × 4.3 × 2)*
Main machinery: 2 diesels; 456 hp *(335 kW)*; 2 shafts
Speed, knots: 8
Guns: 1 Oerlikon 20 mm (can be carried).
Radars: Surface search: Kelvin Hughes; I-band.

Comment: Steel construction. The last two were transferred from the USN on the dates shown and are similar in size. All have *Laguna de* in front of the names. *UPDATED*

LAGUNA DE CUYUTLAN   *6/1994*, Mexican Navy /* 0081253

0 + 20 COMBATBOAT 90 HMN (PCF)

Displacement, tons: 19 full load
Dimensions, feet (metres): 52.2 × 12.5 × 2.6 *(15.9 × 3.8 × 0.8)*
Main machinery: 2 CAT 3406 diesels; 1,104 hp(m) *(812 kW)*; 2 waterjets
Speed, knots: 35. **Range, miles:** 240 at 30 kt
Complement: 3
Guns: 3—12.7 mm MGs.
Radars: Surface search: I-band.

Comment: Ordered from Sweden in 1999 with an option on 20 more. First delivery expected in late 2000. These craft are in service with the Swedish and Norwegian navies and with paramilitary forces in Malaysia and China. *NEW ENTRY*

COMBATBOAT 90H (Malaysian colours)   *12/1999*, Sattler/Steele /* 0081502

5 LAGO CLASS (RIVER PATROL CRAFT) (PB)

Name	No	Builders	Commissioned	
LAGO DE PATZCUARO (ex-AM 04)	P 80 (ex-F 14)	Vera Cruz	9 May	1957
LAGO DE CHAPALA (ex-AM 05)	P 81 (ex-F 15)	Tampico	12 Oct	1959
LAGO DE TEXCOCO (ex-AM 06)	P 81 (ex-F 16)	Vera Cruz	1 Nov	1959
LAGO DE JANITZIO (ex-AM 07)	P 83 (ex-F 17)	Tampico	8 Dec	1961
LAGO DE CUITZEO (ex-AM 08)	P 84 (ex-F 18)	Vera Cruz	8 Dec	1981

Displacement, tons: 37 full load
Dimensions, feet (metres): 56.1 × 13.1 × 3.9 *(17.1 × 4 × 1.2)*
Main machinery: 1 diesel; 320 hp(m) *(235 kW)*; 1 shaft
Speed, knots: 5
Complement: 5
Radars: Surface search: Kelvin Hughes; I-band.

Comment: Steel construction. One already deleted having been replaced by the last of the class which was built 20 years after the others. *UPDATED*

LAGO DE PATZCUARO   *1/1995*, Mexican Navy /* 0081254

13 ARRECIFE (ex-OLMECA II) CLASS (RIVER PATROL CRAFT) (PB)

ALACRAN (ex-*AM-11*) P-90	LA BLANQUILLA (ex-*AM-18*) P-97
SISAL (ex-*AM-12*) P-91	ANEGADA DE ADENTRO (ex-*AM-19*) P-98
TANHUIJO (ex-*AM-13*) P-92	RIZO (ex-*AM-20*) P-99
CABEZO (ex-*AM-14*) P-93	PAJAROS (ex-*AM-21*) P-100
SANTIAGUILLO (ex-*AM-15*) P-94	DE ENMEDIO (ex-*AM-22*) P-101
PALANCAR (ex-*AM-16*) P-95	DE HORNOS (ex-*AM-23*) P-102
LA GALLEGUILLA (ex-*AM-17*) P-96	

Displacement, tons: 18 full load
Dimensions, feet (metres): 54.8 × 14.4 × 3.9 *(16.7 × 4.4 × 1.2)*
Main machinery: 2 Detroit 8V-92TA diesels; 700 hp *(562 kW)* sustained; 2 shafts
Speed, knots: 20. **Range, miles:** 460 at 10 kt
Complement: 15 (2 officers)
Guns: 1—12.7 mm MG.
Radars: Navigation: Raytheon 1900; I-band.

Comment: Built at Acapulco and completed between June 1982 and October 1989 with GRP
 hulls. All have *Arrecife* in front of the names.
UPDATED

ARRECIFE DE HORNOS   3/1997*, John Grima / 0012782

37 + 5 PIRAÑA CLASS (PB) and 10 MAKO MARINE 295 CLASS (PB)

G 1-G 36   C 101-01

Dimensions, feet (metres): 22.3 × 7.5 × 1 *(6.8 × 2.3 × 0.3)*
Main machinery: 2 Johnson outboards; 280 hp *(209 kW)*
Speed, knots: 40. **Range, miles:** 190 at 40 kt
Complement: 2
Guns: 1 or 2—7.62 mm MGs.

Comment: Details are for the G 1-36 Pirañas. Acquired in 1993/94. Carried by 'Admirable' class
 and others. C 101-01 is the 50 kt launch carried in *Démocrata* and more are to be acquired as the
 OPVs enter service. The Mako Marine craft acquired in 1995 are 29 ft boats with twin Mercury
 outboards. There are also five Sea Force 730 RIBs with Hamilton water-jets, also acquired in
 1995-96.
UPDATED

G 19   1994*, Mexican Navy / 0081255

C 101-01   7/1998, Mexican Navy / 0052610

SURVEY AND RESEARCH SHIPS

1 ONJUKU CLASS (SURVEY SHIP) (AGS)

Name	No	Builders	Commissioned
ONJUKU	H 04	Uchida Shipyard	10 Jan 1980

Displacement, tons: 494 full load
Dimensions, feet (metres): 121 × 26.2 × 11.5 *(36.9 × 8 × 3.5)*
Main machinery: 1 Yanmar 6UA-UT diesel; 700 hp(m) *(515 kW)*; 1 shaft
Speed, knots: 12. **Range, miles:** 5,645 at 10.5 kt
Complement: 20 (4 officers)
Radars: Navigation: Furuno; I-band.
Sonars: Furuno; hull-mounted; high frequency active.

Comment: Launched 9 December 1977 in Japan. Sonar is a fish-finder type.
UPDATED

ONJUKU   4/1999*, van Ginderen Collection / 0081256

2 ROBERT D CONRAD CLASS (RESEARCH SHIPS) (AGOR)

Name	No	Builders	Commissioned
ALTAIR (ex-*James M Gilliss*)	H 05 (ex-AGOR 4)	Christy Corp, WI	5 Nov 1962
ANTARES (ex-*S P Lee*)	H 06 (ex-AG 192)	Defoe, Bay City	2 Dec 1962

Displacement, tons: 1,370 full load
Dimensions, feet (metres): 208.9 × 40 × 15.4 *(63.7 × 12.2 × 4.7)*
Main machinery: Diesel-electric; 2 Caterpillar diesel generators; 1,200 hp *(895 kW)*; 2 motors;
 1,000 hp *(746 kW)*; 1 shaft; bow thruster
Speed, knots: 13.5. **Range, miles:** 10,500 at 10 kt
Complement: 41 (12 officers) plus 15 scientists
Radars: Navigation: Raytheon 1025; Raytheon R4iY; I-band.

Comment: *Altair* leased from USA 14 June 1983. Refitted and modernised in Mexico.
 Recommissioned 27 November 1984. Primarily used for oceanography. *Antares* served as an
 AGI with the USN until February 1974 when she transferred on loan to the Geological Survey.
 Acquired by sale 1 December 1992.
UPDATED

ALTAIR   4/1993*, Mexican Navy / 0081257

1 SURVEY SHIP (AGS)

Name	No	Builders	Commissioned
RIO HONDO (ex-*Deer Island*)	H 08 (ex-A 26, ex-YAG 62)	Halter Marine	May 1962

Displacement, tons: 400 full load
Dimensions, feet (metres): 120.1 × 27.9 × 6.9 *(36.6 × 8.5 × 2.1)*
Main machinery: 2 diesels; 2 shafts
Speed, knots: 10. **Range, miles:** 6,000 at 10 kt
Complement: 20

Comment: Acquired from USA on 2 August 1996 and adapted for a support ship role in 1997.
 Converted to Survey Ship in 1999. Used in US service from 1983 as an acoustic research ship to
 test noise reduction equipment. Started life as an oil rig supply tug.
UPDATED

RIO HONDO   4/1999*, M Declerck / 0081258

1 HUMBOLT CLASS (RESEARCH SHIP) (AGOR)

Name	No	Builders	Recommissioned
ALEJANDRO DE HUMBOLT	H 03	JG Hitzler, Elbe	22 June 1987

Displacement, tons: 585 standard; 700 full load
Dimensions, feet (metres): 140.7 × 32 × 13.5 *(42.3 × 9.6 × 4.1)*
Main machinery: 2 diesels; 2 shafts
Speed, knots: 14
Complement: 20 (4 officers)
Radars: Navigation: Kelvin Hughes; I-band.

Comment: Former trawler built in Germany and launched in January 1970. Converted in 1982 to become a hydrographical and acoustic survey ship. Based at Sinaloa.   *VERIFIED*

ALEJANDRO DE HUMBOLT   6/1993, Mexican Navy

AUXILIARIES

Notes: (1) The US LSD *Fort Fisher* (LSD 40) offered for sale in 1999, and the US LST *Newport* (LST 1179) in 2000.
(2) The 'Bolster' class ARS *Matlalcueye* A 64 (ex-*Conserver*) was to have been acquired from the US on 23 July 1998 but did not transfer.

2 LST 511-1152 and 1 FABIUS CLASS (LST)

Name	No	Builders	Commissioned
RIO PANUCO (ex-*Park County*)	A 01	Bethlehem Steel	8 May 1945
RIO PAPALOAPAN (ex-*Manzanillo*, ex-*Clearwater County*)	A 02	Chicago Bridge & Iron Co	31 Mar 1944
RIO GRIJALVA (ex-*Vicente Guerrero*, ex-*Magara*)	A 03 (ex-A 05)	American Bridge	27 June 1945

Displacement, tons: 4,080 full load
Dimensions, feet (metres): 328 × 50 × 14 *(100 × 15.3 × 4.3)*
Main machinery: 2 GM 12-567A diesels; 1,800 hp *(1.34 MW)*; 2 shafts
Speed, knots: 11. **Range, miles:** 6,000 at 11 kt
Complement: 250
Guns: 8 Bofors 40 mm (2 twin, 4 single).

Comment: Transferred from USA 10 September 1971, 17 June 1972 and 10 October 1973 respectively and deployed as SAR and disaster relief ships.   *UPDATED*

RIO PANUCO   7/1991*, Harald Carstens / 0081259

2 USUMACINTA CLASS (AP/AK/AH)

Name	No	Builders	Commissioned
RIO USUMACINTA (ex-*Huasteco*)	A 10 (ex-A 21)	Tampico, Tampa	21 May 1986
RIO COATZACOALCOS (ex-*Zapoteco*)	A 11 (ex-A 22)	Salina Cruz	1 Sep 1986

Displacement, tons: 1,854 standard; 2,650 full load
Dimensions, feet (metres): 227 × 42 × 18.6 *(69.2 × 12.8 × 5.7)*
Main machinery: 1 GM-EMD diesel; 3,600 hp(m) *(2.65 MW)*; 1 shaft
Speed, knots: 14.5. **Range, miles:** 5,500 at 14 kt
Complement: 85 plus 300 passengers
Guns: 1 Bofors 40/60 Mk 3.
Radars: Navigation: I-band.
Helicopters: Platform for 1 MBB BO 105C.

Comment: Can serve as troop transports, supply or hospital ships.   *UPDATED*

RIO USUMACINTA   6/1994*, Mexican Navy / 0081261

1 LOGISTIC SUPPORT SHIP (AK)

Name	No	Builders	Recommissioned
RIO LERMA (ex-*Tarasco*, ex-*Sea Point*, ex-*Tricon*, ex-*Marika*, ex-*Arneb*)	A 22 (ex-A 25)	Solvesborg, Sweden	1 Mar 1990

Displacement, tons: 1,970 full load
Dimensions, feet (metres): 282.2 × 40.7 × 16.1 *(86 × 12.4 × 4.9)*
Main machinery: 1 Kloeckner Humboldt Deutz diesel; 2,100 hp(m) *(1.54 MW)*; 1 shaft
Speed, knots: 14
Complement: 35
Cargo capacity: 778 tons

Comment: Built in 1962 as a commercial ship and taken into the Navy in 1990.   *UPDATED*

RIO LERMA (old number)   1990*, Mexican Navy / 0081260

1 POTRERO DEL LLANO CLASS (AOT)

Name	No	Builders	Recommissioned
POTRERO DEL LLANO (ex-*Alvaro Obregon*)	A 42	Ishikawajima Harima, Nagoya	16 Nov 1993

Displacement, tons: 15,434 standard; 27,432 full load
Dimensions, feet (metres): 560 × 74 × 31 *(170.7 × 22.6 × 9.4)*
Main machinery: 1 IHI/Sulzer diesel; 7,200 hp(m) *(5.29 MW)* sustained; 1 shaft
Speed, knots: 14.6
Complement: 30

Comment: Acquired from the Mexican Merchant Marine. Built in 1968-69 and acquired 1 June 1993. Two others paid off in 1997.   *UPDATED*

POTRERO DEL LLANO (old number)   6/1994*, Mexican Navy / 0081262

1 DURANGO CLASS (TRANSPORT) (AP)

Name	No	Builders	Commissioned
DURANGO	B 01 (ex-128)	Union Naval de Levante, Valencia	14 July 1936

Displacement, tons: 1,600 standard; 2,000 full load
Dimensions, feet (metres): 256.5 × 36.6 × 10.5 *(78.2 × 11.2 × 3.1)*
Main machinery: Diesel-electric; 2 Enterprise DMR-38 diesels; 5,000 hp *(3.73 MW)*; 2 shafts
Speed, knots: 14. **Range, miles:** 3,000 at 12 kt
Complement: 149 (24 officers)
Guns: 1—4 in *(102 mm)*. 2—57 mm. 4 Oerlikon 20 mm.

Comment: Laid down 28 October 1933 and launched 28 June 1935. Originally designed primarily as an armed transport with accommodation for 20 officers and 450 men, then reclassified as a frigate. Became non-operational in the 1970s but has since been refitted as a transport ship. Top speed has reduced.   *VERIFIED*

DURANGO   1992, Mexican Navy

1 SUPPORT SHIP (AK)

Name	No	Builders	Commissioned
— (ex-Seacon)	— (ex-YFNB 33)	Missouri Valley Bridge, Indiana	25 Oct 1945

Displacement, tons: 2,780 full load
Dimensions, feet (metres): 260.2 × 47.9 × 16.4 (79.3 × 14.6 × 5)
Main machinery: 1 GM 12-71 diesel; 2 GM 6-71 diesels; 1,020 hp (761 kW); 3 shafts
Speed, knots: 7
Complement: 10 plus 40 spare

Comment: Former US dumb barge converted in US service as a missile retriever and diver support ship. Acquired in March 1999 as a utility support craft. 25 ton gantry and a towing capacity of 100 tons.   ***VERIFIED***

SEACON   5/1993, Giorgio Arra

1 SUPPORT SHIP (AKS)

Name	No	Builders	Commissioned
RIO SUCHIATE (ex-Monob 1)	A 27 (ex-YAG 61, ex-YW 87)	Zenith Dredge Co	11 Nov 1943

Displacement, tons: 1,390 full load
Dimensions, feet (metres): 191.9 × 33.1 × 15.7 (58.5 × 10.1 × 4.8)
Main machinery: 1 Caterpillar D 398 diesel; 850 hp (634 kW); 1 shaft
Speed, knots: 9. **Range, miles:** 2,500 at 9 kt
Complement: 21

Comment: Acquired from USA on 2 August 1996. The ship was converted from a water carrier to an acoustic research role in 1969, and had four laboratories in US service. Adapted for support ship role in 1997.   ***VERIFIED***

RIO SUCHIATE (US colours)   7/1988, Giorgio Arra

1 LOGISTIC SUPPORT SHIP (AKS)

Name	No	Builders	Recommissioned
RIO NAUTLA (ex-Maya)	A 20 (ex-A 23)	Isla Gran Cayman, Ru	1 June 1988

Displacement, tons: 924 full load
Dimensions, feet (metres): 160.1 × 38.7 × 16.1 (48.8 × 11.8 × 4.9)
Main machinery: 1 MAN diesel; 1 shaft
Speed, knots: 12
Complement: 15 (8 officers)

Comment: First launched in 1962 and acquired for the Navy in 1988. Unarmed.   ***UPDATED***

RIO NAUTLA (old number)   1989*, Mexican Navy / 0081263

1 ADMIRABLE CLASS (SUPPORT SHIP) (AKS)

Name	No	Builders	Launched
ALDEBARAN (ex-DM 20, ex-Harlequin AM 365, ex-ID-20)	A 08 (ex-H 02)	Willamette Iron & Steel	28 Sep 1945

Displacement, tons: 804 full load
Dimensions, feet (metres): 184.5 × 33 × 14.5 (56.3 × 10.1 × 4.4)
Main machinery: 4 Cooper-Bessemer GSB-8 diesels; 1,710 hp (1.26 MW); 2 shafts
Speed, knots: 15. **Range, miles:** 4,300 at 10 kt
Complement: 62 (12 officers)
Guns: 1—3 in (76 mm)/50 Mk 22. 2—7.62 mm MGs.
Radars: Navigation: Kelvin Hughes; I-band.

Comment: Acquired in 1962 and converted for survey work in 1978. Converted again as a Support Ship in 1999, and re-armed.   ***UPDATED***

ALDEBARAN   4/1999*, M Declerck / 0081264

1 LOGISTIC SUPPORT SHIP (AKSL)

Name	No	Builders	Recommissioned
RIO TONALA (ex-Progreso)	A 21 (ex-A 24)	Angulo, Del Carmen	27 Mar 1989

Displacement, tons: 152 full load
Dimensions, feet (metres): 73.8 × 21.7 × 4.9 (22.5 × 6.6 × 1.5)
Main machinery: 1 diesel; 1 shaft
Speed, knots: 10
Complement: 10
Cargo capacity: 57 tons

Comment: First commissioned 27 February 1985. Converted in 1988 and taken into the Navy in 1989.   ***VERIFIED***

RIO TONALA (old number)   1992, Mexican Navy

2 LAS CHOAPAS CLASS (YOG/YO)

Name	No	Builders	Recommissioned
LAS CHOAPAS (ex-Aguascalientes, ex-YOG 6)	A 45 (ex-A 03)	Geo H Mathis Co Ltd, Camden, NJ	25 Nov 1964
AMATLAN (ex-Tlaxcala, ex-YO 107)	A 46 (ex-A 04)	Geo Lawley & Son, Neponset, MA	25 Nov 1964

Displacement, tons: 895 standard; 1,480 full load
Dimensions, feet (metres): 159.2 × 32.9 × 13.3 (48.6 × 10 × 4.1)
Main machinery: 1 Fairbanks-Morse diesel; 500 hp (373 kW); 1 shaft
Speed, knots: 6
Complement: 26 (5 officers)
Cargo capacity: 6,570 barrels
Guns: 1 Oerlikon 20 mm.

Comment: Former US self-propelled fuel oil barges built in 1943. Purchased in August 1964.   ***UPDATED***

AMATLAN   6/1994*, Mexican Navy / 0081265

1 TRANSPORT VESSEL (AKS)

Name	No	Builders	Commissioned
RIO TEHUANTEPEC (ex-*Zacatecas*)	A 24 (ex-B 02)	Ulua SY, Veracruz	12 Mar 1962

Displacement, tons: 785 standard
Dimensions, feet (metres): 158 × 27.2 × 10 *(48.2 × 8.3 × 2.7)*
Main machinery: 1 MAN diesel; 560 hp(m) *(412 kW)*; 1 shaft
Speed, knots: 8
Complement: 50 (13 officers)
Cargo capacity: 400 tons
Guns: 1 Bofors 40 mm/60. 2 Oerlikon 20 mm.

Comment: Cargo ship type employed as a transport.

UPDATED

RIO TEHUANTEPEC   *6/1996** / 0081266

4 FLOATING DOCKS

— (ex-US ARD 2)   — (ex-US ARD 11)   **AR 15** (ex-US ARD 15)   — (ex-US AFDL 28)

Comment: ARD 2 (150 × 24.7 m) transferred 1963 and ARD 11 (same size) 1974 by sale. Lift 3,550 tons. Two 10 ton cranes and one 100 kW generator. ARD 15 has the same capacity and facilities—transferred 1971 by lease. AFDL 28 built in 1944, transferred 1973. Lift, 1,000 tons. ARD 30 may be acquired from US in due course.   *UPDATED*

7 BAHIA CLASS and 14 LAGUNA CLASS (DREDGERS)

BAHIA DE BANDERAS (ex-*Chiapas*) D 01 (ex-A 30)	**LAGUNA DE COYUCA** D 25
BAHIA TODOS SANTOS (ex-*Mazatlan*) D 02 (ex-A 31)	**LAGUNA FARRALLON** D 26
BAHIA MAGDALENA (ex-*Cristobal Colon*) D 03 (ex-A 32)	**LAGUNA DE CHAIREL** D 27
BAHIA ASUNCION (ex-*Isla del Carmen*) D 04 (ex-A 33)	**LAGUNA DE ZAMACH** D 28
BAHIA ALMEJAS (ex-*Isla Azteca*) D 05 (ex-A 34)	**LAGUNA DE TERMINOS** D 29
BAHIA TEPOCA D 06	**LAGUNA CARPINTERO** D 30
BAHIA PETACALCO D 07	**LAGUNA DE TECOMATE** D 31
LAGUNA GUERRERO NEGRO D 21	**LAGUNA DE CHAUTENGO** D 32
LAGUNA DE MINUAYA D 22	**LAGUNA DE TECULAPA** D 33
LAGUNA BACALAR D 23	**LAGUNA DE TAMPAMACHOCO** D 34
LAGUNA DE CHACAGUA D 24	

Comment: First 10 acquired in 1985, remainder in 1994.   *VERIFIED*

TRAINING SHIPS

1 SAIL TRAINING SHIP (AXS)

Name	No	Builders	Launched	Commissioned
CUAUHTEMOC	A 07	Astilleros Talleres Calaya SA, Bilbao	9 Jan 1982	23 Sep 1982

Displacement, tons: 1,662 full load
Dimensions, feet (metres): 296.9 (bowsprit); 220.5 wl × 39.4 × 17.7 *(90.5; 67.2 × 12 × 5.4)*
Main machinery: 1 Detroit 12V-149T diesel; 1,125 hp *(839 kW)*; 1 shaft
Speed, knots: 17 sail; 7 diesel
Complement: 268 (20 officers, 90 midshipmen)
Guns: 2—65 mm Schneider Model 1902 saluting guns.

Comment: Has 2,368 m² of sail. Similar ships in Ecuador, Colombia and Venezuela.   *UPDATED*

CUAUHTEMOC   *7/1999** , Per Kornefeldt / 0081267

TUGS

4 ABNAKI CLASS (ATF)

Name	No	Builders	Commissioned
KUKULKAN (ex-*Otomi*, ex-*Molala* ATF 106)	A 52 (ex-A 17)	United Eng Co, Alameda, CA	29 Sep 1943
EHACATL (ex-*Yaqui*, ex-*Abnaki* ATF 96)	A 53 (ex-A 18)	Charleston SB and DD Co	15 Nov 1943
TONATIUH (ex-*Seri*, ex-*Cocopa* ATF 101)	A 54 (ex-A 19)	Charleston SB and DD Co	25 Mar 1944
CHAC (ex-*Cora*, ex-*Hitchiti* ATF 103)	A 55 (ex-A 20)	Charleston SB and DD Co	27 May 1944

Displacement, tons: 1,640 full load
Dimensions, feet (metres): 205 × 38.5 × 17 *(62.5 × 11.7 × 5.2)*
Main machinery: Diesel-electric; 4 Busch-Sulzer BS-539 diesels; 6,000 hp *(4.48 MW)*; 4 generators; 1 motor; 3,000 hp(m) *(2.24 MW)*; 1 shaft
Speed, knots: 10. **Range, miles:** 6,500 at 10 kt
Complement: 75
Guns: 1 US 3 in *(76 mm)*/50 Mk 22.
Radars: Navigation: Marconi LN66; I-band.

Comment: *Kukulkan* transferred from USA 27 September 1978, remainder 1 October 1978. All by sale. Speed reduced.

UPDATED

EHACATL   *1/1995** , Mexican Navy / 0081268

2 QUEZALCOATL (V 4) CLASS (ATF)

Name	No	Builders	Recommissioned
QUEZALCOATL (ex-*Mayo*, ex-*Montauk*)	A 50 (ex-A 12)	Pendleton Shipyard	1 Nov 1970
HUITILOPOCHTLI (ex-*Mixteco*, ex-*Point Vicente*)	A 51 (ex-A 13)	Levingston Shipyard	1 Nov 1970

Displacement, tons: 1,863 full load
Dimensions, feet (metres): 194.6 × 37.7 × 17.1 *(59.3 × 11.5 × 5.2)*
Main machinery: 2 Nat Supply 8-cyl diesels; 2,250 hp *(1.68 MW)*; 2 Kort nozzle props
Speed, knots: 14. **Range, miles:** 9,000 at 14 kt
Complement: 90
Guns: 1—3 in *(76 mm)*/50. 2 Oerlikon 20 mm *(Quezalcoatl)*.
Radars: Navigation: Kelvin Hughes 14/9; I-band.

Comment: Part of a large class built 1943-45 by US Maritime Administration for civilian use. Not a successful design; most were laid up on completion. In 1968 six were taken from reserve and transferred by sale in June 1969. All originally unarmed—guns fitted in Mexico. *Quezalcoatl* assigned to Gulf area, *Huitilopochtli* to Pacific area. The other four have been scrapped. *Huitilopochtli* is unarmed.

UPDATED

HUITILOPOCHTLI   *1/1995** , Mexican Navy / 0081269

MICRONESIA

Headquarters Appointments	General	Personnel	Bases	Mercantile Marine
Maritime Wing Commander: Commander Steve J Memai	Pacific Islands of the Caroline archipelago comprising the states of Kosral, Pohnpei, Truk and Yap. The Federated States became a self-governing republic on 10 May 1979. The USA maintains responsibility for defence.	2000: 120	Kolonia (main base), Kosral, Moen, Takatik.	*Lloyd's Register of Shipping:* 18 vessels of 9,774 tons gross

PATROL FORCES

3 PACIFIC FORUM TYPE (LARGE PATROL CRAFT) (PC)

Name	No	Builders	Commissioned
PALIKIR	FSM 1	Australian Shipbuilding Industries	28 Apr 1990
MICRONESIA	FSM 2	Australian Shipbuilding Industries	3 Nov 1990
INDEPENDENCE	FSM 5	Transfield	22 May 1997

Displacement, tons: 162 full load
Dimensions, feet (metres): 103.3 × 26.6 × 6.9 *(31.5 × 8.1 × 2.1)*
Main machinery: 2 Caterpillar 3516TA diesels; 4,400 hp *(3.28 MW)* sustained; 2 shafts
Speed, knots: 20. **Range, miles:** 2,500 at 12 kt
Complement: 17 (3 officers)
Radars: Surface search: Furuno 1011; I-band.

Comment: First pair ordered in June 1989 from Australian Shipbuilding Industries. Training and support provided by Australia at Port Kolonia. Third of class negotiated with Transfield (former ASI) in 1997.   ***UPDATED***

MICRONESIA   *11/1990, Royal Australian Navy*

2 CAPE CLASS (LARGE PATROL CRAFT) (PC)

Name	No	Builders	Commissioned
PALUWLAP (ex-*Cape Cross*)	FSM 3	Coast Guard Yard, Curtis Bay	20 Aug 1958
CONSTITUTION (ex-*Cape Corwin*)	FSM 4	Coast Guard Yard, Curtis Bay	14 Nov 1958

Displacement, tons: 148 full load
Dimensions, feet (metres): 95 × 20.2 × 6.6 *(28.9 × 6.2 × 2)*
Main machinery: 2 GM 16V-149TI diesels; 2,070 hp *(1.54 MW)* sustained; 2 shafts
Speed, knots: 20. **Range, miles:** 2,500 at 10 kt
Complement: 14 (3 officers)
Guns: 2—12.7 mm MGs. 2—40 mm mortars.
Radars: Surface search: Raytheon SPS-64; I-band.

Comment: Two former Coast Guard ships transferred from USA on loan in March and September 1991. Re-engined in 1982 and now restricted in speed.   ***VERIFIED***

CAPE (USCG colours)   *1990*

MOROCCO
MARINE ROYALE MAROCAINE

Headquarters Appointments	Personnel	Bases	Aviation	Mercantile Marine
Inspector of the Navy: Captain Mohammed Triki	(a) 2000: 7,800 officers and ratings (including 1,500 Marines) (b) 18 months' national service	Casablanca (HQ), Safi, Agadir, Kenitra, Tangier, Dakhla, Al Hoceima	The Ministry of Fisheries operates 11 Pilatus Britten-Norman Defender maritime surveillance aircraft.	*Lloyd's Register of Shipping:* 496 vessels of 448,455 tons gross

FRIGATES

0 + 2 FLOREAL CLASS (FFG)

Name	No	Builders	Laid down	Launched	Commissioned
—	—	Chantiers de L'Atlantique, St Nazaire	June 1999	Apr 2000	Aug 2001
—	—	Chantiers de L'Atlantique, St Nazaire	Dec 1999	Aug 2000	Feb 2002

Displacement, tons: 2,950 full load
Dimensions, feet (metres): 306.8 × 45.9 × 14.1 *(93.5 × 14 × 4.3)*
Main machinery: CODAD; 4 SEMT-Pielstick 6 PA6 L 280 diesels; 8,820 hp(m) *(6.5 MW)* sustained; 2 shafts; acbLIPS cp props; bow thruster; 340 hp(m) *(250 kW)*
Speed, knots: 20. **Range, miles:** 10,000 at 15 kt
Complement: 86 (10 officers)

Missiles: SSM: 2 Aerospatiale MM 38 Exocet ❶.
SAM: 2 Matra Simbad twin launchers ❷ can replace 20 mm guns or Dagaie launcher.
Guns: 1 Otobreda 76 mm/62 ❸.
2 Giat 20 F2 20 mm ❹.
Countermeasures: Decoys: 2 CSEE Dagaie Mk II ❺; 10-barrelled trainable launchers; chaff and IR flares.
ESM: Thomson-CSF ARBR 17 ❻; radar intercept.
Weapons control: CSEE Najir optronic director ❼.
Radars: Air/surface search: Thomson-CSF Mars DRBV 21A ❽; D-band.
Navigation: 2 Racal Decca 1229 (DRBN 34A) ❾; I-band (1 for helicopter control).

Helicopters: 1 Panther type.

Programmes: Order announced by Alstom on 23 October 1998.
Structure: Details given are for the class in French service. It is likely that the smaller Otobreda 76 mm/62 is to be fitted in place of the 100 mm gun.   ***UPDATED***

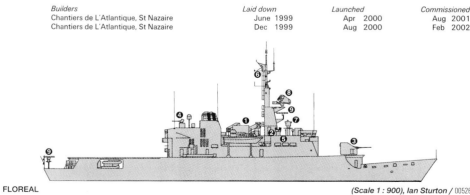

FLOREAL   *(Scale 1 : 900), Ian Sturton / 0052616*

FLOREAL (French colours)
12/1997, G Toremans / 0052615

1 MODIFIED DESCUBIERTA CLASS (FFG)

Name	No	Builders	Laid down	Launched	Commissioned
LIEUTENANT COLONEL ERRHAMANI	501	Bazán, Cartagena	20 Mar 1979	26 Feb 1982	28 Mar 1983

Displacement, tons: 1,233 standard; 1,479 full load
Dimensions, feet (metres): 291.3 × 34 × 12.5
(88.8 × 10.4 × 3.8)
Main machinery: 4 MTU-Bazán 16V 956 TB91 diesels;
15,000 hp(m) (11 MW) sustained; 2 shafts; cp props
Speed, knots: 25.5. **Range, miles:** 4,000 at 18 kt (1 engine)
Complement: 100

Missiles: SSM: 4 Aerospatiale MM 38 Exocet ❶; inertial cruise;
active radar homing to 42 km (23 n miles) at 0.9 Mach;
warhead 165 kg; sea-skimmer. Frequently not embarked.
SAM: Selenia/Elsag Albatros octuple launcher ❷; 24 Aspide;
semi-active radar homing to 13 km (8 n miles) at 2.5 Mach;
height envelope 15-5,000 m (49.2-16,405 ft); warhead 30 kg.
Guns: 1 OTO Melara 3 in (76 mm)/62 compact ❸; 85 rds/min to
16 km (8.6 n miles) anti-surface; 12 km (6.5 n miles) anti-
aircraft; weight of shell 6 kg.
2 Breda Bofors 40 mm/70 ❹; 300 rds/min to 12.5 km (6.7 n
miles); weight of shell 0.96 kg.
Torpedoes: 6—324 mm Mk 32 (2 triple) tubes ❺. Honeywell
Mk 46 Mod 1; anti-submarine; active/passive homing to 11 km
(5.9 n miles) at 40 kt; warhead 44 kg.
A/S mortars: 1 Bofors SR 375 mm twin trainable launcher ❻;
range 3.6 km (1.9 n miles); 24 rockets.
Countermeasures: Decoys: 2 CSEE Dagaie double trainable
mounting; IR flares and chaff; H/J-band.
ESM/ECM: Elettronica ELT 715; intercept and jammer.
Combat data systems: Signaal SEWACO-MR action data
automation. SATCOM.
Radars: Air/surface search: Signaal DA05 ❼; E/F-band (see
Operational).
Surface search: Signaal ZW06 ❽; I-band.
Fire control: Signaal WM25/41 ❾; I/J-band; range 46 km (25 n
miles).
Sonars: Raytheon DE 1160 B; hull-mounted; active/passive;
medium range; medium frequency.

Programmes: Ordered 7 June 1977.
Modernisation: New 40 mm guns fitted in 1995. Refit in Spain in
1996.
Operational: The ship is fitted to carry Exocet but the missiles are
seldom embarked. The air search radar was removed in 1998
but reinstated in 1999.

UPDATED   LIEUTENANT COLONEL ERRHAMANI

LIEUTENANT COLONEL ERRHAMANI   (Scale 1 : 900), Ian Sturton

11/1999*, van Ginderen Collection / 0081270

LIEUTENANT COLONEL ERRHAMANI (without main radar)   6/1998, Diego Quevedo / 0052614

PATROL FORCES

2 OKBA (PR 72) CLASS (LARGE PATROL CRAFT) (PC)

Name	No	Builders	Commissioned
OKBA	302	SFCN, Villeneuve la Garenne	16 Dec 1976
TRIKI	303	SFCN, Villeneuve la Garenne	12 July 1977

Displacement, tons: 375 standard; 445 full load
Dimensions, feet (metres): 188.8 × 25 × 7.1 (57.5 × 7.6 × 2.1)
Main machinery: 4 SACM AGO V16 ASHR diesels; 11,040 hp(m) (8.11 MW); 4 shafts
Speed, knots: 28. **Range, miles:** 2,500 at 16 kt
Complement: 53 (5 officers)
Guns: 1 OTO Melara 3 in (76 mm)/62 compact; 85 rds/min to 16 km (8.6 n miles) anti-surface;
12 km (6.5 n miles) anti-aircraft; weight of shell 6 kg.
1 Bofors 40 mm/70; 300 rds/min to 12.5 km (6.7 n miles); weight of shell 0.96 kg.
Weapons control: 2 CSEE Panda optical directors.
Radars: Surface search: Racal Decca 1226; I-band.

Comment: Ordered June 1973. *Okba* launched 10 October 1975, *Triki* 1 February 1976. Can be
Exocet fitted (with Vega control system).

UPDATED   TRIKI

6/1996*, Moroccan Navy / 0081271

4 LAZAGA CLASS (FAST ATTACK CRAFT—MISSILE) (PCFG)

Name	No	Builders	Commissioned
EL KHATTABI	304	Bazán, San Fernando	26 July 1981
COMMANDANT BOUTOUBA	305	Bazán, San Fernando	2 Aug 1982
COMMANDANT EL HARTY	306	Bazán, San Fernando	20 Nov 1981
COMMANDANT AZOUGGARH	307	Bazán, San Fernando	25 Feb 1982

Displacement, tons: 425 full load
Dimensions, feet (metres): 190.6 × 24.9 × 8.9 *(58.1 × 7.6 × 2.7)*
Main machinery: 2 MTU-Bazán 16V 956 TB91 diesels; 7,500 hp(m) *(5.51 MW)* sustained; 2 shafts
Speed, knots: 30. **Range, miles:** 3,000 at 15 kt
Complement: 41
Missiles: SSM: 4 Aerospatiale MM 38 Exocet; inertial cruise; active radar homing to 42 km *(23 n miles)* at 0.9 Mach; warhead 165 kg; sea-skimmer.
Guns: 1 OTO Melara 3 in *(76 mm)*/62 compact; 85 rds/min to 16 km *(8.6 n miles)* anti-surface; 12 km *(6.5 n miles)* anti-aircraft; weight of shell 6 kg.
 1 Breda Bofors 40 mm/70; 300 rds/min to 12.5 km *(6.7 n miles)*; weight of shell 0.96 kg.
 2 Oerlikon 20 mm/90 GAM-BO1; 800 rds/min to 2 km.
Weapons control: CSEE Panda optical director.
Radars: Surface search: Signaal ZW06; I-band; range 26 km *(14 n miles)*.
Fire control: Signaal WM25; I/J-band; range 46 km *(25 n miles)*.
Navigation: Furuno; I-band.

Comment: Ordered from Bazán, San Fernando (Cadiz), Spain 14 June 1977. New Bofors guns fitted aft in 1996/97. 76 mm gun removed from 305 in 1998.   ***UPDATED***

EL KHATTABI   *8/1997, Diego Quevedo /* 0012784

COMMANDANT EL HARTY   *11/1999*, van Ginderen Collection /* 0081273

4 OSPREY MK II CLASS (LARGE PATROL CRAFT) (PC)

Name	No	Builders	Commissioned
EL HAHIQ	308	Danyard A/S, Frederickshaven	11 Nov 1987
EL TAWFIQ	309	Danyard A/S, Frederickshaven	31 Jan 1988
EL HAMISS	316	Danyard A/S, Frederickshaven	9 Aug 1990
EL KARIB	317	Danyard A/S, Frederickshaven	23 Sep 1990

Displacement, tons: 475 full load
Dimensions, feet (metres): 179.8 × 34 × 8.5 *(54.8 × 10.5 × 2.6)*
Main machinery: 2 MAN Burmeister & Wain Alpha 12V23/30-DVO diesels; 4,440 hp(m) *(3.23 MW)* sustained; 2 water-jets
Speed, knots: 22. **Range, miles:** 4,500 at 16 kt
Complement: 15 plus 20 spare berths
Guns: 1 Bofors 40 mm/60. 2 Oerlikon 20 mm.
Radars: Surface search; Racal Decca; I-band.
Navigation: Racal Decca; I-band.

Comment: First two ordered in September 1986; two more on 30 January 1989. There is a stern ramp with a hinged cover for launching the inspection boat. Used for Fishery Protection duties.   ***UPDATED***

EL HAMISS   *1/1997*, Maritime Photographic /* 0012785

6 CORMORAN CLASS (LARGE PATROL CRAFT) (PC)

Name	No	Builders	Launched	Commissioned
L V RABHI	310	Bázan, San Fernando	23 Sep 1987	16 Sep 1988
ERRACHIQ	311	Bázan, San Fernando	23 Sep 1987	16 Dec 1988
EL AKID	312	Bázan, San Fernando	29 Mar 1988	4 Apr 1989
EL MAHER	313	Bázan, San Fernando	29 Mar 1988	20 June 1989
EL MAJID	314	Bázan, San Fernando	21 Oct 1988	26 Sep 1989
EL BACHIR	315	Bázan, San Fernando	21 Oct 1988	19 Dec 1989

Displacement, tons: 425 full load
Dimensions, feet (metres): 190.6 × 24.9 × 8.9 *(58.1 × 7.6 × 2.7)*
Main machinery: 2 MTU-Bazán 16V 956 TB82 diesels; 8,340 hp(m) *(6.13 MW)* sustained; 2 shafts
Speed, knots: 22. **Range, miles:** 6,100 at 12 kt
Complement: 36 (4 officers) plus 15 spare
Guns: 1 Bofors 40 mm/70. 2 Giat 20 mm.
Weapons control: CSEE Lynx optronic director.
Radars: Surface search; Racal Decca; I-band.

Comment: Three ordered from Bazán, Cadiz in October 1985 as a follow on to the 'Lazaga' class of which these are a slower patrol version with a 10 day endurance. Option on three more taken up. Used for fishery protection.   ***UPDATED***

EL MAHER   *6/1989*, Bazán /* 0081272

5 RAÏS BARGACH CLASS (TYPE OPV 64) (PC)

Name	No	Builders	Launched	Commissioned
RAÏS BARGACH	318	Leroux & Lotz, Lorient	9 Oct 1995	14 Dec 1995
RAÏS BRITEL	319	Leroux & Lotz, Lorient	19 Mar 1996	14 May 1996
RAÏS CHARKAOUI	320	Leroux & Lotz, Lorient	25 Sep 1996	10 Dec 1996
RAÏS MAANINOU	321	Leroux & Lotz, Lorient	7 Mar 1997	21 May 1997
RAÏS AL MOUNASTIRI	322	Leroux & Lotz, Lorient	15 Oct 1997	17 Dec 1997

Displacement, tons: 580 full load
Dimensions, feet (metres): 210 × 37.4 × 9.8 *(64 × 11.4 × 3)*
Main machinery: 2 Wärtsilä Nohab 25 V16 diesels; 10,000 hp(m) *(7.36 MW)* sustained; 2 Leroy auxiliary motors; 326 hp(m) *(240 kW)*; 2 shafts; cp props
Speed, knots: 24; 7 (on motors). **Range, miles:** 4,000 at 12 kt
Complement: 24 (3 officers) + 30 spare
Guns: 1 Bofors 40 mm/60. 1 Oerlikon 20 mm. 4—14.5 mm MGs (2 twin).
Radars: Surface search: Racal Decca Bridgemaster; I-band.

Comment: First pair ordered to a Serter design from Leroux & Lotz, Lorient in December 1993, second pair in October 1994. Option on fifth taken up in 1996. There is a stern door for launching a 7 m RIB, a water gun for firefighting and two passive stabilisation tanks. This version of the OPV 64 does not have a helicopter deck and the armament is fitted after delivery. Manned by the Navy for the Fisheries Department. Based at Agadir. Similar craft built for Mauritania and for France.   ***UPDATED***

RAÏS AL MOUNASTIRI (without main armament)   *7/1999*, H M Steele /* 0081274

6 EL WACIL (P 32) CLASS (COASTAL PATROL CRAFT) (PC)

Name	No	Builders	Launched	Commissioned
EL WACIL	203	CMN, Cherbourg	12 June 1975	9 Oct 1975
EL JAIL	204	CMN, Cherbourg	10 Oct 1975	3 Dec 1975
EL MIKDAM	205	CMN, Cherbourg	1 Dec 1975	30 Jan 1976
EL KHAFIR	206	CMN, Cherbourg	21 Jan 1976	16 Apr 1976
EL HARIS	207	CMN, Cherbourg	31 Mar 1976	30 June 1976
EL ESSAHIR	208	CMN, Cherbourg	2 June 1976	16 July 1976

Displacement, tons: 74 light; 89 full load
Dimensions, feet (metres): 105 × 17.7 × 4.6 *(32 × 5.4 × 1.4)*
Main machinery: 2 SACM MGO 12V BZSHR diesels; 2,700 hp(m) *(1.98 MW)*; 2 shafts
Speed, knots: 28. **Range, miles:** 1,500 at 15 kt
Complement: 17
Guns: 1 Oerlikon 20 mm.
Radars: Surface search: Decca; I-band.

Comment: Ordered in February 1974. In July 1985 a further four of this class were ordered from the same builders but for the Customs Service. Wooden hull sheathed in plastic.   ***UPDATED***

EL WACIL   *6/1988* /* 0081275

AMPHIBIOUS FORCES

1 NEWPORT CLASS (LST)

Name	No	Builders	Commissioned
SIDI MOHAMMED BEN ABDALLAH	407 (ex-1198)	National Steel,	5 Aug 1972
(ex-*Bristol County*)		San Diego	

Displacement, tons: 4,975 light; 8,450 full load
Dimensions, feet (metres): 522.3 (hull) × 69.5 × 17.5 (aft) *(159.2 × 21.2 × 5.3)*
Main machinery: 6 ALCO 16-251 diesels; 16,500 hp *(12.3 MW)* sustained; 2 shafts; cp props; bow thruster
Speed, knots: 20. **Range, miles:** 2,500 at 14 kt
Complement: 257 (13 officers)
Military lift: 400 troops (20 officers); 500 tons vehicles; 3 LCVPs and 1 LCPL on davits
Guns: 1 GE/GD 20 mm 6-barrelled Vulcan Phalanx Mk 15.
Radars: Surface search: Raytheon SPS-67; G-band.
Navigation: Marconi LN66; I/J-band.
Helicopters: Platform only.

Comment: Received from the USA by grant transfer on 16 August 1994. Has replaced *Arrafiq*. The ship was non-operational by late 1995 and although back in service, has so far proved to be a poor bargain. The bow ramp is supported by twin derrick arms. A ramp just forward of the superstructure connects the lower tank deck with the main deck and a vehicle passage through the superstructure provides access to the parking area amidships. A stern gate to the tank deck permits unloading of amphibious tractors into the water, or unloading of other vehicles into an LCU or on to a pier. Vehicle stowage covers 19,000 sq ft. Length over derrick arms is 562 ft *(171.3 m)*; full load draught is 11.5 ft forward and 17.5 ft aft. Based at Casablanca. *UPDATED*

SIDI MOHAMMED BEN ABDALLAH   5/1999*, *Diego Quevedo* / 0081276

3 BATRAL CLASS (LST)

Name	No	Builders	Commissioned
DAOUD BEN AICHA	402	Dubigeon, Normandie	28 May 1977
AHMED ES SAKALI	403	Dubigeon, Normandie	Sep 1977
ABOU ABDALLAH EL AYACHI	404	Dubigeon, Normandie	Mar 1978

Displacement, tons: 750 standard; 1,409 full load
Dimensions, feet (metres): 262.4 × 42.6 × 7.9 *(80 × 13 × 2.4)*
Main machinery: 2 SACM Type 195 V12 CSHR diesels; 3,600 hp(m) *(2.65 MW)* sustained; 2 shafts
Speed, knots: 16. **Range, miles:** 4,500 at 13 kt
Complement: 47 (3 officers)
Military lift: 140 troops; 12 vehicles or 300 tons
Guns: 2 Bofors 40 mm/70. 2—81 mm mortars. 1—12.7 mm MG.
Radars: Surface search: Thomson-CSF DRBN 32 (Racal Decca 1226); I-band.
Helicopters: Platform only.

Comment: Two ordered on 12 March 1975. Third ordered 19 August 1975. Of same type as the French *Champlain*. Vehicle-stowage above and below decks. *Daoud Ben Aicha* was refitted in Lorient by Leroux & Lotz in 1995 and *Abou Abdallah el Ayachi* in 1997. The third of class is expected to refit in due course. *UPDATED*

AHMED ES SAKALI   8/1997, *van Ginderen Collection* / 0012787

1 EDIC CLASS (LCT)

Name	No	Builders	Commissioned
LIEUTENANT MALGHAGH	401	Chantiers Navals Franco-Belges	1965

Displacement, tons: 250 standard; 670 full load
Dimensions, feet (metres): 193.5 × 39.2 × 4.3 *(59 × 12 × 1.3)*
Main machinery: 2 SACM MGO diesels; 1,000 hp(m) *(735 kW)*; 2 shafts
Speed, knots: 8. **Range, miles:** 1,800 at 8 kt
Complement: 16 (1 officer)
Military lift: 11 vehicles
Guns: 2 Oerlikon 20 mm. 1—120 mm mortar.
Radars: Navigation: Decca 1226; I-band.

Comment: Ordered early in 1963. Similar to the former French landing craft of the Edic type built at the same yard. *UPDATED*

LIEUTENANT MALGHAGH   2/1995*, *Diego Quevedo* / 0081277

AUXILIARIES

Notes: (1) There is also a yacht, *Essaouira*, 60 tons, from Italy in 1967, used as a training vessel for watchkeepers.
(2) Bazán delivered a harbour pusher tug, similar to Spanish 'Y 171' class, in December 1993.
(3) There are two sail training craft *Al Massira* and *Boujdour*.
(4) There is a stern trawler used as a utility and diver support vessel *(YFU 14)*.

YFU 14   6/1997* / 0012788

1 LOGISTIC SUPPORT SHIP (AKS)

EL AIGH (ex-*Merc Nordia*) 406

Measurement, tons: 1,500 grt
Dimensions, feet (metres): 252.6 × 40 × 15.4 *(77 × 12.2 × 4.7)*
Main machinery: 1 Burmeister & Wain diesel; 1,250 hp(m) *(919 kW)*; 1 shaft
Speed, knots: 11
Complement: 25
Guns: 2—14.5 mm MGs.

Comment: Logistic support vessel with four 5 ton cranes. Former cargo ship with ice-strengthened bow built by Fredrickshavn Vaerft in 1973 and acquired in 1981. *VERIFIED*

AKS (old number)   5/1994, *M Declerck*

1 DAKHLA CLASS (LOGISTIC SUPPORT SHIP) (AKS)

Name	No	Builders	Launched	Commissioned
DAKHLA	408	Leroux & Lotz, Lorient	5 June 1997	1 Aug 1997

Displacement, tons: 2,160 full load
Dimensions, feet (metres): 226.4 × 37.7 × 13.8 *(69 × 11.5 × 4.2)*
Main machinery: 1 Wärtsilä Nohab 8V25 diesel; 2,300 hp(m) *(1.69 MW)* sustained; 1 shaft; cp prop
Speed, knots: 12. **Range, miles:** 4,300 at 12 kt
Complement: 24 plus 22 spare
Cargo capacity: 800 tons
Guns: 2—12.7 mm MGs.
Radars: Navigation: 2 Racal Decca Bridgemaster ARPA; I-band.

Comment: Ordered from Leroux & Lotz, Nantes in 1995. Side entry for vehicles. One 15 ton crane. Based at Agadir. *UPDATED*

DAKHLA   8/1997*, *Leroux & Lotz* / 0012789

SURVEY AND RESEARCH SHIPS

1 ROBERT D CONRAD CLASS (AGOR)

Name	No	Builders	Commissioned
ABU EL BARAKAT	702 (ex-T-AGOR 13)	Northwest Marine Iron Works,	31 Mar 1969
AL BARBARI		Portland, OR	
(ex-*Bartlett*)			

Displacement, tons: 1,200 light; 1,370 full load
Dimensions, feet (metres): 208.9 × 40 × 15.3 *(63.7 × 12.2 × 4.7)*
Main machinery: Diesel-electric; 2 Caterpillar D 378 diesel generators; 1 motor; 1,000 hp *(746 kW)*; 1 shaft; bow thruster
Speed, knots: 13.5. **Range, miles:** 12,000 at 12 kt
Complement: 41 (9 officers, 15 scientists)
Radars: Navigation: TM 1660/12S; I-band.

Comment: Leased from the USA on 26 July 1993. Fitted with instrumentation and laboratories to measure gravity and magnetism, water temperature, sound transmission in water, and the profile of the ocean floor. Special features include 10 ton capacity boom and winches for handling over-the-side equipment; bow thruster; 620 hp gas turbine (housed in funnel structure) for providing 'quiet' power when conducting experiments; can propel the ship at 6.5 kt.
Ships of this class are in service with Brazil, Mexico, Chile, Tunisia and Portugal.
UPDATED

ABU EL BARAKAT AL BARABARI   *11/1999*, van Ginderen Collection* / 0081278

CUSTOMS/COAST GUARD/POLICE

Note: Four 20 m craft are building at Zamacona, Santurce for delivery in 1999.

4 ERRAID (P 32) CLASS (COASTAL PATROL CRAFT) (PC)

Name	No	Builders	Launched		Commissioned	
ERRAID	209	CMN, Cherbourg	20 Dec	1987	18 Mar	1988
ERRACED	210	CMN, Cherbourg	21 Jan	1988	15 Apr	1988
EL KACED	211	CMN, Cherbourg	10 Mar	1988	17 May	1988
ESSAID	212	CMN, Cherbourg	19 May	1988	4 July	1988

Displacement, tons: 89 full load
Dimensions, feet (metres): 105 × 17.7 × 4.6 *(32 × 5.4 × 1.4)*
Main machinery: 2 SACM MGO 12V BZSHR diesels; 2,700 hp(m) *(1.98 MW)*; 2 shafts
Speed, knots: 28. **Range, miles:** 1,500 at 15 kt
Complement: 17
Guns: 1 Oerlikon 20 mm.
Radars: Navigation: Decca; I-band.

Comment: Similar to the 'El Wacil' class listed under Patrol Forces. Ordered in July 1985.
UPDATED

EL KACED   *6/1999** / 0081279

18 ARCOR 46 CLASS (COASTAL PATROL CRAFT) (PC)

D 01-D 18

Displacement, tons: 15 full load
Dimensions, feet (metres): 47.6 × 13.8 × 4.3 *(14.5 × 4.2 × 1.3)*
Main machinery: 2 SACM UD18V8 M5D diesels; 1,010 hp(m) *(742 kW)* sustained; 2 shafts
Speed, knots: 32. **Range, miles:** 300 at 20 kt
Complement: 6
Guns: 2 Browning 12.7 mm MGs.
Radars: Surface search: Furuno 701; I-band.

Comment: Ordered from Arcor, La Teste in June 1985. GRP hulls. Delivered in groups of three from April to September 1987. Used for patrolling the Mediterranean coastline.
UPDATED

D 09   *8/1994*, Paul Beaver* / 0081280

15 ARCOR 53 CLASS (COASTAL PATROL CRAFT) (PC)

Displacement, tons: 17 full load
Dimensions, feet (metres): 52.5 × 13 × 3.9 *(16 × 4 × 1.2)*
Main machinery: 2 Saab DSI-14 diesels; 1,250 hp(m) *(919 kW)*; 2 shafts
Speed, knots: 35. **Range, miles:** 300 at 20 kt
Complement: 6
Guns: 1—12.7 mm MG.
Radars: Surface search: Furuno; I-band.

Comment: Ordered from Arcor, La Teste in 1990 for the Police Force. Delivered at one a month from October 1992.
UPDATED

ARCOR 53 (Police)   *8/1994*, Paul Beaver* / 0081281

3 SAR CRAFT (PC)

HAOUZ   ASSA   TARIK

Displacement, tons: 40 full load
Dimensions, feet (metres): 63.6 × 15.7 × 4.3 *(19.4 × 4.8 × 1.3)*
Main machinery: 2 diesels; 1,400 hp(m) *(1.03 MW)*; 2 shafts
Speed, knots: 20
Complement: 6

Comment: Rescue craft built by Schweers, Bardenfleth and delivered in 1991.
VERIFIED

MOZAMBIQUE
MARINHA MOÇAMBIQUE

Headquarters Appointments

Head of Navy:
Vice Admiral Pascoal Jose Nhalungo

Personnel

2000: 150

Bases

Maputo (Naval HQ); Nacala; Beira; Pemba (Porto Amelia); Metangula (Lake Malawi); Tete (River Zambesi); Inhambane.

Mercantile Marine

Lloyd's Register of Shipping:
123 vessels of 36,329 tons gross

General

Stability restored by 1997 but all the Russian built Zhuks and Yevgenyas have sunk alongside or been sold. There are some motorboats operational on Lake Malawi, but as yet no funds for new patrol craft. It has been stated that the restoration of the Navy has a high priority.

NAMIBIA

Headquarters Appointments

Head of Maritime Wing:
  Commander Festus Sacharia

General

Maritime Wing established out of the Fishery Protection Service in September 1998. Training being done in Brazil.

Bases

Walvis Bay, Luderitz

Personnel

2000: 250 (50 officers)

Aviation

An F 406 Caravan aircraft and one utility helicopter are in service.

Mercantile Marine

Lloyd's Register of Shipping:
  105 vessels of 55,265 tons gross

DELETIONS

1998   *Cuito Cuanavale* (to Norway)

PATROL FORCES

Notes: (1) There are also three research ships, *Welwitschia, Nautilus II* and *Kuiseb*.
(2) It is planned to acquire patrol craft from Brazil.

1 PATROL SHIP (PC)

Name	No	Builders	Commissioned
ORYX (ex-*S to S*)	—	Burmester/Abeking & Rasmussen	May 1975

Displacement, tons: 406 full load
Dimensions, feet (metres): 149.9 × 28.9 × 7.9 *(45.7 × 8.8 × 2.4)*
Main machinery: 2 Deutz RSBA 16M diesels; 2,000 hp(m) *(1.47 MW)*; 1 shaft; cp prop; bow thruster
Speed, knots: 14. **Range, miles:** 4,100 at 11 kt
Complement: 20 (6 officers)
Guns: 1—12.7 mm MG.
Radars: Surface search: Furuno ARPA FR 1525; I-band.
Navigation: Furuno FR 805D; I-band.

Comment: Built for the Nautical Investment Company, Panama and used as a yacht by the Managing Director of Fiat. Acquired in 1993 by Namibia.   ***UPDATED***

1 OSPREY FV 710 CLASS (PC)

Name	No	Builders	Commissioned
TOBIAS HAINYEKO (ex-*Havørnen*)	—	Frederikshavn Vaerft	July 1979

Displacement, tons: 505 full load
Dimensions, feet (metres): 164 × 34.5 × 9 *(50 × 10.5 × 2.8)*
Main machinery: 2 Burmeister & Wain Alpha 16V23L diesels; 4,640 hp(m) *(3.41 MW)*; 2 shafts; cp props
Speed, knots: 20. **Range, miles:** 4,000 at 15 kt
Complement: 15 plus 20 spare
Radars: Surface search: Furuno ARPA FR 1525; I-band.
Navigation: Furuno FRM 64; I-band.

Comment: Donated by Denmark in late 1993, retaining some Danish crew. Recommissioned 15 December 1994. The helicopter deck can handle up to Lynx size aircraft and there is a slipway on the stern for launching an RIB. Similar ships in service in Greece and Morocco.   ***UPDATED***

ORYX   6/1997* / 0081282

TOBIAS HAINYEKO   12/1994*, *Harald Carstens* / 0081283

NATO

1 RESEARCH SHIP (AGOR)

Name	No	Builders	Launched	Commissioned
ALLIANCE	A 1456	Fincantieri, Muggiano	9 July 1986	6 May 1988

Displacement, tons: 2,466 standard; 3,180 full load
Dimensions, feet (metres): 305.1 × 49.9 × 17.1 *(93 × 15.2 × 5.2)*
Main machinery: Diesel-electric; 2 Fincantieri GMT B 230.12 M diesels; 6,079 hp(m) *(4.47 MW)* sustained; 2 AEG CC 3127 generators; 2 AEG motors; 4,039 hp(m) *(2.97 MW)* sustained; 2 shafts; bow thruster
Speed, knots: 16. **Range, miles:** 7,200 at 11 kt
Complement: 24 (10 officers) plus 23 scientists
Radars: Navigation: 2 Kelvin Hughes ARPA; E/F- and I-bands.
Sonars: TVDS towed active VDS 200 Hz-4 kHz; medium and low frequency passive towed line arrays.

Comment: Built at La Spezia. NATO's first wholly owned ship is a Public Service vessel of the German Navy with a German, British and Italian crew. Designed for oceanography and acoustic research. Based at La Spezia and operated by SACLANT Undersea Research Centre. Facilities include extensive laboratories, position location systems, silent propulsion, and overside deployment equipment. Can tow a 20 ton load at 12 kt. A Kongsberg gas turbine on 02 deck provides silent propulsion power at 1,945 hp *(1.43 MW)* up to speeds of 12 kt. Atlas hydrosweep side scan echo-sounder fitted in 1993. Qubit KH TRAC integrated navigational system fitted in 1995. Carries two Watercraft R6 RIBs. Similar ships in Taiwan Navy and building for Italy.   ***UPDATED***

0 + (1) RESEARCH SHIP (AGOR)

Comment: Coastal vessel of 25 m planned for MCM and shallow water research. Planned to be ordered in 2000 and in service in 2002.   ***NEW ENTRY***

ALLIANCE   4/1999*, *Giorgio Ghiglione* / 0081284

NETHERLANDS

Headquarters Appointments

Chief of Defence Staff:
Admiral L Kroon
Commander in Chief:
Vice Admiral C van Duyvendijk
Deputy Commander in Chief:
Rear Admiral J van der Aa
Director, Material (Navy):
Rear Admiral J W P Spaans
Director, Personnel (Navy):
Rear Admiral L J W E Brand

Commands

Admiral Netherlands Fleet Command:
Vice Admiral L L Buffart
Commander Netherlands Task Group:
Commodore J E A Brandt
Commandant General Royal Netherlands Marine Corps:
Major General E C Klop
Flag Officer Netherlands Antilles:
Brigadier W A J Prins

Diplomatic Representation

Naval Attaché in London and Lisbon:
Captain W T Lansink
Naval Attaché in Madrid:
Captain R E Harte
Naval Attaché in Ankara:
Captain R Blobyendaal
Naval Attaché in Washington:
Commodore P C Kok
Naval Attaché in Oslo, Stockholm and Helsinki:
Captain R A Dwarshuis
Naval Attaché in the Gulf:
Commander T Zwollo
Naval Attaché in Bucharest:
Commander G C de Nooy

Personnel

(a) 2000: 9,830 naval and 3,046 Marines
(b) Voluntary service

Bases

Naval HQ: The Hague
Main Base: Den Helder
Minor Bases: Flushing and Curacao
Fleet Air Arm: NAS Valkenburg (LRMP),
NAS De Kooy (helicopters)
R Neth Marines: Rotterdam, Doorn and Texel

Naval Air Arm

Squadron	Aircraft	Task
7	Lynx (SH-14)	Utility and Transport/ SAR
320/321	P-3C Orion	LRMP
860	Lynx (SH-14D)	Embarked

Royal Netherlands Marine Corps

Four (one in reserve) Marine battalions; one combat support battalion, one logistic battalion and one amphibious support battalion. Based at Doorn and in the Netherlands Antilles and Aruba.

Prefix to Ships' Names

Hr Ms

Strength of the Fleet

Type	Active	Building (Projected)
Submarines	4	—
Destroyers	—	4
Frigates	15	—
Mine Hunters	15	—
Submarine Support Ship	1	—
Amphibious Transport Ship (LPD)	1	(1)
Landing Craft	11	—
Survey Ships	1	(2)
Combat Support Ships	2	(1)
Training Ships	2	—

Fleet Disposition

Operational Control of Belgium and Netherlands surface forces is under Admiral Benelux Command at Den Helder.

(1) Two Task Groups, each with two air defence frigates, four Karel Doormans, two Kortenaers, one AOR, two SSK, 10 helicopters and five MPA.
(2) One amphibious transport ship.
(3) MCMV of 15 'Alkmaar' class.
(4) Marine force of two battalions (arctic trained), one battalion for Antilles and Aruba, one battalion in reserve.
(5) Two hydrographic and one oceanographic vessels.

Mercantile Marine

Lloyd's Register of Shipping:
1,433 vessels of 5,923,426 tons gross

DELETIONS

Frigates

1999   *Tromp* (old)

Mine Warfare Forces

1997   *Naarden*

Auxiliaries

1997   *Pax, Westgat* (to Belgium)
1998   *Dokkum*
1999   *Zeefakkel*
2000   6 LCVP Mk II, *Blommendal, Buyskes*

PENNANT LIST

Submarines

S 802	Walrus
S 803	Zeeleeuw
S 808	Dolfijn
S 810	Bruinvis

Destroyers

F 801	De Zeven Provincien (bldg)
F 802	De Ruyter (bldg) (new)
F 803	Tromp (bldg)
F 804	Evertsen (bldg)

Frigates

F 806	De Ruyter (old)
F 812	Jacob van Heemskerck
F 813	Witte de With
F 823	Philips van Almonde
F 824	Bloys van Treslong
F 825	Jan van Brakel
F 826	Pieter Florisz
F 827	Karel Doorman
F 828	Van Speijk
F 829	Willem van der Zaan
F 830	Tjerk Hiddes
F 831	Van Amstel
F 832	Abraham van der Hulst
F 833	Van Nes
F 834	Van Galen

Mine Warfare Vessels

M 850	Alkmaar
M 851	Delfzyl
M 852	Dordrecht
M 853	Haarlem
M 854	Harlingen
M 855	Scheveningen
M 856	Maassluis
M 857	Makkum
M 858	Middelburg
M 859	Hellevoetsluis
M 860	Schiedam
M 861	Urk
M 862	Zierikzee
M 863	Vlaardingen
M 864	Willemstad

Amphibious Forces

L 800	Rotterdam

Auxiliaries

A 801	Pelikaan
A 832	Zuiderkruis
A 836	Amsterdam
A 851	Cerberus
A 852	Argus
A 853	Nautilus
A 854	Hydra
A 874	Linge
A 875	Regge
A 876	Hunze
A 877	Rotte
A 878	Gouwe
A 887	Thetis
A 900	Mercuur
A 902	Van Kinsbergen
A 906	Tydeman
Y 8005	Nieuwediep
Y 8018	Breezand
Y 8019	Balgzand
Y 8050	Urania
Y 8055	Schelde
Y 8056	Wierbalg
Y 8057	Malzwin
Y 8058	Zuidwal
Y 8059	Westwal
Y 8760	Patria

SUBMARINES

Note: The 'Moray' class is a private design by Rotterdam Drydock with the government giving limited financial support on condition that the company collaborates with developers of air independent systems (AIP).

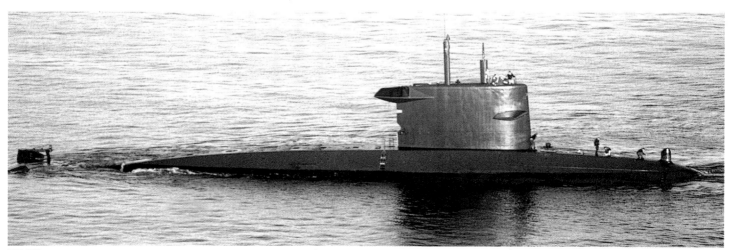

WALRUS

9/1998, B Sullivan / 0052620

4 WALRUS CLASS (SSK)

Name	No	Builders	Laid down	Launched	Commissioned
WALRUS	S 802	Rotterdamse Droogdok Mij, Rotterdam	11 Oct 1979	26 Oct 1985 (13 Sep 1989)	25 Mar 1992
ZEELEEUW	S 803	Rotterdamse Droogdok Mij, Rotterdam	24 Sep 1981	20 June 1987	25 Apr 1990
DOLFIJN	S 808	Rotterdamse Droogdok Mij, Rotterdam	12 June 1986	25 Apr 1990	29 Jan 1993
BRUINVIS	S 810	Rotterdamse Droogdok Mij, Rotterdam	14 Apr 1988	25 Apr 1992	5 July 1994

Displacement, tons: 2,465 surfaced; 2,800 dived
Dimensions, feet (metres): 223.1 × 27.6 × 23
  (67.7 × 8.4 × 7)
Main machinery: Diesel-electric; 3 SEMT-Pielstick 12 PA4 200
  VG diesels; 6,300 hp(m) *(4.63 MW)*; 3 alternators; 2.88 MW;
  1 Holec motor; 6,910 hp(m) *(5.1 MW)*; 1 shaft
Speed, knots: 12 surfaced; 20 dived
Range, miles: 10,000 at 9 kt snorting
Complement: 52 (7 officers)

Missiles: SSM: McDonnell Douglas Sub Harpoon; active radar
  homing to 130 km *(70 n miles)* at 0.9 Mach; warhead 227 kg.
Torpedoes: 4—21 in *(533 mm)* tubes. Honeywell Mk 48 Mod 4;
  wire-guided; active/passive homing to 38 km *(20.5 n miles)*
  active at 55 kt; 50 km *(27 n miles)* passive at 40 kt; warhead
  267 kg and Honeywell NT 37D; wire-guided; active/passive
  homing to 20 km *(10.8 n miles)* at 35 kt; warhead 150 kg; 20
  torpedoes or missiles carried. Mk 19 Turbine ejection pump.
  Mk 67 water-ram discharge.
Mines: 40 in lieu of torpedoes.
Countermeasures: ESM: ARGOS 700; radar warning.
Weapons control: Signaal SEWACO VIII action data automation.
  Signaal Gipsy data system. GTHW integrated Harpoon and
  Torpedo FCS.
Radars: Surface search: Signaal/Racal ZW07; I-band.
Sonars: Thomson Sintra TSM 2272 Eledone Octopus; hull-
  mounted; passive/active search and attack; medium
  frequency.
  GEC Avionics Type 2026; towed array; passive search; very
  low frequency.
  Thomson Sintra DUUX 5; passive ranging and intercept.

Programmes: Contract for the building of the first was signed
  16 June 1979, the second was on 17 December 1979. In
  1981 various changes to the design were made which
  resulted in a delay of one to two years. *Dolfijn* and *Bruinvis*
  ordered 16 August 1985; prefabrication started late 1985.
  Completion of *Walrus* delayed by serious fire 14 August 1986;

DOLFIJN   *6/1999*, van Ginderen Collection* / 0081285

hull undamaged but cabling and computers destroyed. *Walrus*
relaunched 13 September 1989.
Modernisation: A snort exhaust diffuser was fitted to *Zeeleeuw*
  in 1996. The rest of the class have been similarly modified.
Structure: These are improved 'Zwaardvis' class with similar
  dimensions and silhouettes except for X stern. Use of H T steel

increases the diving depth by some 50 per cent. Diving depth,
  300 m *(984 ft)*. Pilkington Optronics CK 24 search and CH 74
  attack periscopes.
Operational: Weapon systems evaluations completed 1990-93.
  Sub Harpoon is not carried.
                                                      UPDATED

DESTROYERS

0 + 4 DE ZEVEN PROVINCIEN CLASS (DDG)

Name	No	Builders	Laid down	Launched	Commissioned
DE ZEVEN PROVINCIEN	F 801	Royal Schelde	1 Sep 1998	8 Apr 2000	Mar 2002
DE RUYTER	F 802	Royal Schelde	3 Sep 1999	2001	2003
TROMP	F 803	Royal Schelde	2000	2002	2004
EVERTSEN	F 804	Royal Schelde	2001	2003	2005

Displacement, tons: 6,048 full load
Dimensions, feet (metres): 473.1 oa; 428.8 wl × 61.7 × 17.1
  (144.2; 130.7 × 18.8 × 5.2)
Flight deck, feet (metres): 88.6 × 61.7 *(27 × 18.8)*
Main machinery: CODOG; 2 RR SM1C Spey; 52,300 hp
  (39 MW) sustained; 2 Stork-Wärtsilä 16V 26 ST diesels;
  13,600 hp(m) *(10 MW)*; 2 shafts; acbLIPS; cp props
Speed, knots: 28. **Range, miles:** 5,000 at 18 kt
Complement: 202 (32 officers) including staff

Missiles: SSM: 8 Harpoon ❶.
  SAM: Mk 41 VLS (40 cells) ❷; Standard SM2-MR Block IIIA;
  Evolved Sea Sparrow (quad pack).
Guns: 1 OTO Breda 5 in *(127 mm)*/54 ❸. 2 Signaal Goalkeeper
  30 mm ❹. 2 Oerlikon 20 mm ❺.
Torpedoes: 4—323 mm (2 twin) Mk 32 Mod 9 fixed launchers ❻
  . Mk 46 Mod 5 torpedoes.
Countermeasures: 4 SRBOC Mk 36 chaff launchers; Nixie
  torpedo decoy.
ESM/ECM: Racal Sabre ❼; intercept/jammer.
Combat data systems: Signaal SEWACO XI; Link 11/16;
  SATCOMS ❽.
Weapons control: Sirius IRST optronic director ❾.
Radars: Air search: Signaal SMART L ❿; 3D; D-band.
  Air/surface search/fire control: Signaal APAR ⓫.
  Surface search: Signaal Scout ⓬; I-band.
  IFF: Mk XII.

Sonars: STN Atlas DSQS 24C; bow-mounted; active search and
  attack; medium frequency.

Helicopters: 1 NFH 90/Lynx ⓭.

Programmes: Project definition awarded to Royal Schelde on
  15 December 1993 with a contract for detailed design
  following on 30 June 1995. Ordered 5 February 1997. The
  second pair are to be without Flag command facilities.
  Shipyards in Germany (ARGE 124 for Type 124) are
  collaborating to achieve some commonality of design and
  equipment.

Structure: As well as the listed equipment the ship is to have an
  electro-optic surveillance system and a navigation radar. The
  Scout radar is a Low Probability Intercept (LPI) set. High
  standards of stealth and NBC protection are part of the design.
  DCN Samahé helicopter handling system.
Operational: The first two ships are to replace the 'Tromp' class
  and the last pair two of the 'Kortenaer' class. NFH 90 helicopter
  planned for 2007. SM-2 Block IVA is a later option.
                                                      UPDATED

DE ZEVEN PROVINCIEN   *(Scale 1 : 1,200), Ian Sturton* / 0052621

DE ZEVEN PROVINCIEN (artist's impression)   *1998, Royal Netherlands Navy* / 0052622

FRIGATES

1 TROMP CLASS (FFG)

Name	No	Builders	Laid down	Launched	Commissioned
DE RUYTER	F 806	Koninklijke Maatschappij De Schelde, Flushing	22 Dec 1971	9 Mar 1974	3 June 1976

Displacement, tons: 3,665 standard; 4,308 full load
Dimensions, feet (metres): 454 × 48.6 × 15.1
(138.4 × 14.8 × 4.6)
Main machinery: COGOG; 2 RR Olympus TM3B gas turbines;
50,880 hp *(37.9 MW)* sustained;
2 RR Tyne RM1C gas turbines; 9,900 hp *(7.4 MW)* sustained;
2 shafts; acbLIPS cp props
Speed, knots: 30. **Range, miles:** 5,000 at 18 kt
Complement: 306 (34 officers)

Missiles: SSM: 8 McDonnell Douglas Harpoon (2 quad)
launchers ❶; active radar homing to 130 km *(70 n miles)* at
0.9 Mach; warhead 227 kg.

SAM: 40 GDC Pomona Standard SM-1MR; Mk 13 Mod 4
launcher ❷; command guidance; semi-active radar homing to
46 km *(25 n miles)* at 2 Mach.
Raytheon Sea Sparrow Mk 29 octuple launcher ❸; semi-active
radar homing to 14.6 km *(8 n miles)* at 2.5 Mach; warhead
39 kg.
Guns: 2 Bofors 4.7 in *(120 mm)*/50 (twin) ❹; 42 rds/min to
20 km *(10.8 n miles)* anti-surface; 12 km *(6.5 n miles)* anti-
aircraft; weight of shell 24 kg.
Signaal SGE-30 Goalkeeper with GE 30 mm ❺; 7-barrelled;
4,200 rds/min combined to 2 km.
2 Oerlikon 20 mm.

Torpedoes: 6—324 mm US Mk 32 (2 triple) tubes ❻. Honeywell
Mk 46 Mod 5; anti-submarine; active/passive homing to 11 km
(5.9 n miles) at 40 kt; warhead 44 kg.
Countermeasures: Decoys: 2 Loral Hycor SRBOC ❼; IR flares
and chaff.
ESM/ECM: Ramses; intercept and jammer.
Combat data systems: Signaal SEWACO I action data
automation; Links 10 and 11. JMCIS. SCOT 1D SATCOM ❽.
Weapons control: Signaal WM25 for guns and missiles.
Radars: Air/surface search: Signaal MTTR/SPS-01 ❾; 3D;
F-band.
Navigation: 2 Decca 1226; I-band.
Fire control: 2 Raytheon SPG-51C ❿; G/I-band.
Signaal WM25 ⓫; I/J-band; range 46 km *(25 n miles)*.
Sonars: CWE 610; hull-mounted; active search and attack;
medium frequency.

Helicopters: 1 Westland SH-14B Lynx ⓬.

Modernisation: Modernisation plans cancelled in 1988 as an
economy measure but partially resurrected in 1990. New
communications fit in 1996.
Operational: Fitted as a Flagship. Second of class paid off in
November 1999, and *De Ruyter* is expected to go by 2003.
Sales: Indonesia has shown an interest in buying at least one of
the class. **UPDATED**

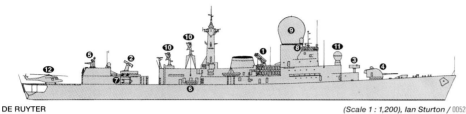

DE RUYTER *(Scale 1 : 1,200), Ian Sturton / 0052625*

DE RUYTER *2/1999 *, M Declerck / 0081286*

4 KORTENAER CLASS (FFG)

Name	No	Builders	Laid down	Launched	Commissioned
PHILIPS VAN ALMONDE	F 823	Dok en Werfmaatschappij Wilton-Fijenoord	3 Oct 1977	11 Aug 1979	2 Dec 1981
BLOYS VAN TRESLONG	F 824	Dok en Werfmaatschappij Wilton-Fijenoord	27 Apr 1978	15 Nov 1980	25 Nov 1982
JAN VAN BRAKEL	F 825	Koninklijke Maatschappij De Schelde, Flushing	16 Nov 1979	16 May 1981	14 Apr 1983
PIETER FLORISZ (ex-*Willem van der Zaan*)	F 826	Koninklijke Maatschappij De Schelde, Flushing	21 Jan 1981	8 May 1982	1 Oct 1983

Displacement, tons: 3,050 standard; 3,630 full load
Dimensions, feet (metres): 428 × 47.9 × 14.1; 20.3 (screws)
(130.5 × 14.6 × 4.3; 6.2)
Main machinery: CODOG; 2 RR Olympus TM3B gas turbines;
50,880 hp *(37.9 MW)* sustained;
2 RR Tyne RM1C gas turbines; 9,900 hp *(7.4 MW)* sustained;
2 shafts; acbLIPS cp props
Speed, knots: 30. **Range, miles:** 4,700 at 16 kt on Tynes
Complement: 176 (18 officers) plus 24 spare berths

Missiles: SSM: 8 McDonnell Douglas Harpoon (2 quad)
launchers ❶; active radar homing to 130 km *(70 n miles)* at
0.9 Mach; warhead 227 kg.
SAM: Raytheon Sea Sparrow Mk 29 octuple launcher ❷; semi-
active radar homing to 14.6 km *(8 n miles)* at 2.5 Mach;
warhead 39 kg; 24 missiles.
Guns: 1 OTO Melara 3 in *(76 mm)*/62 compact ❸; 85 rds/min to
16 km *(8.6 n miles)* anti-surface; 12 km *(6.5 n miles)* anti-
aircraft; weight of shell 6 kg. New 100 rds/min version to be
fitted.
Signaal SGE-30 Goalkeeper with General Electric 30 mm ❹;
7-barrelled; 4,200 rds/min combined to 2 km.
2 Oerlikon 20 mm.
Torpedoes: 4—324 mm US Mk 32 (2 twin) tubes ❺. Honeywell
Mk 46 Mod 5; anti-submarine; active/passive homing to 11 km
(5.9 n miles) at 40 kt; warhead 44 kg.
Countermeasures: Decoys: 2 Loral Hycor SRBOC Mk 36 6-tubed
launchers ❻; chaff distraction or centroid modes.
ESM/ECM: Ramses ❼; intercept and jammer.
Combat data systems: Signaal SEWACO II action data
automation; Link 11. SATCOM ❽.
Radars: Air search: Signaal LW08 ❾; D-band; range 264 km
(145 n miles) for 2 m² target.
Surface search: Signaal ZW06 ❿; I-band.
Fire control: Signaal STIR ⓫; I/J-band; range 140 km *(76 n
miles)* for 1 m² target.
Signaal WM25 ⓬; I/J-band; range 46 km *(25 n miles)*.
Sonars: Westinghouse SQS-509; bow-mounted; active search
and attack; medium frequency.

Helicopters: 2 Westland SH-14B Lynx ⓭.

PIETER FLORISZ *(Scale 1 : 1,200), Ian Sturton*

PHILIPS VAN ALMONDE *7/1999 *, M Declerck / 0081295*

Modernisation: Goalkeeper has replaced the 40 mm gun on the
hangar roof. Plans to fit SMART fire-control radars have been
cancelled. All now fitted with same SATCOM twin aerial as in
the 'Karel Doorman' and 'Jacob van Heemskerck' classes.
Structure: Although only one Lynx is carried there is hangar
accommodation for two. TACTASS is not planned except that
the last two ships had a temporary fit prior to the completion of
the first of the 'Karel Doorman' class. *Jan Van Brakel* had the
trials SMART radar fitted on her hangar roof in 1990 with the
control room in the hangar.

Operational: F 826 planned to decommission in late 2000,
followed by F 825 in late 2001.
Sales: Two sold to Greece during construction, mid-1980 and
mid-1981. *Banckert* to Greece 14 May 1993, *Callenburg*
30 March 1994 and *Van Kinsbergen* 1 February 1995. Sale
agreed for all three on 11 November 1992, including refits by
De Schelde, Flushing and the removal of Goalkeeper CIWS.
Kortenaer to Greece on 15 December 1997, *Abraham
Crijnssen* to UAE on 31 October 1997 and *Piet Heyn* to UAE in
June 1998. **UPDATED**

LEADERSHIP.

Leadership means innovation, experience, flexibility, reliability and quality. It made us the sole supplier to the Royal Netherlands Navy for complex ships like this Air-Defence and Command Frigate with fully automated platform control and integrated communication and weapon systems. A perfect example of high-end technology, resulting in the lowest lifecycle costs in its league. Suitable for all climatic conditions from the poles to the equator. To comply with the Navy's cost-efficient requirements the vessel has a highly economic crew-ship interface to facilitate operations, utilising a minimum crew with low maintenance costs.

This expertise is also used to build other craft, such as Landing Platform Docks and Offshore Patrol Vessels. Closely co-operating with each Defence Agency we actively explore the technical options to arrive at the best cost-performance formula. Customers around the globe turn to Schelde Shipbuilding because they get more for their money.

Glacisstraat 165, P.O. Box 555,
4380 AN Vlissingen,
The Netherlands.
Tel.: +31 118 48 50 00.
Fax +31 118 48 50 50.

SCHELDE SHIPBUILDING

A ROYAL SCHELDE COMPANY

2 JACOB VAN HEEMSKERCK CLASS (FFG)

Name	No	Builders	Laid down	Launched	Commissioned
JACOB VAN HEEMSKERCK	F 812	Koninklijke Maatschappij De Schelde, Flushing	21 Jan 1981	5 Nov 1983	15 Jan 1986
WITTE DE WITH	F 813	Koninklijke Maatschappij De Schelde, Flushing	15 Dec 1981	25 Aug 1984	17 Sep 1986

Displacement, tons: 3,750 full load approx
Dimensions, feet (metres): 428 × 47.9 × 14.1 (20.3 screws)
(130.5 × 14.6 × 4.3 (6.2))
Main machinery: COGOG; 2 RR Olympus TM3B gas turbines;
50,880 hp *(37.9 MW)* sustained
2 RR Tyne RM1C gas turbines; 9,900 hp *(7.4 MW)* sustained;
2 shafts; acbLIPS cp props
Speed, knots: 30. **Range, miles:** 4,700 at 16 kt on Tynes
Complement: 197 (23 officers)

Missiles: SSM: 8 McDonnell Douglas Harpoon (2 quad)
launchers ❶; active radar homing to 130 km *(70 n miles)* at
0.9 Mach; warhead 227 kg.
SAM: 40 GDC Pomona Standard SM-1MR; Block IV; Mk 13 Mod 1
launcher ❷; command guidance; semi-active radar homing to
46 km *(25 n miles)* at 2 Mach.
Raytheon Sea Sparrow Mk 29 octuple launcher ❸; semi-active
radar homing to 14.6 km *(8 n miles)* at 2.5 Mach; warhead
39 kg; 24 missiles.
Guns: 1 Signaal SGE-30 Goalkeeper ❹ with General Electric
30 mm 7-barrelled; 4,200 rds/min combined to 2 km.
2 Oerlikon 20 mm.
Torpedoes: 4—324 mm US Mk 32 (2 twin) tubes ❺. Honeywell
Mk 46 Mod 5; anti-submarine; active/passive homing to 11 km
(5.9 n miles) at 40 kt; warhead 44 kg.
Countermeasures: Decoys: 2 Loral Hycor Mk 36 SRBOC 6-tubed
fixed quad launchers ❻; IR flares and chaff to 4 km *(2.2 n
miles)*.
ESM/ECM: Ramses; intercept and jammer.
Combat data systems: Signaal SEWACO VI action data
automation; Link 11. SHF SATCOM ❼. JMCIS.
Radars: Air search: Signaal LW08 ❽; D-band; range 264 km
(145 n miles) for 2 m² target.
Air/surface search: Signaal Smart; 3D ❾; F-band.
Surface search: Signaal Scout ❿; I-band.
Fire control: 2 Signaal STIR 240 ⓫; I/J/K-band; range 140 km
(76 n miles) for 1 m² target.
Signaal STIR 180 ⓬; I/J/K-band.
Sonars: Westinghouse SQS-509; hull-mounted; active search
and attack; medium frequency.

Modernisation: Planned capability upkeep programme (CUP)
cancelled. Twin SATCOM terminals fitted in 1993 to F 812,
and to F 813 in 1994-95. SMART radar replaced DA05 in F 813
in 1994-95 and in F 812 in 1996-97. The SHF system is based
on the USN WSC-6, with twin aerials providing a 360°
coverage even at high latitudes.
Operational: Air defence frigates with command facilities for a
task group commander and his staff.

UPDATED

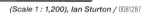

WITTE DE WITH   *(Scale 1 : 1,200), Ian Sturton / 0081287*

JACOB VAN HEEMSKERCK   *3/1999*, Maritime Photographic / 0084270*

WITTE DE WITH   *3/1999*, John Brodie / 0081288*

JACOB VAN HEEMSKERCK   *4/1999*, A Sharma / 0081289*

8 KAREL DOORMAN CLASS (FFG)

Name	No	Builders	Laid down		Launched		Commissioned	
KAREL DOORMAN	F 827	Koninklijke Maatschappij De Schelde, Flushing	26 Feb	1985	20 Apr	1988	31 May	1991
WILLEM VAN DER ZAAN	F 829	Koninklijke Maatschappij De Schelde, Flushing	6 Nov	1985	21 Jan	1989	28 Nov	1991
TJERK HIDDES	F 830	Koninklijke Maatschappij De Schelde, Flushing	28 Oct	1986	9 Dec	1989	3 Dec	1992
VAN AMSTEL	F 831	Koninklijke Maatschappij De Schelde, Flushing	3 May	1988	19 May	1990	27 May	1993
ABRAHAM VAN DER HULST	F 832	Koninklijke Maatschappij De Schelde, Flushing	8 Feb	1989	7 Sep	1991	15 Dec	1993
VAN NES	F 833	Koninklijke Maatschappij De Schelde, Flushing	10 Jan	1990	16 May	1992	2 June	1994
VAN GALEN	F 834	Koninklijke Maatschappij De Schelde, Flushing	7 June	1990	21 Nov	1992	1 Dec	1994
VAN SPEIJK	F 828	Koninklijke Maatschappij De Schelde, Flushing	1 Oct	1991	26 Mar	1994	7 Sep	1995

Displacement, tons: 3,320 full load
Dimensions, feet (metres): 401.2 oa; 374.7 wl × 47.2 × 14.1
(122.3; 114.2 × 14.4 × 4.3)
Flight deck, feet (metres): 72.2 × 47.2 *(22 × 14.4)*
Main machinery: CODOG; 2 RR Spey SM1C; 33,800 hp
(25.2 MW) sustained (early ships of the class will initially only
have SM1A gas generators and 30,800 hp *(23 MW)* sustained
available); 2 Stork-Wärtsilä 12SW280 diesels; 9,790 hp(m)
(7.2 MW) sustained; 2 shafts; acbLIPS cp props
Speed, knots: 30 (Speys); 21 (diesels)
Range, miles: 5,000 at 18 kt
Complement: 156 (16 officers) (accommodation for 163)

Missiles: SSM: 8 McDonnell Douglas Harpoon Block 1C (2 quad)
launchers **❶**; active radar homing to 130 km *(70 n miles)* at
0.9 Mach; warhead 227 kg.
SAM: Raytheon Sea Sparrow Mk 48 vertical launchers **❷**; semi-
active radar homing to 14.6 km *(8 n miles)* at 2.5 Mach;
warhead 39 kg; 16 missiles. Canisters mounted on port side of
hangar.
Guns: 1—3 in *(76 mm)*/62 OTO Melara compact Mk 100 **❸**; 100
rds/min to 16 km *(8.6 n miles)* anti-surface; 12 km *(6.5 n miles)*
anti-aircraft; weight of shell 6 kg. This is the version with an
improved rate of fire.
1 Signaal SGE-30 Goalkeeper with General Electric 30 mm
7-barrelled **❹**; 4,200 rds/min combined to 2 km.
2 Oerlikon 20 mm; 800 rds/min to 2 km.
Torpedoes: 4—324 mm US Mk 32 Mod 9 (2 twin) tubes
(mounted inside the after superstructure) **❺**. Honeywell Mk 46
Mod 5; anti-submarine; active/passive homing to 11 km *(5.9 n
miles)* at 40 kt; warhead 44 kg.
Countermeasures: Decoys: 2 Loral Hycor SRBOC 6-tubed fixed
Mk 36 quad launchers; IR flares and chaff to 4 km *(2.2 n miles)*.
SLQ-25 Nixie towed torpedo decoy.
ESM/ECM: Argo APECS II (includes AR 700 ESM) **❻**; intercept
and jammers.
Combat data systems: Signaal SEWACO VIIB action data
automation; Link 11. SATCOM **❼**. WSC-6 twin aerials.
Weapons control: Signaal IRSCAN infra-red detector (fitted in
F 829 for trials and may be retrofitted in all in due course).
Signaal VESTA helo transponder.
Radars: Air/surface search: Signaal SMART **❽**; 3D; F-band.
Air search: Signaal LW08 **❾**; D-band.
Surface search: Signaal Scout **❿**; I-band.
Navigation: Racal Decca 1226; I-band.
Fire control: 2 Signaal STIR **⓫**; I/J/K-band; range 140 km *(76 n
miles)* for 1 m² target.
Sonars: Signaal PHS-36; hull-mounted; active search and attack;
medium frequency.
Thomson Sintra Anaconda DSBV 61; towed array; passive low
frequency. ATAS in due course.

Helicopters: 1 Westland SH-14 Lynx **⓬**.

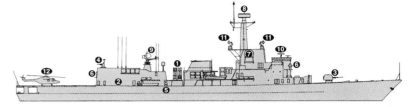

VAN SPEIJK   *(Scale 1 : 1,200), Ian Sturton /* 0012800

TJERK HIDDES   *9/1999*, Findler & Winter /* 0081290

Programmes: Declaration of intent signed on 29 February 1984
although the contract was not signed until 29 June 1985 by
which time the design had been completed. A further four
ordered 10 April 1986. Names have been shuffled to make the
new *Van Speijk* the last of the class but she has retained her
allocated pennant number.
Modernisation: SEWACO VII(A) operational from January 1992
and VII(B) from mid-1994. By 1994 all fitted with APECS II EW
system and DSBV 61 towed array. IRSCAN infrared detector
fitted on hangar roof in *Willem van der Zaan* for trials in 1993.
SHF SATCOM based on the USN WSC-6, with twin aerials
providing a 360° coverage even at high latitudes. Scout radar

fitted on bridge roof in 1997. Four ATAS systems to be ordered
in due course after competitive trials in 1998.
Structure: The VLS SAM is similar to Canadian 'Halifax' and
Greek 'MEKO' classes. The ship is designed to reduce radar
and IR signatures and has extensive NBCD arrangements. Full
automation and roll stabilisation fitted. The APECS jammers
are mounted starboard forward of the bridge and port aft
corner of the hangar. The SAM launchers have been given
added protection and better stealth features with a flat screen
in some of the class.

UPDATED

VAN NES   *11/1999*, Michael Nitz /* 0081291

VAN SPEIJK

3/1999*, Michael Nitz / 0081292

KAREL DOORMAN

10/1999*, Camil Busquets i Vilanova / 0081293

VAN GALEN

7/1999*, H M Steele / 0081294

SHIPBORNE AIRCRAFT

Note: Up to 20 NFH 90 helicopters planned for 2007 to replace Lynx.

Numbers/Type: 21 Westland Lynx Mks 25B/27A/81A.
Operational speed: 125 kt *(232 km/h)*.
Service ceiling: 12,500 ft *(3,810 m)*.
Range: 320 n miles *(590 km)*.
Role/Weapon systems: ASW, SAR and utility helicopter series all converted to SH-14D type. Mk 25B, Mk 27A and Mk 81A can all be embarked for ASW duties in escorts. Sensors: Ferranti Sea Spray radar, Alcatel DUAV-4 dipping sonar, FLIR Model 2000; Ferranti AWARE-3 ESM. Weapons: Two Mk 46 torpedoes or depth bombs.

UPDATED

LYNX   *5/1999*, van Ginderen Collection /* 0081296

LAND-BASED MARITIME AIRCRAFT

Note: Two F-27s based in the Caribbean were withdrawn in 2000.

Numbers/Type: 10 Lockheed P-3C/Update II Orion.
Operational speed: 410 kt *(760 km/h)*.
Service ceiling: 28,300 ft *(8,625 m)*.
Range: 4,000 n miles *(7,410 km)*.
Role/Weapon systems: Long-range MR and NATO area ocean surveillance, particularly for ASW/ASV operations. Three serve in the Antilles. Update for seven aircraft from 1998-2002 includes new radar. The other three may be put in reserve. GPS, ESM and acoustic processors. Sensors: APS-115 radar, AAQ-22 Safire FLIR, AQS-81 MAD, AQA 7 processor, AQS-114 computer, IFF, ECM/ESM, sonobuoys. Weapons: ASW; eight Mk 46 torpedoes, depth bombs or mines. Underwing stations for Harpoon missiles for which procurement is now unlikely.

UPDATED

ORION   *6/1998, J Cislak /* 0052633

MINE WARFARE FORCES

Note: Project definition for an unmanned drone concludes in 2000. The prototype is expected to be of 250 tons and be fitted with magnetic, electric and acoustic influence systems. It is to be built and tested in 2002/03.

15 ALKMAAR (TRIPARTITE) CLASS (MINEHUNTERS) (MHC)

Name	No	Laid down		Launched		Commissioned	
ALKMAAR	M 850	30 Jan	1979	18 May	1982	28 May	1983
DELFZYL	M 851	29 May	1980	29 Oct	1982	17 Aug	1983
DORDRECHT	M 852	5 Jan	1981	26 Feb	1983	16 Nov	1983
HAARLEM	M 853	16 June	1981	6 May	1983	12 Jan	1984
HARLINGEN	M 854	30 Nov	1981	9 July	1983	12 Apr	1984
SCHEVENINGEN	M 855	24 May	1982	2 Dec	1983	18 July	1984
MAASSLUIS	M 856	7 Nov	1982	5 May	1984	12 Dec	1984
MAKKUM	M 857	25 Feb	1983	27 Sep	1984	13 May	1985
MIDDELBURG	M 858	11 July	1983	23 Feb	1985	10 Dec	1986
HELLEVOETSLUIS	M 859	12 Dec	1983	18 July	1985	20 Feb	1987
SCHIEDAM	M 860	6 May	1984	20 Dec	1985	9 July	1986
URK	M 861	1 Oct	1984	2 May	1986	10 Dec	1986
ZIERIKZEE	M 862	25 Feb	1985	4 Oct	1986	7 May	1987
VLAARDINGEN	M 863	6 May	1986	4 Aug	1988	15 Mar	1989
WILLEMSTAD	M 864	3 Oct	1986	27 Jan	1989	20 Sep	1989

Displacement, tons: 562 standard; 595 full load
Dimensions, feet (metres): 168.9 × 29.2 × 8.5 *(51.5 × 8.9 × 2.6)*
Main machinery: 1 Stork Wärtsilä A-RUB 215X-12 diesel; 1,860 hp(m) *(1.35 MW)* sustained; 1 shaft; acbLIPS cp prop; 2 active rudders; 2 motors; 240 hp(m) *(179 kW)*; 2 bow thrusters
Speed, knots: 15 diesel; 7 electric. **Range, miles:** 3,000 at 12 kt
Complement: 29-42 depending on task

Guns: 1 Giat 20 mm (an additional short-range missile system may be added for patrol duties).
Countermeasures: MCM: 2 PAP 104 remote-controlled submersibles. OD 3 mechanical minesweeping gear.
Combat data systems: Signaal Sewaco IX. SATCOM.
Radars: Navigation: Racal Decca TM 1229C or Consilium Selesmar MM 950; I-band.
Sonars: Thomson Sintra DUBM 21A; hull-mounted; minehunting; 100 kHz (± 10 kHz).

Programmes: The two Indonesian ships ordered in 1985 took the place of M 863 and 864 whose laying down was delayed as a result. This class is the Netherlands' part of a tripartite co-operative plan with Belgium and France for GRP hulled minehunters. The whole class built by van der Giessen-de Noord. Ships were launched virtually ready for trials.
Modernisation: New navigation radar being fitted from 1999. The conversion into Troika control ship and the capability update programme are combined into the 'Project Adjusting MCM Capability (PAM)'. This upgrade programme includes a new hull-mounted sonar, the introduction of a self-propelled variable depth sonar, a new command and control system and a new mine identification and disposal system. Linked to this upgrade programme is a plan to build drones (see *Note* at head of section), based on those in use with the German Navy.
Structure: A 5 ton container can be shipped, stored for varying tasks—research; patrol; extended diving; drone control.
Operational: Endurance, 15 days. Automatic radar navigation system. Automatic data processing and display. EVEC 20. Decca Hi-fix positioning system. Alcatel dynamic positioning system. Three are expected to be decommissioned between late 2000 and 2002. Plans to use one ship as a survey vessel have been shelved.
Sales: Two of a modified design to Indonesia, completed March 1988.

UPDATED

ZIERIKZEE   *2/1998, Harald Carstens /* 0052634

AMPHIBIOUS FORCES

5 LCU Mk IX

L 9525-L 9529

Displacement, tons: 200 full load
Dimensions, feet (metres): 89.6 × 21.8 × 5.2 *(27.3 × 6.7 × 1.6)*
Main machinery: Diesel-electric; 2 Caterpillar 3412C diesel generators; 1,496 hp(m) *(1.1 MW)*; 2 Alconza D400 M6 motors; 2 Schottel SPJ 802 pump jets
Speed, knots: 9. **Range, miles:** 400 at 8 kt
Complement: 5 plus 2 spare
Military lift: 130 troops or 2 Warriors or 1 BARV or up to 3 trucks
Guns: 1—12.7 mm MG; 1—7.62 mm MG.
Radars: Navigation: I-band.

Comment: Ordered from Visser Dockyard, Den Helder on 19 July 1996. Steel vessels of which the first commissioned 7 April 1998. The others have been fabricated in Romania and fitted out by Visser in 1999/2000. Embarked in *Rotterdam*.

UPDATED

L 9525   *7/1999*, van Ginderen Collection /* 0081297

6 LCVP Mk III

L 9536-9541

Displacement, tons: 30 full load
Dimensions, feet (metres): 55.4 × 15.7 × 3.6 *(16.9 × 4.8 × 1.1)*
Main machinery: 2 diesels; 750 hp(m) *(551 kW)*; 2 shafts
Speed, knots: 14 (full load); 16.5 (light). **Range, miles:** 200 at 12 kt
Complement: 3
Military lift: 34 troops or 7 tons or 2 Land Rovers or 1 Snowcat
Guns: 1—7.62 mm MG.
Radars: Navigation: Racal Decca 110; I-band.

Comment: Ordered from van der Giessen-de Noord 10 December 1988. First one laid down 10 August 1989, commissioned 16 October 1990. Last one commissioned 19 October 1992.

UPDATED

L 9541   *7/1999*, Findler & Winter /* 0081301

1 + (1) ROTTERDAM CLASS (LPD/ATS)

Name	No	Builders	Laid down	Launched	Commissioned
ROTTERDAM	L 800	Royal Schelde	25 Jan 1996	22 Feb 1997	18 Apr 1998

Displacement, tons: 12,750 full load
Dimensions, feet (metres): 544.6 × 82 × 19.3
(166 × 25 × 5.9)
Flight deck, feet (metres): 183.7 × 82 *(56 × 25)*
Main machinery: Diesel-electric; 4 Stork Wärtsilä 12SW28 diesel generators; 14.6 MW sustained; 2 Holec motors; 16,320 hp(m) *(12 MW)*; 2 shafts; bow thruster; 252 hp(m) *(185 kW)*
Speed, knots: 19. **Range, miles:** 6,000 at 12 kt
Complement: 113 (13 officers) + 611 (41 officers) Marines
Military lift: 611 troops; 170 APCs or 33 MBTs. 6 LCVP Mk 3 or 4 LCU Mk 9 or 4 LCM 8

Guns: 2 Signaal Goalkeeper 30 mm ❶. 4 Oerlikon 20 mm ❷.
Countermeasures: Decoys: 4 SRBOC chaff launchers ❸; Nixie torpedo decoy system.
ESM/ECM: Intercept and jammer.
Combat data systems: SATCOM ❹; Link 11. JMCIS.
Weapons control: Signaal IRSCAN infra-red director.
Radars: Air/surface search: Signaal DA08 ❺; E/F-band.
Surface search: Signaal Scout/Kelvin Hughes ARPA ❻; I-band.
Navigation and CCA: 2 sets; I-band.

Helicopters: 6 NH 90 ❼ or 4 Merlin/Sea King.

Programmes: Project definition for a joint design with Spain completed in December 1993. Contract signed with Royal Schelde 25 April 1994. First steel cut in April 1995. Second of class is to be ordered, to enter service in 2007.
Structure: Facilities to transport a fully equipped Marine battalion with docking facilities for landing craft and a two spot helicopter flight deck with hangar space for six NH 90. 25 ton crane for disembarkation. Full hospital facilities. Built to commercial standards with military command and control and NBCD facilities. Can carry up to 30 torpedoes and 300 sonobuoys.
Operational: Alternative employment as an SAR ship for environmental and disaster relief tasks.

UPDATED

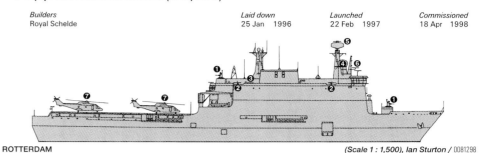

ROTTERDAM
(Scale 1 : 1,500), Ian Sturton / 0081298

ROTTERDAM
*5/1999 *, A Sharma /* 0081299

ROTTERDAM
*10/1999 *, H M Steele /* 0081300

SURVEY SHIPS

Note: There are also four survey boats 8901-8904 completed in 1989-90. Two are carried by A 906.

0 + (2) SURVEY SHIPS (AGS)

Displacement, tons: 1,850 full load
Dimensions, feet (metres): 246.1 × 42 × 13.1 *(75 × 12.8 × 4)*
Main machinery: Diesel electric; 3 diesel generators; 2,652 hp(m) *(1.95 MW)*; 1 motor; 1,360 hp (m) *(1 MW)*; 1 shaft; cp prop
Speed, knots: 13. **Range, miles:** 4,300 at 13 kt
Complement: 12 plus 6 scientists plus 24 spare
Radars: Navigation: E/F- and I-band.
Sonars: Multi and single beam; high frequency; active.

Comment: Both to be built by 2003. Designed for military and civil hydrographic surveys.

NEW ENTRY

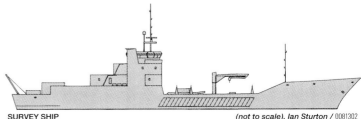

SURVEY SHIP
(not to scale), Ian Sturton / 0081302

1 TYDEMAN CLASS
(HYDROGRAPHIC/OCEANOGRAPHIC SHIP) (AGOR)

Name	No	Builders	Commissioned
TYDEMAN	A 906	Merwede, Hardinxveld, Giessendam	10 Nov 1976

Displacement, tons: 2,977 full load
Dimensions, feet (metres): 295.9 × 47.2 × 15.7 *(90.2 × 14.4 × 4.8)*
Main machinery: Diesel-electric: 3 Stork-Werkspoor 8-FCHD-240 diesel generators; 3,690 hp(m) *(2.71 MW)*; 1 motor; 2,730 hp(m) *(2 MW)*; 1 shaft
1 Paxman diesel; 485 hp(m) *(356 kW)*; 1 active rudder; 300 hp(m) *(220 kW)*; bow thruster; 450 hp(m) *(330 kW)*
Speed, knots: 15. **Range, miles:** 15,700 at 10.3 kt; 10,300 at 13.5 kt
Complement: 62 (8 officers) plus 15 scientists
Radars: Navigation: Racal Decca; I-band.
Sonars: Atlas-Deco 10 echo-sounders with Edig digitisers. KAe Deso 25 replacements.
Kelvin Hughes; hull-mounted; side scan. Klein; towed; side scan.
Elac; bow-mounted; wreck search; trainable in sectors on either bow.

Comment: Ordered in October 1974. Laid down 29 April 1975, launched 18 December 1975. Able to operate oceanographic cables down to 7,000 m. Has six laboratories and two container spaces each for 20 ft standard container. Has forward working deck with wet-hall, midships and after working decks, one 10 ton crane, one 4 ton crane and frames. Diving facilities. Passive stabilisation tank. Decca Hi-fix 6; Digital PDP computer; COMPLOT plotting system. Normally operates in the Atlantic and between March 1991 and March 1992 tested a derivative of the

TYDEMAN   7/1999*, Michael Nitz / 0081303

Thomson Sintra DUBM 41 towed sonar for the detection of mines buried up to 2 m deep. Major refit from April to November 1992 by van der Giessen-de Noord. Carrying out trials with a TSM 2670 2 ton active LF sonar body and passive towed array. Thomson Marconi CAPTAS 20 trials. The flight deck is therefore inoperable.

UPDATED

AUXILIARIES

Note: In addition to the vessels listed there are large numbers of non self-propelled craft with Y pennant numbers, and six harbour launches Y 8200-Y 8205.

1 + (1) AMSTERDAM CLASS (FAST COMBAT SUPPORT SHIP) (AOR)

Name	No	Builders	Laid down	Launched	Commissioned
AMSTERDAM	A 836	Merwede, Hardinxveld, and Royal Schelde, Vlissingen	25 May 1992	11 Sep 1993	2 Sep 1995

Displacement, tons: 17,040 full load
Dimensions, feet (metres): 544.6 × 72.2 × 26.2 *(166 × 22 × 8)*
Main machinery: 2 Bazán/Burmeister & Wain 16V 40/45 diesels; 24,000 hp(m) *(17.6 MW)* sustained; 1 shaft; acbLIPS cp prop
Speed, knots: 20. **Range, miles:** 13,440 at 20 kt
Complement: 160 (23 officers) including 24 aircrew plus 20 spare
Cargo capacity: 6,815 tons dieso; 1,660 tons aviation fuel; 290 tons solids

Guns: 2 Oerlikon 20 mm. 1 Signaal Goalkeeper 30 mm CIWS.
Countermeasures: Decoys: 4 SRBOC Mk 36 chaff launchers. Nixie towed torpedo decoy.
ESM: Ferranti AWARE-4; radar warning.
Weapons control: Signaal IRSCAN infrared director.
Radars: Surface search and helo control: 2 Kelvin Hughes; F-band.

Helicopters: 3 Lynx or 3 SH-3D or 3 NH 90 or 2 EH 101.

Programmes: NP/SP AOR 90 replacement for *Poolster* ordered 14 October 1991. Hull built by Merwede, with fitting out by Royal Schelde from October 1993. A similar ship has been built for the Spanish Navy. A second ship of an improved type is projected with an in-service date of 2006.
Structure: Close co-operation between Dutch Nevesbu and Spanish Bazán led to this design which has maintenance workshops as well as four abeam and one stern RAS/FAS station, and one Vertrep supply station. Built to merchant ship standards but with military NBC damage control.

UPDATED

AMSTERDAM   10/1999*, B Sullivan / 0081304

1 POOLSTER CLASS (FAST COMBAT SUPPORT SHIP) (AOR)

Name	No	Builders	Laid down	Launched	Commissioned
ZUIDERKRUIS	A 832	Verolme Shipyards, Alblasserdam	16 July 1973	15 Oct 1974	27 June 1975

Displacement, tons: 16,900 full load
Measurement, tons: 10,000 dwt
Dimensions, feet (metres): 556 × 66.6 × 27.6 *(169.6 × 20.3 × 8.4)*
Main machinery: 2 Stork-Werkspoor TM410 diesels; 21,000 hp (m) *(15.4 MW)*; 1 shaft; acbLIPS cp props
Speed, knots: 21
Complement: 266 (17 officers)
Cargo capacity: 10,300 tons including 8-9,000 tons oil fuel

Guns: 1 Signaal Goalkeeper 30 mm CIWS. 5 Oerlikon 20 mm.
Countermeasures: Decoys: 2 Loral Hycor SRBOC Mk 36 fixed 6-barrelled launchers; IR flares and chaff.
ESM: Ferranti AWARE-4; radar warning.
Weapons control: Signaal IRSCAN.
Radars: Air/surface search: Racal Decca 2459; F/I-band.
Navigation: 2 Racal Decca TM 1226C; Signaal SCOUT; I-band.

Helicopters: 1 Westland UH-14A Lynx.

Structure: Helicopter deck aft. Funnel heightened by 4.5 m *(14.8 ft)*. 20 mm guns, containerised Goalkeeper CIWS and SATCOM, fitted for operational deployments.
Operational: Capacity for five helicopters with A/S weapons. Two fuelling stations each side for underway replenishment.
Sales: *Poolster* sold to Pakistan in June 1994.   ***UPDATED***

ZUIDERKRUIS   11/1999*, Curt Borgenstam / 0081305

1 ACCOMMODATION SHIP (APB)

THETIS A 887

Displacement, tons: 800 full load
Dimensions, feet (metres): 223 × 39.4 × 5.3 *(68 × 12 × 1.6)*

Comment: Built by Koninklijke Maatschappij De Schelde, Flushing; completed 14 March 1985 and commissioned 27 June 1985; accommodation for 106. Stationed at Den Helder, she provides harbour training for divers and underwater swimmers. **VERIFIED**

1 SUBMARINE SUPPORT SHIP and TORPEDO TENDER (ASL/TRV)

Name	No	Builders	Commissioned
MERCUUR	A 900	Koninklijke Maatschappij de Schelde	21 Aug 1987

Displacement, tons: 1,400 full load
Dimensions, feet (metres): 212.6 × 39.4 × 14.1 *(64.8 × 12 × 4.3)*
Main machinery: 2 Brons 61-20/27 diesels; 1,100 hp(m) *(808 kW)*; 2 shafts; bow thruster
Speed, knots: 14
Complement: 39 (6 officers)
Torpedoes: 3—324 mm (triple) tubes. 1—21 in *(533 mm)* underwater tube.
Mines: Can lay mines.
Radars: Navigation: Racal Decca 1229; I-band.
Sonars: SQR-01; hull-mounted; passive search.

Comment: Replacement for previous ship of same name. Ordered 13 June 1984. Laid down 6 November 1985. Floated out 25 October 1986. Can launch training and research torpedoes above and below the waterline. Services, maintains and recovers torpedoes. **UPDATED**

MERCUUR *6/1999*, Winter & Findler /* 0081306

1 SUPPORT SHIP (ARL)

Name	No	Builders	Commissioned
PELIKAAN (ex-*Kilindoni*)	A 801	Vinholmen, Arendal	1984

Displacement, tons: 505 full load
Dimensions, feet (metres): 151.6 × 34.8 × 9.2 *(46.2 × 10.6 × 2.8)*
Main machinery: 2 Caterpillar 3412T diesels; 1,080 hp *(806 kW)* sustained; 2 shafts
Speed, knots: 10
Complement: 15 plus 40 troops
Guns: 2—12.7 mm MGs.
Radars: Navigation: Racal Decca; I-band.

Comment: Ex-oil platform supply ship acquired 28 May 1990 after being refitted in Curaçao. Serves as tender and transport for marines in the Antilles. Capacity for 40 marines in five accommodation units. **UPDATED**

PELIKAAN *6/1999*, Royal Netherlands Navy /* 0081389

1 TANKER (AOTL)

Name	No	Builders	Commissioned
PATRIA	Y 8760	De Hoop, Schiedam	9 June 1998

Displacement, tons: 681 full load
Dimensions, feet (metres): 145.3 × 22.4 × 8.9 *(44.4 × 6.9 × 2.8)*
Main machinery: 1 Volvo Penta TADM 122A; 381 hp(m) *(280 kW)*; 1 shaft
Speed, knots: 9.5
Complement: 2
Radars: Navigation: Furuno RHRS-2002R; I-band. **NEW ENTRY**

PATRIA *6/1998*, De Hoop /* 0081307

1 SUPPORT SHIP (AP)

Name	No	Builders	Commissioned
NIEUWEDIEP	Y 8005	Akerboom, Leiden	Feb 1972

Displacement, tons: 27 full load
Dimensions, feet (metres): 58.4 × 14.1 × 4.9 *(17.8 × 4.3 × 1.5)*
Main machinery: 2 Volvo Penta diesels; 600 hp(m) *(441 kW)*; 2 shafts
Speed, knots: 10
Complement: 4

Comment: Acquired by the Navy in February 1992 as a passenger craft. **UPDATED**

NIEUWEDIEP *7/1998, van Ginderen Collection /* 0052643

4 CERBERUS CLASS (DIVING TENDERS) (YDT)

Name	No	Builders	Commissioned
CERBERUS	A 851	Visser, Den Helder	28 Feb 1992
ARGUS	A 852	Visser, Den Helder	2 June 1992
NAUTILUS	A 853	Visser, Den Helder	18 Sep 1992
HYDRA	A 854	Visser, Den Helder	20 Nov 1992

Displacement, tons: 223 full load
Dimensions, feet (metres): 89.9 × 27.9 × 4.9 *(27.4 × 8.5 × 1.5)*
Main machinery: 2 Volvo Penta TAMD122A diesels; 760 hp(m) *(560 kW)*; 2 shafts
Speed, knots: 12. Range, miles: 750 at 12 kt
Complement: 8 (2 officers)
Radars: Navigation: Racal Decca; I-band.

Comment: Ordered 29 November 1990. Capable of maintaining 10 kt in Sea State 3. Can handle a 2 ton load at 4 m from the ship's side. *Hydra* lengthened by 10.5 m to provide more accommodation and recommissioned on 13 March 1998. **UPDATED**

HYDRA *4/1999*, van Ginderen Collection /* 0081308

TRAINING SHIPS

Note: Two 'Dokkum' class minesweepers are used by Sea Cadets.

Name	No	Builders	Commissioned
VAN KINSBERGEN	A 902	Damen Shipyards	2 Nov 1999

Displacement, tons: 630 full load
Dimensions, feet (metres): 136.2 × 30.2 × 10.8 *(41.5 × 9.2 × 3.3)*
Main machinery: 2 Caterpillar 3508 BI-TA; 1,572 hp(m) *(1.16 MW)* sustained; 2 shafts; bow thruster; 272 hp(m) *(200 kW)*
Speed, knots: 13
Complement: 5 plus 3 instructors and 16 students
Radars: Navigation: Consilium Selesmar; I-band.

Comment: Launched 30 August 1999. Has replaced *Zeefakkel* as the local training ship at Den Helder. Carries a 25 kt RIB. **NEW ENTRY**

VAN KINSBERGEN *11/1999*, Damen/Flying Focus /* 0081309

Name	No	Builders	Commissioned
URANIA (ex-*Tromp*)	Y 8050	Haarlem	23 Apr 1938

Displacement, tons: 76 full load
Dimensions, feet (metres): 78.4 × 17.4 × 10.5 *(23.9 × 5.3 × 3.2)*
Main machinery: 1 diesel; 65 hp(m) *(48 kW)*; 1 shaft
Speed, knots: 5 diesel; 10 sail
Complement: 17

Comment: Schooner used for training in seamanship.   **UPDATED**

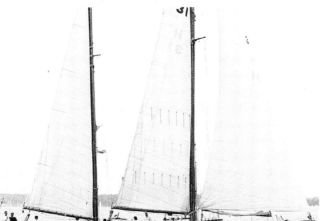

URANIA   *6/1996*, Michael Nitz /* 0081310

TUGS

5 COASTAL TUGS (YTB)

Name	No	Builders	Commissioned
LINGE	A 874	Delta SY, Sliedrecht	20 Feb 1987
REGGE	A 875	Delta SY, Sliedrecht	6 May 1987
HUNZE	A 876	Delta SY, Sliedrecht	20 Oct 1987
ROTTE	A 877	Delta SY, Sliedrecht	20 Oct 1987
GOUWE	A 878	Delta SY, Sliedrecht	21 Feb 1997

Displacement, tons: 380 full load
Dimensions, feet (metres): 90.2 × 27.2 × 8.9 *(27.5 × 8.3 × 2.7)*
Main machinery: 2 Stork-Werkspoor or 2 Caterpillar (A 878) diesels; 1,600 hp(m) *(1.18 MW)*; 2 Kort nozzle props
Speed, knots: 11
Complement: 7
Radars: Racal Decca; I-band.

Comment: Order for first four placed in 1986. Based at Den Helder. A fifth of class was ordered in June 1996 to replace *Westgat*.   **UPDATED**

REGGE   *7/1999*, van Ginderen Collection /* 0081311

7 HARBOUR TUGS (YTL)

BREEZAND Y 8018	SCHELDE Y 8055	ZUIDWAL Y 8058
BALGZAND Y 8019	WIERBALG Y 8056	WESTWAL Y 8059
MALZWIN Y 8057		

Comment: *Breezand* completed December 1989, *Balgzand* January 1990. The others are smaller pusher tugs and were completed December 1986 to February 1987. All built by Delta Shipyard.   **UPDATED**

BALGZAND   *7/1999*, van Ginderen Collection /* 0081312

ARMY

Note: In addition there are three patrol boats with a limited coastal capability, 15 vessels for inland waters and one tank landing craft.

1 DIVING VESSEL (YDT)

RV 50

Dimensions, feet (metres): 121.4 × 29.5 × 4.9 *(37 × 9 × 1.5)*
Main machinery: 2 diesels; 476 hp(m) *(350 kW)*; 2 shafts
Speed, knots: 9
Complement: 21
Radars: Navigation: AP Mk 4; I-band.

Comment: Built by Vervako as a diving training ship and commissioned 3 November 1989. There is a moonpool aft with a 50 m diving bell, and a decompression chamber.   **UPDATED**

RV 50   *5/1997*, van Ginderen Collection /* 0012817

COAST GUARD (KUSTWACHT)

Notes: (1) In 1987 many of the separate maritime services were merged to form a Coast Guard with its own distinctive colours. Included are police craft, customs vessels and assorted craft of the Ministry of Transport and Public Works. Also involved are the Ministries of Finance, Justice, and Agriculture, Nature Control and Fisheries. From 1 June 1995 operational control of the Coast Guard has been exercised by the Navy.
(2) The following lists the major ships and craft under their separate Ministries.
Transport and Public Works: *Waker, Frans Naerebout, Rotterdam, Terschelling, Schuitengat, Vliestroom, Waddenzee, Arca, Nieuwe Diep.*
Finance: *Cor Boersma, Zeevalk.*
Justice: *P 25, P 27, P 56, P 83, P 94, P 96.*

P 27 (Justice)   *4/1999*, van Ginderen Collection /* 0081313

WAKER (Works)   *2/1996*, van Ginderen Collection /* 0081314

ZEEVALK (finance)   *6/1997, RNLN /* 0012820

COAST GUARD (ANTILLES and ARUBA)

Notes: (1) Netherlands Antilles and Aruba Coast Guard (NAACG) formed 23 January 1996. Headquarters is co-located with the RNLN at Parera, Curaçao.
(2) Two Lockheed Orion P3s are available for maritime air patrols.

4 POLICE CRAFT

PB 1–PB 4

Displacement, tons: 35 full load
Dimensions, feet (metres): 57.4 × 15.7 × 5.6 (17.5 × 4.8 × 1.7)
Main machinery: 2 MTU 12V 183 TC91 diesels; 1,190 hp(m) (875 kW); 2 shafts
Speed, knots: 18
Complement: 6

Comment: Built by Schottel in the 1970s. In addition there are six 40 kt RIBs which entered Police service in November 1997.

UPDATED

PB 01 (NAACG)   1/1996*, van Ginderen Collection / 0081316

3 STAN PATROL 4100 CUTTERS

Name	No	Builders	Commissioned
JAGUAR	P 810	Damen Shipyards	2 Nov 1998
PANTER	P 811	Damen Shipyards	18 Jan 1999
POEMA	P 812	Damen Shipyards	19 Mar 1999

Displacement, tons: 205 full load
Dimensions, feet (metres): 140.4 × 22.3 × 8.2 (42.8 × 6.8 × 2.5)
Main machinery: 2 Caterpillar 3516B diesels; 5,685 hp(m) (4.18 MW); 2 shafts; acbLIPS cp props; bow thruster
Speed, knots: 26. **Range, miles:** 2,000 at 12 kt
Complement: 11 plus 6 police
Guns: 1—12.7 mm MG.
Radars: Surface search: Signaal Scout; I-band.
Navigation: Kelvin Hughes; I-band.

Comment: Ordered from Damen shipyards in March 1997 for delivery in late 1998. Equipped with surveillance passive sensors. The cutters have a gas citadel. A 30 kt RIB is launched through a transom door. Based at Willemstad, Curaçao.

UPDATED

POEMA   3/1999*, Damen/Flying Focus / 0081315

NEW ZEALAND

Headquarters Appointments

Chief of Naval Staff:
    Rear Admiral P M McHaffie, OBE
Deputy Chief of Naval Staff:
    Commodore D Ledson
Maritime Commander:
    Commodore M J Wardlaw

Diplomatic Representation

Naval Adviser, London:
    Commander W J Tucker
Naval Adviser, Canberra:
    Commodore A D Clayton-Greene
Naval Adviser, Washington:
    Commander P Sullivan

Personnel

2000: 2,100 regulars and 400 reserves

Bases

Naval Staff: HMNZS Wakefield (Wellington)
Fleet Support: HMNZS Philomel (Auckland)
Training: HMNZS Tamaki (Auckland)
Ship Repair: HMNZ Dockyard (Auckland)

RNZNVR Divisions

Auckland: HMNZS Ngapona
Wellington: HMNZS Olphert
Christchurch: HMNZS Pegasus
Dunedin: HMNZS Toroa

Prefix to Ships' Names

HMNZS

Mercantile Marine

Lloyd's Register of Shipping:
    164 vessels of 264,988 tons gross

DELETIONS

Frigates

1998   *Waikato*
1999   *Wellington* (shore training)

Research and Survey Ships

1997   *Tui*
1998   *Monowai*

Auxiliaries

1999   *Arataki, Tamaki* (civilian)

FRIGATES

TE KAHA   6/1999*, Sattler/Steele / 0081319

2 ANZAC (MEKO 200) CLASS (FF)

Name	No	Builders	Laid down	Launched	Commissioned
TE KAHA	F 77	Transfield Amecon, Williamstown	19 Sep 1994	22 July 1995	22 July 1997
TE MANA	F 111	Transfield Amecon, Williamstown	28 June 1996	10 May 1997	10 Dec 1999

Displacement, tons: 3,600 full load
Dimensions, feet (metres): 387.1 oa; 357.6 wl × 48.6 × 14.3 *(118; 109 × 14.8 × 4.4)*
Main machinery: CODOG; 1 GE LM 2500 gas turbine; 30,172 hp *(22.5 MW)* sustained; 2 MTU 12V 1163 TB83 diesels; 8,840 hp(m) *(6.5 MW)* sustained; 2 shafts; cp props
Speed, knots: 27. **Range, miles:** 6,000 at 18 kt
Complement: 163

Missiles: SAM: Raytheon Sea Sparrow RIM-7P; Lockheed Martin Marietta Mk 41 Mod 5 octuple cell vertical launcher ❶; semi-active radar homing to 14.6 km *(8 n miles)* at 2.5 Mach; warhead 39 kg. ESSM in due course.
Guns: 1 FMC 5 in *(127 mm)*/54 Mk 45 Mod 2 ❷; 20 rds/min to 23 km *(12.6 n miles)*; weight of shell 32 kg.
    1 GE/GD 20 mm Vulcan Phalanx 6 barrelled Mk 15 Mod 11 ❸; 3,000 rds/min combined to 1.5 km.
Torpedoes: 6—324 mm US Mk 32 Mod 5 (2 triple) tubes ❹; Mk 46 Mod 2; anti-submarine; active/passive homing to 11 km *(5.9 n miles)* at 40 kt; warhead 44 kg.
Countermeasures: Decoys: Sea Gnat/SRBOC Mk 36 Mod 1 chaff launcher ❺. Nulka offboard decoys. SLQ-25 torpedo decoy system.
    ESM: Telefunken Telegon 10; Racal Thorn Sceptre A; intercept.
Combat data systems: CelsiusTech 9LV 453 Mk 3. Link 11.
Weapons control: CelsiusTech 9LV 453 optronic director ❻. Raytheon CWI Mk 73 Mod 1 (for SAM).

TE KAHA

(Scale 1 : 1,200), Ian Sturton / 0081317

Radars: Air search: Raytheon SPS-49(V)8 ❼; C/D-band.
    Air/surface search: CelsiusTech 9LV 453 TIR (Ericsson Tx/Rx) ❽; G-band.
    Navigation: Atlas Elektronik 9600 ARPA; I-band.
    Fire control: CelsiusTech 9LV 453 ❾; G-band.
    IFF: Cossor Mk XII.
Sonars: Thomson Sintra Spherion B Mod 5; hull-mounted; active search and attack; medium frequency.
    Towed array; passive; very low frequency; to be fitted.

Helicopters: 1 SH-2G Seasprite ❿. SH-2F until 2000.

Programmes: Contract signed with Amecon consortium on 19 November 1989 to build eight Blohm + Voss designed MEKO 200 ANZ frigates for Australia and two for New Zealand. Options on a third of class were turned down in November 1998. Modules constructed at Newcastle, Australia and Whangarei, New Zealand, and shipped to Melbourne for final assembly. The two New Zealand ships are the second and fourth of the class. First steel cut on *Te Kaha* on 11 February 1993. *Te Kaha* means Prowess. *Te Mana* means Power.
Structure: The ships include space and weight provision for considerable enhancement including canister-launched SSM, an additional fire-control channel and ECM. Signature suppression features are incorporated in the design. All-steel construction. Fin stabilisers. McTaggert Scott Trigon 3 helicopter traversing system. Two RHIBs are carried.
UPDATED

TE KAHA

*8/1999 *, John Mortimer /* 0081318

1 LEANDER (BROAD-BEAMED) CLASS (FF)

Name	No	Builders	Laid down	Launched	Commissioned
CANTERBURY	F 421	Yarrow Ltd, Clyde	12 Apr 1969	6 May 1970	22 Oct 1971

Displacement, tons: 2,474 standard; 2,945 full load
Dimensions, feet (metres): 372 × 43 × 18 *(113.4 × 13.1 × 5.5)*
Main machinery: 2 Babcock & Wilcox boilers; 550 psi *(38.7 kg/cm²)*; 850°F *(454°C)*; 2 White-English Electric turbines; 30,000 hp *(22.4 MW)*; 2 shafts
Speed, knots: 28. **Range, miles:** 5,500 at 15 kt
Complement: 245 (15 officers)

Guns: 2 Vickers 4.5 in *(114 mm)*/45 Mk 6 (twin) ❶; 20 rds/min to 19 km *(10.3 n miles)* anti-surface; 6 km *(3.2 n miles)* anti-aircraft; weight of shell 25 kg.
    1 GE/GD 20 mm Vulcan Phalanx 6-barrelled Mk 15 Mod 11 ❷; 3,000 rds/min combined to 1.5 km.
    4 or 6—12.7 mm MGs.
Torpedoes: 6—324 mm US Mk 32 Mod 5 (2 triple) tubes ❸. Honeywell/Marconi Mk 46 Mod 5; anti-submarine; active/passive homing to 11 km *(5.9 n miles)* at 40 kt; warhead 44 kg.
Countermeasures: Decoys: 2 Loral Hycor SRBOC Mk 36 6-barrelled trainable launchers. Graseby Type 182; towed torpedo decoy.
    ESM/ECM: Argo Phoenix; intercept and jammer. Telegon PST 1288 HVU.
Combat data systems: Plessey/Marconi Nautis F; Link 11.
Weapons control: RCA R-76C5 GFCS.
Radars: Air search: Signaal LW08 ❹; D-band; range 265 km *(145 n miles)* for 2 m² target.
    Air/surface search: Plessey Type 993 ❺; E/F-band.
    Navigation: Kelvin Hughes Type 1006; I-band.
    Fire control: RCA TR 76 ❻; I-band.
    IFF: Cossor Mk XII.
Sonars: Graseby Type 750; hull-mounted; active search and attack; medium frequency.
    Kelvin Hughes Type 162M; hull-mounted; bottom classification; 50 kHz.

Helicopters: 1 SH-2G Seasprite ❼.

Programmes: Ordered in August 1968, arrived in New Zealand in August 1972.
Modernisation: Since 1984 new equipment includes LW08 radar, Telegon HF-DF, Phoenix ESM, a modern gunnery fire-control system, G750 hull-mounted sonar, Mk 32 torpedo

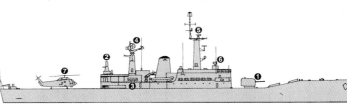

CANTERBURY

(Scale 1 : 1,200), Ian Sturton / 0012826

tubes, Nautis-F system, computer-aided message handling, Mk 36 chaff launchers and replacement ships' boats. Upgrades started in November 1993 include a Whittaker Track Management system, IFF Mk 12, Link 11 and replacement of the HF communications system. Seacat removed in 1993-94; replaced by Phalanx in 1995-96. Hangar enlarged for Seasprite in 1998.

CANTERBURY

*8/1997 *, John Mortimer /* 0012828

Structure: Referred to as a 'broad-beamed' Leander.
Operational: *Canterbury* is scheduled to remain operational and compatible with the Anzacs until 2005. Second of class used for alongside training.
UPDATED

SHIPBORNE AIRCRAFT

Numbers/Type: 4/5 Kaman SH-2F/2G Seasprite.
Operational speed: 130 kt *(241 km/h).*
Service ceiling: 22,500 ft *(6,860 m).*
Range: 367 n miles *(679 km).*
Role/Weapon systems: Four ex-USN SH-2F acquired in 1997/98 pending delivery of new SH-2Gs from mid-2000. Sensors: (SH-2F) Litton LN66 radar; ALR-66 ESM; (SH-2G) Telephonics APS-143 PC radar; AAQ-32 Safire; Litton LR-100 ESM; ALE-47 ECM. Weapons: ASW; 2 Mk 46 torpedoes or Mk 11 depth bomb. ASV; 2 Hughes Maverick AGM-65B; 7.62 mm MG.

UPDATED

SEASPRITE *6/1998, RNZN* / 0052653

LAND-BASED MARITIME AIRCRAFT

Numbers/Type: 6 Lockheed P-3K Orion.
Operational speed: 410 kt *(760 km/h).*
Service ceiling: 28,300 ft *(8,625 m).*
Range: 4,000 n miles *(7,410 km).*
Role/Weapon systems: Purchased in 1966. Long-range surveillance and ASW patrol; update 1981-84 and to Phase II standard 1988-92. Modernisation of airframes done 1995-99 for 20 year extension. If funds are available upgraded ESM, acoustic processors, MAD and Link 11 may be included in due course. Operated by RNZAF. Sensors: APS-134 radar, ASQ-10 MAD, AQH5/AQA1 processor, 3 AYK 14 computers, IFF, ESM, SQ 41/47/SSQ 46 sonobuoys. Weapons: ASW; eight Mk 46 torpedoes, Mk 11 depth bombs or mines, 10 underwing stations for weapons.

UPDATED

PATROL FORCES

4 MOA CLASS (INSHORE PATROL CRAFT) (PC)

Name	No	Builders	Commissioned
MOA	P 3553	Whangarei Engineering and Construction Co Ltd	28 Nov 1983
KIWI	P 3554	Whangarei Engineering and Construction Co Ltd	2 Sep 1984
WAKAKURA	P 3555	Whangarei Engineering and Construction Co Ltd	26 Mar 1985
HINAU	P 3556	Whangarei Engineering and Construction Co Ltd	4 Oct 1985

Displacement, tons: 91.5 standard; 105 full load
Dimensions, feet (metres): 88 × 20 × 7.2 *(26.8 × 6.1 × 2.2)*
Main machinery: 2 Cummins KT-1105M diesels; 710 hp *(530 kW)*; 2 shafts
Speed, knots: 12. **Range, miles:** 1,000 at 11 kt
Complement: 18 (5 officers (4 training))
Guns: 1 Browning 12.7 mm MG.
Radars: Surface search: Racal Decca 916; I-band.
Sonars: Klein 595 Tracpoint; side scan; active high frequency.

Comment: On 11 February 1982 the New Zealand Cabinet approved the construction of four inshore patrol craft. The four IPC are operated by the Reserve Divisions, *Moa* with *Toroa* (Dunedin), *Kiwi* with *Pegasus* (Lyttelton), *Wakakura* with *Olphert* (Wellington), *Hinau* with *Ngapona* (Auckland). Same design as Inshore Survey and Training craft *Kahu* but with a modified internal layout. MCM system fitted in 1993-94. Side scan sonar and MCAIS data system fitted to *Hinau* in 1993; the remainder in 1996.

UPDATED

KIWI *3/1998*, *RNZN* / 0081320

AUXILIARIES

Note: In addition to vessels listed below there are three 12 m sail training craft used for seamanship training: *Paea II, Mako II, Manga II* (sail nos 6911-6913).

1 REPLENISHMENT TANKER (AOR)

Name	No	Builders	Launched	Commissioned
ENDEAVOUR	A 11	Hyundai, South Korea	14 Aug 1998	6 Apr 1988

Displacement, tons: 12,390 full load
Dimensions, feet (metres): 453.1 × 60 × 23 *(138.1 × 18.4 × 7.3)*
Main machinery: 1 MAN-Burmeister & Wain 12V32/36 diesel; 5,780 hp(m) *(4.25 MW)* sustained; 1 shaft; acbLIPS cp prop
Speed, knots: 13.5. **Range, miles:** 8,000 at 13.5 kt
Complement: 49 (10 officers)
Cargo capacity: 7,500 tons dieso; 100 tons Avcat; 20 containers
Radars: Navigation: Racal Decca 1290A/9; ARPA 1690S; I-band.
Helicopters: 1 Kaman Seasprite (not always embarked).

Comment: Ordered July 1986. Laid down 10 April 1987. Completion delayed by engine problems but arrived in New Zealand in May 1988. Two abeam RAS rigs (one QRC, one Probe) and one astern refuelling rig. Fitted with Inmarsat. Standard merchant design modified on building to provide a relatively inexpensive replenishment tanker.

UPDATED

ENDEAVOUR *8/1999*, *John Mortimer* / 0081322

1 MILITARY SEALIFT SHIP (AK/AP/AX)

Name	No	Builders	Recommissioned
CHARLES UPHAM (ex-*Mercandian Queen II*, ex-*Continental Queen*)	A 02	Frederikshavn	18 Oct 1995

Displacement, tons: 7,955 light; 10,500 full load
Dimensions, feet (metres): 432.1 × 69.2 × 20.3 *(131.7 × 21.1 × 6.2)*
Main machinery: 1 MaK M 453AK diesel; 4,890 hp(m) *(3.59 MW)*; 1 shaft; cp prop; bow thruster
Speed, knots: 14. **Range, miles:** 7,000 at 15 kt
Complement: 32 (8 officers)
Military lift: 100 troops; APCs; trucks; 105 mm guns (after 1998)
Guns: 4—12.7 mm MGs.
Countermeasures: Decoys: 2 SRBOC Mk 36 chaff and IR launchers (to be fitted).
Radars: Navigation: 2 sets; I-band.
Helicopters: Platform for 2 medium after full conversion.

Comment: Project Definition Study completed in Autumn 1989 for a logistic support ship to carry equipment and stores for the Army's Ready Reaction Force. Additional roles include disaster relief in the SW Pacific and civil defence in New Zealand. The ship was originally launched in 1984. Purchased in late 1994 and modernised with naval communications. Further modifications including ballast tank refurbishment and installation of an STP occurred prior to the ship being put to charter early in 1998 for two years. Full conversion includes a helicopter platform, accommodation for 65 and facilities for up to 150 troops, and improved sea-keeping qualities. After some doubt, this programme is to go ahead in late 2000 and complete in 2002. The stern ramp is 15.5 × 8.2 m and there is a side entrance (13 × 4.5 m) on the starboard side aft.

UPDATED

CHARLES UPHAM *12/1995*, *RNZN* / 0081324

1 MOA CLASS (TRAINING SHIP) (AXL)

Name	No	Builders	Commissioned
KAHU (ex-*Manawanui*)	A 04 (ex-A 09)	Whangarei Engineering and Construction Co Ltd	28 May 1979

Displacement, tons: 91.5 standard; 105 full load
Dimensions, feet (metres): 88 × 20 × 7.2 *(26.8 × 6.1 × 2.2)*
Main machinery: 2 Cummins KT-1150M diesels; 710 hp *(530 kW)*; 2 shafts
Speed, knots: 12. **Range, miles:** 1,000 at 11 kt
Complement: 16
Radars: Navigation: Racal Decca 916; I-band.

Comment: Same hull design as Inshore Survey Craft and Patrol Craft. Now used for navigation and seamanship training and as a standby diving tender.

UPDATED

KAHU   *6/1999*, RNZN /* 0081325

1 DIVING TENDER (YDT)

Name	No	Builders	Commissioned
MANAWANUI (ex-*Star Perseus*)	A 09	Cochrane, Selby	May 1979

Displacement, tons: 911 full load
Dimensions, feet (metres): 143 × 31.2 × 10.5 *(43.6 × 9.5 × 3.2)*
Main machinery: 2 Caterpillar D 379TA diesels; 1,130 hp *(843 kW)*; 2 shafts; cp props; bow thruster
Speed, knots: 10.7. **Range, miles:** 5,000 at 10 kt
Complement: 24 (2 officers)
Sonars: Klein 595 Tracpoint; side scan; active high frequency.

Comment: North Sea Oil Rig Diving support vessel commissioned into the RNZN on 5 April 1988. Completed conversion in December 1988 and has replaced the previous ship of the same name which proved to be too small for the role. Equipment includes two Phantom HDX remote-controlled submersibles, a decompression chamber (to 250 ft), wet diving bell and 13 ton crane. Fitted with Inmarsat. MCAIS data system, side scan sonar and GPS fitted in 1995. More modifications are planned to enable the ship to do some of the work previously undertaken by *Tui*. This includes a stern gantry and general purpose winches for research including MCM. Used to support RAN submarine trials in 1996/97.

UPDATED

MANAWANUI   *10/1996*, S Farrow, RAN /* 0081323

SURVEY AND RESEARCH SHIPS

1 STALWART CLASS (AGS)

Name	No	Builders	Commissioned
RESOLUTION (ex-*Tenacious*)	A 14 (ex-TAGOS 17)	Halter Marine, Moss Point	29 Sep 1989

Displacement, tons: 2,262 full load
Dimensions, feet (metres): 224 × 43 × 18.7 *(68.3 × 13.1 × 5.7)*
Main machinery: Diesel-electric; 4 Caterpillar D 398B diesel generators; 3,200 hp *(2.39 MW)*; 2 motors; 1,600 hp *(1.2 MW)*; 2 shafts; bow thruster; 550 hp *(410 kW)*
Speed, knots: 11. **Range, miles:** 1,500 at 11 kt
Complement: 26 or 45 (when surveying)
Radars: Navigation: 2 Raytheon; I-band.

Comment: Laid up by USN in 1995 and acquired in September 1996. Reactivated in October 1996 and commissioned into RNZN 13 February 1997 for passage to New Zealand. Conversion commenced mid-1997 to suit the ship for hydrography with secondary role of acoustic research for about three months per year, replacing both *Tui* and *Monowai*. Second stage of conversion to fit Atlas Elektronik MD 2/30 multibeam echo-sounder, completed in January 1999. A fixed dome increased the ship's draught. A DGPS and a towed array fitted for acoustic research. A new survey boat with multibeam echo sounder is to be embarked in 2001. The ship has been repainted in the standard white/buff configuration for survey ships.

UPDATED

RESOLUTION   *4/1998, RNZN /* 0038011

2 INSHORE SURVEY CRAFT (AGSC)

Name	No	Builders	Commissioned
TAKAPU	A 07	Whangarei Engineering and Construction Co Ltd	8 July 1980
TARAPUNGA	A 08	Whangarei Engineering and Construction Co Ltd	9 Apr 1980

Displacement, tons: 112 full load
Dimensions, feet (metres): 88 × 20 × 7.7 *(26.8 × 6.1 × 2.4)*
Main machinery: 2 Cummins KT-1150M diesels; 710 hp *(530 kW)*; 2 shafts
Speed, knots: 12. **Range, miles:** 1,000 at 12 kt
Complement: 11 (2 officers)
Radars: Navigation: Racal Decca 916; I-band.

Comment: Same hull design as Inshore Patrol and Training craft *Kahu* with modified internal layout. Survey equipment: Atlas Deso 20 echo-sounders; Klein 531T *(Takapu)* side scan sonar. Trimble SE 4000 DGPS fitted in 1995. Two Omega power control gearboxes for slow speed running. Survey duties completed in June 1999 and since then the ships have been used for training. Probably to pay off in 2000.

UPDATED

TARAPUNGA   *2/1999*, RNZN /* 0081321

NICARAGUA
FUERZA NAVAL-EJERCITO DE NICARAGUA

Headquarters Appointments

Head of Navy:
Rear Admiral Halleslevens Acevedo

Personnel

2000: 750 officers and men

Bases

Pacific: Corito (HQ), San Juan del Sur, Puerto Sandino, Potosi
Atlantic: Bluefields (HQ), El Bluff, Puerto Cabezas, Corn Islands, San Juan del Norte

Mercantile Marine

Lloyd's Register of Shipping:
28 vessels of 4,293 tons gross

DELETIONS

Patrol Forces

1997-98   4 Sin Hung, 2 Vedette, 1 Yevgenya

PATROL FORCES

2 YEVGENYA CLASS (MINEHUNTERS—INSHORE) (MHI/PC)

501   510

Displacement, tons: 77 standard; 90 full load
Dimensions, feet (metres): 80.7 × 18 × 4.9 *(24.6 × 5.5 × 1.5)*
Main machinery: 2 Type 3-D-12 diesels; 600 hp(m) *(440 kW)* sustained; 2 shafts
Speed, knots: 11. **Range, miles:** 300 at 10 kt
Complement: 10
Guns: 2 USSR 25 mm/80 (twin).
Radars: Surface search/navigation: Don 2; I-band.
Sonars: A small sonar is lifted over stern on crane.

Comment: Transferred from USSR in 1984 and 1986 via Algeria and Cuba. All four refitted in Cuba in 1987-88 but one then sank in the hurricane of 1989 and was subsequently scrapped. Have GRP hulls. Tripod mast. Used as patrol craft. 501 at San Juan, 510 at Corinto. One other is derelict.   *UPDATED*

YEVGENYA 510   *2/1996*, Julio Montes /* 0081326

2 ZHUK (GRIF) (TYPE 1400) CLASS (PC)

315   317

Displacement, tons: 39 full load
Dimensions, feet (metres): 78.7 × 16.4 × 3.9 *(24 × 5 × 1.2)*
Main machinery: 2 Type M 401B diesels; 2,200 hp(m) *(1.6 MW)* sustained; 2 shafts
Speed, knots: 30. **Range, miles:** 1,100 at 15 kt
Complement: 12
Guns: 4 USSR 14.5 mm (2 twin) MGs.
Radars: Surface search: Spin Trough; I-band.

Comment: First transferred April 1982, having previously been sent to Algeria in May 1981. Second transferred 24 July 1983, third in 1984, two more early 1986 and three in late 1986/early 1987 via Cuba. Two more of this class were transferred via Cuba in December 1989 to replace two sunk in the hurricane of October 1989. Both at El Bluff. Operational status doubtful.   *UPDATED*

ZHUK (old number)   *1988* /* 0081327

3 DABUR CLASS (PC)

205   + 2

Displacement, tons: 39 full load
Dimensions, feet (metres): 64.9 × 18 × 5.8 *(19.8 × 5.5 × 1.8)*
Main machinery: 2 GM 12V-71TA; 840 hp *(626 kW)* sustained; 2 shafts
Speed, knots: 19. **Range, miles:** 450 at 13 kt
Complement: 8
Guns: 2—25 mm/80 (twin). 1 Oerlikon 20 mm. 2—12.7 mm MGs.
Radars: Surface search: Decca; I-band.

Comment: Delivered by Israel April 1978 (first pair), May 1978 (second pair) and May 1996 (three). One lost by gunfire in 1985; a second was severely damaged in 1987 and has been deleted and two more paid off in 1996 as soon as the last three were delivered. All are operational on the Atlantic Coast.   *UPDATED*

DABUR 205   *6/1999*, Nicaraguan Navy /* 0081328

40 ASSAULT and RIVER CRAFT (PBF)

Comment: There are at least 24 assault craft of various types mostly built in Nicaragua. Probably belong to the Army. In addition there are about 16 fast motor boats for use on rivers and estuaries.   *UPDATED*

ASSAULT CRAFT   *6/1999*, Nicaraguan Navy /* 0081329

PBF   *6/1999*, Nicaraguan Navy /* 0081330

NIGERIA

Headquarters Appointments

Chief of the Naval Staff:
  Rear Admiral Victor Ombu
Flag Officer Western Command:
  Rear Admiral S O Afolayan
Flag Officer Eastern Command:
  Commodore F C Agbiti

General

In October 1995 the Chief of Naval Staff reported that the Navy was on the verge of collapse due to lack of funds. There were some signs of life in 1996 and two ships judged to be 'beyond economical repair' were restored to the order of battle in 1997.

Personnel

(a) 2000: 5,600 (650 officers) including Coast Guard
(b) Voluntary service

Bases

Apapa—Lagos: Western Naval Command; Dockyard (Wilmot Point, Victoria Island, Lagos)
Calabar: Eastern Naval Command (Naval schools at Lagos, Port Harcourt, Apapa (NNS *Quorra*) and Calabar)
Okemimi, Port Harcourt

Prefix to Ships' Names

NNS

Naval Aviation

The official list includes two Lynx Mk 89, 12 MBB BO 105C, three Fokker F27 and 14 Dornier Do 128-6MPA. It is doubtful if more than a few of these are operational.

Port Security Police

A separate force of 1,600 officers and men in Lagos.

Mercantile Marine

Lloyd's Register of Shipping:
  287 vessels of 432,436 tons gross

FRIGATES

1 MEKO TYPE 360 (FFG)

Name	No	Builders	Laid down	Launched	Commissioned
ARADU (ex-Republic)	F 89	Blohm & Voss, Hamburg	1 Dec 1978	25 Jan 1980	20 Feb 1982

Displacement, tons: 3,360 full load
Dimensions, feet (metres): 412 × 49.2 × 19 (screws)
(125.6 × 15 × 5.8)
Main machinery: CODOG; 2 RR Olympus TM3B gas turbines;
50,880 hp (37.9 MW) sustained; 2 MTU 20V 956 TB92
diesels; 10,420 hp(m) (7.71 MW) sustained; 2 shafts; 2
Kamewa cp props
Speed, knots: 30.5. **Range, miles:** 6,500 at 15 kt
Complement: 195 (26 officers)

Missiles: SSM: 8 OTO Melara/Matra Otomat Mk 1 **①**; active
radar homing to 80 km (43.2 n miles) at 0.9 Mach; warhead
210 kg.
SAM: Selenia Elsag Albatros octuple launcher **②**; 24 Aspide;
semi-active radar homing to 13 km (7 n miles) at 2.5 Mach;
warhead 30 kg.
Guns: 1 OTO Melara 5 in (127 mm)/54 **③**; 45 rds/min to 16 km
(8.7 n miles); weight of shell 32 kg.
8 Breda Bofors 40 mm/70 (4 twin) **④**; 300 rds/min to 12.5 km
(6.8 n miles) anti-surface; weight of shell 0.96 kg.
Torpedoes: 6—324 mm Plessey STWS-1B (2 triple) tubes **⑤**. 18
Whitehead A244S; anti-submarine; active/passive homing to
7 km (3.8 n miles) at 33 kt; warhead 34 kg (shaped charge).
Depth charges: 1 rack.

ARADU

(Scale 1 : 1,200), Ian Sturton / 0081331

Countermeasures: Decoys: 2 Breda 105 mm SCLAR 20-tubed
trainable; chaff to 5 km (2.7 n miles); illuminants to 12 km
(6.6 n miles).
ESM: Decca RDL-2; intercept.
ECM: RCM-2; jammer.
Combat data systems: Sewaco-BV action data automation.
Weapons control: M20 series GFCS. Signaal Vesta ASW.
Radars: Air/surface search: Plessey AWS 5 **⑥**; E/F-band.
Navigation: Racal Decca 1226; I-band.
Fire control: Signaal STIR **⑦**; I/J/K-band. Signaal WM 25 **⑧**; I/J-
band.
Sonars: Atlas Elektronik EA80; hull-mounted; active search and
attack; medium frequency.

Helicopters: 1 Lynx Mk 89 **⑨**.

Modernisation: Refit started at Wilmot Point, Lagos with Blohm
& Voss assistance in 1991 and completed in February 1994.
Operational: Had two groundings and a major collision in 1987
and ran aground again during post refit trials in early 1994.
Assessed as beyond economical repair in 1995 but managed
to go to sea in early 1996, and again in 1997 when she broke
down for several months in Monrovia. Back in Lagos on one
engine in 1998, and it is reported that the builders are assisting
in further repairs. Unlikely that most weapon systems are
operational, although the SSM system was being refurbished
in 1999. ***UPDATED***

ARADU

5/1999* / 0081332

CORVETTES

2 Mk 9 VOSPER THORNYCROFT TYPE (FS)

Name	No	Builders	Commissioned
ERINOMI	F 83	Vosper Thornycroft	29 Jan 1980
ENYMIRI	F 84	Vosper Thornycroft	2 May 1980

Displacement, tons: 680 standard; 780 full load
Dimensions, feet (metres): 226 × 31.5 × 9.8 (69 × 9.6 × 3)
Main machinery: 4 MTU 20V 956 TB92 diesels; 22,140 hp(m) (16.27 MW) sustained; 2 shafts;
2 Kamewa cp props
Speed, knots: 27. **Range, miles:** 2,200 at 14 kt
Complement: 90 (including Flag Officer)

Missiles: SAM: Short Brothers Seacat triple launcher.
Guns: 1 OTO Melara 3 in (76 mm)/62 Mod 6 compact; 85 rds/min to 16 km (8.7 n miles); weight
of shell 6 kg.
1 Breda Bofors 40 mm/70 Type 350; 300 rds/min to 12.5 km (6.8 n miles); weight of shell
0.96 kg.
2 Oerlikon 20 mm.
A/S mortars: 1 Bofors 375 mm twin launcher; range 1,600 or 3,600 m.
Countermeasures: ESM: Decca Cutlass; radar warning.
Weapons control: Signaal WM20 series.
Radars: Air/surface search: Plessey AWS 2; E/F-band.
Navigation: Racal Decca TM 1226; I-band.
Fire control: Signaal WM24; I/J-band; range 46 km (25 n miles).
Sonars: Plessey PMS 26; lightweight; hull-mounted; active search and attack; 10 kHz.

Programmes: Ordered from Vosper Thornycroft 22 April 1975.
Operational: *Erinomi* reported at sea for a short time in 1996, and again in 1998. *Enymiri* assessed
as beyond economical repair in 1996 but is being refurbished in 2000. Seacat system is non-
operational.
UPDATED

ENYMIRI

5/1999* / 0081333

PATROL FORCES

Note: All the Coastal Patrol Craft belong to the Coast Guard. Some 38 craft were acquired in the
mid-1980s from various shipbuilders including Simmoneau, Damen, Swiftships, Intermarine,
Watercraft, Van Mill and Rotork. None of these vessels has been reported at sea in recent years
although some are visible, laid up ashore, and may still be serviceable.

3 EKPE (LÜRSSEN 57) CLASS (LARGE PATROL CRAFT) (PCF)

Name	No	Builders	Commissioned
EKPE	P 178	Lürssen, Vegesack	Aug 1980
DAMISA	P 179	Lürssen, Vegesack	Apr 1981
AGU	P 180	Lürssen, Vegesack	Apr 1981

Displacement, tons: 444 full load
Dimensions, feet (metres): 190.6 × 24.9 × 10.2 (58.1 × 7.6 × 3.1)
Main machinery: 4 MTU 16V 956 TB92 diesels; 17,700 hp(m) (13 MW) sustained; 2 shafts
Speed, knots: 42. **Range, miles:** 2,000 at 10 kt
Complement: 40

Guns: 1 OTO Melara 3 in (76 mm)/62; 60 rds/min to 16 km (8.7 n miles); weight of shell 6 kg.
2 Breda 40 mm/70 (twin); 4 Emerson Electric 30 mm (2 twin).
Radars: Surface search: Racal Decca TM 1226; I-band.
Fire control: Signaal WM28; I/J-band.

Programmes: Ordered in 1977. Major refit in 1984 at Vegesack.
Operational: Not seen at sea for three years from 1994 but *Ekpe* sailed for Sierra Leone in
mid-1997 although she broke down en route. The other pair were reported in 1999 as still being
seaworthy. Otomat SSMs no longer carried.
UPDATED

EKPE

3/1998 / 0052656

3 COMBATTANTE IIIB CLASS
(FAST ATTACK CRAFT—MISSILE) (PCFG)

Name	No	Builders	Commissioned
SIRI	P 181	CMN, Cherbourg	19 Feb 1981
AYAM	P 182	CMN, Cherbourg	11 June 1981
EKUN	P 183	CMN, Cherbourg	18 Sep 1981

Displacement, tons: 385 standard; 430 full load
Dimensions, feet (metres): 184 × 24.9 × 7 *(56.2 × 7.6 × 2.1)*
Main machinery: 4 MTU 16V 956 TB92 diesels; 17,700 hp(m) *(13 MW)* sustained; 2 shafts
Speed, knots: 38. **Range, miles:** 2,000 at 15 kt
Complement: 42

Missiles: SSM: 4 Aerospatiale MM 38 Exocet; inertial cruise; active radar homing to 42 km *(23 n miles)* at 0.9 Mach; warhead 165 kg; sea-skimmer.
Guns: 1 OTO Melara 3 in *(76 mm)*/62; 60 rds/min to 16 km *(8.7 n miles)*; weight of shell 6 kg.
2 Breda 40 mm/70 (twin); 300 rds/min to 12.5 km *(6.8 n miles)*; weight of shell 0.96 kg.
4 Emerson Electric 30 mm (2 twin); 1,200 rds/min combined to 6 km *(3.3 n miles)*; weight of shell 0.35 kg.
Countermeasures: ESM: Decca RDL; radar intercept.
Weapons control: Thomson-CSF Vega system. 2 CSEE Panda optical directors.
Radars: Air/surface search: Thomson-CSF Triton (TRS 3033); G-band.
Navigation: Racal Decca TM 1226; I-band.
Fire control: Thomson-CSF Castor II (TRS 3203); I/J-band.

Programmes: Ordered in late 1977. Finally handed over in February 1982 after delays caused by financial problems.
Modernisation: Major refit and repairs carried out at Cherbourg from March to December 1991 but the ships were delayed by financial problems. Further refits planned.
Operational: *Ekun* sailed with *Aradu* in mid-1997 for Sierra Leone. *Siri* which was reported as beyond economical repair in 1995 was back in service in 1998.
UPDATED

SIRI   *7/1998* / 0052657

MINE WARFARE FORCES

2 LERICI CLASS (MINEHUNTERS/SWEEPERS) (MSC/MHC)

Name	No	Builders	Commissioned
OHUE	M 371	Intermarine SY, Italy	28 May 1987
MARABAI	M 372	Intermarine SY, Italy	25 Feb 1988

Displacement, tons: 540 full load
Dimensions, feet (metres): 167.3 × 32.5 × 9.2 *(51 × 9.9 × 2.8)*
Main machinery: 2 MTU 12V 396 TB83 diesels; 3,120 hp(m) *(2.3 MW)* sustained; 2 water-jets
Speed, knots: 15.5. **Range, miles:** 2,500 at 12 kt
Complement: 50 (5 officers)
Guns: 2 Emerson Electric 30 mm (twin); 1,200 rds/min combined to 6 km *(3.3 n miles)*; weight of shell 0.35 kg.
2 Oerlikon 20 mm GAM-BO1.
Countermeasures: MCM: Fitted with 2 Pluto remote-controlled submersibles, Oropesa 'O' Mis 4 and Ibis V control system.
Radars: Navigation: Racal Decca 1226; I-band.
Sonars: Thomson Sintra TSM 2022; hull-mounted; mine detection; high frequency.

Comment: *Ohue* ordered in April 1983 and *Marabai* in January 1986. *Ohue* laid down 23 July 1984 and launched 22 November 1985, *Marabai* laid down 11 March 1985, launched 6 June 1986. GRP hulls but, unlike Italian and Malaysian versions they do not have separate hydraulic minehunting propulsion. Carry Galeazzi two-man decompression chambers. Both were docked in 1999, after operations off Liberia.
UPDATED

OHUE   *7/1987, Marina Fraccaroli*

AMPHIBIOUS FORCES

2 FDR TYPE RO-RO 1300 (LST)

Name	No	Builders	Commissioned
AMBE	LST 1312	Howaldtswerke, Hamburg	11 May 1979
OFIOM	LST 1313	Howaldtswerke, Hamburg	7 July 1979

Displacement, tons: 1,470 standard; 1,860 full load
Dimensions, feet (metres): 285.4 × 45.9 × 7.5 *(87 × 14 × 2.3)*
Main machinery: 2 MTU 16V 956 TB92 diesels; 8,850 hp(m) *(6.5 MW)* sustained; 2 shafts
Speed, knots: 17. **Range, miles:** 5,000 at 10 kt
Complement: 56 (6 officers)
Military lift: 460 tons and 220 troops long haul; 540 troops or 1,000 troops seated short haul; can carry 5—40 ton tanks
Guns: 1 Breda 40 mm/70. 2 Oerlikon 20 mm.
Radars: Navigation: Racal Decca 1226; I-band.

Comment: Ordered September 1976. Built to a design prepared for the FGN. Have 19 m bow ramps and a 4 m stern ramp. Reported that bow ramps are welded shut. Second of class reported earlier as beyond repair, but both were refitted in 1999.
UPDATED

AMBE   *7/1997** / 0012836

SURVEY SHIPS

Name	No	Builders	Launched	Commissioned
LANA	A 498	Brooke Marine, Lowestoft	4 Mar 1976	18 July 1976

Displacement, tons: 1,088 full load
Dimensions, feet (metres): 189 × 37.5 × 12 *(57.8 × 11.4 × 3.7)*
Main machinery: 2 Lister Blackstone diesels; 2,640 hp *(1.97 MW)*; 2 shafts
Speed, knots: 16. **Range, miles:** 4,500 at 12 kt
Complement: 52 (12 officers)
Radars: Navigation: Decca; I-band.

Comment: Similar to UK 'Bulldog' class. Ordered in 1973. Not reported active since 1997, but back in reasonable condition in 1999.
UPDATED

LANA   *5/1999** / 0081334

TUGS

3 COASTAL TUGS (YTB/YTL)

COMMANDER APAYI JOE A 499   **DOLPHIN MIRA**   **DOLPHIN RIMA**

Comment: A 499 is of 310 tons and was built in 1983. The two Dolphin tugs are under repair.
UPDATED

COMMANDER APAYI JOE   *11/1983, Hartmut Ehlers*

NORWAY

Headquarters Appointments

Chief of Naval Staff:
  Rear Admiral H K Svensholt
Commander Naval Material Command:
  Rear Admiral J G Jaeger
Deputy Chief of Naval Staff:
  Commodore J Børresen
Inspector Coast Artillery:
  Commodore T Eriksen
Inspector Coast Guard:
  Commodore A Klepsvik
Commander Coast Fleet and Commodore Sea Training:
  Commodore A Sandbekk

Diplomatic Representation

Defence Attaché in Helsinki:
  Captain J Søland
Defence Attaché in London:
  Colonel P Baerøy
Defence Attaché in Moscow:
  Colonel R Bratland
Defence Attaché in Paris:
  Captain Gunnar Mjell
Defence Attaché in Stockholm:
  Captain Arne Langeland
Defence Attaché in Washington:
  Major General O Bjerke
Defence Attaché in Warsaw:
  Colonel H Brenna

Personnel

(a) 2000: 5,800 officers and ratings
(b) 9 to 12 months' national service (up to 40 per cent of ships complement)

Naval Home Guard

The Naval Home Guard numbers some 8,000 men and women on mobilisation, assigned to seven naval districts and manning 200 craft.

Coast Defence

Nine coastal forts, all with co-ordinated radar stations and guns (75 mm and 120 mm), and six torpedo batteries, and/or controlled minefields. All are equipped with RB 70 SAM missiles. Nine RBS 17 Hellfire Shore Defence Systems being delivered from 1997.

Coast Guard

Founded April 1977 with operational command held by Norwegian Defence Command. Main bases at Sortland (North) and Haakonsvern (South).

Bases

Karl Johansvern (Horten)—HQ Østlandet District
Haakonsvern (Bergen)—HQ Vestlandet District
Laksevag (Bergen)—Submarine Repair and Maintenance
Ramsund—Supply/Repair/Maintenance
Olavsvern (Tromsø)—HQ Tromsø District

Air Force Squadrons (see *Shipborne* and *Land-based Aircraft*)

Aircraft (Squadron)	Location	Duties
Sea King Mk 43 (330)	Bodø, Banak, Sola, Ørland	SAR
Orion P-3N/C (333)	Andøya	LRMP
Lynx (337)	Coast Guard vessels/Bardufoss	MP
Bell 412 (719, 339 & 720)	Bodø, Rygge, Bardufoss	Army Transport

Prefix to Ships' Names

KNM (Naval)
K/V (Coast Guard)

Strength of the Fleet

Type	Active	Building (Projected)
Submarines—Coastal	12	(4)
Frigates	3	(5)
Fast Attack Craft—Missile	15	(6)
Minelayers	3	—
Minesweepers/Hunters	9	—
LCTs	5	—
Depot Ship	1	—
Auxiliaries	3	—
Naval District Auxiliaries	21	—
Coast Guard Vessels	10	1
Survey Vessels	7	—

Mercantile Marine

Lloyd's Register of Shipping:
  2,350 vessels of 23,446,259 tons gross

DELETIONS

Frigates

1999 *Stavanger* (reserve)

Patrol Forces

2000 *Blink, Kjekk, Djerv, Skudd, Steil, Hvass, Brask, Gnist*

Auxiliaries

1999 *Sarpen, Draug*

Coast Guard

1997 *Volstadjr, Grimsholm*
1999 *Nysleppen*

PENNANT LIST

Note: Naval District Auxiliaries are listed on page 488.

Submarines

S 300	Ula
S 301	Utsira
S 302	Utstein
S 303	Utvaer
S 304	Uthaug
S 305	Uredd
S 306	Skolpen
S 308	Stord
S 309	Svenner
S 314	Sklinna
S 318	Kobben
S 319	Kunna

Frigates

F 301	Bergen
F 302	Trondheim
F 304	Narvik

Minesweepers/Hunters

M 340	Oksøy
M 341	Karmøy
M 342	Måløy
M 343	Hinnøy
M 350	Alta
M 351	Otra
M 352	Rauma
M 353	Orkla
M 354	Glomma

Minelayers

N 50	Tyr
N 52	Vidar
N 53	Vale

Patrol Forces

P 358	Hessa
P 359	Vigra

P 960	Skjold
P 986	Hauk
P 987	Ørn
P 988	Terne
P 989	Tjeld
P 990	Skarv
P 991	Teist
P 992	Jo
P 993	Lom
P 994	Stegg
P 995	Falk
P 996	Ravn
P 997	Gribb
P 998	Geir
P 999	Erle

Amphibious Forces

L 4502	Reinøysund
L 4503	Sørøysund
L 4504	Maursund
L 4505	Rotsund
L 4506	Tjeldsund

Auxiliaries

A 530	Horten
A 533	Norge
A 535	Valkyrien

Coast Guard

W 300	Nornen
W 303	Svalbard (bldg)
W 311	Lance
W 312	Ålesund
W 313	Tromsö
W 314	Stålbas
W 315	Nordsjøbas
W 317	Lafjord
W 319	Thorsteinson
W 320	Nordkapp
W 321	Senja
W 322	Andenes

SUBMARINES

Note: A new generation submarine is required. A Viking project in collaboration with Sweden and Denmark is at the design stage.
Four 50 m submarines are projected with a first in-service date of 2007. The Norwegian hulls are likely to be 5 m longer than those required for Sweden and Denmark.

UTSTEIN

10/1998*, E & M Laursen / 0052658

6 ULA CLASS (SSK)

Name	No
ULA	S 300
UREDD	S 305
UTVAER	S 303
UTHAUG	S 304
UTSTEIN	S 302
UTSIRA	S 301

Builders	Laid down		Launched		Commissioned	
Thyssen Nordseewerke, Emden	29 Jan	1987	28 July	1988	27 Apr	1989
Thyssen Nordseewerke, Emden	23 June	1988	22 Sep	1989	3 May	1990
Thyssen Nordseewerke, Emden	8 Dec	1988	19 Apr	1990	8 Nov	1990
Thyssen Nordseewerke, Emden	15 June	1989	18 Oct	1990	7 May	1991
Thyssen Nordseewerke, Emden	6 Dec	1989	25 Apr	1991	14 Nov	1991
Thyssen Nordseewerke, Emden	15 June	1990	21 Nov	1991	30 Apr	1992

Displacement, tons: 1,040 surfaced; 1,150 dived
Dimensions, feet (metres): 193.6 × 17.7 × 15.1
(59 × 5.4 × 4.6)
Main machinery: Diesel-electric; 2 MTU 16V 396 SB83 diesels;
2,700 hp(m) *(1.98 MW)* sustained; 1 Siemens motor;
6,000 hp(m) *(4.41 MW)*; 1 shaft
Speed, knots: 11 surfaced; 23 dived
Range, miles: 5,000 at 8 kt
Complement: 21 (5 officers)

Torpedoes: 8—21 in *(533 mm)* bow tubes. 14 AEG DM 2A3
Sehecht; dual purpose; wire-guided; active/passive homing to
28 km *(15 n miles)* at 23 kt; 13 km *(7 n miles)* at 35 kt;
warhead 260 kg; depth to 460 m.
Countermeasures: ESM: Racal Sealion; radar warning.
Weapons control: Kongsberg MSI-90(U) TFCS.
Radars: Surface search: Kelvin Hughes 1007; I-band.

Sonars: Atlas Elektronik CSU 83; active/passive intercept search
and attack; medium frequency.
Thomson Sintra; flank array; passive; low frequency.

Programmes: Contract signed on 30 September 1982. This was
a joint West German/Norwegian effort known as Project 210
in Germany. Although final assembly was at Thyssen a number
of pressure hull sections were provided by Norway.
Structure: Diving depth, 250 m *(820 ft)*. The basic command
and weapon control systems are Norwegian, the attack sonar
is German but the flank array, based on piezoelectric polymer
antenna technology, was developed in France and
substantially reduces flow noise. Calzoni Trident modular
system of non-penetrating masts has been installed. Zeiss
periscopes.

UPDATED

UREDD   6/1998, A Sharma / 0050722

ULA   9/1999*, Michael Nitz / 0081335

6 MODERNISED KOBBEN CLASS (TYPE 207) (SSK)

Name	No
SKLINNA	S 314 (ex-S 305)
SKOLPEN	S 306
STORD	S 308
SVENNER	S 309
KOBBEN	S 318
KUNNA	S 319

Builders	Laid down		Launched		Commissioned	
Rheinstahl-Nordseewerke, Emden	17 Aug	1965	21 Jan	1966	27 May	1966
Rheinstahl-Nordseewerke, Emden	1 Nov	1965	24 Mar	1966	17 Aug	1966
Rheinstahl-Nordseewerke, Emden	1 Apr	1966	2 Sep	1966	14 Feb	1967
Rheinstahl-Nordseewerke, Emden	8 Sep	1966	27 Jan	1967	12 June	1967
Rheinstahl-Nordseewerke, Emden	9 Dec	1963	25 Apr	1964	17 Aug	1964
Rheinstahl-Nordseewerke, Emden	3 Mar	1964	16 July	1964	29 Oct	1964

Displacement, tons: 459 standard; 524 dived
Dimensions, feet (metres): 155.5 × 15 × 14
(47.4 × 4.6 × 4.3)
Main machinery: Diesel-electric; 2 MTU 12V 493 AZ80 GA31L
diesels; 1,200 hp(m) *(880 kW)* sustained; 1 motor; 1,800 hp
(m) *(1.32 MW)* sustained; 1 shaft
Speed, knots: 12 surfaced; 18 dived
Range, miles: 5,000 at 8 kt (snorting)
Complement: 21 (5 officers)

Torpedoes: 8—21 in *(533 mm)* bow tubes. 8 mix of (a) FFV Type
61; anti-surface; wire-guided; passive homing to 25 km *(13.7 n
miles)* at 45 kt; warhead 240 kg and (b) Honeywell NT37C;
dual purpose; wire-guided; active/passive homing to 20 km
(10.8 n miles) at 35 kt; warhead 150 kg.
Countermeasures: ESM: Argo radar warning.
Weapons control: Kongsberg MSI-90(U) TFCS.
Radars: Surface search: Kelvin Hughes 1007; I-band.
Sonars: Atlas Elektronik CSU 83; passive search and attack;
medium/high frequency.

Programmes: It was announced in July 1959 that the USA and
Norway would equally share the cost of these submarines.
They are a development of IKL Type 205 (West German U4-
U8) with increased diving depth. *Kobben* was the name of the
first submarine in the Royal Norwegian Navy. Commissioned
on 28 November 1909.
Modernisation: All modernised at Urivale Shipyard, Bergen, to a
similar standard to the three sold to Denmark including
lengthening and new communications, navigation and fire-
control equipment. Modernisation completion programme

KOBBEN   5/1997, Per Kornefeldt / 0012837

was S 314 January 1989, S 306 October 1989, S 308 August
1990, S 318 May 1991, S 319 December 1991, S 309 April
1992.
Structure: Diving depth, 200 m *(650 ft)*. *Svenner's* second
periscope for COs training operations is 1 m longer. Pilkington
Optronics CK 30 search periscope.

Operational: Two are planned to pay off in 2000.
Sales: *Utvaer, Uthaug* and *Kya* sold to Denmark and modernised
to the same standard as the Norwegian programme. *Kaura*
also sold to Denmark to be cannibalised to repair *Saelen*, which
was flooded after conversion.

UPDATED

FRIGATES

3 OSLO CLASS (FFG)

Name	No	Builders	Laid down	Launched		Commissioned	
BERGEN	F 301	Marinens Hovedverft, Horten	1964	23 Aug	1965	15 June	1967
TRONDHEIM	F 302	Marinens Hovedverft, Horten	1963	4 Sep	1964	2 June	1966
NARVIK	F 304	Marinens Hovedverft, Horten	1964	8 Jan	1965	30 Nov	1966

Displacement, tons: 1,650 standard; 1,950 full load
Dimensions, feet (metres): 317 × 36.8 × 18 (screws)
(96.6 × 11.2 × 5.5)
Main machinery: 2 Babcock & Wilcox boilers; 600 psi
(42.18 kg/cm²); 850°F *(454°C)*; 1 set De Laval Ljungstrom
PN20 geared turbines; 20,000 hp(m) *(14.7 MW)*; 1 shaft
Speed, knots: 25+. **Range, miles:** 4,500 at 15 kt
Complement: 125 (11 officers)

Missiles: SSM: 4 Kongsberg Penguin Mk 1 ❶; IR homing to
20 km *(10.8 n miles)* at 0.7 Mach; warhead 120 kg.
SAM: Raytheon NATO RIM-7M Sea Sparrow Mk 29 octuple
launcher ❷; semi-active radar homing to 14.6 km *(8 n miles)* at
2.5 Mach; warhead 39 kg; 24 cell magazine.
Guns: 2 US 3 in *(76 mm)*/50 Mk 33 (twin) ❸; 50 rds/min to
12.8 km *(7 n miles)*; weight of shell 6 kg.
1 Bofors 40 mm/70 ❹; 300 rds/min to 12 km *(6.6 n miles)*;
weight of shell 0.96 kg
2 Rheinmetall 20 mm/20 (not in all); 1,000 rds/min to 2 km.
Torpedoes: 6—324 mm US Mk 32 (2 triple) tubes ❺. Marconi
Stingray; anti-submarine; active/passive homing to 11 km
(5.9 n miles) at 45 kt; warhead 32 kg (shaped charge); depth to
750 m *(2,460 ft)*.
A/S mortars: Kongsberg Terne III 6-tubed trainable ❻; range
pattern from 400-5,000 m; warhead 70 kg. Automatic
reloading in 40 seconds.
Mines: Laying capability.
Countermeasures: Decoys: 2 chaff launchers.
ESM: Argo AR 700; intercept.
Combat data systems: NFT MSI-3100 (supplemented by
Siemens ODIN) action data automation; Link 11 and 14.
SATCOM ❼.

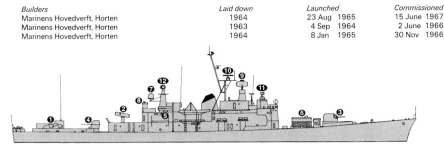

TRONDHEIM
(Scale 1 : 900), Ian Sturton / 0012838

Weapons control: Mk 91 MFCS. TVT 300 tracker ❾.
Radars: Air search: Siemens/Plessey AWS-9 ❾; 2D; E/F-band.
Surface search: Racal Decca TM 1226 ❿; I-band.
Fire control: NobelTech 9LV 218 Mk 2 ⓫; I-band (includes
search).
Raytheon Mk 95 ⓬, I/J-band (for Sea Sparrow).
Navigation: Decca; I-band.
Sonars: Thomson Sintra/Simrad TSM 2633; combined hull and
VDS; active search and attack; medium frequency.
Simrad Terne III; active attack; high frequency.

Programmes: Built under the five year naval construction
programme approved by the Norwegian Storting (Parliament)
late in 1960. Although all the ships of this class were
constructed in the Norwegian Naval Dockyard, half the cost
was borne by Norway and the other half by the USA.
Modernisation: All ships modernised with improvements in
weapons control and habitability; new countermeasures
equipment includes two chaff launchers; Spherion TSM-2633

sonar (with VDS) (a joint Thomson Sintra/Simrad-Subsea
(Norway) project); the after 76 mm mounting replaced by a
Bofors 40 mm/70; and MSI 3100 action data automation.
Modernisation completion programme: F 302 30 November
1987, F 304 21 October 1988, F 301 4 April 1990. Plessey
AWS-9 radar fitted in 1996-98 together with Link 11 and GPS.
Structure: The hull and propulsion design of these ships is based
on that of the 'Dealey' class destroyer escorts (now deleted) of
the US Navy, but considerably modified to suit Norwegian
requirements. The hulls became stressed by towing VDS in
heavy seas and were strengthened in 1995-96 increasing
displacement by over 200 tons.
Operational: The fifth of class *Oslo* sank under tow south of
Bergen in January 1994, after an engine failure had caused her
to run aground in heavy weather. *Stavanger* laid up in 1999
and unlikely to go to sea again. Complements have been
reduced.

UPDATED

NARVIK
11/1999*, Michael Nitz / 0081336

TRONDHEIM
6/1999*, H M Steele / 0081337

0 + (5) NEW ESCORT VESSELS (FFG)

Displacement, tons: 3,700 full load
Dimensions, feet (metres): 419.9 × 55.8 × 19.7
(128 × 17 × 6)
Speed, knots: 27
Complement: 120 plus 25 spare

Missiles: SSM: Kongsberg NSM.
SAM: Evolved Sea Sparrow (ESSM).
Guns: 2—3 in *(76 mm)*/50 (twin). 2 Rheinmetall 20 mm.
Torpedoes: 6—324 mm (2 triple) tubes.
Combat data systems: MSI-2005F; Link 11/22.
Radars: Air search: Lockheed Martin SPY-1F.
Sonars: Thomson Marconi Spherion MRS 2000 and Captas
Mk 2 VDS; combined hull mounted and VDS.

Helicopters: 1 Lynx or similar.

Programmes: Project SMP 6088 for a class of new escort
vessels. Design definition started in March 1997. Bazán with
Lockheed Martin selected in March 2000. First contract
expected in mid-2000 with an in-service date of 2005.
Structure: Some details are speculative but the plan is to transfer
some of the armament from the 'Oslo' class.   **UPDATED**

NEW ESCORT VESSEL (computer graphic)

1999*, Bazán / 0048442

SHIPBORNE AIRCRAFT

Numbers/Type: 6 Westland Lynx Mk 86.
Operational speed: 125 kt *(232 km/h).*
Service ceiling: 12,500 ft *(3,810 m).*
Range: 320 n miles *(590 km).*
Role/Weapon systems: Operated by Air Force on behalf of the Coast Guard for fishery protection,
offshore oil protection and SAR; embarked in CG vessels and shore-based. Sensors: Search radar,
FLIR may be fitted, ESM. Weapons: Generally unarmed.   **UPDATED**

LYNX

6/1996*, H M Steele / 0081338

LAND-BASED MARITIME AIRCRAFT

Note: The Air Force has F-16 Falcons armed with Penguin 3 ASMs.

Numbers/Type: 4 Lockheed P-3C Orion.
Operational speed: 410 kt *(760 km/h).*
Service ceiling: 28,300 ft *(8,625 m).*
Range: 4,000 n miles *(7,410 km).*
Role/Weapon systems: Long-range MR and oceanic surveillance duties in peacetime, with ASW
added as a war role. Updated in 1998-99 with new radars and new tactical computers. P-3Ns
used by Coast Guard paid off in 1999. Sensors: APS-137(V)5 radar, ASQ-81 MAD, AQS-212
processor and computer, IFF, AAR-36 IR detection; AAR-47 ESM; ALE 47 countermeasures;
sonobuoys. Weapons: ASW; 8 MUSL Stingray torpedoes, depth bombs or mines. ASV; Penguin
NFT Mk 3 ASM.   **VERIFIED**

Numbers/Type: 12 Westland Sea King Mk 43B.
Operational speed: 125 kt *(232 km/h).*
Service ceiling: 10,500 ft *(3,200 m).*
Range: 630 n miles *(1,165 km).*
Role/Weapon systems: SAR, surface search and surveillance helicopter; supplemented by civil
helicopters in wartime. Two 43B delivered in May 1996; remainder updated to 43B standard.
Sensors: FLIR 2000 and dual Bendix radars RDR 1500 and RDR 1300. Weapons: Generally
unarmed.   **VERIFIED**

PATROL FORCES

Note: The patrol craft *Hitra* is a sea-going museum ship used in the summer for training cruises.

HITRA

8/1996*, Erik Laursen / 0081339

14 HAUK CLASS (FAST ATTACK CRAFT—MISSILE) (PCFG)

Name	No	Builders (see *Programmes*)	Commissioned
HAUK	P 986	Bergens Mek Verksteder	17 Aug 1977
ØRN	P 987	Bergens Mek Verksteder	19 Jan 1979
TERNE	P 988	Bergens Mek Verksteder	13 Mar 1979
TJELD	P 989	Bergens Mek Verksteder	25 May 1979
SKARV	P 990	Bergens Mek Verksteder	17 July 1979
TEIST	P 991	Bergens Mek Verksteder	11 Sep 1979
JO	P 992	Bergens Mek Verksteder	1 Nov 1979
LOM	P 993	Bergens Mek Verksteder	15 Jan 1980
STEGG	P 994	Bergens Mek Verksteder	18 Mar 1980
FALK	P 995	Bergens Mek Verksteder	30 Apr 1980
RAVN	P 996	Westamarin A/S, Alta	20 May 1980
GRIBB	P 997	Westamarin A/S, Alta	10 July 1980
GEIR	P 998	Westamarin A/S, Alta	16 Sep 1980
ERLE	P 999	Westamarin A/S, Alta	10 Dec 1980

Displacement, tons: 120 standard; 160 full load
Dimensions, feet (metres): 120 × 20.3 × 5.9 *(36.5 × 6.2 × 1.8)*
Main machinery: 2 MTU 16V 538 TB92 diesels; 6,820 hp(m) *(5 MW)* sustained; 2 shafts
Speed, knots: 32. **Range, miles:** 440 at 30 kt
Complement: 24 (6 officers)

Missiles: SSM: Up to 6 Kongsberg Penguin Mk 2 Mod 5; IR homing to 27 km *(14.6 n miles)* at
0.8 Mach; warhead 120 kg.
SAM: Twin Simbad launcher for Matra Sadral; IR homing to 4 km *(2.2 n miles)*; warhead 3 kg.
Guns: 1 Bofors 40 mm/70; 300 rds/min to 12 km *(6.6 n miles)*; weight of shell 0.96 kg.
Torpedoes: 2—21 in *(533 mm)* tubes. FFV Type 613; passive homing to 27 km *(14.5 n miles)* at
45 kt; warhead 240 kg.
Countermeasures: Decoys: Chaff launcher.
ESM: Argo intercept.
Combat data systems: DCN SENIT 2000 (from late 2000).
Weapons control: Kongsberg MSI-80S or Sagem VIGY-20 optronic director.
Radars: Surface search/navigation: 2 Racal Decca TM 1226; I-band.

Programmes: Ordered 12 June 1975.
Modernisation: Simbad twin launchers for SAM fitted from 1994 to replace 20 mm gun. Being
upgraded further with SENIT 2000 combat data system with a first in-service date of late 2000.
Operational: Penguin missiles are sometimes not embarked.   **UPDATED**

GEIR

5/1999*, Findler & Winter / 0081341

TJELD

5/1999*, L-G Nilsson / 0081342

1 + (6) SKJOLD CLASS (PCFG)

Name	No	Builders	Launched	Commissioned
SKJOLD	P 960	Kvaerner Mandal	22 Sep 1998	17 Apr 1999

Displacement, tons: 260 full load
Dimensions, feet (metres): 153.5 × 44.3 × 7.5; 2.6 on cushion *(46.8 × 13.5 × 2.3; 0.8)*
Main machinery: 2 Allison 571-K gas turbines; 16,320 hp(m) *(12 MW)*; 2 MTU 183 cruise diesels; 1,632 hp(m) *(1.2 MW)*; 2 Kamewa water-jets
2 MTU 12V 183 TE92 diesels (lift); 2,000 hp(m) *(1.47 MW)*
Speed, knots: 57; 44 in Sea State 3. **Range, miles:** 800 at 40 kt
Complement: 15

Missiles: 8 SSM; 8 Kongsberg NSM (from 2004).
SAM: Manpad; IR homing to 6 km *(3.3 n miles)* at 2.5 Mach; warhead 3 kg.
Guns: 1 Otobreda 76 mm/62. Super Rapid; 120 rds/min to 16 km *(8.7 n miles)*; weight of shell 6 kg.
Countermeasures: Decoys: Chaff and IR flare launcher.
ESM: Intercept.
Combat data systems: DCN Senit 2000; Link 11/14.
Weapons control: Sagem VIGX-20 optronic director.
Radars: Air/surface search: Ericsson Sea Giraffe; E/F-band.
Navigation: I-band.
Fire control: CelsiusTech Ceros 2000; I/J-band.

Programmes: Project SMP 6081. A preproduction version ordered 30 August 1996. A decision on whether to order more of the class is expected in 2000. It is vulnerable to the priority being given to the new frigates.
Structure: SES hull with advanced stealth technology including anechoic coatings. SSMs embarked in two twin launchers in the bow and four in the stern. The diesel propulsion is to be used for loiter speeds. Six consoles for weapon systems control. Heavyweight torpedoes may also be included.

UPDATED

SKJOLD   *9/1999*, H M Steele /* 0081340

MINE WARFARE FORCES

2 VIDAR CLASS (COASTAL MINELAYERS) (ML)

Name	No	Builders	Launched	Commissioned
VIDAR	N 52	Mjellem and Karlsen, Bergen	18 Mar 1977	21 Oct 1977
VALE	N 53	Mjellem and Karlsen, Bergen	5 Aug 1977	10 Feb 1978

Displacement, tons: 1,500 standard; 1,673 full load
Dimensions, feet (metres): 212.6 × 39.4 × 13.1 *(64.8 × 12 × 4)*
Main machinery: 2 Wichmann 7AX diesels; 4,200 hp(m) *(3.1 MW)*; 2 shafts; auxiliary motor; 425 hp(m) *(312 kW)*; bow thruster
Speed, knots: 15
Complement: 50

Guns: 2 Bofors 40 mm/70; 300 rds/min to 12 km *(6.6 n miles)*; weight of shell 0.96 kg.
Torpedoes: 6—324 mm US Mk 32 (2 triple) tubes. Honeywell Mk 46; anti-submarine; active/passive homing to 11 km *(5.9 n miles)* at 40 kt; warhead 44 kg.
Mines: 300-400 (dependent on type) on 3 decks with an automatic lift between. Loaded through hatches forward and aft, each served by 2 cranes.
Weapons control: TVT optronic director.
Radars: Surface search: 2 Racal Decca TM 1226; I-band.
Sonars: Simrad; hull-mounted; search and attack; medium/high frequency.

Programmes: Ordered 11 June 1975.
Operational: Versatile ships that can perform a number of roles in addition to minelaying. *Vidar* modified for a command and control role to become a Flagship in May 1998.

UPDATED

VIDAR   *5/1999*, E & M Laursen /* 0081343

---

9 OKSØY/ALTA CLASS
(MINEHUNTERS/SWEEPERS) (MHC/MSC)

Name	No	Builders	Commissioned
Hunters			
OKSØY	M 340	Kvaerner Mandal	24 Mar 1994
KARMØY	M 341	Kvaerner Mandal	24 Oct 1994
MÅLØY	M 342	Kvaerner Mandal	24 Mar 1995
HINNØY	M 343	Kvaerner Mandal	8 Sep 1995
Sweepers			
ALTA	M 350	Kvaerner Mandal	12 Jan 1996
OTRA	M 351	Kvaerner Mandal	8 Nov 1996
RAUMA	M 352	Kvaerner Mandal	2 Dec 1996
ORKLA	M 353	Kvaerner Mandal	4 Apr 1997
GLOMMA	M 354	Kvaerner Mandal	1 July 1997

Displacement, tons: 375 full load
Dimensions, feet (metres): 181.1 × 44.6 × 8.2 (2.76 cushion) *(55.2 × 13.6 × 2.5 (0.84))*
Main machinery: 2 MTU 12V 396 TE84 diesels; 3,700 hp(m) *(2.72 MW)* sustained; 2 Kvaerner Eureka water-jets; 2 MTU 8V 396 TE54 diesels; 1,740 hp(m) *(1.28 MW/60 Hz)* sustained; lift engines
Speed, knots: 20.5. **Range, miles:** 1,500 at 20 kt
Complement: 38 (12 officers) (minehunters); 32 (10 officers) (minesweepers)

Missiles: SAM: Matra Sadral twin launcher; Mistral; IR homing to 4 km *(2.2 n miles)*; warhead 3 kg.
Guns: 1 or 2 Rheinmetall 20 mm. 2—12.7 mm MGs.
Countermeasures: MCMV: 2 Pluto submersibles (minehunter) (see *Modernisation*); mechanical, Agate (air gun and transducer equipment) acoustic and Elma magnetic sweep (minesweepers). Minesweeper mini torpedoes can be carried.
Radars: Navigation: 2 Racal Decca; I-band.
Sonars: Thomson Sintra/Simrad TSM 2023N; hull-mounted (minehunters); high frequency. Simrad Subsea SA 950; hull-mounted (minesweepers); high frequency.

Programmes: Order placed with Kvaerner on 9 November 1989. Four are minehunters, the remainder minesweepers.
Modernisation: Kongsberg Minesniper Mk 2 being evaluated. The ROV has a range of 6 km at 6 kt and can deliver a shaped charge.
Structure: Design developed by the Navy in Bergen with the Defence Research Institute and Norsk Veritas and uses an air cushion created by the surface effect between two hulls. The hull is built of Fibre Reinforced Plastics (FRP) in sandwich configuration. The ROVs are carried in a large hangar and are launched by two hydraulic cranes. The minesweeper has an A frame aft for the sweep gear. SAM launcher mounted forward of the bridge.
Operational: Simrad Albatross tactical system including mapping; Cast/Del Norte mobile positioning system with GPS. The catamaran design is claimed to give higher transit speeds with lesser installed power than a traditional hull design. Other advantages are lower magnetic and acoustic signatures, clearer water for sonar operations and less susceptibility to shock.

UPDATED

HINNØY   *5/1999*, Per Kornefeldt /* 0081344

ALTA   *5/1999*, L-G Nilsson /* 0081345

KARMØY   *11/1999*, Michael Nitz /* 0081346

1 MINELAYER (ML)

Name	No	Builders	Commissioned
TYR (ex-Standby Master)	N 50	Alesund Mekaniske Verksted	1981

Displacement, tons: 495 full load
Dimensions, feet (metres): 138.8 × 33.1 × 11.5 *(42.3 × 10.1 × 3.5)*
Main machinery: 2 Deutz SBA12M816 diesels; 1,300 hp(m) *(956 kW)*; 1 shaft; cp prop; 1 MWM diesel; 150 hp(m) *(110 kW)*; bow and stern thrusters
Speed, knots: 12
Complement: 22 (7 officers)
Mines: 2 rails.
Radars: Navigation: Furuno 711 and Furuno 1011; I-band.

Comment: Former oil rig pollution control ship. Acquired in December 1993 and converted by Mjellum & Karlsen, Bergen. Recommissioned 7 March 1995 as a minelayer, and for the maintenance of controlled minefields. Carries a ROV.   **UPDATED**

TYR   *6/1995*, Royal Norwegian Navy /* 0081347

AMPHIBIOUS FORCES

5 REINØYSUND/TJELDSUND CLASS (LCT)

Name	No	Builders	Commissioned
REINØYSUND	L 4502	Mjellem & Karlsen, Bergen	Jan 1972
SØRØYSUND	L 4503	Mjellem & Karlsen, Bergen	May 1972
MAURSUND	L 4504	Mjellem & Karlsen, Bergen	Sep 1972
ROTSUND	L 4505	Mjellem & Karlsen, Bergen	Nov 1972
TJELDSUND (ex-Borgsund)	L 4506	Mjellem & Karlsen, Bergen	Feb 1973

Displacement, tons: 595 (4502 and 4505); 850 (remainder) full load
Dimensions, feet (metres): 171 (4502 and 4505); 198.5 (remainder) × 33.8 × 5.9 *(52.1; 60.5 × 10.3 × 1.8)*
Main machinery: 2 MTU MD (4502 and 4505) or 2 Deutz MWM TBD 234 V12 (remainder) diesels; 1,350 hp(m) *(992 kW)*; 2 shafts
Speed, knots: 11.5
Complement: 10 (2 officers)
Military lift: 7 tanks; 200 troops
Guns: 3 Rheinmetall 20 mm/20.

Comment: Same design as deleted 'Kvalsund' class. L 4503, 4504 and 4506 modernised and lengthened in 1995-96 and are now known as the 'Tjeldsund' class. The other pair were given a technical update in 1996-97. Two of the class are being used as diving tenders.   **UPDATED**

MAURSUND   *5/1999*, E & M Laursen /* 0081348

22 + (16) COMBATBOAT 90N (LCA)

TRONDENES KA 1	KJØKØY KA 14	BRETTINGEN KA 21
HYSNES KA 2	MORVIKA KA 15	LØKHAUG KA 22
HELLEN KA 3	KOPAS KA 16	SØRVIKNES KA 23
TORAS KA 4	TANGEN KA 17	BJØRGVIN KA 30
MØVIK KA 5	ODDANC KA 18	OSTERNES KA 31
SKROLSVIK KA 11	MALMØYA KA 19	FJELL KA 32
KRÅKENES KA 12	NIDAROS KA 20	LERØY KA 33
STANGNES KA 13		

Displacement, tons: 19 full load
Dimensions, feet (metres): 52.2 × 12.5 × 2.6 *(15.9 × 3.8 × 0.8)*
Main machinery: 2 SAAB Scania DSI 14 diesels; 1,104 hp(m) *(812 kW)* or 1,251 hp(m) *(920 kW)* (KA 21-43) sustained; 2 FF 450 water-jets or 2 Kamewa FF 410 (KA 21-43)
Speed, knots: 35 or 40; 20 in Sea State 3. **Range, miles:** 240 at 20 kt
Complement: 3
Military lift: 2.8 tons or 20 troops
Guns: 3—12.7 mm MGs.
Weapons control: Optronic director.
Radars: Navigation: I-band.

Comment: Ordered from Dockstavarvet, Sweden. Four Batch 1 units delivered for trials in July and October 1996. Three more of the class delivered in 1997, 13 in 1998 and two more in early 1999. A further 16 are planned when funds are available. Batch 2 have an uprated propulsion system. Used to carry mobile light missile units. Similar in most details to the Swedish Coastal Artillery craft. Names are mostly taken from Coastal Fortresses.   **UPDATED**

BRETTINGEN   *9/1997*, Dockstavarvet /* 0012942

SURVEY AND RESEARCH SHIPS

1 RESEARCH SHIP (AGI)

Name	Builders	Launched	Commissioned
MARJATA	Tangern Verft A/S	18 Dec 1992	July 1994

Displacement, tons: 7,560 full load
Dimensions, feet (metres): 267.4 × 130.9 × 19.7 *(81.5 × 39.9 × 6)*
Main machinery: Diesel-electric; 2 MTU Siemens 16V 396 TE diesels; 7,072 hp(m) *(5.2 MW)*; 2 Dresser Rand/Siemens gas-turbine generators; 9,792 hp(m) *(7.2 MW)*; 2 Siemens motors; 8,160 hp(m) *(6 MW)*; 2 Schottel 3030 thrusters. 1 Siemens motor; 2,720 hp(m); *(2 MW)*; 1 Schottel thruster (forward)
Speed, knots: 15
Complement: 14 plus 31 scientists

Comment: Ordered in February 1992 from Langsten Slip og Batbyggeri to replace the old ship of the same name. Called Project Minerva. Design developed by Ariel A/S, Horten. The three main superstructure-mounted cupolas contain ELINT and SIGINT equipment. Hull-reinforced to allow operations in fringe ice. Equipment includes Sperry radars, Elac sonars, Siemens TV surveillance, and a fully equipped helicopter flight deck. The unconventional hull which gives the ship an extraordinary length to beam ratio of 2:1 is said to give great stability and dynamic qualities. White hull and superstructure.   **VERIFIED**

MARJATA   *1994, Royal Norwegian Navy*

6 SURVEY SHIPS (AGS)

Name	Displacement tons	Launched	Officers	Crew
LANCE W 311	960	1978	7	8
OLJEVERN 01-04	200	1978	2	6
GEOFJORD	364	1958	2	6

Comment: Under control of Ministry of Environment based at Stavanger. *Oljevern 01* and *03* have red hulls and work for the Pollution Control Authority. *Lance* is owned by the Polar Institute and chartered by the Coast Guard for eight months a year.   **UPDATED**

OLJEVERN 01   *7/1995*, Harald Carstens /* 0081349

TRAINING SHIPS

2 TRAINING SHIPS (AXL)

Name	No	Builders	Commissioned
HESSA (ex-*Hitra*, ex-*Marsteinen*)	P 358	Fjellstrand, Omastrand	Jan 1978
VIGRA (ex-*Kvarven*)	P 359	Fjellstrand, Omastrand	July 1978

Displacement, tons: 39 full load
Dimensions, feet (metres): 77 × 16.4 × 3.5 *(23.5 × 5 × 1.1)*
Main machinery: 2 GM 12V-71 diesels; 1,800 hp *(1.34 MW)*; 2 shafts
Speed, knots: 20
Complement: 5 plus 13 trainees
Guns: 1—12.7 mm Browning MG.
Radars: Navigation: Racal Decca; I-band.

Comment: The vessels are designed for training students at the Royal Norwegian Naval Academy in navigation, manoeuvring and seamanship. All-welded aluminium hulls. Also equipped with an open bridge and a blind pilotage position below deck. 18 berths.

VERIFIED

HESSA   *8/1998, van Ginderen Collection /* 0052670

AUXILIARIES

1 DEPOT SHIP (ASL)

Name	No	Builders	Commissioned
HORTEN	A 530	A/S Horten Verft	Apr 1978

Displacement, tons: 2,530 full load
Dimensions, feet (metres): 287 × 42.6 × 16.4 *(87.5 × 13 × 5)*
Main machinery: 2 Wichmann 7AX diesels; 4,200 hp(m) *(3.1 MW)*; 2 shafts; bow thruster
Speed, knots: 16.5
Complement: 86
Guns: 2 Bofors 40 mm/70.
Radars: Navigation: 2 Decca; I-band.
Helicopters: Platform only.

Comment: Contract signed 30 March 1976. Laid down 28 January 1977; launched 12 August 1977. Serves both submarines and fast attack craft. Quarters for 45 extra and can cater for 190 extra.

UPDATED

HORTEN   *6/1999*, Flottenkommando /* 0081350

1 SUPPLY AND RESCUE VESSEL (AKS/ATS)

Name	No	Builders	Commissioned
VALKYRIEN	A 535	Ulstein Hatlo	1981

Displacement, tons: 3,000 full load
Dimensions, feet (metres): 223.1 × 47.6 × 16.4 *(68 × 14.5 × 5)*
Main machinery: Diesel-electric; 4 diesels; 10,560 hp(m) *(7.76 MW)* sustained; 2 motors; 3.14 MW; 2 shafts; 2 bow thrusters; 1,600 hp(m) *(1.18 MW)*; 1 stern thruster; 800 hp(m) *(588 kW)*
Speed, knots: 16
Complement: 13
Radars: Navigation: 2 Furuno; H/I-band.

Comment: Tug/supply ship acquired in 1994 for supply and SAR duties. Bollard pull 128 tons. Can carry a 700 ton deck load. Oil recovery equipment is also carried.

UPDATED

VALKYRIEN   *5/1999*, Findler & Winter /* 0081351

29 NAVAL DISTRICT COASTAL VESSELS

Note: A number of coastal vessels are attached to the naval districts. They can have bow numbers prefaced by two letters: HT (torpedo recovery), HM (multirole), HS (tenders), HD (diving), HP (personnel), HR (reserve). All are less than 300 tons displacement. Names on 1 January 2000:

Name	No	Speed, knots	Commissioned	Role
TRSD	HD 1	10	1977	Diving vessel
VIKEN	HD 2	12	1984	Cargo (4 tons)/Passengers (40)
ROTVÆR	HM 1	23	1994	Cargo (34 tons)/Passengers (35)
KRØTTØY	HM 2	12	1995	Cargo (100 tons)/Passengers (50)
TORPEN	HM 3	12	1977	Cargo (100 tons)/Passengers (15)
WISTING	HM 5	12	1978	Cargo (150 tons)/Passengers (75)
RAMNES	HM 6	12	1994	Cargo (120 tons)/Passengers (35)
KJEØY	HM 7	10	1993	Training ship/Passengers (30)
MÅGØY	HP 1	20	1989	Passengers (12)
FJØLØY	HP 2	16	1993	Passengers (26)
HYSNES	HP 3	24	1987	Passengers (30)
ODIN	HP 4	17	1989	Passengers (11)
OSCARSBORG I	HP 6	9	1968	Passengers (55)
NORDEP	HP 7	12.5	1987	Cargo (6 tons)/Passengers (60)
WELDING	HP 8	17	1974	Passengers (14)
AMØY	HP 9	13.5	1993	Passengers (50)
FOLDEN	HP 10	12	1974	Cargo (3 tons)/Passengers (80)
MARSTEINEN	HP 14	32	1994	Passengers (11)
BRIMSE	HP 16	16	1982	Cargo (1.5 tons)/Passengers (25)
ULSNES	HP 17	17	1993	Passengers (11)
ROGIN	HP 18	18	1987	Passengers (5)
MERMAID	HP 19	17	1989	Passengers (12)
ELLIDA	HP 20	24	1995	Passengers (12)
OSCARSBORG II	HP 21	11	1999	Cargo (5 tons)/Passengers (200)
KVARVEN	HS 1	11	1987	Tug/Cargo (3 tons)/Passengers (12)
BØGØY	HS 2	10.5	1993	Tug/Cargo (4 tons)
VSD 8	HS 3	10	1967	Tug
VERNØY	HT 1	14	1978	TRV/Cargo (19.5 tons)
KARLSØY	HT 3	12	1978	Cargo (87 tons)/Passengers (31)

UPDATED

ROYAL YACHTS

Name	No	Builders	Commissioned
NORGE (ex-*Philante*)	A 533	Camper & Nicholson's Ltd, Southampton	1937

Displacement, tons: 1,786 full load
Dimensions, feet (metres): 263 × 38 × 15.2 *(80.2 × 11.6 × 4.6)*
Main machinery: 2 Bergen KRMB-8 diesels; 4,850 hp(m) *(3.6 MW)* sustained; 2 shafts
Speed, knots: 17
Complement: 50 (18 officers)
Radars: Navigation: 2 Decca; I-band.

Comment: Built to the order of the late T O M Sopwith as an escort and store vessel for the yachts *Endeavour I* and *Endeavour II*. Launched on 17 February 1937. Served in the Royal Navy as an anti-submarine escort during the Second World War, after which she was purchased by the Norwegian people for King Haakon and reconditioned as a Royal Yacht at Southampton. Can accommodate about 50 people in addition to crew. Repaired after serious fire on 7 March 1985.

UPDATED

NORGE   *8/1999*, Michael Nitz /* 0081352

COAST GUARD

(KYSTVAKT)

0 + 1 ARCTIC CLASS (OPV)

Name	No	Builders	Commissioned
SVALBARD	W 303	Tangen Verft, Krager	Dec 2001

Displacement, tons: 6,100 full load
Dimensions, feet (metres): 337.9 × 62.7 × 21.3 *(103 × 19.1 × 6.5)*
Main machinery: Diesel electric; 4 diesel generators; 8 MW; 2 azimuth pods
Speed, knots: 17. **Range, miles:** 10,000 at 13 kt
Complement: 50
Guns: 1 Bofors 57 mm/70.
Helicopters: 1 light.

Comment: Project definition completed in 1997 for an ice-reinforced vessel equipped with a helicopter. Contract placed 7 January 2000 with Langsten Slip. Studies so far indicate a ship with much the same armament and combat data system as the upgraded 'Nordkapp' class.
UPDATED

SVALBARD (artist's impression)   *1999*, Royal Norwegian Navy /* 0081353

1 NORNEN CLASS (OPV)

Name	No	Builders	Commissioned
NORNEN	W 300	Mjellem & Karlsen, Bergen	1963

Displacement, tons: 1,030 full load
Dimensions, feet (metres): 201.8 × 32.8 × 15.8 *(61.5 × 10 × 4.8)*
Main machinery: 4 diesels; 3,500 hp(m) *(2.57 MW)*; 1 shaft
Speed, knots: 17
Complement: 32
Guns: 1 Bofors 40 mm/70.
Radars: Surface search: I-band.

Comment: Launched 20 August 1962. Modernised in 1978 with increased tonnage. Engines refitted in 1995. To be deleted when *Svalbard* enters service in 2002.   *UPDATED*

NORNEN   *7/1995*, Harald Carstens /* 0081355

6 CHARTERED SHIPS (OPV)

Name	No	Tonnage	Completion
ÅLESUND	W 312	1,357	1996
TROMSÖ	W 313	1,970	1997
STÅLBAS	W 314	498	1955
NORDSJØBAS	W 315	814	1978
LAFJORD	W 317	814	1978
THORSTEINSON	W 319	272	1960

Comment: *Stålbas* chartered in 1977; *Lafjord* and *Nordsjøbas* in 1980 and *Thorsteinson* in 1999. All armed with one 40 mm/60 gun. Two more ships have been built to Coast Guard requirements and leased for 10 years with an option to buy after five. *Tromsö* operates around north Norway while *Ålesund* is based in the south. Some ships are operated with two crews, changing over every three weeks. In addition *Lance* W 311 is listed under *Survey Ships*.
UPDATED

NORDSJØBAS   *5/1998, Per Kornefeldt /* 0052673

3 NORDKAPP CLASS (OPV)

Name	No	Builders	Launched	Commissioned
NORDKAPP	W 320	Bergens Mek Verksteder	2 Apr 1980	25 Apr 1981
SENJA	W 321	Horten Verft	16 Mar 1980	6 Mar 1981
ANDENES	W 322	Haugesund Mek Verksted	21 Mar 1981	30 Jan 1982

Displacement, tons: 3,240 full load
Dimensions, feet (metres): 346 × 47.9 × 16.1 *(105.5 × 14.6 × 4.9)*
Main machinery: 4 Wichmann 9AXAG diesels; 16,163 hp(m) *(11.9 MW)*; 2 shafts
Speed, knots: 23. **Range, miles:** 7,500 at 15 kt
Complement: 52 (6 aircrew)

Missiles: SSM: Fitted for 6 Kongsberg Penguin II but not embarked.
Guns: 1 Bofors 57 mm/70; 200 rds/min to 17 km *(9.3 n miles)*; weight of shell 2.4 kg.
4 Rheinmetall 20 mm/20; 1,000 rds/min to 2 km.
Torpedoes: 6—324 mm US Mk 32 (2 triple) tubes. Honeywell Mk 46; anti-submarine; active/passive homing to 11 km *(5.9 n miles)* at 40 kt; warhead 44 kg. Mountings only in peacetime.
Depth charges: 1 rack.
Countermeasures: Decoys: 2 chaff launchers.
Combat data systems: Navkis or EDO (after modernisation). SATCOM can be carried.
Weapons control: THORN EMI MEOSS optronic director to be fitted.
Radars: Air/surface search: Plessey AWS 5; E/F-band or DRS Technologies SPS 67(V)3; G-band.
Navigation: 2 Racal Decca 1226; I-band.
Fire control: Philips 9LV 218 Mk 2; J-band.
Sonars: Simrad SS 105; hull-mounted; active search and attack; 14 kHz.

Helicopters: 1 Westland Lynx Mk 86.

Programmes: In November 1977 the Coast Guard budget was cut resulting in a reduction of the building programme from seven to three ships.
Modernisation: The ships are to be upgraded including an optronic director, new air search radar and combat data system. Most of the work is to be done during refits starting in 2001.
Structure: Ice strengthened. Fitted for firefighting, anti-pollution work, all with two motor cutters and a Gemini-type dinghy. SATCOM fitted for Gulf deployment.
Operational: Bunks for 109. War complement increases to 76.
UPDATED

NORDKAPP   *8/1999*, van Ginderen Collection /* 0081354

14 FISHERY PROTECTION SHIPS

Name	No	Tonnage	Completion
TITRAN	KV 1	184	1992
KONGSØY	KV 2	331	1958
STURE GØRAN	KV 3	193	1969
ICE LADY	KV 4	442	1959
AGDER	KV 5	140	1974
GARSØY	KV 6	195	1988
ÄHAV	KV 7	50	1981
POLARVAKT	KV 21	290	1965
BARENTSHAV	KV 22	318	1957
NORVAKT	KV 23	197	1959
LOFOTHAV	KV 24	271	1954
SJØVEIEN	KV 25	339	1964
SJØFAREREN	KV 27	180	1966
NYSLEPPEN	KV 28	343	1967

Comment: An Inshore Patrol Force was established in January 1997. This comprises mostly chartered ships with KV pennant numbers. KV 1-KV 7 are coastal cutters. KV 21-KV 28 are used as fishing gear protection ships.
NEW ENTRY

ÄHAV   *8/1999*, van Ginderen Collection /* 0081357

OMAN

Headquarters Appointments

Commander Royal Navy of Oman:
Rear Admiral (Liwaa Bahry) H H Sayyid Shihab bin Tarik bin Taimur Al Said
Principal Staff Officer:
Commodore (Ameed) Salem bin Abdulla bin Rashid Al Alwi
Director General Operations and Plans:
Commodore (Ameed) Rashed bin Hamdan bin Abdullah Al Obaidi
Commander Coast Guard:
Captain (Aqeed Bahry) Hamdan bin Marhoon Al Mamary
Commander Royal Yacht Squadron:
Commodore (Ameed) J M Knapp

Bases

Qa'Adat Said Bin Sultan Albahria, Wudam (main base, dockyard and shiplift)
Mina Salalah (advanced naval base), Salalah
Jazirat Ghanam (advanced naval base), Musandam
Muaskar al Murtafa'a (headquarters)

Personnel

(a)   2000: 4,500 officers and men
(b)   Voluntary service

Mercantile Marine

Lloyd's Register of Shipping:
25 vessels of 16,694 tons gross

DELETIONS

Patrol Forces		Auxiliaries	
1997	*Vortex Q2*	1997	*Al Munassir* (reserve)

CORVETTES

2 QAHIR CLASS (FSG)

Name	No	Builders	Laid down	Launched	Commissioned
QAHIR AL AMWAJ	Q 31	Vosper Thornycroft, Woolston	21 May 1993	21 Sep 1994	3 Sep 1996
AL MUA'ZZAR	Q 32	Vosper Thornycroft, Woolston	4 Apr 1994	26 Sep 1995	13 Apr 1997

Displacement, tons: 1,450 full load
Dimensions, feet (metres): 274.6 oa; 249.3 wl × 37.7 × 11.8 *(83.7; 76 × 11.5 × 3.6)*
Main machinery: CODAD; 4 Crossley SEMT-Pielstick 16 PA6 V 280 STC; 28,160 hp(m) *(20.7 MW)* sustained; 2 shafts; Kamewa cp props
Speed, knots: 28. **Range, miles:** 4,000 at 10 kt
Complement: 76 (14 officers) plus 3 spare

Missiles: SSM: 8 Aerospatiale MM 40 Block 2 Exocet ❶; inertial cruise; active radar homing to 70 km *(40 n miles)* at 0.9 Mach; warhead 165 kg; sea-skimmer.
SAM: Thomson-CSF Crotale NG octuple launcher ❷; 16 VT1; command line of sight guidance; radar/IR homing to 13 km *(7 n miles)* at 2.4 Mach; warhead 14 kg.
Guns: 1 OTO Melara 3 in *(76 mm)*/62 Super Rapid ❸; 120 rds/min to 16 km *(8.7 n miles)*; weight of shell 6 kg.
2 Oerlikon/Royal Ordnance 20 mm GAM-BO1 ❹.
Torpedoes: 6—324 mm (2 triple) tubes may be fitted in due course.
Countermeasures: Decoys: 2 Barricade 12-barrelled chaff and IR launchers ❺.
ESM: Thomson-CSF DR 3000 ❻; intercept.

Combat data systems: Signaal/Thomson-CSF TACTICOS; Link Y; SATCOM.
Weapons control: Signaal STING optronic and radar tracker ❼; 2 Signaal optical directors.
Radars: Air/surface search: Signaal MW08 ❽; G-band.
Fire control: Signaal STING ❼; I/J-band.
Thomson-CSF DRBV 51C ❾; J-band (for Crotale).
Navigation: Kelvin Hughes 1007; I-band.
Sonars: Thomson Sintra/BAeSEMA ATAS; towed array; active search; 3 kHz (may be fitted).

Helicopters: Platform for 1 Super Puma type ❿.

Programmes: Vosper Thornycroft signed the Muheet Project contract on 5 April 1992. First steel cut 23 September 1992. Q 31 accepted on 27 March 1996, and Q 32 on 26 November 1996. Commissioned after operational work up in the UK, and on return to Oman. Names mean Conqueror of the Waves, and The Supported.
Structure: The ship is based on the 'Vigilance' class design with enhanced stealth features. It is possible lightweight torpedo tubes may be fitted. The towed array, if fitted, adds another 8 tons on the stern but does not affect the helicopter deck. RAM (Radar Absorbent Material) is widely used on the superstructure.
Operational: The helicopter platform can support a Super Puma sized aircraft.

UPDATED

QAHIR AL AMWAJ   *(Scale 1 : 900), Ian Sturton*

QAHIR AL AMWAJ   6/1996* / 0012853

AL MUA'ZZAR   1/1997*, H M Steele / 0012854

1 PATROL SHIP (FS/AXL/AGS)

Name	No	Builders	Commissioned
AL MABRUKAH (ex-*Al Said*)	Q 30 (ex-A 1)	Brooke Marine, Lowestoft	1971

Displacement, tons: 900 full load
Dimensions, feet (metres): 203.4 × 35.1 × 9.8 *(62 × 10.7 × 3)*
Main machinery: 2 Paxman Valenta 12CM diesels; 5,000 hp *(3.73 MW)* sustained; 2 shafts
Speed, knots: 12
Complement: 39 (7 officers) plus 32 trainees
Guns: 1 Bofors 40 mm/70. 2 Oerlikon 20 mm A41A.
Countermeasures: Decoys: Wallop Barricade 18-barrelled chaff launcher.
ESM: Racal Cutlass; radar warning.
Radars: Surface search: Racal Decca TM 1226; I-band.
Helicopters: Platform only.

Comment: Built by Brooke Marine, Lowestoft. Launched 7 April 1970 as a yacht for the Sultan of Oman. Carried on board is one Rotork landing craft. Converted to training/patrol ship in 1983 with enlarged helicopter deck, additional accommodation and armament. Re-classified as a corvette and pennant number changed in 1997. Being fitted with survey equipment in 2000, as an additional role.

UPDATED

AL MABRUKAH   *6/1999*, Royal Navy of Oman* / 0081358

PATROL FORCES

Note: Three 54 m OPVs are to be acquired by 2005.

3 AL BUSHRA CLASS (OPV)

Name	No	Builders	Laid down	Launched	Commissioned
AL BUSHRA	B 1	CMN, Cherbourg/Wudam Dockyard	10 Nov 1993	3 May 1995	15 June 1995
AL MANSOOR	B 2	CMN, Cherbourg/Wudam Dockyard	12 Apr 1994	3 May 1995	10 Aug 1995
AL NAJAH	B 3	CMN, Cherbourg/Wudam Dockyard	27 June 1994	5 Mar 1996	15 Apr 1996

Displacement, tons: 475 full load
Dimensions, feet (metres): 178.6 × 26.2 × 8.9 *(54.5 × 8 × 2.7)*
Main machinery: 2 MTU 16V 538 TB93 diesels; 8,000 hp(m) *(5.88 MW)* sustained; 2 shafts
Speed, knots: 24. **Range, miles:** 2,400 at 15 kt
Complement: 43 (8 officers)

Guns: 1 OTO Melara 76 mm/62 Super Rapid; 120 rds/min to 16 km *(8.7 n miles)*; weight of shell 6 kg.
2 Oerlikon/Royal Ordnance 20 mm GAM-BO1. 2—12.7 mm MGs.
Countermeasures: Decoys: Plessey Barricade chaff launcher.
ESM: Thomson-CSF DR 3000; intercept.
Weapons control: CelsiusTech 9LV 207 Mk 3 command system and optronic director.
Radars: Surface search: Kelvin Hughes 1007 ARPA; I-band.

Programmes: Project Mawj order for three, with an option on five more, on 1 September 1993. The ships have had additional weapon systems fitted in Wudam dockyard.
Structure: Same hull design as the French 'P 400' class. 20 mm guns, and countermeasures were not fitted at Cherbourg and

AL BUSHRA   *9/1998*, Royal Navy of Oman* / 0043443

are planned to be installed in 2000. 76 mm guns were fitted from 1998 from deleted 'Al Waafi' class. The plan to fit torpedoes and sonars has been shelved.

Operational: First pair arrived in Oman on 28 September 1995, last one on 29 June 1996.

UPDATED

---

4 DHOFAR (PROVINCE) CLASS
(FAST ATTACK CRAFT—MISSILE) (PCFG)

Name	No	Builders	Launched	Commissioned
DHOFAR	B 10	Vosper Thornycroft	14 Oct 1981	7 Aug 1982
AL SHARQIYAH	B 11	Vosper Thornycroft	2 Dec 1982	5 Dec 1983
AL BAT'NAH	B 12	Vosper Thornycroft	4 Nov 1982	18 Jan 1984
MUSSANDAM	B 14	Vosper Thornycroft	19 Mar 1988	31 Mar 1989

Displacement, tons: 311 light; 394 full load
Dimensions, feet (metres): 186 × 26.9 × 7.9 *(56.7 × 8.2 × 2.4)*
Main machinery: 4 Paxman Valenta 18CM diesels; 15,000 hp *(11.2 MW)* sustained; 4 shafts; auxiliary propulsion; 2 motors; 200 hp *(149 kW)*
Speed, knots: 38. **Range, miles:** 2,000 at 18 kt
Complement: 45 (5 officers) plus 14 trainees

Missiles: SSM: 8 Aerospatiale MM 40 Exocet; inertial cruise; active radar homing to 70 km *(40 n miles)* at 0.9 Mach; warhead 165 kg; sea-skimmer.
Guns: 1 OTO Melara 3 in *(76 mm)*/62 compact; 85 rds/min to 16 km *(8.7 n miles)*; weight of shell 6 kg.
2 Breda 40 mm/70 (twin); 300 rds/min to 12.5 km *(6.8 n miles)*; weight of shell 0.96 kg.
2—12.7 mm MGs.
Countermeasures: Decoys: 2 Wallop Barricade fixed triple barrels; for chaff and IR flares.
ESM: Racal Cutlass; radar warning.
ECM: Scorpion; jammer.
Weapons control: Sperry Sea Archer (B 10). Philips 9LV 307 (remainder).
Radars: Air/surface search: Plessey AWS 4 or AWS 6; E/F-band.
Fire control: Philips 9LV 307; I/J-band.
Navigation: KH 1007 ARPA; I-band.

Programmes: First ordered in 1980, two more in January 1981 and fourth in January 1986.
Structure: Similar to Kenyan 'Nyayo' class. Mast structures are different dependent on radars fitted.

UPDATED

MUSSANDAM   *3/1997*, J W Currie* / 0012857

AL BATNAH   *3/1997*, J W Currie* / 0012856

4 SEEB (VOSPER 25) CLASS (COASTAL PATROL CRAFT) (PC)

Name	No	Builders	Commissioned
SEEB	B 20	Vosper Private, Singapore	15 Mar 1981
SHINAS	B 21	Vosper Private, Singapore	15 Mar 1981
SADH	B 22	Vosper Private, Singapore	15 Mar 1981
KHASSAB	B 23	Vosper Private, Singapore	15 Mar 1981

Displacement, tons: 74 full load
Dimensions, feet (metres): 82.8 × 19 × 5.2 *(25 × 5.8 × 1.6)*
Main machinery: 2 MTU 12V 331 TC92 diesels; 2,660 hp(m) *(1.96 MW)* sustained; 2 shafts
1 Cummins N-855M diesel for slow cruising; 189 hp *(141 kW)* sustained; 1 shaft
Speed, knots: 25; 8 (Cummins diesel). **Range, miles:** 750 at 14 kt
Complement: 13
Guns: 1 Oerlikon 20 mm GAM-BO1. 2—7.62 mm MGs.
Radars: Surface search: Racal Decca 1226; I-band.

Comment: Arrived in Oman on 19 May 1981 having been ordered one month earlier. The craft were built on speculation and completed in 1980.

UPDATED

SHINAS   *9/1999*, Royal Navy of Oman* / 0081359

AMPHIBIOUS FORCES

Note: There are also some French-built Havas Mk 8 two-man SDVs in service.

1 LANDING SHIP—LOGISTIC (LSL)

Name	No	Builders	Commissioned
NASR AL BAHR	L 2	Brooke Marine, Lowestoft	6 Feb 1985

Displacement, tons: 2,500 full load
Dimensions, feet (metres): 305 × 50.8 × 8.5 *(93 × 15.5 × 2.6)*
Main machinery: 2 Paxman Valenta 18 CM diesels; 7,500 hp *(5.6 MW)* sustained; 2 shafts; cp props
Speed, knots: 16. **Range, miles:** 5,000 at 15 kt
Complement: 81 (13 officers)
Military lift: 7 MBT or 400 tons cargo; 240 troops; 2 LCVPs
Guns: 4 Breda 40 mm/70 (2 twin). 2 Oerlikon 20 mm GAM-BO1. 2—12.7 mm MGs.
Countermeasures: Decoys: Wallop Barricade double layer chaff launchers.
Weapons control: PEAB 9LV 107 GFCS and CSEE Lynx optical sight.
Radars: Surface search/navigation: 2 Racal Decca 1226; I-band.
Helicopters: Platform for Super Puma.

Comment: Ordered 18 May 1982. Launched 16 May 1984. Carries one 16 ton crane. Bow and stern ramps. Full naval command facilities. The forward ramp is of two sections measuring length 59 ft (when extended) × 16.5 ft breadth *(18 × 5 m)*, and the single section stern ramp measures 14 × 16.5 ft *(4.3 × 5 m)*. Both hatches can support a 60 ton tank. The tank deck side bulkheads extend 7.5 ft *(2.25 m)* above the upper deck between the forecastle and the forward end of the superstructure, and provides two hatch openings to the tank deck below. Positioned between the hatches is a 2 ton crane with athwartship travel. New funnel fitted in 1997, and the ship may have been re-engined at the same time.

UPDATED

NASR AL BAHR   *4/1997* */ 0012858*

3 LCMs

Name	No	Builders	Commissioned
SABA AL BAHR	L 8 (ex-C 8)	Vosper Private, Singapore	17 Sep 1981
AL DOGHAS	L 9 (ex-C 9)	Vosper Private, Singapore	10 Jan 1983
AL TEMSAH	L 10 (ex-C 10)	Vosper Private, Singapore	12 Feb 1983

Displacement, tons: 230 full load
Dimensions, feet (metres): 108.2 (83.6, C 8) × 24.3 × 4.3 *(33 (25.5) × 7.4 × 1.3)*
Main machinery: 2 Caterpillar 3408TA diesels; 1,880 hp *(1.4 MW)* sustained; 2 shafts
Speed, knots: 8. **Range, miles:** 1,400 at 8 kt
Complement: 11
Military lift: 100 tons
Radars: Navigation: Furuno 701; I-band.

Comment: First one launched 30 June 1981. Second pair similar but not identical ships, launched 12 November and 15 December 1982.

UPDATED

SABA AL BAHR   *6/1999* */ Royal Navy of Oman / 0081360*

1 LCU

Name	No	Builders	Commissioned
AL NEEMRAN	L 7 (ex-C 7)	Lewis Offshore, Stornoway	1979

Measurement, tons: 85 dwt
Dimensions, feet (metres): 84 × 24 × 6 *(25.5 × 7.4 × 1.8)*
Main machinery: 2 diesels; 300 hp *(220 kW)*; 2 shafts
Speed, knots: 7/8
Complement: 6
Radars: Navigation: Furuno; I-band.

Comment: Second of class deleted in 1993.

UPDATED

AL NEEMRAN   *10/1997*, *Royal Navy of Oman / 0012859*

AUXILIARIES

Note: In addition to the listed vessels there are four 12 m Cheverton Work boats (W 41-W 44) and eight 8 m Work boats (W 4-W 11).

1 SUPPLY SHIP (AKS)

Name	No	Builders	Launched	Commissioned
AL SULTANA	S 2 (ex-A 2)	Conoship, Groningen	18 May 1975	4 June 1975

Measurement, tons: 1,380 dwt
Dimensions, feet (metres): 215.6 × 35 × 13.5 *(65.7 × 10.7 × 4.2)*
Main machinery: 1 Mirrlees Blackstone diesel; 1,120 hp(m) *(835 kW)*; 1 shaft
Speed, knots: 11
Complement: 20
Radars: Navigation: Racal Decca TM 1226; I-band.

Comment: Major refit in 1992. Has a 1 ton crane. Pennant number changed in 1997.

UPDATED

AL SULTANA   *4/1999*, *Schaeffer/Marsan / 0081361*

1 SURVEY CRAFT (AGSC)

AL RAHMANNIYA H 1

Displacement, tons: 23.6 full load
Dimensions, feet (metres): 50.8 × 13.1 × 4.3 *(15.5 × 4 × 1.3)*
Main machinery: 2 Volvo TMD120A diesels; 604 hp(m) *(444 kW)* sustained; 2 shafts
Speed, knots: 13.5. **Range, miles:** 500 at 12 kt
Complement: 10
Radars: Navigation: Furuno; I-band.

Comment: Built by Watercraft, Shoreham, UK and completed in April 1981.

UPDATED

AL RAHMANNIYA   *10/1997*, *Royal Navy of Oman / 0012860*

3 HARBOUR CRAFT (YDT/YTL)

R 1   T 2   T 3

Displacement, tons: 13 full load
Dimensions, feet (metres): 59 × 12.4 × 3.6 *(18 × 3.8 × 1.1)*
Main machinery: 2 Volvo Penta diesels; 430 hp(m) *(316 kW)* sustained; 2 shafts
Speed, knots: 20
Complement: 4
Guns: 2—7.62 mm MGs.

Comment: Details given are for *R 1* which is a Rotork type acquired in 1991. Used as a diver's boat. Similar to Police craft also used for divers. *T 2* and *T 3* are Damen Pushy Cat 1500 tugs acquired in 1990-91.

UPDATED

T 2   *10/1992, Hartmut Ehlers*

TRAINING SHIPS

1 SAIL TRAINING SHIP (AXS)

Name	No	Builders	Recommissioned
SHABAB OMAN	S 1	Herd and Mackenzie,	1979
(ex-*Captain Scott*)		Buckie, Scotland	

Displacement, tons: 386 full load
Dimensions, feet (metres): 144.3 × 27.9 × 15.1 *(44 × 8.5 × 4.6)*
Main machinery: 2 Gardner diesels; 460 hp *(343 kW)*; 2 shafts
Speed, knots: 10 (diesels)
Complement: 20 (5 officers) plus 3 officers and 24 trainees

Comment: Topsail schooner built in 1971 and taken over from Dulverton Trust in 1977 used for sail training. Name means Omani Youth.

UPDATED

SHABAB OMAN   *6/1999*, Royal Navy of Oman /* 0081362

ROYAL YACHTS

Notes: (1) The Royal Yacht Squadron is based at Mina Qabus.
(2) There is also a Royal Dhow *Zinat Al Bihaar*.

ZINAT AL BIHAAR   *4/1996*, Royal Navy of Oman /* 0081363

Name	No	Builders	Commissioned
AL SAID	—	Picchiotti SpA, Viareggio	July 1982

Displacement, tons: 3,800 full load
Dimensions, feet (metres): 340.5 × 53.2 × 16.4 *(103.8 × 16.2 × 5)*
Main machinery: 2 GMT A 420.6 H diesels; 8,400 hp(m) *(6.17 MW)* sustained; 2 shafts; cp props; bow thruster
Speed, knots: 18
Complement: 156 (16 officers)
Radars: Navigation: Decca TM 1226C; ACS 1230C; I-band.

Comment: This ship is an independent command manned by naval personnel but is not part of the Omani Navy. Fitted with helicopter deck and fin stabilisers. Carries three Puma C service launches and one Rotork beach landing craft.

UPDATED

AL SAID   *7/1996*, Camil Busquets i Vilanova /* 0081364

Name	No	Builders	Launched	Commissioned
FULK AL SALAMAH	—	Bremer-Vulkan	29 Aug 1986	3 Apr 1987
(ex-*Ghubat Al Salamah*)				

Measurement, tons: 10,864 grt; 5,186 net
Dimensions, feet (metres): 447.5 × 68.9 × 19.7 *(136.4 × 21 × 6)*
Main machinery: 4 Fincantieri GMT A 420.6 H diesels; 16,800 hp(m) *(12.35 MW)* sustained; 2 shafts; cp props
Speed, knots: 19.5
Military lift: 240 troops
Radars: Navigation: 2 Racal Decca; I-band.
Helicopters: Up to 2 AS 332C Super Pumas.

Comment: Support ship and transport with side doors for heavy loading. Part of the Royal Yacht Squadron and the old pennant number L 3 has been removed. Marisat fitted.

UPDATED

FULK AL SALAMAH   *7/1996*, Camil Busquets i Vilanova /* 0081365

POLICE

Notes: (1) In addition to the vessels listed below there are several harbour craft including a Cheverton 8 m work boat *Zahra 24* and a fireboat pennant number *10*. There are also two Pilatus aircraft for SAR.
(2) 15 FPBs between 11 and 30 m may be ordered in due course. These could be for the Navy if it takes over Fishery Protection duties from the Police.

3 CG 29 TYPE (COASTAL PATROL CRAFT) (PC)

HARAS VII   HARAS IX   HARAS X

Displacement, tons: 84 full load
Dimensions, feet (metres): 94.8 × 17.7 × 4.3 *(28.9 × 5.4 × 1.3)*
Main machinery: 2 MTU 12V 331 TC92 diesels; 2,660 hp(m) *(1.96 MW)* sustained; 2 shafts
Speed, knots: 25. **Range, miles:** 600 at 15 kt
Complement: 13
Guns: 2 Oerlikon 20 mm GAM-BO1.
Radars: Navigation: Racal Decca 1226; I-band.

Comment: Built by Karlskrona Varvet. Commissioned in 1981-82. GRP Sandwich hulls.
VERIFIED

HARAS X   *10/1992, Hartmut Ehlers*

1 P 1903 TYPE (COASTAL PATROL CRAFT) (PC)

HARAS VIII

Displacement, tons: 32 full load
Dimensions, feet (metres): 63 × 15.7 × 5.2 *(19.2 × 4.8 × 1.6)*
Main machinery: 2 MTU 8V 331 TC92 diesels; 1,770 hp(m) *(1.3 MW)*; 2 shafts
Speed, knots: 30. **Range, miles:** 1,650 at 17 kt
Complement: 10
Guns: 2—12.7 mm MGs.
Radars: Navigation: Racal Decca 1226; I-band.

Comment: Built by Le Comte, Netherlands. Commissioned August 1981. Type 1903 Mk III.
VERIFIED

HARAS VI   *10/1992, Hartmut Ehlers*

HARAS VIII   *10/1992, Hartmut Ehlers*

1 CG 27 TYPE (COASTAL PATROL CRAFT) (PC)

HARAS VI

Displacement, tons: 53 full load
Dimensions, feet (metres): 78.7 × 18 × 6.2 *(24 × 5.5 × 1.9)*
Main machinery: 2 MTU 12V 331 TC92 diesels; 2,660 hp(m) *(1.96 MW)* sustained; 2 shafts
Speed, knots: 25
Complement: 11
Guns: 1 Oerlikon 20 mm GAM-BO1.
Radars: Navigation: Furuno 701; I-band.

Comment: Completed in 1980 by Karlskrona Varvet. GRP hull.
VERIFIED

1 P 2000 TYPE (COASTAL PATROL CRAFT) (PC)

DHEEB AL BAHAR I

Displacement, tons: 80 full load
Dimensions, feet (metres): 68.2 × 19 × 5 *(20.8 × 5.8 × 1.5)*
Main machinery: 2 MTU 12V 396 TB93 diesels; 3,260 hp(m) *(2.4 MW)* sustained; 2 shafts
Speed, knots: 40. **Range, miles:** 423 at 36 kt; 700 at 18 kt
Guns: 1—12.7 mm MG.
Radars: Surface search: Furuno 701; I-band.

Comment: Delivered January 1985 by Watercraft Ltd, Shoreham, UK. GRP hull. Carries SATNAV.
VERIFIED

DHEEB AL BAHAR I (with *Dheeb Al Bahar II*)   *10/1992, Hartmut Ehlers*

2 D 59116 TYPE (COASTAL PATROL CRAFT) (PC)

DHEEB AL BAHAR II and **III**

Displacement, tons: 65 full load
Dimensions, feet (metres): 75.5 × 17.1 × 3.9 *(23 × 5.2 × 1.2)*
Main machinery: 2 MTU 12V 396 TB93 diesels; 3,260 hp(m) *(2.4 MW)* sustained; 2 shafts
Speed, knots: 36. **Range, miles:** 420 at 30 kt
Complement: 11
Guns: 1—12.7 mm MG.
Radars: Surface search: Furuno 711-2; Furuno 2400; I-band.

Comment: Built by Yokohama Yacht Co, Japan. Commissioned in 1988.

UPDATED

DHEEB AL BAHAR II   *1988*, Royal Oman Police / 0081366*

3 WATERCRAFT TYPE and 2 EMSWORTH TYPE
(INSHORE PATROL CRAFT) (PC)

ZAHRA 14	ZAHRA 15	ZAHRA 17	ZAHRA 18	ZAHRA 21

Displacement, tons: 16; 18 (*Zahra 18* and *21*) full load
Dimensions, feet (metres): 45.6 × 14.1 × 4.6 *(13.9 × 4.3 × 1.4)*
  52.5 × 13.8 × 7.5 *(16 × 4.2 × 2.3)* (*Zahra 18* and *21*)
Main machinery: 2 Cummins VTA-903M diesels; 643 hp *(480 kW)*; 2 shafts
Speed, knots: 36. **Range, miles:** 510 at 22 kt
Complement: 5-6
Guns: 1 or 2—7.62 mm MGs.
Radars: Navigation: Decca 101; I-band.

Comment: *Zahra 14, 15* and *17* built by Watercraft, Shoreham, UK and completed in 1981. *Zahra 21* completed by Emsworth SB in 1987 to a slightly different design. *Zahra 18* built Lecomte in 1987.   ***UPDATED***

ZAHRA 18   *10/1992, Hartmut Ehlers*

1 DIVING CRAFT (YDT)

ZAHRA 27

Displacement, tons: 13 full load
Dimensions, feet (metres): 59 × 12.4 × 3.6 *(18 × 3.8 × 1.1)*
Main machinery: 2 Volvo Penta AQD70D diesels; 430 hp(m) *(316 kW)* sustained; 2 shafts
Speed, knots: 20
Complement: 4
Guns: 2—7.62 mm MGs.

Comment: Rotork Type, the last of several logistic support craft, delivered in 1981 and now used as a diving boat. Similar craft used by the Navy.

VERIFIED

ZAHRA 27   *10/1992, Hartmut Ehlers*

PAKISTAN

Headquarters Appointments

Chief of the Naval Staff:
  Vice Admiral Abdul Aziz Mirza HI(M), S. Bt
Vice Chief of Naval Staff:
  Admiral Mazhar Masood Biabini SI(M), S. Bt

Senior Appointments

Commander Pakistan Fleet:
  Rear Admiral Gul Zaman Malik, S J, SI(M)
Commander Karachi:
  Rear Admiral S A Baqar SI(M)
Commander North:
  Commodore Ubaid Sadiq S. Bt, TJ
Director General Maritime Security Agency:
  Rear Admiral Muhammad Jameel Akhtar, SI(M), T. Bt

Diplomatic Representation

Naval Adviser in London:
  Commodore Javed Ahmed Khan
Naval Attaché in Paris:
  Captain M Abid Saleem
Defence Attaché in Muscat (Oman):
  Captain Faheem Ahmed
Naval Attaché in Tehran:
  Captain Syed Muhammad Obaid Ullah
Naval Attaché in Beijing:
  Captain Naveed Mumtaz
Naval Attaché in Kuala Lumpur:
  Commander M Fahim Khan

Personnel

(a) 2000: 25,100 (2,300 officers) including 1,200 Marines and 1,000 (75 officers) seconded to the MSA
(b) Voluntary service
(c) Reserves 5,000

Bases

PNS *Haider* (Fleet HQ); PNS *Akram* (Gwadar Naval Base); PNS *Iqbal* (Commando Base); PNS *Jahanger* (Port Qasim); PNS *Jinna* (Port Ormara); PNS *Mehran* (Karachi Naval Air Station)

Prefix to Ships' Names

PNS

Maritime Security Agency

Set up in 1986. Main purpose is to patrol the EEZ in co-operation with the Navy and the Army-manned Coast Guard.

Marines

A Marine Commando Unit was formed at PNS *Iqbal*, Karachi in 1991.

Mercantile Marine

Lloyd's Register of Shipping:
  55 vessels of 307,908 tons gross

Strength of the Fleet

Type	Active	Building
Submarines—Patrol	7	2
Submarines—Midget	3	—
Destroyers/Frigates	8	(2)
Fast Attack Craft—Missile	5	1 (1)
Large Patrol Craft	2	(1)
Minehunters	3	—
Survey Ship	1	(1)
Tankers	5	3
Maritime Security Agency		
Destroyers	1	—
Large Patrol Craft	4	—
Fast Attack Craft—Gun	2	—

DELETIONS

Destroyers

1998	*Alamgir, Tughril* (to MSA)
1999	*Taimur*

Patrol Forces

1997	*Jalalat*
1998	*Haibat, Jurat, Shujaat, Pishin, Bahawalpur, Azmat*

Auxiliaries

1998	*Rustom*

PENNANT LIST

Submarines

S 131	Hangor
S 132	Shushuk
S 133	Mangro
S 134	Ghazi
S 135	Hashmat
S 136	Hurmat
S 137	Khalid
S 138	Saad (bldg)
S 139	Ghazi (bldg)

Destroyers/Frigates

D 181	Tariq
D 182	Babur
D 183	Khaibar
D 184	Badr
D 185	Tippu Sultan
D 186	Shahjahan
F 262	Zulfiquar
F 263	Shamsher

Mine Warfare Forces

M 163	Muhafiz
M 166	Munsif
M 164	Mujahid

Patrol Forces

P 140	Rajshahi
P 157	Larkana
P 1022	Jalalat
P 1024	Shujaat
P 1026	Dehshat
P 1027	Himmat
P 1028	Quwwat

Maritime Security Agency

D 156	Nazim
1060	Barkat
1061	Rehmat

1062	Nusrat
1063	Vehdat
1066	Sabqat
1068	Rafaqat
1069	Pishin
1070	Bahawalpur

Auxiliaries

A 20	Moawin
A 21	Kalmat
A 40	Attock
A 44	Bholu
A 45	Gama
A 47	Nasr
A 49	Gwadar
—	Janbaz

SUBMARINES

1 + 2 KHALID (AGOSTA 90B) CLASS (SSK)

Name	No	Builders	Laid down	Launched	Commissioned
KHALID	S 137	DCN, Cherbourg	1997	8 Aug 1998	6 Sep 1999
SAAD	S 138	DCN, Cherbourg/PN Dockyard, Karachi	1998	2001	Feb 2002
GHAZI	S 139	PN Dockyard, Karachi	2000	2002	Dec 2002

Displacement, tons: 1,510 surfaced; 1,760 dived (1,960 with MESMA)

Dimensions, feet (metres): 221.7 × 22.3 × 17.7 *(67.6 × 6.8 × 5.4)*

Main machinery: Diesel-electric; 2 SEMT-Pielstick 16 PA4 V 185 VG diesels; 3,600 hp(m) *(2.65 MW)*; 2 Jeumont Schneider alternators; 1.7 MW; 1 Jeumont motor; 2,992 hp(m) *(2.2 MW)*; 1 cruising motor; 32 hp(m) *(23 kW)*; 1 shaft

Speed, knots: 12 surfaced; 20 dived

Range, miles: 8,500 at 9 kt snorting; 350 at 3.5 kt dived

Complement: 36 (7 officers)

Missiles: SSM: 4 Aerospatiale Exocet SM 39; inertial cruise; active radar homing to 50 km *(27 n miles)* at 0.9 Mach; warhead 165 kg.

Torpedoes: 4—21 in *(533 mm)* bow tubes. 16 ECAN F17P Mod 2; wire-guided; active/passive homing to 20 km *(10.8 n miles)* at 40 kt; warhead 250 kg. Total of 20 weapons.

Mines: Stonefish.

Countermeasures: ESM: Thomson-CSF DR-3000U; intercept.

Weapons control: Thomson Sintra SUBTICS Mk 2.

Radars: Surface search: KH 1007; I-band.

Sonars: Thomson Sintra TSM 2233 suite; bow cylindrical, passive ranging and intercept, and clip-on towed arrays.

Programmes: A provisional order for a second batch of three more Agostas was reported in September 1992 and this was confirmed on 21 September 1994. First one built in France. Parts for S 138 sent to Pakistan in April 1998 and for S 139 in September 1998.

Structure: The last of the class is planned to have a 200 kW MESMA liquid oxygen AIP system which would extend the hull by 9 m, if it is fitted. The MESMA AIP system has a power output of 200 kW which would quadruple dived performance at 4 kt. Testing of the production system started in late 1999 and installation in S 139 is planned in 2001. Hulls also have much improved acoustic quietening and a full integrated sonar suite including flank, intercept and towed arrays. SOPOLEM J 95 search and STS 95 attack periscopes. Sagem integrated navigation system. HLES 80 steel. Diving depth of 320 m *(1,050 ft)*.

Operational: *Khalid* completed 29 April 1999 and sailed for Pakistan in November 1999.

Opinion: This is an ambitious programme, given the unhappy history of licence-built submarines in other medium-sized navies. The introduction of AIP is also ambitious and likely to be costly. Shipbuilders understandably downplay the risks of introducing this new technology, and the Pakistan Navy is an experienced operator of submarines. Nonetheless, the operational advantages of AIP have to be balanced against potential technical risks.

UPDATED

KHALID   *6/1999*, DCN/SIRPA /* 0081367

2 HASHMAT (AGOSTA) CLASS (SSK)

Name	No	Builders	Laid down	Launched	Commissioned
HASHMAT (ex-*Astrant*)	S 135	Dubigeon Normandie, Nantes	15 Sep 1976	14 Dec 1977	17 Feb 1979
HURMAT (ex-*Adventurous*)	S 136	Dubigeon Normandie, Nantes	18 Sep 1977	1 Dec 1978	18 Feb 1980

Displacement, tons: 1,490 surfaced; 1,740 dived

Dimensions, feet (metres): 221.7 × 22.3 × 17.7 *(67.6 × 6.8 × 5.4)*

Main machinery: Diesel-electric; 2 SEMT-Pielstick 16 PA4 V 185 VG diesels; 3,600 hp(m) *(2.65 MW)*; 2 Jeumont Schneider alternators; 1.7 MW; 1 motor; 4,600 hp(m) *(3.4 MW)*; 1 cruising motor; 32 hp(m) *(23 kW)*; 1 shaft

Speed, knots: 12 surfaced; 20 dived

Range, miles: 8,500 at 9 kt snorting; 350 at 3.5 kt dived

Complement: 59 (8 officers)

Missiles: SSM: McDonnell Douglas Sub Harpoon; active radar homing to 130 km *(70 n miles)* at 0.9 Mach; warhead 227 kg.

Torpedoes: 4—21 in *(533 mm)* bow tubes. ECAN F17P; wire-guided; active/passive homing to 20 km *(10.8 n miles)* at 40 kt; warhead 250 kg; water ram discharge gear. E14, E15 and L3 torpedoes are also available. Total of 20 torpedoes and missiles.

Mines: Stonefish.

Countermeasures: ESM: ARUD; intercept and warning.

Radars: Surface search: Thomson-CSF DRUA 33; I-band.

Sonars: Thomson Sintra TSM 2233D; passive search; medium frequency.

Thomson Sintra DUUA 2B; active/passive search and attack; 8 kHz active.

Thomson Sintra TSM 2933D towed array; passive; very low frequency.

Programmes: Purchased from France in mid-1978 after United Nations' ban on arms sales to South Africa. *Hashmat* arrived Karachi 31 October 1979, *Hurmat* arrived 11 August 1980.

Structure: Diving depth, 300 m *(985 ft)*. Both were modified to fire Harpoon in 1985 but may have had to acquire the missiles through a third party.

UPDATED

HURMAT   *6/1998 /* 0052677

4 HANGOR (DAPHNE) CLASS (SSK)

Name	No
HANGOR	S 131
SHUSHUK	S 132
MANGRO	S 133
GHAZI (ex-*Cachalote*)	S 134

Builders	Laid down	Launched	Commissioned
Arsenal de Brest	1 Dec 1967	28 June 1969	12 Jan 1970
CN Ciotat, Le Trait	1 Dec 1967	30 July 1969	12 Jan 1970
CN Ciotat, Le Trait	8 July 1968	7 Feb 1970	8 Aug 1970
Dubigeon, Normandie, Nantes	12 May 1967	23 Sep 1968	1 Oct 1969

Displacement, tons: 700 standard; 869 surfaced; 1,043 dived
Dimensions, feet (metres): 189.6 × 22.3 × 15.1
 (57.8 × 6.8 × 4.6)
Main machinery: Diesel-electric; 2 SEMT-Pielstick 12 PA4 V 185 diesels; 2,450 hp(m) *(1.8 MW)*; 2 Jeumont Schneider alternators; 1.7 MW; 2 motors; 2,600 hp(m) *(1.9 MW)*; 2 shafts
Speed, knots: 13 surfaced; 15.5 dived
Range, miles: 4,500 at 5 kt; 3,000 at 7 kt snorting
Complement: 53 (7 officers)

Missiles: SSM: McDonnell Douglas Sub Harpoon; active radar homing to 130 km *(70 n miles)* at 0.9 Mach; warhead 227 kg.
Torpedoes: 12—21.7 in *(550 mm)* (8 bow, 4 stern). E14, E15, L3 and Z16 torpedoes are available. Total of 12 weapons, no reloads.
Mines: Stonefish.
Countermeasures: ESM: ARUD; intercept and warning.
Radars: Surface search: Thomson-CSF DRUA 31; I-band.
Sonars: Thomson Sintra TSM 2233D; hull-mounted; passive search; medium frequency.
 DUUA 1; active/passive search and attack.

MANGRO   6/1998 / 0052678

Programmes: The first three were built in France. The Portuguese 'Daphne' class *Cachalote* was bought by Pakistan in December 1975.
Structure: They are broadly similar to the submarines built in France for Portugal and South Africa and the submarines constructed to the Daphne design in Spain, but slightly modified internally. Diving depth 300 m *(985 ft)*. SSM capability added in late 1980s.
Operational: Being replaced by 'Khalid' class and first one is planned to pay off in 2000.   **UPDATED**

3 MIDGET SUBMARINES

Displacement, tons: 118 dived
Dimensions, feet (metres): 91.2 × 18.4
 (27.8 × 5.6)
Speed, knots: 7 dived
Range, miles: 2,200 surfaced; 60 dived
Complement: 8 + 8 swimmers
Torpedoes: 2—21 in *(533 mm)* tubes; 2 AEG SUT; wire-guided; active homing to 12 km *(6.5 n miles)* at 35 kt; passive homing to 28 km *(15 n miles)* at 23 kt; warhead 250 kg plus either two short range active/passive homing torpedoes or two SDVs.
Mines: 12 Mk 414 Limpet type.
Sonars: Hull mounted; active/passive; high frequency.

Comment: MG 110 type built in Pakistan under supervision by Cosmos. These are enlarged SX 756 of Italian Cosmos design. Diving depth of 150 m and can carry eight swimmers with 2 tons of explosives as well as two CF2 FX 60 SDVs (swimmer delivery vehicles). Pilkington Optronics CK 39 periscopes. Reported as having a range of 1,000 n miles and an endurance of 20 days. All have been upgraded since 1995 with improved sensors and weapons. All are active.   **UPDATED**

MIDGET SUBMARINE   1993* / 0081368

FRIGATES

Note: Negotiations resumed again in 1999 to buy 'Jiangwei II' class frigates from China. Progress delayed by funding problems.

2 LEANDER CLASS (FF)

Name	No
ZULFIQUAR (ex-*Apollo*)	F 262
SHAMSHER (ex-*Diomede*)	F 263

Builders	Laid down	Launched	Commissioned
Yarrows, Glasgow	1 May 1969	15 Oct 1970	28 May 1972
Yarrows, Glasgow	30 Jan 1968	15 Apr 1969	2 Apr 1971

Displacement, tons: 2,500 standard; 2,962 full load
Dimensions, feet (metres): 360 wl; 372 oa × 43 × 14.8 (keel); 18 (screws) *(109.7; 113.4 × 13.1 × 4.5; 5.5)*
Main machinery: 2 Babcock & Wilcox boilers; 550 psi *(38.7 kg/cm²)*; 850°F *(454°C)*; 2 White/English Electric turbines; 30,000 hp *(22.4 MW)*; 2 shafts
Speed, knots: 28. **Range, miles:** 4,000 at 15 kt
Complement: 235 (15 officers)

Guns: 2 Vickers 4.5 in *(114 mm)*/45 Mk 6 (twin) ❶; 20 rds/min to 19 km *(10.3 n miles)* anti-surface; 6 km *(3.3 n miles)* anti-aircraft; weight of shell 25 kg.
 6—25 mm/60 (3 twin) ❷; 270 rds/min to 3 km *(1.6 n miles)*; weight of shell 0.34 kg.
A/S mortars: 3-barrelled UK MoD Mortar Mk 10 ❸; automatic loading; range 1 km; warhead 92 kg.
Countermeasures: Decoys: Graseby Type 182; towed torpedo decoy.
 2 Vickers Corvus 8-barrelled trainable chaff launchers ❹.
 ESM: UA-8/9/13; radar warning.
 ECM: Type 668; jammer.
Weapons control: MRS 3 system for 114 mm guns.
Radars: Air search: Marconi Type 966 ❺; A-band; AKE-1.
 Surface search: Plessey Type 994 ❻; E/F-band.
 Navigation: 1 Kelvin Hughes Type 1006 and 1 Kelvin Hughes Type 1007; I-band.
 Fire control: Plessey Type 904 (for 114 mm guns) ❼; I/J-band.
Sonars: Kelvin Hughes Type 162M; hull-mounted; bottom classification; 50 kHz.
 Graseby Type 170B; hull-mounted; active search and attack; 15 kHz.
 Graseby Type 184P; hull-mounted; active search and attack; 6-9 kHz.

Helicopters: 1 SA 319B Alouette III ❽.

Programmes: Transferred from UK 15 July 1988 (*Shamsher*) and 14 October 1988 (*Zulfiquar*). Both ships are from the Batch 3B broad-beamed group of this class.
Modernisation: Seacat and 20 mm guns replaced by twin 25 mm mountings. Additional navigation radar mounted on bridge roof.
Operational: Both ships sailed for Pakistan in August and December 1988 respectively. Extensive refits carried out 1991-93.   **VERIFIED**

SHAMSHER   (Scale 1 : 1,200), Ian Sturton

SHAMSHER   3/1997 / 0012864

6 TARIQ (AMAZON) CLASS (TYPE 21) (DDG/DD/FFG/FF)

Name	No	Builders	Laid down		Launched		Commissioned		Recommissioned	
TARIQ (ex-*Ambuscade*)	D 181 (ex-F 172)	Yarrow Shipbuilders, Glasgow	1 Sep	1971	18 Jan	1973	5 Sep	1975	28 July	1993
BABUR (ex-*Amazon*)	D 182 (ex-F 169)	Vosper Thornycroft, Woolston	6 Nov	1969	26 Apr	1971	11 May	1974	30 Sep	1993
KHAIBAR (ex-*Arrow*)	D 183 (ex-F 173)	Yarrow Shipbuilders, Glasgow	28 Sep	1972	5 Feb	1974	29 July	1976	1 Mar	1994
BADR (ex-*Alacrity*)	D 184 (ex-F 174)	Yarrow Shipbuilders, Glasgow	5 Mar	1973	18 Sep	1974	2 July	1977	1 Mar	1994
TIPPU SULTAN (ex-*Avenger*)	D 185 (ex-F 185)	Yarrow Shipbuilders, Glasgow	30 Oct	1974	20 Nov	1975	19 July	1978	23 Sep	1994
SHAHJAHAN (ex-*Active*)	D 186 (ex-F 171)	Vosper Thornycroft, Woolston	23 July	1971	23 Nov	1972	17 June	1977	23 Sep	1994

Displacement, tons: 3,100 standard; 3,700 full load
Dimensions, feet (metres): 384 oa; 360 wl × 41.7 × 19.5
(screws) *(117; 109.7 × 12.7 × 5.9)*
Main machinery: COGOG; 2 RR Olympus TM3B gas turbines;
50,000 hp *(37.3 MW)* sustained; 2 RR Tyne RM1C gas
turbines (cruising); 9,900 hp *(7.4 MW)* sustained; 2 shafts;
cp props
Speed, knots: 30; 18 on Tynes
Range, miles: 4,000 at 17 kt; 1,200 at 30 kt
Complement: 175 (13 officers) (accommodation for 192)

Missiles: SSM: 4 McDonnell Douglas Harpoon 1C ❶ fitted in
D 186, D 184 and D 182.
SAM: China LY 60N sextuple launchers ❷ semi-active radar
homing to 13 km *(7 n miles)* at 2.5 Mach; warhead 33 kg
(D 185, D 181 and D 183).
Guns: 1 Vickers 4.5 in *(114 mm)*/55 Mk 8 ❸; 25 rds/min to
22 km *(11.9 n miles)* anti-surface; 6 km *(3.3 n miles)* anti-
aircraft; weight of shell 21 kg.
4—25 mm/60 (2 twin) ❹; 270 rds/min to 3 km *(1.6 n miles)*;
weight of shell 0.34 kg.

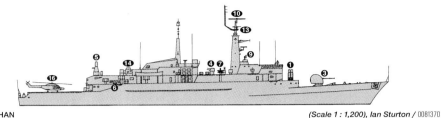

SHAHJAHAN   *(Scale 1 : 1,200), Ian Sturton /* 0081370

Hughes 20 mm Vulcan Phalanx Mk 15 ❺; 3,000 rds/min to
1.5 km.
2 or 4 Oerlikon 20 mm Mk 7A; 1 MSI DS 30B 30 mm/75 and 2
GAM-BO1 20 mm may be fitted in lieu.
Torpedoes: 6—324 mm Plessey STWS Mk 2 (2 triple) tubes ❻
(D 184 and D 186); all being fitted with Bofors Type 43X2
single or quad launchers for Swedish torpedoes in due course.

Countermeasures: Decoys: Graseby Type 182; towed torpedo
decoy.
2 Vickers Corvus 8-tubed trainable launchers ❼ or Mk 36
SRBOC ❽ (D 185, D 181, D 183 and D 182).
ESM: Thomson-CSF DR 3000S; intercept; being fitted.
Combat data systems: CAAIS combat data system with Ferranti
FM 1600B computers (D 186 and D 184). CelsiusTech 9LV
Mk 3 including Link Y (in remainder).
Weapons control: Ferranti WSA-4 digital fire-control system.
CSEE Najir Mk 2 optronic director ❾ fitted in at least three of
the class.
Radars: Air/surface search: Marconi Type 992R ❿; E/F-band.
Replaced by Signaal DA08 ⓫; F-band (D 185, D 181 and
D 183).
Surface search: Kelvin Hughes Type 1007 ⓬ or Type 1006 ⓭
(D 184 and D 186); I-band.
Fire control: 1 Selenia Type 912 (RTN 10X) ⓮; I/J-band.
1 China LL-1 ⓯ (for LY 60N); I/J-band (D 185, D 181 and
D 183).
Sonars: Graseby Type 184P; hull-mounted; active search and
attack; medium frequency.
Kelvin Hughes Type 162M; hull-mounted; bottom
classification; 50 kHz.
Thomson Marconi ATAS; active; medium frequency.

Helicopters: 1 Westland Lynx HAS 3 ⓰.

Programmes: Acquired from the UK in 1993-94. *Tariq* arrived in
Karachi 1 November 1993 and the last pair in January 1995.
These ships replaced the 'Garcia' and 'Brooke' classes and
have been classified as destroyers.
Modernisation: Exocet, torpedo tubes and Lynx helicopter
facilities were all added in RN service, but torpedo tubes were
subsequently removed in all but *Badr* and *Shahjahan* and all
are being retrofitted by Pakistan using Swedish equipment.
Exocet was not transferred and the obsolete Seacat SAM
system has been replaced by Phalanx taken from the Gearings.
Chinese LY 60N, which is a copy of Aspide, has been fitted in
three of the class, Harpoon in three others. New EW equipment
has been installed and ATAS sonar has been acquired (two
sets only). There are still plans to update the hull sonars. Other
equipment upgrades include a DA08 search radar in three of
the class, an optronic director, new 30 mm and 20 mm guns,
SRBOC chaff launchers. An improved combat data system
with a datalink to shore HQ is also fitted in four of the class.
Structure: Due to cracking in the upper deck structure large
strengthening pieces have been fixed to the ships' side at the
top of the steel hull as shown in the illustration. The addition of
permanent ballast to improve stability has increased
displacement by about 350 tons. Further hull modifications to
reduce noise and vibration started in 1988 and completed in all
of the class by 1992.

UPDATED

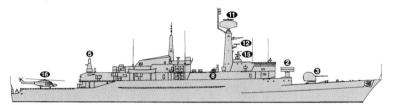

TARIQ   *(Scale 1 : 1,200), Ian Sturton /* 0081369

TARIQ   *12/1999*, Sattler/Steele /* 0081371

TARIQ   *12/1999*, Sattler/Steele /* 0081371

SHIPBORNE AIRCRAFT

Numbers/Type: 3 Westland Lynx HAS 3.
Operational speed: 120 kt *(222 km/h)*.
Service ceiling: 10,000 ft *(3,048 m)*.
Range: 320 n miles *(593 km)*.
Role/Weapon systems: Two delivered August 1994 and one in April 1995. Option on three more. Sensors: Ferranti Sea Spray radar, Orange Crop ESM. Weapons: ASW; two Mk 46 torpedoes. ASV; 2—12.7 mm MG pods; possibly Sea Skua ASM.

UPDATED

LYNX   *8/1994*, Michael Nitz* / 0081373

Numbers/Type: 2/4 Aerospatiale SA 319B/SA 316 Alouette III.
Operational speed: 113 kt *(210 km/h)*.
Service ceiling: 10,500 ft *(3,200 m)*.
Range: 290 n miles *(540 km)*.
Role/Weapon systems: Reconnaissance helicopter. Second four acquired in 1994. Sensors: Weather/search radar MAD (in two). Weapons: ASW; Mk 11 depth charges, one Mk 46 torpedo.

VERIFIED

Numbers/Type: 6 Westland Sea King Mk 45.
Operational speed: 125 kt *(232 km/h)*.
Service ceiling: 10,500 ft *(3,200 m)*.
Range: 630 n miles *(1,165 km)*.
Role/Weapon systems: Sensors: MEL search radar, Marconi Type 2069 dipping sonar (two sets), AQS-928G acoustic processors. Weapons: ASW; two Mk 46 torpedoes; Mk 11 depth charges. ASV; one AM 39 Exocet missile.

UPDATED

SEA KING   *1990*, Pakistan Navy* / 0081374

LAND-BASED MARITIME AIRCRAFT

Note: The Maritime Security Agency operates two Britten-Norman Maritime Defenders. with Bendix RDR 1400C radars.

DEFENDER   *8/1996*, MSA* / 0081375

Numbers/Type: 2 Lockheed P-3C Orion (Update II).
Operational speed: 410 kt *(760 km/h)*.
Service ceiling: 28,300 ft *(8,625 m)*.
Range: 4,000 n miles *(7,410 km)*.
Role/Weapon systems: Order completed in 1991 but held up by the Pressler amendment, until delivery in December 1996. May be used for Elint. Sensors: APS-115 search radar; up to 100 sonobuoys; ASQ 81 MAD; ESM. Weapons: four Mk 46 torpedoes or Mk 11 depth charges for ASW; four Harpoon for ASV (may be carried).

UPDATED

Numbers/Type: 5 Fokker F27-200.
Operational speed: 250 kt *(463 km/h)*.
Service ceiling: 29,500 ft *(8,990 m)*.
Range: 2,700 n miles *(5,000 km)*.
Role/Weapon systems: Acquired in 1994-96 for maritime surveillance. Sensors: APS 504(V)2 radar, Thomson-CSF DR 3000A ESM.

VERIFIED

Numbers/Type: 3 Breguet Atlantic 1.
Operational speed: 355 kt *(658 km/h)*.
Service ceiling: 32,800 ft *(10,000 m)*.
Range: 4,855 n miles *(8,995 km)*.
Role/Weapon systems: Long-range MR/ASW cover for Arabian Sea; ex-French and Dutch stock. Upgraded in 1992-93. Three more acquired in 1994 for spares. Sensors: Thomson-CSF Ocean Master radar, Thomson-CSF DR 3000A ESM, MAD, sonobuoys, Sadang 1C sonobuoy signal processor. Weapons: ASW; nine Mk 46 torpedoes, Mk 11 depth bombs, mines. ASV; two AS 12 or AM 39 Exocet missiles.

UPDATED

Numbers/Type: 12 AMD-BA Mirage III.
Operational speed: 750 kt *(1,390 km/h)*.
Service ceiling: 59,055 ft *(18,000 m)*.
Range: 740 n miles *(1,370 km)*.
Role/Weapon systems: Operated by the Air Force, and all can be used for maritime strike. Sensors: Thomson-CSF radar. Weapons: ASV; two AM 39 Exocet or Harpoon; two 30 mm DEFA.

VERIFIED

PATROL FORCES

Note: Eight Mekat type catamarans ordered in late 1997. These are probably for Customs.

2 + 1 (1) JALALAT CLASS
(FAST ATTACK CRAFT—MISSILE) (PCFG)

Name	No	Builders	Launched		Commissioned	
JALALAT	1022	PN Dockyard, Karachi	17 Nov	1996	15 Aug	1997
SHUJAAT	1024	PN Dockyard, Karachi	6 Mar	1999	30 Sep	2000
—	—	PN Dockyard, Karachi	June	2000	Mar	2001

Displacement, tons: 185 full load
Dimensions, feet (metres): 128 × 22 × 5.7 *(39 × 6.7 × 1.8)*
Main machinery: 2 MTU diesels; 5,984 hp(m) *(4.4 MW)* sustained; 2 shafts
Speed, knots: 23. **Range, miles:** 2,000 at 17 kt
Complement: 31 (3 officers)
Missiles: SSM: 4 China C 802 Saccade (2 twin); active radar homing to 120 km *(66 n miles)* at 0.9 Mach; warhead 165 kg; sea skimmer.
Guns: 2—37 mm/63 (twin); 180 rds/min to 8.5 km *(4.6 n miles)*; weight of shell 1.42 kg.
Countermeasures: Decoys: chaff launcher. ESM.
Radars: Surface search: Kelvin Hughes Type 756; I-band.
Fire control: Type 47G (for gun); Type SR-47 A/R (for SSM); I-band.

Comment: Series production with Chinese assistance to replace deleted 'Hegu' class. Former designation of Jalalat II has been dropped. Same hull as *Larkana*.

UPDATED

JALALAT II   *8/1997, Pakistan Navy* / 0007268

3 HUANGFEN CLASS (FAST ATTACK CRAFT—MISSILE) (PCFG)

DEHSHAT P 1026   **HIMMAT** P 1027   **QUWWAT** P 1028

Displacement, tons: 171 standard; 205 full load
Dimensions, feet (metres): 126.6 × 24.9 × 8.9 *(38.6 × 7.6 × 2.7)*
Main machinery: 3 Type 42-160 diesels; 12,000 hp(m) *(8.8 MW)* sustained; 3 shafts
Speed, knots: 35. **Range, miles:** 800 at 30 kt
Complement: 28
Missiles: SSM: 4 HY-2; active radar or IR homing to 80 km *(43.2 n miles)* at 0.9 Mach; warhead 513 kg.
Guns: 4 Norinco 25 mm/80 (2 twin); 270 rds/min to 3 km *(1.6 n miles)*; weight of shell 0.34 kg.
Radars: Surface search/target indication: Square Tie (352); I-band.

Comment: Transferred from China April 1984. Chinese version of the Soviet 'Osa II' class. Being paid off as 'Jalalat' class enters service.

UPDATED

DEHSHAT   *8/1994*, van Ginderen Collection* / 0081376

1 TOWN CLASS (LARGE PATROL CRAFT) (PC)

Name	No	Builders	Commissioned
RAJSHAHI	P 140	Brooke Marine	1965

Displacement, tons: 115 standard; 143 full load
Dimensions, feet (metres): 107 × 20 × 6.9 (32.6 × 6.1 × 2.1)
Main machinery: 2 MTU 12V 538 diesels; 3,400 hp(m) (2.5 MW); 2 shafts
Speed, knots: 24
Complement: 19
Guns: 2 Bofors 40 mm/70. 2—12.7 mm MGs.
Radars: Surface search: Pot Head; I-band.

Comment: The last survivor in Pakistan of a class of four built by Brooke Marine in 1965. Steel hull and aluminium superstructure.

UPDATED

RAJSHAHI   6/1990*, Pakistan Navy / 0081378

1 LARKANA CLASS (LARGE PATROL CRAFT) (PC)

Name	No	Builders	Commissioned
LARKANA	P 157	Karachi Shipyard	6 June 1994

Displacement, tons: 180 full load
Dimensions, feet (metres): 128 × 22 × 5.4 (39 × 6.7 × 1.7)
Main machinery: 2 MTU diesels; 5,984 hp(m) (4.4 MW) sustained; 2 shafts
Speed, knots: 23. **Range, miles:** 2,000 at 17 kt
Complement: 25 (3 officers)
Guns: 2 Type 76A 37 mm/63 (twin). 4—25 mm/60 (2 twin).
Depth charges: 2 Mk 64 launchers.
Radars: Surface search: Kelvin Hughes Type 756; I-band.

Comment: Ordered in 1991 and started building in October 1992. Has replaced the last of the 'Hainan' class. The missile version on the same hull has taken priority but more may be built.

UPDATED

LARKANA   2/1996* / 0081377

MARITIME SECURITY AGENCY

Notes: (1) All ships are painted white with a distinctive diagonal blue and red band and MSA on each side.
(2) One Britten-Norman Maritime Defender acquired in 1993 and a second in 1994. Based near Karachi with 93 Squadron.

1 GEARING (FRAM 1) CLASS (DD)

Name	No	Builders	Commissioned
NAZIM (ex-*Tughril*)	D 156 (ex-D 167)	Todd Pacific	4 Aug 1945

Displacement, tons: 2,425 standard; 3,500 full load
Dimensions, feet (metres): 390.5 × 41.2 × 19 (119 × 12.6 × 5.8)
Main machinery: 4 Babcock & Wilcox boilers; 600 psi (43.3 kg/cm²); 850°F (454°C); 2 GE turbines; 60,000 hp (45 MW); 2 shafts
Speed, knots: 32. **Range, miles:** 4,500 at 16 kt
Complement: 180 (15 officers)
Guns: 2 US 5 in (127 mm)/38 (twin) Mk 38; 15 rds/min to 17 km (9.3 n miles) anti-surface; 11 km (5.9 n miles); anti-aircraft; weight of shell 25 kg.
Countermeasures: Decoys: 2 Plessey Shield 6-barrelled fixed launchers; chaff and IR flares in distraction, decoy or centroid modes.
Weapons control: Mk 37 for 5 in guns. OE 2 SATCOM.
Radars: Surface search: Raytheon/Sylvania; SPS-10; G-band.
Navigation: KH 1007; I-band.
Fire control: Western Electric Mk 25; I/J-band.

Comment: Transferred from the US on 30 September 1980 to the Navy. Passed on to the MSA in 1998 and renamed. This is the third Gearing to be renamed *Nazim*, the previous pair having been sunk as targets. All weapon systems removed except the main gun. Serves as the MSA Flagship.

UPDATED

NAZIM   6/1999*, Maritime Security Agency / 0081379

2 SHANGHAI II CLASS (FAST ATTACK CRAFT—GUN) (PCF)

SABQAT P 1066   **RAFAQAT** P 1068

Displacement, tons: 131 full load
Dimensions, feet (metres): 127.3 × 17.7 × 5.6 (38.8 × 5.4 × 1.7)
Main machinery: 2 Type L12-180 diesels; 2,400 hp(m) (1.76 MW) (forward); 2 Type 12-D-6 diesels; 1,820 hp(m) (1.34 MW) (aft); 4 shafts
Speed, knots: 30. **Range, miles:** 700 at 16.5 kt
Complement: 34
Guns: 4—37 mm/63 (2 twin). 4—25 mm/80 (2 twin).
Depth charges: 2 projectors; 8 weapons.
Mines: Fitted with mine rails for approx 10 mines.
Radars: Surface search: Anritsu ARC-32A; I-band.

Comment: Four of the class were transferred from the Navy in 1986 and two more in 1998. The last pair were then replaced by naval craft. All were originally acquired from China 1972-1976.

UPDATED

SABQAT   6/1999*, Maritime Security Agency / 0081381

4 BARKAT CLASS (OPV)

Name	No	Builders	Commissioned
BARKAT	1060 (ex-P 60)	China Shipbuilding Corp	29 Dec 1989
REHMAT	1061 (ex-P 61)	China Shipbuilding Corp	29 Dec 1989
NUSRAT	1062 (ex-P 62)	China Shipbuilding Corp	13 June 1990
VEHDAT	1063 (ex-P 63)	China Shipbuilding Corp	13 June 1990

Displacement, tons: 435 full load
Dimensions, feet (metres): 190.3 × 24.9 × 7.5 (58 × 7.6 × 2.3)
Main machinery: 4 MTU 16V 396 TB93 diesels; 8,720 hp(m) (6.4 MW) sustained; 4 shafts
Speed, knots: 27. **Range, miles:** 1,500 at 12 kt
Complement: 50 (5 officers)
Guns: 2—37 mm/63 (twin). 4—25 mm/60 (2 twin).
Radars: Surface search: 2 Anritsu ARC-32A; I-band.

Comment: Type P58A patrol craft built in China for the MSA. First two arrived in Karachi at the end of January 1990, second pair in August 1990. Some of this type of ship are in service with Chinese paramilitary forces.

UPDATED

VEHDAT   6/1994*, Maritime Security Agency / 0081380

SURVEY SHIPS

Note: In 1997 the Institute of Oceanography asked the Navy to procure an oceanographic ship.

1 SURVEY SHIP (AGS/AGOR)

Name	No	Builders	Launched	Commissioned
BEHR PAIMA	34	Ishikawajima, Japan	7 July 1982	17 Dec 1982

Measurement, tons: 1,183 gross
Dimensions, feet (metres): 200.1 × 38.7 × 12.1 (61 × 11.8 × 3.7)
Main machinery: 2 Daihatsu 6DSM-22 diesels; 2,000 hp(m) (1.47 MW); 2 shafts; cp props; bow thruster
Speed, knots: 13.7. **Range, miles:** 5,400 at 12 kt
Complement: 84 (16 officers)

Comment: Ordered in November 1981. Laid down 16 February 1982. Dynamic positioning system. Has seismic, magnetic and gravity survey equipment. DESO 20 deep echo sounder. There is a second survey ship *Jatli* under civilian control.

UPDATED

BEHR PAIMA   4/1996* / 0081382

MINE WARFARE FORCES

3 MUNSIF (ÉRIDAN) CLASS (MINEHUNTERS) (MHC)

Name	No	Builders	Launched	Commissioned
MUNSIF (ex-*Sagittaire*)	M 166	Lorient Dockyard	9 Nov 1988	27 July 1989
MUHAFIZ	M 163	Lorient Dockyard	8 July 1995	15 May 1996
MUJAHID	M 164	Lorient/Karachi	28 Jan 1997	9 July 1998

Displacement, tons: 562 standard; 595 full load
Dimensions, feet (metres): 168.9 × 29.2 × 9.5 *(51.5 × 8.9 × 2.9)*
Main machinery: 1 Stork Wärtsilä A-RUB 215X-12 diesel; 1,860 hp(m) *(1.37 MW)* sustained; 1 shaft; acbLIPS cp prop; Auxiliary propulsion; 2 motors; 240 hp(m) *(179 kW)*; 2 active rudders; 2 bow thrusters
Speed, knots: 15; 7 on auxiliary propulsion. **Range, miles:** 3,000 at 12 kt
Complement: 46 (5 officers)
Guns: 1 GIAT 20F2 20 mm; 1—12.7 mm MG.
Countermeasures: MCM; 2 PAP 104 Mk 5 systems; mechanical sweep gear. Elesco MKR 400 acoustic sweep; MRK 960 magnetic sweep.
Combat data systems: Thomson-CSF TSM 2061 Mk 2 tactical system in the last pair.
Radars: Navigation: Racal Decca 1229 (M 166) or Kelvin Hughes 1007; I-band.
Sonars: Thomson Sintra DUBM 21B or 21D (163 and 164); hull-mounted; active; high frequency; 100 kHz (±10 kHz).
Thomson Sintra TSM 2054 MCM towed array may be included.

Comment: Contract signed with France 17 January 1992. The first recommissioned into the Pakistan Navy on 24 September 1992 after active service in the Gulf with the French Navy in 1991. Sailed for Pakistan in November 1992. The second was delivered in April 1996. The last one was transferred to Karachi by transporter ship in April 1995 with a final package following in November 1995. ***UPDATED***

MUNSIF   *9/1992*, B Sullivan / 0081383

AUXILIARIES

Note: Two oil barges *Janbaz* and *Kalmat* are not naval.

1 FUQING CLASS (AOR)

Name	No	Builders	Commissioned
NASR (ex-*X-350*)	A 47	Dalian Shipyard	27 Aug 1987

Displacement, tons: 7,500 standard; 21,750 full load
Dimensions, feet (metres): 561 × 71.5 × 30.8 *(171 × 21.8 × 9.4)*
Main machinery: 1 Sulzer 8RLB66 diesel; 13,000 hp(m) *(9.56 MW)*; 1 shaft
Speed, knots: 18. **Range, miles:** 18,000 at 14 kt
Complement: 130 (during visit to Australia in October 1988 carried 373 (23 officers) including 100 cadets)
Cargo capacity: 10,550 tons fuel; 1,000 tons dieso; 200 tons feed water; 200 tons drinking water
Guns: 1 GE/GD Vulcan Phalanx CIWS. 2—37 mm. 2—12.7 mm MGs.
Countermeasures: Decoys: SRBOC Mk 36 chaff launcher.
Radars: Navigation: 1 Kelvin Hughes 1007; 1 SPS 66; I-band.
Helicopters: 1 SA 319B Alouette III.

Comment: Similar to Chinese ships of the same class. Two replenishment at sea positions on each side for liquids and one for solids. Phalanx fitted on the hangar roof in 1995. ***UPDATED***

NASR   *12/1999*, Sattler/Steele / 0081386

2 COASTAL TANKERS (AOTL)

Name	No	Builders	Commissioned
GWADAR	A 49	Karachi Shipyard	1984
KALMAT	A 21	Karachi Shipyard	29 Aug 1992

Measurement, tons: 831 grt
Dimensions, feet (metres): 206 × 37.1 × 9.8 *(62.8 × 11.3 × 3)*
Main machinery: 1 Sulzer diesel; 550 hp(m) *(404 kW)*; 1 shaft
Speed, knots: 10
Complement: 25
Cargo capacity: 340 m³ fuel or water

Comment: Second of class launched 6 June 1991. ***UPDATED***

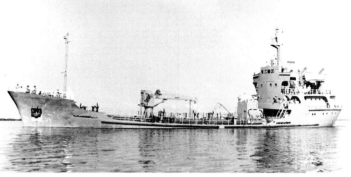

GWADAR   *3/1996*, Pakistan Navy / 0081384

1 POOLSTER CLASS (AOR)

Name	No	Builders	Commissioned	Recommissioned
MOAWIN	A 20	Rotterdamse	10 Sep 1964	28 July 1994
(ex-*Poolster*)	(ex-A 835)	Droogdok Mij		

Displacement, tons: 16,800 full load
Measurement, tons: 10,000 dwt
Dimensions, feet (metres): 552.2 × 66.6 × 26.9 *(168.3 × 20.3 × 8.2)*
Main machinery: 2 boilers; 2 turbines; 22,000 hp(m) *(16.2 MW)*; 1 shaft
Speed, knots: 21
Complement: 200 (17 officers)
Cargo capacity: 10,300 tons including 8-9,000 tons oil fuel
Guns: 1 GE/GD 6-barrelled Vulcan Phalanx Mk 15 or 2 Oerlikon 20 mm.
Countermeasures: Decoys: SRBOC Mk 36 chaff launcher.
Radars: Air/surface search: Racal Decca 2459; F/I-band.
Navigation: Racal Decca TM 1229C; I-band.
Sonars: Signaal CWE 10; hull-mounted; active search; medium frequency.
Helicopters: 1 Sea King.

Comment: Acquired from the Netherlands Navy. Helicopter deck aft. Funnel heightened by 4.5 m *(14.8 ft)*. Capacity for five Lynx sized helicopters. Two fuelling stations each side for underway replenishment. Phalanx to be fitted in due course.
UPDATED

MOAWIN   *4/1997*, Michael Nitz / 0012886

1 TANKER (AOT)

ATTOCK A 40

Displacement, tons: 1,200 full load
Dimensions, feet (metres): 177.2 × 32.3 × 15.1 *(54 × 9.8 × 4.6)*
Main machinery: 2 diesels; 800 hp(m) *(276 kW)*; 2 shafts
Speed, knots: 8
Complement: 18
Cargo capacity: 550 tons fuel
Guns: 2 Oerlikon 20 mm.

Comment: Built in Italy in 1957.

UPDATED

ATTOCK   *6/1995* / 0081385

COAST GUARD AND CUSTOMS SERVICE

Note: Unlike the Maritime Security Agency which comes under the Defence Ministry, the official Coast Guard was set up in 1985 and is manned by the Army and answerable to the Ministry of the Interior. Customs craft are naval manned. Vessels include *Saif*, a 20 m Swallow craft built in South Korea in 1986, and about 20 Crestitalia 16 m craft most of which belong to Customs. All are armed with MGs.

TUGS

Note: There are three more general purpose tugs plus two harbour tugs *Goga* and *Jhara*, and two more started building at Karachi in 1998.

3 COASTAL TUGS (YTB)

Name	No	Builders	Commissioned
BHOLU	A 44	Giessendam Shipyard, Netherlands	Apr 1991
GAMA	A 45	Giessendam Shipyard, Netherlands	Apr 1991
JANBAZ	—	Karachi Shipyard	Sep 1990

Displacement, tons: 265 full load
Dimensions, feet (metres): 85.3 × 22.3 × 9.5 *(26 × 6.8 × 2.9)*
Main machinery: 2 Cummins KTA38-M diesels; 1,836 hp *(1.26 MW)* sustained; 2 shafts
Speed, knots: 12
Complement: 6

Comment: First pair ordered from Damen in 1990. Have replaced the two old tugs of the same name and pennant numbers.

VERIFIED

BHOLU   *1991, Pakistan Navy*

PALAU

General

Self-governing Republic in free association with the USA. Member of the South Pacific Forum.

Coast Guard

An obsolete ex-US Coast Guard 'Cape' class craft was replaced by a 'Pacific Forum' class in mid-1996.

PATROL FORCES

1 PACIFIC FORUM PATROL CLASS (PC)

Name	No	Builders	Commissioned
PRESIDENT H I REMELIIK	001	Transfield Shipbuilding	May 1996

Displacement, tons: 162 full load
Dimensions, feet (metres): 103.3 × 26.6 × 6.9 *(31.5 × 8.1 × 2.1)*
Main machinery: 2 Caterpillar 3516 TA diesels; 4,400 hp *(3.28 MW)* sustained; 2 shafts
Speed, knots: 20. **Range, miles:** 2,500 at 12 kt
Complement: 17 (3 officers)
Guns: 1—12.7 mm MG.
Radars: Surface search: Furuno 1011; I-band.

Comment: Ordered in 1995. This was the twenty-first hull in the Pacific Patrol programme.
UPDATED

PRESIDENT H I REMELIIK
5/1996*, Transfield Shipbuilding / 0081387

PANAMA

Headquarters Appointments

Director General of the Coast Guard:
  Captain José Antonio Isaza Ros

General

A force which became a naval service in 1983 and is split between both coasts. Aircraft are all Air Force operated.

Personnel

(a) 2000: 620
(b) Voluntary service

Bases

Isla Flamenco (HQ) (Punta Brujas — HQ designate), Quebrada de Piedra, Largo Remo (under construction), Punta Cocos (air), Kuna Yala (air) (under construction)

Mercantile Marine

Lloyd's Register of Shipping:
  6,143 vessels of 105,248,069 tons gross

DELETIONS

Patrol Forces

1997   *Barracuda, Centollo, Chepillo, Castillo*

Auxiliaries

1998   *Puerto Escoces, Rolando Martinez, Libertad*

PATROL FORCES

2 VOSPER TYPE (COASTAL PATROL CRAFT) (PC)

Name	No	Builders	Commissioned
PANQUIACO	P 301 (ex-GC 10)	Vospers, Portsmouth	July 1971
LIGIA ELENA	P 302 (ex-GC 11)	Vospers, Portsmouth	July 1971

Displacement, tons: 96 standard; 145 full load
Dimensions, feet (metres): 103 × 18.9 × 5.8 *(31.4 × 5.8 × 1.8)*
Main machinery: 2 Detroit diesels; 5,000 hp *(3.73 MW)*; 2 shafts
Speed, knots: 18. **Range, miles:** 1,500 at 14 kt
Complement: 17 (3 officers)
Guns: 2—7.62 mm MGs.
Radars: Surface search: Raytheon R-81; I-band.

Comment: *Panquiaco* launched on 22 July 1970, *Ligia Elena* on 25 August 1970. Hull of welded mild steel and upperworks of welded or buck-bolted aluminium alloy. Vosper fin stabiliser equipment. P 302 was sunk in December 1989, but subsequently recovered. Both vessels had major repairs in the Coco Solo shipyard from September 1992. This included new engines, a new radar and replacement guns. Pacific Flotilla.
VERIFIED

PANQUIACO   *11/1998, Panama Coast Guard /* 0052684

1 COASTAL PATROL CRAFT (PC)

Name	No	Builders	Commissioned
NAOS (ex-*Erline*)	P 303 (ex-RV 821)	Equitable, NO	Dec 1964

Displacement, tons: 120 full load
Dimensions, feet (metres): 105 × 24.9 × 6.9 *(32 × 7.6 × 2.1)*
Main machinery: 2 Caterpillar diesels; 2 shafts
Speed, knots: 10. **Range, miles:** 550 at 8 kt
Complement: 11 (2 officers)
Guns: 2—7.62 mm MGs.
Radars: Surface search: Raymarx 2600; I-band.

Comment: Served as a support/research craft at the US Underwater Systems establishment at Bermuda. Transferred from USA in July 1992 and recommissioned in December 1992. Refitted in 1997 with new engines. Pacific Flotilla. **VERIFIED**

NAOS   *12/1998, Panama Coast Guard /* 0052685

1 COASTAL PATROL CRAFT (PC)

FLAMENCO (ex-*Scheherazade*) P 304 (ex-WB 831)

Displacement, tons: 220 full load
Dimensions, feet (metres): 105 × 25 × 6.9 *(32 × 7.6 × 2.1)*
Main machinery: 2 Caterpillar diesels; 2 shafts
Speed, knots: 10
Complement: 11 (2 officers)
Guns: 2—7.62 mm MGs.
Radars: Surface search: Furuno FCR 1411; I-band.

Comment: Built in 1963. Transferred from USA 22 July 1992 and commissioned in December 1992. Former US wooden hulled COOP craft. Refitted in Panama in 1994. **VERIFIED**

FLAMENCO   *12/1998, Panama Coast Guard /* 0052686

1 COASTAL PATROL CRAFT (PC)

ESCUDO DE VERAGUAS (ex-*Aun Sin Nombre*, ex-*Kathyuska Kelly*) P 305 (ex-P 206)

Displacement, tons: 158 full load
Dimensions, feet (metres): 90.5 × 24.1 × 6.1 *(27.6 × 7.3 × 1.9)*
Main machinery: 2 Detroit 12V-71 diesels; 840 hp *(627 kW)* sustained; 2 shafts
Speed, knots: 10
Complement: 10 (2 officers)
Guns: 1—12.7 mm MG.
Radars: Surface search: Raytheon; I-band.

Comment: Confiscated drug runner craft taken into service in 1996. Caribbean Flotilla. **VERIFIED**

ESCUDO DE VERAGUAS   *11/1998, Panama Coast Guard /* 0052687

1 SWIFTSHIPS 65 ft TYPE (COASTAL PATROL CRAFT) (PC)

Name	No	Builders	Commissioned
GENERAL ESTEBAN HUERTAS	P 201	Swiftships, Morgan City	July 1982
(ex-*Comandante Torrijos*)	(ex-GC 16)		

Displacement, tons: 35 full load
Dimensions, feet (metres): 65 × 18.5 × 6 *(19.8 × 5.6 × 1.8)*
Main machinery: 2 Detroit 12V-71TA diesels; 840 hp *(627 kW)* sustained; 2 shafts
Speed, knots: 13. **Range, miles:** 500 at 8 kt
Complement: 10 (2 officers)
Guns: 2—7.62 mm MGs.
Radars: Surface search: Raytheon; I-band.

Comment: Aluminium hull. Second of class sunk in 1989. Reverted to its former name in 1996 and was extensively refitted. Caribbean Flotilla. **UPDATED**

GENERAL ESTEBAN HUERTAS   *6/1999*, Panama Coast Guard /* 0084271

1 NEGRITA CLASS (COASTAL PATROL CRAFT) (PC)

CACIQUE NOME (ex-*Negrita*) P 203

Displacement, tons: 68 full load
Dimensions, feet (metres): 80 × 15 × 6 *(24.4 × 4.6 × 1.8)*
Main machinery: 2 Detroit 12V-71 diesels; 840 hp *(627 kW)*; 2 shafts
Speed, knots: 13. **Range, miles:** 250 at 10 kt
Complement: 8 (2 officers)
Guns: 2—7.62 mm MGs.
Radars: Surface search: Raytheon 71; I-band.

Comment: Completely rebuilt in the Coco Solo shipyard and recommissioned 5 May 1993. Pacific Flotilla. **VERIFIED**

CACIQUE NOME   *8/1998, Panama Coast Guard /* 0052688

3 POINT CLASS (COASTAL PATROL CRAFT)

Name	No	Builders	Commissioned
3 DE NOVIEMBRE (ex-*Point Barrow*)	P 204	CG Yard, MD	4 Oct 1964
10 DE NOVIEMBRE (ex-*Point Huron*)	P 206	CG Yard, MD	17 Feb 1967
28 DE NOVIEMBRE (ex-*Point Frances*)	P 207	CG Yard, MD	3 Feb 1967

Displacement, tons: 69 full load
Dimensions, feet (metres): 83 × 17.2 × 5.8 *(25.3 × 5.2 × 1.8)*
Main machinery: 2 Cummins V-12-900M diesels; 1,600 hp *(1.18 MW)*; 2 shafts
Speed, knots: 18. **Range, miles:** 1,500 at 8 kt
Complement: 10 (2 officers)
Guns: 2—7.62 mm MGs.
Radars: Surface search: Raytheon Pathfinder; I-band.

Comment: First one transferred from US Coast Guard 7 June 1991 and recommissioned 10 July 1991. Second pair transferred 22 April 1999. Carry a RIB with a 40 hp engine. Caribbean Flotilla. **UPDATED**

10 DE NOVIEMBRE   *6/1999*, Panama Coast Guard /* 0084272

1 MSB 29 CLASS (COASTAL PATROL CRAFT) (PC)

Name	No	Builders	Commissioned
PUNTAMALA (ex-*MSB 29*)	P 205	John Trumpy, Annapolis	1954

Displacement, tons: 80 full load
Dimensions, feet (metres): 87 × 19 × 5.5 *(26.5 × 5.8 × 1.7)*
Main machinery: 2 Packard 2D850 diesels; 600 hp *(448 kW)*; 2 shafts
Speed, knots: 11. **Range, miles:** 1,500 at 10 kt
Complement: 11 (2 officers)
Guns: 2—7.62 mm MGs.
Radars: Surface search: Raytheon 1900; I-band.

Comment: Built in 1954 as an enlarged MSB 5 design. Paid off in 1992 and transferred from USA to Panama in March 1993 after refit. Wooden hull. Recommissioned in May 1993. Used only as a patrol craft. Pacific Flotilla.

UPDATED

PUNTAMALA   *8/1994*, Panama Coast Guard /* 0081507

3 COASTAL PATROL CRAFT (PC)

CHIRIQUI P 841   **VERAGUAS** P 842   **BOCAS DEL TORO** P 843

Displacement, tons: 46 full load
Dimensions, feet (metres): 73.8 × 17.3 × 2.9 *(22.5 × 5.3 × 0.9)*
Main machinery: 3 Detroit 12V 71 diesels; 1,260 hp *(940 kW)* sustained; 3 shafts
Speed, knots: 20
Complement: 7 (1 officer)
Guns: 2—7.62 mm MGs.
Radars: Surface search: Furuno 1411; I-band.

Comment: Transferred from the US in March 1998. Used for drug prevention patrols in both Flotillas.

VERIFIED

CHIRIQUI   *11/1998, Panama Coast Guard /* 0052689

2 HARBOUR PATROL CRAFT (PB)

PANAMA P 101   **CALAMAR** P 102 (ex-PC 3602)

Displacement, tons: 11 full load
Dimensions, feet (metres): 36 × 13 × 3 *(11 × 4 × 0.9)*
Main machinery: 1 Detroit 6-71T diesel; 300 hp *(224 kW)*; 1 shaft
Speed, knots: 15. **Range, miles:** 160 at 12 kt
Complement: 5
Guns: 1—7.62 mm MG.

Comment: P 102 in service from December 1992, P 101 from February 1998. Pacific flotilla.

VERIFIED

CALAMAR   *8/1996, Panama Coast Guard*

11 FAST PATROL BOATS (PBF)

BPC 2201-2205   **BPC 1801-1806**

Dimensions, feet (metres): 22.3 × 7.5 × 2 *(6.8 × 2.3 × 0.6)*
Main machinery: 2 Johnson outboards; 280 hp *(209 kW)*
Speed, knots: 35
Complement: 4
Guns: 1—7.62 mm MG.

Comment: BPC 2201-2205 are Boston Whaler 'Pirana' class acquired between June 1991 and October 1992. *BPC 1801-1806* are slightly smaller at 6 m and were acquired November 1995 to December 1998.

VERIFIED

BPC 2203   *11/1998, Panama Coast Guard /* 0052690

12 FAST PATROL BOATS (PBF)

BPC 3201-3210   **BPC 2902-2903**

Dimensions, feet (metres): 33.5 × 7.5 × 2 *(10.2 × 2.3 × 0.6)*
Main machinery: 2 Yamaha outboards; 400 hp(m) *(294 kW)*
Speed, knots: 35
Complement: 4
Guns: 1—7.62 mm MG.

Comment: Acquired between June 1995 and October 1998. First ten are in Caribbean Flotilla, the other pair in the Pacific.

VERIFIED

BPC 3201   *11/1998, Panama Coast Guard /* 0052691

AUXILIARIES

2 MSB 5 CLASS (YAG)

NOMBRE DE DIOS (ex-*MSB 25*) L 16   **SANTA CLARA** (ex-*MSB 30*) L 15

Displacement, tons: 44 full load
Dimensions, feet (metres): 57.2 × 15.5 × 4 *(17.4 × 4.7 × 1.2)*
Main machinery: 2 Detroit diesels; 600 hp *(448 kW)*; 2 shafts
Speed, knots: 12
Complement: 6 (1 officer)
Guns: 1—7.62 mm MG.
Radars: Navigation: Raytheon Raystar; I-band.

Comment: Built between 1952 and 1956. Former US minesweeping boats. Served in the canal area until 1992 and were transferred from USA to Panama in December 1992 after refits. Wooden hulls, new engines. Used as logistic craft. A third of class has been scrapped. Pacific flotilla.

UPDATED

SANTA CLARA   *8/1994*, Panama Coast Guard /* 0081508

5 SUPPORT CRAFT (YAG)

BUCARO (ex-*Orient Express*) BA 051   **DORADO I** BA 055   **ANGUILLA** BA 057
ORCA BA 054   **DORADO II** BA 056

Comment: *Bucaro* is a 19 m single masted yacht confiscated in 1996 and used for training. *Orca* acquired in 1997 and used as a SAR craft in the Pacific Flotilla. *Dorado I* and *II* acquired in February 1998 and are used as 40 kt supply craft. *Anguilla* is a confiscated 50 kt power boat taken into service in November 1998.

VERIFIED

DORADO I   *12/1998, Panama Coast Guard /* 0052692

1 LOGISTIC CRAFT (YAG)

TRINIDAD (ex-*Endeavour*) L 11

Displacement, tons: 120 full load
Dimensions, feet (metres): 75 × 14 × 7 *(22.9 × 4.3 × 2.1)*
Main machinery: 1 Caterpillar diesel; 365 hp *(270 kW)*; 1 shaft
Speed, knots: 12
Complement: 7 (1 officer)
Radars: Navigation: Furuno; I-band.

Comment: Acquired in September 1991. Pacific flotilla.

VERIFIED

LAND-BASED MARITIME AIRCRAFT

Numbers/Type: 3 CASA C-212 Aviocar.
Operational speed: 190 kt *(353 km/h)*.
Service ceiling: 24,000 ft *(7,315 m)*.
Range: 1,650 n miles *(3,055 km)*.
Role/Weapon systems: Air Force operated coastal patrol aircraft for EEZ protection and anti-smuggling duties. Sensors: APS-128 radar, limited ESM. Weapons: ASW; two Mk 44/46 torpedoes. ASV; two rocket or machine gun pods.

VERIFIED

Numbers/Type: 1 Pilatus Britten-Norman Islander.
Operational speed: 150 kt *(280 km/h)*.
Service ceiling: 18,900 ft *(5,760 m)*.
Range: 1,500 n miles *(2,775 km)*.
Role/Weapon systems: Air Force operated coastal surveillance duties. Sensors: Search radar. Weapons: Unarmed.

VERIFIED

PAPUA NEW GUINEA

General	Bases	Prefix to Ships' Names	Mercantile Marine
The Navy is known as the Defence Force Maritime Element.	Port Moresby (HQ PNGDF and PNGDF Landing Craft Base); Lombrum (Manus) Buka and Alotau (one Pacific Forum Patrol Craft at each)	HMPNGS	*Lloyd's Register of Shipping:* 105 vessels of 64,842 tons gross

PATROL FORCES

Note: Plans to transfer three 'Vosper' class from Singapore in 1997, and three ex-German Type 331B minesweepers in 1998, have been postponed indefinitely.

4 PACIFIC FORUM TYPE (LARGE PATROL CRAFT) (PC)

Name	No	Builders	Commissioned
TARANGAU	01	Australian Shipbuilding Industries	16 May 1987
DREGER	02	Australian Shipbuilding Industries	31 Oct 1987
SEEADLER	03	Australian Shipbuilding Industries	29 Oct 1988
BASILISK	04	Australian Shipbuilding Industries	1 July 1989

Displacement, tons: 162 full load
Dimensions, feet (metres): 103.3 × 26.6 × 6.9 *(31.5 × 8.1 × 2.1)*
Main machinery: 2 Caterpillar 3516TA diesels; 4,400 hp *(3.3 MW)* sustained; 2 shafts
Speed, knots: 20. **Range, miles:** 2,500 at 12 kt
Complement: 17 (3 officers)
Guns: 1 Oerlikon GAM-BO1 20 mm. 2—7.62 mm MGs.
Radars: Surface search: Furuno 1011; I-band.

Comment: Contract awarded in 1985 to Australian Shipbuilding Industries (Hamilton Hill, West Australia) under Australian Defence co-operation. These are the first, third, sixth and seventh of the class and some of the few to be armed. All upgraded in Australia with new radars and navigation support systems in 1997/98.

UPDATED

SEEADLER   *8/1999*, John Mortimer /* 0081509

AUXILIARIES

2 LANDING CRAFT (LSM)

Name	No	Builders	Commissioned
SALAMAUA	31	Walkers Ltd, Maryborough	19 Oct 1973
BUNA	32	Walkers Ltd, Maryborough	7 Dec 1973

Displacement, tons: 310 light; 503 full load
Dimensions, feet (metres): 146 × 33 × 6.5 *(44.5 × 10.1 × 1.9)*
Main machinery: 2 GM diesels; 2 shafts
Speed, knots: 10. **Range, miles:** 3,000 at 10 kt
Complement: 15 (2 officers)
Military lift: 160 tons
Guns: 2—12.7 mm MGs.
Radars: Navigation: Racal Decca RM 916; I-band.

Comment: Transferred from Australia in 1975. Underwent extensive refits 1985-86. Both are still active.

UPDATED

SALAMAUA   *12/1990*, James Goldrick /* 0081510

LAND-BASED MARITIME AIRCRAFT

Numbers/Type: 6 GAF N22B Missionmaster.
Operational speed: 168 kt *(311 km/h)*.
Service ceiling: 21,000 ft *(6,400 m)*.
Range: 730 n miles *(1,352 km)*.
Role/Weapon systems: Coastal surveillance and transport duties. Sensors: Search radar. Weapons: Unarmed.

VERIFIED

PARAGUAY
ARMADA NACIONAL

Headquarters Appointments

Chief of Defence Staff:
   Admiral José Ramón Ocampos Alfaro
Commander-in-Chief of the Navy:
   Vice Admiral Miguel Angel Candia Fleitas
Chief of Staff:
   Rear Admiral R Benitez

Personnel

(a) 2000: 3,200 including Coast Guard and 450 marines and
      50 naval air
(b) 12 months' national service to be abolished by 2001

Training

Specialist training is done with Argentina (Operation Sirena),
Brazil (Operation Ninfa) and USA (Operation Unitas).

Bases

Base Naval de Bahia Negra (BNBN) (on upper Paraguay river)
Base Aeronaval de Pozo Hondo (BANPH) (on upper Pilcomayo
river)
Base Naval de Saltos del Guaira (BNSG) (on upper Parana river)
Base Naval de Ciudad del Este (BNCE) (on Parana river)
Base Naval de Encarnacion (BNE) (on Parana river)
Base Naval de Ita-Piru (BNIP) (on Parana river)

Marine Corps

BIM 1 (COMIM). BIM 2 (Bahia Negra). BIM 3 (Cuartel Gral del
Comando de la Armada). BIM 4 (Prefectura Gral Naval). BIM 5
(BNBN - BANPH - BNIP). BIM 8 (BNSG - BNCE - BNE).

Coast Guard

Prefectura General Naval

Mercantile Marine

Lloyd's Register of Shipping:
   45 vessels of 43,361 tons gross

DELETIONS

Auxiliaries

1997   *Boqueron*, BT1, BT2

PATROL FORCES

Note: There are also two 16.5 m GRP craft *Yhaguy* and *Tebicuary* fast patrol boats acquired as gifts
from Taiwan in June 1999.

2 RIVER DEFENCE VESSELS (PGR)

Name	No	Builders	Commissioned
PARAGUAY	C 1	Odero, Genoa	May 1931
HUMAITA	C 2	Odero, Genoa	May 1931

Displacement, tons: 636 standard; 865 full load
Dimensions, feet (metres): 231 × 35 × 5.3 *(70 × 10.7 × 1.7)*
Main machinery: 2 boilers; 2 Parsons turbines; 3,800 hp *(2.83 MW)*; 2 shafts
Speed, knots: 17. **Range, miles:** 1,700 at 16 kt
Complement: 86
Guns: 4—4.7 in *(120 mm)* (2 twin). 2 or 3—3 in *(76 mm)*. 2—40 mm. 2—20 mm.
Mines: 6.
Radars: Navigation *(Paraguay)*; I-band.

Comment: Both refitted in 1975. Have 0.5 in side armour plating and 0.3 in on deck. Still in
   restricted operational service with boiler problems. There are plans to re-engine with diesels.
   Both ships have two twin 120 mm guns. *Paraguay* has three single 76 mm and two single
   40 mm, while *Humaita* has two single 76 mm, a twin 40 mm in B position and two single
   Oerlikons.

UPDATED

PARAGUAY   *12/1997*, Hartmut Ehlers / 0081511

HUMAITA   *9/1993* / 0081512

1 ITAIPÚ CLASS (RIVER DEFENCE VESSEL) (PGR)

Name	No	Builders	Commissioned
ITAIPÚ	P 05 (ex-P 2)	Arsenal de Marinha, Rio de Janeiro	2 Apr 1985

Displacement, tons: 365 full load
Dimensions, feet (metres): 151.9 × 27.9 × 4.6 *(46.3 × 8.5 × 1.4)*
Main machinery: 2 MAN V6V16/18TL diesels; 1,920 hp(m) *(1.41 MW)*; 2 shafts
Speed, knots: 14. **Range, miles:** 6,000 at 12 kt
Complement: 40 (9 officers) plus 30 marines
Guns: 1 Bofors 40 mm/60. 2—81 mm mortars. 6—12.7 mm MGs.
Radars: Navigation: I-band.
Helicopters: Platform for 1 HB 350B or equivalent.

Comment: Ordered late 1982. Launched 16 March 1984. Same as Brazilian 'Roraima' class. Has
   some hospital facilities.

UPDATED

ITAIPÚ   *6/1990*, Paraguay Navy / 0081513

2 BOUCHARD CLASS (PATROL SHIPS) (PGR)

Name	No	Builders	Commissioned
NANAWA	P 02 (ex-P 01, ex-M 1)	Rio Santiago Naval Yard	27 Jan 1937
(ex-*Bouchard* M 7)			
TENIENTE FARINA	P 04 (ex-P 03, ex-M 3)	Rio Santiago Naval Yard	1 July 1939
(ex-*Py* M 10)			

Displacement, tons: 450 standard; 620 normal; 650 full load
Dimensions, feet (metres): 197 × 24 × 8.5 *(60 × 7.3 × 2.6)*
Main machinery: 2 sets MAN 2-stroke diesels; 2,000 hp(m) *(1.47 MW)*; 2 shafts
Speed, knots: 16. **Range, miles:** 6,000 at 12 kt
Complement: 70
Guns: 4 Bofors 40 mm/60 (2 twin). 2—12.7 mm MGs.
Mines: 1 rail.
Radars: Navigation: I-band.

Comment: Former Argentinian minesweepers of the 'Bouchard' class. Launched on 20 March
   1936 and 31 March 1938 respectively. Transferred from the Argentine Navy to the Paraguayan
   Navy; *Nanawa* recommissioned 14 March 1964; *Teniente Farina* 6 May 1968.   *UPDATED*

NANAWA   *6/1990*, Paraguay Navy / 0081514

1 RIVER PATROL CRAFT (PGR)

Name	No	Builders	Commissioned
CAPITAN CABRAL	P 01 (ex-P 04, ex-A 1)	Werf-Conrad, Haarlem	1908
(ex-*Triunfo*)			

Displacement, tons: 180 standard; 206 full load
Dimensions, feet (metres): 107.2 × 23.5 × 5.8 *(32.7 × 7.2 × 1.7)*
Main machinery: 1 Caterpillar 3408 diesel; 360 hp *(269 kW)*; 1 shaft
Speed, knots: 9
Complement: 25
Guns: 1 Bofors 40 mm/60. 2 Oerlikon 20 mm. 2—12.7 mm MGs.
Radars: Navigation: I-band.

Comment: Former tug. Launched in 1907. Still in excellent condition. Vickers guns were replaced
   and a diesel engine fitted by Arsenal de Marina in 1984.   *UPDATED*

CAPITAN CABRAL   *6/1990*, Paraguay Navy / 0081515

2 + (4) MODIFIED HAI OU CLASS (PCF)

CAPITAN ORTIZ P 06   **TENIENTE ROBLES** P 07

Displacement, tons: 47 full load
Dimensions, feet (metres): 70.8 × 18 × 3.3 *(21.6 × 5.5 × 1)*
Main machinery: 2 MTU 12V 331 TC82 diesels; 2,605 hp(m) *(1.92 MW)* sustained; 2 shafts
Speed, knots: 36. **Range, miles:** 700 at 32 kt
Complement: 10
Guns: 1—20 mm Type 75. 2—12.7 mm MGs.
Radars: Surface search: I-band.

Comment: Developed by Taiwan from 'Dvora' class hulls and presented as a gift in 1996. It is possible that one of these craft was one of the two original Dvora hulls acquired by Taiwan. More of the class may be acquired as Taiwan decommissions them.

UPDATED

TENIENTE ROBLES   *12/1997*, Hartmut Ehlers /* 0012869

5 RODMAN 55 CLASS (PB)

Displacement, tons: 16 full load
Dimensions, feet (metres): 54.1 × 12.5 × 2.3 *(16.5 × 3.8 × 0.7)*
Main machinery: 2 MAN diesels; 850 hp(m) *(625 kW)*; 2 water-jets
Speed, knots: 25
Complement: 6
Guns: 1—7.62 mm MG.
Radars: Surface search: I-band.

Comment: Ordered from Rodman Polyships, Vigo, Spain on 19 September 1995. These craft are in service with the Spanish Police but with more high-powered engines. There were also plans for two Rodman 101s but the contract was suspended.

UPDATED

RODMAN 55 (Spanish colours)   *8/1998*, A Sharma /* 0081516

13 RIVER PATROL CRAFT (PBR)

P 08-P 20

Displacement, tons: 18 full load
Dimensions, feet (metres): 48.2 × 10.2 × 4.6 *(14.7 × 3.1 × 1.4)*
Main machinery: 2 GM 6-71 diesels; 340 hp *(254 kW)*; 2 shafts
Speed, knots: 12. **Range, miles:** 240 at 12 kt
Complement: 4
Guns: 2—12.7 mm MGs.

Comment: Built by Arsenal de Marina, Paraguay. One launched in 1989, then two each year up to 1995.

UPDATED

P 08   *3/1991*, Paraguay Navy /* 0081517

2 TYPE 701 CLASS (PBR)

LP 101   LP 102

Displacement, tons: 15 full load
Dimensions, feet (metres): 42.5 × 12.8 × 3 *(13 × 3.9 × 0.9)*
Main machinery: 2 diesels; 500 hp *(373 kW)*; 2 shafts
Speed, knots: 20
Complement: 7
Guns: 2—12.7 mm MGs.

Comment: Built by Sewart in 1970. Paid off in 1995 but now back in service with new pennant numbers. There may be a third of class.

UPDATED

LP 102   *12/1997*, Hartmut Ehlers /* 0012870

LAND-BASED MARITIME AIRCRAFT

Note: In addition there are eight Cessnas and 2 Bell 47G helicopters.

Numbers/Type: 2 Helibras HB 350B Esquilo.
Operational speed: 125 kt *(232 km/h)*.
Service ceiling: 10,000 ft *(3,050 m)*.
Range: 390 n miles *(720 km)*.
Role/Weapon systems: Support helicopter for riverine patrol craft. Delivered in July 1985.

VERIFIED

AUXILIARIES

Note: In addition there is a Presidential Yacht *3 de Febrero*, a survey vessel *Lancha Ecografa* of 50 tons, and three LCVPs, *EDVP 1-3*.

3 DE FEBERO   *12/1997*, Hartmut Ehlers /* 0012871

1 TRAINING SHIP/TRANSPORT (AK/AX)

Name	No	Builders	Commissioned
GUARANI	—	Tomas Ruiz de Velasco, Bilbao	Feb 1968

Measurement, tons: 714 gross; 1,047 dwt
Dimensions, feet (metres): 240.3 × 36.3 × 11.9 *(73.6 × 11.1 × 3.7)*
Main machinery: 1 MWM diesel; 1,300 hp(m) *(956 kW)*; 1 shaft
Speed, knots: 13
Complement: 21
Cargo capacity: 1,000 tons

Comment: Refitted in 1975 after a serious fire in the previous year off the coast of France. Used to spend most of her time acting as a freighter on the Asunción-Europe run, commercially operated for the Paraguayan Navy. Since 1991 she has only been used for river service and for training cruises Asunción-Montevideo.

UPDATED

GUARANI   *12/1997*, Hartmut Ehlers /* 0012872

1 RIVER TRANSPORT (AKL)

TENIENTE HERREROS (ex-*Presidente Stroessner*) T 1

Displacement, tons: 420 full load
Dimensions, feet (metres): 124 × 29.5 × 7.2 *(37.8 × 9 × 2.2)*
Main machinery: 2 MWM diesels; 330 hp(m) *(243 kW)*
Speed, knots: 10
Complement: 10
Cargo capacity: 120 tons

Comment: Built by Arsenal de Marina in 1964.

TUGS

5 COASTAL TUGS (YTM/YTL)

R 2   R 4   R 6   R 7   ANGOSTURA R 5

Displacement, tons: 70 full load
Dimensions, feet (metres): 65 × 16.4 × 7.5 *(19.8 × 5 × 2.3)*
Main machinery: 1 Caterpillar 3408 diesel; 360 hp *(269 kW)*; 1 shaft
Speed, knots: 9
UPDATED   **Complement:** 5

Comment: Harbour tugs transferred under MAP in the 1960s and 1970s. Details given are for *R 4* and *R 5*. The others are smaller 20 ton vessels.

UPDATED

TENIENTE HERREROS   *5/1991*, Paraguay Navy /* 0081518

ANGOSTURA   *4/1992*, Paraguay Navy /* 0081519

PERU
ARMADA PERÚANA

Headquarters Appointments

Commander of the Navy:
  Admiral Antonio Ibarcena Amico
Chief of the Naval Staff:
  Vice Admiral Moisés Woll Torres
Chief of Naval Operations:
  Vice Admiral Luis Jaureguy
Flag Officer Commanding Marines:
  Rear Admiral Carlos Sanguinetti

Personnel

(a) 2000: 27,000 (2,450 officers)
(b) 2 years' national service

Marines

There is one brigade of 5,000 men, armed with amphibious vehicles (twin Oerlikon, 88 mm rocket launchers) and armoured cars. Headquarters at Ancón. First Battalion—Guarnicion de Marina; Second Battalion—Guardia Chalaca; Third Battalion—Punta Malpelo; Fourth Battalion—Ucayali.

Bases and Organisation

There are Five Naval Zones: 1st Piura, 2nd Callao, 3rd Arequipa, 4th Puerto Maldonado, 5th Iquitos
Pacific Naval Force (HQ Callao)
Amazon River Force (HQ Iquitos)
Lake Titicaca Patrol Force (HQ at Puno)
Callao—Main naval base; dockyard with shipbuilding capacity, 1 dry dock, 3 floating docks, 1 floating crane; training schools
Iquitos—River base for Amazon Flotilla; small building yard, repair facilities, floating dock
La Punta (naval academy), San Lorenzo (submarine base), Chimbote, Paita, Talara, Puno (Lake Titicaca), Madre de Dios (river base), Piura, El Salto, Bayovar, Pimental, Pacasmayo, Salaverry, Mollendo, Matarani, Ilo, Puerto Maldonado, Inapari, Pucallpa and El Estrecho.

Prefix to Ships' Names

BAP (Buque Armada Peruana). PC (Coastal Patrol). PL (Lake Patrol). PP (Port Patrol). PF (River Patrol).

Coast Guard

A separate service set up in 1975 with a number of light forces transferred from the Navy.

Mercantile Marine

Lloyd's Register of Shipping:
  724 vessels of 284,858 tons gross

DELETIONS

Destroyers

1999 *Ferré*

Auxiliaries

1997 *Matarini, Bayovar*
1999 *Zorritos*

PENNANT LIST

Submarines

SS 31	Casma
SS 32	Antofagasta
SS 33	Pisagua
SS 34	Chipana
SS 35	Islay
SS 36	Arica
SS 41	Dos de Mayo
SS 42	Abtao

Cruisers

CLM 81	Almirante Grau
CH 84	Aguirre (reserve)

Frigates

FM 51	Carvajal
FM 52	Villavicencio
FM 53	Montero
FM 54	Mariategui

Patrol Forces

CF 11	Amazonas
CF 12	Loreto
CF 13	Marañon
CF 14	Ucayali
CM 21	Velarde
CM 22	Santillana
CM 23	De los Heros
CM 24	Herrera
CM 25	Larrea
CM 26	Sanchez Carrillon

Survey Ships

AH 171	Carrasco
AH 172	Stiglich
AH 174	Macha
AH 175	Carrillo
AH 176	Melo

Amphibious Forces

DT 141	Paita
DT 142	Pisco
DT 144	Eten

Auxiliaries

ACA 110	Mantilla
ACA 111	Calayeras
ACP 118	Noguera
ACP 119	Gauden
ARB 120	Mejia
ARB 121	Huerta
ARB 123	Guardian Rios
ARB 126	Duenas
ARB 128	Olaya
ARB 129	Selendon
ATC 131	Ilo
ATP 152	Talara
ATP 157	Supe
ATP 159	Lobitos
ABH 302	Morona
ABH 306	Puno
ART 322	San Lorenzo
ABA 332	Barcasa Cisterna de Agua

SUBMARINES

6 CASMA (TYPE 209) CLASS (TYPE 1200) (SSK)

Name	No	Builders	Laid down	Launched	Commissioned
CASMA	SS 31	Howaldtswerke, Kiel	15 July 1977	31 Aug 1979	19 Dec 1980
ANTOFAGASTA	SS 32	Howaldtswerke, Kiel	3 Oct 1977	19 Dec 1979	20 Feb 1981
PISAGUA	SS 33	Howaldtswerke, Kiel	15 Aug 1978	19 Oct 1980	12 July 1983
CHIPANA	SS 34	Howaldtswerke, Kiel	1 Nov 1978	19 May 1981	20 Sep 1982
ISLAY	SS 35	Howaldtswerke, Kiel	15 Mar 1971	11 Oct 1973	29 Aug 1974
ARICA	SS 36	Howaldtswerke, Kiel	1 Nov 1971	5 Apr 1974	21 Jan 1975

Displacement, tons: 1,185 surfaced; 1,290 dived
Dimensions, feet (metres): 183.7 × 20.3 × 17.9
(56 × 6.2 × 5.5)
Main machinery: Diesel-electric; 4 MTU 12V 493 AZ80 GA31L diesels; 2,400 hp(m) *(1.76 MW)* sustained; 4 Siemens alternators; 1.7 MW; 1 Siemens motor; 4,600 hp(m) *(3.38 MW)* sustained; 1 shaft
Speed, knots: 11 surfaced/snorting; 21.5 dived
Range, miles: 240 at 8 kt
Complement: 35 (5 officers) *(Islay* and *Arica)*; 31 (others)

Torpedoes: 8—21 in *(533 mm)* tubes. 14 Whitehead A184; dual purpose; wire-guided; active/passive homing to 25 km *(13.7 n miles)* at 24 kt; 17 km *(9.2 n miles)* at 38 kt; warhead 250 kg. Swim-out discharge.
Countermeasures: ESM: Radar warning.
Weapons control: Sepa Mk 3 or Signaal Sinbad M8/24 *(Casma* and *Antofagasta).*
Radars: Surface search: Thomson-CSF Calypso; I-band.
Sonars: Atlas Elektronik CSU 3; active/passive search and attack; medium/high frequency.
Thomson Sintra DUUX 2C or Atlas Elektronik PRS 3; passive ranging.

CHIPANA 10/1997 / 0052694

Programmes: First pair ordered 1969. Two further boats ordered 12 August 1976 and two more ordered 21 March 1977. Designed by Ingenieurkontor, Lübeck for construction by Howaldtswerke, Kiel and sale by Ferrostaal, Essen all acting as a consortium.
Modernisation: Sepa Mk 3 fire control fitted progressively from 1986. A184 torpedoes supplied from 1990 to replace SST-4.
Structure: A single-hull design with two ballast tanks and forward and after trim tanks. Fitted with snort and remote machinery control. The single screw is slow revving, very high-capacity batteries with GRP lead-acid cells and battery cooling—by Wilh Hagen and VARTA. Fitted with two periscopes and Omega receiver. Foreplanes retract. Diving depth, 250 m *(820 ft).*
Operational: Endurance, 50 days. Four are in service, two in refit or reserve at any one time.

VERIFIED

2 ABTAO CLASS (SS)

Name	No	Builders	Laid down	Launched	Commissioned
DOS DE MAYO (ex-*Lobo*)	SS 41	General Dynamics (Electric Boat), Groton, Connecticut	12 May 1952	6 Feb 1954	14 June 1954
ABTAO (ex-*Tiburon*)	SS 42	General Dynamics (Electric Boat), Groton, Connecticut	12 May 1952	27 Oct 1953	20 Feb 1954

Displacement, tons: 825 standard; 1,400 dived
Dimensions, feet (metres): 243 × 22 × 14
(74.1 × 6.7 × 4.3)
Main machinery: Diesel-electric; 2 GM 12-278A diesels; 2,400 hp *(1.8 MW)*; 2 motors; 2 shafts
Speed, knots: 16 surfaced; 10 dived
Range, miles: 5,000 at 10 kt surfaced
Complement: 40

Guns: 1—5 in *(127 mm)*/25; manual control; line of sight range.
Torpedoes: 6—21 in *(533 mm)* (4 bow, 2 stern) tubes. Westinghouse Mk 37 Type; typically active/passive homing to 8 km *(4.4 n miles)* at 24 kt; warhead 150 kg.
Countermeasures: ESM: Radar warning.
Radars: Navigation: SS-2A; I-band.
Sonars: Thomson Sintra Eledone 1102/5; active/passive intercept search and attack; medium frequency.

Programmes: They are of modified US 'Mackerel' class. One deleted in 1990 and a second in 1993.

ABTAO 1/1999* / 0081520

Modernisation: New batteries shipped in 1981. Since then engineering and electrical systems have been modernised and Eledone sonar fitted.
Operational: Used for training; reduced diving depth and seldom go to sea, but are still in full commission.

UPDATED

CRUISERS

ALMIRANTE GRAU 4/1997*, Peruvian Navy / 0084273

1 DE RUYTER CLASS (CG/CLM)

Name	No	Builders	Laid down	Launched	Commissioned
ALMIRANTE GRAU (ex-*De Ruyter*)	CLM 81	Wilton-Fijenoord, Schiedam	5 Sep 1939	24 Dec 1944	18 Nov 1953

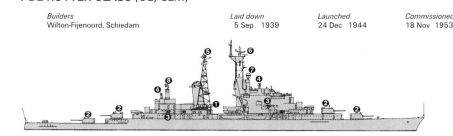

Displacement, tons: 12,165 full load
Dimensions, feet (metres): 624.5 × 56.7 × 22
(190.3 × 17.3 × 6.7)
Main machinery: 4 Werkspoor-Yarrow boilers; 2 De Schelde-
Parsons turbines; 85,000 hp *(62.5 MW)*; 2 shafts
Speed, knots: 32. **Range, miles:** 7,000 at 12 kt
Complement: 953 (49 officers)

Missiles: SSM: 8 OTO Melara/Matra Otomat Mk 2 (TG 1) ❶;
active radar homing to 80 km *(43.2 n miles)* at 0.9 Mach;
warhead 210 kg; sea-skimmer for last 4 km *(2.2 n miles)*.
Guns: 8 Bofors 6 in *(152 mm)*/53 (4 twin) ❷; 15 rds/min to
26 km *(14 n miles)*; weight of shell 46 kg.
8 Bofors 40 mm/70 ❸; 300 rds/min to 12 km *(6.6 n miles)*;
weight of shell 0.96 kg.
Countermeasures: Decoys: 2 Dagaie and 1 Sagaie chaff
launchers.
Combat data systems: Signaal Sewaco PE SATCOM.
Weapons control: 2 Lirod 8 optronic directors ❹.
Radars: Air search: Signaal LW08 ❺; D-band.
Surface search/target indication: Signaal DA08 ❻; E/F-band.
Navigation: Racal Decca 1226; I-band.
Fire control: Signaal WM25 ❼; I/J-band (for 6 in guns); range
46 km *(25 n miles)*.
Signaal STIR ❽; I/J/K-band; range 140 km *(76 n miles)* for 1 m²
target.

Programmes: Transferred by purchase from Netherlands
7 March 1973 and commissioned to Peruvian Navy 23 May
1973.
Modernisation: Taken in hand for a two and a half year
modernisation at Amsterdam Dry Dock Co in March 1985. This
was to include reconditioning of mechanical and electrical
engineering systems, fitting of SSM and SAM, replacement of
electronics and fitting of one CSEE Sagaie and two Dagaie
launchers. In 1986 financial constraints limited the work but
much had been done to update sensors and fire-control
equipment. Sailed for Peru 23 January 1988 without her
secondary gun armament, which was completed at Sima Yard,
Callao. The plan is to retrofit Exocets from the 'Daring' class to
replace the Otomat launchers, but there seems to be no
funding available. Sonar has been removed. SATCOM fitted
aft.

UPDATED

ALMIRANTE GRAU *(Scale 1 : 1,800)*, Ian Sturton / 0081522

ALMIRANTE GRAU
1/1999 * / 0081521

1 DE RUYTER CLASS (CH)

Name	No	Builders	Laid down	Launched	Commissioned
AGUIRRE (ex-*De Zeven Provincien*)	CH 84	Rotterdamse Droogdok Maatschappij	19 May 1939	22 Aug 1950	17 Dec 1953

Displacement, tons: 12,250 full load
Dimensions, feet (metres): 609 × 56.7 × 22
(185.6 × 17.3 × 6.7)
Flight deck, feet (metres): 115 × 56 *(35 × 17)*
Main machinery: 4 Werkspoor-Yarrow boilers; 2 De Schelde-
Parsons turbines; 85,000 hp *(62.5 MW)*; 2 shafts
Speed, knots: 32. **Range, miles:** 7,000 at 12 kt
Complement: 953 (49 officers)

Guns: 4 Bofors 6 in *(152 mm)*/53 (2 twin) ❶; 15 rds/min to
26 km *(14 n miles)*; weight of shell 46 kg.
6 Bofors 57 mm/60 (3 twin) ❷; 130 rds/min to 14 km *(7.7 n
miles)*; weight of shell 2.6 kg.
4 Bofors 40 mm/70 ❸; 300 rds/min to 12 km *(6.6 n miles)*;
weight of shell 0.96 kg.
Weapons control: 1 Lirod 8 optronic director ❹.
Radars: Air search: Signaal LW02 ❺; D-band.
Surface search/target indication: Signaal DA02 ❻; E/F-band.
Surface search: Signaal ZW03; I/J-band.
Fire control: 3 Signaal M45 ❼; I/J-band. One Signaal M25 ❽;
I/J-band.
Navigation: 2 Racal Decca 1226; I-band.

AGUIRRE *(Scale 1 : 1,800)*, Ian Sturton / 0012876

Helicopters: 3 Agusta ASH-3D Sea Kings ❾.

Programmes: Bought from the Netherlands in August 1976 and
taken in hand by her original builders for conversion to a
helicopter cruiser. Conversion completed 31 October 1977. In
1986 *Aguirre* assumed the name *Almirante Grau* and the
former *Almirante Grau* became *Proyecto 01*, while refitting in
Amsterdam. Former names were resumed as soon as *Grau*
started sea trials in November 1987.

Modernisation: Boilers retubed and underwent major refit
completing in mid-1986. Sonar has been removed.
Structure: Terrier missile system replaced by hangar (67 × 54 ft)
and flight deck built from midships to the stern. Second
landing spot on hangar roof.
Operational: Helicopters carry AM 39 Exocet missiles. In reserve
in 1992-93 with only a caretaker crew, but was back in the
operational Fleet in 1994. In reserve again in late 1999 and
may be scrapped.

UPDATED

AGUIRRE
1/1999 * / 0081523

FRIGATES

4 CARVAJAL (LUPO) CLASS (FFG)

Name	No	Builders	Laid down	Launched	Commissioned
CARVAJAL	FM 51	Fincantieri, Riva Trigoso	8 Aug 1974	17 Nov 1976	5 Feb 1979
VILLAVICENCIO	FM 52	Fincantieri, Riva Trigoso	6 Oct 1976	7 Feb 1978	25 June 1979
MONTERO	FM 53	SIMA, Callao	Oct 1978	8 Oct 1982	25 July 1984
MARIATEGUI	FM 54	SIMA, Callao	1979	8 Oct 1984	10 Oct 1987

Displacement, tons: 2,208 standard; 2,500 full load
Dimensions, feet (metres): 371.3 × 37.1 × 12.1
    (113.2 × 11.3 × 3.7)
Main machinery: CODOG; 2 GE/Fiat LM 2500 gas turbines;
    50,000 hp *(37.3 MW)* sustained; 2 GMT A 230.20 M diesels;
    8,000 hp(m) *(5.88 MW)* sustained; 2 shafts; acbLIPS cp props
Speed, knots: 35. **Range, miles:** 3,450 at 20.5 kt
Complement: 185 (20 officers)

Missiles: SSM: 8 OTO Melara/Matra Otomat Mk 2 (TG 1) ❶;
    active radar homing to 80 km *(43.2 n miles)* at 0.9 Mach;
    warhead 210 kg; sea-skimmer for last 4 km *(2.2 n miles)*.
SAM: Selenia Elsag Albatros octuple launcher ❷; 8 Aspide; semi-
    active radar homing to 13 km *(7 n miles)* at 2.5 Mach; height
    envelope 15-5,000 m *(49.2-16,405 ft)*; warhead 30 kg.
    An SA-N-10 launcher (MPG-86) may be fitted on the stern.
Guns: 1 OTO Melara 5 in *(127 mm)*/54 ❸; 45 rds/min to 16 km
    (8.7 n miles); weight of shell 32 kg.
    4 Breda 40 mm/70 (2 twin) ❹; 300 rds/min to 12.5 km *(6.8 n
    miles)*; weight of shell 0.96 kg.
Torpedoes: 6—324 mm ILAS (2 triple) tubes ❺. Whitehead
    A244; anti-submarine; active/passive homing to 7 km *(3.8 n
    miles)* at 33 kt; warhead 34 kg (shaped charge).
Countermeasures: Decoys: 2 Breda 105 mm SCLAR 20-
    barrelled trainable launchers ❻; multipurpose; chaff to 5 km
    (2.7 n miles); illuminants to 12 km *(6.6 n miles)*; HE
    bombardment.
ESM: Elettronica Lambda; intercept.

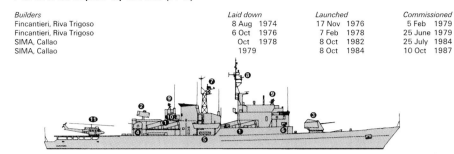

MONTERO   *(Scale 1 : 1,200), Ian Sturton*

Combat data systems: Selenia IPN-10 action data automation.
Weapons control: 2 Elsag Mk 10 Argo with NA-21 directors.
    Dardo system for 40 mm.
Radars: Air search: Selenia RAN 10S ❼; E/F-band.
Surface search: Selenia RAN 11LX ❽; D/I-band.
Navigation: SMA 3 RM 20R; I-band.
Fire control: 2 RTN 10X ❾; I/J-band.
    2 RTN 20X ❿; I/J-band (for Dardo).
Sonars: EDO 610E; hull-mounted; active search and attack;
    medium frequency.

Helicopters: 1 Agusta AB 212ASW ⓫.

Programmes: *Montero* and *Mariategui* were the first major
    warships to be built on the Pacific Coast of South America,
    although some equipment was provided by Fincantieri.

Modernisation: Three of the class were scheduled to have main
    engines changed in 1997-98 but this has not been confirmed.
    It is reported that Russian MGP-8 SAM launchers have been
    fitted on the stern.
Structure: In the design for the pair built by Servicios Industriales
    de la Marina, Callao (SIMA) the two 40 mm guns are mounted
    higher and reloading of the Albatros is by hand not power. Also
    the hangar is fixed and the flight deck does not come flush to
    the stern of the ship.
Operational: Helicopter provides an over-the-horizon targeting
    capability for SSM. HIFR facilities fitted in 1989 allow refuelling
    of Sea King helicopters.

UPDATED

CARVAJAL   *1/1999* * / 0081525

MONTERO   *7/1998* / 0052695

SHIPBORNE AIRCRAFT

Note: There are also four Bell 206B training, and two Bell 412EP SAR helicopters.

Numbers/Type: 6 Agusta AB 212ASW.
Operational speed: 106 kt *(196 km/h)*.
Service ceiling: 14,200 ft *(4,330 m)*.
Range: 230 n miles *(425 km)*.
Role/Weapon systems: ASW and surface search helicopter for smaller escorts. Sensors: Selenia search radar, Bendix ASQ-18 dipping sonar, ECM. Weapons: ASW; two Mk 46 or 244/S torpedoes or depth bombs.

UPDATED

AB 212   *6/1994*, Peruvian Navy /* 0081527

Numbers/Type: 3 Agusta-Sikorsky ASH-3D Sea King.
Operational speed: 120 kt *(222 km/h)*.
Service ceiling: 12,200 ft *(3,720 m)*.
Range: 630 n miles *(1,165 km)*.
Role/Weapon systems: ASW helicopter; embarked in *Aguirre*. Sensors: Selenia search radar, Bendix ASQ-18 dipping sonar, sonobuoys. Weapons: ASW; four Mk 46 or 244/S torpedoes or depth bombs or mines. ASV; two AM 39 Exocet missiles.

UPDATED

SEA KING   *8/1994*, Peruvian Navy /* 0081526

LAND-BASED MARITIME AIRCRAFT (FRONT LINE)

Notes: (1) There are also three Mi-8T transport helicopters.
(2) Three Fokker F-27-200 are used by the Coast Guard for maritime surveillance.

Numbers/Type: 5 Beechcraft Super King Air 200T.
Operational speed: 282 kt *(523 km/h)*.
Service ceiling: 35,000 ft *(10,670 m)*.
Range: 2,030 n miles *(3,756 km)*.
Role/Weapon systems: Coastal surveillance and EEZ patrol duties. Sensors: Search radar, cameras. Weapons: Unarmed.

VERIFIED

PATROL FORCES

6 VELARDE (PR-72P) CLASS
(FAST ATTACK CRAFT—MISSILE) (CM/PCFG)

Name	No	Builders	Launched		Commissioned	
VELARDE	CM 21	SFCN, France	16 Sep	1978	25 July	1980
SANTILLANA	CM 22	SFCN, France	11 Sep	1978	25 July	1980
DE LOS HEROS	CM 23	SFCN, France	20 May	1979	17 Nov	1980
HERRERA	CM 24	SFCN, France	16 Feb	1979	10 Feb	1981
LARREA	CM 25	SFCN, France	12 May	1979	16 June	1981
SANCHEZ CARRILLON	CM 26	SFCN, France	28 June	1979	14 Sep	1981

Displacement, tons: 470 standard; 560 full load
Dimensions, feet (metres): 210 × 27.4 × 5.2 *(64 × 8.4 × 2.6)*
Main machinery: 4 SACM AGO 240 V16 M7 or 4 MTU 12V 595 diesels; 22,200 hp(m) *(16.32 MW)* sustained; 4 shafts
Speed, knots: 37. **Range, miles:** 2,500 at 16 kt
Complement: 36 plus 10 spare

Missiles: SSM; 4 Aerospatiale MM 38 Exocet; inertial cruise; active radar homing to 42 km *(23 n miles)* at 0.9 Mach; warhead 165 kg; sea-skimmer.
SAM: An SA-N-10 launcher (MPG-86) may be fitted on the stern.
Guns: 1 OTO Melara 3 in *(76 mm)*/62; 85 rds/min to 16 km *(8.7 n miles)*; weight of shell 6 kg.
2 Breda 40 mm/70 (twin); 300 rds/min to 12.5 km *(6.8 n miles)*; weight of shell 0.96 kg.
Countermeasures: ESM: Thomson-CSF DR 2000; intercept.
Weapons control: CSEE Panda director. Vega system.
Radars: Surface search: Thomson-CSF Triton; G-band; range 33 km *(18 n miles)* for 2 m² target.
Navigation: Racal Decca 1226; I-band.
Fire control: Thomson-CSF/Castor II; I/J-band; range 15 km *(8 n miles)* for 1 m² target.

Programmes: Ordered late 1976. Hulls of *Velarde, De Los Heros, Larrea* subcontracted to Lorient Naval Yard, the others being built at Villeneuve-la-Garenne. Classified as corvettes.
Modernisation: A Russian SA-N-10 launcher may be carried. Two of the class being re-engined in 2000. Remainder to follow.

UPDATED

SANCHEZ CARRILLON   *1/1999* /* 0081528

2 MARAÑON CLASS (RIVER GUNBOATS) (CF/PGR)

Name	No	Builders	Commissioned	
MARAÑON	CF 13 (ex-CF 401)	John I Thornycroft & Co Ltd	July	1951
UCAYALI	CF 14 (ex-CF 402)	John I Thornycroft & Co Ltd	June	1951

Displacement, tons: 365 full load
Dimensions, feet (metres): 154.8 wl × 32 × 4 *(47.2 × 9.7 × 1.2)*
Main machinery: 2 British Polar M 441 diesels; 800 hp *(597 kW)*; 2 shafts
Speed, knots: 12. **Range, miles:** 6,000 at 10 kt
Complement: 40 (4 officers)
Guns: 2—3 in *(76 mm)*/50. 3 Bofors 40 mm/60. 4 Oerlikon 20 mm (2 twin).

Comment: Ordered early in 1950 and launched 7 March and 23 April 1951 respectively. Employed on police duties in Upper Amazon. Superstructure of aluminium alloy. Based at Iquitos.

UPDATED

MARAÑON   *1995*, Peruvian Navy /* 0081529

UCAYALI   *1993*, Peruvian Navy /* 0081530

2 LORETO CLASS (RIVER GUNBOATS) (CF/PGR)

Name	No	Builders	Commissioned
AMAZONAS	CF 11 (ex-CF 403)	Electric Boat Co, Groton	1935
LORETO	CF 12 (ex-CF 404)	Electric Boat Co, Groton	1935

Displacement, tons: 250 standard
Dimensions, feet (metres): 145 × 22 × 4 *(44.2 × 6.7 × 1.2)*
Main machinery: 2 diesels; 750 hp(m) *(551 kW)*; 2 shafts
Speed, knots: 15. **Range, miles:** 4,000 at 10 kt
Complement: 35 (5 officers)
Guns: 1—3 in *(76 mm)*. 3 Bofors 40 mm/60. 1 Oerlikon 20 mm.

Comment: Launched in 1934. In Upper Amazon Flotilla, based at Iquitos. The after 3 in gun has been replaced by a third 40 mm.
UPDATED

LORETO   *4/1997*, Peruvian Navy /* 0012880

AMPHIBIOUS FORCES

Note: There are plans for up to three 300 ft LSLs to be locally built when funds are available.

3 PAITA (TERREBONNE PARISH) CLASS (LST)

Name	No	Builders	Commissioned
PAITA (ex-*Walworth County* LST 1164)	DT 141	Ingalls SB	26 Oct 1953
PISCO (ex-*Waldo County* LST 1163)	DT 142	Ingalls SB	17 Sep 1953
ETEN (ex-*Traverse County* LST 1160)	DT 144	Bath Iron Works	19 Dec 1953

Displacement, tons: 2,590 standard; 5,800 full load
Dimensions, feet (metres): 384 × 55 × 17 *(117.1 × 16.8 × 5.2)*
Main machinery: 4 GM 16-278A diesels; 6,000 hp *(4.48 MW)*; 2 shafts
Speed, knots: 15. **Range, miles:** 15,000 at 9 kt
Complement: 116
Military lift: 2,000 tons; 395 troops
Guns: 5 Bofors 40 mm/60 (2 twin, 1 single).
Radars: Navigation: I-band.

Comment: Four transferred from USA on loan 7 August 1984, recommissioned 4 March 1985. Have small helicopter platform. Original 3 in guns replaced by 40 mm. Lease extended by grant aid in August 1989, again in August 1994, and again in April 1999. All are active. Fourth of class *Callao* cannibalised for spares after *Pisco* was returned to service.
UPDATED

ETEN   *1/1999* /* 0081531

SURVEY AND RESEARCH SHIPS

Note: AH 177 is a 5 ton fast survey craft.

1 INSHORE SURVEY CRAFT (AGSC/EH)

Name	No	Builders	Commissioned
MACHA	EH 174	SIMA, Chimbote	Apr 1982

Displacement, tons: 53 full load
Dimensions, feet (metres): 64.9 × 17.1 × 3 *(19.8 × 5.2 × 0.9)*
Main machinery: 2 diesels; 2 shafts
Speed, knots: 13
Complement: 8 (2 officers)

Comment: Side scan sonar for plotting bottom contours. EH (Embarcacion Hidrográfica).
VERIFIED

1 DOKKUM CLASS (AGSC/AH)

Name	No	Builders	Commissioned
CARRASCO (ex-*Abcoude*)	AH 171 (ex-M 810)	Smulders, Schiedam	18 May 1956

Displacement, tons: 373 standard; 453 full load
Dimensions, feet (metres): 152.9 × 28.9 × 7.5 *(46.6 × 8.8 × 2.3)*
Main machinery: 2 Fijenoord MAN V64 diesels; 2,500 hp(m) *(1.84 MW)*; 2 shafts
Speed, knots: 16. **Range, miles:** 2,500 at 10 kt
Complement: 27-36
Radars: Navigation: Racal Decca TM 1229C; I-band.

Comment: Service with the Netherlands Navy as a minesweeper included modernisation in the mid-1970s and a life prolonging refit in the late 1980s. *Carrasco* placed in reserve in 1993 and transferred to Peru 16 July 1994. The ship has been acquired for hydrographic duties. Two more were planned to follow in mid-1996 but the transfer was cancelled.
UPDATED

CARRASCO   *10/1994*, Peruvian Navy /* 0081532

2 VAN STRAELEN CLASS (AGSC/AH)

Name	No	Builders	Commissioned
CARRILLO (ex-*van Hamel*)	AH 175	De Vries, Amsterdam	14 Oct 1960
MELO (ex-*van der Wel*)	AH 176	De Vries, Amsterdam	6 Oct 1961

Displacement, tons: 169 full load
Dimensions, feet (metres): 108.6 × 18.2 × 5.2 *(33.1 × 5.6 × 1.6)*
Main machinery: 2 GM diesels; 1,100 hp(m) *(808 kW)* sustained; 2 shafts
Speed, knots: 13
Complement: 17 (2 officers)

Comment: Both built as inshore minesweepers. Acquired 23 February 1985 for conversion with new engines and survey equipment.
VERIFIED

MELO   *1989, Peruvian Navy*

2 RIVER VESSELS (AGSC/ABH)

Name	No	Builders	Commissioned
MORONA	ABH 302	Sima, Iquitos	1976
STIGLICH	AH 172	McLaren, Niteroi	1981

Displacement, tons: 230 full load
Dimensions, feet (metres): 112.2 × 25.9 × 5.6 *(34.2 × 7.9 × 1.7)*
Main machinery: 2 Detroit 12V-71TA diesels; 840 hp *(616 kW)* sustained; 2 shafts
Speed, knots: 15
Complement: 28 (2 officers)

Comment: *Stiglich* is based at Iquitos for survey work on the Upper Amazon. *Morona* is used as a hospital craft and has a red cross on her superstructure.
UPDATED

STIGLICH   *6/1999*, Peruvian Navy /* 0081533

AUXILIARIES

Notes: (1) All auxiliaries may be used for commercial purposes if not required for naval use.
(2) There is also an ex-US auxiliary fuel lighter *Supe* ATP 157 acquired in 1996.

1 ILO CLASS (TRANSPORT) (AF/ATC)

Name	No	Builders	Commissioned
ILO	ATC 131	SIMA, Callao	15 Dec 1971

Displacement, tons: 18,400 full load
Measurement, tons: 13,000 dwt
Dimensions, feet (metres): 507.7 × 67.3 × 27.2 *(154.8 × 20.5 × 8.3)*
Main machinery: 1 Burmeister & Wain 6K47 diesel; 11,600 hp(m) *(8.53 MW)*; 1 shaft
Speed, knots: 15.6
Complement: 60
Cargo capacity: 13,000 tons

Comment: Sister ship *Rimac* is on permanent commercial charter.

UPDATED

ILO   6/1997* / 0012882

1 TALARA CLASS (REPLENISHMENT TANKER) (AOT/ATP)

Name	No	Builders	Launched	Commissioned
TALARA	ATP 152	SIMA, Callao	9 July 1976	23 Jan 1978

Displacement, tons: 30,000 full load
Measurement, tons: 25,000 dwt
Dimensions, feet (metres): 561.5 × 82 × 31.2 *(171.2 × 25 × 9.5)*
Main machinery: 2 Burmeister & Wain 6K47EF diesels; 12,000 hp(m) *(8.82 MW)*; 1 shaft
Speed, knots: 15.5
Cargo capacity: 35,662 m³

Comment: Capable of underway replenishment at sea from the stern. *Bayovar* of this class, launched 18 July 1977 having been originally ordered by Petroperu (State Oil Company) and transferred to the Navy while building. Sold back to Petroperu in 1979 and renamed *Pavayacu*. A third, *Trompeteros*, of this class has been built for Petroperu.

UPDATED

TALARA   4/1997*, Peruvian Navy / 0012883

1 SEALIFT CLASS (TANKER) (AOT)

Name	No	Builders	Commissioned
LOBITOS (ex-*Sealift Caribbean*)	ATP 159 (ex-*TAOT 174*)	Bath Iron Works	10 Feb 1975

Displacement, tons: 34,100 full load
Measurement, tons: 27,648 dwt; 15,979 grt
Dimensions, feet (metres): 587 × 84 × 34.6 *(178.9 × 24.6 × 10.6)*
Main machinery: 2 Colt Pielstick 14 PC-2V400 diesels; 14,000 hp(m) *(10.3 MW)* sustained; 1 shaft; cp prop; bow thruster
Speed, knots: 15. **Range, miles:** 7,500 at 15 kt
Complement: 24
Cargo capacity: 185,000 barrels oil

Comment: Originally built for the US Military Sealift Command. Returned to owners in 1995 and acquired by Peru in 1998. No RAS gear.

VERIFIED

LOBITOS (US colours)   1987, Giorgio Arra / 0052696

5 HARBOUR TANKERS (FUEL/WATER) (YW/YO)

MANTILLA ACA 110 (ex-*YW 122*)   **NOGUERA** ACP 118 (ex-*YO 221*)   **ABA 332** (ex-*113*)
CALAYERAS ACA 111 (ex-*YW 128*)   **GAUDEN** ACP 119 (ex-*YO 171*)

Displacement, tons: 1,235 full load
Dimensions, feet (metres): 174 × 32 × 13.3 *(52.3 × 9.8 × 4.1)*
Main machinery: 1 GM diesel; 560 hp *(418 kW)*; 1 shaft
Speed, knots: 8
Complement: 23
Cargo capacity: 200,000 gallons
Radars: Navigation: Raytheon; I-band.

Comment: Details given are for first four. *YW 122* transferred from USA to Peru July 1963; *YO 221* January 1975; *YO 171* 20 January 1981; *YW 128* 26 January 1985. *ABA 332* is a water tanker built in Peru in 1972, capacity 300 tons.

VERIFIED

GAUDEN   1988, Peruvian Navy

1 TORPEDO RECOVERY VESSEL (TRV/ART)

Name	No	Builders	Commissioned
SAN LORENZO	ART 322	Lürssen/Burmeister	1 Dec 1981

Displacement, tons: 58 standard; 65 full load
Dimensions, feet (metres): 82.7 × 18.4 × 5.6 *(25.2 × 5.6 × 1.7)*
Main machinery: 2 MTU 8V 396 TC82 diesels; 1,740 hp(m) *(1.28 MW)* sustained; 2 shafts
Speed, knots: 19. **Range, miles:** 500 at 15 kt
Complement: 9

Comment: Can carry four long or eight short torpedoes.

UPDATED

SAN LORENZO   9/1981, Lürssen Werft / 0081534

1 LAKE HOSPITAL CRAFT (ABH)

Name	No	Builders	Commissioned
PUNO (ex-*Yapura*)	ABH 306	J Watt Co, Thames Iron Works	18 May 1872

Comment: Stationed on Lake Titicaca. 500 grt and has a diesel engine. Sadly the second of the class was finally paid off in 1990.

UPDATED

PUNO   8/1999*, A Campanera i Rovira / 0081535

5 FLOATING DOCKS

ADF 104   106-109

Displacement, tons: 1,900 *(106)*; 5,200 *(107)*; 600 *(108)*; 18,000 *(109)*; 4,500 tons *(104)*

Comment: *106* (ex-US *AFDL 33*) transferred 1959; *107* (ex-US *ARD 8*) transferred 1961; *108* built in 1951; *109* built in 1979; *104* built in 1991.

VERIFIED

TUGS

Note: There are also five small harbour tugs *Mejia* ARB 120, *Huertas* ARB 121, *Duenas* ARB 126, *Olaya* ARB 128 and *Selendon* ARB 129.

1 CHEROKEE CLASS (SALVAGE TUG) (ARA/ATF)

Name	No	Builders	Commissioned
GUARDIAN RIOS (ex-*Pinto* ATF 90)	ARB 123	Cramp, Philadelphia, PA	1 Apr 1943

Displacement, tons: 1,640 full load
Dimensions, feet (metres): 205 × 38.5 × 17 *(62.5 × 11.7 × 5.2)*
Main machinery: Diesel-electric; 4 GM 12-278 diesels; 4,400 hp *(3.28 MW)*; 4 generators; 1 motor; 3,000 hp *(2.24 MW)*; 1 shaft
Speed, knots: 16.5. **Range, miles:** 6,500 at 16 kt
Complement: 99

Comment: Transferred from USA on loan in 1960, sold 17 May 1974. Fitted with powerful pumps and other salvage equipment. ***UPDATED***

GUARDIAN RIOS   *1993, Peruvian Navy*

COAST GUARD

Note: Six 'Dauntless' class river patrol craft ordered from SeaArk Marine under the FMS programme. To be delivered in the second half of 2000.

5 RIO CANETE CLASS (LARGE PATROL CRAFT) (PC)

Name	No	Builders	Commissioned
RIO NEPEÑA	PC 243	SIMA, Chimbote	1 Dec 1981
RIO TAMBO	PC 244	SIMA, Chimbote	1982
RIO OCOÑA	PC 245	SIMA, Chimbote	1983
RIO HUARMEY	PC 246	SIMA, Chimbote	1984
RIO ZAÑA	PC 247	SIMA, Chimbote	12 Feb 1985

Displacement, tons: 296 full load
Dimensions, feet (metres): 167 × 24.8 × 5.6 *(50.9 × 7.4 × 1.7)*
Main machinery: 4 Bazán MAN V8V diesels; 5,640 hp(m) *(4.15 MW)*; 2 shafts
Speed, knots: 23. **Range, miles:** 3,050 at 17 kt
Complement: 39 (4 officers)
Guns: 1 Bofors 40 mm/60. 1 Oerlikon 20 mm.
Radars: Surface search: Decca 1226; I-band.

Comment: Have aluminium alloy superstructures. The prototype craft was scrapped in 1990. *Rio Ocoña* completed refit in July 1996 and the rest of the class were refitted at one per year. ***UPDATED***

RIO TAMBO   *1989, Peruvian Navy*

1 PGM 71 CLASS (LARGE PATROL CRAFT) (PC)

Name	No	Builders	Commissioned
RIO CHIRA	PC 223 (ex-*PGM 111*)	SIMA, Callao	June 1972

Displacement, tons: 147 full load
Dimensions, feet (metres): 101 × 21 × 6 *(30.8 × 6.4 × 1.8)*
Main machinery: 2 diesels; 1,450 hp *(1.08 MW)*; 2 shafts
Speed, knots: 18. **Range, miles:** 1,500 at 10 kt
Complement: 15
Guns: 1 Bofors 40 mm/60. 2 Oerlikon 20 mm.
Radars: Surface search: Raytheon; I-band.

Comment: Acquired from the Navy in 1975. Paid off in 1994 but back in service again in 1997, with refurbished engines. ***VERIFIED***

RIO CHIRA   *1987, Peruvian Navy*

1 RIVER PATROL CRAFT (PC)

Name	No	Builders	Commissioned
RIO PIURA	PC 242 (ex-P 252)	Viareggio, Italy	5 Sep 1960

Displacement, tons: 37 full load
Dimensions, feet (metres): 65.7 × 17 × 3.2 *(20 × 5.2 × 1)*
Main machinery: 2 GM 8V-71 diesels; 460 hp *(344 kW)* sustained; 2 shafts
Speed, knots: 18. **Range, miles:** 1,000 at 16 kt
Complement: 7 (1 officer)
Guns: 1 Bofors 40 mm/60. 1 Oerlikon 20 mm.
Radars: Navigation: Raytheon; I-band.

Comment: Ordered in 1959. Armament changed in 1992.

UPDATED

RIO PIURA   *6/1994*, Peruvian Navy /* 0012888

7 LAKE and RIVER PATROL CRAFT (PL/PF)

RIO HULLAGA	PF 260	RIO RAMIS	PL 290
RIO SANTIAGO	PF 261	RIO ILAVE	PL 291
RIO NANAY	PF 263	RIO AZANGARO	PL 292
RIO TAMBOPATA	PF 274		

Displacement, tons: 5 full load
Dimensions, feet (metres): 32.8 × 11.2 × 2.6 *(10 × 3.4 × 0.8)*
Main machinery: 2 Perkins diesels; 480 hp *(358 kW)*; 2 shafts
Speed, knots: 29. **Range, miles:** 450 at 28 kt
Complement: 4
Guns: 1—12.7 mm MG.
Radars: Surface search: Raytheon 2800; I-band.

Comment: Details given are for *PL 290-292*. Based at Puno on Lake Titicaca. GRP hulls built in 1982. The others are all older and smaller river craft. ***UPDATED***

RIO AZANGARO   *8/1999*, A Campanera i Rovira /* 0081536

11 PORT PATROL CRAFT (PP)

RIO ZARUMILLA PP 209	HUAURA PP 213	RIO MAJES PP 233
RIO SUPE PP 210	QUILCA PP 214	RIO VIRU PP 235
RIO VITOR PP 211	PUCUSANA PP 215	RIO LURIN PP 236
MANCORA PP 212	RIO SANTA PP 232	

Comment: PP 209-215 acquired in 1996, PP 232-236 in 1999. All are between 12 and 15 m in length and carry MGs. ***UPDATED***

PORT PATROL CRAFT   *1/1999* /* 0081537

PHILIPPINES

Headquarters Appointments

Flag Officer-in-Command:
   Vice Admiral Luisito Fernandez
Vice Commander:
   Rear Admiral Onofre Q Marcelo
Commander Fleet:
   Rear Admiral Eriberto C Varona
Commandant Coast Guard:
   Rear Admiral Manuel I de Leon
Commandant Marines:
   Brigadier Edgardo V Espinosa

Diplomatic Representation

Defence Attaché in London:
   Colonel P I Inserto

Personnel

(a)   2000: 10,300 Navy; 7,600 Marines; 3,000 Coast Guard
(b)   Reserves: 18,000

Marine Corps

Marines comprise three tactical brigades composed of 10 tactical battalions, one support regiment, a service group, a guard battalion and a reconnaissance battalion. Headquarters at Ternate, Manila Bay. Deployed in Mindanao and Palawan.

Organisation

The Navy is organised into three major commands: Fleet, Coast Guard and Marines. From 1996 there are four operational commands composed of Naval Forces North (Cagayan), Naval Forces West ((Palawan), Naval Forces Central (Cebu) and Naval Forces South (Tawi-Tawi). Philippine Coast Guard has eight Coast Guard Districts, 47 Stations and 154 Coast Guard Detachment units that are strategically located in the different parts of the country. The Navy and the Coast Guard are interchangeable and often share duties. In addition there are three Naval construction battalions and 30 SEAL teams deployed in Naval districts. There were plans to devolve the Coast Guard to the Department of Transport in 1998 but this has not yet been confirmed.

Bases

Main: Cavite.
Operational: San Vicente, Mactan, Ternate.
Stations: Cebu, Davao, Legaspi, Bonifacio, Tacloban, San Miguel, Ulugan, Balabne, Puerto Princesa, Pagasa.

Prefix to Ships' Names

BRP: Barko Republika Pilipinas

Mercantile Marine

Lloyd's Register of Shipping:
   1,897 vessels of 7,650,058 tons gross

Strength of the Fleet

Type	Active	Building
Frigates	(1)	—
Corvettes	13	(2)
Fast Attack Craft	6	—
Large Patrol Craft	5	1 (3)
Coastal Patrol Craft	37	2
LST/LSV Transports	8	—
LCM/LCU/RUC/LCVP	44	—
Repair Ship	1	—
Tankers	4	—
Coast Guard		
Tenders	4	—
Patrol Craft	58	1

DELETIONS

Auxiliaries

1999   *Sierra Madre* (aground)

PENNANT LIST

Frigates

PF 11	Rajah Humabon

Corvettes

PS 19	Miguel Malvar
PS 20	Magat Salamat
PS 22	Sultan Kudarat
PS 23	Datu Marikudo
PS 28	Cebu
PS 29	Negros Occidental
PS 31	Pangasinan
PS 32	Iloilo
PS 35	Emilio Jacinto
PS 36	Apolinario Mabini
PS 37	Artemio Ricarte
PS 70	Quezon
PS 74	Rizal

Patrol Forces

PG 101	Kagitingan
PG 102	Bagong Lakas
PG 104	Bagong Silang

PG 110	Tomas Batilo
PG 111	Bonny Serrano
PG 112	Bienvenido Salting
PG 114	Salvador Abcede
PG 115	Ramon Aguirre
PG 140	Emilo Aguinaldo
PG 141	Antonio Luna
PG 370	José Andrada
PG 371	Enrique Jurado
PG 372	Alfredo Peckson
PG 374	Simeon Castro
PG 375	Carlos Albert
PG 376	Heracleo Alano
PG 377	Liberato Picar
PG 378	Hilario Ruiz
PG 379	Rafael Pargas
PG 380	Nestor Reinoso
PG 381	Diocoro Papa
PG 382	—
PG 383	Ismael Lomibao
PG 384	Leovigildo Gantioque
PG 385	Federico Martir
PG 386	Filipino Flojo
PG 387	Anastacio Cacayorin
PG 388	Manuel Gomez
PG 389	Testimo Figuracion
PG 390	José Loor SR

PG 392	—
PG 393	Florenca Nuno
PG 394	—
PG 395	—
PG 840	Conrado Yap
PG 842	Tedorico Dominado Jr
PG 843	Cosme Acosta
PG 844	José Artiaga Jr
PG 845	—
PG 846	Nicanor Jimenez
PG 847	Leopoldo Regis
PG 848	Leon Tadina
PG 849	Loreto Danipog
PG 851	Apollo Tiano
PG 852	—
PG 853	Sulpicio Hernandez

Auxiliaries

LT 86	Zamboanga Del Sur
LT 87	South Cotabato
LT 501	Laguna
LT 504	Lanao Del Norte
LT 507	Benguet
LT 516	Kalinga Apayao
LC 550	Bacolod City

LC 551	Dagupan City
AT 25	Ang Pangulo
AW 33	Lake Bulusan
AW 34	Lake Paoay
AF 72	Lake Taal
AF 78	Lake Buhi
AC 90	Mactan
AD 617	Yakal

Coast Guard

AE 46	Cape Bojeador
PG 61	Agusan
PG 62	Catanduanes
PG 63	Romblon
PG 64	Palawan
AT 71	Mangyan
AU 75	Bessang Pass
AE 79	Limasawa
AG 89	Kalinga
AU 100	Tirad Pass
419	Don Emilio
001	San Juan

FRIGATES

Notes: (1) *Rajah Lakandula*, paid off in 1988, is still afloat as an alongside HQ and depot ship.
(2) The US has offered to lease an 'Oliver Perry' class, and France a 'D'Estienne D'Orves class frigate.

1 CANNON CLASS (FF)

Name	No	Builders	Laid down	Launched	Commissioned
RAJAH HUMABON (ex-*Hatsuhi* DE 263, ex-*Atherton* DE 169)	PF 11 (ex-PF 78)	Norfolk Navy Yard, Portsmouth, VA	14 Jan 1943	27 May 1943	29 Aug 1943

Displacement, tons: 1,390 standard; 1,750 full load
Dimensions, feet (metres): 306 × 36.6 × 14
   (93.3 × 11.2 × 4.3)
Main machinery: Diesel-electric; 4 GM 16-278A diesels; 6,000 hp *(4.5 MW)*; 4 generators; 2 motors; 2 shafts
Speed, knots: 18. **Range, miles:** 10,800 at 12 kt
Complement: 165

Guns: 3 US 3 in *(76 mm)*/50 Mk 22; 20 rds/min to 12 km *(6.6 n miles)*; weight of shell 6 kg.
   6 US/Bofors 40 mm/56 (3 twin). 4 Oerlikon 20 mm/70; 2—12.7 mm MGs.
A/S mortars: 1 Hedgehog Mk 10; range 250 m; warhead 13.6 kg; 24 rockets.
Depth charges: 8 K-gun Mk 6 projectors; range 160 m; warhead 150 kg; 1 rack.
Weapons control: Mk 52 GFCS with Mk 41 rangefinder for 3 in guns. 3 Mk 51 Mod 2 GFCS for 40 mm.
Radars: Surface search: Raytheon SPS-5; G/H-band.
   Navigation: RCA/GE Mk 26; I-band.
Sonars: SQS-17B; hull-mounted; active search and attack; medium/high frequency.

Programmes: *Hatsuhi* originally transferred by the USA to Japan 14 June 1955 and paid off June 1975 reverting to US Navy. Transferred to Philippines 23 December 1978. Towed to South Korea 1979 for overhaul and modernisation. Recommissioned 27 February 1980. A sister ship *Datu Kalantiaw* lost during Typhoon Clara 20 September 1981.
Modernisation: There are plans to fit an SSM system. May also be re-engined when funds are available.

UPDATED

RAJAH HUMABON

5/1998, Sattler/Steele / 0052698

CORVETTES

3 JACINTO (PEACOCK) CLASS (FS)

Name	No	Builders	Launched	Commissioned	Recommissioned
EMILIO JACINTO (ex-Peacock)	PS 35 (ex-P 239)	Hall Russell, Aberdeen	1 Dec 1982	14 July 1984	4 Aug 1997
APOLINARIO MABINI (ex-Plover)	PS 36 (ex-P 240)	Hall Russell, Aberdeen	12 Apr 1983	20 July 1984	4 Aug 1997
ARTEMIO RICARTE (ex-Starling)	PS 37 (ex-P 241)	Hall Russell, Aberdeen	11 Sep 1983	10 Aug 1984	4 Aug 1997

Displacement, tons: 763 full load
Dimensions, feet (metres): 204.1 × 32.8 × 8.9
(62.6 × 10 × 2.7)
Main machinery: 2 Crossley Pielstick 18 PA6 V 280 diesels;
14,000 hp(m) *(10.6 MW)* sustained; 2 shafts; 1 retractable
Schottel prop; 181 hp *(135 kW)*
Speed, knots: 25. **Range, miles:** 2,500 at 17 kt
Complement: 31 (6 officers) plus 7 spare berths

Guns: 1—3 in *(76 mm)*/62 OTO Melara compact; 85 rds/min to
16 km *(8.6 n miles)* anti-surface; 12 km *(6.5 n miles)* anti-
aircraft; weight of shell 6 kg.
4 FN 7.62 mm MGs.
Weapons control: BAe Sea Archer GSA-7 for 76 mm gun.
Radars: Navigation: Kelvin Hughes Type 1006; I-band.

Programmes: Letter of Intention to purchase from the UK signed
in November 1996. Transferred 1 August 1997 after sailing
from Hong Kong on 1 July 1997. Others of the class in service
with the navy of the Irish Republic.
Modernisation: SSM launchers may be fitted in due course.
Structure: Fitted with telescopic cranes, loiter drive and
replenishment at sea equipment. In UK service, two fast
pursuit craft were carried.
Operational: Based at Cavite.

UPDATED   APOLINARIO MABINI

12/1999*, Sattler/Steele / 0081538

2 AUK CLASS (FS)

Name	No	Builders	Laid down	Launched	Commissioned
RIZAL (ex-Murrelet MSF 372)	PS 74 (ex-PS 69)	Savannah Machine & Foundry Co, GA	24 Aug 1944	29 Dec 1944	21 Aug 1945
QUEZON (ex-Vigilance MSF 324)	PS 70	Associated Shipbuilders, Seattle, WA	28 Nov 1942	5 Apr 1943	28 Feb 1944

Displacement, tons: 1,090 standard; 1,250 full load
Dimensions, feet (metres): 221.2 × 32.2 × 10.8
(67.4 × 9.8 × 3.3)
Main machinery: Diesel-electric; 2 GM 12-278 diesels; 2,200 hp
(1.64 MW); 2 generators; 2 motors; 2 shafts
Speed, knots: 18. **Range, miles:** 5,700 at 16 kt
Complement: 80 (5 officers)

Guns: 2 US 3 in *(76 mm)*/50 Mk 26; 20 rds/min to 12 km *(6.6 n
miles)*; weight of shell 6 kg.
4 US/Bofors 40 mm/56 (2 twin); 160 rds/min to 11 km *(5.9 n
miles)*; weight of shell 0.9 kg.
2 Oerlikon 20 mm (twin). 2—12.7 mm MGs.
Torpedoes: 3—324 mm US Mk 32 (triple) tubes. Honeywell
Mk 44; anti-submarine; active homing to 5.5 km *(3 n miles)* at
30 kt; warhead 34 kg.
A/S mortars: 1 Hedgehog Mk 10; range 250 m; warhead
13.6 kg; 24 rockets.
Depth charges: 2 Mk 9 racks.
Radars: Surface search: Raytheon SPS-5C; G/H-band.
Navigation: DAS 3; I-band.
Sonars: SQS-17B; hull-mounted; active search and attack; high
frequency.

Programmes: *Rizal* transferred from the USA to the Philippines
on 18 June 1965 and *Quezon* on 19 August 1967.
Modernisation: There are plans to fit SSMs. May also be re-
engined.

QUEZON

5/1998, John Mortimer / 0052700

Structure: Upon transfer the minesweeping gear was removed
and a second 3 in gun fitted aft; additional anti-submarine
weapons also fitted.

Operational: Both ships were to have been deleted in 1994 but
have been retained until new class of OPVs is built.
UPDATED

8 PCE 827 CLASS (FS)

Name	No	Builders	Commissioned
MIGUEL MALVAR (ex-Ngoc Hoi, ex-Brattleboro PCER 852)	PS 19	Pullman Standard Car Co, Chicago	26 May 1944
MAGAT SALAMAT (ex-Chi Lang II, ex-Gayety MSF 239)	PS 20	Winslow Marine Co, Seattle, WA	14 June 1944
SULTAN KUDARAT (ex-Dong Da II, ex-Crestview PCER 895)	PS 22	Willamette Iron & Steel Corporation, Portland, OR	30 Oct 1943
DATU MARIKUDO (ex-Van Kiep II, ex-Amherst PCER 853)	PS 23	Pullman Standard Car Co, Chicago	16 June 1944
CEBU (ex-PCE 881)	PS 28	Albina E and M Works, Portland, OR	31 July 1944
NEGROS OCCIDENTAL (ex-PCE 884)	PS 29	Albina E and M Works, Portland, OR	30 Mar 1944
PANGASINAN (ex-PCE 891)	PS 31	Willamette Iron & Steel Corp, Portland, OR	15 June 1944
ILOILO (ex-PCE 897)	PS 32	Willamette Iron & Steel Corp, Portland, OR	6 Jan 1945

Displacement, tons: 640 standard; 914 full load
Dimensions, feet (metres): 184.5 × 33.1 × 9.5 *(56.3 × 10.1 × 2.9)*
Main machinery: 2 GM 12-278A diesels; 2,200 hp *(1.64 MW)*; 2 shafts
Speed, knots: 15. **Range, miles:** 6,600 at 11 kt
Complement: 85 (8 officers)

Guns: 1 US 3 in *(76 mm)*/50; 20 rds/min to 12 km *(6.6 n miles)*; weight of shell 6 kg.
2 to 6 US/Bofors 40 mm/56 (single or 1-3 twin); 160 rds/min to 11 km *(5.9 n miles)*; weight of
shell 0.9 kg.
2 Oerlikon 20 mm/70; 800 rds/min to 2 km.
Radars: Surface search: SPS-50 (PS 23). SPS-21D (PS 19, 28). CRM-NIA-75 (PS 29, 31, 32).
SPS-53A (PS 20).
Navigation: RCA SPN-18; I/J-band.

Programmes: Five transferred from the USA to the Philippines in July 1948 (PS 28-32); PS 22 to
South Vietnam from US Navy on 29 November 1961, PS 20 in April 1962, PS 19 on 11 July
1966, and PS 23 in June 1970. PS 19, 20 and 22 to Philippines November 1975 and PS 23
5 April 1976.
Modernisation: PS 19, 22, 31 and 32 refurbished in 1990-91, PS 23 and 28 in 1992 and the last
pair in 1996/97.
Structure: First three were originally fitted as rescue ships (PCER). A/S equipment has been
removed or is inoperable. PS 20 has some minor structural differences having been built as an
'Admirable' class MSF.
UPDATED

MIGUEL MALVAR

8/1995* / 0081539

LAND-BASED MARITIME AIRCRAFT

Numbers/Type: 7 PADC (Pilatus Britten-Norman) Islander F27MP.
Operational speed: 150 kt *(280 km/h)*.
Service ceiling: 18,900 ft *(5,760 m)*.
Range: 1,500 miles *(2,775 km)*.
Role/Weapon systems: Short-range MR and SAR aircraft. Purchased at the rate of one per year
from 1989. Three more transferred from the Air Force. Sensors: Search radar, cameras.
Weapons: Unarmed.
UPDATED

Numbers/Type: 7 PADC (MBB) BO 105C.
Operational speed: 145 kt *(270 km/h)*.
Service ceiling: 17,000 ft *(5,180 m)*.
Range: 355 n miles *(657 km)*.
Role/Weapon systems: Sole shipborne helicopter; some shore-based for SAR; some commando
support capability. Purchased at the rate of one per year from 1986 to 1992. Sensors: Some
fitted with search radar. Weapons: Unarmed.
UPDATED

PATROL FORCES

Note: The Navy operates two Mk 1 (50 ft) and three Mk 2 (65 ft) coastal patrol craft. Details under identical craft operated by the Coast Guard.

0 + (3) OFFSHORE PATROL VESSELS (OPV)

Displacement, tons: 1,200 full load
Dimensions, feet (metres): 278.9 × 32.8 × 9.8 *(85 × 10 × 3)*
Main machinery: CODAD; 4 diesels; 2 shafts
Speed, knots: 24. **Range, miles:** 3,500 at 12 kt
Complement: 84 (14 officers)
Guns: 1 Otobreda 3 in *(76 mm)*/62 Super Rapid.
   4 Emerlec 30 mm (2 twin). 2—12.7 mm MGs.
Weapons control: Optronic director.
Radars: Air/surface search. Navigation.
Helicopters: 1 BO 105C.

Comment: Invitations to tender issued in April 1996 and repeated in April 1998. In August 1998 it was confirmed that the project was shelved for the time being because of lack of funds, but remains a high priority. Specifications are subject to tender, but the details are very close to a helicopter fitted South Korean 'Po Hang' class. Other competing designs include a VLS missile system on either side of the hangar.

VERIFIED

2 + 1 AGUINALDO CLASS (LARGE PATROL CRAFT) (PC)

Name	No	Builders	Commissioned
EMILIO AGUINALDO	PG 140	Cavite, Sangley Point	21 Nov 1990
ANTONIO LUNA	PG 141	Cavite, Sangley Point	27 May 1999
—	PG 142	Cavite, Sangley Point	2001

Displacement, tons: 279 full load
Dimensions, feet (metres): 144.4 × 24.3 × 5.2 *(44 × 7.4 × 1.6)*
Main machinery: 4 Detroit 12V-92TA diesels; 2,040 hp *(1.52 MW)* sustained; 2 shafts
Speed, knots: 25. **Range, miles:** 1,100 at 18 kt
Complement: 58 (6 officers)
Guns: 2 Bofors 40 mm/60. 2 Oerlikon 20 mm. 4—12.7 mm MGs.
Radars: Surface search: Raytheon; I-band.

Comment: First of class launched 23 June 1984 but only completed in 1990. Second laid down 2 December 1990 and launched 23 June 1992, and the keel laid of PG 142 14 February 1994. The plan is a total of six but the programme has been slowed down and may not be completed. Steel hulls of similar design to *Tirad Pass* (see Coast Guard). The intention is to upgrade the armament in due course to include a SAM and an OTO Melara 76 mm/62 gun. This now seems unlikely.

UPDATED

EMILIO AGUINALDO   *6/1993* / 0081540

3 KAGITINGAN CLASS (LARGE PATROL CRAFT) (PC)

Name	No	Builders	Commissioned
KAGITINGAN	P 101	Hamelin SY, Germany	9 Feb 1979
BAGONG LAKAS	PG 102 (ex-P 102)	Hamelin SY, Germany	9 Feb 1979
BAGONG SILANG	PG 104 (ex-P 104)	Hamelin SY, Germany	July 1979

Displacement, tons: 148 full load
Dimensions, feet (metres): 121.4 × 20.3 × 5.6 *(37 × 6.2 × 1.7)*
Main machinery: 2 MTU MB 12V 493 TZ60 diesels; 1,360 hp(m) *(1 MW)* sustained; 2 shafts
Speed, knots: 16
Complement: 30 (4 officers)
Guns: 2—30 mm (twin). 4—12.7 mm MGs. 2—7.62 mm MGs.
Radars: Surface search: I-band.

Comment: Based at Cavite. P 103 paid off and used for spares. All still in service.

VERIFIED

BAGONG LAKAS   *1993, Philippine Navy*

6 TOMAS BATILO (SEA DOLPHIN) CLASS (FAST ATTACK CRAFT) (PCF)

TOMAS BATILO PG 110	**BIENVENIDO SALTING** PG 112	**RAMON AGUIRRE** PG 115
BONNY SERRANO PG 111	**SALVADOR ABCEDE** PG 114	— PG 116

Displacement, tons: 170 full load
Dimensions, feet (metres): 121.4 × 22.6 × 5.6 *(37 × 6.9 × 1.7)*
Main machinery: 2 MTU 16V 538 TB90 diesels; 6,000 hp(m) *(4.41 MW)* sustained; 2 shafts
Speed, knots: 34. **Range, miles:** 600 at 20 kt
Complement: 31 (5 officers)
Guns: 2 Emerson Electric 30 mm (twin); 1,200 rds/min combined to 6 km *(3.2 n miles)*; weight of shell 0.35 kg.
   1 Bofors 40 mm/60. 2 Oerlikon 20 mm.
Weapons control: Optical director.
Radars: Surface search: Raytheon 1645; I-band.

Comment: Transferred from South Korea on 15 June 1995. Part of the PKM 200 series. Different armament to South Korean ships of the same class.

VERIFIED

BIENVENIDO SALTING   *6/1996, Philippines Navy*

24 JOSÉ ANDRADA CLASS (COASTAL PATROL CRAFT) (PC)

JOSÉ ANDRADA PG 370	**RAFAEL PARGAS** PG 379	**ANASTACIO CACAYORIN** PG 387
ENRIQUE JURADO PG 371	**NESTOR REINOSO** PG 380	**MANUEL GOMEZ** PG 388
ALFREDO PECKSON PG 372	**DIOSCORO PAPA** PG 381	**TESTIMO FIGURACION** PG 389
SIMEON CASTRO PG 374	— PG 382	**JOSÉ LOOR SR** PG 390
CARLOS ALBERT PG 375	**ISMAEL LOMIBAO** PG 383	— PG 392
HERACLEO ALANO PG 376	**LEOVIGILDO GANTIOQUE** PG 384	**FLORENCA NUNO** PG 393
LIBERATO PICAR PG 377	**FEDERICO MARTIR** PG 385	— PG 394-395
HILARIO RUIZ PG 378	**FILIPINO FLOJO** PG 386	

Displacement, tons: 56 full load
Dimensions, feet (metres): 78 × 20 × 5.8 *(23.8 × 6.1 × 1.8)*
Main machinery: 2 Detroit 16V-92TA diesels; 1,380 hp *(1.03 MW)* sustained; 2 shafts
Speed, knots: 28. **Range, miles:** 1,200 at 12 kt
Complement: 8 (1 officer)
Guns: 1 Breda 25 mm or Bofors 40 mm/60.
   4—12.7 mm Mk 26 MGs. 2—7.62 mm M60 MGs.
Radars: Surface search: Raytheon SPS-64(V)2; I-band.

Comment: First four ordered from Halter Marine in August 1989 under FMS and built at Equitable Shipyards, New Orleans, as were a further four ordered in 1990. Eight more ordered in March 1993 with co-production between Halter Marine and Cavite, and a further eight in 1995. Built to Coast Guard standards with an aluminium hull and superstructure. The main gun may be fitted in all after some delay. PG 392 delivered in March 1998 and PG 393 in May 1998; the last pair in 2000.

UPDATED

HILARIO RUIZ   *5/1998, John Mortimer* / 0081541

FLORENCA NUNO   *6/1999* / 0081542

12 CONRADO YAP (SEA HAWK/KILLER) CLASS (COASTAL PATROL CRAFT) (PCF)

CONRADO YAP PG 840	**LEOPOLDO REGIS** PG 847
TEDORICO DOMINADO JR PG 842	**LEON TADINA** PG 848
COSME ACOSTA PG 843	**LORETO DANIPOG** PG 849
JOSÉ ARTIAGA JR PG 844	**APOLLO TIANO** PG 851
— PG 845	— PG 852
NICANOR JIMENEZ PG 846	**SULPICIO FERNANDEZ** PG 853

Displacement, tons: 74.5 full load
Dimensions, feet (metres): 83.7 × 17.7 × 6.2 *(25.5 × 5.4 × 1.9)*
Main machinery: 2 MTU 16V 638 TB96 diesels; 7,200 hp(m) *(5.29 MW)*; 2 shafts
Speed, knots: 38. **Range, miles:** 500 at 20 kt
Complement: 15 (3 officers)
Guns: 1 Bofors 40 mm/60. 2 Oerlikon 20 mm (twin) Mk 16.
Radars: Surface search: Raytheon 1645; I-band.

Comment: Type PK 181 built by Korea Tacoma and Hyundai 1975-78. All transferred from South Korea 19 June 1993. There may be some armament variations. The last pair were to be named on completion of refits which have been delayed by lack of funds, and they may be scrapped.
VERIFIED

PG 852 *1993, Philippine Navy*

SURVEY AND RESEARCH SHIPS

Notes: (1) Survey ships are operated by Coast and Geodetic Survey of Ministry of National Defence and are not naval.
(2) Two research ships *Fort San Antonio* (AM 700) and *Fort Abad* (AM 701) were acquired in 1993.

AUXILIARIES

Notes: (1) All LSTs, LSVs, LCMs and LCUs are classified as Transports.
(2) The ex-US 'Stalwart' class *Triumph* TAGOS-4 may be acquired in due course.

2 BACOLOD CITY (FRANK S BESSON) CLASS (LSV)

Name	*No*	*Builders*	*Commissioned*
BACOLOD CITY	LC 550	Moss Point Marine	1 Dec 1993
DAGUPAN CITY (ex-*Cagayan De Oro City*)	LC 551	Moss Point Marine	5 Apr 1994

Displacement, tons: 4,265 full load
Dimensions, feet (metres): 272.8 × 60 × 12 *(83.1 × 18.3 × 3.7)*
Main machinery: 2 GM EMD 16-645E2 diesels; 3,900 hp *(2.9 MW)* sustained; 2 shafts; bow thruster; 250 hp *(187 kW)*
Speed, knots: 11.6. **Range, miles:** 6,000 at 11 kt
Complement: 30 (6 officers)
Military lift: 2,280 tons (900 for amphibious operations) of vehicles, containers or cargo, plus 150 troops; 2 LCVPs on davits
Radars: Navigation: Raytheon SPS-64(V)2; I-band.
Helicopters: Platform for 1 BO 105C.

Comment: Contract announced by Trinity Marine 3 April 1992 for two ships with an option on a third which was not taken up. Ro-ro design with 10,500 sq ft of deck space for cargo. Capable of beaching with 4 ft over the ramp on a 1 : 30 offshore gradient with a 900 ton cargo. Similar to US Army vessels but with only a bow ramp. The stern ramp space is used for accommodation for 150 troops and a helicopter platform is fitted over the stern. ***UPDATED***

DAGUPAN CITY *12/1999*, Sattler/Steele* / 0081543

DAGUPAN CITY *12/1999*, Sattler/Steele* / 0081544

6 LST 512-1152 CLASS (TRANSPORT SHIPS) (LST)

Name	*No*	*Commissioned*
ZAMBOANGA DEL SUR (ex-*Cam Ranh*, ex-*Marion County* LST 975)	LT 86	3 Feb 1945
SOUTH COTABATO (ex-*Cayuga County* LST 529)	LT 87	28 Feb 1944
LAGUNA (ex-*T-LST 230*)	LT 501	3 Nov 1943
LANAO DEL NORTE (ex-*T-LST 566*)	LT 504	29 May 1944
BENGUET (ex-*Davies County* T-LST 692)	LT 507	10 May 1944
KALINGA APAYAO (ex-*Can Tho*, ex-*Garrett County* AGP 786, ex-LST 786)	LT 516 (ex-AE 516)	28 Aug 1944

Displacement, tons: 1,620 standard; 2,472 beaching; 4,080 full load
Dimensions, feet (metres): 328 × 50 × 14 *(100 × 15.2 × 4.3)*
Main machinery: 2 GM 12-567A diesels; 1,800 hp *(1.34 MW)*; 2 shafts
Speed, knots: 10
Complement: Varies—approx 60-110 (depending upon employment)
Military lift: 2,100 tons. 16 tanks or 10 tanks plus 200 troops

Guns: 6 US/Bofors 40 mm (2 twin, 2 single) or 4 Oerlikon 20 mm (in refitted ships).
Radars: Navigation: Raytheon SPS-64(V)2; I-band.

Programmes: Transferred from US Navy in 1976 with exception of LT 57 and LT 516 which were used as light craft repair ships in South Vietnam and have retained amphibious capability (transferred to Vietnam 1970 and to Philippines 1976, acquired by purchase 5 April 1976). LT 86 transferred (grant aid) 17 November 1975. LT 501 and 504 commissioned in Philippine Navy 8 August 1978 and LT 507 on 18 October 1978.
Modernisation: Several have had major refits including replacement of frames and plating as well as engines and electrics and provision for four 20 mm guns to replace the 40 mm guns.
Structure: Some of the later ships have tripod masts, others have pole masts.
Operational: All are used for general cargo work in Philippine service. Fourteen were deleted in 1989 and one sank in 1991. Two paid off in 1992 and one in 1993. *South Cotabato* was also paid off in 1993 but brought back in to service in 1994. *Benguet* broke down in the South China Sea in April 1995 and had to be taken in tow. One other grounded in the Spratley Islands in November 1999 and after a month on the rocks is probably beyond economical repair. Replacements are needed but have not been given priority.
UPDATED

LANAO DEL NORTE *1993, Philippine Navy*

1 ACHELOUS CLASS (REPAIR SHIP) (AR)

Name	*No*	*Builders*	*Commissioned*
YAKAL (ex-*Satyr* ARL 23, ex-*LST 852*)	AD 617 (ex-AR 517)	Chicago Bridge & Iron	20 Nov 1944

Displacement, tons: 4,342 full load
Dimensions, feet (metres): 328 × 50 × 14 *(100 × 15.2 × 4.3)*
Main machinery: 2 GM 12-567A diesels; 1,800 hp *(1.34 MW)*; 2 shafts
Speed, knots: 11.6
Complement: 220 approx
Guns: 4 US/Bofors 40 mm (quad). 10 Oerlikon 20 mm (5 twin).

Comment: Transferred from the USA to the Philippines on 24 January 1977 by sale. (Originally to South Vietnam 30 September 1971.) Converted during construction. Extensive machine shop, spare parts stowage, and logistic support.
UPDATED

YAKAL *1994*, Philippine Navy* / 0081545

47 LCM/LCU

Comment: Ex-US minor landing craft mostly transferred in the mid-1970s. 11 LCM 6, five LCM 8, eight LCU, 14 RUC and two LCVP. More LCVP are building at Cavite and two LCUs were reported delivered from South Korea in late 1995. More LCMs are planned. Used as transport vessels.

UPDATED

LCU 286   *5/1998*, van Ginderen Collection / 0052706

1 ALAMOSA CLASS (SUPPLY SHIP) (AK)

Name	No	Builders	Commissioned
MACTAN (ex-*Kukui*, ex-*Colquith*)	AC 90 (ex-TK 90)	Froemming, Milwaukee	22 Sep 1944

Displacement, tons: 2,500 light; 7,570 full load
Dimensions, feet (metres): 338.5 × 50 × 18 *(103.2 × 15.2 × 5.5)*
Main machinery: 1 Nordberg diesel; 1,700 hp *(1.27 MW)*; 1 shaft
Speed, knots: 11
Complement: 85
Guns: 2—12.7 mm MGs.

Comment: Transferred from the US Coast Guard on 1 March 1972. Used to supply military posts and lighthouses in the Philippine archipelago. Was to have been paid off in 1994 but has been kept in service.

VERIFIED

MACTAN   *4/1996, Philippine Navy*

1 TRANSPORT VESSEL (AP)

Name	No	Builders	Commissioned
ANG PANGULO (ex-*The President*, ex-*Roxas*, ex-*Lapu-Lapu*)	AT 25 (ex-TP 777)	Ishikawajima, Japan	1959

Displacement, tons: 2,239 standard; 2,727 full load
Dimensions, feet (metres): 257.6 × 42.6 × 21 *(78.5 × 13 × 6.4)*
Main machinery: 2 Mitsui DE642/VBF diesels; 5,000 hp(m) *(3.68 MW)*; 2 shafts
Speed, knots: 18. **Range, miles:** 6,900 at 15 kt
Complement: 81 (8 officers)
Guns: 3 Oerlikon 20 mm/70 Mk 4. 8—7.62 mm MGs.
Radars: Navigation: RCA CRMN-1A-75; I-band.

Comment: Built as war reparation; launched in 1958. Was used as presidential yacht and command ship with accommodation for 50 passengers. Originally named *Lapu-Lapu* after the chief who killed Magellan; renamed *Roxas* on 9 October 1962 after the late Manuel Roxas, the first President of the Philippines Republic, renamed *The President* in 1967 and *Ang Pangulo* in 1975. One 15 ton crane. In early 1997 she was planned to bring President Marcos to Hong Kong to transfer to an old Italian liner and set up as an exiled president. The ship is now used as an attack transport, and also as a Presidential Yacht.

UPDATED

ANG PANGULO   *5/1998*, John Mortimer / 0081546

2 YW TYPE (WATER TANKERS) (AWT)

Name	No	Builders	Commissioned
LAKE BULUSAN	AW 33 (ex-YW 111)	Marine Iron, Duluth	1 Aug 1945
LAKE PAOAY	AW 34 (ex-YW 130)	Leathem D Smith, Sturgeon Bay	28 Aug 1945

Displacement, tons: 1,237 full load
Dimensions, feet (metres): 174 × 32.7 × 13.2 *(53 × 10 × 4)*
Main machinery: 2 GM 8-278A diesels; 1,500 hp *(1.12 MW)*; 2 shafts
Speed, knots: 7.5
Complement: 29
Cargo capacity: 200,000 gallons
Guns: 1 Bofors 40/60. 1 Oerlikon 20 mm.

Comment: Basically similar to YOG type but adapted to carry fresh water. Transferred from the USA to the Philippines on 16 July 1975.

VERIFIED

LAKE PAOAY   *5/1998, van Ginderen Collection / 0052708*

2 YOG TYPE (TANKERS) (YO)

Name	No	Builders	Commissioned
LAKE BUHI (ex-*YOG 73*)	AF 78 (ex-YO 78)	Puget Sound, Bremerton	28 Nov 1944
LAKE TAAL (ex-*YOG*)	AF 72 (ex-YO 72)	Puget Sound, Bremerton	14 Apr 1945

Displacement, tons: 447 standard; 1,400 full load
Dimensions, feet (metres): 174 × 32.7 × 13.2 *(53 × 10 × 4)*
Main machinery: 2 GM 8-278A diesels; 1,500 hp *(1.12 MW)*; 2 shafts
Speed, knots: 8
Complement: 28
Cargo capacity: 6,570 barrels dieso and gasoline
Guns: 2 Oerlikon 20 mm/70 Mk 4.

Comment: Former US Navy gasoline tankers. Transferred in July 1967 on loan and by purchase 5 March 1980.

VERIFIED

LAKE BUHI   *1993, Philippine Navy*

4 FLOATING DOCKS

YD 200 (ex-*AFDL 24*)   **YD 204** (ex-*AFDL 20*)   **YD 205** (ex-*AFDL 44*)   — (ex-*AFDL 40*)

Comment: Floating steel dry docks built in the USA; all are former US Navy units with *YD 200* transferred in July 1948, *YD 204* in October 1961 (sale 1 August 1980), *YD 205* in September 1969 and *AFDL 40* in 1994.
Capacities: *YD 205*, 2,800 tons; *YD 200* and *YD 204*, 1,000 tons. In addition there are two floating cranes, *YU 206* and *YU 207*, built in USA in 1944 and capable of lifting 30 tons.

VERIFIED

TUGS

Note: A number of harbour tugs have been acquired from the US. The latest type is ex-Army of 390 tons, a speed of 12 kt and a bollard pull of 12 tons.

HARBOUR TUG   *5/1998, John Mortimer / 0052709*

COAST GUARD

Notes: (1) Some of the PCF craft listed are manned by the Navy as is the buoy tender *Mangyan*.
(2) The Coast Guard also operates one LCM 6 (BM 270), one LCVP (BV 182) and a River Utility Craft VU 463.
(3) A buoy tender *Corregidor* of 731 dwt was commissioned 2 March 1998. Built by Niigata Engineering, she is civilian manned.

1 + 1 SAN JUAN CLASS (PC)

Name	No	Builders	Commissioned
SAN JUAN	001	Tenix Defence Systems	July 2000
DON EMILIO	419	Tenix Defence Systems	Dec 2000

Displacement, tons: 500 full load
Dimensions, feet (metres): 183.7 × 34.5 × 9.8 *(56 × 10.5 × 3)*
Main machinery: 2 Caterpillar 3612 diesels; 4,800 hp(m) *(3.53 MW)* sustained; 2 shafts
Speed, knots: 24.5. **Range, miles:** 3,000 at 15 kt
Complement: 38
Radars: Navigation: I-band.
Helicopters: Platform for one light.

Comment: First reported ordered in mid-1997. Construction started in February 1999. Steel hull and aluminium superstructure. Primarily used for SAR with facilities for 300 survivors. Fire-fighting and pollution control equipment included.

NEW ENTRY

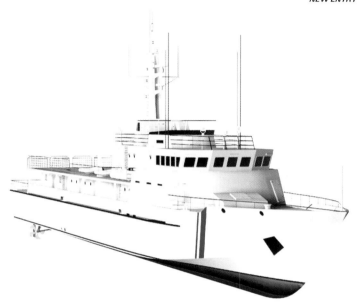

SAN JUAN (artist's impression)   *1999*, Tenix Defence Systems* / 0081547

1 BALSAM CLASS (TENDER) (AKL)

Name	No	Builders	Commissioned
KALINGA (ex-*Redbud, WAGL 398*, ex-*Redbud, T-AKL 398*)	AG 89	Marine Iron, Duluth	2 May 1944

Displacement, tons: 950 standard; 1,041 full load
Dimensions, feet (metres): 180 × 37 × 13 *(54.8 × 11.3 × 4)*
Main machinery: Diesel-electric; 2 diesels; 1,710 hp *(1.28 MW)*; 2 generators; 1 motor; 1,200 hp *(895 kW)*; 1 shaft
Speed, knots: 12. **Range, miles:** 3,500 at 7 kt
Complement: 53
Guns: 2—12.7 mm MGs.
Radars: Navigation: Sperry SPS-53; I/J-band.
Helicopters: Platform for 1 light.

Comment: Originally US Coast Guard buoy tender (WAGL 398). Transferred to US Navy on 25 March 1949 as AG 398 and then to the Philippine Navy 1 March 1972. One 20 ton derrick. New engines fitted.

VERIFIED

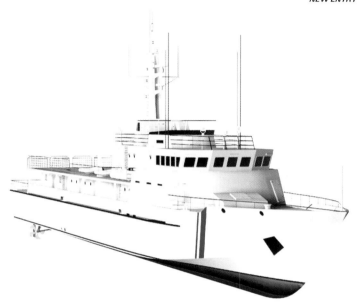

KALINGA   *1994, Philippine Navy*

3 BUOY TENDERS (ABU)

CAPE BOJEADOR (ex-*FS 203*) AE 46 (ex-TK 46)
LIMASAWA (ex-*Nettle* WAK 129, ex-*FS 169*) AE 79 (ex-TK 79)
MANGYAN (ex-*Nasami*, ex-*FS 408*) AT 71 (ex-AE 71, ex-AS 71)

Displacement, tons: 470 standard; 950 full load
Dimensions, feet (metres): 180 × 32 × 10 *(54.9 × 9.8 × 3)*
Main machinery: 2 GM 6-278A diesels; 1,120 hp *(836 kW)*; 2 shafts
Speed, knots: 10. **Range, miles:** 4,150 at 10 kt
Complement: 50
Cargo capacity: 400 tons
Guns: 1—12.7 mm MG can be carried.
Radars: Navigation: RCA CRMN 1A 75; I-band.

Comment: Former US Army FS 381 and FS 330 type freight and supply ships built in 1943-44. First two are employed as tenders for buoys and lighthouses. *Mangyan* transferred 24 September 1976 by sale. *Limasawa* acquired by sale 31 August 1978. One 5 ton derrick. *Cape Bojeador* paid off in 1988 but was back in service in 1991 after a major overhaul. *Mangyan* reclassified AT in 1993 and belongs to the Navy. Masts and superstructures have minor variations.

VERIFIED

CAPE BOJEADOR   *1993, Philippine Navy*

2 LARGE PATROL CRAFT (PC)

Name	No	Builders	Commissioned
TIRAD PASS	AU 100 (ex-SAR 100)	Sumidagawa, Japan	1974
BESSANG PASS	AU 75 (ex-SAR 99)	Sumidagawa, Japan	1974

Displacement, tons: 279 full load
Dimensions, feet (metres): 144.3 × 24.3 × 4.9 *(44 × 7.4 × 1.5)*
Main machinery: 2 MTU 12V 538 TB82 diesels; 4,050 hp(m) *(2.98 MW)*; 2 shafts
Speed, knots: 27.5. **Range, miles:** 2,300 at 14 kt
Complement: 32
Guns: 4—12.7 mm (2 twin) MGs.

Comment: Paid for under Japanese war reparations. Similar type as *Emilio Aguinaldo*. *Bessang Pass* grounded in 1983 but was recovered. May be replaced by 'San Juan' class.

UPDATED

TIRAD PASS   *1992*, Phillippine Navy* / 0081548

1 POINT CLASS (PC)

Name	No	Builders	Commissioned
— (ex-*Point Evans*)	— (ex-82354)	CG Yard, Maryland	10 Jan 1967

Displacement, tons: 67 full load
Dimensions, feet (metres): 83 × 17.2 × 5.8 *(25.3 × 5.2 × 1.8)*
Main machinery: 2 Caterpillar 3412 diesels; 1,600 hp *(1.19 MW)*; 2 shafts
Speed, knots: 23. **Range, miles:** 1,500 at 8 kt
Complement: 10
Guns: 2—12.7 mm MGs.
Radars: Surface search: Furuno; I-band.

Comment: Transferred from US Coast Guard 16 October 1999. This class is in service with many other navies.

NEW ENTRY

POINT (US colours)   *4/1992*, van Ginderen Collection* / 0081549

4 PGM-39 CLASS (LARGE PATROL CRAFT) (PC)

Name	No	Builders	Commissioned
AGUSAN (ex-PGM 39)	PG 61	Tacoma, WA	Mar 1960
CATANDUANES (ex-PGM 40)	PG 62	Tacoma, WA	Mar 1960
ROMBLON (ex-PGM 41)	PG 63	Peterson Builders, WI	June 1960
PALAWAN (ex-PGM 42)	PG 64	Tacoma, WA	June 1960

Displacement, tons: 124 full load
Dimensions, feet (metres): 100.3 × 18.6 × 6.9 *(30.6 × 5.7 × 2.1)*
Main machinery: 2 MTU MB 12V 493 TY57 diesels; 2,200 hp(m) *(1.6 MW)* sustained; 2 shafts
Speed, knots: 17. **Range, miles:** 1,400 at 11 kt
Complement: 26-30
Guns: 2 Oerlikon 20 mm. 2—12.7 mm MGs. 1—81 mm mortar.
Radars: Surface search: Alpelco DFR-12; I/J-band.

Comment: Steel-hulled craft built under US military assistance programmes. Assigned US PGM-series numbers while under construction. Transferred upon completion. These craft are lengthened versions of the US Coast Guard 95 ft 'Cape' class patrol boat design. *UPDATED*

AGUSAN   *1994*, Philippine Navy /* 0081550

10 PCF 46 CLASS (COASTAL PATROL CRAFT) (PC)

DB 411	DB 417	DB 422	DB 429	DB 432
DB 413	DB 419	DB 426	DB 431	DB 435

Displacement, tons: 21 full load
Dimensions, feet (metres): 45.9 × 14.5 × 3.3 *(14 × 4.4 × 1)*
Main machinery: 2 Cummins diesels; 740 hp *(552 kW)*; 2 shafts
Speed, knots: 25. **Range, miles:** 1,000 at 15 kt
Complement: 8
Guns: 2—12.7 mm (twin) MGs. 1—7.62 mm M60 MG.
Radars: Surface search: Kelvin Hughes 17; I-band.

Comment: Survivors of a class built by de Havilland Marine, Sydney NSW between 20 November 1974 and 8 February 1975 (DF series). In August 1975 further craft of this design (DB series) were ordered from Marcelo Yard, Manila to be delivered 1976-78 at the rate of two per month. By the end of 1976, 25 more had been completed but a serious fire in the shipyard destroyed 14 new hulls and halted production. Many deleted. *VERIFIED*

DB 435   *1993, Philippine Navy*

15 PCF 50 (SWIFT Mk 1 and Mk 2) CLASS (COASTAL PATROL CRAFT) (PC)

DF 300-303	DF 305	DF 307-316

Displacement, tons: 22.5 full load
Dimensions, feet (metres): 50 × 13.6 × 4 *(15.2 × 4.1 × 1.2)* (Mk 1) 51.3 × 13.6 × 4 *(15.6 × 4.1 × 1.2)* (Mk 2)
Main machinery: 2 GM 12-71 diesels; 680 hp *(504 kW)* sustained; 2 shafts
Speed, knots: 28. **Range, miles:** 685 at 16 kt
Complement: 6
Guns: 2—12.7 mm (twin) MGs. 2 M-79 40 mm grenade launchers.
Radars: Surface search: Decca 202; I-band.

Comment: Most built in the USA. Built for US military assistance programmes and transferred in the late 1960s. Some built in 1970 in the Philippines (ferro-concrete) with enlarged superstructure. DF 303, 309, 311 and 312 belong to the Navy. *UPDATED*

DF 308   *5/1998*, van Ginderen Collection /* 0081552

14 PCF 65 (SWIFT Mk 3) CLASS (COASTAL PATROL CRAFT) (PC)

DF 325-332	DF 334	DF 347	DF 351-354

Displacement, tons: 29 standard; 37 full load
Dimensions, feet (metres): 65 × 16 × 3.4 *(19.8 × 4.9 × 1)*
Main machinery: 3 GM 12V-71TI diesels; 840 hp *(616 kW)* sustained; 3 shafts
Speed, knots: 25
Complement: 8
Guns: 4 Oerlikon 20 mm. 2—12.7 mm MG (twin).
Radars: Surface search: Koden; I-band.

Comment: Improved Swift type inshore patrol boats built by Sewart for the Philippine Navy. Delivered 1972-76. DF 351-354 belong to the Navy. Some that were laid up have been returned to service. New radars fitted. *UPDATED*

DF 347 (Coast Guard)   *5/1998, Sattler & Steele /* 0052711

DF 354 (Navy)   *5/1998*, John Mortimer /* 0081551

3 DE HAVILLAND CLASS (PC)

DF 321-323

Displacement, tons: 25 full load
Dimensions, feet (metres): 54.8 × 16.4 × 4.3 *(16.7 × 5 × 1.3)*
Main machinery: 2 diesels; 740 hp *(552 kW)*; 2 shafts
Speed, knots: 25. **Range, miles:** 450 at 14 kt
Complement: 8
Guns: 2—12.7 mm MGs.

Comment: Locally built in the mid-1980s. Others of this type have been paid off and numbers are uncertain. *VERIFIED*

DF 321   *5/1998, van Ginderen Collection /* 0052713

11 CUTTERS (PB)

CGC 103	CGC 110	CGC 115	CGC 128-130	CGC 132-136

Displacement, tons: 13 full load
Dimensions, feet (metres): 40 × 13.6 × 3 *(12.2 × 4.1 × 0.9)*
Main machinery: 2 Detroit diesels; 560 hp *(418 kW)*; 2 shafts
Speed, knots: 28
Complement: 5
Guns: 1—12.7 mm MG. 1—7.62 mm MG.

Comment: Built at Cavite Yard from 1984. One deleted in 1994. Used for harbour patrols. There are also some small unarmed Police craft. *UPDATED*

CGC 130   *1994*, Philippine Navy /* 0081553

POLAND
MARYNARKA WOJENNA

Headquarters Appointments

Commander-in-Chief:
  Admiral Ryszard Lukasik
Chief of the Naval Staff:
  Vice Admiral Jedrzej Czajkowski
Chief of Naval Training:
  Rear Admiral Zbigniew Badenski
Chief of Naval Logistics:
  Rear Admiral Zbigniew Popek

Diplomatic Representation

Defence and Naval Attaché in London:
  Colonel A Adamowicz

Personnel

(a) 2000: 17,000
(b) 12 months' national service

Prefix to Ships' Names

ORP, standing for *Okręt Rzeczypospolitej Polskiej*

Strength of the Fleet

Type	Active	Building
Submarines—Patrol	3	(2)
Destroyer	1	—
Frigates	2	1
Corvettes	7	(6)
Fast Attack Craft—Missile	7	
Large Patrol Craft	8	—
Coastal Patrol Craft	11	—
Minesweepers—Coastal	15	—
Minehunters—Coastal	7	—
LSTs	7	—
LCUs	3	—
Survey and Research Ships	3	—
AGIs	2	—
Training Ships	3	—
Salvage Ships	4	—
Tankers	4	—

Sea Department of the Border Guard (MOSG)

A para-naval force, subordinate to the Minister of the Interior.

Bases

Gdynia (3rd Flotilla), Hel (9th Flotilla), Swinoujscie (8th Flotilla), Kolobrzeg, Gdansk (Frontier Guard)

Naval Aviation

HQ at Gdynia
Division 1 at Gdynia (MiG-21, W-3, An-28)
Division 2 at Darlowo (Mi-14, Mi-2)
Division 3 at Siemirowice-Cewice (TS-11, An-2, An-28)

Coast Defence

Two divisions with 24—57 mm guns.

Mercantile Marine

Lloyd's Register of Shipping:
  439 vessels of 1,319,063 tons gross

DELETIONS

Training Ships

1999   *Gryf* (reserve)

Maritime Frontier Guard

1997   *Szkwal*
1999   *Zorza*, 6 Wisloka, 3 Pilica, 2 B 306

PENNANT LIST

Submarines

291	Orzel
292	Wilk
293	Dzik

Destroyers

271	Warszawa

Frigates

240	Kaszub
272	Pulawski
273	Kosciuszkol

Corvettes

421	Orkan
422	Piorun
423	Grom
434	Gornik
435	Hutnik
436	Metalowiec
437	Rolnik

Patrol Forces

351	Grozny
352	Wytrwaly

353	Zreczny
354	Zwinny
355	Zwrotny
356	Zawziety
357	Nieugiety
358	Czujny
427	Puck
428	Ustka
429	Oksywie
430	Darlowo
431	Swinoujscie
432	Dziwnów
433	Wladyslawowo

Mine Warfare Forces

622	Rybitwa
623	Mewa
624	Czajka
625	TR 25
626	TR 26
630	Goplo
631	Gardno
632	Bukowo
633	Dabie
634	Jamno
635	Mielno
636	Wicko
637	Resko
638	Sarbsko
639	Necko
640	Naklo

641	Druzno
642	Hancza
643	Mamry
644	Wigry
645	Sniardwy
646	Wdzydze

Amphibious Forces

810	Cedynia
811	Grunwald
821	Lublin
822	Gniezno
823	Krakow
824	Poznan
825	Torun
851	KD-11
852	KD-12
853	KD-13

Survey Ships and AGIs

261	Kopernik
262	Nawigator
263	Hydrograf
265	Heweliusz
266	Arctowski

Auxiliaries

251	Wodnik
253	Iskra
711	Podchorazy
712	Kadet
713	Elew
281	Piast
282	Lech
R 11	Gniewko
R 12	Bolko
R 13	Semko
R 14	Zbyszko
R 15	Macko
K 18	Bryza
Z 1	Baltyk
Z 3	Krab
Z 8	Meduza
Z 9	Slimak

Maritime Frontier Guard

311	Kaper I
312	Kaper II
323	Zefir
325	Tecza

SUBMARINES

Note: It is reported that German 206A or French 'Agosta' class may be acquired to replace the Foxtrots.

1 KILO CLASS (TYPE 877E) (SSK)

Name	No	Builders	Commissioned
ORZEL	291	Sudomekh, Leningrad	21 June 1986

Displacement, tons: 2,325 surfaced; 3,076 dived
Dimensions, feet (metres): 242.1 × 32.5 × 21.7
  (73.8 × 9.9 × 6.6)
Main machinery: Diesel-electric; 2 DL 42M diesels; 3,650 hp(m) *(2.68 MW)*; 2 generators; 6 MW; 1 PG 141 motor; 5,900 hp (m) *(4.34 MW)*; 1 shaft; 2 auxiliary motors; 204 hp(m) *(150 kW)*; 1 economic speed motor; 130 hp *(95 kW)*
Speed, knots: 10 surfaced; 17 dived; 9 snorting
Range, miles: 6,000 at 7 kt snorting; 400 at 3 kt dived
Complement: 60 (16 officers)

Missiles: SAM: 8 SA-N-5 (Strela 2M).
Torpedoes: 6—21 in *(533 mm)* tubes. Combination of 53-65; anti-surface; passive/wake homing to 19 km *(10.3 n miles)* at 45 kt; warhead 300 kg and TEST-71; anti-submarine; active/passive homing to 15 km *(8.1 n miles)* at 40 kt; warhead 205 kg. 53-56 BA and SET 53 m can also be carried. Total of 18 torpedoes.
Mines: 24 in lieu of torpedoes.
Countermeasures: ESM: Brick Group (MRP-25); radar warning; Quad Loop HF D/F.
Weapons control: Murena MWU 110 TFCS.
Radars: Surface search: Snoop Tray (MRP-25); I-band.
Sonars: Shark Teeth (MGK-400); hull-mounted; passive search and attack (some active capability); low/medium frequency. Mouse Roar (MG 519); active attack; high frequency.

ORZEL   *9/1998, J Cislak /* 0052714

Programmes: This was the second transfer of this class, the first being to India and others have since gone to Romania, Algeria, Iran and China. It was expected that more than one would be acquired as part of an exchange deal with the USSR for Polish-built amphibious ships, but this class is considered too large for Baltic operations and subsequent transfers were of the 'Foxtrot' class.
Structure: Diving depth, 240 m *(787 ft)*. Both have two torpedo tubes modified for wire guided anti-submarine torpedoes.
Operational: Based at Gdynia.   *UPDATED*

2 FOXTROT CLASS (TYPE 641) (SS)

Name	No	Builders	Laid down	Launched	Recommissioned
WILK	292	Sudomekh, Leningrad	30 Oct 1961	31 Jan 1962	3 Nov 1987
DZIK	293	Sudomekh, Leningrad	24 Sep 1965	16 Nov 1966	7 Dec 1988

Displacement, tons: 1,952 surfaced; 2,475 dived
Dimensions, feet (metres): 299.5 × 24.6 × 19.7
  (91.3 × 7.5 × 6)
Main machinery: Diesel-electric; 3 Type 37-D diesels; 6,000 hp
  (m) *(4.4 MW)*; 3 motors; 5,400 hp(m) (1 × 2,700 and 2 ×
  1,350) *(3.97 MW)*; 3 shafts; 1 auxiliary motor; 140 hp(m)
  (103 kW)
Speed, knots: 16 surfaced; 15 dived; 9 snorting
Range, miles: 20,000 at 8 kt surfaced; 380 at 2 kt dived
Complement: 73 (12 officers)

Torpedoes: 10—21 in *(533 mm)* (6 bow, 4 stern) tubes.
  Combination of 53-56 WA; anti-surface; passive homing to
  15 km *(8.1 n miles)* at 29 kt; warhead 400 kg and SET-53M;
  anti-submarine; passive homing to 15 km *(8.1 n miles)* at
  29 kt; warhead 100 kg. Total of 22 weapons.
Mines: 32 AMD-100 in lieu of torpedoes.
Countermeasures: ESM: Stop Light (MRP-25); radar warning.
Weapons control: Leningrad 641 TFCS.
Radars: Surface search: Snoop Tray (RLK 101); I-band.
Sonars: Herkules (MG 10, MG 13/15); hull-mounted; passive/
  active search and attack; high frequency.

Programmes: Both originally leased from the former USSR and
  purchased outright in 1993.
Structure: Diving depth, 250 m (820 ft).
Operational: The Polish Navy considers that this is about the
  largest practical size of submarine for Baltic operations. *Wilk*
  given a six month refit in 1993. Both based at Gdynia. Planned
  deletions in 2001 and 2002 unless replaced by ex-German
  Type 206A before then.

  UPDATED

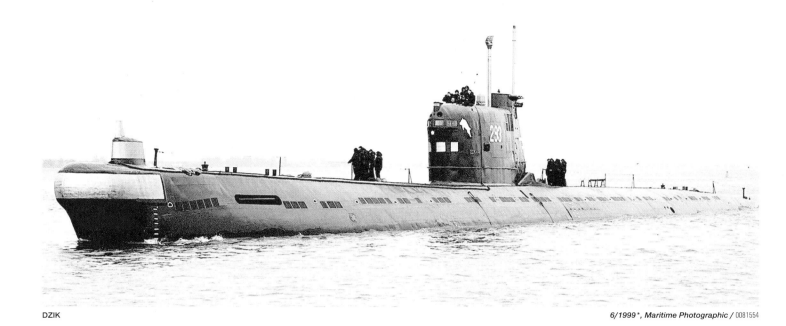

DZIK   *6/1999*, Maritime Photographic /* 0081554

DESTROYERS

1 MODIFIED KASHIN CLASS (TYPE 61MP) (DDG)

Name	No	Builders	Laid down	Launched	Commissioned	Recommissioned
WARSZAWA (ex-*Smely*)	271	Nikolaev 61	15 Nov 1966	6 Feb 1968	27 Nov 1969	9 Jan 1988

Displacement, tons: 4,010 standard; 4,974 full load
Dimensions, feet (metres): 479.7 × 51.8 × 15.7
  (146.2 × 15.8 × 4.8)
Main machinery: COGAG; 4 DE 59 gas turbines; 72,000 hp(m)
  (53 MW); 2 shafts
Speed, knots: 32. **Range, miles:** 2,600 at 30 kt; 4,000 at 18 kt
Complement: 315 (29 officers)

Missiles: SSM: 4 SS-N-2C Styx ❶; active radar or IR homing to
  83 km *(45 n miles)* at 0.9 Mach; warhead 513 kg; sea-skimmer
  at end of run; no reloads.
SAM: 2 SA-N-1 Goa (ZIF 101) twin launchers ❷; command
  guidance to 31.5 km *(17 n miles)* at 2 Mach; warhead 60 kg;
  32 missiles. Some SSM capability.
Guns: 4—3 in *(76 mm)*/60 AK 726 (2 twin) ❸; 90 rds/min to
  15 km *(8 n miles)*; weight of shell 6.8 kg.
  4—30 mm/65 AK 630 ❹; 6 barrels per mounting ❹; 3,000 rds/
  min combined to 2 km.
Torpedoes: 5—21 in *(533 mm)* (quin) tubes ❺. SET-53M; active/
  passive homing to 15 km *(8.1 n miles)* at 29 kt; warhead
  100 kg.
A/S mortars: 2 RBU 6000 12-tubed trainable ❻; range 6,000 m;
  warhead 31 kg; 120 rockets.
Countermeasures: Decoys: 4 PK 16 chaff launchers. 2 towed
  torpedo decoys.
ESM/ECM: 2 Bell Shroud. 2 Bell Squat (MP 401).
Weapons control: 2 Tee Plinth and 4 Tilt Pot optronic directors.
Radars: Air/surface search: Big Net (MR 500U) ❼; C-band.
  Head Net C (MR 310A); 3D; E-band ❽; range 128 km *(70 n
  miles)*.
Navigation: 2 SRN 7453 and 1 SRN 207; I-band.
Fire control: 2 Peel Group ❾; H/I-band (for SA-N-1). 2 Bass Tilt ❿;
  H/I-band (for 30 mm). 2 Owl Screech ⓫; G-band (for guns).
IFF: Salt Pot.
Sonars: Bull Nose (MG 335); hull-mounted; active search and
  attack; medium frequency.
  Mare Tail VDS; active search; medium frequency.

Helicopters: Platform for 1 medium.

Programmes: Converted to Type 61MP in 1976-77 and refitted
  at Riga 1982-85. Transferred from the USSR to the Polish Navy
  at the port of Oksywie after a lengthy refit in St Petersburg.
  Purchased outright in 1993.
Structure: No changes were made to the armament before the
  transfer, except that Polish navigation radars were fitted.
Operational: The Flagship of the Polish Navy. Based at Gdynia.
  The ship is expensive to maintain and seldom goes to sea.
  Planned to be replaced by 'Oliver Perry' class frigate.

  UPDATED

WARSZAWA   *(Scale 1 : 1,200), Ian Sturton*

WARSZAWA   *8/1999*, J Cislak /* 0081555

FRIGATES

1 + 1 OLIVER HAZARD PERRY CLASS (FFG)

Name	No	Builders	Laid down	Launched	Commissioned
GENERAL KAZIMIERZ PULAWSKI (ex-Clark)	272 (ex-FFG 11)	Bath Iron Works	17 July 1978	24 Mar 1979	9 May 1980
KOSCIUSZKOL (?) (ex-John H Sides)	273 (ex-FFG 14)	Todd Shipyards, San Pedro	7 Aug 1978	19 May 1979	30 May 1981

Displacement, tons: 2,750 light; 3,638 full load
Dimensions, feet (metres): 445 × 45 × 14.8; 24.5 (sonar)
(135.6 × 13.7 × 4.5; 7.5)
Main machinery: 2 GE LM 2500 gas turbines; 41,000 hp
(30.59 MW) sustained; 1 shaft; cp prop
2 auxiliary retractable props; 650 hp *(484 kW)*
Speed, knots: 29. **Range, miles:** 4,500 at 20 kt
Complement: 200 (15 officers) including 19 aircrew

Missiles: SSM: 4 McDonnell Douglas Harpoon; active radar
homing to 130 km *(70 n miles)* at 0.9 Mach; warhead 227 kg.
SAM: 36 GDC Standard SM-1MR; command guidance; semi-
active radar homing to 46 km *(25 n miles)* at 2 Mach.
1 Mk 13 Mod 4 launcher for both SSM and SAM missiles ❶.
Guns: 1 OTO Melara 3 in *(76 mm)*/62 Mk 75 ❷; 85 rds/min to
16 km *(8.7 n miles)* anti-surface; 12 km *(6.6 n miles)* anti-
aircraft; weight of shell 6 kg.
1 General Electric/General Dynamics 20 mm/76 6-barrelled
Mk 15 Vulcan Phalanx ❸; 3,000 rds/min combined to 1.5 km.
2 McDonnell Douglas 25 mm Mk 38 guns can be fitted
amidships. 4—12.7 mm MGs.
Torpedoes: 6—324 mm Mk 32 (2 triple) tubes ❹. 24 Honeywell
Mk 46 Mod 5; anti-submarine; active/passive homing to 11 km
(5.9 n miles) at 40 kt; warhead 44 kg.
Countermeasures: Decoys: 2 Loral Hycor SRBOC 6-barrelled
fixed Mk 36 ❺; IR flares and chaff to 4 km *(2.2 n miles)*.
T—Mk 6 Fanfare/SLQ-25 Nixie; torpedo decoy.
ESM/ECM: SLQ-32(V)2 ❻; radar warning. Sidekick modification
adds jammer and deception system.
Combat data systems: NTDS with Link 11 and 14. SATCOM
SRR-1, WSC-3 (UHF).
Weapons control: SWG-1 Harpoon LCS. Mk 92 (Mod 4), WCS
with CAS (Combined Antenna System). The Mk 92 is the US
version of the Signaal WM28 system. Mk 13 weapon direction
system. 2 Mk 24 optical directors.
Radars: Air search: Raytheon SPS-49(V)4 ❼; C/D-band.
Surface search: ISC Cardion SPS-55 ❽; I-band.
Fire control: Lockheed STIR (modified SPG-60) ❾; I/J-band.
Sperry Mk 92 (Signaal WM28) ❿; I/J-band.
Navigation: Furuno; I-band.
Tacan: URN 25. IFF Mk XII AIMS UPX-29.
Sonars: SQQ 89(V)2 (Raytheon SQS 56 and Gould SQR 19); hull-
mounted active search and attack; medium frequency and
passive towed array; very low frequency.

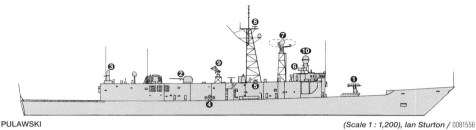

PULAWSKI *(Scale 1 : 1,200), Ian Sturton* / 0081556

PULAWSKI (US colours) *5/1999*, van Ginderen Collection* / 0081557

Helicopters: 2 medium.

Programmes: First one approved for transfer from US by grant in
1999. Recommissioned in April 2000. Second one scheduled
to follow in 2001.

Structure: Details given are for the ship in service with the US
Navy except for helicopter links. The type of helicopter to be
carried is not known.

NEW ENTRY

1 KASZUB CLASS (TYPE 620) (FF)

Name	No	Builders	Laid down	Launched	Commissioned
KASZUB	240	Northern Shipyard, Gdansk	9 June 1984	11 May 1986	15 Mar 1987

Displacement, tons: 1,051 standard; 1,183 full load
Dimensions, feet (metres): 270 × 32.8 × 10.2; 16.1 (sonar)
(82.3 × 10 × 3.1; 4.9)
Main machinery: CODAD; 4 Cegielski-Sulzer AS 16V 25/30
diesels; 16,900 hp(m) *(12.42 MW)*; 2 shafts; cp props
Speed, knots: 27. **Range, miles:** 3,500 at 14 kt; 350 at 26 kt
Complement: 67 (23 officers)

Missiles: SAM: 2 SA-N-5 quad launchers ❶; IR homing to 10 km
(5.5 n miles) at 1.5 Mach. VLS system to replace after 23 mm
gun.
Guns: 1 USSR 3 in *(76 mm)*/66 AK 176 ❷; 120 rds/min to 15 km
(8 n miles); weight of shell 7 kg.
6 ZU-23-2M Wrobel 23 mm/87 (3 twin) ❸; 400 rds/min
combined to 2 km.
Torpedoes: 4—21 in *(533 mm)* (2 twin) tubes ❹. SET-53M;
passive homing to 15 km *(8.1 n miles)* at 29 kt; warhead
100 kg.
A/S mortars: 2 RBU 6000 12-tubed trainable ❺; range 6,000 m;
warhead 31 kg; 120 rockets.
Depth charges: 2 rails. 24 charges.
Mines: 20
Countermeasures: Decoys: 1-10 barrelled 122 mm Jastrzab
launcher ❻ for chaff.
ESM: Intercept.
Weapons control: Drakon TFCS.

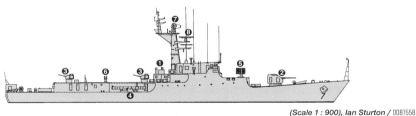

KASZUB *(Scale 1 : 900), Ian Sturton* / 0081558

Radars: Air/surface search: Strut Curve (MR 302) ❼; F-band.
Surface search: Nogat SRN 7453 ❽; I-band.
Navigation: SRN 441XT; I-band.
IFF: Square Head.
Sonars: MG 322T; hull-mounted; active search; medium
frequency.
MG 329M; stern-mounted dipping type mounted on the
transom; active; high frequency.

Programmes: Second of class cancelled in 1989 and a class of
up to ten more ships based on the Kaszub hull and specialised
for anti-submarine warfare has been shelved.

Structure: Design based on 'Grisha' class but with many
alterations. The 76 mm gun was fitted in late 1991. New decoy
system fitted in 1999. There is space for a fire-control director
on the bridge roof.
Operational: Finally achieved operational status in 1990. Based
at Hel with the Border Guard in 1990 but returned to the Navy
in 1991. The ship has to stop to use stern-mounted sonar.

UPDATED

KASZUB *6/1999*, J Cislak* / 0081559

CORVETTES

0 + (6) TYPE 924 (MEKO A 100) CLASS (FSG)

Displacement, tons: 1,900 full load
Dimensions, feet (metres): 297.2 × 44 × 11.2
  (90.6 × 13.4 × 3.4)
Main machinery: CODAG; 1 gas turbine; 2 diesels; 2 shafts
Speed, knots: 30. **Range, miles:** 4,000 at 15 kt
Complement: 94

Missiles: SSM: 8 Harpoon or RBS-15 Mk 3 ❶.
  SAM: Sea Sparrow or Evolved Sea Sparrow; VLS ❷.
Guns: 1-3 in *(76 mm)*/62 ❸. 2—35 mm. Goalkeeper or RAM ❹.
A/S mortars: 2 ASW 601 ❺.
Countermeasures: Decoys: ESM/ECM.
Combat data systems: Signaal TACTICOS.
Radars: Air/surface search ❻; fire control ❼; navigation.
Sonars: Hull mounted; active; medium frequency.
Helicopters: 1 medium ❽.

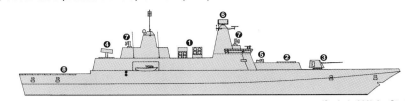

MEKO A 100   *(Scale 1 : 900), Ian Sturton /* 0081560

Programmes: Design definition by German Naval Consortium (Blohm + Voss, Thyssen and HDW) from May to November 1999. First order expected in 2000, to be built at Gdynia with first in-service date in 2003.

Structure: The design is based on the MEKO A 100 but all details are still speculative.

NEW ENTRY

3 ORKAN (SASSNITZ) CLASS (TYPE 660 (ex-151)) (FSG)

Name	No	Builders	Launched	Commissioned
ORKAN	421	Peenewerft/Northern Shipyard, Gdansk	29 Sep 1990	18 Sep 1992
PIORUN	422	Peenewerft/Northern Shipyard, Gdansk	19 Oct 1990	11 Mar 1994
GROM (ex-*Huragan*)	423	Peenewerft/Northern Shipyard, Gdansk	11 Dec 1990	28 Mar 1995

Displacement, tons: 331 standard; 326 full load
Dimensions, feet (metres): 163.4 oa; 147.6 wl × 28.5 × 7.2
  (49.8; 45 × 8.7 × 2.2)

Main machinery: 3 Type M 520T diesels; 14,670 hp(m)
  (10.78 MW) sustained; 3 shafts
Speed, knots: 37. **Range, miles:** 1,600 at 18 kt; 2,400 at 13 kt
Complement: 36 (4 officers)

Missiles: SSM: 8 (2 quad) launchers; RBS-15 Mk 3 missiles being fitted from 2000.
  SAM: SA-N-5 Grail quad launcher; manual aiming; IR homing to 6 km *(3.2 n miles)* at 1.5 Mach; warhead 1.5 kg.
Guns: 1 USSR 3 in *(76 mm)*/66 AK 176; 120 rds/min to 15 km *(8 n miles)*; weight of shell 7 kg.
  1—30 mm/65 AK 630; 6 barrels; 3,000 rds/min combined to 2 km.
Countermeasures: Decoys: 4-9 barrelled DERKACZ 81 mm and 1-10 barrelled Jastrzab 122 mm chaff and IR launchers.
Combat data systems: Signaal TACTICOS (see *Modernisation*).
Radars: Surface search: NUR-27XA; I-band.
  Fire control: Bass Tilt MR-123; H/I-band.
  Navigation: SRN 443XTA; I-band.
  IFF: Square Head; Salt Pot.

Programmes: Originally six of this former GDR 'Sassnitz' class were to be built at Peenewerft for Poland. Three units were acquired and completed at Gdansk.
Modernisation: The class is being upgraded with an SSM and TACTICOS combat data system. *Orkan* is to be the first to complete by 2001 followed by the other pair. A new 76 mm compact gun may also be fitted.
Structure: The prototype vessel had two quadruple SSM launchers with an Exocet type (SS-N-25) of missile and the plan is to fit eight SSM in due course. Plank Shave radar has been replaced by a Polish set. Unlike the German Coast Guard vessels of the same class, these ships have retained three engines.
Operational: Based at Gdynia.

UPDATED

PIORUN
6/1999*, J Cislak / 0081562

GROM   *6/1999*, L-G Nilsson /* 0081563

4 GORNIK (TARANTUL I) CLASS (TYPE 1241RE) (FSG)

Name	No	Builders	Commissioned
GORNIK	434	River Shipyard 341, Rybinsk	28 Dec 1983
HUTNIK	435	River Shipyard 341, Rybinsk	31 Mar 1984
METALOWIEC	436	River Shipyard 341, Rybinsk	13 Feb 1988
ROLNIK	437	River Shipyard 341, Rybinsk	4 Feb 1989

Displacement, tons: 385 standard; 455 full load
Dimensions, feet (metres): 184.1 × 37.7 × 8.2
  (56.1 × 11.5 × 2.5)
Main machinery: COGAG; 2 Type M 70 gas turbines; 24,000 hp
  (m) *(17.65 MW)* sustained; 2 M 75 gas turbines with reversible
  gearbox; 8,000 hp(m) *(5.88 MW)* sustained; 2 shafts
Speed, knots: 42. **Range, miles:** 1,650 at 14 kt
Complement: 46 (6 officers)

Missiles: SSM: 4 SS-N-2C Styx (2 twin) launchers; active radar or
  IR homing to 83 km *(45 n miles)* at 0.9 Mach; warhead 513 kg;
  sea-skimmer in terminal flight.
SAM: SA-N-5 Grail quad launcher; manual aiming; IR homing to
  6 km *(3.2 n miles)* at 1.5 Mach; warhead 1.5 kg.
Guns: 1—3 in *(76 mm)*/60 AK 176; 120 rds/min to 15 km *(8 n miles)*; weight of shell 7 kg.
  2—30 mm/65 AK 630 6-barrelled type; 3,000 rds/min
  combined to 2 km.
Countermeasures: Decoys: 2 PK 16 chaff launchers.
Weapons control: Korall-E WFCS; PMK 453 optronic director.
Radars: Air/surface search: Plank Shave (Garpun E); E-band.
Navigation: Pechora (436 and 437); Kivach (434 and 435);
  I-band.
Fire control: Bass Tilt (MR-123); H/I-band.
IFF: Square Head.
Sonars: Foal Tail; VDS; active; high frequency.

Programmes: Transferred from the USSR.
Structure: Similar to others of the class exported to India,
  Yemen, Romania and Vietnam.
Operational: Based at Gdynia.

UPDATED   GORNIK   *6/1999*, Maritime Photographic /* 0081561

LAND-BASED MARITIME AIRCRAFT (FRONT LINE)

Notes: (1) In addition there are 6 TS-11R Iskra reconnaissance, and 12 TS training aircraft.
(2) 26 MiG-21 with ASMs allocated to the maritime role.

MiG 21   *6/1998*, J Cislak /* 0081564

Numbers/Type: 2/5 PZL Swidnik W-3 Sokol/W-3RM Anakonda.
Operational speed: 119 kt *(220 km/h).*
Service ceiling: 15,256 ft *(4,650 m).*
Range: 335 n miles *(620 km).*
Role/Weapon systems: Replacing the Haze. Total of 24 planned for SAR and a variant for ASW
  (W-3UI Alligator) between 2003 and 2005.   *UPDATED*

ANAKONDA   *6/1999*, Maritime Photographic /* 0081565

Numbers/Type: 5 PZL Mielec An-28RM Bryza (Cash).
Operational speed: 181 kt *(335 km/h).*
Service ceiling: 19,685 ft *(6,000 m).*
Range: 736 n miles *(1,365 km).*
Role/Weapon systems: Based on the USSR Cash light transport and used for maritime patrol and
  SAR. First one delivered in January 1995. Thirteen planned in due course. Sensors: Search radar
  ARS 100/ARS 400; ESM. Weapons: 2 SAB 100 bombs.   *UPDATED*

Numbers/Type: 9/3 Mil Mi-14PL/PS Haze A.
Operational speed: 120 kt *(222 km/h).*
Service ceiling: 15,000 ft *(4,570 m).*
Range: 240 n miles *(445 km).*
Role/Weapon systems: PL for ASW, PS for SAR. PL operates in co-operation with surface units;
  supported by five Mi-2 Hoplite helicopters in same unit. Can be carried in *Warszawa.* Sensors:
  I-2ME search radar; APM-60, MAD, sonobuoys, MGM 329M VDS. Weapons: ASV; internal
  torpedoes, depth bombs and mines.
                                                                UPDATED

HAZE PL   *9/1998, J Cislak /* 0052721

CASH   *3/1999*, J Cislak /* 0081566

HOPLITE   *6/1998, J Cislak /* 0052722

PATROL FORCES

7 PUCK (OSA I) CLASS (TYPE 205)
(FAST ATTACK CRAFT—MISSILE) (PCFG)

Name	No	Builders	Commissioned
PUCK	427	Leningrad	26 Oct 1967
USTKA	428	Leningrad	25 Sep 1968
OKSYWIE	429	Leningrad	9 Dec 1971
DARLOWO	430	Leningrad	20 Jan 1972
SWINOUJSCIE	431	Leningrad	13 Jan 1973
DZIWNÓW	432	Leningrad	27 Jan 1975
WLADYSLAWOWO	433	Leningrad	13 Nov 1975

Displacement, tons: 171 standard; 210 full load
Dimensions, feet (metres): 126.6 × 24.9 × 8.8 *(38.6 × 7.6 × 2.7)*
Main machinery: 3 Type M 503A diesels; 8,025 hp(m) *(5.9 MW)* sustained; 3 shafts
Speed, knots: 35. **Range, miles:** 800 at 30 kt
Complement: 30

Missiles: SSM: 4 SS-N-2A Styx; active radar or IR homing to 46 km *(25 n miles)* at 0.9 Mach; warhead 513 kg.
SAM: SA-N-5 quad launcher.
Guns: 4—30 mm/65 (2 twin) AK 230 automatic; 500 rds/min to 5 km *(2.7 n miles)*; weight of shell 0.54 kg.
Radars: Surface search: Square Tie; I-band.
Fire control: Drum Tilt (MR-104); H/I-band.
Navigation: SRN 207M; I-band.

Programmes: All date from early to mid-1960s and are running out of operational life.
Structure: Pennant numbers are carried on sideboards on the bridge. By the end of 1992 six transferred to Frontier Guard and subsequently deleted.
Operational: Based at Gdynia.

UPDATED

WLADYSLAWOWO   *4/1998* / 0052724

8 MODIFIED OBLUZE CLASS (TYPE 912M)
(LARGE PATROL CRAFT) (PC)

Name	No	Builders	Commissioned
GROZNY	351	Naval Shipyard, Gdynia	8 Feb 1970
WYTRWALY	352	Naval Shipyard, Gdynia	8 Feb 1970
ZRECZNY	353	Naval Shipyard, Gdynia	30 Dec 1970
ZWINNY	354	Naval Shipyard, Gdynia	30 Dec 1970
ZWROTNY	355	Naval Shipyard, Gdynia	4 July 1971
ZAWZIETY	356	Naval Shipyard, Gdynia	10 Oct 1971
NIEUGIETY	357	Naval Shipyard, Gdynia	7 July 1972
CZUJNY	358	Naval Shipyard, Gdynia	30 Sep 1972

Displacement, tons: 237 full load
Dimensions, feet (metres): 135.5 × 20.7 × 6.6 *(41.3 × 6.3 × 2)*
Main machinery: 2 Type 40-D diesels; 4,400 hp(m) *(3.23 MW)* sustained; 2 shafts
Speed, knots: 24. **Range, miles:** 410 at 23 kt; 1,200 at 16 kt
Complement: 27

Guns: 4—30 mm/65 AK 230 (2 twin) automatic; 500 rds/min to 5 km *(2.7 n miles)*; weight of shell 0.54 kg.
Depth charges: 2 racks. 12 charges.
Radars: Surface search: SRN 231; I-band.
Fire control: Drum Tilt (MR-104); H/I-band.
IFF: Two Square Head. High Pole.
Sonars: Tamir II (MG 11); hull-mounted; active attack; high frequency.

Comment: All based at Hel. Drum Tilt radar has been removed from some ships.

UPDATED

ZAWZIETY   *6/1999*, J Cislak* / 0081568

11 PILICA CLASS (TYPE 918M) (COASTAL PATROL CRAFT) (PC)

KP-166—KP-176 166-176

Displacement, tons: 93 full load
Dimensions, feet (metres): 93.8 × 19 × 4.6 *(28.6 × 5.8 × 1.4)*
Main machinery: 3 M 50-F7 diesels; 3,604 hp(m) *(2.65 MW)*; 3 shafts
Speed, knots: 27. **Range, miles:** 1,160 at 12 kt
Complement: 14 (1 officer)
Guns: 2 ZU-23-2M Wrobel 23 mm/87 (twin); 400 rds/min to 2 km.
Torpedoes: 2—21 in *(533 mm)* tubes; SET 53M; active/passive homing to 14 km *(7.6 n miles)* at 29 kt; warhead 90 kg.
Radars: Surface search: SRN 301; I-band.
Sonars: MG 329M; dipping VDS.

Comment: Built at Naval Shipyard, Gdynia. First one commissioned 23 April 1977 and the last 24 February 1983. Based at Kolobrzeg. First batch of five, without torpedo tubes are part of the Maritime Frontier Guard. Guns replaced 1986-90.

UPDATED

KP 171   *6/1999*, J Cislak* / 0081567

MINE WARFARE FORCES

3 KROGULEC CLASS (TYPE 206F) (MHC/MSC)

Name	No	Builders	Commissioned
RYBITWA	622	Gdynia Shipyard	15 Apr 1967
MEWA	623	Gdynia Shipyard	25 May 1967
CZAJKA	624	Gdynia Shipyard	23 June 1976

Displacement, tons: 507 full load
Dimensions, feet (metres): 190.9 × 25.3 × 6.9 *(58.2 × 7.7 × 2.1)*
Main machinery: 2 Sulzer/Cegielski 6AL 25/30 diesels; 2,203 hp(m) *(1.62 MW)*; 2 shafts; acbLIPS cp props
Speed, knots: 18. **Range, miles:** 2,000 at 12 kt
Complement: 53 (5 officers)
Missiles: SAM: 2 Fasta-4M quad launchers. SA-N-5/8.
2 SA-N-10 (Grom) to be fitted in due course.
Guns: SAM/guns: 2 Wrobel ZU-23-2MR 23 mm (twin) with 2 SA-N-5 missiles.
Depth charges: 2 racks.
Mines: 8 or 16.
Countermeasures: Decoys: 6—9-barrelled Derkach 2 launchers for chaff.
ECM: PIT Bren system being fitted.
MCM: 2 Bofors MT2 mechanical, 1 TEM-PE-2M magnetic and 1 BGAT acoustic sweeps. CTM Ukwial ROV with sonar, TV and charges. 10 ZHH 230 sonobuoys.
Combat data systems: CTM Pstrokosz command support system.
Radars: Navigation: Racal Decca Bridgemaster; I-band.
Sonars: CTM SHL-100MA hull mounted; active minehunting; high frequency; Politechnica Gdansk SHL-200 VDS.

Comment: All taken out of service in 1997 but returned between May 1999 and April 2000 with new armament and minehunting equipment installed. Divers recompression chamber carried.

UPDATED

MEWA   *5/1999*, J Cislak* / 0081569

13 GOPLO (NOTEC) CLASS (TYPE 207P/207M)
(MINESWEEPERS/HUNTERS—COASTAL) (MSC)

Name	No	Builders	Launched		Commissioned	
GOPLO	630	Naval Shipyard, Gdynia	16 Apr	1981	13 Mar	1982
GARDNO	631	Naval Shipyard, Gdynia	23 June	1993	31 Mar	1984
BUKOWO	632	Naval Shipyard, Gdynia	28 July	1984	23 June	1985
DABIE	633	Naval Shipyard, Gdynia	24 May	1985	11 May	1986
JAMNO	634	Naval Shipyard, Gdynia	11 Feb	1986	11 Oct	1986
MIELNO	635	Naval Shipyard, Gdynia	27 June	1986	9 May	1987
WICKO	636	Naval Shipyard, Gdynia	20 Mar	1987	12 Oct	1987
RESKO	637	Naval Shipyard, Gdynia	1 Oct	1987	26 Mar	1988
SARBSKO	638	Naval Shipyard, Gdynia	10 May	1988	12 Oct	1988
NECKO	639	Naval Shipyard, Gdynia	21 Nov	1988	9 May	1989
NAKLO	640	Naval Shipyard, Gdynia	29 May	1989	2 Mar	1990
DRUZNO	641	Naval Shipyard, Gdynia	29 Nov	1989	21 Sep	1990
HANCZA	642	Naval Shipyard, Gdynia	9 July	1990	1 Mar	1991

Displacement, tons: 225 full load
Dimensions, feet (metres): 126.3 × 24.3 × 5.9 (38.5 × 7.4 × 1.8)
Main machinery: 2 M 401A1 diesels; 1,874 hp(m) (1.38 MW) sustained; 2 shafts
Speed, knots: 14. **Range, miles:** 1,100 at 9 kt
Complement: 30 (4 officers)
Guns: 2 Wrobel ZU-23-2M 23 mm (twin); 400 rds/min combined to 2 km.
Depth charges: 24
Mines: 24
Countermeasures: MCM: MMTK1 mechanical; MTA 1 acoustic and TEM-PE 1 magnetic sweeps.
Radars: Navigation: SRN 302; I-band.
Sonars: MG 89 or MG 79; active minehunting; high frequency.

Comment: *Goplo* is an experimental prototype numbered 207D. The 23 mm guns have replaced the original 25 mm. GRP hulls. All are to be upgraded to 207M for minehunting, and to carry divers. Named after lakes and based at Hel.

UPDATED

RESKO   6/1999*, *Maritime Photographic* / 0081570

4 MAMRY (NOTEC II) CLASS (TYPE 207M)
(MINESWEEPERS/HUNTERS—COASTAL) (MSC/MHC)

Name	No	Builders	Launched		Commissioned	
MAMRY	643	Naval Shipyard, Gdynia	30 Sep	1991	25 Sep	1992
WIGRY	644	Naval Shipyard, Gdynia	28 Nov	1992	14 May	1993
SNIARDWY	645	Naval Shipyard, Gdynia	18 June	1993	28 Jan	1994
WDZYDZE	646	Naval Shipyard, Gdynia	24 June	1994	2 Dec	1994

Displacement, tons: 225 full load
Dimensions, feet (metres): 125.7 × 23.6 × 5.9 (38.3 × 7.2 × 1.6)
Main machinery: 2 M 401A diesels; 1,874 hp(m) (1.38 MW); 2 shafts
2 auxiliary motors; 816 hp(m) (60 kW)
Speed, knots: 13. **Range, miles:** 790 at 14 kt
Complement: 24 (4 officers)
Missiles: SAM/Guns: 2 ZU-23-2MR 23 mm Wrobel II (twin); combination of 2 SA-N-5 missiles; IR homing to 6 km (3.2 n miles) at 1.5 Mach; warhead 1.5 kg and guns; 400 rds/min combined to 2 km.
Mines: 6-24 depending on type.
Countermeasures: MCM: MMTK 1m mechanical, MTA 2 acoustic and TEM-PE 1m magnetic sweeps.
Radars: Navigation: SRN 401XTA; I-band.
Sonars: SHL 100/200; hull mounted/VDS; active minehunting; high frequency.

Comment: Modified version of the 207P and equipped to carry divers. Identical hull to the 207P. All based at Hel. An enlarged design, the Type 207 MCMV with a length of 43.5 m, is a longer term project.

UPDATED

SNIARDWY   11/1999*, J Cislak / 0081571

2 LENIWKA CLASS (TYPE 410S)
(MINESWEEPERS—COASTAL) (MSC)

Name	No	Builders	Commissioned
TR 25	625	Ustka Shipyard	12 Oct 1983
TR 26	626	Ustka Shipyard	12 Oct 1983

Displacement, tons: 269 full load
Dimensions, feet (metres): 84.6 × 23.6 × 8.9 (25.8 × 7.2 × 2.7)
Main machinery: 1 Puck-Sulzer 6AL20/24 diesel; 570 hp(m) (420 kW); 1 shaft; cp prop
Speed, knots: 11. **Range, miles:** 3,200 at 10 kt
Complement: 16
Countermeasures: MCM: MT-3U mechanical, SEMT 1 magnetic and BAT 2 acoustic sweeps.
Radars: Navigation: SRN 311; I-band.

Comment: Project 410S modified stern trawlers. Sweeping is done by using strung-out charges. The ships can carry 40 tons of cargo or 40 people. Based at Swinoujscie.

UPDATED

TR 26   7/1996*, J Cislak / 0081572

AMPHIBIOUS FORCES

1 MODIFIED POLNOCHNY C CLASS (TYPE 776) (LST)

Name	No	Builders	Commissioned
GRUNWALD	811	Northern Shipyard, Gdansk	28 Apr 1973

Displacement, tons: 1,253 full load
Dimensions, feet (metres): 266.7 × 31.8 × 7.9 (81.3 × 9.7 × 2.4)
Main machinery: 2 Type 40-D diesels; 4,400 hp(m) (3.2 MW) sustained; 2 shafts
Speed, knots: 18. **Range, miles:** 1,000 at 18 kt; 2,600 at 12 kt
Complement: 45 plus 54 flag staff
Military lift: 2 light trucks
Missiles: SAM: 2 Fasta 4M quad launchers for SA-N-5.
Guns: 4—30 mm (2 twin). 2—140 mm rocket launchers.
Radars: Navigation: SRN 7453 Nogat; I-band.
Fire control: Drum Tilt (MR-104); H/I-band.

Comment: *Grunwald* converted to an amphibious command vessel. Command and electronic equipment fitted on the vehicle deck leaving a small area behind the bow doors for two light trucks or jeeps. Based at Swinoujscie.

UPDATED

GRUNWALD   7/1996*, J Cislak / 0081573

1 CEDYNIA CLASS (LST)

Name	No	Builders	Commissioned
CEDYNIA	810	Northern Shipyard, Gdansk	10 Oct 1971

Displacement, tons: 836 full load
Dimensions, feet (metres): 246.7 × 29.5 × 6.9 (75.2 × 9 × 2.1)
Main machinery: 2 DM 40 diesels; 5,000 hp(m) (3.68 MW); 2 shafts
Speed, knots: 18. **Range, miles:** 1,200 at 16 kt
Complement: 37 (5 officers)
Military lift: 6 T55 tanks or 230 tons
Radars: Navigation: SRN 7453 Nogat; SRN 207; I-band.

Comment: Based at Swinoujscie and used as an ammunition transport ship.

UPDATED

CEDYNIA   6/1997*, Marek Twardowski / 0012905

5 LUBLIN CLASS (TYPE 767) (LST/MINELAYER) (LST/ML)

Name	No	Builders	Launched		Commissioned	
LUBLIN	821	Northern Shipyard, Gdansk	12 July	1988	12 Oct	1989
GNIEZNO	822	Northern Shipyard, Gdansk	7 Dec	1988	23 Feb	1990
KRAKOW	823	Northern Shipyard, Gdansk	7 Mar	1989	27 June	1990
POZNAN	824	Northern Shipyard, Gdansk	5 Jan	1990	8 Mar	1991
TORUN	825	Northern Shipyard, Gdansk	8 June	1990	24 May	1991

Displacement, tons: 1,350 standard; 1,745 full load
Dimensions, feet (metres): 313 × 35.4 × 6.6 *(95.4 × 10.8 × 2)*
Main machinery: 3 Cegielski 6ATL25D diesels; 5,390 hp(m) *(3.96 MW)* sustained; 3 shafts
Speed, knots: 16. **Range, miles:** 1,400 at 16 kt
Complement: 37 (5 officers)
Military lift: 9 Type T-72 tanks or 9 APC or 7 amphibious tanks. 135 troops plus equipment
Missiles: SAM/Guns: 8 ZU-23-2MR 23 mm Wrobel II (4 twin); combination of 2 SA-N-5 missiles; IR homing to 6 km *(3.2 n miles)* at 1.5 Mach; warhead 1.5 kg and guns; 400 rds/min combined.
Depth charges: 9 throwers for counter-mining.
Mines: 50-134.
Countermeasures: Decoys: 2 12-barrelled 70 mm Derkacz chaff launchers.
Radars: Navigation: SRN 7453 and SRN 443XTA; I-band.

Comment: Designed with a through deck from bow to stern and can be used as minelayers as well as for amphibious landings. Folding bow and stern ramps and a stern anchor are fitted. The ship has a pressurised citadel for NBC defence and an upper deck washdown system. Mining capabilities upgraded in 1997/98. Based at Swinoujscie. *UPDATED*

GNIEZNO 6/1999*, J Cislak / 0081575

3 DEBA CLASS (TYPE 716) (LCU)

Name	No	Builders	Launched		Commissioned	
KD-11	851	Naval Shipyard, Gdynia	13 Nov	1987	7 Aug	1988
KD-12	852	Naval Shipyard, Gdynia	2 July	1990	2 Jan	1991
KD-13	853	Naval Shipyard, Gdynia	26 Oct	1990	3 May	1991

Displacement, tons: 176 full load
Dimensions, feet (metres): 122 × 23.3 × 5.6 *(37.2 × 7.1 × 1.7)*
Main machinery: 3 Type M 401A diesels; 3,000 hp(m) *(2.2 MW)*; 3 shafts
Speed, knots: 20. **Range, miles:** 430 at 16 kt
Complement: 12
Military lift: 1 tank or 2 vehicles up to 20 tons and 50 troops
Guns: 2 ZU-23-2M Wrobel 23 mm (twin).
Radars: Surface search: SRN 207A; I-band.

Comment: The plan was to build 12 but the programme was suspended at three through lack of funds. A similar design has been assembled in Iran. Can carry up to six launchers for strung-out charges. Based at Swinoujscie. *UPDATED*

KD-12 8/1996*, Marek Twardowski / 0081574

SURVEY AND RESEARCH SHIPS

2 MODIFIED FINIK 2 CLASS (TYPE 874) (AGS)

Name	No	Builders	Launched		Commissioned	
HEWELIUSZ	265	Northern Shipyard, Gdansk	11 Sep	1981	27 Nov	1982
ARCTOWSKI	266	Northern Shipyard, Gdansk	20 Nov	1981	27 Nov	1982

Displacement, tons: 1,135 standard; 1,218 full load
Dimensions, feet (metres): 202.1 × 36.7 × 10.8 *(61.6 × 11.2 × 3.3)*
Main machinery: 2 Cegielski-Sulzer 6AL25/30 diesels; 1,920 hp(m) *(1.4 MW)*; 2 auxiliary motors; 204 hp(m) *(150 kW)*; 2 shafts; cp props; bow thruster
Speed, knots: 13. **Range, miles:** 5,900 at 11 kt
Complement: 49 (10 officers)
Radars: Navigation: SRN 7453 Nogat; SRN 743X; I-band.

Comment: Sister ships to Russian class which were built in Poland, except that *Heweliusz* and *Arctowski* have been modified and have no buoy handling equipment. Equipment includes Atlas Deso, Atlas Ralog and Atlas Dolog survey. Both ships are based at Gdynia. Two sister ships, *Zodiak* and *Planeta*, are civilian operated. *UPDATED*

HEWELIUSZ 11/1999*, J Cislak / 0081577

ARCTOWSKI 5/1999*, J Cislak / 0081576

1 MOMA CLASS (TYPE 861K) (AGS)

Name	No	Builders	Commissioned	
KOPERNIK	261	Northern Shipyard, Gdansk	20 Feb	1971

Displacement, tons: 1,540 full load
Dimensions, feet (metres): 240.5 × 36.8 × 12.8 *(73.3 × 11.2 × 3.9)*
Main machinery: 2 Zgoda-Sulzer 6TD48 diesels; 3,300 hp(m) *(2.43 MW)* sustained; 2 shafts; cp props
Speed, knots: 17. **Range, miles:** 9,000 at 12 kt
Complement: 20 (8 officers) plus 40 scientists
Radars: Navigation: SRN 7453 Nogat; SRN 743X; I-band.

Comment: Forward crane removed in 1983. Based at Gdynia. *UPDATED*

KOPERNIK 6/1999*, J Cislak / 0081578

2 SURVEY CRAFT (TYPE 4234) (AGSC)

Name	Builders	Commissioned	
K-10	Wisla, Gdansk	6 Feb	1989
K-4	Wisla, Gdansk	25 Sep	1989

Displacement, tons: 45 full load
Dimensions, feet (metres): 62 × 14.4 × 4.9 *(18.9 × 4.4 × 1.5)*
Main machinery: 1 Wola DM 150 diesel; 160 hp(m) *(117 kW)* sustained; 1 shaft
Speed, knots: 9
Complement: 10
Radars: Navigation: SRN 207A; I-band.

Comment: Coastal survey craft based at Gdynia. There are a number of survey launches and buoy tenders listed under *Auxiliaries*. *UPDATED*

K-10 5/1998, J Cislak / 0052729

5 SURVEY CRAFT (TYPE III/C) (AGSC)

M 35   M 37-M 40

Displacement, tons: 10 full load
Dimensions, feet (metres): 36.1 × 10.5 × 2.3 *(11 × 3.2 × 0.7)*
Main machinery: 1 Puck Rekin SW 400/MZ diesel; 95 hp(m) *(70 kW)*; 1 shaft
Speed, knots: 8. **Range, miles:** 184 at 8 kt
Complement: 5
Radars: Navigation: SRN 207A; I-band.

Comment: Based at Gdynia and Swinoujscie (M 35).   ***UPDATED***

M 38   *8/1997*, Marek Twardowski /* 0012909

INTELLIGENCE VESSELS

2 MODIFIED MOMA CLASS (TYPE 863) (AGI)

Name	No	Builders	Commissioned
NAWIGATOR	262	Northern Shipyard, Gdansk	17 Feb 1975
HYDROGRAF	263	Northern Shipyard, Gdansk	8 May 1976

Displacement, tons: 1,677 full load
Dimensions, feet (metres): 240.5 × 35.4 × 12.8 *(73.3 × 10.8 × 3.9)*
Main machinery: 2 Zgoda-Sulzer 6TD48 diesels; 3,300 hp(m) *(2.43 MW)* sustained; 2 shafts
Speed, knots: 17. **Range, miles:** 7,200 at 12 kt
Complement: 87 (10 officers)
Countermeasures: ESM/ECM: intercept and jammer.
Radars: Navigation: 2 SRN 7453 Nogat; I-band.

Comment: Much altered in the upperworks and unrecognisable as Momas. The forecastle in *Hydrograf* is longer than in *Nawigator* and one deck higher. Both fitted for but not with two twin 25 mm gun mountings. Forward radome replaced by a cylindrical type in *Nawigator* and after ones removed on both ships. Based at Gdynia.   ***UPDATED***

NAWIGATOR   *6/1999*, Maritime Photographic /* 0081579

HYDROGRAF   *7/1999*, J Cislak /* 0081580

TRAINING SHIPS

Note: The three masted sailing ship *Dar Mlodziezy* is civilian owned and operated but also takes naval personnel for training.

1 WODNIK CLASS (TYPE 888) (AXT)

Name	No	Builders	Launched	Commissioned
WODNIK	251	Northern Shipyard, Gdansk	19 Nov 1975	28 May 1976

Displacement, tons: 1,697 standard; 1,820 full load
Dimensions, feet (metres): 234.3 × 38.1 × 14.8 *(71.4 × 11.6 × 4.5)*
Main machinery: 2 Zgoda-Sulzer 6TD48 diesels; 2,650 hp(m) *(1.95 MW)* sustained; 2 shafts; cp props
Speed, knots: 16. **Range, miles:** 7,200 at 11 kt
Complement: 56 (24 officers) plus 101 midshipmen
Guns: 4 ZU-23-2MR Wrobel 23 mm (2 twin). 2 *(Wodnik)* or 4 *(Gryf)* 30 mm AK 230 (1 or 2 twin).
Radars: Navigation: 2 SRN 7453 Nogat; I-band.
Helicopters: Platform for 1 light.

Comment: Sister to former GDR *Wilhelm Pieck* and two Russian ships. Converted to a hospital ship (150 beds) in 1990 for deployment to the Gulf. Armament removed as part of the conversion but partially restored in 1992. Based at Gdynia. Second of class in reserve from 1999.   ***UPDATED***

WODNIK   *7/1999*, A Campanera i Rovira /* 0081581

1 BRYZA (TYPE 722) and 3 ELEW (TYPE 722U) CLASSES (AXL)

Name	No	Builders	Launched	Commissioned
BRYZA	K 18	Wisla Shipyard, Gdansk	28 Dec 1964	8 Oct 1965
PODCHORAZY	711	Wisla Shipyard, Gdansk	6 Apr 1974	30 Nov 1974
KADET	712	Wisla Shipyard, Gdansk	11 Apr 1975	19 July 1975
ELEW	713	Wisla Shipyard, Gdansk	19 Nov 1975	5 Mar 1976

Displacement, tons: 180 (167, *Bryza*) full load
Dimensions, feet (metres): 94.5 × 21.7 × 6.4 *(28.8 × 6.6 × 2)*
Main machinery: 2 Wola DM 150 diesels; 300 hp(m) *(220 kW)*; 2 shafts
Speed, knots: 10. **Range, miles:** 1,100 at 10 kt
Complement: 11 plus 29 cadets
Radars: Navigation: 2 SRN 743X; I-band.

Comment: *Bryza* has a lighter superstructure than remainder but is built on the same hull. The class is similar to Russian vessels. *Bryza* is used only as a personnel transport ship. Based at Hel (711), Gdynia (K 18 and 713) and Swinoujscie (712).   ***UPDATED***

PODCHORAZY   *6/1997*, Marek Twardowski /* 0012912

1 ISKRA CLASS (TYPE B79) (SAIL TRAINING SHIP) (AXS)

Name	No	Builders	Launched	Commissioned
ISKRA	253	Gdansk Shipyard	6 Mar 1982	11 Aug 1982

Displacement, tons: 498 full load
Dimensions, feet (metres): 160.8 × 26.6 × 12.1 *(49 × 8.1 × 3.7)*
Main machinery: 1 Wola 68H12 diesel; 310 hp(m) *(228 kW)*; 1 auxiliary shaft; cp prop
Speed, knots: 9 (diesel)
Complement: 13 (5 officers) plus 50 cadets
Radars: Navigation: SRN 206; I-band.

Comment: Barquentine with 1,040 m² of sail. Used by the Naval Academy for training with a secondary survey role. Based at Gdynia.   ***UPDATED***

ISKRA   *7/1999*, Per Kornefeldt /* 0081582

AUXILIARIES

1 BALTYK CLASS (TYPE ZP 1200) (TANKER) (AORL)

Name	No	Builders	Commissioned
BALTYK	Z 1	Naval Shipyard, Gdynia	11 Mar 1991

Displacement, tons: 2,918 standard; 2,984 full load
Dimensions, feet (metres): 278.2 × 43 × 15.4 *(84.8 × 13.1 × 4.7)*
Main machinery: 2 Cegielski 8 ASL 25 diesels; 4,025 hp(m) *(2.96 MW)*; 2 shafts; cp props
Speed, knots: 15. **Range, miles:** 4,250 at 12 kt
Complement: 32 (4 officers)
Cargo capacity: 1,184 tons fuel, 97 tons lub oil
Guns: 4 ZU-23-2M Wrobel 23 mm (2 twin).
Radars: Navigation: SRN 7453 and SRN 207A; I-band.

Comment: Beam replenishment stations, one each side. First of a projected class of four, of which the others were cancelled. Based at Gdynia.

UPDATED

BALTYK   *8/1999*, J Cislak /* 0081583

3 MOSKIT CLASS (TYPE B 199) (TANKERS) (AOT)

Name	No	Builders	Launched	Commissioned
KRAB	Z 3	Rzeczna, Wroclaw Shipyard	22 July 1969	23 Sep 1970
MEDUZA	Z 8	Rzeczna, Wroclaw Shipyard	14 Sep 1969	21 July 1970
SLIMAK	Z 9	Wisla Shipyard, Gdansk	1 Aug 1970	15 May 1971

Displacement, tons: 1,225 full load
Dimensions, feet (metres): 189.3 × 31.2 × 11.2 *(57.7 × 9.5 × 3.4)*
Main machinery: 1 Magdeburg diesel; 850 hp(m) (Z 3 and Z 8); 1,060 hp(m) (Z 9) *(625; 780 kW)*; 1 shaft
Speed, knots: 10. **Range, miles:** 1,200 at 10 kt
Complement: 23 (2 officers)
Cargo capacity: 656 tons (Z 3 and Z 8); 599 tons (Z 9)
Guns: 4 ZU-23-2M Wrobel 23 mm (2 twin) (Z 3 and Z 8); 2—25 mm M3 (Z 9).
Radars: Navigation: SRN 206; I-band.

Comment: First two carry oil, the other one water. Names are unofficial. Z 3 based at Swinoujscie, Z 8 at Hel and Z 9 at Gdynia.

UPDATED

MEDUZA   *5/1999*, J Cislak /* 0081584

2 KORMORAN CLASS (TRV)

Name	Builders	Launched	Commissioned
K 8	Naval Shipyard, Gdynia	26 Aug 1970	3 July 1971
K 11	Naval Shipyard, Gdynia	23 June 1971	11 Dec 1971

Displacement, tons: 149 full load
Dimensions, feet (metres): 114.8 × 19.7 × 5.2 *(35 × 6 × 1.6)*
Main machinery: 2 Type M 50F5 diesels; 2,200 hp(m) *(1.6 MW)*; 2 shafts
Speed, knots: 21. **Range, miles:** 550 at 15 kt
Complement: 18
Guns: 2 ZU-23-2M Wrobel 23 mm (twin).
Radars: Navigation: SRN 206/301; I-band.

Comment: Armament updated in 1993. Both based at Gdynia.

UPDATED

K 11   *8/1999*, van Ginderen Collection /* 0081585

3 MROWKA CLASS (TYPE B 208) (DEGAUSSING VESSELS) (YDG)

Name	No	Builders	Commissioned
WRONA	SD 11	Naval Shipyard, Gdynia	10 Oct 1971
RYS	SD 12	Naval Shipyard, Gdynia	25 June 1972
—	SD 13	Naval Shipyard, Gdynia	16 Dec 1972

Displacement, tons: 595 full load
Dimensions, feet (metres): 145.3 × 26.6 × 7.5 *(44.3 × 8.1 × 2.3)*
Main machinery: 1 6NV D48 diesel; 957 hp(m) *(704 kW)*; 1 shaft
Speed, knots: 9.5. **Range, miles:** 2,230 at 9.5 kt
Complement: 25
Guns: 2—25 mm (twin) (SD 11 and 13); 2 ZU-23-2M Wrobel 23 mm (twin) (SD 12).
Radars: Navigation: SRN 206; I-band.

Comment: Names are unofficial. SD 12 based at Swinoujscie, remainder at Gdynia.

UPDATED

WRONA   *8/1999*, van Ginderen Collection /* 0081586

2 PIAST CLASS (TYPE 570) (SALVAGE SHIPS) (ARS)

Name	No	Builders	Commissioned
PIAST	281	Northern Shipyard, Gdansk	26 Jan 1974
LECH	282	Northern Shipyard, Gdansk	30 Nov 1974

Displacement, tons: 1,887 full load
Dimensions, feet (metres): 238.5 × 38.1 × 13.1 *(72.7 × 11.6 × 4)*
Main machinery: 2 Zgoda-Sulzer 6TD48 diesels; 3,300 hp(m) *(2.43 MW)* sustained; 2 shafts; cp props
Speed, knots: 15. **Range, miles:** 3,000 at 12 kt
Complement: 56 (8 officers) plus 12 spare
Missiles: SAM: 2 Fasta 4M twin launchers for SA-N-5.
Guns: 8—25 mm (4 twin) or 4—23 mm Wrobel ZU-23 (2 twin) can be carried.
Radars: Navigation: 2 SRN 7453 Nogat; I-band.

Comment: Basically a 'Moma' class hull with towing and firefighting capabilities. Ice-strengthened hulls. Wartime role as hospital ships. Carry three-man diving bells capable of 100 m depth and a decompression chamber. ROV added and other salvage improvements made in 1997/98. Based at Gdynia. Guns may not be carried.

UPDATED

PIAST   *8/1999*, van Ginderen Collection /* 0081587

2 ZBYSZKO CLASS (TYPE B 823) (SALVAGE SHIPS) (ARS)

Name	No	Builders	Commissioned
ZBYSZKO	R 14	Ustka Shipyard	8 Nov 1991
MACKO	R 15	Ustka Shipyard	20 Mar 1992

Displacement, tons: 380 full load
Dimensions, feet (metres): 114.8 × 26.2 × 9.8 *(35 × 8 × 3)*
Main machinery: 1 Sulzer 6AL20/24D; 750 hp(m) *(551 kW)*; 1 shaft
Speed, knots: 11. **Range, miles:** 3,000 at 10 kt
Complement: 15
Radars: Navigation: SRN 402X; I-band.

Comment: Type B-823 ordered 30 May 1988. Carries a decompression chamber and two divers. Mobile gantry crane on the stern. Based at Kolobrzeg.

UPDATED

MACKO   *8/1999*, van Ginderen Collection /* 0081588

3 PLUSKWA CLASS (TYPE R-30) (SALVAGE TUGS) (ATS)

Name	No	Builders	Commissioned
GNIEWKO	R 11	Naval Shipyard, Gdynia	29 Sep 1981
BOLKO	R 12	Naval Shipyard, Gdynia	7 Nov 1982
SEMKO	R 13	Naval Shipyard, Gdynia	9 May 1987

Displacement, tons: 365 full load
Dimensions, feet (metres): 105 × 29.2 × 10.2 (32 × 8.9 × 3.1)
Main machinery: 1 Cegielski-Sulzer 6AL25/30 diesel; 1,470 hp(m) (1.08 MW); 1 shaft
Speed, knots: 12. **Range, miles:** 4,000 at 7 kt
Complement: 18
Radars: Navigation: SRN 823; I-band.

Comment: Gniewko based at Hel, the others at Swinoujscie. Bollard pull 15 tons.

UPDATED

GNIEWKO   6/1999*, J Cislak / 0081589

9 DIVING TENDERS AND TRANSPORTS (YDT/YFB)

K 1   K 5   K 7   K 9   K 12-14   K 20-21

Displacement, tons: 50 full load
Dimensions, feet (metres): 61.7 × 14.4 × 4.9 (18.8 × 4.4 × 1.5)
Main machinery: 1 Wola diesel; 103 hp(m) (74 km); 1 shaft
Speed, knots: 9
Complement: 4-10
Radars: Navigation: SRN 301 or SRN 207A; I-band.

Comment: K 1-K 14 harbour craft used for various purposes. Built between 1976 and 1989. K 20-21 are small launches built in 1989 and used for survey work.

UPDATED

K 13   9/1999*, J Cislak / 0081590

3 TRANSPORT CRAFT (YFB)

M 1   M 3   M 32

Displacement, tons: 74 full load
Dimensions, feet (metres): 94.2 × 19 × 7.2 (28.7 × 5.8 × 2.2)
Main machinery: 3 M50F5 diesels; 3,600 hp(m) (2.65 MW); 3 shafts
Speed, knots: 27
Complement: 4 plus 30
Radars: Navigation: SRN 207A; I-band.

Comment: Details given are for M 1 built at Gdynia. The other two are similar but slower and smaller. All can be used as emergency patrol craft. M 1 based at Gdynia as an Admirals launch.

UPDATED

M 1   5/1999*, J Cislak / 0081591

15 MISCELLANEOUS HARBOUR CRAFT

B 1-3, B 5-7, B 11-13, W 2, M 5, M 12, M 22, M 30, M41

Comment: M numbers are patrol launches; B numbers are freighters and oil lighters; W 2 is a floating workshop.

UPDATED

B 7   8/1999*, van Ginderen Collection / 0081592

TUGS

2 H 960 CLASS (ATA)

H 6   H 8

Displacement, tons: 332 full load
Dimensions, feet (metres): 91.2 × 26.2 × 12.1 (27.8 × 8 × 3.7)
Main machinery: 1 Sulzer GATL 25 D diesels; 1,306 hp(m) (960 kW); 1 shaft
Speed, knots: 11. **Range, miles:** 1,150 at 12 kt
Complement: 17 (1 officer)
Radars: Navigation: SRN 207A; I-band.

Comment: Built at Nauta Ship Repair Yard, Gdynia and commissioned 25 September 1992 and 19 March 1993 respectively. Based at Hel (H 6) and Gdynia (H 8).

UPDATED

H 8   6/1999*, J Cislak / 0081593

2 MOTYL CLASS (TYPE B 65) (ATA)

H 12   H 20

Displacement, tons: 439 full load
Dimensions, feet (metres): 103.7 × 27.6 × 11.5 (31.6 × 8.4 × 3.5)
Main machinery: 1 Sulzer 5TD48 diesel; 1,500 hp(m) (1.1 MW); 1 shaft
Speed, knots: 13. **Range, miles:** 1,500 at 12 kt
Complement: 22
Radars: Navigation: SRN 206; I-band.

Comment: Built at Northern Shipyard, Gdansk and commissioned 3 January 1964 and 12 September 1964 respectively. Have some ice breaking capability. Bollard pull 15 tons. Based at Hel (H 12) and Swinoujscie (H 20).

UPDATED

H 12   9/1996*, Marek Twardowski / 0081594

8 HARBOUR TUGS (TYPES H 900, H 800, H 820) (YTB/YTM)

H 1-2 (Type 800)   H 3-5, H 7 (Type 900)   H 9-10 (Type 820)

Displacement, tons: 218 full load
Dimensions, feet (metres): 84 × 22.3 × 11.5 (25.6 × 6.8 × 3.5)
Main machinery: 1 Cegielski-Sulzer 6AL20/24H diesel; 935 hp(m) (687 kW); 1 shaft
Speed, knots: 11. **Range, miles:** 1,500 at 10 kt
Complement: 17
Radars: Navigation: SRN 206; I-band.

Comment: Details given are for H 3, 4, 5 and 7. Completed 1979-81. Have firefighting capability except H 9-10. H 1-2 completed 1970 and H 9-10 in 1993.   **UPDATED**

H 7   6/1999 *, J Cislak / 0081595

SEA DEPARTMENT OF THE BORDER GUARD (MOSG)

Headquarters Appointments

Commandant MOSG:
    Rear Admiral Konrad Wisniowskki
Deputy Commandant:
    Captain Marek Borkowski
Deputy Commandant:
    Commander Wlodzimierz Gryc

Bases

Gdansk (HQ and Kaszubski Division)
Kolobrzeg (Baltycki Division)
Swinoujscie (Pomorski Division)

General

MOSG (Morski Oddzial Strazy Granicznej) formed on 12 June 1991. Vessels have blue hulls with red and yellow striped insignia. Superstructures are painted white.

PATROL FORCES

2 OBLUZE CLASS (TYPE 912) (LARGE PATROL CRAFT) (PC)

Name	No	Builders	Commissioned
ZEFIR	SG 323	Naval Shipyard, Gdynia	10 June 1967
TECZA	SG 325	Naval Shipyard, Gdynia	31 Jan 1968

Displacement, tons: 236 full load
Dimensions, feet (metres): 135.5 × 21.3 × 7 (41.3 × 6.5 × 2.1)
Main machinery: 2 40DM diesels; 4,400 hp(m) (3.24 MW) sustained; 2 shafts
Speed, knots: 24. **Range, miles:** 1,200 at 12 kt
Complement: 19
Guns: 4 AK 230 30 mm (2 twin) (SG 323). 2 AK 230 30 mm (twin) (SG 325).
Depth charges: 2 internal racks.
Radars: Surface search: SRN 207; I-band.
Sonars: Tamir II (MG 11); hull-mounted; active attack; high frequency.

Comment: First of class *Fala* is now a museum ship. Both based at Kolobrzeg.   **UPDATED**

TECZA   6/1999 *, Maritime Photographic / 0081596

2 KAPER CLASS (TYPE SKS-40) (LARGE PATROL CRAFT) (PC)

Name	No	Builders	Commissioned
KAPER I	SG 311	Wisla Yard, Gdansk	21 Jan 1991
KAPER II	SG 312	Wisla Yard, Gdansk	3 Apr 1992

Displacement, tons: 470 full load
Dimensions, feet (metres): 139.4 × 27.6 × 9.2 (42.5 × 8.4 × 2.8)
Main machinery: 2 Sulzer 8ATL25/30 diesels; 4,720 hp(m) (3.47 MW); 2 shafts; cp props
Speed, knots: 17. **Range, miles:** 2,800 at 14 kt
Complement: 15
Guns: 2—7.62 mm MGs.
Radars: Surface search: SRN 207; I-band.
Navigation: Racal Decca; I-band.

Comment: Kaper I completed at Wisla Yard, Gdansk in January 1991, Kaper II on 1 October 1994. Have Simrad fish-finding sonars fitted. Used for Fishery Protection. 311 based at Gdansk and 312 at Kolobrzeg.   **UPDATED**

KAPER I   11/1999 *, J Cislak / 0081597

6 WISLOKA CLASS (TYPE 90) (COASTAL PATROL CRAFT) (PC)

SG 142   SG 144-146   SG 150   SG 152

Displacement, tons: 45 full load
Dimensions, feet (metres): 69.6 × 14.8 × 5.2 (21.2 × 4.5 × 1.6)
Main machinery: 2 Wola 31 ANM28 H12A diesels; 1,000 hp(m) (735 kW); 2 shafts
Speed, knots: 18. **Range, miles:** 300 at 18 kt
Complement: 6
Guns: 2—12.7 mm MGs (twin) and 1 ZM rocket launcher.
Radars: Surface search: SRN 207; I-band.

Comment: Built at Wisla Shipyard, Gdansk and completed between October 1973 and August 1977. Three are based at Gdansk and three at Swinoujscie.   **UPDATED**

SG 150   6/1999 *, M Kosycarz/MOSG / 0081598

2 PILICA CLASS (TYPE 918) (COASTAL PATROL CRAFT)

SG 161   SG 164

Displacement, tons: 93 full load
Dimensions, feet (metres): 94.8 × 19 × 4.6 (28.9 × 5.8 × 1.4)
Main machinery: 3 M 50-F6 diesels; 3,604 hp(m) (2.65 MW); 3 shafts
Speed, knots: 27. **Range, miles:** 1,160 at 12 kt
Complement: 12
Guns: 2 ZU-23-2M Wrobel 23 mm (twin).
Radars: Surface search: SRN 231; I-band.

Comment: Same as naval craft but without the torpedo tubes and sonar. Built by Naval Shipyard, Gdynia and completed between June 1973 and October 1974. One based at Swinoujscie and one at Gdansk.   **UPDATED**

SG 161   11/1999 *, J Cislak / 0081599

8 INSHORE PATROL CRAFT (PBI) and 1 TUG (YTM)

SG 002-005   SG 006   SG 008   SG 011   SG 036

Comment: Most are harbour patrol craft except *011* which is a 40 ton coastal craft built in 1976 and *036* which is a river tug. The latest craft are *SG 002-005* which are RIBs built at Szcecin in 1996. Nine transferred to Lithuania in 1996-97.

UPDATED

SG 008   *11/1999*, J Cislak* / 0081600

SG 036   *11/1999*, J Cislak* / 0084274

SG 005
5/1998*, J Cislak / 0084275

PORTUGAL
MARINHA PORTUGUESA

Headquarters Appointments

Chief of Naval Staff:
  Admiral Nuno Gonçalo Vieira Matias
Deputy Chief of Naval Staff:
  Vice Admiral Alexandre Daniel Cunha Reis Rodrigues
Naval Commander:
  Vice Admiral Manuel Lucas Mota E Silva
Azores Maritime Zone Commander:
  Rear Admiral Carlos Monteiro da Silva
Madeira Maritime Zone Commander:
  Captain José Mota Texeira de Agullar
Marine Corps Commander:
  Captain Vasco Manuel Teixeira da Cunha Brazao

Diplomatic Representation

Defence and Naval Attaché in London and Dublin:
  Captain Joaquim Manuel Santana de Mendonça
Naval Attaché in Washington, Ottawa and NLR SACLANT:
  Captain Fernando Manuel de Oliveira Vargas de Matos
Defence Attaché in Luanda:
  Captain José Armando Rodrigues Leite
Defence Attaché in Maputo, Lillongwe, Harare and Dar-Es-Salam:
  Captain Fernando Alberto dos Santos Lourenço
Defence Attaché in Madrid and Athens:
  Captain João Manuel Ribeiro Ferreira
Defence Attaché in S. Tomé and Libreville:
  Commander Arménio Cunha

Personnel

(a) 2000: 11,600 (1,690 officers) including 1,460 marines
(b) 4 months national service

Prefix to Ships' Names

NRP

Bases

Main Base: Lisbon—Alfeite
Dockyard: Arsenal do Alfeite
Fleet Support: Porto, Portimão, Funchal, Ponta Delgada
Air Base: Montijo (Lisbon)

Naval Air

The helicopter squadron was formally activated on 23 September 1993 at Montijo air force base, Lisbon. Operational and logistic procedures are similar to the air force.

Strength of the Fleet

Type	Active (Reserve)	Building (Projected)
Submarines (Patrol)	3	(3)
Frigates	6	—
Corvettes	10	—
Large Patrol Craft	9	(10)
Coastal/River Patrol Craft	15	—
LCTs/LST	1	(1)
Survey Ships and Craft	10	—
Sail Training Ships	4	—
Replenishment Tanker	1	—
Buoy Tenders	2	—

Naval Police

Formed in 1996 for harbour and environmental security duties. This may evolve into a Coast Guard in due course.

Mercantile Marine

Lloyd's Register of Shipping:
  462 vessels of 1,164,767 tons gross

DELETIONS

Frigates

1998   *Commandante Roberto Ivens*

Patrol Forces

1997   *Mandovi, Dom Jeremias*

Amphibious Forces

1997   *Bombarda, Alabarda, LDM 120-121*

Auxiliaries

1997   *Ribeira Grande*
1999   *Almeido Carvalho*

PENNANT LIST

Submarines		Corvettes		Patrol Forces (P list)		Amphibious Forces	
S 163	Albacora	F 471	Antonio Enes	P 1144	Cuanza	LDG 203	Bacamarte
S 164	Barracuda	F 475	João Coutinho	P 1145	Geba		
S 166	Delfim	F 476	Jacinto Candido	P 1146	Zaire		
		F 477	Gen Pereira d'Eça	P 1147	Zambeze	**Service Forces**	
		F 484	Augusto de Castilho	P 1150	Argos		
		F 485	Honorio Barreto	P 1151	Dragão	A 520	Sagres
		F 486	Baptista de Andrade	P 1152	Escorpião	A 521	Schultz Xavier
		F 487	João Roby	P 1153	Cassiopeia	A 522	D Carlos 1
Frigates		F 488	Afonso Cerqueira	P 1154	Hidra	A 523	Almirante Gago Coutinho
		F 489	Oliveira e Carmo	P 1155	Centauro	A 5201	Vega
F 330	Vasco da Gama			P 1156	Orion	A 5203	Andromeda
F 331	Alvares Cabral			P 1157	Pegaso	A 5204	Polar
F 332	Corte Real	**Patrol Forces**		P 1158	Sagitario	A 5205	Auriga
F 480	Comandante João Belo			P 1160	Limpopo	A 5210	Berrio
F 481	Comandante Hermenegildo	P 370	Rio Minho	P 1161	Save		
	Capelo	P 1140	Cacine	P 1162	Albatroz		
F 483	Comandante Sacadura Cabral	P 1141	Cunene	P 1163	Açor		
		P 1143	Rovuma	P 1164	Andorinha		
				P 1165	Aguia		
				P 1167	Cisne		

SUBMARINES

Note: Project Definition for three replacement submarines completed in early 2000. Orders are expected probably for the 'Scorpene' class, in January 2001 with a first delivery date of September 2005.

3 ALBACORA (DAPHNÉ) CLASS (SSK)

Name	No	Builders	Laid down		Launched		Commissioned	
ALBACORA	S 163	Dubigeon-Normandie, Nantes	6 Sep	1965	13 Oct	1966	1 Oct	1967
BARRACUDA	S 164	Dubigeon-Normandie, Nantes	19 Oct	1965	24 Apr	1967	4 May	1968
DELFIM	S 166	Dubigeon-Normandie, Nantes	14 May	1967	23 Sep	1968	1 Oct	1969

Displacement, tons: 869 surfaced; 1,043 dived
Dimensions, feet (metres): 189.6 × 22.3 × 17.1
(57.8 × 6.8 × 5.2)
Main machinery: Diesel-electric; 2 SEMT-Pielstick 12 PA4 V 185
diesels; 2,450 hp(m) *(1.8 MW)*; 2 Jeumont Schneider
alternators; 1.7 MW; 2 motors; 2,600 hp(m) *(1.9 MW)*;
2 shafts
Speed, knots: 13.5 surfaced; 16 dived. **Range, miles:** 2,710 at
12.5 kt surfaced; 2,130 at 10 kt snorting
Complement: 55 (8 officers)

Torpedoes: 12—21.7 in *(550 mm)* (8 bow, 4 stern) tubes. ECAN
E14/15; anti-surface; passive homing to 12 km *(6.6 n miles)* at
25 kt; warhead 300 kg or ECAN L3; anti-submarine; active
homing to 5.5 km *(3 n miles)* at 25 kt; warhead 200 kg.
No reloads.
Countermeasures: ESM: ARUR; radar warning.
Weapons control: DLT D3 torpedo control.
Radars: Surface search: Kelvin Hughes KH 1007; I-band.
Sonars: Thomson Sintra DSUV 2; passive search and attack;
medium frequency.
DUUA 2; active search and attack; 8.4 kHz.

Programmes: Designs are in hand for replacements which may
be ordered in 1999.
Modernisation: Similar to French 'Daphne' class but without the
external modification to the hull. New radar fitted in 1993-94.
Structure: Diving depth, 300 m *(984 ft)*.

UPDATED

BARRACUDA

7/1999*, B Sullivan / 0081601

FRIGATES

3 COMANDANTE JOÃO BELO CLASS (FF)

Name	No	Builders	Laid down		Launched		Commissioned	
COMANDANTE JOÃO BELO	F 480	At et Ch de Nantes	6 Sep	1965	22 Mar	1966	1 July	1967
COMANDANTE HERMENEGILDO CAPELO	F 481	At et Ch de Nantes	13 May	1966	29 Nov	1966	26 Apr	1968
COMANDANTE SACADURA CABRAL	F 483	At et Ch de Nantes	18 Aug	1967	15 Mar	1968	25 July	1969

Displacement, tons: 1,750 standard; 2,250 full load
Dimensions, feet (metres): 336.9 × 38.4 × 14.4
(102.7 × 11.7 × 4.4)
Main machinery: 4 SEMT-Pielstick 12 PC2.2 V 400 diesels;
16,000 hp(m) *(11.8 MW)* sustained; 2 shafts
Speed, knots: 25. **Range, miles:** 7,500 at 15 kt
Complement: 201 (15 officers)

Guns: 2 Creusot-Loire 3.9 in *(100 mm)*/55 Mod 1953 ❶; 60 rds/
min to 17 km *(9 n miles)* anti-surface; 8 km *(4.4 n miles)* anti-
aircraft; weight of shell 13.5 kg.
2 Bofors 40 mm/60 ❷; 300 rds/min to 12 km *(6.6 n miles)*;
weight of shell 0.89 kg.
Torpedoes: 6—324 mm Mk 32 Mod 5 (2 triple) tubes ❸;
Honeywell Mk 46 Mod 5; active/passive homing to 11 km
(5.9 n miles) at 40 kt; warhead 44 kg.
Countermeasures: Decoys: 2 Loral Hycor Mk 36 SRBOC
6-barrelled chaff launchers.
SLQ-25 Nixie; towed torpedo decoy.
ESM: Argo APECS II; intercept.
Combat data systems: Sewaco FD; Link 11.
Weapons control: C T Analogique. Sagem DMA optical director.
Radars: Air search: Thomson-CSF DRBV 22A ❹; D-band.
Surface search: Thomson-CSF DRBV 50 ❺; G-band.
Navigation: Kelvin Hughes KH 1007; I-band.
Fire control: Thomson-CSF DRBC 31D ❻; I-band.
Sonars: CDC SQS-510; hull-mounted; active search and attack;
medium frequency.
Thomson Sintra DUBA 3A; hull-mounted; active search; high
frequency.

Modernisation: Modernisation of external communications,
sensors and electronics completed 1987-90. Chaff launchers
installed in 1989. Further modernisation started in 1993. The
hull sonar has been replaced, torpedo tubes updated, the A/S
mortar removed, towed torpedo decoy installed and ESM

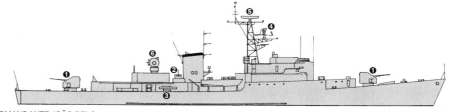

COMANDANTE JOÃO BELO

(Scale 1 : 900), Ian Sturton

COMANDANTE HERMENEGILDO CAPELO

8/1996, Portuguese Navy / 0052745

equipment changed. F 481 completed in 1995, F 480 in 1996
and F 483 in 1999. A combat data system with Link 11 has
been added, compatible with the 'Vasco da Gama' class. The
plan to have one or both after guns replaced either by flight

deck and hangar for helicopter or by SSM has been shelved,
but X turret is removed.
Operational: Designed for tropical service. A fourth of class has
been cannibalised for spares.

VERIFIED

3 VASCO DA GAMA (MEKO 200) CLASS (FFG)

Name	No	Builders	Laid down	Launched	Commissioned
VASCO DA GAMA	F 330	Blohm + Voss, Hamburg	1 Feb 1989	26 June 1989	18 Jan 1991
ALVARES CABRAL	F 331	Howaldtswerke, Kiel	2 June 1989	6 June 1990	24 May 1991
CORTE REAL	F 332	Howaldtswerke, Kiel	24 Nov 1989	6 June 1990	22 Nov 1991

Displacement, tons: 2,700 standard; 3,300 full load
Dimensions, feet (metres): 380.3 oa; 357.6 pp × 48.7 × 20
(115.9; 109 × 14.8 × 6.1)
Main machinery: CODOG; 2 GE LM 2500 gas turbines;
53,000 hp *(39.5 MW)* sustained; 2 MTU 12V 1163 TB83
diesels; 8,840 hp(m) *(6.5 MW)*; 2 shafts; cp props
Speed, knots: 32 gas; 20 diesel
Range, miles: 4,900 at 18 kt; 9,600 at 12 kt
Complement: 182 (23 officers) (including aircrew of 16 (4
officers)) plus 16 Flag Staff

Missiles: SSM: 8 McDonnell Douglas Harpoon (2 quad)
launchers ❶; active radar homing to 130 km *(70 n miles)* at
0.9 Mach; warhead 227 kg.
SAM: Raytheon Sea Sparrow Mk 29 Mod 1 octuple launcher ❷;
RIM-7M; semi-active radar homing to 14.6 km *(8 n miles)* at
2.5 Mach; warhead 39 kg. Space left for VLS Sea Sparrow ❸.
Guns: 1 Creusot-Loire 3.9 in *(100 mm)*/55 Mod 68 CADAM ❹;
60 rds/min to 17 km *(9 n miles)* anti-surface; 8 km *(4.4 n miles)*
anti-aircraft; weight of shell 13.5 kg.

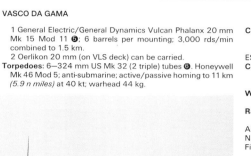

VASCO DA GAMA

(Scale 1 : 1,200), Ian Sturton

1 General Electric/General Dynamics Vulcan Phalanx 20 mm
Mk 15 Mod 11 ❺; 6 barrels per mounting; 3,000 rds/min
combined to 1.5 km.
2 Oerlikon 20 mm (on VLS deck) can be carried.
Torpedoes: 6—324 mm US Mk 32 (2 triple) tubes ❻. Honeywell
Mk 46 Mod 5; anti-submarine; active/passive homing to 11 km
(5.9 n miles) at 40 kt; warhead 44 kg.

Countermeasures: Decoys: 2 Loral Hycor Mk 36 SRBOC
6-barrelled chaff launchers ❼. Sea Gnat.
SLQ-25 Nixie; towed torpedo decoy.
ESM/ECM: Argo AR 700/APECS II; intercept and jammer.
Combat data systems: Signaal SEWACO action data
automation with STACOS tactical command; Link 11 and 14.
Matra Marconi SCOT 3 SATCOM ❽ (1 set between 3 ships).
Weapons control: SWG 1A(V) for SSM. Vesta Helo transponder
with datalink for OTHT.
Radars: Air search: Signaal MW08 (derived from Smart 3D) ❾;
3D; G-band.
Air/surface search: Signaal DA08 ❿; F-band.
Navigation: Kelvin Hughes Type 1007; I-band.
Fire control: 2 Signaal STIR ⓫; I/J/K-band; range 140 km *(76 n
miles)* for 1 m² target.
IFF Mk 12 Mod 4.
Sonars: Computing Devices (Canada) SQS-510(V); hull-
mounted; active search and attack; medium frequency.

Helicopters: 2 Super Sea Lynx Mk 95 ⓬.

Programmes: The contract for all three was signed on 25 July
1986. These are Meko 200 type ordered from a consortium of
builders. As well as Portugal, which provided 40 per cent of the
cost, assistance was given by NATO with some missile, CIWS
and torpedo systems being provided by the USA.
Structure: All-steel construction. Stabilisers fitted. Full RAS
facilities. Space has been left for a sonar towed array and for
VLS Sea Sparrow.
Operational: Designed primarily as ASW ships. SCOT SATCOM
rotated between the three ships. 20 mm guns can be mounted
on the VLS deck.

UPDATED

CORTE REAL

7/1999*, M Declerck / 0081602

CORTE REAL

4/1999*, Michael Nitz / 0081603

VASCO DA GAMA

6/1998, G Toremans / 0052747

CORVETTES

4 BAPTISTA DE ANDRADE CLASS (FS)

Name	No	Builders	Laid down		Launched		Commissioned	
BAPTISTA DE ANDRADE	F 486	Empresa Nacional Bazán, Cartagena	1 Sep	1972	13 Mar	1973	19 Nov	1974
JOÃO ROBY	F 487	Empresa Nacional Bazán, Cartagena	1 Dec	1972	3 June	1973	18 Mar	1975
AFONSO CERQUEIRA	F 488	Empresa Nacional Bazán, Cartagena	10 Mar	1973	6 Oct	1973	26 June	1975
OLIVEIRA E CARMO	F 489	Empresa Nacional Bazán, Cartagena	1 June	1973	22 Feb	1974	28 Oct	1975

Displacement, tons: 1,203 standard; 1,380 full load
Dimensions, feet (metres): 277.5 × 33.8 × 10.2
   (84.6 × 10.3 × 3.1)
Main machinery: 2 OEW Pielstick 12 PC2.2 V 400 diesels;
   12,000 hp(m) *(8.82 MW)* sustained; 2 shafts
Speed, knots: 22. **Range, miles:** 5,900 at 18 kt
Complement: 122 (11 officers)

Guns: 1 Creusot-Loire 3.9 in *(100 mm)*/55 Mod 1968 ❶; 80 rds/
   min to 17 km *(9 n miles)* anti-surface; 8 km *(4.4 n miles)* anti-
   aircraft; weight of shell 13.5 kg.
   2 Bofors 40 mm/70 ❷; 300 rds/min to 12 km *(6.6 n miles)*;
   weight of shell 0.96 kg.
Torpedoes: 6—324 mm US Mk 32 (2 triple) tubes ❸ being
   removed.
Weapons control: Vega GFCS. Panda optical director.
Radars: Air/surface search: Plessey AWS 2 ❹; E/F-band.
   Navigation: Kelvin Hughes; I-band.
   Fire control: Thomson-CSF Pollux ❺; I/J-band.

Helicopters: Platform for 1 Lynx.

Programmes: Originally intended for South Africa. Reclassified
   as corvettes.
Modernisation: Communications equipment updated 1988-91.
   Previous modernisation programme was abandoned in 1998.
   Between 1999 and 2001 all ASW equipment is being
   withdrawn, and radars updated.
Operational: On completion of modernisation programme the
   class is to be used for Fishery Protection duties.
                                              UPDATED

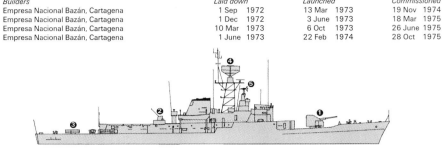

BAPTISTA DE ANDRADE   *(Scale 1 : 900), Ian Sturton*

OLIVEIRA E CARMO   *8/1998, Winter & Findler /* 0052749

6 JOÃO COUTINHO CLASS (FS)

Name	No	Builders	Laid down		Launched		Commissioned	
ANTONIO ENES	F 471	Empresa Nacional Bazán, Cartagena	10 Apr	1968	16 Aug	1969	18 June	1971
JOÃO COUTINHO	F 475	Blohm + Voss, Hamburg	24 Dec	1968	2 May	1969	28 Feb	1970
JACINTO CANDIDO	F 476	Blohm + Voss, Hamburg	10 Feb	1969	16 June	1969	29 May	1970
GENERAL PEREIRA D'EÇA	F 477	Blohm + Voss, Hamburg	21 Apr	1969	26 July	1969	10 Oct	1970
AUGUSTO DE CASTILHO	F 484	Empresa Nacional Bazán, Cartagena	15 Oct	1968	4 July	1969	14 Nov	1970
HONORIO BARRETO	F 485	Empresa Nacional Bazán, Cartagena	20 Feb	1968	11 Apr	1970	15 Apr	1971

Displacement, tons: 1,203 standard; 1,380 full load
Dimensions, feet (metres): 277.5 × 33.8 × 10.8
   (84.6 × 10.3 × 3.3)
Main machinery: 2 OEW Pielstick 12 PC2.2 V 400 diesels;
   12,000 hp(m) *(8.82 MW)* sustained; 2 shafts
Speed, knots: 22. **Range, miles:** 5,900 at 18 kt
Complement: 77 (9 officers)

Guns: 2 US 3 in *(76 mm)*/50 (twin) Mk 33 ❶; 50 rds/min to
   12.8 km *(7 n miles)*; weight of shell 6 kg.
   2 Bofors 40 mm/60 (twin) ❷; 300 rds/min to 12 km *(6.6 n
   miles)*; weight of shell 0.89 kg.
Mines: 2 rails.
Weapons control: Mk 51 GFCS for 40 mm. Mk 63 for 76 mm.
Radars: Air/surface search: Kelvin Hughes ❸; I-band.
   Navigation: Racal Decca RM 1226C; I-band.
   Fire control: Western Electric SPG-34 ❹; I/J-band.

Helicopters: Platform only.

Programmes: Reclassified as corvettes.
Modernisation: A programme for this class to include SSM and
   PDMS has been shelved. In 1989-91 the main radar was
   updated and SATCOMS installed. Also fitted with SIFICAP
   which is a Fishery Protection data exchange system by satellite
   to the main database ashore.
Operational: A/S equipment no longer operational and laid apart
   on shore. Crew reduced by 23 as a result.
                                              VERIFIED

JOÃO COUTINHO   *(Scale 1 : 900), Ian Sturton*

ANTONIO ENES   *7/1994, van Ginderen Collection /* 0052750

SHIPBORNE AIRCRAFT

Numbers/Type: 5 Westland Super Navy Lynx Mk 95.
Operational speed: 125 kt *(231 km/h).*
Service ceiling: 12,000 ft *(3,660 m).*
Range: 320 n miles *(593 km).*
Role/Weapon systems: Ordered 2 November 1990 for MEKO 200 frigates; two are updated HAS
   3 and three were new aircraft, all delivered in August and November 1993. Sensors: Bendix
   1500B radar; Bendix AQS-18V dipping sonar; Racal RNS 252 datalink. Weapons: Mk 46
   torpedoes.   ***UPDATED***

SUPER LYNX   *8/1999*, J Cislak /* 0081604

LAND-BASED MARITIME AIRCRAFT

Note: All Air Force manned.

Numbers/Type: 10 Aerospatiale SA 330C Puma.
Operational speed: 151 kt *(280 km/h).*
Service ceiling: 15,090 ft *(4,600 m).*
Range: 343 n miles *(635 km).*
Role/Weapon systems: For SAR and surface search. Sensors: Omera search radar. Weapons:
   Unarmed except for pintle-mounted 12.7 mm machine guns.   ***VERIFIED***

Numbers/Type: 5/2 CASA C-212-200/300 Aviocar.
Operational speed: 190 kt *(353 km/h).*
Service ceiling: 24,000 ft *(7,315 m).*
Range: 1,650 n miles *(3,055 km).*
Role/Weapon systems: The first five are for short-range SAR support and transport operations.
   The last pair were ordered in February 1993 for maritime patrol and fisheries surveillance off the
   Azores and Madeira. Sensors: Search radar and MAD. FLIR and datalink (last pair). Weapons:
   Unarmed.   ***VERIFIED***

Numbers/Type: 6 Lockheed P-3P Orion.
Operational speed: 410 kt *(760 km/h).*
Service ceiling: 28,300 ft *(8,625 m).*
Range: 4,000 n miles *(7,410 km).*
Role/Weapon systems: Long-range surveillance and ASW patrol aircraft; acquired with NATO
   funding from RAAF update programme and modernised by Lockheed to 3P standard starting in
   1987. Sensors: APS-134/137 radar, ASQ-81 MAD, AQS-901 sonobuoy processor, AQS-114
   computer, IFF, ALR-66 ECM/ESM. Weapons: ASW; eight Mk 46 torpedoes, depth bombs or
   mines; ASV; 10 underwing stations for Harpoon. AGM 65 Maverick in due course.   ***VERIFIED***

PATROL FORCES

Note: Twelve 16 m fast reaction craft ordered from Conafi in 1998. Delivered between September 1999 and September 2001 for Department of Internal Affairs.

0 + (10) NPO 2000 CLASS (PG)

Comment: Planned to be ordered from Arsenal do Alfeite in late 2000 to replace 'Cacine' class. Up to ten of the class are required.

NEW ENTRY

NPO 2000   *(not to scale), Ian Sturton /* 0081605

9 CACINE CLASS (LARGE PATROL CRAFT) (PG)

Name	No	Builders	Commissioned
CACINE	P 1140	Arsenal do Alfeite	May 1969
CUNENE	P 1141	Arsenal do Alfeite	June 1969
ROVUMA	P 1143	Arsenal do Alfeite	Nov 1969
CUANZA	P 1144	Estaleiros Navais do Mondego	May 1969
GEBA	P 1145	Estaleiros Navais do Mondego	May 1970
ZAIRE	P 1146	Estaleiros Navais do Mondego	Nov 1970
ZAMBEZE	P 1147	Estaleiros Navais do Mondego	Jan 1971
LIMPOPO	P 1160	Arsenal do Alfeite	Apr 1973
SAVE	P 1161	Arsenal do Alfeite	May 1973

Displacement, tons: 292.5 standard; 310 full load
Dimensions, feet (metres): 144 × 25.2 × 7.1 *(44 × 7.7 × 2.2)*
Main machinery: 2 MTU 12V 538 TB80 diesels; 3,750 hp(m) *(2.76 MW)* sustained; 2 shafts
Speed, knots: 20. **Range, miles:** 4,400 at 12 kt
Complement: 33 (3 officers)
Guns: 1 Bofors 40 mm/60. 1 Oerlikon 20 mm/65.
Radars: Surface search: Kelvin Hughes Type 1007; I/J-band.

Comment: Originally mounted a second Bofors aft but most have been removed as has the 37 mm rocket launcher. Have SIFICAP satellite data handling system for Fishery Protection duties. An RIB is carried. Two of the class are based at Madeira. To be replaced by new class from 2002.
UPDATED

CUNENE   *11/1999*, van Ginderen Collection /* 0081606

CUANZA   *6/1998, M Verschaeve /* 0052752

5 ALBATROZ CLASS (COASTAL PATROL CRAFT) (PC)

Name	No	Builders	Commissioned
ALBATROZ	P 1162	Arsenal do Alfeite	9 Dec 1974
AÇOR	P 1163	Arsenal do Alfeite	9 Dec 1974
ANDORINHA	P 1164	Arsenal do Alfeite	20 Dec 1974
AGUIA	P 1165	Arsenal do Alfeite	28 Feb 1975
CISNE	P 1167	Arsenal do Alfeite	31 Mar 1976

Displacement, tons: 45 full load
Dimensions, feet (metres): 77.4 × 18.4 × 5.2 *(23.6 × 5.6 × 1.6)*
Main machinery: 2 Cummins diesels; 1,100 hp *(820 kW)*; 2 shafts
Speed, knots: 20. **Range, miles:** 2,500 at 12 kt
Complement: 8 (1 officer)
Guns: 1 Oerlikon 20 mm/65. 2—12.7 mm MGs.
Radars: Surface search: Decca RM 316P; I-band.

Comment: One other is used for harbour patrol duties.

UPDATED

CISNE   *10/1994*, van Ginderen Collection /* 0081608

9 ARGOS CLASS (COASTAL PATROL CRAFT) (PC)

Name	No	Builders	Commissioned
ARGOS	P 1150	Arsenal do Alfeite	2 July 1991
DRAGÃO	P 1151	Arsenal do Alfeite	18 Oct 1991
ESCORPIÃO	P 1152	Arsenal do Alfeite	26 Nov 1991
CASSIOPEIA	P 1153	Conafi	11 Nov 1991
HIDRA	P 1154	Conafi	18 Dec 1991
CENTAURO	P 1155	Arsenal do Alfeite	1 Feb 2000
ORION	P 1156	Estaleiros Navais do Mondego	3 Apr 2000
PEGASO	P 1157	Arsenal do Alfeite	May 2000
SAGITÁRIO	P 1158	Estaleiros Navais do Mondego	July 2000

Displacement, tons: 94 full load
Dimensions, feet (metres): 89.2 × 19.4 × 4.6 *(27.2 × 5.9 × 1.4)*
Main machinery: 2 MTU 12V 396 TE84 diesels (P 1150-1154); 3,700 hp(m) *(2.73 MW)* sustained; 2 shafts
2 Cummins KTA-50-M2 (P 1155-1158); 3,600 hp(m) *(2.64 MW)* sustained; 2 shafts
Speed, knots: 26. **Range, miles:** 1,350 at 15 kt
Complement: 9 (1 officer)
Guns: 2—12.7 mm MGs (1150-1154). 1 Oerlikon 20 mm (1155-1158)
Radars: Navigation: Furuno 1505 DA or Furuno FR 1411; I-band.

Comment: First five ordered in 1989 and 50 per cent funded by the EC. Capable of full speed operation up to Sea State 3. Carries a RIB with a 37 hp outboard engine. The boat is recoverable via a stern well at up to 10 kt. Four more were ordered in 1998 with minor differences. They are 1 m longer and the RIB has a 50 hp outboard engine.

UPDATED

ESCORPIÃO   *6/1998*, Harald Carstens /* 0081607

1 RIO MINHO CLASS (RIVER PATROL CRAFT) (PC)

Name	No	Builders	Commissioned
RIO MINHO	P 370	Arsenal do Alfeite	1 Aug 1991

Displacement, tons: 72 full load
Dimensions, feet (metres): 73.5 × 19.7 × 2.6 *(22.4 × 6 × 0.8)*
Main machinery: 2 KHD-Deutz diesels; 664 hp(m) *(488 kW)*; 2 Schottel pumpjets
Speed, knots: 9.5. **Range, miles:** 420 at 7 kt
Complement: 8 (1 officer)
Guns: 1—7.62 mm MG.
Radars: Navigation: Furuno FR 1505DA; I-band.

Comment: River patrol craft which has replaced *Atria* on the River Minho.

UPDATED

RIO MINHO   *8/1994*, van Ginderen Collection /* 0081609

AMPHIBIOUS FORCES

Note: A multipurpose Logistic Ship (LPD) is a high priority. A new ship is to be procured in due course.

1 BOMBARDA CLASS (LCT/LDG)

Name	No	Builders	Commissioned
BACAMARTE	LDG 203	Arsenal do Alfeite	Dec 1985

Displacement, tons: 652 full load
Dimensions, feet (metres): 184.3 × 38.7 × 6.2 *(56.2 × 11.8 × 1.9)*
Main machinery: 2 MTU MB diesels; 910 hp(m) *(669 kW)*; 2 shafts
Speed, knots: 9.5. **Range, miles:** 2,600 at 9 kt
Complement: 21 (3 officers)
Military lift: 350 tons
Guns: 2 Oerlikon 20 mm.
Radars: Navigation: Decca RM 316P; I-band.

Comment: Similar to French EDIC.   *UPDATED*

BOMBARDA (old number)   *3/1991*, van Ginderen Collection /* 0081610

SURVEY SHIPS

2 STALWART CLASS (AGS)

Name	No	Builders	Commissioned
D CARLOS 1 (ex-*Audacious*, ex-*Dauntless*)	A 522 (ex-T-AGOS 11)	Tacoma Boat	18 June 1989
ALMIRANTE GAGO COUTINHO (ex-*Assurance*)	A 523 (ex-T-AGOS 5)	Tacoma Boat	1 May 1985

Displacement, tons: 2,285 full load
Dimensions, feet (metres): 224 × 43 × 15.9 *(68.3 × 13.1 × 4.6)*
Main machinery: Diesel-electric; 4 Caterpillar D 398B diesel generators; 3,200 hp *(2.39 MW)*; 2 GE motors; 1,600 hp *(1.2 MW)*; 2 shafts; bow thruster; 550 hp *(410 kW)*
Speed, knots: 11. **Range, miles:** 4,000 at 11 kt; 6,450 at 3 kt
Complement: 31 (6 officers) plus 15 scientists
Radars: Navigation: 2 Raytheon; I-band.

Comment: Paid off from USN in November 1995. First one acquired 21 July 1996. Refitted to serve as a hydrographic ship, operating predominantly off the west coast of Africa. Recommissioned 28 February 1997. A second of class acquired by gift 30 September 1999 and has been similarly refitted.

UPDATED

D CARLOS 1   *8/1997*, Portuguese Navy /* 0012931

2 ANDROMEDA CLASS (AGS)

Name	No	Builders	Commissioned
ANDROMEDA	A 5203	Arsenal do Alfeite	1 Feb 1987
AURIGA	A 5205	Arsenal do Alfeite	1 July 1987

Displacement, tons: 245 full load
Dimensions, feet (metres): 103.3 × 25.4 × 8.2 *(31.5 × 7.7 × 2.5)*
Main machinery: 1 MTU 12V 396 TC62 diesel; 1,200 hp(m) *(880 kW)* sustained; 1 shaft
Speed, knots: 12. **Range, miles:** 1,980 at 10 kt
Complement: 17 (3 officers)
Radars: Navigation: Decca RM 914C; I-band.

Comment: Both ordered in January 1984. *Auriga* has a research submarine ROV Phantom S2 and a Klein side scan sonar. Mostly used for oceanography.

UPDATED

ANDROMEDA   *8/1997*, van Ginderen Collection /* 0012932

6 SURVEY CRAFT (AGSC)

CORAL UAM 801	**ACTINIA** UAM 803	**FISALIA** UAM 805
ATLANTA (ex-*Hidra*) UAM 802	**SICANDRA** UAM 804	**SAVEL** UAM 830

Comment: 801, 802 and 805 are of 36 tons and were launched in 1980. 803 and 804 are converted fishing vessels (803 of 90 tons, 804 of 70 tons) of different designs mostly used as lighthouse tenders. 830 is of 7 tons and was built by Conafi in 1992-93.

UPDATED

FISALIA   *3/1992*, van Ginderen Collection /* 0081611

TRAINING SHIPS

1 SAIL TRAINING SHIP (AXS)

Name	No	Builders	Commissioned
SAGRES (ex-*Guanabara*, ex-*Albert Leo Schlageter*)	A 520	Blohm + Voss, Hamburg	10 Feb 1938

Displacement, tons: 1,725 standard; 1,940 full load
Dimensions, feet (metres): 231 wl; 295.2 oa × 39.4 × 17 *(70.4; 90 × 12 × 5.2)*
Main machinery: 2 MTU 12V 183 TE92 auxiliary diesels; 1 shaft
Speed, knots: 10.5. **Range, miles:** 5,450 at 7.5 kt on diesel
Complement: 162 (12 officers)
Radars: Navigation: 2 Racal Decca; I-band.

Comment: Former German sail training ship launched 30 October 1937. Sister of US Coast Guard training ship *Eagle* (ex-German *Horst Wessel*) and Soviet *Tovarisch* (ex-German *Gorch Fock*). Taken by the USA as a reparation after the Second World War in 1945 and sold to Brazil in 1948. Purchased from Brazil and commissioned in the Portuguese Navy on 2 February 1962 at Rio de Janeiro and renamed *Sagres*. Sail area, 20,793 sq ft. Height of main mast, 142 ft. Phased refits 1987-88 and again in 1991-92 which included new engines, improved accommodation, hydraulic crane and updated navigation equipment.

UPDATED

SAGRES   *6/1999*, Michael Nitz /* 0081612

1 SAIL TRAINING SHIP (AXS)

Name	No	Builders	Commissioned
CREOULA	UAM 201	Lisbon Shipyard	1937

Displacement, tons: 818 standard; 1,055 full load
Dimensions, feet (metres): 221.1 × 32.5 × 13.8 (67.4 × 9.9 × 4.2)
Main machinery: 1 MTU 8V 183 TE92 auxiliary diesel; 665 hp(m) (490 kW); 1 shaft

Comment: Ex-deep sea sail fishing ship used off the coast of Newfoundland for 36 years. Bought by Fishing Department in 1976 to turn into a museum ship but because she was still seaworthy it was decided to convert her to a training ship. Recommissioned in the Navy in 1987. Refit completed in 1992 including a new engine and improved accommodation. **UPDATED**

CREOULA   9/1991*, van Ginderen Collection / 0081613

2 SAIL TRAINING YACHTS (AXS)

VEGA (ex-Arreda) A 5201   **POLAR** (ex-Anne Linde) A 5204

Displacement, tons: 70 (60, Vega)
Dimensions, feet (metres): 75 × 16 × 8.2 (22.9 × 4.9 × 2.5) (Polar)
65 × 14.1 × 8.2 (19.8 × 4.3 × 2.5) (Vega)
Radars: Navigation: Raytheon; I-band.

Comment: Sail numbers are displayed. Vega is P-165 and Polar is P-551.   **VERIFIED**

POLAR   6/1998, G Toremans / 0052754

AUXILIARIES

1 ROVER CLASS (REPLENISHMENT TANKER) (AOL)

Name	No	Builders	Launched	Commissioned
BÉRRIO (ex-Blue Rover)	A 5210 (ex-A 270)	Swan Hunter	11 Nov 1969	15 July 1970

Displacement, tons: 4,700 light; 11,522 full load
Dimensions, feet (metres): 461 × 63 × 24 (140.6 × 19.2 × 7.3)
Main machinery: 2 SEMT-Pielstick 16 PA4 185 diesels; 15,360 hp(m) (11.46 MW); 1 shaft; Kamewa cp prop; bow thruster
Speed, knots: 19. **Range, miles:** 15,000 at 15 kt
Complement: 54 (7 officers)
Cargo capacity: 6,600 tons fuel
Guns: 2 Oerlikon 20 mm.
Countermeasures: Decoys: 2 Vickers Corvus launchers. 2 Plessey Shield launchers. 1 Graseby Type 182; towed torpedo decoy.
Radars: Navigation: Kelvin Hughes Type 1006; I-band.
Helicopters: Platform for 1 medium.

Comment: Transferred from UK 31 March 1993. Small fleet tanker designed to replenish oil and aviation fuel, fresh water, limited dry cargo and refrigerated stores under all conditions while under way. Full refit in 1990-91 gives a service life expectancy until about 2004. No hangar but helicopter landing platform is served by a stores lift, to enable stores to be transferred at sea by 'vertical lift'. Capable of HIFR. Can pump fuel at 600 m³/h. Others of the class in service in Indonesia and the UK. **VERIFIED**

BÉRRIO   6/1998, M Verschaeve / 0052755

1 BUOY TENDER (ABU)

Name	No	Builders	Commissioned
SCHULTZ XAVIER	A 521	Alfeite Naval Yard	14 July 1972

Displacement, tons: 900 full load
Dimensions, feet (metres): 184 × 33 × 12.5 (56 × 10 × 3.8)
Main machinery: 2 diesels; 2,400 hp(m) (1.76 MW); 2 shafts
Speed, knots: 14.5. **Range, miles:** 3,000 at 12.5 kt
Complement: 54 (4 officers)

Comment: Used for servicing navigational aids and as an occasional tug.   **VERIFIED**

SCHULTZ XAVIER   5/1998, Diego Quevedo / 0052756

1 BUOY TENDER (ABU)

Name	No	Builders	Commissioned
GUIA	UAM 676	S Jacinto, Aveiro	30 Jan 1985

Displacement, tons: 70 full load
Dimensions, feet (metres): 72.2 × 25.9 × 7.2 (22 × 7.9 × 2.2)
Main machinery: 1 Deutz MWM SBA6M816 diesel; 465 hp(m) (342 kW) sustained; 1 Schottel Navigator prop
Speed, knots: 8.5 (3.5 on auxiliary engine)
Complement: 6

Comment: Belongs to the Lighthouse Service.   **UPDATED**

GUIA   5/1993*, van Ginderen Collection / 0081614

8 CALMARIA CLASS (PB)

CALMARIA UAM 642	**MONCÃO** UAM 645	**PREIA-MAR** UAM 648
CIRRO UAM 643	**SUÃO** UAM 646	**BAIXA-MAR** UAM 649
VENDAVAL UAM 644	**MACAREO** UAM 647	

Displacement, tons: 12 full load
Dimensions, feet (metres): 39 × 12.5 × 2.3 (11.9 × 3.8 × 0.7)
Main machinery: 2 Bazán MAN 2866 LXE diesels; 881 hp(m) (648 kW); 2 water-jets
Speed, knots: 32. **Range, miles:** 275 at 20 kt
Complement: 3
Guns: 1—7.62 mm MG.
Radars: Surface search: Furuno 1830; I-band.

Comment: Harbour patrol craft similar to Spanish Guardia Civil del Mar Saetta II craft. Ordered from Bazán, Cadiz on 8 January 1993. First pair completed 30 November 1993, third one on 18 January 1994. Remainder delivered between August and December 1994. GRP hulls. **UPDATED**

CALMARIA   8/1998*, Schaeffer/Marsan / 0081615

19 + 2 HARBOUR CRAFT

SURRIADA UAM 602	**VENTANTE** UAM 636	**RAINHA D AMÉLIA** UAM 689
MARESIA UAM 608	**TUFÃO** UAM 639	**P M MACATRÃO** UAM 690
BOLINA UAM 611	**PATRÃO FAUSTINO** UAM 659	**N S DA BOA VIAGEM** UAM 691
BONANCA UAM 612	**JOÃO DA SILVA** UAM 672	**DUQUE DA RIBEIRA** UAM 692
MAR CHÃO UAM 613	**BOA VIAGEM** UAM 683	**N S DA CONCEIÇÃO** UAM 693
CONDOR UAM 630	**VAZANTE** UAM 687	**N S DAS SALVAS** UAM 694
LEVANTE UAM 631	**ENCHENTE** UAM 688	

Comment: Harbour craft of different types. Some have *Marinha* on the side, others of the same type have *Guarda Fiscal*. Six Rodman 46 craft acquired in 1997 for SAR with two more for delivery in 2000. Twelve 15 m fast craft being sought by Customs. Some of these may transfer to the Naval Police.

UPDATED

VENTANTE　　　　　　　　　　　　　　4/1992 *, van Ginderen Collection / 0084276

DUQUE DA RIBEIRA　　　　　9/1998 *, Schaeffer/Marsan / 0081616

MAR CHÃO　　　　　　　　　3/1992 *, van Ginderen Collection / 0084277

QATAR

Headquarters Appointments

Commander Naval Force:
  Brigadier Said Muhammad Al Sowaidi

Personnel

(a) 2000: 1,800 officers and men (including Marine Police)
(b) Voluntary service

Bases

Doha (main); Halul Island (secondary)

Coast Defence

Two truck-mounted batteries of Exocet MM 40 quad launchers.

Prefix to Ships' Names

QENS (Qatar Emiri Navy)

Mercantile Marine

Lloyd's Register of Shipping:
  66 vessels of 748,901 tons gross

DELETIONS

Patrol Forces

1997　*Barzan* (old), *Huwar* (old)
1998　*That Assuari, Al Wusail, Fateh-al-Khair*
1999　*Tariq*

PATROL FORCES

HUWAR　　　　　　　　　　　　　　　　7/1997 *, H M Steele / 0081618

4 BARZAN (VITA) CLASS (PGFG)

Name	No	Builders	Laid down	Launched	Completed
BARZAN	Q04	Vosper Thornycroft	Feb 1994	1 Apr 1995	9 May 1996
HUWAR	Q05	Vosper Thornycroft	Aug 1994	15 July 1995	10 June 1996
AL UDEID	Q06	Vosper Thornycroft	Mar 1995	21 Mar 1996	16 Dec 1996
AL DEEBEL	Q07	Vosper Thornycroft	Aug 1995	31 Aug 1996	3 July 1997

Displacement, tons: 376 full load
Dimensions, feet (metres): 185.7 × 29.5 × 8.2
  (56.3 × 9 × 2.5)
Main machinery: 4 MTU 20V 538 TB93 diesels; 18,740 hp(m)
  (13.8 MW) sustained; 4 shafts
Speed, knots: 35. **Range, miles:** 1,800 at 12 kt
Complement: 35 (7 officers)

Missiles: SSM: 8 Aerospatiale MM 40 Exocet (Block II) ❶; inertial
  cruise; active radar homing to 70 km *(40 n miles)* at 0.9 Mach;
  warhead 165 kg; sea-skimmer.
SAM: Matra Sadral sextuple launcher for Mistral ❷; IR homing to
  4 km *(2.2 n miles)*; warhead 3 kg.
Guns: 1 OTO Melara 76 mm/62 Super Rapid ❸; 120 rds/min to
  16 km *(8.7 n miles)*; weight of shell 6 kg.
  1 Signaal Goalkeeper 30 mm ❹; 7 barrels; 4,200 rds/min
  combined to 2 km. 2—12.7 mm MGs.
Countermeasures: Decoys: CSEE Dagaie Mk 2 ❺ for chaff and IR
  flares.
ESM: Thomson-CSF DR 3000S ❻; intercept.
ECM: Dassault Salamandre ARBB 33 ❼; jammer.
Combat data systems: Signaal SEWACO FD with Thomson-CSF
  TACTICOS; Link Y.
Weapons control: Signaal STING optronic director. Signaal
  IRSCAN electro-optical tracker ❽.
Radars: Air/surface search; Thomson-CSF MRR ❾; C-band.
Navigation: Kelvin Hughes 1007 ❿; I-band.
Fire control: Signaal STING ⓫; I/J-band.

Programmes: Order announced on 4 June 1992 by Vosper
  Thornycroft. First steel cut 20 July 1993.
Structure: Vita design derivative based on the hull used for
  Oman and Kenya in the 1980s. Steel hull and aluminium
  superstructure. CSEE Sidewind EW management system is
  installed and a Racal Thorn data distribution system is used.
  Baffles have been added around the ECM aerials to prevent
  mutual interference with other sensors. An advanced
  machinery control and surveillance system allows one-man
  operation of main propulsion, electrical generation and
  auxiliary systems from the bridge. The bridge staff are also able
  to monitor the state of all compartments for damage control
  purposes.
Operational: First pair arrived in the Gulf in August 1997, second
  pair in May 1998. All of the class carry 40 kt RIBs with twin
  60 hp outboards.

UPDATED

BARZAN   *(Scale 1 : 600), Ian Sturton /* 0012934

AL UDEID   *5/1998, Camil Busquets i Vilanova /* 0052759

3 DAMSAH (COMBATTANTE III M) CLASS
(FAST ATTACK CRAFT—MISSILE) (PGFG)

Name	No	Builders	Launched	Commissioned
DAMSAH	Q 01	CMN, Cherbourg	17 Nov 1982	10 Nov 1982
AL GHARIYAH	Q 02	CMN, Cherbourg	23 Sep 1982	10 Feb 1983
RBIGAH	Q 03	CMN, Cherbourg	22 Dec 1982	11 May 1983

Displacement, tons: 345 standard; 395 full load
Dimensions, feet (metres): 183.7 × 26.9 × 7.2 *(56 × 8.2 × 2.2)*
Main machinery: 4 MTU 20V 538 TB93 diesels; 18,740 hp(m) *(13.8 MW)* sustained; 4 shafts
Speed, knots: 38.5. **Range, miles:** 2,000 at 15 kt
Complement: 41 (6 officers)

Missiles: SSM: 8 Aerospatiale MM 40 Exocet; inertial cruise; active radar homing to 70 km *(40 n
  miles)* at 0.9 Mach; warhead 165 kg; sea-skimmer.
Guns: 1 OTO Melara 3 in *(76 mm)*/62; 60 rds/min to 16 km *(8.7 n miles)*; weight of shell 6 kg.
  2 Breda 40 mm/70 (twin); 300 rds/min to 12.5 km *(6.8 n miles)*; weight of shell 0.96 kg.
  4 Oerlikon 30 mm/75 (2 twin); 650 rds/min to 10 km *(5.5 n miles)*.
Countermeasures: Decoys: CSEE Dagaie trainable single launcher; 6 containers; IR flares and
  chaff; H/J-band.
ESM/ECM: Racal Cutlass/Cygnus.
Weapons control: Vega system. 2 CSEE Naja optical directors.
Radars: Surface search: Thomson-CSF Triton; G-band.
Navigation: Racal Decca 1226; I-band.
Fire control: Thomson-CSF Castor II; I/J-band; range 15 km *(8 n miles)* for 1 m² target.

Programmes: Ordered in 1980. All arrived at Doha July 1983. All refitted in 1996/98.

VERIFIED

RBIGAH   1993

3 DAMEN POLYCAT 1450 CLASS (COASTAL PATROL CRAFT) (PC)

Q 31-Q 36 series

Displacement, tons: 18 full load
Dimensions, feet (metres): 47.6 × 15.4 × 4.9 *(14.5 × 4.7 × 2.1)*
Main machinery: 2 Detroit 12V-71TA diesels; 840 hp *(627 kW)* sustained; 2 shafts
Speed, knots: 26
Complement: 11
Guns: 1 Oerlikon 20 mm.
Radars: Navigation: Racal Decca; I-band.

Comment: Six delivered February-May 1980.

UPDATED

Q 33   *3/1980*, Damen SY / 0081617

AUXILIARIES

Note: There are a number of amphibious craft including an LCT *Rabha* of 160 ft *(48.8 m)* with a
capacity for three tanks and 110 troops, acquired in 1986-87. Also four Rotork craft and 30 Sea
Jeeps in 1985. It is not clear how many of the smaller craft are for civilian use.

POLICE

Notes: (1) Requirements have been reported for patrol craft, two of 24 m, two of 22 m and 19 of 12 m. Also for two hovercraft.
(2) Two Halmatic 18 m pilot boats ordered in May 1999.

3 HALMATIC M 160 CLASS (PB)

Displacement, tons: 20 full load
Dimensions, feet (metres): 52.5 × 15.4 × 4.6 *(16 × 4.7 × 1.4)*
Main machinery: 2 MTU diesels; 520 hp(m) *(388 kW)* sustained; 2 shafts
Speed, knots: 27. **Range, miles:** 500 at 17 kt
Complement: 6
Guns: 1—7.62 mm MG.
Radars: Surface search: Racal Decca; I-band.

Comment: Order confirmed on 11 October 1995. Delivered to Police in November 1996. Similar to Police craft obtained by Caribbean countries.

UPDATED

4 CRESTITALIA MV-45 CLASS (PB)

RG 91-RG 94

Displacement, tons: 17 full load
Dimensions, feet (metres): 47.6 × 12.5 × 2.6 *(14.5 × 3.8 × 0.8)*
Main machinery: 2 diesels; 1,270 hp(m) *(933 kW)*; 2 shafts
Speed, knots: 32. **Range, miles:** 275 at 29 kt
Complement: 6
Guns: 1 Oerlikon 20 mm. 2—7.62 mm MGs.
Radars: Surface search: I-band.

Comment: Built by Crestitalia and delivered in mid-1989. GRP construction.

VERIFIED

3 WATERCRAFT P 1200 TYPE (PB)

Displacement, tons: 12.7 full load
Dimensions, feet (metres): 39 × 13.4 × 3.6 *(11.9 × 4.1 × 1.1)*
Main machinery: 2 Wizeman Mercedes 400 diesels; 660 hp(m) *(485 kW)*; 2 shafts
Speed, knots: 29
Complement: 4
Guns: 2—7.62 mm MGs.

Comment: Built by Watercraft, Shoreham, UK in 1980. Four have been deleted, replaced by Halmatic craft.

UPDATED

M 160   *11/1996*, Halmatic /* 0081619

P 1200   *1980, Watercraft /* 0012937

ROMANIA

Headquarters Appointments

Commander-in-Chief of the Navy:
  Rear Admiral Traian Atanasiu

Personnel

(a)   2000: 11,000 Navy plus 10,000 Naval Infantry
(b)   Reserves: 18,000
(c)   Numbers are to be reduced to 9,100 by 2005.

Organisation

The Navy is composed of the Missile Brigade, Torpedo Brigade, Submarine Brigade, ASW Brigade, Minesweeper Brigade and Danube Flotilla. There is also a Naval Infantry Corps.

Bases

Black Sea—Mangalia (HQ and Training); Constanta (Coastal Defence and Naval Aviation), Midia
Danube—Bräila (HQ), Giurgiu, Galati, Tulcea, Drobeta Turnu-Severin

Border Guard

Responsible for land and sea borders and has four brigades, two of which have sea forces based at Orsova and Constanta.

Coast Defence

Four battalions with 130 mm guns, and six battalions with 57 mm, 37 mm and 30 mm guns.

Strength of the Fleet

Type	Active (Reserve)
Submarine	(1)
Destroyer	1
Frigates	6
Corvettes	7
River Monitors	9
Fast Attack Craft (Missile)	3
Fast Attack Craft (Torpedo)	31
River Patrol Craft	18
Minelayer/MCM Support	2
Minesweepers (Coastal and River)	29
Training Ship	1
Survey Ships	2

Mercantile Marine

Lloyd's Register of Shipping:
  325 vessels of 1,220,556 tons gross

DELETIONS

Patrol Forces

1997   3 Osa I, 9 Shanghai, 1 Huchuan
1998   7 Shanghai
1999   4 Huchuan

Mine Warfare Forces

1997   5 T 301
1999   7 T 301

Auxiliaries

1997   YO 132
2000   YO 131

PENNANT LIST

Submarines

521	Delfinul

Destroyers

111	Marasesti

Frigates

260	Admiral Petre Barbuneanu
261	Vice Admiral Vasile Scodrea
262	Vice Admiral Vasile Urseanu
263	Vice Admiral Eugeniu Rosca
264	Contre Admiral Eustatiu Sebastian
265	Admiral Horia Macelariu

Corvettes

13	Vice Admiral Mihai Gavrilescu
14	Vice Admiral Ioan Balanescu
15	Vice Admiral Emil Grecescu
16	Vice Admiral Ioan Georgescu
188	Zborul
189	Pescarusul
190	Lastunul

Patrol Forces

45	Mikhail Kogalniceanu 45
46	I C Bratianu
47	Lascar Catargiu
94	Grivita
96	Rahova
177	Opanez

178	Smirdan
179	Posada
180	Rovine
195	Vulturul
198	Eretele
199	Albatrosul
201	Naluca
202	Smeul
203	Viforul
204	Vijelia
205	Viscolul
206	Virtejul
207	Fulgerul
208	Vintul
209	Vulcanul
210	Furtuna
211	Trasnetul
212	Tornada

Mine Warfare Forces

29	Lieutenant Dimitrie Nicolescu
30	Sub Lieutenant Alexandru Axente
271	Vice Admiral Ioan Murgescu
274	Vice Admiral Constantin Balescu

Auxiliaries

112	Eugen Stihi
113	Ion Ghiculescu
281	Constanta
283	Midia
295	Automatica
296	Electronica
297	Energetica
298	Magnetica
500	Grozavu

SUBMARINES

1 KILO CLASS (TYPE 877E) (SSK)

DELFINUL 521

Displacement, tons: 2,325 surfaced; 3,076 dived
Dimensions, feet (metres): 238.2 × 32.8 × 21.7
(72.6 × 10 × 6.6)
Main machinery: Diesel-electric; 2 diesels; 3,650 hp(m)
(2.68 MW); 2 generators; 1 motor; 5,900 hp(m) *(4.34 MW)*;
1 shaft; 2 auxiliary MT-168 motors; 204 hp(m) *(150 kW)*;
1 economic speed motor; 130 hp(m) *(95 kW)*
Speed, knots: 10 surfaced; 20 dived; 9 snorting
Range, miles: 6,000 at 7 kt surfaced; 400 at 3 kt dived
Complement: 52 (12 officers)

Torpedoes: 6—21 in *(533 mm)* tubes. Combination of Russian
53-65; anti-surface; passive wake homing to 19 km *(10.3 n miles)* at 45 kt; warhead 300 kg or TEST-71; anti-submarine;
active/passive (optional wire-guided) homing to 15 km *(8.1 n miles)* warhead 205 kg. Total of 18 weapons.
Mines: 24 in lieu of torpedoes.
Countermeasures: ESM: Brick Group; radar warning. Quad Loop
D/F.
Radars: Surface search: Snoop Tray; I-band.
Sonars: Shark Teeth/Shark Fin; hull-mounted; passive search
and attack; medium frequency.
Mouse Roar; active attack; high frequency.

Programmes: Transferred from USSR in December 1986.

DELFINUL 8/1996 / 0052761

Structure: Diving depth, 240 m *(785 ft)*. Two torpedo tubes
probably capable of firing wire-guided torpedoes. There is a
well between the snort and W/T masts for a containerised
portable SAM launcher for SA-N-5/8.

Operational: Based at Constanta and in need of a refit which may
not be funded.

VERIFIED

DESTROYERS

1 MARASESTI CLASS (DDG)

Name	No	Builders	Laid down	Launched	Commissioned
MARASESTI (ex-*Muntenia*)	111	Mangalia Shipyard	1979	Apr 1981	3 June 1985

Displacement, tons: 5,790 full load
Dimensions, feet (metres): 474.4 × 48.6 × 23
(144.6 × 14.8 × 7)

Main machinery: 4 diesels; 32,000 hp(m) *(23.5 MW)*; 4 shafts
Speed, knots: 27
Complement: 270 (25 officers)

Missiles: SSM: 8 SS-N-2C Styx ❶; active radar or IR homing to
83 km *(45 n miles)* at 0.9 Mach; warhead 513 kg.
Guns: 4 USSR 3 in *(76 mm)*/60 (2 twin) ❷; 90 rds/min to 15 km
(8 n miles); weight of shell 6.8 kg.
4—30 mm/65 ❸; 6 barrels per mounting; 3,000 rds/min to
2 km.
Torpedoes: 6—21 in *(533 mm)* (2 triple) tubes ❹. Russian 53-65;
passive/wake homing to 25 km *(13.5 n miles)* at 50 kt;
warhead 300 kg.
A/S mortars: 2 RBU 6000 ❺; 12-tubed trainable; range
6,000 m; warhead 31 kg.
Countermeasures: Decoys: 2 PK 16 chaff launchers.
ESM/ECM: 2 Watch Dog; intercept. Bell Clout and Bell Slam.
Radars: Air/surface search: Strut Curve ❻; F-band.
Surface search: Plank Shave ❼; E-band.
Fire control: Two Drum Tilt ❽; H/I-band.
Hawk Screech ❾; I-band.
Navigation: Nayada (MR 212); Racal Decca; I-band.
IFF: High Pole B.
Sonars: Hull-mounted; active search and attack; medium
frequency.

Helicopters: 2 IAR-316 Alouette III ❿.

Modernisation: Attempts have been made to modernise some of
the electronic equipment. Also topweight problems have been
addressed by reducing the height of the mast structures and
lowering the Styx missile launchers by one deck. Two RBU
6000s have replaced the RBU 1200.
Structure: A distinctive Romanian design. Originally thought to
be powered by gas turbines but a diesel configuration
including four shafts is now confirmed.
Operational: Deactivated in June 1988 due to manpower and
fuel shortages but modernisation work was done from 1990 to
1992 and sea trials started in mid-1992. Carried out a major
naval exercise in September 1993, which included firing the
Styx missile. Deployed to the Mediterranean in September
1994 for a short cruise, in 1995 on two occasions and again in
March 1998. Based at Constanta.

UPDATED

MARASESTI *(Scale 1 : 1,200), Ian Sturton* / 0012965

MARASESTI 7/1995, Diego Quevedo / 0052762

MARASESTI 11/1995 / 0052763

FRIGATES

4 TETAL CLASS (FF)

Name	No	Builders	Launched	Commissioned
ADMIRAL PETRE BARBUNEANU	260	Mangalia Shipyard	1981	4 Feb 1983
VICE ADMIRAL VASILE SCODREA	261	Mangalia Shipyard	1982	3 Jan 1984
VICE ADMIRAL VASILE URSEANU	262	Mangalia Shipyard	1983	3 Jan 1985
VICE ADMIRAL EUGENIU ROSCA	263	Mangalia Shipyard	1985	23 Apr 1987

Displacement, tons: 1,440 full load
Dimensions, feet (metres): 303.1 × 38.4 × 9.8
(92.4 × 11.7 × 3)
Main machinery: 4 diesels; 13,000 hp(m) *(9.6 MW)*; 4 shafts
Speed, knots: 24
Complement: 98

Guns: 4 USSR 3 in *(76 mm)*/60 (2 twin) ❶; 90 rds/min to 15 km
(8 n miles); weight of shell 6.8 kg.
4 USSR 30 mm/65 (2 twin) ❷; 500 rds/min to 4 km *(2.2 n miles)*; weight of shell 0.54 kg.
2—14.5 mm MGs.
Torpedoes: 4—21 in *(533 mm)* (2 twin) tubes ❸. Russian 53-65;
passive/wake homing to 25 km *(13.5 n miles)* at 50 kt;
warhead 300 kg.
A/S mortars: 2 RBU 2500 16-tubed trainable ❹; range 2,500 m;
warhead 21 kg.
Countermeasures: Decoys: 2 PK 16 chaff launchers.
ESM: 2 Watch Dog; intercept.
Radars: Air/surface search: Strut Curve ❺; F-band.
Fire control: Drum Tilt ❻; H/I-band. Hawk Screech ❼; I-band.
Navigation: Nayada; I-band.
IFF: High Pole.
Sonars: Hercules (MG 322); Hull-mounted; active search and
attack; medium frequency.

Programmes: Building terminated in 1987 in favour of the
improved design with a helicopter platform.
Structure: A modified Soviet Koni design.
Operational: All based at Constanta.

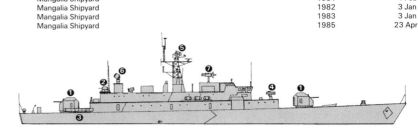

ADMIRAL PETRE BARBUNEANU

(Scale 1 : 900), Ian Sturton

UPDATED   VICE ADMIRAL VASILE SCODREA

*4/1999 *, Fafio* / 0081620

ADMIRAL PETRE BARBUNEANU

7/1998 / 0050723

ADMIRAL PETRE BARBUNEANU

10/1998, C D Yaylali / 0052764

2 IMPROVED TETAL CLASS (FF)

Name	No	Builders	Launched	Commissioned
CONTRE ADMIRAL EUSTATIU SEBASTIAN	264	Mangalia Shipyard	1988	30 Dec 1989
ADMIRAL HORIA MACELARIU	265	Mangalia Shipyard	1994	29 Sep 1997

Displacement, tons: 1,500 full load
Dimensions, feet (metres): 303.1 × 38.4 × 10
   (92.4 × 11.7 × 3.1)
Main machinery: 4 diesels; 13,000 hp(m) *(9.6 MW);* 4 shafts
Speed, knots: 24
Complement: 95

Guns: 1 USSR 3 in *(76 mm/60)* ❶; 120 rds/min to 15 km *(8 n miles);* weight of shell 6.8 kg.
   2—30 mm/65 AK 630 ❷; 6 barrels per mounting; 3,000 rds/min to 2 km.
   2—30 mm/65 AK 306 ❸; 6 barrels per mounting; 3,000 rds/min to 2 km.
Torpedoes: 4—21 in *(533 mm)* (2 twin) tubes ❹. Russian 53-65; passive/wake homing to 25 km *(13.5 n miles)* at 50 kt; warhead 300 kg.
A/S mortars: 2 RBU 6000 ❺; 12-tubed trainable; range 6,000 m; warhead 31 kg.
Countermeasures: Decoys: 2 PK 16 chaff launchers ❻.
ESM: 2 Watch Dog; intercept.
Radars: Air/surface search; Strut Curve ❼; F-band.
Fire control: Drum Tilt ❽; H/I-band.
Navigation: Nayada; I-band.
IFF: High Pole.
Sonars: Hull-mounted; active search and attack; medium frequency.

Helicopters: 1 IAR-316 Aloutte III ❾.

Programmes: Follow on to 'Tetal' class. Second of class was delayed when work stopped for a time in 1993-94.
Structure: As well as improved armament and a helicopter deck, there are superstructure changes from the original Tetals, but the hull and propulsion machinery are the same.
Operational: Both based at Constanta.

UPDATED

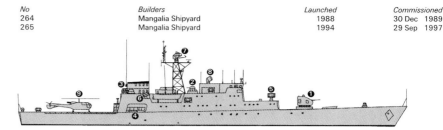

CONTRE ADMIRAL EUSTATIU SEBASTIAN   *(Scale 1 : 900), Ian Sturton*

CONTRE ADMIRAL EUSTATIU SEBASTIAN   *7/1995, C D Yaylali* / 0052765

CORVETTES

4 DEMOCRATIA (M 40) CLASS (Ex-MINESWEEPERS) (FS)

Name	No	Builders	Commissioned
VICE ADMIRAL MIHAI GAVRILESCU (ex-*Democratia*)	13	Galatzi	1954
VICE ADMIRAL IOAN BALANESCU (ex-*Descatusaria*)	14	Galatzi	1954
VICE ADMIRAL EMIL GRECESCU (ex-*Desrobirea*)	15	Galatzi	1955
VICE ADMIRAL IOAN GEORGESCU (ex-*Dreptatea*)	16	Galatzi	1956

Displacement, tons: 543 standard; 775 full load
Dimensions, feet (metres): 206.5 × 28 × 7.5 *(62.3 × 8.5 × 2.3)*
Main machinery: 2 diesels; 2,400 hp(m) *(1.76 MW);* 2 shafts
Speed, knots: 15. **Range, miles:** 1,400 at 10 kt
Complement: 80
Guns: 4—37 mm (2 twin). 4—14.5 mm (2 twin) MGs.
A/S mortars: 2 RBU 1200; 5-tubed fixed; range 1,200 m; warhead 34 kg.
Radars: Surface search: Don 2; I-band.
Sonars: Hull mounted; active attack; high frequency.

Comment: German 'M Boote' class originally designed as coal-burning minesweepers. The appearance of this class changed drastically during refits at Mangalia Shipyard between 1976 and 1983. Referred to locally as Corvettes. All minesweeping gear removed. A small helicopter platform has been fitted aft on *Georgescu*. Based at Constanta.

VERIFIED

3 ZBORUL (TARANTUL I) CLASS (TYPE 1241 RE) (FSG)

Name	No	Builders	Commissioned
ZBORUL	188	Petrovsky Shipyard	Dec 1990
PESCARUSUL	189	Petrovsky Shipyard	Feb 1992
LASTUNUL	190	Petrovsky Shipyard	Feb 1992

Displacement, tons: 385 standard; 455 full load
Dimensions, feet (metres): 184.1 × 37.7 × 8.2 *(56.1 × 11.5 × 2.5)*
Main machinery: COGAG; 2 Type DR 77 gas turbines; 16,016 hp(m) *(11.77 MW)* sustained; 2 Nikolayev Type DR 76 gas turbines with reversible gearboxes; 4,993 hp(m) *(3.67 MW)* sustained; 2 shafts
Speed, knots: 36. **Range, miles:** 2,000 at 20 kt; 400 at 36 kt
Complement: 41 (5 officers)
Missiles: 4 SS-N-2C Styx (2 twin); active radar or IR homing to 83 km *(45 n miles)* at 0.9 Mach; warhead 513 kg.
Guns: 1 USSR 3 in *(76 mm)*/60; 120 rds/min to 15 km *(8 n miles);* weight of shell 7 kg.
   2—30 mm/65 AK 630; 6 barrels per mounting; 3,000 rds/min to 2 km.
Countermeasures: 2 PK 16 chaff launchers.
ESM: 2 Watch Dog; intercept.
Weapons control: Hood Wink optronic director.
Radars: Air/surface search: Plank Shave; E-band.
Fire control: Bass Tilt; H/I-band.
Navigation: Spin Trough; I-band.
IFF: Square Head. High Pole.

Comment: Built in 1985 and later transferred from the USSR. Export version similar to those built for Poland, India and Yemen. Based at Mangalia.

VERIFIED

VICE ADMIRAL MIHAI GAVRILESCU   *6/1997* / 0052767   LASTUNUL   *6/1998, Valentino Cluru* / 0052766

SHIPBORNE AIRCRAFT

Numbers/Type: 6 IAR-316B Alouette III.
Operational speed: 113 kt *(210 km/h).*
Service ceiling: 10,500 ft *(3,200 m).*
Range: 290 n miles *(540 km).*
Role/Weapon systems: ASW helicopter. Sensors: Nose-mounted search radar. Weapons: ASW; two lightweight torpedoes.

VERIFIED

LAND-BASED MARITIME AIRCRAFT

Numbers/Type: 5 Mil Mi-14PL Haze A.
Operational speed: 124 kt *(230 km/h).*
Service ceiling: 15,000 ft *(4,570 m).*
Range: 432 n miles *(800 km).*
Role/Weapon systems: Medium-range ASW helicopter. Sensors: Short Horn search radar, dipping sonar, MAD, sonobuoys. Weapons: ASW; internally stored torpedoes, depth mines and bombs.

VERIFIED

PATROL FORCES

Note: There is a total of about 20 river patrol boats. These include three 27 ft Boston Whalers presented by the USA in March 1993 for Customs/Police patrols on the Danube in support of UN sanctions operations. There is also a hovercraft built at Mangalia in 1998.

6 BRUTAR CLASS (RIVER MONITORS) (PGR)

Name	No	Builders	Commissioned
GRIVITA	94	Mangalia Shipyard	21 Nov 1986
RAHOVA	96	Mangalia Shipyard	14 Apr 1988
OPANEZ	177	Mangalia Shipyard	24 July 1990
SMIRDAN	178	Mangalia Shipyard	24 July 1990
POSADA	179	Mangalia Shipyard	14 May 1992
ROVINE	180	Mangalia Shipyard	30 June 1993

Displacement, tons: 410 full load
Dimensions, feet (metres): 150 × 26.4 × 4.9 *(45.7 × 8 × 1.5)*
Main machinery: 2 diesels; 2,700 hp(m) *(2 MW)*; 2 shafts
Speed, knots: 16
Guns: 1—100 mm (tank turret). 2—30 mm (twin). 10—14.5 mm (2 quad, 2 single) MGs. 2—122 mm BM-21 rocket launchers; 40-tubed trainable.
Radars: Navigation; I-band.

Comment: Operational with the Danube Flotilla. The first two are Brutar Is and are based at Turnu-Severin. The second pair are Brutar IIs based at Tulcea and the last two are Brutar IIs based at Mangalia.

UPDATED

OPANEZ   *6/1999*, Romanian Navy* / 0081621

3 KOGALNICEANU CLASS (RIVER MONITORS) (PGR)

Name	No	Builders	Recommissioned
MIKHAIL KOGALNICEANU	45	Mangalia Shipyard	19 Dec 1993
I C BRATIANU	46	Mangalia Shipyard	28 Dec 1994
LASCAR CATARGIU	47	Mangalia Shipyard	22 Nov 1996

Displacement, tons: 575 full load
Dimensions, feet (metres): 170.6 × 29.5 × 5.6 *(52 × 9 × 1.7)*
Main machinery: 2 diesels; 4,900 hp(m) *(3.6 MW)*; 2 shafts
Speed, knots: 18
Guns: 2—100 mm (tank turrets). 4—30 mm (2 twin). 4—14.5 mm (2 twin). 2—122 mm BM-21 rocket launchers.
Radars: Navigation: I-band.

Comment: Based at Braila.

UPDATED

I C BRATIANU   *6/1999*, Romanian Navy* / 0081622

15 HUCHUAN CLASS (FAST ATTACK CRAFT—TORPEDO) (PHT)

320-325   51-77 series

Displacement, tons: 39 standard; 45 full load
Dimensions, feet (metres): 71.5 × 20.7 oa; 11.8 hull × 3.3 *(21.8 × 6.3; 3.6 × 1)*
Main machinery: 3 Type M 50 diesels; 3,300 hp(m) *(2.4 MW)* sustained; 3 shafts
Speed, knots: 50 foilborne. **Range, miles:** 500 at 30 kt
Complement: 11
Guns: 4—14.5 mm/93 (2 twin) MGs.
Torpedoes: 2—21 in *(533 mm)* tubes; anti-surface.
Depth charges: 2 rails.
Radars: Surface search: Type 753; I-band.

Comment: Hydrofoils of the same class as the Chinese. Three imported from China have been deleted. *51-68* built at Mangalia Shipyard 1974-1983. *320-325* was a repeat order also built at Mangalia 1988-1990. Ten deleted so far and others are of doubtful operational status. Based at Mangalia.

UPDATED

HUCHUAN 53   *6/1999*, Romanian Navy* / 0081624

3 OSA I CLASS (TYPE 205)
(FAST ATTACK CRAFT—MISSILE) (PCFG)

Name	No	Builders	Commissioned
VULTURUL	195	USSR	3 Nov 1964
ERETELE	198	USSR	1 Jan 1965
ALBATROSUL	199	Mangalia Shipyard	25 Feb 1981

Displacement, tons: 171 standard; 210 full load
Dimensions, feet (metres): 126.6 × 24.9 × 8.8 *(38.6 × 7.6 × 2.7)*
Main machinery: 3 Type M 503A diesels; 8,025 hp *(5.9 MW)* sustained; 3 shafts
Speed, knots: 35. **Range, miles:** 400 at 34 kt
Complement: 30

Missiles: SSM: 4 SS-N-2 Styx; active radar or IR homing to 46 km *(25 n miles)* at 0.9 Mach; warhead 513 kg.
Guns: 4 USSR 30 mm/65 (2 twin); 500 rds/min to 5 km *(2.7 n miles)*; weight of shell 0.54 kg.
Radars: Surface search: Square Tie; I-band.
Fire control: Drum Tilt; H/I-band.
IFF: High Pole. Square Head.

Programmes: Six transferred by the USSR in 1964. One deleted and replaced in 1981 by a locally built vessel.
Operational: Last three survivors are based at Mangalia. Others of the class used for spares.

UPDATED

ERETELE   *6/1999*, Romanian Navy* / 0081623

12 NALUCA CLASS (FAST ATTACK CRAFT—TORPEDO) (PCF)

Name	No	Builders	Commissioned
NALUCA	201	Mangalia Shipyard	19 May 1979
SMEUL	202	Mangalia Shipyard	25 Oct 1979
VIFORUL	203	Mangalia Shipyard	14 Jan 1980
VIJELIA	204	Mangalia Shipyard	7 Feb 1980
VISCOLUL	205	Mangalia Shipyard	30 Apr 1980
VIRTEJUL	206	Mangalia Shipyard	1 Sep 1980
FULGERUL	207	Mangalia Shipyard	30 Dec 1980
VINTUL	208	Mangalia Shipyard	25 May 1981
VULCANUL	209	Mangalia Shipyard	26 Oct 1981
FURTUNA	210	Mangalia Shipyard	13 Jan 1982
TRASNETUL	211	Mangalia Shipyard	15 June 1982
TORNADA	212	Mangalia Shipyard	5 Oct 1982

Displacement, tons: 215 full load
Dimensions, feet (metres): 120.7 × 24.9 × 5.9 *(36.8 × 7.6 × 1.8)*
Main machinery: 3 Type M 503A diesels; 8,025 hp *(5.9 MW)* sustained; 3 shafts
Speed, knots: 36. **Range, miles:** 500 at 35 kt
Complement: 22 (4 officers)
Guns: 4—30 mm/65 (2 twin) AK 230.
Torpedoes: 4—21 in *(533 mm)* tubes; anti-surface.
Radars: Surface search: Pot Drum; H/I-band.
Fire control: Drum Tilt; H/I-band.
IFF: High Pole A.

Comment: Based on the 'Osa' class hull with torpedo tubes in lieu of SSMs. Based at Mangalia. Some are non-operational.

UPDATED

SMEUL   *6/1999*, Romanian Navy* / 0081625

18 VB 76 MONITOR CLASS (RIVER PATROL CRAFT) (PC)

VB 76-VB 93

Displacement, tons: 127 full load
Dimensions, feet (metres): 106.3 × 15.8 × 3 *(32.4 × 4.8 × 0.9)*
Main machinery: 2 diesels; 1,700 hp(m) *(1.25 MW)*; 2 shafts
Speed, knots: 17
Complement: 25
Guns: 1—76 mm. 4—14.5 mm (2 twin). 1—81 mm mortar.

Comment: Built in Mangalia Shipyard from 1974-77. Belong to Danube Flotilla. 76-78 based at Sulina, 79-90 at Braila and 91-93 at Tulcea. All are reported as being in service.
UPDATED

VB 91   *6/1999*, Romanian Navy /* 0081626

MINE WARFARE FORCES

2 CORSAR CLASS (MINELAYER/MCM SUPPORT SHIPS) (ML/MCS)

Name	No	Builders	Commissioned
VICE ADMIRAL IOAN MURGESCU	271	Mangalia Shipyard	30 Dec 1980
VICE ADMIRAL CONSTANTIN BALESCU	274	Mangalia Shipyard	16 Nov 1981

Displacement, tons: 1,450 full load
Dimensions, feet (metres): 259.1 × 34.8 × 11.8 *(79 × 10.6 × 3.6)*
Main machinery: 2 diesels; 6,400 hp(m) *(4.7 MW)*; 2 shafts
Speed, knots: 19
Complement: 75
Guns: 1—57 mm/70. 4—30 mm/65 (2 twin) AK 230. 8—14.5 mm (2 quad) MGs.
A/S mortars: 2 RBU 1200 5-tubed fixed; range 1,200 m; warhead 34 kg.
Mines: 200.
Countermeasures: ESM: Watch Dog; intercept.
Radars: Air/surface search: Strut Curve; F-band.
Navigation: Don 2; I-band.
Fire control: Muff Cob; G/H-band. Drum Tilt; H/I-band.
Sonars: Tamir II; hull-mounted; active search; high frequency.

Comment: 271 has a helicopter platform for one IAR-316 Alouette III. 274 has a large crane on the after deck. Similar to survey ship *Grigore Antipa*. Based at Constanta.
UPDATED

VICE ADMIRAL CONSTANTIN BALESCU   *6/1999*, Romanian Navy /* 0081627

4 MUSCA CLASS (MINESWEEPERS—COASTAL) (MSC)

Name	No	Builders	Commissioned
LIEUTENANT REMUS LEPRI	24	Mangalia Shipyard	23 Apr 1987
LIEUTENANT LUPU DUNESCU	25	Mangalia Shipyard	6 Jan 1989
LIEUTENANT DIMITRIE NICOLESCU	29	Mangalia Shipyard	7 Dec 1989
SUB LIEUTENANT ALEXANDRU AXENTE	30	Mangalia Shipyard	7 Dec 1989

Displacement, tons: 790 full load
Dimensions, feet (metres): 194.2 × 31.1 × 9.2 *(59.2 × 9.5 × 2.8)*
Main machinery: 2 diesels; 4,800 hp(m) *(3.5 MW)*; 2 shafts
Speed, knots: 17
Complement: 60
Missiles: SAM: 2 quad SA-N-5 launchers.
Guns: 4—30 mm/65 (2 twin) AK 230.
A/S mortars: 2 RBU 1200 5-tubed fixed; range 1,200 m; warhead 34 kg.
Radars: Surface search: Krivach; I-band.
Fire control: Drum Tilt; H/I-band.
Navigation: Nayada; I-band.
Sonars: Hull-mounted; active search; high frequency.

Comment: Reported as having a secondary mining capability but this is not confirmed. Based at Musca.
UPDATED

LIEUTENANT REMUS LEPRI   *6/1997* /* 0081628

25 VD 141 CLASS (RIVER MINESWEEPERS) (MSC)

141-165

Displacement, tons: 97 full load
Dimensions, feet (metres): 109 × 15.7 × 2.8 *(33.3 × 4.8 × 0.9)*
Main machinery: 2 diesels; 870 hp(m) *(640 kW)*; 2 shafts
Speed, knots: 13
Guns: 4—14.5 mm (2 twin) MGs.
Mines: 6.
Radars: Navigation: Nayada; I-band.

Comment: Built in Romania at Dobreta Severin Shipyard 1976-84. Belong to the Danube Flotilla. Four based at Giurgiu, three at Sulina, four at Tulcea, seven at Galati and seven at Turnu-Severin.
UPDATED

VD 150   *6/1999*, Romanian Navy /* 0081629

SURVEY AND RESEARCH SHIPS

Name	No	Builders	Commissioned
GRIGORE ANTIPA	—	Mangalia Shipyard	25 May 1980

Displacement, tons: 1,450 full load
Dimensions, feet (metres): 259.1 × 34.8 × 11.8 *(79 × 10.6 × 3.6)*
Main machinery: 2 diesels; 6,400 hp(m) *(4.7 MW)*; 2 shafts
Speed, knots: 19
Complement: 75
Radars: Navigation: Nayada; I-band.

Comment: Large davits aft for launching manned submersible. Same hull as 'Corsar' class. Used mostly as an AG1. Based at Constanta.
VERIFIED

GRIGORE ANTIPA   *5/1998, Diego Quevedo /* 0052770

Name	No	Builders	Commissioned
EMIL RACOVITA	—	Drobeta Severin Shipyard	30 Oct 1977

Displacement, tons: 1,900 full load
Dimensions, feet (metres): 229.9 × 32.8 × 12.7 *(70.1 × 10 × 3.9)*
Main machinery: 1 diesel; 3,285 hp(m) *(2.4 MW)*; 1 shaft
Speed, knots: 11
Complement: 80

Comment: Modernised in the mid-1980s. Used mostly as an AGI. Based at Constanta.
VERIFIED

TRAINING SHIPS

Note: *Neptun* belongs to the Merchant Navy.

Name	No	Builders	Launched	Commissioned
MIRCEA	—	Blohm + Voss, Hamburg	29 Sep 1938	29 Mar 1939

Displacement, tons: 1,604 full load
Dimensions, feet (metres): 206; 266.4 (with bowsprit) × 39.3 × 16.5 *(62.8; 81.2 × 12 × 5.2)*
Main machinery: 1 MaK 6M 451 auxiliary diesel; 1,000 hp(m) *(735 kW)*; 1 shaft
Speed, knots: 8. **Range, miles:** 5,000 at 8 kt
Complement: 83 (5 officers) plus 140 midshipmen
Radars: Navigation: Decca 202; I-band.

Comment: Refitted at Hamburg in 1966. Sail area, 5,739 sq m *(18,830 sq ft)*. A smaller version of US Coast Guard cutter *Eagle*, German *Gorch Fock* and Portuguese *Sagres*. Based at Constanta.
UPDATED

MIRCEA   *7/1993*, Aldo Fraccaroli /* 0081630

AUXILIARIES

2 CROITOR CLASS (LOGISTIC SUPPORT SHIPS) (AE)

Name	No	Builders	Commissioned
CONSTANTA	281	Braila Shipyard	15 Sep 1980
MIDIA	283	Braila Shipyard	26 Feb 1982

Displacement, tons: 2,850 standard; 3,500 full load
Dimensions, feet (metres): 354.3 × 44.3 × 12.5 *(108 × 13.5 × 3.8)*
Main machinery: 2 diesels; 6,500 hp(m) *(4.8 MW)*; 2 shafts
Speed, knots: 16
Missiles: SAM: 2 SA-N-5 Grail quad launchers; manual aiming; IR homing to 6 km *(3.2 n miles)* at 1.5 Mach; warhead 1.5 kg.
Guns: 2—57 mm/70 (twin). 4—30 mm/65 (2 twin). 8—14.5 mm (2 quad) MGs.
A/S mortars: 2 RBU 1200 5-tubed fixed; range 1,200 m; warhead 34 kg.
Countermeasures: ESM: 2 Watch Dog; intercept.
Radars: Air/surface search: Strut Curve; F-band.
Navigation: Krivach; I-band.
Fire control: Muff Cob; G/H-band. Drum Tilt; H/I-band.
Sonars: Tamir II; hull-mounted; active attack; high frequency.
Helicopters: 1 IAR-316 Alouette III type.

Comment: These ships are a scaled down version of Soviet 'Don' class. Forward crane for ammunition replenishment. Some ASW escort capability. Can carry Styx missiles and torpedoes. Based at Constanta.
UPDATED

MIDIA   *8/1999*, van Ginderen Collection /* 0081633

2 FRIPONNE CLASS (SUPPLY SHIPS) (AG)

EUGEN STIHI (ex-*Mignonne*) 112   **ION GHICULESCU** (ex-*Impatiente*) 113

Displacement, tons: 440 full load
Dimensions, feet (metres): 200.1 × 23 × 8.2 *(61 × 7 × 2.5)*
Main machinery: 2 Sulzer diesels; 1,800 hp(m) *(1.32 MW)*; 2 shafts
Speed, knots: 12. **Range, miles:** 3,000 at 10 kt
Complement: 50
Guns: 1—37 mm/63. 4—14.5 mm (2 twin) MGs.
A/S mortars: 2 RBU 1200 5-tubed fixed; range 1,200 m; warhead 34 kg.
Radars: Navigation: 2 sets.
Sonars: Tamir II; hull-mounted; active attack; high frequency.

Comment: Originally built at Brest and Lorient in 1916-17 as French minesweepers. The armament listed above reflects the latest conversion which also included a smoother bridge form. Painted white. Based at Constanta.
UPDATED

EUGEN STIHI   *6/1999*, Romanian Navy /* 0081631

8 BRAILA CLASS (RIVER TRANSPORTS) (AG)

203	205	207-8	415	416	419-20

Displacement, tons: 240 full load
Dimensions, feet (metres): 125.7 × 28.2 × 3.3 *(38.3 × 8.6 × 1)*
Main machinery: 2 diesels; 300 hp(m) (220 kW); 2 shafts
Speed, knots: 4
Cargo capacity: 160 tons

Comment: Used by civilian as well as naval authorities. Built at Braila Shipyard 1967-70. Danube Flotilla. Based at Turnul Magurele.
UPDATED

BRAILA 419   *1987* /* 0081634

2 TANKERS (AOT)

532	201

Displacement, tons: 2,170 full load
Dimensions, feet (metres): 250.4 × 41 × 16.4 *(76.3 × 12.5 × 5)*
Main machinery: 2 diesels; 4,800 hp(m) *(3.5 MW)*; 2 shafts
Speed, knots: 16
Cargo capacity: 1,200 tons oil
Guns: 2—30 mm/65 (twin). 4—14.5 mm (2 twin) MGs.

Comment: First one built by Tulcea Shipyard and commissioned 24 December 1992. Second of class reported in 1997. Based at Constanta.
UPDATED

532   *7/1995* /* 0081635

4 DEGAUSSING SHIPS (ADG/AGI)

Name	No	Builders	Commissioned
AUTOMATICA	295	Braila Shipyard	9 Dec 1972
ELECTRONICA	296	Braila Shipyard	6 Aug 1973
ENERGETICA	297	Braila Shipyard	20 Oct 1973
MAGNETICA	298	Mangalia Shipyard	18 Dec 1989

Displacement, tons: 299 full load
Dimensions, feet (metres): 134 × 21.6 × 10.7 *(40.8 × 6.6 × 3.2)*
Main machinery: Diesel-electric; 1 diesel generator; 600 kW; 1 shaft
Speed, knots: 12.5
Complement: 18
Guns: 2—14.5 mm (twin) MGs. 2—12.7 mm MGs.

Comment: Built for degaussing ships up to 3,000 tons displacement. Electronica is used as an AGI. All based at Tulcea.

UPDATED

MAGNETICA   *6/1999*, Romanian Navy /* 0081632

2 COASTAL TANKERS (AOTL)

530   531

Displacement, tons: 1,042 full load
Dimensions, feet (metres): 181.2 × 30.9 × 13.4 *(55.2 × 9.4 × 4.1)*
Main machinery: 2 diesels; 1,800 hp(m) *(1.3 MW)*; 2 shafts
Speed, knots: 12.5
Cargo capacity: 500 tons oil
Guns: 1—37 mm. 2—12.7 mm MGs.

Comment: Built by Braila Shipyard and both commissioned 15 June 1971. Based at Constanta.

UPDATED

531   *6/1999*, Romanian Navy /* 0081636

1 FLAG OFFICERS BARGE

RINDUNICA

Displacement, tons: 40 full load
Dimensions, feet (metres): 78.7 × 16.4 × 3.6 *(24 × 5 × 1.1)*
Main machinery: 2 diesels; 2,200 hp(m) *(1.6 MW)*; 2 shafts
Speed, knots: 28
Complement: 6

Comment: Used as a barge by the Commander-in-Chief.

UPDATED

RINDUNICA   *1/1995* /* 0081637

TUGS

Note: There are also a number of harbour and river tugs, some of which are armed. These include two Roslavl (101 and 106) at Mangalia.

2 OCEAN TUGS (ATA)

GROZAVU 500   **+ 1**

Displacement, tons: 3,600 full load
Dimensions, feet (metres): 212.6 × 47.9 × 18 *(64.8 × 14.6 × 5.5)*
Main machinery: 2 diesels; 5,000 hp(m) *(3.7 MW)*; 2 shafts
Speed, knots: 12
Guns: 2—30 mm (twin). 8—14.5 mm (2 quad) MGs.

Comment: First one built at Oltenitza Shipyard and commissioned 29 June 1993. A second of class completed in 1995. Based at Constanta.

VERIFIED

HARBOUR TUG 570   *12/1994* /* 0081638

RUSSIA
ROSIYSKIY VOENNOMORSKY FLOT

Headquarters Appointments

Commander-in-Chief and Deputy Minister of Defence:
   Admiral of the Fleet V Kuroyedov
Chief of Naval Staff:
   Admiral A Kravchenko
Chief of Operations:
   Vice Admiral V Patrushev
Commander Naval Units Border Guard:
   Vice Admiral I I Nalyotov

Northern Fleet
Commander:
   Admiral V A Popov
First Deputy Commander:
   Vice Admiral V
      Dovbroskochenko

Pacific Fleet
Commander:
   Admiral M G Zakharenko
1st Deputy Commander:
   Vice Admiral V Chirkov

Black Sea Fleet
Commander:
   Vice Admiral V P Komoyedov
1st Deputy Commander:
   Vice Admiral G A Suchkov

Baltic Fleet
Commander:
   Admiral V G Yegorov
1st Deputy Commander:
   Vice Admiral V Valuev

Caspian Flotilla
Commander:
   Vice Admiral V V Masorin
1st Deputy Commander:
   Vice Admiral V Anisimov

Personnel

(a) 2000: 171,500 including naval aviation and naval infantry. The approximate division is 55,000 in the North and Pacific, 30,000 in the Baltic, 23,500 in the Black Sea and 8,000 in the Caspian.
(b) Approximately 30 per cent volunteers (officers and senior ratings)—remainder two years' national service (or three years if volunteered)
(c) Stated aim to reduce to 100,000 by the year 2000, has not been achieved because of inability to meet retirement conditions.

Associated States

The Soviet Union was dissolved in December 1991. In 1992 a Commonwealth of Independent States was formed from the Republics of the former Union, but without the Baltic States. In the Baltic the Russian flotilla had withdrawn from the former East German and Polish ports by 1993 and from the Baltic Republics by the end of 1994. The Caspian flotilla divided with some units going to Azerbaijan, Kazakhstan and Turkmenistan. In the Black Sea the division of the Fleet between Russia and Ukraine was finally implemented in 1997. Facilities are shared in some Crimean ports.

Main Bases (Russian unless indicated otherwise)

North: Severomorsk (HQ), Motovsky Gulf, Polyarny, Severodvinsk, Gremika, Nerpichya, Yagelnaya, Olenya
Baltic: Kaliningrad (HQ), St Petersburg, Kronshtadt, Baltiysk
Black Sea: Sevastopol (HQ) (Crimea), Tuapse, Novorssiysk, Feodosiya
Caspian: Astrakhan (HQ)
Pacific: Vladivostok (HQ), Sovetskaya Gavan, Magadan, Petropavlovsk, Komsomolsk, Racovaya

Operational

Since 1991 a shortage of funds to pay for dockyard repairs, spare parts and fuel has meant that many major surface warships have rarely been to sea, and few have operated away from their local exercise areas. Since 1996 some ships have been 'selected' to go to sea but many remain in commission but permanently in harbour. Marginally more activity was reported in 1999.

Coast Defence

The Command of Naval Infantry and Coastal Artillery and Missiles includes a Division of Coastal Artillery and three Mechanised Infantry (Coastal Defence Troops) Brigades, an Artillery Self-Propelled Brigade, plus the units of Naval Infantry (five Brigades and one Division) and a number of minor units. The force of Coastal Artillery includes 19 Missile Batallions (SSC-1 Sepal SS-C-3 Styx) and 11 Gun Batallions (130 mm and 152 mm). Many of these units are in reserve.

Pennant Numbers

The Navy had changes of pennant numbers as a matter of routine every three years and when ships change fleet. The last major overall change of numbers took place in May 1990 and the Pacific and Northern Fleets changed again in May 1993. Since then there have been no changes except when ships change Fleets. Pennant numbers shown are those in force in early 2000.

Class and Weapon Systems Names

Most Russian ship class names differ from those allocated by NATO. In such cases the Russian name is placed in brackets after the NATO name. Type or Project numbers are also placed in brackets. Weapon systems retain their NATO names with the Russian name, when known, placed in brackets. Some equipment now has three names - NATO, Russian Navy and Russian export.

Civilian Support Ships

Previously, civilian manned research ships and some icebreakers were effectively under naval control and were therefore included in the former Soviet/Russian section. These ships have been removed as all are now employed solely for commercial purposes.

Strength of the Fleet

Type	Active	Building
Submarines (SSBN)	18	1
Submarines (SSGN)	8	1
Submarines (SSN)	20	2
Submarines (SSK)	18	2
Auxiliary Submarines (SSA(N))	8	—
Aircraft Carriers (CV)	1	—
Battle Cruisers (CGN)	2	—
Cruisers (CG)	5	1
Destroyers (DDG)	17	—
Frigates (FFG)	17	1
Frigates (FF and FFL)	37	—
Corvettes	50	—
Hydrofoils (Missile)	1	—
Patrol Forces	110	—
Minehunters—Ocean	2	—
Minesweepers—Ocean	12	—
Minesweepers—Coastal	30	—
Minehunters—Coastal	26	—
Minesweeping Boats/Drones	8	—
LPDs	1	—
LSTs	23	—
Hovercraft (Amphib)	14	—
Replenishment Tankers	15	—
Hospital Ships	3	—

Note: There are large numbers of most classes 'in reserve', and flying an ensign so that skeleton crews may still be paid. The list above reflects only those units assessed as having some realistic operational capability.

Mercantile Marine

Lloyd's Register of Shipping:
   4,694 vessels of 10,648,965 tons gross

TORPEDOES

Note: There are several torpedo types in service. The following table lists characteristics.

Type/Designator	Diameter/Length	Role	Launch Platform	Propulsion	Speed/Range	Guidance	Warhead	Remarks
35 (APR-2)	35 cm/3.7 m	ASW	1. Aircraft 2. Helicopters	Rocket	62 kt/2 km	Active/passive	100 kg	Export as APR-2E
APR-3	35 cm/3.7 m	ASW	1. Aircraft 2. Helicopters	Waterjet	Controlled speed	Active/passive	100 kg	Under development
SET-72	40 cm/4.5 m	ASW/ASV	1. Submarines 2. Escorts	Electric	30 kt/10 km	Active/passive	100 kg	Upgraded version of USET-95 (see Note 1)
UMGT-1M (E40-79)	40 cm/3.8 m	ASW	1. Aircraft 2. Helicopters 3. SS-N-14 4. SS-N-15 5. SS-N-16	Electric	40 kt/15 km	Active/passive	60 kg	Export as APSET-95 or UMGT-1ME
VTT-1 (E45-75)	45 cm/3.9 m	ASW	1. Aircraft 2. Helicopters	Electric	30 kt/15 km	Active/passive	70 kg	
AT-2 (E53-72)	53 cm/4.7 m	ASW	1. Aircraft 2. Helicopters 3. SS-N-14	Electric	40 kt/10 km	Active/passive	80 kg	Alternative to Type 40
SAET-60 M	53 cm/7.8 m	ASV	1. Submarines 2. Surface ships	Electric	40 kt/15 km	Passive	205 kg	Nuclear variant available
SET 65M (E53-76) (see Note 2)	53 cm/7.8 m	ASW	1. Submarines 2. Surface ships	Electric	40 kt/15 km	Active/passive	205 kg	Export as SET-65E/92 K
TEST-71 (see Note 3)	53 cm/8.2 m	ASW	1. Submarines 2. Surface ships	Electric	40 kt/15 km 25 kt/20 km	Active/passive Wire-guided	220 kg	Export as TEST-71ME
USET/-80	53 cm/8.2 m	ASW	1. Submarines 2. Surface ships	Electric	45 kt/19 km	Active/passive and wake homing	250 kg	TE-2 is wire-guided variant for Type 636 SSKs
53-65	53 cm/7.8 m	ASV	1. Submarines 2. Surface ships	Turbine	45 kt/19 km	Wake	305 kg	Nuclear variant available
65 (65-76)	65 cm/11 m	ASV	Submarines (Victor III, Akula, Sierra, Oscar)	Turbine	50 kt/50 km	Wake	450 kg	Nuclear variant available. Export as DT or DST
Shkval (WA III)	53 cm/8 m	ASW/ASV	Submarines Surface ships	Rocket	200 kt/10 km	Gyro	210 kg	Export non-nuclear as Shkval-E Nuclear variant available

Notes: (1) Export USET-95 has ASV wake homing option. Also known as Latush.
(2) SET-65M superseded by torpedo promoted for export as SET-92K (53 cm/7.8 m, ASW, active/passive).
(3) TEST-71 superseded by torpedo promoted for export as TEST-96 (53 cm/8 m, ASW/ASV, wire-guided, active/passive/wake homing) (submarines and surface ships).
(4) MG 34/44 are torpedo tube launched acoustic countermeasures. Run time is advertised as 45 minutes.

Fleet Disposition (1 January 2000)

Type	Northern	Baltic	Black Sea	Pacific	Caspian	Type	Northern	Baltic	Black Sea	Pacific	Caspian
SSBN	12	–	–	6	–	CGN	2	–	–	–	–
SSGN	4	–	–	4	–	CG	1	–	3	1	–
SSN	15	–	–	5	–	DDG	6	2	2	7	–
SSK	6	3	1	8	–	FFG	2	4	2	9	–
SSA(N)	8	–	–	–	–	FF and FFL	12	11	7	7	–
CV	1	–	–	–	–	Corvettes	4	14	17	13	2
						LPD	1	–	–	–	–
						LST	7	5	6	5	–

Note: MCMV are divided evenly between the four main Fleets plus a few in the Caspian Sea.

DELETIONS

Note: Some of the ships listed are still theoretically 'laid up', and some still fly an ensign so that skeleton crews may be paid. None have been to sea for some years.

Submarines

1997   3 Delta III (SSBN), 1 Delta I (SSBN), 1 Charlie II (SSGN), 1 Akula I (SSN), 1 Sierra I (SSN), 7 Victor III (SSN), 6 Kilo (SSK), 4 Tango (SSK)
1998   3 Typhoon (SSBN), 2 Delta III (SSBN), 2 Delta I (SSBN), 2 Oscar II (SSGN), 1 Akula I (SSN), 3 Victor III, 1 Beluga (SSA), 2 Losos (SSA)
1999   1 Typhoon (SSBN), 1 Oscar II (SSGN), 1 Akula I (SSN), 1 Victor III (SSN), 6 Kilo (SSK), 2 Tango (SSK)

Aircraft Carriers

1997   *Admiral Gorshkov* (reserve)

Cruisers

1997   *Admiral Ushakov* (reserve), *Admiral Lazarev* (reserve)
1998   *Azov*

Destroyers

1997   5 Sovremenny *(Sovremenny, Otlichnny, Osmotritelny, Stoyky, Okrylenny)*, 1 Kashin *(Skory)*
1998   1 Sovremenny *(Bezuprechny)*
1999   1 Udaloy *(Vasilevsky)*, 3 Sovremenny *(Boyevoy, Gremyashchy, Rastoropny)*

Frigates

1997   2 Krivak I *(Bodry, Bezukorizenny)* (to Ukraine), 3 Krivak II *(Bessmenny* (to Ukraine), *Grozyashchy, Razitelny)* (to Ukraine), 1 Grisha I, 1 Grisha III
1998   1 Krivak I *(Razumny)*, 4 Grisha I, 11 Grisha III, 3 Grisha II
1999   1 Krivak *(Zharky)*, 1 Krivak II *(Rezvy)*, 1 Grisha I, 5 Grisha II, 8 Grisha III, 7 Grisha V, 1 Parchim

Corvettes (Missile)

1997   3 Nanuchka I, 2 Tarantul I
1998   3 Nanuchka I, 2 Nanuchka III, 12 Tarantul II, 4 Tarantul III
1999   1 Nanuchka III

Patrol Forces

1997   8 Turya, 5 Pauk I, 5 Muravey (three to Ukraine), 6 Svetlyak, 11 Stenka (five to Ukraine), 17 Zhuk (12 to Ukraine)
1998   3 Turya, 1 Pauk I, 3 Pauk II, 10 Shmel
1999   1 Babochka, 3 Stenka, 3 Pauk I, 3 Muravey

Mine Warfare Vessels

1997   4 Natya, 5 Yurka, 5 T 43, 21 Sonya, 5 Vanya, 6 Yevgenya, 1 Ilyusha
1998   1 Yurka, 9 Natya I, 1 Natya II, 11 Sonya, 5 Vanya, 2 Mod Vanya, 3 Yevgenya, 9 Lida, 3 Ilyusha
1999   2 Natya I, 1 Yurka, 1 Vanya, 3 Yevgenya, 1 Olya, *Barentsevo More*

Amphibious Forces

1997   *Ivan Rogov, Aleksandr Nikolayev, Sergey Lazo,* 18 Polnochny, 2 Vydra
1998   2 Ropucha I, 1 Ondatra
1999   1 Alligator, 2 Polnochny, 1 Vydra

Hovercraft

1997   3 Pomornik, 2 Aist, 6 Tsaplya, 6 Lebed
1998   2 Pomornik
1999   5 Lebed

AGIs

1997   *Zaporozhye, Pelorus, Arkhipelag, Seliger,* OS 104
1998   *Pribaltika, Vega*
1999   *Azija*

Naval Survey and Research Ships

1997   *Mikhail Krupsky, Bashkiriya, Fedor Litke, Nikolai Zubov,* 4 Yug, 4 Moma, 3 Finik, 4 Biya, 2 Kamenka, 2 Onega, 9 T 43
1998   *Vladimirsky, Kruzenshtern, Abkhaziya, Baykal, Balkhash, Polyus,* OS 572, 1 Moma, 1 Finik, 1 Kamenka, 13 Onega, 6 T 43, *Marshal Nedelin, Kamchatka, Ural*
1999   *Adzhariya, Moldavia,* 1 Biya

Auxiliaries

1997   *Ivan Kolyshikin, Ivan Vakhrameev,* 4 Lama, 4 Amur I, 3 Oskol (one to Ukraine), *Boris Chilikin* (to Ukraine), *Sventa* (to Ukraine), 11 Voda (one to Ukraine), *Akhtyuba* (to Philippines), *Rossosh,* 3 Luza, *Tsna* (to Ukraine), *Katun, Nepryadva* (to Estonia), 1 Sura (to Ukraine), 2 Muna, 2 Iva, 10 Pozharny, 2 Pelym, 1 Bereza (to Ukraine), 2 Katun, 1 Goryn (to Ukraine), 3 Sorum, 3 Roslavl, 4 Mir (civilian)
1998   8 Petrushka, *Kamchatsky Komsomolets, Brykin, Amga,* 3 Belyanka, 11 Amur I, 1 Oskol, 2 Tomba, *Berezina, Irkut, Desna, Konda,* 2 Vala, *Ob, Tavda, Emba,* 5 Sura, *Dvina,* 3 Muna, 4 Pozharny, 10 Dobrynya Nikitich, 2 Pamir, 3 Neftegaz, 2 Goryn, 4 Sorum, 7 Roslavl, *General Ryabakov, Ivan Susanin, Elbrus*
1999   *Gangut, Khasan,* 6 Bolva, *Kola, Dnepr,* 1 Voda, 4 Vala, *Ingul, Biriusa, Yauza,* 7 Dobrynya Nikitich, 2 Goryn, 3 Sorum, 3 Okhtensky, 1 Oskol, *Pechenga* (civilian), *Manych* (civilian), *Ivan Golubets, Sovietsky Pogranichnik, Barguzin, Oka, Angara,* 2 Pelym

PENNANT LIST

	Aircraft Carriers		620	Bespokoiny		**Corvettes**		738	Zaryad
			650	Admiral Chabanenko				806	Motorist
063	Admiral Kuznetsov		678	Admiral Kharlamov		409	Moroz	824	Navodchik
			715	Bystry		423	Smerch	834	Polemetchik
	Battle Cruisers		754	Bezboyazenny		432	Inez	844	Barentsevo More
			778	Burny		450	Razliv	855	Machinist
080	Admiral Nakhimov		804	Sderzhanny		520	Rassvet	901	A Zheleznyakov
099	Pyotr Velikiy		810	Smetlivy		524	Uragan	909	Turbinist
						526	Nakat	911	Zhukov
						536	Churban	913	Snaypr
	Cruisers					551	Liven	914	Vinogradov
						555	Geyzer		
011	Varyag		**Frigates**			560	Zyb		
055	Marshal Ustinov					562	Priliv		
118	Admiral Golovko		052	Vorovsky (BG)		566	Burun		**Amphibious Forces**
121	Moskva		060	Anadyr (BG)		570	Passat		
711	Kerch		057	Dzerzhinksky (BG)		575	Samum	020	Mitrofan Moskalenko
			103	Kedrov (BG)		577	Storm	081	Nikolay Vilkov
			104	Pskov (BG)		590	Meteor	119	Donetsky Shakhter
	Destroyers		113	Menzhinsky (BG)		615	Bora	148	Ilya Azarov
			156	Orel (BG)		617	Miras	150	Voronezhsky
406	Bezuderzhny		661	Letuchy		620	Shtyl	152	Nikolay Filchenkov
434	Besstrashny		663	Storozhevoy		621	Briz		
543	Marshal Shaposhnikov		702	Pylky					
548	Admiral Panteleyev		712	Neustrashimy					
564	Admiral Tributs		731	Neukrotimy		**Mine Warfare Forces**			**Auxiliaries**
572	Admiral Vinogradov		754	Druzhny					
605	Admiral Levchenko		801	Ladny		119	V Gumanenko	200	Perekop
610	Nastoychivy		808	Pytlivy		610	Svyazist	210	Smolny
619	Severomorsk		930	Legky		718	Semen Roshak	874	Voronesh
			955	Zadorny		719	Desantnik	879	Volga

SUBMARINES

Strategic Missile Submarines (SSBN)

0 + 1 (1) BOREY CLASS (TYPE 955) (SSBN)

Name	No
YURI DOLGORUKY	—

	Builders	Laid down	Launched	Commissioned
	Severodvinsk Shipyard	2 Nov 1996	2005	2008

Displacement, tons: 17,000 dived
Dimensions, feet (metres): 557.7 × 42.7 × 34.4 *(170 × 13 × 10.5)*
Main machinery: Nuclear; 2 PWR; 2 turbines; 1 shaft
Speed, knots: 26 dived
Complement: 130

Missiles: SLBM: 12 SS-27 Topol-M or SS-N-23 Skiff.
A/S: SS-N-15 from torpedo tubes.
Torpedoes: 6—21 in *(533 mm)* tubes.

Countermeasures: Decoys. ESM.
Radars: Surface search.
Sonars: Bow, flank and towed arrays.

Programmes: Rubin design. The revised building schedule looks optimistic given the major problems confronting both the shipyard and equipment manufacturers. The submarine was reported as no more than 25 per cent completed in early 2000, and delays have been caused by both economic and missile selection problems. The latter has caused some redesign work.

Structure: Some of the features of the *Severodvinsk* are to be incorporated. After the cancellation of the SS-N-28 programme, the ship may be fitted with a maritime variant of the SS-27.
Opinion: Production is so slow that there must be doubts about the eventual completion of this project if there are further delays.

UPDATED

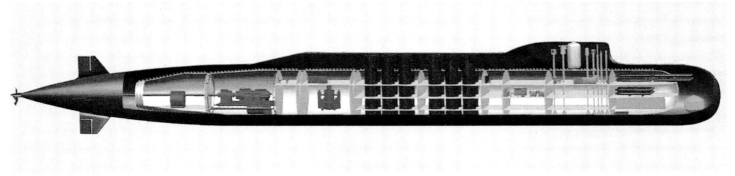

YURI DOLGORUKY

1996, US Navy / 0019001

2 TYPHOON (AKULA) CLASS (TYPE 941) (SSBN)

No	Builders	Laid down	Launched	Commissioned
TK 17	Severodvinsk Shipyard	24 Feb 1985	Aug 1986	6 Nov 1987
TK 20	Severodvinsk Shipyard	6 Jan 1987	July 1988	4 Sep 1989

Displacement, tons: 18,500 surfaced; 26,500 dived
Dimensions, feet (metres): 562.7 oa; 541.3 wl × 80.7 × 42.7 *(171.5; 165 × 24.6 × 13)*
Main machinery: Nuclear; 2 VM-5 PWR; 380 MW; 2 GT3A turbines; 81,600 hp(m) *(60 MW)*; 2 emergency motors; 517 hp(m) *(380 kW)*; 2 shafts; shrouded props; 2 thrusters (bow and stern); 2,860 hp(m) *(1.5 MW)*
Speed, knots: 25 dived; 12 surfaced
Complement: 175 (55 officers)

Missiles: SLBM: 20 Makeyev SS-N-20 (RSM 52/3M20) Sturgeon; three-stage solid fuel rocket; stellar inertial guidance to 8,300 km *(4,500 n miles)*; warhead nuclear 10 MIRV each of 200 kT; CEP 500 m. 2 missiles fired from the first of class in 15 seconds.
SAM: SA-N-8 SAM capability when surfaced.
A/S: Novator SS-N-15 Starfish; inertial flight to 45 km *(24.3 n miles)*; warhead nuclear 200 kT or Type 40 torpedo.
Torpedoes: 6—21 in *(533 mm)* tubes. Combination of torpedoes (see table at front of section). The weapon load includes a total of 22 torpedoes and A/S missiles.
Mines: Could be carried in lieu of torpedoes.
Countermeasures: Decoys: MG 34/44 tube launched decoys. ESM: Rim Hat (Nakat M); radar warning. Park Lamp D/F.
Weapons control: 3R65 data control system.
Radars: Surface search: Snoop Pair (Albatros); I/J-band.
Sonars: Shark Gill; hull-mounted; passive/active search and attack; low/medium frequency.
Shark Rib flank array; passive; low frequency.
Mouse Roar; hull-mounted; active attack; high frequency.
Pelamida towed array; passive search; very low frequency.

Modernisation: First of class TK 208 started refit at Severodvinsk in 1994 with plans to fit the now cancelled SS-N-28 missile. It is unlikely the refit will be completed unless the submarine becomes the test vessel for the naval variant of the Topol-M SLBM.
Structure: This is the largest type of submarine ever built. Two separate 7.2 m diameter hulls covered by a single outer free-flood hull with anechoic Cluster Guard tiles plus separate 6 m diameter pressure-tight compartments in the fin and fore-ends. There is a 1.2 m separation between the outer and inner hulls along the sides. The unique features of Typhoon are her enormous size and the fact that the missile tubes are mounted forward of the fin. The positioning of the launch tubes mean a fully integrated weapons area in the bow section leaving space abaft the fin for the provision of two nuclear reactors, one in each hull. The fin configuration indicates a designed capability to break through ice cover up to 3 m thick; the retractable forward hydroplanes, the rounded hull and the shape of the fin are all related to under-ice operations. Diving depth, 1,000 ft *(300 m)*. It is now confirmed that all six torpedo tubes are 533 mm.
Operational: Strategic targets are within range from anywhere in the world. Two VLF/ELF communication buoys are fitted. VLF navigation system for under-ice operations. Pert Spring SATCOM mast, Cod Eye radiometric sextant and Kremmny 2 IFF. Both based in the Northern Fleet at Litsa Guba. *TK 17* damaged by fire during a missile loading accident in 1992 but the damage has been repaired. First of class TK 208 has been in refit for six years and there are unconfirmed reports that it

TK 20

1/1997* / 0081639

may return to service in 2000. The next three TK 202, TK 12 and TK 13 await formal decommissioning. The US Navy has agreed to help with reactor decommissioning and breaking up the hulls.

Opinion: These ships are costly in manpower and maintenance. It is probable that these last two will be deleted as they come up for refuelling, if not before.

UPDATED

7 DELTA IV (DELFIN) CLASS (TYPE 667BDRM) (SSBN)

No	Builders	Laid down	Launched	Commissioned
K 51	Severodvinsk Shipyard	Feb 1981	Jan 1985	Dec 1985
K 84	Severodvinsk Shipyard	Sep 1984	Dec 1985	Feb 1987
K 64	Severodvinsk Shipyard	Nov 1985	Feb 1986	Feb 1988
K 114	Severodvinsk Shipyard	Dec 1986	Jan 1987	Jan 1989
K 117	Severodvinsk Shipyard	Sep 1987	Feb 1988	Mar 1990
K 18	Severodvinsk Shipyard	Sep 1988	Feb 1989	Sep 1991
K 407	Severodvinsk Shipyard	Nov 1989	Mar 1990	20 Feb 1992

Displacement, tons: 10,800 surfaced; 13,500 dived
Dimensions, feet (metres): 544.6 oa; 518.4 wl × 39.4 × 28.5
(166; 158 × 12 × 8.7)
Main machinery: Nuclear; 2 VM-4 PWR; 180 MW; 2 GT3A-365
turbines; 37,400 hp(m) *(27.5 MW)*; 2 emergency motors;
612 hp(m) *(450 kW)*; 2 shafts
Speed, knots: 24 dived; 14 surfaced
Complement: 135 (40 officers)

Missiles: SLBM: 16 Makeyev SS-N-23 (RSM 54) Skiff (Shtil);
3-stage liquid fuel rocket; stellar inertial guidance to 8,300 km
(4,500 n miles); warhead nuclear 4-10 MIRV each of 100 kT;
CEP 500 m. Same diameter as SS-N-18 but longer.
A/S: Novator SS-N-15 Starfish; inertial flight to 45 km *(24.3 n
miles)*; warhead nuclear 200 kT or Type 40 torpedo.
Torpedoes: 4—21 in *(533 mm)* tubes. Combination of 53 cm
torpedoes (see table at front of section). Total of 18 weapons.
Countermeasures: ESM: Brick Pulp/Group; radar warning. Park
Lamp D/F.
Radars: Surface search: Snoop Tray; I-band.
Sonars: Shark Gill; hull-mounted; passive/active search and
attack; low/medium frequency.
Shark Hide flank array; passive; low frequency.
Mouse Roar; hull-mounted; active attack; high frequency.
Pelamida towed array; passive search; very low frequency.

Programmes: Construction first ordered 10 December 1975.
First of class launched February 1984 and commissioned later
that year. This programme completed in late 1990.
Structure: A slim fitting is sited on the after fin which is
reminiscent of a similar tube in one of the 'November' class in
the early 1980s. This is a dispenser for a sonar thin line towed
array. The other distinguishing feature, apart from the size
being greater than Delta III, is the pressure-tight fitting on the
after end of the missile tube housing, which may be a TV
camera to monitor communications buoy and wire retrieval
operations. This is not fitted in all of the class. Brick Spit
optronic mast. Diving depth, 1,000 ft *(300 m)*. The outer
casing has a continuous acoustic coating and fewer free flood
holes than the Delta III.
Operational: Two VLF/ELF communication buoys. Navigation
systems include SATNAV, SINS, Cod Eye. Pert Spring
SATCOM. A modified and more accurate version of SS-N-23
was tested at sea in 1988 bringing the CEP down from 900 to
500 m. Missile launch is conducted at keel depth 55 m and at
a speed of 6 kt. All operational units based in the Northern
Fleet at Saida Guba. K 51 completed a five year refit in 1999.
K 84 and K 64 are both in refit at Severodvinsk. K 407
launched a German commercial satellite on 7 July 1998 from
the Barents Sea.
Opinion: Given the severe building problems associated with the
'Borey' class, the Delta IV represents the core programme if the
seaborne strategic deterrent is to maintain long term
credibility. It can therefore be assumed that refits have a high
priority.

DELTA IV   8/1996

UPDATED   DELTA IV   10/1993

K 117   4/1996, B Lemachko

7 DELTA III (KALMAR) CLASS (TYPE 667BDR) (SSBN)

No	Builders	Laid down	Launched		Commissioned
K 490	Severodvinsk Shipyard	1975	Jan	1977	1978
K 44	Severodvinsk Shipyard	1975	July	1977	1978
K 496	Severodvinsk Shipyard	1976	Jan	1978	1979
K 506	Severodvinsk Shipyard	1977	Jan	1979	1979
K 211	Severodvinsk Shipyard	1977	Jan	1979	1980
K 180	Severodvinsk Shipyard	1978	Dec	1980	1980
K 129	Severodvinsk Shipyard	1979	Dec	1981	1981

Displacement, tons: 10,550 surfaced; 13,250 dived
Dimensions, feet (metres): 524.9 oa; 498.7 wl × 39.4 × 28.5
(160; 152 × 12 × 8.7)
Main machinery: Nuclear; 2 VM-4 PWR; 180 MW; 2 GT3A-635
turbines; 37,400 hp(m) *(27.5 MW)*; 2 emergency motors;
612 hp(m) *(450 kW)*; 2 shafts
Speed, knots: 24 dived; 14 surfaced
Complement: 130 (40 officers)

Missiles: SLBM: 16 Makeyev SS-N-18 (RSM 50) Stingray
(Volna); 2-stage liquid fuel rocket with post boost vehicle (PBV);
stellar inertial guidance; 3 variants:
  Mod 1; range 6,500 km *(3,500 n miles)*; warhead nuclear
  3 MIRV each of 200 kT; CEP 900 m.
  Mod 2; range 8,000 km *(4,320 n miles)*; warhead nuclear
  450 kT; CEP 900 m.
  Mod 3; range 6,500 km *(3,500 n miles)*; warhead nuclear
  7 MIRV 100 kT; CEP 900 m.
  Mods 1 and 3 were the first MIRV SLBMs in Soviet service.
Torpedoes: 4—21 in *(533 mm)* and 2—400 mm tubes.
Combination of torpedoes (see table at front of section). Total
of 16 weapons.
Countermeasures: ESM: Brick Pulp/Group; radar warning. Park
Lamp D/F.
Radars: Surface search: Snoop Tray; I-band.

Sonars: Shark Teeth; hull-mounted; passive/active search and
attack; low/medium frequency.
  Shark Hide flank array; passive; low frequency.
  Mouse Roar; hull-mounted; active attack; high frequency.
  Pelamida towed array; passive search; very low frequency.

Modernisation: The dispenser tube on the after fin has been
fitted to most of the class. It was planned to retrofit SS-N-23
but this was shelved.
Structure: The missile casing is higher than in 'Delta II' class to
accommodate SS-N-18 missiles which are longer than the SS-
N-8 of the 'Delta II' class. The outer casing has a continuous
'acoustic' coating but is less streamlined and has more free
flood holes than the Delta IV. Brick Spit optronic mast. Diving
depth, 1,000 ft *(300 m)*.
Operational: ELF/VLF communications with floating aerial and
buoy; UHF and SHF aerials. Navigation equipment includes
Cod Eye radiometric sextant, SATNAV, SINS and Omega. Pert
Spring SATCOM. Kremmny 2 IFF. K 44 and K 496 are based at
Saida Guba in the Northern Fleet, the remainder at Tarya Bay in
the Pacific. Another hull of the class K 433 converted to a
DSRV carrier with missile tubes removed. First of class paid off
in 1996, three more in 1997, two more in 1998. Six others are
laid up in Fleet bases.

UPDATED

DELTA III   *8/1996* * / 0081642

DELTA III   *6/1998* *, S Breyer / 0081641*

2 DELTA I (MURENA) CLASS (TYPE 667B) (SSBN)

No	Builders	Laid down	Launched		Commissioned	
K 447	Severodvinsk Shipyard	1971	Sep	1972	July	1973
K 530	Komsomolsk Shipyard	1976	July	1977	May	1978

Displacement, tons: 8,700 surfaced; 10,200 dived
Dimensions, feet (metres): 459.3 oa; 446.2 wl × 39.4 × 28.5
(140; 136 × 12 × 8.7)
Main machinery: Nuclear; 2 VM-2 PWR; 155 MW; 2 GT3A-365
turbines; 37,400 hp(m) *(27.5 MW)*; 2 shafts
Speed, knots: 25 dived; 19 surfaced
Complement: 120 (38 officers)

Missiles: SLBM: 12 Chelomey SS-N-8 (RSM 40) Sawfly (Vysota);
2-stage liquid fuel rocket; stellar inertial guidance; 2 variants:
  Mod 1; range 7,800 km *(4,210 n miles)*; warhead nuclear
  800 kT; CEP 400 m.
  Mod 2; range 9,100 km *(4,910 n miles)*; warhead nuclear
  2 MIRV each of 500 kT; CEP 400 m.
Torpedoes: 4—21 in *(533 mm)* and 2—16 in *(400 mm)* tubes.

Combination of torpedoes (see table at front of section). Total
of 18.
Countermeasures: ESM: Brick Pulp/Group; radar warning. Park
Lamp D/F.
Radars: Surface search: Snoop Tray; I-band.
Sonars: Shark Teeth; hull-mounted; passive/active search and
attack; low/medium frequency.
  Mouse Roar; hull-mounted; active attack; high frequency.

Programmes: The first of this class, an advance on the 'Yankee'
class SSBNs, was laid down at Severodvinsk in 1969 and
completed in 1972. Programme completed in 1974. Building
yards—Severodvinsk 402 (10) and Komsomolsk (8).
Structure: The longer range SS-N-8 missiles are of greater length
than the SS-N-6s and, as this length cannot be accommodated

below the keel, they stand several feet proud of the after-
casing. At the same time the need to compensate for the
additional top-weight would seem to be the reason for the
reduction to 12 missiles in this class. The outer casing has a
continuous 'acoustic' coating. Diving depth, 1,000 ft *(300 m)*.
Operational: ELF/VLF communications with floating aerial and
buoy; UHF and SHF aerials. Cod Eye radiometric sextant.
Kremmny 2 IFF. In common with all the 'Delta' class variations,
this submarine is ill designed for under-ice operations. First of
this class paid off in 1992, three in 1993, six in 1994, one in
1995, two in 1996, one in 1997, and two in 2000. Some are
laid up at operational bases in the North and Pacific. K 530 is
based at Strelok in the Pacific and K 447 at Saida Guba in the
North. Both are expected to pay off by 2001.

UPDATED

DELTA I   *6/1999* * / 0081640

Attack Submarines (SSN/SSGN)

Note: Attack submarines are coated with Cluster Guard anechoic tiles. All submarines are capable of laying mines from their torpedo tubes. All SSNs are fitted with non-acoustic environmental sensors for measuring discontinuities caused by the passage of a submarine in deep water.

0 + 1 YASEN CLASS (TYPE 885) (SSN/SSGN)

Name	No	Builders	Laid down	Launched	Commissioned
SEVERODVINSK	—	Severodvinsk Shipyard	21 Dec 1993	2003	2005

Displacement, tons: 5,900 surfaced; 8,600 dived
Dimensions, feet (metres): 364.2 × 39.4 × 27.6
   (111 × 12 × 8.4)
Main machinery: Nuclear; 1 PWR; 195 MW; 2 GT3A turbines;
   43,000 hp(m) *(31.6 MW)*; 1 shaft; 2 spinners
Speed, knots: 28 dived; 17 surfaced
Complement: 55 (22 officers)

Missiles: SLCM/SSM: Novator Alfa SS-N-27.
   8 VLS launchers in after casing. Total of 24 missiles.
   A/S: SS-N-15. Fired from torpedo tubes.
Torpedoes: 8—21 in *(533 mm)* tubes. Inclined outwards. Total of
   about 30 weapons.
Countermeasures: ESM: Radar warning.
Radars: Surface search: I-band.

Sonars: Irtysh Amfora system includes bow-mounted spherical
   array; passive/active search and attack; low frequency.
   Flank and towed arrays; passive; very low frequency.

Programmes: Malakhit design. Confirmed building in 1993.
   Reported plans are for seven of the class described as
   multipurpose SSNs derived from the 'Akula II' class. Building is
   currently severely affected by shipyard funding problems and
   the first of class was reported as being only 30 per cent
   complete in early 2000. The government owes the shipyard
   huge sums and subsidiary suppliers are existing on credit. It
   has been reported that an improved version of this class is
   already being designed.
Structure: Some of the details given are speculative. VLS
   launchers for SSMs, canted torpedo tubes and spherical bow
   sonars are all new to Russian designs.
Opinion: Progress is slow to the point where the programme is in
   doubt. Unless shipyard workers are regularly paid and
   equipment manufacturers supported by industry, these
   submarines will take a very long time to complete.

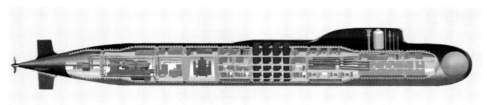

SEVERODVINSK
1996, US Navy / 0019006

UPDATED

2 SIERRA II (KONDOR) CLASS (TYPE 945A) (SSN)

Name	No	Builders	Launched	Commissioned
PSKOW	B 336	Nizhny Novgorod	July 1989	28 Dec 1990
NIZNY-NOVGOROD	B 534	Nizhny Novgorod	Aug 1992	12 Aug 1993

Displacement, tons: 7,600 surfaced; 9,100 dived
Dimensions, feet (metres): 364.2 × 46.6 × 28.9
   (111 × 14.2 × 8.8)
Main machinery: Nuclear; 1 VM-5 PWR; 190 MW; 1 GT3A
   turbine; 47,500 hp(m) *(70 MW)*; 2 emergency motors;
   2,004 hp(m) *(1.5 MW)*; 1 shaft; 2 spinners; 1,006 hp(m)
   (740 kW)
Speed, knots: 32 dived; 10 surfaced
Complement: 61 (31 officers)

Missiles: SLCM: Raduga SS-N-21 Sampson (Granat) fired from
   21 in *(533 mm)* tubes; land-attack; inertial/terrain-following to
   3,000 km *(1,620 n miles)* at 0.7 Mach; warhead nuclear
   200 kT. CEP 150 m. Flies at a height of about 200 m.
   SAM: SA-N-5/8 Strela portable launcher; 12 missiles.
   A/S: Novator SS-N-15 Starfish (Tsakra) fired from 53 cm tubes;
   inertial flight to 45 km *(24.3 n miles)*; warhead nuclear 200 kT
   or Type 40 torpedo.
   Novator SS-N-16 Stallion fired from 65 cm tubes; inertial flight
   to 100 km *(54 n miles)*; payload nuclear 200 kT (Vodopad) or
   Type 40 torpedo (Veder).
Torpedoes: 4—25.6 in *(650 mm)* and 4—21 in *(533 mm)* tubes.
   Combination of 65 and 53 cm torpedoes (see table at front of
   section). Total of 40 weapons.
Mines: 42 in lieu of torpedoes.
Countermeasures: ESM: Rim Hat; intercept. Park Lamp D/F.
Radars: Surface search: Snoop Pair with back-to-back ESM
   aerial.
Sonars: Shark Gill; hull-mounted; passive/active search and
   attack; low/medium frequency.
   Shark Rib flank array; passive; low frequency.
   Mouse Roar; hull-mounted; active attack; high frequency.
   Skat 3 towed array; passive; very low frequency.

Programmes: A third of class *Mars*, was scrapped before
   completion in July 1992.
Structure: A follow-on class to the Sierra I. Apart from larger
   overall dimensions the Sierra II has a longer fin by some 16.5 ft
   (5 m) and an almost flat surface at the leading-edge. Titanium
   hulls. The towed communications buoy has been recessed. A
   10 point environmental sensor is fitted at the front end of the
   fin. The standoff distance between hulls is considerable and

PSKOW
*4/1999 *, Ships of the World /* 0081643

SIERRA II
8/1998 / 0050009

has obvious advantages for radiated noise reduction and
damage resistance. Diving depth, 2,460 ft *(750 m)*. Numbers
and sizes of torpedo tubes are uncertain with different figures
given by Russian sources.

Operational: Pert Spring SATCOM. Both based in the Northern
   Fleet, one at Ara Guba and one at Litsa South.

UPDATED

SIERRA II
6/1997 / 0019009

8 + 1 OSCAR II (ANTYEY) (TYPE 949A) (SSGN)

Name	No	Builders	Launched	Commissioned
VERONESH	K 173	Severodvinsk Shipyard	Dec 1988	Dec 1989
SMOLENSK	K 410	Severodvinsk Shipyard	Jan 1990	Dec 1990
CELJABINSK	K 442	Severodvinsk Shipyard	June 1990	Jan 1991
WILIUCZINSK (ex-*Kasatka*)	K 456	Severodvinsk Shipyard	July 1991	Nov 1992
OREL (ex-*Severodvinsk*)	K 266	Severodvinsk Shipyard	May 1992	Jan 1993
OMSK	K 186	Severodvinsk Shipyard	May 1993	Oct 1993
KURSK	K 141	Severodvinsk Shipyard	May 1994	Jan 1995
ST GEORGE THE VICTORIOUS (ex-*Tomsk*)	K 512	Severodvinsk Shipyard	18 July 1996	May 1997
BELGOROD	K 530	Severodvinsk Shipyard	Aug 1999	—

Displacement, tons: 13,900 surfaced; 18,300 dived
Dimensions, feet (metres): 505.2 × 59.7 × 29.5
(154 × 18.2 × 9)
Main machinery: Nuclear; 2 VM-5 PWR; 380 MW; 2 GT3A turbines; 98,000 hp(m) *(72 MW)*; 2 shafts; 2 spinners
Speed, knots: 28 dived; 15 surfaced
Complement: 107 (48 officers)

Missiles: SSM: 24 Chelomey SS-N-19 Shipwreck (Granit) (improved SS-N-12 with lower flight profile); inertial with command update guidance; active radar homing to 20-550 km *(10.8-300 n miles)* at 1.6 Mach; warhead 750 kg HE or 500 kT nuclear. Novator Alfa SS-N-27 may be carried in due course.
A/S: Novator SS-N-15 Starfish (Tsakra) fired from 53 cm tubes; inertial flight to 45 km *(24.3 n miles)*; warhead nuclear 200 kT or Type 40 torpedo.
Novator SS-N-16 Stallion fired from 65 cm tubes; inertial flight to 100 km *(54 n miles)*; payload nuclear 200 kT (Vodopad) or Type 40 torpedo (Veder).

Torpedoes: 4—21 in *(533 mm)* and 2—26 in *(650 mm)* tubes. Combination of 65 and 53 cm torpedoes (see table at front of section). Total of 28 weapons including tube-launched A/S missiles.
Mines: 32 can be carried.
Countermeasures: ESM: Rim Hat; intercept.
Weapons control: Punch Bowl for third party targeting.
Radars: Surface search: Snoop Pair or Snoop Half; I-band.
Sonars: Shark Gill; hull-mounted; passive/active search and attack; low/medium frequency.
Shark Rib flank array; passive; low frequency.
Mouse Roar; hull-mounted; active attack; high frequency.
Pelamida towed array; passive search; very low frequency.

Programmes: There is some doubt whether K 530 will be completed. Name/Number attribution is still uncertain, and *Omsk* may have been renamed *Petropavlosk Kamchatsky*.

Structure: SSM missile tubes are in banks of 12 either side and external to the 8.5 m diameter pressure hull; they are inclined at 40° with one hatch covering each pair, the whole resulting in the very large beam. The position of the missile tubes provides a large gap of some 4 m between the outer and inner hulls. Diving depth, 1,000 ft *(300 m)* although 2,000 ft *(600 m)* is claimed.
Operational: ELF/VLF communications buoy. All have a tube on the rudder fin as in Delta IV which is used for dispensing a thin line towed sonar array. Pert Spring SATCOM. K 173, K 410, K 266 and K 141 are based at Litsa South in the Northern Fleet and the remainder at Tarya Bay in the Pacific. In 1999 one Northern Fleet unit deployed for the first Russian SSGN patrol in the Mediterranean for ten years. At the same time a Pacific Fleet unit sailed to the western seaboard of the United States. The first three of the class K 148, K 132 and K 119 are laid up awaiting disposal. The only two Oscar Is are laid up in the Northern Fleet.

UPDATED

OSCAR II

3/1998 / 0050004

OSCAR II

6/1998 / 0081644

OSCAR II   *3/1998* / 0050005

OSCAR II   *9/1996* / 0019005

2 AKULA II and 8 + 1 AKULA I (BARS) CLASS (TYPE 971/971M) (SSN)

Name	No	Builders	Launched		Commissioned
DOLPHIN	K 263	Komsomolsk Shipyard	30 Apr	1986	Sep 1986
KIT	K 391	Komsomolsk Shipyard	Apr	1989	July 1989
NARWHAL	K 331	Komsomolsk Shipyard	5 June	1990	Sep 1990
WOLF	K 461	Severodvinsk Shipyard	11 June	1991	Dec 1991
COUGAR	K 419	Komsomolsk Shipyard	May	1992	Aug 1992
LEOPARD	K 328	Severodvinsk Shipyard	6 Oct	1992	Oct 1992
TIGER	K 157	Severodvinsk Shipyard	10 July	1993	Oct 1993
DRAGON	K 295	Komsomolsk Shipyard	15 July	1994	29 July 1995
NERPA	K 267	Komsomolsk Shipyard	May	1994	—
VIPER (II)	—	Severodvinsk Shipyard	10 Dec	1994	July 1995
GEPARD (II)	—	Severodvinsk Shiyard	18 Aug	1999	June 2000

Displacement, tons: 7,500 surfaced; 9,100 (9,500 Akula II) dived

Dimensions, feet (metres): 360.1 oa; 337.9 wl × 45.9 × 34.1 *(110; 103 × 14 × 10.4)*

Main machinery: Nuclear; 1 VM-5 PWR; 190 MW; 2 GT3A turbines; 47,600 hp(m) *(35 MW)*; 2 emergency propulsion motors; 750 hp(m) *(552 kW)*; 1 shaft; 2 spinners; 1,006 hp(m) *(740 kW)*

Speed, knots: 28 dived; 10 surfaced

Complement: 62 (31 officers)

Missiles: SLCM/SSM: Reduga SS-N-21 Sampson (Granat) fired from 21 in *(533 mm)* tubes; land-attack; inertial/terrain-following to 3,000 km *(1,620 n miles)* at 0.7 Mach; warhead nuclear 200 kT. CEP 150 m. Flies at a height of about 200 m. Novator Alfa SS-N-27 subsonic flight with supersonic boost for terminal flight; 180 km *(97 mm)*; warhead 200 kg. May be fitted in due course.
SAM: SA-N-5/8 Strela portable launcher. 18 missiles.
A/S: Novator SS-N-15 Starfish (Tsakra) fired from 53 cm tubes; inertial flight to 45 km *(24.3 n miles)*; warhead nuclear 200 kT or Type 40 torpedo.

Novator SS-N-16 Stallion fired from 650 mm tubes; inertial flight to 100 km *(54 n miles)*; payload nuclear 200 kT (Vodopad) or Type 40 torpedo (Veder).

Torpedoes: 4—21 in *(533 mm)* and 4—25.6 in *(650 mm)* tubes. Combination of 53 and 65 cm torpedoes (see table at front of section). Tube liners can be used to reduce the larger diameter tubes to 533 mm. Total of 40 weapons. In addition the Improved Akulas and Akula IIs have six additional 533 mm external tubes in the upper bow area.

Countermeasures: ESM: Rim Hat; intercept.

Radars: Surface search: Snoop Pair or Snoop Half with back-to-back aerials on same mast as ESM.

Sonars: Shark Gill (Skat MGK 503); hull-mounted; passive/active search and attack; low/medium frequency.
Mouse Roar; hull-mounted; active attack; high frequency.
Skat 3 towed array; passive; very low frequency.

Programmes: Malakhit design. From K 461 onwards, the Akula Is were 'improved'. *Viper* was the first Akula II to complete, and the second II is expected to commission in mid-2000. Akula I K 267 has been building for ten years at Komsomolsk and may never be completed. A possible sale to China has been reported but not confirmed.

Structure: The very long fin is particularly notable. Has the same broad hull as Sierra and has reduced radiated noise levels by comparison with Victor III of which she is the traditional follow-on design. A number of prominent non-acoustic sensors appear on the fin leading-edge and on the forward casing in the later Akulas. These are similar to devices tested on a 'Hotel II' class from the early 1980s. The engineering standards around the bridge and casing are noticeably to a higher quality than other classes. The design has been incrementally improved with reduced noise levels, boundary layer suppression and active noise cancellation reported in the later units. The Improved hulls have an additional six external torpedo tubes and the Akula IIs have been lengthened by 3.7 m to incorporate further noise reduction developments. Operational diving depth, 1,476 ft *(450 m)*.

Operational: Pert Spring SATCOM. Komsomolsk built ships serve in the Pacific at Tarya Bay, and the Northern Fleet units are at Saida Guba and Sevr. The first Akula I was paid off in 1996, a second in 1997, a third in 1998 and one more in 1999. Some of the names are translations of the Russian equivalent.

UPDATED

VIPER (Akula II)   *4/1998* / 0050008

VIPER (Akula II)   *4/1998** / 0081645

AKULA I   10/1993

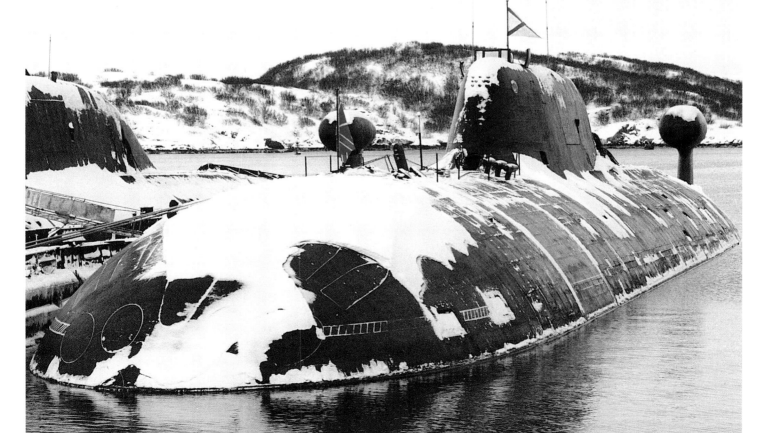

TIGER (Improved Akula)   2/1996, B Lemachko

1 SIERRA I (BARRACUDA) CLASS (TYPE 945) (SSN)

Name	No	Builders	Laid down	Launched	Commissioned
TULA (ex-*Karp*)	K 239	Gorky Shipyard/Severodvinsk Shipyard	Aug 1983	July 1986	Sep 1987

Displacement, tons: 7,200 surfaced; 8,100 dived
Dimensions, feet (metres): 351 × 41 × 28.9
(107 × 12.5 × 8.8)
Main machinery: Nuclear; 1 VM-5 PWR; 190 MW; 1 GT3A
turbine; 47,500 hp(m) *(70 MW)*; 2 emergency motors;
2,004 hp(m) *(1.5 MW)*; 1 shaft; 2 spinners; 1,006 hp(m)
(740 kW)
Speed, knots: 34 dived; 10 surfaced
Complement: 61 (31 officers)

Missiles: SLCM: Raduga SS-N-21 Sampson (Granat) fired from
21 in *(533 mm)* tubes; land-attack; inertial/terrain-following to
3,000 km *(1,620 n miles)* at 0.7 Mach; warhead nuclear
200 kT. CEP 150 m. Probably flies at a height of about 200 m.
SAM: SA-N-5/8 Strela portable launcher; 12 missiles.
A/S: Novator SS-N-15 Starfish (Tsakra) fired from 53 cm tubes;
inertial flight to 45 km *(24.3 n miles)*; warhead nuclear 200 kT
or Type 40 torpedo.
Novator SS-N-16 Stallion fired from 65 cm tubes; inertial flight
to 100 km *(54 n miles)*; payload nuclear 200 kT (Vodopad) or
Type 40 torpedo (Veder).
Torpedoes: 4—25.6 in *(650 mm)* and 4—21 in *(533 mm)* tubes.
Combination of 65 and 53 cm torpedoes (see table at front of
section). Total of 40 weapons.
Mines: 42 in lieu of torpedoes.
Countermeasures: ESM: Rim Hat/Bald Head; intercept. Park
Lamp D/F.
Radars: Surface search: Snoop Pair with back-to-back ESM
aerial.
Sonars: Shark Gill; hull-mounted; passive/active search and
attack; low/medium frequency.
Shark Rib flank array; passive; low frequency.
Mouse Roar; hull-mounted; active attack; high frequency.
Skat 3 towed array; passive; very low frequency.

Programmes: Launched at Gorky (Nizhny Novgorod), and fitted
out at Severodvinsk.
Structure: Has a Titanium hull which makes it much more
expensive than Akula and a logical successor to the deleted
'Alfa' class. The pod on the after fin is larger than that in Victor
III. The standoff distance between hulls is considerable and has
obvious advantages for radiated noise reduction and damage

SIERRA I   1990

resistance. There is a V-shaped casing on the port side of the fin
which covers the releasable escape chamber. This submarine
also has a bulbous casing at the after end of the fin for a towed
communications buoy. Diving depth, 2,460 ft *(750 m)*.

Operational: Pert Spring SATCOM. Based in the Northern Fleet
at Ara Guba. Second of class laid up in 1997 but this one
remains operational although probably not for much longer.
UPDATED

1 YANKEE NOTCH (GROSHA) CLASS (TYPE 667AR/AT) (SSN, ex-SSBN)

K 395

Displacement, tons: 8,500 surfaced; 10,300 dived
Dimensions, feet (metres): 464.2 × 38.1 × 26.6
(141.5 × 11.6 × 8.1)
Main machinery: Nuclear; 2 VM-4 PWR; 155 MW; 2 GT3A-635
turbines; 52,000 hp(m) *(38.2 MW)*; 2 shafts
Speed, knots: 26 dived; 16 surfaced
Complement: 109 (18 officers)

Missiles: SLCM: 35 Raduga SS-N-21 Sampson (Granat) fired
from 6 additional 21 in *(533 mm)* tubes; land attack; inertial/
terrain-following to 3,000 km *(1,620 n miles)* at 0.7 Mach;
warhead nuclear 200 kT. CEP 150 m. Flies at a height of about
200 m.

Torpedoes: 6—21 in *(533 mm)* tubes; combination of 53 cm
torpedoes (see table at front of section). Total of 18 weapons.
Countermeasures: ESM: Brick Group; intercept. Park Lamp D/F.
Radars: Surface search: Snoop Tray; I-band.
Sonars: Shark Teeth; hull-mounted; passive/active search and
attack; low/medium frequency.
Mouse Roar; hull-mounted; active attack; high frequency.

Programmes: The SALT limits of 62 SSBNs and 950 SLBMs
were adhered to by the Soviet Navy and this resulted in the
conversion of 'Yankee' class as well as the deleted 'Hotel' and
'Golf' classes. The Yankee conversion to SSN was first seen in
1983. The conversion took about two years and it seemed to

be the intention to convert about 10 of the class until the
programme fell victim to financial cuts in 1989-90. See also
Auxiliary Submarine section.
Structure: In spite of the removal of the ballistic missile section
the overall length of the hull has increased by 39.4 ft *(12 m)*
with the insertion of a 'notch waisted' central section. This new
section houses three tubes amidships on each side and the
magazine holds up to 35 SS-N-21s or additional torpedoes and
mines. Brick Spit optronic mast. Diving depth, 1,050 ft
(320 m).
Operational: Based in the Northern Fleet at Saida Guba. Two
others have paid off to reserve.
VERIFIED

K 395   4/1998 / 0050006

7 VICTOR III (SCHUKA) CLASS (TYPE 671RTM) (SSN)

No	Builders	Launched	Commissioned
K 138	Admiralty, Leningrad	Aug 1977	1978
K 255	Admiralty, Leningrad	July 1982	1983
K 388	Admiralty, Leningrad	July 1983	1984
K 502	Admiralty, Leningrad	June 1988	1989
K 507	Admiralty, Leningrad	Aug 1989	1990
K 524	Admiralty, Leningrad	Aug 1990	1991
K 527	Admiralty, Leningrad	Oct 1991	1993

Displacement, tons: 4,850 surfaced; 6,300 dived
Dimensions, feet (metres): 351.1 × 34.8 × 24.3
(107 × 10.6 × 7.4)
Main machinery: Nuclear; 2 VM-4 PWR; 150 MW; 2 turbines;
31,000 hp(m) *(22.7 MW)*; 1 shaft; 2 spinners; 1,020 hp(m)
(750 kW)
Speed, knots: 30 dived; 10 surfaced
Complement: 98 (17 officers)

Missiles: SLCM: Raduga SS-N-21 Sampson (Granat) fired from
21 in *(533 mm)* tubes; land-attack; inertial/terrain-following to
3,000 km *(1,620 n miles)* at 0.7 Mach; warhead nuclear
200 kT. CEP 150 m. Probably flies at a height of about 200 m.
A/S: Novator SS-N-15 Starfish (Tsakra) fired from 53 cm tubes;
inertial flight to 45 km *(24.3 n miles)*; warhead nuclear 200 kT
or Type 40 torpedo.
Novator SS-N-16 Stallion fired from 65 cm tubes; inertial flight
to 100 km *(54 n miles)*; payload nuclear 200 kT (Vodopad) or
Type 40 torpedo (Veder).
Torpedoes: 4—21 in *(533 mm)* and 2—25.6 in *(650 mm)* tubes.
Combination of 53 and 65 cm torpedoes (see table at front of
section). Can carry up to 24 weapons. Liners can be used to
reduce 650 mm tubes to 533 mm.
Mines: Can carry 36 in lieu of torpedoes.
Countermeasures: ESM: Brick Group (Brick Spit and Brick Pulp);
intercept. Park Lamp D/F.
Radars: Surface search: Snoop Tray; I-band.
Sonars: Shark Gill; hull-mounted; passive/active search and
attack; low/medium frequency.
Shark Rib flank array; passive; low frequency.
Mouse Roar; hull-mounted; active attack; high frequency.
Scat 3 towed array; passive; very low frequency.

Programmes: An improvement on Victor II, the first of class
being completed at Komsomolsk in 1978. With construction
also being carried out at Admiralty Yard, Leningrad, there was
a very rapid building programme up to the end of 1984.
Construction then continued only at Leningrad and at a rate of
about one per year which terminated in 1991. The last of the
class completed sea trials in October 1992.
Structure: The streamlined pod on the stern fin is a towed sonar
array dispenser. Water environment sensors are mounted at
the front of the fin and on the forward casing as in the 'Akula'
and 'Sierra' classes. One of the class has the trials SS-N-21
SLCM mounted on the forward casing and is sometimes
known as the Victor IV (Type 671RTMK). Incremental
improvements were made to the design and the last nine of the
class are reported as being quieter than the others. Diving
depth, 1,300 ft *(400 m)*.
Operational: VLF communications buoy. VHF/UHF aerials.
Navigation equipment includes SINS and SATNAV. Pert Spring
SATCOM. Kremmny 2 IFF. Much improved acoustic quietening
puts the radiated noise levels at the upper limits of the USN
'Los Angeles' class. All remaining operational units are based
in the Northern Fleet at Litsa South or Ara Guba. Nineteen have
paid off so far although up to nine of these are in reserve and
laid up at anchorages in both Fleets. A recent innovation is
pennant numbers on the fin.

UPDATED

VICTOR III   *7/1997* / 0019010

VICTOR III   *8/1998* / 0050010

VICTOR III   *10/1997* / 0050011

Patrol Submarines (SSK)

0 + 2 LADA AMUR CLASS (TYPE 1677) (SSK)

Name	Builders	Laid down	Launched	Commissioned
ST PETERSBURG	Admiralty, St Petersburg	26 Dec 1997	2001	2002
—	Admiralty, St Petersburg	26 Dec 1997	2001	2002

Displacement, tons: 1,765 surfaced; 2,650 dived
Dimensions, feet (metres): 223.1 × 23.6 × 14.4
(68 × 7.2 × 4.4)
Main machinery: Diesel-electric; 2 diesel generators; 3,400 hp
(m) *(2.5 MW)*; 1 motor; 5,576 hp(m) *(4.1 MW)*; 1 shaft

Speed, knots: 21 dived; 10 surfaced
Range, miles: 6,000 at 7 kt snorting
Complement: 37

Torpedoes: 6—21 in *(533 mm)* tubes. 18 weapons.

Mines: In lieu of torpedoes.
Countermeasures: ESM: Intercept.
Radars: Surface search: I-band.
Sonars: Hull and flank arrays; active/passive; medium frequency.

Programmes: Started building at Admiralty Yard, St Petersburg
in 1996. First keel laid for the Russian Navy, at the same time
as a second of class started for export possibly for India or
China, although this has not been confirmed. Because of the
Russian Navy's financial problems, the export version may
complete first. Plans for opening a second production line at
Severodvinsk have probably been abandoned.
Structure: This is a Rubin design at the top end of the Amur
range. A fuel cell plug (for AIP) of about 12 m can be inserted to
allow installation of AIP in the Russian vessel, although this is
unlikely in the near future.
Diving depth: 820 ft *(250 m)*. A non-hull penetrating optronic
periscope is being fitted.   **UPDATED**

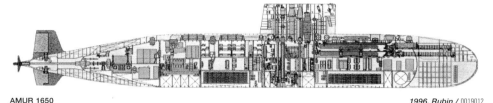

AMUR 1650   *1996, Rubin* / 0019012

6 KILO and 6 KILO 4B (VASHAVYANKA) CLASS (TYPE 877/877K/877M/636) (SSK)

Displacement, tons: 2,325 surfaced; 3,076 dived
Dimensions, feet (metres): 238.2; 242.1 (Type 4B) × 32.5 ×
21.7 *(72.6; 73.8 × 9.9 × 6.6)*
Main machinery: Diesel-electric; Type 4-2DL-42M 2 diesels
(Type 4-2AA-42M in 4B); 3,650 hp(m) *(2.68 MW)*; 2
generators; 1 motor; 5,900 hp(m) *(4.34 MW)*; 1 shaft; 2
auxiliary MT-168 motors; 204 hp(m) *(150 kW)*; 1 economic
speed motor; 130 hp(m) *(95 kW)*
Speed, knots: 17 dived; 10 surfaced; 9 snorting
Range, miles: 6,000 at 7 kt snorting; 400 at 3 kt dived
Complement: 52 (13 officers)

Missiles: SSM: Novator Alfa SS-N-27 may be fitted in due course.
SAM: 6-8 SA-N-5/8; IR homing from 600 to 6,000 m at
1.65 Mach; warhead 2 kg; portable launcher stowed in a well
in the fin between snort and W/T masts.
Torpedoes: 6—21 in *(533 mm)* tubes. 18 combinations of 53 cm
torpedoes (see table at front of section). USET-80 is wire-
guided in the 4B version (from 2 tubes).
Mines: 24 in lieu of torpedoes.
Countermeasures: ESM: Squid Head or Brick Pulp; radar
warning. Quad Loop D/F.
Weapons control: MVU-110EM or MVU-119EM Murena
torpedo fire-control system.
Radars: Surface search: Snoop Tray (MRP-25); I-band.
Sonars: Shark Teeth/Shark Fin (MGK-400); hull-mounted;
passive/active search and attack; medium frequency.
Mouse Roar; hull-mounted; active attack; high frequency.

Programmes: First launched in 1979 at Komsomolsk and
commissioned 12 September 1982. Subsequent construction
also at Nizhny Novgorod and Admiralty Yard, Leningrad. A
total of 24 were built for Russia.
Structure: Has a better hull form than the Foxtrot or Tango but is
still fairly basic by comparison with modern Western designs.
Diving depth, 790 ft *(240 m)* normal. Battery has a
9,700 kW/h capacity. The basic Kilo is the Type 877; 877K
has an improved fire-control system and 877M includes wire-
guided torpedoes from two tubes. Type 4B is the later design
with uprated diesels, a propulsion motor rotating at half the
speed and an automated combat information system capable
of providing simultaneous fire-control data on two targets.
Pressure hull length is 51.8 m *(170 ft)* or 53 m for Type 4B.
Foreplanes are on the hull just forward of the fin. Six of the

KILO   *2/1999** / 0081646

class are reported to be of the Type 4B variant, which has
higher standards of noise reduction than the export Type 636.
Type 4B can be identified on the surface by a vertical cut off to
the after casing.
Operational: With a reserve of buoyancy of 32 per cent and a
heavily compartmented pressure hull, this class is capable of
being holed and still surviving. One based in the Black Sea, one
in the Baltic, two in the North at Polyarny and eight in the
Pacific at Rakovaya. Of the six Type 4B, two are in the North,
one is in the Baltic and three are in the Pacific. Twelve of the

class have been paid off so far but some are held in reserve and
could be re-activated. The Black Sea unit was reported as doing
trials with water-jet propulsion in 1998.
Sales: Exported to Poland (one), Romania (one), India (ten),
Algeria (two), Iran (three) and China (four). Export versions
have the letter E after the type or project designator, or are of
the Type 636 with improved propulsion and fire-control
systems. Russian made main batteries have been a constant
source of problems in warm water operations.

UPDATED

KILO   *6/1998, 92 Wing RAAF* / 0050013

4 TANGO (SOM) CLASS (TYPE 641B) (SSK)

Displacement, tons: 3,100 surfaced; 3,800 dived
Dimensions, feet (metres): 298.6 × 29.9 × 23.6
(91 × 9.1 × 7.2)
Main machinery: Diesel-electric; 3 diesels (2 × 1.4 MW and 1 ×
1.8 MW); 6,256 hp(m) *(4.6 MW)*; 3 motors (2 × 1 MW and 1 ×
1.8 MW); 5,168 hp(m) *(3.8 MW)*; 3 shafts
Speed, knots: 16 dived; 13 surfaced
Range, miles: 500 at 3 kt dived; 14,000 at 7 kt snorting
Complement: 62 (12 officers)

Torpedoes: 6—21 in *(533 mm)* bow tubes. Combination of
24—53 cm torpedoes (see table at front of section). There are
no stern tubes.
Mines: In lieu of torpedoes.
Countermeasures: ESM: Squid Head or Brick Group; radar
warning. Quad Loop D/F.
Radars: Surface search: Snoop Tray; I-band.
Sonars: Shark Teeth/Shark Fin (MGK-400); hull-mounted;
passive/active search and attack; medium frequency.
Mouse Roar; hull-mounted; active attack; high frequency.

Programmes: This class was first seen at the Sevastopol Review
in July 1973 and, immediately succeeding the 'Foxtrot' class,
showed a continuing commitment to non-nuclear-propelled
boats. The building rate rose to two a year at Gorky (Nizhny
Novgorod) and the programme finished in 1982.
Structure: There is a marked increase in the internal capacity of
the hull used to improve battery capacity and habitability
compared with Foxtrot. Diving depth, 820 ft *(250 m)* normal.

TANGO (with towed array tube)   *7/1996*

The casing and fin have a continuous acoustic coating. One
unit was fitted with a towed array stern tube and a reel
mounted in the casing forward of the fin in 1992 and is
referred to as a Modified Tango. There are no stern torpedo
tubes.
Operational: Long-range operational capability as shown by
former deployments to the Mediterranean and to West Africa.

All operational submarines are based in the Northern Fleet at
Polyarny. The first two were paid off in 1995, six more in 1996,
four more in 1997 and two in 1999. These are all laid up with
five in the Baltic, one in the Black Sea, and the remainder in the
North. As with the 'Kilo' class, main batteries have been a
constant source of problems.
UPDATED

TANGO with BELUGA and BRAVO   *9/1998, Hartmut Ehlers* / 0050014

2 FOXTROT CLASS (TYPE 641) (SS)

Displacement, tons: 1,952 surfaced; 2,475 dived
Dimensions, feet (metres): 299.5 × 24.6 × 19.7
(91.3 × 7.5 × 6)
Main machinery: Diesel-electric; 3 Type 37-D diesels; 6,000 hp
(m) *(4.4 MW)*; 3 motors (1 × 2,700 and 2 × 1,350); 5,400 hp
(m) *(3.97 MW)*; 3 shafts; 1 auxiliary motor; 140 hp(m)
(103 kW)
Speed, knots: 16 surfaced; 15 dived; 9 snorting
Range, miles: 20,000 at 8 kt surfaced; 380 at 2 kt dived
Complement: 75 (12 officers)

Torpedoes: 10—21 in *(533 mm)* (6 bow, 4 stern) tubes.
Combination of 22—53 cm torpedoes (see table at front of
section).
Mines: 32 in lieu of torpedoes.
Countermeasures: ESM: Stop Light (Nakat M); radar warning.
Weapons control: Leningrad 642 TFCS.
Radars: Surface search: Snoop Tray or Snoop Plate; I-band.
Sonars: Pike Jaw; hull-mounted; passive/active search and
attack; high frequency.

Programmes: Built in 1971 at Sudomekh. Production continued
until 1984 for transfer to other countries. Only 60 out of a total
programme of 160 were completed as the changeover to
nuclear boats took effect. A most successful class which has
been deployed worldwide, forming the bulk of the submarine
force in the Mediterranean in the 1960s and 1970s.
Operational: This last pair are used for basic anti-submarine
training in the Baltic. A Black Sea Fleet unit is non-operational.
At least two others are museum ships.
Sales: Transferred to Poland, Cuba, India, Libya and Ukraine,
since when many have been deleted.   ***UPDATED***

FOXTROT   *8/1997* / 0016631

Auxiliary Submarines (SSA(N))

Notes: (1) The 'Lima' and 'India' classes are all unserviceable and are being scrapped. 'Losos' and 'Beluga' are still flying ensigns in the Baltic and Black Sea Fleets respectively but are awaiting disposal. The three remaining target submarines of the 'Bravo' class are laid up in the Black Sea.
(2) There are a number of Swimmer Delivery Vessels (SDV) in service including Siren (three-man) and Triton, Sever and Elbrus types.

BRAVO laid up   *6/1999* / 0081647

1 YANKEE SSAN (TYPE 09744) and 1 YANKEE STRETCH (TYPE 09780) CLASS (SSAN)

K 403 (SSAN)   **K 411** (Stretch)

Displacement, tons: 9,800 dived (Yankee SSAN); 11,700 dived (Yankee Stretch)
Dimensions, feet (metres): 440.6 (SSAN); 528.2 (Stretch) × 38 × 26.6 *(134.3; 161 × 11.6 × 8.1)*
Main machinery: Nuclear; 2 VM-4 PWR; 180 MW; 2 turbines; 37,400 hp(m) *(27.5 MW)*; 2 shafts
Speed, knots: 26 dived; 20 surfaced
Complement: 120 (20 officers)
Torpedoes: 4—21 in *(533 mm)* bow tubes.
Countermeasures: ESM: Brick Pulp; radar warning.
Radars: Surface search: Snoop Tray; I-band.
Sonars: Shark Gill; hull-mounted; passive/active search and attack.

Comment: As well as the Yankee Notch SSN and inactive Yankee SSGN conversions, two other hulls have been converted for research and development roles. The Yankee SSAN formerly known as the Yankee Pod was launched in 1983 and was used for sonar trials. The prototype Pod towed array was fitted at the stern in 1984 but after refit in 1993-94 the submarine emerged in 1995 without the Pod but with a bulbous bow sonar which is likely to be the prototype for the *Severodvinsk* (Type 885). The other conversion is the Yankee Stretch which completed conversion in June 1990 and has a lengthened central section extending the hull which is used for underwater research. This includes submarine operations using the 'Paltus' class. The Yankee SSAN and the Yankee Stretch are based in the Northern Fleet at Yagri Island and Olenya Guba respectively. Both are very active.   **UPDATED**

YANKEE STRETCH   *1993*

YANKEE STRETCH and PALTUS (artist's impression)   *1997* / 0019014

1 DELTA III STRETCH (TYPE 667 BDR) (SSAN)

K 433 (Stretch)

Dimensions, feet (metres): 666 × 39.4 × 28.5
(203 × 12 × 8.7)
Main machinery: Nuclear: 2 VM-4 PWR; 180 MW; 2 GT 3A-635 turbines; 37,400 hp(m) *(27.5 MW)*; 2 emergency motors; 612 hp(m) *(450 kW)*; 2 shafts
Speed, knots: 24 dived 14 surfaced
Complement: 130 (40 officers)
Torpedoes: 4—21 in *(533 mm)* and 2—400 mm tubes.
Countermeasures: ESM: Brick Pulp/Group; radar warning.
Radars: Surface search: Snoop Tray; I-band.
Sonars: Shark Teeth; hull mounted; active/passive search; low/medium frequency.
Shark Hide; flank array; passive low frequency.
Mouse Roar; hull mounted; active high frequency.

DELTA III (before conversion)   *8/1997*, JMSDF /* 0019003

Comment: Originally launched in 1981, this former SSBN has been converted with an added central section extending the hull by 43 m. Expected to be back in service in 2000 it may augment or replace the Yankee Stretch for underwater research operations; acting as a mother ship for the 'Paltus' class in the Northern Fleet.

NEW ENTRY

2 PALTUS CLASS (TYPE 1851) (SSAN) and 1 X-RAY CLASS (TYPE 678) (SSA)

Displacement, tons: 730 dived
Dimensions, feet (metres): 173.9 × 12.5 × 13.8
(53 × 3.8 × 4.2)
Main machinery: Nuclear; 1 reactor; 10 MW; 1 shaft; ducted thrusters
Speed, knots: 6 dived
Complement: 14

Comment: Details given are for the 'Paltus' class. The first was launched at Sudomekh, St Petersburg in April 1991, a second of class in September 1994 and a third was started but not completed. This is a follow-on to the single 520 ton 'X-Ray' (Type 678) class which was first seen in 1984 and after a long spell out of service was back in operation in 1999. Paltus probably owes much to the USN NR 1. Paltus is associated with the Yankee Stretch SSAN which acts as a mother ship for special operations. The Delta Stretch SSAN may serve the same role. Titanium hulled and very deep diving to 1,000 m *(3,280 ft)*. Paltus based in the Northern Fleet at Olenya Guba, X-Ray at Yagri Island.

UPDATED

PALTUS (artist's impression)   1994

3 UNIFORM (KASHALOT) CLASS (TYPE 1910) (SSAN)

No	Builders	Launched	Commissioned
AS 15	Sudomekh, Leningrad	Nov 1982	July 1983
AS 16	Sudomekh, Leningrad	Apr 1988	Nov 1989
AS 17	Sudomekh, St Petersburg	Dec 1993	Feb 1995

Displacement, tons: 1,340 surfaced; 1,580 dived
Dimensions, feet (metres): 239.5 × 20 × 17.1
(73 × 6.1 × 5.2)
Main machinery: Nuclear; 1 PWR; 15 MW; 2 turbines; 10,000 hp(m) *(7.35 MW)*; 1 shaft; 2 thrusters
Speed, knots: 10 surfaced; 28 dived

Complement: 36
Radars: Navigation: Snoop Slab; I-band.

Comment: Research and development nuclear-powered submarines. All have single hulls and 'wheel' arches either side of the fin which house side thrusters. These are titanium hulled and very deep diving submarines (possibly down to 700 m *(2,300 ft)*), based in the Northern Fleet at Olenya Guba, and are used mainly for ocean bed operations. Plans to build more of the class have been shelved.

UPDATED

UNIFORM   *8/1996 /* 0016660

AIRCRAFT CARRIERS

Note: The modified Kiev (Type 1143.4) *Admiral Gorshkov* has not been fully operational since 1988 and is at Severodvinsk Shipyard. India continues to be reported to be interested. If this sale goes ahead, it would involve a three year refit in which the flight deck would be extended the length of the ship.

1 KUZNETSOV (OREL) CLASS (TYPE 1143.5/6) (CV)

Name	No	Builders	Laid down	Launched	Commissioned
ADMIRAL KUZNETSOV (ex-*Tbilisi*, ex-*Leonid Brezhnev*)	063	Nikolayev South, Ukraine	22 Feb 1983	5 Dec 1985	21 Jan 1991

Displacement, tons: 45,900 standard; 58,500 full load
Dimensions, feet (metres): 999 oa; 918.6 wl × 229.7 oa; 121.4 wl × 34.4 *(304.5; 280 × 70; 37 × 10.5)*
Flight deck, feet (metres): 999 × 229.7 *(304.5 × 70)*
Main machinery: 8 boilers; 4 turbines; 200,000 hp(m) *(147 MW)*; 4 shafts
Speed, knots: 30. **Range, miles:** 3,850 at 29 kt; 8,500 at 18 kt
Complement: 1,960 (200 officers) plus 626 aircrew plus 40 Flag staff

Missiles: SSM: 12 Chelomey SS-N-19 Shipwreck (Granit 4K-80) launchers (flush mounted) **①**; inertial guidance with command update; active radar homing to 20-450 km *(10.8-243 n miles)* at 1.6 Mach; warhead 500 kT nuclear or 750 kg HE.
SAM: 4 Altair SA-N-9 Gauntlet (Klinok) sextuple vertical launchers (192 missiles) **②**; command guidance and active radar homing to 12 km *(6.5 n miles)* at 2 Mach; warhead 15 kg. 24 magazines; 192 missiles; 4 channels of fire.
SAM/Guns: 8 Altair CADS-N-1 (Kortik/Kashtan) **③**; each has a twin 30 mm Gatling combined with 8 SA-N-11 (Grisson) and Hot Flash/Hot Spot fire-control radar/optronic director. Laser beam-riding guidance for missiles to 8 km *(4.4 n miles)*; warhead 9 kg; 9,000 rds/min combined to 2 km (for guns).
Guns: 6—30 mm/65 **④** AK 630; 6 barrels per mounting; 3,000 rds/min combined to 2 km. Probably controlled by Hot Flash/Hot Spot on CADS-N-1.
A/S mortars: 2 RBU 12,000 **⑤**; range 12,000 m; warhead 80 kg. UDAV-1M; torpedo countermeasure.

Countermeasures: Decoys: 10 PK 10 and 4 PK 2 chaff launchers.
ESM/ECM: 8 Foot Ball. 4 Wine Flask (intercept). 4 Flat Track. 10 Ball Shield A and B.
Weapons control: 3 Tin Man optronic trackers. 2 Punch Bowl SATCOM datalink **⑥**. 2 Low Ball SATNAV **⑦**. 2 Bell Crown and 2 Bell Push datalinks.

Radars: Air search: Sky Watch; four Planar phased arrays **⑧**; 3D.
Air/surface search: Top Plate B **⑨**; D/E-band.
Surface search: 2 Strut Pair **⑩**; F-band.
Navigation: 3 Palm Frond; I-band.
Fire control: 4 Cross Sword (for SAM) **⑪**; K-band. 8 Hot Flash; J-band.
Aircraft control: 2 Fly Trap B; G/H-band.
Tacan: Cake Stand **⑫**.
IFF: 4 Watch Guard.
Sonars: Bull Horn and Horse Jaw; hull-mounted; active search and attack; medium/low frequency.

Fixed-wing aircraft: 18 Su-33 Flanker D; 4 Su-25 UTG Frogfoot.
Helicopters: 15 Ka-27 Helix. 2 Ka-31 RLD Helix AEW.

Programmes: This is a logical continuation of the deleted 'Kiev' class. A second of class was between 70 and 80 per cent complete by early 1993 at Nikolayev in the Ukraine. Building was then terminated after an unsuccessful attempt by the Navy to fund completion. The full name of *Kuznetsov* is *Admiral Flota Sovietskogo Sojuza Kuznetsov*.
Structure: The hangar is 183 × 29.4 × 7.5 m and can hold up to 18 Flanker aircraft. There are two starboard side lifts, a ski jump of 14° and an angled deck of 7°. There are four arrester wires. The SSM system is in the centre of the flight deck forward with flush deck covers. The class has some 16.5 m of freeboard. There is no Bass Tilt radar and the ADG guns are controlled by Kashtan fire-control system. The ship suffers from severe water distillation problems.
Operational: AEW, ASW and reconnaissance tasks undertaken by Helix helicopters. The aircraft complement listed is based on the number which might be embarked for normal operations but the Russians claim a top limit of 60. *Kuznetsov* conducted extensive flight operations throughout the second half of both 1993 and 1994, and was at sea again by September 1995 after a seven month refit. Deployed to the Mediterranean for 80 days in early 1996 before returning to the Northern Fleet. Based alongside at Rosta from mid-1996 to mid-1998. Sailed for a VIP demonstration in August 1998 and then continued trials and training in-area. The plan is to deploy again when funds become available in 2000.

ADMIRAL KUZNETSOV   *6/1999* */ 0081648

ADMIRAL KUZNETSOV   *1/1996*

UPDATED

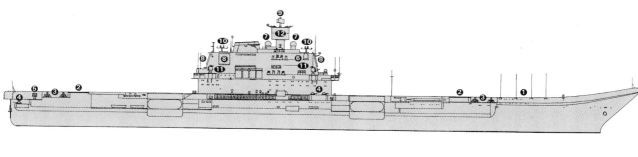

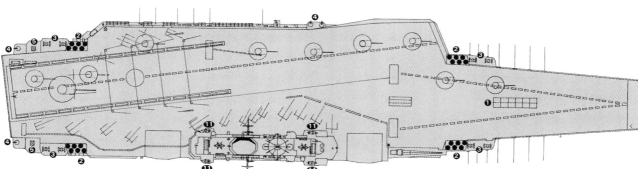

ADMIRAL KUZNETSOV

(Scale 1 : 1,800), Ian Sturton

ADMIRAL KUZNETSOV   2/1996 / 0050015

ADMIRAL KUZNETSOV   2/1996 / 0019019

BATTLE CRUISERS

2 KIROV (ORLAN) CLASS (TYPE 1144.1/1144.2) (CGN)

Name	No	Builders	Laid down	Launched	Commissioned
ADMIRAL NAKHIMOV (ex-*Kalinin*)	080	Baltic Yard 189, Leningrad	6 May 1983	26 Apr 1986	30 Dec 1988
PYOTR VELIKIY (ex-*Yuri Andropov*)	099 (ex-183)	Baltic Yard 189, St Petersburg	25 Apr 1986	25 Apr 1989	18 Apr 1998

Displacement, tons: 19,000 standard; 24,300 full load
Dimensions, feet (metres): 826.8; 754.6 wl × 93.5 × 29.5 *(252; 230 × 28.5 × 9.1)*
Main machinery: CONAS; 2 KN-3 PWR; 300 MW; 2 oil-fired boilers; 2 GT3A-688 turbines; 140,000 hp(m) *(102.9 MW)*; 2 shafts
Speed, knots: 30. **Range, miles:** 14,000 at 30 kt
Complement: 726 (82 officers) plus 18 aircrew

Missiles: SSM: 20 Chelomey SS-N-19 Shipwreck (3M 45) (Granit) (improved SS-N-12 with lower flight profile) **❶**; inertial guidance with command update; active radar homing to 20-450 km *(10.8-243 n miles)* at 1.6 Mach; warhead 350 kT nuclear or 750 kg HE; no reloads.
SAM: 12 SA-N-6 Grumble (Rif) vertical launchers *(Nakhimov)*; 8 rounds per launcher; command guidance; semi-active radar homing to 100 km *(54 n miles)*; warhead 90 kg (or nuclear?); altitude 27,432 m *(90,000 ft)*; 96 missiles.
12 SA-NX-20 vertical launchers *(Velikiy)* **❷**; semi-active radar homing to 90 km *(48.6 n miles)*; warhead 133 kg or nuclear; 128 missiles.
2 SA-N-4 Gecko twin launchers **❸**; semi-active radar homing to 15 km *(8 n miles)* at 2.5 Mach; warhead 50 kg; altitude 9.1-3,048 m *(30-10,000 ft)*; 40 missiles.
2 SA-N-9 Gauntlet (Klinok) octuple vertical launchers **❹**; command guidance; active radar homing to 12 km *(6.5 n miles)* at 2 Mach; warhead 15 kg; altitude 3.4-12,192 m *(10-40,000 ft)*; 128 missiles; 4 channels of fire.
SAM/Guns: 6 CADS-N-1 (Kortik/Kashtan) **❺**; each has a twin 30 mm Gatling combined with 8 SA-N-11 (Grisson) and Hot Flash/Hot Spot fire-control radar/optronic director. Laser beam-riding guidance for missiles to 8 km *(4.4 n miles)*; warhead 9 kg; 9,000 rds/min combined to 2 km (for guns).
A/S: Novator SS-N-15 (Starfish); inertial flight to 45 km *(24.3 n miles)*; payload Type 40 torpedo or nuclear warhead; fired from fixed torpedo tubes behind shutters in the superstructure.

Guns: 2—130 mm/70 (twin) AK 130 **❻**; 35/45 rds/min to 29 km *(16 n miles)*; weight of shell 33.4 kg.
Torpedoes: 10—21 in *(533 mm)* (2 quin) tubes. Combination of 53 cm torpedoes (see table at front of section). Mounted in the hull adjacent the RBU 1000s on both quarters. Fixed tubes behind shutters can fire either SS-N-15 (see *Missiles A/S*) or Type 40 torpedoes.
A/S mortars: 1 RBU 12,000 **❼**; 10 tubes per launcher; range 12,000 m; warhead 80 kg.
2 RBU 1000 6-tubed aft **❽**; range 1,000 m; warhead 55 kg. UDAV-1M; torpedo countermeasures.
Countermeasures: Decoys: 2 twin PK 2 150 mm chaff launchers. Towed torpedo decoy.
ESM/ECM: 8 Foot Ball. 4 Wine Flask (intercept). 8 Bell Bash. 4 Bell Nip. Half Cup (laser intercept).
Weapons control: 4 Tin Man optronic trackers **❾**. 2 Punch Bowl C SATCOM **❿**. 4 Low Ball SATNAV. 2 Bell Crown and 2 Bell Push datalinks.
Radars: Air search: Top Pair (Top Sail + Big Net) **⓫**; 3D; C/D-band; range 366 km *(200 n miles)* for bomber, 183 km *(100 n miles)* for 2 m² target.
Air/surface search: Top Plate **⓬**; 3D; D/E-band.
Navigation: 3 Palm Frond; I-band.
Fire control: Cross Sword **⓭**; K-band (for SA-N-9). 1 *(Velikiy)* or 2 Top Dome for SA-N-6 **⓮**; Tomb Stone *(Velikiy)* E-band (for SA-NX-20) **⓯**. 2 Pop Group, F/H/I-band (for SA-N-4) **⓰**. Kite Screech **⓱**; H/I/K-band (for main guns). 6 Hot Flash for CADS-N-1; I/J-band.
Aircraft control: Flyscreen B; I-band.
IFF: Salt Pot A and B.
Tacan: 2 Round House B **⓲**.
Sonars: Horse Jaw (Polinom); hull-mounted; active search and attack; low/medium frequency.
Horse Tail; VDS; active search; medium frequency. Depth to 150-200 m *(492.1-656.2 ft)* depending on speed.

Helicopters: 3 Ka-27 Helix **⓳**.

Programmes: Design work started in 1968. Type name is *atomny raketny kreyser* meaning nuclear-powered missile cruiser. A fifth of class, to be called *Kuznetsov*, was scrapped before being launched in 1989.
Structure: The first Russian surface warships with nuclear propulsion. In addition to the nuclear plant a unique maritime combination with an auxiliary oil-fuelled system has been installed. This provides a superheat capability, boosting the normal steam output by some 50 per cent. The SS-N-19 tubes are set at an angle of about 45°. CADS-N-1 with a central fire-control radar on six mountings, each of which has two cannon and eight missile launchers. Two are mounted either side of the SS-N-19 forward and four on the after superstructure. Same A/S system as the frigate *Neustrashimy* with fixed torpedo tubes in ports behind shutters in the superstructure for firing SS-N-15 or Type 45 torpedoes. These ships are reported as carrying about 500 SAM of different types. *Velikiy* has a Tomb Stone fire-control radar instead of the forward Top Dome for SA-N-20 which is a maritime variant of SA-10C. There are still some equipment deficiencies particularly in fire-control radars which are fitted for but not with.
Operational: Over-the-horizon targeting for SS-N-19 provided by SATCOM or helicopter. Both are in the Northern Fleet. Pennant number for *Velikiy* changed in July 1998. Two others of the class *Admiral Ushakov* and *Admiral Lazarev* have been inactive in the Northern and Pacific Fleets respectively, for some years and although there are reported attempts to restore them, both are likely to be scrapped.

UPDATED

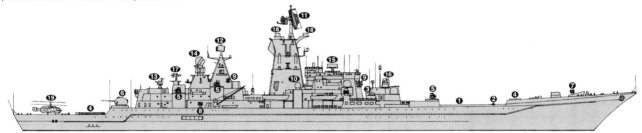

PYOTR VELIKIY

(Scale 1 : 1,500), Ian Sturton / 0019016

ADMIRAL NAKHIMOV

3/1997 / 0019017

PYOTR VELIKIY (old number) *8/1996, H M Steele* / 0016661

PYOTR VELIKIY (with Tomb Stone radar) *11/1996* / 0019018

PYOTR VELIKIY *4/1999* * / 0081649

CRUISERS

3 + 1 SLAVA (ATLANT) CLASS (TYPE 1164) (CG)

Name	No	Builders	Laid down		Launched		Commissioned	
MOSKVA (ex-*Slava*)	121	Nikolayev North (61 Kommuna)	5 Nov	1976	27 July	1979	30 Dec	1982
MARSHAL USTINOV	055	Nikolayev North (61 Kommuna)	5 Oct	1978	25 Feb	1982	15 Sep	1986
VARYAG (ex-*Chervona Ukraina*)	011	Nikolayev North (61 Kommuna)	31 July	1979	28 Aug	1983	25 Dec	1989
ADMIRAL LOBOV (ex-*Ukraina*)	—	Nikolayev North (61 Kommuna)	29 Aug	1984	11 Aug	1990	—	

Displacement, tons: 9,380 standard; 11,490 full load
Dimensions, feet (metres): 611.5 × 68.2 × 27.6
  (186.4 × 20.8 × 8.4)
Main machinery: COGAG; 4 gas-turbines; 88,000 hp(m)
  (64.68 MW); 2 M-70 gas-turbines; 20,000 hp(m) *(14.7 MW)*;
  2 shafts
Speed, knots: 32. **Range, miles:** 2,200 at 30 kt; 7,500 at 15 kt
Complement: 476 (62 officers)

Missiles: SSM: 16 Chelomey SS-N-12 (8 twin) Sandbox (Bazalt)
  launchers ❶; inertial guidance with command update; active
  radar homing to 550 km *(300 n miles)* at 1.7 Mach; warhead
  nuclear 350 kT or HE 1,000 kg. Possible SS-N-27 in *Admiral
  Lobov.*
SAM: 8 SA-N-6 Grumble (Rif) vertical launchers ❷; 8 rounds per
  launcher; command guidance; semi-active radar homing to
  100 km *(54 n miles)*; warhead 90 kg (or nuclear?); altitude
  27,432 m *(90,000 ft)*. 64 missiles.
  2 SA-N-4 Gecko twin launchers ❸; semi-active radar homing to
  15 km *(8 n miles)* at 2.5 Mach; warhead 50 kg; altitude 9.1-
  3,048 m *(30-10,000 ft)*; 40 missiles.
Guns: 2—130 mm/70 (twin) AK 130 ❹; 35/45 rds/min to
  29 km *(16 n miles)*; weight of shell 33.4 kg.
  6—30 mm/65 AK 650; ❺ 6 barrels per mounting; 3,000 rds/
  min to 2 km.
Torpedoes: 10—21 in *(533 mm)* (2 quin) tubes ❻. Combination
  of 53 cm torpedoes (see table at front of section).
A/S mortars: 2 RBU 6000 12-tubed trainable ❼; range 6,000 m;
  warhead 31 kg.
Countermeasures: Decoys: 2 PK 2 or 12 PK 10 *(Lobov)* chaff
  launchers.
ESM/ECM: 8 Side Globe (jammers). 4 Rum Tub (intercept).
Weapons control: 2 Tee Plinth and 3 Tilt Pot optronic directors.
  2 Punch Bowl satellite data receiving/targeting systems. 2 Bell
  Crown and 2 Bell Push datalinks.
Radars: Air search: Top Pair (Top Sail + Big Net) ❽; 3D; C/D-
  band; range 366 km *(200 n miles)* for bomber, 183 km *(100 n
  miles)* for 2 m² target.
Air/surface search: Top Steer or Top Plate ❾ *(Varyag and Admiral
  Lobov)*; 3D; D/E-band.
Navigation: 3 Palm Frond; I-band.
Fire control: Front Door ❿; F-band (for SS-N-12). Top Dome ⓫;
  J-band (for SA-N-6). 2 Pop Group ⓬; F/H/I-band (for SA-N-4).
  3 Bass Tilt ⓭; H/I-band (for Gatlings). Kite Screech ⓮; H/I/K-
  band (for 130 mm).
IFF: Salt Pot A and B. 2 Long Head.
Sonars: Bull Horn and Steer Hide (Platina); hull-mounted; active
  search and attack; low/medium frequency.

MARSHAL USTINOV   *1/1998* / 0050018

Helicopters: 1 Ka-27 Helix ⓯.

Programmes: Built at the same yard as the 'Kara' class. This is a
smaller edition of the dual-purpose surface warfare/ASW
Kirov, designed as a conventionally powered back-up for that
class. The fourth ship, originally being completed for Ukraine,
was transferred back to Russia in July 1995 and renamed
again. It is still intended to complete her possibly again for
Ukraine which is reported to have taken the ship back again in
February 1999. A fifth of class was started but cancelled in
October 1990.
Structure: The notable gap abaft the twin funnels (SA-N-6 area)
is traversed by a large crane which stows between the funnels.
The hangar is recessed below the flight deck with an inclined
ramp. The torpedo tubes are behind shutters in the hull below
the Top Dome radar director aft. Air conditioned citadels for

NBCD. There is a bridge periscope. *Admiral Lobov* has a single
funnel casing.
Operational: The SA-N-6 system effectiveness is diminished by
having only one radar director. Over-the-horizon targeting for
SS-N-12 provided by helicopter or Punch Bowl SATCOM.
Moskva is based in the Black Sea Fleet at Sevastopol and is
likely to become the Black Sea Fleet flagship in 2000 after a
nine-year refit beset by payment problems. Some funds have
been provided by the city of Moscow. *Marshal Ustinov*
deployed to the Northern Fleet in March 1987 and completed
refit at St Petersburg in May 1995 where she remained until
January 1998, when she transferred back to the Northern Fleet
and is based at Severomorsk. *Varyag* transferred to
Petropavlovsk in the Pacific in October 1990.

UPDATED

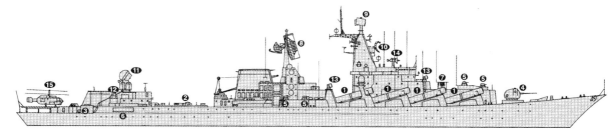

MOSKVA

(Scale 1 : 1,200), Ian Sturton / 0050017

MOSKVA   *8/1999*, Oleg Leus* / 0081650

1 KARA (BERKOT-B) CLASS (TYPE 1134B) (CG)

Name	No	Builders	Laid down	Launched	Commissioned
KERCH	711	Nikolayev North (61 Kommuna)	30 Apr 1971	21 July 1972	26 Dec 1974

Displacement, tons: 7,650 standard; 9,900 full load
Dimensions, feet (metres): 568 × 61 × 22
(173.2 × 18.6 × 6.7)
Main machinery: COGAG; 4 gas turbines; 108,800 hp(m)
(80 MW); 2 gas turbines; 13,600 hp(m) *(10 MW)*; 2 shafts
Speed, knots: 32
Range, miles: 9,000 at 15 kt cruising turbines; 3,000 at 32 kt
Complement: 390 (49 officers)

Missiles: SAM: 2 SA-N-3 Goblet twin launchers ❶; semi-active radar homing to 55 km *(30 n miles)* at 2.5 Mach; warhead 80 kg; altitude 91.4-22,860 m *(300-75,000 ft)*; 72 missiles.
2 SA-N-4 Gecko twin launchers (twin either side of mast) ❷; semi-active radar homing to 15 km *(8 n miles)* at 2.5 Mach; warhead 50 kg; altitude 9.1-3,048 m *(30-10,000 ft)*; 40 missiles.
A/S: 2 Raduga SS-N-14 Silex (Rastrub) quad launchers ❸; command guidance to 55 km *(30 n miles)* at 0.95 Mach; payload nuclear 5 kT or Type 40 torpedo or E53-72 torpedo. SSM version; range 35 km *(19 n miles)*; warhead 500 kg.
Guns: 4—3 in *(76 mm)*/60 (2 twin) ❹; 90 rds/min to 15 km *(8 n miles)*; weight of shell 6.8 kg.
4—30 mm/65 ❺; 6 barrels per mounting; 3,000 rds/min combined to 2 km.
Torpedoes: 10—21 in *(533 mm)* (2 quin) tubes ❻. Combination of 53 cm torpedoes (see table at front of section).
A/S mortars: 2 RBU 6000 12-tubed trainable ❼; range 6,000 m; warhead 31 kg.
2 RBU 1000 6-tubed (aft) ❽; range 1,000 m; warhead 55 kg; torpedo countermeasures.
Countermeasures: Decoys: 2 PK 2 chaff launchers. 1 BAT-1 torpedo decoy.
ESM/ECM: 8 Side Globe (jammers). 2 Bell Slam. 2 Bell Clout. 4 Rum Tub (intercept) (fitted on mainmast).
Weapons control: 4 Tilt Pot optronic directors. Bell Crown, Bike Pump and Hat Box datalinks.
Radars: Air search: Flat Screen ❾; E/F-band.
Air/surface search: Head Net C ❿; 3D; E-band; range 128 km *(70 n miles)*.
Navigation: 2 Don Kay; I-band. Don 2 or Palm Frond; I-band.
Fire control: 2 Head Light B/C ⓫; F/G/H-band (for SA-N-3 and SS-N-14). 2 Pop Group ⓬; F/H/I-band (for SA-N-4). 2 Owl Screech ⓭; G-band (for 76 mm). 2 Bass Tilt ⓮; H/I-band (for 30 mm).
Tacan: Fly Screen A or Fly Spike.
IFF: High Pole A. High Pole B.
Sonars: Bull Nose (Titan 2-MG 332); hull-mounted; active search and attack; low/medium frequency.
Mare Tail; VDS (Vega-M 325) ⓯; active search; medium frequency.

Helicopters: 1 Ka-27 Helix ⓰.

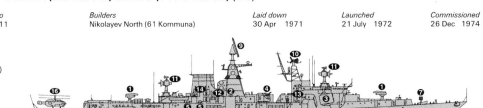

KERCH
(Scale 1 : 1,500), Ian Sturton / 0081651

KERCH
9/1998, T Gander / 0050021

Programmes: Apart from the specialised 'Moskva' class this was the first class of large cruisers to join the Soviet Navy since the 'Sverdlov' class—designed specifically for ASW. Type name is *bolshoy protivolodochny korabl*, meaning large anti-submarine ship.
Modernisation: The Flat Screen air search radar, replaced Top Sail.
Structure: The helicopter is raised to flight deck level by a lift. In addition to the 8 tubes for the SS-N-14 A/S system and the pair of twin launchers for SA-N-3 system with Goblet missiles, 'Kara' class mounts the SA-N-4 system in 2 silos, either side of the mast. The SA-N-3 system has only 2 loading doors per launcher and a larger launching arm.

Operational: Two of the class started refits in July 1987 and have been scrapped by the Ukraine. One more was scrapped in the Pacific in 1996. Two others *Ochakov* and *Petropavlovsk* are laid up in the Black Sea and Pacific respectively and are unlikely to go to sea again although there are unconfirmed reports of *Ochakov* being worked on. *Azov* was cannibalised for spares in 1998. *Kerch* is based in the Black Sea at Sevastopol.

UPDATED

1 KYNDA CLASS (TYPE 58) (CG)

Name	No		Builders	Laid down	Launched	Commissioned
ADMIRAL GOLOVKO	118		Zhdanov, Leningrad	20 Apr 1961	18 July 1962	30 Dec 1964

Displacement, tons: 4,265 standard; 5,412 full load
Dimensions, feet (metres): 468.2 × 52.5 × 13.5
(142.7 × 16 × 4.1)
Main machinery: 4 KWN 95/64 boilers; 2 TW 12 turbines; 90,000 hp(m) *(66.15 MW)*; 2 shafts
Speed, knots: 34. **Range, miles:** 3,610 at 18 kt
Complement: 339 (27 officers)

Missiles: SSM: 8 SS-N-3B Sepal (2 quad) launchers ❶; inertial guidance; active radar homing to 460 km *(250 n miles)* at 1.1 Mach; warhead nuclear 350 kT or HE 900 kg; 8 reloads.

SAM: SA-N-1 Goa twin launcher ❷; command guidance to 31.5 km *(17 n miles)* at 2 Mach; warhead 60 kg; altitude 91.4-22,860 m *(300-75,000 ft)*; 16 missiles. Some SSM capability.
Guns: 4—3 in *(76 mm)*/60 (2 twin) ❸; 90 rds/min to 15 km *(8 n miles)*; weight of shell 6.8 kg.
4—30 mm/65 ❹; 6 barrels per mounting; 3,000 rds/min combined to 2 km.
Torpedoes: 6—21 in *(533 mm)* (2 triple) tubes ❺. Combination of 53 cm torpedoes (see table at front of section).
A/S mortars: 2 RBU 6000 12-tubed trainable ❻; range 6,000 m; warhead 31 kg.

Countermeasures: ESM/ECM: 4 Top Hat. 1 Bell Clout. 1 Bell Tap. 1 Bell Slam.
Weapons control: 2 Tee Plinth; 2 Plinth Net ❼ optronic directors.
Radars: Air search: 2 Head Net A ❽; E-band.
Surface search and Navigation: 2 Don 2; I-band.
Fire control: 2 Scoop Pair ❾; E-band (for SS-N-3B). Peel Group ❿; H/I-band (for SAM). Owl Screech ⓫; G-band (for 76 mm). 2 Bass Tilt ⓬; H/I-band (for 30 mm).
IFF: High Pole B.
Sonars: Herkules-2N (GS 372); hull-mounted; active search and attack; medium frequency.

Helicopters: Platform only.

Programmes: This class was designed for surface warfare and was the first class of missile cruisers built. The role made it the successor of the 'Sverdlov' class. Type name is *raketny kreyser* meaning missile cruiser.
Modernisation: Modernised in the early 1980s, including the four 30 mm Gatling mounts, with two associated Bass Tilt radars and a twin level deckhouse abaft the forward funnel.
Operational: One of the class deleted in 1990, one in 1992, one in 1993. *Admiral Golovko* was laid up in 1995 but somewhat surprisingly was reactivated as the Black Sea Fleet flagship in 1996. Expected to be replaced by *Moskva* (ex-*Slava*) as flagship in due course. Based at Sevastopol. ***UPDATED***

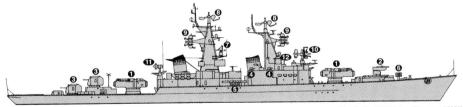

ADMIRAL GOLOVKO
(Scale 1 : 1,200), Ian Sturton / 0081652

ADMIRAL GOLOVKO
*9/1998 *, T Gander /* 0081653

DESTROYERS

1 UDALOY II (FREGAT) CLASS (TYPE 1155.1) (DDG)

Name	No	Builders	Laid down	Launched	Commissioned
ADMIRAL CHABANENKO	650 (ex-437)	Yantar, Kaliningrad 820	15 Sep 1988	12 Dec 1992	13 Sep 1995

Displacement, tons: 7,700 standard; 8,900 full load
Dimensions, feet (metres): 536.4 × 63.3 × 24.6
(163.5 × 19.3 × 7.5)
Main machinery: COGAG; 2 gas turbines; 48,600 hp(m)
(35.72 MW); 2 gas turbines; 24,200 hp(m) *(17.79 MW)*;
2 shafts
Speed, knots: 28. **Range, miles:** 4,000 at 18 kt
Complement: 249 (29 officers)

Missiles: SSM: 8 Raduga SS-N-22 Sunburn (3M-82 Moskit)
(2 quad) ❶; active/passive radar homing to 160 km *(87 n
miles)* at 2.5 Mach (4.5 for attack); warhead nuclear or HE
300 kg; sea-skimmer.
SAM: 8 SA-N-9 Gauntlet (Klinok) vertical launchers ❷; command
guidance; active radar homing to 12 km *(6.5 n miles)* at
2 Mach; warhead 15 kg. 64 missiles; 4 channels of fire.
SAM/Guns: 2 CADS-N-1 (Kashtan) ❸; each with twin 30 mm
Gatling; combined with 8 SA-N-11 (Grisson) and Hot Flash/Hot
Spot fire-control radar/optronic director. Laser beam guidance
for missiles to 8 km *(4.4 n miles)*; warhead 9 kg; 9,000 rds/
min combined to 1.5 km for guns.
A/S: Novator SS-N-15 (Starfish); inertial flight to 45 km *(24.3 n
miles)*; payload Type 40 torpedo or nuclear, fired from torpedo
tubes.
Guns: 2—130 mm/70 (twin) AK 130 ❹; 35-45 rds/min to
29.5 km *(16 n miles)*; weight of shell 33.4 kg.
Torpedoes: 8—21 in *(533 mm)* (2 quad tubes) ❺. Combination of
53 cm torpedoes (see table at front of section). The tubes are
protected by flaps in the superstructure.
A/S mortars: 2 RBU 6000 ❻. 12-tubed trainable; range
6,000 m; warhead 31 kg.
Countermeasures: 8 PK 10 and 2 PK 2 chaff launchers ❼.
ESM/ECM: 2 Wine Glass (intercept). 2 Bell Shroud. 2 Bell Squat.
4 Half Cup laser warner. 2 Shot Dome.
Weapons control: M 145 radar and optronic system. 2 Bell
Crown datalink. Band Stand ❽ datalink for SS-N-22; 2 Light
Bulb, 2 Round House and 1 Bell Nest datalinks.

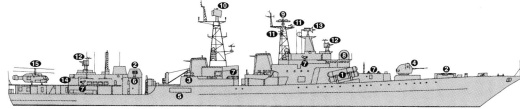

ADMIRAL CHABANENKO

Radars: Air Search: Strut Pair II ❾; F-band.
Top Plate ❿; 3D; D/E-band.
Surface Search: 3 Palm Frond ⓫; I-band.
Fire control: 2 Cross Swords ⓬; K-band (for SA-N-9). Kite
Screech ⓭; H/I/K-band (for 100 mm gun).
CCA: Fly Screen B ⓮.
IFF: Salt Pot B and C.
Sonars: Horse Jaw (Polinom); hull-mounted; active search and
attack; medium/low frequency.
Horse Tail; VDS; active search; medium frequency.

Helicopters: 2 Ka-27 Helix A ⓯.

Programmes: A single ship follow-on class from the Udaloys.
NATO designator Balcom 12. At least two more were
projected with names *Admiral Basisty* and *Admiral Kucherov*;
Basisty was scrapped in March 1994, and *Kucherov* was never
started.
Structure: Similar size to the Udaloy and has the same
propulsion machinery. Improved combination of weapon
systems owing something to both the 'Sovremenny' and the
'Neustrashimy' classes. The distribution of SA-N-9 launchers
may be the same as 'Udaloy' class. The torpedo tubes are
protected by a hinged flap in the superstructure.
Operational: Short trials done in late 1993 but further progress
delayed until sea trials started on 14 September 1995 from
Baltiysk. Deployed to the Northern Fleet in March 1999 when
the pennant number changed. Based at Severomorsk.

3/1999* / 0081654

UPDATED

ADMIRAL CHABANENKO

(Scale 1 : 1,200), Ian Sturton

1 KASHIN (TYPE 61) and 1 MODIFIED KASHIN (TYPE 61M) CLASSES (DDG)

Name	No	Builders	Laid down	Launched	Commissioned
SMETLIVY	810	Nikolayev North	15 July 1966	26 Aug 1967	25 Sep 1969
SDERZHANNY	804	Nikolayev North	20 Oct 1970	29 Feb 1972	30 Dec 1973

Displacement, tons: 4,010 standard; 4,750 full load (Kashin);
4,974 (mod Kashin)
Dimensions, feet (metres): 472.4 (479.7 mod) × 51.8 × 15.4
(144 (146.2) × 15.8 × 4.7)
Main machinery: COGAG; 4 DE 59 gas turbines; 72,000 hp(m)
(52.9 MW); 2 shafts

Speed, knots: 32. **Range, miles:** 4,000 at 18 kt; 1,520 at 32 kt
Complement: 280 (25 officers)

Missiles: SSM: 8 Zvezda SS-N-25 (KH 35 Uran) (2 quad)
(Smetlivy). 4 SS-N-2C Styx *(Sderzhanny)* ❶; missiles are not
fitted.

SAM: 2 SA-N-1 Goa twin launchers ❷; command guidance to
31.5 km *(17 n miles)* at 2 Mach; warhead 72 kg; altitude 91.4-
22,860 m *(300-75,000 ft)*; 32 missiles.
Guns: 2 or 4—3 in *(76 mm)*/60 (1 or 2 twin) ❸; 90 rds/min to
15 km *(8 n miles)*; weight of shell 6.8 kg.
4—30 mm/65 *(Sderzhanny)* ❹; 6 barrels per mounting; 3,000
rds/min combined to 2 km.
Torpedoes: 5—21 in *(533 mm)* (quin) tubes ❺. Combination of
53 cm torpedoes (see table at front of section).
A/S mortars: 2 RBU 6000 12-tubed trainable ❻; range 6,000 m;
warhead 31 kg; 120 rockets.
Countermeasures: Decoys: PK 16 chaff launchers (modified).
2 towed torpedo decoys.
ESM/ECM: 2 Bell Shroud. 2 Bell Squat *(Sderzhanny)*. 2 Watch
Dog *(Smetlivy)*.
Weapons control: 3 Tee Plinth and 4 Tilt Pot optronic directors.
Radars: Air/surface search: Head Net C ❼; 3D; E-band.
Big Net ❽; C-band.
Navigation: 2 Don 2/Don Kay/Palm Frond; I-band.
Fire control: 2 Peel Group ❾; H/I-band (for SA-N-1). 1 or 2 Owl
Screech ❿; G-band (for guns). 2 Bass Tilt *(Sderzhanny)* ⓫;
H/I-band (for 30 mm).
IFF: High Pole B.
Sonars: Bull Nose (MGK 336) or Wolf Paw; hull-mounted; active
search and attack; medium frequency.
Mare Tail; or Vega *(Smetlivy)* VDS; active search; medium
frequency.

Helicopters: Platform only ⓬ *(Sderzhanny)*.

Programmes: The first class of warships in the world to rely
entirely on gas-turbine propulsion. *Sderzhanny*, last of the
class, was the only one to be built to a modified design. Type
name is *bolshoy protivolodochny korabl*, meaning large anti-
submarine ship.
Modernisation: *Smetlivy* has been modernised with a VDS aft,
vice the after gun, and been fitted for SS-N-25 in place of the
RBU 1000 launchers.
Operational: Both based in the Black Sea. *Smetlivy* was in refit
from 1990 to 1996 but was back in service in 1997 replacing
Skory which sank alongside in Sevastopol in November 1997.
Neither ship carries SSMs.
Sales: Additional ships of a modified design built for India. First
transferred September 1980, the second in June 1982, the
third in 1983, the fourth in August 1986 and the fifth and last in
January 1988. *Smely* transferred to Poland 9 January 1988.

SDERZHANNY

(Scale 1 : 1,200), Ian Sturton / 0019048

SDERZHANNY

6/1999*, S Breyer / 0081655

UPDATED

7 UDALOY (FREGAT) CLASS (TYPE 1155) (DDG)

Name	No	Builders	Laid down	Launched	Commissioned
ADMIRAL TRIBUTS	564	Zhdanov Yard, Leningrad 190	19 Apr 1980	26 Mar 1983	30 Dec 1985
MARSHAL SHAPOSHNIKOV	543	Yantar, Kaliningrad 820	8 May 1983	30 Dec 1984	30 Dec 1985
SEVEROMORSK (ex-*Simferopol*, ex-*Marshal Budienny*)	619	Yantar, Kaliningrad 820	12 June 1984	24 Dec 1985	30 Dec 1987
ADMIRAL LEVCHENKO (ex-*Kharbarovsk*)	605	Zhdanov Yard, Leningrad 190	27 Jan 1982	21 Feb 1985	30 Sep 1988
ADMIRAL VINOGRADOV	572	Yantar, Kaliningrad 820	5 Feb 1986	4 June 1987	30 Dec 1988
ADMIRAL KHARLAMOV	678	Yantar, Kaliningrad 820	7 Aug 1986	29 June 1988	30 Dec 1989
ADMIRAL PANTELEYEV	548	Yantar, Kaliningrad 820	28 Apr 1988	7 Feb 1990	19 Dec 1991

Displacement, tons: 6,700 standard; 8,500 full load
Dimensions, feet (metres): 536.4 × 63.3 × 24.6
(163.5 × 19.3 × 7.5)
Flight deck, feet (metres): 65.6 × 59 *(20 × 18)*
Main machinery: COGAG; 2 gas turbines; 55,500 hp(m)
(40.8 MW); 2 gas turbines, 13,600 hp(m) *(10 MW)*; 2 shafts
Speed, knots: 29. **Range, miles:** 2,600 at 30 kt; 7,700 at 18 kt
Complement: 249 (29 officers)

Missiles: SAM: 8 SA-N-9 Gauntlet (Klinok) vertical launchers ❶;
command guidance; active radar homing to 12 km *(6.5 n miles)* at 2 Mach; warhead 15 kg; altitude 3.4-12,192 m *(10-40,000 ft)*; 64 missiles; four channels of fire.
The launchers are set into the ships' structures with 6 ft diameter cover plates—4 on the forecastle, 2 between the torpedo tubes and 2 at the forward end of the after deckhouse between the RBUs.
A/S: 2 Raduga SS-N-14 Silex (Rastrub) quad launchers ❷;
command guidance to 55 km *(30 n miles)* at 0.95 Mach; payload nuclear 5 kT or Type 40 torpedo or Type E53-72 torpedo. SSM version; range 35 km *(19 n miles)*; warhead 500 kg.
Guns: 2—3.9 in *(100 mm)*/59 ❸; 60 rds/min to 15 km *(8.2 n miles)*; weight of shell 16 kg.
4—30 mm/65 AK 630 ❹; 6 barrels per mounting; 3,000 rds/min combined to 2 km.
Torpedoes: 8—21 in *(533 mm)* (2 quad) tubes ❺. Combination of 53 cm torpedoes (see table at front of section).
A/S mortars: 2 RBU 6000 12-tubed trainable ❻; range 6,000 m; warhead 31 kg.
Mines: Rails for 26 mines.
Countermeasures: Decoys: 2 PK-2 and 8 PK-10 chaff launchers. US Masker type noise reduction.
ESM/ECM: 2 Foot Ball B (*Levchenko* onwards); 2 Wine Glass (intercept). 6 Half Cup laser warner (*Levchenko* onwards); 2 Bell Squat (jammers).
Weapons control: MP 145 radar and optronic system. 2 Bell Crown and Round House C datalink.
Radars: Air search: Strut Pair ❼; F-band.
Top Plate ❽; 3D; D/E-band.
Surface search: 3 Palm Frond ❾; I-band.
Fire control: 2 Eye Bowl ❿; F-band (for SS-N-14). 2 Cross Sword ⓫; K-band (for SA-N-9). Kite Screech ⓬; H/I/K-band (for 100 mm guns). 2 Bass Tilt ⓭; H/I/K-band (for 30 mm guns).
IFF: Salt Pot A and B. Box Bar A and B.
Tacan: 2 Round House.
CCA: Fly Screen B (by starboard hangar) ⓮. 2 Fly Spike B.
Sonars: Horse Jaw (Polinom); hull-mounted; active search and attack; low/medium frequency.
Mouse Tail; VDS; active search; medium frequency.

Helicopters: 2 Ka-27 Helix A ⓯.

Programmes: Design approved in October 1972. Successor to 'Kresta II' class but based on 'Krivak' class. Type name is *bolshoy protivolodochny korabl* meaning large anti-submarine ship. Programme stopped at 12 in favour of 'Udaloy II' class (Type 1155.1).
Structure: The two hangars are set side by side with inclined elevating ramps to the flight deck. Has pre-wetting NBCD equipment and replenishment at sea gear. Active stabilisers are fitted. The chaff launchers are on both sides of the foremast and inboard of the torpedo tubes. Cage Flask aerials are

SEVEROMORSK

4/1998 */ 0081656*

ADMIRAL PANTELEYEV

9/1999, Hachiro Nakai / 0081657*

mounted on the mainmast spur and on the mast on top of the hangar. There are indications of a nuclear release mechanism, or interlock, on the lower tubes of the SS-N-14 launchers.
Operational: A general purpose ship with the emphasis on ASW and complementary to 'Sovremenny' class. Good sea-keeping and endurance have been reported. Based as follows: Northern Fleet—*Severomorsk*, *Kharlamov* and *Levchenko*; Pacific Fleet—*Shaposhnikov*, *Panteleyev*, *Vinogradov* and *Tributs*.

Severomorsk deployed to St Petersburg for refit in June 1998 and *Levchenko* followed in November 1999. Both may not be seen again. The fourth of class, *Zakharov*, was scrapped after a fire in March 1992. *Tributs* was in reserve in 1994 and had a machinery space fire in September 1995 but was back in service in mid-1999. *Udaloy*, *Spiridonov*, *Kulakov* and *Vasilevsky* have been laid up or scrapped.

UPDATED

SEVEROMORSK

(Scale 1 : 1,200), Ian Sturton

ADMIRAL LEVCHENKO

10/1999 */ 0081658*

7 SOVREMENNY (SARYCH) CLASS (TYPE 956/956A) (DDG)

Name	No	Builders	Laid down		Launched		Commissioned	
BURNY	778	Zhdanov Yard, Leningrad	4 Nov	1983	30 Dec	1986	30 Sep	1988
BYSTRY	715	Zhdanov Yard, Leningrad	29 Oct	1985	28 Nov	1987	30 Sep	1989
BEZBOYAZNENNY	754	Zhdanov Yard, Leningrad	8 Jan	1987	18 Feb	1989	28 Nov	1990
BEZUDERZHNY	406	Zhdanov Yard, Leningrad	24 Feb	1987	30 Sep	1989	25 June	1991
BESPOKOINY	620	Zhdanov Yard, Leningrad	18 Apr	1987	22 Feb	1992	29 Dec	1993
NASTOYCHIVY (ex-Moskowski Komsomolets)	610	North Yard, St Petersburg	7 Apr	1988	June	1992	27 Mar	1993
BESSTRASHNY	434	North Yard, St Petersburg	16 Apr	1988	30 Dec	1993	17 Apr	1994

Displacement, tons: 6,600 standard; 7,940 full load
Dimensions, feet (metres): 511.8 × 56.8 × 21.3
(156 × 17.3 × 6.5)
Main machinery: 4 KVN boilers; 2 GTZA-674 turbines;
99,500 hp(m) *(73.13 MW)* sustained; 2 shafts; bow thruster
Speed, knots: 32. **Range, miles:** 2,400 at 32 kt; 6,500 at 20 kt;
14,000 at 14 kt
Complement: 296 (25 officers) plus 60 spare

Missiles: SSM: 8 Raduga SS-N-22 Sunburn (3M-80 Zubr) (2
quad) launchers ❶; active/passive radar homing to 110 km
(60 n miles) at 2.5 (4.5 for attack) Mach; warhead nuclear
200 kT or HE 300 kg; sea-skimmer. From *Bespokoiny* onwards
the launchers are longer and fire a modified missile (3M-82
Moskit) with a range of 160 km *(87 n miles)*.
SAM: 2 SA-N-7 Gadfly 3K 90 (Uragan) ❷; command/semi-active
radar and IR homing to 25 km *(13.5 n miles)* at 3 Mach;
warhead 70 kg; altitude 15-14,020 m *(50-46,000 ft)*; 44
missiles. Multiple channels of fire. From *Bespokoiny* onwards
the same launcher is used for the SA-N-17 Grizzly/SA-N-12
Yezh.
Guns: 4—130 mm/70 (2 twin) AK 130 ❸; 35-45 rds/min to
29.5 km *(16 n miles)*; weight of shell 33.4 kg.
4—30 mm/65 AK 630 ❹; 6 barrels per mounting; 3,000 rds/
min combined to 2 km.
Torpedoes: 4—21 in *(533 mm)* (2 twin) tubes ❺. Combination of
53 cm torpedoes (see table at front of section).
A/S mortars: 2 RBU 1000 6-barrelled ❻; range 1,000 m;
warhead 55 kg; 120 rockets carried. Torpedo
countermeasure.
Mines: Mine rails for up to 40.
Countermeasures: Decoys: 8 PK 10 and 2 PK 2 chaff launchers.
ESM/ECM: 4 Foot Ball (some variations including 2 Bell Shroud
and 2 Bell Squat). 6 Half Cup laser warner.
Combat data systems: Sapfir-U.
Weapons control: 1 Squeeze Box optronic director and laser
rangefinder ❼. Band Stand ❽ datalink for SS-N-22. Bell Nest,
2 Light Bulb and 2 Tee Pump datalinks.
Radars: Air search: Top Plate ❾; 3D; D/E-band.
Surface search: 3 Palm Frond ❿; I-band.
Fire control: 6 Front Dome ⓫; F-band (for SA-N-7/17). Kite
Screech ⓬; H/I/K-band (for 130 mm guns). 2 Bass Tilt ⓭;
H/I-band (for 30 mm guns).
IFF: Salt Pot A and B. High Pole A and B. Long Head.
Tacan: 2 Light Bulb.

BESPOKOINY   *7/1998, H M Steele /* 0050025

Sonars: Bull Horn (MGK-335 Platina) and Whale Tongue; hull-
mounted; active search and attack; medium frequency.

Helicopters: 1 Kamov Ka-27 Helix ⓮.

Programmes: Zhdanov was renamed North Yard in 1989. Type
name is *eskadrenny minonosets* meaning destroyer. From
Bespokoiny onwards the class is known as 956A. Total of 17
built for Russia, two (hulls 18 and 19) for China, and one more
(Bulny) which is unlikely to be completed unless for export.
Structure: Telescopic hangar. The fully automatic 130 mm gun
was first seen in 1976. Chaff launchers are fitted on both sides
of the foremast and either side of the after SAM launcher. A

longer range version of SS-N-22 has been introduced in the
Type 956A. This has slightly longer launch tubes. Also the
SAM system has been improved to take the SA-N-17. There are
also some variations in the EW fit.
Operational: A specialist surface warfare ship complementing
the ASW-capable 'Udaloy' class. Based as follows: Northern
Fleet—*Bezuderzhny* and *Besstrashny*. Pacific Fleet—*Burny*,
Bystry and *Bezboyaznenny*. Baltic Fleet—*Nastoychivy* and
Bespokoiny. So far ten others have paid off or are non-
operational.
Sales: Two others which were near completion in 1996, have
been sold to China.

UPDATED

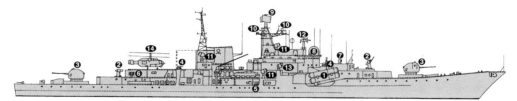

BOYEVOY   *(Scale 1 : 1,200), Ian Sturton /* 0019027

NASTOYCHIVY   *6/1997 * /* 0081659

BESPOKOINY   7/1998, H M Steele / 0050028

BESPOKOINY   7/1998*, H M Steele / 0081660

BESPOKOINY   7/1998* / 0081661

FRIGATES

7 KRIVAK I (BUREVESTNIK) (TYPE 1135), 2 KRIVAK II (TYPE 1135M) and 7 KRIVAK III (NEREY) (TYPE 1135MP) CLASSES
(FFG/FF/FFH)

Name	Type	No	Builders	Launched	Commissioned
STOROZHEVOY	I	663	Yantar, Kaliningrad	21 Mar 1973	30 Dec 1973
DRUZHNY	I	754	Zhdanov, Leningrad	30 May 1975	30 Sep 1975
LEGKY	I Mod	930	Zhdanov, Leningrad	1 Apr 1977	29 Sep 1977
NEUKROTIMY	II	731	Yantar, Kaliningrad	27 June 1977	30 Dec 1977
LETUCHY	I	661	Zhdanov, Leningrad	19 Mar 1978	20 Aug 1978
PYLKY	I Mod	702	Zhdanov, Leningrad	20 Aug 1978	28 Dec 1978
ZADORNY	I	955	Zhdanov, Leningrad	25 May 1979	31 Aug 1979
LADNY	I	801	Kamish-Burun, Kerch	7 May 1980	29 Dec 1980
PYTLIVY	II	808	Yantar, Kaliningrad	16 Apr 1981	30 Nov 1981
MENZHINSKY	III	113	Kamish-Burun, Kerch	1983	Dec 1983
DZERZHINSKY	III	057	Kamish-Burun, Kerch	1984	May 1985
OREL (ex-Imeni XXVII Sezda KPSS)	III	156	Kamish-Burun, Kerch	1986	Nov 1986
PSKOV (ex-Imeni LXX Letiya VCHK-KGB)	III	104	Kamish-Burun, Kerch	1987	Dec 1987
ANADYR (ex-Imeni LXX Letiya Pogranvoysk)	III	060	Kamish-Burun, Kerch	1988	Dec 1988
KEDROV	III	103	Kamish-Burun, Kerch	1989	Dec 1989
VOROVSKY	III	052	Kamish-Burun, Kerch	1990	Dec 1990

Displacement, tons: 3,100 standard; 3,650 full load
Dimensions, feet (metres): 405.2 × 46.9 × 24 (sonar)
(123.5 × 14.3 × 7.3)
Main machinery: COGAG; 2 M8K gas-turbines; 55,500 hp(m)
(40.8 MW); 2 M 62 gas-turbines; 13,600 hp(m) *(10 MW)*;
2 shafts
Speed, knots: 32. **Range, miles:** 4,000 at 14 kt; 1,600 at 30 kt
Complement: 194 (18 officers)

Missiles: SSM: 8 Zvezda SS-N-25 (KH 35 Uran) (2 quad) ❶;
(Krivak I after modernisation); fitted for but not with.
SAM: 2 SA-N-4 Gecko (Zif 122) twin launchers (1 in Krivak III) ❷;
Osa-M semi-active radar homing to 15 km *(8 n miles)* at
2.5 Mach; warhead 50 kg; altitude 9.1-3,048 m *(30-10,000 ft)*;
40 missiles (20 in Krivak III).
A/S: Raduga SS-N-14 Silex quad launcher (not in Krivak III) ❸;
command guidance to 55 km *(30 n miles)* at 0.95 Mach;
payload nuclear 5 kT or Type 40 torpedo or Type E53-72
torpedo. SSM version; range 35 km *(19 n miles)*; warhead
500 kg.
Guns: 4—3 in *(76 mm)*/60 (2 twin) (Krivak I) ❹; 90 rds/min to
15 km *(8 n miles)*; weight of shell 6.8 kg.
2—3.9 in *(100 mm)*/59 (Krivak II) (1 in Krivak III) ❺; 60 rds/min
to 15 km *(8.2 n miles)*; weight of shell 16 kg.
2—30 mm/65 (Krivak III) ❻; 6 barrels per mounting;
3,000 rds/min combined to 2 km.
Torpedoes: 8—21 in *(533 mm)* (2 quad) tubes ❼. Combination of
53 cm torpedoes (see table at front of section).
A/S mortars: 2 RBU 6000 12-tubed trainable ❽; (not in
modernised Krivak I); range 6,000 m; warhead 31 kg. MRG-7
55 mm grenade launcher (Krivak III).
Mines: Capacity for 16.
Countermeasures: Decoys: 4 PK 16 or 10 PK 10 chaff launchers.
Towed torpedo decoy.
ESM/ECM: 2 Bell Shroud. 2 Bell Squat. Half Cup laser warning (in
some).
Radars: Air search: Head Net C ❾; 3D; E-band; or Top Plate
(Krivak I mod and Krivak III) ❿.
Surface search: Don Kay or Palm Frond or Don 2 or Spin Trough
⓫; I-band.
Peel Cone ⓬; I-band (Krivak III).
Fire control: 2 Eye Bowl (not in Krivak III) ⓭; F-band
(for SS-N-14). 2 Pop Group (one in Krivak III) ⓮; F/H/I-band
(for SA-N-4). Owl Screech (Krivak I) ⓯; G-band. Kite Screech
(Krivak II and III) ⓰; H/I/K-band. Bass Tilt (Krivak III) ⓱; H/I-
band. Plank Shave (Harpoon-B) (for SS-N-25) to be fitted.
IFF: High Pole B. Salt Pot (Krivak III).
Sonars: Bull Nose (MGK-335S or MG-332); hull-mounted; active
search and attack; medium frequency.
Mare Tail (MGK-345) or Steer Hide (some Krivak Is after
modernisation); VDS (MG 325) ⓲; active search; medium
frequency.

Helicopters: 1 Ka-27 Helix (Krivak III) ⓳.

Programmes: Type name was originally *bolshoy protivolodochny
korabl*, meaning large anti-submarine ship. Changed in
1977-78 to *storozhevoy korabl* meaning escort ship. The
eighth Krivak III belongs to Ukraine.
Modernisation: Two Krivak Is have been modernised with SS-
N-25 quadruple launchers replacing RBU mountings forward
of the bridge. No ship has yet been reported with missiles
embarked and the associated fire-control radar is still to be
fitted. Top Plate radar has replaced Head Net in some and a
more modern VDS is also fitted. Ships converted with SS-N-25
launchers are *Legky* and *Pylky*. This programme has stopped.

KRIVAK I (mod) *(Scale 1 : 1,200), Ian Sturton*

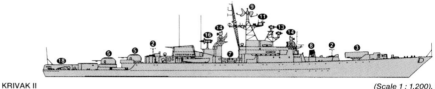

KRIVAK II *(Scale 1 : 1,200), Ian Sturton*

KRIVAK III *(Scale 1 : 1,200), Ian Sturton*

ZADORNY (I) *6/1999* */ 0081664*

Structure: 'Krivak II' class has Y-gun mounted higher and the
break to the quarterdeck further aft apart from other variations
noted. 'Krivak III' class built for the former KGB but now under
Border Guard. The removal of SS-N-14 and one SA-N-4
mounting compensates for the addition of a hangar and flight
deck.

Operational: Krivak Is and IIs are being scrapped. Northern Fleet:
Zadorny, Legky. Black Sea: *Ladny, Pytlivy*. Baltic: *Druznhy,
Pylky, Neukrotimy*. Pacific: *Letuchy, Storozhevoy*. All Krivak IIIs
are in the Pacific.
Sales: An improved version of the Krivak III is being built for India.
Three of the class transferred to Ukraine in July 1997.

UPDATED

DRUZHNY (I) *6/1998, Michael Nitz / 0050035*

VOROVSKY (III)   10/1991

PYLKY (I Mod)   5/1998 / 0050034

NEUKROTIMY (II)   6/1999* / 0081665

0 + 1 GROM (TYPE 1244.1) CLASS (FFG)

Name	No	Builders	Laid down	Launched	Commissioned
NOVIK	—	Yantar, Kaliningrad	26 July 1997	—	—

Displacement, tons: 3,600 full load
Dimensions, feet (metres): 397 × 46.3 × 30.5 (sonar)
(121 × 14.1 × 9.3)
Main machinery: CODAG; 2 M62M gas turbines; 2 diesels;
2 shafts
Speed, knots: 31. **Range, miles:** 4,800 at 12 kt, 2,500 at 20 kt
Complement: 165 (21 officers)

Missiles: SSM: 6 VLS triple launchers ❶ for Oniks.
SAM: 4 octuple Polinet ❷.
A/S: 2 quad Medveka launchers ❸.
Guns: 1—4 in *(100 mm)* A 190 ❹.
2—30 mm AK 630 M1 *(twin)* ❺.
Countermeasures: Decoys: 4 PK 16 chaff launchers.
Radars: Air/surface search: Top Plate (Fregat M) ❻ 3D; D/E-
band.
Surface search: Cross Dome (MR-352) ❼; E/F-band.
Fire control: Bass Tilt (MR-123) ❽; H/I-band.
Navigation: Vaygach; I-band.
Sonars: MGK-335 MS hull-mounted and VDS.

NOVIK

Helicopters: 1 Kamov Ka-27 Helix ❾.

Programmes: Almaz Central Marine Design Bureau. Keel laid
with much publicity in 1997. By early 2000 the ship was only
about 20 per cent complete and was authorised for sale.

(Scale 1 : 1,200), Ian Sturton / 0081663

Structure: Most details are speculative based on a published
export design. The SSM launchers are in two groups of three
either side of the hangar. Stealth features are part of the
specification.

UPDATED

1 NEUSTRASHIMY (JASTREB) CLASS (TYPE 1154) (FFG)

Name	No	Builders	Laid down	Launched	Commissioned
NEUSTRASHIMY	712	Yantar, Kaliningrad	Apr 1986	May 1988	24 Jan 1993

Displacement, tons: 3,450 standard; 4,250 full load
Dimensions, feet (metres): 430.4 oa; 403.5 wl × 50.9 × 15.7
(131.2; 123 × 15.5 × 4.8)
Main machinery: COGAG; 2 gas turbines; 48,600 hp(m)
(35.72 MW); 2 gas turbines; 24,200 hp(m) *(17.79 MW)*;
2 shafts
Speed, knots: 30. **Range, miles:** 4,500 at 16 kt
Complement: 210 (35 officers)

Missiles: SSM: Fitted for but not with 16 SS-N-25 (4 quad).
SS-CX-5 Sapless (possibly a version of SS-N-22 (Moskit M))
may be carried (see *Torpedoes*).
SAM: 4 SA-N-9 Gauntlet (Klinok) sextuple vertical launchers ❶;
command guidance; active radar homing to 12 km *(6.5 n
miles)* at 2 Mach; warhead 15 kg. 32 missiles.
SAM/Guns: 2 CADS-N-1 (Kortik/Kashtan) ❷; each has a twin
30 mm Gatling combined with 8 SA-N-11 (Grisson) and Hot
Flash/Hot Spot fire-control radar/optronic director. Laser
beam guidance for missiles to 8 km *(4.4 n miles)*; warhead
9 kg; 9,000 rds/min (combined) to 1.5 km (for guns).
A/S: SS-N-15/16; inertial flight to 120 km *(65 n miles)*; payload
Type 40 torpedo or nuclear warhead; fired from torpedo tubes.
Guns: 1—3.9 in *(100 mm)*/59 ❸; 60 rds/min to 15 km *(8.2 n
miles)*; weight of shell 16 kg.
Torpedoes: 6—21 in *(533 mm)* tubes combined with A/S
launcher ❹; can fire SS-N-15/16 missiles with Type 40 anti-
submarine torpedoes or 53 cm torpedoes (see table at front of
section).
A/S mortars: 1 RBU 12,000 ❺; 10-tubed trainable; range
12,000 m; warhead 80 kg.
Mines: 2 rails.
Countermeasures: Decoys: 8 PK 10 and 2 PK 16 chaff launchers.
ESM/ECM: Intercept and jammers. 2 Foot Ball; 2 Half Hat; 4 Half
Cup laser intercept.
Weapons control: 2 Bell Crown datalink.
Radars: Air/surface search: Top Plate ❻ 3D; D/E-band.
Navigation: 2 Palm Frond; I-band.
Fire control: Cross Sword ❼ (for SAM); K-band. Kite Screech B ❽
(for SSM and guns); I-band.
IFF: 2 Salt Pot; 4 Box Bar.
Sonars: Ox Yoke and Whale Tongue; hull-mounted; active search
and attack; medium frequency.
Ox Tail; VDS ❾ or towed sonar array.

Helicopters: 1 Ka-27 Helix ❿.

NEUSTRASHIMY

(Scale 1 : 1,200), Ian Sturton

NEUSTRASHIMY

6/1999 * / 0081662*

Programmes: The first of class started sea trials in the Baltic in
December 1990. Second of class was launched in May 1991,
but in October 1998 the shipyard stated the hull would be sold
for scrap to pay outstanding debts. By early 2000, the ship was
still at Kaliningrad but not being worked on. The third was
launched in July 1993 with only the hull completed and work
stopped in December 1997 without any further work being
done.
Structure: Slightly larger than the Krivak and has a helicopter
which is a standard part of the armament of modern Western
frigates. There are three horizontal launchers at main deck
level on each side of the ship, angled at 18° from forward.

These double up for A/S missiles of the SS-N-15/16 type using
a 'plunge-fly-plunge' launch and flight and normal torpedoes.
Similar launchers are behind shutters in the last three of the
'Kirov' class. The helicopter deck extends across the full width
of the ship. The after funnel is unusually flush decked but both
funnels have been slightly extended after initial sea trials.
Attempts have been made to incorporate stealth features.
Main propulsion is the same as the 'Udaloy II' class. Reported
as having a basic computerised combat data system.
Operational: Based in the Baltic at Baltiysk.

UPDATED

NEUSTRASHIMY

9/1997 / 0050033

1 GEPARD (TYPE 11661) CLASS (FFG)

Name	No	Builders	Laid down	Launched	Completed
YASTREB	—	Zelenodolsk, Kazan, Tartarstan	1991	July 1993	Dec 1994

Displacement, tons: 1,930 full load
Dimensions, feet (metres): 334.6 × 44.6 × 14.4
(102 × 13.6 × 4.4)
Main machinery: CODOG; 2 gas turbines; 58,600 hp(m)
(43.07 MW); 1 Type 61 diesel; 8,000 hp(m) *(5.88 MW)*; 2
shafts; cp props
Speed, knots: 26 (18 on diesels). **Range, miles:** 3,500 at 18 kt
Complement: 110 plus 21 spare

Missiles: SSM: 8 Zvezda SS-N-25 (KH 35 Ural) (2 quad) **❶**; IR or
radar homing to 130 km *(70.2 n miles)* at 0.9 Mach; warhead
145 kg; sea-skimmer.
SAM: 1 SA-N-4 Gecko twin launcher **❷**; semi-active radar homing
to 15 km *(8 n miles)* at 2.5 Mach; warhead 50 kg. 20 weapons.
Guns: 1—3 in *(76 mm)/60* **❸**; 120 rds/min to 15 km *(8 n miles)*;
weight of shell 7 kg.
2—30 mm/65 ADG 630 **❹**; 6 barrels per mounting; or
4—30 mm (2 twin) AK 230.
Torpedoes: 4—21 in *(533 mm)* (2 twin) tubes **❺**. Combination of
53 cm torpedoes (see table at front of section).
A/S mortars: 1 RBU 6000 12-tubed trainable **❻**; range 6,000 m;
warhead 31 kg.
Mines: 2 rails. 48 mines.

Countermeasures: Decoys: 4 PK 16 chaff launchers.
ESM/ECM: 2 Bell Shroud. 2 Bell Squat. Intercept and jammers.
Weapons control: 2 Light Bulb datalink. Hood Wink and Odd Box
optronic systems. Band Stand **❽** datalink.
Radars: Air/surface search: Cross Dome **❼**; E/F-band.
Fire control: Bass Tilt **❾**; H/I-band (for guns). Pop Group **❿**; F/H/
I-band (for SAM). Harpun-B (for SSM); I/J-band.
Navigation: Nayada; I-band.
IFF: 2 Square Head. 1 Salt Pot B.
Sonars: Ox Yoke; hull-mounted; active search and attack;
medium frequency.
Ox Tail; VDS **⓫**; active search and attack; medium frequency.

Programmes: Successor to the 'Koni' class. Although long since
completed, the first ship has not found a buyer. Second of class
with a helicopter platform has been scrapped. An improved
follow-on design with better armament is projected. Available
for export possibly to Algeria and not included in the Russian
Fleet strength.
Structure: A logical development of existing light frigate classes
with the addition of SS-N-25. Steel hull with aluminium
superstructure. Stealth features are claimed and the ship has
roll stabilisers and air conditioned spaces.

Operational: Planned to deploy to naval exhibitions in 1995, but
failed to show, and remains at the shipyard.
Sales: It is reported that the original order was for India. Algeria
and Bangladesh have also shown an interest.

UPDATED

YASTREB 1994, Zelenodolsk Shipyard

YASTREB *(Scale 1 : 900), Ian Sturton*

11 PARCHIM II CLASS (TYPE 1331) (FFL)

MPK 67	301	MPK 192	304	MPK 216	258	MPK 224	243
MPK 99	308	MPK 205	321	MPK 219	209	MPK 229	232
MPK 105	245	MPK 213	222	MPK 223	218		

Displacement, tons: 769 standard; 960 full load
Dimensions, feet (metres): 246.7 × 32.2 × 14.4
(75.2 × 9.8 × 4.4)
Main machinery: 3 Type M 504A diesels; 10,812 hp(m)
(7.95 MW) sustained; 3 shafts
Speed, knots: 26. **Range, miles:** 2,500 at 12 kt
Complement: 70 (8 officers)

Missiles: SAM: 2 SA-N-5 Grail quad launchers **❶**; manual aiming;
IR homing to 6 km *(3.2 n miles)* at 1.5 Mach; altitude to
2,500 m *(8,000 ft)*; warhead 1.5 kg.
Guns: 1—3 in *(76 mm)/66* AK 176 **❷**; 120 rds/min to 15 km *(8 n
miles)*; weight of shell 7 kg.
1—30 mm/65 AK 630 **❸**; 6 barrels; 3,000 rds/min combined
to 2 km.
Torpedoes: 4—21 in *(533 mm)* (2 twin) tubes **❹**. Combination of
53 cm torpedoes (see table at front of section).
A/S mortars: 2 RBU 6000 12-tubed trainable **❺**; range 6,000 m;
warhead 31 kg. 96 weapons.
Depth charges: 2 racks.
Mines: Rails fitted.
Countermeasures: Decoys: 2 PK 16 chaff launchers.
ESM: 2 Watch Dog; intercept.
Weapons control: Hood Wink and Odd Box optronic systems.

PARCHIM II *(Scale 1 : 600), Ian Sturton*

Radars: Air/surface search: Cross Dome **❻**; E/F-band.
Navigation: TSR 333 or Nayala or Kivach III; I-band.
Fire control: Bass Tilt **❼**; H/I-band.
IFF: High Pole A.
Sonars: Bull Horn; hull-mounted; active search and attack;
medium frequency.
Lamb Tail; helicopter type VDS; high frequency.

Programmes: Built in the GDR at Peenewerft, Wolgast for the
USSR. First one commissioned 19 December 1986 and the last

on 6 April 1990. MPK 229 is named *Kalmykia* and MPK 205
Kazaniets.
Structure: Similar design to the ex-GDR 'Parchim I' class now
serving with the Indonesian Navy but some armament
differences.
Operational: All operate in the Baltic. All of the class refitted at
Rostock in 1994-95. One more (MPK 228) damaged by fire in
1999 and is unlikely to be repaired.

UPDATED

PARCHIM II 9/1997 / 0050037

1 GRISHA I (TYPE 1124), 2 GRISHA III (TYPE 1124M), 1 GRISHA IV (TYPE 1124K) and 23 GRISHA V (TYPE 1124EM) (ALBATROS) CLASSES (FFL)

Displacement, tons: 950 standard; 1,200 full load
Dimensions, feet (metres): 233.6 × 32.2 × 12.1
(71.2 × 9.8 × 3.7)
Main machinery: CODAG; 1 gas-turbine; 15,000 hp(m) *(11 MW)*;
2 diesels; 16,000 hp(m) *(11.8 MW)*; 3 shafts
Speed, knots: 30. **Range, miles:** 2,500 at 14 kt; 1,750 at 20 kt
diesels; 950 at 27 kt
Complement: 70 (5 officers) (Grisha III); 60 (Grisha I)

Missiles: SAM: SA-N-4 Gecko twin launcher ❶; semi-active radar
homing to 15 km *(8 n miles)* at 2.5 Mach; warhead 50 kg;
altitude 9.1-3,048 m *(30-10,000 ft)*; 20 missiles (see *Structure*
for SA-N-9).
Guns: 2—57 mm/80 (twin) ❷; 120 rds/min to 6 km *(3.3 n miles)*;
weight of shell 2.8 kg.
1—3 in *(76 mm)*/60 (Grisha V) ❸; 120 rds/min to 15 km *(8 n
miles)*; weight of shell 7 kg.
1—30 mm/65 (Grisha III and V classes) ❹; 6 barrels; 3,000
rds/min combined to 2 km.
Torpedoes: 4—21 in *(533 mm)* (2 twin) tubes ❺. Combination of
53 cm torpedoes (see table at front of section).
A/S mortars: 2 RBU 6000 12-tubed trainable ❻; range 6,000 m;
warhead 31 kg. (Only 1 in Grisha Vs.)
Depth charges: 2 racks (12).
Mines: Capacity for 18 in lieu of depth charges.
Countermeasures: Decoys: 4 PK 10 or 2 PK 16 chaff launchers.
ESM: 2 Watch Dog.
Radars: Air/surface search: Strut Curve (Strut Pair in early Grisha
Vs) ❼; F-band; range 110 km *(60 n miles)* for 2 m² target.
Half Plate Bravo (in later Grisha Vs); E/F-band.
Navigation: Don 2; I-band.
Fire control: Pop Group ❽; F/H/I-band (for SA-N-4). Muff Cob
(Grisha I) ❾; G/H-band (for 57 mm). Bass Tilt (Grisha III and V)
❿; H/I-band (for 57/76 mm and 30 mm).
IFF: High Pole A or B. Square Head. Salt Pot.
Sonars: Bull Nose; hull-mounted; active search and attack; high/
medium frequency.
Elk Tail; VDS ⓫; active search; high frequency. Similar to
Hormone helicopter dipping sonar.

Programmes: Grisha I series production 1968-75; Grisha III
1973-85; Grisha V 1982-1996 onwards. All were built at
Kiev, Kharbarovsk and Zelenodolsk. Type name is

GRISHA I
(Scale 1 : 900), Ian Sturton

GRISHA III
(Scale 1 : 900), Ian Sturton

GRISHA V
(Scale 1 : 900), Ian Sturton

maly protivolodochny korabl meaning small anti-submarine
ship.
Structure: 'Grisha III' class has Muff Cob radar removed, Bass Tilt
and 30 mm ADG (fitted aft), and Rad-haz screen removed from
abaft funnel as a result of removal of Muff Cob. Grisha V is
similar to Grisha III with the after twin 57 mm mounting
replaced by a single Tarantul type 76 mm gun. One Grisha III in
the Black Sea was modified as the trials unit for the SA-N-9/
Cross Swords SAM system in the early 1980s and is
sometimes known as Grisha IV.

Operational: The only surviving Grisha I is in the Northern Fleet
with eleven Grisha Vs. The Black Sea has two III, one IV and
four Vs; the remainder are in the Pacific. All Grisha IIs have paid
off.
Sales: Two Grisha III to Lithuania in November 1992. One
Grisha V in 1994 and four Grisha II in 1996 to Ukraine.

UPDATED

GRISHA I
7/1994

GRISHA III
5/1995, van Ginderen Collection

GRISHA IV
6/1998*, S Breyer / 0081666

GRISHA V
4/1997 / 0019032

SHIPBORNE AIRCRAFT

Notes: (1) Kamov Ka-40 and Ka-60 helicopters are being developed.
(2) Haze B helicopters have all been placed in reserve as have all Ka-25 Hormones.

Numbers/Type: 22/1 Sukhoi Su-33 Flanker D/Su-33 Kub.
Operational speed: 1,345 kt *(2,500 km/h)*.
Service ceiling: 59,000 ft *(18,000 m)*.
Range: 2,160 + n miles *(4,000 km)*.
Role/Weapon systems: Fleet air defence fighter. The first two seater Kub delivered in 1999. More
are being built. All based in the Northern Fleet. Most training is done from a simulated flight deck
ashore. Sensors: Track-while-scan pulse Doppler radar, IR scanner. Weapons: One 30 mm
cannon, 10 AAMs (AA-12, AA-11, AA-8).

UPDATED

FLANKER
2/1996

Numbers/Type: 8 Sukhoi Su-25UT Frogfoot UTG.
Operational speed: 526 kt *(975 km/h)*.
Service ceiling: 22,965 ft *(7,000 m)*.
Range: 675 n miles *(1,250 km)*.
Role/Weapon systems: The UTG version is the two seater ground attack aircraft used for deck training in the carrier *Kuznetsov*. About 40 more of these aircraft are Air Force. Sensors: Laser rangefinder, ESM, ECM. Weapons: One 30 mm cannon, AAMs (AA-8), rockets, bombs.
UPDATED

FROGFOOT   *2/1996*

Numbers/Type: 2 Kamov Ka-31 Helix RLD.
Operational speed: 119 kt *(220 km/h)*.
Service ceiling: 11,480 ft *(3,500 m)*.
Range: 162 n miles *(300 km)*.
Role/Weapon systems: AEW conversions with a solid-state radar under the fuselage. Four sold to India. Sensors: Oko E-801 Surveillance radar, datalinks. Weapons: Unarmed.   *UPDATED*

HELIX RLD   *9/1995*

Numbers/Type: 60/15/12 Kamov Ka-27PL/Ka-29/Ka-32 Helix A/B/D.
Operational speed: 135 kt *(250 km/h)*.
Service ceiling: 19,685 ft *(6,000 m)*.
Range: 432 n miles *(800 km)*.
Role/Weapon systems: ASW helicopter; three main versions—'A' for ASW, 'B' for assault and D for SAR; deployed to surface ships and some shore stations. Sensors: Osminog Splash Drop search radar, VGS-3 dipping sonar, sonobuoys, MAD, ESM. Weapons: ASW; three APR-2 torpedoes, nuclear or conventional S3V depth bombs or mines. Assault type: Two UV-57 rocket pods (2 × 32).   *UPDATED*

LAND-BASED MARITIME AIRCRAFT (FRONT LINE)

Notes: (1) The MiG-29 Fulcrum D has been abandoned by the Navy and the Ka-34 Hokum is not in production. Yak-41 Freestyle is not being developed but the prototype is for sale. Fitter C/D, Badgers and Bear D aircraft were out of service by 1995, Blinders and Bear G by 1997, and Mail and Haze A/C by 1999 (except for a few still active in the Black Sea Fleet).
(2) Tu-204P under development for long-range reconnaissance, OTHT and ASW. Possibly in service by 2005.

Numbers/Type: 3 Ilyushin Il-20 Coot A/B.
Operational speed: 364 kt *(675 km/h)*.
Service ceiling: 32,800 ft *(10,000 m)*.
Range: 3,508 n miles *(6,500 km)*.
Role/Weapon systems: Long-range Elint and MR for naval forces' intelligence gathering. Sensors: SLAR, weather radar, cameras, Elint equipment. Weapons: Unarmed.
VERIFIED

Numbers/Type: 25 Ilyushin Il-38 May.
Operational speed: 347 kt *(645 km/h)*.
Service ceiling: 32,800 ft *(10,000 m)*.
Range: 3,887 n miles *(7,200 km)*.
Role/Weapon systems: Long-range MR and ASW. 10 in the North, 15 in the Pacific. An upgrade programme started in 1998 but is making very slow progress. Sensors: Wet Eye search/weather radar, MAD, sonobuoys. Weapons: ASW; internal storage for 6 tons weapons.
UPDATED

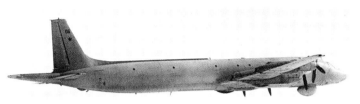

MAY   *6/1999* / 0081667

Numbers/Type: 7 Antonov An-12 Cub ('Cub B/C/D') ('Cub C/D' ECM/ASW).
Operational speed: 419 kt *(777 km/h)*.
Service ceiling: 33,500 ft *(10,200 m)*.
Range: 3,075 n miles *(5,700 km)*.
Role/Weapon systems: Used either for intelligence gathering (B) or electronic warfare (C, D); is versatile with long range. Sensors: Search/weather radar, three EW blisters (B), tail-mounted EW/Elint equipment in addition (C/D). Weapons: Self-defence; two 23 mm cannon (B and D only).
UPDATED

Numbers/Type: 40 Tupolev Tu-22 M Backfire C.
Operational speed: 2.0 Mach.
Service ceiling: 60,000 ft *(18,300 m)*.
Range: 2,500 n miles *(4,630 km)*.
Role/Weapon systems: Medium-range nuclear/conventional strike and reconnaissance. About 20 are operational. Sensors: Down Beat search/Fan Tail attack radars, EW. Weapons: ASV; 12 tons of 'iron' bombs or standoff missiles AS-4 Kitchen (Kh 22N(A)) and AS-6 Kickback (Kh 15P). Self-defence; two 23 mm cannon.
UPDATED

Numbers/Type: 33/12 Tupolev/Tu-142 Bear F/J.
Operational speed: 500 kt *(925 km/h)*.
Service ceiling: 60,000 ft *(18,300 m)*.
Range: 6,775 n miles *(12,550 km)*.
Role/Weapon systems: Multimission long-range aircraft (ASW and communications variants). 36 in the North, remainder Pacific. Sensors: Wet Eye search radar, ESM; search radar, sonobuoys, EW, MAD (F), ELINT systems (J). Weapons: ASW; various torpedoes, depth bombs and/or mines (F). Self-defence; some have two 23 mm or more cannon.
UPDATED

Numbers/Type: 40 Sukhoi Su-24 Fencer D/E.
Operational speed: 1.15 Mach.
Service ceiling: 57,400 ft *(17,500 m)*.
Range: 950 n miles *(1,755 km)*.
Role/Weapon systems: Maritime reconnaissance and strike. Sensors: Radar and EW. Weapons: 30 mm Gatling gun; various ASM missiles and bombs; some have 23 mm cannon.
UPDATED

HELIX   *7/1998, H M Steele* / 0050038

CORVETTES

2 DERGACH (SIVUCH) (TYPE 1239) CLASS (PGGF/PGGA)

Name	No	Builders	Launched	Commissioned
BORA (MRK 27)	615	Zelenodolsk, Kazan	1987	20 May 1997
SAMUM (MRK 17)	575 (ex-890)	Zelenodolsk, Kazan	1992	31 Dec 1995

Displacement, tons: 1,050 full load
Dimensions, feet (metres): 211.6 × 55.8 × 12.5
(64.5 × 17 × 3.8)
Main machinery: CODOG; 2 gas turbines; 55,216 hp(m)
(40.6 MW); 2 diesels; 10,064 hp(m) *(7.4 MW)*; 2 hydroprops;
2 auxiliary diesels; 2 props on retractable pods
Speed, knots: 53 foil; 12 hullborne
Range, miles: 600 at 50 kt; 2,500 at 12 kt
Complement: 67 (8 officers)

Missiles: SSM: 8 SS-N-22 (2 quad) Sunburn (3M-82 Moskit)
launchers ❶; active radar homing to 160 km *(87 n miles)* at
2.5 Mach; warhead nuclear or 200 kT or HE 300 kg; sea-
skimmer.
SAM: SA-N-4 Gecko twin launcher ❷; semi-active radar homing
to 15 km *(8 n miles)* at 2.5 Mach; warhead 50 kg; 20 missiles.
Guns: 1—3 in *(76 mm)*/60 AK 176 ❸; 120 rds/min to 7 km *(3.8 n miles)*; weight of shell 16 kg.
2—30 mm/65 AK 630 ❹; 6 barrels per mounting; 3,000 rds/
min combined to 2 km.
Countermeasures: Decoys: 2 PK 16 and 2 PK 10 chaff launchers.
ESM/ECM: 2 Foot Ball A. 2 Half Hats.
Weapons control: 2 Light Bulb datalink ❺. Band Stand ❻
datalink for SS-N-22; Bell Nest.
Radars: Air/surface search: Cross Dome ❼; E/F-band.
Fire control: Bass Tilt ❽; H/I-band (for guns).
Pop Group ❾; F/H/I-band (for SAM).
Navigation: SRN-207; I-band.
IFF: Square Head. Salt Pot.

Programmes: Almaz design approved 24 December 1980.
Classified as a PGGA (Guided Missile Patrol Air Cushion
Vessels). Both did trials from 1989 (Bora) and 1993 *(Samum)*
before being accepted into service.
Structure: Twin-hulled surface effect design. The auxiliary
diesels are for slow speed operations.
Operational: *Bora* in the Black Sea at Sevastopol, *Samum* in the
Baltic. The design was unreliable but efforts were made in
1996/97 to restore both to an operational state. *Bora* has a
camouflaged hull. *Samum* changed pennant number in 1999.
UPDATED

BORA   *(Scale 1 : 600), Ian Sturton*

BORA   *9/1998 *, T Gander /* 0081668

1 TARANTUL I (TYPE 1241.1), 5 TARANTUL II (TYPE 1241.1M), 23 TARANTUL III (TYPE 1241.1MP), and 1 MOD TARANTUL III (TYPE 1242.1) (MOLNYA) CLASSES (FSG)

Tarantul I:	860							
Tarantul II:	820	832	833	852	962			
Tarantul III:	819	825	855	860	874	921	924	953
	935	937	940	944	946	954	955	870
	964	971	978	991	994	995	952	

Displacement, tons: 385 standard; 455 full load
Dimensions, feet (metres): 184.1 × 37.7 × 8.2 *(56.1 × 11.5 × 2.5)*
Main machinery: COGAG; 2 Nikolayev Type DR 77 gas turbines; 16,016 hp(m) *(11.77 MW)*
sustained; 2 Nikolayev Type DR 76 gas turbines with reversible gearboxes; 4,993 hp(m)
(3.67 MW) sustained; 2 shafts or CODOG with 2 CM 504 diesels; 8,000 hp(m) *(5.88 MW)*,
replacing second pair of gas-turbines in Tarantul IIIs.
Speed, knots: 36. **Range, miles:** 400 at 36 kt; 1,650 at 14 kt
Complement: 34 (5 officers)

Missiles: SSM: 4 Raduga SS-N-2D Styx (2 twin) launchers (Tarantul I and Tarantul II); active radar or
IR homing to 83 km *(45 n miles)* at 0.9 Mach; warhead 513 kg; sea-skimmer.
4 Raduga SS-N-22 Sunburn (3M-82 Moskit) (2 twin) launchers (Tarantul III); active radar homing
to 160 km *(87 n miles)* at 2.5 Mach; warhead nuclear 200 kT or HE 300 kg; sea-skimmer.
Modified version in Type 1242.1.
SAM: SA-N-5 Grail quad launcher; manual aiming; IR homing to 6 km *(3.2 n miles)* at 1.5 Mach;
altitude to 2,500 m *(8,000 ft)*; warhead 1.5 kg.
SAM/Guns: 1 CADS-N-1 (Kashtan) (Tarantul II 962); twin 30 mm Gatling combined with 8 SA-N-11
and Hot Flash/Hot Spot fire control radar/optronic director; laser beam guidance for missiles to
8 km *(4.4 n miles)*; 4,500 rds/min combined to 1.5 km (for guns).
Guns: 1—3 in *(76 mm)*/60; 120 rds/min to 15 km *(8 n miles)*; weight of shell 7 kg.
2—30 mm/65; 6 barrels per mounting; 3,000 rds/min to 2 km (not in CADS-N-1 Tarantul II).
Countermeasures: Decoys: 2 PK 16 or 4 PK 10 (Tarantul III) chaff launchers.
ESM: 2 Foot Ball, 2 Half Hat (in some).

Weapons control: Hood Wink optronic director. Light Bulb datalink. Band Stand; datalink for SSM
(II and III); Bell Nest.
Radars: Air/surface search: Plank Shave or Positiv E (Tarantul 874); I-band.
Navigation: Kivach III; I-band.
Fire control: Bass Tilt; H/I-band.
IFF: Square Head. High Pole B.
Sonars: Foal Tail; VDS; active search; high frequency.

Programmes: The first Tarantul I was completed in 1978 at Petrovsky, Leningrad. A single
experimental Tarantul III with four SS-N-22 was completed at Petrovsky in 1981. Tarantul II were
built at Kolpino, Petrovsky, Leningrad and in the Pacific in 1980-86. Production ceased in 1995
but one more was launched in September 1997 at Rybinsk, and a Tarantul III at Kolpino
completed in December 1999 for the Baltic Fleet. Three more are building probably for export.
Type name is *raketny kater* meaning missile cutter.
Modernisation: Tarantul III 874 served as a trials platform for a modified version of SS-N-22 with a
longer range; the missile is distinguished by end caps on the launcher doors. Tarantul II 962
served as a trials platform for the CADS-N-1 point defence system in the Black Sea.
Structure: Basically same hull as 'Pauk' class, without extension for sonar. The single Type 1242.1
has a Positiv E radar.
Operational: The Tarantul I, four IIs and five IIIs are in the Baltic, one II (962) and three IIIs are in the
Black Sea and the remainder in the Pacific.
Sales: 'Tarantul I' class—one to Poland 28 December 1983, second in April 1984, third in March
1988 and fourth in January 1989. One to GDR in September 1984, second in December 1984,
third in September 1985, fourth in January 1986 and fifth in November 1986 (all deleted or sold
including one which is doing trials with the US Navy). One to India in April 1987, second in
January 1988, third in December 1988, fourth in November 1989 and fifth in January 1990. Two
to Yemen in November 1990 and January 1991. One to Romania in December 1990, two more
in February 1992. One Tarantul II to Bulgaria in March 1990. Two Tarantul Is to Vietnam in 1996.
Four Tarantul IIIs building, possibly for Vietnam.
UPDATED

TARANTUL I (old number)   *7/1992, J Kürsener /* 0081669

TARANTUL II (with Kashtan)   *7/1996, Marcin Schiele*

MOD TARANTUL III   *6/1999 * /* 0081670   TARANTUL III   *6/1998 /* 0050039

3 NANUCHKA I (BURYA) (TYPE 1234), 14 NANUCHKA III (VETER) (TYPE 1234.1) and 1 NANUCHKA IV (NAKAT) (TYPE 1234.2) CLASSES
(FSG)

Nanuchka I:	STORM 577	BRIZ 621	MOLNIYA 535				
Nanuchka III:	METEOR 590	PRILIV 562	PASSAT 570	SMERCH 423	MOROZ 409	INEZ 432	RAZLIV 450
	ZYB 560	LIVEN 551	BURUN 566	GEYZER 555	RASSVET 520	MIRAS 617	SHTYL 620
Nanuchka IV:	NAKAT 526						

Displacement, tons: 660 full load
Dimensions, feet (metres): 194.5 × 38.7 × 8.5
(59.3 × 11.8 × 2.6)
Main machinery: 6 M 504 diesels; 26,112 hp(m) *(19.2 MW)*;
3 shafts
Speed, knots: 33. **Range, miles:** 2,500 at 12 kt; 900 at 31 kt
Complement: 42 (7 officers)

Missiles: SSM: 6 Chelomey SS-N-9 Siren (Malakhit) (2 triple)
launchers ❶; command guidance and IR and active radar
homing to 110 km *(60 n miles)* at 0.9 Mach; warhead nuclear
250 kT or HE 500 kg. Nanuchka IV has 2 sextuple launchers
for trials of SS-NX-26; radar homing to 300 km *(161.9 n miles)*
at Mach 2-3.5.
SAM: SA-N-4 Gecko twin launcher ❷; semi-active radar homing
to 15 km *(8 n miles)* at 2.5 Mach; warhead 50 kg; altitude 9.1-
3,048 m *(30-10,000 ft)*; 20 missiles. Some anti-surface
capability.
Guns: 2—57 mm/80 (twin) (Nanuchka I) ❸; 120 rds/min to 6 km
(3.3 n miles); weight of shell 2.8 kg.
1—3 in *(76 mm)*/60 (Nanuchka III and IV) ❹; 120 rds/min to
7 km *(3.8 n miles)*; weight of shell 7 kg.
1—30 mm/65 (Nanuchka III and IV) ❺; 6 barrels; 3,000 rds/
min combined to 2 km.
Countermeasures: Decoys: 2 PK 16 or 4 PK 10 (Nanuchka III)
chaff launchers ❻.
ESM: Bell Tap (Is) or Foot Ball and Half Hat A and B (IIIs). 4 Half
Cup laser warners (IIIs).
Weapons control: 2 Bell Nest or Light Bulb (later IIIs) (datalinks).
Band Stand ❼ datalink for SS-N-9.
Radars: Air/surface search: Peel Pair ❽; I-band (in early units) or
Plank Shave (later IIIs); I-band.
Fire control: Muff Cob (Nanuchka I) ❾; G/H-band. Bass Tilt
(Nanuchka III) ❿; H/I-band. Pop Group ⓫; F/H/I-band (for
SA-N-4).
Navigation: Nayada; I-band.
IFF: High Pole. Square Head. Spar Stump. Salt Pot A and B.

Programmes: Built from 1969 onwards at Petrovsky, Leningrad
and in the Pacific (Nanuchka III only). Nanuchka III, first seen in
1978. Nanuchka IV completed in 1987 as a trials ship. Type
name is *maly raketny korabl* meaning small missile ship.
Structure: The Nanuchka IV is similar in detail to Nanuchka III
except that she is the trials vehicle for SS-NX-26.
Operational: Intended for deployment in coastal waters although
formerly deployed in the Mediterranean (in groups of two or
three), North Sea and Pacific. Some have been scrapped.
Nanuchka III: three in the North Sea, seven in the Baltic, two in
the Black Sea and two in the Pacific. Nanuchka I: one in the
Black Sea, two in the Baltic, Nanuchka IV is in the Northern
Fleet.
Sales: Three of a modified version of Nanuchka I (Nanuchka II)
with four SS-N-2B missiles supplied to India in 1977-78, three
to Algeria in 1980-82, one to Libya in 1981, a second in
February 1983, a third in February 1984 and a fourth in
September 1985.

UPDATED

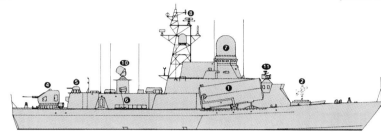

NANUCHKA I   *(Scale 1 : 600), Ian Sturton*

NANUCHKA III   *(Scale 1 : 600), Ian Sturton*

BRIZ   *9/1998, T Gander / 0050040*

PASSAT   *5/1999*, Per Kornefeldt / 0081671*

PATROL FORCES

3 MATKA (VEKHR) CLASS (TYPE 206MP)
(FAST ATTACK CRAFT—MISSILE HYDROFOIL) (PHG)

995	966	822

Displacement, tons: 225 standard; 260 full load
Dimensions, feet (metres): 129.9 × 24.9 (41 over foils) × 6.9 (13.1 over foils)
(39.6 × 7.6 (12.5) × 2.1 (4))
Main machinery: 3 Type M 504 diesels; 10,800 hp(m) *(7.94 MW)* sustained; 3 shafts
Speed, knots: 40. **Range, miles:** 600 at 35 kt foilborne; 1,500 at 14 kt hullborne
Complement: 33

Missiles: SSM: 2 SS-N-2C/D Styx; active radar or IR homing to 83 km *(45 n miles)* at 0.9 Mach; warhead 513 kg; sea-skimmer at end of run.
8 SS-N-25 (in *966*); radar homing to 130 km *(70.2 n miles)* at 0.9 Mach; warhead 145 kg; seaskimmer.
Guns: 1—3 in *(76 mm)*/60; 120 rds/min to 15 km *(8 n miles)*; weight of shell 7 kg.
1—30 mm/65 AK 630; 6 barrels per mounting; 3,000 rds/min to 2 km.
Countermeasures: Decoys: 2 PK 16 chaff launchers.
ESM: Clay Brick; intercept.
Weapons control: Hood Wink optronic directors.
Radars: Air/surface search: Plank Shave; E-band.
Navigation: SRN-207; I-band.
Fire control: Bass Tilt; H/I-band.
IFF: High Pole B or Salt Pot B and Square Head.

Programmes: In early 1978 the first of class was seen. Built at Kolpino Yard, Leningrad. Production stopped in 1983 being superseded by 'Tarantul' class. Type name is *raketny kater* meaning missile cutter.
Structure: Similar hull to the deleted 'Osa' class with similar single hydrofoil system to 'Turya' class. The combination has produced a better sea-boat than the 'Osa' class. *966* in the Black Sea is the trials craft for the SS-N-25.
Operational: *822* is in the Baltic, the other pair in the Black Sea. Four Black Sea Fleet units transferred to Ukraine in 1996.
UPDATED

MATKA 966   *6/1999*, Oleg Leus /* 0081672

2 TURYA (STORM) CLASS (TYPE 206M)
(FAST ATTACK CRAFT—TORPEDO HYDROFOIL) (PTH)

300	373

Displacement, tons: 190 standard; 250 full load
Dimensions, feet (metres): 129.9 × 24.9 (41 over foils) × 5.9 (13.1 over foils)
(39.6 × 7.6 (12.5) × 1.8 (4))
Main machinery: 3 Type M 504 diesels; 10,800 hp(m) *(7.94 MW)* sustained; 3 shafts
Speed, knots: 40 foilborne; 18 hullborne
Range, miles: 600 at 35 kt foilborne; 1,450 at 14 kt hullborne
Complement: 21

Guns: 2—57 mm/80 (twin, aft); 120 rds/min to 6 km *(3.3 n miles)*; weight of shell 2.8 kg.
2—25 mm/80 (twin, fwd); 270 rds/min to 3 km *(1.6 n miles)*; weight of shell 0.34 kg.
1—14.5 mm MG.
Torpedoes: 4—21 in *(533 mm)* tubes. For torpedo details, see table at front of section.
Depth charges: 1 rack.
Countermeasures: ESM: Brick Plug; intercept.
Radars: Surface search: Pot Drum; H/I-band.
Fire control: Muff Cob; G/H-band.
Navigation: SRN 207; I-band.
IFF: High Pole B. Square Head.
Sonars: Foal Tail; VDS; active search and attack; high frequency. Similar to Hormone dipping sonar. This sonar is not fitted in most export versions.

Programmes: The second class of hydrofoil with single foil forward (after 'Matka' class). Has a naval orientation rather than the earlier 'Pchela' class of the Border Guard. Entered service from 1972 to 1978—built at Petrovsky, Kolpino, Leningrad and Vladivostok. Basically Osa hull. Type name is *torpedny kater* meaning torpedo cutter. Production ended in 1987.
Operational: This last pair are in the Caspian Sea.
Sales: Two to Cuba 9 February 1979, two in February 1980, two in February 1981, two in January 1983 and one in November 1983; one to Ethiopia in early 1985 and one in March 1986; one to Kampuchea in mid-1984 and one in early 1985; one to Seychelles in April 1986 (no tubes or sonar); two to Vietnam in mid-1984, one in late 1984 and two in early 1986.
UPDATED

TURYA 300   *7/1996*, B Lemachko /* 0081673

23 PAUK I (MOLNYA) (TYPE 1241P) CLASS
(FAST ATTACK CRAFT—PATROL) (PCF)

Displacement, tons: 440 full load
Dimensions, feet (metres): 189 × 33.5 × 10.8 *(57.6 × 10.2 × 3.3)*
Main machinery: 2 Type M 521 diesels; 16,184 hp(m) *(11.9 MW)* sustained; 2 shafts
Speed, knots: 32. **Range, miles:** 2,400 at 14 kt
Complement: 38

Missiles: SAM: SA-N-5 Grail quad launcher; manual aiming; IR homing to 6 km *(3.2 n miles)* at 1.5 Mach; altitude to 2,500 m *(8,000 ft)*; warhead 1.5 kg; 8 missiles.
Guns: 1—3 in *(76 mm)*/60; 120 rds/min to 15 km *(8 n miles)*; weight of shell 7 kg.
1—30 mm/65 AK 630; 6 barrels; 3,000 rds/min combined to 2 km.
Torpedoes: 4—16 in *(406 mm)* tubes. For torpedo details see table at front of section.
A/S mortars: 2 RBU 1200 5-tubed fixed; range 1,200 m; warhead 34 kg.
Depth charges: 2 racks (12).
Countermeasures: Decoys: 2 PK 16 or 4 PK 10 chaff launchers.
ESM: 3 Brick Plug and 2 Half Hat; radar warning.
Weapons control: Hood Wink optronic director.
Radars: Air/surface search: Peel Cone; E/F-band.
Surface search: Kivach or Pechora or SRN 207; I-band.
Fire control: Bass Tilt; H/I-band.
Sonars: Foal Tail; VDS (mounted on transom); active attack; high frequency.

Programmes: First laid down in 1977 and completed in 1979. In series production at Yaroslavl in the Black Sea and at Vladivostok until 1988 when the 'Svetlyak' class took over. Type name is *maly protivolodochny korabl* meaning small anti-submarine ship. An improved version building at Kharbarovsk in 1995 was not completed.
Structure: An ASW version of the 'Tarantul' class having the same hull form with a 1.8 m extension for dipping sonar. First three of class have a lower bridge than successors. A modified version (Pauk II) with a longer superstructure, two twin 533 mm torpedo tubes and a radome similar to the 'Parchim' class built for export.
Operational: 17 of the craft are operated by the Border Guard. Four naval craft are in the Baltic two more in the Black Sea.
Sales: All Pauk II: First one to India in March 1989, second in January 1990, third in December 1990 and fourth in February 1991. One Pauk I to Bulgaria in September 1989 and a second in December 1990. Two Pauk I to Ukraine in 1996.
UPDATED

PAUK I   *7/1996*, Michael Nitz /* 0081674

PAUK I (Border Guard)   *6/1998 /* 0081675

1 MUKHA (SOKOL) (TYPE 1145) CLASS
(FAST ATTACK CRAFT—PATROL HYDROFOIL) (PHT)

VLADIMIRETS 060

Displacement, tons: 400 full load
Dimensions, feet (metres): 164 × 27.9 (33.5 over foils) × 13.1 (19.4 foils)
(50 × 8.5 (10.2.) × 4 (5.9))
Main machinery: CODOG; 2 Type NK-12M gas turbines; 23,046 hp(m) *(16.95 MW)* sustained; 2 diesels; 2,400 hp(m) *(1.76 MW)*; 2 shafts
Speed, knots: 40; 12 hullborne
Complement: 45

Guns: 1—3 in *(76 mm)*/60; 120 rds/min to 15 km *(8 n miles)*; weight of shell 7 kg.
2—30 mm/65 AK 630; 6 barrels per mounting; 3,000 rds/min combined to 2 km.
Torpedoes: 8—16 in *(406 mm)* (2 quad) tubes. SAET-40; anti-submarine; active/passive homing to 10 km *(5.4 n miles)* at 30 kt; warhead 100 kg.
Countermeasures: Decoys: 2 PK 16 chaff launchers.
ESM: Radar warning.
Radars: Surface search: Peel Cone; E-band.
Navigation: SRN 206; I-band.
Fire control: Bass Tilt; H/I-band.
Sonars: Foal Tail; VDS; active search; high frequency.

Structure: Features include a hydrofoil arrangement with a single fixed foil forward, large gas-turbine exhausts aft, and trainable torpedo mountings.
Operational: Based in the Black Sea and used by the Border Guard. The ship of the class which was used as a trials platform for the Medveka ASW guided weapon, has been paid off. *UPDATED*

VLADIMIRETS   *9/1998, T Gander /* 0050043

6 MURAVEY (ANTARES) (TYPE 133) CLASS
(FAST ATTACK CRAFT—PATROL HYDROFOIL)

DELFIN   RIBA   + 4

Displacement, tons: 180 standard; 230 full load
Dimensions, feet (metres): 126.6 × 24.9 × 6.2; 14.4 (foils) *(38.6 × 7.6 × 1.9; 4.4)*
Main machinery: 2 gas turbines; 8,000 hp(m) *(5.88 MW)*; 2 shafts
Speed, knots: 40. **Range, miles:** 900 at 12 kt
Complement: 30
Guns: 1—3 in *(76 mm)*/60; 120 rds/min to 15 km *(8 n miles)*; weight of shell 7 kg.
    1—30 mm/65 AK 630; 6 barrels; 3,000 rds/min combined to 2 km.
Torpedoes: 2—16 in *(406 mm)* tubes; SAET-40; anti-submarine; active/passive homing to 10 km *(5.4 n miles)* at 30 kt; warhead 100 kg.
Depth charges: 6.
Weapons control: Hood Wink optronic director.
Radars: Surface search: Peel Cone; E-band.
Fire control: Bass Tilt; H/I-band.
IFF: High Pole B. Square Head. Salt Pot.
Sonars: Rat Tail; VDS; active attack; high frequency; dipping sonar.

Comment: Built at Feodosiya. First seen in 1983. Programme terminated in 1988. Assigned to Border Guard, all six in the Black Sea. Three others transferred to Ukraine in 1997.   **UPDATED**

MURAVEY   *6/1997, MoD Bonn /* 0019040

18 SVETLYAK (TYPE 1041Z) CLASS
(FAST ATTACK CRAFT—PATROL) (PCF)

Displacement, tons: 375 full load
Dimensions, feet (metres): 159.1 × 30.2 × 11.5 *(48.5 × 9.2 × 3.5)*
Main machinery: 3 diesels; 14,400 hp(m) *(10.58 MW)*; 3 shafts
Speed, knots: 31. **Range, miles:** 2,200 at 13 kt
Complement: 36 (4 officers)
Missiles: SAM; SA-N-5 Grail quad launcher; manual aiming; IR homing to 6 km *(3.2 n miles)* at 1.5 Mach; warhead 1.5 kg.
Guns: 1—3 in *(76 mm)*/60; 120 rds/min to 15 km *(8 n miles)*; weight of shell 7 kg.
    1 or 2—30 mm/65 AK 630; 6 barrels; 3,000 rds/min combined to 2 km; 12 missiles.
Torpedoes: 2—16 in *(406 mm)* tubes; SAET-40; anti-submarine; active/passive homing to 10 km *(5.4 n miles)* at 30 kt; warhead 100 kg.
Depth charges: 2 racks; 12 charges.
Countermeasures: Decoys; 2 PK 16 chaff launchers.
Weapons control: Hood Wink optronic director.
Radars: Air/surface search: Peel Cone; E-band.
Fire control: Bass Tilt (MP 123); H/I-band.
Navigation: Palm Frond B; I-band.
IFF: High Pole B. Square Head.
Sonars: Rat Tail; VDS; active search; high frequency.

Comment: A class of attack craft for the Border Guard built at Vladivostok, St Petersburg and Yaroslavl. Series production after first of class trials in 1989, but although at least six were of the class were completed, they were not delivered because of lack of funds to pay for them. One has a second AK 630 gun vice the 76 mm and no Bass Tilt radars. Sales to Sri Lanka are possible. One in the Northern Fleet, four in the Baltic, nine in the Pacific, three in the Caspian and one in the Black Sea.   **UPDATED**

SVETLYAK   *8/1999* / 0081676

36 STENKA (TARANTUL) (TYPE 205P) CLASS
(FAST ATTACK CRAFT—PATROL) (PCF)

Displacement, tons: 211 standard; 253 full load
Dimensions, feet (metres): 129.3 × 25.9 × 8.2 *(39.4 × 7.9 × 2.5)*
Main machinery: 3 Type M 517 or M 583 diesels; 14,100 hp(m) *(10.36 MW)*; 3 shafts
Speed, knots: 37. **Range, miles:** 800 at 24 kt; 500 at 35 kt; 2,300 at 14 kt
Complement: 25 (5 officers)
Guns: 4—30 mm/65 (2 twin) AK 230.
Torpedoes: 4—16 in *(406 mm)* tubes.
Depth charges: 2 racks.
Radars: Surface search: Pot Drum or Peel Cone; H/I- or E-band.
Fire control: Drum Tilt; H/I-band.
Navigation: Palm Frond; I-band.
IFF: High Pole. 2 Square Head.
Sonars: Stag Ear or Foal Tail; VDS; high frequency; Hormone type dipping sonar.

Comment: Based on the hull design of the 'Osa' class. Construction started in 1967 and continued at a rate of about five a year at Petrovsky, Leningrad and Vladivostok for the Border Guard. Programme terminated in 1989 at a total of 133 hulls. Type name is *pogranichny storozhevoy korabl* meaning border patrol ship. Most serve in the Baltic. Many are being scrapped. Transfers include: Cuba, two in February 1985 and one in August 1985. Four to Cambodia in October 1985 and November 1987. Five transferred to Azerbaijan control in November 1992 and 10 more to Ukraine. Operational units include 14 in the Baltic, nine in the Pacific, five in the Caspian and eight in the Black Sea.   **UPDATED**

STENKA   *7/1996* / 0081677

20 ZHUK (GRIF) (TYPE 199/1400) CLASS
(COASTAL PATROL CRAFT) (PC)

Displacement, tons: 39 full load
Dimensions, feet (metres): 78.7 × 16.4 × 3.9 *(24 × 5 × 1.2)*
Main machinery: 2 Type M 401B diesels; 2,200 hp(m) *(1.6 MW)* sustained; 2 shafts
Speed, knots: 30. **Range, miles:** 1,100 at 15 kt
Complement: 11 (3 officers)
Guns: 2—14.5 mm (twin, fwd) MGs. 1—12.7 mm (aft) MG.
Radars: Surface search: Spin Trough; I-band.

Comment: Under construction from 1976. Manned by the Border Guard. Export versions (Type 1400) have twin (over/under) 14.5 mm aft. Some have twin guns forward and aft. Ukraine Border Guard and has received 12 from the Russians. 16 are in the Baltic and four in the Black Sea serve with the Russian Border Guard.
Transfers: Algeria (one in 1981), Angola (one in 1977), Benin (four in 1978-80), Bulgaria (five in 1977), Cape Verde (one in 1980), Congo (three in 1982), Cuba (40 in 1971-88), Equatorial Guinea (two in 1974-75), Ethiopia (two in October 1982 and two in June 1990), Guinea (two in July 1987), Iraq (five in 1974-75), Kampuchea (three in 1985-87), Mauritius (two in January 1990), Mozambique (five in 1978-80), Nicaragua (eight in 1982-86), Seychelles (one in 1981, one in October 1982), Somalia (one in 1974), Syria (six in 1981-84), Vietnam (nine in 1978-88 (at least one passed on to Cambodia), five in 1990 and two in 1995), North Yemen (five in 1978-87), South Yemen (two in 1975). Many have been deleted.   **UPDATED**

ZHUK   *7/1996*, J Cislak / 0081678

RIVER PATROL FORCES

Notes: (1) Attached to Black Sea and Pacific Fleets for operations on the Danube, Amur and Usuri Rivers, and to the Caspian Flotilla. Belong to the Maritime Border Guard or Regional Border Districts. Operational numbers are uncertain.
(2) Three obsolete SO 1 patrol craft are still in use in the Caspian Sea.

11 YAZ (SLEPEN) (TYPE 1208) CLASS (PGR)

Displacement, tons: 440 full load
Dimensions, feet (metres): 180.4 × 29.5 × 4.9 *(55 × 9 × 1.5)*
Main machinery: 3 diesels; 11,400 hp(m) *(8.39 MW)*; 3 shafts
Speed, knots: 24. **Range, miles:** 1,000 at 10 kt
Complement: 32 (4 officers)
Guns: 2—115 mm tank guns (TB 62) or 100 mm/56.
    2—30 mm/65 AK 630; 6 barrels per mounting.
    4—12.7 mm MGs (2 twin).
    2—40 mm mortars on after deckhouse.
Mines: Laying capability.
Radars: Surface search: Spin Trough; I-band.
Fire control: Bass Tilt; H/I-band.
IFF: High Pole B. Square Head.

Comment: First entered service in Amur Flotilla 1978. Built at Khabarovsk until 1987. Some have a quad SA-N-5/8 mounting for SAM. All have MAK numbers and are operated by the Border Guard. Twelve of an earlier version deleted in 1994-95.   **VERIFIED**

YAZ   *5/1995, van Ginderen Collection*

7 PIYAVKA (TYPE 1249) CLASS (PGR)

Displacement, tons: 229 full load
Dimensions, feet (metres): 136.5 × 20.7 × 2.9 *(41.6 × 6.3 × 0.9)*
Main machinery: 3 diesels; 3,300 hp(m) *(2.42 MW)*; 2 shafts
Speed, knots: 17
Complement: 30 (4 officers)
Guns: 1—30 mm/65 AK 630; 6 barrels. 2—14.5 mm (twin) MGs.
Radars: Surface search: Spin Trough; I-band.

Comment: Built at Khabarovsk 1979-84. Amur Flotilla. Have PSKR numbers in the 50-57 series and are operated by the Border Guard.

VERIFIED

PIYAVKA   *1992, B Lemachko*

40 SHMEL (TYPE 1204) CLASS (PGR)

Displacement, tons: 77 full load
Dimensions, feet (metres): 90.9 × 14.1 × 3.9 *(27.7 × 4.3 × 1.2)*
Main machinery: 2 Type M 50 diesels; 2,200 hp(m) *(1.6 MW)* sustained; 2 shafts
Speed, knots: 25. **Range, miles:** 600 at 12 kt
Complement: 12 (4 officers)
Guns: 1—3 in *(76 mm)*/48 (tank turret). 1—25 mm/70 (later ships). 2—14.5 mm (twin) MGs (earlier ships). 5—7.62 mm MGs. 1 BP 6 rocket launcher; 18 barrels.
Mines: Can lay 9.
Radars: Surface search: Spin Trough; I-band.

Comment: Completed at Kerch and Khabarovsk 1967-74. Some of the later ships also mount one or two multibarrelled rocket launchers amidships. The 7.62 mm guns fire through embrasures in the superstructure with one mounted on the 76 mm. Can be carried on land transport. Type name is *artillerisky kater* meaning artillery cutter. About 50 have been scrapped so far. Have AK numbers and are based in the Black Sea (Danube Flotilla), in the Caspian and on the Amur River. Transfers: Four to Cambodia (1984-85). Some have been taken over by Belorussian forces, and others allocated to Ukraine.

VERIFIED

SHMEL (with 14.5 mm gun)   *10/1994, van Ginderen Collection*

SHMEL (with 25 mm gun)   *6/1995, van Ginderen Collection*

7 VOSH (MOSKIT) (TYPE 1248) CLASS (PGR)

Displacement, tons: 229 full load
Dimensions, feet (metres): 140.1 × 20.7 × 3.3 *(42 × 6.3 × 1)*
Main machinery: 3 diesels; 3,300 hp(m) *(2.42 MW)*; 3 shafts
Speed, knots: 17
Complement: 34 (3 officers)
Guns: 1—3 in *(76 mm)*/48 (tank turret). 1—30 mm/65 AK 630. 2—12.7 mm (twin) MGs.
Countermeasures: 1 twin barrel decoy launcher.
Radars: Surface search: Spin Trough; I-band.

Comment: Built at Khabarovsk 1980-84. Have BAK numbers and are operated by the Border Guard. Based on Amur River. Same hull as Piyavka.

VERIFIED

VOSH   *1992, B Lemachko*

MINE WARFARE FORCES

Notes: (1) A new MHO *Valentin Pikul* is expected to be completed at Nevsky in due course. This may be a Minehunter version of the 'Natya' class. Little progress in being made.
(2) Some 40 to 50 craft of various dimensions, some with cable reels, some self-propelled and unmanned, some towed and unmanned are reported including the 8 m Kater and Volga unmanned mine clearance craft.

12 NATYA I (AKVAMAREN) (TYPE 266M) CLASS
(MINESWEEPER—OCEAN) (MSO)

PULEMETCHIK 834	TURBINIST 909	VINOGRADOV 914	SEMEN ROSHAL 718
NAVODCHIK 824	ZHUKOV 911	SVYAZIST 610	MACHINIST 855
MOTORIST 806	SNAYPR 913	DESANTNIK 719	ZARYAD 738

Displacement, tons: 804 full load
Dimensions, feet (metres): 200.1 × 33.5 × 9.8 *(61 × 10.2 × 3)*
Main machinery: 2 Type M 504 diesels; 5,000 hp(m) *(3.67 MW)* sustained; 2 shafts; cp props
Speed, knots: 16. **Range, miles:** 3,000 at 12 kt
Complement: 67 (8 officers)

Missiles: SAM: 2 SA-N-5/8 Grail quad launchers (in some); manual aiming; IR homing to 6 km *(3.2 n miles)* at 1.5 Mach; altitude to 2,500 m *(8,000 ft)*; warhead 1.5 kg; 18 missiles.
Guns: 4—30 mm/65 (2 twin) AK 306; 500 rds/min to 5 km *(2.7 n miles)*; weight of shell 0.54 kg or 2—30 mm/65 AK 630; 6 barrels per mounting; 3,000 rds/min combined to 2 km.
4—25 mm/80 (2 twin); 270 rds/min to 3 km *(1.6 n miles)*; weight of shell 0.34 kg.
A/S mortars: 2 RBU 1200 5-tubed fixed; range 1,200 m; warhead 34 kg.
Depth charges: 62.
Mines: 10.
Countermeasures: MCM: 1 or 2 GKT-2 contact sweeps; 1 AT-2 acoustic sweep; 1 TEM-3 magnetic sweep.
Radars: Surface search: Don 2 or Low Trough; I-band.
Fire control: Drum Tilt; H/I-band (not in all).
IFF: 2 Square Head. High Pole B.
Sonars: MG 79/89; hull-mounted; active minehunting; high frequency.

Programmes: First reported in 1970, as successor to the 'Yurka' class. Built at Kolpino and Khabarovsk. Type name is *morskoy tralshchik* meaning seagoing minesweeper. A new type, fitted for minehunting, is expected in due course, possibly based on the modified Natya II which was deleted in 1998.
Structure: Some have hydraulic gantries aft. Have aluminium/steel alloy hulls. Some have Gatling 30 mm guns and a different radar configuration without Drum Tilt.
Operational: Usually operate in home waters but have deployed to the Mediterranean, Indian Ocean and West Africa. Sweep speed is 14 kt. Of the remaining operational units, four are based in the Black Sea (900 series), four in the North (800 series), three in the Pacific (700 series) and one in the Baltic (610).
Sales: India (two in 1978, two in 1979, two in 1980, one in August 1986, two in 1987, three in 1988). Libya (two in 1981, two in February 1983, one in August 1983, one in January 1984, one in January 1985, one in October 1986). Syria (one in 1985). Yemen (one in 1991). Ethiopia (one in 1991). Some have been deleted.

UPDATED

MACHINIST   *6/1999* * / 0081679

2 GORYA (TYPE 12660) CLASS (MINEHUNTERS—OCEAN) (MHO)

Name	No	Builders	Commissioned
A ZHELEZNYAKOV	901	Kolpino Yard, Leningrad	30 Dec 1988
V GUMANENKO	119	Kolpino Yard, Leningrad	9 Jan 1994

Displacement, tons: 1,130 full load
Dimensions, feet (metres): 216.5 oa; 200.1 wl × 36.1 × 10.8 *(66; 61 × 11 × 3.3)*
Main machinery: 2 diesels; 5,000 hp(m) *(3.7 MW)*; 2 shafts
Speed, knots: 15
Complement: 65

Missiles: 2 SA-N-5 Grail quad launchers; IR homing to 6 km *(3.2 n miles)* at 1.5 Mach.
Guns: 1—3 in *(76 mm)*/60 AK 176; 120 rds/min to 15 km *(8 n miles)*; weight of shell 7 kg.
  1—30 mm/65 AK 630; 6 barrels; 3,000 rds/min to 2 km.
Countermeasures: Decoys: 2 PK 16 chaff launchers.
ESM: Cross Loop; Long Fold.
Radars: Surface search: Palm Frond; I-band.
Navigation: Nayada; I-band.
Fire control: Bass Tilt; H/I-band.
IFF: Salt Pot C. 2 Square Head.
Sonars: Hull-mounted; active search; high frequency.

Programmes: A third of class was started but has been scrapped.
Structure: Appears to carry mechanical, magnetic and acoustic sweep gear and may have accurate positional fixing equipment. A remote-controlled submersible is housed behind the sliding doors in the superstructure below the ADG gun mounting. Two 406 mm torpedo tubes are reported as used for mine countermeasures.
Operational: 901 is based in the Black Sea, 119 in the Baltic. Neither are reported as active.

UPDATED

A ZHELEZNYAKOV   *6/1996, B Lemachko /* 0019042

27 SONYA (YAKHONT) (TYPE 12650/1265M) CLASS
(MINESWEEPERS—HUNTERS/COASTAL) (MSC)

Displacement, tons: 450 full load
Dimensions, feet (metres): 157.4 × 28.9 × 6.6 *(48 × 8.8 × 2)*
Main machinery: 2 Kolomna Type 9-D-8 diesels; 2,000 hp(m) *(1.47 MW)* sustained; 2 shafts
Speed, knots: 15. **Range, miles:** 3,000 at 10 kt
Complement: 43 (5 officers)
Missiles: SAM: 2 quad SA-N-5 launchers (in some).
Guns: 2—30 mm/65 AK 630 or 2—30 mm/65 (twin) and 2—25 mm/80 (twin).
Mines: 8.
Radars: Surface search: Don 2 or Kivach or Nayada; I-band.
IFF: 2 Square Head. High Pole B.
Sonars: MG 69/79; hull-mounted; active minehunting; high frequency.

Comment: Wooden hull with GRP sheath. Built at about two a year in St Petersburg and at Ulis, Vladivostok (Pacific). First reported 1973 and the last one commissioned in January 1995. Type name is *bazovy tralshchik* meaning base minesweeper. Some have two twin 30 mm Gatling guns, others one 30 mm/65 (twin) plus one 25 mm (twin). Early models are being scrapped. Operational hulls include five based in the Pacific, eight in the North, eight in the Baltic, four in the Black Sea and two in the Caspian. In addition there are a further 40 in reserve, many of them in the Pacific.
Transfers: Bulgaria, four in 1981-85. Cuba, four in 1980-85. Syria, one in 1986. Vietnam, one in February 1987, one in February 1988, one in July 1989 and one in February 1990. Ethiopia, one in February 1991. Ukraine, two in 1996.

UPDATED

SONYA   *8/1997* / 0016632

3 TOLYA (TYPE 696) CLASS (MINESWEEPER—COASTAL) (MSI)

Displacement, tons: 95 full load
Dimensions, feet (metres): 78.7 × 17.7 × 7.2 *(24 × 5.4 × 2.2)*
Main machinery: 2 diesels; 500 hp(m) *(367 kW)*; 2 shafts
Speed, knots: 12. **Range, miles:** 300 at 10 kt
Complement: 15
Guns: 2—12.7 mm MGs.
Mines: 20.
Radars: Navigation: Spin Trough; I-band.

Comment: First reported in 1990. The first ship commissioned in January 1992 and the second pair in early 1993. All are based in the Baltic and little has been seen of them since 1994, so the design may not have been successful. The ships may also be capable of drone control.

UPDATED

TOLYA   *7/1996*, Hartmut Ehlers /* 0081680

12 YEVGENYA (KOROND) (TYPE 1258) CLASS
(MINEHUNTERS—COASTAL) (MHC)

Displacement, tons: 77 standard; 90 full load
Dimensions, feet (metres): 80.7 × 18 × 4.9 *(24.6 × 5.5 × 1.5)*
Main machinery: 2 Type 3-D-12 diesels; 600 hp(m) *(440 kW)* sustained; 2 shafts
Speed, knots: 11. **Range, miles:** 300 at 10 kt
Complement: 10 (1 officer)
Guns: 2—14.5 mm (twin) MGs or 2—25 mm/80 (twin) (in some later ships).
Mines: 8 racks.
Radars: Surface search: Spin Trough or Mius; I-band.
IFF: Salt Pot.
Sonars: A small MG-7 sonar is lifted over stern on crane; a TV system may also be used.

Comment: GRP hulls. Production started in 1967 and completed in 1988 at Kolpino. Type name is *reydny tralshchik* meaning roadstead minesweeper. Some are painted a blue/grey colour. Three based in each of the four Fleets. Two belong to Azerbaijan in the Caspian Sea.
Transfers: Two to Angola (September 1987), three to Bulgaria (1976-77), 10 to Cuba (1977-82), six to India (1983-84), three to Iraq (1975), three to Mozambique (1985-86), eight to Nicaragua (1984-88), five to Syria (1978-86), three to North Yemen (May 1982-November 1987), three to Vietnam (December 1986-November 1987), three to South Yemen in March 1990, one to Ukraine in 1996. Some of these have been deleted.

VERIFIED

YEVGENYA   *1991*

14 LIDA (SAPFIR) (TYPE 1259.2) CLASS
(MINEHUNTERS—COASTAL) (MHC)

Displacement, tons: 135 full load
Dimensions, feet (metres): 103.3 × 21.3 × 5.2 *(31.5 × 6.5 × 1.6)*
Main machinery: 3 D12MM diesels; 900 hp(m) *(690 kW)*; 3 shafts
Speed, knots: 12. **Range, miles:** 650 at 10 kt
Complement: 14 (1 officer)
Guns: 1—30 mm/65 AK 630; 6 barrels; 3,000 rds/min to 2 km.
Countermeasures: MCM: AT-6 acoustic, SEMT-1 magnetic and GKT-3M wire sweeps.
Radars: Surface search: Pechora; MR241; I-band.
Sonars: Kabarga I; minehunting; high frequency.

Comment: A follow-on to the 'Yevgenya' class started construction in 1989 at Kolpino Yard, St Petersburg. Similar in appearance to Yevgenya. Building rate was about three a year to 1992 and then slowed to one a year until 1995. Some are painted a blue/grey colour. Eleven are based in the Baltic and three in the Black Sea.

UPDATED

LIDA   *6/1995* / 0081682

2 OLYA (MALAKHIT) (TYPE 1259) CLASS
(MINESWEEPERS—INSHORE) (MSB)

Displacement, tons: 64 full load
Dimensions, feet (metres): 84.6 × 14.9 × 3.3 *(25.8 × 4.5 × 1)*
Main machinery: 2 Type 3D 6S11/235 diesels; 471 hp(m) *(364 kW)*; 2 shafts
Speed, knots: 12. **Range, miles:** 500 at 10 kt
Complement: 15
Guns: 2—25 mm/80 (twin).
Radars: Surface search: Don 2; I-band.
IFF: Salt Pot.

Comment: Built 1973-75. Type name is *reydny tralshchik* meaning roadstead minesweeper. Being
   deleted. These last two are based in the Baltic at Baltiysk.   ***UPDATED***

OLYA   *8/1991, MoD Bonn* / 0081681

6 TANYA (PRORYVATEL) (TYPE 1300) CLASS
(MINESWEEPERS—DRONES) (MSD)

Displacement, tons: 73 full load
Dimensions, feet (metres): 87 × 13 × 5 *(26.5 × 4 × 1.5)*
Main machinery: 1 diesel; 270 hp(m) *(200 kW)*; 1 shaft
Speed, knots: 10
Complement: 6
Radars: Surface search: Spin Trough; I-band.

Comment: Built at Kolpino Yard. First operational in 1987, second and third in 1989-90. Probably
   designed to replace the deleted 'Ilyusha' class as radio-controlled drones but the programme
   stopped at six hulls. Based in the Baltic at Baltiysk, and probably non-operational.
                                                                        VERIFIED

TANYA   *6/1996, MoD Bonn* / 0050045

AMPHIBIOUS FORCES

1 IVAN ROGOV (YEDNOROG) (TYPE 1174) CLASS (LPD)

Name	*No*	*Builders*	*Launched*	*Commissioned*
MITROFAN MOSKALENKO	020	Yantar, Kaliningrad	July 1989	Mar 1991

Displacement, tons: 8,260 standard; 14,060 full load
Dimensions, feet (metres): 516.7 × 80.2 × 21.2 (27.8 flooded)
   (157.5 × 24.5 × 6.5 (8.5))
Main machinery: 2 M8K gas-turbines; 39,998 hp(m) *(29.4 MW)*;
   2 shafts
Speed, knots: 19. **Range, miles:** 7,500 at 14 kt
Complement: 239 (37 officers)
Military lift: 522 troops (battalion); 20 tanks or equivalent weight
   of APCs and trucks; 3 'Lebed' class ACVs or 6 'Ondatra' class
   LCM in docking bay

Missiles: SAM: SA-N-4 Gecko twin launcher ❶; semi-active radar
   homing to 15 km *(8 n miles)* at 2.5 Mach; warhead 50 kg;
   altitude 9.1-3,048 m *(30-10,000 ft)*; 20 missiles.
   2 SA-N-5 Grail quad launchers; manual aiming; IR homing to
   6 km *(3.2 n miles)* at 1.5 Mach; warhead 1.5 kg.
Guns: 2—3 in *(76 mm)*/60 (twin) ❷; 60 rds/min to 15 km *(8 n
   miles)*; weight of shell 6.8 kg.
   1—122 mm BM-22 (naval); 2—20-barrelled rocket launcher;
   range 20 km *(10.8 n miles)*.
   4—30 mm/65 AK 630 ❸; 6 barrels per mounting; 3,000 rds/
   min combined to 2 km.
Countermeasures: Decoys: 16 PK 10 and 4 PK 16 chaff
   launchers.
ESM: 3 Bell Shroud; intercept.
ECM: 2 Bell Squat; jammers.
Weapons control: 2 Squeeze Box optronic directors ❹.
Radars: Air/surface search: Top Plate A ❺; 3D; E-band.
Navigation: 2 Don Kay or 2 Palm Frond; I-band.
Fire control: Owl Screech ❻; G-band (for 76 mm). 2 Bass Tilt ❼;
   H/I-band (for 30 mm). Pop Group ❽; F/H/I-band (for SA-N-4).
CCA: Fly Screen ❾ and Fly Spike; I-band.
IFF: Salt Pot B.
Tacan: 2 Round House ❿.
Sonars: Mouse Tail VDS; active search; high frequency.

Helicopters: 4 Ka-29 Helix B ⓫.

Programmes: This was the third of class. Fourth of class was not
   completed. Type name is *bolshoy desantny korabl* meaning
   large landing ship.
Structure: Has bow ramp with beaching capability leading from
   a tank deck 200 ft long and 45 ft wide. Cargo capacity 2,500
   tons Stern doors open into a docking bay 250 ft long and 45 ft

MITROFAN MOSKALENKO   *10/1996* * / 0019045

wide. A helicopter spot forward has a flying-control station and
the after helicopter deck and hangar is similarly fitted.
Helicopters can enter the hangar from both front and rear.
Positions arranged on main superstructure for replenishment
of both fuel and solids. Has been reported streaming a VDS
from the stern door and has also conducted unidentified
missile trials.

Operational: Based in the Northern Fleet at Severomorsk. Two
   Pacific Fleet units were paid off in 1996 and 1997. Reported
   that one of these is being overhauled in Vladivostok for
   possible foreign sale to Indonesia.
                                                    UPDATED

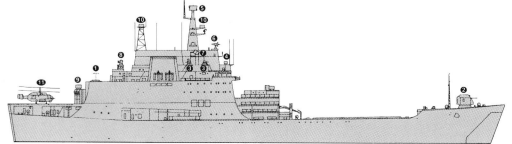

MITROFAN MOSKALENKO   *(Scale 1 : 1,200), Ian Sturton*

15 ROPUCHA I (TYPE 775) and 3 ROPUCHA II (TYPE 775M) CLASSES (LST)

North:	012	016	023	027	031	035	039	Black:	151 (II)	156	158	
Baltic:	110	125	127	130 (II)				Pacific:	055	066	070	077 (II)

Displacement, tons: 4,400 full load
Dimensions, feet (metres): 369.1 × 49.2 × 12.1
(112.5 × 15 × 3.7)
Main machinery: 2 Zgoda-Sulzer 16ZVB40/48 diesels;
19,230 hp(m) *(14.14 MW)* sustained; 2 shafts
Speed, knots: 17.5. **Range, miles:** 3,500 at 16 kt; 6,000 at 12 kt
Complement: 95 (7 officers)
Military lift: 10 MBT plus 190 troops or 24 AFVs plus 170 troops
or mines

Missiles: SAM: 4 SA-N-5 Grail quad launchers (in at least two
ships); manual aiming; IR homing to 6 km *(3.2 n miles)* at
1.5 Mach; altitude to 2,500 m *(8,000 ft)*; warhead 1.5 kg; 32
missiles.
Guns: 4—57 mm/80 (2 twin) ❶ (Ropucha I); 120 rds/min to
6 km *(3.3 n miles)*; weight of shell 2.8 kg.
1—76 mm/60 (Ropucha II) ❷; 60 rds/min to 15 km *(8 n miles)*;
weight of shell 6.8 kg.
2—30 mm/65 AK 630 (Ropucha II).
2—122 mm BM-21 (naval) (in some). 2—20-barrelled rocket
launchers; range 9 km *(5 n miles)*.
Mines: 92 contact type.
Weapons control: 2 Squeeze Box optronic directors ❸. Hood
Wink and Odd Box.
Radars: Air/surface search: Strut Curve ❹ (Ropucha I) or Cross
Dome (Ropucha II); F-band.
Navigation: Don 2 or Nayada; I-band.
Fire control: Muff Cob ❺ (Ropucha I); G/H-band.
Bass Tilt (Ropucha II); H/I-band.
IFF: 2 High Pole A or Salt Pot A.
Sonars: Mouse Tail VDS can be carried.

Programmes: Ropucha Is completed at Northern Shipyard,
Gdansk, Poland in two spells from 1974-78 (12 ships) and
1980-88. Ropucha IIs started building in 1987 with the first
one commissioning in May 1990. The third and last of the class
completed in January 1992. Type name is *bolshoy desantny
korabl* meaning large landing ship.
Structure: A ro-ro design with a tank deck running the whole
length of the ship. All have very minor differences in
appearance. These ships have a higher troop-to-vehicle ratio
than the 'Alligator' class. At least five of the class have rocket
launchers at the after end of the forecastle. The second type
have a 76 mm gun forward in place of one twin 57 mm and an
ADG aft instead of the second. Radar and EW suites are also
different. The after mast has been replaced by a solid extension
to the superstructure.
Operational: All have BDK numbers. Six more have been deleted
so far.
Sales: One to South Yemen in 1979, returned to Russia in late
1991 for refit and was back in Aden in 1993. One to Ukraine in
1996.

UPDATED

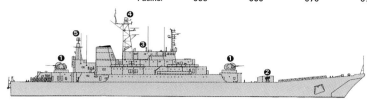

ROPUCHA I

(Scale 1 : 1,200), Ian Sturton

ROPUCHA I

7/1999*, G Toremans / 0081683

ROPUCHA II

6/1999* / 0081684

5 ALLIGATOR (TAPIR) (TYPE 1171) CLASS (LST)

VORONEZHSKY 150	ILYA AZAROV 148	DONETSKY SHAKHTER 119	NIKOLAY FILCHENKOV 152	NIKOLAY VILKOV 081 (IV)

Displacement, tons: 3,400 standard; 4,700 full load
Dimensions, feet (metres): 370.7 × 50.8 × 14.7
(113 × 15.5 × 4.5)
Main machinery: 2 diesels; 9,000 hp(m) *(6.6 MW)*; 2 shafts
Speed, knots: 18. **Range, miles:** 10,000 at 15 kt
Complement: 100
Military lift: 300 troops; 1,750 tons including about 20 tanks and
various trucks; 40 AFVs

Missiles: SAM: 2 or 3 SA-N-5 Grail twin launchers; manual
aiming; IR homing to 6 km *(3.2 n miles)* at 1.5 Mach; altitude to
2,500 m *(8,000 ft)*; warhead 1.5 kg; 16 missiles.
Guns: 2—57 mm/70 (twin); 120 rds/min to 8 km *(4.4 n miles)*;
weight of shell 2.8 kg.
4—25 mm/80 (2 twin) (Type 4); 270 rds/min to 3 km *(1.6 n
miles)*; weight of shell 0.34 kg.
1—122 mm BM-21; 2—20-barrelled rocket launchers (in Types
3 and 4); range 9 km *(5 n miles)*.
Weapons control: 1 Squeeze Box optronic director (Types 3 and
4).
Radars: Surface search: 2 Don 2; I-band.

Programmes: First ship commissioned in 1966 at Kaliningrad.
Last of class completed in 1976. Type name is *bolshoy
desantny korabl* meaning large landing ship. One more Type 3
in service with Ukraine.

NIKOLAY VILKOV

6/1995* / 0081685

Structure: These ships have ramps on the bow and stern. In Type
3 the bridge structure has been raised and a forward deck
house has been added to accommodate shore bombardment
rocket launchers. Type 4 is similar to Type 3 with the addition
of two twin 25 mm gun mountings on centreline abaft the
bridge superstructure. As well as a tank deck 300 ft long
stretching right across the hull there are two smaller deck
areas and a hold.

Operational: In the 1980s the class operated regularly off West
Africa, in the Mediterranean and in the Indian Ocean, usually
with Naval Infantry units embarked. Half the class have been
scrapped or laid up. Of the remainder, *Vilkov* is in the Pacific,
Shakhter in the Baltic, and the others in the Black Sea.
Sales: One to Ukraine in 1995.

UPDATED

DONETSKY SHAKHTER

8/1998* / 0081686

1 POLNOCHNY B CLASS (TYPE 771) (LSM)

Displacement, tons: 760 standard; 834 full load
Dimensions, feet (metres): 246.1 × 31.5 × 7.5 *(75 × 9.6 × 2.3)*
Main machinery: 2 Kolomna Type 40-D diesels; 4,400 hp(m) *(3.2 MW)* sustained; 2 shafts
Speed, knots: 19. **Range, miles:** 1,000 at 18 kt
Complement: 40-42
Military lift: 180 troops; 350 tons including 6 tanks
Missiles: SAM: 4 SA-N-5 Grail quad launchers.
Guns: 2 or 4—30 mm (1 or 2 twin).
    2—140 mm rocket launchers; 18 barrels.
Weapons control: PED-1 system.
Radars: Surface search: Spin Trough; I-band.
Fire control: Drum Tilt; H/I-band (for 30 mm guns).
IFF: High Pole A. Square Head.

Comment: Built in Poland in 1970. The last survivor serves in the Northern Fleet as a logistic
    support ship. Others of the class are all in reserve or derelict or scrapped. Tank deck 45.7 × 5.2 m
    (150 × 17 ft).

UPDATED

POLNOCHNY   *7/1996, van Ginderen Collection /* 0019047

3 ONDATRA (AKULA) (TYPE 1176) CLASS (LCMs)

Displacement, tons: 145 full load
Dimensions, feet (metres): 78.7 × 16.4 × 4.9 *(24 × 5 × 1.5)*
Main machinery: 2 diesels; 300 hp(m) *(220 kW)*; 2 shafts
Speed, knots: 10. **Range, miles:** 500 at 5 kt
Complement: 5
Military lift: 1 MBT

Comment: First completed in 1979 and associated with *Ivan Rogov.* 32 deleted so far. Tank deck of
    45 × 13 ft. Two to Yemen in 1983. These last three are in the Baltic.

UPDATED

ONDATRA   *9/1995*, Hartmut Ehlers /* 0081687

1 SERNA CLASS (LCU)

747

Displacement, tons: 105 full load
Dimensions, feet (metres): 86.3 × 19 × 5.2 *(26.3 × 5.8 × 1.6)*
Main machinery: 2 M 503A3 diesels; 5,522 hp(m) *(4.06 MW)*; 2 shafts
Speed, knots: 30. **Range, miles:** 100 at 30 kt; 600 at 22 kt
Complement: 6
Military lift: 45 tons or 100 troops

Comment: High-speed utility landing craft capable of beaching. Has an 'air-lubricated' hull.
    Designed for both military and civilian use by the R Alexeyev Central Design Bureau and has been
    building since 1993 at Nizhny Novgorod. Can be armed. Operational in the Baltic Fleet. Others
    have been sold commercially.

UPDATED

SERNA   *7/1996*, J Cislak /* 0081688

4 POMORNIK (ZUBR) (TYPE 1232.2) CLASS (ACV)

717   770   782   795

Displacement, tons: 550 full load
Dimensions, feet (metres): 189 × 84 *(57.6 × 25.6)*
Main machinery: 5 Type NK-12MV gas-turbines; 2 for lift, 23,672 hp(m) *(17.4 MW)* nominal; 3 for
    drive, 35,508 hp(m) *(26.1 MW)* nominal
Speed, knots: 63. **Range, miles:** 300 at 55 kt
Complement: 31 (4 officers)
Military lift: 3 MBT or 10 APC plus 230 troops (total 130 tons)
Missiles: SAM: 2 SA-N-5 Grail quad launchers; manual aiming; IR homing to 6 km *(3.2 n miles)* at
    1.5 Mach; altitude to 2,500 m *(8,000 ft)*; warhead 1.5 kg.
Guns: 2—30 mm/65 AK 630; 6 barrels per mounting; 3,000 rds/min combined to 2 km.
    2 retractable 122 mm rocket launchers (not in first of class).
Mines: 2 rails can be carried for 80.
Countermeasures: Decoys: MS227 chaff launcher.
    ESM: Tool Box; intercept.
Weapons control: Quad Look (DWU-3) (modified Squeeze Box) optronic director.
Radars: Air/surface search: Cross Dome; I-band.
Fire control: Bass Tilt; H/I-band.
IFF: Salt Pot A/B. Square Head.

Comment: First of class delivered 1986, commissioned in 1988. Last of class launched December
    1994. Produced at St Petersburg and at Feodosiya. Bow and stern ramps for ro-ro working. Last
    survivors are in the Baltic and four more are held by Ukraine. Four to Greece in 2000/01.

UPDATED

POMORNIK (with Cross Dome)   *9/1995*, Hartmut Ehlers /* 0081689

5 AIST (DZHEYRAN) (TYPE 1232.1) CLASS (ACV)

505   615   700   722   730

Displacement, tons: 298 full load
Dimensions, feet (metres): 155.2 × 58.4 *(47.3 × 17.8)*
Main machinery: 2 Type NK-12M gas turbines driving 4 axial lift fans and 4 propeller units for
    propulsion; 19,200 hp(m) *(14.1 MW)* nominal
Speed, knots: 70. **Range, miles:** 120 at 50 kt
Complement: 15 (3 officers)
Military lift: 80 tons or 4 light tanks plus 50 troops or 2 medium tanks plus 200 troops or 3 APCs
    plus 100 troops
Guns: 4—30 mm/65 (2 twin) AK 630; 6 barrels per mounting; 3,000 rds/min combined to 2 km.
Countermeasures: Decoys: 2 PK 16 chaff launchers.
Radars: Surface search: Kivach; I-band.
Fire control: Drum Tilt; H/I-band.
IFF: High Pole B. Square Head.

Comment: First produced at Leningrad in 1970, subsequent production at rate of about six every
    four years. The first large hovercraft for naval use. Similar to UK SR. N4. Type name is *maly
    desantny korabl na vozdushnoy podushke* meaning small ACV. Modifications have been made to
    the original engines and some units have been reported as carrying two SA-N-5 quadruple SAM
    systems and chaff launchers. Three are based in the Baltic, two in the Caspian. Remainder have
    been deleted.

UPDATED

AIST   *7/1996*, J Cislak /* 0081690

1901-2001

100 YEARS ON THE WAY OF PROGRESS & QUALITY

CENTRAL DESIGN BUREAU
FOR MARINE ENGINEERING
90 Marata, Saint-Petersburg
191119 Russia
Phone: (812) 113-5132
Fax: (812) 164-3749
E-mail: neptun@ckb-rubin.spb.su

RUBIN

1 LEBED (KALMAR) (TYPE 1206) CLASS (ACV)

533

Displacement, tons: 87 full load
Dimensions, feet (metres): 80.1 × 36.7 *(24.4 × 11.2)*
Main machinery: 2 Ivchenko AI-20K gas turbines for lift and propulsion; 8,000 hp(m) *(5.88 MW)*
Speed, knots: 50. **Range, miles:** 100 at 50 kt
Complement: 6 (2 officers)
Military lift: 2 light tanks or 40 tons cargo or 120 troops
Guns: 2—30 mm (twin) MGs.
Radars: Navigation: Kivach; I-band.

Comment: First entered service 1975. Can be carried in 'Ivan Rogov' class. Has a bow ramp with gun on starboard side and the bridge to port. This last unit is in the Black Sea, although there may be one more in the Caspian.

UPDATED

LEBED (old number) *4/1995*, Eric Grove / 0081691*

4 CZILIM (TYPE 20910) CLASS (ACV)

Displacement, tons: 8.6 full load
Dimensions, feet (metres): 39.4 × 19 *(12 × 5.8)*
Main machinery: 2 Deutz BF 6M 1013 diesels; 435 hp(m) *(320 kW)* sustained; for lift and propulsion
Speed, knots: 33. **Range, miles:** 300 n miles at 30 kt
Complement: 2 + 6 Border Guard
Guns: 1—7.62 mm MG. 1—40 mm RPG.
Radars: Navigation: I-band.

Comment: Ordered from Jaroslawski Sudostroiteinyj Zawod to an Almaz design for Russian Border Guard. First one laid down 24 February 1998. Planned to be in service in late 1999 but probably delayed.

NEW ENTRY

CZILIM (artist's impression) *6/1999*, JaSZ / 0033563*

INTELLIGENCE VESSELS

Notes: (1) About half the AGIs are fitted with SA-N-5/8 SAM launchers.
(2) SSV in pennant numbers of some AGIs is a contraction of *sudno svyazy* meaning communications vessel.
(3) GS in pennant numbers of some AGIs is a contraction of *gidrograficheskoye sudno* meaning survey ship.
(4) Activity reported in all Fleet areas, as well as in the Mediterranean, in 1999.
(5) 'Okean' class *Krenometr* GS 440 was reported in the Northern Fleet in 1998/99.

1 BALZAM (ASIA) (TYPE 1826) CLASS (AGI)

Name	No	Builders	Commissioned
BELOMORE	SSV 571	Yantar, Kaliningrad	Dec 1987

Displacement, tons: 4,500 full load
Dimensions, feet (metres): 344.5 × 50.9 × 16.4 *(105 × 15.5 × 5)*
Main machinery: 2 diesels; 18,000 hp(m) *(13.2 MW)*; 2 shafts
Speed, knots: 20. **Range, miles:** 7,000 at 16 kt
Complement: 200
Missiles: SAM: 2 SA-N-5 Grail quad launchers; manual aiming; IR homing to 6 km *(3.2 n miles)* at 1.5 Mach; altitude to 2,500 m *(8,000 ft)*; warhead 1.5 kg; 16 missiles.
Guns: 1—30 mm/65 AK 630; 6 barrels per mounting.
Radars: Surface search: Palm Frond and Don Kay; I-band.
Sonars: Lamb Tail/Mouse Tail VDS can be fitted.

Comment: Notable for twin radomes. Full EW and optronic fits. The first class of AGI to be armed. Based in the Northern Fleet. This is the last of the class. Capable of underway replenishment.

UPDATED

BELOMORE *4/1994* / 0081694*

7 VISHNYA (TYPE 864) CLASS (AGI)

Name	No	Builders	Commissioned
TAVRIYA	SSV 169	Northern Shipyard, Gdansk	Dec 1987
ODOGRAF	SSV 175	Northern Shipyard, Gdansk	July 1988
PRIAZOVE	SSV 201	Northern Shipyard, Gdansk	Jan 1987
KURILY	SSV 208	Northern Shipyard, Gdansk	Apr 1987
PELENGATOR	SSV 231	Northern Shipyard, Gdansk	Apr 1989
MERIDIAN	SSV 520	Northern Shipyard, Gdansk	July 1986
KARELIYA	SSV 535	Northern Shipyard, Gdansk	July 1987

Displacement, tons: 3,470 full load
Dimensions, feet (metres): 309.7 × 47.9 × 14.8 *(94.4 × 14.6 × 4.5)*
Main machinery: 2 Zgoda 12AV25/30 diesels; 4,406 hp(m) *(3.24 MW)* sustained; 2 auxiliary electric motors; 286 hp(m) *(210 kW)*; 2 shafts; cp props
Speed, knots: 16. **Range, miles:** 7,000 at 14 kt
Complement: 146
Missiles: SAM: 2 SA-N-5 Grail quad launchers; manual aiming; IR homing to 6 km *(3.2 n miles)* at 1.5 Mach; altitude to 2,500 m *(8,000 ft)*; warhead 1.5 kg.
Guns: 2—30 mm/65 AK 630; 6 barrels per mounting. 2—72 mm 4-tubed rocket launchers.
Radars: Surface search: 2 Nayada; I-band.
Sonars: Lamb Tail VDS can be carried.

Comment: SSV 231 and 520 based in the Baltic, SSV 201 in the Black Sea, SSV 169 and SSV 175 in the Northern Fleet and SSV 208 and 535 in the Pacific. All have a full EW fit plus optronic systems and datalinks. Punch Bowl is fitted in SSV 231 and possibly in others. Some superstructure differences in all of the class. NBC pressurised citadels. Ice-strengthened hulls. All are comparatively active.

UPDATED

PELENGATOR *9/1997* / 0019049*

ODOGRAF *4/1998 / 0050050*

2 PRIMORYE (TYPE 394B) CLASS (AGI)

KRYM SSV 590   **KAVKAZ** SSV 591

Displacement, tons: 3,700 full load
Dimensions, feet (metres): 278 × 46 × 23 *(84.7 × 14 × 7)*
Main machinery: 2 diesels; 4,000 hp(m) *(2.94 MW)*; 2 shafts
Speed, knots: 12. **Range, miles:** 10,000 at 10 kt
Complement: 120
Missiles: SAM: 1 or 2 SA-N-5 Grail quad launchers; manual aiming; IR homing to 6 km *(3.2 n miles)* at 1.5 Mach; altitude to 2,500 m *(8,000 ft)*; warhead 1.5 kg; 16 missiles.
Radars: Surface search: 2 Nayada and 2 Don Kay; I-band.

Comment: The first custom-built class of AGIs and the first to have an onboard analysis capability. First unit built 1968-70 to the same hull design as the 'Mayakovsky' class of stern trawlers. Mast arrangements and electronic fits vary between ships. Both in the Black Sea at Sevastopol and may be scrapped in 2000.

UPDATED

KRYM   *6/1994* */ 0081692*

KAVKAZ   *9/1997* */ 0016633*

4 MOMA (TYPE 861M) CLASS (AGI)

EKVATOR   **LIMAN**   **KILDIN** (mod)   **NAKHODKA** SSV 506

Displacement, tons: 1,240 standard; 1,600 full load
Dimensions, feet (metres): 240.5 × 36.8 × 12.8 *(73.3 × 11.2 × 3.9)*
Main machinery: 2 Zgoda-Sulzer 6TD48 diesels; 3,300 hp(m) *(2.43 MW)*; 2 shafts; cp props
Speed, knots: 17. **Range, miles:** 9,000 at 11 kt
Complement: 66 plus 19 scientists
Missiles: SAM: 2 SA-N-5 Grail quad launchers in some.
Radars: Surface search: 2 Don 2; I-band.

Comment: The two modernised ships have a foremast in the fore well-deck and a low superstructure before the bridge. Non-modernised ships retain their cranes in the forward well-deck. Similar class operates as survey ships. Built at Gdansk, Poland between 1968-72. *Ekvator, Kildin* and *Liman* in the Black Sea and two of these ships were active in the Adriatic during NATO operations against Serbia in 1999. *Nakhodka* in Northern Fleet may be laid up. One to Ukraine in 1996.

UPDATED

LIMAN   *5/1999*, A Sharma / 0081693*

3 ALPINIST (TYPE 503M/R) CLASS (AGI)

GS 7   **GS 19**   **GS 39**

Displacement, tons: 1,260 full load
Dimensions, feet (metres): 177.1 × 34.4 × 13.1 *(54 × 10.5 × 4)*
Main machinery: 1 SKL 8 NVD 48 A2U diesel; 1,320 hp(m) *(970 kW)* sustained; 1 shaft; bow thruster
Speed, knots: 13. **Range, miles:** 7,000 at 13 kt
Complement: 50
Missiles: SAM: 1 SA-N-5 Grail quad launcher *(GS 39)*.
Countermeasures: ESM: 2 Watch Dog; intercept.
Radars: Surface search: Nayada and Kivach; I-band.
Sonars: Paltus; active; high frequency.

Comment: Similar to Alpinist stern-trawlers which were built at about 10 a year at the Leninskaya Kuznitsa yard at Kiev and at the Volvograd shipyard. These AGIs were built at Kiev. In 1987 and 1988 forecastle was extended further aft and the electronics fit upgraded. *GS 7* in the Pacific, the other two in the Baltic. A fourth of class converted for ASW training was laid up in 1997.

UPDATED

GS 19   *6/1999* */ 0081695*

SURVEY AND RESEARCH SHIPS

Note: Civilian research ships are now all used for commercial purposes only or are laid up, and are no longer naval associated. The former section has therefore been deleted since 1998.

14 YUG (TYPE 862) CLASS (AGS/AGI/AGE)

V ADM VORONTSOV (ex-*Briz*)	**STRELETS**	**TAYGA**
GIDROLOG	**STVOR**	**PEGAS**
GORIZONT	**SSV 328**	**MARSHAL GELOVANI**
TEMRYUK SSV 703 (ex-*Mangyshlak*)	**SENEZH**	**DONUZLAV**
PERSEY	**NIKOLAY MATUSEVICH**	

Displacement, tons: 2,500 full load
Dimensions, feet (metres): 270.6 × 44.3 × 13.1 *(82.5 × 13.5 × 4)*
Main machinery: 2 Zgoda-Sulzer Type 6TD48 diesels; 3,300 hp(m) *(2.43 MW)* sustained; 2 auxiliary motors; 272 hp(m) *(200 kW)*; 2 shafts; cp props; bow thruster; 300 hp *(220 kW)*
Speed, knots: 15. **Range, miles:** 9,000 at 12 kt
Complement: 46 (8 officers) plus 20 scientists
Guns: 6—25 mm/80 (3 twin) (fitted for but not with).
Radars: Navigation: Palm Frond or Nayada; I-band.

Comment: Built at Northern Shipyard, Gdansk 1977-83. Have 4 ton davits at the stern and two survey craft. Others have minor variations around the stern area. *Strelets* has been taken over by the Arctic Border Guard. Four are based in the Pacific, two in the Black Sea, four in the North and two in the Baltic. *SSV 328* and *SSV 703* are classified as AGEs. Both are in the Northern Fleet.

UPDATED

STRELETS (Border Guard)   *8/1997*, E & M Laursen / 0019052*

GIDROLOG   *7/1998 / 0050052*

2 SIBIRIYAKOV (TYPE 865) CLASS (AGS)

SIBIRIYAKOV   **ROMZUALD MUKLEVITCH**

Displacement, tons: 3,422 full load
Dimensions, feet (metres): 281.2 × 49.2 × 16.4 *(85.7 × 15 × 5)*
Main machinery: Diesel-electric; 2 Cegielski-Sulzer 12AS25 diesels; 6,480 hp(m) *(4.44 MW)*
  sustained; 2 motors; 2 shafts; cp props; bow and stern thrusters
Speed, knots: 14. **Range, miles:** 11,000 at 14 kt
Complement: 58 plus 12 scientists
Guns: 1—30 mm AK 630 can be carried.
Radars: Navigation: 2 Nayada; I-band.

Comment: Built in Northern Shipyard, Gdansk 1990-92. Has a pressurised citadel for NBC
defence, and a degaussing installation. Six separate laboratories for hydrographic and
geophysical research. Two submersibles can be embarked. Both ships are very active,
Sibiriyakov in the Baltic at Kronstadt, and *Muklevitch* in the North.   ***UPDATED***

SIBIRIYAKOV   *9/1995*, J Cislak* / 0081697

1 AKADEMIK KRYLOV (TYPE 852/856) CLASS (AGOR)

LEONID DEMIN

Displacement, tons: 9,100 full load
Dimensions, feet (metres): 482.3 × 60.7 × 20.3 *(147 × 18.5 × 6.2)*
Main machinery: 4 Sulzer diesels; 14,500 hp(m) *(10.7 MW)*; 2 shafts; bow and stern thrusters
Speed, knots: 20. **Range, miles:** 36,000 at 15 kt
Complement: 120
Radars: Navigation: Nayada, Palm Frond and Don 2; I-band.
Helicopters: 1 Hormone.

Comment: Built in Szczecin 1974-79. Carry two survey launches and have 26 laboratories. Based
in the Baltic at Kronstadt. One of the class sold to Greece in 1993 and now flies the Cyprus flag.
Two others are laid up in the Baltic.   ***UPDATED***

LEONID DEMIN   *5/1994** / 0081696

4 NIKOLAY ZUBOV (TYPE 850) CLASS (AGS)

ANDREY VILKITSKY   **BORIS DAVIDOV**   **SEMEN DEZHNEV**   **FADDEY BELLINGSGAUZEN**

Displacement, tons: 2,674 standard; 3,021 full load
Dimensions, feet (metres): 294.2 × 42.7 × 15 *(89.7 × 13 × 4.6)*
Main machinery: 2 Zgoda-Sulzer 8TD48 diesels; 4,400 hp(m) *(3.23 MW)* sustained; 2 shafts
Speed, knots: 16.5. **Range, miles:** 11,000 at 14 kt
Complement: 50
Radars: Navigation: Palm Frond or Don 2; I-band.

Comment: Oceanographic research ships built at Szczecin Shipyard, Poland in 1964-68. Also
employed on navigational, sonar and radar trials. Has nine laboratories and small deck aft for
hydromet-balloon work. Carry two to four survey launches. Three based in the Northern Fleet and
Bellingsgauzen in the Black Sea returned to service in 1999.   ***UPDATED***

BORIS DAVIDOV   *6/1994** / 0081698

10 MOMA (TYPE 861) CLASS (AGS)

ANTARES	**ASKOLD**	**SEVER** (AGE)	**ANDROMEDA**
ANTARKTYDA	**OKEAN**	**KRILON**	**ARKTIKA**
ELTON	**MARS**		

Displacement, tons: 1,550 full load
Dimensions, feet (metres): 240.5 × 36.8 × 12.8 *(73.3 × 11.2 × 3.9)*
Main machinery: 2 Zgoda-Sulzer 6TD48 diesels; 3,300 hp(m) *(2.43 MW)* sustained; 2 shafts;
  cp props
Speed, knots: 17. **Range, miles:** 9,000 at 11 kt
Complement: 55
Radars: Navigation: Nayada and Don 2; I-band.
IFF: High Pole A.

Comment: Built at Northern Shipyard, Gdansk 1967-72. Some of the class are particularly active in
ASW research associated operations. Four laboratories. One survey launch and a 7 ton crane.
The AGEs are fitted with bow probes. Three in the Northern Fleet, three in the Pacific, one in the
Black and three in the Baltic. One transferred to Ukraine.   ***UPDATED***

ANTARKTYDA   *6/1996** / 0081699

8 SAMARA (TYPE 860) CLASS (AGS)

DEVIATOR	**GIGROMETR**	**GLUBOMYR**	**VOSTOK**
VAYGACH	**AZIMUT**	**ZENIT**	**TROPIK**

Displacement, tons: 1,050 standard; 1,270 full load
Dimensions, feet (metres): 193.5 × 34.4 × 12.5 *(59 × 10.5 × 3.8)*
Main machinery: 2 Zgoda-Sulzer Type 6TD48 diesels; 3,300 hp(m) *(2.43 MW)* sustained; 2 shafts;
  cp props
Speed, knots: 15. **Range, miles:** 6,200 at 10 kt
Complement: 45
Radars: Navigation: Don 2; I-band.
IFF: High Pole B.

Comment: Built at Northern Shipyard, Gdansk, 1962-65 for hydrographic surveying and research.
Has laboratories and one survey launch and a 5 ton crane. *Vaygach* has additional
accommodation around the base of the crane and has been fitted with a bow probe. One
transferred to Estonia in 1996. Four in the Baltic and two each in the North and Pacific.   ***UPDATED***

SAMARA   *4/1992, van Ginderen Collection*

2 MUNA (TYPE 1824B) CLASS (AGS/AGE)

GIROSCOP   **UGLOMER**

Displacement, tons: 690 full load
Dimensions, feet (metres): 165 × 26.9 × 9.5 *(50.3 × 8.2 × 2.9)*
Main machinery: 1 diesel; 300 hp(m) *(220 kW)*; 1 shaft
Speed, knots: 10. **Range, miles:** 3,000 at 10 kt
Complement: 40
Radars: Navigation: Kivach; I-band.

Comment: Built as transport ships in the 1970s and converted at Nikolayev in 1990. *Giroscop* is
based at Baltiysk, *Uglomer* is in the Pacific Fleet. Others of the class in service as auxiliaries have
been paid off.   ***VERIFIED***

GIROSCOP   *9/1995, Hartmut Ehlers*

20 FINIK (TYPE 872) CLASS (AGS/AGE)

North:	87	260	278	297	392	405
Pacific:	44	84	272	296	397	404
Black:	86	402				
Baltic:	270	301	388	399	400	403

Displacement, tons: 1,200 full load
Dimensions, feet (metres): 201.1 × 35.4 × 10.8 *(61.3 × 10.8 × 3.3)*
Main machinery: 2 Cegielski-Sulzer 6AL25/30 diesels; 1,920 hp(m) *(1.4 MW)*; auxiliary propulsion; 2 motors; 204 hp(m) *(150 kW)*; 2 shafts; cp props; bow thruster
Speed, knots: 13. **Range, miles:** 3,000 at 13 kt
Complement: 26 (5 officers) plus 9 scientists
Radars: Navigation: Kivach B; I-band.

Comment: Improved 'Biya' class. Built at Northern Shipyard, Gdansk 1978-83. Fitted with 7 ton crane for buoy handling. Can carry two self-propelled pontoons and a boat on well-deck. Ships of same class serve in the Polish Navy. Three transferred to Ukraine in 1997.

UPDATED

FINIK GS 87   *6/1995, van Ginderen Collection*

11 BIYA (TYPE 870/871) CLASS (AGS)

192	194	206	271	275	269
193	200	202	210	214	

Displacement, tons: 766 full load
Dimensions, feet (metres): 180.4 × 32.1 × 8.5 *(55 × 9.8 × 2.6)*
Main machinery: 2 diesels; 1,200 hp(m) *(882 kW)*; 2 shafts; cp props
Speed, knots: 13. **Range, miles:** 4,700 at 11 kt
Complement: 25
Radars: Navigation: Don 2; I-band.

Comment: Built at Northern Shipyard, Gdansk 1972-76. With laboratory and one survey launch and a 5 ton crane. Three based in the Pacific, two in the Baltic, five in the North and one, *GS 202*, in the Caspian. Two transferred to Ukraine in 1997.

UPDATED

BIYA   *4/1997*, Riku Lehtinen /* 0081700

8 KAMENKA (TYPE 870/871) CLASS (AGS)

66	74	107	113
118	199	207	211

Displacement, tons: 760 full load
Dimensions, feet (metres): 175.5 × 29.8 × 8.5 *(53.5 × 9.1 × 2.6)*
Main machinery: 2 Sulzer diesels; 1,800 hp(m) *(1.32 MW)*; 2 shafts; cp props
Speed, knots: 14. **Range, miles:** 4,000 at 10 kt
Complement: 25
Radars: Navigation: Don 2; I-band.
IFF: High Pole.

Comment: Built at Northern Shipyard, Gdansk 1968-69. A 5 ton crane forward. They do not carry a survey launch but have facilities for handling and stowing buoys. Three in the Baltic and five in the Pacific. One transferred to Vietnam in 1979, one to Estonia in 1996 and one to Ukraine in 1997.

UPDATED

KAMENKA   *6/1984*

2 ONEGA (TYPE 1806) CLASS (AGS)

AKADEMIK SEMINIKHIN   **AKADEMIK ISANIN**

Displacement, tons: 2,150 full load
Dimensions, feet (metres): 265.7 × 36 × 13.7 *(81 × 11 × 4.2)*
Main machinery: 2 gas turbines; 8,000 hp(m) *(5.88 MW)*; 1 shaft
Speed, knots: 20
Complement: 45
Radars: Navigation: Nayada; I-band.

Comment: Built at Zelenodolsk and first seen in September 1973. Helicopter platform but no hangar in earlier ships of the class but in later hulls the space is taken up with more laboratory accommodation. Used as hydroacoustic monitoring ships. *Akademik Seminikhin* was completed in October 1992 and may be armed. One to Ukraine in 1997. Others are laid up in each of the four Fleets.

VERIFIED

ONEGA   *9/1998, T Gander /* 0050053

2 VINOGRAD CLASS (AGOR)

GS 525   **GS 526**

Displacement, tons: 498 full load
Dimensions, feet (metres): 108.3 × 34.1 × 9.1 *(33 × 10.4 × 2.8)*
Main machinery: Diesel-electric; 2 diesels; 2 motors; 1,200 hp(m) *(882 kW)*; 2 trainable props
Speed, knots: 9. **Range, miles:** 1,000 at 6 kt
Complement: 19

Comment: Built by Rauma-Repola 1985-87 as hydrographic research ships. *GS 525* commissioned 12 November 1985 and *GS 526* on 17 December 1985. *525* is in the Pacific and *526* in the North. Both have side scan sonars.

UPDATED

GS 525   *6/1998, Hartmut Ehlers /* 0050054

1 MARSHAL NEDELIN (TYPE 1914) CLASS
(MISSILE RANGE SHIPS) (AGM)

MARSHAL KRYLOV

Displacement, tons: 24,500 full load
Dimensions, feet (metres): 695.5 × 88.9 × 25.3 *(212 × 27.1 × 7.7)*
Main machinery: 2 gas turbines; 54,000 hp(m) *(40 MW)*; 2 shafts
Speed, knots: 20. **Range, miles:** 22,000 at 16 kt
Complement: 450
Radars: Air search: Top Plate.
Navigation: 3 Palm Frond; I-band.
Helicopter control: Fly Screen B; I-band.
Space trackers: End Tray (balloons). Quad Leaf. 3 Quad Wedge. 4 smaller aerials.
Tacan: 2 Round House.
Helicopters: 2-4 Ka-32 Helix C.

Comment: Completed at Admiralty Yard, Leningrad 23 February 1990. Fitted with a variety of space and missile associated electronic systems. Fitted for but not with six twin 30 mm/65 ADG guns and three Bass Tilt fire-control radars. Naval subordinated, the task is monitoring missile tests with a wartime role of command ship. The Ship Globe radome is for SATCOM. Based in the Pacific. Second of class deleted.

VERIFIED

MARSHAL KRYLOV   *10/1995, van Ginderen Collection*

TRAINING SHIPS

Notes: (1) The 'Mir' class sail training ships have no military connections.
(2) The 'Ugra II' class depot ship *Gangut* was transferred to the Border Guard in the Baltic in 1998 as a Command Ship but is not sea-going.

2 SMOLNY (TYPE 887) CLASS (AX)

PEREKOP 200   **SMOLNY** 210

Displacement, tons: 9,150 full load
Dimensions, feet (metres): 452.8 × 53.1 × 21.3 *(138 × 16.2 × 6.5)*
Main machinery: 2 Zgoda Sulzer 12ZV 40/48 diesels; 15,000 hp(m) *(11 MW)*; 2 shafts
Speed, knots: 20. **Range, miles:** 9,000 at 15 kt
Complement: 137 (12 officers) plus 330 cadets
Guns: 4—3 in *(76 mm)*/60 (2 twin). 4—30 mm/65 (2 twin).
A/S mortars: 2 RBU 2500.
Countermeasures: ESM: 2 Watch Dog; radar warning.
Radars: Air/surface search: Head Net C; 3D; E-band; range 128 km *(70 n miles)*.
Navigation: 4 Don 2; I-band. Don Kay *(Perekop)*; I-band.
Fire control: Owl Screech; G-band. Drum Tilt; H/I-band.
IFF: 2 High Pole A. Square Head.
Sonars: Mouse Tail VDS; active; high frequency.

Comment: Built at Szczecin, Poland. *Smolny* completed in 1976, *Perekop* in 1977. Have considerable combatant potential. Both are active in the Baltic.   **UPDATED**

SMOLNY   6/1999* / 0081701

6 PETRUSHKA (DRAKON) CLASS (AXL)

MIERNYK   **ORSON**   **+ 4**

Displacement, tons: 335 full load
Dimensions, feet (metres): 129.3 × 27.6 × 7.2 *(39.4 × 8.4 × 2.2)*
Main machinery: 2 Wola H12 diesels; 756 hp(m) *(556 kW)*; 2 shafts
Speed, knots: 11. **Range, miles:** 1,000 at 11 kt
Complement: 13 plus 30 cadets

Comment: Training vessels built at Wisla Shipyard, Poland; first one commissioned in 1989. Used for seamanship and navigation training and may be commercially owned. There is also a version used as a hospital ship. Three are active in the Pacific, and three in the Baltic with a further eight laid up.   **UPDATED**

PETRUSHKA   5/1995*, L-G Nilsson / 0081702

AUXILIARIES

1 UGRA (TYPE 1886.2) CLASS (SUBMARINE DEPOT SHIP) (AS)

VOLGA 879

Displacement, tons: 6,750 standard; 9,650 full load
Dimensions, feet (metres): 462.6 × 57.7 × 23 *(141 × 17.6 × 7)*
Main machinery: Diesel-electric; 4 Kolomna Type 2-D-42 diesel generators; 2 motors; 8,000 hp(m) *(5.88 MW)*; 2 shafts
Speed, knots: 17. **Range, miles:** 5,000 at 13 kt
Complement: 220 (18 officers)
Missiles: SAM: 2 SA-N-5 Grail quad launchers.
Guns: 8—57 mm/70 (4 twin).
Countermeasures: ESM: 2 Watch Dog.
Radars: Air/surface search: Strut Curve; F-band.
Navigation: 2 Don 2; I-band.
Fire control: 2 Muff Cob; G/H-band.
IFF: 2 Square Head. High Pole B.

Comment: Built at Nikolayev in 1970. Type name is *plavuchaya baza* meaning floating base. Equipped with workshops. Provided with a helicopter platform. Has mooring points in hull about 100 ft apart, and has baggage ports for coastal craft and submarines. Two 10 ton and two 5 ton cranes. Based in the Black Sea. One of this class transferred to India in 1969. Another ship of this class acts as a Border Guard command vessel in the Baltic but is not sea-going.   **UPDATED**

VOLGA   9/1998, T Gander / 0050056

2 AMGA (TYPE 1791) CLASS (MISSILE SUPPORT SHIPS) (AEM)

VETLUGA   **DAUGAVA**

Displacement, tons: 6,100 *(Vetluga)*, 6,350 *(Daugava)* full load
Dimensions, feet (metres): 354.3 × 59 × 14.8 *(108 × 18 × 14.5)* *(Vetluga)*
Main machinery: 2 diesels; 9,000 hp(m) *(6.6 MW)*; 2 shafts
Speed, knots: 16. **Range, miles:** 4,500 at 14 kt
Complement: 210
Guns: 4—25 mm/80 (2 twin).
Radars: Surface search: Strut Curve; F-band.
Navigation: Don 2; I-band.
IFF: High Pole B.

Comment: Built at Gorkiy. Ships with similar duties to the 'Lama' class. Fitted with a large 55 ton crane forward and thus capable of handling much larger missiles than their predecessors. Each ship has a different length and type of crane to handle later types of missiles. Designed for servicing submarines. *Vetluga* completed in 1976 and *Daugava* (5 m longer than *Vetluga*) in 1981. Both are in the Pacific Fleet. A third of class is laid up in the North.   **UPDATED**

VETLUGA   7/1996* / 0081703

3 MALINA (TYPE 2020) CLASS
(NUCLEAR SUBMARINE SUPPORT SHIPS) (AS)

PM 63   **PM 74**   **PM 12**

Displacement, tons: 10,500 full load
Dimensions, feet (metres): 449.5 × 68.9 × 18.4 *(137 × 21 × 5.6)*
Main machinery: 4 gas turbines; 60,000 hp(m) *(44 MW)*; 2 shafts
Speed, knots: 17
Complement: 260
Radars: Navigation: 2 Palm Frond or 2 Nayada; I-band.

Comment: Built at Nikolayev. First deployed to the Northern Fleet in October 1984, second *(PM 74)* to Pacific in 1986, and third to the Northern Fleet in 1991. A fourth of class *(PM 16)* launched early in 1992, was not completed. Designed to support nuclear-powered submarines and surface ships. Carry two 15 ton cranes. Only the Pacific unit is active, but the other pair are still in commission and reported as being full of low level radiation waste products.   **UPDATED**

PM 74   7/1996* / 0081704

2 BELYANKA (TYPE 11510) CLASS (SPECIAL TANKERS) (AOS)

AMUR   **PINEGA**

Displacement, tons: 8,250 full load
Dimensions, feet (metres): 416.7 × 57.1 × 21.3 *(127 × 17.4 × 6.5)*
Main machinery: 2 diesels; 9,000 hp(m) *(6.62 MW)*; 2 shafts
Speed, knots: 15. **Range, miles:** 4,000 at 14 kt
Complement: 86
Cargo capacity: 1,070 tons
Radars: Navigation: 2 Kivach; I-band.

Comment: Built at Vyborg. *Amur* commissioned 29 November 1984 and went to the Northern Fleet. *Pinega* commissioned 17 July 1987, and transferred to the Pacific in 1989. Both used for the dispersal of low-level radioactive waste. Three more of a similar design were building at Severodvinsk from 1996 but were not completed.   **UPDATED**

AMUR   1994, B Lemachko

1 LAMA (TYPE 323/323B) CLASS
(MISSILE SUPPORT SHIP) (AEM)

VORONESH   874

Displacement, tons: 4,600 full load
Dimensions, feet (metres): 370 × 49.2 × 14.4 *(112.8 × 15 × 4.4)*
Main machinery: 2 diesels; 4,800 hp(m) *(3 MW)*; 2 shafts
Speed, knots: 14. **Range, miles:** 6,000 at 10 kt
Complement: 200
Missiles: SAM: 4 SA-N-5 Grail quad launchers.
Guns: 4—25 mm/80.
Radars: Surface search: Strut Curve; F-band.
Navigation: Don 2; I-band.
IFF: 2 Square Head. High Pole A.

Comment: Built 1968 at Nikolayev. The engines are sited aft to allow for a very large and high
hangar or hold amidships for carrying missiles or weapons' spares for submarines, surface ships
and missile craft. This is about 12 ft high above the main deck. There are doors at the forward
end with rails leading in and a raised turntable gantry or 20 ton travelling cranes for armament
supply. The well-deck is about 40 ft long, enough for most missiles to fit horizontally before being
lifted for loading. Type name is *plavuchaya masterskaya* meaning floating workshop. Based in
the Black Sea.   ***UPDATED***

VORONESH   *9/1998, Hartmut Ehlers /* 0050057

8 AMUR I (TYPE 304) and 5 AMUR II (TYPE 304M) CLASS
(REPAIR SHIPS) (AR)

AMUR I
PM 9, PM 56, PM 75, PM 138, 40, 64, 140, 156
AMUR II
59, 69, 86, 92, 97

Displacement, tons: 5,500 full load
Dimensions, feet (metres): 400.3 × 55.8 × 16.7 *(122 × 17 × 5.1)*
Main machinery: 1 Zgoda 8 TAD-48 diesel; 3,000 hp(m) *(2.2 MW)*; 1 shaft
Speed, knots: 12. **Range, miles:** 13,000 at 8 kt
Complement: 145
Radars: Navigation: Kivach or Palm Frond or Nayada; I-band.

Comment: 'Amur I' class general purpose depot and repair ships completed 1968-83 in Szczecin,
Poland. Successors to the 'Oskol' class. Carry two 5 ton cranes and have accommodation for 200
from ships alongside. 'Amur II' class similar in design. Built at Szczecin 1983-85. Three Amur IIs
are based in the Pacific, one in the North and one in the Baltic. Two Amur Is are in the Pacific, two
in the Black Sea, and four in the North. Most are inactive.   ***VERIFIED***

PM 56 (Amur I)   *9/1998, T Gander /* 0050058

6 OSKOL (TYPE 300/301) CLASS (REPAIR SHIPS) (AR)

PM 20   PM 21   PM 26   PM 51   PM 146   PM 148

Displacement, tons: 2,550 (3,500, Oskol IV) full load
Dimensions, feet (metres): 300.1 × 40 × 13.1 *(91.5 × 12.2 × 4)*
Main machinery: 1 Skoda diesel; 2,200 hp(m) *(1.62 MW)*; 1 shaft
Speed, knots: 12. **Range, miles:** 8,000 at 10 kt
Complement: 100
Radars: Navigation: Don 2; I-band.
IFF: High Pole.

Comment: Four series: 'Oskol I' class, well-decked hull, no armament; 'Oskol II' class, well-decked
hull, open promenade deck aft and twin 14.5 mm MGs forward; 'Oskol III' class, well-decked hull,
armed with two 57 mm guns (one twin forward) and four 25 mm guns (2 twin aft); 'Oskol IV'
class, flush-decked hull with no armament and a bridge one deck higher than other types.
General purpose tenders and repair ships with one or two 3.5 ton cranes. Built from 1963 to
1970 in Poland. Type name is *plavuchaya masterskaya* meaning floating workshop. Of the six
survivors, two are operational in the Northern Fleet, the remainder are laid up in the North, the
Pacific and in the Black Sea. One to Ukraine in 1997.   ***UPDATED***

OSKOL III PM 24   *4/1991* /* 0081705

1 TOMBA (TYPE 802) CLASS (SUPPORT SHIPS) (AG)

ENS 244

Displacement, tons: 5,820 full load
Dimensions, feet (metres): 351 × 55.8 × 16.4 *(107 × 17 × 5)*
Main machinery: Diesel-electric; 3 diesel generators; 1 motor; 5,500 hp(m) *(4 MW)*; 1 shaft
Speed, knots: 18. **Range, miles:** 7,000 at 14 kt
Complement: 50
Radars: Navigation: Don 2 and Spin Trough; I-band.
IFF: High Pole B.

Comment: Built at Szczecin, Poland in 1974. *ENS 244* is operational in the Northern Fleet. There is
a donkey funnel on forecastle. Two 3 ton cranes. Type name is *elektrostantsiye nalivatelnoye
sudno* meaning electricity supply ship. Originally built to support aircraft carriers.
                                                                                  VERIFIED

TOMBA   *10/1982*

4 VYTEGRALES II (TYPE 596P) CLASS (SUPPLY SHIPS) (AK/AGF)

APSHERON	**DAURIYA**	**SEVAN**	**YAMAL**
(ex-*Vagales*)	(ex-*Vyborgles*)	(ex-*Siverles*) 208	(ex-*Tosnoles*) 206

Displacement, tons: 6,150 full load
Dimensions, feet (metres): 400.3 × 55.1 × 22.3 *(122.1 × 16.8 × 6.8)*
Main machinery: 1 Burmeister & Wain 950VTBF diesel; 5,200 hp(m) *(3.82 MW)*; 1 shaft
Speed, knots: 15
Complement: 46
Radars: Navigation: Nayada or Palm Frond or Spin Trough; I-band.
CCA: Fly Screen.
Helicopters: 1 Ka-25 Hormone C (not in *Yamal*).

Comment: Standard timber carriers of a class of 27. These ships were modified for naval use in
1966-68 with helicopter flight deck. Built at Zhdanov Yard, Leningrad between 1963 and 1966.
Sevan fitted as squadron Flagship in support of Indian Ocean detachments. Variations exist
between ships of this class; *Dauriya* has a deckhouse over the aft hold. All have two Vee Cone
communications aerials. *Yamal* had her flight deck removed in 1995. The first of class,
completed in 1962, was originally *Vytegrales*, but this was later changed to *Kosmonaut Pavel
Belyayev* and, with three other ships of this class, converted to Space Support Ships. Four others
(*Borovichi* and so on) received a different conversion for the same purpose. The civilian-manned
ships together with these naval ships are often incorrectly called 'Vostok' or 'Baskunchak' class.
First pair are in the Black Sea, the other two in the Baltic. Two others transferred to Ukraine in
1996.
                                                                                  VERIFIED

SEVAN   *6/1998 /* 0050059

5 BORIS CHILIKIN (TYPE 1559V) CLASS (REPLENISHMENT SHIPS) (AOR)

BORIS BUTOMA	IVAN BUBNOV	SEGEY OSIPOV (ex-*Dnestr*)	VLADIMIR KOLECHITSKY	GENRICH GASANOV

Displacement, tons: 23,450 full load
Dimensions, feet (metres): 531.5 × 70.2 × 33.8
(162.1 × 21.4 × 10.3)
Main machinery: 1 diesel; 9,600 hp(m) *(7 MW)*; 1 shaft
Speed, knots: 17. **Range, miles:** 10,000 at 16 kt

Complement: 75 (without armament)
Cargo capacity: 13,000 tons oil fuel and dieso; 400 tons
ammunition; 400 tons spares; 400 tons victualling stores;
500 tons fresh water

Guns: 4—57 mm/80 (2 twin). Most are fitted for but not with the
guns.
Radars: Air/surface search/fire control: Strut Curve (fitted for
but not with).
Muff Cob (fitted for but not with).
Navigation: 2 Nayada or Palm Frond (plus Don 2 in *V Kolechitsky*);
I-band.
IFF: High Pole B.

Programmes: Based on the Veliky Oktyabr merchant ship tanker
design. Built at the Baltic Yard, Leningrad; *Vladimir Kolechitsky*
completed in 1972, *Osipov* in 1973, *Ivan Bubnov* in 1975,
Genrich Gasanov in 1977. Last of class *Boris Butoma*
completed in 1978.
Structure: This is the only class of purpose-built underway fleet
replenishment ships for the supply of both liquids and solids.
Although most operate in merchant navy paint schemes, all
wear naval ensigns.
Operational: Earlier ships can supply solids on both sides
forward. Later ships supply solids to starboard, liquids to port
forward. All can supply liquids either side aft and astern. *Osipov*
and *Gasanov* are based in the North, *Bubnov* in the Black Sea,
Butoma and *Kolechitsky* in the Pacific. *Boris Chilikin* transferred
to Ukraine in 1997.

UPDATED

GENRICH GASANOV   10/1997* / 0019063

6 BOLVA 1 (TYPE 688), 16 BOLVA 2 and 8 BOLVA 3 (TYPE 688A) CLASSES (BARRACKS SHIPS) (APB)

Displacement, tons: 6,500
Dimensions, feet (metres): 560.9 × 45.9 × 9.8 *(110 × 14 × 3)*
Cargo capacity: 350-400 tons

Comment: A total of 59 built by Valmet Oy, Helsinki between 1960 and 1984. Used for
accommodation of ships' companies during refit and so on. The Bolva 2 and 3 have a helicopter
pad. Have accommodation facilities for about 400 people. No means of propulsion but can be
steered. In addition there are several other types of Barracks Ships including five ex-'Atrek' class
depot ships as well as converted merchant ships and large barges. At least 18 have been
scrapped.

UPDATED

5 MOD ALTAY CLASS (REPLENISHMENT TANKERS) (AOL)

PRUT	YELNYA	ILIM	YEGORLYK	IZHORA

Displacement, tons: 7,250 full load
Dimensions, feet (metres): 348 × 51 × 22 *(106.2 × 15.5 × 6.7)*
Main machinery: 1 Burmeister & Wain BM550VTBN110 diesel; 3,200 hp(m) *(2.35 MW)*; 1 shaft
Speed, knots: 14. **Range, miles:** 8,600 at 12 kt
Complement: 60
Cargo capacity: 4,400 tons oil fuel; 200 m³ solids
Radars: Navigation: 2 Don 2 or 2 Spin Trough; I-band.

Comment: Built from 1967-72 by Rauma-Repola, Finland. Modified for alongside replenishment.
This class is part of 38 ships, being the third group of Rauma types built in Finland in 1967. *Ilim*
and *Yegorlik* transferred to civilian companies in 1996/97. *Prut* in the North, *Yelnya* in the Baltic
and the other three in the Pacific.

UPDATED

BOLVA 3   6/1996* / 0019060

MOD ALTAY   1/1997, van Ginderen Collection / 0019062

1 DUBNA CLASS (REPLENISHMENT TANKER) (AOL)

DUBNA

Displacement, tons: 11,500 full load
Dimensions, feet (metres): 426.4 × 65.6 × 23.6 *(130 × 20 × 7.2)*
Main machinery: 1 Russkiy 8DRPH23/230 diesel; 6,000 hp(m) *(4.4 MW)*; 1 shaft
Speed, knots: 16. **Range, miles:** 7,000 at 16 kt
Complement: 70
Cargo capacity: 7,000 tons fuel; 300 tons fresh water; 1,500 tons stores
Radars: Navigation: 2 Nayada; I-band.

Programmes: Completed 1974 at Rauma-Repola, Finland.
Structure: Has 1 ton replenishment stations forward. Normally painted in merchant navy colours.
Operational: Can refuel on either beam and astern. Based in North. One of the class transferred to
Ukraine in 1997 and another sold commercially in 1999 in the Pacific.

UPDATED

2 OLEKMA CLASS (REPLENISHMENT TANKER) (AORL)

OLEKMA (mod)	IMAN

Displacement, tons: 7,300 full load
Dimensions, feet (metres): 344.5 × 47.9 × 22 *(105.1 × 14.6 × 6.7)*
Main machinery: 1 Burmeister & Wain diesel; 2,900 hp(m) *(2.13 MW)*; 1 shaft
Speed, knots: 14. **Range, miles:** 8,000 at 14 kt
Complement: 40
Cargo capacity: 4,500 tons oil fuel; 180 m³ solids
Radars: Navigation: Don 2 or Nayada and Spin Trough; I-band.

Comment: Part of the second group of 34 tankers built by Rauma-Repola, Finland between 1960
and 1966. *Olekma* is modified for replenishment with refuelling rig abaft the bridge as well as
astern refuelling. *Olekma* in the Baltic, *Iman* in the Black Sea after a refit in Bulgaria in 1997/98.

UPDATED

IMAN   9/1998*, Hartmut Ehlers / 0081706

DUBNA   7/1996, van Ginderen Collection / 0019061

OLEKMA   6/1998 / 0050062

5 UDA CLASS (TYPE 577D) (REPLENISHMENT TANKERS) (AOL)

DUNAY   LENA   TEREK   VISHERA   SHEKSNA

Displacement, tons: 5,500 standard; 7,126 full load
Dimensions, feet (metres): 400.3 × 51.8 × 20.3 *(122.1 × 15.8 × 6.2)*
Main machinery: 2 diesels; 9,000 hp(m) *(6.6 MW)*; 2 shafts
Speed, knots: 17. **Range, miles:** 4,000 at 15 kt
Complement: 85
Cargo capacity: 2,900 tons oil fuel; 100 m³ solids
Radars: Navigation: 2 Don 2 or Nayada/Palm Frond; I-band.
IFF: High Pole A.

Comment: Built between 1962 and 1967 at Vyborg Shipyard. All have a beam replenishment capability. Guns removed. *Dunay* and *Vishera* in the Pacific, *Terek* in the Northern Fleet and the other two in the Baltic.

UPDATED

LENA   *4/1998 / 0050061*

1 KALININGRADNEFT CLASS (SUPPORT TANKER) (AORL)

VYAZMA

Displacement, tons: 8,600 full load
Dimensions, feet (metres): 380.5 × 56 × 21 *(116 × 17 × 6.5)*
Main machinery: 1 Russkiy Burmeister & Wain 5DKRP50/110-2 diesel; 3,850 hp(m) *(2.83 MW)*; 1 shaft
Speed, knots: 14. **Range, miles:** 5,000 at 14 kt
Complement: 32
Cargo capacity: 5,400 tons oil fuel and other liquids
Radars: Navigation: Okean; I-band.

Comment: Built by Rauma-Repola, Finland in 1982. Can refuel alongside or astern. At least an additional 20 of this class operate with the fishing fleets. Operational in the Northern Fleet.

VERIFIED

KALININGRADNEFT   *11/1991, G Jacobs*

1 KONDA CLASS (SUPPORT TANKERS) (AORL)

YAKHROMA

Displacement, tons: 2,090 full load
Dimensions, feet (metres): 226.3 × 33 × 14.1 *(69 × 10.1 × 4.3)*
Main machinery: 1 diesel; 1,600 hp(m) *(1.18 MW)*; 1 shaft
Speed, knots: 12. **Range, miles:** 2,200 at 11.5 kt
Complement: 36
Cargo capacity: 1,000 tons oil fuel
Radars: Navigation: Don 2; I-band. Spin Trough; I-band.

Comment: Originally of the 'Iskra' class of merchant tankers built in 1955. Has a stern refuelling capability. Icebreaker bow. Operational, in the Baltic.

VERIFIED

KONDA   *5/1990*

1 LUZA (TYPE 1541) CLASS (SPECIAL TANKER) (AOS)

ALAMBAI

Displacement, tons: 1,900 full load
Dimensions, feet (metres): 205 × 35.1 × 14.1 *(62.5 × 10.7 × 4.3)*
Main machinery: 1 diesel; 1,000 hp(m) *(735 kW)*; 1 shaft
Speed, knots: 12. **Range, miles:** 2,000 at 11 kt
Complement: 60
Radars: Navigation: Don 2; I-band. Spin Trough; I-band.
IFF: High Pole B.

Comment: Completed at Kolpino 1970. Used for transporting special liquids such as missile fuel. This last one is in the Pacific. Six others are laid up and are unlikely to go to sea again.

UPDATED

ALAMBAI   *10/1996* / 0019065*

TOPLIVO AND KHOBI SERIES (HARBOUR TANKERS) (AOL)

Comment: There are three Toplivo versions. Toplivo 1, total of 36 built in Poland, are of 420 tons full load and 34.4 m long. Toplivo 2, some of which were built in Egypt but the majority in the USSR, are of 1,200 tons full load and 53 m long. Toplivo 3, built in the USSR, are of 1,300 tons full load and 52.7 m long with a very different appearance from Toplivo 2. Total of 27 Toplivo 2 and 3 built. Four of the 'Khobi' class are also reported as still being in service. These are 1,500 ton tankers capable of carrying 550 tons of fuel. Three *(Cheremshan, Shacha* and *Sysola)* are in the North and one *(Lovat)* in the Baltic. These ships are used in many bases for the transport of all forms of liquids. Operational numbers are uncertain and many have been deleted.

UPDATED

TOPLIVO III   *6/1991 / 0081707*

KHOBI   *6/1994 / 0081708*

3 OB (TYPE 320) CLASS (HOSPITAL SHIPS) (AH)

YENISEI   SVIR   IRTYSH

Displacement, tons: 11,570 full load
Dimensions, feet (metres): 499.7 × 63.6 × 20.5 *(152.3 × 19.4 × 6.3)*
Main machinery: 2 Zgoda-Sulzer 12ZV40/48; 15,600 hp(m) *(11.47 MW)* sustained; 2 shafts; cp props
Speed, knots: 19. **Range, miles:** 10,000 at 18 kt
Complement: 124 plus 83 medical staff
Radars: Navigation: 3 Don 2 or 3 Nayada; I-band.
IFF: High Pole A.
Helicopters: 1 Ka-25 Hormone C.

Comment: Built at Szczecin, Poland. *Yenisei* completed 1981 and is based in the Black Sea. *Svir* completed in early 1989 and transferred to the Northern Fleet in September 1989. *Irtysh* completed in June 1990, was stationed in the Gulf in 1990-91 and is now based in the Pacific. A fourth of class is derelict and a fifth was cancelled. Have 100 beds and seven operating theatres. The first purpose-built hospital ships in the Navy, a programme which may have been prompted by the use of several merchant ships off Angola for Cuban casualties in the 'war of liberation.' NBC pressurised citadel. Ship stabilisation system. Decompression chamber. All are in use, mostly as alongside medical faculties.

UPDATED

IRTYSH   *8/1996* / 0019066*

4 KLASMA (TYPE 1274) CLASS (CABLE SHIPS) (ARC)

DONETS   INGURI   YANA   ZEYA

Displacement, tons: 6,000 standard; 6,900 full load
Measurement, tons: 3,400 dwt; 5,786 gross
Dimensions, feet (metres): 427.8 × 52.5 × 19 *(130.5 × 16 × 5.8)*
Main machinery: Diesel-electric; 5 Wärtsilä Sulzer 624TS diesel generators (4 in *Ingul* and *Yana*); 5,000 hp(m) *(3.68 MW)*; 2 motors; 2,150 hp(m) *(1.58 MW)*; 2 shafts
Speed, knots: 14. **Range, miles:** 12,000 at 14 kt
Complement: 118
Radars: Navigation: Spin Trough and Nayada; I-band.

Comment: *Yana* built by Wärtsilä, Helsingforsvarvet, Finland in 1962; *Donets* at the Wärtsilä, Åbovarvet in 1968-69; *Zeya* in 1970. *Donets* and *Zeya* are of slightly modified design. *Inguri* completed in 1978. All are ice strengthened and can carry 1,650 miles of cable. *Yana* is distinguished by gantry right aft. *Donets* is in the Baltic, and the other three are in the North. Can be leased for commercial use. One to Ukraine in 1997.
UPDATED

KLASMA   3/1992* / 0081709

2 EMBA I (TYPE 1172) and 1 EMBA II (TYPE 1175) CLASSES (CABLE SHIPS) (ARC)

SETUN (I)   NEPRYADAVA (I)   KEMJ (II)

Displacement, tons: 2,050 full load (Group I); 2,400 (Group II)
Dimensions, feet (metres): 249 × 41.3 × 9.8 *(75.9 × 12.6 × 3)* (Group I)
282.4 × 41.3 × 9.9 *(86.1 × 12.6 × 3)* (Group II)
Main machinery: Diesel-electric; 2 Wärtsilä Vasa 6R22 diesel alternators; 2,350 kVA 60 Hz; 2 motors; 1,360 hp(m) *(1 MW)*; 2 shafts (Group I)
2 Wärtsilä Vasa 8R22 diesel alternators; 3,090 kVA 60 Hz; 2 motors; 2,180 hp(m) *(1.6 MW)*; 2 shafts (Group II)
The 2 turnable propulsion units can be inclined to the ship's path giving, with a bow thruster, improved turning movement
Speed, knots: 11
Complement: 40
Radars: Navigation: Kivach and Don 2; I-band.

Comment: Both Emba Is built in 1981. Designed for shallow water cable-laying. Carry 380 tons of cable. Order placed with Wärtsilä in January 1985 for two larger (Group II) ships; *Kemj* completed on 23 October 1986. Can lay about 600 tons of cable. Designed for use off Vladivostok but also capable of operations in inland waterways. *Setun* is in the Caspian Sea, *Nepryadava* in the Baltic, and *Kemj* in the Pacific.
UPDATED

KEMJ (Emba II)   1986*, Wärtsilä / 0081710

4 MIKHAIL RUDNITSKY (TYPE 05360/1) CLASS (SALVAGE AND MOORING VESSELS) (ARS)

MIKHAIL RUDNITSKY   GEORGY KOZMIN   GEORGY TITOV   SAYANY

Displacement, tons: 10,700 full load
Dimensions, feet (metres): 427.4 × 56.7 × 23.9 *(130.3 × 17.3 × 7.3)*
Main machinery: 1 S5DKRN62/140-3 diesel; 6,100 hp(m) *(4.48 MW)*; 1 shaft
Speed, knots: 16. **Range, miles:** 12,000 at 15.5 kt
Complement: 72 (10 officers)
Radars: Navigation: Palm Frond; Nayada; I-band.
Sonars: MG 89 *(Sayany)*.

Comment: Built at Vyborg, based on 'Moskva Pionier' class merchant ship hull. First completed 1979, second in 1980, third in 1983 and fourth in 1984. Fly flag of Salvage and Rescue Service. Have two 40 ton and one 20 ton lift with cable fairleads forward and aft. This lift capability would be adequate for handling small submersibles, one of which is carried in the centre hold. *Sayany* is also described as a research ship and has a sonar. *Rudnitsky* and *Titov* in the Northern Fleet and the other two in the Pacific.
UPDATED

MIKHAIL RUDNITSKY   6/1992* / 0081711

8 KASHTAN (TYPE 141) CLASS (BUOY TENDERS) (ABU/ASR/AGL)

KIL 926	**KIL 143**	**KIL 164**	**KIL 498**
KIL 927	**KIL 158**	**SS 750** (ex-*KIL 140*)	**KIL 168**

Displacement, tons: 4,600 full load
Dimensions, feet (metres): 313.3 × 56.4 × 16.4 *(95.5 × 17.2 × 5)*
Main machinery: 4 Wärtsilä diesels; 29,000 hp(m) *(2.31 MW)*; 2 shafts
Speed, knots: 13.5
Complement: 51 plus 20 spare berths
Radars: Navigation: 2 Nayada; I-band.

Comment: Enlarged 'Sura' class built at the Neptun Shipyard, Rostock. Ordered 29 August 1986; *926* handed over in June 1988 and is classified as an AGL in the Baltic; *927* to the Pacific in July 1989; *143* to the North in July 1989; *158* to the Black Sea in November 1989; *164* to the North in January 1990; *498* to the Pacific in November 1990 and *168* to the Pacific in mid-1991. Lifting capacity: one 130 ton lifting frame, one 100 ton derrick, one 12.5 ton crane and one 10 ton derrick. All are civilian operated except *SS 750* in the Baltic.
UPDATED

SS 750   9/1999* / 0081712

4 SURA (TYPE 145) CLASS (BUOY TENDERS) (ABU)

KIL 21   KIL 22   KIL 27   KIL 31

Displacement, tons: 2,370 standard; 3,150 full load
Dimensions, feet (metres): 285.4 × 48.6 × 16.4 *(87 × 14.8 × 5)*
Main machinery: Diesel-electric; 4 diesel generators; 2 motors; 2,240 hp(m) *(1.65 MW)*; 2 shafts
Speed, knots: 12. **Range, miles:** 2,000 at 11 kt
Complement: 40
Cargo capacity: 900 tons cargo; 300 tons fuel for transfer
Radars: Navigation: 2 Don 2; I-band.

Comment: Heavy lift ships built as mooring and buoy tenders at Rostock in East Germany between 1965 and 1976. Lifting capacity: one 65 ton derrick and one 65 ton stern cage. Have been seen to carry 12 m DSRVs. *KIL 27* and *KIL 21* are in the Pacific, the other pair in the North. Three others are laid up. One to Ukraine in 1997.
VERIFIED

KIL 31   4/1996, van Ginderen Collection

1 ELBRUS (OSIMOL) (TYPE 537) CLASS (SUBMARINE RESCUE SHIP) (ASR)

ALAGEZ

Displacement, tons: 19,000 standard; 22,500 full load
Dimensions, feet (metres): 575.8 × 80.4 × 27.9 *(175.5 × 24.5 × 8.5)*
Main machinery: Diesel-electric; 4 diesel generators; 2 motors; 20,000 hp(m) *(14.7 MW)*; 2 shafts
Speed, knots: 17. **Range, miles:** 14,500 at 15 kt
Complement: 420
Guns: 4—30 mm/65 (2 twin).
Radars: Navigation: 2 Nayada and 2 Palm Frond; I-band.
Helicopters: 1 Ka-25 Hormone C.

Comment: Very large submarine rescue and salvage ship with icebreaking capability, possibly in view of under-ice capability of some SSBNs. Built at Nikolayev, and completed in 1982. Can carry two submersibles in store abaft the funnel which are launched from telescopic gantries. Based in the Pacific.
UPDATED

ALAGEZ   9/1991, G Jacobs

1 NEPA (TYPE 530) CLASS (SUBMARINE RESCUE SHIP) (ASR)

KARPATY

Displacement, tons: 9,800 full load
Dimensions, feet (metres): 424.9 × 63 × 21 *(129.5 × 19.2 × 6.4)*
Main machinery: Diesel-electric; 4 diesel generators; 2 motors; 8,000 hp(m) *(5.88 MW)*; 2 shafts
Speed, knots: 16. Range, miles: 8,000 at 14 kt
Complement: 270
Radars: Navigation: 2 Don 2; I-band.
IFF: High Pole B.

Comment: Commissioned 29 March 1967 at Nikolayev. Submarine rescue and salvage ship with a special high stern which extends out over the water for rescue manoeuvres. Has two 750 ton lifts which can work in tandem. Also one 100 ton lift, one 60 ton derrick and two 10 ton derricks. Carries a rescue bell, two submersibles and a number of recompression chambers. Based in the Baltic at Kronstadt since November 1988.

UPDATED

KARPATY   4/1996, van Ginderen Collection

8 ANTONOV (TYPE 1595) CLASS (TRANSPORTS) (AK)

NEON ANTONOV	VICTOR DENISOV	IVAN YEVTEYEV
IVAN LEDNEV	MIKHAIL KONOVALOV	SERGEY SUDETSKY
NIKOLAY SIPYAGIN	NICOLAY STARSHINOV	

Displacement, tons: 6,400 full load
Dimensions, feet (metres): 311.7 × 48.2 × 21.3 *(95 × 14.7 × 6.5)*
Main machinery: 2 diesels; 7,000 hp(m) *(5.15 MW)*; 2 shafts
Speed, knots: 17. Range, miles: 8,500 at 13 kt
Complement: 45
Cargo capacity: 2,500 tons
Missiles: SAM: 2 SA-N-5 Grail twin launchers; manual aiming; IR homing to 6 km *(3.2 n miles)* at 1.5 Mach; altitude to 2,500 m *(8,000 ft)*; warhead 1.5 kg.
Guns: 2—30 mm/65 (twin). 4—14.5 mm (2 twin) MGs. 4—12.7 mm MGs.
Radars: Navigation: Don Kay; Spin Trough or Palm Frond; I-band.

Comment: Ten of the class built at Nikolayev from 1975 to early 1980s. All operated by the Border Guard in the Pacific. Have two small landing craft aft. Armament is not normally mounted. One *(Irbit)* sold for civilian use in 1995.

UPDATED

MIKHAIL KONOVALOV   4/1996* / 0019068

5 TYPE 16900A (AKL)

CHANTIJ-MANSISK	JURGA	ARCHANGELSK	KANIN	PSKR 491

Comment: Built in the Pacific since 1996 for the Border Guard.

UPDATED

CHANTIJ-MANSISK   10/1997, B Lemachko / 0019077

SHELON I/II (TYPE 1388/1388M) CLASS (TRV/YAG)

Displacement, tons: 270 full load
Dimensions, feet (metres): 150.9 × 19.7 × 6.6 *(46 × 6 × 2)*
Main machinery: 2 diesels; 8,976 hp(m) *(6.6 MW)*; 2 shafts
Speed, knots: 26. Range, miles: 1,500 at 10 kt
Complement: 14
Radars: Navigation: Spin Trough or Kivach; I-band.

Comment: Type I built 1978-84. Built-in weapon recovery ramp aft. Type II built 1985-87. Type IIs can be used as environmental monitoring ships. Probably about 20 are still in use, one as an Admirals yacht in the Baltic.

UPDATED

SHELON I   2/1998 / 0050064

SHELON II   7/1996, J Cislak / 0081714

FLAMINGO (TYPE 1415) CLASS (TENDERS) (YDT)

Displacement, tons: 42 full load
Dimensions, feet (metres): 72.8 × 12.8 × 4.6 *(22.2 × 3.9 × 1.4)*
Main machinery: 1 Type 3-D-12 diesel; 300 hp(m) *(220 kW)* sustained; 1 shaft
Speed, knots: 12
Complement: 8

Comment: Successor to Nyryat II as a diving tender and for miscellaneous harbour duties by the Border Guard. Numbers unknown. VK number means used as diving craft; RK are workboats; MGK are buoy tenders.

UPDATED

FLAMINGO   7/1996*, B Lemachko / 0081715

FLAMINGO   7/1996*, Michael Nitz / 0081716

POLUCHAT I, II and III CLASSES (TRV)

Displacement, tons: 70 standard; 100 full load
Dimensions, feet (metres): 97.1 × 19 × 4.8 *(29.6 × 5.8 × 1.5)*
Main machinery: 2 M 50 diesels; 2,200 hp(m) *(1.6 MW)* sustained; 2 shafts
Speed, knots: 20. **Range, miles:** 1,500 at 10 kt
Complement: 15
Guns: 2—14.5 mm (twin) MGs (in some).
Radars: Navigation: Spin Trough; I-band.

Comment: Employed as specialised or dual-purpose torpedo recovery vessels and/or patrol boats. They have a stern slipway. Several exported as patrol craft. Some used by the Border Guard. Transfers: Algeria, Angola, Congo (three), Ethiopia (one), Guinea-Bissau, India, Indonesia (three), Iraq (two), Mozambique, Somalia (six), Syria, Tanzania, Vietnam (five), North Yemen (two), South Yemen. About 25 remain in service.

UPDATED

POLUCHAT I　　　　　　　　　　　　　*11/1991*, MoD Bonn /* 0081713

PO 2 and NYRYAT 2 (TYPE 1896) CLASSES (TENDERS) (YDT)

Displacement, tons: 56 full load
Dimensions, feet (metres): 70.5 × 11.5 × 3.3 *(21.5 × 3.5 × 1)*
Main machinery: 1 Type 3-D-12 diesel; 300 hp(m) *(220 kW)* sustained; 1 shaft
Speed, knots: 12
Complement: 8
Guns: Some carry 1—12.7 mm MG on the forecastle.

Comment: This 1950s design of hull and machinery has been used for a wide and diverse number of adaptations. Steel hull. Nyryat 2 have the same characteristics but are used as diving tenders (RVK), inshore survey craft (MGK) and workboats (RK).
Transfers: Albania, Bulgaria, Cuba, Guinea, Iraq. Many deleted.

VERIFIED

NYRYAT 2　　　　　　　　　　　　　*9/1998, T Gander /* 0050065

NYRYAT I (TYPE 522) CLASS (TENDERS) (YDT)

Displacement, tons: 120 full load
Dimensions, feet (metres): 93 × 18 × 5.5 *(28.4 × 5.5 × 1.7)*
Main machinery: 1 diesel; 450 hp(m) *(331 kW)*; 1 shaft
Speed, knots: 12.5. **Range, miles:** 1,500 at 10 kt
Complement: 15
Guns: 1—12.7 mm MG (in some).

Comment: Built from 1955. Can operate as patrol craft or diving tenders with recompression chamber. Similar hull and propulsion used for inshore survey craft. Some have BGK, VM or GBP (survey craft) numbers.
Transfers: Albania, Algeria, Cuba, Egypt, Iraq, North Yemen. Many deleted.

VERIFIED

NYRYAT I　　　　　　　　　　*6/1998, van Ginderen Collection /* 0050066

15 SK 620 CLASS (TENDERS) (YH/YFL)

Displacement, tons: 236 full load
Dimensions, feet (metres): 108.3 × 24.3 × 6.9 *(33 × 7.4 × 2.1)*
Main machinery: 2 56ANM30-H12 diesels; 620 hp(m) *(456 kW)* sustained; 2 shafts
Speed, knots: 12. **Range, miles:** 1,000 at 12 kt
Complement: 14 plus 3 spare

Comment: Built at Wisla Shipyard, Poland as a smaller version of the 'Petrushka' class training ship. PSK series serve as harbour ferries. Mostly used as hospital tenders capable of carrying 15 patients. Numbers uncertain.

UPDATED

SK 620　　　　　　　　　　　　　*7/1996, Hartmut Ehlers*

13 YELVA (KRAB) (TYPE 535M) CLASS (DIVING TENDERS) (YDT)

VM 143, 146, 159, 250, 266, 268, 413, 414, 416, 420, 425, 807, 809

Displacement, tons: 295 full load
Dimensions, feet (metres): 134.2 × 26.2 × 6.6 *(40.9 × 8 × 2)*
Main machinery: 2 Type 3-D-12A diesels; 630 hp(m) *(463 kW)* sustained; 2 shafts
Speed, knots: 12.5. **Range, miles:** 1,870 at 12 kt
Complement: 30
Radars: Navigation: Spin Trough; I-band.

Comment: Diving tenders built 1971-83. Carry a 1 ton crane and diving bell. Some have submersible recompression chamber. Ice strengthened. One to Cuba 1973, one to Libya 1977. Operational numbers are uncertain.

UPDATED

YELVA 159　　　　　　　　　　*4/1996, van Ginderen Collection*

16 POZHARNY I (TYPE 364) CLASS (FIREFIGHTING CRAFT) (YTR)

Displacement, tons: 180 full load
Dimensions, feet (metres): 114.5 × 20 × 6 *(34.9 × 6.1 × 1.8)*
Main machinery: 2 Type M 50 diesels; 2,200 hp(m) *(1.6 MW)* sustained; 2 shafts
Speed, knots: 12. **Range:** 250 at 12 kt
Complement: 26
Guns: 4—12.7 mm (2 twin) MGs (in some).

Comment: Total of 84 built from mid-1950s to mid-1960s. Harbour fire boats but can be used for patrol duties. One transferred to Iraq (now deleted) and two to Ukraine.

UPDATED

POZHARNY I　　　　　　　　　　　*7/1996, Hartmut Ehlers /* 0081718

7 IVA (MORKOV) (TYPE 1461.3) CLASS (FIRE/PATROL CRAFT)

PZHK 415, 900, 1514, 1544, 1547, 1859, 1680

Displacement, tons: 320 full load
Dimensions, feet (metres): 119.8 × 25.6 × 7.2 *(36.5 × 7.8 × 2.2)*
Main machinery: 2 diesels; 1,040 hp(m) *(764 kW)*; 2 shafts
Speed, knots: 12.5. **Range:** 250 at 12 kt
Complement: 20

Comment: Carry four water monitors. Completed in 1984-86 at Rybinsk. Can be used for patrol/towage. Some are under civilian control.

UPDATED

IVA 900   *6/1999* * / 0081717

16 PELYM (TYPE 1799) CLASS (DEGAUSSING SHIPS) (YDG)

SR 26	SR 203	SR 221	SR 276	SR 344	SR 409
SR 179	SR 215	SR 222	SR 280	SR 407	SR 455
SR 180	SR 218	SR 233	SR 281		

Displacement, tons: 1,370 full load
Dimensions, feet (metres): 214.8 × 38 × 11.2 *(65.5 × 11.6 × 3.4)*
Main machinery: 1 diesel; 1,536 hp(m) *(1.13 MW)*; 1 shaft
Speed, knots: 14. **Range, miles:** 1,000 at 13 kt
Complement: 70
Radars: Navigation: Don 2; I-band.

Comment: Built from 1970 to 1987 at Khabarovsk and Gorokhovets. Earlier ships have stump mast on funnel, later ships a tripod main mast and a platform deck extending to the stern. Type name is *sudno razmagnichivanya* meaning degaussing ship. One to Cuba 1982. Several in reserve.

UPDATED

SR 26   *9/1998, T Gander* / 0050067

HARBOUR CRAFT (YP)

Comment: There are numerous types of harbour launches, training cutters and trials vessels in all of the major Fleet bases. Class names include Nachimovec (Type 286), Bryza (Type 722), Yaroslavec (Type 376), Admiralec (Type 371), Krym, Albatros, Amurec and Saigak. Some used by Border Guard.

UPDATED

ALBATROS   *4/1997* * / 0019070

17 BEREZA (TYPE 18061) CLASS (DEGAUSSING SHIPS) (YDG)

SR 23	SR 74	SR 216	SR 479	SR 569	SR 936
SR 28	SR 120	SR 245	SR 541	SR 570	SR 939
SR 59	SR 137	SR 478	SR 548	SR 933	

Displacement, tons: 1,850 standard; 2,051 full load
Dimensions, feet (metres): 228 × 45.3 × 13.1 *(69.5 × 13.8 × 4)*
Main machinery: 2 Zgoda-Sulzer 8AL25/30 diesels; 2,938 hp(m) *(2.16 MW)* sustained; 2 shafts; cp props
Speed, knots: 13. **Range, miles:** 1,000 at 13 kt
Complement: 48
Radars: Navigation: Kivach; I-band.

Comment: First completed at Northern Shipyard, Gdansk 1984-1991. One transferred to Bulgaria in 1988. Have NBC citadels and three laboratories. *SR 933* based in the Caspian Sea. Several in reserve. One to Ukraine in 1997. One laid up in Poland (SR 938) and may be taken over by the Polish Navy.

UPDATED

SR 137   *9/1998, T Gander* / 0050068

ICEBREAKERS

Note: Only military icebreakers are shown in this section. Other icebreakers come under civilian management and are now used predominantly for commercial purposes. Operational civilian ships include the nuclear powered *Taymyr, Vaygach, Arktika, Sibir, Rossiya, S Soyuz, Yamal* and *50 Let Pobeda* (ex-*Ural*) (still building). Diesel powered ships include *A Makarov, Krasin, K Sorokin, K Nikolayev, K Dranitsyn* and *K Khlebnikov. Arktika* and *Sibir* are planned to pay off in 2000/01.

2 DOBRYNYA NIKITICH CLASS (AGB)

IVAN KRUZENSHTERN (ex-*Ledokol 6*)   **VLADIMIR KAVRAYSKY**

Displacement, tons: 2,995 full load
Measurement, tons: 2,254 gross; 1,118 dwt; 50 net
Dimensions, feet (metres): 222.1 × 59.4 × 20 *(67.7 × 18.1 × 6.1)*
Main machinery: Diesel-electric; 3 Type 13-D-100 or 3 Wärtsilä 6L 26 *(Kruzenshtern)* diesel generators; 3 motors; 5,400 hp(m) *(4 MW)*; 3 shafts (1 fwd, 2 aft)
Speed, knots: 14.5. **Range, miles:** 5,500 at 12 kt
Complement: 45
Guns: 2—57 mm/70 (twin). 2—37 mm/63.
Radars: Navigation: 2 Don 2; I-band.

Comment: Both built at Admiralty Yard, Leningrad between 1960 and 1971. *Kavraysky* is in the Northern Fleet. *Kruzenshtern* was re-engined in 1997 and is in the Pacific. Fourteen others of the class are non-naval.

UPDATED

IVAN KRUZENSHTERN   *9/1997, Harald Carstens* / 0019071

7 IVAN SUSANIN (TYPE 97P) CLASS
(ARMED ICEBREAKERS/PATROL SHIPS) (PG/AGB)

AISBERG   DUNAY   NEVA   VOLGA   RUSLAN   ANADYR   IRTYSH

Displacement, tons: 3,567 full load
Dimensions, feet (metres): 229.7 × 59.4 × 21 *(70 × 18.1 × 6.4)*
Main machinery: Diesel-electric; 3 Type 13-D-150 diesel generators; 3 motors; 5,400 hp(m) *(4 MW)*; 3 shafts (1 fwd, 2 aft)
Speed, knots: 14.5. **Range, miles:** 5,500 at 12.5 kt
Complement: 45
Guns: 2—3 in *(76 mm)*/60 (twin). 2—30 mm/65 AK 630 (not in all).
Radars: Surface search: Strut Curve; F-band.
Navigation: 2 Don Kay or Palm Frond; I-band.
Fire control: Hawk Screech; I-band.
Helicopters: Platform only.

Comment: Built at Admiralty Yard, Leningrad. Generally similar to 'Dobrynya Nikitich' class though larger with a tripod mast and different superstructure. Operated by the Border Guard primarily as patrol ships. Three in the Pacific and four in the Northern Fleet. One deleted so far.   ***UPDATED***

AISBERG   8/1991*, Bryan Hird / 0081719

TUGS

Notes: (1) SB means *Spasatelny Buksir* or Salvage Tug. MB means *Morskoy Buksir* or Seagoing Tug.
(2) One 'Prut' class ARS is reported as still active in the Black Sea.

3 INGUL (TYPE 1453) CLASS (SALVAGE TUGS) (ATS)

PAMIR   MASHUK   ALTAY (ex-*Karabakh*)

Displacement, tons: 4,050 full load
Dimensions, feet (metres): 304.4 × 50.5 × 19 *(92.8 × 15.4 × 5.8)*
Main machinery: 2 Type 58-D-4R diesels; 6,000 hp(m) *(4.4 MW)*; 2 shafts; cp props
Speed, knots: 19. **Range, miles:** 9,000 at 19 kt
Complement: 71 plus salvage party of 18
Radars: Navigation: 2 Palm Frond; I-band.
IFF: High Pole. Square Head.

Comment: Built at Admiralty Yard, Leningrad in 1975-84. NATO class name the same as one of the 'Klasma' class cable-ships. Naval-manned arctic salvage and rescue tugs. Two more, *Yaguar* (Murmansk) and *Bars* (Vladivostok), operate with the merchant fleet. Carry salvage pumps, diving and firefighting gear as well as a high-line for transfer of personnel. Fitted for guns but these are not carried. *Pamir* and *Altay* in the North, *Mashuk* in the Pacific.   ***UPDATED***

ALTAY   4/1997* / 0019072

3 SLIVA (TYPE 712) CLASS (SALVAGE TUGS) (ATS)

SB 406   PARADOKS SB 921   **SHAKHTER** SB 922

Displacement, tons: 3,050 full load
Dimensions, feet (metres): 227 × 50.5 × 16.7 *(69.2 × 15.4 × 5.1)*
Main machinery: 2 Russkiy SEMT-Pielstick 6 PC2.5 L 400 diesels; 7,020 hp(m) *(5.2 MW)* sustained; cp props; bow thruster
Speed, knots: 16. **Range:** 6,000 at 16 kt
Complement: 43 plus 10 salvage party
Radars: Navigation: 2 Nayada; I-band.

Comment: Built at Rauma-Repola, Finland. Based on Goryn design. *SB 406* completed 20 February 1984. Second pair ordered 1984 *SB 921* completed 5 July 1985 and *SB 922* on 20 December 1985. *SB 922* named *Shakhter* in 1989. A fourth of class, *Iva* SB 408, was sold illegally to a Greek company in March 1993 and now flies the flag of Cyprus but is operated as a 'joint venture' with the Russian Navy. Diving facilities to 60 m. Bollard pull 60 tons. *SB 406* based in the Northern Fleet, *SB 921* in the Baltic and *SB 922* in the Black Sea.   ***UPDATED***

PARADOKS   10/1996*, M Nalecz / 0081720

7 KATUN I (TYPE 1893) and 2 KATUN II (TYPE 1993) CLASSES
(SALVAGE TUGS) (ATS)

Katun I: PZHS 96, 98, 123, 209, 273, 279, 282
Katun II: PZHS 64, 92

Displacement, tons: 1,005 (Katun I); 1,220 (Katun II) full load
Dimensions, feet (metres): 205.3 × 33.1 × 11.5 *(62 × 10.1 × 3.5)* (Katun I)
Main machinery: 2 diesels; 5,000 hp(m) *(3.68 MW)*; 2 shafts
Speed, knots: 17. **Range, miles:** 2,000 at 17 kt
Complement: 32
Radars: Navigation: Spin Trough or Kivach (Katun II); I-band.
IFF: High Pole A.

Comment: Katun I built at Kolpino 1970-78. Equipped for firefighting and rescue. *PZHS 64, 92,* and *95*, all Katun II, were completed in 1982—3 m *(9.8 ft)* longer than Katun I with an extra bridge level and lattice masts. Some may have a PDS prefix to their pennant numbers. *273* and *279* are based in the Caspian Sea, *92* and *209* in the Pacific, *64* and *98* in the North, *96* and *282* in the Baltic and *123* in the Black Sea. Four others are laid up.   ***UPDATED***

KATUN 123   8/1991, van Ginderen Collection

1 BAKLAZHAN (TYPE 5757) CLASS (ARS)

NIKOLAI CHIKER SB 131

Displacement, tons: 7,300 full load
Dimensions, feet (metres): 324.8 × 64 × 23.6 *(99 × 19.5 × 7.2)*
Main machinery: 4 Wärtsilä Vasa 12V32 diesels; 24,160 hp(m) *(17.76 MW)*; 2 shafts; cp props; bow thruster; 1,360 hp(m) *(1 MW)*
Speed, knots: 18. **Range, miles:** 11,000 at 16 kt
Complement: 51 plus 20 spare berths
Radars: Navigation: 2 Nyada; I-band.

Comment: Built by Hollming (Rauma), Helsinki and completed 12 April 1989. A second of class *A Krylov* SB 135 completed 30 June 1989 but was sold illegally to Greece in March 1993 and for a short time renamed *Tsavliris Giant*. These are the largest salvage tugs in the world with a 250 ton bollard pull on each of two towing winches with a third 60 ton winch. The crew includes two divers and there are two decompression chambers. Four firefighting foam/water guns are fitted on the bridge/mast. Designed to operate in extreme temperatures. *SB 131* is in the Northern Fleet.   ***UPDATED***

NIKOLAI CHIKER   3/1995* / 0081721

8 GORYN (TYPE 714) CLASS (ARS/ATA)

MB 15	MB 38	MB 119	SB 522 (ex-*MB 62*)
MB 32	MB 105	SB 521 (ex-*MB 61*)	SB 523 (ex-*MB 64*)

Displacement, tons: 2,240 standard; 2,600 full load
Dimensions, feet (metres): 208.3 × 46.9 × 16.7 *(63.5 × 14.3 × 5.1)*
Main machinery: 2 Russkiy SEMT-Pielstick 6 PC2.5 L 400 diesels; 7,020 hp(m) *(5.2 MW)* sustained; 2 shafts; cp props; bow thruster
Speed, knots: 15
Complement: 43 plus 16 spare berths
Radars: Navigation: 2 Don 2 or Nayada or Kivach; I-band.

Comment: Built by Rauma-Repola 1977-83. Have sick-bay. First ships have goalpost mast with 10 and 5 ton derricks and bollard pull of 35 tons. Remainder have an A-frame mast with a 15 ton crane and bollard pull of 45 tons. SB number indicates a 'rescue' tug. Three in the North, four in the Pacific and one in the Black Sea. One transferred to Ukraine in 1997.
UPDATED

MB 38   5/1999* / 0081722

29 SORUM (TYPE 745/1454) CLASS (ATA/PG)

AMUR	SAKHALIN	MB 5	MB 58
BREST	TAYMIR	MB 6	MB 61
BUG	URAL	MB 28	MB 100
CHUKOTKA	V KINGISEPP	MB 31	MB 110
DON	BAYKAL (ex-*Yan Berzin*)	MB 37	MB 148
KAMCHATKA	YENISEY	MB 56	MB 307
KARELIA	ZABAYKALYE		
LADOGA	ZAPOLARYE		
PRIMORYE			

Displacement, tons: 1,660 full load
Dimensions, feet (metres): 190.2 × 41.3 × 15.1 *(58 × 12.6 × 4.6)*
Main machinery: Diesel-electric; 2 Type 5-2-DW2 diesel generators; 2,900 hp(m) *(2.13 MW)*; 1 motor; 2,000 hp(m) *(1.47 MW)*; 1 shaft
Speed, knots: 14. **Range, miles:** 3,500 at 13 kt
Complement: 35
Guns: 4—30 mm/65 (2 twin) (all fitted for, but only Border Guard ships carry them).
Radars: Navigation: 2 Don 2 or Nayada; I-band.
IFF: High Pole B.

Comment: A class of ocean tugs with firefighting and diving capability. Named ships are used as patrol vessels and are Border Guard operated in the North, Pacific, Baltic and Caspian. Only 12 of the PGs are active. Built in Yaroslavl and Oktyabskoye from 1973 to 1989, design used for Ministry of Fisheries rescue tugs.
UPDATED

ZABAYKALYE   6/1996* / 0019075

MB 110   6/1996* / 0081723

12 OKHTENSKY (TYPE 733/733S) CLASS (ARS/ATA)

NEPTUN	MB 12	MB 165
ORION	MB 21	LOKSA MB 171
POCHETNY	SPUTNIK MB 52	MB 176
SB 6	MB 160	SATURN MB 178

Displacement, tons: 948 full load
Dimensions, feet (metres): 156.1 × 34 × 13.4 *(47.6 × 10.4 × 4.1)*
Main machinery: Diesel-electric; 2 BM diesel generators; 1 motor; 1,500 hp(m) *(1.1 MW)*; 1 shaft
Speed, knots: 13. **Range, miles:** 8,000 at 7 kt; 6,000 at 13 kt
Complement: 40
Guns: 2—57 mm/70 (twin) or 2—25 mm/80 (twin) (Border Guard only).
Radars: Navigation: 1 or 2 Don 2 or Spin Trough; I-band.
IFF: High Pole B.

Comment: Ocean-going salvage and rescue tugs. First of a total of 62 completed 1958. Fitted with powerful pumps and other apparatus for salvage. Five named ships are operated by the Border Guard and are armed; others have either SB or MB numbers and some have names as well. Two to Ukraine in 1997. Many have been scrapped.
UPDATED

MB 160   9/1998, T Gander / 0050070

HARBOUR TUGS

Displacement, tons: 189 full load
Dimensions, feet (metres): 98.4 × 21.3 × 9.8 *(30 × 6.5 × 3)*
Main machinery: 1 RGDV 148 K10 diesel; 1 shaft
Speed, knots: 10

Comment: Details given are for the 'Scholle' (Type 98057) class. There are numerous other types including 'Tugur' (Type 730) class, Sidehole I and II (Type 745) classes, Mazin (Type 498) and MB 70 (Type 192). Some have BUK designators. Many are laid up.
UPDATED

HARBOUR TUG   8/1999* / 0081724

RUSSIAN FEDERAL BORDER SERVICE
(ex-Maritime Border Guard)

Notes: (1) The Border Guard operates a considerable fleet of warships which would be integrated with naval operations in a crisis. Formerly run by the KGB, the force came under the Ministry of Defence in October 1991 and was then given to the Ministry of Interior in December 1993. Some of the vessels have been devolved to the individual Republics with coastal regions. Class names are listed here for convenience—details of the classes are in the sections preceding.
(2) From 1993 the Border Guard started to fly its own ensign which is the St Andrews Cross with a white border on a green background. Diagonal stripes are painted on the hull in white/blue/red. So far these colours have been seen in all Fleets except the Black Sea.
(3) Roles include Law Enforcement, Port Security, Counter Intelligence, Counter Terrorism and Fishery Protection.
(4) The Fisheries Protection Service became part of the Border Service in 1998.

Frigates	*Patrol Forces*	*Armed Icebreakers*
'Krivak III' class	'Pauk' class	'Ivan Susanin' class
'Grisha III' class	'Stenka' class	
	'Muravey' class	*Auxiliaries*
River Monitors	'Zhuk' class	'Antonov' class
'Piyavka' class	'Svetlyak' class	'Yug' class
'Vosh' class	'Sorum' class	Type 16900A
'Yaz' class	'Okhtensky' class	
'Schmel' class	'Flamingo' class	

Comment: In addition there are large numbers of harbour launches and two 220 ton Presidential Yachts *Krim* and *Kavkaz* based in the Black Sea.
UPDATED

4 KOMANDOR CLASS (FISHERY CONTROL SHIPS)

KOMANDOR   SHKIPER GYEK   HERLUF BIDSTRUP   MANCHZHUR

Displacement, tons: 2,435 full load
Dimensions, feet (metres): 289.7 × 44.6 × 15.4 *(88.3 × 13.6 × 4.7)*
Main machinery: 2 Russkiy SEMT-Pielstick 6 PC2.5 L 400 diesels; 7,020 hp(m) *(5.2 MW)* sustained; 1 shaft; bow thruster; 1,500 hp(m) *(1.1 MW)*
Speed, knots: 19. **Range, miles:** 7,000 at 19 kt
Complement: 42
Radars: Navigation: Furuno; I-band.
Helicopters: 2 Helix type for SAR.

Comment: Built by Danyard A/S for the Ministry of Fisheries. Contract signed in December 1987 and the ships were completed between August 1989 and April 1990. The hull is ice strengthened. The helicopter deck has a lift serving the double hangar below. Based in the Pacific. *VERIFIED*

HERLUF BIDSTRUP   5/1992, 92 Wing RAAF

1 MUSTANG-2 CLASS (FISHERY CONTROL CRAFT)

MUSTANG-2

Displacement, tons: 36 full load
Dimensions, feet (metres): 65.6 × 14.8 × 3.6 *(20 × 4.5 × 1.1)*
Main machinery: 2 Zvezda M470 diesels; 2,992 hp(m) *(2.2 MW)*; 2 Kamewa FF550 waterjets
Speed, knots: 45. **Range, miles:** 350 at 40 kt
Complement: 10

Comment: Built by Redan Shipyard, St Petersburg and delivered in November 1998 for use in the Baltic. More may be ordered. *VERIFIED*

CUSTOMS

Note: Five air cushioned craft built at Kharbarovsk Shipyard. These 50 kt craft are for use in the Pacific Fleet. First one delivered in September 1998, remainder in 1999.

3 MIRAZH (TYPE 14310) CLASS
(FAST ATTACK CRAFT—PATROL) (PCF)

P 201   P 202   P 203

Displacement, tons: 126 full load
Dimensions, feet (metres): 111.5 × 21.7 × 8.9 *(34 × 6.6 × 2.7)*
Main machinery: 2 M 521 diesels; 16,184 hp(m) *(11.9 MW)*; 2 shafts
Speed, knots: 48. **Range, miles:** 1,500 at 8 kt
Complement: 12 (2 officers)
Guns: 1—30 mm AK 306.
    2—7.62 mm MGs.
Radars: Surface search: I-band.

Comment: Series production being built by Vympel Shipbuilding in Rybinsk on the Volga. First one completed final trials in late 1996. Deliveries slowed by lack of funds. Hard chine hull. Accommodation is air conditioned. A portable SAM twin launcher can be set up aft with six reloads. The missile is capable of firing to 3,500 m height and has a range of 5 km. There is also a luxury motor cruiser version of this craft for export, and numerous Customs craft and launchers. *VERIFIED*

MIRAZH type   4/1997 / 0050087

ST KITTS-NEVIS

Headquarters Appointments	General	Bases	Personnel	Mercantile Marine
Commanding Officer Coast Guard: Major Patrick Wallace	Formerly part of the Police Force, but from 1 October 1997 transferred to the Regular Corps of the Defence Force.	Basseterre	2000: 45	*Lloyd's Register of Shipping:* 1 vessel of 300 tons

COAST GUARD

Note: There is also a 40 kt RIB number *C 420*.

1 SWIFTSHIPS 110 ft CLASS (PC)

STALWART C 253

Displacement, tons: 100 normal
Dimensions, feet (metres): 116.5 × 25 × 7 *(35.5 × 7.6 × 2.1)*
Main machinery: 4 Detroit 12V-71TA diesels; 1,680 hp *(1.25 MW)* sustained; 4 shafts
Speed, knots: 21. **Range, miles:** 1,800 at 15 kt
Complement: 14
Guns: 2—12.7 mm MGs. 2—7.62 mm MGs.
Radars: Surface search: Raytheon; I-band.
Navigation: Furuno; I-band

Comment: Built by Swiftships, Morgan City, and delivered August 1985. Aluminium alloy hull and superstructure. *VERIFIED*

STALWART   3/1998 / 0050088

1 DAUNTLESS CLASS (PB)

ARDENT C 421

Displacement, tons: 11 full load
Dimensions, feet (metres): 40 × 14 × 4.3 *(12.2 × 4.3 × 1.3)*
Main machinery: 2 Caterpillar 3208TA diesels; 870 hp *(650 kW)*; 2 shafts
Speed, knots: 27. **Range, miles:** 600 at 18 kt
Complement: 4
Guns: 1—7.62 mm MG.
Radars: Surface search: Raytheon; I-band.

Comment: Built by SeaArk Marine under FMS funding and commissioned 8 August 1995. *UPDATED*

ARDENT   8/1996*, St Kitts-Nevis Police / 0081725

1 FAIREY MARINE SPEAR CLASS (PB)

RANGER I

Displacement, tons: 4.3 full load
Dimensions, feet (metres): 29.8 × 9.5 × 2.8 *(9.1 × 2.8 × 0.9)*
Main machinery: 2 Ford Mermaid diesels; 360 hp *(268 kW)*; 2 shafts
Speed, knots: 20
Complement: 2
Guns: Mountings for 2—7.62 mm MGs.

Comment: Ordered for the police in June 1974—delivered 10 September 1974. Refitted 1986. Considerably slower than when new but still in service.

UPDATED

RANGER I   *1992*, St Kitts-Nevis Police* / 0081726

2 BOSTON WHALERS (PB)

ROVER I C 087   ROVER II C 088

Displacement, tons: 3 full load
Dimensions, feet (metres): 22 × 7.5 × 2 *(6.7 × 2.3 × 0.6)*
Main machinery: 1 Johnson outboard; 223 hp *(166 kW)*
Speed, knots: 35. **Range, miles:** 70 at 35 kt
Complement: 2

Comment: Delivered in May 1988.

UPDATED

ROVER I   *1990*, St Kitts-Nevis Police* / 0081727

ST LUCIA

Headquarters Appointments	Bases	Personnel	Mercantile Marine	DELETIONS
Coast Guard Commander: Superintendent André Cox	Castries, Vieux-Fort	2000: 49	*Lloyd's Register of Shipping:* 5 vessels of 1,421 tons gross	1997 *Vigilant II*

COAST GUARD

1 POINT CLASS (PC)

ALPHONSE REYNOLDS (ex-*Point Turner*)   P 01 (ex-WPB 82365)

Displacement, tons: 66 full load
Dimensions, feet (metres): 83 × 17.2 × 5.8 *(25.3 × 5.2 × 1.8)*
Main machinery: 2 Caterpillar 3412 diesels; 1,600 hp *(1.19 MW)*; 2 shafts
Speed, knots: 23. **Range, miles:** 1,500 at 8 kt
Complement: 10
Guns: 2—12.7 mm MGs.
Radars: Surface search: Raytheon SPS-64(V)1; I-band.

Comment: Ex-US Coast Guard ship transferred on 3 April 1998. Originally built at Curtis Bay and first commissioned 14 April 1967.

UPDATED

ALPHONSE REYNOLDS   *10/1999*, St Lucia CG* / 0081728

1 SWIFT 65 ft CLASS (PC)

DEFENDER P 02

Displacement, tons: 42 full load
Dimensions, feet (metres): 64.9 × 18.4 × 6.6 *(19.8 × 5.6 × 2)*
Main machinery: 2 Detroit 12V-71 diesels; 680 hp *(507 kW)* sustained; 2 shafts
Speed, knots: 22. **Range, miles:** 1,500 at 18 kt
Complement: 7
Radars: Surface search: Furuno; I-band.

Comment: Ordered from Swiftships, Morgan City in November 1983. Commissioned 3 May 1984. Similar to craft supplied to Antigua and Dominica. Has a blue hull and white superstructure. New radar in 1997.

UPDATED

DEFENDER   *10/1999*, St Lucia CG* / 0081729

1 DAUNTLESS CLASS

PROTECTOR P 04

Displacement, tons: 11 full load
Dimensions, feet (metres): 40 × 14 × 4.3 *(12.2 × 4.3 × 1.3)*
Main machinery: 2 Caterpillar 3208TA diesels; 870 hp *(650 kW)*; 2 shafts
Speed, knots: 27. **Range, miles:** 600 at 18 kt
Complement: 4
Radars: Surface search: Raytheon; I-band.

Comment: Ordered October 1994. Built by SeaArk Marine under FMS funding and commissioned 9 October 1995.
UPDATED

PROTECTOR (alongside *Defender*)   *7/1997*, St Lucia CG* / 0019078

4 HARBOUR CRAFT

P 03   P 05   P 06   P 07

Comment: P 03 is a 35 kt Boston Whaler acquired in July 1988. P 05 is a 35 kt Hurricane RIB acquired in June 1993 and P 06 and P 07 are 45 kt Mako craft acquired in November 1995.
UPDATED

P 07   7/1997*, St Lucia CG / 0019080

P 05   7/1997*, St Lucia CG / 0019081

ST VINCENT AND THE GRENADINES

Headquarters Appointments	Bases	Personnel	Mercantile Marine
Coast Guard Commander: Lieutenant Commander D V Robin	Calliaqua	2000: 60	*Lloyd's Register of Shipping:* 1,333 vessels of 7,105,479 tons gross

COAST GUARD

1 SWIFTSHIPS 120 ft CLASS (PC)

CAPTAIN MULZAC SVG 01

Displacement, tons: 101
Dimensions, feet (metres): 120 × 25 × 7 (36.6 × 7.6 × 2.1)
Main machinery: 4 Detroit 12V-71TA diesels; 1,360 hp (1.01 MW) sustained; 4 shafts
Speed, knots: 21. **Range, miles:** 1,800 at 15 kt
Complement: 14 (4 officers)
Guns: 2—12.7 mm MGs. 2—7.62 mm MGs.
Radars: Surface search: Furuno 1411 Mk II; I/J-band.

Comment: Ordered in August 1986. Built by Swiftships, Morgan City and delivered 13 June 1987. Carries a RIB with a 40 hp outboard. **UPDATED**

CAPTAIN MULZAC   6/1994*, St Vincent Coast Guard / 0081730

1 VOSPER THORNYCROFT 75 ft CLASS (PC)

GEORGE McINTOSH SVG 05

Displacement, tons: 70 full load
Dimensions, feet (metres): 75 × 19.5 × 8 (22.9 × 6 × 2.4)
Main machinery: 2 Caterpillar D 348 diesels; 1,450 hp (1.08 MW) sustained; 2 shafts
Speed, knots: 24.5. **Range, miles:** 1,000 at 11 kt; 600 at 20 kt
Complement: 11 (3 officers)
Guns: 1 Oerlikon 20 mm.
Radars: Surface search: Furuno 1411 Mk III; I/J-band.

Comment: Handed over 23 March 1981. GRP hull. **UPDATED**

GEORGE McINTOSH   6/1992*, St Vincent Coast Guard / 0081731

1 DAUNTLESS CLASS (PB)

HAIROUN SVG 04

Displacement, tons: 11 full load
Dimensions, feet (metres): 40 × 14 × 4.3 (12.2 × 4.3 × 1.3)
Main machinery: 2 Caterpillar 3208TA diesels; 870 hp (650 kW); 2 shafts
Speed, knots: 27. **Range, miles:** 600 at 18 kt
Complement: 4
Guns: 1—7.62 mm MG.
Radars: Surface search: Raytheon; I-band.

Comment: Ordered October 1984. Built by SeaArk Marine under FMS funding and commissioned 8 June 1995. **UPDATED**

HAIROUN   7/1997* / 0019082

4 HARBOUR CRAFT

SVG 03   **LARIKAI** SVG 06   **BRIGHTON** SVG 07   **CHATHAM BAY** SVG 08

Comment: SVG 03 is a 30 kt Zodiac RIB. SVG 06 and 07 are 23 kt Buhler craft acquired in 1991. SVG 08 is a 30 kt Boston Whaler acquired in 1994. The Buhler craft are in poor condition.
UPDATED

BRIGHTON   6/1991*, St Vincent Coast Guard / 0081732

SAUDI ARABIA

Headquarters Appointments

Chief of Naval Staff:
  Vice Admiral Talal Salem Al Mofadhi
Commander Eastern Fleet:
  Rear Admiral Mohammad Abdul Khalij Al Asseri
Commander Western Fleet:
  Rear Admiral Muhammad Abdullah Al-Ajalen
Director Frontier Force (Coast Guard):
  Lieutenant General Mujib bin Muhammad Al-Qahtani

Personnel

(a) 2000: 13,500 officers and men (including 1,500 marines)
(b) Voluntary service

Bases

Naval HQ: Riyadh
Main bases: Jiddah (HQ Western Fleet), Al Jubail (HQ Eastern Fleet), Aziziah (Coast Guard). Jizan (Red Sea) building from May 1996
Minor bases (Naval and Coast Guard): Ras Tanura, Al Dammam, Yanbo, Ras al-Mishab, Al Wajh, Al Qatif, Haqi, Al Sharmah, Qizan, Duba

General

Funding for the Navy has the lowest defence service priority. New programmes are slow to come forward, and the operational status of existing ships is very variable.

Command and Control

The USA provided an update of command and control capabilities during the period 1991-95, including a commercial datalink to improve interoperability.

Coast Defence

Truck-mounted Otomat batteries.

Coast Guard

Part of the Frontier Force under the Minister for Defence and Aviation. 5,500 officers and men. It is not always clear which ships belong to the Navy and which to the Coast Guard.

Strength of the Fleet

Type	Active	Building
Frigates	4	3
Corvettes—Missile	4	—
Fast Attack Craft—Missile	9	—
Patrol Craft	56	—
Minehunters	3	—
Minesweepers—Coastal	4	—
Replenishment Tankers	2	—

Mercantile Marine

Lloyd's Register of Shipping:
  272 vessels of 1,207,508 tons gross

SUBMARINES

Notes: (1) Orders for patrol submarines are a low priority although training has been done in France and Pakistan.
(2) Previous reports of Midget Submarines being acquired are not correct, although there is much interest.

FRIGATES

HOFOUF

11/1997*, J Y Robert / 0019083

4 MADINA (TYPE F 2000S) CLASS (FFG)

Name	No	Builders	Laid down	Launched	Commissioned
MADINA	702	Lorient (DTCN)	15 Oct 1981	23 Apr 1983	4 Jan 1985
HOFOUF	704	CNIM, Seyne-sur-Mer	14 June 1982	24 June 1983	31 Oct 1985
ABHA	706	CNIM, Seyne-sur-Mer	7 Dec 1982	23 Dec 1983	4 Apr 1986
TAIF	708	CNIM, Seyne-sur-Mer	1 Mar 1983	25 May 1984	29 Aug 1986

Displacement, tons: 2,000 standard; 2,870 full load
Dimensions, feet (metres): 377.3 × 41 × 16 (sonar)
   (115 × 12.5 × 4.9)
Main machinery: CODAD; 4 SEMT-Pielstick 16 PA6 280V BTC
   diesels; 38,400 hp(m) *(28 MW)* sustained; 2 shafts
Speed, knots: 30
Range, miles: 8,000 at 15 kt; 6,500 at 18 kt
Complement: 179 (15 officers)

Missiles: SSM: 8 OTO Melara/Matra Otomat Mk 2 (2 quad) ❶;
   active radar homing to 160 km *(86.4 n miles)* at 0.9 Mach;
   warhead 210 kg; sea-skimmer for last 4 km *(2.2 n miles)*.
   ERATO system allows mid-course guidance by ship's
   helicopter.
SAM: Thomson-CSF Crotale Naval octuple launcher ❷;
   command line of sight guidance; radar/IR homing to 13 km
   (7 n miles) at 2.4 Mach; warhead 14 kg; 26 missiles.
Guns: 1 Creusot-Loire 3.9 in *(100 mm)*/55 compact Mk 2 ❸; 20/
   45/90 rds/min to 17 km *(9.3 n miles)* weight of shell 13.5 kg.
   4 Breda 40 mm/70 (2 twin) ❹; 300 rds/min to 12.5 km *(6.8 n
   miles)*; weight of shell 0.96 kg.
Torpedoes: 4—21 in *(533 mm)* tubes ❺. ECAN F17P; anti-
   submarine; wire-guided; active/passive homing to 20 km
   (10.8 n miles) at 40 kt; warhead 250 kg.
Countermeasures: Decoys: CSEE Dagaie double trainable
   mounting ❻; IR flares and chaff; H/J-band.
ESM: Thomson-CSF DR 4000; intercept; HF/DF.
ECM: Thomson-CSF Janet; jammer.

Combat data systems: Thomson-CSF TAVITAC action data
   automation; capability for Link W.
Weapons control: Vega system. 3 CSEE Naja optronic directors.
   Alcatel DLT for torpedoes.
Radars: Air/surface search/IFF: Thomson-CSF Sea Tiger (DRBV
   15) ❼; E/F-band; range 110 km *(60 n miles)* for 2 m² target.
   Navigation: 2 Racal Decca TM 1226; I-band.
Fire control: Thomson-CSF Castor IIB/C ❽; I/J-band; range 15 km
   (8 n miles) for 1 m² target.
   Thomson-CSF DRBC 32 ❾; I/J-band (for SAM).
Sonars: Thomson Sintra Diodon TSM 2630; hull-mounted;
   active search and attack with integrated Sorel VDS ❿; 11, 12
   or 13 kHz.

Helicopters: 1 SA 365F Dauphin 2 ⓫.

Programmes: Ordered in 1980, the major part of the Sawari I
   contract. Agreement for France to provide supplies and
   technical help.
Modernisation: The class are being upgraded. The work is being
   done by DCN Toulon, *Madina* completed in April 1997. *Hofouf*
   in mid-1998. *Abha* in late 1999, and *Taif* in mid-2000.
   Improvements include updating TAVITAC, Otomat missiles,
   both sonars and fitting a Samahé 110 helo handling system.
Structure: Fitted with Snach/Saphir folding fin stabilisers.
Operational: Navigation: CSEE Sylosat. Helicopter can provide
   mid-course guidance for SSM. All based at Jiddah. Only a few
   weeks a year are spent at sea.

UPDATED

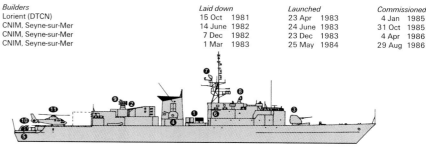

MADINA   *(Scale 1 : 1,200), Ian Sturton*

MADINA   *11/1999 * / 0084278*

0 + 3 ARRIYAD (MODIFIED LA FAYETTE) CLASS (TYPE F-3000S) (FFG)

Name	No	Builders	Laid down	Launched	Commissioned
ARRIYAD	812	DCN, Lorient	29 Sep 1999	June 2000	July 2002
—	814	DCN, Lorient	June 2000	Apr 2001	June 2003
—	816	DCN, Lorient	Feb 2001	Jan 2003	Mar 2005

Displacement, tons: 4,650 full load
Dimensions, feet (metres): 436.4 × 56.4 × 13.5
   (133 × 17.2 × 4.1)
Main machinery: CODAD; 4 SEMT-Pielstick 16 PA6 STC diesels;
   28,000 hp(m) *(20.58 MW)* sustained; 2 shafts; acbLIPS cp
   props; bow thruster
Speed, knots: 25. **Range, miles:** 7,000 at 15 kt
Complement: 181 (25 officers)

Missiles: SSM: 8 Aerospatiale MM 40 Block II Exocet ❶; inertial
   cruise; active radar homing to 70 km *(40 n miles)* at 0.9 Mach;
   warhead 165 kg; sea-skimmer.
SAM: Eurosam SAAM ❷; 2 octuple Sylver VLS for Aster 15;
   command guidance active radar homing to 15 km *(8.1 n miles)*
   anti-missile, at 30 km *(16.2 n miles)* anti-aircraft. 16 missiles.
   2 twin Sadral launchers may be fitted on hangar roof.

Guns: 1 Giat Industries 3.9 in *(100 mm)*/55 Compact Mk 2 ❸;
   90 rds/min to 17.4 km *(9.4 n miles)*; weight of shell 13.5 kg.
   2 Giat 15A 20 mm ❹; 800 rds/min to 3 km; weight of shell
   0.1 kg.
   2—12.7 mm MGs.
Torpedoes: 4—21 in *(533 mm)* tubes; ECAN F17P; anti-
   submarine; wire-guided active/passive homing to 20 km
   (10.8 n miles) at 40 kt; warhead 250 kg.
Countermeasures: Decoys: 2 Matra Dagaie Mk 2 ❺; 10-
   barrelled trainable launchers; chaff and IR flares. SLAT anti-
   wake homing torpedoes system (when available).
ESM: Thomson-CSF (DR 3000-S2) ❻; intercept. Sagem Telegon
   10.
ECM: 2 CSEE Salamandre; jammers.
Combat data systems: Thomson-CSF TAVITAC 2000. OPSMER
   Senit 7 combat support system. Link W.

Weapons control: Thomson-CSF CTM radar/IR system.
   2 Sagem VIGY-105 optronic directors.
Radars: Air search: Thomson-CSF DRBV 26C Jupiter II ❼;
   D-band.
   Surveillance/Fire control: Thomson-CSF Arabel 3D ❽; I/J-band.
   Fire control: Thomson-CSF Castor II UJ ❾; J-band; range 15 km
   (8 n miles) for 1 m² target.
   Navigation: 2 Racal Decca 1226 ❿; I-band. A second set fitted
   for helicopter control.
Sonars: Thomson Marconi CAPTAS 20; active low frequency;
   towed array.

Helicopters: 1 Aerospatiale SA 365 Dauphin 2 ⓫.

Programmes: A provisional order was made on 11 June 1989,
   but this was not finally confirmed until 22 November 1994
   when a contract for two ships was authorised under the Sawari
   II programme. Thomson-CSF is the prime contractor. On 25
   May 1997 an order for a third ship was placed together with a
   substantial enhancement of the weapon systems in all three.
   First steel cut 13 December 1997.
Structure: The design has changed considerably from the basic
   French *La Fayette*, and changed again since the contract was
   first signed in 1994. Space and weight included for two more
   octuple SAM launchers. Provision is made for a larger NH 90
   type helicopter in the future, DCN Samahé helo handling
   system. STAF stabilisers.
Operational: OTHT link for helicopters and Air Force F-15s.

UPDATED

ARRIYAD   *(Scale 1 : 1,200), Ian Sturton / 0019084*

CORVETTES

4 BADR CLASS (FSG)

Name	No	Builders	Laid down		Launched		Commissioned	
BADR	612	Tacoma Boatbuilding Co, Tacoma	6 Oct	1979	26 Jan	1980	30 Nov	1980
AL YARMOOK	614	Tacoma Boatbuilding Co, Tacoma	3 Jan	1980	13 May	1980	18 May	1981
HITTEEN	616	Tacoma Boatbuilding Co, Tacoma	19 May	1980	5 Sep	1980	3 Oct	1981
TABUK	618	Tacoma Boatbuilding Co, Tacoma	22 Sep	1980	18 June	1981	10 Jan	1983

Displacement, tons: 870 standard; 1,038 full load
Dimensions, feet (metres): 245 × 31.5 × 8.9
 (74.7 × 9.6 × 2.7)
Main machinery: CODOG; 1 GE LM 2500 gas turbine; 23,000 hp
 (17.2 MW) sustained; 2 MTU 12V 652 TB91 diesels; 3,470 hp
 (m) (2.55 MW) sustained; 2 shafts; cp props
Speed, knots: 30 gas; 20 diesels. **Range, miles:** 4,000 at 20 kt
Complement: 58 (7 officers)

Missiles: SSM: 8 McDonnell Douglas Harpoon (2 quad)
 launchers ❶; active radar homing to 130 km (70 n miles) at
 0.9 Mach; warhead 227 kg.
Guns: 1 FMC/OTO Melara 3 in (76 mm)/62 Mk 75 Mod 0 ❷;
 85 rds/min to 16 km (8.7 n miles); weight of shell 6 kg.
 1 General Electric/General Dynamics 20 mm 6-barrelled
 Vulcan Phalanx ❸; 3,000 rds/min combined to 2 km.
 2 Oerlikon 20 mm/80 ❹.
 1—81 mm mortar. 2—40 mm Mk 19 grenade launchers.
Torpedoes: 6—324 mm US Mk 32 (2 triple) tubes ❺. Honeywell
 Mk 46; anti-submarine; active/passive homing to 11 km (5.9 n
 miles) at 40 kt; warhead 44 kg.
Countermeasures: Decoys: 2 Loral Hycor SRBOC 6-barrelled
 fixed Mk 36 ❻; IR flares and chaff to 4 km (2.2 n miles).
 ESM: SLQ-32(V)1 ❼; intercept.
Weapons control: Mk 24 optical director ❽. Mk 309 for
 torpedoes. Mk 92 Mod 5 GFCS. FSI Safire FLIR.
Radars: Air search: Lockheed SPS-40B ❾; E/F-band; range
 320 km (175 n miles).
Surface search: ISC Cardion SPS-55 ❿; I/J-band.
Fire control: Sperry Mk 92 ⓫; I/J-band.
Sonars: Raytheon SQS-56 (DE 1164); hull-mounted; active
 search and attack; medium frequency.

Modernisation: Refitting done in Saudi Arabia with US
 assistance. FLIR being fitted from 1998.
Structure: Fitted with fin stabilisers.
Operational: All based at Al Jubail on the east coast and spend
 little time at sea.

VERIFIED

BADR   (Scale 1 : 600), Ian Sturton

AL YARMOOK   2/1997, van Ginderen Collection / 0019085

PATROL FORCES

9 AL SIDDIQ CLASS (PCFG)

Name	No	Builders	Launched		Commissioned	
AL SIDDIQ	511	Peterson, WI	22 Sep	1979	15 Dec	1980
AL FAROUQ	513	Peterson, WI	17 May	1980	22 June	1981
ABDUL AZIZ	515	Peterson, WI	23 Aug	1980	3 Sep	1981
FAISAL	517	Peterson, WI	15 Nov	1980	23 Nov	1981
KHALID	519	Peterson, WI	23 Mar	1981	11 Jan	1982
AMYR	521	Peterson, WI	13 June	1981	21 June	1982
TARIQ	523	Peterson, WI	23 Sep	1981	11 Aug	1982
OQBAH	525	Peterson, WI	12 Dec	1981	18 Oct	1982
ABU OBAIDAH	527	Peterson, WI	3 Apr	1982	6 Dec	1982

Displacement, tons: 495 full load
Dimensions, feet (metres): 190.5 × 26.5 × 6.6
 (58.1 × 8.1 × 2)
Main machinery: CODOG; 1 GE LM 2500 gas turbine; 23,000 hp
 (17.2 MW) sustained; 2 MTU 12V 652 TB91 diesels; 3,470 hp
 (m) (2.55 MW) sustained; 2 shafts; cp props
Speed, knots: 38 gas; 25 diesel. **Range, miles:** 2,900 at 14 kt
Complement: 38 (5 officers)

Missiles: SSM: 4 McDonnell Douglas Harpoon (2 twin)
 launchers; active radar homing to 130 km (70 n miles) at
 0.9 Mach; warhead 227 kg.

Guns: 1 FMC/OTO Melara 3 in (76 mm)/62 Mk 75 Mod 0;
 85 rds/min to 16 km (8.7 n miles); weight of shell 6 kg.
 1 General Electric/General Dynamics 20 mm 6-barrelled
 Vulcan Phalanx; 3,000 rds/min combined to 2 km.
 2 Oerlikon 20 mm/80; 800 rds/min to 2 km anti-aircraft.
 2—81 mm mortars. 2—40 mm Mk 19 grenade launchers.
Countermeasures: Decoys: 2 Loral Hycor SRBOC 6-barrelled
 fixed Mk 36; IR flares and chaff to 4 km (2.2 n miles).
 ESM: SLQ-32(V)1; intercept.
Weapons control: Mk 92 mod 5 GFCS. FSI Safire FLIR. Link W.

Radars: Surface search: ISC Cardion SPS-55; I/J-band.
Fire control: Sperry Mk 92; I/J-band.

Modernisation: Safire FLIR and Link W being fitted.
Operational: *Amyr* and *Tariq* operate from Jiddah, the remainder
 are based at Al Jubail. *Faisal* damaged in the Gulf War in 1991
 and was operational again in 1994.

UPDATED

AL FAROUQ   1/1997* / 0080562

17 HALTER TYPE (COASTAL PATROL CRAFT) (PC)

Displacement, tons: 56 full load
Dimensions, feet (metres): 78 × 20 × 5.8 *(23.8 × 6.1 × 1.8)*
Main machinery: 2 Detroit 16V-92TA diesels; 1,380 hp *(1.03 MW)* sustained; 2 shafts
Speed, knots: 28. **Range, miles:** 1,200 at 12 kt
Complement: 8 (2 officers)
Guns: 2—25 mm Mk 38. 2—7.62 mm MGs.
Radars: Surface search: Raytheon SPS-64; I-band.

Comment: Ordered from Halter Marine 17th February 1991. Last delivered in January 1993. Same type for Philippines.   **UPDATED**

HALTER TYPE   *8/1990*, Trinity Marine /* 0080563

39 SIMMONEAU 51 TYPE (INSHORE PATROL CRAFT) (PB)

Displacement, tons: 22 full load
Dimensions, feet (metres): 51.8 × 15.7 × 5.9 *(15.8 × 4.8 × 1.8)*
Main machinery: 4 outboards; 2,400 hp(m) *(1.76 MW)*
Speed, knots: 33. **Range, miles:** 375 at 25 kt
Guns: 1—12.7 mm MG. 2—7.62 mm MGs.
Radars: Surface search: Furuno; I-band.

Comment: First 20 ordered from France in June 1988 and delivered in 1989-90. A second batch of 20 ordered in 1991. Used by naval commandos. These craft were also reported as Panhards. One deleted so far.   **VERIFIED**

SIMMONEAU TYPE   *1989, Simmoneau Marine*

SHIPBORNE AIRCRAFT

Numbers/Type: 15/6 Aerospatiale SA 365F/N Dauphin 2.
Operational speed: 140 kt *(260 km/h).*
Service ceiling: 15,000 ft *(4,575 m).*
Range: 410 n miles *(758 km).*
Role/Weapon systems: SA 365F is the ASV/ASW helicopter; procured for embarked naval aviation force; surface search/attack is the primary role. Sensors: Thomson-CSF Agrion 15 radar; Crouzet MAD. Weapons: ASV; four AS/15TT missiles. ASW; 2 Mk 46 torpedoes. SA 365N is for SAR. Sensors: Omera DRB 32 search radar. Weapons: Unarmed.   **UPDATED**

LAND-BASED MARITIME AIRCRAFT

Notes: (1) Six P-3C Orion or CASA CN-235 may be acquired in due course.
(2) Five Boeing E3-A AEW aircraft in service with Air Force.

Numbers/Type: 18 Aerospatiale AS 332SC Super Puma.
Operational speed: 150 kt *(280 km/h).*
Service ceiling: 15,090 ft *(4,600 m).*
Range: 335 n miles *(620 km).*
Role/Weapon systems: First pair delivered in August 1989. Total of 18 by the end of 1996. Shared with the Coast Guard. Sensors: 12 have Omera search radar Safire AAQ-22 FLIR from 1998. Weapons: ASV; six have Giat 20 mm cannon; 12 have AM39 Exocet or Sea Eagle ASM.   **VERIFIED**

MINE WARFARE FORCES

4 ADDRIYAH (MSC 322) CLASS
(MINESWEEPERS/HUNTERS—COASTAL) (MSC)

Name	No	Builders	Launched		Commissioned	
ADDRIYAH	MSC 412	Peterson, WI	20 Dec	1976	6 July	1978
AL QUYSUMAH	MSC 414	Peterson, WI	26 May	1977	15 Aug	1978
AL WADEEAH	MSC 416	Peterson, WI	6 Sep	1977	7 Sep	1979
SAFWA	MSC 418	Peterson, WI	7 Dec	1977	2 Oct	1979

Displacement, tons: 320 standard; 407 full load
Dimensions, feet (metres): 153 × 26.9 × 8.2 *(46.6 × 8.2 × 2.5)*
Main machinery: 2 Waukesha L1616 diesels; 1,200 hp *(895 kW)*; 2 shafts
Speed, knots: 13
Complement: 39 (4 officers)
Guns: 1 Oerlikon 20 mm.
Radars: Surface search: ISC Cardion SPS-55; I/J-band.
Sonars: GE SQQ-14; VDS; active minehunting; high frequency.

Comment: Ordered on 30 September 1975 under the International Logistics Programme. Wooden structure. Fitted with fin stabilisers, wire and magnetic sweeps and also for minehunting. *Addriyah* based at Jiddah, the remainder at Al Jubail. Expected to be replaced by arrival of Sandowns but all are still in service mostly as patrol craft.   **VERIFIED**

AL QUYSUMAH   *6/1996, van Ginderen Collection /* 0019090

3 AL JAWF (SANDOWN) CLASS
(MINEHUNTERS—COASTAL) (MHC)

Name	No	Builders	Launched		Commissioned	
AL JAWF	420	Vosper Thornycroft	2 Aug	1989	12 Dec	1991
SHAQRA	422	Vosper Thornycroft	15 May	1991	7 Feb	1993
AL KHARJ	424	Vosper Thornycroft	8 Feb	1993	7 Aug	1997

Displacement, tons: 450 standard; 480 full load
Dimensions, feet (metres): 172.9 × 34.4 × 6.9 *(52.7 × 10.5 × 2.1)*
Main machinery: 2 Paxman 6RP200E diesels; 1,500 hp *(1.12 MW)* sustained; Voith-Schneider propulsion; 2 shafts; 2 Schöttel bow thrusters
Speed, knots: 13 diesels; 6 electric drive. **Range, miles:** 3,000 at 12 kt
Complement: 34 (7 officers) plus 6 spare berths
Guns: 2 Electronics & Space Emerlec 30 mm (twin); 1,200 rds/min combined to 6 km *(3.3 n miles)*; weight of shell 0.35 kg.
Countermeasures: Decoys: 2 Loral Hycor SRBOC Mk 36 Mod 1 6-barrelled chaff launchers.
ESM: Thomson-CSF Shiploc; intercept.
MCM: ECA mine disposal system; 2 PAP 104 Mk 5.
Combat data systems: Plessey Nautis M action data automation.
Weapons control: Contraves TMEO optronic director (Seahawk Mk 2).
Radars: Navigation: Kelvin Hughes Type 1007; I-band.
Sonars: Plessey/MUSL Type 2093; VDS; high frequency.

Comment: Three ordered 2 November 1988 from Vosper Thornycroft with option for three more not taken up. GRP hulls. Combines vectored thrust units with bow thrusters and Remote Controlled Mine Disposal System (RCMDS). *Al Jawf* sailed for Saudi Arabia in November 1995, *Shaqra* in November 1996, and *Al Kharj* in August 1997. All based at Al Jubail.   **UPDATED**

AL KHARJ   *8/1997, Vosper Thornycroft /* 0050091

AUXILIARIES

2 MOD DURANCE CLASS (REPLENISHMENT SHIPS) (AOR)

Name	No	Builders	Launched		Commissioned	
BORAIDA	902	La Ciotat, Marseilles	22 Jan	1983	29 Feb	1984
YUNBOU	904	La Ciotat, Marseilles	20 Oct	1984	29 Aug	1985

Displacement, tons: 11,200 full load
Dimensions, feet (metres): 442.9 × 61.3 × 22.9 *(135 × 18.7 × 7)*
Main machinery: 2 SEMT-Pielstick 14 PC2.5 V 400 diesels; 18,200 hp(m) *(13.4 MW)* sustained; 2 shafts; acbLIPS cp props
Speed, knots: 20.5. **Range, miles:** 7,000 at 15 kt
Complement: 129 plus 11 trainees
Cargo capacity: 4,350 tons diesel; 350 tons AVCAT; 140 tons fresh water; 100 tons victuals; 100 tons ammunition; 70 tons spares
Guns: 4 Breda Bofors 40 mm/70 (2 twin); 300 rds/min to 12.5 km *(6.8 n miles)*; weight of shell 0.96 kg.
Weapons control: 2 CSEE Naja optronic directors. 2 CSEE Lynx optical sights.
Radars: Navigation: 2 Decca; I-band.
Helicopters: 2 SA 365 F Dauphin or 1 AS 332SC Super Puma.

Comment: Contract signed October 1980 as part of Sawari I programme. Both upgraded by DCN at Toulon; *Boraida* in 1996/97, followed by *Yunbou*, in 1997/98. Refuelling positions: Two alongside, one astern. Also serve as training ships and as depot and maintenance ships. Helicopters can have ASM or ASW armament. Both based at Jiddah.   **UPDATED**

BORAIDA   *1/1998* /* 0016635

4 LCU 1610 CLASS (TRANSPORTS) (YFU)

AL QIAQ (ex-SA 310) 212		AL ULA (ex-SA 312) 216	
AL SULAYEL (ex-SA 311) 214		AFIF (ex-SA 313) 218	

Displacement, tons: 375 full load
Dimensions, feet (metres): 134.9 × 29 × 6.1 (41.1 × 8.8 × 1.9)
Main machinery: 4 GM diesels; 1,000 hp (746 kW); 2 Kort nozzles
Speed, knots: 11. **Range, miles:** 1,200 at 8 kt
Complement: 14 (2 officers)
Military lift: 170 tons; 20 troops
Guns: 2—12.7 mm MGs.
Radars: Navigation: Marconi LN66; I-band.

Comment: Built by Newport Shipyard, Rhode Island. Transferred from USA June/July 1976. Based at Al Jubail.
UPDATED

LCU 1610 (US colours)   9/1997*, Hachiro Nakai / 0016483

4 LCM 6 CLASS (TRANSPORTS) (YFU)

DHEBA 220	UMLUS 222	AL LEETH 224	AL QUONFETHA 226

Displacement, tons: 62 full load
Dimensions, feet (metres): 56.2 × 14 × 3.9 (17.1 × 4.3 × 1.2)
Main machinery: 2 GM diesels; 450 hp (336 kW); 2 shafts
Speed, knots: 9. **Range, miles:** 130 at 9 kt
Complement: 5
Military lift: 34 tons or 80 troops
Guns: 2—40 mm Mk 19 grenade launchers.

Comment: Four transferred July 1977 and four in July 1980. The first four have been cannibalised for spares. Based at Jiddah.
VERIFIED

TUGS

13 COASTAL TUGS (YTB/YTM)

RADHWA 1-6, 14-15	TUWAIG 113	DAREEN 111	RADHWA 12, 16, 17

Comment: Radhwa 12, 16 and 17 are 43 m YTMs built in 1982-83. Tuwaig and Dareen are ex-US YTB transferred in October 1975. These two are used to tow targets for weapons firing exercises and are based at Al Jubail and Damman respectively. The remainder are all of about 35 m built in Singapore and the Netherlands between 1981 and 1983.
UPDATED

YTB TYPE (US colours)   9/1992*, Jürg Kürsener / 0080564

ROYAL YACHTS

Note: There is also a Royal Yacht in the Coast Guard section.

Name	No	Builders	Commissioned
AL YAMAMAH	—	Elsinore, Denmark	Feb 1981

Displacement, tons: 1,660 full load
Dimensions, feet (metres): 269 × 42.7 × 10.8 (82 × 13 × 3.3)
Main machinery: 2 MTU 12V 1163 TB82 diesels; 6,000 hp(m) (4.41 MW); 2 shafts; cp props; bow thruster; 300 hp(m) (221 kW)
Speed, knots: 19
Complement: 42 plus 56 spare
Helicopters: Platform for 1 medium.

Comment: Ordered by Iraq but not delivered because of the war with Iran. Given to Saudi Arabia by Iraq in 1988. Based at Dammam.
VERIFIED

1 PEGASUS CLASS (HYDROFOIL)

AL AZIZIAH

Displacement, tons: 115 full load
Dimensions, feet (metres): 89.9 × 29.9 × 6.2 (27.4 × 9.1 × 1.9)
Main machinery: 2 Allison 501-KF20A gas turbines; 8,660 hp (6.46 MW) sustained; 2 waterjets (foilborne); 2 Detroit 8V92 diesels; 606 hp (452 kW) sustained; 2 shafts (hullborne)
Speed, knots: 46. **Range, miles:** 890 at 42 kt
Guns: 2 General Electric 20 mm Sea Vulcan.
Weapons control: Kollmorgen GFCS; Mk 35 optronic director.

Comment: Ordered in 1984 from Lockheed and subcontracted to Boeing, Seattle; delivered in August 1985. Mostly used as a tender to the Royal Yacht.
VERIFIED

COAST GUARD

2 SEA GUARD CLASS (PCF)

AL RIYADH 304	ZULURAB 305

Displacement, tons: 56 full load
Dimensions, feet (metres): 73.8 × 18.4 × 5.6 (22.5 × 5.6 × 1.7)
Main machinery: 2 MTU 12V 331 TC92 diesels; 2,920 hp(m) (21.46 MW); 2 shafts
Speed, knots: 35
Complement: 10
Guns: 2 Giat 20 mm (twin). 2—7.62 mm MGs.
Radars: Surface search: Racal Decca; I-band.
Fire control: Thomson-CSF Agrion; J-band.

Comment: Built by Simonneau Marine and delivered by SOFREMA in April 1992. Aluminium construction. Both based at Jiddah. The SSM launcher shown in the picture is not fitted.
UPDATED

ZULURAB   1992*, Simonneau Marine / 0080565

4 AL JOUF CLASS (PCF)

AL JOUF 351	TURAIF 352	HAIL 353	NAJRAN 354

Displacement, tons: 210 full load
Dimensions, feet (metres): 126.6 × 26.2 × 6.2 (38.6 × 8 × 1.9)
Main machinery: 3 MTU 16 V 538 TB93 diesels; 11,265 hp(m) (8.28 MW) sustained; 3 shafts
Speed, knots: 38. **Range, miles:** 1,700 at 15 kt
Complement: 20 (4 officers)
Guns: 2 Oerlikon GAM-BO1 20 mm. 2—12.7 mm MGs.
Radars: Surface search: Racal S 1690 ARPA; I-band.
Navigation: Racal Decca RM 1290A; I-band.

Comment: Ordered on 18 October 1987 from Blohm + Voss. First two completed 15 June 1989; second pair 20 August 1989. Steel hulls with aluminium superstructure. Hail and Najran based at Jiddah in the Red Sea and the others at Aziziah.
UPDATED

AL JOUF   6/1989*, Blohm + Voss / 0080566

2 AL JUBATEL CLASS (PCF)

AL JUBATEL	SALWA

Displacement, tons: 95 full load
Dimensions, feet (metres): 86 × 19 × 6.9 (26.2 × 5.8 × 2.1)
Main machinery: 2 MTU 16V 396 TB94 diesels; 5,800 hp(m) (4.26 MW) sustained; 2 shafts
Speed, knots: 34. **Range, miles:** 1,100 at 25 kt
Complement: 12 (4 officers)
Guns: 1 Oerlikon/GAM-BO1 20 mm. 2—12.7 mm MGs.
Radars: Surface search: Racal Decca AC 1290; I-band.

Comment: Built by Abeking & Rasmussen, completed in April 1987. Smaller version of Turkish SAR 33 Type. One based at Jizan and one at Al Wajh.
UPDATED

AL JUBATEL   1987*, Abeking & Rasmussen / 0080567

3 SLINGSBY SAH 2200 HOVERCRAFT

Dimensions, feet (metres): 34.8 × 13.8 *(10.6 × 4.2)*
Main machinery: 1 Deutz BF6L913C diesel; 192 hp(m) *(141 kW)* sustained; lift and propulsion
Speed, knots: 40. **Range, miles:** 500 at 40 kt
Complement: 2
Military lift: 2.2 tons or 16 troops
Guns: 1—7.62 mm MG.

Comment: Supplied by Slingsby Amphibious Hovercraft, York in December 1990. Have Kevlar armour. These craft have replaced the SRN type. Five more may be acquired in due course.
UPDATED

SAH 2200   *1990*, Slingsby /* 0080568

INSHORE PATROL CRAFT (PB)

Type	Date	Speed
Rapier 15.2 m	1976	28
Enforcer, USA, 9.4 m	1980s	30
Simonneau SM 331, 9.3 m	1992	40
Boston Whalers, 8.3 m	1980s	30
Catamarans, 6.4 m	1977	30
Task Force Boats, 5.25 m	1976	20
Viper, 5.1 m	1980s	25
Cobra, 3.9 m	1984	40

Comment: About 500 mostly Task Force Boats. Many are based at Jiddah with the rest spread around the other bases. Most are armed with MGs and the larger craft have I-band radars.
UPDATED

SIMONNEAU SM 331   *6/1992*, Simonneau Marine /* 0080569

1 ROYAL YACHT (YAC)

Name	No	Builders	Commissioned
ABDUL AZIZ	—	Halsingør Waerft, Denmark	12 June 1984

Displacement, tons: 5,200 full load
Measurement, tons: 1,450 dwt
Dimensions, feet (metres): 482.2 × 59.2 × 16.1 *(147 × 18 × 4.9)*
Main machinery: 2 Lindholmen-Pielstick 12 PC2.5 V diesels; 15,600 hp(m) *(11.47 MW)* sustained; 2 shafts
Speed, knots: 22
Complement: 65 plus 4 Royal berths and 60 spare
Helicopters: 1 Bell 206B JetRanger type.

Comment: Completed March 1983 for subsequent fitting out at Vosper's Ship Repairers, Southampton. Helicopter hangar set in hull forward of bridge—covers extend laterally to form pad. Swimming pool. Stern ramp leading to garage. Based at Jiddah. There is also a Royal Yacht listed under the Navy.
VERIFIED

ABDUL AZIZ   *5/1994, van Ginderen Collection*

1 TRAINING SHIP (AXL)

TABBOUK

Displacement, tons: 585 full load
Dimensions, feet (metres): 196.8 × 32.8 × 5.8 *(60 × 10 × 1.8)*
Main machinery: 2 MTU MD 16V 538 TB80 diesels; 5,000 hp(m) *(3.68 MW)* sustained; 2 shafts
Speed, knots: 20. **Range, miles:** 3,500 at 12 kt
Complement: 26 (6 officers) plus 70 trainees
Guns: 1 Oerlikon GAM-BO1 20 mm.
Radars: Surface search: Racal Decca TM 1226; I-band.
Navigation: Racal Decca 2690BT; I-band.

Comment: Built by Bayerische, Germany and commissioned 1 December 1977. Based at Jiddah.
VERIFIED

3 SMALL TANKERS (YO)

AL FORAT   DAJLAH   AL NIL

Displacement, tons: 233 full load
Dimensions, feet (metres): 94.2 × 21.3 × 6.9 *(28.7 × 6.5 × 2.1)*
Main machinery: 2 Caterpillar D343 diesels; 2 shafts
Speed, knots: 12. **Range, miles:** 500 at 12 kt
Radars: Navigation: Decca 110; I-band.

Comment: *Al Nil* based at Aziziah, the others at Jiddah.
VERIFIED

SENEGAL
MARINE SÉNÉGALAISE

Headquarters Appointments	Personnel	General	Bases	Mercantile Marine
Head of Navy: Captain Moustapha Thioubou	(a) 2000: 700 officers and men (b) 2 years' conscript service	On 1 February 1982 the two countries of Senegal and Gambia united to form the confederation of Senegambia, which included merging the armed forces. Confederation was cancelled on 30 September 1989 and the forces again became national and independent of each other.	Dakar, Casamance	*Lloyd's Register of Shipping:* 194 vessels of 47,635 tons gross

PATROL FORCES

1 IMPROVED OSPREY 55 CLASS (LARGE PATROL CRAFT) (PC)

Name	No	Builders	Commissioned
FOUTA	—	Danyard A/S, Fredrikshavn	1 June 1987

Displacement, tons: 470 full load
Dimensions, feet (metres): 180.5 × 33.8 × 8.5 *(55 × 10.3 × 2.6)*
Main machinery: 2 MAN Burmeister & Wain Alpha 12V23/30-DVO diesels; 4,400 hp(m) *(3.23 MW)* sustained; 2 shafts; cp props
Speed, knots: 20. **Range, miles:** 4,000 at 16 kt
Complement: 38 (4 officers) plus 8 spare
Guns: 1 Hispano Suiza 30 mm. 1 Giat 20 mm.
Radars: Surface search: Furuno FR 1411; I-band.
Navigation: Furuno FR 1221; I-band.

Comment: Ordered in 1985. Intended for patrolling the EEZ rather than as a warship, hence the modest armament. A 25 kt rigid inflatable boat can be launched from a stern ramp which has a protective hinged door. Similar vessels built for Morocco, Greece, Mauritania and Burma.
VERIFIED

FOUTA   *6/1998 /* 0050092

1 PR 72M CLASS (PC)

Name	No	Builders	Commissioned
NJAMBUUR	P 773	SFCN, Villeneuve-la-Garenne	Feb 1983

Displacement, tons: 451 full load
Dimensions, feet (metres): 192.5 × 24.9 × 7.2 *(58.7 × 7.6 × 2.2)*
Main machinery: 4 SACM AGO 195 V16 RVR diesels; 11,760 hp(m) *(8.64 MW)* sustained; 4 shafts
Speed, knots: 29. **Range, miles:** 2,500 at 16 kt
Complement: 39 plus 7 passengers
Guns: 2 OTO Melara 3 in *(76 mm)*/62 compact; 85 rds/min to 16 km *(8.7 n miles)*; weight of shell 6 kg. 2 Giat 20 mm F2.
Weapons control: 2 CSEE Naja optical directors.
Radars: Surface search: Racal Decca 1226; I-band.

Comment: Ordered in 1979 and launched 23 December 1980. Completed September 1981 for shipping of armament at Lorient. **VERIFIED**

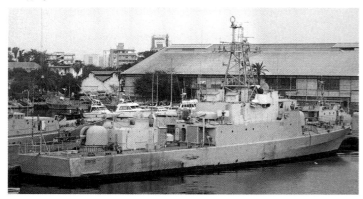

NJAMBUUR *6/1997, M Declerck /* 0050093

3 PR 48 CLASS (LARGE PATROL CRAFT) (PC)

Name	No	Builders	Launched	Commissioned
SAINT LOUIS	—	SFCN, Villeneuve-la-Garenne	5 Aug 1970	1 Mar 1971
POPENGUINE	—	SFCN, Villeneuve-la-Garenne	22 Mar 1974	10 Aug 1974
PODOR	—	SFCN, Villeneuve-la-Garenne	20 July 1976	13 July 1977

Displacement, tons: 250 full load
Dimensions, feet (metres): 156 × 23.3 × 8.1 *(47.5 × 7.1 × 2.5)*
Main machinery: 2 SACM AGO V12 CZSHR diesels; 4,340 hp(m) *(3.2 MW)*; 2 shafts
Speed, knots: 23. **Range, miles:** 2,000 at 16 kt
Complement: 33 (3 officers)
Guns: 2 Bofors 40 mm/70. 2—7.62 mm MGs.
Radars: Surface search: Racal Decca 1226; I-band.

Comment: First one ordered in 1969, second in 1973 and third in 1975. *Saint Louis* may be non-operational. **VERIFIED**

POPENGUINE *6/1998 /* 0050094

3 INTERCEPTOR CLASS (COASTAL PATROL CRAFT) (PCF)

Name	No	Builders	Commissioned
SÉNÉGAL II	—	Les Bateaux Turbec Ltd, Sainte Catherine, Canada	Feb 1979
SINE-SALOUM II	—	Les Bateaux Turbec Ltd, Sainte Catherine, Canada	16 Nov 1979
CASAMANCE II	—	Les Bateaux Turbec Ltd, Sainte Catherine, Canada	Aug 1979

Displacement, tons: 62 full load
Dimensions, feet (metres): 86.9 × 19.3 × 5.2 *(26.5 × 5.8 × 1.6)*
Main machinery: 2 diesels; 2,700 hp *(2.01 MW)*; 2 shafts
Speed, knots: 32.5
Guns: 1 Giat 20 mm.
Radars: Surface search: Furuno; I-band.

Comment: Used for EEZ patrol. All still in service with new radars. **VERIFIED**

CASAMANCE II *6/1997, M Declerck /* 0050095

2 PETERSON Mk 4 CLASS (PC)

Name	No	Builders	Commissioned
MATELOT ALIOUNE SAMB	—	Peterson Builders Inc	28 Oct 1993
MATELOT OUMAR NDOYE	—	Peterson Builders Inc	4 Nov 1993

Displacement, tons: 22 full load
Dimensions, feet (metres): 51.3 × 14.8 × 4.3 *(15.6 × 4.5 × 1.3)*
Main machinery: 2 Detroit 6V-92TA diesels; 520 hp *(388 kW)*; 2 shafts
Speed, knots: 24. **Range, miles:** 500 at 20 kt
Complement: 6
Guns: 2—12.7 mm (twin) MGs. 2—7.62 mm (twin) MGs.
Radars: Surface search: Furuno; I-band.

Comment: Ordered in September 1992. Same type delivered to Cape Verde, Gambia and Guinea-Bissau under FMS. Carries an RIB on the stern. **UPDATED**

MATELOT ALIOUNE SAMB *6/1999* / 0080570

LAND-BASED MARITIME AIRCRAFT

Numbers/Type: 1 de Havilland Canada DHC-6 Twin Otter.
Operational speed: 168 kt *(311 km/h)*.
Service ceiling: 23,200 ft *(7,070 m)*.
Range: 1,460 n miles *(2,705 km)*.
Role/Weapon systems: MR for coastal surveillance but effectiveness limited. Backed up by a French Navy Breguet Atlantique based at Dakar. Sensors: Search radar. Weapons: Unarmed. **VERIFIED**

CUSTOMS

2 TYPE DS-01 (COASTAL PATROL CRAFT) (PC)

DS-01   DS-02

Displacement, tons: 26 full load
Dimensions, feet (metres): 52.5 × 15.1 × 7.5 *(16 × 4.6 × 2.3)*
Main machinery: 2 GM diesels; 970 hp *(724 kW)*; 2 shafts
Speed, knots: 20
Complement: 8
Guns: 1—12.7 mm MG.
Radars: Surface search: Raytheon; I-band.

Comment: Ordered A T Celaya, Bilbao March 1981. Delivered 9 February 1982. There are also some small harbour craft. **UPDATED**

DS-02 *6/1995* / 0080571

AMPHIBIOUS FORCES

1 LCM

CTM 5

Displacement, tons: 150 full load
Dimensions, feet (metres): 78 × 21 × 4.2 *(23.8 × 6.4 × 1.3)*
Main machinery: 2 Poyaud 520 V8 diesels; 225 hp(m) *(165 kW)*; 2 shafts
Speed, knots: 9.5. **Range, miles:** 350 at 8 kt
Complement: 6
Military lift: 90 tons

Comment: Transferred from French Navy in September 1999. Has a bow ramp.
NEW ENTRY

CTM (French colours)   *9/1995*, B Sullivan* / 0080572

2 EDIC 700 CLASS (LCT)

Name	No	Builders	Launched	Commissioned
KARABANE	841	SFCN, Villeneuve-la-Garenne	6 Mar 1986	30 Jan 1987
JAVELINE	— (ex-L 9070)	SFCN, Villeneuve-la-Garenne	1966	1967

Displacement, tons: 736 full load
Dimensions, feet (metres): 193.5 × 39 × 5.6 *(59 × 11.9 × 1.7)*
Main machinery: 2 SACM MGO 175 V12 ASH diesels; 1,200 hp(m) *(882 kW)* sustained; 2 shafts
Speed, knots: 12; 8 *(Javeline)*. **Range, miles:** 1,800 at 10 kt
Complement: 18 (33 spare billets)
Military lift: 12 trucks; 340 tons equipment
Guns: Fitted for 2 Giat 20 mm.
Radars: Navigation: Racal Decca 1226; I-band.

Comment: *Karabane* ordered May 1985, delivered 23 June 1986 from France. Second of class *(L 9070)* transferred from the French Navy and arrived 16 October 1995, returned to France in June 1996 and was then transferred back again on 7 February 1999. *UPDATED*

KARABANE   *6/1997, M Verschaeve* / 0019095

SEYCHELLES

Headquarters Appointments

Commander of the Coast Guard:
   Lieutenant Colonel Andre Ciseau

Bases

Port Victoria, Mahé

Personnel

2000: 300 including 80 air wing and 100 marines

Mercantile Marine

Lloyd's Register of Shipping:
   19 vessels of 23,991 tons gross

DELETIONS

Patrol Forces

1997   *Topaz, Cinq Juin* (civilian from 1997)

COAST GUARD

Note: The ex-Russian 'Turya' class *Zoroaster* is a decommissioned hulk.

1 ZHUK (TYPE 1400M) CLASS (COASTAL PATROL CRAFT) (PC)

Name	No	Builders	Commissioned
FORTUNE	604	USSR	6 Nov 1982

Displacement, tons: 39 full load
Dimensions, feet (metres): 78.7 × 16.4 × 3.9 *(24 × 5 × 1.2)*
Main machinery: 2 Type M 401B diesels; 2,200 hp *(1.6 MW)* sustained; 2 shafts
Speed, knots: 30. **Range, miles:** 1,100 at 15 kt
Complement: 12 (3 officers)
Guns: 4—14.5 mm (2 twin) MGs.
Radars: Surface search: Furuno; I-band.

Comment: Two transferred from USSR. Second of class paid off in 1996 and used for spares.
VERIFIED

FORTUNE   *6/1998, Seychelles Coast Guard* / 0050097

1 TYPE FPB 42 (LARGE PATROL CRAFT) (PC)

Name	No	Builders	Commissioned
ANDROMACHE	605	Picchiotti, Viareggio	10 Jan 1983

Displacement, tons: 268 full load
Dimensions, feet (metres): 137.8 × 26 × 8.2 *(41.8 × 8 × 2.5)*
Main machinery: 2 Paxman Valenta 16 CM diesels; 6,650 hp *(5 MW)* sustained; 2 shafts
Speed, knots: 26. **Range, miles:** 3,000 at 16 kt
Complement: 22 (3 officers)
Guns: 1 Oerlikon 25 mm. 2—7.62 mm MGs.
Radars: Surface search: 2 Furuno; I-band.

Comment: Ordered from Inma, La Spezia in November 1981. A second of class reported ordered in 1991 but the order was not confirmed.
UPDATED

ANDROMACHE   *3/1997** / 0019096

LAND-BASED MARITIME AIRCRAFT

Numbers/Type: 2 Pilatus Britten-Norman BN-42 Maritime Defender.
Operational speed: 150 kt *(280 km/h).*
Service ceiling: 18,900 ft *(5,760 m).*
Range: 1,500 n miles *(2,775 km).*
Role/Weapon systems: Coastal surveillance and surface search aircraft. Sensors: Search radar.
  Weapons: Provision for rockets or guns.

UPDATED

BN2T-4S (Irish Police colours)
8/1997* / 0016662

SIERRA LEONE

Headquarters Appointments

Senior Officer, Navy:
  Captain Sessay

Personnel

(a)   2000: 140 officers and men
(b)   Voluntary service

Bases

Freetown

Mercantile Marine

Lloyd's Register of Shipping:
  48 vessels of 17,430 tons gross

DELETIONS

Note: The last three craft were all non-operational by late 1998. *Farandugu* may be repairable if funds can be found.

Patrol Forces

1997   *Naimbana* (old) (sunk)
1998   *Moa, Naimbana, Farandugu,* 2 CAT 900S

SINGAPORE

Headquarters Appointments

Chief of the Navy:
  Rear Admiral Lui Tuck Yew
Deputy Chief of Navy:
  Rear Admiral Simon Ong
Fleet Commander:
  Rear Admiral Larry Loon Leong Yoon
Command Police Coast Guard:
  Assistant Commissioner Foo Kia Juah

Personnel

(a)   2000: 4,500 officers and men including 1,800 conscripts
(b)   National Service: two and a half years for Corporals and above; two years for the remainder
(c)   5,000 reservists

Bases

Pulau Brani, Tuas (Jurong), Changi, Sembawang

Prefix to Ships' Names

RSS

Organisation

Four Commands: Fleet, Coastal Command, Naval Logistics Command and Training Command.
Fleet: First Flotilla (six Victory, six Sea Wolf, 12 Fearless).
    Third Flotilla (three LSTs, Fast Craft at Civil Squadron).
Coastal Command: (four Bedok, 12 PBs, *Jupiter*)

Police Coast Guard

Organised into four paramilitary squadrons: Coastal Patrol and Special Task Squadron using ex-naval craft; Port for routine security and Interceptor for preventing drug smuggling and illegal immigrants. All vessels have Police Coast Guard on the superstructure and a white-red-white diagonal stripe on the hull except for Interceptor craft which have dark blue hulls with grey superstructures. Personnel numbers are about 1,000.

Mercantile Marine

Lloyd's Register of Shipping:
  1,736 vessels of 21,780,112 tons gross

Strength of the Fleet

Type	Active	Building (Projected)
Submarines	3	1
Missile Corvettes	6	(6)
Offshore Patrol Vessels	12	—
Fast Attack Craft—Missile	6	—
Inshore Patrol Craft	12	—
Minehunters	4	—
LST/LSL/LPD	6	1
LCMs	6	—
Diving Support Ship	1	—

DELETIONS

Patrol Forces

1997   *Sovereignty* (old), *Independence* (old), *Freedom* (old), *Justice* (old)

Amphibious Forces

1998   *Resolution* (old), *Persistence*

SUBMARINES

3 + 1 SJÖORMEN (A 12) CLASS (SSK)

Name	Builders	Laid down	Launched		Commissioned	
CHALLENGER (ex-*Sjöbjörnen*)	Karlskronavarvet	1967	6 Aug	1968	28 Feb	1969
CENTURION (ex-*Sjöormen*)	Kockums	1965	25 Jan	1967	31 July	1968
CONQUEROR (ex-*Sjölejonet*)	Kockums	1966	29 June	1967	16 Dec	1968
— (ex-*Sjöhunden*])	Kockums	1966	21 Mar	1968	25 June	1969

Displacement, tons: 1,130 surfaced; 1,210 dived
Dimensions, feet (metres): 167.3 × 20 × 19
(51 × 6.1 × 5.8)
Main machinery: Diesel-electric; 2 Hedemora-Pielstick V12A/A2/15 diesels; 2,200 hp(m) *(1.62 MW)*; 1 ASEA motor; 1,500 hp(m) *(1.1 MW)*; 1 shaft
Speed, knots: 12 surfaced; 20 dived
Complement: 23 (7 officers)

Torpedoes: 4—21 in *(533 mm)* bow tubes. 10 FFV Type 613; anti-surface; wire-guided; passive homing to 15 km *(8.2 n miles)* at 45 kt; warhead 250 kg.

2—16 in *(400 mm)* tubes: 4 FFV Type 431; anti-submarine; wire-guided; active/passive homing to 20 km *(10.8 n miles)* at 25 kt; warhead 45 kg shaped charge.
Mines: Minelaying capability.
Weapons control: Ericsson IPS-12 data automation.
Radars: Navigation: Terma; I-band.
Sonars: Plessey Hydra; hull-mounted; passive search and attack; medium frequency.

Programmes: It was announced on 23 September 1995 that a submarine would be acquired from Sweden for training purposes only. Three more of the same class acquired in July 1997 for conversion plus one more *(Sjöhasten)* for spares.
Structure: Albacore hull. Twin-decked. Diving depth, 150 m *(492 ft)*. Air conditioning added for tropical service, together with battery cooling.
Operational: *Challenger* re-launched on 26 September 1997, the next pair 28 May 1999, and the last one started conversion in late 1999. *Challenger* remains in Sweden as a training/trials ship. *Conqueror* was the first to sail to Singapore by transportership on 30 March 2000. The next to go will be *Centurion* in 2001. Based at Changi.

UPDATED

CONQUEROR

3/2000*, Per Körnefeldt / 0084434

FRIGATES

Note: Six Modified 'La Fayette' class frigates ordered from DCN International on 6 March 2000. These ships are to be 360.1 ft *(110 m)* in length with a speed of 27 kt. First one to be built in France, remainder in Singapore. This contract replaces the NGPV corvette design.

CORVETTES

6 VICTORY CLASS (FSG)

Name	No	Builders	Launched	Commissioned
VICTORY	P 88	Lürssen Werft, Bremen	8 June 1988	18 Aug 1990
VALOUR	P 89	Singapore SB and Marine	10 Dec 1988	18 Aug 1990
VIGILANCE	P 90	Singapore SB and Marine	27 Apr 1989	18 Aug 1990
VALIANT	P 91	Singapore SB and Marine	22 July 1989	25 May 1991
VIGOUR	P 92	Singapore SB and Marine	1 Dec 1989	25 May 1991
VENGEANCE	P 93	Singapore SB and Marine	23 Feb 1990	25 May 1991

Displacement, tons: 595 full load
Dimensions, feet (metres): 204.7 oa; 190.3 wl × 27.9 × 10.2 *(62.4; 58 × 8.5 × 3.1)*
Main machinery: 4 MTU 16V 538 TB93 diesels; 15,020 hp(m) *(11 MW)* sustained; 4 shafts
Speed, knots: 35. **Range, miles:** 4,000 at 18 kt
Complement: 49 (8 officers)

Missiles: SSM: 8 McDonnell Douglas Harpoon ❶; active radar homing to 130 km *(70 n miles)* at 0.9 Mach; warhead 227 kg.
SAM: 2 Octuple IAI/Rafael Barak I ❷ radar or optical guidance to 10 km *(5.5 m)* at 2 Mach; warhead 22 kg.
Guns: 1 OTO Melara 3 in *(76 mm)*/62 Super Rapid ❸; 120 rds/min to 16 km *(8.7 n miles)*; weight of shell 6 kg.
4 CIS 50 12.7 mm MGs.
Torpedoes: 6—324 mm Whitehead B 515 (2 triple) tubes ❹. Whitehead A 244S; anti-submarine; active/passive homing to 7 km *(3.8 n miles)* at 33 kt; warhead 34 kg (shaped charge).
Countermeasures: Decoys: 2 Plessey Shield 9-barrelled chaff launchers ❺. 4 Rafael (2 twin) long-range chaff launchers to be fitted below the bridge wings.
ESM: Elisra SEWS ❻; intercept.
ECM: Rafael RAN 1101; ❼ jammer.
Combat data systems: Elbit command system. SATCOM ❽.
Weapons control: Elbit MSIS optronic director ❾.
Radars: Surface search: Ericsson/Radamec Sea Giraffe 150HC ❿; G/H-band.
Navigation: Kelvin Hughes 1007; I-band.
Fire control: 2 Elta EL/M-2221(X) ⓫; I/J/K-band.

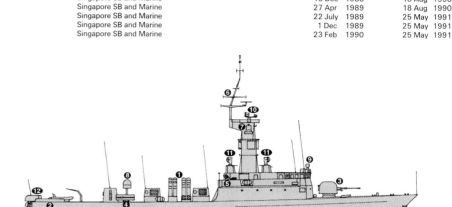

VICTORY

(Scale 1 : 600), Ian Sturton / 0019098

Sonars: Thomson Sintra TSM 2064; VDS ⓬; active search and attack.

Programmes: Ordered in June 1986 to a Lürssen MGB 62 design similar to Bahrain and UAE vessels.
Modernisation: Barak launchers fitted on either side of the VDS, together with a second fire-control radar on the platform aft of

the mast and an optronic director on the bridge roof. Rudder roll stabilisation retrofitted to improve sea-keeping qualities.
Operational: Form Squadron 188. Designated Missile Corvettes (MCV). First live Barak firing in September 1997.

UPDATED

VALIANT

8/1999*, John Mortimer / 0080573

PATROL FORCES

12 FEARLESS CLASS (OPV)

Name	No	Builders	Launched		Commissioned	
FEARLESS	94	Singapore STEC	18 Feb	1995	5 Oct	1996
BRAVE	95	Singapore STEC	9 Sep	1995	5 Oct	1996
COURAGEOUS	96	Singapore STEC	9 Sep	1995	5 Oct	1996
GALLANT	97	Singapore STEC	27 Apr	1996	3 May	1997
DARING	98	Singapore STEC	27 Apr	1996	3 May	1997
DAUNTLESS	99	Singapore STEC	23 Nov	1996	3 May	1997
RESILIENCE	82	Singapore STEC	23 Nov	1996	7 Feb	1998
UNITY	83	Singapore STEC	19 July	1997	7 Feb	1998
SOVEREIGNTY	84	Singapore STEC	19 July	1997	7 Feb	1998
JUSTICE	85	Singapore STEC	18 Oct	1997	7 Feb	1998
FREEDOM	86	Singapore STEC	18 Oct	1997	22 Aug	1998
INDEPENDENCE	87	Singapore STEC	18 Apr	1998	22 Aug	1999

Displacement, tons: 500 full load
Dimensions, feet (metres): 180.4 × 28.2 × 8.9 *(55 × 8.6 × 2.7)*
Main machinery: 2 MTU 12V 595 TE90 diesels; 8,554 hp(m) *(6.29 MW)* sustained; 2 Kamewa water-jets
Speed, knots: 20
Complement: 32 (5 officers)

Missiles: SAM: Matra Simbad twin launcher; Mistral; IR homing to 4 km *(2.2 n miles)*; warhead 3 kg.
Guns: 1 OTO Melara 3 in *(76 mm)*/62 Super Rapid; 120 rds/min to 16 km *(8.7 n miles)*; weight of shell 6 kg. 4 CIS 50 12.7 mm MGs.
Torpedoes: 6—324 mm Whitehead B515 (triple) tubes; (94-99) Whitehead A244S; active/passive homing to 7 km *(3.8 m)* at 33 kt; warhead 34 kg (shaped charge).
Countermeasures: Decoys: 2 GEC Marine Shield III 102 mm sextuple fixed chaff launchers.
ESM: Elisra NS-9010C; intercept.
Weapons control: ST 3100 WCS. Elbit MSIS optronic director being fitted.
Radars: Surface search and fire control: Elta EL/M-2228(X); E/F-band.
Navigation: Kelvin Hughes 1007; I-band.
Sonars: Thomson Sintra TSM 2362 Gudgeon; hull-mounted; active attack; medium frequency (94-99 only).

Programmes: Contract awarded on 27 February 1993 for 12 patrol vessels to Singapore Shipbuilding and Engineering.
Structure: First six are ASW specialist ships. All have water-jet propulsion. Second batch were to have been fitted with Gabriel II SSMs but this plan has been shelved. MSIS director being fitted.
Operational: First six serve with 189 Squadron; second six with 182 Squadron. *Unity* is to be used as a test bed for new technologies including an Indep 21 combat system.

UPDATED

DARING   *12/1999*, Sattler/Steele /* 0084279

6 SEA WOLF CLASS (FAST ATTACK CRAFT—MISSILE) (PCFG)

Name	No	Builders	Commissioned
SEA WOLF	P 76	Lürssen Werft, Vegesack	1972
SEA LION	P 77	Lürssen Werft, Vegesack	1972
SEA DRAGON	P 78	Singapore SBEC	1974
SEA TIGER	P 79	Singapore SBEC	1974
SEA HAWK	P 80	Singapore SBEC	1975
SEA SCORPION	P 81	Singapore SBEC	29 Feb 1976

Displacement, tons: 226 standard; 254 full load
Dimensions, feet (metres): 147.3 × 23 × 8.2 *(44.9 × 7 × 2.5)*
Main machinery: 4 MTU 16V 538 TB92 diesels; 13,640 hp(m) *(10 MW)* sustained; 4 shafts
Speed, knots: 35. **Range, miles:** 950 at 30 kt; 1,800 at 15 kt
Complement: 41 (5 officers)

Missiles: SSM: 4 McDonnell Douglas Harpoon (2 twin); active radar homing to 130 km *(70 n miles)* at 0.9 Mach; warhead 227 kg.
4 IAI Gabriel I launchers; radar or optical guidance; semi-active radar homing to 20 km *(10.8 n miles)* at 0.7 Mach; warhead 75 kg.
SAM: 1 Matra Simbad twin launcher; Mistral; IR homing to 4 km *(2.2 n miles)*; warhead 3 kg.
Guns: 1 Bofors 57 mm/70; 200 rds/min to 17 km *(9.3 n miles)*; weight of shell 2.4 kg.
Countermeasures: Decoys: 2 Hycor Mk 137 sextuple RBOC chaff launchers. 4 Rafael (2 twin) long-range chaff launchers.
ESM/ECM: RQN 3B (INS-3) intercept and jammer. TDF-205 DF.
Weapons control: Elbit MSIS optronic director to be fitted.
Radars: Surface search: Racal Decca; I-band.
Fire control: Signaal WM28/5; I/J-band; range 46 km *(25 n miles)*.

Programmes: Lürssen Werft FPB 45 type. Designated Missile Gunboats (MGB).
Modernisation: *Sea Hawk* was the first to complete refit in January 1988 with two sets of twin Harpoon launchers replacing the triple Gabriel launcher. The remainder were converted by December 1990 with the exception of *Sea Wolf* which finished refit in Spring 1991. ECM equipment has also been fitted on a taller mast. SATCOM and GPS installed. There have also been some superstructure changes. The Bofors 40 mm gun has been replaced with a Matra Simbad SAM launcher. Life extension programme started at Singapore Shipbuilders in 1994. Gabriel may be withdrawn from this class in due course. MSIS optronic director to be fitted.

UPDATED

SEA LION   *3/1999*, van Ginderen Collection /* 0080577

12 INSHORE PATROL CRAFT (PB/FB)

FB 31-FB 42

Displacement, tons: 20 full load
Dimensions, feet (metres): 47.6 × 13.8 × 3.6 *(14.5 × 4.2 × 1.1)*
Main machinery: 2 MTU 12V 183 TC91 diesels; 1,200 hp(m) *(882 kW)*; 2 Hamilton water-jets
Speed, knots: 30
Complement: 4
Guns: 1—40 mm grenade launcher. 1—12.7 mm MG.
Radars: Surface search: Racal Decca; I-band.

Comment: Built by Singapore SBEC and delivered in 1990-91. Based at Brani and Tuas. Designated Fast Boats (FB). Some are kept in storage at Tuas. Similar to Police 'PT' class. ***UPDATED***

FB 42   *1991*, Singapore SBEC /* 0080578

SOVEREIGNTY   *3/1999*, van Ginderen Collection /* 0080575

LAND-BASED MARITIME AIRCRAFT

Notes: (1) The Air Force also has 50 A4-SU Skyhawks, 7 F-16A/B and 18 F-16C/D with 30 more on order.
(2) There are also six CH-47D used for maritime tasks.

Numbers/Type: 4 Grumman E-2C Hawkeye.
Operational speed: 323 kt *(598 km/h).*
Service ceiling: 30,800 ft *(9,390 m).*
Range: 1,000 n miles *(1,850 km).*
Role/Weapon systems: Delivered in 1987 for surveillance of shipping in sea areas around Singapore and South China Sea; understood to have priority assistance from US Government. Sensors: APS-125 or APS-138 radar; datalink for SSM targeting. Weapons: Unarmed.

UPDATED

HAWKEYE   *9/1998*, David Boey /* 0080579

Numbers/Type: 5 Fokker F50 Mk 2S Enforcer.
Operational speed: 220 kt *(463 km/h).*
Service ceiling: 29,500 ft *(8,990 m).*
Range: 2,700 n miles *(5,000 km).*
Role/Weapon systems: In service from September 1995. Part of Air Force 121 Squadron but with mixed crews and under naval op con. Sensors: Texas Instruments APS-134(V)7 radar; GEC FLIR; Elta ESM. Weapons: Harpoon ASM; mines; A-244S torpedoes.

UPDATED

FOKKER F 50   *9/1998*, David Boey /* 0080580

MINE WARFARE FORCES

4 BEDOK (LANDSORT) CLASS (MINEHUNTERS) (MHC)

Name	No	Builders	Launched		Commissioned	
BEDOK	M 105	Kockums/Karlskrona	24 June	1993	7 Oct	1995
KALLANG	M 106	Singapore Shipbuilding	29 Jan	1994	7 Oct	1995
KATONG	M 107	Singapore Shipbuilding	8 Apr	1994	7 Oct	1995
PUNGGOL	M 108	Singapore Shipbuilding	16 July	1994	7 Oct	1995

Displacement, tons: 360 full load
Dimensions, feet (metres): 155.8 × 31.5 × 7.5 *(47.5 × 9.6 × 2.3)*
Main machinery: 4 Saab Scania diesels; 1,592 hp(m) *(1.17 MW)*; coupled in pairs to 2 Voith Schneider props
Speed, knots: 15. **Range, miles:** 2,000 at 10 kt
Complement: 31 (5 officers)

Guns: 1 Bofors 40 mm/70. 4—12.7 mm MGs.
Mines: 2 rails.
Weapons control: Thomson-CSF TSM 2061 Mk II minehunting and mine disposal system. Signaal WM20 director.
Radars: Navigation: Norcontrol DB 2000; I-band.
Sonars: Thomson-CSF TSM 2022; hull-mounted; minehunting; high frequency.

Programmes: Kockums/Karlskrona design ordered in February 1991. *Bedok* started trials in Sweden in December 1993, and was shipped to Singapore in early 1994 to complete. Prefabrication work done for the other three in Sweden with assembly and fitting out in Singapore at Benoi Basin.
Structure: GRP hulls. Two PAP 104 Mk V ROVs embarked. Racal Precision Navigation system. Two sets of Swedish SAM minesweeping system. Magnavox GPS.
Operational: Based at Tuas.

UPDATED

PUNGGOL   *7/1996*, van Ginderen Collection /* 0084280

PUNGGOL   *4/1997*, Maritime Photographic /* 0019103

AMPHIBIOUS FORCES

Note: The Tiger 40 hovercraft acquired in 1997 is beyond repair but the design may be used again for a repeat order in due course.

1 SIR LANCELOT CLASS (LSL)

Name	No	Builders	Laid down	Launched	Commissioned
PERSEVERANCE (ex-*Sir Lancelot*, ex-*Lowland Lancer*)	L 206 (ex-L 3029)	Fairfield, Glasgow	Mar 1962	25 June 1963	16 Jan 1964

Displacement, tons: 3,270 light; 5,674 full load
Dimensions, feet (metres): 412.1 × 59.8 × 13 *(125.6 × 18.2 × 4)*
Main machinery: 2 Ruston diesels; 9,400 hp *(7.01 MW)*; 2 shafts; bow thruster
Speed, knots: 15. **Range, miles:** 8,000 at 15 kt
Complement: 61 (6 officers)
Military lift: 340 troops (534 hard lying); 16 MBTs; 34 mixed vehicles; 120 tons POL; 30 tons ammunition; 1—20 ton crane; 2—4.5 ton cranes

Missiles: SAM: 4 Matra Simbad twin launchers for Mistral.
Guns: 1 Bofors 40 mm/70. 6—12.7 mm MGs.
Radars: Navigation: Norcontrol DB 2000; I-band.

Helicopters: Platform for 2 medium.

Programmes: Built for the British Army but transferred to the Royal Fleet Auxiliary Service in 1970. Paid off from the Royal Navy in 1989 and used commercially for survey work and for a short time as an offshore casino at Cape Town in 1991. Acquired by Singapore in October 1992. Recommissioned 5 May 1994 with new engines.
Structure: Refitted to upgrade accommodation and fit a 40 mm gun and Mistral SAM. Fitted for bow and stern loading with drive-through facilities and deck-to-deck ramps. Facilities provided for onboard maintenance of vehicles and for laying

PERSEVERANCE   *10/1998, John Mortimer /* 0050101

out pontoon equipment. Mexeflote self-propelled floating platforms can be strapped one on each side. Carries 850 tons of oil fuel.

Operational: The ship is also used in the training role for cruises of up to five weeks.

VERIFIED

3 + 1 ENDURANCE CLASS (LPD/LST)

Name	No	Builders	Laid down	Launched	Commissioned
ENDURANCE	L 207	Singapore Technologies Marine, Banoi	26 Mar 1997	14 Mar 1998	18 Mar 2000
RESOLUTION	L 208	Singapore Technologies Marine, Banoi	22 Oct 1997	1 Aug 1998	18 Mar 2000
PERSISTENCE	L 209	Singapore Technologies Marine, Banoi	3 Apr 1998	13 Mar 1999	Mar 2001
ENDEAVOUR	L 210	Singapore Technologies Marine, Banoi	15 Oct 1998	12 Feb 2000	Mar 2001

Displacement, tons: 8,500 full load
Dimensions, feet (metres): 462.6 pp × 68.9 × 16.4
(141 × 21 × 5)
Main machinery: 2 Ruston 16RK 270 diesels; 12,000 hp(m)
(8.82 MW); 2 shafts; Kamewa cp props; bow thruster
Speed, knots: 15. **Range, miles:** 10,400 at 12 kt
Complement: 65 (8 officers)
Military lift: 350 troops; 18 tanks; 20 vehicles; 4 LCVP

Missiles: SAM: 2 Matra Simbad twin launchers for Mistral; IR
homing to 4 km *(2.2 n miles)*; warhead 3 kg. 2 Barak octuple
launchers may be fitted in due course.
Guns: 1 Otobreda 76 mm/62 Super Rapid; 120 rds/min to
16 km *(8.7 n miles)*; weight of shell 6 kg.
5—12.7 mm MGs.
Countermeasures: Decoys: 2 GEC Marine Shield III 102 mm
sextuple fixed chaff launcher.
ESM/ECM: Rafael RAN 1101; intercept and jammer.
Weapons control: CS Defense NAJIR 2000 optronic director.
Radars: Air/surface search: Ericsson; E/F-band.
Navigation: Kelvin Hughes Type 1007; I-band.

Helicopters: Platform for 2 Super Puma.

Programmes: Ordered in September 1994 and confirmed in
mid-1996.
Structure: US drive through design with bow and stern ramps.
Single intermediate deck with three hydraulic ramps.
Helicopter platform aft. Indal ASIST helo handling system.
Dockwell for four LCUs and davits for four LCVPs. Two 25 ton
cranes. The second pair may be to an improved design with
ro-ro and advanced hull design.
Operational: Sea trials for *Endurance* started in March 1999.
Commissioning dates are projected approximately one year
after completion.

UPDATED

ENDURANCE
5/1999*, STM / 0080581

ENDURANCE

6/1999*, Sattler/Steele / 0080582

2 LST 511-1152 CLASS (LST)

Name	No	Builders	Commissioned
EXCELLENCE (ex-*LST 629*)	L 202 (ex-A 81)	Chicago Bridge & Iron Co	28 July 1944
INTREPID (ex-*LST 579*)	L 203 (ex-A 83)	Missouri Valley B and I Co	21 July 1944

Displacement, tons: 1,653 light; 4,080 full load
Dimensions, feet (metres): 328 × 50 × 14 *(100 × 15.2 × 4.3)*
Main machinery: 2 MTU diesels; 1,800 hp *(1.34 MW)*; 2 shafts
Speed, knots: 9. **Range, miles:** 19,000 at 9 kt
Complement: 72 (6 officers)
Military lift: 1,500 tons general; 500 tons beaching; 440 m² tank deck; 500 m² main deck storage;
can carry 125 troops on long haul; 2—5 ton cranes; 2 LCVPs on davits

Missiles: SAM: 2 twin Matra Simbad launchers for Mistral.
Guns: 1 Bofors 40 mm/70. 6—12.7 mm MGs.
Radars: Navigation: Norcontrol DB 2000; I-band.
IFF: UPX 12.

Helicopters: Platform only.

Programmes: Both transferred 4 June 1976 and recommissioned 28 October 1978.
Modernisation: Both modernised since 1977. This included new electrics, new communications,
an enclosed bridge and updated command facilities. *Excellence* has a helicopter pad aft. Both
have been re-engined.

EXCELLENCE
4/1999*, Hachiro Nakai / 0080583

Operational: Used as Command ships and in support of the Army and for occasional training
cruises. One more of the class is in reserve and laid up at Tuas and could be activated in an
emergency. Being replaced by the new LSTs. Complement reduced.

UPDATED

4 RPL TYPE (LCM)

RPL 60-RPL 63

Displacement, tons: 151 standard
Dimensions, feet (metres): 120.4 × 28 × 5.9 (36.7 × 8.5 × 1.8)
Main machinery: 2 MAN D2540MLE diesels; 860 hp(m) (632 kW); 2 Schottel props
Speed, knots: 10.7
Complement: 6
Military lift: 2 tanks or 450 troops or 110 tons cargo (fuel or stores)

Comment: First pair built at North Shipyard Point, second pair by Singapore SBEC. First two launched August 1985, next two in October 1985. Cargo deck 86.9 × 21.6 ft (26.5 × 6.6 m). Bow ramp suitable for beaching. Reports of a third pair were not confirmed.   ***UPDATED***

RPL 63   *7/1993*, David Boey /* 0080584

30 LANDING CRAFT UTILITY (LCU/FCU)

Dimensions, feet (metres): 75.4 × 19.7 × 2.6 (23 × 6 × 0.8)
Main machinery: 2 MAN 2842 LZE diesels; 4,400 hp(m) (3.23 MW); 2 Kamewa water-jets
Speed, knots: 20. **Range, miles:** 180 at 15 kt
Complement: 4
Military lift: 18 tons
Guns: 2—12.7 mm MGs or 40 mm grenade launchers.

Comment: This is a larger and much faster version of the LCVPs. Being built from 1993. Designated Fast Craft Utility (FCU). Pennant numbers in the 300 series.   ***UPDATED***

FCUs 397 and 378   *8/1998*, David Boey /* 0080585

100 LANDING CRAFT (LCVP/FCEP)

Displacement, tons: 4 full load
Dimensions, feet (metres): 44.6 × 12.1 × 2 (13.6 × 3.7 × 0.6)
Main machinery: 2 MAN D2866 LE diesels; 816 hp(m) (600 kW); sustained; 2 Hamilton 362 water-jets
Speed, knots: 20. **Range, miles:** 100 at 20 kt
Complement: 3
Military lift: 4 tons or 30 troops

Comment: Fast Craft, Equipment and Personnel (FCEP), built by Singapore SBEC from 1989 and are used to transport troops around the Singapore archipelago. They have a single bow ramp and can carry a rifle platoon. More than 25 are in service and the rest in storage. Have numbers in the 500 and 800 series except for those carried in LSTs.   ***UPDATED***

LCVP (*Excellence* number)   *10/1999*, John Mortimer /* 0080586

10 DIVING SUPPORT CRAFT

Comment: Boston Whalers used by the Naval Diving Unit. Armed with 7.62 mm MGs and 40 mm grenade launchers. Tenders closed in November 1995 for replacement 12 m craft, but there has been no confirmation of an order.   ***UPDATED***

BOSTON WHALER   *7/1995*, David Boey /* 0080587

450 ASSAULT CRAFT

Dimensions, feet (metres): 17.7 × 5.9 × 2.3 (5.4 × 1.8 × 0.7)
Main machinery: 1 outboard; 50 hp(m) (37 kW)
Speed, knots: 12
Military lift: 12 troops
Guns: 1—7.62 mm MG or 40 mm grenade launcher.

Comment: Built by Singapore SBEC. Man-portable craft which can carry a section of troops in the rivers and creeks surrounding Singapore island. Numbers are approximate.   ***UPDATED***

ASSAULT CRAFT   *9/1995*, David Boey /* 0080588

AUXILIARIES

Notes: (1) An oil rig supply ship MV *Ocean Explorer* has been chartered as an unarmed training vessel. Orange hull with white superstructure.
(2) There are two Floating Docks with a lift of 600 tons. *FD 1* is at Tuas and *FD 2* at Brani.

1 DIVING SUPPORT SHIP (YDT)

Name	No	Builders	Launched	Commissioned
JUPITER	A 102	Singapore SBEC	3 Apr 1990	19 Aug 1991

Displacement, tons: 170 full load
Dimensions, feet (metres): 117.5 × 23.3 × 7.5 (35.8 × 7.1 × 2.3)
Main machinery: 2 Deutz MWM TBD234V12 diesels; 1,360 hp(m) (1 MW) sustained; 2 shafts; bow thruster
Speed, knots: 14. **Range, miles:** 200 at 14 kt
Complement: 33 (5 officers)
Guns: 1 Oerlikon 20 mm GAM-BO1. 4—12.7 mm MGs.
Radars: Navigation: Racal Decca; I-band.

Comment: Designed for underwater search and salvage operations and built to German naval standards. Secondary role of surveying. Equipped with a precise navigation system, towed side scan sonar and an ECA PAP Mk V remotely operated vehicle (ROV). The ship's diving support equipment comprises two high-pressure compressors, a two-man decompression chamber, an RIB with 40 hp outboard motor and a 1.5 ton SWL crane.   ***UPDATED***

JUPITER   *6/1994*, van Ginderen Collection /* 0084281

POLICE COAST GUARD

12 SWIFT CLASS

BLUE SHARK (ex-*Swift Lancer*) PH 50 (ex-P 12)
MAKO SHARK (ex-*Swift Swordsman*) PH 51 (ex-P 14)
WHITE SHARK (ex-*Swift Archer*) PH 52 (ex-P 16)
HAMMERHEAD SHARK (ex-*Swift Combatant*) PH 53 (ex-P 18)
TIGER SHARK (ex-*Swift Knight*) PH 54 (ex-P 11)
BASKING SHARK (ex-*Swift Warrior*) PH 55 (ex-P 15)
SANDBAR SHARK (ex-*Swift Conqueror*) PH 56 (ex-P 21)
THRESHER SHARK (ex-*Swift Chieftain*) PH 57 (ex-P 23)
WHITETIP SHARK (ex-*Swift Warlord*) PH 58 (ex-P 17)
BLACKTIP SHARK (ex-*Swift Challenger*) PH 59 (ex-P 19)
GOBLIN SHARK (ex-*Swift Cavalier*) PH 60 (ex-P 20)
SCHOOL SHARK (ex-*Swift Centurion*) PH 61 (ex-P 22)

Displacement, tons: 45.7 full load
Dimensions, feet (metres): 74.5 × 20.3 × 5.2 *(22.7 × 6.2 × 1.6)*
Main machinery: 2 Deutz BA16M816 diesels; 2,680 hp(m) *(1.96 MW)* sustained; 2 shafts
Speed, knots: 32. **Range, miles:** 550 at 20 kt; 900 at 10 kt
Complement: 15
Guns: 1 Oerlikon 20 mm GAM-BO1. 2 CIS 90 12.7 mm MGs.
Radars: Surface search: Decca 1226; I-band.

Comment: Built by Singapore SBEC and all completed 20 October 1981 for the Navy. First four transferred from the Navy on 15 February 1993, second four on 8 April 1994, last four on 7 November 1996. All to be fitted with ARPA radar in due course.   *UPDATED*

GOBLIN SHARK   *7/1999*, van Ginderen/B Morrison /* 0080589

33 PATROL CRAFT

PX 1-PX 33

Displacement, tons: 11 full load
Dimensions, feet (metres): 37 × 10.5 × 1.6 *(11 × 3.2 × 0.5)*
Main machinery: 2 MTU diesels; 770 hp(m) *(566 kW)*; 2 shafts
Speed, knots: 30
Complement: 3
Guns: 1—7.62 mm MG.

Comment: Completed 1981 by Sembawang SY. Being replaced by new craft.   *UPDATED*

PX 17   *7/1999*, David Boey /* 0080590

20 PATROL CRAFT

PT 20-PT 39

Dimensions, feet (metres): 59.1 × 17.7 × 3 *(18 × 5.4 × 0.9)*
Main machinery: 2 diesels; 2 waterjets
Speed, knots: 40
Complement: 5

Comment: Order placed 7 January 1998 with Asia Pacific Singapore for two Command craft and 18 patrol craft built by Geraldton Boats, Australia. These have been called after Rays.   *UPDATED*

PT 22   *7/1999*, David Boey /* 0080591

19 PATROL CRAFT

PT 1-PT 19

Displacement, tons: 20 full load
Dimensions, feet (metres): 47.6 × 13.8 × 3.9 *(14.5 × 4.2 × 1.2)*
Main machinery: 2 MAN D2542MLE diesels; 1,076 hp(m) *(791 kW)*; or MTU 12V 183 TC91 diesels; 1,200 hp(m) *(882 kW)* maximum; 2 shafts
Speed, knots: 30. **Range, miles:** 310 at 22 kt
Complement: 4 plus 8 spare berths
Guns: 1—7.62 mm MG.
Radars: Surface search: Furuno or Racal Decca Bridgemaster; I-band.

Comment: First 13 completed by Singapore SBEC between January and August 1984, two more completed February 1987 and eight more (including two Command Boats) in 1989. Of aluminium construction. Four are operated by Customs and Excise. There are differences in the deckhouses between earlier and later vessels.   *UPDATED*

PT 7   *5/1999*, van Ginderen/B Morrison /* 0080592

11 INTERCEPTOR CRAFT

SAILFISH PK 10   BILLFISH PK 30   SPIKEFISH PK 50
SPEARFISH PK 20   SWORDFISH PK 40   PK 23 + 5

Dimensions, feet (metres): 42 × 10.5 × 1.6 *(12.8 × 3.2 × 0.5)*
Main machinery: 3 Mercruiser 502 Magnum diesels; 3 shafts
Speed, knots: 50
Complement: 5
Guns: 1—7.62 mm MG.

Comment: First five built locally and delivered in 1995. Colours have been changed to dark blue hulls and grey superstructures, to make the craft less visible at sea. Six more ordered from Pro Marine/North Shipyard in 1999 to a slightly different design, with twin outboard motors.   *UPDATED*

PK 40   *7/1999*, David Boey /* 0080593

PK 23   *1/2000*, David Boey /* 0080594

HARBOUR CRAFT

Comment: There are large numbers of harbour craft, many of them armed, with PC numbers. These include four RIBs with Yamaha 200 hp outboards capable of 43 kt, and with pennant numbers PJ 1-PJ 4. Twenty more PC craft are to be ordered in 2000, capable of 42 kt.

UPDATED

HARBOUR CRAFT   *1/2000*, David Boey /* 0080595

CUSTOMS

Note: Customs Craft include CE 1-4 and CE 5-8, the latter being sisters to PT 1 Police Craft.

CE 8   *8/1999*, David Boey /* 0080596

SLOVENIA
SLOVENSKI MORNARJI

Headquarters Appointments	General	Personnel	Bases	Mercantile Marine
Chief of Navy: Captain Marijan Meršak	Navy formed in January 1993.	2000: 38	Ankaran	*Lloyd's Register of Shipping:* 10 vessels of 1,767 tons gross

PATROL FORCES

1 + (1) SUPER DVORA Mk II (PCF)

Name	No	Builders	Commissioned
ANKARAN	HPL 21	IAI Ramta	Aug 1996

Displacement, tons: 58 full load
Dimensions, feet (metres): 82 × 18.4 × 3.6 *(25 × 5.6 × 1.1)*
Main machinery: 2 MTU 12V 396 TE94 diesels; 4,570 hp(m) *(3.36 MW)*; 2 ASD 15 surface drives
Speed, knots: 45. **Range, miles:** 700 at 30 kt
Complement: 15 (2 officers)
Guns: 2—12.7 mm MGs.
Weapons control: Elop MSIS optronic director.
Radars: Surface search: Koden; I-band.

Comment: First one delivered in August 1996 at Isola base. Second planned for 2001.

UPDATED

ANKARAN   *6/1999*, Slovenian Navy /* 0080597

POLICE

Note: In addition there is a 40 kt cabin cruiser P 101 and two RIBs.

1 HARBOUR PATROL CRAFT (FPB)

Name	No	Builders	Commissioned
LADSE	P 111	Aviotechnica	21 June 1995

Displacement, tons: 44 full load
Dimensions, feet (metres): 65.3 × 16.4 × 3 *(19.9 × 5 × 0.9)*
Main machinery: 2 MTU 8V 396 TE84 diesels; 2,400 hp(m) *(1.76 MW)*; 2 shafts
Speed, knots: 40. **Range, miles:** 270 at 38 kt
Complement: 10
Guns: 1—7.62 mm MG.
Radars: Surface search: I-band.

Comment: Acquired from Italy in 1995.

UPDATED

LADSE   *10/1997* /* 0080598

SOLOMON ISLANDS

Personnel	Prefix to Ships' Names	Mercantile Marine	DELETIONS	
2000: 60 (14 officers)	RSIPV	*Lloyd's Register of Shipping:* 31 vessels of 10,372 tons gross	1998 2000	*Savo* *Tulagi*

POLICE

AUKI   *1/1994*, van Ginderen Collection /* 0080599

2 PACIFIC FORUM TYPE (PC)

Name	No	Builders	Commissioned
LATA	03	Australian Shipbuilding Industries	3 Sep 1988
AUKI	04	Australian Shipbuilding Industries	2 Nov 1991

Displacement, tons: 162 full load
Dimensions, feet (metres): 103.3 × 26.6 × 7.5 *(31.5 × 8.1 × 2.3)*
Main machinery: 2 Caterpillar 3516TA diesels; 4,400 hp *(3.28 MW)* sustained; 2 shafts
Speed, knots: 20. **Range, miles:** 2,230 at 12 kt
Complement: 14 (1 officer)
Guns: 3—12.7 mm MGs.
Radars: Surface search: Furuno 8100-D; I-band.

Comment: Built under the Australian Defence Co-operation Programme. Training, operational and technical assistance provided by the Royal Australian Navy. Aluminium construction. Nominal endurance of 10 days.

UPDATED

SOUTH AFRICA

Headquarters Appointments

Chief of the Navy:
Vice Admiral R C Simpson-Anderson
Chief Director Maritime Support:
Rear Admiral H J M Trainor
Chief Director Maritime Warfare:
Rear Admiral A N Howell
Flag Officer Fleet:
Rear Admiral E M Green

Diplomatic Representation

Naval Attaché in Washington:
Captain R W Higgs
Naval Attaché in Paris:
Captain L O Reeders
Defence Attaché in Buenos Aires:
Captain S L Pillay
Defence Attaché in Santiago:
Captain A H de Vries
Defence Attaché in Nairobi:
Captain N H Snyman

Personnel

2000:
(a) 4,709 naval
(b) 2,984 reserves

Prefix to Ships' Names

SAS (South African Ship)

Bases

Simon's Town (main); Durban.
Saldanha Bay (basic training), Gordon's Bay (officer training).

Mercantile Marine

Lloyd's Register of Shipping:
192 vessels of 379,280 tons gross

DELETIONS

Submarines

1999 *Spear*

Patrol Forces

1998 *Jan Smuts*
1999 *Shakha, Sekhukune* (both reserve)

Mine Warfare Forces

1999 *Kimberley, Windhoek* (both reserve)

Auxiliaries

1998 P 1551

SUBMARINES

0 + (3) 209 CLASS (TYPE 1400) (SSK)

Displacement, tons: 1,454 surfaced; 1,594 dived
Dimensions, feet (metres): 201.5 × 24.7 × 18.8
(62 × 7.6 × 5.8)
Main machinery: Diesel electric: 4 MTU 12V 396 diesels;
3,800 hp(m) *(2.8 MW)*; 4 alternators; 1 Siemens motor;
5,032 hp(m) *(3.7 MW)*; 1 shaft
Speed, knots: 10 surfaced; 21.5 dived
Complement: 30

Torpedoes: 8—21 in *(533 mm)* bow tubes.
Countermeasures: ESM: intercept.
Weapons control: STN Atlas ISUS 90 TFCS.
Radars: Surface search: I-band.
Sonars: Hull mounted and flank arrays.

Programmes: To be acquired from the German Submarine
Consortium. Final approval given on 15 September 1999. The
submarines are to be built by HDW and TNSW with a first
delivery date of April 2005, and then at 12 month intervals.
Structure: Diving depth 280 m *(820 ft)*.

NEW ENTRY

TYPE 209 (1400) (Turkish colours)   *3/1999*, Diego Quevedo /* 0080600

2 DAPHNE CLASS (SSK)

Name	No	Builders	Laid down	Launched	Commissioned
UMKHONTO (ex-*Emily Hobhouse*)	S 98	Dubigeon—Normandie, Nantes-Chantenay	18 Nov 1968	24 Oct 1969	25 Jan 1971
ASSEGAAI (ex-*Johanna van der Merwe*)	S 99	Dubigeon—Normandie, Nantes-Chantenay	24 Apr 1969	21 July 1970	21 July 1971

Displacement, tons: 869 surfaced; 1,043 dived
Dimensions, feet (metres): 189.6 × 22.3 × 15.1
(57.8 × 6.8 × 4.6)
Main machinery: Diesel-electric; 2 SEMT-Pielstick 12 PA4 V 185
diesels; 2,450 hp(m) *(1.8 MW)*; 2 Jeumont Schneider
alternators; 1.7 MW; 2 motors; 2,600 hp(m) *(1.9 MW)*; 2
shafts
Speed, knots: 13.5 surfaced; 16 dived
Range, miles: 4,500 at 5 kt snorting; 2,700 at 12.5 kt surfaced
Complement: 47 (6 officers)

Torpedoes: 12—21.7 in *(550 mm)* (8 bow, 4 stern) tubes. ECAN
E15; dual purpose; passive homing to 12 km *(6.6 n miles)* at

25 kt; warhead 300 kg; or ECAN L4/L5 to 9.5 km *(5.1 n miles)*.
No reloads.
Countermeasures: ESM: ARUD; radar warning upgraded by
Grinaker Electronics.
Weapons control: Trivetts-UEC weapon control system. DCSC-2
being fitted.
Radars: Surface search: Thomson-CSF Calypso II; I-band.
Sonars: Thomson Sintra DUUA 2; hull-mounted; active/passive
search and attack; 8.4 kHz active.
Thomson Sintra DUUX 2 or UEC; passive rangefinding.
Thomson Sintra DSUV 2 or UEC; passive search; medium
frequency.

Programmes: Ordered from France in 1967.
Modernisation: Weapon systems upgrading (including sonar) as
well as improved habitability as part of a mid-life improvement
programme. *Umkhonto* completed in July 1988, *Assegaai*
late 1990. *Assegaai* completed a four year refit on 19 May
1999, and *Umkhonto* is expected to be operational again in
2000 after a short refit.
Structure: French Daphne design, similar to those built in France
for that country, Pakistan and Portugal and also built in Spain.
Diving depth, 300 m *(985 ft)*.

UPDATED

ASSEGAAI   *5/1999*, South African Navy /* 0053491

CORVETTES

0 + 4 MEKO A-200 TYPE (CORVETTES) (FSG)

Displacement, tons: 3,590 full load
Dimensions, feet (metres): 397 × 53.8 × 20.3
(121 × 16.4 × 6.2)
Main machinery: CODAG; 1 GE LM 2500 gas turbine; 2 MTU
16V 1163 diesels; 2 shafts; cp props; 1 Kamewa waterjet
(centreline)
Speed, knots: 28. **Range, miles:** 7,700 at 15 kt
Complement: 92 plus 8 aircrew plus 20 spare

Missiles: SSM: 8 Exocet MM 40 Block 2 ❶.
SAM: Umkhonto 16 cell VLS ❷.
Guns: 1 Otobreda 76 mm/62 compact ❸.
2 LIW Veldor 35 mm (twin) ❹. 2 LIW 20 mm Mk 1.
Torpedoes: 4 or 6—324 mm tubes ❺.
Countermeasures: Decoys: 2 Super Barricade chaff launchers
❻.
ESM/ECM: intercept and jammer ❼.

Combat data systems: Thomson-CSF.
Weapons control: 2 optronic trackers.
Radars: Air/surface search: Thomson-CSF ❽ 3D; E/F-band.
Fire control: 2 sets ❾; I/J-band.
Navigation/Helicopter control: 2 sets ❿; I-band.
Sonars: Hull mounted, active search; medium frequency.

Helicopters: 2 Oryx or Super Lynx ⓫ in due course.

Programmes: Tenders first closed in August 1994. Approval
finally given on 15 September 1999 for contracts to be placed
with ESACC which includes African Defence Systems,
Thomson-CSF, Blohm + Voss and HDW. Two are to be built by
Blohm + Voss, Hamburg, and two by HDW, Kiel. Hulls are to be
delivered in 2002/03 for fitting out and weapon systems
integration in South Africa by African Defence Systems and
Thomson-CSF. The plan is to complete the first of class in 2004
and the last by 2006.
Structure: The design is a MEKO A-200 derivative, adapted for
South African requirements.
Operational: Westland Super Lynx helicopters selected, but not
ordered at the same time as the ships. ***UPDATED***

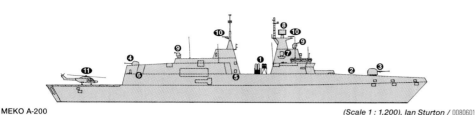

MEKO A-200

(Scale 1 : 1,200), Ian Sturton / 0080601

PATROL FORCES

6 WARRIOR (EX-MINISTER) CLASS
(FAST ATTACK CRAFT—MISSILE) (PCFG)

Name	No	Builders	Commissioned
ADAM KOK (ex-*Frederic Creswell*)	P 1563	Haifa Shipyard	6 Apr 1978
ISAAC DYOBHA (ex-*Frans Erasmus*)	P 1565	Sandock Austral, Durban	27 July 1979
RENÉ SETHREN (ex-*Oswald Pirow*)	P 1566	Sandock Austral, Durban	4 Mar 1980
GALESHEWE (ex-*Hendrik Mentz*)	P 1567	Sandock Austral, Durban	11 Feb 1983
JOB MASEKO (ex-*Kobie Coetsee*)	P 1568	Sandock Austral, Durban	11 Feb 1983
MAKHANDA (ex-*Magnus Malan*)	P 1569	Sandock Austral, Durban	4 July 1986

Displacement, tons: 430 full load
Dimensions, feet (metres): 204 × 25 × 8 *(62.2 × 7.8 × 2.4)*
Main machinery: 4 Maybach MTU 16V 965 TB91 diesels; 15,000 hp(m) *(11 MW)* sustained;
4 shafts
Speed, knots: 32. **Range, miles:** 1,500 at 30 kt; 3,600+ at economical speed
Complement: 52 (7 officers)

Missiles: SSM: 6 Skerpioen; active radar or optical guidance; semi-active radar homing to 36 km
(19.4 n miles) at 0.7 Mach; warhead 75 kg. Another pair may be mounted. Skerpioen is an Israeli
Gabriel II built under licence in South Africa.
Guns: 1 or 2 OTO Melara 3 in *(76 mm)*/62 compact; 85 rds/min to 16 km *(8.7 n miles)*; weight of
shell 6 kg; 500 rounds per gun.
2 LIW Vektor 35 mm (twin); 550 rds/min; may replace one 76 mm gun in one craft for trials.
2 LIW Mk 1 20 mm. 2—12.7 mm MGs.
Countermeasures: Decoys: 4 ACDS launchers for chaff.
ESM: Elta; radar warning; being replaced by Delcon (ADS/Sysdel) EW system.
ECM: Elta Rattler; jammer.
Combat data systems: ADS Diamant (after upgrade). Mini action data automation with Link.
Radars: Air/surface search: Elta EL/M 2208; E/F-band.
Fire control: Selenia RTN 10X; I/J-band.

Programmes: Contract signed with Israel in late 1974 for this class, similar to 'Saar 4' class. Three
built in Haifa and reached South Africa by July 1978. The ninth craft launched June 1986.
Three more improved vessels of this class were ordered but subsequently cancelled. The last of
the class was finally christened in March 1992. Pennant numbers restored to the ships side and
stern in 1994.
Modernisation: P 1568 modernised in July 1988; P 1566 in May 1989. The postponement of the
corvette replacements in 1991 led to the expansion of the upgrade programme into a major ship-
life extension. This includes a new communications refit, improvements to EW sensors, a third-
generation target designation assembly, a computer-assisted action information system served
by datalinks, improvements to fire control, a complete overhaul of the Skerpioen missiles, and a
new engine room monitoring system. P 1563 was the first to undergo this upgrade and
completed in mid-1996. P 1565 completed in April 1999, P 1567 in March 2000 and P 1569 by
mid-2000. P 1568 is planned to complete in mid-2001 and P 1566 in early 2002.
Operational: In addition, P 1562 and P 1564 are in reserve and unlikely to go to sea again.

UPDATED

3 COASTGUARD CLASS (PB)

Name	No	Builders	Commissioned
TOBIE	P 1552	T Craft International, Cape Town	June 1992
TERN	P 1553	T Craft International, Cape Town	June 1996
TEKWANE	P 1554	T Craft International, Cape Town	Dec 1996

Displacement, tons: 36 full load
Dimensions, feet (metres): 72.2 × 23 × 3 *(22 × 7 × 0.9)*
Main machinery: 2 ADE 444 TI 12V diesels; 2,000 hp *(1.5 MW)*; 2 Castoldi water-jets
Speed, knots: 32. **Range, miles:** 530 at 22 kt
Complement: 16 (1 officer)
Guns: 1—12.7 mm MG. 6—107 mm mortars.
Weapons control: Hesis optical director.
Radars: Surface search: Racal Decca; I-band.

Comment: Twin hulled catamarans of GRP sandwich construction. Capable of carrying up to 15
people. Ordered in mid-1991. Carries an RIB in the stern well. Three of this type built for Israel in
1997.

UPDATED

TERN

4/1997, Michael Nitz / 0050110

28 NAMACURRA CLASS (INSHORE PATROL CRAFT) (PB)

Y 1501-1519   Y 1521-1529

Displacement, tons: 5 full load
Dimensions, feet (metres): 29.5 × 9 × 2.8 *(9 × 2.7 × 0.8)*
Main machinery: 2 Yamaha outboards; 380 hp(m) *(279 kW)*
Speed, knots: 32. **Range, miles:** 180 at 20 kt
Complement: 4
Guns: 1—12.7 mm MG. 2—7.62 mm MGs.
Depth charges: 1 rack.
Radars: Surface search: Furuno; I-band.

Comment: Built in South Africa in 1980-81. Can be transported by road. One transferred to Malawi
in October 1988 and one has sunk at sea.

VERIFIED

JOB MASEKO

6/1997, *Michael Nitz / 0016640*

NAMACURRA

4/1997, Robert Pabst / 0050109

SHIPBORNE AIRCRAFT

Note: Four Westland Super Lynx are to be ordered for the new corvettes to coincide with the first corvette in-service date.

Numbers/Type: 8 Aerospatiale SA 330E/H/J Oryx.
Operational speed: 139 kt *(258 km/h).*
Service ceiling: 15,750 ft *(4,800 m).*
Range: 297 n miles *(550 km).*
Role/Weapon systems: Support helicopter; allocated by SAAF for naval duties and can be embarked in both AORs and in *Agulhas.* Sensors: Doppler navigation, some with search radar. Weapons: Unarmed but can mount Armscor 30 mm Ratler.

UPDATED

ORYX   *3/1995*, Mike Gething /* 0080602

LAND-BASED MARITIME AIRCRAFT

Note: There are also some utility Alouette helicopters.

Numbers/Type: 13 Douglas Turbodaks.
Operational speed: 161 kt *(298 km/h).*
Service ceiling: 24,000 ft *(7,315 m).*
Range: 1,390 n miles *(2,575 km).*
Role/Weapon systems: A number of Dakotas has been converted for MR/SAR and other tasks. Additional fuel tanks extend the range to 2,620 n miles *(4,800 km).* Sensors: Elta M-2022 search radar and FLIR; Sysdel ESM; sonobuoy acoustic processor. Weapons: Unarmed.

VERIFIED

SURVEY AND RESEARCH SHIPS

Note: As well as *S A Agulhas,* the Department of Environmental Affairs has three research vessels: *Africana* of 2,471 grt, *Algoa* of 760 grt and *Sardinops* of 255 grt.

1 HECLA CLASS (AGS)

Name	No	Builders	Commissioned
PROTEA	A 324	Yarrow (Shipbuilders) Ltd	23 May 1972

Displacement, tons: 2,733 full load
Dimensions, feet (metres): 260.1 × 49.1 × 15.6 *(79.3 × 15 × 4.7)*
Main machinery: Diesel-electric; 3 MTU diesels; 3,840 hp *(2.68 MW)* sustained; 3 generators; 1 motor; 2,000 hp *(1.49 MW);* 1 shaft; cp prop; bow thruster
Speed, knots: 14. **Range, miles:** 12,000 at 11 kt
Complement: 124 (10 officers)
Radars: Navigation: Racal Decca; I-band.
Helicopters: 1 Alouette III.

Comment: Laid down 20 July 1970. Launched 14 July 1971. Equipped for hydrographic survey with limited facilities for the collection of oceanographical data and for this purpose fitted with special communications equipment, Polaris survey system, survey launches and facilities for helicopter operations. Hull strengthened for navigation in ice and fitted with a passive roll stabilisation system. New engines and full overhaul in 1995-96. Carries EGNG sidescan sonar and two survey boats. Fitted for two 20 mm guns.

UPDATED

PROTEA   *4/1997*, Robert Pabst /* 0019118

1 ANTARCTIC SURVEY AND SUPPLY VESSEL (AGOB)

Name	Builders	Launched	Commissioned
S A AGULHAS	Mitsubishi, Shimonoseki	30 Sep 1977	31 Jan 1978

Measurement, tons: 5,353 gross
Dimensions, feet (metres): 358.3 × 59 × 19 *(109.2 × 18 × 5.8)*
Main machinery: 2 Mirrlees-Blackstone K6 major diesels; 6,600 hp *(4.49 MW);* 1 shaft; bow and stern thrusters
Speed, knots: 14. **Range, miles:** 8,200 at 14 kt
Complement: 40 plus 92 spare berths
Radars: Navigation: Racal Decca; I-band.
Helicopters: 2 SA 330J Puma.

Comment: Red hull and white superstructure. A Department of Environmental Affairs vessel, civilian manned. Major refit March to October 1992; 25 ton crane moved forward, transverse thrusters and roll damping fitted, improved navigation and communications equipment. A hinged hatch has been fitted at the stern to recover towed equipment.

UPDATED

S A AGULHAS   *11/1999*, Robert Pabst /* 0080603

MINE WARFARE FORCES

Note: Negotiations started in early 1999 for the possible transfer of the Type 351 Troika control ships *Paderborn* and *Ulm* from Germany. Delays caused by the German government in November 1999, but the transfer is expected to go ahead in 2000/01.

4 RIVER CLASS (COASTAL MINEHUNTERS) (MHC)

Name	No	Builders	Commissioned
UMKOMAAS (ex-*Navors I*)	M 1499	Abeking & Rasmussen/ Sandock Austral	13 Jan 1981
UMGENI (ex-*Navors II*)	M 1213	Abeking & Rasmussen/ Sandock Austral	1 Mar 1981
UMZIMKULU (ex-*Navors III*)	M 1142	Sandock Austral	30 Oct 1981
UMHLOTI (ex-*Navors IV*)	M 1212	Sandock Austral	15 Dec 1981

Displacement, tons: 380 full load
Dimensions, feet (metres): 157.5 × 27.9 × 8.2 *(48 × 8.5 × 2.5)*
Main machinery: 2 MTU 12V 652 TB81 diesels; 4,515 hp(m) *(3.32 MW);* 2 Voith Schneider props
Speed, knots: 16. **Range, miles:** 2,000 at 13 kt
Complement: 40 (7 officers)
Guns: 1 Oerlikon 20 mm GAM-BO1. 2—12.7 mm MGs.
Countermeasures: MCM: 2 PAP 104 remote-controlled submersibles.
Radars: Navigation: Decca; I-band.
Sonars: Klein VDS; side scan; high frequency.

Comment: Ordered in 1978 as Research Vessels to be operated by the Navy for the Department of Transport. The lead ship *Navors I* was shipped to Durban from Germany in the heavy lift ship *Uhenfels* in June 1980 for fitting out, shortly followed by the second. The last pair were built in Durban. The vessels were painted blue with white upperworks and formed the First Research Squadron. Painted grey and renamed in 1982 but continued to fly the national flag and not the naval ensign. The prefix RV was only changed to SAS on 3 February 1988 when they were formally accepted as naval ships. Minehunting capability could be enhanced by substituting the diving container on the after deck with lightweight mechanical and acoustic sweeping gear. Carry an RIB and a decompression chamber. The plan is to give them a second generation minehunting system.

VERIFIED

UMZIMKULU   *5/1998 /* 0050112

2 TON CLASS (MINESWEEPERS) (MSC)

Name	No	Builders	Commissioned
WALVISBAAI (ex-*Packington*)	M 1214	Harland & Wolff, Belfast	20 Sep 1959
EAST LONDON (ex-*Chilton*)	M 1215	Cook Welton and Gemmell	28 Oct 1958

Displacement, tons: 360 standard; 440 full load
Dimensions, feet (metres): 153 × 28.9 × 8.2 *(46.6 × 8.8 × 2.5)*
Main machinery: 2 Paxman Deltic 18A-7A diesels; 3,000 hp *(2.24 MW)*; 2 shafts
Speed, knots: 15. **Range, miles:** 2,300 at 13 kt
Complement: 39
Guns: 1 Bofors 40 mm/60; 120 rds/min to 10 km *(5.5 n miles)*; weight of shell 0.89 kg.
2—12.7 mm (twin). 6—7.62 mm MGs.
Radars: Navigation: Racal Decca; I-band.

Comment: The last two survivors of a class of 10. Six were paid off in 1987 because of a shortage of trained personnel. Two year major modernisation started in 1991 with a new MCM control system and a major renewal of decks and frames. *Walvisbaai* completed modernisation 13 April 1993 and *East London* 12 February 1999. Two others are in reserve and the plan is to replace them with ex-German Type 351 class. ***UPDATED***

WALVISBAAI   *4/1997*, Michael Nitz /* 0019116

AUXILIARIES

1 FLEET REPLENISHMENT SHIP (AOR)

Name	No	Builders	Launched	Commissioned
DRAKENSBERG	A 301	Sandock Austral, Durban	24 Apr 1986	11 Nov 1987

Displacement, tons: 6,000 light; 12,500 full load
Dimensions, feet (metres): 482.3 × 64 × 25.9 *(147 × 19.5 × 7.9)*
Main machinery: 2 diesels; 16,320 hp(m) *(12 MW)*; 1 shaft; cp prop; bow thruster
Speed, knots: 20+. **Range, miles:** 8,000 at 15 kt
Complement: 96 (10 officers) plus 10 aircrew plus 22 spare
Cargo capacity: 5,500 tons fuel; 750 tons ammunition and dry stores; 2 Delta 80 LCUs
Guns: 4 Oerlikon 20 mm GAM-BO1. 6—12.7 mm MGs.
Helicopters: 2 SA 330H/J Oryx.

Comment: The largest ship built in South Africa and the first naval vessel to be completely designed in that country. In addition to her replenishment role she is employed on SAR, patrol and surveillance with a considerable potential for disaster relief. As well as LCUs carries two diving support boats and two RIBs. Two abeam positions and astern fuelling, jackstay and vertrep. Two helicopter landing spots. Can be used as a mother ship for small craft and for troop transport. ***UPDATED***

DRAKENSBERG   *4/1997*, van Ginderen Collection /* 0019121

1 DIVING SUPPORT SHIP (YDT)

Name	No	Builders	Launched	Commissioned
FLEUR	P 3148	Dorman Long, Durban	30 June 1969	3 Dec 1969

Displacement, tons: 220 standard; 257 full load
Dimensions, feet (metres): 121.5 × 27.5 × 11.1 *(37 × 8.4 × 3.4)*
Main machinery: 2 Paxman 6YJCM diesels; 1,400 hp *(1.04 MW)* sustained; 2 shafts
Speed, knots: 14. **Range:** 2,300 at 14 kt
Complement: 31 (4 officers)
Guns: 2—12.7 mm MGs. 2—7.62 mm MGs.
Radars: Navigation: Decca; I-band.

Comment: Combined torpedo recovery vessel and diving tender with recompression chamber. Can also serve as a submarine tender. ***VERIFIED***

FLEUR   *4/1997, Michael Nitz /* 0050114

---

1 COMBAT SUPPORT SHIP (AP)

Name	No	Builders	Commissioned
OUTENIQUA (ex-*Juvent*, ex-*Aleksander Sledzyuk*)	A 302	Kherson Shipyard, Ukraine	3 Apr 1992

Displacement, tons: 21,025 full load
Dimensions, feet (metres): 545.6 × 74.1 × 29.5 *(166.3 × 22.6 × 9)*
Main machinery: 1 MAN Burmeister & Wain 8DKRN-60/195 diesel; 17,512 hp(m) *(12.87 MW)*; 1 shaft; cp prop
Speed, knots: 17. **Range, miles:** 8,000 at 15 kt
Complement: 126 (17 officers) including aircrew
Military lift: 4 Delta 80 LCU; 10 vehicles; 600 troops
Guns: 2 Oerlikon 20 mm GAM-BO1. 6—12.7 mm MGs.
Radars: Navigation: 2 Racal; I-band.
Helicopters: 2 SA 330H/J Oryx.

Comment: Launched on 6 September 1991 as the *Aleksander Sledzyuk* and renamed *Juvent* on 4 April 1992 when ownership was transferred to a shipping company. This company operated her until 26 February 1993 when she was bought by the Navy, through Armscor and recommissioned 8 July 1993. Built as an Arctic supply vessel with an icebreaking capability of 1 m thick ice at a constant speed of 2 kt. Refit in 1994 to allow alterations to flight deck and hangars to take Oryx helicopters, and to fit light armament and RAS gear. Further work done from May to September 1996, and again from May to September 1997. Helicopter handling system installed in 1998. Primary role is troop transport. Secondary roles include replenishment, Antarctic support, SAR and relief work. ***UPDATED***

OUTENIQUA   *1/1999*, South African Navy /* 0080604

8 DELTA 80 CLASS (LCU)

Displacement, tons: 5.5 full load
Dimensions, feet (metres): 27.2 × 10.2 × 3 *(8.3 × 3.1 × 0.9)*
Main machinery: 2 outboards; 350 hp *(261 kW)*
Speed, knots: 37. **Range, miles:** 150 at 35 kt
Complement: 5

Comment: Built in the 1980s. Two each can be carried in *Drakensberg* and *Outeniqua*. ***UPDATED***

DELTA 80   *1993*, South African Navy /* 0080605

TUGS

Note: There are also two harbour tugs *De Neys* and *Umalusi*.

1 COASTAL TUG (YTB)

DE MIST

Displacement, tons: 275 full load
Dimensions, feet (metres): 112.5 × 25.6 × 11.1 *(34.3 × 7.8 × 3.4)*
Main machinery: 2 Mirlees-Blackstone diesels; 2,440 hp *(1.82 MW)*; 2 Voith-Schneider props
Speed, knots: 12
Complement: 11

Comment: Completed by Dorbyl Long, Durban on 23 December 1978. ***VERIFIED***

DE MIST   *9/1997, van Ginderen Collection /* 0050116

SPAIN
ARMADA ESPAÑOLA

Headquarters Appointments

Chief of the Naval Staff:
Admiral Antonio Moreno Barbera
Second Chief of the Naval Staff:
Vice Admiral Juan José González-Irún Sánchez
Chief of Fleet Support:
Admiral Nicolás J Lapique Dobarro

Commands

Commander-in-Chief of the Fleet:
Admiral Francisco Rapallo Comendador
Commander-in-Chief, Cantabrian Zone:
Admiral Rafael de Morales Romero
Commander-in-Chief, Straits Zone:
Vice Admiral Alfonso Mosquera Areces
Commander-in-Chief, Mediterranean Zone:
Admiral Adolfo Baturone Santiago
Commander-in-Chief, Canarian Islands Zone:
Vice Admiral José A Zea Salguero
Commander-in-Chief, Central Zone:
Admiral Marcelino Garcia Teibel
Commandant General, Marines:
Lieutenant General Francisco Gonzales Mūnoz

Diplomatic Representation

Naval Attaché in Bonn:
Captain Alvaro Fernandez Navarro de los Paños
Naval Attaché in Brasilia:
Captain Martin Maañon López-Leyton
Naval Attaché in Lisbon:
Captain Alberto Ladriñan Diaz
Naval Attaché in London:
Captain José C Iglesias Bermudez
Naval Attaché in Paris:
Commander Manuel Cela Murais
Naval Attaché in Rabat:
Commander Francisco Aviles Beriguistain
Naval Attaché in Rome:
Commander Manuel Garcia de Quesada Fort
Naval Attaché in Santiago:
Captain Aurelio Fernandez Diz
Naval Attaché in Washington:
Captain José Manuel Palencia Luaces
Naval Attaché in The Hague, Oslo and Copenhagen:
Captain José Maria Agúndez Betelu
Naval Attaché in Bangkok:
Captain Carlos Marquez Montero
Naval Attaché in Pretoria:
Captain José M Gárate Martinez

Personnel

(a) 2000: Navy: 22,863 (2,700 officers)
Marines: 8,895 (491 officers)
(b) 9 months' national service (approx quarter of the total numbers) to end by 2003

Bases

Ferrol: Cantabrian Zone HQ—Ferrol arsenal, support centre at La Graña, naval school at Marín, Pontevedra, electronics school at Vigo, Pontevedra
Cádiz: Straits Zone HQ—La Carraca arsenal, fleet command HQ and naval air base at Rota, amphibious base at Puntales, Tarifa small ships' base
Cartagena: Mediterranean Zone HQ—Cartagena arsenal, underwater weapons and divers school at La Algameca; support base at Mahón, Minorca and at Soller and Porto Pi, Majorca, submarine weapons schools at La Algameca and Porto Pi base, Majorca
Las Palmas: Canaries Zone HQ—Las Palmas arsenal

Naval Air Service

Type	Escuadrilla
AB 212	3
Cessna Citation II	4
Sikorsky SH-3D/G Sea King	
Sikorsky SH-3E Sea King (AEW)	5
Hughes 500M (Training)	6
EAV-8B Harrier II/Harrier Plus	9
Sikorsky SH-60B Seahawk	10

Guardia Civil del Mar

Started operations in 1992. For details, see end of section.

Fleet Deployment

(1) Fleet
(a) Grupo Aeronaval Alfa: (based at Rota)
Principe de Asturias with appropriate escorts
(b) Escuadrillas de Escoltas:
21st Squadron; 6 'Descubierta' class (based at Cartagena)
31st Squadron; 5 'Baleares' class (based at Ferrol)
41st Squadron; 6 'Santa María' class (based at Rota)
(c) Grupo Anfibio Delta: (based at Puntales, Cádiz)
All Amphibious Forces
(d) Fuerza de Medidas contra Minas: (based at Cartagena)
8 MSCs and 3 MSOs
(e) Flotilla de Submarinos: (based at Cartagena)
All submarines
(2) Support units, Cantabrian Zone:
1 Ocean Tug, 8 Tugs, 4 Patrol Ships, 5 Large Patrol Craft, 7 Coastal Patrol Craft, 4 Sail Training Ships, 5 Training Craft
(3) Support units, Straits Zone:
6 Oceanographic Ships, 1 Sail Training Ship, 4 Fast Attack Craft, 1 Transport, 1 Ocean Tug, 7 Tugs, 1 Water-boat
(4) Support units, Mediterranean Zone:
4 Fast Attack Craft, 1 Water-boat, 7 Tugs, 1 Frogman Support Ship
(5) Support units, Canaries Zone:
1 Water-boat, 2 Ocean Tugs, 2 Tugs, 2 LCTs

Strength of the Fleet

Type	Active	Building (Planned)
Submarines—Patrol	8	(3)
Aircraft Carriers	1	—
Frigates	11	4
Corvettes	6	—
Offshore Patrol Vessels	4	—
Fast Attack Craft—Gun	6	—
Large Patrol Craft	12	—
Coastal Patrol Craft	8	—
Inshore Patrol Craft	2	—
LPDs	2	(1)
LSTs	2	—
LCTs	2	—
Minesweepers	7	(4)
Minehunters	4	(4)
Survey and Research Ships	8	—
Replenishment Tankers	2	—
Tankers	15	—
Transport Ships	2	—
Training Ships	11	—

Mercantile Marine

Lloyd's Register of Shipping:
1,562 vessels of 1,903,081 tons gross

DELETIONS

Amphibious Forces

1998   *Castilla* (old), LCT AO7

Mine Warfare Forces

1998   *Guadalete*
1999   *Guadiana, Duero, Miño*
2000   *Guadalmedina*

Amphibious Warfare Forces

2000   *Aragon*

Auxiliaries

1998   *Nereida*
1999   *Poseidón* (to Mauritania)

PENNANT LIST

Submarines

S 61	Delfín
S 62	Tonina
S 63	Marsopa
S 64	Narval
S 71	Galerna
S 72	Siroco
S 73	Mistral
S 74	Tramontana

Aircraft Carriers

R 11	Príncipe de Asturias

Frigates

F 71	Baleares
F 72	Andalucía
F 73	Cataluña
F 74	Asturias
F 75	Extremadura
F 81	Santa María
F 82	Victoria
F 83	Numancia
F 84	Reina Sofía
F 85	Navarra
F 86	Canarias
F 101	Alvaro de Bazán (bldg)
F 102	Roger de Lauria (bldg)
F 103	Blas de Lezo (bldg)
F 104	Mendez Nuñez (bldg)

Corvettes

F 31	Descubierta
F 32	Diana
F 33	Infanta Elena
F 34	Infanta Cristina
F 35	Cazadora
F 36	Vencedora

Patrol Forces

P 11	Barceló
P 12	Laya
P 13	Javier Quiroga
P 14	Ordóñez
P 15	Acevedo
P 16	Cándido Pérez
P 21	Anaga
P 22	Tagomago
P 23	Marola
P 24	Mouro
P 25	Grosa
P 26	Medas
P 27	Izaro
P 28	Tabarca
P 29	Deva
P 30	Bergantín
P 31	Conejera
P 32	Dragonera
P 33	Espalmador
P 34	Alcanada
P 61	Chilreu
P 62	Alboran
P 71	Serviola
P 72	Centinela

P 73	Vigia
P 74	Atalaya
P 81	Toralla
P 82	Formentor
P 201	Cabo Fradera

Amphibious Forces

L 41	Hernán Cortés
L 42	Pizarro
L 51	Galicia
L 52	Castilla

Mine Warfare Forces

M 21	Júcar
M 22	Ebro
M 24	Tajo
M 25	Genil
M 26	Odiel
M 27	Sil
M 31	Segura
M 32	Sella
M 33	Tambre
M 34	Turia
M 43	Guadalquivir

Survey Ships

A 21	Castor
A 22	Pollux
A 23	Antares

A 24	Rigel
A 31	Malaspina
A 32	Tofiño
A 33	Hespérides
A 111	Alerta

Auxiliaries

A 01	Contramaestre Casado
A 04	Martín Posadillo (Army)
A 05	El Camino Español
A 11	Marqués de la Ensenada
A 14	Patiño
A 20	Neptuno
A 31	Ferrol
A 51	Mahón
A 52	Las Palmas
A 53	La Graña
A 63	Torpédista Hernández
A 65	Marinero Jarano
A 66	Condestable Zaragoza
A 71	Juan Sebastián de Elcano
A 72	Arosa
A 73	Hispania
A 74	La Graciosa
A 75	Sisargas
A 76	Giralda
A 81	Guardiamarina Barrutia
A 82	Guardiamarina Salas
A 83	Guardiamarina Godínez
A 84	Guardiamarina Rull
A 85	Guardiamarina Chereguini
A 101	Mar Caribe
Y 563	Proserpina

SUBMARINES

Note: Three or four Scorpène S 80 submarines with MESMA AIP are to be ordered. Displacement about 1,870 tons submerged, and 70 m in length. First in-service date planned for 2005.

4 GALERNA (AGOSTA) CLASS (SSK)

Name	No	Builders	Laid down	Launched	Commissioned
GALERNA	S 71	Bazán, Cartagena	5 Sep 1977	5 Dec 1981	22 Jan 1983
SIROCO	S 72	Bazán, Cartagena	27 Nov 1978	13 Nov 1982	5 Dec 1983
MISTRAL	S 73	Bazán, Cartagena	30 May 1980	14 Nov 1983	5 June 1985
TRAMONTANA	S 74	Bazán, Cartagena	10 Dec 1981	30 Nov 1984	27 Jan 1986

Displacement, tons: 1,490 surfaced; 1,740 dived
Dimensions, feet (metres): 221.7 × 22.3 × 17.7 *(67.6 × 6.8 × 5.4)*
Main machinery: Diesel-electric; 2 SEMT-Pielstick 16 PA4 V 185 VG diesels; 3,600 hp(m) *(2.7 MW)*; 2 Jeumont Schneider alternators; 1.7 MW; 1 motor; 4,600 hp(m) *(3.4 MW)*; 1 cruising motor; 32 hp(m) *(23 kW)*; 1 shaft
Speed, knots: 12 surfaced; 20 dived; 17.5 sustained
Range, miles: 8,500 snorting at 9 kt; 350 dived on cruising motor at 3.5 kt
Complement: 54 (6 officers)

Torpedoes: 4—21 in *(533 mm)* tubes. 20 combination of
(a) ECAN L5 Mod 3/4; dual purpose; active/passive homing to 9.5 km *(5.1 n miles)* at 35 kt; warhead 150 kg; depth to 550 m *(1,800 ft)*.
(b) ECAN F17 Mod 2; wire-guided; active/passive homing to 20 km *(10.8 n miles)* at 40 kt; warhead 250 kg; depth 600 m *(1,970 ft)*.
Mines: 19 can be carried if torpedo load is reduced to 9.
Countermeasures: ESM: THORN EMI/Inisel Manta E; radar warning.
Weapons control: DLA-2A TFCS.
Radars: Surface search: Thomson-CSF DRUA 33C; I-band.
Sonars: Thomson Sintra DSUV 22; passive search and attack; medium frequency.
Thomson Sintra DUUA 2A/2B; active search and attack; 8 or 8.4 kHz active.
DUUX 2A/5; passive; rangefinding. Eledone; intercept.
SAES Solarsub towed passive array; low frequency.

Programmes: First two ordered 9 May 1975 and second pair 29 June 1977. Built with some French advice. About 67 per cent of equipment and structure from Spanish sources.
Modernisation: Modernised with improved torpedo fire control, new ESM and IR enhanced periscopes. New main batteries installed with central control monitoring. *Galerna* started in April 1993 and completed in late 1994, *Siroco* in mid-1995,

MISTRAL
5/1999*, A Campanera i Rovira / 0080607

Tramontana in early 1997, and *Mistral* in 2000. The plan to fit SSM has been shelved. Solarsub towed arrays are being fitted to all of the class during overhauls.

Structure: Diving depth, 300 m *(984 ft)*.
Operational: Endurance, 45 days.

UPDATED

4 DELFÍN (DAPHNE) CLASS (SSK)

Name	No	Builders	Laid down	Launched	Commissioned
DELFÍN	S 61	Bazán, Cartagena	13 Aug 1968	25 Mar 1972	3 May 1973
TONINA	S 62	Bazán, Cartagena	2 Mar 1970	3 Oct 1972	10 July 1973
MARSOPA	S 63	Bazán, Cartagena	19 Mar 1971	15 Mar 1974	12 Apr 1975
NARVAL	S 64	Bazán, Cartagena	24 Apr 1972	14 Dec 1974	22 Nov 1975

Displacement, tons: 869 surfaced; 1,043 dived
Dimensions, feet (metres): 189.6 × 22.3 × 15.1 *(57.8 × 6.8 × 4.6)*
Main machinery: Diesel-electric; 2 SEMT-Pielstick 12 PA4 V 185 diesels; 2,450 hp(m) *(1.8 MW)*; 2 Jeumont Schneider alternators; 1.7 MW; 2 motors; 2,600 hp(m) *(1.9 MW)*; 2 shafts
Speed, knots: 13.5 surfaced; 15.5 dived
Range, miles: 4,300 snorting at 7.5 kt; 2,710 surfaced at 12.5 kt
Complement: 47 (6 officers)

Torpedoes: 12—21.7 in *(550 mm)* (8 bow, 4 stern) tubes. 12 combination of (a) ECAN L5 Mod 3/4; dual purpose; active/

passive homing to 9.5 km *(5.1 n miles)* at 35 kt; warhead 150 kg; depth to 550 m *(1,800 ft)*.
(b) ECAN F17 Mod 2; wire-guided; active/passive homing to 20 km *(10.8 n miles)* at 40 kt; warhead 250 kg; depth 600 m *(1,970 ft)*.
Mines: 12 in lieu of torpedoes.
Countermeasures: ESM: THORN EMI Manta; radar warning.
Weapons control: DLT-3A TFCS.
Radars: Surface search: Thomson-CSF DRUA 31 or 33A; I-band.
Sonars: Thomson Sintra DSUV 22; passive search and attack; medium frequency.
Thomson Sintra DUUA 2A; active search and attack; 8 or 8.4 kHz active.

Programmes: First pair ordered 26 December 1966 and second pair in March 1970. Built with extensive French assistance.
Modernisation: The class was taken in hand from 1983 for modernisation of sonar (DUUA 2A for DUUA 1), updating of fire control and torpedo handling. Torpedo tubes were also linered to 21 in *(533 mm)*. Last one completed at the end of 1988. ESM updated in 1990-91. Torpedo fire control updated for the F17 wire-guided weapons starting with *Marsopa* in 1994-95. *Narval*'s refit was delayed with fears that she may be paid off, but overhaul was started in early 1995 and completed in December 1995. *Delfín* similarly refitted in 1996. *Tonina* may not now be done.
Structure: Diving depth, 300 m *(984 ft)*.

UPDATED

TONINA
1/1999*, Diego Quevedo / 0080606

AIRCRAFT CARRIERS

1 PRÍNCIPE DE ASTURIAS CLASS (CVS)

Name	No	Builders	Laid down	Launched	Commissioned
PRÍNCIPE DE ASTURIAS	R 11	Bazán, Ferrol	8 Oct 1979	22 May 1982	30 May 1988
(ex-*Almirante Carrero Blanco*)					

Displacement, tons: 17,188 full load
Dimensions, feet (metres): 642.7 oa; 615.2 pp × 79.7 × 30.8 *(195.9; 187.5 × 24.3 × 9.4)*
Flight deck, feet (metres): 575.1 × 95.1 *(175.3 × 29)*
Main machinery: 2 GE LM 2500 gas turbines; 46,400 hp *(34.61 MW)* sustained; 1 shaft; acbLIPS cp prop; 2 motors; 1,600 hp(m) *(1.18 MW)*; retractable prop
Speed, knots: 25 (4.5 on motors). **Range, miles:** 6,500 at 20 kt
Complement: 555 (90 officers) plus 208 (Flag Staff (7 officers) and Air Group)

Guns: 4 Bazán Meroka Mod 2A/2B 12-barrelled 20 mm/120 ❶; 3,600 rds/min combined to 2 km.
2 Rheinmetall 37 mm saluting guns.
Countermeasures: Decoys: 4 Loral Hycor SRBOC 6-barrelled fixed Mk 36; IR flares and chaff to 4 km *(2.2 n miles)*.
SLQ-25 Nixie; towed torpedo decoy.
US Prairie/Masker; hull noise/blade rate suppression.
ESM/ECM: Elettronica Nettunel; intercept and jammers.
Combat data systems: Tritan Digital Command and Control System NTDS; Links 11 and 14. Marconi Matra SCOT 3 Secomsat ❷.
Weapons control: 4 Selenia directors (for Meroka). Radamec 2000 series.
Radars: Air search: Hughes SPS-52C/D ❸; 3D; E/F-band; range 439 km *(240 n miles)*.
Surface search: ISC Cardion SPS-55 ❹; I/J-band.
Aircraft control: ITT SPN-35A ❺; J-band.
Fire control: 4 Sperry/Lockheed VPS 2 ❻; I-band (for Meroka).
RTN 11L/X; I/J-band; missile warning.
Selenia RAN 12L (target designation); I/J-band.
Tacan: URN 25.

Fixed-wing aircraft: 6-12 AV-8B Harrier II/Harrier Plus.
Helicopters: 6-10 SH-3 Sea Kings; 2-4 AB 212EW; 2 SH-60B Seahawks.

Programmes: Ordered on 29 June 1977. Associated US firms were Gibbs and Cox, Dixencast, Bath Iron Works and Sperry SM. Commissioning delays caused by changes to command and control systems and the addition of a Flag Bridge.

PRÍNCIPE DE ASTURIAS

9/1998, Diego Quevedo / 0050120

Modernisation: After two years' service some modifications were made to the port after side of the island, to improve briefing rooms and provide sheltered parking space for FD vehicles. Also improved accommodation has been added on for six officers and 50 specialist ratings.
Structure: Based on US Navy Sea Control Ship design. 12° ski-jump of 46.5 m. Two flight deck lifts, one right aft. Two LCVPs carried. Two pairs of fin stabilisers. The hangar is 24,748 sq ft *(2,300 m²)*. The Battle Group Commander occupies the lower bridge. Two saluting guns have been mounted on the port quarter.

Operational: Three Sea Kings have Searchwater AEW radar. Aircraft complement could be increased to 37 (parking on deck) in an emergency but maximum operational number is 29 (17 in hangar, 12 on deck). A typical air wing includes eight Harriers and 10 Seahawks/Sea Kings (including two AEW). Ship is based at Rota.
Sales: Modified design built for Thailand.

VERIFIED

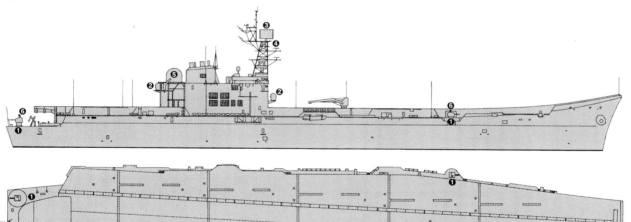

PRÍNCIPE DE ASTURIAS

(Scale 1 : 1,200), Ian Sturton

PRÍNCIPE DE ASTURIAS

8/1996, H M Steele / 0019130

FRIGATES

Note: The 'Descubierta' class are to be replaced by an F 110 design in due course.

6 SANTA MARÍA CLASS (FFG)

Name	No	Builders	Laid down	Launched	Commissioned
SANTA MARÍA	F 81	Bazán, Ferrol	23 May 1982	24 Nov 1984	12 Oct 1986
VICTORIA	F 82	Bazán, Ferrol	16 Aug 1983	23 July 1986	11 Nov 1987
NUMANCIA	F 83	Bazán, Ferrol	8 Jan 1986	30 Jan 1987	8 Nov 1988
REINA SOFÍA (ex-*América*)	F 84	Bazán, Ferrol	12 Dec 1987	19 July 1989	18 Oct 1990
NAVARRA	F 85	Bazán, Ferrol	15 Apr 1991	23 Oct 1992	30 May 1994
CANARIAS	F 86	Bazán, Ferrol	15 Apr 1992	21 June 1993	14 Dec 1994

Displacement, tons: 3,610 standard; 3,969 full load
Dimensions, feet (metres): 451.2 × 46.9 × 24.6
(137.7 × 14.3 × 7.5)
Main machinery: 2 GE LM 2500 gas turbines; 41,000 hp
(30.59 MW) sustained; 1 shaft; cp prop
2 auxiliary retractable props; 650 hp *(484 kW)*
Speed, knots: 29. **Range, miles:** 4,500 at 20 kt
Complement: 223 (13 officers)

Missiles: SSM: 8 McDonnell Douglas Harpoon; active radar
homing to 130 km *(70 n miles)* at 0.9 Mach; warhead 227 kg.

SAM: 32 GDC Pomona Standard SM-1MR; Mk 13 Mod 4
launcher ❶; command guidance; semi-active radar homing to
46 km *(25 n miles)* at 2 Mach.
Both missile systems share a common magazine.
Guns: 1 OTO Melara 3 in *(76 mm)*/62 ❷; 85 rds/min to 16 km
(8.7 n miles); weight of shell 6 kg.
1 Bazán 20 mm/120 12-barrelled Meroka Mod 2A or 2B ❸;
3,600 rds/min combined to 2 km. 2—12.7 mm MGs.
Torpedoes: 6—324 mm US Mk 32 (2 triple) tubes ❹. Honeywell/
Alliant Mk 46 Mod 5; anti-submarine; active/passive homing
to 11 km *(5.9 n miles)* at 40 kt; warhead 44 kg.

Countermeasures: Decoys: 4 Loral Hycor SRBOC 6-barrelled
fixed Mk 37 Mod 1/2 ❺; IR flares and chaff to 4 km *(2.2 n miles)*.
Prairie/Masker: hull noise/blade rate suppression.
SLQ-25 Nixie; torpedo decoy.
ESM/ECM: Elettronica Nettunel or Mk 3000 Neptune (F 84-86);
intercept and jammer.
Combat data systems: IPN 10 action data automation; Link 11.
SSQ 28 LAMPS III helo datalink. Saturn and SCOT 3 Secomsat
❻ being fitted.
Weapons control: Loral Mk 92 Mod 2 (Mod 6 with CORT in F 85
and 86). Enosa optronic tracker for Meroka 2B.
Radars: Air search: Raytheon SPS-49(V)5 ❼; C/D-band; range
457 km *(250 n miles)*.
Surface search: Raytheon SPS-55 ❽; I-band.
Navigation: Raytheon 1650/9 or SPS-67; I/J-band.
Fire control: RCA Mk 92 Mod 2/6 ❾; I/J-band.
Signaal STING ❿; I/J-band.
Selenia RAN 30L/X (RAN 12L + RAN 30X) ⓫; I-band (for
Meroka). Sperry/Lockheed VPS 2 ⓬ (for Meroka); I-band.
Tacan: URN 25.
Sonars: Raytheon SQS-56 (DE 1160); hull-mounted; active
search and attack; medium frequency.
Gould SQR-19(V)2; tactical towed array (TACTASS); passive;
very low frequency.

Helicopters: 2 Sikorsky S-70L ⓭ (only one normally embarked).

Programmes: Three ordered 29 June 1977. The execution of
this programme was delayed due to the emphasis placed on
the carrier construction. The fourth ship was ordered on
19 June 1986, and numbers five and six on 26 December
1989.
Modernisation: All are being modified with a combined RAN 12L
and RAN 30X fire-control radar for Meroka. The combined
system is called RAN 30L/X. Last two are fitted with Meroka
Mod 2B which includes an Enosa optronic tracker. Dorna
optronic and fire-control radar (includes Signaal STING to
replace STIR) tested in 1995 for 76 mm gun. Remainder
retrofitted. SCOT 3 SATCOM is also being fitted, first in
Navarra, and *Reina Sofía*.
Structure: Based on the US FFG 7 'Oliver Perry' class although
broader in the beam and therefore able to carry more
topweight. Fin stabilisers fitted. RAST helicopter handling
system. *Navarra* and *Canarias* have an indigenous combat data
system thereby increasing national inputs to 75 per cent. They
also have improved fire-control systems.
Operational: All based at Rota as the 41st Squadron. **UPDATED**

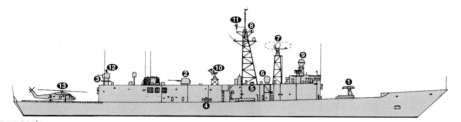

REINA SOFÍA

(Scale 1 : 1,200), Ian Sturton / 0019131

REINA SOFÍA

4/1998, Michael Nitz / 0050123

NAVARRA

*7/1999 *, A Campanera i Rovira /* 0080608

5 BALEARES (F 70) CLASS (FFG)

Name	No	Builders	Laid down		Launched		Commissioned	
BALEARES	F 71	Bazán, Ferrol	31 Oct	1968	20 Aug	1970	24 Sep	1973
ANDALUCÍA	F 72	Bazán, Ferrol	2 July	1969	30 Mar	1971	23 May	1974
CATALUÑA	F 73	Bazán, Ferrol	20 Aug	1970	3 Nov	1971	16 Jan	1975
ASTURIAS	F 74	Bazán, Ferrol	30 Mar	1971	13 May	1972	2 Dec	1975
EXTREMADURA	F 75	Bazán, Ferrol	3 Nov	1971	21 Nov	1972	10 Nov	1976

Displacement, tons: 3,350 standard; 4,177 full load
Dimensions, feet (metres): 438 × 46.9 × 15.4; 25.6 (sonar)
  (133.6 × 14.3 × 4.7; 7.8)
Main machinery: 2 Combustion Engineering V2M boilers; 1,200
  psi *(84.4 kg/cm²)*; 950°F *(510°C)*; 1 Westinghouse turbine;
  35,000 hp(m) *(25.7 MW)*; 1 shaft
Speed, knots: 28. **Range, miles:** 4,500 at 20 kt
Complement: 256 (15 officers)

Missiles: SSM: 8 McDonnell Douglas Harpoon (4 normally
  carried) **❶**; active radar homing to 130 km *(70 n miles)* at
  0.9 Mach; warhead 227 kg.
SAM: 16 GDC Pomona Standard SM-1MR; Mk 22 Mod 0
  launcher **❷**; command guidance; semi-active radar homing to
  46 km *(25 n miles)* at 2 Mach.
A/S: Honeywell ASROC Mk 112 octuple launcher **❸** (except
  F 71); 8 reloads; inertial guidance to 1.6-10 km *(1-5.4 n miles)*;
  payload Mk 46 torpedo.
Guns: 1 FMC 5 in *(127 mm)*/54 Mk 42 Mod 9 **❹**; dual purpose;
  20-40 rds/min to 24 km *(13 n miles)* anti-surface; 14 km *(7.7 n
  miles)* anti-aircraft; weight of shell 32 kg; 600 rounds in
  magazine.
  2 Bazán 20 mm/120 12-barrelled Meroka **❺**; 3,600 rds/min
  combined to 2 km. 2—12.7 mm MGs.
Torpedoes: 4—324 mm US Mk 32 fixed tubes (fitted internally
  and angled at 45° **❻**. Honeywell/Alliant Mk 46 Mod 5; anti-
  submarine; active/passive homing to 11 km *(5.9 n miles)* at
  40 kt; warhead 44 kg.
  2—484 mm US Mk 25 stern tubes **❼**; no longer in use.

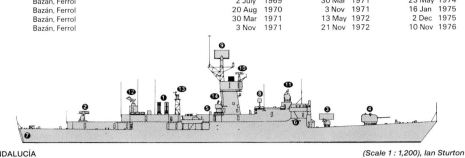

ANDALUCÍA   *(Scale 1 : 1,200), Ian Sturton*

Countermeasures: Decoys: 4 Loral Hycor SRBOC Mk 36 Mod 2
  6-barrelled chaff launchers.
ESM: Ceselsa Deneb; or Mk 1600; intercept.
ECM: Ceselsa Canopus; or Mk 1900; jammer.
Combat data systems: Tritan 1 action data automation; Link 11.
  Saturn SATCOM **❽**.
Weapons control: Mk 68 GFCS. Mk 74 missile system with Mk
  73 director. Mk 114 torpedo control. Dorna GFCS on trial
  (F 71).
Radars: Air search: Hughes SPS-52B **❾**; 3D; E/F-band; range
  439 km *(240 n miles)*.
Surface search: Raytheon SPS-10 **❿**; G-band.
Navigation: Raytheon Marine Pathfinder; I/J-band.
Fire control: Western Electric SPG-53B **⓫**; I/J-band (for Mk 68).
  Raytheon SPG-51C **⓬**; G/I-band (for Mk 73).

Selenia RAN 12L **⓭**; I-band (for Meroka). 2 Sperry VPS 2 **⓮**
  (for Meroka).
Tacan: SRN 15A.
Sonars: Raytheon SQS-56 (DE 1160); hull-mounted; active
  search and attack; medium frequency.
  EDO SQS-35V; VDS; active search and attack; medium
  frequency.

Programmes: This class resulted from a very close co-operation
  between Spain and the USA. Programme was approved
  17 November 1964, technical support agreement with USA
  being signed 31 March 1966. US Navy supplied weapons and
  sensors. Major hull sections, turbines and gearboxes made at
  El Ferrol, superstructures at Alicante, boilers, distilling plants
  and propellers at Cádiz.
Modernisation: The mid-life update programme was done in two
  stages; all had completed the first stage by the end of 1987
  and *Asturias* was the first to be fully modernised in 1988;
  Extremadura completed in May 1989, *Cataluña* in early 1990,
  Baleares in July 1990 and *Andalucía* in February 1991.
  Changes included the fitting of two Meroka 20 mm CIWS, Link
  11, Tritan data control, Deneb passive EW systems, four Mk 36
  SRBOC chaff launchers and replacing SQS-23 with DE 1160
  sonar. The stern torpedo tubes have been blanked off. ASROC
  removed and GFCS (for F 100) on trial in *Baleares*.
Structure: Generally similar to US Navy's 'Knox' class although
  they differ in the missile system and lack of helicopter facilities.
Operational: All based at Ferrol, forming the 31st Squadron. May
  be paid off early due to steam plant problems.
  UPDATED

EXTREMADURA
*11/1999 *, Michael Nitz* / 0080609

CATALUÑA   *7/1999 *, H M Steele* / 0080610

6 DESCUBIERTA CLASS (FFG/FSG)

Name	No	Builders	Laid down		Launched		Commissioned	
DESCUBIERTA	F 31	Bazán, Cartagena	16 Nov	1974	8 July	1975	18 Nov	1978
DIANA	F 32	Bazán, Cartagena	8 July	1975	26 Jan	1976	30 June	1979
INFANTA ELENA	F 33	Bazán, Cartagena	26 Jan	1976	14 Sep	1976	12 Apr	1980
INFANTA CRISTINA	F 34	Bazán, Cartagena	11 Sep	1976	25 Apr	1977	24 Nov	1980
CAZADORA	F 35	Bazán, Ferrol	14 Dec	1977	17 Oct	1978	20 July	1982
VENCEDORA	F 36	Bazán, Ferrol	1 June	1978	27 Apr	1979	18 Mar	1983

Displacement, tons: 1,233 standard; 1,666 full load
Dimensions, feet (metres): 291.3 × 34 × 12.5
  (88.8 × 10.4 × 3.8)
Main machinery: 4 MTU-Bazán 16V 956 TB91 diesels;
  15,000 hp(m) *(11 MW)* sustained; 2 shafts; cp props
Speed, knots: 25. **Range, miles:** 4,000 at 18 kt; 7,500 at 12 kt
Complement: 118 (10 officers) plus 30 marines

Missiles: SSM: 8 McDonnell Douglas Harpoon (2 quad)
  launchers ❶; active radar homing to 130 km *(70 n miles)* at
  0.9 Mach; warhead 227 kg. Normally only 2 pairs are
  embarked.
  SAM: Selenia Albatros octuple launcher ❷; 24 Raytheon Sea
  Sparrow/Selenia Aspide; semi-active radar homing to 14.6 km
  (8 n miles) at 2.5 Mach; height envelope 15-5,000 m *(49.2-
  16,405 ft)*; warhead 39 kg.
Guns: 1 OTO Melara 3 in *(76 mm)*/62 compact ❸; 85 rds/min to
  16 km *(8.7 n miles)*; weight of shell 6 kg.
  1 or 2 Bofors 40 mm/70 ❹; 300 rds/min to 12.5 km *(6.8 n
  miles)*; weight of shell 0.96 kg.
Torpedoes: 6—324 mm US Mk 32 (2 triple) tubes ❺. Honeywell/
  Alliant Mk 46 Mod 5; anti-submarine; active/passive homing
  to 11 km *(5.9 n miles)* at 40 kt; warhead 44 kg.
A/S mortars: 1 Bofors 375 mm twin-barrelled trainable ❻;
  automatic loading; range 3,600 m.
Countermeasures: Decoys: 2 Loral Hycor SRBOC 6-barrelled
  Mk 36 for chaff and IR flares.
  US Prairie Masker; blade rate suppression.
  ESM: Elsag Mk 1000 (part of Deneb system); or Mk 1600;
  intercept.
  ECM: Ceselsa Canopus; or Mk 1900; jammer.
Combat data systems: Tritan IV; Link 11 (in some). Saturn
  SATCOM ❼.
Weapons control: Signaal WM22/41 or WM25; GM 101.
Radars: Air/surface search: Signaal DA05/2 ❽; E/F-band; range
  137 km *(75 n miles)* for 2 m² target.
  Surface search: Signaal ZW06 ❾; I-band.
  Navigation ❿: I-band.
  Fire control: Signaal WM22/41 or WM25 system ⓫; I/J-band;
  range 46 km *(25 n miles)*.
Sonars: Raytheon 1160B; hull-mounted; active search and
  attack; medium frequency.

Programmes: Officially rated as Corvettes. *Diana* (tenth of the
  name) originates with the galley *Diana* of 1570. Infanta Elena
  and Cristina are the daughters of King Juan Carlos. Approval
  for second four ships given on 21 May 1976. First four ordered
  7 December 1973 (83 per cent Spanish ship construction
  components) and two more from Bazán, Ferrol on 25 May
  1976.
Modernisation: The 40 mm gun aft of the mainmast was
  planned to be replaced by Meroka with associated fire-control
  radars but this update has been shelved. SRBOC chaff
  launchers fitted and EW equipment updated. Link 11 added.
  WM25 fire-control system may be updated in four of the class
  in due course. Tritan command data system has replaced
  SEWACO.
Structure: Original Portuguese 'João Coutinho' design by
  Comodoro de Oliveira PN developed by Blohm + Voss and
  considerably modified by Bazán including use of Y-shaped
  funnel. Harpoon fitted between bridge and funnel. Noise
  reduction measures include Masker fitted to shafts, propellers
  (five types tested) under trial for four years, auxiliary gas-
  turbine generator fitted on upper deck for use during passive
  sonar search, all main and auxiliary diesels sound-mounted.
  Fully stabilised. Automatic computerised engine and alternator
  control; two independent engine rooms; normal running on
  two diesels.
Operational: All based at Cartagena, forming 21st Squadron.
Sales: F 37 and F 38 sold to Egypt prior to completion. One to
  Morocco in 1983.

UPDATED

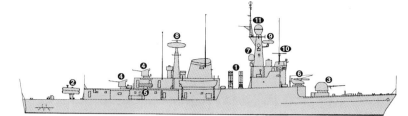

DESCUBIERTA   *(Scale 1 : 900), Ian Sturton*

DIANA   *11/1999*, Diego Quevedo / 0080611*

VENCEDORA   *1/1999, Diego Quevedo / 0050124*

DESCUBIERTA   *12/1999*, Camil Busquets i Vilanova / 0080612*

0 + 4 ALVARO DE BAZÁN CLASS (FFG)

Name	No	Builders	Laid down	Launched	Commissioned
ALVARO DE BAZÁN	F 101	Bazán, Ferrol	14 June 1999	Oct 2000	Sep 2002
ROGER DE LAURIA	F 102	Bazán, Ferrol	Feb 2001	Feb 2002	Nov 2003
BLAS DE LEZO	F 103	Bazán, Ferrol	May 2002	June 2003	Dec 2004
MENDEZ NUÑEZ	F 104	Bazán, Ferrol	Aug 2003	Sep 2004	Feb 2006

Displacement, tons: 5,853 full load
Dimensions, feet (metres): 481.3 oa; 437 pp × 61 × 16.1
(146.7; 133.2 × 18.6 × 4.9)
Flight deck, feet (metres): 86.6 × 56 *(26.4 × 17)*
Main machinery: CODOG; 2 GE LM 2500 gas turbines;
47,328 hp(m) *(34.8 MW)* sustained; 2 Bazán/Caterpillar
diesels; 12,240 hp(m) *(9 MW)* sustained; 2 shafts; acbLIPS
cp props
Speed, knots: 28. **Range, miles:** 4,500 at 18 kt
Complement: 218 plus 11 aircrew plus 16 Flag

Missiles: SSM: 8 Harpoon Block II ❶.
SAM: Mk 41 VLS for Evolved Sea Sparrow (ESSM) and Standard
SM-2MR Block IIIA; 48 cells ❷.
Guns: 1 FMC 5 in *(127 mm)*/54 Mk 45 Mod 2 ❸ (ex-US).
1 Bazán 20 mm/120 Meroka 2B ❹. 2 Oerlikon 20 mm.
Torpedoes: 4—323 mm (2 twin) Mk 32 Mod 5 fixed launchers
❺. 24 torpedoes. Mk 46 Mod 5.
A/S mortars: 2 ABCAS/SSTDS launchers.
Countermeasures: Decoys: 4 SRBOC Mk 36 Mod 2 chaff
launchers ❻. SLQ-25A Nixie torpedo decoy.
ESM: Ceselsa Elnath; intercept.
ECM: Ceselsa Aldebaran; jammer.
Combat data systems: Lockheed Aegis Baseline 5 Phase III
(DANCS); Link 11/16. SATCOM. JMCIS.
Weapons control: Sirius optronic director ❼; FABA Dorna GFCS.
Sainsel DLT 309 TFCS. SQR-4 helo datalink.
Radars: Air/surface search: Aegis SPY-1D/F ❽.
Surface search: DRS SPS-67 (RAN 12S) ❾.
Fire control: 2 Mk 99 (for SAM) ❿.
Sonars: Raytheon DE 1160 LF; hull-mounted; active search and
attack; medium frequency. Possible ATAS active towed sonar.

Helicopters: 1 SH-70L Seahawk Lamps III ⓫.

Programmes: Project definition from September 1992 to July
1995, and then extended to July 1996 to incorporate Aegis.
Design collaboration with German and Netherlands shipyards
started 27 January 1994. Spain withdrew from the APAR air
defence radar project in June 1995 and decided to incorporate
Aegis SPY-1D into the design. Production order agreed on
21 October 1996 and building approved 24 January 1997.
FSC in November 1997.
Structure: The inclusion of SPY-1D radar has increased the size
of the ship and caused major changes to the shape of the
superstructure. Stealth technology incorporated. Indal RAST
helicopter system. Hangar for two helicopters but only one to
be carried. 127 mm gun for gunfire support to land forces, to
be taken from USN *Tarawa* class. RAM may be fitted vice
Meroka.
Opinion: This class has the potential to carry both Tomahawk
SLCM and SM-2 Block IVA ATBM systems, although neither
are currently intended.

UPDATED

ALVARO DE BAZÁN   *(Scale 1 : 1,200), Ian Sturton /* 0019137

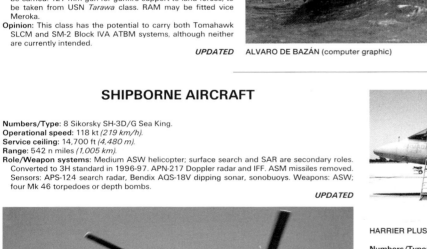

ALVARO DE BAZÁN (computer graphic)   *1996, Bazán /* 0019138

SHIPBORNE AIRCRAFT

Numbers/Type: 8 Sikorsky SH-3D/G Sea King.
Operational speed: 118 kt *(219 km/h).*
Service ceiling: 14,700 ft *(4,480 m).*
Range: 542 n miles *(1,005 km).*
Role/Weapon systems: Medium ASW helicopter; surface search and SAR are secondary roles.
Converted to 3H standard in 1996-97. APN-217 Doppler radar and IFF. ASM missiles removed.
Sensors: APS-124 search radar, Bendix AQS-18V dipping sonar, sonobuoys. Weapons: ASW;
four Mk 46 torpedoes or depth bombs.

UPDATED

HARRIER PLUS   *4/1999*, Diego Quevedo /* 0080613

Numbers/Type: 3 Sikorsky SH-3D Sea King AEW.
Operational speed: 110 kt *(204 km/h).*
Service ceiling: 14,700 ft *(4,480 m).*
Range: 542 n miles *(1,005 km).*
Role/Weapon systems: Three Sea King helicopters were taken in hand in 1986 for conversion to
AEW role to provide organic cover; first entered service August 1987. Sensors: THORN EMI
Searchwater radar, ESM. Weapons: Unarmed.

UPDATED

SEA KING   *1/1999*, Camil Busquets i Vilanova /* 0080615

Numbers/Type: 9/8 BAe/McDonnell Douglas EAV-8B (Harrier II)/EAV-8B (Harrier Plus).
Operational speed: 562 kt *(1,041 km/h).*
Service ceiling: Not available.
Range: 480 n miles *(889 km).*
Role/Weapon systems: First batch delivered in 1987-88. The plan is to update them to AV-8B
Harrier Plus standard with APG-65 radar plus FLIR in due course. Eight new EAV-8B delivered
from January 1996 to July 1997, replaced the Matadors. Sensors: ECM; ALQ 164. Weapons:
Strike; two 25 mm GAU-12/U cannon, two or four AIM-9L Sidewinders, two or four AGM-65E
Mavericks; up to 16 GP bombs. AMRAAM AIM-120 in updated aircraft.

UPDATED

SEA KING AEW   *1/1999*, A Campanera i Rovira /* 0080614

Numbers/Type: 6 Sikorsky SH-70L Seahawk (LAMPS III).
Operational speed: 135 kt *(249 km/h)*.
Service ceiling: 10,000 ft *(3,050 m)*.
Range: 600 n miles *(1,110 km)*.
Role/Weapon systems: ASW helicopter; delivery in 1988-89 for FFG 7 frigates. Six more Block 1 to be acquired in 2002 for new frigates, and the existing six to be upgraded to Block 1. Sensors: Search radar, sonobuoys, ECM/ESM. Weapons: ASW; two Mk 46 torpedoes or depth bombs. ASV; AGM-119B Penguin to be fitted.

UPDATED

AB 212   *11/1999*, Diego Quevedo /* 0080616

Numbers/Type: 10 Hughes 500MD.
Operational speed: 110 kt *(204 km/h)*.
Service ceiling: 10,000 ft *(3,050 m)*.
Range: 203 n miles *(376 km)*.
Role/Weapon systems: Used for training; secondary role is SAR and surface search. ASW role removed. Sensors: Some may have search radar, MAD.

VERIFIED

SEA HAWK   *4/1999*, Diego Quevedo /* 0080617

Numbers/Type: 10 Agusta AB 212.
Operational speed: 106 kt *(196 km/h)*.
Service ceiling: 14,200 ft *(4,330 m)*.
Range: 230 n miles *(426 km)*.
Role/Weapon systems: Surface search; four are equipped for Fleet ECM support and have a datalink and six for Assault operations with the Amphibious Brigade. All ASW equipment and ASM missiles removed. Sensors: Selenia search radar, Mk 2000 EW system (in four); Elmer ECM.

UPDATED   500 MD   *2/1998, Diego Quevedo /* 0050133

LAND-BASED MARITIME AIRCRAFT (FRONT LINE)

Notes: (1) There are also three Cessna 550 Citation II used for transport and 14 AS 332 Super Pumas used for SAR.
(2) The Air Force F/A-18 Hornet (C.15) can be armed with Harpoon ASM. Air Force CN-235 are not used for maritime role.

Numbers/Type: 2/5 Lockheed P-3A/B Orion.
Operational speed: 410 kt *(760 km/h)*.
Service ceiling: 28,300 ft *(8,625 m)*.
Range: 4,000 n miles *(7,410 km)*.
Role/Weapon systems: Air Force operation for long-range MR/ASW; P-3A supplemented in 1988 by P-3B Orions from Norway after Lockheed modernisation. All further upgraded in 1995-97 and further combat system improvements planned for 2002. Sensors: APS-134 (Searchwater 2000 in due course); FLIR; search radar, AQS-81 MAD, ALR 66 V(3) ECM/ESM, 87 sonobuoys. Weapons: ASW; eight torpedoes or depth bombs internally; 10 underwing stations. ASV; four Harpoon or 127 mm rockets.

UPDATED

Numbers/Type: 3 Fokker F27 Maritime.
Operational speed: 250 kt *(463 km/h)*.
Service ceiling: 29,500 ft *(8,990 m)*.
Range: 2,700 n miles *(5,000 km)*.
Role/Weapon systems: Canaries and offshore patrol by Air Force. May be replaced by CN-235 in due course. Sensors: APS-504 search radar, cameras. Weapons: ASW; torpedoes or depth bombs.

VERIFIED

Numbers/Type: 14 CASA C-212 Aviocar.
Operational speed: 190 kt *(353 km/h)*.
Service ceiling: 24,000 ft *(7,315 m)*.
Range: 1,650 n miles *(3,055 km)*.
Role/Weapon systems: Mediterranean and Atlantic surveillance is carried out by detached flights from the Air Force; SAR is secondary role. Six are used by Customs. Sensors: APS-128 radar, MAD, sonobuoys and ESM. Weapons: ASW; Mk 46 torpedoes or depth bombs. ASV; two rockets or machine gun pods.

VERIFIED

PATROL FORCES

4 SERVIOLA CLASS (OFFSHORE PATROL VESSELS) (OPV)

Name	No	Builders	Laid down		Launched		Commissioned	
SERVIOLA	P 71	Bazán, Ferrol	17 Oct	1989	10 May	1990	22 Mar	1991
CENTINELA	P 72	Bazán, Ferrol	12 Dec	1989	30 Mar	1990	24 Sep	1991
VIGÍA	P 73	Bazán, Ferrol	30 Oct	1990	12 Apr	1991	24 Mar	1992
ATALAYA	P 74	Bazán, Ferrol	14 Dec	1990	22 Nov	1991	29 June	1992

Displacement, tons: 1,147 full load
Dimensions, feet (metres): 225.4; 206.7 pp × 34 × 11 *(68.7; 63 × 10.4 × 3.4)*
Main machinery: 2 MTU-Bazán 16V 956 TB91 diesels; 7,500 hp (m) *(5.5 MW)* sustained; 2 shafts; acbLIPS cp props
Speed, knots: 19. **Range, miles:** 8,000 at 12 kt
Complement: 42 (8 officers) plus 6 spare berths

Guns: 1 US 3 in *(76 mm)*/50 Mk 27; 20 rds/min to 12 km *(6.6 n miles)*; weight of shell 6 kg.
2—12.7 mm MGs.
Countermeasures: ESM; ULQ-13 (in P 71).
Weapons control: Bazán Alcor or MSP 4000 (P 73) optronic director. Hispano mini combat system. SATCOM.
Radars: Surface search: Racal Decca 2459; I-band.
Navigation: Racal Decca ARPA 2690 BT; I-band.

Helicopters: Platform for 1 AB 212.

Programmes: Project B215 ordered from Bazán, Ferrol in late 1988. The larger Milano design was rejected as being too expensive.
Modernisation: The guns are old stock refurbished but could be replaced by an OTO Melara 76 mm/62 or a Bofors 40 mm/70 Model 600 if funds can be found. Other equipment fits could include four Harpoon SSM, Meroka CIWS, Sea Sparrow SAM or a Bofors 375 mm ASW rocket launcher. No plans to carry out any of these improvements so far. EW equipment fitted in Serviola for training.
Structure: A modified 'Halcón' class design similar to ships produced for Argentina and Mexico. Helicopter facilities enabling operation in up to Sea State 4 using non-retractable stabilisers. Three firefighting pumps.

VIGÍA   *1/1999*, Camil Busquets i Vilanova /* 0080619

Operational: For EEZ patrol. *Vigía* based at Cádiz, *Serviola* and *Atalaya* at Ferrol and *Centinela* at Las Palmas.   *UPDATED*

1 PESCALONSO CLASS (LARGE PATROL CRAFT) (PG)

Name	No	Builders	Commissioned
CHILREU (ex-*Pescalonso 2*)	P 61	Gijon, Asturias	30 Mar 1992

Displacement, tons: 2,101 full load
Dimensions, feet (metres): 222.4 × 36.1 × 15.4 *(67.8 × 11 × 4.7)*
Main machinery: 1 MaK 6M-453K diesel; 2,460 hp(m) *(1.81 MW)* sustained; 1 shaft; cp prop
Speed, knots: 12. **Range, miles:** 1,500 at 12 kt
Complement: 35 (7 officers)
Guns: 1—12.7 mm MG.
Radars: Surface search: Racal Decca; I-band.

Comment: Launched 2 May 1988 and purchased by the Fisheries Department for the Navy to use as a Fishery Protection vessel based at Ferrol. Former stern ramp trawler. Inmarsat fitted.
VERIFIED

CHILREU   *12/1997, Diego Quevedo /* 0019148

1 ALBORAN CLASS (LARGE PATROL CRAFT) (PG)

Name	No	Builders	Commissioned
ALBORAN	P 62	Freire, Vigo	8 Jan 1997

Displacement, tons: 1,848 full load
Dimensions, feet (metres): 216.2 × 34.4 × 14.4 *(65.9 × 10.5 × 4.4)*
Main machinery: 1 Krupp MaK 6 M 453C diesel; 2,400 hp(m) *(1.76 MW)* sustained; 1 diesel generator and motor for emergency propulsion; 462 hp(m) *(340 kW)*; 1 shaft
Speed, knots: 13 (3.5 on emergency motor). **Range, miles:** 20,000 at 13 kt
Complement: 37 (7 officers) plus 9 spare
Guns: 2—12.7 mm MGs.
Radars: Surface search: Furuno FAR-2825; I-band.
Navigation: Furuno FR-2130S; I-band.
Helicopters: Platform for 1 light.

Comment: Launched in 1991 and purchased by the Fisheries Department to use as a Fishery Protection vessel based at Cartagena.
VERIFIED

ALBORAN   *7/1997, A Campanera i Rovira /* 0050135

6 BARCELÓ CLASS (FAST ATTACK CRAFT—GUN) (PCF)

Name	No	Builders	Commissioned
BARCELÓ	P 11	Lürssen, Vegesack	20 Mar 1976
LAYA	P 12	Bazán, La Carraca	23 Dec 1976
JAVIER QUIROGA	P 13	Bazán, La Carraca	4 Apr 1977
ORDÓÑEZ	P 14	Bazán, La Carraca	7 June 1977
ACEVEDO	P 15	Bazán, La Carraca	14 July 1977
CÁNDIDO PÉREZ	P 16	Bazán, La Carraca	25 Nov 1977

Displacement, tons: 145 full load
Dimensions, feet (metres): 118.7 × 19 × 6.2 *(36.2 × 5.8 × 1.9)*
Main machinery: 2 MTU-Bazán MD 16V 538 TB90 diesels; 6,000 hp(m) *(4.41 MW)* sustained; 2 shafts
Speed, knots: 36. **Range, miles:** 1,200 at 17 kt
Complement: 19 (3 officers)
Guns: 1 Breda 40 mm/70. 1 Oerlikon 20 mm/85. 2—12.7 mm MGs.
Torpedoes: Fitted for 2—21 in *(533 mm)* tubes.
Weapons control: CSEE optical director.
Radars: Surface search: Raytheon 1220/6XB; I/J-band.

Comment: Ordered 5 December 1973. All manned by the Navy although building cost was borne by the Ministry of Commerce. Of Lürssen TNC 36 design. Reported as able to take two or four surface-to-surface missiles instead of 20 mm gun and torpedo tubes. Plans to transfer to the Guardia Civil del Mar have been shelved.
UPDATED

ORDÓÑEZ   *1/1999 *, Diego Quevedo /* 0080618

10 ANAGA CLASS (LARGE PATROL CRAFT) (PC)

Name	No	Builders	Commissioned
ANAGA	P 21	Bazán, La Carraca	14 Oct 1980
TAGOMAGO	P 22	Bazán, La Carraca	30 Jan 1981
MAROLA	P 23	Bazán, La Carraca	4 June 1981
MOURO	P 24	Bazán, La Carraca	14 July 1981
GROSA	P 25	Bazán, La Carraca	15 Sep 1981
MEDAS	P 26	Bazán, La Carraca	16 Oct 1981
IZARO	P 27	Bazán, La Carraca	9 Dec 1981
TABARCA	P 28	Bazán, La Carraca	30 Dec 1981
DEVA	P 29	Bazán, La Carraca	3 June 1982
BERGANTÍN	P 30	Bazán, La Carraca	28 July 1982

Displacement, tons: 319 full load
Dimensions, feet (metres): 145.6 × 21.6 × 8.2 *(44.4 × 6.6 × 2.5)*
Main machinery: 1 MTU-Bazán 16V 956 SB90 diesel; 4,000 hp(m) *(2.94 MW)* sustained; 1 shaft; cp prop
Speed, knots: 20. **Range, miles:** 4,000 at 13 kt
Complement: 25 (3 officers)
Guns: 1 FMC 3 in *(76 mm)*/50 Mk 22. 1 Oerlikon 20 mm Mk 10. 2—7.62 mm MGs.
Radars: Surface search: 1 Racal Decca 1226; I-band.
Navigation: Sperry; I-band.

Comment: Ordered from Bazán, Cádiz on 22 July 1978. For fishery and EEZ patrol duties. Rescue and firefighting capability.
UPDATED

DEVA   *2/1999 *, Diego Quevedo /* 0080620

4 CONEJERA CLASS (COASTAL PATROL CRAFT) (PC)

Name	No	Builders	Commissioned
CONEJERA	P 31	Bazán, Ferrol	31 Dec 1981
DRAGONERA	P 32	Bazán, Ferrol	31 Dec 1981
ESPALMADOR	P 33	Bazán, Ferrol	10 May 1982
ALCANADA	P 34	Bazán, Ferrol	10 May 1982

Displacement, tons: 85 full load
Dimensions, feet (metres): 106.6 × 17.4 × 4.6 *(32.2 × 5.3 × 1.4)*
Main machinery: 2 MTU-Bazán MA 16V 362 SB80 diesels; 2,450 hp(m) *(1.8 MW)*; 2 shafts
Speed, knots: 25. **Range, miles:** 1,200 at 15 kt
Complement: 12
Guns: 1 Oerlikon 20 mm Mk 10. 1—12.7 mm MG.
Radars: Surface search: Furuno; I-band.

Comment: Ordered in 1978, funded jointly by the Navy and the Ministry of Commerce. Naval manned.
UPDATED

ESPALMADOR   *6/1999 *, Camil Busquets i Vilanova /* 0080621

2 TORALLA CLASS (COASTAL PATROL CRAFT) (PC)

Name	No	Builders	Commissioned
TORALLA	P 81	Viudes, Barcelona	27 Feb 1987
FORMENTOR	P 82	Viudes, Barcelona	23 June 1988

Displacement, tons: 102 full load
Dimensions, feet (metres): 93.5 × 21.3 × 5.9 *(28.5 × 6.5 × 1.8)*
Main machinery: 2 MTU-Bazán 8V 396 TB93 diesels; 2,100 hp(m) *(1.54 MW)* sustained; 2 shafts
Speed, knots: 19. **Range, miles:** 1,000 at 12 kt
Complement: 13
Guns: 1 Browning 12.7 mm MG.
Radars: Surface search: Racal Decca RM 1070; I-band.
Navigation: Racal Decca RM 270; I-band.

Comment: Wooden hull with GRP sheath. *Formentor* refitted in 1996-97.
UPDATED

FORMENTOR   *7/1999 *, Diego Quevedo /* 0080622

2 P 101 CLASS (COASTAL PATROL CRAFT) (PB)

P 114   **P 111**

Displacement, tons: 18.5 standard; 20.8 full load
Dimensions, feet (metres): 44.9 × 14.4 × 4.3 *(13.7 × 4.4 × 1.3)*
Main machinery: 2 Baudouin-Interdiesel DNP-350; 768 hp(m) *(564 kW)*; 2 shafts
Speed, knots: 23.3. **Range, miles:** 430 at 18 kt
Complement: 6
Guns: 1—12.7 mm MG.
Radars: Surface search: Decca 110; I-band.

Comment: Ordered under the programme agreed 13 May 1977, funded jointly by the Navy and the Ministry of Commerce. Built to the Aresa LVC 160 design by Aresa, Arenys de Mar, Barcelona. GRP hull. 11 of the class transferred to harbour auxiliary duties with Y numbers, the remainder paid off in 1993. One of the class transferred back again to patrol duties in 1996. *VERIFIED*

P 114   *6/1998, Diego Quevedo / 0050139*

1 INSHORE/RIVER PATROL LAUNCH (PBR)

Name	No	Builders	Commissioned
CABO FRADERA	P 201	Bazán, La Carraca	25 Feb 1963

Displacement, tons: 21 full load
Dimensions, feet (metres): 58.3 × 13.8 × 3 *(17.8 × 4.2 × 0.9)*
Main machinery: 2 diesels; 280 hp(m) *(206 kW)*; 2 shafts
Speed, knots: 11
Complement: 9
Guns: 1—7.62 mm MG.
Radars: Surface search: Furuno; I-band.

Comment: Based at Tui on River Miño for border patrol with Portugal. There is also a small launch P 221 on the same river.
UPDATED

CABO FRADERA (P 221 outboard)   *5/1999*, A Campanera i Rovira / 0080623*

AMPHIBIOUS FORCES

Note: It is planned to construct a third 'Galicia' class with a modified structure and through-deck flight deck similar to Italian *San Giusto*.

2 GALICIA CLASS (LPD)

Name	No	Builders	Laid down	Launched	Commissioned
GALICIA	L 51	Bazán, Ferrol	31 May 1996	21 July 1997	30 Apr 1998
CASTILLA	L 52	Bazán, Ferrol	11 Dec 1997	14 June 1999	July 2000

Displacement, tons: 13,815 full load
Dimensions, feet (metres): 524.9 oa; 465.9 pp × 82 × 19.3 *(160; 142 × 25 × 5.9)*
Flight deck, feet (metres): 196.9 × 82 *(60 × 25)*
Main machinery: 2 Bazán/Caterpillar 3612 diesels; 12,512 hp (m) *(9.2 MW)*; 2 shafts; acbLIPS cp props; bow thruster 680 hp (m) *(500 kW)*
Speed, knots: 19. **Range, miles:** 6,000 at 12 kt
Complement: 115 plus 12 spare; 179 (L 52)
Military lift: 543 or 404 (L 52) fully equipped troops and 72 (staff and aircrew)
6 LCVP or 4 LCM or 1 LCU and 1 LCVP. 130 APCs or 33 MBTs.

Guns: 2 Bazán 20 mm/120 12-barrelled Meroka; 3,600 rds/min combined to 2 km. 4 Oerlikon 20 mm.
Countermeasures: Decoys: 4 SRBOC chaff launchers.
ESM: Intercept.
Combat data systems: SICOA (L 52); SATCOM; Link 11.
Radars: Air/surface search: Signaal DA08 or TRS 3D/16 (L 52); E/F-band.
Surface search: Kelvin Hughes ARPA; I-band.
Navigation and helo control: I-band.

Helicopters: 6 NH 90 or 4 EH 101.

Programmes: Originally started as a national project by the Netherlands. In 1990 the ATS was seen as a possible solution to fulfil the requirements for a new LPD. Joint project definition study announced in July 1991 and completed in December 1993 and the first ship was authorised on 29 July 1994. The second of class ordered 9 May 1997. A third to a modified design is planned to be ordered in 2000/01.

GALICIA (without main radar and guns)   *2/1999*, Diego Quevedo / 0080624*

Structure: Able to transport a fully equipped battalion of marines providing a built-in dock for landing craft and a helicopter flight deck for debarkation in offshore conditions. Docking well is 885 m²; vehicle area 1,010 m². Access hatch on the port side. Hospital facilities. Built to commercial standards with military command and control and NBCD facilities. Second of class has improved command and control facilities with two operations centres, one for amphibious and one for a combat group.
Operational: Alternatively can also be used for a general logistic support for both military and civil operations, including environmental and disaster relief tasks.
UPDATED

GALICIA (without main radar and guns)   *1/1999*, A Campanera i Rovira / 0080625*

2 NEWPORT CLASS (LST)

Name	No	Builders	Laid down	Launched	Commissioned
HERNÁN CORTÉS (ex-Barnstable County)	L 41 (ex-L 1197)	National Steel, San Diego	19 Dec 1970	2 Oct 1971	27 May 1972
PIZARRO (ex-Harlan County)	L 42 (ex-L 1196)	National Steel, San Diego	7 Nov 1970	24 July 1971	8 Apr 1972

Displacement, tons: 4,975 light; 8,550 full load
Dimensions, feet (metres): 522.3 (hull) × 69.5 × 18.2 (aft)
   (159.2 × 21.2 × 5.5)
Main machinery: 6 Alco 16-251 diesels; 16,500 hp (12.3 MW)
   sustained; 2 shafts; cp props; bow thruster
Speed, knots: 20. **Range, miles:** 2,500 at 14 kt
Complement: 255 (15 officers)
Military lift: 374 troops; (20 officers) 500 tons vehicles; 2 LCVPs
   and 2 LCPLs on davits

Guns: 1 General Electric/General Dynamics 20 mm Vulcan
   Phalanx Mk 15. 2 Oerlikon 20 mm/85. 4—12.7 mm MGs.
Countermeasures: ESM: Celesa Deneb.
Radars: Surface search: Raytheon SPS-10F/67; G-band.
Navigation: Marconi LN66; I-band.

Helicopters: Platform only for 3 AB 212.

Programmes: First one transferred from the USA and
   recommissioned 26 August 1994, the second one transferred
   14 April 1995. Leases have been renewed.
Structure: The 3 in guns removed on transfer. The ramp is
   supported by twin derrick arms. A ramp just forward of the
   superstructure connects the lower tank deck with the main
   deck and a vehicle passage through the superstructure
   provides access to the parking area amidships. A stern gate to
   the tank deck permits unloading of amphibious tractors into
   the water, or unloading of other vehicles into an LCU or on to a
   pier. Vehicle stowage covers 19,000 sq ft. Length over derrick
   arms is 562 ft (171.3 m); full load draught is 11.5 ft forward and
   17.5 ft aft. Bow thruster fitted to hold position offshore while
   unloading amphibious tractors. Meroka may replace Phalanx
   or be fitted on the former 3 in gun platform. SCOT 3 SATCOM
   fitted in 1995-96. Can carry four Mexeflotes, two of them
   powered.

UPDATED   PIZARRO

11/1998, Diego Quevedo / 0050141

2 EDIC CLASS (LCT)

A 06   A 08

Displacement, tons: 279 standard; 665 full load
Dimensions, feet (metres): 193.5 × 39 × 4.3 (59 × 11.9 × 1.3)
Main machinery: 2 MTU-Bazán MA 6 R 362 SB70 diesels; 1,120 hp(m) (823 kW); 2 shafts
Speed, knots: 9.5. **Range, miles:** 1,500 at 9 kt
Complement: 23
Military lift: 300 tons; 35 troops
Guns: 2—12.7 mm MGs. 1—81 mm mortar.
Radars: Navigation: Decca; I-band.

Comment: Built by Bazán, La Carraca to the French EDIC design and commissioned in December
   1966. Rated as logistic craft and used as transports in the Canary Islands.   *UPDATED*

A 06   11/1999 *, van Ginderen Collection / 0080626

2 LCUs

L 071 (ex-LCU 11, ex-LCU 1, ex-LCU 1471)   **L 072** (ex-LCU 12, ex-LCU 2, ex-LCU 1491)

Displacement, tons: 360 full load
Dimensions, feet (metres): 119.7 × 31.5 × 5.2 (36.5 × 9.6 × 1.6)
Main machinery: 3 Gray Marine 64 YTL diesels; 675 hp (504 kW); 3 shafts
Speed, knots: 8
Complement: 14
Military lift: 160 tons
Radars: Navigation: Furuno; I-band.

Comment: Transferred from USA June 1972. Purchased August 1976. Both refitted 1993-94.
   UPDATED

L 071   4/1999 *, Diego Quevedo / 0080627

8 LCM 8

L 81-86 (ex-LCM 81-86, ex-E 81-86)   **L 87-88**

Displacement, tons: 115-120 full load
Dimensions, feet (metres): 74.5 × 21.7 × 5.9 (22.7 × 6.6 × 1.8)
Main machinery: 4 GM 6-71 diesels; 696 hp (519 kW) sustained; 2 shafts
Speed, knots: 11
Complement: 5

Comment: First six ordered from Oxnard, California in 1974. Assembled in Spain. Commissioned in
   June-September 1975. Two more built by Bazán, San Fernando, and completed in April 1989.
   UPDATED

L 87   4/1999 *, Diego Quevedo / 0080628

0 + 8 LCM (X)

Displacement, tons: 108 full load
Dimensions, feet (metres): 76.5 × 21 × 3.4 (23.3 × 6.4 × 1.1)
Main machinery: 2 diesels; 2,200 hp(m) (1.62 MW); 2 waterjets
Speed, knots: 14. **Range, miles:** 160 at 12 kt
Complement: 3
Military lift: 100 tons

Comment: Being built to a Bazán design at San Fernando. Bow and stern ramps. To be carried in
   the LPDs from late 2000.
   NEW ENTRY

45 LANDING CRAFT

Comment: Apart from those used for divers there are 16 LCM 6 (L 161-167, L 261-267, L 601-602),
   17 LCVP and 8 LCP. All of the LCM 6, eight of the LCVPs and most of the LCPs were built in
   Spanish Shipyards 1986-88. There are also two tug pontoons (mexeflotes) (L 91-L 92) completed
   in 1995. Some of these craft are laid up.
   VERIFIED

LCM L 162   10/1993, Diego Quevedo

MINE WARFARE FORCES

4 + (4) SEGURA CLASS (MINEHUNTERS) (MHC)

Name	No	Builders	Launched	Commissioned
SEGURA	M 31	Bazán, Cartagena	25 July 1997	27 Apr 1999
SELLA	M 32	Bazán, Cartagena	6 July 1998	28 May 1999
TAMBRE	M 33	Bazán, Cartagena	5 Mar 1999	18 Feb 2000
TURIA	M 34	Bazán, Cartagena	22 Nov 1999	Sep 2000

Displacement, tons: 530 full load
Dimensions, feet (metres): 177.2 oa; 167.3 wl × 35.1 × 7.2 *(54; 51 × 10.7 × 2.2)*
Main machinery: 2 MTU-Bazán 6V 396 TB83 diesels; 1,523 hp(m) *(1.12 MW)*; 2 motors (for hunting); 200 kW; 2 Voith Schneider props; 2 side thrusters; 150 hp(m) *(110 kW)*
Speed, knots: 14; 7 (hunting). **Range, miles:** 2,000 at 12 kt
Complement: 41 (7 officers)
Guns: 1 Bazán/Oerlikon 20 mm GAM-BO1.
Countermeasures: MCM: FABA/Inisel system. 2 Gayrobot Pluto Plus ROVs.
Combat data systems: FABA/SMYC Nautis.
Radars: Navigation: I-band.
Sonars: Raytheon/ENOSA SQQ-32 multifunction VDS mine detection; high frequency.

Comment: On 4 July 1989 a technology transfer contract was signed with Vosper Thornycroft to allow Bazán to design a new MCM vessel based on the 'Sandown' class. The order for four of the class was authorised on 7 May 1993, and an agreement signed on 26 November 1993 between DCN and Bazán provided for training in GRP technology. The first of class laid down 30 May 1995. Four more are expected to be ordered in as soon as the fourth ship is completed in 2000. Sonar includes side scanning, and a towed body tracking and positioning system. A further four sweepers are also needed.
UPDATED

TAMBRE *9/1999*, Diego Quevedo /* 0080629

1 GUADALETE (AGGRESSIVE) CLASS
(MINESWEEPER—OCEAN) (MSO)

Name	No	Builders	Commissioned
GUADALQUIVIR (ex-*Persistant* MSO 491)	M 43	Tacoma, Seattle, WA	3 Feb 1956

Displacement, tons: 860 full load
Dimensions, feet (metres): 172.5 × 35 × 14.1 *(52.6 × 10.7 × 4.3)*
Main machinery: 4 Packard ID-1700 diesels; 2,280 hp *(1.7 MW)*; 2 shafts; cp props
Speed, knots: 12. **Range, miles:** 3,000 at 10 kt
Complement: 74 (6 officers)
Guns: 2 Oerlikon 20 mm (twin). 2—7.62 mm MGs.
Countermeasures: Pluto ROVs.
Radars: Surface search: Racal Decca 1226; I-band.
Navigation: Decca 626; I-band.
Sonars: General Electric SQQ-14; VDS; active minehunting; high frequency.

Comment: Transferred from USA and commissioned on 1 July 1971. Modernisation completed in 1984-86 to extend service lives. Two Pluto ROVs acquired in 1989 in order to gain experience for the new MCMVs. This last of class is based at Cartagena and is to pay off in 2001.
UPDATED

GUADALQUIVIR *2/1999, Diego Quevedo /* 0050145

6 ADJUTANT, REDWING and MSC 268 CLASSES
(MINESWEEPERS—COASTAL) (MSC)

Name	No	Builders	Commissioned
JÚCAR (ex-*MSC 220*)	M 21	Bellingham SY	22 June 1956
EBRO (ex-*MSC 269*)	M 22	Bellingham SY	19 Dec 1958
TAJO (ex-*MSC 287*)	M 24	Tampa Marine Corporation	9 July 1959
GENIL (ex-*MSC 279*)	M 25	Tacoma, Seattle, WA	11 Sep 1959
ODIEL (ex-*MSC 288*)	M 26	Tampa Marine Corporation	9 Oct 1959
SIL (ex-*Redwing* MSC 200)	M 27	Tampa Marine Corporation	16 Jan 1959

Displacement, tons: 390 full load
Dimensions, feet (metres): 144 × 28 × 8.2 *(43.9 × 8.5 × 2.5)*
Main machinery: 2 GM 8-268A diesels; 880 hp *(656 kW)*; 2 shafts
Speed, knots: 13. **Range, miles:** 2,700 at 10 kt
Complement: 39 (3 officers)
Guns: 2 Oerlikon 20 mm (twin).
Radars: Navigation: Decca TM 626 or RM 914; I-band.
Sonars: UQS-1; active minehunting; high frequency.

Comment: Transferred from USA. Wooden hulled. Two sub-types: M 22, M 24, M 25 and M 26 with no mainmast but crane abreast the funnel. M 21 and M 27 have derrick on mainmast. Three others of the class transferred to Patrol Ship duties in 1980 and deleted in 1993. All based at Cartagena.
UPDATED

ODIEL *7/1999*, Diego Quevedo /* 0080630

SURVEY AND RESEARCH SHIPS

1 DARSS CLASS (RESEARCH SHIP) (AGI/AGOR)

Name	No	Builders	Launched
ALERTA (ex-*Jasmund*)	A 111	Peenewerft, Wolgast	27 Feb 1982

Displacement, tons: 2,292 full load
Dimensions, feet (metres): 250.3 × 39.7 × 13.8 *(76.3 × 12.1 × 4.2)*
Main machinery: 1 Kolomna Type 40-DM diesel; 2,200 hp(m) *(1.6 MW)* sustained; 1 shaft; cp prop
Speed, knots: 12. **Range, miles:** 1,000 at 12 kt
Complement: 60
Guns: Fitted for 3 twin 25 mm/70. 2—12.7 mm MGs.
Radars: Navigation: Racal Decca; I-band.

Comment: Former GDR depot ship converted to an AGI, with additional accommodation replacing much of the storage capacity. Was to have transferred to Ecuador in 1991 but the sale was cancelled. Commissioned in the Spanish Navy on 6 December 1992 and sailed from Wilhelmshaven for a refit at Las Palmas prior to being based at Cartagena and used as an AGI and equipment trials ship. Saturn 35 SATCOM.
UPDATED

ALERTA *6/1997*, Diego Quevedo /* 0019160

1 RESEARCH SHIP (AGOB)

Name	No	Builders	Commissioned
HESPÉRIDES (ex-*Mar Antártico*)	A 33	Bazán, Cartagena	16 May 1991

Displacement, tons: 2,738 full load
Dimensions, feet (metres): 270.7; 255.2 × 46.9 × 14.8 *(82.5; 77.8 × 14.3 × 4.5)*
Main machinery: Diesel-electric; 4 MAN-Bazán 14V20/27 diesels; 6,860 hp(m) *(5 MW)* sustained; 4 generators; 2 AEG motors; 3,800 hp(m) *(2.8 MW)*; 1 shaft; bow and stern thrusters; 350 hp(m) *(257 kW)* each
Speed, knots: 15. **Range, miles:** 12,000 at 13 kt
Complement: 39 (9 officers) plus 30 scientists
Radars: Surface search: Racal/Hispano ARPA 2690; I-band.
Navigation: Racal 2690 ACS; F-band.
Helicopters: 1 AB 212.

Comment: Ordered in July 1988 from Bazán, Cartagena, by the Ministry of Education and Science. Laid down in 1989, launched 12 March 1990. Has 330 sq m of laboratories, Simbad ice sonar. Dome in keel houses several sensors. Ice-strengthened hull capable of breaking first year ice up to 45 cm at 5 kt. The main task is to support the Spanish base at Livingston Island, Antarctica. Manned and operated by the Navy. Has a telescopic hangar. **UPDATED**

HESPÉRIDES   *10/1999**, *Diego Quevedo* / 0080631

4 CASTOR CLASS (SURVEY SHIPS) (AGS)

Name	No	Builders	Commissioned
CASTOR	A 21 (ex-H 4)	Bazán, La Carraca	10 Nov 1966
POLLUX	A 22 (ex-H 5)	Bazán, La Carraca	6 Dec 1966
ANTARES	A 23	Bazán, La Carraca	21 Nov 1974
RIGEL	A 24	Bazán, La Carraca	21 Nov 1974

Displacement, tons: 363 full load
Dimensions, feet (metres): 125.9 × 24.9 × 10.2 *(38.4 × 7.6 × 3.1)*
Main machinery: 1 Sulzer 4TD36 diesel; 720 hp(m) *(530 kW)*; 1 shaft
Speed, knots: 11.5. **Range, miles:** 3,620 at 8 kt
Complement: 36 (4 officers)
Radars: Navigation: Raytheon 1620; I/J-band.

Comment: Fitted with Raydist, Omega and digital presentation of data. A 21 and 22 have gaps in the gunwhale aft for Oropesa sweep for side scan mapping sonar. In A 23 and 24 this is a full run to the stern. **UPDATED**

ANTARES   *2/1997**, *Diego Quevedo* / 0019161

2 MALASPINA CLASS (SURVEY SHIPS) (AGS)

Name	No	Builders	Commissioned
MALASPINA	A 31	Bazán, La Carraca	21 Feb 1975
TOFIÑO	A 32	Bazán, La Carraca	23 Apr 1975

Displacement, tons: 820 standard; 1,090 full load
Dimensions, feet (metres): 188.9 × 38.4 × 12.8 *(57.6 × 11.7 × 3.9)*
Main machinery: 2 San Carlos MWM TbRHS-345-61 diesels; 3,600 hp(m) *(2.64 MW)*; 2 shafts; acbLIPS cp props
Speed, knots: 15. **Range, miles:** 4,000 at 12 kt; 3,140 at 14.5 kt
Complement: 63 (9 officers)
Guns: 2 Oerlikon 20 mm.
Radars: Navigation: Raytheon 1220/6XB; I/J-band.

Comment: Ordered mid-1972. Both named after their immediate predecessors. Developed from British 'Bulldog' class. Fitted with two Atlas DESO-10 AN 1021 (280-1,400 m) echo-sounders, retractable Burnett 538-2 sonar for deep sounding, Egg Mark B side scan sonar, Raydist DR-S navigation system, Hewlett Packard 2100A computer inserted into Magnavox Transit satellite navigation system, active rudder with fixed pitch auxiliary propeller. *Malaspina* used for a NATO evaluation of a Ship's Laser Inertial Navigation System (SLINS) produced by British Aerospace. **UPDATED**

TOFIÑO   *6/1999**, *Paul Jackson* / 0080632

AUXILIARIES

1 PATIÑO CLASS (FLEET LOGISTIC TANKER) (AOR)

Name	No	Builders	Launched	Commissioned
PATIÑO	A 14	Bazán, Ferrol	22 June 1994	16 June 1995

Displacement, tons: 5,762 light; 17,045 full load
Dimensions, feet (metres): 544.6 × 72.2 × 26.2 *(166 × 22 × 8)*
Main machinery: 2 Bazán/Burmeister & Wain 16V40/45 diesels; 24,000 hp(m) *(17.6 MW)* sustained; 1 shaft; acbLIPS cp prop
Speed, knots: 20. **Range, miles:** 13,440 at 20 kt
Complement: 146 plus 19 aircrew plus 20 spare
Cargo capacity: 6,815 tons dieso; 1,660 tons aviation fuel; 500 tons solids
Guns: 2 Bazán 20 mm/120 Meroka CIWS (fitted for). 2 Oerlikon 20 mm/90.
Countermeasures: Decoys: 4 SRBOC chaff launchers. Nixie torpedo decoy.
ESM/ECM: Aldebaran intercept and jammer.
Radars: 3 navigation/helo control; I-band.
Helicopters: 3 SH-3D Sea King size.

Comment: The Bazán design AP 21 was rejected in favour of this joint Netherlands/Spain design. Ordered on 26 December 1991. Laid down 1 July 1993. One supply station each side for both liquids and solids. Stern refuelling. One Vertrep supply station, and workshops for aircraft maintenance. Medical facilities. Built to merchant ship standards with military NBC. Accommodation for up to 50 female crew members. SCOT 3 SATCOM to be fitted. **UPDATED**

PATIÑO   *1/1999*, *Diego Quevedo* / 0050149

1 TRANSPORT SHIP (AP)

Name	No	Builders	Recommissioned
CONTRAMAESTRE CASADO (ex-*Thanasis-K*, ex-*Fortuna Reefer*, ex-*Bonzo*, ex-*Bajamar*, ex-*Leeward Islands*)	A 01	Eriksberg-Göteborg, Sweden	15 Dec 1982

Displacement, tons: 2,272 full load
Dimensions, feet (metres): 343.4 × 46.9 × 29.2 *(104.7 × 14.3 × 8.9)*
Main machinery: 1 Burmeister & Wain diesel; 3,600 hp(m) *(2.65 MW)*; 1 shaft
Speed, knots: 16. **Range, miles:** 8,000 at 15 kt
Complement: 72
Guns: 2 Oerlikon 20 mm.
Radars: Navigation: Racal Decca 1226 and 626; I-band.

Comment: Built in the 1950s. Impounded as smuggler. Delivered after conversion 6 December 1983. Has a helicopter deck. **VERIFIED**

CONTRAMAESTRE CASADO   *2/1998*, *Diego Quevedo* / 0050150

8 HARBOUR TANKERS (YO)

No	Displacement, tons	Dimensions metres	Cargo, tons fuel	Commissioned
Y 231	524	34 × 7 × 2.9	300	1981
Y 251	830	42.8 × 8.4 × 3.1	500	1981
Y 256	200	28 × 5.2 × 1.9	100	1959
Y 237	344	34.3 × 6.2 × 2.5	193	1965
Y 252	337	34.3 × 6.2 × 2.5	193	1965
Y 253	337	34.3 × 6.2 × 2.5	193	1965
Y 254	214.7	24.5 × 5.5 × 2.2	100	1981
Y 255	524	34 × 7 × 2.9	300	1981

Comment: All built by Bazán at Cádiz and Ferrol. **UPDATED**

Y 231   *1/1999**, *Camil Busquets i Vilanova* / 0080634

1 TRANSPORT SHIP (AP)

Name	No	Builders	Commissioned
EL CAMINO ESPAÑOL	A 05 (ex-ET 03)	Maua, Rio de Janeiro	Oct 1984
(ex-Araguary, ex-Cyndia)			

Displacement, tons: 4,560 full load
Dimensions, feet (metres): 306.9 × 59.8 × 15.2 *(93.5 × 18.3 × 4.6)*
Main machinery: 2 Sulzer diesels; 6,482 hp(m) *(4.76 MW)*; 2 shafts
Speed, knots: 15
Complement: 24 (3 officers) plus 40 Army
Military lift: 24 tanks plus 15 trucks and 102 jeeps
Radars: Navigation: I-band.

Comment: Acquired by the Army in early 1999 but commissioned into the Navy on 21 September 1999. RoRo design converted for military use by Bazán in Cartagena. Used for logistic supply of the Canary Islands. Has two 25 ton cranes.

NEW ENTRY

EL CAMINO ESPAÑOL   9/1999 *, Diego Quevedo / 0080633

1 FLEET TANKER (AORL)

Name	No	Builders	Launched	Commissioned
MARQUÉS DE LA ENSENADA	A 11	Bazán, Ferrol	3 Oct 1990	3 June 1991
(ex-Mar del Norte)				

Displacement, tons: 13,592 full load
Dimensions, feet (metres): 403.9 oa; 377.3 wl × 64 × 25.9 *(123.1; 115 × 19.5 × 7.9)*
Main machinery: 1 MAN-Bazán 18V40/50A; 11,247 hp(m) *(8.27 MW)* sustained; 1 shaft
Speed, knots: 16. **Range, miles:** 10,000 at 15 kt
Complement: 80 (11 officers)
Cargo capacity: 7,498 tons dieso; 1,746 tons JP-5; 120 tons deck cargo
Guns: 2—12.7 mm MGs.
Radars: Surface search: Racal Decca 2459; I/F-band.
Navigation: Racal Decca ARPA 2690/9; I-band.
Helicopters: 1 AB 212 or similar.

Comment: Ordered 30 December 1988; laid down 16 November 1989. The deletion of the *Teide* left a serious deficiency in the Fleet's at sea replenishment capability which has been restored by the *Patiño*. In addition, and as a stop gap, this tanker was built at one third of the cost of the larger support ship. Two Vertrep stations and a platform for a Sea King size helicopter. Replenishment stations on both sides and one astern. Provision for Meroka CIWS behind the bridge and four chaff launchers as well as ESM. Has a small hospital.

VERIFIED

MARQUÉS DE LA ENSENADA   5/1998, H M Steele / 0050151

2 LOGISTIC SUPPORT SHIPS (ATF)

Name	No	Builders	Commissioned
MAR CARIBE (ex-Amatista)	A 101	Duro Felguera, Gijon	24 Mar 1975
NEPTUNO (ex-Mar Rojo, ex-Amapola)	A 20 (ex-A 102)	Duro Felguera, Gijon	24 Mar 1975

Displacement, tons: 1,860 full load
Dimensions, feet (metres): 176.4 × 38.8 × 14.8 *(53.8 × 11.8 × 4.5)*
Main machinery: 2 Echevarria-Burmeister & Wain 18V23HU diesels; 4,860 hp(m) *(3.57 MW)*; 2 shafts; bow thruster
Speed, knots: 12. **Range, miles:** 6,000 at 10 kt
Complement: 44

Comment: Two offshore oil rig support tugs were acquired and commissioned into the Navy 14 December 1988. Bollard pull, 80 tons. *Neptuno* converted as a diver support vessel. She has a dynamic positioning system and carries a side scan mine detection high-frequency sonar as well as a semi-autonomous remote-controlled DSRV. The control cable restricts operations to within 75 m of an auxiliary diving unit. The DSRV is launched and recovered by a hydraulic arm. *Mar Caribe* works with Amphibious Forces.

UPDATED

MAR CARIBE   8/1999 *, Diego Quevedo / 0080635

NEPTUNO   12/1999 *, Camil Busquets i Vilanova / 0080636

1 WATER TANKER (AWT)

Name	No	Builders	Commissioned
TORPÉDISTA HERNÁNDEZ	A 63 (ex-AA 22, ex-A 10)	Bazán, La Carraca	24 Jan 1963

Displacement, tons: 584 full load
Dimensions, feet (metres): 146.9 × 24.9 × 9.8 *(44.8 × 7.6 × 3)*
Main machinery: 1 diesel; 700 hp(m) *(514 kW)*; 1 shaft
Speed, knots: 10. **Range, miles:** 1,000 at 8 kt
Complement: 17
Cargo capacity: 350 tons
Radars: Navigation: Furuno; I-band.

Comment: Ocean-going. Was to have been deleted in 1994 but was reprieved when two others of the class paid off in December 1993.

UPDATED

TORPÉDISTA HERNÁNDEZ   6/1997 *, Diego Quevedo / 0019167

1 WATER TANKER (AWT)

Name	No	Builders	Commissioned
MARINERO JARANO	A 65 (ex-AA 31)	Bazán, Cádiz	16 Mar 1981

Displacement, tons: 549 full load
Dimensions, feet (metres): 123 × 23 × 9.8 *(37.5 × 7 × 3)*
Main machinery: 1 diesel; 600 hp(m) *(441 kW)*; 1 shaft
Speed, knots: 10
Complement: 13
Cargo capacity: 300 tons

Comment: Similar to Y 231 and Y 255 (harbour tankers).

VERIFIED

MARINERO JARANO   4/1998 / 0050152

1 WATER TANKER (AWT)

Name	No	Builders	Commissioned
CONDESTABLE ZARAGOZA	A 66 (ex-AA 41)	Bazán, Cádiz	16 Oct 1981

Displacement, tons: 895 full load
Dimensions, feet (metres): 152.2 × 27.6 × 11.2 *(46.4 × 8.4 × 3.4)*
Main machinery: 1 diesel; 700 hp(m) *(515 kW)*; 1 shaft
Speed, knots: 10
Complement: 16
Cargo capacity: 600 tons

UPDATED

CONDESTABLE ZARAGOZA   *2/1995*, Diego Quevedo /* 0080637

1 DIVING SUPPORT VESSEL (YDT)

PROSERPINA Y 563 (ex-*YBZ 12*)

Displacement, tons: 103.5 full load
Dimensions, feet (metres): 70.5 × 19.2 × 9.5 *(21.5 × 5.9 × 2.9)*
Main machinery: 1 Sulzer diesel; 200 hp(m) *(147 kW)*; 1 shaft
Speed, knots: 9
Complement: 6

Comment: Built by Bazán, Cartagena. Frogmen support craft.

VERIFIED

PROSERPINA   *9/1998, Diego Quevedo /* 0050153

39 HARBOUR CRAFT

Y 501-512	Y 574	Y 529-530	Y 571-572	Y 540
Y 515	Y 521-527	Y 545-548	Y 580-587	Y 577

Comment: Some used as divers boats, others as harbour ferries. Some are former patrol craft of the 'P 101' and 'P 202' class. *Y 540* is an Admirals' Yacht.

UPDATED

Y 586   *7/1999*, Diego Quevedo /* 0080638

Y 540   *3/1999*, Diego Quevedo /* 0080639

36 BARGES (YO/YE)

Comment: Have Y numbers. Four in 200 series carry fuel, 29 in 300 for ammunition and general stores, three in 400 for anti-pollution. Some floating pontoons have L numbers.   *UPDATED*

Y 257   *3/1998, Diego Quevedo /* 0050155

TRAINING SHIPS

6 SAIL TRAINING SHIPS (AXS)

Name	No	Builders	Commissioned
JUAN SEBASTIAN DE ELCANO	A 71	Echevarrieta, Cádiz	17 Aug 1928
AROSA	A 72	Inglaterra	1 Apr 1981
HISPANIA	A 73	Palma Mallorca	27 July 1988
LA GRACIOSA (ex-*Dejá Vu*)	A 74	—	30 June 1988
GIRALDA (ex-*Southern Cross*)	A 76	Morris & Mortimer, Argyll	23 Aug 1993
SISARGAS	A 75	Novo Glass, Polinya	19 Sep 1995

Displacement, tons: 3,420 standard; 3,656 full load
Dimensions, feet (metres): 308.5 oa × 43.3 × 24.6 *(94.1 × 13.15 × 7.46)*
Main machinery: 1 Deutz MWM KHD 6M diesel; 1,950 hp(m) *(1.43 MW)*; 1 shaft
Speed, knots: 9. **Range, miles:** 10,000 at 9 kt
Complement: 347 (students 120)
Guns: 2—37/80 mm Bazán saluting guns.
Radars: Navigation: 2 Racal Decca; I-band.

Comment: Details are for A 71 which is a four masted top-sail schooner—near sister of Chilean *Esmeralda*. Named after the first circumnavigator of the world (1519-22) who succeeded to the command of the expedition led by Magellan after the latter's death. Laid down 24 November 1925. Launched on 5 March 1927. Carries 230 tons oil fuel. Engine replaced in 1992. The other five are a ketch (A 72) (52 tons and 22.84 m in length), a cruiser of regattas (A 73) (37.8 tons and 24.5 m in length), a schooner (A 74) (16.8 m in length) used by the Naval School, a 90 tons ketch (A 75) launched in 1958 and formerly owned by the father of King Juan Carlos I and presented to the Naval School at Marin (Pontevedra) in 1993, an ex-yacht (A 76), and a bermudian yacht (A 75) built near Barcelona.   *UPDATED*

JUAN SEBASTIAN DE ELCANO   *7/1996, A Campanera i Rovira*

5 TRAINING CRAFT (AXL)

Name	No	Builders	Commissioned
GUARDIAMARINA BARRUTIA	A 81	Cartagena	14 Sep 1982
GUARDIAMARINA SALAS	A 82	Cartagena	10 May 1983
GUARDIAMARINA GODÍNEZ	A 83	Cartagena	4 July 1984
GUARDIAMARINA RULL	A 84	Cartagena	11 June 1984
GUARDIAMARINA CHEREGUINI	A 85	Cartagena	11 June 1984

Displacement, tons: 56 full load
Dimensions, feet (metres): 62 × 16.7 × 5.2 *(18.9 × 5.1 × 1.6)*
Speed, knots: 13
Complement: 15; 22 (A 81)
Radars: Navigation: Halcon 948; I-band.

Comment: Tenders to Naval School. A 81 has an operations centre.   *UPDATED*

GUARDIAMARINA CHEREGUINI   *1/2000*, Diego Quevedo /* 0085027

TUGS

2 OCEAN TUGS (ATA)

Name	No	Builders	Commissioned
MAHÓN (ex-Circos)	A 51	Astilleros Atlántico, Santander	1978
LAS PALMAS (ex-Somiedo)	A 52	Astilleros Atlántico, Santander	1978

Displacement, tons: 1,450 full load
Dimensions, feet (metres): 134.5 × 38.1 × 18 *(41 × 11.6 × 5.5)*
Main machinery: 2 AESA/Sulzer 16ASV25/30 diesels; 7,744 hp(m) *(5.69 MW)*; 2 shafts
Speed, knots: 13. **Range, miles:** 27,000 at 12 kt (A 52)
Complement: 33 (8 officers) plus 45 scientists
Guns: 2—12.7 mm MGs.
Radars: Navigation: 2 Racal Decca; I-band.

Comment: Built for Compania Hispano Americana de Offshore SA. Commissioned in the Navy 30 July 1981. *Las Palmas* converted in 1988 for Polar Research Ship duties in Antarctica with an ice strengthened bow, an enlarged bridge and two containers aft for laboratories. Based at Las Palmas and used as a tug.

UPDATED

MAHÓN   *2/1997*, Camil Busquets i Vilanova /* 0019170

1 OCEAN TUG (ATA)

Name	No	Builders	Commissioned
LA GRAÑA (ex-Punta Amer)	A 53 (ex-Y 119)	Astilleros Luzuriaga, San Sebastian	1982

Displacement, tons: 664 full load
Dimensions, feet (metres): 102.4 × 27.6 × 10.5 *(31.2 × 8.4 × 3.2)*
Main machinery: 1 diesel; 3,240 hp(m) *(2.38 MW)*; 1 Voith Schneider prop
Speed, knots: 13. **Range, miles:** 1,750 at 12 kt
Complement: 28

Comment: Former civilian tug, now designated as ocean-going.

VERIFIED

LA GRAÑA   *6/1998, Diego Quevedo /* 0050157

1 OCEAN TUG (ATA/ATS)

Name	No	Builders	Commissioned
FERROL	A 31 (ex-A 43, ex-AR 45, ex-RA 5)	Bazán, La Carraca	11 Apr 1964

Displacement, tons: 951 standard; 1,069 full load
Dimensions, feet (metres): 183.5 × 32.8 × 13.1 *(55.9 × 10 × 4)*
Main machinery: 2 Sulzer diesels; 3,200 hp *(2.53 MW)*; 1 shaft; cp prop
Speed, knots: 15. **Range, miles:** 4,640 at 14 kt
Complement: 49; 60 (A 12)
Guns: 2 or 4 Oerlikon 20 mm (single or twin).
Radars: Navigation: 2 Decca TM 626; I-band.

Comment: Second of class *Poseidón* transferred to Mauritania in January 2000.

UPDATED

FERROL   *6/1999*, Paul Jackson /* 0080640

20 COASTAL and HARBOUR TUGS (YTB/YTM/YTL)

No	Displacement tons (full load)	HP/speed	Commissioned
Y 111	227	800/10	1963
Y 116-117	422	1,500/12	1981
Y 118, Y 121-123	236	1,560/14	1989-91
Y 120 (ex-Punta Roca)	260	1,750/12	1973
Y 131-132, Y 140	70	200/8	1965-67
Y 141-142	229	800/11	1981
Y 143	133	600/10	1961
Y 144-145	195	2,030/11	1983
Y 147-148	87	400/10	1987/1999
Y 171-173	10	440/11	1982/1985

Comment: *Y 143* has a troop carrying capability. *Y 171-173* are pusher tugs for submarines. *Y 118, Y 119-123* have Voith Schneider propulsion.

UPDATED

Y 121   *1/1999*, A Campanera i Rovira /* 0080641

ARMY

Note: In addition there is a second vessel *Santa Teresa de Avila* ET-01 of 92 tons built in 1974.

1 TRANSPORT SHIP (AP)

MARTÍN POSADILLO (ex-*Rivanervión*, ex-*Cala Portals*) A 04 (ex-ET-02)

Displacement, tons: 1,920 full load
Dimensions, feet (metres): 246.1 × 42.7 × 14.1 *(75 × 13 × 4.3)*
Main machinery: 1 BMW diesel; 2,400 hp(m) *(1.77 MW)*; 1 shaft
Speed, knots: 10
Complement: 18
Military lift: 42 trucks plus 25 jeeps

Comment: RoRo ship built in 1973, taken on by the Army in 1990. Pennant number changed in early 2000.

NEW ENTRY

MARTÍN POSADILLO   *1/2000*, Diego Quevedo /* 0085028

POLICE (GUARDIA CIVIL DEL MAR)

Note: Created by Royal decree on 22 February 1991. Bases at La Coruña, Barcelona, Valencia, Tarragona, Baleares, Cantabria, Almeira, Malaga, Murcia and, Algeciras. Personnel strength 1,000 (35 officers). The force has taken over the anti-terrorist role and some general patrol duties as a peacetime paramilitary organisation coming under the Ministry of Defence in war. BO 105 helicopters are used for coastal patrols. All vessels are armed.

BO 105   *10/1998, Diego Quevedo* / 0050159

14 RODMAN 55 CLASS (INSHORE PATROL CRAFT—PM)

M 01-M 14

Displacement, tons: 15.7 full load
Dimensions, feet (metres): 54.1 × 12.5 × 2.3 *(16.5 × 3.8 × 0.7)*
Main machinery: 2 MAN D2848-LXE diesels; 1,360 hp(m) *(1 MW)* sustained; 2 Hamilton water-jets
Speed, knots: 35. **Range, miles:** 500 at 25 kt
Complement: 7
Guns: 1—12.7 mm MG.
Radars: Surface search: Ericsson; I-band.

Comment: GRP hulls built by Rodman, Vigo. First five in service in 1992, three in 1993, and six more in 1995-96. Five of this type sold to Paraguay.   *UPDATED*

M 04   *1/1999*, Diego Quevedo* / 0080643

12 SAETA-12 CLASS (INSHORE PATROL CRAFT—PL)

L 01-L 12

Displacement, tons: 14 full load
Dimensions, feet (metres): 39 × 12.5 × 2.3 *(11.9 × 3.8 × 0.7)*
Main machinery: 2 MAN D2848-LXE diesels; 1,360 hp(m) *(1 MW)* sustained; 2 Hamilton water-jets
Speed, knots: 38. **Range, miles:** 300 at 25 kt
Complement: 4
Guns: 1—7.62 mm MG.
Radars: Surface search: Ericsson; I-band.

Comment: GRP hulls built by Bazán and delivered in 1993-97.   *UPDATED*

L 11   *1/1999*, A Campanera i Rovira* / 0080644

CUSTOMS

Note: All carry ADUANAS on ships' sides. In addition to the listed vessels there are a number of fast boats. Some of the larger vessels are armed with machine guns. There are also four MBB-105 and one MBB 117 helicopters. Six CASA C-212 patrol aircraft were transferred to the Air Force in 1997.

Name	Displacement tons (full load)	HP/speed	Commissioned
ÁGUILA	80	2,700/29	1974
ALBATROS 2 and 3	85	2,700/29	1964-69
ALCA 1 and 3	24	2,000/45	1987-88
ALCAVARÁN 1-5	85	3,920/28	1984-87
CÁRABO	57	1,350/16	1977
GAVILÁN 1	63	2,700/28	1975-76
GAVILÁN 2-4	65	3,200/30	1983-87
HALCÓN 2-3	68	3,200/28	1980-83
HJ 1, HJ 3-11	20	2,000/50	1986
VA 2-5	23	1,400/27	1985
CORMORÁN	22	2,970/65	1990
CONDOR 5	20	1,300/35	1992
NEBLÍ 1	50	3,480/53	1993
PETREL 1	1,600	1,200/12	1994
CONDOR 6 and 8	20	1,360/35	1998

Comment: There are also six fast patrol boats IPP 1-3 and IMP 1-3.
     UPDATED

VA 5   *7/1998, Diego Quevedo* / 0050162

CONDOR 6   *9/1999*, Diego Quevedo* / 0080645

MARITIME RESCUE AND SAFETY

Note: A service under the direction of the Merchant Marine, called the SSSM (Sociedad de Salvamento y Securidad Maritima), may come under a future Coast Guard service in due course. 11 salvage tugs and 14 fast launches, four harbour pollution craft and four Sea King SAR helicopters.

ANTARTICO   *6/1999*, Diego Quevedo* / 0080646

SEA KING   *11/1998*, Diego Quevedo* / 0080647

SRI LANKA

Headquarters Appointments

Commander of the Navy:
  Vice Admiral Cecil Tissera, VSV, USP
Chief of Staff:
  Rear Admiral D W K Sandagiri, VSV, USP
Commander East Area:
  Rear Admiral J T G Sundaram, USP
Commander South Area:
  Commodore S P Weerasekera
Commander North Area:
  Commodore H S Rathnakeerthi, USP
Commander North Central Command:
  Commodore L D Dharmapriya, USP
Commander West Area:
  Rear Admiral A H M Razeek, USP

General

The Royal Ceylon Navy was formed on 9 December 1950 when the Navy Act was proclaimed. Called the Sri Lanka Navy since Republic Day 22 May 1972. The Tamil insurgency in Sri Lanka had a major impact on the naval programme. The main area of maritime importance is the Palk Strait between India and the primarily Tamil area of northern Sri Lanka. This area has many small creeks—the main requirement is the support of shallow draught fast craft, a very different task from EEZ patrols.

Personnel

2000
(a) 17,993 (978 officers) regulars
(b) SLVNF: 1,993 (160 officers)
(c) Naval reservists: 160 (9 officers)

Bases

Main Naval Base at Trincomalee (East).
(HQ and West) Colombo, Welisara, Kalpitiya.
(North) Karainagar, Kankasanthuari, Thalaimmanner, Madagal, Kayts, Mandativu, Pungndutivu.
(North Central) Poonewa, Mankulam, Mamaduwa.
(South) Tangalle, Galle, Boossa.
(East) Nilaweli.
There are five Area Commands—North, North Central, South, East and West.

Pennant Numbers

Patrol craft in the 400 series were given new pennant numbers in November 1996.

Prefix to Ships' Names

SLNS.

Mercantile Marine

Lloyd's Register of Shipping:
  64 vessels of 194,585 tons gross

DELETIONS

Patrol Forces

1999   *P 174* (sunk)

Amphibious Forces

1998   *Pabbatha* (sunk)

PATROL FORCES

Note: Two ex-Israeli 'SAAR 4' class attack craft are expected to transfer in mid-2000.

1 JAYASAGARA CLASS (OFFSHORE PATROL VESSEL) (OPV)

Name	No	Builders	Launched	Commissioned
JAYASAGARA	P 601	Colombo Dockyard	26 May 1983	9 Dec 1983

Displacement, tons: 330 full load
Dimensions, feet (metres): 130.5 × 23 × 7 *(39.8 × 7 × 2.1)*
Main machinery: 2 MAN 8L20/27 diesels; 2,180 hp(m) *(1.6 MW)* sustained; 2 shafts
Speed, knots: 15. **Range, miles:** 3,000 at 11 kt
Complement: 52 (4 officers)
Guns: 2 China 25 mm/80 (twin). 2 China 14.5 mm (twin) MGs.
Radars: Surface search: Anritsu RA 723; I-band.

Comment: Ordered from Colombo Dockyard on 31 December 1981. Second of class sunk by Tamil forces in September 1994.   ***UPDATED***

JAYASAGARA   *6/1996*, Sri Lanka Navy /* 0080691

1 HAIQING (TYPE 037/1G) CLASS
(FAST ATTACK CRAFT—GUN) (PCF)

Name	No	Builders	Commissioned
PARAKRAMABAHU	P 351	Qingdao Shipyard	22 May 1996

Displacement, tons: 478 full load
Dimensions, feet (metres): 206 × 23.6 × 7.9 *(62.8 × 7.2 × 2.4)*
Main machinery: 4 PR 230ZC diesels; 4,000 hp(m) *(2.94 MW)*; 4 shafts
Speed, knots: 28. **Range, miles:** 1,300 at 15 kt
Complement: 71
Guns: 4 China 37 mm/63 (2 twin) Type 76A; 4 China 14.5 mm (2 twin) MGs Type 69.
A/S mortars: 2 Type 87 6-tubed launchers.
Radars: Surface search: Anritsu RA 273; I-band.
Sonars: Stag Ear; hull mounted; active search and attack; high frequency.

Comment: Ordered in March 1994 from China and delivered on 13 December 1995. This is a Houxin hull with a different armament to the Chinese vessels of the same class.   ***UPDATED***

PARAKRAMABAHU   *5/1996*, Sri Lanka Navy /* 0080692

6 SHANGHAI II (TYPE 062) CLASS
(FAST ATTACK CRAFT—GUN) (PCF)

WEERAYA P 311	RANAKAMEE P 312	JAGATHA P 315	P 316-P 318
(ex-P 3141)	(ex-P 3142)	(ex-P 3146)	

Displacement, tons: 139 full load
Dimensions, feet (metres): 127.3 × 17.7 × 5.2 *(38.8 × 5.4 × 1.6)*
Main machinery: 4 Type L12-180 diesels; 4,800 hp(m) *(3.53 MW)*; 4 shafts
Speed, knots: 28. **Range, miles:** 750 at 16 kt
Complement: 34 (3 officers)
Guns: 4 Royal Ordnance GCM-AO3 30 mm (2 twin).
  4 China 14.5 mm (2 twin) MG.
Radars: Surface search: Koden MD 3220 Mk 2; I-band.
Navigation: Furuno 825 D; I-band.

Comment: The first three transferred by China on 30 November 1980. Three more built at Qinxin shipyard and commissioned on 31 July 1998. Armament and radars updated.   ***UPDATED***

P 317   *3/1999, Sri Lanka Navy /* 0053485

1 RANARISI (MOD SHANGHAI II) CLASS
(FAST ATTACK CRAFT—GUN) (PCF)

Name	No	Builders	Commissioned
RANARISI	P 322	Guijiang Shipyard	14 July 1992

Displacement, tons: 150 full load
Dimensions, feet (metres): 134.5 × 17.7 × 5.2 *(41 × 5.4 × 1.6)*
Main machinery: 4 diesels; 4,800 hp(m) *(3.53 MW)*; 4 shafts
Speed, knots: 29. **Range, miles:** 750 at 16 kt
Complement: 28 (4 officers)
Guns: 4 China 37 mm/63 (2 twin) Type 76 or 4 Royal Ordnance GCM-AO3 30 mm (2 twin).
  4 China 14.5 mm (twin) Type 69.
Radars: Surface search: Racal Decca; I-band.

Comment: Acquired from China in September 1991. Automatic guns and improved habitability. Two others destroyed by Tamil guerrillas.   ***UPDATED***

RANARISI   *6/1996*, Sri Lanka Navy /* 0080694

2 LUSHUN (TYPE 062/1G) CLASS
(FAST ATTACK CRAFT—GUN) (PCF)

P 340   P 341

Displacement, tons: 212 full load
Dimensions, feet (metres): 149 × 21 × 5.6 *(45.5 × 6.4 × 1.7)*
Main machinery: 4 Type Z12V 190 BCJ diesels; 4,800 hp(m) *(3.53 MW)*; 4 shafts
Speed, knots: 28. **Range, miles:** 750 at 16 kt
Complement: 30 (3 officers)
Guns: 4 China 37 mm/63 (2 twin) Type 76.
  4 China 14.5 mm (2 twin) Type 82 MGs.
Radars: Surface search: Racal Decca RM 1070A; I-band.

Comment: Built at Lushun Dockyard, Darlin. Commissioned on 2 March 1998. Larger version of 'Haizhui' class.

UPDATED

P 340   *3/1999*, Sri Lanka Navy* / 0080699

3 RANAJAYA (HAIZHUI CLASS) (TYPE 062/1) (PC)

Name	No	Builders	Commissioned
RANAJAYA	P 330	Guijiang Shipyard	9 Sep 1996
RANADEERA	P 331	Guijiang Shipyard	9 Sep 1996
RANAWICKRAMA	P 332	Guijiang Shipyard	9 Sep 1996

Displacement, tons: 170 full load
Dimensions, feet (metres): 134.5 × 17.4 × 5.9 *(41 × 5.3 × 1.8)*
Main machinery: 4 Type L12-180A diesels; 4,400 hp(m) *(3.22 MW)* sustained; 4 shafts
Speed, knots: 21
Complement: 44
Guns: 4 China 37 mm/63 (2 twin). 4 China 25 mm/60 (2 twin).
Radars: Surface search: Anritsu 726UA; I-band.

Comment: Transferred from China by lift ship after delivery on 22 May 1996.

UPDATED

RANAJAYA   *9/1996*, Sri Lanka Navy* / 0080693

10 COLOMBO CLASS (FAST ATTACK CRAFT—GUN) (PCF)

P 450-P 455   P 494-P 497

Displacement, tons: 56 full load
Dimensions, feet (metres): 81.4 × 19.7 × 3.9 *(24.8 × 6 × 1.2)*
Main machinery: 2 MTU 12V 396 TE94 diesels; 4,570 hp(m) *(3.36 MW)*; ASD 16 surface drives
Speed, knots: 45. **Range, miles:** 850 at 16 kt
Complement: 15
Guns: 1 Rafael Typhoon 20 mm. 1 Oerlikon 20 mm. 2—12.7 mm MGs. 2—7.62 mm MGs.
Weapons control: Elop MSIS optronic director; Typhoon GFCS.
Radars: Surface search: Furuno FR 8250 or Corden Mk 2; I-band.

Comment: Built by Colombo Dockyard to the Israeli Shaldag design. First one launched 3 February 1996, second 10 June 1996 and third 27 July 1996. First four delivered in 1997-98. Six more in 1998-99.

UPDATED

COLOMBO   *11/1999** / 0080695

3 DVORA CLASS (FAST ATTACK CRAFT—GUN) (PCF)

P 420 (ex-P 453)   P 421 (ex-P 454)   P 422 (ex-P 455)

Displacement, tons: 47 full load
Dimensions, feet (metres): 70.8 × 18 × 5.8 *(21.6 × 5.5 × 1.8)*
Main machinery: 2 MTU 12V 331 TC81 diesels; 2,605 hp(m) *(1.91 MW)* sustained; 2 shafts
Speed, knots: 36. **Range, miles:** 1,200 at 17 kt
Complement: 12
Guns: 2 Oerlikon 20 mm. 2—12.7 mm MGs.
Radars: Surface search: Anritsu 721UA; I-band.

Comment: First pair transferred from Israel early 1984, next four in October 1986. Built by Israel Aircraft Industries. One sunk by Tamil forces on 29 August 1995 and second on 30 March 1996. One more deleted in late 1996.

VERIFIED

DVORA (old number)   *1992, Sri Lanka Navy*

4 SUPER DVORA CLASS (FAST ATTACK CRAFT—GUN) (PCF)

P 440-P 443 (ex-P 465-P 468)

Displacement, tons: 54 full load
Dimensions, feet (metres): 73.5 × 18 × 5.8 *(22.4 × 5.5 × 1.8)*
Main machinery: 2 MTU 12V 396 TB93 diesels; 3,260 hp(m) *(2.4 MW)* sustained; 2 shafts
Speed, knots: 46. **Range, miles:** 1,200 at 17 kt
Complement: 12 (1 officer)
Guns: 2 Oerlikon 20 mm. 2—12.7 mm MGs.
Radars: Surface search: Decca 926; I-band.

Comment: Ordered from Israel Aircraft Industries in October 1986 and delivered in 1987-88. A more powerful version of the 'Dvora' class. P 464 was destroyed by Tamil guerrillas on 29 August 1993 and P 463 on 29 August 1995. These craft have a deeper draft than the Mk II version with surface drives.

UPDATED

SUPER DVORA   *6/1992*, Sri Lanka Navy* / 0080696

6 SUPER DVORA MK II CLASS
(FAST ATTACK CRAFT—GUN) (PCF)

P 460 (ex-P441)   P 461 (ex-P 496)   P 462 (ex-P 497)   P 463-P 465

Displacement, tons: 64 full load
Dimensions, feet (metres): 82 × 18.4 × 3.6 *(25 × 5.6 × 1.1)*
Main machinery: 2 MTU 12V 396 TE94 diesels; 4,570 hp(m) *(3.36 MW)*; ASD16 surface drives
Speed, knots: 50. **Range, miles:** 700 at 30 kt
Complement: 10 (1 officer)
Guns: 1 Rafael Typhoon 20 mm or 2 Royal Ordnance GCM-AO3 30 mm (twin). 2—12.7 mm MGs. 2—7.62 mm MGs.
Weapons control: Elop MSIS optronic director; Typhoon GFCS.
Radars: Surface search: Koden MD 3220; I-band.

Comment: First four ordered from Israel Aircraft Industries Ramta in early 1995. A slightly larger version of the Mk 1. First one delivered 5 November 1995, second 30 April 1996, third 22 June 1996 and fourth in December 1996. Two more were acquired on 9 June 1999 and 15 September 1999 respectively. The engines are an improved version of those fitted in the Israeli Navy craft.

UPDATED

SUPER DVORA Mk II   *11/1999** / 0080697

3 SOUTH KOREAN KILLER CLASS
(FAST ATTACK CRAFT—GUN) (PCF)

P 430 (ex-P 473)   **P 431** (ex-P 474)   **P 432** (ex-P 475)

Displacement, tons: 56 full load
Dimensions, feet (metres): 75.5 × 17.7 × 5.9 *(23 × 5.4 × 1.8)*
Main machinery: 2 MTU 396 TB93 diesels; 3,260 hp(m) *(2.4 MW)* sustained; 2 shafts
Speed, knots: 40
Complement: 12
Guns: 2 Oerlikon 20 mm. 2—12.7 mm MGs.
Radars: Surface search: Racal Decca 926; I-band.

Comment: Built by Korea SB and Eng, Buson. All commissioned February 1988.

UPDATED

P 430   *8/1996*, Sri Lanka Navy /* 0080698

3 + 2 SHALDAG CLASS (FAST ATTACK CRAFT—GUN) (PCF)

P 470 (ex-P 491)   **P 471** (ex-P 492)   **P 472**

Displacement, tons: 56 full load
Dimensions, feet (metres): 81.4 × 19.7 × 3.9 *(24.8 × 6 × 1.2)*
Main machinery: 2 Deutz/MWM TBO 604 BV16 diesels; 5,000 hp(m) *(3.68 MW)*; 2 Riva Calzoni water-jets
Speed, knots: 45. **Range, miles:** 850 at 16 kt
Complement: 15
Guns: 2 Oerlikon 20 mm. 2—12.7 mm MGs.
Radars: Surface search: MD 3220 Mk II; I-band.

Comment: First one acquired from the Israeli Shipyards, Haifa on 24 January 1996, second 20 July 1996 and third on 16 February 2000. More are planned. Originally launched in December 1989, this class was not bought by the Israeli Navy. Same hull used for the 'Colombo' class. Also in service in Cyprus.

UPDATED

SHALDAG 470   *2/1996*, Sri Lanka Navy /* 0080700

6 TRINITY MARINE CLASS (FAST ATTACK CRAFT—GUN) (PCF)

P 480   **P 481**   **P 482**   **P 483**   **P 484**   **P 485**

Displacement, tons: 68 full load
Dimensions, feet (metres): 81.7 × 17.7 × 4.9 *(24.9 × 5.4 × 1.5)*
Main machinery: 2 MTU 12V 396 TE94 diesels; 4,570 hp(m) *(3.36 MW)* sustained; 2 water-jets
Speed, knots: 47. **Range, miles:** 600 at 17 kt
Complement: 12
Guns: 2 Oerlikon 20 mm. 2—12.7 mm MGs. 1 Grenade launcher.
Radars: Surface search: Raytheon R 1210; I-band.

Comment: All built at Equitable Shipyard, New Orleans. First three delivered in January 1997; second three in September 1997. Kevlar reinforced GRP hulls.

UPDATED

TRINITY P 480   *1/1997*, Sri Lanka Navy /* 0080701

3 COASTAL PATROL CRAFT (PC)

P 241-P 243

Displacement, tons: 40 full load
Dimensions, feet (metres): 66 × 18 × 7 *(20 × 5.5 × 2.1)*
Main machinery: 2 Detroit 12V-71TA diesels; 840 hp *(626 kW)* sustained; 2 shafts
Speed, knots: 22. **Range, miles:** 1,500 at 14 kt
Complement: 10 (1 officer)
Guns: 2 Oerlikon 20 mm. 2—12.7 mm MGs.
Radars: Surface search: Furuno FR 2010; I-band.

Comment: Ordered from Colombo Dockyard and completed in 1982. All refitted 1988-89. Two sunk on 10 June 1996.

UPDATED

P 241   *1993*, Sri Lanka Navy /* 0080702

4 COASTAL PATROL CRAFT (PC)

P 201   **P 211**   **P 214**   **P 215**

Displacement, tons: 21 full load
Dimensions, feet (metres): 46.6 × 12.8 × 3.3 *(14.2 × 3.9 × 1)*
Main machinery: 2 Detroit 8V-71 diesels; 460 hp *(343 kW)*; 2 shafts
Speed, knots: 20. **Range, miles:** 450 at 14 kt
Complement: 6 (1 officer)
Guns: 1—12.7 mm MGs.
Radars: Surface search: Furuno FR 2010; I-band.

Comment: Built by Colombo DY and commissioned in 1982 *(P 201)*, June 1986 *(P 211 and P 214)* and 1993 *(P 215)*. Some of the earlier craft have been paid off.

UPDATED

P 211   *6/1996*, Sri Lanka Navy /* 0080703

4 SIMMONEAU CLASS (PCF)

P 410 (ex-P 483)   **P 411** (ex-P 484)   **P 412** (ex-P 485)   **P 413** (ex-P 486)

Displacement, tons: 28 full load
Dimensions, feet (metres): 56.8 × 16.1 × 4.6 *(17.3 × 4.9 × 1.4)*
Main machinery: 2 MTU 12V 183 TE93 diesels; 2,300 hp(m) *(1.69 MW)*; 2 Hamilton water-jets
Speed, knots: 42. **Range, miles:** 500 at 35 kt
Complement: 8
Guns: 1 DCN 20 mm. 1—12.7 mm MG. 2—7.62 mm MGs.
Radars: Surface search: Racal Decca; I-band.

Comment: Simmoneau Marine Type 508 craft. First pair completed in December 1993 and shipped to Colombo in 1994. Second pair built in Colombo and completed in 1995. The plan to build more was shelved.

UPDATED

P 410 (old number)   *6/1994*, D A Cromby /* 0080704

4 COASTAL PATROL CRAFT (PC)

P 221-P 224 (ex-*P 421-424*)

Displacement, tons: 22 full load
Dimensions, feet (metres): 55.9 × 14.8 × 3.9 *(17 × 4.5 × 1.2)*
Main machinery: 2 Detroit 8V-71TA diesels; 460 hp *(343 kW)*; 2 shafts
Speed, knots: 23. **Range, miles:** 1,000 at 12 kt
Complement: 7
Guns: 1—12.7 mm MG.
Radars: Surface search: Racal Decca 110; I-band.

Comment: Used for general patrol duties. Built by Cheverton Workboats, UK and commissioned in
1977. One paid off in 1996.

UPDATED

P 224   *3/1996*, Sri Lanka Navy* / 0080705

4 COUGAR CLASS (INSHORE PATROL CRAFT) (PB)

P 101   P 102   P 107   P 109

Displacement, tons: 7.4 full load
Dimensions, feet (metres): 34.1 × 9.5 × 2.6 *(10.4 × 2.9 × 0.8)*
Main machinery: 2 Sabre diesels; 500 hp *(373 kW)*; 2 shafts
Speed, knots: 30
Complement: 4
Guns: 1—12.7 mm MG.

Comment: First ordered in 1984 for trials from Cougar Marine, order for eight more placed in
1985. Five paid off or sunk so far.

UPDATED

COUGAR (old number)   *6/1992*, Sri Lanka Navy* / 0080706

25 INSHORE PATROL CRAFT (PB)

P 151-P 152   P 161-P 173   P 175-P 178   P 180   P 189-P 194   P 196-P 198

Displacement, tons: 10 full load
Dimensions, feet (metres): 44.3 × 9.8 × 1.6 *(13.5 × 3 × 0.5)*
Main machinery: 2 Cummins 6BTA5.9-M2; 584 hp *(436 kW)* sustained; 2 water-jets
Speed, knots: 33. **Range, miles:** 330 at 25 kt
Complement: 5
Guns: 2—12.7 mm MGs. 2—7.62 mm MGs.
Radars: Surface search: Furuno 1941; I-band.

Comment: First pair built by TAOS Yacht Company, Colombo, and delivered in 1991. Next fifteen
built by Blue Star Marine, Colombo and delivered in 1994-95 and seven more in 1997/98. There
are minor superstructure differences between the first pair and the rest. More being built. One
sunk in 1999.

UPDATED

P 189   *7/1999** / 0080707

3 INSHORE PATROL CRAFT (PB)

P 111-P 113

Displacement, tons: 5 full load
Dimensions, feet (metres): 44 × 9.8 × 1.6 *(13.4 × 3 × 0.5)*
Main machinery: 2 Yamaha D 343 diesels; 730 hp(m) *(544 kW)* sustained; 2 shafts
Speed, knots: 26
Complement: 5
Guns: 1—12.7 mm MG.
Radars: Surface search: Furuno FR 1941; I-band.

Comment: Built by Consolidated Marine Engineers, Sri Lanka. First nine delivered in 1988; four
more in 1992 and two more in 1994. Most of these craft have been destroyed.

UPDATED

P 111   *1992*, Sri Lanka Navy* / 0080708

9 INSHORE PATROL CRAFT (PB)

P 140-P 142   P 144-P 149

Displacement, tons: 3.5 full load
Dimensions, feet (metres): 42 × 8 × 1.6 *(12.8 × 2.4 × 0.5)*
Main machinery: 2 outboard motors; 280 hp *(209 kW)*
Speed, knots: 30
Complement: 4
Guns: 1—12.7 mm MG.

Comment: Acquired in 1988 from Blue Star Marine. Similar to *P 111* but with outboard engines.
P 150 was mined and sunk in August 1991, *P 143* sunk in 1995.

UPDATED

P 150 (old number)   *1989*, Sri Lanka Navy* / 0080709

AMPHIBIOUS FORCES

Note: There is a civilian ferry *Vaalampuri* which is sometimes used by the Navy.

1 YUHAI (WUHU-A) (TYPE 074) CLASS (LSM)

Name	No	Builders	Commissioned
SHAKTHI	L 880	China	22 May 1996

Displacement, tons: 799 full load
Dimensions, feet (metres): 191.6 × 34.1 × 8.9 *(58.4 × 10.4 × 2.7)*
Main machinery: 2 MAN 8 L 20/27 diesels; 4,900 hp(m) *(3.6 MW)*; 2 shafts
Speed, knots: 14. **Range, miles:** 1,000 at 12 kt
Complement: 56
Military lift: 150 tons
Guns: 10—14.5 mm/93 (5 twin) MGs. 6—12.7 mm MGs.
Radars: Navigation: Racal Decca; I-band.

Comment: Transferred by lift ship from China arriving 13 December 1995. A planned second of
class was built but not acquired.

UPDATED

SHAKTHI   *5/1996*, Sri Lanka Navy* / 0080710

2 LANDING CRAFT (LCM)

Name	No	Builders	Commissioned
RANAGAJA (ex-*Gajasingha*)	L 839	Colombo Dockyard	15 Nov 1991
RANAVIJAYA	L 836	Colombo Dockyard	21 July 1994

Displacement, tons: 268 full load
Dimensions, feet (metres): 108.3 × 26 × 4.9 *(33 × 8 × 1.5)*
Main machinery: 2 Caterpillar diesels; 1,524 hp *(1.14 MW)*; 2 shafts
Speed, knots: 8. **Range, miles:** 1,800 at 8 kt
Complement: 12 (2 officers)
Guns: 4 China 14.5 mm (2 twin) *(Ranagaja)* or 2 Oerlikon 20 mm. 2—12.7 mm MGs.
Radars: Navigation: Furuno FCR 1421; I-band.

Comment: Two built in 1983 and acquired in October 1985. Third of the class taken over by the Navy in September 1991 and a fourth in March 1992. *Kandula* sank in October 1992 and was salvaged in mid-December. *Ranagaja* damaged by gunfire in October 1995. *Pabbatha* sank in February 1998.   ***UPDATED***

PABBATHA (with 20 mm guns)   *1992* */ 0080711*

2 FAST PERSONNEL CARRIERS (LCP)

Name	No	Builders	Commissioned
HANSAYA	A 540 (ex-*Offshore Pioneer*)	Sing Koon Seng, Singapore	20 Dec 1987
LIHINIYA	A 541 (ex-*Offshore Pride*)	Sing Koon Seng, Singapore	20 Dec 1987

Displacement, tons: 154 full load
Dimensions, feet (metres): 98.4 × 36.8 × 7.7 *(30 × 11.2 × 2.3)*
Main machinery: 2 Paxman Vega 12 diesels; 1,800 hp(m) *(1.32 MW)*; 2 shafts
Speed, knots: 30
Complement: 12 (2 officers)
Military lift: 60 tons; 120 troops
Guns: 1 Oerlikon 20 mm. 2—12.7 mm MGs.
Radars: Navigation: Furuno FR 1012; I-band.

Comment: Acquired in January 1986 from Aluminium Shipbuilders. Catamaran hulls built as oil rig tenders. Now used as fast transports.   ***UPDATED***

LIHINIYA   *6/1996* *, Sri Lanka Navy / 0080712*

2 YUNNAN CLASS (TYPE 067) (LCU)

L 820   L 821

Displacement, tons: 135 full load
Dimensions, feet (metres): 93.8 × 17.7 × 4.9 *(28.6 × 5.4 × 1.5)*
Main machinery: 2 diesels; 600 hp(m) *(441 kW)*; 2 shafts
Speed, knots: 12. **Range, miles:** 500 at 10 kt
Complement: 12 (2 officers)
Military lift: 46 tons
Guns: 4—14.5 mm (2 twin) MGs.
Radars: Surface search: Fuji; I-band.

Comment: First one acquired from China in May 1991, second in May 1995.
UPDATED

L 820   *1992* *, Sri Lanka Navy / 0080713*

1 M 10 CLASS HOVERCRAFT (UCAC)

A 530

Displacement, tons: 18 full load
Dimensions, feet (metres): 67.6 × 28.9 *(20.6 × 8.8)*
Main machinery: 2 Deutz diesels; 1,050 hp(m) *(772 kW)*
Speed, knots: 40; 7 with cushion deflated. **Range, miles:** 600 at 30 kt
Complement: 3
Military lift: 56 troops or 20 troops plus 2 vehicles
Guns: 1—12.7 mm MG.
Radars: Navigation: Furuno; I-band.

Comment: Acquired from ABS Hovercraft/Vosper Thornycroft in April 1998 and designated a Utility Craft Air Cushion (UCAC). Has a Kevlar superstructure. More may be ordered in due course.
UPDATED

A 530   *4/1998* *, ABS Hovercraft / 0033561*

SUDAN

Personnel	Establishment	Bases	General	Mercantile Marine
(a) 2000: 1,300 officers and men (b) Voluntary service	The Navy was established in 1962 to operate on the Red Sea coast and on the River Nile.	Port Sudan (HQ). Flamingo Bay (Red Sea), Khartoum (Nile).	In spite of Iranian assistance, this Navy is ineffective even on the Nile.	*Lloyd's Register of Shipping:* 19 vessels of 43,078 tons gross

PATROL FORCES

2 COASTAL PATROL CRAFT (PC)

KADIR (ex-*Shahpar*) 129   KARARI (ex-*Shahram*) 130

Displacement, tons: 70 full load
Dimensions, feet (metres): 75.2 × 16.5 × 6 *(22.9 × 5 × 1.8)*
Main machinery: 2 MTU diesels; 2,200 hp(m) *(1.62 MW)*; 2 shafts
Speed, knots: 27
Complement: 19 (3 officers)
Missiles: SSM: 2 YJ-1 may be fitted.
Guns: 1 Oerlikon 20 mm.
Radars: Surface search: I-band.

Comment: Built for Iran by Abeking & Rasmussen in 1970. Transferred to Iranian Coast Guard 1975 and to Sudan later that year. *Sheikan* (128) was cannibalised for spares but then refurbished in 1994 with Iranian assistance. Out of service again in 1995. Both still seaworthy but no recent reports of activity.
UPDATED

KADIR   *2/1990* */ 0080714*

4 KURMUK (TYPE 15) CLASS (INSHORE PATROL CRAFT) (PBR)

KURMUK 502	QAYSAN 503	RUMBEK 504	MAYOM 505

Displacement, tons: 19.5 full load
Dimensions, feet (metres): 55.4 × 12.8 × 2.3 (16.9 × 3.9 × 0.7)
Main machinery: 2 diesels; 330 hp(m) (243 kW); 2 shafts
Speed, knots: 16. Range, miles: 160 at 12 kt
Complement: 6
Guns: 1 Oerlikon 20 mm; 2—7.62 mm MGs.

Comment: Delivered by Yugoslavia on 18 May 1989 for operations on the White Nile. All may be operational at Khartoum.
VERIFIED

KURMUK   1989, G Jacobs

4 SEWART CLASS (INSHORE PATROL CRAFT) (PB)

MAROUB 1161	FIJAB 1162	SALAK 1163	HALOTE 1164

Displacement, tons: 9.1 full load
Dimensions, feet (metres): 40 × 12.1 × 3.3 (12.2 × 3.7 × 1)
Main machinery: 2 GM diesels; 348 hp (260 kW); 2 shafts
Speed, knots: 31
Complement: 6
Guns: 1—12.7 mm MG.

Comment: Transferred by Iranian Coast Guard in 1975. All are based at Flamingo Bay, and all are active.
VERIFIED

8 ASHOORA I CLASS (INSHORE PATROL CRAFT) (PB)

Displacement, tons: 3 full load
Dimensions, feet (metres): 26.6 × 8 × 1.6 (8.1 × 2.4 × 0.5)
Main machinery: 2 Yamaha outboards; 400 hp(m) (294 kW)
Speed, knots: 42
Complement: 2
Guns: 1—7.62 mm MG.

Comment: Acquired from Iran in 1992-94. Based at Flamingo Bay.
UPDATED

ASHOORA I   1992*, IRI Marine Industries / 0080715

AUXILIARIES

Notes: (1) In addition there are two small miscellaneous support ships. *Baraka* 21 a water boat, and a Rotork 512 craft. Both restored with Iranian assistance.
(2) Five Type II LCVPs were delivered from Yugoslavia in 1991 and are based at Kosti.

2 SUPPLY SHIPS (AFL)

SOBAT 221	DINDER 222

Displacement, tons: 410 full load
Dimensions, feet (metres): 155.1 × 21 × 7.5 (47.3 × 6.4 × 2.3)
Main machinery: 3 Gray Marine diesels; 495 hp (369 kW); 3 shafts
Speed, knots: 9
Complement: 15
Guns: 1 Oerlikon 20 mm. 2—12.7 mm MGs.

Comment: Two Yugoslav 'MFPD' class LCTs transferred in 1969. Used for transporting ammunition, petrol and general supplies. Both are active.
VERIFIED

SURINAM

Personnel

2000: 240 (25 officers)

Bases

Kruktu Tere

Aircraft

Two CASA C-212-400 Aviocar aircraft acquired for maritime patrol in 1998/99.

Mercantile Marine

Lloyd's Register of Shipping:
   20 vessels of 6,482 tons gross

DELETIONS

1997	C 301, C 303
1998	P 401-P 403

PATROL FORCES

3 RODMAN 101 CLASS (PC)

JARABAKKA P 01	SPARI P 02	GRAMORGU P 03

Displacement, tons: 46 full load
Dimensions, feet (metres): 98.4 × 19 × 5.9 (30 × 5.8 × 1.8)
Main machinery: 2 MTU 12V 2000 diesels; 2,900 hp (2.16 MW) sustained; 2 Hamilton 571 water-jets
Speed, knots: 30. Range, miles: 800 at 12 kt
Complement: 9
Guns: 1—40 mm grenade launcher.
Radars: Surface search: 2 Furuno; I-band.

Comment: Ordered in December 1997, from Rodman, Vigo. First one delivered in February 1999, second and third on 3 July 1999. Carry a RIB with twin outboards.
UPDATED

SPARI   9/1999*, A Campanera i Rovira / 0080716

5 RODMAN 55 CLASS (PBR)

P 04-P 08

Displacement, tons: 16 full load
Dimensions, feet (metres): 57.1 × 12.8 × 2.3 (17.4 × 3.9 × 0.7)
Main machinery: 2 MAN D2848-LXE diesels; 1,360 hp(m) (1 MW) sustained; 2 Hamilton water-jets
Speed, knots: 35. Range, miles: 500 at 25 kt
Complement: 7
Guns: 1—12.7 mm MG.
Radars: Surface search: Furuno; I-band.

Comment: Ordered in December 1997 from Rodman, Vigo. First one delivered in October 1998, remainder in April 1999. Carry a RIB with a single outboard engine.
UPDATED

P 06   4/1999* / 0080717

SWEDEN
SVENSKA MARINEN

Headquarters Appointments

Inspector General of the Navy:
  Rear Admiral Torsten Lindh
Deputy Inspector General of the Navy:
  Brigadier S Fagrell

Diplomatic Representation

Naval Attaché in London:
  Colonel Mats Engman
Naval Attaché in Moscow:
  Commander Christian Allerman
Naval Attaché in Washington:
  Colonel Göran Boijsen
Defence Attaché in Paris:
  Captain Sven Rudberg
Defence Attaché in Copenhagen:
  Captain Christer Nordling
Naval Attaché in Singapore:
  Commander Magnus Waldenström
Defence Attaché in Berlin:
  Colonel Håkan Beskow

Organisation

There are four naval commands: North, East, South and West. The Navy and Coastal Artillery (combined in 1998) has two Surface Attack Flotillas, three MCMV Flotillas and one Submarine Flotilla.

Personnel

(a) 2000: 9,100 officers and men made up of 3,100 regulars and 6,000 national servicemen (4,100 new and the remainder refreshers)
(b) 10-17¼ months' national service

Coast Defence

The Coastal Artillery is divided into four Territorial Regiments, six Territorial Battalions, four Minelayer Divisions, and two Mobile Brigades. The Territorial units consist of fixed 120, 105 and 75 mm guns, remote-controlled mines and underwater surveillance systems, short-range land-sea missiles (RBS 17 Hellfire), infantry units, 120 and 81 mm mortar units, and supply and logistics units.

The Mobile Brigades consist of three Mobile Artillery Battalions with eight 120 mm guns each, one Missile Battalion with lorry-mounted RBS 15 Mk 2, six Amphibious Battalions with 800 troops divided into two Coast Ranger Companies, one Mortar Company (81 mm), and one Amphibious Company with remote-controlled mines, underwater surveillance systems, and short-range land-sea missiles (RBS 17 Hellfire). Each Amphibious Battalion has 35 Combat Boat 90H, 13 Combat Boat 90E, four small tenders, 26 group landing craft, and 19 Klepper collapsible kayaks.

Strength of the Fleet

Type	Active	Building (Planned)
Submarines—Patrol	9	—
Missile Corvettes	6	6
Fast Attack Craft—Missile	14	—
Coastal Patrol Craft	4	—
Inshore Patrol Craft	22	—
Minelayers	2	—
MCM Support Ship	1	—
Minelayers—Coastal	7	—
Minelayers—Small	21	—
Minesweepers/Hunters—Coastal	8	—
Minesweepers—Inshore	15	—
Sonobuoy Craft	4	—
LCMs	20	—
Survey Ships	2	—
Electronic Surveillance Ship	1	—
Transport Ships	4	(10)
Repair and Support Ships	19	—
Tankers	2	—

Bases

Muskö (Stockholm), Hårsfjärden (Stockholm), Karlskrona. Minor bases at Härnösand, Göteborg and Furosund.

Mercantile Marine

Lloyd's Register of Shipping:
  570 vessels of 2,946,851 tons gross

DELETIONS

Submarines

1997 *Sjöhästen, Sjölejonet, Sjöhunden* (all to Singapore)
1998 *Neptun*

Patrol Forces

1997 *Norrtälje, Varberg, Västerås, Västervik, Umeå, Strömstad, Äggskär, Flaggskär*
1998 *Smyge* (museum)
1999 *Hugin, Munin, Mode, Vidar*

Mine Warfare Forces

1997 *Nämdö, Gillöga, Svartlöga*
1998 *Rödlöga*

Auxiliaries

1997 *Minören, Skagul*
1998 *Johan Nordenankar* (to Norway)
2000 *Njord, Tor*

Coast Guard

1998 KBV 171 (to Belgium)

PENNANT LIST

Corvettes		V 11	Østhammar	M 11	Styrsö	B 02	Krickan
		V 150	Jägaren	M 12	Spårö	B 03	Svärtan
K 11	Stockholm	63	Ekeskär	M 13	Skaftö	B 04	Viggen
K 12	Malmö	64	Skifteskär	M 14	Sturkö		
K 21	Göteborg	65	Gråskär	M 20-22	MSI		
K 22	Gävle	67	Vitaskär	M 24-25	MSI	**Auxiliaries**	
K 23	Kalmar	68	Altaskär	M 31	Gåssten		
K 24	Sundsvall	70	Hojskär	M 32	Norsten	A 201	Orion
—	Visby (bldg)	74	Bredskär	M 33	Viksten	A 212	Ägir
		75	Sprängskär	M 43	Hisingen	A 213	Nordanö
		76	Hamnskär	M 44	Blackan	A 214	Belos III
Patrol Forces		77	Huvudskär	M 45	Dämman	A 229	Eldaren
		81	Tapper	M 46	Galten	A 241	Urd
P 159	Kaparen	82	Djärv	M 71	Landsort	A 247	Pelikanen
P 160	Väktaren	83	Dristig	M 72	Arholma	A 248	Pingvinen
P 161	Snapphanen	84	Händig	M 73	Koster	A 251	Achilles
P 162	Spejaren	85	Trygg	M 74	Kullen	A 253	Hermes
P 163	Styrbjörn	86	Modig	M 75	Vinga	A 261	Utö
P 164	Starkodder	87	Hurtig	M 76	Ven	A 262	Skredsvik
P 165	Tordön	88	Rapp	M 77	Ulvön	A 263	Gålö
P 166	Tirfing	89	Stolt	MUL 11	Kalvsund	A 264	Trossö
R 131	Norrköping	90	Ärlig	MUL 12	Arkösund	A 322	Heros
R 132	Nynäshamn	91	Munter	MUL 13	Kalmarsund	A 323	Hercules
R 138	Piteå	92	Orädd	MUL 15	Grundsund	A 324	Hera
R 139	Luleå			MUL 17	Skramsösund	A 330	Atlas
R 140	Halmstad	**Mine Warfare Forces**		MUL 18	Fårösund	A 343	Sleipner
R 142	Ystad			MUL 19	Barösund	A 344	Loke II
V 09	Dalarö	M 03	Visborg	MUL 20	Furusund	S 01	Gladan
V 10	Sandhamn	M 04	Carlskrona	502-516	Small Minelayers	S 02	Falken
				B 01	Ejdern		

ÖSTERGÖTLAND

10/1999*, Winter & Findler / 0084409

SUBMARINES

Note: The Viking project involves collaboration with Norway and Denmark for a 45 m submarine class to be in service around 2010.

4 VÄSTERGÖTLAND (A 17) CLASS (SSK)

Name	No	Builders	Laid down		Launched		Commissioned	
VÄSTERGÖTLAND	—	Kockums, Malmö	10 Jan	1983	17 Sep	1986	27 Nov	1987
HÄLSINGLAND	—	Kockums, Malmö	1 Jan	1984	31 Aug	1987	20 Oct	1988
SÖDERMANLAND	—	Kockums, Malmö	2 Feb	1985	12 Apr	1988	21 Apr	1989
ÖSTERGÖTLAND	—	Kockums, Malmö	15 Oct	1985	9 Dec	1988	10 Jan	1990

Displacement, tons: 1,070 surfaced; 1,143 dived
Dimensions, feet (metres): 159.1 × 20 × 18.4
(48.5 × 6.1 × 5.6)
Main machinery: Diesel-electric; 2 Hedemora V12A/15 diesels; 2,200 hp(m) *(1.62 MW)*; 1 Jeumont Schneider motor; 1,800 hp(m) *(1.32 MW)*; 1 shaft; acbLIPS prop
Speed, knots: 10 surfaced; 20 dived
Complement: 28 (5 officers)

Torpedoes: 6—21 in *(533 mm)* tubes. 12 FFV Type 613; anti-surface; wire-guided; passive homing to 20 km *(10.8 n miles)* at 45 kt; warhead 240 kg. Swim-out discharge.
3—15.75 in *(400 mm)* tubes. 6 FFV Type 431/451; anti-submarine; wire-guided; active/passive homing to 20 km *(10.8 n miles)* at 25 kt; warhead 45 kg shaped charge or a small charge anti-intruder version is available.
Mines: Capability for 48 mines in an external girdle.
Countermeasures: ESM: Argo AR-700-S5; or Condor CS 3701; intercept.
Weapons control: Ericsson IPS-17 (Sesub 900A) TFCS.
Radars: Navigation: Terma; I-band.
Sonars: Atlas Elektronik CSU 83; hull-mounted; passive search and attack; medium frequency.
Flank array; passive search; low frequency.

Programmes: Design contract awarded to Kockums, Malmö on 17 April 1978. Contract for construction of these boats signed 8 December 1981. Kockums built midship section and carried out final assembly while Karlskrona built bow and stern sections.
Modernisation: The plan is to insert a 10 m plug in the pressure hull to receive Stirling Mk 3 AIP for the last two of the class. Work starts in late 2000 to complete in 2004. ESM being replaced.
Structure: Single hulled with an X type rudder/after hydroplane design. Reported that SSM were considered but rejected as non-cost-effective weapons in the context of submarine

SÖDERMANLAND   *9/1999*, J Cislak /* 0080718

operations in the Baltic. Equipped with Pilkington Optronics CK 38 electro-optic search periscope. Diving depth 300 m *(984 ft)*. Anechoic coating.

Operational: The first pair may be leased to Denmark in due course.

UPDATED

SÖDERMANLAND   *6/1999*, Maritime Photographic /* 0080719

3 GOTLAND (A 19) CLASS (SSK)

Name	No	Builders	Laid down		Launched		Commissioned	
GOTLAND	—	Kockums, Malmö	20 Nov	1992	2 Feb	1995	2 Sep	1996
UPPLAND	—	Kockums, Malmö	14 Jan	1994	9 Feb	1996	1 May	1997
HALLAND	—	Kockums, Malmö	21 Oct	1994	27 Sep	1996	1 Oct	1997

Displacement, tons: 1,240 surfaced; 1,494 dived
Dimensions, feet (metres): 198.2 × 20.3 × 18.4
(60.4 × 6.2 × 5.6)
Main machinery: Diesel-stirling-electric; 2 MTU diesels; 2 Kockums V4-275R Stirling AIP; 204 hp(m) *(150 kW)*; 1 Jeumont Schneider motor; 1 shaft; acbLIPS prop
Speed, knots: 10 surfaced; 20 dived
Complement: 25 (5 officers)

Torpedoes: 4—21 in *(533 mm)* bow tubes; 12 FFV Type 613/62; anti-surface; wire-guided; passive homing to 20 km *(10.8 n miles)* at 45 kt; warhead 240 kg or Bofors Type 62 (2000); wire-guided; active/passive homing to 50 km *(27 n miles)* at 20-50 kt; warhead 250 kg. Swim-out discharge.
2—15.75 in *(400 mm)* bow tubes; 6 Swedish Ordnance Type 432/451; anti-submarine; wire-guided; active/passive homing to 20 km *(10.8 n miles)* at 25 kt; warhead 45 kg. Shaped charge or a small charge anti-intruder version.
Mines: Capability for 48 in an external girdle or 12 Type 47 swim-out mines in lieu of torpedoes.
Countermeasures: ESM: Racal THORN Manta S; radar warning.
Weapons control: CelsiusTech IPS-19 (Sesub 940A); TFCS.
Radars: Navigation: Terma Scanter; I-band.
Sonars: STN/Atlas Elektronik CSU 90-2; hull-mounted; bow, flank and intercept arrays; passive search and attack.

Programmes: In October 1986 a research contract was awarded to Kockums for a design to replace the 'Sjöormen' class. Ordered on 28 March 1990.

GÖTLAND   *9/1999*, E & M Laursen /* 0080720

Structure: The design has been developed on the basis of the Type A 17 series but this class is the first to be built with Air Independent Propulsion as part of the design. This type of AIP runs on liquid oxygen and diesel in a helium environment. Space has been reserved to fit two more V4-275R engines in due course. Single electro-optic periscope. The periscope is the only hull penetrating mast. Anechoic coatings are being applied. The four 21 in torpedo tubes are mounted over the smaller 15.75 in tubes. The smaller tubes can be tandem-loaded with two torpedoes per tube.

Operational: Reported as being able to patrol at 5 kt for several weeks without snorting. The Type 47 mine swims out to a predetermined position before laying itself on the bottom.

UPDATED

2 NÄCKEN (A 14) CLASS (SSK)

Name	No	Builders	Laid down	Launched	Commissioned
NÄCKEN	—	Kockums, Malmö	Nov 1972	17 Apr 1978	25 Apr 1980
NAJAD	—	Kockums, Malmö/Karlskronavarvet	Sep 1973	6 Dec 1978	26 June 1981

Displacement, tons: 1,015 surfaced; 1,085 dived
Dimensions, feet (metres): 162.4 (188.6, *Näcken*) × 18.7 × 18 *(49.5 (57.5) × 5.7 × 5.5)*
Main machinery: Diesel-electric; 1 MTU 16V 652 MB80 diesel; 1,730 hp(m) *(1.27 MW)*; 2 Stirling V4-275R engines (*Näcken*); 150 kW; 1 Jeumont Schneider motor; 1,800 hp(m) *(1.32 MW)*; 1 shaft; acbLIPS prop
Speed, knots: 10 surfaced; 20 dived
Complement: 27 (5 officers)

Torpedoes: 6—21 in *(533 mm)* tubes. 8 FFV Type 613; anti-surface; wire-guided; passive homing to 20 km *(10.8 n miles)* at 45 kt; warhead 250 kg.
2—15.75 in *(400 mm)* tubes. 4 FFV Type 431; anti-submarine; wire-guided; active/passive homing to 20 km *(10.8 n miles)* at 25 kt; warhead 45 kg shaped charge.
Mines: Minelaying capability including an external girdle of 48 mines.
Countermeasures: ESM: Argo AR-700-S5; radar warning.
Weapons control: Ericsson IPS-17 (Sesub 900C) TFCS.
Radars: Navigation: Terma; I-band.
Sonars: Thomson Sintra; hull-mounted and flank arrays; passive search and attack; medium frequency.

Modernisation: *Näcken* was taken in hand by Kockums in November 1987 for the installation of a closed-circuit Tillma Stirling diesel which provides non-nuclear propulsion without requiring access to the atmosphere. This involved the ship being lengthened and she was relaunched on 6 September 1988. The new section which is neutrally buoyant contains the Stirling generators, two LOX supply tanks and control systems. Work started in 1993 to update all of the class with new weapon control systems, torpedo tube automation and new sonars, to extend service lives into the next century. This work completed in 1996.
Structure: Has large bow-mounted sonar. Main accommodation space is abaft the control room with machinery spaces right aft. A central computer provides both attack information and data on main machinery. Single periscope. Diving depth 300 m *(984 ft)*.
Operational: The Stirling engine is primarily for slow submerged speed patrolling without much use of battery power. Liquid oxygen (LOX) provides the combustible air. Exhaust products

NÄCKEN   9/1998, J Cislak / 0050167

dissolve in water. It is claimed that fully submerged endurance is possible up to 14 days. Trials started on 23 November 1988 and the submarine returned to operational service on 11 April 1989. These last two of the class were planned to remain in service until 2007 but are now to be paid off early.

UPDATED

NÄCKEN   9/1999*, J Cislak / 0080721

CORVETTES

0 + 6 VISBY CLASS (FSG)

Name	No	Builders	Laid down	Launched	Commissioned
VISBY	—	Karlskronavarvet	Dec 1996	June 2000	Mar 2001
HELSINGBORG	—	Karlskronavarvet	June 1997	Nov 2001	June 2002
HÄRNÖSAND	—	Karlskronavarvet	Dec 1997	Sep 2002	June 2003
NYKÖPING	—	Karlskronavarvet	June 1998	Aug 2003	Mar 2004
KARLSTAD	—	Karlskronavarvet	Dec 1999	June 2004	Mar 2005
UDDEVALLA	—	Karlskronavarvet	June 2000	June 2005	Mar 2006

Displacement, tons: 620 full load
Dimensions, feet (metres): 236.2 × 34.1 × 8.2 *(72 × 10.4 × 2.5)*
Main machinery: CODOG; 4 AlliedSignal TF 50A gas turbines; 21,760 hp(m) *(16 MW)*; 2 MTU 16V N90 diesels; 3,536 hp(m) *(2.6 MW)*; 2 Kamewa 125 water-jets; bow thruster
Speed, knots: 35; 15 (diesels)
Complement: 43 (6 officers)

Missiles: SSM: 8 RBS 15 Mk II (Batch 2).
Guns: 1 Bofors 57 mm/70 SAK Mk 3.
Torpedoes: 4 fixed 400 mm tubes. Type 43/45 anti-submarine.
A/S mortars: Saab 601 127 mm rocket-powered grenades; range 1,200 m.
Countermeasures: MCMV: STN Atlas Seafox Combat (C) or Inspector (I) sonar/TV sensor; range 500 m at 6 kt; shaped charge.
ESM/ECM: Condor Systems CS 701; intercept and jammer.
Combat data systems: CelsiusTech 9LV Mk 3E CETRIS with Link.
Radars: Air/surface search: Ericsson Sea Giraffe 3D; C-band.
Surface search: I-band.
Fire control: CEROS 200 Mk 3; I/J-band.
Sonars: Computing Devices Canada (CDC) Hydra; bow mounted active high frequency plus passive towed array and VDS active.

VISBY   *(Scale 1 : 600), Ian Sturton*

Helicopters: 1 AB 206A.

Programmes: Order for first two with an option on two more on 17 October 1995. Second pair ordered on 17 December 1996, and third pair in mid-1999. First batch of four ASW/MCM specialised, second batch of two for anti-surface warfare with SSM.
Structure: Stealth features developed from the trials vessel *Smyge* but without the twin hull design for which this ship was considered too large. A hangar for the helicopter is included. The hull is of Fibre Reinforced Plastic used in a sandwich construction and the superstructure is covered with RAM. An ROV with active sonar is carried in the MCM role as well as expendable mini torpedoes for mine countermeasures. Plans for a SAM system have been shelved.
Operational: First of class is scheduled for delivery for trials in 2001.

UPDATED

4 GÖTEBORG CLASS (FSG)

Name	No	Builders	Laid down	Launched	Commissioned
GÖTEBORG	K 21	Karlskronavarvet	10 Feb 1987	14 Apr 1989	15 Feb 1990
GÄVLE	K 22	Karlskronavarvet	21 Mar 1988	23 Mar 1990	1 Feb 1991
KALMAR	K 23	Karlskronavarvet	21 Nov 1988	1 Nov 1990	1 Sep 1991
SUNDSVALL	K 24	Karlskronavarvet	20 Nov 1989	29 Nov 1991	7 July 1993

Displacement, tons: 300 standard; 399 full load
Dimensions, feet (metres): 187 × 26.2 × 6.6
(57 × 8 × 2)
Main machinery: 3 MTU 16V 396 TB94 diesels; 8,700 hp(m)
(6.4 MW) sustained; Kamewa 80562-6 water-jets
Speed, knots: 30
Complement: 36 (7 officers) plus 4 spare berths

Missiles: SSM: 8 Saab RBS 15 (4 twin) launchers ❶; inertial guidance; active radar homing to 70 km *(37.8 n miles)* at 0.8 Mach; warhead 150 kg. Being upgraded to Mk II; range 110 km *(59.4 n miles)*.
Guns: 1 Bofors 57 mm/70 Mk 2 ❷; 220 rds/min to 17 km *(9.3 n miles)*; weight of shell 2.4 kg.
   1 Bofors 40 mm/70 ❸; 330 rds/min to 12.5 km *(6.8 n miles)*; weight of shell 0.96 kg.
Torpedoes: 4—15.75 in *(400 mm)* tubes ❹. Swedish Ordnance Type 43/45; anti-submarine.
A/S mortars: 4 Saab 601 ❺ 9-tubed launchers; range 1,200 m; shaped charge.
Depth charges: On mine rails.
Mines: Minelaying capability.
Countermeasures: Decoys: 4 Philips Philax fixed launchers; IR flares and chaff grenades. A/S mortars have also been adapted to fire IR/chaff decoys.
ESM: Racal; intercept.
Combat data systems: CelsiusTech 9LV Mk 3 SESYM. Datalink.
Weapons control: 2 Bofors Electronics 9LV 200 Mk 3 Sea Viking or Signaal IRST (K 24) optronic directors. Bofors Electronics 9LV 450 GFCS. RC1-400 MFCS. 9AU-300 ASW control system with AQS 928G/SM sonobuoy processor. Bofors 9EW 400 EW control.
Radars: Air/surface search: Ericsson Sea Giraffe 150 HC ❻; G/H-band.
Navigation: Terma PN 612; I-band
Fire control: 2 Bofors Electronics 9GR 400 ❼; I/J-band.
Sonars: Thomson Sintra TSM 2643 Salmon ❽; VDS; active search; medium frequency.
Simrad SA 950; hull-mounted; active attack.
STN Atlas passive towed array; low frequency.

Programmes: Ordered 1 December 1985 as replacements for 'Spica I' class.
Modernisation: An improved A/S mortar fitted in 1998-99. All are to be retrofitted with CDS Hydra sonar in due course. Passive towed arrays are being installed. An IRST director is fitted aft of the mast for trials in K 24.
Structure: Efforts have been made to reduce radar and IR signatures.
Operational: Trials were done with a Sea Trinity 40 mm gun, but each ship has reverted to the standard Bofors 40 mm/70.

UPDATED

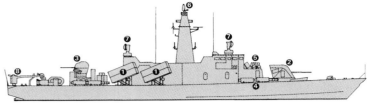

GÖTEBORG   *(Scale 1 : 600), Ian Sturton*

SUNDSVALL (with IRST)   *6/1999 *, L-G Nilsson /* 0080723

KALMAR   *6/1999 *, Maritime Photographic /* 0080724

KALMAR (with RBS Mk II launcher)   *9/1999 *, John Brodie /* 0080725

2 STOCKHOLM CLASS (FSG)

Name	No	Builders	Laid down	Launched	Commissioned
STOCKHOLM	K 11	Karlskronavarvet	1 Aug 1982	24 Aug 1984	22 Feb 1985
MALMÖ	K 12	Karlskronavarvet	14 Mar 1983	22 Mar 1985	10 May 1985

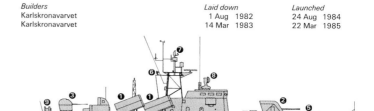

STOCKHOLM

(Scale 1 : 600), Ian Sturton

Displacement, tons: 310 standard; 335 full load
Dimensions, feet (metres): 164 × 24.6 × 6.9 *(50 × 7.5 × 2.1)*
Main machinery: CODAG; 1 GM/Allison 570-KF gas turbine; 6,540 hp(m) *(4.74 MW)* sustained; 2 MTU 16V 396 TB93 diesels; 4,200 hp(m) *(3.1 MW)* sustained; 3 shafts; Kamewa props
Speed, knots: 32 gas; 20 diesel
Complement: 30 (7 officers)

Missiles: SSM: 8 Saab RBS 15 Mk II (4 twin) launchers ❶; inertial guidance; active radar homing to 110 km *(54 n miles)* at 0.8 Mach; warhead 150 kg.
Guns: 1 Bofors 57 mm/70 Mk 2 ❷; 220 rds/min to 17 km *(9.3 n miles)*; weight of shell 2.4 kg.
1 Bofors 40 mm/70 ❸; 300 rds/min to 12.5 km *(6.8 n miles)*; weight of shell 0.96 kg.
Torpedoes: 2—21 in *(533 mm)* tubes ❹. FFV Type 613; wire-guided; passive homing to 15 km *(8.2 n miles)* at 45 kt; warhead 240 kg. 2-6 can be fitted in lieu of missiles.
4—15.75 in *(400 mm)* tubes; Swedish Ordnance Type 43/45; anti-submarine.
A/S mortars: 4 Saab 601 ❺ 9-tubed launchers; range 1,200 m; shaped charge.
Depth charges: On mine rails.
Mines: Minelaying capability.
Countermeasures: Decoys: 2 Philips Philax fixed launchers; 4 magazines each holding 36 IR/chaff grenades; fired in groups of nine.
ESM: Argo Systems AR 700; radar intercept.
Combat data systems: Ericsson MARIL 880; datalink.
Weapons control: Philips 9LV 300 GFCS including a 9LV 100 optronic director ❻.
Radars: Air/surface search: Ericsson Sea Giraffe 50HC ❼; G-band.
Navigation: Terma PN 612; I-band.
Fire control: Philips 9LV 200 Mk 3 ❽; J-band.
Sonars: Simrad SA 950; hull-mounted; active attack.
Thomson Sintra TSM 2642 Salmon ❾; VDS; search; medium frequency.

Programmes: Orders placed in September 1981. Developed from 'Spica II' class.
Modernisation: RBS 15 missile upgraded from 1994. Improved A/S mortar fitted in 1998-99. There are plans for a mid-life upgrade at Karlskrona. These include a new Allied Signal

MALMÖ

6/1998, Curt Borgenstam / 0050169

TF 50A gas turbine and MTU TB94 diesels, the 9LV Mk 3E CETRIS combat data systems and a Condor Systems CS-701 EW outfit. To complete in February and August 2002 respectively.

Operational: Some flexibility in weapon fit depending on mission. The A/S mortar is designed to surface a submarine even if it does not sink it.

UPDATED

STOCKHOLM

6/1999*, Maritime Photographic / 0080722

LAND-BASED MARITIME AIRCRAFT (FRONT LINE)

Notes: (1) In addition 12 AS 332 Super Puma helicopters are used for SAR.
(2) SH-37 Viggen aircraft are Air Force operated and can be used for maritime strike.

Numbers/Type: 7/7 Boeing 107-II-5/Kawasaki KV 107-II. All to HKP-4C/D standard.
Operational speed: 137 kt *(254 km/h).*
Service ceiling: 8,500 ft *(2,590 m).*
Range: 300 n miles *(555 km).*
Role/Weapon systems: ASW and surface search helicopter; updated with avionics, TM2D engines, radar, sonar, datalink for SSM targeting, MARIL 920 combat information system. The Nordic Standard helicopter is expected to start replacing these aircraft from 2005. Sensors: BEAB Omera radar, Thomson Sintra DUAV-4 dipping sonar. Weapons: ASW; six Type 11/51 depth charges and/or two Type 45 torpedoes.

UPDATED

Numbers/Type: 10 Agusta-Bell 206A JetRanger (HKP-6B).
Operational speed: 115 kt *(213 km/h).*
Service ceiling: 13,500 ft *(4,115 m).*
Range: 368 n miles *(682 km).*
Role/Weapon systems: Primarily operated in a liaison and training role and for secondary ASW, SAR and surface search helicopter operations. Replacements are needed. Weapons: ASW; four Type 11 or depth charges.

UPDATED

AB 206A

8/1998, Per Kornefeldt / 0050172

Numbers/Type: 1 CASA C-212 Aviocar.
Operational speed: 190 kt *(353 km/h).*
Service ceiling: 24,000 ft *(7,315 m).*
Range: 1,650 n miles *(3,055 km).*
Role/Weapon systems: For ASW and surface surveillance. Two others belong to the Coast Guard. Sensors: Omera radar, Sonobuoys/Lofar, CDC sonobuoy processor, FLIR, datalink. Weapons: ASW; depth charges.

VERIFIED

BOEING 107

5/1999*, Per Kornefeldt / 0080726

PATROL FORCES

Note: The experimental craft *Smyge* V 02 is no longer an operational naval unit.

8 KAPAREN CLASS (FAST ATTACK CRAFT—MISSILE) (PCFG)

Name	No	Builders	Commissioned
KAPAREN	P 159	Bergens MV, Norway	7 Aug 1980
VÄKTAREN	P 160	Bergens MV, Norway	19 Sep 1980
SNAPPHANEN	P 161	Bergens MV, Norway	14 Jan 1980
SPEJAREN	P 162	Bergens MV, Norway	21 Mar 1980
STYRBJÖRN	P 163	Bergens MV, Norway	15 June 1980
STARKODDER	P 164	Bergens MV, Norway	24 Aug 1981
TORDÖN	P 165	Bergens MV, Norway	26 Oct 1981
TIRFING	P 166	Bergens MV, Norway	23 Jan 1982

Displacement, tons: 120 standard; 170 full load
Dimensions, feet (metres): 120 × 20.7 × 5.6 *(36.6 × 6.3 × 1.7)*
Main machinery: 2 MTU 16V 396 TB94; 5,800 hp(m) *(4.26 MW)* sustained; 2 shafts; 2 hydraulic motors for slow speed propulsion
Speed, knots: 36. **Range, miles:** 550 at 36 kt
Complement: 22 (3 officers)

Missiles: SSM: 6 Kongsberg Penguin Mk 2; IR homing to 27 km *(14.6 n miles)* at 0.8 Mach; warhead 120 kg.
Guns: 1 Bofors 57 mm/70 Mk 1; 200 rds/min to 17 km *(9.3 n miles)*; weight of shell 2.4 kg. 57 mm illuminant launchers on either side of mounting.
A/S mortars: 4 Saab Elma 9-tubed launchers; range 400 m; warhead 4.2 kg shaped charge or Saab 601 9-tubed launchers; range 1,200 m; shaped charge.
Depth charges: 2 racks.
Mines: 24. Mine rails extend from after end of bridge superstructure with an extension over the stern. Use of these would mean the removal of missiles in the ratio of 8 mines for each pair of missiles.
ESM: Saab Scania EWS 905; radar intercept.
Radars: Surface search: Skanter 16 in Mk 009; I-band.
Fire control: Philips 9LV 200 Mk 2; J-band.
Sonars: Simrad SA 950; hull-mounted; active attack; high frequency.
Simrad ST 570 VDS; active; high frequency.

Programmes: In the early 1970s it was decided to build fast attack craft similar to the Norwegian 'Hauk' class. Prototype *Jägaren* underwent extensive trials and, on 15 May 1975, an order for a further 16 was placed.
Modernisation: Half-life modernisation between 1991 and 1994. The update included new engines with improved loiter capability and new sonars including the Simrad Toadfish VDS. Saab ASW-601 multibarrel grenade launcher being fitted.
Operational: The VDS can be operated down to 100 m as a dipping sonar, or towed at speeds up to 16 kt. Eight unmodernised craft of this type are laid up and unlikely to go to sea again.

UPDATED

TORDÖN   *6/1999*, Michael Nitz /* 0080727

STYRBJÖRN   *6/1999*, L-G Nilsson /* 0080728

STARKODDER   *6/1999*, J Cislak /* 0084410

6 NORRKÖPING CLASS (FAST ATTACK CRAFT—MISSILE) (PCFG)

Name	No	Builders	Commissioned
NORRKÖPING	R 131	Karlskronavarvet	11 May 1973
NYNÄSHAMN	R 132	Karlskronavarvet	28 Sep 1973
PITEÅ	R 138	Karlskronavarvet	12 Sep 1975
LULEÅ	R 139	Karlskronavarvet	28 Nov 1975
HALMSTAD	R 140	Karlskronavarvet	9 Apr 1976
YSTAD	R 142	Karlskronavarvet	10 Jan 1976

Displacement, tons: 190 standard; 230 full load
Dimensions, feet (metres): 143 × 23.3 × 7.4 *(43.6 × 7.1 × 2.4)*
Main machinery: 3 RR Proteus gas turbines; 12,750 hp *(9.5 MW)* sustained; 3 shafts; Kamewa props
Speed, knots: 40.5. **Range, miles:** 500 at 40 kt
Complement: 27 (7 officers)

Missiles: SSM: 8 Saab RBS 15; active radar homing to 70 km *(37.8 n miles)* at 0.8 Mach; warhead 150 kg.
Guns: 1 Bofors 57 mm/70 Mk 1; 200 rds/min to 17 km *(9.3 n miles)*; weight of shell 2.4 kg. 8 launchers for 57 mm illuminants on side of mounting.
Torpedoes: 6—21 in *(533 mm)* tubes (2-6 can be fitted at the expense of missile armament); Swedish Ordnance Type 613; anti-surface; wire-guided passive homing to 15 km *(8.2 n miles)* at 45 kt; warhead 240 kg.
Mines: Minelaying capability.
Countermeasures: Decoys: 2 Philips Philax fixed launchers; IR flares and chaff.
ESM: Argo Systems AR 700 or MEL Susie; radar intercept.
Combat data systems: MARIL 2000 datalink.
Radars: Air/surface search: Ericsson Sea Giraffe 50HC; G/H-band.
Fire control: Philips 9LV 200 Mk 1; J-band.

Modernisation: Programme included missile launchers, new fire-control equipment, modernised electronics and new 57 mm guns. A/S mortars removed. All completed by late 1984. These last six have had some weapon systems upgrading to keep them in service until 2010. All completed by August 1999. The plan to fit new engines has been shelved.
Structure: Similar to the original 'Spica' class from which they were developed.
Operational: The six unmodernised craft have paid off and these last six are likely to follow soon.

UPDATED

YSTAD   *6/1999*, Michael Nitz /* 0080729

1 JÄGAREN CLASS (COASTAL PATROL CRAFT) (PC)

Name	No	Builders	Commissioned
JÄGAREN	V 150	Bergens MV, Norway	24 Nov 1972

Displacement, tons: 120 standard; 150 full load
Dimensions, feet (metres): 120 × 20.7 × 5.6 *(36.6 × 6.3 × 1.7)*
Main machinery: 2 Cummins KTA50-M; 2,500 hp *(1.87 MW)* sustained; 2 shafts
Speed, knots: 20. **Range, miles:** 550 at 20 kt
Complement: 15 (3 officers)
Guns: 1 Bofors 40 mm/70.
Mines: 2 rails.
Radars: Surface search: Terma Scanter 009; I-band.

Comment: This was the prototype for the deleted 'Hugin' class and up to 1988 was used for training and testing. In 1988 new engines were installed and the craft recommissioned for patrol and minelaying duties. Has no torpedo tubes, fire-control radar, ESM or sonar.

UPDATED

JÄGAREN   *8/1997*, Frank Behling /* 0019191

3 DALARÖ CLASS (COASTAL PATROL CRAFT) (PC)

Name	No	Builders	Commissioned
DALARÖ	V 09	Djupviksvarvet	21 Sep 1984
SANDHAMN	V 10	Djupviksvarvet	5 Dec 1984
ÖSTHAMMAR	V 11	Djupviksvarvet	1 Mar 1985

Displacement, tons: 50 full load
Dimensions, feet (metres): 76.8 × 16.7 × 5.9 *(23.4 × 5.1 × 1.8)*
Main machinery: 2 MTU 8V 396 TB83 diesels; 2,100 hp(m) *(1.54 MW)* sustained; 2 shafts
Speed, knots: 30
Complement: 7 (3 officers)
Guns: 1 Oerlikon 20 mm. 2—7.62 mm MGs.
Mines: Rails fitted.
Radars: Surface search: Terma 610; I-band.

Comment: Ordered 28 February 1983 for anti-intruder patrols. Categorised as part of the Mine Warfare forces. 40 mm gun has been replaced by 20 mm. Carry AQS-928 acoustic processors for sonobuoys. **UPDATED**

ÖSTHAMMAR   6/1999*, E & M Laursen / 0080730

10 INSHORE PATROL CRAFT (PC)

EKESKÄR 63	VITASKÄR 67	BREDSKÄR 74	HAMNSKÄR 76
SKIFTESKÄR 64	ALTASKÄR 68	SPRÄNGSKÄR 75	HUVUDSKÄR 77
GRÅSKÄR 65	HOJSKÄR 70		

Displacement, tons: 30 full load
Dimensions, feet (metres): 69.2 × 15 × 4.3 *(21.1 × 4.6 × 1.3)*
Main machinery: 3 diesels; 3 shafts
Speed, knots: 18 *(61-67)*; 22 *(68-77)*
Guns: 1—12.7 mm MG.
Depth charges: Carried in all of the class.
Radars: Surface search: Decca RM 914; I-band.
Sonars: Simrad; hull-mounted; active search; high frequency.

Comment: The 60 series launched in 1960-61 and 70 series in 1966-67. Modernised in the 1980s with a tripod mast and radar mounted over the bridge. Now called Type 72. All except 67, 68 and 76 have been modernised. **UPDATED**

EKESKÄR   6/1994*, Curt Borgenstam / 0080731

12 TAPPER CLASS (PC)

TAPPER 81	HÄNDIG 84	HURTIG 87	ÄRLIG 90
DJÄRV 82	TRYGG 85	RAPP 88	MUNTER 91
DRISTIG 83	MODIG 86	STOLT 89	ORÄDD 92

Displacement, tons: 57 full load
Dimensions, feet (metres): 71.9 × 17.7 × 4.9 *(21.9 × 5.4 × 1.5)*
Main machinery: 2 MWM TBD234V16 diesels; 1,812 hp(m) *(1.33 MW)* sustained; 2 shafts
Speed, knots: 25
Complement: 9
Guns: 2—12.7 mm MGs.
A/S mortars: 4 Elma/Saab grenade launchers; range 300 m; warhead 4.2 kg shaped charge.
Depth charges: 18.
Mines: 2 rails (in four of the class).
Radars: Surface search: 2 Racal Decca; I-band.
Sonars: Simrad; hull-mounted; active search; high frequency.

Comment: Seven Type 80 ordered from Djupviksvarvet in early 1992, and delivered between February 1993 and December 1995. Five more ordered in 1995 for delivery at six month intervals between December 1996 and January 1999. A Phantom HD-2 ROV is carried. This is equipped with a Tritech ST 525 imaging sonar. **VERIFIED**

TRYGG   8/1998, Per Kornefeldt / 0050178

3 TORPEDO BOATS

T 26   T 38   T 46

Comment: These are vintage 1942 and 1952 privately owned torpedo craft which are not part of the Swedish Navy, but are seen sufficiently often at sea to need inclusion for recognition purposes. **UPDATED**

T 46   8/1998*, E & M Laursen / 0080732

T 26   8/1998, E & M Laursen / 0050180

MINE WARFARE FORCES

Note: A transportable COOP system was ordered in 1991. The unit can be shifted from one ship to another and comprises a container, processing module and tactical display, an underwater positioning system, sonar, Sea Eagle ROV and mine disposal charge. Optimised for shallow water surveillance and can be used in conjunction with other MCM systems. The primary role is route survey.

1 CARLSKRONA CLASS (MINELAYER) (ML/AXT)

Name	No	Builders	Launched	Commissioned
CARLSKRONA	M 04	Karlskronavarvet	28 June 1980	11 Jan 1982

Displacement, tons: 3,300 standard; 3,550 full load
Dimensions, feet (metres): 346.7 × 49.9 × 13.1 *(105.7 × 15.2 × 4)*
Main machinery: 4 Nohab F212 D825 diesels; 10,560 hp(m) *(7.76 MW)*; 2 shafts; cp props
Speed, knots: 20
Complement: 50 plus 136 trainees. Requires 118 as operational minelayer
Guns: 2 Bofors 57 mm/70. 2 Bofors 40 mm/70.
Mines: Can lay 105.
Countermeasures: 2 Philips Philax chaff/IR launchers.
ESM: Argo AR 700; intercept.
Radars: Air/surface search: Ericsson Sea Giraffe 50HC; G/H/I-band.
Surface search: Raytheon; E/F-band.
Fire control: 2 Philips 9LV 200 Mk 2; I/J-band.
Navigation: Terma Scanter 009; I-band.
Helicopters: Platform only.

Comment: Ordered 25 November 1977, laid down in sections late 1979 and launched at the same time as Karlskrona celebrated its tercentenary. Midshipmen's Training Ship as well as a minelayer; also a 'padded' target for exercise torpedoes. Sonar removed. Name is an older form of Karlskrona. **UPDATED**

CARLSKRONA   4/1999*, van Ginderen Collection / 0080733

1 ÄLVSBORG CLASS (MINELAYER/SUPPORT SHIP) (ML/AGF/AS)

Name	No	Builders	Launched	Commissioned
VISBORG	M 03	Karlskronavarvet	25 Jan 1975	6 Feb 1976

Displacement, tons: 2,400 standard; 2,650 full load
Dimensions, feet (metres): 303.1 × 48.2 × 13.2 *(92.4 × 14.7 × 4)*
Main machinery: 2 Nohab-Polar diesels; 4,200 hp(m) *(3.1 MW)*; 1 shaft; cp prop; bow thruster; 350 hp(m) *(257 kW)*
Speed, knots: 16
Complement: 95 plus 158 Flag staff
Guns: 3 Bofors 40 mm/70 SAK 48.
Mines: 300.
Countermeasures: 2 Philips Philax chaff/IR launchers.
ESM: Argo 700; intercept.
Radars: Surface search: Raytheon; E/F-band.
Fire control: Philips 9LV 200 Mk 2; I/J-band.
Navigation: Terma Scanter 009; I-band.
Helicopters: Platform only.

Comment: Laid down on 16 October 1973, acts as a Command Ship.   **UPDATED**

VISBORG   *6/1999*, J Cislak / 0080734

1 FURUSUND CLASS (COASTAL MINELAYER) (MLC)

Name	No	Builders	Launched	Commissioned
FURUSUND	MUL 20	ASI Verken	16 Dec 1982	10 Oct 1983

Displacement, tons: 225 full load
Dimensions, feet (metres): 106.9 × 26.9 × 7.5 *(32.6 × 8.2 × 2.3)*
Main machinery: Diesel-electric; 2 Scania GAS 1 diesel generators; 2 motors; 416 hp(m) *(306 kW)*; 2 shafts
Speed, knots: 11.5
Complement: 24
Guns: 1—12.7 mm MG.
Mines: 22 tons.
Radars: Navigation: Racal Decca 1226; I-band.

Comment: Built for the former Coastal Artillery. Carries a Mantis type ROV.   **UPDATED**

FURUSUND   *6/1999*, Royal Swedish Navy / 0080936

6 ARKÖSUND CLASS (COASTAL MINELAYERS) (MLC)

ARKÖSUND MUL 12	**GRUNDSUND** MUL 15	**FÅRÖSUND** (ex-*Öresund*) MUL 18
KALMARSUND MUL 13	**SKRAMSÖSUND** MUL 17	**BARÖSUND** MUL 19

Displacement, tons: 200 standard; 245 full load
Dimensions, feet (metres): 102.3 × 24.3 × 10.2 *(31.2 × 7.4 × 3.1)*
Main machinery: Diesel-electric; 2 Nohab/Scania diesel generators; 2 motors; 460 hp(m) *(338 kW)*; 2 shafts
Speed, knots: 10.5
Complement: 24
Guns: 2—12.7 mm MGs.
Mines: 2 rails; 26 tons.
Radars: Navigation: Racal Decca 1226; I-band.

Comment: All completed by 1954-1957. Former Coastal Artillery craft for laying and maintaining minefields. One deleted in 1992, one in 1996 and *Skramsösund* has been reclassified as an auxiliary. 40 mm guns removed.   **VERIFIED**

BARÖSUND   *4/1998*, van Ginderen Collection / 0050182

1 COASTAL MINELAYER (MLC)

KALVSUND MUL 11

Displacement, tons: 200 full load
Dimensions, feet (metres): 98.4 × 23.6 × 11.8 *(30 × 7.2 × 3.6)*
Main machinery: 2 MAN Atlas diesels; 300 hp(m) *(221 kW)*; 2 shafts
Speed, knots: 10
Complement: 24
Guns: 2—12.7 mm MGs.
Mines: 2 rails; 21 tons.
Radars: Navigation: Terma Skanter 009; I-band.

Comment: Commissioned in 1947. Former Coastal Artillery craft. Reclassified as an auxiliary in 1993.   **VERIFIED**

KALVSUND   *9/1998*, Per Kornefeldt / 0050183

15 SMALL MINELAYERS (MLI)

M 502-516

Displacement, tons: 15 full load
Dimensions, feet (metres): 47.9 × 13.8 × 2.9 *(14.6 × 4.2 × 0.9)*
Main machinery: 2 diesels; 2 shafts
Speed, knots: 14
Complement: 7
Mines: 2 rails; 12.
Radars: Navigation: Racal Decca; I-band.

Comment: Ordered in 1969. Mines are laid from rails or by crane on the stern. Former Coastal Artillery craft.   **UPDATED**

M 509   *5/1995*, Curt Borgenstam / 0080735

5 SAM CLASS (MCM DRONES)

SAM 01-SAM 05

Displacement, tons: 20 full load
Dimensions, feet (metres): 59.1 × 20 × 5.2 *(18 × 6.1 × 1.6)*
Main machinery: 1 Volvo Penta TAMD70D diesel; 210 hp(m) *(154 kW)*; 1 Schottel prop
Speed, knots: 8. **Range, miles:** 330 at 8 kt

Comment: Built by Karlskronavarvet in 1983. *SAM 03* and *05* sold to the USA for Gulf operation in March 1991 and replaced in 1992/93. Remote-controlled catamaran magnetic and acoustic sweepers operated by the 'Landsort' and 'Styrsö' classes. Two delivered to Japan in February 1998 and two more in December 1998.   **VERIFIED**

SAM 01   *8/1998*, Curt Borgenstam / 0050184

7 LANDSORT CLASS (MINEHUNTERS) (MHC)

Name	No	Builders	Launched		Commissioned	
LANDSORT	M 71	Karlskronavarvet	2 Nov	1982	19 Apr	1984
ARHOLMA	M 72	Karlskronavarvet	2 Aug	1984	23 Nov	1984
KOSTER	M 73	Karlskronavarvet	16 Jan	1986	30 May	1986
KULLEN	M 74	Karlskronavarvet	15 Aug	1986	28 Nov	1986
VINGA	M 75	Karlskronavarvet	14 Aug	1987	27 Nov	1987
VEN	M 76	Karlskronavarvet	10 Aug	1988	12 Dec	1988
ULVÖN	M 77	Karlskronavarvet	4 Mar	1992	9 Oct	1992

Displacement, tons: 270 standard; 360 full load
Dimensions, feet (metres): 155.8 × 31.5 × 7.3 *(47.5 × 9.6 × 2.2)*
Main machinery: 4 Saab-Scania DSI 14 diesels; 1,592 hp(m) *(1.17 MW)* sustained; coupled in pairs to 2 Voith Schneider props
Speed, knots: 15. **Range, miles:** 2,000 at 12 kt
Complement: 29 (12 officers) plus 4 spare

Missiles: SAM: Saab Manpads.
Guns: 1 Bofors 40 mm/70 Mod 48; 240 rds/min to 12.5 km *(6.8 n miles)*; weight of shell 0.96 kg. Bofors Sea Trinity CIWS trial carried out in *Vinga* (fitted in place of 40 mm/70). 2—7.62 mm MGs.
A/S mortars: 4 Saab Elma 9-tubed launchers; range 400 m; warhead 4.2 kg shaped charge or Saab 601 9-tubed launchers; range 1,200 m; shaped charge.
Countermeasures: Decoys: 2 Philips Philax fixed launchers can be carried with 4 magazines each holding 36 grenades; IR/chaff.
ESM: Matilda; intercept.
MCM: This class is fitted for mechanical sweeps for moored mines as well as magnetic and acoustic sweeps. In addition it is possible to operate two SAM drones (see separate entry). Fitted with 2 Sutec Sea Eagle or Double Eagle remote-controlled units with 600 m tether and capable of 350 m depth.
Weapons control: Philips 9LV 100 optronic director. Philips 9 MJ 400 minehunting system.
Radars: Navigation: Thomson-CSF Terma; I-band.
Sonars: Thomson-CSF TSM-2022; Racal Decca 'Mains' control system; hull-mounted; minehunting; high frequency.

Programmes: The first two of this class ordered in early 1981. Second four in 1984 and the seventh in 1989.
Structure: The GRP mould for the hull has also been used for the Coast Guard former 'KBV 171' class.
Operational: The integrated navigation and action data automation system developed by Philips and Racal Decca.
Sales: Four built for Singapore.

UPDATED

VEN   *10/1999*, Maritime Photographic /* 0080736

KULLEN   *10/1999*, E & M Laursen /* 0080737

0 + (3) SAM II CLASS (MCM DRONES)

Displacement, tons: 56 full load
Dimensions, feet (metres): 73.8 × 38.4 *(22.5 × 11.7)* (on cushion)
Main machinery: 2 Lycoming TF40B gas turbines; 31,100 hp(m) *(22.87 MW)*; 2 ducted air props
Speed, knots: 40 (transit); 25 (operating)

Comment: Contract awarded to Karlskronavarvet in 1995 to develop a design of air cushion MCM drone for remote control by 'Styrsö' class. Dimensions given are for the craft on cushion, the hard structure is 20 × 5.2 m. Acoustic, magnetic and possibly electric influence sweeps will be fitted. This was a joint venture with the USN who dropped out in 1996. Alternative systems (MACVACS and NEWSAM) are being evaluated. Progress is very slow.

UPDATED

4 STYRSÖ CLASS
(MINESWEEPERS/HUNTERS—INSHORE) (MSI)

Name	No	Builders	Launched		Commissioned	
STYRSÖ	M 11	Karlskronavarvet	8 Mar	1996	20 Sep	1996
SPÅRÖ	M 12	Karlskronavarvet	30 Aug	1996	21 Feb	1997
SKAFTÖ	M 13	Karlskronavarvet	20 Jan	1997	13 June	1997
STURKÖ	M 14	Karlskronavarvet	27 June	1997	19 Dec	1997

Displacement, tons: 175 full load
Dimensions, feet (metres): 118.1 × 25.9 × 7.2 *(36 × 7.9 × 2.2)*
Main machinery: 2 Saab Scania DSI 14 diesels; 1,104 hp(m) *(812 kW)*; 2 shafts; bow thruster
Speed, knots: 13
Complement: 17 (8 officers)
Guns: 2—12.7 mm MGs.
Countermeasures: MCM: AK-90 acoustic, EL-90 magnetic, and mechanical sweeps. 2 Sutec Sea Eagle/Double Eagle ROVs equipped with Tritech SE 500 sonar and mine disposal charges.
Combat data systems: Ericsson tactical data system with datalink.
Radars: Navigation: Racal Bridgemaster: I-band.
Sonars: Reson Sea Bat 8100; mine avoidance; active; high frequency. EG & G side scan; active for route survey; high frequency.

Comment: Contract awarded to KKV and Erisoft AB on 11 February 1994. Capable of operating two SAM drones. These ships are also used for inshore surveillance patrols.

UPDATED

STYRSÖ   *9/1999*, Michael Nitz /* 0080739

4 HISINGEN CLASS (MINESWEEPERS—INSHORE) (MSI/YDT)

Name	No	Commissioned	
HISINGEN	M 43	18 Aug	1960
BLACKAN	M 44	19 Jan	1961
DÄMMAN	M 45	17 Dec	1960
GALTEN	M 46	21 Nov	1960

Displacement, tons: 130 standard; 150 full load
Dimensions, feet (metres): 78.7 × 21.3 × 11.5 *(24 × 6.5 × 3.5)*
Main machinery: 1 diesel; 380 hp(m) *(279 kW)*; 1 shaft
Speed, knots: 10
Complement: 12
Guns: 1 Bofors 20 mm.
Radars: Navigation: Terma Scanter 009; I-band.

Comment: Trawler type with wooden hulls. Now used as diver support ships for mine clearance.
VERIFIED

GALTEN   *8/1998, Curt Borgenstam /* 0050188

3 GÅSSTEN CLASS (MINESWEEPERS—INSHORE) (MSI)

Name	No	Builders	Commissioned
GÅSSTEN	M 31	Knippla Skeppsvarv	16 Nov 1973
NORSTEN	M 32	Hellevikstrands Skeppsvarv	12 Oct 1973
VIKSTEN	M 33	Karlskronavarvet	15 July 1974

Displacement, tons: 120 standard; 135 full load
Dimensions, feet (metres): 78.7 × 21.3 × 11.5 *(24 × 6.5 × 3.5)*
Main machinery: 1 diesel; 460 hp(m) *(338 kW)*; 1 shaft
Speed, knots: 11
Complement: 9
Guns: 1 Bofors 20 mm.
Radars: Navigation: Terma; I-band.

Comment: Ordered 1972. *Viksten* built of GRP, as a forerunner to new minehunters building at Karlskrona. Others have wooden hulls. These are repeat 'Hisingen' class.
VERIFIED

VIKSTEN   *8/1998, E & M Laursen* / 0050189

5 M 15 CLASS (MINESWEEPERS—INSHORE) (MSI)

M 20   M 21   M 22   M 24   M 25

Displacement, tons: 94 full load
Dimensions, feet (metres): 90.9 × 16.5 × 6.6 *(27.7 × 5 × 2)*
Main machinery: 2 diesels; 320 hp(m) *(235 kW)* sustained; 2 shafts
Speed, knots: 12
Complement: 10
Radars: Navigation: Terma; I-band.

Comment: All launched in 1941 and now used as platforms for mine clearance divers. *M 20* of this class was re-rated as tender and renamed *Skuld*, but was converted back again in 1993. All five were modernised in 1992-93 and are also used for navigation training.
UPDATED

M 24   *8/1996*, Erik Laursen* / 0080738

4 EJDERN CLASS (SONOBUOY CRAFT) (MSI)

EJDERN B 01   KRICKAN B 02   SVÄRTAN B 03   VIGGEN B 04

Displacement, tons: 36 full load
Dimensions, feet (metres): 65.6 × 15.7 × 4.3 *(20 × 4.8 × 1.3)*
Main machinery: 2 Volvo Penta TAMD122 diesels; 366 hp(m) *(269 kW)* sustained; 2 shafts
Speed, knots: 15
Complement: 9 (2 officers)
Guns: 1—7.62 mm MG.
Radars: Navigation: Terma; I-band.

Comment: Built by Djupviksvarvet and completed in 1991. GRP hulls. Classified as mine warfare vessels. Used for laying and monitoring sonobuoys to detect intruders in Swedish territorial waters. Carry an AQS-928 acoustic processor.
UPDATED

KRICKAN   *5/1997*, Curt Borgenstam* / 0019204

AMPHIBIOUS FORCES

3 GRIM CLASS (LCM)

BORE   GRIM   HEIMDAL

Displacement, tons: 340 full load
Dimensions, feet (metres): 124 × 28.2 × 8.5 *(37.8 × 8.6 × 2.6)*
Main machinery: 2 diesels; 800 hp(m) *(588 kW)*; 2 shafts
Speed, knots: 12
Military lift: 325 troops
Guns: 2—12.7 mm MGs.
Radars: Navigation: Terma; I-band.

Comment: Launched in 1961 *(Grim)* and other two in 1966. Former Coastal Artillery craft and used to transport guns. There are some superstructure and funnel shape differences.
VERIFIED

BORE   *6/1997, Per Kornefeldt* / 0050190

145 COMBATBOAT 90H (STRIDSBÅT) (LCA)

803-947

Displacement, tons: 19 full load
Dimensions, feet (metres): 52.2 × 12.5 × 2.6 *(15.9 × 3.8 × 0.8)*
Main machinery: 2 Saab Scania DSI 14 diesels; 1,104 hp(m) *(812 kW)*; 2 Kamewa water-jets
Speed, knots: 35-50; 20 (Sea State 3). **Range, miles:** 240 at 30 kt
Complement: 3
Military lift: 20 troops plus equipment or 2.8 tons
Missiles: SSM; Rockwell RBS 17 Hellfire; semi-active laser guidance to 5 km *(3 n miles)* at 1.0 Mach; warhead 8 kg.
Guns: 3—12.7 mm MGs.
Mines: 4 (or 6 depth charges).
Radars: Navigation: Racal Decca; RD 360 or Furuno 8050; I-band.

Comment: The first two prototypes ordered in January 1988 are no longer in service, although one is used as a trials craft and is fitted with a twin 120 mm mortar. Twelve more built in 1991-92. 63 more ordered from Dockstavarvet and Gotlands Varv in mid-January 1992, with an option for 35 more which was taken up in 1994. The building period for these completed in mid-1997. 22 more Batch 2C ordered in August 1996 for delivery by March 2001. This craft has a large hatch forward to aid disembarkation. All have a 20° deadrise and all carry four six-man inflatable rafts. Some of these craft are on loan to the Swedish Police. Twenty-two of the class delivered to Norway by 1999.
UPDATED

COMBATBOAT 900   *6/1999*, Curt Borgenstam* / 0080741

COMBATBOAT 887   *5/1999*, Per Kornefeldt* / 0080740

52 COMBATBOAT 90E (STRIDSBÅT) (LCP)

101-152

Displacement, tons: 9 full load
Dimensions, feet (metres): 39 × 9.5 × 2.3 *(11.9 × 2.9 × 0.7)*
Main machinery: 1 Scania AB DSI 14 diesel; 398 hp(m) *(293 kW)* sustained; FFJet 410 water-jet
Speed, knots: 40; 37 (laden)
Complement: 2
Military lift: 2 tons or 6-10 troops
Radars: Navigation: Furuno 8050; I-band.

Comment: First batch ordered from Storebro Royal Cruiser AB in 1995 for delivery from August 1995-98. Second batch ordered in 1997 for delivery in 1998-99. These are ambulance boats but may also be used for stores. Two more ordered for Chinese Customs and three for Malaysian Customs in April 1997.

VERIFIED

COMBATBOAT 139   *8/1998, Per Kornefeldt /* 0050192

17 LCMs (TROSSBÅT)

603-612   652-658

Displacement, tons: 55 full load
Dimensions, feet (metres): 68.9 × 19.7 × 4.9 *(21 × 6 × 1.5)*
Main machinery: 2 Saab DSI 11/40 M2 diesels; 340 hp(m) *(250 kW)*; 2 Schottel props
Speed, knots: 10
Military lift: 30 tons
Radars: Navigation: Racal Decca 914C; I-band.

Comment: Completed from 1980-88. Classified as Trossbåt (support boat). Built by Djupviksvarvet.

UPDATED

LCM 657   *6/1998, Curt Borgenstam /* 0050193

70 LCUs

| 207-208 | 211-217 | 219-226 | 228 | 230-239 | 241-277 | 280-284 |

Displacement, tons: 31 full load
Dimensions, feet (metres): 70.2 × 13.8 × 4.2 *(21.4 × 4.2 × 1.3)*
Main machinery: 3 diesels; 600 hp(m) *(441 kW)*; 3 shafts
Speed, knots: 18
Military lift: 40 tons; 40 troops
Guns: 3 to 8—6.5 mm MGs.
Mines: Minelaying capability *(280-284 only)*.

Comment: Built between 1960 and 1987. 35 modernised 1989-93; 12 more 1997-98.

VERIFIED

LCU 247   *8/1998, E & M Laursen /* 0050194

2 + (10) TRANSPORTBÅT 2000

451   452

Displacement, tons: 43 full load
Dimensions, feet (metres): 77.1 × 16.7 × 3.3 *(23.5 × 5.1 × 1)*
Main machinery: 3 Saab Scania DSI 14 diesels or 3 Volvo Penta 163 diesels; 1,194 hp(m) *(878 kW)* sustained; 3 FFJet 450 or 3 Kamewa K40 waterjets
Speed, knots: 25
Complement: 3
Military lift: 45 troops or 10 tons
Guns: 2—12.7 mm MGs.
Radars: Navigation: Terma; I-band.

Comment: Two similar prototypes ordered from Djupviks Shipyard in 1997. *452* is configured for troop carrying, and *451* as a command boat. Each has a different propulsion system which are in competition to be fitted in seven more troop carriers and three more command boats to be ordered in 2000.

UPDATED

TRANSPORTBÅT 451   *5/1999*, E & M Laursen /* 0080742

1 + (3) M 10 CLASS HOVERCRAFT

Displacement, tons: 26 full load
Dimensions, feet (metres): 61.8 × 29 *(18.8 × 8.8)*
Main machinery: 2 Scania diesels; 1,224 hp(m) *(900 kW)*
Speed, knots: 40; 7 with cushion deflated. **Range, miles:** 600 at 30 kt
Complement: 3
Military lift: 10 tons or 50 troops
Radars: Navigation: I-band.

Comment: ABS design built at Karlskronavarvet under licence and started trials in June 1998 which included ice trials in early 1999. Has a Kevlar superstructure. Three more are planned for delivery at one a year from 2001.

UPDATED

M 10   *8/1999*, Per Kornefeldt /* 0080743

80 RAIDING CRAFT (GRUPPBÅT) (LCVP)

Displacement, tons: 3 full load
Dimensions, feet (metres): 26.2 × 6.9 × 1 *(8 × 2.1 × 0.3)*
Main machinery: 1 Volvo Penta TAMD 42WJ diesel; 230 hp(m) *(169 kW)*; 1 Kamewa 240 water-jet
Speed, knots: 30
Complement: 2
Military lift: 1 ton

Comment: Small raiding craft are used throughout the Archipelago. Some have been replaced.

UPDATED

GRUPPBÅT   *8/1998, Per Kornefeldt /* 0050196

ICEBREAKERS

Note: All Icebreakers are manned by the Navy.

1 ODEN CLASS (PGB/ML)

Name	Builders	Launched	Commissioned
ODEN	Gotaverken Arendal, Göteborg	25 Aug 1988	29 Jan 1989

Displacement, tons: 12,900 full load
Dimensions, feet (metres): 352.4 × 102 × 27.9 *(107.4 × 31.1 × 8.5)*
Main machinery: 4 Sulzer ZAL40S8L diesels; 23,940 hp(m) *(17.6 MW)* sustained; 2 shafts; cp props
Speed, knots: 17. **Range, miles:** 30,000 at 13 kt
Complement: 32 plus 17 spare berths
Guns: 4 Bofors 40 mm/70 can be fitted.

Comment: Ordered in February 1987, laid down 19 October 1987. Can break 1.8 m thick ice at 3 kt. Towing winch aft with a pull of 150 tons. Helicopter platform 73.5 × 57.4 ft *(22.4 × 17.5 m)*. The main hull is only 25 m wide but the full width is at the bow. Also equipped as a minelayer.

UPDATED

ODEN *8/1999*, Royal Swedish Navy /* 0080937

3 ATLE CLASS (PGB/ML)

Name	Builders	Launched	Commissioned
ATLE	Wärtsilä, Helsinki	27 Nov 1973	21 Oct 1974
FREJ	Wärtsilä, Helsinki	3 June 1974	30 Sep 1975
YMER	Wärtsilä, Helsinki	3 Sep 1976	25 Oct 1977

Displacement, tons: 7,900 standard; 9,500 full load
Dimensions, feet (metres): 343.1 × 78.1 × 23.9 *(104.6 × 23.8 × 7.3)*
Main machinery: 5 Wärtsilä-Pielstick diesels; 22,000 hp(m) *(16.2 MW)*; 4 Strömberg motors; 22,000 hp(m) *(16.2 MW)*; 4 shafts (2 fwd, 2 cp aft)
Speed, knots: 19
Complement: 50 (16 officers)
Guns: 4 Bofors 40 mm/70.
Helicopters: 2 light.

Comment: Similar to Finnish 'Urho' class. Also equipped as minelayers.

UPDATED

FREJ *8/1994*, E & M Laursen /* 0080744

Name	Builders	Launched	Commissioned
ALE	Wärtsilä, Helsinki	1 June 1973	19 Dec 1973

Displacement, tons: 1,550
Dimensions, feet (metres): 154.2 × 42.6 × 16.4 *(47 × 13 × 5)*
Main machinery: 2 diesels; 4,750 hp(m) *(3.49 MW)*; 2 shafts
Speed, knots: 14
Complement: 32 (8 officers)
Guns: 1 Bofors 40 mm/70 (not embarked).

Comment: Built for operations on Lake Vänern. Is also used as a survey ship.

VERIFIED

ALE *9/1998, van Ginderen Collection /* 0050197

INTELLIGENCE VESSELS

1 ELECTRONIC SURVEILLANCE SHIP (AGI)

Name	No	Builders	Launched	Commissioned
ORION	A 201	Karlskronavarvet	30 Nov 1983	7 June 1984

Displacement, tons: 1,400 full load
Dimensions, feet (metres): 201.1 × 32.8 × 9.8 *(61.3 × 10 × 3)*
Main machinery: 2 Hedemora V8A diesels; 1,800 hp(m) *(1.32 MW)* sustained; 2 shafts; cp props
Speed, knots: 15
Complement: 35
Radars: Navigation: Terma Scanter 009; I-band.
Helicopters: Platform for 1 light.

Comment: Ordered 23 April 1982. Laid down 28 June 1982. The communications aerials are inside the elongated dome.

UPDATED

ORION *8/1999*, E & M Laursen /* 0080745

SURVEY SHIPS

Notes: (1) Owned by the National Maritime Administration but manned and operated by the Navy.
(2) There is a research ship *Argos*. Civilian manned and owned by the National Board of Fisheries. A second civilian ship *Ocean Surveyor* belongs to the Geological Investigation but has been leased as a Support Ship on occasions.
(3) The Board of Navigation owns two buoy tenders *Scandica* and *Baltica* built in 1982 and two lighthouse tenders *Fyrbyggaren* and *Fyrbjörn*.

FYRBYGGAREN *5/1999*, Curt Borgenstam /* 0080746

JACOB HÄGG

Displacement, tons: 192 standard
Dimensions, feet (metres): 119.8 × 24.6 × 5.6 *(36.5 × 7.5 × 1.7)*
Main machinery: 4 Saab Scania DSI 14 diesels; 1,592 hp(m) *(1.17 MW)* sustained; 2 shafts
Speed, knots: 16
Complement: 13 (5 officers)

Comment: Laid down April 1982 at Djupviks Shipyard. Launched 12 March 1983. Completed 16 May 1983. Aluminium hull.

VERIFIED

JACOB HÄGG *5/1998, J Cislak /* 0050199

NILS STRÖMCRONA

Displacement, tons: 210 full load
Dimensions, feet (metres): 98.4 × 32.8 × 5.9 *(30 × 10 × 1.8)*
Main machinery: 4 Saab Scania DSI 14 diesels; 1,592 hp(m) *(1.17 MW)* sustained; 2 shafts; bow and stern thrusters
Speed, knots: 12
Complement: 14 (5 officers)

Comment: Completed 28 June 1985. Of catamaran construction—each hull of 3.9 m made of aluminium.

UPDATED

NILS STRÖMCRONA   *3/1999*, Per Kornefeldt /* 0080747

AUXILIARIES

Note: A rescue submersible, *Urf (Ubåts Räddnings Farkost)*, of 52 tons with a diving depth of 1,500 ft *(460 m)*, was launched 17 April 1978. Similar to US Navy DSRV she has a capacity for 35 men on each dive.

URF   *9/1998, J Cislak /* 0050200

1 MIDGET SUBMARINE

SPIGGEN II

Displacement, tons: 17 dived
Dimensions, feet (metres): 34.8 × 5.6 × 4.6 *(10.6 × 1.7 × 1.4)*
Main machinery: 1 Volvo Penta diesel; 1 shaft
Speed, knots: 5 dived; 6 surfaced
Complement: 4

Comment: Launched 19 June 1990 by Försvarets Materielverk. Has an endurance of 14 days and a diving depth of 100 m *(330 ft)*, and is used as a target for ASW training. Refitted by Kockums and back in service in December 1996.

UPDATED

SPIGGEN II   *8/1998, Per Kornefeldt /* 0050201

1 TRANSPORT (AKL)

Name	No	Builders	Commissioned
SLEIPNER (ex-*Ardal*)	A 343	Bergen	1980

Displacement, tons: 1,049 full load
Dimensions, feet (metres): 163.1 × 36.1 × 11.5 *(49.7 × 11 × 3.5)*
Main machinery: 1 Normo diesel; 1,300 hp(m) *(956 kW)*; 1 shaft
Speed, knots: 12
Complement: 12
Cargo capacity: 260 tons

Comment: Acquired in 1992 from a Norwegian Shipping Company.

UPDATED

SLEIPNER   *10/1999*, van Ginderen Collection /* 0080748

1 + 1 AKADEMIK SHULEYKIN CLASS (SUPPORT SHIP) (ARL)

Name	No	Builders	Commissioned
TROSSÖ (ex-*Arnold Viemer*, ex-*Livonia*)	A 264	Valmet, Finland	1984

Displacement, tons: 2,140 full load
Dimensions, feet (metres): 234.9 × 42 × 14.8 *(71.6 × 12.8 × 4.5)*
Main machinery: 2 Russkiy G74 36/45 diesels; 3,084 hp(m) *(2.27 MW)*; 2 shafts
Speed, knots: 14
Complement: 64

Comment: Built as a survey ship for the USSR and used in the Baltic as an AGOR. Taken on by the Estonian Marine Institute and then transferred to Sweden on 23 September 1996. Converted as a depot ship for corvettes and patrol craft and back in service in 1997. Can act as a Headquarters Ship. A second of class may be acquired.

UPDATED

TROSSÖ   *5/1999*, Curt Borgenstam /* 0080749

1 REPAIR SHIP (ARL)

Name	No	Builders	Commissioned
GÅLÖ (ex-*Herjolfur*)	A 263	Bergen	1976

Displacement, tons: 1,200 full load
Dimensions, feet (metres): 196.9 × 39.4 × 14.4 *(60 × 12 × 4.4)*
Main machinery: 1 Wichman diesel; 2,400 hp(m) *(1.76 MW)*; 1 shaft; 2 bow thrusters
Speed, knots: 12
Complement: 24

Comment: Built as a ferry for Iceland. Acquired in 1993 as a repair and maintenance ship for patrol craft. May be deleted soon.

UPDATED

GÅLÖ   *10/1999*, Curt Borgenstam /* 0080750

1 MCM SUPPORT SHIP (AS)

Name	No	Builders	Commissioned
UTÖ (ex-*Smit Manila*, ex-*Seaford* ex-*Seaforth Challenger*)	A 261	Cochrane Shipyard, Selby	1974

Displacement, tons: 1,800 full load
Dimensions, feet (metres): 182.1 × 40.4 × 14.1 *(55.5 × 12.3 × 4.3)*
Main machinery: 2 Hedemora diesels; 3,000 hp(m) *(22 MW)*; 2 shafts; cp props
Speed, knots: 12
Complement: 32 plus 33 staff
Guns: 2 Bofors 20 mm.

Comment: Ex-supply ship converted by Pan United Ltd, Singapore and recommissioned in April 1989 as an MCM tender and command ship.

UPDATED

UTÖ   5/1999*, Curt Borgenstam / 0080751

1 DIVER SUPPORT SHIP (YDT)

Name	No	Builders	Commissioned
SKREDSVIK (ex-*KBV 172*)	A 262 (ex-*M 70*)	Karlskronavarvet	Oct 1981

Displacement, tons: 375 full load
Dimensions, feet (metres): 164 × 27.9 × 7.9 *(50 × 8.5 × 2.4)*
Main machinery: 2 Hedemora V16A diesels; 4,500 hp(m) *(3.3 MW)*; 2 shafts
Speed, knots: 18. **Range, miles:** 3,000 at 12 kt
Complement: 15
Radars: Navigation: 2 Racal Decca; I-band.
Helicopters: Platform for 1 light.

Comment: Transferred from the Coast Guard in 1991 and used as a Diver Support ship for mine clearance operations after a refit from October 1992 to February 1993. Employed for Command and Control in war. Has a Simrad high-frequency active sonar.

UPDATED

SKREDSVIK   7/1996*, Per Kornefeldt / 0080752

1 DIVER SUPPORT SHIP (YDT)

ÄGIR (ex-*Bloom Syrveyor*)   A 212

Displacement, tons: 117 full load
Dimensions, feet (metres): 82 × 24.9 × 6.6 *(25 × 7.6 × 2)*
Main machinery: 2 GM diesels; 2 shafts
Speed, knots: 11
Complement: 15
Radars: Navigation: Terma; I-band.

Comment: Built in Norway in 1984. Acquired in 1989.

UPDATED

ÄGIR   6/1996*, E & M Laursen / 0080753

1 DIVER SUPPORT SHIP (YDT)

NORDANÖ (ex-*Sjöjungfrun*)   A 213

Displacement, tons: 148 full load
Dimensions, feet (metres): 80.1 × 24.9 × 8.9 *(24.4 × 7.6 × 2.7)*
Main machinery: 2 Volvo Penta TAMD diesels; 767 hp(m) *(564 kW)*; 2 shafts
Speed, knots: 10
Complement: 15

Comment: Launched in 1983 and bought by the Navy in 1992.

UPDATED

NORDANÖ   7/1996*, E & M Laursen / 0080754

1 SALVAGE SHIP (ARS)

Name	No	Builders	Recommissioned
BELOS III (ex-*Energy Supporter*)	A 214	De Hoop, Netherlands	Nov 1992

Measurement, tons: 5,096 grt
Dimensions, feet (metres): 344.2 × 59.1 × 16.7 *(104.9 × 18 × 5.1)*
Main machinery: 5 MAN 9ASL 25/30 diesel alternators; 8.15 MW; 2 motors; 5,110 hp(m) *(3.76 MW)*; 2 shafts
Speed, knots: 14
Complement: 35

Comment: Bought from Midland and Scottish Resources in mid-1992 and arrived in Sweden in November 1992. Replaced the previous ship of the same name which paid off in April 1993. Ice-strengthened hull and fitted with a helicopter platform.

VERIFIED

BELOS III (with URF on deck)   9/1998, J Cislak / 0050203

1 TORPEDO AND MISSILE RECOVERY VESSEL (TRV)

Name	No	Builders	Commissioned
PELIKANEN	A 247	Djupviksvarvet	26 Sep 1963

Displacement, tons: 144 full load
Dimensions, feet (metres): 108.2 × 19 × 7.2 *(33 × 5.8 × 2.2)*
Main machinery: 2 MTU MB diesels; 1,040 hp(m) *(764 kW)*; 2 shafts
Speed, knots: 14
Complement: 14
Radars: Navigation: Terma; I-band.

Comment: Torpedo recovery and rocket trials vessel.

VERIFIED

PELIKANEN   9/1998, J Cislak / 0050204

1 TORPEDO AND MISSILE RECOVERY VESSEL (TRV)

Name	No	Builders	Commissioned
PINGVINEN	A 248	Lunde Varv-och Verstads	20 Mar 1975

Displacement, tons: 191 full load
Dimensions, feet (metres): 109.3 × 20 × 7.2 *(33.3 × 6.1 × 2.2)*
Main machinery: 2 MTU diesels; 1,140 hp(m) *(838 kW)*; 2 shafts
Speed, knots: 13
Complement: 14
Radars: Navigation: Terma; I-band.

Comment: Recovery vessel for trials firings.

UPDATED

PINGVINEN   *10/1996*, Michael Nitz /* 0080755

1 TANKER (AOTL)

Name	No	Builders	Commissioned
ELDAREN (ex-*Brotank*)	A 229	Asiverken, Åmål	Apr 1959

Measurement, tons: 320 dwt
Dimensions, feet (metres): 122 × 21.3 × 9.5 *(37.2 × 6.5 × 2.9)*
Main machinery: 1 Volvo Penta diesel; 300 hp(m) *(220 kW)*; 1 shaft; cp prop
Speed, knots: 9
Cargo capacity: 300 tons oil fuel; 10 tons water
Radars: Navigation: Terma; I-band.

Comment: Civilian tanker purchased from A F Karlsson in May 1981.

UPDATED

ELDAREN   *6/1997*, Per Kornefeldt /* 0019215

1 SUPPORT SHIP (AKL)

Name	No	Builders	Commissioned
LOKE	A 344	Oskarsham Shipyard	Sep 1994

Displacement, tons: 455 full load
Dimensions, feet (metres): 117.8 × 29.5 × 8.6 *(35.9 × 9 × 2.7)*
Main machinery: 2 Scania diesels; 2 shafts
Speed, knots: 12
Complement: 8
Cargo capacity: 50 tons or 50 passengers
Radars: Navigation: Terma; I-band.

Comment: General support craft which can be used as a ferry. Landing craft bow.

VERIFIED

LOKE   *8/1998, E & M Laursen /* 0050205

1 TENDER (YAG)

URD (ex-*Capella*) A 241

Displacement, tons: 63 standard; 90 full load
Dimensions, feet (metres): 73.8 × 18.3 × 9.2 *(22.5 × 5.6 × 2.8)*
Main machinery: 1 diesel; 200 hp(m) *(147 kW)*; 1 shaft; bow thruster
Speed, knots: 8
Complement: 6

Comment: Experimental vessel added to the official list in 1970. Launched in 1929. *UPDATED*

URD   *5/1997*, H M Steele /* 0019217

16 SUPPORT VESSEL (TROSSBÅT)

662-677

Displacement, tons: 60 full load
Dimensions, feet (metres): 80.1 × 17.7 × 4.6 *(24.4 × 5.4 × 1.4)*
Main machinery: 3 Saab Scania DSI 14 diesels; 1,194 hp(m) *(878 kW)* sustained; 3 FFJet 450 water-jets
Speed, knots: 25; 13 (laden)
Complement: 3
Military lift: 22 tons
Guns: 1—12.7 mm MG.
Radars: Navigation: Terma; I-band.

Comment: Prototype Trossbåt-built at Holms Shipyard in 1991 and capable of carrying 15 tons of deck cargo and 9 tons internal cargo or 17 troops plus mines. Aluminium hull with a bow ramp. Some ice capability. A second prototype delivered in late 1993, and the first production vessel in 1996. *UPDATED*

TROSSBÅT 676   *5/1999*, Per Kornefeldt /* 0080756

TRAINING SHIPS

2 SAIL TRAINING SHIPS (AXS)

Name	No	Builders	Commissioned
GLADAN	S 01	Naval Dockyard, Stockholm	1947
FALKEN	S 02	Naval Dockyard, Stockholm	1947

Displacement, tons: 225 standard
Dimensions, feet (metres): 112.8 × 23.6 × 13.8 *(34.4 × 7.2 × 4.2)*
Main machinery: 1 diesel; 120 hp(m) *(88 kW)*; 1 shaft

Comment: Sail training ships. Two masted schooners. Sail area, 512 sq m. Both had major overhauls in 1986-88 in which all technical systems were replaced. *UPDATED*

FALKEN   *5/1997*, Marek Twardowski /* 0019218

TUGS

Note: There is also a 35 ton harbour tug *Atlas* A 330 which can carry mines.

ACHILLES A 251

Displacement, tons: 450 full load
Dimensions, feet (metres): 108.2 × 28.9 × 15.1 *(33 × 8.8 × 4.6)*
Main machinery: 1 diesel; 1,650 hp(m) *(1.2 MW)*; 1 shaft
Speed, knots: 12
Complement: 12
Radars: Navigation: Racal Decca 1226C; I-band.

Comment: Launched in 1962. Icebreaking tug.

VERIFIED

ACHILLES   *4/1991, Hartmut Ehlers*

| **HERMES** A 253 | **HEROS** A 322 | **HERCULES** A 323 | **HERA** A 324 |

Displacement, tons: 185 standard; 215 full load
Dimensions, feet (metres): 80.5 × 22.6 × 13.1 *(24.5 × 6.9 × 4)*
Main machinery: 1 diesel; 600 hp(m) *(441 kW)*; 1 shaft
Speed, knots: 11
Complement: 8

Comment: Details given for the first pair launched 1953-57. Second pair are smaller at 127 tons and were launched in 1969-71. All are icebreaking tugs.

UPDATED

HERMES   *8/1998, Per Kornefeldt / 0050207*

A 701-705, 751-756

Displacement, tons: 42 full load
Dimensions, feet (metres): 50.9 × 16.4 × 8.9 *(15.5 × 5 × 2.7)*
Main machinery: 1 diesel; 1 shaft
Speed, knots: 9.5
Complement: 6

Comment: Can carry 40 people. Icebreaking tugs. *701-703* used by Coastal Artillery. All can carry mines.

UPDATED

A 752   *8/1997*, Curt Borgenstam / 0019220*

COAST GUARD
(KUSTBEVAKNING)

Establishment: Established in 1638, and for 350 years was a part of the Swedish Customs administration. From 1 July 1988 the Coast Guard became an independent civilian authority with a Board supervised by the Ministry of Defence. Organised in four regions with a central Headquarters.

Duties: Responsible for civilian surveillance of Swedish waters, fishery zone and continental shelf. Supervises and enforces fishing regulations, customs, dumping and pollution regulations, environmental protection and traffic regulations. Also concerned with prevention of drug running and forms part of the Swedish search and rescue organisation.

Headquarters Appointments

Director General:
  Marie Hafstrom

Personnel: 2000: 560

Aircraft: Three CASA 212.

Ships: Tv pennant numbers replaced by KBV in 1988 but the KBV is not displayed. Vessels are not normally armed.

1 KBV 181 CLASS (HIGH ENDURANCE CUTTER)

KBV 181

Displacement, tons: 991 full load
Dimensions, feet (metres): 183.7 oa; 167.3 wl × 33.5 × 15.1 *(56; 51 × 10.2 × 4.6)*
Main machinery: 2 Wärtsilä Vasa 8R22 diesels; 3,755 hp(m) *(2.76 MW)* sustained; 1 shaft; Kamewa cp prop; bow thruster
Speed, knots: 16. **Range, miles:** 2,800 at 15 kt
Complement: 11
Guns: 1 Oerlikon 20 mm (if required).
Radars: Navigation: Furuno FAR 2830; I-band.
Sonars: Simrad Subsea; active search; high frequency.

Comment: Ordered from Rauma Shipyards in August 1989 and built at Uusikaupunki. Commissioned 30 November 1990. Unarmed in peacetime. Equipped as a Command vessel for SAR and anti-pollution operations. All-steel construction similar to Finnish *Tursas*.

UPDATED

KBV 181   *6/1996*, Michael Nitz / 0080757*

4 KBV 101 CLASS (MEDIUM ENDURANCE CUTTER)

KBV 102-KBV 105

Displacement, tons: 65 full load
Dimensions, feet (metres): 87.6 × 16.4 × 7.2 *(26.7 × 5 × 2.2)*
Main machinery: 2 Cummins KTA38-M diesels; 2,120 hp *(1.56 MW)*; 2 shafts
Speed, knots: 21. **Range, miles:** 1,000 at 15 kt
Complement: 5 plus 2 spare
Sonars: Hull-mounted; active search; high frequency.

Comment: Built 1969-73 at Djupviksvarvet. Class A cutters. All-welded aluminium hull and upperworks. Equipped for salvage divers. All modernised with new diesels, a new bridge and new electronics completed in 1988. *KBV 101* transferred to Lithuania in 1996.

UPDATED

KBV 102   *5/1994*, E & M Laursen / 0080758*

0 + 2 KBV 201 CLASS (HIGH ENDURANCE CUTTER)

KBV 201   KBV 202

Displacement, tons: 468 full load
Dimensions, feet (metres): 170.6 × 28.2 × 7.9 *(52 × 8.6 × 2.4)*
Main machinery: 2 MWM 610 diesels; 5,440 hp(m) *(4 MW)*; 2 MWM 616 diesels; 1,904 hp(m)
   (1.4 MW); 2 shafts; Kamewa cp props; 2 bow thruster 424 hp(m) *(312 kW)*
Speed, knots: 22. **Range, miles:** 1,340 at 16 kt
Complement: 9
Radars: Navigation: E/F- and I-band.

Comment: Ordered from Kockums in January 1999 and building at Karlskrona. First one to be
   delivered in October 2000, second a year later. Steel hulls. Multirole vessels for surveillance and
   environmental protection. Stern ramp for launching a RIB.

UPDATED

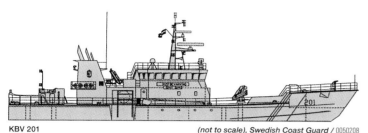

KBV 201   *(not to scale), Swedish Coast Guard /* 0050208

10 KBV 281 CLASS (MEDIUM ENDURANCE CUTTER)

KBV 281-290

Displacement, tons: 45 full load
Dimensions, feet (metres): 68.9 × 16.4 × 6.2 *(21 × 5 × 1.9)*
Main machinery: 2 Cummins KTA38-M or MWM diesels; 2,120 hp *(1.56 MW)*; 2 shafts
Speed, knots: 27
Complement: 4
Radars: Navigation: Furuno; I-band.

Comment: Built by Djupviksvarvet and delivered at one a year from 1979. Last one commissioned
   6 December 1990. Aluminium hulls. Some of the class have an upper bridge.

UPDATED

KBV 290   *5/1999*, Per Kornefeldt /* 0080759

11 KBV 301 CLASS (MEDIUM ENDURANCE CUTTER)

KBV 301-311

Displacement, tons: 35 full load
Dimensions, feet (metres): 65.6 × 15.1 × 3.6 *(20 × 4.6 × 1.1)*
Main machinery: 2 MTU 183 TE92 diesels; 1,830 hp(m) *(1.35 MW)* sustained; 2 MTP 7500S or
   Kamewa water-jets
Speed, knots: 34. **Range, miles:** 500 at 25 kt
Complement: 4
Radars: Navigation: 2 Kelvin Hughes 6000; I-band.

Comment: Built at Karlskronavarvet. First one delivered in May 1993 and the remainder ordered in
   December 1993. Three delivered in 1995, four in 1996 and the last three in 1997.

UPDATED

KBV 301   *8/1999*, Per Kornefeldt /* 0080760

3 KBV 591 (GRIFFON 2000 TDX) CLASS (HOVERCRAFT)

KBV 591-593

Displacement, tons: 3.5 full load
Dimensions, feet (metres): 38.4 × 19.4 *(11.7 × 5.9)*
Main machinery: 1 Deutz BF8L diesel; 350 hp(m) *(235 kW)*
Speed, knots: 35. **Range, miles:** 450 at 35 kt
Complement: 3
Radars: Navigation: Furuno 7010 D; I-band.

Comment: Built by Griffon Hovercraft, Southampton and delivered in 1992-93. Aluminium hulls.

UPDATED

KBV 593   *7/1996*, E & M Laursen /* 0080761

60 COAST GUARD PATROL CRAFT (SMALL)

KBV 401-408   + 52

Comment: *KBV 401-408* built in 1994-95. There is a total of some 60 speed boats with Raytheon
   radars.

UPDATED

SPEED BOAT   *7/1995*, E & M Laursen /* 0080762

POLLUTION CONTROL CRAFT

Number	Displacement (tons)	Comment
KBV 044	52	Steel hulled. Class B sea trucks built
KBV 045-049	340	1972-1983 by Lunde SY. Complement
KBV 050-051	316	includes salvage divers. 050 jumboised in 1993 and 051 in 1996.
KBV 003	471	Steel hulled support ship. Class A built 1971-76 by Lunde SY. Complement includes salvage divers.
KBV 004	440	Built by Lunde SY in 1978. Carries salvage divers.
KBV 005	990	Ice Class 1A built in 1980 and acquired in 1993.
KBV 010	430	Built by Lunde SY 1985. Sea Truck.
KBV 020	85	Aluminium catamaran hull. Class D.

UPDATED

KBV 005   *7/1996*, E & M Laursen /* 0080763

SWITZERLAND

Diplomatic Representation

Defence Attaché in London:
  Colonel W Knüsli

General

The patrol boats are manned by the Army and split between Lakes Constance, Geneva and Maggiore; one company to each.

Mercantile Marine

Lloyd's Register of Shipping:
  21 vessels of 439,140 tons gross

ARMY

Note: There are also large numbers of flat bottomed raiding craft powered by single 40 hp outboard engines.

11 AQUARIUS CLASS (Patrouillenboot 80) (PBR)

ANTARES	AQUARIUS	ORION	SATURN
URANUS	CASTOR	PERSEUS	SIRIUS
VENUS	MARS	POLLUX	

Displacement, tons: 7 full load
Dimensions, feet (metres): 35.1 × 10.8 × 3 *(10.7 × 3.3 × 0.9)*
Main machinery: 2 Volvo KAD 42 diesels; 460 hp(m) *(338 kW)*; 2 shafts
Speed, knots: 35
Complement: 8
Guns: 2—12.7 mm MGs.
Radars: Surface search: JFS Electronic 364; I-band.

Comment: Builders Müller AG, Spiez. GRP hulls, wooden superstructure. *Aquarius* commissioned in 1978, *Pollux* in 1984, the remainder in 1981. Re-engined with diesels which have replaced the former petrol engines.

UPDATED   AQUARIUS

10/1997, Swiss Army / 0019223

SYRIA

Headquarters Appointments

Commander-in-Chief Navy:
  Vice Admiral Abdul Nasser Waell
Director of Naval Operations:
  Rear Admiral Hamed Makrin

Personnel

(a)   2000: 3,200 officers and men (2,500 reserves)
(b)   18 months' national service

Bases

Latakia, Tartous, Al-Mina-al-Bayda, Baniyas

Submarines

One 'Romeo' class hull is moored at Tartous and two at Latakia, but none has been to sea for seven years.

Coast Defence

12 missile batteries with SS-C-1 Sepal and SS-C-3 Styx in sites at Tartous (2), Baniyas and Latakia. In addition there are 36—130 mm guns and 12—100 mm guns plus a radar surveillance battalion. Coastal Artillery has been under naval control since 1984.

Mercantile Marine

Lloyd's Register of Shipping:
  223 vessels of 440,056 tons gross

DELETIONS

Patrol Forces

1996-97   3 Komar, 2 Osa I, 2 Osa II

Mine Warfare Forces

1996-97   2 Yevgenya, 2 Vanya

FRIGATES

2 PETYA III CLASS (FFL)

1-508 (ex-*12*)   **2-508** (ex-*14*)

Displacement, tons: 950 standard; 1,180 full load
Dimensions, feet (metres): 268.3 × 29.9 × 9.5 *(81.8 × 9.1 × 2.9)*
Main machinery: CODAG; 2 gas turbines; 30,000 hp(m) *(22 MW)*; 1 Type 61V-3 diesel; 5,400 hp(m) *(3.97 MW)* sustained (centre shaft); 3 shafts
Speed, knots: 32. **Range, miles:** 4,870 at 10 kt; 450 at 29 kt
Complement: 98 (8 officers)

Guns: 4—3 in *(76 mm)*/60 (2 twin) ❶; 90 rds/min to 15 km *(8 n miles)*; weight of shell 6.8 kg.
Torpedoes: 5—16 in *(400 mm)* (quin) tubes ❷. SAET-40; active/passive homing to 10 km *(5.5 n miles)* at 30 kt; warhead 100 kg.
A/S mortars: 4 RBU 2500 16-tubed trainable ❸; range 2,500 m; warhead 21 kg.
Depth charges: 2 racks.
Mines: Can carry 22.
Radars: Surface search: Slim Net ❹; E/F-band.
Navigation: Don 2; I-band.
Fire control: Hawk Screech ❺; I-band.
IFF: High Pole B. 2 Square Head.
Sonars: Herkules; hull-mounted; active search and attack; high frequency.

Programmes: Transferred by the USSR in July 1975 and March 1975.
Operational: Based at Tartous. *2-508* in dock in mid-1998 and still there in early 2000. Both in a poor state but still in commission.

UPDATED

PETYA 1-508   *(Scale 1 : 900), Ian Sturton*

LAND-BASED MARITIME AIRCRAFT

Numbers/Type: 11/2 Mil Mi-14P Haze A/C.
Operational speed: 124 kt *(230 km/h)*.
Service ceiling: 15,000 ft *(4,570 m)*.
Range: 432 n miles *(800 km)*.
Role/Weapon systems: Medium-range ASW helicopter. Sensors: Short Horn search radar, dipping sonar, MAD, sonobuoys. Weapons: ASW; internally stored torpedoes, depth mines and bombs.
VERIFIED

Numbers/Type: 2 Kamov Ka-28 Helix.
Operational speed: 135 kt *(250 km/h)*.
Service ceiling: 19,685 ft *(6,000 m)*.
Range: 432 n miles *(800 km)*.
Role/Weapon systems: ASW helicopter. Delivered in February 1990. Sensors: Splash Drop search radar, dipping sonar, sonobuoys, MAD, ECM. Weapons: ASW; 3 torpedoes, depth bombs, mines.
VERIFIED

PATROL FORCES

8 OSA II CLASS (FAST ATTACK CRAFT—MISSILE) (PCFG)

33-40

Displacement, tons: 245 full load
Dimensions, feet (metres): 126.6 × 24.9 × 8.8 *(38.6 × 7.6 × 2.7)*
Main machinery: 3 Type M 504 diesels; 10,800 hp(m) *(9.94 MW)* sustained; 3 shafts
Speed, knots: 37. **Range, miles:** 500 at 35 kt
Complement: 25 (3 officers)

Missiles: SSM: 4 SS-N-2C; active radar or IR homing to 83 km *(43 n miles)* at 0.9 Mach; warhead 513 kg; sea-skimmer at end of run.
Guns: 4—30 mm/65 (2 twin); 500 rds/min to 5 km *(2.7 n miles)*; weight of shell 0.54 kg.
Countermeasures: Decoys: PK 16 chaff launcher.
Radars: Surface search: Square Tie; I-band.
Fire control: Drum Tilt; H/I-band.
IFF: 2 Square Head. High Pole A or B.

Programmes: Delivered: October 1979 (two), November 1979 (two), August 1982 (one), September 1982 (one) and May 1984 (two). Others have already been deleted.
Structure: Two are modified (Nos 39 and 40).
Operational: Based at Latakia. At least four are still fully operational. Two Osa Is (31 and 32) at Tartous are non-operational.
UPDATED

OSA II 38   6/1998 / 0050214

8 ZHUK (GRIF) (TYPE 1400M) CLASS (COASTAL PATROL CRAFT) (PC)

1-8   2-8   3-8   4-8   5-8   6-8   7-8   8-8

Displacement, tons: 39 full load
Dimensions, feet (metres): 78.7 × 16.4 × 3.9 *(24 × 5 × 1.2)*
Main machinery: 2 Type M 401B diesels; 2,200 hp(m) *(1.6 MW)* sustained; 2 shafts
Speed, knots: 30. **Range, miles:** 1,100 at 15 kt
Complement: 11 (3 officers)
Guns: 4—14.5 mm (2 twin) MGs.
Radars: Surface search: Spin Trough; I-band.

Comment: Three transferred from USSR in August 1981, three on 25 December 1984 and two more in the late 1980s. All based at Tartous and some are non-operational.
VERIFIED

ZHUK 5-8   6/1998 / 0050215

AMPHIBIOUS FORCES

3 POLNOCHNY B CLASS (TYPE 771) (LSM)

1-114   2-114   3-114

Displacement, tons: 760 standard; 834 full load
Dimensions, feet (metres): 246.1 × 31.5 × 7.5 *(75 × 9.6 × 2.3)*
Main machinery: 2 Kolomna Type 40-D diesels; 4,400 hp(m) *(3.2 MW)* sustained; 2 shafts
Speed, knots: 19. **Range, miles:** 1,500 at 15 kt
Complement: 40
Military lift: 180 troops; 350 tons cargo
Guns: 4—30 mm/65 (2 twin); 500 rds/min to 5 km *(2.7 n miles)*; weight of shell 0.54 kg.
2—140 mm rocket launchers; 18 barrels per launcher; range 9 km *(5 n miles)*.
Radars: Surface search: Spin Trough; I-band.
Fire control: Drum Tilt; H/I-band.

Comment: Built at Northern Shipyard, Gdansk. First transferred from USSR January 1984, two in February 1985 from Black Sea. All based at Tartous and still active.
VERIFIED

POLNOCHNY B (Russian colours)   1988

MINE WARFARE FORCES

1 NATYA (TYPE 266M) CLASS (MSC/AGOR)

642

Displacement, tons: 804 full load
Dimensions, feet (metres): 200.1 × 33.5 × 10.8 *(61 × 10.2 × 3)*
Main machinery: 2 Type 504 diesels; 5,000 hp(m) *(3.67 MW)* sustained; 2 shafts
Speed, knots: 16. **Range, miles:** 3,000 at 12 kt
Complement: 65
Missiles: SAM: 2 SA-N-5 Grail quad launchers; manual aiming; IR homing to 6 km *(3.2 n miles)* at 1.5 Mach; altitude to 2,500 m *(8,000 ft)*; warhead 1.5 kg; 16 missiles.
Guns: 4—30 mm/65 (2 twin) can be fitted.
Radars: Surface search: Don 2; I-band.
Fire control: Drum Tilt; H/I-band.

Comment: Arrived in Tartous from USSR in January 1985. Has had sweeping gear and guns removed and converted to serve as an AGOR. Painted white. Based at Latakia in reasonable condition.
UPDATED

NATYA 642   6/1996 * / 0080764

1 T 43 CLASS (MINESWEEPER—OCEAN) (MSO/PG)

504

Displacement, tons: 580 full load
Dimensions, feet (metres): 196.8 × 27.6 × 6.9 *(60 × 8.4 × 2.1)*
Main machinery: 2 Kolomna Type 9-D-8 diesels; 2,000 hp(m) *(1.47 MW)* sustained; 2 shafts
Speed, knots: 15. **Range, miles:** 3,000 at 10 kt
Complement: 65
Guns: 4—37 mm/63 (2 twin). 2—14.5 mm MGs (twin).
Mines: Can carry 16.
Radars: Surface search: Ball End; E/F-band.
Navigation: Don 2; I-band.
IFF: Square Head. High Pole A.
Sonars: Stag Ear (MG 11); hull-mounted; active minehunting; high frequency.

Comment: Two transferred from USSR in 1959. The second of this class was sunk in the Israeli October 1973 war. Refurbished in 1995 and used as a patrol ship. Based at Latakia and of doubtful operational status. Reported as being named *Hittin* but this is incorrect.
UPDATED

T 43 504   4/1996 * / 0080765

1 SONYA (TYPE 1265) CLASS (MSC)

532

Displacement, tons: 450 full load
Dimensions, feet (metres): 157.4 × 28.9 × 6.6 *(48 × 8.8 × 2)*
Main machinery: 2 Kolomna Type 9-D-8 diesels; 2,000 hp(m) *(1.47 MW)* sustained; 2 shafts
Speed, knots: 15. **Range, miles:** 3,000 at 10 kt
Complement: 43
Guns: 2—30 mm/65 (twin) or 2—30 mm/65 AK 630. 2—25 mm/80 (twin).
Mines: 8.
Radars: Surface search: Don 2; I-band.
IFF: 2 Square Head. 1 High Pole B.
Sonars: MG 69; hull-mounted; active; high frequency.

Comment: Wooden hull. Made passage from USSR in December 1985, transferred January 1986. Based at Tartous.

VERIFIED

SONYA (Russian colours)   *4/1992, van Ginderen Collection*

3 YEVGENYA CLASS (MINESWEEPERS—INSHORE) (MSI/PC)

6-507   7-507   8-507

Displacement, tons: 77 standard; 90 full load
Dimensions, feet (metres): 80.7 × 18 × 4.9 *(24.6 × 5.5 × 1.5)*
Main machinery: 2 Type 3-D-12 diesels; 600 hp(m) *(444 kW)*; 2 shafts
Speed, knots: 11. **Range, miles:** 300 at 10 kt
Complement: 10
Guns: 2—14.5 mm (twin) MGs (first pair). 2—25 mm/80 (twin) (second pair).
Radars: Surface search: Spin Trough; I-band.
IFF: High Pole.
Sonars: MG-7; stern-mounted VDS; active; high frequency.

Comment: First transferred from USSR 1978, two in 1985 and two in 1986. Second pair by Roflow from Baltic in February 1985 being new construction with tripod mast. All based at Tartous. Two others have been deleted.

VERIFIED

YEVGENYA (Russian colours)   *1991*

AUXILIARIES

1 SEKSTAN CLASS (YDG)

SR 153

Displacement, tons: 400 full load
Dimensions, feet (metres): 133.8 × 30.5 × 14.1 *(40.8 × 9.3 × 4.3)*
Main machinery: 1 diesel; 400 hp(m) *(2.94 MW)*; 1 shaft
Speed, knots: 11. **Range, miles:** 1,000 at 11 kt
Complement: 24
Cargo capacity: 115 tons

Comment: Initially belonged to and was used by the Soviet Mediterranean Squadron. Transferred to the Syrian Navy in December 1983. Wooden construction. The upper hull is slowly decaying. Based at Latakia.

UPDATED

SR 153   *4/1996* / 0080766*

1 POLUCHAT CLASS (YDT)

Displacement, tons: 100 full load
Dimensions, feet (metres): 97.1 × 19 × 4.8 *(29.6 × 5.8 × 1.5)*
Main machinery: 2 Type M 50 diesels; 2,200 hp(m) *(1.6 MW)* sustained; 2 shafts
Speed, knots: 20. **Range, miles:** 1,500 at 10 kt
Complement: 15
Guns: 2—14.5 mm (twin) MGs.
Radars: Surface search: Spin Trough; I-band.

Comment: Used as divers' base-ship. Transferred from USSR September 1967. Based at Al-Mina-al-Bayda.

VERIFIED

POLUCHAT (Russian colours)   *1991, van Ginderen Collection*

TRAINING SHIPS

AL ASSAD

Displacement, tons: 3,500 full load
Dimensions, feet (metres): 344.5 × 56.4 × 13.1 *(105 × 17.2 × 4)*
Main machinery: 2 Zgoda-Sulzer 6ZL40/48 diesels; 8,700 hp(m) *(6.4 MW)*; 2 shafts; bow thruster
Speed, knots: 16. **Range, miles:** 4,500 at 15 kt
Complement: 56 plus 140 cadets
Radars: Navigation: E/F- and I-band.

Comment: Built in Polnochny Shipyard, Gdansk and launched 18 February 1987. Delivered in late 1988. Ro-ro design used as a naval training ship. Unarmed but has minelaying potential. Based at Latakia and occasionally deploys on cruises.

UPDATED

AL ASSAD   *6/1999*, A Campanera i Rovira / 0080767*

AL ASSAD   *6/1999*, Camil Busquets i Vilanova / 0084411*

TAIWAN
REPUBLIC OF CHINA

Headquarters Appointments

Commander-in-Chief:
   Admiral Chieh Li
Deputy Commander-in-Chief:
   Vice Admiral Fang-Hsiang Shen
Commandant of Marine Corps:
   Lieutenant General Bon Chih Chen
Director of Logistics:
   Vice Admiral Feng-Shiang Jin
Commander of ASW:
   Vice Admiral Chi-Chiang Wong
Director of Political Warfare:
   Vice Admiral Hai-Ping Chang

Senior Flag Officers

Fleet Commander:
   Vice Admiral Chai-Kwei Hu
Director of Logistics:
   Vice Admiral Ke-Chiang Gan
Commander of East Command:
   Vice Admiral Chi-Chiang Wang

Personnel

(a) 2000: 31,500 (and 32,500 reserves) in Navy, 15,000 (and 35,000 reserves) in Marine Corps
(b) 2 years' conscript service

Bases

Tsoying: HQ First Naval District (Southern Taiwan, Pratas and Spratly). Main Base, HQ of Fleet Command, Naval Aviation Group and Marine Corps. Base of southern patrol and transport squadrons. Officers and ratings training, Naval Academy, Naval shipyard.
Kaohsiung; Naval shipyard.
Makung (Pescadores): HQ Second Naval District (Pescadores, Quemoy and Wu Ch'iu). Base for attack squadrons. Naval shipyard and training facilities.
Keelung: HQ Third Naval District (Northern Taiwan and Matsu group). Base of northern patrol and transport squadrons. Naval shipyard.
Hualien: Naval Aviation Command.
Suao: East Coast Command, submarine depot and shipyard.
Minor bases at Hualien, Tamshui, Hsinchu, Wuchi and Anping.
Building: Taitung.

Organisation

1. Fleet Command:
124th Attack squadron, based at Tsoying
131st Patrol squadron, based at Keelung
142nd Support squadron, based at Kaohsiung
146th Attack squadron, based at Pescadores
151st Amphibious squadron, based at Tsoying
168th Patrol squadron, based at Suao
192nd Mine Warfare squadron, based at Tsoying
256th Submarine Unit, based at Tsoying.

2. Naval Aviation Command: Two helicopter squadrons and two S-2E/T Tracker squadrons, the latter supported logistically from the ROCAF. Land bases include Tsoying, Hualien, Hsinchu and Pintung.

Coast Defence

The land-based SSM command has six squadrons equipped with Hsiung-Feng II SSM at Tonying Island of the Matsu Group, Siyu Island of the Pescadores, Shiao Liuchiu off Kaohsiung, north of Keelung harbour, Tsoying naval base and Hualien. The ROCMC deploy eight SAM Platoons, equipped with Chaparral SAM quad-launchers, to the offshore island of Wuchiu, and Pratas islets in the South China Sea. There are also a number of 127 mm guns.

Marine Corps

Reduced to two brigades by mid-2000 supported by one amphibious regiment and one logistics regiment. Equipped with M-116, M-733, LARC-5, LVTP5 personnel carriers and LVTH6 armour tractors. Based at Tsoying and in southern Taiwan with a detachment at Pratas in the South China Sea. Spratly detachment provided by the Coast Guard from 1 January 2000.

Coast Guard

Formerly the Maritime Security Police but name changed on 1 January 2000. Comes under the Minister of the Interior but its numerous patrol boats are integrated with the Navy for operational purposes.

Pennant Numbers

Pennant numbers were changed in early 1987.

Mercantile Marine

Lloyd's Register of Shipping:
   684 vessels of 5,371,388 tons gross

Strength of the Fleet

Type	Active (Reserve)	Building/ Transfer (Planned)
Submarines	4	(6)
Destroyers	11	(4)
Frigates	21	1
Corvettes	—	(10)
Fast Attack Craft (Missile)	48	(29)
Large Patrol Craft	15	4
Ocean Minesweepers	4	—
Coastal Minesweepers/Hunters	8	(2)
LSD	2	1
Landing Ships (LST and LSM)	17	4
LCUs	18	—
Survey Ships	1	—
Combat Support Ships	1	—
Transports	4	3
Salvage Ships	3	1
Support Tankers	2	—
Customs	10+	—

DELETIONS

Destroyers

1998   *Tsi Yang* (930), *Lai Yang* (920)
1999   *Yue Yang* (905), *Dang Yan* (911), *Kuei Yang* (908), *Chin Yang* (909), *Huei Yang* (906), *Han Yang* (915), *An Yang* (918), *Kun Yang* (919)
2000   *Loa Yang* (914)

Corvettes

1997   *Yu Shan* (832), *Shou Shan* (837), *Tai Shan* (838)
1998   *Ping Ching* (870), *Wu Sheng* (866), *Chu Yung* (867)

Amphibious Forces

1997   *Chung Hsing, Chung Yung, Chung Fu, Ho Teng, Ho Chang*
1998   *Ho Feng* (civilian)
1999   *Cheng Hai, Ho Tsung*

Auxiliaries

1998   *Yu Tai, Tai Wu, Wan Shou, Ta Teng, Ta Peng* (old)
1999   *Ling Yuen*

PENNANT LIST

Submarines

791	Hai Shih
792	Hai Bao
793	Hai Lung
794	Hai Hu

Destroyers

907	Fu Yang
912	Chien Yang
917	Nan Yang
921	Liao Yang
923	Shen Yang
924	Kai Yang
925	Te Yang
926	Shuei Yang
927	Yun Yang
928	Chen Yang
929	Shao Yang

Frigates

932	Chin Yang
933	Fong Yang
934	Feng Yang
935	Yen Yang
936	Hae Yang
937	Hwai Yang
938	Ning Yang
939	Yi Yang
1101	Cheng Kung
1103	Cheng Ho
1105	Chi Kuang
1106	Yueh Fei
1107	Tzu-I
1108	Pan Chao
1110	Tien Tan (bldg)
1109	Chang Chien
1202	Kang Ding
1203	Si Ning
1205	Kun Ming
1206	Di Hua
1207	Wu Chang
1208	Chen Te

Patrol Forces

601	Lung Chiang
602	Sui Chang
603	Jin Chiang
605	Tan Chiang
606	Hsin Chiang
607	Fong Chiang
608	Tseng Chiang
615	—
609	Kao Chiang
610	Hsiang Chiang
611	Tsi Chiang
612	Po Chiang
613	Chan Chiang
615	Chu Chiang

Amphibious Forces

191	Chung Cheng
193	Shiu Hai
201	Chung Hai
205	Chung Chien
208	Chung Shun
216	Chung Kuang
217	Chung Chao
219 (LCC 1)	Kao Hsiung
221	Chung Chuan
226	Chung Chih
227	Chung Ming
230	Chung Pang
231	Chung Yeh
232	Chung Ho
233	Chung Ping
341	Mei Chin
347	Mei Sung
353	Mei Ping
356	Mei Lo
401	Ho Chi
402	Ho Huei
403	Ho Yao
406	Ho Chao
481	Ho Shun
484	Ho Chung
488	Ho Shan
489	Ho Chuan
490	Ho Seng

491	Ho Meng
492	Ho Mou
493	Ho Shou
494	Ho Chun
495	Ho Yung
496	Ho Chien
SB 1	Ho Chie
SB 2	Ho Ten

Mine Warfare Forces

158	Yung Chuan
162	Yung Fu
163	Yung Ching
165	Yung Chung
1301	Yung Feng
1302	Yung Chia
1303	Yung Ting
1305	Yung Shun
1306	Yung Yang
1307	Yung Tzu
1308	Yung Ku
1309	Yung Teh

Auxiliaries and Survey Ships

507	Hsin Lung
515	Lung Chuan
523	Wan An
524	Yuen Feng
525	Wu Kang
526	Hsin Kang
530	Wu Yi
552	Ta Hu
1601	Ta Kuan

Tugs

548	Ta Tung
549	Ta Peng
550	Ta De
551	Ta Wan
553	Ta Han
554	Ta Kang
555	Ta Fung
563	Ta Tai

SUBMARINES

Notes: (1) There are plans to acquire up to six patrol submarines, down in 1997 from the originally planned twelve. In January 1993 the export of German-built hulls was blocked by the Federal Security Council. France has been similarly discouraged although DCN has tried to sell the 'Agosta' class. In February 1992 the Netherlands Government also refused permission to build in Dutch shipyards. The assembly under US supervision of a German S 209 design is the latest proposal, with the first one to be in service by 2005.

(2) A German-built midget submarine was acquired in 1984 for research. Named *Sea Horse* it has a 52 ton dived displacement, 14.5 × 2.3 m, diesel-electric propulsion generating 80 kW, speed 5 kt and a range of 400 n miles surfaced and 35 n miles dived. Crew of four plus two divers. A second of class due in 1987 was cancelled by Germany because of protests from China.

2 HAI LUNG CLASS (SSK)

Name	No	Builders	Laid down	Launched	Commissioned
HAI LUNG	793	Wilton Fijenoord, Netherlands	Dec 1982	6 Oct 1986	9 Oct 1987
HAI HU	794	Wilton Fijenoord, Netherlands	Dec 1982	20 Dec 1986	9 Apr 1988

Displacement, tons: 2,376 surfaced; 2,660 dived
Dimensions, feet (metres): 219.6 × 27.6 × 22
(66.9 × 8.4 × 6.7)
Main machinery: Diesel-electric; 3 Bronswerk D-RUB 215-12 diesels; 4,050 hp(m) *(3 MW)*; 3 alternators; 2.7 MW; 1 Holec motor; 5,100 hp(m) *(3.74 MW)*; 1 shaft
Speed, knots: 12 surfaced; 20 dived
Range, miles: 10,000 at 9 kt surfaced
Complement: 67 (8 officers)

Torpedoes: 6—21 in *(533 mm)* bow tubes. 20 AEG SUT; dual purpose; wire-guided; active/passive homing to 12 km *(6.6 n miles)* at 35 kt; warhead 250 kg.
Countermeasures: ESM: Argo AR 700SF and Elbit Timnex 4CH (V)2; intercept.
Weapons control: Sinbads M TFCS.
Radars: Surface search: Signaal ZW06; I-band.
Sonars: Signaal SIASS-Z; hull-mounted; passive/active intercept search and attack; low/medium frequency.
Fitted for but not with towed passive array.

Programmes: Order signed with Wilton Fijenoord in September 1981 for these submarines with variations from the standard Netherlands Zwaardvis design. Construction was delayed by the financial difficulties of the builders but was resumed in 1983. Sea trials of *Hai Lung* in March 1987 and *Hai Hu* in January 1988 and both submarines were shipped out on board a heavy dock vessel. The names mean *Sea Dragon* and *Sea Tiger*.

HAI HU   6/1996* / 0080768

Structure: The four horns on the forward casing are Signaal sonar intercept transducers. Torpedoes manufactured under licence in Indonesia.

Operational: Hsiung Feng II submerged launch SSMs are planned to be part of the weapons load and a torpedo tube launched version is being developed, although no recent progress has been reported.   **UPDATED**

2 GUPPY II CLASS (SS)

Name	No	Builders	Laid down	Launched	Commissioned
HAI SHIH (ex-*Cutlass* SS 478)	791 (ex-SS 91)	Portsmouth Navy Yard	22 July 1944	5 Nov 1944	17 Mar 1945
HAI BAO (ex-*Tusk* SS 426)	792 (ex-SS 92)	Federal SB & DD Co, Kearney, New Jersey	23 Aug 1943	8 July 1945	11 Apr 1946

Displacement, tons: 1,870 standard; 2,420 dived
Dimensions, feet (metres): 307.5 × 27.2 × 18
(93.7 × 8.3 × 5.5)
Main machinery: Diesel-electric; 3 Fairbanks-Morse diesels; 4,500 hp *(3.3 MW)*; 2 Elliott motors; 5,400 hp *(4 MW)*; 2 shafts
Speed, knots: 18 surfaced; 15 dived
Range, miles: 8,000 at 12 kt surfaced
Complement: 75 (7 officers)

Torpedoes: 10—21 in *(533 mm)* (6 fwd, 4 aft) tubes. AEG SUT; active/passive homing to 12 km *(6.5 n miles)* at 35 kt; 28 km *(15 n miles)* at 23 kt; warhead 250 kg.
Countermeasures: ESM: WLR-1/3; radar warning.
Radars: Surface search: US SS 2; I-band.
Sonars: EDO BQR 2B; hull-mounted; passive search and attack; medium frequency.
Raytheon/EDO BQS 4C; adds active capability to BQR 2B.
Thomson Sintra DUUG 1B; passive ranging.

Programmes: Originally fleet-type submarines of the US Navy's 'Tench' class; extensively modernised under the Guppy II programme. *Hai Shih* transferred in April 1973 and *Hai Bao* in October the same year.
Structure: After 55 years in service diving depth is very limited.
Operational: Used for anti-submarine training exercises. Kept in service because of difficulty in buying replacements, but effectiveness is questionable.   **UPDATED**

HAI SHIH   8/1990, DTM / 0053450

DESTROYERS

Notes: (1) Fully operational numbers of destroyers, frigates, corvettes and PGGs are restricted to a total of 48. As a new ship commissions, one of the older ships is paid off.
(2) Negotiations are in hand for the acquisition of four *Arleigh Burke* Aegis destroyers to be in service after 2006. A budget may be allocated in 2000. To be known as the 'Shentun' class.

3 GEARING (WU CHIN I and II CONVERSIONS) (FRAM I and II) CLASS (DDG)

Name	No	Builders	Laid down	Launched	Commissioned
FU YANG (ex-*Ernest G Small* DD 838) (FRAM II)	907	Bath Iron Works Corporation	30 Jan 1945	14 June 1945	21 Aug 1945
KAI YANG (ex-*Richard B Anderson* DD 786)	924	Todd Pacific SY, Seattle, WA	1 Dec 1944	7 July 1945	26 Oct 1945
SHUEI YANG (ex-*Hawkins* DD 873)	926	Consolidated Steel Corporation	14 May 1944	7 Oct 1944	10 Feb 1945

Displacement, tons: 2,425 standard; 3,500 approx full load
Dimensions, feet (metres): 390.5 × 41.2 × 19
(119 × 12.6 × 5.8)
Main machinery: 4 Babcock & Wilcox boilers; 600 psi *(43.3 kg/cm²)*; 850°F *(454°C)*; 2 GE turbines; 60,000 hp *(45 MW)*; 2 shafts
Speed, knots: 32.5. **Range, miles:** 5,800 at 15 kt
Complement: 275 approx

Missiles: SSM: 5 Hsiung Feng I or II or Gabriel II ❶ (1 triple, 2 single); radar or optical guidance (HFI); inertial guidance and active radar or IR homing (HF II) to 36 km *(19.4 n miles)*; warhead 75 kg (I) or 80 km *(43.2 n miles)* (II) at 0.7 Mach (I) and 0.85 Mach (II); warhead 190 kg (II). 4 Hsiung Feng II ❷ *(Fu Yang)* (2 twin).
1 Sea Chaparral quad launcher ❸; Sidewinder missile; IR homing to 3 km *(1.6 n miles)* supersonic; warhead 5 kg; 16 reloads.
A/S: Honeywell ASROC Mk 112 octuple launcher ❹ *(Shuei Yang)*; inertial guidance to 1.6-10 km *(1-5.4 n miles)*; payload Mk 46 torpedo.
Guns: 2 or 4 USN 5 in *(127 mm)*/38 (1 or 2 twin) Mk 38 ❺; 15 rds/min to 17 km *(9.3 n miles)*; weight of shell 25 kg.
1 OTO Melara 3 in *(76 mm)*/62 ❻; 85 rds/min to 16 km *(8.7 n miles)*; weight of shell 6 kg.
2 or 4 Bofors 40 mm/70 (2 single or 2 twin) ❼. 4 or 6—12.7 mm MGs.
Torpedoes: 6—324 mm US Mk 32 (2 triple) tubes ❽. Honeywell Mk 46; anti-submarine; active/passive homing to 11 km *(5.9 n miles)* at 40 kt; warhead 44 kg.
Countermeasures: Decoys: 4 Kung Fen 6 16-tubed chaff launchers (mounted abreast after funnel and on the quarterdeck).
Mk T-6 Fanfare torpedo decoy.
ESM/ECM: ULQ-6 jammers and WLR-1 and WLR-3 passive warning receivers or Chang Feng II combined intercept and jammers.
Combat data systems: Elbit; action data automation (Wu Chin II). SATCOM in some.
Weapons control: Honeywell H 930 with 2 RCA HR 76 directors for SSM. Mk 37 GFCS with Kollmorgen electro-optical sight ❾ for 127 mm or IAI Galileo optronic director Mk 114 system (for ASROC).
Radars: Air search: Lockheed SPS-40 ❿; E/F-band or Westinghouse SPS-29 ⓫; B/C-band.
Surface search: Raytheon SPS-10/SPS-58 ⓬; G-band or Israeli Elta 1040 ⓭ (Wu Chin II).
Fire control: Western Electric Mk 25 ⓮ or Selenia RTN-10X ⓯ (Wu Chin II); I/J-band.
2 RCA HR 76 ⓰; I/J-band (for SSM and guns).
Tacan: SRN 15.
Sonars: Atlas Elektronik DSQS-21CZ *(Fu Yang)* or Raytheon SQS-23H; hull-mounted; active search and attack; medium frequency.

Helicopters: 1 Hughes MD 500 ⓱.

Programmes: *Fu Yang* transferred from the USA 5 February 1971; *Kai Yang*, 10 June 1977 by sale; *Shuei Yang*, 10 March 1978.

Modernisation: (a) Wu Chin I: Installation of SSM and Honeywell H 930 Mod 1 fire-control system with twin lattice masts topped by HR 76 directors in *Fu Yang* and *Shuei Yang*. Developed by Honeywell and Chung-Shan Institute. Can track eight targets simultaneously and attack three with a 20 second response time.
(b) Wu Chin II: *Kai Yang* separately upgraded with the Elbit Naval Tactical Command and Control System. Developed by IAI, Israel and Chung-Shan Institute. Can track up to 12 targets simultaneously and attack three with a 20 second response time. Each ship also received an OTO Melara 76 mm gun, two

Bofors 40 mm/70 single mounts, a quad Sea Chaparral SAM launcher and five (two single and one triple) Gabriel II or Hsiung Feng missile launchers. An RTN-10X on a lattice mast and an Officine Galileo optronic director replaced the Mk 37 fire-control director on the bridge. The SPS-10 surface search radar was replaced by an Elta EL-1040. *Fu Yang* has Hsiung Feng II SSM.
Operational: *Fu Yang* is the Fleet Flagship. Two others paid off in 1998, and one more in 1999. *Shuei Yang* is expected to go in 2000.

UPDATED

FU YANG
(Scale 1 : 1,200), Ian Sturton / 0050218

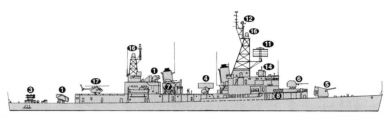

SHUEI YANG
(Scale 1 : 1,200), Ian Sturton / 0080769

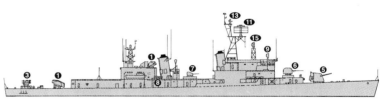

KAI YANG
(Scale 1 : 1,200), Ian Sturton / 0080770

SHUEI YANG
12/1994, C Chung / 0050220

7 GEARING (WU CHIN III CONVERSION) (FRAM I) CLASS (DD)

Name	No	Builders	Laid down		Launched		Commissioned	
CHIEN YANG (ex-*James E Kyes* DD 787)	912	Todd Pacific SY, Seattle, WA	27 Dec	1944	4 Aug	1945	8 Feb	1946
LIAO YANG (ex-*Hanson* DD 832)	921	Bath Iron Works Corporation	7 Oct	1944	11 Mar	1945	11 May	1945
SHAO YANG (ex-*Hollister* DD 788)	929	Todd Pacific SY, Seattle, WA	18 Jan	1945	9 Oct	1945	26 Mar	1946
TE YANG (ex-*Sarsfield* DD 837)	925	Bath Iron Works Corporation	15 Jan	1945	27 May	1945	31 July	1945
CHEN YANG (ex-*Johnston* DD 821)	928	Consolidated Steel Corporation	6 May	1945	19 Oct	1945	10 Oct	1946
SHEN YANG (ex-*Power* DD 839)	923	Bath Iron Works Corporation	26 Feb	1945	30 June	1945	13 Sep	1945
YUN YANG (ex-*Hamner* DD 718)	927	Federal SB and DD Co	5 Apr	1945	24 Nov	1945	11 July	1946

Displacement, tons: 2,425 standard; 3,540 full load
Dimensions, feet (metres): 390.5 × 41.2 × 19
(119 × 12.6 × 5.8)
Main machinery: 4 Babcock & Wilcox boilers; 600 psi *(43.3 kg/ cm²)*; 850°F *(454°C)*; 2 GE turbines; 60,000 hp *(45 MW)*; 2 shafts
Speed, knots: 30. **Range, miles:** 6,080 at 15 kt
Complement: 275 approx

Missiles: SSM: 4 Hsiung Feng II (quad) ❶; active radar/IR homing to 80 km *(43.2 n miles)* at 0.85 Mach; warhead 190 kg.
SAM: 10 General Dynamics Standard SM1-MR (2 triple ❷; 2 twin ❸); command guidance; semi-active radar homing to 46 km *(25 n miles)* at 2 Mach.
A/S: Honeywell ASROC Mk 112 octuple launcher ❹; inertial guidance to 1.6-10 km *(1-5.4 n miles)*; payload Mk 46 torpedo.
Guns: 1 OTO Melara 3 in *(76 mm)*/62 ❺; 85 rds/min to 16 km *(8.7 n miles)*; weight of shell 6 kg.
1 GE/GD 20 mm Vulcan Phalanx Block 1 6-barrelled Mk 15 ❻; 3,000 rds/min combined to 1.5 km.
2 Bofors 40 mm/70 ❼. 4 or 6—12.7 mm MGs.
Torpedoes: 6—324 mm US Mk 32 (2 triple) tubes ❽. Honeywell Mk 46, anti-submarine; active/passive homing to 11 km *(5.9 n miles)* at 40 kt; warhead 44 kg. Some Mk 44s are still in service.
Countermeasures: Decoys: 4 Kung Fen 6 16-tubed chaff launchers ❾.
Mk T-6 Fanfare torpedo decoy.
ESM/ECM: Chang Feng III (Hughes SLQ-17/SLQ-31) intercept and jammers.
Combat data systems: Ta Chen tactical datalink.
Weapons control: Honeywell H 930 MFCS Mk 114 system (for ASROC).
Radars: Air search: Signaal DA08 (with DA05 aerial) ❿; E/F-band.
Surface search: Raytheon SPS-58 ⓫; G/I-band.
Fire control: Signaal STIR ⓬; I/J-band (for Standard and 76 mm).
Westinghouse W-160 ⓭; I-band (for Bofors).
Navigation: I-band.
Tacan: SRN 15.
Sonars: Raytheon SQS-23H; hull-mounted; active search and attack; medium frequency.

Helicopters: 1 McDonnell Douglas MD 500 ⓮.

Programmes: *Chien Yang* transferred 18 April 1973; *Liao Yang*, 18 April 1973; *Te Yang* and *Shen Yang*, 1 October 1977 by sale; *Yun Yang*, December 1980; *Chen Yang* by sale 27 February 1981; *Shao Yang* by sale 3 March 1983. There has been some confusion over the English translation of some names. These are now correct.
Modernisation: All ships converted to area air defence ships under the Wu Chin III programme. This upgrade involved the installation of the H 930 Modular Combat System (MCS) with a Signaal DA08 air search radar (employing a lightweight DA05 antenna) and a Signaal STIR missile control radar directing 10 box-launched Standard SM-1 surface-to-air missiles (two twin in 'B' position, two triple facing either beam aft). The system can track 24 targets simultaneously and attack four with an 8 second response time. An OTO Melara 76 mm is fitted to 'A' position, one Bofors 40 mm/70 is mounted forward of the

LIAO YANG   *(Scale 1 : 1,200), Ian Sturton*

CHEN YANG   *11/1998*, C Chung /* 0080771

seaboat on the starboard side, one abaft the ASROC magazine on the port side and a Mk 15 Block 1 Phalanx CIWS is aft between two banks of Standard launchers. A Westinghouse W-160 is mounted on a lattice mast on the hangar to control the Bofors. The amidships ASROC launcher is retained, its Mk 114 fire-control system is integrated with the H 930 MCS via a digital-analogue interface. The SQS-23 sonar has also been upgraded to the H standard using a Raytheon solid-state transmitter. The Chang Feng III EW system was developed jointly by Taiwan's Chung-Shan Institute of Science and Technology (CSIST) with the assistance of Hughes. The Chang Feng III employs phased-array antennas which resemble those of the Hughes SLQ-17, it is capable of both deception and noise jamming. An eighth ship, *Lao Yang*, was to have been given the same conversion but missed the programme after a grounding incident in 1987 and has since been deleted. Ta Chen datalink fitted from 1994. Four Hsiung Feng II SSM launchers (quad) are fitted aft of the ASROC launcher.

UPDATED

SHAO YANG   *6/1994*, R N Lane /* 0080772

1 ALLEN M SUMNER CLASS (DDG)

Name	No
NAN YANG (ex-*Thomason* DD 760)	917

Builders	Laid down	Launched	Commissioned
Bethlehem Steel, San Francisco, CA	21 Nov 1944	30 Sep 1944	11 Oct 1945

Displacement, tons: 2,100 standard; 3,050 full load
Dimensions, feet (metres): 376.5 × 39.5 × 18
  (114.8 × 12 × 5.5)
Main machinery: 4 Babcock & Wilcox boilers; 600 psi *(43.3 kg/
  cm²)*; 850°F *(454°C)*; 2 GE/Allis Chalmers/Westinghouse
  turbines; 60,000 hp *(45 MW)*; 2 shafts
Speed, knots: 35. **Range, miles:** 3,750 at 14 kt
Complement: 270

Missiles: SSM: 5 Hsiung Feng I (1 triple ❶ and 2 single ❷); radar
  or optical guidance to 36 km *(19.4 n miles)* at 0.7 Mach;
  warhead 75 kg.
  SAM: 1 Sea Chaparral quad launcher ❸; Sidewinder missile; IR
  homing to 3 km *(1.6 n miles)* supersonic; warhead 5 kg; 16
  reloads.
Guns: 1 or 2 USN 5 in *(127 mm)*/38 Mk 30 ❹; 15 rds/min to
  17 km *(9.3 n miles)*; weight of shell 25 kg. Some may still have
  3—5 in *(127 mm)* instead of the 76 mm.
  1 OTO Melara 3 in *(76 mm)*/62 ❺; 85 rds/min to 16 km *(8.8 n
  miles)*; weight of shell 6 kg.
  2 Bofors 40 mm/70 (in some).
Torpedoes: 6—324 mm US Mk 32 (2 triple) tubes ❻. Honeywell
  Mk 46; anti-submarine; active/passive homing to 11 km *(5.9 n
  miles)* at 40 kt; warhead 44 kg.
A/S mortars: 2 Hedgehog Mk 10 24-tubed fixed ❼; range
  250 m; warhead 13.6 kg.
Depth charges: 1 rack.
Mines: 1 rail.
Countermeasures: Decoys: 4 Kung Fen 6 16-barrelled chaff
  launchers.
  ESM/ECM: Argo 680/681; intercept and jammer.
Weapons control: Honeywell H 930 for SSM. Mk 37 GFCS with
  Kollmorgen electro-optical sight ❽ for 127 mm.
Radars: Air search: Lockheed SPS-40 ❾; E/F-band.
  Air/surface search: Westinghouse SPS-58 ❿; D-band.
  Fire control: Two RCA HR 76 ⓫; I/J-band (for SSM and guns).
Sonars: Atlas Elektronik DSQS-21CZ; hull-mounted; active
  search and attack; medium frequency.

Helicopters: Platform for Hughes MD 500 ⓬ (in some).

Programmes: Transferred from the US in the 1970s.
Modernisation: Conversion made under the Wu Chin I
  programme.

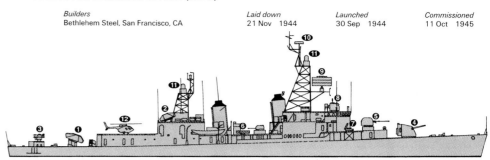

NAN YANG   *(Scale 1 : 900), Ian Sturton /* 0050216

NAN YANG   *7/1995*, L J Lamb /* 0080773

Operational: Classified as being in active service but with
reduced operational status. This means mainly used for Fishery
Protection purposes with reduced crew, and only the gun
armament is operational. This last one is the only survivor of
the 'Allen M Sumner' class.

UPDATED

FRIGATES

8 KNOX CLASS (FFG)

Name	No	Builders	Laid down		Launched		Commissioned		Recommissioned	
CHIN YANG (ex-*Robert E Peary*)	932 (ex-FF 1073)	Lockheed Shipbuilding	20 Dec	1970	23 June	1971	23 Sep	1972	6 Oct	1993
FONG YANG (ex-*Brewton*)	933 (ex-FF 1086)	Avondale Shipyards	2 Oct	1970	24 July	1971	8 July	1972	6 Oct	1993
FENG YANG (ex-*Kirk*)	934 (ex-FF 1087)	Avondale Shipyards	4 Dec	1970	25 Sep	1971	9 Sep	1972	6 Oct	1993
LAN YANG (ex-*Joseph Hewes*)	935 (ex-FF 1078)	Avondale Shipyards	15 May	1969	7 Mar	1970	22 Apr	1971	4 Aug	1995
HAE YANG (ex-*Cook*)	936 (ex-FF 1083)	Avondale Shipyards	20 Mar	1970	23 Jan	1971	18 Dec	1971	4 Aug	1995
HWAI YANG (ex-*Barbey*)	937 (ex-FF 1088)	Avondale Shipyards	5 Feb	1971	4 Dec	1971	11 Nov	1972	4 Aug	1995
NING YANG (ex-*Aylwin*)	938 (ex-FF 1081)	Avondale Shipyards	13 Nov	1969	29 Aug	1970	18 Sep	1971	18 Oct	1999
YI YANG (ex-*Pharris*)	939 (ex-FF 1094)	Avondale Shipyards	11 Feb	1972	16 Dec	1972	26 Jan	1974	18 Oct	1999

Displacement, tons: 3,011 standard; 3,877 (932, 935), 4,260
  (933, 934) full load
Dimensions, feet (metres): 439.6 × 46.8 × 15; 24.8 (sonar)
  (134 × 14.3 × 4.6; 7.8)
Main machinery: 2 Combustion Engineering/Babcock & Wilcox
  boilers; 1,200 psi *(84.4 kg/cm²)*; 950°F *(510°C)*; 1 turbine;
  35,000 hp *(26 MW)*; 1 shaft
Speed, knots: 27. **Range, miles:** 4,000 at 22 kt on 1 boiler
Complement: 288 (17 officers) including aircrew

Missiles: SSM: 8 McDonnell Douglas Harpoon; active radar
  homing to 130 km *(70 n miles)* at 0.9 Mach; warhead 227 kg.
A/S: Honeywell ASROC Mk 16 octuple launcher with reload
  system (has 2 cells modified to fire Harpoon) ❶; inertial
  guidance from 1.6-10 km *(1-5.4 n miles)*; payload Mk 46 Mod 5
  Neartip.
Guns: 1 FMC 5 in *(127 mm)*/54 Mk 42 Mod 9 ❷; 20-40 rds/min
  to 24 km *(13 n miles)* anti-surface; 14 km *(7.7 n miles)* anti-
  aircraft; weight of shell 32 kg.
  1 General Electric/General Dynamics 20 mm/76 6-barrelled
  Mk 15 Vulcan Phalanx ❸; 3,000 rds/min combined to 1.5 km.
  4 Type 75 20 mm.
Torpedoes: 4—324 mm Mk 32 (2 twin) fixed tubes ❹. 22
  Honeywell/Alliant Mk 46 Mod 5; anti-submarine; active/
  passive homing to 11 km *(5.9 n miles)* at 40 kt; warhead 44 kg.
  May be replaced by 2 triple tubes.

CHIN YANG   *(Scale 1 : 1,200), Ian Sturton*

Countermeasures: Decoys: 2 Loral Hycor SRBOC 6-barrelled
  fixed Mk 36 ❺; IR flares and chaff to 4 km *(2.2 n miles)*. T Mk 6
  Fanfare/SLQ-25 Nixie; torpedo decoy. Prairie Masker hull and
  blade rate noise suppression.
  ESM/ECM: SLQ-32(V)2 ❻; radar warning. Sidekick modification
  adds jammer and deception system.
Combat data systems: Link 14 receive only. Link W may be
  fitted. FFISTS (Frigate Integrated Shipboard Tactical System).
Weapons control: SWG-1A Harpoon LCS. Mk 68 GFCS. Mk 114
  ASW FCS. Mk 1 target designation system. SRQ-4 for LAMPS I.
Radars: Air search: Lockheed SPS-40B ❼; E/F-band; range
  320 km *(175 n miles)*.

Surface search: Raytheon SPS-10 or Norden SPS-67 ❽; G-band.
Navigation: Marconi LN66; I-band.
Fire control: Western Electric SPG-53A/D/F ❾; I/J-band.
Tacan: SRN 15. IFF: UPX-12.
Sonars: EDO/General Electric SQS-26CX; bow-mounted; active
  search and attack; medium frequency.
  EDO SQR-18A(V)1; passive towed array.

Helicopters: 1 SH-2F LAMPS I ❿ when available or 1 MD 500.

Programmes: *Chin Yang* leased from the USA on 2 July 1993,
  Fong Yang 23 July 1993 and *Feng Yang* 6 August 1993. *Lan
  Yang* leased 30 June 1994; *Hae Yang* 3 March 1994 and *Hwai
  Yang* 31 May 1994. The second batch were overhauled and
  upgraded by Long Beach Shipyard, California. Two more
  transferred by sale on 28 April 1998, and refitted at Denton
  Shipyard, South Carolina. One more (*Valdez* 1096) transferred
  30 September 1998 for spares possibly to be followed by two
  more (*Whipple* 1062 and *Downes* 1070) also for spares. The
  first six are to be purchased outright.
Structure: ASROC-torpedo reloading capability (note slanting
  face of bridge structure immediately behind ASROC). Four
  Mk 32 torpedo tubes are fixed in the midships structure, two to
  a side, angled out at 45°. The arrangement provides improved
  loading capability over exposed triple Mk 32 torpedo tubes. A
  4,000 lb lightweight anchor is fitted on the port side and an
  8,000 lb anchor fits into the after section of the sonar.
Operational: Seasprite helicopters are planned to be embarked
  in due course and when funds are available. All of the class are
  assigned to 168 Patrol Squadron at Suao. *Lan Yang* is the
  Flagship.

YI YANG   *9/1999*, van Ginderen Collection /* 0080777

UPDATED

7 + 1 CHENG KUNG CLASS (KWANG HUA 1 PROJECT) (FFG)

Name	No	Builders	Laid down	Launched	Commissioned
CHENG KUNG	1101	China SB Corporation, Kaohsiung	7 Jan 1990	5 Oct 1991	7 May 1993
CHENG HO	1103	China SB Corporation, Kaohsiung	21 Dec 1990	15 Oct 1992	28 Mar 1994
CHI KUANG	1105	China SB Corporation, Kaohsiung	4 Oct 1991	27 Sep 1993	4 Mar 1995
YUEH FEI	1106	China SB Corporation, Kaohsiung	5 Sep 1992	26 Aug 1994	7 Feb 1996
TZU-I	1107	China SB Corporation, Kaohsiung	7 Aug 1994	13 July 1995	9 Jan 1997
PAN CHAO	1108	China SB Corporation, Kaohsiung	25 July 1995	4 July 1996	16 Dec 1997
CHANG CHIEN	1109	China SB Corporation, Kaohsiung	4 Dec 1995	14 May 1997	1 Dec 1998
TIEN TAN	1110	China SB Corporation, Kaohsiung	Apr 2000	2002	2003

Displacement, tons: 2,750 light; 4,105 full load
Dimensions, feet (metres): 453 × 45 × 14.8; 24.5 (sonar)
  (138.1 × 13.7 × 4.5; 7.5)
Main machinery: 2 GE LM 2500 gas turbines; 41,000 hp
  (30.59 MW) sustained; 1 shaft; cp prop
  2 auxiliary retractable props; 650 hp *(484 kW)*
Speed, knots: 29. **Range, miles:** 4,500 at 20 kt
Complement: 234 (15 officers) including 19 aircrew

Missiles: SSM: 8 Hsiung Feng II ❶ (2 quad); inertial guidance;
  active radar/IR homing to 80 km *(43.2 n miles)* at 0.85 Mach;
  warhead 190 kg.
  SAM: 40 GDC Standard SM1-MR; Mk 13 launcher ❷; command
  guidance; semi-active radar homing to 46 km *(25 n miles)* at
  2 Mach.
Guns: 1 OTO Melara 76 mm/62 Mk 75 ❸; 85 rds/min to 16 km
  (8.7 n miles); weight of shell 6 kg.
  2 Bofors 40 mm/70 ❹. 3—20 mm Type 75 (on hangar roof
  when fitted).
  1 GE/GD 20 mm/76 Vulcan Phalanx 6-barrelled Mk 15 ❺;
  3,000 rds/min combined to 1.5 km.
Torpedoes: 6—324 mm Mk 32 (2 triple) tubes ❻. Honeywell/
  Alliant Mk 46 Mod 5; anti-submarine; active/passive homing
  to 11 km *(5.9 n miles)* at 40 kt; warhead 44 kg.
Countermeasures: Decoys: 4 Kung Fen 6 chaff launchers or
  locally produced version of RBOC (114 mm).
  ESM/ECM: Chang Feng IV (locally produced version of
  SLQ-32(V)2 with Sidekick); combined radar warning and
  jammers.
Combat data systems: Norden SYS-2(V)2 action data
  automation with UYK 43 computer. Ta Chen link (from *Chi
  Kuang* onwards and being backfitted).
Weapons control: Loral Mk 92 Mod 6. Mk 13 Mod 4 weapon
  direction system. Mk 114 ASW. 2 Mk 24 optical directors.
  Mk 309 TFCS.
Radars: Air search: Raytheon SPS-49(V)5 or SPS-49A (1108-9)
  ❼; C/D-band.
  Surface search: ISC Cardion SPS-55 ❽ or Raytheon Chang Bai;
  I/J-band.
  Fire control: USN UD 417 STIR ❾; I/J-band.
  Unisys Mk 92 Mod 6 ❿; I/J-band.
Sonars: Raytheon SQS-56/DE 1160P; hull-mounted; active
  search and attack; medium frequency.
  SQR-18A(V)2; passive towed array or BAe/Thomson Sintra
  ATAS active towed array (from *Chi Kuang* onwards).

Helicopters: 2 Sikorsky S-70C(M) ⓫ (only 1 embarked).

Programmes: First two ordered 8 May 1989. Named after
  Chinese generals and warriors. An eighth of class was ordered
  in late July 1999. Originally this ship was planned to be the first
  of a Flight II design, which was scrapped.

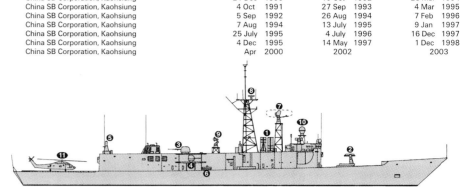

CHENG KUNG   *(Scale 1 : 1,200), Ian Sturton / 0019226*

CHENG KUNG   *1/1999*, van Ginderen Collection / 0080774*

Structure: Similar to the USS *Ingraham*. RAST helicopter
hauldown. The area between the masts had to be
strengthened to take the Hsiung Feng II missiles. Prairie
Masker hull acoustic suppression system fitted. A PDMS may
be fitted vice the 40 mm guns. RAM is a possibility.
Operational: Form the 124th Attack Squadron.   ***UPDATED***

PAN CHAO   *10/1999*, Sattler/Steele / 0080775*

6 KANG DING (LA FAYETTE) CLASS (KWANG HUA 2 PROJECT) (FFG)

Name	No	Builders	Laid down		Launched		Commissioned	
KANG DING	1202	Lorient Dockyard/Kaohsiung Shipyard	26 Aug	1993	12 Mar	1994	24 May	1996
SI NING	1203	Lorient Dockyard/Kaohsiung Shipyard	27 Apr	1994	5 Nov	1994	15 Sep	1996
KUN MING	1205	Lorient Dockyard/Kaohsiung Shipyard	7 Nov	1994	13 May	1995	26 Feb	1997
DI HUA	1206	Lorient Dockyard/Kaohsiung Shipyard	1 July	1995	27 Nov	1995	14 Aug	1997
WU CHANG	1207	Lorient Dockyard/Kaohsiung Shipyard	1 July	1995	27 Nov	1995	16 Dec	1997
CHEN TE	1208	Lorient Dockyard/Kaohsiung Shipyard	27 Dec	1995	2 Aug	1996	16 Jan	1998

Displacement, tons: 3,800 full load
Dimensions, feet (metres): 407.5 × 50.5 × 18 (screws)
(124.2 × 15.4 × 5.5)
Main machinery: CODAD; 4 SEMT-Pielstick 12 PA6 V 280 STC diesels; 23,228 hp(m) *(17.08 MW)*; 2 shafts; acbLIPS cp props
Speed, knots: 25. **Range, miles:** 7,000 at 15 kt
Complement: 134 (15 officers) plus 25 spare

Missiles: SSM: 8 Hsiung Feng II (2 quad) ❶; inertial guidance; active radar/IR homing to 80 km *(43.2 n miles)* at 0.85 Mach; warhead 190 kg.
SAM: 1 Sea Chaparral quad launcher ❷; IR homing to 3 km *(1.6 n miles)* supersonic; warhead 5 kg.
Guns: 1 OTO Melara 76 mm/62 Mk 75 ❸; 85 rds/min to 16 km *(8.7 n miles)*; weight of shell 6 kg.

1 Hughes 20 mm/76 Vulcan Phalanx Mk 15 Mod 2 ❹.
2 Bofors 40 mm/70 ❺. 2 CS 20 mm Type 75.
Torpedoes: 6—324 mm Mk 32 (2 triple) tubes ❻; Alliant Mk 46 Mod 5; active/passive homing to 11 km *(5.9 n miles)* at 40 kt; warhead 44 kg.
Countermeasures: Decoys: 2 CSEE Dagaie chaff launchers ❼.
ESM: Thomson-CSF DR 3000S; intercept and jammer.
Combat data systems: Thomson-CSF TACTICOS. Link W (Ta Chen).
Weapons control: CSEE Najir Mk 2 optronic director ❽.
Radars: Air/surface search: Thomson-CSF DRBV-26D Jupiter II (with LW08 aerial) ❾; D-band.
Surface search: Thomson-CSF Triton G ❿; G-band.
Fire control: 2 Thomson-CSF Castor IIC ⓫; I/J-band.
Navigation and helo control: 2 Racal Decca 20V90; I-band.

Sonars: BAe/Thomson Sintra ATAS (V)2; active towed array. Thomson Sintra Spherion B; bow-mounted; active search; medium frequency.

Helicopters: 1 Sikorsky S-70C(M)1 ⓬ Thunderhawk.

Programmes: Sale of up to 16 of the class authorised by the French Government in August 1991. Contract for six signed with Thomson-CSF in early 1992, manufactured in France with some weapon assembly by China SB Corporation at Kaohsiung in Taiwan. First one to Taiwan in March 1996 and the last in January 1998. Names are those of Chinese cities. Second batch of 10 to be built by China SB Corporation was planned but this now seems unlikely.
Modernisation: There are plans to move Phalanx to the bridge roof and fit two 10-round RAM launchers on the hangar.
Structure: There are considerable differences with the French 'La Fayette' design in both superstructure and weapon systems. A comprehensive ASW fit has been added as well as additional gun armament. There is also no stern hatch for launching RIBs. Some of the weapons were fitted after arrival in Taiwan. DCN Samahé helicopter landing gear installed.
UPDATED

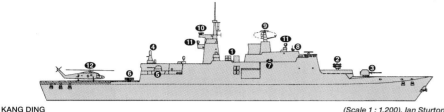

KANG DING
(Scale 1 : 1,200), Ian Sturton / 0019229

DI HUA
8/1997, C Chung / 0019230

KANG DING
7/1999*, Ships of the World / 0080776

SHIPBORNE AIRCRAFT

Numbers/Type: (12) Kaman SH-2F Seasprite (LAMPS I).
Operational speed: 130 kt *(241 km/h)*.
Service ceiling: 22,500 ft *(6,860 m)*.
Range: 367 n miles *(679 km)*.
Role/Weapon systems: ASW and OTHT helicopter; were to have transferred from USN in August 1993 but have been delayed through lack of funds and there is no sign of it being given a higher priority. In LAMPS I programme, acts as ASW information relay for surface ships. Sensors: LN66/HP radar, ALR-66 ESM, ASN-123 tactical navigation, ASQ-81(V)2 MAD, AAQ-16 night vision system; ARR-57 sonobuoy receivers; 15 sonobuoys. Weapons: ASW; two Mk 46 Mod 5 torpedoes, eight Mk 25 smoke markers. ASV; 1 Penguin; 1—7.62 mm MG M60.
UPDATED

Numbers/Type: 9 Hughes MD 500/ASW.
Operational speed: 110 kt *(204 km/h)*.
Service ceiling: 16,000 ft *(4,880 m)*.
Range: 203 n miles *(376 km)*.
Role/Weapon systems: Short-range ASW helicopter with limited surface search capability. 501 ASW Squadron. Sensors: Search radar, Texas Instruments ASQ 81(V)2 MAD. Weapons: ASW; one Mk 46 Mod 5 torpedo or two depth bombs. ASV; could carry machine gun pod.
UPDATED

MD 500   *1/1995, L J Lamb /* 0080778

Numbers/Type: 9 + 11 Sikorsky S-70C(M)1 Thunderhawks.
Operational speed: 145 kt *(269 km/h)*.
Service ceiling: 19,000 ft *(5,790 m)*.
Range: 324 n miles *(600 km)*.
Role/Weapon systems: Delivered in 1991. This is a variant of the SH-60B and became seaborne with the first 'Cheng Kung' and 'Kang Ding' class frigates. 701 ASW Squadron. Two modified for EW and Sigint role. Eleven more ordered in late 1996. Another 14 S-70B/C SAR and assault aircraft belong to the Air Force. Sensors: APS 128 search radar; Litton ALR 606(V)2 ESM; ARR 84 sonobuoy receiver with Litton ASN 150 datalink; Allied AQS 18(V)3 dipping sonar; ASQ 504 MAD. Ta Chen datalink to be fitted. Weapons: ASW; two Hughes Mk 46 Mod 5 torpedoes or two Mk 64 depth bombs. ASV; could carry ASM.
UPDATED

THUNDERHAWK   *7/1995*, L J Lamb /* 0080779

LAND-BASED MARITIME AIRCRAFT

Notes: (1) Maritime patrol aircraft and A3 fighter-bombers may be acquired by the Naval Aviation Command.
(2) Four Grumman E-2T Hawkeye AEW aircraft were acquired by the Air Force in February 1995.

Numbers/Type: 3/21 Grumman S-2E/T (Turbo) Trackers.
Operational speed: 130 kt *(241 km/h)*.
Service ceiling: 25,000 ft *(7,620 m)*.
Range: 1,350 n miles *(2,500 km)*.
Role/Weapon systems: Patrol and ASW tasks transferred to the Navy in July 1998; 21 aircraft updated with turboprop engines and new sensors. Based at Pintung. Sensors: APS 504 search radar, ESM, MAD, AAS 40 FLIR, SSQ-41B, SSQ-47B sonobuoys; AQS 902F sonobuoy processor; ASN 150 datalink. Weapons: ASW; four Mk 44 torpedoes, Mk 54 depth charges or Mk 64 depth bombs or mines. ASV; Hsiung Feng II ASM; six 127 mm rockets.
VERIFIED

CORVETTES

Note: A Kwang Hua 5 Project of ten 1,500 ton corvettes (PCEG) is planned, but has a lower priority than the KH 3 project. The ships are to be equipped with Hsiung Feng II SSM. Orders for first four are expected, with the first one to be acquired from a Western shipbuilder and the remainder constructed locally.

PATROL FORCES

Note: All coastal patrol craft were transferred to the Maritime Police on 8 December 1992. The Maritime Police became the Coast Guard 1 January 2000.

7 + 4 JIN CHIANG CLASS (LARGE PATROL CRAFT) (PGG)

Name	No	Builders	Launched		Commissioned	
JIN CHIANG	603	Lien-Ho, Kaohsiung	1 May	1994	1 Dec	1994
TAN CHIANG	605	China SB, Kaohsiung	18 June	1998	7 Sep	1999
HSIN CHIANG	606	China SB, Kaohsiung	14 Aug	1998	7 Sep	1999
FONG CHIANG	607	China SB, Kaohsiung	16 Nov	1998	29 Oct	1999
TSENG CHIANG	608	China SB, Kaohsiung	15 Dec	1998	29 Oct	1999
KAO CHIANG	609	China SB, Kaohsiung	25 Mar	1999	Feb	2000
HSIANG CHIANG	610	China SB, Kaohsiung	16 July	1999	Feb	2000
TSI CHIANG	611	China SB, Kaohsiung	Oct	1999	Sep	2000
PO CHIANG	612	China SB, Kaohsiung	Jan	2000	Dec	2000
CHAN CHIANG	613	China SB, Kaohsiung	Apr	2000	Mar	2001
CHU CHIANG	615	China SB, Kaohsiung	June	2000	May	2001

Displacement, tons: 680 full load
Dimensions, feet (metres): 201.4 × 31.2 × 9.5 *(61.4 × 9.5 × 2.9)*
Main machinery: 2 MTU 20V 1163 TB93 diesels; 20,128 hp(m) *(14.79 MW)*; 2 shafts
Speed, knots: 25. **Range, miles:** 4,150 at 15 kt
Complement: 50 (7 officers)

Missiles: SSM: 4 Hsiung Feng I; radar or optical guidance to 36 km *(19.4 n miles)* at 0.7 Mach; warhead 75 kg.
Guns: 1 Bofors 40 mm/70. 1 CS 20 mm Type 75. 2—12.7 mm MGs.
Depth charges: 2 racks.
Mines: 2 rails for Mk 6.
Weapons control: Honeywell H 930 Mod 2 MFCS. Contraves WCS. Rafael Sea Eye FLIR; range out to 3 km.
Radars: Air/surface search: Marconi LN66; I-band.
Fire control: Hughes HR-76C5; I/J-band.
Navigation: Racal Decca Bridgemaster; I-band.
Sonars: Simrad; search and attack; high frequency.

Programmes: Kwang Hua Project 3 design by United Ship Design Centre. First one laid down 25 June 1993. Ten more ordered 26 June 1997. Last of class laid down 31 March 1999.
Structure: The ship looks like an enlarged version of *Sui Chiang*.
UPDATED

JIN CHIANG   *1/1995*, L J Lamb /* 0080780

2 LUNG CHIANG CLASS (FAST ATTACK CRAFT—MISSILE) (PCFG)

Name	No	Builders	Commissioned
LUNG CHIANG	601 (ex-PGG 581)	Tacoma Boatbuilding, WA	15 May 1978
SUI CHIANG	602 (ex-PGG 582)	China SB Corporation, Kaohsiung	31 Dec 1981

Displacement, tons: 270 full load
Dimensions, feet (metres): 164.5 × 23.1 × 9.5 *(50.2 × 7.3 × 2.9)*
Main machinery: CODAG; 3 Avco Lycoming TF-40A gas turbines; 12,000 hp *(8.95 MW)* sustained; 3 Detroit 12V-149TI diesels; 2,736 hp *(2.04 MW)* sustained; 3 shafts; cp props
Speed, knots: 20 kt diesels; 38 kt gas. **Range, miles:** 3,100 at 12 kt on 1 diesel; 800 at 36 kt
Complement: 38 (5 officers)

Missiles: SSM: 4 Hsiung Feng I; radar or optical guidance to 36 km *(19.4 n miles)* at 0.7 Mach; warhead 75 kg.
Guns: 1 OTO Melara 3 in *(76 mm)*/62; 60 rds/min to 16 km *(8.7 n miles)*; weight of shell 6 kg. 2 Emerlec 30 mm (twin). 2—12.7 mm MGs.
Countermeasures: Decoys: 4 Israeli AV2 (601) or SMOC-4 (602) chaff launchers.
ESM: WD-2A; intercept.
Combat data systems: IPN 10 action data automation.
Weapons control: NA 10 Mod 0 GFCS. Honeywell H 930 Mod 2 MFCS (602).
Radars: Surface/air search: Selenia RAN 11 L/X; D/I-band.
Fire control: RCA HR 76; I/J-band (for SSM) (602). Selenia RAN IIL/X; I/J-band for SSM (601).
Navigation: SPS-58(A); I-band.

Programmes: Similar to the US Patrol Ship Multi-Mission Mk 5 (PSMM Mk 5). Second of class was built to an improved design. A much larger number of this class was intended, all to be armed with Harpoon. However at that time the US ban on export of Harpoon to Taiwan coupled with the high cost and doubts about seaworthiness caused the cancellation of this programme.
Structure: Fin stabilisers were fitted to help correct the poor sea-keeping qualities of the design. Both have had engine room fires caused by overheating in GT gearboxes.
Operational: *Lung Chiang* may be non-operational.
UPDATED

SUI CHIANG   *4/1997*, Ships of the World /* 0019231

48 HAI OU CLASS (FAST ATTACK CRAFT—MISSILE) (PCFG)

FABG 7-12   FABG 14-21   FABG 23-30   FABG 32-39   FABG 41-58

Displacement, tons: 47 full load
Dimensions, feet (metres): 70.8 × 18 × 3.3 *(21.6 × 5.5 × 1)*
Main machinery: 2 MTU 12V 331 TC82 diesels; 2,605 hp(m) *(1.92 MW)* sustained; 2 shafts
Speed, knots: 30. **Range, miles:** 700 at 32 kt
Complement: 10 (2 officers)

Missiles: SSM: 2 Hsiung Feng I; radar or optical guidance to 36 km *(19.4 n miles)* at 0.7 Mach; warhead 75 kg.
Guns: 1 CS 20 mm Type 75. 2—12.7 mm MGs.
Countermeasures: Decoys: 4 Israeli AV2 chaff launchers.
ESM: WD-2A; intercept.
Weapons control: Kollmorgen Mk 35 optical director.
Radars: Surface search: Marconi LN66; I-band.
Fire control: RCA R76 C5; I-band.

Programmes: This design was developed by Sun Yat Sen Scientific Research Institute from the basic Israeli Dvora plans. Built by China SB Corporation (Tsoying SY), Kaohsiung except for the first pair which were the original 'Dvora' class hulls and were commissioned on 31 December 1977. These two were probably the pair transferred to Paraguay in 1996.
Structure: Aluminium alloy hulls. The first series had a solid mast and the missiles were nearer the stern. Second series changed to a lattice mast and moved the missiles further forward allowing room for two 12.7 mm MGs right aft. One 20 mm has been added on the stern.
Operational: The prototype reached 45 kt on trials but top speeds are now reported as 25 to 30 kt. These craft often carry shoulder-launched SAMs. One task is to provide exercise high-speed targets in shallow waters. From 1997 organised in five divisions based at Makung, Anping, Tsoying, Suao and Keelung. Not all are operational.
Sales: Two to Paraguay in 1996.   *UPDATED*

FABG 21   *2/1998* / 0050224

0 + (29) KWANG HUA 6 CLASS (PCFG)

Displacement, tons: 180 standard
Dimensions, feet (metres): 131.2 × 23 × 6.2 *(40 × 7 × 1.9)*
Main machinery: 2 diesels; 2 shafts
Speed, knots: 30. **Range, miles:** 1,150 at 22 kt
Complement: 14
Missiles: SSM: 4 Hsiung Feng II.
Guns: 1 CS 20 mm Type 75.
Countermeasures: Decoys: Chaff launchers. ESM.
Weapons control: Optronic director.
Radars: Surface search. Fire control.

Comment: Funds allocated for the budget period July 1998 to June 2003 to build these craft in Taiwan to replace the 'Hai Ou' class. Contract expected to be given to CSBC in 2000. This project replaced the 50 craft of the Kwang Hua 5 proposal.   *UPDATED*

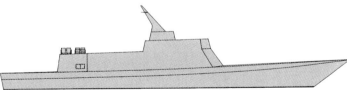

KWANG HUA 6   *(not to scale), Ian Sturton* / 0050225

8 NING HAI CLASS (LARGE PATROL CRAFT) (PC)

NING HAI PCL 1   AN HAI PCL 2   PCL 3   PCL 5-9

Displacement, tons: 143 full load
Dimensions, feet (metres): 105 × 29.5 × 5.9 *(32 × 9 × 1.8)*
Main machinery: 3 MTU 12V 396 TB93 diesels; 4,890 hp(m) *(3.6 MW)* sustained; 3 shafts
Speed, knots: 40
Complement: 16 (3 officers)
Guns: 1 Bofors 40 mm/60. 1 CS 20 mm Type 75.
Depth charges: 2 racks.
Radars: Surface search: Decca; I-band.
Sonars: Hull-mounted; active search and attack; high frequency.

Comment: Built to Vosper QAF design by China SB Corporation, Kaohsiung in 1987-90. Previously reported numbers had been exaggerated. They are used mainly for harbour defence against midget submarines and frogmen and also for Fishery protection tasks.   *UPDATED*

AN HAI   *6/1999** / 0080781

AMPHIBIOUS FORCES

1 + 1 ANCHORAGE CLASS (LSD)

Name	No	Builders	Commissioned
SHIU HAI (ex-*Pensacola*)	LSD 193 (ex-LSD 38)	General Dynamics, Quincy	27 Mar 1971
— (ex-*Fort Fisher*)	— (ex-LSD 40)	General Dynamics, Quincy	9 Dec 1972

Displacement, tons: 8,600 light; 13,700 full load
Dimensions, feet (metres): 553.3 × 84 × 20 *(168.6 × 25.6 × 6)*
Main machinery: 2 Foster-Wheeler boilers; 600 psi *(42.3 kg/cm²)*; 870°F *(467°C)*; 2 De Laval turbines; 24,000 hp *(18 MW)*; 2 shafts
Speed, knots: 22. **Range, miles:** 14,800 at 12 kt
Complement: 374 (24 officers)
Military lift: 366 troops (18 officers); 2 LCU or 18 LCM 6 or 9 LCM 8 or 50 LVT; 1 LCM 6 on deck; 2 LCPL and 1 LCVP on davits. Aviation fuel, 90 tons
Guns: 2 General Electric/General Dynamics 20 mm/76 6-barrelled Vulcan Phalanx Mk 15; 3,000 rds/min combined to 1.5 km.
2—25 mm Mk 38. 6—12.7 mm MGs.
Countermeasures: Decoys: 4 Loral Hycor SRBOC 6-barrelled Mk 36; IR flares and chaff to 4 km *(2.2 n miles)*.
ESM: SLQ-32(V)1; intercept.
Radars: Air search: Lockheed SPS-40B; E/F-band.
Surface search: Raytheon SPS-10F; G-band.
Navigation: Marconi LN66; I-band.
Helicopters: Platform only.

Comment: First one acquired from US Navy 30 September 1999 and is expected to transfer in 2000. Possibly a second of class to follow in due course. Has a docking well 131.1 × 15.2 m and two 50 ton cranes.   *UPDATED*

TAN HAI (US colours)   *1/1998, van Ginderen Collection* / 0050226

4 LSM 1 CLASS

MEI LO (ex-*LSM 362*) 356 (ex-637)   MEI PING (ex-*LSM 471*) 353 (ex-659)
MEI CHIN (ex-*LSM 155*) 341 (ex-649)   MEI SUNG (ex-*LSM 431*) 347 (ex-694)

Displacement, tons: 1,095 full load
Dimensions, feet (metres): 203.5 × 34.2 × 8.3 *(62.1 × 10.4 × 2.5)*
Main machinery: 2 Fairbanks Morse 38D8-1/8-10 diesels; 3,540 hp *(2.64 MW)* sustained (356 and 353); 4 GM 16-278A diesels; 3,000 hp *(2.24 MW)* (341 and 347); 2 shafts
Speed, knots: 13. **Range, miles:** 2,500 at 12 kt
Complement: 65-75
Guns: 2 Bofors 40 mm/56 (twin). 4 or 8 Oerlikon 20 mm (4 single or 4 twin).
Radars: Surface search: SO 8; I-band.

Comment: All built in 1945. *Mei Chin* and *Mei Sung* transferred from USA 1946, *Mei Ping* in 1956 and *Mei Lo* in 1962. Rebuilt in Taiwan and bear little resemblance to 1970s photographs.   *VERIFIED*

MEI SUNG   *5/1995, C Chung*

2 + 1 NEWPORT CLASS (LST)

Name	No	Builders	Commissioned
CHUNG HO (ex-*Manitowic*)	232 (ex-LST 1180)	Philadelphia Shipyard	24 Jan 1970
CHUNG PING (ex-*Sumter*)	233 (ex-LST 1181)	Philadelphia Shipyard	20 June 1970
— (ex-*Schenectady*)	— (ex-LST 1185)	National Steel, San Diego	13 June 1970

Displacement, tons: 4,975 light; 8,450 full load
Dimensions, feet (metres): 522.3 × 69.5 × 17.5 *(159.2 × 21.2 × 5.3)*
Main machinery: 6 ALCO 16-251 diesels; 16,500 hp *(12.3 MW)* sustained; 2 shafts; cp props; bow thruster
Speed, knots: 20. **Range, miles:** 2,500 at 14 kt
Complement: 257 (13 officers)
Military lift: 400 troops; 500 tons vehicles; 3 LCVPs and 1 LCPL on davits
Guns: 1 General Electric/General Dynamics 20 mm Vulcan Phalanx Mk 15.
Radars: Surface search: Raytheon SPS-67; G-band.
Navigation: Marconi LN66; I-band.
Helicopters: Platform only.

Comment: First pair transferred from USA by lease confirmed for both ships on 1 July 1995. Refitted at Newport News and recommissioned 8 May 1997, sailing for Taiwan after a short operational work-up. A third of class approved for transfer in 2000, possibly with others to follow. These ships unload by a 112 ft ramp over their bow. The ramp is supported by twin derrick arms. A ramp just forward of the superstructure connects the lower tank deck with the main deck and a vehicle passage through the superstructure provides access to the parking area amidships. A stern gate to the tank deck permits unloading of amphibious tractors into the water, or unloading of other vehicles into an LCU or on to a pier. Vehicle stowage covers 19,000 sq ft. Length over derrick arms is 562 ft *(171.3 m)*; full load draught is 11.5 ft forward and 17.5 ft aft. Bow thruster fitted to hold position offshore while unloading amphibious tractors.

UPDATED

CHUNG HO   *10/1997 *, C Chung /* 0019234

1 CABILDO CLASS (LSD)

Name	No	Builders	Commissioned
CHUNG CHENG (ex-*Comstock*)	191 (ex-LSD 19)	Newport News, Virginia	2 July 1945

Displacement, tons: 4,790 standard; 9,375 full load
Dimensions, feet (metres): 475 × 76.2 × 18 *(144.8 × 23.2 × 5.5)*
Main machinery: 2 boilers; 435 psi *(30.6 kg/cm²)*; 740°F *(393°C)*; 2 turbines; 7,000 hp *(5.22 MW)*; 2 shafts
Speed, knots: 15.4. **Range, miles:** 8,000 at 15 kt
Complement: 316
Military lift: 3 LCUs or 18 LCMs or 32 LVTs in docking well
Missiles: SAM: 1 Sea Chaparral quadruple launcher.
Guns: 12 Bofors 40 mm/56 (2 quad, 2 twin).
Weapons control: US Mk 26 Mod 4.
Radars: Surface search: Raytheon SPS-5; G/H-band.
Navigation: Marconi LN66; I-band.

Comment: Launched 28 April 1945 and transferred to Taiwan on 1 October 1985 having been bought from a ship breaker. SAM system fitted in 1992. Second of class scrapped in mid-1999.

UPDATED

CHUNG CHENG   *5/1997, van Ginderen Collection /* 0050227

10 LST 1-510 and 511-1152 CLASSES (LST)

CHUNG HAI (ex-*LST 755*) 201 (ex-697)	CHUNG CHIH (ex-*Sagadahoc County* LST 1091) 226 (ex-655)
CHUNG CHIEN (ex-*LST 716*) 205 (ex-679)	
CHUNG SHUN (ex-*LST 732*) 208 (ex-624)	CHUNG MING (ex-*Sweetwater County* LST 1152) 227 (ex-681)
CHUNG KUANG (ex-*LST 503*) 216 (ex-646)	
CHUNG CHAO (ex-*Bradley County* LST 400) 217 (ex-667)	CHUNG PANG (ex-*LST 578*) 230 (ex-629)
CHUNG CHUAN (ex-*LST 1030*) 221 (ex-651)	CHUNG YEH (ex-*Sublette County* LST 1144) 231 (ex-699)

Displacement, tons: 1,653 standard; 4,080 (3,640, 1-510 class) full load
Dimensions, feet (metres): 328 × 50 × 14 *(100 × 15.2 × 4.3)*
Main machinery: 2 GM 12-567A diesels; 1,800 hp *(1.34 MW)*; 2 shafts
Speed, knots: 11.6. **Range, miles:** 15,000 at 10 kt
Complement: Varies—100-125 in most ships
Guns: Varies—up to 10 Bofors 40 mm/56 (2 twin, 6 single) with some modernised ships rearmed with 2 USN 3 in *(76 mm)*/50 and 6—40 mm (3 twin). Several Oerlikon 20 mm (twin or single).
Radars: Navigation: US SO 1, 2 or 8; I-band.

Comment: Constructed between 1943 and 1945. These ships have been rebuilt in Taiwan. Six transferred from USA in 1946; two in 1947; one in 1948; eight in 1958; one in 1959; two in 1960; and one in 1961. Some have davits forward and aft. Pennant numbers have reverted to those used in the 1960s. One deleted in 1990, six more in 1993, one more in 1995 after going aground, and three more in 1997. Being replaced by locally built AKs. The midships deck is occasionally used as a helicopter platform.

UPDATED

CHUNG SHUN   *4/1999 *, C Chung /* 0080782

1 LST 511-1152 CLASS (FLAGSHIP) (AGC)

Name	No	Builders	Commissioned
KAO HSIUNG (ex-*Chung Hai*, ex-*Dukes County* LST 735)	LCC 1 (ex-219, ex-663)	Dravo Corporation, Neville Island, Penn	26 Apr 1944

Displacement, tons: 1,653 standard; 3,675 full load
Dimensions, feet (metres): 328 × 50 × 14 *(100 × 15.2 × 4.3)*
Main machinery: 2 GM 12-567A diesels; 1,800 hp *(1.34 MW)*; 2 shafts
Speed, knots: 11.6. **Range, miles:** 11,200 at 10 kt
Complement: 195
Guns: 8 Bofors 40 mm/56 (3 twin, 2 single).
Radars: Air search: Raytheon SPS 58; D-band.
Surface search: Raytheon SPS-10; G-band.

Comment: Launched on 11 March 1944. Transferred from USA in May 1957 for service as an LST. Converted to a flagship for amphibious operations and renamed and redesignated (AGC) in 1964. Purchased November 1974. Note lattice mast above bridge structure, modified bridge levels, and antenna mountings on main deck. Redesignated as Command and Control Ship LCC 1.

UPDATED

KAO HSIUNG   *6/1999 * /* 0080783

10 LCU 501 CLASS (LCU)

HO CHI (ex-*LCU 1212*) 401	HO SHUN (ex-*LCU 892*) 481	HO YUNG (ex-*LCU 1271*) 495
HO HUEI (ex-*LCU 1218*) 402	HO CHUNG (ex-*LCU 849*) 484	HO CHIE (ex-*LCU 700*) SB 1
HO YAO (ex-*LCU 1244*) 403	HO CHUN (ex-*LCU 1225*) 494	HO TEN (ex-*LCU 1367*) SB 2
HO CHAO (ex-*LCU 1429*) 406		

Displacement, tons: 158 light; 309 full load
Dimensions, feet (metres): 119 × 32.7 × 5 *(36.3 × 10 × 1.5)*
Main machinery: 3 GM 6-71 diesels; 522 hp *(390 kW)* sustained; 3 shafts
Speed, knots: 10
Complement: 10-25
Guns: 2 Oerlikon 20 mm. Some also may have 2—12.7 mm MGs.

Comment: Built in USA in the 1940s and transferred in 1959. *SB 1* and *SB 2* are used as auxiliaries. *Ho Feng* 405 converted for ferry duties in 1998 and serves Matzu island.

UPDATED

HO CHIE   *6/1994 * /* 0080784

6 LCU 1466 CLASS (LCU)

HO SHAN (ex-*LCU 1596*) 488 **HO SENG** (ex-*LCU 1598*) 490 **HO MOU** (ex-*LCU 1600*) 492
HO CHUAN (ex-*LCU 1597*) 489 **HO MENG** (ex-*LCU 1599*) 491 **HO SHOU** (ex-*LCU 1601*) 493

Displacement, tons: 180 light; 360 full load
Dimensions, feet (metres): 119 × 34 × 6 *(36.3 × 10.4 × 1.8)*
Main machinery: 3 Gray Marine 64 YTL diesels; 675 hp *(504 kW)*; 3 shafts
Speed, knots: 10. **Range, miles:** 800 at 11 kt
Complement: 15-25
Military lift: 167 tons or 300 troops
Guns: 3 Oerlikon 20 mm. Some may also have 2—12.7 mm MGs.

Comment: Built by Ishikawajima Heavy Industries Co, Tokyo, Japan, for transfer to Taiwan; completed in March 1955. All originally numbered in 200 series; subsequently changed to 400 series.   **VERIFIED**

HO CHUAN   1991

2 TAIWAN TYPE LCU

LCU 497   LCU 498

Displacement, tons: 190 light; 439 full load
Dimensions, feet (metres): 135.5 × 29.9 × 6.9 *(41.3 × 9.1 × 2.1)*
Main machinery: 4 Detroit diesels; 1,200 hp *(895 kW)*; 2 Kort nozzle props
Speed, knots: 11. **Range, miles:** 1,200 at 10 kt
Complement: 16
Military lift: 180 tons or 350 troops
Guns: 2—12.7 mm MGs.

Comment: Locally built versions of US types. Ramps at both ends.
                                                                        VERIFIED

LCU 497   *8/1998, Ships of the World /* 0050228

180 LCM 6 CLASS (LCM)

Displacement, tons: 57 full load
Dimensions, feet (metres): 56.4 × 13.8 × 3.9 *(17.2 × 4.2 × 1.2)*
Main machinery: 2 diesels; 450 hp *(336 kW)*; 2 shafts
Speed, knots: 9
Military lift: 34 tons
Guns: 1—12.7 mm MG.

Comment: Some built in the USA, some in Taiwan. 20 were exchanged for torpedoes with Indonesia. Some 45 have been deleted in the last four years.
                                                                        UPDATED

LCM 6   *2/1993*, C Chung /* 0080785

100 LCVPs and ASSAULT CRAFT

Comment: Some ex-US, and some built in Taiwan. Most are armed with one or two 7.62 mm MGs. Two transferred to Indonesia in 1988. About 20 deleted in the last three years and 30 transferred to Honduras in 1996 for River operations. There are also a number of amphibious reconnaissance boats in the ARP 1000, 2000 and 3000 series.   **VERIFIED**

TYPE 272   *1989, DTM (Raymond Cheung)*

MINE WARFARE FORCES

Note: A new class of minehunters is planned. Tenders may be invited in when funds are available.

4 AGGRESSIVE CLASS (MINESWEEPERS) (MSO)

Name	No	Builders	Commissioned
YUNG YANG (ex-*Implicit*)	1306 (ex-455)	Wilmington Boat	10 Mar 1954
YUNG TZU (ex-*Conquest*)	1307 (ex-488)	Martenac, Tacoma	20 July 1955
YUNG KU (ex-*Gallant*)	1308 (ex-489)	Martenac, Tacoma	14 Sep 1955
YUNG TEH (ex-*Pledge*)	1309 (ex-492)	Martenac, Tacoma	20 Apr 1956

Displacement, tons: 720 standard; 780 full load
Dimensions, feet (metres): 172.5 × 35.1 × 14.1 *(52.6 × 10.7 × 4.3)*
Main machinery: 4 Packard ID-1700 or Waukesha diesels; 2,280 hp *(1.7 MW)*; 2 shafts; cp props
Speed, knots: 14. **Range, miles:** 3,000 at 10 kt
Complement: 86 (7 officers)
Guns: 2—12.7 mm MGs.
Radars: Navigation: Sperry SPS-53L; I/J-band.
Sonars: General Electric SQQ-14; VDS; active minehunting; high frequency.

Comment: Transferred by sale to Taiwan from the USN 3 August and 30 September 1994. Delivery was delayed into 1995 while replanking work was carried out in the USA. All recommissioned 1 March 1995. Second batch of three planned to transfer but were subsequently scrapped after cannibalisation for spares. All are fitted with SLQ-37 mechanical acoustic and magnetic sweeps and can carry an ROV. The plan is to update the class with a Unisys SYQ-12 minehunting system and Pluto ROVs.   **UPDATED**

YUNG TZU   *8/1996, Ships of the World*

4 ADJUTANT and MSC 268 CLASSES
(MINESWEEPERS—COASTAL) (MSC)

YUNG CHUAN (ex-*MSC 278*) 158   **YUNG CHING** (ex-*Eekloo*, ex-*MSC 101*) 163
YUNG FU (ex-*Macaw*, ex-*MSC 77*) 162   **YUNG CHUNG** (ex-*Maaseik*, ex-*MSC 78*) 165

Displacement, tons: 375 full load
Dimensions, feet (metres): 144 × 27.9 × 8 *(43.9 × 8.5 × 2.4)*
Main machinery: 2 GM 8-268A diesels; 880 hp *(656 kW)*; 2 shafts
Speed, knots: 13. **Range, miles:** 2,500 at 12 kt
Complement: 35
Guns: 2 Oerlikon 20 mm (twin).
Radars: Navigation: Decca 707; I-band.
Sonars: Simrad 950; hull-mounted; minehunting; high frequency.

Comment: Non-magnetic, wood-hulled minesweepers built in the USA in the 1950s specifically for transfer to allied navies. All refitted 1984-86. All are in very poor condition. Several deleted so far. Two put back in service in 1996 and one in 1997 to replace three others paid off.   **UPDATED**

ADJUTANT (old number)

4 YUNG FENG (MWV 50) CLASS
(MINEHUNTERS—COASTAL) (MHC)

YUNG FENG 1301   **YUNG CHIA** 1302   **YUNG TING** 1303   **YUNG SHUN** 1305

Displacement, tons: 500 full load
Dimensions, feet (metres): 163.1 × 28.5 × 10.2 *(49.7 × 8.7 × 3.1)*
Main machinery: 2 MTU 8V 396 TB93 diesels; 2,180 hp(m) *(1.6 MW)* sustained; 2 shafts
Speed, knots: 14. **Range, miles:** 3,500 at 14 kt
Complement: 45 (5 officers)
Guns: 1 Bofors 40 mm/60. 2—12.7 mm MGs.
Radars: Navigation: I-band.
Sonars: TSM-2022; hull-mounted; active minehunting; high frequency.

Comment: Built for the Chinese Petroleum Corporation by Abeking & Rasmussen at Lemwerder, Germany. First four delivered in 1991 as offshore oil rig support ships and then converted for minehunting in Taiwan. Thomson Sintra IBIS V minehunting system is fitted and two STN Pinguin B3 ROVs are carried. The civilian livery has been abandoned. Two more reported building in 1993 in Taiwan but this is not confirmed. These ships spend little time at sea.
UPDATED

YUNG SHUN   *12/1998*, C Chung* / 0080786

SURVEY AND RESEARCH SHIPS

1 ALLIANCE CLASS (AGS)

Name	No	Builders	Launched	Commissioned
TA KUAN	1601	Fincantieri, Muggiano	17 Dec 1994	27 Sep 1995

Displacement, tons: 2,466 standard; 3,180 full load
Dimensions, feet (metres): 305.1 × 49.9 × 16.7 *(93 × 15.2 × 5.1)*
Main machinery: Diesel-electric; 3 MTU/AEG diesel generators; 5,712 hp(m) *(4.2 MW)*; 2 AEG motors; 5,100 hp(m) *(3.75 MW)*; 2 shafts; bow thruster; stern trainable and retractable thruster
Speed, knots: 15. **Range, miles:** 12,000 at 12 kt
Complement: 82
Guns: 2—12.7 mm MGs.
Radars: Navigation: H/I-band.

Comment: Ordered in June 1993 and laid down 8 April 1994. Almost identical to the NATO vessel. Designed for oceanography and hydrographic research. Facilities include laboratories, position location systems, and overside deployment equipment. Equipment includes a Simrad side scan sonar EM 1200, deep and shallow echo-sounders, two radars, Navsat and Satcom, an ROV for remote inspection, and a dynamic positioning system with bow thruster and stern positioning propeller.
UPDATED

TA KUAN   *8/1997*, C Chung* / 0019239

AUXILIARIES

1 ATTACK TRANSPORT (AK)

Name	No	Builders	Launched	Commissioned
WAN AN	523	CSBC, Keelung	22 July 1978	26 Jan 1979

Displacement, tons: 2,591 standard, 4,262 full load
Dimensions, feet (metres): 334 × 54.1 × 15.1 *(101.8 × 16.5 × 4.6)*
Main machinery: 1 diesel; 1 shaft
Speed, knots: 17. **Range, miles:** 5,800 at 10 kt
Complement: 61 (11 officers)
Guns: 2 Type 75 20 mm. 2—12.7 mm MGs.

Comment: Can carry 600 troops. *Wan An* was extensively damaged in a collision in March 1997 but has been repaired. One other deleted in 1998, and one in 1999.
UPDATED

WAN AN   *5/1999** / 0080788

1 COMBAT SUPPORT SHIP (AOE)

Name	No	Builders	Launched	Commissioned
WU YI	530	China SB Corporation, Keelung	4 Mar 1989	23 June 1990

Displacement, tons: 7,700 light; 17,000 full load
Dimensions, feet (metres): 531.8 × 72.2 × 28 *(162.1 × 22 × 8.6)*
Main machinery: 2 MAN 14-cyl diesels; 25,000 hp(m) *(18.37 MW)*; 2 shafts
Speed, knots: 21. **Range, miles:** 9,200 at 10 kt
Cargo capacity: 9,300 tons
Missiles: SAM: 1 Sea Chaparral quad launcher.
Guns: 2 Bofors 40 mm/70. 2 Oerlikon 20 mm GAM-BO1. 4—12.7 mm MGs.
Countermeasures: Decoys: 2 chaff launchers.
ESM: Radar warning.
Radars: 2 navigation; I-band.
Helicopters: Platform for CH-47 or S-70C(M)1.

Comment: Largest unit built so far for the Taiwanese Navy. Design assisted by the United Shipping Design Center in the USA. Beam replenishment rigs on both sides. SAM system on forecastle, 40 mm guns aft of the funnels.
UPDATED

WU YI   *5/1999*, van Ginderen Collection* / 0080787

3 + 3 WU KANG CLASS (ATTACK TRANSPORTS) (AK)

Name	No	Builders	Commissioned
YUEN FENG	524	China SB Corporation, Keelung	10 Sep 1982
WU KANG	525	China SB Corporation, Keelung	9 Oct 1984
HSIN KANG	526	China SB Corporation, Keelung	30 Nov 1988
—	527	China SB Corporation, Keelung	2000
—	528	China SB Corporation, Keelung	2001
—	529	China SB Corporation, Keelung	2002

Displacement, tons: 2,804 standard; 4,845 full load
Dimensions, feet (metres): 334 × 59.1 × 16.4 *(101.8 × 18 × 5)*
Main machinery: 2 diesels; 2 shafts; bow thruster
Speed, knots: 20. **Range, miles:** 6,500 at 12 kt
Complement: 61 (11 officers)
Military lift: 1,400 troops
Missiles: SAM: 1 Sea Chaparral quad launcher.
Guns: 2 Bofors 40 mm/60. 2 or 4—12.7 mm MGs.
Countermeasures: ESM: WD-2A (524 only); intercept.

Comment: First three were built and then the programme stopped. Restarted with the fourth of class laid down in July 1994. The plan was to build at about one a year to a final total of seven, but the programme has been delayed by the priority given to the lease of amphibious ships. With a helicopter platform, stern docking facility and davits for four LCVP, the design resembles an LPD. Used mostly for supplying garrisons in offshore islands, and on the Spratley and Pratas islands in the South China Sea. SAM launcher is mounted aft of the foremast. Accommodation is air conditioned. *Hsin Kang* was badly damaged in harbour in collision with a merchant ship in March 1996, but was back in service by mid-1999.
UPDATED

HSIN KANG   *1/1999, van Ginderen Collection* / 0050230

2 PATAPSCO CLASS (SUPPORT TANKERS) (AOTL)

Name	No	Builders	Commissioned
HSIN LUNG (ex-*Elkhorn* AOG 7)	507	Cargill, Inc, Savage, Minnesota, MN	12 Feb 1944
LUNG CHUAN (ex-*Endeavour*, ex-*Namakagon* AOG 53)	515	Cargill, Inc, Savage, Minnesota, MN	10 May 1945

Displacement, tons: 1,850 light; 4,335 full load
Dimensions, feet (metres): 310.8 × 48.5 × 15.7 *(94.8 × 14.8 × 4.8)*
Main machinery: 2 GM 16-278A diesels; 3,000 hp *(2.24 MW)*; 2 shafts
Speed, knots: 14. **Range, miles:** 7,000 at 12 kt
Complement: 124
Cargo capacity: 2,000 tons
Guns: 1 USN 3 in *(76 mm)*/50. 2 Bofors 40 mm/60.
Radars: Navigation: Raytheon SPS-21; G/H-band.

Comment: *Lung Chuan* was launched on 4 November 1944 and transferred from the USA to New Zealand on 5 October 1962 for use as an Antarctic resupply ship; strengthened for polar operations and renamed *Endeavour*; returned to the US Navy on 29 June 1971 and retransferred to Taiwan the same date. *Hsin Lung* was launched on 15 May 1943 and was transferred to Taiwan on 1 July 1972. Both transferred by sale 19 May 1976.
UPDATED

HSIN LUNG
5/1999 * / 0080789

3 + 1 SALVAGE SHIPS (ARS)

Name	No	Builders	Commissioned
TA HU (ex-*Grapple*)	552 (ex-ARS 7)	Basalt Rock, USA	16 Dec 1943
TA PENG (ex-*Hoist*)	549 (ex-ARS 40)	Basalt Rock, USA	21 July 1945
TA DE (ex-*Recovery*)	550 (ex-ARS 43)	Basalt Rock, USA	15 May 1946
TA TUEN (ex-*Conserver*)	551 (ex-ARS 39)	Basalt Rock, USA	9 June 1945

Displacement, tons: 1,557 standard; 1,745 full load
Dimensions, feet (metres): 213.5 × 39 × 15 *(65.1 × 11.9 × 4.6)*
Main machinery: Diesel-electric; 4 Cooper Bessemer GSB-8 diesels; 3,420 hp *(2.55 MW)*; 2 generators; 2 motors; 2 shafts
Speed, knots: 14. **Range, miles:** 8,500 at 13 kt
Complement: 85
Guns: 2 Oerlikon 20 mm.
Radars: Navigation: SPS-53; I-band.

Comment: Fitted for salvage, towing and compressed-air diving. *Ta Hu* transferred from USA 1 December 1977 by sale. The second pair which are of the slightly beamier 'Bolster' class (13.4 m width), but otherwise very similar, transferred from the US in 1999. A fourth is planned for 2000.
UPDATED

TA HU
1/1999, van Ginderen Collection / 0050231

6 FLOATING DOCKS

HAY TAN (ex-*AFDL 36*) AFDL 1
KIM MEN (ex-*AFDL 5*) AFDL 2
HAN JIH (ex-*AFDL 34*) AFDL 3

FO WU 5 (ex-*ARD 9*) ARD 5
FO WU 6 (ex-*Windsor* ARD 22) ARD 6
FO WU 7 (ex-*AFDM 6*)

Comment: Former US Navy floating dry docks. *Hay Tan* transferred in March 1947, *Kim Men* in January 1948, *Han Jih* in July 1959, *Fo Wu 5* in June 1971, *Fo Wu 6* in June 1971. *Fo Wu 6* by sale 19 May 1976 and *Fo Wu 5* on 12 January 1977. *Fo Wu 7* transferred by sale in 1999.
VERIFIED

TUGS

6 CHEROKEE CLASS (ATF/ARS)

TA TUNG (ex-*Chickasaw*) ATF 548
TA WAN (ex-*Apache*) ATF 551
TA HAN (ex-*Tawakoni*) ATF 553

TA KANG (ex-*Achomawi*) ATF 554
TA FUNG (ex-*Narragansett*) ATF 555
TA TAI (ex-*Shakori*) ATF 563

Displacement, tons: 1,235 standard; 1,731 full load
Dimensions, feet (metres): 205 × 38.5 × 17 *(62.5 × 11.7 × 5.2)*
Main machinery: Diesel-electric; 4 GM 12-278 diesels; 4,400 hp *(3.28 MW)*; 4 generators; 1 motor; 3,000 hp *(2.24 MW)*; 1 shaft
Speed, knots: 15. **Range, miles:** 6,000 at 14 kt
Complement: 85
Guns: 1 Bofors 40 mm/70. Several 12.7 mm MGs.

Comment: All built between 1943 and 1945. *Ta Tung* transferred from USA in January 1966 and by sale 19 May 1976; *Ta Wan* in June 1974; *Ta Han* in June 1978; and the last three in June 1991 together with two more which were cannibalised for spares.
UPDATED

TA HAN
4/1995 * / 0080790

7 HARBOUR TUGS (YTL)

YTL 30　　YTL 36-38　　YTL 42-43　　YTL 45

Comment: Replacements for the old US Army type which were scrapped in 1990/91.
UPDATED

YTL 36
5/1997 *, van Ginderen Collection / 0019242

COAST GUARD

Notes: (1) The 2,220 man Coast Guard General Bureau (formerly the Peace Preservation Police Corps), commands two patrol groups of small craft for its duties of anti-smuggling, anti-insurgency and fishery protection. The northern group, based at Tamshui, has four squadrons with depots at Hualien, Suao, Keelung, and Hsinchu; the southern group, based at Kaohsiung, has five squadrons with depots at Wuchi, Makung, Anping, and Kenting. Many of these craft were transferred from the Navy on 8 December 1992. A helicopter detachment with SWAT team was formed in 1995. In addition to the vessels listed below there are 26 assault craft.
(2) Four offshore patrol vessels of up to 1,500 tons and eight of 500 tons are planned to build when funds are available.

6 COASTAL PATROL CRAFT

PP 901-PP 906

Displacement, tons: 91 full load
Dimensions, feet (metres): 91.9 × 20.3 × 7.9 *(28 × 6.2 × 2.4)*
Main machinery: 2 Paxman 12V P185 diesels; 6,645 hp(m) *(4.89 MW)* sustained; 2 shafts; cp props
Speed, knots: 40. **Range, miles:** 600 at 25 kt
Complement: 12
Guns: 2—12.7 mm MGs.
Radars: Surface search: 2 Racal Decca; I-band.

Comment: Built by Lung Teh Shipyard, Taiwan from March 1996 and all delivered by March 1997. GRP hulls with some Kevlar protection. Can carry a 6.5 m RIB. May be given new pennant numbers in 2000.
UPDATED

PP 902
11/1996 *, Lung Teh / 0019243

12 LARGE PATROL CRAFT

PP 1001-1002   PP 1005-1014

Displacement, tons: 140 full load
Dimensions, feet (metres): 90 × 28.6 × 6 *(27.4 × 8.7 × 1.8)*
Main machinery: 2 MTU diesels; 6,000 hp(m) *(4.4 MW)*; 2 shafts
Speed, knots: 30
Guns: 2—12.7 mm MGs (aft).
Radars: Surface search: Decca; I-band.

Comment: The first pair were former naval craft transferred 8 December 1992. Two more completed in October 1994, three more by February 1995 and the last five by November 1998. May be given new pennant numbers in 2000.

UPDATED

59 COASTAL PATROL CRAFT

No/Type	Displacement, tons	Pennant Numbers series
10 PP 821	55	PP 821-830
12 PP 801	50	PP 801-817
2 PP 501	35	PP 501-502
21 PP 601	35	PP 602-630
14 PP 701	30	PP 701-719

Comment: These are all armed with 12.7 mm MGs and capable of speeds up to 35 kt. The pennant numbers are not consecutive, as some have been deleted. *P 805* sunk in November 1997. May be given new pennant numbers in 2000.

UPDATED

PP 802   *1994*, Taiwan Police /* 0080791

CUSTOMS

Notes: (1) Director General Kuo-An Chao.
(2) Three ships were deleted in 1997.
(3) In addition to the ships listed below, there are large numbers of small harbour launches.

2 HO HSING CLASS (LARGE PATROL CRAFT)

HO HSING   WEI HSING

Displacement, tons: 1,823 full load
Dimensions, feet (metres): 270 × 38.1 × 13.5 *(82.3 × 11.6 × 4.1)*
Main machinery: 2 MTU 16V 1163 TB93 diesels; 13,310 hp(m) *(9.78 MW)* sustained; 2 shafts; cp props; bow thruster
Speed, knots: 22. **Range, miles:** 7,000 at 16 kt
Complement: 80 (18 officers)
Guns: 2—12.7 mm MGs.
Radars: Surface search: Racal Decca; I-band.

Comment: Built by the China SB Corporation, Keelung, to a Tacoma design and both delivered 26 December 1991. Four high-speed interceptor boats are carried on individual davits. This is a variant of the US Coast Guard 'Bear' class.

UPDATED

WEI HSING   *6/1996*, Taiwan Customs /* 0080792

2 PAO HSING CLASS (COASTAL PATROL CRAFT)

PAO HSING   CHIN HSING

Displacement, tons: 550 full load
Dimensions, feet (metres): 189.6 × 25.6 × 6.9 *(57.8 × 7.8 × 2.1)*
Main machinery: 2 MAN 12V25/30 diesels; 7,183 hp(m) *(5.28 MW)* sustained; 2 shafts
Speed, knots: 20
Complement: 40
Guns: 2—12.7 mm MGs.
Radars: Surface search: JRC; I-band.

Comment: First delivered 20 May 1980; second 23 May 1985. Built by Keelung yard of China SB Corporation.

UPDATED

PAO HSING   *1994*, Taiwan Customs /* 0080793

2 COASTAL PATROL CRAFT

MOU HSING   FU HSING

Displacement, tons: 917 full load
Dimensions, feet (metres): 214.6 × 31.5 × 10.5 *(65.4 × 9.6 × 3.2)*
Main machinery: 2 MTU 16V 1163 TB93 diesels; 13,310 hp(m) *(9.78 MW)* sustained; 2 shafts
Speed, knots: 28. **Range, miles:** 4,500 at 12 kt
Complement: 54
Guns: 2—12.7 mm MGs.
Radars: Surface search: Racal Decca; I-band.

Comment: Ordered from Wilton Fijenoord in September 1986, and commissioned 14 June 1988.

UPDATED

MOU HSING   *1994*, Taiwan Customs /* 0080794

1 YUN HSING CLASS (COASTAL PATROL CRAFT)

YUN HSING

Displacement, tons: 964 full load
Dimensions, feet (metres): 213.3 × 32.8 × 9.5 *(65 × 10 × 2.9)*
Main machinery: 2 MAN 12V 25/30 diesels; 7,183 hp(m) *(5.28 MW)*; 2 shafts
Speed, knots: 18
Complement: 67
Guns: 2—12.7 mm MGs.
Radars: Surface search: JRC; I-band.

Comment: Built by China SB Corporation and delivered 28 December 1987.

UPDATED

YUN HSING   *5/1997*, van Ginderen Collection /* 0019244

1 HSUN HSING CLASS (COASTAL PATROL CRAFT)

HSUN HSING

Displacement, tons: 264 full load
Dimensions, feet (metres): 146 × 24.6 × 5.8 *(44.5 × 7.5 × 1.7)*
Main machinery: 3 MTU 16V 396 TB93 diesels; 6,540 hp(m) *(4.81 MW)* sustained; 3 shafts
Speed, knots: 28. **Range, miles:** 1,500 at 20 kt
Complement: 41
Guns: 3 Oerlikon 20 mm.
Radars: Surface search: JRC; I-band.

Comment: Built by China SB Corporation and delivered 15 December 1985.

UPDATED

HSUN HSING   *1993, Taiwan Customs /* 0080795

1 HAI PING CLASS (INSHORE PATROL CRAFT)

HAI PING

Displacement, tons: 96 full load
Dimensions, feet (metres): 85.3 × 18.4 × 3.6 *(26 × 5.6 × 1.1)*
Main machinery: 2 MTU 8V 331 TC81 diesels; 1,740 hp(m) *(1.28 MW)* sustained; 2 shafts
Speed, knots: 28
Complement: 18
Guns: 1 Oerlikon 20 mm.
Radars: Surface search: JRC; I-band.

Comment: Built by China SB Corporation, Keelung and delivered 28 February 1979. Two others
   scrapped in 1997.
UPDATED

HAI PING   *6/1999*, G Toremans /* 0080796

1 HAI WEI CLASS (INSHORE PATROL CRAFT)

HAI WEI

Displacement, tons: 70 full load
Dimensions, feet (metres): 78.7 × 18.4 × 4.9 *(24 × 5.6 × 1.5)*
Main machinery: 2 Detroit 12V-71TA diesels; 840 hp *(627 kW)* sustained; 2 shafts
Speed, knots: 19
Complement: 17 (5 officers)
Guns: 1 Oerlikon 20 mm.
Radars: Surface search: JRC; I-band.

Comment: Built by Halter Marine, New Orleans. Purchased in 1977. Steel hull. Second of class
   scrapped in 1997.
UPDATED

HAI WEI   *1994*, Taiwan Customs /* 0080797

TANZANIA

Headquarters Appointments	Personnel	Bases	DELETIONS
Commander of the Navy: Brigadier L G Sande	(a) 2000: 1,050 (including Zanzibar) (b) Voluntary service	Dar Es Salaam, Zanzibar, Mwanza (Lake Victoria). Mtwara (Lake Victoria). Kigoma (Lake Tanganyika).	**Patrol Forces** 1997-98 2 Kimjin, 1 Vosper 75, 2 Huchuan 1999 1 Vosper 75
General			
There is a small Coastguard Service (KMKM), based on Zanzibar, which uses small boats for anti-smuggling patrols.	**Coast Defence** 85 mm mobile gun battery.	**Mercantile Marine** *Lloyd's Register of Shipping:* 56 vessels of 36,238 tons gross	

PATROL FORCES

Note: The Police have four 'Yulin' class patrol boats which are probably non-operational.

2 SHANGHAI II CLASS (FAST ATTACK CRAFT—GUN) (PCF)

MZIZI JW 9867   **MZIA** JW 9868

Displacement, tons: 134 full load
Dimensions, feet (metres): 127.3 × 17.7 × 5.6 *(38.8 × 5.4 × 1.7)*
Main machinery: 2 Type L12-180 diesels; 2,400 hp(m) *(1.76 MW)* (forward); 2 Type 12-D-6
   diesels; 1,820 hp(m) *(1.34 MW)* (aft); 4 shafts
Speed, knots: 30. **Range, miles:** 700 at 16.5 kt
Complement: 38
Guns: 4—37 mm/63 (2 twin). 4—25 mm/80 (2 twin).
Radars: Surface search: Skin Head; I-band.

Comment: Six transferred by the People's Republic of China in 1971-72, two more in June 1992.
   These last two are still seaworthy, the remainder have been scrapped.
UPDATED

SHANGHAI II (old number)   *1990*

2 HUCHUAN CLASS (FAST ATTACK CRAFT—TORPEDO) (PHT)

JW 9843   JW 9844

Displacement, tons: 39 standard; 45.8 full load
Dimensions, feet (metres): 71.5 × 20.7 oa × 11.8 (hullborne) *(21.8 × 6.3 × 3.6)*
Main machinery: 3 Type M 50 diesels; 3,300 hp(m) *(2.4 MW)* sustained; 3 shafts
Speed, knots: 50. **Range, miles:** 500 at 30 kt
Complement: 16
Guns: 4—14.5 mm (2 twin) MGs.
Torpedoes: 2—21 in *(533 mm)* tubes.
Radars: Surface search: Skin Head; I-band.

Comment: Four transferred from the People's Republic of China 1975. After a major effort in 1992,
   were all operational and reported to be in good condition but by 1998 two had been laid up. This
   last pair are based at Kigoma on Lake Tanganyika. One gun mounting is forward of the bridge.
UPDATED

HUCHUAN (Chinese colours)   *1993* /* 0080798

2 VOSPER THORNYCROFT 75 ft TYPE (COASTAL PATROL CRAFT)

Displacement, tons: 70 full load
Dimensions, feet (metres): 75 × 19.5 × 8 *(22.9 × 6 × 2.4)*
Main machinery: 2 Caterpillar D 348 diesels; 1,450 hp *(1.08 MW)* sustained; 2 shafts
Speed, knots: 24.5. **Range, miles:** 800 at 20 kt
Complement: 11
Guns: 2 Oerlikon 20 mm GAM-BO1.
Radars: Surface search: Furuno; I-band.

Comment: First pair delivered 6 July 1973, second pair 1974. Used for anti-smuggling patrols off
   Zanzibar. These two still operational.
UPDATED

VOSPER 75 ft (Oman colours)   *1984, N Overington*

AUXILIARIES

2 YUNNAN (TYPE 067) CLASS (LCU)

Displacement, tons: 135 full load
Dimensions, feet (metres): 93.8 × 17.7 × 4.9 *(28.6 × 5.4 × 1.5)*
Main machinery: 2 diesels; 600 hp(m) *(441 kW)*; 2 shafts
Speed, knots: 12. **Range, miles:** 500 at 10 kt
Complement: 12
Military lift: 46 tons
Guns: 4—14.5 mm (2 twin) MGs.
Radars: Navigation: Fuji; I-band.

Comment: Transferred from China in 1995 probably to replace the Police Yuchai transport craft. Based at Dar-es-Salaam.

UPDATED   YUNNAN (Sri Lanka colours)   *1992* */ 0080713*

THAILAND

Headquarters Appointments

Commander-in-Chief of the Navy:
  Admiral Thira Hao-Charoen
Deputy Commander-in-Chief:
  Admiral Preecha Poungsuwan
Assistant Commander-in-Chief:
  Admiral Prasert Boonsong
Chief of Staff:
  Admiral Pallop Suntrapai
Deputy Chief of Staff:
  Vice Admiral Daweesak Somabha

Senior Appointments

Commander-in-Chief, Fleet:
  Admiral Narong Yuthavong
Deputy Commander-in-Chief, Fleet:
  Vice Admiral Somchai Tarvornpanich
Deputy Commander-in-Chief:
  Vice Admiral Preecha Prayodyothin
Chief of Staff, Fleet:
  Vice Admiral Chai Suvannaparb

Diplomatic Representation

Naval Attaché in London:
  Captain Supot Pruksa
Naval Attaché in Washington:
  Captain Narongpol Nabangchang
Naval Attaché in Paris:
  Captain Pachara Pumpiched
Naval Attaché in Canberra:
  Captain Komin Komuthanon
Naval Attaché in Madrid:
  Captain Pairoat Kaensarn
Naval Attaché in New Delhi:
  Captain Pasomtsup Kuanoon
Naval Attaché in Singapore:
  Captain Srivisuthi Ratarun
Naval Attaché in Kuala Lumpur:
  Captain Choomnoom Ardwong
Naval Attaché in Beijing:
  Captain Polwat Sirodom
Naval Attaché in Rome:
  Captain Narong Pipatanasai

Personnel

(a) 2000: Navy, 74,000 (including 2,000 Naval Air Arm, 11,000 Marines and Coastal Defense Command)
(b) 2 years' national service (28,000 conscripts)

Organisation

First naval area command (East Thai Gulf)
Second naval area command (West Thai Gulf)
Third naval area command (Andaman Sea)

Bases

Bangkok, Sattahip, Songkhla, Phang-Nga (west coast)

Naval Aviation

First air wing (U-Tapao)
Second air wing (Songkhla)
101 Sqdn   MPA/ASW
102 Sqdn   MPA/ASuW
103 Sqdn   Utility
104 Sqdn   Maritime Strike
105 Sqdn   Matador
201 Sqdn   Central Patrol
202 Bell Helos
203 Sikorsky Helos

Pennant Numbers

Ships over 150 tons displacement which had single digit numbers, had new numbers allocated in 1994-95.

Strength of the Fleet

Type	Active	Building (Projected)
Aircraft Carriers	1	—
Frigates	14	—
Corvettes	7	1
Fast Attack Craft (Missile)	6	—
Fast Attack Craft (Gun)	3	—
Large Patrol Craft	6	—
Coastal Patrol Craft	49	(7)
MCM Support Ship	1	—
Minehunters	4	(6)
Coastal Minesweepers	2	—
MSBs	12	—
LSTs	6	—
LSMs	2	—
Hovercraft	3	—
Survey Vessels	5	—
Replenishment Ship	1	—
MCMV Depot Ship	1	—
Tankers/Transports	8	—
Training Ships	2	(1)

Prefix to Ships' Names

HTMS

Coast Guard

A trial coastal unit of one frigate, eight patrol craft and four aircraft was established on 1 April 1989. The Coast Guard Squadron was officially authorised on 29 September 1992. Armed Sea Rangers in converted Fishing Vessels are being used to counter pirates. Ships and aircraft are rotated monthly from the Navy.

Coast Defence

Coastal Defence Command was rapidly expanded to the 1992 two Division level after the government charged the RTN with the responsibility of defending the entire Eastern Seaboard Development Project on the east coast of the Gulf of Thailand in 1988. Equipment includes 10 batteries of truck-mounted Exocet MM 40, 155 and 130 mm guns for coastal defence, 76, 40, 37, 20 mm guns and PL-9B SAM for air defence.

Marine Police

Acts as a Coast Guard in inshore waters with some 60 armed patrol craft and another 65 equipped with small arms only.

Submarines

By 1996 plans to acquire submarines had moved to the point of proposals being requested from seven different countries. Since then the project has again been cancelled, but a force of five submarines is still projected by 2006.

Mercantile Marine

Lloyd's Register of Shipping:
  551 vessels of 1,956,057 tons gross

DELETIONS

Amphibious Forces

1999   *Aungthong*

PENNANT LIST

Aircraft Carriers

911	Chakri Naruebet

Frigates

411	Tachin
412	Prasae
413	Pin Klao
421	Naresuan
422	Taksin
431	Tapi
432	Khirirat
433	Makut Rajakumarn
455	Chao Phraya
456	Bangpakong
457	Kraburi
458	Saiburi
461	Phuttha Yotfa Chulalok
462	Phuttha Loetia Naphalai

Corvettes

441	Rattanakosin
442	Sukothai
531	Khamronsin
532	Thayanchon
533	Longlom
541	Hua Hin
542	Klaeng
543	Si Racha (bldg)

Patrol Forces

311	Prabparapak
312	Hanhak Sattru
313	Suphairin
321	Ratcharit
322	Witthayakhom
323	Udomdet
331	Chon Buri
332	Songkhla
333	Phuket
521	Sattahip
522	Klongyai
523	Takbai
524	Kantang
525	Thepha
526	Taimuang

Mine Warfare Forces

612	Bangkeo
613	Donchedi

621	Thalang
631	Bang Rachan
632	Nongsarai
633	Lat Ya
634	Tha Din Daeng

Amphibious Forces

712	Chang
713	Pangan
714	Lanta
715	Prathong
721	Sichang
722	Surin
731	Kut
732	Kram
741	Prab
742	Satakut
751	Nakha
761	Mataphon
762	Rawi
763	Adang
764	Phetra
766	Talibong
771	Thong Kaeo
772	Thong Lang
773	Wang Nok
774	Wang Nai
775	Man Nok (bldg)
776	Man Klang (bldg)
777	Man Nal (bldg)

Auxiliaries

811	Chanthara
812	Suk
821	Suriya
831	Chula
832	Samui
833	Prong
834	Proet
835	Samed
841	Chuang
842	Chik
851	Klueng Baden
852	Marn Vichai
853	Rin
854	Rang
855	Samaesan
856	Raet
861	Kled Keo
871	Similan

AIRCRAFT CARRIERS

1 CHAKRI NARUEBET CLASS (CVS)

Name	No	Builders	Laid down	Launched	Commissioned
CHAKRI NARUEBET	911	Bazán, Ferrol	12 July 1994	20 Jan 1996	27 Mar 1997

Displacement, tons: 11,485 full load
Dimensions, feet (metres): 599.1 oa; 538.4 wl × 100.1 oa; 73.8 wl × 20.3 *(182.6; 164.1 × 30.5; 22.5 × 6.2)*
Flight deck, feet (metres): 572.8 × 90.2 *(174.6 × 27.5)*
Main machinery: CODOG; 2 GE LM 2500 gas turbines; 44,250 hp *(33 MW)* sustained; 2 MTU 16V 1163 TB83 diesels; 11,780 hp(m) *(8.67 MW)*; 2 shafts; acbLIPS cp props
Speed, knots: 26; 16 (diesels). **Range, miles:** 10,000 at 12 kt
Complement: 455 (62 officers) plus 146 aircrew plus 4 (Royal family)

Missiles: SAM: 1 Mk 41 LCHR 8 cell VLS launcher ❶; Sea Sparrow missiles. To be fitted.
3 Matra Sadral sextuple launchers for Mistral; IR homing to 4 km *(2.2 n miles)*; warhead 3 kg.
Guns: 4 Vulcan Phalanx CIWS ❷. 2—30 mm. To be fitted.
Countermeasures: Decoys: 4 Tracor Mk 137 chaff launchers.
ESM: Indra Aldebaran; intercept.
ECM: Raytheon SLQ-32(V)3; jammer.
Combat data systems: Tritan derivative with Unisys UYK-3 and 20 computers.
Radars: Air search: Hughes SPS-52C ❸; E/F-band.
Surface search: SPS-64 ❹; I-band. To be fitted.
Fire control: Signaal STIR ❺; I/J/K-band.
Navigation: Kelvin Hughes; I-band.
Aircraft control: Kelvin Hughes; E/F-band.
Tacan: URN 25.
Sonars: Hull-mounted; active search; medium frequency.

Fixed-wing aircraft: 6 AV-8S Matador (Harrier).
Helicopters: 6 S-70B7 Seahawk; Chinook capable.

Programmes: An initial contract for a 7,800 ton vessel with Bremer Vulcan was cancelled on 22 July 1991 and replaced on 27 March 1992 with a government to government contract for a larger ship to be built by Bazán. Fabrication started in October 1993. Sea trials conducted from November 1996 to January

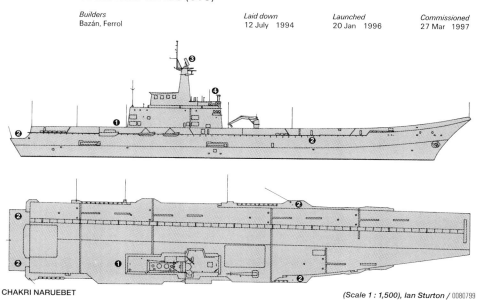

CHAKRI NARUEBET   (Scale 1 : 1,500), Ian Sturton / 0080799

1997 followed by an aviation work-up at Rota from April 1997. The ship arrived in Thailand on 10 August 1997.
Structure: Similar to Spanish *Príncipe de Asturias*. 12° ski jump and two 20 ton aircraft lifts. Many of the weapon systems are being fitted in Bangkok and some of these have been delayed by funding problems. They include SAM, CIWS,

countermeasures, surface search and fire-control radars and sonar. Hangar can take up 10 Sea Harrier or Seahawk aircraft.
Operational: Main tasks are SAR co-ordination and EEZ surveillance. Secondary role is air support for all maritime operations. Fixed-wing aircraft flying has been mostly limited to shore based operations.   **UPDATED**

CHAKRI NARUEBET   5/1997, S G Gaya / 0019250

CHAKRI NARUEBET   8/1997, Thai Navy League / 0050232

CHAKRI NARUEBET   5/1997, S G Gaya / 0019245

FRIGATES

2 NARESUAN CLASS (TYPE 25T) (FFG)

Name	No	Builders	Laid down	Launched	Commissioned
NARESUAN	421 (ex-621)	Zhonghua SY, Shanghai	Feb 1992	24 July 1993	15 Dec 1994
TAKSIN	422 (ex-622)	Zhonghua SY, Shanghai	Nov 1992	14 May 1994	28 Sep 1995

Displacement, tons: 2,500 standard; 2,980 full load
Dimensions, feet (metres): 393.7 × 42.7 × 12.5
(120 × 13 × 3.8)
Main machinery: CODOG; 2 GE LM 2500 gas turbines; 44,250 hp *(33 MW)* sustained; 2 MTU 20 V 1163 TB83 diesels; 11,780 hp(m) *(8.67 MW)* sustained; 2 shafts; acbLIPS cp props

Speed, knots: 32. **Range, miles:** 4,000 at 18 kt
Complement: 150

Missiles: SSM: 8 McDonnell Douglas Harpoon (2 quad) launchers ❶; active radar homing to 130 km *(70 n miles)* at 0.9 Mach; warhead 227 kg.

SAM: Mk 41 LCHR 8 cell VLS launcher ❷ Sea Sparrow; semi-active radar homing to 14.6 km *(8 n miles)* at 2.5 Mach; warhead 39 kg.
Guns: 1 FMC 5 in *(127 mm)*/54 Mk 45 Mod 2 ❸; 20 rds/min to 23 km *(12.6 n miles)*; weight of shell 32 kg.
4 China 37 mm/76 (2 twin) H/PJ 76 A ❹; 180 rds/min to 8.5 km *(4.6 n miles)* anti-aircraft; weight of shell 1.42 kg.
Torpedoes: 6—324 mm Mk 32 Mod 5 (2 triple) tubes ❺. Honeywell Mk 46; active/passive homing to 11 km *(5.9 n miles)* at 40 kt; warhead 44 kg.
Countermeasures: Decoys: 4 China Type 945 GPJ 26-barrelled launchers ❻; chaff and IR.
ESM/ECM: Elettronica Newton Beta EW System; intercept and jammer.
Weapons control: 1 JM-83H Optical Director ❼.
Radars: Air search: Signaal LW08 ❽; D-band.
Surface search: China Type 360 ❾; E/F-band.
Navigation: 2 Raytheon SPS-64(V)5; I-band.
Fire control: 2 Signaal STIR ❿; I/J/K-band (for SSM and 127 mm). After one to be fitted.
China 374 G ⓫ (for 37 mm).
Sonars: China SJD-7; hull-mounted; active search and attack; medium frequency.

Helicopters: 1 SH-2G Seasprite ⓬ in due course or 1 Sikorsky S-70B7 Seahawk.

Programmes: Contract signed 21 September 1989 for construction of two ships by the China State SB Corporation (CSSC) with delivery in 1994. US and European weapon systems were fitted as funds became available. The first ship sailed for Bangkok without most weapon systems in January 1995 with the second following in October 1995.
Structure: Jointly designed by the Royal Thai Navy and China State Shipbuilding Corporation (CSSC). This is a design incorporating much Western machinery and equipment and provides enhanced capabilities by comparison with the four 'Type 053' class. The anti-aircraft guns are Breda 40 mm types with 37 mm ammunition and they are controlled by a Chinese RTN-20 Dardo tracker.
Operational: *Naresuan* acted as one of the escorts for the aircraft carrier during her aviation work-up in Spanish waters in 1997.
UPDATED

NARESUAN
(Scale 1 : 1,200), Ian Sturton / 0080801

NARESUAN
6/1997, Luis Adell / 0050233

NARESUAN
8/1997, Thai Navy League / 0019246

TAKSIN
7/1998, Hachiro Nakai / 0050234

4 CHAO PHRAYA CLASS (TYPES 053 HT and 053 HT (H)) (FFG)

Name	No	Builders	Laid down	Launched		Commissioned	
CHAO PHRAYA	455	Hudong SY, Shanghai	1989	24 June	1990	5 Apr	1991
BANGPAKONG	456	Hudong SY, Shanghai	1989	25 July	1990	20 July	1991
KRABURI	457	Hudong SY, Shanghai	1990	28 Dec	1990	16 Jan	1992
SAIBURI	458	Hudong SY, Shanghai	1990	27 Aug	1991	4 Aug	1992

Displacement, tons: 1,676 standard; 1,924 full load
Dimensions, feet (metres): 338.5 × 37.1 × 10.2
(103.2 × 11.3 × 3.1)
Main machinery: 4 MTU 20V 1163 TB83 diesels; 29,440 hp(m)
(21.6 MW) sustained; 2 shafts; acbLIPS cp props
Speed, knots: 30. **Range, miles:** 3,500 at 18 kt
Complement: 168 (22 officers)

Missiles: SSM: 8 Ying Ji (Eagle Strike) (C-801) **❶**; active radar/IR
homing to 85 km *(45.9 n miles)* at 0.9 Mach; warhead 165 kg;
sea-skimmer. This is the extended range version.
SAM: 1 HQ-61 launcher for PL-9 or Matra Sadral for Mistral to be
fitted.
Guns: 2 (457 and 458) or 4 China 100 mm/56 (1 or 2 twin) **❷**;
25 rds/min to 22 km *(12 n miles)*; weight of shell 15.9 kg.
8 China 37 mm/76 (4 twin) H/PJ 76 A **❸**; 180 rds/min to
8.5 km *(4.6 n miles)* anti-aircraft; weight of shell 1.42 kg.
A/S mortars: 2 RBU 1200 (China Type 86) 5-tubed fixed
launchers **❹**; range 1,200 m.
Depth charges: 2 BMB racks.
Countermeasures: Decoys: 2 China Type 945 GPJ 26-barrelled
chaff launchers.
ESM: China Type 923(1); intercept.
ECM: China Type 981(3); jammer.

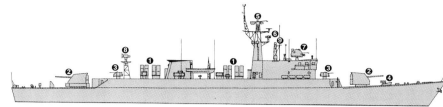

CHAO PHRAYA

(Scale 1 : 900), Ian Sturton / 0080802

Combat data systems: China Type ZKJ-3 or STN Atlas mini
COSYS action data automation being fitted.
Radars: Air/surface search: China Type 354 Eye Shield **❺**;
E-band.
Surface search/fire control: China Type 352C Square Tie **❻**;
I-band (for SSM).
Fire control: China Type 343 Sun Visor **❼**; I-band (for 100 mm).
China Type 341 Rice Lamp **❽**; I-band (for 37 mm).
Navigation: Racal Decca 1290 A/D ARPA and Anritsu
RA 71CA **❾**; I-band.
IFF: Type 651.

Sonars: China Type SJD-5A; hull-mounted; active search and
attack; medium frequency.

Helicopters: Platform for 1 Bell 212 (457 and 458) **❿** or SH-2G
Seasprite in due course.

Programmes: Contract signed 18 July 1988 for four modified
'Jianghu' class ships to be built by the China State SB
Corporation (CSSC).
Modernisation: A mini COSYS system was acquired for two of
the class in 1999.
Structure: Thailand would have preferred only the hulls but
China insisted on full armament. Two of the ships are the Type
III variant with 100 mm guns, fore and aft, and the other two
are a variation with a helicopter platform replacing the after
100 mm gun. German communication equipment fitted. The
EW fit is Italian designed.
Operational: On arrival in Thailand each ship was docked to
make good poor shipbuilding standards and improve damage
control capabilities. The ships are mostly used for rotating
monthly to the Coast Guard, and for training, although *Kraburi*
was part of the escort force for the aircraft carrier in Spanish
waters in 1997.

KRABURI

(Scale 1 : 900), Ian Sturton / 0080803

UPDATED

KRABURI

5/1998, Ships of the World / 0050235

BANGPAKONG

6/1999 /* 0080804

2 KNOX CLASS (FFG)

Name	No	Builders	Laid down	Launched	Commissioned
PHUTTHA YOTFA CHULALOK (ex-*Truett*)	461 (ex-FF 1095)	Avondale Shipyards	27 Apr 1972	3 Feb 1973	1 June 1974
PHUTTHA LOETIA NAPHALAI (ex-*Ouellet*)	462 (ex-FF 1077)	Avondale Shipyards	15 Jan 1969	17 Jan 1970	12 Dec 1970

Displacement, tons: 3,011 standard; 4,260 full load
Dimensions, feet (metres): 439.6 × 46.8 × 15; 24.8 (sonar)
(134 × 14.3 × 4.6; 7.8)
Main machinery: 2 Combustion Engineering/Babcock & Wilcox boilers; 1,200 psi *(84.4 kg/cm²)*; 950°F *(510°C)*; 1 turbine; 35,000 hp *(26 MW)*; 1 shaft
Speed, knots: 27. **Range, miles:** 4,000 at 22 kt on 1 boiler
Complement: 288 (17 officers)

Missiles: SSM: 8 McDonnell Douglas Harpoon; active radar homing to 130 km *(70 n miles)* at 0.9 Mach; warhead 227 kg.
A/S: Honeywell ASROC Mk 16 octuple launcher with reload system (has 2 cells modified to fire Harpoon) ❶; inertial guidance to 1.6-10 km *(1-5.4 n miles)*; payload Mk 46.
Guns: 1 FMC 5 in *(127 mm)*/54 Mk 42 Mod 9 ❷; 20-40 rds/min to 24 km *(13 n miles)* anti-surface; 14 km *(7.7 n miles)* anti-aircraft; weight of shell 32 kg.
1 General Electric/General Dynamics 20 mm/76 6-barrelled Mk 15 Vulcan Phalanx ❸; 3,000 rds/min combined to 1.5 km.
Torpedoes: 4—324 mm Mk 32 (2 twin) fixed tubes ❹. 22 Honeywell Mk 46; anti-submarine; active/passive homing to 11 km *(5.9 n miles)* at 40 kt; warhead 44 kg.
Countermeasures: Decoys: 2 Loral Hycor SRBOC 6-barrelled fixed Mk 36 ❺; IR flares and chaff to 4 km *(2.2 n miles)*. T Mk-6 Fanfare/SLQ-25 Nixie; torpedo decoy. Prairie Masker hull and blade rate noise suppression.
ESM/ECM: SLQ-32(V)2 ❻; radar warning. Sidekick modification adds jammer and deception system.
Combat data systems: Link 14 receive only.
Weapons control: SWG-1A Harpoon LCS. Mk 68 GFCS. Mk 114 ASW FCS. Mk 1 target designation system. MMS target acquisition sight (for mines, small craft and low-flying aircraft).
Radars: Air search: Lockheed SPS-40B ❼; E/F-band; range 320 km *(175 n miles)*.
Surface search: Raytheon SPS-10 or Norden SPS-67 ❽; G-band.
Navigation: Marconi LN66; I-band.
Fire control: Western Electric SPG-53A/D/F ❾; I/J-band.
Tacan: SRN 15. IFF: UPX-12.
Sonars: EDO/General Electric SQS-26CX; bow-mounted; active search and attack; medium frequency.

Helicopters: 1 Bell 212 or SH-2G Seasprite ❿ in due course.

Programmes: The first ship transferred on five year lease from the USA on 30 July 1994. This was renewed by grant in 1999. The second transferred on lease 27 November 1996 and arrived in Thailand in November 1998.
Structure: Four Mk 32 torpedo tubes are fixed in the midships structure, two to a side, angled out at 45°. The arrangement

PHUTTHA YOTFA CHULALOK

(Scale 1 : 1,200), Ian Sturton / 0080805

PHUTTHA LOETIA NAPHALAI

11/1998, Thai Navy League / 0043441

provides improved loading capability over exposed triple Mk 32 torpedo tubes. A 4,000 lb lightweight anchor is fitted on the port side and an 8,000 lb anchor fits into the after section of the sonar dome.

Operational: Towed sonar array and helicopter facilities are uncertain but the acquisition of these ships adds emphasis to the need for an ASW helicopter.

UPDATED

1 YARROW TYPE (TRAINING SHIP) (FF/AX)

Name	No	Builders	Laid down	Launched	Commissioned
MAKUT RAJAKUMARN	433 (ex-7)	Yarrow Shipbuilders	11 Jan 1970	18 Nov 1971	7 May 1973

Displacement, tons: 1,650 standard; 1,900 full load
Dimensions, feet (metres): 320 × 36 × 18.1
(97.6 × 11 × 5.5)
Main machinery: CODOG; 1 RR Olympus TM3B gas turbine; 22,500 hp *(16.8 MW)* sustained; 1 Crossley-SEMT-Pielstick 12 PC2.2 V 400 diesel; 6,000 hp(m) *(4.4 MW)* sustained; 2 shafts
Speed, knots: 26 gas; 18 diesel
Range, miles: 5,000 at 18 kt; 1,200 at 26 kt
Complement: 140 (16 officers)

Guns: 2 Vickers 4.5 in *(114 mm)*/55 Mk 8 ❶; 25 rds/min to 22 km *(12 n miles)* anti-surface; 6 km *(3.3 n miles)* anti-aircraft; weight of shell 21 kg.
2 Bofors 40 mm/70 (twin) ❷; 300 rds/min to 12.5 km *(6.8 n miles)*; weight of shell 0.96 kg.
2 Oerlikon 20 mm.
Torpedoes: 6 Plessey PMW 49A tubes ❸ Mk 46; active/passive homing to 11 km *(5.9 n miles)* at 40 kt; warhead 44 kg.
A/S mortars: 1 Limbo 3-tubed Mk 10 ❹; non-operational.
Depth charges: 1 rack.

Countermeasures: Decoys: 2 Loral Mk 135 chaff launchers.
ESM/ECM: Elettronica Newton ❺; intercept and jammer. WLR-1; radar warning.
Combat data systems: Signaal Sewaco TH.
Radars: Air/surface search: Signaal DA05 ❻; E/F-band; range 137 km *(75 n miles)* for 2 m² target.
Surface search: Signaal ZW06 ❼; I-band.
Fire control: Signaal WM22/61 ❽; I/J-band; range 46 km *(25 n miles)*.
Navigation: Racal Decca; I-band.
Sonars: Atlas Elektronik DSQS-21C; hull-mounted; active search and attack; medium frequency.

Programmes: Ordered on 21 August 1969.
Modernisation: A severe fire in February 1984 resulted in extensive work including replacement of the Olympus gas turbine, a new ER control room and central electric switchboard. Further modifications included the removal of Seacat SAM system and the installation of new EW equipment in 1993. In 1997 two Bofors 40 mm were fitted on the old Seacat mounting, and torpedo tubes replaced the old Bofors abreast the funnel.
Operational: The ship is largely automated with a consequent saving in complement, and has been most successful in service. Has lost its Flagship role to one of the Chinese-built frigates and become a training ship.

UPDATED

MAKUT RAJAKUMARN

(Scale 1 : 900), Ian Sturton / 0080806

MAKUT RAJAKUMARN

7/1999, John Mortimer / 0080807*

2 TAPI (PF 103) CLASS (FF)

Name	No
TAPI	431 (ex-5)
KHIRIRAT	432 (ex-6)

Builders	Laid down	Launched	Commissioned
American SB Co, Toledo, OH	1 July 1970	17 Oct 1970	19 Nov 1971
Norfolk SB & DD Co	18 Feb 1972	2 June 1973	10 Aug 1974

Displacement, tons: 885 standard; 1,172 full load
Dimensions, feet (metres): 275 × 33 × 10; 14.1 (sonar)
  (83.8 × 10 × 3; 4.3)
Main machinery: 2 Fairbanks-Morse 38TD8-1/8-9 diesels;
  5,250 hp *(3.9 MW)* sustained; 2 shafts
Speed, knots: 20. **Range, miles:** 2,400 at 18 kt
Complement: 135 (15 officers)

Guns: 1 OTO Melara 3 in *(76 mm)*/62 compact ❶; 85 rds/min to
  16 km *(8.7 n miles)* anti-surface; 12 km *(6.6 n miles)* anti-
  aircraft; weight of shell 6 kg.
  1 Bofors 40 mm/70 ❷; 300 rds/min to 12.5 km *(6.8 n miles)*;
  weight of shell 0.96 kg.
  2 Oerlikon 20 mm ❸. 2—12.7 mm MGs.
Torpedoes: 6—324 mm US Mk 32 (2 triple) tubes ❹. Honeywell
  Mk 46; anti-submarine; active/passive homing to 11 km *(5.9 n
  miles)* at 40 kt; warhead 44 kg.
Depth charges: 1 rack.
Combat data systems: Signaal Sewaco TH.
Radars: Air/surface search: Signaal LW04 ❺; E/F-band; range
  137 km *(75 n miles)* for 2 m² target.
Surface search: Raytheon SPS-53E ❻; I-band.
Fire control: Signaal WM22-61 ❼; I/J-band; range 46 km *(25 n
  miles)*.
IFF: UPX-23.
Sonars: Atlas Elektronik DSQS-21C; hull-mounted; active search
  and attack; medium frequency.

Programmes: *Tapi* was ordered on 27 June 1969. *Khirirat* was
  ordered on 25 June 1971.
Modernisation: *Tapi* completed 1983 and *Khirirat* in 1987. This
  included new gunnery and radars and a slight heightening of
  the funnel. Further modernisation in 1988-89 mainly to
  external and internal communications.
Structure: Of similar design to the Iranian ships of the 'Bayandor'
  class.
Operational: Used for EEZ patrols.

VERIFIED

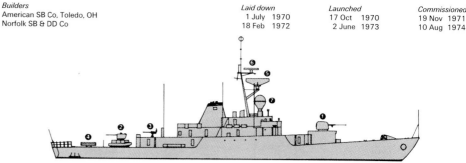

TAPI

(Scale 1 : 900), Ian Sturton

KHIRIRAT

10/1996, L-G Nilsson / 0050237

1 CANNON CLASS (FF)

Name	No
PIN KLAO (ex-*Hemminger* DE 746)	413 (ex-3, ex-1)

Builders	Laid down	Launched	Commissioned
Western Pipe & Steel Co	1943	12 Sep 1943	30 May 1944

Displacement, tons: 1,240 standard; 1,930 full load
Dimensions, feet (metres): 306 × 36.7 × 14
  (93.3 × 11.2 × 4.3)
Main machinery: Diesel-electric; 4 GM 16-278A diesels;
  6,000 hp *(4.5 MW)*; 4 generators; 2 motors; 2 shafts
Speed, knots: 20
Range, miles: 10,800 at 12 kt; 6,700 at 19 kt
Complement: 192 (14 officers)

Guns: 3 USN 3 in *(76 mm)*/50 Mk 22; 20 rds/min to 12 km
  (6.6 n miles); weight of shell 6 kg.
  6 Bofors 40 mm/60 (3 twin); 120 rds/min to 10 km *(5.5 n
  miles)*; weight of shell 0.89 kg.

Torpedoes: 6—324 mm US Mk 32 (2 triple) tubes; anti-
  submarine.
A/S mortars: 1 Hedgehog Mk 10 multibarrelled fixed; range
  250 m; warhead 13.6 kg; 24 rockets.
Depth charges: 8 projectors; 2 racks.
Countermeasures: ESM: WLR-1; radar warning.
Weapons control: Mk 52 radar GFCS for 3 in guns. Mk 63 radar
  GFCS for aft gun only. 2 Mk 51 optical GFCS for 40 mm.
Radars: Air/surface search: Raytheon SPS-5; G/H-band.
Navigation: Raytheon SPS-21; G/H-band.
Fire control: Western Electric Mk 34; I/J-band.
  RCA/General Electric Mk 26; I/J-band.
IFF: SLR 1.

Sonars: SQS-11; hull-mounted; active attack; high frequency.

Programmes: Transferred from US Navy at New York Navy
  Shipyard in July 1959 under MDAP and by sale 6 June 1975.
Modernisation: The three 21 in torpedo tubes were removed and
  the 20 mm guns were replaced by 40 mm. The six A/S
  torpedo tubes were fitted in 1966.
Operational: Used mostly as a training ship.

VERIFIED

PIN KLAO

6/1997, Royal Thai Navy / 0019254

2 TACHIN (TACOMA) CLASS (FF)

Name	No	Builders	Laid down	Launched	Commissioned
TACHIN (ex-*Glendale* PF 36)	411 (ex-1)	Consolidated Steel Corporation, LA	6 Apr 1943	28 May 1943	1 Oct 1943
PRASAE (ex-*Gallup* PF 47)	412 (ex-2)	Consolidated Steel Corporation, LA	18 Aug 1943	17 Sep 1943	29 Feb 1944

Displacement, tons: 1,430 standard; 2,454 full load
Dimensions, feet (metres): 304 × 37.5 × 12.5
(92.7 × 11.4 × 4.1)
Main machinery: 2 boilers; 2 reciprocating engines; 5,500 ihp
(4.1 MW); 2 shafts
Speed, knots: 18. **Range, miles:** 7,200 at 12 kt; 5,400 at 15 kt
Complement: 214 (13 officers)

Guns: 3 USN 3 in *(76 mm)*/50; 20 rds/min to 12 km *(6.6 n
miles)*; weight of shell 6 kg.
2 Bofors 40 mm/60; 120 rds/min to 10 km *(5.5 n miles)*;
weight of shell 0.89 kg.
9 Oerlikon 20 mm/70.
Radars: Air search: Westinghouse SPS-6C; D-band.
Surface search: Raytheon SPS-5 *(Tachin)*; G/H-band.
Raytheon SPS-10 *(Prasae)*; G/H-band.
Navigation: Decca; I-band.
Fire control: Mk 51; I/J-band.
IFF: UPX 12B.

Programmes: Delivered from the USA on 29 October 1951. The
last active survivors of the US equivalent of the British and
Canadian 'River' class.
Operational: Used in Training Squadron and in rotation for
coastguard duties. All ASW equipment either removed or non-
operational. Planned to decommission in 1998 but are still in
service.

UPDATED

TACHIN   *6/1999 * / 0080808*

CORVETTES

2 RATTANAKOSIN CLASS (FSG)

Name	No	Builders	Laid down	Launched	Commissioned
RATTANAKOSIN	441 (ex-1)	Tacoma Boatbuilders, WA	6 Feb 1984	11 Mar 1986	26 Sep 1986
SUKHOTHAI	442 (ex-2)	Tacoma Boatbuilders, WA	26 Mar 1984	20 July 1986	10 June 1987

Displacement, tons: 960 full load
Dimensions, feet (metres): 252 × 31.5 × 8
(76.8 × 9.6 × 2.4)
Main machinery: 2 MTU 20V 1163 TB83 diesels; 14,730 hp(m)
(10.83 MW) sustained; 2 shafts; Kamewa cp props
Speed, knots: 26. **Range, miles:** 3,000 at 16 kt
Complement: 87 (15 officers) plus Flag Staff

Missiles: SSM: 8 McDonnell Douglas Harpoon (2 quad)
launchers ❶; active radar homing to 130 km *(70 n miles)* at
0.9 Mach; warhead 227 kg (84A) or 258 kg (84B/C).

SAM: Selenia Elsag Albatros octuple launcher ❷; 24 Aspide;
semi-active radar homing to 13 km *(7 n miles)* at 2.5 Mach;
height envelope 15-5,000 m *(49.2-16,405 ft)*; warhead 30 kg.
Guns: 1 OTO Melara 3 in *(76 mm)*/62 ❸; 60 rds/min to 16 km
(8.7 n miles); weight of shell 6 kg.
2 Breda 40 mm/70 (twin) ❹; 300 rds/min to 12.5 km *(6.8 n
miles)*; weight of shell 0.96 kg.
2 Oerlikon 20 mm ❺.
Torpedoes: 6—324 mm US Mk 32 (2 triple) tubes ❻. MUSL
Stingray; active/passive homing to 11 km *(5.9 n miles)* at

45 kt; warhead 35 kg (shaped charge); depth to 750 m
(2,460 ft).
Countermeasures: Decoys: CSEE Dagaie 6- or 10-tubed
trainable; IR flares and chaff; H- to J-band.
ESM: Elettronica; intercept.
Weapons control: Signaal Sewaco TH action data automation.
Lirod 8 optronic director ❼.
Radars: Air/surface search: Signaal DA05 ❽; E/F-band; range
137 km *(75 n miles)* for 2 m² target.
Surface search: Signaal ZW06 ❾; I-band.
Navigation: Decca 1226; I-band.
Fire control: Signaal WM25/41 ❿; I/J-band; range 46 km *(25 n
miles)*.
Sonars: Atlas Elektronik DSQS-21C; hull-mounted; active search
and attack; medium frequency.

Programmes: Contract signed with Tacoma on 9 May 1983.
Intentions to build a third were overtaken by the Vosper
corvettes.
Structure: There are some similarities with the missile corvettes
built for Saudi Arabia five years earlier. Space for Phalanx aft of
the Harpoon launchers, but there are no plans to fit.

UPDATED

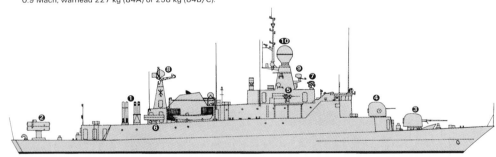

RATTANAKOSIN
(Scale 1 : 600), Ian Sturton

RATTANAKOSIN   *8/1997, John Mortimer / 0019257*

3 KHAMRONSIN CLASS (FS)

Name	No	Builders	Laid down	Launched	Commissioned
KHAMRONSIN	531 (ex-1)	Ital Thai Marine, Bangkok	15 Mar 1988	15 Aug 1989	29 July 1992
THAYANCHON	532 (ex-2)	Ital Thai Marine, Bangkok	20 Apr 1988	7 Dec 1989	5 Sep 1992
LONGLOM	533 (ex-3)	Bangkok Naval Dockyard	15 Mar 1988	8 Aug 1989	2 Oct 1992

Displacement, tons: 630 full load
Dimensions, feet (metres): 203.4 oa; 186 wl × 26.9 × 8.2
(62; 56.7 × 8.2 × 2.5)
Main machinery: 2 MTU 12V 1163 TB93; 9,980 hp(m)
(7.34 MW) sustained; 2 Kamewa cp props
Speed, knots: 25. **Range, miles:** 2,500 at 15 kt
Complement: 57 (6 officers)

Guns: 1 OTO Melara 76 mm/62 Mod 7 ❶; 60 rds/min to 16 km
(8.7 n miles); weight of shell 6 kg.
2 Breda 30 mm/70 (twin) ❷; 800 rds/min to 12.5 km *(6.8 n
miles)*; weight of shell 0.37 kg.
2—12.7 mm MGs.
Torpedoes: 6 Plessey PMW 49A (2 triple) launchers ❸; MUSL
Stingray; active/passive homing to 11 km *(5.9 n miles)* at
45 kt; warhead 35 kg shaped charge.

Combat data systems: Plessey Nautis P action data automation.
Weapons control: British Aerospace Sea Archer 1A Mod 2
optronic GFCS ❹.
Radars: Air/surface search: Plessey AWS 4 ❺; E/F-band.
Navigation: Racal Decca 1226; I-band.
Sonars: Atlas Elektronik DSQS-21C; hull-mounted; active search
and attack; medium frequency.

Programmes: Contract signed on 29 September 1987 with Ital
Thai Marine of Bangkok for the construction of two ASW
corvettes and for technical assistance with a third to be built in
Bangkok Naval Dockyard. A fourth of the class with a different
superstructure and less armament was ordered by the Police in
September 1989.
Structure: The vessels are based on a Vosper Thornycroft
'Province' class 56 m design stretched by increasing the frame
spacing along the whole length of the hull. Depth charge racks
and mine rails may be added.

UPDATED

KHAMRONSIN

(Scale 1 : 600), Ian Sturton

THAYANCHON

12/1999*, Sattler/Steele / 0080809

2 + 1 HUA HIN CLASS (FS)

Name	No	Builders	Laid down	Launched	Commissioned
HUA HIN	541	Asimar, Samut Prakarn	Mar 1997	3 May 1999	25 Mar 2000
KLAENG	542	Asimar, Samut Prakarn	May 1997	19 Apr 1999	Aug 2000
SI RACHA	543	Bangkok Naval Dockyard	Dec 1997	6 Sep 1999	Feb 2001

Displacement, tons: 645 full load
Dimensions, feet (metres): 203.4 × 29.2 × 8.9
(62 × 8.9 × 2.7)
Main machinery: 3 Paxman 12VP 185 diesels; 10,372 hp(m)
(7.63 MW) sustained; 3 shafts; 1 acbLIPS cp prop (centreline)
Speed, knots: 25. **Range, miles:** 2,500 at 15 kt
Complement: 45 (11 officers)

Guns: 1 Otobreda 3 in *(76 mm)*/62 compact ❶; 85 rds/min to
16 km *(8.7 n miles)*; weight of shell 6 kg.
1 Bofors 40 mm/70 ❷; 2 Oerlikon 20 mm GAM-BO1 ❸.
2—12.7 mm MGs.
Weapons control: Optronic director ❹.
Radars: Surface search: Sperry Rascar ❺; E/F-band.
Navigation: Sperry Apar; I-band.

Programmes: Ordered in September 1996 from Asian Marine.
Delayed and reported cancelled by the Thai Navy in late 1997
as a result of shortage of funds but the programme continued
in spite of delays.
Structure: Derived from the Khamronsin design.

UPDATED

HUA HIN

(Scale 1 : 600), Ian Sturton / 0080810

HUA HIN
3/1999*, Royal Thai Navy / 0084412

SHIPBORNE AIRCRAFT

Note: 10 SH-2G Seasprite helicopters are required when funds are available.

Numbers/Type: 7/2 BAe/McDonnell Douglas AV-8S/TAV-8S Matador (Harrier).
Operational speed: 640 kt *(1,186 km/h)*.
Service ceiling: 51,200 ft *(15,600 m)*.
Range: 800 n miles *(1,480 km)*.
Role/Weapon systems: AV-8S supplied via USA to Spain and transferred in 1996. Sensors: None.
Weapons: Strike; two 30 mm Aden cannon, two AIM-9 Sidewinder or 20 mm/127 mm rockets
and 'iron' bombs.

UPDATED

MATADOR
6/1999* / 0080811

Numbers/Type: 6 Sikorsky S-70B7 Seahawk.
Operational speed: 135 kt *(250 km/h)*.
Service ceiling: 10,000 ft *(3,050 m)*.
Range: 600 n miles *(1,110 km)*.
Role/Weapon systems: Multimission helicopters delivered by June 1997. ASW equipment is to be acquired. Sensors: Telephonics APS-143(V)3 radar; ASN 150 databus; provision for sonobuoys and dipping sonar; ALR 606(V)2 ESM. Weapons: Provision for ASM and MUSL Stingray torpedoes.

UPDATED

SEAHAWK   8/1997, Thai Navy League / 0019260

Numbers/Type: 8 Bell 212.
Operational speed: 100 kt *(185 km/h)*.
Service ceiling: 13,200 ft *(4,025 m)*.
Range: 200 n miles *(370 km)*.
Role/Weapon systems: Commando assault and general support. May be sold to help pay for Seasprites. Mostly based ashore but operate from 'Normed' class and frigates. Weapons: Pintle-mounted M60 machine guns.

VERIFIED

BELL 212   1993, Royal Thai Navy / 0050240

LAND-BASED MARITIME AIRCRAFT (FRONT LINE)

Note: 25 Cessna transports, four UH-1H and eight Bell 214ST utility helicopters are in service in the support role.

Numbers/Type: 4 Sikorsky S-76B.
Operational speed: 145 kt *(269 km/h)*.
Service ceiling: 6,500 ft *(1,980 m)*.
Range: 357 n miles *(661 km)*.
Role/Weapon systems: Six originally acquired in 1996 for maritime surveillance and utility purposes. Sensors: Weather radar. Weapons: Unarmed.

UPDATED

S-76   8/1996, Royal Thai Navy / 0050241

Numbers/Type: 2/1 Lockheed P-3T/UP-3T Orion.
Operational speed: 411 kt *(761 km/h)*.
Service ceiling: 28,300 ft *(8,625 m)*.
Range: 4,000 n miles *(7,410 km)*.
Role/Weapon systems: Delivered in 1996. Two for ASW and one utility. Two more are required. Sensors: APS-115 radar, ECM/ESM. Weapons: ASW; Mk 46 or Stingray torpedoes. ASV; four Harpoon.

VERIFIED

ORION   8/1997, Royal Thai Navy / 0019261

Numbers/Type: 14/4 A-7E/TA-7E Corsair II.
Operational speed: 600 kt *(1,112 km/h)*.
Service ceiling: 50,000 ft *(15,240 m)*.
Range: 2,000 n miles *(3,705 km)*.
Role/Weapon systems: Delivered in 1996-97 from the US. Not all are operational. Weapons: AIM-9L Sidewinder; 1—20 mm cannon.

UPDATED

CORSAIR II   8/1996, Royal Thai Navy / 0053451

Numbers/Type: 3/2 Fokker F27 Maritime 200ME/400M.
Operational speed: 250 kt *(463 km/h)*.
Service ceiling: 25,000 ft *(7,620 m)*.
Range: 2,700 n miles *(5,000 km)*.
Role/Weapon systems: Increased coastal surveillance and response is provided, including ASW and ASV action by 200ME. 400M is for transport. Sensors: APS-504 search radar, Bendix weather radar, ESM and MAD equipment. Weapons: ASW; four Mk 46 or Stingray torpedoes or depth bombs or mines. ASV; two Harpoon ASM.

VERIFIED

FOKKER 400   1994, Royal Thai Navy / 0053452

Numbers/Type: 5 GAF Searchmaster B (Nomad).
Operational speed: 168 kt *(311 km/h)*.
Service ceiling: 21,000 ft *(6,400 m)*.
Range: 730 n miles *(1,352 km)*.
Role/Weapon systems: Short-range MR for EEZ protection and anti-smuggling operations. Sensors: Search radar, cameras. Weapons: Unarmed.

VERIFIED

Numbers/Type: 6 Dornier 228.
Operational speed: 200 kt *(370 km/h)*.
Service ceiling: 28,000 ft *(8,535 m)*.
Range: 940 n miles *(1,740 km)*.
Role/Weapon systems: Coastal surveillance and EEZ protection. Three acquired in 1991, three more in 1996. Sensors: APS-128/504 search radar.

VERIFIED

DORNIER 228   6/1996, Royal Thai Navy / 0019262

Numbers/Type: 2 Canadair CL-215.
Operational speed: 206 kt *(382 km/h)*.
Service ceiling: 10,000 ft *(3,050 m)*.
Range: 1,125 n miles *(2,085 km)*.
Role/Weapon systems: Used for general purpose transport and SAR.

VERIFIED

CL-215   1993, Royal Thai Navy / 0053453

PATROL FORCES

3 RATCHARIT CLASS (FAST ATTACK CRAFT—MISSILE) (PCFG)

Name	No	Builders	Commissioned
RATCHARIT	321 (ex-4)	CN Breda (Venezia)	10 Aug 1979
WITTHAYAKHOM	322 (ex-5)	CN Breda (Venezia)	12 Nov 1979
UDOMDET	323 (ex-6)	CN Breda (Venezia)	21 Feb 1980

Displacement, tons: 235 standard; 270 full load
Dimensions, feet (metres): 163.4 × 24.6 × 7.5 *(49.8 × 7.5 × 2.3)*
Main machinery: 3 MTU MD 20V 538 TB91 diesels; 11,520 hp(m) *(8.47 MW)* sustained; 3 shafts; Kamewa cp props
Speed, knots: 37. **Range, miles:** 2,000 at 15 kt
Complement: 45 (7 officers)

Missiles: SSM: 4 Aerospatiale MM 38 Exocet; inertial cruise; active radar homing to 42 km *(23 n miles)* at 0.9 Mach; warhead 165 kg; sea-skimmer.
Guns: 1 OTO Melara 3 in *(76 mm)*/62 compact; 85 rds/min to 16 km *(8.7 n miles)* anti-surface; 12 km *(6.6 n miles)* anti-aircraft; weight of shell 6 kg.
   1 Bofors 40 mm/70; 300 rds/min to 12.5 km *(6.8 n miles)*; weight of shell 0.96 kg.
Countermeasures: ESM: Racal RDL-2; intercept.
Radars: Surface search: Decca; I-band.
Fire control: Signaal WM25; I/J-band; range 46 km *(25 n miles)*.

Programmes: Ordered June 1976. *Ratcharit* launched 30 July 1978, *Witthayakhom* 2 September 1978 and *Udomdet* 28 September 1978.
Structure: Standard Breda BMB 230 design.

UPDATED

RATCHARIT   *6/1997*, Royal Thai Navy /* 0019263

3 PRABPARAPAK CLASS (FAST ATTACK CRAFT—MISSILE) (PCFG)

Name	No	Builders	Commissioned
PRABPARAPAK	311 (ex-1)	Singapore SBEC	28 July 1976
HANHAK SATTRU	312 (ex-2)	Singapore SBEC	6 Nov 1976
SUPHAIRIN	313 (ex-3)	Singapore SBEC	1 Feb 1977

Displacement, tons: 224 standard; 268 full load
Dimensions, feet (metres): 149 × 24.3 × 7.5 *(45.4 × 7.4 × 2.3)*
Main machinery: 4 MTU 16V 538 TB92 diesels; 13,640 hp(m) *(10 MW)* sustained; 4 shafts
Speed, knots: 40. **Range, miles:** 2,000 at 15 kt; 750 at 37 kt
Complement: 41 (5 officers)

Missiles: SSM: 5 IAI Gabriel I (1 triple, 2 single) launchers; radar or optical guidance; semi-active radar homing to 20 km *(10.8 n miles)* at 0.7 Mach; warhead 75 kg.
Guns: 1 Bofors 57 mm/70; 200 rds/min to 17 km *(9.3 n miles)*; weight of shell 2.4 kg. 8 rocket illuminant launchers on either side of 57 mm gun.
   1 Bofors 40 mm/70; 300 rds/min to 12 km *(6.6 n miles)*; weight of shell 2.4 kg.
Countermeasures: ESM: Racal RDL-2; intercept.
Radars: Surface search: Kelvin Hughes Type 17; I-band.
Fire control: Signaal WM28/5 series; I/J-band.

Programmes: Ordered June 1973. Built under licence from Lürssen. Launch dates—*Prabparapak* 29 July 1975, *Hanhak Sattru* 28 October 1975, *Suphairin* 20 February 1976.
Modernisation: There are plans to replace Gabriel possibly by RBS 15.
Structure: Same design as Lürssen standard 45 m class built for Singapore. Normally only three Gabriel SSM are carried.

UPDATED

PRABPARAPAK   *10/1995*, Royal Thai Navy /* 0080812

3 CHON BURI CLASS (FAST ATTACK CRAFT—GUN) (PCF)

Name	No	Builders	Commissioned
CHON BURI	331 (ex-1)	CN Breda (Venezia) Mestre	22 Feb 1983
SONGKHLA	332 (ex-2)	CN Breda (Venezia) Mestre	15 July 1983
PHUKET	333 (ex-3)	CN Breda (Venezia) Mestre	13 Jan 1984

Displacement, tons: 450 full load
Dimensions, feet (metres): 198 × 29 × 15 *(60.4 × 8.8 × 4.5)*
Main machinery: 3 MTU 20V 538 TB92 diesels; 12,795 hp(m) *(9.4 MW)* sustained; 3 shafts; cp props
Speed, knots: 30. **Range, miles:** 2,500 at 18 kt; 900 at 30 kt
Complement: 41 (6 officers)
Guns: 2 OTO Melara 3 in *(76 mm)*/62; 85 rds/min to 16 km *(8.7 n miles)*; weight of shell 6 kg. 2 Breda 40 mm/70 (twin).
Countermeasures: Decoys: 4 Hycor Mk 135 chaff launchers.
ESM: Elettronica Newton; intercept.
Weapons control: Signaal Lirod 8 optronic director.
Radars: Surface search: Signaal ZW06; I-band.
Fire control: Signaal WM22/61; I/J-band; range 46 km *(25 n miles)*.

Comment: Ordered in 1979 (first pair) and 1981. Laid down—*Chon Buri* 15 August 1981 (launched 29 November 1982), *Songkhla* 15 September 1981 (launched 6 September 1982), *Phuket* 15 December 1981 (launched 3 February 1983). Steel hulls, alloy superstructure. Can be adapted to carry SSMs.

UPDATED

PHUKET   *6/1999*, Sattler/Steele /* 0080813

SONGKHLA   *3/1999*, G Toremans /* 0080814

6 SATTAHIP (PSMM Mk 5) CLASS (LARGE PATROL CRAFT) (PC)

Name	No	Builders	Commissioned
SATTAHIP	521 (ex-4)	Ital Thai (Samutprakarn) Ltd	16 Sep 1983
KLONGYAI	522 (ex-5)	Ital Thai (Samutprakarn) Ltd	7 May 1984
TAKBAI	523 (ex-6)	Ital Thai (Samutprakarn) Ltd	18 July 1984
KANTANG	524 (ex-7)	Ital Thai (Samutprakarn) Ltd	14 Oct 1985
THEPHA	525 (ex-8)	Ital Thai (Samutprakarn) Ltd	17 Apr 1986
TAIMUANG	526 (ex-9)	Ital Thai (Samutprakarn) Ltd	17 Apr 1986

Displacement, tons: 270 standard; 300 full load
Dimensions, feet (metres): 164.5 × 23.9 × 5.9 *(50.1 × 7.3 × 1.8)*
Main machinery: 2 MTU 16V 538 TB92 diesels; 6,820 hp(m) *(5 MW)* sustained; 2 shafts
Speed, knots: 22. **Range, miles:** 2,500 at 15 kt
Complement: 56
Guns: 1 OTO Melara 3 in *(76 mm)*/62 (in 521-523). 1 USN 3 in *(76 mm)*/50 Mk 26 (in 524-526).
   1 Bofors 40 mm/70 or 40 mm/60. 2 Oerlikon 20 mm GAM-BO1. 2—12.7 mm MGs.
Weapons control: NA 18 optronic director (in 521-523).
Radars: Surface search: Decca; I-band.

Comment: First four ordered 9 September 1981, *Thepha* on 27 December 1983 and *Taimuang* on 31 August 1984.

UPDATED

TAKBAI   *10/1999*, Royal Thai Navy /* 0080815

3 + (7) T 81 CLASS (COASTAL PATROL CRAFT) (PC)

T 81   T 82   T 83

Displacement, tons: 120 full load
Dimensions, feet (metres): 98.8 × 20.7 × 5.6 *(30.1 × 6.3 × 1.7)*
Main machinery: 2 MTU 16V 2000 TE90 diesels; 3,600 hp(m) *(2.56 MW)*; 2 shafts
Speed, knots: 25. **Range, miles:** 1,300 at 15 kt
Complement: 28 (3 officers)
Guns: 1 Bofors 40 mm/70. 1 Oerlikon 20 mm. 2—12.7 mm MGs.
Radars: Surface search: Sperry SM 5000; I-band.

Comment: Ordered in October 1996 from ASC Silkline in Pranburi. First one commissioned 5 August 1999, second 9 December 1999 and the third planned for mid-2000. Plans for seven more may be shelved.

UPDATED

T 81   3/1999, ASC/Silkline / 0048072

7 PGM 71 CLASS (COASTAL PATROL CRAFT) (PC)

T 14-19   T 110

Displacement, tons: 130 standard; 147 full load
Dimensions, feet (metres): 101 × 21 × 6 *(30.8 × 6.4 × 1.9)*
Main machinery: 2 GM diesels; 1,800 hp *(1.34 MW)*; 2 shafts
Speed, knots: 18.5. **Range, miles:** 1,500 at 10 kt
Complement: 30
Guns: 1 Bofors 40 mm/60. 1 Oerlikon 20 mm. 2—12.7 mm MGs.
  In some craft the 20 mm gun has been replaced by an 81 mm mortar/12.7 mm combined mounting aft.
Radars: Surface search: Decca 303 *(T 11* and *12)* or Decca 202 (remainder); I-band.

Comment: Built by Peterson Inc between 1966 and 1970. Transferred from USA. To be replaced by T 81 class.

UPDATED

T 16   10/1999*, Royal Thai Navy / 0080816

9 T 91 CLASS (COASTAL PATROL CRAFT) (PC)

T 91-99

Displacement, tons: 87.5 *(T 91)*, 130 (remainder) standard
Dimensions, feet (metres): 104.3 × 17.5 × 5.5 *(31.8 × 5.3 × 1.7)* *(T 91)*
  118 × 18.7 × 4.9 *(36 × 5.7 × 1.5)* (remainder)
Main machinery: 2 MTU 12V 538 TB81/82 diesels; 3,300 hp(m) *(2.43 MW)*/4,430 hp(m) *(3.26 MW)* sustained; 2 shafts
Speed, knots: 25. **Range, miles:** 700 at 21 kt
Complement: 21; 23 *(T 93-94)*; 25 *(T 99)*
Guns: 1 or 2 Bofors 40 mm/60. 1—20 mm GAM-BO1 (in some). 2—12.7 mm MGs.
Weapons control: Sea Archer 1A optronic director *(T 99* only).
Radars: Surface search: Raytheon SPS-35 (1500B); I-band.

Comment: Built by Royal Thai Naval Dockyard, Bangkok. *T 91* commissioned in 1965; *T 92-93* in 1973; *T 94-98* between 1981 and 1984; *T 99* in 1987. *T 91* has an extended upperworks and a 20 mm gun in place of the after 40 mm. *T 99* has a single Bofors 40/70, one Oerlikon 20 mm and two MGs. There may be other armament variations in the group *T 94-98*. Major refits from 1983-86 for earlier vessels of the class.

UPDATED

T 98   6/1999*, Sattler/Steele / 0080817

12 SWIFT CLASS (COASTAL PATROL CRAFT) (PC)

T 21-29   T 210-212

Displacement, tons: 22 full load
Dimensions, feet (metres): 50 × 13 × 3.5 *(15.2 × 4 × 1.1)*
Main machinery: 2 Detroit diesels; 480 hp *(358 kW)*; 2 shafts
Speed, knots: 25. **Range, miles:** 400 at 25 kt
Complement: 8 (1 officer)
Guns: 2—81 mm mortars. 2—12.7 mm MGs.
Radars: Surface search: Raytheon Pathfinder; I-band.

Comment: Transferred from US Navy from 1967-75. *T 210-212* are Sea Spectre ex-PB Mk III and have three engines and a slightly larger hull.

UPDATED

T 26   8/1998*, P Marsan / 0080818

18 T 213 CLASS (COASTAL PATROL CRAFT) (PC)

T 213-226   T 227-230

Displacement, tons: 35 standard
Dimensions, feet (metres): 64 × 17.5 × 5 *(19.5 × 5.3 × 1.5)*
Main machinery: 2 MTU diesels; 715 hp(m) *(526 kW)*; 2 shafts
Speed, knots: 25
Complement: 8 (1 officer)
Guns: 1 Oerlikon 20 mm. 1—81 mm mortar with 12.7 mm MG.
Radars: Surface search: Racal Decca 110; I-band.

Comment: Built by Ital Thai Marine Ltd. Commissioned—*T 213-215*, 29 August 1980; *T 216-218*, 26 March 1981; *T 219-223*, 16 September 1981; *T 224*, 19 November 1982; *T 225* and *T 226*, 28 March 1984; *T 227-230* in 1990/91. Of alloy construction. Used for fishery patrol and coastal control duties.

UPDATED

T 223   6/1999*, Sattler/Steele / 0080819

13 PBR Mk II (RIVER PATROL CRAFT) (PBR)

T 240 series

Displacement, tons: 8 full load
Dimensions, feet (metres): 32.1 × 11.5 × 2.3 *(9.8 × 3.5 × 0.7)*
Main machinery: 2 Detroit diesels; 430 hp *(321 kW)*; 2 Jacuzzi water-jets
Speed, knots: 25. **Range, miles:** 150 at 23 kt
Complement: 4
Guns: 2—12.7 mm (twin) MGs. 2—6.72 mm MGs. 1—60 mm mortar.
Radars: Surface search: Raytheon SPS-66; I-band.

Comment: Transferred from USA from 1967-73. Employed on Mekong River. Reported to be getting old, numbers are reducing and maximum speed has been virtually halved. All belong to the Riverine Squadron.

VERIFIED

T 242   5/1997, A Sharma / 0050242

90 ASSAULT BOATS

Displacement, tons: 0.4 full load
Dimensions, feet (metres): 16.4 × 6.2 × 1.3 *(5 × 1.9 × 0.4)*
Main machinery: 1 outboard; 150 hp *(110 kW)*
Speed, knots: 24
Complement: 2
Guns: 1—7.62 mm MG.

Comment: Part of the Riverine Squadron with the PBRs and two PCFs. Can carry six people. Numbers uncertain.

UPDATED

ASSAULT BOAT   *1991*, Royal Thai Navy /* 0080820

MINE WARFARE FORCES

1 MCM SUPPORT SHIP (MST)

Name	No	Builders	Commissioned
THALANG	621 (ex-1)	Bangkok Dock Co Ltd	4 Aug 1980

Displacement, tons: 1,000 standard
Dimensions, feet (metres): 185.5 × 33 × 10 *(55.7 × 10 × 3.1)*
Main machinery: 2 MTU diesels; 1,310 hp(m) *(963 kW)*; 2 shafts
Speed, knots: 12
Complement: 77
Guns: 1 Bofors 40 mm/70. 2 Oerlikon 20 mm. 2—12.7 mm MGs.
Radars: Surface search: Racal Decca 1226; I-band.

Comment: Has minesweeping capability. Two 3 ton cranes provided for change of minesweeping gear in MSCs—four sets carried. Design by Ferrostaal, Essen. Has dormant minelaying capability.

UPDATED

THALANG   *5/1997*, Maritime Photographic /* 0019269

2 + (6) LAT YA (GAETA) CLASS
(MINEHUNTERS/SWEEPERS) (MHC/MSC)

Name	No	Builders	Launched	Commissioned
LAT YA	633	Intermarine, Sarzana	30 Mar 1998	18 June 1999
THA DIN DAENG	634	Intermarine, Sarzana	31 Oct 1998	18 Dec 1999

Displacement, tons: 680 full load
Dimensions, feet (metres): 172.1 × 32.4 × 9.4 *(52.5 × 9.9 × 2.9)*
Main machinery: 2 MTU 8V 396 TE74K diesels; 1,600 hp(m) *(1.18 MW)* sustained; 2 Voith Schneider props; auxiliary propulsion; 2 hydraulic motors
Speed, knots: 14. **Range, miles:** 2,000 at 12 kt
Complement: 50 (8 officers)
Guns: 1 MSI 30 mm.
Countermeasures: MCM: Atlas MWS 80-6 minehunting system. Magnetic, acoustic and mechanical sweeps; ADI Mini Dyad, Noise Maker, Bofors MS 106, 2 Pluto Plus ROVs.
Radars: Navigation: Atlas Elektronik 9600M (ARPA); I-band.
Sonars: Atlas Elektronik DSQS-11M; hull-mounted; active; high frequency.

Comment: Invitations to tender lodged by 3 April 1996. Ordered 19 September 1996. Specifications include hunting at up to 6 kt and sweeping at 10 kt. Up to eight ships are required.

UPDATED

THA DIN DAENG   *1/2000*, Giorgio Ghiglione /* 0080821

2 BANG RACHAN CLASS
(MINEHUNTERS/SWEEPERS) (MHC/MSC)

Name	No	Builders	Commissioned
BANG RACHAN	631 (ex-2)	Lürssen Vegesack	29 Apr 1987
NONGSARAI	632 (ex-3)	Lürssen Vegesack	17 Nov 1987

Displacement, tons: 444 full load
Dimensions, feet (metres): 161.1 × 30.5 × 8.2 *(49.1 × 9.3 × 2.5)*
Main machinery: 2 MTU 12V 396 TB83 diesels; 3,120 hp(m) *(2.3 MW)* sustained; 2 shafts; Kamewa cp props; auxiliary propulsion; 1 motor
Speed, knots: 17; 7 (electric motor). **Range, miles:** 3,100 at 12 kt
Complement: 33 (7 officers)
Guns: 3 Oerlikon GAM-BO1 20 mm.
Countermeasures: MCM: MWS 80R minehunting system. Acoustic, magnetic and mechanical sweeps. 2 Gaymarine Pluto 15 remote-controlled submersibles.
Radars: Navigation: 2 Atlas Elektronik 8600 ARPA; I-band.
Sonars: Atlas Elektronik DSQS-11H; hull-mounted; minehunting; high frequency.

Comment: First ordered from Lürssen late 1984, arrived Bangkok 22 October 1987. Second ordered 5 August 1985 and arrived in Bangkok May 1988. Amagnetic steel frames and deckhouses, wooden hull. Motorola Miniranger MRS III precise navigation system. Draeger decompression chamber. It is planned to upgrade the sonar to 11M when funds are available.

UPDATED

BANG RACHAN   *8/1997*, Royal Thai Navy /* 0019270

2 BLUEBIRD CLASS (MINESWEEPERS—COASTAL) (MSC)

Name	No	Builders	Commissioned
BANGKEO (ex-*MSC 303*)	612 (ex-6)	Dorchester SB Corporation, Camden	9 July 1965
DONCHEDI (ex-*MSC 313*)	613 (ex-8)	Peterson Builders Inc, Sturgeon Bay, WI	17 Sep 1965

Displacement, tons: 317 standard; 384 full load
Dimensions, feet (metres): 145.3 × 27 × 8.5 *(44.3 × 8.2 × 2.6)*
Main machinery: 2 GM 8-268 diesels; 880 hp *(656 kW)*; 2 shafts
Speed, knots: 13. **Range, miles:** 2,750 at 12 kt
Complement: 43 (7 officers)
Guns: 2 Oerlikon 20 mm/80 (twin).
Countermeasures: MCM: US Mk 4 (V). Mk 6. US Type Q2 magnetic.
Radars: Navigation: Decca TM 707; I-band.
Sonars: UQS-1; hull-mounted; minehunting; high frequency.

Comment: Constructed for Thailand. One paid off in 1992, one in 1995 and the last two are in limited operational service. Being replaced by 'Lat Ya' class in 2000.

UPDATED

BANGKEO   *5/1997*, Maritime Photographic /* 0019271

12 MSBs

MLM 6-10　　　**MSB 11-17**

Displacement, tons: 25 full load
Dimensions, feet (metres): 50.2 × 13.1 × 3 *(15.3 × 4 × 0.9)*
Main machinery: 1 Gray Marine 64 HN9 diesel; 165 hp *(123 kW)*; 1 shaft
Speed, knots: 8
Complement: 10
Guns: 2—7.62 mm MGs.

Comment: Three transferred from USA in October 1963 and two in 1964. More were built locally from 1994. Wooden hulled, converted from small motor launches. Operated on Chao Phraya river.

UPDATED

MSB 11　　　　　　　　　　　　　　*10/1995*, Royal Thai Navy /* 0080822

AMPHIBIOUS FORCES

Note: Ex-US 'Newport' class LST *Schenectady* authorised for transfer on lease but is no longer required.

2 NORMED CLASS (LST)

Name	No	Builders	Launched	Commissioned
SICHANG	721 (ex-LST 6)	Ital Thai	14 Apr 1987	9 Oct 1987
SURIN	722 (ex-LST 7)	Bangkok Dock Co Ltd	12 Apr 1988	16 Dec 1988

Displacement, tons: 3,540 standard; 4,235 full load
Dimensions, feet (metres): 337.8; 357.6 (722) × 51.5 × 11.5 *(103; 109 × 15.7 × 3.5)*
Main machinery: 2 MTU 20V 1163 TB82 diesels; 11,000 hp(m) *(8.1 MW)* sustained; 2 shafts; cp props
Speed, knots: 16. **Range, miles:** 7,000 at 12 kt
Complement: 53
Military lift: 348 troops; 14 tanks or 12 APCs or 850 tons cargo; 3 LCVP; 1 LCPL
Guns: 1 Bofors 40 mm/70. 2 Oerlikon GAM-CO1 20 mm. 2—12.7 mm MGs. 1—81 mm mortar.
Weapons control: 2 BAe Sea Archer Mk 1A optronic directors.
Radars: Navigation: Racal Decca 1226; I-band.
Helicopters: Platform for 2 Bell 212.

Comment: First ordered 31 August 1984 to a Chantier du Nord (Normed) design. Second ordered to a modified design and lengthened to accommodate a battalion. The largest naval ships yet built in Thailand. Have bow doors and a 17 m ramp.

UPDATED

SURIN　　　　　　　　　　　　　　　　　　*6/1997* /* 0080823

SICHANG　　　　　　　　　　　　　*10/1995*, Royal Thai Navy /* 0080824

4 LST 511-1152 CLASS (LST)

Name	No	Builders	Commissioned
CHANG (ex-*Lincoln County* LST 898)	712 (ex-LST 2)	Dravo Corporation	29 Dec 1944
PANGAN (ex-*Stark County* LST 1134)	713 (ex-LST 3)	Chicago Bridge and Iron Co, ILL	7 Apr 1945
LANTA (ex-*Stone County* LST 1141)	714 (ex-LST 4)	Chicago Bridge and Iron Co, ILL	9 May 1945
PRATHONG (ex-*Dodge County* LST 722)	715 (ex-LST 5)	Jefferson B & M Co, Ind	13 Sep 1944

Displacement, tons: 1,650 standard; 3,640/4,145 full load
Dimensions, feet (metres): 328 × 50 × 14 *(100 × 15.2 × 4.4)*
Main machinery: 2 GM 12-567A diesels; 1,800 hp *(1.34 MW)*; 2 shafts
Speed, knots: 11.5. **Range, miles:** 9,500 at 9 kt
Complement: 80; 157 (war)
Military lift: 1,230 tons max; 815 tons beaching
Guns: 8 Bofors 40 mm/60 (2 twin, 4 single) (can be carried).
　2—12.7 mm MGs *(Chang)*. 2 Oerlikon 20 mm (others).
Weapons control: 2 Mk 51 GFCS. 2 optical systems.
Radars: Navigation: Racal Decca 1229; I/J-band.

Comment: *Chang* transferred from USA in August 1962. *Pangan* 16 May 1966, *Lanta* on 15 August 1973 (by sale 1 March 1979) and *Prathong* on 17 December 1975. *Chang* has a reinforced bow and waterline. *Lanta, Prathong* and *Chang* have mobile crane on the well-deck. All have tripod mast.

UPDATED

PANGAN　　　　　　　　　　*5/1997, Maritime Photographic /* 0050246

2 LSM 1 CLASS (LSM)

Name	No	Builders	Commissioned
KUT (ex-*LSM 338*)	731 (ex-LSM 1)	Pullman Std Car Co, Chicago	10 Jan 1945
KRAM (ex-*LSM 469*)	732 (ex-LSM 3)	Brown SB Co, Houston, TX	17 Mar 1945

Displacement, tons: 743 standard; 1,107 full load
Dimensions, feet (metres): 203.5 × 34.5 × 9.9 *(62 × 10.5 × 3)*
Main machinery: 2 Fairbanks-Morse 38D8-1/8-10 diesels; 3,540 hp *(2.64 MW)* sustained; 2 shafts
Speed, knots: 12.5. **Range, miles:** 4,500 at 12.5 kt
Complement: 91 (6 officers)
Military lift: 452 tons beaching; 50 troops with vehicles
Guns: 2 Bofors 40 mm/60 Mk 3 (twin). 4 Oerlikon 20 mm/70.
Weapons control: Mk 51 Mod 2 optical director *(Kram)*.
Radars: Surface search: Raytheon SPS-5 *(Kram)*; G/H-band.
Navigation: Raytheon 1500 B; I-band.

Comment: Former US landing ships of the LCM, later LSM (Medium Landing Ship) type. *Kram* was transferred to Thailand under MAP on 25 May 1962, *Kut* in October 1946.

UPDATED

KUT　　　　　　　　　　　　*6/1998, Royal Thai Navy /* 0050244

0 + 3 MAN NOK CLASS (LCU)

Name	No	Builders	Commissioned
MAN NOK	775	Pranburi, Kra Isthmus	2000
MAN KLANG	776	Pranburi, Kra Isthmus	2001
MAN NAI	777	Pranburi, Kra Isthmus	2001

Displacement, tons: 170 light; 315 full load
Dimensions, feet (metres): 131.2 × 27.9 × 5.9 *(40 × 8.5 × 1.8)*
Main machinery: 2 MAN 2842 LE 403 V12 diesels; 700 hp(m) *(515 kW)*; 2 shafts
Speed, knots: 12. **Range, miles:** 1,500 at 10 kt
Complement: 30 (3 officers)
Military lift: 2 M60 tanks or 25 tons vehicles
Guns: 2 Oerlikon 20 mm.
Radars: Navigation: I-band.

Comment: Ordered from Silkline ASC in 1997. Launch dates are planned for 2000/01.

UPDATED

2 LSIL 351 CLASS (LCM)

PRAB 741 (ex-LSIL 1)   **SATAKUT** 742 (ex-LSIL 2)

Displacement, tons: 230 standard; 399 full load
Dimensions, feet (metres): 157 × 23 × 6 *(47.9 × 7 × 1.8)*
Main machinery: 4 GM diesels; 2,320 bhp *(1.73 MW)*; 2 shafts
Speed, knots: 15. **Range, miles:** 5,600 at 12.5 kt
Complement: 49 (7 officers)
Military lift: 101 tons or 76 troops
Guns: 1 US 3 in *(76 mm)*/50 or 1 Bofors 40 mm/60. 2 Oerlikon 20 mm/70.
Radars: Surface search: Raytheon SPS-35 (1500B); I-band.

Comment: Built in 1944-45, transferred from USA May 1947. A second of class was repaired and
was back in service in 1997.

UPDATED

PRAB   *2/1998*, Thai Navy League / 0019275

1 LCG TYPE (LSL)

NAKHA 751 (ex-LSSL 102, ex-LSSL 3)

Displacement, tons: 233 standard; 393 full load
Dimensions, feet (metres): 158.1 × 23.6 × 6.2 *(48.2 × 7.2 × 1.9)*
Main machinery: 2 GM diesels; 1,320 hp *(985 kW)*; 2 shafts
Speed, knots: 15. **Range, miles:** 5,000 at 6 kt
Complement: 60
Guns: 1 USN 3 in *(76 mm)*/50. 4 Bofors 40 mm/60 (2 twin). 4 Oerlikon 20 mm/70 (2 twin).
6—81 mm mortars. 2—12.7 mm MGs.
Radars: Navigation: Raytheon 1500 B; I-band.

Comment: Built by Commercial Ironworks, Oregon in 1945. Transferred from USA in 1966.
Acquired when Japan returned her to the USA.

VERIFIED

NAKHA   *8/1996, L Holland, USN*

4 THONG KAEO CLASS (LCU)

Name	No	Builders	Commissioned
THONG KAEO	771 (ex-7)	Bangkok Dock Co Ltd	23 Dec 1982
THONG LANG	772 (ex-8)	Bangkok Dock Co Ltd	19 Apr 1983
WANG NOK	773 (ex-9)	Bangkok Dock Co Ltd	16 Sep 1983
WANG NAI	774 (ex-10)	Bangkok Dock Co Ltd	11 Nov 1983

Displacement, tons: 193 standard; 396 full load
Dimensions, feet (metres): 134.5 × 29.5 × 6.9 *(41 × 9 × 2.1)*
Main machinery: 2 GM 16V-71 diesels; 1,400 hp *(1.04 MW)*; 2 shafts
Speed, knots: 10. **Range, miles:** 1,200 at 10 kt
Complement: 31 (3 officers)
Military lift: 3 lorries; 150 tons equipment
Guns: 2 Oerlikon 20 mm. 2—7.62 mm MGs.

Comment: Ordered in 1980.

UPDATED

WANG NAI   *5/1997*, Maritime Photographic / 0019276

5 MATAPHON CLASS (LCU)

MATAPHON 761 (ex-LCU 1)   **ADANG** 763 (ex-LCU 3)   **TALIBONG** 766 (ex-LCU 6)
RAWI 762 (ex-LCU 2)   **PHETRA** 764 (ex-LCU 4)

Displacement, tons: 145 standard; 330 full load
Dimensions, feet (metres): 120.4 × 32 × 4 *(36.7 × 9.8 × 1.2)*
Main machinery: 3 Gray Marine 65 diesels; 675 hp *(503 kW)*; 3 shafts
Speed, knots: 10. **Range, miles:** 650 at 8 kt
Complement: 13
Military lift: 150 tons or 3-4 tanks or 250 troops
Guns: 2 Oerlikon 20 mm/80.
Radars: Navigation: Raytheon Pathfinder; I-band.

Comment: Transferred from USA 1946-47. Employed as transport ferries.

UPDATED

TALIBONG   *6/1999* / 0080825

24 LCM 6 + 12 LCVP + 4 LCA

Displacement, tons: 56 full load
Dimensions, feet (metres): 56.1 × 14.1 × 3.9 *(17.1 × 4.3 × 1.2)*
Main machinery: 2 Gray Marine 64 HN9 diesels; 330 hp *(264 kW)*; 2 shafts
Speed, knots: 9. **Range, miles:** 135 at 9 kt
Complement: 5
Military lift: 34 tons

Comment: Details given are for the ex-US LCMs delivered in 1965-69. The ex-US LCVPs can lift
40 troops and are of 1960s vintage. The LCAs can lift 35 troops and were built in 1984 in
Bangkok.

VERIFIED

LCM 208   *11/1998, Thai Navy League* / 0050247

3 GRIFFON 1000 TD HOVERCRAFT

401–403

Dimensions, feet (metres): 27.6 × 12.5 *(8.4 × 3.8)*
Main machinery: 1 Deutz BF6L913C diesel; 190 hp(m) *(140 kW)*
Speed, knots: 33. **Range, miles:** 200 at 27 kt
Complement: 2
Cargo capacity: 1,000 kg plus 9 troops
Radars: Navigation: Raytheon; I-band.

Comment: Acquired in mid-1990 from Griffon Hovercraft. Although having an obvious amphibious
capability they are also used for rescue and flood control.

UPDATED

GRIFFON 401   *6/1999*, Royal Thai Navy / 0084413

TRAINING SHIPS

Note: A 3,500 ton ship Carlskrona type is wanted for training and as a support ship.

1 ALGERINE CLASS (AXL)

Name	No	Builders	Commissioned
PHOSAMTON (ex-*Minstrel*)	415 (ex-MSF 1)	Redfern Construction Co	9 June 1945

Displacement, tons: 1,040 standard; 1,335 full load
Dimensions, feet (metres): 225 × 35.5 × 11.5 *(68.6 × 10.8 × 3.5)*
Main machinery: 2 boilers; 2 reciprocating engines; 2,000 ihp *(1.49 MW)*; 2 shafts
Speed, knots: 16. **Range, miles:** 4,000 at 10 kt
Complement: 103
Guns: 1 USN 3 in *(76 mm)*/50. 1 Bofors 40 mm/60. 2 Oerlikon 20 mm.
Radars: Navigation: Raytheon Pathfinder; I-band.

Comment: Transferred from UK in April 1947. Received engineering overhaul in 1984. Minesweeping gear replaced by a deckhouse to increase training space. Vickers 4 in gun replaced.

UPDATED

PHOSAMTON   *8/1999*, Royal Thai Navy* / 0080827

SURVEY AND RESEARCH SHIPS

Note: There is also a civilian research vessel *Chulab Horn* which completed in 1986.

1 OCEANOGRAPHIC SHIP (AGOR)

Name	No	Builders	Commissioned
SUK	812	Bangkok Dock Co Ltd	3 Mar 1982

Displacement, tons: 1,450 standard; 1,526 full load
Dimensions, feet (metres): 206.3 × 36.1 × 13.4 *(62.9 × 11 × 4.1)*
Main machinery: 2 MTU diesels; 2,400 hp(m) *(1.76 MW)*; 2 shafts
Speed, knots: 15
Complement: 86 (20 officers)
Guns: 2 Oerlikon 20 mm. 2—7.62 mm MGs.
Radars: Navigation: Racal Decca 1226; I-band.

Comment: Laid down 27 August 1979, launched 8 September 1981. Designed for oceanographic and survey duties.

UPDATED

SUK   *5/1999*, van Ginderen Collection* / 0080828

1 SURVEY SHIP (AGS)

Name	No	Builders	Commissioned
CHANTHARA	811 (ex-AGS 11)	Lürssen Werft	30 May 1961

Displacement, tons: 870 standard; 996 full load
Dimensions, feet (metres): 229.2 × 34.5 × 10 *(69.9 × 10.5 × 3)*
Main machinery: 2 KHD diesels; 1,090 hp(m) *(801 kW)*; 2 shafts
Speed, knots: 13.25. **Range, miles:** 10,000 at 10 kt
Complement: 68 (8 officers)
Guns: 2 Bofors 40 mm/60.

Comment: Laid down on 27 September 1960. Launched on 17 December 1960. Has served as a Royal Yacht.

UPDATED

CHANTHARA   *5/1997*, Maritime Photographic* / 0019280

1 OCEANOGRAPHIC SHIP (AGOR)

Name	No	Builders	Commissioned
SURIYA	821	Bangkok Dock Co Ltd	15 Mar 1979

Displacement, tons: 690 full load
Dimensions, feet (metres): 177.8 × 33.5 × 10.2 *(54.2 × 10.2 × 3.1)*
Main machinery: 2 MTU diesels; 1,310 hp(m) *(963 kW)*; 2 shafts; bow thruster; 135 hp(m) *(99 kW)*
Speed, knots: 12
Complement: 60 (12 officers)
Radars: Navigation: Racal Decca; I-band.

Comment: Mostly used as a buoy tender to service navigational aids. Can carry 20 mm guns.

UPDATED

SURIYA   *6/1997** / 0019278

AUXILIARIES

1 SIMILAN (HUDONG) CLASS (TYPE R22T)
(REPLENISHMENT SHIP) (AOR)

Name	No	Builders	Launched	Commissioned
SIMILAN	871	Hudong Shipyard, Shanghai	9 Nov 1995	12 Sep 1996

Displacement, tons: 23,000 full load
Dimensions, feet (metres): 562.3 × 80.7 × 29.5 *(171.4 × 24.6 × 9)*
Main machinery: 2 HD-SEMT-Pielstick 16 PC2 6V400; 24,000 hp(m) *(17.64 MW)*; 2 shafts; Kamewa cp props
Speed, knots: 19. **Range, miles:** 10,000 at 15 kt
Complement: 130 plus 53 spare
Cargo capacity: 9,000 tons fuel, water, ammunition and stores
Guns: 8—37 mm/63 (4 twin) Type 76A.
Radars: Air/surface search: Eye Shield (Type 354); E/F-band.
Navigation: Racal Decca 1290 ARPA; I-band.
Fire control: Rice Lamp (Type 341); I/J-band.
Helicopters: 2 Seahawk type.

Comment: Contract signed with China State Shipbuilding Corporation on 29 September 1993. Fabrication started in December 1994. Two replenishment at sea positions each side and facilities for Vertrep. This ship complements the carrier and the new frigates to give the Navy a full deployment capability. Guns to be fitted when funds are available.

UPDATED

SIMILAN   *10/1998, Thai Navy League* / 0050248

1 REPLENISHMENT TANKER (AOR)

Name	No	Builders	Launched
CHULA	831 (ex-2)	Singapore SEC	24 Sep 1980

Displacement, tons: 2,000 full load
Measurement, tons: 960 dwt
Dimensions, feet (metres): 219.8 × 31.2 × 14.4 *(67 × 9.5 × 4.4)*
Main machinery: 2 MTU 12V 396 TC62 diesels; 2,400 hp(m) *(1.76 MW)* sustained; 2 shafts
Speed, knots: 14
Complement: 39 (7 officers)
Cargo capacity: 800 tons oil fuel
Guns: 2 Oerlikon 20 mm.
Radars: Navigation: Racal Decca 1226; I-band.

Comment: Replenishment is done by a hose handling crane boom.

VERIFIED

CHULA   *6/1998, Royal Thai Navy /* 0050249

3 HARBOUR TANKERS (YO)

PROET 834 (ex-YO 9)   **SAMED** 835 (ex-YO 10)   **CHIK** 842 (ex-YO 11)

Displacement, tons: 360 standard; 485 full load
Dimensions, feet (metres): 122.7 × 19.7 × 8.7 *(37.4 × 6 × 2.7)*
Main machinery: 1 GM 8-268A diesel; 500 hp(m) *(368 kW)*; 1 shaft
Speed, knots: 9
Cargo capacity: 210 tons

Comment: Built by Bangkok Naval Dockyard. *Proet* commissioned 27 January 1967, remainder the same year.

UPDATED

SAMED   *5/1999* / 0080829

2 HARBOUR TANKERS (YO)

SAMUI 832 (ex-YOG 60, ex-YO 4)   **PRONG** 833 (ex-Y 05)

Displacement, tons: 1,420 full load
Dimensions, feet (metres): 174.5 × 32 × 15 *(53.2 × 9.7 × 4.6)*
Main machinery: 1 Union diesel; 600 hp *(448 kW)*; 1 shaft
Speed, knots: 8
Complement: 29
Cargo capacity: 985 tons fuel
Guns: 2 Oerlikon 20 mm can be carried.
Radars: Navigation: Raytheon Pathfinder; I-band.

Comment: Both laid up in the 1980s but back in service.

VERIFIED

SAMUI   *12/1995*

1 WATER TANKER (YW)

Name	No	Builders	Commissioned
CHUANG	841 (ex-YW 5)	Royal Thai Naval Dockyard, Bangkok	1965

Displacement, tons: 305 standard; 485 full load
Dimensions, feet (metres): 136 × 24.6 × 10 *(42 × 7.5 × 3.1)*
Main machinery: 1 GM diesel; 500 hp *(373 kW)*; 1 shaft
Speed, knots: 11
Complement: 29
Guns: 1 Oerlikon 20 mm.

Comment: Launched on 14 January 1965.

UPDATED

CHUANG (alongside *Proet*)   *5/1997*, Maritime Photographic /* 0019284

1 TRANSPORT SHIP (AKS)

Name	No	Builders	Commissioned
KLED KEO	861 (ex-AF-7)	Norfjord, Norway	1948

Displacement, tons: 450 full load
Dimensions, feet (metres): 150.1 × 24.9 × 14 *(46 × 7.6 × 4.3)*
Main machinery: 1 CAT diesel; 900 hp(m) *(662 kW)*; 1 shaft
Speed, knots: 12
Complement: 54 (7 officers)
Guns: 3 Oerlikon 20 mm.

Comment: Former Norwegian transport acquired in 1956. Paid off in 1990 but back in service in 1997. Operates with the patrol boat squadron.

VERIFIED

KLED KEO   *6/1998, Royal Thai Navy /* 0050250

TUGS

2 COASTAL TUGS (YTB)

RIN 853 (ex-ATA 5)   **RANG** 854 (ex-ATA 6)

Displacement, tons: 350 standard
Dimensions, feet (metres): 106 × 29.7 × 15.2 *(32.3 × 9 × 4.6)*
Main machinery: 1 MWM TBD441V/12K diesel; 2,100 hp(m) *(1.54 MW)*; 1 shaft
Speed, knots: 12. **Range, miles:** 1,000 at 10 kt
Complement: 19

Comment: Launched 12 and 14 June 1980 at Singapore Marine Shipyard. Both commissioned 5 March 1981. Bollard pull 22 tons.

UPDATED

RANG   *1992*, Royal Thai Navy /* 0080830

2 SAMAESAN CLASS (COASTAL TUGS) (YTB)

SAMAESAN 855   **RAET** 856

Displacement, tons: 300 standard
Dimensions, feet (metres): 82 × 27.9 × 7.9 *(25 × 8.5 × 2.4)*
Main machinery: 2 Caterpillar 3512TA diesels; 2,350 hp(m) *(1.75 MW)* sustained; 2 Aquamaster
    US 901 props
Speed, knots: 10
Complement: 6

Comment: Contract signed 23 September 1992 for local construction at Thonburi Naval
    dockyard. Completed in December 1993. Equipped for firefighting.
                                                                                    VERIFIED

RAET   5/1997, A Sharma / 0050251

2 YTL 422 CLASS (YTL)

KLUENG BADEN 851 (ex-YTL 2)   **MARN VICHAI** 852 (ex-YTL 3)

Displacement, tons: 63 standard
Dimensions, feet (metres): 64.7 × 16.5 × 6 *(19.7 × 5 × 1.8)*
Main machinery: 1 diesel; 240 hp *(179 kW)*; 1 shaft
Speed, knots: 8

Comment: Built by Central Bridge Co, Trenton and bought from Canada 1953.
                                                                                    UPDATED

KLUENG BADEN   5/1999* / 0080831

POLICE

Notes: (1) There is also a Customs service which operates unarmed patrol craft with CUSTOMS on
the hull, and a Fishery Patrol Service also unarmed but vessels are painted blue with broad white
and narrow gold diagonal stripes on the hull. Two Hydrofoil craft are on loan from the Police to the
Customs service.
(2) There are large numbers of RIBs in service.

1 VOSPER THORNYCROFT TYPE (LARGE PATROL CRAFT) (PG)

SRINAKARIN 1804

Displacement, tons: 630 full load
Dimensions, feet (metres): 203.4 × 26.9 × 8.2 *(62 × 8.2 × 2.5)*
Main machinery: 2 Deutz MWM BV16M628 diesels; 9,524 hp(m) *(7 MW)* sustained; 2 shafts;
    Kamewa cp props
Speed, knots: 25. **Range, miles:** 2,500 at 15 kt
Complement: 45
Guns: 1 Breda 30 mm/82. 2 Oerlikon 20 mm. GAM-BO1.
Radars: Surface search: Racal Decca 1226; I-band.

Comment: Ordered in September 1989 from Ital Thai Marine. Same hull as the 'Khamronsin' class
    corvettes for the Navy but much more lightly armed. Delivered in April 1992. ***UPDATED***

SRINAKARIN   6/1997* / 0019286

2 HAMELN TYPE (LARGE PATROL CRAFT) (PG)

DAMRONG RACHANUPHAT 1802   **LOPBURI RAMAS** 1803

Displacement, tons: 430 full load
Dimensions, feet (metres): 186 × 26.6 × 8 *(56.7 × 8.1 × 2.4)*
Main machinery: 4 MTU diesels; 4,400 hp(m) *(3.23 MW)*; 2 shafts
Speed, knots: 23
Complement: 45
Guns: 2 Oerlikon 30 mm/75 (twin). 2 Oerlikon 20 mm (twin).
Radars: Surface search: Racal Decca 1226; I-band.

Comment: Delivered by Schiffwerft Hameln, Germany, on 3 January 1969 and 10 December
    1972 respectively.
                                                                                    UPDATED

LOPBURI RAMAS   1993*, Marine Police / 0080832

2 SUMIDAGAWA TYPE (COASTAL PATROL CRAFT) (PC)

CHASANYABADEE 1101   **PHROMYOTHEE** 1103

Displacement, tons: 130 full load
Dimensions, feet (metres): 111.5 × 19 × 9.1 *(34 × 5.8 × 2.8)*
Main machinery: 3 Ikegai diesels; 4,050 hp(m) *(2.98 MW)*; 3 shafts
Speed, knots: 32
Complement: 23
Guns: 2—12.7 mm MGs.
Radars: Surface search: Racal Decca; I-band.

Comment: Commissioned in August 1972 and May 1973 respectively.
                                                                                    UPDATED

PHROMYOTHEE   1990*, Marine Police / 0080833

1 YOKOHAMA TYPE (COASTAL PATROL CRAFT) (PC)

CHAWENGSAK SONGKRAM 1102

Displacement, tons: 190 full load
Dimensions, feet (metres): 116.5 × 23 × 11.5 *(35.5 × 7 × 3.5)*
Main machinery: 4 Ikegai diesels; 5,400 hp(m) *(3.79 MW)*; 2 shafts
Speed, knots: 32
Complement: 18
Guns: 2 Oerlikon 20 mm.

Comment: Commissioned 13 April 1973. A second of class operates for the Customs with the
    number 1201.
                                                                                    UPDATED

CHAWENGSAK SONGKRAM   1990*, Marine Police / 0080834

1 ITAL THAI MARINE TYPE (COASTAL PATROL CRAFT) (PC)

SRIYANONT 901

Displacement, tons: 52 full load
Dimensions, feet (metres): 90 × 16 × 6.5 *(27.4 × 4.9 × 2)*
Main machinery: 2 Deutz BA16M816 diesels; 2,680 hp(m) *(1.97 MW)* sustained; 2 shafts
Speed, knots: 23
Complement: 14
Guns: 1 Oerlikon 20 mm. 2—7.62 mm MGs.
Radars: Surface search: Racal Decca; I-band.

Comment: Commissioned 12 June 1986.

UPDATED

SRIYANONT (alongside *Phromyothee*)   *5/1997, Maritime Photographic /* 0019287

1 BURESPADOONGKIT CLASS (COASTAL PATROL CRAFT) (PC)

BURESPADOONGKIT 813

Displacement, tons: 65 full load
Dimensions, feet (metres): 80.5 × 19.4 × 6 *(24.5 × 5.9 × 1.8)*
Main machinery: 2 SACM UD 23 V12 M5D diesels; 2,534 hp(m) *(1.86 MW)* sustained; 2 shafts
Speed, knots: 28. **Range, miles:** 650 at 20 kt
Complement: 14
Guns: 1 Oerlikon GAM-CO1 20 mm; 2—7.62 mm MGs.

Comment: Built by Matsun, Thailand and commissioned 9 August 1995.

NEW ENTRY

BURESPADOONGKIT   *6/1999*, Marine Police /* 0080835

3 CUTLASS CLASS (COASTAL PATROL CRAFT) (PC)

PHRAONGKAMROP 807   **PICHARNPHOLAKIT** 808   **RAMINTHRA** 809

Displacement, tons: 34 full load
Dimensions, feet (metres): 65 × 17 × 8.3 *(19.8 × 5.2 × 2.5)*
Main machinery: 3 Detroit 12V-71TA diesels; 1,020 hp(m) *(761 kW)* sustained; 3 shafts
Speed, knots: 25
Complement: 14
Guns: 1 Oerlikon 20 mm. 2—7.62 mm MGs.

Comment: Delivered by Halter Marine, New Orleans, and all commissioned on 9 March 1969. Aluminium hulls.

UPDATED

PICHARNPHOLAKIT   *6/1999* /* 0080836

3 TECHNAUTIC TYPE (COASTAL PATROL CRAFT) (PC)

810-812

Displacement, tons: 50 full load
Dimensions, feet (metres): 88.6 × 19.4 × 6.2 *(27 × 5.9 × 1.9)*
Main machinery: 3 Isotta Fraschini diesels; 2,500 hp(m) *(1.84 MW)*; 3 Castoldi hydrojets
Speed, knots: 27
Complement: 14
Guns: 1 Oerlikon 20 mm GAM-BO1. 2—7.62 mm MGs.

Comment: Delivered by Technautic, Bangkok in 1984.

UPDATED

812   *1990*, Marine Police /* 0080837

5 ITAL THAI MARINE TYPE (COASTAL PATROL CRAFT) (PC)

625-629

Displacement, tons: 42 full load
Dimensions, feet (metres): 64 × 17.5 × 5 *(19.5 × 5.3 × 1.5)*
Main machinery: 2 MAN D2842LE diesels; 1,350 hp(m) *(992 kW)* sustained; 2 shafts
Speed, knots: 27
Complement: 14
Guns: 1—12.7 mm MG.

Comment: Built in Bangkok 1987-90. Aluminium hulls. More of the class operated by the Fishery Patrol Service.

UPDATED

ITAL THAI 625   *6/1999*, Marine Police /* 0080838

8 MARSUN TYPE (COASTAL PATROL CRAFT) (PC)

630-637

Displacement, tons: 38 full load
Dimensions, feet (metres): 65.6 × 18.2 × 5 *(20 × 5.6 × 1.5)*
Main machinery: 2 MAN D2840LXE diesels; 1,640 hp(m) *(1.2 MW)* sustained; 2 shafts
Speed, knots: 25
Complement: 11
Guns: 1—12.7 mm MG.

Comment: Built by Marsun, Thailand and commissioned from 2 August 1994.

NEW ENTRY

MARSUN 637   *6/1999*, Marine Police /* 0080839

17 TECHNAUTIC TYPE (COASTAL PATROL CRAFT) (PC)

608-624

Displacement, tons: 30 full load
Dimensions, feet (metres): 60 × 16 × 2.9 *(18.3 × 4.9 × 0.9)*
Main machinery: 2 Isotta Fraschini ID 36 SS 8V diesels; 1,760 hp(m) *(1.29 MW)* sustained;
    2 Castoldi hydrojets
Speed, knots: 27
Complement: 11
Guns: 1—12.7 mm MG.

Comment: Built from 1983-87 in Bangkok.   *UPDATED*

TECHNAUTIC 619 (alongside 810)   *5/1997*, Maritime Photographic /* 0080840

2 MARSUN TYPE (PB)

539-540

Displacement, tons: 30 full load
Dimensions, feet (metres): 57 × 16 × 3 *(17.4 × 4.9 × 0.9)*
Main machinery: 2 Detroit 12V-71TA diesels; 840 hp *(627 kW)* sustained; 2 shafts
Speed, knots: 25
Complement: 8
Guns: 1—12.7 mm MG.

Comment: Built in Thailand. Both commissioned 26 March 1986.   *UPDATED*

MARSUN 539   *5/1997*, Maritime Photographic /* 0019289

26 SUMIDAGAWA TYPE (RIVER PATROL CRAFT) (PBR)

513-538

Displacement, tons: 18 full load
Dimensions, feet (metres): 54.1 × 12.5 × 2.3 *(16.5 × 3.8 × 0.7)*
Main machinery: 2 Cummins diesels; 800 hp *(597 kW)*; 2 shafts
Speed, knots: 23
Complement: 6
Guns: 1—12.7 mm MG.

Comment: First 21 built by Sumidagawa, last five by Captain Co, Thailand 1978-79.

                                                                          UPDATED

SUMIDAGAWA 529   *6/1999*, Marine Police /* 0080841

20 CAMCRAFT TYPE (RIVER PATROL CRAFT) (PBR)

415-440 series

Displacement, tons: 13 full load
Dimensions, feet (metres): 40 × 12 × 3.2 *(12.2 × 3.7 × 1)*
Main machinery: 2 Detroit diesels; 540 hp *(403 kW)*; 2 shafts
Speed, knots: 25
Complement: 6

Comment: Delivered by Camcraft, Louisiana. Aluminium hulls. Numbers uncertain.
                                                                          UPDATED

CAMCRAFT 435   *6/1999*, Marine Police /* 0080842

34 RIVER PATROL CRAFT (PBR)

Displacement, tons: 5 full load
Dimensions, feet (metres): 37 × 11 × 6 *(11.3 × 3.4 × 1.8)*
Main machinery: 2 diesels; 2 shafts
Speed, knots: 25
Complement: 4

Comment: Numbers in the 300 series. Details given are for *339* built in 1990. The remainder are
    similar.   *UPDATED*

RIVER PATROL CRAFT 338   *6/1999*, Marine Police /* 0080843

TOGO

Headquarters Appointments	Personnel	Bases	Mercantile Marine

Commanding Officer, Navy:
   Commander Lucien Laval
	(a) 2000: 105
	(b) Voluntary service
		Lome	*Lloyd's Register of Shipping:*
			   12 vessels of 42,823 tons gross

PATROL FORCES

2 COASTAL PATROL CRAFT (PC)

Name	No	Builders	Launched
KARA	P 761	Chantiers Navals de l'Esterel, Cannes	18 May 1976
MONO	P 762	Chantiers Navals de l'Esterel, Cannes	16 June 1976

Displacement, tons: 80 full load
Dimensions, feet (metres): 105 × 19 × 5.3 *(32 × 5.8 × 1.6)*
Main machinery: 2 MTU MB 12V 493 TY60 diesels; 2,000 hp(m) *(1.47 MW)* sustained; 2 shafts
Speed, knots: 30. **Range, miles:** 1,500 at 15 kt
Complement: 17 (1 officer)
Missiles: SSM: Aerospatiale SS 12M; wire-guided to 5 km *(3 n miles)* subsonic; warhead 30 kg.
Guns: 1 Bofors 40 mm/70. 1 Oerlikon 20 mm.
Radars: Surface search: Decca 916; I-band.

Comment: Both craft in good condition.

                                        VERIFIED

MONO   *6/1998 /* 0050252

TONGA

Headquarters Appointments	Personnel	Bases	Prefix to Ships' Names	Mercantile Marine
Commander Defence Services: Colonel F Tupou *Commanding Officer, Navy:* Commander Toni Fonokalafi	2000: 115	Touliki Base, Nuku'alofa (HMNB *Masefield*)	VOEA (Vaka O Ene Afio)	*Lloyd's Register of Shipping:* 19 vessels of 25,071 tons gross

PATROL FORCES

Note: A Beech 18 aircraft was acquired in May 1995 for maritime surveillance.

3 PACIFIC FORUM TYPE (LARGE PATROL CRAFT) (PC)

Name	No	Builders	Commissioned
NEIAFU	P 201	Australian Shipbuilding Industries	28 Oct 1989
PANGAI	P 202	Australian Shipbuilding Industries	30 June 1990
SAVEA	P 203	Australian Shipbuilding Industries	23 Mar 1991

Displacement, tons: 162 full load
Dimensions, feet (metres): 103.3 × 26.6 × 6.9 *(31.5 × 8.1 × 2.1)*
Main machinery: 2 Caterpillar 3516TA diesels; 2,820 hp *(2.1 MW)* sustained; 2 shafts
Speed, knots: 20. **Range, miles:** 2,500 at 12 kt
Complement: 17 (3 officers)
Guns: 2—12.7 mm MGs.
Radars: Surface search: Furuno 1101; I-band.

Comment: Part of the Pacific Forum Australia Defence co-operation. First laid down 30 January 1989, second 2 October 1989, third February 1990. *Savea* has a hydrographic survey capability. ***UPDATED***

SAVEA   *1/2000*, Sattler/Steele /* 0080844

AUXILIARIES

1 LCM

Name	No	Builders	Commissioned
LATE (ex-*1057*)	C 315	North Queensland, Cairns	1 Sep 1982

Displacement, tons: 116 full load
Dimensions, feet (metres): 73.5 × 21 × 3.3 *(22.4 × 6.4 × 1)*
Main machinery: 2 Detroit 12V-71 diesels; 680 hp *(507 kW)* sustained; 2 shafts
Speed, knots: 10. **Range, miles:** 480 at 10 kt
Complement: 5
Cargo capacity: 54 tons
Guns: 1—7.62 mm MG can be carried.
Radars: Surface search: Koden MD 305; I-band.

Comment: Acquired from the Australian Army for inter-island transport. ***UPDATED***

LATE   *6/1999*, Tongan Navy /* 0084414

1 TANKER (AOTL)

Name	No	Builders	Commissioned
LOMIPEAU (ex-*Punaruu*, ex-*Bow Cecil*)	A 301 (ex-A 632)	Norway	16 Nov 1971

Displacement, tons: 4,050 full load
Dimensions, feet (metres): 272.2 × 45.6 × 19 *(83 × 13.9 × 5.8)*
Main machinery: 2 Normo LSMC-8 diesels; 2,050 hp(m) *(1.51 MW)*; 1 shaft; cp prop; bow thruster
Speed, knots: 12. **Range, miles:** 8,000 at 11 kt
Complement: 28 (4 officers)
Cargo capacity: 2,500 m³
Radars: Navigation: Racal Decca 1226; I-band.

Comment: Transferred from France on 1 October 1995 and recommissioned on 30 November 1995 after being modified at Tahiti. Naval manned but the intention is to train a civilian crew. ***UPDATED***

LOMIPEAU   *8/1997*, van Ginderen/B Morrison /* 0019291

1 ROYAL YACHT (PC)

TITILUPE

Displacement, tons: 10 full load
Dimensions, feet (metres): 34.1 × 9.8 × 3.3 *(10.4 × 3 × 1)*
Main machinery: 1 Ford diesel; 1 shaft
Speed, knots: 8
Complement: 4

Comment: GRP. Also used as a patrol craft. ***UPDATED***

TITILUPE   *1/1997*, van Ginderen Collection /* 0019292

TRINIDAD AND TOBAGO

Headquarters Appointments	Personnel	Prefix to Ships' Names	DELETIONS
Commanding Officer, Coast Guard: Commander Kayam Mohammed, ED	(a) 2000: 650 (55 officers) (b) Voluntary service	TTS	**Patrol forces** 1999 *Carenage*

Aircraft

The Coast Guard operates three Cessna (Types 172, 402B and 310R) for surveillance and two C26B acquired in 1999. These aircraft can be backed by Air Division Gazelle and Sikorsky S-76 helicopters when necessary.

Bases

Staubles Bay (HQ)
Hart's Cut, Tobago, Point Fortin (all from 1989)
Piarco (Air station), Cedros (from 1992)
Galeota (from 1995)

Mercantile Marine

Lloyd's Register of Shipping:
56 vessels of 21,558 tons gross

Auxiliaries

1997 *Cedros, Speyside*

COAST GUARD

Note: The ex-UK 'Island' class OPV *Orkney* may be acquired in 2000.

2 TYPE CG 40 (LARGE PATROL CRAFT) (PC)

Name	No	Builders	Commissioned
BARRACUDA	CG 5	Karlskronavarvet	15 June 1980
CASCADURA	CG 6	Karlskronavarvet	15 June 1980

Displacement, tons: 210 full load
Dimensions, feet (metres): 133.2 × 21.9 × 5.2 *(40.6 × 6.7 × 1.6)*
Main machinery: 2 Paxman Valenta 16CM diesels; 6,700 hp *(5 MW)* sustained; 2 shafts
Speed, knots: 30. **Range, miles:** 3,000 at 15 kt
Complement: 25
Guns: 1 Bofors 40 mm/70. 1 Oerlikon 20 mm.
Weapons control: Optronic GFCS.
Radars: Surface search: Racal Decca 1226; I-band.

Comment: Ordered in Sweden mid-1978. Laid down early 1979. Fitted with foam-cannon oil pollution equipment and for oceanographic and hydrographic work. Nine spare berths. The hull is similar to Swedish 'Spica' class but with the bridge amidships. One refitted in 1988, the other in 1989. *Cascadura* refitted again in 1998/99.

UPDATED

CASCADURA   *1/1994, Maritime Photographic*

2 POINT CLASS (COASTAL PATROL CRAFT) (PC)

Name	No	Builders	Commissioned
COROZAL POINT (ex-*Point Heyer*)	CG 7 (ex-WPB 82369)	J Martinac, Tacoma	3 Aug 1967
CROWN POINT (ex-*Point Bennett*)	CG 8 (ex-WPB 82351)	Coast Guard Yard, Curtis Bay	19 Dec 1966

Displacement, tons: 66 full load
Dimensions, feet (metres): 83 × 17.2 × 5.8 *(25.3 × 5.2 × 1.8)*
Main machinery: 2 Caterpillar 3412 diesels; 1,600 hp *(1.19 MW)*; 2 shafts
Speed, knots: 23. **Range, miles:** 1,500 at 8 kt
Complement: 10
Guns: 2—7.62 mm MGs.
Radars: Surface search: Raytheon SPS-64(V)I and Raytheon SPS 69AN; I-band.

Comment: Transferred from US Coast Guard 12 February 1999. Others of the class being distributed throughout Latin America and the Caribbean.

UPDATED

CROWN POINT   *6/1999*, Trinidad and Tobago Coast Guard /* 0080846

4 SOUTER WASP 17 METRE CLASS
(COASTAL PATROL CRAFT) (PC)

Name	No	Builders	Commissioned
PLYMOUTH	CG 27	WA Souter, Cowes	27 Aug 1982
CARONI	CG 28	WA Souter, Cowes	27 Aug 1982
GALEOTA	CG 29	WA Souter, Cowes	27 Aug 1982
MORUGA	CG 30	WA Souter, Cowes	27 Aug 1982

Displacement, tons: 20 full load
Dimensions, feet (metres): 55.1 × 13.8 × 4.6 *(16.8 × 4.2 × 1.4)*
Main machinery: 2 MANN 8V diesels; 1,470 hp *(1.1 MW)*; 2 shafts
Speed, knots: 32. **Range, miles:** 500 at 18 kt
Complement: 7 (2 officers)
Guns: 1—7.62 mm MG.
Radars: Surface search: Raytheon SPS 69AN; I-band.

Comment: GRP hulls. All refitted from September 1997 with new engines.

UPDATED

MORUGA   *6/1996, Trinidad and Tobago Coast Guard*

2 WASP 20 METRE CLASS (COASTAL PATROL CRAFT) (PC)

Name	No	Builders	Commissioned
KAIRI (ex-*Sea Bird*)	CG 31	WA Souter, Cowes	Dec 1982
MORIAH (ex-*Sea Dog*)	CG 32	WA Souter, Cowes	Dec 1982

Displacement, tons: 32 full load
Dimensions, feet (metres): 65.8 × 16.5 × 5 *(20.1 × 5 × 1.5)*
Main machinery: 2 MANN 12V diesels; 2,400 hp *(1.79 MW)*; 2 shafts
Speed, knots: 30. **Range, miles:** 450 at 30 kt
Complement: 6 (2 officers)
Guns: 2—7.62 mm MGs.
Radars: Surface search: Decca 150; I-band.

Comment: Ordered 30 September 1981. Aluminium alloy hull. Transferred from the Police in June 1989. New engines in 1999.

UPDATED

MORIAH   *6/1996*, Trinidad and Tobago Coast Guard /* 0080847

1 SWORD CLASS (COASTAL PATROL CRAFT) (PC)

Name	No	Builders	Commissioned
MATELOT (ex-*Sea Skorpion*)	CG 33	SeaArk Marine	May 1979

Displacement, tons: 15.5 full load
Dimensions, feet (metres): 44.9 × 13.4 × 4.3 *(13.7 × 4.1 × 1.3)*
Main machinery: 2 GM diesels; 850 hp *(634 kW)*; 2 shafts
Speed, knots: 28. **Range, miles:** 500 at 20 kt
Complement: 6
Guns: 1—7.62 mm MG.
Radars: Surface search: Decca 150; I-band.

Comment: Two transferred from the Police 30 June 1989, one scrapped in 1990. Refitted in 1998.

VERIFIED

MATELOT   *1/1994, Maritime Photographic*

3 DAUNTLESS CLASS (PB)

Name	No	Builders	Commissioned
SOLDADO	CG 38	SeaArk Marine, Monticello	14 June 1995
ROXBOROUGH	CG 39	SeaArk Marine, Monticello	14 June 1995
MAYARO	CG 40	SeaArk Marine, Monticello	14 June 1995

Displacement, tons: 11 full load
Dimensions, feet (metres): 40 × 14 × 4.3 *(12.2 × 4.3 × 1.3)*
Main machinery: 2 Caterpillar 3208TA diesels; 870 hp *(650 kW)* sustained; 2 shafts
Speed, knots: 27. **Range, miles:** 600 at 18 kt
Complement: 4
Guns: 1—7.62 mm MG.
Radars: Surface search: Raytheon R40; I-band.

Comment: Several of these craft provided to Caribbean navies through FMS funding. Used as utility boats.   ***UPDATED***

SOLDADO   *6/1995*, SeaArk Marine /* 0080848

2 BOWEN CLASS and 3 RHIB (FAST INTERCEPTOR CRAFT) (PB)

CG 001   CG 002   CG 004-CG 006

Comment: The first pair are 31 ft fast patrol boats acquired in May 1991. Capable of 40 kt. The last three are 25 ft RHIBs with twin Johnson outboards acquired from the US in 1993. Capable of 45 kt.   ***UPDATED***

CG 001   *1991*, Trinidad and Tobago Coast Guard /* 0080849

2 AUXILIARY VESSELS

NAPARIMA (ex-*CG 26*) A 01   REFORM A 04

Comment: Used for Port Services and other support functions.   ***VERIFIED***

TUNISIA

Headquarters Appointments

Naval Chief of Staff:
Rear Admiral Mohamed Chedly Cherif

Bases

Bizerte, Sfax, La Goulette, Kelibia

Personnel

(a) 2000: 4,800 officers and men (including 800 conscripts)
(b) 1 year's national service

Mercantile Marine

Lloyd's Register of Shipping:
79 vessels of 199,547 tons gross

DELETIONS

Patrol Forces

1997   *Gafsah, Amilcar*
1999   *Tazarika, Menzel Bourguiba*

PATROL FORCES

Note: Two 30 m and two 12 m patrol craft are required as soon as funds are available.

3 COMBATTANTE III M CLASS
(FAST ATTACK CRAFT—MISSILE) (PCFG)

Name	No	Builders	Launched	Commissioned
LA GALITÉ	501	CMN, Cherbourg	16 June 1983	27 Feb 1985
TUNIS	502	CMN, Cherbourg	27 Oct 1983	27 Mar 1985
CARTHAGE	503	CMN, Cherbourg	24 Jan 1984	29 Apr 1985

Displacement, tons: 345 standard; 425 full load
Dimensions, feet (metres): 183.7 × 26.9 × 7.2 *(56 × 8.2 × 2.2)*
Main machinery: 4 MTU 20V 538 TB93 diesels; 18,740 hp(m) *(13.8 MW)* sustained; 4 shafts
Speed, knots: 38.5. **Range, miles:** 700 at 33 kt; 2,800 at 10 kt
Complement: 35

Missiles: SSM: 8 Aerospatiale MM 40 Exocet (2 quad) launchers; inertial cruise; active radar homing to 70 km *(40 n miles)* at 0.9 Mach; warhead 165 kg; sea-skimmer.
Guns: 1 OTO Melara 3 in *(76 mm)*/62; 55-65 rds/min to 16 km *(8.7 n miles)*; weight of shell 6 kg.
2 Breda 40 mm/70 (twin); 300 rds/min to 12.5 km *(6.8 n miles)*; weight of shell 0.96 kg.
4 Oerlikon 30 mm/75 (2 twin); 650 rds/min to 10 km *(5.5 n miles)*; weight of shell 1 kg or 0.36 kg.

TUNIS   *4/1999*, C E Castle /* 0080850

Countermeasures: Decoys: 1 CSEE Dagaie trainable launcher; IR flares and chaff.
ESM: Thomson-CSF; DR 2000; intercept.
Combat data systems: Tavitac action data automation.
Weapons control: 2 CSEE Naja optronic directors for 30 mm. Thomson-CSF Vega II for SSM, 76 mm and 40 mm.
Radars: Air/surface search: Thomson-CSF Triton S; G-band; range 33 km *(18 n miles)* for 2 m² target.
Fire control: Thomson-CSF Castor II; I/J-band; range 31 km *(17 n miles)* for 2 m² target.

Programmes: Ordered 27 June 1981.
Operational: CSEE Sylosat navigation system. All three ships need refits.   ***UPDATED***

TUNIS   *4/1999*, C E Castle /* 0080851

3 MODIFIED HAIZHUI CLASS (LARGE PATROL CRAFT) (PC)

UTIQUE P 207   **JERBA** P 208   **KURIAT** P 209

Displacement, tons: 120 full load
Dimensions, feet (metres): 114.8 × 17.7 × 5.9 *(35 × 5.4 × 1.8)*
Main machinery: 4 MWM TB 604 BV12 diesels; 4,400 hp(m) *(3.22 MW)* sustained; 4 shafts
Speed, knots: 28. Range, miles: 750 at 17 kt
Complement: 39
Guns: 4 China 25 mm/80 (2 twin).
Radars: Surface search: Pot Head; I-band.

Comment: Delivered from China in March 1994. These craft resemble a smaller version of the 'Haizhui' class in service with the Chinese Navy but with a different armament and some superstructure changes. Built to Tunisian specifications.

UPDATED

KURIAT   *4/1995* * / 0080852*

3 BIZERTE CLASS (TYPE PR 48) (LARGE PATROL CRAFT) (PC)

Name	No	Builders	Commissioned
BIZERTE	P 301	SFCN, Villeneuve-la-Garenne	10 July 1970
HORRIA (ex-*Liberté*)	P 302	SFCN, Villeneuve-la-Garenne	Oct 1970
MONASTIR	P 304	SFCN, Villeneuve-la-Garenne	25 Mar 1975

Displacement, tons: 250 full load
Dimensions, feet (metres): 157.5 × 23.3 × 7.5 *(48 × 7.1 × 2.3)*
Main machinery: 2 MTU 16V 652 TB81 diesels; 4,600 hp(m) *(3.4 MW)* sustained; 2 shafts
Speed, knots: 20. Range, miles: 2,000 at 16 kt
Complement: 34 (4 officers)
Missiles: SSM: 8 Aerospatiale SS 12M; wire-guided to 5.5 km *(3 n miles)* subsonic; warhead 30 kg.
Guns: 4—37 mm/63 (2 twin).
Radars: Surface search: Thomson-CSF DRBN 31; I-band.

Comment: First pair ordered in 1968, third in August 1973. Guns changed in 1994. All are active.

VERIFIED

BIZERTE   *7/1998, A Campanera i Rovira / 0050255*

BIZERTE   *8/1998, A Sharma / 0050256*

4 COASTAL PATROL CRAFT (PC)

Name	No	Builders	Commissioned
ISTIKLAL (ex-*VC 11, P 761*)	P 201	Ch Navals de l'Esterel	Apr 1957
JOUMHOURIA	P 202	Ch Navals de l'Esterel	Jan 1961
AL JALA	P 203	Ch Navals de l'Esterel	Nov 1963
REMADA	P 204	Ch Navals de l'Esterel	July 1967

Displacement, tons: 60 standard; 80 full load
Dimensions, feet (metres): 104 × 19 × 5.3 *(31.5 × 5.8 × 1.6)*
Main machinery: 2 MTU MB 12V 493 TY70 diesels; 2,200 hp(m) *(1.62 MW)* sustained; 2 shafts
Speed, knots: 30. Range, miles: 1,500 at 15 kt
Complement: 17 (3 officers)
Guns: 2 Oerlikon 20 mm.
Radars: Surface search: Racal Decca 1226; I-band.

Comment: *Istiklal* transferred from France March 1959. Wooden hulls. At least one may belong to the Coast Guard.

UPDATED

REMADA   *4/1997* * / 0019295*

6 COASTAL PATROL CRAFT (PC)

V 101-106

Displacement, tons: 38 full load
Dimensions, feet (metres): 83 × 15.6 × 4.2 *(25 × 4.8 × 1.3)*
Main machinery: 2 Detroit 12V-71TA diesels; 840 hp *(627 kW)* sustained; 2 shafts; acbLIPS cp props
Speed, knots: 23. Range, miles: 900 at 15 kt
Complement: 11
Guns: 1 Oerlikon 20 mm.
Radars: Surface search: Racal Decca 1226; I-band.

Comment: Built by Chantiers Navals de l'Esterel and commissioned in 1961-63. Two further craft of the same design *(Sabaq el Bahr* T 2 and *Jaouel el Bahr* T 1) but unarmed were transferred to the Fisheries Administration in 1971—same builders. Refitted in 1997/98. *V 102* is Coast Guard.

UPDATED

V 106   *1/1995* * / 0080853*

TRAINING/SURVEY SHIPS

1 WILKES CLASS (AGS)

Name	No	Builders	Launched	Completed
KHAIREDDINE	A 700	Defoe SB Co, Bay City, MI	31 July 1969	28 June 1971
(ex-*Wilkes*)	(ex-T-AGS 33)			

Displacement, tons: 2,843 full load
Dimensions, feet (metres): 285.3 × 48 × 15.1 *(87 × 14.6 × 4.6)*
Main machinery: Diesel-electric; 2 Alco diesel generators; 1 Westinghouse/GE motor; 3,600 hp *(2.69 MW)*; 1 shaft; bow thruster; 350 hp *(261 kW)*
Speed, knots: 15. Range, miles: 8,000 at 13 kt
Complement: 37
Radars: Navigation: RM 1650/9X; I-band.

Comment: Decommissioned on 29 August 1995 and transferred from the USA by grant aid on 29 September 1995. Designed specifically for surveying operations. Bow propulsion unit for precise manoeuvrability and station keeping. Second of class planned for transfer but not confirmed.

UPDATED

KHAIREDDINE   *7/1999* *, H M Steele / 0080854*

1 ROBERT D CONRAD CLASS (AGOR/AX)

Name	No	Builders	Launched	Commissioned
N N O SALAMMBO	A 701	Northwest Iron Works,	13 June 1966	28 Feb 1969
(ex-*De Steiguer*)	(ex-T-AGOR 12)	Portland		

Displacement, tons: 1,370 full load
Dimensions, feet (metres): 208.9 × 40 × 15.3 *(63.7 × 12.2 × 4.7)*
Main machinery: Diesel-electric; 2 Cummins diesel generators; 1 motor; 1,000 hp *(746 kW)*;
1 shaft; bow thruster; 350 hp *(257 kW)*
Speed, knots: 13. **Range, miles:** 12,000 at 12 kt
Complement: 40
Radars: Navigation: Raytheon 1650/6X; I-band.

Comment: Transferred from USA on 2 November 1992 and recommissioned on 11 February
1993. Built as an oceanographic research ship. Special features include a 10 ton boom, and a
gas turbine for quiet propulsion up to 6 kt. Used primarily for training having replaced the frigate
Inkadh, which is now an accommodation hulk. ***UPDATED***

N N O SALAMMBO   *7/1997*, Camil Busquets i Vilanova /* 0019296

2 WHITE SUMAC CLASS (BUOY TENDERS)

Name	No	Launched	Recommissioned
TABARKA (ex-*White Heath*)	— (ex-WLM 545)	21 July 1943	31 Mar 1998
TURQUENNESS	— (ex-WLM 546)	28 July 1943	31 Mar 1998
(ex-*White Lupine*)			

Displacement, tons: 485 full load
Dimensions, feet (metres): 133 × 31 × 9 *(40.5 × 9.5 × 2.7)*
Main machinery: 2 Caterpillar diesels; 600 hp *(448 kW)*; 2 shafts
Speed, knots: 9
Complement: 24
Radars: Navigation: Raytheon; I-band.

Comment: Former US Coast Guard vessels transferred by gift on 10 June 1998. Arrived in Tunisia
one month later. ***UPDATED***

TURQUENNESS (US colours)   *9/1997*, Harald Carstens /* 0012986

COAST GUARD

Notes: (1) *Tazarke* P 205 and *Menzel Bourguiba* P 206 may have transferred from the Navy to the
Coast Guard but this is not confirmed.
(2) A Rodman 11 m craft acquired by Customs in 2000. Capable of 30 kt.

5 KONDOR I CLASS (PC)

RAS EL BLAIS (ex-*Demmin*) 601   **RAS EL MANOURA** (ex-*Templin*) 604
RAS AJDIR (ex-*Malchin*) 602   **RAS ENGHELA** (ex-*Ahrenshoop*) 605
RAS EL EDRAK (ex-*Altentreptow*) 603

Displacement, tons: 377 full load
Dimensions, feet (metres): 170.3 × 23.3 × 7.2 *(51.9 × 7.1 × 2.2)*
Main machinery: 2 Russki/Kolomna 40-DM; 4,408 hp(m) *(3.24 MW)* sustained; 2 shafts; cp props
Speed, knots: 20. **Range, miles:** 1,800 at 15 kt
Complement: 24
Guns: 2—25 mm (twin) can be carried.
Radars: Navigation: TSR 333 or Racal Decca 360; I-band.

Comment: Former GDR minesweepers built at Peenewerft, Wolgast in 1969. First four transferred
in May 1992 and the last one in August 1992. In German service they were fitted with a twin
25 mm gun and a hull-mounted sonar. These ships may belong to the Navy. Ships of the same
class acquired by Malta and Guinea-Bissau. ***UPDATED***

RAS ENGHELA   *8/1997, Diego Quevedo /* 0050258

5 BREMSE CLASS (PC)

SBEITLA (ex-*G 32*)   **UTIQUE** (ex-*G 37*)   **SELEUTA** (ex-*G 39*)
BULLARIJIA (ex-*G 36*)   **UERKOUANE** (ex-*G 38*)

Displacement, tons: 42 full load
Dimensions, feet (metres): 74.1 × 15.4 × 3.6 *(22.6 × 4.7 × 1.1)*
Main machinery: 2 SKL 6VD 18/5 AL-1 diesels; 944 hp(m) *(694 kW)* sustained; 2 shafts
Speed, knots: 14
Complement: 6
Guns: 2—14.5 mm (twin) MGs can be carried.
Radars: Navigation: TSR 333; I-band.

Comment: Built in 1971-72 for the ex-GDR GBK. Transferred from Germany in May 1992. Others
of the class sold to Malta and Cyprus. ***UPDATED***

BREMSE (Malta colours)   *10/1995*, van Ginderen Collection /* 0080855

11 COASTAL PATROL CRAFT (PC)

ASSAD BIN FOURAT   + 10

Displacement, tons: 32 full load
Dimensions, feet (metres): 67.3 × 15.4 × 4.3 *(20.5 × 4.7 × 1.3)*
Main machinery: 2 diesels; 1,000 hp(m) *(735 kW)*; 2 shafts
Speed, knots: 28. **Range, miles:** 500 at 20 kt
Complement: 8
Guns: 1—12.7 mm MG.

Comment: Details given are for the first one built by Socomena Bizerte, with assistance from South
Korea, and completed 2 March 1986. The remainder are probably ARCOR 38 craft of which five
belong to the Coast Guard and five to the National Guard. ***UPDATED***

ASSAD BIN FOURAT   *8/1994* /* 0080856

4 GABES CLASS (PB)

GABES   **JERBA**   **KELIBIA**   **TABARK**

Displacement, tons: 18 full load
Dimensions, feet (metres): 42.3 × 12.5 × 3 *(12.9 × 3.8 × 0.9)*
Main machinery: 2 diesels; 800 hp(m) *(588 kW)*; 2 shafts
Speed, knots: 38. **Range, miles:** 250 at 15 kt
Complement: 6
Guns: 2—12.7 mm MGs.

Comment: Built by SBCN, Loctudy in 1988-89. ***UPDATED***

GABES   *1/1995* /* 0080857

TURKEY
TÜRK DENIZ KUVVETLERI

Headquarters Appointments

Commander-in-Chief, Turkish Naval Forces:
    Admiral Ilhami Erdil
Chief of Naval Staff:
    Vice Admiral Yener Karahanoğlu
Chief of Coast Guard:
    Rear Admiral Yalçin Ertuna

Flag Officers

Fleet Commander (Aksaz):
    Admiral Bülent Alpkaya
Comsarnorth (Istanbul):
    Vice Admiral Özden Örnek
Comsarsouth (Izmir):
    Vice Admiral Atilla Şenkul
Combastraining:
    Vice Admiral Altaç Atilan
Comiststrait (Istanbul):
    Rear Admiral Metin Açimuz
Comcanstrait (Çanakkale):
    Rear Admiral Mustafa Ültanur
Comeageanzone (Izmir):
    Rear Admiral Hüseyin Hoşgit
Commedzone (Mersin):
    Rear Admiral Mehmet Otuzbiroğlu
Comebaseiskenderun (Iskenderun):
    Rear Admiral Hasan Hoşgit
Combaseaksaz (Aksaz):
    Rear Admiral Engin Heper
Comblackzone (Ereğli):
    Rear Admiral Ruhsar Sümer
Comseaguard (Coast Guard) (Ankara):
    Rear Admiral Yalçin Ertuna
Comsur (Aksaz):
    Rear Admiral Metin Atac
Comsubgrup (Aksaz):
    Rear Admiral Engin Baykal
Comminesgrup (Aksaz):
    Rear Admiral Uğur Yiğit
Comamphibigrup (Foça-Izmir):
    Rear Admiral Lütfü Sancar
Comfastgrup (Istanbul):
    Rear Admiral Taner Ezgü

Diplomatic Representation

Naval Attaché in London:
    Captain A Niyazi Senol

Personnel

(a) 2000: 51,000 (4,200 officers) including 34,500 conscripts,
     3,000 Marines and 900 Air Arm (reserves 70,000)
(b) 18 months' national service

Organisation

Fleet HQ (Ankara), Fleet Command (Aksaz), Northern Area
Command (Black Sea and Marmara), Southern Area Command
(Aegean and Mediterranean), Naval Training Command.

Bases

Headquarters: Ankara
Black Sea: Ereğli, Bartin, Samsun, Trabzon
Marmara: Istanbul, Erdek, Çanakkale
Mediterranean: Izmir, Foça, Antalya, Mersin, Iskenderun, Aksaz
Dockyards: Gölcük, Pendik (Istanbul), Izmir

Strength of the Fleet (including Coast Guard)

Type	Active	Building (Planned)
Submarines—Patrol	14	4
Frigates	22	1 (6)
Fast Attack Craft—Missile	21	—
Fast Attack Craft—Gun	1	—
Large Patrol Craft	25	—
Coastal Patrol Craft	4	(12)
Minelayers—Large	1	—
Minelayers—Tenders	3	—
Minesweepers/Hunters—Coastal	17	6
Minesweepers—Inshore	4	—
Minehunting Tenders	8	—
LSTs/Minelayers	7	—
LCTs	30	—
Survey Vessels/AGI	5	—
Training Ships	4	6
Fleet Support Ships	2	—
Tankers	19	—
Transports—Large and small	35	—
Salvage Ships	3	—
Boom Defence Vessels	2	—

Pennant Numbers

From mid-1997 all pennant numbers have been repainted in non-reflective paint.

Marines

Total: 3,000
One brigade of HQ company, three infantry battalions, one
artillery battalion, support units.

Coast Guard (Sahil Güvenlik)

Formed in July 1982 from the naval wing of the Jandarma. Prefix
J replaced by SG and paint scheme is very light grey with a
diagonal stripe forward. About 1,700 officers and men.

Mercantile Marine

Lloyd's Register of Shipping:
    1,152 vessels of 6,324,631 tons gross

DELETIONS

Submarines

1998 *Çanakkale* (old), *Birinci Inönü*
1999 *Çerbe*

Destroyers

1997 *Anittepe*
1998 *Yücetepe, Alçitepe, Kiliç Ali Paşa*
1999 *Piyale Paşa*

Frigates

1999 *Berk*

Patrol Forces

1998 *AB 30* (to Georgia)
1999 *AB 32, AB 34*

Mine Warfare Forces

1997 *Mersin*
1998 *Selçuk, Seyhan*

Amphibious Forces

1998 EDIC 110, LCU 205 and 211, LCM 305 and 318
1999 *Çakabey*, EDIC 114
2000 EDIC 118, C119, C121

Auxiliaries

1997 *AG 4, Halas, Öncü* (old)
1998 *Albay Hakki Burak* (old), *Havuz-7, Önder* (old)
1999 *Şarköy, Umurbey*

PENNANT LIST

Submarines

S 336	Muratreis
S 338	Uluçalireis
S 342	Hizirreis
S 343	Pirireis
S 347	Atilay
S 348	Saldiray
S 349	Batiray
S 350	Yildiray
S 351	Doğanay
S 352	Dolunay
S 353	Preveze
S 354	Sakarya
S 355	18 Mart
S 356	Anafartalar
S 357	Gür (bldg)
S 358	Çanakkale

Frigates

D 359	Peyk
F 240	Yavuz
F 241	Turgutreis
F 242	Fatih
F 243	Yildirim
F 244	Barbaros
F 245	Orucreis
F 246	Salihreis
F 247	Kemalreis
F 250	Muavenet
F 251	Adatepe
F 252	Kocatepe
F 253	Zafer
F 254	Trakya
F 255	Karadeniz
F 256	Ege
F 257	Akdeniz
F 490	Gaziantep
F 491	Giresun
F 492	Gemlik
F 493	Gelibolu
F 494	Gökçeada

Mine Warfare Forces (Layers)

N 110	Nusret

Mine Warfare Forces (Sweepers/Hunters)

M 260	Edincik
M 261	Edremit
M 262	Enez
M 263	Erdek
M 264	Erdemli
M 500	Foça
M 501	Fethiye
M 502	Fatsa
M 503	Finike
M 510	Samsun
M 511	Sinop
M 512	Sümene
M 513	Seddülbahir
M 514	Silifke
M 515	Saros
M 516	Sigacik
M 517	Sapanca
M 518	Sariyer
M 520	Karamürsel
M 521	Kerempe
M 522	Kilimli
P 312-19	MTB 2-9

Amphibious Forces

L 401	Ertuğrul
L 402	Serdar
NL 120	Bayraktar
NL 121	Sancaktar
NL 123	Sarucabey
NL 124	Karamürselbey
NL 125	Osman Gazi

Patrol Forces

P 111	Sultanhisar
P 112	Demirhisar
P 113	Yarhisar
P 114	Akhisar
P 115	Sivrihisar
P 116	Koçhisar
P 140	Girne
P 301	Kozlu
P 302	Kuşadasi
P 321	Denizkuşu
P 322	Atmaca
P 323	Şahin
P 324	Kartal
P 326	Pelikan
P 327	Albatros
P 328	Şimşek
P 329	Kasirga
P 330	Kiliç
P 331	Kalkan
P 332	Mizrak
P 339	Bora
P 340	Doğan
P 341	Marti
P 342	Tayfun
P 343	Volkan
P 344	Rüzgar
P 345	Poyraz
P 346	Gurbet
P 347	Firtina
P 348	Yildiz
P 349	Karayel
P 530	Trabzon
P 531	Terme

Auxiliaries

P 305	AG 5
P 306	AG 6
A 570	Taşkizak
A 571	Albay Hakki Burak
A 572	Yuzbasi Ihsan Tolunay
A 573	Binbaşi Sadettin Gürcan
A 575	Inebolu
A 576	Değirmendere
A 577	Sokullu Mehmet Paşa
A 578	Darica
A 579	Cezayirli Gazi Hasan Paşa
A 580	Akar
A 581	Çinar
A 582	Kemer
A 583	Aksaz
A 584	Kurtaran
A 585	Akin
A 586	Akbas
A 587	Gazal
A 589	Işin
A 590	Yunus
A 591	Çesme
A 592	Karadeniz Ereğlisi
A 593	Eceabat
A 594	Çubuklu
A 595	Yarbay Kudret Güngör
A 596	Ulubat
A 597	Van
A 598	Söğüt
A 600	Kavak
A 601	Tekirdağ
A 1531	E 1
A 1532	E 2
A 1533	E 3
A 1534	E 4
A 1535	E 5
A 1536	E 6
A 1542	Söndüren 2
A 1543	Söndüren 3

SUBMARINES

4 + 4 PREVEZE (209) CLASS (TYPE 1400) (SSK)

Name	No	Builders	Laid down		Launched		Commissioned	
PREVEZE	S 353	Gölcük, Kocaeli	12 Sep	1989	22 Oct	1993	28 July	1994
SAKARYA	S 354	Gölcük, Kocaeli	1 Feb	1990	28 July	1994	21 Dec	1995
18 MART	S 355	Gölcük, Kocaeli	28 July	1994	25 Aug	1997	28 June	1998
ANAFARTALAR	S 356	Gölcük, Kocaeli	1 Aug	1995	1 Sep	1998	22 July	1999
GÜR	S 357	Gölcük, Kocaeli/Pendik	24 July	1998	May	2002	Feb	2004
ÇANAKKALE	S 358	Gölcük, Kocaeli/Pendik	22 July	1999	Aug	2002		June 2004

Displacement, tons: 1,454 surfaced; 1,586 dived
Dimensions, feet (metres): 203.4 × 20.3 × 18
  (62 × 6.2 × 5.5)
Main machinery: Diesel-electric; 4 MTU 12V 396 SB83 diesels; 3,800 hp(m) *(2.8 MW)* sustained; 4 alternators; 1 Siemens motor; 4,000 hp(m) *(3.38 MW)* sustained; 1 shaft
Speed, knots: 10 surfaced/snorting; 21.5 dived
Range, miles: 8,200 at 8 kt surfaced; 400 at 4 kt dived
Complement: 30 (8 officers)

Missiles: SSM: McDonnell Douglas Sub Harpoon; active radar homing to 130 km *(70 n miles)* at 0.9 Mach; warhead 227 kg.
Torpedoes: 8—21 in *(533 mm)* bow tubes. GEC-Marconi Tigerfish Mk 24 Mod 2; wire-guided; active/passive homing to 13 km *(7 n miles)* at 35 kt active; 29 km *(15.7 n miles)* at 24 kt passive; warhead 134 kg or STN Atlas DM 2A4 (S 357 onwards). Total of 14 torpedoes and missiles.
Mines: In lieu of torpedoes.
Countermeasures: ESM: Racal Porpoise or Racal Sealion (UAP) (S 357 onwards); intercept.
Weapons control: Atlas Elektronik ISUS 83-2 TFCS. Link 11 receive only.
Radars: Surface search; I-band.
Sonars: Atlas Elektronik CSU 83; passive/active search and attack; medium/high frequency.
  Atlas Elektronik TAS-3; towed array; passive low frequency.
  STN Atlas flank array; passive low frequency.

Programmes: Order for first two signed in Ankara on 17 November 1987 with option on two more taken up in 1993. Four more ordered 22 July 1998. All built with HDW prefabrication and assembly at Gölcük. The last four are to complete at one a year from 2004 and are to be called the 'Gür' class. The programme has been slowed by the earthquake damage to Gölcük in 1999. The first four names commemorate Turkish victories. 18 March 1915 marks a victory in the Dardanelles and *Anafartalar* is a hill in Gallipoli.
Structure: Diving depth, 280 m *(820 ft)*. Kollmorgen masts. Four torpedo tubes can be used for SSM. STN Atlas flank arrays fitted in 1998/99 to the first four.
Operational: Endurance, 50 days.

UPDATED

18 MART   *11/1999*, Selim San* / 0084415

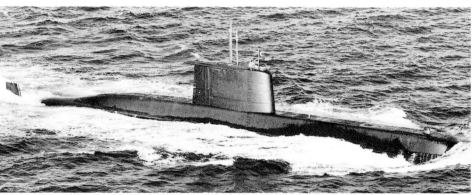

SAKARYA   *11/1998*, Michael Nitz* / 0080858

PREVEZE   *5/1999*, John Brodie* / 0080859

6 ATILAY (209) CLASS (TYPE 1200) (SSK)

Name	No	Builders	Laid down	Launched	Commissioned
ATILAY	S 347	Howaldtswerke, Kiel	1 Dec 1972	23 Oct 1974	12 Mar 1976
SALDIRAY	S 348	Howaldtswerke, Kiel	2 Jan 1973	14 Feb 1975	15 Jan 1977
BATIRAY	S 349	Howaldtswerke, Kiel	1 June 1975	24 Oct 1977	7 Nov 1978
YILDIRAY	S 350	Gölcük, Izmit	1 May 1976	20 July 1979	20 July 1981
DOĞANAY	S 351	Gölcük, Izmit	21 Mar 1980	16 Nov 1983	16 Nov 1984
DOLUNAY	S 352	Gölcük, Izmit	9 Mar 1981	22 July 1988	29 June 1990

Displacement, tons: 980 surfaced; 1,185 dived
Dimensions, feet (metres): 200.8 × 20.3 × 17.9
(61.2 × 6.2 × 5.5)
Main machinery: Diesel-electric; 4 MTU 12V 493 TY60 diesels;
2,400 hp(m) *(1.76 MW)* sustained; 4 alternators; 1.7 MW;
1 Siemens motor; 4,600 hp(m) *(3.38 MW)* sustained; 1 shaft
Speed, knots: 11 surfaced; 22 dived
Range, miles: 7,500 at 8 kt surfaced
Complement: 38 (9 officers)

Torpedoes: 8—21 in *(533 mm)* tubes. 14 AEG SST 4; wire-
guided; active/passive homing to 28 km *(15.3 n miles)* at
23 kt; 12 km *(6.6 n miles)* at 35 kt; warhead 260 kg. Swim-out
discharge.
Countermeasures: ESM: Thomson-CSF DR 2000 or Racal
Sealion (UAP) or Racal Porpoise; intercept
Weapons control: Signaal M8 (S 347-348). Signaal Sinbads
(remainder). Link 11 receive.
Radars: Surface search: S 63B; I-band.
Sonars: Atlas Elektronik CSU 3; hull-mounted; passive/active
search and attack; medium/high frequency.

Programmes: Designed by Ingenieurkontor, Lübeck for
construction by Howaldtswerke, Kiel and sale by Ferrostaal,
Essen, all acting as a consortium. Last three built in Turkey with
assistance given by HDW.
Modernisation: Mid-life upgrades planned to include fire-control
system starting with the first pair. Possibly by STN Elektronik to
'Preveze' class standards. Programme drawn up in July 1995
and started with first pair being fitted with a new ESM in 1999.

YILDIRAY   *12/1998*, Selim San* / 0080860

Structure: A single-hull design with two ballast tanks and
forward and after trim tanks. Fitted with snort and remote
machinery control. The single screw is slow revving. Very high-
capacity batteries with GRP lead-acid cells and battery
cooling—by Wilh Hagen. Active and passive sonar, sonar
detection equipment, sound ranging gear and underwater
telephone. Fitted with two periscopes, radar and Omega
receiver. Fore-planes retract. Diving depth, 250 m *(820 ft)*.
Operational: Endurance, 50 days. Some US Mk 37 torpedoes
may also be carried.

UPDATED

2 GUPPY IIA CLASS (SS)

Name	No	Builders	Laid down	Launched	Commissioned	Recommissioned
MURATREIS (ex-*Razorback* SS 394)	S 336	Portsmouth Navy Yard	9 Sep 1943	27 Jan 1944	3 Apr 1944	17 Dec 1971
ULUÇALIREIS (ex-*Thornback* SS 418)	S 338	Portsmouth Navy Yard	5 Apr 1944	7 July 1944	13 Oct 1944	1 July 1974

Displacement, tons: 1,848 surfaced; 2,440 dived
Dimensions, feet (metres): 306 × 27 × 17
(93.2 × 8.2 × 5.2)
Main machinery: Diesel-electric; 3 Fairbanks-Morse 38D8-1/
8-10 diesels; 4,500 hp *(3.4 MW)*; 2 motors; 4,800 hp
(3.6 MW); 2 shafts
Speed, knots: 17 surfaced; 14-15 dived
Range, miles: 12,000 at 10 kt surfaced
Complement: 85 (9 officers)

Torpedoes: 10—21 in *(533 mm)* (6 bow, 4 stern) tubes; 21 US
Mk 37; active/passive homing to 8 km *(4.4 n miles)* at 24 kt;
warhead 150 kg.
Mines: 40 in lieu of torpedoes.
Weapons control: Mk 106 TFCS.
Radars: Surface search: SS 2A; I-band.
Sonars: EDO BQR 2B; hull-mounted; passive search and attack;
medium frequency.
EDO BQS 4; adds active capability to BQR 2B.
Sperry/Raytheon BQG 3; passive ranging.

Programmes: This last pair of survivors were transferred from
the US in the early 1970s.
Operational: Diving probably restricted to periscope depth, and
used for training.

UPDATED

ULUÇALIREIS   *12/1998*, Selim San* / 0080861

2 TANG CLASS (SS)

Name	No	Builders	Laid down	Launched	Commissioned	Recommissioned
HIZIRREIS (ex-*Gudgeon* SS 567)	S 342	Portsmouth Navy Yard	20 May 1950	11 June 1952	21 Nov 1952	30 Sep 1983
PIRIREIS (ex-*Tang* SS 563)	S 343	Portsmouth Navy Yard	18 Apr 1949	27 Apr 1952	25 Oct 1952	21 Apr 1980

Displacement, tons: 2,100 surfaced; 2,700 dived
Dimensions, feet (metres): 287 × 27.3 × 19
(87.4 × 8.3 × 5.8)
Main machinery: Diesel-electric; 3 Fairbanks-Morse 38D8-1/
8-10 diesels; 4,500 hp *(3.4 MW)*; 2 Westinghouse motors;
5,600 hp *(4.2 MW)*; 2 shafts
Speed, knots: 16 surfaced; 16 dived
Range, miles: 7,600 at 15 kt surfaced
Complement: 87 (8 officers)

Torpedoes: 8—21 in *(533 mm)* (6 fwd, 2 aft) tubes. 21
Westinghouse Mk 37; active/passive homing to 8 km *(4.4 n
miles)* at 24 kt; warhead 150 kg.
Mines: In lieu of torpedoes.
Countermeasures: ESM: WLR-1; radar warning.
Weapons control: Mk 106 torpedo FCS.
Radars: Surface search: Fairchild BPS 12; I-band.

Sonars: EDO BQR 2B; hull-mounted; passive search and attack;
medium frequency.
EDO BQS 4; adds active capability to BQR 2B.
Sperry/Raytheon BQG 4; passive ranging.

Programmes: S 343 transferred by lease from USA January
1980, S 342 September 1983. Both finally purchased in June
1987.

VERIFIED

PIRIREIS   *11/1998, Michael Nitz* / 0050263

FRIGATES

Note: An Invitation To Tender (ITT) was issued in 1998 for up to six TF 2000 air defence frigates, to be fitted with Standard SM-2. There is some doubt about whether this project may be overtaken by an order for up to 12 corvettes, for which an ITT is expected in 2000.

5 + 1 GAZIANTEP (OLIVER HAZARD PERRY) CLASS (FFG)

Name	No	Builders	Laid down		Launched		Commissioned		Recommissioned	
GAZIANTEP (ex-*Clifton Sprague*)	F 490 (ex-FFG 16)	Bath Iron Works	30 Sep	1979	16 Feb	1980	21 Mar	1981	24 July	1998
GIRESUN (ex-*Antrim*)	F 491 (ex-FFG 20)	Todd Shipyards, Seattle	21 June	1978	27 Mar	1979	26 Sep	1981	24 July	1998
GEMLIK (ex-*Flatley*)	F 492 (ex-FFG 21)	Bath Iron Works	13 Nov	1979	15 May	1980	20 June	1981	24 July	1998
GELIBOLU (ex-*Reid*)	F 493 (ex-FFG 30)	Todd Shipyards, San Pedro	8 Oct	1980	27 June	1981	19 Feb	1983	22 July	1999
GÖKÇEADA (ex-*Mahlon S Tisdale*)	F 494 (ex-FFG 27)	Todd Shipyards, San Pedro	19 Mar	1980	7 Feb	1981	27 Nov	1982	8 June	2000
— (ex-*John A Moore*)	F 495 (ex-FFG 19)	Todd Shipyards, San Pedro	19 Dec	1978	20 Oct	1979	14 Nov	1981		2000

Displacement, tons: 2,750 light, 3,638 full load
Dimensions, feet (metres): 445 × 45 × 14.8; 24.5 (sonar)
(135.6 × 13.7 × 4.5; 7.5)
Main machinery: 2 GE LM 2500 gas turbines; 41,000 hp
(30.59 MW) sustained; 1 shaft; cp prop
2 auxiliary retractable props; 650 hp *(484 kW)*
Speed, knots: 29. **Range, miles:** 4,500 at 20 kt
Complement: 206 (13 officers) including 19 aircrew

Missiles: SSM: 4 McDonnell Douglas Harpoon; active radar homing to 130 km *(70 n miles)* at 0.9 Mach; warhead 227 kg.
SAM: 36 GDC Standard SM-1MR; command guidance; semi-active radar homing to 46 km *(25 n miles)* at 2 Mach.
1 Mk 13 Mod 4 launcher for both SSM and SAM missiles ❶.
Guns: 1 OTO Melara 3 in *(76 mm)*/62 Mk 75 ❷; 85 rds/min to 16 km *(8.7 n miles)* anti-surface; 12 km *(6.6 n miles)* anti-aircraft; weight of shell 6 kg.
1 General Electric/General Dynamics 20 mm/76 6-barrelled Mk 15 Vulcan Phalanx ❸; 3,000 rds/min combined to 1.5 km.
4—12.7 mm MGs.
Torpedoes: 6—324 mm Mk 32 (2 triple) tubes ❹. 24 Honeywell Mk 46 Mod 5; anti-submarine; active/passive homing to 11 km *(5.9 n miles)* at 40 kt; warhead 44 kg.
Countermeasures: Decoys: 2 Loral Hycor SRBOC 6-barrelled fixed Mk 36 ❺; IR flares and chaff to 4 km *(2.2 n miles)*.
T—Mk-6 Fanfare/SLQ-25 Nixie; torpedo decoy.
ESM/ECM: SLQ-32(V)2 ❻; radar warning. Sidekick modification adds jammer and deception system.
Combat data systems: NTDS with Link 11 and 14. SATCOM.

Weapons control: SWG-1 Harpoon LCS. Mk 92 Mod 4 WCS with CAS (Combined Antenna System). The Mk 92 is the US version of the Signaal WM28 system. Mk 13 weapon direction system.
2 Mk 24 optical directors.
Radars: Air search: Raytheon SPS-49(V)4 ❼; C/D-band.
Surface search: ISC Cardion SPS-55 ❽; I-band.
Fire control: Lockheed STIR (modified SPG-60) ❾; I/J-band.
Sperry Mk 92 (Signaal WM28) ❿; I/J-band.
Navigation: Furuno; I-band.
Tacan: URN 25.
Sonars: Raytheon SQS-56; hull-mounted; active search and attack; medium frequency.

Helicopters: 1 S-70B Seahawk ⑪ to be carried from 2002.

GAZIANTEP   *(Scale 1 : 1,200), Ian Sturton* / 0019307

Programmes: Three approved for transfer by grant aid. Transfer delayed by Greek objections, and Turkish sailors were sent home from the USA in mid-1996. Congress authorised the go-ahead again on 27 August 1997. Two more approved for transfer by sale 30 September 1998 and one more in February 2000. At least one other *Duncan* FFG 10 for spares.
Structure: Flight deck extension is needed to embark S-70B helicopters.
Operational: F 490 arrived at Gölcük in March 1998, second pair in April 1998, fourth and fifth 5 April 1999 and 27 September 1999 respectively. Sonar towed arrays were not transferred. Seahawk helicopters are expected to be embarked by 2002.
UPDATED

GIRESUN   *10/1998*, Selim San* / 0050269

GAZIANTEP   *8/1998, Maritime Photographic* / 0050270

8 TEPE (KNOX) CLASS (FFG)

Name	No	Builders	Laid down		Launched		Commissioned		Recommissioned	
MUAVENET (ex-*Capodanno*)	F 250 (ex-1093)	Avondale Shipyards	12 Oct	1971	21 Oct	1972	17 Nov	1973	12 Sep	1993
ADATEPE (ex-*Fanning*)	F 251 (ex-1076)	Todd Shipyards	7 Dec	1968	24 Jan	1970	23 July	1971	27 Sep	1993
KOCATEPE (ex-*Reasoner*)	F 252 (ex-1063)	Lockheed Shipbuilding	6 Jan	1969	1 Aug	1970	31 July	1971	28 Aug	1993
ZAFER (ex-*Thomas C Hart*)	F 253 (ex-1092)	Avondale Shipyards	8 Oct	1971	12 Aug	1972	28 July	1973	30 Aug	1993
TRAKYA (ex-*McCandless*)	F 254 (ex-1084)	Avondale Shipyards	4 June	1970	20 Mar	1971	18 Mar	1972	6 May	1994
KARADENIZ (ex-*Donald B Beary*)	F 255 (ex-1085)	Avondale Shipyards	24 July	1970	22 May	1971	22 July	1972	20 May	1994
EGE (ex-*Ainsworth*)	F 256 (ex-1090)	Avondale Shipyards	11 June	1971	15 Apr	1972	31 Mar	1973	27 May	1994
AKDENIZ (ex-*Bowen*)	F 257 (ex-1079)	Avondale Shipyards	11 July	1969	2 May	1970	22 May	1971	3 June	1994

Displacement, tons: 3,011 standard; 4,260 full load
Dimensions, feet (metres): 439.6 × 46.8 × 15; 24.8 (sonar) *(134 × 14.3 × 4.6; 7.8)*
Main machinery: 2 Combustion Engineering/Babcock & Wilcox boilers; 1,200 psi *(84.4 kg/cm²)*; 950°F *(510°C)*; 1 Westinghouse turbine; 35,000 hp *(26 MW)*; 1 shaft
Speed, knots: 27. **Range, miles:** 4,000 at 22 kt on 1 boiler
Complement: 288 (20 officers)

Missiles: SSM: 8 McDonnell Douglas Harpoon; active radar homing to 130 km *(70 n miles)* at 0.9 Mach; warhead 227 kg.
A/S: Honeywell ASROC Mk 16 octuple launcher with reload system (has 2 cells modified to fire Harpoon) ❶; inertial guidance to 1.6-10 km *(1-5.4 n miles)*; payload Mk 46 Mod 5 Neartip.
Guns: 1 FMC 5 in *(127 mm)*/54 Mk 42 Mod 9 ❷; 20-40 rds/min to 24 km *(13 n miles)* anti-surface; 14 km *(7.7 n miles)* anti-aircraft; weight of shell 32 kg.
1 General Electric/General Dynamics 20 mm/76 6-barrelled Mk 15 Vulcan Phalanx ❸; 3,000 rds/min combined to 1.5 km.
Torpedoes: 4—324 mm Mk 32 (2 twin) fixed tubes ❹. 22 Honeywell Mk 46 Mod 5; anti-submarine; active/passive homing to 11 km *(5.9 n miles)* at 40 kt; warhead 44 kg.
Countermeasures: Decoys: 2 Loral Hycor SRBOC 6-barrelled fixed Mk 36 ❺; IR flares and chaff to 4 km *(2.2 n miles)*. T Mk-6 Fanfare/SLQ-25 Nixie; torpedo decoy. Prairie Masker hull and blade rate noise suppression.
ESM: SLQ-32(V)2 ❻; intercept.
Combat data systems: Signaal Sigma K5 with Link 11.
Weapons control: SWG-1A Harpoon LCS. Mk 68 Mod 3 GFCS. Mk 114 Mod 6 ASW FCS. Mk 1 target designation system. MMS target acquisition sight (for mines, small craft and low-flying aircraft).
Radars: Air search: Lockheed SPS-40B ❼; E/F-band.
Surface search: Raytheon SPS-10 or Norden SPS-67 ❽; G-band.
Navigation: Marconi LN66; I-band.
Fire control: Western Electric SPG-53D/F ❾; I/J-band.
Tacan: SRN 15.
Sonars: EDO/General Electric SQS-26CX; bow-mounted; active search and attack; medium frequency.

Helicopters: 1 AB 212ASW ❿.

Programmes: In late 1992 the USA offered Turkey four of the class. A proposal was put to Congress in June 1993 and four approved for transfer on a five year lease, plus one more for spares, *Elmer Montgomery*, on a grant basis under the Foreign Assistance Act. The latter replaced the former destroyer *Muavenet* which was scrapped after being hit by a Sea Sparrow missile. The second batch of four transferred in 1994. Three more were offered in 1996. This was overtaken by the transfer of the 'Oliver Perry' class, but they have been taken by grant aid for spares (FF 1059, 1080 and 1091) in 1998. All eight operational ships are being purchased outright.

MUAVENET   *(Scale 1 : 1,200), Ian Sturton*

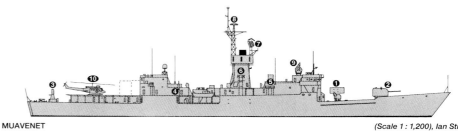

AKDENIZ   *4/1998*, Michael Nitz* / 0080865

Modernisation: Hangar and flight deck enlarged. In 1979 a programme was initiated to fit 3.5 ft bow bulwarks and spray strakes adding 9.1 tons to a displacement. Sea Sparrow SAM replaced by Phalanx 1982-88. Link 11 fitted after transfer.
Structure: Improved ASROC torpedo reloading capability (note slanting face of bridge structure immediately behind ASROC). Four Mk 32 torpedo tubes are fixed in the midships structure, two to a side, angled out at 45°. The arrangement provides improved loading capability over exposed triple Mk 32 torpedo tubes. A 4,000 lb lightweight anchor is fitted on the port side and an 8,000 lb anchor fits into the after section of the sonar dome.

UPDATED

EGE   *11/1999*, Guy Toremans* / 0080866

4 YAVUZ CLASS (MEKO 200 TYPE) (FFG)

Name	No	Builders	Laid down	Launched	Commissioned
YAVUZ	F 240	Blohm + Voss, Hamburg	30 May 1985	7 Nov 1985	17 July 1987
TURGUTREIS (ex-*Turgut*)	F 241	Howaldtswerke, Kiel	20 May 1985	30 May 1986	4 Feb 1988
FATIH	F 242	Gölcük, Izmit	1 Jan 1986	24 Apr 1987	28 Aug 1988
YILDIRIM	F 243	Gölcük, Izmit	24 Apr 1987	22 July 1988	17 Nov 1989

Displacement, tons: 2,414 standard; 2,919 full load
Dimensions, feet (metres): 378.9 × 46.6 × 13.5
  (115.5 × 14.2 × 4.1)
Main machinery: CODAD; 4 MTU 20V 1163 TB93 diesels;
  29,940 hp(m) *(22 MW)* sustained; 2 shafts; cp props
Speed, knots: 27. **Range, miles:** 4,100 at 18 kt
Complement: 180 (24 officers)

Missiles: SSM: 8 McDonnell Douglas Harpoon (2 quad)
  launchers ❶; active radar homing to 130 km *(70 n miles)* at
  0.9 Mach; warhead 227 kg.
  SAM: Raytheon Sea Sparrow Mk 29 Mod 1 octuple launcher ❷;
  24 Selenia Elsag Aspide; semi-active radar homing to 13 km
  (7 n miles) at 2.5 Mach; warhead 39 kg.
Guns: 1 FMC 5 in *(127 mm)*/54 Mk 45 Mod 1 ❸; 20 rds/min to
  23 km *(12.6 n miles)* anti-surface; 15 km *(8.2 n miles)* anti-
  aircraft; weight of shell 32 kg.
  3 Oerlikon-Contraves 25 mm Sea Zenith ❹; 4 barrels per
  mounting; 3,400 rds/min combined to 2 km.
Torpedoes: 6—324 mm Mk 32 (2 triple) tubes ❺. Honeywell Mk
  46 Mod 5; anti-submarine; active/passive homing to 11 km
  (5.9 n miles) at 40 kt; warhead 44 kg.
Countermeasures: Decoys: 2 Loral Hycor 6-tubed fixed Mk 36
  Mod 1 SRBOC ❻; IR flares and chaff to 4 km *(2.2 n miles)*.
  Nixie SLQ-25; towed torpedo decoy.
ESM/ECM: Signaal Rapids/Ramses; intercept and jammer.
Combat data systems: Signaal STACOS-TU; action data
  automation; Link 11. WSC 3V(7) SATCOMs. Marisat.
Weapons control: 2 Siemens Albis optronic directors (for Sea
  Zenith). SWG-1A for Harpoon.
Radars: Air search: Signaal DA08 ❼; F-band.
  Air/surface search: Plessey AWS 6 Dolphin ❽; G-band.
  Fire control: Signaal STIR ❾; I/J/K-band (for SAM); range 140 km
  (76 n miles) for 1 m² target.
  Signaal WM25 ❿; I/J-band (for SSM and 127 mm).
  2 Contraves Seaguard ⓫; I/J-band (for 25 mm).
  Navigation: Racal Decca TM 1226; I-band.
Tacan: URN 25. IFF Mk XII.
Sonars: Raytheon SQS-56 (DE 1160); hull-mounted; active
  search and attack; medium frequency.

Helicopters: 1 AB 212ASW ⓬.

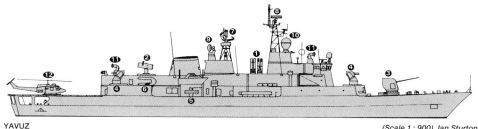

YAVUZ

(Scale 1 : 900), Ian Sturton

TURGUTREIS

6/1999*, John Brodie / 0080862

Programmes: Ordered 29 December 1982 with builders and
Thyssen Rheinstahl Technik of Dusseldorf. Meko 200 type
similar to Portuguese frigates. *Turgutreis* was renamed on
14 February 1988.

Operational: Helicopter has Sea Skua anti-ship missiles.
  UPDATED

YILDIRIM

11/1998*, Michael Nitz / 0080863

TURGUTREIS

10/1999*, H M Steele / 0080864

4 BARBAROS CLASS (MODIFIED MEKO 200 TYPE) (FFG)

Name	No	Builders	Laid down	Launched	Commissioned
BARBAROS	F 244	Blohm + Voss, Hamburg	18 Mar 1993	29 Sep 1993	16 Mar 1995
ORUCREIS	F 245	Gölcük, Kocaeli	15 Sep 1993	28 July 1994	10 May 1996
SALIHREIS	F 246	Blohm + Voss, Hamburg	24 July 1995	26 Sep 1997	17 Dec 1998
KEMALREIS	F 247	Gölcük, Kocaeli	4 Apr 1997	24 July 1998	8 June 2000

Displacement, tons: 3,380 full load
Dimensions, feet (metres): 387.1 × 48.6 × 14.1; 21 (sonar) *(118 × 14.8 × 4.3; 6.4)*
Main machinery: CODOG; 2 GE LM 2500 gas turbines; 60,000 hp *(44.76 MW)* sustained; 2 MTU 16V 1163 TB83 diesels; 11,780 hp(m) *(8.67 MW)* sustained; 2 shafts; Escher Wyss; cp props
Speed, knots: 32. **Range, miles:** 4,100 at 18 kt
Complement: 187 (22 officers) plus 9 aircrew plus 8 spare

Missiles: SSM: 8 McDonnell Douglas Harpoon (2 quad) launchers ❶; active radar homing to 130 km *(70 n miles)* at 0.9 Mach; warhead 227 kg.
SAM: Raytheon Sea Sparrow Mk 29 Mod 1 octuple launcher ❷ (F 244 and F 245) and VLS Mk 41 Mod 8 ❸ (F 246 and F 247); 24 Selenia Elsag Aspide; semi-active radar homing to 13 km *(7 n miles)* at 2.5 Mach; warhead 39 kg. Evolved Sea Sparrow (ESSM) in due course.
Guns: 1 FMC 5 in *(127 mm)*/54 Mk 45 Mod 1/2 ❹; 20 rds/min to 23 km *(12.6 n miles)* anti-surface; 15 km *(8.2 n miles)* anti-aircraft; weight of shell 32 kg.
3 Oerlikon-Contraves 25 mm Sea Zenith ❺; 4 barrels per mounting; 3,400 rds/min combined to 2 km.
Torpedoes: 6—324 mm Mk 32 Mod 5 (2 triple) tubes ❻. Honeywell Mk 46 Mod 5; anti-submarine; active/passive homing to 11 km *(5.9 n miles)* at 40 kt; warhead 44 kg.
Countermeasures: Decoys: 2 Loral Hycor 6-tubed fixed Mk 36 Mod 1 SRBOC ❼; IR flares and chaff to 4 km *(2.2 n miles)*. Nixie SLQ-25; towed torpedo decoy.
ESM/ECM: Racal Cutlass/Scorpion; intercept and jammer.
Combat data systems: Thomson-CSF/Signaal STACOS Mod 3; Link 11. WSC 3V(7) SATCOMs. Marisat.
Weapons control: 2 Siemens Albis optronic directors ❽. SWG-1A for Harpoon.
Radars: Air search: Siemens/Plessey AWS 9 (Type 996) ❾; 3D; E/F-band.
Air/surface search: Plessey/BAe AWS 6 Dolphin ❿; G-band.
Fire control: 1 or 2 (F 246-247) Signaal STIR ⓫; I/J/K-band (for SAM); range 140 km *(76 n miles)* for 1 m² target.
Contraves TMKu (F 244-245) ⓬; I/J-band (for SSM and 127 mm).
2 Contraves Seaguard ⓭; I/J-band (for 25 mm).
Navigation: Racal Decca 2690 BT ARPA; I-band.
Tacan: URN 25. IFF Mk XII Mod 4.
Sonars: Raytheon SQS-56 (DE 1160); hull-mounted; active search and attack; medium frequency.

Helicopters: 1 AB 212ASW ⓮ or S-70B Seahawk.

Programmes: First pair ordered 19 January 1990, second pair authorised 14 December 1992. Programme started 5 November 1991 with construction commencing in June

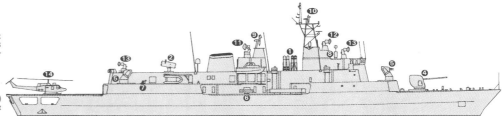

BARBAROS   *(Scale 1 : 900), Ian Sturton / 0019315*

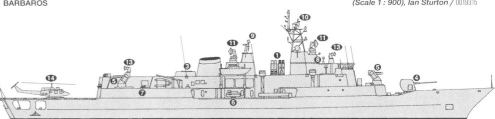

SALIHREIS   *(Scale 1 : 900), Ian Sturton / 0050273*

SALIHREIS   *2/1999 *, Michael Nitz / 0080867*

1992 in Germany. Completion of the last one delayed by the Gölcük earthquake in 1999.
Structure: An improvement on the 'Yavuz' class. Mk 29 Sea Sparrow launchers fitted in the first two, while the second pair have Mk 41 VLS aft of the funnel, which will be retrofitted in the first two in due course. The ships have CODOG propulsion

for a higher top speed. Other differences with *Yavuz* include a full command system, improved radars and a citadel for NBCD protection. A bow bulwark has been added in the second pair.
Operational: Helicopter has Sea Skua anti-ship missiles. The first pair used as Flagships.

UPDATED

ORUCREIS   *11/1999 *, Guy Toremans / 0080868*

BARBAROS   *10/1999 *, A Campanera i Rovira / 0080869*

1 BERK CLASS (FF)

Name	No	Builders	Laid down	Launched	Commissioned
PEYK	D 359	Gölcük Naval Yard	18 Jan 1968	7 June 1972	15 Apr 1976

Displacement, tons: 1,450 standard; 1,950 full load
Dimensions, feet (metres): 311.7 × 38.7 × 18.1
(95 × 11.8 × 5.5)
Main machinery: 4 Fiat-Tosi Type 3-016-RSS diesels; 24,000 hp
(m) *(17.7 MW)*; 1 shaft
Speed, knots: 25
Complement: 164 (14 officers)

Guns: 4 USN 3 in *(76 mm)*/50 (2 twin) ❶; 50 rds/min to 12.8 km
(7 n miles); weight of shell 6 kg.
Torpedoes: 6—324 mm US Mk 32 (2 triple) tubes ❷. Honeywell
Mk 46; anti-submarine; active/passive homing to 11 km *(5.9 n
miles)* at 40 kt; warhead 44 kg.
A/S mortars: 2 Mk 11 Hedgehog 24 rocket launchers ❸; range
250 m; warhead 13.6 kg.
Depth charges: 1 rack.
Countermeasures: ESM: WLR 1; radar warning.
Weapons control: 2 Mk 63 GFCS.
Radars: Air search: Lockheed SPS-40 ❹; E/F-band; range
320 km *(175 n miles)*.
Surface search: Raytheon SPS-10 ❺; G-band.
Navigation: Racal Decca 1226; I-band.
Fire control: 2 Western Electric Mk 34 ❻; I/J-band (for guns).
Sonars: Sangamo SQS-29/31 series; hull-mounted; active
search and attack; high frequency.

Helicopters: Platform only for AB 212ASW ❼.

Programmes: First major class of warships built in Turkey.
Named after a famous ship of the Ottoman Navy.
Structure: Of modified US Claud Jones design (now Indonesian
'Samadikun' class).
UPDATED

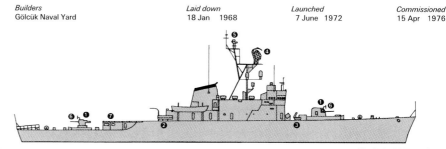
PEYK
(Scale 1 : 900), Ian Sturton

PEYK
6/1999*, Selim San / 0080870

SHIPBORNE AIRCRAFT

Notes: (1) There are three AB 204 utility aircraft.
(2) Five AB 412 SAR helicopters fitted with radar and FLIR are to be delivered in 2001.

Numbers/Type: 13 Agusta AB 212ASW.
Operational speed: 106 kt *(196 km/h)*.
Service ceiling: 14,200 ft *(4,330 m)*.
Range: 230 n miles *(426 km)*.
Role/Weapon systems: ASV/ASW helicopter with updated systems. Sensors: BAe Ferranti Sea
Spray Mk 3 radar, ECM/ESM, MAD, Bendix ASQ-18 dipping sonar. Weapons: ASW; two Mk 46
or 244/S torpedoes. AVS; two Sea Skua missiles.
UPDATED

AB 212
7/1999*, A Sharma / 0080871

Numbers/Type: 8 Sikorsky S-70B Seahawk.
Operational speed: 135 kt *(250 km/h)*.
Service ceiling: 10,000 ft *(3,050 m)*.
Range: 600 n miles *(1,110 km)*.
Role/Weapon systems: Contracts placed 3 June 1998 for first four to be delivered by February
2001. Second contract for four more on 31 December 1998. Helras ASW weapon systems
ordered. Sensors: APS-124 search radar; Helras dipping sonar. Weapons: ASW: 2 Mk 46
torpedoes; AGM-114B Hellfire II ASM.
UPDATED

SEAHAWK S-70B (Thai colours)
8/1997*, Thai Navy League / 0019260

LAND-BASED MARITIME AIRCRAFT

Note: The plan was to acquire P-3 Orion aircraft from the USA but this has been overtaken by the
cheaper option of Air Force CASA CN-235M aircraft converted by IPTN for maritime use. At least
seven maritime patrol aircraft are needed for the Navy and three for the Coast Guard. Project
completion is scheduled for 2004.

PATROL FORCES

Note: *Kozlu* P 301 and *Kuşadasi* P 302 are listed under 'Vegesack' class in Mine Warfare section.

8 DOĞAN CLASS (FAST ATTACK CRAFT—MISSILE) (PCFG)

Name	No	Builders	Commissioned
DOĞAN	P 340	Lürssen, Vegesack	23 Dec 1977
MARTI	P 341	Taşkizak Yard, Istanbul	1 Aug 1978
TAYFUN	P 342	Taşkizak Yard, Istanbul	9 Aug 1979
VOLKAN	P 343	Taşkizak Yard, Istanbul	25 July 1980
RÜZGAR	P 344	Taşkizak Yard, Istanbul	24 May 1985
POYRAZ	P 345	Taşkizak Yard, Istanbul	28 Aug 1986
GURBET	P 346	Taşkizak Yard, Istanbul	24 July 1988
FIRTINA	P 347	Taşkizak Yard, Istanbul	14 Oct 1988

Displacement, tons: 436 full load
Dimensions, feet (metres): 190.6 × 25 × 8.8 *(58.1 × 7.6 × 2.7)*
Main machinery: 4 MTU 16V 956 TB92 diesels; 17,700 hp(m) *(13 MW)* sustained; 4 shafts
Speed, knots: 38. **Range, miles:** 1,050 at 30 kt
Complement: 40 (5 officers)

Missiles: SSM: 8 McDonnell Douglas Harpoon (2 quad) launchers; active radar homing to 130 km
(70 n miles) at 0.9 Mach; warhead 227 kg.
Guns: 1 OTO Melara 3 in *(76 mm)*/62 compact; 85 rds/min to 16 km *(8.7 n miles)* anti-surface;
12 km *(6.6 n miles)* anti-aircraft; weight of shell 6 kg.
2 Oerlikon 35 mm/90 (twin); 550 rds/min to 6 km *(3.3 n miles)*; weight of shell 1.55 kg.
Countermeasures: Decoys: 2 Mk 36 SRBOC chaff launchers.
ESM: MEL Susie; intercept.
Combat data systems: Signaal mini TACTICOS.
Weapons control: LIOD Mk 2 optronic director.
Radars: Surface search: Racal Decca 1226; I-band.
Fire control: Signaal WM28/41; I/J-band.

Programmes: First ordered 3 August 1973 to a Lürssen FPB 57 design.
Structure: Aluminium superstructure; steel hulls. The last pair were built with optronic directors
which are being retrofitted in all, together with an improved Signaal combat data system.
UPDATED

DOĞAN
11/1999*, Selim San / 0080874

POYRAZ
11/1998, Michael Nitz / 0050280

3 KILIÇ CLASS (FAST ATTACK CRAFT—MISSILE) (PCFG)

Name	No	Builders	Launched		Commissioned
KILIÇ	P 330	Lürssen, Vegesack	15 July	1997	17 Mar 1998
KALKAN	P 331	Taşkizak, Istanbul	22 Sep	1998	22 July 1999
MIZRAK	P 332	Taşkizak, Istanbul	5 Apr	1999	June 2000

Displacement, tons: 550 full load
Dimensions, feet (metres): 204.6 × 27.2 × 8.5 (62.4 × 8.3 × 2.6)
Main machinery: 4 MTU 16V 956 TB91 diesels; 15,120 hp(m) (11.1 MW) sustained; 4 shafts
Speed, knots: 38. **Range, miles:** 1,050 at 30 kt
Complement: 46 (12 officers)

Missiles: SSM: 8 McDonnell Douglas Harpoon (2 quad) launchers; active radar homing to 130 km
    (70 n miles) at 0.9 Mach; warhead 227 kg.
Guns: 1 Otobreda 3 in (76 mm)/62 compact; 85 rds/min to 16 km (8.7 n miles) anti-surface; 12 km
    (6.6 n miles) anti-aircraft; weight of shell 6 kg.
    2 Otobreda 40 mm/70 (twin); 300 rds/min to 12 km (6.6 n miles); weight of shell 0.96 kg.
Countermeasures: Decoys: 2 Mk 36 SRBOC chaff launchers.
ESM: Racal Cutlass; intercept.
Combat data systems: Signaal/Thomson-CSF STACOS.
Weapons control: LIOD Mk 2 optronic director; Vesta helo datalink/transponder.
Radars: Surface search: Signaal MW08; G-band.
Fire control: Signaal STING; I/J-band.
Navigation: KH 1007; I-band.

Programmes: Contract first signed in May 1993 but there was a delay in confirming it. Last pair laid
    down on 5 July 1996.
Structure: Essentially the same hull and propulsion as the *Yildiz* but with a reduced radar cross-
    section mast and a redesigned bow to improve sea-keeping. The after gun and radars are also
    different to *Yildiz*.
Operational: First of class arrived in Turkey in April 1998.   ***UPDATED***

KALKAN   *11/1999*, Selim San /* 0080873

2 YILDIZ CLASS (FAST ATTACK CRAFT—MISSILE) (PCFG)

Name	No	Builders	Commissioned
YILDIZ	P 348	Taşkizak Yard, Istanbul	3 June 1996
KARAYEL	P 349	Taşkizak Yard, Istanbul	19 Sep 1996

Displacement, tons: 433 full load
Dimensions, feet (metres): 189.6 oa; 178.5 wl × 25 × 8.8 (57.8; 54.4 × 7.6 × 2.7)
Main machinery: 4 MTU 16V 956 TB91 diesels; 15,120 hp(m) (11.1 MW) sustained; 4 shafts
Speed, knots: 38. **Range, miles:** 1,050 at 30 kt
Complement: 45 (6 officers)

Missiles: SSM: 8 McDonnell Douglas Harpoon (2 quad) launchers; active radar homing to 130 km
    (70 n miles) at 0.9 Mach; warhead 227 kg.
Guns: 1 OTO Melara 3 in (76 mm)/62 compact; 85 rds/min to 16 km (8.7 n miles) anti-surface;
    12 km (6.6 n miles) anti-aircraft; weight of shell 6 kg.
    2 Oerlikon 35 mm/90 (twin); 550 rds/min to 6 km (3.3 n miles); weight of shell 1.55 kg.
Countermeasures: Decoys: 2 Mk 36 SRBOC chaff launchers.
ESM: Racal Cutlass; intercept.
Combat data systems: Signaal/Thomson-CSF TACTICOS.
Weapons control: LIOD Mk 2 optronic director; Vesta helo datalink/transponder.
Radars: Surface search: Siemens/Plessey AW 6 Dolphin; G-band.
Fire control: Oerlikon/Contraves TMX; I/J-band.
Navigation: Racal Decca TM 1226; I-band.

Programmes: Ordered in June 1991. *Karayel* launched 20 June 1995.
Structure: 'Doğan' class hull with much improved weapon systems. A second batch is sufficiently
    different to merit a separate entry.   ***UPDATED***

KARAYEL   *11/1999*, Selim San /* 0080872

8 KARTAL CLASS (FAST ATTACK CRAFT—MISSILE) (PCF)

Name	No	Builders	Commissioned
DENIZKUŞU	P 321 (ex-*P 336*)	Lürssen, Vegesack	9 Mar 1967
ATMACA	P 322 (ex-*P 335*)	Lürssen, Vegesack	9 Mar 1967
ŞAHIN	P 323 (ex-*P 334*)	Lürssen, Vegesack	3 Nov 1966
KARTAL	P 324 (ex-*P 333*)	Lürssen, Vegesack	3 Nov 1966
PELIKAN	P 326	Lürssen, Vegesack	11 Feb 1970
ALBATROS	P 327 (ex-*P 325*)	Lürssen, Vegesack	18 Mar 1970
ŞIMŞEK	P 328 (ex-*P 332*)	Lürssen, Vegesack	6 Nov 1969
KASIRGA	P 329 (ex-*P 338*)	Lürssen, Vegesack	25 Nov 1967

Displacement, tons: 160 standard; 190 full load
Dimensions, feet (metres): 139.4 × 23 × 7.9 (42.5 × 7 × 2.4)
Main machinery: 4 MTU MD 16V 538 TB90 diesels; 12,000 hp(m) (8.82 MW) sustained; 4 shafts
Speed, knots: 42. **Range, miles:** 500 at 40 kt
Complement: 39 (4 officers)

Missiles: SSM: 2 or 4 Kongsberg Penguin Mk 2; IR homing to 27 km (14.6 n miles) at 0.8 Mach;
    warhead 120 kg.
Guns: 2 Bofors 40 mm/70; 300 rds/min to 12 km (6.6 n miles); weight of shell 0.96 kg.
Torpedoes: 2—21 in (533 mm) tubes; anti-surface.
Mines: Can carry 4.
Radars: Surface search: Racal Decca 1226; I-band.

Operational: *Meltem* sunk in collision with Soviet naval training ship *Khasan* in Bosphorus in 1985.
    Subsequently salvaged but beyond repair. This class is nearing the end of its operational life.
                                                  UPDATED

KASIRGA   *11/1998*, Selim San /* 0080875

1 GIRNE CLASS (FAST ATTACK CRAFT—GUN) (PCF)

Name	No	Builders	Commissioned
GIRNE	P 140	Taşkizak Naval Yard	7 June 1977

Displacement, tons: 341 standard; 399 full load
Dimensions, feet (metres): 190.6 × 24.9 × 9.2 (58.1 × 7.6 × 2.8)
Main machinery: 2 MTU 16V 956 SB90 diesels; 8,000 hp(m) (5.9 MW) sustained; 2 shafts
Speed, knots: 36. **Range, miles:** 4,200 at 16 kt
Complement: 54 (6 officers)
Guns: 2 Bofors 40 mm/70. 2 Oerlikon 20 mm.
A/S mortars: 2 Mk 20 Mousetrap 4 rocket launchers; range 200 m; warhead 50 kg.
Depth charges: 2 projectors; 2 racks.
Weapons control: CSEE Naja optronic director.
Radars: Surface search: Racal Decca 1226; I-band.
Sonars: Plessey PMS 26; hull-mounted; active attack; high frequency.

Comment: Unsuccessful prototype of an ASW patrol boat on a Lürssen 57 hull. Started building in
    October 1973. The mast was modified in 1986.   ***UPDATED***

GIRNE   *4/1999*, Selim San /* 0080876

1 ASHEVILLE CLASS (LARGE PATROL CRAFT) (PGF)

Name	No	Builders	Commissioned
BORA (ex-*Surprise* PG 97)	P 339	Petersons, Wisconsin	17 Oct 1969

Displacement, tons: 225 standard; 245 full load
Dimensions, feet (metres): 164.5 × 23.8 × 9.5 (50.1 × 7.3 × 2.9)
Main machinery: CODAG; 1 GE LM 1500 gas turbine; 13,300 hp (9.92 MW); 2 Cummins VT12-
    875M diesels; 1,450 hp (1.08 MW); 2 shafts
Speed, knots: 36 gas; 16 diesels. **Range, miles:** 320 at 38 kt
Complement: 37 (5 officers)
Guns: 1 USN 3 in (76 mm)/50 Mk 34; 50 rds/min to 12.8 km (7 n miles); weight of shell 6 kg.
    1 Bofors 40 mm/56 Mk 10. 4—12.7 mm (2 twin) MGs.
Weapons control: Mk 63 GFCS.
Radars: Surface search: Sperry SPS-53; I/J-band.
Fire control: Western Electric SPG-50; I/J-band.

Comment: Launched 15 November 1968. Transferred from USA on 28 February 1973 on loan and
    purchased outright in June 1987. Commissioned in the Turkish Navy 9 March 1973.
                                                  UPDATED

BORA   *5/1999*, Selim San /* 0080877

6 HISAR (PC 1638) CLASS (LARGE PATROL CRAFT) (PG)

Name	No	Builders	Commissioned
SULTANHISAR (ex-*PC 1638*)	P 111	Gunderson, Portland	May 1964
DEMIRHISAR (ex-*PC 1639*)	P 112	Gunderson, Portland	Apr 1965
YARHISAR (ex-*PC 1640*)	P 113	Gunderson, Portland	Sep 1964
AKHISAR (ex-*PC 1641*)	P 114	Gunderson, Portland	Dec 1964
SIVRIHISAR (ex-*PC 1642*)	P 115	Gunderson, Portland	June 1965
KOÇHISAR (ex-*PC 1643*)	P 116	Gölcük Dockyard	July 1965

Displacement, tons: 325 standard; 477 full load
Dimensions, feet (metres): 173.7 × 23 × 10.2 (53 × 7 × 3.1)
Main machinery: 2 Fairbanks-Morse diesels; 2,800 hp (2.09 MW); 2 shafts
Speed, knots: 19. **Range, miles:** 6,000 at 10 kt
Complement: 31 (3 officers)
Guns: 2 Bofors 40 mm/60.
Depth charges: 4 projectors; 1 rack (9).
Radars: Surface search: Decca 707; I-band.

Comment: Transferred from the USA on build. ASW equipment removed. P 112 to be paid off
    in 2000.   ***UPDATED***

DEMIRHISAR   *4/1999*, Selim San /* 0080878

3 TRABZON CLASS (LARGE PATROL CRAFT) (PG/AGI)

TRABZON (ex-*Gaspe*) P 530 (ex-M 530)   **TEKIRDAĞ** (ex-*Ungava*) A 601 (ex-M 533)
TERME (ex-*Trinity*) P 531 (ex-M 531)

Displacement, tons: 370 standard; 470 full load
Dimensions, feet (metres): 164 × 30.2 × 9.2 *(50 × 9.2 × 2.8)*
Main machinery: 2 GM 12-278A diesels; 2,200 hp *(1.64 MW)*; 2 shafts
Speed, knots: 15. **Range, miles:** 4,500 at 11 kt
Complement: 35 (4 officers)
Guns: 1 Bofors 40 mm/60. 2—12.7 mm MGs.
Radars: Surface search: Racal Decca 1226; I-band.

Comment: All transferred from Canada and recommissioned 31 March 1958. Built by Davie SB Co 1951-53. Of similar type to British 'Ton' class. *Tekirdag* has been fitted with ECM pods abaft mast and used as an AGI since 1991. Pennant numbers changed in 1991 reflecting use as patrol ships with all minesweeping gear removed. **UPDATED**

TEKIRDAĞ   6/1999*, Selim San / 0080879

9 TURK CLASS (LARGE PATROL CRAFT) (PC)

Name	No	Builders	Commissioned
AB 25	P 125 (ex-P 1225)	Haliç Shipyard	2 Feb 1969
AB 26	P 126 (ex-P 1226)	Haliç Shipyard	6 Feb 1970
AB 27	P 127 (ex-P 1227)	Haliç Shipyard	27 June 1969
AB 28	P 128 (ex-P 1228)	Haliç Shipyard	Apr 1969
AB 29	P 129 (ex-P 1229)	Haliç Shipyard	21 Feb 1969
AB 31	P 131 (ex-P 1231)	Haliç Shipyard	17 Nov 1971
AB 33	P 133 (ex-P 1233)	Camialti Shipyard	15 May 1970
AB 35	P 135 (ex-P 1235)	Taşkizak Shipyard	13 Apr 1976
AB 36	P 136 (ex-P 1236)	Taşkizak Shipyard	13 Apr 1976

Displacement, tons: 170 full load
Dimensions, feet (metres): 132 × 21 × 5.5 *(40.2 × 6.4 × 1.7)*
Main machinery: 4 SACM-AGO V16CSHR diesels; 9,600 hp(m) *(7.06 MW)*
2 cruise diesels; 300 hp(m) *(220 kW)*; 2 shafts
Speed, knots: 22
Complement: 31 (3 officers)
Guns: 1 or 2 Bofors 40 mm/70.
1 Oerlikon 20 mm (in those with 1—40 mm). 2—12.7 mm MGs.
A/S mortars: 1 Mk 20 Mousetrap 4 rocket launcher; range 200 m; warhead 50 kg.
Depth charges: 1 rack.
Radars: Surface search: Racal Decca; I-band.
Sonars: Plessey PMS 26; hull-mounted; active search and attack; high frequency.

Comment: Pennant numbers changed in 1991. Similar to *SG 21* Coast Guard class. One to Georgia in December 1998. **UPDATED**

AB 33   11/1998, Selim San / 0050287

4 PGM 71 CLASS (LARGE PATROL CRAFT) (PC)

AB 21-AB 24 (ex-*PGM 104-PGM 108*) P 121-P 124 (ex-P 1221-P 1224)

Displacement, tons: 130 standard; 147 full load
Dimensions, feet (metres): 101 × 21 × 7 *(30.8 × 6.4 × 2.1)*
Main machinery: 8 GM diesels 2,040 hp *(1.52 MW)*; 2 shafts
Speed, knots: 18.5. **Range, miles:** 1,500 at 10 kt
Complement: 31 (3 officers)
Guns: 1 Bofors 40 mm/60. 4 Oerlikon 20 mm (2 twin). 1—7.62 mm MG.
A/S mortars: 2 Mk 22 Mousetrap 8 rocket launchers; range 200 m; warhead 50 kg.
Depth charges: 2 racks (4).
Radars: Surface search: Raytheon 1500B; I-band.
Sonars: EDO SQS-17A; hull-mounted; active attack; high frequency.

Comment: Built by Peterson, Sturgeon Bay and commissioned 1967-68. Transferred from USA almost immediately after completion. Pennant numbers changed in 1991. **UPDATED**

AB 21   6/1997*, Michael Nitz / 0019325

4 COAST GUARD TYPE (COASTAL PATROL CRAFT) (PC)

LS 1-LS 4 P 141-P 144 (ex-P 1209-P 1212)

Displacement, tons: 63 full load
Dimensions, feet (metres): 83 × 14 × 5 *(25.3 × 4.3 × 1.6)*
Main machinery: 2 Cummins diesels; 1,100 hp *(820 kW)*; 2 shafts
Speed, knots: 13
Complement: 17 (3 officers)
Guns: 1 Oerlikon 20 mm.
A/S mortars: 2 Mk 20 Mousetrap 8 rocket launchers; range 200 m; warhead 50 kg.
Radars: Surface search: Racal Decca; I-band.
Sonars: QBE-3; hull-mounted; active attack; high frequency.

Comment: Transferred from USCG on 25 June 1953. All built by US Coast Guard Yard, Curtis Bay, Maryland. Engines changed. Pennant numbers changed in 1991. **UPDATED**

LS 1   1992*, Turkish Navy / 0080880

MINE WARFARE FORCES

Note: Minelayers: see *Bayraktar*, *Sancaktar*, *Sarucabey* and *Karamürselbey* under Amphibious Forces.

1 MINELAYER (ML)

Name	No	Builders	Commissioned
NUSRET	N 110 (ex-N 108)	Frederikshavn Dockyard, Denmark	16 Sep 1964

Displacement, tons: 1,880 standard
Dimensions, feet (metres): 252.7 × 41 × 11 *(77 × 12.6 × 3.4)*
Main machinery: 2 GM EMD 16-567 diesels; 2,800 hp *(2.1 MW)*; 2 shafts; cp props
Speed, knots: 16
Complement: 153 (13 officers)
Guns: 4 USN 3 in *(76 mm)* (2 twin) Mk 33; 50 rds/min to 12.8 km *(7 n miles)*; weight of shell 6 kg.
Mines: 400.
Weapons control: 2 Mk 63 GFCS.
Radars: Air/surface search: Selenia RAN 7S; E/F-band.
Navigation: Racal Decca; I-band.
Fire control: Western Electric Mk 34; I/J-band.

Comment: Laid down in 1962, launched in 1964. Similar to Danish 'Falster' class. **UPDATED**

NUSRET   2/1994*, Turkish Navy / 0080881

3 MINELAYER TENDERS (MLI)

ŞAMANDIRA 1 Y 81 (ex-Y 131, ex-Y 1148)   **ŞAMANDIRA 12** Y 92 (ex-Y 1150)
ŞAMANDIRA 11 Y 91 (ex-Y 132, ex-Y 1149)

Displacement, tons: 72 full load
Dimensions, feet (metres): 64.3 × 18.7 × 5.9 *(19.6 × 5.7 × 1.8)*
Main machinery: 1 Gray Marine 64 HN9 diesel; 225 hp *(168 kW)*; 1 shaft
Speed, knots: 10
Complement: 8

Comment: Acquired in 1959. Used for laying and recovering mine distribution boxes. Third of class put back into service in 1994. **VERIFIED**

ŞAMANDIRA 11 (old number)   9/1991, Erik Laursen

5 EDINCIK (CIRCÉ) CLASS (MINEHUNTERS) (MHC)

Name	No	Builders	Commissioned	Recommissioned
EDINCIK (ex-Cybèle)	M 260 (ex-M 712)	CMN, Cherbourg	28 Sep 1972	24 July 1998
EDREMIT (ex-Calliope)	M 261 (ex-M 713)	CMN, Cherbourg	28 Sep 1972	28 Aug 1998
ENEZ (ex-Cérès)	M 262 (ex-M 716)	CMN, Cherbourg	7 Mar 1973	30 Oct 1998
ERDEK (ex-Circé)	M 263 (ex-M 715)	CMN, Cherbourg	18 May 1972	4 Dec 1998
ERDEMLI (ex-Clio)	M 264 (ex-M 714)	CMN, Cherbourg	18 May 1972	15 Jan 1999

Displacement, tons: 460 standard; 495 normal; 510 full load
Dimensions, feet (metres): 167 × 29.2 × 11.2 *(50.9 × 8.9 × 3.4)*
Main machinery: 1 MTU diesel; 1,800 hp(m) *(1.32 MW)*; 2 active rudders; 1 shaft
Speed, knots: 15. **Range, miles:** 3,000 at 12 kt
Complement: 48 (5 officers)
Guns: 1 Oerlikon 20 mm.
Countermeasures: MCM: DCN Mintac minehunting system with PAP Plus ROV.
Radars: Navigation: Racal Decca 1229; I-band.
Sonars: Thomson Sintra DUBM 20B; hull-mounted; active search; high frequency.

Comment: Acquired from France on 24 September 1997. Full refits included installation of Mintac system before being handed over.   ***UPDATED***

EDREMIT   *10/1999*, Diego Quevedo /* 0080882

0 + 6 MODIFIED TYPE 332 (MHC/MSC)

Displacement, tons: 715 full load
Dimensions, feet (metres): 178.8 × 31.8 × 8.5 *(54.5 × 9.7 × 2.6)*
Main machinery: 2 MTU 8V 396 TB84 diesels; 2 Voith-Schneider props; 2 Schottel bow thrusters
Speed, knots: 14
Complement: 53 (6 officers)
Guns: 1 Otobreda 30 mm. 2—12.7 mm MGs.
Countermeasures: MCM: 2 ECA PAP 104 Mk 5. 1 Oropesa mechanical sweep.
Combat data systems: Plessey Nautis-M.
Radars: Navigation: KH 1007; I-band.
Sonars: Thomson Marconi Type 2093; VDS; active high frequency.

Comment: Ordered from Abeking & Rasmussen and Lürssen on 30 July 1999. First one building in Bremen, remainder at Taskizak and Pendik shipyards in Turkey. The design is based on the German Type 332 but with different propulsion and mine countermeasures equipment. First in-service date planned for mid-2003, all to complete by 2007.
                                                                 NEW ENTRY

MODIFIED TYPE 332 (computer graphic)   *1999*, Abeking & Rasmussen /* 0080883

6 VEGESACK CLASS (MSC/AGS/PC)

Name	No	Builders	Commissioned
KARAMÜRSEL (ex-Worms M 1253)	M 520	Amiot, Cherbourg	30 Apr 1960
KEREMPE (ex-Detmold M 1252)	M 521	Amiot, Cherbourg	20 Feb 1960
KILIMLI (ex-Siegen M 1254)	M 522	Amiot, Cherbourg	9 July 1960
KOZLU (ex-Hameln M 1251)	P 301 (ex-M 523)	Amiot, Cherbourg	15 Oct 1959
KUŞADASI (ex-Vegesack M 1250)	P 302 (ex-M 524)	Amiot, Cherbourg	19 Sep 1959
KEMER (ex-Passau M 1255)	A 582 (ex-M 525)	Amiot, Cherbourg	15 Oct 1960

Displacement, tons: 362 standard; 378 full load
Dimensions, feet (metres): 155.1 × 28.2 × 9.5 *(47.3 × 8.6 × 2.9)*
Main machinery: 2 MTU MB diesels; 1,500 hp(m) *(1.1 MW)*; 2 shafts; cp props
Speed, knots: 15
Complement: 33 (2 officers)
Guns: 2 Oerlikon 20 mm (twin).
Radars: Navigation: Decca 707; I-band.
Sonars: Simrad; active mine detection; high frequency.

Comment: Transferred by West Germany and recommissioned in the mid-1970s. Sonars were fitted from 1989. *Kemer* paid off in 1998 but returned as a survey ship in 1999. *Kozlu* and *Kuşadasi* similarly refitted as patrol ships in 1999.
                                                                 UPDATED

KILIMLI   *4/1996*, van Ginderen Collection /* 0080884

9 ADJUTANT, MSC 268 and MSC 294 CLASSES
(MINESWEEPERS—COASTAL) (MSC)

SAMSUN (ex-*MSC 268*) M 510		**SAROS** (ex-*MSC 305*) M 515	
SINOP (ex-*MSC 270*) M 511		**SIGACIK** (ex-*MSC 311*) M 516	
SÜMENE (ex-*MSC 271*) M 512		**SAPANCA** (ex-*MSC 312*) M 517	
SEDDÜLBAHIR (ex-*MSC 272*) M 513		**SARIYER** (ex-*MSC 315*) M 518	
SILIFKE (ex-*MSC 304*) M 514			

Displacement, tons: 320 standard; 370 full load
Dimensions, feet (metres): 141 × 26 × 8.3 *(43 × 8 × 2.6)*
Main machinery: 4 GM 6-71 diesels; 696 hp *(519 kW)* sustained; 2 shafts (M 510-M 513)
2 Waukesha L 1616 diesels; 1,200 hp *(895 kW)*; 2 shafts (M 514-M 518)
Speed, knots: 14. **Range, miles:** 2,500 at 10 kt
Complement: 35 (2 officers)
Guns: 2 Oerlikon 20 mm (twin).
Radars: Navigation: Racal Decca 1226; I-band.
Sonars: UQS-1D; hull-mounted mine search; high frequency.

Comment: Built 1955-59 (M 510-M 513) and 1965-67 (M 514-M 518). Transferred from US. Commissioning dates in the Turkish Navy were respectively: 4 September 1979, 4 September 1970, 3 October 1958, 7 February 1959, 30 March 1959, 1 May 1959, 21 March 1966, 25 October 1966, 20 December 1965, 20 December 1965 and 7 December 1967. Height of funnels and bridge arrangements vary.   ***UPDATED***

SINOP   *8/1999*, C D Yaylali /* 0080885

SILIFKE   *10/1998, Selim San /* 0050289

4 COVE CLASS (MINESWEEPERS—INSHORE) (MSI)

Name	No	Builders	Commissioned
FOÇA (ex-*MSI 15*)	M 500	Peterson, WI	19 Apr 1968
FETHIYE (ex-*MSI 16*)	M 501	Peterson, WI	24 Apr 1968
FATSA (ex-*MSI 17*)	M 502	Peterson, WI	21 Mar 1968
FINIKE (ex-*MSI 18*)	M 503	Peterson, WI	26 Apr 1968

Displacement, tons: 180 standard; 235 full load
Dimensions, feet (metres): 111.9 × 23.5 × 7.9 *(34 × 7.1 × 2.4)*
Main machinery: 4 GM 6-71 diesels; 696 hp *(520 kW)* sustained; 2 shafts
Speed, knots: 13. **Range, miles:** 900 at 11 kt
Complement: 25 (3 officers)
Guns: 1—12.7 mm MG.
Radars: Navigation: I-band.

Comment: Built in USA and transferred under MAP at Boston, Massachusetts, August-December 1967.   ***VERIFIED***

FETHIYE   *10/1998, Selim San /* 0050290

8 MINEHUNTING TENDERS (YAG/YDT)

DALGIÇ 2 (ex-*MTB 2*) P 312	MTB 5 P 315	MTB 8 P 318
MTB 3 P 313	MTB 6 P 316	MTB 9 P 319
MTB 4 P 314	MTB 7 P 317	

Displacement, tons: 70 standard
Dimensions, feet (metres): 71.5 × 13.8 × 8.5 *(21.8 × 4.2 × 2.6)*
Main machinery: 2 diesels; 2,000 hp(m) *(1.47 MW)*; 2 shafts
Speed, knots: 20
Guns: 1 Oerlikon 20 mm or 1—12.7 mm MG (aft) (in some).

Comment: All launched in 1942. Now employed as minehunting base ships (P 313-319) and diver support craft (P 312).

UPDATED

MTB 6   *7/1995*, van Ginderen Collection* / 0080886

AMPHIBIOUS FORCES

Note: The prefix 'Ç' for smaller amphibious vessels stands for 'Çikartma Gemisi' (landing vessel) and indicates that the craft are earmarked for national rather than NATO control.

1 OSMAN GAZI CLASS (LST)

Name	No	Builders	Launched	Commissioned
OSMAN GAZI	NL 125	Taşkizak Yard, Istanbul	20 July 1990	27 July 1994

Displacement, tons: 3,773 full load
Dimensions, feet (metres): 344.5 × 52.8 × 15.7 *(105 × 16.1 × 4.8)*
Main machinery: 2 MTU 12V 1163 TB73 diesels; 8,800 hp(m) *(6.47 MW)*; 2 shafts
Speed, knots: 17. **Range, miles:** 4,000 at 15 kt
Military lift: 900 troops; 15 tanks; 4 LCVPs
Guns: 2 Oerlikon 35 mm/90 (twin). 4 Bofors 40 mm/60 (2 twin). 2 Oerlikon 20 mm.
Radars: Navigation: Racal Decca; I-band.
Helicopters: Platform for 1 large.

Comment: Laid down 7 July 1989. Full NBCD protection. Equipped with a support weapons co-ordination centre to control amphibious operations. The ship has about a 50 per cent increase in military lift capacity compared with the 'Sarucabey' class. Second of class cancelled in 1991 and *Osman Gazi* took a long time to complete. Marisat fitted.

UPDATED

OSMAN GAZI   *5/1998, Diego Quevedo* / 0050291

OSMAN GAZI   *5/1998, Diego Quevedo* / 0050292

2 ERTUĞRUL (TERREBONNE PARISH) CLASS (LST)

Name	No	Builders	Commissioned
ERTUĞRUL (ex-*Windham County* LST 1170)	L 401	Christy Corporation	15 Dec 1954
SERDAR (ex-*Westchester County* LST 1167)	L 402	Christy Corporation	10 Mar 1954

Displacement, tons: 2,590 light; 5,800 full load
Dimensions, feet (metres): 384 × 55 × 17 *(117.1 × 16.8 × 5.2)*
Main machinery: 4 GM 16-278A diesels; 6,000 hp *(4.48 MW)*; 2 shafts; cp props
Speed, knots: 15
Complement: 163 (14 officers)
Military lift: 395 troops; 2,200 tons cargo; 4 LCVPs
Guns: 6 USN 3 in *(76 mm)*/50 (3 twin).
Weapons control: 2 Mk 63 GFCS.
Radars: Surface search: Racal Decca 1226; I-band.
Fire control: 2 Western Electric Mk 34; I/J-band.

Comment: Transferred by USA and recommissioned 3 October 1973 and 24 February 1975 respectively. Purchased outright 6 August 1987. Marisat fitted.

UPDATED

ERTUĞRUL   *9/1998, Selim San* / 0050293

2 LST 512-1152 CLASS (LST/ML)

Name	No	Commissioned
BAYRAKTAR (ex-*Bottrop*, ex-*Saline County* LST 1101)	NL 120 (ex-N-111, ex-A 579, ex-L 403)	26 Jan 1945
SANCAKTAR (ex-*Bochum*, ex-*Rice County* LST 1089)	NL 121 (ex-N-112, ex-A 580, ex-L 404)	14 Mar 1945

Displacement, tons: 1,653 standard; 4,080 full load
Dimensions, feet (metres): 328 × 50 × 14 *(100 × 15.2 × 4.3)*
Main machinery: 2 GM 12-567A diesels; 1,800 hp *(1.34 MW)*; 2 shafts; cp props
Speed, knots: 11. **Range, miles:** 15,000 at 9 kt
Complement: 125 (12 officers)
Guns: 6 Bofors 40 mm/60 (2 twin, 2 single). 2 Oerlikon 20 mm.
Mines: 4 rails.
Radars: Navigation: Kelvin Hughes 14/9; I-band.

Comment: Transferred by USA to West Germany in 1961 and then to Turkey 13 December 1972. Converted into minelayers in West Germany 1962-64. Minelaying gear removed 1974-75 and replaced in 1979. Now dual-purpose ships.

VERIFIED

BAYRAKTAR   *4/1997, Turkish Navy* / 0050294

2 SARUCABEY CLASS (LST/ML)

Name	No	Builders	Launched	Commissioned
SARUCABEY	NL 123	Taşkizak Naval Yard	30 July 1981	17 July 1984
KARAMÜRSELBEY	NL 124	Taşkizak Naval Yard	26 July 1984	19 June 1987

Displacement, tons: 2,600 full load
Dimensions, feet (metres): 301.8 × 45.9 × 7.5 *(92 × 14 × 2.3)*
Main machinery: 3 diesels; 4,320 hp *(3.2 MW)*; 3 shafts
Speed, knots: 14
Military lift: 600 troops; 11 tanks; 12 jeeps; 2 LCVPs
Guns: 3 Bofors 40 mm/70. 4 Oerlikon 20 mm (2 twin).
Mines: 150 in lieu of amphibious lift.
Radars: Navigation: Racal Decca 1226; I-band.
Helicopters: Platform only.

Comment: *Sarucabey* is an enlarged Çakabey design more suitable for naval requirements. First one launched 30 July 1981, second 26 July 1984. Dual-purpose minelayers. NL 124 has superstructure one deck lower.

UPDATED

SARUCABEY   *4/1996*, C D Yaylali* / 0080887

4 EDIC TYPE (LCT)

Ç 108, 113, 117, 120

Displacement, tons: 580 full load
Dimensions, feet (metres): 186.9 × 39.4 × 4.6 *(57 × 12 × 1.4)*
Main machinery: 3 GM 6-71 diesels; 522 hp *(390 kW)* sustained; 3 shafts
Speed, knots: 8.5. **Range, miles:** 600 at 10 kt
Complement: 15
Military lift: 100 troops; up to 5 tanks
Guns: 2 Oerlikon 20 mm. 2—12.7 mm MGs.
Radars: Navigation: Racal Decca; I-band.

Comment: Built at Gölcük Naval Shipyard 1966-73. French EDIC type.

UPDATED

Ç 108   *2/1996 *, C D Yaylali* / 0080888

26 LCT

Ç 122-129, 132-135, 137-150

Displacement, tons: 600 standard
Dimensions, feet (metres): 195.5 × 38 × 10.5 *(59.6 × 11.6 × 3.2)*
Main machinery: 3 GM 6-71 diesels; 522 hp *(390 kW)* sustained; 3 shafts *(119-138)*
   or 3 MTU diesels; 900 hp(m) *(662 kW)*; 3 shafts *(139-150)*
Speed, knots: 8.5. **Range, miles:** 600 at 8 kt
Complement: 17 (1 officer)
Military lift: 100 troops; 5 tanks
Guns: 2 Oerlikon 20 mm. 2—12.7 mm MGs.
Radars: Navigation: Racal Decca; I-band.

Comment: Follow-on to the *Ç 107* type started building in 1977. *Ç 130* and *Ç 131* transferred to Libya January 1980 and *Ç 136* sunk in 1985. The delivery rate was about two per year from the Taşkizak and Gölcük yards until 1987. Then two launched in July 1987 and commissioned in 1991. Last three completed in 1992. Dimensions given are for *Ç 139* onwards, earlier craft are 3.6 m shorter and have less freeboard.

UPDATED

Ç 129   *8/1995 *, Selçuk Emre* / 0080889

20 LCM 8 TYPE

Ç 302-303, 308-309, 312-314, 316, 319, 321-331

Displacement, tons: 58 light; 113 full load
Dimensions, feet (metres): 72 × 20.5 × 4.8 *(22 × 6.3 × 1.4)*
Main machinery: 4 GM 6-71 diesels; 696 hp *(520 kW)* sustained; 2 shafts
Speed, knots: 9.5
Complement: 9
Military lift: 60 tons or 140 troops
Guns: 2—12.7 mm MGs.

Comment: Up to *Ç 319* built by Taşkizak and Haliç in 1965-66. *Ç 321-331* built by Taşkizak and Naldöken in 1987-89.

VERIFIED

Ç 308   *10/1989, Hartmut Ehlers*

INTELLIGENCE VESSELS

Name	No	Builders	Commissioned
YUNUS (ex-*Alster*, ex-*Mellum*)	A 590 (ex-A 50)	Unterweser, Bremen	21 Mar 1961

Displacement, tons: 1,497 full load
Dimensions, feet (metres): 275.5 × 34.4 × 18.4 *(84 × 10.5 × 5.6)*
Main machinery: Diesel-electric; 1 Deutz diesel; 1,800 hp(m) *(1.32 MW)*; 1 shaft
Speed, knots: 15
Complement: 90
Radars: Navigation: Kelvin Hughes 14/7; I-band.

Comment: Ex-trawler, purchased by West German Navy in 1965. Conversion at Blohm + Voss and commissioned for naval service on 19 October 1971. Transferred in February 1989. Planned to be paid off in 2000.

UPDATED

YUNUS   *12/1999 *, Selim San* / 0084416

SURVEY SHIPS

Note: *Kemer* A 582 (ex-M 525) is listed under 'Vegesack' class in Mine Warfare Forces.

1 SILAS BENT CLASS (AGS)

Name	No	Builders	Commissioned
ÇESME (ex-*Silas Bent*)	A 591 (ex-TAGS 26)	American SB Co, Lorain	23 July 1965

Displacement, tons: 2,843 full load
Dimensions, feet (metres): 285.3 × 48 × 15.1 *(87 × 14.6 × 4.6)*
Main machinery: Diesel-electric; 2 Alco diesel generators; 1 Westinghouse/GE motor; 3,600 hp *(2.69 MW)*; 1 shaft; cp prop; bow thruster 350 hp *(261 kW)*
Speed, knots: 15. **Range, miles:** 12,000 at 14 kt
Complement: 31 plus 28 spare
Radars: Navigation: RM 1650/9X; I-band.

Comment: Transferred from US on 28 October 1999.

NEW ENTRY

ÇESME (US colours)   *6/1998 ** / 0053397

1 SURVEY SHIP (AGS)

Name	No	Builders	Launched	Commissioned
ÇUBUKLU (ex-*Y 1251*)	A 594	Gölcük	17 Nov 1983	24 June 1987

Displacement, tons: 680 full load
Dimensions, feet (metres): 132.8 × 31.5 × 10.5 *(40.5 × 9.6 × 3.2)*
Main machinery: 1 MWM diesel; 820 hp(m) *(603 kW)*; 1 shaft; cp prop
Speed, knots: 11
Complement: 37 (6 officers)
Guns: 2 Oerlikon 20 mm.
Radars: Navigation: Racal Decca; I-band.

Comment: Qubit advanced integrated navigation and data processing system fitted in 1991.

VERIFIED

ÇUBUKLU   *6/1997, Turkish Navy* / 0050296

2 SURVEY CRAFT (AGSC)

MESAHA 1 Y 35   **MESAHA 2** Y 36

Displacement, tons: 38 full load
Dimensions, feet (metres): 52.2 × 14.8 × 4.3 *(15.9 × 4.5 × 1.3)*
Main machinery: 2 GM 6-71 diesels; 348 hp *(260 kW)* sustained; 2 shafts
Speed, knots: 10. **Range, miles:** 600 at 10 kt
Complement: 9

Comment: Completed in 1994 and took the names and pennant numbers of their deleted predecessors.

UPDATED

SOKULLU MEHMET PAŞA   *11/1998*, Selim San / 0080891*

MESAHA 2   *9/1994*, C D Yaylali / 0080890*

6 + 2 TRAINING CRAFT (AXL)

Name	No	Builders	Commissioned
E 1	A 1531	Bora-Duzgit	22 July 1999
E 2	A 1532	Bora-Duzgit	22 July 1999
E 3	A 1533	Bora-Duzgit	8 June 2000
E 4	A 1534	Bora-Duzgit	8 June 2000
E 5	A 1535	Bora-Duzgit	8 June 2000
E 6	A 1536	Bora-Duzgit	8 June 2000

Displacement, tons: 94 full load
Dimensions, feet (metres): 94.5 × 19.7 × 6.2 *(28.8 × 6 × 1.9)*
Main machinery: 1 MTU diesel; 1 shaft
Speed, knots: 12. **Range, miles:** 240 at 12 kt
Complement: 15

Comment: Naval Academy training craft ordered in 1998.

NEW ENTRY

TRAINING SHIPS

2 RHEIN CLASS (AX)

Name	No	Builders	Commissioned
CEZAYIRLI GAZI HASAN PAŞA (ex-*Elbe*)	A 579	Schliekerwerft, Hamburg	17 Apr 1962
SOKULLU MEHMET PAŞA (ex-*Donau*)	A 577	Schlichting, Travemünde	23 May 1964

Displacement, tons: 2,370 standard; 2,940 full load
Dimensions, feet (metres): 322.1 × 38.8 × 14.4 *(98.2 × 11.8 × 4.4)*
Main machinery: Diesel-electric; 6 MTU MD diesels; 14,400 hp(m) *(10.58 MW)*; 2 Siemens motors; 11,400 hp(m) *(8.38 MW)*; 2 shafts
Speed, knots: 20.5. **Range, miles:** 1,625 at 15 kt
Complement: 188 (15 officers)
Guns: 2 Creusot-Loire 3.9 in *(100 mm)*/55. 4 Bofors 40 mm/60.
Radars: Surface search: Signaal DA02; E/F-band.
Fire control: 2 Signaal M 45; I/J-band.

Comment: *Elbe* transferred from Germany on 15 March 1993, taking over the same name and pennant number as the former *Ruhr*. *Donau* transferred 13 March 1995 taking the same name and pennant number as the deleted *Isar*.

UPDATED

E 1   *7/1999*, Selçuk Emre / 0080892*

AUXILIARIES

Note: *Tekirdağ* A 601 is listed under 'Trabzon' class in *Patrol Forces*.

2 FLEET SUPPORT SHIPS (AOR)

Name	No	Builders	Laid down	Launched	Commissioned
AKAR	A 580	Gölcük Naval Dockyard	5 Aug 1982	17 Nov 1983	9 Sep 1987
YARBAY KUDRET GÜNGÖR	A 595	Sedef Shipyard, Istanbul	5 Nov 1993	15 Nov 1994	24 Oct 1995

Displacement, tons: 19,350 full load
Dimensions, feet (metres): 475.9 × 74.8 × 27.6 *(145.1 × 22.8 × 8.4)*
Main machinery: 1 diesel; 6,500 hp(m) *(4.78 MW)*; 1 shaft
Speed, knots: 16. **Range, miles:** 6,000 at 14 kt
Complement: 203 (14 officers)
Cargo capacity: 16,000 tons oil fuel (A 580); 9,980 tons oil fuel (A 595); 2,700 tons water (A 595); 80 tons hub oil (A 595); 500 m³ stores (A 595)
Guns: 2—3 in *(76 mm)*/50 (twin) Mk 34 (A 580). 1—20 mm/76 Mk 15 Vulcan Phalanx (A 595). 2 Bofors 40 mm/70.
Weapons control: Mk 63 GFCS (A 580).
Radars: Fire control: SPG-34; I-band (A 580).
Navigation: Racal Decca 1226; I-band.
Helicopters: Platform for 1 medium.

Comment: Helicopter flight deck aft. *Akar* is primarily a tanker whereas the second ship of the same type is classified as logistic support vessel. *Güngör* was the first naval ship to be built at a civilian yard in Turkey.

UPDATED

YARBAY KUDRET GÜNGÖR   *10/1996* / 0080897*

1 SUPPORT TANKER (AOL)

Name	No	Builders	Launched	Commissioned
TAŞKIZAK	A 570	Taşkizak Naval DY, Istanbul	28 July 1983	14 Aug 1985

Displacement, tons: 1,440 full load
Dimensions, feet (metres): 211.9 × 30.8 × 11.5 *(64.6 × 9.4 × 3.5)*
Main machinery: 1 diesel; 1,400 hp(m) *(1.03 MW)*; 1 shaft
Speed, knots: 13
Complement: 57
Cargo capacity: 800 tons
Guns: 1 Bofors 40 mm/60. 2 Oerlikon 20 mm.
Radars: Navigation: Racal Decca 1226; I-band.

Comment: Laid down 20 July 1983.

UPDATED

TAŞKIZAK ('Doğan' class in background)   *5/1990*, A Sheldon Duplaix / 0080893*

2 SUPPORT TANKERS (AOL)

Name	No	Builders	Commissioned
ALBAY HAKKI BURAK	A 571	RMK Tusla, Istanbul	21 Nov 1999
YUZBASI IHSAN TOLUNAY	A 572	RMK Tusla, Istanbul	8 June 2000

Displacement, tons: 3,300 full load
Dimensions, feet (metres): 267.1 × 40 × 16.4 *(81.4 × 12.2 × 5)*
Main machinery: 2 Caterpillar 3606TA diesels; 5,522 hp(m) *(4.06 MW)*; 2 shafts
Speed, knots: 15
Complement: 50
Cargo capacity: 2,355 m³ dieso

Comment: Ordered in 1998.

NEW ENTRY

ALBAY HAKKI BURAK   11/1999*, Selim San / 0080894

1 SUPPORT TANKER (AOL)

Name	No	Builders	Commissioned
BINBAŞI SADETTIN GÜRCAN	A 573	Taşkizak Naval DY, Istanbul	4 Sep 1970

Displacement, tons: 1,505 standard; 4,460 full load
Dimensions, feet (metres): 294.2 × 38.7 × 17.7 *(89.7 × 11.8 × 5.4)*
Main machinery: Diesel-electric; 4 GM 16-567A diesels; 5,600 hp *(4.12 MW)*; 4 generators; 2 motors; 4,400 hp *(3.28 MW)*; 2 shafts
Speed, knots: 16
Complement: 63
Guns: 2 Oerlikon 20 mm.
Radars: Navigation: E/F-band.

Comment: Main armament removed. Can be used for replenishment at sea.

UPDATED

BINBAŞI SADETTIN GÜRCAN   6/1995*, Turkish Navy / 0080895

1 SUPPORT TANKER (AOT)

Name	No	Builders	Commissioned
INEBOLU (ex-*Bodensee* A 1406, ex-*Unkas*)	A 575	Lindenau, Kiel	26 Mar 1959

Displacement, tons: 1,840 full load
Measurement, tons: 1,238 dwt
Dimensions, feet (metres): 219.8 × 32.1 × 14.1 *(67 × 9.8 × 4.3)*
Main machinery: 1 MaK diesel; 1,050 hp(m) *(772 kW)*; 1 shaft
Speed, knots: 12. **Range, miles:** 6,200 at 12 kt
Complement: 26
Cargo capacity: 1,230 tons
Guns: 2 Oerlikon 20 mm (on bridge).
Radars: Navigation: Kelvin Hughes 14/9; I-band.

Comment: Launched 19 November 1955. Of 'Bodensee' class. Transferred 25 August 1977 at Wilhelmshavn, under West German military aid programme. Has replenishment at sea capability.

UPDATED

INEBOLU   6/1995*, Turkish Navy / 0080896

3 WATER TANKERS (AWT)

SÖĞÜT (ex-*FW 2*) A 598 (ex-Y 1217)   KAVAK (ex-*FW 4*) A 600   ÇINAR (ex-*FW 1*) A 581

Displacement, tons: 626 full load
Dimensions, feet (metres): 144.4 × 25.6 × 8.2 *(44.1 × 7.8 × 2.5)*
Main machinery: 1 MWM diesel; 230 hp(m) *(169 kW)*; 1 shaft
Speed, knots: 9.5. **Range, miles:** 2,150 at 9 kt
Complement: 12
Cargo capacity: 340 tons

Comment: *Söğüt* acquired from West Germany and commissioned 12 March 1976. Pennant number changed in 1991. *Kavak* transferred from Germany 12 April 1991 and *Çinar* in early 1996.

UPDATED

KAVAK   4/1997*, C D Yaylali / 0019332

2 WATER TANKERS (AWT)

Name	No	Builders	Commissioned
VAN	A 597 (ex-Y 1208)	Camialti Shipyard	12 Aug 1968
ULUBAT	A 596 (ex-Y 1209)	Camialti Shipyard	3 July 1969

Displacement, tons: 1,250 full load
Dimensions, feet (metres): 174.2 × 29.5 × 9.8 *(53.1 × 9 × 3)*
Main machinery: 1 diesel; 650 hp(m) *(478 kW)*; 1 shaft
Speed, knots: 14
Complement: 39 (3 officers)
Cargo capacity: 700 tons
Guns: 1 Oerlikon 20 mm.
Radars: Racal Decca 707; I-band.

Comment: Pennant numbers changed in 1991.

VERIFIED

VAN   7/1995, Selim San

6 WATER TANKERS (YO)

PINAR 1-6 Y 111-Y 116 (ex-Y 1211-Y 1216)

Displacement, tons: 300 full load
Dimensions, feet (metres): 110.2 × 27.9 × 5.9 *(33.6 × 8.5 × 1.8)*
Main machinery: 1 GM diesel; 225 hp *(168 kW)*; 1 shaft
Speed, knots: 11
Complement: 12
Cargo capacity: 150 tons

Comment: Built by Taşkizak Naval Yard. Details given for last four, sisters to harbour tankers H 500-502. First pair differ from these particulars and are individually different. *Pinar 1* (launched 1938) of 490 tons displacement with one 240 hp *(179 kW)* diesel, and *Pinar 2* built in 1958 of 1,300 tons full load, 167.3 × 27.9 ft *(51 × 8.5 m)*.

UPDATED

PINAR 1   6/1994*, Turkish Navy / 0080899

PINAR 5   10/1996*, Selim San / 0080900

3 HARBOUR TANKERS (YO)

H 500-H 502 Y 140-Y 142 (ex-Y 1231-1233)

Displacement, tons: 300 full load
Dimensions, feet (metres): 110.2 × 27.9 × 5.9 *(33.6 × 8.5 × 1.8)*
Main machinery: 1 GM diesel; 225 hp(m) *(165 kW)*; 1 shaft
Speed, knots: 11
Complement: 12
Cargo capacity: 150 tons

Comment: Sisters of water tankers of Pinar series. Built at Taşkizak in early 1970s.

UPDATED

H 500   *6/1994*, Turkish Navy /* 0080901

1 HARBOUR TANKER (YO)

GÖLCÜK Y 50

Displacement, tons: 310 full load
Dimensions, feet (metres): 108.8 × 19.2 × 9.2 *(33.2 × 5.8 × 2.8)*
Main machinery: 1 diesel; 550 hp(m) *(404 kW)*; 1 shaft
Speed, knots: 12
Complement: 12

UPDATED

GÖLCÜK   *7/1992*, Selçuk Emre /* 0080898

1 DIVER CLASS (SALVAGE SHIP) (ARS)

Name	No	Builders	Launched	Commissioned
IŞIN (ex-*Safeguard* ARS 25)	A 589	Basalt Rock, Napa	20 Nov 1943	31 Oct 1944

Displacement, tons: 1,530 standard; 1,970 full load
Dimensions, feet (metres): 213.5 × 41 × 13 *(65.1 × 12.5 × 4)*
Main machinery: Diesel-electric; 4 Cooper-Bessemer GSB-8 diesels; 3,420 hp *(2.55 MW)*; 4 generators; 2 motors; 2 shafts
Speed, knots: 14.8
Complement: 110
Guns: 2 Oerlikon 20 mm.

Comment: Transferred from USA 28 September 1979 and purchased outright 6 August 1987.

UPDATED

IŞIN   *10/1997*, C D Yaylali /* 0019333

1 CHANTICLEER CLASS (SUBMARINE RESCUE SHIP) (ASR)

Name	No	Builders	Launched	Commissioned
AKIN (ex-*Greenlet* ASR 10)	A 585	Moore SB & DD Co	12 July 1942	29 May 1943

Displacement, tons: 1,653 standard; 2,321 full load
Dimensions, feet (metres): 251.5 × 44 × 16 *(76.7 × 13.4 × 4.9)*
Main machinery: Diesel-electric; 4 Alco 539 diesels; 3,532 hp *(2.63 MW)*; 4 generators; 1 motor; 1 shaft
Speed, knots: 15
Complement: 111 (9 officers)
Guns: 1 Bofors 40 mm/60. 4 Oerlikon 20 mm (2 twin).
Radars: Navigation: Racal Decca 1226; I-band.

Comment: Transferred from USA, recommissioned 23 December 1970 and purchased 15 February 1973. Carries a Diving Bell.

UPDATED

AKIN   *4/1996*, van Ginderen Collection /* 0080902

1 BLUEBIRD CLASS (SUBMARINE RESCUE SHIP) (ASR)

Name	No	Builders	Commissioned
KURTARAN (ex-*Bluebird* ASR 19, ex-*Yurak* AT 165)	A 584	Charleston Shipyard	28 May 1946

Displacement, tons: 1,294 standard; 1,675 full load
Dimensions, feet (metres): 205 × 38.5 × 11 *(62.5 × 12.2 × 3.5)*
Main machinery: Diesel-electric; 4 GM 12-278A diesels; 4,400 hp *(3.28 MW)*; 4 generators; 1 motor; 3,000 hp *(2.24 MW)*; 1 shaft
Speed, knots: 16. **Range, miles:** 6,000 at 15 kt
Complement: 100
Guns: 1 USN 3 in *(76 mm)*/50. 2 Oerlikon 20 mm.
Radars: Navigation: I-band.

Comment: Former salvage tug adapted as a submarine rescue vessel in 1947. Transferred from the US Navy and recommissioned 25 August 1950. Carries a Diving Bell.

UPDATED

KURTARAN   *10/1994*, van Ginderen Collection /* 0080903

2 TRANSPORTS (AKS/AWT)

Name	No	Builders	Completed
KARADENIZ EREĞLISI	A 592 (ex-Y 1157)	Erdem	30 Aug 1982
ECEABAT	A 593 (ex-Y 1165)	Taşkazik	4 Nov 1968

Displacement, tons: 820 full load
Dimensions, feet (metres): 166.3 × 26.2 × 9.2 *(50.7 × 8 × 2.8)*
Main machinery: 1 diesel; 1,440 hp *(1.06 MW)*; 1 shaft
Speed, knots: 10
Complement: 23 (3 officers)
Cargo capacity: 300 tons
Guns: 1 Oerlikon 20 mm.

Comment: Funnel-aft coaster type. Pennant numbers changed in 1991. *Karadeniz Ereğlisi* is a stores ship, *Eceabat* is a water carrier.

UPDATED

ECEABAT   *11/1999*, Selim San /* 0084417

2 BARRACK SHIPS (APB)

NAŞIT ÖNGEREN (ex-US *APL 47*) Y 38 (ex-Y 1204)
BINBAŞI NETIN SÜLÜS (ex-US *APL 53*) Y 39 (ex-Y 1205)

Comment: Ex-US barrack ships transferred on lease: Y 1204 in October 1972 and Y 1205 on
6 December 1974. Y 1204 based at Ereğli and Y 1205 at Gölcük. Purchased outright June 1987.
Pennant numbers changed in 1991.   ***VERIFIED***

31 SMALL TRANSPORTS (YFB/YE)

SALOPA 1-14 Y 21-24 (ex-Y 1031-1044)
LAYTER 1-4 and **6-7** Y 101-104 and Y 106-107
PONTON 1-7 (ex-Y 1061-1067)
ARSLAN Y 75 (ex-Y 1112)
YAKIT Y 139
CEPHANE 2 Y 97 (ex-Y 1195)

Comment: Of varying size and appearance. Pennant numbers changed in 1991.   ***UPDATED***

CEPHANE 2   *6/1994*, Turkish Navy* / 0080905

2 BOOM DEFENCE VESSELS (ABU)

Name	No	Builders	Commissioned
AG 6 (ex-*AN 93*,	P 306	Bethlehem Steel	10 Nov 1952
ex-Netherlands *Cerberus* A 895)		Corporation, Staten Island, NY	

Displacement, tons: 780 standard; 855 full load
Dimensions, feet (metres): 165 × 33 × 10 *(50.3 × 10.1 × 3)*
Main machinery: Diesel-electric; 2 GM 8-268A diesels; 880 hp *(656 kW)*; 2 generators; 1 motor;
1 shaft
Speed, knots: 12.8. **Range, miles:** 5,200 at 12 kt
Complement: 32 (3 officers)
Guns: 1 USN 3 in *(76 mm)*/50. 4 Oerlikon 20 mm.
Radars: Navigation: Racal Decca 1226; I-band.

Comment: Netlayer. Transferred from USA to Netherlands in December 1952. Used first as a
boom defence vessel and latterly as salvage and diving tender since 1961 but retained her
netlaying capacity. Handed back to US Navy on 17 September 1970 but immediately turned over
to the Turkish Navy under grant aid.   ***UPDATED***

AG 6   *7/1995*, Frank Behling* / 0080906

Name	No	Builders	Commissioned
AG 5 (ex-*AN 104*)	P 305	Kröger, Rendsburg	25 Feb 1962

Displacement, tons: 960 full load
Dimensions, feet (metres): 173.8 × 35 × 13.5 *(53 × 10.7 × 4.1)*
Main machinery: Diesel-electric; 1 MAN G7V40/60 diesel generator; 1 motor; 1,470 hp(m)
(1.08 MW); 1 shaft
Speed, knots: 12. **Range, miles:** 6,500 at 11 kt
Complement: 32 (3 officers)
Guns: 1 Bofors 40 mm/60. 3 Oerlikon 20 mm.
Radars: Navigation: Racal Decca 1226; I-band.

Comment: Netlayer P 305 built in US offshore programme for Turkey.   ***UPDATED***

AG 5   *6/1995*, Turkish Navy* / 0080907

3 TORPEDO RETRIEVERS (TRV)

TORPITO TENDERI Y 95 (ex-Y 1051)   **TAKIP** Y 98 (ex-Y 1052)   **Y 44**

Comment: Of different types.   ***VERIFIED***

Y 44   *9/1998, C D Yaylali* / 0050297

1 FLAG OFFICERS' YACHT (YAC)

GÜL Y 76 (ex-Y 1103)

Comment: Pennant number not displayed. There is also an Admiral's Barge named *Kaplan*.
VERIFIED

GÜL   *7/1995, van Ginderen Collection*

11 FLOATING DOCKS/CRANES

Name	Lift	Name	Lift
HAVUZ 1 Y 121 (ex-Y 1081)	16,000 tons	**HAVUZ 5** Y 125 (ex-Y 1085)	400 tons
HAVUZ 2 Y 122 (ex-Y 1082)	12,000 tons	**HAVUZ 6** Y 126 (ex-Y 1086)	3,000 tons
HAVUZ 3 Y 123 (ex-Y 1083)	2,500 tons	**HAVUZ 8-10** Y 128-130	700 tons
(ex-US AFDL)		(ex-Y 1088-1090)	
HAVUZ 4 Y 124 (ex-Y 1084)	4,500 tons	**LEVENT** Y 59 (ex-Y 1022)	—
ALGARNA 3 Y 60	—		
(ex-Y 1021)			

Comment: *Algarna* and *Levent* are ex-US floating cranes.
VERIFIED

TUGS

1 CHEROKEE CLASS (ATF)

GAZAL (ex-*Sioux* ATF 75) A 587

Displacement, tons: 1,235 standard; 1,675 full load
Dimensions, feet (metres): 205 × 38.5 × 17 *(62.5 × 11.7 × 5.2)*
Main machinery: Diesel-electric; 4 GM 12-278 diesels; 4,400 hp *(3.28 MW)*; 4 generators;
1 motor; 3,000 hp *(2.24 MW)*; 1 shaft
Speed, knots: 16. **Range, miles:** 15,000 at 8 kt
Complement: 85
Guns: 1 USN 3 in *(76 mm)*/50. 2 Oerlikon 20 mm.
Radars: Navigation: Racal Decca; I-band.

Comment: Originally completed on 6 December 1942. Transferred from USA and commissioned
9 March 1973. Purchased 15 August 1973. Can be used for salvage. 3 in gun removed in 1987
but has since been restored.
UPDATED

GAZAL   *6/1995*, Turkish Navy* / 0080908

1 TENACE CLASS (ATA)

Name	No	Builders	Commissioned
DEĞIRMENDERE (ex-*Centaure*)	A 576 (ex-A 674)	Chantiers de la Rochelle	14 May 1974

Displacement, tons: 1,454 full load
Dimensions, feet (metres): 167.3 × 37.8 × 18.6 *(51 × 11.5 × 5.7)*
Main machinery: 2 SACM AGO 240 V12 diesels; 4,600 hp(m) *(3.38 MW)*; 1 shaft; Kort nozzle
Speed, knots: 13. **Range, miles:** 9,500 at 13 kt
Complement: 37 (3 officers)
Radars: Navigation: Racal Decca RM 1226 and Racal Decca 060; I-band.

Comment: Transferred from French Navy 16 March 1999. Recommissioned after refit 22 July 1999. Bollard pull 60 tons.

UPDATED

DEĞIRMENDERE   *4/1999*, Diego Quevedo /* 0080909

16 COASTAL/HARBOUR TUGS (YTB/YTM/YTL)

Name	No	Displacement, tons/ Speed, knots	Commissioned
AKDAS	A 586	1660/14	1978
SÖNDÜREN 3	A 1543	—	1999
SÖNDÜREN 2	A 1542	—	1998
SÖNDÜREN 1	Y 51 (ex-Y 1117)	128/12	1954
KUVVET	Y 53 (ex-Y 1122)	390/10	1962
DOĞANARSLAN	Y 52 (ex-Y 1123)	500/12	1985
ATIL	Y 55 (ex-Y 1132)	300/10	1962
ERSEN BAYRAK	Y 64 (ex-Y 1134)	30/9	1946
KUDRET	Y 54 (ex-Y 1229)	128/12	1957
KEPEZ	Y 57	—	1992
AKSAZ (ex-*Koos*)	A 583 (ex-Y 1651, ex-A 08)	320/11	1962
ÖNDER	Y 160	230/12	1998
ÖNCÜ	Y 161	230/12	1998
ÖZGEN	Y 162	230/12	1999
ÖDEV	Y 163	230/12	1999
ÖZGÜR	Y 164	230/12	2000

Comment: In addition there are 47 Katir pusher berthing tugs. *Koos* was transferred from Germany on 7 October 1996.

UPDATED

DOĞANARSLAN   *7/1996*, Frank Behling /* 0080911

SÖNDÜREN 3   *7/1999*, Selçuk Emre /* 0080912

1 OCEAN TUG (ATR)

DARICA A 578 (ex-Y 1125)

Displacement, tons: 750 full load
Dimensions, feet (metres): 134.2 × 32.2 × 12.8 *(40.9 × 9.8 × 3.9)*
Main machinery: 2 ABC diesels; 4,000 hp *(2.94 MW)*; 2 shafts
Speed, knots: 14. **Range, miles:** 2,500 at 14 kt

Comment: Built at Taşkizak Naval Yard and commissioned 13 June 1991. Equipped for firefighting and as a torpedo tender. Pennant number changed in 1991.

UPDATED

DARICA   *11/1994*, van Ginderen Collection /* 0080910

COAST GUARD (SAHIL GÜVENLIK)

Notes: (1) Three patrol craft are based in North Cyprus. These are *Raif Denktas,* and *SG 102* and *103.*
(2) Five AB 412EP helicopters ordered 15 April 1999 for delivery by May 2001.
(3) Four 'Vigilante' class Boston Whalers were acquired by the Police in September 1999.

8 + 4 LARGE PATROL CRAFT

SG 80-SG 91

Displacement, tons: 195 full load
Dimensions, feet (metres): 133.5 × 23.3 × 7.2 *(40.7 × 7.1 × 2.2)*
Main machinery: 2 diesels; 5,700 hp(m) *(4.19 MW)*; 2 shafts
Speed, knots: 27
Complement: 25
Guns: 1 Breda 40 mm/70. 2—12.7 mm MGs.
Radars: Surface search: Racal Decca; I-band.

Comment: *SG 80* and *81* launched 3 June 1994 at Taşkizak Shipyard. First three completed in 1996, second three in 1997, and the next two in 1999. Two more are planned for late 2000 and the last pair in 2001.

UPDATED

SG 80   *7/1998, C D Yaylali /* 0050299

14 LARGE PATROL CRAFT

SG 21-34

Displacement, tons: 180 full load
Dimensions, feet (metres): 132 × 21 × 5.5 *(40.2 × 6.4 × 1.7)*
131.2 × 21.3 × 4.9 *(40 × 6.5 × 1.5)* (SG 30-34)
Main machinery: 2 SACM AGO 195 V16 CSHR diesels; 4,800 hp(m) *(3.53 MW)* sustained
2 cruise diesels; 300 hp(m) *(220 kW)*; 2 shafts
Speed, knots: 22
Complement: 25
Guns: 1 or 2 Bofors 40 mm/60. 2—12.7 mm MGs.
Radars: Surface search: Racal Decca 1226; I-band.

Comment: *SG 21* and *22* built by Gölcük Naval Yard, remainder by Taşkizak Naval Yard. *SG 34* commissioned in 1977, remainder 1968-71. *SG 30-34* have minor modifications—knuckle at bow, radar stirrup on bridge and MG on superstructure sponsons. These are similar craft to the 'Turk' class listed under *Patrol Forces* for the Navy.

UPDATED

SG 34   *5/1998* /* 0080913

10 SAR 33 TYPE (LARGE PATROL CRAFT)

SG 61-70

Displacement, tons: 180 full load
Dimensions, feet (metres): 113.5 × 28.3 × 9.7 *(34.6 × 8.6 × 3)*
Main machinery: 3 SACM AGO 195 V16 CSHR diesels; 7,200 hp(m) *(5.29 MW)* sustained; 3 shafts; cp props
Speed, knots: 33. **Range, miles:** 450 at 24 kt; 550 at 18 kt
Complement: 24
Guns: 1 Bofors 40 mm/60. 2—12.7 mm MGs.
Radars: Surface search: Racal Decca; I-band.

Comment: Prototype Serter design ordered from Abeking & Rasmussen, Lemwerder in May 1976. The remainder were built at Taşkizak Naval Yard, Istanbul between 1979 and 1981. Fourteen of this class were to have been transferred to Libya but the order was cancelled. Two delivered to Saudi Arabia. The engines have been governed back and the top speed correspondingly reduced from the original 12,000 hp and 40 kt.

UPDATED

SG 65   *11/1998*, Michael Nitz /* 0080914

4 SAR 35 TYPE (LARGE PATROL CRAFT)

SG 71-74

Displacement, tons: 210 full load
Dimensions, feet (metres): 120 × 28.3 × 6.2 *(36.6 × 8.6 × 1.9)*
Main machinery: 3 SACM AGO 195 V16 CSHR diesels; 7,200 hp(m) *(5.29 MW)* sustained; 3 shafts; cp props
Speed, knots: 33. **Range, miles:** 450 at 24 kt; 550 at 18 kt
Complement: 24
Guns: 1 Bofors 40 mm/70. 2—12.7 mm MGs.
Radars: Surface search: Racal Decca 1226; I-band.

Comment: A slightly enlarged version of the Serter designed SAR 33 Type built by Taşkizak Shipyard between 1985 and 1987. Restricted to less than designed speed.

UPDATED

SG 74   *6/1995*, Turkish Coast Guard /* 0080915

0 + 10 SEAGUARD CLASS (LARGE PATROL CRAFT)

Displacement, tons: 90 full load
Dimensions, feet (metres): 97.1 × 20.7 × 4.9 *(29.6 × 6.3 × 1.5)*
Main machinery: 2 MTU 16V 400 M90 diesels; 7,398 hp(m) *(5.44 MW)*; 2 MJP 750 waterjets
Speed, knots: 45. **Range, miles:** 750 at 20 kt
Complement: 13 plus 7 spare
Guns: 1 Bofors 40 mm/70. 1 Oerlikon 20 mm.
Radars: Surface search: I-band.

Comment: Ordered from Onuk Taşit Sanayii/Yonea AS/Yurtsan AS in October 1998. First to be delivered in late 2000. Onuk MRTP 29 design.

UPDATED

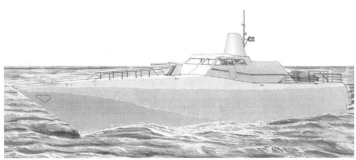

SEAGUARD (artist's impression)   *1998, Onuk /* 0050301

8 KW 15 CLASS (LARGE PATROL CRAFT)

SG 12-16, 18-20

Displacement, tons: 70 full load
Dimensions, feet (metres): 94.8 × 15.4 × 4.6 *(28.9 × 4.7 × 1.4)*
Main machinery: 2 MTU diesels; 2,700 hp(m) *(1.98 MW)*; 2 shafts
Speed, knots: 20. **Range, miles:** 550 at 16 kt
Complement: 16
Guns: 1 Bofors 40 mm/60. 2 Oerlikon 20 mm.
Radars: Surface search: Racal Decca; I-band.

Comment: Built by Schweers, Bardenfleth. Commissioned 1961-62.

VERIFIED

SG 12   *8/1998, A Sharma /* 0050302

12 KAAN CLASS (FAST INTERVENTION CRAFT)

TCSG 1-TCSG 12

Displacement, tons: 19 full load
Dimensions, feet (metres): 49.4 × 13.3 × 3.3 *(15.1 × 4 × 1)*
Main machinery: 2 MTU 12V 183 TE93 diesels; 2,300 hp(m) *(1.69 MW)*; 2 Arneson ASD 12 B1L surface drives
Speed, knots: 54. **Range, miles:** 300 at 40 kt
Complement: 4
Guns: 2—12.7 mm MGs.
Radars: Surface search: Raytheon; I-band.

Comment: Contract for first six with Yonca Technical Investment signed in May 1997, second order for six more in February 1999. All built at Tuzla-Istanbul shipyard. Three delivered in 1998, seven in 1999 and the last pair in early 2000. Onuk MRTP 15 design. Fibreglass hulls.

UPDATED

TCSG 4   *8/1998, Turkish Coast Guard /* 0050303

12 COASTAL PATROL CRAFT

SG 50-59   SG 102-103

Displacement, tons: 29 full load
Dimensions, feet (metres): 47.9 × 13.7 × 3.6 *(14.6 × 4.2 × 1.1)*
Main machinery: 2 diesels; 700 hp(m) *(514 kW)*; 2 shafts
Speed, knots: 15
Complement: 7
Guns: 1—12.7 mm MG or 1 Breda-Oerlikon 25 mm *(SG 102-103)*.
Radars: Surface search: Raytheon; I-band.

Comment: SG 102 and 103 were built for North Cyprus and have been based there since August 1990 and July 1991 respectively. Both these craft were given a heavier gun in 1992. Second batch of three completed by Taşkizak in October 1992, three more in June 1993, four more in December 1993.

VERIFIED

SG 56   *10/1998, Selim San /* 0050304

1 INSHORE PATROL CRAFT

RAIF DENKTAS 74

Displacement, tons: 10 full load
Dimensions, feet (metres): 38 × 11.5 × 2.4 *(11.6 × 3.5 × 0.7)*
Main machinery: 2 Volvo Aquamatic AQ200F petrol engines; 400 hp(m) *(294 kW)*; 2 shafts
Speed, knots: 28. **Range, miles:** 250 at 25 kt
Complement: 6
Guns: 1—12.7 mm MG.
Radars: Surface search: Raytheon; I-band.

Comment: Built by Protekson, Istanbul. Transferred to North Cyprus 23 September 1988. Can be equipped with a rocket launcher.

VERIFIED

RAIF DENKTAS (North Cyprus)   *9/1988, Selçuk Emre*

2 HARBOUR PATROL CRAFT

SG 1-2

Displacement, tons: 35 *(SG 1)*; 15 *(SG 2)* full load
Dimensions, feet (metres): 55.8 × 16.4 × 3.3 *(17 × 5 × 1) (SG 1)*
    47.5 × 14.4 × 2.3 *(14.5 × 4.4 × 0.7) (SG 2)*
Main machinery: 2 diesels; 1,050 hp(m) *(771 kW) (SG 1)*
    2 diesels; 700 hp(m) *(515 kW) (SG 2)*
Speed, knots: 20 *(SG 1)*; 18 *(SG 2)*
Complement: 7
Radars: Surface search: I-band.

Comment: High-speed patrol boats for anti-smuggling duties. Probably confiscated drug smuggling craft.

UPDATED

SG 1   *6/1995*, *Turkish Coast Guard* / 0080916

TUVALU

General	Bases	Mercantile Marine
A Pacific Island midway between Fiji and Kiribati.	Funafuti	*Lloyd's Register of Shipping:* 10 vessels of 43,109 tons gross

PATROL FORCES

1 PACIFIC FORUM TYPE (PC)

Name	No	Builders	Commissioned
TE MATAILI	—	Transfield Shipbuilding, WA	8 Oct 1994

Displacement, tons: 165 full load
Dimensions, feet (metres): 103.3 × 26.6 × 6.9 *(31.5 × 8.1 × 2.1)*
Main machinery: 2 Caterpillar 3516TA diesels; 4,400 hp *(3.28 MW)* sustained; 2 shafts
Speed, knots: 18. **Range, miles:** 2,500 at 12 kt
Complement: 18 (3 officers)
Guns: Can carry 1—12.7 mm MG but is unarmed.
Radars: Navigation: Furuno 1011; I-band.

Comment: This is the 18th of the class to be built by the Australian Government for EEZ patrols in the Pacific islands. The programme originally terminated at 15 but was re-opened on 19 February 1993 to include construction of five more craft for Fiji, Kiribati and Tuvalu. Training and support assistance is given by the Australian Navy.

VERIFIED

PACIFIC FORUM (Samoan colours)   *1991, John Mortimer*

UGANDA

Headquarters Appointments	Personnel	Bases	DELETIONS	
Commander, Army Marine Unit: Captain Saleh Agondoa	2000: 150	HQ: Fort Bell Entebbe, Sese Isles, Gaba, Jinja, Majinji, Bukakata (all on Lake Victoria).	1997 1998	2 Kimjins 3 Yugoslav AL8K Type

ARMY

14 GRP PATROL CRAFT (PBR)

Comment: These are fast motor boats used on the minor lakes and waterways. Some are armed with 7.62 mm MGs. GRP hulls.   *VERIFIED*

3 YUGOSLAV AL8K TYPE (PBR)

801-806 series

Displacement, tons: 6.3 full load
Dimensions, feet (metres): 36.6 × 12.3 × 1.5 *(11.2 × 3.7 × 0.5)*
Main machinery: 2 diesels; 300 hp(m) *(220 kW)*; 2 shafts
Speed, knots: 25
Complement: 3
Guns: 1—12.7 mm MG.
Radars: Surface search: Furuno; I-band.

Comment: Six acquired in September 1988. Aluminium hulls. Designed for patrol work on rivers and lakes. At least three others are out of the water and derelict.   *UPDATED*

LAKE PATROL CRAFT 801   *1989* / 0080917

UKRAINE

Headquarters Appointments

Commander of the Navy:
  Vice Admiral Mikhallo Yezhel
Deputy Commanders of the Navy:
  Vice Admiral Victor Fomin
  Rear Admiral Vyzcheslav Sychov

Senior Officers

Commander Southern Region:
  Rear Admiral Borys Rekuts
Commander Western Region:
  Rear Admiral D Ukrainetz
Commander Border Guard, Navy:
  Rear Admiral I V Alferyev

Bases

Sevastopol (HQ), Donuzlav (Southern Region), Odessa (Western Region), Nikolayev, Feodosiya, Izmail, Balaklava, Kerch

Personnel

2000: 12,500 navy

General

On 3 August 1992 a joint agreement signed by Russia and Ukraine, declared that all Black Sea Fleet units would be jointly operated by the two states until 1995, by which time the division of the Fleet should have been agreed. Stage One of the division of the Fleet was agreed at Sochi in November 1995 and has been implemented. The Stage Two agreement reached at Teesovets in April 1996 was implemented in May 1997. Many of the ships transferred were beyond economical repair.

Border Guard

The Maritime Border Guard is an independent subdivision of the State Committee for Border Guards, and is not part of the Navy. It has four cutter brigades to patrol the 827 mile coastline and two river brigades, which include a gunship squadron, a minesweeping squadron, an auxiliary ship group and a training division.

Mercantile Marine

Lloyd's Register of Shipping:
  936 vessels of 1,775,161 tons gross

DELETIONS

Frigates

1999   *Sevastopol*

Patrol forces

1999   *Konotop* (to Georgia), *Tsurupinsk*

Amphibious forces

1999   *Kirovograd*

Auxiliaries

1999   *Chernivsky, Ivano Frankivsk* (both civilian)

PENNANT LIST

Submarines			Auxiliaries		Survey Ships	
U 01	Zaporizya	U 156 Kremenchuk	U 510	Slavutich	U 851	Novy Bug
		U 170 Skadovsk	U 533	Kolomiya	U 852	Sostka
		U 207 Uzhgorod	U 540	Chernivici	U 853	Arciz
Frigates		U 208 Khmelnitsky	U 541	Suvar	U 861	Svitlovodsk
			U 542	Akar	U 891	Monastirisze
U 130	Hetman Sagaidachny	**Mine Warfare Forces**	U 701	Krab	U 947	Krasnoperekovsk
U 133	Mikolaiv		U 705	Kremenets		
U 134	Dnipropetrovsk	U 310 Zhovti Vody	U 706	Izyaslav	**Survey Ships**	
U 205	Chernigiv	U 311 Cherkasy	U 707	Brodi		
U 206	Vinnitsa	U 330 Mezitopol	U 722	Borshev	U 511	Simferopol
U 207	Lutsk	U 331 Mariupol	U 728	Evpatoriya	—	Pereyaslov
U 209	Sumy	U 360 Genichesk	U 753	Berdjansk	U 603	Alchevsk
U 210	Kherson		U 756	Sudak	U 635	Skvyra
			U 757	Makivka	U 754	Dzhankoi
Patrol Forces		**Amphibious Forces**	U 758	Kerch	U 755	Yalta
			U 759	Krasnodon	U 812	Severodonetsk
U 152	Uman	U 400 Rivne	U 800	Malin		
U 153	Priluki	U 402 Konstantin Olshansky	U 811	Balta		
U 154	Kahovka	U 420 Donetsk	U 812	Severodonetsk		
U 155	Nicopol	U 422 Kramatorsk	U 830	Korets		
		U 423 Gorlivka	U 831	Kovel		
		U 424 Artimivsk				

SUBMARINES

Note: Four submarines were transferred from the Black Sea Fleet, three Foxtrot and one Tango. Only one of these is confirmed as operational.

1 FOXTROT CLASS (TYPE 641) SS

ZAPORIZYA (ex-B 435) U 01

Displacement, tons: 1,952 surfaced; 2,475 dived
Dimensions, feet (metres): 299.5 × 24.6 × 19.7
  (91.3 × 7.5 × 6)
Main machinery: Diesel-electric; 3 Type 37-D diesels; 6,000 hp
  (m) *(4.4 MW)*; 3 motors (1 × 2,700 and 2 × 1,350); 5,400 hp
  (m) *(3.97 MW)*; 3 shafts; 1 auxiliary motor; 140 hp(m)
  (103 kW)
Speed, knots: 16 surfaced; 15 dived; 9 snorting

Range, miles: 20,000 at 8 kt surfaced; 380 at 2 kt dived
Complement: 75

Torpedoes: 10—21 in *(533 mm)* (6 bow, 4 stern) tubes.
  Combination of 22—53 cm torpedoes.
Mines: 44 in lieu of torpedoes.
Countermeasures: ESM: Stop Light; radar warning.
Radars: Surface search: Snoop Tray; I-band.

Sonars: Pike Jaw; hull-mounted; passive/active search and
  attack; high frequency.

Programmes: Transferred from Russia with two others of the
  class.
Operational: Based at Balaklava, this is the only submarine that
  has any prospect of becoming operational. In refit and needs a
  new main battery.

UPDATED

ZAPORIZYA

9/1998, Hartmut Ehlers / 0050305

FRIGATES

Note: Reports that Ukraine is to commission the fourth 'Slava' class missile cruiser have yet to be confirmed. Details on this ship are in the Russian section.

1 KRIVAK III (NEREY) CLASS (TYPE 1135.1) (FFH)

Name	No	Builders	Laid down	Launched	Commissioned
HETMAN SAGAIDACHNY	U 130 (ex-201)	Kamysh-Burun, Kerch	5 Oct 1990	29 Mar 1992	5 July 1993

Displacement, tons: 3,100 standard; 3,650 full load
Dimensions, feet (metres): 405.2 × 46.9 × 16.4
 (123.5 × 14.3 × 5)
Main machinery: COGAG; 2 gas turbines; 55,500 hp(m)
 (40.8 MW); 2 gas turbines, 13,600 hp(m) *(10 MW)*; 2 shafts
Speed, knots: 32
Range, miles: 4,600 at 20 kt; 1,600 at 30 kt
Complement: 180 (18 officers)

Missiles: SAM: 1 SA-N-4 Gecko twin launcher ❶; semi-active
 radar homing to 15 km *(8.1 n miles)* at 2.5 Mach; warhead
 50 kg; altitude 9.1-3,048 m *(30-10,000 ft)*; 20 missiles. The
 launcher retracts into the mounting for stowage and
 protection, rising to fire and retracting to reload. The two
 mountings are forward of the bridge and abaft the funnel.
Guns: 1—3.9 in *(100 mm)*/59 ❷; 60 rds/min to 15 km *(8.1 n
 miles)*; weight of shell 16 kg.
 2—30 mm/65 ❸; 6 barrels per mounting; 3,000 rds/min
 combined to 2 km.
Torpedoes: 8—21 in *(533 mm)* (2 quad) tubes ❹. Combination of
 Russian 53 cm torpedoes.
A/S mortars: 2 RBU 6000 12-tubed trainable ❺; range 6,000 m;
 warhead 31 kg.
Countermeasures: Decoys: 4 PK 16 chaff launchers. Towed
 torpedo decoy.
 ESM: 2 Bell Shroud; intercept.
 ECM: 2 Bell Squat; jammers.
Radars: Air search: Top Plate ❻; 3D; D/E-band.
 Surface search: Spin Trough ❼; I-band. Peel Cone ❽; I-band.
 Fire control: Pop Group ❾; F/H/I-band (for SA-N-4). Kite Screech
 ❿; H/I/K-band. Bass Tilt (Krivak III) ⓫; H/I-band.
 Navigation: Kivach; I-band.
 IFF: Salt Pot (Krivak III).
Sonars: Bull Nose (MGK 335MS); hull-mounted; active search
 and attack; medium frequency.

Helicopters: 1 Ka-25 Hormone or Ka-27 Helix ⓬.

Programmes: This is the last of the 'Krivak IIIs' originally
 designed for the USSR Border Guard. The seven others are
 based in the Russian Pacific Fleet. A ninth of class was not
 completed.
Operational: *Sagaidachny* has so far not been sighted with a
 helicopter embarked. Deployed to the Mediterranean in 1994
 and late 1995, to the Indian Ocean in early 1995 and to the
 USA in late 1996. Other Krivak transfers are being used for
 spares.

VERIFIED

HETMAN SAGAIDACHNY   *(Scale 1 : 1,200), Ian Sturton*

HETMAN SAGAIDACHNY   *9/1998, Hartmut Ehlers /* 0050308

HETMAN SAGAIDACHNY
3/1995, H M Steele / 0016644

2 KRIVAK I (TYPE 1135) CLASS (FF)

MIKOLAIV (ex-*Bezukoriznenny*) U 133   **DNIPROPETROVSK** (ex-*Bezzavetny*) U 134

Displacement, tons: 3,100 standard; 3,650 full load
Dimensions, feet (metres): 405.2 × 46.9 × 16.4
 (123.5 × 14.3 × 5)
Main machinery: COGAG; 2 gas turbines; 55,000 hp(m)
 (40.8 MW); 2 gas turbines, 13,600 hp(m) *(10 MW)*; 2 shafts
Speed, knots: 32. **Range, miles:** 4,600 at 20 kt; 1,600 at 30 kt
Complement: 194 (18 officers)

Missiles: SAM: 2 SA-N-4 Gecko twin launchers ❶ semi-active
 radar homing to 15 km *(8 n miles)* at 2.5 Mach; warhead 50 kg;
 altitude 9.1-3,048 m *(30-10,000 ft)*; 40 missiles (20 in Krivak
 III). The launcher retracts into the mounting for stowage and
 protection, rising to fire and retracting to reload. The two
 mountings are forward of the bridge and abaft the funnel.
A/S: Raduga SS-N-14 Silex quad launcher ❷ command guidance
 to 55 km *(30 n miles)* at 0.95 Mach; payload nuclear 5 kT or
 Type 40 torpedo or Type E53-72 torpedo. SSM version; range
 35 km *(19 n miles)*; warhead 500 kg.
Guns: 4—3 in *(76 mm)*/60 (2 twin) ❸; 90 rds/min to 15 km *(8 n
 miles)*; weight of shell 6.8 kg.
Torpedoes: 8—21 in *(533 mm)* (2 quad) tubes ❹. Combination of
 53 cm torpedoes.
A/S mortars: 2 RBU 6000 12-tubed trainable ❺; range 6,000 m;
 warhead 31 kg.
Mines: Capacity for 20.
Countermeasures: Decoys: 4 PK 16 or 10 PK 10 chaff launchers.
 Towed torpedo decoy.
 ESM/ECM: 2 Bell Shroud. 2 Bell Squat.
Radars: Air search: Head Net C ❻; 3D; E-band; range 128 km
 (70 n miles).
 Surface search: Don Kay ❼; I-band.
 Fire control: 2 Eye Bowl ❽; F-band (for SS-N-14). 2 Pop Group ❾;
 F/H/I-band (for SA-N-4). Owl Screech ❿; G-band.
 IFF: High Pole B.
Sonars: Bull Nose; hull-mounted; active search and attack;
 medium frequency.
 Mare Tail VDS active search; medium frequency.

Programmes: Built in the 1970s. Transferred from Russia in
 1997.
Operational: Both are in refit with *Dnipropetrovsk* possibly being
 cannibalised. Neither ship has been reported at sea since being
 transferred. A single Krivak II *Sevastopol* was broken up in
 mid-1999.

UPDATED

MIKOLAIV   *(Scale 1 : 1,200), Ian Sturton /* 0019338

MIKOLAIV   *9/1998, T Gander /* 0050306

1 GRISHA V (TYPE 1124EM), 2 GRISHA II (TYPE 1124P) and 2 GRISHA I CLASSES (FFL)

LUTSK U 200 (ex-*400*)
VINNITSA (ex-*Dnepr*) U 206
KHERSON (ex-*MPK 52*) U 210

CHERNIGIV (ex-*Izmail*) U 205
SUMY (ex-ex-*MPK 43*) U 209

Displacement, tons: 950 standard; 1,150 full load
Dimensions, feet (metres): 233.6 × 32.2 × 12.1
(71.2 × 9.8 × 3.7)
Main machinery: CODAG; 1 gas turbine; 15,000 hp(m) *(11 MW)*;
2 diesels; 16,000 hp(m) *(11.8 MW)*; 3 shafts
Speed, knots: 30. **Range, miles:** 2,500 at 14 kt; 1,750 at 20 kt
diesels; 950 at 27 kt
Complement: 70 (5 officers)

LUTSK

(Scale 1 : 900), Ian Sturton

Missiles: SAM: SA-N-4 Gecko twin launcher ❶ *(Lutsk)*; semi-
active radar homing to 15 km *(8 n miles)* at 2.5 Mach; warhead
50 kg; altitude 9.1-3,048 m *(30-10,000 ft)*; 20 missiles.
Guns: 1—3 in *(76 mm)*/60 ❷; *(Lutsk)*; 120 rds/min to 15 km *(8 n
miles)*; weight of shell 7 kg.
2 or 4—57 mm/80 (twin) (1 in 'Grisha II' and 2 in 'Grisha I');
120 rds/min to 6 km *(3.3 n miles)*; weight of shell 2.8 kg.
1—30 mm/65 ❸; *(Lutsk)*; 6 barrels; 3,000 rds/min combined
to 2 km.
Torpedoes: 4—21 in *(533 mm)* (2 twin) tubes ❹. SAET-60;
passive homing to 15 km *(8.1 n miles)* at 40 kt; warhead
400 kg.
A/S mortars: 1 or 2 RBU 6000 12-tubed trainable ❺; range
6,000 m; warhead 31 kg.
Depth charges: 2 racks (12).
Mines: Capacity for 18 in lieu of depth charges.
Countermeasures: ESM: 2 Watch Dog. 2 PK 16 chaff launchers.
Radars: Air/surface search: Half Plate B ❻; *(Lutsk)*; E/F-band.
Strut Curve (remainder); F-band.
Navigation: Don 2; I-band.
Fire control: Pop Group ❼; *(Lutsk)*; F/H/I-band (for SA-N-4). Bass
Tilt ❽; *(Lutsk)*; H/I-band (for 76 mm and 30 mm).
Muff Cobb (remainder); G/H-band.
IFF: High Pole A or B. Square Head. Salt Pot.
Sonars: Bull Nose (MGK 335MS); hull-mounted; active search
and attack; high/medium frequency.
Elk Tail VDS ❾; active search; high frequency.

Programmes: *Lutsk* is a 'Grisha V' launched 12 May 1993 and
completed 27 November 1993. U 205 and U 206 are 'Grisha II'
ex-Russian Border Guard ships transferred in 1996. U 209 and
U 210 are 'Grisha I'. A second 'Grisha V' stopped building in
1997.
Operational: The two Grisha Is have not been reported at sea
since being transferred from Russia in 1997.   *UPDATED*

CHERNIGIV

4/1997, Ukraine Navy / 0019339

LUTSK

2/1998, Ukraine Navy / 0050309

PATROL FORCES

Note: In addition there are two 'Tarantul I' class, *Nicopol* U 155 and *Kremenchuk* U 156, and 'Zhuk' class *Skadovsk* U 170, which are not fully operational but may be refitted if funds are available.

2 PAUK I (MOLNYA) (TYPE 1241P) CLASS (PCF)

UZHGOROD (ex-*MPK 93*) U 207   **KHMELNITSKY** (ex-*MPK 116*) U 208

Displacement, tons: 440 full load
Dimensions, feet (metres): 189 × 33.5 × 10.8 *(57.6 × 10.2 × 3.3)*
Main machinery: 2 Type M 521 diesels; 16,184 hp(m) *(11.9 MW)* sustained; 2 shafts
Speed, knots: 32. **Range, miles:** 2,400 at 14 kt
Complement: 32

Missiles: SAM: SA-N-5 Grail quad launcher; manual aiming; IR homing to 6 km *(3.2 n miles)* at
1.5 Mach; altitude to 2,500 m *(8,000 ft)*; warhead 1.5 kg; 8 missiles.
Guns: 1—3 in *(76 mm)*/60; 120 rds/min to 15 km *(8 n miles)*; weight of shell 7 kg.
1—30 mm/65 AK 630; 6 barrels; 3,000 rds/min combined to 2 km.
Torpedoes: 4—16 in *(406 mm)*.
A/S mortars: 2 RBU 1200 5-tubed fixed; range 1,200 m; warhead 34 kg.
Depth charges: 2 racks (12).
Countermeasures: Decoys: 2 PK 16 or 4 PK 10 chaff launchers.
ESM: 3 Brick Plug and 2 Half Hat; radar warning.
Weapons control: Hood Wink optronic director.
Radars: Air/surface search: Peel Cone; E/F-band.
Surface search: Kivach or Pechora; I-band.
Fire control: Bass Tilt; H/I-band.
Sonars: Foal Tail; VDS (mounted on transom); active attack; high frequency.

Programmes: Transferred from Black Sea Fleet Border Guard in 1996. Others of this class are in the
Ukraine Border Guard.
Structure: ASW version of the Russian 'Tarantul' class.
Operational: *Uzhgorod* is probably non-operational.   *VERIFIED*

KHMELNITSKY

4/1997, Ukraine Navy / 0003115

3 MATKA (VEKHR) CLASS (TYPE 206MP)
(FAST ATTACK CRAFT—MISSILE HYDROFOIL) (PHG)

UMAN (ex-R-260) U 152   **PRILUKI** (ex-R-262) U 153   **KAHOVKA** (ex-R-265) U 154

Displacement, tons: 225 standard; 260 full load
Dimensions, feet (metres): 129.9 × 24.9 (41 over foils) × 6.9 (13.1 over foils)
  (39.6 × 7.6 (12.5) × 2.1 (4))
Main machinery: 3 Type M 504 diesels; 10,800 hp(m) *(7.94 MW)* sustained; 3 shafts
Speed, knots: 40. **Range, miles:** 600 at 35 kt foilborne; 1,500 at 14 kt hullborne
Complement: 33
Missiles: SSM: 2 SS-N-2C/D Styx; active radar or IR homing to 83 km *(45 n miles)* at 0.9 Mach;
  warhead 513 kg; sea-skimmer at end of run.
Guns: 1—3 in *(76 mm)*/60; 120 rds/min to 15 km *(8 n miles)*; weight of shell 7 kg.
  1—30 mm/65 AK 630; 6 barrels per mounting; 3,000 rds/min to 2 km.
Countermeasures: Decoys: 2 PK 16 chaff launchers.
ESM: Clay Brick; intercept.
Weapons control: Hood Wink optronic directors.
Radars: Air/surface search: Plank Shave; E-band.
Navigation: SRN-207; I-band.
Fire control: Bass Tilt; H/I-band.
IFF: High Pole B or Salt Pot B and Square Head.

Comment: Five Russian Black Sea Fleet units transferred in 1996. Built between 1978 and 1983
  with similar hulls to the 'Osa' class. One was transferred to Georgia in 1999 and one other has
  been cannibalised for spares.

UPDATED

KAHOVKA   6/1999*, Oleg Leus / 0080918

MINE WARFARE FORCES

2 NATYA I CLASS (MSO)

ZHOVTI VODY (ex-*Zenitchik*) U 310   **CHERKASY** (ex-*Razvedchik*) U 311

Displacement, tons: 804 full load
Dimensions, feet (metres): 200.1 × 33.5 × 9.8 *(61 × 10.2 × 3)*
Main machinery: 2 Type M 504 diesels; 5,000 hp(m) *(3.67 MW)* sustained; 2 shafts; cp props
Speed, knots: 16. **Range, miles:** 3,000 at 12 kt
Complement: 67 (8 officers)

Missiles: SAM: 2 SA-N-5/8 Grail quad launchers.
Guns: 4—30 mm/65 (2 twin) AK 306 or 2—30 mm/65 AK 630; 4—25 mm/80 (2 twin).
A/S mortars: 2 RBU 1200 5-tubed fixed.
Depth charges: 62.
Mines: 10.
Countermeasures: MCM: 1 or 2 GKT-2 contact sweeps; 1 AT-2 acoustic sweep.
  1 TEM-3 magnetic sweep.
Radars: Surface search: Low Trough; I-band.
Fire control: Drum Tilt; H/I-band.
IFF: 2 Square Head. High Pole B.
Sonars: MG 79/89; hull-mounted; active minehunting; high frequency.

Comment: Transferred from Russia in 1996. Both are operational.

UPDATED

NATYA I (Russian colours)   10/1996, van Ginderen Collection / 0019043

2 SONYA (YAKHONT) (TYPE 1265) CLASS (MSC/MHC)

MELITOPOL (ex-BT 79) U 330   **MARIUPOL** (ex-BT 126) U 331

Displacement, tons: 460 full load
Dimensions, feet (metres): 157.4 × 28.9 × 6.6 *(48 × 8.8 × 2)*
Main machinery: 2 Kolomna diesels; 2,000 hp(m) *(1.47 MW)* sustained; 2 shafts
Speed, knots: 15. **Range, miles:** 3,000 at 10 kt
Complement: 43
Guns: 2—30 mm/65 (twin). 2—25 mm/80 (twin).
Mines: 8.
Radars: Surface search: Don 2; I-band.
IFF: Two Square Head.
Sonars: MG 69/79; hull-mounted; active; high frequency.

Comment: Transferred from Russia in 1996. Wooden hulls. *Melitopol* is operational.

VERIFIED

SONYA (Russian colours)   9/1995, Hartmut Ehlers

1 YEVGENYA (KOROND) (TYPE 1258) CLASS (MHC)

GENICHESK (ex-RT 214) U 360

Displacement, tons: 77 standard; 90 full load
Dimensions, feet (metres): 80.7 × 18 × 4.9 *(24.6 × 5.5 × 1.5)*
Main machinery: 2 Type 3-D-12 diesels; 600 hp(m) *(440 kW)* sustained; 2 shafts
Speed, knots: 11. **Range, miles:** 300 at 10 kt
Complement: 10
Guns: 2—14.5 mm (twin) MGs.
Mines: 8 racks.
Radars: Surface search: Spin Trough or Mius; I-band.
IFF: Salt Pot.
Sonars: A small MG-7 sonar is lifted over stern on crane; a TV system may also be used.

Comment: Transferred from Russia in 1996. Fully operational.

VERIFIED

YEVGENYA (Russian colours)   1991 / 0019342

AMPHIBIOUS FORCES

1 ROPUCHA I (TYPE 775) CLASS (LST)

KONSTANTIN OLSHANSKY (ex-BDK 56) U 402

Displacement, tons: 4,400 full load
Dimensions, feet (metres): 370.7 × 47.6 × 11.5 *(113 × 14.5 × 3.6)*
Main machinery: 2 Zgoda-Sulzer 16ZVB40/48 diesels; 19,230 hp(m) *(14.14 MW)* sustained;
  2 shafts
Speed, knots: 17.5. **Range, miles:** 3,500 at 16 kt
Complement: 95 (7 officers)
Military lift: 10 MBT plus 190 troops or 24 AFVs plus 170 troops
Missiles: SAM: 4 SA-N-5 Grail quad launchers.
Guns: 4—57 mm/80 (2 twin); 120 rds/min to 6 km *(3.3 n miles)*; weight of shell 2.8 kg.
Weapons control: 2 Squeeze Box optronic directors.
Radars: Air/surface search: Strut Curve; F-band.
Navigation: Don 2; I-band.
Fire control: Muff Cob; G/H-band.
IFF: High Pole B.

Comment: Built at Gdansk, Poland in 1978 and transferred from Russia in 1996. Can be used to
  carry mines. Ro-ro design with 540 m² of parking space between the stern gate and the bow
  doors. Fully operational.

UPDATED

KONSTANTIN OLSHANSKY   9/1996*, Winter & Findler / 0019343

1 ALLIGATOR (TYPE 1171) CLASS (LST)

RIVNE U 400

Displacement, tons: 4,700 full load
Measurement, tons: 370.7 × 50.8 × 14.7 (113 × 15.5 × 4.5)
Main machinery: 2 diesels; 9,000 hp(m) (6.6 MW); 2 shafts
Speed, knots: 18. **Range, miles:** 10,000 at 15 kt
Complement: 100
Military lift: 300 troops; 1,700 tons including about 20 tanks and various trucks; 40 AFVs
Radars: Surface search: 2 Don 2; I-band.

Comment: Launched in 1971 and transferred from Russian Fleet in 1994. This is the Type 2 variant of this class. Disarmed in 1997, in refit in 1999, but may now be operational. Previously wrongly reported as the ex-*Ilya Azarov*. **UPDATED**

RIVNE 4/1997*, Ukraine Navy / 0019345

4 POMORNIK (ZUBR) (TYPE 1232.2) CLASS (ACV)

DONETSK U 420	KRAMATORSK (ex-MDK-57) U 422	GORLIVKA (ex-MDK-123) U 423	ARTEMIVSK (ex-MDK-93) U 424

Displacement, tons: 550 full load
Dimensions, feet (metres): 189 × 70.5 (57.6 × 21.5)
Main machinery: 5 Type NK-12MV gas turbines; 2 for lift, 23,672 hp(m) (17.4 MW) nominal; 3 for drive, 35,508 hp(m) (26.1 MW) nominal
Speed, knots: 60. **Range, miles:** 300 at 55 kt
Complement: 31 (4 officers)
Military lift: 3 MBT or 10 APC plus 230 troops (total 170 tons)
Missiles: SAM: 2 SA-N-5 Grail quad launchers; manual aiming; IR homing to 6 km (3.2 n miles) at 1.5 Mach; altitude to 2,500 m (8,000 ft); warhead 1.5 kg.
Guns: 2—30 mm/65 AK 630; 6 barrels per mounting; 3,000 rds/min combined to 2 km. 2 retractable 122 mm rocket launchers.
Mines: 80.
Countermeasures: Decoys: TSP 41 chaff.
ESM: Tool Box; intercept.
Weapons control: Quad Look (modified Squeeze Box) (DWU 3) optronic director.
Radars: Air/surface search: Cross Dome (Ekran); I-band.
Fire control: Bass Tilt MR 123; H/I-band.
IFF: Salt Pot A/B. Square Head.

Comment: *Donetsk* was completed by Morye, Feodosiya on 20 July 1993. The other three were acquired from Russia in 1996. A fifth of class was building in 1997 but has been cancelled. *Donetsk* is operational. The other three have not been reported at sea since being transferred. **UPDATED**

DONETSK 6/1999*, Oleg Leus / 0080919

AUXILIARIES

Note: Other ships transferred from Russia in 1997, and possibly in limited service, are a 'Keyla II' class tanker *Berdjansk* U 753, a 'Voda' class tanker *Sudak* U 756, two 'Pozharny' class ATR *Borshev* U 722 and *Evpatoriya* U 728, an 'Amur' class support ship *Krasnodon* U 759, and a 'Sura' class buoy tender *Sostka* U 852. Smaller craft include a 'Nyryat I' class *Brodi* U 707, two 'Shelon' class *Malin* U 800 and *Monastirisze* U 891, a 'Potok' class *Arciz* U 853, and a 'T 43' class *Svitlovodsk* U 861.

BORIS CHILIKIN (TYPE 1559V) CLASS (AOR)

MAKIVKA (ex-*Boris Chilikin*) U 757

Displacement, tons: 23,450 full load
Dimensions, feet (metres): 531.5 × 70.2 × 33.8 (162.1 × 21.4 × 10.3)
Main machinery: 1 diesel; 9,600 hp(m) (7 MW); 1 shaft
Speed, knots: 17. **Range, miles:** 10,000 at 16 kt
Complement: 75 (without armament)
Cargo capacity: 13,000 tons oil fuel and dieso; 400 tons ammunition; 400 tons spares; 400 tons victualling stores; 500 tons fresh water
Radars: Navigation: 2 Nayada or Palm Frond; I-band.
IFF: High Pole B.

Comment: Built at Baltic Yard, Leningrad in 1971. Transferred from Russia in 1997. Capable of underway replenishment on both sides. Probably non-operational. **VERIFIED**

MAKIVKA 9/1998, Hartmut Ehlers / 0050310

1 DUBNA CLASS (AOL)

KERCH (ex-*Sventa*) U 758

Displacement, tons: 11,500 full load
Dimensions, feet (metres): 426.4 × 65.6 × 23.6 (130 × 20 × 7.2)
Main machinery: 1 Russkiy 8DRPH23/230 diesel; 6,000 hp(m) (4.4 MW); 1 shaft
Speed, knots: 16. **Range, miles:** 7,000 at 16 kt
Complement: 70
Cargo capacity: 7,000 tons fuel; 300 tons fresh water; 1,500 tons stores
Radars: Navigation: 2 Nayada; I-band.

Comment: Transferred in 1997 from Russia. Built by Rauma Repola, Finland and completed in April 1979. Underway refuelling on either beam or astern. **UPDATED**

KERCH 8/1997*, W Globke / 0019349

1 LAMA CLASS (TYPE 323) (AEM)

KOLOMIYA U 533

Displacement, tons: 4,600 full load
Dimensions, feet (metres): 370 × 49.2 × 14.4 (112.8 × 15 × 4.4)
Main machinery: 2 diesels; 4,800 hp(m) (3 MW); 2 shafts
Speed, knots: 14. **Range, miles:** 6,000 at 10 kt
Complement: 200
Guns: 4—57 mm/70 (2 twin). 4—25 mm/80.
Radars: Surface search: Slim Net; E/F-band.
Navigation: Don 2; I-band.
Fire control: 2 Hawk Screech; I-band.

Comment: Transferred in 1997 from Russia. Missile support ship and floating workshop. Probably used for its alongside maintenance facilities and is unlikely to be fully manned. **VERIFIED**

KOLOMIYA 9/1998, T Gander / 0050311

1 KLASMA CLASS (TYPE 1274) (ARC)

NOVY BUG (ex-*Tsna*) U 851

Displacement, tons: 6,000 standard; 6,900 full load
Measurement, tons: 3,400 dwt; 5,786 gross
Dimensions, feet (metres): 427.8 × 52.5 × 19 *(130.5 × 16 × 5.8)*
Main machinery: Diesel-electric; 5 Wärtsilä Sulzer 624TS diesel generators; 5,000 hp(m) *(3.68 MW)*; 2 motors; 2,150 hp(m) *(1.58 MW)*; 2 shafts
Speed, knots: 14. **Range, miles:** 12,000 at 14 kt
Complement: 118
Radars: Navigation: Spin Trough and Nayada; I-band.

Comment: Built by Wärtsilä Äbovarvet in Finland in 1969. Cable laying ship transferred from Russia in 1997.   ***VERIFIED***

NOVY BUG   *9/1998, T Gander /* 0050312

1 BEREZA CLASS (TYPE 18061) (YDG)

BALTA U 811 (ex-*SR 568*)

Displacement, tons: 1,850 standard; 2,051 full load
Dimensions, feet (metres): 228 × 45.3 × 13.1 *(69.5 × 13.8 × 4)*
Main machinery: 2 Zgoda-Sulzer 8AL25/30 diesels; 2,938 hp(m) *(2.16 MW)* sustained; 2 shafts
Speed, knots: 14. **Range, miles:** 1,000 at 14 kt
Complement: 88
Radars: Navigation: Kivach; I-band.

Comment: Built at Northern Shipyard, Gdansk in 1987. Transferred from Russia in 1997. Degaussing vessel with an NBC citadel and three laboratories. Not seen at sea since being transferred but may be in use.   ***UPDATED***

BALTA   *9/1998, Hartmut Ehlers /* 0050313

1 BAMBUK (TYPE 1288) CLASS (AGF)

Name	*No*	*Builders*	*Launched*	*Commissioned*
SLAVUTICH	U 510 (ex-800, ex-SSV 189)	Nikolayev	12 Oct 1990	28 July 1992

Displacement, tons: 5,403 full load
Dimensions, feet (metres): 350.1 × 52.5 × 19.7 *(106.7 × 16 × 6)*
Main machinery: 2 Skoda 6L2511 diesels; 6,100 hp(m) *(4.5 MW)*; 2 shafts
Speed, knots: 16. **Range, miles:** 8,000 at 12 kt
Complement: 178
Missiles: SAM: 2 SA-N-5/8 Grail quad launchers; manual aiming; IR homing to 6 km *(3.2 n miles)* at 1.5 Mach; altitude to 2,500 m *(8,000 ft)*; warhead 1.5 kg.
Guns: 2—30 mm/65 AK 630; 6 barrels per mounting.
Countermeasures: Decoys: 2 PK 16 chaff launchers.
Radars: Navigation: 3 Palm Frond; I-band.
CCA: Fly Screen; I-band.
Tacan: 2 Round House.
Helicopters: 2 Ka-25 Hormone C.

Comment: Laid down on 20 March 1988. Second of a class built for acoustic research but taken over before completion and used as a command ship.   ***VERIFIED***

SLAVUTICH   *9/1998, T Gander /* 0050314

1 YELVA (TYPE 535M) CLASS (DIVING TENDER) (YDT)

KRAB U 701

Displacement, tons: 295 full load
Dimensions, feet (metres): 134.2 × 26.2 × 6.6 *(40.9 × 8 × 2)*
Main machinery: 2 Type 3-D-12A diesels; 630 hp(m) *(463 kW)* sustained; 2 shafts
Speed, knots: 12.5. **Range, miles:** 1,870 at 12 kt
Complement: 30
Radars: Navigation: Spin Trough; I-band.

Comment: Diving tender built in mid-1970s. Transferred from Russia in 1997. Carries a 1 ton crane and diving bell. Operational.   ***VERIFIED***

KRAB   *6/1998, van Ginderen Collection /* 0050315

SURVEY SHIPS

Notes: (1) Also transferred in 1997 but not confirmed as operational are a 'Mod Mayak' class *Yalta* U 755, a 'Muna' class AGI *Dzhankoi* U 754, and an 'Onega' class *Severodonetsk* U 812.
(2) Ten former Russian civilian research ships were transferred in 1996/97. All are now in commercial service.

1 MOMA (TYPE 861M) CLASS (AGS)

SIMFEROPOL (ex-*Jupiter*) U 511

Displacement, tons: 1,600 full load
Dimensions, feet (metres): 240.5 × 36.8 × 12.8 *(73.3 × 11.2 × 3.9)*
Main machinery: 2 Zgoda-Sulzer diesels; 3,300 hp(m) *(2.43 MW)* sustained; 2 shafts; cp props
Speed, knots: 17. **Range, miles:** 9,000 at 11 kt
Complement: 56
Radars: Navigation: Don 2; I-band.

Comment: Transferred from Russia in February 1996 and is active.   ***UPDATED***

SIMFEROPOL   *4/1997*, Ukraine Navy /* 0019347

3 FINIK (TYPE 872) CLASS (AGS)

PEREYASLAV — (ex-*GS 401*)   **ALCHEVSK** U 603 (ex-*GS 402*)   **SKVYRA** U 635 (ex-*OS 265*)

Displacement, tons: 1,200 full load
Dimensions, feet (metres): 201.1 × 35.4 × 10.8 *(61.3 × 10.8 × 3.3)*
Main machinery: 2 Cegielski-Sulzer 6AL25/30 diesels; 1,920 hp(m) *(1.4 MW)*; auxiliary propulsion; 2 motors; 204 hp(m) *(150 kW)*; 2 shafts; cp props; bow thruster
Speed, knots: 13. **Range, miles:** 3,000 at 13 kt
Complement: 26 (5 officers) plus 9 scientists
Radars: Navigation: Kivach B; I-band.

Comment: Improved 'Biya' class. Built at Northern Shipyard, Gdansk 1978-83. Transferred from Russia in 1997. Fitted with 7 ton crane for buoy handling. Can carry two self-propelled pontoons and a boat on well-deck. Not reported as active.   ***UPDATED***

PEREYASLAV   *1/1997, van Ginderen Collection /* 0019355

2 BIYA (TYPE 870) CLASS (AGS)

U 601 (ex-*GS 273*)   **U 602** (ex-*GS 212*)

Displacement, tons: 766 full load
Dimensions, feet (metres): 180.4 × 32.1 × 8.5 *(55 × 9.8 × 2.6)*
Main machinery: 2 diesels; 1,200 hp(m) *(882 kW)*; 2 shafts; cp props
Speed, knots: 13. **Range, miles:** 4,700 at 11 kt
Complement: 25
Radars: Navigation: Don 2; I-band.

Comment: Built at Northern Shipyard, Gdansk 1972-76. Transferred from Russia in 1997. Laboratory and one survey launch, and a 5 ton crane. Probably not operational.

UPDATED

U 601   *8/1997*, W Globke /* 0019356

TUGS

Note: There are four tugs: one 'Okhtensky' class *Izyaslav* U 706, the others are 'Sorum' class *Korets* U 830, 'Goryn' class *Kremenets* U 705, and *Krasnoperekovsk* U 947.

TRAINING SHIPS

3 PETRUSHKA (DRAKON) CLASS (AXL)

SUVAR U 541   **AKAR** U 542   **CHERNIVICI** U 540

Displacement, tons: 335 full load
Dimensions, feet (metres): 129.3 × 27.6 × 7.2 *(39.4 × 8.4 × 22)*
Main machinery: 2 Wola H12 diesels; 756 hp(m) *(556 kW)*; 2 shafts
Speed, knots: 11. **Range, miles:** 1,000 at 11 kt
Complement: 13 plus 30 cadets

Comment: Training vessels built at Wisla Shiyard, Poland in 1989. Transferred from Russia in 1997. Used for seamanship and navigation training.

UPDATED

SUVAR and AKAR   *8/1997*, W Globke /* 0019353

2 BRYZA (TYPE 722) CLASS (AXL)

U 543   U 544

Displacement, tons: 167 full load
Dimensions, feet (metres): 94.5 × 21.7 × 6.4 *(28.8 × 6.6 × 2)*
Main machinery: 2 Wola DM 150 diesels; 300 hp(m) *(220 kW)*; 2 shafts
Speed, knots: 10. **Range, miles:** 1,100 at 10 kt
Complement: 11 plus 29 spare
Radars: Navigation: 2 SRN; I-band.

Comment: Transferred from Russia in 1997. Used for training.

VERIFIED

BRYZA U 544   *6/1998, van Ginderen Collection /* 0050316

---

1 MIR CLASS (SAIL TRAINING SHIP) (AXS)

Name	No	Builders	Commissioned
KHERSONES	—	Northern Shipyard, Gdansk	10 June 1988

Measurement, tons: 2,996 grt
Dimensions, feet (metres): 346.1 × 45.9 × 19.7 *(105.5 × 14 × 6)*
Main machinery: 1 Sulzer 8AL20/24 diesels; 1,500 hp(m) *(1.1 MW)*; 1 shaft
Speed, knots: 17
Complement: 55 plus 144 trainees

Comment: One of five of a class ordered in July 1985. Civilian manned.

UPDATED

KHERSONES   *7/1999*, Per Kornefeldt /* 0080920

BORDER GUARD

Notes: (1) There are plans to build new patrol cutters of the 'Kordon' (47 m) and 'Afalina' (44 m) classes, and new patrol boats of the 'Scif' (26 m) class. These new designs are also on offer for export by the Feodosiya Shipbuilding Association Morye. A 67 m OPV design by Nikolayev 61 Kommuna shipyard, is also in the export market.
(2) The river brigades also include four minesweeping boats, and 16 training craft. Not all of these are operational.
(3) Border Guard vessels are painted dark grey with a thick yellow and thin blue diagonal line on the hull. From 1999 pennant numbers are preceded by the letters BG.

3 PAUK I (MOLNYA) CLASS (TYPE 1241) (PCF)

GRIGORY KUROPIATNIKOV 012   **POLTAVA** 013
GRIGORY GNATENKO 014

Displacement, tons: 475 full load
Dimensions, feet (metres): 189 × 33.5 × 10.8 *(57.6 × 10.2 × 3.3)*
Main machinery: 2 Type M 521 diesels; 16,184 hp(m) *(11.9 MW)* sustained; 2 shafts
Speed, knots: 32. **Range, miles:** 1,260 at 14 kt
Complement: 44 (7 officers)

Guns: 1—3 in *(76 mm)*/60; 120 rds/min to 15 km *(8 n miles)*; weight of shell 7 kg.
  1—30 mm/65 AK 630; 6 barrels; 3,000 rds/min combined to 2 km.
Torpedoes: 4—16 in *(406 mm)* tubes. SAET-40; anti-submarine; active/passive homing to 10 km *(5.4 n miles)* at 30 kt; warhead 100 kg.
A/S mortars: 2 RBU 1200 5-tubed fixed; range 1,200 m; warhead 34 kg.
Depth charges: 2 racks (12).
Countermeasures: Decoys: 2 PK 16 or 4 PK 10.
ESM: Brick Plug and Half Hat; radar warning.
Weapons control: Hood Wink optronic director.
Radars: Air/surface search: Peel Cone; E/F-band.
Surface search: Kivach or Pechora or SRN 207; I-band.
Fire control: Bass Tilt; H/I-band.
Sonars: Foal Tail; VDS (mounted on transom); active attack; high frequency.

Comment: Built at Yaroslavl in the early 1980s and transferred from Russian Black Sea Fleet.

UPDATED

GRIGORY KUROPIATNIKOV   *3/1998, Ukraine Coast Guard /* 0050318

12 STENKA (TARANTUL) CLASS (TYPE 205P) (PCF)

— 019	— 030	BUKOVINA 034
VOLIN 020	ZAKARPATTIYA 031	DONBASS 035
— 021	ZHANOROZHSKAYA SEC 032	PODOLIE 036
NIKOLAYEV 023	ODESSA 033	PAVEL DERZHAVIN 037

Displacement, tons: 253 full load
Dimensions, feet (metres): 129.3 × 25.9 × 8.2 *(39.4 × 7.9 × 2.5)*
Main machinery: 3 Type M 517 or M 583 diesels; 14,100 hp(m) *(10.36 MW)*; 3 shafts
Speed, knots: 37. **Range, miles:** 500 at 35 kt; 1,540 at 14 kt
Complement: 30 (5 officers)
Guns: 4—30 mm/65 (2 twin) AK 230.
Torpedoes: 4—16 in *(406 mm)* tubes.
Depth charges: 2 racks (12).
Radars: Surface search: Pot Drum or Peel Cone; H/I- or E-band.
Fire control: Drum Tilt; H/I-band.
Navigation: Palm Frond; I-band.
IFF: High Pole. 2 Square Head.
Sonars: Stag Ear or Foal Tail; VDS; high frequency; Hormone type dipping sonar.

Comment: Similar hull to the 'Osa' class. Built in the 1970s and 1980s. A further 13 hulls were transferred from Russia and are used for spares. *UPDATED*

NIKOLAYEV *3/1998, Ukraine Coast Guard /* 0050320

1 SSV-10 CLASS (SUPPORT SHIP) (ARL)

DUNAI 500

Displacement, tons: 340 full load
Dimensions, feet (metres): 129.3 × 23 × 3.9 *(39.4 × 7 × 1.2)*
Main machinery: 2 diesels; 2 shafts
Speed, knots: 12
Complement: 20 (4 officers)

Comment: Headquarters ship built in 1940. Taken over from the Russian Danube Flotilla and now acts as the command ship for the river brigades. *UPDATED*

DUNAI *4/1998, Ukraine Coast Guard /* 0050322

3 MURAYVEY (ANTARES) CLASS (TYPE 133) (PCFH)

008 (ex-025) **009** (ex-026) **GALICHINA** 010 (ex-027)

Displacement, tons: 212 full load
Dimensions, feet (metres): 126.6 × 24.9 × 6.2; 14.4 (foils) *(38.6 × 7.6 × 1.9; 4.4)*
Main machinery: 2 gas turbines; 22,600 hp(m) *(16.6 MW)*; 2 shafts
Speed, knots: 60. **Range, miles:** 410 at 12 kt
Complement: 30 (5 officers)
Guns: 1—3 in *(76 mm)*/60; 120 rds/min to 15 km *(8 n miles)*; weight of shell 7 kg.
1—30 mm/65 AK 630; 6 barrels; 3,000 rds/min combined to 2 km.
Torpedoes: 2—16 in *(406 mm)* tubes; SAET-40; anti-submarine; active/passive homing to 10 km *(5.4 n miles)* at 30 kt; warhead 100 kg.
Depth charges: 6.
Weapons control: Hood Wink optronic director.
Radars: Surface search: Peel Cone; E-band.
Fire control: Bass Tilt; H/I-band.
Sonars: Rat Tail; VDS; active attack; high frequency; dipping sonar.

Comment: Built at Feodosiya in the mid-1980s for the USSR Border Guard. High speed hydrofoil craft. *UPDATED*

20 ZHUK (GRIF) CLASS (TYPE 1400M) (PC)

600	610	627	682	687
601	613	630	683	691
608	623	631	685	692
609	626	681	686	693

Displacement, tons: 39 full load
Dimensions, feet (metres): 78.7 × 16.4 × 3.9 *(24 × 5 × 1.2)*
Main machinery: 2 Type M 401B diesels; 2,200 hp(m) *(1.6 MW)* sustained; 2 shafts
Speed, knots: 30. **Range, miles:** 1,100 at 15 kt
Complement: 13 (1 officer)
Guns: 2—14.5 mm (twin, fwd) MGs. 1—12.7 mm (aft) MG.
Radars: Surface search: Spin Trough; I-band.

Comment: Russian Border Guard vessel built in the 1980s and transferred in 1996. Not all are operational. *UPDATED*

BG 687 *4/1998, Ukraine Coast Guard /* 0050321

10 SHMEL CLASS (TYPE 1204) (PGR)

LUBNY 171	KANIV 173	175-180
NIZYN 172	IZMAYIL 174	

Displacement, tons: 77 full load
Dimensions, feet (metres): 90.9 × 14.1 × 3.9 *(27.7 × 4.3 × 1.2)*
Main machinery: 2 Type M 50 diesels; 2,200 hp(m) *(1.6 MW)* sustained; 2 shafts
Speed, knots: 25. **Range, miles:** 600 at 12 kt
Complement: 12 (4 officers)
Guns: 1—3 in *(76 mm)*/48 (tank turret). 2—14.5 mm (twin) MGs. 5—7.62 mm MGs. 1 BP 6 rocket launcher; 18 barrels.
Mines: Can lay 9.
Radars: Surface search: Spint Trough; I-band.

Comment: Built at Kerch from 1967-74. Now part of the river brigade having been transferred from the Russian Danube flotilla. Probably only the named ships are operational. *UPDATED*

LUBNY *4/1998, Ukraine Coast Guard /* 0050323

BG 025 (old number) *3/1998, Ukraine Coast Guard /* 0050319

UNITED ARAB EMIRATES

Headquarters Appointments

Commander, Naval Forces:
  Brigadier Suhail Shaheen Al-Murar
Deputy Commander, Naval Forces:
  Colonel Mohammad Mehmood Al-Madni
Director General, Coast Guard:
  Colonel Abdullah Rahman Saleh Shelwah

Bases

Abu Dhabi (main base).
Mina Rashid and Mina Jebel Ali (Dubai),
Mina Saqr (Ras al Khaimah), Mina Sultan (Sharjah),
Khor Fakkan (Sharjah-East Coast).

General

This federation of the former Trucial States (Abu Dhabi, Ajman, Dubai, Fujairah, Ras al Khaimah, Sharjah, Umm al Qaiwan) was formed under a provisional constitution in 1971 with a new constitution coming into effect on 2 December 1976.
Following a decision of the UAE Supreme Defence Council on 6 May 1976 the armed forces of the member states were unified and the organisation of the UAE armed forces was furthered by decisions taken on 1 February 1978.

Personnel

(a) 2000: 2,400 (200 officers) Navy. 1,200 (110 officers) Coast Guard.
(b) Voluntary service

Mercantile Marine

Lloyd's Register of Shipping:
  322 vessels of 786,455 tons gross

DELETIONS

Auxiliaries

1997 *Ghagha II* (civilian)
1998 2 *Serna* (civilian)

SUBMARINES

Note: Two ex-German Type 206 may be acquired and some training is being done.

FRIGATES

2 KORTENAER CLASS (FFG)

Name	No	Builders	Laid down	Launched	Commissioned
ABU DHABI (ex-*Abraham Crijnssen*)	F 01 (ex-F 816)	Koninklijke Maatschappij De Schelde, Flushing	25 Oct 1978	16 May 1981	27 Jan 1983
AL EMIRAT (ex-*Piet Heyn*)	F 02 (ex-F 811)	Koninklijke Maatschappij De Schelde, Flushing	28 Apr 1977	3 June 1978	14 Apr 1981

Displacement, tons: 3,050 standard; 3,630 full load
Dimensions, feet (metres): 428 × 47.9 × 14.1; 20.3 (screws) *(130.5 × 14.6 × 4.3; 6.2)*
Main machinery: CODOG; 2 RR Olympus TM3B gas turbines; 50,880 hp *(37.9 MW)* sustained
  2 RR Tyne RM1C gas turbines; 9,900 hp *(7.4 MW)* sustained; 2 shafts; cp props
Speed, knots: 30. **Range, miles:** 4,700 at 16 kt on Tynes
Complement: 176 (18 officers) plus 24 spare berths

Missiles: SSM: 8 McDonnell Douglas Harpoon (2 quad) launchers ❶; active radar homing to 130 km *(70 n miles)* at 0.9 Mach; warhead 227 kg.
SAM: Raytheon Sea Sparrow Mk 29 octuple launcher ❷; semi-active radar homing to 14.6 km *(8 n miles)* at 2.5 Mach; warhead 39 kg; 24 missiles.
Guns: 1 OTO Melara 3 in *(76 mm)*/62 compact ❸; 85 rds/min to 16 km *(8.6 n miles)* anti-surface; 12 km *(6.5 n miles)* anti-aircraft; weight of shell 6 kg.
  1 Signaal SGE-30 Goalkeeper with General Electric 30 mm ❹; 7-barrelled; 4,200 rds/min combined to 2 km.
  2 Oerlikon 20 mm.
Torpedoes: 4—324 mm US Mk 32 (2 twin) tubes ❺. Honeywell Mk 46 or Whitehead A-244S Mod 1.

AL EMIRAT   *3/1998*, John Brodie* / 0016646

Countermeasures: Decoys: 2 Loral Hycor SRBOC Mk 36 6-tubed launchers ❻; chaff distraction or centroid modes.
ESM/ECM: Ramses ❼; intercept and jammer.
Combat data systems: Signaal SEWACO II action data automation; Link 11.
Radars: Air search: Signaal LW08 ❽; D-band; range 264 km *(145 n miles)* for 2 m² target.

Surface search: Signaal Scout ❾; I-band.
Fire control: Signaal STIR ❿; I/J-band; range 140 km *(76 n miles)* for 1 m² target.
  Signaal WM25 ⓫; I/J-band; range 46 km *(25 n miles)*.
Sonars: Westinghouse SQS-505; bow-mounted; active search and attack; medium frequency.

Helicopters: 2 Eurocopter AS 565 Panther ⓬.

Programmes: Contract signed on 2 April 1996 to transfer two Netherlands frigates, after refits by Royal Schelde. First one recommissioned in December 1997, second one in May 1998. Two more are wanted and may become available in 2000/01.
Structure: Harpoon SSM and Goalkeeper CIWS has been purchased separately, as have the Scout radars. Additional air conditioning has been fitted.
Operational: Training done for the crews in the Netherlands. Both based at Jebel Ali.

UPDATED

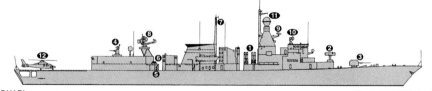

ABU DHABI   (Scale 1 : 1,200), Ian Sturton

ABU DHABI   *9/1997, John Brodie* / 0019359

CORVETTES

Note: Project Fallah (LEWA 2) is for 90 m multirole corvettes.

2 MURAY JIB (MGB 62) CLASS (FSG)

Name	No	Builders	Launched	Commissioned
MURAY JIB	CM 01 (ex-P 6501)	Lürssen, Bremen	Mar 1989	Nov 1990
DAS	CM 02 (ex-P 6502)	Lürssen, Bremen	May 1989	Jan 1991

Displacement, tons: 630 full load
Dimensions, feet (metres): 206.7 × 30.5 × 8.2 -
 (63 × 9.3 × 2.5)
Main machinery: 4 MTU 16V 538 TB92 diesels; 13,640 hp(m)
 (10 MW) sustained; 4 shafts
Speed, knots: 32. **Range, miles:** 4,000 at 16 kt
Complement: 43

Missiles: SSM: 8 Aerospatiale MM 40 Exocet (Block II) ❶; inertial
 cruise; active radar homing to 70 km *(40 n miles)* at 0.9 Mach;
 warhead 165 kg; sea-skimmer.
 SAM: Thomson-CSF modified Crotale Navale octuple
 launcher ❷; radar guidance; IR homing to 13 km *(7 n miles)* at
 2.4 Mach; warhead 14 kg.

Guns: 1 OTO Melara 3 in *(76 mm)*/62 Super Rapid ❸; 120 rds/
 min to 16 km *(8.7 n miles)*; weight of shell 6 kg.
 1 Signaal Goalkeeper with GE 30 mm 7-barrelled ❹; 4,200
 rds/min combined to 2 km.
Countermeasures: Decoys: 2 Dagaie launchers ❺; IR flares and
 chaff.
ESM/ECM: Racal Cutlass/Cygnus ❻; intercept/jammer.
Weapons control: CSSE Najir optronic director ❼.
Radars: Air/surface search: Bofors Ericsson Sea Giraffe 50HC ❽;
 G-band.
 Navigation: Racal Decca 1226; I-band.
 Fire control: Bofors Electronic 9LV 223 ❾; J-band (for gun and
 SSM).
 Thomson-CSF DRBV 51C ❿; J-band (for Crotale).

Helicopters: 1 Aerospatiale Alouette SA 316 ⓫.

Programmes: Ordered in late 1986. Similar vessels to Bahrain
 craft. Delivery in October 1991.
Structure: Lürssen design adapted for the particular conditions
 of the Gulf. This class has good air defence and a considerable
 anti-ship capability. The helicopter hangar is reached by flight
 deck lift.   ***UPDATED***

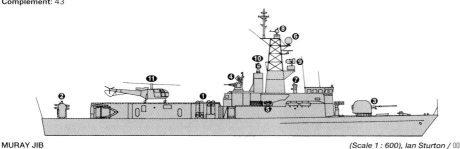

MURAY JIB   *(Scale 1 : 600)*, Ian Sturton / 0080921

DAS   5/1998 / 0050325

DAS   6/1999* / 0080922

PATROL FORCES

Notes: (1) Project LEWA 1 revised and submitted in 1998. This is for up to eight 65 m attack craft with helicopter facilities and has a high priority.
(2) Contract for 12 LEWA 3 patrol craft given to CMN Cherbourg on 8 December 1999. The first is to be built in France and the remainder at Abu Dhabi Shipbuilding, with equipment supplied by France. These craft are to have 32 m GRP hulls.

2 MUBARRAZ CLASS (FAST ATTACK CRAFT—MISSILE) (PCFG)

Name	No	Builders	Commissioned
MUBARRAZ	P 4401	Lürssen, Bremen	Aug 1990
MAKASIB	P 4402	Lürssen, Bremen	Aug 1990

Displacement, tons: 260 full load
Dimensions, feet (metres): 147.3 × 23 × 7.2 *(44.9 × 7 × 2.2)*
Main machinery: 2 MTU 20V 538 TB93 diesels; 9,370 hp(m) *(6.9 MW)* sustained; 2 shafts
Speed, knots: 40. **Range, miles:** 500 at 38 kt
Complement: 40 (5 officers)

Missiles: SSM: 4 Aerospatiale MM 40 Exocet; inertial cruise; active radar homing to 70 km *(40 n miles)* at 0.9 Mach; warhead 165 kg; sea-skimmer.
SAM: 1 Matra Sadral sextuple launcher; Mistral; IR homing to 4 km *(2.2 n miles)*; warhead 3 kg.
Guns: 1 OTO Melara 3 in *(76 mm)*/62 Super Rapid; 120 rds/min to 16 km *(8.7 n miles)*; weight of shell 6 kg.
  2 Rheinmetall 20 mm.
Countermeasures: Decoys: 2 Dagaie launchers; IR flares and chaff.
ESM/ECM: Racal Cutlass/Cygnus; intercept/jammer.
Weapons control: CSEE Najir optronic director (for SAM).
Radars: Air/surface search: Bofors Ericsson Sea Giraffe 50HC; G-band.
Navigation: Racal Decca 1226; I-band.
Fire control: Bofors Electronic 9LV 223; J-band (for gun and SSM).

Programmes: Ordered in late 1986 from Lürssen Werft at the same time as the two Type 62 vessels. Delivered in February 1991.
Structure: This is a modified TNC 38 design, with the first export version of Matra Sadral. The radome houses the jammer. The 20 mm guns are mounted on the bridge deck aft of the mast.
UPDATED

MUBARRAZ   *6/1997*, van Ginderen Collection / 0080923*

MAKASIB   *5/1995* / 0080924*

0 + 3 FAST INTERCEPT CRAFT (PBF)

Displacement, tons: 8 full load
Dimensions, feet (metres): 52.5 × 9.3 × 3.3 *(16 × 2.8 × 1)*
Main machinery: 2 diesels; 1,400 hp *(1.03 MW)*; 2 surface drives
Speed, knots: 55
Complement: 3

Comment: Reported ordered from Halmatic in 1999 for delivery in 2000. Similar to craft in service with the UK. VSV wave piercing hull. There may be some minor variations on the details given. Two 7.62 mm MGs can be mounted, and the cabin can take up to 14 troops.
NEW ENTRY

FIC (UK colours)   *6/1998*, Halmatic / 0080925*

6 BAN YAS (TNC 45) CLASS
(FAST ATTACK CRAFT—MISSILE) (PCFG)

Name	No	Builders	Commissioned
BAN YAS	P 4501	Lürssen Vegesack	Nov 1980
MARBAN	P 4502	Lürssen Vegesack	Nov 1980
RODQM	P 4503	Lürssen Vegesack	July 1981
SHAHEEN	P 4504	Lürssen Vegesack	July 1981
SAGAR	P 4505	Lürssen Vegesack	Sep 1981
TARIF	P 4506	Lürssen Vegesack	Sep 1981

Displacement, tons: 260 full load
Dimensions, feet (metres): 147.3 × 23 × 8.2 *(44.9 × 7 × 2.5)*
Main machinery: 4 MTU 16V 538 TB92 diesels; 13,640 hp(m) *(10 MW)* sustained; 4 shafts
Speed, knots: 40. **Range, miles:** 500 at 38 kt
Complement: 40 (5 officers)

Missiles: SSM: 4 Aerospatiale MM 40 Exocet; inertial cruise; active radar homing to 70 km *(40 n miles)* at 0.9 Mach; warhead 165 kg; sea-skimmer.
Guns: 1 OTO Melara 3 in *(76 mm)*/62; 60 rds/min to 16 km *(8.7 n miles)*; weight of shell 6 kg.
  2 Breda 40 mm/70 (twin); 300 rds/min to 12.5 km *(6.8 n miles)*; weight of shell 0.96 kg.
  2—7.62 mm MGs.
Countermeasures: Decoys: 1 CSEE trainable Dagaie; IR flares and chaff.
ESM: Racal Cutlass; intercept.
Weapons control: 1 CSEE Panda director for 40 mm. PEAB low-light USFA IR and TV tracker.
Radars: Surface search: Bofors Ericsson Sea Giraffe 50HC; G-band.
Navigation: Signaal Scout; I-band.
Fire control: Philips 9LV 200 Mk 2/3; J-band.

Programmes: Ordered in late 1977. First two shipped in September 1980 and four more in Summer 1981. This class was the first to be fitted with MM 40.
Modernisation: Upgrade contract for ship and propulsion systems given to Newport News. Work done by Abu Dhabi Shipbuilding Company. First pair completed in late 1998, second pair in mid-1999 and the third pair in mid-2000. Combat data system modernisation to start on completion.
UPDATED

SHAHEEN   *7/1997* / 0019361*

6 ARDHANA CLASS (LARGE PATROL CRAFT) (PC)

Name	No	Builders	Commissioned
ARDHANA	P 3301 (ex-P 1101)	Vosper Thornycroft	24 June 1975
ZURARA	P 3302 (ex-P 1102)	Vosper Thornycroft	14 Aug 1975
MURBAN	P 3303 (ex-P 1103)	Vosper Thornycroft	16 Sep 1975
AL GHULLAN	P 3304 (ex-P 1104)	Vosper Thornycroft	16 Sep 1975
RADOOM	P 3305 (ex-P 1105)	Vosper Thornycroft	1 July 1976
GHANADHAH	P 3306 (ex-P 1106)	Vosper Thornycroft	1 July 1976

Displacement, tons: 110 standard; 175 full load
Dimensions, feet (metres): 110 × 21 × 6.6 *(33.5 × 6.4 × 2)*
Main machinery: 2 Paxman 12CM diesels; 5,000 hp *(3.73 MW)* sustained; 2 shafts
Speed, knots: 30. **Range, miles:** 1,800 at 14 kt
Complement: 26
Guns: 2 Oerlikon/BMARC 30 mm/75 A32 (twin); 650 rds/min to 10 km *(5.5 n miles)*; weight of shell 1 kg or 0.36 kg.
  1 Oerlikon/BMARC 20 mm/80 A41A; 800 rds/min to 2 km.
  2—51 mm projectors for illuminants.
Radars: Surface search: Racal Decca TM 1626; I-band.

Comment: A class of round bilge steel hull craft. Originally operated by Abu Dhabi. New pennant numbers in 1996. To be replaced by the LEWA 3 ships from 2001.
UPDATED

AL GHULLAN   *2/1997, A Sharma / 0019362*

8 ARCTIC 28 RIBs and 12 AL-SHAALI TYPE

Displacement, tons: 4 full load
Dimensions, feet (metres): 27.9 × 9.7 × 2 *(8.5 × 3 × 0.6)*
Main machinery: 2 outboards; 450 hp *(336 kW)*
Speed, knots: 38
Complement: 1 plus 11 troops

Comment: RIBs ordered from Halmatic, Southampton in June 1992 and delivered in mid-1993. GRP hulls. Speed given is fully laden. Used by Special Forces. The Al-Shaali type were ordered in 1994 and built in Dubai.

UPDATED

ARCTIC   3/1995*, H M Steele / 0080926

SHIPBORNE AIRCRAFT

Numbers/Type: 4 Aerospatiale SA 316/319S Alouette.
Operational speed: 113 kt *(210 km/h)*.
Service ceiling: 10,500 ft *(3,200 m)*.
Range: 290 n miles *(540 km)*.
Role/Weapon systems: Reconnaissance and general purpose helicopters. Sensors: radar. Weapons: Unarmed.

UPDATED

Numbers/Type: 7 Eurocopter AS 565 Panthers.
Operational speed: 165 kt *(305 km/h)*.
Service ceiling: 16,700 ft *(5,100 m)*.
Range: 483 n miles *(895 km)*.
Role/Weapon systems: Ordered in March 1995 and delivered from 1998. Sensors: Thomson-CSF Agrion radar. Weapons: ASV; Aerospatiale AS 15TT ASM.

UPDATED

COUGAR   6/1994* / 0080927

LAND-BASED MARITIME AIRCRAFT

Note: Four IPTN CN 235 MPA or four Bombardier aircraft with Thomson-CSF avionics are being acquired.

Numbers/Type: 7 Aerospatiale AS 535 Cougar/Super Puma.
Operational speed: 150 kt *(280 km/h)*.
Service ceiling: 15,090 ft *(4,600 m)*.
Range: 335 n miles *(620 km)*.
Role/Weapon systems: Former transport helicopters. Five updated from 1995 with ASW equipment. Two used as VIP transports. Sensors: Omera ORB 30 radar; Thomson Marconi HS 312 dipping sonar. Weapons: ASV; one AM 39 Exocet ASM. ASW; A 244S torpedoes and mines.

VERIFIED

Numbers/Type: 2 Pilatus Britten-Norman Maritime Defender.
Operational speed: 150 kt *(280 km/h)*.
Service ceiling: 18,900 ft *(5,760 m)*.
Range: 1,500 n miles *(2,775 km)*.
Role/Weapon systems: Coastal patrol and surveillance aircraft although seldom used in this role. Sensors: Nose-mounted search radar, underwing searchlight. Weapons: Underwing rocket and gun pods.

VERIFIED

MINE WARFARE FORCES

Note: Three MHCs out to tender on 10 December 1997. No report of a contract.

AUXILIARIES

Notes: (1) There are also four civilian LCM ships, *El Nasirah 2, Baava 1, Makasib* and *Ghagha II*, and two 'Serna' class LCUs are also civilian owned.
(2) Two Damen harbour tugs acquired in 1997-98.

2 + 2 LCT

L 6401   L 6402

Comment: Built at Abu Dhabi Naval Base and completed in 1996. Details are uncertain but the ships are reported as being 65 m in length. Two more were reported ordered in late 1998.

UPDATED

L 6402   8/1996* / 0080928

3 AL FEYI CLASS (LSL)

AL FEYI L 5401   **DAYYINAH** L 5402   **JANANAH** L 5403

Displacement, tons: 650 full load
Dimensions, feet (metres): 164 × 36.1 × 9.2 *(50 × 11 × 2.8)*
Main machinery: 2 diesels; 1,248 hp *(931 kW)*; 2 shafts
Speed, knots: 11. **Range, miles:** 1,800 at 11 kt
Complement: 10
Military lift: 4 vehicles
Guns: 2—12.7 mm MGs.

Comment: *Al Feyi* built by Siong Huat, Singapore; completed 4 August 1987. The other pair built by Argos Shipyard, Singapore to a similar design and completed in December 1988. Used mostly as transport ships.

UPDATED

DAYYINAH   6/1996* / 0080929

1 DIVING TENDER (YDT)

D 1051

Displacement, tons: 100 full load
Dimensions, feet (metres): 103 × 22.6 × 3.6 *(31.4 × 6.9 × 1.1)*
Main machinery: 2 MTU 12V 396 TB93 diesels; 3,260 hp(m) *(2.4 MW)* sustained; 2 water-jets
Speed, knots: 26. **Range, miles:** 390 at 24 kt
Complement: 6

Comment: Ordered from Crestitalia in December 1985 for Abu Dhabi and delivered in July 1987. GRP hull. Used primarily for mine clearance but also for diving training, salvage and SAR. Fitted with a decompression chamber and diving bell. Lengthened version of Italian *Alcide Pedretti*.
UPDATED

ANNAD
6/1994* / 0080930

D 1051
3/1997* / 0019363

1 COASTAL TUG (YTB)

ANNAD A 3501

Displacement, tons: 795 full load
Dimensions, feet (metres): 114.8 × 32.2 × 13.8 *(35 × 9.8 × 4.2)*
Main machinery: 2 Caterpillar 3606TA diesels; 4,180 hp *(3.12 MW)* sustained; 2 shafts; cp props; bow thruster; 362 hp *(266 kW)*
Speed, knots: 14. **Range, miles:** 2,500 at 14 kt
Complement: 14 (3 officers)
Radars: Navigation: Racal Decca 2070; I-band.

Comment: Built by Dunston, Hessle, and completed in April 1989. Bollard pull, 55 tons. Equipped for SAR and is also used for logistic support.
UPDATED

COAST GUARD

Note: Under control of Minister of Interior. In addition to the vessels listed below there is a number of Customs and Police launches including three Swedish Boghammar 13 m craft of the same type used by Iran and delivered in 1985, two Baglietto police launches acquired in 1988, about 10 elderly 'Dhafeer' and 'Spear' class of 12 and 9 m respectively, and two Halmatic 'Arun' class Pilot craft delivered in 1990-91; some of these launches carry light machine guns.

2 PROTECTOR CLASS (PC)

1101   1102

Displacement, tons: 180 full load
Dimensions, feet (metres): 108.3 × 22 × 6.9 *(33 × 6.7 × 2.1)*
Main machinery: 2 MTU 16V 396 TE94 diesels; 5,911 hp(m) *(4.35 MW)* sustained; 2 shafts; acbLIPS props
Speed, knots: 33
Complement: 14
Guns: 1 Mauser 20 mm. 2—12.7 mm MGs.
Weapons control: 1 SAGEM optronic director.
Radars: Surface search: I-band.

Comment: Ordered from FBM Marine, Cowes in 1998. Aluminium hulls. First one laid down 15 June 1998. Both delivered in late 1999. More may be built by Abu Dhabi Shipbuilders. Similar to Bahamas and Chilean naval craft.
UPDATED

PROTECTOR 1101
7/1999*, Per Kornefeldt / 0080932

5 CAMCRAFT 77 ft (COASTAL PATROL CRAFT) (PC)

753-757

Displacement, tons: 70 full load
Dimensions, feet (metres): 76.8 × 18 × 4.9 *(23.4 × 5.5 × 1.5)*
Main machinery: 2 GM 12V-71TA diesels; 840 hp *(627 kW)* sustained; 2 shafts
Speed, knots: 25
Complement: 8
Guns: 2 Lawrence Scott 20 mm (not always embarked).
Radars: Surface search: Racal Decca; I-band.

Comment: Completed 1975 by Camcraft, New Orleans. Not always armed.
UPDATED

CAMCRAFT 755   6/1997* / 0019364

16 CAMCRAFT 65 ft (COASTAL PATROL CRAFT) (PC)

650-655

Displacement, tons: 50 full load
Dimensions, feet (metres): 65 × 18 × 5 *(19.8 × 5.5 × 1.5)*
Main machinery: 2 MTU 6V 396 TB93 diesels; 1,630 hp(m) *(1.2 MW)* sustained; 2 shafts (in 14)
2 Detroit 8V-92TA diesels; 700 hp *(522 kW)* sustained; 2 shafts (in 2)
Speed, knots: 25
Complement: 8
Guns: 1 Oerlikon 20 mm GAM-BO1.
Radars: Surface search: Racal Decca; I-band.

Comment: Built by Camcraft, New Orleans and delivered by September 1978.
UPDATED

CAMCRAFT 650   5/1995* / 0080933

6 BAGLIETTO GC 23 TYPE (COASTAL PATROL CRAFT) (PCF)

758-763

Displacement, tons: 50.7 full load
Dimensions, feet (metres): 78.7 × 18 × 3 *(24 × 5.5 × 0.9)*
Main machinery: 2 MTU 12V 396 TB93 diesels; 3,260 hp(m) *(2.4 MW)* sustained; 2 Kamewa water-jets
Speed, knots: 43. Range, miles: 700 at 20 kt
Complement: 9
Guns: 1 Oerlikon 20 mm. 2—7.62 mm MGs.
Radars: Surface search: I-band.

Comment: Built by Baglietto, Varazze. First two completed in March and May 1986, second pair in July 1987 and two more in 1988. All were delivered to UAE Coast Guard in Dubai.
UPDATED

BAGLIETTO 758   1987*, UAE Coast Guard / 0080934

3 BAGLIETTO 59 ft (COASTAL PATROL CRAFT) (PCF)

501-503

Displacement, tons: 22 full load
Dimensions, feet (metres): 59.4 × 13.9 × 2.3 *(18.1 × 4.3 × 0.7)*
Main machinery: 2 MTU 12V 183 TE92 diesels; 2 shafts
Speed, knots: 40
Complement: 6
Guns: 2—7.62 mm MGs.
Radars: Surface search: Racal Decca; I-band.

Comment: Ordered in 1992 and delivered in late 1993.
UPDATED

BAGLIETTO 503   10/1993*, UAE Coast Guard / 0080935

6 WATERCRAFT 45 ft (COASTAL PATROL CRAFT) (PC)

Displacement, tons: 25 full load
Dimensions, feet (metres): 45 × 14.1 × 4.6 *(13.7 × 4.3 × 1.4)*
Main machinery: 2 MAN D2542 diesels; 1,300 hp(m) *(956 kW)*; 2 shafts
Speed, knots: 26. Range, miles: 380 at 18 kt
Complement: 5
Guns: Mounts for 2—7.62 mm MGs.
Radars: Surface search: Racal Decca; I-band.

Comment: Ordered from Watercraft, UK in February 1982. Delivery in early 1983. Four deleted. Two similar craft built by Halmatic were delivered to the Dubai Port Authority in October 1997.
VERIFIED

WATERCRAFT 45 ft   1984, UAE Coast Guard

35 HARBOUR PATROL CRAFT (PB/YDT)

Comment: The latest are 11 Shark 33 built by Shaali Marine, Dubai and delivered in 1993-94. The remainder are a mixture of Baracuda 30 ft and FPB 22 ft classes. All are powered by twin outboard engines and most carry a 7.62 mm MG and have a Norden radar. There are also two Rotork craft used as diving tenders. Customs boats are operated separately by each of the UAE states. Some have been built for Kuwait.
UPDATED

BARACUDA 271   5/1995*, UAE Coast Guard / 0080931

UNITED KINGDOM

Headquarters Appointments

Chief of the Naval Staff and First Sea Lord:
Admiral Sir Michael Boyce, GCB, OBE
Commander-in-Chief, Fleet:
Admiral Sir Nigel Essenhigh, KCB
Chief of Naval Personnel and Commander-in-Chief, Naval Home Command:
Vice Admiral P Spencer
Chief of Fleet Support:
Rear Admiral B B Perowne
Controller of the Navy:
Rear Admiral N C F Guild
Assistant Chief of the Naval Staff:
Rear Admiral J M Burnell-Nugent, CBE

Flag Officers

Deputy Commander-in-Chief, Fleet:
Vice Admiral F M Malbon
Flag Officer, Surface Flotilla:
Rear Admiral I A Forbes, CBE
Flag Officer, Submarines:
Rear Admiral R P Stevens
Flag Officer, Maritime Aviation:
Rear Admiral I R Henderson, CBE
Commander, UK Task Group:
Rear Admiral S R Meyer
Flag Officer, Sea Training:
Rear Admiral A R Backus, OBE
Commandant-General, Royal Marines:
Major General R H G Fulton
Flag Officer, Scotland, Northern England and Northern Ireland:
Rear Admiral D J Anthony
Flag Officer, Training and Recruiting:
Rear Admiral J Chadwick
Hydrographer of the Navy:
Rear Admiral J P Clarke, CB, LVO, MBE
Commodore Mine Warfare and Fishery Protection:
Commodore B A L Goldman
Commodore Royal Fleet Auxiliaries:
Commodore P J Lannin

Royal Marines Operational Units

HQ 3 Commando Brigade RM; 40 Commando RM; 42 Commando RM; 45 Commando Group (RM/Army); 3 Commando Logistic Regiment RM (RN/RM/Army); 3 Commando Brigade HQ and Signal Squadron RM including Air Defence Troop RM (Rapier), EW Troop RM, Tactical Air Command Posts RM (3 regular, 1 reserve); 539 Assault Squadron RM (hovercraft, landing craft and raiding craft); Brigade Patrol Troop (reconnaissance); Special Boat Service RM; Comacchio Group RM (security); T Company RMR; 29 Commando Regiment RA (Army); 59 Independent Commando Squadron RE (Army); 289 Commando Battery RA (Volunteers); 131 Independent Squadron RE (Volunteers).

Fleet Disposition

Submarine Flotilla
1st Squadron (*Neptune,* Faslane) 5 Attack submarines, 4 Strategic submarines
2nd Squadron (*Defiance,* Devonport) 7 Attack submarines

Surface Flotilla
2nd Frigate Squadron (Devonport) Type 22
3rd Destroyer Squadron (Portsmouth) Type 42
4th Frigate Squadron (Portsmouth) Type 23
5th Destroyer Squadron (Portsmouth) Type 42
6th Frigate Squadron (Devonport) Type 23

MCM Flotilla
1st Squadron (Portsmouth), 2nd Squadron (Portsmouth)
3rd Squadron (Faslane)

Fishery Protection Squadron (Portsmouth)
Surveying Squadron (Devonport)

Diplomatic Representation

Naval Attaché in Ankara:
Colonel S M Pegg
Naval Attaché in Athens:
Captain J L Milnes
Naval Attaché in Berlin:
Captain C V Ellison
Naval Attaché in Brasilia:
Captain R B Turner
Naval Adviser in Bridgetown:
Captain P Jackson
Naval Attaché in Brunei:
Captain P A Jones, OBE
Naval Attaché in Cairo:
Commander J A Barltrop
Defence Adviser in Canberra:
Commodore A J Lyall MBE
Defence Attaché in Copenhagen:
Commander A C Gordon Lennox
Naval Attaché in The Hague:
Captain R St J S Bishop
Naval Attaché in Islamabad:
Captain M J Broadhurst
Defence Attaché in Kiev:
Captain M N Littleboy
Assistant Defence Adviser in Kuala Lumpur:
Lieutenant Commander M P O'Riordan
Defence Attaché in Lisbon:
Commander A J Bull
Naval Attaché in Madrid:
Captain P J Pacey
Naval Attaché in Manama:
Commander M Dodds
Defence Attaché in Manila:
Captain C Peach
Naval Attaché in Moscow:
Captain G A R McCready, MBE
Naval Adviser in New Delhi:
Captain K Ridland
Naval Attaché in Oslo:
Commander D L Stanesby
Naval Adviser in Ottawa:
Group Captain T J Williams, AFC
Naval Attaché in Paris:
Captain A A S Adair
Naval Attaché in Peking:
Captain A A Ainslie
Naval Attaché in Pretoria:
Commander D L W Sim
Naval Attaché in Riyadh:
Commander I A Vosper
Naval Attaché in Rome:
Captain A Sinclair
Defence Attaché in Santiago:
Captain P J Ellis
Naval Attaché in Seoul:
Captain C P Robinson, MBE
Naval Attaché in Singapore:
Commander P D Doyne-Ditmas, MBE
Naval Attaché in Stockholm:
Commander G Bateman
Naval Attaché in Tokyo:
Captain J A Boyd
Naval Attaché in Warsaw:
Lieutenant Colonel P R P Swanson, MBE
Naval Attaché in Washington:
Commodore D J Anthony, MBE
Defence Attaché in Wellington:
Captain D A Wines

Bases

Northwood (*Warrior*); C-in-C Fleet; FO Submarines
Portsmouth; C-in-C Navhome; HQ Royal Marines; FO Surface Flotillas
Devonport; FO Sea Training
Faslane; FO Scotland, Northern England and Northern Ireland
Gibraltar; CBF Gibraltar

Personnel

2000:
(a) Regulars: RN 35,833 (6,884 officers)
                RM 6,725 (682 officers)
(b) Volunteer Reserves: RN 3,121 (958 officers)
                RM 913 (81 officers)

Strength of the Fleet

Type	Active (Reserve)	Building (Projected)
SSBNs	4	—
Submarines—Attack	12	3 (2)
Aircraft Carriers	2 (1)	(2)
Destroyers	11	(12)
Frigates	20	2
Assault Ships (LPD)	1	2
Helicopter Carriers (LPH)	1	—
LSLs (RFA)	5	(2)
Offshore Patrol Vessels	7	—
Patrol/Training Craft	33	—
Minehunters/Minesweepers	11	—
Minehunters	10	2
Repair/Maintenance Ships (RFA)	1	—
Survey Ships	6	2
Antarctic Patrol Ships	1	—
Large Fleet Tankers (RFA)	2	2
Support Tankers (RFA)	4	—
Small Fleet Tankers (RFA)	3	—
Aviation Training Ships (RFA)	1	—
Fleet Replenishment Ships (RFA)	4	—
Transport Ro-ro (RFR)	2	(6)

Mercantile Marine

Lloyd's Register of Shipping:
1,765 vessels of 10,677,594 tons gross

DELETIONS

Destroyers

1999   *Birmingham*

Frigates

1997   *Battleaxe* (to Brazil)
1999   *London, Boxer, Beaver, Brave*

Amphibious Forces

1999   *Arakan, Ardennes* (both Army), *Intrepid*

Mine Warfare Forces

1998   *Blackwater, Itchen, Spey, Arun* (all to Brazil)
2000   *Bicester* (to Greece)
2001   *Berkeley* (to Greece)

Patrol Forces

1997   *Peacock, Plover, Starling* (all to Philippines)
1999   *Orkney*

Auxiliaries

1997   *Resource, Britannia, Loyal Watcher, Loyal Chancellor, Watercourse, Mary, Elkstone, Grasmere, Sultan Venturer, Magnet, Beddgelert*
1998   *Northella, Oilman, Lilah, Epworth, Ettrick, Holmwood, Datchet, Appleby, Alnmouth*
1999   *Sea Chieftain* (not completed), *Arrochar, Cairn, Dunster*
2000   *Hambledon, Harlech, Headcorn, Hever, Horning, Lamlash, Lechlade*

Fleet Air Arm Squadrons (see *Shipborne Aircraft* section) on 1 May 2000

F/W Aircraft		Role	Deployment	Squadron no
6	Sea Harrier	FA 2	*Invincible*	800
6	Sea Harrier	FA 2	*Illustrious*	801

F/W Aircraft		Role	Deployment	Squadron no
16	Sea Harrier (FA. Mk 2/T8)	Aircrew Training	Yeovilton, *Heron*	899
13	Jetstream	Aircrew Training	Culdrose, *Seahawk*	750

Helicopters		Role	Deployment	Squadron no
4	Merlin HM Mk 1	ASW/ASUW	Culdrose	700M
8	Merlin HM Mk 1	ASW/ASUW	Culdrose	824
9 {	Sea King AEW 2	Aircrew Training	Culdrose, *Seahawk*	849 HQ
	Sea King AEW 2	AEW	*Invincible*	849 A flight
	Sea King AEW 2	AEW	*Illustrious*	849 B flight
7	Sea King HAS 6	ASW	*Invincible*	814
7	Sea King HAS 6	ASW	*Illustrious*	820
9	Sea King HAS 5/6	ASW	Prestwick, *Gannet*	819
14	Sea King HAS 5/6	Aircrew Training	Culdrose, *Seahawk*	810
10	Sea King HC 4	Commando Assault	Yeovilton, *Heron*	845
10	Sea King HC 4	Commando Assault	Yeovilton, *Heron*	846
9	Sea King HC 4	Aircrew Training/ Special Task	Yeovilton, *Heron*	848

Helicopters		Role	Deployment	Squadron no
5	Sea King HAS. Mk 5	SAR	Culdrose, *Seahawk*	771
6	Sea King HC 4	SAR	Yeovilton, *Heron*	772
38	Lynx HMA. Mk 3/8	ASUW/ASW	Yeovilton, *Heron*	815
12	Lynx HAS. Mk 3	Aircrew Training	Yeovilton, *Heron*	702
6 {	Lynx Mk 7	Commando Support	Yeovilton, *Heron*	847
9	Gazelle AH-1			

Notes: (1) Training and Liaison aircraft not listed under the *Shipborne* or *Land-based Aircraft* sections include Sea Harrier T8, Gazelle HT 2, Jetstream, Falcon 20 (under contract).
(2) FA = Fighter Attack. HMA = Helicopter Medium Attack.
(3) 800 and 801 to RAF Wittering and 899 to RAF Cottesmore in 2003.

PENNANT LIST

Note: Numbers are not displayed on Submarines.

Aircraft Carriers

R 05	Invincible
R 06	Illustrious
R 07	Ark Royal

Destroyers

D 87	Newcastle
D 88	Glasgow
D 89	Exeter
D 90	Southampton
D 91	Nottingham
D 92	Liverpool
D 95	Manchester
D 96	Gloucester
D 97	Edinburgh
D 98	York
D 108	Cardiff

Frigates

F 78	Kent
F 79	Portland (bldg)
F 80	Grafton
F 81	Sutherland
F 82	Somerset
F 83	St Albans (bldg)
F 85	Cumberland
F 86	Campbeltown
F 87	Chatham
F 96	Sheffield
F 98	Coventry
F 99	Cornwall
F 229	Lancaster
F 230	Norfolk
F 231	Argyll
F 233	Marlborough
F 234	Iron Duke
F 235	Monmouth
F 236	Montrose
F 237	Westminster
F 238	Northumberland
F 239	Richmond

Amphibious Warfare Forces

L 10	Fearless
L 12	Ocean
L 14	Albion (bldg)
L 15	Bulwark (bldg)
L 105	Arromanches

L 107	Andalsnes
L 109	Akyab
L 110	Aachen
L 111	Arezzo
L 113	Audemer
L 3004	Sir Bedivere
L 3005	Sir Galahad
L 3027	Sir Geraint
L 3036	Sir Percivale
L 3505	Sir Tristram

Mine Warfare Forces

M 29	Brecon
M 30	Ledbury
M 31	Cattistock
M 32	Cottesmore
M 33	Brocklesby
M 34	Middleton
M 35	Dulverton
M 37	Chiddingfold
M 38	Atherstone
M 39	Hurworth
M 41	Quorn
M 101	Sandown
M 102	Inverness
M 103	Cromer
M 104	Walney
M 105	Bridport
M 106	Penzance
M 107	Pembroke
M 108	Grimsby
M 109	Bangor
M 110	Ramsey
M 111	Blythe (bldg)
M 112	Shoreham (bldg)
M 2011	Orwell (training)

Patrol Forces

P 163	Express
P 164	Explorer
P 165	Example
P 167	Exploit
P 258	Leeds Castle
P 264	Archer
P 265	Dumbarton Castle
P 270	Biter
P 272	Smiter
P 273	Pursuer
P 274	Tracker
P 275	Raider
P 277	Anglesey

P 278	Alderney
P 279	Blazer
P 280	Dasher
P 291	Puncher
P 292	Charger
P 293	Ranger
P 294	Trumpeter
P 297	Guernsey
P 298	Shetland
P 300	Lindisfarne

Survey Ships

H 86	Gleaner
H 130	Roebuck
H 131	Scott
H 138	Herald
H 317	Bulldog
H 319	Beagle

Auxiliaries

A 72	Cameron
A 81	Brambleleaf
A 83	Melton
A 84	Menai
A 87	Meon
A 91	Milford
A 96	Sea Crusader
A 98	Sea Centurion
A 109	Bayleaf
A 110	Orangeleaf
A 111	Oakleaf
A 122	Olwen
A 123	Olna
A 127	Torrent
A 129	Dalmatian
A 132	Diligence
A 135	Argus
A 140	Tornado
A 142	Tormentor
A 147	Frances
A 148	Fiona
A 149	Florence
A 150	Genevieve
A 170	Kitty
A 171	Endurance
A 172	Lesley
A 178	Husky
A 180	Mastiff
A 182	Saluki
A 185	Salmoor
A 186	Salmaster

A 187	Salmaid
A 189	Setter
A 190	Joan
A 191	Bovisand
A 192	Cawsand
A 198	Helen
A 199	Myrtle
A 201	Spaniel
A 205	Norah
A 216	Bee
A 221	Forceful
A 222	Nimble
A 223	Powerful
A 224	Adept
A 225	Bustler
A 226	Capable
A 227	Careful
A 228	Faithful
A 230	Cockchafer
A 231	Dexterous
A 232	Adamant
A 250	Sheepdog
A 253	Ladybird
A 269	Grey Rover
A 271	Gold Rover
A 273	Black Rover
A 280	Newhaven
A 281	Nutbourne
A 282	Netley
A 283	Oban
A 284	Oronsay
A 285	Omagh
A 286	Padstow
A 308	Ilchester
A 309	Instow
A 328	Collie
A 344	Impulse
A 345	Impetus
A 367	Newton
A 368	Warden
A 378	Kinterbury
A 385	Fort Rosalie
A 386	Fort Austin
A 387	Fort Victoria
A 388	Fort George
A 389	Wave Knight (bldg)
A 390	Wave Ruler (bldg)
Y 01	Petard
Y 02	Falconet
Y 21	Oilpress
Y 32	Moorhen
Y 33	Moorfowl

SUBMARINES

VIGILANT

6/1996 / 0053455

Strategic Missile Submarines (SSBN)

4 VANGUARD CLASS (SSBN)

Name	No	Builders	Laid down		Launched		Commissioned	
VANGUARD	S 28	Vickers Shipbuilding & Engineering, Barrow-in-Furness	3 Sep	1986	4 Mar	1992	14 Aug	1993
VICTORIOUS	S 29	Vickers Shipbuilding & Engineering, Barrow-in-Furness	3 Dec	1987	29 Sep	1993	7 Jan	1995
VIGILANT	S 30	Vickers Shipbuilding & Engineering, Barrow-in-Furness	16 Feb	1991	14 Oct	1995	2 Nov	1996
VENGEANCE	S 31	Vickers Shipbuilding & Engineering, Barrow-in-Furness	1 Feb	1993	19 Sep	1998	27 Nov	1999

Displacement, tons: 15,900 dived
Dimensions, feet (metres): 491.8 × 42 × 39.4
  (149.9 × 12.8 × 12)
Main machinery: Nuclear; 1 RR PWR 2; 2 GEC turbines;
  27,500 hp *(20.5 MW)*; 1 shaft; pump jet propulsor; 2 auxiliary
  retractable propulsion motors; 2 WH Allen turbo generators;
  6 MW; 2 Paxman diesel alternators; 2,700 hp *(2 MW)*
Speed, knots: 25 dived
Complement: 135 (14 officers)

Missiles: SLBM: 16 Lockheed Trident 2 (D5) 3-stage solid fuel
  rocket; stellar inertial guidance to 12,000 km *(6,500 n miles)*;
  thermonuclear warhead of up to 8 MIRV of 100-120 kT; cep
  90 m. The D5 can carry up to 12 MIRV but under plans
  announced in November 1993 each submarine carried a
  maximum of 96 warheads (of UK manufacture). This is
  reducing to 48 in 1999. Substrategic low yield nuclear
  warheads introduced in 1996.
Torpedoes: 4—21 in *(533 mm)* tubes. Marconi Spearfish; dual
  purpose; wire-guided; active/passive homing to 26 km *(14 n
  miles)* at 65 kt; or 31.5 km *(17 n miles)* at 50 kt; attack speed
  55 kt; warhead 300 kg directed charge.
Countermeasures: Decoys: 2 SSE Mk 10 launchers for Type
  2066 and 2071 decoys.
ESM: Racal UAP 3; intercept.
Combat data systems: Dowty Sema SMCS.
Weapons control: Dowty tactical control system. SAFS 3 FCS.
Radars: Navigation: Kelvin Hughes Type 1007; I-band.
Sonars: Marconi/Plessey Type 2054 composite multifrequency
  sonar suite includes Marconi/Ferranti Type 2046 towed array,
  Type 2043 hull-mounted active/passive search and Type
  2082 passive intercept and ranging.

Programmes: On 15 July 1980 the decision was made to buy
  the US Trident I (C4) weapon system. On 11 March 1982 it
  was announced that the government had opted for the
  improved Trident II weapon system, with the D5 missile, to be
  deployed in a force of four submarines, in the mid-1990s.
  Vanguard ordered 30 April 1986; *Victorious* 6 October 1987;
  Vigilant 13 November 1990 and *Vengeance* 7 July 1992. The
  original programme anticipated ordering one per year for the
  first three years so there has been much stretching out of the
  building programme.
Structure: Refit and recore interval is anticipated at eight to nine
  years. The outer surface of the submarine is covered with
  conformal anechoic noise reduction coatings. The limits
  placed on warhead numbers leaves spare capacity within the
  Trident system. This capacity is used for a non-strategic
  warhead variant which has been available since 1996. Fitted
  with Pilkington Optronics CK 51 search and CH 91 attack
  periscopes.
Operational: Three successful submerged launched firings of the
  D5 missile from USS *Tennessee* in December 1989 and the US
  missile was first deployed operationally in March 1990.
  Vanguard started sea trials in October 1992; the first UK
  missile firing was on 26 May 1994 and the first operational
  patrol early in 1995. At least one SSBN has been at immediate
  readiness to fire ballistic missiles since 1969, but as a result of
  the Strategic Defence Review in 1998, readiness to fire has
  been relaxed 'to days rather than minutes'. Plans to phase out

VENGEANCE   9/1999*, BAE Systems / 0075768

the two crew system have been cancelled. Submarines on
patrol can be given secondary tasks without compromising
security.

Opinion: The intention not to use the full capacity of the Trident
system in the present calmer international strategic deterrent
climate, has allowed the development of a number of substrategic options. At the same time the option remains
available to increase the strategic weapon load at some time in

the future, should the threat once again merit a greater
capability. The US Navy reported firing a D5 missile in October
1993 to test the feasibility of increasing accuracy by the use of
GPS navigational hardware mounted on the missile. This is a
step towards the aim of developing a conventional kinetic
energy weapon. The UK Government has said it has no plans to
deploy conventional warheads on Trident.

UPDATED

VENGEANCE   6/1999*, A Sharma / 0075769

VICTORIOUS

Attack Submarines (SSN)

7 TRAFALGAR CLASS (SSN)

Name	No	Builders	Laid down		Launched		Commissioned	
TRAFALGAR	S 107	Vickers Shipbuilding & Engineering, Barrow-in-Furness	25 Apr	1979	1 July	1981	27 May	1983
TURBULENT	S 87	Vickers Shipbuilding & Engineering, Barrow-in-Furness	8 May	1980	1 Dec	1982	28 Apr	1984
TIRELESS	S 88	Vickers Shipbuilding & Engineering, Barrow-in-Furness	6 June	1981	17 Mar	1984	5 Oct	1985
TORBAY	S 90	Vickers Shipbuilding & Engineering, Barrow-in-Furness	3 Dec	1982	8 Mar	1985	7 Feb	1987
TRENCHANT	S 91	Vickers Shipbuilding & Engineering, Barrow-in-Furness	28 Oct	1985	3 Nov	1986	14 Jan	1989
TALENT	S 92	Vickers Shipbuilding & Engineering, Barrow-in-Furness	13 May	1986	15 Apr	1988	12 May	1990
TRIUMPH	S 93	Vickers Shipbuilding & Engineering, Barrow-in-Furness	2 Feb	1987	16 Feb	1991	12 Oct	1991

Displacement, tons: 4,740 surfaced; 5,208 dived
Dimensions, feet (metres): 280.1 × 32.1 × 31.2
(85.4 × 9.8 × 9.5)
Main machinery: Nuclear; 1 RR PWR 1; 2 GEC turbines; 15,000 hp *(11.2 MW)*; 1 shaft; pump jet propulsor; 2 WH Allen turbo generators; 3.2 MW; 2 Paxman diesel alternators; 2,800 hp *(2.09 MW)*; 1 motor for emergency drive; 1 auxiliary retractable prop
Speed, knots: 32 dived
Complement: 130 (18 officers)

Missiles: SLCM: Hughes Tomahawk Block IIIC; Tercom aided inertial navigation system with GPS back-up to 1,700 km *(918 n miles)* at 0.7 Mach; warhead 318 kg shaped charge or submunitions. Being fitted to all from 1999.
SSM: McDonnell Douglas UGM-84B Sub Harpoon Block 1C; active radar homing to 130 km *(70 n miles)* at 0.9 Mach; warhead 227 kg.
Torpedoes: 5—21 in *(533 mm)* bow tubes. Marconi Spearfish; wire-guided; active/passive homing to 26 km *(14 n miles)* at 65 kt; or 31.5 km *(17 n miles)* at 50 kt; attack speed 55 kt; warhead 300 kg directed charge. Marconi Tigerfish Mk 24 Mod 2; wire-guided; active/passive homing to 13 km *(7 n miles)* at 35 kt active; 29 km *(15.7 n miles)* at 24 kt passive; warhead 134 kg; 20 reloads.

Mines: Can be carried in lieu of torpedoes.
Countermeasures: Decoys: 2 SSE Mk 8 launchers. Type 2066 and 2071 torpedo decoys.
ESM: Racal UAP; passive intercept.
Combat data systems: Ferranti/Gresham/Dowty DCB/DCG or Dowty Sema SMCS tactical data handling system. BAeSEMA Link 11 being fitted.
Weapons control: Dowty tactical control system.
Radars: Navigation: Kelvin Hughes Type 1007; I-band.
Sonars: Marconi 2072; hull-mounted; flank array; passive; low frequency.
Plessey Type 2020 or Marconi/Plessey 2074 or Ferranti/ Thomson Sintra 2076 (see *Modernisation*); hull-mounted; passive/active search and attack; low frequency.
Ferranti Type 2046; towed array; passive search; very low frequency.
Thomson Sintra Type 2019 PARIS or THORN EMI 2082; passive intercept and ranging.
Marconi Type 2077; short-range classification; active; high frequency.

Programmes: *Trafalgar* ordered 7 April 1977; *Turbulent* 28 July 1978; *Tireless* 5 July 1979; *Torbay* 26 June 1981; *Trenchant* 22 March 1983; *Talent* 10 September 1984; *Triumph* 3 January 1986.

Modernisation: All being updated with Type 2076 sonar systems, integrated with SMCS and countermeasures. Sonar 2076 is to replace 2074 and 2046. This update also includes Marconi Type 2077, short-range classification sonar. Tomahawk capability is being progressively fitted and started with *Triumph* and *Trafalgar* in 2000. *Trafalgar* completed first refuel in December 1995 with SMCS and Spearfish. *Turbulent* refuelled by mid-1997 with sonar 2074, SMCS and Spearfish. *Tireless* completed modernisation and refuelling in January 1999, followed by *Torbay* by February 2001. Link 11 is being fitted to all. Non-hull penetrating optronic mast fitted in *Trenchant* for trials in 1998. Dry deck shelters may be carried from 2000.
Structure: The pressure hull and outer surfaces are covered with conformal anechoic noise reduction coatings. Retractable forward hydroplanes and strengthened fins for under ice operations. Diving depth in excess of 300 m *(985 ft)*. Fitted with Pilkington Optronics CK 34 search and CH 84 or CM 010 attack optronic periscopes.
Operational: *Trafalgar* was the trials submarine for Spearfish which started full production in 1992 and was first embarked operationally in *Trenchant* in early 1994. All of the class belong to the Second Submarine Squadron based at Devonport. Two are usually in refit.

UPDATED

TALENT
7/1999*, B Sullivan / 0075765

TRAFALGAR
4/1999* / 0075767

TRENCHANT   *7/1998* / 0053185

5 SWIFTSURE CLASS (SSN)

Name	No	Builders	Laid down		Launched		Commissioned	
SOVEREIGN	S 108	Vickers Shipbuilding & Engineering, Barrow-in-Furness	18 Sep	1970	17 Feb	1973	11 July	1974
SUPERB	S 109	Vickers Shipbuilding & Engineering, Barrow-in-Furness	16 Mar	1972	30 Nov	1974	13 Nov	1976
SCEPTRE	S 104	Vickers Shipbuilding & Engineering, Barrow-in-Furness	19 Feb	1974	20 Nov	1976	14 Feb	1978
SPARTAN	S 105	Vickers Shipbuilding & Engineering, Barrow-in-Furness	26 Apr	1976	7 Apr	1978	22 Sep	1979
SPLENDID	S 106	Vickers Shipbuilding & Engineering, Barrow-in-Furness	23 Nov	1977	5 Oct	1979	21 Mar	1981

Displacement, tons: 4,000 light; 4,400 standard; 4,900 dived
Dimensions, feet (metres): 272 × 32.3 × 28
(82.9 × 9.8 × 8.5)
Main machinery: Nuclear; 1 RR PWR 1; 2 GEC turbines; 15,000 hp *(11.2 MW)*; 1 shaft; pump jet propulsor; 2 WH Allen turbo generators; 3.6 MW; 1 Paxman diesel alternator; 1,900 hp *(1.42 MW)*; 1 motor for emergency drive; 1 auxiliary retractable prop
Speed, knots: 30+ dived
Complement: 116 (13 officers)

Missiles: SLCM: Hughes Tomahawk Block III; Tercom aided inertial navigation system with GPS back-up to 1,700 km *(918 n miles)* at 0.7 Mach; warhead 318 kg shaped charge or submunitions. Being fitted in all.
SSM: McDonnell Douglas UGM-84B Sub Harpoon; active radar homing to 130 km *(70 n miles)* at 0.9 Mach; warhead 227 kg.
Torpedoes: 5—21 in *(533 mm)* bow tubes. Marconi Spearfish; wire-guided; active/passive homing to 26 km *(14 n miles)* at 65 kt; or 31.5 km *(17 n miles)* at 50 kt; attack speed 55 kt; warhead 300 kg directed charge. Marconi Tigerfish Mk 24 Mod 2; wire-guided; active/passive homing to 13 km *(7 n miles)* at 35 kt active; 29 km *(15.7 n miles)* at 24 kt passive; warhead 134 kg; 20 reloads.
Mines: Can be carried in lieu of torpedoes.
Countermeasures: Decoys: 2 SSE Mk 6 launchers. Type 2066 and 2071 torpedo decoys.
ESM: Racal UAP; passive intercept.
Combat data systems: Ferranti/Gresham/Dowty DCB/DCG or Dowty Sema SMCS tactical data handling system. Link 11 can be fitted.
Radars: Navigation: Kelvin Hughes Type 1007; I-band.
Sonars: Marconi/Plessey Type 2074; hull-mounted; active/passive search and attack; low frequency.
Marconi 2072; flank array; passive; low frequency.
Ferranti Type 2046; towed array; passive search; very low frequency.
Thomson Sintra Type 2019 PARIS or THORN EMI 2082; passive intercept and ranging.
Marconi Type 2077; short-range classification; active; high frequency.

SUPERB   *8/1999 *, B Sullivan /* 0075758

Programmes: *Sovereign* ordered 16 May 1969; *Superb,* 20 May 1970; *Sceptre,* 1 November 1971; *Spartan,* 7 February 1973; *Splendid,* 26 May 1976.
Modernisation: *Sceptre* finished refit in 1987, *Spartan* in 1989, *Splendid* in 1993, *Sovereign* in 1997 with full tactical weapons system upgrade and Spearfish, and *Superb* in April 1998, each fitted with a PWR 1 Core Z giving a 12 year life cycle although refits/refuel cycles will remain at eight to nine year intervals. *Sceptre* started refit again in early 1997 and is expected to complete in June 2000. Other improvements included acoustic elastomeric tiles, sonar processing equipment and improved decoys. Marconi Type 2077, short-range classification sonar is also fitted. Marconi/Plessey 2074 sonar has replaced 2020 and 2001. In 1994 *Spartan* had a trial non-acoustic sensor fitted to the port side of the fin. First full

warload of Tomahawk missiles in *Splendid,* with first live firing in October 1998; *Spartan* fitted in 1999.
Structure: The pressure hull in the 'Swiftsure' class maintains its diameter for much greater length than previous classes. Control gear by MacTaggart, Scott & Co Ltd for: attack and search periscopes, snort induction and exhaust, radar and ESM masts. The forward hydroplanes house within the casing. Fitted with Pilkington Optronics CK 33 search and CH 83 attack electro-optic periscopes. Link 11 can be fitted.
Operational: All belong to the First Submarine Squadron based at Faslane. As a result of budget cuts *Swiftsure* paid off in 1992 after less than 20 years' service, *Splendid* is planned to go in 2003.

UPDATED

SPARTAN   *9/1998, Maritime Photographic /* 0053186

SPLENDID   *5/1997, John Brodie /* 0016219

0 + 3 (2) ASTUTE CLASS (SSN)

Name	No	Builders	Laid down	Launched	Commissioned
ASTUTE	S 20	BAE Systems, Barrow	Oct 1999	Sep 2004	June 2005
AMBUSH	S 21	BAE Systems, Barrow	2001	2005	2007
ARTFUL	S 22	BAE Systems, Barrow	2002	2006	2008

Displacement, tons: 6,500 surfaced; 7,200 dived
Dimensions, feet (metres): 318.2 × 35.1 × 32.8
   (97 × 10.7 × 10)
Main machinery: Nuclear; 1 RR PWR 2; 2 Alsthom turbines; 1 shaft; pump jet propulsor; 2 turbo generators; 2 diesel alternators; 2 motors for emergency drive; 1 auxiliary retractable prop
Speed, knots: 29 dived
Complement: 98 (12 officers) plus 12 spare

Missiles: SLCM: Tomahawk.
SSM: Sub Harpoon.

Torpedoes: 6—21 in *(533 mm)* tubes for Tomahawk, Sub Harpoon and Spearfish torpedoes. Total of 38 weapons.
Mines: In lieu of torpedoes.
Countermeasures: Decoys. ESM: Racal UAP 4; intercept.
Combat data systems: BAeSEMA SMCS tactical data handling system. Links 11/16.
Radars: Navigation: I-band.
Sonars: Thomson Marconi 2076 integrated suite with reelable towed array.

Programmes: Invitations to tender issued on 14 July 1994 to build three of the class with an option on two more. GEC-

Marconi selected as prime contractor in December 1995. Contract to start building the first three placed on 17 March 1997. Option for two more was confirmed in mid-1998. First steel cut late 1999.
Structure: An evolution of the Trafalgar design with increased weapon load and reduced radiated noise but with overall performance similar to Trafalgar after full modernisation. The fin is slightly longer and there are two Pilkington Optronics CM010 non-hull-penetrating periscopes.
Operational: Nuclear refuelling will not be necessary in the lifetime of the submarine.

UPDATED

ASTUTE (computer graphic)   *1999*, BAE Systems* / 0075757

AIRCRAFT CARRIERS

Note: Combat design study awarded to EDS Defence in July 1995 for prefeasibility studies for two replacement carriers. Invitation to Tender for an initial assessment issued in January 1999. Prime contractor to be selected in 2004 with first steel cut in 2005 and first of class trials in 2010. Design options include short take off and vertical landing (STOVL), short take off and arrested recovery (STOBAR) and a conventional angled deck design (CTOL). Up to 50 aircraft are to be carried.

INVINCIBLE   *3/2000*, Maritime Photographic* / 0084418

3 INVINCIBLE CLASS (CVS)

Name	No	Builders	Laid down	Launched	Commissioned
INVINCIBLE	R 05	Vickers Shipbuilding & Engineering, Barrow-in-Furness	20 July 1973	3 May 1977	11 July 1980
ILLUSTRIOUS	R 06	Swan Hunter Shipbuilders, Wallsend	7 Oct 1976	1 Dec 1978	20 June 1982
ARK ROYAL	R 07	Swan Hunter Shipbuilders, Wallsend	14 Dec 1978	2 June 1981	1 Nov 1985

Displacement, tons: 20,600 full load
Dimensions, feet (metres): 685.8 oa; 632 wl × 118 oa; 90 wl × 26 (screws) *(209.1; 192.6 × 36; 27.5 × 8)*
Flight deck, feet (metres): 550 × 44.3 *(167.8 × 13.5)*
Main machinery: COGAG; 4 RR Olympus TM3B gas turbines; 97,200 hp *(72.5 MW)* sustained; 2 shafts
Speed, knots: 28. **Range, miles:** 7,000 at 19 kt
Complement: 685 (60 officers) plus 366 (80 officers) aircrew plus up to 600 marines

Guns: 3 Signaal/General Electric 30 mm 7-barrelled Gatling Goalkeeper **❶**; 4,200 rds/min to 1.5 km.
2 Oerlikon/BMARC 20 mm GAM-BO1 **❷**.
Countermeasures: Decoys: Outfit DLJ; 8 Sea Gnat 6-barrelled 130 mm/102 mm dispensers **❸**. Prairie Masker noise suppression system.
ESM: Racal Thorn UAT **❹**; intercept.
ECM: THORN EMI Type 675(2); jammer.
Combat data systems: ADAWS 10 (with ADIMP) action data automation; Links 10, 11, 14 and Siemens Plessey JTIDS Link 16. JMCIS. Matra Marconi SCOT 2D SATCOM **❺**.
Weapons control: GWS 30 Mod 2 for SAM.
Radars: Air search: Marconi/Signaal Type 1022 **❻**; D-band.
Surface search: Plessey Type 996 **❼**; E/F-band.
Navigation: 2 Kelvin Hughes Type 1007; I-band.
Fire control: 2 Marconi Type 909(1) (R 06) **❽**; I/J-band.
Sonars: Plessey Type 2016; hull-mounted; active search and attack; medium frequency.

Fixed-wing aircraft: 8 BAe Sea Harrier FA 2 **❾** and 8 Harrier GR 7.

INVINCIBLE

Helicopters: 2 Westland Sea King HAS 6 **❿** or Merlin HM Mk 1; 4 Westland Sea King AEW 2.

Programmes: The first of class, the result of many compromises, was ordered from Vickers on 17 April 1973. The order for the second ship was placed on 14 May 1976, the third in December 1978.

Modernisation: In January 1989 R 05 completed modernisation which included a 12° ski ramp, space and support facilities for at least 21 aircraft, three Goalkeeper systems, Sonar 2016, Sea Gnat decoys, 996 radar, Flag and Command facilities and accommodation for an additional 120 aircrew and Flag Staff. In February 1994 R 06 completed a similar modernisation to bring her to the same standard, but with additional command and weapon system improvements. In addition R 06 has a modified main mast and sponsons for chaff launchers. Ski ramp has been increased to 13°. Both ships are equipped as Joint Force HQ ships. In 1998 R 06 was modified to operate Harrier GR 7 aircraft. This included the removal of Sea Dart, increasing the flight deck area by 7 per cent, (23 × 18 m) and fitting GR 7 support facilities. All of the above modifications were done in R 05 by April 2000, and are being done to R 07 from May 1999 to May 2001. The Type 909 radars are being removed.
Structure: In 1976-77 an amendment was incorporated to allow for the transport and landing of an RM Commando. The forward end of the flight deck (ski ramp) allows STOVL aircraft of greater all-up weight to operate more efficiently.
Operational: The role of this class, apart from its primary task of providing a command, control and communications facility, is the operation of both helicopters and STOVL aircraft. Air Force Harrier GR. Mk 7s are embarked for operations requiring ground attack aircraft. Provision has been made for sufficiently large lifts and hangars to accommodate the next generation of both these aircraft. The aircraft numbers shown are for the combined shore support operational role. Only two of the class are fully operational at any one time, the third either being in refit, working-up or on standby.

ILLUSTRIOUS

UPDATED

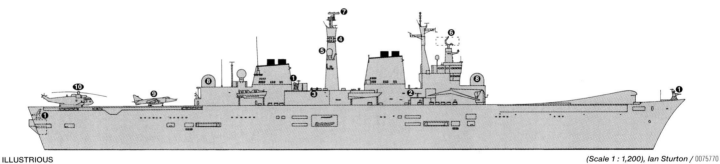

ILLUSTRIOUS

ILLUSTRIOUS

ILLUSTRIOUS

ILLUSTRIOUS

7/1999 * / 0075774

DESTROYERS

Note: *Bristol* (D 23) is an immobile tender used for training in Portsmouth Harbour.

11 TYPE 42 CLASS (DDG)

Batch 1

Name	No	Builders	Laid down		Launched		Commissioned	
NEWCASTLE	D 87	Swan Hunter Shipbuilders, Wallsend-on-Tyne	21 Feb	1973	24 Apr	1975	23 Mar	1978
GLASGOW	D 88	Swan Hunter Shipbuilders, Wallsend-on-Tyne	16 Apr	1974	14 Apr	1976	24 May	1979
CARDIFF	D 108	Vickers Shipbuilding & Engineering, Barrow-in-Furness	6 Nov	1972	22 Feb	1974	24 Sep	1979

Batch 2

Name	No	Builders	Laid down		Launched		Commissioned	
EXETER	D 89	Swan Hunter Shipbuilders, Wallsend-on-Tyne	22 July	1976	25 Apr	1978	19 Sep	1980
SOUTHAMPTON	D 90	Vosper Thornycroft, Woolston	21 Oct	1976	29 Jan	1979	31 Oct	1981
NOTTINGHAM	D 91	Vosper Thornycroft, Woolston	6 Feb	1978	18 Feb	1980	14 Apr	1983
LIVERPOOL	D 92	Cammell Laird, Birkenhead	5 July	1978	25 Sep	1980	1 July	1982

Displacement, tons: 3,500 standard; 4,100 full load
Dimensions, feet (metres): 412 oa; 392 wl × 47 × 19 (screws) *(125; 119.5 × 14.3 × 5.8)*
Main machinery: COGOG; 2 RR Olympus TM3B gas turbines; 50,000 hp *(37.3 MW)* sustained; 2 RR Tyne RM1C gas turbines (cruising); 9,900 hp *(7.4 MW)* sustained; 2 shafts; cp props
Speed, knots: 29. **Range, miles:** 4,000 at 18 kt
Complement: 253 (24 officers) (accommodation for 312)

Missiles: SAM: British Aerospace Sea Dart twin launcher ❶; radar/semi-active radar guidance to 40 km *(21.5 n miles)* at 2 Mach; height envelope 100-18,300 m *(328-60,042 ft)*; 22 missiles; limited anti-ship capability.
Guns: 1 Vickers 4.5 in *(114 mm)*/55 Mk 8 ❷; 25 rds/min to 22 km *(11.9 n miles)* anti-surface; 6 km *(3.3 n miles)* anti-aircraft; weight of shell 21 kg.
2 or 4 Oerlikon/BMARC 20 mm GAM-BO1 ❸ and ❹; 1,000 rds/min to 2 km.
2 Oerlikon 20 mm Mk 7A ❹ (in those with only 2 GAM-BO1); 800 rds/min to 2 km; weight of shell 0.24 kg.
2 General Electric/General Dynamics 20 mm Vulcan Phalanx Mk 15 ❺; 6 barrels per launcher; 3,000 rds/min combined to 1.5 km.
Torpedoes: 4—324 mm Plessey STWS Mk 3 (2 twin) tubes ❻. Fitted for, but not with.

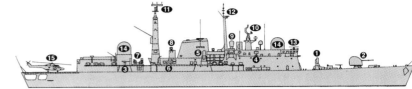

NOTTINGHAM

(Scale 1 : 1,200), Ian Sturton / 0075777

Countermeasures: Decoys: Outfit DLB; 4 Sea Gnat 130 mm/102 mm 6-barrelled launchers ❼. Barricade IR decoy launchers. Irvin DLF 2/3 offboard decoys.
Graseby Type 182 or SLQ-25A; towed torpedo decoy.
ESM: MEL UAA-2 or Racal Thorn UAT 1; intercept.
ECM: Type 675(2) (Batch 2) ❽; jammer.
Combat data systems: ADAWS 7 or 8 action data automation. 2 Matra Marconi SCOT 1C SATCOMs ❾; Links 10, 11 and 14. JTIDS. Link 16 in due course.
Weapons control: GWS 30 Mod 2; GSA 1 secondary system. 2 Radamec 2100 series optronic surveillance directors. Radamec 1000N optronic director (can be fitted on bridge roof).

Radars: Air search: Marconi/Signaal Type 1022 ❿; D-band.
Air/surface search: Plessey Type 996 ⓫; E/F-band.
Navigation: Kelvin Hughes Type 1007 ⓬; I-band and Racal Decca Type 1008 ⓭; E/F-band.
Fire control: 2 Marconi Type 909 ⓮; or 9091; I/J-band.
Sonars: Ferranti/Thomson Type 2050 or Plessey Type 2016; hull-mounted; active search and attack; medium frequency.

Helicopters: 1 Westland Lynx HMA 3/8 ⓯.

GLASGOW

7/1999*, Sattler/Steele / 0075776

EXETER

7/1999* / 0075778

Batch 3

Name	No	Builders	Laid down	Launched	Commissioned
MANCHESTER	D 95	Vickers Shipbuilding & Engineering, Barrow-in-Furness	19 May 1978	24 Nov 1980	16 Dec 1982
GLOUCESTER	D 96	Vosper Thornycroft, Woolston	29 Oct 1979	2 Nov 1982	11 Sep 1985
EDINBURGH	D 97	Cammell Laird, Birkenhead	8 Sep 1980	14 Apr 1983	17 Dec 1985
YORK	D 98	Swan Hunter Shipbuilders, Wallsend-on-Tyne	18 Jan 1980	21 June 1982	9 Aug 1985

Displacement, tons: 3,500 standard; 4,675 full load
Dimensions, feet (metres): 462.8 oa; 434 wl × 49 × 19 (screws) *(141.1; 132.3 × 14.9 × 5.8)*
Main machinery: COGOG; 2 RR Olympus TM3B gas turbines; 43,000 hp *(32 MW)* sustained; 2 RR Tyne RM1C gas turbines (cruising); 10,680 hp *(8 MW)* sustained; 2 shafts; cp props
Speed, knots: 30+. **Range, miles:** 4,000 at 18 kt
Complement: 301 (26 officers)

Missiles: SAM: British Aerospace Sea Dart twin launcher ❶; radar/semi-active radar guidance to 40 km *(21 n miles)*; warhead HE; 22 missiles; limited anti-ship capability.
Guns: 1 Vickers 4.5 in *(114 mm)*/55 Mk 8 ❷; 25 rds/min to 22 km *(11.9 n miles)* anti-surface; 6 km *(3.3 n miles)* anti-aircraft; weight of shell 21 kg.
2 or 4 Oerlikon/BMARC 20 mm GAM-BO1 ❸; 1,000 rds/min to 2 km.
2 Oerlikon 20 mm Mk 7A ❹ (in those with only 2 GAM-BO1); 50° elevation; 800 rds/min to 2 km; weight of shell 0.24 kg.
2 General Electric/General Dynamics 20 mm Vulcan Phalanx Mk 15 ❺; 6 barrels per launcher; 3,000 rds/min combined to 1.5 km.

Torpedoes: 6—324 mm STWS Mk 2 (2 triple) tubes ❻. Marconi Stingray; active/passive homing to 11 km *(5.9 n miles)* at 45 kt; warhead 35 kg shaped charge.
Countermeasures: Outfit DLB; 4 Sea Gnat 130 mm/102 mm 6-barrelled launchers ❼. DLF-3 offboard decoys. Graseby Type 182 or SLQ-25A; towed torpedo decoy.
ESM: Racal Thorn UAT; intercept.
ECM: Type 675(2) ❽; jammer.
Combat data systems: ADAWS 8 (ADIMP) action data automation. Matra Marconi SCOT 1C SATCOM ❾; Links 10, 11 and 14. JTIDS. Link 16.
Weapons control: GWS 30 Mod 2 (for SAM); GSA 1 secondary system. 2 Radamec 2100 series optronic surveillance directors.
Radars: Air search: Marconi/Signaal Type 1022 ❿; D-band.
Air/surface search: Plessey Type 996 ⓫; E/F-band.
Navigation: Kelvin Hughes Type 1007 ⓬; I-band and Racal Decca Type 1008 ⓭; E/F-band.
Fire control: 2 Marconi Type 909 or 909 Mod 1 ⓮; I/J-band.
Sonars: Ferranti/Thomson Type 2050 or Plessey Type 2016; hull-mounted; active search and attack.

Helicopters: 1 Westland Lynx HMA 3/8 ⓯.

Batches 1, 2 and 3

Programmes: Designed to provide area air defence for a task force. The completion of later ships was delayed to allow for some modifications resulting from experience in the Falklands' campaign (1982).
Modernisation: Vulcan Phalanx replaced 30 mm guns 1987-89. All have Plessey Type 996 radar in place of Type 992, and Type 909(1) fire-control radars with improved Tx/Rx circuits. STWS Mk 3 can be fitted in Batch 2. D 97 had a partial conversion completing in 1990 with the Phalanx moved forward and a protective visor fitted around the bow of the ship. D 97 reverted to the standard armament in late 1994. All Batch 2 and 3 ships have had a command system update. Sea Gnat decoy launchers can fire a variety of devices. JTIDS (Link 16) fitted in D 97 in 1996, followed by all Batch 3 by 1999. Batch 2 ships being fitted from 1998.
Structure: All have two pairs of stabilisers and twin rudders. Advantages of gas-turbine propulsion include ability to reach maximum speed with great rapidity, reduction in space and weight and 25 per cent reduction in technical manpower. The stretched Batch 3 have been fitted with a strengthening beam on each side which increases displacement by 50 tons and width by 2 ft.
Operational: The helicopter carries the Sea Skua air-to-surface weapon for use against lightly defended surface ship targets. Ships may be fitted with DEC laser dazzle sight, additional decoy flare launchers and optronic surveillance sights on operational deployments.

UPDATED

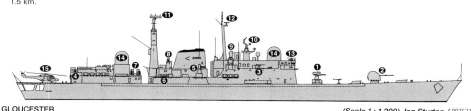

GLOUCESTER

(Scale 1 : 1,200), Ian Sturton / 0075779

EDINBURGH

3/2000, Maritime Photographic / 0084420*

MANCHESTER

10/1999, H M Steele / 0075780*

0 + (12) D CLASS (TYPE 45) (DDG)

Name	No	Builders	Laid down	Launched	Commissioned
DEFENDER (?)	—	BAE Systems Marine (YSL), Scotstoun	2002	2005	2007

DEFENDER   (Scale 1 : 1,200), Ian Sturton / 0084421

Displacement, tons: 6,900 full load
Dimensions, feet (metres): 494.3 oa; 462.9 wl × 65.2 × 17.4
  (150.7; 141.1 × 19.9 × 5.3)
Main machinery: Integrated Electric Propulsion; 2 RR WR-21 gas
  turbine alternators; 42 MW; 2 diesel generators; 4 MW; 2
  motors; 40 MW; 2 shafts; cp props
Speed, knots: 29. **Range, miles:** 7,000 at 18 kt
Complement: 190 plus 45 spare

Missiles: SSM: 8 Harpoon (2 quad) ❶.
  SAM: 6 DCN Sylver A 50 VLS ❷ PAAMS (principal anti-air missile
  system); 16 Aster 15 and 32 Aster 30 weapons or
  combination.
Guns: 1 Vickers 4.5 in (114 mm)/55 Mk 8 Mod 1 ❸.
  2—20 mm Vulcan Phalanx ❹. 2—30 mm ❺.
Torpedoes: 4 (2 twin) fixed launchers ❻. Stingray torpedoes.
Countermeasures: Decoys: 4 chaff/IR flare launchers ❼. SSTD
  torpedo defence system.
  ESM/ECM ❽. IR detector.
Combat data systems: BAE Systems; Links 11, 16 STDL and 22.
  SATCOM ❾.
Weapons control: GSA 8/GPEOD WCS.
Radars: Air/surface search: Signaal/Marconi S1850M ❿;
  D-band.
  Surveillance/fire control: BAE Systems Sampson ⓫; E/F-band;
  multifunction.
  Surface search ⓬. E/F-band.
  Navigation: E/F- and I-band.
Sonars: Ferranti/Thomson Sintra Type 2050; hull-mounted;
  active search and attack; medium frequency.

Helicopters: 1 Merlin HM 1 ⓭ or Lynx HMA 3/8.

Programmes: The ship started as a three-nation project for a new
  air defence ship with Italy, France and UK signing a
  Memorandum of Understanding on 11 July 1994. On 25 April
  1999, the UK withdrew from the project but continues to
  support PAAMS. A national design has replaced Horizon with
  BAE Systems as prime contractor. Shipyard contracts for the
  first batch of two or three ships are planned for early 2001.
  Ship names may include Defender, Daring, Dorsetshire, Dover,
  Dauntless, Dragon, Demon, Duncan, Dreadnought, Diamond,
  Despatch and Decoy. The original first of class in-service date
  for Horizon has slipped from 2002 to 2007 for the 'D' class.
Structure: Some details are still speculative but the urgency to
  get these ships built will mean incremental changes being
  made to later units of the class possibly including a 155 mm
  gun, and improved CIWS. OTC facilities are to be included.

UPDATED

DEFENDER (computer graphic)   2000*, BAE Systems / 0084480

DEFENDER (computer graphic)   2000*, BAE Systems / 0084481

FRIGATES

Notes: (1) The Defence Evaluation and Research Agency (DERA) is building a 1,200 ton trimaran hull for trials in late 2000. Details in the *Government Agency* section.
(2) Project Definition assessment starts mid-2000 for a Future Surface Combatant (FSC) of about 9,000 tons. Twenty ships are required with a first in-service date of 2012.

2 BROADSWORD CLASS (TYPE 22 BATCH 2) (FFG)

Name	No	Builders	Laid down	Launched	Commissioned
SHEFFIELD	F 96	Swan Hunter Shipbuilders, Wallsend-on-Tyne	29 Mar 1984	26 Mar 1986	26 July 1988
COVENTRY	F 98	Swan Hunter Shipbuilders, Wallsend-on-Tyne	29 Mar 1984	8 Apr 1986	14 Oct 1988

Displacement, tons: 4,100 standard; 4,800 full load
Dimensions, feet (metres): 480.5 × 48.5 × 21
(146.5 × 14.8 × 6.4)
Main machinery: COGOG; 2 RR Olympus TM3B gas turbines; 50,000 hp *(37.3 MW)* sustained; 2 RR Tyne RM1C gas turbines; 9,900 hp *(7.4 MW)* sustained; 2 shafts; acbLIPS; cp props
Speed, knots: 30; 18 on Tynes
Range, miles: 4,500 at 18 kt on Tynes
Complement: 273 (30 officers) plus 23 spare

Missiles: SSM: 4 Aerospatiale MM 38 Exocet ❶; inertial cruise; active radar homing to 42 km *(23 n miles)* at 0.9 Mach; warhead 165 kg; sea-skimmer.
SAM: 2 British Aerospace Seawolf GWS 25 Mod 3 ❷; command line of sight with 2 channel radar tracking to 5 km *(2.7 n miles)* at 2+ Mach; warhead 14 kg; 32 rounds.
Guns: 4 Oerlikon/BMARC GCM-A03 30 mm/75 (2 twin) ❸; 650 rds/min to 10 km *(5.5 n miles)*; weight of shell 0.36 kg.
2 Oerlikon/BMARC 20 mm GAM-BO1 ❹; 1,000 rds/min to 2 km.
Torpedoes: 6—324 mm Plessey STWS Mk 2 (2 triple) tubes ❺. Marconi Stingray; active/passive homing to 11 km *(5.9 n miles)* at 45 kt; warhead 35 kg shaped charge.
Countermeasures: Decoys: Outfit DCH; 4 Sea Gnat 130 mm/102 mm 6-barrelled fixed launchers ❻. Graseby Type 182; towed torpedo decoy.
ESM: MEL UAA-2 or Racal Thorn UAT; intercept.
ECM: Type 670; jammers.
Combat data systems: Ferranti CACS 5; Links 11 and 14. Matra Marconi SCOT 1C SATCOM ❼. Marisat.
Weapons control: GWS 25 Mod 3 (for SAM); GWS 50.
Radars: Air/surface search: Marconi Type 968 ❽; D/E-band.
Navigation: Kelvin Hughes Type 1007; I-band.
Fire control: 2 Marconi Type 911 ❾; I/Ku-band (for Seawolf).
Sonars: Ferranti/Thomson Sintra Type 2050; hull-mounted; search and attack.
Dowty Type 2031Z; towed array; passive search; very low frequency.

Helicopters: 2 Westland Lynx HMA 3/8 ❿; or 1 Westland Sea King HAS 5 or Merlin HM 1.

Programmes: Originally planned as successors to the 'Leander' class. Order for the first of class was placed on 8 February 1974.
Modernisation: Seawolf GWS 25 progressively upgraded. Sonar 2016 replaced by Sonar 2050. Bofors 40 mm/60 have been replaced by Oerlikon 30 mm guns. Sea Gnat is the standard launcher for a variety of distraction and seduction decoys. EDS Command Support System fitted in F 96 in 1997.
Structure: Batch 2 ships were lengthened on build to give more space for EW equipment. Both have enlarged flight decks to take Sea King helicopters.

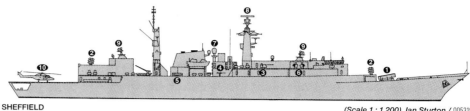

SHEFFIELD

(Scale 1 : 1,200), Ian Sturton / 0053197

COVENTRY

8/1999*, J Cislak / 0075786

Operational: This class is primarily designed for ASW operations and is capable of acting as OTC. One Lynx normally embarked. Ships are fitted with DEC laser dazzle device, and additional EW equipment mounted forward of the foremast, on operational deployments. Both are in the 2nd Frigate Squadron. *Coventry* is planned to pay off in 2001.
Sales: All Batch 1 to Brazil; *Broadsword* 30 June 1995, *Brilliant* and *Brazen* 30 August 1996 and *Battleaxe* 30 April 1997.

UPDATED

SHEFFIELD

7/1999*, B Sullivan / 0075787

14 + 2 DUKE CLASS (TYPE 23) (FFG)

Name	No	Builders	Laid down		Launched		Commissioned	
NORFOLK	F 230	Yarrow Shipbuilders, Glasgow	14 Dec	1985	10 July	1987	1 June	1990
ARGYLL	F 231	Yarrow Shipbuilders, Glasgow	20 Mar	1987	8 Apr	1989	31 May	1991
LANCASTER	F 229 (ex-F 232)	Yarrow Shipbuilders, Glasgow	18 Dec	1987	24 May	1990	1 May	1992
MARLBOROUGH	F 233	Swan Hunter Shipbuilders, Wallsend-on-Tyne	22 Oct	1987	21 Jan	1989	14 June	1991
IRON DUKE	F 234	Yarrow Shipbuilders, Glasgow	12 Dec	1988	2 Mar	1991	20 May	1993
MONMOUTH	F 235	Yarrow Shipbuilders, Glasgow	1 June	1989	23 Nov	1991	24 Sep	1993
MONTROSE	F 236	Yarrow Shipbuilders, Glasgow	1 Nov	1989	31 July	1992	2 June	1994
WESTMINSTER	F 237	Swan Hunter Shipbuilders, Wallsend-on-Tyne	18 Jan	1991	4 Feb	1992	13 May	1994
NORTHUMBERLAND	F 238	Swan Hunter Shipbuilders, Wallsend-on-Tyne	4 Apr	1991	4 Apr	1992	29 Nov	1994
RICHMOND	F 239	Swan Hunter Shipbuilders, Wallsend-on-Tyne	16 Feb	1992	6 Apr	1993	22 June	1995
SOMERSET	F 82	Yarrow Shipbuilders, Glasgow	12 Oct	1992	25 June	1994	20 Sep	1996
GRAFTON	F 80	Yarrow Shipbuilders, Glasgow	13 May	1993	5 Nov	1994	29 May	1997
SUTHERLAND	F 81	Yarrow Shipbuilders, Glasgow	14 Oct	1993	9 Mar	1996	4 July	1997
KENT	F 78	Yarrow Shipbuilders, Glasgow	16 Apr	1997	27 May	1998	Sep	2000
PORTLAND	F 79	Yarrow Shipbuilders, Glasgow	14 Jan	1998	15 May	1999	Jan	2001
ST ALBANS	F 83	Yarrow Shipbuilders, Glasgow	18 Apr	1999	6 May	2000	Apr	2002

Displacement, tons: 3,500 standard; 4,200 full load
Dimensions, feet (metres): 436.2 × 52.8 × 18 (screws); 24 (sonar) *(133 × 16.1 × 5.5; 7.3)*
Main machinery: CODLAG; 2 RR Spey SM1A (F 229-F 236) or SM1C (F 237 onwards) gas turbines (see *Structure*); 31,100 hp *(23.2 MW)* sustained; 4 Paxman 12CM diesels; 8,100 hp *(6 MW)*; 2 GEC motors; 4,000 hp *(3 MW)*; 2 shafts
Speed, knots: 28; 15 on diesel-electric
Range, miles: 7,800 miles at 15 kt
Complement: 181 (13 officers)

Missiles: SSM: 8 McDonnell Douglas Harpoon (2 quad) launchers ❶; active radar homing to 130 km *(70 n miles)* at 0.9 Mach; warhead 227 kg (84C). 4 normally carried.
SAM: British Aerospace Seawolf GWS 26 Mod 1 VLS ❷; command line of sight (CLOS) radar/TV tracking to 6 km *(3.3 n miles)* at 2.5 Mach; warhead 14 kg; 32 canisters.
Guns: 1 Vickers 4.5 in *(114 mm)*/55 Mk 8 ❸; 25 rds/min to 22 km *(11.9 n miles)* anti-surface; 6 km *(3.3 n miles)* anti-aircraft; weight of shell 21 kg.
2 DES/MSI DS 30B 30 mm/75 ❹; 650 rds/min to 10 km *(5.4 n miles)* anti-surface; 3 km *(1.6 n miles)* anti-aircraft; weight of shell 0.36 kg.
Torpedoes: 4 Cray Marine 324 mm fixed (2 twin) tubes ❺. Marconi Stingray; active/passive homing to 11 km *(5.9 n miles)* at 45 kt; warhead 35 kg (shaped charge); depth to 750 m *(2,460 ft)*. Automatic reload in 9 minutes.
Countermeasures: Decoys: Outfit DLB; 4 Sea Gnat 6-barrelled 130 mm/102 mm launchers ❻. DLF 2/3 offboard decoys. Type 182 or SLQ-25A; towed torpedo decoy.
ESM: Racal Thorn UAT ❼; intercept.
ECM: Type 675(2) or Racal Scorpion; jammer.
Combat data systems: BAeSEMA DNA 1; Links 11, 14 and JTIDS 16 in due course. Matra Marconi SCOT 1D SATCOMs ❽.
Weapons control: BAe GSA 8B/GPEOD optronic director ❾. GWS 60 (for SSM). GWS 26 (for SAM).
Radars: Air/surface search: Plessey Type 996(I) ❿; 3D; E/F-band.
Surface search: Racal Decca Type 1008 ⓫; E/F-band.
Navigation: Kelvin Hughes Type 1007; I-band.
Fire control: 2 Marconi Type 911 ⓬; I/Ku-band.
IFF: 1010/1011.
Sonars: Ferranti/Thomson Sintra Type 2050; bow-mounted; active search and attack.
Dowty Type 2031Z (F 229-F 239); towed array; passive search; very low frequency. To be replaced by Type 2087 from late 2004; active low-frequency towed body with a passive array.

Helicopters: 1 Westland Lynx HMA 3/8 or 1 Merlin HM 1 ⓭.

MARLBOROUGH

(Scale 1 : 1,200), Ian Sturton / 0016230

GRAFTON

10/1999*, A Campanera i Rovira / 0075782

Programmes: The first of this class was ordered from Yarrows on 29 October 1984. Next three in September 1986, with four more out to tender in October 1987 but only three ordered in July 1988. Again four out to tender in late 1988 and only three ordered 19 December 1989. Long lead items for another six ordered in 1990 but contracts were not placed until 23 January 1992 when three more were ordered. The last three were put out to tender on 29 November 1994, and after several delays were ordered on 28 February 1996. Planned final total was 23 but is now unlikely to exceed 16. F 229 pennant number changed because 232 was considered unlucky as it is the RN report form number for collisions and groundings.

Modernisation: Mid-life update for Sea Wolf from 2001 to include an improved I-band radar and the addition of an optronic tracking channel to the I/K-band fire-control radar. Flight deck modifications are needed for the Merlin helicopter.
Structure: Incorporates stealth technology to minimise acoustic, magnetic, radar and IR signatures. The design includes a 7° slope to all vertical surfaces, rounded edges, reduction of IR emissions and a hull bubble system to reduce radiated noise. The combined diesel electric and GT propulsion system provides quiet motive power during towed sonar operations. The SM1C engines although capable of 41 MW of power combined are constrained by output into the gearbox. MacTaggart Scott Helios helo landing system. SSCS (DNA 1)

software Phase II installed in *Westminster* on build and is being retrofitted in earlier ships which were built without an integrated data system. Subsequent Phases III to V are being fitted on build to all the later ships with full capability introduced from 1997. The Type 2031 towed array is fitted in the first 10 ships, but the replacement Type 2087 LFAS will not be available until 2004. This means the last six ships have no sonar towed arrays.
Operational: F 233, F 229, F 234, F 237, F 239 and F 80 are based at Portsmouth (4th Frigate Squadron), with the remainder, up to F 81, at Devonport (6th Frigate Squadron).
UPDATED

SOMERSET

7/1999*, H M Steele / 0075783

ARGYLL

6/1999*, H M Steele / 0075785

GRAFTON

8/1999*, Maritime Photographic / 0075784

4 BROADSWORD CLASS (TYPE 22 BATCH 3) (FFG)

Name	No
CORNWALL	F 99
CUMBERLAND	F 85
CAMPBELTOWN	F 86
CHATHAM	F 87

Builders	Laid down	Launched	Commissioned
Yarrow Shipbuilders, Glasgow	14 Dec 1983	14 Oct 1985	23 Apr 1988
Yarrow Shipbuilders, Glasgow	12 Oct 1984	21 June 1986	10 June 1989
Cammell Laird, Birkenhead	4 Dec 1985	7 Oct 1987	27 May 1989
Swan Hunter Shipbuilders, Wallsend-on-Tyne	12 May 1986	20 Jan 1988	4 May 1990

Displacement, tons: 4,200 standard; 4,900 full load
Dimensions, feet (metres): 485.9 × 48.5 × 21
(148.1 × 14.8 × 6.4)
Main machinery: COGOG; 2 RR Spey SM1A gas turbines; 29,500 hp (22 MW) sustained; 2 RR Tyne RM3C gas turbines; 10,680 hp (8 MW) sustained; 2 shafts; acbLIPS; cp props
Speed, knots: 30; 18 on Tynes.
Range, miles: 4,500 at 18 kt on Tynes.
Complement: 250 (31 officers) (accommodation for 301)

Missiles: SSM: 8 McDonnell Douglas Harpoon Block 1C (2 quad) launchers ❶; preprogrammed; active radar homing to 130 km (70 n miles) at 0.9 Mach; warhead 227 kg.
SAM: 2 British Aerospace Seawolf GWS 25 Mod 3 ❷; command line of sight (CLOS) with 2 channel radar tracking to 5 km (2.7 n miles) at 2+ Mach; warhead 14 kg.
Guns: 1 Vickers 4.5 in (114 mm)/55 Mk 8 ❸; 25 rds/min to 22 km (11.9 n miles) anti-surface; 6 km (3.3 n miles) anti-aircraft; weight of shell 21 kg.
1 Signaal/General Electric 30 mm 7-barrelled Goalkeeper ❹; 4,200 rds/min combined to 1.5 km.
2 DES/MSI DS 30B 30 mm/75 ❺; 650 rds/min to 10 km (5.5 n miles); weight of shell 0.36 kg or 2 Oerlikon 20 mm.
Torpedoes: 6—324 mm Plessey STWS Mk 2 (2 triple) tubes ❻. Marconi Stingray; active/passive homing to 11 km (5.9 n miles) at 45 kt; warhead 35 kg shaped charge.
Countermeasures: Decoys: Outfit DCH; 4 Sea Gnat 6-barrelled 130 mm/102 mm fixed launchers ❼.
Graseby Type 182 or SLQ-25A; towed torpedo decoy.
ESM: Racal Thorn UAT 1; intercept.
ECM: Type 675(2); jammer.

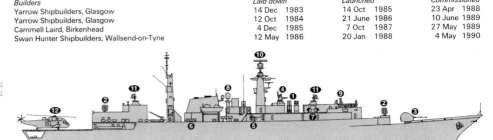

CORNWALL

(Scale 1 : 1,200), Ian Sturton / 0053201

Combat data systems: CACS 5 action data automation; Links 11 and 14. 2 Matra Marconi SCOT 1C SATCOMs ❽. ICS-3 integrated comms. Marisat. JMICS being fitted.
Weapons control: 2 BAe GSA 8B GPEOD Sea Archer optronic directors with TV and IR imaging and laser rangefinders ❾. GWS 60. GWS 25 Mod 3 (for SAM).
Radars: Air/surface search: Marconi Type 967/968 ❿; D/E-band.
Surface search: Racal Decca Type 2008; E/F-band; being fitted.
Fire control: 2 Marconi Type 911 ⓫; I/Ku-band (for Seawolf).
Navigation: Kelvin Hughes Type 1007; I-band.
Sonars: Ferranti/Thomson Sintra Type 2050; hull-mounted; active search and attack.
Dowty Type 2031; towed array; passive search; very low frequency.

Helicopters: 2 Westland Lynx HMA 3/8; or 1 Westland Sea King HAS 5 ⓬.

Modernisation: Seawolf GWS 25 progressively upgraded. Sonar 2016 replaced by Sonar 2050. EW fit is being updated and Sea Gnat is the standard launcher for a variety of distraction and seduction decoys. EDS Command Support System fitted by 2008. From 2001 an improved I-band radar is to be fitted to Sea Wolf, and the fire-control radar is to have an additional optronic tracker. Type 2008 radar from 2000.
Structure: All have enlarged flight decks to take Sea King helicopters.
Operational: This class is primarily designed for ASW operations and is capable of acting as OTC. All have facilities for Flag and staff. One Lynx normally embarked. Ships are fitted with DEC laser dazzle device, and additional EW equipment mounted forward of the foremast, on operational deployments. All are in the 2nd Frigate Squadron.

UPDATED

CUMBERLAND

3/1999*, C E Castle / 0075789

CORNWALL

3/1999*, John Brodie / 0075788

SHIPBORNE AIRCRAFT

Notes: (1) Memorandum of Understanding signed with USA in December 1995 for a four year concept demonstration phase of the US Joint Advanced Strike Technology (JAST) programme. This could lead to a Sea Harrier replacement in about 2012.
(2) Joint Force Harrier formed 1 April 2000 combines Air Force Harrier GR 7 and Naval Sea Harrier FA 2.
(3) Dauphin 2 helicopters with Royal Naval markings are leased by FOST for staff transfers. Painted red.

SEA HARRIER FA 2   *2/1999*, Maritime Photographic* / 0075791

Numbers/Type: 47/7 British Aerospace Sea Harrier FA 2/T 8.
Operational speed: 540 kt *(1,000 km/h)*.
Service ceiling: 45,000 ft *(13,716 m)*.
Range: 800 n miles *(1,480 km)*.
Role/Weapon systems: Air defence, ground attacks, reconnaissance and maritime attack. Sensors: Blue Vixen radar, GEC-Marconi Sky Guardian ESM, ALE 40 chaff/IR flares, camera, IFF Mk 12; JTIDS Link 16 in 2003. Weapons: ASV. Strike; 1,000 lb and 540 lb bombs; Paveway II laser-guided bombs. AD; four AIM-9M Sidewinder or Hughes AIM-120 AMRAAM (FA 2); two 30 mm Aden cannon.

UPDATED

HARRIER GR 7 (Air Force)   *10/1999*, H M Steele* / 0075792

Numbers/Type: 12 Westland/Agusta Merlin HM Mk 1.
Operational speed: 160 kt *(296 km/h)*.
Service ceiling: 15,000 ft *(4,572 m)*.
Range: 550 n miles *(1,019 km)*.
Role/Weapon systems: Primary anti-submarine role with secondary anti-surface and troop-carrying capabilities. Contract for 44 signed 9 October 1991. First four in service in late 1998. Sensors: GEC-Marconi Blue Kestrel 5000 radar, Thomson Marconi Flash AQS 960 dipping sonar, GEC-Marconi sonobuoy acoustic processor AQS-903, Racal Orange Reaper ESM, ECM. Weapons: ASW; four Stingray torpedoes or Mk 11 Mod 3 depth bombs. ASV; OTHT for ship-launched SSM.

UPDATED

MERLIN   *6/1999*, Maritime Photographic* / 0075794

Numbers/Type: 41 Westland Sea King HAS 5/6.
Operational speed: 112 kt *(207 km/h)*.
Service ceiling: 10,000 ft *(3,050 m)*.
Range: 400 n miles *(925 km)*.
Role/Weapon systems: Embarked and shore-based medium ASW helicopter in front-line and training squadron service; Mk 6 entered service in June 1989. Sensors: MEL Sea Searcher radar, 'Orange Crop' ESM, Ferranti 2069 (HAS 6) replacing Type 195M dipping sonar, combined sonar processor AQS 902G-DS Mk 6 replacing 902C. Weapons: ASW; two Stingray torpedoes or Mk 11 depth bombs. ASV; OTHT for SSM.

UPDATED

SEA KING HAS 6   *10/1999*, H M Steele* / 0075795

Numbers/Type: 59 Westland Lynx HAS 3/HMA 3/HMA 8.
Operational speed: 120 kt *(222 km/h)*.
Service ceiling: 10,000 ft *(3,048 m)*.
Range: 320 n miles *(593 km)*.
Role/Weapon systems: Primarily anti-surface helicopter with short-range ASW capability; embarked in all modern RN escorts; update with Sea Owl passive identification and centralised tactical system. Sensors: Ferranti Sea Spray Mk 1 radar, 'Orange Crop' ESM, chaff and flare dispenser. Weapons: ASW; two Stingray torpedoes or Mk 11 Mod 3 depth bombs. ASV; four Sea Skua missiles; two 12.7 mm MG pods.

UPDATED

LYNX HMA 8   *1/1999, Maritime Photographic* / 0053209

LYNX HAS 3   *5/1999*, H M Steele* / 0075793

Numbers/Type: 10 Westland Sea King AEW 2/7.
Operational speed: 110 kt *(204 km/h)*.
Service ceiling: 10,000 ft *(3,050 m)*.
Range: 660 n miles *(1,220 km)*.
Role/Weapon systems: Primarily used for airborne early warning organic to the Fleet, with EW, surface search and OTHT secondary roles; modified from ASW version. AEW 7 contract in October 1996 for all 10 aircraft plus three surplus HAS 5 to be fitted with Racal Thorn Searchwater 2000 radar. Link 16 being fitted from 2000. Sensors: Searchwater AEW radar, Racal MIR-2 'Orange Crop' ESM, IFF Mk XII. Weapons: Unarmed.

UPDATED

SEA KING AEW   *10/1999*, H M Steele* / 0075796

Numbers/Type: 29 Westland Sea King HC. Mk 4.
Operational speed: 112 kt *(208 km/h)*.
Service ceiling: 10,000 ft *(3,050 m)*.
Range: 664 n miles *(1,230 km)*.
Role/Weapon systems: 24 commando support and five training/special task helicopters; capable of carrying most Commando Force equipment underslung. Expected to remain in service to 2010. Sensors: Prophet 2 plus AAR-47 ESM; jammer, chaff and IR flares ECM. Weapons: Can fit 7.62 mm GPMG or similar.

UPDATED

SEA KING HC4   *1/2000*, A Sharma* / 0075797

Numbers/Type: 9 Westland Gazelle AH Mk 1.
Operational speed: 130 kt *(242 km/h).*
Service ceiling: 9,350 ft *(2,850 m).*
Range: 361 n miles *(670 km).*
Role/Weapon systems: For observation with 847 Squadron. Sensors: Roof-mounted sight. Weapons: Normally unarmed.   *VERIFIED*

GAZELLE   *8/1994, Ash Amliwala*

Numbers/Type: 6 Westland Lynx AH Mk 7.
Operational speed: 140 kt *(259 km/h).*
Service ceiling: 10,600 ft *(3,230 m).*
Range: 340 n miles *(630 km).*
Role/Weapon systems: Military general purpose and anti-tank with 847 Squadron. Sensors: Day/ thermal imaging sight. Weapons: Up to eight Hughes TOW anti-tank missiles.   *VERIFIED*

LYNX AH MK 7   *6/1998 / 0053215*

LAND-BASED MARITIME AIRCRAFT (FRONT LINE)

Notes: (1) All Air Force manned.
(2) 24 Tornado GR. 1B are equipped for tactical air support of maritime operations (TASMO) with Sea Eagle ASMs.

Numbers/Type: 25 Hawker Siddeley Nimrod MR 2/2P/4.
Operational speed: 500 kt *(926 km/h).*
Service ceiling: 42,000 ft *(12,800 m).*
Range: 5,000 n miles *(9,265 km).*
Role/Weapon systems: ASW but with ASV, OTHT and control potential at long range from shore bases; three are modified for EW; duties include SAR, maritime surveillance. Contract in July 1996 to convert and upgrade 21 aircraft with first delivery in 2005. New equipment includes Searchwater 2000MR radar, Elta ER-8300 and ALR-56M ESM. Sensors: THORN EMI Searchwater radar, ECM, ESM, cameras, MAD, sonobuoys, AQS-901 acoustic processor. Weapons: ASW; 6.1 tons of Stingray torpedoes or depth bombs or mines. ASV; four Harpoon missiles. Self-defence; four AIM-9L Sidewinder.   *UPDATED*

NIMROD   *6/1999*, Maritime Photographic / 0075798*

Numbers/Type: 7 Boeing E-3D Sentry AEW Mk 1.
Operational speed: 460 kt *(853 km/h).*
Service ceiling: 36,000 ft *(10,973 m).*
Range: 870 n miles *(1,610 km).*
Role/Weapon systems: Air defence early warning aircraft with secondary role to provide coastal AEW for the Fleet; 6 hours endurance at the range given above. Sensors: Westinghouse APY-2 surveillance radar, Bendix weather radar, Mk XII IFF, Yellow Gate, ESM, ECM. Weapons: Unarmed.   *VERIFIED*

MINE WARFARE FORCES

Note: There are plans to procure a remote-controlled minesweeping system using a concept similar to the German drone. In service date is projected as 2006.

11 HUNT CLASS
(MINESWEEPERS/MINEHUNTERS—COASTAL) (MSC/MHC)

Name	No	Builders	Launched	Commissioned
BRECON	M 29	Vosper Thornycroft, Woolston	21 June 1978	21 Mar 1980
LEDBURY	M 30	Vosper Thornycroft, Woolston	5 Dec 1979	11 June 1981
CATTISTOCK	M 31	Vosper Thornycroft, Woolston	22 Jan 1981	16 June 1982
COTTESMORE	M 32	Yarrow Shipbuilders, Glasgow	9 Feb 1982	24 June 1983
BROCKLESBY	M 33	Vosper Thornycroft, Woolston	12 Jan 1982	3 Feb 1983
MIDDLETON	M 34	Yarrow Shipbuilders, Glasgow	27 Apr 1983	15 Aug 1984
DULVERTON	M 35	Vosper Thornycroft, Woolston	3 Nov 1982	4 Nov 1983
CHIDDINGFOLD	M 37	Vosper Thornycroft, Woolston	6 Oct 1983	10 Aug 1984
ATHERSTONE	M 38	Vosper Thornycroft, Woolston	1 Mar 1986	30 Jan 1987
HURWORTH	M 39	Vosper Thornycroft, Woolston	25 Sep 1984	2 July 1985
QUORN	M 41	Vosper Thornycroft, Woolston	23 Jan 1988	21 Apr 1989

Displacement, tons: 615 light; 750 full load
Dimensions, feet (metres): 187 wl; 197 oa × 32.8 × 9.5 (keel); 11.2 (screws)
(57; 60 × 10 × 2.9; 3.4)
Main machinery: 2 Ruston-Paxman 9-59K Deltic diesels; 1,900 hp *(1.42 MW);* 1 Deltic Type 9-55B diesel for pulse generator and auxiliary drive; 780 hp *(582 kW);* 2 shafts; bow thruster
Speed, knots: 15 diesels; 8 hydraulic drive. **Range, miles:** 1,500 at 12 kt
Complement: 45 (5 officers)

Guns: 1 DES/MSI DS 30B 30 mm/75; 650 rds/min to 10 km *(5.4 n miles)* anti-surface; 3 km *(1.6 n miles)* anti-aircraft; weight of shell 0.36 kg.
2 Oerlikon/BMARC 20 mm GAM-CO1 (enhancement); 900 rds/min to 2 km.
2—7.62 mm MGs.
Countermeasures: MCM: 2 PAP 104/105 remotely controlled submersibles, MS 14 magnetic loop, Sperry MSSA Mk 1 Towed Acoustic Generator and conventional Mk 8 Oropesa sweeps.
Decoys: Outfit DLK; 2 Barricade Mk III; 6 sets of triple barrels per mounting.
2 Irvin Replica RF; passive decoys.
ESM: MEL Matilda UAR 1; Marconi Mentor A (in some).
Combat data systems: CAAIS DBA 4 action data automation.
Radars: Navigation: Kelvin Hughes Type 1006 or Type 1007; I-band.
Sonars: Plessey 193M Mod 1; hull-mounted; minehunting; 100/300 kHz.
Mil Cross mine avoidance sonar; hull-mounted; active; high frequency.
Type 2059 to track PAP 104/105.

Programmes: A class of MCM Vessels combining both hunting and sweeping capabilities.
Modernisation: Ten PAP 105 were acquired in 1988-89 to replace the 104s. They have a range of 600 m *(1,968 ft)* down to 300 m *(984 ft)* depth and a speed of 6 kt; weight 700 kg. 30 mm gun has replaced the Bofors 40 mm. Racal Mk 53 navigation system ordered in August 1990 for all ships. Mid-life update plans have been cut back and now include minor improvements to the command system, a wideband capability added to the 193M sonar. Plans for a possible replacement PAP or mine disposal UUV or ADI AMASS influence sweep have been shelved. *Cottesmore, Dulverton,* and *Brecon* modified as Northern Ireland patrol ships. Sweep gear in these three ships has been displaced by three RIBs, but can be replaced if required.
Structure: Hulls of GRP.
Operational: For operational deployments fitted with enhanced weapons systems, Inmarsat SATCOMs and some have the SCARAB remote-control floating mine towing device which helps the safe destruction of moored mines once they have been cut from their moorings. Ships of this class can be used for Fishery Protection duties as well as Northern Ireland patrols.
Sales: One of the class to Greece in July 2000, second in February 2001.   *UPDATED*

MIDDLETON   *7/1999*, Michael Nitz / 0075800*

10 + 2 SANDOWN CLASS (MINEHUNTERS) (MHC/SRMH)

Name	No	Builders	Launched	Commissioned
SANDOWN	M 101	Vosper Thornycroft, Woolston	16 Apr 1988	9 June 1989
INVERNESS	M 102	Vosper Thornycroft, Woolston	27 Feb 1990	24 Jan 1991
CROMER	M 103	Vosper Thornycroft, Woolston	6 Oct 1990	7 Apr 1992
WALNEY	M 104	Vosper Thornycroft, Woolston	25 Nov 1991	20 Feb 1993
BRIDPORT	M 105	Vosper Thornycroft, Woolston	30 July 1992	6 Nov 1993
PENZANCE	M 106	Vosper Thornycroft, Woolston	11 Mar 1997	14 May 1998
PEMBROKE	M 107	Vosper Thornycroft, Woolston	15 Dec 1997	6 Oct 1998
GRIMSBY	M 108	Vosper Thornycroft, Woolston	10 Aug 1998	25 Sep 1999
BANGOR	M 109	Vosper Thornycroft, Woolston	16 Apr 1999	July 2000
RAMSEY	M 110	Vosper Thornycroft, Woolston	25 Nov 1999	Sep 2000
BLYTHE	M 111	Vosper Thornycroft, Woolston	May 2000	Feb 2001
SHOREHAM	M 112	Vosper Thornycroft, Woolston	Feb 2001	Nov 2001

Displacement, tons: 450 standard; 484 full load
Dimensions, feet (metres): 172.2 × 34.4 × 7.5 *(52.5 × 10.5 × 2.3)*
Main machinery: 2 Paxman Valenta 6RP200E/M diesels; 1,523 hp *(1.14 MW)* sustained; Voith-Schneider propulsion; 2 Schottel bow thrusters
Speed, knots: 13 diesels; 6.5 electric drive. **Range, miles:** 2,500 at 12 kt
Complement: 34 (5 officers) plus 6 spare berths

Guns: 1 DES/MSI DS 30B 30 mm/75; 650 rds/min to 10 km *(5.4 n miles)* anti-surface; 3 km *(1.6 n miles)* anti-aircraft; weight of shell 0.36 kg.

Countermeasures: MCM: ECA mine disposal system, 2 PAP 104 Mk 5 (RCMDS 2). These craft can carry 2 mine wire cutters, a charge of 100 kg and a manipulator with TV/projector. Control cables are either 1,000 m (high capacity) or 2,000 m (low capacity) and the craft can dive to 300 m at 6 kt with an endurance of 5e 20 minute missions.
Decoys: Outfit DLK; 2 Barricade (fitted for deployment).
Combat data systems: Plessey Nautis M action data automation.
Radars: Navigation: Kelvin Hughes Type 1007; I-band.
Sonars: Marconi Type 2093; VDS; VLF-VHF multifunction with 5 arrays; mine search and classification.

Programmes: A class designed for hunting and destroying mines and for operating in deep and exposed waters. Single role minehunter (SRMH) complements the 'Hunt' class. On 9 January 1984 the Vosper Thornycroft design for this class was approved. First one ordered August 1985, four more on 23 July 1987. A contract was to have been placed for a second batch in 1990 but this was deferred twice, until an order for seven more was placed in July 1994.
Structure: GRP hull. Combines vectored thrust units with bow thrusters and Remote-Control Mine Disposal System (RCMDS). The sonar is deployed from a well in the hull. Batch 2 have larger diameter (1.8 m) Voith-Schneider props and an improved two-man decompression chamber. The new ships have a larger Gemini crane for RCMDS vehicle launch and recovery. All of the class are to be retrofitted in due course.
Operational: Racal Hyperfix. Decca Navigation Mk 21. Kelvin Hughes NAVPAC system integrates all navigational aids to give an accuracy of 9 m. Allocation: All to 3rd MCM Squadron.
Sales: Three to Saudi Arabia. *Cromer* is planned to be sold in November 2001.

UPDATED

WALNEY   *6/1999* / 0075799

AMPHIBIOUS FORCES

Notes: (1) Further amphibious ships and craft covered in RFA and RLC (ex-RCT) sections. These include a Helicopter Support Ship, five LSLs, and six LCLs.
(2) There are also four Swimmer Delivery Vehicles (SDV) Mk 8 and three SDVs Mk 8 Mod 1 in service and a number of very high speed low profile Marine delivery surface craft.

0 + 2 ALBION CLASS (ASSAULT SHIPS) (LPD)

Name	No	Builders	Laid down	Launched	Commissioned
ALBION	L 14	BAE Systems, Barrow	22 May 1998	Mar 2001	Mar 2003
BULWARK	L 15	BAE Systems, Barrow	27 Jan 2000	Dec 2001	Dec 2003

Displacement, tons: 19,560 full load
Dimensions, feet (metres): 577.4 × 98.1 × 22
(176 × 29.9 × 6.7)
Main machinery: Diesel-electric; 2 Wärtsilä Vasa 16V 32LNE diesel generators; 17,000 hp(m) *(12.5 MW)*; 2 Wärtsilä Vasa 4R 32LNE diesel generators; 4,216 hp(m) *(3.1 MW)*; 2 motors; 2 shafts; acbLIPS props; 1 bow thruster; 1,176 hp(m) *(865 kW)*
Speed, knots: 20. **Range, miles:** 8,000 at 15 kt
Complement: 325
Military lift: 305 troops; overload 710 troops; 67 support vehicles; 4 LCU Mk 10 or 2 LCAC (dock); 4 LCVP Mk 5 (davits)

Guns: 8—30 mm (4 twin) ❶. 2 Goalkeeper CIWS ❷.
Countermeasures: Decoys: Outfit DLJ; 8 Sea Gnat launchers ❸ and DLH offboard decoys.
ESM/ECM: Racal Thorn UAT 1/4.
Combat data systems: ADAWS 2000. Thomson-CSF/Redifon/BAeSEMA/CS comms system. Marconi Matra SCOT 2D SATCOM ❹.
Radars: Air/surface search: Siemens Plessey Type 996 ❺; E/F-band.
Surface search ❻: E/F-band.
Navigation/aircraft control: 2 Racal Marine Type 1007 ❼; I-band.
IFF: Type 1016/1017.

Helicopters: Platform for 3 Merlin EH 101. Chinook capable.

Programmes: A decision was taken in mid-1991 to replace both existing LPDs. Project definition studies by YARD completed in February 1994 after a year's delay caused by attempts to introduce commercial shipbuilding standards without compromising safety. Invitations to tender for design and build of two ships were issued to VSEL and Yarrow on 18 August 1994 with an additional tender package to Vosper Thornycroft in November 1994. In March 1995 it was announced that only VSEL would bid, conforming to the rules governing non-competitive tenders. The contract to build the ships was awarded on 18 July 1996. First steel cut 17 November 1997.

ALBION   *(Scale 1 : 1,500), Ian Sturton*

ALBION (computer graphic)   *1999*, BAE Systems* / 0075806

Structure: The design shown in the drawing has emerged from contract negotiations. Two helicopter landing spots. Substantial command and control facilities included within a large combined operation room. The configuration is similar to *Fearless* with a well dock and stern gate but with side ramp access as well. The ships are being built to military damage control standards.

UPDATED

1 HELICOPTER CARRIER (LPH)

Name	No	Builders	Laid down	Launched	Commissioned
OCEAN	L 12	Vickers Shipbuilding/Kvaerner Govan	30 May 1994	11 Oct 1995	30 Sep 1998

Displacement, tons: 21,758 full load
Dimensions, feet (metres): 667.3 oa; 652.2 pp × 112.9 × 21.3 *(203.4; 198.8 × 34.4 × 6.6)*
Flight deck, feet (metres): 557.7 × 104 *(170 × 31.7)*
Main machinery: 2 Crossley Pielstick 16 PC2.6 V 400 diesels; 18,360 hp(m) *(13.5 MW)* sustained; 2 shafts; Kamewa cp props; bow thruster; 612 hp *(450 kW)*
Speed, knots: 19. **Range, miles:** 8,000 at 15 kt
Complement: 285 plus 206 aircrew plus up to 830 Marines
Military lift: 4 LCVP Mk 5 (on davits); 2 Griffon hovercraft; 40 vehicles and equipment for most of a marine commando battalion

Guns: 8 Oerlikon/BMARC 20 mm GAM-B03 (4 twin) ❶. 650 rds/min to 10 km *(5.4 n miles)* anti-surface; 3 km *(1.6 n miles)* anti-aircraft; weight of shell 0.36 kg.
3 Vulcan Phalanx Mk 15 ❷. 6 barrels per launcher; 3,000 rds/min combined to 1.5 km.
Countermeasures: Decoys: Outfit DLJ; 8 Sea Gnat 130 mm/102 mm launchers ❸ and DLH offboard decoys.
ESM: Racal Thorn UAT; intercept.
Combat data systems: Ferranti ADAWS 2000 Mod 1; Link 11, 14 and 16 in due course; Marconi Matra SATCOM 1D ❹; Merlin computer link. JMCIS from 2000.
Radars: Air/surface search: Plessey Type 996 ❺; E/F-band.
Surface search/aircraft control: 2 Kelvin Hughes Type 1007 ❻; I-band.
IFF: Type 1010/1011.

Helicopters: 12 Sea King HC Mk 4/Merlin plus 6 Lynx (or Apache by 2005).

Programmes: Initial invitations to tender were issued in 1987. Tenders submitted in July 1989 were allowed to lapse and it was not until 11 May 1993 that a contract was placed. The hull was built on the Clyde by Kvaerner Govan and sailed under its own power to Vickers at Barrow in November 1996 for the installation of military equipment.
Structure: The hull form is based on the 'Invincible' class with a modified superstructure. The deck is strong enough to take Chinook helicopters. Six landing and six parking spots for the aircraft. Accommodation for 972 plus 303 bunk overload. The combat data system is compatible with other frontline RN ships.

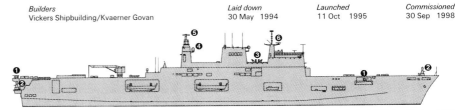

OCEAN

(Scale 1 : 1,800), Ian Sturton / 0053220

OCEAN

8/1999*, van Ginderen Collection / 0075803

Operational: The LPH provides a helicopter lift and assault capability. The prime role of the vessel is embarking, supporting and operating a squadron of helicopters and carrying a Royal Marine Commando including vehicles, arms and ammunition. Up to 20 Sea Harriers can be carried but not supported. Operational sea trials started in June 1998 and completed in February 1999. Twin 20 mm guns are not always carried and may be replaced by single 20 mm.

UPDATED

OCEAN

12/1999*, Maritime Photographic / 0075804

OCEAN

8/1999*, B Sullivan / 0075805

1 FEARLESS CLASS (LPD)

Name	No
FEARLESS	L 10

Builders	Laid down	Launched	Commissioned
Harland & Wolff, Belfast	25 July 1962	19 Dec 1963	25 Nov 1965

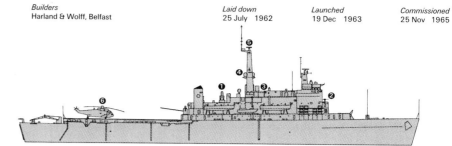

FEARLESS

(Scale 1 : 1,500), Ian Sturton

Displacement, tons: 11,060 standard; 12,120 full load; 16,950 dock flooded

Dimensions, feet (metres): 500 wl; 520 oa × 80 × 20.5 (32 flooded) *(152.4; 158.5 × 24.4 × 6.2 (9.8))*

Main machinery: 2 Babcock & Wilcox boilers; 550 psi *(38.66 kg/cm²)*; 850°F *(454°C)*; 2 English Electric turbines; 22,000 hp *(16.4 MW)*; 2 shafts

Speed, knots: 21. **Range, miles:** 5,000 at 20 kt

Complement: 550 (50 officers) plus 22 (3 officers) air group plus 88 (3 officers) RM

Military lift: 380-400 troops; overload 1,000 troops; 15 MBTs; 7—3 ton trucks; 20¼ ton trucks (specimen load) Landing craft: 4 LCU Mk 9 (dock); 4 LCVP Mk 3 (davits)

Guns: 2 GE/GD 20 mm Mk 15 Vulcan Phalanx ❶; 6 barrels per launcher; 3,000 rds/min combined to 1.5 km. 2 Oerlikon/BMARC 20 mm GAM-BO1 ❷.

Countermeasures: Decoys: Outfit DLB; 4 Sea Gnat 130 mm/102 mm 6-barrelled fixed launchers ❸. ESM: Marconi Mentor A; radar warning.

Combat data systems: Plessey Nautis M. Marconi Matra SCOT 1D SATCOM ❹.

Radars: Surface search: Plessey Type 994 ❺; E/F-band. Navigation: Kelvin Hughes Type 1006; I-band.

Helicopters: Platform for up to 4 Westland Sea King HC 4 ❻.

Modernisation: *Fearless* completed a two year refit in November 1990 with two Vulcan Phalanx 20 mm gun mountings and new decoy launchers.

Structure: The two funnels are staggered across the beam of the ship. Landing craft are floated through the open stern by flooding compartments of the ship and lowering her in the water. They are able to deploy tanks, vehicles and men and have sea-keeping qualities much superior to those of tank landing ships as well as greater speed and range. The helicopter platform is also the deckhead of the dock and has two landing spots.

Operational: Fitted out as a Naval Assault Group/Brigade Headquarters with an Assault Operations Room. Required to be available until *Albion* enters service in 2003.

UPDATED

FEARLESS

4/1999*, Maritime Photographic / 0075801

FEARLESS

4/1999* / 0075802

2 + 8 (2) LCU MK 10

L 1001-1010

Displacement, tons: 170 light; 240 full load
Dimensions, feet (metres): 97.8 × 24.3 × 5.6 *(29.8 × 7.4 × 1.7)*
Main machinery: 2 MAN diesels; 2 Schottel propulsors; bow thruster
Speed, knots: 12. **Range, miles:** 600 at 12 kt
Complement: 7
Military lift: 1 MBT or 4 vehicles or 120 troops
Radars: Navigation: I-band.

Comment: Ordered in 1998 from Ailsa Troon Yard. First pair delivered in November 1999, then eight more planned from December 2001 to February 2003 after trials of the first two. To be embarked in the 'Albion' class LPDs. Bow and stern ramps.

UPDATED

LCU MK 10 (artist's impression)   *1998 */ 0053458*

14 LCU Mk 9M/9R/9S

L 700-702   L 704-711   L 713-715

Displacement, tons: 115 light; 175 full load
Dimensions, feet (metres): 90.2 × 21.5 × 5 *(27.5 × 6.8 × 1.6)*
Main machinery: 2 Paxman or Dorman diesels; 474 hp *(354 kW)* sustained; Kort nozzles or Schottel propulsors
Speed, knots: 10. **Range, miles:** 300 at 9 kt
Complement: 7
Military lift: 1 MBT or 60 tons of vehicles/stores or 90 troops
Radars: Navigation: Raytheon; I-band.

Comment: First 11 (Mk 9M) built in the mid-1960s, last three (Mk 9R) in 1986. Operated by the Royal Marines. Four in each LPD. *L 710* is a trials craft for the next generation LCU Mk 10 and was fitted in 1993 with two Schottel flush hulled propulsors. Six Mk 9M upgraded with Schottel propulsors and re-designated Mk 9S.

UPDATED

LCU 714   *6/1998 *, John Brodie / 0053226*

4 GRIFFON 2000 TDX(M) (LCAC(L))

C 21-C 24

Displacement, tons: 6.8 full load
Dimensions, feet (metres): 36.1 × 15.1 *(11 × 4.6)*
Main machinery: 1 Deutz BF8L513 diesel; 320 hp *(239 kW)* sustained
Speed, knots: 33. **Range, miles:** 300 at 25 kt
Complement: 2
Military lift: 16 troops plus equipment or 2 tons
Guns: 1—7.62 mm MG.
Radars: Navigation: Raytheon; I-band.

Comment: Ordered 26 April 1993. Design based on 2000 TDX(M) hovercraft. Aluminium hulls. Capable of being embarked in an LCU. Speed indicated is at Sea State 3 with a full load. There is also a requirement for three LCACs with a 40 to 50 ton lift.

UPDATED

GRIFFON TDX   *1/2000 *, John Brodie / 0075807*

23 LCVP Mk 4

LCVP 8031   8401-8420   8621   8622

Displacement, tons: 10.5 light; 16 full load
Dimensions, feet (metres): 43.8 × 10.9 × 2.8 *(13.4 × 3.3 × 0.8)*
Main machinery: 2 Perkins T6.3544 diesels; 290 hp *(216 kW)*; 2 shafts
Speed, knots: 15. **Range, miles:** 150 at 14 kt
Complement: 3
Military lift: 20 Arctic equipped troops or 5.5 tons

Comment: Built by Souters and McTays. Introduced into service in 1986. Fitted with removable arctic canopies across well-deck. Operated by the Royal Marines. *LCVPs 8402, 8409, 8419* and *8420* built for the Royal Logistic Corps. These serve in rotation between the Falklands and UK.

UPDATED

LCVP Mk 4   *9/1998 *, H M Steele / 0053230*

7 + (8) LCVP Mk 5

LCVP 9473   9673-9676   9707   9708

Displacement, tons: 25 full load
Dimensions, feet (metres): 50.9 × 13.8 × 3 *(15.5 × 4.2 × 0.9)*
Main machinery: 2 Volvo Penta TAMD 72 WJ diesels; 2 PP 170 water-jets
Speed, knots: 25. **Range, miles:** 210 at 18 kt
Complement: 3
Military lift: 35 troops plus 2 tons equipment or 8 tons vehicles and stores
Radars: Navigation: Raytheon 40; I-band.

Comment: Contract placed with Vosper Thornycroft on 31 January 1995 for one craft which was handed over on 17 January 1996. Four more ordered on 23 October 1996 for *Ocean* were delivered 6 December 1997; and two more for RM Poole in October 1998. Eight more may be ordered in 2000. Can beach fully laden on a 1 : 120 gradient. Speed 15 kt at full load.

UPDATED

LCVP Mk 5   *7/1999 *, H M Steele / 0075808*

FAST INTERCEPT CRAFT

Comment: Two main types in service. Both around 15 m in length and powered by two 750 hp diesels to give speeds up to 55 kt. One has a VSV wave piercing hull which can maintain fast speeds in high sea states. Both types can be transported by air.

UPDATED

VSV   *10/1999 *, H M Steele / 0069031*

FIC 145   *8/1998 *, H M Steele / 0053229*

RRC and RIB

Comment: (1) 38 RRC Mk 2: 1.31 tons and 6.5 m *(21.3 ft)*; powered by either a single or twin Suzuki 140 hp *(104 kW)* outboard; 30 kt fully laden (50 light); carry 10 troops plus 1,500 lbs of equipment or 20 troops. In service 1993-96 and with the Army from 1997.
(2) 36 RRC Mk 3: 2.6 tons and 7.4 m *(24.2 ft)* powered by single Yamaha 220 hp *(162 kW)* diesel; 36 kt fully laden (40 light); carry 8 troops. Some used by the Army. In service 1996-98.
(3) RIBs: Halmatic Arctic 22/Pacific 22/Arctic 28/Pacific 28. Rolling contract for all four types. Capable of carrying 10 to 15 fully laden troops at speeds of 26 to 35 kt.

UPDATED

RRC   *6/1999*, A Sharma* / 0075809

RIBs   *5/1999*, John Brodie* / 0075810

PATROL FORCES

Note: Two 'Archer' class, *Ranger* and *Trumpeter*, are used as Gibraltar Guard Ships (details in *Training Ships* section).'

1 ANTARCTIC PATROL SHIP (AGOB)

Name	No	Builders	Commissioned
ENDURANCE (ex-*Polar Circle*)	A 171 (ex-A 176)	Ulstein Hatlo, Norway	21 Nov 1991

Displacement, tons: 6,500 full load
Dimensions, feet (metres): 298.6 × 57.4 × 27.9 *(91 × 17.9 × 8.5)*
Main machinery: 2 Bergen BRM8 diesels, 8,160 hp(m) *(6 MW)* sustained; 1 shaft; cp prop; bow and stern thrusters
Speed, knots: 15. **Range, miles:** 6,500 at 12 kt
Complement: 112 (15 officers) plus 14 Royal Marines
Radars: Surface search: Raytheon R 84 and M 34 ARG; E/F- and I-bands.
Navigation: Kelvin Hughes Type 1007; I-band.
IFF: Type 1011.
Helicopters: 2 Westland Lynx HAS 3.

Comment: Leased initially in late 1991 and then bought outright in early 1992 as support ship and guard vessel for the British Antarctic Survey. Hull is painted red. Inmarsat fitted. Main machinery is resiliently mounted. Ice-strengthened hull capable of breaking 1 m thick ice at 3 kt. Helicopter hangar is reached by lift from the flight deck. Accommodation is to standards previously unknown in the Royal Navy. Name and pennant number changed during refit in mid-1992. Sonars 2053, 2090 and 60-88.

UPDATED

2 CASTLE CLASS (OFFSHORE PATROL VESSELS Mk 2) (OPV)

Name	No	Builders	Launched	Commissioned
LEEDS CASTLE	P 258	Hall Russell, Aberdeen	29 Oct 1980	27 Oct 1981
DUMBARTON CASTLE	P 265	Hall Russell, Aberdeen	3 June 1981	26 Mar 1982

Displacement, tons: 1,427 full load
Dimensions, feet (metres): 265.7 × 37.7 × 11.8 *(81 × 11.5 × 3.6)*
Main machinery: 2 Ruston 12RKC diesels; 5,640 hp *(4.21 MW)* sustained; 2 shafts; cp props
Speed, knots: 19.5. **Range, miles:** 10,000 at 12 kt
Complement: 45 (6 officers) plus austerity accommodation for 25 Royal Marines
Guns: 1 DES/MSI DS 30B 30 mm/75; 650 rds/min to 10 km *(5.4 n miles)*; weight of shell 0.36 kg.
Mines: Can lay mines.
Countermeasures: Decoys: Outfit DLE; 2 or 4 Plessey Shield 102 mm 6-tubed launchers.
ESM: 'Orange Crop'; intercept.
Combat data systems: Racal CANE DEA-3 action data automation; SATCOM.
Weapons control: Radamec 2000 series optronic director.
Radars: Surface search: Plessey Type 994; E/F-band.
Navigation: Kelvin Hughes Type 1006; I-band.
Helicopters: Platform for operating Sea King or Lynx.

Comment: Started as a private venture. Ordered 8 August 1980. Design includes an ability to lay mines. Inmarsat commercial terminals fitted. Two Avon Sea Rider high-speed craft are embarked. P 258 is part of the Fishery Protection Squadron, P 265 based in the Falklands.

UPDATED

LEEDS CASTLE   *1/1998** / 0075812

5 ISLAND CLASS (OFFSHORE PATROL VESSELS) (OPV)

Name	No	Builders	Commissioned
ANGLESEY	P 277	Hall Russell, Aberdeen	1 June 1979
ALDERNEY	P 278	Hall Russell, Aberdeen	6 Oct 1979
GUERNSEY	P 297	Hall Russell, Aberdeen	28 Oct 1977
SHETLAND	P 298	Hall Russell, Aberdeen	14 July 1977
LINDISFARNE	P 300	Hall Russell, Aberdeen	3 Mar 1978

Displacement, tons: 925 standard; 1,260 full load
Dimensions, feet (metres): 176 wl; 195.3 oa × 36 × 15 *(53.7; 59.5 × 11 × 4.5)*
Main machinery: 2 Ruston 12RKC diesels; 5,640 hp *(4.21 MW)* sustained; 1 shaft; cp prop
Speed, knots: 16.5. **Range, miles:** 7,000 at 12 kt
Complement: 35 (5 officers)
Guns: 1 BMARC Oerlikon 20 mm GAM-BO1 or DES/MSI DS 30B 30 mm/75 Mk 1. 2 FN 7.62 mm MGs can be carried.
Countermeasures: ESM: 'Orange Crop'; intercept.
Combat data systems: Racal CANE DEA-1 action data automation.
Weapons control: Radamec 1000N optronic sight (may be fitted).
Radars: Navigation: Kelvin Hughes Type 1006; I-band.

Comment: Order for first five placed 2 July 1975. Two more ordered 21 October 1977. The earlier ships were retrofitted and the remainder built with enlarged bilge keels to damp down their motion in heavy weather. Fitted with stabilisers and water ballast arrangement. Operate in the Fishery Protection Squadron. The 40 mm guns replaced by 20 or 30 mm. Can carry small RM detachment and two Avon Sea Rider semi-rigid craft with 85 hp motor, for boarding. One paid off in December 1993 and was sold to Bangladesh. A second is laid up and is also for sale.

UPDATED

ENDURANCE   *5/1999*, Maritime Photographic* / 0075811

ALDERNEY   *6/1999*, T Gander* / 0075813

TRAINING SHIPS

1 RIVER CLASS (MINESWEEPER/PATROL CRAFT) (MSC/PC)

Name	No	Builders	Launched	Commissioned
ORWELL	M 2011	Richards Ltd (GY)	7 Feb 1985	27 Nov 1985

Displacement, tons: 770 full load
Dimensions, feet (metres): 156 × 34.5 × 9.5 *(47.5 × 10.5 × 2.9)*
Main machinery: 2 Ruston 6RKC diesels; 3,100 hp *(2.3 MW)* sustained; 2 shafts
Speed, knots: 14. **Range, miles:** 4,500 at 10 kt
Complement: 30 (7 officers)
Radars: Navigation: 2 Racal Decca TM 1226C; I-band.

Comment: The last of a class of 12 ships designed as EDATS wire sweep minesweepers manned by the Reserves. Four subsequently used as Northern Ireland patrol ships. Four of the class sold to Bangladesh in 1994; three to Brazil in 1995 followed by four more in 1997-98. This sole survivor has been used as the Britannia Naval College training ship since September 1994, with the Bofors 40 mm gun removed. **UPDATED**

ORWELL   7/1999*, Maritime Photographic / 0075815

16 ARCHER CLASS (TRAINING and PATROL CRAFT) (PB/AXL)

ARCHER P 264	PUNCHER P 291	EXAMPLE P 165 (ex-A 153)
BITER P 270	CHARGER P 292	EXPLORER P 164 (ex-A 154)
SMITER P 272	RANGER P 293	EXPLOIT P 167 (ex-A 167)
PURSUER P 273	TRUMPETER P 294	TRACKER P 274
BLAZER P 279	EXPRESS P 163 (ex-A 163)	RAIDER P 275
DASHER P 280		

Displacement, tons: 49 full load
Dimensions, feet (metres): 68.2 × 19 × 5.9 *(20.8 × 5.8 × 1.8)*
Main machinery: 2 RR CV 12 M800T diesels; 1,590 hp *(1.19 MW)*; or 2 MTU diesels; 2,000 hp(m) *(1.47 MW)* (P 274-275); 2 shafts
Speed, knots: 22 or 25 (P 274-275). **Range, miles:** 550 at 15 kt
Complement: 11 (3 officers)
Guns: 1 Oerlikon 20 mm (can be fitted).
Radars: Navigation: Racal Decca 1216; I-band.

Comment: First 14 ordered from Watercraft Ltd, Shoreham. Commissioning dates: *Archer*, August 1985; *Example*, September 1985; *Explorer*, January 1986; *Biter* and *Smiter*, February 1986. The remaining nine were incomplete when Watercraft went into liquidation in 1986 and were towed to Portsmouth for completion in 1988 by Vosper Thornycroft. Initially allocated for RNR training but underused in that role and now employed as University Naval Units (URNU)—*Puncher* (London), *Blazer* (Southampton), *Smiter* (Glasgow), *Charger* (Liverpool), *Dasher* (Bristol), *Archer* (Aberdeen), *Pursuer* (Sussex), *Biter* (Manchester and Salford), *Exploit* (Birmingham), *Express* (Wales), *Example* (Newcastle) and *Explorer* (Hull). The four ex-RNXS ships (P 163-P 167) are also part of the Inshore Training Squadron and are based at Gosport, Ipswich and Penarth. *Ranger* and *Trumpeter* are used as Gibraltar guard ships. Similar craft built for the Indian and Omani Coast Guards. Two more ordered from BMT in early 1997 to a modified design and built at Ailsa, Troon. *Tracker* and *Raider* commissioned January 1998 for Oxford and Cambridge University respectively. **UPDATED**

PURSUER   6/1999*, I J Plokker / 0075814

EXPLORER   7/1998*, Michael Nitz / 0053237

SURVEY SHIPS

Notes: (1) In addition to the ships listed below some work is done by chartered vessels with Naval Parties embarked. These include *Proud Seahorse* (of MFV type) which operates for the Hydrographer with Naval Party 1016 embarked and *Marine Explorer* with Naval Party 1008. These NPs are to be retained.
(2) All RN survey vessels painted grey in 1997-98 and given H pennant numbers.

PROUD SEAHORSE   8/1993* / 0075816

MARINE EXPLORER   6/1999*, Eidesvik Shipping / 0084422

1 SCOTT CLASS (AGS)

Name	No	Builders	Launched	Commissioned
SCOTT	H 131	Appledore Shipbuilders, Bideford	13 Oct 1996	30 June 1997

Displacement, tons: 13,500 full load
Dimensions, feet (metres): 430.1 × 70.5 × 29.5 *(131.1 × 21.5 × 9)*
Main machinery: 2 Krupp MaK 9M32 9-cyl diesels; 10,800 hp(m) *(7.94 MW)*; 1 shaft; acbLIPS cp prop; retractable bow thruster
Speed, knots: 17.5
Complement: 62 (12 officers) (see *Comment*)
Radars: Navigation: Kelvin Hughes ARPA 1626; I-band.
Helicopters: Platform for 1 light.

Comment: Designed by BAeSEMA/YARD and ordered 20 January 1995 to replace *Hecla*. Ice-strengthened bow. Foredeck strengthened for helicopter operations. The centre of the OSV surveying operations consists of an integrated navigation suite, the Sonar Array Sounding System (SASS) and data processing equipment. Additional sensors include gravimeters, a towed proton magnetometer and the Sonar 2090 ocean environment sensor. The SASS IV multibeam depth-sounder is capable of gathering 121 individual depth samples concurrently over a 120° swathe, producing a three-dimensional image of the seabed. 8,000 tons of seawater ballast can be used to achieve a sonar trim. The ship is at sea for 300 days a year with a crew of 42 embarked, rotating with the other 20 ashore. Can be used as an MCMV support ship. **UPDATED**

SCOTT   9/1999*, John Brodie / 0075817

0 + 2 (1) ECHO CLASS (AGS)

Displacement, tons: 3,500 full load
Dimensions, feet (metres): 295.3 × 52.5 × 18 *(90 × 16 × 5.5)*
Main machinery: Diesel electric; 4 MW; 2 azimuth thrusters
Speed, knots: 15. **Range, miles:** 9,000 at 12 kt
Complement: 69
Radars: Navigation: 2 sets; I-band.

Comment: Contract expected by mid-2000 for two new hydrographic and oceanographic ships with a secondary role of MCMV support. Vosper Thornycroft selected as preferred bidder in February 2000. First in-service date planned for September 2002 and second in February 2003. Names are likely to be *Echo* and *Enterprise.*

NEW ENTRY

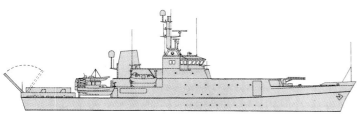

ECHO   *(not to scale), Ian Sturton /* 0084423

1 IMPROVED HECLA CLASS (AGS)

Name	No	Builders	Launched	Commissioned
HERALD	H 138	Robb Caledon, Leith	9 Nov 1972	31 Oct 1974

Displacement, tons: 2,945 full load
Dimensions, feet (metres): 259.8 × 49.2 × 18 *(79.2 × 15.4 × 5.5)*
Main machinery: Diesel-electric; 3 Paxman 12YJCZ diesels; 3,600 hp *(2.68 MW)* sustained; 3 generators; 1 motor; 2,000 hp *(1.49 MW)*; 1 shaft; bow thruster
Speed, knots: 14. **Range, miles:** 12,000 at 11 kt
Complement: 128 (12 officers)
Guns: 2 Oerlikon 20 mm (can be fitted). 2—12.7 mm MGs.
Countermeasures: ESM: UAR 1; intercept.
Radars: Navigation: Kelvin Hughes Type 1006; Racal Decca ARPA 1626C; I-band.
Helicopters: 1 Westland Lynx HAS 3.

Comment: Laid down 9 November 1972. Fitted with Qubit SIPS(S) integrated navigation and survey system, Hyperfix, SINS Mk 2, computerised data logging, gravimeter, magnetometer, sonars, echo-sounders, an oceanographic winch, passive stabilisation tank and two 35 ft surveying motorboats. Completed refit in January 1988 with a strengthened and extended flight deck for Lynx. Conducted trials of Scarab remote-controlled mine clearance device. Works in the North Norwegian Sea and North Atlantic when not required as an MCM support ship. Aqua shuttle towed vehicle acquired in 1995. This has a comprehensive oceanographic suite which undulates from the surface to 150 m depth, while being towed at 8 to 14 kt. Sonars 2090, 2094 and Simrad EA 500.

UPDATED

HERALD   *8/1999*, Maritime Photographic /* 0075818

2 BULLDOG CLASS (AGS)

Name	No	Builders	Launched	Commissioned
BULLDOG	H 317	Brooke Marine, Lowestoft	12 July 1967	21 Mar 1968
BEAGLE	H 319	Brooke Marine, Lowestoft	7 Sep 1967	9 May 1968

Displacement, tons: 1,159 full load
Dimensions, feet (metres): 189.6 × 37.4 × 12 *(57.8 × 11.4 × 3.7)*
Main machinery: 4 Lister-Blackstone ERS8M diesels; 2,640 hp *(1.97 MW)*; 2 shafts; cp props
Speed, knots: 15. **Range, miles:** 4,500 at 12 kt
Complement: 42 (5 officers)
Guns: Fitted for 2 Oerlikon 20 mm or 2—12.7 mm MGs.
Radars: Navigation: Kelvin Hughes Type 1007; I-band.

Comment: Originally designed for duty overseas, working in pairs although normally now employed in home waters. Built to commercial standards. Fitted with passive tank stabiliser, precision ranging radar, automatic steering. Qubit SIPS(S) integrated navigation and survey system. This allows chart processing in real time as the data is acquired. Air conditioned throughout. Sonars 2094 and 2060. Carry 9 m surveying motorboat. *Bulldog* completed refit including new radar and UHF in early 1985.

UPDATED

BEAGLE   *10/1999*, H M Steele /* 0075819

1 ROEBUCK CLASS (AGS)

Name	No	Builders	Launched	Commissioned
ROEBUCK	H 130	Brooke Marine, Lowestoft	14 Nov 1985	3 Oct 1986

Displacement, tons: 1,477 full load
Dimensions, feet (metres): 210 × 42.6 × 13 *(63.9 × 13 × 4)*
Main machinery: 4 Mirrlees Blackstone ESL8 Mk 1 diesels; 3,040 hp *(2.27 MW)*; 2 shafts; cp props
Speed, knots: 14. **Range, miles:** 4,000 at 10 kt
Complement: 46 (6 officers)
Radars: Navigation: Nautilus 6000C ARPA; I-band.

Comment: Designed for hydrographic surveys to full modern standards on UK continental shelf. Passive tank stabiliser. Qubit SIPS(S) integrated navigation and survey system. Air conditioned. Carries two 9 m surveying motor boats and one 4.5 m RIB. Acts as an MCM support ship when required.

UPDATED

ROEBUCK   *7/1999*, van Ginderen Collection /* 0075820

1 GLEANER CLASS (YFS)

Name	No	Builders	Launched	Commissioned
GLEANER	H 86	Emsworth Shipyard	18 Oct 1983	5 Dec 1983

Displacement, tons: 26 full load
Dimensions, feet (metres): 48.6 × 15.4 × 5.2 *(14.8 × 4.7 × 1.6)*
Main machinery: 2 Volvo Penta TMD 112; 524 hp(m) *(391 kW)*; 2 shafts
Speed, knots: 14 diesels; 7 centre shaft only
Complement: 5 plus 1 spare bunk
Radars: Navigation: Raytheon R40SX; I-band.

Comment: This craft is prefixed HMSML—HM Survey Motor Launch. Sonar 2094 and Atlas Fansweep multibeam echo sounder.

UPDATED

GLEANER   *4/1999*, John Brodie /* 0075821

4 NESBITT CLASS (YFS/SMB)

NESBITT 9423	PAT BARTON 9424	COOK 9425	OWEN 9426

Displacement, tons: 11 full load
Dimensions, feet (metres): 34.8 × 9.4 × 3.3 *(10.6 × 2.9 × 1)*
Main machinery: 2 Perkins Sabre 185C diesels; 430 hp(m) *(316 kW)* sustained; 2 shafts
Speed, knots: 15. **Range, miles:** 300 at 8 kt
Complement: 2 plus 10 spare

Comment: Delivered by Halmatic, Southampton by September 1996. Fitted with GPS, Ultra 3000 Side scan sonar and Qubit SIPS. In service at the Hydrographic School and are likely to be carried in new survey vessels in due course.

VERIFIED

NESBITT   *11/1998, John Brodie /* 0053244

ROYAL FLEET AUXILIARY SERVICE

Personnel

1 January 2000: 2,274 (891 officers)

General

The Royal Fleet Auxiliary Service is a civilian-manned fleet under the command of the Commander in Chief Fleet from 1 April 1993. Its main task is to supply warships at sea with fuel, food, stores and ammunition. It also provides aviation platforms, amphibious support for the

Navy and Marines and sea transport for Army units. All ships take part in operational sea training. An order in council on 30 November 1989 changed the status of the RFA service to government-owned vessels on non-commercial service.

Ships taken up from Trade

The following ships taken up from trade: *Proud Seahorse* and *Marine Explorer* operate in home waters under the Hydrographer. *Oil Mariner*

(supply), *St Brandan* (ferry), *Indomitable* (tug), all operate in the Falkland Islands; *Maersk Ascension* and *Maersk Gannet* as tankers to Ascension Island; *St Angus* as Gulf supply ship.

New Construction

(1)   Two new LSLs are planned to enter service in 2003/04. Contracts planned for 2001 after tenders in October 2000. Military lift to be 350 troops and 70 tons stores. To

have a helicopter platform and carry mexeflotes. Possible names are *Lyme Bay* and *Largs Bay*.

(2)   Six RoRo ships identified in 1998 as being required are likely to be commercially operated and managed. To be in service in 2002/03.

2 OL CLASS (LARGE FLEET TANKERS) (AO)

Name	No	Builders	Launched	Commissioned
OLWEN	A 122	Hawthorn Leslie, Hebburn-on-Tyne	10 July 1964	21 June 1965
OLNA	A 123	Hawthorn Leslie, Hebburn-on-Tyne	28 July 1965	1 Apr 1966

Displacement, tons: 9,367 light; 36,000 full load
Measurement, tons: 25,100 dwt; 18,600 gross
Dimensions, feet (metres): 648 × 84 × 36.4
(197.5 × 25.6 × 11.1)
Main machinery: 2 Babcock & Wilcox boilers; 750 psi
(52.75 kg/cm²); 950°F *(510°C)*; Pametrada turbines;
26,500 hp *(19.77 MW)*; 1 shaft
Speed, knots: 20
Complement: 94 (28 officers) plus 40 aircrew
Cargo capacity: 16,000 tons diesel; 125 tons lub oil; 2,750 tons
Avcat; 375 tons fresh water
Guns: 2 Oerlikon 20 mm. 2—7.62 mm MGs.
Countermeasures: Decoys: 2 Corvus or Plessey Shield chaff
launchers.
Radars: Surface search and Navigation: 2 Kelvin Hughes; I-band.
Helicopters: 2 Westland Sea King HAS 6.

Comment: Designed for underway replenishment both alongside and astern (fuel only) or by helicopter. Specially

OLNA   *6/1999*, A Sharma /* 0075822

strengthened for operations in ice, fully air conditioned. *Olna* has an improved design of replenishment-at-sea systems. Inmarsat SATCOM system fitted. Hangar accommodation for

two helicopters port side of funnel. Both ships are to be replaced by 'Wave' class in 2002.   **UPDATED**

0 + 2 WAVE CLASS (LARGE FLEET TANKERS) (AO)

Name	No	Builders	Laid down	Launched	Commissioned
WAVE KNIGHT	A 389	BAE Systems, Barrow	22 Oct 1998	Sep 2000	Feb 2002
WAVE RULER	A 390	Govan, Clyde	10 Feb 2000	Mar 2001	Oct 2002

Displacement, tons: 30,300 full load
Measurement, tons: 18,200 dwt
Dimensions, feet (metres): 596 × 88 × 32.8
(181.7 × 26.9 × 10)
Main machinery: Diesel-electric: 4 Wärtsilä 12V 32E/GECLM
diesel generators; 25,514 hp(m) *(18.76 MW)*; 2 GECLM
motors; 19,040 hp(m) *(14 MW)*; 1 shaft; Kamewa bow and
stern thrusters.
Speed, knots: 18. **Range, miles:** 8,000 at 16 kt
Complement: 80 plus 22 aircrew

Cargo capacity: 15,000 m³ total liquids plus 3,000 m³ aviation
fuel; 8—20 ft refrigerated containers plus 500 m³ solids
Guns: 2 Vulcan Phalanx CIWS; fitted for but not with.
2—30 mm. 4—7.62 mm MGs.
Countermeasures: Decoys: Outfit DLJ.
Radars: Surface search: E/F-band.
Navigation: KH 1007; I-band.
IFF: Type 1017.
Helicopters: 1 Merlin HM Mk 1.

Comment: Feasibility studies by BAeSEMA/YARD completed in early 1995. Draft invitation to tender issued 10 October 1995 followed by full tender on 26 June 1996. Contracts to build placed with VSEL (BAE Systems) on 12 March 1997. One spot flight deck with full hangar facilities for one Merlin. Enclosed bridge including bridge wings. Double hull construction. Inclined RAS gear with three rigs and one crane.
                                                        UPDATED

WAVE KNIGHT (computer graphic)   *1999*, BAE Systems /* 0075823

1 OAKLEAF CLASS (SUPPORT TANKER) (AOT)

Name	No	Builders	Commissioned	Recommissioned
OAKLEAF (ex-*Oktania*)	A 111	Uddevalla, Sweden	1981	14 Aug 1986

Displacement, tons: 49,648 full load
Measurement, tons: 37,328 dwt
Dimensions, feet (metres): 570 × 105.6 × 36.7
(173.7 × 32.2 × 11.2)
Main machinery: 1 Burmeister & Wain 4L80MCE diesel;
10,800 hp(m) *(7.96 MW)* sustained; 1 shaft; cp prop; bow and
stern thrusters
Speed, knots: 14
Complement: 35 (14 officers)
Cargo capacity: 43,000 m³ fuel
Guns: 2—7.62 mm MGs.
Countermeasures: Decoys: 2 Plessey Shield chaff launchers can
be fitted.
Radars: Navigation: Racal Decca 1226 and 1229; I-band.

Comment: Acquired in July 1985 and converted by Falmouth Ship Repairers to include full RAS rig and extra accommodation. Handed over on completion and renamed. Ice-strengthened hull. Marisat fitted. Major refit in 1994-95.
                                                        UPDATED

OAKLEAF   *3/1999*, M Declerck /* 0075824

3 APPLELEAF CLASS (SUPPORT TANKERS) (AOT)

Name	No	Builders	Launched		Commissioned	
BRAMBLELEAF (ex-Hudson Deep)	A 81	Cammell Laird, Birkenhead	22 Jan	1976	3 Mar	1980
BAYLEAF	A 109	Cammell Laird, Birkenhead	27 Oct	1981	26 Mar	1982
ORANGELEAF (ex-Balder London, ex-Hudson Progress)	A 110	Cammell Laird, Birkenhead	—		2 May	1984

Displacement, tons: 37,747 full load (A 109-110); 40,870 (A 81)
Measurement, tons: 20,761 gross; 11,573 net; 29,999 dwt
Dimensions, feet (metres): 560 × 85 × 36.1
(170.7 × 25.9 × 11)
Main machinery: 2 Pielstick 14 PC2.2 V 400 diesels; 14,000 hp
(m) *(10.29 MW)* sustained; 1 shaft
Speed, knots: 15.5; 16.3 (A 109)
Complement: 56 (19 officers)
Cargo capacity: 22,000 m³ dieso; 3,800 m³ Avcat
Guns: 2 Oerlikon 20 mm. 4—7.62 mm MGs.
Countermeasures: Decoys: 2 Corvus or 2 Plessey Shield
launchers.
Radars: Navigation: Racal Decca 1226 and 1229; I-band.

Comment: *Brambleleaf* chartered in 1979-80 and converted,
completing Autumn 1979. Part of a four-ship order cancelled
by Hudson Fuel and Shipping Co, but completed by the
shipbuilders, being the only mercantile order then in hand.
Bayleaf built under commercial contract to be chartered by
MoD. *Orangeleaf* major refit September 1985 to fit full RAS
capability and extra accommodation. *Appleleaf* sold to
Australia in September 1989.

UPDATED

BAYLEAF
7/1999*, A Sharma / 0075825

3 ROVER CLASS (SMALL FLEET TANKERS) (AOL)

Name	No	Builders	Launched		Commissioned	
GREY ROVER	A 269	Swan Hunter Shipbuilders, Wallsend-on-Tyne	17 Apr	1969	10 Apr	1970
GOLD ROVER	A 271	Swan Hunter Shipbuilders, Wallsend-on-Tyne	7 Mar	1973	22 Mar	1974
BLACK ROVER	A 273	Swan Hunter Shipbuilders, Wallsend-on-Tyne	30 Oct	1973	23 Aug	1974

Displacement, tons: 4,700 light; 11,522 full load
Measurement, tons: 6,692 (A 271, 273), 6,822 (A 269) dwt;
7,510 gross; 3,185 net
Dimensions, feet (metres): 461 × 63 × 24
(140.6 × 19.2 × 7.3)
Main machinery: 2 SEMT-Pielstick 16 PA4 185 diesels;
15,360 hp(m) *(11.46 MW)*; 1 shaft; Kamewa cp prop; bow
thruster
Speed, knots: 19. **Range, miles:** 15,000 at 15 kt
Complement: 48 (17 officers) (A 269); 55 (18 officers) (A 271,
273)
Cargo capacity: 6,600 tons fuel
Guns: 2 Oerlikon 20 mm. 2—7.62 mm MGs.
Countermeasures: Decoys: 2 Corvus and 2 Plessey Shield
launchers. 1 Graseby Type 182; towed torpedo decoy.
Radars: Navigation: Racal Decca 52690 ARPA; Racal Decca
1690; I-band.
Helicopters: Platform for Westland Sea King HAS 5 or HC 4.

Comment: Small fleet tankers designed to replenish HM ships at
sea with fuel, fresh water, limited dry cargo and refrigerated
stores under all conditions while under way. No hangar but
helicopter landing platform is served by a stores lift, to enable
stores to be transferred at sea by 'vertical lift'. Capable of HIFR.
Siting of SATCOM aerial varies. *Green Rover* sold in September
1992 to Indonesia. *Blue Rover* to Portugal in March 1993.

UPDATED

GREY ROVER
1/2000*, Robert Pabst / 0075826

2 FORT VICTORIA CLASS (FLEET REPLENISHMENT SHIPS) (AOR)

Name	No	Builders	Laid down		Launched		Commissioned	
FORT VICTORIA	A 387	Harland & Wolff/Cammell Laird	4 Apr	1988	12 June	1990	24 June	1994
FORT GEORGE	A 388	Swan Hunter Shipbuilders, Wallsend-on-Tyne	9 Mar	1989	1 Mar	1991	16 July	1993

Displacement, tons: 36,580 full load
Dimensions, feet (metres): 667.7 oa; 607 wl × 99.7 × 32
(203.5; 185 × 30.4 × 9.8)
Main machinery: 2 Crossley SEMT-Pielstick 16 PC2.6 V 400
diesels; 23,904 hp(m) *(17.57 MW)* sustained; 2 shafts
Speed, knots: 20
Complement: 134 (95 RFA plus 15 RN plus 24 civilian stores
staff) plus 154 (28 officers) aircrew
Cargo capacity: 12,505 m³ liquids; 6,234 m³ solids

Guns: 2 DES/MSI DS 30B 30 mm/75.
2 Vulcan Phalanx 20 mm Mk 15.

Countermeasures: Decoys: 4 Plessey Shield or 4 Sea Gnat
6-barrelled 130 mm/102 mm launchers. Graseby Type 182;
towed torpedo decoy.
ESM: Marconi Racal Thorn UAT; intercept.
Combat data systems: Marconi Matra SCOT 1D SATCOM.
Radars: Air search: Plessey Type 996; 3D; E/F-band (can be
fitted).
Navigation: Kelvin Hughes Type 1007; I-band.
Aircraft control: Kelvin Hughes NUCLEUS; E/F-band.

Helicopters: 5 Westland Sea King/Merlin helicopters.

Programmes: The requirement for these ships is to provide fuel
and stores support to the Fleet at sea. *Fort Victoria* ordered

23 April 1986 and *Fort George* on 18 December 1987. *Fort
Victoria* delayed by damage during building and entered
Cammell Laird Shipyard for post sea trials completion in July
1992. The original plan for six of this class was progressively
eroded and no more of this type will be built.
Structure: Four dual-purpose abeam replenishment rigs for
simultaneous transfer of liquids and solids. Stern refuelling.
Repair facilities for Merlin helicopters. The plan to fit Seawolf
GWS 26 VLS has been abandoned in favour of Phalanx CIWS
fitted in 1998/99 to both ships.
Operational: Two helicopter spots. There is a requirement to
provide an emergency landing facility for Sea Harriers.

UPDATED

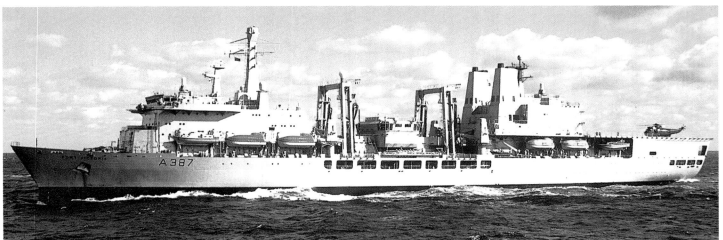

FORT VICTORIA
10/1999*, H M Steele / 0075828

2 FORT GRANGE CLASS (FLEET REPLENISHMENT SHIPS) (AFS)

Name	No	Builders	Laid down	Launched	Commissioned
FORT ROSALIE (ex-Fort Grange)	A 385	Scott-Lithgow, Greenock	9 Nov 1973	9 Dec 1976	6 Apr 1978
FORT AUSTIN	A 386	Scott-Lithgow, Greenock	9 Dec 1975	9 Mar 1978	11 May 1979

Displacement, tons: 23,384 full load
Measurement, tons: 8,300 dwt
Dimensions, feet (metres): 603 × 79 × 28.2
(183.9 × 24.1 × 8.6)
Main machinery: 1 Sulzer RND90 diesel; 23,200 hp(m)
(17.05 MW); 1 shaft; 2 bow thrusters
Speed, knots: 22. **Range, miles:** 10,000 at 20 kt
Complement: 114 (31 officers) plus 36 RNSTS (civilian supply staff) plus 45 RN aircrew

Cargo capacity: 3,500 tons armament, naval and victualling stores in 4 holds of 12,800 m³
Guns: 2 Oerlikon 20 mm. 4—7.62 mm MGs.
Countermeasures: Decoys: 2 Corvus or 2 Plessey Shield launchers (upper bridge).
Radars: Navigation: Kelvin Hughes Type 1007; I-band.
Helicopters: 4 Westland Sea King.

Comment: Ordered in November 1971. Fitted for SCOT SATCOMs but carry Marisat. Normally only one helicopter is embarked. ASW stores for helicopters carried on board. Emergency flight deck on the hangar roof. There are six cranes, three of 10 tons lift and three of 5 tons. A 385 relieved *Resource* at Split from early 1997 until early 2000 as a support ship for UK forces in the Balkans.
UPDATED

FORT AUSTIN

3/1999*, C E Castle / 0075827

1 STENA TYPE (FORWARD REPAIR SHIP) (AR)

Name	No	Builders	Commissioned	Recommissioned
DILIGENCE (ex-Stena Inspector)	A 132	Oresundsvarvet AB, Landskrona, Sweden	1981	12 Mar 1984

Displacement, tons: 10,765 full load
Measurement, tons: 6,550 gross; 4,939 dwt
Dimensions, feet (metres): 367.5 × 67.3 × 22.3
(112 × 20.5 × 6.8)
Flight deck, feet (metres): 83 × 83 *(25.4 × 25.4)*
Main machinery: Diesel-electric; 5 V16 Nohab-Polar diesel generators; 2,650 kW; 4 NEBB motors; 6,000 hp(m) *(4.41 MW)*; 1 shaft; Kamewa cp prop; 2 Kamewa bow tunnel thrusters; 3,000 hp(m) *(2.2 MW)*; 2 azimuth thrusters (aft); 3,000 hp(m) *(2.2 MW)*
Speed, knots: 12. **Range, miles:** 5,000 at 12 kt
Complement: 38 (15 officers) plus accommodation for 147 plus 55 temporary
Cargo capacity: Long-jib crane SWL 5 tons; maximum lift, 40 tons

Guns: 4 Oerlikon 20 mm. 4—7.62 mm MGs.
Countermeasures: Decoys: Outfit DLE; 4 Plessey Shield 102 mm 6-tubed launchers.

Helicopters: Facilities for up to Boeing Chinook HC 1 (medium lift) size.

Programmes: *Stena Inspector* was designed originally as a Multipurpose Support Vessel for North Sea oil operations, and completed in January 1981. Chartered on 25 May 1982 for use as a fleet repair ship during the Falklands War. Purchased from Stena (UK) Line in October 1983, and converted for use as Forward Repair Ship in the South Atlantic (Falkland Islands). Conversion by Clyde Dock Engineering Ltd, Govan from 12 November 1983 to 29 February 1984.
Modernisation: Following items added during conversion: large workshop for hull and machinery repairs (in well-deck);

DILIGENCE (in the Falkland Islands)

4/1999* / 0075829

accommodation for naval Junior Rates (new accommodation block); accommodation for crew of conventional submarine (in place of Saturation Diving System); extensive craneage facilities; overside supply of electrical power, water, fuel, steam, air, to ships alongside; large naval store (in place of cement tanks); armament and magazines; Naval Communications System; decompression chamber.
Structure: Four 5 ton anchors for four-point mooring system. Strengthened for operations in ice (Ice Class 1A). Kongsberg

Albatross Positioning System has been retained in full. Uses bow and stern thrusters and main propeller to maintain a selected position to within a few metres, up to Beaufort Force 9. Controlled by Kongsberg KS 500 computers.
Operational: Falkland Islands support team (Naval Party 2010) embarked when the ship is in the South Atlantic. Has also been used as MCMV support ship in the Gulf.
UPDATED

1 AVIATION TRAINING SHIP (HSS/ATS)

Name	No	Builders	Commissioned	Recommissioned
ARGUS (ex-Contender Bezant)	A 135	CNR Breda, Venice	1981	1 June 1988

Displacement, tons: 18,280 standard; 26,421 full load
Measurement, tons: 9,965 dwt
Dimensions, feet (metres): 574.5 × 99.7 × 27
(175.1 × 30.4 × 8.2)
Main machinery: 2 Lindholmen SEMT-Pielstick 18 PC2.5 V 400 diesels; 23,400 hp(m) *(17.2 MW)* sustained; 2 shafts
Speed, knots: 18. **Range, miles:** 20,000 at 19 kt
Complement: 80 (22 officers) plus 35 permanent RN plus 137 RN aircrew
Military lift: 3,300 tons dieso; 1,100 tons aviation fuel; 138 4 ton vehicles in lieu of aircraft

Guns: 4 BMARC 30 mm Mk 1. 4—7.62 mm MGs.
Countermeasures: Decoys: Outfit DLB; 4 Sea Gnat 130 mm/102 mm launchers. Graseby Type 182; torpedo decoy.
ESM: THORN EMI Guardian; radar warning.
Combat data systems: Racal CANE DEB-1 data automation. Inmarsat SATCOM communications. Marisat.
Radars: Air search: Type 994 MTI; E/F-band.
Air/surface search: Kelvin Hughes Type 1006; I-band.
Navigation: Racal Decca Type 994; I-band.

Fixed-wing aircraft: Provision to transport 12 BAe Sea Harrier FA-2.
Helicopters: 6 Westland Sea King HAS 5/6 or similar.

Programmes: Ro-ro container ship whose conversion for her new task was begun by Harland and Wolff in March 1984 and completed on 3 March 1988.
Structure: Uses former ro-ro deck as hangar with four sliding WT doors able to operate at a speed of 10 m/min. Can replenish

ARGUS

10/1999*, B Sullivan / 0075830

other ships underway. One lift port midships, one abaft funnel. Domestic facilities are very limited if she is to be used in the Command support role. Flight deck is 372.4 ft *(113.5 m)* long and has a 5 ft thick concrete layer on its lower side. First RFA to be fitted with a command system.

Operational: Deployed to the Gulf in 1990-91 as a Primary Casualty Receiving Ship (PCRS) with the hangar converted into hospital accommodation. Deployed to the Adriatic as a Helicopter Support Ship. Obvious shortcomings in this role added impetus to the ordering of a properly designed LPH.
UPDATED

1 TRANSPORT (AK)

Name	No	Builders	Commissioned
SEA CRUSADER	A 96	Kawasaki Heavy Industries	Oct 1996

Measurement, tons: 23,986 grt; 9,677 dwt
Dimensions, feet (metres): 528.2 × 82 × 21.3
(161 × 25 × 6.5)
Main machinery: 2 Kawasaki MAN diesels; 13,382 hp(m)
(9.84 MW); 2 shafts; cp props; 2 bow thrusters; 2,000 hp(m)
(1.47 MW)
Speed, knots: 18
Complement: 17
Radars: Navigation: Raytheon; E/F-band and Raytheon ARPA;
I-band.

Comment: Leased in 1996 and lease extended until at least April
2001. This is a ro-ro general cargo ship built to commercial
standards. There are 2,300 lane metres of space and a stern
ramp capacity of 150 tons. Available for use by the Joint Rapid
Deployment Force and used for MoD general freighting duties.
Not equipped to enter a war zone. Based at Southampton.
UPDATED

SEA CRUSADER

6/1999 * / 0075831

1 TRANSPORT (AK)

Name	No	Builders	Completed
SEA CENTURION	A 98	SEC, Viareggio	Sep 1998

Measurement, tons: 12,350 dwt
Dimensions, feet (metres): 599.1 × 84.6 × 24
(182.6 × 25.8 × 7.3)
Main machinery: 4 Sulzer 8ZA40S diesels; 31,334 hp(m)
(23.04 MW) sustained; 2 shafts; acbLIPS cp props; 2 bow
thrusters; 2,720 hp(m) *(2 MW)*
Speed, knots: 22. **Range, miles:** 6,000 at 12 kt
Complement: 18
Cargo capacity: 800 × 20 ft and 268 × 40 ft containers plus
211 × 40 ft trailers

Comment: Leased from Stena RoRo in October 1998 until at
least January 2001. A second of class A 97 was planned to be
leased in April 1999 but the shipyard was unable to finish the
contract. 2,715 lane metres of space. Available for Joint Rapid
Deployment Force and for MOD freighting. Up to six RoRos are
expected to be earmarked for leasing when required. Based at
Southampton.

UPDATED

SEA CENTURION
1/1999 * / 0075832

4 SIR BEDIVERE CLASS (LANDING SHIPS LOGISTIC) (LSL)

Name	No	Builders	Laid down	Launched	Commissioned
SIR BEDIVERE	L 3004	Hawthorn Leslie, Hebburn-on-Tyne	Oct 1965	20 July 1966	18 May 1967
SIR GERAINT	L 3027	Alex Stephen, Glasgow	June 1965	26 Jan 1967	12 July 1967
SIR PERCIVALE	L 3036	Hawthorn Leslie, Hebburn-on-Tyne	Apr 1966	4 Oct 1967	23 Mar 1968
SIR TRISTRAM	L 3505	Hawthorn Leslie, Hebburn-on-Tyne	Feb 1966	12 Dec 1966	14 Sep 1967

Displacement, tons: 3,270 light; 5,674 full load
6,700 full load (SLEP)
Dimensions, feet (metres): 412.1; 441.1 (SLEP) × 59.8 × 13
(125.6; 134.4 × 18.2 × 4)
Main machinery: 2 Mirrlees 10-ALSSDM diesels; 9,400 hp
(7.01 MW) or 2 Wärtsilä 280 V12 diesels; 9,928 hp(m) *(7.3
MW)* sustained (SLEP); 2 shafts; bow thruster; 980 hp(m)
(720 kW) (SLEP)
Speed, knots: 17. **Range, miles:** 8,000 at 15 kt
Complement: 51 (18 officers); 49 (15 officers) (SLEP)
Military lift: 340 troops (534 hard lying); 17 or 18 (SLEP) MBTs;
34 mixed vehicles; 120 tons POL; 30 tons ammunition;
1—25 ton crane; 2—4.5 ton cranes. Increased capacity for 20
helicopters (11 tank deck and 9 vehicle deck) after SLEP
Guns: 2 or 4 Oerlikon 20 mm. 4—7.62 mm MGs.
Countermeasures: Decoys: 2 Plessey Shield chaff launchers.
Radars: Navigation: Kelvin Hughes Type 1006 or Racal Decca
2690; I-band.
Aircraft control: Kelvin Hughes Type 1007; I-band (SLEP).
Helicopters: Platforms to operate Gazelle or Lynx or Chinook
(SLEP) or Sea King.

Comment: Fitted for bow and stern loading with drive-through
facilities and deck-to-deck ramps. Facilities provided for
onboard maintenance of vehicles and for laying out pontoon
equipment. Mexeflote self-propelled floating platforms can be
strapped one on each side. On 8 June 1982 *Sir Tristram* was
severely damaged off the Falkland Islands. Tyne Shiprepairers
were given a contract to repair and modify her. This included
lengthening by 29 ft, an enlarged flight deck capable of taking
Chinooks, a new bridge and twin masts. The aluminium
superstructure was replaced by steel and the provision of new

SIR GERAINT
6/1999 *, A Sharma / 0075833

communications, an EMR, SATCOM, new navigation systems
and helicopter control radar greatly increase her effectiveness.
Completed 9 October 1985. *Sir Bedivere* had a similar SLEP in
Rosyth from December 1994 to January 1998, including new
main engines, a new bridge, and the helicopter platform
lowered by one deck, which has reduced the size of the stern

ramp. The other pair are to be replaced by two new ships
planned to enter service in 2003/04. Based at Southampton.
All deployed to the Gulf in 1991 with additional 20 mm guns,
decoy systems and navigation equipment. One of the class in
service in Singapore Navy.
UPDATED

SIR BEDIVERE
12/1999 *, G Toremans / 0075834

1 SIR GALAHAD CLASS (LSL)

Name	No	Builders	Laid down	Launched	Commissioned
SIR GALAHAD	L 3005	Swan Hunter Shipbuilders, Wallsend-on-Tyne	12 May 1985	13 Dec 1986	25 Nov 1987

Displacement, tons: 8,585 full load
Dimensions, feet (metres): 461 × 64 × 14.1
(140.5 × 19.5 × 4.3)
Main machinery: 2 Mirrlees-Blackstone diesels; 13,320 hp
(9.94 MW); 2 shafts; cp props
Speed, knots: 18. **Range, miles:** 13,000 at 15 kt
Complement: 49 (15 officers)
Military lift: 343 troops (537 hard-lying); 18 MBT; 20 mixed
vehicles; ammunition, fuel and stores
Guns: 2 Oerlikon 20 mm GAM-BO3. 2—12.7 mm MGs.
Countermeasures: Decoys: 4 Plessey Shield 102 mm 6-tubed
launchers.
Combat data systems: Racal CANE data automation.
Radars: Navigation: Kelvin Hughes Type 1007; I-band.
Helicopters: 1 Westland Sea King HC 4.

Comment: Ordered on 6 September 1984 as a replacement for
Sir Galahad, sunk as a war grave after air attack at Bluff Cove,
Falkland Islands on 8 June 1982. Has bow and stern ramps
with a visor bow gate. One 25 ton and three 8.6 ton cranes. Up
to four (total) Mexeflote pontoons can be attached on both
sides of the hull superstructure. Based at Southampton.

UPDATED   SIR GALAHAD

5/1999*, Maritime Photographic / 0075835

ROYAL MARITIME AUXILIARY AND GOVERNMENT AGENCY SERVICES

Notes: (1) In early 2000, a total of 12 vessels were still operated by the RMAS. The remainder of ships in this section are MoD assets and retain the RMAS markings but are operated either by SERCO-Denholm, and fly the Government Services (GS) ensign, or are classified as Government Furnished Equipment (GFE) and operated by contractors shown, or are Defence Research Agency vessels.
(2) Two hospital ships with 200 beds are planned to be in-service by 2005.

3 SAL CLASS (SALVAGE AND MOORING SHIPS) (ARSD)

Name	No	Builders	Commissioned
SALMOOR	A 185	Hall Russell, Aberdeen	12 Nov 1985
SALMASTER	A 186	Hall Russell, Aberdeen	10 Apr 1986
SALMAID	A 187	Hall Russell, Aberdeen	28 Oct 1986

Displacement, tons: 1,605 light; 2,225 full load
Dimensions, feet (metres): 253 × 48.9 × 12.5 *(77 × 14.9 × 3.8)*
Main machinery: 2 Ruston 8RKC diesels; 4,000 hp *(2.98 MW)* sustained; 1 shaft; cp prop
Speed, knots: 15
Complement: 17 (4 officers) plus 27 spare billets
Radars: Navigation: Racal Decca; I-band.

Comment: Ordered on 23 January 1984. *Salmoor* on the Clyde and *Salmaid* at Devonport are
RMAS ships. *Salmaster* on the Clyde is GS. Lift, 400 tons; 200 tons on horns. Can carry
submersibles including LR 5.

UPDATED

SALMAID

6/1999*, A Sharma / 0075836

1 SUPPORT SHIP (AR)

Name	No	Builders	Commissioned
NEWTON	A 367	Scott-Lithgow, Greenock	17 June 1976

Displacement, tons: 3,140 light; 4,652 full load
Dimensions, feet (metres): 323.5 × 53 × 18.5 *(98.6 × 16 × 5.7)*
Main machinery: Diesel-electric; 3 Mirrlees-Blackstone diesel generators; 4,350 hp *(3.25 MW)*;
1 GEC motor; 2,040 hp *(1.52 MW)*; Kort nozzle; bow thruster
Speed, knots: 14. **Range, miles:** 5,000 at 14 kt
Complement: 64 including 12 scientists
Radars: Navigation: Kelvin Hughes 1006; I-band.

Comment: Passive tank stabilisation. Prime duty was sonar propagation trials but now converted
to a support ship for special forces. Can serve as cable-layer with large cable tanks. Special winch
system. Low noise level electric propulsion system. RMAS ship based at Devonport.

UPDATED

3 MOORHEN CLASS (SALVAGE AND MOORING SHIPS) (ARS)

Name	No	Builders	Commissioned
MOORHEN	Y 32	McTay, Bromborough	26 Apr 1989
MOORFOWL	Y 33	McTay, Bromborough	30 June 1989
CAMERON	A 72	Dunston, Hessle	31 May 1991

Displacement, tons: 530 full load
Dimensions, feet (metres): 106 × 37.7 × 6.6 *(32.3 × 11.5 × 2)*
Main machinery: 2 Cummins KT19-M diesels; 730 hp *(545 kW)* sustained; 2 Aquamasters; bow
thruster
Speed, knots: 8
Complement: 10 (2 officers) plus 2 divers

Comment: Classified as powered mooring lighters. The whole ship can be worked from a 'flying
bridge' which is constructed over a through deck. Day mess for five divers. *Moorhen* at
Portsmouth, *Moorfowl* at Devonport are RMAS vessels. *Cameron* works for DERA (Maritime) and
is modified as a trials support vessel.

UPDATED

MOORFOWL

5/1999*, John Brodie / 0075837

1 OILPRESS CLASS (COASTAL TANKER) (AOTL)

Name	No	Builders	Launched
OILPRESS	Y 21	Appledore Ferguson	29 Aug 1968

Displacement, tons: 280 standard; 530 full load
Dimensions, feet (metres): 139.5 × 30 × 8.3 *(42.5 × 9 × 2.5)*
Main machinery: 1 Lister-Blackstone ES6 diesel; 405 hp *(302 kW)*; 1 shaft
Speed, knots: 9
Complement: 8 (3 officers)
Cargo capacity: 250 tons dieso

Comment: Ordered on 10 May 1967. GS ship on the Clyde.

UPDATED

NEWTON

9/1999*, John Brodie / 0075838

OILPRESS

10/1998*, M Declerck / 0053258

1 TRIALS SHIP

Name	No	Builders	Launched	Commissioned
TRITON	—	Vosper Thornycroft, Woolston	6 May 2000	Sep 2000

Displacement, tons: 1,100 full load
Dimensions, feet (metres): 321.5 × 73.8 × 10.5 *(98 × 22.5 × 3.2)*
Main machinery: Diesel electric; 2 Paxman 12V 185 diesel generators; 4 MW; 1 HMA motor 3.5 MW; 1 shaft (centreline); 2 HMA motors; 700 kW; 2 Schottel propulsors (outer hulls)
Speed, knots: 20; 8 (outer hulls only). **Range, miles:** 3,000 at 12 kt
Complement: 12 plus 12 scientists
Radars: Navigation: Racal Bridgemaster ARPA; E/F- and I-band.
Helicopters: Platform for 1 Lynx.

Comment: Contract placed in July 1998 for a trimaran demonstrator vessel. First steel cut 11 January 1999. The side hulls have an overall length of 111.5 ft *(34 m)*. This is the trials vessel for a possible 7,000 ton future frigate of 175 × 30 m. The ship is to be run by the Defence Evaluation Research Agency (DERA). Phase 1 US/UK trials are scheduled from late 2000 until March 2002. Instrumentation system supplied by USN. Provision has been made for a 5 MW magnetic propulsion motor.   ***UPDATED***

TRITON (computer graphic)   *1999*, DERA /* 0075839

1 RESEARCH SHIP (AGOR)

Name	No	Builders	Commissioned
COLONEL TEMPLER (ex-*Criscilla*)	—	Hall Russell, Aberdeen	1966

Displacement, tons: 1,300 full load
Dimensions, feet (metres): 185.4 × 36 × 18.4 *(56.5 × 11 × 5.6)*
Main machinery: Diesel-electric; 2 Cummins KTA-38G4M diesels; 2,557 hp(m) *(1.88 MW)* sustained; 2 Newage HC M734E1 generators; 1 Amsaldo DH 560S motor; 2,312 hp(m) *(1.7 MW)*; 1 Aquamaster azimuth thruster with contra rotating props
Speed, knots: 13.5
Complement: 14 plus 12 scientists
Radars: Navigation: Racal Decca 2690 ARPA; I-band.

Comment: Built as a stern trawler. Converted in 1980 for use at RAE Farnborough as an acoustic research ship. After a major rebuild in 1992 she is operated by Vosper Thornycroft for the Defence Research Agency. Re-engined in early 1997 with a raft mounted diesel-electric plant to reduce noise and vibration. Carries a 9 m workboat *Quest* Q 26. Well equipped laboratories. Capable of deploying and recovering up to 5 tons of equipment from deck winches and a 5 ton hydraulic A frame.   ***UPDATED***

COLONEL TEMPLER   *7/1999*, Maritime Photographic /* 0075840

2 TORNADO CLASS (TORPEDO RECOVERY VESSELS) (TRV)

Name	No	Builders	Commissioned
TORNADO	A 140	Hall Russell, Aberdeen	15 Nov 1979
TORMENTOR	A 142	Hall Russell, Aberdeen	29 Apr 1980

Displacement, tons: 698 full load
Dimensions, feet (metres): 154.5 × 31.3 × 11.3 *(47.1 × 9.6 × 3.4)*
Main machinery: 2 Mirrlees-Blackstone ESL8 MCR diesels; 2,200 hp *(1.64 MW)*; 2 shafts
Speed, knots: 14. **Range, miles:** 3,000 at 14 kt
Complement: 14
Radars: Navigation: Kelvin Hughes 1006; I-band.

Comment: Ordered on 1 July 1977. GS vessels on the Clyde. Can lay and recover exercise mines.   ***UPDATED***

TORNADO   *12/1999*, W Sartori /* 0075841

1 TORPEDO RECOVERY VESSEL (TRV)

Name	No	Builders	Commissioned
TORRENT	A 127	Cleland SB, Wallsend-on-Tyne	10 Sep 1971

Displacement, tons: 550 gross
Dimensions, feet (metres): 162 × 31 × 11.5 *(49.4 × 9.5 × 3.5)*
Main machinery: 2 Mirrlees-Blackstone diesels; 700 hp *(522 kW)*; 2 shafts
Speed, knots: 10. **Range, miles:** 1,500 at 10 kt
Complement: 18
Radars: Navigation: Kelvin Hughes 1006; I-band.

Comment: Has a stern ramp for torpedo recovery—can carry 22 torpedoes in hold and 10 on deck. Torpedo maintenance and repair facilities. RMAS ship based at Kyle of Loch Alsh. Planned to pay off in late 2000.   ***UPDATED***

TORRENT   *1991, RMAS*

1 ARMAMENT STORE CARRIER (AKF)

Name	No	Builders	Commissioned
KINTERBURY	A 378	Appledore Ferguson SB	Nov 1980

Displacement, tons: 2,207 full load
Measurement, tons: 1,150 dwt
Dimensions, feet (metres): 231.2 × 39 × 15 *(70.5 × 11.9 × 4.6)*
Main machinery: 2 Mirrlees-Blackstone diesels; 3,000 hp *(2.24 MW)*; 1 shaft
Speed, knots: 14.5. **Range, miles:** 4,000 at 11 kt
Complement: 24 (8 officers)
Radars: Navigation: Kelvin Hughes 1006; I-band.

Comment: Carries armament stores in two holds. RMAS ship based at Portsmouth. One of the class sold to Ecuador in 1992.   ***UPDATED***

KINTERBURY   *11/1998, M Declerck /* 0053261

9 ADEPT CLASS (COASTAL TUGS) (YTB)

FORCEFUL A 221	**ADEPT** A 224	**CAREFUL** A 227
NIMBLE A 222	**BUSTLER** A 225	**FAITHFUL** A 228
POWERFUL A 223	**CAPABLE** A 226	**DEXTEROUS** A 231

Displacement, tons: 450
Dimensions, feet (metres): 127.3 × 30.8 × 11.2 *(38.8 × 9.4 × 3.4)*
Main machinery: 2 Ruston 6RKC diesels; 3,000 hp *(2.24 MW)* sustained; 2 Voith-Schneider props
Speed, knots: 12
Complement: 10

Comment: 'Twin unit tractor tugs' (TUTT). First four ordered from Richard Dunston (Hessle) on 22 February 1979 and next five on 8 February 1984. Primarily for harbour work with coastal towing capability. Nominal bollard pull, 27.5 tons. *Adept* accepted 28 October 1980, *Bustler* 15 April 1981, *Capable* 11 September 1981, *Careful* 12 March 1982, *Forceful* 18 March 1985, *Nimble* 25 June 1985, *Powerful* 30 October 1985, *Faithful* 21 December 1985, *Dexterous* 23 April 1986. *Powerful* and *Bustler* at Portsmouth, *Forceful, Faithful, Adept* and *Careful* at Devonport, *Nimble* and *Dexterous* on the Clyde. All are GS vessels except *Capable* at Gibraltar.   ***UPDATED***

NIMBLE   *6/1999*, A Sharma /* 0075842

8 DOG CLASS (7 TUGS + 1 RANGE TRIALS VESSEL) (YTM)

DALMATIAN A 129	SALUKI A 182	SHEEPDOG A 250
HUSKY A 178	SETTER A 189	COLLIE A 328
MASTIFF A 180	SPANIEL A 201	

Displacement, tons: 248 full load
Dimensions, feet (metres): 94 × 24.5 × 12 *(28.7 × 7.5 × 3.7)*
Main machinery: 2 Lister-Blackstone ERS8 MCR diesels; 1,320 hp *(985 kW)*; 2 shafts
Speed, knots: 10. **Range, miles:** 2,236 at 10 kt
Complement: 7

Comment: Harbour berthing tugs. Nominal bollard pull, 17.5 tons. Completed 1962-72. *Collie* operates at Kyle of Loch Alsh as RMAS Range trials vessel and has had towing gear removed. The remainder are GS vessels serving at Portsmouth, Devonport and on the Clyde. Appearance varies considerably, some with mast, some with curved upper-bridge work, some with flat monkey-island. **UPDATED**

SETTER   *6/1999*, van Ginderen Collection / 0075843

5 TRITON CLASS (YTL)

KITTY A 170	LESLEY A 172	JOAN A 190	MYRTLE A 199	NORAH A 205

Displacement, tons: 107.5 standard
Dimensions, feet (metres): 57.7 × 18 × 7.9 *(17.6 × 5.5 × 2.4)*
Main machinery: 1 diesel; 330 hp *(264 kW)*; 1 shaft
Speed, knots: 7.5
Complement: 4

Comment: All completed by August 1974 by Dunstons. 'Water-tractors' with small wheelhouse and adjoining funnel. Later vessels have masts stepped abaft wheelhouse. Voith-Schneider vertical axis propellers. Nominal bollard pull, 3 tons. All are GS vessels divided between Devonport and Portsmouth. **VERIFIED**

NORAH   *5/1998*, Maritime Photographic / 0053264

5 FELICITY CLASS (YTL)

FRANCES A 147	FLORENCE A 149	HELEN A 198
FIONA A 148	GENEVIEVE A 150	

Displacement, tons: 144 full load
Dimensions, feet (metres): 70 × 21 × 9.8 *(21.5 × 6.4 × 3)*
Main machinery: 1 Mirrlees-Blackstone ESM8 diesel; 615 hp *(459 kW)*; 1 Voith-Schneider cp prop
Speed, knots: 10
Complement: 4
Radars: Navigation: Raytheon; I-band.

Comment: Four completed 1973 by Hancocks. A 147, 149 and 150 ordered early 1979 from Richard Dunston (Thorne) and completed by end 1980. Nominal bollard pull, 5.7 tons. All are GS vessels divided between Devonport, Portsmouth and the Clyde. **UPDATED**

GENEVIEVE   *7/1999*, Per Körnefeldt / 0075844

1 RANGE SUPPORT VESSEL (YAG)

WARDEN A 368

Displacement, tons: 900 full load
Dimensions, feet (metres): 159.4 × 34.4 × 8.2 *(48.6 × 10.5 × 2.5)*
Main machinery: 2 Ruston 8RKC diesels; 4,000 hp *(2.98 MW)* sustained; 1 shaft; cp prop
Speed, knots: 15
Complement: 11 (4 officers)
Radars: Navigation: Racal Decca RM 1250; I-band.
Sonars: Dowty 2053; high frequency.

Comment: Built by Richards, Lowestoft and completed 20 November 1989. Reverted in 1998 to being an RMAS ship at Kyle of Lochalsh in support of BUTEC. **UPDATED**

WARDEN   *5/1997*, B Sullivan / 0075845

2 RANGE SUPPORT VESSELS (YAG)

FALCONET (ex-*Alfred Herring V C*) Y 02 (ex-Y 497)
PETARD (ex-*Michael Murphy V C*) Y 01 (ex-519)

Displacement, tons: 70 full load
Dimensions, feet (metres): 77.7 × 18 × 4.9 *(23.7 × 5.5 × 1.5)*
Main machinery: 2 Paxman 8 CM diesels; 2,000 hp *(1.49 MW)* sustained; 2 shafts
Speed, knots: 20
Complement: 4

Comment: Range Safety Craft built by James and Stone, Brightlingsea. Similar design to 'Spitfire' class. Transferred from the RCT on 30 September 1988. *Falconet* commissioned 1978 serves at Whitehaven Cumbria; *Petard* commissioned 1983 serves at the Royal Artillery Range in the Outer Hebrides. GFE vessels operated by Smit Internat. **UPDATED**

PETARD   *1/1994*, van Ginderen Collection

12 RANGE SAFETY CRAFT (YAG)

RSC 7713 (ex-*Samuel Morley VC*)	RSC 7820 (ex-*Richard Masters VC*)
RSC 7821 (ex-*Joseph Hughes GC*)	RSC 7822 (ex-*James Dalton VC*)
RSC 8125 (ex-*Sir Paul Travers*)	RSC 8128 (ex-*Sir Reginald Kerr*)
RSC 8126 (ex-*Sir Cecil Smith*)	RSC 8129 (ex-*Sir Humfrey Gale*)
RSC 8487 (ex-*Geoffrey Rackman GC*)	RSC 8488 (ex-*Walter Cleal GC*)
RSC 8489 (ex-*Sir Evan Gibb*)	SIR WILLIAM ROE 8127

Displacement, tons: 20.2 full load
Dimensions, feet (metres): 48.2 × 11.5 × 4.3 *(14.7 × 3.5 × 1.3)*
Main machinery: 2 RR C8M 410 or Volvo Penta TAMD-122A diesels; 820 hp *(612 kW)*; 2 shafts
Speed, knots: 22. **Range, miles:** 300 at 20 kt
Complement: 3
Radars: Navigation: Furuno; I-band.

Comment: Range Safety Craft of the 'Honours' and 'Sirs' classes, built by Fairey Marine, A R P Whitstable and Halmatic. All completed 1982-86. Transferred from the RCT on 30 September 1988. All GFE vessels operated by Smit Internat except *Sir William Roe* which is based in Cyprus and has remained with the Royal Logistic Corps. The remainder are based at Whitehaven, Pembroke Dock, Hebrides, Dover and Portland. Now known only by their pennant numbers. New engines fitted from 1993. Three similar craft were built in 1991 as pilot cutters. **VERIFIED**

RSC 8129   *3/1995*, W Sartori

2 SUBMARINE BERTHING TUGS (YTL)

Name	No	Builders	Completed
IMPULSE	A 344	Dunston, Hessle	11 Mar 1993
IMPETUS	A 345	Dunston, Hessle	28 May 1993

Displacement, tons: 530 full load
Dimensions, feet (metres): 106.7 × 34.2 × 11.5 *(32.5 × 10.4 × 3.5)*
Main machinery: 2 WH Allen 8S12 diesels; 3,400 hp *(2.54 MW)* sustained; 2 Aquamaster Azimuth thrusters; 1 Jastrom bow thruster
Speed, knots: 12
Complement: 6

Comment: Ordered 28 January 1992 for submarine berthing duties. There are two 10 ton hydraulic winches forward and aft with break capacities of 110 tons. Bollard pull 38.6 tons ahead, 36 tons astern. Fitted with firefighting and oil pollution equipment. Designed for one-man control from the bridge with all round vision and a comprehensive Navaids fit. *Impulse* launched 10 December 1992; *Impetus* 9 February 1993. GS vessels based on the Clyde.

UPDATED

IMPULSE   *1/2000*, A Sharma* / 0075846

4 TOWED ARRAY TENDERS (YAG)

TARV 8611   **OHMS LAW** 8612   — 8613   **SAPPER** 8614

Dimensions, feet (metres): 65.9 × 19.7 × 7.9 *(20.1 × 6 × 2.4)*
Main machinery: 2 Perkins diesels; 400 hp *(298 kW)*; 2 Kort nozzles
Speed, knots: 12
Complement: 8
Radars: Navigation: Racal Decca; I-band.

Comment: First three built by McTay Marine, Bromborough in 1986. *Sapper* completed in February 1999. Used for transporting clip-on towed arrays from submarine bases Faslane and Devonport. Also used as divers support craft. Naval manned.

UPDATED

SAPPER   *7/1999*, Per Körnefeldt* / 0075847

1 SUBMARINE TENDER (YFB)

Name	No	Builders	Commissioned
ADAMANT	A 232	FBM, Cowes	18 Jan 1993

Dimensions, feet (metres): 101 × 25.6 × 3.6 *(30.8 × 7.8 × 1.1)*
Main machinery: 2 Cummins KTA-19M2 diesels; 970 hp *(724 kW)* sustained; 2 water-jets
Speed, knots: 23. **Range, miles:** 250 at 22 kt
Complement: 5 plus 36 passengers plus 1 ton stores

Comment: Twin-hulled support ship ordered in 1991 and launched 8 October 1992. A GS vessel used for personnel and stores transfers in the Firth of Clyde. In addition to the passengers, half a ton of cargo can be carried. Capable of top speed up to Sea State 3 and able to transit safely up to Sea State 6.

VERIFIED

ADAMANT   *10/1998, M Verschaeve* / 0053268

2 STORM CLASS (YFB)

Name	No	Builders	Commissioned
CAWSAND	A 192	FBM Marine, Cowes	July 1997
BOVISAND	A 191	FBM Marine, Cowes	Sep 1997

Dimensions, feet (metres): 78.4 × 36.4 × 7.5 *(23.9 × 11.1 × 2.3)*
Main machinery: 2 diesels; 1,224 hp(m) *(900 kW)*; 2 shafts
Speed, knots: 14
Complement: 5 plus 75 passengers

Comment: GS vessels for the use of FOST staff at Devonport. Swath design with hydraulically operated telescopic gangways. Have replaced *Fionan of Skellig*.

UPDATED

BOVISAND   *6/1999*, A Sharma* / 0075848

2 SEAL CLASS (YAG)

Name	No	Builders	Commissioned
SEAL	5000	Brooke Marine, Lowestoft	Aug 1967
SEAGULL	5001	Fairmile Construction, Berwick-on-Tweed	1970

Displacement, tons: 159 full load
Dimensions, feet (metres): 120.3 × 23.5 × 6.5 *(36.6 × 7.2 × 2)*
Main machinery: 2 Paxman 16YJCM diesels; 4,000 hp *(2.98 MW)* sustained; 2 shafts
Speed, knots: 21. **Range, miles:** 2,200 at 12 kt
Complement: 8

Comment: Long-range recovery and support craft (LRRSC). All-welded steel hull. Aluminium alloy superstructure. Used for weapon recovery, target towing, search and rescue. Both are GFE vessels operated by VT Marine Services at Invergordon.

UPDATED

SEAL (old number)   *6/1987** / 0084424

6 SPITFIRE CLASS (YAG)

Name	No	Builders	Commissioned
SPITFIRE	4000	James and Stone, Brightlingsea	1972
HALIFAX	4003	James and Stone, Brightlingsea	1977
HAMPDEN	4004	James and Stone, Brightlingsea	1980
HURRICANE	4005	James and Stone, Brightlingsea	1980
LANCASTER	4006	James and Stone, Brightlingsea	1981
WELLINGTON	4007	James and Stone, Brightlingsea	1981

Displacement, tons: 70.2 full load
Dimensions, feet (metres): 78.7 × 18 × 4.9 *(24.1 × 5.5 × 1.5)*
Main machinery: 2 Paxman 8YJCM diesels; 2,000 hp *(1.49 MW)* sustained; 2 shafts
Speed, knots: 22
Complement: 6

Comment: Rescue target towing launches (RTTL). GFE vessels operated by VT Marine Services. All-welded steel hulls; aluminium alloy superstructure. *Spitfire* has twin funnels, remainder none. Devonport: *Spitfire* and *Hurricane*. Great Yarmouth: *Hampden* and *Wellington*. Holyhead: *Halifax*. Pembroke Dock: *Lancaster*. All used for helicopter winch training, SAR drills, target towing and torpedo recovery, except *Lancaster* which is primarily a Range Safety craft.

UPDATED

SPITFIRE   *1/2000*, John Brodie* / 0075849

2 PINNACES 1300 SERIES (YAG)

1374   **1392**

Displacement, tons: 28.3 full load
Dimensions, feet (metres): 63 × 15.5 × 5 *(19.2 × 4.7 × 1.5)*
Main machinery: 2 RR C6 diesels; 190 hp *(142 kW)*; 2 shafts
Speed, knots: 13
Complement: 6
Radars: Navigation: Furuno; I-band.

Comment: Hard chine, wooden hulls. Built by Groves and Gutteridge, Robertsons (Dunoon) and
Dorset Yacht Co (Poole) in 1955-65. GFE vessels operated by VT Marine Services. Of 5 ton cargo
capacity. *1374* at Holyhead; *1392* at Plymouth. Used for helicopter winch training and SAR drills.
UPDATED

1392   *1/2000*, John Brodie /* 0075850

3 INSECT CLASS (YAG)

BEE A 216   **COCKCHAFER** A 230   **LADYBIRD** A 253

Displacement, tons: 475 full load
Dimensions, feet (metres): 111.8 × 28 × 11 *(34.1 × 8.5 × 3.4)*
Main machinery: 1 Lister-Blackstone ERS8 MCR diesel; 660 hp *(492 kW)*; 1 shaft
Speed, knots: 11.3. Range, miles: 3,000 at 10 kt
Complement: 7

Comment: First two built as stores carriers, and third as armament carrier. All commissioned
between 1970 and 1973. *Cockchafer* is an RMAS vessel at Kyle of Loch Alsh, the other pair are
GS ships used for training aircrew at Devonport. Of 200 ton cargo capacity and 2 ton crane.
VERIFIED

LADYBIRD   *7/1998, B Sullivan /* 0053272

3 OBAN CLASS (YFL)

OBAN A 283   **ORONSAY** A 284   **OMAGH** A 285

Displacement, tons: 230 full load
Dimensions, feet (metres): 90.9 × 24 × 12.3 *(27.7 × 7.3 × 3.8)*
Main machinery: 2 Cummins N14M diesels; 1,017 hp(m) *(748 kW)*; 2 Kort-Nozzles
Speed, knots: 10
Complement: 7

Comment: Built by McTay Marine and completed January to July 2000. Capable of carrying 60
passengers. Based on the Clyde.
NEW ENTRY

OBAN   *1/2000*, McTay Marine /* 0084425

4 PADSTOW AND NEWHAVEN CLASSES (YFL)

PADSTOW A 286   **NEWHAVEN** A 280   **NUTBOURNE** A 281   **NETLEY** A 282

Displacement, tons: 125 full load
Dimensions, feet (metres): 60 × 22.3 × 6.2 *(18.3 × 6.8 × 1.9)*
Main machinery: 2 Cummins 6 CTA diesels; 710 hp(m) *(522 kW)*; 2 shafts
Speed, knots: 10
Complement: 3

Comment: Built by Aluminium Shipbuilders at Fishbourne, Isle of Wight and completed May to
November 2000. Capable of carrying 60 passengers and based at Devonport (A 286) and
Portsmouth. Catamaran hulls.
NEW ENTRY

2 DIVING TENDERS (YDT)

ILCHESTER A 308   **INSTOW** A 309

Displacement, tons: 143 full load
Dimensions, feet (metres): 80 × 21 × 6.6 *(24.1 × 6.4 × 2)*
Main machinery: 2 Gray Marine diesels; 450 hp *(336 kW)*; 2 shafts
Speed, knots: 12
Complement: 6

Comment: Similar to 'Clovelly' class. Built by Gregson Ltd, Blyth and commissioned in 1974. GS
vessels based on the Clyde. Carry a decompression chamber.
VERIFIED

INSTOW   *8/1989, Wright & Logan*

4 MANLY CLASS (YAG)

MELTON A 83   **MENAI** A 84   **MEON** A 87   **MILFORD** A 91

Displacement, tons: 143 full load
Dimensions, feet (metres): 80 × 21 × 6.6 *(24.4 × 6.4 × 2)*
Main machinery: 1 Lister-Blackstone ESR4 MCR diesel; 320 hp *(239 kW)*; 1 shaft
Speed, knots: 10. Range, miles: 600 at 10 kt
Complement: 6 (1 officer)

Comment: All built by Richard Dunston, Hessle. All completed by early 1983. *Melton* is an RMAS
vessel at Kyle of Loch Alsh, the remainder are GS ships at Devonport.
UPDATED

MILFORD   *6/1999*, A Sharma /* 0075851

1 FBM CATAMARAN CLASS (YFL)

8837

Displacement, tons: 21 full load
Dimensions, feet (metres): 51.8 × 18 × 4.9 *(15.8 × 5.5 × 1.5)*
Main machinery: 2 Mermaid Turbo 4 diesels; 280 hp *(209 kW)*; 2 shafts
Speed, knots: 13. Range, miles: 400 at 10 kt
Complement: 2

Comment: Built by FBM Marine in 1989. Can carry 30 passengers or 2 tons stores. First of a
catamaran type designed to replace some of the older harbour launches but no more have been
ordered. GS vessel.
UPDATED

8837   *7/1999*, Per Körnefeldt /* 0075852

1 VOSPER CRAFT (AXL)

MARGHERITA (ex-*Tresham*)

Comment: Former 'Ham' class built in 1955 at Teignmouth. Bought by Vosper Thornycroft in 1994, refitted as a training vessel and run by VT Marine Services for the Navy.

UPDATED

MARGHERITA   *8/1998, Maritime Photographic* / 0053276

ARMY (ROYAL LOGISTIC CORPS)

Notes: (1) Four LCVPs are listed in the RN section.
(2) One Range Safety Craft is listed in RMAS section.
(3) Up to 30 new Combat Support Boats are planned to be delivered by 2002. These are 8.8 m craft, road transportable and with a top speed of 30 kt. Two prototypes are being built by RTK Marine for delivery in November 2000.
(4) The RLC is based at Marchwood, Southampton.

6 RAMPED CRAFT, LOGISTIC (LCL/RCL)

Name	No	Builders	Commissioned
ANDALSNES	L 107	James and Stone, Brightlingsea	22 May 1984
AKYAB	L 109	James and Stone, Brightlingsea	15 Dec 1984
AACHEN	L 110	James and Stone, Brightlingsea	12 Feb 1987
AREZZO	L 111	James and Stone, Brightlingsea	26 Mar 1987
ARROMANCHES	L 105	James and Stone, Brightlingsea	12 June 1987
(ex-*Agheila*)	(ex-L 112)		
AUDEMER	L 113	James and Stone, Brightlingsea	21 Aug 1987

Displacement, tons: 290 full load
Dimensions, feet (metres): 109.2 × 27.2 × 4.9 *(33.3 × 8.3 × 1.5)*
Main machinery: 2 Dorman 8JTCWM diesels; 504 hp *(376 kW)* sustained; 2 shafts
Speed, knots: 10. **Range, miles:** 900 at 10 kt
Complement: 6 (2 NCOs)
Military lift: 96 tons
Radars: Navigation: Racal Decca; I-band.

Comment: *Andalsnes* and *Akyab* based in Cyprus, remainder at Southampton.

UPDATED

AUDEMER   *8/1998, Maritime Photographic* / 0053277

6 WORK BOATS (YAG)

BREAM WB 03   **ROACH** WB 05   **PERCH** WB 06   **MILL REEF** WB 08   + 2

Displacement, tons: 27 full load
Dimensions, feet (metres): 48.6 × 14.1 × 4.2 *(14.8 × 4.3 × 1.3)*
Main machinery: 2 Gardner diesels; 640 hp *(460 kW)*; 2 shafts
Speed, knots: 10. **Range, miles:** 500 at 10 kt
Complement: 4
Radars: Navigation: Raytheon; I-band.

Comment: First three built 1966-71; fourth one built in 1987 and last pair in late 1990s.

UPDATED

PERCH   *8/1998, Maritime Photographic* / 0053278

SCOTTISH FISHERIES PROTECTION AGENCY

Notes: (1) The Agency has a complement of 260.
(2) There are two Cessna F-406 Caravan II aircraft with Bendix 1500 radars.

SULISKER   **VIGILANT**   **NORNA**

Displacement, tons: 1,566 (1,586 *Norna*) full load
Dimensions, feet (metres): 234.3 × 38 × 17.6 *(71.4 × 11.6 × 5.4)*
Main machinery: 2 Ruston 6AT350 diesels; 6,000 hp *(4.48 MW)* sustained *(Norna)*; 2 Ruston 12 RK 3 diesels; 5,600 hp *(4.18 MW)* sustained; 2 shafts; cp props; bow thruster; 450 hp *(336 kW)*
Speed, knots: 18. **Range, miles:** 7,000 at 13 kt
Complement: 15 (6 officers) plus 6 spare bunks
Radars: Navigation: 2 Racal Decca Bridgemaster; I-band.

Comment: First pair built by Appledore Ferguson, Port Glasgow. *Sulisker* completed 1981, *Vigilant* completed June 1982. *Norna* built by Richards, Lowestoft and completed in June 1988. There are some structural differences in *Norna* including an A frame aft.

UPDATED

NORNA   *6/1998, SFPA* / 0053279

VIGILANT   *6/1998, SFPA* / 0053280

WESTRA

Displacement, tons: 778 light; 1,285 full load
Measurement, tons: 1,017 gross
Dimensions, feet (metres): 194.9 × 36.1 × 13.5 *(59.4 × 11 × 4.1)*
Main machinery: 2 British Polar SP112VS-F diesels; 4,200 hp *(3.13 MW)*; 1 shaft; cp prop
Speed, knots: 16.5. **Range, miles:** 10,000 at 12 kt
Complement: 15 (6 officers)
Radars: Navigation: 2 Decca Bridgemaster; E/F- and I-band.

Comment: Launched on 6 August 1974 by Hall Russell, Aberdeen. Similar to RN 'Island' class.

UPDATED

WESTRA   *6/1998, SFPA* / 0053281

MOIDART   **MORVEN**

Displacement, tons: 48 full load
Dimensions, feet (metres): 65 × 18.9 × 6.6 *(19.8 × 5.8 × 2)*
Main machinery: 2 Detroit 8V-92TA diesels; 850 hp *(635 kW)* sustained; 2 shafts
Speed, knots: 20
Complement: 5 (3 officers)

Comment: Cheverton patrol craft completed 31 January 1983 at Cowes. GRP hulls. Endurance is four days. Third engine and centre shaft removed in 1997.

VERIFIED

MORVEN   *11/1996, M Declerck*

SKUA

Displacement, tons: 7.5 full load
Dimensions, feet (metres): 38 × 12.1 × 3.9 *(11.6 × 3.7 × 1.2)*
Main machinery: 2 Sabre 212 diesels; 424 hp *(316 kW)*; 2 shafts
Speed, knots: 24
Complement: 3 (2 officers)
Radars: Navigation: Furuno; I-band.

Comment: 'Pacific 36' class RIB built by Osborne Marine and completed in April 1984. Dimensions given include the inflatable flotation collar.

VERIFIED

VENTUROUS   7/1999*, John Brodie / 0084426

SKUA   6/1994, SFPA

SENTINEL   6/1998, John Brodie / 0053283

CUSTOMS

Note: The Customs and Excise (Marine Branch) of HM Treasury operates a considerable number of craft around the UK: two Brooke Marine 33 m craft *(Searcher, Seeker)*; four FBM Marine 26 m craft *(Vigilant, Valiant, Venturous* and *Vincent)*; one Vosper 36 m craft *(Sentinel)*; one Halmatic 20 m craft *(Swift)*; five Cheverton 8.2 m craft *(Avocet, Bittern, Courser, Diver* and *Egret)*; two Halmatic 13 m craft *(Hunter* and *Panther)*; plus 60 small craft ranging from 4 m Seariders to 10 m harbour launches. None of these vessels is armed.

VINCENT   1/2000*, John Brodie / 0075854

TRINITY HOUSE

Note: A number of vessels of varying types — offshore support craft and lighthouse tenders — may be met throughout the waters of the UK.

SEEKER   6/1999*, A Sharma / 0075853

THV MERMAID   7/1999*, Maritime Photographic / 0084427

UNITED STATES OF AMERICA

Headquarters Appointments

Chief of Naval Operations:
  Admiral Vernon E Clark
Vice Chief of Naval Operations:
  Admiral Donald L Pilling
Director, Naval Nuclear Propulsion Programme, Naval Sea Systems Command:
  Admiral Frank L Bowman
Chief of Naval Personnel:
  Vice Admiral Norbert Ryan Jr
Commander, Military Sealift Command:
  Rear Admiral Gordon S Holder
Commander, Naval Air Systems Command:
  Vice Admiral John A Lockard
Commander, Space and Naval Warfare Systems Command:
  Rear Admiral John A Gauss

Commanders-in-Chief

Commander-in-Chief, Joint Forces and NATO Supreme Allied Commander, Atlantic:
  Admiral Harold W Gehman Jr
Commander-in-Chief, Pacific Command:
  Admiral Dennis C Blair
Commander-in-Chief, Pacific Fleet:
  Admiral Thomas B Fargo
Commander-in-Chief, Naval Forces, Europe, and Allied Forces, Southern Europe:
  Admiral James O Ellis Jr

Marine Corps

Commandant:
  General James L Jones Jr
Assistant Commandant:
  General Terence Dake
Commander, Fleet Marine Force, Atlantic:
  Lieutenant General Raymond P Ayres Jr
Commander, Fleet Marine Force, Pacific:
  Lieutenant General Frank Libutti

Flag Officers (Atlantic Area)

Commander, Second Fleet, Atlantic Fleet and Striking Fleet, Atlantic:
  Vice Admiral William J Fallon
Commander, Surface Force, Atlantic Fleet:
  Vice Admiral Henry C Giffin III
Commander, Sixth Fleet and Striking and Support Forces, Southern Europe:
  Vice Admiral Daniel J Murphy Jr
Commander, Submarine Force, Atlantic Fleet and Submarine Allied Command, Atlantic:
  Vice Admiral Edmund P Giambastiani
Commander, Naval Air Force, Atlantic Fleet:
  Rear Admiral Joseph S Mobley
Commander, Fleet Air, Keflavik and Iceland Defense Force:
  Rear Admiral David Architzel
Commander, Southern Command:
  Rear Admiral Kevin P Green
Commander, Mine Warfare Command:
  Rear Admiral Jose L Betancourt

Flag Officers (Pacific Area)

Commander, Seventh Fleet:
  Vice Admiral Walter F Doran
Commander, Naval Surface Force, Pacific Fleet:
  Vice Admiral Edward Moore Jr
Commander, Third Fleet:
  Vice Admiral Dennis V McGinn
Commander, Naval Air Force, Pacific Fleet:
  Vice Admiral Michael L Bowman
Commander, US Naval Forces, Japan:
  Rear Admiral Donald A Weiss
Commander, Submarine Force, Pacific Fleet:
  Rear Admiral Albert H Konetzni Jr
Commander, US Naval Forces, Korea:
  Rear Admiral William D Sullivan

Flag Officer (Central Area)

Commander, Central Command and Fifth Fleet:
  Vice Admiral Charles W Moore Jr

Territorial Seas

On 27 December 1988, the USA claimed territorial seas were extended from 3 to 12 n miles. The USA exercises sovereignty over waters, seabed and airspace out to 12 n miles. This extension also applies to the Commonwealth of Puerto Rico, Guam, American Samoa, the US Virgin Islands, the Commonwealth of the Northern Mariana Islands and any other territory or possession over which the USA exercises sovereignty.

The USA continues to recognise the right of all ships to conduct innocent passage and, in the case of international straits, the right of all ships and aircraft to conduct transit passage through its territorial sea.

Personnel

	1 Jan 1998	1 Jan 1999	1 Jan 2000
Navy			
Officers	55,611	53,564	53,538
Enlisted	327,876	313,106	315,158
Marine Corps			
Officers	17,773	17,892	17,897
Enlisted	153,904	155,250	154,744

Mercantile Marine

Lloyd's Register of Shipping:
  5,642 vessels of 12,025,775 tons gross

Strength of the Fleet (1 June 2000)

Type	Active (NRF) (Reserve)	Building (Projected) + Conversion/SLEP	Type	Active (NRF) (Reserve)	Building (Projected) + Conversion/SLEP
SHIPS OF THE FLEET			**Auxiliaries**		
			AGSS Auxiliary Research Submarine	1	—
Strategic Missile Submarines			AOE Fast Combat Support Ships	8	—
SSBN (Ballistic Missile Submarines) (nuclear-powered)	18	—	ARS Salvage Ships	4	—
			AS Submarine Tenders	2	—
Attack Submarines					
SSN Submarines (nuclear-powered)	55	5 (2)	**NAVAL RESERVE FORCE**		
			FFG Guided Missile Frigates	10	—
Aircraft Carriers			LST Tank Landing Ships	2	—
CVN Multipurpose Aircraft Carriers (nuclear-powered)	9	2 (1)	MCM/MHC Mine Warfare Ships	14	—
CV Multipurpose Aircraft Carriers (conventionally powered)	2 (1)	—	**MILITARY SEALIFT COMMAND INVENTORY**		
			Naval Fleet Auxiliary Force		
Cruisers			T-ADC Dry Cargo	—	(12)
CG Guided Missile Cruisers	27	—	T-AE Ammunition	7	—
			T-AFS Combat Stores	6	—
			T-AH Hospital	2	—
Destroyers			T-AO Oilers	14	—
DDG Guided Missile Destroyers	30	22 (5)	T-ATF Fleet Ocean Tugs	5	—
DD Destroyers	24	—			
			Special Mission Ships		
Frigates			T-AG/T-AGM Miscellaneous	3	—
FFG Guided Missile Frigates	27 (8)	—	T-AGOS Surveillance/Patrol	14	—
			T-AGS Surveying	8	1
			T-ARC Cable Repair	1	—
Patrol Forces					
PC Coastal Defense Ships	14	—	**Sealift Force**		
			T-AKR Vehicle Cargo	8	—
			T-AOT Tankers	5	—
Command Ships			T-AKR Large, Medium-Speed, Ro-ro ships	9	3
LCC Command Ships	2	—			
AGF Command Ships	2	—	**Prepositioning Programme**		
			T-AK FLO/FLO	1	—
			T-AK Container	4	—
Amphibious Warfare Forces			T-AK Cargo	4	—
LHA Amphibious Assault Ships (general purpose)	5	—	T-AK LASH	2	—
LHD Amphibious Assault Ships (multipurpose)	6	2	T-AK Vehicle Cargo	13	—
LPD Amphibious Transport Docks	11	4 (8)	T-AKR Large, Medium-Speed, Ro-ro ships	5	2
LPH Amphibious Assault Ships (helicopter)/MCM Support Ship	1/1	—	T-AOT Tankers	3	—
LSD Dock Landing Ships	15	—	T-AVB Aviation Logistic	2	—
LST Tank Landing Ships	(2)	—			
			Ready Reserve Force		
			T-ACS Auxiliary Crane	10	—
			T-AK Break Bulk	28	—
Mine Warfare Forces			T-AKR Ro-ro	31	—
MCM Mine Countermeasures Ships	10 (4)	—	T-AOT/T-AOG Product Tankers	8	—
MHC Minehunters (Coastal)	2 (10)	—	T-AK/T-AP Miscellaneous	9	—

Special Notes

To provide similar information to that included in other major navies' Deployment Tables the fleet assignment (abbreviated 'F/S') status of each ship in the US Navy has been included. The assignment appears in a column immediately to the right of the commissioning date. In the case of the Floating Dry Dock section this system is not used. The following abbreviations are used to indicate fleet assignments:

AA	active Atlantic Fleet
Active	active under charter with MSC
AR	in reserve Out of Commission, Atlantic Fleet
ASA	active In Service, Atlantic Fleet
ASR	in reserve Out of Service, Atlantic Fleet
Bldg	building
CONV	ship undergoing conversion
LOAN	ship or craft loaned to another government, or non-government agency, but US Navy retains title and the ship or craft is on the NVR
MAR	in reserve Out of Commission, Atlantic Fleet and laid up in the temporary custody of the Maritime Administration
MPR	same as 'MAR', but applies to the Pacific Fleet
NRF	assigned to the Naval Reserve Force (ships so assigned are listed in a special table for major warships and amphibious ships)
Ord	the contract for the construction of the ship has been let, but actual construction has not yet begun
PA	active Pacific Fleet
PR	in reserve Out of Commission, Pacific Fleet
Proj	the ship is scheduled for construction at some time in the immediate future
PSA	active In Service, Pacific Fleet
PSR	in reserve Out of Service, Pacific Fleet
ROS	reduced Operating Status
TAA	active Military Sealift Command, Atlantic Fleet
TAR	in Ready Reserve, Military Sealift Command, Atlantic Fleet
TPA	active Military Sealift Command, Pacific Fleet
TPR	in Ready Reserve, Military Sealift Command, Pacific Fleet
TWWR	active Military Sealift Command, Worldwide Routes

Ship Status Definitions

In Commission: as a rule any ship, except a Service Craft, that is active, is in commission. The ship has a Commanding Officer and flies a commissioning pennant. 'Commissioning date' as used in this section means the date of being 'in commission' rather than 'completion' or 'acceptance into service' as used in some other navies.

In Service: all service craft (dry docks and with classifications that start with 'Y'), with the exception of *Constitution,* that are active, are 'in service'. The ship has an Officer-in-Charge and does not fly a commissioning pennant.

Ships 'in reserve, out of commission' or 'in reserve, out of service' are put in a state of preservation for future service. Depending on the size of the ship or craft, a ship in 'mothballs' usually takes from 30 days to nearly a year to restore to full operational service. The above status definitions do not apply to the Military Sealift Command.

Approved Fiscal Year 2000 Programme

	Appropriations (US dollars millions)
1 'Virginia' class (SSN 776) (advance procurement)	746.6
3 'Arleigh Burke' class (DDG 97-99)	2,674.7
2 'San Antonio' class (LPD 19-20)	1,504.4
1 'Nimitz' class (CVN 77)	749.6
1 ADC(X)	438.8
1 'Nimitz' class refuelling	344.7
1 'Wasp' class (LHD-8) (increment)	356.2

Proposed Fiscal Year 2001 Programme

	Appropriations (US dollars millions)
1 'Virginia' class (SSN 776)	1,203
1 'Virginia' class (SSN 777) advance procurement	508.2
3 'Arleigh Burke' class (DDG 100-103)	2,713.6
2 'San Antonio' class (LPD 21-22)	1,489.3
1 'Nimitz' class (CVN 77)	4,053.7

Naval Aviation

Naval Aviation had an active inventory of 4,108 aircraft as of 1 January 2000, with approximately 31 per cent of those being operated by the US Marine Corps. The principal aviation organisations are 10 active carrier air wings and one reserve, 12 active maritime patrol squadrons and seven reserve, and three Marine aircraft wings and one reserve.

Fighter Attack: 24 (3) Naval and 14 (4) Marine squadrons with F/A-18 Hornets. 12 Navy squadrons for F-14 Tomcats.
Attack: Seven Marine squadrons with AV-8B Harriers.
Airborne Early Warning: 10 (2) Navy squadrons with E-2C Hawkeyes.
Electronic Warfare: 15 Navy and four Marine squadrons with EA-6B Prowlers.
Anti-Submarine: 10 Navy squadrons with S-3B Vikings.
Maritime Patrol: 14 (7) Navy squadrons with P-3C Orions.
Helicopter Anti-Submarine: 23 Navy squadrons with SH-60B, SH-60F and HH-60H Seahawks.
Helicopter Mine Countermeasures: Two Navy squadrons with MH-53E Sea Dragons.
Helicopter Support: Six Navy squadrons with UH-46D Sea Knights and MH-53E Sea Dragons.
Electronic Reconnaissance: Two Navy squadrons with EP-3E Orions and two with ES-3A Vikings.
Communications Relay: Two Navy squadrons with E-6A Tacamos.
Helicopter Gunship: Eight Marine squadrons with AH-1W SuperCobras.

Helicopter Transport: 15 (2) Marine squadrons with CH-46S Sea Knights, four with CH-53D Sea Stallions and six (two) CH-53E Super Stallions.

Aircraft Procurement Plan FY2000-2002

	00	01	02
AV-8B Harrier	12	10	—
F/A-18E/F Super Hornet	36	42	45
V-22 Osprey	10	16	20
T-45TS Goshawk	15	15	—
E-2C Hawkeye	3	5	5
CH-60	13	18	24

Note: AV-8Bs are remanufactured aircraft. The CH-60 is a Vertrep helicopter.

Naval Special Warfare

The Naval Special Warfare Command was commissioned 16 April 1987.

SEAL (Sea Air Land) teams are manned at a nominal 10 platoons per team, with 30 platoons on each coast based at Coronado (Group 1) and Little Creek, Virginia (Group 2). Assigned directly to CinC US Special Operations Command, platoons are allocated to theatre commanders during operational deployments. Total numbers 5,000 of whom 2,300 are SEALs.

Bases

Naval Air Stations and Air Facilities

Naval Air Warfare Center Weapons Division (NAWS) China Lake, CA; Naval Air Facility (NAF) Centro, CA; Naval Air Station (NAS) Lemoore, CA; NAS Point Magu, CA; NAS North Island (San Diego), CA; NAF Washington, DC; NAS Jacksonville, FL; NAS Key West, FL; NAS Whiting Field (Milton), FL; NAS Soufley Field (Pensacola), FL; NAS Pensacola, FL; NAS San Diego, FL; NAS Atlanta (Marietta), GA; PMRF Barking Sands, HI; NAS New Orleans, LA; NAS Brunswick, ME; NAS Patuxent River, MD; NAS Meridian, MS; NAS Fallon, NV; Naval Air Engineering Center (NAEC) Lakehurst, NJ; NAS Willow Grove, PA; NAS Corpus Christi, TX; NAS Fort Worth, TX; NAS Kingsville, TX; NAS Oceana, VA; NAS Whidbey Island (Oak Harbor), WA.
NAS Keflavik, Iceland; NAS Sigonella, Italy; NAS Atsugi, Japan; NAF Missawa, Japan; NAF Okinawa, Japan.

Naval Stations and Naval Bases

NS San Diego, CA; NB (Amphibious) Coronado, CA; NS Mayport, FL; NS Pearl Harbor, HI; NS Annapolis, MD; NS Pascagoula, MS; NS Ingleside, TX; NS Roosevelt Roads, OR; NS Newport, RI; NB (Amphibious) Little Creek, VA; NS Norfolk, VA; NS Bremerton, WA; NS Everett, WA.
Naval Base (NB) Guantanamo Bay, Cuba; Fleet Activities (FA) Okinawa, Japan; FA Sasebo, Japan; FA Chinhae, Korea; NS Rota, Spain.

Naval Support Facilities

NSA Monterey Bay, CA; NSA Washington, DC; NSA New Orleans, LA; NSA Mid-South (Millington), TN.
NSA Diego Garcia, BIOT; NA Guam (Apra) GM; NSA Souda Bay, Greece; NSA Gaeta, Italy; NSA La Maddalena, Italy; NSA Naples, Italy, NA United Kingdom (London), UK.

Strategic Missile Submarine Bases

Bangor, WA (West Coast); Kings Bay, GA (East Coast).

Naval Shipyards

Pearl Harbor, HI; Puget Sound, Bremerton, WA; Norfolk, VA; Portsmouth, NH (located in Kittery, ME).

Naval Ship Repair Facilities

Yokosuka, Japan; Lumut, Malaysia.

Marine Corps Air Stations and Helicopter Facilities

MCAS: Beaufort, SC; Yuma, AZ; Kaneohe Bay, Oahu, HI; Quantico, VA; Cherry Point, NC; Iwakuni, Honshu, Japan; New River (Jacksonville), NC. Futema, Okinawa.

Marine Corps Bases

Camp Pendleton, CA; Twentynine Palms, CA; Camp H M Smith (Oahu), HI; Camp Lejeune, NC; Camp Smedley D Butler (Kawasaki), Okinawa, Japan.

Communications and Data Systems

Advanced Combat Direction System (ACDS)

ACDS is a centralised, automated command and control system. It upgrades the Naval Tactical Data System (NTDS) for non-AEGIS surface warships, aircraft carriers and amphibious ships to enable identification and classification of targets, to vector interceptor aircraft to targets, and to exchange targeting information and engagement orders within the battlegroup and among different service components, US and foreign.

ACDS is in two phases. The Block 0 interim system replaces obsolete NTDS computers and display consoles and incorporates both upgraded and new NTDS software. Block 1 will operate with the Block 0 equipment but will advance software performance. Block 1 upgrades include modifiable doctrine, Joint Tactical Information Distribution (JTIDS) and Link 16 for joint and allied interoperability, increased range and track capability, multisource identification, up-to-date digital maps and embedded training.

Automated Digital Network System (ADNS)

The ADNS system provides a data delivery service based on the incorporation of commercial- and government-off-the-shelf (COTS/GOTS) hardware and software, such as IP routers and ISDN and ATM switches.
ADNS comprises three functional elements: integrated network manager (INM), routeing and switching (R&S), and channel access protocols (CAPs). The system will operate at the Secret High General Service (GENSER) classification. Initially, multiple security levels from unclassified to top secret special compartments information (SCI) will be enforced by cryptographic separation using the Network Encryption System (NES). In successive builds, NES will be replaced by the Embedded INFOSEC Product (EIP).

Challenge Athena

The Challenge Athena Commercial Wideband Satellite Communications Program is a full-duplex, high-data-rate (1.544 Mbps) communications link (wideband) providing access to high-volume primary national imagery dissemination; intelligence database transfers; video tele-conferencing, tele-medicine, tele-training and telephone services; and other computer data systems. Challenge Athena also supports tactical strike and Tomahawk Land-Attack Cruise Missile mission planning, the Defence Information Support Network (DISN) Joint Interoperable Networks, including Joint Worldwide Intelligence Communications System (JWICS), Unclassified/Secret Internet Protocol Router Networks, and Air Tasking Order/Mission Data Update (ATO/MDU) transmissions. The programme makes use of commercial satellite connectivity, COTS and non-developmental items (NDI) to augment existing, over-burdened military satellite communications systems. The initial focus has been to get Challenge Athena terminals to Joint Task Force command-capable warships (for example, carriers and air-capable amphibious assault ships).

Common High Band Data Link - Shipboard Terminal (CHBDL-ST)

This programme provides a common data terminal for the receipt of signal and imagery intelligence data from remote sensors and transmission of link and sensor control data to airborne platforms. CHBDL-ST interfaces with shipboard processors of the Joint Services Imagery Processing System - Navy (JSIPS-N) and the Battle Group Passive Horizon Extension System - Surface Terminal (BGPHES-ST), and links with BGPHES or Advanced Tactical Airborne Reconnaissance System (ATARS) aircraft configured with Modular Interoperable Data Link (MIDL) terminals. The BGPHES-ST (AN/ULQ-20) controls remote receivers in an aircraft sensor payload to relay radio transmissions via CHBDL-ST; the primary aircraft for these tasks are ES-3As and USAF U-2s.

Co-operative Engagement Capability (CEC)

CEC improves battle force anti-air warfare (AAW) capability by integrating the sensor data of each ship and aircraft into a single, real-time, fire-control quality composite track picture. CEC also provides the interfaces with the weapons of each CEC-equipped warship in the battlegroup to provide an integrated engagement capability that enhances Force Threat Evaluation and Weapons Assignment (F-TEWA).
By simultaneously distributing sensor data on AAW threats to each warship within the battlegroup, CEC extends the range at which a ship can engage hostile missiles well beyond the radar horizon. CEC may enable a battlegroup or joint taskforce to act as a single 'theatre air dominance' combat system.
Initially focused on defeating cruise missiles, CEC is being extended to support the Navy's area- and theatre-wide ballistic missile defence systems, and is seen as a key element in the 'Ring of Fire' concepts for enhanced Naval Surface Fire Support.

Global Broadcast Service (GBS)

GBS augments and interfaces with other communications systems to provide a continuous, high-speed, one-way flow of high-volume multimedia information supporting routine operations, training and exercises, special activities, crisis-response, situational awareness, weapons targeting, intelligence, and the transition to and conduct of operations short of nuclear war. A joint Navy-Air Force-Army and Defense Information Systems Agency (DISA) programme, the GBS space segment is being implemented in three phases. The second phase comprises the Navy-sponsored interim-GBS capability hosted on the UHF Follow-On communications satellites, 8, 9 and 10.

Global Command and Control System (GCCS)

GCCS is a comprehensive, worldwide network-centric system which provides the National Command Authority (NCA), Joint Chiefs of Staff, combatant and functional unified commands, Services, Defense Agencies, Joint Task Forces and their Service components, and others with information processing and dissemination capabilities necessary to conduct Command and Control (C²) of forces. GCCS is a means to implement the Command, Control, Communications, Computers, and Intelligence for the Warrior (C⁴IFTW) concept. GCCS provides the operational commanders with a near-realtime Common

Operational Picture, intelligence information, collaborative joint operational planning and execution tools, and other information necessary for the execution of joint operations.

Global Command and Control System (Maritime) (GCCS-M) (ex-JMCIS)

As the naval implementation of GCCS, GCCS-Maritime (GCCS-M) is the Office of the Secretary of Defense (OSD) designated command and control (C^2) migration system for the Navy, representing the evolutionary integration of many previous C^2 and intelligence systems. It supports multiple warfighting, manpower and logistics missions for commanders at every echelon, in all afloat, ashore, and tactical naval environments, and for joint, coalition, and allied forces, provides a complete command and control solution to the Fleet with appropriate Navy specific software applications, with interfaces to a variety of communications, databases and computer systems.

GCCS-M meets the Joint and Service requirements for a single, integrated, scaleable Command, Control, Computer, and Intelligence (C^3I) system that receives, displays, correlates, fuses and maintains geo-locational track information on friendly, hostile, and neutral land, sea and air forces and integrates it with available intelligence and environmental information. The product of GCCS-M is a near-realtime, fused situational awareness picture that supports C^2 requirements for decision makers through every level of conflict from peace-time through war. Key capabilities include:

- Multisource information management
- Display and dissemination through extensive communications interfaces
- Multisource data fusion and analysis/decision making tools
- Force co-ordination

GCCS-M is implemented afloat (formerly referred to as Navy Tactical Command System-Afloat (NTCS-A) and Joint Maritime Command Information System (JMCIS) Afloat), at ashore fixed command centers (formerly referred to as Operational Support System (OSS) and JMCIS Ashore), and as the command and control (C^2) portion of mobile command centers (formerly known as Tactical Support Center (TSC) and JMCIS Tactical-Mobile). GCCS-M now refers to all three GCCS-M implementations.

Integrated Broadcast Service/Joint Tactical Terminal (IBS/JTT)

This programme supports indications and warning (I&W), surveillance and targeting data requirements of operational commanders and targeting staffs across all naval warfare areas. Comprising broadcast receiver/transponder equipment that provides target-quality data to tactical users, IBS is a 'system of systems' that will migrate TRAP Data Dissemination System (TDDS), Tactical Information Broadcast Service (TIBS), Tactical Reconnaissance Intelligence Exchange System (TRIXS) and Tactical Data Exchange - B (TACIXS-B) UHF broadcasts into an integrated service with a common format. IBS will also be able to send data via other communications paths, such as SHF, EHF and GBS. The US Army-procured Joint Tactical Terminal will receive, decrypt, process, format and distribute tactical data according to preset user-defined criteria across open-architecture equipment.

Joint Service Imagery Processing System (JSIPS)

JSIPS-N is the component of the joint programme to receive and exploit infra-red and electro-optical imagery from tactical airborne reconnaissance systems. The Navy is calling for JSIPS to be installed on all aircraft carriers and amphibious assault ships, and requirements for command ships have also been addressed. JSIPS will also provide the USMC with an 'amphibious' — afloat/ashore — processing facility that can be deployed as an integral element of Marine Air-Ground Task Forces (MAGTFs). JSIPS upgrades being considered include a common radar processor for both tactical and theatre-level radars, and an automated capability to insert and process mapping, charting and geodesy products.

Joint Surveillance Target Attack Radar System (JSTARS)

JSTARS is described as a 'bulletproof anti-jam datalink', utilising omnidirectional broadcast on UHF SATCOM. It receives and transmits real time MTI/FTI/SAR data via a secure uplink and downlink. It is used to demonstrate 'sensor to shooter' technology.

Joint Tactical Information Distribution System (JTIDS)/Link 16

This high-capacity digital information distribution system provides rapid, secure, jam-resistant/frequency-hopping communications, navigation and identification capabilities up to and including secret information. JTIDS provides Navy aircraft, ships and submarines and USMC units with crypto-secure, jam-resistant and low-probability-of-exploitation tactical data and voice communications. Upgrades will provide capabilities for common-grid navigation and automatic communications relay. In service since 1995, JTIDS has also been identified as the preferred communications link for Navy and other-service theatre ballistic missile defence programmes. JTIDS is the first element in the overall implementation of the Joint Message Standard (TADIL-J), and will provide the single, real-time, joint datalink network. Several NATO countries are participating in the JTIDS/ Link 16 programme.

Land Attack Warfare System (LAWS)

This system networks all shooters (tactical air, shore artillery and seaborne fire support) into a Battle Local Area Network (Battle LAN) known as the 'Ring of Fire'. This automatically assigns fire missions to the most capable unit in the Battle LAN. LAWS controls preplanned missions, including Tomahawk, as well as time critical calls for fire from land forces. Fleet Battle Experiment ALFA was the initial test of this system.

Link Eleven Improvement Program (LEIP)

This programme improves Link 11 connectivity and reliability and supports NILE (NATO Improved Link 11 and Link 22). Link 11 will be the common datalink for all US Navy and allied ships (seven NATO navies) not equipped with JTIDS/Link 16. NILE/ Link 22 is an element of the TADIL-J family. LEIP thus provides improvements in fleet support, training, commonality and interoperability. In addition to NILE, the programme comprises the Common Shipboard Data Terminal Set (CSDTS), Mobile Universal Link Translator System (MULTS), and Multiple Unit Link 11 Test and Operational Training System (MULTOTS). Some 190 CSDTS installations are planned.

Miniature Demand Assigned Multiple Access (Mini-DAMA)

In 2000, the Navy completes installations for submarines AV(2) and mine warfare ships V(2). Aircraft installations V(3) continue beyond 2000. These mini-DAMA radio installations provide the channel utilisation efficiencies by employing time division multiple access methods that have been achieved for surface warfare ships and shore stations equipped with the larger version TD-1271 DAMA multiplexer.

Mission Data System (MDS)

This system allows planners to view Tomahawk Land Attack Missile information. MDS receives via TADIXS A or OTCIXS I digital Mission Data Updates (MDUs) from the Cruise Missile Support Activity (CMSA) and stores preplanned TLAM strike plans. Initial TLAM mission data fill is distributed via magnetic tape media provided by the CMSA.

Multifunctional Information Distribution - Low Volume Terminal (MIDS-LVT)

This is a multinational co-operative development programme to design, develop and produce a tactical distribution system equivalent to JTIDS but in a low-volume, low-weight, compact terminal for aircraft. US Navy/USMC procurement is targeted for the F/A-18 Hornet aircraft and attack submarines. Other NATO participants in the programme include France, Germany, Italy and Spain. MIDS-LVT will employ the Link 16 (TADIL-J) message standards.

NTCS - A Intelligence Processing System (NIPS)

This is a comprehensive military database which provides characteristics and performance data on Red, White and Blue units, weapons and sensor suites. It can be automatically updated.

Ocean Surveillance Information System (OSIS) Baseline Upgrade/Evolutionary Development (OBU/OED)

The OSIS Baseline Upgrade (OBU) programme is a shore-based intelligence system providing on-line, automated, near-realtime netted C^2 support to the Unified Commanders in Chief, JTF commanders afloat and ashore, individual ships and allies. It receives, processes and disseminates all-source information on fixed and mobile targets at sea and on land. OBU provides a multilevel secure system at message level and automated event-by-event reporting. It is evolving into a JMCIS-compliant system, the OSIS Evolutionary Development (OED) system, which will employ JMCIS software and hardware (TAC-X series). Land-based sites operate in the US, at US facilities overseas, and in Australia and the UK.

Radiant Mercury

Radiant Mercury is a rules-driven (Boolean logic), multilevel security (MLS) system meeting operational requirements to sanitise highly classified data automatically and provide it as SI-GENSER-Releasable to the shooters while protecting sources, methods, national sensitivities and foreign releasability of the tactical picture. In order to enhance interoperability, Radiant Mercury can transliterate a message or a field to another format, permitting rapid sharing of data within commands and among coalition forces.

Tactical Intelligence Information Exchange Subsystem, Phase II (TACINTEL II+)

TACINTEL II is a computer-based message communications system for automatic receipt and transmission of Special Intelligence (SI) and Special Compartmented Information (SCI) messages geared primarily to contact reports and other tactically useful information.

TACINTEL II+ extends the Phase II system by implementing the Copernicus vision for joint C^4I interoperability using open-architecture standards. The full-up capability will include voice, message and data transfer among SCI-capable ships and aircraft, with gateways to shore nodes. TACINTEL II+ is the lead implementing programme for the Communications Support System (CSS).

Major Commercial Shipyards

Avondale Industries, New Orleans, Louisiana
Bath Iron Works, Bath, Maine (General Dynamics)
Baltimore Marine (ex-Bethlehem Steel), Sparrows Point, Maryland
Bender Shipbuilding, Mobile, Alabama
Bollinger Shipyards, Lockport, Louisiana
General Dynamics Corporation, Electric Boat Division, Groton, Connecticut
Halter Marine Inc, Moss Point, Mississippi
Ingalls Shipbuilding (Litton), Pascagoula, Mississippi
Intermarine USA, Savannah, Georgia
McDermott Marine, Morgan City, Louisiana
National Steel & Shipbuilding Company, San Diego, California
Newport News Shipbuilding Company, Newport News, Virginia
Textron Marine Systems, New Orleans, Louisiana
Todd Pacific Shipyards, Seattle, Washington

Note: All the yards mentioned have been involved in naval shipbuilding, overhaul, or modernisation except for the General Dynamics/Electric Boat yard which is engaged only in submarine work. Newport News is the only US shipyard capable of building nuclear-powered aircraft carriers.

Major Warships Taken Out of Service 1997 to mid-2000

Submarines

1997 *Groton, Birmingham, Tautog, Grayling, Baltimore, Pintado, Archerfish, Tunny, Cavalla, Phoenix*
1998 *Sand Lance, Indianapolis, Batfish*
1999 *Boston, Atlanta, Pogy, Narwhal, Trepang, Billfish, James K Polk, William H Bates, Hawkbill*

Aircraft Carriers

1999 *Independence*

Cruisers

1997 *Arkansas*
1998 *California, South Carolina*

Destroyers

1997 *Merrill, Leftwich*
1998 *Comte de Grasse, Conolly, John Rodgers, Harry W Hill, Ingersoll, Kidd, Callaghan, Scott*
1999 *Chandler*

Frigates

1997 *Oliver Hazard Perry, Aubrey Fitch*
1998 *Reid* (to Turkey), *Fahrion* (to Egypt), *Lewis B Puller* (to Egypt)
1999 *Stark*
2000 *Clark* (to Poland), *John A Moore* (to Turkey)

Amphibious Forces

1997 *New Orleans*
1998 *Fort Fisher, Guam*
1999 *Pensacola* (to Taiwan)

Auxiliaries

1997 *Maury* (AGS), *Turtle* (DSV), *Mars* (AFS), *San Diego* (AFS), *Wyman* (AGS), *Range Sentinel* (AGM), *American Merlin* (AK)
1998 *Cimarron* (AO), *Merrimack* (AO), *Simon Lake* (AS), *Powhatan* (ATF), *Vanguard* (AG), *American Osprey* (AOT)
1999 *Willamette* (AO), *McKee* (AS), *Mount Hood* (AE), *Narragansett* (ATF); *Platte* (AO), *Monongahela* (AO)

HULL NUMBERS

Note: Ships in reserve not included.

SUBMARINES

Ballistic Missile Submarines

Ohio class
SSBN 726	Ohio
SSBN 727	Michigan
SSBN 728	Florida
SSBN 729	Georgia
SSBN 730	Henry M Jackson
SSBN 731	Alabama
SSBN 732	Alaska
SSBN 733	Nevada
SSBN 734	Tennessee
SSBN 735	Pennsylvania
SSBN 736	West Virginia
SSBN 737	Kentucky
SSBN 738	Maryland
SSBN 739	Nebraska
SSBN 740	Rhode Island
SSBN 741	Maine
SSBN 742	Wyoming
SSBN 743	Louisiana

Attack Submarines

Benjamin Franklin class
SSN 642	Kamehameha

Seawolf class
SSN 21	Seawolf
SSN 22	Connecticut
SSN 23	Jimmy Carter

Sturgeon class
SSN 683	Parche
SSN 686	L Mendel Rivers

Los Angeles class
SSN 688	Los Angeles
SSN 690	Philadelphia
SSN 691	Memphis
SSN 698	Bremerton
SSN 699	Jacksonville
SSN 700	Dallas
SSN 701	La Jolla
SSN 705	City of Corpus Christi
SSN 706	Albuquerque
SSN 707	Portsmouth
SSN 708	Minneapolis—Saint Paul
SSN 709	Hyman G Rickover
SSN 710	Augusta
SSN 711	San Francisco
SSN 713	Houston
SSN 714	Norfolk
SSN 715	Buffalo
SSN 716	Salt Lake City
SSN 717	Olympia
SSN 718	Honolulu
SSN 719	Providence
SSN 720	Pittsburgh
SSN 721	Chicago
SSN 722	Key West
SSN 723	Oklahoma City
SSN 724	Louisville
SSN 725	Helena
SSN 750	Newport News
SSN 751	San Juan
SSN 752	Pasadena
SSN 753	Albany
SSN 754	Topeka
SSN 755	Miami
SSN 756	Scranton
SSN 757	Alexandria
SSN 758	Asheville
SSN 759	Jefferson City
SSN 760	Annapolis
SSN 761	Springfield
SSN 762	Columbus
SSN 763	Santa Fe
SSN 764	Boise
SSN 765	Montpelier
SSN 766	Charlotte
SSN 767	Hampton
SSN 768	Hartford
SSN 769	Toledo
SSN 770	Tucson
SSN 771	Columbia
SSN 772	Greeneville
SSN 773	Cheyenne

Virginia class
SSN 774	Virginia
SSN 775	Texas
SSN 776	Hawaii

SURFACE COMBATANTS

Aircraft Carriers

Kitty Hawk class
CV 63	Kitty Hawk
CV 64	Constellation

John F Kennedy class
CV 67	John F Kennedy

Enterprise class
CVN 65	Enterprise

Nimitz class
CVN 68	Nimitz
CVN 69	Dwight D Eisenhower
CVN 70	Carl Vinson
CVN 71	Theodore Roosevelt
CVN 72	Abraham Lincoln
CVN 73	George Washington
CVN 74	John C Stennis
CVN 75	Harry S Truman
CVN 76	Ronald Reagan

Cruisers

Ticonderoga class
CG 47	Ticonderoga
CG 48	Yorktown
CG 49	Vincennes
CG 50	Valley Forge
CG 51	Thomas S Gates
CG 52	Bunker Hill
CG 53	Mobile Bay
CG 54	Antietam
CG 55	Leyte Gulf
CG 56	San Jacinto
CG 57	Lake Champlain
CG 58	Philippine Sea
CG 59	Princeton
CG 60	Normandy
CG 61	Monterey
CG 62	Chancellorsville
CG 63	Cowpens
CG 64	Gettysburg
CG 65	Chosin
CG 66	Hue City
CG 67	Shiloh
CG 68	Anzio
CG 69	Vicksburg
CG 70	Lake Erie
CG 71	Cape St George
CG 72	Vella Gulf
CG 73	Port Royal

Destroyers

Spruance class
DD 963	Spruance
DD 964	Paul F Foster
DD 965	Kinkaid
DD 966	Hewitt
DD 967	Elliott
DD 968	Arthur W Radford
DD 969	Peterson
DD 970	Caron
DD 971	David R Ray
DD 972	Oldendorf
DD 973	John Young
DD 975	O'Brien
DD 977	Briscoe
DD 978	Stump
DD 980	Moosbrugger
DD 981	John Hancock
DD 982	Nicholson
DD 985	Cushing
DD 987	O'Bannon
DD 988	Thorn
DD 989	Deyo
DD 991	Fife
DD 992	Fletcher
DD 997	Hayler

Arleigh Burke class
DDG 51	Arleigh Burke
DDG 52	Barry
DDG 53	John Paul Jones
DDG 54	Curtis Wilbur
DDG 55	Stout
DDG 56	John S McCain
DDG 57	Mitscher
DDG 58	Laboon
DDG 59	Russell
DDG 60	Paul Hamilton
DDG 61	Ramage
DDG 62	Fitzgerald
DDG 63	Stethem
DDG 64	Carney
DDG 65	Benfold
DDG 66	Gonzalez
DDG 67	Cole
DDG 68	The Sullivans
DDG 69	Milius
DDG 70	Hopper
DDG 71	Ross
DDG 72	Mahan
DDG 73	Decatur
DDG 74	McFaul
DDG 75	Donald Cook
DDG 76	Higgins
DDG 77	O'Kane
DDG 78	Porter
DDG 79	Oscar Austin
DDG 80	Roosevelt
DDG 81	Winston Churchill
DDG 82	Lassen
DDG 83	Howard
DDG 84	Bulkeley
DDG 85	McCampbell
DDG 86	Shoup
DDG 87	Mason
DDG 88	Preble
DDG 89	Mustin
DDG 90	Chaffee

Frigates

Oliver Hazard Perry class
FFG 8	McInerney
FFG 9	Wadsworth
FFG 12	George Philip
FFG 13	Samuel Eliot Morison
FFG 14	John H Sides
FFG 15	Estocin
FFG 28	Boone
FFG 29	Stephen W Groves
FFG 32	John L Hall
FFG 33	Jarrett
FFG 36	Underwood
FFG 37	Crommelin
FFG 38	Curts
FFG 39	Doyle
FFG 40	Halyburton
FFG 41	McClusky
FFG 42	Klakring
FFG 43	Thach
FFG 45	De Wert
FFG 46	Rentz
FFG 47	Nicholas
FFG 48	Vandegrift
FFG 49	Robert G Bradley
FFG 50	Taylor
FFG 51	Gary
FFG 52	Carr
FFG 53	Hawes
FFG 54	Ford
FFG 55	Elrod
FFG 56	Simpson
FFG 57	Reuben James
FFG 58	Samuel B Roberts
FFG 59	Kauffman
FFG 60	Rodney M Davis
FFG 61	Ingraham

Coastal Patrol Craft

Cyclone class
PC 1	Cyclone
PC 2	Tempest
PC 3	Hurricane
PC 4	Monsoon
PC 5	Typhoon
PC 6	Sirocco
PC 7	Squall
PC 8	Zephyr
PC 9	Chinook
PC 10	Firebolt
PC 11	Whirlwind
PC 12	Thunderbolt
PC 13	Shamal
PC 14	Tornado

COMMAND SHIPS

Blue Ridge class
LCC 19	Blue Ridge
LCC 20	Mount Whitney

Raleigh and Austin class
AGF 3	La Salle
AGF 11	Coronado

AMPHIBIOUS FORCES

Amphibious Assault Ships

Wasp class
LHD 1	Wasp
LHD 2	Essex
LHD 3	Kearsage
LHD 4	Boxer
LHD 5	Bataan
LHD 6	Bonhomme Richard
LHD 7	Iwo Jima

Tarawa class
LHA 1	Tarawa
LHA 2	Saipan
LHA 3	Belleau Wood
LHA 4	Nassau
LHA 5	Peleliu

Amphibious Transport Docks

Austin class
LPD 4	Austin
LPD 5	Ogden
LPD 6	Duluth
LPD 7	Cleveland
LPD 8	Dubuque
LPD 9	Denver
LPD 10	Juneau
LPD 12	Shreveport
LPD 13	Nashville
LPD 14	Trenton
LPD 15	Ponce

San Antonio class
LPD 17	San Antonio
LPD 18	New Orleans

Amphibious Cargo Ships

Anchorage class
LSD 36	Anchorage
LSD 37	Portland
LSD 39	Mount Vernon

Whidbey Island class
LSD 41	Whidbey Island
LSD 42	Germantown
LSD 43	Fort McHenry
LSD 44	Gunston Hall
LSD 45	Comstock
LSD 46	Tortuga
LSD 47	Rushmore
LSD 48	Ashland

Harpers Ferry class
LSD 49	Harpers Ferry
LSD 50	Carter Hall
LSD 51	Oak Hill
LSD 52	Pearl Harbor

Tank Landing Ships

Newport class
LST 1184	Frederick
LST 1194	La Moure County

MINE WARFARE FORCES

Command Ship

Iwo Jima class
MCS 12	Inchon

Mine Countermeasures Ships

Avenger class
MCM 1	Avenger
MCM 2	Defender
MCM 3	Sentry
MCM 4	Champion
MCM 5	Guardian
MCM 6	Devastator
MCM 7	Patriot
MCM 8	Scout
MCM 9	Pioneer
MCM 10	Warrior
MCM 11	Gladiator
MCM 12	Ardent
MCM 13	Dextrous
MCM 14	Chief

Osprey class
MHC 51	Osprey
MHC 52	Heron
MHC 53	Pelican
MHC 54	Robin
MHC 55	Oriole
MHC 56	Kingfisher
MHC 57	Cormorant
MHC 58	Black Hawk
MHC 59	Falcon
MHC 60	Cardinal
MHC 61	Raven
MHC 62	Shrike

UNDERWAY REPLENISHMENT SHIPS

Fast Combat Support Ships

Sacramento class
AOE 1	Sacramento
AOE 2	Camden
AOE 3	Seattle
AOE 4	Detroit

Supply class
AOE 6	Supply
AOE 7	Rainier
AOE 8	Arctic
AOE 10	Bridge

MATERIAL SUPPORT SHIPS

Submarine Tenders

Emory S Land class
AS 39	Emory S Land
AS 40	Frank Cable

Salvage Ships

Safeguard class
ARS 50	Safeguard
ARS 51	Grasp
ARS 52	Salvor
ARS 53	Grapple

MISCELLANEOUS

Auxiliary Research Submarine

Dolphin class
AGSS 555	Dolphin

Oceanographic Research Ships

AGOR 14	Melville
AGOR 15	Knorr
AGOR 21	Gyre
AGOR 23	Thomas G Thompson
AGOR 24	Roger Revelle
AGOR 25	Atlantis
(AGOR 26)	Ronald H Brown

MILITARY SEALIFT COMMAND

NAVAL FLEET AUXILIARY FORCE

Ammunition Ships

T-AE 26	Kilauea
T-AE 27	Butte
T-AE 28	Santa Barbara
T-AE 32	Flint
T-AE 33	Shasta
T-AE 34	Mount Baker
T-AE 35	Kiska

Combat Stores Ships

T-AFS 3	Niagara Falls
T-AFS 5	Concord
T-AFS 7	San Jose
T-AFS 8	Sirius
T-AFS 9	Spica
T-AFS 10	Saturn

Hospital Ships

T-AH 19	Mercy
T-AH 20	Comfort

Oilers

Henry J Kaiser class
T-AO 187	Henry J Kaiser (PREPO)
T-AO 189	John J Lenthall
T-AO 193	Walter S Diehl
T-AO 194	John Ericsson
T-AO 195	Leroy Grumman
T-AO 196	Kanawha
T-AO 197	Pecos
T-AO 198	Big Horn
T-AO 199	Tippecanoe
T-AO 200	Guadalupe
T-AO 201	Patuxent
T-AO 202	Yukon
T-AO 203	Laramie
T-AO 204	Rappahannock

Fleet Ocean Tugs

Powhatan class
T-ATF 168	Catawba
T-ATF 169	Navajo
T-ATF 170	Mohawk
T-ATF 171	Sioux
T-ATF 172	Apache

SPECIAL MISSION SHIPS

Acoustic Survey Ship

T-AG 195	Hayes

Cable Repair Ship

T-ARC 7	Zeus

Counter-drug Surveillance

T-AGOS 1	Stalwart
T-AGOS 3	Vindicator
T-AGOS 6	Persistent
T-AGOS 7	Indomitable
T-AGOS 16	Capable

Missile Range Instrumentation Ship

T-AGM 23	Observation Island

Navigation Test/Launch Area Support Ships

T-AG 45	Waters

Surveillance Ships

T-AGOS 8	Prevail
T-AGOS 9	Assertive
T-AGOS 10	Invincible
T-AGOS 12	Bold
T-AGOS 19	Victorious
T-AGOS 20	Able
T-AGOS 21	Effective
T-AGOS 22	Loyal
T-AGOS 23	Impeccable

Surveying Ships

T-AGS 27	Kane
T-AGS 51	John McDonnell
T-AGS 52	Littlehales
T-AGS 60	Pathfinder
T-AGS 61	Sumner
T-AGS 62	Bowditch
T-AGS 63	Henson
T-AGS 64	Bruce C Heezen
T-AGS 65	Mary Spears

PREPOSITIONING PROGRAMME

Container Ships

T-AK 4296	Capt Steven L Bennett
T-AK 4396	Maj Bernard F Fisher
T-AK 4397	Lt Col Calvin P Titus
T-AK 4398	SP5 Eric G Gibson

Flo-Flo Ship

T-AK 2026	American Cormorant

Cargo Ships

T-AK 9881	Buffalo Soldier
T-AK 9655	Green Ridge
T-AK 9205	Strong Virginian

LASH

T-AK 2064	Green Harbour
T-AK 9204	Jeb Stuart

Large, Medium-Speed, Ro-ro

T-AKR 310	Watson
T-AKR 311	Sisler
T-AKR 312	Dahl
T-AKR 313	Red Cloud
T-AKR 314	Charlton
T-AKR 315	Watkins
T-AKR 316	Pomeroy

Tankers

T-AOT 9101	Petersburg
T-AOT 181	Potomac

Aviation Logistic Ships

T-AVB 3	Wright
T-AVB 4	Curtiss

Crane

T-ACS 4	Gopher State

Maritime Prepositioning Ships

T-AK 3000	CPL Louis J Hauge, Jr
T-AK 3001	PFC William B Baugh
T-AK 3002	PFC James Anderson, Jr
T-AK 3003	1st Lt Alex Bonnyman
T-AK 3004	PVT Franklin J Phillips
T-AK 3005	SGT Matej Kocak
T-AK 3006	PFC Eugene A Obregon
T-AK 3007	MAJ Stephen W Pless
T-AK 3008	2nd Lt John P Bobo
T-AK 3009	PFC Dewayne T Williams
T-AK 3010	1st Lt Baldomero Lopez
T-AK 3011	1st Lt Jack Lummus
T-AK 3012	SGT William R Button
T-AK 3015	1st Lt Harry L Martin
T-AK 3016	L/Cpl Roy M Wheat

SEALIFT FORCE

Fast Sealift Ships

T-AKR 287	Algol
T-AKR 288	Bellatrix
T-AKR 289	Denebola
T-AKR 290	Pollux
T-AKR 291	Altair
T-AKR 292	Regulus
T-AKR 293	Capella
T-AKR 294	Antares

Large, Medium-speed Ro-ro

T-AKR 295	Shughart
T-AKR 296	Gordon
T-AKR 297	Yano
T-AKR 298	Gilliland (PREPO)
T-AKR 299	Soderman
T-AKR 300	Bob Hope
T-AKR 301	Fisher
T-AKR 302	Seay
T-AKR 303	Mendonca
T-AKR 304	Pililaau
T-AKR 305	Brittin
T-AKR 306	—

Tankers

T-AOT 1121	Gus W Darnell
T-AOT 1122	Paul Buck
T-AOT 1123	Samuel L Cobb
T-AOT 1124	Richard G Matthieson
T-AOT 1125	Lawrence H Gianella

READY RESERVE FORCE
(see pages 839 and 840)

Attack Submarines (SSN)

Notes: (1) **Deep submergence vehicles:** The Deep Submergence Vehicles (DSV), including the nuclear-propelled *NR-1*, are rated as Service Craft and are listed at the end of the 'Special Vessels' section following the MSC section.

(2) **Swimmer-Seal Delivery Vehicles (SDVs):** There are 10 Mk VIII Mod 1 six-man mini submarines in service for naval commando units. These SDVs have a speed of 8 kt and can be carried by suitably modified SSNs. Range 35 n miles at up to 150 ft. All have been SLEPed from 1995 to improve performance. A new design **ASDS** (Advanced Swimmer Delivery System) with electric propulsion was ordered from Northrop Grumman in September 1994. Trials started in October 1999 and complete in 2000. One unit is then to be assigned to Pearl Harbor, with a second to Little Creek a year later. These are dry submersibles capable of deploying from a mother submarine to a hostile shore. 65 × 10 ft with a crew of two and space for eight SEALs. Range is 125 n miles at 8 kt using a 55 hp motor and four thrusters. Optical and comms periscopes are fitted plus a small

sonar. The craft can be air transported. The plan is to have three in service by 2001 with one more to follow in 2003.

(3) **Unmanned Undersea Vehicles (UUVs):** Two prototype surface ship-launched vehicles were built under joint ARPA/Navy UUV programmes. Operational testing of the second vehicle, the Mine Search System (MSS), was completed in 1993. The MSS vehicle is 35 ft long and has a titanium hull with a diameter of 44 in. The payload is housed in an internal pressure hull. The propulsion motor is free flooding and develops 12 hp from two battery sections. MSS operational trials demonstrated the performance of mine detection sonars and the ability of a UUV to survey designated areas with precise navigation.

Another semi-autonomous vehicle is the Advanced Unmanned Search System (AUSS), which was developed by NRaD, San Diego, and is operated by the Navy Supervisor of Salvage. AUSS was designed for search operations to 20,000 ft and is controlled by an acoustic datalink from a surface support ship. AUSS is 17 ft long and 31 in in diameter with a graphite epoxy

pressure hull weighing 2,800 lb. Two main thrusters provide forward and aft propulsion and steering with two vertical thrusters for altitude control. Endurance is 10 hours at 5 kt on silver-zinc batteries. Sensors include a side-looking sonar and a CCD camera which transmits images to the surface via an acoustic datalink.

UUVs capable of remote control from either surface ships or submarines are being researched. Roles are limitless but remote sensing and acoustic deception are two obvious front runners. Operating difficulties should not be underestimated.

(4) **Autonomous Undersea Vehicles (AUVs):** Research work is being done with the aim of producing torpedo-launched remote-controlled vehicles for a range of tasks including surveillance, communications and mine warfare. An NMRS (Near-term Mine Reconnaissance System) prototype was ordered in 1995 from Westinghouse. This is tube-launched, controlled and recovered.

ASDS   *10/1999*, Northrop Grumman* / 0085296

SDV Mk VIII   *10/1997, A McKaskle, USN* / 0053312

0 + 4 (2) VIRGINIA CLASS (SSN)

Name	No
VIRGINIA	SSN 774
TEXAS	SSN 775
HAWAII	SSN 776
—	SSN 777

Builders	Start date	Launched	Commissioned
General Dynamics (Electric Boat)	2 Sep 1999	2003	2004
Newport News Shipbuilding	2000	2005	2006
General Dynamics (Electric Boat)	2001	2006	2007
Newport News Shipbuilding	2002	2007	2008

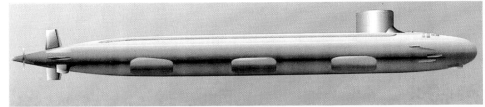

Displacement, tons: 7,800 dived
Dimensions, feet (metres): 377 × 34 × 30.5
(114.9 × 10.4 × 9.3)
Main machinery: Nuclear; 1 GE PWR S9G; 2 turbines; 40,000 hp
(29.84 MW); 1 shaft; pump jet propulsor; 1 secondary
propulsion submerged motor
Speed, knots: 34 dived
Complement: 134

Missiles: SLCM Tomahawk. ATMS possibly.
SSM: 12 VLS tubes for cruise missiles.
Torpedoes: 4—21 in *(533 mm)* tubes. Mk 48 ADCAP Mod 6;
total of 38 weapons including SSM, torpedoes and UUVs.
Mines: Mk 48 Advanced Mobile mines in lieu of torpedoes.
Countermeasures: Decoys: 14 external and 1 internal
(reloadable). Anti-torpedo torpedo.
ESM: WLQ-4(V); BLQ-10; intercept.
Combat data systems: Lockheed Martin CCSM (Command and
Control System Module) compatible with JMCIS.
Radars: Navigation: BPS 16; I-band.
Sonars: Bow spherical active/passive array; wide aperture flank
passive arrays; high-frequency active keel and fin arrays; TB 16
and TB 29 towed arrays.

Programmes: Advanced funding in FY96 programme and this
continued into FY98. Second of class funding in FY99, third in
FY01 and then one a year is planned. In February 1997,

VIRGINIA (artist's impression)

1998, Electric Boat / 0053313

a teaming agreement was reached with Newport News to co-
operatively build the first four NSSNs. Electric Boat is the lead
design yard, and constructs the engine room modules,
command and control modules, and seven other sections of
each ship. It also performs final assembly, testing, outfitting,
and delivery of the first and third submarines. Newport News
constructs the sail, the habitability and auxiliary machinery
room modules, and six other sections. It also performs final
assembly, testing, outfitting, and delivery of the second and
fourth submarines. Reactor compartments built by the delivery
yard in each case. A total of 30 hulls has been identified as
required by the Navy. A scale version (0.294) LSV-2 is listed
under *Deep Submergence Vehicles*.

Structure: Seawolf level quietening. Acoustic hull cladding. The
reactor core will last the life of the ship. The integral nine-man
lock out chamber can be used with the Advanced SEAL
Delivery System mini submarine or a dry deck shelter, and the
torpedo magazine can be adapted to provide 2,400 ft³ of
space for up to 40 SEALs and equipment. Non-hull-penetrating
mast with eight antenna packages depending on the role. Test
depth 488 m *(1,600 ft)*.
Operational: To be capable of both deep ocean ASW and
shallow water operations of all types. Advanced UUVs, wake
detection equipment and a deployable bistatic source are all to
be available.

UPDATED

2 STURGEON CLASS (SSN)

Name	No
PARCHE	SSN 683
L MENDEL RIVERS	SSN 686

Builders	Laid down	Launched	Commissioned	F/S
Ingalls Shipbuilding	10 Dec 1970	13 Jan 1973	17 Aug 1974	PA
Newport News Shipbuilding	26 June 1971	2 June 1973	1 Feb 1975	AA

Displacement, tons: 4,250; 4,460 standard; 4,780; 4,960 dived
(see *Structure*); 7,800 dived *(Parche)*
Dimensions, feet (metres): 302.2; or 393 *(Parche)* × 31.8 ×
28.9 *(92.1; or 119.8 × 9.7 × 8.8)*
Main machinery: Nuclear; 1 Westinghouse PWR S5W;
2 turbines; 15,000 hp *(11.2 MW)*; 1 shaft
Speed, knots: 15 surfaced; 30 dived
Complement: 107 (12 officers); 179 (22 officers) *(Parche)*

Missiles: SLCM: GDC Tomahawk (TLAM-N); land attack; Tercom
aided inertial navigation system (TAINS) to 2,500 km *(1,400 n
miles)* at 0.7 Mach; altitude 15-100 m; nuclear warhead
200 kT; CEP 80 m. There are also two versions (TLAM-C/D)
with either a single 454 kg HE warhead or a single warhead
with submunitions; range 900 km *(485 n miles)*; CEP 10 m.
Nuclear warheads are not normally carried. TLAM-C Block III
increases range to 1,700 km *(918 n miles)*, adds GPS back-up
to TAINS and substitutes a 318 kg shaped charge warhead.

SSM: GDC Tomahawk (TASM); anti-ship; inertial guidance; active
radar/anti-radiation homing to 460 km *(250 n miles)* at
0.7 Mach; warhead 454 kg.
McDonnell Douglas Harpoon; active radar homing to 130 km
(70 n miles) at 0.9 Mach; warhead 227 kg (84A) or 258 kg
(84B/C).
Torpedoes: 4—21 in *(533 mm)* Mk 63 tubes midships. Gould
Mk 48 ADCAP; wire-guided (option); active/passive homing to
50 km *(27 n miles)*/38 km *(21 n miles)* at 40/55 kt; warhead
267 kg; depth to 900 m *(2,950 ft)*.
Total of 23 weapons, for example 4 Harpoon, 4 Tomahawk
and 15 torpedoes. Up to 8 Tomahawk can be carried in place
of other weapons.
Mines: Mk 67 Mobile and Mk 60 Captor can be carried.
Countermeasures: Decoys: Emerson Electric Mk 2; torpedo
decoy launchers.
ESM: WLQ-4; radar warning.
Weapons control: Mk 117 torpedo fire-control system.
Radars: Surface search/navigation/fire control: Sperry BPS 15
or Raytheon BPS 14; I/J-band.
Sonars: IBM BQQ 5; passive/active search and attack; low
frequency.
EDO BQS 8 or Raytheon BQS 14A; ice detection; high
frequency.
Raytheon BQS 13; active/passive array.
BQR 15; towed array; passive search; very low frequency.

Structure: Sail-mounted diving planes rotate to vertical for
breaking through ice when surfacing in arctic regions.
L Mendel Rivers can carry a dry deck shelter. *Parche* modified
1987-91 with an additional section for special equipment
designed for seabed operations. The sail planes are higher up
and there is a marked hump in the casing forward of the sail for
a cable reel. Diving depth is 400 m *(1,320 ft)*.
Operational: Operational life was expected to be 30 years but
many of the class decommissioned early as a result of defence
cutbacks. Subroc phased out in 1990. Nuclear warheads are
not carried. *Rivers* scheduled to decommission in late 2000,
Parche at the end of 2003.

UPDATED

L MENDEL RIVERS (with dry deck shelter)
4/1999*, Jürg Kürsener / 0084085

1 BENJAMIN FRANKLIN CLASS (SSN)

Name	No
KAMEHAMEHA	SSN (ex-SSBN) 642

Builders	Laid down	Launched	Commissioned	F/S
Mare Island Naval Shipyard	2 May 1963	16 Jan 1965	10 Dec 1965	PA

Displacement, tons: 7,330 surfaced; 8,250 dived
Dimensions, feet (metres): 425 × 33 × 31.5
(129.5 × 10.1 × 9.6)
Main machinery: Nuclear; 1 Westinghouse PWR S5W;
2 turbines; 15,000 hp *(11.2 MW)*; 1 shaft
1 Magnetek auxiliary prop motor; 325 hp *(242 kW)*
Speed, knots: 18 surfaced; 25 dived
Complement: 120 (13 officers) plus 180 troops

Torpedoes: 4—21 in *(533 mm)* Mk 65 bow tubes. Gould Mk 48;
ADCAP; wire-guided (option); active/passive homing to 50 km
(27 n miles)/38 km *(21 n miles)* at 40/55 kt; warhead 267 kg;
depth to 900 m *(2,950 ft)*.
Countermeasures: Decoys: 8 Emerson Electric Mk 2 launchers;
torpedo decoy.
ESM: WLR-8; intercept. WLR-10; radar warning.
Weapons control: Mk 113 Mod 9 torpedo fire-control system.
Radars: Surface search/navigation: BPS 15; I/J-band.
Sonars: EDO BQR 7E; passive search.
Western Electric; BQR 15; passive towed array.
Raytheon BQR 19; active for navigation; high frequency.
Honeywell BQR 21 (Dimus); passive array.
Raytheon BQS 4; active search and classification.

KAMEHAMEHA

6/1999*, van Ginderen Collection / 0084086

Programmes: Last survivor of the class, except for *Daniel
Webster* and *Sam Rayburn* which are used as moored nuclear
reactor training ships.
Modernisation: Converted to dry deck shelter (DDS) SSN and
equipped for special operations, supporting SEALs. Former
missile spaces have been converted into accommodation,
stores and recreation rooms.

Structure: Diesel-electric standby machinery, snorts, and
'outboard' auxiliary propeller for emergency use. Diving depth
is approximately 300 m *(984 ft)*.
Operational: Two dry deck shelters carried side by side can carry
one SDV Mk 8 each for up to six SEALs, and the submarine has
berths for up to 65 troops and SEALs. Second of class was
similarly converted but paid off in early 1999. This one is
expected to go in late 2001.

UPDATED

2 + 1 SEAWOLF CLASS (SSN)

Name	No	Builders	Start date	Launched	Commissioned	F/S
SEAWOLF	SSN 21	General Dynamics (Electric Boat)	25 Oct 1989	24 June 1995	19 July 1997	AA
CONNECTICUT	SSN 22	General Dynamics (Electric Boat)	14 Sep 1992	1 Sep 1997	11 Dec 1998	AA
JIMMY CARTER	SSN 23	General Dynamics (Electric Boat)	12 Dec 1995	June 2004	Dec 2005	Bldg

Displacement, tons: 8,060 surfaced; 9,142 dived
Dimensions, feet (metres): 353 × 42.3 × 35.8
  (107.6 × 12.9 × 10.9) (see *Modernisation*)
Main machinery: Nuclear; 1 Westinghouse PWR S6W; 2 turbines; 45,000 hp *(33.57 MW)*; 1 shaft; pumpjet propulsor; 1 Westinghouse secondary propulsion submerged motor
Speed, knots: 39 dived
Complement: 134 (14 officers)

Missiles: SLCM: Hughes Tomahawk (TLAM-N); land attack; Tercom Aided Inertial Navigation System (TAINS) to 2,500 km *(1,400 n miles)* at 0.7 Mach; altitude 15-100 m; nuclear warhead 200 kT; CEP 80 m. There are also 2 versions (TLAM-C/D) with either a single 454 kg HE warhead or a single warhead with submunitions; range 900 km *(485 n miles)*; CEP 10 m.

Nuclear warheads are not normally carried. Block III missiles increase TLAM-C range to 1,700 km *(918 n miles)*, add GPS back-up to TAINS and substitute a 318 kg shaped charge warhead.
SSM: GDC/Hughes Tomahawk (TASM); anti-ship; inertial guidance; active radar/anti-radiation homing to 460 km *(250 n miles)* at 0.7 Mach; warhead 454 kg. May be carried in due course.
Torpedoes: 8—26 in *(660 mm)* tubes (external measurement is 30 in *(762 mm)*); Gould Mk 48 ADCAP; wire-guided (option); active/passive homing to 50 km *(27 n miles)*/38 km *(21 n miles)* at 40/55 kt; warhead 267 kg; depth to 900 m *(2,950 ft)*. Air turbine discharge. Total of 50 tube-launched missiles and torpedoes, and UUVs in due course.
Mines: 100 in lieu of torpedoes.

Countermeasures: Decoys: torpedo decoys. WLY-1 system in due course.
ESM: WLQ-4(V)1; BLD-1; intercept.
Combat data systems: General Electric BSY-2 system. USC-38 EHF. JMCIS.
Weapons control: Raytheon Mk 2 FCS
Radars: Navigation: BPS 16; I-band.
Sonars: BQQ 5D suite with bow spherical active/passive array and wide aperture passive flank arrays; TB 16 and TB 29 surveillance and tactical towed arrays.
  BQS 24; active close range detection; high frequency.

Programmes: First of class ordered on 9 January 1989; second of class on 3 May 1991 and third on 30 April 1996. Design changes to *Carter* contracted in late 1999 have delayed the launch by four years.
Modernisation: *Carter*'s hull is being lengthened behind the sail for insertion of an Ocean Interface section with larger payload apertures to the sea. Modular architecture allows configuration for specific missions. Payloads could include standoff vehicles, distributed sensors and leave-behind weapons that would be activated after the submarine has left the area. It also supports Special Operations Forces including Dry Deck Shelter (DDS) and the Advanced SEAL Delivery System (ASDS). *Carter* retains all of the 'Seawolf' class's original war-fighting capability.
Structure: The modular design has more weapons, a higher tactical speed, better sonars and an ASW mission effectiveness 'three times better than the improved 'Los Angeles' class' according to the Navy. It is estimated that over a billion dollars has been allocated for research and development including the S6W reactor system. Full acoustic cladding fitted. Mk 21 Air turbine torpedo discharge pump. There are no external weapons. Emphasis has been put on sub-ice capabilities including retractable bow planes. Test depth 1,950 ft *(594 m)*.
Operational: A quoted 'silent' speed of 20 kt. Other operational advantages include greater manoeuvrability and space for subsequent weapon systems development. Delay in commissioning *Seawolf* caused by panels pulling away from the wide aperture sonar array during sea trials. The panels have been redesigned. There were also torpedo tube door closure problems leading to the doors being replaced.
Opinion: This submarine was intended to restore the level of acoustic advantage (in the one to one nuclear submarine engagement against the Russians) which the USN has enjoyed for the last three decades. At the same time the larger capacity of the magazine enhances overall effectiveness in a number of other roles. The decision to discontinue building this one very expensive design was the inevitable result of falling defence budgets, technical problems and a much diminished Russian threat.

SEAWOLF

9/1996, Electric Boat / 0016301

UPDATED

CONNECTICUT

6/1998, Electric Boat / 0044058

51 LOS ANGELES CLASS (SSN)

Name	No	Builders	Laid down	Launched	Commissioned	F/S
LOS ANGELES	SSN 688	Newport News Shipbuilding	8 Jan 1972	6 Apr 1974	13 Nov 1976	PA
PHILADELPHIA	SSN 690	General Dynamics (Electric Boat Div)	12 Aug 1972	19 Oct 1974	25 June 1977	AA
MEMPHIS	SSN 691	Newport News Shipbuilding	23 June 1973	3 Apr 1976	17 Dec 1977	AA
BREMERTON	SSN 698	General Dynamics (Electric Boat Div)	8 May 1976	22 July 1978	28 Mar 1981	PA
JACKSONVILLE	SSN 699	General Dynamics (Electric Boat Div)	21 Feb 1976	18 Nov 1978	16 May 1981	AA
DALLAS	SSN 700	General Dynamics (Electric Boat Div)	9 Oct 1976	28 Apr 1979	18 July 1981	AA
LA JOLLA	SSN 701	General Dynamics (Electric Boat Div)	16 Oct 1976	11 Aug 1979	24 Oct 1981	PA
CITY OF CORPUS CHRISTI	SSN 705	General Dynamics (Electric Boat Div)	4 Sep 1979	25 Apr 1981	8 Jan 1983	AA
ALBUQUERQUE	SSN 706	General Dynamics (Electric Boat Div)	27 Dec 1979	13 Mar 1982	21 May 1983	AA
PORTSMOUTH	SSN 707	General Dynamics (Electric Boat Div)	8 May 1980	18 Sep 1982	1 Oct 1983	PA
MINNEAPOLIS-SAINT PAUL	SSN 708	General Dynamics (Electric Boat Div)	30 Jan 1981	19 Mar 1983	10 Mar 1984	AA
HYMAN G RICKOVER	SSN 709	General Dynamics (Electric Boat Div)	24 July 1981	27 Aug 1983	21 July 1984	AA
AUGUSTA	SSN 710	General Dynamics (Electric Boat Div)	1 Apr 1982	21 Jan 1984	19 Jan 1985	AA
SAN FRANCISCO	SSN 711	Newport News Shipbuilding	26 May 1977	27 Oct 1979	24 Apr 1981	PA
HOUSTON	SSN 713	Newport News Shipbuilding	29 Jan 1979	21 Mar 1981	25 Sep 1982	PA
NORFOLK	SSN 714	Newport News Shipbuilding	1 Aug 1979	31 Oct 1981	21 May 1983	AA
BUFFALO	SSN 715	Newport News Shipbuilding	25 Jan 1980	8 May 1982	5 Nov 1983	PA
SALT LAKE CITY	SSN 716	Newport News Shipbuilding	26 Aug 1980	16 Oct 1982	12 May 1984	PA
OLYMPIA	SSN 717	Newport News Shipbuilding	31 Mar 1981	30 Apr 1983	17 Nov 1983	PA
HONOLULU	SSN 718	Newport News Shipbuilding	10 Nov 1981	24 Sep 1983	6 July 1985	PA
PROVIDENCE	SSN 719	General Dynamics (Electric Boat Div)	14 Oct 1982	4 Aug 1984	27 July 1985	AA
PITTSBURGH	SSN 720	General Dynamics (Electric Boat Div)	15 Apr 1983	8 Dec 1984	23 Nov 1985	AA
CHICAGO	SSN 721	Newport News Shipbuilding	5 Jan 1983	13 Oct 1984	27 Sep 1986	PA
KEY WEST	SSN 722	Newport News Shipbuilding	6 July 1983	20 July 1985	12 Sep 1987	AA
OKLAHOMA CITY	SSN 723	Newport News Shipbuilding	4 Jan 1984	2 Nov 1985	9 July 1988	AA
LOUISVILLE	SSN 724	General Dynamics (Electric Boat Div)	16 Sep 1984	14 Dec 1985	8 Nov 1986	PA
HELENA	SSN 725	General Dynamics (Electric Boat Div)	28 Mar 1985	28 June 1986	11 July 1987	PA
NEWPORT NEWS	SSN 750	Newport News Shipbuilding	3 Mar 1984	15 Mar 1986	3 June 1989	AA
SAN JUAN	SSN 751	General Dynamics (Electric Boat Div)	16 Aug 1985	6 Dec 1986	6 Aug 1988	AA
PASADENA	SSN 752	General Dynamics (Electric Boat Div)	20 Dec 1985	12 Sep 1987	11 Feb 1989	PA
ALBANY	SSN 753	Newport News Shipbuilding	22 Apr 1985	13 June 1987	7 Apr 1990	AA
TOPEKA	SSN 754	General Dynamics (Electric Boat Div)	13 May 1986	23 Jan 1988	21 Oct 1989	AA
MIAMI	SSN 755	General Dynamics (Electric Boat Div)	24 Oct 1986	12 Nov 1988	30 June 1990	AA
SCRANTON	SSN 756	Newport News Shipbuilding	29 June 1986	3 July 1989	26 Jan 1991	AA
ALEXANDRIA	SSN 757	General Dynamics (Electric Boat Div)	19 June 1987	23 June 1990	29 June 1991	AA
ASHEVILLE	SSN 758	Newport News Shipbuilding	1 Jan 1987	28 Oct 1989	28 Sep 1991	PA
JEFFERSON CITY	SSN 759	Newport News Shipbuilding	21 Sep 1987	24 Mar 1990	29 Feb 1992	PA
ANNAPOLIS	SSN 760	General Dynamics (Electric Boat Div)	15 June 1988	18 May 1991	11 Apr 1992	AA
SPRINGFIELD	SSN 761	General Dynamics (Electric Boat Div)	29 Jan 1990	4 Jan 1992	9 Jan 1993	PA
COLUMBUS	SSN 762	General Dynamics (Electric Boat Div)	7 Jan 1991	1 Aug 1992	24 July 1993	PA
SANTA FE	SSN 763	General Dynamics (Electric Boat Div)	9 July 1991	12 Dec 1992	8 Jan 1994	AA
BOISE	SSN 764	Newport News Shipbuilding	25 Aug 1988	20 Oct 1990	7 Nov 1992	AA
MONTPELIER	SSN 765	Newport News Shipbuilding	19 May 1989	6 Apr 1991	13 Mar 1993	AA
CHARLOTTE	SSN 766	Newport News Shipbuilding	17 Aug 1990	3 Oct 1992	16 Sep 1994	PA
HAMPTON	SSN 767	Newport News Shipbuilding	2 Mar 1990	28 Sep 1991	6 Nov 1993	AA
HARTFORD	SSN 768	General Dynamics (Electric Boat Div)	27 Apr 1992	4 Dec 1993	10 Dec 1994	AA
TOLEDO	SSN 769	Newport News Shipbuilding	6 May 1991	28 Aug 1993	24 Feb 1995	AA
TUCSON	SSN 770	Newport News Shipbuilding	15 Aug 1991	19 Mar 1994	9 Sep 1995	PA
COLUMBIA	SSN 771	General Dynamics (Electric Boat Div)	24 Apr 1993	24 Sep 1994	9 Oct 1995	PA
GREENEVILLE	SSN 772	Newport News Shipbuilding	28 Feb 1992	17 Sep 1994	16 Feb 1996	PA
CHEYENNE	SSN 773	Newport News Shipbuilding	6 July 1992	4 Apr 1995	13 Sep 1996	PA

Displacement, tons: 6,082 standard; 6,927 dived
Dimensions, feet (metres): 362 × 33 × 32.3 *(110.3 × 10.1 × 9.9)*
Main machinery: Nuclear; 1 GE PWR S6G; 2 turbines; 35,000 hp *(26 MW)*; 1 shaft; 1 Magnetek auxiliary prop motor; 325 hp *(242 kW)*
Speed, knots: 32 dived
Complement: 133 (13 officers)

Missiles: SLCM: GDC/Hughes Tomahawk (TLAM-N); land attack; Tercom aided inertial navigation system (TAINS) to 2,500 km *(1,400 n miles)* at 0.7 Mach; altitude 15-100 m; nuclear warhead 200 kT; CEP 80 m. There are also 2 versions (TLAM-C/D) with either a single 454 kg HE warhead or a single warhead with submunitions; range 900 km *(485 n miles)*; CEP 10 m.
Nuclear warheads are not normally carried. Block III missiles, installed from 1994, increase TLAM-C range to 1,700 km *(918 n miles)*, add GPS back-up to TAINS and substitute a 318 kg shaped charge warhead.
SSM: GDC/Hughes Tomahawk (TASM); anti-ship; inertial guidance; active radar/anti-radiation homing to 460 km *(250 n miles)* at 0.7 Mach; warhead 454 kg.
From SSN 719 onwards all are equipped with the Vertical Launch System, which places 12 launch tubes external to the pressure hull behind the BQQ 5 spherical array forward.
McDonnell Douglas Harpoon; active radar homing to 130 km *(70 n miles)* at 0.9 Mach; warhead 227 kg.
Torpedoes: 4—21 in *(533 mm)* tubes midships. Gould Mk 48; ADCAP Mod 5/6; wire-guided (option); active/passive homing to 50 km *(27 n miles)*/38 km *(21 n miles)* at 40/55 kt; warhead 267 kg; depth to 900 m *(2,950 ft)*. Air Turbine Pump discharge.
Total of 26 weapons can be tube-launched, for example—8 Tomahawk, 4 Harpoon, 14 torpedoes.
Mines: Can lay Mk 67 Mobile and Mk 60 Captor mines.
Countermeasures: Decoys: Emerson Electric Mk 2; torpedo decoy. MOSS based Mk 48 torpedo with noise maker.
ESM: BRD-7; direction finding. WLR-1H (in 771-773). WLR-8(V)2/6; intercept. WSQ-5 (periscope) and WLR-10; radar warning. BLQ-10 being fitted in some.
Combat data systems: CCS Mk 2 (688-750) with UYK 7 computers; IBM BSY-1 (751-773) with UYK 43/UYK 44 computers. JOTS, BGIXS and TADIX-A can be fitted. USC-38 EHF (in some). Link 11; Link 16 being fitted.
Weapons control: Mk 117 torpedo fire-control system. Mk 81 Mod 3 OTHT.
Radars: Surface search/navigation/fire control: Sperry BPS 15 H/16; I/J-band.
Sonars: IBM BQQ 5D/E; passive/active search and attack; low frequency.
BQG 5D wide aperture flank array (SSN 710 and SSN 751 onwards).
TB 23/29 thin line array or TB 16 and TB 93; passive towed array.
Ametek BQS 15; active close range including ice detection; high frequency.
MIDAS (mine and ice detection avoidance system) (SSN 751 onwards); active high frequency.
Raytheon SADS-TG active detection system (being retrofitted).

ALBUQUERQUE *7/1999*, Diego Quevedo* / 0084087

Programmes: Various major improvement programmes and updating design changes caused programme delays in the late 1980s. From SSN 751 onwards the class is prefixed by an 'I' for 'improved'. Programme terminated at 62 hulls. Eleven paid off by mid-1999 with one more planned to go in FY2001 and three in FY2002.
Modernisation: Mk 117 TFCS backfitted in earlier submarines of the class. WLY-1 acoustic intercept and countermeasures system is replacing WLR 9A/12 acoustic intercept in the late 1990s. EHF communications and Link 16 are being fitted. BQQ 5E and TB 29 fitted in all from SSN 751 onwards. From 1998 a fibre optic cable controlled NMRS (Near-term Mine Reconnaissance System), with AQS 14 side scan sonar, can be carried. Launch and recovery from a torpedo tube. An ARCI (Acoustic Rapid COTS Insertion) programme from 1997 to 2002 to backfit BQQ 5 sonars with open system architecture. Five of the class are fitted with DDS (SSN 688, 690, 700, 701 and 715). Four others are being fitted to operate ASDS (SSN 772, 766 (in 1999), 762 (in 2001) and 768 (in 2003)). C-303 acoustic jammer in one of the class for trials in 1998.
Structure: Every effort has been made to improve sound quieting and from SSN 751 onwards the class has acoustic tile cladding to augment the 'mammalian' skin which up to then had been the standard USN outer casing coating. Also from SSN 751 the forward hydro planes are fitted forward instead of on the fin. The planes are retractable mainly for surfacing through ice. The S6G reactor is a modified version of the D2G type. The towed sonar array is stowed in a blister on the side of the casing. Reactor core life between refuellings is estimated at 10 years. Diving depth is 450 m *(1,475 ft)*. *Memphis* was withdrawn from active service in late 1989 to become an interim research platform for advanced submarine technology. Early trials did not involve major changes to the submarine but tests started in September 1990 for optronic non-hull-penetrating masts and a major overhaul included installation of a large diameter tube for testing UUVs and large torpedoes. An after casing hangar is fitted for housing larger UUVs and towed arrays. Many other ideas are being evaluated with the main aim of allowing contractors easy access for trials at sea of new equipment. *Augusta* was the trials platform for the BQQ-5D wide aperture array passive sonar system. Various staged design improvements have added some 220 tons to the class displacement between 668 and 773.
Operational: Emphasis on the ability to operate under the Arctic ice has led to improvements in ice detection sensors, navigation and communications equipment as well as strengthening the sail and placing the sailplanes forward in later units of the class. *Norfolk* fired the first ADCAP torpedo on 23 July 1988 and sank the destroyer *Jonas K Ingram*. Normally eight Tomahawk missiles are carried internally (in addition to the external tubes in 719 onwards) but this load can be increased depending on the mission. Subroc phased out in 1990. Nuclear weapons disembarked but still available. Predator and Sea Ferret UAV trials done in two of the class in 1996-97 and may become available for launching from a sub-Harpoon canister in due course.

UPDATED

LOS ANGELES

11/1999*, D Yates, RAN / 0084088

GREENEVILLE

10/1998, John Mortimer / 0053316

Strategic Missile Submarines (SSBN)

Note: Trident: The Trident fitted SSBN force provides the principal US strategic deterrent. Land- and air-based systems have been sharply reduced since 1991. The current treaty is the Strategic Arms Reduction Treaty (START). START is to be fully implemented in December 2001 with a combined limit of SLBM and ICBM re-entry bodies (RBs) of 4,900. The second treaty, called START II, was signed in 1993 and ratified by the US Senate in 1996. The total number of SLBM RBs is limited first to 2,160 and finally to 1,750. The original START II called for an implementation date in 2003, however, the Russian Duma has yet to ratify the treaty. In 1997, as an incentive for Russian ratification of START II, the two Presidents agreed to extend the final implementation date to the end of 2007. These treaty limits are achieved by attributing the launch tubes on SSBNs with a certain number of RBs. This tube limit must be uniform for each weapon system and/or for each coast. The whole force comes under the US Strategic Command Headquarters at Offut Air Force Base, Nebraska.

18 OHIO CLASS (SSBN)

Name	No	Builders	Launched		Commissioned		F/S
OHIO	SSBN 726	General Dynamics (Electric Boat Div)	7 Apr	1979	11 Nov	1981	PA
MICHIGAN	SSBN 727	General Dynamics (Electric Boat Div)	26 Apr	1980	11 Sep	1982	PA
FLORIDA	SSBN 728	General Dynamics (Electric Boat Div)	14 Nov	1981	18 June	1983	PA
GEORGIA	SSBN 729	General Dynamics (Electric Boat Div)	6 Nov	1982	11 Feb	1984	PA
HENRY M JACKSON	SSBN 730	General Dynamics (Electric Boat Div)	15 Oct	1983	6 Oct	1984	PA/Conv
ALABAMA	SSBN 731	General Dynamics (Electric Boat Div)	19 May	1984	25 May	1985	PA/Conv
ALASKA	SSBN 732	General Dynamics (Electric Boat Div)	12 Jan	1985	25 Jan	1986	PA/Conv
NEVADA	SSBN 733	General Dynamics (Electric Boat Div)	14 Sep	1985	16 Aug	1986	PA/Conv
TENNESSEE	SSBN 734	General Dynamics (Electric Boat Div)	13 Dec	1986	17 Dec	1988	AA
PENNSYLVANIA	SSBN 735	General Dynamics (Electric Boat Div)	23 Apr	1988	9 Sep	1989	AA
WEST VIRGINIA	SSBN 736	General Dynamics (Electric Boat Div)	14 Oct	1989	20 Oct	1990	AA
KENTUCKY	SSBN 737	General Dynamics (Electric Boat Div)	11 Aug	1990	13 July	1991	AA
MARYLAND	SSBN 738	General Dynamics (Electric Boat Div)	10 Aug	1991	13 June	1992	AA
NEBRASKA	SSBN 739	General Dynamics (Electric Boat Div)	15 Aug	1992	10 July	1993	AA
RHODE ISLAND	SSBN 740	General Dynamics (Electric Boat Div)	17 July	1993	9 July	1994	AA
MAINE	SSBN 741	General Dynamics (Electric Boat Div)	16 July	1994	29 July	1995	AA
WYOMING	SSBN 742	General Dynamics (Electric Boat Div)	15 July	1995	13 July	1996	AA
LOUISIANA	SSBN 743	General Dynamics (Electric Boat Div)	27 July	1996	6 Sep	1997	AA

Displacement, tons: 16,600 surfaced; 18,750 dived
Dimensions, feet (metres): 560 × 42 × 36.4
(170.7 × 12.8 × 11.1)
Main machinery: Nuclear; 1 GE PWR S8G; 2 turbines; 60,000 hp
(44.8 MW); 1 shaft; 1 Magnetek auxiliary prop motor; 325 hp
(242 kW)
Speed, knots: 24 dived
Complement: 155 (15 officers)

Missiles: SLBM: 24 Lockheed Trident I (C4) (726-733); stellar inertial guidance to 7,400 km *(4,000 n miles)*; thermonuclear warhead of up to 8 MIRV Mk 4 with W76 warhead of 100 kT; CEP 450 m. Trident I is being phased out (see *Modernisation*) from 2000.
24 Lockheed Trident II (D5) (734 onwards); stellar inertial guidance to 12,000 km *(6,500 n miles)*; thermonuclear warheads of up to 12 MIRVs of either Mk 4 with W76 of 100 kT each, or Mk 5 with W88 of 300-475 kT each; CEP 90 m. A limit of 8 RVs was set in 1991 under the START counting rules but this may reduce to 4 or 5 under START II.
Torpedoes: 4—21 in *(533 mm)* Mk 68 bow tubes. Gould/ Westinghouse Mk 48; ADCAP; wire-guided (option); active/ passive homing to 50 km *(27 n miles)*/38 km *(21 n miles)* at 40/55 kt; warhead 267 kg; depth to 900 m *(2,950 ft)*.
Countermeasures: Decoys: 8 launchers for Emerson Electric Mk 2; torpedo decoy.
ESM: WLR-8(V)5; intercept. WLR-10; radar warning.
Combat data systems: CCS Mk 2 Mod 3 with UYK 43/UYK 44 computers.
Weapons control: Mk 118 digital torpedo fire-control system. Mk 98 missile control system.
Radars: Surface search/navigation/fire control: BPS 15A; I/J- band.
Sonars: IBM BQQ 6; passive search.
Raytheon BQS 13; spherical array for BQQ 6.
Ametek BQS 15; active/passive for close contacts; high frequency.
Western Electric BQR 15 (with BQQ 9 signal processor); passive towed array. TB 23 thin line array being fitted.
Raytheon BQR 19; active for navigation; high frequency.

Programmes: Under START II, the size of the SSBN forces is to be limited to 14 hulls.
Modernisation: WLY-1 acoustic intercept and countermeasures system is to be fitted in the late 1990s. This is an automatic response system designed for defence against torpedo attack. Four of the first eight hulls are being upgraded to take Trident II missiles starting with *Alaska* and *Nevada* in May 2000 and February 2001 respectively, and followed by *Jackson* and *Alabama* in FY2005/06. The first four hulls may be modified with 22 silos able to launch up to 154 non-nuclear T-LAM or

MARYLAND

6/1999*, van Ginderen Collection / 0084084

LASM missiles, and two silos for wet/dry launch of SEALs. If approved, work is to start in FY2003, if not the four submarines are to be taken out of service in 2002/03.
Structure: The size of the Trident submarine is dictated primarily by the 24 vertically launched Trident missiles and the larger reactor plant to drive the ship. The reactor has a nuclear core life of about 15 years between refuellings. Diving depth is 244 m *(800 ft)*. Kollmorgen Type 152 and Type 82 periscopes. Mk 19 Air Turbine Pump for torpedo discharge.
Operational: Pacific Fleet units with C4 missiles are based at Bangor, Washington, while the D5 submarines in the Atlantic

Fleet are based at King's Bay, Georgia. In the current more relaxed state of worldwide tensions, a modified alert status has been implemented. Single crews were considered but rejected. Hull life of the class is extended to 42 years.
In October 1993 *Nebraska* fired a Trident missile to test the use of GPS hardware for fixing the location of the re-entry vehicles. This was part of a series of trials leading up to the development of a mid-course guidance package to produce the pinpoint accuracy required to use the missile for carrying a conventional kinetic energy payload.

UPDATED

OHIO

9/1997, Findler & Winter / 0016649

AIRCRAFT CARRIERS

8 + 2 NIMITZ CLASS (CVN)

Name	No	Builders	Laid down	Launched	Commissioned	F/S
NIMITZ	CVN 68	Newport News Shipbuilding	22 June 1968	13 May 1972	3 May 1975	Conv/AA
DWIGHT D EISENHOWER	CVN 69	Newport News Shipbuilding	15 Aug 1970	11 Oct 1975	18 Oct 1977	AA/Conv
CARL VINSON	CVN 70	Newport News Shipbuilding	11 Oct 1975	15 Mar 1980	13 Mar 1982	PA
THEODORE ROOSEVELT	CVN 71	Newport News Shipbuilding	13 Oct 1981	27 Oct 1984	25 Oct 1986	AA
ABRAHAM LINCOLN	CVN 72	Newport News Shipbuilding	3 Nov 1984	13 Feb 1988	11 Nov 1989	PA
GEORGE WASHINGTON	CVN 73	Newport News Shipbuilding	25 Aug 1986	21 July 1990	4 July 1992	AA
JOHN C STENNIS	CVN 74	Newport News Shipbuilding	13 Mar 1991	13 Nov 1993	9 Dec 1995	PA
HARRY S TRUMAN (ex-*United States*)	CVN 75	Newport News Shipbuilding	29 Nov 1993	14 Sep 1996	25 July 1998	AA
RONALD REAGAN	CVN 76	Newport News Shipbuilding	12 Feb 1998	Dec 2000	Dec 2002	Bldg
—	CVN 77	Newport News Shipbuilding	Dec 2003	Dec 2006	Dec 2008	Ord

Displacement, tons: 72,916 (CVN 68-70), 73,973 (CVN 71)
light; 91,487 (CVN 68-70), 96,386 (CVN 71), 102,000 (CVN
72-76) full load
Dimensions, feet (metres): 1,040 pp; 1,092 oa × 134 wl × 37
(CVN 68-70); 38.7 (CVN 71); 39 (CVN 72-76)
(317; 332.9 × 40.8 × 11.3; 11.8; 11.9)
Flight deck, feet (metres): 1,092; 779.8 (angled) × 252
(332.9; 237.7 × 76.8)
Main machinery: Nuclear; 2 Westinghouse/GE PWR A4W/A1G;
4 turbines; 260,000 hp *(194 MW)*; 4 emergency diesels;
10,720 hp *(8 MW)*; 4 shafts
Speed, knots: 30+
Complement: 3,360 (160 officers); 2,500 aircrew (366
officers); Flag 70 (25 officers)

Missiles: SAM: 2 or 3 Raytheon GMLS Mk 29 octuple launchers;
NATO Sea Sparrow; semi-active radar homing to 14.6 km *(8 n
miles)* at 2.5 Mach; warhead 39 kg. ESSM in due course.
RAM to be fitted with SSDS in due course.
Guns: 4 General Electric/General Dynamics 20 mm Vulcan
Phalanx 6-barrelled Mk 15 (3 in CVN 68 and 69); 3,000 rds/
min (or 4,500 in Block 1) combined to 1.5 km. To be replaced
by RAM.
Countermeasures: Decoys: 4 Loral Hycor SRBOC 6-barrelled
fixed Mk 36; IR flares and chaff to 4 km *(2.2 n miles)*. SSTDS
(torpedo defence system). SLQ-36 Nixie (Phase I).
ESM/ECM: SLQ-32(V)4/SLY-2 intercept and jammers. WLR-1H.
Combat data systems: ACDS Block 0 or 1 naval tactical and
advanced combat direction systems; Links 4A, 11, 14 and 16.
GCCS (M). SATCOMS: SSQ-82, SRR-1, WSC-3 (UHF), WSC-6
(SHF), USC-38 (EHF) (see Data Systems at front of section).
SSDS Mk 2 (CVN 76, and to be back fitted in all.)
Weapons control: 3 Mk 91 Mod 1 MFCS directors (part of the
NSSMS Mk 57 SAM system).
Radars: Air search: ITT SPS-48E; 3D; E/F-band.
Raytheon SPS-49(V)5; C/D-band.
Hughes Mk 23 TAS; D-band or SPQ-9B with SSDS in due
course.
Surface search: Norden SPS-67V; G-band.
CCA: SPN-41, SPN-43B, SPN-44, 2 SPN-46; J/K/E/F-band.
Navigation: Raytheon SPS-64(V)9; Furuno 900; I/J-band.
Fire control: 6 Mk 95; I/J-band (for SAM).
Tacan: URN 25.

Fixed-wing aircraft: 50 TACAIR air wing depends on mission
and includes: up to 20 F-14D Tomcat; 36 F/A-18 Hornet; 4
EA-6B Prowler; 4 E-2C Hawkeye; 6 S-3B Viking; 2 ES-3A
Shadow.
Helicopters: 4 SH-60F and 2 HH-60H Seahawk.

Programmes: *Nimitz* was authorised in FY67, *Dwight D
Eisenhower* in FY70, *Carl Vinson* in FY74, *Theodore Roosevelt*
in FY80 and *Abraham Lincoln* and *George Washington* in
FY83. Construction contracts for *John C Stennis* and *Harry S
Truman* were awarded in June 1988 and for *Ronald Reagan* in
December 1994. Authorisation for CVN 77 advanced
procurement in FY99 with construction scheduled to start in
2002. The propulsion system will remain the same, although
there could be changes to the island structure, and in many
other systems throughout the ship. A step change to a new

CARL VINSON

7/1998*, RAN / 0084090

design CVX has been abandoned in favour of incremental
improvements to CVN 77. These could include a new type of
catapult that would not need steam to activate it.
Requirements for handling the Joint Strike Fighter now under
development also could have a bearing on the ship's design.
Modernisation: ACDS Block 1 Level 2 in CVN 68 and CVN 69.
ACDS to be replaced by SSDS Mk 2 from 2002. This includes
fitting RAM, ESSM and SPQ-9B radar vice Mk 23 TAS. RAM
replaces one Mk 29 and all Phalanx launchers. CVN 68 started
a three year refuel in May 1998 and is also having a reshaped
island. CVN 69 in 2001. SLY-2 intercept equipment replacing
part of the SLQ-32 system from 1999.
Structure: Damage control measures include sides with system
of full and empty compartments (full compartments can
contain aviation fuel), approximately 2.5 in Kevlar plating over
certain areas of side shell, box protection over magazine and
machinery spaces. Aviation facilities include four lifts, two at

the forward end of the flight deck, one to starboard abaft the
island and one to port at the stern. There are four steam
catapults (C13-1) and four (or three) Mk 7 Mod 3 arrester
wires. Launch rate is one every 20 seconds. The hangar can
hold less than half the full aircraft complement, deckhead is
25.6 ft. Aviation fuel, 9,000 tons. Tactical Flag Command
Centre for Flagship role. Mk 32 triple torpedo tubes were fitted
for anti-wake homing torpedo trials, but the programme was
cancelled and the tubes removed.
Operational: Multimission role of 'attack/ASW'. From CVN 70
onwards ships have an A/S control centre and A/S facilities;
CVN 68 and 69 are backfitted. Endurance of 16 days for
aviation fuel (steady flying). 15 years' theoretical life for
nuclear reactors; 800,000 to 1 million miles between
refuelling. Ships' complements and air wings can be changed
depending on the operational task.

UPDATED

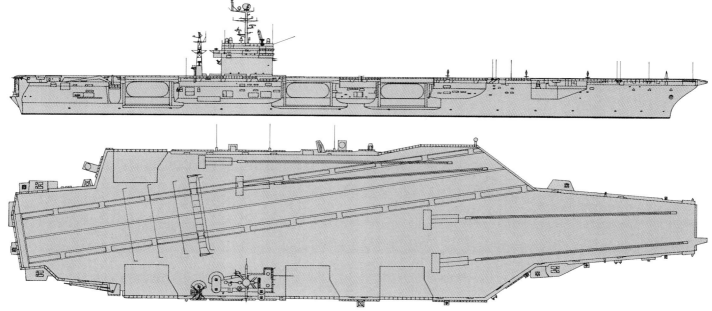

CARL VINSON

(Scale 1 : 1,800), Ian Sturton / 0016327

ABRAHAM LINCOLN

10/1999*, Findler & Winter / 0084091

GEORGE WASHINGTON

9/1999*, US Navy / 0084092

JOHN C STENNIS

4/1998*, Maritime Photographic / 0084093

JOHN C STENNIS

4/1998, Maritime Photographic / 0053321

CARL VINSON

1/1999*, C E Castle / 0084094

3 KITTY HAWK and JOHN F KENNEDY CLASSES (CV)

Name	No	Builders	Laid down	Launched	Commissioned	F/S
KITTY HAWK	CV 63	New York Shipbuilding	27 Dec 1956	21 May 1960	29 Apr 1961	PA
CONSTELLATION	CV 64	New York Naval Shipyard	14 Sep 1957	8 Oct 1960	27 Oct 1961	PA
JOHN F KENNEDY	CV 67	Newport News Shipbuilding	22 Oct 1964	27 May 1967	7 Sep 1968	NRF

KITTY HAWK   8/1999*, Vic Jeffery / 0084095

Displacement, tons: 83,960 full load; 81,430 full load (CV 67)
Dimensions, feet (metres): 1,062.5 (CV 63); 1,072.5 (CV 64);
1,052 (CV 67) × 130 × 37.4
(323.6; 326.9; 320.6 × 39.6 × 11.4)
Flight deck, feet (metres): 1,046 × 252 *(318.8 × 76.8)*
Main machinery: 8 Foster-Wheeler boilers; 1,200 psi *(83.4 kg/
cm²)*; 950°F *(510°C)*; 4 Westinghouse turbines; 280,000 hp
(209 MW); 4 shafts
Speed, knots: 32
Range, miles: 4,000 at 30 kt; 12,000 at 20 kt
Complement: 2,930 (155 officers); aircrew 2,480 (320
officers); Flag 70 (25 officers)

Missiles: SAM: 3 Raytheon GMLS Mk 29 octuple launchers;
NATO Sea Sparrow; semi-active radar homing to 14.6 km *(8 n
miles)* at 2.5 Mach; warhead 39 kg. ESSM in due course.
Guns: 3 or 4 General Electric/General Dynamics 20 mm Vulcan
Phalanx 6-barrelled Mk 15; 3,000 rds/min (or 4,500 in Block
1) combined to 1.5 km. Two mountings to be replaced by RAM
in CV 63 and CV 67.
Countermeasures: Decoys: 4 Loral Hycor SRBOC 6-barrelled
fixed Mk 36; IR flares and chaff to 4 km *(2.2 n miles)*. SSTDS
(Surface Ship Torpedo Defence System). SLQ-36 Nixie
(Phase I).
ESM/ECM: SLQ-32(V)4/SLY-2 intercept and jammers. WLR-1H.
Combat data systems: ACDS Block 0 (Block 1 Level 1 in CV 67)
naval tactical and advanced combat direction systems Links
4A, 11, 14 and 16. GCCS (M) SATCOMS: SSQ-82, SRR-1,
WSC-3 (UHF), WSC-6 (SHF), USC-38 (EHF) (see Data Systems
at front of section).
Weapons control: 3 Mk 91 MFCS directors (part of NSSMS
Mk 57 SAM system).

Radars: Air search: ITT SPS-48E; 3D; E/F-band.
Raytheon SPS-49(V)5; C/D-band.
Hughes Mk 23 TAS; D-band. SPQ-9B in due course.
Surface search: Norden SPS-67; G-band.
CCA: SPN-41, SPN-43A; 2 SPN-46; J/K/E/F-band.
Navigation: Raytheon SPN-64(V)9; Furuno 900; I-band.
Fire control: 6 Mk 95; I/J-band (for SAM).
Tacan: URN 25.

Fixed-wing aircraft: 50 TACAIR air wing depends on mission
and includes: up to 20 F-14D Tomcat; 36 F/A-18 Hornet; 4
EA-6B Prowler; 4 E-2C Hawkeye; 6 S-3B Viking; 2 ES-3A
Shadow.
Helicopters: 4 SH-60F and 2 HH-60H Seahawk.

Programmes: *Kitty Hawk* was authorised in FY56, *Constellation*
in FY57, and *John F Kennedy* in FY63.
Modernisation: Service Life Extension Programme (SLEP): *Kitty
Hawk* completed in February 1991 and *Constellation* in
December 1992. A 'complex overhaul' of *Kennedy* completed
in September 1995 and she retains her operational status
within the NRF. ACDS Block 1 trials done in *Kennedy* in 1998.
SSDS Mk 2 to be fitted in CV 63 and CV 67 in due course
including RAM, ESSM and SPQ-9B radar.
Structure: These ships were built to an improved Forrestal
design. They have two deck-edge lifts forward of the
superstructure, a third lift aft of the structure, and the port-side
lift on the after quarter. Four C13 steam catapults (with one
C13-1 in *Kennedy*) and four arrester wires. Aviation fuel of
5,882 tons carried.
Operational: *Kitty Hawk* based in Yokosuka from July 1998. Air
wings are changed depending on the operational role.
Constellation to pay off in 2003.   **UPDATED**

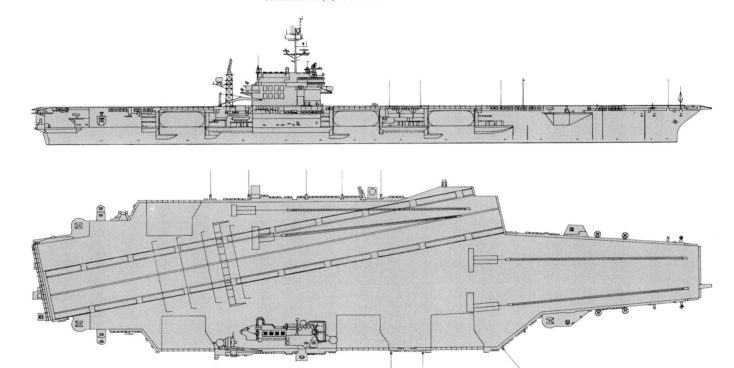

CONSTELLATION   *(Scale 1 : 1,800), Ian Sturton / 0016331*

KITTY HAWK   *8/1998, Ships of the World / 0053326*

CONSTELLATION   4/1997*, Neil Sheinbaum, US Navy / 0084096

JOHN F KENNEDY   11/1997, A Campanera i Rovira / 0053327

1 ENTERPRISE CLASS (CVN)

Name	No	Builders	Laid down	Launched	Commissioned	F/S
ENTERPRISE	CVN 65	Newport News Shipbuilding	4 Feb 1958	24 Sep 1960	25 Nov 1961	AA

Displacement, tons: 73,502 light; 75,700 standard; 93,970 full load

Dimensions, feet (metres): 1,123 × 133 × 39 *(342.3 × 40.5 × 11.9)*

Flight deck, feet (metres): 1,088 × 252 *(331.6 × 76.8)*

Main machinery: Nuclear; 8 Westinghouse PWR A2W; 4 Westinghouse turbines; 280,000 hp *(209 MW)*; 4 emergency diesels; 10,720 hp *(8 MW)*; 4 shafts

Speed, knots: 33

Complement: 3,215 (171 officers); 2,480 aircrew (358 officers); Flag 70 (25 officers)

Missiles: SAM: 3 Raytheon GMLS Mk 29 octuple launchers; NATO Sea Sparrow; semi-active radar homing to 14.6 km *(8 n miles)* at 2.5 Mach; warhead 39 kg. ESSM in due course.

Guns: 3 General Electric/General Dynamics 20 mm Vulcan Phalanx 6-barrelled Mk 15; 3,000 rds/min (or 4,500 in Block 1) combined to 1.5 km. May be replaced by RAM.

Countermeasures: Decoys: 4 Loral Hycor SRBOC 6-barrelled fixed Mk 36; IR flares and chaff to 4 km *(2.2 n miles)*. SSTDS (Surface Ship Torpedo Defence System). SLQ-36 Nixie. ESM/ECM: SLQ-32(V)4/SLY-2; intercept and jammers. WLR-1H.

Combat data systems: ACDS Block 0 naval tactical and advanced combat direction systems; Links 4A, 11, 14 and 16. GCCS (M) SATCOMS: SSQ-82, SRR-1, WSC-3 (UHF), WSC-6 (SHF), USC-38 (EHF) (see Data Systems at front of section).

Weapons control: 3 Mk 91 Mod 1 MFCS directors (part of NSSMS Mk 57 SAM system).

Radars: Air search: ITT SPS-48E; 3D; E/F-band. Raytheon SPS-49(V)5; C/D-band. Hughes Mk 23 TAS; D-band. SPQ-9B in due course. Surface search: Norden SPS-67; G-band. CCA: SPN-41, SPN-43A; 2 SPN-46; J/K/E/F-band. Navigation: Raytheon SPS-64(V)9; Furuno 900; I/J-band. Fire control: 6 Mk 95; I/J-band (for SAM). Tacan: URN 25.

Fixed-wing aircraft: 50 TACAIR air wing depends on mission and includes: up to 20 F-14 Tomcat; 36 F/A-18 Hornet; 4 EA-6B Prowler; 4 E-2C Hawkeye; 6 S-3B Viking; 2 ES-3A Shadow.

Helicopters: 4 SH-60F and 2 HH-60H Seahawk.

Programmes: Authorised in FY58. Underwent a refit/overhaul at Puget Sound Naval SY, Bremerton, Washington from January 1979 to March 1982. Latest complex overhaul including refuelling started at Newport News in early 1991 and completed 27 September 1994. Minor refit again in 1997.

Modernisation: Mk 25 Sea Sparrow was installed in late 1967 and this has been replaced by first two and then three Mk 29 and supplemented with three 20 mm Mk 15 CIWS. A reshaping of the island took place in her 1979-82 refit. This included a replacement mast similar to the 'Nimitz' class with SPS-48C and 49 radars. Improvements during latest overhaul included SPS-48E and Mk 23 TAS air search radars, SPN-46 precision approach and landing radar and C³ and EW systems. ESSM and RAM may be fitted in due course, plus radar SPQ-9B vice Mk 23 TAS.

Structure: Built to a modified 'Forrestal' class design. *Enterprise* was the world's second nuclear-powered warship (the cruiser *Long Beach* was completed a few months earlier). Aviation facilities include four deck edge lifts, two forward and one each side abaft the island. There are four 295 ft C 13 Mod 1 catapults. Hangars cover 216,000 sq ft with 25 ft deck head. Aviation fuel, 8,500 tons.

Operational: 12 days' aviation fuel for intensive flying. Air wing depends on the operational role.

UPDATED

ENTERPRISE

7/1998*, M W Pendergrass, US Navy / 0084089

ENTERPRISE

8/1998, C E Castle / 0053323

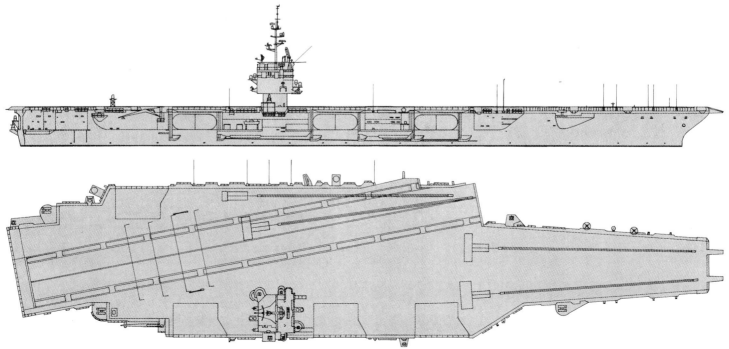

ENTERPRISE

(Scale 1 : 1,800), Ian Sturton / 0016325

CRUISERS

Note: The Smart Ship. A Naval Research Advisory Committee recommendation to undertake an initiative aimed at demonstrating reduced manning technologies and concepts led to the formation of the Smart Ship project in December 1995. The Project was endorsed in February 1996 and *Yorktown* (CG 48) was selected as the first Smart Ship. By November 1996, 47 workload reduction initiatives had been approved for implementation. *Yorktown* completed a five month deployment in June 1997, undergoing testing and evaluation of the Smart Ship initiatives. An additional 14 initiatives were installed during July 1997. Core systems included an Integrated Bridge System, Integrated Condition Assessment System, Machinery Control System, Damage Control System, Fiber Optic Local Area Network, and an Internal cordless Communications System. *Yorktown's* experience validated that these technologies, combined with changes in policies and procedures and adoption of new watch routines, could generate a substantial workload reduction. Smart Ship-type systems are also being evaluated in dock landing ship US *Rushmore* (LSD 47) and the plan is to include them in *Rainier* AOE 7 in due course. What is now called the Integrated Ship Controls (ISC) Upgrade has been fitted in CG 47, and operational evaluation started in early 2000. Full ISC is being fitted in CG 48, CG 57 and CG 61 in 2000. All of the class are to be equipped by 2005. Aegis destroyers are to follow, and the Integrated Bridge System will be fitted on build to destroyers. The equipment programme is costly and has been criticised not least because fewer sailors means less operational flexibility during low intensity operations, and when the ship is damaged in war.

27 TICONDEROGA CLASS: GUIDED MISSILE CRUISERS (AEGIS) (CG)

Name	*No*	*Builder/Programme*	*Laid down*	*Launched*	*Commissioned*	*F/S*
TICONDEROGA	CG 47 (ex-DDG 47)	Ingalls Shipbuilding	21 Jan 1980	25 Apr 1981	22 Jan 1983	AA
YORKTOWN	CG 48	Ingalls Shipbuilding	19 Oct 1981	17 Jan 1983	4 July 1984	AA
VINCENNES	CG 49	Ingalls Shipbuilding	20 Oct 1982	14 Jan 1984	6 July 1985	PA
VALLEY FORGE	CG 50	Ingalls Shipbuilding	14 Apr 1983	23 June 1984	18 Jan 1986	PA
THOMAS S GATES	CG 51	Bath Iron Works	31 Aug 1984	14 Dec 1985	22 Aug 1987	PA
BUNKER HILL	CG 52	Ingalls Shipbuilding	11 Jan 1984	11 Mar 1985	20 Sep 1986	PA
MOBILE BAY	CG 53	Ingalls Shipbuilding	6 June 1984	22 Aug 1985	21 Feb 1987	PA
ANTIETAM	CG 54	Ingalls Shipbuilding	15 Nov 1984	14 Feb 1986	6 June 1987	PA
LEYTE GULF	CG 55	Ingalls Shipbuilding	18 Mar 1985	20 June 1986	26 Sep 1987	AA
SAN JACINTO	CG 56	Ingalls Shipbuilding	24 July 1985	14 Nov 1986	23 Jan 1988	AA
LAKE CHAMPLAIN	CG 57	Ingalls Shipbuilding	3 Mar 1986	3 Apr 1987	12 Aug 1988	PA
PHILIPPINE SEA	CG 58	Bath Iron Works	8 May 1986	12 July 1987	18 Mar 1989	AA
PRINCETON	CG 59	Ingalls Shipbuilding	15 Oct 1986	2 Oct 1987	11 Feb 1989	PA
NORMANDY	CG 60	Bath Iron Works	7 Apr 1987	19 Mar 1988	9 Dec 1989	AA
MONTEREY	CG 61	Bath Iron Works	19 Aug 1987	23 Oct 1988	16 June 1990	AA
CHANCELLORSVILLE	CG 62	Ingalls Shipbuilding	24 June 1987	15 July 1988	4 Nov 1989	PA
COWPENS	CG 63	Bath Iron Works	23 Dec 1987	11 Mar 1989	9 Mar 1991	PA
GETTYSBURG	CG 64	Bath Iron Works	17 Aug 1988	22 July 1989	22 June 1991	AA
CHOSIN	CG 65	Ingalls Shipbuilding	22 July 1988	1 Sep 1989	12 Jan 1991	PA
HUE CITY	CG 66	Ingalls Shipbuilding	20 Feb 1989	1 June 1990	14 Sep 1991	AA
SHILOH	CG 67	Bath Iron Works	1 Aug 1989	8 Sep 1990	2 July 1992	PA
ANZIO	CG 68	Ingalls Shipbuilding	21 Aug 1989	2 Nov 1990	2 May 1992	AA
VICKSBURG	CG 69	Ingalls Shipbuilding	30 May 1990	2 Aug 1991	14 Nov 1992	AA
LAKE ERIE	CG 70	Bath Iron Works	6 Mar 1990	13 July 1991	24 July 1993	PA
CAPE ST GEORGE	CG 71	Ingalls Shipbuilding	19 Nov 1990	10 Jan 1992	12 June 1993	AA
VELLA GULF	CG 72	Ingalls Shipbuilding	22 Apr 1991	13 June 1992	18 Sep 1993	AA
PORT ROYAL	CG 73	Ingalls Shipbuilding	18 Oct 1991	20 Nov 1992	9 July 1994	PA

Displacement, tons: 9,590 (CG 47-48); 9,407 (CG 49-51); 9,957 (remainder) full load
Dimensions, feet (metres): 567 × 55 × 31 (sonar) *(172.8 × 16.8 × 9.5)*
Main machinery: 4 GE LM 2500 gas turbines; 86,000 hp *(64.16 MW)* sustained; 2 shafts; cp props
Speed, knots: 30+. **Range, miles:** 6,000 at 20 kt
Complement: 358 (24 officers); accommodation for 405 total
312 (24 officers) (CG 48)

Missiles: SLCM: GDC Tomahawk (CG 52 onwards); Tercom aided guidance to 1,300 km *(700 n miles)* (TLAM-C and D) or 1,853 km *(1,000 n miles)* (TLAM-C Block III) at 0.7 Mach; warhead 454 kg (TLAM-C) or 347 kg shaped charge (TLAM-C Blocks II and III) or submunitions (TLAM-D). TLAM-C has GPS back-up to Tercom and a CEP of 10 m.
SSM: 8 McDonnell Douglas Harpoon (2 quad) ❶; active radar homing to 130 km *(70 n miles)* at 0.9 Mach; warhead 227 kg. Extended range SLAM can be fired from modified Harpoon canisters.
SAM: 68 (CG 47-51); 122 (CG 52 onwards) GDC Standard SM-2MR; command/inertial guidance; semi-active radar homing to 73 km *(40 n miles)* at 2 Mach. SM-2 Block IIIB uses an IR seeker. SM-2 Block IVA (TBMD) has a Mk 72 booster for extended range. SAM and ASROC missiles are fired from 2 twin Mk 26 Mod 5 launchers ❷ (CG 47-51) and 2 Mk 41 Mod 0 vertical launchers ❸ (61 missiles per launcher) (CG 52 onwards). Tomahawk is carried in CG 52 onwards with 8 missiles in each VLS launcher and 12 reloads. Quad pack Evolved Sea Sparrow in designated Mk 41 cells in due course. Phalanx to be replaced by RAM Block I from 2001. Standard LASM may be fitted from 2003 in 12 of the class.
A/S: Honeywell ASROC (CG 47-55) and Loral ASROC VLA (CG 56 onwards and CG 52-55 from 1998). VLA has a range of 16.6 km *(9 n miles)*; inertial guidance of 1.6-10 km *(1-5.4 n miles)*; payload Mk 46 Mod 5 Neartip or Mk 50.
Guns: 2 FMC 5 in *(127 mm)*/54 Mk 45 (Mod 0 (CG 47-50); Mod 1 (CG 51 onwards)) ❹; 20 rds/min to 23 km *(12.6 n miles)* anti-surface; weight of shell 32 kg. Modified 5 in *(127 mm)*/62 barrel to be fitted from 2002 to take ERGM (extended-range guided munitions); GPS guidance to about 140 km *(75.6 n miles)*; warhead 72 bomblets; cep 10 m.
2 General Electric/General Dynamics 20 mm/76 Vulcan Phalanx 6-barrelled Mk 15 Mod 2 ❺; 3,000 rds/min (4,500 in Block 1) combined to 1.5 km. Can be fitted with high-definition thermal imagers (HDTI) for tracking small craft.
2 McDonnell Douglas 25 mm. 4—12.7 mm MGs.
Torpedoes: 6—324 mm Mk 32 (2 triple) Mod 14 tubes (fitted in the ship's side aft) ❻. 36 Honeywell Mk 46 Mod 5; anti-submarine; active/passive homing to 11 km *(5.9 n miles)* at 40 kt; warhead 44 kg or Alliant/Westinghouse Mk 50; active/passive homing to 15 km *(8.1 n miles)* at 50 kt; warhead 45 kg shaped charge.
Countermeasures: Decoys: Up to 8 Loral Hycor SRBOC 6-barrelled fixed Mk 36 Mod 2 ❼; IR flares and chaff. Nulka being acquired. SLQ-25 Nixie; towed torpedo decoy.
ESM/ECM: Raytheon SLQ-32V(3)/SLY-2 ❽; intercept, jammers.
Combat data systems: CEC being fitted 1996-2007 starting with CG 66 and 69. NTDS with Links 4A, 11, 14. GCCS (M) and Link 16 being fitted. Link 22 in due course. SATCOM WRN-5, WSC-3 (UHF), USC-38 (EHF). UYK 7 and 20 computers (CG 47-58); UYK 43/44 (CG 59 onwards and being backfitted to CG 56-58). SQQ-28 for LAMPS sonobuoy datalink ❾ (see Data Systems at front of section).

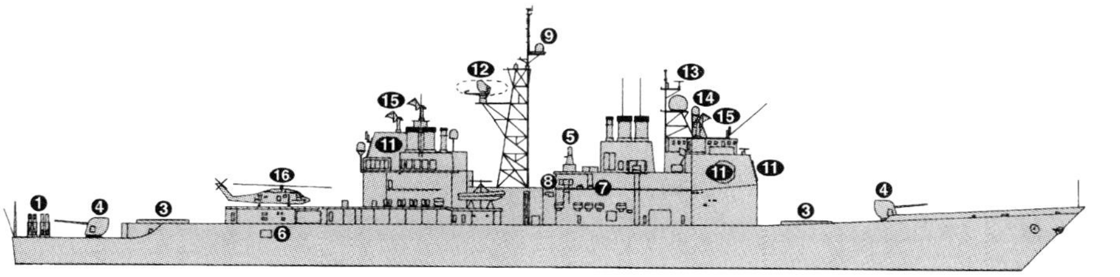

BUNKER HILL *(Scale 1 : 1,500), Ian Sturton* / 0016356

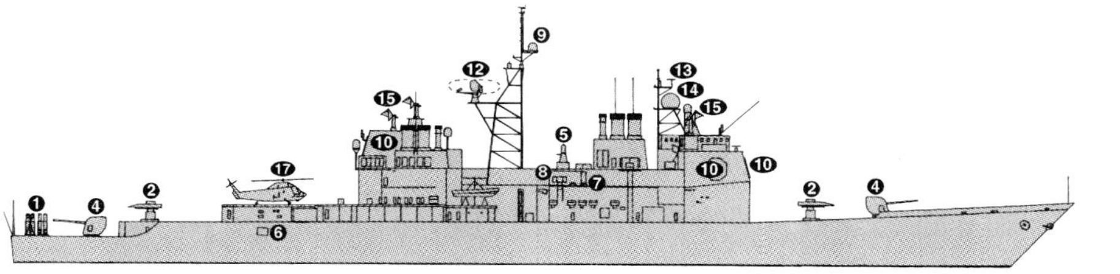

TICONDEROGA *(Scale 1 : 1,500), Ian Sturton* / 0016357

Weapons control: SWG-3 Tomahawk WCS. SWG-1A Harpoon LCS. Aegis Mk 7 Mod 4 multitarget tracking with Mk 99 MFCS (includes 4 Mk 80 illuminator directors); has at least 12 channels of fire. Singer Librascope Mk 116 Mod 6 (53B) or Mod 7 (53C) FCS for ASW. Lockheed Mk 86 Mod 9 GFCS.
Radars: Air search/fire control: RCA SPY-1A phased arrays ❿; 3D; E/F-band (CG 47-58).
Raytheon SPY-1B phased arrays ⓫; 3D; E/F-band (CG 59 on).
Air search: Raytheon SPS-49(V)7 or 8 ⓬; C/D-band; range 457 km *(250 n miles)*.
Surface search: ISC Cardion SPS-55 ⓭; I/J-band.
Navigation: Raytheon SPS-64(V)9; I-band.
Fire control: Lockheed SPQ-9A/B ⓮; I/J-band.
Four Raytheon SPG-62 ⓯; I/J-band.
Tacan: URN 25. IFF Mk XII AIMS UPX-29.
Sonars: General Electric/Hughes SQS-53B (CG 47-51); bow-mounted; active search and attack; medium frequency.
Gould SQR-19 (CG 54-55); passive towed array (TACTAS).
Gould/Raytheon SQQ-89(V)3 (CG 52 onwards); combines hull-mounted active SQS-53B (CG 52-67) or SQS-53C (CG 68-73) and passive towed array SQR-19.

Helicopters: 2 SH-60B Seahawk LAMPS III ⓰; 2 SH-2F LAMPS I (CG 47-48) ⓱. UAV in due course.

Modernisation: Four baselines were planned and seven have evolved. *Ticonderoga*, equipped with LAMPS I, represents Baseline 0. Baseline I starts with *Vincennes* equipped with LAMPS III, RAST haul-down flight deck system and Block 2 Standard missiles. Baseline II, beginning with *Bunker Hill*, adds Tomahawk, and the Vertical Launch System. Baseline III starting with *San Jacinto* adds the SQQ-89 sonar. Baseline IV, beginning with *Princeton* (CG 59), incorporates the advanced AN/SPY-1B radar on UYQ-21 displays and includes the upgraded computers UYK-43/44 which are retrofitted in Baseline III ships. *Lake Champlain* fired the first SLAM missile from a Harpoon canister in June 1990. *Lake Erie* carried out first SM-2 Block IV trials in mid-1994. Baseline V incorporates SM-2 Block IV and JTIDS Link 16. Baseline VI adds ESSM, CEC and improved CDS for TBMD. Baseline VII upgrades Tomahawk fire control and adds TBMD advance processing including COTS computers. Phalanx is being fitted with an IR tracker for targeting small craft at close range but is to be replaced by RAM from 2001. The Co-operative Engagement Capability (CEC) and Theatre Ballistic Missile Defences are being installed in up to 22 of the class. ASROC VLA and SQQ-89 fitted in CG 52-55 from 1998. From late 1996 CG 48 carries advanced automation in navigation, damage control and machinery control systems. This reduces the crew by 46 people. (See Note under Cruisers.) CG 47, CG 61 and CG 57 fitted in 2000, and the rest of the class by 2005. Plans to fit VLS in the first five of the class have been abandoned. Twelve ships are to be upgraded to improve land attack capabilities from 2003. This may include Standard LASM.
Structure: The 'Ticonderoga' class design is a modification of the 'Spruance' class. The same basic hull is used, with the same gas-turbine propulsion plant although the overall length is slightly increased. The design includes Kevlar armour to protect vital spaces. No stabilisers. *Vincennes* and later ships have a lighter tripod mainmast vice the square quadruped of the first two.
Operational: A combination of Aegis and an upgraded Standard missile is to give the first naval defence against ballistic missiles. CG 67 conducted first SM 3 firings on 24 September 1999. The first ships to be fully fitted are CG 70 and CG 73 for user evaluation in 2001/02. Two of the class are based at Yokosuka, Japan.

UPDATED

VALLEY FORGE   10/1999*, Findler & Winter / 0084097

VELLA GULF   7/1999*, A Campanera i Rovira / 0084098

ANTIETAM   3/1999*, C E Castle / 0084099

THOMAS S GATES   4/1999*, M Declerck / 0085297

VICKSBURG   6/1999*, Maritime Photographic / 0085298

MONTEREY   4/1999*, Michael Nitz / 0085299

DESTROYERS

Note: As a result of Congressional funding cuts and general scepticism about both the cost and the concept, the Maritime Fire Support Demonstrator (Arsenal Ship) project was cancelled in late 1997. Some of the design work has been carried forward to the Land Attack Destroyer (DD 21) which is scheduled for a design contract for three years starting in 2001. About three ships a year are planned with a first in-service date of 2010. A crew of about 95 is the objective. Equipment includes electric drive propulsion, 155 mm guns and advanced stealth characteristics. The aim is a total of 32 ships.

2 + 22 (5) ARLEIGH BURKE CLASS (FLIGHT IIA): GUIDED MISSILE DESTROYERS (AEGIS) (DDG)

Name	No	Builders	Laid down		Launched		Commissioned		F/S
OSCAR AUSTIN	DDG 79	Bath Iron Works	9 Oct	1997	7 Nov	1998	Aug	2000	AA
ROOSEVELT	DDG 80	Ingalls Shipbuilding	15 Dec	1997	10 Jan	1999	Oct	2000	AA
WINSTON S CHURCHILL	DDG 81	Bath Iron Works	9 May	1998	17 Apr	1999	Jan	2001	Bldg/AA
LASSEN	DDG 82	Ingalls Shipbuilding	24 Aug	1998	16 Oct	1999	Dec	2000	Bldg/PA
HOWARD	DDG 83	Bath Iron Works	12 Dec	1998	20 Nov	1999	June	2001	Bldg/PA
BULKELEY	DDG 84	Bath Iron Works	10 May	1999	June	2000	May	2001	Bldg/AA
McCAMPBELL	DDG 85	Ingalls Shipbuilding	16 July	1999	July	2000	Jan	2002	Bldg
SHOUP	DDG 86	Ingalls Shipbuilding	13 Dec	1999	Nov	2000	Jan	2002	Bldg
MASON	DDG 87	Bath Iron Works	20 Jan	2000	Dec	2000	Sep	2002	Bldg
PREBLE	DDG 88	Ingalls Shipbuilding	June	2000	June	2001	Sep	2002	Bldg
MUSTIN	DDG 89	Ingalls Shipbuilding	Jan	2001	Dec	2001	Mar	2003	Bldg
CHAFFEE	DDG 90	Bath Iron Works	Nov	2000	Mar	2002	Mar	2003	Bldg
PINCKNEY	DDG 91	Ingalls Shipbuilding	July	2001	June	2002	May	2003	Bldg
—	DDG 92	Bath Iron Works	Feb	2001	July	2002	June	2003	Bldg
—	DDG 93	Ingalls, Shipbuilding	Nov	2001	Dec	2002	Apr	2004	Ord
—	DDG 94	Bath Iron Works	Mar	2002	Aug	2003	Aug	2004	Ord
—	DDG 95	Ingalls Shipbuilding	Aug	2002	Sep	2003	Mar	2005	Ord
—	DDG 96	Bath Iron Works	Apr	2003	Sep	2004	Sep	2005	Ord
—	DDG 97	Ingalls Shipbuilding	Jan	2004	Dec	2004	Mar	2005	Ord
—	DDG 98	Ingalls Shipbuilding	July	2004	July	2005	Dec	2005	Ord

Displacement, tons: 9,238 full load
Dimensions, feet (metres): 509.5 oa; 471 wl × 66.9 × 20.7; 32.7 (sonar) *(155.3; 143.6 × 20.4 × 6.3; 9.9)*
Main machinery: 4 GE LM 2500-30 gas turbines; 105,000 hp *(78.33 MW)* sustained; 2 shafts; cp props
Speed, knots: 31. **Range, miles:** 4,400 at 20 kt
Complement: 344 plus 22 spare

Missiles: SLCM: GCD/Hughes Tomahawk; Tercom aided guidance to 1,300 km *(700 n miles)* (TLAM-C and D) or 1,853 km *(1,000 n miles)* (TLAM-C Block III) at 0.7 Mach; warhead 454 kg (TLAM-C) or 347 kg shaped charge (TLAM-C Blocks II and III) or submunitions (TLAM-D). TLAM-C has GPS back-up to Tercom and a CEP of 10 m. Tactical Tomahawk from 2003.
SSM: 8 Hughes Harpoon (2 quad) can be fitted.
SAM: GDC Standard SM-2ER Block 4; command/inertial guidance; semi-active radar homing to 137 km *(74 n miles)*. 2 Lockheed Martin Mk 41 Vertical Launch Systems (VLS) for Tomahawk, Standard and ASROC VLS **❶**; 2 magazines; 32 missiles forward, 64 aft. Quad pack ESSM from designated cells in due course. LASM conversion for SM-2 Block II/III; GPS guidance to 333 km *(180 n miles)*; Mk 125 warhead for land attack, from 2003.
A/S: Loral ASROC VLA; inertial guidance to 1.6-16.6 km *(1-9 n miles)*; payload Mk 46 Mod 5 Neartip.

Guns: 1 United Defense 5 in *(127 mm)*/54 Mk 45 Mod 2 (DDG 79-80) **❷**; 20 rds/min to 23 km *(12.6 n miles)*; weight of shell 32 kg.
United Defense 5 in *(127 mm)*/62 (DDG 81 onwards); 20 or 10 (ERGM) rds/min; GPS guidance to 116.7 km *(63 n miles)*; warhead 72 bomblets; cep 10 m.
2 Hughes 20 mm Vulcan Phalanx 6-barrelled Mk 15 **❸**; 4,500 rds/min combined to 1.5 km. Fitted with IR detectors for tracking small craft. To be replaced by RAM from 2004.
Torpedoes: 6—324 mm Mk 32 Mod 14 (2 triple) tubes **❹**. Alliant Mk 46 Mod 5; anti-submarine; active/passive homing to 11 km *(5.9 n miles)* at 40 kt; warhead 44 kg or Alliant/Westinghouse Mk 50; active/passive homing to 15 km *(8.1 n miles)* at 50 kt; warhead 45 kg shaped charge.
Countermeasures: Decoys: 2 Loral Hycor SRBOC 6-barrelled fixed Mk 36 Mod 12 **❺**; IR flares and chaff to 4 km *(2.2 n miles)*. SLQ-25 Nixie; torpedo decoy. NATO Sea Gnat. SLQ-95 AEB. SLQ-39 chaff buoy.
ESM/ECM: Raytheon SLQ-32(V)3/SLY-2 **❻**; intercept and jammer.
Combat data systems: TADIX-B and TADIL-J. CEC. Links 4, 11 and 16. (See Data Systems at front of section.) Link 22 in due course. CDS upgrade for DDG 91.
Weapons control: SWG-3 Mk 37 Tomahawk WCS. Aegis multitarget tracking with Mk 99 Mod 3 MFCS and three Mk 80 illuminators. GWS 34 GFCS (includes Mk 160 Mod 8 computing system and Kollmorgen Mk 46 optronic sight). Singer Librascope Mk 116 FCS for ASW.
Radars: Air search/fire control: RCA SPY-1D phased arrays **❼**; 3D; E/F-band.
Surface search: DRS SPS-67(V)3 **❽**; G-band.
Navigation: Raytheon SPS-64(V)9; I-band.
Fire control: Three Raytheon/SPG-62 **❾**; I/J-band.
Tacan: URN 25 **❿**. IFF Mk XII AIMS UPX-29.
Sonars: Lockheed Martin SQQ-89(V)10; combines SQS-53C; bow-mounted; active search and attack with SQR 19B passive towed array (TACTAS); low frequency. Kingfisher; mine detection; active; high frequency.

Helicopters: 2 LAMPS III SH-60B/F helicopters **⓫**. UAV in due course.

Programmes: First ship of revised 'Arleigh Burke' class design was authorised in the FY94 budget. Funding for three provided in FY95 and a further two in FY96 plus partial funding for a third. Balance for this third ship plus three more in FY97 and four in FY98. Multiyear contracts were awarded on 6 March 1998, six to Bath Iron Works and eight to Ingalls. Two more to Ingalls on 14 December 1998. Total of 29 of the class seems likely.
Structure: The upgrade from Flight II includes two hangars for embarked helicopters and an extended transom to increase the size of a dual RAST fitted flight deck at the expense of SQR-19 TACTAS. Vertical launchers are increased at each end by three cells are able to fire the agile Evolved Sea Sparrow missile. Harpoon may be fitted for, but not with. Other changes include the Kingfisher minehunting sonar, a reconfiguration of the SPY-1D arrays and the inclusion of a Track Initiation Processor in the Aegis radar system. Use of fibre optic technology should reduce weight and improve reliability. A Kollmorgen optronic bridge periscope is fitted. A remote minehunting system WLD-1 is to be installed from DDG 91 onwards. DDG 83 is scheduled to be the first ship to include 'Smart Ship' technology.
Operational: The helicopter is to carry Penguin and Hellfire missiles. Tactical Tomahawk and LASM planned from 2003.

UPDATED

OSCAR AUSTIN

(Scale 1 : 1,500), Ian Sturton / 0016362

ROOSEVELT

3/2000*, Ingalls Shipbuilding / 0084100

28 ARLEIGH BURKE CLASS (FLIGHTS I and II): GUIDED MISSILE DESTROYERS (AEGIS) (DDG)

Name	No	Builders	Laid down		Launched		Commissioned		F/S
ARLEIGH BURKE	DDG 51	Bath Iron Works	6 Dec	1988	16 Sep	1989	4 July	1991	AA
BARRY (ex-John Barry)	DDG 52	Ingalls Shipbuilding	26 Feb	1990	10 May	1991	12 Dec	1992	AA
JOHN PAUL JONES	DDG 53	Bath Iron Works	8 Aug	1990	26 Oct	1991	18 Dec	1993	PA
CURTIS WILBUR	DDG 54	Bath Iron Works	12 Mar	1992	16 May	1992	4 Apr	1994	PA
STOUT	DDG 55	Ingalls Shipbuilding	8 Aug	1991	16 Oct	1992	13 Aug	1994	AA
JOHN S McCAIN	DDG 56	Bath Iron Works	3 Sep	1991	26 Sep	1992	2 July	1994	AA
MITSCHER	DDG 57	Ingalls Shipbuilding	12 Feb	1992	7 May	1993	10 Dec	1994	AA
LABOON	DDG 58	Bath Iron Works	23 Mar	1992	20 Feb	1993	18 Mar	1995	AA
RUSSELL	DDG 59	Ingalls Shipbuilding	24 July	1992	20 Oct	1993	20 May	1995	PA
PAUL HAMILTON	DDG 60	Bath Iron Works	24 Aug	1992	24 July	1993	27 May	1995	PA
RAMAGE	DDG 61	Ingalls Shipbuilding	4 Jan	1993	11 Feb	1994	22 July	1995	AA
FITZGERALD	DDG 62	Bath Iron Works	9 Feb	1993	29 Jan	1994	14 Oct	1995	PA
STETHEM	DDG 63	Ingalls Shipbuilding	11 May	1993	17 June	1994	21 Oct	1995	PA
CARNEY	DDG 64	Bath Iron Works	3 Aug	1993	23 July	1994	13 Apr	1996	AA
BENFOLD	DDG 65	Ingalls Shipbuilding	27 Sep	1993	9 Nov	1994	30 Mar	1996	PA
GONZALEZ	DDG 66	Bath Iron Works	3 Feb	1994	18 Feb	1995	12 Oct	1996	AA
COLE	DDG 67	Ingalls Shipbuilding	28 Feb	1994	10 Feb	1995	8 June	1996	AA
THE SULLIVANS	DDG 68	Bath Iron Works	27 July	1994	12 Aug	1995	19 Apr	1997	AA
MILIUS	DDG 69	Ingalls Shipbuilding	8 Aug	1994	1 Aug	1995	23 Nov	1996	PA
HOPPER	DDG 70	Bath Iron Works	23 Feb	1995	6 Jan	1996	6 Sep	1997	PA
ROSS	DDG 71	Ingalls Shipbuilding	10 Apr	1995	23 Mar	1996	28 June	1997	AA
MAHAN	DDG 72	Bath Iron Works	17 Aug	1995	29 June	1996	14 Feb	1998	AA
DECATUR	DDG 73	Bath Iron Works	11 Jan	1996	10 Nov	1996	29 Aug	1998	PA
McFAUL	DDG 74	Ingalls Shipbuilding	26 Jan	1996	18 Jan	1997	25 Apr	1998	AA
DONALD COOK	DDG 75	Bath Iron Works	9 July	1996	3 May	1997	4 Dec	1998	AA
HIGGINS	DDG 76	Bath Iron Works	14 Nov	1996	4 Oct	1997	24 Apr	1999	PA
O'KANE	DDG 77	Bath Iron Works	5 May	1997	28 Mar	1998	23 Oct	1999	PA
PORTER	DDG 78	Ingalls Shipbuilding	2 Dec	1996	12 Nov	1997	20 Mar	1999	AA

Displacement, tons: 8,422; 9,033 (from DDG 72) full load
Dimensions, feet (metres): 504.5 oa; 466 wl × 66.9 × 20.7; 32.7 (sonar) *(153.8; 142 × 20.4 × 6.3; 9.9)*
Main machinery: 4 GE LM 2500 gas turbines; 105,000 hp *(78.33 MW)* sustained; 2 shafts; cp props
Speed, knots: 32. **Range, miles:** 4,400 at 20 kt
Complement: 346 (22 officers)

Missiles: SLCM: 56 GDC/Hughes Tomahawk; Tercom aided guidance to 1,300 km *(700 n miles)* (TLAM-C and D) or 1,853 km *(1,000 n miles)* (TLAM-C Block III) at 0.7 Mach; warhead 454 kg (TLAM-C) or 347 kg shaped charge (TLAM-C Blocks II and III) or submunitions (TLAM-D). TLAM-C has GPS back-up to Tercom and a CEP of 10 m.
SSM: 8 McDonnell Douglas Harpoon (2 quad) ❶; active radar homing to 130 km *(70 n miles)* at 0.9 Mach; warhead 227 kg.
SAM: GDC Standard SM-2MR Block 4; command/inertial guidance; semi-active radar homing to 73 km *(40 n miles)* at 2 Mach. SM-2ER extended range to 137 km *(74 n miles)* from DDG 72 onwards. 2 Martin Marietta Mk 41 (Mod 0 forward, Mod 1 aft) Vertical Launch Systems (VLS) for Tomahawk, Standard and ASROC VLA ❷; 2 magazines; 29 missiles forward, 61 aft. Mod 2 from DDG 59 onwards. Quad pack ESSM from designated cells in due course.
A/S: Loral ASROC VLA; inertial guidance to 1.6-16.6 km *(1-9 n miles)*; payload Mk 46 Mod 5 Neartip.
Guns: 1 FMC/UDLP 5 in *(127 mm)*/54 Mk 45 Mod 1 or 2 ❸; 20 rds/min to 23 km *(12.6 n miles)*; weight of shell 32 kg. Modified 5 in *(127 mm)*/62 barrel may be fitted from 2000 to take ERGM (extended-range guided munitions); GPS guidance to 116.7 km *(63 n miles)*; warhead 72 bomblets; cep 10 m.
2 General Electric/General Dynamics 20 mm Vulcan Phalanx 6-barrelled Mk 15 ❹; 3,000 rds/min (4,500 in Block 1) combined to 1.5 km. Being fitted with IR detectors for tracking small craft. To be replaced by RAM from 2004.
Torpedoes: 6—324 mm Mk 32 Mod 14 (2 triple) tubes ❺. Alliant Mk 46 Mod 5; anti-submarine; active/passive homing to 11 km *(5.9 n miles)* at 40 kt; warhead 44 kg or Alliant/Westinghouse Mk 50; active/passive homing to 15 km *(8.1 n miles)* at 50 kt; warhead 45 kg shaped charge.
Countermeasures: Decoys: 2 Loral Hycor SRBOC 6-barrelled fixed Mk 36 Mod 12 ❻; IR flares and chaff to 4 km *(2.2 n miles)*. SLQ-25 Nixie; torpedo decoy. NATO Sea Gnat. SLQ-95 AEB. SLQ-39 chaff buoy. Nulka being acquired.
ESM/ECM: Raytheon SLQ-32(V)2 ❼ or SLQ-32(V)3/SLY-2 (from DDG 72 and being backfitted); radar warning. Sidekick modification adds jammer and deception system to (V)2. SRS-1 DF (from DDG 72).
Combat data systems: CEC being fitted. NTDS Mod 5 with Links 4A, 11, 14 and 16 (from DDG 72) and being back fitted. SATCOM SRR-1, WSC-3 (UHF), USC-38 (EHF). SQQ-28 for LAMPS processor datalink. TADIX B Tactical Information

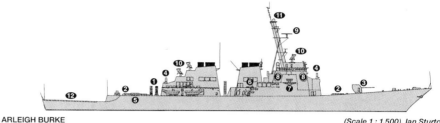

ARLEIGH BURKE

(Scale 1 : 1,500), Ian Sturton / 0053331

STOUT

*1/1999 *, Maritime Photographic /* 0084102

Exchange System (from DDG 72). Link 22 in due course (see Data Systems at front of section).
Weapons control: SWG-3 Mk 37 Tomahawk WCS. SWG-1A Harpoon LCS. Aegis multitarget tracking with Mk 99 Mod 3 MFCS and three Mk 80 illuminators. GWS 34 Mod 0 GFCS (includes Mk 160 Mod 4 computing system and Kollmorgen Mk 46 Mod 0/1 optronic sight). Singer Librascope Mk 116 Mod 7 FCS for ASW.

Radars: Air search/fire control: RCA SPY-1D phased arrays ❽; 3D; E/F-band.
Surface search: Norden/DRS SPS-67(V)3 ❾; G-band.
Navigation: Raytheon SPS-64(V)9; I-band.
Fire control: Three Raytheon/RCA SPG-62 ❿; I/J-band.
Tacan: URN 25 ⓫. IFF Mk XII AIMS UPX-29.
Sonars: Gould/Raytheon/GE SQQ-89(V)6; combines SQS-53C; bow-mounted; active search and attack with SQR-19B passive towed array (TACTAS) low frequency.

Helicopters: Platform and facilities to fuel and rearm LAMPS III SH-60B/F helicopters ⓬. UAV in due course.

Programmes: First ship authorised in FY85, last pair in FY94. The first 21 are Flight I and the next seven are Flight II.
Modernisation: TBMD lower tier may be fitted from 2003. Quad pack ESSM from designated Mk 41 cells in 2003 and RAM from 2004 vice Phalanx.
Structure: The ship, except for the aluminium funnels, is constructed of steel. 70 tons of armour provided to protect vital spaces. This is the first class of US Navy warship designed with a 'collective protection system' for defense against the fallout associated with NBC warfare'. The ship's crew are protected by double air-locked hatches, fewer accesses to the weatherdecks and positive pressurisation of the interior of the ship to keep out contaminants. All incoming air is filtered and more reliance placed on recirculating air inside the ship. All accommodation compartments have sprinkler systems. Stealth technology includes angled surfaces and rounded edges to reduce radar signature and IR signature suppression plus Prairie Masker hull/blade rate suppression. The Ops room is below the waterline and electronics are EMP hardened. The original upright mast design has been changed to increase separation between electronic systems and the forward funnel. Differences in Flight II starting with DDG 72 include Link 16, SLQ-32(V)3 EW suite, extended-range SAM missiles and improved tactical information exchange systems. The topmast is vertical to take the SRS-1. There is also an increase in displacement caused by using more space to carry fuel.
Operational: Two of the class are based at Yokosuka in Japan.

UPDATED

HIGGINS

*5/1999 *, M Declerck /* 0084101

O'KANE   5/1999*, *Bath Iron Works* / 0084103

PAUL HAMILTON   2/1999*, *van Ginderen/B Morrison* / 0084104

FITZGERALD   9/1999*, *J Montes* / 0084105

McFAUL   *4/1998, Ingalls Shipbuilding* / 0053475

STOUT   *3/1999, Maritime Photographic* / 0053476

24 SPRUANCE CLASS: DESTROYERS (DD/DDG)

Name	No	Builders	Laid down	Launched	Commissioned	F/S
SPRUANCE	DD 963	Ingalls Shipbuilding	17 Nov 1972	10 Nov 1973	20 Sep 1975	AA
PAUL F FOSTER	DD 964	Ingalls Shipbuilding	6 Feb 1973	23 Feb 1974	21 Feb 1976	PA
KINKAID	DD 965	Ingalls Shipbuilding	19 Apr 1973	25 May 1974	10 July 1976	PA
HEWITT	DD 966	Ingalls Shipbuilding	23 July 1973	24 Aug 1974	25 Sep 1976	PA
ELLIOTT	DD 967	Ingalls Shipbuilding	15 Oct 1973	19 Dec 1974	22 Jan 1977	PA
ARTHUR W RADFORD	DD 968	Ingalls Shipbuilding	14 Jan 1974	1 Mar 1975	16 Apr 1977	AA
PETERSON	DD 969	Ingalls Shipbuilding	29 Apr 1974	21 June 1975	9 July 1977	AA
CARON	DD 970	Ingalls Shipbuilding	1 July 1974	24 June 1975	1 Oct 1977	AA
DAVID R RAY	DD 971	Ingalls Shipbuilding	23 Sep 1974	23 Aug 1975	19 Nov 1977	PA
OLDENDORF	DD 972	Ingalls Shipbuilding	27 Dec 1974	21 Oct 1975	4 Mar 1978	PA
JOHN YOUNG	DD 973	Ingalls Shipbuilding	17 Feb 1975	7 Feb 1976	20 May 1978	PA
O'BRIEN	DD 975	Ingalls Shipbuilding	9 May 1975	8 July 1976	3 Dec 1977	PA
BRISCOE	DD 977	Ingalls Shipbuilding	21 July 1975	15 Dec 1976	3 June 1978	AA
STUMP	DD 978	Ingalls Shipbuilding	25 Aug 1975	29 Jan 1977	19 Aug 1978	AA
MOOSBRUGGER	DD 980	Ingalls Shipbuilding	3 Nov 1975	23 July 1977	16 Dec 1978	AA
JOHN HANCOCK	DD 981	Ingalls Shipbuilding	16 Jan 1976	29 Oct 1977	10 Mar 1979	AA
NICHOLSON	DD 982	Ingalls Shipbuilding	20 Feb 1976	11 Nov 1977	12 May 1979	AA
CUSHING	DD 985	Ingalls Shipbuilding	27 Dec 1976	17 June 1978	20 Oct 1979	PA
O'BANNON	DD 987	Ingalls Shipbuilding	21 Feb 1977	25 Sep 1978	15 Dec 1979	AA
THORN	DD 988	Ingalls Shipbuilding	29 Aug 1977	14 Nov 1978	16 Feb 1980	AA
DEYO	DD 989	Ingalls Shipbuilding	14 Oct 1977	27 Jan 1979	22 Mar 1980	AA
FIFE	DD 991	Ingalls Shipbuilding	6 Mar 1978	1 May 1979	31 May 1980	PA
FLETCHER	DD 992	Ingalls Shipbuilding	24 Apr 1978	16 June 1979	12 July 1980	PA
HAYLER	DD 997	Ingalls Shipbuilding	20 Oct 1980	27 Mar 1982	5 Mar 1983	AA

Displacement, tons: 5,770 light; 8,040 full load
Dimensions, feet (metres): 563.2 × 55.1 × 19; 29 (sonar)
(171.7 × 16.8 × 5.8; 8.8)
Main machinery: 4 GE LM 2500 gas turbines; 86,000 hp
(64.16 MW) sustained; 2 shafts; cp props
Speed, knots: 33. **Range, miles:** 6,000 at 20 kt
Complement: 319-339 (20 officers)

Missiles: SLCM: GDC Tomahawk; Tercom aided guidance to
1,300 km *(700 n miles)* (TLAM-C and D) or 1,853 km *(1,000 n
miles)* (TLAM-C Block III) at 0.7 Mach; warhead 454 kg
(TLAM-C) or 347 kg shaped charge (TLAM-C Blocks II and III)
or submunitions (TLAM-D). TLAM-C has GPS back-up to
Tercom and a CEP of 10 m.
  Mk 41 Mod 0 VLS ❶ with one 61 missile magazine combining
45 Tomahawk and ASROC in some.
  8 McDonnell Douglas Harpoon (2 quad) ❷; active radar
homing to 130 km *(70 n miles)* at 0.9 Mach; warhead 227 kg.
SAM: Raytheon GMLS Mk 29 octuple launcher ❸; 24 Sea
Sparrow; semi-active radar homing to 14.6 km *(8 n miles)* at
2.5 Mach; warhead 39 kg.
  GDC RAM quadruple launcher ❹; passive IR/anti-radiation
homing to 9.6 km *(5.2 n miles)* at 2 Mach; warhead 9.1 kg.
Being fitted in 12 of the class.
A/S: Loral ASROC VLA can be carried; inertial guidance to
16.6 km *(9 n miles)*; payload Mk 46 Mod 5 Neartip.
Guns: 2 FMC 5 in *(127 mm)*/54 Mk 45 Mod 0/1 ❺; 20 rds/min
to 23 km *(12.6 n miles)* anti-surface; 15 km *(8.2 n miles)* anti-
aircraft; weight of shell 32 kg.
  2 General Electric/General Dynamics 20 mm/76 6-barrelled
Mk 15 Vulcan Phalanx ❻; 3,000 rds/min (4,500 in Batch 1)
combined to 1.5 km.
  4—12.7 mm MGs.
Torpedoes: 6—324 mm Mk 32 (2 triple) tubes ❼. 14 Honeywell
Mk 46; anti-submarine; active/passive homing to 11 km *(5.9 n
miles)* at 40 kt; warhead 44 kg or Alliant/Westinghouse Mk
50; active/passive to 15 km *(8.1 n miles)* at 50 kt; warhead
45 kg shaped charge. The tubes are inside the superstructure
to facilitate maintenance and reloading. Torpedoes are fired
through side ports.
Countermeasures: Decoys: 4 Loral Hycor SRBOC 6-barrelled
fixed Mk 36 ❽; IR flares and chaff to 4 km *(2.2 n miles)*. SLQ-39
chaff buoy.
  SLQ-25 Nixie; torpedo decoy. Prairie/Masker hull/blade rate
noise suppression system. Remote Minehunting System
(RMS) can be carried; endurance 24 hours at 12 kt.
ESM/ECM: SLQ-32(V)2 ❾; radar warning. Sidekick modification
adds jammer and deception system. WLR-1 (in some).
Combat data systems: NTDS with Links 11 and 14. SATCOMS
❿ SRR-1, WSC-3 (UHF), USC-38 (EHF) (in some). SQQ-28 for
LAMPS datalink. SYQ-17 RAIDS (see *Modernisation*) being
fitted.
Weapons control: SWG-3 Tomahawk WCS. SWG-1A Harpoon
LCS. Mk 116 Mod 7 FCS ASW. Mk 86 Mod 3 GFCS. Mk 91
MFCS. SRQ-4 LAMPS III. SAR-8 IR director (DD 965).
Radars: Air search: Lockheed SPS-40B/C/D (not in DD 997) ⓫;
E/F-band; range 320 km *(175 n miles)*.
  Raytheon SPS-49V (DD 997); C/D-band; range 457 km *(250 n
miles)*.
  Hughes Mk 23 TAS ⓬; D-band.
Surface search: ISC Cardion SPS-55 ⓭; I/J-band.
Navigation: Raytheon SPS-64(V)9; I-band.
Fire control: Lockheed SPG-60 ⓮; I/J-band.
  Lockheed SPQ-9A ⓯ or 9B (DD 972); I/J-band.
  Raytheon Mk 95 ⓰; I/J-band (for SAM).
Tacan: URN 20 or URN 25 (D 997). IFF Mk XII AIMS UPX-25.

OLDENDORF
(Scale 1 : 1,500), Ian Sturton / 0016370

NICHOLSON (with RAM)
3/1999*, Diego Quevedo / 0084106

Sonars: SQQ-89(V)6 including GE/Hughes SQS-53B/C; bow-
mounted; active search and attack; medium frequency; and
Gould SQR-19 (TACTAS); passive towed array.

Helicopters: 2 SH-60B LAMPS III ⓱ or SH-2G Seasprite.

Programmes: Funds approved between FY70 and FY78.
Modernisation: Beginning with FY86 overhauls, major
improvements have been made. These included the
installation of VLS, upgrading of EW to SLQ-32V(2) plus
sidekick; LAMPS III and the recovery, assist, secure and
traverse system (RAST), the Halon 1301 firefighting system
and anti-missile and target acquisition systems. All are capable
of launching Standard SM-2MR for control by Aegis fitted
vessels. RAIDS (Rapid Anti-ship missile Integrated Defence
System) evaluated in DD 963, and installed in all of the class in
1996-97. RAM launcher being fitted on the stern in 12 of the
class. DD 968 was fitted with an Advanced Enclosed Mast
Sensor System in 1997. This structure is designed for greater

stealth and to provide a better operational and maintenance
environment for the enclosed sensors. It weighs 40 tons and is
88 ft high. SPQ-9B in DD 972 for trials in 2000. Plans to fit
ESSM have been cancelled.
Structure: Extensive use of the modular concept has been used
to facilitate construction and block modernisation. There is a
high level of automation. These were the first large US
warships to employ gas-turbine propulsion and advanced self-
noise reduction features. Kevlar internal coating in all vital
spaces.
Operational: Three of the class are based at Yokosuka, Japan.
DD 978-987 (six) and 989 have helicopters equipped with
SSM. DD 973 has operated a remote-controlled semi-
submersible with AQS 14 VDS sonar for minehunting. This is
available for all of the class. The seven of the class not
converted to VLS placed in Category B reserve from end FY98.
DD 981, DD 980 and DD 966 are scheduled to pay off in 2001.
UPDATED

JOHN HANCOCK
10/1999*, Melanie Rovery / 0084107

SPRUANCE

4/1999*, Michael Nitz / 0084109

OLDENDORFF

3/1999*, C E Castle / 0084108

ARTHUR W RADFORD

7/1998, Maritime Photographic / 0053339

FRIGATES

35 OLIVER HAZARD PERRY CLASS: GUIDED MISSILE FRIGATES (FFG)

Name	No	Builders	Laid down	Launched	Commissioned	F/S
McINERNEY	FFG 8	Bath Iron Works	7 Nov 1977	4 Nov 1978	15 Dec 1979	AA
WADSWORTH	FFG 9	Todd Shipyards, San Pedro	13 July 1977	29 July 1978	28 Feb 1980	NRF
GEORGE PHILIP	FFG 12	Todd Shipyards, San Pedro	14 Dec 1977	16 Dec 1978	15 Nov 1980	NRF
SAMUEL ELIOT MORISON	FFG 13	Bath Iron Works	4 Dec 1978	14 July 1979	11 Oct 1980	NRF
JOHN H SIDES	FFG 14	Todd Shipyards, San Pedro	7 Aug 1978	19 May 1979	30 May 1981	NRF
ESTOCIN	FFG 15	Bath Iron Works	2 Apr 1979	3 Nov 1979	10 Jan 1981	NRF
BOONE	FFG 28	Todd Shipyards, Seattle	27 Mar 1979	16 Jan 1980	15 May 1982	NRF
STEPHEN W GROVES	FFG 29	Bath Iron Works	16 Sep 1980	4 Apr 1981	17 Apr 1982	NRF
JOHN L HALL	FFG 32	Bath Iron Works	5 Jan 1981	24 July 1981	26 June 1982	AA
JARRETT	FFG 33	Todd Shipyards, San Pedro	11 Feb 1981	17 Oct 1981	2 July 1983	PA
UNDERWOOD	FFG 36	Bath Iron Works	3 Aug 1981	6 Feb 1982	29 Jan 1983	AA
CROMMELIN	FFG 37	Todd Shipyards, Seattle	30 May 1980	1 July 1981	18 June 1983	PA
CURTS	FFG 38	Todd Shipyards, San Pedro	1 July 1981	6 Mar 1982	8 Oct 1983	NRF
DOYLE	FFG 39	Bath Iron Works	16 Nov 1981	22 May 1982	21 May 1983	AA
HALYBURTON	FFG 40	Todd Shipyards, Seattle	26 Sep 1980	15 Oct 1981	7 Jan 1984	AA
McCLUSKY	FFG 41	Todd Shipyards, San Pedro	21 Oct 1981	18 Sep 1982	10 Dec 1983	PA
KLAKRING	FFG 42	Bath Iron Works	19 Feb 1982	18 Sep 1982	20 Aug 1983	AA
THACH	FFG 43	Todd Shipyards, San Pedro	10 Mar 1982	18 Dec 1982	17 Mar 1984	PA
De WERT	FFG 45	Bath Iron Works	14 June 1982	18 Dec 1982	19 Nov 1983	AA
RENTZ	FFG 46	Todd Shipyards, San Pedro	18 Sep 1982	16 July 1983	30 June 1984	PA
NICHOLAS	FFG 47	Bath Iron Works	27 Sep 1982	23 Apr 1983	10 Mar 1984	AA
VANDEGRIFT	FFG 48	Todd Shipyards, Seattle	13 Oct 1981	15 Oct 1982	24 Nov 1984	PA
ROBERT G BRADLEY	FFG 49	Bath Iron Works	28 Dec 1982	13 Aug 1983	11 Aug 1984	AA
TAYLOR	FFG 50	Bath Iron Works	5 May 1983	5 Nov 1983	1 Dec 1984	AA
GARY	FFG 51	Todd Shipyards, San Pedro	18 Dec 1982	19 Nov 1983	17 Nov 1984	PA
CARR	FFG 52	Todd Shipyards, Seattle	26 Mar 1982	26 Feb 1983	27 July 1985	AA
HAWES	FFG 53	Bath Iron Works	22 Aug 1983	18 Feb 1984	9 Feb 1985	AA
FORD	FFG 54	Todd Shipyards, San Pedro	16 July 1983	23 June 1984	29 June 1985	PA
ELROD	FFG 55	Bath Iron Works	21 Nov 1983	12 May 1984	6 June 1985	AA
SIMPSON	FFG 56	Bath Iron Works	27 Feb 1984	21 Aug 1984	9 Nov 1985	AA
REUBEN JAMES	FFG 57	Todd Shipyards, San Pedro	19 Nov 1983	8 Feb 1985	22 Mar 1986	PA
SAMUEL B ROBERTS	FFG 58	Bath Iron Works	21 May 1984	8 Dec 1984	12 Apr 1986	AA
KAUFFMAN	FFG 59	Bath Iron Works	8 Apr 1985	29 Mar 1986	21 Feb 1987	AA
RODNEY M DAVIS	FFG 60	Todd Shipyards, San Pedro	8 Feb 1985	11 Jan 1986	9 May 1987	PA
INGRAHAM	FFG 61	Todd Shipyards, San Pedro	30 Mar 1987	25 June 1988	5 Aug 1989	PA

Displacement, tons: 2,750 light; 3,638; 4,100 (FFG 8, 15, 28, 29, 32, 36-61) full load

Dimensions, feet (metres): 445; 453 (FFG 8, 15, 28, 29, 32, 36-61) × 45 × 14.8; 24.5 (sonar) *(135.6; 138.1 × 13.7 × 4.5; 7.5)*

Main machinery: 2 GE LM 2500 gas turbines; 41,000 hp *(30.59 MW)* sustained; 1 shaft; cp prop
2 auxiliary retractable props; 650 hp *(484 kW)*

Speed, knots: 29. **Range, miles:** 4,500 at 20 kt

Complement: 200 (15 officers) including 19 aircrew

Missiles: SSM: 4 McDonnell Douglas Harpoon; active radar homing to 130 km *(70 n miles)* at 0.9 Mach; warhead 227 kg.
SAM: 36 GDC Standard SM-1MR; command guidance; semi-active radar homing to 46 km *(25 n miles)* at 2 Mach.
1 Mk 13 Mod 4 launcher for both SSM and SAM missiles **❶**.

Guns: 1 OTO Melara 3 in *(76 mm)*/62 Mk 75 **❷**; 85 rds/min to 16 km *(8.7 n miles)* anti-surface; 12 km *(6.6 n miles)* anti-aircraft; weight of shell 6 kg.
1 General Electric/General Dynamics 20 mm/76 6-barrelled Mk 15 Vulcan Phalanx **❸**; 3,000 rds/min (4,500 in Block 1) combined to 1.5 km. Block 1B with anti-surface capability.
2 Boeing 25 mm Mk 38 guns can be fitted amidships. 4—12.7 mm MGs.

Torpedoes: 6—324 mm Mk 32 (2 triple) tubes **❹**. 24 Honeywell Mk 46 Mod 5; anti-submarine; active/passive homing to 11 km *(5.9 n miles)* at 40 kt; warhead 44 kg or Alliant/Westinghouse Mk 50; active/passive homing to 15 km *(8.1 n miles)* at 50 kt; warhead 45 kg shaped charge.

Countermeasures: Decoys: 2 Loral Hycor SRBOC 6-barrelled fixed Mk 36 **❺**; IR flares and chaff to 4 km *(2.2 n miles)*.
T—Mk 6 Fanfare/SLQ-25 Nixie; torpedo decoy.
ESM/ECM: SLQ-32(V)2 **❻**; radar warning. Sidekick modification adds jammer and deception system.

Combat data systems: NTDS with Link 11 and 14. Link 14 only (NRF ships). SATCOM **❼** SRR-1, WSC-3 (UHF). SQQ-28 for LAMPS III datalink.

Weapons control: SWG-1 Harpoon LCS. Mk 92 (Mod 4 or Mod 6 (FFG 61 and during modernisation in 11 others of the class)). WCS with CAS (Combined Antenna System). The Mk 92 is the US version of the Signaal WM28 system. Mk 13 weapon direction system. 2 Mk 24 optical directors. SYS 2(V)2 IADT (FFG 61 and in 11 others of the class - see *Modernisation*). SRQ-4 for LAMPS III, SKR-4A for LAMPS I.

Radars: Air search: Raytheon SPS-49(V)4 or 5 (FFG 61 and during modernisation of others) **❽**; C/D-band; range 457 km *(250 n miles)*.
Surface search: ISC Cardion SPS-55 **❾**; I-band.
Fire control: Lockheed STIR (modified SPG-60) **❿**; I/J-band; range 110 km *(60 n miles)*.
Sperry Mk 92 (Signaal WM28) **⓫**; I/J-band.
Navigation: Furuno; I-band.
Tacan: URN 25. IFF Mk XII AIMS UPX-29.

Sonars: SQQ 89(V)2 (Raytheon SQS 56 and Gould SQR 19); hull-mounted active search and attack; medium frequency and passive towed array; very low frequency.

Helicopters: 2 SH-2G LAMPS I (NRF ships) or 2 SH-60B LAMPS III **⓬**.

Programmes: The lead ship was authorised in FY73. On 31 January 1984 the first of this class transferred to the Naval Reserve Force.

Modernisation: To accommodate the helicopter landing system (RAST), the overall length of the ship was increased by 8 ft *(2.4 m)* by increasing the angle of the ship's transom, between the waterline and the fantail, from virtually straight up to a 45° angle outwards. LAMPS III support facilities and RAST were fitted in all ships authorised from FFG 36 onwards, during construction and have been backfitted to all except FFG 9-14 and 33. The remainder can operate this aircraft without landing facilities. FFG 61 has much improved Combat Data and Fire-Control equipment which has been retrofitted in FFG 36, 47, 48, 50-55, 57 and 59. SQS-56 is modified for mine

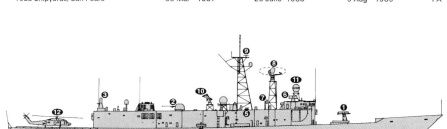
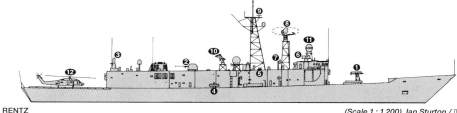

RENTZ   *(Scale 1 : 1,200), Ian Sturton /* 0016376

STEPHEN W GROVES   *8/1999*, J Cislak /* 0084110

detection. Block 1B Phalanx fitted first in FFG 36 in October 1999. This has a capability against high speed surface craft at short range. Plans to fit RAM have been shelved. Two more are planned to go in each of 2001 and 2002.

Structure: The original single hangar has been changed to two adjacent hangars. Provided with 19 mm Kevlar armour protection over vital spaces. 25 mm guns can be fitted for some operational deployments.

Operational: Ships of this class were the first Navy experience in implementing a design-to-cost acquisition concept. Many of their limitations were manifest during the intense fires which resulted from *Stark* (FFG 31) being struck by two Exocet

missiles in the Persian Gulf 17 May 1987. Since then there have been many improvements in firefighting and damage control doctrine and procedures and equipment to deal with residual missile propellant-induced fires. On 14 April 1988, *Samuel B Roberts* (FFG 58), was mined in the Gulf. Penguin SSM can be carried in some LAMPS III helicopters. Two of the class are based at Yokosuka. Several have paid off.

Sales: Australia bought four of the class and has built two more. Spain has six and Taiwan eight. Transfers include six to Turkey plus one for spares, four to Egypt, one to Bahrain, and one to Poland plus one more planned for 2001.

UPDATED

JARRETT   *10/1999*, Findler & Winter* / 0084111

HALYBURTON   *3/1999*, M Declerck* / 0084112

McCLUSKY   *3/1999*, Maritime Photographic* / 0084113

Combatant Naval Reserve Force Frigates

Name/Hull No	NRF Homeport	Assignment		Name/Hull No	NRF Homeport	Assignment
WADSWORTH (FFG 9)	San Diego, CA	June 1985		**ESTOCIN** (FFG 15)	Norfolk, VA	Sep 1986
GEORGE PHILIP (FFG 12)	San Diego, CA	Jan 1986		**STEPHEN W GROVES** (FFG 29)	Pascagoula, MI	Mar 1997
SAMUEL ELIOT MORISON (FFG 13)	Mayport, FL	June 1986		**BOONE** (FFG 28)	Mayport, FL	May 1998
JOHN H SIDES (FFG 14)	San Diego, CA	Aug 1986		**CURTS** (FFG 38)	San Diego, CA	Sep 1998

SHIPBORNE AIRCRAFT (FRONT LINE)

Note: Numbers given are for 1 January 2000.

Numbers/Type: 76/73/46 Grumman F-14A/B/D Tomcat.
Operational speed: 1,342 kt *(2,485 km/h).*
Service ceiling: 56,000 ft *(17,070 m).*
Range: 1,735 n miles *(3,220 km).*
Role/Weapon systems: Standard fleet fighter (VF) aircraft for long-range air defence of task groups; undergoing phased improvements; F-14D in-service date of 1990. Sensors: AWG-9 or APG-71 (D type) radar, ALQ-126 jammer, ASN-92 nav or ASN-139 (D type), ALR-45 or Litton ALR-67 (B and D type) RWR; IRST and JTIDS (Link 16) (D type). Weapons: AD; one 20 mm cannon, six AIM-54 Phoenix (ASV); AGM-88 HARM and AGM-84 Harpoon/SLAM may be added. CAP; one 20 mm cannon, four Phoenix, two AIM-7M Sparrow, two AIM-9M Sidewinder, Recce; one 20 mm cannon, two AIM-7M, two AIM-9M.

UPDATED

TOMCAT   *9/1999*, M Kadota /* 0084114

TOMCAT   *3/1998, Maritime Photographic /* 0053345

Numbers/Type: 194/32/410/139 McDonnell Douglas F/A-18A/B/C/D Hornet.
Operational speed: 1,032 kt *(1,910 km/h).*
Service ceiling: 50,000 ft *(15,240 m).*
Range: 1,000 n miles *(1,850 km).*
Role/Weapon systems: Strike interdictor (VFA) for USN/USMC air groups. Some are used for EW support with ALQ-167 jammers. Sensors: ESM: Litton ALR 67, ALQ 165 ASPJ jammer (18D), APG-65 or APG-73 radar, AAS-38 FLIR, ASQ-173 tracker. Weapons: ASV; four Harpoon or SLAM (18D) or AGM-88 HARM (18D) missiles. Strike; up to 7.7 tons of bombs (or LGM). AD; one 20 mm Vulcan cannon, nine AIM-7/AIM-9 missiles. Typical ASV load might include 20 mm gun, 7.7 ton bombs including AGM 154A JSOW, two AIM-9 missiles. Typical AAW load might include 20 mm gun, four AIM-7, two AIM-9 missiles. 18C/D includes AIM-120 AMRAAM and AGM-65 Maverick or AGM 62 Walleye capability.

UPDATED

HORNET   *8/1998, Hachiro Nakai /* 0053344

Numbers/Type: 9/6 Boeing F/A-18E/F Super Hornet.
Operational speed: 1,032 kt *(1,910 km/h).*
Service ceiling: 50,000 ft *(15,240 m).*
Range: 1,320 n miles *(2,376 km).*
Role/Weapon systems: Strike interdictor for USN/USMC. First one rolled out in September 1995. First sea trials January 1997. In service from 2001. First 12 production aircraft ordered in FY97. Sensors: APG-73 radar. Weapons: 11 wing stations for 8,051 kg of weapons (same armament as C/D) plus 20 mm guns.

UPDATED

SUPER HORNET   *1/1997, Adam Plantz, US Navy /* 0016382

Numbers/Type: 156/1/19 Boeing/British Aerospace AV-8B/AV-8B II Plus/TAV-8B Harrier II.
Operational speed: 562 kt *(1,041 km/h).*
Service ceiling: 50,000 ft *(15,240 m).*
Range: 800 n miles *(1,480 km).*
Role/Weapon systems: CAS (VMA) for USMC operational from 1985. A total of 72 AV-8B Plus conversions scheduled to complete in 2002. Sensors: FLIR, laser spot tracker and ECM; Litton ALR-67 ESM; APG-65 radar (AV-8B II Plus). Weapons: Strike; up to 4.2 tons of 'iron' bombs or Paveway II LGM, AGM-62 Walleye or AGM-65 Maverick. Self-defence; one GAU-12/U 25 mm cannon and four AIM-9L Sidewinder.

UPDATED

HARRIER   *3/1999*, M Declerck /* 0084115

Numbers/Type: 114 Lockheed SSB Viking/Shadow.
Operational speed: 450 kt *(834 km/h).*
Service ceiling: 35,000 ft *(10,670 m).*
Range: 2,000 n miles *(3,706 km).*
Role/Weapon systems: Standard ASW/ASV (VS) aircraft; works in concert with towed array escorts; first S-3B flew in 1987; conversion to B type at the rate of about 30 a year completed in 1994. Link 11/16 fitted. Sensors: APS-137(V)1 radar; APN-200 radar, FLIR, OR-263AA, MAD, ASQ-81(V)1, 60 sonobuoys; ARR-78 sonobuoy receiver with AYS 1 acoustic processor; ESM: ALR-76; ECM ALE 47; ALE 39 chaff. Weapons: ASW; four Mk 54 depth charges, four Mk 46/Mk 50 torpedoes. ASV; two Harpoon Block 1C; mines.

UPDATED

VIKING   *8/1998, Hachiro Nakai /* 0053346

Numbers/Type: 124 Grumman EA-6B Prowler.
Operational speed: 566 kt *(1,048 km/h)*.
Service ceiling: 41,200 ft *(12,550 m)*.
Range: 955 n miles *(1,769 km)*.
Role/Weapon systems: EW and jamming aircraft (VAQ) to accompany strikes and armed reconnaissance. First of 20 modified aircraft delivered in January 1999, remainder by mid-2000. Further update planned with first in service in 2004. Sensors: APS-130 or APS-145 radar; ALQ-99F, VSQ-113 jammers. ALR-73 ESM. Weapons: AGM-88 HARM anti-radiation missile capable.

UPDATED

PROWLER   *9/1998, Diego Quevedo* / 0053348

Numbers/Type: 75 Grumman E-2C Hawkeye.
Operational speed: 323 kt *(598 km/h)*.
Service ceiling: 37,000 ft *(11,278 m)*.
Range: 1,540 n miles *(2,852 km)*.
Role/Weapon systems: Used for direction of AD and strike operations; (VAW); 16 Group II upgrades from 1995-2000 included APS 145 radar and Link 16. Sensors: ESM: ALR-73 PDS; Airborne tactical data system with Links 4A, 11 or 16; CEC from 2000. APS-125/138/145 radar; Mk XII IFF. Weapons: Unarmed.

UPDATED

HAWKEYE   *9/1999*, M Kadota* / 0084116

Numbers/Type: 161/75/1 Sikorsky SH-60B/F/R Seahawk (LAMPS Mk III/CV).
Operational speed: 135 kt *(250 km/h)*.
Service ceiling: 10,000 ft *(3,050 m)*.
Range: 600 n miles *(1,110 km)*.
Role/Weapon systems: LAMPS Mk III (HSL) air vehicle for medium-range ASW and ASUW; SH-60B operated from 'DDH', 'FFGH' and 'CGH' class Surface Combatants. SH-60F (HS) is derived CV model which replaced the Sea King. 243 aircraft are being remanufactured to the Seahawk Block II upgrade (SH-60R) which includes Telephonics APS-147 radar, Hughes AQS-22 low frequency dipping sonar, UYS-2 acoustic processor, upgraded ESM and Integrated Self Defense (ISD). First five in service in 2001. Current sensors: SH-60B; APS-124 search radar, AAS-44 FLIR with laser designator, ASQ-81(V) MAD, 25 sonobuoys, ALQ-142 ESM, ALQ-144 IR suppressor and ALE-39 chaff and flare dispenser. SH-60F; AQS-13F dipping sonar. Weapons: ASW; three Mk 46 or Mk 50 torpedoes. ASUW; SH-60B/R only, one Penguin Mk 2 Mod 7 AGM-119B missile, one 7.62 mm MG M60 or 12.7 mm MG, AGM-114B/K Hellfire missile (87 SH-60B from 1998; all SH-60R).

UPDATED

SEAHAWK   *3/1997, Maritime Photographic* / 0016383

Numbers/Type: 12 Kaman SH-2G Seasprite (LAMPS Mk I).
Operational speed: 130 kt *(241 km/h)*.
Service ceiling: 22,500 ft *(6,860 m)*.
Range: 367 n miles *(697 km)*.
Role/Weapon systems: ASW and OTHT helicopter (HSL) flown in the Naval Reserve; acts as ASW information relay and attack platform for surface combatants. Sensors: LN66/HP radar, ALR-66 ESM, ALE-39 ECM, ASN-150 tactical nav, AQS-81(V)2 MAD, AAQ-16 FLIR AAR-47 IR detection; ARR-57/84 sonobuoy receivers, 15 sonobuoys, Magic Lantern laser mine detector. Weapons: ASW; two Mk 46/Mk 50 torpedoes, eight Mk 25 smoke markers. ASV; one 7.62 mm MG M60, one Penguin Mk 2 Mod 7.

UPDATED

SEASPRITE 2G (with Penguin ASM)   *1995, Kaman*

Numbers/Type: 39 Sikorsky HH-60H Seahawk.
Operational speed: 147 kt *(272 km/h)*.
Service ceiling: 10,000 ft *(3,050 m)*.
Range: 600 n miles *(1,110 km)*.
Role/Weapon systems: Strike, special warfare support and SAR derivative (HCS) of the SH-60F. Sensors: APR-39A radar, AVR-2 LWR and AA 47 MAW, FLIR, AAQ-16, ALE-47 chaff dispenser, ALQ-144 ECM. Weapons: ASV; Hellfire AGM-114; two 7.62 mm MGs.

UPDATED

SEAHAWK HH-60H   *4/1998, Maritime Photographic* / 0053350

Numbers/Type: 2 (4) Sikorsky CH-60S Knighthawk.
Operational speed: 135 kt *(250 km/h)*.
Service ceiling: 10,000 ft *(3,050 m)*.
Range: 600 n miles *(1,110 km)*.
Role/Weapon systems: Derived from the SH-60 as a combat support helicopter. More than 200 are required. First two delivered for operational testing in late 1999, four more in mid-2000. Fitted with the same external stores system as the Army Blackhawk.

NEW ENTRY

KNIGHTHAWK   *12/1999*, Sikorsky* / 0084117

Numbers/Type: 5/51 Sikorsky SH-3H/UH-3 Sea King.
Operational speed: 144 kt *(267 km/h)*.
Service ceiling: 12,200 ft *(3,720 m)*.
Range: 630 n miles *(1,166 km)*.
Role/Weapon systems: Used for liaison and SAR tasks having been replaced in CV service by SH-60F. Sensors: ALR 606B ESM.

UPDATED

SEA KING   *8/1998, Hachiro Nakai* / 0053351

Numbers/Type: 42/26/231/11 Boeing HH-46D/CH-46D/E/UH-46D Sea Knight.
Operational speed: 137 kt *(254 km/h).*
Service ceiling: 8,500 ft *(2,590 m).*
Range: 180 n miles *(338 km).*
Role/Weapon systems: Support/assault (HMM) for 18 Marines and resupply (USN) helicopter. To be replaced by AV-22 in due course. Can lift 1.3 or 4.5 tons in a cargo net or sling. Sensors: None. Weapons: Unarmed.

UPDATED

SEA KNIGHT
3/1999*, M Declerck / 0084118

Numbers/Type: 7 Bell Boeing MV-22 Osprey.
Operational speed: 270 kt *(500 km/h).*
Service ceiling: 25,000 ft *(7,620 m).*
Range: 1,200 n miles *(2,224 km)* (VTO).
Role/Weapon systems: Replacement for CH-46E/CH-53D for assault/support for Marines (MV) and special operations (HV). First four in FY97 budget. Total of 425 (MV) and 48 (HV) projected. Sensors: AAR-47 ESM; APQ-174C radar; AAQ-16 FLIR. APR 39A(V)2 ESM. Weapons: 12.7 mm MG or self-defence gun.

UPDATED

OSPREY
1993, Bell Helicopter / 0039397

Numbers/Type: 49 Sikorsky CH-53D Sea Stallion.
Operational speed: 130 kt *(241 km/h).*
Service ceiling: 21,000 ft *(6,400 m).*
Range: 540 n miles *(1,000 km).*
Role/Weapon systems: Assault, support and transport helicopters (MMH); can carry 38 Marines. Sensors: None. Weapons: Up to three 12.7 mm machine guns.

UPDATED

SEA STALLION
1994, Julio Montes / 0039396

Numbers/Type: 153 Sikorsky CH-53E Super Stallion.
Operational speed: 170 kt *(315 km/h).*
Service ceiling: 18,500 ft *(5,640 m).*
Range: 1,000 n miles *(1,850 km).*
Role/Weapon systems: Uprated, three-engined version of Sea Stallion (MMH) with support (USN) and transport (USMC) roles. Carries 55 Marines. Sensors: None. Weapons: Up to three 12.7 mm machine guns.

UPDATED

SUPER STALLION
5/1999*, A Sharma / 0084119

Numbers/Type: 43 Sikorsky MH-53E Sea Dragon.
Operational speed: 170 kt *(315 km/h).*
Service ceiling: 18,500 ft *(5,640 m).*
Range: 1,000 n miles *(1,850 km).*
Role/Weapon systems: Three-engined AMCM helicopter (HM) similar to Super Stallion; tows ALQ-166 (Mod 4 by 2001) MCM sweep equipment; self-deployed if necessary. Sensors: Northrop Grumman AQS-14A or AQS-20 (in due course) dipping sonar. Weapons: Two 12.7 mm guns for self-defence.

VERIFIED

SEA DRAGON
1995, Grumman

Numbers/Type: 197 Bell AH-1W Super Cobra.
Operational speed: 149 kt *(277 km/h).*
Service ceiling: 12,200 ft *(3,718 m).*
Range: 317 n miles *(587 km).*
Role/Weapon systems: Close support helicopter (HMA); uprated and improved version, with own air-to-air capability. Four-bladed rotor to be fitted from 2004, plus new engines giving speed of 158 kt. Sensors: NTS (laser and FLIR nightsight) retrofitted from 1993 at the rate of 24 aircraft per year. Weapons: Strike/assault; one triple 20 mm cannon, eight TOW or Hellfire missiles and gun. AAW; two AIM-9L Sidewinder missiles.

UPDATED

SUPER COBRA
2/1998, A Campanera i Rovira / 0053353

Numbers/Type: 101 Bell UH-1N Iroquois. Twin Huey.
Operational speed: 110 kt *(204 km/h).*
Service ceiling: 15,000 ft *(4,570 m).*
Range: 250 n miles *(463 km).*
Role/Weapon systems: Utility of C² and support and logistics helicopter (HMLA) for USMC operations afloat and ashore. Can carry 16 marines. Upgrade improves speed to 160 kt. Sensors: None. Weapons: Can be armed with 12.7 mm or 7.62 mm machine guns and 2.75 in rockets.

UPDATED

TWIN HUEY
5/1999*, A Sharma / 0084120

Numbers/Type: 45 Pioneer UAV.
Operational speed: 65 kt *(120 km/h).*
Service ceiling: 15,000 ft *(4,570 m).*
Range: 200 n miles *(370 km).*
Role/Weapon systems: Nine systems in service. Six are available for LPDs, two for Marine Shore units and one for Navy training. Sensors: Optronic surveillance with Link terminal.

UPDATED

Numbers/Type: 3 Northrop Grumman Firescout UAV.
Operational speed: 104 kt *(193 km/h)*.
Service ceiling: 18,000 ft *(5,486 m)*.
Range: 110 n miles *(205 km)*.
Role/Weapon systems: Selected in February 2000 as the next generation UAV. One system comprising three air vehicles, two control stations and three payloads including optronic sensors is scheduled for operational testing in late 2002. 12 systems are required by the Navy and 11 by the Marines. Endurance is more than six hours. All flight deck fitted ships could be capable in due course.

UPDATED

FIRESCOUT   *6/1999*, Northrop Grumman /* 0067526

LAND-BASED MARITIME AIRCRAFT (FRONT LINE)

Note: There are also 38/14 Lockheed KC-130F/R Hercules tankers.

Numbers/Type: 11 Lockheed EP-3E Orion.
Operational speed: 411 kt *(761 km/h)*.
Service ceiling: 28,300 ft *(8,625 m)*.
Range: 4,000 n miles *(7,410 km)*.
Role/Weapon systems: Electronic warfare and intelligence gathering aircraft (VQ). Sensors: EW equipment including AN/ALR-60, AN/ALQ-76, AN/ALQ-78, AN/ALQ-108 and AN/ASQ-114. Weapons: Unarmed.

UPDATED

Numbers/Type: 228 Lockheed P-3C Orion.
Operational speed: 411 kt *(761 km/h)*.
Service ceiling: 28,300 ft *(8,625 m)*.
Range: 4,000 n miles *(7,410 km)*.
Role/Weapon systems: 111 in active (49 in reserve) operational squadrons (VP) deployed worldwide; primary ASW/ASUW; ASUW update III conversions to 146 airframes by end 2000. Sensors: APS-115 search radar or APS-137(V)3 fitted in 18 aircraft, ASQ-81 MAD, UYS-1 acoustic suite, up to 100 sonobuoys, AAR-36 FLIR, cameras, ALR-66 ESM. AAR 47 ESM and ALE 47 chaff/IR dispenser in Update II. 18 Counter-Drug Upgrade (CDU) aircraft employ APG-66 air-to-air radar and AVX-1 Electro-Optics. Up to 68 ASUW Improvement Program (AIP) aircraft employ the APS-137B(V)5 ISAR/SAR radar, AVX-1 Electro-Optics, UYS-1 acoustics, OASIS III/OTCIXS communications suite, and SATCOM. Weapons: ASW; four Mk 46/50 torpedoes or depth bombs. ASUW; four AGM-84C Harpoon, AGM-65F Maverick, AGM-84E SLAM, six Mk 55/56 mines.

UPDATED

ORION   *1/1998, A Sharma /* 0016388

Numbers/Type: 8/8 Boeing E-6A/6B Mercury/TACAMO/ABNCP.
Operational speed: 455 kt *(842 km/h)*.
Service ceiling: 42,000 ft *(12,800 m)*.
Range: 6,350 n miles *(11,760 km/h)*.
Role/Weapon systems: First flew in February 1987 (VQ). Strategic Command Airborne Command Post (ABNCP). EMP hardened against nuclear bursts. Eight converted to B standard by 2000 and carry an airborne battle staff. Remainder to be converted to 6B in due course. Sensors: Radar Bendix APS-133; ALR-68(V)4 ESM; supports Trident Fleet radio communications with up to 28,000 ft of VLF trailing wire antenna. Weapons: Unarmed.

UPDATED

TACAMO   *1997, Chrysler Technologies /* 0016389

COMMAND SHIPS

2 BLUE RIDGE CLASS: COMMAND SHIPS (LCC)

Name	No	Builders	Laid down		Launched		Commissioned		F/S
BLUE RIDGE	LCC 19	Philadelphia Naval Shipyard	27 Feb	1967	4 Jan	1969	14 Nov	1970	PA
MOUNT WHITNEY	LCC 20	Newport News Shipbuilding	8 Jan	1969	8 Jan	1970	16 Jan	1971	AA

Displacement, tons: 16,790 light; 18,372 full load *(Blue Ridge)* 16,100 light; 18,646 full load *(Mount Whitney)*
Dimensions, feet (metres): 636.5 × 107.9 × 28.9 *(194 × 32.9 × 8.8)*
Main machinery: 2 Foster-Wheeler boilers; 600 psi *(42.3 kg/cm²)*; 870°F *(467°C)*; 1 GE turbine; 22,000 hp *(16.4 MW)*; 1 shaft
Speed, knots: 23. **Range, miles:** 13,000 at 16 kt
Complement: 821 (43 officers); Flag 253 (127 officers).
Military lift: 700 troops; 3 LCPs; 2 LCVPs

Guns: 2 General Electric/General Dynamics 20 mm/76 6-barrelled Vulcan Phalanx Mk 15; 3,000 rds/min (4,500 in Block 1) combined to 1.5 km.
Countermeasures: Decoys: 4 Loral Hycor SRBOC 6-barrelled fixed Mk 36; IR flares and chaff to 4 km *(2.2 n miles)*. SLQ-25 Nixie; torpedo decoy.
ESM/ECM: SLQ-32(V)3; combined radar intercept, jammer and deception system.

BLUE RIDGE   *6/1999* /* 0084122

Combat data systems: GCCS (M) Link 4A, Link 11 and Link 14. Contingency Theater Air Control System Automated Planning System (CTAPS). Wide band commercial SATCOM, USC-38 SATCOM, WSC-3 EHF SATCOM, WSC-6(V)1 and 5, and WSC-6A(V)4 SHF SATCOM. High Frequency Radio Group (HFRG). Mission Display System (MDS). Demand Assigned Multiple Access (DAMA QUAD). (See Data Systems at front of section.)
Radars: Air search: ITT SPS-48C; 3D; E/F-band.
Lockheed SPS-40E; E/F-band.
Surface search: Raytheon SPS-65(V)1; G-band.
Navigation: Marconi LN66; Raytheon SPS-64(V)9; I-band.
Tacan: URN 25. IFF: Mk XII AIMS UPX-29.

Helicopters: 1 Sikorsky SH-3H Sea King.

Programmes: Authorised in FY65 and 1966. Originally designated Amphibious Force Flagships (AGC); redesignated Command Ships (LCC) on 1 January 1969.
Modernisation: Modernisation completed FY87. 3 in guns removed in 1996/97 and Sea Sparrow missile launchers have been disembarked. Mk 23 TAS and RAM are not now to be fitted.
Structure: General hull design and machinery arrangement are similar to the 'Iwo Jima' class assault ships. Accommodation for 250 officers and 1,300 enlisted men.
Operational: These are large force command ships of post-Second World War design. They can provide integrated command and control facilities for sea, air and land commanders in all types of operations. *Blue Ridge* is the Seventh Fleet flagship, based at Yokosuka, Japan. *Mount Whitney* has served since January 1981 as flagship Second Fleet, based at Norfolk, Virginia.

UPDATED

MOUNT WHITNEY   *8/1999*, Camil Busquets i Vilanova /* 0084121

1 CONVERTED AUSTIN CLASS: COMMAND SHIP (AGF)

Name	No	Builders	Laid down	Launched	Commissioned	F/S
CORONADO	AGF 11 (ex-LPD 11)	Lockheed SB & Construction Co	3 May 1965	30 July 1966	23 May 1970	PA

Displacement, tons: 11,482 light; 16,912 full load
Dimensions, feet (metres): 570 × 100 × 23
(173.8 × 30.5 × 7)
Main machinery: 2 Foster-Wheeler boilers; 600 psi *(42.2 kg/cm²)*; 870°F *(467°C)*; 2 De Laval turbines; 24,000 hp *(17.9 MW)*; 2 shafts .
Speed, knots: 21. **Range, miles:** 7,700 at 20 kt
Complement: 485 (25 officers) plus 181 Flag Staff
Guns: 2 General Electric/General Dynamics 20 mm Vulcan Phalanx Mk 15. 2—12.7 mm MGs.
Countermeasures: Decoys: 4 Loral Hycor SRBOC 6-barrelled Mk 36; IR flares and chaff.
ESM: SLQ-32V(2); WLR-1; intercept.
Combat data systems: GCCS (M) Link 11 and Link 16 (receive only). Contingency Theater Air Control System Automated

Planning System (CTAPS). Land Attack Warfare System (LAWS). Wide band commercial SATCOM, USC-38 SATCOM, WSC-3 EHF SATCOM, WSC-6 SHF SATCOM. High Frequency Radio Group (HFRG). Single Channel Ground Air Radio System. (See Data Systems at front of section.)
Radars: Air search: Lockheed SPS-40E; E/F-band; range 320 km *(175 n miles)*.
Surface search: Raytheon SPS-10F; G-band.
Navigation: Raytheon SPS-64(V)9; I-band.
Tacan: URN 25.
Helicopters: 2 Light.

Comment: A former LPD of the 'Austin' class. Authorised in FY64. Converted in late 1980 as a temporary replacement for *La Salle* (AGF 3), as flagship, Middle East Force, so *La Salle*

could be overhauled. When *Coronado* was relieved by *La Salle* in early 1983, it was planned for her to be reconverted back to an LPD. Due to the shortage of fleet flagships, however, she continued in the flagship role. When relieved by *Belknap* as Sixth Fleet flagship in July 1986, she deployed to the Pacific to become the flagship of the Third Fleet then in Hawaii. She is now based at San Diego. 3 in guns removed. Completed further 18 month conversion in mid-1997 to serve as Joint Force Command Ship. The well deck has been converted to offices, with a three deck command facility and additional accommodation for up to four Flag Officers with a combined staff of 259. The stern gate has gone.

UPDATED

CORONADO

8/1998, J G McCarter, US Navy / 0084123

1 CONVERTED RALEIGH CLASS: COMMAND SHIP (AGF)

Name	No	Builders	Laid down	Launched	Commissioned	F/S
LA SALLE	AGF 3 (ex-LPD 3)	New York Naval Shipyard	2 Apr 1962	3 Aug 1963	22 Feb 1964	AA

Displacement, tons: 9,670 light; 14,650 full load
Dimensions, feet (metres): 519.7 × 84 × 21
(158.4 × 25.6 × 6.4)
Main machinery: 2 Babcock & Wilcox boilers; 600 psi *(42.2 kg/cm²)*; 870°F *(467°C)*; 2 De Laval turbines; 24,000 hp *(17.9 MW)*; 2 shafts
Speed, knots: 20. **Range, miles:** 9,600 at 16 kt
Complement: 440 (25 officers) plus 59 Flag Staff (12 officers)
Guns: 2 General Electric/General Dynamics 20 mm Vulcan Phalanx Mk 15.
2 Bushmaster 25 mm Mk 38. 2—40 mm saluting guns. 2—12.7 mm MGs.
Countermeasures: Decoys: 4 Loral Hycor SRBOC Mk 36; chaff and IR flares.
ESM: SLQ-32(V)3; WLR-1; intercept and jammer.
Combat data systems: GCCS (M) Link 11 and Link 14 (receive only). Contingency Theater Air Control System Automated Planning System (CTAPS). Wide band commercial SATCOM, USC-38 SATCOM, WSC-3 EHF SATCOM, WSC-6 SHF SATCOM, Mission Display System (MDS). Demand Assigned Multiple Access (DAMA HEXA). (See Data Systems at front of section.)
Radars: Air search: Lockheed SPS-40; E/F-band.
Surface search: Raytheon SPS-10F; G-band.
Navigation: Raytheon SPS-64(V)9; I-band.
Tacan: URN 25.
Helicopters: 1 light.

Comment: A former amphibious transport dock (LPD) of the 'Raleigh' class. Authorised in FY61. She served as an amphibious ship until converted in 1972 at Philadelphia Navy

LA SALLE

5/1999, van Ginderen Collection / 0084124

Yard. Flag command and communications facilities installed; additional air conditioning fitted. Helicopter hangar installed on the port side of the flight deck. Deck landing spots for heavy helicopters. Reclassified as a flagship and designated AGF 3 on 1 July 1972 keeping previous '3' hull number. Has served as flagship for the US Commander, Middle East Force, operating

in the Persian Gulf, Arabian Sea and Indian Ocean. Refitted again in 1993-94 and again at Toulon from June to December 1999. Took over as Sixth Fleet Flagship in November 1994 at Gaeta in Italy.

UPDATED

AMPHIBIOUS FORCES

Notes: (1) Additional capacity is provided by the maritime pre-positioning ships (see listing under *Military Sealift Command* (MSC) section) which are either new construction or conversions of commercial ships. One squadron is maintained on station in the Atlantic, a second at Guam, and a third at Diego Garcia. Each carries equipment to support a Marine Expeditionary Force.

Since 1992 there has been a constant presence in the Adriatic in indirect support of UN operations in Bosnia, and more recently in Kosovo.
(2) **Minesweeping:** Several of the larger amphibious ships have been used as operating bases for minesweeping helicopters. *Inchon* has been converted to become a dedicated support ship.

(3) Five decommissioned LKAs and four LSTs are kept in an inactive reduced maintenance status (ROS). These are *Fresno* (LST 1182), *Tuscaloosa* (LST 1187), *Boulder* (LST 1190), *Racine* (LST 1191), *Charleston* (LKA 113), *Durham* (LKA 114), *Mobile* (LKA 115), *St Louis* (LKA 116) and *El Paso* (LKA 117).

0 + 4 (8) SAN ANTONIO CLASS: AMPHIBIOUS TRANSPORT DOCKS (LPD)

Name	No	Builders	Laid down		Launched		Commissioned		F/S
SAN ANTONIO	LPD 17	Avondale	Dec	2000	Mar	2002	Sep	2003	Bldg
NEW ORLEANS	LPD 18	Avondale	July	2001	Oct	2002	May	2004	Bldg
—	LPD 19	Bath Iron Works	Sep	2001	Apr	2003	Aug	2004	Ord
—	LPD 20	Avondale	Mar	2002	May	2003	Dec	2004	Ord

Displacement, tons: 25,300 full load
Dimensions, feet (metres): 683.7 × 104.7 × 23 *(208.4 × 31.9 × 7)*
Main machinery: 4 Colt Pielstick PC 2.5 diesels; 40,000 hp *(29.84 MW)*; 2 shafts; cp props
Speed, knots: 22
Complement: 362 (25 officers) plus 34 spare
Military lift: 720 troops; 2 LCACs, 15 AAAVs

Missiles: SAM: Mk 41 VLS for 2 octuple cell Evolved Sea Sparrow ❶. 64 missiles. May be fitted later. 2 Mk 31 Mod 1 RAM launchers ❷.
Guns: 2—30 mm Mk 46. 4—12.7 mm MGs.
Countermeasures: Decoys: 6 Mk 53 Mod 4 Nulka and chaff launcher ❸. SLQ-25A Nixie towed torpedo decoy.
ESM/ECM: SLQ-32A(V)2 ❹; intercept and jammer.
Combat data systems: SSDS Mk 2; GCCS (M), CEC, JTIDS (Link 16), AADS (see Data Systems at front of section).
Weapons control: 2 Mk 95 NSSMs optronic directors ❺.
Radars: Air search: ITT SPS-48E ❻; C/D-band.
Surface search: Raytheon SPS 67(V)3 ❼; G-band.
Fire control: Lockheed SPQ-9B ❽; I-band.
Navigation: Raytheon SPS 64(V)9; I-band.

Helicopters: 2 CH-53E Sea Stallion or 4 CH-46E Sea Knight or 2 MV-22 Osprey or 4 UH-1.

Programmes: The LPD 17 (ex-LX) programme was first approved by the Defense Acquisition Board on 11 January 1993. It is expected to replace four classes of amphibious ships: LPD 4s, LSTs, LKAs and LSD 36s. Contract for first ship, with an option on two more, awarded to Avondale on 17 December 1996. A protest about the award delayed the effective contract date to April 1997. Second ship authorised in FY99 budget and two more in FY2000. Total of 12 ships to be in service by 2009, four to be built by Bath and eight by Avondale.
Structure: LPD 17 is a Panama Canal-capable ship able to control and support landing forces disembarking either via surface craft such as LCACs or by VTOL aircraft, principally helicopters. The ship design supports a lift capability of 25,000 sq ft of deck space for vehicles, 36,000 cu ft of cargo below decks,

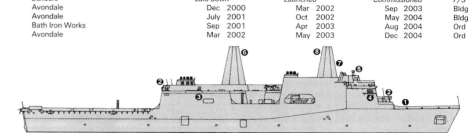

SAN ANTONIO *(Scale 1 : 1,800), Ian Sturton / 0084135*

SAN ANTONIO (computer graphic) *1998*, Raytheon / 0016653*

720 embarked Marines, two LCACs, and two CH-53 helicopters, with a hangar able to support one CH-53. It will not have the flag configuration of LPDs or the heavy over-the-side lift capability of LKAs. Well-deck and stern gate arrangements similar to 'Wasp' class. 24 bed hospital. The three vehicle decks have a capacity of 2,360 m³. There is a crane on board for support of boat operations. The ship lacks the capability to

offload over a beach. Otherwise, it has most of the capabilities of the four classes of ships it is replacing. Numbers of helicopters listed are those for which there is hangar space. Flight deck spots double the number. Advanced Enclosed Mast System being fitted in all. Space and weight reserved for Mk 41 VLS.

UPDATED

3 ANCHORAGE CLASS: DOCK LANDING SHIPS (LSD)

Name	No	Builders	Laid down		Launched		Commissioned		F/S
ANCHORAGE	LSD 36	Ingalls Shipbuilding	13 Mar	1967	5 May	1968	15 Mar	1969	PA
PORTLAND	LSD 37	General Dynamics, Quincy	21 Sep	1967	20 Dec	1969	3 Oct	1970	AA
MOUNT VERNON	LSD 39	General Dynamics, Quincy	29 Jan	1970	17 Apr	1971	13 May	1972	PA

Displacement, tons: 8,600 light; 13,700 full load
Dimensions, feet (metres): 553.3 × 84 × 20 *(168.6 × 25.6 × 6)*
Main machinery: 2 Foster-Wheeler boilers (Combustion Engineering in LSD 36); 600 psi *(42.3 kg/cm²)*; 870°F *(467°C)*; 2 De Laval turbines; 24,000 hp *(18 MW)*; 2 shafts
Speed, knots: 22. **Range, miles:** 14,800 at 12 kt
Complement: 374 (24 officers)

Military lift: 366 troops (18 officers); 3 LCUs or 3 LCACs or 18 LCM 6 or 9 LCM 8 or 50 LVTs; 1 LCM 6 on deck; 2 LCPLs and 1 LCVP on davits. Aviation fuel, 90 tons

Guns: 2 General Electric/General Dynamics 20 mm/76 6-barrelled Vulcan Phalanx Mk 15 ❶; 3,000 rds/min combined to 1.5 km.
2 Bushmaster 25 mm Mk 38. 6—12.7 mm MGs.

Countermeasures: Decoys: 4 Loral Hycor SRBOC 6-barrelled Mk 36; IR flares and chaff to 4 km *(2.2 n miles)*.
ESM: SLQ-32(V)1; intercept. May be updated to (V)2.
Combat data systems: SATCOM SRR-1, WSC-3 (UHF).
Radars: Air search: Lockheed SPS-40B ❷; E/F-band.
Surface search: Raytheon SPS-10F ❸; G-band.
Navigation: Raytheon SPS-64(V)9; I-band.

Helicopters: Platform only.

Structure: Helicopter platform aft with docking well partially open; helicopter platform can be removed. Docking well approximately 430 × 50 ft *(131.1 × 15.2 m)*. Two 50 ton capacity cranes. 3 in guns have been removed.
Operational: One of the class paid off in February 1998 and one in mid-1999.
Sales: One to Taiwan in 2000, possibly a second to follow.

UPDATED

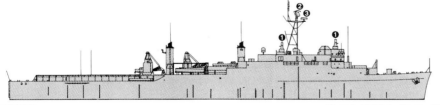

ANCHORAGE *(Scale 1 : 1,500), Ian Sturton / 0016477*

MOUNT VERNON *8/1998, van Ginderen Collection / 0053366*

6 + 2 WASP CLASS: AMPHIBIOUS ASSAULT SHIPS (LHD)

Name	No	Builders	Laid down		Launched		Commissioned		F/S
WASP	LHD 1	Ingalls Shipbuilding	30 May	1985	4 Aug	1987	29 July	1989	AA
ESSEX	LHD 2	Ingalls Shipbuilding	20 Mar	1989	4 Jan	1991	17 Oct	1992	PA
KEARSARGE	LHD 3	Ingalls Shipbuilding	6 Feb	1990	26 Mar	1992	16 Oct	1993	AA
BOXER	LHD 4	Ingalls Shipbuilding	8 Apr	1991	13 Aug	1993	11 Feb	1995	PA
BATAAN	LHD 5	Ingalls Shipbuilding	22 June	1994	15 Mar	1996	20 Sep	1997	AA
BONHOMME RICHARD	LHD 6	Ingalls Shipbuilding	18 Apr	1995	14 Mar	1997	15 Aug	1998	PA
IWO JIMA	LHD 7	Ingalls Shipbuilding	12 Dec	1997	4 Feb	2000	July	2001	Bldg
—	LHD 8	Ingalls Shipbuilding	June	2001	Apr	2003	Jan	2005	Proj

Displacement, tons: 28,233 light; 40,532 full load
Dimensions, feet (metres): 844 oa; 788 wl × 140.1 oa; 106 wl × 26.6 *(257.3; 240.2 × 42.7; 32.3 × 8.1)*
Flight deck, feet (metres): 819 × 106 *(249.6 × 32.3)*
Main machinery: 2 Combustion Engineering boilers; 600 psi *(42.3 kg/cm²)*; 900°F *(482°C)*; 2 Westinghouse turbines; 70,000 hp *(52.2 MW)*; 2 shafts
Speed, knots: 22. **Range, miles:** 9,500 at 18 kt
Complement: 1,077 (98 officers)
Military lift: 1,870 troops; 12 LCM 6s or 3 LCACs; 1,232 tons aviation fuel; 4 LCPL

Missiles: SAM: 2 Raytheon GMLS Mk 29 octuple launchers ❶; 16 Sea Sparrow; semi-active radar homing to 14.6 km *(8 n miles)* at 2.5 Mach; warhead 39 kg. ESSM in due course.
2 GDC Mk 49 RAM; 21 rounds per launcher ❷; passive IR/anti-radiation homing to 9.6 km *(5.2 n miles)* at 2 Mach; warhead 9.1 kg.
Guns: 2 or 3 General Electric/General Dynamics 20 mm 6-barrelled Vulcan Phalanx Mk 15 ❸; 3,000 rds/min (4,500 in Batch 1) combined to 1.5 km.
3 Boeing Bushmaster 25 mm Mk 38. 4 or 8—12.7 mm MGs.
Countermeasures: Decoys: 4 or 6 Loral Hycor SRBOC 6-barrelled fixed Mk 36; IR flares and chaff to 4 km *(2.2 n miles)*.
SLQ-25 Nixie; acoustic torpedo decoy system. NATO Sea Gnat. SLQ-49 chaff buoys. AEB SSQ-95.
ESM/ECM: SLQ-32(V)3/SLY-2; intercept and jammers. Raytheon ULQ-20.
Combat data systems: ACDS Block 1 level 2 (LHD 1) and Block 0 (in remainder). Integrated Tactical Amphibious Warfare Data System (ITAWDS) and Marine Tactical Amphibious C² System (MTACCS). Links 4A, 11 (modified), 14 and 16. SATCOMS ❹ SSR-1, WSC-3 (UHF), USC-38 (EHF). SMQ-11 Metsat (see Data Systems at front of section). Advanced Field Artillery TDS (LHD 6 and 7).
Weapons control: 2 Mk 91 MFCS. SYS-2(V)3 IADT.
Radars: Air search: ITT SPS-48E ❺; 3D; E/F-band.
Raytheon SPS-49(V)9 ❻; C/D-band.
Hughes Mk 23 TAS ❼; D-band.
Surface search: Norden SPS-67 ❽; G-band.
Navigation: SPS-64(V)9; I-band.
CCA: SPN-35A and SPN-43B. SPN-46 in due course.
Fire control: 2 Mk 95; I/J-band. SPQ-9B to be fitted.
Tacan: URN 25. IFF: CIS Mk XV UPX-29.

Fixed-wing aircraft: 6-8 AV-8B Harriers or up to 20 in secondary role. V22 Osprey in due course.
Helicopters: Capacity for 42 CH-46E Sea Knight but has the capability to support: AH-1W Super Cobra, CH-53E Super Stallion, CH-53D Sea Stallion, UH-1N Twin Huey, AH-1T Sea Cobra, and SH-60B Seahawk helicopters. UAV in due course.

BONHOMME RICHARD   *9/1999*, M Prendergast* / 0084126

Programmes: Eighth of class being funded incrementally by Senate intervention and approved in FY2000 budget. No further funding planned by Navy until 2005.
Modernisation: RAM launchers retrofitted in all vice the forward Phalanx (which may be moved to the bridge roof) and at the stern. LHD 5 and 6 have the SPS 52 radar mounted on the cross trees at the head of the foremast and RAM fitted on build. UAVs are a priority.
Structure: Two aircraft elevators, one to starboard and aft of the 'island' and one to port amidships; both fold for Panama canal transits. The well-deck is 267 × 50 ft and can accommodate up to three LCACs. The flight deck has nine helicopter landing spots. Cargo capacity is 101,000 cu ft total with an additional 20,000 sq ft to accommodate vehicles. Vehicle storage is

available for five M1 tanks, 25 LAVs, eight M 198 guns, 68 trucks, 10 logistic vehicles and several service vehicles. The bridge is two decks lower than that of an LHA, command, control and communication spaces having been moved inside the hull to avoid 'cheap kill' damage. Fitted with a 60 bed capacity hospital and four operating rooms. HY-100 steel covers the flight deck. Three 32 ft monorail trains each carrying 6,000 lbs, deliver material to the well-deck at 6.8 mph.
Operational: A typical complement of aircraft is a mix of 30 helicopters and six to eight Harriers (AV-8B). In the secondary role as a sea control ship the most likely mix is 20 AV-8B Harriers and four to six SH-60B Seahawk helicopters.

UPDATED

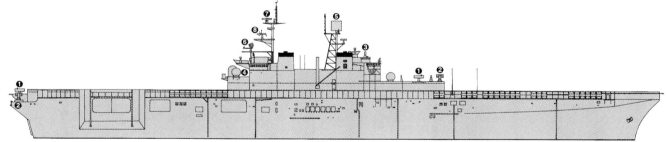

BONHOMME RICHARD   *(Scale 1 : 1,500), Ian Sturton* / 0084128

BATAAN   *2/1999*, M Declerck* / 0084127

ESSEX

10/1999 *, Findler & Winter / 0084129

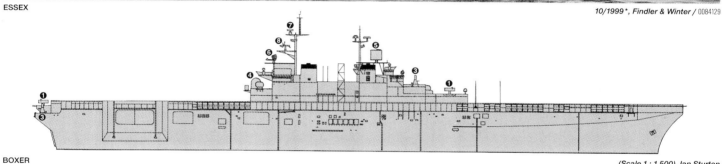

BOXER

(Scale 1 : 1,500), Ian Sturton

BONNEHOMME RICHARD

6/1998, Ingalls / 0053359

5 TARAWA CLASS: AMPHIBIOUS ASSAULT SHIPS (LHA)

Name	No	Builders	Laid down	Launched	Commissioned	F/S
TARAWA	LHA 1	Ingalls Shipbuilding	15 Nov 1971	1 Dec 1973	29 May 1976	PA
SAIPAN	LHA 2	Ingalls Shipbuilding	21 July 1972	18 July 1974	15 Oct 1977	AA
BELLEAU WOOD	LHA 3	Ingalls Shipbuilding	5 Mar 1973	11 Apr 1977	23 Sep 1978	PA
NASSAU	LHA 4	Ingalls Shipbuilding	13 Aug 1973	21 Jan 1978	28 July 1979	AA
PELELIU (ex-Da Nang)	LHA 5	Ingalls Shipbuilding	12 Nov 1976	25 Nov 1978	3 May 1980	PA

Displacement, tons: 39,967 full load
Dimensions, feet (metres): 834 × 131.9 × 25.9
(254.2 × 40.2 × 7.9)
Flight deck, feet (metres): 820 × 118.1 *(250 × 36)*
Main machinery: 2 Combustion Engineering boilers; 600 psi
(42.3 kg/cm²); 900°F *(482°C)*; 2 Westinghouse turbines;
70,000 hp *(52.2 MW)*; 2 shafts; bow thruster; 900 hp
(670 kW)
Speed, knots: 24. **Range, miles:** 10,000 at 20 kt
Complement: 930 (56 officers)
Military lift: 1,703 troops; 4 LCU 1610 type or 2 LCU and 2 LCM
8 or 17 LCM 6 or 45 LVT tractors; 1,200 tons aviation fuel.
1 LCAC may be embarked. 4 LCPL

Missiles: SAM: 2 GDC Mk 49 RAM ❶; 21 rounds per launcher;
passive IR/anti-radiation homing to 9.6 km *(5.2 n miles)* at
2 Mach; warhead 9.1 kg.
Guns: 2 General Electric/General Dynamics 20 mm/76
6-barrelled Vulcan Phalanx Mk 15 ❷; 3,000 rds/min (4,500 in
Block 1) combined to 1.5 km.
6 Mk 242 25 mm automatic cannons. 8—12.7 mm MGs.
Countermeasures: Decoys: 4 Loral Hycor SRBOC 6-barrelled
fixed Mk 36; IR flares and chaff to 4 km *(2.2 n miles)*.
SLQ-25 Nixie; acoustic torpedo decoy system. NATO Sea Gnat.
SLQ-49 chaff buoys. AEB SSQ-95.
ESM/ECM: SLQ-32V(3); intercept and jammers.

Combat data systems: ACDS Block 0. Integrated Tactical
Amphibious Warfare Data System (ITAWDS) to provide
computerised support in control of helicopters and aircraft,
shipboard weapons and sensors, navigation, landing craft
control and electronic warfare. Links 4A, 11, 14 and 16 in due
course. SATCOM SRR-1, WSC-3 (UHF), USC-38 (EHF) (LHA 2
and 4). SMQ-11 Metsat (see Data Systems at front of section).
Weapons control: Mk 86 Mod 4 GFCS. 2 optronic directors.
Radars: Air search: ITT SPS-48E ❸; E/F-band.
 Lockheed SPS-40E ❹; E/F-band.
 Hughes Mk 23 TAS ❺; D-band.
Surface search: Raytheon SPS-67(V)3 ❻; G-band.
Navigation: Raytheon SPS-64(V)9; I-band.
CCA: SPN-35A; SPN-43B.
Fire control: Lockheed SPG-60 ❼; I/J-band.
 Lockheed SPQ-9A ❽; I/J-band.
Tacan: URN 25. IFF: CIS Mk XV/UPX-36.

Fixed-wing aircraft: Harrier AV-8B VSTOL aircraft in place of
some helicopters as required. V22 Osprey in due course.
Helicopters: 19 CH-53D Sea Stallion or 26 CH-46D/E Sea
Knight. UAV in due course.

Programmes: Originally intended to be a class of nine ships.
LHA 1 was authorised in FY69, LHA 2 and LHA 3 in FY70 and
LHA 4 and LHA 5 in FY71.
Modernisation: Two Vulcan Phalanx CIWS replaced the GMLS
Mk 25 Sea Sparrow launchers. Programme completed in early
1991. RAM launchers fitted to all of the class 1993-95. One
launcher is above the bridge offset to port, and the other on the
starboard side at the after end of the flight deck. Mk 23 TAS
target acquisition radar fitted in LHA 3 and 5 in 1992, LHA 4 in
1993 and the last pair in 1994. SPS-48E started replacing
SPS-52D in 1994 to improve low altitude detection of missiles
and aircraft. ACDS Block 0 in 1996. 5 in guns removed in
1997/98. Plans to fit SSDS have been shelved.
Structure: There are two lifts, one on the port side aft and one at
the stern. Beneath the after elevator is a floodable docking well
measuring 268 ft in length and 78 ft in width which is capable
of accommodating four LCU 1610 type landing craft. Also
included is a large garage for trucks and AFVs and troop
berthing for a reinforced battalion. 33,730 sq ft available for
vehicles and 116,900 cu ft for palletted stores. Extensive
medical facilities including operating rooms, X-ray room,
hospital ward, isolation ward, laboratories, pharmacy, dental
operating room and medical store rooms.
Operational: The flight deck can operate a maximum of nine
CH-53D Sea Stallion or 12 CH-46D/E Sea Knight helicopters or
a mix of these and other helicopters at any one time. With
some additional modifications, ships of this class can
effectively operate AV-8B aircraft. The normal mix of aircraft
allows for six AV-8Bs. The optimum aircraft configuration
is dependent upon assigned missions. Unmanned
Reconnaissance Vehicles (URVs) can be operated. *Belleau
Wood* is based at Sasebo, Japan. Topweight problems as a
result of modernisation programmes may lead to an earlier
than planned replacement of these ships.

UPDATED

NASSAU   1/1999 *, Camil Busquets i Vilanova / 0084130

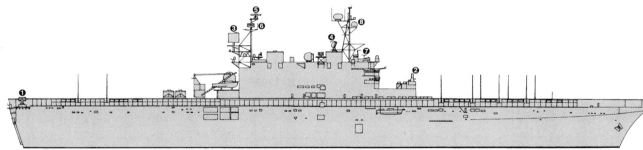

TARAWA   (Scale 1 : 1,500), Ian Sturton / 0016467

BELLEAU WOOD   2/1999 *, Maritime Photographic / 0084131

11 AUSTIN CLASS: AMPHIBIOUS TRANSPORT DOCKS (LPD)

Name	No	Builders	Laid down	Launched	Commissioned	F/S
AUSTIN	LPD 4	New York Naval Shipyard	4 Feb 1963	27 June 1964	6 Feb 1965	AA
OGDEN	LPD 5	New York Naval Shipyard	4 Feb 1963	27 June 1964	19 June 1965	PA
DULUTH	LPD 6	New York Naval Shipyard	18 Dec 1963	14 Aug 1965	18 Dec 1965	PA
CLEVELAND	LPD 7	Ingalls Shipbuilding	30 Nov 1964	7 May 1966	21 Apr 1967	PA
DUBUQUE	LPD 8	Ingalls Shipbuilding	25 Jan 1965	6 Aug 1966	1 Sep 1967	PA
DENVER	LPD 9	Lockheed SB & Construction Co	7 Feb 1964	23 Jan 1965	26 Oct 1968	PA
JUNEAU	LPD 10	Lockheed SB & Construction Co	23 Jan 1965	12 Feb 1966	12 July 1969	PA
SHREVEPORT	LPD 12	Lockheed SB & Construction Co	27 Dec 1965	25 Oct 1966	12 Dec 1970	AA
NASHVILLE	LPD 13	Lockheed SB & Construction Co	14 Mar 1966	7 Oct 1967	14 Feb 1970	AA
TRENTON	LPD 14	Lockheed SB & Construction Co	8 Aug 1966	3 Aug 1968	6 Mar 1971	AA
PONCE	LPD 15	Lockheed SB & Construction Co	31 Oct 1966	20 May 1970	10 July 1971	AA

Displacement, tons: 9,130 light; 16,500-17,244 full load
Dimensions, feet (metres): 570 × 100 (84 hull) × 23
(173.8 × 30.5 (25.6) × 7)
Main machinery: 2 Foster-Wheeler boilers (Babcock & Wilcox in LPD 5 and 12); 600 psi *(42.3 kg/cm²)*; 870°F *(467°C)*; 2 De Laval turbines; 24,000 hp *(18 MW)*; 2 shafts
Speed, knots: 21. **Range, miles:** 7,700 at 20 kt.
Complement: 420 (24 officers); Flag 90 (in LPD 7-13)
Military lift: 930 troops (840 only in LPD 7-13); 9 LCM 6s or 4 LCM 8s or 2 LCAC or 20 LVTs. 4 LCPL/LCVP

Guns: 2 General Electric/General Dynamics 20 mm/76 6-barrelled Vulcan Phalanx Mk 15 ❶; 3,000 rds/min (4,500 in Block 1) combined to 1.5 km.
2—25 mm Mk 38. 8—12.7 mm MGs.
Countermeasures: Decoys: 4 Loral Hycor SRBOC 6-barrelled Mk 36; IR flares and chaff to 4 km *(2.2 n miles)*.
ESM: SLQ-32(V)1; intercept. May be updated to (V)2.
Combat data systems: SATCOM ❷, WSC-3 (UHF) (see Data Systems at front of section).
Radars: Air search: Lockheed SPS-40B/C ❸; E/F-band.
Surface search: Norden SPS-67 ❹; G-band.
Navigation: Raytheon SPS-64(V)9; I-band.
Tacan: URN 25. IFF: Mk XII UPX-29.

Helicopters: Up to 6 CH-46D/E Sea Knight can be carried. Hangar for only 1 light (not in LPD 4).

Programmes: LPD 4-6 were authorised in the FY62 new construction programme, LPD 7-10 in FY63, LPD 12 and 13 in FY64, LPD 14 and LPD 15 in FY65.
Modernisation: Modernisation carried out in normal maintenance periods from FY87. This included fitting two Phalanx, SPS-67 radar replacing SPS-10 and updating EW capability. 3 in guns have been removed.
Structure: LPD 7-13 have an additional bridge and are fitted as flagships. One small telescopic hangar. There are structural variations in the positions of guns and electronic equipment in different ships of the class. Flight deck is 168 ft *(51.2 m)* in length. Well-deck 394 × 50 ft *(120.1 × 15.2 m)*. Communications domes are not uniformly fitted.
Operational: A typical operational load might include one Seahawk, two Sea Knight, two Twin Huey, four Sea Cobra helicopters and one Cyclone patrol craft. Pioneer UAV carried in six ships (LPDs 4, 7, 9, 10, 12 and 15). *Juneau* is based in Japan.

UPDATED

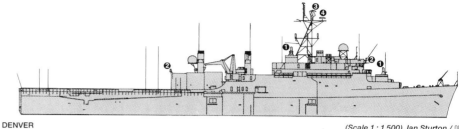

DENVER   *(Scale 1 : 1,500), Ian Sturton / 0016471*

PONCE   *4/1999*, Jürg Kürsener / 0084125*

TRENTON   *6/1998, C D Yaylali / 0053357*

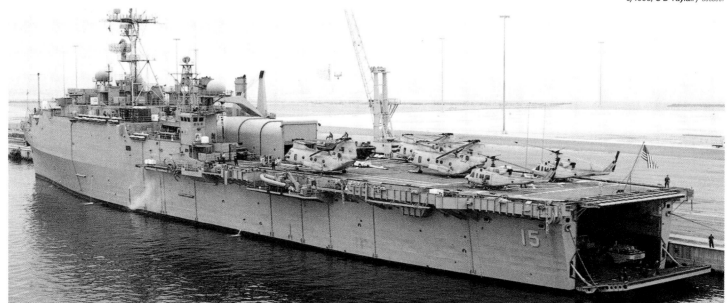

PONCE   *5/1999*, A Sharma / 0085300*

8 WHIDBEY ISLAND and 4 HARPERS FERRY CLASSES: DOCK LANDING SHIPS (LSD and LSD-CV)

Name	No	Builders	Laid down		Launched		Commissioned		F/S
WHIDBEY ISLAND	LSD 41	Lockheed SB & Construction Co	4 Aug	1981	10 June	1983	9 Feb	1985	AA
GERMANTOWN	LSD 42	Lockheed SB & Construction Co	5 Aug	1982	29 June	1984	8 Feb	1986	PA
FORT McHENRY	LSD 43	Lockheed SB & Construction Co	10 June	1983	1 Feb	1986	8 Aug	1987	PA
GUNSTON HALL	LSD 44	Avondale Industries	26 May	1986	27 June	1987	22 Apr	1989	AA
COMSTOCK	LSD 45	Avondale Industries	27 Oct	1986	16 Jan	1988	3 Feb	1990	PA
TORTUGA	LSD 46	Avondale Industries	23 Mar	1987	15 Sep	1988	17 Nov	1990	AA
RUSHMORE	LSD 47	Avondale Industries	9 Nov	1987	6 May	1989	1 June	1991	PA
ASHLAND	LSD 48	Avondale Industries	4 Apr	1988	11 Nov	1989	9 May	1992	AA
HARPERS FERRY	LSD 49	Avondale Industries	15 Apr	1991	16 Jan	1993	7 Jan	1995	PA
CARTER HALL	LSD 50	Avondale Industries	11 Nov	1991	2 Oct	1993	30 Sep	1995	AA
OAK HILL	LSD 51	Avondale Industries	21 Sep	1992	11 June	1994	8 June	1996	AA
PEARL HARBOR	LSD 52	Avondale Industries	27 Jan	1995	24 Feb	1996	30 May	1998	PA

Displacement, tons: 11,125 light; 15,726 (LSD 41-48), 16,740 (LSD 49 onwards) full load

Dimensions, feet (metres): 609.5 × 84 × 20.5 *(185.8 × 25.6 × 6.3)*

Main machinery: 4 Colt SEMT-Pielstick 16 PC2.5 V 400 diesels; 37,440 hp(m) *(27.5 MW)* sustained; 2 shafts; cp props

Speed, knots: 22. **Range, miles:** 8,000 at 18 kt

Complement: 340 (21 officers)

Military lift: 500 troops; 2 (CV) or 4 LCACs, or 9 (CV) or 21 LCM 6, or 1 (CV) or 3 LCUs, or 64 LVTs. 2 LCPL

Cargo capacity: 5,000 cu ft for marine cargo, 12,500 sq ft for vehicles (including four preloaded LCACs in the well-deck). The 'cargo version' has 67,600 cu ft for marine cargo, 20,200 sq ft for vehicles but only two or three LCACs. Aviation fuel, 90 tons.

Missiles: 1 or 2 GDC/Hughes Mk 49 RAM ❶; passive IR/anti-radiation homing to 9.6 km *(5.2 n miles)* at 2 Mach; warhead 9.1 kg. Being fitted in all.

Guns: 2 General Electric/General Dynamics 20 mm/76 6-barrelled Vulcan Phalanx Mk 15 ❷; 3,000 rds/min (4,500 in Block 1) combined to 1.5 km.
2—25 mm Mk 38. 8—12.7 mm MGs.

Countermeasures: Decoys: 4 Loral Hycor SRBOC 6-barrelled Mk 36 and Mk 50; IR flares and chaff. SLQ-25 Nixie.
ESM: SLQ-32(V)1 or (V)2; intercept. SLQ-49.

Combat data systems: SATCOM SRR-1, WSC-3 (UHF) (see Data Systems at front of section). SSDS Mk 1 being fitted.

Radars: Air search: Raytheon SPS-49(V)5 ❸; C/D-band.
Surface search: Norden SPS-67V ❹; G-band.
Navigation: Raytheon SPS-64(V)9; I/J-band.
Tacan: URN 25. IFF: Mk XII UPX-29/UPX-36.

Helicopters: Platform only for 2 CH-53 Sea Stallion.

Programmes: Originally it was planned to construct six ships of this class as replacements for the 'Thomaston' class LSDs. Eventually, the level of 'Whidbey Island' class ships was established at eight, with four additional cargo-carrying variants of that class to be built to provide increased cargo-carrying capability. The first cargo variant, LSD 49, was authorised and funded in the FY88 budget; LSD 50 in FY89 and LSD 51 in FY91. The fourth was authorised in FY92 but not ordered until 12 October 1993.

Modernisation: A Quick Reaction Combat System (QRCC)/Ship Self-Defense System (SSDS) was installed and successfully demonstrated in LSD 41 in 1993. During the QRCC demonstrations, the ship's SPS-49, SLQ-32, RAM and Phalanx were successfully integrated via SSDS. All ships of the class fitted except LSD 43 and 51 to be done in 2001, and LSD 47 in 2002.

Structure: Based on the earlier 'Anchorage' class. One 60 and one 20 ton crane. Well-deck measures 440 × 50 ft *(134.1 × 15.2 m)* in the LSD but is shorter in the Cargo Variant (CV). The cargo version is a minimum modification to the LSD 41 design. Changes in that design include additional air conditioning, piping and hull structure; the forward Phalanx is forward of the bridge, RAM is on the bridge roof, and there is only one crane. There is approximately 90 per cent commonality between the two ships.

Operational: LSDs 42 and 43 are based at Sasebo. *Rushmore* is being used to test 'smart ship' concepts allowing technology to reduce crew size. The plan is to retrofit the rest of the 'Whidbey Island' class by 2004.

UPDATED

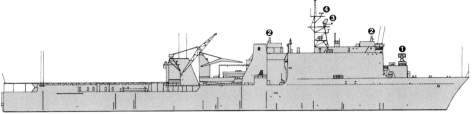

ASHLAND   *(Scale 1 : 1,500), Ian Sturton* / 0053362

GUNSTON HALL   *7/1999*, M Declerck* / 0084132

RUSHMORE   *11/1999*, John Mortimer* / 0084133

PEARL HARBOR   *10/1999*, Findler & Winter* / 0084134

2 NEWPORT CLASS: TANK LANDING SHIPS (LST)

Name	No	Builders	Laid down	Launched	Commissioned	F/S
FREDERICK	LST 1184	National Steel & Shipbuilding Co	13 Apr 1968	8 Mar 1969	11 Apr 1970	NRF
LA MOURE COUNTY	LST 1194	National Steel & Shipbuilding Co	22 May 1970	13 Feb 1971	18 Dec 1971	NRF

Displacement, tons: 4,975 light; 8,450 full load
Dimensions, feet (metres): 522.3 (hull) × 69.5 × 17.5 (aft) *(159.2 × 21.2 × 5.3)*
Main machinery: 6 ALCO 16-251 diesels; 16,500 hp *(12.3 MW)* sustained; 2 shafts; cp props; bow thruster
Speed, knots: 20. **Range, miles:** 2,500 at 14 kt
Complement: 257 (13 officers)
Military lift: 400 troops (20 officers); 500 tons vehicles; 3 LCVPs and 1 LCPL on davits

Guns: 1 General Electric/General Dynamics 20 mm Vulcan Phalanx Mk 15.
Combat data systems: SATCOM SRR-1, WSC-3 (UHF).
Radars: Surface search: Raytheon SPS-67; G-band.
Navigation: Marconi LN66 or Raytheon CRP 3100 Pathfinder (LST 1194); I/J-band.

Helicopters: Platform only.

Structure: The hull form required to achieve 20 kt would not permit bow doors, thus these ships unload by a 112 ft ramp over their bow. The ramp is supported by twin derrick arms. A ramp just forward of the superstructure connects the lower tank deck with the main deck and a vehicle passage through the superstructure provides access to the parking area amidships. A stern gate to the tank deck permits unloading of amphibious tractors into the water, or unloading of other vehicles into an LCU or on to a pier. Vehicle stowage covers 19,000 sq ft. Length over derrick arms is 562 ft *(171.3 m)*; full load draught is 11.5 ft forward and 17.5 ft aft. Bow thruster fitted to hold position offshore while unloading amphibious tractors.

LA MOURE COUNTY

6/1999*, van Ginderen Collection / 0084136

Operational: Of these last two *Frederick* is based at Pearl Harbor and *La Moure County* at Little Creek, Virginia. Four others are in a 180 day reduced maintenance status (ROS) three at Pearl Harbor and one at Portsmouth, Virginia.
Sales: Two sold to Australia in September 1994, one leased to Brazil in August 1994, one sold to Malaysia in December 1994, one by grant aid to Morocco August 1994, one leased to Spain in August 1994 and a second in April 1995, one to Chile in September 1995 and two to Taiwan in 1997.

UPDATED

91 LANDING CRAFT AIR CUSHION (LCAC/MCAC)

Displacement, tons: 87.2 light; 170-182 full load
Dimensions, feet (metres): 88 oa (on-cushion) (81 between hard structures) × 47 beam (on-cushion) (43 beam hard structure) × 2.9 draught (off-cushion) *(26.8 (24.7) × 14.3 (13.1) × 0.9)*
Main machinery: 4 Avco-Lycoming TF-40B gas turbines; 2 for propulsion and 2 for lift; 16,000 hp *(12 MW)* sustained; 2 shrouded reversible-pitch airscrews (propulsion); 4 double entry fans, centrifugal or mixed flow (lift)
Speed, knots: 40 (loaded). **Range, miles:** 300 at 35 kt; 200 at 40 kt
Complement: 5
Military lift: 24 troops; 1 MBT or 60-75 tons

Guns: 2—12.7 mm MGs or 30 mm Gatling (GPU-5).
Radars: Navigation: Marconi LN66; I-band.

Programmes: Built by Textron Marine Systems and Avondale Gulfport. 33 funded FY82-86, 15 in FY89, 12 in each of FY90, 1991 and 1992 and seven more in FY93. Some of the craft are being designated as MCAC and evaluated for mine clearance and other tasks. The completion of the last pair was delayed until late 1998.
Modernisation: There are plans to SLEP 27 of the class from 2000 to 2005 and the remainder by 2016.
Structure: Incorporates the best attributes of the JEFF(A) and JEFF(B) learned from over five years of testing the two prototypes. Bow ramp 28.8 ft, stern ramp 15 ft. Cargo space capacity is 1,809 sq ft. Noise and dust levels are high and if disabled the craft is not easy to tow. Spray suppressors have been added to the skirt to reduce interference with the driver's vision. 30 mm Gatling guns can be fitted.
Operational: Ship classes capable of carrying the LCAC are Wasp (three), Tarawa (one), Anchorage (four), Austin (one), Whidbey (four), Modified Whidbey (two) and San Antonio (two). Eight minesweeping kits were acquired in 1994-95. 12M58 line charges for MCM are being used as is AQS-14 towfish sonar. A transport model can seat 180 personnel. According to the USMC the craft can cross 70 per cent of the world's coastlines compared to about 15 per cent for conventional landing craft. Some limitations in very rough seas. Shore bases on each coast at Little Creek, Virginia and Camp Pendleton, California.
Sales: Two to Japan. One of a similar type built by South Korea.

UPDATED

6 FRANK S BESSON CLASS: LOGISTIC SUPPORT VESSELS (LSV-ARMY)

Name	No	Builders	Completed
GENERAL FRANK S BESSON JR	LSV 1	Moss Point Marine, MS	18 Dec 1987
CW 3 HAROLD C CLINGER	LSV 2	Moss Point Marine, MS	20 Feb 1988
GENERAL BREHON B SOMERVELL	LSV 3	Moss Point Marine, MS	2 Apr 1988
LT GENERAL WILLIAM B BUNKER	LSV 4	Moss Point Marine, MS	18 May 1988
MAJOR GENERAL CHARLES P GROSS	LSV 5	Moss Point Marine, MS	30 Apr 1991
SPECIALIST 4 JAMES A LOUX	LSV 6	Moss Point Marine, MS	16 Dec 1994

Displacement, tons: 4,265 full load
Dimensions, feet (metres): 272.8 × 60 × 12 *(83.1 × 18.3 × 3.7)*
Main machinery: 2 GM EMD 16-645E2 diesels; 3,900 hp *(2.9 MW)* sustained; 2 shafts; Schottel bow thruster; 250 hp *(187 kW)*
Speed, knots: 11.6. **Range, miles:** 8,300 at 11 kt
Complement: 30 (6 officers)
Military lift: 2,280 tons of vehicles including 26 M-1 tanks, containers or general cargo
Radars: Navigation: Raytheon SPS-64(V)2; I-band.

Comment: First one approved in FY85, second in FY87, remainder from Army reserve funds. Army owned ro-ro design with 10,500 sq ft of deck space for cargo. Capable of beaching with 4 ft over the ramp on a 1:30 offshore gradient with a payload of 900 tons of cargo. Three are based at Fort Eustis, Virginia, two in Hawaii and LSV-3 is with the National Guard at Tacoma, Washington. Two modified ships of the class built for the Philippines Navy in 1993-94.

UPDATED

MAJOR GENERAL CHARLES P GROSS

9/1996*, van Ginderen Collection / 0084139

38 MECHANISED LANDING CRAFT: LCM 6 TYPE

Displacement, tons: 64 full load
Dimensions, feet (metres): 56.2 × 14 × 3.9 *(17.1 × 4.3 × 1.2)*
Main machinery: 2 Detroit 6-71 diesels; 348 hp *(260 kW)* sustained or 2 Detroit 8V-71 diesels; 460 hp *(344 kW)* sustained; 2 shafts
Speed, knots: 9. **Range, miles:** 130 at 9 kt
Complement: 5
Military lift: 34 tons or 80 troops

Comment: Welded steel construction. Used for various utility tasks. Numbers are reducing.
UPDATED

LCAC 76

10/1999*, Findler & Winter / 0084137

LCAC 19

1/2000*, A Sharma / 0084138

LCM 6

6/1997*, J W Currie / 0016482

35 LCU 2000 CLASS: UTILITY LANDING CRAFT (LCU-ARMY)

LCU 2001-2035

Displacement, tons: 1,102 full load
Dimensions, feet (metres): 173.8 × 42 × 8.5 *(53 × 12.8 × 2.6)*
Main machinery: 2 Cummins KTA50-M diesels; 2,500 hp *(1.87 MW)* sustained; 2 shafts; bow thruster
Speed, knots: 11.5. **Range, miles:** 4,500 at 11.5 kt
Complement: 13 (2 officers)
Military lift: 350 tons
Radars: Navigation: 2 Raytheon SPS-64; I-band.

Comment: Order placed with Lockheed by US Army 11 June 1986. First one completed 21 February 1990 by Moss Point Marine. The 2000 series have names, some of which duplicate naval ships. These are the first LCUs to have been built to an Army specification. 14 are active, 12 in reserve, eight prepositioned and one used for training.

UPDATED

49 LCU 1600 CLASS: UTILITY LANDING CRAFT
(LCU-ARMY (13) and NAVY (38))

Displacement, tons: 200 light; 375 (437, LCU 1680-81) full load
Dimensions, feet (metres): 134.9 × 29 × 6.1 *(41.1 × 8.8 × 1.9)*
Main machinery: 4 Detroit 6-71 diesels; 696 hp *(519 kW)* sustained; 2 shafts; Kort nozzles
2 Detroit 12V-71 diesels (LCU 1680-1681); 680 hp *(508 kW)* sustained; 2 shafts; Kort nozzles
Speed, knots: 11. **Range, miles:** 1,200 at 8 kt
Complement: 14 (2 officers)
Military lift: 170 tons; 3 M103 (64 tons) or M48 (48 tons) tanks or 350 troops
Guns: 2—12.7 mm MGs.
Radars: Navigation: LN66 or SPS-53; I-band.

Comment: Improved steel hulled landing craft, larger than previous series. Versatile craft used for a variety of tasks. Pennant numbers are in the 1600 series. Most were built between the mid-1960s and mid-1980s. There are no plans for more of this type. At least three converted as ASDV 1 to 3, 1 and 3 based in San Diego and 2 in Little Creek. LCU 1641 carries a chute over a cutaway stern and is used as a mine recovery tender at Charleston, South Carolina. Two of an earlier type to Bangladesh in 1991. A contract is planned for 2004 for an LCU(X) of 200 tons, and capable of 20 kt.

UPDATED

LCU 2024   *5/1999 *, M Declerck /* 0084140

LCU 1681   *4/1999 *, M Declerck /* 0084141

LCU 2003   *7/1998 *, John Brodie /* 0053368

89 MECHANISED LANDING CRAFT: LCM 8 TYPE

Displacement, tons: 111 full load (aluminium)
Dimensions, feet (metres): 73.7 × 21 × 5.2 *(22.5 × 6.4 × 1.6)*
Main machinery: 2 Detroit 6-71 diesels; 348 hp *(260 kW)* sustained or 2 Detroit 12V-71 diesels; 680 hp *(508 kW)* sustained; 2 shafts
Speed, knots: 11. **Range, miles:** 271 at 9 kt full load
Complement: 5
Military lift: 54 tons or 1 tank or 200 troops

Comment: Naval craft are Mk 7 all-aluminium new construction types for use in amphibious ships. The last 12 were built in 1993-94. 90 similar craft are used by the Army. The advanced amphibious assault vessel (AAAV) is planned to replace the older Army units from 2004.

UPDATED

ASDV 1   *9/1997 *, Winter & Findler /* 0016484

120 LANDING CRAFT PERSONNEL (LCPL)

Displacement, tons: 11 full load
Dimensions, feet (metres): 36 × 12.1 × 3.8 *(11 × 3.7 × 1.2)*
Main machinery: 1 GM 8V-71TI diesel; 425 hp *(317 kW)* sustained; 1 shaft
Speed, knots: 20. **Range, miles:** 150 at 20 kt
Complement: 3
Military lift: 17 troops
Radars: Navigation: Marconi LN66; I-band.

Comment: There are 105 Mk 12 and 15 Mk 13. Details given are for eight Mk 13 of GRP construction, ordered from Bollinger Shipyard in FY89 and delivered in 1991, and seven from Peterson Builders ordered in October 1992 and delivered in 1994. Some have navigation radar. For use as control craft and carried aboard LHA, LPD, LSD and LST classes. A new 13 m craft is being designed for *San Antonio*.

UPDATED

LCM 8   *6/1999 *, van Ginderen Collection /* 0084142

LCPL Mk 13   *4/1991 *, Bollinger /* 0084143

MINE WARFARE FORCES

Notes: (1) There are no surface minelayers. Mining is done by carrier-based aircraft, land-based aircraft and submarines. The mine inventory includes Mk 56 moored influence mines, the Mk 60 CAPTOR, the Mk 67 submarine launched mobile mine (SLMM) and the Quickstrike series of bottom mines. Mk 56 and Mk 60 are being phased out.
(2) NRF ships are manned by composite active/reserve crews.
(3) MH-53E Sea Dragon helicopters are deployed in amphibious assault ships or by C-5 aircraft for mine countermeasures.

(4) The Near-term Mine Reconnaissance System (NMRS) uses a torpedo tube-launched prototype UUV, connected by fibre optic cable to a 'Los Angeles' class SSN. This is being followed by a contract to Boeing to produce six LMRS (Long-term Mine Reconnaissance Systems) by 2004.
(5) Marine Mammal Systems (MMS) uses trained dolphins and sea lions for mine detection, swimmer protection, and recovery of exercise mines and torpedoes. The dolphins can be transported by C-5 aircraft. The MMS is the

only operational method of detecting and neutralising buried mines.
(6) A Remote Minehunting System (RMS) is being developed for Arleigh Burke Flight IIA destroyers. The system is an unmanned semi-submersible, diesel powered. There is an over-the-horizon radio link and an AQS-20X VDS. The RMS is 23 ft, weighs 15,000 lb and has an endurance of 24 hours at 12 kt.

1 IWO JIMA CLASS: (MCS)

Name	No	Builders	Laid down	Launched	Commissioned	F/S
INCHON	MCS 12	Ingalls Shipbuilding	8 Apr 1968	24 May 1969	20 June 1970	NRF

Displacement, tons: 19,600 full load
Dimensions, feet (metres): 602.3 × 104 × 31.7
  (183.7 × 31.7 × 9.7)
Flight deck, feet (metres): 602.3 × 104 *(183.7 × 31.7)*
Main machinery: 2 Combustion Engineering boilers; 600 psi
  (42.3 kg/cm²); 900°F *(482°C)*; 1 Westinghouse turbine;
  23,000 hp *(17.2 MW)*; 1 shaft
Speed, knots: 23. **Range, miles:** 10,000 at 20 kt
Complement: 1,443 (122 officers)

Guns: 2 General Electric/General Dynamics 20 mm 6-barrelled
  Vulcan Phalanx Mk 15; 4,500 rds/min combined to 1.5 km.
  2 Bushmaster 25 mm Mk 38. 8—12.7 mm MGs.
Countermeasures: Decoys: 4 Loral Hycor SRBOC 6-barrelled
  fixed Mk 36; IR flares and chaff to 4 km *(2.2 n miles)*. SLQ-25A
  torpedo countermeasures.
ESM/ECM: SLQ-32(V)3 intercept and jammer. SLQ-25 Nixie.
Combat data systems: GCCS and Link 11 (Tadil A). SHF
  SATCOM.
Radars: Air search: Lockheed SPS-40E; E/F-band.
Surface search: Norden SPS-67(V)1; G-band.
Navigation: Raytheon SPS-64(V)9; I-band.
CCA: SPN-43B.
Tacan: URN 25. IFF: Mk XII UPX-29.

Helicopters: 8 MH-53E Sea Stallion.

Modernisation: Completed conversion on 24 May 1996 to a
  Mine Countermeasures Command, Control and Support Ship
  (MCS). Up to eight MCMV are able to tie up alongside. Hangar
  space provided for eight MH-53E Sea Dragon helicopters.
  Workshop spaces are much improved and new cranes are
  fitted on the upper deck. Fitted for fuelling MCMVs. Command
  and weapon systems upgrades included GCCS, Naval Tactical
  Command System (NTCS) and improved radar and EW
  countermeasures.

INCHON   *2/1998, A Campanera i Rovira /* 0053370

Structure: Two deck-edge lifts, one to port opposite the bridge
  and one to starboard aft of island. Two small elevators carry
  cargo from holds to flight deck. Fitted with extensive medical
  facilities.

Operational: Based at Ingleside, Texas. Hand held Stinger SAMs
  can be embarked. More aircraft can be carried on the flight
  deck. Deployed to the Adriatic for the NATO campaign against
  Serbia in 1999.   ***UPDATED***

12 OSPREY CLASS (MINEHUNTERS COASTAL) (MHC)

Name	No	Builders	Launched		Commissioned		F/S
OSPREY	MHC 51	Intermarine, Savannah	23 Mar	1991	20 Nov	1993	AA
HERON	MHC 52	Intermarine, Savannah	21 Mar	1992	6 Aug	1994	NRF
PELICAN	MHC 53	Avondale Industries	27 Feb	1993	18 Nov	1995	NRF
ROBIN	MHC 54	Avondale Industries	11 Sep	1993	11 May	1996	NRF
ORIOLE	MHC 55	Intermarine, Savannah	22 May	1993	13 Sep	1995	NRF
KINGFISHER	MHC 56	Avondale Industries	18 June	1994	26 Oct	1996	NRF
CORMORANT	MHC 57	Avondale Industries	21 Oct	1995	12 Apr	1997	NRF
BLACK HAWK	MHC 58	Intermarine, Savannah	27 Aug	1994	11 May	1996	NRF
FALCON	MHC 59	Intermarine, Savannah	3 June	1995	26 Oct	1997	NRF
CARDINAL	MHC 60	Intermarine, Savannah	9 Mar	1996	17 Oct	1997	NRF
RAVEN	MHC 61	Intermarine, Savannah	28 Sep	1996	4 Apr	1998	NRF
SHRIKE	MHC 62	Intermarine, Savannah	24 May	1997	13 Mar	1999	NRF

Displacement, tons: 959 full load
Dimensions, feet (metres): 187.8 × 35.9 × 9.5
  (57.2 × 11 × 2.9)
Main machinery: 2 Isotta Fraschini ID 36 SS 8V AM diesels;
  1,600 hp(m) *(1.18 MW)* sustained; 2 Voith-Schneider props;
  3 Isotta Fraschini ID 36 diesel generators; 984 kW; 2 motors
  (slow speed); 360 hp(m) *(265 kW)*; bow thruster 180 hp(m)
  (132 kW)
Speed, knots: 12. **Range, miles:** 1,500 at 10 kt
Complement: 51 (5 officers)

Guns: 2—12.7 mm MGs.
Countermeasures: MCM: Alliant SLQ-48 mine neutralisation
  system ROV (with 1,070 m cable). Degaussing DGM-4.

Combat data systems: Unisys SYQ 13 and SYQ 109; integrated
  combat and machinery control system. USQ-119(V) NTCS-A,
  UHF Dama, and OTCIXS provide GCCS connectivity.
Radars: Surface search: Raytheon SPS-64(V)9 or SPS-73; I-band.
Navigation: R41XX; I-band.
Sonars: Raytheon/Thomson Sintra SQQ-32(V)3; VDS; active
  minehunting; high frequency.

Programmes: A design contract for 'Lerici' class mine hunters
  was awarded in August 1986 followed by a construction
  contract in May 1987 for the lead ship of the class. Intermarine
  SpA established Intermarine USA and purchased Sayler
  Marine Corporation in Savannah, Georgia. On 2 October 1989
  Avondale, Gulfport was named as the second construction

source. Plans for a lengthened version have been shelved.
  Engine modifications in *Osprey* delayed completion and the
  whole programme suffered progressive delays.
Modernisation: Integrated Combat Weapon System (ICWS) to
  replace existing system from 2000. New search radar also
  being fitted.
Structure: Construction is of monocoque GRP throughout hull,
  with frames eliminated. Main machinery is mounted on GRP
  cradles and provided with acoustic enclosures. SQQ-32 is
  deployed from a central well forward. Fitted with Voith
  cycloidal propellers which eliminate need for forward thrusters
  during station keeping.
Operational: All are NRF except MHC 51.
                                           UPDATED

RAVEN   *7/1998, van Ginderen Collection /* 0053372

14 AVENGER CLASS: MINE COUNTERMEASURES VESSELS (MCM/MSO/MHO)

Name	No	Builders	Laid down		Launched		Commissioned		F/S
AVENGER	MCM 1	Peterson Builders Inc	3 June	1983	15 June	1985	12 Sep	1987	NRF
DEFENDER	MCM 2	Marinette Marine Corp	1 Dec	1983	4 Apr	1987	30 Sep	1989	NRF
SENTRY	MCM 3	Peterson Builders Inc	8 Oct	1984	20 Sep	1986	2 Sep	1989	NRF
CHAMPION	MCM 4	Marinette Marine Corp	28 June	1984	15 Apr	1989	27 July	1991	NRF
GUARDIAN	MCM 5	Peterson Builders Inc	8 May	1985	20 June	1987	16 Dec	1989	PA
DEVASTATOR	MCM 6	Peterson Builders Inc	9 Feb	1987	11 June	1988	6 Oct	1990	AA
PATRIOT	MCM 7	Marinette Marine Corp	31 Mar	1987	15 May	1990	18 Oct	1991	PA
SCOUT	MCM 8	Peterson Builders Inc	8 June	1987	20 May	1989	15 Dec	1990	AA
PIONEER	MCM 9	Peterson Builders Inc	5 June	1989	25 Aug	1990	7 Dec	1992	AA
WARRIOR	MCM 10	Peterson Builders Inc	25 Sep	1989	8 Dec	1990	7 Apr	1993	AA
GLADIATOR	MCM 11	Peterson Builders Inc	7 July	1990	29 June	1991	18 Sep	1993	AA
ARDENT	MCM 12	Peterson Builders Inc	22 Oct	1990	16 Nov	1991	18 Feb	1994	AA
DEXTROUS	MCM 13	Peterson Builders Inc	11 Mar	1991	20 June	1992	9 July	1994	AA
CHIEF	MCM 14	Peterson Builders Inc	19 Aug	1991	12 June	1993	5 Nov	1994	AA

Displacement, tons: 1,312 full load
Dimensions, feet (metres): 224.3 × 38.9 × 12.2
(68.4 × 11.9 × 3.7)
Main machinery: 4 Waukesha L-1616 diesels (MCM 1-2);
2,600 hp(m) *(1.91 MW)* or 4 Isotta Fraschini ID 36 SS 6V AM
diesels (MCM 3 onwards); 2,280 hp(m) *(1.68 MW)* sustained;
2 Hansome Electric motors; 400 hp(m) *(294 kW)* for hovering;
2 shafts; cp props; 1 Omnithruster hydrojet; 350 hp *(257 kW)*
Speed, knots: 13.5. **Range, miles:** 2,500 at 10 kt
Complement: 81 (6 officers)

Guns: 2—12.7 mm Mk 26 MGs.
Countermeasures: MCM: 2 SLQ-48; includes Honeywell/
Hughes ROV mine neutralisation system, capable of 6 kt
(1,500 m cable with cutter (MP1), and countermining charge)
(MP 2). SLQ-37(V)3; magnetic/acoustic influence sweep
equipment. Oropesa SLQ-38 Type 0 Size 1; mechanical sweep.
Combat data systems: SATCOM SRR-1; WSC-3 (UHF). GEC/
Marconi Nautis M in last two ships (and to be fitted in all),
includes SSN 2 (being replaced by ICWS) PINS command
system and control. USQ-119(V) NTCS-A, UHF Dama and
OTCIXS provide JMCIS connectivity.
Radars: Surface search: ISC Cardion SPS-55; I/J-band.
Navigation: Raytheon SPS-66(V)9 or LN66; I-band. Both being
replaced by SPS-73.
Sonars: General Electric SQQ-30 or Raytheon/Thomson Sintra
SQQ-32 (in MCM 10 onwards and being retrofitted); VDS;
active minehunting; high frequency.

Programmes: The contract for the prototype MCM was awarded
in June 1982. The last three were funded in FY90.
Modernisation: Integrated Combat Weapon System (ICWS) is
replacing SSN 2. New radar being fitted.
Structure: The hull is constructed of oak, Douglas fir and Alaskan
cedar, with a thin coating of fibreglass on the outside, to permit
taking advantage of wood's low magnetic signature. A
problem of engine rotation on the Waukesha diesels in MCM
1-2 was resolved; however, those engines have been replaced
in the rest of the class by low magnetic engines manufactured
by Isotta-Fraschini of Milan, Italy. Fitted with SSN2(V) Precise
Integrated Navigation System (PINS).

DEVASTATOR
4/1999*, A Campanera i Rovira / 0084144

Operational: *Avenger* fitted with the SQQ-32 for Gulf operations
in 1991 and all of the class are being retrofitted. Two
transferred to NRF in 1995 and two more in 1996. *Ardent* and
Dextrous permanently stationed in the Gulf from March 1996
with crew rotation, and *Guardian* and *Patriot* are at Sasebo,
Japan. The remainder are based at Ingleside, Texas. Early
problems of unreliability are reported to have been overcome.
UPDATED

PATROL FORCES

14 CYCLONE CLASS (PATROL COASTAL SHIPS) (PCF)

Name	No	Builders	Commissioned		F/S
CYCLONE	PC 1	Bollinger, Lockport	7 Aug	1993	AA
TEMPEST	PC 2	Bollinger, Lockport	21 Aug	1993	AA
HURRICANE	PC 3	Bollinger, Lockport	15 Oct	1993	PA
MONSOON	PC 4	Bollinger, Lockport	22 Jan	1994	PA
TYPHOON	PC 5	Bollinger, Lockport	12 Feb	1994	AA
SIROCCO	PC 6	Bollinger, Lockport	11 June	1994	AA
SQUALL	PC 7	Bollinger, Lockport	4 July	1994	PA
ZEPHYR	PC 8	Bollinger, Lockport	15 Oct	1994	PA
CHINOOK	PC 9	Bollinger, Lockport	28 Jan	1995	AA
FIREBOLT	PC 10	Bollinger, Lockport	10 June	1995	AA
WHIRLWIND	PC 11	Bollinger, Lockport	1 July	1995	AA
THUNDERBOLT	PC 12	Bollinger, Lockport	7 Oct	1995	AA
SHAMAL	PC 13	Bollinger, Lockport	27 Jan	1996	AA
TORNADO	PC 14	Bollinger, Lockport	15 May	2000	AA

Displacement, tons: 334 full load; 360 full load (PC 2, 8, 13, 14)
Dimensions, feet (metres): 170.3; 179 (PC 2, 8, 13, 14) × 25.9 × 7.9 *(51.9; 54.6 × 7.9 × 2.4)*
Main machinery: 4 Paxman Valenta 16RP200CM diesels; 13,400 hp *(10 MW)* sustained; 4 shafts
Speed, knots: 35. **Range, miles:** 2,500 at 12 kt
Complement: 28 (4 officers) plus 8 SEALs
Missiles: SAM: 1 sextuple Stinger mounting.
Guns: 1 Bushmaster 25 mm Mk 38. 1 Bushmaster 25 mm/87 Mk 96 (aft). 4—12.7 mm MGs.
4—7.62 mm MGs. 2—40 mm Mk 19 grenade launchers (MGs and grenade launchers are
interchangeable).
Countermeasures: Decoys: 2 Mk 52 sextuple and/or Wallop Super Barricade Mk 3 chaff
launchers.
ESM: Privateer APR-39; radar warning.
Weapons control: Marconi VISTAR IM 405 IR system.
Radars: Surface search: 2 Sperry RASCAR; E/F/I/J-band.
Sonars: Wesmar; hull-mounted; active; high frequency.

WHIRLWIND
4/1999*, M Declerck / 0084145

Comment: Contract awarded for eight in August 1990 and five more in July 1991. The last one
was ordered by Congress on 15 August 1997. The design is based on the Vosper Thornycroft
'Ramadan' class modified to meet US Navy requirements with 1 in armour on the superstructure.
Shoulder-launched Stinger SAM may be carried. The craft have a slow speed loiter capability.
Can be operated in pairs with a 12-man maintenance team in two vans ashore. Based at Norfolk,
Virginia and San Diego, California. PC 12 wore Coast Guard colours for a trial period in 1998/99.
A stabilised weapons platform system has been developed for Stinger. Two SEAL raiding craft
and one RIB can be 'launched' from a platform at the stern. Swimmers can be 'launched' from a platform at the stern. Currently
being used for drug interdiction operations in the Caribbean and have been deployed to the
Mediterranean, and northern Europe. The last of class is fitted with enhanced ESM, a rocket
launcher, better communications and a Mk 96 stabilised weapons platform. It has also been
lengthened at the stern to improve launch and recovery of 11 m raiding craft. Three others PC 2,
8 and 13 similarly lengthened in 2000 and others may follow in due course.
UPDATED

TYPHOON
8/1999*, van Ginderen Collection / 0084146

20 + 20 PEGASUS CLASS Mk V (SOC/PBF)

Displacement, tons: 57 full load
Dimensions, feet (metres): 81.2 × 17.5 × 4.3 *(24.7 × 5.3 × 1.3)*
Main machinery: 2 MTU 12V 396 TE94 diesels; 4,506 hp *(3.36 MW)* sustained; 2 Kamewa water-jets
Speed, knots: 45. **Range, miles:** 515 at 35 kt
Complement: 5 plus 4 spare
Military lift: 16 fully equipped troops
Guns: 5 Mk 46 Mod 4 mountings for twin 12.7 mm or 7.6 mm MGs, 1 Mk 19 40 mm grenade launcher. 3 Bushmaster 25 mm Mk 38.
Radars: Navigation: Furuno; I-band.
IFF: APX-100(V).

Comment: This was the winning design of a competition held in 1994 to find a high-speed craft to insert and withdraw Navy SEAL teams and other special operations forces personnel. Fourteen delivered by mid-1998 and six more by mid-1999. All built at the Halter Marine Equitable Shipyard in New Orleans. The craft has an aluminium hull and is transportable by C-5 aircraft. Stinger missiles may be carried and gun armaments can be varied. A variant with three engines is in service with the Mexican Navy. An improved version is being developed based on the Halmatic fast wave piercing craft (VSV) in service in the UK and capable of 55 kt. Up to 20 may be acquired.

UPDATED

PEGASUS   7/1999*, A Campanera i Rovira / 0084147

PEGASUS   4/1999*, Diego Quevedo / 0084148

VSV (UK colours)   2/1998*, Terje Eggum / 0016257

10 MINI ARMOURED TROOP CARRIERS (ATC)

Displacement, tons: 14.8 full load
Dimensions, feet (metres): 36 × 12.7 × 3.5 *(11 × 3.9 × 1.1)*
Main machinery: 2 Detroit 6V-92TA diesels; 445 hp *(332 kW)* sustained; 2 Jacuzzi 20YJ water-jets
Speed, knots: 33. **Range, miles:** 280 at 28 kt
Complement: 3
Military lift: 16 SEALs
Guns: 7—12.7 mm MGs.
Radars: Navigation: Marconi LN66; I-band.

Comment: Built by Sewart, Louisiana 1972-73. A small troop carrier for riverine and SEAL operations; aluminium hull; ceramic armour. Draught 1 ft when under way at high speed. Used by Special Boat Forces of the NRF. To be replaced by new craft from 2001.

UPDATED

MINI ATC   10/1996*, van Ginderen Collection / 0084149

44 (+26) RIBs (RIGID INFLATABLE BOATS)

Displacement, tons: 8 full load
Dimensions, feet (metres): 36.1 × 10.5 × 3 *(11 × 3.2 × 0.9)*
Main machinery: 2 Caterpillar 3126 diesels; 940 hp *(700 kW)*; 2 Kamewa FF 280 water-jets
Speed, knots: 33. **Range, miles:** 200 at 33 kt
Complement: 3 plus 8 SEALs
Guns: 1—12.7 mm MG, 1—7.62 mm MG or Mk 19 Mod 3 grenade launcher.

Comment: Capable of carrying eight Seals at 32 kt. Details given are for the latest type being built by USMI, New Orleans. First six in service in early 1998 and the plan is to acquire up to 70 to replace all front line RIBs over the next few years. In addition there are 26 smaller 24 ft craft able to carry four SEALs at 28 kt.

UPDATED

RIB   1/1998*, US Navy / 0016492

16 COUNTER DRUG PATROL BOATS (PBL)

Displacement, tons: 3.3 full load
Dimensions, feet (metres): 25 × 8.6 × 1.5 *(7.6 × 2.6 × 0.5)*
Main machinery: 2 OMC outboards; 300 hp *(224 kW)*
Speed, knots: 35
Complement: 3
Guns: 3—12.7 mm MGs. 1—7.62 mm MG.
Radars: Surface search: Furuno 1731; I-band.

Comment: Built by Boston Whaler for US Special Operations Command. Air transportable. Glass fibre hulls. To be replaced from 2001.

UPDATED

PBL-CD   1996*, Boston Whaler / 0084150

70 HARBOUR SECURITY CRAFT

Displacement, tons: 3.9 full load
Dimensions, feet (metres): 24 × 8 × 3.3 *(7.3 × 2.4 × 1)*
Main machinery: 1 Volvo Penta AQAD41A diesel; 330 hp(m) *(243 kW)* sustained; 1 Type 290 outdrive
Speed, knots: 22
Complement: 3
Guns: 1—7.62 mm MG.
Radars: Surface search: Furuno; I-band.

Comment: Built by Peterson, Wisconsin and delivered between 29 February 1988 and 12 May 1989 in batches of 50, 25 and 10. Used for protecting naval installations, ports, harbours and anchorages. Some have been deleted. In addition there are large numbers of other small craft used in similar roles.

UPDATED

HARBOUR SECURITY CRAFT   2/1999*, Maritime Photographic / 0084151

AUXILIARIES

Notes: (1) The current plan is to be able to provide support in two regional crises simultaneously. This plan is based on the availability of some storage depots on foreign territory, and the use of Military Sealift Ships to carry fuels, munitions and the stores from the USA or overseas sources for transfer to UNREP (Underway Replenishment) ships in overseas areas. Some 16 to 18 UNREP ships are normally forward deployed in the Mediterranean, Western Pacific and Indian Ocean areas in support of the 5th, 6th and 7th Fleets, respectively.

Fleet support ships provide primarily maintenance and related towing and salvage services at advanced bases and at ports in the USA. These ships normally do not provide fuel, munitions, or other supplies except when ships are alongside for maintenance. Most fleet support ships operate from bases in the USA.

(2) A few underway replenishment ships and fleet support ships are Navy manned and armed, but most are operated by the Military Sealift Command (MSC) with civilian crews and are unarmed. The latter ships have T-prefix before their designations and are listed in the next section.

4 SUPPLY CLASS: FAST COMBAT SUPPORT SHIPS (AOE)

Name	No	Builders	Laid down		Launched		Commissioned		F/S
SUPPLY	AOE 6	National Steel & Shipbuilding Co	24 Feb	1989	6 Oct	1990	26 Feb	1994	AA
RAINIER	AOE 7	National Steel & Shipbuilding Co	31 May	1990	28 Sep	1991	21 Jan	1995	PA
ARCTIC	AOE 8	National Steel & Shipbuilding Co	2 Dec	1991	30 Oct	1993	16 Sep	1995	AA
BRIDGE	AOE 10	National Steel & Shipbuilding Co	16 Sep	1993	25 Aug	1996	5 Aug	1998	PA

Displacement, tons: 19,700 light; 49,000 full load
Dimensions, feet (metres): 753.7 × 107 × 38
   (229.7 × 32.6 × 11.6)
Main machinery: 4 GE LM 2500 gas turbines; 105,000 hp
   (78.33 MW) sustained; 2 shafts
Speed, knots: 25. **Range, miles:** 6,000 at 22 kt
Complement: 531 (28 officers) plus 136 spare
Cargo capacity: 156,000 barrels of fuel; 1,800 tons ammunition; 400 tons refrigerated cargo; 250 tons general cargo; 20,000 gallons water
Missiles: SAM: Raytheon GMLS Mk 29 octuple launcher; NATO Sea Sparrow.
Guns: 2 General Electric/General Dynamics 20 mm Vulcan Phalanx Mk 15.
   2 Hughes 25 mm Mk 88. 4—12.7 mm MGs.
Countermeasures: Decoys: 4 Loral Hycor SRBOC 6-barrelled Mk 36; IR flares and chaff. SLQ-25 Nixie torpedo decoy.
ESM/ECM: SLQ-32(V)3; combined intercept and jammer.
Weapons control: Mk 91 MFCS.
Radars: Air search: Hughes Mk 23 TAS; D-band.
Air/surface search: Norden SPS-67; G-band.
Navigation: Raytheon SPS-64(V)9; I-band.
Fire control: 2 Raytheon Mk 95; I/J-band.
Tacan: URN 25.
Helicopters: 3 UH-46E Sea Knight.

Comment: Modified 'Sacramento' class. Construction of *Supply* started in June 1988 and the second and third in August 1989 and July 1990 respectively. Funds for fourth of class were

ARCTIC

3/1999*, M Declerck / 0084152

rescinded in FY92 but restored in FY93. The aim was one ship per carrier air group but by 1994 there were no plans to build more. The ships have six RAS stations, four 10 ton cargo booms and two Vertrep positions. *Rainier* is being used to test 'smart ship' concepts using technology to allow complement reductions.

UPDATED

4 SACRAMENTO CLASS: FAST COMBAT SUPPORT SHIPS (AOE)

Name	No	Builders	Laid down		Launched		Commissioned		F/S
SACRAMENTO	AOE 1	Puget Sound SY	30 June	1961	14 Sep	1963	14 Mar	1964	PA
CAMDEN	AOE 2	New York Shipbuilding	17 Feb	1964	29 May	1965	1 Apr	1967	PA
SEATTLE	AOE 3	Puget Sound SY	1 Oct	1965	2 Mar	1968	5 Apr	1969	AA
DETROIT	AOE 4	Puget Sound SY	29 Nov	1966	21 June	1969	28 Mar	1970	AA

Displacement, tons: 19,200 light; 51,400-53,600 full load
Dimensions, feet (metres): 793 × 107 × 39.3
   (241.7 × 32.6 × 12)
Main machinery: 4 Combustion Engineering boilers; 600 psi
   (42.2 kg/cm²); 900°F *(480°C)*; 2 GE turbines; 100,000 hp
   (76.4 MW); 2 shafts
Speed, knots: 26. **Range, miles:** 6,000 at 25 kt; 10,000 at 17 kt
Complement: 601 (24 officers)
Cargo capacity: 177,000 barrels of fuel; 2,150 tons munitions; 500 tons dry stores; 250 tons refrigerated stores
Missiles: SAM: Raytheon NATO Sea Sparrow Mk 29 octuple launcher.
Guns: 2 General Electric/General Dynamics 20 mm Vulcan Phalanx Mk 15. 4—12.7 mm MGs.
Countermeasures: Decoys: Loral Hycor SRBOC 6-barrelled Mk 36; IR flares and chaff to 4 km *(2.2 n miles)*. SLQ-25 towed torpedo decoy.
ESM/ECM: SLQ-32(V)3; combined intercept and jammer.
Weapons control: Mk 91 Mod 1 MFCS.
Radars: Air search: Lockheed SPS-40E, Westinghouse SPS-58A (AOE 1 and 2), SPS-58A only (AOE 4); E/F- and D-band (SPS-58). Hughes Mk 23 TAS (AOE 3); D-band.
Surface search: Raytheon SPS-10F; G-band.
Navigation: Raytheon SPS-64(V)9; I-band.
Fire control: 2 Raytheon Mk 95; I/J-band (for SAM).
Tacan: URN 25.
Helicopters: 2 UH-46E Sea Knight normally assigned.

SACRAMENTO

8/1999*, John Mortimer / 0084154

Comment: Designed to provide rapid replenishment at sea of petroleum, munitions, provisions, and fleet freight. Fitted with large hangar for vertical replenishment operations (VERTREP).

Camden used as the trials ship for improved replenishment at sea equipment.

UPDATED

2 EMORY S LAND CLASS: SUBMARINE TENDERS (AS)

Name	No	Builders	Laid down		Launched		Commissioned		F/S
EMORY S LAND	AS 39	Lockheed SB & Construction Co, Seattle	2 Mar	1976	4 May	1977	7 July	1979	AA
FRANK CABLE	AS 40	Lockheed SB & Construction Co, Seattle	2 Mar	1976	14 Jan	1978	5 Feb	1980	PA

Displacement, tons: 13,840 standard; 23,493 full load
Dimensions, feet (metres): 643.8 × 85 × 28.5
   (196.2 × 25.9 × 8.7)
Main machinery: 2 Combustion Engineering boilers; 620 psi
   (43.6 kg/cm²); 860°F *(462°C)*; 1 De Laval turbine; 20,000 hp
   (14.9 MW); 1 shaft
Speed, knots: 20. **Range, miles:** 10,000 at 12 kt
Complement: 535 (52 officers) plus Flag Staff 69 (25 officers)
Guns: 4 Oerlikon 20 mm Mk 67.
Radars: Navigation: ISC Cardion SPS-55; I/J-band.
Helicopters: Platform only.

Comment: The first US submarine tenders designed specifically for servicing nuclear-propelled attack submarines. Each ship can simultaneously provide services to four submarines moored alongside. Carry one 30 ton crane and two 5 ton mobile cranes. Have a 23 bed sick bay. *Frank Cable* is based at Guam and *Emory S Land* in the Mediterranean.

UPDATED

EMORY S LAND

4/1999*, Jürg Kürsener / 0084155

4 SAFEGUARD CLASS: SALVAGE SHIPS (ARS)

Name	No	Builders	Commissioned	F/S
SAFEGUARD	ARS 50	Peterson Builders	16 Aug 1985	PA
GRASP	ARS 51	Peterson Builders	14 Dec 1985	AA
SALVOR	ARS 52	Peterson Builders	14 June 1986	PA
GRAPPLE	ARS 53	Peterson Builders	15 Nov 1986	AA

Displacement, tons: 2,880 full load
Dimensions, feet (metres): 255 × 51 × 17 *(77.7 × 15.5 × 5.2)*
Main machinery: 4 Caterpillar diesels; 4,200 hp *(3.13 MW)*; 2 shafts; cp Kort nozzle props; bow thruster; 500 hp *(373 kW)*
Speed, knots: 14. **Range, miles:** 8,000 at 12 kt
Complement: 90 (6 officers)
Guns: 2 Oerlikon 20 mm Mk 67.
Radars: Navigation: Raytheon SPS-69 and SPS-64(V)9; I-band.

Comment: Prototype approved in FY81, two in FY82 and one in FY83. The procurement of the fifth ARS was dropped on instructions from Congress. The design follows conventional commercial and Navy criteria. Equipped with recompression chamber. Bollard pull, 65.5 tons. Using beach extraction equipment the pull increases to 360 tons. 150 ton deadlift.

UPDATED

SAFEGUARD   *4/1999*, van Ginderen Collection / 0084153

1 DOLPHIN CLASS (AGSS)

Name	No	Builders	Launched	Commissioned	F/S
DOLPHIN	AGSS 555	Portsmouth Naval Shipyard	8 June 1968	17 Aug 1968	PA

Displacement, tons: 860 standard; 948 full load
Dimensions, feet (metres): 165 × 19.3 × 18 *(50.3 × 5.9 × 5.5)*
Main machinery: Diesel-electric; 2 Detroit 12V-71 diesels; 840 hp *(616 kW)* sustained; 2 generators; 1 motor; 1 shaft
Fitted with 330 cell silver-zinc battery
Speed, knots: 15+ dived; 7 surfaced
Complement: 29 (3 officers) plus 4-7 scientists
Radars: Navigation: Sperry SPS-53 portable; I/J-band.
Sonars: Ametek BQS 15; active close-range detection; high frequency.
EDO BQR 2; passive search; low frequency.
Acoustic arrays towed at up to 4,000 ft astern.

Comment: Authorised in FY61. Has a constant diameter cylindrical pressure hull approximately 15 ft in outer diameter closed at both ends with hemispherical heads. Pressure hull fabricated of HY-80 steel with aluminium and fibreglass used in secondary structures to reduce weight. No conventional hydroplanes are mounted, improved rudder design and other features provide manoeuvring control and hovering capability. Fitted for deep-ocean sonar and oceanographic research. The digital-computer submarine safety system monitors equipment and provides data on closed-circuit television screens; malfunctions in equipment set off an alarm and if they are not corrected within the prescribed time the system, unless overridden by an operator, automatically brings the submarine to the surface. There are several research stations for scientists and she is fitted to take water samples down to her operating depth. Assigned to Submarine Development Group 1 at San Diego. Designed for deep diving operations. Submerged endurance is approximately 24 hours with an at-sea endurance of 14 days. Refitted in 1993. Based at San Diego.

UPDATED

DOLPHIN   *7/1997*, A Sharma / 0016494

FLOATING DRY DOCKS

Notes: (1) The US Navy operates a number of floating dry docks to supplement dry dock facilities at major naval activities, and to provide repair capabilities in forward combat areas. The larger floating dry docks are made sectional to facilitate movement overseas and to render them self-docking. The ARD-type docks have the forward end of their docking well closed by a structure resembling the bow of a ship to facilitate towing. Berthing facilities, repair shops and machinery are housed in sides of larger docks. None is self-propelled.
(2) Each section of the AFDB docks has a lifting capacity of about 10,000 tons and is 256 × 80 ft, with wing walls 83 ft high; the wing walls, which contain compartments, fold down when the sections are towed.

LARGE AUXILIARY FLOATING DRY DOCKS (AFDB)

Name/No	Completed	Capacity (tons)	Construction*	Status
ARTISAN (AFDB 1)	1943	36,000	Steel (4)	Pearl Harbor (D), active
AFDB 2	1944	36,000	Steel (10)	Pearl Harbor (D), active

* Figures in brackets indicate the number of sections of each dock remaining.

UPDATED

AFDB   *8/1996*, van Ginderen collection / 0084156

MEDIUM AUXILIARY FLOATING DRY DOCKS (AFDM)

Name/No	Completed	Capacity (tons)	Construction	Status
AFDM 3 (ex-YFD 6)	1943	12,000	Steel (3)	Commercial lease (to Oct 2000), Bender SY, Mobile, AL
RESOLUTE (AFDM 10)	1945	10,000	Steel (3)	Active, Norfolk, VA

Sales: AFDM 2 to Dominican Republic in 1999. Another offered to Greece in 1999.

UPDATED

RESOLUTE   *3/1999*, M Declerck / 0084157

SMALL AUXILIARY FLOATING DRY DOCKS (AFDL)

Name/No	Completed	Capacity (tons)	Construction	Status
DYNAMIC (AFDL 6)	1944	950	Steel	Little Creek, VA
ADEPT (AFDL 23)	1944	1,770	Steel	Commercial lease, Ingleside, TX
RELIANCE (AFDL 47)	1946	7,000	Steel	Commercial lease, Deytens, SC

Sales: AFDL 1 to Dominican Republic; 4, Brazil; 5, Taiwan; 11, Kampuchea; 20, Philippines; 22, Vietnam; 24, Philippines; 26, Paraguay; 28, Mexico; 33, Peru; 34 and 36, Taiwan; 39, Brazil; 40 and 44, Philippines.

VERIFIED

DYNAMIC   *6/1986*, Giorgio Arra

AUXILIARY REPAIR DRY DOCKS and MEDIUM AUXILIARY REPAIR DRY DOCKS (ARD and ARDM)

Name/No	Completed	Capacity (tons)	Construction	Status
OAK RIDGE (ARDM 1) (ex-ARD 19)	1944	7,500	Steel	New London, CT
SHIPPINGPORT (ARDM 4)	1979	7,800	Steel	New London, CT
ARCO (ARDM 5)	1986	7,800	Steel	San Diego, CA

Sales: ARD 2 to Mexico; 5, Chile; 6, Pakistan; 8, Peru; 9, Taiwan; 11, Mexico; 12, Turkey; 13, Venezuela; 14, Brazil; 15, Mexico; 17, Ecuador; 22 (Windsor), Taiwan; 23, Argentina; 24, Ecuador; 25, Chile; 28, Colombia; 29, Iran; 32, Chile. **UPDATED**

ARCO   3/1998, van Ginderen Collection / 0053381

YARD FLOATING DRY DOCKS (YFD)

Name/No	Completed	Capacity (tons)	Construction	Status
YFD 54	1943	5,000	Wood	Commercial lease, Todd Pacific SY, Seattle, WA
YFD 69	1945	15,000	Steel (3)	Commercial lease, Port of Portland, OR
YFD 70	1945	15,000	Steel (3)	Commercial lease, Todd Pacific SY, Seattle, WA
YFD 83 (ex-AFDL 31)	1943	1,000	Steel	US Coast Guard

VERIFIED

UNCLASSIFIED MISCELLANEOUS (IX)

Notes: (1) In addition to the vessels listed below, one of the ex-'Forrest Sherman' class, *Decatur*, completed conversion on 21 October 1994 as a Self-Defence testing-ship, including high-energy laser trials. Tests with HFSWR (high-frequency surface wave radar) started mid-1997.
(2) *Mercer* IX 502 and *Nueces* IX 503 are barrack ships of mid-1940s vintage.
(3) IX 516 is a decommissioned SSBN used for propulsion plant training and IX 509 is a research barge.
(4) IX 517 is a submarine sea trials escort vessel *(Gosport)* and IX 518 is the decommissioned submarine tender *Proteus* used for accommodation at Puget Sound.
(5) IX 519 is used as a boat platform for *La Salle*. IX 520 is an accommodation barge and IX 523 is used for training, both at Norfolk, VA.

Name	Builders	Launched	Under Way	F/S
CONSTITUTION	Hartt Shipyard, Boston	21 Oct 1797	22 July 1798	AA

Displacement, tons: 2,200
Dimensions, feet (metres): 316 oa; 175 wl × 43.5 × 21 (96.3; 53.3 × 13.2 × 6.4)
Speed, knots: 12 under sail
Complement: 62 (2 officers)

Comment: The oldest ship remaining on the Navy List. One of six frigates authorised 7 March 1794. Best remembered for her service in the war of 1812, in which she earned the nickname 'Old Ironsides'. Following extensive restoration (1927-30), went on a three year goodwill tour around the United States (1931-34), travelling over 22,000 miles and receiving over 4 million visitors. Open to the public in her homeport of Boston, the ship receives over a million visitors a year. The most recent overhaul was conducted at the Charlestown Naval Shipyard, Boston from 1992-96. Under fighting sails (jibs, topsails and spanker) *Constitution* sailed for the first time in 116 years on 21 July 1997 as part of her bicentennial celebration. Armament is 32 × 24 pounder guns and 20 × 32 pounder carronades. Sail area 42,710 sq ft (13,018 m²). **UPDATED**

CONSTITUTION   7/1997*, Todd Stevens, US Navy / 0016501

Name	No	Builders	Commissioned	F/S
ORCA	IX 508 (ex-LCU 1618)	Gunderson Bros, Portland	1959	PSA

Comment: For general characteristics, see under 'LCU 1600' class in the *Amphibious Warfare* section. Conversion and overhaul in 1977 included installation of a bow thruster, a bridge and pilot-house, and a hangar type enclosed storage area in the well-deck, for the support of the Center's recovery vehicles CURV I and CURV II and installation of a crane. Reclassified as IX on 1 December 1979. Assigned to the Naval Command, Control and Ocean Surveillance Center at San Diego, CA. Is being used for range support of test and evaluation programmes. **UPDATED**

ORCA   8/1999*, van Ginderen Collection / 0084158

Name	Builders	Commissioned
IX 514 (ex-*YFU 79*)	Pacific Coast Eng, Alameda	1968

Displacement, tons: 380 full load
Dimensions, feet (metres): 125 × 36 × 7.5 (38.1 × 10.9 × 2.3)
Main machinery: 4 GM 6-71 diesels; 696 hp (519 kW) sustained; 2 shafts
Speed, knots: 8
Radars: Navigation: Racal Decca; I-band.

Comment: Harbour utility craft converted in 1986 with a flight deck covering two thirds of the vessel and a new bridge and flight control position at the forward end. Used for basic helicopter flight training at Pensacola, Florida. Similar craft *IX 501* deleted. **VERIFIED**

IX 514   12/1994, van Ginderen Collection

Name	Builders	Commissioned
IX 515 (SES-200) (ex-USCG *Dorado*)	Bell Halter, New Orleans	Feb 1979

Displacement, tons: 243 full load
Dimensions, feet (metres): 159.1 × 42.6 × 6; 3 on cushion (48.5 × 13 × 1.8; 0.9)
Main machinery: 2 MTU 16V 396 TB94 diesels (propulsion); 5,800 hp(m) (4.26 MW) sustained; 2 Kamewa 71 water-jets
2 MTU 6V 396 TB83 diesels (lift); 1,560 hp(m) (1.15 MW) sustained
Speed, knots: 45. **Range, miles:** 2,950 at 30 kt
Complement: 22 (2 officers)

Comment: The *IX 515* is a waterborne, air-supported craft with catamaran-style rigid sidewalls. It uses a cushion of air trapped between the sidewalls and flexible bow and stern seals to lift a large part of the hull clear of the water to reduce drag. A portion of the sidewall remains in the water to aid in stability and manoeuvrability. Modifications to the advanced ride control system were made in 1989. Serve as a high-performance test platform for weapon system development programmes, and as operational demonstrator for an advanced naval vehicle hullform. Trials of ALISS (Advanced Lightweight Influence Sweep System) in 1996-97. Based in Norfolk, VA. **VERIFIED**

IX 515   9/1998, Findler & Winter / 0053382

MINOR AUXILIARIES

Note: As of January 2000, the US Navy had about 600 active and inactive service craft, primarily small craft, on the US Naval Vessel Register. A majority of them provide services to the fleet in various harbours and ports. Others are ocean-going ships that provide services to the fleet in the research area. Most of the service craft are rated as 'active, in service', but a few are rated as 'in commission'. Some are accommodation ships.

2 DIVING TENDERS (YDT)

NEPTUNE YDT 17   **POSEIDON** YDT 18

Displacement, tons: 275 full load
Dimensions, feet (metres): 136 × 27 × 5.2 *(41.5 × 5.2 × 1.6)*
Main machinery: 2 Caterpillar diesels; 2,600 hp *(1.91MW)*; 2 Hamilton waterjets
Speed, knots: 20
Complement: 8 plus 7 divers

Comment: Tenders used to support shallow-water diving operations and are based at Panama City, FL. Ordered from Swiftships in July 1997 and delivered in April 1999.   *UPDATED*

NEPTUNE   *8/1999*, US Navy /* 0084159

3 HARBOUR UTILITY CRAFT LCU TYPE (YFU)

YFU 81   **YFU 83**   **YFU 91** (ex-LCU 1608)

Comment: Former utility landing craft employed primarily as harbour and coastal cargo craft (see Landing Craft for basic characteristics). Based at Roosevelt Roads.   *UPDATED*

YFU 91   *5/1999*, M Declerck /* 0084160

26 PATROL CRAFT (YP)

YP 676-YP 677   **YP 679-YP 702**

Displacement, tons: 167 full load
Dimensions, feet (metres): 108 × 24 × 5.9 *(32.9 × 7.3 × 1.8)*
Main machinery: 2 Detroit 12V-71 diesels; 680 hp *(507 kW)* sustained; 2 shafts
Speed, knots: 13.3. **Range, miles:** 1,500 at 12 kt
Complement: 6 (2 officers) plus 24 midshipmen
Radars: Navigation: I-band.

Comment: Built in the 1980s by Peterson Builders and Marinette Marine, both in Wisconsin. Twenty are based at the Naval Academy, Annapolis; three at the Naval air station, Pensacola; two at Naval Underwater Warfare Centre, Keyport; and two at the USCG Academy. Some earlier versions converted for mine countermeasures operations and assigned to the former COOP project which was discontinued in 1995.   *UPDATED*

YP 698   *4/1999*, van Ginderen Collection /* 0084161

2 TORPEDO TRIALS CRAFT (YTT)

BATTLE POINT YTT 10   **DISCOVERY BAY** YTT 11

Displacement, tons: 1,168 full load
Dimensions, feet (metres): 186.5 × 40 × 10.5 *(56.9 × 12.2 × 3.2)*
Main machinery: 1 Cummins KTA50-M diesel; 1,250 hp *(932 kW)* sustained; 1 shaft; 1 bow thruster; 400 hp *(298 kW)*; 2 stern thrusters; 600 hp *(448 kW)*
Speed, knots: 11. **Range, miles:** 1,000 at 10 kt
Complement: 31 plus 9 spare berths

Comment: Built by McDermott Shipyard, Morgan City, and delivered in 1991-92. Fitted with two 21 in Mk 59 and three (one triple) 12.75 in Mk 32 Mod 5 torpedo tubes. YTT 10 is used for torpedo trials and development at Keyport, Washington. A battery is fitted for limited duration operations with the diesel shutdown. YTT 11 assigned to National Oceanographic as a ROV carrier for research into US coastal waters until 2004. Two others of the class are in reserve. Underwater recovery vessels SORD 4, TROV and CURV.   *UPDATED*

YTT   *9/1999*, van Ginderen Collection /* 0084162

22 TORPEDO RETRIEVERS (TR)

Comment: Five different types spread around the Fleet bases and at AUTEC. There are 3 × 65 ft, 5 × 72 ft, 5 × 85 ft, 3 × 100 ft and 8 × 120 ft.   *VERIFIED*

TR 3   *9/1998, Findler & Winter /* 0053386

TUGS

38 LARGE HARBOUR TUGS (YTB)

NATICK	YTB 760	MASSAPEQUA	YTB 807
MUSKEGON	YTB 763	WENATCHEE	YTB 808
OKMULGEE	YTB 765	ANOKA	YTB 810
WAPAKONETA	YTB 766	ACCONAC	YTB 812
APALACHICOLA	YTB 767	NEODESHA	YTB 815
CHESANING	YTB 769	MECOSTA	YTB 818
DAHLONEGA	YTB 770	WANAMASSA	YTB 820
KEOKUK	YTB 771	TONTOGANY	YTB 821
WAUWATOSA	YTB 775	PAWHUSKA	YTB 822
MANISTEE	YTB 782	CANONCHET	YTB 823
REDWING	YTB 783	SANTAQUIN	YTB 824
KALISPELL	YTB 784	CATAHECASSA	YTB 828
KITTANNING	YTB 787	METACOM	YTB 829
TOMAHAWK	YTB 789	DEKANAWIDA	YTB 831
MARINETTE	YTB 791	PETALESHARO	YTB 832
PIQUA	YTB 793	SHABONEE	YTB 833
SACO	YTB 796	NEWGAGON	YTB 834
TAMAQUA	YTB 797	SKENANDOA	YTB 835
OPELIKA	YTB 798	POKAGON	YTB 836

Displacement, tons: 356 full load
Dimensions, feet (metres): 109 × 30 × 13.8 *(33.2 × 9.1 × 4.2)*
Main machinery: 1 Fairbanks-Morse 38D8-1/8 diesel; 2,000 hp *(1.49 MW)* sustained; 1 shaft
Speed, knots: 12. **Range, miles:** 2,000 at 12 kt
Complement: 10-12
Radars: Navigation: Marconi LN66; I-band.

Comment: Built between 1959 and 1975. Two transferred to Saudi Arabia in 1975. Most are to be taken out of service by late 2000 and tugs are being provided by MSC charter.   *UPDATED*

MARINETTE   *3/1999*, M Declerck /* 0085301

RESEARCH SHIPS

Note: There are many naval associated research vessels which are civilian manned and not carried on the US Naval Vessel Register. In addition civilian ships are leased for short periods to support a particular research project or trial. Some of those employed include *RSB-1* (missile booster recovery), *Acoustic Pioneer* and *Acoustic Explorer* (acoustic research).

ACOUSTIC PIONEER   3/1996*, W H Clements / 0085302

SLICE

Displacement, tons: 180 full load
Dimensions, feet (metres): 105 × 55.5 × 14 *(32 × 16.9 × 4.3)*
Main machinery: 2 MTU 16V 396 TB94 diesels; 13,700 hp(m) *(10.07 MW)*; 2 shafts; acbLIPS cp props
Speed, knots: 30
Complement: 12

Comment: Technology demonstrator built by Pacific Marine and owned by Lockheed Martin. Based in Honolulu completing sea trials in December 1997. The ship has been used for deck trials of helicopters and UAVs. Currently in use for mid-range tracking of surface-to-air missiles.
NEW ENTRY

SLICE   6/1999*, US Navy / 0084163

SEA SHADOW

Displacement, tons: 560 full load
Dimensions, feet (metres): 160 × 70 × 14 *(48.8 × 21.3 × 4.3)*
Main machinery: Diesel-electric; 2 Detroit 12V-149TI diesels; 2 shafts
Speed, knots: 13. **Range, miles:** 2,250 at 9 kt
Complement: 12

Comment: Built by Lockheed in 1983-84. Testing started in 1985 but the ship was then laid up until April 1993 when testing resumed off Santa Cruz island, southern California. This is a stealth ship prototype of SWATH design with sides angled at 45° to minimise the radar cross-section. Operated by Lockheed for testing all aspects of stealth technology and reactivated for a six year programme at San Diego in early 1999.
UPDATED

SEA SHADOW   9/1999*, van Ginderen Collection / 0084164

3 ASHEVILLE CLASS

ATHENA (ex-*Chehalis*)   **ATHENA II** (ex-*Grand Rapids*)   **LAUREN** (ex-*Douglas*)

Displacement, tons: 245 full load
Dimensions, feet (metres): 164.5 × 23.8 × 9.5 *(50.1 × 7.3 × 2.9)*
Main machinery: CODOG; 1 GE LM 1500 gas-turbine; 12,500 hp *(9.3 MW)*; 2 Cummins VT12-875 diesels; 1,450 hp *(1.07 MW)*; 2 shafts; cp props
Speed, knots: 16. **Range, miles:** 1,700 at 16 kt
Complement: 22

Comment: All built 1969-71. Work for the Carderock Division, Naval Surface Warfare Center, at Panama City, Florida. Disarmed except *Lauren* which has maintained its military appearance.
VERIFIED

ATHENA II   6/1993, Giorgio Arra

RESEARCH OCEANOGRAPHIC SHIPS

2 MELVILLE CLASS (AGOR)

Name	No	Builders	Completed	F/S
MELVILLE	AGOR 14	Defoe SB Co, Bay City, MI	27 Aug 1969	Loan
KNORR	AGOR 15	Defoe SB Co, Bay City, MI	14 Jan 1970	Loan

Displacement, tons: 2,670 full load
Dimensions, feet (metres): 278.9 × 46.3 × 15.1 *(85 × 14.1 × 4.6)*
Main machinery: Diesel-electric; 4 Caterpillar 3516 diesel generators; 3 motors; 3,000 hp *(2.24 MW)*; 3 shafts (2 aft, 1 fwd)
Speed, knots: 14. **Range, miles:** 12,000 at 12 kt
Complement: 58 (9 officers) plus 33 scientists

Comment: *Melville* operated by Scripps Institution of Oceanography and *Knorr* by Woods Hole Oceanography Institution for the Office of Naval Research, under technical control of the Oceanographer of the Navy. Fitted with internal wells for lowering equipment, underwater lights and observation ports. Facilities for handling small research submersibles. Problems with the propulsion system have led to major modifications including electric drive (vice the original mechanical) and the insertion of a 34 ft central section increasing the displacement from the original 1,915 tons and allowing better accommodation and improved laboratory spaces. The forward propeller is retractable. These ships are highly manoeuvrable for precise position keeping.
UPDATED

KNORR   10/1997*, Harald Carstens / 0016554

1 GYRE CLASS (AGOR)

Name	No	Builders	Completed	F/S
GYRE	AGOR 21	Halter Marine	14 Nov 1973	Loan

Displacement, tons: 1,427 full load
Dimensions, feet (metres): 174 × 36 × 13 *(53 × 11 × 4)*
Main machinery: 2 Caterpillar diesels; 1,700 hp *(1.27 MW)*; 2 shafts; cp props; bow thruster; 150 hp *(112 kW)*
Speed, knots: 11.5. **Range, miles:** 12,000 at 10 kt
Complement: 13 plus 19 scientists

Comment: Based on a commercial ship design. Open deck aft provides space for equipment vans to permit rapid change of mission capabilities. Single hard-chine hulls. Assigned for operation to Texas A & M University. Second of class *Moana Wave* paid off in 1999 and may be taken up by the State of Alaska.
UPDATED

MOANA WAVE   1991*, van Ginderen Collection / 0084166

0 + 1 AGOR-26 CLASS (AGOR)

Name	No	Builders	Completed
—	AGOR 26	Atlantic Marine, Jacksonville	Oct 2001

Displacement, tons: 2,500 full load
Dimensions, feet (metres): 182 × 88 × - *(55.5 × 26.8 × -)*

Comment: Lockheed Martin SWATH ship design to be loaned to the University of Hawaii.
NEW ENTRY

4 THOMAS G THOMPSON CLASS (AGOR)

Name	No	Builders	Launched	Completed	F/S
THOMAS G THOMPSON	AGOR-23	Halter Marine	27 July 1990	8 July 1991	Loan
(ex-Ewing)					
ROGER REVELLE	AGOR-24	Halter Marine	20 Apr 1995	11 June 1996	Loan
ATLANTIS	AGOR-25	Halter Marine	1 Feb 1996	3 Mar 1997	Loan
RONALD H BROWN	— (ex-AGOR-26)	Halter Marine	30 May 1996	25 Apr 1997	NOAA
(ex-Researcher)					

Displacement, tons: 3,251 full load
Dimensions, feet (metres): 274 oa; 246.8 wl × 52.5 × 19 *(83.5; 75.2 × 16 × 5.6)*
Main machinery: Diesel-electric; 6 Caterpillar diesel generators; 6.65 MW (3 1.5 MW and 3 715 kW); 2 motors; 6,000 hp *(4.48 MW)*; 2 shafts; bow thruster; 1,140 hp *(850 kW)*
Speed, knots: 15. **Range, miles:** 11,300 at 12 kt
Complement: 22 plus 37 scientists
Sonars: Atlas Elektronik Hydrographic.

Comment: *Thomas G Thompson* is the first of a class of oceanographic research vessels capable of operating worldwide in all seasons and suitable for use by navy laboratories, contractors and academic institutions. Dynamic positioning system enables station to be held within 300 ft of a point. 4,000 sq ft of laboratories. Loaned to the University of Washington and sponsored by the Chief of Naval Research, these ships are not part of the MSC. Ships in this series are able to meet changing oceanographic requirements for general, year-round, worldwide research. This includes launching, towing and recovering a variety of equipment. The ships are also involved in hydrographic data collection. *Roger Revelle* was authorised in FY92, ordered 11 January 1993 and is operated by the Scripps Institute of Oceanography. The third and fourth were ordered from Trinity Marine on 15 February 1994 and are 9 ft longer than the first pair and can carry *Alvin* DSV 2. *Atlantis* is operated by the Woods Hole Oceanographic Institution. *Ronald H Brown* by NOAA.
UPDATED

THOMAS G THOMPSON   *3/1996*, Robert Pabst /* 0084165

DEEP SUBMERGENCE VEHICLES

(Included in US Naval Vessel Register)

Notes: (1) Deep submergence vehicles and other craft and support ships are operated by Submarine Development Group One at San Diego, California. The Group is a major operational command that includes advanced diving equipment; divers trained in 'saturation' techniques; DSRV-1, DSRV-2; the submarine *Dolphin* (AGSS 555) and several submarine rescue ships. Two unmanned vessels CURV (Cable Controlled Underwater Remote Vehicle) Super Scorpios made test dives to 5,000 ft *(1,524 m)* and ATV (Advanced Tethered Vehicle) to 20,000 ft *(6,100 m)* in late 1990.
(2) There are also four naval ROVs operated by the Supervisor of Salvage and Diving. These are air-transportable and can be operated from most warships.
(3) A contract was placed with Newport News on 15 February 1999 to build *Cutthroat* LSV-2. This is a 0.294 scale model of *Virginia* SSN 774 designed to evaluate technologies planned for the 'Virginia' class SSNs. The ship is being built by Electric Boat. 196 tons displacement, 110 × 10 ft and has a 3,000 hp *(2.21 MW)* electric drive motor. There are plans to increase the power of the electric drive to 6,000 hp. Delivery is scheduled for January 2001 and the craft is to be based at Bayview, Idaho.

2 DEEP SUBMERGENCE RESCUE VEHICLES

Name	No	Builders	In service	F/S
MYSTIC	DSRV 1	Lockheed Missiles and Space Co,	7 Aug 1971	PSA
AVALON	DSRV 2	Sunnyvale, CA	28 July 1972	ASA

Displacement, tons: 30 surfaced; 38 dived
Dimensions, feet (metres): 49.2 × 8 *(15 × 2.4)*
Main machinery: Electric motors; silver/zinc batteries; 1 prop (movable control shroud); 4 ducted thrusters (2 fwd, 2 aft)
Speed, knots: 4. **Range, miles:** 24 at 3 kt
Complement: 4 (pilot, co-pilot, 2 rescue sphere operators) plus 24 rescued men
Sonars: Search and navigational sonar, and closed-circuit television (supplemented by optical devices) are installed in the DSRV to determine the exact location of a disabled submarine within a given area and for pinpointing the submarine's escape hatches. Side-looking sonar can be fitted for search missions.

Comment: The DSRV is intended to provide a quick-reaction worldwide, all-weather capability for the rescue of survivors in a disabled submarine. Transportable by road, aircraft (in C-141 and C-5 jet cargo aircraft), surface ship, and specially modified SSNs.
The carrying submarine will launch and recover the DSRV while submerged and, if necessary, while under ice. A total of six DSRVs were planned, but only two were funded. They alternate their duties every two months.
The outer hull is constructed of formed fibreglass. Within this outer hull are three interconnected spheres which form the main pressure capsule. Each sphere is 7.5 ft in diameter and is constructed of HY-140 steel. The forward sphere contains the vehicle's control equipment and is manned by the pilot and co-pilot, the centre and after spheres accommodate 24 passengers and a third crewman. Under the DSRV's centre sphere is a hemispherical protrusion or 'skirt' which seals over the disabled submarine's hatch. During the mating operation the skirt is pumped dry to enable personnel to transfer. Operating depth, 1,525 m *(5,000 ft)*. Names are not 'official'. Both have been upgraded with modern electronics and navigation systems.
Avalon carried out trials with the British SSBN *Victorious* in November 1995.   ***UPDATED***

MYSTIC   *11/1998, van Ginderen Collection /* 0053388

AVALON   *3/1999*, van Ginderen Collection /* 0085303

1 DEEP SUBMERGENCE VEHICLE: ALVIN TYPE

Name	No	Builders	F/S
ALVIN	DSV 2	General Mills Inc, Minneapolis	PSA

Displacement, tons: 18 full load
Dimensions, feet (metres): 26.5 × 8.5 *(8.1 × 2.6)*
Main machinery: 6 brushless DC motors; 6 thrusters; 2 vertical-motion thrusters (located near the centre of gravity); 2 horizontally (near stern) (1 directed athwartships, 1 directed longitudinally); 2 on rotatable shaft near stern for vertical or longitudinal motion
Speed, knots: 2. **Range, miles:** 3 at 0.5 kt
Complement: 3 (1 pilot, 2 observers)

Comment: Built for operation by the Woods Hole Oceanographic Institution for the Office of Naval Research. Original configuration had an operating depth of 6,000 ft. Named for Allyn C Vine of Woods Hole Oceanographic Institution. *Alvin* accidentally sank in 5,051 ft of water on 16 October 1968; subsequently raised in August 1969; refurbished 1970-71 in original configuration. Placed in service on Navy List 1 June 1971. Subsequently refitted with titanium pressure sphere to provide increased depth capability and again operational in November 1973. She has two banks of lead acid batteries, 120 V DC system with 47 kW/h capacity. Operating depth, 4,000 m *(13,120 ft)*. Two other DSVs were placed out of service in 1997/98, one transferred to the Woods Hole Institute.
VERIFIED

1 NUCLEAR-POWERED OCEAN ENGINEERING AND RESEARCH VEHICLE

Name	Builders	In service	F/S
NR 1	General Dynamics (Electric Boat Div)	27 Oct 1969	ASA

Displacement, tons: 380 surfaced; 700 dived
Dimensions, feet (metres): 147 × 12.4 × 14.6 *(44.8 × 3.8 × 4.5)*
Main machinery: Nuclear; 1 PWR; 1 turbo-alternator; 2 motors (external to the hull); 2 props; 4 ducted thrusters (2 vertical, 2 horizontal)
Complement: 13 (3 officers, 2 scientists)

Comment: NR 1 was built primarily to serve as a test platform for a small nuclear propulsion plant; however, the craft additionally provides an advanced deep submergence ocean engineering and research capability. She was the only Naval deep submergence vehicle to be used in the recovery of the wreckage of the space shuttle *Challenger* January to April 1986. Laid down on 10 June 1967; launched on 25 January 1969. Commanded by an officer-in-charge vice commanding officer. First nuclear-propelled service craft. Overhauled and refuelled in 1993. Refitted with a new bow which extended her length by 9.6 ft, and new sonars and cameras. In 1995 and again in 1997 she was used for an archaeological survey of the Carthage-Ostia trade route.
The NR 1 has wheels beneath the hull to permit 'bottom crawling' and she is fitted with external lights, external television cameras, a remote-controlled manipulator, and various recovery devices. No periscopes, but fixed television mast. Diving depth, 3,000 ft *(914 m)*. A surface 'mother' ship is required to support her.
UPDATED

NR 1   *7/1996*, van Ginderen Collection /* 0016582

MILITARY SEALIFT COMMAND (MSC)

Notes: (1) The Military Sealift Command is responsible for providing sea transportation, logistics forces and special mission ships for the Department of Defense.
(2) Headquarters are in the Washington Navy Yard, Washington DC. The organisation is commanded by a Rear Admiral, and its five principal area commands by Captains.
(3) MSC ships are assigned standard hull designations with the added prefix 'T'. All are unarmed. Ships' funnels have black, grey, blue and gold horizontal bands.
(4) On 1 October 1987, the transportation elements of the Army, Navy and Air Force were merged into the US Transportation Command, a unified command with headquarters at Scott Air Force Base, Ill. In 1992, based on lessons learned during Desert Shield/Desert Storm, USTRANSCOM was designated as the single manager for defence transportation in peace and war.

NAVAL FLEET AUXILIARY FORCE

0 + (12) AUXILIARY DRY CARGO SHIP (ADC(X))

Displacement, tons: 17,871 light; 34,416 full load
Dimensions, feet (metres): 689 × 100 × 28.9 *(210 × 30.5 × 8.9)*
Main machinery: 2 diesels or 2 gas turbines; 2 shafts
Speed, knots: 20. **Range, miles:** 11,535 at 20 kt
Complement: 120
Cargo capacity: 5,463 tons dry; 2,390 tons fuel
Helicopters: 2 UH 46D Sea Knight.

Comment: Design and construction contract planned for late 2000, with a first order in 2002 for completion in 2005. Three RAS stations each side. To be built to commercial standards and to replace existing AE and AFS ships for the provision of dry cargo and ammunition at sea. ***NEW ENTRY***

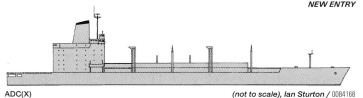

ADC(X) *(not to scale), Ian Sturton /* 0084168

3 MARS CLASS: COMBAT STORE SHIPS (AFS)

Name	No	Builders	Commissioned	F/S
CONCORD	T-AFS 5	National Steel & Shipbuilding Co	27 Nov 1968	TPA
SAN JOSE	T-AFS 7	National Steel & Shipbuilding Co	23 Oct 1970	TAA
NIAGARA FALLS	T-AFS 3	National Steel & Shipbuilding Co	29 Apr 1967	TPA

Displacement, tons: 9,200 light; 15,900-18,663 full load
Dimensions, feet (metres): 581 × 79 × 26 *(177.1 × 24.1 × 7.9)*
Main machinery: 3 Babcock & Wilcox boilers; 580 psi *(40.8 kg/cm²)*; 825°F *(440°C)*; 1 De Laval turbine (Westinghouse in AFS 6); 22,000 hp *(16.4 MW)*; 1 shaft
Speed, knots: 20. **Range, miles:** 10,000 at 18 kt
Complement: 125 civilians plus 51 naval
Cargo capacity: 2,625 tons dry stores; 1,300 tons refrigerated stores (varies with specific loadings)
Radars: Navigation: 2 Raytheon; I-band.
Tacan: URN 25.
Helicopters: 2 UH-46E Sea Knight normally assigned or 2 K-MAX.

Comment: *Concord* transferred to MSC on 15 October 1992 after disarming and conversion to a civilian crew. *San Jose* followed on 2 November 1993 and *Niagara Falls* on 23 September 1994. All have accommodation improvements and stores lifts installed. These ships carry comprehensive inventories of aviation spare parts as well as the cargo listed above. Two others of the class de-activated in 1997. ***UPDATED***

SAN JOSE *10/1999*, John Mortimer /* 0084170

7 KILAUEA CLASS: AMMUNITION SHIPS (AE)

Name	No	Builders	Commissioned	F/S
KILAUEA	T-AE 26	General Dynamics, Quincy	10 Aug 1968	TPA
BUTTE	T-AE 27	General Dynamics, Quincy	14 Dec 1968	TAA/ROS
SANTA BARBARA	T-AE 28	Bethlehem Steel	11 July 1970	TAA/ROS
FLINT	T-AE 32	Ingalls Shipbuilding	20 Nov 1971	TPA
SHASTA	T-AE 33	Ingalls Shipbuilding	26 Feb 1972	TPA
MOUNT BAKER	T-AE 34	Ingalls Shipbuilding	22 July 1972	TAA
KISKA	T-AE 35	Ingalls Shipbuilding	16 Dec 1972	TPA

Displacement, tons: 9,340 light; 19,940 full load
Dimensions, feet (metres): 564 × 81 × 28 *(171.9 × 24.7 × 8.5)*
Main machinery: 3 Foster-Wheeler boilers; 600 psi *(42.3 kg/cm²)*; 870°F *(467°C)*; 1 GE turbine; 22,000 hp *(16.4 MW)*; 1 shaft
Speed, knots: 20. **Range, miles:** 10,000 at 18 kt
Complement: 125 civilians plus 24 naval
Radars: Navigation: 2 Raytheon; I-band.
Tacan: URN 25.
Helicopters: 2 UH-46E Sea Knight (cargo normally embarked).

Comment: *Kilauea* transferred to MSC 1 October 1980, *Flint* in August 1995, *Butte* in June 1996, *Kiska* in August 1996, *Mount Baker* in December 1996, *Shasta* in October 1997 and *Santa Barbara* in September 1998. An eighth of class was to have transferred in 1999, but has been decommissioned. Pacific Fleet units may carry 12.7 mm MGs to discourage pirates. Ships undergo a civilian modification overhaul during which accommodation is improved. Main armament taken out. Seven UNREP stations operational: four port, three starboard. ***VERIFIED***

KILAUEA *3/1998, A Sharma /* 0053389

3 SIRIUS (LYNESS) CLASS: COMBAT STORES SHIP (AFS)

Name	No	Builders	Commissioned	F/S
SIRIUS (ex-*Lyness*)	T-AFS 8	Swan Hunter & Wigham Richardson Ltd, Wallsend-on-Tyne	22 Dec 1966	TAA
SPICA (ex-*Tarbatness*)	T-AFS 9	Swan Hunter & Wigham Richardson Ltd, Wallsend-on-Tyne	21 Mar 1967	TPA
SATURN (ex-*Stromness*)	T-AFS 10	Swan Hunter & Wigham Richardson Ltd, Wallsend-on-Tyne	10 Aug 1967	TAA

Displacement, tons: 9,010 light; 16,792 full load
Measurement, tons: 7,782 dwt; 12,359 gross; 4,744 net
Dimensions, feet (metres): 524 × 72 × 22 *(159.7 × 22 × 6.7)*
Main machinery: 1 Wallsend-Sulzer 8RD76 diesel; 11,520 hp *(8.59 MW)*; 1 shaft
Speed, knots: 18. **Range, miles:** 12,000 at 16 kt
Complement: 124 civilian plus 51 naval
Cargo capacity: 8,313 m³ dry; 3,921 m³ frozen
Radars: Navigation: 2 Raytheon; I-band.
Tacan: URN 25.
Helicopters: 2 UH-46E Sea Knight.

Comment: After a period of charter *Sirius* was purchased from the UK on 1 March 1982, *Spica* on 30 September 1982 and *Saturn* on 1 October 1983. All refitted from August 1992-96 to improve communications, RAS facilities and cargo handling equipment. ***UPDATED***

SATURN *5/1999*, Giorgio Ghiglione /* 0084171

14 HENRY J KAISER CLASS: OILERS (AO)

Name	No	Builders	Laid down	Completed	F/S
HENRY J KAISER	T-AO 187	Avondale	22 Aug 1984	19 Dec 1986	PREPO
JOHN J LENTHALL	T-AO 189	Avondale	15 July 1985	2 June 1987	TAA
WALTER S DIEHL	T-AO 193	Avondale	8 July 1986	13 Sep 1988	TPA
JOHN ERICSSON	T-AO 194	Avondale	15 Mar 1989	18 Mar 1991	TPA
LEROY GRUMMAN	T-AO 195	Avondale	7 June 1987	2 Aug 1989	TAA
KANAWHA	T-AO 196	Avondale	13 July 1989	6 Dec 1991	TAA
PECOS	T-AO 197	Avondale	17 Feb 1988	6 July 1990	TPA
BIG HORN	T-AO 198	Avondale	9 Oct 1989	31 July 1992	TAA
TIPPECANOE	T-AO 199	Avondale	19 Nov 1990	26 Mar 1993	TPA
GUADALUPE	T-AO 200	Avondale	9 July 1990	26 Oct 1992	TPA
PATUXENT	T-AO 201	Avondale	16 Oct 1991	21 June 1995	TAA
YUKON	T-AO 202	Avondale	13 May 1991	11 Dec 1993	TPA
LARAMIE	T-AO 203	Avondale	1 Oct 1994	24 May 1996	TAA
RAPPAHANNOCK	T-AO 204	Avondale	29 June 1992	7 Nov 1995	TPA

Displacement, tons: 40,700; 42,000 (T-AO 201, 203-204) full load
Dimensions, feet (metres): 677.5 × 97.5 × 35 *(206.5 × 29.7 × 10.7)*
Main machinery: 2 Colt-Pielstick 10 PC4.2 V 570 diesels; 34,422 hp(m) *(24.3 MW)* sustained; 2 shafts; cp props
Speed, knots: 20. **Range, miles:** 6,000 at 18 kt
Complement: 82 civilian (18 officers); 23 naval (1 officer) plus 21 spare
Cargo capacity: 180,000; 159,500 (T-AO 201, 203-204) barrels of fuel oil or aviation fuel
Guns: 1 Vulcan Phalanx CIWS (fitted for).
Countermeasures: Decoys: SLQ-25 Nixie; towed torpedo decoy.
Radars: Navigation: 2 Raytheon; I-band.
Helicopters: Platform only.

Comment: Construction was delayed initially by design difficulties, by excessive vibration at high speeds and other problems encountered in the first ship of the class. There are stations on both sides for underway replenishment of fuel and solids. Fitted with integrated electrical auxiliary propulsion. T-AOs 201, 203 and 204 were delayed by the decision to fit double hulls to meet the requirements of the Oil Pollution Act of 1990. This modification increases construction time from 32 to 42 months and reduces cargo capacity by 17 per cent although this can be restored in an emergency. Hull separation is 1.83 m at the sides and 1.98 m on the bottom. T-AOs 191 and 192 were transferred from Penn Ship (when the yard became bankrupt) to Tampa. Tampa's contract was also cancelled on 25 August 1993, with both vessels still incomplete. T-AO 192 was removed from the Register in late 1997. T-AO 187 has become part of the PREPO force at Diego Garcia and carries aviation fuel. T-AO 188 and 190 were laid up in mid-1996 and T-AO 189 in September 1997, but the latter was back in service in January 1999. It is likely that more of this class will be reactivated in due course. ***UPDATED***

PECOS *10/1999*, Findler & Winter /* 0084169

2 MERCY CLASS: HOSPITAL SHIPS (AH)

Name	No	Builders	Completed	F/S
MERCY (ex-SS *Worth*)	T-AH 19	National Steel & Shipbuilding Co	1976	ROS/TPA
COMFORT (ex-SS *Rose City*)	T-AH 20	National Steel & Shipbuilding Co	1976	ROS/TAA

Displacement, tons: 69,360 full load
Measurement, tons: 54,367 gross; 35,958 net
Dimensions, feet (metres): 894 × 105.6 × 32.8 *(272.6 × 32.2 × 10)*
Main machinery: 2 boilers; 2 GE turbines; 24,500 hp *(18.3 MW)*; 1 shaft
Speed, knots: 17. **Range, miles:** 13,420 at 17 kt
Complement: 73 civilian crew; 820 naval medical staff; 387 naval support staff
Radars: Navigation: SPS-67; I-band.
Tacan: URN 25.
Helicopters: Platform only.

Comment: Converted 'San Clemente' class tankers. *Mercy* was commissioned 19 December 1986; *Comfort* on 30 November 1987. Each ship has 1,000 beds and 12 operating theatres. Normally, the ships are kept in a reduced operating status in Baltimore, MD, and San Diego, CA, by a small crew of civilian mariners and active duty Navy medical and support personnel. Each ship can be fully activated and crewed within five days.

UPDATED

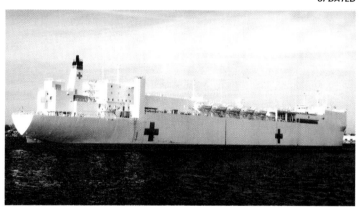
MERCY *3/1999*, van Ginderen Collection / 0084172*

5 POWHATAN CLASS: FLEET OCEAN TUGS (ATF)

Name	No	Laid down	Completed	F/S
CATAWBA	T-ATF 168	14 Dec 1977	28 May 1980	TPA
NAVAJO	T-ATF 169	14 Dec 1977	13 June 1980	TPA
MOHAWK	T-ATF 170	22 Mar 1979	16 Oct 1980	TAA
SIOUX	T-ATF 171	22 Mar 1979	1 May 1981	TPA
APACHE	T-ATF 172	22 Mar 1979	30 July 1981	TAA

Displacement, tons: 2,260 full load
Dimensions, feet (metres): 240.2 × 42 × 15 *(73.2 × 12.8 × 4.6)*
Main machinery: 2 GM EMD 20-645F7B diesels; 7,250 hp(m) *(5.41 MW)* sustained; 2 shafts; Kort nozzles; cp props; bow thruster; 300 hp *(224 kW)*
Speed, knots: 14.5. **Range, miles:** 10,000 at 13 kt
Complement: 21 (17 civilians, 4 naval communications technicians)
Guns: Space provided to fit 2—20 mm and 2—12.7 mm MGs.
Radars: Navigation: Raytheon 1660/12 and SPS-64(V)9; I-band.

Comment: Built at Marinette Marine Corp, Wisconsin patterned after commercial offshore supply ship design. Originally intended as successors to the 'Cherokee' and 'Abnaki' class ATFs. All transferred to MSC upon completion. 10 ton capacity crane and a bollard pull of at least 54 tons. A 'deck grid' is fitted aft which contains 1 in bolt receptacles spaced 24 in apart. This allows for the bolting down of a wide variety of portable equipment. There are two GPH fire pumps supplying three fire monitors with up to 2,200 gallons of foam per minute. A deep module can be embarked to support naval salvage teams. Two others of the class deactivated for commercial lease in 1999.

UPDATED

APACHE *6/1999*, van Ginderen Collection / 0084173*

SPECIAL MISSION SHIPS

Notes: (1) Civilian operated but some technical work, communications and research is done by naval personnel. Average of 25 days a month are spent at sea.
(2) There are also four chartered vessels: *Carolyn Chouest* (NR-1 support ship), *Kellie Chouest* and *Dolores Chouest* (both deep submergence submarine support ships), and *Cory Chouest* (support ship for IFA TAGOS trials). These ships are owned and operated by Edison Chouest.

CAROLYN CHOUEST *6/1999*, van Ginderen Collection / 0084174*

1 HAYES CLASS: ACOUSTIC RESEARCH SHIP (AG)

Name	No	Builders	Completed	F/S
HAYES	T-AG 195 (ex-AGOR 16)	Todd Shipyards, Seattle, WA	21 July 1971	TAA

Displacement, tons: 4,037 full load
Dimensions, feet (metres): 256.5 × 75 (see *Comment*) × 22 *(78.2 × 22.9 × 6.7)*
Main machinery: Diesel-electric; 2 Caterpillar 3516TA diesels; 3,620 hp *(2.7 MW)* sustained; 2 generators; 2 Westinghouse motors; 2,400 hp *(1.79 MW)*; 2 auxiliary diesels (for creep speed); 330 hp *(246 kW)*; 2 shafts; acbLIPS cp props
Speed, knots: 10. **Range, miles:** 2,000 at 10 kt
Complement: 19 civilian plus 29 scientists
Radars: Navigation: Raytheon TM 1650/6X and TM 1660/12S; I-band.

Comment: Catamaran hull. Laid down 12 November 1969; launched 2 July 1970. To Ready Reserve 10 June 1983 and transferred to James River (Maritime Administration) for lay-up in 1984 having been too costly to operate. Under FY86 programme was converted to Acoustic Research Ship (AG); reclassified T-AG 195 and completed in early 1992 after five years' work in two shipyards. Mission is to transport, deploy and retrieve acoustic arrays, to conduct acoustic surveys in support of the submarine noise reduction programme and to carry out acoustic testing. Catamaran hull design provides large deck working area, centre well for operating equipment at great depths, and removes laboratory areas from main propulsion machinery. Each hull is 246 ft long and 24 ft wide (maximum). There are three 36 in diameter instrument wells in addition to the main centre well.

VERIFIED

HAYES *2/1992*

1 ZEUS CLASS: CABLE REPAIRING SHIP (ARC)

Name	No	Builders	Completed	F/S
ZEUS	T-ARC 7	National Steel & Shipbuilding Co	19 Mar 1984	TPA

Displacement, tons: 8,370 light; 14,934 full load
Dimensions, feet (metres): 513 × 73 × 25 *(156.4 × 22.3 × 7.6)*
Main machinery: Diesel-electric; 5 GM EMD 20-645F7B diesel generators; 14.32 MW sustained; 2 motors; 10,200 hp *(7.51 MW)*; 2 shafts; cp props; bow thrusters (forward and aft)
Speed, knots: 15.8. **Range, miles:** 10,000 at 15 kt
Complement: 51 civilians plus 6 Navy plus 10 scientists

Comment: Ordered 7 August 1979. Remotely manned engineering room controlled from the bridge. Can lay up to 1,000 miles of cable in depths of 9,000 ft. As well as cable laying the ship is equipped for oceanographic survey.

UPDATED

ZEUS *3/1999*, M Declerck / 0084175*

1 CONVERTED COMPASS ISLAND CLASS:
MISSILE RANGE INSTRUMENTATION SHIP (AGM)

Name	No	Builders	Commissioned	F/S
OBSERVATION ISLAND	T-AGM 23	New York	5 Dec 1958	TPA
(ex-*Empire State Mariner*)	(ex-AG 154, ex-YAG 57)	Shipbuilding		

Displacement, tons: 13,060 light; 17,015 full load
Dimensions, feet (metres): 564 × 76 × 25 *(171.6 × 23.2 × 7.6)*
Main machinery: 2 Foster-Wheeler boilers; 600 psi *(42.3 kg/cm²)*; 875°F *(467°C)*; 1 GE turbine; 19,250 hp *(14.36 MW)*; 1 shaft
Speed, knots: 20. **Range, miles:** 17,000 at 15 kt
Complement: 66 civilians plus 59 scientists
Missiles: SLBM: She fired the first ship-launched Polaris missile at sea on 27 August 1959. Refitted to fire the improved Poseidon missile in 1969 and launched the first Poseidon test missile fired afloat on 16 December 1969.
Radars: Navigation: Raytheon 1650/9X and 1660/12S; I-band.
Tacan: URN 25.

Comment: Built as a 'Mariner' class merchant ship (C4-S-A1 type); launched on 15 August 1953; acquired by the Navy on 10 September 1956 for use as a Fleet Ballistic Missile (FBM) test ship. Converted at Norfolk Naval Shipyard. In reserve from September 1972. On 18 August 1977, *Observation Island* was reacquired by the US Navy from the Maritime Administration and transferred to the Military Sealift Command. Reclassified AGM 23 on 1 May 1979. Converted to Missile Range Instrumentation Ship from July 1979-April 1981 at Maryland SB and DD Co to carry an Air Force shipborne phased-array radar system (Cobra Judy and Cobra Gemini from 1999) for collection of data on foreign ballistic missile tests. Operated by the Navy in the North Pacific for the US Air Force Intelligence Command, Patrick Air Force Base, Florida.

UPDATED

OBSERVATION ISLAND   *11/1996*, Robert Pabst /* 0084178

9 STALWART CLASS:
OCEAN SURVEILLANCE/COUNTER DRUG PATROL SHIPS
(AGOS/AGM)

Name	No	Laid down		Completed		F/S
STALWART	T-AGOS 1	3 Apr	1982	9 Nov	1984	TAA
VINDICATOR	T-AGOS 3	14 Apr	1983	20 Nov	1984	TAA
PERSISTENT	T-AGOS 6	22 Oct	1984	14 Aug	1985	TAA
INDOMITABLE	T-AGOS 7	26 Jan	1985	26 Nov	1985	TAA
PREVAIL	T-AGOS 8	13 Mar	1985	5 Mar	1986	TAA
ASSERTIVE	T-AGOS 9	30 July	1985	12 Sep	1986	TPA
INVINCIBLE	T-AGOS 10	8 Nov	1985	3 Feb	1987	TPA
BOLD (ex-*Vigorous*)	T-AGOS 12	13 June	1988	20 Oct	1989	TAA
CAPABLE	T-AGOS 16	17 Oct	1987	8 July	1989	TAA

Displacement, tons: 2,285 full load
Dimensions, feet (metres): 224 × 43 × 14.9 *(68.3 × 13.1 × 4.5)*
Main machinery: Diesel-electric; 4 Caterpillar D 398B diesel generators; 3,200 hp *(2.39 MW)*; 2 motors; 1,600 hp *(1.2 MW)*; 2 shafts; bow thruster; 550 hp *(410 kW)*
Speed, knots: 11; 3 when towing. **Range, miles:** 4,000 at 11 kt; 6,450 at 3 kt
Complement: 23 (18 civilian, 5 Navy) (T-AGOS 8, 9 and 12)
38 (18 civilian; 20 Navy/CG) (T-AGOS 1, 3, 6, 7 and 16)
Radars: Air search: SPS-49 (T-AGOS 1, 3, 6, 7 and 16); E/F-band; Cobra Gemini (T-AGOS 10); dual band; E/F and I (T-AGOS 10).
Surface search: Furuno (T-AGOS 1, 3, 6, 7 and 16); E/F-band.
Navigation: Furuno (T-AGOS 1, 3, 6, 7 and 16); I-band. 2 Raytheon (T-AGOS 8, 9 and 12); I-band.
IFF: UPX-36 (in some).
Sonars: SURTASS (T-AGOS 8, 9 and 12); towed array; passive surveillance.
WQT-2; low frequency active transmitter.

Comment: All built by Tacoma except *Capable* which was built by Halter Marine. Oceanographic and hydrographic surveys, underwater surveillance, acoustic research, submarine support, space tracking and Coast Guard support are just a few of the services these ships provide. Operated and maintained by civilian contractors. The Surveillance Towed Array Sensor is a linear array of 8.575 ft *(2.614 m)* deployed on a 6,000 ft *(1,829 m)* tow cable and neutrally buoyant. The array can operate at depths between 500 and 1,500 ft. Information from the array is relayed via WSC-6 (SHF) SATCOM link to the shore. WQT-2 is a 72 ton active transmitter. SURTASS LFA trials from 2000. *Bold* fitted with an experimental twin line array for shallow water. *Stalwart*, *Indomitable* and *Capable* have been modified for drug interdiction patrols supporting Joint Interagency Task Force (East); radars have been replaced. *Vindicator* and *Persistent* modified for a similar role with the Coast Guard and carry 50 kt pursuit boats. *Invincible* was converted as an AGM in early 1999 and is used to support *Observation Island* in this role. Others of the class are laid up. One to New Zealand and two to Portugal in 1997/99.

UPDATED

ASSERTIVE (SURTASS)   *8/1999*, Hachiro Nakai /* 0084176

STALWART (patrol)   *9/1997*, US Navy /* 0016556

INVINCIBLE (space)   *6/1999*, Ships of the World /* 0084177

1 WATERS CLASS: TEST SUPPORT SHIP (AGM)

Name	No	Builders	Completed	F/S
WATERS	T-AG 45	Avondale Industries	26 May 1993	TPA

Displacement, tons: 12,208 full load
Dimensions, feet (metres): 455 × 68.9 × 21 *(138.7 × 21 × 6.4)*
Main machinery: Diesel-electric; 5 GM EMD diesels; 7,400 hp *(5.45 MW)*; 2 Westinghouse motors; 6,800 hp *(15.07 MW)*; 2 shafts; 4 thrusters
Speed, knots: 12. **Range, miles:** 6,500 at 12 kt
Complement: 66 civilians plus 59 scientists
Radars: Navigation: 2 Raytheon; E/F- and I-bands.

Comment: Ordered 4 April 1990. Laid down 16 May 1991 and launched 6 June 1992. Carried out oceanographic and acoustic surveys in support of the Integrated Underwater Surveillance System. Converted in 1998 to support submarine navigation system testing and missile tracking. In 1999 has replaced *Vanguard* and *Range Sentinel*, both of which have been deactivated.

VERIFIED

WATERS   *4/1994, Giorgio Arra*

4 VICTORIOUS CLASS: OCEAN SURVEILLANCE SHIPS (AGOS)

Name	No	Builders	Completed		F/S
VICTORIOUS	T-AGOS 19	McDermott Marine	5 Sep	1991	TPA
ABLE	T-AGOS 20	McDermott Marine	22 July	1992	TAA
EFFECTIVE	T-AGOS 21	McDermott Marine	27 Jan	1993	TPA
LOYAL	T-AGOS 22	McDermott Marine	1 July	1993	TAA

Displacement, tons: 3,396 full load
Dimensions, feet (metres): 234.5 × 93.6 × 24.8 *(71.5 × 28.5 × 7.6)*
Main machinery: Diesel-electric; 4 Caterpillar 3512TA diesels; 5,440 hp *(4 MW)* sustained; 2 GE motors; 3,200 hp *(2.39 MW)*; 2 shafts; 2 bow thrusters; 2,400 hp *(1.79 MW)*
Speed, knots: 16; 3 when towing
Complement: 22 civilian plus 5 Navy
Radars: Navigation: 2 Raytheon; I-band.
Sonars: SURTASS and LFA; towed array; passive/active surveillance.

Comment: All of SWATH design because of its greater stability at slow speeds in high latitudes under adverse weather conditions. A contract for the first SWATH ship, T-AGOS 19, was awarded in November 1986, and options for the next three were exercised in October 1988. Same WSC-6 communications, links and operating procedures as the 'Stalwart' class. T-AGOS 20 conducted trials with a Reduced Diameter Array (RDA) with an enhanced signal processor. The Low Frequency Active component produces both mono and bistatic performance against submerged diesel submarines in shallow water. Short thin-line twin arrays have also been developed.

VERIFIED

LOYAL   *1/1999, van Ginderen Collection / 0053396*

1 IMPECCABLE CLASS: OCEAN SURVEILLANCE SHIP (AGOS)

Name	No	Builders	Completed	F/S
IMPECCABLE	T-AGOS 23	Tampa Shipyard/Halter Marine	July 2000	TAA

Displacement, tons: 5,370 full load
Dimensions, feet (metres): 281.5 × 95.8 × 26 *(85.8 × 29.2 × 7.9)*
Main machinery: Diesel-electric; 3 GM EMD 12-645F7B diesel generators; 5.48 MW *(60 Hz)* sustained; 2 Westinghouse motors; 5,000 hp *(3.73 MW)*; 2 shafts; 2 omni-thruster hydrojets; 1,800 hp *(1.34 MW)*
Speed, knots: 12; 3 when towing. **Range, miles:** 3,000 at 12 kt
Complement: 20 civilians plus 5 scientists plus 20 Navy
Radars: Navigation: Raytheon; I-band.
Sonars: SURTASS; passive surveillance towed array.

Comment: Hull form based on that of *Victorious*. Acoustic systems include an active low frequency towed array (LFA), which has a series of modules each of which houses two high-powered active transducers. These can be used with either mono or bistatic receivers. The payload is lowered through a centre well. Laid down 2 February 1993. Ship was 60 per cent complete when shipyard encountered difficulties that led to termination in October 1993 of the contract for completion of two 'Kaiser' class oilers. Work stopped on *Impeccable*, and the construction contract was also cancelled. The contract was sublet to Halter Marine on 20 April 1995 to complete the ship. Launched in April 1998. WSC-3(V)3 and WSC-6 communications fitted.

UPDATED

IMPECCABLE (artist's impression)   *1997*, Halter Marine / 0016555*

2 JOHN McDONNELL CLASS: SURVEYING SHIPS (AGS)

Name	No	Builders	Completed		F/S
JOHN McDONNELL	T-AGS 51	Halter Marine	16 Dec	1991	TAA
LITTLEHALES	T-AGS 52	Halter Marine	1 Jan	1992	TAA

Displacement, tons: 2,054 full load
Dimensions, feet (metres): 208 × 45 × 14 *(63.4 × 13.7 × 4.3)*
Main machinery: 1 GM EMD 12-645E6 diesel; 2,550 hp *(1.9 MW)* sustained; 1 auxiliary diesel; 230 hp *(172 kW)*; 1 shaft
Speed, knots: 12. **Range, miles:** 13,800 at 12 kt
Complement: 22 civilians plus 11 scientists

Comment: Laid down on 3 August 1989 and 25 October 1989 respectively. *McDonnell* launched 15 August 1990, *Littlehales* 14 February 1991. Carry 34 ft survey launches for data collection in coastal regions with depths between 10 and 600 m and in deep water to 4,000 m. A small diesel is used for propulsion at towing speeds of up to 6 kt. Simrad high-frequency active hull-mounted and side scan sonars are carried.

UPDATED

JOHN McDONNELL   *4/1999*, A Sharma / 0084180*

5 + 1 PATHFINDER CLASS: SURVEYING SHIPS (AGS)

Name	No	Builders	Launched		Completed		F/S
PATHFINDER	T-AGS 60	Halter Marine	7 Oct	1993	5 Dec	1994	TAA
SUMNER	T-AGS 61	Halter Marine	19 May	1994	30 May	1995	TAA
BOWDITCH	T-AGS 62	Halter Marine	15 Oct	1994	30 Dec	1995	TAA
HENSON	T-AGS 63	Halter Marine	21 Oct	1996	20 Feb	1998	TAA
BRUCE C HEEZEN	T-AGS 64	Halter Marine	17 Dec	1998	13 Jan	2000	TAA
MARY SEARS	T-AGS 65	Halter Marine	Sep	2000	Dec	2001	Bldg

Displacement, tons: 4,762 full load
Dimensions, feet (metres): 328.5 × 58 × 19 *(100.1 × 17.7 × 5.8)*
Main machinery: Diesel-electric; 4 EMD/Baylor diesel generators; 11,425 hp *(8.52 MW)*; 2 GE CDF 1944 motors; 8,000 hp *(5.97 MW)* sustained; 6,000 hp *(4.48 MW)*; 2 shafts; bow thruster; 1,500 hp *(1.19 MW)*
Speed, knots: 16. **Range, miles:** 12,000 at 12 kt
Complement: 28 civilians plus 27 oceanographers

Comment: Contract awarded in January 1991 for two ships with an option for a third which was taken up on 29 May 1992. A fourth ship was ordered in October 1994 with an option for two more. Fifth ordered 15 January 1997 and sixth on 6 January 1999. There are three multipurpose cranes and five winches plus a variety of oceanographic equipment including multibeam echo-sounders, towed sonars and expendable sensors. ROVs may be carried. Replacements for 'Robert D Conrad' class, all of which have been paid off or leased to other countries.

UPDATED

HENSON   *6/1998, Halter Marine / 0053398*

PATHFINDER   *1/1997*, Camil Busquets i Vilanova / 0016561*

1 SILAS BENT CLASS: SURVEYING SHIP (AGS)

Name	No	Builders	Completed	F/S
KANE	T-AGS 27	Christy Corp, Sturgeon Bay	19 May 1967	TAA

Displacement, tons: 2,550-2,843 full load
Dimensions, feet (metres): 285.3 × 48 × 15.1 *(87 × 14.6 × 4.6)*
Main machinery: Diesel-electric; 2 Alco diesel generators; 1 Westinghouse/GE motor; 3,600 hp *(2.69 MW)*; 1 shaft; cp prop; bow thruster; 350 hp *(261 kW)*
Speed, knots: 15. **Range, miles:** 12,000 at 14 kt
Complement: 31 civilians plus 28 scientists
Radars: Navigation: RM 1650/9X and TM 1660/12S; I-band.

Comment: Designed specifically for surveying operations. Bow propulsion unit for precise manoeuvrability and station keeping. Operated for the Oceanographer of the Navy under technical control of the Naval Oceanographic Office. One of the class transferred to Tunisia in 1995, and one to Turkey in 1999. This last one is planned to pay off in May 2001.
UPDATED

KANE   *1/1999*, C E Castle /* 0084179

SEALIFT FORCE

Note: These ships provide ocean transportation for Defense and other government agencies. As well as those listed below, there are two tankers, two down-range support and four freighting merchant ships under contract to MSC to support the Sealift Force in early 2000. These numbers vary with the operational requirement.

3 SHUGHART CLASS:
LARGE, MEDIUM-SPEED, RO-RO (LMSR) SHIPS (AKR)

Name	No	Completed	F/S
SHUGHART (ex-*Laura Maersk*)	T-AKR 295	7 May 1996	TPA
YANO (ex-*Leise Maersk*)	T-AKR 297	8 Feb 1997	TPA
SODERMAN (ex-*Lica Maersk*)	T-AKR 299	11 Nov 1997	TPA

Measurement, tons: 54,298 grt
Dimensions, feet (metres): 906.8 × 105.5 × 34.4 *(276.4 × 32.2 × 10.5)*
Main machinery: 1 Burmeister & Wain 12L90 GFCA diesel; 46,653 hp(m) *(34.29 MW)*; 1 shaft; bow and stern thrusters
Speed, knots: 24. **Range, miles:** 12,000 at 24 kt
Complement: 26-45 civilian; up to 50 Navy
Cargo capacity: 260,779 sq ft plus 51,682 sq ft deck cargo
Radars: Navigation: 2 Sperry ARPA; I-band.
Helicopters: Platform for 1 heavy *(Soderman)*.

Comment: All three were container ships built in Denmark in 1981 and lengthened by Hyundai in 1987. Conversion contract awarded to National Steel and Shipbuilding in July 1993. All are fitted with a stern slewing ramp, side accesses and cranes for both roll-on/roll-off and lift-on/lift-off capabilities. Two twin 55 ton cranes. Conversion for *Shughart* started in June 1994; *Yano* in May 1995; and *Soderman* in October 1995. *Soderman* again being converted in 2000/01 with a flight deck and wet stern ramp, plus accommodation for 50 marines.
UPDATED

SHUGART   *4/1999*, van Ginderen Collection /* 0084184

2 GORDON CLASS:
LARGE, MEDIUM-SPEED, RO-RO (LMSR) SHIPS (AKR)

Name	No	Completed	F/S
GORDON (ex-*Selandia*)	T-AKR 296	23 Aug 1996	PREPO/TPA
GILLILAND (ex-*Jutlandia*)	T-AKR 298	24 May 1997	PREPO

Measurement, tons: 55,422 grt
Dimensions, feet (metres): 956 × 105.8 × 36.3 *(291.4 × 32.2 × 11.9)*
Main machinery: 1 Burmeister & Wain 12K84EF diesel; 26,000 hp(m) *(19.11 MW)*; 2 Burmeister & Wain 9K84EF diesels; 39,000 hp(m) *(28.66 MW)*; 3 shafts (centre cp prop); bow thruster
Speed, knots: 24. **Range, miles:** 12,000 at 24 kt
Complement: 26-45 civilian; 50 Navy
Cargo capacity: 284,064 sq ft plus 49,991 sq ft deck cargo
Radars: Navigation: 2 Sperry ARPA; I-band.

Comment: Built in Denmark in 1972 and lengthened by Hyundai in 1984. Conversion contract given to Newport News Shipbuilding on 30 July 1993. Both fitted with a stern slewing ramp, side accesses and improved craneage. Conversion started for both ships on 15 October 1993. *Gilliland* operates as part of Afloat Prepositioning Squadron Two out of Diego Garcia.
UPDATED

GILLILAND   *2/2000*, A Sharma /* 0085304

8 ALGOL CLASS: FAST SEALIFT SHIPS (AKR)

Name	No	Builders	Delivered
ALGOL (ex-SS *Sea-Land Exchange*)	T-AKR 287	Rotterdamsche DD Mij NV, Rotterdam	7 May 1973
BELLATRIX (ex-SS *Sea-Land Trade*)	T-AKR 288	Rheinstahl Nordseewerke, Emden, West Germany	6 Apr 1973
DENEBOLA (ex-SS *Sea-Land Resource*)	T-AKR 289	Rotterdamsche DD Mij NV, Rotterdam	4 Dec 1973
POLLUX (ex-SS *Sea-Land Market*)	T-AKR 290	A G Weser, Bremen, West Germany	20 Sep 1973
ALTAIR (ex-SS *Sea-Land Finance*)	T-AKR 291	Rheinstahl Nordseewerke, Emden, West Germany	17 Sep 1973
REGULUS (ex-SS *Sea-Land Commerce*)	T-AKR 292	A G Weser, Bremen, West Germany	30 Mar 1973
CAPELLA (ex-SS *Sea-Land McLean*)	T-AKR 293	Rotterdamsche DD Mij NV, Rotterdam	4 Oct 1972
ANTARES (ex-SS *Sea-Land Galloway*)	T-AKR 294	A G Weser, Bremen, West Germany	27 Sep 1972

Displacement, tons: 55,355 full load
Measurement, tons: 25,389 net; 27,051-28,095 dwt
Dimensions, feet (metres): 946.2 × 106 × 34.8 *(288.4 × 32.3 × 10.6)*
Main machinery: 2 Foster-Wheeler boilers; 875 psi *(61.6 kg/cm²)*; 950°F *(510°C)*; 2 GE MST-19 steam turbines; 120,000 hp *(89.5 MW)*; 2 shafts
Speed, knots: 30. **Range, miles:** 12,200 at 27 kt
Complement: 42 (as merchant ship); 24 (minimum); 18 (ROS)
Helicopters: Platform only.

Comment: All were originally built as container ships for Sea-Land Services, Port Elizabeth, NJ, but used too much fuel to be cost-effective as merchant ships. Six ships of this class were approved for acquisition in FY81 and the remaining two in FY82. The purchase price included 4,000 containers and 800 container chassis for use in container ship configuration. All eight were converted to Fast Sealift Ships, which are vehicle cargo ships. Conversion included the addition of roll-on/roll-off features. The area between the forward and after superstructures allows for a helicopter flight deck. Capacities are as follows: (sq ft) 150,016 to 166,843 ro-ro; 43,407 lift-on/lift-off; and either 44 or 46 20 ft containers. In addition to one ro-ro ramp port and starboard, twin 35 ton pedestal cranes are installed between the deckhouses and twin 50 ton cranes are installed aft. Ninety-three per cent of a US Army mechanised division can be lifted using all eight ships. Seven of the class moved nearly 9 per cent of all the cargo transported between the US and Saudi Arabia during and after the Gulf War. Six were activated for the Somalian operation in December 1992 and all have been used in various operations and exercises since then. All based in Atlantic and Gulf of Mexico ports.
UPDATED

CAPELLA   *6/1999*, van Ginderen Collection /* 0084183

4 + 3 BOB HOPE CLASS:
LARGE, MEDIUM-SPEED, RO-RO (LMSR) SHIPS (AKR)

Name	No	Builders	Launched		Completed		F/S
BOB HOPE	T-AKR 300	Avondale	27 Mar	1997	18 Nov	1998	TPA/PREPO
FISHER	T-AKR 301	Avondale	21 Oct	1997	4 Aug	1998	TPA
SEAY	T-AKR 302	Avondale	25 June	1998	30 Mar	2000	TPA
MENDONCA	T-AKR 303	Avondale	25 May	1999	7 Oct	2000	Bldg
PILILAAU	T-AKR 304	Avondale	18 Jan	2000	Jan	2001	Bldg
BRITTIN	T-AKR 305	Avondale	July	2000	July	2001	Bldg
—	T-AKR 306	Avondale	Jan	2001	Jan	2002	Bldg

Displacement, tons: 62,069 full load
Dimensions, feet (metres): 951.4 × 106 × 35 *(290 × 32.3 × 11)*
Main machinery: 4 Colt Pielstick 10 PC4.2 V diesels; 65,160 hp(m) *(47.89 MW)*; 2 shafts; cp props
Speed, knots: 24. **Range, miles:** 12,000 at 24 kt
Complement: 26-45 civilian; up to 50 Navy
Cargo capacity: 397,413 sq ft. 13,250 tons

Comment: Contract awarded in 1993; options for additional ships exercised in 1994, 1995, 1996 and 1997. All fitted with a stern slewing ramp, side accesses and cranes for both roll-on/roll-off and lift-on/lift-off capabilities. Ramps extend to 130 ft *(40 m)*, and two twin 55 ton cranes are installed.
UPDATED

BOB HOPE   *6/1999*, Findler & Winter /* 0084181

5—T 5 TYPE: TANKERS (AOT)

Name	No	Builders	Commissioned
GUS W DARNELL	T-AOT 1121	American SB Co, Tampa, FL	11 Sep 1985
PAUL BUCK	T-AOT 1122	American SB Co, Tampa, FL	11 Sep 1985
SAMUEL L COBB	T-AOT 1123	American SB Co, Tampa, FL	15 Nov 1985
RICHARD G MATTHIESON	T-AOT 1124	American SB Co, Tampa, FL	18 Feb 1986
LAWRENCE H GIANELLA	T-AOT 1125	American SB Co, Tampa, FL	22 Apr 1986

Displacement, tons: 39,624 full load
Dimensions, feet (metres): 615 × 90 × 34 *(187.5 × 27.4 × 10.4)*
Main machinery: 1 Sulzer 5RTA76 diesel; 18,400 hp(m) *(13.52 MW)* sustained; 1 shaft
Speed, knots: 16. **Range, miles:** 12,000 at 16 kt
Complement: 23 (9 officers)
Cargo capacity: 238,400 barrels of oil fuel

Comment: Built for Ocean Carriers Inc, Houston, Texas specifically for long-term time charter to the Military Sealift Command (20 years) as Ocean Transportation ships. The last two are able to rig underway replenishment gear.

UPDATED

RICHARD G MATTHIESON   *8/1998, A Sharma /* 0053402

PREPOSITIONING PROGRAMME

Notes: (1) Military Sealift Command's Afloat Prepositioning Force (APF) improves US capabilities to deploy forces rapidly in any area of conflict. The APF comprises: the Maritime Prepositioning Force (MPF), Logistics Prepositioning Ships (LPS) and Combat Prepositioning Ships (CPS). Together these ships preposition equipment and supplies for the Marine Corps, Navy, Air Force and the Defense Logistics Agency.
(2) The Carter Administration initially created a force comprised of elements of all three services and named it the Rapid Deployment Joint Task Force. Initially containing seven MSC ships, the RDJTF was first deployed to Diego Garcia in July 1980. For a time, it was expanded to 17 ships, and carried tactical equipment, ammunition, fuel and supplies to sustain combat operations until reinforcements could be shipped from the US.
(3) The MPF includes 13 ships which are loaded with equipment and supplies for the US Marine Corps.
(4) The nine LPS are mostly tankers and dry cargo vessels. They preposition cargo for the Defense Logistics Agency, US Air Force and Navy.
(5) The 15 CPS preposition equipment and supplies for a US Army heavy brigade and combat support/combat service support elements.
(6) The Afloat Prepositioning Force (APF) includes long-term chartered commercial vessels, activated Ready Reserve Force ships and government ships and includes vehicle/cargo carriers, container ships, a crane ship, heavy lift ships, float-on/float-off ship, an oiler/tanker, and Large, Medium-Speed, Roll-on/roll-off (LMSR) ships.
(7) The Afloat Prepositioning Force has been essential in the Gulf War, Somalia and Kosovo operations in the 1990s.

5 + 3 WATSON CLASS:
LARGE, MEDIUM-SPEED, RO-RO (LMSR) SHIPS (AKR)

Name	No	Builders	Launched		Completed		F/S
WATSON	T-AKR 310	NASSCO	26 July	1997	23 June	1998	PREPO
SISLER	T-AKR 311	NASSCO	28 Feb	1998	1 Dec	1998	PREPO
DAHL	T-AKR 312	NASSCO	2 Oct	1998	13 July	1999	PREPO
RED CLOUD	T-AKR 313	NASSCO	7 Aug	1999	19 Jan	2000	PREPO
CHARLTON	T-AKR 314	NASSCO	13 Dec	1999	23 May	2000	PREPO
WATKINS	T-AKR 315	NASSCO	July	2000	Nov	2000	Bldg
POMEROY	T-AKR 316	NASSCO	Mar	2001	June	2001	Bldg
—	T-AKR 317	NASSCO	Apr	2002	July	2002	Bldg

Displacement, tons: 62,968 full load
Dimensions, feet (metres): 951.4 × 106 × 35 *(290 × 32.3 × 11)*
Main machinery: 2 GE Marine LM gas turbines; 64,000 hp *(47.7 MW)*; 2 shafts; cp props
Speed, knots: 24. **Range, miles:** 12,000 at 24 kt
Complement: 26-45 civilian; up to 50 Navy
Cargo capacity: 394,673 sq ft. 13,000 tons

Comment: Contract awarded in 1993; options for additional ships exercised at one a year to 2000. All are fitted with a stern slewing ramp, side accesses and cranes for both roll-on/roll-off and lift-on/lift-off capabilities. Ramps extend to 130 ft *(40 m)*, and two twin 55 ton cranes are installed.
UPDATED

SISLER   *8/1999 *, van Ginderen Collection /* 0084182

2 T-AVB 3 CLASS: AVIATION LOGISTIC SHIPS (AVB)

Name	No	Builders	Completed	F/S
WRIGHT (ex-SS *Young America*)	T-AVB 3	Ingalls Shipbuilding	1970	PREPO/ROS
CURTISS (ex-SS *Great Republic*)	T-AVB 4	Ingalls Shipbuilding	1969	PREPO/ROS

Displacement, tons: 23,872 full load
Measurement, tons: 11,757 gross; 6,850 net; 15,946 dwt
Dimensions, feet (metres): 602 × 90.2 × 29.8 *(183.5 × 27.5 × 9.1)*
Main machinery: 2 Combustion Engineering boilers; 2 GE turbines; 30,000 hp *(22.4 MW)*; 1 shaft
Speed, knots: 23. **Range, miles:** 9,000 at 22 kt
Complement: 41 crew and 1 Aircraft Maintenance Detachment totalling 366 men

Comment: To reinforce the capabilities of the Maritime Prepositioning Ship programme, conversion of two ro-ro ships into maintenance aviation support ships was approved in FY85 and FY86. *Wright* was completed 14 May 1986, *Curtiss* 18 August 1987. Both conversions took place at Todd Shipyards, Galveston, Texas. Each ship has side ports and three decks aft of the bridge superstructure and has the capability to load the vans and equipment of a Marine Aviation Intermediate Maintenance Activity. The ships' mission is to service aircraft until their containerised units can be offloaded. They can then revert to a standard sealift role if required. Maritime Administration hull design is C5-S-78a. They are operated by American Overseas Marine and maintained in a reduced operating status.
UPDATED

CURTISS   *6/1999 *, MSC /* 0075712

1 LASH TYPE: CARGO SHIP, BARGE (AKB)

Name	No	Builders	Completed	F/S
JEB STUART (ex-*Atlantic Forest*)	T-AKB 924	Sumitomo Shipbuilding	1969	PREPO

Displacement, tons: 66,629 full load
Dimensions, feet (metres): 857 × 106 × 40 *(261.2 × 32.3 × 12.2)*
Main machinery: 1 Sulzer 9RND90 diesel; 26,000 hp(m) *(19.1 MW)*; 1 shaft
Speed, knots: 16. **Range, miles:** 26,000 at 16 kt
Complement: 23
Cargo capacity: 1,191,683 cu ft

Comment: Acquired 8 December 1992 for Army PREPO and assigned to Atlantic. Owned and operated by Waterman Steamship Company.
UPDATED

JEB STUART   *6/1998, MSC /* 0053406

1 LASH TYPE: CARGO SHIPS, BARGE (AKB)

Name	No	Builders	Completed	F/S
GREEN HARBOUR	T-AK 2064	Avondale Shipyards	Feb 1974	PREPO

Measurement, tons: 26,406 gross; 39,277 dwt
Dimensions, feet (metres): 820 × 100 × 40.7 *(249.9 × 30.4 × 12.4)*
Main machinery: 2 Combustion Engineering boilers; 1,100 psi *(77.3 kg/cm²)*; 2 De Laval turbines; 32,000 hp *(23.9 MW)*; 1 shaft
Speed, knots: 16
Complement: 23
Cargo capacity: 1,248,663 cu ft (77 bales)

Comment: Acquired 20 October 1985 and operates in the Indian Ocean.
UPDATED

GREEN HARBOUR   *6/1999 *, MSC /* 0075711

3 CONTAINER SHIPS (AK)

Name	No	Builders	Completed	F/S
MAJ BERNARD F FISHER (ex-Sea Fox)	T-AK 4396	Odense	1985	PREPO
LT COL CALVIN P TITUS (ex-Sea wolf)	T-AK 4397	Odense	1984	PREPO
SP5 ERIC G GIBSON (ex-Sea lion)	T-AK 4398	Odense	1985	PREPO

Displacement, tons: 48,012 full load
Dimensions, feet (metres): 652.2 × 105.6 × 36.1 (198.1 × 32.2 × 11)
Main machinery: 1 BMW diesel; 1 shaft
Speed, knots: 19
Complement: 24
Cargo capacity: 1,466 TEUs with 10,227 sq ft garage space for ro-ro cargo

Comment: Titus and Gibson are owned and operated by Osprey Acomarit Ship Management. Acquired in 1998, both ships carry US Army supplies and sustainment cargo. Fisher is owned and operated by Sealift, Inc. Acquired in 1998, it is used to preposition US Air Force war stocks at sea.

UPDATED

MAJ BERNARD F FISHER   6/1999*, US Navy / 0084185

1 CONTAINER SHIP (AK)

Name	No	Builders	Completed	F/S
CAPT STEVEN L BENNETT (ex-Sea Pride)	T-AK 4296	Samsung Shipbuilding	1984	PREPO

Displacement, tons: 53,727.26 full load
Dimensions, feet (metres): 687 × 99.7 × 49.9 (209.4 × 30.4 × 15.2)
Main machinery: 1 diesel; 1 shaft
Speed, knots: 16.5
Complement: 21 civilian
Cargo capacity: 520 TEU (on deck within cocoons); 1,006 TEU (under deck); 422 TEU (reefer)

Comment: The ship is owned and operated by Sealift Inc, under charter to Military Sealift Command. When fully loaded, Bennett carries over 1,500 20 ft containers of various aviation munitions intended to resupply forward-deployed fighter and attack squadrons. The ship is fitted with an extensive cocoon system enabling it to maintain deck-loaded munitions in an environmentally controlled atmosphere. While lightweight and easy to maintain, the fabric cocoon system is able to withstand gusts of up to 90 kt. Bennett is assigned to MPSRON One in the Mediterranean.

UPDATED

CAPT STEVEN L BENNETT   6/1999*, US Navy / 0016575

1 FLOAT-ON/FLOAT-OFF TYPE CARGO SHIP, SEMI-SUBMERSIBLE (AKF)

Name	No	Builders	Completed	F/S
AMERICAN CORMORANT (ex-Ferncarrier)	T-AK 2062	Eriksbergs Mekaniska Verkstads AB	Sep 1974	PREPO

Displacement, tons: 69,555 full load
Measurement, tons: 10,196 gross; 47,230 dwt
Dimensions, feet (metres): 738 × 135 × 35.1 (225 × 41.1 × 10.7)
Main machinery: 1 Eriksberg/Burmeister & Wain 10K84EF diesel; 19,900 hp(m) (14.6 MW); 1 shaft; 2 thrusters; 3,000 hp(m) (2.2 MW)
Speed, knots: 16. Range, miles: 23,700 at 13 kt
Complement: 21
Cargo capacity: 10,000 barrels of fuel; 44,000 tons deck cargo

Comment: Converted in 1982. Acquired on time charter 25 November 1985 for Army. Owned by Cormorant Shipholding and operated by Osprey Ship Management. Cargo includes Army watercraft and port support equipment. Rated as a heavy lift ship and stationed at Diego Garcia.

UPDATED

AMERICAN CORMORANT   11/1994*, van Ginderen Collection / 0084186

1 RO-RO CONTAINER: CARGO SHIP (AK)

Name	No	Builders	Completed	F/S
BUFFALO SOLDIER (ex-CGM Monet)	T-AK 322	Chantiers Navigation de la Ciotat	1978	PREPO

Displacement, tons: 40,357 full load
Dimensions, feet (metres): 670 × 87 × 34.5 (204.2 × 26.5 × 10.5)
Main machinery: 2 SEMT-Pielstick 18 PC2.5 V diesels; 23,400 hp(m) (17.2 MW); 1 shaft; bow thruster
Speed, knots: 16
Complement: 23
Cargo capacity: 1,447,517 cu ft

Comment: Reflagged French Government Line ship. Buffalo Soldier owned by RR and VO Partnership and operated by Red River Shipping. Air Force PREPO. Carries ammunition under MPS-2 control.

UPDATED

BUFFALO SOLDIER   6/1999*, MSC / 0075710

1 RO-RO CONTAINER: CARGO SHIP (AK)

Name	No	Builders	Completed	F/S
STRONG VIRGINIAN (ex-Saint Magnus)	T-AKR 9205	Bremer-Vegesach, Germany	1984	PREPO

Displacement, tons: 31,390 full load
Dimensions, feet (metres): 512 × 105 × 29.6 (156.1 × 32 × 9)
Main machinery: 2 MAK 6M601 diesels; 16,320 hp(m) (12 MW); 2 shafts; cp props; bow thruster
Speed, knots: 23
Complement: 33
Cargo capacity: 855,859 cu ft

Comment: Reflagged Antigua/Barbuda flag with heavy lift capability. Stationed at Diego Garcia with Army watercraft and 10,000 BBLS of fuel aboard. Owned by Kaoampanttv Corp and operated by Van Ommeren Ship.

UPDATED

STRONG VIRGINIAN   8/1998, W Sartori / 0053409

1 TANKER TYPE: TRANSPORT OILER (AOT)

Name	No	Builders	Commissioned	F/S
POTOMAC	T-AOT 181	Sun Shipbuilding	Jan 1957	PREPO

Displacement, tons: 34,700 full load
Dimensions, feet (metres): 614.5 × 83.5 × 33.7 (187.3 × 25.5 × 10.3)
Main machinery: 2 boilers; 2 turbines; 20,460 hp (15.3 MW); 2 shafts
Speed, knots: 15
Complement: 42
Cargo capacity: 1,700,069 cu ft liquids; 30,400 cu ft solids

Comment: Acquired in 1991. Operated by Bay Ship Management and owned by MARAD. Under MPS-2 control.

UPDATED

POTOMAC   3/1997*, John Mortimer / 0016576

1 RO-RO CONTAINER: CARGO SHIP (AK)

Name	No	Builders	Completed	F/S
1st LT HARRY L MARTIN (ex-*Tarago*)	T-AK 3015	Tarago Shipyard	21 Apr 2000	PREPO

Displacement, tons: 47,777 full load
Dimensions, feet (metres): 754.3 × 106 × 36.1 *(229.9 × 32.3 × 11)*
Main machinery: 1 MAN K7-SZ-90/160 diesel; 25,690 hp(m) *(18.88 MW)*; 1 shaft
Speed, knots: 21. **Range, miles:** 16,000 at 21 kt
Complement: 36 plus 100 marines
Cargo capacity: 127,000 sq ft. 767 TEU

Comment: Acquired in February 1997 for conversion at Atlantic Drydock, Jacksonville. Joined the Maritime Prepositioning Force in June 2000. Can carry a detachment of marines.   *UPDATED*

1 RO-RO CONTAINER: CARGO SHIP (AK)

Name	No	Builders	Completed	F/S
L/CPL ROY M WHEAT (ex-*Bazaluja*)	T-AK 3016	Bender Shipbuilding	Jan 2001	PREPO

Displacement, tons: 50,101 full load
Dimensions, feet (metres): 863.8 × 98.4 × 34.8 *(263.3 × 30 × 10.6)*
Main machinery: 2 gas turbines; 47,020 hp(m) *(34.56 MW)*; 2 shafts
Speed, knots: 21. **Range, miles:** 40,000 at 21 kt
Complement: 42 plus 100 marines
Cargo capacity: 127,000 sq ft. 960 TEU

Comment: Acquired in March 1997 for conversion for Maritime Prepositioning Force by Bender Shipbuilding, Mobile. The ship has been lengthened by 117 ft and joins the force in November 2000.   *UPDATED*

1 TANKER TYPE: TRANSPORT OILER (AOT)

Name	No	Builders	Completed	F/S
PETERSBURG	T-AOT 9101	Bethlehem Steel	1963	PREPO

Displacement, tons: 48,993 full load
Dimensions, feet (metres): 736 × 102 × 36.1 *(224.3 × 31.1 × 11)*
Main machinery: 1 diesel; 1 shaft
Speed, knots: 15
Complement: 38
Comment: Acquired by MARAD to replace *American Osprey* in 1998. Comes under MPS-3 control.   *UPDATED*

PETERSBURG   *6/1998, MSC /* 0053405

5 CPL LOUIS J HAUGE, JR CLASS: VEHICLE CARGO SHIPS (AK)

Name	No	Builders	Completed	F/S
CPL LOUIS J HAUGE, JR (ex-MV *Estelle Maersk*)	T-AK 3000	Odense Staalskibsvaerft A/S, Lindo	Oct 1979	Sqn 2
PFC WILLIAM B BAUGH (ex-MV *Eleo Maersk*)	T-AK 3001	Odense Staalskibsvaerft A/S, Lindo	Apr 1979	Sqn 2
PFC JAMES ANDERSON, JR (ex-MV *Emma Maersk*)	T-AK 3002	Odense Staalskibsvaerft A/S, Lindo	July 1979	Sqn 2
1st LT ALEX BONNYMAN (ex-MV *Emilie Maersk*)	T-AK 3003	Odense Staalskibsvaerft A/S, Lindo	Jan 1980	Sqn 2
PVT FRANKLIN J PHILLIPS (ex-*Pvt Harry Fisher*, ex-MV *Evelyn Maersk*)	T-AK 3004	Odense Staalskibsvaerft A/S, Lindo	Apr 1980	Sqn 2

Displacement, tons: 46,552 full load
Dimensions, feet (metres): 755 × 90 × 37.1 *(230 × 27.4 × 11.3)*
Main machinery: 1 Sulzer 7RND76M diesel; 16,800 hp(m) *(12.35 MW)*; 1 shaft; bow thruster
Speed, knots: 17.5. **Range, miles:** 10,800 at 16 kt
Complement: 27 plus 10 technicians
Cargo capacity: Containers, 361; ro-ro, 121,595 sq ft; JP-5 bbls, 17,128; DF-2 bbls, 10,642; Mogas bbls, 3,865; stable water, 2,022; cranes, 3 twin 30 ton; 92,831 cu ft breakbulk
Helicopters: Platform only.

Comment: Converted from five Maersk Line ships by Bethlehem Steel, Sparrow Point, MD. Conversion work included the addition of 157 ft *(47.9 m)* amidships. All based at Diego Garcia and operated by Maersk Line Ltd.   *VERIFIED*

CPL LOUIS J HAUGE JR   *3/1998, A Sharma /* 0053410

3 SGT MATEJ KOCAK CLASS: VEHICLE CARGO SHIPS (AK)

Name	No	Builders	Completed	F/S
SGT MATEJ KOCAK (ex-SS *John B Waterman*)	T-AK 3005	Pennsylvania SB Co, Chester, PA	14 Mar 1981	Sqn 1
PFC EUGENE A OBREGON (ex-SS *Thomas Heywood*)	T-AK 3006	Pennsylvania SB Co, Chester, PA	1 Nov 1982	Sqn 1
MAJ STEPHEN W PLESS (ex-SS *Charles Carroll*)	T-AK 3007	General Dynamics Corp, Quincy, MA	14 Mar 1983	Sqn 1

Displacement, tons: 48,754 full load
Dimensions, feet (metres): 821 × 105.6 × 32.3 *(250.2 × 32.2 × 9.8)*
Main machinery: 2 boilers; 2 GE turbines; 30,000 hp *(22.4 MW)*; 1 shaft
Speed, knots: 20. **Range, miles:** 13,000 at 20 kt
Complement: 29 plus 10 technicians
Cargo capacity: Containers, 532; ro-ro, 152,236 sq ft; JP-5 bbls, 20,290; DF-2 bbls, 12,355; Mogas bbls, 3,717; stable water, 2,189; cranes, 2 twin 50 ton and 1—30 ton gantry
Helicopters: Platform only.

Comment: Converted from three Waterman Line ships by National Steel and Shipbuilding, San Diego. Delivery dates T-AK 3005, 1 October 1984; T-AK 3006, 16 January 1985; T-AK 3007, 15 May 1985. Conversion work included the addition of 157 ft *(47.9 m)* amidships. Operated by Waterman SS Corp.   *UPDATED*

SGT MATEJ KOCAK   *1/2000*, A Sharma /* 0084187

5 2nd LT JOHN P BOBO CLASS: VEHICLE CARGO SHIPS (AK)

Name	No	Builders	Completed	F/S
2nd LT JOHN P BOBO	T-AK 3008	General Dynamics, Quincy	14 Feb 1985	Sqn 1
PFC DEWAYNE T WILLIAMS	T-AK 3009	General Dynamics, Quincy	6 June 1985	Sqn 3
1st LT BALDOMERO LOPEZ	T-AK 3010	General Dynamics, Quincy	20 Nov 1985	Sqn 3
1st LT JACK LUMMUS	T-AK 3011	General Dynamics, Quincy	6 Mar 1986	Sqn 3
SGT WILLIAM R BUTTON	T-AK 3012	General Dynamics, Quincy	27 May 1986	Sqn 3

Displacement, tons: 44,330 full load
Dimensions, feet (metres): 675.2 × 105.5 × 29.6 *(205.8 × 32.2 × 9)*
Main machinery: 2 Stork-Wärtsilä Werkspoor 16TM410 diesels; 27,000 hp(m) *(19.84 MW)* sustained; 1 shaft; bow thruster; 1,000 hp *(746 kW)*
Speed, knots: 18. **Range, miles:** 12,840 at 18 kt
Complement: 30 plus 10 technicians
Cargo capacity: Containers, 530; ro-ro, 152,185 sq ft; JP-5 bbls, 20,776; DF-2 bbls, 13,334; Mogas bbls, 4,880; stable water, 2,357; cranes, 1 single and 2 twin 39 ton
Helicopters: Platform only.

Comment: Built for MPS operations. Owned and operated by American Overseas Marine.   *UPDATED*

2nd LT JOHN P BOBO   *1/2000*, A Sharma /* 0084188

READY RESERVE FORCE (RRF)

Notes: (1) The Ready Reserve Force was created in 1976, due to a shrinking US-flagged commercial fleet, to support military sea transportation needs. Composed of merchant ships that are no longer commercially useful, the RRF is designed to be made available quickly for military sealift operations.
(2) On 1 January 2000 the RRF consisted of 78 ships, including roll-on/roll-off ships, breakbulk ships, auxiliary crane ships, heavy lift barge carriers, tankers and troop ships. These ships are maintained in various stages of readiness and able to get underway in four, five, 10 or 20 days. The ships are located in various ports along the US East, West and Gulf Coasts and in Japan. Numbers are to reduce to 62 in due course.
(3) The Department of Transportation's Maritime Administration (MARAD) is responsible for the maintenance and administration of the ships when they are not operating. Military Sealift Command assumes operational control once the ships are activated. More than 75 per cent of the RRF was used during Operation Desert Shield/Storm in 1990/91. RRF ships were used during 1994 to support camps at Guantanamo Bay, Cuba, and in Haiti. In 1995 and 1996, some ships were activated to support UN and NATO actions in Bosnia. Several of the RRF ro-ros have also been used to support the at-sea prepositioning requirements of the Army.
(4) RRF ships have red, white and blue funnel stripes.

8 PRODUCT TANKERS

NODAWAY T-AOG 78	**MISSION CAPISTRANO** T-AOT 5005
ALATNA T-AOG 81	**AMERICAN OSPREY** T-AOT 5075
CHATTAHOOCHEE T-AOG 82	**MOUNT WASHINGTON** T-AOT 5076
MISSION BUENAVENTURA T-AOT 1012	**CHESAPEAKE** T-AOT 5084

UPDATED

CHESAPEAKE   *10/1999*, Findler & Winter /* 0084191

10 KEYSTONE STATE CLASS: AUXILIARY CRANE SHIPS (ACS)

Name	No	Builders	Conversion Completed
KEYSTONE STATE (ex-SS *President Harrison*)	T-ACS 1	Defoe SB Co, Bay City	1984
GEM STATE (ex-SS *President Monroe*)	T-ACS 2	Defoe SB Co, Bay City	1985
GRAND CANYON STATE (ex-SS *President Polk*)	T-ACS 3	Dillingham SR, Portland	1986
GOPHER STATE (ex-*Export Leader*)	T-ACS 4	Norshipco, Norfolk	Oct 1987
FLICKERTAIL STATE (ex-*Export Lightning*)	T-ACS 5	Norshipco, Norfolk	Dec 1987
CORNHUSKER STATE (ex-*Staghound*)	T-ACS 6	Norshipco, Norfolk	Mar 1988
DIAMOND STATE (ex-*President Truman*)	T-ACS 7	Tampa SY	Jan 1989
EQUALITY STATE (ex-*American Banker*)	T-ACS 8	Tampa SY	May 1989
GREEN MOUNTAIN STATE (ex-*American Altair*)	T-ACS 9	Norshipco, Norfolk	Sep 1990
BEAVER STATE (ex-*American Draco*)	T-ACS 10	Kreith Ship Repair, New Orleans	4 May 1997

Displacement, tons: 31,500 full load
Dimensions, feet (metres): 668.6 × 76.1 × 33.5 *(203.8 × 23.2 × 10.2)*
Main machinery: 2 boilers; 2 GE turbines; 19,250 hp *(14.4 MW)*; 1 shaft
Speed, knots: 20. **Range, miles:** 13,000 at 20 kt
Complement: 89
Cargo capacity: 300+ standard containers

Comment: Auxiliary crane ships are container ships to which have been added up to three twin boom pedestal cranes which will lift containerised or other cargo from itself or adjacent vessels and deposit it on a pier or into lighterage. Since a significant portion of the US merchant fleet is composed of non-self-sustaining container ships lacking integral cranes, thus needing a fully developed port to unload, a requirement exists for crane ships that can unload others in areas of the world which have very simple, damaged or no developed port facilities. Funds provided in the FY88 budget for conversion of T-ACS 9 and 10 were transferred to other Navy SCN accounts. Funding for T-ACS 9 was then taken from Maritime Administration budgets. The 10th ship on which work had stopped in 1991 because of shortage of funds, was completed with money from the MSC FY96-97 budgets. There are minor dimensional differences between some of the class. Five of the ships were deployed to the Gulf in 1990-91 but the excellent Saudi harbour facilities meant that dockside cranes were available to unload cargoes, so their particular talents were not required other than as standard cargo ships. T-ACS 4 was activated to serve as a temporary Army PREPO ship at Diego Garcia in early 1994.

UPDATED

30 RO-RO SHIPS

COMET T-AKR 7
METEOR T-AKR 9
CAPE ISLAND (ex-*Mercury*) T-AKR 10
CAPE INTREPID T-AKR 11
CAPE TEXAS (ex-*Lyra*) T-AKR 112
CAPE TAYLOR (ex-*Cygnus*) T-AKR 113
ADM WM H CALLAGHAN T-AKR 1001
CAPE ORLANDO (ex-*American Eagle*) T-AKR 2044
CAPE DUCATO T-AKR 5051
CAPE DOUGLAS T-AKR 5052
CAPE DOMINGO T-AKR 5053
CAPE DECISION T-AKR 5054
CAPE DIAMOND T-AKR 5055
CAPE ISABEL T-AKR 5062
CAPE HUDSON T-AKR 5066
CAPE HENRY T-AKR 5067
CAPE HORN T-AKR 5068
CAPE EDMONT T-AKR 5069
CAPE INSCRIPTION T-AKR 5076
CAPE LAMBERT T-AKR 5077
CAPE LOBOS T-AKR 5078
CAPE KNOX T-AKR 5082
CAPE VINCENT (ex-*Taabo Italia*) T-AKR 9666
CAPE RISE (ex-*Saudi Riyadh*) T-AKR 9678
CAPE RAY (ex-*Saudi Makkah*) T-AKR 9679
CAPE VICTORY (ex-*Merzario Britania*) T-AKR 9701
CAPE TRINITY (ex-*Santos*) T-AKR 9711
CAPE RACE (ex-*G&C Admiral*) T-AKR 9960
CAPE WASHINGTON (ex-*Hual Transporter*) T-AKR 9961
CAPE WRATH (ex-*Hual Trader*) T-AKR 9962

UPDATED

COMET   *10/1999*, Findler & Winter /* 0084189

8 MISCELLANEOUS SHIPS

Lash ships	Troopships	Heavy lift ships
CAPE FEAR T-AK 5061	EMPIRE STATE T-AP 1001	CAPE MAY T-AKR 5063
CAPE FLATTERY T-AK 5070		CAPE MENDOCINO T-AKR 5064
CAPE FLORIDA T-AK 5071		CAPE MOHICAN T-AKR 5065
CAPE FAREWELL T-AK 5073		

UPDATED

DIAMOND STATE   *6/1999*, van Ginderen Collection /* 0084190

24 BREAK BULK SHIPS

CAPE NOME T-AK 1014
PIONEER COMMANDER T-AK 2016
PIONEER CONTRACTOR T-AK 2018
GULF TRADER T-AK 2036
CAPE GIRARDEAU T-AK 2039
GULF BANKER T-AK 5044
CAPE ANN T-AK 5009
CAPE ALEXANDER T-AK 5010
CAPE ARCHWAY T-AK 5011
CAPE ALAVA T-AK 5012
CAPE AVINOF T-AK 5013
LAKE T-AK 5016

SCAN T-AK 5018
COURIER T-AK 5019
CAPE COD T-AK 5041
BANNER T-AK 5008
CAPE BRETON T-AKR 5056
CAPE BOVER T-AK 5057
CAPE BORDA T-AK 5058
CAPE BON T-AK 5059
CAPE BLANCO T-AK 5060
CAPE CATAWBA T-AK 5074
NORTHERN LIGHT T-AKR 284
CAPE JACOB T-AK 5029

Comment: *Cape Jacob* is currently serving as an Ammunition ship for the USN.

UPDATED

CAPE MOHICAN   *3/1999*, van Ginderen Collection /* 0084193

CAPE GIRARDEAU   *9/1999*, Winter & Findler /* 0084192

COAST GUARD

Headquarters Appointments

Commandant:
Admiral James M Loy
Commander, Atlantic Area:
Vice Admiral John E Shkor
Commander, Pacific Area:
Vice Admiral Thomas Collins

Establishment

The United States Coast Guard was established by an Act of Congress approved 28 January 1915, which consolidated the Revenue Cutter Service (founded in 1790) and the Life Saving Service (founded in 1848). The act of establishment stated the Coast Guard "shall be a military service and a branch of the armed forces of the USA at all times. The Coast Guard shall be a service in the Treasury Department except when operating as a service in the Navy".
Congress further legislated that in time of national emergency or when the President so directs, the Coast Guard operates as a part of the Navy. The Coast Guard did operate as a part of the Navy during the First and Second World Wars.
The Lighthouse Service (founded in 1789) was transferred to the Coast Guard on 1 July 1939 and the Bureau of Navigation and Steamboat Inspection on 28 February 1942.
The Coast Guard was transferred to the newly established Department of Transportation on 1 April 1967.

Missions

The Coast Guard has five strategic aims:
Safety: Eliminate deaths, injuries, and property damage associated with maritime transportation, fishing and recreational boating.
National Defense: Defend the nation as one of the five US Armed Services. Enhance regional stability in support of the National Security Strategy.
Maritime Security: Protect maritime borders from all intrusions by (a) halting the flow of illegal drugs, aliens, and contraband into the United States through maritime routes; (b) preventing illegal fishing; and (c) suppressing violations of federal law in the maritime arena.
Mobility: Facilitate maritime commerce and eliminate interruptions and impediments to the economical movement of goods and people, while maximizing recreational access and enjoyment of the water.
Protection of Natural Resources: Eliminate environmental damage and natural resource degradation associated with maritime transportation, fishing, and recreational boating.

Personnel

2000: 5,509 officers, 1,433 warrant officers, 27,593 enlisted, 8,000 reserves

Category/Classification		Active	Building (Projected)
Cutters			
WHEC	High Endurance Cutters	12	—
WMEC	Medium Endurance Cutters	32	—
Icebreakers			
WAGB	Icebreakers	4	—
WTGB	Icebreaking Tugs	8	—
Patrol Forces			
WPB	Patrol Craft	94	26
Training Cutters			
WIX	Training Cutters	2	—
Buoy Tenders			
WLB	Buoy Tenders, Seagoing	19	11
WLM	Buoy Tenders, Coastal	15	—
WLI	Buoy Tenders, Inland	6	—
WLR	Buoy Tenders, River	18	—
Construction Tenders			
WLIC	Construction Tenders, Inland	13	—
Harbour Tugs			
WYTL	Harbour Tugs, Small	11	—

Cutter Strength

All Coast Guard vessels over 65 ft in length and that have adequate crew accommodation are referred to as 'cutters'. All names are preceded by USCG. The first two digits of the hull number for all Coast Guard vessels under 100 ft in length indicates the approximate length overall.
There are plans under a Deepwater contract to place orders in 2002 for the first of a new class of cutter to enter service in 2005. Approximately 2,000 standard and non-standard boats are in service ranging in size from 11 ft skiffs to 55 ft aids-to-navigation craft.

DELETIONS

Medium Endurance Cutters

1996 *Yacona*

Patrol Forces

1997 *Point Richmond, Point Turner* (to St Lucia)
1998 *Point Ledge, Point Franklin* (to Venezuela), *Point Bennett* (to Trinidad), *Point Steel* (to Antigua), *Point Hever* (to Trinidad)
1999 *Point Huron, Point Francis, Point Hobart* (to Argentina), *Point Martin* (to Dominican Republic), *Point Batan* (to Dominican Republic), *Point Nowell* (to Jamaica), *Point Barnes* (to Jamaica), *Point Camden* (to Costa Rica), *Point Evans* (to Philippines)

Tenders and Tugs

1997 *Spar, Mallow, White Lupine* (to Tunisia), *Bittersweet, Hornbeam, Planetree*
1998 *White Heath* (to Tunisia), *Morro Bay, Gentian, Basswood, Red Birch* (to Argentina), *White Holly* (to Dominican Republic), *Rambler*
1999 *Red Cedar, Red Wood* (both to Argentina), *Primrose, White Pine, Laurel*
2000 *Sumac*

HIGH ENDURANCE CUTTERS

Note: The Deepwater Project aims to place a production contract for a new design cutter in January 2002. The ship must be capable of 28 kt, have a 60 day endurance and a range of 12,000 n miles.

12 HAMILTON and HERO CLASSES (WHEC)

Name	No	Builders	Laid down		Launched		Commissioned		F/S
HAMILTON	WHEC 715	Avondale Shipyards	Jan	1965	18 Dec	1965	20 Feb	1967	PA
DALLAS	WHEC 716	Avondale Shipyards	7 Feb	1966	1 Oct	1966	1 Oct	1967	AA
MELLON	WHEC 717	Avondale Shipyards	25 July	1966	11 Feb	1967	22 Dec	1967	PA
CHASE	WHEC 718	Avondale Shipyards	27 Oct	1966	20 May	1967	1 Mar	1968	PA
BOUTWELL	WHEC 719	Avondale Shipyards	5 Dec	1966	17 June	1967	14 June	1968	PA
SHERMAN	WHEC 720	Avondale Shipyards	23 Jan	1967	23 Sep	1967	23 Aug	1968	PA
GALLATIN	WHEC 721	Avondale Shipyards	27 Feb	1967	18 Nov	1967	20 Dec	1968	AA
MORGENTHAU	WHEC 722	Avondale Shipyards	17 July	1967	10 Feb	1968	14 Feb	1969	PA
RUSH	WHEC 723	Avondale Shipyards	23 Oct	1967	16 Nov	1968	3 July	1969	PA
MUNRO	WHEC 724	Avondale Shipyards	18 Feb	1970	5 Dec	1970	10 Sep	1971	PA
JARVIS	WHEC 725	Avondale Shipyards	9 Sep	1970	24 Apr	1971	30 Dec	1971	PA
MIDGETT	WHEC 726	Avondale Shipyards	5 Apr	1971	4 Sep	1971	17 Mar	1972	PA

Displacement, tons: 3,050 full load
Dimensions, feet (metres): 378 × 42.8 × 20
(115.2 × 13.1 × 6.1)
Flight deck, feet (metres): 88 × 40 *(26.8 × 12.2)*
Main machinery: CODOG; 2 Pratt & Whitney FT4A-6 gas turbines; 36,000 hp *(26.86 MW)*; 2 Fairbanks-Morse 38TD8-1/8-12 diesels; 7,000 hp *(5.22 MW)* sustained; 2 shafts; cp props; retractable bow propulsor; 350 hp *(261 kW)*
Speed, knots: 29
Range, miles: 14,000 at 11 kt diesels; 2,400 at 29 kt gas
Complement: 167 (19 officers)

Guns: 1 OTO Melara 3 in *(76 mm)*/62 Mk 75 Compact; 85 rds/min to 16 km *(8.7 n miles)* anti-surface; 12 km *(6.6 n miles)* anti-aircraft; weight of shell 6 kg.
2 Boeing 25 mm/87 Mk 38 Bushmaster.
1 GE/GD 20 mm Vulcan Phalanx 6-barrelled Mk 15; 3,000 rds/min combined to 1.5 km. 4—12.7 mm MGs.
Countermeasures: Decoys: 2 Loral Hycor SRBOC 6-barrelled fixed Mk 36; IR flares and chaff.
ESM: WLR-1C, WLR-3; intercept.
Combat data systems: SCCS includes OTCIXS satellite link.
Weapons control: Mk 92 Mod 1 GFCS.
Radars: Air search: Lockheed SPS-40B; D/E-band.
Surface search: Hughes/Furuno SPS-73; E/F- and I-bands.
Fire control: Sperry Mk 92; I/J-band.
Tacan: URN 25.

Helicopters: 1 HH-65A or 1 HH-60J or 1 MH-90.

Programmes: In the Autumn of 1977 *Gallatin* and *Morgenthau* were the first of the Coast Guard ships to have women assigned as permanent members of the crew.
Modernisation: FRAM programme for all 12 ships in this class from October 1985 to October 1992. Work included standardising the engineering plants, improving the clutching systems, replacing SPS-29 air search radar with SPS-40 radar

MELLON
4/1999*, van Ginderen Collection / 0084195

and replacing the Mk 56 fire-control system and 5 in/38 gun mount with the Mk 92 system and a single 76 mm OTO Melara Compact gun. In addition Harpoon and Phalanx CIWS fitted to five of the class by 1992 and CIWS to all by late 1993. The flight deck and other aircraft facilities upgraded to handle a Jay Hawk helicopter including a telescopic hangar. URN 25 Tacan added along with the SQR-4 and SQR-17 sonobuoy receiving set and passive acoustic analysis systems. SRBOC chaff launchers were also fitted but not improved ESM which has been shelved. All missiles, torpedo tubes, sonar and ASW equipment removed in 1993-94. 25 mm Mk 38 guns replaced the 20 mm Mk 67. Shipboard Command and Control System

(SCCS) fitted to all of the class by 1996. Surface search radar replaced 1997-99.
Structure: These ships have clipper bows, twin funnels enclosing a helicopter hangar, helicopter platform aft. All are fitted with elaborate communications equipment. Superstructure is largely of aluminium construction. Bridge control of manoeuvring is by aircraft-type joystick rather than wheel.
Operational: Ten of the class are based in the Pacific, leaving only two on the East Coast. The removal of SSMs and all ASW equipment sensibly refocuses on Coast Guard roles.

UPDATED

MEDIUM ENDURANCE CUTTERS

Note: Two 'Stalwart' class T-AGOS ships *Persistent* and *Vindicator* reactivated on 26 August 1999 with civilian crews and a 17 person Coast Guard detachment. Both ships carry 50 kt pursuit boats. Details in MSA section.

13 FAMOUS CUTTER CLASS (WMEC)

Name	No	Builders	Laid down	Launched	Commissioned	F/S
BEAR	WMEC 901	Tacoma Boatbuilding Co	23 Aug 1979	25 Sep 1980	4 Feb 1983	AA
TAMPA	WMEC 902	Tacoma Boatbuilding Co	3 Apr 1980	19 Mar 1981	16 Mar 1984	AA
HARRIET LANE	WMEC 903	Tacoma Boatbuilding Co	15 Oct 1980	6 Feb 1982	20 Sep 1984	AA
NORTHLAND	WMEC 904	Tacoma Boatbuilding Co	9 Apr 1981	7 May 1982	17 Dec 1984	AA
SPENCER	WMEC 905	Robert E Derecktor Corp	26 June 1982	17 Apr 1984	28 June 1986	AA
SENECA	WMEC 906	Robert E Derecktor Corp	16 Sep 1982	17 Apr 1984	4 May 1987	AA
ESCANABA	WMEC 907	Robert E Derecktor Corp	1 Apr 1983	6 Feb 1985	27 Aug 1987	AA
TAHOMA	WMEC 908	Robert E Derecktor Corp	28 June 1983	6 Feb 1985	6 Apr 1988	AA
CAMPBELL	WMEC 909	Robert E Derecktor Corp	10 Aug 1984	29 Apr 1986	19 Aug 1988	AA
THETIS	WMEC 910	Robert E Derecktor Corp	24 Aug 1984	29 Apr 1986	30 June 1989	AA
FORWARD	WMEC 911	Robert E Derecktor Corp	11 July 1986	22 Aug 1987	4 Aug 1990	AA
LEGARE	WMEC 912	Robert E Derecktor Corp	11 July 1986	22 Aug 1987	4 Aug 1990	AA
MOHAWK	WMEC 913	Robert E Derecktor Corp	15 Mar 1987	5 May 1988	20 Mar 1991	AA

Displacement, tons: 1,825 full load
Dimensions, feet (metres): 270 × 38 × 13.9
(82.3 × 11.6 × 4.2)
Main machinery: 2 Alco 18V-251 diesels; 7,290 hp *(5.44 MW)* sustained; 2 shafts; cp props
Speed, knots: 19.5
Range, miles: 10,250 at 12 kt, 3,850 at 19.5 kt
Complement: 100 (14 officers) plus 5 aircrew

Guns: 1 OTO Melara 3 in *(76 mm)*/62 Mk 75; 85 rds/min to 16 km *(8.7 n miles)* anti-surface; 12 km *(6.6 n miles)* anti-aircraft; weight of shell 6 kg.
2—12.7 mm MGs or 2—40 mm Mk 19 grenade launchers.
Countermeasures: Decoys: 2 Loral Hycor SRBOC 6-barrelled fixed Mk 36; IR flares and chaff.
ESM/ECM; SLQ-32(V)2; radar intercept.

Combat data systems: SCCS-270; OTCIXS satellite link.
Radars: Surface search: Hughes/Furuno SPS-73; I-band.
Fire control: Sperry Mk 92 Mod 1; I/J-band.
Tacan: URN 25.

Helicopters: 1 HH-65A or HH-60J or MH-90.

Programmes: The contract for construction of WMEC 905-913 was originally awarded to Tacoma Boatbuilding Co on 29 August 1980. However, under lawsuit from the Robert E Derecktor Corp, Middletown, Rhode Island, the contract to Tacoma was determined by a US District Court to be invalid and was awarded to Robert E Derecktor Corp on 15 January 1981.
Modernisation: OTCIXS satellite link fitted from 1992.

Structure: They are the only medium endurance cutters with a helicopter hangar (which is telescopic) and the first cutters with automated command and control centre. Fin stabilisers fitted. Plans to fit SSM and/or CIWS have been abandoned as has towed array sonar and sonobuoy datalinks. New radars fitted 1997-99.
Operational: Bases are at Portsmouth, New Bedford, Key West and Boston. Very lively in heavy seas because the length to beam ratio is unusually small for ships required to operate in Atlantic conditions.

UPDATED

LEGARE

6/1999*, van Ginderen Collection / 0084196

16 RELIANCE CLASS (WMEC)

Name	No	Builders	Commissioned	MMA completion	F/S
RELIANCE	WMEC 615	Todd Shipyards	20 June 1964	Jan 1989	AA (Newcastle)
DILIGENCE	WMEC 616	Todd Shipyards	26 Aug 1964	Mar 1992	AA (Wilmington)
VIGILANT	WMEC 617	Todd Shipyards	3 Oct 1964	Aug 1990	AA (Cape Canaveral)
ACTIVE	WMEC 618	Christy Corp	17 Sep 1966	Feb 1987	PA (Port Angeles)
CONFIDENCE	WMEC 619	Coast Guard Yard, Baltimore	19 Feb 1966	June 1988	AA (Cape Canaveral)
RESOLUTE	WMEC 620	Coast Guard Yard, Baltimore	8 Dec 1966	Mar 1996	AA (New London)
VALIANT	WMEC 621	American Shipbuilding Co	28 Oct 1967	July 1993	AA (Miami)
COURAGEOUS	WMEC 622	American Shipbuilding Co	10 Apr 1968	Mar 1990	AA (Panama City)
STEADFAST	WMEC 623	American Shipbuilding Co	25 Sep 1968	Feb 1994	AA (Baltimore)
DAUNTLESS	WMEC 624	American Shipbuilding Co	10 June 1968	Mar 1995	AA (Galveston)
VENTUROUS	WMEC 625	American Shipbuilding Co	16 Aug 1968	Sep 1995	AA (St Petersburg)
DEPENDABLE	WMEC 626	American Shipbuilding Co	22 Nov 1968	Aug 1997	AA (Baltimore)
VIGOROUS	WMEC 627	American Shipbuilding Co	2 May 1969	Jan 1993	AA (Cape May)
DURABLE	WMEC 628	Coast Guard Yard, Baltimore	8 Dec 1967	Jan 1989	AA (St Petersburg)
DECISIVE	WMEC 629	Coast Guard Yard, Baltimore	23 Aug 1968	Sep 1998	AA (Baltimore)
ALERT	WMEC 630	Coast Guard Yard, Baltimore	4 Aug 1969	Sep 1994	PA (Astoria)

Displacement, tons: 1,129 full load (WMEC 620-630)
1,110 full load (WMEC 618, 619)
Dimensions, feet (metres): 210.5 × 34 × 10.5
(64.2 × 10.4 × 3.2)
Main machinery: 2 Alco 16V-251 diesels; 6,480 hp *(4.83 MW)* sustained; 2 shafts; acbLIPS cp props
Speed, knots: 18. **Range, miles:** 6,100 at 14 kt; 2,700 at 18 kt
Complement: 75 (12 officers)

Guns: 1 Boeing 25 mm/87 Mk 38 Bushmaster; 200 rds/min to 6.8 km *(3.4 n miles)*. 2—12.7 mm MGs.
Radars: Surface search: 2 Raytheon SPS-64(V)1; I-band being replaced by Hughes/Furuno SPS-73; I-band.

Helicopters: 1 HH-65A embarked as required.

Modernisation: All 16 cutters have undergone a Major Maintenance Availability (MMA). The exhausts for main engines, ship service generators and boilers have been run in a new vertical funnel which reduces flight deck size. Completion dates are listed above. 76 mm guns have been replaced by 25 mm Mk 38. New radars being fitted 1997-2000.
Structure: Designed for search and rescue duties. Design features include 360° visibility from bridge; helicopter flight deck (no hangar); and engine exhaust vent at stern which has

been replaced by a funnel during MMA. Capable of towing ships up to 10,000 tons. Air conditioned throughout except engine room; high degree of habitability.

VALIANT

6/1999*, M Declerck / 0084197

Operational: Normally operate within 500 miles of the coast. Primary roles are SAR, law enforcement and defence operations.

UPDATED

1 EDENTON CLASS (WMEC)

Name	No	Builders	Commissioned	F/S
ALEX HALEY	WMEC 39 (ex-ATS 1)	Brooke Marine, Lowestoft	23 Jan 1971	PA
(ex-*Edenton*)				

Displacement, tons: 2,929 full load
Dimensions, feet (metres): 282.6 × 50 × 15.1 *(86.1 × 15.2 × 4.6)*
Main machinery: 4 Caterpillar 3516 DITAWJ diesels; 6,000 hp(m) *(4.41 MW)*; 2 shafts; cp props; bow thruster
Speed, knots: 16. **Range, miles:** 10,000 at 13 kt
Complement: 99 (9 officers)
Guns: 2 McDonnell Douglas 25 mm/87 Mk 38; 200 rds/min to 6.8 km *(3.4 n miles)*. 2—12.7 mm MGs.
Radars: Surface search: Hughes/Furuno SPS-73; I-band.
Helicopters: Platform for 1 HH-65A or 1 HH-60J.

Comment: Former Navy salvage ship paid off in 1996 and taken on by the Coast Guard in November 1997 for conversion. All diving and salvage gear removed, flight deck installed, and upgraded navigation and communications. Armed with 25 mm guns. Used in the Bering Sea, Gulf of Alaska and North Pacific for fisheries protection from 16 December 1999.
UPDATED

ALEX HALEY   *12/1999*, USCG /* 0084198

1 DIVER CLASS (WMEC)

Name	No	Builders	USN Comm	F/S
ACUSHNET	WMEC 167	Basalt Rock Co,	5 Feb 1944	PA
(ex-*Shackle*)	(ex-WAGO 167,	Napa, CA		
	ex-WAT 167, ex-ARS 9)			

Displacement, tons: 1,557 standard; 1,745 full load
Dimensions, feet (metres): 213.5 × 39 × 15 *(65.1 × 11.9 × 4.6)*
Main machinery: 4 Fairbanks-Morse diesels; 3,000 hp *(2.24 MW)* sustained; 2 shafts
Speed, knots: 15.5. **Range, miles:** 9,000 at 15 kt
Complement: 75 (7 officers)
Radars: Navigation: 2 Raytheon SPS-64; I-band.

Comment: Large, steel-hulled salvage ship transferred from the Navy to the Coast Guard and employed in tug and oceanographic duties. Modified for handling environmental data buoys and reclassified WAGO in 1968 and reclassified WMEC in 1980. Major renovation work completed in 1983 and now used for SAR and law enforcement operations.
UPDATED

ACUSHNET   *7/1995*, van Ginderen Collection /* 0084199

1 STORIS CLASS (WMEC)

Name	No	Builders	Commissioned	F/S
STORIS (ex-*Eskimo*)	WMEC 38 (ex-WAGB 38)	Toledo Shipbuilding	30 Sep 1942	PA

Displacement, tons: 1,715 standard; 1,925 full load
Dimensions, feet (metres): 230 × 43 × 15 *(70.1 × 13.1 × 4.6)*
Main machinery: Diesel-electric; 3 GM EMD diesel generators; 1 motor; 3,000 hp *(2.24 MW)*; 1 shaft
Speed, knots: 14. **Range, miles:** 22,000 at 8 kt; 12,000 at 14 kt
Complement: 106 (10 officers)
Guns: 1 Boeing 25 mm/87 Mk 38 Bushmaster.
Radars: Navigation: Raytheon SPS-64; I-band.

Comment: Laid down on 14 July 1941; launched on 4 April 1942 as ice patrol tender. Strengthened for ice navigation but no longer employed as icebreaker. Employed in Alaskan service for search, rescue and law enforcement. Completed a major maintenance availability in June 1986, during which main engines were replaced with EMD diesels and living quarters expanded. Gun changed in 1994. Planned to be paid off in 2001.
UPDATED

STORIS   *3/1998, van Ginderen Collection /* 0053416

SHIPBORNE AIRCRAFT

Numbers/Type: 94 Aerospatiale HH-65A Dolphin.
Operational speed: 165 kt *(300 km/h)*.
Service ceiling: 11,810 ft *(3,600 m)*.
Range: 400 n miles *(741 km)*.
Role/Weapon systems: Short-range rescue and recovery (SRR) helicopter. 80 aircraft are operational. Sensors: Bendix RDR 1300 radar and Collins mission management system. Weapons: Unarmed.
UPDATED

DOLPHIN   *5/1999*, van Ginderen Collection /* 0084200

Numbers/Type: 42 Sikorsky HH-60J Jayhawk.
Operational speed: 140 kt *(259 km/h)*.
Service ceiling: 17,200 ft *(5,240 m)*.
Range: 700 n miles *(1,296 km)*.
Role/Weapon systems: Coast Guard version of Seahawk, first flew in 1988, and has replaced HH-3F in MRR role. Sensors: Bendix RDR-1300C weather/search radar. AAQ-15 FLIR. Weapons: Unarmed.
UPDATED

JAYHAWK   *6/1996*, Harald Carstens /* 0084201

Numbers/Type: 2 Boeing MH-90 Enforcer.
Operational speed: 138 kt *(263 km/h)*.
Service ceiling: 10,000 ft *(3,048 m)*.
Range: 302 n miles *(559 km)*.
Role/Weapon systems: There are plans for eight of the type to counter high-speed smuggling craft. Sensors: Mk III FLIR and weather radar. Weapons: 7.62 MG or 12.7 mm disabling rifle.
NEW ENTRY

ICEBREAKERS

1 HEALY CLASS (WAGB)

Name	No	Builders	Commissioned	F/S
HEALY	WAGB 20	Avondale, New Orleans	29 Oct 1999	PA

Displacement, tons: 16,700 full load
Dimensions, feet (metres): 420 oa; 397.8 wl × 82 × 32 (128; 121.2 × 25 × 9.8)
Main machinery: Diesel-electric; 4 Westinghouse/Sulzer 12ZA 40S diesels; 42,400 hp (31.16 MW); 4 Westinghouse alternators; 2 motors; 30,000 hp (22.38 MW); 2 shafts; bow thruster; 2,200 hp (1.64 MW)
Speed, knots: 17. **Range, miles:** 16,000 at 12.5 kt
Complement: 75 (12 officers) plus 35 scientists
Helicopters: 2 HH-65A.

Comment: In response to the 1984 Interagency Polar Icebreaker Requirements Study and Congressional mandate, approval was given for the construction of a new icebreaker as a replacement for two 'Wind' class which were then decommissioned in 1988. However, no action was taken to provide funds for the new ship until Congress included it in the Navy's FY91 ship construction budget and after further delays the ship was ordered 15 July 1993. Icebreaking capability of 4.5 ft at 3 kt. Launched 15 November 1997.

UPDATED

HEALY   10/1999*, USCG / 0084202

2 POLAR CLASS (WAGB)

Name	No	Builders	Launched	Commissioned	F/S
POLAR STAR	WAGB 10	Lockheed SB	17 Nov 1973	19 Jan 1976	PA
POLAR SEA	WAGB 11	Lockheed SB	24 June 1975	23 Feb 1978	PA

Displacement, tons: 13,190 full load
Dimensions, feet (metres): 399 × 86 × 32 (121.6 × 26.2 × 9.8)
Main machinery: CODOG; diesel-electric (AC/DC); 6 Alco 16V-251F/Westinghouse AC diesel generators; 21,000 hp (15.66 MW) sustained; 3 Westinghouse DC motors; 18,000 hp (13.42 MW) sustained; 3 Pratt & Whitney FT4A-12 gas turbines; 60,000 hp (44.76 MW) sustained; 3 Philadelphia 75 VMGS gears; 60,000 hp (44.76 MW) sustained; 3 shafts; cp props
Speed, knots: 18. **Range, miles:** 28,275 at 13 kt
Complement: 142 (15 officers) plus 33 scientists and 12 aircrew
Guns: 2—7.62 mm MGs.
Radars: Navigation: 2 Raytheon SPS-64; I-band.
Tacan: SRN 15.
Helicopters: 2 HH-65A.

Comment: Both are based at Seattle, Washington. At a continuous speed of 3 kt, they can break ice 6 ft (1.8 m) thick, and by ramming can break 21 ft (6.4 m) pack. Conventional icebreaker hull form with 'White' cutaway bow configuration and well-rounded body sections to prevent being trapped in ice. The ice belt is 1.75 in (44.45 mm) thick supported by framing at 16 in (0.4 m) centres. Three heeling systems assist icebreaking and ship extraction. Two 15 ton capacity cranes fitted aft; one 3 ton capacity crane fitted forward. Two over-the-side oceanographic winches, one over-the-stern trawl/core winch. Deck fixtures for scientific research vans, and research laboratories provided for arctic and oceanographic research. Between 1986-92, science facilities were upgraded including habitability, lab spaces and winch capabilities. *Polar Sea* went to the North Pole in August 1994.

VERIFIED

POLAR SEA   6/1998, Ships of the World / 0053421

1 MACKINAW CLASS (WAGB)

Name	No	Builders	Commissioned	F/S
MACKINAW	WAGB 83	Toledo Shipbuilding	20 Dec 1944	GLA

Displacement, tons: 5,252 full load
Dimensions, feet (metres): 290 × 74 × 19 (88.4 × 22.6 × 5.8)
Main machinery: Diesel-electric; 6 Fairbanks-Morse 38D8-1/8-12 diesel generators; 8.7 MW sustained; Elliot electric drive; 10,000 hp (7.46 MW); 3 shafts (1 fwd, 2 aft)
Speed, knots: 18.7. **Range, miles:** 41,000 at 11.5 kt; 10,000 at 18.7 kt
Complement: 74 (8 officers)
Radars: Navigation: 2 Raytheon SPS-64; I-band.

Comment: Specially designed and constructed for service as icebreaker on the Great Lakes. Equipped with two 5 ton capacity cranes. Clear area for helicopter is provided on the quarterdeck, the aircraft being called for from shore Coast Guard station. First scheduled to be paid off in FY88 but pressure from members of Congress from states bordering the Great Lakes resulted in her being placed in an 'In Commission, Special' status. Operational again in Spring 1988. Again scheduled for decommissioning in December 1994 after 50 years' service but again extended indefinitely.

UPDATED

MACKINAW   2/1995*, USCG / 0084203

8 BAY CLASS (TUGS—WTGB)

Name	No	Laid down	Commissioned	F/S
KATMAI BAY	WTGB 101	7 Nov 1977	8 Jan 1979	GLA
BRISTOL BAY	WTGB 102	13 Feb 1978	5 Apr 1979	GLA
MOBILE BAY	WTGB 103	13 Feb 1978	6 May 1979	GLA
BISCAYNE BAY	WTGB 104	29 Aug 1978	8 Dec 1979	GLA
NEAH BAY	WTGB 105	6 Aug 1979	18 Aug 1980	GLA
PENOBSCOT BAY	WTGB 107	24 July 1983	4 Sep 1984	AA
THUNDER BAY	WTGB 108	20 July 1984	29 Dec 1985	AA
STURGEON BAY	WTGB 109	9 July 1986	20 Aug 1988	AA

Displacement, tons: 662 full load
Dimensions, feet (metres): 140 × 37.6 × 12.5 (42.7 × 11.4 × 3.8)
Main machinery: Diesel-electric; 2 Fairbanks-Morse 38D8-1/8-10 diesel generators; 2.4 MW sustained; Westinghouse electric drive; 2,500 hp (1.87 MW); 1 shaft
Speed, knots: 14.7. **Range, miles:** 4,000 at 12 kt
Complement: 17 (3 officers)
Radars: Navigation: Raytheon SPS-64(V)1; I-band.

Comment: The size, manoeuvrability and other operational characteristics of these vessels are tailored for operations in harbours and other restricted waters and for fulfilling present and anticipated multimission requirements. All units are ice strengthened for operation on the Great Lakes, coastal waters and in rivers and can break 24 in of ice continuously and up to 8 ft by ramming. A self-contained portable bubbler van and system reduces hull friction. First six built at Tacoma Boatbuilding, Tacoma. WTGB 107-109 built in Tacoma by Bay City Marine, San Diego. *Bristol Bay* and *Mobile Bay* have had their bows reinforced to push the two aids-to-navigation barges on the Great Lakes. One deleted in 1998.

VERIFIED

STURGEON BAY   7/1998, van Ginderen Collection / 0053422

PATROL FORCES

49 ISLAND CLASS (WPB)

Name	No	Commissioned	Home Port
FARALLON	WPB 1301	21 Feb 1986	Miami, FL
MANITOU	WPB 1302	28 Feb 1986	Miami, FL
MATAGORDA	WPB 1303	24 Apr 1986	Miami, FL
MAUI	WPB 1304	9 May 1986	Miami, FL
MONHEGAN	WPB 1305	16 June 1986	Key West, FL
NUNIVAK	WPB 1306	4 July 1986	San Juan, PR
OCRACOKE	WPB 1307	4 Aug 1986	San Juan, PR
VASHON	WPB 1308	15 Aug 1986	San Juan, PR
AQUIDNECK	WPB 1309	26 Sep 1986	Portsmouth, VA
MUSTANG	WPB 1310	3 Dec 1986	Seward, AK
NAUSHON	WPB 1311	5 Dec 1986	Ketchikan, AK
SANIBEL	WPB 1312	28 May 1987	Woods Hole, MA
EDISTO	WPB 1313	27 Mar 1987	San Diego, CA
SAPELO	WPB 1314	14 May 1987	Key West, FL
MATINICUS	WPB 1315	19 June 1987	San Juan, PR
NANTUCKET	WPB 1316	10 Aug 1987	Key West, FL
ATTU	WPB 1317	9 May 1988	San Juan, PR
BARANOF	WPB 1318	25 May 1988	Miami, FL
CHANDELEUR	WPB 1319	8 June 1988	Miami, FL
CHINCOTEAGUE	WPB 1320	8 Aug 1988	Mobile, AL
CUSHING	WPB 1321	8 Aug 1988	San Juan, PR
CUTTYHUNK	WPB 1322	5 Oct 1988	Port Angeles, WA
DRUMMOND	WPB 1323	19 Oct 1988	Port Canaveral, FL
KEY LARGO	WPB 1324	24 Dec 1988	Savannah, GA
METOMPKIN	WPB 1325	12 Jan 1989	Charleston, SC
MONOMOY	WPB 1326	19 May 1989	Woods Hole, MA
ORCAS	WPB 1327	14 Apr 1989	Coos Bay, OR
PADRE	WPB 1328	21 Apr 1989	Key West, FL
SITKINAK	WPB 1329	31 May 1989	Key West, FL
TYBEE	WPB 1330	4 Aug 1989	San Diego, CA
WASHINGTON	WPB 1331	6 Oct 1989	Honolulu, HI
WRANGELL	WPB 1332	15 Sep 1989	South Portland, ME
ADAK	WPB 1333	17 Nov 1989	Sandy Hook, NJ
LIBERTY	WPB 1334	22 Sep 1989	Auke Bay, AK
ANACAPA	WPB 1335	13 Jan 1990	Petersburg, AK
KISKA	WPB 1336	21 Apr 1990	Hilo, HI
ASSATEAGUE	WPB 1337	15 June 1990	Honolulu, HI
GRAND ISLE	WPB 1338	19 Apr 1991	Gloucester, MA
KEY BISCAYNE	WPB 1339	23 Apr 1991	Corpus Christi, TX
JEFFERSON ISLAND	WPB 1340	16 Aug 1991	South Portland, ME
KODIAK ISLAND	WPB 1341	21 June 1991	Panama City, FL
LONG ISLAND	WPB 1342	27 Aug 1991	Monterey, CA
BAINBRIDGE ISLAND	WPB 1343	20 Sep 1991	Sandy Hook, NJ
BLOCK ISLAND	WPB 1344	22 Nov 1991	Atlantic Beach, NC
STATEN ISLAND	WPB 1345	22 Nov 1991	Atlantic Beach, NC
ROANOKE ISLAND	WPB 1346	8 Feb 1992	Homer, AK
PEA ISLAND	WPB 1347	29 Feb 1992	Mayport, FL
KNIGHT ISLAND	WPB 1348	22 Apr 1992	Freeport, TX
GALVESTON ISLAND	WPB 1349	5 June 1992	Apra Harbor, Guam

Displacement, tons: 168 (A series); 154 (B series); 134 (C series) full load
Dimensions, feet (metres): 110 × 21 × 7.3 *(33.5 × 6.4 × 2.2)*
Main machinery: 2 Paxman Valenta 16RP 200M diesels (A and B series); 6,246 hp *(4.62 MW)*, sustained; 2 Caterpillar 3516 DITA diesels (C series); 5,596 hp *(4.17 MW)* sustained; 2 shafts
Speed, knots: 26. **Range, miles:** 3,928 at 10 kt
Complement: 16 (2 officers)
Guns: 1 McDonnell Douglas 25 mm/87 Mk 38. 2—12.7 mm M60 MGs.
Radars: Navigation: Hughes/Furuno SPS-73; I-band.

Comment: All built by the Bollinger Machine Shop and Shipyard at Lockport, Louisiana. The design is based upon the 110 ft patrol craft built by Vosper Thornycroft, UK, in service in Venezuela, Qatar, UAE and Singapore, but modified to meet Coast Guard needs. Vosper Thornycroft supplied design support, stabilisers, propellers, and steering gear. Batches: A 1301-1316, B 1317-1337, C 1338-1349. Radars replaced by 1999. **UPDATED**

MATINICUS   6/1999*, M Declerck / 0084204

EDISTO   10/1999*, Findler & Winter / 0084205

24 + 26 MARINE PROTECTOR CLASS (WPB)

Name	No	Launched	Home Port
BARRACUDA	87301	18 Jan 1998	Eureka, CA
HAMMERHEAD	87302	11 May 1998	Woods Hole, MA
MAKO	87303	22 June 1998	Cape May, NJ
MARLIN	87304	14 Sep 1998	Fort Meyers, FL
STINGRAY	87305	21 Sep 1998	Mobile, AL
DORADO	87306	7 Dec 1998	Crescent City, CA
OSPREY	87307	18 Jan 1999	Port Townsend, WA
CHINOOK	87308	1 Mar 1999	New London, CT
ALBACORE	87309	6 Apr 1999	Little Creek, VA
TARPON	87310	18 May 1999	Savannah, GA
COBIA	87311	15 June 1999	Mobile, AL
HAWKSBILL	87312	27 July 1999	Oceanside, CA
CORMORANT	87313	24 Aug 1999	Fort Pierce, FL
FINBACK	87314	21 Sep 1999	Cape May, NJ
AMBERJACK	87315	19 Oct 1999	Port Isabel, TX
KITTIWAKE	87316	16 Nov 1999	Nawiliwilli, HI
BLACKFIN	87317	14 Dec 1999	Santa Barbara, CA
BLUEFIN	87318	11 Jan 2000	Fort Pierce, FL
YELLOWFIN	87319	8 Feb 2000	Charleston, SC
MANTA	87320	7 Mar 2000	Freeport, TX
COHO	87321	4 Apr 2000	Panama City, FL
KINGFISHER	87322	May 2000	Mayport, FL
SEAHAWK	87323	May 2000	Clearwater, FL
STEELHEAD	87324	June 2000	Nokomis, FL
BELUGA	87325	July 2000	Wrightsville, FL
BLACKTIP	87326	Aug 2000	Oxnard, CA
PELICAN	87327	Sep 2000	Morgan City, LA
RIDLEY	87328	Oct 2000	Montauk, NY
COCHITO	87329	Nov 2000	Little Creek, VA
MANOWAR	87330	Dec 2000	Galveston, TX
MORAY	87331	Jan 2001	Jonesport, ME
RAZORBILL	87332	Feb 2001	Gulfport, MS
ADELIE	87333	Mar 2001	Everett, WA
GANNET	87334	Apr 2001	Cape Canaveral, FL
NARWHAL	87335	May 2001	Fort Lauderdale, FL
STURGEON	87336	May 2001	Newport Beach, CA
SOCKEYE	87337	June 2001	Grand Isle, LA
OBOS	87338	July 2001	Bodega Bay, CA
POMPANO	87339	Aug 2001	Cape May, NJ
HALIBUT	87340	Sep 2001	Gulfport, MS
BONITO	87341	Oct 2001	Marina Del Ray, CA
SHRIKE	87342	Nov 2001	Pensacola, FL
TERN	87343	Dec 2001	San Francisco, CA
HERON	87344	Jan 2002	Sabine, TX
WAHOO	87345	Feb 2002	Cape May, NJ
FLYINGFISH	87346	Mar 2002	Newport, RI
HADDOCK	87347	Apr 2002	San Diego, CA
BRANT	87348	Apr 2002	Half Moon Bay, CA
SHEARWATER	87349	May 2002	Port Angelos, WA
PETREL	87350	June 2002	Little Creek, VA

Displacement, tons: 91 full load
Dimensions, feet (metres): 86.9 × 19 × 5.2 *(26.5 × 5.8 × 1.6)*
Main machinery: 2 MTU 8V 396 TE94 diesels; 2,680 hp(m) *(1.97 MW)* sustained; 2 shafts
Speed, knots: 25. **Range, miles:** 800 at 8 kt
Complement: 10 (1 officer)
Guns: 2—12.7 mm MGs.
Radars: Navigation: I-band.

Comment: Designed by David M Cannell based on the hull of the Damen Stan Patrol 2600 which is in service with the Hong Kong police. Steel hull built by Bollinger with GRP superstructure by Halmatic. A stern ramp is used for launching a 5.5 m RIB. **UPDATED**

BLACKFIN   1/2000*, Bollinger / 0084206

BARRACUDA   4/1998*, Bollinger / 0084207

21 POINT CLASS (WPB)

Name	No	F/S	Name	No	F/S
C Series					
POINT HIGHLAND	82333	AA	POINT HANNON	82355	AA
POINT COUNTESS	82335	PA	POINT STUART	82358	PA
POINT GLASS	82336	AA	POINT WINSLOW	82360	PA
POINT BRIDGE	82338	PA	POINT LOBOS	82366	AA
POINT CHICO	82339	PA	POINT WARDE	82368	AA
POINT BAKER	82342	AA			
POINT WELLS	82343	AA			
POINT ESTERO	82344	AA	D Series		
POINT BONITA	82347	AA	POINT BROWER	82372	PA
POINT SPENCER	82349	AA	POINT CARREW	82374	PA
POINT SAL	82352	AA	POINT DORAN	82375	PA
POINT MONROE	82353	AA	POINT JACKSON	82378	AA

Displacement, tons: 66 (C series); 69 (D series) full load
Dimensions, feet (metres): 83 × 17.2 × 5.8 *(25.3 × 5.2 × 1.8)*
Main machinery: 2 Caterpillar 3412 diesels; 1,600 hp *(1.19 MW)*; 2 shafts
Speed, knots: 23.5; 22.6 (D series). **Range, miles:** 1,500 at 8 kt; 1,200 at 8 kt (D series)
Complement: 10 (1 officer)
Guns: 2—12.7 mm MGs.
Radars: Surface search: Hughes/Furuno SPS-73; I-band.

Comment: Steel-hulled craft with aluminium superstructures designed for patrol and search and rescue. C series built in 1961-67, and D series in 1970. Some of the cutters operate with an officer assigned, the rest with all-enlisted crews. All re-engined. Some of the class are in service with navies of Costa Rica, Panama, Mexico, Venezuela, Ecuador, St Lucia, Antigua, Trinidad, Jamaica, Argentina, Dominican Republic and·Philippines. Radars replaced.

UPDATED

POINT BROWER   *3/1998, van Ginderen Collection /* 0053424

44 GUARDIAN CLASS (TPSB)

Displacement, tons: 3 full load
Dimensions, feet (metres): 24.6 × 8.2 × 0.4 *(7.5 × 2.5 × 0.4)*
Main machinery: 2 Evinrude outboards; 350 hp *(261 kW)*
Speed, knots: 35
Complement: 4
Guns: 1—12.7 mm MG. 2—7.62 mm MGs.
Radars: Navigation: Raytheon; I-band.

Comment: Transportable Port Security Boats (TPSB) which serve with the six Port Security Units and a Training Detachment. Can be transported by aircraft.

UPDATED

GUARDIAN   *6/1999*, USCG /* 0084208

GUARDIAN   *6/1998, Boston Whaler /* 0053426

SEAGOING TENDERS

15 BALSAM CLASS (BUOY TENDERS—WLB/WIX)

Name	No	Launched	F/S	Name	No	Launched	F/S
A Series				C Series			
COWSLIP	WLB 277	1942	AA	BRAMBLE	WLB 392	1944	GLA
GENTIAN	WIX 290	1942	AA	FIREBUSH	WLB 393	1944	PA
CONIFER	WLB 301	1943	PA	SASSAFRAS	WLB 401	1944	PA
MADRONA	WLB 302	1943	AA	SEDGE	WLB 402	1944	PA
				SUNDEW	WLB 404	1944	GLA
B Series				SWEETBRIER	WLB 405	1944	PA
IRONWOOD	WLB 297	1943	PA	ACACIA	WLB 406	1944	GLA
BUTTONWOOD	WLB 306	1943	PA	WOODRUSH	WLB 407	1944	PA
SWEETGUM	WLB 309	1943	AR				

Displacement, tons: 757 standard; 1,034 full load
Dimensions, feet (metres): 180 × 37 × 12 *(54.9 × 11.3 × 3.8)*
Main machinery: Diesel-electric; 2 diesels; 1,402 hp *(1.06 MW)* or 1,800 hp *(1.34 MW)* (404); 1 motor; 1,200 hp *(895 kW)*; 1 shaft; bow thruster (except in 395 and 396)
Speed, knots: 13. **Range, miles:** 8,000 at 12 kt
Complement: 53 (6 officers)
Guns: 2—12.7 mm MGs (except 392, 406 and 404).
Radars: Navigation: Raytheon SPS-64(V)1; I-band.

Comment: Seagoing buoy tenders. *Ironwood* built by Coast Guard Yard at Curtis Bay, Maryland; others by Marine Iron & Shipbuilding Co, Duluth, Minnesota, or Zenith Dredge Co, Duluth, Minnesota. Completed 1943-45. All have 20 ton capacity booms.
  Modernisation and Service Life Extension Programmes: *Cowslip, Conifer, Madrona, Sweetgum* and *Buttonwood* completed an 18 month SLEP. Work included replacement of main engines, improvement of electronics, navigation and weight-handling systems, and improved habitability. *Ironwood, Bramble, Firebush, Sassafras, Sedge, Sundew, Sweetbrier, Acacia* and *Woodrush* all underwent major renovation in the mid- to late 1970s which was not as extensive as the SLEPs. However, in the 1988-91 period all of these cutters received same main engines as those installed in cutters receiving SLEP. The last 20 mm guns removed in 1993. *Sundew's* main engines are the same as the others but are 'ungoverned' because of her icebreaking capability. Being replaced by new classes. One transferred to Estonia in 1997. *Gentian* brought back into service on 27 July 1999 to support former USCG craft transferred to Caribbean countries. The ship has a complement of 45 including people from eight different countries. The whole of this class are available for transfer and sale in 2000/01.

UPDATED

GENTIAN   *7/1999*, USCG /* 0084209

MADRONA   *3/1999*, M Declerck /* 0084210

5 + 11 JUNIPER CLASS (BUOY TENDERS—WLB)

Name	No	Builders	Launched		Commissioned	
JUNIPER	WLB 201	Marinette Marine	24 June	1995	10 Apr	1997
WILLOW	WLB 202	Marinette Marine	15 June	1996	10 Apr	1997
KUKUI	WLB 203	Marinette Marine	3 May	1997	1 Sep	1998
ELM	WLB 204	Marinette Marine	24 Jan	1998	20 Nov	1998
WALNUT	WLB 205	Marinette Marine	22 Aug	1998	22 Feb	1999
SPAR	WLB 206	Marinette Marine	July	2000	Jan	2001
MAPLE	WLB 207	Marinette Marine	Sep	2000	Apr	2001
ASPEN	WLB 208	Marinette Marine	Oct	2000	June	2001
SYCAMORE	WLB 209	Marinette Marine	Jan	2001	Sep	2001
CYPRESS	WLB 210	Marinette Marine	Mar	2001	Jan	2002
OAK	WLB 211	Marinette Marine	Oct	2001	June	2002
HICKORY	WLB 212	Marinette Marine	Jan	2002	Sep	2002
FIR	WLB 213	Marinette Marine	Mar	2002	Jan	2003
SEQUOIA	WLB 214	Marinette Marine	Oct	2002	June	2003
HOLLYHOCK	WLB 215	Marinette Marine	Jan	2003	Sep	2003
ALDER	WLB 216	Marinette Marine	Apr	2003	Jan	2004

Displacement, tons: 2,032 full load
Dimensions, feet (metres): 225 × 46 × 13 *(68.6 × 14 × 4)*
Main machinery: 2 Caterpillar 3608 diesels; 6,200 hp *(4.6 MW)* sustained; 1 shaft; cp prop; bow;
   460 hp *(343 kW)* and stern; 550 hp *(410 kW)* thrusters
Speed, knots: 15. **Range, miles:** 6,000 at 12 kt
Complement: 40 (6 officers)
Guns: 1—25 mm/87 Mk 38; 2—12.7 mm MGs.
Radars: Navigation: SPS-73; I-band.

Comment: On 18 February 1993, the Coast Guard awarded Marinette Marine of Marinette, WI, a
   contract to construct the first of a new class of seagoing buoy tenders. Capable of breaking 14 in
   of ice at 3 kt or a minimum of 3 ft by ramming. Main hoist can lift 20 tons, secondary 5 tons. The
   class is named after the first *Juniper*, which was built in 1940 and decommissioned in 1975.
   UPDATED

WILLOW   *6/1998, Harald Carstens /* 0053427

COASTAL TENDERS

14 KEEPER CLASS (BUOY TENDERS—WLM)

Name	No	Builders	Launched		Completed	
IDA LEWIS	WLM 551	Marinette Marine	14 Oct	1995	1 Nov	1996
KATHERINE WALKER	WLM 552	Marinette Marine	14 Sep	1996	27 June	1997
ABIGAIL BURGESS	WLM 553	Marinette Marine	5 Apr	1997	19 Sep	1997
MARCUS HANNA	WLM 554	Marinette Marine	23 Aug	1997	26 Nov	1997
JAMES RANKIN	WLM 555	Marinette Marine	25 Apr	1998	26 Aug	1998
JOSHUA APPLEBY	WLM 556	Marinette Marine	8 Aug	1998	20 Nov	1998
FRANK DREW	WLM 557	Marinette Marine	5 Dec	1998	17 June	1999
ANTHONY PETIT	WLM 558	Marinette Marine	30 Jan	1999	1 July	1999
BARBARA MABRITY	WLM 559	Marinette Marine	27 Mar	1999	29 July	1999
WILLIAM TATE	WLM 560	Marinette Marine	8 May	1999	16 Sep	1999
HARRY CLAIBORNE	WLM 561	Marinette Marine	26 June	1999	28 Oct	1999
MARIA BRAY	WLM 562	Marinette Marine	28 Aug	1999	6 Apr	2000
HENRY BLAKE	WLM 563	Marinette Marine	20 Nov	1999	18 May	2000
GEORGE COBB	WLM 564	Marinette Marine	18 Dec	1999	22 June	2000

Displacement, tons: 916 full load
Dimensions, feet (metres): 175 × 36 × 7.9 *(53.3 × 11 × 2.4)*
Main machinery: 2 Caterpillar 3508TA diesels; 1,920 hp *(1.43 MW)* sustained; 2 Ulstein Z-drives;
   bow thruster; 460 hp *(343 kW)*
Speed, knots: 12. **Range, miles:** 2,000 at 10 kt
Complement: 18 (1 officer)
Radars: Navigation: Raytheon SPS-64; I-band.

Comment: Contract awarded 22 June 1993 for first of class with an option for 13 more. Capable of
   breaking 9 in of ice at 3 kt or 18 in by ramming. Named after Lighthouse Keepers for the
   Lighthouse Service, one of the predecessors of the modern Coast Guard. The ship is a scaled
   down model of the 'Juniper' class for coastal service. Main hoist to lift 10 tons, secondary
   3.75 tons. Able to skim and recover surface oil pollution.   *UPDATED*

MARCUS HANNA   *11/1997, Marinette Marine /* 0053428

1 WHITE SUMAC CLASS (BUOY TENDERS—WLM)

Name	No	Builders	Launched	F/S
WHITE SUMAC	WLM 540	Niagara Shipyard, Buffalo	14 June 1943	AA

Displacement, tons: 435 standard; 485 full load
Dimensions, feet (metres): 133 × 31 × 9 *(40.5 × 9.5 × 2.7)*
Main machinery: 2 Caterpillar diesels; 600 hp *(448 kW)*; 2 shafts
Speed, knots: 9.8
Complement: 24 (1 officer)

Comment: Former US Navy YF, adapted for the Coast Guard. Fitted with 10 ton capacity boom. To
   be paid off in 2000. Two to Tunisia in June 1998, one to Dominican Republic in 1999.
   UPDATED

WHITE SUMAC   *1/1992, Giorgio Arra*

BUOY TENDERS (INLAND—WLI)

Name	No	Builders	Launched		F/S
BLUEBELL	WLI 313	Birchfield Shipyard, Tacoma	28 Sep	1944	PA
BUCKTHORN	WLI 642	Mobile Shipyard, Mobile	18 Aug	1963	GLA

Displacement, tons: 226 (174 *Bluebell*) full load
Dimensions, feet (metres): 100 × 24 × 5 *(30.5 × 7.3 × 1.5)* (*Buckthorn* draught 4 *(1.2)*)
Main machinery: 2 Caterpillar diesels; 600 hp *(448 kW)*; 2 shafts
Speed, knots: 11.9; 10.5 *(Bluebell)*
Complement: 14 (1 officer)

Comment: Different vintage but similar in design.
   UPDATED

BUCKTHORN   *3/2000*, US Coast Guard /* 0085029

Name	No	Builders	F/S
BLACKBERRY	WLI 65303	Dubuque Shipyard, Iowa	AA
CHOKEBERRY	WLI 65304	Dubuque Shipyard, Iowa	AA
BAYBERRY	WLI 65400	Reliable Shipyard, Olympia	PA
ELDERBERRY	WLI 65401	Reliable Shipyard, Olympia	PA

Displacement, tons: 68 full load
Dimensions, feet (metres): 65 × 17 × 4 *(19.8 × 5.2 × 1.2)*
Main machinery: 1 or 2 *(Bayberry* and *Elderberry)* GM diesels; 1 or 2 shafts
Speed, knots: 11
Complement: 9

Comment: First two completed in August 1946, second two in June 1954.
   UPDATED

BAYBERRY   *5/1999*, Hartmut Ehlers /* 0084211

BUOY TENDERS (RIVER) (WLR)

Notes: (1) All are based on rivers of USA especially the Mississippi and the Missouri and its tributaries.
(2) Two ATON (aids to navigation) barges completed in 1991-92 by Marinette Marine. For use on the Great Lakes in conjunction with icebreaker tugs *Bristol Bay* and *Mobile Bay*.

ATON I and Icebreaker Tug (WGTB)   *1991*, Marinette Marine* / 0084214

18 BUOY TENDERS (WLR)

WEDGE WLR 75307	**GREENBRIAR** WLR 75501	**SANGAMON** WLR 65506
GASCONADE WLR 75401	**KICKAPOO** WLR 75406	**OUACHITA** WLR 65501
MUSKINGUM WLR 75402	**KANAWHA** WLR 75407	**SCIOTO** WLR 65504
WYACONDA WLR 75403	**PATOKA** WLR 75408	**CIMARRON** WLR 65502
CHIPPEWA WLR 75404	**CHENA** WLR 75409	**OSAGE** WLR 65505
CHEYENNE WLR 75405	**KANKAKEE** WLR 75500	**OBION** WLR 65503

Displacement, tons: 145 full load
Dimensions, feet (metres): 75 × 22 × 4 *(22.9 × 6.7 × 1.2)*
Main machinery: 2 Caterpillar diesels; 660 hp *(492 kW)*; 2 shafts
Speed, knots: 9. **Range, miles:** 1,500 at 8 kt
Complement: 12

Comment: WLR 75401-09 built 1964-70 and WLR 65501-06 in 1960-62. WLR 75500-01 were completed in early 1990 and more of this type may be built. Details given are for the WLR 75401 series, but all are much the same size.   *UPDATED*

TRAINING CUTTERS

Note: *Gentian* WIX 290 is listed under 'Balsam' class.

1 EAGLE CLASS (WIX)

Name	*No*	*Builders*	*Commissioned*	*F/S*
EAGLE (ex-*Horst Wessel*)	WIX 327	Blohm + Voss, Hamburg	15 May 1946	AA

Displacement, tons: 1,816 full load
Dimensions, feet (metres): 231 wl; 293.6 oa × 39.4 × 16.1 *(70.4; 89.5 × 12 × 4.9)*
Main machinery: 1 Caterpillar D 399 auxiliary diesel; 1,125 hp *(839 kW)* sustained; 1 shaft
Speed, knots: 10.5; 18 sail. **Range, miles:** 5,450 at 7.5 kt diesel only
Complement: 245 (19 officers, 180 cadets)
Radars: Navigation: SPS-73; I-band.

Comment: Former German training ship. Launched on 13 June 1936. Taken by the USA as part of reparations after the Second World War for employment in US Coast Guard Practice Squadron. Taken over at Bremerhaven in January 1946; arrived at home port of New London, Connecticut, in July 1946. (Sister ship *Albert Leo Schlageter* was also taken by the USA in 1945 but was sold to Brazil in 1948 and re-sold to Portugal in 1962. Another ship of similar design, *Gorch Fock*, transferred to the USSR in 1946 and survives as *Tovarisch*.) *Eagle* was extensively overhauled 1981-82. When the Coast Guard added the orange-and-blue marking stripes to cutters in the 1960s *Eagle* was exempted because of their effect on her graceful lines; however, in early 1976 the stripes and words 'Coast Guard' were added in time for the July 1976 Operation Sail in New York harbour. During the Coast Guard's year long bicentennial celebration, which ended 4 August 1990, *Eagle* visited each of the 10 ports where the original revenue cutters were homeported: Baltimore, Maryland; New London, Connecticut; Washington, North Carolina; Savannah, Georgia; Philadelphia, Pennsylvania; Newburyport, Maryland; Portsmouth, New Hampshire; Charleston, South Carolina; New York, New York; and Hampton, Virginia. Fore and main masts 150.3 ft *(45.8 m)*; mizzen 132 ft *(40.2 m)*; sail area, 25,351 sq ft.   *VERIFIED*

EAGLE   *7/1998, van Ginderen Collection* / 0053430

CONSTRUCTION TENDERS (INLAND) (WLIC)

Note: All, although operating on inland waters, are administered by the Atlantic Area.

4 PAMLICO CLASS (WLIC)

PAMLICO WLIC 800   **HUDSON** WLIC 801   **KENNEBEC** WLIC 802   **SAGINAW** WLIC 803

Displacement, tons: 459 full load
Dimensions, feet (metres): 160.9 × 30 × 4 *(49 × 9.1 × 1.2)*
Main machinery: 2 Caterpillar diesels; 1,000 hp *(746 kW)*; 2 shafts
Speed, knots: 11.5
Complement: 15 (1 officer)
Radars: Navigation: Raytheon SPS-69; I-band.

Comment: Completed in 1976 at the Coast Guard Yard, Curtis Bay, Maryland. These ships maintain structures and buoys in bay areas along the Atlantic and Gulf coasts.   *VERIFIED*

HUDSON   *12/1989, Giorgio Arra*

1 COSMOS CLASS (WLIC)

SMILAX WLIC 315

Displacement, tons: 178 full load
Dimensions, feet (metres): 100 × 24 × 5 *(30.5 × 7.3 × 1.5)*
Main machinery: 2 Caterpillar D 353 diesels; 425 hp *(317 kW)* sustained; 2 shafts
Speed, knots: 10.5
Complement: 15 (1 officer)
Radars: Navigation: Raytheon SPS-69; I-band.

Comment: Completed in 1944. Primary areas of operation are intercoastal waters from Virginia to Georgia.   *UPDATED*

COSMOS   *7/1990, van Ginderen Collection*

8 ANVIL/CLAMP CLASSES (WLIC)

ANVIL WLIC 75301	**MALLET** WLIC 75304	**HATCHET** WLIC 75309
HAMMER WLIC 75302	**VISE** WLIC 75305	**AXE** WLIC 75310
SLEDGE WLIC 75303	**CLAMP** WLIC 75306	

Displacement, tons: 145 full load
Dimensions, feet (metres): 75 (76—WLIC 75306-75310) × 22 × 4 *(22.9 (23.2) × 6.7 × 1.2)*
Main machinery: 2 Caterpillar diesels; 660 hp *(492 kW)*; 2 shafts
Speed, knots: 10
Complement: 13 (1 officer in *Mallet, Sledge* and *Vise)*

Comment: Completed 1962-65. Primary areas of operation are intercoastal waters from Texas to New Jersey.   *UPDATED*

CLAMP   *10/1999*, Marsan/Schaeffer* / 0084215

HARBOUR TUGS

11 65 ft CLASS (WYTL)

CAPSTAN WYTL 65601	**PENDANT** WYTL 65608	**WIRE** WYTL 65612
CHOCK WYTL 65602	**SHACKLE** WYTL 65609	**BOLLARD** WYTL 65614
TACKLE WYTL 65604	**HAWSER** WYTL 65610	**CLEAT** WYTL 65615
BRIDLE WYTL 65607	**LINE** WYTL 65611	

Displacement, tons: 72 full load
Dimensions, feet (metres): 65 × 19 × 7 *(19.8 × 5.8 × 2.1)*
Main machinery: 1 Caterpillar 3412TA diesel; 475 hp *(637 kW)* sustained; 1 shaft
Speed, knots: 10. **Range, miles:** 850 at 10 kt
Complement: 10
Radars: Navigation: Raytheon SPS-69; I-band.

Comment: Built between 1961 and 1967. All active in the Atlantic Fleet. Re-engined 1993-96.
VERIFIED

LINE *5/1998, John Grima* / 0053431

1610 + RESCUE AND UTILITY CRAFT

Note: Craft of several different types. All carry five or six figure numbers of which the first two figures reflect the craft's length in feet.

179 UTILITY BOATS

Displacement, tons: 15 full load
Dimensions, feet (metres): 41.3 × 14.1 × 4.1 *(12.6 × 4.3 × 1.3)*
Main machinery: 2 diesels; 636 hp *(474 kW)* sustained; 2 shafts
Speed, knots: 26. **Range, miles:** 300 miles at 18 kt
Complement: 3

Comment: Built by Coast Guard Yard, Baltimore 1973-83. Aluminium hull with a towing capacity of 100 tons. Used for fast multimission response in weather conditions up to moderate.
UPDATED

41420 *5/1998, John Grima* / 0053432

73 MOTOR LIFEBOATS

Displacement, tons: 20 full load
Dimensions, feet (metres): 47.9 × 14.5 × 4.5 *(14.6 × 4.4 × 1.4)*
Main machinery: 2 Detroit diesels; 850 hp *(634 kW)* sustained; 2 shafts
Speed, knots: 25. **Range, miles:** 220 at 25 kt
Complement: 4

Comment: Built by Textron Marine, New Orleans. The prototype completed trials in mid-1991. Five production boats delivered in 1994. More ordered in September 1995. Replacing the ageing fleet of 44 ft lifeboats. Aluminium hulls, self-righting with a 9,000 lb bollard pull and a towing capability of 150 tons. Primarily a lifeboat but it has a multimission capability.
UPDATED

MOTOR LIFEBOAT *10/1999*, Findler & Winter* / 0084216

NATIONAL OCEANIC AND ATMOSPHERIC ADMINISTRATION (NOAA)

Headquarters Appointments

Under Secretary of Commerce for Oceans and Atmosphere:
  Dr James Baker
Director, NOAA Corps Operations:
  Rear Admiral Evelyn J Fields
Director, Atlantic and Pacific Marine Centers:
  Rear Admiral Nicholas Prah

Establishment and Missions

NOAA has been the largest component of the US Department of Commerce, with a diverse set of responsibilities in environmental sciences. These responsibilities have in years past included the Office of NOAA Corps Operations, the National Ocean Service, the National Weather Service, the National Marine Fisheries Service, the National Environment Satellite, Data, and Information Service, and the Office of Oceanic and Atmospheric Research. Its research vessels normally conduct operations in hydrography, bathymetry, oceanography, atmospheric research,

fisheries surveys and research, and related programmes in marine resources. Larger research vessels have operated in international waters; and smaller ones primarily in Atlantic and Pacific coastal waters, the Gulfs of Mexico and Alaska, and the five US Great Lakes. NOAA also has conducted diving operations and has operated fixed-wing and rotary-wing aircraft for reconnaissance, oceanographic and atmospheric research, and in support of aerial mapping and charting and hurricane monitoring.

Proposals to merge NOAA with other organisations have been made since 1995, but in October 1998 Congress passed a funding bill and the Commissioned Officer Corps is to be retained.

NOAA's fleet remains at 15 ships, some of which are old and require costly maintenance. One new ship, the *Ronald H Brown* (ex-AGOR 26) has been constructed since 1980, but two ex-naval T-AGOS ships have been acquired and are used for oceanographic research *(Ka'imimoana)*, and fisheries research *(Gordon Gunter)*. *Miller Freeman* was SLEPed in 1999. Funds approved in FY2000 to acquire the first of several new fisheries research ships.

Ships

The following ships may be met with at sea.
Oceanographic Research Ships: *Ronald H Brown, Ka'imimoana.*
Multipurpose Oceanographic/Coastal Research Ships: *McArthur, Ferrel*
Hydrographic Survey Ships: *Rainier, Rude, Whiting.*
Fisheries Research Ships: *Miller Freeman, Oregon II, Albatross IV, Delaware II, Townsend Cromwell, David Starr Jordan, John N Cobb, Gordon Gunter.*

Personnel

2000: 250 officers plus 12,000 civilians.

Bases

Major: Norfolk, VA and Seattle, WA.
Minor: Woods Hole, MA; Pascagoula, MS; Honolulu, HI; Charleston, SC; San Diego, CA.

ALBATROSS IV   *10/1997, Harald Carstens* / 0053484

GORDON GUNTER   *6/1998, NOAA* / 0053433

FERREL   *10/1997, Harald Carstens* / 0053434

D S JORDAN   *6/1998, van Ginderen Collection* / 0053483

URUGUAY

Headquarters Appointments

Commander-in-Chief of the Navy:
  Vice Admiral Francisco Pazos Maresca
Commander Sea Forces:
  Rear Admiral Raul Lecumbory

Diplomatic Representation

Naval Attaché in London:
  Captain Juan Herrera

Personnel

(a) 2000: 5,000 (500 officers) (including 500 naval infantry,
     300 naval air and 1,800 Coast Guard)
(b) Voluntary service

Prefectura Nacional Naval (PNN)

Established in 1934 primarily for harbour security and coastline guard duties. In 1991 it was integrated with the Navy but some patrol craft still retain Prefectura markings. There are three regions: Atlantic, Rio de la Plata, and Rio Uruguay.

Bases

Montevideo: Main naval base with two dry docks and a slipway at Punta Lobos
La Paloma: Naval station *(Ernesto Motto)*
Paysandu: River base
Laguna del Sauce, Maldonado: Naval air station *(Capitan Carlos A Curbelo)*

Marines

Cuerpo de Fusileros Navales consisting of 500 men in three units plus a command company of 100.

Prefix to Ships' Names

ROU

Mercantile Marine

Lloyd's Register of Shipping:
  90 vessels of 61,806 tons gross

DELETIONS

Patrol forces

1999   *Salto*

Auxiliaries

1997   *Zapican* (immobile tender), *LD 40*
1999   *Presidente Rivera*

FRIGATES

Note: Replacement frigates are needed. Ex-UK Type 22 *Brave* and an ex-French Type A 69 are possible.

3 COMMANDANT RIVIÈRE CLASS (FFG)

Name	No	Builders	Laid down	Launched	Commissioned	Recommissioned
URUGUAY (ex-*Commandant Bourdais*)	1	Lorient Naval Dockyard	Apr 1959	15 Apr 1961	10 Mar 1962	20 Aug 1990
GENERAL ARTIGAS (ex-*Victor Schoelcher*)	2	Lorient Naval Dockyard	Oct 1957	11 Oct 1958	15 Oct 1962	9 Jan 1989
MONTEVIDEO (ex-*Amiral Charner*)	3 (ex-4)	Lorient Naval Dockyard	Nov 1958	12 Mar 1960	14 Dec 1962	28 Jan 1991

Displacement, tons: 1,750 standard; 2,250 full load
Dimensions, feet (metres): 336.9 × 38.4 × 14.1
(102.7 × 11.7 × 4.3)
Main machinery: 4 SEMT-Pielstick 12 PC series diesels;
16,000 hp(m) *(11.8 MW)*; 2 shafts
Speed, knots: 25. **Range, miles:** 7,500 at 15 kt
Complement: 159 (9 officers)

Missiles: SSM: 4 Aerospatiale MM 38 Exocet ❶; active radar
homing to 42 km *(23 n miles)* at 0.9 Mach; warhead 165 kg;
sea-skimmer.
Guns: 2 DCN 3.9 in *(100 mm)*/55 Mod 1953 automatic ❷; dual
purpose; 60 rds/min to 17 km *(9 n miles)* anti-surface; 8 km
(4.4 n miles) anti-aircraft; weight of shell 13.5 kg.
2 Hispano Suiza 30 mm/70 ❸; 600 rds/min to 8.5 km *(4.8 n
miles)* anti-aircraft.
Torpedoes: 6—21.7 in *(550 mm)* (2 triple) tubes ❹ ECAN L3; anti-
submarine; active homing to 5.5 km *(3 n miles)* at 25 kt;
warhead 200 kg; depth to 300 m *(985 ft)*.
A/S mortars: 1 Mortier 305 mm 4-barrelled launcher ❺.
Countermeasures: ESM: ARBR 16; radar warning.
Weapons control: C T Analogique. Sagem DMAA optical
director.
Radars: Air/surface search: Thomson-CSF DRBV 22A ❻; D-band.
Navigation: Racal Decca 1226 ❼; I-band.
Fire control: Thomson-CSF DRBC 32C ❽; I-band.

Sonars: EDO SQS-17; hull-mounted; active search; medium
frequency.
Thomson Sintra DUBA 3; active attack; high frequency.

Programmes: First one bought from France through SOFMA on
30 September 1988, second pair 14 March 1990. All refitted
before transfer.
Structure: Exocet and Dagaie removed before transfer but SSM
casings were retained and missiles restored in 1991-92.
40 mm guns replaced by 30 mm.
Operational: Can carry a Flag Officer and staff. In French service
this class sometimes embarked up to 80 soldiers and two
LCPs. The A/S mortar is non-operational. *Montevideo* had SSM
launchers removed after refit in 1999.

UPDATED

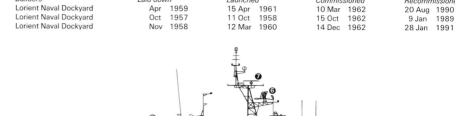
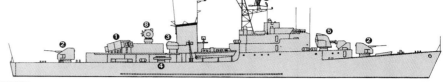

URUGUAY

(Scale 1 : 900), Ian Sturton

MONTEVIDEO (without SSM)

7/1999*, A E Galarce / 0084217

URUGUAY

4/1997, Robert Pabst / 0050724

LAND-BASED MARITIME AIRCRAFT

Note: In addition to those listed there are also six helicopters (one Bell 47G, five Westland Wessex HC Mk 2 and 3 Wessex 60). There are also six fixed-wing aircraft, three Beech T-34B, one Beech B-200T and two Jetstream T2. The latter were bought from the UK in 1998 for use as maritime patrol aircraft.

JETSTREAM   6/1999*, Uruguay Navy / 0084218

Numbers/Type: 1 Grumman S-2G Tracker.
Operational speed: 130 kt *(241 km/h)*.
Service ceiling: 25,000 ft *(7,620 m)*.
Range: 1,350 n miles *(2,500 km)*.
Role/Weapon systems: ASW and surface search with improved systems. Sensors: Search radar, MAD, sonobuoys. Weapons: ASW; torpedoes, depth bombs or mines. ASV; rockets underwing.
UPDATED

PATROL FORCES

3 VIGILANTE CLASS (LARGE PATROL CRAFT) (PC)

Name	No	Builders	Commissioned
15 de NOVIEMBRE	5	CMN, Cherbourg	25 Mar 1981
25 de AGOSTO	6	CMN, Cherbourg	25 Mar 1981
COMODORO COÉ	7	CMN, Cherbourg	25 Mar 1981

Displacement, tons: 190 full load
Dimensions, feet (metres): 137 × 22.4 × 5.2 *(41.8 × 6.8 × 1.6)*
Main machinery: 2 MTU 12V 538 TB91 diesels; 4,600 hp(m) *(3.4 MW)* sustained; 2 shafts
Speed, knots: 28. **Range, miles:** 2,400 at 15 kt
Complement: 28 (5 officers)
Gun: 1 Bofors 40 mm/70.
Weapons control: CSEE Naja optronic director.
Radars: Surface search: Racal Decca TM 1226C; I-band.

Comment: Ordered in 1979. Steel hull. First launched 16 October 1980, second 11 December 1980 and third 27 January 1981.
UPDATED

COMODORO COÉ   7/1999*, A E Galarce / 0084220

2 CAPE CLASS (LARGE PATROL CRAFT) (PC)

Name	No	Builders	Commissioned
COLONIA (ex-*Cape Higgon*)	10	Coast Guard Yard, Curtis Bay	14 Oct 1953
RIO NEGRO (ex-*Cape Horn*)	11	Coast Guard Yard, Curtis Bay	3 Sep 1958

Displacement, tons: 98 standard; 148 full load
Dimensions, feet (metres): 95 × 20.2 × 6.6 *(28.9 × 6.2 × 2)*
Main machinery: 2 GM 16V-149TI diesels; 2,322 hp *(1.73 MW)* sustained; 2 shafts
Speed, knots: 20. **Range, miles:** 2,500 at 10 kt
Complement: 14 (1 officer)
Guns: 2—12.7 mm MGs.
Radars: Surface search: Raytheon SPS-64; I-band.

Comment: Designed for port security and search and rescue. Steel hulled. During modernisation in 1974 received new engines, electronics and deck equipment. Superstructure modified or replaced, and habitability improved. Transferred from the US Coast Guard 25 January 1990. Both based at Paysandu.
UPDATED

COLONIA   6/1999*, Uruguay Navy / 0084219

1 COASTAL PATROL CRAFT (PC)

Name	No	Builders	Commissioned
PAYSANDU	12 (ex-PR 12)	Sewart, USA	Nov 1968

Displacement, tons: 58 full load
Dimensions, feet (metres): 83 × 18 × 6 *(25.3 × 5.5 × 1.8)*
Main machinery: 2 GM 16V-71 diesels; 811 hp *(605 kW)* sustained; 2 shafts
Speed, knots: 22. **Range, miles:** 800 at 20 kt
Complement: 8
Guns: 3—12.7 mm MGs.
Radars: Surface search: Raytheon 1500B; I-band.

Comment: Formerly incorrectly listed under Coast Guard. Based at Paysandu.
UPDATED

PAYSANDU   6/1999*, Uruguay Navy / 0084221

3 COASTGUARD PATROL CRAFT (PC)

70   71   72

Displacement, tons: 90 full load
Dimensions, feet (metres): 72.2 × 16.4 × 5.9 *(22 × 5 × 1.8)*
Main machinery: 2 GM diesels; 400 hp *(298 kW)*; 2 shafts
Speed, knots: 12
Complement: 8

Comment: Built in 1957 at Montevideo. These are Coast Guard craft.
UPDATED

PREFECTURA 72   12/1997*, Hartmut Ehlers / 0016606

9 TYPE 44 CLASS (PBI)

441-449

Displacement, tons: 18 full load
Dimensions, feet (metres): 44 × 12.8 × 3.6 *(13.5 × 3.9 × 1.1)*
Main machinery: 2 Detroit 6V-38 diesels; 185 hp *(136 kW)*; 2 shafts
Speed, knots: 14. **Range, miles:** 215 at 10 kt
Complement: 3

Comment: Acquired from the US in 1999 and operated by the Coast Guard primarily as SAR craft.
NEW ENTRY

446 *11/1999*, A E Galarce /* 0084225

MINE WARFARE FORCES

4 KONDOR II CLASS (MINESWEEPERS—COASTAL) (MSC)

Name	No	Builders	Launched		Recommissioned	
TEMERARIO (ex-*Riesa*)	31	Peenewerft, Wolgast	2 Oct	1972	11 Oct	1991
VALIENTE (ex-*Eilenburg*)	32	Peenewerft, Wolgast	31 Aug	1972	11 Oct	1991
FORTUNA (ex-*Bernau*)	33	Peenewerft, Wolgast	3 Aug	1972	11 Oct	1991
AUDAZ (ex-*Eisleben*)	34	Peenewerft, Wolgast	2 Jan	1973	11 Oct	1991

Displacement, tons: 310 full load
Dimensions, feet (metres): 186 × 24.6 × 7.9 *(56.7 × 7.5 × 2.4)*
Main machinery: 2 Russki/Kolomna Type 40-DM diesels; 4,408 hp(m) *(3.24 MW)* sustained; 2 shafts; cp props
Speed, knots: 17. **Range, miles:** 2,000 at 15 kt
Complement: 31 (6 officers)
Guns: 1 Hispano Suiza 30 mm/70.
Mines: 2 rails.
Radars: Surface search: TSR 333 or Raytheon 1900; I-band.

Comment: Belonged to the former GDR Navy. Transferred without armament. Minesweeping gear retained including MSG-3 variable depth sweep device. *UPDATED*

FORTUNA *1/1999* /* 0084222

SURVEY AND RESEARCH SHIPS

1 AUK CLASS (AGOR)

Name	No	Builders	Commissioned
COMANDANTE PEDRO CAMPBELL (ex-*Chickadee*, MSF 59)	24 (ex-4, ex-MS 31, ex-MSF 1)	Defoe B & M Works	9 Nov 1942

Displacement, tons: 1,090 standard; 1,250 full load
Dimensions, feet (metres): 221.2 × 32.2 × 10.8 *(67.5 × 9.8 × 3.3)*
Main machinery: Diesel-electric; 4 Alco 539 diesels; 3,532 hp *(2.63 MW)*; 4 generators; 2 motors; 2 shafts
Speed, knots: 18. **Range, miles:** 4,300 at 10 kt
Complement: 105
Guns: 1 Bofors 40 mm/60. 2 Oerlikon 20 mm.

Comment: Former US fleet minesweeper. Launched on 20 July 1942. Transferred on loan and commissioned at San Diego on 18 August 1966. Purchased 15 August 1976. Sweeping gear removed and classified as a corvette. Refitted again at Montevideo naval yard in 1988-89 and then recommissioned for Antarctic service without armament. Now classified as a 'Buque de Adiestramiento', has been renamed and is painted grey. *UPDATED*

COMANDANTE PEDRO CAMPBELL *6/1999*, Uruguay Navy /* 0084224

1 HELGOLAND (TYPE 720B) CLASS (AGS)

Name	No	Builders	Commissioned
OYARVIDE (ex-*Helgoland*)	22 (ex-A 1457)	Unterweser, Bremerhaven	8 Mar 1966

Displacement, tons: 1,310 standard; 1,643 full load
Dimensions, feet (metres): 223.1 × 41.7 × 14.4 *(68 × 12.7 × 4.4)*
Main machinery: Diesel-electric; 4 MWM 12-cyl diesel generators; 2 motors; 3,300 hp(m) *(2.43 MW)*; 2 shafts
Speed, knots: 17. **Range, miles:** 6,400 at 16 kt
Complement: 34
Radars: Navigation: Raytheon; I-band.
Sonars: High definition, hull-mounted for wreck search.

Comment: Former German ocean-going tug launched on 25 November 1965. Paid off in 1997 and recommissioned on 21 September 1998 after being fitted out as a survey ship. Ice strengthened hull. Fitted for twin 40 mm guns. *UPDATED*

OYARVIDE *1/1999* /* 0084223

TRAINING SHIPS

1 SAIL TRAINING SHIP (AXS)

Name	No	Builders	Commissioned
CAPITAN MIRANDA	20 (ex-GS 10)	SECN Matagorda, Cádiz	1930

Displacement, tons: 839 full load
Dimensions, feet (metres): 209.9 × 26.3 × 12.4 *(64 × 8 × 3.8)*
Main machinery: 1 GM diesel; 750 hp *(552 kW)*; 1 shaft
Speed, knots: 10
Complement: 49
Radars: Navigation: Racal Decca TM 1226C; I-band.

Comment: Originally a diesel-driven survey ship with pronounced clipper bow. Converted for service as a three-masted schooner, commissioning as cadet training ship in 1978. Major refit by Bazán, Cadiz from June 1993 to March 1994, including a new diesel engine and a 5 m extension to the superstructure. Now has 853.4 m² of sail. *UPDATED*

CAPITAN MIRANDA *8/1999*, A Campanera i Rovira /* 0084226

AUXILIARIES

2 LCVPs

LD 44   **LD 45**

Displacement, tons: 15 full load
Dimensions, feet (metres): 46.5 × 11.6 × 2.7 *(14.1 × 3.5 × 0.8)*
Main machinery: 1 GM 4-71 diesel; 115 hp *(86 kW)* sustained; 1 shaft
Speed, knots: 9. **Range, miles:** 580 at 9 kt
Military lift: 10 tons

Comment: Built at Naval Shipyard, Montevideo and completed 1980. These are Coast Guard craft. *UPDATED*

LD 45 (PNN 631 alongside) *12/1997, Hartmut Ehlers /* 0016610

1 PIAST CLASS (TYPE 570) (SALVAGE SHIP) (ARS)

Name	No	Builders	Commissioned
VANGUARDIA	26 (ex-A 441)	Northern Shipyard, Gdansk	29 Dec 1976
(ex-*Otto Von Guericke*)			

Displacement, tons: 1,732 full load
Dimensions, feet (metres): 240 × 39.4 × 13.1 *(73.2 × 12 × 4)*
Main machinery: 2 Zgoda diesels; 3,800 hp(m) *(2.79 MW)*; 2 shafts; cp props
Speed, knots: 16. **Range, miles:** 3,000 at 12 kt
Complement: 61
Radars: Navigation: 2 TSR 333; I-band.

Comment: Acquired from Germany in October 1991 and sailed from Rostock in January 1992 after a refit at Neptun-Warnow Werft. Carries extensive towing and firefighting equipment plus a diving bell forward of the bridge. Armed with four 25 mm twin guns when in service with the former GDR Navy.

UPDATED

VANGUARDIA   6/1999*, Uruguay Navy / 0084227

1 BUOY TENDER (ABU)

SIRIUS 21

Displacement, tons: 290 full load
Dimensions, feet (metres): 115.1 × 32.8 × 5.9 *(35.1 × 10 × 1.8)*
Main machinery: 2 Detroit 12V-71TA diesels; 840 hp *(626 kW)* sustained; 2 shafts
Speed, knots: 11
Complement: 15

Comment: Buoy tender built at Montevideo Naval Yard and completed in 1988. Endurance, five days.

UPDATED

SIRIUS   6/1999*, Uruguay Navy / 0084228

3 LCM CLASS

LD 41   LD 42   LD 43

Displacement, tons: 24 light; 57 full load
Dimensions, feet (metres): 56.1 × 14.1 × 3.9 *(17.1 × 4.3 × 1.2)*
Main machinery: 2 Gray Marine 64 HN9 diesels; 330 hp *(264 kW)*; 2 shafts
Speed, knots: 9. **Range, miles:** 130 at 9 kt
Complement: 5
Military lift: 30 tons

Comment: First one transferred on lease from USA October 1972. Lease extended in October 1986. Second pair were built in Uruguay. Details given are for *LD 41* and *42*. *LD 43* is a smaller craft at 13 tons full load and is subordinate to the Fleet Air Arm Flying School at Laguna del Sauce.

UPDATED

LD 41   8/1999*, P Marsan / 0084229

TUGS

1 COASTAL TUG (YTB)

Name	No	Builders	Commissioned
BANCO ORTIZ	27 (ex-7, ex-Y 1655)	Peenewerft, Wolgast	10 Sep 1959
(ex-*Zingst*, ex-*Elbe*)			

Displacement, tons: 261 full load
Dimensions, feet (metres): 100 × 26.6 × 10.8 *(30.5 × 8.1 × 3.3)*
Main machinery: 1 R6 DV 148 diesel; 550 hp(m) *(404 kW)*; 1 shaft
Speed, knots: 10
Complement: 12

Comment: Ex-GDR Type 270 tug acquired in October 1991. 10 ton bollard pull.

VERIFIED

BANCO ORTIZ   7/1998, A E Galarce / 0050728

VANUATU

Headquarters Appointments	General	Bases	Mercantile Marine
Commander, Maritime Wing: Superintendent B Timbari	Originally the New Hebrides. Achieved independence on 30 July 1980, having previously been under Franco-British condominium.	Port Vila, Efate Island	*Lloyd's Register of Shipping:* 299 vessels of 1,444,160 tons gross

POLICE

1 PACIFIC FORUM PATROL CRAFT (PC)

Name	No	Builders	Commissioned
TUKORO	02	Australian Shipbuilding Industries	13 June 1987

Displacement, tons: 165 full load
Dimensions, feet (metres): 103.3 × 26.6 × 6.9 *(31.5 × 8.1 × 2.1)*
Main machinery: 2 Caterpillar 3516TA diesels; 4,400 hp *(3.28 MW)* sustained; 2 shafts
Speed, knots: 18. **Range, miles:** 2,500 at 12 kt
Complement: 18 (3 officers)
Guns: 1—12.7 mm MG. 1—7.62 mm MG.
Radars: Navigation: Furuno 1011; I-band.

Comment: Under the Defence Co-operation Programme Australia has provided one Patrol Craft to the Vanuatu Government. Training and operational and technical assistance is also given by the Royal Australian Navy. Ordered 13 September 1985 and launched 20 May 1987. Used for Fishery Patrol and EEZ surveillance including Customs.

UPDATED

TUKORO   7/1990*, J Goldrick, RAN / 0084230

VENEZUELA
ARMADA DE VENEZUELA

Headquarters Appointments

Commander General of the Navy (Chief of Naval Operations):
Vice Admiral Oswaldo Quintana Castro
Inspector General of the Navy:
Vice Admiral Jorge Sierralta
Chief of Naval Staff:
Vice Admiral Bernabé Carrero Cuberos
Commander of Naval Operations:
Rear Admiral Alvaro Martin Fossa
Commander of Naval Personnel:
Rear Admiral Vicente Quevedo Moreno
Commander of Naval Logistics:
Rear Admiral Julio Cordero Fornerino
Commander, Coast Guard:
Rear Admiral Hector Ramirez Pérez

Diplomatic Representation

Naval Attaché in London:
Captain Luis Vargas Lander

Personnel

(a) 2000: 18,300 including 7,800 Marines and 400 naval aviation
(b) 2 years' national service

Fleet Organisation

The fleet is split into 'Type' squadrons—all the frigates together (except GC 11 and 12) and the same for submarines, light and amphibious forces. Service Craft Squadron composed of RA 33, BO 11 and BE 11. The Fast Attack Squadron of the 'Constitución' class is subordinate to the Fleet Command. There is also a River Forces (Fluvial) Command.

Marines

The Comando de Infantería de Marina has two Amphibious Commands, organised as light brigades. The Amphibious Command 1 consists of two Combat Tactic Units: UTACBO *Libertador Simon Bolivar* at *Mariscal Juán Crisótomo Falcón* Naval Base and UTACUR *General Rafael Urdaneta* at the *Base Naval at Contralmirante Agustín Armario* Naval Base in Puerto Cabello, one Artillery Group, one Vehicle Unit and one Support Unit; The Amphibious Command 2 consists of one Combat Tactic Unit *Mariscal Antonio José de Sucre* at Carúpano, one Support Unit, one Artillery Group. The Combat Tactic Unit *Mariscal Antonio José de Sucre* has two Fluvial Frontier Commands at Puerto Ayacucho (Amazonas State) and a Special Operations Command at Turiamo.

Coast Guard

Formed in August 1982. It is part of the Navy. Its Headquarters are at La Guaira (Vargas State). Its primary task is the surveillance of the 200 mile Exclusive Economic Zone and other jurisdictional areas of the Venezuelan waters. Coast Guard Squadron includes the frigates GC 11 and GC 12 and several patrol craft.

Naval Aviation

Headquarters are at Puerto Cabello (Carabobo State). There are four Squadrons: Training, ASW, Patrol and Transport.

Naval Bases

Caracas: Navy Headquarters and *La Carlota* Naval Aviation Facility.
Vargas State: Comando de Infantería de Marina (Marines) HQ and Naval Academy at Mamo; OCHINA (Hydrography) and OCAMAR (Marines Support) HQ and the Coast Guard Command HQ at La Guaira.
Puerto Cabello (Carabobo State): Fleet Command HQ, Marines Amphibious Command No 1 at *Contralmirante Agustín Armario*

Naval Base and Naval Aviation Command at *General Salom* Airport, Naval Schools and Dockyard.
Punto Fijo (Falcón State): Western Naval Zone HQ, Patrol Ships Squadron and UTC *Simón Bolívar* Marines Combat Tactical Unit at *Mariscal Juán Crisóstomo Falcón* Naval Base.
Carúpano (Sucre State): Eastern Naval Zone HQ, Marines Amphibious Command No 2 and Marines Training Centre.
Ciudad Bolívar (Bolívar): Fluvial Command HQ at *Capitán de Fragata Tomás Machado* Naval Base, with several Naval Posts along the Orinoco River.
Turiamo (Aragua State): *Generalísimo Francisco de Miranda* Marines Special Operation Command at the *Teniente de Navío Tomás Vega* Naval Station.
Puerto Ayacucho (Amazonas State): Marine Fluvial Frontier Command *General de Brigada Franz Rízquez Iribarren* with several Naval Posts along Orinoco and Meta rivers.
El Amparo (Apure State): Fluvial Frontier Command HQ *Teniente de Navío Jacinto Muñoz*, with several Naval Posts along Arauca and Barinas rivers.
Puerto de Nutrias (Barinas State): Fluvial Post.
La Orchila (Caribbean Sea): Minor Naval Base and Naval Aviation Station.
Puerto Hierro (Sucre State): Minor Naval Base.
Maracaibo (Zulia State), Güiria (Sucre State), Guanta (Anzoátegui State) and Margarita Island (Nueva Esparta State): Main Coast Guard Stations.
Los Monjes (Gulf of Venezuela), Los Testigos, Aves de Sotavento, La Tortuga and La Blanquilla Island (Caribbean Sea): Secondary Coast Guard Stations.

Prefix to Ships' Names

ARV (Armada de la República de Venezuela)

Mercantile Marine

Lloyd's Register of Shipping:
250 vessels of 657,380 tons gross

SUBMARINES

2 SÁBALO (209) CLASS (TYPE 1300) (SSK)

Name	No	Builders	Laid down	Launched	Commissioned
SÁBALO	S 31 (ex-S 21)	Howaldtswerke, Kiel	2 May 1973	1 July 1975	6 Aug 1976
CARIBE	S 32 (ex-S 22)	Howaldtswerke, Kiel	1 Aug 1973	6 Nov 1975	11 Mar 1977

Displacement, tons: 1,285 surfaced; 1,600 dived
Dimensions, feet (metres): 200.1 × 20.3 × 18 *(61.2 × 6.2 × 5.5)*
Main machinery: Diesel-electric; 4 MTU 12V 493 AZ80 GA31L diesels; 2,400 hp(m) *(1.76 MW)* sustained; 4 alternators; 1.7 MW; 1 Siemens motor; 4,600 hp(m) *(3.38 MW)* sustained; 1 shaft
Speed, knots: 10 surfaced; 22 dived
Range, miles: 7,500 at 10 kt surfaced
Complement: 33 (5 officers)

Torpedoes: 8—21 in *(533 mm)* bow tubes. AEG SST 4; anti-surface; wire-guided; active/passive homing to 12 km *(6.6 n miles)* at 35 kt or 28 km *(15.3 n miles)* at 23 kt; warhead 260 kg. 14 torpedoes carried. Swim-out discharge.

Countermeasures: ESM: Thomson-CSF DR 2000; intercept.
Weapons control: Atlas Elektronik ISUS TFCS.
Radars: Navigation: Terma Scanter Mil; I-band.
Sonars: Atlas Elektronik CSU 3-32; hull-mounted; passive/active search and attack; medium frequency.
Thomson Sintra DUUX 2; passive ranging.

Programmes: Type 209, IK81 designed by Ingenieurkontor Lübeck for construction by Howaldtswerke, Kiel and sale by Ferrostaal, Essen, all acting as a consortium. Both refitted at Kiel in 1981 and 1984 respectively. There are plans for two more of the class.
Modernisation: Carried out by HDW at Kiel. *Sábalo* started in April 1990 and left in November 1992 without fully completing the refit. *Caribe* docked in Kiel throughout 1993

but was back in the water in mid-1994, and completed in 1995. The hull is slightly lengthened and new engines, fire control, sonar and attack periscopes fitted.
Structure: A single-hull design with two main ballast tanks and forward and after trim tanks. The additional length is due to the new sonar dome similar to German Type 206 system. Fitted with snort and remote machinery control. Slow revving single screw. Very high-capacity batteries with GRP lead-acid cells and battery-cooling. Diving depth 250 m *(820 ft)*.
Operational: Endurance, 50 days patrol. Both are active.

UPDATED

CARIBE

6/1999 * / 0084231

FRIGATES

6 MODIFIED LUPO CLASS (FFG)

Name	No	Builders	Laid down	Launched	Commissioned
MARISCAL SUCRE	F 21	Fincantieri, Riva Trigoso	19 Nov 1976	28 Sep 1978	10 May 1980
ALMIRANTE BRIÓN	F 22	Fincantieri, Riva Trigoso	June 1977	22 Feb 1979	7 Mar 1981
GENERAL URDANETA	F 23	Fincantieri, Riva Trigoso	23 Jan 1978	23 Mar 1979	8 Aug 1981
GENERAL SOUBLETTE	F 24	Fincantieri, Riva Trigoso	26 Aug 1978	4 Jan 1980	5 Dec 1981
GENERAL SALOM	F 25	Fincantieri, Riva Trigoso	7 Nov 1978	13 Jan 1980	3 Apr 1982
ALMIRANTE GARCIA (ex-*José Felix Ribas*)	F 26	Fincantieri, Riva Trigoso	21 Aug 1979	4 Oct 1980	30 July 1982

Displacement, tons: 2,208 standard; 2,520 full load
Dimensions, feet (metres): 371.3 × 37.1 × 12.1
(113.2 × 11.3 × 3.7)
Main machinery: CODOG; 2 Fiat/GE LM 2500 gas turbines;
50,000 hp *(37.3 MW)* sustained; 2 GMT A230.20M or 2 MTU
20V 1163 (F 21 and F 22) diesels; 8,000 hp(m) *(5.97 MW)*
sustained; 2 shafts; acbLIPS cp props
Speed, knots: 35; 21 on diesels. **Range, miles:** 5,000 at 15 kt
Complement: 185

Missiles: SSM: 8 OTO Melara/Matra Otomat Teseo Mk 2 TG1 ❶;
active radar homing to 80 km *(43.2 n miles)* at 0.9 Mach;
warhead 210 kg; sea-skimmer for last 4 km *(2.2 n miles)*.
SAM: Selenia Elsag Albatros octuple launcher ❷; 8 Aspide; semi-
active radar homing to 13 km *(7 n miles)* at 2.5 Mach; height
envelope 15-5,000 m *(49.2-16,405 ft)*; warhead 30 kg.
Guns: 1 OTO Melara 5 in *(127 mm)*/54 ❸; 45 rds/min to 16 km
(8.7 n miles); weight of shell 32 kg.
4 Breda 40 mm/70 (2 twin) ❹; 300 rds/min to 12.5 km *(6.8 n
miles)*; weight of shell 0.96 kg.
Torpedoes: 6—324 mm ILAS 3 (2 triple) tubes ❺. Whitehead
A244S; anti-submarine; active/passive homing to 7 km *(3.8 n
miles)* at 33 kt; warhead 34 kg (shaped charge).
Countermeasures: Decoys: 2 Breda 105 mm SCLAR 20-
barrelled trainable ❻; chaff to 5 km *(2.7 n miles)*; illuminants to
12 km *(6.6 n miles)*. Can be used for HE bombardment.
ESM: Elisra NS 9003/9005; intercept.
Combat data systems: Elbit system (F 21 and F 22) or Selenia
IPN 10.
Weapons control: 2 Elsag NA 10 MFCS. 2 Dardo GFCS for
40 mm. IAI GFCS (F 21 and 22).
Radars: Air/surface search: Selenia RAN 10S or Elta 223 (F 21
and 22) ❼; E/F-band.
Surface search: Selenia RAN 11X; I-band.
Fire control: 2 Selenia Orion 10XP ❽; I/J-band.
2 Selenia RTN 20X ❾; I/J-band.
Navigation: SMA 3RM20; I-band.
Tacan: SRN 15A.
Sonars: EDO SQS-29 (Mod 610E) or Northrop Grumman 21 HS-7
(F 21 and F 22); hull-mounted; active search and attack;
medium frequency.

Helicopters: 1 AB 212ASW ❿.

Programmes: All ordered on 24 October 1975. Similar to ships in
the Italian and Peruvian navies.
Modernisation: The first two of the class were scheduled to start
a refit by Litton's Ingalls Shipyard in September 1992 but this
contract was suspended in October 1994 because of
contractural problems. Two year refits finally started in
February 1998 and included upgrading the gas turbines,
replacing the diesels, improving the combat data system,
updating sonar and ESM, and overhauling all weapon systems.
F 23 and F 24 are to be refitted in Venezuela starting in 2000.
Structure: Fixed hangar means no space for Aspide reloads.
Fully stabilised.

UPDATED

GENERAL SALOM   *(Scale 1 : 900), Ian Sturton*

GENERAL SALOM   *6/1999*, Venezuelan Navy /* 0084232

GENERAL SALOM   *7/1996, Venezuelan Navy /* 0050729

GENERAL URDANETA   *7/1996 /* 0050730

SHIPBORNE AIRCRAFT

Note: Four Bell 412EP acquired in 1999 for SAR and Utility. There are also three Bell 206B.

Numbers/Type: 7 Agusta AB 212ASW.
Operational speed: 106 kt *(196 km/h)*.
Service ceiling: 14,200 ft *(4,330 m)*.
Range: 230 n miles *(426 km)*.
Role/Weapon systems: ASW helicopter with secondary ASV role. Sensors: APS-705 search radar, Bendix AQS-18A dipping sonar. Weapons: ASW; two Mk 46 or A244/S torpedoes or depth bombs. ASV; mid-course guidance to Teseo Mk 2 missiles.

UPDATED

LAND-BASED MARITIME AIRCRAFT (FRONT LINE)

Note: There are also two Beech King Air and four Cessnas used for utility and transport.

Numbers/Type: 1/2/2 CASA C-212 S 43/S 200/S 400 Aviocar.
Operational speed: 190 kt *(353 km/h)*.
Service ceiling: 24,000 ft *(7,315 m)*.
Range: 1,650 n miles *(3,055 km)*.
Role/Weapon systems: Medium-range MR and coastal protection aircraft; limited armed action. Acquired in 1981-82 and 1985-86. Three modernised and augmented in 1998 by S 400 type. Previous numbers have reduced. Sensors: APS-128 radar. Weapons: ASW; depth bombs. ASV; gun and rocket pods.

UPDATED

AB 212ASW

6/1999*, Venezuelan Navy / 0084233

CASA S 43

6/1999*, Venezuelan Navy / 0084234

PATROL FORCES

Note: Invitation to Tender issued in February 1999 for six 30 kt craft. First one ordered from Bazán in September 1999. To be fitted with Harpoon SSM and Otobreda 76 mm/62 guns. Remainder are planned to be built in Venezuela.

6 CONSTITUCIÓN CLASS (FAST ATTACK CRAFT—MISSILE AND GUN) (PCFG/PCF)

Name	No	Builders	Laid down	Launched	Commissioned
CONSTITUCIÓN	PC 11	Vosper Thornycroft	Jan 1973	1 June 1973	16 Aug 1974
FEDERACIÓN	PC 12	Vosper Thornycroft	Aug 1973	26 Feb 1974	25 Mar 1975
INDEPENDENCIA	PC 13	Vosper Thornycroft	Feb 1973	24 July 1973	20 Sep 1974
LIBERTAD	PC 14	Vosper Thornycroft	Sep 1973	5 Mar 1974	12 June 1975
PATRIA	PC 15	Vosper Thornycroft	Mar 1973	27 Sep 1973	9 Jan 1975
VICTORIA	PC 16	Vosper Thornycroft	Mar 1974	3 Sep 1974	22 Sep 1975

Displacement, tons: 170 full load
Dimensions, feet (metres): 121 × 23.3 × 6
(36.9 × 7.1 × 1.8)
Main machinery: 2 MTU MD 16V 538 TB90 diesels; 6,000 hp (m) *(4.4 MW)* sustained; 2 shafts
Speed, knots: 31. **Range, miles:** 1,350 at 16 kt
Complement: 20 (4 officers)

Missiles: SSM: 2 OTO Melara/Matra Otomat Teseo Mk 2 TG1 *(Federación, Libertad* and *Victoria)*; active radar homing to 80 km *(43.2 n miles)* at 0.9 Mach; warhead 210 kg.

Guns: 1 OTO Melara 3 in *(76 mm)*/62 compact *(Constitución, Independencia* and *Patria)*; 85 rds/min to 16 km *(8.7 n miles)*; weight of shell 6 kg.
1 Breda 30 mm/70 *(Federación, Libertad* and *Victoria)*; 800 rds/min; weight of shell 0.37 kg.
Weapons control: Elsag NA 10 Mod 1 GFCS (gunships). Alenia Elsag Medusa optronic director (missile ships).
Radars: Surface search: SMA SPQ-2D; E/F-band.
Fire control: Selenia RTN 10X (in 76 mm ships); I/J-band.
Navigation: Racal; I-band.

Programmes: Transferred from the Navy in 1983 to the Coast Guard but now back again with Fleet Command.
Modernisation: Single Breda 30 mm guns replaced the 40 mm guns in the missile craft in 1989. All were refitted at Puerto Cabello 1992-1995.
Operational: To be replaced in due course by a new class of 30 kt attack craft.

UPDATED

VICTORIA

7/1999*, Venezuelan Navy / 0084235

AMPHIBIOUS FORCES

4 CAPANA (ALLIGATOR) CLASS (LST)

Name	No	Builders	Commissioned
CAPANA	T 61	Korea Tacoma Marine	24 July 1984
ESEQUIBO	T 62	Korea Tacoma Marine	24 July 1984
GOAJIRA	T 63	Korea Tacoma Marine	20 Nov 1984
LOS LLANOS	T 64	Korea Tacoma Marine	20 Nov 1984

Displacement, tons: 4,070 full load
Dimensions, feet (metres): 343.8 × 50.5 × 9.8 *(104.8 × 15.4 × 3)*
Main machinery: 2 SEMT-Pielstick 16 PA6 V 280 diesels; 12,800 hp(m) *(9.41 MW)*; 2 shafts
Speed, knots: 14. **Range, miles:** 5,600 at 11 kt
Complement: 117 (13 officers)
Military lift: 202 troops; 1,600 tons cargo; 4 LCVPs
Guns: 2 Breda 40 mm/70 (twin). 2 Oerlikon 20 mm GAM-BO1.
Weapons control: Selenia NA 18/V; optronic director.
Helicopters: Platform only.

Comment: Ordered in August 1982. Version III of Korea Tacoma Alligator type. Each has a 50 ton tank turntable and a lift between decks. Similar to Indonesian and South Korean LSTs. *Goajira* was out of service from June 1987 to May 1993 after a serious fire.

UPDATED

CAPANA   6/1998*, *Venezuelan Navy* / 0084236

ESEQUIBO   3/1999* / 0084237

2 AJEERA CLASS (LCU)

Name	No	Builders	Commissioned
MARGARITA	T 71	Swiftships Inc, Morgan City	20 Jan 1984
LA ORCHILA	T 72	Swiftships Inc, Morgan City	11 May 1984

Displacement, tons: 428 full load
Dimensions, feet (metres): 129.9 × 36.1 × 5.9 *(39.6 × 11 × 1.8)*
Main machinery: 2 Detroit 16V-149 diesels; 1,800 hp *(1.34 MW)* sustained; 2 shafts
Speed, knots: 13. **Range, miles:** 1,500 at 10 kt
Complement: 26 (4 officers)
Military lift: 150 tons cargo; 100 tons fuel
Guns: 3—12.7 mm MGs.
Radars: Navigation: Raytheon 6410; I-band.

Comment: Both serve in Fluvial Command for the Marines. Have a 15 ton crane.

UPDATED

MARGARITA   6/1999*, *Venezuelan Navy* / 0084238

AUXILIARIES

1 LOGISTIC SUPPORT SHIP (AK)

Name	No	Builders	Commissioned
PUERTO CABELLO	T 44	Drammen Slip & Verk,	1972
(ex-M/V *Sierra Nevada*)		Drammen	

Displacement, tons: 13,500 full load
Measurement, tons: 6,682 gross; 9,218 dwt
Dimensions, feet (metres): 461.3 × 59 × 29.5 *(140.6 × 18 × 9)*
Main machinery: 1 Sulzer diesel; 13,200 hp(m) *(9.7 MW)*; 1 shaft
Speed, knots: 22.5
Complement: 40
Cargo capacity: 7,466 tons

Comment: Commissioned in the Navy 22 May 1986. Former refrigerated cargo ship.

UPDATED

PUERTO CABELLO   10/1998, *E & M Laursen* / 0050733

0 + 1 LOGISTIC SUPPORT SHIP (AK)

Name	No	Builders	Commissioned
CIUDAD BOLIVAR	T 81	Hyundai, Ulsan	2002

Displacement, tons: 9,750 full load
Dimensions, feet (metres): 451.8 × 59 × 31.2 *(137.7 × 18 × 9.5)*
Main machinery: 2 Caterpillar 3616 diesels; 2 shafts
Speed, knots: 18
Complement: 78
Guns: 2 Bofors 40 mm/70. 2—12.7 mm MGs.

Comment: Ordered from Hyundai, South Korea, in February 1999. Laid down in early 2000 for delivery in 2002.

NEW ENTRY

SURVEY SHIPS

1 CHEROKEE CLASS (PG/AGS)

Name	No	Builders	Commissioned
MIGUEL RODRIGUEZ	RA 33	Charleston SB and DD Co	9 Nov 1945
(ex-*Salinan* ATF 161)	(ex-R 23)		

Displacement, tons: 1,235 standard; 1,675 full load
Dimensions, feet (metres): 205 × 38.5 × 17 *(62.5 × 11.7 × 5.2)*
Main machinery: Diesel-electric; 4 GM 16-278A diesels; 4,400 hp *(3.28 MW)*; 4 generators; 1 motor; 3,000 hp *(2.24 MW)*; 1 shaft
Speed, knots: 15. **Range, miles:** 7,000 at 15 kt.
Complement: 85
Guns: 2—12.7 mm MGs.
Radars: Navigation: Sperry SPS-53; I/J-band.

Comment: Acquired from USA on 1 September 1978. Last of a class of three. Assigned to OCHINA (Hydrographic department).

UPDATED

MIGUEL RODRIGUEZ   6/1998 / 0050735

1 SURVEY AND RESEARCH SHIP (AGOR)

Name	No	Builders	Launched	Commissioned
PUNTA BRAVA	BO 11	Bazán, Cartagena	9 Mar 1990	14 Mar 1991

Displacement, tons: 1,170 full load
Dimensions, feet (metres): 202.4 × 39 × 12.1 *(61.7 × 11.9 × 3.7)*
Main machinery: 2 Bazán-MAN 7L20/27 diesels; 2,500 hp(m) *(1.84 MW);* 2 shafts; bow thruster
Speed, knots: 13. **Range, miles:** 8,000 at 13 kt
Complement: 49 (6 officers) plus 6 scientists
Radars: Navigation: ARPA; I-band.

Comment: Ordered in September 1988. Developed from the Spanish 'Malaspina' class. A multipurpose ship for oceanography, marine resource evaluation, geophysical and biological research. Equipped with Qubit hydrographic system. Carries two survey launches. EW equipment is fitted. Assigned to the OCHINA (Hydrographic department). **UPDATED**

PUNTA BRAVA (former CG colours)   4/1996*, Venezuelan Navy / 0084239

2 SURVEY CRAFT (AGSC)

Name	No	Builders	Commissioned
GABRIELA (ex-*Peninsula de Araya*)	LH 11	Abeking & Rasmussen	5 Feb 1974
LELY (ex-*Peninsula de Paraguana*)	LH 12	Abeking & Rasmussen	7 Feb 1974

Displacement, tons: 90 full load
Dimensions, feet (metres): 88.6 × 18.4 × 4.9 *(27 × 5.6 × 1.5)*
Main machinery: 2 MTU diesels; 2,300 hp(m) *(1.69 MW);* 2 shafts
Speed, knots: 20
Complement: 9 (1 officer)

Comment: LH 12 laid down 28 May 1973, launched 12 December 1973 and LH 11 laid down 10 March 1973, launched 29 November 1973. Acquired in September 1986 from the Instituto de Canalizaciones. LH 11 is assigned to the Fluvial Command, LH 12 to the Coast Guard. **UPDATED**

GABRIELA (alongside *Alcatraz* PG 32)   1/1994, Maritime Photographic

TRAINING SHIPS

1 SAIL TRAINING SHIP (AXS)

Name	No	Builders	Launched	Commissioned
SIMÓN BOLÍVAR	BE 11	AT Celaya, Bilbao	21 Nov 1979	6 Aug 1980

Displacement, tons: 1,260 full load
Measurement, tons: 934 gross
Dimensions, feet (metres): 270.6 × 34.8 × 14.4 *(82.5 × 10.6 × 4.4)*
Main machinery: 1 Detroit 12V-149T diesel; 875 hp *(652 kW)* sustained; 1 shaft
Speed, knots: 10
Complement: 93 (17 officers) plus 102 trainees

Comment: Ordered in 1978. Three-masted barque; near sister to *Guayas* (Ecuador). Sail area (23 sails), 1,650 m². Highest mast, 131.2 ft *(40 m)*. Has won several international sail competitions including Cutty Sark '96. **UPDATED**

SIMÓN BOLÍVAR   7/1999*, Per Körnefeldt / 0084240

COAST GUARD

4 + 4 PETREL (POINT) CLASS (PC)

Name	No	Builders	Commissioned
PETREL (ex-*Point Knoll*)	PG 31	US Coast Guard Yard, Curtis Bay	26 June 1967
ALCATRAZ (ex-*Point Judith*)	PG 32	US Coast Guard Yard, Curtis Bay	26 July 1966
ALBATROS (ex-*Point Franklin*)	PG 33	US Coast Guard Yard, Curtis Bay	14 Nov 1966
PELÍCANO (ex-*Point Ledge*)	PG 34	US Coast Guard Yard, Curtis Bay	18 July 1962

Displacement, tons: 68 full load
Dimensions, feet (metres): 83 × 17.2 × 5.8 *(25.3 × 5.2 × 1.8)*
Main machinery: 2 Caterpillar diesels; 1,600 hp *(1.19 MW);* 2 shafts
Speed, knots: 23.5. **Range, miles:** 1,500 at 8 kt
Complement: 10 (1 officer)
Guns: 2—12.7 mm MGs.
Radars: Surface search: Raytheon SPS-64; I-band.

Comment: *Petrel* transferred from USCG on 18 November 1991 and *Alcatraz* on 15 January 1992, *Albatros* on 23 June 1998 and *Pelícano* on 3 August 1998. Four more are to be acquired in 2000/01. **UPDATED**

ALCATRAZ   4/1999* / 0084242

12 GAVION CLASS (PC)

GAVION	PG 401	CORMORAN	PG 405	NEGRON	PG 409
ALCA	PG 402	COLIMBO	PG 406	PIGARGO	PG 410
BERNACLA	PG 403	FARDELA	PG 407	PAGAZA	PG 411
CHAMAN	PG 404	FUMAREL	PG 408	SERRETA	PG 412

Displacement, tons: 48 full load
Dimensions, feet (metres): 80 × 17 × 4.8 *(24.4 × 5.2 × 1.5)*
Main machinery: 2 Detroit 12V-92TA diesels; 2,160 hp *(1.61 MW)* sustained; 2 shafts
Speed, knots: 26. **Range, miles:** 1,000 at 12 kt
Complement: 10
Guns: 2—12.7 mm MGs. 2—7.62 mm MGs. 1—40 mm Mk 19 grenade launcher.
Radars: Surface search: Raytheon R1210; I-band.

Comment: Ordered from Halter Marine 24 April 1998 and delivered from late 1999 to early 2000. Aluminium construction. **UPDATED**

ALCA   10/1999*, Halter Marine / 0084243

2 ALMIRANTE CLEMENTE CLASS (FS)

Name	No	Builders	Laid down	Launched	Commissioned
ALMIRANTE CLEMENTE	GC 11	Ansaldo, Leghorn	5 May 1954	12 Dec 1954	1956
GENERAL JOSÉ TRINIDAD MORAN	GC 12	Ansaldo, Leghorn	5 May 1954	12 Dec 1954	1956

Displacement, tons: 1,500 full load
Dimensions, feet (metres): 325.1 × 35.5 × 12.2
(99.1 × 10.8 × 3.7)
Main machinery: 2 GMT 16-645E7C diesels; 6,080 hp(m)
(4.47 MW) sustained; 2 shafts
Speed, knots: 22. **Range, miles:** 3,500 at 15 kt
Complement: 142 (12 officers)

Guns: 2 OTO Melara 3 in *(76 mm)*/62 compact ❶; 85 rds/min to
16 km *(8.7 n miles)*; weight of shell 6 kg.
2 Breda 40 mm/70 (twin) ❷; 300 rds/min to 12.5 km *(6.8 n
miles)*; weight of shell 0.96 kg.
Torpedoes: 6—324 mm ILAS 3 (2 triple) tubes ❸. Whitehead
A 244S; anti-submarine; active/passive homing to 7 km *(3.8 n
miles)* at 33 kt; warhead 34 kg (shaped charge).
Depth charges: 2 throwers.
Weapons control: Elsag NA 10 Mod 1 GFCS.
Radars: Air search: Plessey AWS 4 ❹; D-band.
Surface search: Racal Decca 1226 ❺; I-band.
Fire control: Selenia RTN 10X ❻; I/J-band.
Sonars: Plessey PMS 26; hull-mounted; active search and attack;
10 kHz.

Programmes: Survivors of a class of six ordered in 1953.
Modernisation: Both ships were refitted by Cammell Laird/
Plessey group in April 1968. 4 in guns replaced by 76 mm.
Both refitted again in Italy in 1983-85, prior to transfer to Coast
Guard duties in 1986.
Structure: Fitted with Denny-Brown fin stabilisers and air
conditioned throughout the living and command spaces.

UPDATED

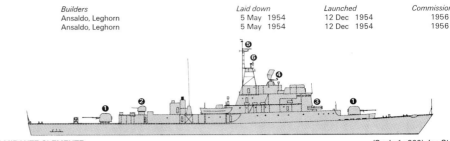

ALMIRANTE CLEMENTE   *(Scale 1 : 900), Ian Sturton*

ALMIRANTE CLEMENTE   *4/1999* * / 0084241*

GENERAL JOSÉ TRINIDAD MORAN   *10/1998, E & M Laursen / 0050734*

2 UTILITY CRAFT (YAG)

LOS TAQUES LG 11   **LOS CAYOS** LG 12

Displacement, tons: 350 full load
Dimensions, feet (metres): 87.3 × 23.3 × 4.9 *(26.6 × 7.1 × 1.5)*
Main machinery: 1 diesel; 850 hp(m) *(625 kW)*; 1 shaft
Speed, knots: 8
Complement: 10
Comment: Former trawlers. Commissioned 15 May 1981 and 17 July 1984 respectively. Used for
salvage and SAR tasks.

UPDATED

4 MANAURE and 3 TEREPAIMA CLASS (PBR/PBF)

MANAURE PF 21	**GUAICAIPURO** PF 23	**TEREPAIMA** PF 31
MARA PF 22	**TAMANACO** PF 24	**YARACUY** PF 33
		SOROCAIMA PF 34

Displacement, tons: 15 full load
Dimensions, feet (metres): 54.1 × 14.1 × 4.3 *(16.5 × 4.3 × 1.3)*
Main machinery: 2 diesels; 2 shafts
Speed, knots: 10
Complement: 8
Guns: 1—12.7 mm MG.
Radars: Surface search: Raytheon 6410; I-band.

Comment: River craft used by the Marines. Details given are for the larger 'Manaure' class. The
other three are 10 m fast craft capable of 45 kt.

UPDATED

LOS CAYOS   *3/1999* *, Venezuelan Navy / 0084244*

MANAURE   *6/1998, Venezuelan Navy / 0050737*

18 INSHORE PATROL BOATS (PB)

CONSTANCIA LRG 001	HONESTIDAD LRG 003	INTEGRIDAD LRG 005
PERSEVERANCIA LRG 002	TENACIDAD LRG 004	LEALTAD LRG 006

Displacement, tons: 11 full load
Dimensions, feet (metres): 39.4 × 9.2 × 5.6 *(12 × 2.8 × 1.7)*
Main machinery: 2 diesels; 640 hp(m) *(470 kW)*; 2 shafts
Speed, knots: 38
Complement: 4
Guns: 2—7.62 mm MGs.
Radars: Surface search: I-band.

Comment: First three speed boat type with GRP hulls delivered from a local shipyard in December 1991. Fourth completed in August 1993. Details given are for *Integridad* which is the first of two built at Guatire, and delivered in 1997/98. GRP construction. The twelve un-named craft are Boston Whaler 'Guardian' class capable of 25 kt, mounting 2—12.7 mm and 2—6.72 mm MGs, and with Raytheon radars. These were donated by the US. All of these craft are used by Marines.
UPDATED

GUARDIAN   *4/1999*, Venezuelan Navy / 0084245

6 PUNTA MACOLLA CLASS (PBF)

PUNTA MACOLLA LSM 001	CHARAGATO LSM 003	BAJO ARAYA LSM 005
FARALLÓN CENTINELA LSM 002	BAJO BRITO LSM 004	CARECARE LSM 006

Displacement, tons: 5 full load
Dimensions, feet (metres): 41.7 × 9.2 × 6.6 *(12.7 × 2.8 × 2)*
Main machinery: 2 diesels; 2 shafts
Speed, knots: 30
Complement: 4
Guns: 1—12.7 mm MG.
Radars: Surface search: Raytheon; I-band.

Comment: Built in Venezuela by Intermarine. Used by OCHINA (Hydrographic department) and for SAR.
NEW ENTRY

BAJO ARAYA   *3/1999*, Venezuelan Navy / 0084246

7 POLARIS CLASS (PBF)

POLARIS LG 21	ALDEBARAN LG 24	CANOPUS LG 25
SIRIUS LG 22	ANTARES LG 25	ALTAIR LG 26
RIGEL LG 23		

Displacement, tons: 5 full load
Dimensions, feet (metres): 26 wl × 8.5 × 2.6 *(7.9 × 2.6 × 0.8)*
Main machinery: 1 diesel outdrive; 400 hp(m) *(294 kW)*
Speed, knots: 50
Complement: 10
Guns: 1—12.7 mm MG.
Radars: Surface search: Raytheon; I-band.

Comment: Used by the Coast Guard for drug interdiction.
NEW ENTRY

ALDEBARAN   *4/1999*, Venezuelan Navy / 0084247

1 SUPPORT SHIP (AK)

Name	No	Builders	Commissioned
FERNANDO GOMEZ (ex-*José Felix Ribas*, ex-*Oswegatchie*)	RP 21 (ex-R 13)	Commercial Iron Works, Portland	14 Dec 1945

Displacement, tons: 345 full load
Dimensions, feet (metres): 100.1 × 25.9 × 9.5 *(30.5 × 7.9 × 2.9)*
Main machinery: 2 diesels; 1,270 hp *(947 kW)*; 1 shaft
Speed, knots: 10
Complement: 12
Guns: 2—12.7 mm MGs.
Radars: Navigation: Raytheon; I-band.

Comment: Former tugs, originally acquired from the US in 1965. Out of service for some years but now employed as a logistic support ship and for occasional patrol and SAR.
UPDATED

FERNANDO GOMEZ   *6/1998*, Venezuelan Navy / 0050738

2 RIVER TRANSPORT CRAFT (LCM/LCU)

CURIAPO LC 21	YOPITO LC 01

Displacement, tons: 115 full load
Dimensions, feet (metres): 241.8 × 68.9 × 17.1 *(73.7 × 21 × 5.2)*
Main machinery: 2 Detroit diesels; 850 hp *(625 kW)*; 2 shafts
Speed, knots: 9
Complement: 5
Cargo capacity: 60 tons or 200 Marines
Guns: 2—12.7 mm MGs.

Comment: Details given are for *Curiapo* which is a former LCM. *Yopito* is a former LCU of 18 m. Both are used by the Marines. There are also 12 11 m LCVPs.
NEW ENTRY

YOPITO   *7/1999*, Venezuelan Navy / 0084248

NATIONAL GUARD
(FUERZAS ARMADAS DE COOPERACIÓN)

10 RIO ORINOCO II CLASS (PC)

Displacement, tons: 30 full load
Dimensions, feet (metres): 54 × 14 × 4.6 *(16.5 × 4.3 × 1.4)*
Main machinery: 2 MTU 12V 183 TE93 diesels; 2,268 hp(m) *(1.67 MW)* sustained; 2 shafts
Speed, knots: 36. **Range, miles:** 750 at 28 kt
Complement: 5
Guns: 2—12.7 mm MGs. 2—7.62 mm MGs.
Radars: Surface search: Raytheon R1210; I-band.

Comment: Ordered from Halter Marine 24 April 1998. All delivered by late 1999. Aluminium construction. These craft may have replaced some of the Rio Orinoco type built in the 1970s.
UPDATED

ORINOCO II   *1/1999*, Halter Marine / 0050739

8 ITALIAN TYPE (COASTAL PATROL CRAFT) (PC)

Displacement, tons: 48 full load
Dimensions, feet (metres): 75.4 × 19 × 8.5 *(23 × 5.8 × 2.6)*
Main machinery: 2 MTU Series 183 diesels; 1,500 hp(m) *(1.1 MW)*; 2 shafts
Speed, knots: 30. **Range, miles:** 500 at 25 kt
Complement: 8
Guns: 1—12.7 mm MG.
Radars: Navigation: Furuno FR 24 or FR 711; I-band.

Comment: Built at La Spezia and at Puerto Cabello in the mid-1970s. The Italian-built craft are slightly broader in the beam. Re-engined in 1996-97. Many others deleted.   *UPDATED*

ITALIAN TYPE   1989

10 LAGO CLASS (RIVER PATROL CRAFT) (PBR)

LAGO 1 A 6901	**RIO CABRIALES** A 7918	**RIO TUY** A 7921
LAGO 2 A 6902	**RIO CHAMA** A 7919	**MANATI** A 7929
LAGO 3 A 6903	**RIO CARIBE** A 7920	**GOAIGOAZA** A 8223
LAGO 4 A 6904		

Displacement, tons: 1.5 full load
Dimensions, feet (metres): 20.7 × 7.9 × 1 *(6.3 × 2.4 × 0.3)*
Main machinery: 2 Evinrude outboard petrol engines; 230 hp *(172 kW)*
Speed, knots: 30. **Range, miles:** 120 at 15 kt
Complement: 4
Guns: 1—12.7 mm MG.
Radars: Navigation: Furuno FR 10; I-band.

Comment: Built by SeaArk Marine, Monticello. All delivered 6 August 1984. Sometimes used as pusher tugs. The last pair are classified as Yachts.   *VERIFIED*

12 PUNTA and 12 PROTECTOR CLASS (PB)

Displacement, tons: 15 full load
Dimensions, feet (metres): 43 × 13.4 × 3.9 *(13.1 × 4.1 × 1.2)*
Main machinery: 2 MTU Series 183 diesels; 1,500 hp *(1.1 MW)*; 2 shafts
Speed, knots: 34. **Range, miles:** 390 at 25 kt
Complement: 4
Guns: 2—12.7 mm MGs.
Radars: Navigation: Raytheon; I-band.

Comment: Details given for the 'Punta' class. Ordered 24 January 1984. Built by Bertram Yacht, Miami, Florida. Names begin with *Punta*. Aluminium hulls. Completed from July-December 1984. Re-engined in 1996-97. The 'Protector' class are the same size, but are slower at 28 kt. They were built by SeaArk Marine and completed in 1984. Some are probably non-operational. Names begin with *Rio*.

UPDATED

PROTECTOR   *2/1996*, van Ginderen Collection /* 0084249

VIETNAM

Headquarters Appointments	Personnel	Bases	Coast Guard	Mercantile Marine

Chief of Naval Forces:
  Vice Admiral Mai Xuan Binh
Deputy Chief of Naval Forces:
  Captain Tran Quang Khue
	(a) 2000: 9,000 regulars
	(b) Additional conscripts on three to four year term (about 3,000)
	(c) 25,000 naval infantry
		Hanoi (HQ), Cam Ranh Bay, Cân Tho, Hai Phong, Hue, Da Nang, Ha Tou, Vung Tau	A Coast Guard was formed on 1 September 1998. It is subordinate to the Navy and may take on Customs duties.	*Lloyd's Register of Shipping:*
				  640 vessels of 864,722 tons gross

FRIGATES

Note: Ex-Russian light frigates of the 'Parchim' class may be acquired.

5 PETYA (TYPE 159) CLASS (FFL)

HQ 09,11 (Type III)   **HQ 13, 15, 17 (Type II)**

Displacement, tons: 950 standard; 1,180 full load
Dimensions, feet (metres): 268.3 × 29.9 × 9.5
  (81.8 × 9.1 × 2.9)
Main machinery: CODAG; 2 gas turbines; 30,000 hp(m) *(22 MW)*; 1 Type 61V-3 diesel; 5,400 hp(m) *(3.97 MW)* sustained; centre shaft; 3 shafts
Speed, knots: 32. **Range, miles:** 4,870 at 10 kt; 450 at 29 kt
Complement: 98 (8 officers)

Guns: 4 USSR 3 in *(76 mm)*/60 (2 twin); 90 rds/min to 15 km *(8 n miles)*; weight of shell 6.8 kg.
Torpedoes: 3—21 in *(533 mm)* (triple) tubes (Petya III). SAET-60; passive homing to 15 km *(8.1 n miles)* at 40 kt; warhead 400 kg.
  10—16 in *(406 mm)* (2 quin) tubes (Petya II). SAET-40; active/passive homing to 10 km *(5.5 n miles)* at 30 kt; warhead 100 kg.
A/S mortars: 4 RBU 6000 12-tubed trainable (Petya II); range 6,000 m; warhead 31 kg.
  4 RBU 2500 16-tubed trainable (Petya III); range 2,500 m; warhead 21 kg.
Depth charges: 2 racks.
Mines: Can carry 22.
Countermeasures: ESM: 2 Watch Dog; radar warning.
Radars: Air/surface search: Strut Curve; F-band.
Navigation: Don 2; I-band.
Fire control: Hawk Screech; I-band.
IFF: High Pole B. 2 Square Head.
Sonars: Vychada MG 311; hull-mounted; active attack; high frequency.

Programmes: Two Petya III (export version) transferred from USSR in December 1978 and three Petya IIs, two in December 1983 and one in December 1984.
Modernisation: Refitted and updated 1994 to 1999. The RBUs replaced by 25 mm guns and the torpedo tubes by 37 mm guns in some of the class.
Structure: The Petya IIIs have the same hulls as the Petya IIs but different armament.
Operational: All are reported active between the coast and the Spratley Islands.   *UPDATED*

HQ 17   *9/1995, G Toremans*

HQ 09   *9/1995, G Toremans*

1 BARNEGAT CLASS (FF)

Name	No	Builders	Commissioned
PHAM NGU LAO (ex-*Absecon*)	HQ 01 (ex-WHEC 374)	Lake Washington SY	28 Jan 1943

Displacement, tons: 1,766 standard; 2,800 full load
Dimensions, feet (metres): 310.8 × 41.1 × 13.5 *(94.7 × 12.5 × 4.1)*
Main machinery: 2 Fairbanks-Morse 38D8-1/8-10 diesels; 3,540 hp *(2.64 MW)* sustained; 2 shafts
Speed, knots: 18. **Range, miles:** 20,000 at 12 kt
Complement: 200 approximately

Guns: 1 USN 5 in *(127 mm)*/38; 15 rds/min to 17 km *(9.3 n miles)*; weight of shell 25 kg.
   3—37 mm/63. 4—25 mm (2 twin). 2—81 mm mortars.
Radars: Surface search: Raytheon SPS-28; G/H-band.
Fire control: RCA/GE Mk 26; I/J-band.

Programmes: Last of a group built as seaplane tenders for the US Navy. Transferred to US Coast Guard in 1948, initially on loan designated WAVP and then on permanent transfer, subsequently redesignated as high endurance cutter (WHEC). Transferred from US Coast Guard to South Vietnamese Navy in 1971.
Modernisation: Styx SSMs mounted aft and close-range armament fitted in the mid-1980s. The SSMs have probably been removed.
Operational: Still seaworthy but may be non-operational.

UPDATED

BARNEGAT (Italian colours)   *1991, van Ginderen Collection*

SUBMARINES

2 YUGO CLASS (MIDGET SUBMARINES)

Displacement, tons: 90 surfaced; 110 dived
Dimensions, feet (metres): 65.6 × 10.2 × 15.1 *(20 × 3.1 × 4.6)*
Main machinery: 2 diesels; 320 hp(m) *(236 kW)*; 1 shaft
Speed, knots: 12 surfaced; 8 dived
Range, miles: 550 at 10 kt surfaced; 50 at 4 kt dived
Complement: 4 plus 6/7 divers

Comment: Transferred from North Korea in 1997. May be fitted with two short torpedo tubes and a snort mast, but used primarily for diver related operations. The conning tower acts as a wet/dry diver compartment.

UPDATED

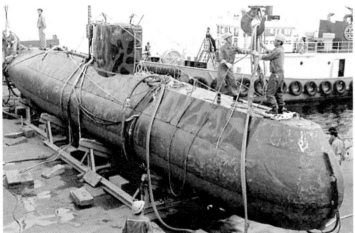

YUGO (North Korean colours)   *6/1998 *, Ships of the World /* 0052525

CORVETTES

Note: Ex-US 'Admirable' class *HQ 07* is an alongside training hulk.

0 + (1) KBO 2000 (TYPE 2100) CLASS (FSG)

Displacement, tons: 2,000 full load
Main machinery: 2 diesels or 2 gas turbines; 2 shafts
Speed, knots: 26
Complement: 110
Missiles: SSM: 4 or 8 SS-N-25 (KH-35) ❶.
SAM: 1 SA-N-9 (Klinok) sextuple vertical launcher ❷.
Guns: 1 USSR 3.9 in *(100 mm)* 59 ❸.
   2—30 mm/65 AK 630 ❹.
Radars: Air/surface search: Top Plate (Fregat-M) ❺; D/E-band.
Fire control: Cross Sword (for SAM) ❻; K-band.
   Plank Shave (for SSM) ❼.
Helicopters: Platform only.

Programmes: Being designed with Severnoye assistance. Construction may start by 2001 if funds are available.
Structure: All details are speculative but the design is similar to the Russian 'Gepard' class which has not yet found a buyer.

NEW ENTRY

KBO 2000   *(not to scale), Ian Sturton /* 0084251

1 + 1 (2) HO-A (TYPE 1241A) CLASS (FSG)

Displacement, tons: 517 full load
Dimensions, feet (metres): 203.4 × 36.1 × 8.2 *(62 × 11 × 2.5)*
Main machinery: 2 MTU diesels; 19,600 hp(m) *(14.41 MW)*; 2 Kamewa waterjets
Speed, knots: 32. **Range, miles:** 2,200 at 14 kt
Complement: 28

Missiles: SSM: 8 Zvezda SS-N-25 (KH-35 Uran) (2 quad) ❶; active radar homing to 130 km *(70.1 n miles)* at 0.9 Mach; warhead 145 kg.
SAM: SA-N-10. 24 missiles.
Guns: 1—3 in *(76 mm)*/60 ❷; 120 rds/min to 15 km *(8 n miles)*; weight of shell 7 kg.
   1—30 mm/65 AK 630 ❸; 6 barrelled; 3,000 rds/min combined to 2 km.
   2—12.7 mm MGs.
Countermeasures: Decoys: 2 chaff launchers ❹.
Weapons control: Optronic director ❺.
Radars: Air/surface search: Cross Dome ❻; E/F-band.
Navigation: I-band.
Fire control: Bass Tilt ❼; H/I-band.

Programmes: Severnoye design ordered in 1996 and started building in April 1997 at a shipyard near Ho Chi Minh City. First one launched in June 1998 and in service in August 1999. Second of class planned for 2001/02, with two more funded. Up to 10 may be ordered in due course.
Structure: Improved Pauk design produced by Russia for export.

UPDATED

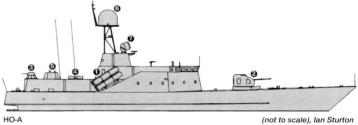

HO-A   *(not to scale), Ian Sturton*

4 TARANTUL CLASS (TYPE 1241) (FSG)

HQ 371	HQ 372	HQ 373	HQ 374

Displacement, tons: 385 standard; 450 full load
Dimensions, feet (metres): 184.1 × 37.7 × 8.2 *(56.1 × 11.5 × 2.5)*
Main machinery: 2 Nikolayev Type DR 77 gas turbines; 16,016 hp(m) *(11.77 MW)* sustained; 2 Nikolayev Type DR 76 gas turbines with reversible gearboxes; 4,993 hp(m) *(3.67 MW)* sustained; 2 shafts
Speed, knots: 36. **Range, miles:** 2,000 at 20 kt; 400 at 36 kt
Complement: 41 (5 officers)

Missiles: SSM: 4 SS-N-2D Styx; IR homing to 83 km *(45 n miles)* at 0.9 Mach; warhead 513 kg; sea-skimmer at end of run.
SAM: SA-N-5 Grail quad launcher; manual aiming; IR homing to 6 km *(3.2 n miles)* at 1.5 Mach; warhead 1.5 kg.
Guns: 1—3 in *(76 mm)*/60; 120 rds/min to 15 km *(8 n miles)*; weight of shell 7 kg.
   2—30 mm/65 AK 630; 6 barrels per mounting; 3,000 rds/min combined to 2 km.
Countermeasures: Decoys: 2 PK 16 chaff launchers.
Weapons control: Hood Wink optronic director.
Radars: Air/surface search: Plank Shave; E-band.
Navigation: Pechora; I-band.
Fire control: Bass Tilt; H/I-band.
IFF: Salt Pot, Square Head A.
Sonars: Foal Tail; active; high frequency.

Programmes: First pair ordered in October 1994. These are new hulls exported at a favourable price and completed by 1996. Some delay in delivery because of late payments, but both were in service by April 1996. Two more of the Tarantul II (Type 1241RE) built at Rybinsk and transferred in mid-1999.
Structure: Details given are for the 'Tarantul I' class in Russian service.
Operational: All based at Da Nang.

UPDATED

HQ 372   *4/1998 /* 0050740

LAND-BASED MARITIME AIRCRAFT

Note: Air Force Flankers and Filters can be used for maritime surveillance.

Numbers/Type: 3 Beriev Be-12 Mail.
Operational speed: 328 kt *(608 km/h)*.
Service ceiling: 37,000 ft *(11,280 m)*.
Range: 4,050 n miles *(7,500 km)*.
Role/Weapon systems: Long-range ASW/MR amphibian. Sensors: Short Horn search radar, MAD, EW. Weapons: ASW; 5 tons of depth bombs, mines or torpedoes. ASV; limited missile and rocket armament.

UPDATED

MAIL (Russian colours)   7/1996*, J Cislak / 0084250

PATROL FORCES

Notes: (1) At least one 'Shanghai II' class PC may still be operational.
(2) Some of the craft listed may be transferred to the Coast Guard.
(3) Two 34 m patrol craft may be ordered in late 2000.

8 OSA II CLASS (FAST ATTACK CRAFT—MISSILE) (PCFG)

Displacement, tons: 245 full load
Dimensions, feet (metres): 126.6 × 24.9 × 8.8 *(38.6 × 7.6 × 2.7)*
Main machinery: 3 Type M 504 diesels; 10,800 hp(m) *(7.94 MW)* sustained; 3 shafts
Speed, knots: 37. **Range, miles:** 500 at 35 kt
Complement: 30
Missiles: SSM: 4 SS-N-2B Styx; active radar or IR homing to 46 km *(25 n miles)* at 0.9 Mach; warhead 513 kg.
Guns: 4 USSR 30 mm/65 (2 twin); 500 rds/min to 5 km *(2.7 n miles)*; weight of shell 0.54 kg.
Radars: Surface search: Square Tie; I-band.
Fire control: Drum Tilt; H/I-band.
IFF: High Pole. 2 Square Head.

Comment: Transferred from USSR: two in October 1979, two in September 1980, two in November 1980 and two in February 1981. Operational status doubtful.

UPDATED

OSA II (Bulgarian colours)   9/1999, E & M Laursen / 0056634

5 TURYA (TYPE 206M) CLASS
(FAST ATTACK CRAFT—HYDROFOIL) (PHT)

HQ 331-HQ 335

Displacement, tons: 190 standard; 250 full load
Dimensions, feet (metres): 129.9 × 29.9 (41 over foils) × 5.9 (13.1 over foils) *(39.6 × 7.6 (12.5) × 1.8 (4))*
Main machinery: 3 Type M 504 diesels; 10,800 hp(m) *(7.94 MW)* sustained; 3 shafts
Speed, knots: 40. **Range, miles:** 600 at 35 kt foilborne; 1,450 at 14 kt hullborne
Complement: 30
Guns: 2 USSR 57 mm/70 (twin, aft); 120 rds/min to 8 km *(4.4 n miles)*; weight of shell 2.8 kg.
2 USSR 25 mm/80 (twin, fwd); 270 rds/min to 3 km *(1.6 n miles)*; weight of shell 0.34 kg.
Torpedoes: 4—21 in *(533 mm)* tubes (not in all).
Depth charges: 2 racks.
Radars: Surface search: Pot Drum; H/I-band.
Fire control: Muff Cob; G/H-band.
IFF: High Pole B. Square Head.
Sonars: Foal Tail (not in all); VDS; high frequency.

Comment: Transferred from USSR: two in mid-1984, one in late 1984, two in January 1986. Two more acquired from Russia. Two of the five do not have torpedo tubes or sonar. Two scrapped so far, the remainder are probably non-operational.

UPDATED

TURYA (Russian colours)   6/1992* / 0084252

5 SHERSHEN CLASS (FAST ATTACK CRAFT) (PCF)

HQ 301   HQ 334   HQ 354   HQ 359   HQ 360

Displacement, tons: 145 standard; 170 full load
Dimensions, feet (metres): 113.8 × 22 × 4.9 *(34.7 × 6.7 × 1.5)*
Main machinery: 3 Type 503A diesels; 8,025 hp(m) *(5.9 MW)* sustained; 3 shafts
Speed, knots: 45. **Range, miles:** 850 at 30 kt; 460 at 42 kt
Complement: 23
Missiles: SAM: 1 SA-N-5 Grail quad launcher; manual aiming; IR homing to 6 km *(3.2 n miles)* at 1.5 Mach; altitude to 2,500 m *(8,000 ft)*; warhead 1.5 kg.
Guns: 4 USSR 30 mm/65 (2 twin); 500 rds/min to 5 km *(2.7 n miles)*; weight of shell 0.54 kg.
Torpedoes: 4—21 in *(533 mm)* tubes (not in all).
Depth charges: 2 racks (12).
Mines: Can carry 6.
Radars: Surface search: Pot Drum; H/I-band.
Fire control: Drum Tilt; H/I-band.
IFF: High Pole A. Square Head.

Comment: Transferred from USSR: two in 1973, two in April 1979 (without torpedo tubes), two in September 1979, two in August 1980, two in October 1980, two in January 1983 and four in June 1983. Some have been cannibalised for spares.

UPDATED

SHERSHEN (Bulgarian colours)   8/1998, E & M Laursen / 0017644

4 + (12) STOLKRAFT CLASS (PC)

HQ 56-HQ 59

Displacement, tons: 44 full load
Dimensions, feet (metres): 73.5 × 24.6 × 3.9 *(22.4 × 7.5 × 1.2)*
Main machinery: 2 MTU 12V 183 TE93 diesels; 2,301 hp(m) *(1.69 MW)* sustained; 2 Doen waterjets
1 Volvo Penta diesel; 360 hp(m) *(265 kW)*; 1 shaft
Speed, knots: 30
Complement: 7
Guns: 1 Oerlikon 20 mm.

Comment: First four built by Oceanfast Marine, Western Australia and delivered in early 1997. Trimaran construction forward, transforming into a catamaran at the stern. Shallow draft needed for inshore and river operations. The centreline single shaft is used for loitering. The craft show the colours of the Customs department. Up to twelve more may be built in Vietnam, when funds are available.

UPDATED

4 SO 1 CLASS (LARGE PATROL CRAFT) (PC)

Displacement, tons: 170 standard; 215 full load
Dimensions, feet (metres): 137.8 × 19.7 × 5.9 *(42 × 6 × 1.8)*
Main machinery: 3 Kolomna Type 40-D diesels; 6,600 hp(m) *(4.8 MW)* sustained; 3 shafts
Speed, knots: 28. **Range, miles:** 1,100 at 13 kt; 350 at 28 kt
Complement: 31
Guns: 4 USSR 25 mm/80 (2 twin); 270 rds/min to 3 km *(1.6 n miles)*; weight of shell 0.34 kg.
A/S mortars: 4 RBU 1200 5-tubed fixed; range 1,200 m; warhead 34 kg.
Depth charges: 2 racks (24).
Mines: 10.
Radars: Surface search: Pot Head; I-band.
IFF: High Pole A. Dead Duck.

Comment: Transferred from USSR: two in March 1980, two in September 1980, two in May 1981, and two in September 1983. Four more of this class were transferred in 1960-63 but have been deleted, as have four others.

VERIFIED

SO 1   1984

14 ZHUK (TYPE 1400M) CLASS (PC)

Displacement, tons: 39 full load
Dimensions, feet (metres): 78.7 × 16.4 × 3.9 *(24 × 5 × 1.2)*
Main machinery: 2 Type M 401B diesels; 2,200 hp(m) *(1.6 MW)* sustained; 2 shafts
Speed, knots: 30. **Range, miles:** 1,100 at 15 kt
Complement: 11 (3 officers)
Guns: 4—14.5 mm (2 twin) MGs.
Radars: Surface search: Spin Trough; I-band.

Comment: Transferred: three in 1978, three in November 1979, three in February 1986, two in January 1990, three in August 1990, three in January 1996, two in January 1998 and two in April 1998. So far seven have been deleted but operational numbers are uncertain. Some may be allocated to the Coast Guard.   *UPDATED*

ZHUK   *6/1994*, T Hollingsbee / 0084253

2 POLUCHAT CLASS (COASTAL PATROL CRAFT) (PC)

Displacement, tons: 100 full load
Dimensions, feet (metres): 97.1 × 19 × 4.8 *(29.6 × 5.8 × 1.5)*
Main machinery: 2 Type M 50 diesels; 2,200 hp(m) *(1.6 MW)* sustained; 2 shafts
Speed, knots: 20. **Range, miles:** 1,500 at 10 kt
Complement: 15
Guns: 2—12.7 mm MGs.
Radars: Navigation: Spin Trough; I-band.

Comment: Both transferred from USSR in January 1990. Can be used as torpedo recovery vessels.   *VERIFIED*

POLUCHAT (Russian colours)   *7/1993, Hartmut Ehlers*

RIVER PATROL CRAFT

Comment: There are large numbers of river patrol boats, mostly armed with MGs. A 14.5 m craft ordered from Singapore TSE in 1994. More are being built locally with Volvo Penta engines.   *VERIFIED*

RIVER CRAFT   *1991, B Lemachko*

AMPHIBIOUS FORCES

3 POLNOCHNY CLASS (TYPE 771) (LSM)

HQ 511   HQ 512   HQ 513

Displacement, tons: 760 standard; 834 full load
Dimensions, feet (metres): 246.1 × 31.5 × 7.5 *(75 × 9.6 × 2.3)*
Main machinery: 2 Kolomna Type 40-D diesels; 4,400 hp(m) *(3.2 MW)* sustained; 2 shafts
Speed, knots: 19
Complement: 40
Guns: 2 or 4 USSR 30 mm/65 (1 or 2 twin). 2—140 mm rocket launchers.
Radars: Surface search: Spin Trough; I-band.
Fire control: Drum Tilt; H/I-band.

Comment: Transfers from USSR: one in May 1979 (B), one in November 1979 (A) and one in February 1980 (B). Details are for 'Polnochny B' class. Two are reported to be in poor condition.   *UPDATED*

HQ 512 and 513   *6/1995*, Giorgio Arra / 0084254

1 LST 1-510 and 2 LST 511-1152 CLASSES (LST)

DA NANG (ex-*Maricopa County* LST 938) HQ 501   **VUNG TAU** (ex-*Cochino County* LST 603) HQ 503
QUI NONH (ex-*Bulloch County* LST 509) HQ 502

Displacement, tons: 2,366 beaching; 4,080 full load
Dimensions, feet (metres): 328 × 50 × 14 *(100 × 15.2 × 4.3)*
Main machinery: 2 GM 12-567A diesels; 1,800 hp *(1.34 MW)*; 2 shafts
Speed, knots: 11. **Range, miles:** 6,000 at 10 kt
Complement: 110
Guns: 6 Bofors 40 mm/60 (2 twin, 2 single). 4 Oerlikon 20 mm.

Comment: Built in 1943-44. Transferred from USA to South Vietnam in mid-1960s. Seldom seen at sea.   *UPDATED*

DA NANG   *1994*, T Hollingsbee / 0084255

30 LANDING CRAFT (LCM and LCU)

Comment: About five LCUs, 12 LCM 8 and LCM 6, and three LCVPs remain of the 180 minor landing craft left behind by the USA in 1975. In addition there are about 10 T4 LCUs acquired from the USSR in 1979.   *VERIFIED*

MINE WARFARE FORCES

2 YURKA (RUBIN) (TYPE 266) CLASS
(MINESWEEPER—OCEAN) (MSO)

HQ 851   HQ 885

Displacement, tons: 540 full load
Dimensions, feet (metres): 171.9 × 30.8 × 8.5 *(52.4 × 9.4 × 2.6)*
Main machinery: 2 Type M 503 diesels; 5,350 hp(m) *(3.91 MW)* sustained; 2 shafts
Speed, knots: 17. **Range, miles:** 1,500 at 12 kt
Complement: 45
Guns: 4 USSR 30 mm/65 (2 twin); 500 rds/min to 5 km *(2.7 n miles)*; weight of shell 0.54 kg.
Mines: 10.
Radars: Surface search: Don 2; I-band.
Fire control: Drum Tilt; H/I-band.
Sonars: Stag Ear; hull-mounted; active minehunting; high frequency.

Comment: Transferred from USSR December 1979. Steel-hulled, built in early 1970s.   *UPDATED*

YURKA (Egyptian colours)   *10/1998*, F Sadek / 0017818

4 SONYA (YAKHONT) (TYPE 1265) CLASS
(MINESWEEPER/HUNTER—COASTAL) (MSC)

HQ 864   + 3

Displacement, tons: 450 full load
Dimensions, feet (metres): 157.4 × 28.9 × 6.6 *(48 × 8.8 × 2)*
Main machinery: 2 Kolomna 9-D-8 diesels; 2,000 hp(m) *(1.47 MW)* sustained; 2 shafts
Speed, knots: 15. **Range, miles:** 3,000 at 10 kt
Complement: 43
Guns: 2 USSR 30 mm/65 AK 630. 2—25 mm/80 (twin).
Mines: 8.
Radars: Surface search: Nayada; I-band.
Sonars: MG 69/79; active; high frequency.

Comment: First one transferred from USSR 16 February 1987, second in February 1988, third in July 1989, fourth in March 1990. Two based at Da Nang. **UPDATED**

SONYA (Bulgarian colours)   7/1997, Frank Behling / 0012957

2 YEVGENYA (KOROND) (TYPE 1258) CLASS
(MINEHUNTER—INSHORE) (MHI)

Displacement, tons: 90 full load
Dimensions, feet (metres): 80.7 × 18 × 4.9 *(24.6 × 5.5 × 1.5)*
Main machinery: 2 Type 3-D-12 diesels; 600 hp(m) *(440 kW)* sustained; 2 shafts
Speed, knots: 11. **Range, miles:** 300 at 10 kt
Complement: 10
Guns: 2 USSR 25 mm/80 (twin).
Mines: 8.
Radars: Surface search: Spin Trough; I-band.
Sonars: MG 7; active; high frequency.

Comment: First transferred from USSR in October 1979; two in December 1986. One deleted in 1990. **VERIFIED**

YEVGENYA (Russian colours)   1993, B Lemachko

5 K 8 CLASS (MINESWEEPING BOATS) (MSB)

Displacement, tons: 26 full load
Dimensions, feet (metres): 55.4 × 10.5 × 2.6 *(16.9 × 3.2 × 0.8)*
Main machinery: 2 Type 3-D-6 diesels; 300 hp(m) *(220 kW)* sustained; 2 shafts
Speed, knots: 18
Complement: 6
Guns: 2—14.5 mm (twin) MGs.

Comment: Transferred from USSR in October 1980. Probably used as river patrol craft. **VERIFIED**

SURVEY SHIPS

Note: A new survey ship of 2,500 tons is required.

1 KAMENKA (TYPE 870) CLASS (AGS)

Displacement, tons: 760 full load
Dimensions, feet (metres): 175.5 × 29.8 × 8.5 *(53.5 × 9.1 × 2.6)*
Main machinery: 2 Sulzer diesels; 1,800 hp(m) *(1.32 MW)*; 2 shafts; cp props
Speed, knots: 14. **Range, miles:** 4,000 at 10 kt
Complement: 25
Radars: Navigation: Don 2; I-band.

Comment: Transferred from USSR December 1979. Built at Northern Shipyard, Gdansk in the late 1960s. **VERIFIED**

KAMENKA (Russian colours)   1984

AUXILIARIES

Note: In addition to the vessels listed below there are two YOG 5 fuel lighters, two floating cranes and two ex-USSR unarmed Nyryat 2 diving tenders.

20 TRUONG CLASS (AK)

Displacement, tons: 1,000 full load
Dimensions, feet (metres): 231.6 × 38.7 × 13.1 *(70.6 × 11.8 × 4)*
Main machinery: 1 diesel; 1 shaft
Speed, knots: 12
Complement: 30

Comment: HQ 966 launched at Halong Shipyard in June 1994. This is one of a group of 20 freighters reported as used by the Navy for coastal transport, and to service the Spratleys garrison. The ships may not all be similar. **NEW ENTRY**

HQ 608   3/1997* / 0050742

2 FLOATING DOCKS

Comment: One has a lift capacity of 8,500 tons. Transferred from USSR August 1983. Second one *(Khersson)* has a lift capacity of 4,500 tons and was supplied in 1988. **VERIFIED**

VIRGIN ISLANDS

Headquarters Appointments	Bases	General
Commissioner of British Virgin Islands Police: Vernon E Malone	Road Town, Tortola	The British Virgin Islands and US Virgin Islands are separate territories.

POLICE

1 HALMATIC M 140 PATROL CRAFT (PBI)

ST URSULA

Displacement, tons: 17 full load
Dimensions, feet (metres): 50.6 × 12.8 × 3.9 *(15.4 × 3.9 × 1.2)*
Main machinery: 2 Detroit 6V-92TA diesels; 520 hp *(388 kW)* sustained; 2 shafts
Speed, knots: 27. **Range, miles:** 300 at 20 kt
Complement: 6
Guns: 2—7.62 mm MGs.
Radars: Surface search: Racal Decca; I-band.

Comment: Built by Halmatic with funds provided by the UK and commissioned 4 July 1988 by the BVI. Large davit aft for rapid launch and recovery of a rigid inflatable boat. Refit in 1995. **VERIFIED**

ST URSULA   6/1998 / 0050743

2 DAUNTLESS CLASS (PBI)

Displacement, tons: 12 full load
Dimensions, feet (metres): 40 × 14 × 4.3 *(12.2 × 4.3 × 1.3)*
Main machinery: 3 Cummins diesels; 900 hp *(671 kW)*; 3 water-jets
Speed, knots: 31. **Range, miles:** 500 at 18 kt
Complement: 5
Guns: 2—7.62 mm MGs.
Radars: Surface search: Raytheon; I-band.

Comment: First one built by SeaArk Marine and commissioned in January 1994 by the USVI after
transfer by US grant aid from the Border Patrol. Unusually for this class, three engines were fitted
to give a higher top speed. Second of class delivered in January 1999 and used as a Pilot craft.
UPDATED

PB 1 (US colours)
1993*, SeaArk Marine / 0084256

WESTERN SAMOA

General

After 48 years of New Zealand occupation, mandate and
trusteeship, Western Samoa achieved independence in 1962.

Bases

Apia

Mercantile Marine

Lloyd's Register of Shipping:
6 vessels of 3,111 tons gross

PATROL FORCES

1 PACIFIC FORUM PATROL CRAFT (PC)

Name	No	Builders	Commissioned
NAFANUA	—	Australian Shipbuilding Industries	5 Mar 1988

Displacement, tons: 165 full load
Dimensions, feet (metres): 103.3 × 26.6 × 6.9 *(31.5 × 8.1 × 2.1)*
Main machinery: 2 Caterpillar 3516TA diesels; 4,400 hp *(3.28 MW)* sustained; 2 shafts
Speed, knots: 20. **Range, miles:** 2,500 at 12 kt
Complement: 17 (3 officers)
Guns: Can carry 1 Oerlikon 20 mm and 2—7.62 mm MGs.
Radars: Surface search: Furuno 1011; I-band.

Comment: Under the Defence Co-operation Programme Australia has provided a number of these
craft to Pacific islands. Training, operational and technical assistance is provided by the Royal
Australian Navy. Ordered 3 October 1985.
UPDATED

NAFANUA

1/1996*, van Ginderen Collection / 0084257

YEMEN

Headquarters Appointments

Chief of Navy:
Admiral Abdel-Karim Yahya Moharrem

General

In May 1990 the North and South Yemen republics were
reunited to form the Republic of Yemen. The two former states
engaged in civil war from May to July 1994 which ended in
victory for the north. The destruction of base facilities affected
operational availability and little has been done to repair them.

Personnel

2000: 1,700 naval plus 500 marines

Bases

Main: Aden, Hodeida
Secondary: Mukalla, Perim, Socotra, Al Katib
Coast Defence regions: Al Ghaydah, Aden and Cameron Island

Coast Defence

Two mobile SS-C-3 Styx batteries. Some 100 mm guns installed
in tank turrets at Perim Island.

Mercantile Marine

Lloyd's Register of Shipping:
45 vessels of 25,267 tons gross

DELETIONS

Patrol Forces

1997   *Ramadan, Sana'a, Zhuks 303* and *304*
1998   *Tarantul 976*
1999   *26 September* (beyond repair)

Amphibious Forces

1999   *Ropucha 139* (beyond repair)

Auxiliaries

1998   *Shabwah, Al Mahrah* (both civilian)

PATROL FORCES

Note: Two 'Osa IIs', 122 and 124, may still be seaworthy. The SSM system is non-operational.

2 ZHUK CLASS (TYPE 1400M) (PC)

202   203

Displacement, tons: 39 full load
Dimensions, feet (metres): 78.7 × 16.4 × 3.9 *(24 × 5 × 1.2)*
Main machinery: 2 Type M 401B diesels; 2,200 hp(m) *(1.6 MW)* sustained; 2 shafts
Speed, knots: 30. **Range, miles:** 1,100 at 15 kt
Complement: 11 (3 officers)
Guns: 4—14.5 mm (2 twin) MGs.
Radars: Surface search: Spin Trough; I-band.

Comment: Two delivered from USSR in December 1984 and three in January 1987. Three have
been cannibalised for spares. One based at Aden, one at Al Katib. Used as utility craft including
target towing.
UPDATED

ZHUK

3/1990* / 0084258

1 TARANTUL I CLASS (TYPE 1241) (FSG)

971

Displacement, tons: 385 standard; 580 full load
Dimensions, feet (metres): 184.1 × 37.7 × 8.2 *(56.1 × 11.5 × 2.5)*
Main machinery: 2 Nikolayev Type DR 77 gas turbines; 16,016 hp(m) *(11.77 MW)* sustained;
  2 Nikolayev Type DR 76 gas turbines with reversible gearboxes; 4,993 hp(m) *(3.67 MW)*
  sustained; 2 shafts
Speed, knots: 36. **Range, miles:** 400 at 36 kt; 2,000 at 20 kt
Complement: 50

Missiles: SSM: 4 SS-N-2C Styx (2 twin) launchers; active radar or IR homing to 83 km *(45 n miles)*
  at 0.9 Mach; warhead 513 kg; sea-skimmer at end of run.
  SAM: SA-N-5 Grail quad launcher; manual aiming; IR homing to 10 km *(5.4 n miles)* at 1.5 Mach;
  altitude to 2,500 m *(8,000 ft)*; warhead 1.1 kg.
Guns: 1—3 in *(76 mm)*/60; 120 rds/min to 7 km *(3.8 n miles)*; weight of shell 7 kg.
  2—30 mm/65 AK 630; 6 barrels per mounting; 3,000 rds/min to 2 km.
Countermeasures: Decoys: 2 PK 16 chaff launchers.
Weapons control: Hood Wink optronic director.
Radars: Air/surface search: Plank Shave (also for missile control); E-band.
  Navigation: Spin Trough; I-band.
  Fire control: Bass Tilt; H/I-band.
  IFF: Square Head. High Pole.

Programmes: First one delivered from USSR 7 December 1990, second on 15 January 1991. This
  is the standard export version.
Operational: Facilities for servicing missiles in Aden were destroyed in mid-1994 but one of the
  class is still operational probably without missiles.   *UPDATED*

TARANTUL 971   10/1995* / 0016612

3 HUANGFEN (TYPE 021) CLASS
(FAST ATTACK CRAFT—MISSILE) (PCFG)

126   127   128

Displacement, tons: 171 standard; 205 full load
Dimensions, feet (metres): 126.6 × 24.9 × 8.9 *(38.6 × 7.6 × 2.7)*
Main machinery: 3 Type 42-160 diesels; 12,000 hp(m) *(8.8 MW)* sustained; 3 shafts
Speed, knots: 35. **Range, miles:** 800 at 30 kt
Complement: 28
Missiles: SSM: 4 YJ-1 (Eagle Strike) (C-801); inertial cruise; active radar homing to 40 km *(22 n*
  miles) at 0.9 Mach; warhead 165 kg; sea-skimmer.
Guns: 4 USSR 25 mm/60 (2 twin); 270 rds/min to 3 km *(1.6 n miles)* anti-aircraft.
Radars: Surface search: Square Tie; I-band.
  Fire control: Rice Lamp; H/I-band.
  IFF: 2 Square Head. High Pole A.

Comment: Modified Huangfen type. Delivered on 6 June 1995 at Aden having been built by the
  China Shipbuilding Corporation and completed in 1993. Payment was delayed by the Yemeni
  civil war. Based at Al Katib. *128* ran aground in September 1997 but was salvaged and may be
  operational again. All three are in poor condition.   *VERIFIED*

HUANGFEN 126   5/1995

6 BAKLAN CLASS (PCF)

BAKLAN 1201	**ZUHRAB** 1203	**HUNAISH** 1205
SIYAN 1202	**AKISSAN** 1204	**ZAKR** 1206

Displacement, tons: 12 full load
Dimensions, feet (metres): 50.9 × 9.8 × 2.6 *(15.5 × 3 × 0.8)*
Main machinery: 2 diesels; 2 surface drives
Speed, knots: 55. **Range, miles:** 400 at 30 kt
Complement: 4
Guns: 2—12.7 mm MGs.
Radars: Surface search: Furuno; I-band.

Comment: Ordered from CMN Cherbourg on 3 March 1996. First five were delivered 1 August
  1996 and the last one in mid-1997. Top speed in Sea States up to 3. Composite hull
  construction.   *UPDATED*

BAKLAN   8/1996*, C M N Cherbourg / 0084259

AMPHIBIOUS FORCES

Note: Ropucha 139 is an alongside hulk and is to be replaced by a 1,300 ton LCM ordered from
Poland in late 1999.

0 + 3 DEBA CLASS (TYPE 716) (LCU)

Displacement, tons: 176 full load
Dimensions, feet (metres): 122 × 23.3 × 5.6 *(37.2 × 7.1 × 1.7)*
Main machinery: 3 diesels; 3,000 hp(m) *(2.2 MW)*; 3 shafts
Speed, knots: 20. **Range, miles:** 430 at 16 kt
Complement: 12
Military lift: 20 tons and 50 troops
Guns: 2—23 mm (twin).
Radars: Navigation: I-band.

Comment: Ordered from Poland in October 1999 for delivery in 2002. Details given are for the
  ships in service with the Polish Navy.
                                                                                NEW ENTRY

DEBA (Polish colours)   8/1996*, Marek Twardowski / 0081574

2 ONDATRA (TYPE 1176) CLASS (LCUs)

13   14

Displacement, tons: 145 full load
Dimensions, feet (metres): 78.7 × 16.4 × 4.9 *(24 × 5 × 1.5)*
Main machinery: 1 diesel; 300 hp(m) *(221 kW)*; 1 shaft
Speed, knots: 10. **Range, miles:** 500 at 5 kt
Complement: 4
Military lift: 1 MBT
Radars: Navigation: Spin Trough; I-band.

Comment: Transferred from USSR January 1983. Has a tank deck of 45 × 13 ft.
                                                                                VERIFIED

ONDATRA 14   1990

1 T4 CLASS (LCU)

134

Displacement, tons: 93 full load
Dimensions, feet (metres): 65.3 × 18.4 × 4.6 *(19.9 × 5.6 × 1.4)*
Main machinery: 2 diesels; 316 hp(m) *(232 kW)*; 2 shafts
Speed, knots: 10
Complement: 4

Comment: Reported to have paid off in 1995 but still in service.

UPDATED

T4 134   *1/1990* */ 0016614*

MINE WARFARE FORCES

1 NATYA CLASS (TYPE 266ME) (MINESWEEPERS—OCEAN) (MSO)

201

Displacement, tons: 804 full load
Dimensions, feet (metres): 200.1 × 33.5 × 10.8 *(61 × 10.2 × 3)*
Main machinery: 2 Type M 504 diesels; 5,000 hp(m) *(3.67 MW)* sustained; 2 shafts; cp props
Speed, knots: 16. **Range, miles:** 3,000 at 12 kt
Complement: 67
Guns: 4—30 mm/65 (2 twin); 500 rds/min to 5 km *(2.7 n miles)*; weight of shell 0.54 kg.
    4—25 mm/80 (2 twin); 270 rds/min to 3 km *(1.6 n miles)*; weight of shell 0.34 kg.
A/S mortars: 2 RBU 1200 five-tubed fixed launchers; range 1,200 m; warhead 34 kg.
Mines: 10
Countermeasures: MCM: Carries contact, acoustic and magnetic sweeps.
Radars: Surface search: Don 2; I-band.
Sonars: MG 69/79; hull-mounted; active minehunting; high frequency.

Comment: Transferred from USSR in February 1991. Operational status doubtful. A second of
    class was delivered to Ethiopia in October 1991 but sheltered in Aden for a time in 1992.

VERIFIED

NATYA 201   *5/1996*

5 YEVGENYA (TYPE 1258) CLASS (MINEHUNTERS) (MHC)

11	12	15	20	+ 1

Displacement, tons: 90 full load
Dimensions, feet (metres): 80.7 × 18 × 4.9 *(24.6 × 5.5 × 1.5)*
Main machinery: 2 Type 3-D-12 diesels; 600 hp(m) *(440 kW)* sustained; 2 shafts
Speed, knots: 11. **Range, miles:** 300 at 10 kt
Complement: 10
Guns: 2—25 mm/80 (twin).
Radars: Navigation: Spin Trough; I-band.
Sonars: MG 7 small transducer lifted over stern on crane.

Comment: GRP hulls. Two transferred from USSR in May 1982, third in November 1987 and three
    more in March 1990. One deleted in 1994. Two based at Aden and three at Al Katib. At least two
    are fully operational.   *UPDATED*

YEVGENYA 20   *2/1997* */ 0016615*

AUXILIARIES

Notes: (1) A 4,500 ton Floating Dock acquired from the USSR. (2) A 14 m Hydrographic craft
acquired from Cougar Marine in 1988.

2 TOPLIVO CLASS (TANKERS) (AOTL)

135	140

Displacement, tons: 1,029 full load
Dimensions, feet (metres): 176.2 × 31.8 × 10.5 *(53.7 × 9.7 × 3.2)*
Main machinery: 1 6DR 30/50-5 diesel; 600 hp(m) *(441 kW)*; 1 shaft
Speed, knots: 10.5. **Range, miles:** 400 at 7 kt
Complement: 23
Cargo capacity: 500 tons
Radars: Navigation: Don; I-band.

Comment: Two small harbour tankers acquired in the early 1980s. *135* carries water, *140* oil. Both
    based at Aden and at least one is still in service.   *VERIFIED*

TOPLIVO   *1990, van Ginderen Collection*

YUGOSLAVIA
FEDERATION OF SERBIA AND MONTENEGRO

Headquarters Appointments

Commander-in-Chief:
    Admiral Milan Zec
Chief of Staff:
    Rear Admiral Milan Radović
Fleet Commander:
    Rear Admiral Pavlović Milivoj

Kosovo War 1999

The Navy remained largely unaffected by the NATO Kosovo
campaign in 1999. Most ships remained alongside and passive
in Montenegro ports, although the potential submarine threat
was taken seriously by NATO forces in the Adriatic.

Personnel

2000: 5,000 (3,500 conscripts)

Bases

Headquarters: Bar
Main bases: Tivat, Bar, Valdanos (planned)

Organisation

Fleet: Submarines Tactical Group, Frigates Tactical Group,
Missile FAC Brigade, Patrol Craft Brigade, Minesweeper Brigade,
Auxiliary Brigade. The Riverine Flotilla (Novi Sad) responds to the
Commander 1st Army.

Naval ground forces: 81 Bde Coast Defence (Kumbor), 83 Bde
Coast Defence (Bar), 16 Bde Naval Border Guard, 85 Bde Light
Infantry (Bar), 82 Center Combat Divers (Kumbor), 61 Bn Signal,
49 Bn Logistic/Medical. Usually Brigades have the strength of a
battalion (600-800 men).

Coast Defence

Truck-mounted twin SS-C-3 Styx SSM launchers and a number of
Coastal Artillery units with 130 mm, 122 mm and 88 mm guns.

Mercantile Marine

Lloyd's Register of Shipping:
    8 vessels of 4,416 tons gross

DELETIONS

Submarines

1998   *Drava, Uskok* (both reserve)

Frigates

1999   *Beograd* (reserve)

Mine Warfare Forces

1997   *Olib, Panonsko More*

Auxiliaries

1997   *Galeb, Jadran* (civilian)
1998   *Kit, PN 26, Alga, Jastog* (all reserve)

SUBMARINES

1 SAVA CLASS (PATROL SUBMARINE) (SS)

Name	No	Builders	Laid down	Launched	Commissioned
SAVA	831	S and DE Factory, Split	1975	1977	1978

Displacement, tons: 830 surfaced; 960 dived
Dimensions, feet (metres): 182.7 × 23.6 × 16.7
(55.7 × 7.2 × 5.1)
Main machinery: Diesel-electric; 2 Sulzer diesels; 1,600 hp(m)
(1.18 MW); 2 generators; 1 MW; 1 motor; 2,040 hp(m)
(1.5 MW); 1 shaft
Speed, knots: 10 surfaced; 16 dived
Complement: 35

Torpedoes: 6—21 in *(533 mm)* bow tubes. 10 TEST-71ME; wire-guided active/passive homing to 15 km *(8.1 n miles)* at 40 kt or 20 km *(10.8 n miles)* at 25 kt; warhead 220 kg.
Mines: 20 in lieu of torpedoes.
Countermeasures: ESM: Stop Light; radar warning.
Radars: Surface search: Snoop Group; I-band.
Sonars: Atlas Elektronik PRS-3; hull-mounted; active/passive search and attack; medium frequency.

Structure: An improved version of the 'Heroj' class. Diving depth, 300 m *(980 ft)*, built with USSR electronic equipment and armament. Pressure hull is 42.7 × 5.05 m and the casing is made of GRP. Accommodation is poor, suggesting the design was intended for only short periods at sea.
Operational: *Sava* is operational. Second of class *Drava* is laid up and unlikely to go to sea again.

UPDATED

SAVA   2/1998, Yugoslav Navy / 0050744

1 HEROJ CLASS (PATROL SUBMARINE) (SSC)

Name	No	Builders	Laid down	Launched	Commissioned
HEROJ	821	Uljanik Shipyard, Pula	1964	1967	1968

Displacement, tons: 615 surfaced; 705 dived
Dimensions, feet (metres): 165.4 × 15.4 × 14.8
(50.4 × 4.7 × 4.5)
Main machinery: Diesel-electric; 2 Rade Končar diesel generators; 1,200 hp(m) *(880 kW)*; 1 motor; 1,560 hp(m) *(1.15 MW)*; 1 shaft; auxiliary motor
Speed, knots: 10 surfaced; 15 dived
Range, miles: 4,100 at 10 kt dived and snorting
Complement: 31

Torpedoes: 4—21 in *(533 mm)* bow tubes. 6 SET-65E; active/passive homing to 15 km *(8.1 n miles)* at 40 kt; warhead 205 kg.
Mines: 12 in lieu of torpedoes.
Countermeasures: ESM: Stop Light; radar warning.
Radars: Surface search: Snoop Group; I-band.
Sonars: Thomson Sintra Eledone; hull-mounted; passive ranging; medium frequency.

Structure: Diving depth 150 m *(500 ft)*.

HEROJ   1982

Operational: *Heroj* operational, with second of class *Uskok* laid up at Tivat and unlikely to go to sea again. Capable of only short periods at sea and not much seen.

Sales: This type probably provided the basic design for some North Korean coastal submarines.

UPDATED

5 UNA CLASS (MIDGET SUBMARINES)

TISA 911   **UNA** 912   **ZETA** 913   **KUPA** 915   **VARDAR** 916

Displacement, tons: 76 surfaced; 88 dived
Dimensions, feet (metres): 61.7 × 9 × 8.2
(18.8 × 2.7 × 2.5)
Main machinery: 2 motors; 49 hp(m) *(36 kW)*; 1 shaft
Speed, knots: 6 surfaced; 7 dived
Range, miles: 200 at 4 kt
Complement: 6 plus 4 swimmers
Sonars: Atlas Elektronik; passive/active search; high frequency.

Comment: Building yard, Split. First of class commissioned May 1985; last two in 1989. Exit/re-entry capability with mining capacity. Can carry six combat swimmers, plus four Swimmer Delivery Vehicles (SDV) and limpet mines. Diving depth: 120 m *(394 ft)*. Batteries can only be charged from shore or from a depot ship. *Velebit* 914 to Croatia in 1991 and since fitted with a diesel generator. All based at Tivat. *Una* and *Tisa* reported cannibalised in 1997 but both were back in service in 1999.

UPDATED

VARDAR   2/1998, Yugoslav Navy / 0050745

2 R-2 MALA CLASS (TWO-MAN SWIMMER DELIVERY VEHICLES)

Displacement, tons: 1.4
Dimensions, feet (metres): 16.1 × 4.6 × 4.3
(4.9 × 1.4 × 1.3)
Main machinery: 1 motor; 4.5 hp(m) *(3.3 kW)*; 1 shaft
Speed, knots: 4.4
Range, miles: 18 at 4.4 kt; 23 at 3.7 kt
Complement: 2
Mines: 250 kg of limpet mines.

Comment: This is a free-flood craft with the main motor, battery, navigation pod and electronic equipment housed in separate watertight cylinders. Instrumentation includes aircraft type gyrocompass, magnetic compass, depth gauge (with 0 to 100 m scale), echo-sounder, sonar and two searchlights. Constructed of light aluminium and plexiglass, it is fitted with

fore and after-hydroplanes, the tail being a conventional cruciform with a single rudder abaft the screw. Large perspex windows give a good all-round view. Operating depth, 60 m *(196.9 ft)*, maximum. A second pair are laid up. A number of these craft has been sold to Russia. Six transferred to Libya. Sweden has also taken delivery of both two- and one-man versions of this type.

Note: Yugoslavia also operates a number of R-1 'wet chariots'. Can be transported in submarine torpedo tubes. Crewed by one man. Propulsion 1 kW electric motor; 24 v silver-zinc batteries. Normal operating depth 60 m *(196.9 ft)*. Range 6 n miles at 3 kt. Weight 145 kg. Dimensions 12.2 × 3.45 × 0.8 ft *(3.72 × 1.05 × 0.26 m)*.

VERIFIED

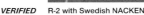

R-2 with Swedish NACKEN   12/1988, Gilbert Gyssels

FRIGATES

1 SPLIT (KONI) and 2 KOTOR CLASSES (FFG)

Name	No	Builders	Launched	Commissioned
PODGORICA (ex-Kopar)	32	Zelenodolsk Shipyard	1981	5 Dec 1982
KOTOR	33	Tito Shipyard, Kraljevica	21 May 1985	Jan 1987
NOVI SAD (ex-Pula)	34	Tito Shipyard, Kraljevica	18 Dec 1986	Nov 1988

Displacement, tons: 1,870 full load
Dimensions, feet (metres): 317.3 × 42 × 13.7 *(96.7 × 12.8 × 4.2)*
Main machinery: CODAG; 1 SGW Nikolayev gas turbine; 18,000 hp(m) *(13.2 MW)*; 2 Russki B-68 diesels; 15,820 hp (m) *(11.63 MW)* sustained (32); 2 SEMT-Pielstick 12 PA6 V 280 diesels; 9,600 hp(m) *(7.1 MW)* sustained (33 and 34); 3 shafts
Speed, knots: 27 gas; 22 diesel. **Range, miles:** 1,800 at 14 kt
Complement: 110

Missiles: SSM: 4 SS-N-2C Styx ❶; active radar or IR homing to 83 km *(45 n miles)* at 0.9 Mach; warhead 513 kg; sea-skimmer at end of run.
SAM: SA-N-4 Gecko twin launcher ❷; semi-active radar homing to 15 km *(8 n miles)* at 2.5 Mach; height envelope 9-3,048 m *(29.5-10,000 ft)*; warhead 50 kg.
Guns: 4 USSR 3 in *(76 mm)*/60 (2 twin) (1 mounting only in 33 and 34) ❸; 90 rds/min to 15 km *(8 n miles)*; weight of shell 6.8 kg.
4 USSR 30 mm/65 (2 twin) ❹; 500 rds/min to 5 km *(2.7 n miles)*; weight of shell 0.54 kg.
A/S mortars: 2 RBU 6000 12-barrelled trainable ❺; range 6,000 m; warhead 31 kg.
Mines: Can lay mines.
Countermeasures: Decoys: 2 Wallop Barricade double layer chaff launchers.
Radars: Air/surface search: Strut Curve ❻; F-band; range 110 km *(60 n miles)* for 2 m² target.
Navigation: Don 2 (32); I-band. Palm Frond (33 and 34); I-band.
Fire control: Owl Screech ❼; G-band (32). PEAB 9LV200 ❽; I-band (33 and 34) (for 76 mm and SSM).
Drum Tilt ❾; H/I-band (for 30 mm).
Pop Group ❿; F/H/I-band (for SAM).
IFF: High Pole; 2 Square Head.

Sonars: Hercules (32) or Bull Nose (33 and 34); hull-mounted; active search and attack; medium frequency.

Programmes: First two transferred from the USSR. Second pair built under licence. Type name, VPB (Veliki Patrolni Brod).
Structure: Although the hulls are identical to the 'Koni' class there are some equipment, and considerable structural differences between the USSR- and Yugoslav-built ships. The ex-USSR ship has the SS-N-2C missiles aft of midships and facing aft. The second pair have the same missiles level with the forward end of the bridge facing forward. The Yugoslav-built ship probably has the same gas-turbine engines as the other pair but there are different diesels. There is also a different arrangement of the bridge superstructure which is similar to the training frigate sold to Indonesia.
Operational: Based at Tivat. One other cannibalised for spares in 1999.

UPDATED

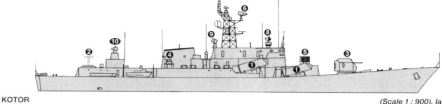

KOTOR

(Scale 1 : 900), Ian Sturton

PODGORICA

(Scale 1 : 900), Ian Sturton

SPLIT (old number)

6/1998, Yugoslav Navy / 0050747

KOTOR

6/1998, Yugoslav Navy / 0050746

LAND-BASED MARITIME AIRCRAFT

Notes: (1) Operational numbers of aircraft are uncertain but they include about three Mi-14 Haze ASW helicopters.
(2) The Air Force has a naval brigade with approximately 35 Galeb/Jastreb fighter-bombers and 10 Orao reconnaissance.

Numbers/Type: 2 Kamov Ka-25 Hormone A.
Operational speed: 104 kt *(193 km/h)*.
Service ceiling: 11,500 ft *(3,500 m)*.
Range: 217 n miles *(400 km)*.
Role/Weapon systems: ASW within Yugoslavian waters in support of submarine flotilla. Sensors: Short Horn search radar, MAD, dipping sonar, sonobuoys. Weapons: ASW; two torpedoes or depth bombs. ASV; four locally produced wire-guided missiles.

UPDATED

Numbers/Type: 3 Kamov Ka-27 Helix A.
Operational speed: 110 kt *(204 km/h)*.
Service ceiling: 12,000 ft *(3,658 m)*.
Range: 270 n miles *(500 km)*.
Role/Weapon systems: ASW within territorial waters, to supplement Ka-25. Sensors: Splash Drop search radar, MAD, dipping sonar, sonobuoys. Weapons: ASW only; two torpedoes or depth bombs.

UPDATED

PATROL FORCES

5 KONČAR CLASS (TYPE 240) (PCFG)

Name	No	Builders	Launched	Commissioned
RADE KONČAR	401	Tito Shipyard, Kraljevica	16 Oct 1976	Apr 1977
RAMIZ SADIKU	403	Tito Shipyard, Kraljevica	24 Apr 1978	Sep 1978
HASAN ZAFIROVIĆ-LACA	404	Tito Shipyard, Kraljevica	9 Nov 1978	Dec 1978
JORDAN NIKOLOV ORCE	405	Tito Shipyard, Kraljevica	26 Apr 1979	Aug 1979
ANTE BANINA	406	Tito Shipyard, Kraljevica	23 Nov 1979	Nov 1980

Displacement, tons: 271 full load
Dimensions, feet (metres): 147.6 × 27.6 × 8.5 *(45 × 8.4 × 2.6)*
Main machinery: CODAG; 2 RR Proteus gas turbines; 7,100 hp *(5.29 MW)* sustained; 2 MTU 16V 538 TB91 diesels; 6,000 hp(m) *(4.41 MW)* sustained; 4 shafts; cp props
Speed, knots: 38. **Range, miles:** 490 at 38 kt; 870 at 23 kt (diesels)
Complement: 30 (5 officers)

Missiles: SSM: 2 SS-N-2B Styx; active radar or IR homing to 46 km *(25 n miles)* at 0.9 Mach; warhead 513 kg.
Guns: 2 Bofors 57 mm/70; 200 rds/min to 17 km *(9.3 n miles)*; weight of shell 2.4 kg.
2—128 mm rocket launchers for illuminants.
2—30 mm/65 (twin) may be fitted in place of the after 57 mm.
Countermeasures: 2 Wallop Barricade double layer chaff launchers.
Weapons control: PEAB 9LV 202 GFCS.
Radars: Surface search: Decca 1226; I-band.
Fire control: Philips TAB; I/J-band.

Programmes: Type name, Raketna Topovnjaca. All names have probably been changed as they are of Croatian, Albanian and Bosnian origin.
Structure: Aluminium superstructure. Designed by the Naval Shipping Institute in Zagreb based on Swedish 'Spica' class with bridge amidships like Malaysian boats. The after 57 mm gun is replaced by a twin 30 mm mounting in some of the class.
Operational: 402 was taken by Croatia in 1991 and 401 was badly damaged but has been repaired. Based at Tivat. At least one of these five has been cannibalised for spares.

UPDATED

HASAN ZAFIROVIĆ-LACA   *2/1998, Yugoslav Navy* / 0050748

5 OSA I CLASS (TYPE 205)
(FAST ATTACK CRAFT—MISSILE) (PCFG)

STEVAN FILIPOVIĆ STEVA 304		JOSIP MAŽAR SOSA 307
ŽIKICA JOVANOVIĆ-ŠPANAC 305		KARLO ROJC 308
NIKOLA MARTINOVIĆ 306		

Displacement, tons: 171 standard; 210 full load
Dimensions, feet (metres): 126.6 × 24.9 × 8.8 *(38.6 × 7.6 × 2.7)*
Main machinery: 3 Type M 503A diesels; 8,025 hp(m) *(5.9 MW)* sustained; 3 shafts
Speed, knots: 35. **Range, miles:** 400 at 34 kt
Complement: 30 (4 officers)

Missiles: SSM: 4 SS-N-2A Styx; active radar or IR homing to 46 km *(25 n miles)* at 0.9 Mach; warhead 513 kg.
Guns: 4 USSR 30 mm/65 (2 twin); 500 rds/min to 5 km *(2.7 n miles)*; weight of shell 0.54 kg.
Radars: Surface search: Square Tie; I-band.
Fire control: Drum Tilt; H/I-band.
IFF: High Pole. 2 Square Head.

Programmes: Transferred from USSR in the late 1960s. Named after war heroes. Type name, Raketni Čamac. 306 and 308 have probably had name changes.
Operational: One more of the class held by Croatia and converted to a minelayer. Four others cannibalised for spares. All are operational.

UPDATED

JOSIP MAŽAR SOSA   *2/1998, Yugoslav Navy* / 0050749

6 MIRNA CLASS (TYPE 140) (PCF)

POHORJE 172	GRMEČ 175	KOSMAJ 178
UČKA 174	FRUŠKA GORA 177	ZELENGORA 179

Displacement, tons: 142 full load
Dimensions, feet (metres): 104.9 × 22 × 7.5 *(32 × 6.7 × 2.3)*
Main machinery: 2 SEMT-Pielstick 12 PA4 200 VGDS diesels; 5,292 hp(m) *(3.89 MW)* sustained; 2 shafts
Speed, knots: 28. **Range, miles:** 400 at 20 kt
Complement: 19 (3 officers)
Missiles: SAM: 1 SA-N-5 Grail quad mounting; manual aiming; IR homing to 6 km *(3.2 n miles)* at 1.5 Mach; altitude to 2,500 m *(8,000 ft)*; warhead 1.5 kg.
Guns: 1 Bofors 40 mm/70. 1 Oerlikon 20 mm. 2—128 mm illuminant launchers.
Depth charges: 8 DCs.
Radars: Surface search: Racal Decca 1216C; I-band.
Sonars: Simrad SQS-3D/3F; active; high frequency.

Comment: Builders, Kraljevica Yard. Launched between June 1981 and December 1983. An unusual feature of this design is the fitting of an electric outboard motor giving a speed of up to 6 kt. One sunk possibly by a limpet mine in November 1991. Four held by Croatia. Others have paid off and been cannibalised. 172 and 174 have probably had name changes.

UPDATED

POHORJE   *1988*, Yugoslav Navy* / 0084260

6 TYPE 20 (RIVER PATROL CRAFT) (PBR)

PC 211-PC 216

Displacement, tons: 55 standard
Dimensions, feet (metres): 71.5 × 17 × 3.9 *(21.8 × 5.3 × 1.2)*
Main machinery: 2 diesels; 1,156 hp(m) *(850 kW)*; 2 shafts
Speed, knots: 16. **Range, miles:** 200 at 15 kt
Complement: 10
Guns: 2 Oerlikon 20 mm.
Radars: Surface search: Decca 110; I-band.

Comment: Completed in the late 1980s. Steel hull with GRP superstructure. All active with the Riverine Flotilla.

UPDATED

TYPE 20   *1988*, Yugoslav Navy* / 0084261

1 BOTICA CLASS (TYPE 16) (RIVER PATROL CRAFT) (PBR)

PC 303

Displacement, tons: 23 full load
Dimensions, feet (metres): 55.8 × 11.8 × 2.8 *(17 × 3.6 × 0.8)*
Main machinery: 2 diesels; 464 hp(m) *(340 kW)*; 2 shafts
Speed, knots: 15. **Range, miles:** 340 at 14 kt
Complement: 7
Military lift: 3 tons
Guns: 1 Oerlikon 20 mm. 7—7.62 mm MGs.
Radars: Surface search: Decca 110; I-band.

Comment: Can carry up to 30 troops. This is the last surviving member of the class. Active with the Riverine Flotilla. ***UPDATED***

TYPE 16 (model) *1988*, Yugoslav Navy* / 0084262

11 TYPE 15 (RIVER PATROL CRAFT) (PBR)

Displacement, tons: 19.5 full load
Dimensions, feet (metres): 55.4 × 12.8 × 2.3 *(16.9 × 3.9 × 0.7)*
Main machinery: 2 diesels; 330 hp(m) *(242 kW)*; 2 shafts
Speed, knots: 16. **Range, miles:** 160 at 12 kt
Complement: 6
Guns: 1 Oerlikon 20 mm; 2—7.62 mm MGs.
Radars: Surface search: Racal Decca 110; I-band.

Comment: Built in Yugoslavia in the late 1980s for use in shallow water. Steel hulls with GRP superstructure. Four air conditioned craft were delivered to Sudan on 18 May 1989. One deleted so far, the rest are still operational with the Riverine Flotilla. ***UPDATED***

TYPE 15 *1989*, Yugoslav Navy* / 0084263

MINE WARFARE FORCES

2 SIRIUS CLASS
(MINESWEEPERS/HUNTERS) (MSC/MHC)

Name	No	Builders	Commissioned
PODGORA (ex-*Smeli*)	M 152 (ex-D 26)	A Normand, France	Sep 1957
BLITVENICA* (ex-*Slobodni*)	M 153 (ex-D 27)	A Normand, France	Sep 1957
*Hunter			

Displacement, tons: 365 standard; 424 full load
Dimensions, feet (metres): 152 × 28 × 8.2 *(46.4 × 8.6 × 2.5)*
Main machinery: 2 SEMT-Pielstick PA1 175 diesels; 1,620 hp(m) *(1.19 MW)*; 2 shafts
Speed, knots: 15. **Range, miles:** 3,000 at 10 kt
Complement: 40
Guns: 2 Oerlikon 20 mm.
Countermeasures: MCMV: PAP 104 (minehunter); remote-controlled submersibles.
Radars: Navigation: Thomson-CSF DRBN 30; I-band.
Sonars: Thomson Sintra TSM 2022 (minehunter); hull-mounted; active minehunting; high frequency.

Comment: Built to a British design as US 'offshore' orders. *Blitvenica* converted to minehunter in 1980-81. Decca Hi-fix. One more acquired by Croatia in 1991 and has been scrapped. These two are based at Tivat and are both operational. Names have probably been changed, being of Croatian origin. ***UPDATED***

BLITVENICA *10/1999*, van Ginderen/Heine* / 0085305

1 HAM CLASS (MINESWEEPER—INSHORE) (MSI)

BRSEČ M 142

Displacement, tons: 120 standard; 159 full load
Dimensions, feet (metres): 106.5 × 21.3 × 5.5 *(32.5 × 6.5 × 1.7)*
Main machinery: 2 Paxman YHAXM diesels; 1,100 hp *(821 kW)*; 2 shafts
Speed, knots: 14. **Range, miles:** 2,000 at 9 kt
Complement: 22
Guns: 2 Oerlikon 20 mm (twin).

Comment: Built in Yugoslavia 1964-66 under the US Military Aid Programme. Wooden hulls. One more acquired by Croatia in 1991 and has since been scrapped. Based at Tivat. Name probably changed. This ship was used to lay mines in 1999. ***UPDATED***

HAM (old number) *1988, Yugoslav Navy*

7 NESTIN CLASS (RIVER MINESWEEPERS) (MSI)

Name	No	Builders	Commissioned
NESTIN	M 331	Brodotehnika, Belgrade	20 Dec 1975
MOTAJICA	M 332	Brodotehnika, Belgrade	18 Dec 1976
BELEGIŠ	M 333	Brodotehnika, Belgrade	1976
BOČUT	M 334	Brodotehnika, Belgrade	1979
VUČEDOL	M 335	Brodotehnika, Belgrade	1979
DJERDAP	M 336	Brodotehnika, Belgrade	1980
NOVI SAD	M 341	Brodotehnika, Belgrade	8 June 1996

Displacement, tons: 65 full load
Dimensions, feet (metres): 88.6 × 21.7 × 5.2 *(27 × 6.3 × 1.6)*
Main machinery: 2 diesels; 520 hp(m) *(382 kW)*; 2 shafts
Speed, knots: 15. **Range, miles:** 860 at 11 kt
Complement: 17
Guns: 5 Hispano 20 mm (quad fwd, single aft). Some may still have a 40 mm gun forward.
Mines: 24 can be carried.
Countermeasures: MCMV: Magnetic, acoustic and explosive sweeping gear.
Radars: Surface search: Racal Decca 1226; I-band.

Comment: Some transferred to Hungary and Iraq. One more completed in 1996. The class is based at Novi Sad as part of the Riverine Flotilla. One deleted in 1997. One more building is unlikely to be completed. ***UPDATED***

BOČUT *10/1997, Yugoslav Navy* / 0050750

AMPHIBIOUS FORCES

1 SILBA CLASS (LCT/ML)

Name	No	Builders	Commissioned
— (ex-*Silba*)	DBM 241	Brodosplit Shipyard, Split	1990

Displacement, tons: 880 full load
Dimensions, feet (metres): 163.1 oa; 144 wl × 33.5 × 8.5 *(49.7; 43.9 × 10.2 × 2.6)*
Main machinery: 2 Burmeister & Wain Alpha 10V23L-VO diesels; 3,100 hp(m) *(2.28 MW)* sustained; 2 shafts; cp props
Speed, knots: 12. **Range, miles:** 1,200 at 12 kt
Complement: 33 (3 officers)
Military lift: 460 tons or 6 medium tanks or 7 APCs or 4—130 mm guns plus towing vehicles or 300 troops with equipment
Missiles: SAM: 1 SA-N-5 Grail quad mounting.
Guns: 4—30 mm/65 (2 twin) AK 230.
4—20 mm M75 (quad). 2—128 mm illuminant launchers.
Mines: 94 Type SAG-1.
Radars: Surface search: Racal Decca; I-band.

Comment: Ro-ro design with bow and stern ramps. Can be used for minelaying, transporting weapons or equipment and troops. Based at Tivat. A second of class was launched in July 1992 and a third in September 1994 both for the Croatian Navy. ***UPDATED***

DBM 241 *6/1998, MoD Bonn* / 0050751

4 DSM 501 TYPE (LCT/ML)

DSM 513   **+3**

Displacement, tons: 260 full load
Dimensions, feet (metres): 78.2 × 41.5 × 3.6 *(25.8 × 13.7 × 1.2)*
Main machinery: 2 diesels; 200 hp(m) *(147 kW)*; 2 shafts
Speed, knots: 8
Complement: 15
Military lift: 100 tons
Guns: 2 Hispano Suiza 20 mm M71.
Mines: Can carry 64.

Comment: Unlike other tank landing craft in that the centre part of the bow drops to form a ramp down which the tanks go ashore, the vertical section of the bow being articulated to form outer end of ramp. Built in Yugoslavia. Can also act as minelayer. Based at Tivat. Two sold to Sudan in 1969. Some of the class acquired by Croatia in 1991. Three others laid up by 1996 were restored to service in 1999.

UPDATED

DSM (Croatian colours)   *6/1996*, Tomislav Brandt /* 0012244

8 TYPE 22 (LCU)

DJC 621, 625-628, 630-632

Displacement, tons: 48 full load
Dimensions, feet (metres): 73.2 × 15.7 × 3.3 *(22.3 × 4.8 × 1)*
Main engines: 2 MTU diesels; 1,740 hp(m) *(1.28 MW)*; 2 water-jets
Speed, knots: 35. **Range, miles:** 320 at 22 kt
Complement: 8
Military lift: 40 troops or 15 tons cargo
Guns: 2—20 mm M71.
Radars: Navigation: Decca 101; I-band.

Comment: Built of polyester and glass fibre. Last one completed in 1987. Three held by Croatia of which one has paid off. *DJC 621, 625* and *632* based in the Danube Flotilla from 1995; *DJC 628, 630* and *631* from 1996.

UPDATED

DJC 627   *1989*, Yugoslav Navy /* 0084264

6 TYPE 21 (LCU)

DJC 613-DJC 618

Displacement, tons: 32 full load
Dimensions, feet (metres): 69.9 × 15.7 × 5.2 *(21.3 × 4.8 × 1.6)*
Main machinery: 1 diesel; 1,450 hp(m) *(1.07 MW)*; 1 shaft
Speed, knots: 23. **Range, miles:** 320 at 22 kt
Complement: 6
Military lift: 6 tons
Guns: 1—20 mm M71.

Comment: The survivors of a class of 30 built between 1976 and 1979. Four held by Croatia in 1991 of which three have paid off. Others sunk or scrapped. Some of these may be laid up.

UPDATED

DJC 618   *2/1998, Yugoslav Navy /* 0050752

11 TYPE 11 (LCVP)

DJC 602-DJC 612

Displacement, tons: 10 full load
Dimensions, feet (metres): 37 × 10.2 × 1.6 *(11.3 × 3.1 × 0.5)*
Main machinery: 2 diesels; 2 water-jets
Speed, knots: 23. **Range, miles:** 100 at 15 kt
Complement: 2
Military lift: 4.8 tons of equipment or troops
Guns: 1—7.62 mm MG.
Radars: Navigation: Decca 101; I-band.

Comment: GRP construction building at Vela Luka from 1986. Some that had been in reserve were brought back into service in 1999.

UPDATED

LCVP TYPE 11   *1990*, Yugoslav Navy /* 0084265

AUXILIARIES

Note: The sail training ship *Jadran* is active but civilian manned.

1 KOZARA CLASS (HEADQUARTERS SHIP) (PG)

KOZARA (ex-*Oregon*, ex-*Kriemhild*) PB 34 (ex-PB 30)

Displacement, tons: 695 full load
Dimensions, feet (metres): 219.8 × 31.2 × 4.6 *(67 × 9.5 × 1.4)*
Main machinery: 2 Deutz RV6M545 diesels; 800 hp(m) *(588 kW)*; 2 shafts
Speed, knots: 12
Guns: 9 Hispano Suiza 20 mm (3 triple).

Comment: Former Presidential Yacht on Danube. Built in Austria in 1940. Acts as Flagship of the Riverine Flotilla. A similar ship served in the Russian Black Sea Fleet before being transferred to Ukraine.

VERIFIED

KOZARA (old number)   *1982, Yugoslav Navy*

1 VIS CLASS (HEADQUARTERS SHIP) (PG)

VIS BB 35 (ex-*Vis* PB 35)

Displacement, tons: 680 full load
Dimensions, feet (metres): 187 × 27.9 × 11.5 *(57 × 8.5 × 3.5)*
Main machinery: 2 diesels; 2,000 hp(m) *(1.47 MW)*; 2 shafts
Speed, knots: 17
Complement: 35
Guns: 6 Hispano 20 mm (1 quad, 2 single).

Comment: Built in 1956 as one of a group of passenger ferries. Based at Bar. Name probably changed.

UPDATED

VIS   *4/1992, Livio Černjul /* 0016618

1 DRINA CLASS (AOTL)

SIPA PN 27

Displacement, tons: 430 full load
Dimensions, feet (metres): 151 × 23.6 × 10.2 *(46 × 7.2 × 3.1)*
Main machinery: 1 diesel; 300 hp(m) *(220 kW)*; 1 shaft
Speed, knots: 7
Complement: 12
Missiles: SAM: 1 SA-N-5.
Guns: 6 Hispano 20 mm (1 quad, 2 single).

Comment: Built at Kraljevic in mid-1950s. The last survivor of the class. Based at Tivat.

UPDATED

SIPA   *6/1998, MoD Bonn* / 0050753

1 SABAC CLASS (DEGAUSSING VESSEL) (YDG)

RSRB 36

Displacement, tons: 110 standard
Dimensions, feet (metres): 105.6 × 23.3 × 3.9 *(32.2 × 7.1 × 1.2)*
Main machinery: 1 diesel; 528 hp(m) *(388 kW)*; 1 shaft
Speed, knots: 10. **Range, miles:** 660 at 10 kt
Complement: 20
Guns: 2—20 mm M71.
Radars: Navigation: Decca 101; I-band.

Comment: Built in 1985. Used to degauss River vessels up to a length of 50 m. Part of the Riverine Flotilla.

UPDATED

36   *1987*, Yugoslav Navy* / 0084266

TENDERS

Displacement, tons: 51 full load
Dimensions, feet (metres): 69 × 14.8 × 4.6 *(21 × 4.5 × 1.4)*
Main machinery: 2 diesels; 304 hp(m) *(224 kW)*; 2 shafts
Speed, knots: 12. **Range, miles:** 400 at 10 kt
Guns: 2—20 mm M71 can be carried.
Radars: Navigation: Decca; I-band.

Comment: A number of tenders which, as transports, can carry up to 130 people or 15 tons of cargo and also act as diving tenders. A new type BMR-5 seen in 1997 with a 20 mm cannon mounted on the bow. Some have been sold for commercial use. There is also a training tender BS 22 of 72 tons capable of 11 kt.

UPDATED

TENDER   *6/1998*, Zvonimir Freivogel* / 0084267

TUGS

Note: There are three coastal tugs PR 37, PR 38 and PR 48, and two harbour tugs LR 72 and LR 77. All are active. Two others acquired by Croatia in 1991.

COASTAL TUG   *1988*, Yugoslav Navy* / 0084268

INDEXES

Indexes

Country Abbreviations

Alb	Albania	Dom	Dominica	Jpn	Japan	Rom	Romania
Alg	Algeria	DPRK	Korea, Democratic	Kaz	Kazakhstan	Rus	Russia
Ana	Anguilla		People's Republic (North)	Ken	Kenya	SA	South Africa
Ang	Angola	DR	Dominican Republic	Kir	Kiribati	SAr	Saudi Arabia
Ant	Antigua and Barbuda	Ecu	Ecuador	Kwt	Kuwait	Sen	Senegal
Arg	Argentina	Egy	Egypt	Lat	Latvia	Sey	Seychelles
Aus	Austria	ElS	El Salvador	Lby	Libya	Sin	Singapore
Aust	Australia	EqG	Equatorial Guinea	Leb	Lebanon	SL	Sierra Leone
Az	Azerbaijan	Eri	Eritrea	Lit	Lithuania	Slo	Slovenia
Ban	Bangladesh	Est	Estonia	Mad	Madagascar	Sol	Solomon Islands
Bar	Barbados	Fae	Faeroes	Mex	Mexico	Spn	Spain
Bdi	Burundi	Fij	Fiji	MI	Marshall Islands	Sri	Sri Lanka
Bel	Belgium	Fin	Finland	Mic	Micronesia	StK	St Kitts
Ben	Benin	Fl	Falkland Islands	Mld	Maldive Islands	StL	St Lucia
Bhm	Bahamas	Fra	France	Mlt	Malta	StV	St Vincent and the Grenadines
Bhr	Bahrain	Gab	Gabon	Mlw	Malawi	Sud	Sudan
Blz	Belize	Gam	The Gambia	Mly	Malaysia	Sur	Surinam
Bmd	Bermuda	GB	Guinea-Bissau	Mor	Morocco	Swe	Sweden
Bol	Bolivia	Ger	Germany	Moz	Mozambique	Swi	Switzerland
Bru	Brunei	Geo	Georgia	Mrt	Mauritius	Syr	Syria
Brz	Brazil	Gha	Ghana	Mtn	Mauritania	Tan	Tanzania
Bul	Bulgaria	Gn	Guinea	Nam	Namibia	Tld	Thailand
Bur	Burma	Gra	Grenada	NATO	NATO	Tog	Togo
Cam	Cameroon	Gre	Greece	Nic	Nicaragua	Ton	Tonga
Can	Canada	Gua	Guatemala	Nig	Nigeria	TT	Trinidad and Tobago
Cay	Cayman Islands	Guy	Guyana	Nld	Netherlands	Tun	Tunisia
Chi	Chile	Hai	Haiti	Nor	Norway	Tur	Turkey
CI	Cook Islands	HK	Hong Kong	NZ	New Zealand	Tuv	Tuvalu
Cmb	Cambodia	Hon	Honduras	Omn	Oman	UAE	United Arab Emirates
Col	Colombia	Hun	Hungary	Pak	Pakistan	Uga	Uganda
Com	Comoro Islands	IC	Ivory Coast	Pan	Panama	UK	United Kingdom
Con	Congo	Ice	Iceland	Par	Paraguay	Ukr	Ukraine
ConD	Congo, Democratic Republic	Ind	India	Per	Peru	Uru	Uruguay
CPR	China, People's Republic	Indo	Indonesia	Plp	Philippines	USA	United States of America
CpV	Cape Verde	Iran	Iran	PNG	Papua New Guinea	Van	Vanuatu
CR	Costa Rica	Iraq	Iraq	Pal	Palau	Ven	Venezuela
Cro	Croatia	Ire	Irish Republic	Pol	Poland	VI	Virgin Islands
Cub	Cuba	Isr	Israel	Por	Portugal	Vtn	Vietnam
Cypr	Cyprus, Republic	Ita	Italy	Qat	Qatar	WS	Western Samoa
Den	Denmark	Jam	Jamaica	RoC	Taiwan	Yem	Yemen
Dji	Djibouti	Jor	Jordan	RoK	Korea, Republic (South)	Yug	Yugoslavia

Named Ships

* shows the vessel is listed in a **Note** at the beginning of the section. † shows the vessel is referred to in a **Comment** following the entry for another vessel. Vessel names commencing with initials are indexed under the surname. Ranks and forenames continue to be the primary entry.

1st Lt Alex Bonnyman (USA) 839
1st Lt Baldomero Lopez (USA) 839
1st Lt Harry L Martin (USA) 839
1st Lt Jack Lummus (USA) 839
2nd Lt John P Bobo (USA) 839
3 de Febrero (Par) 507*
3 de Noviembre (Pan) 503
5 de Augusto (Ecu) 184
9 de Octubre (Ecu) 184
10 de Noviembre (Pan) 503
15 de Enero (Gua) 283*
15 de Noviembre (Uru) 852
18 Mart (Tur) 713
24 de Mayo (Ecu) 184
25 de Agosto (Uru) 852
25 de Julio (Ecu) 185
27 de Febrero (Ecu) 184
27 de Octubre (Ecu) 184
28 de Noviembre (Pan) 503
50 Let Pobeda (Rus) 604*

A

A 06-A 08 (Spn) 640
A 33-A 35 (Lby) 428
A 41 (Ger) 259
A 71, A 72 (Ind) 308
A 534 (Sri) 651
A 641 (Alg) 6
Aachen (UK) 781
AB 21-24 (Tur) 721
AB 25-36 (Tur) 721
AB 1050-1, 1053, 1055-6, 1058-67 (Aust) 34

ABA 332 (Per) 514
Abad (Iran) 333
Abadia Mendez (Col) 153*
Abdul Aziz (fast attack craft) (SAr) 612
Abdul Aziz (YAC) (SAr) 615
Abdul Halim Perdanakusuma (Indo) 312
Abdul Rahman Al Fadel (Bhr) 40
Abeille Flandre (Fra) 236*
Abeille Languedoc (Fra) 236*
Abeille Supporter (Fra) 236*
Abha (SAr) 611
Abhay (Ind) 303
Abigail Burgess (USA) 847
Able (USA) 835
Abnegar (Iran) 331*
Abou Abdallah El Ayachi (Mor) 461
Aboubekr Ben Amer (Mtn) 444
Abraham Crijnssen (Nld) .... 466†
Abraham Lincoln (USA) 793, 794
Abraham van der Hulst (Nld) 468
Abrolhos (Brz) 67
Abtao (Per) 509
Abu Bakr (Ban) 44
Abu Dhabi (UAE) 740
Abu El Barakat Al Barbari (Mor) 462
Abu El Ghoson (Egy) 191
Abu Obaidah (SAr) 612
Abu Qir (Egy) 187
Abukuma (Abukuma class) (Jpn) 377

Abukuma (Bihoro class) (Jpn) 390
Acacia (USA) 846
Acanthe (Fra) 239
Acchileus (Gre) 280
Acevedo (Spn) 638
Acharné (Fra) 241
Achernar (Brz) 69
Achéron (Fra) 234
Achilles (Swe) 668
Achimota (Gha) 265
Acolhua (Mex) 453
Aconcagua (Chi) 114
Aconit (Fra) 226
Açor (Por) 539
Acoustic Explorer (USA) 830*
Acoustic Pioneer (USA) 830*
Acquario (Col) 152
Acre (Bol) 56
Actinia (Por) 540
Active (USA) 842
Acushnet (USA) 843
Adak (USA) 845
Adam Kok (SA) 627
Adamant (UK) 779
Adamastos (Gre) 280
Adang (Tld) 701
Adatepe (Tur) 716
Addriyah (SAr) 613
Adelaide (Aust) 26
Adept (UK) 777
Adept (USA) 827
ADF 104, 106-9 (Per) 514
ADG 40 (Cub) 162*
Adhara II (Arg) 21
Aditya (Ind) 308
Adm Wm H Callaghan (USA) 840
Admiral Basisty (Rus) ...... 574†

Admiral Branimir Ormanov (Bul) 79
Admiral Chabanenko (Rus) 574
Admiral Golovko (Rus) ... 573
Admiral Gorshkov (Rus) 293, 568*
Admiral Horia Macellaru (Rom) 547
Admiral Kharlamov (Rus) 575
Admiral Kucherov (Rus) .... 574†
Admiral Kuznetsov (Rus) 568, 569
Admiral Lazarev (Rus) ..... 570†
Admiral Levchenko (Rus) 575
Admiral Lobov (Rus) 572
Admiral Makarov (Rus) 604*
Admiral Nakhimov (Rus) 570
Admiral Panteleyev (Rus) 575
Admiral Petre Barbuneanu (Rom) 546
Admiral Spiridonov (Rus) .... 575†
Admiral Tributs (Rus) 575
Admiral Ushakov (Rus) .... 570†
Admiral Vinogradov (Rus) 575
Admiral Zakharov (Rus) .... 575†
ADRI XXXII-ADRI LVIII (Indo) 324
Adrias (Gre) 270
Advent (Can) 101
Aegean (Gre) 270
Aegeon (Gre) .... 278†
Aegeus (Gre) 280

Aegir (Ice) 290
AFDB 2 (USA) 827
AFDM 2 (USA) .... 827†
AFDM 3 (USA) 827
Afif (SAr) 614
Afonso Cerqueira (Por) 538
Africana (SA) 628*
AG 5 (Tur) 728
AG 6 (Tur) 728
Al Agami (Egy) 192
Agaral (Ind) 309
Agder (Nor) 489
Agdlek (Den) 171
Ägir (Swe) 666
Agnadeen (Iraq) 333*
Agon (Gre) 272
Agpa (Den) 171
Agray (Ind) 303
Agu (Nig) 480
Aguia (Por) 539
Águila (Spn) 646
Aguirre (Per) 509
S A Agulhas (SA) ...... 628, 628†
Agusan (Plp) 522
AH 177 (Per) 513*
Ahalya Bai (Ind) 310
Ahmad El Fateh (Bhr) 40
Ahmad Yani (Indo) 312
Al-Ahmadi (Kwt) 420
Ahmed Es Sakali (Mor) 461
Ahti (Est) 198
Al Ahweirif (Lby) 428
Aias (Gre) 280
Aida IV (Egy) 194*
Aidon (Gre) 277
Aigle (Fra) 234
Aiguière (Fra) 241
Ailette (Fra) 236*
Aina Vao Vao (Mad) 431
Airone (Ita) 352*
Aisberg (Rus) 605

Named Classes

* shows the class is referred to in a **Note** at the beginning of the section. † shows the class is referred to in a *Comment* following the entry for another vessel or class. A Country abbreviation is only added if the nation is currently operating a vessel of the class.

To help users of this title evaluate the published data, *Jane's Information Group* has divided entries into three categories.
[N] NEW ENTRY Information on new equipment and/or systems appearing for the first time in the title.
[V] VERIFIED The editor has made a detailed examination of the entry's content and checked its relevancy and accuracy for publication in the new edition to the best of his ability.
[U] UPDATED During the verification process, significant changes to content have been made to reflect the latest position known to *Jane's* at the time of publication.

2nd Lt John P Bobo (USA) 839 [N]
65 ft WYTL (USA) 849 [V]
300 Ton (Jpn) 382 [N]
600, 700, 800 (Ita) 364*
980 Ton (Jpn) 385 [N]

A

A 12 (Sin, Swe) 618 [U]
A 14 (Swe) 655 [U]
A 17 (Swe) 654†, 654 [U]
A 19 (Swe) 654 [U]
A 69 (Arg, Fra) 12 [U], 227 [U]
AAAV (Advanced Amphibious Assault Vessel) (USA) 815†, 822†
Abhay (Pauk II) (Ind) 303 [U]
Abnaki (Mex) 457 [U], 833†
Abtao (Per) 509 [U]
Abukuma (Jpn) 377 [U]
Achelous (CPR, Indo, Plp) 141 [U], 321 [V], 519 [U]
Actif (Fra) 241 [U]
Addriyah (MSC 322) (SAr) 613 [V]
Adelaide (Oliver Hazard Perry) (Aust) 26 [U]
Adept (UK) 777 [U]
Adjutant (Gre, Spn, RoC, Tur) 277 [U], 641 [U], 683 [U], 722 [U]
Admirable (Bur, DR, Mex) 80 [U], 177 [U], 452†, 452 [U], 454†, 456 [U], 863*
Admiralec (Rus) 604†
Advanced Amphibious Assault Vessel (USA) 815†, 822†
Advanced Swimmer-Seal Delivery System (USA) 787*, 788†, 789†
Advanced Unmanned Search System (USA) 787*
Afalina (Ukr) 738*
AFDM (Gre, USA) 278†
Agave (Ita) 353 [U], 357 [U]
Agdlek (Den) 171 [U]
Aggressive (Bel, Ita, Spn, RoC) 52 [U], 234†, 354 [U], 641 [U], 683 [U]
AGOR-26 (USA) 830 [N]
Agosta 90B (Pak) 496 [U]
Agosta (Fra, Pak, Spn) 217 [U], 496 [U], 523*, 631 [U], 674*
Aguinaldo (Plp) 518 [U], 520†
Ahmad El Fateh (FPB 45) (Bhr) 40 [U]
Ahmad Yani (Van Speijk) (Indo) 312 [U]
Aigrette (Mad) 432*
Aist (Dzheyran) (Rus) 592 [U]
Ajeera (Bhr, Ven) 40 [U], 858 [U]
Akademik Fersman (Rus) 320*
Akademik Krylov (Rus) 595 [U]
Akademik Shuleykin (Swe) 665 [U]
Akagi (Jpn) 391 [U]
Akizuki (Jpn) 392 [U]
Akshay (Ban) 46 [U]
Aktion (Gre) 277 [U]
Akula I (Bars) (Rus) 117*, 560 [U], 562†
Akula II (Rus) 560 [U], 563†
Akula (Ondatra) (Rus, Yem) 592 [U], 868 [V]
Akula (Typhoon) (Rus) 554 [U]
Akvamaren (Natya) (Rus) 588 [U]
Al Bushra (Omn) 491 [V]
Al Feyi (UAE) 743 [U]
Al Hussein (Hawk) (Jor) 397 [U]
Al Jarim (FPB 20) (Bhr) 40 [V]
Al Jawf (Sandown) (SAr) 613 [U]
Al Jouf (SAr) 614 [U]
Al Jubatel (SAr) 614 [U]
Al Manama (FPB 62) (Bhr) 39 [U]
Al Riffa (FPB 38) (Bhr) 40 [U]
Al Shaheed (Kwt) 421 [U]
Al Siddiq (SAr) 612 [U]
Al Tahaddy (Kwt) 422 [V]
Al Waafi (Omn) 491†
Al-Shaali (Kwt, UAE) 421 [V], 743 [U]
Alamosa (Plp) 520 [V]
Albacora (Daphne) (Por) 536 [U]
Albatros (Grisha) (Lit, Rus, Ukr) 429 [U], 582 [U], 734 [U]
Albatros (Ita) 352*
Albatros (Type 143B) (Ger) 254 [U]
Albatros (YP) (Rus) 604†
Albatroz (Por) 539 [U]
Albion (UK) 765 [U], 768†
Alboran (Spn) 638 [V]
Alcotan 30 (Ang) 8†
Alcotan (ElS) 195†
Alfa (Lira) (Rus) 562†
Alfeite (GB) 285 [U]
Algerine (Tld) 702 [U]
Algol (USA) 836 [U]
Aliya (Saar 4.5) (Isr) 338 [U]
Alkmaar (Tripartite) (Indo, Nld) 318 [U], 469*, 470 [U]
Alkyon (MSC 294) (Gre) 277 [U]
Allen M Sumner (Fram II) (RoC) 677 [U]
Alliance (Ita, Nato, RoC) 356 [N], 463 [U], 684 [U]
Alligator (Indo, RoK, Ven) 317 [U], 414†, 414 [U], 858 [U]
Alligator (Tapir) (Rus, Ukr) 591†, 591 [U], 736 [U]
Almirante Brown (MEKO 360) (Arg) 11 [U]
Almirante Clemente (Ven) 860 [U]
Almirante Guilhem (Brz) 73 [V]
Almirante Padilla (Type FS 1500) (Col) 149 [U], 434†
Alpinist (Rus) 594 [U]
Alpino (Ita) 351 [U]
Alta/Oksøy (Nor) 486 [U]
Altay (modified) (Rus) 599 [U]
Alucat 850 (Arg) 21 [U]
Alucat 1050 (Arg) 20 [U]
Alvand (Vosper Mk 5) (Iran) 326 [U]
Alvaro De Bazán (F 100) (Spn) 636 [U]
Alvin (USA) 831 [V]
Älvsborg (Chi, Swe) 113 [V], 660 [U]
Amami (Jpn) 389 [U]
Amazon (Type 21) (Pak) 498 [U]
Amga (Rus) 597 [U]
Amorim Do Valle (River) (Brz) 69 [V]
Amsterdam (Nld, Spn) 472 [U], 642†
Amur I, II (Rus, Ukr) 118*, 119†, 598 [V], 736*
Amur (Lada) (Rus) 292*, 564 [U]
Amurec (Rus) 604†
AN-2 (Hun) 289 [U]
Anaga (Spn) 638 [U]
Anchorage (RoC, USA) 681 [U], 815 [U], 820†, 821†
Andrea Doria (Ita) 346†
Andromeda (Por) 540 [U]
Animoso (De La Penne) (Ita) 347 [U]
Anninos (La Combattante II) (Gre) 273 [U]
Antarès (BRS) (Fra) 234 [U]
Antares (Mlw) 432 [V]
Antares (Muravey) (Rus, Ukr) 587 [U], 739 [U]
Antonio Zara (Ita) 363 [U]
Antonov (Rus) 602 [U], 606*
Antyey (Oscar II) (Rus) 558 [U]
Anvil (USA) 848 [U]
Anzac (MEKO 200) (Aust, NZ) 25 [U], 27†, 476†, 476 [U]
AP.1-88/200 (Can) 102 [U]
AP.1-88/400 (Can) 10 [V]
Appleleaf (Aust, UK) 773 [U]
Aquamaster/Drago (Ita) 364*
Aquarius (Swi) 670 [U]
Aragosta (Ham) (Ita) 357†, 362 [U]
Aratú (Schütze) (Brz) 67 [V]
Arauca (Col) 150 [U]
Archer (UK) 310†, 769*, 770 [U]
Arcor 38 (Tun) 711†
Arcor 46 (Mor) 462 [U]
Arcor 53 (Mor) 462 [U]
Arctic 22/24 ft RIB (Bmd, UK) 55†, 769†
Arctic 28 (UAE, UK) 743 [U], 769†
Arctic (Nor) 489 [U]
ARD 12 (Ecu, Iran) 183 [U], 331†
Ardhana (Vosper 33) (UAE) 742 [U]
Aresa LVC 160 (P 101) (Spn) 639†
Argos (Por) 539 [U]
Argus (Brz) 68 [V]
Argus (UK) 138†
Ariel (Fra) 238 [U]
Arkösund (Swe) 660 [V]
Arleigh Burke (Flight I and II) (USA) 675*, 802†, 803 [U], 804 [U], 805 [U], 822*
Arleigh Burke (Flight IIA) (USA) 784*, 802 [U]
Arleigh Burke (improved) (Jpn) 370†
Armatolos (Gre) 274 [U]
Arnala (Petya II) (Ind) 300 [U]
Arrecife (Olmeca II) (Mex) 454 [U]
Arriyad (Modified La Fayette) (SAr) 611 [U]
Arsenal Ships (USA) 802*
Artigliere (Lupo) (Ita, Per, Ven) 350†, 351 [U], 352†, 511 [U], 856 [U]
Arun Type 300A (UAE) 744*
Arun Type 300B (Can) 101†
Asagiri (Jpn) 372†, 373 [U]
ASDS (Advanced Swimmer-Seal Delivery System) (USA) 787*, 788†, 789†
Ashdod (Isr) 340 [U]
Asheville (Col, Gre, RoK, Tur, USA) 151 [U], 275 [U], 413†, 720 [U], 830 [V]
Ashoora I (Iran, Sud) 330 [U], 652 [U]
ASI 315 (HK) 287 [U]
Asia (Balzam) (Rus) 593 [U]
Asmar Protector (Chi, ElS) 114 [U], 194†, 195 [U]
Asogiri (Jpn) 393 [U]
Assad (Mly) 435 [U]
Astute (UK) 753 [N]
ASU 81 (Jpn) 385 [U]
Asuka (Jpn) 39 [U]
Atilay (209) (Tur) 714 [U]
Atlant (Slava) (Rus) 572 [U]
Atle (Swe) 207†, 664 [U]
Atrek (Rus) 599†
ATS (Nld) 645†
Atsumi (Jpn) 380 [U]
Attack (Indo) 317 [U]
Attacker (Leb) 424 [U]
Audace (Ita) 347†, 348 [V]
Auk (Mex, Plp, Uru) 451 [U], 458†, 517 [U], 853 [U]
AUSS (Advanced Unmanned Search System) (USA) 787*
Austin (converted) (USA) 814 [U]
Austin (USA) 814†, 819 [U], 821†
Autonomous Undersea Vehicles (USA) 787*
AUV (Autonomous Undersea Vehicles) (USA) 787*
Avenger (USA) 381†, 824 [U]
Avon Sea Rider (Dji, Ire, Ger, Mrt, UK) 176*, 263†, 334†, 446†, 769† *bis*, 782*
Azteca (Mex) 453 [U]

B

Bacolod City (Frank S Besson) (Plp) 519 [U]
Badr (SAr) 612 [V]
Baglietto 59 ft (UAE) 745 [U]
Baglietto GC 23 (UAE) 745 [U]
Baglietto Type 20 (Alg) 7 [V]
Bahamas (Bhm) 36†, 36 [U]
Bahia (Mex) 457 [V]
Bakassi (P 48S) (Cam) 87 [U]
Baklan (Yem) 868 [U]
Baklazhan (Rus) 605 [U]
Balcom 10 (Ger) 263†
Baleares (F 70) (Spn) 634 [U]
Balsam (DR, Est, Plp, USA) 177 [U], 199 [U], 521 [V], 846 [U]
Balsam (USA) 848*
Baltyk (Pol) 532 [U]
Balzam (Rus) 593 [U]
Bambu (Agave) (Ita) 353 [U], 354†
Bambuk (Ukr) 737 [V]
Ban Yas (Lürssen TNC 45) (UAE) 742 [U]
Bang Rachan (Tld) 699 [U]
Bango (Indo) 324*
Baptista de Andrade (Por) 538 [U]
Baracuda 30 ft (UAE) 745†
Baradero (Dabur) (Arg) 16 [V]
Barbaros (Mod MEKO 200) (Tur) 718 [U]
Barceló (Spn) 638 [U]
Barkat (Pak) 500 [U]
Barnegat (Vtn) 863 [U]
Barracuda Project (Fra) 213†, 214†, 216*
Barracuda (Sierra I) (Rus) 562 [U]
Barroso (Brz) 62 [U]
Barroso Pereira (Brz) 71 [U]
Bars (Akula I) (Rus) 560 [U]
Baruna Jaya (AGS) (Indo) 319 [V]
Baruna Jaya (Indo) 319 [U], 324*
Barzan (Vita) (Qat) 543 [U]
Basento (Ita) 359 [U]
Baskunchak (Rus) 598†
Batral (Chi, Fra, Gab, IC, Mor) 112 [U], 230 [U], 243 [U], 365 [U], 461 [U]
Bay (Aust) 30 [U], 34 [N]
Bay (USA) 844 [V]
Bayandor (PF 103) (Iran) 327 [V], 693†
Bazan 39 (Arg) 20 [U]
Bear (USA) 686†
Bedok (Landsort) (Sin) 621 [U]
Bélier (Fra) 240 [U]
Bellatrix (DR) 178 [U]
Beluga (Rus) 565 [U], 566*
Belyanka (Rus) 597 [U]
Benjamin Franklin (USA) 788 [U]
Bereza (Bul, Rus, Ukr) 79 [U], 604 [U], 737 [U]
Bergamini (Ita) 354†
Berk (Claud Jones) (Tur) 719 [U]
Berkot-B (Kara) (Rus) 573 [U]
Berlin (Ger) 257 [U]
BH 2 (Fra) 235 [U]
BH 7 (Iran) 331 [U]
Bigliani (Ita) 363†, 363 [V]
Bihoro (Jpn) 390 [U]
Bima VIII (Indo) 322*
BIP (Fra) 230*
Biya (Type 870/871) (Cub, Rus, Ukr) 162 [U], 596†, 596 [U], 738 [U]
Bizerte (PR 48) (Cam, Sen, Tun) 87 [U], 616 [V], 710 [V]
Black Swan (Egy) 186*
Blohm + Voss Z-28 (Arg) 20†
Blue Ridge (USA) 813 [U]
Bluebird (Tld, Tur) 699 [U], 727 [U]
Bob Hope (USA) 836 [U]
Bobcat (Coastguard) (Isr) 340 [U]
Bodan (Ger) 262*, 262 [V]
Bodensee (Tur) 726†
Boghammar (Dji, Iran, UAE) 176*, 329 [U], 744*
Bolster (Mex, RoC) 455*, 685†
Bolva 1, 2, 3 (Rus) 599 [U]
Bombarda (Por) 540 [U]
Borey (Rus) 554 [U], 555†
Boris Chilikin (Rus, Ukr) 599 [U], 736 [V]
Bormida (Ita) 359 [V]
Boston Whaler (Ana, Ant, Arg, Bar, Bhm, Bmd, Bol, Bul, Col, CR, Dom, ElS, Gra, Gua, Hon, HK, Iran, Jam, Kaz, Mex, Pan, Rom, StK, StL, StV, SAr, Sin, Tur, USA, Ven) 8 [V], 16*, 37 [U], 50†, 55†, 56 [U], 77*, 152†, 156*, 176†, 195†, 283 [U], 284 [U], 286†, 288†, 330 [V], 366*, 397*, 452† *bis*, 504†, 548*, 608 [U], 609†, 615†, 623†, 729*, 825†, 846†, 861*
Botica (Yug) 873 [U]
Bouchard (Par) 506 [U]
Bougainville (Fra) 230 [U]
Bowen (TT) 709 [U]

Aircraft by Countries

NOTES

NOTES